Also from
Visible Ink Press

**VideoHound's® Cult Flicks & Trash Pics,
2nd Edition**

**VideoHound's Horror Show:
999 Hair-Raising, Hellish, and Humorous Movies**

**VideoHound's Independent Film Guide,
2nd Edition**

VideoHound's Sci-Fi Experience

**VideoHound's War Movies:
Classic Conflict on Film**

**VideoHound's World Cinema:
The Adventurer's Guide to Movie Watching**

The St. James Film Directors Encyclopedia

**The St. James Women Filmmakers Encyclopedia:
Women on the Other Side of the Camera**

Dedication

This book is dedicated to two individuals who lost their lives while it was being written, and one who saved mine.

Lo Lieh passed away from a heart attack in November 2002. He was the first Asian action star to have a big hit in America, when in the spring of 1973 *Five Fingers of Death* was released across the country, preceding Bruce Lee's *Fists of Fury* and the *Kung Fu* TV series by several months. Aside from being a pioneer, Lo appeared in around 200 films, including *Executioners from Shaolin, Black Magic, Supercop, Miracles, Secret of Chinese Kung Fu, Fists of the White Lotus, Fists and Guts, Abbot of Shaolin, Mad Monkey Kung Fu, Born Invincible, Killer from Above,* and his final film, *Glass Tears.* He always lent his role some extra effort, no matter the circumstances, impressing those who met him with his gracious nature and rich reverberating voice.

Kinji Fukasaku was a dedicated writer and director who was racing the reaper to complete *Battle Royale 2* when he succumbed to prostate cancer in January 2003. Able to work in any genre, he did impressive work in all of them, making a movie star of Sonny Chiba in *The Drifting Detective* and *Vigilante in the Funky Hat,* creating star wars in *Battle in Outer Space* and *Message from Space,* exploring space creepers in *The Green Slime,* building a web of secrets in *Sure Death,* or camping it up in *Black Lizard.* He headed the Director's Guild of Japan and was awarded the government's Medal with Purple Ribbon for his cinematic achievements. It's ironic that he left us just as he was achieving worldwide prominence.

Kristin Yates Thomas is my lovely and brilliant wife, who has been supportive and encouraging throughout this endeavor, even as the months of writing stretched into a year and our home filled up with DVDs and videotapes.

I thank you all.

VideoHound's Dragon

VideoHound's Dragon

Asian Action & Cult Flicks

BRIAN THOMAS

Detroit

VideoHound's®
Dragon
Asian Action
& Cult Flicks

Copyright © 2003 by Visible Ink Press®

Published by Visible Ink Press
43311 Joy Rd., Ste. 414
Canton, MI 48187-2075

Most Visible Ink books are available at special quantity discounts when purchased in bulk by corporations, organizations, or groups. Customized printings, special imprints, messages, and excerpts can be produced to meet your needs. For more information, contact Special Markets Manager, Visible Ink Press, 43311 Joy Rd., Ste. 414, Canton, MI 48187-2075.

Art Direction: Mary Claire Krzewinski
Typesetting: Graphix Group

Cover/back cover photos:
Gamera, Guardian of the Universe (The Kobal Collection), *Supercop* (The Kobal Collection / Golden Harvest), *Crouching Tiger, Hidden Dragon* (The Kobal Collection / Columbia / Sony), *Legend of the 7 Golden Vampires* (The Kobal Collection / Hammer / Shaw), *Akira* (The Kobal Collection / Akira), *Mothra vs. Godzilla* (The Kobal Collection).

Library of Congress Cataloging-in-Publication Data

ISBN 1-57859-141-4
Printed in the United States of America
All rights reserved

10 9 8 7 6 5 4 3 2 1

A Cunning Canine Production™

Contents

Foreword by Cynthia Rothrock   *ix*

Introduction   *xiii*

Acknowledgments   *xix*

Contributors   *xxi*

Glossary   *xxv*

Anatomy of an Entry   *xxviii*

The Reviews

An A to Z Collection, with photos, quotes, and sidebars   *1*

MST3K Goes to Japan
703

Dragon Connections
709

Alternative Titles Index
715

Cast Index
745

Director Index
823

Writer Index
833

Cinematographer Index
847

Composer Index
855

Category Index
863

DragonHound Salutes

Alternate Versions 16

Dubs and Subs 22

John Woo 38

China 60

Bruceploitation: Too Many Fists of Fury! 72

Tsui Hark 94

Planet Chang: The Bizarre Martial Arts
    World of Chang Cheh 100

Chow Yun-fat 106

Maggie Cheung 112

Kung Fu Movie Dynasties: Seven
    Little Fortunes 142

Donnie Yen 152

The Jackie Chan Story Part 1 162

Kung Fu through the Ages 168

Bruce Lee vs. Sammo Hung: Battle of
    the Century? .182

Kung Fu Movie Dynasties: The Yuens 186

Bruce Lee 214

That's Bruceploitation: The Clones
    of Bruce Lee .224

Friend to All Children: The Saga of
    Supermonster Gamera 244

Hail King Ghidorah 250

Stephen Chow 258

Godzilla Conquers the World 262

continued...

DragonHound Salutes
continued...

Godzilla Marching Orders: Music in
Toho's Kaiju Epics 268

Kung Fu Movie Dynasties: The Laus 278

The Philippines 302

Michelle Yeoh 306

Hong Kong 314

Bollywood 320

Kung Fu Movie Dynasties:
Spring and Autumn 326

Japan 342

Korea 368

Kung Fu Movie Dynasties: The Venoms 374

Lone Wolf and Cub 390

Taiwan 414

Hip Hop Vampires of China 428

Ninja Ninja Ninja! 452

Wong Fei-hung: Kung Fu Hero Number One . . .464

Peking Opera 474

Sammo Hung 492

Godfrey Ho and the Mystery
of Tomas Tang 522

Four Sky Kings of Cantopop 542

The Shaolin Temple 558

Jet Li 564

Sonny Chiba 590

The Jackie Chan Story Part 2 596

Akira Kurosawa 616

Enter the Yakuza .626

The Ultraman Family 644

Once upon a Time in Triad Society 688

Shintaro Katsu *Is* Zatoichi 694

Foreword
How I Kicked My Way to Hong Kong and Back
By Cynthia Rothrock

It is my pleasure to write the foreword for *VideoHound's Dragon* because I grew up watching Hong Kong movies. Every week, I would drive from Scranton, Pennsylvania, to New York City to train with my teacher, Shum Leung. After four hours of training we would go into Chinatown, have dinner, and see an Asian action film. I grew up watching the old Jackie Chan movies. I just loved watching them and they always gave me an inspiration to train harder. I would go home and practice the more difficult stunts Chan did.

My love for martial arts was strong. I was undefeated forms champion for five straight years. After five years I retired from competition because I felt it was a record no one could break. **The record still stands.** In 1982, I was ranked number one in the males weapons division. This is the first time a woman dominated the men's division—I had to compete with the men because back in the '80s there was not a separate women's division.

I was a member of the West Coast Demonstration Team headed by Ernie Reyes. He received a call saying that a Hong Kong company was holding auditions for a male to star in some action films. He decided to bring the girls along as well. The auditions were held at a karate school in Los Angeles. I have never seen so many martial artists gathered in one room. When it was my turn, I did some forms, weapons, and self-defense techniques. I received a call saying that they decided to go with me instead of a **male.** I had a three-year contract to do three films, but two years went by and I did not hear anything from the company. By this time in my life, I'd been ranked number one for four years. Peter Jennings from *World News Tonight* did a piece on me. It stated how I was signed to do a movie in Hong Kong, and ended the show, "look out Hong Kong—here she comes." When the piece aired in Hong Kong, Sammo Hung saw it and asked who I was. Yuen Kwei

was in Los Angeles for the auditions and told him who I had a contract with. Sammo bought my contract from them, and in June 1985 I was on a plane to HK to shoot my first film.

I knew nothing about filming. I knew no one in Hong Kong. I kept imagining *Enter the Dragon* and I was going to this competition. I thought they would dress me up in Chinese clothes, give me a black wig with pigtails, and I would fight non-stop. I was surprised when I got there and they said, "No, you will play an inspector from England and will wear jeans."

The first day of shooting they wanted me to say my lines in Chinese. I was so nervous that I didn't think I could say them in English! I gave it a shot. They gave me my line in Chinese, but I forgot it and just started saying, "humma humma humma," and no one took any notice. They thought I was speaking English. I found out it didn't matter what you said—they shot with no sound and dubbed it all later. I also found it interesting that the actors didn't dub their own dialogue. I asked why, and they said I'm just an actor; someone else has a better voice than I.

My first movie was *Yes, Madam,* directed by Yuen Kwei (Cory Yuen). I never knew pain until I started shooting Hong Kong movies. In *Yes, Madam,* I was hit in the nose with a sword when we were shooting the ending fight scene. I was fighting quite a few people at one time, and timing was crucial. Tears started rolling out of my eyes, even though I tried to stop them. Yuen Kwei came up to me and said my nose now looked better. That was my introduction to pain. During the same movie I was hit so hard in the jaw that my ear started bleeding. I thought I was going to die because I remembered hearing if blood comes out of your ear you could die. They took me to the doctor, and he said my internal ear was split open and it needed stitching, but it was too deep to get into. They took me back to the set to continue shooting. Each movie I did in Hong Kong, the stunts became harder and harder. I got to the point I thought I was going to get killed on set. I would say this is my last movie—then I would heal, see the finished product, and couldn't wait until the next one began.

My second movie was *Millionaire's Express* with Sammo Hung directing. I heard he was in a bad mood because he'd lost a lot of money gambling. I had to fight his double, and my move was a wheel kick to the head. The stuntman kept coming in too close so I would kick over his head, and after doing this four times, Sammo started getting mad. He told me to kick the guy in the head. So I did the kick slow, told the translator to tell the stuntman this is where my foot is coming, and if he stays here he is going to get kicked. Sammo yells action, I kick, the guy comes in close, and I hit him in the head. I see blood. I feel so bad, but Sammo is happy. Another stuntman comes up to me and says, "Don't feel bad, that's the guy who hit you in the nose on *Yes, Madam.*"

My best movies were the ones I made in Hong Kong. The action is amazing. There is quite a difference in making movies in America and Hong Kong.

In America, you get a script to study. In Hong Kong, the writer sometimes comes to the set to write the scene you are going to shoot. In America, you cannot hit the actors. In Hong Kong, you can never hit them hard enough. An American fight scene can take one day to shoot. In Hong Kong, the ending of *Yes, Madam* took a month. In America, action is thought out and practiced beforehand. In Hong Kong, you work out the movements on the set.

In America, they don't want you to do dangerous stunts. Here are some of the stunts I had to do myself: In *Blonde Fury,* I had to jump off a 30-foot building, in heels and a skirt, with a fake baby in my arms, and a huge explosion behind me. If I didn't jump on "action," the flames would have hit me— and I didn't land on a fancy air bag that you would have here in America, but a bunch of boxes with a mattress on top. I had to do a fight scene on a very high net; every time I bounced into the ropes I got rope burns. I had to hang from a moving truck upside down, with my ankle strapped in the window of the car and my face by the wheel.

In *Millionaire's Express,* we had a scene to do with lots of horses. The day before the scene the actors were going to practice riding their horses. These horses weren't tame ones either; they were retired racehorses. Mine was so big that they decided to get me a smaller one. Besides, he was ornery and kept bucking up. My new horse never arrived, however, and the next day he was late getting there, so I had no time to practice. Sammo tells me: whatever you do, don't fall off the horse, because there are a hundred horses behind you, and if you fall off you will get trampled. I'm as nervous as can be. Sammo calls "action" and forgets to tell us that all the electric fans alongside of us were going to have sand thrown into them to give the effect that we would be riding out of a cloud of dust. We all felt like someone threw a handful of sand right into our eyes, horses included. No one could see and we ended up all over the place. All I kept thinking was, don't fall off.

I had to fight on pillars in *Prince of the Sun.* It gets a little scary knowing that your life is in the hands of two guys holding a wire attached to you in case you fall so they can pull you up. In *Yes, Madam,* I sat on a wall in a split for three hours. I couldn't walk for four days.

Even now, I get excited telling you these stories and crave the Hong Kong action. I guess it's the challenge to yourself to see how far you can go.

About ten years ago, I tried to get the rights for my films. I thought that if American people could see these films they would be amazed. It wasn't until Ang Lee did his film that Hollywood took interest. For a time, all you saw was wirework in movies like *The Matrix, Charlie's Angels, X-Men,* and so on. Jackie Chan is more popular than ever, and Jet Li has done quite a few successful movies. It's just plain fun to watch. I think now we finally have an international exchange of action from the masters of Asia.

Have fun finding all the films listed in this book. I guarantee you will have much excitement, laughter, and just plain fun in your movie-watching days ahead. Keep this book as your guide to the incredible world of Asian filmmaking at its best.

Cynthia Rothrock

A bona fide martial arts champion, during her years in Hong Kong Cynthia Rothrock appeared in some of the all-time classics of Asian action cinema, working with some of the greatest stars in the business, and even starred in Indonesian pictures. In 1990, Golden Harvest began producing her movies in the U.S., beginning with her title role in China O'Brien. *Since then, she's appeared in action films all over the world, earning legions of fans with her acting talent, athletic ability, and personal charm. In all, she's starred in over 40 features, and made guest appearances on TV shows like* Hercules *and even video games. You can catch up with her on her official website at* cynthiarothrock.org, *or write to her fan club:* Rothrock-In, 2633 Lincoln Blvd. #103, Santa Monica, CA 90405.

Introduction
The Big Feast and the Hunger Afterward

Most cinephiles will tell you they're well versed in the cinema of Asia—after all, they're familiar with the work of Juzo Itami and Zhang Yimou. But ask them about Lau Kar-Leung or Ishiro Honda and you're likely to get blank stares. (I may be getting a blank stare from you right now, but hold on, please.) They've heard of Bruce Lee, of course, but weren't all of his films made in America?

The art-house community has served a certain level of Asian film very well for the last 50 years or so. But what about movies that might not have a pedigree, a scrapbook full of glowing reviews from high-class critics, or a few international film festival awards? Akira Kurosawa's films may have gotten onto the North American continent through festivals and art houses, but it was their subsequent wider releases in dubbed and edited form that placed them firmly in the public consciousness. Asian action and cult flicks—"genre" films to academia, "psychotronic movies" to the hipsters—have been sneaking into America through the back door for years, peddled by lower-level distributors and seedy exhibitors until the films acquired an unwholesome reputation. *Gammera the Invincible* lured innocent children into a matinee double bill just to shock their senses when the second feature, Mario Bava's bloody *Knives of the Avenger,* flashed across the screen. Teenagers tramped into unsanitary downtown fleapit theatres to see *four* back-to-back kung fu features, only to emerge and find themselves in a dangerous neighborhood after dark. And who was safe with *King Kong vs. Godzilla* thundering across their area drive-in screen? Asian cinema came from a culture as far away from our own as it could be without being extraterrestrial. While *The Makioka Sisters* were making diplomatic inroads uptown, we were getting our minds blown in the back row as the *Five Deadly Venoms* tore each other apart.

To be fair, art-film bastions like the Film Center of the Art Institute of Chicago (now the Gene Siskel Film Center) did their part to push the door open a little wider. Jackie Chan tried to crack the American market twice and failed, but when festivals of Hong Kong films started to play in art houses in

the late 1980s, word of mouth about stars like Chan, Sammo Hung, Brigitte Lin, and Chow Yun-fat began to spread.

But what really made the cult of Asian action cinema spread like wildfire is home video. Converts began haunting the darker aisles of video stores searching out whatever titles they could find. Those lucky enough to live in a large city made frequent trips into Chinatown to plunder the imported tapes in video stores where no one spoke English, and when that failed to satisfy their appetites, turned to mail-order companies.

And now the cult has gone mainstream. Every time a Jackie Chan (or Sonny Chiba, or Chow Yun-fat, or Jet Li) film plays somewhere, somebody sees him for the first time and wants to see more. This process has been repeated so many times that we are now a nation that's very hungry for Asian movies, and every time we see one, the hunger returns.

It's an old cliché, if not an outright slur, that you're hungry again an hour after eating Chinese food. This belief is probably based more on the Americanized version of Chinese food than the real thing, but with Asian movies it's just the opposite. When you get the uncut stuff straight from the source, you want another fix as soon as you can get it. This is a book for everybody who went to see a film like *Crouching Tiger, Hidden Dragon* and came out with their heads spinning, wondering just what it was they'd just experienced. And how they can make it happen again.

What do you mean by "Asian Action & Cult Flicks"?

One of the most frequent requests from readers of VideoHound's best-selling guide *Cult Flicks & Trash Pics* has been that we include more Asian movies in future editions. Not every film from Asia is a cult flick or a trash pic, but a vampire movie is just a bit more exotic when it comes from Hong Kong. Don't think so? Then check out some of the vampire movies in this book.

When Visible Ink Press first proposed I write this book, it was to be just about Hong Kong action films. But the more I thought about it, the more sure I was that we'd need to expand the scope. Not that there isn't enough material—there are more titles from Hong Kong represented here than any other country, with more being released on video every week. But too many titles were co-produced with Japan or filmed in Thailand but financed by Korea—it just became too restrictive. And so, movies from all Asian countries have been accepted. The "action & cult flicks" label is a bit harder to explain—perhaps you'll have a better idea after you read the book. (You ARE going to read it, aren't you? You didn't buy it just to read this intro, did you?) We've also included selected reviews of films made by American studios with Asian stars, just so you know what they're up to when they come to visit.

Why is *X* included but *Y* is not?

Well the short and snarky answer is that there is a movie named *X* (look for it under, um, *X*) but there isn't one named *Y.*

The more complex answer is that certain criteria were enforced for inclusion in this volume. One was that the film had to be made in an Asian country (see list in the "Anatomy of an Entry" on p. xxviii). The film also had to be available on home video to viewers in the U.S. and Canada, either in English dubbed form or with English subtitles, in a format compatible with typical U.S. equipment (VHS tape or Region 1/0 DVD). Initially, it was thought that this only meant films available from U.S. video distributors, but the world is getting much more accessible to each of us every day. Region-free DVDs from Asian countries are easily available via the Internet from a variety of sources, and are sometimes much cheaper and more complete than the U.S. releases. We even found that while some Asian DVDs are marked Region 3 on the packaging, they don't bother adding the region codes to the actual disc.

There are also some exceptions in the book I call "crystal ball entries"—movies not yet available according to the above categories, but likely to be soon. When the reviews of the three Gamera movies made in the 1990s were written, they were unavailable, but sure enough, as I write this they've been announced and will likely be for sale before the book goes on sale. There are also titles that will be available the day after I write this that I would've liked to include, but didn't know about them.

Another reason is that the reviews were written based on the availability of the films. We don't believe in reviewing movies we haven't seen, and neither should you. Certain titles that likely should be here either were not provided by their video label, or we couldn't find them in time. Some titles that you'd think you could find anywhere just happened to be absent while the book was being written, and we had to stop writing and publish the darn thing at some point!

The Name Game: Your review of *Challenge of Death* says it stars Wang Tao, but elsewhere the credits say Don Wong—what gives?

One of the biggest editorial challenges of this project has been Asian names. Jackie Chan has been known by at least 10 names in his life, and has been credited onscreen under several of them. I've seen names of Korean actors presented differently in ads, on screen, on video box copy, in reviews, and in subtitles—all for the same film! I made a list of these and showed them to a Korean restaurant manager I know to find out which is "correct." She seemed confused, too, not knowing whether to give me the surname at the end, as she thought we wanted it in the U.S., or whether it should be in the middle, as presented in Korean. I ended up keeping them close to the surname-then-hyphenated-given-name style we've used for most Chinese names—at least the *Chinese* Chinese names.

Our "rule of them" has been to decide which name is most familiar to the American audience and stick with it throughout the text, listing every alternative name we find in the Cast Index. In most cases, for Chinese names this means the English version of the name—most modern Chinese in Hong Kong choose an English given name when they reach their teens—but not always. I found many more films crediting Chan Lung than Peter Chan. Since most Japanese are known by their "reversed" (surname last) Western-style names, we've stuck with those.

One of my favorite old kung fu movies is *When Taekwondo Strikes,* but you don't have a review for it!

Yes, we do—under the title *Sting of the Dragon Masters.* Asian films, like Asian actors, are usually known by more than one name, too. In some cases, we've used the title found in the most current and well-known video release, so *Drunken Master 2* is reviewed under its U.S. release title, *Legend of the Drunken Master,* and *Fong Sai-yuk* is listed as *The Legend.* However, I refused to use the title *Legend of the Red Dragon* for a film that's been known and available in the U.S. as *New Legend of Shaolin* for years. I've also decided to list most Toho Studios monster movies under their official international titles, even though *Ebirah, Horror of the Deep* is much better known here as *Godzilla vs. the Sea Monster.* Personally, I've loved the title *Monster Zero* ever since I saw it in a theatre on a twin bill with *War of the Gargantuas,* but if Toho wants people to call the movie *Invasion of Astro Monster,* well, I bow to their efforts to simplify. Hopefully, they'll make it worthwhile some day by setting up a U.S. video label and releasing all these movies in deluxe edition DVDs (or authorizing someone else to do the job).

Why aren't there any Russian/Soviet movies included?

Russia is historically as much a part of Europe as Asia, and Russian film is more oriented toward European culture. We hope to include Russian films in a follow-up VideoHound guide to European cult flicks.

What's this I see where some entries are marked "Asians in the USA"?

Just as it was difficult to confine our subject to just one country, it's been tough to keep it contained to just Asia. When people read a book that reviews almost every Jackie Chan movie, they don't want you to ignore *The Protector.* If we got too picky, we'd have to leave out *Enter the Dragon* because it was produced by Warner Bros. We didn't go so far as to hunt down every American film with a Asian actor, and there are a few we missed that we should have included, but I think we got a nice representation of the career continuity we were looking for.

Hey, you got any cartoons in here?

Another big request we got after the first edition of *Cult Flicks* was that we include some anime titles. By definition, Japanese animation is even more important to this book. Hopefully, we'll be bringing you a whole Video-Hound title dedicated to animation soon, but in the meantime we wanted to make sure anime was represented here.

Heh. Heh. How about some porn?

Okay, so there a lot of very weird Japanese "pink" films out there in which people are having sex with robots and space monsters and stuff. We're aware of it, and we've even included some of the more interesting titles. But, geez, we want this to be a family publication, and even if you're family is less repressed than mine, we want our moms to be able to read the book, y'know?

Hey, you screwed up! I found a mistake in...

What? A "mistake"? In tihs book?

The cinema of Asia is more difficult to research than that of any other region. That's not an excuse—just a fact. Even in Hong Kong, where the film business has been healthy for over 50 years, studios did not make a practice of keeping full records on all their films. And even if they had some data, it's unlikely to have been translated into English. However, our knowledge of Asian cinema increases daily, especially with the Internet. Our best hope is that this book has collected together knowledge from many different sources, while minimizing whatever misinformation is passed on. It's hoped that an expanded and updated edition of *VideoHound's Dragon* will be available every few years, and that you'll let us know if there's a mistake we should fix or a title we should make sure we include. If you'd like to write me, I can be reached in care of the Visible Ink Press offices, or at this e-mail address: dragon@visibleink.com.

It's our sincere hope that this book causes you many sleepless nights. You know—the good kind. The kind that makes you want more.

Brian Thomas
Chicago, Illinois, USA

Acknowledgments

There are many people that made this project a whole lot easier and we want to make sure you know that by mentioning them here. I've been using the Internet Movie Database since before the first web browser was invented. It has its flaws, but one of the best things about it is that it's so malleable and can be improved so easily. It's still the largest and most useful storehouse of movie information that exists. More particularly, a thousand thanks go out Ryan Law, Dave Rolsky, Joseph Au, and all those folks around the world who contribute to the Hong Kong Movie Database, which has been another invaluable resource. I always make sure to check any Hong Kong movie information with the published work of the brilliant John Charles, either in his massive book *Hong Kong Filmography, 1977–1997,* in the pages of *Video Watchdog* (which I read religiously), or on his Hong Kong Digital website. The Japanese Horror Movie Database is another valuable resource for extra info, and I have a feeling my visits to the IndoFilms website will only become more frequent (it's not only a store, but a database of Indian movies). And I thank the good people at the Gene Siskel Film Center, whose annual Hong Kong Festival introduced me to so much.

More resources are listed in the back pages in the "Dragon Connections." The following have provided screeners and help throughout the course of this project, for which we are humbly thankful: James Veronico and Crash Cinema; Kavita Smith, John Singh, and Columbia/Tristar Home Entertainment; Spencer Savage and Image Entertainment; Rod Peters and ADV Films; Anita Thomas and AnimEigo; Amalia McPartlon, Danny Duran, and Buena Vista Home Entertainment; Lisa Petrucci, Mike Vraney, and Something Weird Video; Brentwood Home Video; Mike Mayo; Mark Lance and Ground Zero Entertainment; Manga Video; Ric Meyers; MTI Home Video; Stephen S. Biro and Unearthed Films; Don May and Synapse Films; Kent Mak; MySTies worldwide, especially Carlis; Wellspring Media; American Cinematheque; Artisan Entertainment; Central Park Media; Bandai Entertainment; Anchor Bay Entertainment; BFS Entertainment; Media Blasters; Ed Baran Public Relations; Right Stuf International; New Line Home Video; and last but far from least, Jon Soo, Frank Djeng, and Tai Seng Video, who provided DVDs beyond the call of duty.

Contributors

Author

Although some may argue the point, it's been said that Brian Thomas was conceived (if not born) at the drive-in, most likely during a double feature of *Attack of the Giant Leeches* and *A Bucket of Blood.* His first exposure to Asian cinema was watching the *Astro Boy* TV series, after which he was caught sketching a portrait of the robot hero—on a coffee table in red crayon. His first exposure to an Asian feature film was catching the last half of *Mothra vs. Godzilla* (playing as *Godzilla vs. the Thing*) after school on TV. It's possible he saw Bruce Lee performing kung fu on the *Green Hornet* show the same week. While becoming secretly famous drawing and writing hundreds of comic books—including *Teenage Mutant Ninja Turtles, Speed Racer,* and *Astro Boy*—he was privy to the pop culture hotline available to those in the field, sampling imported bootlegs of animation, gory horror films and martial arts action thrillers from the Far East, often hunting down videos in the backs of Chinatown dress shops and upstairs from sushi restaurants. He is a founding member of the Psychotronic Film Society [www.psychotronic.com], in which he still participates as House Critic and Propaganda Minister of the Sinister. As a writer and columnist, he has contributed to many print and online film journals, including *Cinescape* [www.cinescape.com] and *Video Watchdog,* as well as VideoHound's *Cult Flicks & Trash Pics, DVD Guide,* and *Sci-Fi Experience.* He has also contributed to the cult hit mutant TV talk show *Abductions with the Alter Boy* as a writer and actor. Brian Thomas currently resides in his hometown, Chicago, Illinois. In the zoo.

No great sin is committed alone—one needs collaborators! Aiding and abetting the author in his crime were the following individuals, who should share in the punishment:

Co-editor

As a child, **Carol Schwartz** had a crush on Speed Racer and flat-out wanted to marry Kimba the White Lion. Carol grew up, appeared in a few indie film efforts, and then compiled *VideoHound's Cult Flicks & Trash Pics* [www.cultflicksandtrashpics.com], through which she met the new love of her life, Jimmy O (see below), at—appropriately—a video store. Carol also edited *VideoHound's Sci-Fi Experience,* and has managed several other *VideoHound* books on horror movies, direct-to-video features, indie film, and DVDs, as well as other reference books on unrelated and uninteresting topics.

Contributing Writers

Jeff Bond (JB) is executive editor of *Cinefantastique* and *Femmes Fatales* magazines, senior editor of *Film Score Monthly* magazine, and a contributor to *The Hollywood Reporter, Cinescape, Star Trek Communicator,* and *Pulse.* He is the author of *The Music of Star Trek* and has written liner notes for soundtrack album CDs from Capitol/EMI and Varese Sarabande Records. He resides in Burbank, California.

Jason Henderson (JH) [www.jasonhenderson.com] has written several novels, including *The Incredible Hulk: Abominations, X-Men & Spider-Man: Time's Arrow, The Iron Thane,* and *The Spawn of Loki.* He's the screenwriter and writer for the national #1-selling games *Command & Conquer: Red Alert 2* and *Command & Conquer: Renegade.* In comics, Jason has written for *Vampire: The Masquerade* and is the creator of the "Hard-edged Horror" series *Sword of Dracula* [www.swordofdracula.com]. He's written extensively on horror and Asian cinema and uses their influence in all his work.

As a child, **Peter A. Martin** (PM) was captivated by Bruce Lee in *The Green Hornet* and by Godzilla and Rodan in Japanese monster movies. As a teenager, he was hooked by martial arts movies on Saturday afternoon television. As an adult, he was thrilled by the action and artistry of Jackie Chan, John Woo, and Wong Kar-Wai. One great film led to another, and soon he found himself happily buried in videos and DVDs from all corners of Asia. He created A Better Tomorrow [www.abtdvd.com], a web site devoted to news and reviews about the Hong Kong film industry, in August 2000. Peter started writing "Hollywood to Hong Kong Express," a weekly movie column, for Mobius Home Video Forum [www.mhvf.net], in September 2002. His preferred method of supporting his addiction to movies is by writing about them, though he also works as an editor and researcher in the technology field [www.peteramartin.com]. He is based in Los Angeles, California.

Jim Olenski (JO) owns the coolest video store in the world, Thomas Video & DVD [www.thomasvideo.com], in Clawson, Michigan, a fabulous enterprise that specializes in hard-to-find, cult, foreign, indie, anime, and classic film. Jim is a frequent contributor to *VideoHound* books, and has penned liner notes for several Anchor Bay DVDs. Jim's pseudo-elite and sometimes abrasive critical style spawned from the same punk ethic demonstrated in his 25 years as lead guitarist for Detroit's oldest yet least mature punk band, Cynecide.

Stephen D. Sullivan (SS) is the Origins Award–winning author of *The Lion* as well as two other samurai fantasy books in the *Legend of the Five Rings*

series: *The Scorpion* and *The Phoenix*. He's also written a huge number of comic books over the years, including working on *Speed Racer, Teenage Mutant Ninja Turtles,* and *Astro Boy* with artist/author Brian Thomas. Steve has also worked on many non-oriental projects, including a long stint contributing to *Dungeons & Dragons* and other role-playing games. He's also ghost written nine detective novels for children (probably ten by the time you read this). Steve's most recent projects include the novel *Dragonlance Crossroads: The Dragon Isles,* and a story in the 2002 *Simpsons Treehouse of Horrors* comic. He's also written a *Magic: The Gathering* short story ("The Crucible") for the *Monsters of Magic* anthology. Don't tell anyone, but it's really a Godzilla tale in disguise. (Steve's always wanted to write a Godzilla story but hasn't been able to talk anyone into letting him do it yet.) Steve is proud of his contributions to this book, and wants everyone to know that writing a big bunch of movie reviews is—as Brian told him at the outset—not as easy as one would think. More information on what Steve's been up to lately can be found at www.sdsullivan.com or www.alliterates.com.

Bill White (BW) was a contributing editor for *Video Eyeball* in the mid-90s. Among his other credits are pieces for *Boston Rock, Eye Magazine, Musicomet,* and *Earshot Jazz*; as well as several entries in *Videohound's Cult Flicks & Trash Pics.* He currently is a regular contributor to the Seattle *Post-Intelligencer*'s arts section, reviewing music, theatre, and film. He is also seeking a publisher for his first novel, *Blinkers.*

And also:

Mary Claire Krzewinski, Jeff Muhr, Susan Salter, Bob Huffman, Jeff Hermann, Melissa Hill, and **Christine Slovey.**

Glossary

action director (also **action coordinator, stunt director**) person responsible for stunts, fights, and other action scenes—which sometimes is most of the film!

Beggar So famous Drunken Master hero, head of Beggar's Guild, and member of Ten Tigers of Kwangtung

Bollywood Indian film industry

Cantonese modern, flexible Chinese dialect

Canto-pop Hong Kong pop music, much like American "bubble gum"

Category III for persons aged 18 or above only (similar to U.S. "NC-17")

Category IIB suitable for young persons and children (similar to U.S. "R")

CGI computer-generated imagery

chambara historical Japanese action film; the word comes from the sound of striking weapons

CID Central Intelligence Division (detective arm of Hong Kong Police)

congee rice porridge dish

daikaiju giant monster

dojo martial arts training school/gymnasium

feng shui fortune-telling and superstition based on position of objects and elements

fever HK slang for wild sex

Fong Sai-yuk famous folk hero, member of Ten Tigers of Kwangtung, and mama's boy

14K powerful Hong Kong triad society

Girls with Guns action movie subgenre featuring strong modern females kicking butt

glossary a list of often difficult or specialized words with their definitions

Golden Triangle Vietnam, Cambodia, and Thailand, in reference to production of opium and other drugs

gweilo (also **kwei-lo, gwailo**) "white devil"—a sometimes derogatory term for Westerners

Heisei "the achievement of complete peace on earth and in the heavens"—refers to the reign of Emperor Akihito (and film series entries during same), beginning in 1989 (see also **Shinsei** and **Showa**)

Hentai Japanese for "pervert," the term has come to refer to adults-only anime by American fans

hex errors computer programming term applied by writer Stefan Hammond to amusing mistranslations in film subtitles; with generally more careful subtitling on DVDs, you don't see them as much, though they still occur

Hongkie Hong Kong native

Hong Kong "fragrant harbor" island nation in possession of British for 100 years

I.C.A.C. Independent Commission Against Corruption (HK government anti-bribery department)

kaiju monster (Japanese)

katana a samurai's main weapon, a sword distinguished by its extremely sharp edge and slightly curved blade

Kowloon "9 dragons"—peninsula across bay from Hong Kong island known for its casinos

kowtow showing deference and respect, specifically via bowing

kumite martial arts fighting tournament

kyonsi (also **gyonsi**) Chinese vampire (see sidebar on p. 428)

Manchu invaders who overthrew the Ming Dynasty and established the Ching

Mandarin dominant Chinese dialect

mo lai tau "nine follows eight, but nine doesn't have anything to do with eight"—nonsense comedy style commonly practiced by Stephen Chow

Mongkok busy, turbulent district of Kowloon

1997 year of Britain's handover of Hong Kong to China

nokuta! "Fight!" (something to shout at sumo matches)

nunchakus Japanese weapon: two hardwood sticks joined by a chain or cord, possibly originated in Taiwan, where they were adapted from a farm tool

OAV (OVA) Original Anime Video

OCTB Organized Crime & Triad Bureau of the HK Police

old school traditional kung fu movies

otaku obsessed fan, usually associated with anime

pinku eiga "pink movie"—Japanese pornographic films

Portland Street area of Kowloon known for prostitution

queue "pigtail" hairstyle required during Ching Dynasty

RHKP Royal Hong Kong Police

rickshaw two-wheeled taxi cart pulled by human

ronin samurai without a master

ryu (also **ryo**) archaic Japanese currency unit, worth 4,000 mon or 4 kan, or about 6.5 ounces of gold

SDU Special Duty Unit (a section of the Hong Kong Police Tactical Unit, roughly equivalent to U.S. SWAT). Established in 1974 with only 30 members, at first duties were mainly to counter terrorist activities and provide VIP protection, has become more involved in providing service on criminal cases.

sensei "master" (Japanese)

Shaolin ancient Chinese Buddhist clerical order dating from seventh century, often considered the heart of kung fu development

Shinsei era following end of Heisei in 1998

Showa era preceding Heisei

shuriken "dagger hidden in palm"—a small throwing blade, most often star shaped, associated with ninjas

sifu "master" (Chinese)

suit-mation monster roles performed by a man in a suit, as opposed to animation or CGI

taekwondo (also **tae kwon do**) "trample fist way"—Korean martial arts style similar to karate

tonfa straight club/baton with a perpendicular handle near one end, adapted by Japanese workers from machine crank into weapon, now common to police officers

triad Chinese "secret" societies, often engaged in criminal activity

TVB Television Broadcasting Limited (HK channel owned by Shaw Bros.)

wirework stunts aided by wire-hoisted actors (also **wire fu**)

wu shu generic term for Chinese martial arts, usually referring to demonstration

Wu Tang a clan of Buddhist monks, usually portrayed as specializing in swordsmanship and rivals/enemies of the Shaolin Temple

wuxia Chinese swordplay genre, or hero of same

yakuza Japanese organized crime, or member of same

Anatomy of an Entry

Alphabetization

Titles are arranged on a word-by-word basis, including articles and prepositions, but ignoring punctuation marks such as colons and commas. Leading articles (A, An, The) are ignored in English-language titles. The equivalent foreign articles are not ignored (because so many people—not you, of course—don't recognize them as articles) Acronyms appear alphabetically as if regular words; for example, *I.K.U.* is alphabetized as "IKU," and *A*P*E* can be found as "APE." Common abbreviations in titles file as if they were spelled out, so *Mr. Vampire* will be alphabetized as "Mister Vampire." Movie titles with numbers, such as *36 Crazy Fists,* are alphabetized as if the number were spelled out—so this early stunt job by Jackie Chan would appear in the Ts as if it were "Thirty-Six Crazy Fists."

Bone Ratings

Movies are rated by the Hound's patented bone rating system. In this book, "good" movies are either 1) good, or 2) so bad they're good, or 3) cult classics.

🦴🦴🦴🦴	The best of the best, as well as the best of the beasts
🦴🦴🦴	Worthy efforts, high in artistic merit and *demerit*
🦴🦴	More mundane mongrel movies
🦴	Dime-a-dozen trash flicks
WOOF!	Not worth *anyone*'s time

Country of Origin Codes

The country of origin codes indicate the country or countries in which a film was produced or financed. A listing of films by country may also be found in the **Category Index** under the appropriate term below.

CB	Cambodia
CA	Canada
CH	China
FR	France
HK	Hong Kong
IN	India
IT	Italy
JP	Japan
KO	Korea
PH	Philippines
RU	Russia
TW	Taiwan
TH	Thailand
UK	United Kingdom
US	United States
VN	Vietnam

Anatomy of an Entry

Sample Review

Each review contains up to 15 tidbits of information, as enumerated below. Please realize that we faked a bit of info in this review for demonstration purposes.

1. The label "asians in usa" indicates films made in the United States, but featuring Asian stars.
2. Title (see also #4 below)
3. The TV icon appearing after a title means that the video comprises one or more episodes from a TV series.
4. Our DragonHound girl denotes anime features.
5. Synopsis/review
6. Byline of reviewer; see **Contributors**, p. xxi
7. Alternative titles—we've listed all the alternate titles we could find, including the original language titles. An easy look-up Alternative Titles Index is located in the back of the book.
8. Critical rating of the movie (𝄫 to 𝄫𝄫𝄫𝄫, or **WOOFI**, 𝄫𝄫𝄫𝄫 being the ultimate praise)
9. Year movie was released
10. MPAA rating (if any)
11. Length in minutes
12. Black and white (BW) or color (C)
13. Country of origin; see previous page
14. Credits, including cast, voice cast (V), narrator (N), director (D), screenwriter (W), cinematographer (C), and music composer/lyricist (M).
15. Video formats (VHS and/or DVD)

---

①
asians in usa

②
The Big Heat 📺 **③**

④ **⑤** Tough Hong Kong copper John Wong Wai-pong (Waise Lee) learns that nerve damage is affecting his gun hand. He's about to turn in his resignation from the force, when his chief (Ken Boyle) tells him that his former partner Skinny Tse has been murdered in Malaysia by triad boss Han Ching (Paul Chu). He delays his resignation, and his wedding, to take on the case, bringing clumsy rookie Lun Kwok-keung (Matthew Wong) to work with his assistant Tangerine Kam (Phillip Kwok). Tse was killed trying to blackmail Han and shipping company president Ho Ka-nin (Stuart Ong), and copies he made of incriminating evidence are found in his bag. Han, who is blackmailing Ho himself, turns the tables on the cops by sending hit men (including Michael Chow) after Wong and his team, while using his influence to stymie their investigation. Playing rough, Wong uses some illegal tactics to get Ho to testify. However, Han's thugs invade the hospital and go all out to kill Ho.

From the opening shot of a drill bit going through a man's hand, you know this is one hard-edged police thriller, which combines illustration of straightforward police procedures with gory violence. Thugs don't just get shot in this movie—they get their hands blown off and then get run over by trucks. One expects Danny Lee to pop up in every other scene. Paul Chu plays one of the most relentlessly evil drug lords in movie history. This may contain the first use of the "shoot the hostage in the leg" technique on film. Not surprisingly, action director Phillip Kwok takes on a lot of the rough-and-tumble stuff himself. **⑥** —MM **AKA:** **⑦** *Sing Si Dak Ging; Cheng Shi Te Jing.* **⑧** 𝄫𝄫𝄫𝄫

⑨ 1988 **⑩** (R) **⑪** 105m **⑫** C **⑬** HK **⑭** Waise Lee, Joey Wong, Phillip Kwok, Paul Chu, Stuart Ong, Peter Lai, Matthew Wong, Roy Cheung, Michael Chow, Robin Shou, Ken Boyle, Che-kirk Wong, Aaron Kwok; **D:** Andrew Kam, Johnny To; **W:** Gordon Chan; **C:** Horace Wong; **M:** Lo Tai-yu. **⑮** **VHS, DVD**

Aakhri Adalat

The crime kingpins of Bombay are up in arms, as a stranger in black—with motorcycle helmet to match—has been killing their men. What's more, dynamic police inspector Amar Kaushal (Vinod Khanna) seems to know their every move. When boss Bansi goes to make a cocaine sale, Kaushal is there to bust him. However, Bansi gets off on a technicality, leading the frustrated Kaushal to declare that someday a fanatic will kill such men. As if on cue, the Black Biker appears soon after to shoot Bansi dead. Frustrating Kaushal further in his investigation is the assignment of his new assistant, accident-prone sub-inspector Reema Kapoor (former child star Dimple Kapadia). Also on the trail of the killer is intrepid reporter Nitin Sinha (Jackie Shroff), who is similarly hampered in his efforts by his clingy girlfriend Nisha (Sonam).

When known syndicate hit man Raghu and mobster Bosco Gonsalves are acquitted in court, the killer strikes again, always one step ahead of police. Both murders were witnessed by nightclub singer Rita Chowdhary, and the remaining two mob bosses interrogate her, but boss Girja Shivsaran (Gulshan Grover) goes too far and drowns the woman. However, when her body is found, clutched in her hand is a gold chain with Shivsaran's name on it. While Kaushal is out arresting Shivsaran, Reema makes a surprising discovery in her boss's closet.

A typical Bollywood mixture of action, drama, suspense, and musical numbers from the Mehra brothers, *Aakhri Adalat* gives us car chases, fistfights, courtroom theatrics, and slapstick comedy. Both macho heroes, it should be noted, live with their mothers. When it becomes obvious that officers Kaushal and Kapoor share an attraction, in no time at all Kaushal's mom is contacting Reema's relatives to plan the engagement party. The action scenes are all pretty ham-fisted, with obvious stunt doubles and sloppy editing. An early sequence is copied directly from Jackie Chan's bus scene in *Police Story*. Still, the filmmaker's relentless efforts to entertain overcome all obstacles, keeping the show going throughout its long running time. *AKA: The Last Judgment.* 🐉🐉

1988 160m/C IN Vinod Khanna, Dimple Kapadia, Jackie Shroff, Sonam, Vinod Mehra, Shafi Inamdar, Gulshan Grover, Roopesh Kumar, Amrit Pal, Sharat Saxena, Mahaveer Shah, Seema Deo, Sushma Seth, Paresh Rawal. **D:** Rajiv Mehra. **W:** Ravi Kapoor, Javed Siddique, Mohan Kaul (story). **C:** S.M. Anwar. **M:** Anu Malik. **DVD**

Abbot White

Little student Mo-fat goes to clean in the forbidden top floor of the Shaolin Holy Tower (played by the famous Chung Hsing Tower, often seen in movies lensed in Taiwan), and carelessly sets free the demon Devil Claw Yu Kin-san, who has been imprisoned in a trunk for 30 years. Taking possession of the little monk, his first act is to toss a fellow student off of the tower, and soon after runs away from the temple. He grows to manhood studying Demon Kung Fu in solitude. On a return visit, one touch from Mo-fat (Kwan Chung) is enough to kill the old abbot. The Devil Claw, dressed in white robes, becomes a suspect in several murders in the area. Chi-ying,

Wong-fong, and other fighters from the Tai Chi Academy form patrols for the killer, but find his supernatural martial arts make his skin impervious to swords, and even their sifu is no match for his Demon Kung Fu. Master Yu Tin-shou (Cheung Fong-ha), Devil Claw's brother, is suspected of participating in the crimes, and reports of an assassin give Officer Ling-si an excuse to search the house. Because she fancies him, daughter Lin Tsiu-fun (Pan Yingzi) hides the intruder named Tin-chun, putting him up in the bedroom of servant Chen-yi. Finding the rumors of Yu's guilt false, the stranger leaves, but Tsiu-fun follows him. His sister Si Shou-chi (Lee Siu-Kei) and hunchback Uncle Chan (Frank Wong) are also searching for him. (This heroic brother disappears from the film completely, said to have died in an offscreen duel!) All the various fighters band together against their evil adversary.

For most of the film, Devil Claw stalks around like Dracula, killing old foes like Ching-wan Golden Crown and raping virgins. However, sometimes his early Buddhist values come through—when he sees a special pendant that Shou-chi wears, the possession leaves Mo-fat with no memory of his other identity. During one

of these periods, he rescues her from thugs of the Mountain Yellow Gang, and she finds herself defending the suspect from his attackers. Kwan Chung *(Shaolin Disciple)* is only partially effective at portraying this Jekyll/Hyde character. He's great as the evil master, but since Mo-fat has no memory of growing up, shouldn't he think more like a kid? Or are they representing him as the man he would have become? Though too much time is spent on various subplots, once the action gets going, all is forgiven. In addition to the fine choreography and athleticism on display, many of the fighters are given amusing special gimmicks. Not only does the hunchback have the usual "Iron Hump," but he can launch it at enemies like a yo-yo. Devil Claw's powers include intangibility and invisibility, which he uses only to amuse himself, since his strength and skill are enough to lay waste to most of the cast.

This rare Taiwanese flick recently resurfaced after 20 years in a dubbed version. All the dubbing actors speak heavily accented English, and it's difficult to understand them. It's also difficult to understand what market the dub was intended for, though it has the effect of making it appear that the actors dubbed their own voices. The sound is very uneven, and sometimes the

Chinese dialogue bleeds through the mix, while obscuring some sound effects. Some of the music cues were taken from the *Planet of the Apes* soundtrack. **AKA:** *Shaolin Legend.* ♪♪♪▽

1982 88m/C *TW* Kwan Chung, Cheung Fong-ha, Lee Siu-Kei, Pan Yingzi, Frank Wong, Chen Hung Lieh, Chui Chung Hei. **VHS, DVD**

The Accidental Spy

The plot of this Jackie Chan adventure bears some resemblance to such Hitchcock thrillers as *North by Northwest* and *Saboteur,* in which an innocent is drawn by chance into a perilous web of intrigue. Jackie is Buck Yuen, an exercise equipment salesman at a Hong Kong mall. On his lunch hour, he gets caught in the middle of a bank robbery; in trying to help, he ends up fleeing with the loot, with both the crooks and the cops after him. Yuen ends up climbing across a construction crane—which is sent crashing *through* a building. He becomes a bit of a celebrity for his daring, drawing the attention of a strange little detective named Many Liu (Eric Tsang), who is seeking out orphan men born in 1958 for a client (which *should* leave out Chan by a good four years!). The client firm is trying to find the heir of a dying Korean man, and Yuen is sent to Seoul as one of the finalists.

While there, he finds out from American reporter Carmen Wong (Kim Min-jeong) that his father Park Won-jung was a notorious North Korean spy in the 1950s who defected to work for the South. (Some of the basics of the plot could have been taken from Chan's own life. In recent years he's learned of how his parents met while fleeing the Communist takeover after World War II, each leaving behind previous marriages and children whom Jackie knew nothing about.) Among the small inheritance left to Yuen is a mysterious key. However, others seem to be after the key, and Yuen often finds himself fighting for his life (fortunately, he studied kung fu at the orphanage). A clue left at his mother's grave leads him to the Istanbul Bank, where the key opens a safe deposit box holding a pile of cash and a miniature Bible. But the mysterious thugs continue to pursue him. In one of Chan's most daring (if not dangerous) stunt sequences, he flees attackers in a Turkish bath, only to lose his towel. While fighting through a street market, each time he grabs an item to cover himself he somehow loses it, falling through baskets of spices and other hazards.

Carmen introduces him to CIA agent Phillip Ashley (Tony Jones), who says a certain Mr. Zen (Wu Hsing-kuo), AKA "The Fixer," is behind the men who are after him. Zen is also the boss of Yong (Vivian Hsu), a bewitching young lady Yuen met the day before. They believe Yuen holds the

recipe for a new super-virus known as Anthrax II, and the CIA wants to use him to catch Zen and retrieve the hidden virus. Yuen finds the virus, but uses it to trade for the drug-enslaved Yong's freedom. But Yong dies of an overdose soon afterward, and Yuen decides to try to retrieve the virus and even the score.

Jackie Chan here deviates slightly from his usual straight-arrow screen persona, delighting in his inherited wealth and dealing drugs to arms dealers. It's refreshing to see some flaws in his character now and then. Some of the action scenes reprise elements Chan has used before, but he comes up with some ingenious twists on them, while creating some fresh new stunts never before attempted. However, much like *Crime Story,* this is one of those rare outings for Chan in which action takes a backseat to intrigue and drama—at least until the fantastic thrill-packed climax, which features a plane crash, a car/motorcycle chase, Chan fighting JC Action Team member Brad Allan all over a speeding convertible, and a variation on *Speed* involving an ignited gas tanker. This last gives us Chan leaping off the truck and onto a car while both vehicles are moving (and while carrying a real kid!), with the whole sequence engineered by stunt-driving expert Jean-Claude Lagniez *(Ronin).*

The U.S. version changes the lead character's name to "Jackie Chan," and Zen is given a more believable translation, becoming "Lee Tsung-jan," who is now after a super-opium recipe rather than the more topical anthrax. Some scenes have been cut or rearranged slightly, and about 20 minutes of footage has been cut to quicken the pace, sacrificing suspense and flavor. In either version, it makes absolutely no sense for Chan to become involved in the main plot, since he really has nothing to do with it. But both versions are highly entertaining, above any of Chan's recent Hong Kong films. **AKA:** *Te Wu Mi Cheng; Tak Mo Mai Sing.* ♪♪♪▽

2001 (PG-13) 108/87m/C *HK* Jackie Chan, Eric Tsang, Vivian Hsu, Kim Min-jeong, Wu Hsing-kuo, Tony Jones, Brad Allan, Alfred Cheung, Lillian Ho, Cheung Tat-Ming, Vincent Kok, Fletcher Poon, Paulyn Sun, Ha Ping, Ken Chang, Eric Lee, Glory Simon, Scott Adkins. **D:** Teddy Chan. **W:** Ivy Ho. **C:** Horace Wong. **M:** Peter Kam, Michael Wandmacher (U.S.). **VHS, DVD**

Aces Go Places

Sam Hui had always been the Zeppo of the Hui Brothers comedies. He didn't have a hilarious comic character like his brothers, but he was athletic and good-looking, and had a fine singing voice (with many hit records to show for it). Former New York electrical engineer Karl Maka studied film at New York University, and was assistant director on *Goldfinger*. Returning to Hong Kong, he was very busy throughout the 1970s as director and producer, but as an actor, he was cast only in comic character roles. When Maka formed Cinema City Productions with Raymond Wong and Dean Shek in 1980, both he and Hui found breakout roles in this lively action comedy vehicle.

The plot is very similar to that of the British comedy *Get Charlie Tully* (AKA *Ooh, You Are Awful*) starring Dick Emery. At a triad meeting in a Hong Kong skyscraper, a deal between mobsters Szeto (Gam Biu) and Monterosso for a fortune in diamonds is interrupted by internationally infamous thief King Kong (Sam Hui), who swipes the gems and leaves behind his white-glove calling card. Aided by his bumbling mechanic Gigolo Joe (Dean Shek), he makes a daring escape via motorcycle and glider. Since Peter Sellers isn't available (!), Sergeant Albert Au, AKA Kodojak (Karl Maka), is given three months to catch White Glove, or face dismissal from the force. Tough cop Superintendent Ho (Sylvia Chang) and her assistant Danny Chan are assigned to keep an eye on him. Squealie Ming (Hon Gwok-choi) identifies King Kong as their culprit, but also looking for the diamond thief is a suave Mafia burglar—who wears white gloves. Joe hides the diamonds, but is killed by thug Mad Max (Chan Sing) before he can tell King Kong where. Put in a fix, Kong is forced to cooperate with the cops to find the girls Joe had clues tattooed on and recover the loot. Merry mix-ups, car chases, stunts, gunfights, and fisticuffs ensue.

With four cinematographers, it's not exactly a consistent visual masterpiece, but some of the stunts are still impressive, and the stars' personalities make the corny gags work. A gigantic hit in Asia, *Aces* failed to capture the Western audience it was hoping for, but spawned several sequels. Maka tied with Sammo Hung for Best Actor in the Hong Kong Film Awards. *AKA: Jui Gaai Paak Dong; Zui Jia Pai Dang; Mad Mission; Diamondfinger.* ♫♫♫

1982 93m/C *HK* Sam Hui, Karl Maka, Dean Shek, Sylvia Chang, Chan Sing, Tsui Hark, Walter Cho, Lindsay Chan, Raymond Wong, George Lam, Carroll Gordon, Gam Biu, Hon Gwok-choi, Ho Pak Kwong. **D:** Eric Tsang. **W:** Raymond Wong, Wellington Fung Wing. **C:** Yip Pak-ying, Ho Ming, Arthur Wong, Chow Kin-ming. **M:** Sam Hui, Teddy Robin Kwan. **VHS, DVD**

Aces Go Places 2

In the opening 10 minutes of this sequel, reformed master thief King Kong (Sam Hui) is attacked by a big black robot, shot at by hit man Black Gloves, and chased around Hong Kong by a motorcycle squad—all while whistling the cheerful *Aces Go Places* theme song. In New York, Mafia godfather representative Henry Kissinger hires Filthy Harry (Joe Dimmick) to go to Hong Kong to make a deal with Bull (Yasuaki Kurata), and incidentally, kill King Kong and his sometimes partner Sergeant Albert Au (Karl Maka). Meanwhile, kooky Eurasian beauty Juju tricks Kong into unknowingly helping her rob a bank. But Albert is in real trouble: he's about to get married to temperamental Superintendent Nancy Ho (Sylvia Chang). Kong is able to save his pal from that fate. On a tip from Squealie (Hon Gwok-choi), they learn Juju and her brother Bull head up a new gang in town. They go after the gang, but only end up tricked into helping Juju rob a jewelry store.

The comedy is funnier and the stunts are both more plentiful and more exciting this time around, though the climax does go a little too far into cartoon territory. Kong and Au are captured by Bull's gang, and forced into going to buy diamonds from Harry (AKA Black Gloves) with time bombs strapped to their bodies. The cash they're carrying is revealed as counterfeit right off, and the exchange soon turns into a ridiculous war between robots, gadget-loaded cars, and other gimmicks. The series is at its funniest when it plays more on the characters than on gimmicks, especially from the underrated Sylvia Chang. However, a section in the middle that includes a musical interlude and more romantic comedy runs too long. A running gag with Tsui Hark as a lunatic who thinks he's an FBI man actually becomes integral to the plot. Director Eric Tsang is almost unrecognizable under a wig and false mustache. With another smash hit, the boys moved quickly on to *Part 3*. *AKA: Jui Gaai Paak Dong Daai Hin Sang Tun; Zui Jia Pai Dang Da Xian Sheng Tong; Mad Mission Part 2: Aces Go Places.* ♫♫♫

1983 102m/C *HK* Sam Hui, Karl Maka, Sylvia Chang, Tsui Hark, Yasuaki Kurata, Charlie Cho, Raymond Wong, Walter Cho, Lee Ka-ting, Eric Tsang, Billy Lau, Hon Gwok-choi, Joe Dimmick, Yip Ha-lei, Wong Jing. **D:** Eric Tsang. **W:** Raymond Wong. **C:** Abdul M. Rumjahn, Peter Ngor, Johnny Koo, Arthur Wong. **M:** Sam Hui, Teddy Robin Kwan, Ha On Chia. **VHS, DVD**

Aces Go Places 3

The third entry in the series is the most ambitious yet, this time going all-out (or as all-out as they could on a Hong Kong budget) as a spy movie spoof. While girl-watching in Paris, King Kong (Sam Hui) becomes the target of a beautiful female assassin. Chasing her up the Eiffel Tower, he's attacked by Odd Job (Tsunehara Sogiyama) and Jaws (Richard Kiel). He escapes, but is captured by a giant mechanical shark captained by superspy Mr. Bond (Sean

Connery look-alike Jean Marchent). Bond tells him that the Royal Crown Jewels have been stolen and traced to Hong Kong, and the queen needs him to covertly steal them back before there's a scandal. To help out Her Majesty (Huguette Funfrock)—and the gorgeous Agent 701 (Naomi Otsubo) sent to assist him—Kong agrees to come out of retirement. However, the jewel he's supposed to steal happens to be in the vault underneath police headquarters, meaning he has to make sure his old pal Albert Au (Karl Maka) isn't implicated, and provides him with an alibi as well. While 701 distracts Albert with her charms, Kong uses his inventions to pull off the heist, escaping on a motorized skateboard. Though Albert suspects him, Kong and a squad of flying Santas provide a diversion while 701 steals the final jewel. After a wild chase, Albert arrests Kong, but they both find out that Bond isn't who he says he is, and Kong has been fooled into the thefts. The Man from Bond Street (Peter Graves) arrives to fill them in and send them on an impossible mission to intercept the sale of the crown to a mad Arab sheik.

Some may find the domestic comedy antics of Albert and Nancy Ho (Sylvia Chang) a distraction, but they give the series heart and bring the characters down to earth amid the action and special effects. Those effects are occasionally hokey, but imaginative and enjoyable nonetheless. There are plenty of the series' trademark goofy gadgets, vehicle stunts, and guest stars. Albert and Nancy's bouncing bald baby Junior could have been a disastrously cute addition, but enough sour is put in with the sweet to make the little devil amusing, even spoofing how kids like him are added to such successful series. Plus, he's not spared the stunts, getting tossed around by friend and foe alike, and even accidentally shooting a gun in one scene. And yes, the catchy whistling Aces theme song is much in evidence. *AKA: Jui Gaai Paak Dong Lui Wong Mat Lim; Zui Jai Pai Dang Nu Huang Mi Ling; Mad Mission Part III: Our Man from Bond Street.* 🐶🐶🐶

1984 95m/C *HK* Sam Hui, Karl Maka, Sylvia Chang, Jean Marchent, Naomi Otsubo, Richard Kiel, Ricky Hui, Walter Cho, Charlie Cho, John Sham, Peter Graves, Lowell Lo, Tsui Hark, Tsunehara Sogiyama, Huguette Funfrock. *D:* Tsui Hark. *W:* Raymond Wong. *C:* Bill Wong, Yiu Yau-hung. *M:* Noel Quinlan. **VHS, DVD**

Aces Go Places 4

While the third entry in the series spoofed spy films, this one takes on *Raiders of the Lost Ark* in that the action rarely stops, and they even

cast Ronald Lacey in essentially the same villainous role. In New Zealand, King Kong (Sam Hui) volunteers to be the guinea pig in an experiment using a special prism for electronic hypnosis, the aim being to unlock the subject's brain to make him superhuman. A squad of killers attacks the lab, intent on stealing the prism. Kong and Sally (Sally Yeh), the daughter of the professor in charge (Roy Chiao), escape with the prism, while the thieves get away with the professor's notes. After one of the series' best chase scenes (featuring an exploding helicopter—always a good thing in action movies), they both make their way to Hong Kong, where Detective Au (Karl Maka) is playing in a hockey match (!) between the HK Police and Interpol (!!).

The Interpol team is coached by Shih Kien (Han from *Enter the Dragon*), while the cops' coach is none other than Kwan Tak-hing, from the classic Wong Fei-hung movies! Kong arrives to get in on the game, after which Albert escapes from the attacking thugs with the prism. Having identified Albert, the bad guys kidnap his wife Nancy Ho (Sylvia Chang) and try to get his son, little Baldy Jr. (who has plenty of toy guns, and is involved in some stunts that would make Jackie Chan cringe). Kong, Albert, and Junior go to New Zealand to save Nancy (unaccountably called "Sylvia" in the subtitles). Upon arrival, Albert and Junior are captured, along with the prism, leaving it up to Kong and his new girlfriend to rescue everyone from the headquarters of the purple-uniformed bad guys (who fly the Canadian flag). But first, they get captured themselves, and the villains use the prism to transform Albert into a super-strong monster.

The Professor uses his dying breath to betroth Sally to Kong, adding an extra angle to this entry's romantic comedy element. The stunts are terrific, more impressive than the previous films' reliance on mediocre special effects, since King Kong is kept away from his beloved gadgets. Included is a roof-to-roof car jump that ends in the kitchen of a restaurant, a plane crash-landing into a bus, and an extended burn scene performed by Karl Maka. What f/x there are, are much better than before. Sam Hui even gets into some good martial arts battles. Ringo Lam likes to say he directed this as a returned favor to Cinema City for giving him his first directing job, but he really has nothing to be ashamed of with this entertaining show. *AKA: Jui Gaai Paak Dong Chin Lee Gau Cha Poh; Zui Jai Pai Dang Qian Li Jiu Cha Po; Mad Mission IV: You Never Die Twice.* 🐶🐶🐶

1986 85m/C *HK* Sam Hui, Karl Maka, Sylvia Chang, Sally Yeh, Ricky Hui, Walter Cho, Ronald Lacey, Fung Ging Man, Roy Chiao, Shih Kien, Kwan Tak-hing. *D:* Ringo Lam. *W:* Karl Maka, Ringo Lam. *C:* Sander Lee. *M:* Tony Lo. **VHS, DVD**

Aces Go Places 5: The Terracotta Hit

The last of the real "Best Partners" adventures tries to breathe life into the series by introducing new characters and losing old ones—not *always* a bad idea. But almost always. In a village in Thailand, King Kong (Sam Hui) and Albert (Karl Maka) are hired to abduct a bride from a wedding procession, only to find out that Mr. Sombut, the man who hired them, was her fiancé in name only and she was eloping with her true love—until they interrupted. The Aces make things right, but argue over how they got into such a mess and part company. Three years later, Wong (Melvin Wong) steals the famous Terracotta Army, plus the "Chinese Excaliber" green sword, from China for his boss White Gloves (Brad Kerner, who wears a cat hand-puppet). Brother (Leslie Cheung, anticipating his role in *Once a Thief*) and Sister (Nina Li Chi) steal the sword from the thieves, while disguised as Kong and Albert.

With a national treasure rivaling the Great Wall hijacked, Chief Wah (Walter Cho) calls in the Chinese Rambo (Conan Lee) on the case. Kong is broke and using the name "Chow Wai Fatt" to hide from creditors, with only his faithful secretary Ellen (Ellen Chan) to stand by his side when Rambo attacks. Albert is in similar straits, having sent his wife and son to Canada, and is hiding out with his niece (Fennie Yuen) down by the docks. Both elude the police, but are captured by the villains, who think they have the sword. They escape and catch the new Best Partners, only to be arrested with them by the Chinese National Security Force and thrown in a mainland prison. But the prison is only a senseless ruse (complete with Danny Lee in a funny bit part as a con executed for "whoremongering") to get the four Best Partners to sign on for a mission to get the Terracotta Army back for China.

The brother-and-sister thieves are cute enough, but Sylvia Chang and Baldy Jr. are missed, and were jettisoned needlessly as a few scenes with them could have been included. As could be expected with Lau Kar-Leung directing (and action direction by brother Lau Kar-Wing), the focus of the action in this entry shifts from gadgets to the martial arts. This is emphasized by the climax, in which the heroes must do without guns so as not to damage the precious statues. The result is an entertaining sequence skewed more to series comedy. At times it seems like the plot was lifted from a straight action film and grafted onto the Aces format. The series was revived eight years later for *97 Aces Go Places* with an entirely different cast of characters. Some of Nina Li Chi's screen persona is lost on Western viewers, as much has been made of her accented Cantonese, which affected her career as a TV star before they started to play off it by casting her as foreigners (much like Michael Wong). *AKA: Sanj Jui Gaai Paak Dong; Xin Zui Jia Pai Dang; Mad Mission V.* 🐉🐉🐉

1989 98m/C *HK* Sam Hui, Karl Maka, Leslie Cheung, Nina Li Chi, Conan Lee, Ellen Chan, Melvin Wong, Roy Cheung, Danny Lee, Walter Cho, Ha Chi-chun, Deborah Grant, Fennie Yuen, Billy Chong, Maria Cordero, Mark Houghton, Brad Kerner, Montatip Keawprasert. **D:** Lau Kar-Leung. **W:** Tsang Kwok-chi. **C:** Paul Chan. **M:** Richard Lo, Teddy Robin Kwan. **VHS, DVD**

Adrenaline Drive

Meek rental-car clerk Suzuki Satoru (Masanobu Ando) bumps into Yakuza Kuroiwa's (Tutaka Matsushige) car because his boss is teasing him. Forced to go the gang's office, he's told he has to pay for the car. Just then, there's a gas explosion.

Meek nurse Sato Shizuko (Hikari Ishida of *Battle Royale*) is "too busy" studying for boyfriends. Away from the hospital on an errand, she comes to help after the explosion as paramedics arrive. When the frantic gangster crashes their ambulance, Suzuki decides to take a case full of money, and Shizuko decides to help him. The first problem is how to deal with such a load of cash, illustrated by a nice visual pun involving literal money laundering. Their second problem is that the big mean Kuroiwa survived both the explosion and the crash somehow, and though in intensive care, he suspects what the pair have done. He sends a gang of low-echelon hoods after them, and our heroes are chased all over the countryside. And wouldn't you know it, there's nothing like being on the run from a gang of crooks to make a young man and woman fall in love.

Director Shinobu Yaguchi gives his little adventure just the right understated tone, keeping things light—but not to the point of total caricature, and full of surprises. Much of the humor comes from the antics of the too-dumb thugs. Ishida is especially good as the little nurse busting loose for the first time in her life. *AKA: Adorenarin Doraibui.* 🐉🐉🐉

1999 111m/C *JP* Hikari Ishida, Masanobu Ando, Jovi Jova, Kazue Tsunogae, Kirina Mano, Yu Tokui, Kouichi Ueda, Yutaka Matsushige. **D:** Shinobu Yaguchi. **W:** Shinobu Yaguchi. **C:** Takeshi Hamada. **M:** Seichi Yamamoto, Rashinban. **VHS, DVD**

The Adventurers

With a title like this, an Indiana Jones–style action flick is expected, or at least a lot of fast-paced chases and fights, especially if you know Ringo Lam *(Full Contact)* is the director. But instead we have this relatively tame revenge saga.

In 1975, little Wai Lok-yan sees his mother and father (Phillip Ko) murdered by the traitorous Ray Lui (Paul Chun), who is looking for a certain document meant for the CIA. Uncle Shang (David Chiang) arrives too late with the army to help, and takes the orphan in. Twenty years pass, and Yan (Andy Lau) is now a jet fighter pilot in Thailand under Shang's command. Lui is a billionaire in Hong Kong, with large investments and properties all over Asia. Burning for revenge, Yan gets a gun and tries to kill Lui at a party thrown by General Buboei (William Ho). But his gun jams as he goes for the kill, and Lui escapes by hiding behind his mistress Mona (Rosamund Kwan), whom Yan had met earlier in the day.

Yan escapes with Mona's help, and Shang sends him to San Francisco, where his old friends in the CIA can use Yan in their plans to stop Lui's illegal activities. Their plan is for Yan to get close to Lui's daughter Crystal (Jacqueline Wu), posing as the grandson of Tong leader Uncle Nine (Victor Wong). Back in Hong Kong, Yan and Crystal have a huge wedding onboard one of Lui's casino ships, while Mona keeps her mouth shut about Yan, hoping he'll save her. When Buboei's son Major Bodar (John Ching) is killed in a shootout with police, Yan agrees to go with Lui to Cambodia to explain what happened, hoping to learn the location of his arms-smuggling operation. But Lui plans to use Yan as a scapegoat in Bodar's death, and it's sure that for one of them, it'll be a one-way trip.

To be sure, there's plenty of action and adventure, with big battle scenes staged on location in the Philippines and some in the U.S., along with complex situations and interesting characters. But it has none of the style and heated excitement associated with Lam's other films, lacking his usual focus and intensity. It's odd but fitting to see Asian-American actors like Victor Wong cast in the San Francisco scenes. This was Andy Lau and Jacqueline Wu's third film together—their chemistry is hard to explain, but it works. **AKA:** Dai Mak Him Ka; Da Mao Xian Jia; Great Adventurers. 🐉🐉🐉

1995 107m/C HK Andy Lau, Jacqueline Wu, Rosamund Kwan, Paul Chun, David Chiang, Ben Ng, William Ho, John Ching, Victor Wong, George Kee, Phillip Ko, Parkman Wong, Wong Kam-Kong, Lee Siu-Kei, Nam Yin. **D:** Ringo Lam. **W:** Ringo Lam, Yip Kong-yam, Sandy Shaw. **C:** Arthur Wong, Ardy Lam. **M:** Teddy Robin Kwan. **DVD**

Adventures of a Blind Man

The ninth entry in the Zatoichi series has a bit more complicated plot than most, but otherwise satisfies with the requisite mix of drama, humor, and dazzling swordplay.

On his way to Kasama for the New Year's festival, blind masseur Ichi (Shintaro Katsu) is given a note by a stranger and asked to deliver it to a maid named Sen at Musashi Inn. Ichi complies and, due to the festival crowds, is asked to share the room occupied by the maid's mistress Saki. Both ladies are in peril—Saki's father, headman of neighboring Ota village, has been causing trouble for the typically corrupt local politicos by going to Edo on a mission to petition for tax relief, but has failed to return. Sen's brother Shinzuko, who sent the note, escaped from an island prison after being convicted of murder. Behind it all is the usual scheming Boss and sinister Intendent, Jinbei and Kajime, who tricked Shinzuko into killing Saki's dad and are extorting the peasants through increased taxes and merchant fees. To help Sen get the cash Shinzuko needs, Ichi makes this episode's visit to a casino, and exposes this episode's cheating diceman. This brings him an audience with the villains, including their enforcer samurai, Gounosuke. Another bit of light-speed swordwork leaves the stinkers aghast and Gounosuke itching for a duel.

One nice touch here comes in the form of an eyeless daruma doll, a gift to Ichi that draws him closer to Saki. Another subplot introduces Ichi's notion that an old drunk named Giju may be his long-lost papa, whom he hasn't heard from since he was a child. This hope is rudely dashed when Giju betrays them all into an ambush, which leaves Shinzuko dead and Saki captured. Having had enough, Zatoichi draws his sword to bring heaven's justice to the new year. **AKA:** Zatoichi Sekishoyaburi; Blind Swordsman: Adventures of Zatoichi. 🐉🐉🐉

1964 87m/C JP Shintaro Katsu, Miwa Takada, Eiko Taki. **D:** Kimiyoshi Yasuda. **W:** Shozaburo Asai, Kan Shimozawa (story). **M:** Akira Ifukube. **VHS**

The Adventures of Milo and Otis

The cycle-of-life story of the first year of a cat and dog is told in this charming children's film from Japan. Milo is a mischievous kitten, living on a farm in an area not too far from both forest and sea. He becomes the best friend of pug puppy Otis, playing games and getting into trouble around the farm. But the word "adventures" in the title is not to be taken lightly, as our furry heroes soon get into more nasty scrapes than Indiana Jones. Milo finds himself floating down a river, with his doggy friend in dogged pursuit. The cat is swept down rapids to the sea, is adopted by a family of pigs, and survives encounters with a bear, a screech owl, a snake, and angry seagulls. Otis fights the aforementioned bear, is rescued from high tide by a sea turtle, and saves Milo from starving in a pit. Both animals struggle through hunger and harsh terrain to eventually find true love, followed by some birth footage that is not for the squeamish.

An innocuous little picture, *Milo and Otis* nevertheless scored at the boxoffice both in Japan and during an American release in 1989. The English version is narrated by Dudley Moore in the vigorous style of the best grampa in the world reading a storybook to a captive tot audience. Masanori Hata put his skills as a documentary filmmaker to work, capturing natural animal performances, while manipulating the action to fit his script. Building on the work done for Disney pictures like *The Incredible Journey*, Hata's meticulousness (filming lasted four years) pays off in a film that is an adorable fantasy throughout, but with the threatening edge of real life as a subtext. In several scenes, it appears that the animal actors are in real danger, though whether that was the case is a matter of conjecture. But Milo looks like he's in real enough pain when a crab nips his nose. *Milo and Otis* set the stage for later animal films like *The Bear* and *Babe*. *AKA: Koneko Monogatari; The Adventures of Chatran, Milo and Otis.* 🦴🦴🦴🦴🦴

1986 (G) 75m/C *JP* Milo, Otis, Gloria. **D:** Masanori Hata. **W:** Mark Saltzman, Masanori Hata (story). **C:** Hideo Fujii, Shinji Tomita. **M:** Ryuichi Sakamoto, Michael Boddicker (U.S. version). **VHS, DVD**

The Adventures of the Master and His Servant

Singapore jeweler Jia (Chen Weirong) goes on a trip to Shanghai in 1941, taking his servant San (Liu Liu) with him. The Japanese and communists both threaten to take over. Special Commissioner Long fears that Japanese intelligence will send their super-agent, The Condor, in advance to disrupt operations and gain intelligence. Because of a wager, master and servant pose as each other, and San is treated like royalty.

Jia's mission is to deliver funds to the communists. The military sends the actress Miss Luo (Yu Xiaohui) to seduce Jia (who is being impersonated by San). A cop from Singapore is after Jia, too. Miss Luo and the cop both turn out to be Japanese agents. Another agent (with a monkey) seems to be after Jia, too. They get help from pretty communist agent Xue (Pan Jie), but when the Japanese attack Pearl Harbor and invade Shanghai, pandemonium erupts. Intrigues, mix-ups, slapstick, gun battles, romance, wild kung fu, swordplay, and car chases follow. It's almost as if the Mainland Changchun Film Studio made this with the Hong Kong audience in mind, trying to look like a Tsui Hark adventure with Communist Party good guys (Tsui's *Peking Opera Blues* had communist heroes as well). Some of the action is a bit lethargic, while the later fight scenes are ridiculously undercranked and feature exaggerated wirework. 🦴🦴

1996 90m/C *CH* Chen Weirong, Liu Liu, Yu Xiaohui, Pan Jie, Zhang Jibo. **D:** Sun Zingguo. **W:** Zhao Yansen. **C:** Sun Guangwen, Lu Beiyu. **M:** Liang Qing. **VHS**

After Life

Bureaucracy lives on, even after death! Kawashima (Susumu Terajima), Shiori (Erika Oda), Mochizuki (Arata), and Sugie (Takashi Naito) all work in a plain old office building, processing those who have recently died. Entrants stay at the processing center for a week, and during the first three days they have an important requirement to fulfill: the selection of a memory, one perfect and most moving moment from their lives. The staff then takes the rest of the week to re-create that moment on film, which will be the only thing they can take with them into the afterlife. With a setup like that, the film naturally acts as a medium of self-examination, much like Albert Brooks's *Defending Your Life,* only more so, since the focus is not on a single character. The interview portions are very much like a documentary; some of the characters seem real. All have interesting—or interestingly, even not so interesting—stories to tell. Many of the older people relate wartime memories. A teenage girl (Yusuki Iseya) talks about a trip to Disneyland—apparently a common choice for teen girls. Some have trouble locating any good candidates and are even provided videotapes of their lives. One stubborn young man outright refuses to choose, bucking the system beyond his last breath.

But just as fascinating are the reactions of the staff members, who function just like any other office full of people, complete with attractions, gossip, and arguments. The film's mystery (until well in) is what exactly they are supposed to be—they're all certainly dead, but haven't passed on, and were somehow hired for this job. There are also a few other mysteries and surprises revealed before the end. Their film re-creations are woefully underfinanced, thrown together far too quickly, short on talent, but kind of fun. Some feel completely inadequate and a cheat to the entrant. With the videotapes available, why they need to bother making the films is open to conjecture. But then, conjecture and introspection are what the film is all about. It would be a great rental for a

third or fourth date—just the thing to encourage deep, revealing conversation afterward. **AKA:** *Wandafuru Raifu; Afterlife.* 🎵🎵🎵💃

1998 118m/C *JP* Erika Oda, Susumu Terajima, Taketoshi Naito, Kyoko Kagawa, Kei Tani, Takashi Naito, Sadao Abe, Yusuke Iseya, Sayaka Yoshino, Arata. *D:* Hirokazu Koreeda. *W:* Hirokazu Koreeda. *C:* Yutaka Yamazaki. *M:* Yasuhiro Kasamatsu. **VHS, DVD**

Akira

Ever since its debut in 1988, *Akira* has been the film most referenced when talking about anime features. At least this is the case in America, where *Akira*'s artistry, scope, and advance underground buzz led Streamline Pictures to give it a limited theatrical run. Word of mouth and critical raves gave the film an ever-growing cult following. No wonder; within its story of a gang of youths in a future metropolis who discover that they're already deeply involved in a government plot to create mutant supermen, *Akira* combines elements from the biker, monster, JD, action, sci-fi, and horror genres—all illustrated in painstaking detail with hyperkinetic power.

In MegaTokyo, a city that has suffered numerous disasters and rebirths to become a sprawling megalopolis, secret government experiments on children with ESP go awry, resulting in a cataclysmic explosion. Akira, the most powerful of the children, is kept in cryogenic suspension under strict security. Though the city is constantly being rebuilt, many of the same old problems remain. Though shining new buildings reach for the skies, much of the city is mired in urban decay. Kaneda is leader of one of the many street gangs that roam the slums and highways. His best friend Tetsuo becomes the target of government goons—it seems Tetsuo is part of a secret experiment in genetic mutation, and has vast untapped powers of telekinetic manipulation that the government team wants under their control. They already have a small group of powerful but physically vulnerable children at work. But Kaneda is unwilling to part with his friend without a fight, especially after he meets Kei, a young revolutionary working against the Big Brother powers that be. The wild card in the situation is Akira; a mutant kept in stasis by the government because his powers are far beyond their ability to control.

Director Katsuhiro Otomo adapted *Akira* from his own very popular manga series, and one of the film's great strengths is how closely it follows his densely detailed narrative—in a visual sense at least. Since the movie began production before his epic was finished, Otomo decided to complete the manga version with a different ending. Otomo's obsessive attention to detail shows in every frame—at one time, nearly every animation studio in southeast Asia worked on *Akira*. The work pays off with an exciting, impressive spectacle, although the complex plot is often perplexing. The well-rounded characters are sometimes lost in all the gadgetry. While conceptually it tends to wander at times, the movie still packs a punch with its awesome visuals. Among a group of films selected for re-release in 2001 while Hollywood jittered over an impending writers' strike, *Akira* was given a thorough image and sound clean-up, and brought back to theatres and video looking and sounding better than ever before. 🦴🦴🦴🦴

1988 (R) 124m/C *JP* **V:** Mitsuo Iwata, Nozomu Sasaki, Mami Koyama. **D:** Katsuhiro Otomo. **W:** Izo Hashimoto, Katsuhiro Otomo (manga). **C:** Katsuji Misawa. **M:** Shoji Yamashiro. **VHS, DVD**

Akira Kurosawa's Dreams

Dreams is a collection of stories based on actual dreams from the mind of the great director. The tales are largely unconnected, save in themes, and follow a rough journey of the director's life from childhood to old age. Wandering travelers are featured in a number of the tales, and perhaps these pilgrims represent Kurosawa himself. There are eight segments in the film:

1) "Sunshine through the Rain"—A young boy is told not to go out when it rains on a sunny day, as that's when the foxes have their weddings. Foxes are jealous creatures, and don't like to be watched. The boy goes out anyway and sees a beautiful fox wedding. When he returns home, his mother won't let him in. The foxes were offended, and now he must kill himself.

2) "The Peach Orchard"—In a house with an elaborate doll display, a boy sees a woman no one else sees. He follows her to a hillside, and finds living replicas of the dolls on display in his home. The dolls tell him that they are the spirits of the peach trees that his family cut down over the years.

3) "The Blizzard"—An expedition is lost in a terrible blizzard on a mountainside. When an avalanche rumbles down on them, it seems that they are doomed. One by one, the men suc-

cumb to the cold. As the expedition leader falls, he is visited by a strange woman who tells him that the wind is hot and the snow is warm; she covers him with a frosty blanket.

4) "The Tunnel"—A wandering soldier is harassed by a dog and walks through a strange dark tunnel. When he gets to the other side, the man is confronted by the ghost of a soldier he once knew. The ghost asks the wanderer to visit his parents, who still don't believe he is dead. Then a whole platoon of ghosts comes out of the tunnel.

5) "Crows"—A museum-goer is very much taken by the paintings of Vincent Van Gogh—so much so that he actually steps into one of the paintings *(The Bridge at Arles*—if memory serves) for a stroll. He wanders the countryside, looking for the great, mad painter (played by Martin Scorsese), and the two discuss life and painting.

6) "Mount Fuji in Red"—A traveler wanders through the streets of a dying city in the shadow of Mount Fuji. Huge explosions are detonating on the mountainside. Someone tells him that the nuclear power plants are blowing up. People are trying to escape, though they know there's nowhere to run. Ironically, the technocrats have color-coded the radiation, so they know what's killing them—though they still cannot stop it.

7) "The Weeping Demon"—A traveler meets a one-horned demon on a blasted, deserted mountainside. The demon tells him that radiation has ruined the world. Men ruined nature, and thus ruined themselves. Every night, the demons cry because the horns on their heads hurt like cancer.

8) "Village of the Watermills"—A tourist wanders through a sylvan river landscape dotted with watermills. The people who live there have forsaken the trappings of modern life, conveniences that dull the mind—electric lights, for instance. The tourist sees that mankind can live in harmony with nature, and this village is an example.

Dreams is a brilliant meditation on the things that concerned Akira Kurosawa. Understandably, given their source, all the pieces are dreamlike in their content and laden with symbolism. The shorts are emotion-packed, eerie, beautiful, and thought-provoking. Kurosawa's worries about ecology and the destiny of humankind are clearly manifest. Kurosawa, ironically, was having trouble bankrolling his movies in his native land. Thus, we get Americans helping out—"Steven Spielberg presents..." at the front of the film, Scorsese playing a part in it, and ILM (George Lucas) contributing the special effects. If none of these gentlemen did anything else in their lives, we would still owe them a debt for helping make this marvelous motion picture. —*SS* **AKA:** *Yume; Konna Yume Wo Mita; Dreams; I Saw a Dream Like This; Such Dreams I Have Dreamed.* 🦴🦴🦴🦴

1990 (PG) 120m/C *JP* Akira Terao, Mitsuko Baisho, Toshie Negishi, Meiko Harada, Mitsunori Isaki, Toshiko Nakano, Yoshitaka Zushi, Hisashi Igawa, Chosuke Ikariya, Chisu Ryu, Martin Scorsese, Masayaki Yui, Misato Tate, Ryojiro Oki, Masaru Sakurai, Sakae Kimura, Tetsu Watanabe, Haruko Togo, Junpei Natsuki, Shigeo Kato, Saburo Kadowaki, Sachio Sakai. *D:* Akira Kurosawa, Ishiro Honda. *W:* Akira Kurosawa, Ishiro Honda. *C:* Takao Saito, Masaharu Ueda, Kazutami Hara. *M:* Shinichiro Ikebe. **VHS, DVD**

All About Ah-Long

Ten-year-old Porky Yeung (Wong Kwan-yuen) is late for school again. His father, Ah-Long (Chow Yun-fat) races with him to get ready for his job as a truck driver for a construction company. The apartment is a cluttered mess, and breakfast is eaten on the run as the two zip through the streets of Hong Kong on Pop's battered old motorcycle. Still, it's clear that father and son share a close, affectionate, and playful bond. Their relationship is tested when Porky is chosen by Sylvia Poon (Sylvia Chang) to star in a bicycle commercial.

When Ah-Long comes to the ad agency's office to sign the contracts, he is shocked to see Sylvia. It's clear that they share a significant history, but she coolly calls him Mr. Yeung and insists that he call her Miss Poon. Through flashbacks, we learn that Sylvia was involved with Ah-Long 10 years in the past, when she used her given name, Por-Por. Her mother disapproved of the relationship and threw Por-Por out of the house. Judging by appearances, it's not hard to see why—Ah-Long was a long-haired motorcycle racer. But maybe Por-Por's mother was right—Por-Por catches him cheating on her while she's pregnant. She confronts him, and he beats her up, resulting in an accidental fall down a flight of stairs. Por-Por's mother tells her that her baby was born dead, and she leaves the country. Ah-Long cracks up his motorcycle, suffers a career-ending injury, and is imprisoned for two years. Upon his release, he reclaims his son from the orphanage where Por-Por's mother placed the infant. Ah-Long assumed that Por-Por abandoned her son; she thought he was dead. Now that the truth is known, Ah-Long hopes to reunite with Por-Por. But sometimes the past leaves scars that can never be healed. Por-Por doesn't want Ah-Long back, but she does want to make up for lost time and take Porky back with her to the United States. That sets up a supremely melodramatic and heart-wrenching conclusion.

Above all, the three lead performances allow the audience to invest in the characters, even though some very hard choices must be made. Though bearing some plot resemblances to Hollywood's *Kramer vs. Kramer,* the film differs significantly. Ah-Long had to give up his dreams of motorcycle racing and raise his son by himself. There's evidence that he has made changes for the better, and wants the best for his son. The contrast between Por-Por's wealthier lifestyle and Ah-Long's modest abode is sharply drawn. The climax might be overwrought for a Hollywood film, but here it seems strangely fitting. Philip Cheng wrote the screenplay, based on a story by Chow and Chang. Ng Man-Tat plays a supporting role as Dragon, a longtime friend of Ah-Long. —PM **AKA:** *A Long Dik Goo Si; A Lang De Gu Shi.* 🐉🐉🐉

1989 95m/C *HK* Chow Yun-fat, Sylvia Chang, Wong Kwan-yuen, Ng Man-Tat, Wong Tin Lam. *D:* Johnny To. *W:* Philip Cheng. *C:* Horace Wong. *M:* Richard Lo, Law Dai-yau. **VHS, DVD**

All Men Are Brothers: Blood of the Leopard

This classic Chinese swordplay story, a section of the epic novel *All Men Are Brothers,* was filmed previously in 1972 by Ching Kong under the title *Pursuit* (with another section serving as *Seven Soldiers of Kung Fu* in 1975), but this ambitious independent production misses the mark, annoying rather than entertaining. Commander Lin Chung (Tony Leung Ka-Fai), known as the Leopard, is sent by his master General Kao (Lau Shun) to retrieve his irritating son Kao Jr. (Pal Sin). To avoid bloodshed, he defeats the enemy commander (Austin Wai) in a one-on-one duel. As coach of military training, Lin is a better fighter than administrator, always putting off paperwork to practice kung fu. When he meets drunken monk Ru Chi-Shen (Elvis Tsui), the two great martial artists become great friends, and practice kung fu together day and night.

Having scolded Kao Jr. for his lecherous ways, Ru Chi-Shen makes himself a target for Kao, and so soon takes his leave rather than cause his friend trouble. Soon Lin has a new playmate though, when the young warrior Tso Wu (Lau Ching-Wan) arrives for a visit, bearing the famous Dew Saber with him. Kao and the traitorous Lu Chien (Lam Wai) trick Lin Chung into carrying the Saber into the sacred Tiger Hall, but the Prime Minister (Wu Ma) brings troops to prevent a lynching. Lin is sent to the capitol for legal trial, but Kao hedges his bets by forcing soldiers to kill the prisoner before he gets there. Fortunately, Ru saves him, while Tso Wu unsuccessfully attempts to protect Lin's wife (Joey Wong) from Junior.

"Broad" doesn't begin to describe the style of this film, in which the actors never stand when they can pose and never speak when they can shout. On Elvis Tsui, this looks O.K., but others don't come off as well, especially Pal Sin as the insufferably bratty general's son. Tony Leung Ka-Fai, on the other hand, fails to give his character much personality at all. The locations look great, but are shot in an ordinary way. The superpowered martial arts sequences are imaginative, but use editing and movement rather than any kind of real performance or choreography. William Woo's cheap synth score drains whatever grandeur there is in the production. *AKA: Sui Woo Juen Ji Ying Hung Boon Sik; Shui Hu Zhuan Zi Ying Xiong Ben Se; Waterside Story: Heroic Character; True Colors of a Hero.* 🐶🐶

1993 96m/C *HK* Tony Leung Ka-Fai, Elvis Tsui, Joey Wong, Lau Shun, Lam Wai, Pal Sin, Lau Ching-Wan, Austin Wai, Wu Ma, Billy Ching. **D:** Billy Chan. **W:** Johnny Lee. **C:** Joe Chan. **M:** William Woo. **VHS, DVD**

All Monsters Attack

The extravaganza *Destroy All Monsters* was supposed to be the last Godzilla film, a grand send-off for a series that had begun to slip in popularity during the late 1960s. However, *DAM* made money for Toho Studios, while the kid-oriented Gamera series, as well as giant monster superheroes on TV, were becoming extremely popular. To stay in the game, Toho produced this, the first Godzilla film aimed directly at children, best known in the U.S. as *Godzilla's Revenge*. As children's movies go, this is a pretty grim one.

Ichiro Miki (Tomonori Yazaki) is a latchkey kid living in an industrialized urban wasteland. His railroad-man father (Kenji Sahara) and innkeeper mother (Machiko Naka) are away from home much of the day, leaving Ichiro to hang out with his toy inventor neighbor Shinpei (Eisei Amamoto) or daydreaming by himself. These daydreams take him far away from his dreary world of gray skies and menacing schoolyard bullies to Monster Island, where Godzilla's son Minilla ("Little Man" Machan) is his best pal, and they can spend all day watching stock footage of Godzilla (Haruo Nakajima) fighting monsters like Ebirah and Kumonga. But Minilla—who can shrink to Ichiro's size and talk in a goofy voice—has bully problems of his own. A warty, cackling ogre named Gabara (Hiroshi Sekita) harasses poor Minilla constantly, until (with a little help from Ichiro and Godzilla) he finds the courage to stand up for himself. The lessons Ichiro learns during his Monster Island fantasies come in handy when he wanders into an abandoned building and is held captive by a gang of bank robbers hiding out there.

Like an urban version of *The Wizard of Oz*, it might have been better if the "real world" scenes had been filmed in black and white. *All Monsters Attack* seems to be an attack on a modern society where children need to grow up fast on their own. It also teaches young children that even the company that makes their favorite monster movies might sell them a picture packed with scenes from other movies. Cost-conscious Toho even had director Ishiro Honda directing the special-effects scenes. Gabara, with his painful electric jolts and hair-raising howls, is a pretty scary monster for a kid flick. Too bad Toho didn't bring him back for an encore—the silly 1970s entries in the series could've used a jolt. *AKA: Gojira, Minira, Gabara: Oru Kaiju Daishingeki; Godzilla's Revenge; Minya: Son of Godzilla.* 🐶🐶🐶

1970 (G) 70m/C *JP* Tomonori Yazaki, Eisei Amamoto, Kenji Sahara, Machiko Naka, Sachio Sakai, Kazuo Suzuki, Shigeki Ishida, Yoshifumi Tajima, Chotaro Togin, Yutaka Sada, Ikio Sawamura, Haruo Nakajima, "Little Man" Machan, Hiroshi Sekita. **D:** Ishiro Honda. **W:** Shinichi Sekizawa. **C:** Sokei Tomioka. **M:** Kunio Miyauchi. **VHS, DVD**

All Monsters Attack!

The movie trailer (or "Coming Attractions" ad) is an art form in itself, often more entertaining than the feature it's rigorously hawking to the public. This DVD collection of trailers from All Day Entertainment includes over 50 giant-monster movie trailers, for features like *King Kong, Dinosaurus,* and *The Valley of Gwangi.* Of course, a large section is devoted to trailers for the U.S. releases of Japanese monster movies, most of them in letterboxed format. The lineup includes: the classic *Godzilla, King of the Monsters; Varan the Unbelievable; Rodan; King Kong vs. Godzilla; Godzilla vs. the Thing; Gammera the Invincible* (with Brian Donlevy and Albert Dekker); *Ghidorah the Three-Headed Monster;* the super-submarine epic *Atragon; King Kong Escapes; Destroy All Monsters;* a semi-serious ad for *Godzilla vs. the Smog Monster; Yog, Monster from Space;* and the spectacular *The Mysterians.* Among the more rare entries are both a black-and-white pre-release and final letterboxed trailers for *Mothra.* The pre-release version is made up entirely of production design artwork, and bears the title *Mothra, the Monster God.* In all, it's an excellent collection and a great party disc. The only thing that would be better is a collection that included all the Japanese trailers as well. 🐶🐶🐶

2002 120m/C/BW *US/UK/JP* **DVD**

All's Well End's Well

The movie got some extra publicity when triads stole part of the negative, but this all-star New Year's comedy hardly needed it, as it went on to be a boxoffice sensation, spawning several sequels. The minimal plot concerns a crazy family and their romantic misadventures, similar to *Eighth Happiness,* but what it's really about is watching top Hong Kong stars go through all sorts of comic shenanigans.

Shang Moon (Raymond Wong) is too busy running around with Miss Hong Kong contestant Sheila (Sheila Chan) to remember the big anniversary luncheon prepared by his ditsy wife Ching (Sandra Ng). Shang So (Leslie Cheung) is Moon's effeminate brother who teaches flower arrangement, and doesn't get along with his biker second cousin Leung Mo-shang (Teresa Mo). Brother Shang Foon (Stephen Chow) is a zany afternoon disc jockey ready to break up with his girlfriend Dolleen (Rachel Lee). He meets even crazier Holliyok Ho (Maggie Cheung) off the station phone lines, but is challenged by the fact that she lives her life according to whatever movie she's currently obsessed with. He finally wins her after following her to Japan for the Tokyo Film Festival. When Moon's affair is exposed, So makes Ching defiantly move out—a move that backfires as Moon moves Sheila in. Still a playboy, Foon stalls Holliyok from catching him with another woman by inventing a movie for them to move on to: *Kennedy with Drunken Fists,* AKA *Kung Fu Sun Yat-san Part 2*! This somehow results in Foon contracting a rare brain disease. Meanwhile, So's mutual annoyance with Mo naturally develops into mutual attraction, Ching becomes a karaoke hostess and gets a makeover, and everyone comes together for mom and dad's anniversary party.

It's a good bet that Stephen Chow had a lot of control over his involvement, since most of his material scores laughs while much of the rest fails. Still, it's hard to deny that the film carries with it a great spirit of fun, even for viewers unfamiliar with any of the stars. Followed by *All's Well End's Well, Too.* **AKA:** *Ga Yau Hei Si; Jia You Xi Shi; Family Happiness.* 🐉🐉🐉

1992 100m/C *HK* Leslie Cheung, Stephen Chow, Maggie Cheung, Teresa Mo, Raymond Wong, Sandra Ng, Rachel Lee, Sheila Chan, Kwan Hoi-san, Lee Heung-kam, Tommy Wong, Clifton Ko, Vincent Kok. **D:** Clifton Ko. **W:** Vincent Kok, Tessa Choi, Raymond Wong (story). **C:** Lee Kin Keung. **M:** Violet Lam. **VHS, DVD**

All's Well End's Well '97

Following 1993's *All's Well End's Well, Too,* Stephen Chow returned for this third entry in this hit-and-miss comedy series. As usual, it's about a wacky family. The patriarch Mr. Lo (Roy Chiao) runs a successful restaurant chain, with the help of eldest son Old Fei (Raymond Wong). Shy middle son Little Fei (Francis Ng) is expected to help in the business, but so far just earns one esoteric degree after another. What he really wants is to be a singer. Youngest son Kung (Stephen Chow) is a lazy playboy whom everyone has nearly given up expecting anything from. Old Fei's unattractive wife Yinsu (Christine Ng, in Canto-comedy makeup) has low self-esteem and just tries to please everyone.

For Kung's birthday, his brothers decide to trick him into thinking he's won $30 million in the lottery. The brothers feel bad when Kung tells them he forgot to buy the ticket with their numbers, but when they learn he lied to them so he wouldn't have to share the prize, they decide to let him make a fool of himself. Kung only learns the truth after borrowing $5,000 from girlfriend Gigi (Gigi Lai), and losing a million dollars to triad member Brother Smartie (Simon Liu) in a dice game. Kung feigns accident-induced insanity to escape from his debt, but when he learns the family is setting up a fund that will have him set for life, he decides to keep up the charade.

When dad finds Little Fei's biker girlfriend Karen (Amanda Lee) too rude, Fei begins dating Shenny (Jacqueline Wu), a girl from a fried chicken shop. Though she seems normal at first, it turns out Shenny fancies herself a fortune-teller, and frequently becomes possessed. However, it's just a scheme to make Karen look better. Of course, Shenny and Little Fei are meant for each other. Romance is in the air for Kung as well, when he meets Suen (Christy Chung), who is also pretending to be an idiot.

Much of this is a retread of the first film's characters and situations—Wong as the unappreciative husband who gets jealous when his wife starts dressing up, Chow getting hit on the head and going nuts, etc. Roy Chiao lends a note of dignity and stability to the proceedings, but too much of the comedy just doesn't work. Christy Chung gets in a surprise action scene, taking on Simon Liu's thugs in a poolroom brawl. A whole bunch of stars show up for cameos at the end. Hong Kong films aren't too shy about their product placements, but this production is downright obnoxious about it, with a prominently placed Pepsi can in nearly every shot. **AKA:** *97 Fung Yau Hei Si; 97 Gu You Xi Shi; All's Well, End's Well 1997.* 🐉🐉

1997 92m/C *HK* Stephen Chow, Roy Chiao, Francis Ng, Raymond Wong, Christine Ng, Jacqueline Wu, Gigi Lai, Emil Chau, Amanda Lee, Simon Liu, Alfred Cheung, Leslie Cheung, Pauline Yeung, Teddy Robin Kwan, Law Kar-Ying, Michael Chan, Christy Chung.

D: Alfred Cheung. **W:** Raymond Wong, Vincent Kok. **C:** Tam Chi-wai. **M:** Tang Siu-lam. **VHS, DVD**

Angel

This simpleminded low-budget Girls with Guns action entry was a surprise smash in Hong Kong, leading to several sequels and imitators. After drug war soldiers burn their Golden Triangle poppy fields, drug cartel chief Madam Yeung (Yukari Oshima) is bloody angry, ordering the assassination or capture of the officers behind it. But she doesn't stop there—when she feels her superiors aren't aggressive enough, she kills them, too, and takes over the business. DEA agent Alex Fong (Alex Fong) goes to Bangkok to investigate, and brings in the Angel Team to help out. Members of this high-priced task force all hold down secret identities when not on assignment. Moon (Moon Lee) is a secretary, Saijo (Hideki Saijo) is a martial arts instructor at Japan's Shaolin Temple, and Elaine (Elaine Lui) is a lounge singer. Leader John Keung (David Chiang) calls them all together in Hong Kong for their assignment: to take down Yeung and her associate Chan Lo (Hwang Jang Lee). After breaking into their executive offices to gather information, the Angel Team stakes out their operations and steals their next drug shipment to draw them into a trap. During a mission to free captured agents, Fong is captured himself, and the Angels declare all-out war on Yeung's headquarters to retrieve him. Then they go after Yeung herself, knowing she's got a big operation planned.

Though not as relentless as future entries in the series, there are still plenty of stunts, fights, shootouts, explosions, and car chases here. The economical script, which resembles an old matinee serial, gives the main characters only enough depth that viewers can tell them apart, leaving room for more action. Oshima steals the show with a flamboyant Dragon Lady routine, cackling as she tortures captives, and then leaping into high-kicking action. A hand-to-hand duel between Oshima and Moon Lee is a terrific highlight, though it's disappointing that David Chiang doesn't get in on the fighting—it would've been nice to see him spar with Hwang Jang Lee. The English-dubbed version gives everyone different names, and begins with a terrific fight scene from *Angel 3* cut in without explanation—a bonus or a detriment, depending on how you look at it. **AKA:** *Tin Si Hang Dung; Tian Shi Hang Dong; Iron Angels; Midnite Angels; Midnight Angels; Martial Angels.* 🐉🐉🐉

1987 93m/C *TW* Moon Lee, Elaine Lui, Hideki Saijo, Yukari Oshima, Alex Fong, David Chiang, Peter Yang, Hwang Jang Lee, Lam Chung, Chan Chi-fai, Eddie Ko, Choi Wang, Wong Chi-cheung, Wong Ching-wai, Chu Dout, Lung Tin Cheng. **D:** Teresa Woo, Raymond Leung. **W:** Teresa Woo. **C:** Sander Lee. **M:** Richard Lo. **VHS**

Angel 2

The first *Angel* was a surprise hit, spawning this quick sequel. After rescuing a kidnapped businessman in typically violent fashion, Moon Lee, Elaine Lui, and Alex Fong (using their own names, except in dubbed versions) head on a vacation to Kuala Lumpur, Malaysia, to visit Alex's rich philanthropist friend Peter Kam (Nathan Chan). The move to a foreign location provides plenty of opportunities for travelogue shots of impressive landmarks. There's also opportunities for romance—as Elaine easily falls for Alex's old college buddy, and intrigue—as his other buddy Marco (Gary Siu) is a CIA agent secretly investigating Peter. But most of all there are opportunities for action and more action, as Peter isn't satisfied with his palm tree empire, fueling his profits into a secret private army bent on overthrowing the Malaysian government and installing him as king. Every other scene has our heroes battling mercenaries, getting into bar brawls with transvestites, or touring palm oil factories. Marco is captured and executed, and after the Angel Team is ordered into action, Elaine disappears as well. Gorgeous Malaysian agent Kharina (Kharina Isa) comes to help the heroes out, providing an arsenal of weaponry to be used in their rescue mission.

Not up to the level of its predecessor, this is still a pretty good Girls with Guns outing, with Lee and Fong providing the best stunts and fights. Kharina would be back for more in *Part 3*, replacing Elaine. Despite a retitle on Xenon Video as *Midnight Angel 2*, this bears no relation to the satirical *Midnight Angel* starring May Lo. The English dubbed version is at least 10 minutes shorter. **AKA:** *Tin Si Hang Dung II Jo Foh Fung Gaau Lung; Tian Shi Xing Dong II Zhi Huo Feng Jiao Long; Angels 2; Midnight Angel 2; Midnight Angels 2; Angels; Iron Angels 2; Fighting Madam 2; Hong Kong Police Madam 2.* 🐉🐉🐲

1988 94m/C *HK* Alex Fong, Moon Lee, Elaine Lui, Nathan Chan, Kharina Isa, Gary Siu, Jacinta Lee, Hussein Abu Hassan. **D:** Teresa Woo. **W:** Teresa Woo, William Hsu (story). **C:** Wong Nico. **M:** John Wong, Tang Siu-lam. **VHS**

Angel on Fire

Mimi (Melanie Marquez), a former model now working for an international crime syndicate, steals a relic from Shaolin Temple—leading to the odd spectacle of the high-cheekboned beauty being chased by the martial monks, all on

bicycles. She double-crosses her partner Rock (Phillip Ko), and flees to Hong Kong. Mainland Officer Wan-li (Sharon Yeung) is sent to Hong Kong to follow up on the case, reporting to Interpol agent Waise Lee—who has only two brief scenes. Agent Hsu Ching (Cynthia Khan) poses as a reporter to trail Mimi, getting photos of the gang threatening her. That night, both Hsu Ching and Wan-li are sent to Manila to follow after Mimi. Hsu Ching misses her connection, instead getting involved with obnoxious cab driver Harry (Ronnie Ricketts). Actually, Mimi's play was a ruse to expose Rock as a traitor. Rock's partners aren't happy about this, and give him three days to get the relic for them.

One of many flicks inspired by the success of Moon Lee's Angel movies, this little potboiler from Phillip Ko gets by on its unusual Philippine locations—most of which are blown up real good—and its willingness to fill the screen with all kinds of mindless mayhem. A gunfight, car chase, or illegal kickboxing match is bound to break out at any given second. With all the various factions and extraneous characters running around, it's difficult to tell who is shooting at who, but Ko keeps things moving constantly, and even adds quite a bit of humor along the way. ♪♪▽

1995 81m/C *PH/HK* Cynthia Khan, Waise Lee, Ronnie Ricketts, Sharon Yeung, Phillip Ko, Melanie Marquez, Ellis Winston, Darren Shahlavi, Tom Tom, Mark Houghton. **D:** Phillip Ko. **W:** Phillip Ko. **C:** Baby Cabrales. **M:** Ringgo Marquez. **VHS, DVD**

Anna Magdalena

Take one part Bach, one part fairy tale, one part romance, mix vigorously and pour. Lonely piano tuner Chan Kar-Fu (Takeshi Kaneshiro) allows charming ne'er-do-well Yau Muk Yan (Aaron Kwok) to move in with him. Mok Man-Yee (Kelly Chan), a lovely piano-playing lady, moves into their building. Chan Kar-Fu falls for her but does nothing; Yau Muk Yan also falls for her but takes action. The two begin a romance while Chan Kar-Fu pines away. He then spins an extended fairy tale in his mind in which he ends up with Mok Man-Yee as they play Cupid-like games to help couples come together.

Director Hai Chung-man's 17 years as an art director are certainly evident in the overall good looks of the film. Music by Bach provides accompaniment and divides the movie into different "movements" (the first two are named after two of the main characters, followed by a "duet" and then "variations," the fantasy sequence) in harmony with the music. The cinematography by Peter Pau looks lovely; the location work for the fantasy sequence (mostly shot in Vietnam) is especially sumptuous. All the surface gloss in the world, though, cannot hide the hollow heart of this production. The characters are not very likable and the performances are less than persuasive. Though the fantasy sequence is a welcome attempt to do something different within the romance subgenre, it's so out of tune with the first part of the film that it doesn't hold together. The ending is equally unsatisfactory. Adventurous viewers can look out for bit parts played by Hong Kong stars Anita Yuen, Leslie Cheung, and Jacky Cheung. —*PM* **AKA:** *On Loh Lut Tak Lin Loh; An Na Ma De Lian Na.* ♪♪

1998 98m/C *HK* Takeshi Kaneshiro, Aaron Kwok, Kelly Chan, Eric Tsang, Anita Yuen, Leslie Cheung, Jacky Cheung, Josie Ho, Jane Chung. **D:** Hai Chung-man. **W:** Ivy Ho. **C:** Peter Pau. **VHS, DVD**

Another Heaven

Inspector Tobitaka (Yoshio Harada) is called to a murder scene, taking with him old Dr. Akagi (Akira Emoto). The victim is found to have his skull sawed open, and Det. Manabu Hayase (Yosuke Eguchi) discovers the killer was making a stew out of the brain. A quick bit of comedy here, as writer/director Joji Iida films the hard-boiled coppers all bolting outside to barf, where they discover another corpse. Before they can puzzle out the case, several more nearly identical murders are discovered. Is it the latest challenge for the Iron Chef? Media commentators are—as ever—quick to blame the violence in the popular arts. Though the killer must have had the strength of a gorilla, the only fingerprints found are small. The latest victim is a special education teacher, and one of his students claimed to have seen what happened. His testimony implicates college student Chizuru Kashiwagi (Yukiko Okamoto), and Manabu is already tending to believe that a woman with supernatural powers raped, killed, and ate all the victims. Incredibly, this idea turns out to be correct when one of Chizuru's intended victims escapes. Chizuru is found at the crime scene, but collapses—and the police discover that her brain is missing as well!

Unlike other entries in the new wave of Japanese horror films, Iida's movie is lively and mischievous, with cartoon wipes and noisy characters. Based (with Kawato Azusa) on Iida's novel, its closest antecedent would probably be the British Quatermass movies, which also followed no-nonsense investigators as they try to unravel the puzzle of inexplicable events, and are inevitably led to a supernatural conclusion. Like *Quatermass, Another Heaven* was also a TV miniseries. Though the feature version feels overlong, perhaps the story would work better divided into chapters. The menace itself is reminiscent of *The Hidden* and *The Borrower,* and Iida treats it with just as much humor and grisly violence. The cast is excellent, considering the

Alternate versions

"My Japanese is a little rusty..."

When you buy a sculpture, you can take satisfaction in the fact that you own *the* sculpture, unique in all the universe. And when you read a book, you usually need not become too concerned that some copies of the book have the chapters rearranged, or that in other copies the characters have different names. But it's not so simple in the case of movies. Watching *Kwaidan* on DVD, you may notice that there are a few more stories in the anthology than on the version you taped from a TV broadcast 12 years ago. Or that when you saw *Operation Condor* in a theatre, it looked and sounded a lot better than when you watched the subtitled version on tape with your roommate after the Bears game 10 years ago, but it just didn't seem to be as good a movie—like something was missing.

When the Japanese monster movie *Gojira* was imported to the U.S. as *Godzilla, King of the Monsters,* the distributor filmed new scenes with American actors that were edited together with existing footage and dubbed or narrated over. The result was a weaker but viable alternate version of the film that played to packed houses across the country in 1956. Naturally, now with a hit *American* film on his hands, the distributor sold it to play subtitled around the world—even in Japan, where it was a hit all over again. But not without some unintentional comedy, as audiences heard Takashi Shimura making a speech, only to hear Raymond Burr's translator tell him he said something completely different!

Giving fuel to the argument that movies are more commerce than art, film is definitely a fluid medium, and prints of a movie playing at two theatres in the same city may have differences. Movies used to be re-edited by local censor boards in every city across the U.S., and local TV station managers would think nothing of chopping 10 random minutes out of a film to make it meet his time slot. Some TV movie hosts were known to cut out material from the films they showed to suit their own tastes. On an international level, a distributor often has the right to do what he wants with a film he's purchased the rights to in a certain territory—edit it, change the title, or show it upside-down if he wants to. Video labels have been known to tamper with the films they distribute, though most don't bother. Some saintly souls even go to great trouble to restore the film to the most complete form and best quality possible. More often, a library of film transfers is released on video without any care whatsoever. Films are released on video with erroneous casts listed on the box, with photos from other movies on the cover, or in at least one case, with an entirely different film on the tape. Dedicated Video Watchdogs report movies in video release in which the print used has a hole burnt in the middle of the frame throughout, dubbing technicians are heard on the soundtrack, or the image isn't framed properly. One commercially available DVD has a station break in the middle of the movie, revealing that the source of the transfer was taped from a local TV broadcast.

It's possible to see the same film over a dozen times and still see new scenes every time. Yes, it's a nightmare, folks, but don't despair. We VideoHounds always urge the reader to seek out the best possible version of a film available, and in these days of high-speed Internet and region-free, multilanguage DVDs, that task has become a whole lot easier. The reason that *Legend of the Drunken Master* and *Iron Monkey* didn't do better in American theatres is because the core target audience had already seen both years before. You say you don't want to buy the DVD of your favorite Jet Li movie dubbed into English (with no other language or subtitle option) and missing five minutes of footage? Well, the import version is likely for sale on the web for half the price. Having alternate versions isn't always such a bad thing, especially if it means you can see the original if you want.

fantastic material they're asked to take seriously, especially Miwako Ichikawa as the ex-con that Manabu reluctantly falls in love with. Akira Emoto's character Dr. Akagi is a reference to his revered performance in Shohei Imamura's film of that name. If *Another Heaven* teaches you one thing, it's that if you have to face the supernatural, remember to bring a towel. 🎵🎵🎵

2000 132m/C *JP* Yosuke Eguchi, Akira Emoto, Yoshio Harada, Miwako Ichikawa, Takashi Kashiwabara, Yukiko Okamoto, Haruhiko Kato, Yasuko Matsuyuki, Kunihiko Iida, Naomasa Musaka, Yoko Oshima, Taro Suwa, Shinmei Tsuji, Go Shimada. **D:** Joji Iida. **W:** Joji Iida. **C:** Hiroshi Takase. **M:** Taro Iwashiro. **VHS**

A*P*E

When Dino De Laurentiis decided to produce a big-budget remake of *King Kong*, he sent Univer-

sal Pictures' legal department into overdrive trying to crush potential competition. They were successful in stopping another studio from proceeding with their own Kong project, but a few little independents still managed to squeeze their crappy knockoffs into theatres, including this supremely awful co-production between the U.S. and South Korea.

An expedition discovers the giant primate of the title, but before they can get it back to civilization, it breaks loose from its transport barge and swims ashore, pausing only to fight with a big rubber shark (in 1976, every other movie had to have a shark in it). Meanwhile, the appealing Joanna Kerns (using the pseudonym Joanna deVarona) plays movie star Marilyn Baker, who comes to Korea to make some crummy movie, followed by Rod Arrants as her reporter boyfriend. Well, we all know that giant apes are irresistibly attracted to blonde actresses, so in no time at all, the monster is lugging around a doll meant to represent Marilyn while smashing poorly constructed miniatures that are supposed to represent Seoul. No attempt is made to convince the audience that the film was shot for any other purpose other than to make a fast buck. As Marilyn whimpers at the end: "Why?! Why?!" **AKA:** *Ape; A*P*E: Attacking Primate Monster; Attack of the Giant Horny Gorilla; Hideous Mutant; The New King Kong; Super Kong.* ⚔

1976 (PG) 87m/C *KO/US* Joanna Kerns, Rod Arrants, Lee Nak-hun, Alex Nicol, Jerry Hartke, Woo Yoin-jang, Paul Leder, Bob Kurcz, Kwan Choi-sung. **D:** Paul Leder. **W:** Paul Leder, Reuben Leder. **C:** Tony Francis. **M:** Bruce MacRae. **VHS, DVD**

Appleseed

 Can humans cope with a perfect world? That's the question asked in this anime feature based on a manga by Masamune Shirow. In a post-apocalyptic Earth after World War III, a group called the General Management Control Office creates the domed city of Olumpos (yes, the subtitles say "Olympus," but that's what it says onscreen). With all city functions controlled by the central computer Gaia, the aim is for the inhabitants to lead lives as trouble-free as possible. Of course, there's always some cranks. A group of terrorists known as the Free Human Liberation Alliance values freedom over security, and wants to stop the government plan to hand over most of the city's security to cyborg "bionoids." Their leader A.J. Sebastian is willing to go to any lengths to accomplish their goals, even if it means massive death and destruction.

Opposing these terrorists is the Olumpos Police Force Special Weapons and Tactics Squad, which uses traditional SWAT weapons as well as robot battle armor in their fight. Our heroes are Deunan Nats, a determined firearms specialist, and her cyborg partner Briareos Hekatonecles.

Sebastian gets supplies through crooked cop Calon, whose wife chose death over living without freedom. After Sebastian's raids claim too many good cops, gung-ho Deunan puts in for a transfer to Special Investigations to go after him. Loyal Briareos puts in for a transfer, too, stating that even if they don't get them, they can hunt the villain on their own time. The pair don't take the city for granted, having been born in the wilderness outside the dome. Their friend Hitomi is responsible for bringing them inside. She's a rich social worker who specializes in bringing survivors in from the wastelands.

Sebastian swipes some robot armor, and his gang goes on a rampage. Though he fears that machines are given too much responsibility and are taking over, he's a cyborg himself and is not above using the technology for his own ends. Inspector General Athena gives Deunan and Briareos a special assignment: assassinate Sebastian. Before they can figure out a plan on how to go about this, Calon and Sebastian kidnap Hitomi, whose brain holds the key to shutting down Gaia, crippling the entire city.

The combo of sexy warrior Deunan and her big lug partner, whose head attachments make him look like a big bunny rabbit, is still the main appeal of this anime. Compared to the original manga, the anime is somewhat of a disappointment. Though it picks up some heat for the climax, the designs of the animation lose most of the dynamism and detail of Shirow's art, and looks more like a generic cartoon. The language of the English dubbed version is much more harsh than the Japanese. **AKA:** *Appurushido.* ⚔⚔

1988 67m/C *JP* **D:** Kazuyoshi Katayama. **W:** Kazuyoshi Katayama, Masamune Shirow (manga). **M:** Norimasa Yamanaka. **VHS, DVD**

Armageddon

The approaching millennium produced a lot of ridiculous apocalyptic thrillers, from *The Omega Code* to the TV movie *Y2K*. This rare sci-fi outing from Hong Kong fits right in with that less-than-elite group, despite the superior star power of the leads. A hit team from MI6 is sent into a cathedral to find a scientist, but he spontaneously combusts before their eyes. Simultaneously, two other scientists die the same way, and an experimental video-on-demand and information system invented by super-genius Dr. Tak Ken (Andy Lau) has a major satellite blowout. Ken's old schoolmate Inspector Louie Chiu Tai-pang (Anthony Wong) from CID, along with Agent James from MI6 and Inspector Ivy Yip (Claudia Lau), is sent to investigate the deaths. A group called the Brotherhood of Technology is suspected, and it's surmised that Ken is either a member, or next on their list. Ken chooses Chiu to be his bodyguard, but his old buddy can't prevent Ken from getting hurt when they try to protect a noodle stand from extortionists.

In the hospital, Ken sees the ghost of his dead fiancée Adele (Michelle Reis). As the team continues to muddle through whatever evidence they can gather after yet another scientist is killed, Adele appears again, this time in front of a room full of people. She leaves them with a clue: two airline tickets to Prague for Ken and Chiu. While the boys are wandering around the ancient city learning to wear yarmulkes, they find Adele again. This time, she sticks around

long enough for dinner and shopping before disappearing again. An enigmatic stranger named Billy Connors (Michael Lambert) gives Ken a ring and implies that Adele is a supernatural hostage of the Brotherhood.

Entirely too much screen time is spent on flashbacks to Ken's office romance with Adele, so even when the focus shifts back to the plot, it seems to take forever to get moving. Writer/director Gordon Chan *(Fist of Legend)* seems more interested in presenting an intimate portrait of a scientist than making a thriller. Filmed before the Hollywood blockbuster of the same name, *Armageddon* gains some points for trying to present some big ideas in a thriller format, but loses more by making a complete muddle of them. *AKA: Tin Dei Hung Sam; Tian Di Xiong Xin.*

1997 112m/C *HK* Anthony Wong, Andy Lau, Michelle Reis, Vincent Kok, Claudia Lau, Jessica Chau, Kim Yip, Michael Lui, Angel Wong, Michael Lambert, Wayne Lai, Kim Penn. **D:** Gordon Chan. **W:** Gordon Chan, Vincent Kok. **C:** Horace Wong. **M:** Comfort Chan. **VHS, DVD**

Armour of God

Inspired by *Raiders of the Lost Ark,* Jackie Chan and Edward Tang cooked up this wild scenario that casts Jackie as globetrotting tomb raider Asian Hawk. In the incredibly goofy backstory, Jackie is in a pop singing group with Alan (singer Alan Tam) and his girlfriend Lorelei (Rosamund Kwan). After Lorelei throws Jackie over for Alan, he leaves the group to take up his first love, the swashbuckling world of archeology. A cult of satanic European monks has two out of the five pieces that make up the legendary relics the Armour of God. Jackie has just procured the other three pieces, and the cult kidnaps Lorelei to demand them as ransom. However, he's already sold them to rich collector Bannon (Bozidar Smiljanic). In exchange for the loan of the Armour, Jackie agrees to steal the monks' pieces for Bannon. Daughter May Bannon (Lola Forner) goes along to keep an eye on daddy's property. With the plot in place, Jackie, Alan, and May head for Europe, where they get involved in a bit of kooky Cantonese comedy, and some of Chan's most exhilarating action sequences of all, including a motorcycle and car chase, a huge fight with the monks (and a quintet of black dominatrixes!) in the cult's mountaintop caverns, and a skydive onto a hot-air balloon.

The flashback to the pop music group "The Losers" must have been even funnier in Hong Kong, where Alan Tam's real group is called "The Wynners." His singing partners Anthony

Chan and Kenny Bee have cameos. Tam and Kwan turn out to be deft comic foils to Jackie's gum-chewing hero.

This is the film in which Chan came closest to losing his life, cracking his skull while making a relatively simple leap. Part of an incredible period of action filmmaking, Chan made this one in between *Police Story* and *Project A 2.* Released on video as a sequel to the later *Operation Condor,* the U.S. version is 10 minutes shorter. *AKA: Lung Hing Foo Dai; Long Xiong Hu Di; Thunderarm; Operation Condor 2: The Armour of God.*

1986 (R) 88m/C *HK* Jackie Chan, Alan Tam, Rosamund Kwan, Lola Forner, Bozidar Smiljanic, Ken Boyle, John Ladalski, Robert O'Brien, Kenny Bee, Bennett Pang, Anthony Chan, Danny Yip, Clarence Fok, Carina Lau. **D:** Jackie Chan. **W:** Jackie Chan, Edward Tang, Lo Kin, John Sheppard. **C:** Peter Ngor, Bob Thompson, Arthur Wong, Cheung Yiu-cho. **M:** Michael Lai, Michael Wandmacher (U.S.). **VHS, DVD**

The Art of Action: Martial Arts in the Movies

While 1990's *The Deadliest Art* was a fine compilation of great fight scenes (many from films that had yet to be released in the United States), this documentary, first broadcast on the Encore cable networks, goes a lot deeper. Jedi Knight Samuel L. Jackson stalks around a wonderful-looking backdrop, expertly reading cue cards that trace martial arts cinema all the way back to the Boxer Rebellion, and even back to the origins of kung fu. From there, we see how the Chinese opera carried on the art form into the movies; how women dominated through the 1950s; the influence of Japanese samurai films on Hong Kong kung fu cinema; the power of directors King Hu, Cheng Cheh, and Lau Kar Leung in the '60s and beyond; the Bruce Lee explosion, and so on.

Interview footage with relevant stars is interspersed with terrific clips to tell the whole story—at least, as much as can be told in 98 minutes. Even clips going back to the silent *Red Errant Knight, My Son Was a Hero,* and *Swordswoman from Huangjiang* are included. Other films represented include *The Shaolin Temple, 36 Chambers of Shaolin,* the *Wong Fei Hung* series, *Peking Opera Blues, Farewell My Concubine, Enter the Dragon, One-Armed Swordsman, Golden Swallow, Seven Samurai, Come Drink with Me, Magnificent Butcher,* the *Once upon a Time in China* series, *Bride with White Hair, Painted*

Faces, The Killer, Drunken Master, Police Story, A Chinese Ghost Story, and even *The Wizard of Oz!* In all, an excellent documentary, marred in the original broadcast version only by the fact that at least 15 minutes is taken up with discussion of *Crouching Tiger, Hidden Dragon.* It's an important film, but come on. 🦴🦴🦴🦴

2002 98m/C *US* Samuel L. Jackson, John Woo, Roger Yuan, Ronny Yu, Lau Kar Leung, Sammo Hung, Jackie Chan, Cheng Pei Pei, David Carradine, Corey Yuen, Raymond Chow, Donnie Yen, Kirk Wong, Cynthia Rothrock, Ang Lee, Mang Hoi. **D:** Keith Clarke. **W:** Keith Clarke, Christopher Sliney. **C:** Steven Finestone. **M:** Steve Rucker. **VHS, DVD**

Ashes of Time

While Jeff Lau made the wild and wacky *Eagle Shooting Heroes,* his friend Wong Kar-Wai was making this wildly different, artistically ambitious film based on the same Jin Yong source novel, using many of the same actors. World-weary swordsman Ouyang Feng (Leslie Cheung) retires from the Martial Arts World to run a desert inn, occupying his time as a freelance "problem solver" to guests. Once a year, his old friend Huang Yaoshi (Tony Leung Ka-Fai) visits. This time Huang has brought a gift: some magic wine that causes amnesia. Ouyang was once hired by Murong Yang (Brigitte Lin) to kill Huang because he broke up with Yang's sister Murong Yin (Lin again). However, Yin also wanted to hire Ouyang, but to kill brother Yang instead. While going back and forth between clients, Ouyang comes to learn that the one is a character played by the other in order to engineer a murder suicide, but Huang and Ouyang became best friends instead. After drinking the wine, Huang can no longer remember either friends or enemies. Ouyang also relates the story of a half-blind swordsman (Tony Leung Chiu-Wai) who completes a mission of vengeance for him, but dies when his sight fails altogether, plus another about Hong Qi (Jacky Cheung), a carefree hero who nevertheless fails to keep his wife (Bai Li) happy because he's always off on adventures.

Some viewers are fascinated by the interplay of characters and relationships presented here, drawn in by the symbolism, and revel in the beauty of Christopher Doyle's golden desert imagery. Others are bored by the sleepwalking characters mouthing endless monotonous dialogue and multiple voice-over, depressing situations, overcomplicated flashbacks, and leaden pace. Some find the blurred, slow-motion action scenes a refreshing change, while others think it needlessly obscures Sammo Hung's choreography. Whether you think it's a triumphant visionary work or disappointing self-indulgent art-crap, this troubled production brought critical attention to the talented Wong, and effectively capped the early '90s swordplay cycle. While Wong edited and re-edited *Ashes,* he dashed off the engaging and more accessible modern meditation *Chungking Express.* One death scene is stolen from *Lone Wolf and Cub 2.* **AKA:** *Dung Che Sai Duk; Dong Xie Xi Du.* 🦴🦴

1994 98m/C *HK* Tony Leung Ka-Fai, Leslie Cheung, Brigitte Lin, Jacky Cheung, Tony Leung Chiu-Wai, Charlie Yeung, Carina Lau, Maggie Cheung, Bai Li, Lau Shun, Ngai Sing, Siu Tak-foo. **D:** Wong Kar-Wai. **W:** Wong Kar-Wai. **C:** Christopher Doyle. **M:** Frankie Chan, Roel A. Garcia. **VHS, DVD**

The Assassin

During the Ming Dynasty, the royal eunuchs wielded great power by training scores of assassins. One such assassin, Tong Po-ka (Zhang Fengyi), becomes a fugitive by attempting to elope with Yiu (Rosamund Kwan). Showing no remorse for the crime of attempting to wed a commoner, Tong is sentenced to "Punishment A," and has his eyes sewn shut until his execution. By order of Grand Eunuch Mi, the condemned prisoners are made to fight to the death in a battle royale. The lone survivor, Tong is chosen for assassin training by Master Assassin Sung Chung, and given the name Tong Jan (the Slasher). Tong does well, and quickly rises to the top of Mi's 19 assassins. But Tong screws up royally on a mission, refusing to kill a Tibetan lama child. Making his evening even worse, he sees Yiu—now a wife and mother—in the crowd. With Tong Jan in hiding, young Wong Kau (Max Mok) takes his place among the assassins. Tong ends up stumbling into the cabin of Yiu's family. Ironically, he finds himself saving a fouling horse's life with his sword, becoming a hero to the farmers. But it's not long before Sung and his assassins come to break the peace.

The entire film has a very striking look to it, courtesy of the unusual high-contrast cinematography by Chiu Fei, and almost has the look of video at times. The action nicely mixes wirework swordplay with bloody violence, and features some nice-looking mainland locations. However, the story and characters are so simple that they hardly rate so much fuss. Rosamund Kwan is wasted in a do-nothing part. Max Mok looks a bit silly in his filthy wig, but accounts for himself nicely in the action department. **AKA:** *Saat Yan Je Tong Jaan; Sha Ren Zhe Tang Zhan.* 🦴🦴

1993 81m/C *HK* Zhang Fengyi, Rosamund Kwan, Max Mok, Cheung Kwok-bak, Ngai Tai-wang. **D:** Billy Chung. **W:** Charcoal Cheung Tan, Roy Szeto, Wen Shui-on (novel). **C:** Chiu Fei. **M:** Wong Bong. **DVD**

Astro Boy

Based on an incredibly popular manga series by Osamu Tezuka, this was the very first anime produced in Japan. Beyond its historical importance, the series is also highly entertaining on its own merits, especially for young children, who are more likely to forgive the primitive black-and-white limited animation. A big fan of both science fiction and Disney animation, Tezuka created *Astro Boy* as a sci-fi version of *Pinocchio*.

Professor Boynton, director of the Institute of Science, is driven mad when his young son is killed in a car accident. Putting the entire resources of the institute to work, he creates an extremely powerful and advanced robot double of his dead son. However, the finished robot's lack of humanity disappoints the mad Boynton and he rejects his artificial son, selling him to Cacciatore's Robot Circus. Astro Boy is a failure there as well, as he is unwilling to "kill" other robots in the arena. During a fire, the rejected robot saves the lives of Cacciatore and the audience. Dr. Elefun (Ray Owens), new head of the institute, pushes a Robot Liberation Act into law, and Astro Boy (Billie Lou Watt) goes to work for the institute as an all-purpose hero.

During the 193-episode run of the series, Astro Boy journeyed to other planets, deep under the sea, and foiled dozens of threats to the Earth. But his greatest triumph was to establish the Japanese animation industry, not only in Japan but worldwide. Shown in its initial run in prime time on the NBC network in the U.S., *Astro Boy* was the number-one show in many markets. Surely both Steven Spielberg and Stanley Kubrick saw a few episodes, long before swiping ideas for *A.I.* Plenty more anime would follow in its wake, all of which have been influenced in large part by Tezuka's groundbreaking work—for his expressive cartoon drawings style, storytelling techniques, and quirky sense of humor. One aspect not imitated as widely was the series' willingness to deal with weighty issues—such as biotechnology, pollution, and civil rights (robots often stood for minorities). Some of the sci-fi concepts dealt with were also beyond children's programs of the day. One episode was built around travel to a parallel universe. Some questioned whether Astro had a soul. There were episodes that borrowed concepts from H.G. Wells and Robert Heinlein—and even Richard Shaver! Only 104 episodes were dubbed prepared for broadcast in the U.S., and only a portion of these is available on video (so far). These include a "lost" episode, one Tezuka had rejected. *AKA: Tetsuwan Atom.* 🐾🐾🐾🐾

1963 /**BW** *JP* **V:** (English) Billie Lou Watt, Ray Owens, Gilbert Mack, Peter Fernandez. **D:** Osamu Tezuka. **W:** Osamu Tezuka. **M:** Tatsuo Takai. **VHS**

Astro Boy

To celebrate the 30th anniversary of their premiere character, Tezuka Productions created this updated anime series. Unlike the classic 1960s series, the new series is in color, but an even bigger difference is the way subsequent technological advances were incorporated into the story and designs. In the '50s, Tezuka could afford to be sketchy in the use of technology in the far-off year of 2000, but couldn't afford more than limited animation. By 1980, audiences were getting used to questioning how things like time guns and Death Stars might work, so pains are taken to show what happens to Astro Boy's feet when he fires up his rockets, and to answer other common questions. Also updated is Tezuka's cartoon drawing style, to a more contemporary look, sacrificing charm for more believable science fiction and finished animation. The original story is expanded to three episodes, which allows for an explanation of things like how Astro got his boots and name, and extra opportunities for him to perform heroic deeds. There is a definite arc over the course of the series, which includes episodes adapting manga stories never attempted in the first series, to how Astro goes from a clumsy child, prone to breaking things and taking speech too literally, to a confidant and powerful robot citizen of his world. All 51 episodes are available on home video. Still available only on bootleg is a primitive live-action *Astro Boy* movie made in 1958, which looks like a black-and-white *Superman* episode shot with half the budget. *AKA: Tetsuwan Atom.* 🐾🐾🐾♡

1980 /**C** *JP* **V:** (English) Richard Ganoung, Bob Gonzalez, Debby Holmes, Del Lewis, David G. Miller, Paul M. Nelson, Brian Parry. **D:** Noboru Ishiguro. **W:** Osamu Tezuka. **C:** Noboyuki Sugaya. **M:** Seiji Suzuki, Nariaki Saegusa, Tatsuo Takai. **VHS**

Atomic Rulers of the World

Highly influenced by the *Superman* television series, superheroes became a staple of children's TV and movies in the 1950s, which evolved into the Ultraman, Kamen Rider, and Power Rangers series of today. Super Giant was the hero of a series of shorter features of about 40–50 minutes, some of which were imported

Dubs and Subs

But still...why does your mouth move one way, and you talk another?

One of the biggest roadblocks between the general American audience and Asian cinema is, of course, language. Throughout the world, where you're often within a dozen miles of another nation, people are used to the fact that the whole planet doesn't speak their language—but we're accustomed to having our entertainment spoon-fed to us. There are two ways around this barrier: dubbing and subtitles. Actually, there used to be three ways—back in the 1930s and before, theatres in many countries would employ a "talker" to narrate foreign films, and even domestic pictures in countries with more than one common language and/or a high rate of illiteracy. Generally, a leather-lunged young man would stand in the theatre and give everyone a play-by-play account of the action and dialogue, sometimes adding a comment or two of his own. Akira Kurosawa's brother was employed as a theatre talker, and the Wong Yu movie *The Young Avenger* gives a pretty apt presentation of a rural Chinese film house with a lively talker. This practice was revived in the U.S. during the 1980s—before the explosion of translated Japanese animation on home video, anime clubs had to rely on members that were bilingual or just knew the story to narrate imported tapes. But let's just concern ourselves with the relevant two methods: subtitles and dubbing.

Subtitles

It was a natural progression to pair movies with reading. Silent films used intertitles to help tell the story, and even a few years into the sound era, movie studios would still prepare silent versions of many films with title cards for theatres still without sound equipment. Some filmmakers actually got quite creative with the design of their title cards to help the atmosphere of a film. Alfred Hitchcock got his start in the movie business creating title cards. But unfortunately, though the quality of subtitles has improved a great deal (yellow type backed in black is so easy on the eyes), no one has yet found a way to make them a part of the film, except as a necessity. Recently, Universal Studios has been experimenting with subtitles on DVDs, moving them under the speaker on-screen, but this is more annoying than useful. Some films have been subtitled with the type flush near the left of the screen rather than the traditional center, allowing the viewer's eye to return to the same spot for each line.

But some people don't like to read subtitles, feeling they're too much bother and too distracting. Others find it too distracting to hear everyone in Osaka speaking English that has been dubbed over by actors inferior to the original performer. Whatever your feeling, American distributors have long considered subtitles the only alternative when they can't afford to dub. In Hong Kong, it became a necessity to both dub *and* subtitle movies for use within their own country. Since it's so noisy in HK, it's much easier to shoot without sync sound. And since there are so many dialects spoken throughout their immediate distribution area, but only one written Chinese language, subtitling in Chinese became the norm. With Hong Kong still under British rule, English was also added under the Chinese subtitles. This became one of the leading factors in the rise in popularity of HK cinema in English-speaking countries, as it was always easy to find English subtitled movies. Not that the subtitles were always legible—far too many films opted for cheap, burned-in white text that would disappear over white backgrounds.

This situation has only improved with DVD, as distributors can release films with nice clear subtitles in a variety of languages, and Chinese can even come in formal and simplified characters. However, that doesn't guarantee a good translation, as you can still catch plenty of garbled grammar, typos, and just plain bizarre lines of dialogue that you know can't really be what was in the script. It's even worse when you watch a movie from one country released on video in another, since the English subtitles are sometimes translated from the distributor's country's language rather than the language of the film.

Dubbing

At first, studios rejected dubbing films into other languages, preferring to shoot versions in different languages. But dubbing took hold fast in countries in which building huge soundstages was found to be expensive and impractical. Looping dialogue (matching speech recorded in a sound studio with the filmed performance) was much more logical, especially since the sound facilities were already a necessary part of production for music and sound effects. From there, it was only a step away to have one actor running around making different movies while another provided his voice. And dubbing in different language tracks for distribution to your neighbors across

Continued on next page...

the border or overseas was that much simpler. While some stars almost always dubbed their own performances domestically, other movie stars have never had their voices recorded.

But the job of dubbing Asian movies into English carries with it specific problems. Asian languages tend to have the reverse sentence structure, making translation into natural-sounding dialogue a difficult creative chore. Plus, their languages tend to end statements with opened-mouth sounds, while English lines usually end with the mouth closed. Depending on the skill of the dubbing team, this may mean that pauses come in odd places, some lines are stretched while others are rushed, and the meaning of lines can be lost or changed. Think about these challenges the next time you complain about "bad" dubbing. This explains why we hear certain dubbing techniques that sound a bit odd over and over in English-dubbed films. The phrase "But still..." can be used to cover up just about any awkward pause in dialogue, and the threat "You must be tired of living!" can cover for a more esoteric regional insult. The voice actors have developed their own tricks over the years to make their lines match lip movements a bit more closely, though this also at times make it seem that characters moan or grunt strangely. Obsessive fans (you know who you are) even get hooked on the sound of certain actors' voices, and try to find out who they are to follow their filmography. What's really odd is when an actor will pick up some cash dubbing early in their careers, only to become stars later.

Of course, in Asia they're used to hearing different voices come out of an actor's mouth in different movies, but most Americans are unaware just how much dubbing takes place even in Hollywood movies, to clarify dialogue, change meaning to accommodate script changes, or just to punch up the soundtrack. But a lot of people are *looking* for the dubbing to be bad when they're watching a dubbed foreign film. Since many imported pictures are senselessly edited anyway "to accommodate American tastes," noting imperfections in the dubbing—which most viewers blame the foreign filmmakers for rather than the domestic distributor—just adds to the impression of a shoddy foreign product. On rare occasions, attentive and talented people have produced American versions of Asian films that meet the intentions of the original filmmakers, and rarer still, sometimes use the extra time and money available to improve the film. But more often distributors are just trying to turn a buck on a picture that was cheap to begin with, using junior high drama clubs to dub English over ancient Chinese monks.

and edited together for television and matinee release in the U.S. by Walter Manley Enterprises in 1964. This feature combines the third and fourth entries: *Invaders from the Planets* and *The Earth in Danger.*

A narrator informs us that the radiation from Earth's nuclear testing has begun to even pollute the far reaches of outer space. On the planet Emerald, the high council (a terrific collection of weird aliens) meets to discuss the matter. One nation (Megolia in the dubbing, though signs clearly spell out "Merapolia") threatens the entire space sector by smuggling nuclear weapons into foreign countries, bringing the Earth to the brink of atomic war. The wristwatch-like "globe meter"—a radiation detector/universal translator, that also gives the wearer the power of flight—is given to the near-indestructible Starman (Ken Utsui) for a mission to Earth to stop the Megolian criminals. After helping a troubled airliner, Starman switches to Earth clothes from his space tights to trail Megolian spies carrying a nuclear weapon into Japan. While the superhero beats up the spies, a gang of orphan kids picks up their guns and the bomb. Catching up with the kids, he picks up the pistols, telling them he's "a friend to all children" (predating Gamera by a decade). Detective Okamoro and his sister Reita think the stranger is more suspicious than heroic.

The spies have abducted little Hiroshi, bringing the boy to their secret base to face their leader Motar D (who looks a bit like Richard Nixon), who forces the boy to tell them where he's hidden the nuclear device. The Megolians plan to conquer Japan on the first day of attack, taking the rest of Asia the second day, America on the third, and finishing up the rest of the world over the weekend. Starman rescues Hiroshi and accompanies the bad guys on their way to get the bomb. But the spies manage to slip away and Okamoro arrests Starman for murder. He has to break out of jail to pursue the spies and keep them from starting a nuclear war.

The fight scenes are halfway between old-fashioned movie serial fisticuffs and the kind of acrobatic battles that would become standard in martial arts films. At one point, Starman engages in a fencing duel with an ambassador. Flying sequences are well done, using tradition-

al f/x techniques. Megolia's secret base looks almost exactly like that of *Doctor No,* except for the huge grinning devil face decorating one wall. The action is split between fantastic sci-fi settings and the dreary industrialized landscape of urban Japan, with children playing amid the wreckage of ruined factories or around dangerous fields of electric towers. **AKA:** *Atomic Rulers; Attack of the Flying Saucers; Super Giant No. 3 & 4.* ♫♫♡

1957 74m/BW *JP* Ken Utsui, Junko Ikeuchi, Minako Yamada, Sachihiro Ohsawa, Shoji Nakayama, Kan Hayashi, Minoru Takada, Utako Mitsuya, Chisako Tahara, Reiko Seto, Akira Tamura, Tomohiko Ohtani, Fumiko Miyata, Johji Ohhara, Kami Ashita, Terumi Hoshi, Shinsuke Mikimoto. **D:** Teruo Ishii, Akira Mitsuwa, Koreyoshi Akasaka. **W:** Ichiro Miyagawa. **C:** Takashi Watanabe. **M:** Michiaki Watanabe. **VHS, DVD**

Attack from Space

In 1965, Walter Manley followed *Atomic Rulers of the World* with this combination of parts 5 and 6 of the Japanese *Super Giant* sci-fi serial as a feature for television.

The Sapphire Galaxy plots to invade Earth, lighting a fire under the Cold War. The High Counsel of the Emerald Planet once again sends superhero Starman to Earth with a globe meter, hoping he can intercept the Sapphire main forces before they reach their target. Landing on a Sapphire warship, his sabotage efforts are hampered by meteor showers, so he instead heads to Earth to ferret out intergalactic traitors. Sapphire agents have been causing mishaps at observatories worldwide, and it's feared the next target will be a spaceship under construction at a secret island base.

Dr. Yamanaka discovers some solenoids in the ship's engine have been destroyed, and sends his children Ichi and Keoru to the mainland for replacements. They find a strange man has bought up all available solenoids, and they trail him to a graveyard. There, Sapphire soldiers capture the kids and take them to their underground lair. The doctor's assistant

Kobayashi is a spy, and forces Yamanaka to help them build an engine for their own spaceship. Starman destroys a Sapphirian space station, and heads for their mothership, while the spies launch their ship from Earth, with the enslaved Yamanakas onboard. On course for the mothership, both the spy ship and Starman have to risk passing near the radioactive flames of the Death Star. Starman is shot down by missiles, and Yamanaka is taken to the enemy mothership to help them build a fleet to conquer Earth and the entire universe. To quash resistance, the aliens destroy downtown Tokyo, New York, and London with rockets. However, the kids plot to sabotage the mothership and escape, and Starman is on his way.

A change in setting from Earth to outer space makes *Attack from Space* a much more dynamic feature than its predecessor. The fight scene pitting Starman against the Sapphirians on the mothership lasts well over 13 minutes, with Ken Utsui hopping around the place throwing punches and occasionally picking soldiers off with their own pistols. The alien mothership is terrific, fittingly looking halfway between a battleship and a futuristic factory. With a huge fleet of their own on the way, it's difficult to understand why the Sapphirians would need Yamanaka and his puny Buck Rogers spaceship for their plans of conquest. Maybe they've spread their forces too thin across the galaxy and need to build more weapons as they go. Or maybe they exhaust their own resources manufacturing their snappy uniforms. Followed by *Invaders from Space* and *Evil Brain from Outer Space*. **AKA:** *Jinko Eisen to Jinrui no Hametsu; Spaceship of Human Destruction; Uchutei to Jinko Eisen no Kekitotsu; Destruction of the Space Fleet; Super Giant No. 5 & 6.* 🗡🗡🗡

1958 75m/BW *JP* Ken Utsui, Sachihiro Ohsawa, Junko Ikeuchi, Minako Yamada, Shoji Nakayama, Kan Hayashi, Minoru Takada, Utako Mitsuya, Chisako Tahara, Reiko Seto, Akira Tamura, Tomohiko Ohtani, Fumiko Miyata, Johji Ohhara, Kami Ashita, Terumi Hoshi, Shinsuke Mikimoto. **D:** Teruo Ishii, Akira Mitsuwa, Koreyoshi Akasaka. **W:** Ichiro Miyagawa. **C:** Takashi Watanabe. **M:** Michiaki Watanabe. **VHS, DVD**

Attack of the Mushroom People

A pleasure cruise on a yacht runs into a storm, stranding seven passengers on a secluded island. There doesn't seem to be any food on the island, save the mushrooms that grow plentifully, though no one dares to eat them. Mystery brews when another ship is found derelict on the beach, its crew vanished. Apparently it was a research vessel conducting experiments on the fungi, but there are no clues as to what became of the crew, except to say that some of them disobeyed orders and ate some mushrooms.

Soon, some of the newcomers begin to succumb to starvation as well, and they too disappear. However, evidence seems to indicate that someone—or something—has been making nightly visits to the ship. Holdout Akira Kubo (who continued with director Ishiro Honda for several more pictures) is confronted with the ghastly truth: those eating the mysterious mushrooms have been turning into oversized killer "shrooms" themselves! Despite the sensationalistic American title, this is a weirdly atmospheric horror film from the director of many Godzilla pictures. The art direction is excellent, as mold and fungus seem to be spreading from the corners of every frame. The drug references are not ignored, as it's made clear that the fungus has a psychological as well as a physical effect. The production is marred by a ridiculous song performed by one of the boatniks before arriving at the island, the only lyrics for which are "La la la!" **AKA:** *Matango; Fungus of Terror; Curse of the Mushroom People.* 🗡🗡🗡

1963 89m/C *JP* Akira Kubo, Kumi Mizuno, Kenji Sahara, Yoshio Tsuchiya, Hiroshi Koizumi, Miki Yashiro, Hiroshi Tachikawa, Eisei Amamoto. **D:** Ishiro Honda. **W:** Masami Fukushima, Shinchiro Hoshi, Takeshi Kimura, William Hope Hodgson (story). **C:** Hajime Koizumi. **M:** Sadao Bekku. **VHS**

Attack the Gas Station!

While not exactly the new *Trainspotting*, this Korean comedy has a lot of the same youthful vigor and satire. The happy staff of a Seoul full-service gas station is interrupted in their night's work by a quartet of bored juvenile delinquents, who set about robbing the owner Kim (Park Yeong-gyu) and smashing things for fun. Soon after, the money spent on sports jackets and ramen, the JDs are stupid enough to return to rob the very same station, and get into more trouble than they thought possible. Minimal security measures have been put into practice, meaning that there's very little money on hand this time. To make their venture profitable, the gang takes the staff hostage and operates the station themselves—but they soon find that running a police state is incredibly complicated, even on a small scale. Troublesome customers are locked in trunks, and when a high-school gang comes by to extort a classmate, they're captured and put in the upstairs office with the staff. One gets away to tell the gang leader Yongari (!), who brings his boys for a rumble. But the thieves are better fighters, and the gang is captured as well. They even force the police to pay for their gas. However, the biggest challenge yet erupts in a war with the triads and Chinese food delivery boys.

Occasional flashbacks show how the gang of four had their dreams crushed, leading to their life of crime—which helps to build the bit of audience sympathy they need, since their actions aren't always righteous. While they're stealing and pushing people around, our four heroes are also righting a few wrongs, standing up for the little guy, building courage in the downtrodden, and helping in the discovery of a new boy band. **AKA:** *Juyuso Seubgyuk Sa Geun.* 🐉🐉🐉🐉

1999 112m/C *KO* Lee Sung-jae, Yu Oh-seong, Kang Seong-jin, Yu Ji-tae, Park Yeong-gyu, Jeong Jun. **D:** Kim Sang-jin. **W:** Kim Sang-jin. **C:** Choi Jung-woo. **M:** Son Mu-hyeon. **VHS, DVD**

Audition

How long should someone wait after the death of a spouse to remarry? Anyone thinking about getting back into the dating pool ought to think twice before viewing this incredibly creepy thriller. Seven years after his wife Ryoko's death, at the urging of friends and his son Shigehiko (Tetsu Sawaki), film producer Shigeharu Aoyama thinks he'd like to get married again, but doesn't quite know how to go about finding the right woman. His associate Yoshikawa (Jun Kunimura) has an idea: they'll produce a new film, as well as a television program called "Heroine of Tomorrow." While auditioning for the leads, their ulterior motive will be to audition for a mate as well. Reading through the applications, Aoyama is impressed by that of a former dancer named Asami Yamazaki (Eihi Shiina). He's even more impressed with her at her audition, though Yoshikawa's instincts tell him there's something wrong with her. He does some checking and finds that one of her references disappeared over a year before. None of her other contacts check out either. Yoshikawa advises Aoyama not to call her again, but of course he does. He begins to feel that quiet, introspective Asami could be the perfect woman for him, and if she has flaws, he's quick to dismiss them. There's not much more to be said without giving too much away, but Aoyama soon finds that Asami is much more than he bargained for.

Most horror films fall all over themselves to let you know they are horror films, turning ridiculously ominous with each foot of film or note on the soundtrack. Part of *Audition*'s effectiveness comes from the fact that it doesn't play fair. For the first half hour, you might think it would turn into a decent drama or light romantic comedy, except there's no obvious cinematic clues to tell the viewer exactly what's going to happen—which is very unsettling, since we're all so used

to that quick shot of a tombstone or tinkling piano to tell us how to feel. The film seems to be about loneliness. As Japan is becoming more and more in touch with other countries, whose emotions are perhaps less repressed, the entire nation of Japan is feeling depressed and lonely, and people feel compelled to reach out somehow, no matter how uncomfortable it might make them. Never before has the fear of human interaction been taken to such harrowing extremes. *Audition* may make even hard-core gorehounds cringe. It makes *Fatal Attraction* look like *Mary Poppins.* **AKA:** *Odishon.* 🐉🐉🐉🐉

1999 (R) 115m/C *JP* Ryo Ishibashi, Eihi Shiina, Tetsu Sawaki, Jun Kunimura, Miyuki Matsuda, Renji Ishibashi, Ren Osugi, Shigeru Saiki, Toshie Negishi, Ken Mitsuishi, Fumiyo Kohinata. **D:** Takashi Miike. **W:** Daisuke Tengan, Ryu Murakami (novel). **C:** Hideo Yamamoto. **M:** Koji Endo. **VHS, DVD**

Avenging Eagle

Outlaw Chi Ming-sing (Ti Lung) stumbles across the desert, until a wanderer (Alexander Fu Sheng) stops to help him. Unexpectedly, Chi attacks him and steals his horse. The man catches up with him by nightfall, and after the customary duel, the two travelers call a truce. At dawn, they're awakened by Han Sung, Eagle Pang, and another of Chi's fellow assassins, who have come to take him back to their clan. Chi has rebelled against the Iron Boat Clan, whose leader Yu Hsi-hung (Ku Feng) raised him and many other orphans he bought to be ruthless killers. Chi was one of the 13 Eagles that survived Yu's deadly training, but on a raid to steal a shipment of gold and ginseng, he was wounded and abandoned by his brothers. Found and cared for by the kindly Chang family, he regains his humanity. But it's discovered that Chang is really lawman Wong Ahn, Yu's hated enemy, and Chi can't stop the Eagles from killing the whole family. Having heard his story, the stranger decides to help Chi make a stand against the Eagles—but just who is he really?

The story suffers due to the start-and-stop pacing brought on by the flashbacks, and though Chi was supposedly once a remorseless killer, they never risk showing star Ti Lung actually doing anything evil. However, the entire picture benefits from the legendary Shaw Brothers facilities—star power, elaborate sets, interesting cinematography, and of course, terrific fight choreography. Fu Sheng and Ti Lung make for a great team, and should have done more films together. **AKA:** *Long Xie Shi San Ying; Cold Blooded Eagles.* 🐉🐉🐉

1978 (R) 93m/C *HK* Alexander Fu Sheng, Ku Feng, Ti Lung, Johnny Wang, Tang Yim-chan, Tu Lung, Lam Fai-wong, Wang Pei-chi, Eddie Ko, Jamie Luk, Yang

Chih-ching, Yang Sha-fei, Yau Tsui-ling, Shih Szu, Jenny Yu Yung, Tang Chia. *D:* Sun Chung. *W:* Ngai Hong, Chin Hung (novel). *C:* Lan Nai-tsai. *M:* Chen Yung-yu. **DVD**

The Avenging Fist

Those who have always wanted to see Yuen Biao and Sammo Hung play superheroes need look no further than this film, though they have only supporting roles. In the future, all weapons have been abolished by international treaty. A hundred policemen are selected for an experiment called the Power Glove Project, an attempt to create a device to unlock the unused portion of human potential, but the project is aborted without explanation. Actually, only three cops survived the project: Dark (Sammo Hung), Thunder (Yuen Biao), and Combat 21 (Roy Cheung). At a martial arts tournament, eight-time champion Iron Surfer (Stephen Fung) finds a worthy challenger in Nova (Wang Lee-hom), a young punk trying to win the prize money so he can buy a black-market Power Glove. Nova wins the fight, much to the displeasure of his mother Aunt Wing (Cecilia Yip), who has forbidden him to use the Avenging Fist style for anything but practice. His late father Thunder developed the Avenging Fist, leaving computer programs for Nova to learn from. Later, Nova—along with his buddy Jazz (Chin Ka-lok) and sister Belle (Kristy Yeung)—meets up with Iron Surfer again at a nightclub. A brawl breaks out, but Inspector Dark arrives with a Power Glove to quell it. Seeing Nova use the Avenging Fist, he brings him his father's Power Glove and Nova learns the truth: Combat 21 went power mad, becoming an evil fascist supervillain who captured Thunder 20 years ago, enslaving him to try to discover the secrets of the Avenging Fist. The enthralled Thunder is ordered to attack during Nova's birthday party, abducting Belle and killing Wing.

But Combat 21 finds that Belle doesn't have the secrets he wants, and sends Thunder back to abduct Nova. Combat 21 also knows that Thunder's children are a result of another experiment, a genetics project designed to unleash superpowers without the use of a Power Glove, as evidenced in Belle's ability to generate heat with a touch. He brainwashes Nova and Belle, and puts Iron Surfer in a cryogenic freeze. He then broadcasts his intention to explode a nerve gas bomb unless all of Region 3 surrenders to him. However, Dark has given Nova a device to counteract Combat 21's brainwashing in advance, allowing him to break free and join with Iron Surfer (revived by Belle's self-sacrifice, her powers transferred to him) and Dark to confront Combat 21 in a final showdown.

Virtually drowning in well-designed digital f/x, *The Avenging Fist* is great eye candy, but fails to make its characters interesting. All the fancy effects and editing only serve to emphasize that the martial arts on display aren't all that exciting. Modern special-effects techniques can successfully embellish fight scenes—see *Blade 2* and *The One*—but here they only look like a light show. Lacking either a compelling story or impressive stunts, the CGI becomes the whole focus, starting with the gorgeous title sequence—all cool bluish liquid shapes that look like microphotography. There's also a pretty cool monster that pops up now and then, though not often enough. A lot of the costumes are nice, too—a glaring exception being Sammo Hung's silly hat. Ekin Cheng guest stars as the young Dark (his weight gain is often blamed as a side-effect of using the Power Glove, but Sammo's funniest line explains that he just "likes to eat"). As a notice in the end credits clearly spells out, this is NOT based on Namco's hit video game franchise Tekken. Well, it is, but Namco changed their minds about selling the rights for this film (maybe because they thought they'd get more money from Hollywood), though in typical Hong Kong fashion, production was already under way. The project was stalled several months while lawyers hashed out the details. *AKA: Kuen San; Quan Shen; Kuen Sun; Fight Zone; God of Fist Style; Legend of Tekken; Legend of the Fist Master.* ♪♪♪♡

2001 96m/C *HK* Wang Lee-hom, Stephen Fung, Kristy Yeung, Gigi Leung, Sammo Hung, Chin Ka-lok, Yuen Biao, Roy Cheung, Ekin Cheng, Cecilia Yip, Yu Ka-ho, Benjamin Yuen, Ron Smoorenburg. *D:* Andrew Lau, Corey Yuen. *W:* Thirteen Chan. *C:* Lai Yiu-fai. **VHS, DVD**

Avenging Warriors of Shaolin

Many films have been made dealing with various heroes who fought the Ching Dynasty and the destruction of Shaolin Temple, but this one focuses on three nobodies who rise up in the aftermath to aid the cause. Ying Cha-po (Phillip Kwok) is a restaurant waiter and Chun Ah-chien (Lo Meng) makes tofu, but they're both more interested in improving their kung fu than their jobs. They're joined in their practice by Chu Tsai (Sun Chien), an outcast from a local kung fu school run by Chi Chu-chou. All three dream of using their skills to become heroes. They get their chance when the renegade monk Pai Mei destroys the Shaolin Temple and sends General Kau Ching-cheung (Lu Feng) to track down the injured hero Hung Hei-kwun (Jason Pai). Hung hides out at Chi's school while searching for rebel leader Han Chi (Chiang Sheng), and meets

Ying, Chun, and Chu when he collapses from his wounds outside the tofu shop. While the lads tend to their guest, Kau and his men track down the fugitive, leading to the inevitable rumble.

More lighthearted than most Chang Cheh movies, this film's trio of heroes at times appears like extensively trained and acrobatically gifted Three Stooges. Their antics—cutting up in the restaurant and tofu shop—sometimes go on too long, but the film pays off when Chang's Five Venoms come together for the mesmerizing final battle. All the combatants seem very young here due to their Beatle-cut-plus-pigtail hairdos. Not his best work, but this was another hit for Chang, and features the expected high level of fight choreography and acrobatics. Hung Hei-kwun is one of China's greatest heroes, his exploits featured in such films as *Executioners from Shaolin* and *New Legend of Shaolin*. *AKA: Gaai Si Ying Hung; Jie Shi Ying Xiong; Avenging Warriors; Shaolin Rescuers.*

1979 107m/C *HK* Phillip Kwok, Lo Meng, Sun Chien, Lu Feng, Chiang Sheng, Jason Pai, Wang Li, Yu Tai-ping, Goo Goon-chung, Yeung Hung, Yang Chih-ching, Chan Shen, Chiang Nan, Walter Cho, Wong Ching Ho, Sai Gwa Pau, Cheng Miu, Tan Chun-tao, Lau Fong-sai, Paul Wong. **D:** Chang Cheh. **W:** Ngai Hong, Chang Cheh, Tsai Kai-pin. **C:** Tsao Hui-chi. **M:** Chen Yung-yu. **VHS, DVD**

The Awaken Punch

Chan Dai-gan (Henry Yu Yung) puts his kung fu to work driving off the gangs collecting protection money in his town, and reluctantly accepts the reward money offered by merchants. He gains a reputation as the area's hero for hire, and when he saves Miss San (Susanna Au Yeung) from some rapists, she attaches herself to him in gratitude, but he rejects her attention. Having failed to find a real job in the city, Chan returns to his little village, where he promises his dying father (Kenneth Tsang) to become a successful farmer and give up fighting. Of course, events conspire to force him to fight. When will these dying fathers wise up and add, "…unless absolutely necessary," to these deathbed vows? As in a classic western plot, richest man in town Wong (Tin Fung) has inside information about the route planned for a new government road project, and sends his emissaries White Fan (Fong Yeh) and Black Fan Lee (San Kwai) to buy the Chan property. When Chan refuses to sell, Wong sends for fighters Han Chu (Fung Hark-On) and Chow (Lee Chiu) to apply pressure. They kidnap visiting San and put her in their brothel, beat up Chan's student friend Ying Ho, and burn down the farm, killing Chan's mother and sister (Suzy Mang). This is

the anticipated last straw that awakens Chan's fists of fury.

Recent video editions tout this flick as starring Chan Sing (who doesn't appear) and for Yuen Woo-ping's contributions as action director. He and brother Yuen Cheung-yan choreograph a number of fine action sequences, including an unusual one in which a hero on bicycle is chased down a mountainside by one of the villains, and ends up nearly run over by a train. Some fight scenes are shot too dark to see the action. Now a popular HK TV star, Susanna Au Yeung was just 18 when she appeared here. The soundtrack steals liberally from the score for *The Godfather* and, less appropriately, an instrumental version of Van Morrison's "Wild Night"! *AKA: Sek Po Tin Geng; Dan Po Tian Jing; Village on Fire; Fury of the Black Belt.*

1973 96m/C *HK* Henry Yu Yung, Susanna Au Yeung, Tin Fung, Suzy Mang, Kenneth Tsang, Fong Yeh, San Kwai, Fung Hark-On, Lee Chiu, Got Heung Ting, Yuen Wah, Nancy Sit, Mars, Sunny Yuen. **D:** Fong Lung-seung. **W:** Cony B. Sarangaya, Fong Lung-seung. **C:** Hwa San. **M:** Chou Fu-liang. **DVD**

Bakery Amour

Lost love letters and a special loaf of bread are the key ingredients in this gentle and openhearted romance. The lovely Lok To (Michelle Reis) recommends a newly vacated apartment in her building to longtime platonic friend Chanty (William So). On the same day, her boyfriend Gala (Convoy Chan), away at a job in France for the past year, writes and tells her that he is breaking up with her because she never responded to any of his previous 99 letters. Lok To is crushed, in part because she never received the letters. After Chanty and his uncle Jet (Francis Ng) move into the building, Jet discovers the letters among the items left behind by the former occupant, who evidently stole them for the collectible stamps. Feeling guilty about reading the letters after he meets Lok To, Jet concocts an elaborate plan to help her reunite with her boyfriend. Abandoning his dream of opening a detective agency, he uses the money to buy the bakery shop where Lok To formerly worked and asks her to run it, confident that eventually Gala will return to Hong Kong and look for her there. Inevitably, however, Jet begins falling for her. What will happen when Gala returns?

At first glance the story appears quite traditional. Adding resonance, though, is that Jet and Chanty are Hakkas, an ethnic group of Chinese people known for their conservative traditions, yet quite willing to migrate. Jet left the village—where he was a revered elder despite his youth—to move to Hong Kong and keep an eye on Chanty. He is inexperienced in love because he was too busy with village responsibilities to romance anyone. Like Chanty, Jet is ready to stretch his wings, and it's fun to watch Francis Ng, an actor renowned for his darker roles, play someone who is so fussy, insecure, and uncertain. It's also a pleasure to watch a variety of emotions wash across Michelle Reis's face like gentle waves breaking on a tropical beach. The script allows the two main characters to develop while giving the supporting players room to breathe. Things get a bit messy, though, when unnecessary complications are introduced late in the game. The fact that the film itself is not overly cute or sentimental is a definite plus and makes up for its overly ambitious second half. —PM **AKA:** *Oi Ching Baak Min Baau; Ai Qing Bai Mian Bao.* 𝄞𝄞♡

2001 101m/C *HK* Francis Ng, Michelle Reis, William So, Convoy Chan, Stephanie Che, Helena Law. **D:** Steven Lo. **W:** Canny Leung. **C:** Chan Chi-ying. **M:** Leung Wai-kin. **DVD**

Ballistic Kiss

Donnie Yen *(Iron Monkey)* directs and stars in this film, written by Bey Logan (author of the book *Hong Kong Action Cinema*). Talk radio personality Simon (Simon Lui) has an enigmatic regular caller named Cat Lee (Yen), who "makes deliveries" for a living. What he delivers is death, as a highly skilled elite contract killer. An early sequence establishes his abilities, showing the bespectacled hit man taking down a penthouse full of bad guys without even breaking a sweat.

Carrie (Annie Wu) is a cop assigned to "Operation Assassin," a project dedicated to the many triad execution cases in Hong Kong. Cat is quite taken with her, as he can see into her apartment window from his own. Cat agrees to one more assignment before going on a vacation—the target is Conroy Chan, playboy film producer who screwed mobster Carl Tsoi out of a chunk of cash. A complication: head of Chan's security Wesley Wong (Yu Rongguang, also in *Iron Monkey*) is Tsoi's inside man. Wong and Cat used to be partners on the NYPD, until Wong framed Cat for his secret criminal activities. Cat makes the hit and shoots Wong for dessert, but his old enemy was wearing a bullet-proof vest. Before long, the two men are involved in their own private war, with Carrie getting mixed up in the middle of it.

Yen is a stylish director; he mixes up film speeds à la John Woo, and paints his screen in monochrome shades for business, wider hues for pleasure. He's a bit too stylish at times, however, obscuring the action and making frequent

rewinds a necessity. **AKA:** *Sha Sha Ren, Tiao Tiao Miu.* 𝄞𝄞𝄞

1998 90m/C *HK* Donnie Yen, Annie Wu, Simon Lui, Yu Rongguang, Vincent Kok, Karen Tong, Lily Chow, Jimmy Wong. **D:** Donnie Yen. **W:** Bey Logan. **C:** Wong Kai Fei. **M:** Yukie Nishimura. **VHS, DVD**

Bangkok Dangerous

Thailand gets in on the action with this kinetic gun fu flick, putting the Pang Brothers (Oxide and Danny) on the list of world-class action directors. In a scenario that recalls *Fallen Angels*, Kong (Pawalit Mongkolpisit) is a deaf young urban contract killer, taking odd jobs from his agent Aom (Patharawarin Timkul, who sometimes narrates), the manager of the Anna a Go-Go strip club. His mentor Joe (Pisek Intrakanchit) brought him into the business after meeting him mopping up at a gun club, and taught him everything; but since Joe took a bullet through his gun hand, he's been feeling burned out and wants to retire. A scar-faced triad ex-boxer courier brings Aom a new job that takes Kong to Hong Kong.

Returning with a cold, Kong meets druggist Fon (Premsinee Ratanasopha). Aom rejects Scarface's advances, and while Kong is busy dating Fon, the thug comes to the club with his stooges and rapes her. Joe kills Scarface in revenge, angering Aom's triad contact, who still hasn't been paid for the Hong Kong hit. When he finds out Joe is responsible, he sends Joe out on a job with blanks in his gun (a plot flaw—professionals always check their guns). Meanwhile, Kong's relationship with Fon hits a bump when his instincts take over and he kills two muggers that try to rob them. Kong finds out who was in on Joe's murder and goes after them. And when Kong completes a hit on a prominent target, it puts his life in danger, too.

The material may be almost trite, but the execution is very good, mixing fancy editing with some genuinely great visual ideas. When Kong stalks the halls of a Japanese restaurant, looking to avenge his mentor, Joe's ghost goes with him. Kong's deafness is often used as not only a plot point, but a point of view. And then there's that shot from a lizard's eye view. The Pang twins started their careers in Hong Kong before bringing the Hong Kong–style filmmaking they'd learned to Bangkok. Like so many young filmmakers around the world, their view is global without losing the local flavor. 𝄞𝄞𝄞

2000 (R) 105m/C *TH* Pawalit Mongkolpisit, Premsinee Ratanasopha, Patharawarin Timkul, Pisek Intrakanchit, Korkiate Limpapat, Piya Roonnak. **D:** Oxide Pang, Danny Pang. **W:** Oxide Pang, Danny

Pang. **C:** Decha Srimantra. **M:** Orange Music. **VHS, DVD**

Barefoot Gen

No more Hiroshimas. That's the simple message of Project Gen, the life work of cartoonist Keiji Nakazawa. It's such a simple message that one might think it doesn't really need to be said, but it's so important a message that it must be said anyway. On August 6, 1945, Nakajima's life—and the world—was forever changed when he was a firsthand witness to the atomic explosion that destroyed his home city. In 1972, he told of that day in a manga story titled "I Saw It," which was so popular that the next year saw the beginning of his much expanded, slightly fictionalized version, *Barefoot Gen*. Ten years later, Masaki Mori directed this animated feature version. On that fateful day, six-year-old Gen Nakaoka and his little brother Shinji only know that they're hungry, and are looking forward to the rice harvest. They don't understand the rationing, and how they and their sister Eiko have to sacrifice a bit so their pregnant mother stays strong, and they can only see that the air raids interrupt their sleep. But for some reason, the bombs never drop on Hiroshima—until the big one comes. It's especially shocking to see the bomb's horrors rendered in Nakazawa's simple cartoon style. It's also startling in its detail, and pulls no punches. Gen is saved only by fate—he's not blinded by the flash because he stoops for a pebble, and a small wall protects him while the girl he was talking to beside him has her right side scorched away in an instant. The aftermath is even worse. Gen awakes to find burnt corpses everywhere. Mobs of horribly disfigured living dead shamble about. Survivors drown in the river while trying to escape the fires. Gen sees his father, brother, and sister die in their burning house, and hours later has to assist in his mother's labor. Radioactive black rain falls all the next day. Brave Gen struggles on in the days ahead, trying to help his mother and save others, and fearing radiation poisoning.

Not as relentlessly depressing as the similar *Grave of the Fireflies*, *Barefoot Gen* is one of those stories full of otherwise "adults only" content that supervised children ought to see, if only so its lessons of intense tragedy and hope will be remembered. It seems incredible, but the Japanese government actually tried to cover up the extent of the Hiroshima damage, refusing to surrender until after the horror was repeated at Nagasaki. *AKA: Hadashi no Gen.* ♫♫♫♪

1983 83m/C *JP* **D:** Masaki Mori. **W:** Keiji Nakazawa. **C:** Kinichi Ishikawa. **M:** Kentaro Haneda. **DVD**

Battle in Outer Space

In the far-off future of 1965, Satellite SJ-1 is attacked and destroyed by alien spaceships. The aliens then cause all sorts of disasters on Earth using gravity manipulation and mind control. Fortunately, scientists Dr. Adachi (Minoru Takada) and Dr. Richardson (Leonard Stanford) have invented a powerful atomic heat ray cannon, and the Japanese military has just finished construction of two new spaceships. International crews take off aboard the ships and head for the moon to look for the enemy base. However, crewman Iwamura (Yoshio Tsuchiya) has been implanted with an alien mind-control device, and periodically tries to sabotage the mission. On the moon, the crews head off in moon buses, leaving Iwamura behind to escape and blow up one of the ships. However, Major Katsumiya (Ryo Ikebe) manages to destroy the alien base with a ray gun, ending the mind control before Iwamura can destroy the second ship. The crew heads back to Earth, fighting all the way, to prepare defenses for the alien attack.

Enthusiasm for the Space Age gripped Japan even harder than the United States—just compare this picture to *The Mysterians,* made just three years before. Then, Earthlings faced the alien threat with an emphasis on finding and exploiting the enemy's weakness. Here, humans have already constructed powerful ships and weapons of their own, and fight it out toe-to-toe with the invaders. Maybe we were able to use technology left behind by the defeated Mysterians, but more likely it was the fact that, by the early 1960s, society had suddenly grown comfortable with the idea that we'd be traveling to Mars almost immediately. Magazines like *Popular Mechanics* regularly featured cover illustrations depicting space stations and moon colonies, right along with articles about how to build your own radio (or bomb shelter), so the future of the space race was taken for granted. At least some things didn't change, as one of the film's astronauts has to be reminded about the lack of gravity in space once in a while. Eiji Tsuburaya's special-effects unit carries the whole show, creating spectacle on the grand scale. Scenes of the alien mothership destroying cities with a gravity ray, and others in which meteors are hurled into landmarks, are still mighty impressive. Another thrilling sequence occurs in a moon cave, where hordes of creepy little aliens attack the astronauts. Ishiro Honda's direction consists almost entirely of organizing teams of people in uniforms to react in concert. A similar plotline would be adopted in *Destroy All Monsters* later on. *AKA: Uchu Daisenso; The Great Space War.* ♫♫♫

1959 90m/C *JP* Ryo Ikebe, Kyoko Anzai, Minoru Takada, Koreya Senda, Hisaya Ito, Yoshio Tsuchiya, Nadao Kirino, Kozo Nomura, Fuyuki Murakami, Ikio Sawamura, Leonard Stanford, Harold Conway, Tadashi Okabe, Yutaka Oka, Yasuhisa Tsutsumi, Koichi Sato, Rinsaku Ogata, Shigeo Kato, Saburo Kadowaki, Yukihiko Gondo, Katsumi Tezuka, Mitsuo Tsuda, Osman Yusuf, Yasuhisa Tsutsumi. *D:* Ishiro Honda. *W:* Shinichi Sekizawa, Jojiro Okami (story). *C:* Hajime Koizumi. *M:* Akira Ifukube. **VHS**

Battle of Shaolin

Another film given a new title with "Shaolin" in it for commercial purposes only. Stagecoach driver Shang-li (Wang Tao) and his kid sidekick Little Rabbit (Lam Siu-foo) are hired by a stranger carrying a birdcage—the infamous killer Sparrow (Man Kong Lung)—for a long trip. While proving his skill with a whip, Shang-li has a run-in with Mr. Wu Chu (Wong Hap), the lackey of local boss Pao Cheng-fang (Lo Lieh). Wu's escort service has been hired to transport $3,000 in silver, but Pao secretly hires bandits of the Three Scars gang to steal the treasure on the way. Shang-li is desperate to make some

money, trying to buy out the debt of prostitute Shou-chui. Though he's proficient at kung fu, his beloved Shou-chui makes him promise to stay out of fights. Sparrow wants to hire Shang-li to help him steal the silver, but though the extra cash is tempting, Shang-li sticks to his promise and agrees only to drive Sparrow to the job. Even though he's recognized as participating in the robbery, Shang-li defends the witnesses, and kills Sparrow when he attacks in self-defense. In over his head, Shang-li flees with the loot, bringing him up against Three Scars (Phillip Ko) and his gang (which is actually run by his wife, played by Angela Mao). Though Shang-li gets out of the scrap with the silver, he still has to get his girlfriend out of the brothel, even though Pao and his men are waiting to ambush him.

This Western-flavored adventure from Kao Pao Shu, the top female director in kung fu cinema, features unusual depth of character, and a heavy dose of pathos and romance. Not that it doesn't have its share of wacky kung fu action—Wang Tao displays his famous backward kicks and leaping punches, and uses a whip like a magician, while Lo Lieh uses a device like the flying guillotine on a chain, and

Angela Mao's bound feet are rigged with mini-circular saws! Some of the flashbacks feel like padding, but it's a generally good story, abetted by great fighting by top kung fu stars. **AKA:** *Bok Meng; Bo Mang; Battle for Shaolin; The Damned; Bandits, Prostitutes and Silver; Snake in the Eagle's Shadow 3; Wu Tang, Hos, Thugs and Scrillah.* 🐉🐉🐉

1977 82m/C HK Wang Tao, Angela Mao, Lo Lieh, Phillip Ko, Wong Hap, Man Kong Lung, Hsueh Fon, Ko Saio Pao, Wu Chia Hsiang, Yuen Sam, Lau Lap Cho, Lam Siu-foo, Sit Hon, Wong Chi Sang, Siu Yiu, Chin Leung, Cheung Pang, Wong Man-chuen, Chen Chiu, Au Lap-bo, Chiang Kam, Chen Shan, Shih Ting Ken, Mau Ging-shun, Ching Kuo-chung. **D:** Kao Pao Shu. **W:** Ngai Hong, Kao Pao Shu. **C:** Chang Wei-hung, Chang Shih-chun. **M:** Chou Fu-liang. **VHS, DVD**

Battle Royale

Ever watch a "reality" TV show like *Survivor* (or *Big Brother* or *The Real World*) and wonder what it would be like if, instead of getting voted off the island, contestants would be put to death? In the Not Too Distant Future, an economic collapse—followed by rocketing unemployment and school boycotts—results in the government passing the Millennium Education Reform Act, allowing the creation of the Battle Royale Survivor Program. Orphaned Nanahara (Tatsuya Fujiwara) finds that his middle-school class trip is a ruse—his class is the latest to be abducted for this year's BR tournament. Drugged, they awake in a different sort of classroom, each of them wearing metal collars. Soldiers surround the building. Their teacher Kitano ("Beat" Takeshi Kitano) appears, introducing two "transfer students": older juvenile delinquents Kawada (Taro Yamamoto) and Kiriyama (Masanobu Ando). He explains the situation to them: Class B has been isolated on a small deserted island. Their instructions are to kill each other until only one is left. To demonstrate the seriousness of the situation, he executes a girl for whispering during the lecture. If they try to escape, or fail to leave the constantly shifting "danger zones" in time, the collars will explode. If there is no winner by the third day, all the collars will explode. Kitano demonstrates this on Nanahara's unruly best friend Nobu. Each student is given a survival kit and a random weapon. Some immediately begin sniping, picking the others off. Some commit suicide. Others band together to defy the game for a while, but mostly to kill stragglers more easily. Nanahara joins with his girlfriend Noriko (Aki Maeda) and tries to figure some way out of the situation. But everyone is inevitably drawn into the bloodshed.

Based on a best-selling novel, *Battle Royale* takes the darkly comic tone of *RoboCop* and turns the lights down a few notches darker. Though the book places the story in an alternate world where Japan won World War II, our own universe is sufficiently violent for the story to work. If it were made about a group of adults, this would have likely been picked up for distribution in the U.S. immediately. But a film in which 15-year-olds run around stabbing and shooting each other is a bit beyond what most Americans can handle, even with *Lord of the Flies* being taught as a literary classic in our schools. As time goes on, the killing is less frequent, but increasingly savage. Even amid the violence, the teens continue their petty crushes and disputes. Even friendships are formed, despite the fact that they may be forced to kill each other when the time comes. Taken as science fiction, action-adventure, or social commentary, *Battle Royale* is a terrific film, full of engaging ideas, thrills, and surprises. The traditional mainstream music soundtrack only makes it more effective. 🐉🐉🐉🐉

2000 113m/C JP "Beat" Takeshi Kitano, Tatsuya Fujiwara, Aki Maeda, Taro Yamamoto, Masanobu Ando, Kou Shibasaki, Chiaki Kuriyama, Yuko Miyamura. **D:** Kinji Fukasaku. **W:** Kenta Fukasaku, Koshun Takami (novel). **C:** Katsumi Yanagishima. **M:** Masamichi Amano. **VHS, DVD**

Beast Cops

Police Detective Sgt. Frank Tung (Anthony Wong) finds that his gambling debts to triad boss Alphonse Fai (Roy Cheung) occasionally compromise his position on the force, but he tries not to let it bother him. When his assistant Sam (Sam Lee) tells him about an XTC deal, he finds himself pointing a gun at Fai when the mainland bumpkin sent to broker the deal panics and turns violent. Alphonse gets out of town until the heat dies down, leaving his girlfriend Yoyo (Kathy Chow) behind when she's late and taking floozy Suzi instead. Straitlaced SDU officer Lt. Michael Cheung (Michael Wong) gets transferred to take over Tung's department after assaulting his boss. After meeting Tung at Alphonse' club, Cheung becomes his roommate, and gets involved romantically with Yoyo. Cheung's disciplined style clashes with sloppy Tung, who can't even pay their rent on time. Under Cheung's watch, Tung is forced to chase robbers and other police duties he'd rather avoid. With Alphonse out of town, other triads are lining up to try to take over chunks of his territory. At the urging of godfather Uncle Tai, gun-crazy underling Pushy-Pin Ted (Patrick Tam) starts protecting the territory by killing off competitors, and even makes a move on Yoyo.

"So today's lesson is...you kill each other off 'til there's only one left. Nothing's against the rules."

—Teacher Kitano introduces the new math to his class in *Battle Royale*

Most of the picture is more concerned with the daily lives of the cops, only giving a bit of plot now and then. Occasionally, Anthony Wong narrates or talks to the camera, as do Michael Wong and Sam Lee. There are scenes of the cops' romantic adventures, and Cheung gets Yoyo pregnant. Cheung comes to learn how fraternizing with the criminal element can yield positive results. But when Pushy-Pin slaps Yoyo, he comes down hard on the crook. The triad sends knife-wielding thugs after Cheung, and when Alphonse returns, the situation explodes. After cruising along for 90 minutes, the violence of the picture increases suddenly and escalates sharply, leading to one of the most savage and ferociously bloody fight scenes ever filmed. Fine performances all around, with another edgy portrayal from Anthony Wong, and a cool, jazzy soundtrack. Avoid the English dubbed version, which makes half the cast sound like cartoon gangsters. *AKA: Yau Sau Ying Ging; Ye Shou Xing Jing; Beast Cop.* 🎝🎝🎝🎝

1998 108m/C *HK* Anthony Wong, Michael Wong, Roy Cheung, Kathy Chow, Sam Lee, Patrick Tam, Stephanie Che, Kam Kong, Michael Lui, Arthur Wong, Daisy Wu, Aaron Chong, Cheung Chu Hong, Chan Nam Wing, Gordon Leung. *D:* Gordon Chan, Dante Lam. *W:* Chan Hing-ka, Gordon Chan. *C:* Tony Cheung. *M:* T2. **VHS, DVD**

Beast of the Yellow Night

Philippines horror specialist Eddie Romero gives us his take on the Faust legend, mixing it with Dr. Jekyll and Mr. Hyde. In 1946, the Philippine army is called in when a maniac is reported butchering folks in the hill country. A strange man (Vic Diaz) tracks down fugitive maniac Langdon (John Ashley) in the woods, feeds him human flesh, and offers protection in exchange for obedience. Decades later, Langdon is still at work—every time he dies, his devilish boss brings him back in someone else's body, the latest being industrialist Phillip Rogers, who died in an accident. Langdon's mission: to bring out the latent evil in people. It's a mission that, even after so many years, has Langdon confused and at times rebellious. When he goes too far, about to enter a church, his master turns him into a savage, cannibalistic monster. After tearing open a groundskeeper and eating his guts, the monster tries to destroy himself by throwing himself in front of a train—an effort that fails. From then on, the film becomes a mostly pedestrian were-monster tale, with Langdon trying to hide his curse and protect his wife Julia (Mary Wilcox) and brother Earl (Ken Metcalfe), while running from a determined police lieutenant (Eddie Garcia). There's a bit of

philosophical discussion with a blind man (Andres Centenera) who takes him in briefly, but for the most part it's a monster dragnet.

This late Romero entry is unusual in many ways. Ashley steps outside his usual hero role, though we don't get to see his Langdon doing enough evil work to make his dilemma really effective. The satanic Vic Diaz plays a role much grander than he normally gets, and his devil appears and disappears in clouds of yellow mist (thus the title), rather than the obvious red color code. Some of the bit players speak Tagalog, whereas usually these productions released to the U.S. drive-in circuit had every line dubbed in English. One feature that's not unusual for a Romero horror flick: the casting of a wooden American blonde as the heroine. 🎝🎝▽

1970 (R) 87m/C *PH* John Ashley, Mary Wilcox, Leopoldo Salcedo, Eddie Garcia, Ken Metcalfe, Vic Diaz, Andres Centenera, Ruben Rustia, Jose Garcia, Johnny Long. *D:* Eddie Romero. *W:* Eddie Romero. *C:* Justo Paulino. *M:* Nestor Robles. **VHS, DVD**

Beautiful Beast

Though not a sequel, this follow-up continues Toei's "XX" series of female-assassin movies. The mysterious Chinese warrior woman Ran (Kaori Shimamura), better known as Black Orchid, arrives in Japan and rubs out mob boss Ishizuka (Yuzo Hayakawa), carving her trademark "X" on his forehead. Fleeing the scene, she hides out with bartender Yoichi Fujinami (Takeshi Yamato). She rewards his hospitality by seducing him. Ishizuka's right-hand man Yaguchi (Takanori Kikuchi) is hot for revenge on Black Orchid, whom he learns is a member of the elite Pasei Ding ("Untouchables"), former Red Guards turned mercenary strike force. Next on her hit list is another yakuza boss, Ho (Hakuryu). She's come on a personal vendetta against Ho and Ishizuka for murdering her little sister. However, she finds that Ho is not as easy to kill, and Yoichi becomes torn between helping his old pal Yaguchi and the mystery girl that he's falling in love with.

Beautiful Beast may not have as strong a villain as its predecessor *Beautiful Hunter* (that blind yakuza priest is tough to beat), but improves on it by foregoing a lot of empty softcore sex in favor of providing more action. Director Toshiharu Ikeda (who contributed the earlier entry *Beautiful Prey*) is no John Woo, but at least Ran's trunk-full of high-powered weaponry provides a little fun. *AKA: XX: Utukushiki Gakuen; XX Beautiful Beast.* 🎝🎝

1995 87m/C *JP* Kaori Shimamura, Takanori Kikuchi, Hakuryu, Minako Ogawa, Shiro Namiki, Mou Kokkyou, Yuzo Hayakawa, Sho Gyogun, Lee Tang, Eiju Kiriyama, Takeshi Yamato. *D:* Toshiharu

Ikeda. **W:** Tamiya Takehashi, Hiroshi Takehashi. **C:** Seizo Sengen. **VHS, DVD**

Beautiful Hunter

Unlike Hong Kong, Canada, and America, Japan never had an official remake of *La Femme Nakita*, but Toei Studios found the female-assassin genre the perfect format for direct-to-video sex and violence features, based on the *XX* novels by Arimasa Osawa.

Blind Father Kano (Koji Shimizu) fully controls the life of his adopted daughter Shion (Makiko Kuno), his "Warrior for God." Shion has been raised since birth to be the perfect assassin and executioner for the Magnificat crime family. A devoutly Catholic gang, they do their criminal business in the vestments of priests and nuns. Shion's First Communion calls for her to execute her first prisoner. Reporters following Kano's activities see Shion at the site when she kills racketeer Ishizaki; photographer Ito (Johnny Okura) gets away just before his partner Sakuma is caught and killed, and his magazine is afraid to publish his photos of the incident. Sent to collect his evidence, the lethal yet naïve Shion finds herself attracted to Ito, and his pleading convinces her to spare his life. Ito's aftershave lotion must be something else, because the mere thought of him has her masturbating with a gun. Yearning for the sort of normal life she's never known, Shion approaches Ito and asks for a date. Father Kano isn't quite so happy about her new boyfriend, and sends Sister Mitsuko (Maiko Kazama) and a squad of killers after them.

Despite its early nunsploitation trappings, *Beautiful Hunter* concentrates mainly on the unconventional love story throughout the first half. It doesn't get down to any really kinky antics until later on, when the captured Shion is subjected to a rather elaborate torture session in the priory basement, which is outfitted with all manner of bondage gear. Kuno looks—well, beautiful, in and out of a series of foxy outfits, but she doesn't perform any kind of martial arts to convince us of her master assassin status. Shimizu *(Prisoner Maria)* makes for a very creepy villain, even dubbed in English. **AKA:** *Jul; XX Beautiful Hunter.* 🐉🐉

1994 91m/C *HK* Makiko Kuno, Koji Shimizu, Katsuo Tokashiki, Johnny Okura, Kenji Mitamura, Maiko Kazama. **D:** Masaru Konuma. **W:** Hiroshi Takahashi, Mangetsu Hanamura (story). **VHS, DVD**

Beauty and the Breast

Shouldn't a comedy about men, breasts, women, and more breasts be a surefire winner? Mario (Francis Ng) is a "brown-noser" at a company that makes ointments; he's developed a well-deserved reputation as a womanizer. He is training co-worker Harper (Daniel Wu) to follow in his footsteps as a lothario, which does not please Harper's girlfriend, Amy (Halina Tam). Mario makes a bet with his boss, Fat (Matt Chow), that he can bed new employee Yuki (Michelle Reis) by the end of the week. Meanwhile, Boss Fat acts outrageously toward everyone and brings in two nasty female executives (Sophie Ngan and Angela Tong) from Bosnia (!) with a new breast-enhancement product. Eventually the good women of the company exact revenge against their oppressors.

From the movie poster and DVD cover art, it appears that the male characters will sprout breasts and learn how to live with them. Alas, it takes the film nearly an hour to arrive at this point. And when it does come to what should be a comedic highlight, the story is gasping for air and soon expires, though a clumsy and extremely extended coda extends the running time considerably.

What went wrong? Judging by the celebrity news items available on the Internet, breast enhancement products have been the rage in Hong Kong for years. So it would seem a natural target for satire, along with trenchant commentary on male chauvinism and various prejudices. Instead, it seems the filmmakers were inspired more by the *idea* behind the much-more successful *La Brassiere* (i.e. men prancing around in women's products) and gave little or no thought to the inherent possibilities of the material. So we have an extremely obnoxious boss behaving badly toward his employees (a faded copy of Andy Lau's character in the runaway boxoffice smash *Needing You*), a pair of attractive women characterized entirely by the size of their breasts and their nasty behavior toward the other, less-endowed women (Sophie Ngan takes the lead here), and an office Don Juan faking cancer to get a woman into bed and thus win a bet. Clearly the film wants to operate in some sort of alternate universe of extreme behavior, but the outrageous antics seem precipitated by the exigencies of the plot rather than as expressions of the characters. Francis Ng and Michelle Reis were much more effective as potential lovers in the previous year's *Bakery Amour.* —PM **AKA:** *Fung Hung Bei Cup; Feng Xiong Mi Cup.* 🐉♡

2002 97m/C *HK* Francis Ng, Michelle Reis, Daniel Wu, Halina Tam, Amanda Strang, Sophie Ngan, Angela Tong, Lam Chi-chung, Matt Chow, Wong Yat-Fei, Wong Tin Lam. **D:** Raymond Yip. **W:** Not a Woman. **C:** Geung Gwok-man. **M:** Lincoln Lo. **DVD**

Beauty Investigator

In this low-budget action comedy, Ellen "Phoenix" Li Min-feng (Moon Lee) and Grace

Chin (Kim Jee-Kee) are a pair of daffy police-women. Despite their penchant for disobeying orders in their enthusiasm for upholding the law, Captain Wong (Melvin Wong) assigns them to undercover duty at Club Vulva (!) in an effort to lure a psycho killer preying on Hong Kong club hostesses. The club's owner, triad underling Bill Tam (Billy Chow), gets ambitious while his boss Hung (Peter Yang) is in prison. He double-crosses some Japanese arms smugglers, then hires Japanese hit woman Tanaka (Yukari Oshima) to kill his superiors Chui Wai (Shum Wai) and Chung Fat (Chung Fat). Grace overhears Bill's plans to assassinate Hung while he's being transferred to a hospital, and the girls decide to try to bust the gang themselves. They end up only wrecking several cars, and Tanaka steals Ellen's gun. They decide to have Grace seduce the club's manager David (Billy Chow) to get a lead on the hit woman, but he turns out to be the psycho. He's got Grace tied up and his animal costume on, when Tanaka steps in and kills him. Bill wants Tanaka to stay on as a bodyguard, but when he won't meet her price, she joins up with the yakuza that are after him. Still snooping around for the gun after a demotion, Grace ends up getting killed by Bill. In a rage, Ellen loads up on artillery (including a nifty wrist rocket launcher) and goes after Bill and his gang.

A lightweight diversion, the main attraction here is another chance to see Lee, Oshima, and Chow kicking each other around. Sophia Crawford, as Bill's bodyguard, was surely hired for her fighting ability, but throws in a gratuitous shower scene for good measure. *AKA: Miu Taam Seung Giu; Miao Tan Shuang Jiao; Beauty Inspectors.*

1992 87m/C *HK* Moon Lee, Yukari Oshima, Melvin Wong, Kim Jee-Kee, Sophia Crawford, Billy Chow, Peter Yang, Shum Wai, Chung Fat, Tai Bo, Chui Jing-yat, Ng Ming Choi. **D:** Lee Tso Nam. **W:** Rico Chung. **C:** Kwan Chi-kan. **M:** Michael Fung. **VHS, DVD**

Beijing Bicycle

Critically acclaimed yet uncomfortable to watch. The backdrop is modern-day China; Guo (Cui Lin) is a country lad newly arrived in the city. He secures a job as a bicycle courier. His pay is meager, though, because he must repay the messenger service for the cost of the bicycle. He works furiously hard, and is fast approaching the time when ownership of the bicycle will transfer to him. One day he is delayed making a pickup, and his bicycle is stolen. He sets off in search of the thief, and thinks he has found him in the person of Jian (Li Bin), a schoolboy out to impress his friends—and a beautiful female schoolmate. Incredibly stubborn, Guo is determined to reclaim his bicycle, despite repeated beatings by Jian's friends, who believe Guo to be the thief. The two teens reach an uneasy agreement that leaves neither one happy.

Though a quick read may remind some of the Italian classic *The Bicycle Thief,* this film, though beautifully shot and well-acted, is incredibly infuriating to watch because it manipulates the audience with a mean spirit. It sets up a certain degree of sympathy for Guo, next questions Guo's character because of his difficult-to-comprehend behavior, reverses course and revels in the unfair beatings he suffers, and then turns around and builds a case for Jian as a misunderstood and persecuted youth. It hides meaningful information from the audience, apparently just to elicit a reaction that's meant to question preconceptions. Instead it feels like the filmmakers are questioning the intelligence and motives of the audience, and makes you wonder why you bothered watching in the first place. —*PM* **AKA:** *Shiqi sui de dan che.*

2001 (PG-13) 113m/C *CH/TW* Cui Lin, Li Bin, Zhou Xun, Gao Yuanyuan, Li Shuang, Zhao Yiwei, Pang Yan, Liu Lei. **D:** Wang Xiaoshuai. **W:** Peggy Chiao, Hsu Hsiao-ming, Tang Danian, Wang Xiaoshuai. **C:** Liu Jie. **M:** Wang Feng. **VHS, DVD**

Beijing Rocks

Awaiting trial for possession of drugs, Michael (Daniel Wu), a Hong Kong pop star, is exiled to mainland China where he becomes a hanger-on in a punk rock entourage fronted by a street-hardened singer Road (Geng Le). He falls for Road's can-can dancing girlfriend Yang Yin (Shu Qi,) who takes him for a nerd, not knowing that he is a big star in Hong Kong. After playing some shows in the city, the band takes to the country where identities and relationships go through the expected changes.

The love triangle, although typical in terms of plot, is sympathetic to each character. Although he doesn't show it, Road is heavily dependant upon Yin, and when Michael threatens their relationship, he is devastated, although he is too cool to show it. The contrast between Hong Kong and China's popular cultures is an eye-opener. In the frustrating and explosive world of Beijing's nightlife, the pop singer learns what proletariat rock and roll is all about. To appreciate the cultural gap in this film, which takes place five years after Hong Kong returned to Chinese rule, imagine Sting roaming about the American countryside with an obscure indie rock band, nobody having the slightest idea of his overseas fame.

Director Mabel Cheung and writer Alex Law are longtime collaborators. Among the films they have done together are *City of Glass* (1998), *The Soong Sisters* (1997), and *Eight Tales of Gold* (1990). Cinematographer Peter Pau *(Crouching Tiger, Hidden Dragon)* illuminates both the urban underworld and scenic countryside with brash color and striking light. In addition to Geng Le's punk rock singing, the soundtrack offers some traditional Chinese music. —BW *AKA: Bakging Lok Yu Lo, Bei Jing le yu lu.* 🎵🎵🎵🎶

2001 109m/C *HK* Daniel Wu, Shu Qi, Geng Le, Richard Ng, Faye Yue. *D:* Mabel Cheung. *W:* Alex Law, Mabel Cheung. *C:* Peter Pau. *M:* Henry Lai. **VHS, DVD**

The Best of the Best

In Asia, this was released as a sequel to *Final Option* (which also spawned the prequel *First Option*), but has no returning characters, and chronicles the adventures of a different bunch through SDU training. Police officer Chan Hiu-tung (Daniel Chan) sees a fellow officer killed and nearly dies himself when the driver they've pulled over for speeding is shot by a Vietnamese hit man. The experience leads him to enter the SDU, but a raid on a terrorist hideout in Yuen Wai Village turns into a massacre, which leaves only Tung unhurt. Tung's dad Commissioner Calvin Chan Lik-wang (Damian Lau) proposes an elite group be formed within SDU, the BoB (Best of the Best), to deal with such threats. Of course, Tung applies, going to camp for a two-week training period under the command of Commander Eagle Cheung (Roy Cheung). For some reason, his fellow trainee Coolman Ho Chi-lum (Julian Cheung) has a grudge against him. Shooting instructor Karen Kook (Karen Mok) is attracted to Coolman, and learns his secret (which turns out to be rather ordinary), though he tries to be cool toward her. The young men eat as much as they want, go swimming and running, shoot guns, play with explosives—it all looks like a summer camp, actually, easier than army basic training. They even get a day off in the middle!

The film is one of the few to address the problem of the Vietnamese Refugee Camp in Hong Kong, showing the squalor the interred lived in, though the opinion offered isn't far above the usual image of non-HK Asians in Hong Kong films. The BoB trainees' final exercise is to spend three days on a deserted island. The island Tung's team is put on turns out to be an exchange point for Vietnamese from the camp buying guns, and they have to fight to survive. Facing repatriation before 1997, the refugees stage an uprising, and the BoB team is called into action for the first time. While functioning as a respectable action drama, *Best of the Best* serves even better as a portrait of the time in which it was filmed. Not to be confused with the kickboxing film of the same title, nor the 1992 Herman Yau comedy. *AKA: Fei Foo Hung Sam 2 Ji Ngo Hei Bei Tin Go; Fei Hu Xiong Xin 2 Zhi Ao Qi Bi Tian Gao.* 🎵🎵🎶

1996 108m/C *HK* Daniel Chan, Julian Cheung, Roy Cheung, Karen Mok, Jerry Lamb, Amanda Lee, Jason Chu, Annie Wu, Damian Lau, Marianne Chan, Blackie Ko, Herman Yau, Michael Tse, Samuel Leung, Benny Lai, Frankie Ng, Yee Tin-hung, William Cho, Wong Tak-ban. *D:* Andrew Lau. *W:* Manfred Wong, Candy Cheng. *C:* Andrew Lau. *M:* Lin Che-yeung. **DVD**

A Better Tomorrow

This crime drama was the first big hit for both director John Woo and star Chow Yun-fat. Sung Tse-ho (Ti Lung) and his friend Mark (Chow) run a successful counterfeiting dynasty until some double-dealing results in a shoot-out, and Ho's father (Tin Fung) is killed. Betrayed, Ho is caught and sent to prison. Even worse punishment comes from his younger brother Kit (Leslie Cheung), who knew nothing of the family crime business (and has even become a cop); Kit turns his back on the older brother who shamed him. On the other hand, an enraged Mark becomes crippled in a gunfight avenging his friend. Their former underling Shing (Waise Lee) ascends to the leadership of the gang, but runs the operation hard, unlike the family crime business the Sungs had built. Ho is released from prison years later to find that Mark has had to endure sustained humiliation to stay in the gang, and Kit still resents him. Learning that Kit will be killed—ambushed during a raid on Shing's operation—Mark and Ho load up their shootin' irons to protect the young cop.

Based on the little seen 1967 film *Story of a Discharged Prisoner,* this is first and foremost a drama about honor, family, and friendship (the HK title translates as "The Essence of a Hero"). However, it's Woo's awesome gun battle sequences (aided by Blackie Ko and Stephen Tung) that made this an enduring hit, and gained worldwide attention for the Hong Kong film industry as a place that produces more than just kung fu flicks. In fact, the film is structured much the same as the martial arts films of Woo's mentor Chang Cheh *(One-Armed Swordsman)* and revived the career of one of Chang's biggest stars, Ti Lung. Chow Yun-fat finally crossed over from being a TV star to a legitimate film star, but it's doubtful he ever expected to gain the worldwide adula-

John Woo

吳宇森

Doves flap their wings in slow motion. Men fly horizontally across the screen, guns blazing from both hands. Bullets tear apart flesh and furniture. Two men face each other with guns drawn.

Such imagery has become the signature of a John Woo action movie. He's become so closely identified with big-budget bombast in his Hollywood career that it's hard to picture him as a director of comedies—yet that's how he first made his mark in Hong Kong. Though several of the films were quite successful, none bore a distinguishable personal touch. The same could be said for the other genre flicks he directed during the mid-1970s to the early 1980s. It's not that he was making bad films; they just weren't *his* films.

Woo had quite a storehouse of stories to tell. He was born in 1946 in China; his family moved to Hong Kong in the early 1950s. The family suffered through hard times, revolving around the frail health of his father (who died when Woo was still a teenager). Movies were an early refuge—Woo fondly recalls musicals like *Seven Brides for Seven Brothers* and *Singing in the Rain* as well as European and Japanese films. As a young man, Woo trained for the priesthood, but clashed with the hypocrisy and politics within the church. Instead of becoming a priest, he became a filmmaker, creating his own short subjects in the late 1960s. He eventually secured a position as an assistant director to the legendary Chang Cheh, and also worked on films directed by Michael Hui, which helps explain his affinity for the comedies he later made with Michael's brother Ricky.

By the mid 1980s Woo was running out of gas, both commercially and creatively. He regrouped in the employ of producer Tsui Hark and made *A Better Tomorrow* in 1986. It was a huge hit and made a film star out of television actor Chow Yun-fat. *The Killer* made international waves in 1989. *Bullet in the Head* was Woo at the top of his form, fusing deeply affecting themes of friendship and loyalty with gut-wrenching blood and bullets. In these films Woo created a substantial body of work that resonated with audiences. He used his personal experiences to flesh out basic narratives. As an example, he often sets epic gun battles within Catholic churches. Setting such violent action in a church is not just chutzpah—it symbolizes his belief that God accepts and forgives even his heroes' sins, as long as they remain pure within their chivalrous hearts.

After the release of *Hard Boiled,* Woo moved to Hollywood. He started by making *Hard Target.* It was deemed too violent and had to be edited in order to secure an "R" rating by the MPAA. Even with the alterations, *Hard Target* is an easy pill to swallow. Woo's next project made him a player. *Broken Arrow* overflowed with sharply paced action sequences. The boxoffice returns more than doubled the reported $65 million budget. In the splashy *Face/Off,* the character conflicts, especially the battle between good and evil that rages within John Travolta's Sean Archer, echoed the identity crisis at the heart of *The Killer* and *Bullet in the Head.* The film gave evidence that Woo might be the rare case of a Hollywood director who could marry complex emotional issues with exciting (and globally appealing) action scenes.

Woo's succeeding films raised more questions than they answered. *Mission: Impossible 2* was even more financially successful, but came in for its share of critical brickbats. Individual sequences were fascinating to watch, but, taken as a whole, the film relies too much on what were now Woo's signature moments (slow-motion and doves). The World War II–era *Windtalkers* took it easy on the familiar imagery but never caught on with audiences, becoming one of the biggest boxoffice bombs of 2002.

As *Windtalkers* demonstrated, projects that require big budgets entail huge risks. Woo has told at least one reporter that he's sworn off action films and wants to explore other avenues. He's long maintained that he wants to make a musical. Even if that dream never comes true, fans can still watch *Once a Thief* and see Chow Yun-fat gliding across a dance floor in a wheelchair as gracefully as any musical dance star of the 1930s. Maybe that should be the signature image for which John Woo is remembered.

tion he's gained from playing Mark. For years after, young men adopted the character's trademark sunglasses and long coat, even if they'd never seen the movie. A sequel, a prequel, and countless imitations followed. Woo and producer Tsui Hark have cameos. *AKA: Ying Hung Boon Sik; Ying Xiong Ben Se; Hung The Color of a Hero; Gangland Boss; True Colors of a Hero.* 🎵🎵🎵♡

1986 95m/C *HK* Ti Lung, Chow Yun-fat, Leslie Cheung, Emily Chu, Waise Lee, Tin Fung, Kenneth Tsang, John Woo, Sek Yin Ji, Shing Fui-on, Tsui Hark, Wong Hap, Lung Ming-yan, Chan Chi-fai. **D:**

John Woo. **W:** John Woo, Chan Hing-ka, Leung Suk-wah. **C:** Horace Wong. **M:** Joseph Koo. **VHS, DVD**

A Better Tomorrow 2

Chow Yun-fat is back, in this sequel to his first big hit with John Woo. What's that, you say? Chow's character died in *A Better Tomorrow*? Woo and Tsui Hark figured it was worth reviving the hoary old twin-brother cliché in order to get Chow back.

Ho is in prison again following the first film's climax, but is offered parole if he helps the police arrest his crime biz mentor Lung (Dean Shek). Ho hesitates, but agrees after learning his cop brother Kit is working under-cover on the case already, dating Lung's daughter Peggy (Regina Kent). Lung is mistak-enly convinced he killed a competitor, and runs off to New York, where he has a nervous break-down after an attempted Mafia hit. He meets up with twin brother Ken (Chow), who runs a Chinese restaurant where neighborhood kids dress like their hero Mark. While Ken tries to nurse Lung back to sanity, Mafia goons come around demanding extortion. When a fight starts, the sound of gunfire brings Lung to his senses, and he helps Ken defeat the mob-sters. To return the favor, Ken goes back to Hong Kong with Lung to reclaim his business from his rival Ko (Kwan San), who has moved into his territory while Lung was busy being insane. Kit and Ho join them for a massive gun battle at Ko's country house.

Cinema City partners Dean Shek and Tsui Hark planned the sequel as an opportunity for Shek to make a comeback, over the objections of director Woo. Their focus on Shek's character Lung throws the whole film out of balance, and Shek's embarrassing histrionics as the insane Lung are a tough act to sit through. Ken's trans-formation from a genial restaurant owner to channeling his dead brother is hard to swallow, too, and the middle part of the film is mostly worthless. However, once Woo shifts the emphasis from mindless melodrama to mind-less mayhem, he regains a lot of points. The sensationally over-the-top gunfight at the end makes it all worthwhile, and points the way to even greater bullet ballet in Woo's following films. One Zen moment, in which Ken and a respected opponent senselessly trade guns in mid-match, is a particular crowd-pleaser. The backstage bickering was enough for Tsui to take over direction of *Part 3* himself, while Woo turned his script into the similar but superior *Bullet in the Head.* **AKA:** *Ying Hung Boon Sik Chuk Chap; Ying Xiong Ben Se Xu Ji; The Color of a Hero II.* 🎵🎵🎵🎝

1987 104m/C *HK* Chow Yun-fat, Ti Lung, Leslie Cheung, Dean Shek, Kwan San, Emily Chu, Kenneth Tsang, Regina Kent, Shing Fui-on, Lau Siu-ming, Lam Chung, Lung Ming-yan, Ng Man-Tat, Ken Boyle, Louis Roth. **D:** John Woo. **W:** John Woo, Tsui Hark, Leung Suk-wah. **C:** Horace Wong. **M:** Joseph Koo, Lowell Lo. **VHS, DVD**

A Better Tomorrow 3

After having the first sequel to his crime thriller classic interfered with by producers Dean Shek and Tsui Hark, John Woo left the series, took his script for Part 3 and reworked it for his incredible *Bullet in the Head.* Tsui Hark decided to go ahead with a similar idea for this prequel, set in 1974, which tells a story from the early days of Chow Yun-fat's antihero Mark Cheung. But surprisingly, in a twist away from anything John Woo would do, it's Anita Mui who domi-nates the feature.

On his way to Saigon to bail his cousin Che-ung Chi-mun (Tony Leung Ka-Fai) out of jail, Mark encounters glamorous smuggler Chow Ying-kit (Mui), who helps him through customs. Needing to raise cash to get Mun's dad (Shih Kien) out of the country, Mark agrees to help Mun in a black-market deal with a new contact—who turns out to be Chow Ying-kit. But their associ-ates in the army double-cross them, and the trio has to shoot their way out of a jam. It's Kit who teaches Mark how to shoot, and even picks out his trademark sunglasses and raincoat (basical-ly creating the icon of a million youths). Though it's obvious Kit likes Mark better, he hangs back to give Mun his chance with her.

Back in Hong Kong, Mark and Mun open a garage together, and the triangle appears again when Kit shows up. Unfortunately, Kit's clout with authorities comes from her gangster boyfriend Ho Cheung-ching (Saburo Takito), who has been in hiding for years but suddenly reap-pears. Ho doesn't take kindly to Kit's new friends, and sends a bomb that nearly kills them all. Kit returns with Ho to Saigon, where she plans to get revenge for them. Mun and Mark follow to help her out and do some dam-age of their own. But with Saigon falling, they all nearly drown in the chaos.

While Tsui Hark is certainly not John Woo's equal when it comes to gun fu (who is?), he's still a creative force to be reckoned with, and his prequel only suffers in comparison to Woo. Well, there's also the lack of suspense that comes with any prequel—we know Mark isn't going to get killed, no matter how dangerous the situation. We also know that some charac-ters are not so invulnerable. Be that as it may, the film still packs an emotional punch, and

there's certainly plenty of gunfire and explosions. The Saigon locations and sets are impressive, too. There are bullet holes everywhere, and everything looks like it's about to fall apart. Followed by *Return to a Better Tomorrow*. **AKA:** *Ying Hung Boon Sik III: Jik Yeung Ji Gor; Ying Xiong Ben Se III: Tzu Yang Tsu Gor; Love and Death in Saigon.* 🦴🦴🦴

1989 130m/C *HK* Chow Yun-fat, Anita Mui, Tony Leung Ka-Fai, Saburo Takito, Shih Kien. **D:** Tsui Hark. **W:** Tsui Hark, Tai Fu-ho, Edward Leung. **C:** Horace Wong. **M:** Lowell Lo. **VHS, DVD**

Beyond Hypothermia

A bloodstained hand reaches for a bullet. Cryptic narration alludes to a mystery woman. The hand is attached to a fierce-looking man. He disappears as we are drawn into the mystery woman's story. She has no name—she was "rescued' from the horrors of war-torn Cambodia in the 1970s only to be turned into an assassin by the equally mysterious Mr. Ming. Ming has recently died, leaving the hit woman

(Ng Sin-Lin, AKA Jacqueline Wu) to the mercies of her manager and mother-figure.

The assassin was born with a body temperature five degrees colder than normal, and that also aptly describes her icy-cold emotional temperament. She feels nothing when she carries out her assignments. Lately, however, she has taken to eating noodles after each hit at a nearby food stall run by Long Shek (Lau Ching-Wan), attracted to the warmth of Long Shek's personality rather than his "ugly" appearance. He is a goodhearted, reformed triad, with no idea of what the woman he calls "pretty ghost" does for a living. She finally starts making an emotional connection to him, something she has never been able to do in the past, but she is constrained by the rules of her profession—no name, no photos, no identity, no past, no permanent place of residence—and it will soon be time for her to move on. Real trouble begins after she kills Mr. Pok, a Japanese crime boss. Pok's security chief, a Korean man named Yichin Cheu (Han Sang-woo), tracks her down in Hong Kong. He is determined to take revenge for the killing. She must deal with real emotions for the first time in her life.

Chow Yun-fat paints Hong Kong red in *A Better Tomorrow 2*.
THE KOBAL COLLECTION

The violence is ugly and extremely bloody. The actions of the hit woman are not romanticized—we see her carrying out multiple murders with heartless efficiency. She appears to be beyond redemption, yet she's also a tragic victim of circumstances—orphaned and forced into a life she did not choose with no way out. Jacqueline Wu creates an indelible character, a believable woman who never experienced a proper childhood, has no conscience, and must now decide whether she is capable of rejoining the human race. Lau Ching-Wan seems naïve but it's really a cover; he's blanked his own past from his mind and represents the possibilities of personal transformation. Director Patrick Leung juxtaposes restless point-of-view shots with objective framing that constantly challenges the assumptions of the viewer. The final sequence is a demented demolition derby that will leave you battered, bruised, and breathless. —*PM* **AKA:** *Lip Jeung 32 Diy; She Shi 32 Du; 32 Degrees Celsius.* 🐾🐾🐾

1996 85m/C *HK* Jacqueline Wu, Lau Ching-Wan, Han Sang-woo, Sally Wong. **D:** Patrick Leung. **W:** Roy Szeto. **C:** Arthur Wong. **M:** Cheung Siu-hung. **VHS, DVD**

Bichunmoo

An epic swordplay adventure in the mold of *Bride with White Hair* or *Crouching Tiger, Hidden Dragon,* this production boasts the highest budget of any Korean film to date. In the late Yuan Dynasty, the Mongolians ruled most of Asia, and there was much conflict between the Mongols, the Hans, and the migrant Koryo people. Jinha (Shin Hyun-joon) is the orphaned son of a Koryo migrant and a master swordsman. He met his true love Sullie (Kim Hee-sun) when they were children, Jinha taught her how to use a sword, and they grew up happily together. But when Sullie's mother falls deathly ill, her father, feared Mongol general Taruga (Kim Hak-chu) comes to be with her. Forced to separate, Sullie gives Jinha half her jade piece and tells him she'll wait every full moon at Yu Hua Pagoda in Shao Xing. Sullie gets into trouble by slapping a boorish visiting Han Lord Namgung Junkwang (Chung Jin-young). Jinha wants to go to her, but his uncle insists he finish his Bichun Secret martial arts training—a technique that allows the master to send a line of destructive force through the ground. After Uncle is dealt a fatal strike in an encounter with assassins (who are the first to die on Jinha's sword), he tells Jinha his true heritage: he's actually a descendant of the Koryu House of Yu, destroyed by General Taruga's forces when the Mongols invaded. His dying wish is that Jinha complete his training

in Bichun Secret Arts and use them to avenge his parents.

On the road to Shao Xing, Jinha and Junkwang meet when assassins attack and they become friends, not knowing that they are actually rivals. Jinha tries to take Sullie away, but he's surrounded by Taruga's warriors, and falls into the sea pierced by several arrows. Resigned to his death, Sullie agrees to make peace between Taruga and the Hans by marrying Junkwang, and bears him a son. Meanwhile, Jinha has survived his fall. He becomes a terrifying warrior called Jahalang, and trains a platoon of powerful assassins to help him wreak vengeance on his enemies.

And that's just in the first half. A generation-spanning saga of romance, action, and intrigue, *Bichunmoo* has enough material in it to fill three movies. With so much invested, the studio probably thought it best to put everything they had into one show. This makes for some pacing problems in the plot, as some sections feel rushed and condensed, while others tend to drag. The performances, costumes, and spectacular action scenes more than make up the difference for these faults. When someone feels the Bichun sword stroke, they don't just spurt blood—they explode! Shots of Jinha and his warriors soaring over rooftops, the lovers playing in fields and waterfalls, an exotic dance number—there are many breathtaking sights in this film. Kim Jun-seon has composed a score for this period film in which electronic instruments don't feel out of place. **AKA:** *Flying Warriors; Dance with Sword.* 🐾🐾🐾🐾

1999 118m/C *KO* Shin Hyun-joon, Kim Hee-sun, Jang Dong-jik, Chung Jin-young, Choi Yoo-jung, Suh Tai-wha, Kim Hak-chu, Jeon Ha-na, Lee Han-garl, Kim Su-roh, Ryoo Hyoun-kyoung, Bang Hyoup, Ki Joo-bong. **D:** Kim Young-jun. **W:** Kim Young-jun, Jung Yong-ki, Kim Hye-rin (story). **C:** Byeon Hee-seong. **M:** Kim Jun-seon. **DVD**

Big Boobs Buster

Long have women around the world suffered rejection, humiliation, and discrimination because of their smaller bra sizes. If only there were a hero to strike back at their oppressors. Well, now there is. High school student Masako (Harumi Kai) is obsessed with a cute boy named Bando (Masakazu Arai), but he won't give her the time of day because he hates flat-chested women. Stunned, she raids the office of the school's health professor (Eisei Amamoto—*King Kong Escapes'* Dr. Who!) to steal the "big boobs list," which records the school's bust sizes. Her first target is Noriko Kijima (Mariko Itsuki), bust size 35 inches. Donning wrap-around shades, falsies, and a pink uniform, Masako becomes the Big Boobs Buster, intent on punishing her classmates who take advantage of their genetic mammary superiority.

Masako waylays and binds Noriko, then makes a quick cast of her bust, threatening "If you should corrupt another man with those huge tits again, I'll parade this bust mold in front of the whole town." When Mitsuko Ueda (Natsuko Kayama), size 39, cuts phys. ed. because of her breast size, she gets the same treatment. Her victims don't report the assaults to the police because they kind of enjoy it. Girls start to strap themselves down with bandages, and they avoid Bando like the plague. But a girl named Sachiko Furubayashi (Marina Matsumoto, bust size unknown—she's not on the list) dares to go on a date with him, though her real motive is to catch the Big Boobs Buster with her big steel bra. Masako is barely able to defeat this challenger, and the encounter has attracted Bando's attention to the avenger's big fake breasts. Track star Kyoko Mitoizumi (Uran Hirosaki), size 36, presents a different challenge: she's an aggressive lesbian who's too tough to beat and learns Big Boob Buster's secret identity. Suffering from an appendectomy, Kyoko forces Masako to take her place against her rival in an upcoming track meet. To her own shock, all that exercise has begun to increase Masako's own bust size.

Those looking for giant breast porn should look elsewhere—this is a Japanese video, after all, and the size never exceeds merely above-average proportions. Besides, while the nudity and subject matter definitely place this enjoyable nonsense in the adults-only category, *Big Boobs Buster* is far too tame for purely prurient pursuits. As it contains a positive message for young girls about looking beyond body image for fulfillment, in essence it would make a good *ABC Afterschool Special*. However, its raunchy humor and erotic content—not to mention the subtitles—would make this unlikely. The action scenes are about what you'd expect from typical teenage girls pretending to fight. The running time includes a hilarious 12-minute behind-the-scenes and blooper reel, with a cheerful narrator that makes gleeful fun of all participants. Toru Minegishi from *Godzilla vs. Biollante* is the "big guest star" playing the heroine's father, with Aya Katsuragi of *Evil Dead Trap* playing the young mom. 🐉🐉🐉

1990 58m/C *JP* Harumi Kai, Mariko Itsuki, Uran Hirosaki, Masakazu Arai, Toru Minegishi, Aya Katsuragi, Eisei Amamoto, Marina Matsumoto, Natsuko Kayama, Asako Sakura, Minori Yoshinaga. **D:** Hisashi Watanabe. **W:** Hisashi Watanabe, Koichiro Yasunaga (story). **C:** Jun Abe. **M:** Yoichi Ogawa. **VHS, DVD**

Jackie Chan takes on a burly opponent in *The Big Brawl*.

asians in usa

The Big Brawl

An amusing attempt to bring Jackie Chan to the U.S., this film didn't quite make it with American audiences. Perhaps the timing just wasn't right, as the film itself holds up pretty well. Jackie is Jerry Kwan, an immigrant working his way up through the U.S. capitalist system in Chicago during the Great Depression. He has a talent for fighting, but his family doesn't want him involved in such things. The Big Brawl fighting contest in Battle Creek, Texas, holds the promise of wealth for Jackie's family, but he resists the temptation—until a relative is kidnapped, and Jackie must participate in the brawl to win her freedom.

The film shows some of the martial arts/humor mix that Jackie is now famous for worldwide. The stunts are good, and the cast is, too. Mako is a lot of fun as Jackie's teacher. However, Chan was very frustrated by the experience—used to years of directing his own stunts and action sequences, he found it difficult to deal with the style of the U.S. stuntmen. An interesting note on the Hong Kong release of this movie is that it completely cuts out the sexual angle of the romance subplots between the heroes (Jackie and Mako) and their American paramours/girlfriends. Not the best Chan flick ever made, but the fights and the roller-skating scene certainly make this film worth a look. Give it a half bone more for the uncut version. Jackie's co-star Kristine DeBell starred in the 1976 "X"-rated version of *Alice in Wonderland*! —SS *AKA: Saai Sau Hiu; Sha Shou Hao; Battle Creek Brawl.* 🐕🐕

1980 (R) 95m/C *US/HK* Jackie Chan, Mako, Jose Ferrer, Kristine DeBell, Rosalind Chao, Chi Chao-Li. **D:** Robert Clouse. **W:** Robert Clouse. **C:** Robert C. Jessup. **M:** Lalo Schifrin. **VHS**

Big Bullet

Most Hong Kong police movies focus on the Organized Crime and Triad Bureau or Special Crimes Unit, but this routine but entertaining action film offers a portrait of the Emergency Unit. After several questionable incidents, righteous cop Bill Zhu (Lau Ching-Wan) is set up by jealous and arrogant superior Guan, and transferred from SCU to the less glamorous EU. Bill enters into his new duties with quite a reputation, and his detective experience makes him very effective, but his relaxed manner brings him into conflict with by-the-book cop Jeff (Jordan Chan, cast against type). Meanwhile, Professor (Yu Rongguang), a U.S. criminal awaiting extradition, is rescued by his associate Bird (Anthony Wong). Zhu and his troops happen to be there when Professor's gang tries to abduct an old enemy Interpol agent, starting a mini-war that leaves Zhu's pal Yang (Francis Ng) dead. Zhu and his team are itching to hunt down Professor and Bird, and suspect they have some larger evil planned, but are restricted to their emergency function. Professor sends teen gangsters throughout HK to cause trouble, diverting attention from their target: $9 million kept in a safe at Interpol headquarters. Zhu catches on to their scheme, and goes against orders to rush to the scene. But because Guan ignores his warning, the thieves get away with the loot and kill a lot of cops. Though Jeff is officially put in charge of the team for Bill's insubordination, they all decide to follow Bill into battle to go after the thieves before they leave town.

Humor and personality, in addition to thrilling action scenes, put this show over, despite the cliché-ridden plot. The villains are completely two-dimensional (Anthony Wong is so bored he has his character speak Italian), but the funny script and fine performances bring the standard cop characters to life. The fun-filled climax has the bad guys and the EU team invading an RAF base, with Lau Ching-Wan fighting Yu Rongguang on top of a taxiing transport plane. The ending brings a surprising and touching finish to a subplot. In all, it succeeds much better than it ought to. Lau's comrades Cheung Tat-Ming, Theresa Lee, and Spencer Lam mix heroism and comedy in just the right amounts. It's easy to see why Theresa Lee is always cast as a Canadian immigrant—her accent is obvious even to non-Chinese. *AKA: Chung Fung Dui Liu Feng Gaai Tau; Chong Feng Dui Nu Huo Jie Tou; EU Strike Force.* 🐕🐕🐕🐕

1996 91m/C *HK* Lau Ching-Wan, Jordan Chan, Cheung Tat-Ming, Theresa Lee, Spencer Lam, Francis Ng, Anthony Wong, Yu Rongguang, Dayo Wong, Vincent Kok, Michael Lambert. **D:** Benny Chan. **W:** Susanne Chan, Joe Ma. **C:** Arthur Wong. **M:** Peter Kam, Clarence Hui. **VHS, DVD**

The Big Heat

Tough Hong Kong copper John Wong Wai-pong (Waise Lee) learns that nerve damage is affecting his gun hand. He's about to turn in his resignation from the force, when his chief (Ken Boyle) tells him that his former partner Skinny Tse has been murdered in Malaysia by triad boss Han Ching (Paul Chu). He delays his resignation, and his wedding, to take on the case, bringing clumsy rookie Lun Kwok-keung (Matthew Wong) to work with his assistant Tangerine Kam (Phillip Kwok). Tse was killed trying to blackmail Han and shipping company president Ho Ka-nin (Stuart Ong), and copies he made of incriminating evidence are found in his bag. Han, who is blackmailing Ho himself, turns the tables on the cops by sending hit men (including Michael Chow) after Wong and his team, while using his influence to stymie their investigation. Playing rough, Wong uses some illegal tactics to get Ho to testify. However, Han's thugs invade the hospital and go all-out to kill Ho.

From the opening shot of a drill bit going through a man's hand, you know this is one hard-edged police thriller, which combines illustration of straightforward police procedures with gory violence. Thugs don't just get shot in this movie—they get their hands blown off and then get run over by trucks. One expects Danny Lee to pop up in every other scene. Paul Chu plays one of the most relentlessly evil drug lords in movie history. This may contain the first use of the "shoot the hostage in the leg" technique on film. Not surprisingly, action director Phillip Kwok takes on a lot of the rough-and-tumble stuff himself. *AKA: Sing Si Dak Ging; Cheng Shi Te Jing.* 🐕🐕🐕

1988 98m/C *HK* Waise Lee, Joey Wong, Phillip Kwok, Paul Chu, Stuart Ong, Peter Lai, Matthew Wong, Roy Cheung, Michael Chow, Robin Shou, Ken Boyle, Kirk Wong, Aaron Kwok. *D:* Andrew Kam, Johnny To. *W:* Gordon Chan. *C:* Horace Wong. *M:* Law Dai-yau. **VHS, DVD**

The Big Sting

Ill-named (to cash in on *The Sting* with Andy Lau), this comic thriller is more about theft for revenge than any sort of a clever swindle. In 1972, a trio of thieves tries to fence the stolen Double-faced Buddha to triad boss Madam Wu Kam (Hu Chin, looking the same as she did in the '70s!). There's an argument over price, and though they cheat, the thieves lose a winner-take-all game of mah-jongg to her. When the trio objects, Kam shoots them all. Dying, the thieves make their pregnant wives promise to have their children bond for revenge, with provisions made for different sex combinations (though none is made for all girls).

Twenty-four years later, son Cheung Yan-lone (Leung Kar-yan) is a petty thief and Lee Ka-shing (Lau Wing) is a cheating gambler. They meet by chance and decide to find third son Leung and get back the Buddha. The boys meet Susie Leung (Angie Leon) at the Hong Kong Club when they try to rob it, and she sees they wear the same charm that she has. But she doesn't let on, since she's got a scheme of her own in mind, working as business manager for the ailing Madam Kam. Disguised as a doctor and nurse, the boys attempt to steal the Buddha, but only cause Kam to die of a heart attack. Son Tony returns to Hong Kong for the funeral, and Susie plays up to him to learn the Buddha's whereabouts: in a safe within a room keyed to Tony's handprint. While Susie keeps Tony at the club, the boys go after the prize—but Tony has kept secret a key feature of the security plan. Finally, the trio try to win the Buddha from Tony in a crooked card game, with Cheung disguised as an Arab prince.

Though the stars have charm, their antics aren't all that interesting, and the situations are trite. Plus, the whole film is shot in a flat, dull style. Despite the presence of old-school kung fu cinema players, the action is minimal. 🎵🎵

1982 94m/C *HK* Leung Kar-yan, Lau Wing, Hu Chin, Wong Yu, Dai Sai Aan, Ng Man-Tat, Angie Leon. *D:* Tony Liu. **VHS**

Bio-Cops

Following up on his success in *Bio Zombie,* Sam Lee returns in this similar horror comedy with a bit bigger budget, the title of which also trades on Lee co-star Stephen Fung's hit *Gen-X Cops.* A Red River, Texas, Army Depot hides a secret laboratory where Dr. Harry (Benny Lai) is developing "painless warriors" for the U.S. military. It's hoped these unstoppable soldiers, who heal immediately from any injury, and don't need food or sleep for long periods, will allow the United States to officially become the world's police force. What he's actually done is accidentally made an artificial copy of the vampire virus, which becomes troublesome when a test subject bites Harry on the leg.

Rural HK cop Marco (Fung) encounters scoundrel Cheap (Lee) in a teashop, and the two immediately antagonize each other, with Cheap facilitating a fight between Marco and his girlfriend May (Chan Wai-ming) so he can videotape their breakup. Infected with the virus, Harry visits his ex-wife Bell (Alice Chan) in Hong Kong to find out how the Russian scientist she originally bought the virus from is dealing with these mutations in his own project. Raging with unearthly hormones, Harry has a violent run-in with Cheap's boss Brother Kow (Frankie Ng), and infects one of his club girls. Breaking up the fight, Marco and his men arrest them all, but Harry's infection continues to spread in jail, and he tears into his cellmates. Peasants come to the police station bearing torches, as Kow's relatives demand his release, and the cops barricade themselves inside. Cheap only escapes undeath by pretending to already be one of Harry's "Zombie New Humans." While May (who came to make up) and Bell (who happens to be May's sister, the film's biggest coincidence) hide out in the basement, Marco and his partner Milky (Ronald Wong) try to find a way out of the nightmare. Their ingenious solution: condom bombs!

Unlike the *Dawn of the Dead* knockoff *Bio Zombie,* there's much more comedy here, and most of the gags are actually funny; the jokes mix with splatter freely. In one exchange, zombie king Harry tells a victim not to object to cannibalism until he's tried it, whereupon the man says he already did, having eaten human pork buns in the events that inspired *The Untold Story!* Some of the material is as old as Abbott and Costello, but it still works. As with most films inspired by George Romero's zombie movies, this one doesn't have a very good ending, but at least it has a good time getting there. *AKA: Sang Dut Dak Ging Ji Song Shut Yam Miu; Sheng Hua Te Jing Zhi Sang Shi Ren Wu.* 🎵🎵🎵

2000 89m/C *HK* Sam Lee, Stephen Fung, Alice Chan, Chan Wai-ming, Benny Lai, Frankie Ng, Hui Siu-hung, Ronald Wong, Samuel Leung, Chin Ka-Lok, Jude Poyer. *D:* Steve Cheng. *W:* Szeto Cheuk Hon. *C:* Joe Chan. *M:* Lincoln Lo. **VHS, DVD**

Bio Zombie

What begins as a typically rude HK slacker comedy ends up tumbling into a cheap version of *Dawn of the Dead,* complete with a poignant, doom-laden ending. Two clerks at a mall VCD shop with the unlikely names Woody Invincible (Jordan Chan of *Downtown Torpedoes*) and Crazy Bee (Sam Lee of *Gen-X Cops*) hang out, try to avoid their boss's wrath, and scam the mall girls. Gruff Woody especially has his eye on salon worker Rolls (Angela Tong, best known in the U.S. as the voice of Dee Dee in the *Dexter's Laboratory* cartoons), though his shallow tough-guy act fails to impress her. She's even less impressed when she begins to suspect it was Woody and Bee who mugged her in the ladies' room.

Meanwhile in the mall's parking garage, underworld figures are making a deal for a powerful new weapon: a bio-toxin smuggled out of a government lab inside a soft-drink bottle. As proof of the goop's effectiveness, a test subject has been brought along as part of the deal. Unfortunately, the crazed bio-zombie is too strong for his shackles, and quickly breaks free to go on a rampage.

Gradually, as the zombie plague spreads through the mall after hours, the flick's awkward comedy gives way to genuine thrills, and all of the characters trapped within gain a bit of range. As in George Romero's zombie pictures, the crisis brings out the best and worst in everyone. Even the zombified sushi boy (Wayne Lai, a regular in the long *Troublesome Night* series) who has a crush on Rolls still has enough of the right stuff to stand up to his fellow zombies and save her.

It's all a bit sloppy, but director Wilson Yip manages to get some momentum going around the midway point, and he builds on it sufficiently to keep your interest through the end. Considering the flatly lit, purposely dull look of the mall setting, this may be one film that is most appropriately viewed on a cheap VCD. *AKA: Sang Dut Sau Shut.* 🎵🎵

1998 94m/C *HK* Jordan Chan, Sam Lee, Angela Tong, Frankie Chan, Wayne Lai, Emotion Cheung. *D:* Wilson Yip. *W:* Matt Chow, So Man-sing, Wilson Yip. *C:* Kwok-Man Keung. *M:* Peter Kam. **VHS, DVD**

Black Cat

Perhaps you think Luc Besson's *La Femme Nikita* is a little too short on action, a little short on sci-fi, or a little too French? Producer/director Stephen Shin was quick to service your needs with this Hong Kong remake, released just a year after the original. Jade Leung stars as tough Chinese-American chick Catherine, who is arrested for murder after a truck stop brawl gets out of hand and she shoots a cop. Her case draws the attention of a top-secret assassination division of the CIA, that fakes her death and forcibly recruits her in their agent training program. She's also implanted with a computer chip, whose code name matches her own: Black Cat. It's designed to unlock her physical and mental potential, while providing her keepers with a handy means of control: it contains a device that will induce a massive hemorrhage on command. Black Cat excels in her studies, able to both follow orders and improvise, as needed. Over time, she and her supervisor Brian (Simon Yam) become a little closer than is recommended for their line of work.

Her final test is a bit more intense than the restaurant Mafia hit that Besson cooked up for his Nikita—without warning, Black Cat is sent to kill the bride at a wedding and escape through woods and down a river, with her escape car disabled. For a graduation present, she's sent to Hong Kong to pose as a photojournalist, taking on assignments whenever and wherever she's ordered. On one such job, she meets Allen Yeung (Thomas Lam), a wildlife officer who intrigues her, and they end up dating (one such occasion finds them at a Chow Yun-fat film).

All seems well, but Cat continues to have doubts about her situation. A fellow agent who refuses an experimental chip upgrade is found dead. And when a childhood friend recognizes her on the street, the friend's apartment is mysteriously firebombed. And her chip-bred headaches don't exactly inspire her confidence. Sent on an assignment in Japan, she begins to think that Allen may become the trip's second intended target.

Leung, a former model in Sweden, reportedly insisted on doing more than her share of stunts (which are terrific), picking up a few minor injuries, while no doubt adding to the intensity of her portrayal. Yam, in between his gigolo period and psycho period, is smooth and manipulative, but still sympathetic. Shin handles both drama and action perfectly—surprising in a director whose expertise was in romances. The only sour note is that the film's ending hinges on a highly unlikely anatomical condition. Followed by an even more action-loaded sequel. *AKA: Hak Mau; Hei Mao.* 🎵🎵🎵🎵🎶

1991 92m/C *HK* Jade Leung, Simon Yam, Thomas Lam. *D:* Stephen Shin. *W:* Lam Wai-Lun, Chan Bo-sun, Lam Tan-Ping. *C:* Lee Kin Keung. *M:* Danny Chung. **VHS, DVD**

Black Jack

In the 1970s, Osamu Tezuka launched a new manga series that owed its origins to a life he'd known way before his world was filled with robots and

adventure. Before his life was taken over by comics, he went to medical school and became a doctor. He may have taken on medicine partially to avoid military service in a war he didn't support, but one can find an interest in the subject cropping up frequently in his work. That interest came to a head with *Black Jack*, a series about an incredibly gifted surgeon who nevertheless doesn't have a license and operates outside the law. The series worked best in short-story format, so the main flaw of this animated movie is that it has to stretch a bit to reach feature length.

The world is thrilled and puzzled when athletes begin to smash one record after another. People in other fields—music, art, science—are making gigantic strides as well. It seems as if the human race has taken a step forward in evolution. Two years later, these members of "super-mankind" begin to succumb to some kind of deadly mystery ailment. Black Jack finds that their organs are aging much more rapidly than normal. His suspicions are aroused when a mysterious young woman named Jo Carol hounds him for his services. When he refuses, the woman—the head of a huge pharmaceuticals company—has his young ward Pinoko (benignly) kidnapped from his mountain cabin.

A word about Pinoko: The movie doesn't go into it because it's not relevant, but this small girl has a very bizarre backstory. In an early story, Black Jack is called in to remove a large growth from an 18-year-old girl. He finds the growth contains an undeveloped twin—and what's more, the twin is alive and conscious. Instead of disposing of them as requested, he assembled the removed parts surgically, and with the aid of a few prosthetics, Pinoko was born!

With no alternative, Black Jack joins a futuristic research center trying to find the cause of the super-mankind ailment, dubbed the Moira Syndrome. He learns that the cause is connected to a strange growth at the base of the brain. He also learns that Jo Carol isn't just funding the search for a cure, but was also the creator of Moira in the first place. Before he can do anything about it, the center is taken over by armed members of a medical ethics group!

The first animated cartoon feature to require a medical supervisor (Akira Nagai), *Black Jack* combines medical drama with larger issues brought up by scientific progress, environmental problems, and economic competition. While the characters designed by animation supervisor Akio Sugino bear a closer resemblance to his other work with director Osamu Dezaki (namely *Golgo 13*) than to Tezuka's bold cartoons, the film maintains some of the same depth and strange flavor. (However, if Tezuka were alive, he would have cut the film by 20 minutes.) Still, it's remarkable that anime this far outside of comfortable genres gets made at all, much less

imported to America. Dezaki and his crew embellish the story with wonderful visual and audio effects. The tale is treated respectfully throughout, resisting the urge to include bits of awkward humor that Tezuka himself sometimes had a weakness for. *AKA: Burakku Jakku.* ♫♫♫

1996 90m/C *JP* **D:** Osamu Dezaki. **W:** Eto Mori, Kihachi Okamoto, Osamu Tezuka (manga). **M:** Eiji Kawamura. **VHS, DVD**

Black Magic M-66

Those who think the robots in *Terminator* movies are too slow and clunky should give this action-packed anime a try. A heli-jet crashes with a top-secret cargo—two state-of-the-art M-66 anti-personnel androids. Curiously, though they haven't been programmed, they disappear from the crash site. Soon, the military find themselves battling their own weapons. Tough reporter Sybel catches the crash info on her military band radio, and with her assistant Leakey, rushes out with a camera to get the story. The army sends for Professor Matthew, the cranky developer of the M-66, and begin their plan to catch the dangerous armored androids. Losing many soldiers, they succeed in netting one of the monsters, triggering its self-destruct response. However, the remaining M-66 continues on the mission contained in the test programming that should have been deleted: killing Matthews's own teenage granddaughter Ferris. Sybel stumbles upon an answering machine message that only the M-66 has seen—one that says where Ferris went for dinner in the city—and goes to the rescue. But even if help reaches Ferris in time, will they be able to save her from the most advanced killer robot ever built?

Unlike his *Appleseed*, here cartoonist Masamune Shirow co-directs an anime adaptation of his manga, assuring a better translation of his distinctive drawing style, with much more eye-pleasing results. While the rest of the cast of characters is rather routine, the M-66 pair are dynamic and frightening. *AKA: Baraku Majikku M-66.* ♫♫♩

1987 47m/C *JP* **V:** (English) Lia Sargent, Doug Stone, Steve Blum, Simon Isaacson. **D:** Masamune Shirow, Hiroyuki Kitakubo. **W:** Masamune Shirow (manga). **M:** Yasunori Honda. **VHS, DVD**

Black Mask

When Jackie Chan finally became a star in America, there was a rush to retool and release his back catalogue, with mixed results. After his role in *Lethal Weapon 4* raised awareness of Jet Li, the same treatment was given to some of his old features. This was the first, although it's atypical of the usual Jet picture. It's a sci-fi action-fest that has Jet playing a former member of a group of super-soldiers called 701 Squad, who left the team when they became too ruthless for his tastes. He goes into hiding and takes a job as a mild-mannered librarian. However, his friendship with police detective Shek (Lau Ching-Wan) draws him back into opposition with 701. The Squad is wiping out drug lords in a complicated plan to earn a serum said to cure a side effect of the super-soldier formula (they only have a few years to live). Not wanting to expose his new identity, Li dons a mask and black uniform to fight the 701, which leads to inevitable comparisons with the Green Hornet's sidekick Kato.

Though most Jet Li films are more akin to old-fashioned westerns with fantastic martial arts (as in the *Once upon a Time in China* series), this one has a much harder edge and is full of blood and guts, despite being cut to earn an "R" rating in the States (the HK version has a bit less gore, but is at least eight minutes longer). The super-soldiers are all super strong and near impervious to pain, which means they get shot, stabbed, and sliced up numerous times and still come back to dish out the same. Scenes in which the disguised Li kidnaps his librarian girlfriend (Karen Mok) in order to protect her have a definite bondage theme. The kung fu scenes (by Yuen Woo-ping)—though enhanced by wirework—are terrific, directed with campy finesse by Daniel Lee. This film actually has better dubbing than most of its contemporaries, with mouth movement closely matching dialogue, and some of the actors (including Francoise Yip) dub their own voices. **AKA:** *Hak Hap; Hei Xia.* 🐉🐉🐉

1996 (R) 92m/C *HK* Jet Li, Lau Ching-Wan, Karen Mok, Francoise Yip, Patrick Lung, Chung King-fai, Moses Chan, Henry Fong, Anthony Wong, Xiong Xinxin, Lawrence Ah Mon. **D:** Daniel Lee. **W:** Tsui Hark, Koan Hui, Teddy Chan, Joe Ma. **C:** Tony Cheung. **M:** Teddy Robin Kwan, Ben Vaughn (U.S.). **VHS, DVD**

Black Tight Killers

The 1960s was a crazy decade for Japanese cinema. It had superheroes fighting space aliens, robot detectives, blind samurai, mushroom people, vengeful statues, and giant mutant monsters, so why not ninja go-go dancers? Combat photographer Daisuke Hondo (Akira Kobayashi) makes a date with flight attendant Yoriko Sawanouchi (Chieko Matsubura) on his flight back to Tokyo from Saigon. That night,

Yoriko is abducted from the restaurant by a mysterious stranger named Fernando Lopez, but she's rescued when three stylish Black Tights ninja girls kill him. Hondo tangles with the trio, but they blind him with their bubble gum(!) and disappear. While Hondo calls the police, some other guys kidnap Yoriko, then frame Hondo for the murder. Luckily, his reporter friend Bill Summers helps him out.

By the next day, Summers manages to find Yoriko's uncle, a researcher named Okada. Hondo is led into an ambush by Lopez's gang, but is saved by a woman named Akiko wielding a golf club. Of course, it turns out she's with the Black Tights, who continue their parade of unusual weapons by trapping him with a trick called the "Octopus Pot," then frame him for the murder of Okada. He and Yoshiro both escape from their clutches, and she reveals that Okada wasn't her uncle at all. Both gangs seem to think Yoshiro is the key to a fortune in World War II loot, and will stop at nothing to get it. More captures and escapes follow, giving the ladies a chance to use lethal 45 records, exploding golf balls, and other items from their jet-age ninja bag of tricks.

The Black Tights, whose turn-ons include jiu-jitsu, driving around in a hearse, and dying in the hero's arms, were precursors to even more eccentric fighting females like the *Sukeban Deka* and *Keikko Mask*. None of them—nor Kobayashi, for that matter—is exactly a likely candidate for the Japan Action Club, but they make up for it with pure style. The wild art direction is fantastic; with such rich colors played against jet blacks, the film emulsion itself should get top billing. Director Yasukaru Hasebe was a former editor who cut many of Seijen Suzuki's films. After this first effort for Nikkatsu Studios, he went on to direct several of their best yakuza thrillers, plus some other fightin' female pictures like *Sukeban Deka: Dirty Mary* and *The Naked Seven*. **AKA:** *Ore Ni Sawaru To Abunaize; Don't Touch Me I'm Dangerous.* 🐉🐉🐉🐲

1966 84m/C *JP* Akira Kobayashi, Chieko Matsubara, Mieko Nishio, Kazue Kamo, Toshiko Saito, Kazuko Kano, Tomoko Hamakawa, Kaku Takashina, Eiji Go, Kan Nihonyanagi, Bin Morizuka, Akemi Kita. **D:** Yasukaru Hasebe. **W:** Michio Tsuzuki, Ryuzo Nakanishi. **C:** Kazue Nagatsuka. **M:** Naozumi Yamamoto. **DVD**

The Blacksheep Affair

His name is Dong—Yim Dong. Vincent Zhao plays heroic Chinese Special Forces officer Yim, who takes out a plane full of would-be hijackers in the opening minutes. In doing so, he disobeyed an order to abort his mission, and is

punished by being transferred to the Chinese embassy in Lithuania. He finds his new duties are hardly less exciting though; no sooner is he greeted by his comrade Hung Wai-kwok (Ken Wong) at the train station, than the two of them are fighting to subdue a gang that just assassinated some Interpol agents. The gang leader turns out to be international criminal Keizo Mishima (Andrew Lin), leader of the Japanese Red Zone terrorist group. However, the Lithuanians don't particularly care for Asians, and Dong and Kwok receive no credit for the arrest.

Wandering the streets that night, Dong is shocked to find his old sweetheart Chan Pun (Shu Qi), who he hasn't seen since the Tiananmen Square riots. Though they still have feelings for each other, he can't forgive her for running out on him. No one talks about Mishima's reason for being in Lithuania—crooked government officials taking orders from Red Zone bigwig Tasta have plans to secretly sell off the nuclear weapons left behind by the Russians, and Red Zone is among the waiting customers. Fearing Mishima will talk, Tasta plans to get rid of him, sending a hit team to kill the Japanese cops sent to take him away. Meanwhile, Red Zone agents attack the Chinese ambassador and explode bombs throughout the city, demanding their leader's release. Frightened citizens begin attacking all Asians, and police use tear gas to quell the riots. The ambassador makes a deal with the Lithuanian minister: he'll lend him Dong and some of his other men to help get Mishima out of the country, if the minister will allow the Red Cross to send aid to hundreds of Chinese refugee boat-people in the harbor. But the snake immediately sends his Italian Mafia friends to kill Mishima, planning to have the Chinese take the blame while they continue their dirty business.

There's obviously more going on in the film than martial arts action, though the fight scenes are powerful—Zhao and Lin destroy the interior of the embassy during their big duel. Most Americans are unaware of how Asians are involved in the political affairs of Europe, and here we get some tips in an action-movie format. One scene even has the Chinese toasting the downfall of the Lithuanian government, hoping for a return to Socialism. There are also a lot of beautifully shot location scenes, a bit of romance, and Vincent Zhou even indulges in some song and dance. Most of the non-Chinese dialogue is dubbed in English. Lithuania is often pronounced "Lavernia"—indicating an attempt to disguise the location. *AKA: Bik Huet Laam Tin; Bi Xie Lan Tian.* 🦴🦴🦴

1998 91m/C *HK* Vincent Zhao, Shu Qi, Ken Wong, Andrew Lin, Kenneth Tsang, Joe Cheung, Xiong Xinxin, Lau Shun, Jude Poyer. *D:* Allun Lam. *W:* Alex Law, Roy Szeto. *C:* Kwen Pak-huen, Puccini yu. *M:* Alex San. **VHS, DVD**

The Blade

Tsai Hark's grim, dark, and twisted version of a traditional swordplay film. Ling (Song Lei) is a dreamy young woman. During a childhood in which her family moved frequently, her father has told her tales of Emprise Field, a place of buying and selling. She can't imagine what Emprise Field is like, but she can conjure up a war for her affections between two young men she fancies. Iron Head (Moses Chan) and Ting On (Vincent Zhao Wen Zhuo) both work for her father at Sharp Manufacturing, a sword factory. Fed up with the troubles caused by a gang of hunters bold enough to kill a monk in a public market-place, Iron Head and Ting On decide they will take vengeance against the gang. Ling's father insists that his men avoid any violence; he points to a broken blade whose power, he feels, has kept the peace for 20 years. The blade belonged to Ting On's father, who was viciously murdered by a tattooed brute named Lung (Xiong Xinxin). Ting On's father insisted that Lung's identity not be revealed for fear that his son would try to take vengeance, but as soon as he learns about this secret, Ting On rides out. At roughly the same time, Iron Head and other co-workers are searching for the gang of hunters.

Trailing behind Ting On, Ling stumbles upon the hunters. Ting On comes to her rescue, but loses an arm in the process and is tossed over a cliff by the hunters. Presumed dead because his body cannot be located, the others mourn for him. What they do not know is that Black Head, a young orphaned farm girl, has dragged him away and nursed him back to health. The proud Ting On is ridiculed for being a "cripple" and is not ready to face his friends. He is still burning to take revenge, though, and begins training with his father's broken blade. Meanwhile, Ling becomes convinced that Ting On is alive, and Iron Head joins her on a journey to find him. Finally, the forces of fate conspire to bring everyone together again.

Clearly inspired by *One-Armed Swordsman*, this is a rendering that kicks butt from start to finish. Traces of melancholy provided by Ling's occasional narration help put things in perspective. Though Vincent Zhao and Moses Chan may be a notch below the top-flight action stars of the past, the action is so intense and feels so messy, spontaneous, and realistic that it doesn't matter. Notable sequences include Ting On's attempted rescue of Ling from the bandits in a thicket of bamboo and animal traps, Ting On's training, and a battle in a guest house that gets rough. The speeded-up action in the final reel feels weirdly out of place and unnecessary, but that's the only false step taken. Valerie Chow memorably portrays a prostitute who attracts attention from both Iron Head and Ling. —PM *AKA: Diy; Dao.* 🦴🦴🦴🦴🦴

1995 101m/C *HK* Vincent Zhao, Xiong Xinxin, Song Lei, Austin Wai, Moses Chan, Chung Bik-ha, Che Hing-wa, Jason Chu, Valerie Chow, Michael Tse, Mama Hung, Chan Chi-fai. *D:* Tsui Hark. *W:* Tsui Hark, So Man-sing, Koan Hui. *C:* Gam Sing. *M:* William Woo, Raymond Wong. **VHS, DVD**

Blade 2

In this sequel to the hit comic-book adaptation, we catch up with vampire-hunter Blade (Wesley Snipes) a few years later as he makes his way around Russia and Eastern Europe searching for his mentor Whistler (Kris Kristofferson), who didn't shoot himself in the previous picture after all. Blade rescues Whistler from being bled in a giant vampire draining center and submits him to a Cold Turkey cure for his vampirism. Whistler barely has time to get into an argument with Blade's new mechanic Scud (Norman Reedus) before their HQ is invaded by representatives of the Vampire Nation. The vampires propose a truce with Blade so they can combine forces to face a common enemy—a new mutation from the pure blood vampire strain called the Reapers, that are nearly indestructible and prey on vampire and human alike.

So what is *Blade 2* doing in this book? Donnie Yen. The fight scenes in the first half of the film, for the most part choreographed by Hong Kong star Donnie Yen *(Iron Monkey)*, have a fluidity and grace that the action in the remaining fights lack, giving way to more traditional professional wrestling and street-fighting moves that the creative team felt were more in keeping with the film's tone. They may be right, but *The Matrix* notwithstanding, there has yet to be a movie made in America that fully embraces Chinese kung fu, and it would be interesting to see that happen. Yen is a marvelous martial artist, who really ought to be a bigger star in the States. Unlike other Asian stars, language is not an obstacle, as he's completely fluent in English. He also plays one of team of vampire warriors in the film—whose disappearance from the story goes completely unexplained in the film. Maybe he'll be back for *Blade 3*. 🎵🎵🎵

2002 (R) 117m/C *US* Wesley Snipes, Kris Kristofferson, Ron Perlman, Leonor Varela, Norman Reedus, Luke Goss, Donnie Yen. **D:** Guillermo Del Toro. **W:** David S. Goyer. **C:** Gabriel Beristain. **M:** Marco Beltrani. **VHS, DVD**

The Blazing Temple

This historical action epic tells the story of the clash between Buddhist monks and the Ching Dynasty emperor, and the subsequent destruction of the Shaolin Temple. General Yim (Liu Ping) informs Emperor Yungzheng (Yee Yuen) that the monks have been seen spying in Peking and are believed to be collaborating with rebel leader Liu. The emperor orders the entire Liu family massacred, putting him in conflict with his old schoolmate Lin (Judy Lee), a daughter of the Lius. A squad of soldiers is sent to arrest the Lius, but Lin throws them out. Outraged, she attacks Yungzheng in one of his own gardens, but is foiled by his Shaolin training, sword-proof vest, and barricaded Panic Pagoda. Cannons and a thousand Manchu troops are sent to destroy Shaolin Temple, where thousands of Ming patriots are in training. Most die in the barrage, but a group of disciples fights their way past the 18 Bronzemen to escape. Others get out when the Abbot (O Yau-man) lifts the stone barrier blocking the escape tunnel. One disciple named Siu (Carter Wong) is entrusted with the scroll containing the treasured Shaolin scripture, Buddha's 18 Lessons, and is instructed to take the survivors and rebuild the temple. A squad of 10 fighting monks goes to Hangchou to kill the visiting emperor—but it's a trap, baited with doubles for Yungzheng. Siu is able to return to their hideout, but is suspected of being a traitor. But it's Fung (Lau Lap Cho) who is the real traitor, revealing their position. On the run, the monks decide to launch a last desperate assault on the palace to kill the tyrant at all costs.

Epic in scope, the film boasts colorful costumes, terrific sets, and locations, and reasonably good special effects. Its weakness is that a great deal of effort goes into establishing Judy Lee as the heroine in the first part of the film, only to forget about her entirely when the monks take the stage, and she doesn't put in another appearance until briefly popping up right at the end. One wonders why she's even in the movie, as her presence is superfluous to the story of the burnt temple and vengeful monks. Except for some slick moves by Carter Wong, there's not much first-class kung fu here, but the standard action and adventure elements—plus some eccentric embellishments of the Shaolin

Temple—are more than enough to hold interest. The 18 Bronzemen, Joseph Kuo's imaginative upgrade of the Shaolin Wooden Men, put in a brief appearance here, following their own *18 Bronzemen Part 2*. **AKA:** *Feng Shui Siu Lam Chi; Huo Shao Shao Lin Si; Burning Shaolin Temple.* 🎵🎵🎵

1976 88m/C *HK* Carter Wong, Judy Lee, Chang Yi, Wong Fei-lung, Barry Chan, Yee Yuen, O Yau-man, Kam Kong, Liu Ping, Chai Kai, Tong Wai, Lau Lap Cho, Ng Ho, Yeung Gam-yuk, Shaw Luo-hui, Yip Mau, Woo Gwong, Che Yuen. **D:** Joseph Kuo. **W:** Joseph Kuo, M.L. Shu, P.S. Chiang (story). **DVD**

Blind Beast

The more sensational works of Japanese mystery pioneer Edogawa Rampo enjoyed resurgence in popularity following the release of *Black Lizard* in 1968, and among the film adaptations to follow is this striking film from Yasuzo Masamura *(Giants and Toys)*. Rampo's horror tale tells the story of a blind sculptor who poses as a masseur in order to abduct women, whom he butchers to use their body parts in his work. The general idea was borrowed for many films, from *Mystery of the Wax Museum* to *A Bucket of Blood*.

To concentrate the psychosexual dynamics—and allay the trembling of Daiei Studios, who felt the material too risky—Masamura scaled the story back to a single abductee. Mako Midori stars as fashion model Aki Shima, flavor of the month for starring in an exhibit of nude photos. Calling for a massage one night, she finds herself kidnapped by the masseur (Eiji Funakoshi from *Giant Monster Gamera),* and awakes in his warehouse studio. There follows a long scene in which the mad sculptor Michio tells his life's story and explains his obsession with touch, and his mad plan to create artwork to entertain the sense of touch only. While this rather convenient exposition continues, the sculptor's studio is gradually revealed to us: the walls covered in oversize body parts, surrounding two gigantic female nude sculptures. Though the script and brave performances are fine, it's hard to imagine that the film would have enjoyed the reputation it has without this amazing set.

An extra angle is added to the story: Michio's domineering mother (Noriko Sengoku from *Invasion of Astro-Monster)* assists him in all he does. Aki manipulates the situation, setting mother against son in a bid for freedom, until a struggle among the three of them results in the mother's death. With her out of the way, Aki and Michio lock themselves in the darkened studio, exploring ever further into sexual sensation, then beyond into sadomasochism, vampirism, and madness. Considering the subject matter, Masamura handles it all rather chastely, rarely venturing into

Mako Midori and Eiji Funakoshi become entangled in a psychosexual game while trapped in a surreal landscape in the weird thriller *Blind Beast.*

what would be considered even an "R"-rated camera angle. Far too bizarre and shocking, the general theatre audience didn't know what to do with it, but *Blind Beast* has been an art-house hit ever since. ***AKA:*** *Moju.* ♪♪♪♫

1969 84m/C *JP* Eiji Funakoshi, Mako Midori, Noriko Sengoku. **D:** Yasuzo Masamura. **W:** Ishio Shirasaka, Edogawa Rampo (story). **C:** Setsuo Kobayashi. **M:** Hikaru Hayashi. **DVD**

Blind Fist of Bruce

This Bruceploitation title combines elements from its contemporary hits *Prodigal Son* and *Drunken Master.* A gang led by Ho Fu-wei (Kong Do) has invaded a small town, beating up the local constables. Some try to rob the bank, but banker Yeh Chen-lung (Bruce Li) is a kung fu expert and thrashes them easily, impressing client Miss Hung (Meg Lam). Yeh takes his two teachers out to dinner at Hung's restaurant to celebrate. However, teacher Su (Chan Lau) hired the robbers to act out the holdup just to make Yeh and his bank look good. They've been teaching the spoiled young man bogus kung fu

to pacify him. But when Ho and his gang come to demand a "loan," Yeh learns just how useless his skills really are. Ho establishes his Fu-wei kung fu school and takes over the area, collecting extortion from merchants. After losing his bank to Ho, Yeh finds that an old blind lyre player (Simon Yuen) knows kung fu far beyond his dishonest teachers, and asks him to take him on as a pupil. Four months later, Yeh learns enough to break training and beat his enemy Ho and get his fortune back. However, Ho calls on his friend Tiger Chen Tao-suen (Tiger Yang) for help. Tiger uses hidden drugs to fight, and is the traitor who blinded the old master years ago, and killed his daughter.

A weaker version of tea we've tasted before, *Blind Fist* has only the personalities of its supporting players to support it. Simon Yuen is charming, but is just blind instead of blind drunk. The fighting is decent, but not all that imaginative—Tiger's blinding toxins are the only exotic element. The script is more like a diagram for a kung fu film than a real story. ***AKA:*** *Mang Quan Gui Shou; Blind Fist of Bruce Lee.* ♪♪

1979 94m/C *TW* Bruce Li, Simon Yuen, Tiger Yang, Meg Lam, Kong Do, Chan Lau, Ho Pak Kwong, Wong

Biu Chan, Tang Yim-chan. **D:** Kam Bo. **W:** Yeung Wai. **VHS, DVD**

1962 95m/BW *JP* Shintaro Katsu, Masayo Banri, Raizo Ichikawa, Chitose Maki, Ryuzu Shimada. **D:** Kenji Misumi. **W:** Minoru Inuzuka, Kan Shimozawa (story). **VHS**

Blind Swordsman: The Tale of Zatoichi

This is the first of the Zatoichi series starring Shintaro Katsu, based on the stories of Kan Shimozawa about a sightless gangster who becomes a masseur, but learns how to handle a sword to regain respect among his brothers. Eventually, the series would span 26 films and 50 television episodes. We're introduced to Ichi as he visits Boss Sukegoro of Iioka. In a scene that would be repeated in various ways throughout the series, Ichi finds a dice game, and uses a gambling trick to take advantage of those trying to take advantage of him. Sukegoro knows and respects Ichi, having witnessed a duel he fought in another town, and welcomes him into his home, assigning Tate to serve him.

Sukegoro has a hidden motive for being hospitable to Ichi: Word is that his rival Boss Shigezo has hired a new samurai, and with the two gangs nearing a fight, he hopes to have the famed Zatoichi on his side. Tate and sister Tane both have romantic trouble—he got a girl pregnant, and she won't take her husband (and Tane's brother gangster) back. While fishing, Ichi meets Shigezo's samurai Hirate (Raizo Ichikawa), who is ill and wants to give up killing; else he'd still be in Edo making a good living. Zatoichi also dislikes using his skills to serve an unjust cause, angering Sukegoro by refusing to do any sword tricks for amusement. However, having the two great swordsmen in their camps just seems to add fuel to the rival boss's competitiveness, and both are looking forward to seeing the titans duel.

Still comfortable among his gangster brothers this early in the series, Ichi lacks much of the charming earthy humor he'd develop in later films. The basic plot of two rival gangs in a small town, each depending on outside help, recalls Kurosawa's *Yojimbo*. However, there's still enough plot machinations, philosophy, and thrilling swordplay to make this an entertaining show, certainly worthy of the sequels to come. Some of director Kenji Misumi's tricks are almost as impressive as Zatoichi's. One scene has a medium shot of several characters discussing the blind man. Suddenly, the camera hops back quickly to reveal Ichi sitting behind a crowd. Ichi's opponent Raizo Ichikawa later starred in the Katsu-produced *Sleepy Eyes of Death* series. **AKA:** *Zatoichi Monogatari; Zatoichi: The Life and Opinion of Masseur Ichi.* 𝄞𝄞𝄞

Blonde Fury

After Cynthia Rothrock's breakout role in *Righting Wrongs,* this fast-moving action feature was built around her. Rothrock stars as San Francisco cop Cindy, who is enlisted by the FBI to investigate a suspected counterfeiting ring working out of a Hong Kong newspaper. Cindy gets in a fight soon after arrival—a pillow fight with her roommate Judy Yu (Elizabeth Lee). Going undercover as a reporter, she finds herself making news as well as reporting it by saving a baby from a burning building, meeting rival newshounds Shorty Hai (director Mang Hoi) and Turbo Tai Pao (Tai Bo) in the process. Hai's dad (Wu Ma), who owns his paper, is in dire financial straits, going so far as to fake murder scene photos to save money. He has his son tail Cindy, hoping to freeload off her investigations for their own paper. He isn't the only father involved in Cindy's business, as she finds that Judy's DA dad (Roy Chiao) has a file on her editor and publisher Huang Te (director Ronny Yu, taking a rare acting job). Hai gets photos of Huang abducting the prosecutor to drug him, earning him the right to tag along when Cindy busts the gang.

Rothrock has never been more appealing than she is here—cute, but not too sweet to be believable, and typically dynamic in action scenes. A long break in filming may account in part for the fact that the plot doesn't make much sense and has little momentum, losing track of Cynthia for stretches to follow other characters. But director/star Mang Hoi makes up for it with excellent fights and stunts, plus little touches of humor—much of which may be lost on Western audiences, as it has to do with Rothrock's role as a fast-driving, cheeseburger-munching American stereotype. Those who enjoyed seeing Tom Green put a mouse in his mouth in *Road Trip* may enjoy Chung Fat topping that trick by holding a much larger rat's head in his mouth. Highlights include Cynthia's battle against thugs on some scaffolding, a tough fight with Billy Chow, and the big climactic battle in a giant spiderweb! It's surprising to see martial arts champ Chow playing himself as a villain, but he apparently had no trouble with damage to his image over it, as he went on to do it again in *Kick Boxer's Tears*. **AKA:** *Si Je Daai Saai; Shi Jie Da Shai; Above the Law 2; Righting Wrongs 2; Lady Reporter; Female Reporter; Born to Fight.* 𝄞𝄞𝄞

"Why are you moving sneakily here?"

—Mang Hoi's movements are questioned in *Blonde Fury*

1989 83m/C *HK* Cynthia Rothrock, Elizabeth Lee, Mang Hoi, Ronny Yu, Roy Chiao, Chin Siu-Ho, Keith Kwan, Wu Ma, Tai Bo, Chung Fat, Billy Chow, Melvin Wong, Jeff Falcon, Vincent Lyn, James Tien, Yip Wing-cho. *D:* Mang Hoi. *W:* Shum Chi-leung. *C:* Bill Wong, Peter Ngor. *M:* Chris Babida. **VHS, DVD**

The Blood Drinkers

Philippine cinema gained one of its best horror characters here in Dr. Marco (Ronald Remy), a vampire king of the European variety. With his full evening wear, cape, and shining bald head, Marco combined elements of both Bela Lugosi's Dracula and Max Schrek's Count Orlock from *Nosferatu.* But this fangster is also remarkably hip, sometimes appearing in a black turtleneck and shades. He may still trundle coffins around in a horse-drawn hearse, but his main ride is a Cadillac. Accompanied by his sexy personal assistant Tanya (Eva Montes), tumbling dwarf Giru, hunchback Gordo, and an oversized bat named Basra, Marco has come to a small village seeking aid for his undead bride Katrina

(Amalia Fuentes), who is dying (again) of a blood disease. With the cooperation of Katrina's still-living mother Marisa (Mary Walter), Marco means to replace Katrina's heart with that of her twin sister Chelito (Fuentes again). The vampires chow down on Chelito's foster parents, leaving the girl vulnerable to Marisa's invitation to come live at her villa. But the arrival of family friends Victor de la Cruz (Eddie Fernandez) and his two sisters offer Chelito unexpected support. The reappearance of Chelito's bloodthirsty former guardians, only driven off by the interruption of Marco, alerts the parish priest (who narrates) that there are undead creatures about.

Based on a comic-book serial, *The Blood Drinkers* is both a throwback to the great Universal Pictures horror movies and a precursor of the romantic vampire stories of Anne Rice. Marco has all the old vampire abilities such as changing into a bat, but also likes to swing a whip, and he can wander around in the daytime as long as he stays out of the sunlight. He's a tragic creature, shown in a fantasy wandering through a flowered garden with his lady, while living in a tomb. There's also a tense triangle going on with Tanya, who obviously would replace Katrina if she could (recently uncovered outtakes show Tanya contemplating her mistress's murder). The priest has a huge book that contains scientific information about vampires that recalls Richard Matheson's *I Am Legend*, but as this is the Philippines, a heavy dose of religion is the main weapon against evil. Director Gerardo de Leon would pour on the religious symbolism even more in his follow-up *Curse of the Vampires*. Many of cinematographer Felipe J. Sacdalan's images are stunningly beautiful, no doubt inspired by European gothic pictures like *Black Sunday*. Many night scenes were shot in black and white, then tinted various colors—but this technique is enhanced by some shots that were shot in color, but fade to tinted monochrome at times. A compelling narrative is all that's lacking here, as Marco and crew just seem to be hanging around instead of getting on with the heart transplant. De Leon would soon team up with partner Eddie Romero to make the infamous Blood Island series. Eva Montes starred in the *Darna* superhero movies. *AKA: Kulay Dugo Ang Gabi; Vampire People.* 🐉🐉🐉

1964 86m/C/BW *PH* Ronald Remy, Amalia Fuentes, Eddie Fernandez, Eva Montes, Celia Rodriguez, Renato Robles, Mary Walter, Paquito Salcedo, Andres Benitez. *D:* Gerardo de Leon. *W:* Cesar Amigo, Rico Bello Omagap (story). *C:* Felipe J. Sacdalan. *M:* Tito Arevalo. **VHS, DVD**

Blood of the Dragon

Rebel patriot Yang and wife are attacked on the road and killed by guardsman Kang Fu (Lung Fei) and his men. But before he dies, Yang makes it into town and gives phony "blind" boy beggar Ni Chiu a bamboo tube to give to Prince Ma Tong at Pei Ping Palace. The bamboo tube contains a regular McGuffin of these old kung fu flicks—a list of rebels and the locations of their meeting places, which is being sought by Mongol Prime Minister Sing Pa Tou (Miu Tin). Ni Chiu and his big sister Yen Mu-tsien (Chiao Chiao) are caught by Kang Fu, but they're saved by the heroic Master Lung Ti (Jimmy Wang Yu), the White Dragon, who defeats the guards with his Wonder Spear and cuts Kang Fu's finger off.

Lung agrees to accompany Ni Chiu on his task, but there's a problem: Lung defeated Ma Tong's father Ma Chin (Tin Yau) and his magic sword in the pre-credit sequence. Ma Tong is in no mood to talk, and Lung learns the hard way the secret of his magic sword—a concealed dagger. He escapes, but is determined to deliver the list as soon as his wounds are healed. Knowing they're no match for the White Dragon, the bad guys try to delay him

until the formidable Red Wolf General Tai (Yee Yuen) arrives.

Looks like there's quite a bit of good swordplay here, but much of it is obscured by dim nighttime photography. Luckily, the sun comes up before the epic final bloody battle, which is worth the wait. At one point, Lung skewers four opponents on his spear like shish kabob.

Distributor Michael Thevis saw fit to provide fresh main credit animation (which gives a lot more space to those involved with the dubbing than the original cast and crew), and a new rock soundtrack for its 1978 U.S. debut. Koa Pao Shu was one of the few women on record to direct a martial arts action movie. *AKA:* Chiu Meng Cheong; Zhui Ming Qiang; The Desperate Chase; The Dangerous Chase. 🐉🐉♡

1971 (R) 96m/C *HK* Jimmy Wang Yu, Lung Fei, Chiao Chiao, Tin Yau, Miu Tin, Yee Yuen, Roy Chiao, Ko Saio Pao. *D:* Kao Pao Shu. *W:* Kao Pao Shu, Ngai Hong. *C:* Kuo Fang Chi. *M:* Flood. **VHS, DVD**

The Blood Rules

Mike Cheng (Michael Wong) heads up a gang of thieves that preys on the triads, pulling off daring robberies of illicit gems and other valuables. His lieutenant Jean (Suki Kwan) secretly loves Mike, though he has a wife and son. Shoot (Lam Suet) loves Jean, but knows she's hopelessly taken with Mike. Their fence Uncle Lam (Wong Tin Lam) always insists they obey the old rules of conduct in their criminal activities, which makes Q (Jackie Lui), the youngest member of the gang, a danger to them all when he tries to buy a flashy sports car to impress a girl. Since Lam still owes them half their money, the gang can't refuse when he proposes a difficult new heist. Chicken Sam (Yeung Hung) of the Taiwanese Chuhung Gang is hiding out in Hong Kong after killing another triad in a gambling dispute. Their mission is to snatch his prized pearl bracelet—and the seven diamonds he keeps attached to his penis. But Q gets greedy and tries to get the loot first. He gets caught, and under torture betrays the others. There's a big shootout, and the gang barely escapes with their lives. But their trouble isn't over yet—Chicken Sam is still on their trail, and Detective Tom Wai (Stephen Au), who has been waiting for a break to catch the gang, is quick to pick up on their scent.

A somewhat predictable tale of a heist gone sour, with only the love triangle and decent action scenes to keep it fresh. As soon as you see that Shoot keeps a tropical fish store as a side business, you just know there's going to be a gun battle there, with all those tempting tanks and lights to smash. There's another beautiful

B

"I don't have time to die right now."

—Busy Jimmy Wang Yu checks his schedule in *Blood of the Dragon*

CGI title sequence from Storm Riders. **AKA:** *Hang Kwai; Hang Gui.* 🎜🎜🎜

2000 96m/C *HK* Michael Wong, Suki Kwan, Jackie Lui, Lam Suet, Wong Tim Lam, Stephen Au, Tin Yue-lai, Lau Wing-wai, Patrick Keung, Yeung Hung, Pauline Yam, Wai Lit, Geung Hiu-man. **D:** Marco Mak. **W:** James Yuen, Andy Law. **C:** Fung Yuen-man. **M:** Lincoln Lo. **VHS, DVD**

Blood: The Last Vampire

 Saya (Youki Kudoh of *Snow Falling on Cedars*) is a little lady with a very sharp sword. She works as a special assassin for an unnamed secret U.S. government agency. Her job is hunting down and wiping out the blood-drinking demons known as "chiropterans." Saya's new assignment is to work undercover as a Japanese schoolgirl at the U.S. Air Force base at Yokota. It's 1966, and a lot of servicemen and their families are stationed there, gearing up for missions to Vietnam. She picks up the trail of her quarry at the school medical office. The school nurse (Rebecca Forstadt, whom some may recognize as the English voice of *Robotech*'s Lynn Minmei) is the intended victim of two demons disguised as Saya's classmates. Saya dispatches one, but the other gets away, hiding among the Halloween revelers. As a witness, the nurse is now a target for the demon—and two more are rapidly approaching the base from town.

Producer Mamoru Oshii (director of *Ghost in the Shell*) and director Hiroyuki Kitakubo *(Roujin Z)* have teamed up to once again to expand the art form of animation. *Blood* merges stylized cel animation seamlessly with CGI settings and effects to create an exciting new look, all in service of a thrilling, action-packed story that mixes *Blade* with *Buffy the Vampire Slayer* by way of *Vampire Princess Miyu*. There is only one thing that will keep *Blood* from joining the likes of *Akira* and *Princess Mononoke* as a modern anime masterpiece: its length. During the 1980s, the OAV (Original Anime Video) release became established as a legitimate and accepted cartoon format in Japan, making projects of intermediate length viable. But at 48 minutes, *Blood* feels unfinished. The story leaves many unanswered questions, such as whether the man Saya killed in the opening sequence was really a vampire or an "acceptable human loss," or how she came to be doing what she's doing. There's no indication as to why it's set against the Vietnam War (other than to give a unique setting for supernatural horror), and there's the feeling that Saya is headed toward an even bigger climax soon after, perhaps in the war zone itself. It begs for a sequel, but why not provide a much more satisfying debut? Make no mistake, though; that 48 minutes is pure anime magic. The wonderful music soundtrack by Yoshohiro Ike also deserves applause. 🎜🎜🎜🎜

2000 48m/C *JP* **V:** Youki Kudoh, Joe Romersa, Rebecca Forstadt. **D:** Hiroyuki Kitakubo. **W:** Kenji Kamiyama. **M:** Yoshohiro Ike. **VHS, DVD**

Blooded Treasury Fight

Ching government man Marshal Chow Kwan-hai (Delon Tan) is leading a gang of fighters to look for the Pai Lin treasure. He's sent to talk to condemned killer Ying kan-tow (David Chiang), offering him freedom and a reward to go on the dangerous mission with him. Ying resists, but changes his mind after learning his old girlfriend Chai-nin (Chan Bik-fung) has signed on rather than be forced into marriage with an old merchant. The team also includes another tough fighter named Shur-tan (Choi Wang) and a burly pickpocket (Fan Mui-Sang). One of the team, however, is secretly one of outlaw Tang Pao's (Michael Chan) men—the gang guarding the treasure at Bloody Mill.

Chow falls into a wolf trap early on and injures his leg, and sends the other four on without him. But it's a ruse—Chow faked his injury to meet up with two brothers for another part of his plan, the first group obviously being used as a distraction. Another of his men, Wai-lan (Wong Chung), poses as a tattoo artist hired by Tang Pao to mark a map of the mill on his leg. They meet up with a traveler who was wounded by bandits, along with nephew Lu-chin (Ko Chiang) and niece Shou-lang (Kim Chin-lin). But his injuries are fake, too—the family is really spying for Tang Pao. While Tang's men are busy capturing Ying's group, Chow sneaks into Bloody Mill to meet up with Wai-lan and find the treasure. Plus, another marshal comes into town on a mission of his own.

With all the various characters and their secret identities, this is almost like a Chang Cheh picture. It has a good story and interesting settings, and should have been better than it is. But outside of Chiang, the stars don't have the presence to keep viewers interested, and the fight scenes are only average. Since Tang doesn't know where the treasure is, it's confusing why he wants the map tattoo. But then, there's a lot of confusion in the complex plot. The climax set in the mill, which gets destroyed by the stars all fighting for the treasure, prefigures the wild, scenery smashing fight scenes in Jet Li movies. **AKA:** *Dragon Devils Die.* 🎜🎜🎜

1979 91m/C *HK* David Chiang, Delon Tan, Michael Chan, Wong Chung, Choi Wang, Fan Mui-Sang, Bruce Lai, Ko Chun, Chan Bik-fung, Kim Chin-lin, Chin Feng, Wong Ching, Wu Ma, Lu Wei, Ko Saio Pao. *D:* Bau Hok-lai. *W:* Ngai Hong, Chin Shu Mei, Chu Yu (story). *C:* Woo Kuo-hsiao. *M:* Chen Hsua Chi. **DVD**

BloodFight

A "kumite" martial arts tournament movie, and not a particularly good one. The fighting isn't bad, especially given the novelty of a wide range of disciplines, but the drama portion is awful. Hong Kong: Masahiko Kai (Yasuaki Kurata of *Return of the Deadly Blade*) works his way up the ranks in the 1989 World Championship of Free Fighting. As the matches continue, he recalls how his wife Suzie (Lum Ken-ming) left him because he wouldn't stop reliving past championships, close his crummy gym, and get a job. He tries to train an angry street punk to be his successor, but the youth remains a boorish bully. When a student/waiter named Ryu Tenmei (Simon Yam) beats Kai's student and his whole gang in a street fight, Kai is determined to make him a martial arts champion. Ryu only wants to play basketball, but changes his mind when the gang returns and ambushes him.

He begins intense training, neglecting his poor girlfriend Milly (Cristina Lawson). Ryu proves himself at the 1987 Championships, beating many opponents, but the brutal Chong Lee (Bolo Yeung) thrashes him soundly, and then delivers a neck-snapping death-blow. Kai goes on a bender, until the Free Fighting Association sends his old friend Jack (John Ladaski) to make him an offer: they want his gym back in the tournament to face Chong Lee, hoping to sell a lot of tickets. He keeps moping, until Milly gives him a pep talk that puts him back into *Rocky*-style training for the title himself.

Aimed at the U.S. video market, this was Kurata's lone effort as a producer, obviously hoping to cash in on the success of Jean-Claude Van Damme's hit *Bloodsport*. Bolo Yeung even plays the same character. The film's lack of English dubbing is actually a detriment, as the Asian cast members all struggle to speak their dialogue in English, with varying levels of comprehensibility—Lum Ken-ming's struggle is especially painful. Bolo Yeung always makes a great villain, though supposedly over-the-hill Kurata is about the same age. 🐉🐉

1989 96m/C *JP/HK* Yasuaki Kurata, Simon Yam, Lum Ken-ming, Cristina Lawson, Bolo Yeung, Shinya Ono, John Ladalski. *D:* Shuji Goto. *W:* Yoshiaki Sawaguchi. *C:* Nobuaki Murano. *M:* Yuji Oguchi. **DVD**

Bloody Beach

Fun slasher movies like *Scream* and *I Know What You Did Last Summer* were big hits in Korea, propagating a crop of fresh imitations there, many of which use the Internet as a plot device. Here, an Internet chat group decides to meet at a beach house for a vacation. However, a dark cloud hovers over the group due to the mysterious death of one of their group, who they only know by the screen name "Sandmanzz" (a cross-language pun for "sender"). Rumor has it that the unpopular Sandmanzz committed suicide because of the group's unkind treatment, and some harbor guilt or resentment because of it. The dead don't rest easy, and some members of the group receive threatening messages. Do-yeon is killed by a mysterious attacker before she gets off the train after receiving a page signed "Sandmanzz." Nam-kyeong (Kim Hyun-jung) dreams of being stabbed in her sleep, but soon there's real blood on the beach. Kim Yu-na (Lee Seung-chae) seduces boastful virgin Jung-min (Jin Tae-seong), and someone slaughters both of them. While searching for the lost couple, the rest of the group sees a man wearing dark overalls walking in the woods, and finds blood in Yu-na's car. But their suspicions shift inside while they wait for police to arrive, as it's discovered that the messages were sent from the beach-house computer. Suspicion falls on nerdy Jae-sung (Yang Dong-kun) when it's learned he was the one sending the messages—but is he the real Sandmanzz?

When the whodunit element is added to the stalk-and-slash formula, the movie doesn't get any more interesting, and has to rely on the slick visual style of veteran horror director Kim In-soo *(The Vengeful Vampire Girl)* to keep things going. There are enough scare and shock moments to make this nothing more or less than a solid little thriller, with a visually unusual climax. *AKA: Haebyeoneuro Gada.* 🐉🐉

2000 89m/C *KO* Kim Hyun-jung, Lee Seung-chae, Yang Dong-kun, Jin Tae-seong, Lee Jeong-jin, Lee Hyun-kyoon, Lee Sae-Eun, Kim Hyeon-jeong. *D:* Kim In-soo. *W:* Baek Seung-jae, Noh Jin-soo, Park Mi-young, Shim Hae-won, Son Kwang-soo. *C:* Kim Yoon-soo. *M:* Bang Jun-seok, Cho Young-ook. **DVD**

Bloody Fight

Horrible editing is the main feature that distinguishes this vintage martial arts film, over and above some good fight choreography by Chan Siu-pang. Here's what we see in this movie: opening credits showing action-packed scenes from other movies. The real opening shows a remote village, with a Japanese samurai reeling around, having just killed several members of

the local martial arts club. The samurai attacks a new student and his sister, and then he's fighting *a totally different character with a moustache.* Apparently somebody else has arrived to beat the villain, and then disappear from the movie for another 20 minutes.

Master Sher Ching Tao-fu then delivers a lecture to the new students, warning them about how his ex-student Chi Shi-hou turned to the Dark Side, though daughter Chi-ling sticks up for him. Japanese boxers Shen Da-kwei (Chen Kuan-tai) and Yuen Yen-au (Eddie Ko) arrive to challenge the school in advance of their boss Chen Cheng (Fong Yeh), who wants a fight to the death with Master Sher. He agrees, and is soundly defeated. While the Japanese are celebrating by breaking down the school's signs, Sher is on his deathbed, making Chi-ling promise to go live with his brother and not seek revenge. Chen Cheng continues his promotional tour of Asia, killing martial arts masters in every town. No sooner has Chi-ling been taken in by Uncle Shih, than Chen Cheng and his gang arrives in *his* village. Visiting Thai fighters Chalaba (the guy who beat the samurai earlier), Sai-koong, and his sister Chao are also on hand for the challenge. Chen Cheng defeats them all, and Shih's son Tin-wah (Alan Tang) proves to be no match for him either. Drunken gambler Ch Shi-hou (Tang Ching) has seen all this, and scurries after the Japanese, challenging them on a picturesque mountainside. He does better than most, but retreats when it becomes obvious that he's no match for Chen Cheng. Shih recovers, and his school goes to work developing new tactics to deal with the enemy. As they work, a love triangle develops among Tin-wah, Chao, and Chi-ling (though she still has feelings for Shi-hou). Their skills improve, but they don't have the ideas necessary to challenge Chen Cheng until black sheep Chi Shi-hou rejoins the family—as Shih says, "Bringing doom with every blow."

Director Ng Tin-chi shows the definite influence of spaghetti westerns. There are some really nicely composed shots throughout the film, making good use of locations available, but the poor editing ruins their effectiveness. The tension of a duel is interrupted at odd moments by reaction shots of side characters. Ng also bears classical traits dating back to silent film days. At one point he presents a flashback that's shot through a hole in a piece of clouded glass. The editing problem is compounded by a lack of focus in the film, which is an ensemble piece without a true lead character. It all doesn't really gel until the third act, when the best fighting begins. The fights get bloody all right, and are nicely designed, though don't expect the kind of fast-paced action that typifies more modern films. **AKA:** *Kuen Moon; Quan Men.* 🐉🐉🐉

1972 92m/C *HK* Alan Tang, Tang Ching, Pai Ying, Lau Lan-ying, Ingrid Hu, Chen Kuan-tai, Fong Yeh, Eddie Ko, Lee Ka-ting, Goo Man-chung. **D:** Ng Tin-chi. **C:** Lin Tsau. **M:** Wong Chu-jen. **VHS, DVD**

The Bloody Fists

This bombastic martial arts picture is generally recognized as the film that made a star out of Chan Sing, and deservedly so. Two years after getting chased out of the village, rascal Pai Chin-san (Suen Lam) returns as a collaborator with some Japanese fighters. The foreigners make a small effort to hide their intentions by claiming that they only want to set up their own martial arts school, but their true aim is obvious: cornering the market on the region's rare Dragon Herb (Dude!), which is sorely needed as a cure for a plague raging across north China, intending to replace the crops with opium. Before long, the Japanese fighters are beating up all the fighters in town for their masked leader Okingawa (Chen Kuan-tai), making their way to the powerful Yu clan. The Japanese issue a public challenge to all fighters in the area to come duel with them, just to make sure everyone knows who the new bosses are. The first challenger is Pai's own brother (action director Yuen Woo-ping) who is quickly beaten. But the Yu brothers and their friend Sun prove tougher to beat, thanks in part to the help of a stranger. This stranger in town is actually the Infamous Fugitive Chan Wu-ger (Chan Sing), who is on the run from the law, specifically Captain Kam. Not long after, Chan falls victim to the plague and is found by mute woodcutter Yabo (Hon Gwok-choi). While Yabo and his grandfather (Kok Lee-yan) use the Herb to cure Chan, the Japanese keep busy torturing the villagers, hoping to learn where the Yus have hidden the stores of Dragon Herb. They also kidnap Shou-lan ("H.K. TVB Star" Hoh Sau-san), the fiancée of young Yu Lang, to force them to cough up the Herb. But by the time the Japanese have the surviving fighters lined up for execution, Chan has recovered and is ready to get some blood on his fists.

Though the martial arts scenes aren't as fancy as those Yuen Woo-ping would create in later years, writer/director Ng See-yuen gives the film a dynamic pace, borrowing ideas from spaghetti westerns and treating it like an epic. Chan Sing brings a lot of charisma to his anti-hero role, carefully combing his hair each time he's about to make with some serious ass-kicking. The film's dramatic quotient is exaggerated considerably by the extensive lifting of soundtrack music from the James Bond series, and even the theme from the soap opera *The Young and the Restless*. **AKA:** *Dong Kau Taan; Dang Kou Tan; Death Beach.* 🐉🐉🐉

1972 97m/C *HK* Chan Sing, Chen Kuan-tai, Henry Yu Yung, Lindy Lin, Hon Gwok-choi, Kok Lee-yan, Hoh Sau-san, Suen Lam, Fong Yeh, San Kwai, Pak Sha-lik, Wong Biu Chan, Shum Wai, Yuen Woo-ping, Wong Yu, Brandy Yuen, Sham Chin-bo. *D:* Ng See-yuen. *W:* Ng See-yuen. *M:* Chou Fu-liang. **DVD**

Blowback: Love and Death

Leisure-suit gunmen Joe (Riki Takeuchi) and Baku (Takashi Matsuyama) are looking forward to spending their pay from a job on some R&R, but they run into an ambush, and are robbed by their own gang. Their driver Lopez (Keishi Hunt) double-crosses them, and shoots Baku; Joe takes a bullet, too, but survives. At a bar in town, he's taken in by the owner, Rei (Mie Yoshida), who fixes up his wounds. She agrees to help him track down Lopez, and they get caught between Lopez and the cops in a shootout. Rei and Joe are rescued by a man named Ratts (Shun Sugata); an ex-cop bounty hunter, he's after the same man who ambushed Joe, a ruthless yakuza boss called Wildcat (Mike Monty). Joe and Ratts follow Lopez's girlfriend (Sheila Lintan), and manage to finally kill him in his go-go bar. But while they're gone, Wildcat finds their hideout and kidnaps Rei. Joe loads up on ammo and heads out to raid Wildcat's compound.

None of it is exceptionally well executed, but there's still plenty of chases and gun battles in this Philippines-based action thriller. The bad guys can't hit the heroes, even shooting at close range. Some of the squib packs are clearly visible beneath clothing before they're detonated. Non-actors play most of the minor roles. On the other hand, Takeuchi displays a great deal of intensity, like he has a bad stomach cramp, and it's a matter of quantity over quality in the action department. Villain Mike Monty is a longtime veteran of international exploitation, having appeared in films like *Frankenstein's Castle of Freaks* and *Escape from Blood Plantation*. **AKA:** *Blow Back 2.* 🎵🎵🎵

1990 88m/C *JP/PH* Riki Takeuchi, Mie Yoshida, Shun Sugata, Keishi Hunt, Takashi Matsuyama, Mike Monty, Sheila Lintan, Nobuyuki Asano, Tony Ogunsanya. *D:* Atsushi Muroga. *W:* Toshimichi Ohkawa. *C:* Toshio Iwaki. *M:* Masanari Abe. **VHS, DVD**

Body Snatcher from Hell

Though sci-fi cinema is full of alien baddies taking possession of poor human brains, it's rare to find one that actually shows a glob from space splitting open somebody's head to climb inside! That showstopping little scene takes place mid-

way through this weird thriller from Hajime Sato, director of *Terror beneath the Sea*. The decade between 1955 and 1965 saw a huge boom in film production in Japan, when studios there churned out twice as many features in a year as in the United States. Perhaps as a result of a cooling-off period, Japanese films of the late 1960s are among the strangest ever made.

A passenger jet passes through strange red clouds, after which there is a bomb threat. A search reveals passenger Taraoka Hirofumi (Hideo Ko) as an assassin who intends to hijack the plane. After an encounter with a glowing UFO, the plane crashes in the desert. The usual cross section of survivors is on hand: a senator (Eizo Kitamura), a young widow (Kathy Horan), an arms dealer (Yuko Kusunoki), and a psychiatrist (Kazuo Kato) and scientist (Masaya Takahashi) to try to explain everything. Everyone bickers while suffering from hunger and dehydration. Taraoka runs off into the dunes, taking stewardess Kuzumi (Tomomi Sato) along as a hostage. Kuzumi escapes when they're confronted with another UFO. An evil space amoeba takes possession of Taraoka, who begins sneaking around killing people and drinking their blood. The aliens, called "Gokemidoro," next take over the arms dealer's wife (Yuko Kusunoki), using her to denounce the human race for their warlike ways and announce their intention to take over the Earth. With everyone else possessed or dead, Kuzumi and pilot (Teruo Yoshida) make a break for civilization, but find even greater surprises in store for them.

A sci-fi version of *Flight of the Phoenix*, this little gem overcomes its low budget and some poor acting with an atmosphere of exotic creepiness. It maintains a steady undercurrent of tension throughout, relieved only by flashes of outright horror. The shock ending prefigures living-dead horror films like *Dawn of the Dead, Zombie,* and *Resident Evil*. **AKA:** *Kyuketsuki Gokemidoro; Goke the Vampire; Goke, Body Snatcher from Hell.* 🎵🎵🎵

1968 (PG) 84m/C *JP* Teruo Yoshida, Tomomi Sato, Hideo Ko, Eizo Kitamura, Kathy Horan, Yuko Kusunoki, Kazuo Kato, Hiroyuki Nishimoto, Masaya Takahashi. *D:* Hajime Sato. *W:* Susumu Tanaka, Kyuzo Kobayashi. *C:* Shizuo Hirase. *M:* Shunsuke Kikuchi. **VHS**

Body Weapon

A trio of sadistic psychos, including one who wears a leather mask, is raping and killing young couples parked on Lovers Lane. The only clues left for Detective Wu Chi-kwun (Vincent Zhao) are video arcade tokens. Kwun beats out his partner Dennis Lee (Stephen Au) to represent the Hong Kong Police Department in an

When we think of Chinese films, we're usually thinking about Hong Kong and Taiwan, but the Chinese cinema began on the mainland. Early centers for film studios were located in Beijing, Canton, and especially Shanghai. During the Japanese invasion and the Communist Cultural Revolution, the commercial business of film gradually moved to the islands, but filmmaking for public entertainment continued in the Peoples Republic of China. While government control was absolute, some who work in Chinese film feel that freedom is relative. Restrictions have less to do with specifying film subjects than with making sure certain negative elements are avoided. While there are strict rules to follow and censorship in effect, there are also restrictions in a free market, and commercial cinema tends to follow commercial subjects. Little thought is given to what will sell in a Chinese film. The focus is on how to best deliver messages that will benefit society—or the government's idea of society.

The state runs the film studios, the film distribution, and the film academies where filmmakers are trained. Film studios produce films to serve their province first, and are more widely distributed if successful. The small number of students at the academies are divided into specialties, with little overlap. In China, film is considered more like literature than a performing art, and prospective directors are first trained in scriptwriting.

All of this has been changing a great deal since the borders of China began to open in the 1970s. As they say, how ya gonna keep 'em down on the collective farm.... More commercial-minded movies began to be made, such as the *Shaolin Temple* films starring Jet Li, with the international market in mind. An avant-garde, independent movement began, and some maverick filmmakers began making films outside of government control—though many were banned in China and only played outside its borders. This situation has accelerated even more rapidly since the reunification with Hong Kong. HK has had just as much effect on the mainland as the mainland has had on HK, and as more of Hong Kong's established industries (including film) have been stretching their legs to take advantage of big, roomy China, the mainland Chinese have been picking up ideas from the "Hongkies," and their Western friends.

annual martial arts tournament, giving Zhao and Au a chance to show off their kicks. Wu and Lee have also been competing for the affection of Officer Miriam Wong Siu-ling (Angie Cheung), a frequent topic of conversation around the precinct. Wong decides to marry Lee, but on their wedding night, the psychos invade their house and assault them, leaving Lee dead. Rather than identify a suspect when he's brought in, Wong decides to let him go and get revenge her own way. A friend (Pinky Cheung) takes her to a gay man (Clarence Fok) who teaches her how to become a body weapon, able to control or destroy any man.

While not exactly the kung fu version of *I Spit on Your Grave*, this surreal cheapie is just as unpleasant, with martial arts awkwardly added to the mix. It'd be tough to pick what part of the script is most offensive—the portrayal of gays, the heroine who needs constant protection, or sadistic acts presented as entertainment. One might think that the nicely shot fight scene at the end could redeem this mess, but then, it also includes a bit of business where Zhao uses another cop's corpse as a puppet to fight his opponent! A feast for those who enjoy Hong Kong cinema at its outrageous worst, and for fans of continuity errors. Anyone who can't guess the identity of the masked psycho in the first act should turn in his or her popcorn. *AKA: Yuen Chi Miu Hei, Yuan Shi Wu Qi.* ♫♪

1999 92m/C *HK* Angie Cheung, Vincent Zhao, Elvis Tsui, Stephen Au, Joe Ma, Sam Wong, Clarence Fok, Benny Lai, Pinky Cheung. **D:** Aman Chang. **W:** Cheung Kwok-yuen. **C:** Choi Sung-fai. **M:** EMP. **VHS, DVD**

The Bodyguard

Don Salvattore Rocco is gunned down on the steps of St. James Cathedral by yakuza hit men. Sonny Chiba, pretty much playing himself, is somehow involved in the investigation. Gangsters take over his Pan Am flight back to Tokyo just to catch him, but he kills all five with his bare hands. At a press conference, he vows to smash the whole drug ring himself, chopping a Coke bottle in half for emphasis. He offers himself as bodyguard to anyone who will step forward to testify against them.

He has a taker—a young woman named Reiko. Proving she's a marked woman, Cosa Nostra killers attack Chiba's sister, Mak Lee. That night, thugs break into Reiko's apartment and torture her for information. Some bodyguard! What Chiba actually wants is someone to act as bait for the bad guys. What Reiko wants is his high-profile protection while she rips off the mob. She was Rocco's girlfriend, and she means to get her revenge, with a big cash

bonus. Her ex-boyfriend/pimp Taka cuts in on her plan, but may be playing both sides. The yakuza ships heroin into the country inside caskets using U.S. Air Force planes, and Reiko swipes a shipment for herself. Chiba agrees to go along with her plan in order to get to the chiefs, but when they find the head of her USAF contact (still blinking a bit) in her car, they know that someone is onto the game.

The script is a bit of a mess, so you'd expect a Chiba picture to pay off with more action. Unfortunately, outside of a few scenes, he does more dodging around than direct fighting. In an otherwise unrelated scene added by U.S. distributor Aquarius, Aaron Banks and Billie Louie argue a bit about Bruce Lee and Sonny Chiba in a 42nd Street karate school, demonstrate a few moves, then get the hell out of the movie. The opening scroll was borrowed by Quentin Tarantino as Samuel L. Jackson's creed in *Pulp Fiction.* **AKA:** *Karate Kiba; Hissatsu Sankaku Tobi; Bodyguard Kiba; Viva Chiba the Bodyguard.* ♫♫

1973/78 (R) 88m/C *JP/US* Sonny Chiba, Judy Lee, Sue Shiomi, Jiro Chiba, Aaron Banks, Bill Louie. **M:** Toshiaki Tsushima. **DVD**

Boiling Point

With his stunning directorial debut *Violent Cop,* Takeshi Kitano expanded the range of the cops-and-robbers thriller. With his second feature, he de-glamorizes the world of yakuza gangsters by setting his criminals within the bounds of dull and ordinary life. Masaki Iguchi (Yurei Yanagi, billed here in his first film as Masahiko Ono) is a disenchanted young gas-station attendant, who can't seem to even work up any enthusiasm for his position on the Eagles amateur baseball team. His bad attitude gets under the skin of a local yakuza underling, and his feeble attempt to fight back only brings him more trouble. Masaki likely picked up his hard head from his father (Takahito Iguchi), a former yakuza who now owns a seedy bar, but still won't take guff from anyone. Seeing his pop straighten things out with the yakuza with some straight negotiation and back-alley violence brightens Masaki's spirits a bit—he starts dating a girl and nearly hits a home run. However, Mr. Iguchi's methods don't take. Gang Boss Otomo (Hisashi Igawa) complains to his superiors, bringing Iguchi a beating.

On a quest for revenge, Masaki heads for Okinawa with a pal to buy a gun. While there, they're befriended by two-fisted bisexual gangster Uehara (Kitano), who's in trouble with his own organization for embezzling. Masaki takes wild man Uehara, with his eagerness to attack anyone whose looks he doesn't like, as almost

a surrogate father figure. Uehara helps Masaki acquire his firearms from a U.S. serviceman, then heads off with his assistant Tamagi (Katsuo Yokashiki) to unleash his own plan for mayhem and vengeance. After spending time with Uehara, seemingly a visitor from a more dramatic and disturbing universe, one would think Masaki would be glad to get back to the smaller-scale fate that awaits him. But with his horizons expanded, Masaki finds it difficult not to think bigger than a mere handgun.

The deadpan delivery that made Kitano a TV comedy star works just as well for him with violent action, and here he takes his technique to extremes in both directions. He uses his straightforward filming style and relaxed pace to keep the audience off balance, never knowing when a sharp sight gag or bone-breaking punch is coming. Sometimes both come together, as when Iguchi clocks an annoying yuppie who comes into his bar. The end result is a film that takes pleasure in a simple ice cream bar, while acknowledging that the universe contains some sudden and unpleasant shocks. **AKA:** *3-4x10 Jugatsu; San Tai Yon Ekkusu Jugatsu; The Third and Fourth of October.* 🎬🎬🎬♡

1990 97m/C JP Yurei Yanagi, Yuriko Ishida, Takahito Iguchi, "Beat" Takeshi Kitano, Minoru Iizuka, Makoto Ashikawa, Hisashi Igawa, Bengal, Johnny Ohkura, Katsuo Tokashiki. **D:** Takeshi Kitano. **W:** Takeshi Kitano. **C:** Katsumi Yanagishima. **VHS, DVD**

Bolo

A kind of spaghetti-western kung fu flick, *Bolo* tells the story of two friends who are taken out of prison to become sheriffs of a frontier town. The town, you see, has trouble keeping its sheriffs alive, and the government is tired of losing good men on the job. Enter Bolo (Bolo Yeung) and Ma (Jason Pai), two rogues who are more than glad to get out of jail free. Bolo and Ma hike through the country to the town in question, where they quickly find that no one much likes either the law or lawmen. The two are welcomed by an ambush in their honor—but they take the trouble in stride. Bolo isn't too bright, and is more than willing to bull ahead no matter what the obstacles. Ma spends most of his time whoring and gambling, and in between, he plots to recover gold from a robbery he pulled years ago. Unknown to anyone, even Bolo, Ma plans to use this money to build a hospital. (Really!)

The corrupt local officials spend a lot of effort trying to get rid of the sheriff-thieves, but can never quite manage. Bolo stomps his way through every attempt to stop him, and Ma plays both sides against each other. It's a comic odyssey, in the traditional "kung fool" mold: some slapstick, some (mild) sex farce, lots of

brawls, and the obligatory goofy cross-eyed guy (actually *two*: To Siu Ming and Yue Tau Wan are both on hand). It all ends up in a big kung fu duel—naturally. Did we mention the sacred turtle fighter?

Bolo Yeung and Jason Pai did the martial arts choreography on this flick, and the fights are—on the whole—pretty good. There's even some prop battles in the mode that Jackie Chan would later make famous. The goofy music, which veers from spaghetti-western choral to Greek bazuki and/or balalaika, is worth mentioning—though hardly worth listening to. All in all, a pretty fun film—much in the spirit of the Italian *Trinity* westerns—and fans of Bolo shouldn't miss it. It's hard to recognize Yeung beneath his scraggly beard, but there's no mistaking his fabulous pecs. Most films featured bodybuilder Bolo as a weightlifting brute, but he was actually also a fine martial artist and acrobat, who as a youth swam to Hong Kong from the mainland. His physique started getting him roles at Shaw Brothers in the late 1960s. After working with Bruce Lee in a Winston cigarette commercial, the two became friends, and Lee cast Bolo in *Enter the Dragon* (their big fight was unfortunately cut). Kung fu fans came to know him through the dozens of roles he played through the '70s, but his popularity exploded when "The Beast from the East" played the villain in *Bloodsport,* and is still busy promoting bodybuilding and appearing in many American action films. *—SS* **AKA:** *Bolo the Brute.* 🎬🎬

1980 90m/C HK Jason Pai, Bolo Yeung, Huang Ha, Chin Yuet Sang, San Kwai, Lau Yat-fan, To Siu Ming, Michelle Lai, Fung Ging Man, Eric Tsang, Chan Lung, Sai Gwa Pau, Dai Sai Aan, Lau Hok Nin, Chin Ti, Yue Tau Wan. **D:** Bolo Yeung. **W:** Yeung Hon-ming. **C:** E Chung. **M:** Chou Fu-liang. **VHS, DVD**

Born Invincible

A HohwaScope kung fu classic from Joseph Kuo, *Born Invincible* begins with a pack of lies. We see Carter Wong practicing various chi kung techniques, which a narrator calls tai chi training, then goes on to tell us how this special training makes the skin impervious, "the voice becomes high in pitch and strange to the ear; the hair loses color, and becomes like snow." He also says it makes those who practice it mean and violent—quite the opposite of most real tai chi masters.

A pair of Hen Tai killers, sent by the Chin Yin clan to capture old enemy Lu Chin (Su Chen Ping) and his daughter Sou-fei, chase down their quarry close to where Yu Ming-tu (Jack Lung) is drilling his martial arts students. They can't help but come to the defense of the weak. Though their teacher Sou Chu arrives to drive off the intruders, one of the students is killed, and Master Lei Ping (Lung Fei) punishes the students who got involved. However, soon after the Chin Yin chiefs Chin Pao (Lo Lieh, wielding a tonfa with some nasty surprises built in) and "Tai Chi expert" Tin Wu-chien (Carter Wong, dubbed in a voice that is indeed "strange to the ear") come calling in person. The two fiends kill Sou Chu, Lei Ping, and Lu Chin before calling it a day. Ming-tu takes command of the school, vowing that they'll all dedicate themselves completely to eliminating the Chin Yin chiefs.

After a few months training, Ming-tu challenges Pao to a duel, from which he barely escapes with his life. He decides to go on a sabbatical to train even harder for at least a year. Before he can leave, the Hen Tai killers come looking for trouble. Though brother Wah Liu-chen (Mark Lung) is still forbidden to fight for another year by the master's order, he's constructed some nifty traps for the intruders that make them easy picking for his fellow students. By the time Ming-tu has returned, he's figured out Pao's tricks and is able to kill him using a few of his own. He is also able to find Chief Tin's weak point, but is unable to exploit it before getting killed. However, he passes on the secret before passing on, so that his brothers can avenge him.

Joseph Kuo's films usually provided excellent kung fu fighting, along with clever gimmicks to spice things up, and *Born Invincible* delivers all of this. With Yuen Woo-ping directing the action, and the likes of Wong, Lo, Nancy Yen, and the Lung Brothers performing, the fight scenes are all top-notch, and there are some interesting training sequences thrown in. As for gimmickry, we have Lo Lieh's tricky tonfa, Mark Lung's traps, a fighter who spits iron balls like a rifle, and other amusements. There are some oddball moments that frequently crop up in these films where the makers basically made up the plot to fit whatever action they come up with, such as when aged guides pop up to offer crucial advice late in the game. The slide whistle sound effects that accompany Carter Wong as he summons his chi energy are just plain silly, and in a realistic note, one character suggests the heroes simply set the invincible villain on fire to kill him! Plenty entertaining—and a must-see for kung fu fans. *AKA: Taai Gik Hei Gung; Tai Ji Qi Gong; Shaolin's Born Invincible.* 🐲🐲🐲🐲

1978 83m/C *HK/TW* Carter Wong, Nancy Yen, Lo Lieh, Chen Pei Ling, Jack Lung, Wang Chu Liang, Mark Lung, Lung Fei, Su Chen Ping, Alan Chui, Corey Yuen, Yuen Sam, Yuen Woo-ping, Chu Siu-wa, Hung Fa-long, Chen Chiu, Cheung Mei-yee. *D:* Joseph Kuo. *W:* Joseph Kuo, Yiu Hing-hong. *C:* Woo Kuo-hsiao. *M:* Chen Shiun-chi. **VHS, DVD**

Born to Defence

Jet Li's patriotism gets a workout in this mainland production, his lone trip to the director's chair, which portrays all Americans as evil monsters. Following the end of World War II, veterans returning to the port of Tsingtao find it swarming with U.S. servicemen. Soldiers Jet and Liu are brushed aside by the crowds welcoming the foreign war heroes. Jet goes to find a place to stay with his lieutenant, Zhang (Zhao Er-kang), joining in his rickshaw business. U.S. Navy captain Hans roars through town in his car, knocking Jet down, and a scrap between them turns into a riot. The fighting continues in a tough saloon, where Jet gets in a match with a Yankee sailor named Bailey (Paulo Tocha) in a boxing ring. Bailey later beats Zhang in a dispute about Zhang's estranged daughter Na. In a hard-to-watch scene, Jet sells his blood to raise money for repairs and medical expenses. Bailey and his crewmates wreck Jet's rickshaw, and Jet goes to work as a "sparring partner" (punching bag) for boxers—including Bailey. Captain Hans—a big man who knows a little kung fu himself—is disgusted with Bailey's behavior and impressed with Jet's stamina. To defend the Navy's honor (he says) the captain pays to fight Jet when he returns to the ring the next day. When the sailors kill Zhang and Na, Jet breaks out of jail to claim his grim revenge.

Too much of the film is taken up with Li getting socked in the head, getting up, and getting socked again, but the film retains a richly gritty atmosphere. Li's bare-knuckle fight with the officer twice his size, with rain pouring down through a leaky roof, is the film's best scene—though their rematch in the empty factory is a killer. The opening battle scenes are really impressive, with lots of great stunts, hundreds of extras, and vintage hardware. The conflict between Zhang and his prostitute daughter makes for effective drama, but feels like an artificial device added to distract from the fact that the film consists of little more than repeated fights between Jet and the sailors. Not a very good movie, but worth catching for the great fight scenes. *AKA: Jung Wa Ying Hung; Zhong Hua Ying Xioung; Chinese Hero; Born to Defend.* 🐲🐲

1988 88m/C *CH/HK* Jet Li, Zhao Er-kang, Song Jia, Kurt Roland Pettersson, Paulo Tocha, Biu Law Do. *D:* Jet Li. *W:* Shi Yang-ping, Jie Er-ge. *C:* Cho Him. *M:* Hou De-jian, Qu Xiao-song. **DVD**

Born Wild

A boxing drama with a murder mystery mixed in. On his 26th birthday, windsurfing instructor Tide Ho (Daniel Wu) learns that his twin brother Tan (Louis Koo) is dead, apparently beaten to death.

Police believe his death was connected to underground boxing. At Tan's apartment, he meets Tan's girlfriend Sandy (Jo Koo), who is losing her sight. She tells him of how Tan stole her away from triad Mann (Patrick Tam) at a karaoke club. After a few run-ins (and a broken nose), Mann was impressed enough with Tan's boxing skills that he offered to be his manager. Tide finds Mann at his day job as a toll taker. Mann takes Tide to where Tan died, and tells him how Tan became a legend in the illegal boxing world, beating one tough foe after another. When Tan refused to take a dive in a match, he was set up against a gigantic black fighter named Arion (Wrath White), and died fighting. Tide goes to promoter Mr. Chu (Felix Lok), looking to get into a grudge fight with Arion himself.

Much time is taken up with meandering psychodrama, romance, and scenes meant to give Patrick Tam a chance to chew the scenery. The fight scenes are well choreographed, but shot with a lot of fast editing that obscures the action—not a good thing for a boxing movie. A lot of jumping around between flashbacks doesn't often work in a movie, but former John Woo assistant Patrick Leung actually pulls that part of the film together quite well. A lot of the shots have the same style as Woo's, but Leung should have quickened the pace. *AKA: Yau Sau Ji Tung; Ye Shou Zhi Tong.* 🐉🐉

2001 109m/C *HK* Louis Koo, Daniel Wu, Patrick Tam, Jo Koo, Felix Lok, Wrath White, Park Ju-chun, Pai Ying, Chang Kuo-chu, Arthur Wong, Ron Smoorenburg, Phyllis Quek, Lawrence Cheng, Cheung Shiu-chit. *D:* Patrick Leung. *W:* Chan Hing-ka, Amy Chin. *C:* Joe Chan. *M:* Chu Tsang-hei, Anthony Chue. **VHS, DVD**

Branded to Kill

Director Seijun Suzuki sets this modern-day samurai tale in a minimalist film noir world where everyone is insane, and you might be, too. Hanada (Joe Shishido) is the #3 contract killer in Japan. Sakura is #2 and Ko is #4—nobody knows who the "phantom #1" is. Needing cash, Hanada agrees to help an old friend, Kasuga (Hiroshi Minami), get back in with the yakuza by taking a bodyguard job with him for Boss Yabuhara (Isao Tamagawa). While trying to get their client to a house in the country, alcoholic Kasuga loses his nerve and gets shot while they go through a gauntlet of killers, including Ko and Sakura. Hanada has his own obsession: He can only make love after getting a whiff of boiled rice.

Having eliminated Sakura during his successful bodyguard gig, Hanada moves up in rank and is quickly assigned to four tricky assassinations, and he pulls off every miracle

shot without a hitch. Misako (Mari Annu), a stern young man-hating woman he met on the road, hires him to kill a foreign man. Hanada muffs the difficult shot when a butterfly settles on his rifle at the crucial split second, making him kill an innocent woman. His reputation smashed, he's marked for death by the yakuza. Even his crazy wife Mami (Mariko Ogawa) turns on him. Injured, with nowhere else to turn, he hides out with the bewitching Misako, whose home is filled with a collection of butterflies, strangely enough. Seemingly trapped in this pressure cooker (or rice cooker) environment with mad Misako, the psychological games begin. When Hanada goes out to kill Mami, Yabuhara abducts Misako, and an even deadlier game begins, as Hanada finds himself the prey of the phantom #1 killer (Koji Nambara).

Suzuki's camera doesn't flinch from gruesome sights, taking in close-ups of bullet wounds, and ironically, even a man getting a new glass eye. But he also has exquisite taste in bizarre, beautiful imagery. Similar to Jean-Pierre Melville's great *Le Samourai* (released the same year), *Branded to Kill* takes the crime thriller genre into surreal territory. Both films would inspire John Woo's *The Killer* to a great degree. After a prolific period that produced *Gate of Flesh* and *Tokyo Drifter,* Suzuki's bosses at Nikkatsu found this picture way too weird for them, and he was fired, spending the next 10 years working mostly in television. Chubby-cheeked Nikkatsu star Joe Shishido also lost favor after this picture, ending up some years later on the goofy *Fugitive Alien* TV series. *AKA: Koroshi no Rakuin.* 🐉🐉🐉🐉

1967 91m/BW *JP* Joe Shishido, Mariko Ogawa, Koji Nanbara, Mari Annu, Isao Tamagawa, Hiroshi Minami. *D:* Seijun Suzuki. *W:* Hachiro Guryu, Takeo Kimura, Chusei Sone, Atsushi Yamatoya. *C:* Kazue Nagatsuka. *M:* Naozumi Yamamoto. **VHS, DVD**

Brassiere

Two men learn that there's more to being a woman than wearing a brassiere. The head of a multinational lingerie company based in Japan decides that the Hong Kong branch should hire men to design a new product, the "ultimate bra." The branch manager, Samantha (Carina Lau), is not happy about it, and neither is the lead designer, Lena (Gigi Leung), but Johnny (Lau Ching-Wan) and Wayne (Louis Koo) come onboard. Trouble is, they are completely clueless about bras. Will they succeed? And, since they are the only men in the formerly all-female company, could love come knocking on their door?

What is it about a comedy that makes it work? If you analyze jokes or humorous situations too closely, the fun goes away and it doesn't sound quite so hilarious. Indeed, a closer look would reveal that *La Brassiere* runs too long and relies too heavily on the charms of its leading characters to really stand on its own as a classic comedy. But you'll be laughing too much to care. Lau Ching-Wan gives a bravura performance as Johnny. The actor made a mark in dark crime films during the late 1990s and then took some time off from the Hong Kong movie scene. This was a triumphant return, and he's at the top of his game here, funny and romantic at the same time. Louis Koo may never have been sillier, but he looks like he had a good time while filming and that's certainly communicated through his performance. He and Lau Ching-Wan display good chemistry.

Based on his long association with John Woo as assistant director and the films he has made on his own, it seems hard to believe that co-director Patrick Leung could have made such a light and frothy piece of entertainment. Yet the pace, alternating between relaxed and snappy, is similar to that exhibited in his earlier *Task Force*. The production design of Ringo Fung stands out. The offices of the bra company are 22nd century in appearance yet completely functional. The sets inspire some of the comedy, in fact. The cinematography of Fletcher Poon is similarly sharp, keeping the light flattering for the romantic leads but also making the sets and locations look great. —*PM* **AKA:** *Chuet Sai Hiu Bra; Jue Shi Hao Bra; La Brassiere; Ultimate Bra.* 🐉🐉🐉

2001 110m/C *HK* Louis Koo, Lau Ching-Wan, Gigi Leung, Carina Lau, Lee San-San, Chikako Aoyama, Higuchi Asuka, GC Goo Bi, Rosemary Vanderbroucke. **D:** Patrick Leung, Chan Hing-Kar. **W:** Chan Hing-ka, Amy Chin Siu-Wai. **C:** Fletcher Poon. **M:** Chiu Tsang-Hei, Anthony Chue. **VHS, DVD**

Brave Archer

Those who think of kung fu flicks as simple revenge fantasies should try this one, the first in a four-part Chang Cheh epic, based on the famous, much-filmed Yin Jong novel *Eagle Shooting Heroes*. Promising a confusing array of characters and situations, but also great kung fu action from the Shaw Brothers' stable of stars, it doesn't disappoint those dogged enough to get through the complex plot. And for a real change of pace, it doesn't end with a fight scene, but a memorization test!

Even the 93-minute dubbed version (which bears the onscreen title *Kung Fu Warlords*) gives its first three minutes up to the credit sequence in an effort to help keep the characters straight, and offers narration over some of the dialogue to try to simplify things. Here's the first chunk: "During the reign of Emperor Ninchung in the Sung Dynasty, the north of China

was occupied by the Chin family. In a small village near the northern border, there lived two young Sung copiers. One was Yang Ti-tsin, the famous General Yang's grandson. The other, Ku Sau-chin, Ku Ching's son. Both learned kung fu from their military ancestors. One day one of the famous Chu Chien priests, Chu Chu-chi, another Sung patriot, arrived in the village, after having hunted down and killed the traitor. The trio became bosom friends."

The scene following shows the priest naming his friends' infant sons Kuo-ching and Yangkhan. Chin guardsmen show up after the priest leaves and find the head of the man he killed, implicating his friends in the killing. Both men are apparently killed in the ensuing fight, though their friends, the Seven Warriors of Changnan, arrive in time to save their families. Chu returns and gets in a disagreement with the warriors' leader Ling (Fan Mui-Sang), and over the corpses of their friends, agree that they'll each train one of the boys in their own martial arts, meeting again in 18 years to prove whose kung fu is best! Guess that's how they did things back then. During all the chitchat, no one notices that Yang (Dick Wei) isn't really dead yet, but by the time he wakes up they're all gone. He changes his name to Lao-yi to avoid capture, and in his travels adopts an orphan girl.

Grown into manhood, Kuo-ching (Alexander Fu Sheng) befriends beggar Wong Yung-er (Tien Niu). In the street, they see Lao-yi offer the hand of his adopted daughter Nin-chi (Kara Hui) to any man who can beat her in a fight. Lord Chou's son does so, but only for fun—which is a good thing, considering he happens to be Yangkhan (James Lee) grown up. Chou captured him and his mother and made her his royal concubine, and monk Chu Chu-chi has been training him in kung fu all his life. Kuo-ching thinks he should follow through on the marriage offer, and picks a fight. A famous trio of fighters—Sao Ting-tun, Ling Si-yun, and monk Ling Chi Suntin—along with Iron Foot Wang Chi-yun are drawn into the conflict. Kuo-ching and Yung-er (who turns out to be a girl!) fall in love, bringing them into conflict with the Seven Warriors, since her estranged father is notorious killer Peach Blossom Wong Lo-su (Goo Goon-chung). Yangkhan turns out to be a worse disappointment, siding with Chou over his real parents (who commit suicide to avoid a fight). One of the seven is killed by Chin Sing-fung with his Skeleton Hand technique. Kuo-ching stabs the killer, accidentally finding his weak point. The young lovers meet up with Hung, the Nine Fingered Beggar (Ku Feng), an old associate of Lan, who teaches them his 18 Palm Strike.

Crippled Lu Cheng-feng holds quite a house party for the kids and Six Warriors—blind Mei Chou-fung (Helen Yiu), who has been teaching Yang-khan "evil" kung fu, crashes the party,

fighting with Lu and Kuo-ching. Yung's dad Peach Blossom Wong, both Lu and Mei's teacher, comes to break things up. Kuo-ching promises to return to fight Wong after getting revenge for his father's death. On the way, he learns some more tricks from mad Cho Kwei-chun (Phillip Kwok), who has a secret kung fu manual. Meanwhile, Wong promises Yung to rich Prince Au Yang-feng (Danny Lee), so Kuo-ching has to break training to try to spoil the wedding, with Hung's help. To settle the rivalry, Wong sets up a three-part contest for the two suitors, which is only partially based on kung fu.

Hard to find, this series is among the many Shaw classics that's definitely due for a restored version release, as the dubbed version is incomprehensible, leaving out even major turns of the plot. The master for the NS Video version was recorded off of a television broadcast! *AKA: Se Diu Ying Hung Juen; She Diao Ying Xiong Zhuan; Kung Fu Warlords; Shaolin Archers.* 🐉🐉🐉

1977 127m/C *HK* Alexander Fu Sheng, Tien Niu, Goo Goon-chung, Helen Yiu, Ti Lung, Danny Lee, Johnny Wang, Wang Ching-liang, Stephan Yip, Ku Feng, Yang Ni-chiu, Li Shiao-hwa, James Lee, Choi Wang, Lam Fai-wong, Liu Huai Liang, Dick Wei, Kara Hui, Phillip Kwok, Fan Mui-Sang, Chao Chung-hsing, Lu Feng, Lo Meng, Chu Ching, Hsu Chin-leung, Henry Yu Yung, Chiang Sheng, Suen Shu-pau, Jamie Luk. *D:* Chang Cheh. *W:* Yin Yong, Ngai Hong. *C:* Kung Mu-to. **DVD**

Breakout from Oppression

This cheap independent kung fu flick from the Lau Brothers introduced adopted brother Gordon Lau. Gordon is rural mailman To Chung, who is mistaken for a prisoner from a work gang on a trip to East Village. He fights free of the guards, but loses all his letters. He continues on his way to explain his loss, but finds a house full of corpses at his destination. A blind woman is the only survivor of the massacre, and can't identify the killer. To Chung comes to suspect the Chang brothers, who are involved in a labor dispute. Ah-sam (Fung Hark-On), a young heir to a factory, has been embezzling salaries from workers. Ah-sam stalls off the angry workers, planning to hire some fighters to eliminate the leading rabble rousers, brothers Chang Choi and Chang Lik (Dean Shek), along with their kung fu teacher Te Chow-ming. To shows up to demonstrate his kung fu skills and is hired on the spot, making Ah-sam's assistant Man-yu jealous. He sends a worker to carry a bomb to the Changs, and when the man rebels, they attack him. To comes to his aid, intensifying his rivalry with Man-yu. While Ah-sam plots to bomb the workers, To lures the

Changs to a remote spot to confront them. But their quarrel is interrupted when the bombs start going off.

The dubbing is extremely awkward, which may at least partially account for the muddled storytelling. It's supposed to be a mystery story, but its difficult enough trying to figure out who the characters are and why they're constantly fighting with each other. Gordon was only about 20 at the time, and looks even younger, but his talent is already apparent. However, the choreography is uninteresting—working with such an obviously low budget, the Laus may just have been grateful to get film in the can. The soundtrack is comprised of a few funky 1970s tracks mixed with some really ancient library music. The 1978 release date is deceiving, as Gordon Lau is obviously much younger. This likely sat on the shelf until he became a star in *Shaolin Master Killer.* *AKA: Sai Chut Chung Wai, Sha Chu Chong Wei; Deadly Strike.* 🐉

1978 79 m/C *HK* Gordon Lau, Maggie Lee, Fung Hark-On, Chow Fai, Dean Shek, Yam Sai-kwoon, Paul Chun, Huang Ha. *D:* Huang Ha. *C:* Cheh Wan. *M:* Chou Fu-liang. **DVD**

The Bride with White Hair

This classic swordplay fantasy was the best of a wave of such films from Hong Kong in the early 1990s. Brigitte Lin stars as the Wolf Girl, a Mowgli-esque warrior raised by a wolf pack from infancy. She's taken in by a blood cult led by back-to-back conjoined twins named Chi Wu-shuang (Elaine Lui, Francis Ng), who use her as their top assassin. Cho Yi-hang (Leslie Cheung) is the top fighter in a clan resisting the Manchurian invasion of Chung Yuan province. This makes them natural enemies—but they find themselves drawn to each other, and sneak off to have a holiday away from the conflicts of their tribes. Cho gives the Wolf Girl the name "Lien Ni-chang," and promises to be true to her always. Lien tells Chi that she's leaving the cult, but as the male twin is in love with her, he demands she walk through a terrible gauntlet to get out. She survives, but the twins spitefully put in motion a plot that will set the lovers against each other again.

First filmed as *The White-Haired Devil Lady* in 1970 (and abused by the outrageous *Wolf Devil Woman*), *Bride with White Hair* takes Leung Yu-sang's fantasy and embellishes it beautifully with stunning visuals and thrilling fight scenes. The story is made more fantastic with the addition of magical elements, and the hermaphrodite villain of the book is made all the more sensational as superpowered Siamese twins. But overwhelmingly, it's the romantic core of the plot that

engages the viewer, making this one of the most memorable pictures to ever come out of Hong Kong. Shot with Asian-gothic atmosphere by Peter Pau, it all seems to take place in a world of its own. *AKA: Baak Faat Moh Nui; Bai Fa Mo Nu; Jiang-Hu: Between Love and Glory.* 🐉🐉🐉🐉

1993 89m/C *HK* Brigitte Lin, Leslie Cheung, Elaine Lui, Francis Ng, Yammie Nam, Pao Fong, Law Loklam, Joseph Cheng, Eddie Ko. *D:* Ronny Yu. *W:* Ronny Yu, David Wu, Lam Kee-to, Elsa Tang, Leung Yu-sang (novel). *C:* Peter Pau. *M:* Richard Yuen. **VHS, DVD**

The Bride with White Hair 2

Although the original film had a perfect, poignant ending, which wrapped up the story with the elegance of a haiku, that never stopped a studio from making a sequel before. Our tragic hero Cho Yi-hang (Leslie Cheung) is still atop Mount Shing Fung, waiting for the magic flower to blossom, believing it will have the power to cure his wronged true love. Meanwhile, Wolf Girl Lien Nichang (Brigitte Lin) has founded her own cult of man-hating witches, dedicated to wiping out the eight clans of Chung Yuan. With the witch decimating the clans, tearing off heads with her long white hair, the Wu Tang Clan looks forward to the wedding of young Fung Chun-kit (Sunny Chan) to Lyre (Joey Man), hoping they'll help replenish their ranks. But the happy wedding night is spoiled by the invading witch, who means to kill the last descendant of Wu Tang. He's saved by his best man Liu Hang (Richard Suen), who knocks him out and pushes him down a garbage chute, and Lien Ni-chang has to be satisfied with kidnapping the bride. Lien puts Lyre in the care of her aide Chen Yuen-yuen (Ruth Winona Tao), planning to brainwash her into the cult and eventually order her to kill Kit herself. Yuen-yuen is the former lover of traitor General Wu (Eddie Ko), who betrayed her and the entire region to the Manchurians. Kit is found by Ling Moon Yee (Christy Chung) of Kwan Lun Clan, who nurses his wounds. The clan descendants—Moon, Kit, Liu of Hung Tung, Siu Lau (Cheung Kwok-leung) of Wah Shan, Lan Long (Ng Chun-fung) of Shaolin, Yee (Yeung Tak-ngai) of Ching Sing, etc.—are gathered to train with old Granny Yip Pak-chow (Lee Heung-kam) of Ngo Mei Clan. Together, they make a desperate raid on Lien's temple, to rescue Lyre and kill the white-haired witch.

Like many sequels, this one gets off track a bit by concentrating too much on the new characters, when fans are mainly interested in the old ones. But as an action-adventure quest to destroy a powerful demon, it's not bad. David Wu, graduating from editing the first feature for Ronny Yu, relies too much on the blurred action

technique, which Wong Kar-wai would wallow in for his *Ashes of Time*. Sources say Yu stepped in to direct the fiery climax himself. Brigitte Lin is stunning in the lead, a luminously beautiful monster. Christy Chung gets to stretch in her role as a sassy tomboy. *AKA: Baak Faat Moh Nui 2; Bai Fa Mo Nu 2; The White-Haired Swordswoman 2; Jiang-Hu: Between Love and Glory 2.* 🐉🐉🐉

1993 89m/C *HK* Brigitte Lin, Leslie Cheung, Sunny Chan, Christy Chung, Joey Man, Ruth Winona Tao, Richard Suen, Lily Chung, Cheung Kwok-leung, Yeung Tak-ngai, Ng Chun-fung, Lee Heung-kam, Helena Law, Eddie Ko. *D:* David Wu. *W:* Raymond To, Ronny Yu, David Wu, Leung Yu-sang (novel). *C:* Joe Chan. *M:* Richard Yuen. **VHS, DVD**

Brides of Blood

While the filmmaking team of Eddie Romero *(Twilight People)* and Gerardo de Leon *(Curse of the Vampires)* introduced Blood Island in the feature *Terror Is a Man,* what came to be known as the Blood Island Trilogy began with this first of three films starring former American teen idol John Ashley. Government agent Jim Ferrell (Ashley) is sent to the remote island with biologist Dr. Paul Henderson (Kent Taylor), who brings along his vixen trophy wife Carla (Beverly Hills, wearing a gigantic hairdo), to investigate reports of mutation in the plant and animal life caused by H-bomb tests. Things get creepy right away as their boat is met by a native funeral procession. When a pallbearer stumbles, several bloody body parts tumble loose! Their guide Arcadio (Andres Centenera) and his lovely granddaughter Alam (Eva Darren) offer a warning: certain recent events have the natives reverting to the Old Ways, and their stay may be unpleasant. They learn the meaning of "unpleasant" that night when, after a civilized meal with wealthy Estaban Powers (Mario Montenegro), Carla is attacked by a hungry banana tree. It seems the jungle gets a lot more animated after dark. They find the villagers tying young girls up in a clearing as sacrifices to the Evil One—a big, lumpy, green monster—resulting in another funeral the next morning. When Alam is chosen as the next sacrifice, Ferrell decides to interfere in the quaint native customs.

This is the best realized of the Blood Island pictures, with plenty of atmosphere and a reasonably original monster-movie plot. The monsters aren't very convincing, but they're well presented, and their howling and grunting sound effects help to put them over. The flick has enough sex and violence to please the drive-in audience, though not that much blood, considering. Once the menace is vanquished, the movie takes its time ending, with a lot of folks dancing around. Followed by *Mad Doctor of Blood Island. AKA: Brides of Blood Island; Brides of Death; Brides of the*

Beast; Grave Desires; Orgy of Blood; Terror on Blood Island; Island of Living Horror. 🐉🐉🐉

1968 97m/C *PH/US* Kent Taylor, John Ashley, Beverly Hills, Eva Darren, Mario Montenegro, Andres Centenera, Bruno Punzalan, Oscar Keesee Jr., Quiel Mendoza, Ely Ramos, Ben Sanchez. *D:* Gerardo de Leon, Eddie Romero. **VHS, DVD**

Bronson Lee, Champion

He's just like Charles Bronson! No, he's just like Bruce Lee! Uh-uh, you're both wrong—he's Bronson Lee! This Japanese production was an early distribution property from New Line Pictures that tried to capture the audience of both stars and failed.

Japanese-American Vietnam vet Bronson (Tadashi Yamashita) spots an item in his local paper about a Budo tournament being held in Japan, and leaves his grandma behind in Ohio (which looks like the Wild West) to enter it. He befriends Sammy Harrah and his sister Suzy, who run a noodle shop with their grandfather, and visits their karate dojo with them. It so happens their Kishin School is owned by karate champ Masafumi Suzuki (the Street Fighter's master, as himself), who is running the tournament. When Bronson helps daughter Reiko defend herself from attacking students of a rival school, she tries to help him get into the competition. Bronson tries to make some room on the card for himself by beating up Japanese master Go Komada, but Suzuki rejects such brash tactics. However, Komada's sponsor Yamatani signs Bronson to take his fighter's place.

Bronson beats Mexican Joe Gonzales and American Gary Samson to advance to the final round, in which he faces Malaysian Nicom "Black Tiger" Prancha. They fight to a draw, meaning they have to have a rematch, giving time for Black Tiger's manager Mr. Tsuju to kidnap Suzy. Bronson and Gary rescue her, but Gary (who looks a bit like Jesus) sacrifices himself for his friend, and Bronson is blinded by fire. With the tournament called off because of the scandal, Bronson and Black Tiger have to fight it out on their own.

Tadashi Yamashita is a classically untalented actor. As a fighter, he makes a lot of noises in imitation of Bruce Lee, but sounds more like Curly Howard. Some of the key blows during the matches are repeated in slow motion so viewers can get a better look at how phony they are. The dubbing is horrible—little

attempt is made to synch with the actors, the dialogue is ridiculous, and it's difficult to decide which sounds sillier: Yamashita with a Texas drawl, or the villain who uses a heavy accent, calling the hero "Blonson Ree"! Today, Tadashi Yamashita operates a string of karate dojos in the U.S. and makes an occasional appearance in American films like *The Game* and *Lethal Weapon 4.* 🐉

1978 (PG) 79m/C *JP* Tadashi Yamashita, Jimmy Yamashiro, Yoko Horikoshi, Chong Men-jo, Albert Tsao, Gofian Huddart, Dale Ferguson, Masafumi Suzuki. *D:* Yukio Noda. *W:* Ken Takata, Masahiro Ishimura. *C:* Ted Masuda. **VHS**

Brother

After his family is decimated in a gang war, Anika Yamamoto ("Beat" Takeshi Kitano) goes to Los Angeles to find his brother Ken (Claude Maki, better known as Kuroudo Maki). When he finds him, the former student has become a small-time dope pusher working for a black thug named Denny (Omar Epps), with whom Anika had a skirmish upon his arrival in L.A. Anika organizes the gang of clumsy hoods into an entity with whom he eventually tries to bring down the Mafia.

While *Brother* is no great development in Takeshi's career, it's no Hollywood sell-out either. In fact, he transplants himself without losing the offbeat existentialism for which he is known. He wears the same Noh-faced mask of indifference when faced with extinction that has marked previous films. As a director, he has a unique vision of the multicultured L.A. Latinos, blacks, and Asians are all caught in each other's alien cultures as they vie for the easy buck. A flashback is an emphatic reminder that Anika, with a samurai's discipline, is a remnant of a more serious, less chaotic age, when action took the place of words. The contrast between his cool demeanor and their strutting incompetence is hilarious. —*BW* 🐉🐉🐉

2000 (R) 113m/C *JP/US/UK* "Beat" Takeshi Kitano, Omar Epps, Kuroudo Maki, Masaya Kato, Susumu Terajima, James Shigeta, Ren Osugi, Ryo Ishibashi, Naomasa Musaka. *D:* Takeshi Kitano. *W:* Takeshi Kitano. *C:* Katsumi Yanagishima. *M:* Jo Hisaishi. **VHS, DVD**

Brother of Darkness

Another HK true-crime horror story, though this one is about the lurid details of a single murder,

"Pits off! Pits off! Pits off! Pits off!"

—To (Hugo Ng) finally gets pitsed off enough to settle with his evil brother in *Brother of Darkness*

Another shot for the wedding scrapbook from *Brides of Blood.*
THE KOBAL COLLECTION / HEMISPHERE

rather than the depravity of a serial killer. Wong Kuen To (Hugo Ng, later a director) has been arrested for the bloody murder of his older step-brother, Wah (William Ho). Court testimony flashbacks explain why he did it; it's not much of a mystery, just a terrific excuse to show a lot of sadism, sex, and violence. The evil brother proves worthy of painful death within the first reel; AKA "The King," he terrorizes everyone in the neighborhood, especially his own family. The only respite the Wong family gets from "The King" is when he's in prison or off in Macau on a gambling trip, though they seem to spend these breaks trembling in fear of his return.

Growing up, To trains in the martial arts to defend himself. He has a girlfriend named Jenny (Lily Chung), and his life would be pretty good without his evil brother, whose behavior gets worse all the time. Wah sells his wife and son to his wife's boyfriend—at a discount because of the wear and tear he's put on her. At their father's birthday party, To finally gets fed up enough to stand up to Wah, and beats him up.

However, Wah's abuse is felt even when he's far away. To is psychologically frustrated in bed, and much is made in court of his "hypogonadism." There's also a long stretch of film in which Jenny tries to "cure" him. When Wah returns from jail this time, he swears to reform, but he's worse than ever. His threats, drug abuse, stealing, and gambling debts make it necessary for the family to move. But he finds them again. To returns home in time to save Jenny from rape, but Wah continues to threaten. Finally, with his mother driven nearly into insanity, To is driven over the edge.

Wah is such a thoroughly nasty villain that it's almost comical, and William Ho hams it up terrifically. As an amusing twist, frequent screen psycho Anthony Wong is cast as the prosecutor. It's all completely sordid. *AKA: Ti Tian Xing Dao Zhi Sha Xiong.* ♫♫

1994 84m/C *HK* Lily Chung, Hugo Ng, William Ho, Tseng Gen Wing, Lai Yee, Chan Pui-Kee, Anthony Wong, Money Lo. *D:* Billy Tang. *W:* Billy Tang, Kong Heung-sang. *C:* Tony Miu. *M:* Wong Bong. **VHS, DVD**

Bruce Lee: A Warrior's Journey

When Bruce Lee died in 1973, he was working on a film many believe would have been his masterpiece, *The Game of Death.* Just how much footage was shot for the film has always been a matter of debate. When producer Raymond Chow ordered the film completed for release from Golden Harvest in the late 1970s, adding new footage using doubles for Lee to fill in the blanks, only 11 minutes of the original film was deemed usable, and the finished product bore little resemblance to Lee's script. Footage from the film has shown up in the many documentaries on Lee, and every once in a while more of the original footage has come to light, leading many Lee fans to form the opinion that Chow was holding back footage to milk it for all that he could. In recent years, John Little has been digging up as much material as possible for a projected seven-volume series of books of Lee's writings, and he suddenly discovered a large cache of original 35mm footage from *Game of Death,* along with Lee's complete written plans for the film. Forty-one minutes of the footage were assembled using Lee's script notes to reflect his vision of the film, or at least the most important part of it, as Lee and his companions fight their way to the top of a five-story pagoda, seeking a fabulous treasure. The first hour of the film consists of an excellent documentary, focusing on his career leading up to *Game of Death,* and concentrating on the philosophy behind it. We get a look at Lee's 1965 screen test, his scrapbook, a wing chun workout, home movies, scenes from his *Longstreet* episode, and clips from all his starring roles in films. There is also a good deal devoted to the development of jeet kune do, his back injury, and other aspects of his personal life and career. But the main purpose is to set up the grand finale: the *Game of Death* footage itself.

It starts with James Tien fighting the Filipino escrima master (Dan Inosanto) in the Hall of the Tiger, after Chieh Yuan has already been defeated. With Tien clearly outmatched, Lee issues a warning and enters the fray, both opponents teasing each other by tapping out "shave-and-a-haircut" (of all things) with their weapons. Lee matches his green bamboo whip against his adversary's clubs, then both switch to nunchakus. Next, the trio ascends to the fourth level to face the hapkido master (Ji Han Jae). Again, Chieh and Tien attack first, and Mr. Hapkido wipes the tatami with them. While Lee takes his turn, Chieh and Tien race up to the next level, where they are both crushed by the black giant (Kareem Abdul-Jabbar). Lee ascends to face a foe that is faster, much larger, and just as adaptable as he is. The color is off for some of the footage, and a bit of dialogue is missing, but the footage has been finished with appropriate music and (for the most part) decent sound effects. It shows an unexpected degree of humor, and clearly outlines and demonstrates Lee's teachings. Much of the dialogue is amusingly dated—Lee requests that an arena be cleared so he and an opponent can "groove." But for the most part, it's all action footage, and damn good, and contains three of the best fight scenes of Bruce Lee's career. It's as close as we're likely to get to Lee's true vision of *The Game of Death,* and should be considered required viewing. *AKA: A Warrior's Journey.* ♫♫♫♫

2000 100m/C *HK/US/KO* Bruce Lee, Kareem Abdul-Jabbar, Grandmaster Ji Han Jae, Dan Inosanto, Taky Kimura, Linda Lee Cadwell, James Tien, Chieh Yuan, James Franciscus. **D:** John Little, Bruce Lee. **W:** John Little, Bruce Lee. **C:** Lee Hoogon. **M:** Wayne Hawkins. **VHS, DVD**

Bruce Lee Fights Back from the Grave

Within a few years of Bruce Lee's untimely death, producers in Hong Kong and all over the world flooded the market with poor imitations and bold rip-offs. Many fans wished that Bruce would dig his way out of his coffin and give the thieves a thrashing. Perhaps the producers of this film sensed their anger and frustration, and decided to give them what they want—by making another imitation! A tacked-on prologue shows a corny-looking Bruce Lee tombstone mock-up. After a lightning strike, a "Leealike" (to use screenwriter Bey Logan's term) bursts out of the ground.

Go Ha Kahn, a kung fu instructor, travels to Los Angeles to seek a new life. Fellow instructor Wong Hang (Bruce Le) goes to visit him, but arrives just in time for the man's funeral. As Wong mourns over his friend's ashes, a bald, black stranger wearing a cape attacks him with a hatchet. Wong is unable to prove he killed the man in self-defense, and the cops hassle him, but rich mobster Scott Lee bails him out to hire him to find a girl. Le recognizes the girl in the picture (Deborah Chaplin) because she was at Go's funeral, and now the circumstances of his friend's death look mighty suspicious to him. Wong tracks the girl down on his own, just in time to save her from a rapist. She tells him how Go was taken advantage of by an unscrupulous lawyer and his business was nearly ruined, until he got involved with five mysterious men. Wong vows to track down the remaining four to make them pay. And the first step in his plan of revenge is to buy a funny leather hat.

Le's acting and martial arts are standard—during slow-motion replays, you can see that he actually misses with kicks by a good 12 inches. Chaplin (later known as Debbie Dutch) is charming enough in the daffy waitress role, offering contrast to the resolute Asian hero. The main attraction should be Le's duels with the five different-styled killers, but they're all sloppy and fake-looking, with stuntmen waiting around to get hit. The producers even think of a way to pad out the running time with footage from a Hollywood Boulevard parade. The bearded main villain is named "Marcus Welby"! Even Italian director Umberto Lenzi *(Nightmare City, Rambo's Revenge)*, who somehow fit this into his schedule in between Tomas Milian crime thrillers, took

his name off it, disguising his credit as "Doo Yong Lee." **AKA:** *The Stranger.* 🐉

1976 (R) 84m/C *HK* Bruce Le, Anthony Bronson, Deborah Chaplin, Steve Mak, Jack Houston, Charlie Chow, Philip Kennedy, Jimmy Sato. **D:** Umberto Lenzi. **W:** Chee Do Hong, Chong Huang Kuok (story). **C:** Albert Wong. **M:** Wong Kuet Yen. **VHS, DVD**

Bruce Lee, The Legend

Raymond Chow produced this special documentary on his Golden Harvest Studios' first star, who put them on the map. One thing this film has that other such docs lack is access to the Golden Harvest archives and film library, and the program seems to be built around whatever footage was available. Sections are devoted to Lee's early years, film career, his kung fu, and death. It begins with clips from Tsui Hark's *Zu, Warriors from Magic Mountain,* which are used to illustrate how the tradition of old legends in China were to be reincarnated in the 20th century with the birth of Bruce Lee in 1940. Scenes and stills from *My Son Ah Cheung* and other films show Lee as a child star. These clips differ from those included in earlier documentaries like *The Real Bruce Lee,* and it's a wonder these films haven't been made available in their entirety, if only to cash in on the name of their boy star. Clips from *Warriors Two* with Casanova Wong and Leung Kar-yan to illustrate Bruce's wing chun instruction. Master Siu Hon-sung reveals how the young Hong Kong cha-cha dancing champ offered to teach him in the dance in exchange for kung fu instruction.

Returning to the States to establish U.S. citizenship after filming of *The Thunderstorm,* Lee settled in Seattle, working in Ruby Chow's restaurant and living in an apartment above. His 1964 screen test is more extensive than shown elsewhere, but is in much worse shape, a fact they try to cover up by tinting the footage. Raymond Chow is seen in clips visiting Sammo Hung (uncredited) on the set of a picture, and tells about how he discovered Lee when he saw him on a TV show. Interview clips from an English Hong Kong TV show document audience reaction to the success of *The Big Boss,* the biggest hit in HK movie history at the time. Another interview features his co-star (and childhood friend) Nora Miao, and discusses his characters in films in depth, illustrated with many clips. There's a bit of discussion of Lee's plans to play more classical roles, including a blind swordsman. This gives the filmmakers a chance to include clips of Shintaro Katsu as Zatoichi, and one from *Duel to the Death.* Clips and outtakes from *Game of Death* that had never been seen at the time are shown. The section on

"Star sinking in a sea of art."

—Banner over Bruce Lee's coffin as shown in *Bruce Lee, The Legend*

TOO MANY FISTS OF FURY!

Bruceploitation

Not only have cinematic graverobbers unleashed an army of Bruce Lee clones, but they feel no ping of conscience when it comes time to slap titles on their new kung fu movies. Here's a rundown of titles that want to be like Lee.

The Bruce Lee Originals:

Fists of Fury (AKA *The Big Boss*)
The Chinese Connection (AKA *Fist of Fury*)
Return of the Dragon (AKA *Way of the Dragon*)
Enter the Dragon Game of Death

The Damning Evidence:

Asian Connection
Big Boss (1982), *Big Boss 2*
The Big Boss Girl and CID
Big Boss of Shanghai
Blind Fist of Bruce
Bruce and Dragon Fist
Bruce and Shaolin Kung Fu, Bruce and Shaolin Kung Fu 2
Bruce and the Iron Finger
Bruce and the Shaolin Bronzemen
Bruce, King of Kung Fu
Bruce, Kung Fu Girls
Bruce Lee—A Dragon Story
Bruce Lee: A Warrior's Journey
Bruce Lee—The Invincible
Bruce Lee—True Story
Bruce Lee We Miss You (AKA *Bruce Li Superdragon, Dragon Dies Hard*)
Bruce Lee's Ways of Kung Fu
Bruce Le's Greatest Revenge (AKA *Bruce Lee's Fists of Vengeance*)
Bruce Li in New Guinea
Bruce's Deadly Fingers
Bruce Strikes Back
Bruce Takes Dragon Town
Bruce the Superhero
Bruce vs. Bill
Chinese Connection 2 (AKA *Fist of Fury 2*)
Clones of Bruce Lee
Crocodile Hero (AKA *Tears of the Dragon*)
Deadly Strike (AKA *Bruce Has Risen*)
Enter the Deadly Dragon
Enter the Fat Dragon
Enter the Game of Death
Enter the Invincible Hero
Enter the Ninja
Enter the Panther
Enter the 36th Chamber of Shaolin
Exit the Dragon, Enter the Tiger
Fist of Fear, Touch of Death
Fist of Fury 1991, Fist of Fury 1991 2
Fist of Fury 3 (AKA *Chinese Connection 3*), *Fist of Fury in China*
Fist of Legend, Fist of Legend 2: Iron Bodyguards
Fist of Unicorn (AKA *Bruce Lee and I*)
Fist of Vengeance
Fists Like Lee
Fists of Bruce Lee
Fists of Dragons
Fists of the Double K (AKA *Fist to Fist*)
Goodbye Bruce Lee: His Last Game of Death
Green Dragon Inn (AKA *Bruce Is Loose*)
Hong Kong Superman (AKA *Bruce, Kung Fu Master*)
Image of Bruce Lee
In the Line of Duty 3 (AKA *Force of the Dragon*)
Jaws of the Dragon

Legend of Bruce Lee
Legendary Heroes 2: The Fist of Fury
Lone Shaolin Avenger (AKA *Bruce against the Odds, Big Boss 2*)
My Name Called Bruce
New Fist of Fury
Ninja Strikes Back (AKA *Eye of the Dragon, Bruce Lee Fights Back*)
Rage of the Dragon
The Real Bruce Lee
Return of Bruce (AKA *Dragon's Return*)
Revenge of Fist of Fury
Shaolin Invincible Sticks (AKA *Fist of Shaolin*)
Spirits of Bruce Lee
Story of the Dragon (AKA *Bruce Lee's Deadly Kung Fu, Bruce Lee's Secret, Bruce Li's Jeet Kun Do*)
They Call Me Bruce, They Still Call Me Bruce
Treasure of Bruce Le
Way of the Black Dragon
Ways of Kung Fu
The Young Bruce Lee

martial arts uses clips and demonstrations by students to show his techniques. The section on his untimely death has a brief interview with girlfriend Betty Ting Pei, footage of stars and family at his funeral, and even footage of his wife Linda taking his body back to the U.S. for a second memorial.

Raymond Chow has taken a lot of flack for his exploitation of Bruce Lee—though detractors should note that exploitation is Chow's profession. This film gave him a chance to both defend himself from these charges, and continue to make money from Lee. A substantial sequence is given to how *Game of Death* was finished post mortem, congratulating those involved for their ingenuity. This follows a section decrying the wave of Lee imitators from other studios. In effect, it says that Chow's own Lee imitators put an end to other Lee imitations, then goes on to plug the new Golden Harvest star Jackie Chan with a clip from *Winners and Sinners*. 🎵🎵🎵

1984 85m/C/BW *HK* **N:** (English) James B. Nicholson. Bruce Lee, Nora Miao, Siu Hon-sung, Betty Ting Pei, Raymond Chow, Gig Young. **D:** Leonard Ho. **W:** Russell Cawthorne. **M:** Avalon Music. **VHS, DVD**

Bruce Lee: The Man, the Myth

Bruce Li had already tired of his career as the top Bruce Lee imitator in movies when producer Pal Ming offered him the lead in what was meant to be the definitive Lee biopic, rising director Ng See-yuen at the helm. A young Bruce (Bruce Li) is upset that his mother is making him leave Hong Kong to study in the U.S., and bids farewell to his master Yip Man (here played by his son Yip Chun). A shot of the New York skyline is labeled "AMERICA," and then more

properly we see "SEATTLE," where Bruce is working his way through college teaching kung fu and pumping gas. Bruce fights off a pair of karate experts working for a loan shark who are hassling his boss Pete. They go running to their master Muriaki, who challenges Bruce to a fight at the college stadium. But Muriaki's thugs attack Bruce on his way there, delaying him, but Bruce shows up in time to whip the Japanese.

The scene shifts to San Francisco, where Bruce begins teaching at his friend Butchie's kung fu school. Chinatown triad boss Sun Taimao tells them not to accept non-Chinese students, but Bruce puts the smack down. Muriaki sends thugs after Bruce again, but he still makes it to Long Beach to win the international martial arts championship. This brings Bruce a contract to play Kato in the *Green Hornet* series, but finding Hollywood resistant to Asians, he heads back to Hong Kong to become a movie star. "I don't know how, but I'm gonna get it," says Bruce. The movie doesn't know how either, cutting straight to Bangkok for the shooting of *The Big Boss* (AKA *Fists of Fury*). Bruce runs into more trouble there, challenged by the Thai boxers hanging around the set. Even when he becomes a big star, Bruce is still challenged by kung fu fighters looking to gain a rep.

The film portrays one such match, combining elements from several true incidents into one fight in which Bruce takes time out to thrash a Mongolian fighter (Lee Hoi-sang). Then it's off to Rome to make *Return of the Dragon*, where one of the stuntmen makes threatening phone calls and challenges in the newspapers before finally attacking Bruce on the set. Bruce's death scene in the home of actress Betty Ting Pei (Betty Chen) while discussing plans to complete *Game of Death* are shown simply, with the cause of death due to illness, though the film goes on to illustrate various rumors about his death, including the one that Bruce faked his death to live as a recluse for 10 years.

Bruce Li trained intensely for this role, and it paid off with some of his best fight scenes to date. Many details of Lee's life that were ignored or changed for the Hollywood bio *Dragon* years later are included here, while other bits are skipped over. Bruce is shown experimenting with electricity to improve his physique, and using bizarre machines to develop his famous "One Inch Punch." Very little time is devoted to Lee's personal life—Linda and the kids show up out of nowhere to wave to Bruce after the premiere of *Big Boss,* and that's about it. But the main flaw is in portraying Lee as an egomaniac, ready to fight anybody without reason. This may have been necessary to get as much action in the film as possible, but it gives the image of Lee as a hothead throughout his life, which is far from the truth. After this film, Bruce Li vowed to abandon his career as a Bruce Lee clone and only work under his own name, Ho Chung Tao. However, distributors demanded more Bruce Li films, and he was forced to comply if he wanted to keep working. *AKA: Lee Siu Lung Chuen Kei; Li Xiao Long Chuan Ji; Bruce Lee—True Story; Behind Bruce Lee; The Dragon Lives.* 🐉🐉🐉

1976 (R) 90m/C *HK* Bruce Li, Fung Hark-On, Chu Chi-ling, Mars, Little Unicorn Chan, Alan Chui, Sham Chin-bo, Fung Ging Man, Lee Hoi-sang, Yip Chun, Betty Chen, Anders Nelson, Caryn White. *D:* Ng See-yuen. *W:* Ng See-yuen. *C:* Chen Wing. **VHS, DVD**

Bruce Lee We Miss You

An interesting entry in the Bruceploitation genre, this film features Bruce Li as Stone, a student dedicated to following the martial arts path of Bruce Lee. Early in the film, Stone learns that Lee has died, but he can't reconcile to it; he feels in his heart that something rotten is involved with the master's death. Convinced by these feelings and a dream in which Bruce Lee (a double) reveals that he died violently, Stone decides to find out what "really" happened.

He visits a monastery where he is told that Lee's restless spirit may be wandering the earth. Stone goes to see Betty Ting (Chan Pooi-ling), who (according to legend) was the last woman to see Bruce Lee alive. Betty seems nice enough, but she's mixed up with some very shifty businessmen who may—or may not—have something to do with Lee's death. Betty notices that, in some situations (low light or from a distance), Stone actually resembles the dead actor. (Li's resemblance to Lee is only fair, but he does a good job of aping the late actor's mannerisms. From certain angles, and in dim light, there *is* a resemblance to the real Bruce

Lee. Naturally, the filmmakers play this up—overplay it, actually.) Stone and his friends find themselves caught between the (relatively harmless) gang backing Betty Ting and a band of ruthless gamblers. The gamblers, it turns out, are the real culprits—and they mistake Stone for Lee. They think Lee faked his own death, and is now back to hassle them again. This leads up to the final battle between Stone and the gang. Will vengeance win out, or will Stone go the way of his fallen "master"?

This film ties together some of the various rumors surrounding the death of Bruce Lee. Amazingly, it does so in a fairly coherent and entertaining narrative. The fights alternate between sloppy imitations of Lee-style brawls, to the kind of stagy over-choreographed action that dominated pre-Lee kung fu epics. The real Bruce was both faster and crisper in his movements than any of his many imitators. There is an interesting attempt at a battle atop a moving bus. It's pre–Jackie Chan, and nowhere near as good as it could be, but the filmmakers get points for the effort. Clearly, the people making this were trying. They even have some decent locations, and a script—unlike many Bruce-ploitation epics. Some of the fights are pretty good, too. Mostly, though, watching this film makes you appreciate just how good the *real* Bruce Lee was and realize that we do, indeed, miss him. —*SS AKA: Gam Sik Tai Yeung; Jin Se Tai Yang; Dragon Dies Hard; Bruce Li, Superdragon; Super Dragon; Golden Sun.* 🐉🐉

1976 (PG) 87m/C *HK* Bruce Li, Chan Pooi-ling, Lung Fei, Shan Mao, Ng Ho, Hei Ying, Woo Gwong, Tong Kar-chun, Cheung Fong-ha. *D:* Lee Koon-chung. *M:* Chou Fu-liang. **VHS**

Brutal Boxer

This previously lost film is one of those footnotes in Jackie Chan's career that he'd probably prefer remained lost. Jackie plays one of many thugs in the employ of villain Chan Sing who gets beaten up repeatedly by the heroes and doesn't have any lines.

Brothers Chang Wu-shing (Ray Lui) and Chang Siu-cheng (Kwan San) come from the mainland to visit their uncle Yu Wu-shang, but find his restaurant under new management. Uncle's friend King Chan (Chan Sing) explains that Yu disappeared a while ago, and offers the brothers jobs. Cheng goes to work in King's lumber mill, and starts to date King's gorgeous adopted daughter Ying-Ying (Tim Lei). Shing runs errands for King and falls in with his thugs, helping out King's other business as a triad boss. He goes along with the gang to pressure the owner of a new restaurant who refuses to pay protection, only to find out the place is owned by his uncle Yu (Got Heung Ting). Yu's son Chin (Mars) and friend Chu Han fight off the thugs, and Shing reunites with his relatives. Meanwhile, in order to get him out of the way (and collect on his life insurance), King Chan has Cheng killed. When she refuses to sign the insurance papers, Ying meets her end, too. Oh, and old Yu is murdered via a knife in his chest. In the extremely bloody climax, Mars and Ray Lui kill about 50 guys (some of them two or three times) before having a final deadly duel with Chan Sing. The video master on the available edition is very poor—the audio is very low during dubbed sections, and the picture drops out briefly at reel changes. **AKA:** *Tong Yan Hak; Tang Ren Ke; Blood Fingers; Bloodfingers.* ♫♫

1972 74m/C *HK* Chan Sing, Raymond Lui, Mars, Kwan San, Tim Lei, Got Heung Ting, Corey Yuen, Wilson Tong, Jackie Chan. **D:** Kwan San. **VHS, DVD**

Bubblegum Crisis

 One of the earliest of the many Japanese anime series set against the backdrop of a future Tokyo, and inspired by actual plans for citywide renovation set to take place over the next 50 years. The nefarious, ever-expanding GENOM Corporation unleashes biomechanical soldiers called Boomers—originally designed for outer-space projects and foreign wars, but now causing havoc within the city as part of a plot for world domination. The AD Police, a special crimes unit assigned to deal with the Boomers, find their resources stretched to the limit as the Boomers become more and more powerful. Only a group of young women calling themselves the Knight Sabres, using hi-tech suits of armor, pose a threat to GENOM's evil plan. Influenced by *Macross* and *Bladerunner* (the rock singing Knight Saber's name is Priss, and her band is The Replicants), this series was in turn highly influential on other anime series for its MegaTokyo setting, mecha designs, and sexy girl heroes battling scary monsters, all set to rocking "J-pop" music. As single episodes, this isn't especially remarkable anime, but interest grows throughout the entire eight-part series, and it deserves kudos for its place in anime history. Followed by sequel series *Bubblegum Crash* and *AD Police Files.* **AKA:** *Baburugamu Kuraishisu.* ♫♫♪

1985 200m/C *JP* **D:** Katsuhito Akiyama, Hiroaki Goda, Hiroki Hayashi, Oobari Masami, Fumihiko Takayama. **W:** Katsuhito Akiyama, Shinji Aramaki, Hideki Kakinuma, Kenichi Matsuzaki, Toshimichi Suzuki. **C:** Kazuhiro Konishi, Akihiko Takahashi. **M:** Kouji Makaino. **VHS, DVD**

The Buddha Assassinator

An introduction, possibly edited in from another flick, explains how kung fu practitioners of the modest Buddha Fist Style came into conflict with those who use the greedy Lo Han Style— or is it the other way around? Everyone is in a flurry of activity because Prince Tsoi is visiting the district. That includes his enemies, the Ming patriots, who are plotting an assassination. Abbot Fung Yung scolds dirty Abbot Sun Lu (Chen Yueh-Sheng) to clean up for the visiting royalty, and his rascal adopted nephew Shao Hai (Mang Hoi) is told to keep out of the way. Luckily, he disobeys, and saves the Prince from the assassins. He's rewarded with a job as the Prince's personal guard. However, the real plan is for the brash Shao Hai to act as bait for the assassins.

Uncle Sun Lu tells Shao Hai to get the Prince to teach him his crazy Lo Han style of kung fu. Afterward, Sun Lu teaches him his own Buddhist Fist style. Eventually, Prince Tsoi faces off against Shao. Can his Five Element Buddha Palm win out over Tsoi's Lo Han Sleeping Kick?

It's not easy trying to figure out who the bad guys are in this kung fu comedy. Both political factions are equally ruthless, and even the monks are a pretty rude bunch. Shao Hai is the designated young hero, but acts like such a jerk for most of the film that it's tough to root for him. Fight scenes are nicely acrobatic, but bear no similarity to any kind of actual fighting. The U.S. version features bad dubbing, cropped and scratched prints, and music stolen from other movies. **AKA:** *Fo Zhang Huang Di; Shogun Massacre.* ♫♪

1979 85m/C *HK* Hwang Jang Lee, Mang Hoi, Chen Yueh-Sheng, Lung Fei, Corey Yuen, Fang Fang. **D:** Tung Kar Wu. **W:** Ngai Hong, Tu Liang-Ti. **C:** Woo Kuo-Hsiao. **M:** Frankie Chan. **VHS, DVD**

The Buddhist Fist

This old-school effort from director Yuen Wooping tells the story of two friends, peasant Shang (Sunny Yuen) and monk Si-ming (Tsui Siuming), who are both trained in martial arts by Master Ti-ying. The blood brothers are separated when Shang has to leave to find work in the city. The evil Chen (Lee Hoi-sang) gets Siu-ming drunk and frames him for the murder of a prostitute, then blackmails the monk in order to get his hands on a valuable jade Buddha. However, the artifact is well guarded by a crafty old monk (Simon Yuen). Shang gets a job as a barber, but he and his buddy Yu (Chan Lung) get fired for shaving half the mustache off a customer. They go back to Shang's homestead, but find Shang's

godfather Goi-shang has disappeared. Shang does find his old friend Si-ming, who is secretly convinced he killed Goi-shang while drunk as well, and is forced to carry out secret missions for the masked Chen. Fearing Shang will catch on to his identity while hunting for his dead godfather, Chen sends a variety of odd assassins to ambush or trap the young master.

Kung fu fans should be delighted by the fantastic fight scenes choreographed by the Yuen Clan, which include everything from acrobatic weapons combat to tabletop chopstick fights. However, the serious nature of the plot is not easily conducive to the film's knockabout comic tone, making for some awkward pacing, and the ending is unsatisfying. Casual viewers may become impatient for the plot to continue while the cast engages in one battle after another, and the masked villain is too easily identified for that mystery to hold interest. The humor is generally subpar—when a cow is raped by a neighboring bull, the victim is blamed (no doubt a script contribution from Wong Jing). The payoff of another gag is some servants getting stabbed by spears. But the action is plentiful, with many familiar faces showing up for the party. This was one of the last roles for Simon Yuen (the *Drunken Master* himself), who died shortly after and is doubled for much of his fight scene. *AKA: Fat Jeung Lo Hon Kuen; Fo Zhang Luo Han Quan; Secret of the Buddhist Fist.* 𝄞𝄞𝄞

1979 87m/C *HK* Sunny Yuen, Tsui Siu-ming, Simon Yuen, Fan Mui-sang, Chan Lung, Lee Hoi-sang, Chan Siu Pang, Brandy Yuen, David Wu, Yuen Cheung-yan, Dai Sai Aan, Ho Pak Kwong, Yuen Yat-chor, San Kwai, Tang Ching. **D:** Yuen Woo-ping. **W:** Lam Chiming, Tsiu Siu-ming, Wong Jing. **C:** Michael Ma. **M:** Frankie Chan. **DVD**

Bullet in the Head

Between the bullet-riddled orgy of brotherhood and violence in *The Killer*, and the giddy thrills of *Once a Thief*, John Woo created this highly emotional, decade-spanning epic. In the tenements of Hong Kong in 1967, rock-and-roll fan Ben (Tony Leung) is growing up fast amid civil unrest. His life of carefree shenanigans with his friends Frank (Jacky Cheung) and Paul (Waise Lee) soon comes to an end. After Frank hocks his family's home to pay for Ben's wedding, the two get into a rumble that ends with gangster Ringo dead. Hunted by police and crooks, the trio of friends agree to smuggle a shipment of contraband into Vietnam. However, their goods are blown up in an assassination attempt on the violent streets, and they lose their passports to the military police. They find the road back to Hong Kong long and extremely hard. In a fix for cash, and influenced by the increasingly greedy Paul, they join up with half-French hit man Luke (Simon

Yam) in an attempt to extort cash from their intended contact, arms-dealing gang boss Y.S. Leong (Lam Chung). Their plan goes sour, but amid the gunfire the gang makes off with a strongbox full of gold. They don't get far before getting caught and, in one of Woo's most harrowing sequences, subjected to the tortures of a Vietcong POW camp. Rescued by Luke and U.S. soldiers, they become separated in the escape. To keep the wounded Frank quiet while the enemy is nearby, cowardly Paul shoots his friend in the head. Years later, Ben comes across Frank on the streets of Saigon, still alive, but left a drooling wretch by the bullet in his head. Ben goes to Paul in Hong Kong, now a rich businessman from his stolen gold, to demand retribution, leading to an explosive modern joust using automobiles and firearms.

From the opening bars of "I'm a Believer" played over the opening montage, this is Woo's most heartbreaking, resonant work. Though packed with violent action, it doesn't have the over-the-top delirium that made his heroic bloodshed epics with Chow Yun-fat more marketable overseas. Overall, its tone is much more desperate, a portrait of a chaotic world in which the only things to cling to are honor, love, and friendship. Numerous variations exist, including a 136-minute director's cut, a butchered 100-minute cut, and at least one with an alternate ending that takes place in the board room of Paul's company. *AKA: Dip Huet Gaai Tau; Die Xie Jie Tou; Bloodshed in the Streets.* 𝄞𝄞𝄞𝄞

1990 126m/C *HK* Tony Leung Chiu-Wai, Jacky Cheung, Waise Lee, Simon Yam, Yolinda Yan, Fennie Yuen, Lam Chung, Chang Gan Wing, Leung Biu Ching, So Hang Suen, Pau Hei-ching, Cheung Jing. **D:** John Woo. **W:** John Woo, Patrick Leung, Janet Chun. **C:** Ardy Lam, Wilson Chan, Somchai Kittikun, Horace Wong. **M:** James Wong, Romeo Diaz. **VHS, DVD**

Bullet Train

Twenty years before *Speed,* the central idea appeared in this Japanese film. A bomb has been planted on a high-speed train carrying 1500 passengers, and if the train's speed drops below 80 kilometers per hour, the bomb will explode. The criminal plot was hatched by Okita (Ken Takakura), Koga (Kei Yamamoto), and Hiroshi, three friends who've never amounted to much of anything in life. They don't mean to kill anybody, but they demand $5 million in ransom money. As a demonstration, they've planted a similar bomb on a freight train; when it blows up after slowing down, the authorities are convinced that the threat is real. They have 10 hours to locate the extortionists before the train reaches the end of the line.

In the railway control room, Kuramochi (Ken Utsui) helps Aoki (Sonny Chiba), the nervous conductor, avoid a collision early on. The next crisis ensues when the train doesn't make its scheduled stop in Nagoya. The passengers begin to panic, some to the point of hysteria. The authorities arrange to make a ransom drop; young Koga goes to pick it up but is killed in an accident after the police give chase. The police next close in on Hiroshi; they fail to apprehend him, although Hiroshi is seriously wounded. Kuramochi begins to question whether the authorities are more interested in making an arrest than in saving the lives of the passengers. Higher-ups in the government grapple with the realization that if the bomb explodes in a populated area, many thousands may perish. The train must be stopped well before the end of the line, and time is running out.

The premise sounds pulse-pounding, but the execution is not. Rather than pace the film like a thriller, director Junya Sato *(The Go Masters)* stages it as a straightforward drama. The railway controller has a crisis of conscience, the criminals turn out to be not so bad after all, and the authorities are portrayed as incompetent and unconcerned about the fate of the train's passengers. As a suspense drama, *Bullet Train* picks up momentum in the latter half of the story before rounding things out with a moralistic coda. Ken Takakura is excellent as the leader of the gang, giving a very measured performance that tightens up as he nears the completion of his plan. Ken Utsui is his equal as the gradually tortured controller. Sonny Chiba has little to do but sweat in a supporting role as the train conductor. A 152-minute print of the film reportedly exists, but is not currently available on video. —PM **AKA:** *Shinkansen daibakuha; Bullet Train Big Explosion.* 🎵🎵

1975 115m/C *JP* Ken Takakura, Ken Utsui, Sonny Chiba, Eiji Go, Takashi Shimura, Tetsuro Tamba, Fumio Watanabe, Sue Shiomi, Kei Yamamoto, Kunie Tanaka. *D:* Junya Sato. *W:* Ryunosuke Ono, Junya Sato. *C:* Masahiko Iimura. *M:* Hachiro Aoyama. **VHS, DVD**

Bullets of Love

Andrew Lau *(Storm Riders)* creates another thriller with a stylish look, here combining the hired-assassin genre with elements of *Vertigo.*

Simon Yam can't stop the bleeding in *Bullet in the Head.*

Inspector Sam Lam (Leon Lai) of OCTB leads his team on what should be a routine raid on a nightclub to arrest the infamous Wong Brothers, leaders of the Sun Ching gang. An unknown shooter starts a gun battle, and Sam's partner Ho Ma (Ronald Cheng)—who of course had just been talking about retiring—gets stabbed by Wong Po (Richard Suen) when he corners Wong Fun (Terence Yin). Po is arrested and sentenced to five years imprisonment for his crimes. Wong Fun hires contract killer You (Asaka Seto) to kill Sam's girlfriend Ann (Seto again), who prosecuted the case. You waits until the couple travels to Paris to kill Ann, and while watching the woman who looks like her with Sam, she develops a desire to not only kill Ann, but to replace her. After the spectacular murder, a devastated Sam quits the force to become a pub owner, living in squalor with Uncle Ho Ngau (Michael Chan) at his Chinese therapy clinic in Tai O. Fortunately, the film doesn't wallow in his grief, injecting some welcome humor via Sam's bandmate buddies. While watching a video of their crushing defeat against a bunch of 10-year-olds, Sam meets a Japanese photographer named You. Sam learns Japanese to get to know her (though they both speak English in the Chinese language version). Naturally he falls for her, haunted by her resemblance and the carefully practiced habits she's copied from Ann. And inevitably, Sam learns that You is really Ann's killer. When the Wong brothers are reunited, Sam heads for HK to seek revenge, but he gets in over his head with the savage criminals, and You is there to help out.

The filmmakers can be forgiven for the preposterous high-concept plot (though it's not so outrageous by Hong Kong standards), since it's so competently enacted. The middle section of the film is as pleasant as first and last acts are thrilling. With location shooting in France, Tai O, and Japan, it's really a much bigger and better-crafted film than the concept deserves. *AKA: Bat Sei Ching Mai; Bu Si Qing Mi.* 🐉🐉♥

2001 103m/C *HK* Leon Lai, Asaka Seto, Ronald Cheng, Terence Yin, Michael Chan, Frankie Ng, Saki Hayawaka, Richard Suen, Tony Ho, Alan Kuo, Benjamin Yuen, Yu Ka-ho, Michael Tse, Alexander Chan, Fletcher Poon. *D:* Andrew Lau. *W:* Thirteen Chan. *C:* Lai Yiu-fai, Andrew Lau. *M:* Comfort Chan. **VHS, DVD**

Bullets over Summer

This stylish thriller was a favorite with the Hong Kong critics. Mike Lai (Francis Ng) and Brian Leung (Louis Koo) are a pair of quirky police detectives, working on the arrest of Dragon (Lo Meng), a vicious bandit whose gang robbed a bank disguised as police, shooting everyone whom they could draw a bead on. Stone, an informant, tells them Dragon is planning a big job. Mike and Brian decide to stake out the most likely arms supplier named Lighter, figuring Dragon's gang will be looking to score some weapons. They coerce an elderly woman (Helena Law) who lives within sight of Lighter's flat to let them use her balcony. Granny, who is a bit addle-brained, takes a liking to responsible Mike. Brian is delighted when Stone sends his cute "godsister" Yen (Michelle Alicia Saram) to stay with them as well. While keeping an eye on Lighter, they get to know the neighbors. Mike helps Tin Yuen (Stephanie Lam), an unwed pregnant laundry woman. Brian continues to try to romance Yen. Mike goes to an owners' meeting, and ends up elected board president. After a long wait and some tense moments, it turns out they were watching the wrong guy. Mike learns he has a rare blood condition called "Harrington Dancing" disorder (according to the subtitles). He begins to try to live his life better, buying Granny a massage chair, and volunteering to help raise Yuen's baby.

Every story is allowed at least one coincidence, or else it's just not realistic. The twist here is that one of the building's units just so happens to be one of Dragon's hideouts. This leads to the inevitable shootouts and chases, but the resolution is a surprising one. Acting and creative directing are more the point here than action, though what gunfights there are here are quite good. Ng and Helena Law both won recognition for their emoting, and the rest of the cast aren't bad either. In all, a distinct improvement over Wilson Yip's previous work. *AKA: Baau Lit Ying Ging; Bao Lie Xing Jing.* 🐉🐉🐉♥

1999 98m/C *HK* Francis Ng, Louis Koo, Helena Law, Michelle Alicia Saram, Stephanie Lam, Wayne Lai, Lo Meng, David Lee, Joe Lee. *D:* Wilson Yip. *W:* Matt Chow, Wilson Yip, Ben Cheung. *C:* Lam Wah-chuen. *D:* Tommy Wai. **VHS, DVD**

Burning Paradise

Within the first five minutes, a man is cut in half and a horse is beheaded—welcome to Ringo Lam's nightmare vision of the Fong Sai-yuk legend. Fong (Willie Chi, who played Wong Fei-hung the same year in *Drunken Master Killer*) is a student at the Shaolin Temple. Soldiers of the corrupt Ching government, led by a man named Crimson (John Ching), sack the temple, taking the monks and their followers into captivity. Fong escapes along with his master Chi Nun, and they hide out in a shack, and encounter Dau Dau (Carman Lee)—the proverbial prostitute with a heart of gold—who was forced into prostitution due to a famine. Now that three years have passed and her entire family has died or been killed, she wants out. Crimson finds the trio, kills Chi Nun, and brings the other two back to Red Lotus Temple.

The mostly subterranean temple has been converted into a prison and is presided over by Elder Kung (Wong Kam-Kong). He is old, corrupt, and jaded, and takes delight in torturing the prisoners, most of whom are Shaolin students. His #2 man is Hung Hei-kwun (Yeung Sing), formerly a Shaolin disciple who has turned to the dark side. His chief female accomplice is Brooke (Lam Chuen)—she is also eager to inflict pain. Fong leads a rebellion of the Shaolin students, but they find that the prison has been baited with countless traps, and escape seems impossible.

It's not for nothing that fires are constantly burning and sunlight is a rare commodity in the Red Lotus Temple. Ringo Lam seems intent on putting Fong Sai-yuk through Hell. After arriving at the temple/prison, Fong tries to save a fellow student from a burning pit. Later he is tossed into "the well of corpses," where dead bodies are tossed to rot away. Still later he battles Crimson in an enflamed battleground. And he must rescue Dau Dau by jumping into a fiery inferno.

Up to 1994, Ringo Lam had created several memorable films in which big cities provided the background for urban warfare—think *City on Fire* or *Full Contact*—and in the two *Prison on Fire* films the battle was taken to a different locale. Though a costumed epic may have seemed an unusual choice for the director, *Burning Paradise* fairly reeks of his sensibilities. The film serves as an effective counterpoint to *Fong Sai-yuk* (AKA *The Legend*) and its sequel, both released the previous year and starring Jet Li. Rather than focus on the heroic aspects of Fong Sai-yuk's character, the most memorable impressions left here are the painful injuries and deaths suffered by nearly everyone in the movie. At least it can be said that the action scenes—many wire-enhanced and choreographed by Chris Lee—are quite well done. Produced by Tsui Hark. —PM **AKA:** *Rape of the Red Temple; Feng Shiu Hung Lin Chi; Huo Shao Gong Lian Si; Burning Paradise in Hell; Destruction of the Red Lotus Temple.* 🐉🐉

1994 104m/C *HK* Willie Chi, Carmen Lee, Wong Kam-Kong, Yeung Sing, Lam Chuen, John Ching, Yuen Kam-fai. **D:** Ringo Lam. **W:** Nam Yin. **M:** Mak Chun-hung. **VHS, DVD**

Bury Me High

An epic adventure film based on the traditional Chinese practice of feng shui, or geomancy, featuring Wisely, who in China is a hero on par with Indiana Jones.

In the tiny nation of Carrinan, megalomaniac millionaire Nguen (Paul Chu) uses geomancy to select the perfect burial site, guaranteeing that his descendants will conquer the world. His associate Wei Tsien-Hsien (Corey Yuen) judges his plan to be against the sacred precepts of geomancy, and takes steps to warn the world. His friend Wong dies helping him escape. Wei vows to bury Wong in a cave of Wealth, and himself in a cave of Wisdom, hoping their children can join forces to stop the madman.

Two dozen years later, daughter Anna Wong (Moon Lee) is in Los Angeles busting hackers as a computer security expert. Her current foe: Wisely Wei (Chin Ka-Lok), who is hacking her corporate client because of broken promises they made to charities. Wisely has not only become a computer expert, but has mastered mathematics and martial arts like his father. Anna decides not to turn him over to the police once she finds out who he is, but x-rays reveal that his recent headaches are due to an inoperable brain tumor. In addition, the once-rich Wong family is on the brink of bankruptcy. Anna believes that Wei's prediction of ill fortune after 24 years may be coming true, and hires Wisely to go to Carrinan with her to move their fathers' graves. Wisely tricks his feng shui–expert friend Chen Chang-Ching (Tsui Siu-Ming) into a fight with a gang so that he'll give up his job teaching at UCLA to help him out in China.

Nguen's daughter (Sibelle Hu) arranges a grand military greeting for the travelers in Carrinan. The night of their arrival, brutal brother General Nguen (Yuen Wah) stages a coup and assassinates the president. In the moveable floors and walls that form the General's puzzle box of a study, the heroes discover his plan to build a city over the five peaks of the Conqueror's Locale, changing the topography in his favor. Soon, the heroes find themselves fighting an all-out revolution before they can approach their goals.

This grand adventure has a lot going for it, including good action scenes, marvelous locations, and the breathtaking camera artistry of Peter Pau *(Crouching Tiger, Hidden Dragon)*. The premise of using topography to influence events is also engaging. However, the story meanders quite a bit. Star Chin has the moves but not the charisma to make an engaging hero, and he's only indirectly involved in too much of the action. Tsui Siu-Ming's character gets more centrally involved in the action, yet he's the sidekick—perhaps a benefit of also being the director. **AKA:** *Wei Si Li Zhi ba Wang Xie Ji; The Legend of Wisely.* 🐉🐉

1990 97m/C *HK* Moon Lee, Chin Ka-Lok, Sibelle Hu, Yuen Wah, Tsui Siu-Ming, Corey Yuen, Paul Chu. **D:** Tsui Siu-Ming. **W:** Tsui Siu-Ming, Cheung Wah Biu, Sit Kar Wah. **C:** Peter Pau. **M:** Chris Babida. **VHS, DVD**

Butterfly and Sword

Well, this one starts out interesting. Somebody flies into a house and slices a guy's face off, which lands in a nest of cobras. We then cut to Tony Leung as he shoots *himself* from a bow, flying straight through a bunch of guardsmen. Tony stars as Sing, a warrior on a mission to kidnap the security officer of the Western Chamber. His partner Lady Ko (Michelle Yeoh) isn't too happy with Sing since he got engaged to the maiden Butterfly (Joey Wong), in his secret identity as a simple merchant. They both work for Eunuch Tsao of the Eastern Chamber, who is having a deadly feud with Eunuch Li Shu-Tin. Li is conspiring with Master Suen Yuk-pa (Elvis Tsui) of Elites Villa Clan to take control of the Martial Arts World after sickly Tsao's imminent death. Li gave Suen a letter outlining their plan of rebellion, which Tsao wants Lady Ko to get for him before the Mid-Autumn Festival. Striking at Suen sits fine with Lady Ko, since her Happy Forest Clan clashed with the Elites Villa 10 years ago, but Tsao sweetens the deal with a promise of a mountain of gold dust. Eunuch Li invites all the best fighters for a tournament in Han Forest, planning to hire the 10 best to send against Tsao. Sing doesn't let Butterfly know that he knows any kung fu, because her father was a master who died in battle. Ko loves Sing, and is loved by their childhood buddy Yip Cheung (Donnie Yen). (Sometimes they take time out in this soap opera to get on with the plot.) Sing goes undercover on a mission to infiltrate Suen's group, while Ko and Yip stage raids on his territory. Befriending Suen, Sing finds another childhood friend Ho Ching (Yip Chuen Chan) is also in the household on a mission for Ko under an assumed name. Meanwhile, thugs set fire to Sing's house, and Yip saves secretly pregnant Butterfly from the burning building. On the eve of Suen's attack, Ko and Yip join Sing to strike at his headquarters first.

Based on a Ku Long novel, and previously filmed as *Killer Clan,* this swordplay entry has plenty of energetic action once it gets going, though much of it is too incoherently dizzy to be satisfying. There are a lot of extremely beautiful shots of people flying around, bouncing off walls and swords, along with some outrageously bloody mayhem. The last act has some wonderfully kooky fights, but there's an hour or so of thick plot to get through to reach it. Pop star Jimmy Lin is on hand to deliver the teenybopper audience, but his appearances are blessedly brief. As ever, it's Michelle Yeoh who comes out looking best, floating above any nonsense and handling both action and drama like a champion. Some sources credit the direction to Kevin Chu Yin-ping *(Fantasy Mission Force)*. **AKA:** *San Lau SingWoo Dip Gim; Xin Liu Xing Hu Die Jian; Butterfly Sword; Comet, Butterfly and Sword.* 🎵🎵🎵

1993 87m/C *TW/HK* Tony Leung Chiu-Wai, Michelle Yeoh, Joey Wong, Donnie Yen, Elvis Tsui, Jimmy Lin, Tok Chung-wah, Yip Chuen Chan, Lee Ka-ting. **D:** Michael Mak. **W:** John Chong Ching. **C:** Chen Rong-shu. **M:** Chris Babida. **VHS, DVD**

The Butterfly Murders

Tsui Hark's very promising directorial debut. The setting is ancient China, a time of war in which 72 forces are arrayed against the Tien Clan, led by Boss Tien (Wong Shu Tong). Fong (Lau Siu-ming) is a scholar, untrained in the martial arts and thus not respected in "the martial world." He makes his living by traveling around China, writing down his observations, and selling them. Eight pages purported to be his memoirs are presented to a print shop owner, who recognizes that the writings have been forged and is killed. His murderer is caught and executed by a representative of the Tien Clan.

Boss Tien assembles his men and tells them that their help has been requested by Shum (Chang Kuo-chu), an old friend. Killer butterflies (!) have attacked Shum Castle. Boss Tien sends Big Eyes, a scout, ahead to the Shum Castle. On the journey, Tien is joined by Green Shadow (Michelle Lai), a mysterious woman with a penchant for flying around. When Tien, his men, and Green Shadow arrive at the deserted castle, they discover Big Eyes's corpse. Soon they find Shum, his wife (JoJo Chan), and Chee (Tsui Siu-ling), the couple's mute maid, hiding under the castle in a labyrinth of chambers, rooms, and tunnels. Shum explains that a murderous attack by butterflies resulted in a mass exodus of his servants from the once highly populated castle. The butterflies return and kill Shum. His will stipulates that the so-called Three Thunders be summoned to the castle for the reading of a letter. The Three Thunders are renowned for their individual expertise with fire, small weapons, and the like—and when they arrive, all hell breaks loose.

For a first-time director, Tsui Hark was certainly ambitious. *The Butterfly Murders* features a convoluted plot, a multitude of characters, and a desire to address complex issues. At least two careful viewings are needed just to figure out

Who is behind the bizarre deaths known as *The Butterfly Murders*? And did he see the old Bela Lugosi thriller *The Devil Bat*? THE KOBAL COLLECTION / SEASONAL FILMS

PRODUCED BY NG SEE YUEN
監製 吳思遠
陳琪琪
黃樹棠
領銜主演
THE BUTTERFLY MURD
蝶變

what's going on. It's hard to get a grip on the story because the characters come and go with little introduction or explanation. Despite any reservations, it's clear from the opening frames that something different is afoot. Arriving at the tail end of the 1970s boom in martial arts films, the story includes several action scenes, but none are shot in a traditional way. The camera moves quickly, and many brief edits cut up the sequences, which adds to the confusion and highlights the danger of the situations. The aspect of the story that sounds the most ridiculous—can you really posit butterflies as vicious killers and expect anyone to believe it?—is treated with the utmost seriousness. In fact, the butterfly attack scenes look absolutely authentic and are poetically powerful. As a dramatic mystery with a small dose of social commentary, the film pointed forward to a remarkable career to come. Tsui Hark demonstrated considerable visual panache and showed he belonged in the director's chair. Not to be confused with the 1984 murder thriller by Yang Tao of the same name. —PM **AKA:** *Dip Bin; Die Ban.* 🐉🐉🐉

1979 87m/C *HK* Lau Siu-ming, Michelle Lai, JoJo Chan, Chang Kuo-chu, Wong Shu Tong, Shih Kwong-li, Tsui Siu-ling, Eddie Ko, Tino Wong, Danny Chow. **D:** Tsui Hark. **W:** Lam Chi-ming. **C:** Fan Jin-yu. **M:** Frankie Chan. **VHS**

Cannonball Run

Jackie Chan went to the U.S. to star in *The Big Brawl,* and stayed to take part in this star-studded, good ol' boy, road-race comedy. Based on an illegal real race, the Cannonball is a no-holds-barred car scramble across the United States, with a huge tax-free cash prize going to the winner. It had already been the subject of two features in 1976, but this was the big hit. J.J. (Burt Reynolds) is a smuggler determined to win. His mechanic Victor (Dom DeLuise) is an oaf with a split personality, sometimes thinking he's a masked superhero called Captain Chaos. They disguise themselves as paramedics, racing an ambulance with their "patient" Farrah Fawcett inside. Dean Martin and Sammy Davis Jr. play gamblers who dress as priests as a cover to enter the race. Seymour Goldfarb Jr. (Roger Moore) is a girdle factory heir who thinks he's Roger Moore, who thinks he's James Bond, who thinks he's in the race on a mission. Chan plays Dragon Racer Jackie Chan, who enters the race with computer genius partner Michael Hui (as his Mr. Boo character in Cantonese) with a car full of high-tech gadgets that don't always work. Jamie Farr is a wacky Arab sheik who loves to drive fast cars with lots of "camel power."

Though brainless, this is hardly any more stupid than a lot of Hong Kong comedies. Jackie

Chan learned three things from this movie. One: Putting a bunch of stars in one big comedy can yield a huge hit, an idea he and Sammo Hung used for *Winners and Sinners.* Two: The audience gets a big kick out of showing outtakes at the end. Three: Be very careful about dealing with Hollywood. Not only did he and Michael Hui have to play Japanese for no good reason, but he also found working with American action directors, crews, and stuntmen extremely frustrating. While short on decent fights, director (and former stuntman) Hal Needham provides plenty of good vehicle stunts, including a jump from an airplane on a motorcycle (performed by paratrooper Dale Clark), and a truck jumping over a freight train. Chan gets to kick a few bikers (including Peter Fonda), and almost crashes while trying to watch *Behind the Green Door* and drive. It's amusing to view the Hong Kong version, which contains a lot of dialogue that differs greatly in the translation, and Don DeLuise' superhero shtick is totally glossed over. Confronted by police, a masked DeLuise introduces himself as "The Godfather," and instead of telling Reynolds, "Say hello, Kato," he says, "We operate at the Bund in Shanghai." Many of the gags are actually funnier in Chinese. 🐉🐉🐉

1981 (PG) 95m/C *US/HK* Burt Reynolds, Dom DeLuise, Roger Moore, Farrah Fawcett, Mel Tillis, Jackie Chan, Michael Hui, Dean Martin, Sammy Davis Jr., Jamie Farr, Burt Convy, Adrienne Barbeau, Jack Elam, Tara Buckman, Terry Bradshaw, Johnny Yune, Peter Fonda, Valerie Perrine, Bianca Jagger. **D:** Hal Needham. **W:** Brock Yates. **C:** Michael Butler. **M:** Al Capps. **VHS, DVD**

Cantonen Iron Kung Fu

Righteous and powerful Third Brother Keung Ah-kam (Leung Kar-yan) refuses offers from Master Lin Pao-hui (Wong Hap) to work at his shipping company in order to keep his present boss from abusing his fellow workers. The master of another shipping company clandestinely sends Master Chow and his fighters to try to take over the business throughout the territory by force, challenging and beating the best workers. When his friend Yeung is killed by Chow, Ah-kam tries to get revenge. But since we're only at the 30-minute mark, the hero isn't ready to win yet, and only escapes death when Master Lin interferes. Lin agrees to teach Ah-kam more kung fu, while Chow kills his friends Strongman Yuen and Ching Yen. He even kills Master Lin, making the murder look like an accident, but his real target is Chin Suen (Wong Chung), an old enemy of his boss who has been hiding among the coolies incognito. By this time Ah-kam is good enough to defeat Chow, earning the nickname Iron

Bridge Keung. After some further training, Ah-kam teams up with Chin Suen to hunt down the mysterious villain, who is (surprise!) their boss Chui Wan-chin (Phillip Ko), previously the fierce bandit Black Eagle.

Director Lei Chiu's follow-up to his debut hit *Ways of Kung Fu* is another feature shot in Taiwan starring Leung Kar-yan. The opening text says this is all about the Ten Tigers of Kwangtung, but nobody ever gets close to them. Dependable Leung can be counted on for some good kung fu, especially during the final clash with Phillip Ko, and showing off a physique in top form during the training sequences. Snatches of music from *Superman* can be heard on the soundtrack. A more historically accurate version can be seen in the *Sam the Iron Bridge* trilogy. **AKA:** *Gong Dung Tit Kiu Saam; Guang Dong Tie Qiao San; Iron Fisted Warrior.* 🐉🐉

1979 (G) 87m/C *HK* Leung Kar-yan, Phillip Ko, Wong Chung, Ting Wa-chung, Wong Hap, Ma Kim-tong, Ching Kuo-chung, Ma Chin-ku, Cheng Fu Hung. **D:** Lee Chiu. **W:** Wei Shin, Lei Chiu. **VHS, DVD**

Casino Raiders

Crab Chan (Andy Lau) gets out of prison, and is picked up by club girl BoBo (Rosamund Kwan) on orders from her boss Sam Law (Alan Tam). The two old partners immediately leave for the U.S. on a job—Lake Tahoe casino owner Lon (Charles Heung) has been hit hard (to the tune of $60 million) by a group of Japanese sharpers, and wants them to find out how it was done. They spot the trick easily, and then spot beautiful heiress Tong Koyan (Idy Chan). Sam impersonates an escort to get a date with her, and then rigs up a fake biker bar brawl to impress her (though how he escapes injury while being thrown around the room is a mystery). While the boys go back to Hong Kong with Koyan, Lon has the Japanese killed. Their yakuza boss Kung (Kenzo Hagiwara) holds Sam responsible, sending Gold Teeth (Eddie Ko) and his thugs to kill him. After Sam is stabbed and Crab loses full use of his left hand to a knife injury, things seem to be settled, and Sam marries Koyan, accepting a job offer from her businessman father. Crab gets involved in a game with Kung's son Taro (Lung Fong), though Sam refuses to help him, as he's promised never to gamble again. But when Crab gets caught cheating, it's Koyan who is kidnapped by Taro, and Crab and BoBo die rescuing her. To avenge his friend, Sam breaks his vow and calls in some favors to declare war on Taro.

Wong Jing scored a hit by returning to the gambling genre of his TV series *The Shell Game* with this feature, but would have even greater success by teaming with Chow Yun-fat for the more bizarre *God of Gamblers* a few months later. This is much more of a straightforward gangster yarn than Wong's fantastic gambling yarns to come, with more drama and gunplay than casino trickery. It's also much more down-beat, and a little overlong. However, it's a solid picture with good performances, and the final big card game is not to be missed. **AKA:** *Ji Juen Mo Seung; Zhi Zun Wu Shuang.* 🐉🐉🐉

1989 125m/C *HK* Alan Tam, Andy Lau, Idy Chan, Rosamund Kwan, Lung Fong, Charles Heung, Kirk Wong, Shum Wai, Eddie Ko, Ronald Wong, Kenzo Hagiwara, Robin Shou, Luk Chuen. **D:** Wong Jing. **W:** Jimmy Heung, Wong Jing. **C:** Henry Chan, Lee Chi-wai. **M:** James Wong, Romeo Diaz. **DVD**

Casino Raiders 2

A sequel in name only, this gambling epic again stars Andy Lau, but this project probably had more to do with the studio's desire to reteam Lau with Jacqueline Wu (to follow their hit *A Moment of Romance*) than to continue *Raiders* as a series. While Lau was saddled with the character name Crab in the first outing, here he plays a guy named Chicken Feet. Wu plays Lin, his bitchy sweetheart. The plot actually spins off from the bigger hit *God of Gamblers*—narration informs us the God gave out two jade pieces before retiring, which can be used by the owner to summon him for help. Chicken Feet manages a gambling boat owned by his crippled mentor Fan (Lau Siu-ming), and is practicing to enter the Asian gambling championship. Chicken's brother Kit (Wang Chieh) was Fan's former student, but got framed for the murder when their opponent James Yamamoto (Kelvin Wong) killed his own father after a game they lost. Knowing James covets his jade piece and will kill to get it, he hides it and sends Chicken Feet on an errand.

Sure enough, James's men attack, and Fan dies rather than be captured by his enemy. Kit returns in time for the funeral, but professes to have quit gambling, refusing all offers and becoming a bartender. His only wish is to retrieve his little daughter Yan, who has gone wild since he left. James kidnaps Yan to make sure Kit is out of his way, to which Kit responds by proving he's done with gambling by cutting off his own hand! The brothers find the stake and jade Fan left to them, but James's gang kills Lin and Chicken barely escapes to gamble again.

The plot suffers some from too many shifts in focus, but director Johnny To maintains the picture's integrity, giving it some visual grace by painting scenes in his rose and blue palette. Though Wong Jing is nowhere to be found here, his spirit lives in some outrageous aspects.

After Kelvin Wong produces a red neon tube out of nowhere and bashes Andy Lau across the face with it, Lau shows up later with a large white bandage across his eyes to gamble in the big game blind. Anthony Wong gets a plum role as a smiling thug named Pow, and even treats us with a bit of singing. *AKA: Ji Juen Mo Seung II; Wing Au Tin Gwong; Zhi Zun Wu Shuang II: Yong Ba Tian Xia.* ♫♫♡

1991 91m/C *HK* Andy Lau, Jacqueline Wu, Wang Chieh, Monica Chan, Anthony Wong, Kelvin Wong, Lau Siu-ming, Lee Siu-Kei, Lau Kong, Tin Fung, Lau Shun. *D:* Johnny To. *W:* Sammy Tsang. *C:* Horace Wong. *M:* William Woo. **VHS, DVD**

Casino Tycoon 2

This sequel is a bit episodic in the first half, with tycoon Andy Lau solving various problems that crop up before getting down to the actual plot. Years have passed, and Mr. Benny Ho Hsin (Lau) and his Casino Lisboa are landmarks in Macau. Some Thai tourists get a gambling geomancer to help them win with feng shui, but it doesn't work more than once. He settles a violent dispute between loan shark gangs with the old "let the leaders face off" technique. Then, he gets held up by a desperate debt-ridden employee, whose family has been taken hostage by gangsters. Ho gets shot in the scuffle during the man's capture—just the first of many trips to the hospital.

While all this is going on, Ho is pursued by pretty TV star Miss Ti Yun (Michelle Reis of *Chinese Ghost Story 2*), who wants to interview him and get him involved in some charity events. At first he brushes her off, but eventually he and the young woman find themselves drawn together. Ho's understanding wheelchair-bound wife (Chingmy Yau) encourages an affair, though guilt keeps them apart.

During a charity walking race, Ho is attacked by knife-wielding thugs and is injured. He suspects a deeper plot against him, but can't figure which of his enemies is behind it. When things get nasty, Ho gets nasty, too—but can his heart stand the stress?

There's not much in the way of action; the film generally carried by the screen power of Lau and the other leads rather than any interest it generates in its story, though the principals from the original have to overcome a ridiculous dusting of white hair paint applied in an effort to make them look older. *AKA: Do Sing Daai Hang II ji ji Juen Mo Dik; Gambling City Magnate II.* ♫♫

1992 114m/C *HK* Andy Lau, Michelle Reis, Chingmy Yau, Alex Man, Lau Siu-Ming, Joey Wong, John Ching, Sandra Ng. *D:* Wong Jing. *W:* Wong Jing. **VHS**

Castle of Cagliostro

Arsene Lupin, the gentleman burglar whose exploits were recorded in a series of stories by Maurice Leblanc, became a sensational pop-culture folk hero in his native France, but is little known today in the United States. He served as inspiration for *To Catch a Thief, The Thomas Crown Affair, Once a Thief*—not to mention TV's *It Takes a Thief.* Cartoonist Monkey Punch was a fan, and decided to update the character for a modern manga series. His hero was the half-Japanese grandson of Arsene Lupin, also known as The Wolf or Rupan, but mostly as Lupin 3. Punch's skills at plot construction and gift for slapstick comedy made the series as big a hit in Japan as the original had been in France.

Master thief Lupin 3 and his hard-boiled sidekick Daisuke Jigen pull off a casino robbery, only to find that the booty is all in counterfeit bills. Lupin recognizes the fakes as coming from an operation in the tiny European kingdom of Cagliostro, which he'd tried to infiltrate years ago. This inspires Lupin to plan their next caper. Traveling to Cagliostro by car, they save the life of a woman under attack. The girl turns out to be Clarisse, the nation's heir to the throne—she's being held prisoner by the evil Count Cagliostro, who has been serving as Regent. The Count plans to force her into a marriage that will make him owner of the castle, and give him free reign to uncover the fabulous fortune which legend states is hidden somewhere in the castle walls.

Lupin, of course, plans to get his hands on the treasure himself, and even announces his plans to rescue the girl in the process. What he hadn't counted on was the Count hiring ninja assassins to eliminate the two foreigners. Lupin sends for their enigmatic samurai friend Goemon Ishikawa to help against the assassins. Lupin also sees that his nemesis, Interpol agent Zenigata, is called into the case, and counts on the lawman's presence to help in his plan to infiltrate the castle. Sneaking inside, Lupin finds his lovely rival Fujiko Mine already there. Our heroes manage to keep one step ahead of the Count, but it's not easy what with the army of creepy ninjas and Interpol on their tails, trying to protect the Princess, falling prey to the castle's many death traps, getting lost in the dungeon full of corpses. Still, it's all in a day's work for the world's foremost super-thief. The action, though unconstrained by the forces of gravity, goes only slightly beyond the point of impossibility, which makes the film thrilling and suspenseful as well as funny.

The Castle of Cagliostro is an early feature directed by master animator Hayao Miyazaki (*Princess Mononoke*), second of eight anime features made adapting the adventures of Lupin 3, each under the guidance of a different director. All of them are great fun—a mix of intrigue, slapstick adventure, and comedy within the heist genre—but this one is a standout due to the craftsmanship, attention to detail, and raw storytelling talent of Miyazaki. *AKA: Rupan Sansei: Kariosutoro no Shiro; Arsene Lupin & the Castle of Cagliostro; Lupin III: Castle of Cagliostro.* ♫♫♫♫

1979 109m/C *JP* **D:** Hayao Miyazaki. **W:** Hayao Miyazaki, Tadashi Yamazaki. **M:** Yuji Ono. **VHS, DVD**

The Cat

Sci-fi author/adventurer Wisely (Waise Lee) relates this wild tale of alien invasion. Pounding from the apartment above annoys his friend Li Tung (Lau Sek Yin). Upstairs is a nebbish of a man, who lives with a bewitching young girl (Gloria Yip) and a black cat. Seeing them moving out the next morning, he decides to have a peek and find out what the hammering was about, and finds bloody intestines left behind. He calls his friend on the police, Wang Cheih-mei (Phillip Kwok), but the evidence turns out to be cat guts. Wang dismisses the case, but Wisely is curious and investigates the trio.

Meanwhile, a gloppy glob from space re-animates a corpse. The girl, the cat, and their friend Errol (Lau Siu-ming) are all extraterrestrials, too, and that night they invade a museum to steal a strange octagon. The corpse arrives to confront them, disgorging a big, slimy monster. The good aliens need two such octagons to defeat the gloppy bad alien, which keeps on growing and raising zombies—including Detective Wang. To catch the cat, Wisely borrows a huge dog from his friend Chen. When the cat shows up to steal the other octagon, the dog takes off in pursuit, leading to the film's best scene. In a junkyard, the cat turns into a feline Jackie Chan, defeating the dog in a martial arts duel but losing its tail. The aliens join forces with Wisely (and the cat rejoins with its tail), just before the glob-possessed Wang arrives and starts blasting away at Wisely's book-loaded house.

There's not much the cast can do with the script, which leaves it up to the uneven special effects to carry the show. The main virtue here is the film's anything-goes spirit. This is one of several Wisely movies based on the novels of Ngai Hong, all played by different actors. *AKA: Lo Maau; Lao Mao; Wai Shut Lee Ji Liu Maau; Wei Si Li Zhi Lao Mao.* ♫♫♫

1991 88m/C *HK* Waise Lee, Phillip Kwok, Gloria Yip, Lau Siu-ming, Lau Sek Yin, Christine Ng. **D:** Siman Nam. **W:** Chan Hing-ka, Gordon Chan. **C:** Mak Hoi-man. **M:** Phil Chan. **VHS, DVD**

Century of the Dragon

As an outstanding cadet in training for the Royal Hong Kong Police Force just before reunification, Wong Chi-sing (Louis Koo) is asked to leave before graduation to take on a special assignment: to go undercover and infiltrate the Hung Hing triad. Once inside, Wong finds triad life much different than he thought—no longer the righteous society of outlaws, but a horde of scramblers ready to "lose face for a dollar." His mission is to become right-hand man to Lone Fai-lone (Andy Lau), who oddly enough is one triad leader who has gone straight. Three years later, he's still with Fai-lone, fighting to remember he's still a policeman. While they celebrate Lone's mother's birthday, his senior Tong Pao (Anthony Wong) is getting shot by a cop during a rumble over pirate VCD sales. Tong Man-chun (Patrick Tam), Pao's psycho son who recently returned from studying in England, says he knows there's cops within the triad, and is assigned to find the traitor. But Chun is just mad with ambition, recruiting the hotheaded Ma (Frankie Ng) and arrogant Fa to help him kill Big Head Man, who really is an undercover, but is loyal to Pao. Sing agrees to help Chun hunt for traitors to keep an eye on him, but is asked to kill Cole, the cop who shot Pao and his superior officer. But Cole has a grudge against Lone, and won't believe young Chun is the real danger. While Sing is tied up trying to reason with Cole, Chun's men kidnap Lone, along with his mother and son. However, the villains haven't reckoned on Fai-lone's wife Daisy (Suki Kwan).

Movies about undercover cops in the triads have been popular in HK the past few years. This one gets a bit too wound up in its own melodrama and intrigue, seeming longer than it is. There are some interesting twists and characters, but the action scenes are poorly executed, draining some of the film's momentum. There's also an unfortunate claustrophobic, set-bound atmosphere to the production that makes it seem more like a TV movie. Andy Lau looks lean and tough, and believable as a mob boss, if only a reformed one. *AKA: Lung Joi Bin Yuen; Long Zai Bian Yuan.* ♫♫

1999 107m/C *HK* Andy Lau, Louis Koo, Patrick Tam, Suki Kwan, Anthony Wong, Joey Man, Lee Siu-Kei, Lau Sek Yin, Pau Hei-ching, Frankie Ng, Eric Wan, Clarence Fok. **D:** Clarence Fok. **W:** Wong Jing. **C:** Fung Yuen-man. **M:** Sammy Ha, Wei Hin-kun. **DVD**

C'est la Vie, Mon Cheri

The multitalented Derek Yee (actor, writer, cinematographer, director, and producer) was the creative force behind this immensely popular and Hong Kong Award–winning film (Best Picture and Best Actress for Anita Yuen). Kit (Lau Ching-Wan) is a moody and dissatisfied musician whose girlfriend (Carina Lau) is a successful pop singer. After they argue, he moves out and ends up in the same building as the preternaturally happy Min (Anita Yuen) and her sprawling musical family. They perform Chinese opera on the street and barely get by, but are happy to be doing what they love most in life. As Min tries to draw Kit out and into her family circle, it turns out that her sunny disposition is, in fact, multilayered. The story takes a darker turn when Min's dormant but terminally serious illness is revealed.

Put aside thoughts of *Love Story*. This film does not rely on easy sentimentality or trite sayings. The setting is grounded closer to real life. Granted, all the main characters are musicians, but the interactions among Min's family, and the loneliness and bitterness that Kit initially feels, ring true. As a whole, it's emotionally draining, but that's a mark of accomplishment. When characters come to life, you can't help but be affected when they must deal with the most painful subject of all. Anita Yuen was 22 when the film was released, and the former Miss Hong Kong was already known as an irresistibly cheerful character from comedies such as *Days of Being Dumb* and *Tom, Dick, and Hairy*. Her magical performance as Min, in which she convincingly essays a three-dimensional human being, solidified her status as a superstar, and is the anchor around which the film revolves. Equally persuasive is Lau Ching-Wan. As Kit, he ranges all over the emotional map, from angry to betrayed to charming to cheerful to sad, et al. A large supporting cast adds believability to their roles. Director Yee creates a rich atmosphere of music, family, and love; look for cameos from a variety of real-life filmmakers and musicians. —*PM* **AKA:** *San Bat Liu Ching; Xin Bu Le Qing; New Endless Love; Endless Love.* 🦴🦴🦴🦴

1993 99m/C *HK* Anita Yuen, Lau Ching-Wan, Paul Chun, Petrina Fung, Carina Lau, Carrie Ng, David Wu, Sherman Wong, Tats Lau, Sylvia Chang, Jacob Cheung, Peter Chan, Herman Yau, Joe Junior, Mama Hung, Jamie Luk. **D:** Derek Yee. **W:** Derek Yee. **C:** Tam Chi-wai, Peter Ngor. **M:** Chris Babida, William Woo. **VHS, DVD**

Challenge of Death

Clashing styles, specifically the Dragon Fist and Snake Fist, form a backdrop for this tale of intrigue in old China, a sequel to *The Hot, the Cool, and the Vicious*. Chen Hsao-lan (Wang Tao), also known as the Golden Snake, is a famous hero, but has a weakness for the ladies. Government Security Corps agent Lu Hsao-yun (Delon Tan), a Dragon fighter, uses this weakness to force Chen to get information from his girlfriend Wu Chin-wah (Lau Ming), a courtesan known to hang out with Manchurian arms dealers, about a deal expected to take place in Li Chi. On arrival, they immediately have a run-in with some thugs belonging to gangster Master Sung Tin-fat (Chang Yi), a master of the exotic Spider Fist, who just happens to be the ammunition dealer they're looking for. Wu Chin-wah is brokering the deal between Sung and Manchurian agent Chow (Sit Hon), but so far Chen is playing it cagey and she hasn't given up any information. Wu and Chen plan to double-cross Sung by winning all of Chow's funds at the gambling table before he can spend it. But Lu breaks in on the dice party, impersonating Chen's mother! Lu and Chen settle their argument in a duel of Snake vs. Dragon, and end up cooperating as friends.

Like its predecessor, there's a definite spaghetti-western influence on display here. Though not the dominant element, there's also a bit of comedy running through this otherwise routine martial arts adventure. Wang Tao's lady-killer activities and the heroes' disguise tactics are amusing, and a scene in which Lau Ming has several callers to her tent on the same evening threatens to turn into a door-slamming bedroom farce. But it seems to take forever for them to get into direct conflict with Sung, and the fight choreography is nothing special. The only unusual thing about the fight scenes are Sung's silly spider tricks, and the fact that the heroes actually plot specific strategies to beat them while learning each other's styles. The English credits are full of typos—the onscreen title is *Challengs of Death*. **AKA:** *Lung Kuen Sau Sau Moon Jeung Chu; Long Quan She Shou Men Zhi Zhu.* 🦴🦴

1978 (R) 92m/C *HK* Delon Tan, Wang Tao, Chang Yi, Lau Ming, Tommy Lee, Lung Fong, Sit Hon, Ma Cheung, Shih Ting Ken, Chui Chung Hei, Man Man, Ko Jan Pang. **D:** Lee Tso Nam. **W:** Chang Seng-yi. **C:** Chuang Yin-ta. **VHS, DVD**

Champ against Champ

Godfrey Ho, the master of bad kung fu movies, presents another flick where there's more chopping in the editing than in the choreography. Master Kai's men attack Li Wan (Dragon Lee) on his way back to his hometown, and are defeated. The evil Kai fears there's a plot against him, and

wants to eliminate all possible opponents, even though he's protected by his magic handmaidens. He rightfully suspects Master Ti is leading the resistance, and is after a list Ti holds of his secret enemies. Li Wan and his father are in town to see to his betrothal to Sing (Doris Tsui), Ti's daughter. When Kai's men injure Ti, Li elder and junior get captured with him. Wan fights his way free, but his dad gets fatally stabbed in the heart. Vowing to save Master Ti and get revenge, Li Wan heads for Devil's Lair to bust some heads. But he's stopped by Kai, who leaves him injured. Sing rescues him, but Li Wan's leg has to be amputated.

After moping a bit (and failing to hide his leg from the camera), Li is inspired by the great one-legged hero Ti Kong, who just happens to have been Sing's grandfather! They find Master Kong's training manual, and with a freshly made steel leg, Li Wan learns the famed 18 Kicking Styles that can grant him victory.

The snowy mountain locations provide a fresh backdrop for the action, but Lee's movements are relatively lacking in grace even before his leg gets cut off, and many of the battles rely on gimmicks like steel legs, fighting rings, fire breathing, and magic bolts. One fight is set to a waltz! Other music is provided by anachronistic cues from '70s action pictures and John Barry's score to *King Kong*. Good for a Saturday afternoon of camp, this one gets an extra bone for sheer goofiness. *AKA: Champ vs. Champ; Wu Tang Champ v. Champ.* 🎵🎵

1983 88m/C *HK* Dragon Lee, Charlie Han, Mike Wong, Doris Tsui, Antonio Sieou, Danny Hung, Stan Yuen, David Yuen, Bobby Mah. *D:* Godfrey Ho. *W:* Richard Sam. *C:* Joey Mah. *M:* Ricky Chan. **VHS, DVD**

Champion

A suspicious midair explosion of a private plane kills fireworks tycoon Nawab Khan and his wife, leaving his young son Abbas (Abishek Sharma) a billionaire orphan—and a likely target if the explosion was due to sabotage. Nazir Ahmad (Rahul Dev), a psychopath whose father committed suicide when Khan exposed his dealings with terrorists, is behind the sabotage. Rajveer Singh (Sunny Deol), an incorruptible green recruit fresh from the police academy (who fantasizes about being a supercop), is assigned to stay with Abbas 24 hours a day, but Abbas and his bratty gang rebel over the strict security measures Rajveer installs. The boy calls in his "special advisor," fashion model "Chief" Sapna (Manisha Koirala) for help, and Rajveer is immediately smitten.

Chief helps the kids bypass security so they can visit a cricket match, where Ahmad sets off

a bomb—no one is hurt, but Rajveer gets in a lot of trouble. After this incident, both the cop and the bed-wetting boy make an effort to cooperate, and Rajveer saves Abbas from another bombing at an award ceremony. Incredibly, the commissioner agrees to Rajveer's request not to add more security in an effort to draw the assassin out. Sure enough, Ahmad comes after the boy again. This time Rajveer can identify the suspect, but since Ahmad is operating as a patient from inside an asylum, with the staff bribed to obey him, the police can't prove his guilt. With Rajveer locked up and suspended for attacking the suspect, Ahmad is free to attack Abbas at will. Rajveer escapes from jail in time to rescue his little friend again, but Ahmad survives, too, and is relentless in his pursuit. With Abbas traumatized, the only way Rajveer can assure his safety is to catch the killer.

Champion offers blockbuster action scenes, slick musical numbers, a scary villain, cute kid comedy, sexy girls, tear-jerking melodrama, macho fight scenes, and a plot hole on every page of the script. A rookie cop is not only given such an important assignment as protecting a minor billionaire, but also allowed to purposely put his charge in danger over and over again. Those able to overlook these flaws for the sake of enjoying the action will surely be rolling their eyes during the jaw-dropping scene in which Rajveer "cures" Abbas's post–traumatic stress disorder. However, it features some terrific cinematography, and is so far over the top that it remains entertaining—the Bollywood something-for-everyone ethic in action. Rahul Dev makes for an intensely creepy psycho. 🎵🎵🎶

2000 152m/C *IN* Sunny Deol, Manisha Koirala, Abishek Sharma, Rahul Dev, Vikram Gokhale, Kashmira Shah, Dina Pathak, Deepak Parasher, Surender Pal, Rana Jung Bahadur, Kamal Chopra, Vivek Shauq. *D:* Padam Kumar. *W:* Padam Kumar. *C:* S. Thiru. *M:* Aadesh Shrivastava, Anu Malik. **DVD**

Cheap Killers

The title refers to assassins Sam Cool (Alex Fong) and his womanizing partner "Yeti" Yat-tiu (Sunny Chan). On the way to an assignment, they stop to pick up weapons from their contact Ma (Ku Feng), and can't help notice his pretty new wife Ling (Kathy Chow) from the mainland. While dispatching a cheating millionaire for client Uncle Doctrine King (Henry Fong), Yat-tiu only wounds bodyguard Blond (Mike Lambert), leaving him alive to help spread their reputation. Ma catches Yat-tiu and Ling together, and a vicious fight leaves Ma dead, and the new couple cover up the murder. But though it looks like Yat-tiu is finally serious about a girl, she bodes ill, flirting with Doctrine and worrying Sam.

Sam's grinning, handsome neighbor Sunny (Stephen Fung), who wants to be a cop, notices her, too. Having left a mess at their last job, police come asking questions and Doctrine turns against them, so the boys plan to flee to Taiwan. But Ling immediately betrays them to Doctrine, and attacks by his new enforcer Blond and his men leave Sam injured, his family dead, and Yat-tiu in an insane asylum. Sam breaks Yat-tiu out and they go underground, with Sam taking on low-budget assassinations to support them while Yat-tiu recovers. Meanwhile, Ling has become Doctrine's dragon lady wife, and Sunny, now a cop, starts dating her sister Charlie (Lillian Ho). Sunny tracks down Sam, too, and hopes they'll forget their triad code and provide evidence against the evil Doctrine. But when Ling kidnaps Sunny, Sam evens the score by stealing her horse!

At one point, the addled Yat-tiu asks Sam why he sticks with him, and it seems a valid question. The film's homosexual subtext gives Sam an excuse, but we're not given any such motivation, and none of the leads is at all likeable. Even Stephen Fung's righteous cop character is a bit too cocky, and while there are some enjoyable action scenes, there are many more unpleasant ones. The film merely provides an excuse for moody cinematography and ham-fisted acting. The film skips over points of continuity, failing to show how Sam gets out of jail for one thing, while spending endless footage on the heroes sobbing and Kathy Chow taking showers (clothed!). *AKA: Yue Doh Laai Yue Ying Hung; Yu Duo La Yu Ying Xiong.*

1998 97m/C *HK* Sunny Chan, Alex Fong, Kathy Chow, Stephen Fung, Lillian Ho, Henry Fong, Ku Feng, Michael Lambert. **D:** Clarence Fok. **W:** Wong Jing. **C:** Fung Yuen-man. **M:** EMP. **VHS, DVD**

The Cheaters

Brother Ho B (Frankie Ng) gathers together a gang to bilk high-roller Tong Ka-Chun (Ken Wong) with loaded dice—at Monopoly! He lets his young friend Wo Tin-Bo (Jordan Chan) in on the scam as a favor, and then quickly loses everyone's money. But Tin-Bo is a confidence man, in league with the "strangers"—Lok (Alex Fong), Wong Chi-wai (Chapman To), and Elsa (Sonija Kwok)—Ho brought into the game, including their "lucky" intended pigeon, Tong. Tin-Bo's talent is in taking on identities and building trust. Elsa's the computer databank expert. She's carrying on an affair with Lok, Tin-Bo's boyhood pal and a financial genius. Tong's talent is recognizing the patterns that point to a potential scam. Chi-wai does odd jobs. Working different scams together every now and then, the group has amassed millions.

Their next project is to infiltrate the Tin Kei Company. They plan to get the company to free collateral for a $20 million loan from an Indonesian bank, and then disappear with all funds. What drew them to the project is the new senior director Cow, who is really the infamous King of Ghosts Lun Yan (Simon Liu). He seems to be working a scam of his own on the company, and thus an easy scapegoat for their smaller scam if things go wrong. The problem is, he may smell something rotten and resent competitors. As feared, Lun Yan detects their plan, and tells them to take the $2 million advance money and clear out.

Another complication pops up when Tin-Bo discovers Michelle (Hera Lam), the girl he's been wooing, is the daughter of the CEO, Mr. Lui. With their plan proceeding, tension builds as they wonder what Lun Yan will do. It doesn't take long to find out that the King of Ghosts plays the game at a more serious and deadly level, as Tong is forced to take a dive from a very high window. It seems their only hope is to make a deal with Mr. Lui to fight together against the mastermind Lun Yan. But is he the real threat?

Those hoping for a twisty puzzle thriller on the order of *Sneakers* should look elsewhere, as the intent here is to place noir drama in some new modern context. Director Billy Chung seems to build his film toward some sort of climax, but instead lets it drift away. It's not as bad as Chung's *Trust Me U Die*, but it's more of a disappointment because the characters and situations have more potential. Jordan Chan is becoming one of the more interesting Hong Kong stars of the past few years. *AKA: Jing Cheung; Zheng Jiang.*

2001 80m/C *HK* Jordan Chan, Alex Fong, Sonija Kwok, Simon Lui, Ken Wong, Chapman To, Hera Lam, Bonnie Law, Frankie Ng, Thomas Lam. **D:** Billy Chung. **W:** Edmond Pang, Paul Chung. **C:** Daniel Chan. **M:** Lincoln Lo. **VHS, DVD**

China Strike Force

After the disastrous *Mr. Magoo*, director Stanley Tong returned to Hong Kong filmmaking with a big-budget bang-up action extravaganza. Shanghai police investigators Darren Tong (Aaron Kwok) and Alex Cheung (Wang Lee-hom) just happen to be on the scene at a lingerie fashion show when a murder is committed. The victim is the brother-in-law of Uncle Ma (Lau Siu-ming), a powerful crime lord in nearby Lang Sheng. Ma is concluding business with Norika (Norika Fujiwara), an outlandishly flirtatious Japanese businesswoman. Norika eludes capture by Alex after she lifts a computer disc from the victim's suit, demonstrating both martial

arts and acrobatic abilities. Darren pursues the assassin (Yuen Jung) on foot into traffic, confiscates a passing motorcycle, defies gravity by riding the motorcycle *straight up* the back of a truck, exchanges punches with the killer on top of a bus, knocks the assassin off the truck, and chases him to the middle of a bridge, where the surely exhausted suspect takes a near-suicidal leap into the water far below. Darren and Alex travel to Lang Sheng and meet with the local sheriff (Paul Chun), who happens to be the father of Alex's girlfriend (Ruby Lin). They try to question Ma, but he is uncooperative. Ma is upset that Tony (Mark Dacascos), the sole surviving male descendant of the family, is working a drug deal with Coolio (strangely enough, played by rap star Coolio) behind his back. As in *The Godfather,* Ma doesn't feel his family should be involved with drugs. On the other hand, Norika is eager to get in on the action with Tony and Coolio—perhaps a little too eager. Darren and Alex chase the suspects around town until Darren finally figures out what's going on.

The plot in action films such as this one serves only to string together the stunt and fighting sequences. While Stanley Tong's direction is not as sharp or stylish as it was in his films with Jackie Chan or Michelle Yeoh *(Supercop, First Strike, Supercop 2),* the action scenes choreographed by Tong and Ailen Sit are fun to watch and are worth multiple looks, including a car chase featuring a Formula One race car sliding back and forth under an 18-wheel truck while in pursuit of a Lamborghini. Special mention must be made of the final sequence, a fight scene staged atop a large pane of glass suspended in mid-air from a high-rise skyscraper. It looks absolutely real, until marred by a cheap special-effects explosion, and may cause viewers to break out in giddy laughter. This is the type of cinematic lunacy that helped put Hong Kong films first in the hearts of action fans. It almost makes you forgive Coolio for repeating "Man, I could get used to this @#$%" in four consecutive scenes. Don't skip the wince-inducing outtakes that play under the closing credits. —*PM* **AKA:** *Lui Ting Chin Ging; Lei Ting Zhan Jing; Thunderous Battle Cops.* ♪♪♪

2000 103m/C *HK* Aaron Kwok, Noriko Fujiwara, Wang Lee-hom, Ruby Lin, Coolio, Mark Dacascos, Paul Chun, Lau Sui-ming, Ken Lo, Yuen Jung, Jackson Liu. **D:** Stanley Tong. **W:** Stanley Tong, Steven Whitney. **C:** Jeffrey Mygatt. **M:** Nathan Wang. **DVD**

Chinatown Kid

In one of his rare Shaw Brothers features with a contemporary setting, Chang Cheh began using a group of talented young Taiwan and Hong Kong opera performers more extensively, and he would go on to cast them as his legendary *5 Deadly Venoms.* Alexander Fu Sheng *(Brave Archer)* stars as Tan Tung, a struggling young refugee in Hong Kong. Using his kung fu grip to squeeze oranges, he and his grandfather (Wong Ching Ho) open an unlicensed juice stand, which attracts unwanted attention from both the cops and Ching Wu triad boss Chu Ho (Johnny Wang). After Tung helps one of Chu's girls (Kara Hui) escape from prostitution, the gangster gets revenge by planting cocaine on him, and Tung has to flee to San Francisco.

Tung shares a room and works with Taiwanese student Yang Ching-wen (Sun Chien), and gets on well until he finds that the triads run things in Chinatown, too. Tung loses his job for beating up gangsters from the Ching Wu Green Tiger triad, but the leader of the White Dragon gang (Phillip Kwok) is quick to hire him. Tung leads a raid on Green Tiger headquarters, getting revenge on the visiting Chu Ho and smashing their operation. While Tan Tung is becoming a big man in the gang, his buddy Yang, under pressures of work and study, becomes a drug addict. This leads Tung to try to stop all of the gang's drug business, putting him at odds with his fellows, who try to get rid of him once and for all.

Chang obviously had intentions of creating more than the usual kung fu picture with this ambitious feature, but too much trite drama and not enough action sink this overlong crime epic, which is a predecessor of so many Hong Kong triad movies to come. No doubt this was an influence on John Woo, a previous assistant to Chang Cheh. The action choreography is surprisingly ordinary, given the caliber of talent involved, but gives an honest portrait of the plight of Chinese refugees. Some versions run as much as 25 minutes shorter. **AKA:** *Tang Yan Gaai Siu Ji; Tang Ren Jie Xiao Zi.* ♪♪♡

1977 (R) 115m/C *HK* Alexander Fu Sheng, Sun Chien, Phillip Kwok, Johnny Wang, Wong Ching Ho, Lo Meng, Ha Ping, Kara Hui, Dick Wei, Chiang Sheng, James Wong, Lu Feng, Shirley Yu, Yang Chihching, Shaw Yin-Yin, Chiang Nan, Goo Goon-chung, Lo Dik, Choi Wang, Suen Shu-pau, Wang Li, Jenny Tseng, Robert Tai, Lee Ka-ting, Jamie Luk, Yu Taiping, Lam Fai-wong. **D:** Chang Cheh. **W:** Ngai Hong, James Wong, Chang Cheh. **C:** Kung Mu-to. **M:** Chen Yung-yu. **VHS, DVD**

The Chinese Connection

Shanghai, 1908. Martial arts master Hua Yin-jia is dead, and his most talented student Chen Jeh (Bruce Lee) shows his distress at the funeral

with a fine display of casket diving. While the Jing Wu School grieves, interpreter Wu (Paul Wei) for Mr. Susuki's Japanese Hom Kiu bushido school arrives to challenge the Chinese, but they resist out of respect for their late master. But later, Chen goes to Hom Kiu School to meet the challenge, humiliating teacher Yoshida (Feng Yi) and every one of them with his fists and nunchakus. This only prompts the Japanese to attack Jing Wu in force while Chen is away, busting up the place and demanding Chen's surrender. Chen agrees to leave town for the sake of the school, but before he does, he learns that Master Hua was really poisoned by the chef Tien (Huang Chung-hsin) and his assistant (and Yoshida's brother) Feng Kwai-sher (Han Ying Chieh), under instructions from Mr. Wu. Chen kills the pair and leaves them hanging from a lamppost, then goes to find out who is issuing instructions through Wu. But before he can get to Susuki (Riki Hoshimoto), he'll have to go through his new teacher from Russia, Petrov (Robert Baker).

This smash hit had a huge influence on martial arts films, far beyond any of Lee's other movies. The setting provided a forum for pure fighting, and it even allowed Lee to adopt several characters and disguises. Much of the action

is motivated by signs: The Japanese insult the Jing Wu School by giving them a sign that reads, "Sick men of Asia," which Chen makes them eat later. Another brawl is touched off by the "No dogs and Chinese allowed" sign at the Japanese settlement, which Chen smashes. Released around the world as *Fist of Fury,* the American distributor got the film mixed up with Lee's *The Big Boss* and gave it this title inspired by *The French Connection.* Jackie Chan and Sammo Hung can be glimpsed doing stunts. ***AKA:*** *Chen Miu Moon; Jing Wu Men; Fist of Fury.* 🦴🦴🦴🦴

1971 (R) 107m/C *HK* Bruce Lee, Nora Miao, Feng Yi, Maria Yi, James Tien, Tin Fung, Huang Chung-hsin, Han Ying Chieh, Lo Wei, Lee Kwan, Robert Baker, Tony Liu, Chin San, Riki Hoshimoto, Jun Arimura, Chen Fu Ching, Paul Wei, Corey Yuen, Mars. ***D:*** Lo Wei. ***W:*** Lo Wei. ***C:*** Chen Ching Chu. ***M:*** Ku Chia Hui. **VHS, DVD**

The Chinese Feast

Family fun has never tasted this good. Chiu Gong-sang (Leslie Cheung) wants to be a great

chef and leave his triad past behind. He's a flop at culinary school, but is able to snag an entry-level restaurant job, where he manages to screw up every task he's given—including a colossal goof that causes a gigantic fish to go squirting all over the restaurant as patrons dive for cover. The owner, Au Siu-fung (Law Kar-Ying), is remarkably tolerant of his apprentice's general incompetence, but keeps on training him because of the younger man's burning desire to succeed. Gong-sang catches the eye of Au Ga-wai (Anita Yuen), the owner's daughter. She is first seen with flame-red hair and a supremely rebellious attitude—she hates the business and will do anything to cause problems. That includes romancing Gong-sang. She changes and rallies to her father's side when he takes ill after being challenged to a multicourse, three-day cooking contest by Wong Wing (Xiong Xinxin), an arrogant rival. The contest winner receives the loser's restaurant.

Ga-wai and Gong-sang don't have what it takes to win the contest—the feast is rarely prepared because the ingredients are quite uncommon, so few cooks have the specialized skills to do so properly. They ask another rival cook (Vincent Zhao), but he too is inadequate to the task. He points them to their only hope: Liu Git (Kenny Bee), a drunken, down-on-his-luck retired master cook. Liu Git is a broken man. He has lost his senses of taste and smell, and his wife has separated from him. Ga-wai and Gong-sang must rehabilitate him and help him to recapture his lost talents. The feast awaits! Anyone for bear paw, elephant trunk, or monkey's brain?

You can compare this to a rousing sports movie where an underdog takes on an unbeatable rival (Rocky). You can compare this to a martial arts movie, where two masters challenge each other, one master falls ill, the stricken master's replacement undergoes intensive training, and the finale is an amazing showdown (too many examples to list). You can even compare this to a political situation wherein a small region is pitted against a superpower (Hong Kong vs. Mainland China). Whatever you compare it to, *just make sure you eat* before watching this one or you'll be salivating too much to enjoy it. The first half is a hodge-podge of comedy and character sketches. The second half, consisting of the training and cooking sequences, is an extraordinary mad dash to the finish line. The contest is presented in all of its festive glory, as extraordinary dishes are prepared with the dynamic grace of supremely skilled martial artists. You'll want to raise a glass to toast the cast and crew at the end. And then you will definitely want to eat. —PM *AKA: Gam Yuk Moon Tong; Jin Yu Man Tang.* ♪♪♪

1995 102m/C *HK* Leslie Cheung, Anita Yuen, Kenny Bee, Vincent Zhao, Law Kar-Ying, Xiong Xin-xin, Joyce Ngai, William Ho, Peter Lai, Lau Shun, Peter Pau, Faan Yik-man, Wong Yat-Fei. **D:** Tsui Hark. **W:** Tsui Hark, Philip Cheng, Ng Man-fai. **C:** Peter Pau. **M:** Lowell Lo. **VHS, DVD**

A Chinese Ghost Story

Tsui Hark (producer) and Ching Siu-tung (director) had a huge hit with this remake of 1960's *The Enchanting Shadow,* using all the special effects and action tricks they could muster. Traveling tax collector Ning Tsai-shen (Leslie Cheung) finds lodging hard to come by in a remote village. A pack of wolves chases the unlucky young man right into the haunted Lo Ran Temple, where a pretty ghost named Nieh Hsiao-tsing (Joey Wong) takes a fancy to him. But Hsiao-tsing is enslaved to the monstrous Tree Devil (Lau Siu-ming), and assigned to lure unsuspecting travelers into the monster's clutches. Touched by Ning's tender heart, she decides to spare him, risking the wrath of her master. However, Ning makes more trouble for her by stumbling into the Devil's villa. Sure enough, the Tree Devil drags Hsiao-tsing off to the netherworld to marry the evil Lord Black. Ning seeks the help of ghostbusting swordsman Yen Che-hsia (Wu Ma) to find a way to get down to Hell to save his ghost lover, and set her free to reincarnate.

Sam Raimi's *Evil Dead* was initially a bigger hit in Asia than back home, and its influence can be seen in the atmosphere of the haunted woods and sinister trees. However, the focus here is on romance and fantasy rather than horror—though the Tree Devil is a scary creature, who enjoys sending its mile-long tongue out to ensnare victims. The warriors and demons all fly around in combat like in any swordplay movie, and all supernatural dealings are strictly according to Chinese folklore. The images are stunningly beautiful, often disguising the fact that the special effects are sometimes a bit clunky. Highly influential, a whole horde of ghost fantasy pictures followed the picture, many of which starred Joey Wong and Wu Ma. However, the magic of this production proved difficult to reproduce by imitators. Tsui made two official sequels and an animated feature as a result. *AKA: Sien Nui Yau Wan; Qian Nu You Hun.* ♪♪♪♡

1987 95m/C *HK* Leslie Cheung, Joey Wong, Wu Ma, Lau Siu-ming, Sit Chi-lun, Lam Wai, David Wu, Wong Jing, Chiang Kam. **D:** Ching Siu-tung. **W:** Yuen Kai-chi, Pu Songling (story). **C:** Poon Hang-sang, Sander Lee, Tom Lau, Horace Wong. **M:** James Wong, Romeo Diaz. **VHS, DVD**

A Chinese Ghost Story 2

This sequel to Tsui Hark's exciting supernatural kung fu film *A Chinese Ghost Story* reunites the original cast in a story that looks and feels the same with a few key differences. The intoxicatingly fragile (and occasionally ass-kicking) Joey Wong—the forlorn ghost of the original—here returns as a woman who might be the original ghost's reincarnation. But Leslie Cheung, the young tax collector of the first film whom we find here still collecting taxes, isn't sure—just as everyone else in the film is convinced that Cheung is actually a long-lost political rabble-rouser, just as Wong, reincarnation or not, is now a member of a team of benevolent highwaymen. The film is awash in mistaken identities that hardly make any sense at all, making *A Chinese Ghost Story 2* one of the most Kafkaesque and sad kung-fu horrors; the early sequences, in which Cheung winds up languishing in prison with an old poet for what seems like an eternity, play like a Chinese riff on *The Count of Monte Christo*.

And yet if one tries to remember the film, it blends so seamlessly in with the original *A Chinese Ghost Story* that the two feel like one long movie, and the reason is that despite the fact that there's not even a *ghost* here, there's still the same gonzo monster kung fu. Having thoroughly depressed the audience in Act I as Cheung wanders through a corrupt China, suddenly a Taoist monk who travels underground like Bugs Bunny shows up to help fight a whole slew of monsters, giant Buddhas, and titanic centipedes summoned by an evil magician to undermine Joey Wong's estranged family. If the message of Kafka's "The Trial" was, "life is an interminable, impenetrable, and dull process from which the only escape is death," Hark's thesis seems to be "life is an interminable, impenetrable, and dull process occasionally interrupted by superpowered monsters vulnerable to Taoist magic and kung fu." That's an improvement, really. The best business? Watch for the scene involving Cheung, the monk, the monster, and a freezing spell. —JH **AKA:** *Yangan Dou; Sinnui yauman II Yan Gaan Diy; Qian Nu You Hun II Ren Jian Dao.* 🎭🎭🎭

1990 104m/C *HK* Leslie Cheung, Joey Wong, Michelle Reis, Jacky Cheung, Wu Ma, Ku Feng, Lau Shun, Lau Siu-ming, Waise Lee, To Siu-chun, Yang Sha-fei, Yeung Ching-Ching, Li Fai, Wong Hung, Tin Kai-man. **D:** Ching Siu-Tung. **W:** Edward Leung, Lam Kee-To, Lau Dai Muk. **C:** Arthur Wong. **M:** James Wong, Romeo Diaz. **VHS, DVD**

A Chinese Ghost Story 3

Whereas *A Chinese Ghost Story 2* spun the characters of the original film off into another non-ghostly monster-fighting adventure in the mad, mad world of Tsui Hark, *A Chinese Ghost Story 3* returns to the themes of forbidden love (occasionally interrupted by mad monster kung fu) of the first film. To do so it gives us a new set of characters while returning to the plot of the Pu Songling story that inspired the original.

The hero here is Tony Leung Chiu-Wai, a young priest training under the sage and powerful (if cranky) older priest Lau Shun. The medieval village they pass through is far too violent a place to bring the golden Buddha statue the pair are carrying, so they decide to spend the night in a creepy old abandoned temple outside of town—which of course, anyone in these movies would do. The reason is plain to the viewer: if you stay there, cute ghosts hit on you, and they're all played by Joey Wong, who here reprises her role of winsome magic girl for the umpteen millionth time. The young priest is sorely tempted by Wong, who's job as a ghost (which this time she embraces enthusiastically) is to tempt men into the waiting arms of the her evil tree witch mistress and her wading pool of bald lesbian water nymphs.

It gets weirder: as Leung and Wong flirt and circle one another and Wong slowly comes over to the side of good, a master swordsman with all the half-baked machismo and barely hidden golden heart of Han Solo joins the fight while evil gangs from town in search of the monks' gold get chopped to pieces by the tree witch's enormous prehensile tongue. Did we mention the old master gives himself a massive power-up by bleeding gold all over himself while he chants and levitates? That he can cover his eyes with his earlobes? *A Chinese Ghost Story 3* in the end is a bigger, louder remake of the first film, giving us the idea that the Tsui's universe spouts adventures like this all the time. That's good, because Tsui's skewed, supernaturally charged world is a wonderful place to visit. —JH **AKA:** *Sin Lui Yau Wan, Sinnui yauman III: Do Do Do; Qian Nu You Hun III Dao Dao Dao.* 🎭🎭🎭

1991 115m/C *HK* Jacky Cheung, Lau Shun, Lau Siu-ming, Tony Leung Chiu-Wai, Nina Li Chi, Joey Wong, Tiffany Liu, Tommy Wong. **D:** Ching Siu-Tung, Tsui Hark. **W:** Roy Szeto, Tsui Hark. **C:** Tom Lau. **M:** James Wong, Romeo Diaz. **VHS, DVD**

Spirited Joey Wong slips hiding beau Leslie Cheung a kiss in *A Chinese Ghost Story.* THE KOBAL COLLECTION

徐克

Xu Wen Guang, who has changed the course of Hong Kong filmmaking more than once, was not unlike other filmmakers in some ways. When he was 13, he got his first 8mm movie camera and immediately started making his own little backyard epics. The difference is that this youngster's backyard was in Vietnam in 1964—not your typical breeding ground for future Spielbergs.

After his family relocated to Hong Kong, Wen Guang began using the more English-friendly shortened Cantonese form of his name (Tsui Hark), and was able to continue his studies at the University of Texas. He then moved to New York in the mid-'70s, where he got involved in Asian newspapers and cable TV programs. Back in Hong Kong, he got a job directing for the TVB network, before eventually breaking out into films with *The Butterfly Murders* in 1979. Tsui Hark really came into his own with the production of the fantasy epic *Zu: Warriors of the Magic Mountain* in 1983. A big, bold, legendary adventure story, *Zu* brought new life to the Hong Kong film industry by combining the most basic and traditional tales out of Chinese culture and rendering them with the hottest stars of the day and Hollywood-style special effects—even using American f/x experts as consultants.

His vision was to make movies that were not just aimed at the local audience, but pictures of value and excitement that the whole world could enjoy. As producer, he backed John Woo's *A Better Tomorrow* series, making the director an instant star, then did the same for Ching Siu-Tung's vibrant *Chinese Ghost Story* films. For his own films as director and producer, he created an individual style that became much copied by his peers. *Peking Opera Blues* is a perfect example—a group of interesting heroes is brought together through chance and circumstance in a romantic setting, and through wits and a series of dynamic action scenes eventually face off with a thoroughly evil villain. In a way, they're reminiscent of the *Star Wars* formula, except in a style that's distinctly Chinese—and distinctly Tsui Hark. With reunification looming in the 1990s, Tsui struck even closer to Chinese traditions by reintroducing the historic hero Wong Fei-Hung in *Once upon a Time in China*. The hit film, and its sequels, made a star of its lead actor, authentic Wu Shu champion Jet Li. For years, all Hong Kong swordplay films had a distinct look, and that look was Tsui Hark's—or as close as they could get to it.

Like many talents of Hong Kong film, Tsui Hark made a stab at Hollywood in 1997. Though inferior to much of his previous work, the films he directed for Jean-Claude Van Damme *(Double Team* and *Knock Off)* were at least among the most interesting of Van Damme's films, and Tsui took the opportunity afforded by larger Hollywood budgets to experiment with new technology. *Knock Off* is a terrible picture, but it has an entrancing hyperkinetic camera, which can go anywhere at any time. Returning to Hong Kong, he went to work on a sequel to *Zu,* incorporated an unorthodox story worthy of Wong Kar-Wai with spectacular action in the underrated *Time and Tide,* as well as directing the second in the superhero series *Black Mask 2.* As writer, producer, director, and even occasional actor, one cannot overestimate the contribution of Tsui Hark to Hong Kong film.

A Chinese Ghost Story: The Tsui Hark Animation

Hong Kong does ghosts the Disney way in this rarity that really shouldn't be one: it's a Hong Kong anime. Hong Kong has remained relatively silent on the subject of animation, which is interesting, considering how cartoonish kung fu thrillers tend to be in the sense of defying all laws of physics. But thankfully there is Tsui Hark, the Vietnamese-born University of Texas alum who set a new standard for live-action kung fu horror in 1987 with his adaptation of the Chinese story "Nieh Hsiao Chien" as the classic film *A Chinese Ghost Story.* Having apparently exhausted the number of times Hark felt he could remake the live-action version of that film, he decided it was time to bring in the kids. And thus we get Hark's anime, *A Chinese Ghost Story: The Tsui Hark Animation,* which is less a remake than an evolution. Rather than merely a haunted Temple, we now have the hapless Ning wander into the teeming metropolis of ghosts—microscopic ghosts, towering skyscraper-sized ghosts, beautiful ghosts, hideous ghosts, ghosts that ride intelligent ghost vehicles. Ning wanders into the city by mistake looking to collect taxes, and quickly falls in love with

Shine, a ghost who is betrothed to a towering rock star demon whose big number is a song about how much he loves himself.

The animation freely mixes cel animation with amazing computer graphics, lending the whole event a distinctly strange feel. A thrilling moment involves the train to reincarnation, here envisioned as a vast snorting dragon with train wheels, a stunning, miles-long creation. The influence from Disney is obvious: characters are painted with broad strokes, every frame is rich with detail, and the final climax is carefully concocted to talking at the heartstrings of all but the most cynical—and why would they be watching anyway? But the story works because at the base of it is still the ancient fable with its themes of forbidden love and the sadness of immortality. —JH *AKA: Xiao Qian; Siu Sin.* 🐉🐉🐉🐉

1997 (G) 83m/C *HK* **V:** (Cantonese version) Jordan Chan, Kelly Chan, Eric Kot, Vivian Lai, Jan Lamb, James Wong, Raymond Wong, Rene Liu, Tsui Hark, Ronald Cheng, Charlie Yeung, Anita Yuen; (Mandarin version) Sylvia Chang, Ronald Cheng, Sammo Hung, Lichun Lee, Rene Liu, Lo Ta-yu, Tommy So, Tsui Hark, Linda Wong, Nicky Wu. **D:** Andrew Chan. **W:** Tsui Hark. **M:** Ricky Ho. **VHS, DVD**

Chinese Hercules

Though it's Bruce Lee's street-fightin' pal Michael Chan who's the star of this martial arts extravaganza, it's Lee's other pal Bolo Yeung who garnered all the attention due to an aggressive ad campaign that emphasized Bolo's broad physique. The martial arts schoolmaster's bullying son Lan pushes orphaned student Sun Weisan (Chan) too far late one night, and is unintentionally killed when they fight. Overcome with guilt, Sun smashes his hand with a rock and vows never to fight again. Under the name Chung San, he takes up work on a loading dock, but blows a month's wages to pay for rice stolen by a couple of kids, and takes a beating besides. Despite Chung's passive nature, foreman Uncle Lok (Huang Chung-hsin)—who also committed manslaughter and made a vow not to fight years ago—can see that he has the look of a fighter. Triad boss Leung (Fong Yeh) arrives and makes the company owner Chan Ho (Tong Lung) an offer he can't refuse in exchange for closing down the pier so they can use it to run drugs. The ousted coolies resist, and their shacks are torn down. When Chan and his thugs beat coolie Chu Han (Lee Tin-ying) to death, Uncle Lok decides to break his vow—and breaks Chan's arms and legs in a fight. This prompts Leung to send his man-monster Pang Tai (Bolo Yeung) into action to break a few things, too. He breaks logs, furniture, Chan's skull, and Lok's neck in short order, then moves on to the rest of the coolies before Sun is convinced to face up to the hulking killer.

Bolo Yeung showed he was capable of fancier kung fu and tai chi moves later in his career, but here he and Michael Chan are just showing raw power through basic karate and street fighting. Action director Corey Yuen provides most of the choreography. Since a lot of the fighting takes place on a rocky shoreline, it looks like tough going for the stars and stuntmen. Boxoffice returns on this feature led to more prominent roles for Bolo from that point on—in the advertising at least. Jackie Chan and Yuen Biao are among the many stuntmen running around. *AKA:* *A Dragon on the Waterfront; Freedom Strikes a Blow.* 🐉🐉

1973 (R) 89m/C *HK* Michael Chan, Bolo Yeung, Fan Chiang, Fong Yeh, Huang Chung-hsin, Tong Lung, Chin Ti, Lee Man Tai, Kong Do, Yuen Miu, Corey Yuen, Wan Fat, Yuen Biao, Jackie Chan, Chung Fat, Yuen Yat-chor, Sunny Yuen, Brandy Yuen, Lee Tin-ying, Alan Chui, Yuen Miu, Ringo Wong. **D:** Choy Tak. **W:** Ngai Hong. **VHS, DVD**

Chinese Iron Man

This Joseph Kuo picture swipes liberally from Bruce Lee's hit *The Chinese Connection*, as well as elements from *Fists of Fury* and *Return of the Dragon*. Once again, competition between Japanese and Chinese martial arts schools leads to trouble during the occupation. Chef Little Tiger Lang Hsiao-hu (Man Kong Lung) has promised not to get into fights, and works in his Uncle Lee's Shanghai Restaurant. But when students from the Japanese Musashi dojo come around causing trouble and bullying his cousins, he can't take anymore; he thrashes the lot of them, sending them crawling like dogs. The Japanese run back to their sifu Tetsuo Kuroki (Lau Lap Cho), who gathers them up to return, but he's told Hsiao-hu has gone back to his own village to avoid more trouble. However, Kuroki doesn't believe this, and threatens more trouble if they don't hand over Little Tiger soon. In fact, Hsiao-hu is out defying Japanese orders by taking his girlfriend Wen Lan (Nancy Yen) and his nephew to a park forbidden to Chinese, where he has another rumble with the Japanese.

Next, the Japanese go looking for Hsiao-hu at the Chung Hua Chinese Boxing Gymnasium, attacking his friends there. The Iron Chef comes running to the rescue, thrashing the villains with his rolling pin. But one of his enemies is accidentally skewered on his buddy's sword during the fight, and the police charge Hsiao-hu with murder. Hsiao-hu goes into hiding, but when the Musashis ambush and kill his friend Liu, he invades the enemy headquarters seeking vengeance from Kuroki and Master Takahashi himself.

The plot is dull and completely derivative, but Kuo shoots it all with a sense of style. The main attraction of course is the fighting, which is all pretty decent, especially when Man goes into action wearing his chef's hat and apron. However, the nonstop fighting gets to be a bit tedious, much like the fisticuffs in an old western or serial. How many times does Man have to hit the same guys? Not to be confused with Chang Cheh's *Iron Man* (1972). *AKA: Chung Gwok Foo Yan; Zhong Guo Fu Ren; Iron Man.* 🐉🐉

1975 90m/C *HK* Man Kong Lung, Nancy Yen, Shih Chung Tien, Lau Lap Cho, Yee Yuen, Liu Ping, Choi Wang, Shaw Luo-hui, O Yau-man, Bruce Li, Su Chen Ping, Ng Tung-kiu, Gam Kim, Yip Mau, Lau Cheungming, Ho Ming-hiu, Chung Seung-man, Lau Chingfat, Heung Yeung, Woo Gwong, Chan Chiu-ming. **D:** Joseph Kuo. **DVD**

A Chinese Odyssey Part 1: Pandora's Box

Jeff Lau *(Eagle Shooting Heroes)* presents the first part of his lavish adaptation of the fantasy novel *Journey to the West*, which is filtered through both the sensibility of a European fairy tale and the insane comedy of superstar Stephen Chow. The film opens in Heaven, as the Monkey King (a typecast Chow) is misbehav-

ing as usual. Because of his antics, his master the Longevity Monk (Law Kar-Ying) and his followers are all banished to Earth. Centuries later, Monkey King is incarnated as bandit chief Joker, whose leadership is threatened by a visit from 30th Madam (Yammie Nam). She and her sister Pak Jing-Jing (Karen Mok) are demons looking for the Monkey King, hoping he can lead them to Longevity Monk—whose flesh is said to grant immortality to whoever eats it. Joker is quite taken with Miss Pak, until Buddha (Jeff Lau)—disguised as a bunch of grapes—gives him a magic mirror that allows him to see her scary true face. Pak—who still carries a torch for the Monkey King from an earlier period—takes pity on Joker, taking sides with him against the spider-demon 30th Madam. Meanwhile, King Bull is looking for any advantage to use against any of them to get to Longevity Monk. With Pak dying from poison, Joker tries to use the Pandora's Box he's found to travel back in time to save her. However, he goes too far and ends up 500 years in the past!

The makeup and special effects are marvelous, creating a credible world of gods, monsters, giant spiders, and pig-faced bandits. It's all wrapped up in fantastic settings and beautifully photographed. But the fabled supernatural figures are difficult to get attached to—the most accessible character is the Assistant Master Bandit played by Ng Man-Tat, who is more sympathetic than he's ever been. It all ends with preview scenes from *Part 2*. **AKA:** *Sai Yau Gei Dai Yat Baak Ling Yat Wooi Ji Yuet Gwong Bo Hap; Xi You Ji Di Yi Bai Ling Yi Hui Zie Yu Guang Bao He; Daiwah Saiyau; A Chinese Odyssey.* 🎵🎵🎶

1995 87m/C *HK* Stephen Chow, Ng Man-Tat, Law Kar-Ying, Yammie Nam, Karen Mok, Jeff Lau, Athena Chu, Law Kar-Ying. **D:** Jeff Lau. **W:** Jeff Lau. **C:** Fletcher Poon. **M:** Chiu Kwai-ping. **VHS, DVD**

A Chinese Odyssey Part 2: Cinderella

The adventures of the Monkey King (Stephen Chow) continue. Lin Zixia (Athena Chu) is one of a pair of sisters who form Buddha's lamp wick, but she sneaks out of Heaven and takes on corporeal form to find her true love—which will be whoever can pull out her sword (insert your own Freudian joke here). At the offhand suggestion of Jester, the reincarnation of Monkey King that just arrived from 500 years in the future, Zixia becomes the Spiderweb Immortal and settles into her new home in Spiderweb Cave. While serving his new mistress, Joker stays close to look for a chance to use the Pandora's Box to get back to the future and save his lover Pak

Jing-Jing (Karen Mok). Being an Immortal in disguise himself, Joker quite easily pulls Zixia's sword from its scabbard, unknowingly marking himself as the love of her life. Zixia has little trouble eluding or defeating the various warriors sent to recapture her, but fears that her sister/enemy Lin Qingxia (Ada Choi) will also escape from Heaven and come after her. Jester's presence at the trial of the Monkey King, and at other junctures in his own past, continues to change history. Next he accidentally helps King Bull catch the Longevity Monk (Law Kar-Ying), earning the "reward" of betrothal to the nasty Lin Qingxia.

As if things weren't already completely confusing, when Qingxia catches Joker with her sister, she casts a spell switching the bodies of the sisters with two of Longevity Monk's disciples (one of whom is Ng Man-Tat in amazing makeup as the arrogant Pig King). Then there's the King Bull's spat with his wife (who is another of Monkey King's old girlfriends), the Longevity Monk unstuck in time, the vampiric Dark Mountain King, Joker meeting up with the Jing-Jing of the past, an army of monkeys battling an army of fleas, and other strange beasties running about. Making matters much worse are the subtitles, which seem to switch some of the characters' names at times. Even so, this episode still has a better sense of direction than its predecessor. Chow is a much more sympathetic protagonist, pulling off the pathos as well as the gags. He also makes for a classic Monkey King. The f/x and makeup folks have a field day again, and it all looks great through the lenses of Fletcher Poon. Never has such stunningly beautiful cinematography been allied so closely with fart jokes. In Hong Kong, *Part 2* was released one month following *Part 1*. **AKA:** *Sai Yau Gei Dai Git Guk Ji Sin Lei Kei Yuen; Xi You Ji Di Jie Ju Zhi Xian Lu Qi Yuan.* 🎵🎵🎵

1995 99m/C *HK* Stephen Chow, Athena Chu, Ada Choi, Ng Man-Tat, Law Kar-Ying, Yammie Nam, Karen Mok, Jeff Lau. **D:** Jeff Lau. **W:** Jeff Lau. **C:** Fletcher Poon. **M:** Chiu Kwai-ping. **VHS, DVD**

Chinese Orthopedist and the Spice Girls

As pessimistic readers might suspect, the title is the best thing about this shot-on-video release. Wah (Cecilia Yip) is a widowed Chinese orthopedist. Her daughter Tweety (Ann Ho) hangs out with her friends, the "Spice Girls" of the English title. Visa (Zoie Tam) is only too happy to pay all the bills the group incurs, because her distant father (Felix Lok) is a wealthy businessman. Sister Mark (Moe Chin)

97
VideoHound's Dragon

appears to be some kind of club girl. Showhand (Sally Tan) loves to gamble, but always loses. Eventually Showhand loses a huge sum of money to Philip (Karel Wong), who just happens to be the boss of Marky (Ronnie Cheung), Tweety's boyfriend. Frustrated that he can no longer communicate with his daughter, Visa's father cuts off her money, and the group has to figure out a way to pay off Showhand's debt. Prostitution—at least for one night—looms large as an option.

It takes nearly an hour for the plot machinations to begin cranking up. Until then, it looks like a slice of daily life—not very compelling and a bit aimless. Even when the "story" begins, it's so routine that viewers may find themselves scrambling for the fast-forward button on the remote control. And the larger problem is that it focuses on the two least interesting characters: Tweety and Visa. Although both have dealt with losing a parent, they seem well adjusted and both have a loving (remaining) parent. The other girls (Showhand and Sister Mark) are more enigmatic—we never learn anything about their family situations—and thus more intriguing, but they are involved in the story in only the most rudimentary fashion. The filmmakers have a vague idea about providing a cautionary tale for young people, but are far too fuzzy to drive any warning points home. So we end up with a production that is far from offensive but equally distant from recommended viewing. —*PM* **AKA:** *Dip Ckui Poh Yue Kwong Mooi; Die Da Po Yu La Mei.* 🐉

2002 85m/C *HK* Cecilia Yip, Ann Ho, Zoie Tam, Sally Tan, Moe Chin, Kenny Bee, Shing Fui-on, Ronnie Cheung, Karel Wong, Turbo Law, Felix Lok. **D:** Chow Jan-wing. **W:** Chow Jan-wing, Lam Wa-fan. **C:** Ng Man-chuen. **M:** Mak Chun-hung. **DVD**

Chinese Samson

During the Tea War, bandits raid the tea convoys running across China. In Red Clay Village, a schoolteacher (John Chang) is constantly picked on because he won't fight. Everyone seems to be against him, except for a kindly widow and her daughter Chun. When he's seen making an innocent visit to her house at night, gossip empties his classroom. Though the teacher vows to continue somehow, he turns to drink, and while drunk meets up with two kung fu fighting fortunetellers. During a strange drunken kung fu and calligraphy practice, the fortunetellers relate that they suspect a visiting trade representative is really one-time bandit Ah Yan (Bolo Yeung), who massacred 15 men in one day years ago, leaving only the two of them as survivors.

While stumbling around, Teacher also meets and befriends the local boss's sister (Candy Yu), who secretly teaches him some kung fu. Win-

ning some money at the cockfights, Teacher vows to make a comeback, but when he loses the cash he has a breakdown. Ah Yan strikes again, killing the widow, her child, and the two fortunetellers (though no one seems to take much notice). An old beggar (Hon Siu) is next on his list, but before succumbing to his fatal wounds, the beggar teaches Teacher his drunken boxing style. The scholar incorporates the various techniques he's learned with his calligraphy moves to develop his own fighting style, and challenges the killer himself.

The musical score featuring accordion and strings gives this Bolo Yeung–directed Taiwanese effort an odd European flavor. We know that eventually the teacher is going to become some sort of kung fu master, yielding extensive training sequences and a final duel with serial killer Bolo, but the movie takes its sweet time getting to it, with precious little action to keep you interested. The stops and starts during the first hour are frustrating (made worse by the poor quality of available prints). But at least it's working toward some unusual kung fu ideas. Yeung's flute-playing psycho is a refreshing change from the brutes he usually plays. **AKA:** *Man Chui; Wan Da; Writing Kung Fu; Hot Dog Kung Fu; Literate Strike.* 🐉🐉

1979 80m/C *TW/HK* John Chang, Bolo Yeung, Candy Yu, Hon Siu. **D:** Bolo Yeung. **VHS, DVD**

Chinese Super Ninjas

While Phillip Kwok and other members of the Venoms team went to Taiwan to make *Ninja in the Deadly Trap*, Chang Cheh made his own ninja movie for Shaw Brothers. When the white-clad martial arts school of Yen Chan meets the Kang school for 10 rounds of combat, Kang (Chen Pei-hsi) brings in a ringer for the final rounds: Japanese samurai Sanyi. Chi Sang (Lo Meng) is able to win the match—and force Kang out of the Martial Arts World—using only his bare hands against Sanyi's sword. Before committing seppuku, Sanyi gives Kang a letter for Ninja Master Chin Yun Munda (Michael Chan), asking that he be avenged. Suspecting a diversion, warriors Chi Sang and Chow Chen-hou (Ricky Cheng) remain behind with Yen Chan to protect the headquarters, while the rest go out to meet the challenge of Chin's Five Element Ninjas. The heroes arrive at locations representing each of five elements—Gold, Wood, Water, Fire, Earth—but since none of the Chinese knows anything about ninjas, they're easily tricked by the Japanese' deceptions and slaughtered. It's feared an invasion of the headquarters will be next, and heavy defenses are erected. Chin Yun responds by sending female

ninja Sanji (Yu Tai-ping) to infiltrate their ranks by pretending to be a damsel in distress. While tidying up the place to earn her keep, the spy makes a full diagram of their fortifications. Using this knowledge, the ninjas storm the heroes' headquarters in a surprise attack. Only one warrior is captured alive, and owing to some ninja tricks taught him once by old Master Tang, he manages to escape. He returns to Master Tang to learn more, and joining with some of Tang's students, prepares to get revenge on the Five Element Ninjas.

Unlike most Chinese ninja movies, the ninja here are portrayed with a degree of authenticity, using many actual ninja tactics, costumes, and weapons, and a minimum of fantasy gimmicks. And though missing most of his Venoms team, this is still a Chang Cheh flick, and the martial arts choreography and performers are first-rate, with action even more violent and bloody than Chang's other pictures. However, the simple story—which uses the familiar structure of a hero learning to counteract a technique that's defeated him in the past—is less compelling, and the action less thrilling, due to the fact that most of the heroes and villains are faceless strangers—three quarters of the team of heroes at the climax aren't even introduced until the third act, and don't even have any dialogue. Chang benefits from standing sets on the Shaw Brothers lot, but this still looks like a cheaper production than his past works. *AKA: Yan Je Mo Dik; Rhen Zhe Wu Di; Super Ninjas; Five Element Ninja.* ♫♫♫

1982 (R) 105m/C *HK* Ricky Cheng, Lung Tin Cheung, Lo Meng, Michael Chan, Chen Pei-hsi, Yu Taiping, Wang Li, Chu Ko, Bruce Lai, Kwan Fung, Chan Shen, Wan Seung-lam. *D:* Chang Cheh. *W:* Chang Cheh, Ngai Hong. **VHS, DVD**

A Chinese Torture Chamber Story

Those who like their Hong Kong movies absolutely insane are sure to enjoy this politically incorrect extravaganza, produced by Wong Jing to take advantage of sets left over from Stephen Chow's *Hail the Judge.* As expected from the title, the story at least marginally concerns some extreme forms of torture, a catalog of which is demonstrated right at the start (and all on the same unfortunate guy!). Some of these tortures are put into practice by the Judge Lau Sek-tung (Lee Siu-Kei) trying to coax a confession in an unusual murder case. Little Cabbage (Yvonne Yung) is found soaked with blood alongside her dead husband Got Siu-tai (Tommy Wong), whose enormous penis exploded after administration of an aphrodisiac. Dr. Yang Ni-mu (Lawrence Ng), who once employed Little Cab-

bage as a maid, is accused of writing the prescription for her, but claims the killer aphrodisiac was added to another Rx. The two young lovers never consummated their passion, due to the fact that Little Cabbage wanted to wait a year to show respect for her parents, recently murdered by loan sharks. Yang's nymphomaniac wife Jane (Ching Mai) was having an affair with wicked Lau Hoi-sing (Wong Tak-ban), the judge's son, and his private confession of guilt guarantees the corrupt judge will convict the framed couple. After Little Cabbage caught them in the act, Mrs. Yang had her married off to the dangerously over-endowed Got Siu-tai to get rid of her. Got gives Lau a beating defending his new wife from the lecher, and Lau responds by buying an invisibility sutra to get his revenge.

A wild mix of suspense, action, sex, comedy, sex comedy, sex action, and physical cruelty, even among Category III features they don't get much weirder than this. Some highlights include nanny Yuen King-Tan's efforts to increase her bust size, a hilarious parody of the potter's-wheel scene from *Ghost,* and an incredible over-the-top martial arts sex duel between heroic Win Chung-lung (Elvis Tsui) and Ki Dan-fung (Julie Lee), shot like a scene from a Tsui Hark swordplay movie, that features such stances as the Wonder Screw and Sparking Ejaculation. Some may flinch at how the more graphic bits are mixed together with more lighthearted bawdy material, but in the right frame of mind, this freak show is highly entertaining. *AKA: Moon Ching Sap Dai Huk Ying; Man Qing Shi Da Ku Xing; Chinese Torture Chamber.* ♫♫♫

1994 93m/C *HK* Yvonne Yung, Lawrence Ng, Tommy Wong, Wong Tak-ban, Elvis Tsui, Julie Lee, Ching Mai, Yuen King-Tan, Lee Siu-Kei. *D:* Bosco Lam. *W:* Cheuk Bing. *C:* Tony Miu. **VHS, DVD**

A Chinese Torture Chamber Story 2

Yolinda Yan *(Bullet in the Head)* returned to the screen after a six-year absence, surprising audiences by showing up in this outrageous Wong Jing Category III epic. Lotus Wong (Yan), wife of Cheung Man-cheong, is convicted of murdering her husband's friend, Governor Ma San-yee (Mark Cheng). Her sentence is to die by Ling-chi—to have 1,000 pieces of flesh cut from her body in ritual torture. Lotus first met Ma during his first trip to the capitol, when Man-cheong (Lam Wai-kin) and her brother Wong Chung (Yeung Hung) tried to rob him. Despite the circumstances, the three men become fast friends, and Ma and Lotus fall for each other. She refuses him however, since she's betrothed to Wong. Her sister-in-law (Yeung Fan) is not so virtuous. Later, Ma gives his friends jobs, and gives them

Planet Chang

The Bizarre Martial Arts World of Chang Cheh

張徹

The films produced by the Shaw Brothers Studios were already imbued with a glossy, artificial look—a combination of huge sets and backlots and some of the world's finest film-processing facilities produced a sheen not unlike the Technicolor wonderland created by MGM in its heyday. Chang Cheh was the Vincent Minnelli—and in some instances the Ed Wood—of that candy-colored world, staging martial arts battles as if they were fabulous song-and-dance numbers. But with plenty of blood. His characters were usually outfitted in costumes unlike those worn in any Chinese period, or anywhere on Earth anytime in history. Chang's characters were, by and large, superheroes whose powers were based in kung fu, and they dressed accordingly in tight-fitting open-front tunics, capes, and sometimes masks. Despite their theatricality and grace, Chang also made some of the most macho martial arts pictures ever.

Born Chang Yi-yang in 1923 in Qingtian, in Zhejiang Province, he fled the Japanese invasion inland with other students. Back in Shanghai, his work for the Department of Education involved staging Chinese operas, dramas, and movie screenings. Through his superiors he became involved in the Cathay and Tai Tung film studios. In 1947, Chang wrote his first film script, *The Girl with the Mask,* for Cathay, which starred David Chiang's father Yim Far; the soundtrack spawned some hit songs. At the age of 26 he co-directed his second script *Storm Cloud over Alishan.* He also wrote the hit theme song. Much of his exterior shooting took place in Taiwan, and he stayed there to do anti-Communist propaganda work for the government through the 1950s. In 1957, Chang went to Hong Kong to direct *Wild Fire,* and he moved there to continue his career as screenwriter, journalist, and pulp novelist. Run Run Shaw was impressed by Chang's film reviews, and in 1962 Chang joined Shaw Brothers as head of the script department.

Chang believed movies in Hong Kong had become too feminine in nature, and thought the studio would do better making more manly films. During this period, his scripts started a craze for swordplay movies, which gave him the clout to direct his hit *Tiger Boy*. He also directed a string of hit swordplay films, and his *One-Armed Swordsman* broke all boxoffice records, making a superstar out of Jimmy Wang Yu.

Success cleared the way for Chang to make films the way he wanted. Working from scripts written in collaboration with ultra-productive pulp writer Ngai Hong, Chang produced one film after another, each one involving amazing martial arts, a touch of mystery, operatic drama, and an increasing preoccupation with violence and fetishism (or shall we say fetishistic violence). Though his films focused energy on fighting and training in authentic kung fu forms (much of the choreography was provided by Lau Kar-Leung and Robert Tai), much like other kung fu films, an outstanding feature is their utter maleness, much like the tough Italian westerns but without the mud and dust. Increasingly, when a woman did play a major role in a Chang movie, she was usually just a distraction to the heroes, or an outright traitor. Chang clearly preferred the company of men (the homosexual subtext to his films couldn't be more obvious), and his films were increasingly filled with brawny he-men. When Jimmy Wang Yu left the Shaws, Chang cast the likes of David Chiang and Ti Lung as his heroes, then brought in Alexander Fu Sheng and the whole Venoms mob officially introduced via *Five Deadly Venoms*.

At the same time, his films' protagonists went from being straitlaced public servants to rugged individualists to vengeful loners. In the 1980s, his movies became increasingly bizarre. His last film for the Shaws was the ironically titled *The Weird Man*. His '80s output is highlighted by the twisted confessional statement *Venom Warrior* (AKA *Dancing Warrior*)—in which Ricky Cheng stars as a youth who just wants to dance, but crooks force him to use his martial arts skills in illegal kickboxing matches—and the completely insane action/horror/fantasy *Nine Demons*.

Whatever demons were driving Chang Cheh throughout his life and career, the result is a bounty of incredibly entertaining action films which are only beginning to find an audience in the U.S.

a tour of the torture chamber. While the brothers-in-law are ineptly leading troops in an attempt to catch the cannibalistic Black Wind bandit gang, Ma and Mrs. Wong engage in naughty S&M games. On her wedding night, Lotus learns that due to tortures he endured while captured by Black Wind, it's extremely painful for Man-cheong to get an erection. On the same night, Wong finds the bruises and bites on his wife's body, and Ma tells him a man named Chu is responsible. Ma finally gets his "pals" out of the way when Wong and Cheung beat the innocent man to death, leading them to arrest and hideous suffering in the torture chamber. Lotus learns what happened from Cheung as he faces execution, and plots her revenge.

Despite the amount of sex, violence, gore, and depravity on display, *Chamber 2* is a rather dull film—at least in between freakish atrocities. Decapitation, dismemberment, whipping, impalement, rope tricks, and other such mischief are among the amusements. Some are repeated to make the most of fake limbs and such. Flashbacks are piled on top of flashbacks just to add some extra scenes of deviltry. One such attempts to explain Ma's psychosis on childhood abuse. One viewer's pleasure is another's torture, so choose wisely. Mark Cheng *(Peking Opera Blues)* was married to Yokari Oshima for a few years. **AKA:** *Moon Ching Sap Daai Huk Ying Ji Chek Law Ling Jeung; Man Qing Shi Da Ku Xing Zhi Chi Luo Ling Chi.* ♪♥

1998 91m/C *HK* Yolinda Yan, Mark Cheng, Lam Wai-kin, Yeung Fan, Yeung Hung, Wong San. **D:** Dik Sang. **W:** Dick Tso. **C:** Chan Chung-yuen. **M:** Lincoln Lo. **DVD**

Chivalrous Legend

The true story of the legendary Taiwanese hero Liao Tien-Ting, told to liberally emphasize his feats of derring-do. In 1894, China signed a treaty with Japan, giving the latter control of Taiwan. The occupation forces proceeded to treat the populous with the usual contempt and brutality afforded foreigners under Japanese rule. Ten-year-old Liao Tien-Ting (Sik Siu-long) has just been released from indenture. He returns home to find his mother's been killed by a Japanese soldier. Trained in the martial arts by his Master, little Tien-Ting uses kung fu to kill the soldier, Now a fugitive, he is taken in by an opera troupe. (The Chinese opera is famous for aiding revolutionaries and keeping Shaolin kung fu alive during oppression, and in Taiwan it was no different.) The troupe is caught performing an anti-Japanese play, and Liao goes on the run again. Caught stealing from a temple to feed his rumbling stomach, he's saved by his sifu Kuang (Blackie Ko). The pair stay alive by entertaining

with kung fu tricks in the streets, and little Liao grows into Taiwan teen idol Jimmy Lin *(Butterfly and Sword)*.

Sifu Kuang is challenged by a Japanese officer and is shot. Liao kills the officer and goes on the run once again. After saving a gambler named Red Turtle, the pair go to work on railroad projects. Things go quietly until Liao is compelled to kill a Japanese who tried to rape his girlfriend. Having taken enough, he decides to fight the empire, taking up the banner of heroes past as the Robin Hood of Taiwan.

Not unusual for film biographies, *Chivalrous Legend* tries to cover too many areas of its subject's life in too short a time, resulting in an episodic, oversimplified portrait. They would have done better by focusing on one part of Liao's life, sketching in whatever other information necessary through flashbacks and such. As it is, the film probably doesn't do the hero justice. **AKA:** *Hup do Jing Chuen; Xia Dao Zheng Chuan; Legend of the Thieving Hero.* ♪♪

1998 96m/C *TW* Jimmy Lin, Vivian Hsu, Blackie Ko, Sik Siu-long. **D:** Chai Yang-Ming. **VHS, DVD**

Chungking Express

During the years it took to film and edit the mysterious swordplay epic *Ashes of Time*, director Wong Kar-Wai felt he needed to cleanse his palette, as it were, so he took time off to make this meditation on life and loneliness in the big city. Two stories are played out in Hong Kong. In the first, a policeman (Takeshi Kaneshiro) mourns the loss of his girlfriend. His path crosses that of a drug smuggler (Brigitte Lin) whose life is on the line. The policeman obsessively eats pineapple and calls his old girlfriends. The drug smuggler organizes her "mules" with ruthless efficiency, making sure the maximum amounts of drugs are secured on their person and in their luggage. She has no hesitation about kidnapping the daughter of a criminal cohort when one of the "mules" disappears. The policeman and the drug smuggler end up spending a few hours in each other's company, their respective occupations unmentioned.

In the second tale, another policeman (Tony Leung) also mourns the loss of his girlfriend, a flight attendant (Valerie Chow) who unexpectedly moves out of his apartment. He stops nightly at a small restaurant, where he encounters a newly hired worker (Faye Wong). After she comes into possession of a key to his apartment, she becomes infatuated with him and starts transforming his life, while he remains oblivious to her attentions.

Wong Kar-Wai's signature techniques are on vivid display here—blurred slow-motion action scenes, enigmatic characters, and repeated use of a few musical themes. At its heart, it's about hope without reason, and how men and women react in different ways to the possibilities of life. The film is anchored by the performances of Brigitte Lin and Tony Leung Chiu-Wai. Lin's expression barely changes (is she being stoic, or is she resigned to her fate?), yet her body language speaks volumes as she sets about her highly dangerous work. Leung's eyes are the key to his performance. Just watch the way he reacts to Faye Wong at different points in the story: at first wary, and then slowly, begrudgingly, curious, and finally, some other feeling entirely. Wong is limited as an actor in her first role of any substance (evidently she also appeared in a supporting part in *Beyond's Diary* in 1990, but she has a beguiling look, and many of her expressions are priceless. Takeshi Kaneshiro also had limited experience in films (this was one of his first parts), but his heartfelt (and not overplayed) emoting belie his inexperience. Valerie Chow is quite attractive as Tony Leung's lost love. The final exchange of dialogue between Leung and Wong is perfect. —PM **AKA:** *Chung Hing Sam Lam; Chong Qing Sen Lin; Chungking Forest.* 🎵🎵🎵🎵

1994 (PG-13) 98m/C *HK* Brigitte Lin, Takeshi Kaneshiro, Tony Leung Chiu-Wai, Faye Wong, Valerie Chow. **D:** Wong Kar-Wai. **W:** Wong Kar-Wai. **C:** Christopher Doyle, Andrew Lau. **M:** Roel A. Garcia, Frankie Chan. **VHS, DVD**

Chushingura

Frequently called the *Gone with the Wind* of Japan, this often-filmed samurai tale has a deep cast of characters and a huge scope. It tells the near-legendary story of the 47 Loyal Retainers, and their doomed lord. The lord is an honest man within a corrupt Japanese bureaucracy; when he lashes out against his dishonest superior, the lord is forced to commit suicide, and his clan is disgraced and disbanded. The lord's vassals go underground, vowing to avenge their master on the anniversary of his death. The retainers swear to meet again in one year to carry out their plan. In the intervening time, they suffer all manner of humiliation as ronin (masterless samurai), often taking demeaning jobs or pretending to be less honorable than they truly are. In this way, they hope to fool their enemy into believing they've forgotten the injustice done and catch him unaware. The plan works, and the resulting battle is an epic part of Japanese history. Equally as interesting is who of the original group carries through with the vow, and why they do so, or fail to do so.

The film is beautiful in costumes, sets, and cinematography. No expense was spared in bringing the tale to vivid life. The cast is very good, if perhaps overly large for a Western audience. It is sometimes difficult to tell one young retainer from another, and the drama does get a bit soapy at times. Still, that's a very small quibble for a film this large and this good. While not, perhaps, up to the standards of Kurosawa's masterpieces, this film still deserves a prominent place in any collection of Far Eastern cinema. After its first run in America, it was re-released in a 108-minute version. The Japanese release was reportedly four hours in length, shown in two parts. —SS **AKA:** *47 Ronin; 47 Samurai; The 47 Loyal Retainers.* 🎵🎵🎵🎵

1962 204m/C *JP* Toshiro Mifune, Yuzo Kayama, Chusa Ichikawa, Yoko Tsukasa, Yosuke Natsuki, Ichiro Arishima, Frankie Sakai, Keiju Kobayashi, Yuriko Hoshi, Makoto Sato, Ryo Ikebe, Daisuke Kato, Yumi Shirakawa, Kumi Mizuno, Akira Takarada, Takashi Shimura, Hiroshi Koizumi, Akira Kubo, Jun Tazaki, Seizaburo Kawazu, Yu Fujiki, Yoshio Kosugi, Akihiko Hirata, Tadao Takashima, Yoshio Tsuchiya, Nadao Kirino, Hisaya Ito, Ren Yamamoto, Kenji Sahara, Sachio Sakai, Kamatari Fujiwara, Ikio Sawamura, Mie Hama, Senkichi Omura, Chieko Nakakita, Susumu Fujita. **D:** Hiroshi Inagaki. **W:** Kazuo Yamada. **C:** Toshio Yasumi. **M:** Akira Ifukube. **VHS, DVD**

City Cop

Another crime thriller produced by Danny Lee's cops-and-robbers film factory. Ng Wai-Hon (Ben Ng of *Thunder Cop*) is a ruthless criminal, leaving behind and in trouble one of the mainlanders he hired for a job. When "Monkey" is stopped by cops, he panics, pulls a gun, and takes hostages. Inspector Jackson Wong (co-producer Parkman Wong) of Serious Crime Unit is on the scene. Off-duty Inspector Chow (Canadian Michael Chow) of SCU is impatient with negotiations, and boldly charges in to make the arrest. Officers Wong and Lee (Danny Lee) both object to Chow's grandstanding, but of course, that afternoon Wong is informed that Chow is his new partner. Yes, before you can say, "I'm getting too old for this!," it's the classic reckless-young-cop-teamed-with-tired-old-cop story. Meanwhile, Ng Wai-Hon is even more reckless than Chow, starting a gunfight during a jewelry-store robbery—even when things are clearly under control—before screeching away in their getaway Mazda.

Monkey helps identify Hon and the others, so Chow and Wong get on their trail. They follow clues to stake out likely targets for the next robbery, but Hon's gang are armed with automatic weapons and the police are simply outgunned on the next shootout. Fortunately, one of the gang gets scared off by Hon's trigger-happy

ways, and decides to head for China. Picked up by the Coast Guard, he's identified as part of the gang, and gives Chow and Wong more leads to the gang's hideout.

Making the most of the cliché situation, this is a solid little policier. Director Herman Yau *(Untold Story)* shoots some scenes to look almost like news footage. There's plenty of action, but none of it goes too far to be believable, and it's all held together nicely by Wong's sympathetic performance. Chow doesn't come off as well, looking wooden in most of his scenes. *AKA: Gung Book II; Gong Pu II; City Cop II.* 🎵🎵🎵

1995 106m/C *HK* Michael Chow, Parkman Wong, Danny Lee, Ben Ng, Peter Yung. *D:* Herman Yau. *W:* Anna Lee. *C:* Puccini Yu. *M:* Brother Hung. **VHS**

City Hunter

This nearly mindless, breezy adaptation of the Tsukasa Hojo's *City Hunter* manga series pairs Hong Kong's top star Jackie Chan with Hong Kong top cheeseball writer/director Wong Jing, with what should have been predicted as mixed results. Chan stars Ryo Saeba, a Tokyo detective whose most apparent attributes are of wolf and glutton, but who somehow always shows his heart's in the right place during his adventures—and never gains an ounce. Rich newspaper publisher Imamura hires Saeba to find his runaway daughter Shizuko (Kumiko Goto). Picking up her trail in Hong Kong, Saeba nearly catches up with her, only to lose her at the pier when she boards a luxury liner. He follows, but learns that keeping Shizuko safe is even more difficult than finding her. His shipmates include a gang of crooks led by sinister Colonel MacDonald (Richard Norton) who take over the ship, planning to hold the hostage millionaires for ransom.

City Hunter is among several solid *Die Hard* knockoffs made in Hong Kong, which would include Wong Jing's later *High Risk*—an action comedy that sends up Jackie Chan in some scenes, and it's generally assumed that this was a direct result of their troubled working relationship on *City Hunter*. Chan is miscast in the leering detective role, and this soon evolves into more of a Jackie Chan movie than a straight adaptation of the character. Due to this conflict of characterization, supporting players like Chingmy Yau and Leon Lai threaten to steal the show at certain points. Wong's influence is felt throughout as well, with everyone mugging their way through one silly gag after another. The high point for many comes when Chan fights Gary Daniels and some other thugs in an arcade, which somehow turns them into characters from the *Streetfighter 2* game—an idea that falls flat for those unfamiliar with the game. Some of these bits work, as when Chan fights a very tall man in a theatre,

while the climax of *Game of Death* screens behind them. However, most of the time the film gets by only on the personalities of the stars, and of course, the action courtesy of the Jackie Chan Stuntmen Association. *AKA: Sing Si Lip Yan; Cheng Shi Lie Ren.* 🎵🎵🎵

1992 95m/C *HK* Jackie Chan, Joey Wong, Chingmy Yau, Kumiko Goto, Leon Lai, Richard Norton, Gary Daniels, Pal Sin, Eric Kot, Jan Lam, Peter Lai, Michael Wong, Ken Lo, Mike Abbott, Louis Roth. *D:* Wong Jing. *W:* Wong Jing. *C:* Gigo Lee, Tom Lau, George Ma. *M:* James Wong, Romeo Diaz. **VHS, DVD**

City Hunter: Secret Service

World-renowned detective Ryo "Joe" Saeba, better known as City Hunter, now has a partner: Kaori, who is as tough as he is and much more disciplined. Assistant Rosa Martinez hires him as an extra bodyguard for her boss James McGuire, a reform candidate for the presidency in the Guinam Republic, now under an oppressive military regime. Though incorrigible horn-dog Saeba insists he only guards women, he changes his tune when he learns threats have been made against McGuire's daughter Anna Shinjo—who also happens to be a secret service agent assigned to McGuire. Saeba and Kaori join the security team, though their secret mission is to protect Anna. Kaori's nemesis Detective Saeko Nogami is also on the case as police representative, and was the one who recommended City Hunter.

With the requisite number of pretty women involved, Saeba has plenty of opportunities to act like a pervert—and Kaori has plenty of reason to clobber him with an oversize mallet. Anna treats her father coldly, believing it was he who shot her mother years before. Of course, it's McGuire's opponent Gonzales who is behind the threats, having hired an assassin named Dunkirk to do his shooting. Despite a change in McGuire's itinerary, some thugs almost kidnap Anna, their attempt only foiled by the dynamic actions of City Hunter. With Anna obviously protected, Gonzales has Rosa kidnapped instead, his real aim being to get McGuire to reveal the location of a rich vein of diamonds. During a rescue attempt, McGuire and Anna are captured as well, leaving it up to City Hunter—along with blind assassin Falcon Umibuzo—to stage their own rescue.

City Hunter is perhaps the most popular detective character in Japanese comics, though there doesn't seem to be anything special about him. He's the same as most American fantasy private eye characters: always surrounded by beautiful women, and better at shooting than he is at deduction. Despite this, he's been a hit in several media, including a Hong Kong feature with Jackie Chan in the lead. The animation here is flat and dull, perhaps in response to the plot, which favors melodrama over action and comedy. The director's name shows up on a tombstone in one shot, a traditional gag among cartoonists. Not so traditional are several symbols that don't translate very well—several times dragonflies or crows make tracks across the screen, most likely signifying a character reaction as nonplussed or confused. *AKA: City Hunter; Secret Police.* 🐉🐉

1996 (R) 90m/C *JP* **D:** Kenji Kodama. **W:** Akinori Endo, Kenji Kodama, Tsukasa Hojo (manga). **C:** Youichi Hasegawa. **M:** Tatsumi Yano. **VHS, DVD**

City of Desire

Social melodrama is fine if the characters are believable and if the story has a fresh take on the dilemma being portrayed. Unfortunately, this film has neither. Sandra Lui (Sandra Ng) returns to Macau from Canada for the first time in 10 years because her businessman father (Law Kar-Ying) has become incapacitated to run the family business. She is dismayed to learn that a few legitimate properties are simply cover for the real moneymakers—gambling, and especially prostitution. She is torn between empathy for the women being victimized—as epitomized by childhood friend turned gambling addict and prostitute Pepper (Josie Ho)—and the huge profits that are generated, as emphasized by her father's lieutenants, Johnny (Alex Fong) and Uncle Motor. Meanwhile, a parallel story plays out as straitlaced police officer Cat (Blackie Ko) finds himself falling for Man Sau (Alice Chan), a deaf and mute prostitute. A man in priestly garb (Anthony Wong) occasionally strolls by to offer perplexing advice.

The script by veteran scribes Manfred Wong and Bryan Chang sets up a decent premise, but fails to create truly sympathetic or realistic inhabitants of the "sinful" Macau scene. The direction by Raymond Yip is too slack, lacking tension. For example: Sandra is unhappy with the situation in which she finds her family's business, but takes little decisive action to change things for the better until far too late in the story; Pepper appears too relaxed to be desperate; neither Johnny nor Uncle Motor demonstrate any real moxie as would befit top underlings in such a sprawling enterprise; and we never see why weary veteran cop Cat begins to fall for Man Sau, other than the allure of her beguiling eyes. Still, the Macau locations are used effectively, and the flavorful musical score by Lincoln Lo is also quite enjoyable. The cinematography by Lai Yiu-fai is fairly attractive con-

sidering that the budget was likely quite low; variety is added by occasional use of documentary-style, handheld video footage. —PM *AKA: Yuk Mong Ji Shing; Yu Wang Zhi Cheng.* 🐉🐉

2001 90m/C *HK* Sandra Ng, Alex Fong, Law Kar-Ying, Josie Ho, Blackie Ko, Alice Chan, Anthony Wong, Kristy Yeung, Cheung Tat-Ming, Lau Siu-ming, Patrick Keung, Charlie Cho. **D:** Raymond Yip. **W:** Manfred Wong, Bryan Chang. **C:** Lai Yiu-fai. **M:** Lincoln Lo. **VHS, DVD**

City on Fire

This suspenseful action drama teamed rising superstar Chow Yun-fat *(A Better Tomorrow)* with 1970s Shaw Brothers contract player Danny Lee *(Inframan)* for the first time, and advanced director Ringo Lam to the "A" list among Hong Kong directors.

Burnt out, his personal life and engagement to Hung (Carrie Ng, in her first film) crumbling from the pressures of long undercover police work, Ko Chow (Chow) sends in his resignation from the force. However, his superior, Lau Ting-kwong (Sun Yueh), won't accept it until they bust the gang already responsible for another cop's death. Sam Fu (Lee) is the leader of the gang of jewelry-store robbers Chow has to infiltrate. When the gang commits a vicious robbery, Lau is forced to work with forceful young Inspector John Chan (Roy Cheung), who's willing to sacrifice cops to advance his career. Chow manages to get into the gang by selling them guns to use on their next job, going through many trials and constantly having to prove his allegiance to both the cops and the crooks. As his mission progresses, the two sides seem to become more and more alike. When a robbery goes sour, and the gang gets pinned down by police gunfire, Chow has to choose which side is truly the more honorable and deserves his allegiance.

Unfortunately, *City on Fire* has gained more recognition for being the controversial basis of Quentin Tarantino's *Reservoir Dogs* than for its own merits. This is a shame, as the distinctions of Ringo Lam's film become more apparent with each viewing. The most important factor is Chow Yun-fat, who gives a finely nuanced performance as the conflicted hero, caught between professional and personal commitments, and the friendships and fears he forms on both sides of the law. Sun Yueh also does excellent work as the mentor who both uses and tries to protect Chow. Teddy Robin Kwan's score in the original is fine, but for a change the rhythms in the U.S. version enhance the steadily building suspense Lam has created. *AKA: Lung Foo Fung Wan; Long Hu Feng Yun.* 🐉🐉🐉🐉

1987 (R) 106m/C *HK* Chow Yun-fat, Danny Lee, Sun Yueh, Roy Cheung, Carrie Ng, Lau Kong, Tommy

Chow Yun-fat

My Gun Barked: Chow Chow Chow!!

周潤發

Chow Yun-fat is possibly the first Hong Kong star you ever heard of who is not known for his martial arts movies. And though he became famous for blasting away with twin automatics in a series of films directed by John Woo, it wasn't the guns that made him a star. It's the *man.* Whatever it is that makes classic movie stars—charisma, charm, magnetism—Chow has it in spades. Anyone who has ever been in the same room with him will tell you that the camera is only a filter for his natural star power.

His story is a Cinderella one, or nearly so. Answering a newspaper ad in 1973, 18-year-old Chow was accepted in TVB's actors' training program, along with his buddy (and future director) Ringo Lam. At TVB, he was cast in more than two dozen series during the next 10 years, scoring hits with *Hotel* and *Shanghai Beach* (AKA *The Bund*). But as a movie actor, his early career could be compared to fellow TV star Bruce Willis—disappointing until he had a hit. Aside from good notices for Ann Hui's *The Story of Woo Viet*, common knowledge states that Chow was boxoffice poison before John Woo's *A Better Tomorrow* in 1985, but none of his movies were really that bad. It's just that, in hindsight, we can see the strengths presented by Woo struggling to find a way out. In movie theatres, both Woo and Chow were known for mediocre comedies. *ABT* changed all that, with Chow suddenly becoming Mark, that classic character in shades and long coat who coolly avenged his family honor against treacherous triad thugs of all stripes—with as many bullets as he could pump out.

A quartet of films with Woo stand at the center of Chow Yun-fat's image, blasting the bad guys to Hell in *A Better Tomorrow, A Better Tomorrow 2, The Killer,* and *Hard Boiled.*

By the time he left Hong Kong behind with *Peace Hotel* in 1995, Chow had racked up some 70 movie roles in all genres. He's won Best Actor awards twice in Taiwan and three times in Hong Kong. Since then, he's fought *The Replacement Killers,* exposed *The Corruptor,* ruled Thailand in *Anna and the King,* and broke a lot

of records with *Crouching Tiger, Hidden Dragon*. Of course we know Chow as *The Killer,* as the *God of Gamblers,* and as an undercover cop in *City on Fire* and *Hard Boiled*—but have you seen him as a jerk soccer player in *100 Ways to Murder Your Wife,* playing dual roles with Maggie Cheung in *The Story of Rose,* a ghostbuster in *The Seventh Curse,* or a psycho killer in the comedy *Scared Stiff?* The man may be picking his roles more carefully these days, but as you can see, he's got quite a back catalogue for fans to dig into— so let's get to it!

Wong, Victor Hon Kwan, Parkman Wong, Elvis Tsui, Fong Yeh, Chan Chi-fai, Maria Cordero. *D:* Ringo Lam. *W:* Tommy Sham. *C:* Andrew Lau. *M:* Teddy Robin Kwan, Jim Klein (U.S. version). **VHS, DVD**

City War

Chow Yun-fat and Ti Lung, the stars of *A Better Tomorrow,* are reunited for another tale of crime and bullets. Though the calm demeanor of Inspector Dick Lee (Chow) has gotten him promoted beyond his hotheaded senior Ken Chow (Ti), Ken's crafty ways still get results. Meanwhile, Ted Yiu (Norman Tsui) comes home to his fiancée Penny (Tien Niu) after a long hard stretch in prison, itching for revenge against Ken, the cop who caught him. Since Ken's partner Ho was killed recently, Ken naturally suspects Ted hired someone to do it, and gets in trouble with his superior Wu (Ricky Yi) when he confronts Ted. Dick does some dirty dancing with Penny, not knowing he's wooing his friend's enemy's girl—though he soon finds out.

Seeing the situation is heating up, Dick negotiates with Ted's grandpa Kuen (Lo Lieh) to get the two men together to talk things out. But Ted smuggles in some mainland killers to attack the Chows. Knowing the killers are coming, Penny tries to lure Dick away, and he gets back in time to save only Ken from getting shot. You know what comes next: Dick and Ken push aside their fussy commander, load up on guns, and go to hunt Ted down like the dog he is.

Old-school kung fu director Sun Chung proves he's still got it, though his action scenes do better with the martial arts than the gun fu, giving the various battles a harsh, violent edge. The atmosphere is satisfyingly gritty, and no one comes out of the movie clean. Plots like this are a dime a dozen, but Ti Lung and Chow Yun-fat manage to raise it all up a notch through sheer personality.

AKA: Sing Si Jin Jaang; Cheng Shi Zhan Zheng; Yi Dam Hung Sun; Yi Dan Hong Chun. ♫♫♫

1988 92m/C *HK* Chow Yun-fat, Ti Lung, Norman Tsui, Tien Niu, Lo Lieh, Michael Chow, Ricky Yi, Robin Shou, Lee Ka-ting, John Ladalski, Eddie Maher, Danny Lee. *D:* Sun Chung. *W:* Tung Lo, Leung Wai-ting, Rico Chung. *C:* Li Hsin-yeh. *M:* Michael Lai. **VHS, DVD**

Clean My Name, Mr. Coroner!

The wacky title hides a very decent crime drama. The titular coroner is Keith Ko (Francis Ng), a buttoned-down, straitlaced, by-the-book kind of guy. As the film opens, we see him take a work-related call that wrecks his dinner date, thanks to a conversation more suited for a morgue than a nice restaurant. No less devoted to his work is Fred Cheung (Nick Cheung), a policeman who's been undercover for five years. When his superior officer, C. K. Lau (Ti Lung), rejects his plan to use a large sum of counterfeit funds to make an arrest, Fred gets drunk and ends up in the apartment of kindhearted bartender Ling (Stephanie Che). She harbors a well-hidden attraction to Fred, her favorite regular customer. The next day, Lau has a change of heart and allows the use of the funny money, but the bust goes bad, and it looks like Fred's partner Herman took off with the cash. Still puzzling over this situation, Fred races to a rendezvous point. En route, he is stopped at a routine police blockade, and is shocked when his fellow cops discover a headless body in his trunk. Fred knows a setup when he sees one, so he goes on the lam. The body is identified as his partner's, but the facts and the evidence don't add up. Fred forcibly enlists coroner Ko to help him "clean his name." The trail points to police corruption and betrayal.

The action scenes are effective and photographed in a fresh way—look for a tersely underplayed foot chase through city streets for a good example—though, overall, the pacing does not build as it should for a straightforward action film. Known mostly for his skill at writing comedies, James Yuen stretched himself admirably in the director's chair in this outing. The acting is good, though, and the combination of action and drama works more than it doesn't. In other words, this is not a pulse-pounding high-octane thriller. The film succeeds as a character-driven police drama. —PM *AKA: Gau Geung Ying Ging; Jiu Jiang Xing Jing.* ♪♪♡

2000 101m/C *HK* Francis Ng, Nick Cheung, Ti Lung, Stephanie Che, Jerry Lamb, Joe Ma, Wayne Lai, Joe Lee, Tin Yue-lai. **D:** James Yuen. **W:** James Yuen. **C:** Fung Yuen-man. **M:** Lincoln Lo. **VHS, DVD**

Clueless

A pleasant alternative to watching reruns of *The X-Files.* In two separate but related episodes, Hong Kong Police Senior Inspector Tang Yat-see (Hacken Lee) and his partner Kim (Elvis Tsui) try to deal with baffling crimes but end up "clueless." Clueless, that is, until Yat-see's girlfriend Helen (Siu Suet) introduces the idea that legends and supernatural forces may be involved. The cleaning lady at the police station, known only as Blind Woman (Helena Law), provides solid clues for Yat-see.

Dividing the film into two episodes is a bit awkward. On the one hand, the plots are not extended unnecessarily and everything is tied up neatly. On the other hand, just when the characters become engaging in the first story, it's time for the mechanics of the second story to begin spinning. The direction by Ally Wong is straightforward; the script by Sam Wong holds a couple of cleverly set-up minor surprises. Hacken Lee and Siu Suet have a relaxed and sometimes playful chemistry that adds to the modest charms of the film. Elvis Tsui is agreeably sharp as Kim; Ben Ng is suitably wacko as the rape suspect Chan Wing-keung in the first episode (a wry reference to his fame playing a rapist in *Red to Kill* and other 1990s horrors). Chan Yiu-ming's cinematography uses blue filters in nearly every scene; the use of blue as a predominant color should mean something integral to the plot or characters, yet here it seems to have been employed merely as a stylistic device. The musical score by Carlton Chu is quite good, mixing a wide variety of styles in an effective manner. —PM *AKA: Bat Gaai Ji Mai; Bue Jie Zhi Mi.* ♪♪

2001 88m/C *HK* Hacken Lee, Siu Suet, Elvis Tsui, Ben Ng, Helena Law, Hui Siu-hung. **D:** Ally Wong. **W:** Sam Wong. **C:** Chan Yiu-ming. **M:** Carlton Chu. **VHS, DVD**

Code of Honor

Released shortly after Chow Yun-fat became an overnight boxoffice success via *A Better Tomorrow,* distributors of this triad picture took full advantage of his minor presence in the cast by plastering his name and image all over the advertising, a trend that continues through its video life and onto DVD. Shot in a gritty style similar to that used for *Long Arm of the Law,* it offers other aspects a bit out of the ordinary other than the style itself, including a subtext dealing with the Vietnamese refugee camps in Hong Kong.

Ho Chen-tung (O Chun Hung) is an aging triad chief who can't stomach the violence of the gangster life anymore, and makes increasing efforts to run his organization as a legitimate business, atoning for past crimes by donating to charities. However, the police squad led by Inspector Mak Chih-chieh (Dick Wei) has been tracking him for decades, and won't give up on any chance to send him to prison. He has just as big a problem with his underlings, some of whom have only known success doing business the old way, and don't see the sense in going straight when it was the easy—though dangerous—life of crime that drew them to their positions in the triad in the first place. When Li Piao (Shing Fui-on) makes a savage attack on Mak's brother in a restaurant, it enables the cop to arrest him and get some leverage on his investigation into Ho's affairs. His associate in Tokyo, Yudaki (Shinichi Ihara), and several others are also arrested, and Ho is shocked when they all cut a deal with the cops and testify against him. Wang Han (Lam Wai), an old non-triad Vietnamese friend loyal to Ho, decides to get even with the squealers by hunting them down and dispatching them in bloody fashion. With the witnesses dead, Ho is released, but Mak continues to pursue Ho, and his main effort is ironically centered on pinning the murders on his quarry.

The standout feature here is the savagery provided by action director Power Lee King-chue for several brutal fights and suspenseful chase scenes. Director Billy Chan gives the film a remarkably even-handed tone, leading the viewer to root for opposing characters at different times, and even within the same sequence. The ensemble cast does wonderful work, adding to the atmosphere of struggle as they all seem to be trying to keep their own kind of order—only to see their efforts result in chaos. Chow has only a small part as O Chun Hung's son, but don't let that stop you from giving this picture a chance. *AKA: Yee Boon Mo Yin; Yi Ben Wu Yan; Brotherhood; Triad Savagers; Triad Savages.* ♪♪♪

1987 88m/C *HK* O Chun Hung, Lam Wai, Dick Wei, Shum Wai, Chow Yun-fat, Shing Fui-on, Dennis

Chan, Lung Ming-yan, Lam Gei-yan, Danny Lee, Shinichi Ihara, Chui Sau-lai, Sunny Fang, William Oscar Sun. **D:** Billy Chan. **W:** Wong Ying, Hoh Cheuk-wing, Billy Chung. **C:** Cheung Tak-wai. **M:** Richard Yuen. **VHS, DVD**

The Cold Mountain Temple

Hanshan (Cold Mountain) Temple is located in Maple Bridge town in the west outskirts of Suzhou. It was first built in the Tianjian period of the Liang dynasty (502–557) with the name of Miaolita Yuan (Miaolita Temple). During the Tang dynasty (618–907), a famous monk named Hanshan was said to have lived and been in charge of the temple, and then the name was changed to Hanshan Temple. The riverway to the Cold Mountain Temple is treacherous. Because of a corrupt Ching Dynasty government, bandits patrol the waters and even devout pilgrims may be attacked. Two merchant families fall victim to one such assault. The elders are killed, and their children barely escape the dark waters with their lives. One child—Tammy—goes to the temple, where she learns amazing wire-induced kung fu techniques (such as performing great leaps and walking on water); another—Leon—finds himself ward of the corrupt bureaucracy (after his only surviving relative is killed). Tammy teams up with rebel Suzie May to recover the stolen lotus cup and bring down the corrupt governor. Leon resists helping, even when it is revealed that the governor was part of the plot that kills his parents. This all leads to a huge mass kung fu battle at the Temple at the end of the film.

Despite distracting anachronistic dubbing by Jalisco, this film is filled with cool martial arts and pretty decent f/x. The plot is a bit choppy, but the action more than makes up for deficiencies on the story front. The box copy doesn't match the dubbed film in terms of character names. —SS **AKA:** *Zhong Ming Han Shan Si; The Bell Tolls in the Cold Mountain Temple; Cold Mountain Temple Master.* 🐉🐉🐲

1991 70m/C CH Wang Zhonliang, Lu Yan, Huang Wei, Zhang Shuyu, Liu Jing. **D:** Tang Yanlin. **W:** Jiang Di-An. **C:** Sun Chang-yi, Xing Pei-xiu. **VHS, DVD**

Cold War

Top professional killer Ka Kui (Simon Yam) is sent to Seoul by his agent Maria (Christy Chung) on an assignment. His target is Taiwanese arms smuggler Chue Chung, though younger brother Yung (Vincent Wan) is the smart and dangerous one. Ka starts to suspect that something is wrong when he learns that his last 12 targets

have all been gangsters in Chue Chung's operation. That means whoever hired him may be taking over once Chue Chung is out of the way—and he may become a target himself to keep him quiet. Indeed, it's Yung who is ordering the hits, and Maria has been ordered to kill Ka herself. Detectives Wu and Jing are after the Chues themselves. Unwittingly, they interrupt the mission by hanging around Chung just as Ka is getting ready to strike. Maria distracts them so Ka can pursue his target. Kinko (Kinko), a shy young prostitute, gets shot trying to save Ka's life, so after shooting Chung, Ka risks his own neck to take her to a hospital. At the rendezvous point, Maria finds she's grown too attached to Ka to pull the trigger. But after Yung reminds her of the loyalty she owes him, she decides to try again. What's more, she admits to Ka that she was the one who killed his wife three years ago. However, she fails again, and dies while she and Yung's lieutenant blast away at each other. Ka is injured, and this time it's Kinko's turn to rescue him. Wu and Jing have been keeping an eye on the lone murder witness, and they're soon closing in on Ka Kui. Forced to go on the run, Ka has time to get to know Kinko better, while plotting his revenge on Chue Yung.

This hit-man thriller is mostly a routine affair, looking like a much older picture than it is, and distinguished only by the novelty of the South Korean locations and actors. Yam does little to define his character—his lone personality trait is the way he stubs out cigarettes. It makes little sense that Yung, now head of a huge criminal organization, would be hunting down a hired assassin on his own, but that's what he does. At least the ending shows a little spirit, but not much. **AKA:** *Laang Chin; Leng Zhan.* 🐲🐲

2000 91m HK/KO Simon Yam, Christy Chung, Vincent Wan, Lee Yak-choi, Yeung On-tung, Kinko, Leung Kar-yan. **D:** Leung Kar-yan. **W:** Leung Kar-yan, Law Kam-fai. **C:** Ross Clarkson. **VHS, DVD**

Color of Pain

Within the first dozen minutes, writer/director Sam Leung references three John Woo classics (*The Killer, A Better Tomorrow, Bullet in the Head*), setting the tone for his take on the "doomed assassin involved with a troubled cop" genre (add *Hard Boiled* to the John Woo reference points). Ryuya, an extremely cool Japanese assassin (Kenya Sawada), is shot in the head on his latest job. He survives, but is told that the bullet will eventually kill him. By chance he happens upon a bank robbery in progress. Volunteering as a hostage, he decides to join the gang (led by Terence Yin as Dino; the other members of the gang are played by Sam Lee as Cat, the comic relief, and Tony Ho as Doggie, the

hothead.). The three thieves are confounded but capitulate because he is such a superior fighter. Meanwhile, Joe (Raymond Wong Ho-yin), a young, intense police sniper, is still dealing with guilt from accidentally shooting a policewoman in the line of duty. After undergoing psychological treatment and doing desk work for months, he is reassigned to field work as a sniper by his tough-as-nails superior (Josie Ho). His unit must track down the gang of thieves. The assassin and the sniper must cross paths and resolve their individual, painful conflicts.

Although numerous sequences are drenched in slow motion, Leung is less interested in Woo-style bravura set-pieces and themes of brotherhood. Instead, he seems to be after something more elusive: what happens to men when faced with pain? That's the ostensible subject matter. Along the way, Leung becomes a bit too preoccupied with style over substance, and sabotages the story. Major lapses in credulity at key turning points do not help. In the first bank robbery, for example, the team need only speed away for two blocks before the threat of arrest is eliminated. But as a young director Lueng shows a lot of promise. And the performances are very good, especially by Sawada and the three members of the gang. Lam Suet delivers a nice bit as a former police sharpshooter relegated to desk work. Adam Chan (Her Name Is Cat, Martial Angels) choreographed the often fierce action. —PM **AKA:** Yau Long; Ye Lang. 🎵🎵🎺

2002 96m/C HK Kenya Sawada, Raymond Wong Ho-yin, Terence Yin, Sam Lee, Tony Ho, Lam Suet, Josie Ho. **D:** Sam Leung. **W:** Sam Leung. **C:** Joe Chan. **M:** Kiyoshi Yoshikawa. **VHS, DVD**

Combo Cops

A nutty comic action film in the traditional Asian kitchen sink style, using cartoon f/x and liberal amounts of pop-culture parody. Mainland Super Cop Hwang Fei (Yu Rongguang of The Enforcer) gets a page—the police are engaged in a huge gun battle with drug-runners on the edge of town. Instantly, Hwang Fei switches from his street clothes to his combat fatigues, jumps on his motorcycle, and rushes off to save the day. His friend Officer Lin becomes a hostage of the last remaining crook, and a miscalculation leaves her infant son severely injured. Hwang is given a cushy assignment in Hong Kong, where his sister Mona (Christine Ng) is also a cop. Officer Lin, not one to spoil her baby, agrees to give him over to the government to raise as the next 007.

Scotland Yard–trained Superintendent James Fok (Michael Wong) has achieved the status of a supercop himself in the HK Royal Police. At a cocktail party initiating the Special Duty Unit, it's love at first sight for James and Mona, as colorful lightning bolts connect their eyes. Disapproving Hwang and Fok are assigned together to train the SDU. With two such strong leaders, half the men decide to follow Fok's Westernized training, while others learn Old World kung fu instruction from Hwang. However, on their first mission, they fail to keep Tiger's (Law Kar-Ying) gang of thieves from stealing a rare painting, and Hwang is shot protecting Fok. Using information coerced from a captured crook, Fok and his team are determined to bust the gang and retrieve the painting in time for its exhibition.

This reunification comedy works in daft send-ups of James Bond, The Seven Year Itch, John Woo movies, Silence of the Lambs, Wong Fei-hung, Organized Crime and Triad Bureau, Untold Story, and dozens of other references unknown to Western viewers. Yuen King-Tan does a bizarre but very funny send-up of an abused but loyal gun moll. **AKA:** Gwok Chaan Suet Gap Wai Lung; Guo Chan Xue Ge Wei Long. 🎵🎵🎺

1996 90m/C HK Michael Wong, Yu Rongguang, Law Kar-Ying, Christine Ng, Manfred Wong, Yuen King-Tan. **D:** Yui Man-Kei, Wong Siu Ming. **W:** So Jing Man. **C:** George Ma. **M:** Tang Siu-lam. **VHS**

Comeuppance

Three men are found dead, killed by cyanide poisoning, in the VIP room of a bar. One of the men is a triad member. Police investigator Michael (Sunny Chan) begins probing the case, which may involve a rival gang. Reporter Hak (Jordan Chan) takes on the job of writing a fictional serial for his newspaper, based on the crime. Soon enough, the killer is revealed to be a former film-processing lab worker named Sung (Patrick Tam). Gangsters continue to be knocked off by Sung using various poisoning methods as the three main characters are inexplicably drawn closer together.

Sunny Chan plays Michael as a calm and experienced detective, not terribly distressed by the killings since the victims are all bad guys, possibly receiving their "comeuppance" as his girlfriend suggests at one point. As the just-trying-to-get-by reporter Hak, Jordan Chan is disheveled and opportunistic. He becomes rattled and nervous when the real killer apparently begins drawing inspiration from Hak's fictional killer's murderous exploits. Patrick Tam roughly parallels Sunny Chan in his calm and deliberate nature. The pace of the film reflects the personalities of its three main characters. For the most part it is unhurried and sometimes a bit slow. On the other hand, the pace allows the story to breathe and the audience to follow the sometimes-tricky plot twists. Director Derek Chiu keeps the camera moving constantly and uses camera angles that are sometimes too clever for their own good—by being so off-the-wall that they distract. Yet it is his inventiveness that keeps interest alive in the drama being played out, and each of his stylized moves seems to be used for a reason. Cinematographer Tony Cheung employs a natural-light approach to emphasize the near-documentary feel. The musical score enlivens without drawing attention to itself. —*PM* **AKA:** *Tin Yau Aan; Tian You Yan; Heaven's Assassin, Heaven Has Eyes.*

2000 102m/C *HK* Jordan Chan, Patrick Tam, Sunny Chan, Wu Hsing-kuo, Joe Lee, Benny Li, Crystal Lui. *D:* Derek Chiu. *W:* Zevia Tong, Derek Chiu, Benny Li. *C:* Tony Cheung. *M:* Chan Sau-pok, Gordon O'Yang, Leung Yiu-pak. **VHS, DVD**

Comic King

Though the comic-book business in America has appeared to be headed toward obsolescence many times since its heyday in the 1940s, in actuality the industry has grown and expanded, developing a tenacious grip on its niche in the entertainment industry. In Asia, where languages and dialects number in the hundreds but pictures speak to everyone, the business exploded, especially in Japan. This HK comedy follows in the footsteps of such U.S. media satires as *Artists and Models* and *The Girl Can't Help It,* wrapping the commentary around a romantic comedy core.

Yip Fung (Eason Chan) is among the young hopefuls that line up and pay (!) for the chance to be hired as assistant artists for the Great Empire comics company, while his slacker friend Mo Wan (Julian Cheung) chooses to skate in the back door, getting them both jobs by dint of his boot-licking skills. Fung's talents and Wan's guile keep them from being ousted by temperamental editor Yeung Lo (Hacken Lee) or the insane boss Lo Siu-fu (Liu Wai-hung, looking like a cartoon himself with huge glasses), and they manage to get their own title (at no extra pay, of course), "The Untouchable." When sales begin to rise, Lo tries to coerce the boys into a lifetime contract and dilute their creativity by giving them each separate titles.

They retaliate by going to Wan's grandmother Queen of Mahjong (Helena Law), who creates a business plan for them to go into publishing for themselves. In order to get Lo to fire them (and collect severance), the boys sabotage their book by killing off a main character. Their first self-published project, "Knife, Sword and Smile" (a definite swipe at *Storm Riders*), is a big success. While they work, both guys fall for editorial assistant Mandy (Ruby Lin), and when Wan gets the idea for another book aimed at the triad audience (lampooning the *Young and Dangerous* series), it deepens the hidden resentment between the two creators. Dividing to conquer, Great Empire publishes the heroic triad book (essentially the same series in a different setting), making a big splash. While Fung founders on his own, Wan finds it hard to keep coming up with ideas by himself, and a toy knife giveaway scheme is a disaster.

Unlike so many others that attempt to portray cartoonists, the filmmakers here have done their homework, getting the nuts and bolts details of the business right. The only real concession to cinema is that everyone works together in an office, instead of freelancing from home. Whereas musicals have used song and dance to illustrate the characters' inner conflicts—and martial arts films have done the same through stylized combat—here the drama between characters is enacted through their comics creations (played by Nicholas Tse, Jerry Lamb, and Tats Lau, with plenty of f/x dazzle). However, the story is the same old show biz plotline, and the comics fantasy sequences come off as a gimmick. It might have worked better to animate these sequences, but for some reason very little artwork is shown—an odd thing for a movie about comic books.

2000 95m/C *HK* Julian Cheung, Eason Chan, Ruby Lin, Nicholas Tse, Hacken Lee, Liu Wai-hung, Spencer Lam, Helena Law, Jerry Lamb, Tats Lau. *D:* O Sing-pui. *W:* Chris Lau. *C:* Chan Siu-gwan. **DVD**

Comrades, Almost a Love Story

A gleamingly beautiful tale that looks at romance from street level. The date is March 1, 1986. Freshly arrived in Hong Kong from his home in Northern China, Li Xiao Jin (Leon Lai) is overwhelmed by the city. He has emigrated to make a better life for himself and for the girlfriend he left behind, the sweet and trusting Xiao-ting (Kristy Yeung). He finds living quarters in the home of Aunt Rosie (Irene Tsu), who works as a Madam. Eventually he forms a friendship and a tentative romance with the lovely and ambitious Li Chiao (Maggie Cheung). She takes advantage of him, and then reluctantly helps him, and then—against her more avaricious instincts—is drawn to him. Their almost-romance is played out over a period of years.

The script is very good, although it takes some too-predictable turns as the story progresses. The direction is brilliant, allowing some scenes to play out in silence and others without music, heightening the impact at certain key points. Maggie Cheung is the emotional core of the film as Li Chiao. Many of her best scenes are extremely quiet as the camera captures the

THE HOUND SALUTES
Maggie Cheung

Can you pick out the moment when Maggie Cheung Man-Yuk's life changed?

She told *Interview* magazine (April 1998): "During the making of Wong Kar-Wai's first film as director, *As Tears Goes By* (1988), I started to realize that if you really want to act, you have to use different kinds of energies and strengths than you do if you're just making a career of being on magazine covers, of being 'well-known.' In a way, Wong Kar-Wai was my first acting teacher."

That's rather a remarkable statement when you realize that Maggie had already acted in more than a dozen films by that point of her career. It's understandable that it might take a while to come to that realization, though, in view of the frenetic pace of the Hong Kong film industry during the 1980s. For example, during the same year in which she was receiving her "first" acting lessons, Maggie appeared in a *dozen* other films!

Maggie never planned on becoming a movie star. Born in Hong Kong in September 1964, Maggie lived in England for a good chunk of her childhood. She remembers *Quadrophenia* as being the first influential film she saw, and loved British ska groups like Madness and the Specials. Offered a modeling contract after returning to Hong Kong in her late teens, her agency put her up for the Miss Hong Kong and Miss World beauty pageants. The contests led to roles on television and then in the movies.

Her big break came via a prototypical "girlfriend" role in Jackie Chan's *Police Story* in 1985. She was adorable as Jackie's long-suffering gal pal and made a very favorable impression with local audiences. She was cast in seven films during the next couple of years—including *Police Story 2*. The offers were pouring in when Wong Kar-Wai implored her to accept a part in his directorial debut. *As Tears Go By* was financially successful but, more importantly, Wong Kar-Wai gave Maggie "the confidence to believe that I could be serious about my work, and that acting could be appreciated as a skill and an art; that there was more to it than facial expressions and reaction shots. He helped me understand that it was more about working from within." Maggie was rewarded with her first Hong Kong Film Awards Best Actress nomination.

Maggie continued to make comedies, dramas, crime flicks, and action epics over the next few years. She won her first Best Actress prize at the Hong Kong Film Awards for *A Fishy Story* in 1989, worked with Wong Kar-Wai again *(Days of Being Wild)*, and won acclaim—and another Best Actress award—for Stanley Kwan's *Centre Stage* (AKA *Actress*) in 1992. She played a super-heroine in Johnny To's *The Heroic Trio* and its sequel *The Executioners*—which led to another turning point in her life.

The busy schedule—an incredible 43 films between 1989 and 1994—was wearing Maggie down. After completing the exhausting and extended production of Wong Kar-Wai's *Ashes of Time,* Maggie took a break that stretched into two years. She traveled, played golf and tennis, and developed her interest in photography.

Having recharged her batteries, she was open to new experiences, but was quite surprised to receive a script in the mail with an offer to play a character named "Maggie Cheung" in a film to be directed by Frenchman Olivier Assayas. Deciding that, at the minimum, she would be able to hang out in France, Maggie accepted the part. *Irma Vep* was her first English-language role (she has a delightful British accent) and also introduced her to the man she would eventually marry, director Assayas.

In the years since, Maggie has been quite selective in deciding which offers to accept, and has so far been resistant to the aggressive self-promotion that a Hollywood career would require. Still, she has won three more Best Actress awards *(Comrades, Almost a Love Story*; *The Soong Sisters*; and Wong Kar-Wai's *In the Mood for Love)* and acted in the English-language *The Chinese Box* and the French-language *Augustin, King of Kung Fu.* Her latest projects include Zhang Yimou's *Hero,* Christophe Gans's *The Adventurer,* and Wong Kar-Wai's *2046.*

Maggie Cheung has grown up on-screen. She has morphed from a baby-faced ingenue into a complex, fully nuanced woman. And she continues to break hearts.

—*PM*

"Are you crazy? We have a huge age difference."

—Andy Lau raises a question that never seems to bother other actors in *The Conman*

look in her eyes and face as she responds to words or actions that are heartrending. Without doing anything to draw attention to herself, she shows the changes in her character's personality over a period of time. As the naïve and well-intentioned Li Xiao-Jin, Leon Lai does not quite measure up to her performance, yet he complements her quite well. Good support is given by Irene Tsu as Aunt Rosie, Eric Tsang as Paau Goh, and Christopher Doyle (best known as Wong Kar-Wai's cinematographer) as Jeremy, an English teacher and later the boyfriend of Cabbage, a prostitute who works for Aunt Rosie. Songs by famed Mainland singer Teresa Teng figure prominently. The cinematography by Jingle Ma is beautiful, making cityscapes look lush. Even Eric Tsang's back glows. —*PM* **AKA:** *Tim Mat Ma; Tian Mi Mi.* 🐉🐉🐉🐲

1996 116m/C *HK* Maggie Cheung, Leon Lai, Kristy Yeung, Christopher Doyle, Eric Tsang, Joe Cheung, Irene Tsu, Ding Yue. **D:** Peter Chan. **W:** Ivy Ho. **C:** Jingle Ma. **M:** Chiu Tsang-Hei. **DVD**

The Conman

Wong Jing goes back to the well one more time with this attempt to do for confidence men what *God of Gamblers* did for punters, using one of the stars of the *GoG* series as his lead. Sharp King (Andy Lau) refuses to let it distract him when his pregnant wife Fanny (Angie Cheung) finds him with his mistress—after all, he's worked too hard to set up a card-game sting on gambler Bad Temper. But the cheat is discovered, resulting in a vicious fight. King comes out of it with a cracked skull and a five-year sentence for killing Bad Temper in self-defense. King uses his time to improve his cheating skills, while both the women in his life disappear, along with his ability to see colors. Cheap gangster Dragon (Nick Cheung) is excited when his boss and King's brother Liang tells him to pick up his idol from prison and show him a good time.

Dragon's sister Ching (Athena Chu) rents him a room, and King soon has his horse-betting system setup, while he schools Dragon in other games. Though he seems intent on finding Fanny, King grows more attracted to Ching, and helps Dragon expose her "Princeton student" boyfriend Raymond Chow (!) as a gigolo. King's ambition is to match wits with his idol, the famed "Macau Mon" Ma Kau-mon (Jack Kao), but runs into trouble when it turns out that Mon's right-hand man, Handsome San Ken (Waise Lee, with his head completely shaved), is Bad Temper's little brother. Handsome, who claims no interest in revenge, forces King to challenge his boss, betraying him for a big score.

Some martial arts films suffer from too much talk and not enough action. This movie is

infected with the same malady, concentrating on the drama when it ought to be constructing complex and clever plots. As Waise Lee says at one point, "It's like a soap opera." It seems that the color-blind angle will become significant at some point, but it never does. The finale is suitably audacious though, involving a faked broadcast of the World Cup Championship, including commercials! Followed by *Conman in Vegas* and *Conman in Tokyo.* **AKA:** *Diy Hap 1999; Du Xia 1999; The Conman 1999.* 🐉🐉🐉

1998 107m/C *HK* Andy Lau, Nick Cheung, Athena Chu, Angie Cheung, Ben Ng, Emotion Cheung, Jack Kao, Waise Lee, Frankie Ng, Karel Wong, Bonnie Law, Wong Jing. **D:** Wong Jing. **W:** Wong Jing. **C:** Ko Chiu-lam. **M:** Lincoln Lo. **DVD**

Conman in Tokyo

Ching Siu-Tung, the celebrated director of such films as *Duel to the Death, A Chinese Ghost Story,* and *Swordsman 2,* did not seem like the obvious choice to direct a late entry in the "conman" series of movies, but he produced an entertaining mish-mash. Jersey (Nick Cheung) aspires to be a great gambler. He appears to have reached the pinnacle of his profession after winning a pool match against his top competition. The jazzy editing as well as the mocking song he and his friends sing help set the tone for this silly flick. An old-timer puts things in perspective by telling Jersey that he's nothing in comparison to Cool, the greatest gambler in all of Asia, legendary for his mastery of "flying cards." Cool disappeared mysteriously three years before. Still pondering this, Jersey agrees to a shopping trip in Japan to appease his girlfriend Nancy (Christy Chung). They end up in a restaurant where they encounter the owner (Louis Koo), who deftly defends himself against local gangsters with a trick reminiscent of the legendary "flying cards." Though he initially denies it, the owner is indeed Cool. He reveals that he retired after his former partner and close friend Yeung (Ben Lam) betrayed him, stealing away and marrying Cool's girlfriend Karen (Athena Chu). Yeung delights in humiliating poor Karen—even urinating in her bath water—but his real desire is to smoke out Cool and defeat him publicly, once and for all.

The plot is easier to follow than to describe and really just serves as an excuse for goofy Wong Jing–style crass comedy and a few nifty "flying card" tricks. All the performers are adequate to the roles they play, and director Ching Siu-Tung keeps the action rolling along, no matter how improbable it sometimes appears—just watch the concluding action set on a moored aircraft carrier for inspired insanity. Despite the jovial tone, much of the violence carries a nasty and violent edge.

The film runs a bit long at 103 minutes and could have lost a couple of scenes. —*PM* *AKA: Chung Wa Diy Hap; Zhong Hua Du Xia.* 🐉🐉💧

2000 103m/C *HK* Nick Cheung, Louis Koo, Christy Chung, Athena Chu, Ben Lam, Leung Kar-yan, Yasuaki Kurata, Joe Cheng. *D:* Ching Siu-Tung. *C:* Ko Chiu-lam. **VHS, DVD**

Contract Killer

Yakuza head man Tsukamoto is murdered by a highly skilled assassin known as the King of Killers, and a reward of $100 million goes into effect automatically. Every killer in Asia tries to get in on the action, though grandson Eiji (Keiji Sato) thinks the family should take care of things themselves, even daring to eat the old man's ashes in contempt of the revenge plan—but Eiji is forced to join the hunt himself as one of the contesting assassins. Martin, the man running the revenge corporation, sells Eiji inside information—before he sells it to the others. In a borrowed suit, down-on-his-luck soldier Fu (Jet Li) goes after the job, too, but only gets his chance through an agent he meets named Norman Liu (Eric Tsang). But Liu is really a con man trying to get in on the assassination game, and Fu is too softhearted to carry out his first hit in front of the target's family.

Lieutenant Chan (Simon Yam) leads a team investigating the murder for the police, while also keeping an eye on the contract killers. There's an oddly out-of-place scene in which Liu's law-student daughter Kiki (Gigi Leung) befriends Fu so that he'll keep an eye on her father, an obvious ploy to generate some audience sympathy. A key figure in the plot is an old man named Leung, who turns out to have hired Liu to kill Tsukamoto in revenge for World War II murders, and when the target really turns up dead, Liu fears that he'll be fingered as the King of Killers. His fears come true, and only Fu can protect him from the legion of contract killers that come gunning for them—though the real King of Killers may lend a hand.

The awkward melodrama only serves to give Eric Tsang another quirky character to play. There's plenty of action, though not enough pure martial arts demonstrations to make this a favorite among Jet Li's fans—more a combination of gun fu with some kicks thrown in. A fight in an elevator shaft is probably the film's best moment. The U.S. version is missing a few minutes and has been given a stupid rap theme, which only serves to annoy and distract from the onscreen action whenever it appears. *AKA: Sat Sau Ji Wong; Hitman; King of Assassins.* 🐉🐉💧

1998 (R) 104m/C *HK* Jet Li, Eric Tsang, Simon Yam, Gigi Leung, Keiji Sato, Paul Rapovski, Kim Yip, Hidari Meiken, Timmy Ho, Kenji Sahara, Frankie Ng, Chen Tung, Hiroshi Kato. *D:* Stephen Tung. *W:* Chan Hing-ka, Vincent Kok, Cheng Kam-fu. *C:* Arthur Wong. *M:* Jussi Tegelman, Teddy Robin Kwan. **VHS, DVD**

Cop on a Mission

When three thugs attempt a restaurant robbery of the King of Pimps, inept patrolman Mike (Daniel Wu) has to shoot everyone, while his partner doesn't even fire a round. Despite the influence of his father's partner, Officer Cheung, Mike is put on suspension. In a video game parlor, Mike makes the acquaintance of triad kingpin Yum King Tin (Eric Tsang). Next day, Cheung asks him to resign as part of an undercover assignment.

Within two months, Mike is working as a valet within the Hung Hing triad organization, where he gets an opportunity to save Tin's wife Pauline (Suki Kwan) from a rival gang raid. Hired by Tin as a bodyguard, Mike is granted control of some territory when he efficiently eliminates a troublesome boss. Pauline's gambling debts go too far, and Mike is called upon to rescue her once again. Tin is impotent from an injury, leaving Pauline bored and lonely. Mike is lonely from his long time undercover, and the two can't resist starting an affair.

Mike's friend Chung (David Lee) is also undercover, yet Mike is forced to kill him when Chung is discovered to protect the operation. But is Mike still working to bust the triad, or has he become one? The longer he plays his role, the more difficult it becomes to be sure of his motivation. In any case, Tin may suspect both his affair and that he's a cop, and he can't decide which secret is more dangerous. When Tin is kidnapped, Mike goes over the edge and finds out where his loyalties really lie.

Director Marco Mak does a fine job in this crime drama, presenting the gradual blurring of the lines between hero and villain. Shot with plenty of 21st-century editing tricks, *Cop on a Mission* is commonly compared with American gang movies such as *GoodFellas*, but you could still draw parallels with much earlier crime flicks like *Public Enemy*. Wu is good in the lead, but Eric Tsang easily walks off with the movie as the noble mob boss. A true veteran of Hong Kong show business, Tsang started out as a stuntman in the 1970s, before co-founding Cinema City and becoming a respected actor, director, and producer. Asian audiences still know him best as a comedian who often hosts game shows and award ceremonies. Lincoln Lo's winsome honky-tonk theme song gets to be annoying. *AKA: Chi Faat Fan Faat; ZhiFa Fan Fa.* 🐉🐉🐉

2001 102m/C *HK* Daniel Wu, Eric Tsang, Suki Kwan, David Lee, Ng An-ya, Frankie Ng, Richard Cheung Kuen, Lam Suet, Tony Ho, Karel Wong, Wong

Shu Tong, Samuel Kwok. **D:** Marco Mak. **W:** Not A Woman. **C:** Tony Miu. **M:** Lincoln Lo. **VHS, DVD**

Cop Shop Babes

From the ads and title, one might mistake this for a sex comedy, but this is more in the way of a small-scale *Charlie's Angels*. Beer (Eason Chan) and Satay (Jerry Lamb) are partner CID officers, a rough parody of those in cop films like *Bullets over Summer*. When they get in a fix trying to arrest a criminal named Rhino and his gang (who happen to be disguised as circus clowns!), their butts are saved by the beautiful kung fu fightin' Cop Shop Babes of the Hong Kong East District Police Station. After their impressive introduction, Beer and Satay immediately put in for transfer to East District. As it happens, they arrive the same day as FBI Agent Katie "Alien" Goodman (Cathy Chui, who always speaks English), who is there studying triads, so we get an easy introduction to the Babes: Peggy "PC" Wong (Lee San-San), Bony (Rachel Fu), AV-King (Yuen King-Tan, in another she-wolf role—though this time dubbed in a sultry voice), Dynamite (Lam Wai-ling), Sis (Lillian Ho), and their supervisor Madam Mona Lui (Carina Lau). The first order of monkey business is for the boys to bust their former informer Eggplant (Cheung Tat-Ming), who is trying to beat an arrest by disguising himself as an abused teenage girl (!), and has convinced Lui, Sis, PC, and Bony to take him home (where Katie is also visiting) for a few days. But the officers soon have bigger problems—there's a mad bomber called Fireball (Tony Ho) operating in the area, and his main target seems to be the Cop Shop Babes.

Though some of the humor is based in local culture, this comedy from Storm Riders is so full of good-natured nonsense that it may have you laughing in spite of yourself. Wong Jing has an odd role as mad Dr. Auyeung—AKA "Mr. Biting," for his habit of biting criminals—who deactivates most of the bombs, and does a Hannibal Lecter routine with Lau. For a movie where buildings and phone booths keep getting blown up, the action is somewhat subdued. **AKA:** *Ching Lui Cha Goon.* 🐉🐉🐲

2001 96m/C *HK* Eason Chan, Jerry Lamb, Carina Lau, Lillian Ho, Lee San-San, Rachel Fu, Cathy Chui, Lam Wai-ling, Yuen King-Tan, Cheung Tat-Ming, Li Fai, Joe Ma, Karel Wong, Tony Ho, Wong Jing, E-Lin. **D:** Aman Chang. **W:** Szeto Cheuk-hon. **C:** Joe Chan. **M:** Lincoln Lo. **VHS, DVD**

Could You Kill My Husband Please?

Body Heat it ain't. Chui San (Jade Leung) has made an effort to be a "traditional" wife to her businessman husband Ching Po. But she has become increasingly dissatisfied by his devotion to work and inattention to her. Desperate, she invites herself along on one of his business trips to Shanghai, thinking they can spend some time together. When Ching Po discovers an irregularity in the branch office finances, he decides to return immediately to Hong Kong to correct matters. Upset, Chui San remains in Shanghai and camps out in a bar. After she's had a few drinks, Wu Man He (Michael Wong) approaches her and subsequently hears her drunken declaration that she wants someone to kill her husband. He decides to take her up on her offer.

Jade Leung looks ravishing and does well with a thankless and poorly written role. Michael Wong's performance as Wu Man He is dreadful—or so it seems. The entire film was post-synched, and the actor chosen to dub Wong's voice has a very deep baritone voice that sounds completely out of place coming from Michael Wong's lips. Some of the music is enjoyable, ranging from a light Spanish guitar to a little techno pop beat. Otherwise the film is entirely without merit. The post-synched dubbing is terrible—it rarely matches with the on-screen performances. The plot is crashingly obvious and boring. As for the direction, let's just say that Michael Wong and the actor who portrays the lead police investigator both look like they can barely keep from laughing at the dialogue. The film never builds to anything, the action scenes are flat, many scenes run on too long, and the others are poorly paced. Despite the brief running time, you'd need artificial stimulation to stay awake. —*PM* 🐲

2001 86m/C *HK* Jade Leung, Michael Wong. **D:** Yiu Tin-hung. **W:** Tam Wai-shing. **DVD**

Crack Shadow Boxers

Pai San (Ku Feng) and Wu Lung (Han Gwok-choi) are a pair of wandering con men, selling fake aphrodisiacs using phony kung fu tricks. One village is being terrorized by a bandit gang, led by Tiger (San Kwai), the chief of Monkey Hill, and the mayor sends for two heroes from the city to save them. Pai and Wu arrive just in time to be mistaken for the mercenaries, and take advantage of the town's hospitality until they can figure out a way to escape without fighting the bandits. The bandits have caught the two real fighters easily on their way into town, and naturally assume they've made a mistake when they learn two heroes have arrived, believing the real McCoy must be much better fighters. The two fakers' reputation grows when they manage to capture two of the bandits—Wu beats Wolf accidentally with his "Stumbling Style," while an

overdose of aphrodisiacs temporarily gives Pai enough extra energy to beat Leopard (Dai Sai Aan). While pretending to make preparations for a showdown, Pai and Wu make a break for it, but have an attack of conscience when they learn Tiger has sent for a terror known as Golden Lion to help.

Pairing Ku Feng and Han Gwok-choi as a comic kung fu duo is a stroke of genius, as they display a lot of screen chemistry. Unfortunately, the Cantonese comedy material they have to work with here gives new meaning to the term broad comedy, with the accent on the broad. A prostitute called the Tigress has photos of her 11 late husbands in her bedroom (including Jack Nicholson, Lo Lieh, and Bruce Lee!), and has her sights on Ku Feng for the 12th spot. Another highlight is the odd performance of San Kwai, whose bandit chief acts a bit crackers since banging his head trying to get in the Tigress's bed. The heroes' method of defeating the Golden Lion is called a Beauty Trap, in which Tigress takes a large part as well. In case you're not sure this is a comedy, the soundtrack is full of "funny" music to point out the fact. A sleeper hit at the HK boxoffice, *Crack Shadow Boxers* helped inspire the kung fu comedy craze that led to Jackie Chan's hits soon after. *AKA: Crack Showdown Boxers.* ♪♪♡

1977 92m/C *HK* Ku Feng, Hon Gwok-choi, San Kwai, Dai Sai Aan, Fong Yeh. *D:* Wen Yao Hua. **VHS, DVD**

Crash Landing

The problem in any disaster movie is that it has to show some disaster without having all the heroes die. This Chinese blockbuster comes up with a clever concept to have it both ways. China Bluesky Airline pilot Captain Li (Shao Bing) finds that not only is he called in to work a flight from Shanghai to Beijing on his day off, but the head flight attendant is his estranged wife Shu (Xu Fan). The passenger list includes the usual cross-section: an elderly couple on their first flight, a single mom with baby, a hotheaded complainer, a man carrying a mysterious suitcase, and a serene kung fu master. First class contains only a jet-lagged American couple. Soon after takeoff, the crew detects a technical problem, and they have to return to Shanghai. With their nose landing gear locked, they try some fancy maneuvers to try to shift it free. Flight engineer Pot even goes down to try to jiggle it loose, but the captain has to request an emergency landing from the airport. The airport officials and manager Liu Yuan (You Yong) discuss their options, and like any good movie should do, it shows us the horrifying results of each choice. A runway landing results in the jet smashing through a terminal and crashing into another jet. A grass landing tears the jet open and flings passengers into the jets. All agree that a runway landing will be more exciting. With precious minutes ticking past until the fuel is used up, fire crews get busy foaming the runway, while the flight attendants try to calm the passengers by collecting their shoes and pantyhose.

Slickly produced, this is an obvious attempt by the Shanghai studio to step into the international marketplace already occupied by their Hong Kong and Korean neighbors. The performances are good, but the focus of the show is more on the details of procedure than action or drama. Outside of a few clunky miniature shots, the special effects are fine, especially in the crash sequences. One shot shows the shadow of the camera crane on the plane. Although it's a well-done thriller, it's tough for American audiences to take this kind of movie with a straight face since *Airplane!* was made. *AKA: Jinji Pojiang.* ♪♪♪

2000 116m/C *CH* Shao Bing, You Yong, Xu Fan. *D:* Zhang Jian-ya. *W:* Hao Jian. *C:* Yang Tao. *M:* Pan Guoxing. **DVD**

Crazy Crooks

Moo Pi-Chide (Dean Shek) is a crazy unemployed inventor with 10 crazy kids and a crazy nagging wife. While riding his crazy motorbike, Moo meets crazy con man Kong Koon-chat (Karl Maka), and they both keep busy trying to trick each other. Hearing that crazy rich man Kung (Ho Pak Kwong) wants to gamble with American money, the two rascals team up to swindle him, with Moo disguised as a crazy gweilo ("Long time no see!"), and Kong as a crazy security chief who busts the game. However, Kung—and everyone else they target to rob—is connected to the real security chief (Sun Yueh) in some way. The two con men manage to steal Kung's counterfeit U.S. bills anyway, prompting Kung to send his two crazy thugs Crazy Horse and Iron Cow to kill them.

The boys also run afoul of martial arts experts Lao Shen, Lady Lan, and Tu (Yue Tau Wan) due to the machinations of crafty street urchin Mak Tou, better known as Black Ink. The crazy kid eventually tires of getting Moo and Kong into trouble and saves them from the crazy killers. He now wants their help since crazy beggars Mok Ming (Chan Lung) and Chi Mao are after him. The reason the two psychos are after Black Ink is complicated—while an old artist was painting their portrait, gangster Tong Szu-niu (Alan Chan) abducted the artist to make the counterfeit bills for him, and pregnant Chi Mao lost the baby in the scuffle. The couple lost their minds and have been wandering about, intent on killing Tong's son ever since. Learning that Black Ink is Tong's long-lost son, Kong and Moo decide to return the boy home, despite the danger.

"Knockabout" doesn't begin to describe the crazy action in this crazy picture. Karl Maka has always specialized in comic fight scenes, but with the help of Dean Shek, he outdoes himself here, as a minute doesn't go by in which someone isn't getting conked on the head, slapped in the face, or sustaining some other bodily injury. This noisy brand of nonsense wears one down over such a long haul, and the "plot" is introduced almost as an afterthought, so it's best to keep one's higher mental processes in check while taking in this epic. Shek's character is one of his most eccentric: with a bowl haircut, large glasses, a Hitler mustache, and his thin frame accentuated, he goes about cackling, showing off his sleight-of-hand tricks, and using strange gadgets—and generally portraying some alien creature more akin to a cartoon character than a human being. As for Maka, he displays his now-familiar persona as the sharpie who's not as sharp as he thinks. This frenetic escapade is guaranteed to keep a houseful of guests either mighty entertained or heading for home. **AKA:** *Fung Kwong Daai Liu Chin; Feng Kuang Da Lao Qian.* ♪♪♪ ♡

1980 95m/C *HK* Karl Maka, Dean Shek, Alan Chan, Chan Lung, Cheung Gwok-wa, Ho Pak Kwong, Chu Chi-ling, Tsang Choh-lam, Sun Yueh, Yue Tau Wan. **D:** Karl Maka. **W:** Raymond Wong. **C:** Ho Ming. **DVD**

Crime of a Beast

One of the earliest shot-on-video releases in Hong Kong, the production is a mass of confusing contradictions. By day Ah Fun (Samuel Leung) is a downtrodden member of a film crew. He lusts after the leading lady, but is ignored and mistreated. By night, Ah Fun commits heinous crimes, raping and killing women. A psychiatrist tries to help, but employs very unorthodox and unsuccessful methods of treatment.

The DVD features an alluringly posed half-naked woman (Grace Lam) on the cover, leading one to expect a sleazy little thriller. Yet it seems the filmmakers wanted to explore a serious issue: To what extent is society to blame for sex crimes against women? A psychiatrist is included in the story, evidently to add legitimacy to the story line. She spends much time tossing around psychological terms, and has the apparent respect of both the film crew and the police, but her actions in one scene that takes place fairly early invalidates her as a character that can be taken seriously. Under the guise of helping a victim of incest to enjoy sexual relations, the psychiatrist unbuttons the patient's blouse, kisses her, and starts caressing her breast. Uh,

what school of psychology is that again? Thus, it's an uphill battle to believe this film is not simply exploiting a serious issue. Speaking of exploitation, certainly you can argue that one or perhaps two rape scenes are required to demonstrate the beastliness of the crime. But the scenes are lingered upon, as though the filmmakers wish the audience to identify, not with the various victims—none of whom are depicted with any great degree of sympathy—but with the leering and nasty rapist. The casting of Samuel Leung as the rapist does not help matters. Leung is an actor who has grown from supporting roles into the occasional lead; he's demonstrated his ability in the past to embody embattled losers who finally erupt when given the chance, as in the thoroughly unappetizing *Naked Poison*. Here, though, he's not able to overcome the limitations of the script, which makes his character, Ah Fun, a lowlife beyond redemption. In fact, it's incomprehensible why his guilt is not as readily apparent to the authorities as it is to the viewer. The last third of the film becomes a jumbled mess to the point that it became difficult to follow the story line, to distinguish what is real, what is a dream, and so forth. By the point that Ah Fun escapes the police wearing a flowered dress taken off a woman he just tried to rape, stops along the way to try to rape a female officer, is dragged off her and beaten, and then resumes trying to rape the hapless woman, well, it's difficult even to laugh at the film's misguided attempts to educate. The only real highlight of the production is the semi-mesmerizing musical score. —PM ♡

2001 87m/C *HK* Samuel Leung, Grace Lam, Natalie Ng, Chan Kwok-Bong, Patrick Keung, Wong Yat-Fei. **D:** David Lau. **W:** Or Siu-lun, Tong Man-kit. **C:** Chang Chi-wing. **DVD**

Crime Story

Another action story where Jackie Chan plays a tough, honest cop, in this entry, he's up against a band of ruthless kidnappers with a difference. Though clearly bad guys, these kidnappers are not out only to line their own pockets, but also to advance the cause of social justice. Their target is corrupt businessman Wong (Law Kar-Ying), who mistreats the workers at his construction sites. Kent Cheng *(The Defender, Wonder 7)* is Chung, the corrupt cop who leads the kidnap gang. Jackie, recovering from a brutal gun-battle, must cope with both the criminals and the effects of post–traumatic stress. His personal trouble causes him to be short-tempered, and even more impulsive than is usual for the HK superstar's cop characters. Despite Jackie's best efforts, the kidnappers succeed in taking Mr. Wong prisoner. A complex ransom

scheme is set up, and then goes bad. Jackie and Chung travel to Taiwan in an attempt to recover the portion of the ransom money that has been lost. The two are supposed to be just "observers," but naturally get caught in the middle of the action. Jackie, of course, is unaware that Chung is a traitor. Many times throughout the film, Chung tips off his confederates just as the police seem about to apprehend the criminals. Eventually, Jackie catches on to the fact that his "pal" isn't such a good guy after all. This doesn't happen, though, until Chung has slain a few of his criminal buddies, dumped Jackie down the interior of a cargo ship, and blamed our hero for crimes that the kidnappers have committed. (A plot thread not adequately explored once it's introduced.)

Originally a Jet Li vehicle, *Crime Story* is darker than most of Jackie's other police flicks. There's also more bloody gunplay than usual—a lot of gunplay for a Chan flick, though not quite as much as in your standard Chow Yun-fat movie. We do get the usual chases, fights, and stunts that one expects from a Jackie Chan movie—though none of it is up to the standard of Jackie's best flicks. There's some good stuff here, but nothing to put *Crime Story* very high in the oeuvre of Chan films. Sometimes *Crime Story* is listed as part of the *Police Story* series, though it definitely is not. It lacks the frenetic (and often comedic) spirit of Chan's other police flicks (*Police Story 1–3*, etc.). Fans of the genre are probably better off seeing those films first, and saving this for later. Ironically, the same true-crime kidnapping case was also the basis of the more factual *Kidnap of Wong Chak Fai*, with Chan's role played by...Kent Cheng! —SS **AKA:** *Chung Ngon Cho; Chong An Zu; New Police Story; Police Dragon; Police Story IV; Serious Crimes Squad.* 🦴🦴🦴

1993 (R) 103m/C *HK* Jackie Chan, Kent Cheng, Christine Ng, Law Kar-Ying, Chung Fat, Susanna Au Yeung, William Duan, James Ha, Cheung Wa, Chan Tat-kwong, Chan Sai-tang, Ken Lo, Wan Fat, Blackie Ko, Nicky Li, Mars, Wan Seung-lam. **D:** Kirk Wong, Jackie Chan. **W:** Chun Tin-nam, Chan Man-keung, Cheung Lia-ling, Cheung Chi-sing, Teddy Chan. **C:** Poon Wai-keung, Ardy Lam, Poon Hang-sang. **M:** James Wong, Mark Lui. **VHS, DVD**

Crippled Masters

Chang Cheh's *Crippled Avengers* (AKA *Return of the 5 Deadly Venoms*) was a hit, and some wily producer decided to go one better by making a film starring actual cripples as the leads. Ling Chang-kung is a local warlord with a chip on his shoulder—or more accurately, a hump on his back. This birth defect, which he has developed into his own Iron Hump kung fu technique, has made him a sadistic bastard who delights in punishing enemies and troublesome underlings by pruning off various parts of their anatomies. Lee Ho is one of his warriors who is punished for a transgression of some sort by having his arms lopped off. He stumbles across the countryside feeling sorry for himself (who wouldn't?) until a friendly farmer finds him eating from his pig trough. The farmer takes him in and makes him a farm han—er, worker.

Meanwhile, Ling thinks that innocent Kung Suh-ching has been spying on him, and responds by burning his legs off with acid. Sometime later, these two unfortunates meet up on the road and get into a fight. As luck would have it, an old beggar is eavesdropping on their quarrel. Like every old beggar in China, the old goat is actually an eccentric kung fu master incognito. He trains them to defend themselves from sand-kicking beach bullies and other threats. When Ling finds the location of their secret headquarters (well, a shack in the sticks), the boys team up with secret government agent A Pao, who has been sent to deal with the Ling problem by getting back the Eight Jade Horses he's stolen. Our handi-capable heroes steal the horses back, and then learn from them how to combine their abilities by forming one mutant body able to beat Ling once and for all.

Though possessed of a freak-show quality, this is actually an effective showcase for overcoming disabilities. The stars, likely discovered performing in a circus or whatnot, are amazing to watch, and they're not too bad at acting either. Hey, who else would you get to play these parts? Those disturbed at all by the deformities are more likely to be grossed out by the malformed appendages sticking out from where actual amputation would leave stumps. If you happen to be missing a couple limbs, this may be your favorite (or least favorite) flick. Other than the unusual stars, this is a substandard outing in all departments. The two protagonists would be paired again less successfully in *Two Crippled Heroes,* and the more serious 1981 modern-day drama *Fighting Life.* A popular screening item for years in Chicago at meetings of the Psychotronic Film Society—so much so that a local band took the movie's title as their name. 🦴🦴🦴

1980 (R) 86m/C *HK* Frankie Shum, Jackie Conn, Ma Cheung, Wong Hap, Ka Hai. **D:** Joe Law. **VHS, DVD**

Crocodile Hunter

Long before a certain Australian zookeeper was chasing snakes on TV, Andy Lau was starring in this Wong Jing action flick of the same name. While rescuing hostages in a movie theatre,

SDU cop Happy Chiu (Andy Lau) gets shot in the head. He wakes up months later, but due to the slug still buried in his noggin, Captain Wei (Lau Kong) transfers him to less hazardous duty. Partnered with cocky cop Bad Odor Chuan (Alex Man), Chao is assigned to interview incarcerated criminal Bitch Ying (Sandra Ng) to get information on her boyfriend Stalled Engine Te (K.K. Cheung) and his gang, who just stole a load of weapons and nearly killed Chuan. Believing that gang member Convulsion (Frankie Chan) has a fixation with TV star Lam Chia-hsin (Alvina Kong), the cops arrive at her place just in time to chase off the maniac, and take Lam into protective custody. The combination of the flaky actress and Ying (who lives up to her name) staying in the same apartment is predictably explosive, especially since they were classmates at school. Attempting to silence Bitch Ying, who knows that computer criminal Te can break open the type of safe the want to rob, the gang comes in blasting at Chiu's apartment, only leaving when they're tricked into thinking they've killed her. Te is understandably upset that his boss Fu (Lung Fong) shot his girlfriend, but plays along with the gang long enough to send a message out as to the place and time of their heist.

If the first half borrows a little from *48 Hrs.*, then the second half borrows even more from *Die Hard*, as the gang takes over a high-rise office building for their robbery, with the heroes—and the girls—inside. Since Wong Jing can't hope to match the Hollywood picture for spectacle, he at least beats it in one way: since cop-with-marriage-trouble Bruce Willis fights thieves barefoot, Wong has cop-with-marriage-trouble Alex Man fight thieves stark-naked for much of the climax. Typically, Wong never lets credibility get in the way of entertainment, so while *Crocodile Hunter* (the title is never explained) doesn't make much sense at times, it's still a lot of fun. *AKA: Juen Diu Daai Ngok; Zhuan Diao Da E.* 🐉🐉🐉

1989 100m/C *HK* Andy Lau, Alex Man, Sandra Ng, Alvina Kong, K.K. Cheung, Lung Fong, Lau Kong, Ricky Yi, Shing Fui-on, Ronald Wong, Charlie Cho, Frankie Chan, Eddie Maher, Maria Cordero, So Hang Suen, Stephen Chan, Jimmy Wong Shu-kei, Chen Jing, Liu Fan, Rosamund Kwan, Yeung Ching-Ching. **D:** Wong Jing. **W:** Wong Jing. **C:** Gigo Lee. **M:** Lowell Lo. **VHS, DVD**

Cross Fire

What if the little girl in Stephen King's *Firestarter* had grown up undiscovered? That's the general premise of this thriller from Shusuke Kaneko (director of the new Gamera movies), which manages to take a concept that looked kind of silly in the Drew Barrymore movie and make something much richer with it.

Ever since a schoolyard incident when she was small, Junko Aoki (Akiko Yada) has had to keep a close watch on her emotions, avoiding friendships and suppressing her passions. Junko can start fires with her mind, and anyone close to her is in danger. Working in a company mailroom, she weakens and accepts an invitation to a party from Tada Kazuki (Hideaki Ito), a nice young man in the office. She befriends Tada's little sister Yukie, and walks her to the train station. However, on her way home Yukie is abducted and murdered by a thrill-seeking gang of vicious delinquents. The gang is quickly caught, but the juveniles have no fear of the law—they all come from wealthy families and can't be prosecuted as adults. Kogure (Hidenori Tokuyama), the gang leader, is the son of the district attorney, and his case gets massive publicity.

Junko's feelings of guilt and sympathy bubble over. She stops Tada from attempting his own vengeance on Kogure, conspiring with him to use her power to kill undetected. Tada in turn stops Junko from going through with the murder, finding he can't consent to it. However, he guesses there's more to Junko's actions than a desire to help him. The truth is that, deep down, she's dying to cut loose with her power, starting a fire that might consume her. But police Detective Ishizu (Kaori Momoi) already suspects Tada and Junko of burning Kogure, her partner Detective Makihara is surprisingly quick to accept the pyrokinesis idea, and Junko hides away from them, convinced she's made a mistake in getting close to anyone. The cops aren't the only ones that know the truth—Junko is tracked down by a young man named Kido, who has pyropsychic powers of his own, and he convinces Junko that they should become vigilantes to stop Kogure's gang before they kill again. Then she meets a third pyropsychic, a younger girl named Kaori Kurata (Masami Nagasawa), who has more power than either of them—which is fortunate, since there's a lot more to Kido than he's let on.

Kaneko once again demonstrates his own special power: to take the fantastic and make it more compelling by exploring every Real World consequence of it. Exceeding genre expectations in every way, not only are the implications of psychic abilities explored, but the story is told through fully imagined and intriguing characters. One can imagine a whole movie about Ishizu, the mature and laconic detective. When Makihara wants to shoot Junko because "she's dangerous," Ishizu is quick to point out that a man with a gun is dangerous, too. Akiko Yada is startlingly good in the lead, giving a performance full of subtle hesitations and releases—she scares you and breaks your heart at the same time. Yada starred in the *Spiral* TV series,

and is currently in the Japanese version of *Friends*. As can be expected from a Kaneko picture, the special effects are excellent, too. *AKA: Kurosufaia; Pyrokinesis; Ross Fire.* ♪♪♪♪

2000 115m/C *JP* Akiko Yada, Hideaki Ito, Ryuji Harada, Masami Nagasawa, Yu Yoshizawa, Hidenori Tokuyama, Toshiyuki Nagashima, Kaori Momoi. **D:** Shusuke Kaneko. **W:** Kota Yamada, Masahiro Yokotani, Shusuke Kaneko, Miyuki Miyabe (novel). **C:** Kenji Takama. **M:** Ko Otani. **VHS, DVD**

Crouching Tiger, Hidden Dragon

Director Ang Lee returned to China for the first time since 1994's *Eat Drink Man Woman,* but this time he surprised everyone. Though this film has the same concern for traditions and the delicate interplay of subtle emotions that have marked all his films, it's also a kick-ass kung fu sock-fest in the tradition of the great sword operas everyone in China grew up with! Based on the novel *Wu Hu Zang Long* by Wang Du Lu, it tells a story from old China about a famed fighter of the Wudan school, named Li Mu Bai (Chow

Yun-fat), who is tired of bloodshed and wants to retire. He asks his old friend, security expert Yu Shu Lien (Michelle Yeoh), to deliver his wonderful sword "Green Destiny" to a friend in Peking, Sir Te (Sihung Lung). He agrees to join her there to present it himself, but his visit's real purpose is to see Yu Shu Lien again, as the two warriors have carried a torch for each other for decades. But first, Li wants to carry out one last mission: taking vengeance on Jade Fox (Cheng Pei-Pei), who killed his master and stole a valued kung fu instruction manual from Wudan 10 years before.

In Peking, Shu Lien befriends the visiting daughter of Governor Yu (Li Fa Zeng), innocent young Jen Yu (Zhang Ziyi). That night, someone steals the Green Destiny, escaping after a fierce battle with Shu Lien. All feel certain this is the work of Jade Fox, but complications set in when a witness spies the thief fleeing into the house of Governor Yu. Li shows up and helps to flush out the thief—which turns out to be Jen! Jade Fox has been hiding out all these years as the girl's maid, and together the pair have plundered the Wudan text's secrets. From there, it's one amazing battle after another, with our two heroes vying with Jade Fox over the new fighting master Jen.

Lethal debutante Zhang Ziyi is ready to bust heads in the Oscar-winning *Crouching Tiger, Hidden Dragon.*
THE KOBAL COLLECTION / COLUMBIA / SONY / CHUEN, CHAN KAM

This is one of the most beautiful films in years, with rich sets, scenery, and costumes competing for one's attention with the fine acting and breathtaking action scenes. Lee succeeds admirably in reproducing the epic excitement of the old classic Chinese films by directors like King Hu *(A Touch of Zen)*. Though Lee takes advantage of digital effects to enhance the image, the fight choreography of Yuen Woo-Ping *(Iron Monkey)* is unapologetic in its use of wirework to make the performers effortlessly defy gravity. The actors run up walls, float over rooftops, and skim lakes like fairies, in gorgeous photography by Peter Pau *(Bride with White Hair)*—who ironically has sometimes been credited as Peter Pan.

We should all be familiar with the work of Chow Yun-fat (from *The Killer* to *God of Gamblers*) and Yeoh (from *Royal Warriors* to *Tomorrow Never Dies*), but Zhang Ziyi was a fresh face in movies, and a welcome one. It's especially thrilling to see her mowing down opponents in the old Golden Harvest bi-level restaurant set, just as so many kung fu stars have before her. Cheng Pei-Pei's presence resonates back to the series of action films she starred in as the "Golden Swallow" during the 1960s. Character actor Sihung Lung is a familiar face from Ang Lee's films, and steals many of his scenes with subtle humor. To fans of Asian cinema, the elements on display here are nothing new, but to see them presented in such a classy package makes all the sword-work and magic seem new again—and indeed, it will be new for the majority of viewers. Sony Pictures Classics deserves high praise for giving this incredible film a wide theatrical release uncut and undubbed. *AKA: Ngo Foo Chong Lung; Wo Hu Cang Long.* ♫♫♫♫

2000 (PG-13) 120m/C *CH/HK/TW/US* Chow Yun-fat, Michelle Yeoh, Zhang Ziyi, Chang Chen, Sihung Lung, Cheng Pei-Pei, Li Fa Zeng. *D:* Ang Lee. *W:* Wang Hui-Ling, James Schamus, Tsai Kuo Jung. *C:* Peter Pau. *M:* Jorge Calandrelli, Tan Dun, King Yong. **VHS, DVD**

Crystal Hunt

This action-packed adventure flick, shot in Thailand, was inspired by the Indiana Jones series, but takes an hour to get out of the city and into the jungle. Triad princess Lisa Li (Carrie Ng) hires Professor Lau to help her on a dangerous expedition to the Sacred Mountain and find the legendary Golden Crystal, which can cure her dying father's rare illness. Lau's shifty assistant Peter Tang is involved in shady deals with gangster Stephen (John Salvitti), and tells them about the Crystal before they murder him, after which they kidnap the professor to lead an expedition of their own. Superintendent Trina Wu

(Sibelle Hu) is assigned the murder case, and brings in her ex-partner, tour guide Bret Chan (Donnie Yen)—who is dating Lau's daughter Winnie (Fujimi Nadeki)—to help. Lisa sends her boyfriend Gordon Chin (Ken Lo) and his goons to find Lau, putting pressure on Winnie for info. Threatened by Stephen as well, Trina, Winnie, and Bret are forced to join Li's expedition to find Lau and the Golden Crystal.

Almost everyone in the cast can fight, and do so often. Although there are plenty of gunfights, they always find a way to get rid of the guns and start kicking. By the time everyone gets out of town, the Sacred Mountain doesn't look any wilder than a national park, and just provides another location for fist and gun battles. The film works best when it abandons melodrama (including the unresolved romantic triangle) for a lighter tone and keeps the action moving. Highlights include Yen's warehouse duel with Salvitti, a tag-team match against big Michael Woods, and Hu and Lau versus Salvitti. One particularly rough-looking stunt is a fall from a cliff against a tree and rocks. The end credits include Jackie Chan–style outtakes, which show some stuntmen getting carted off to the hospital—plus the stars taking some unintentional punishment—giving an indication of how Hong Kong B-movies like this one can be just as dangerous (or more so) than bigger-budget features. *AKA: No Foh Wai Lung; Nu Huo Wei Long; China Heat.* ♫♫♫

1991 86m/C *HK* Donnie Yen, Sibelle Hu, Carrie Ng, Ken Lo, Gordon Lau, Leung Kar-yan, Fujimi Nadeki, Michael Woods, John Salvitti, William Ho, Michael Ryan, Kelvin Leton, Tin Ching, Chui Pak-lam, Tan Chun-tao, Chui Fat, Walter Cho. *D:* Chui Pak-lam. *W:* Hung Hin-pang. *C:* Chan Chuen-lai, Luk Kin-lok. **DVD**

Cure

Detective Kenichi Takabe (Koji Yakusho) investigates a murder scene, and finds the suspect Mr. Kuwada hiding in a crawlspace. It's the third such recent murder—all premeditated and without motive, after which the killers are shocked at what they've done. Some of the victims have a large X cut across their throats. The case is particularly troubling for Takabe, as his wife Fumie (Anna Nakagawa) has been having mental problems.

Schoolteacher Mr. Hanoaka finds an amnesiac on the beach who has trouble retaining any information. The next morning, Hanoaka kills his wife, and has no memory of the visitor. The amnesiac is found by a policeman, who takes him to the local station. The next day, the policeman shoots his partner. Takabe gets the idea that perhaps the murders are caused by hypnotic suggestion, though his psychiatrist friend Sakuma (Tsuyoshi Ujiki) tells him the hypnotist would have to be at a genius level. That seems to be precisely what they're dealing with—next the amnesiac entrances the doctor at the hospital he's been sent to, digging deep to nurture the slightest hidden murderous impulse. The next day, she slices open a man in a public lavatory. Takabe finally catches up with the young man, and manages to learn that the young man's name is Kunihiko Mamiya (Masato Hagiwara), a medical student who was studying mesmerism and animal magnetism. But how do you stop someone who is a psychopathic carrier? And how can you be sure he hasn't infected you while questioning him?

In Japan, as elsewhere, mesmerism has never been completely understood. Its critics, and even some of its early practitioners, believed it to be more magic than science. *Cure,* at the forefront of Japan's new wave of disturbing horror films, takes the line between science and mysticism and blurs it once again, exploring the terrors of mere perception. Are you reading this paragraph, or did someone convince you that you are? Though the film contains the more traditional shocks of bloody violence and spooky shadows, writer/director Kiyoshi Kurosawa uses this kind of question to try to freak you out, and succeeds very well, thank you. **AKA:** *Kyua.* 🐉🐉🐉

1997 111m/C *JP* Koji Yakusho, Tsuyoshi Ujiki, Anna Nakagawa, Masato Hagiwara, Yukijiro Hotaru, Yoriko Douguchi, Denden, Ren Osugi, Masahiro Toda, Masayo Haruki, Akira Otaka, Kae Egawa, Taro Suwa, Makoto Togashi. **D:** Kiyoshi Kurosawa. **W:** Kiyoshi Kurosawa. **C:** Tokusho Kikumura. **M:** Gary Ashiya. **VHS**

Curry & Pepper

Curry is Jacky Cheung and Pepper is Stephen Chow, both still rising stars at the time (having gained fame in other media) whom some genius decided to co-star in a buddy-cop action comedy. To make things even better, it's set at Christmas—which predominantly Buddhist Hong Kong goes unaccountably mad for. Curry and Pepper are easygoing detectives in the scruffy Tsim-shatsui district, which gives them opportunities to make fun of American tourists. Inspector Ma (Michael Dinga) tells Director Chou (Barry Wong) to let his niece, TV reporter Joey Luo (Ann Bridgewater) tag along with the two detectives for a few days, and they both immediately fall for the beauty. When she appears to prefer Curry, it puts a strain on the partners' friendship. Luo sticks with them, even on a stakeout for suspected arms dealers, though it turns out their suspect Dog is an undercover cop. Their

interference ends up getting Dog killed by the arms dealers' scar-faced hit man Abalone (director Blackie Ko), and he and Curry both get hit in the shootout, too. Abalone sees them on the TV special and comes gunning for them, forcing Curry and Pepper to put aside their feud to defend each other from the super-tough gunman.

The section detailing Pepper's heartbreak and jealousy drags on too long, but Stephen Chow definitely comes off better than Jacky Cheung, who has more of a straight man part. Chow is much funnier and portrays more pathos in his role. One of his strong points as a comic has always been his willingness to appear unpleasant, and his wit and charm survive some ugly moments here. Cheung gets in some good bits, too, especially in the party scene when he finds he doesn't fit into Luo's world. The two are so comfortable in their roles that the climactic bloodbath, in which they assault an entire steamship loaded with thugs, seems to take them by surprise as much as it does the audience. Eric Tsang is also good as the small-time crook who goes into danger for his two favorite cops. **AKA:** *Ka Lei Laat Jiu; Ga Li La Jiao.* 🐉🐉🐉

1990 96m/C *HK* Jacky Cheung, Stephen Chow, Blackie Ko, Ann Bridgewater, Barry Wong, Eric Tsang, Michael Dinga, John Sham. **D:** Blackie Ko. **W:** James Yuen. **C:** Andrew Lau. **M:** Richard Lo. **VHS, DVD**

Curse of the Vampires

Don Enrique (Johnny Monteiro), the patron of the Escodero family, has a stroke during a formal party, and makes an unusual request: that his villa be burned to the ground immediately after his passing. This angers eldest son Eduardo (Eddie Garcia), and Don Enrique explains his wishes by revealing to him a hidden passageway to a secret crypt beneath the house. There in a coffin lies his mother Consuela (Mary Walter), who died years before, but became a victim of the curse of the vampires. This is a clever twist on the old gothic tradition (as in *Jane Eyre*) of keeping an insane relative chained up and telling everyone they're dead. Knowing the secret convinces daughter Leonora (Amalia Fuentes) to break off her engagement to Daniel (Romeo Vasquez), fearing she'll pass on the curse. But as Norman Bates said, "A boy's best friend is his mother," and mama's boy Eduardo can't resist getting too close before the vampire can be destroyed.

Before long, Eduardo is sporting pointy fangs, avoiding the daylight, and snacking on local maidens. His first choice is his girlfriend—and Daniel's sister—Christina (Rosario del

Pilar), after which he does the honorable thing and marries her. While the happy couple is picking out His and Hearse towel sets, Eduardo has left the crypt unlocked, letting Consuela run loose. Don Enrique and his servant Jose hunt her down and destroy the beast, but the curse has already been set free. Having shared bodily fluids with his mother, and killed his father, Eduardo embarks on a reign of terror.

In this follow-up to his *Blood Drinkers* (1966), Gerardo de Leon does a fine job of building tension and conveying atmosphere. He throws a shocking red spot on the vampires when the bloodlust is upon them, and otherwise handles the lighting quite well. Some scenes are chilling, campy, and touching at the same time, as when Leonora and Daniel lie dying in a ditch after Eduardo sabotages their carriage. Leonora survives, and is protected from the vampires by Daniel's ghost! The performances are also quite good, given the bizarre circumstances, but the servants in blackface are kind of embarrassing. The old-time religious fervor of the climax is unprecedented in horror films, and has to be seen to be believed. *AKA: Creatures of Evil.* 🐉🐉🐲

1970 81m/C *PH* Amalia Fuentes, Romeo Vasquez, Eddie Garcia, Johnny Monteiro, Rosario del Pilar, Mary Walter, Francisco Cruz, Paquito Salcedo, Quiel Mendoza, Andres Benitez, Luz Angeles, Tessie Hernandez, Linda Rivera. *D:* Gerardo de Leon. *W:* Ben Feleo, Pierre L. Sallas. *C:* Mike Accion. *M:* Tito Arevalo. **DVD**

Cyclo

Gangster flicks meet the art-house world in this independent Vietnamese movie, co-produced by the French Canal+. Cyclo (Le Van Loc) is a young pedicab driver in the steaming slums of Ho-Chi-Min City. His elder Sister (Tran Nu Yen-Khe) works as a cook, while his younger sister shines shoes, and their grandfather pumps tires, but Cyclo's ride is the family's main source of income. Victimized by street gangs who steal his pedicab, Cyclo is introduced by his boss to Poet (Tony Leung Chiu-Wai), a pimp who hides him in a pit of an apartment, and he's slowly drawn into the gangster world. Very slowly. *Cyclo* may offer an unusual setting, fine performances, and excellent photography, but its entertainment value is sabotaged by its lethargic pace.

Poet seduces Sister into becoming one of his girls as well, serving fetish customers, and Cyclo is sent by the boss on an arson job, burning a warehouse full of rice. Poet tries to discourage Cyclo by taking him to see Mr. Lullaby (Van Day Nguyen), an executioner who sings as he kills. Still drawn in, the boy moves on to learning more of the business, from transporting pig car-

casses stuffed with drugs, to assassination. There are plenty of fresh twists on the old gangster story here, and some unique sights, such as when a scrap army helicopter falls off of a truck and blocks traffic. But unless you have an incredible amount of patience, you'll end up looking more bored and depressed than Tony Leung looks throughout the film. Banned in its native country. *AKA: Xich Lo.* 🐉🐉

1995 120m/C VN Le Van Loc, Tony Leung Chiu-Wai, Tran Nu Yen-Khe, Nguyen Nhu Quynh, Van Day Nguyen. *D:* Tran Anh Hung. *W:* Tran Anh Hung, Nguyen Trung Binh. *C:* Benoit Delhomme, Laurence Tremolet. *M:* Tiet Ton-That. **VHS**

Dagora the Space Monster

Satellites are disappearing in orbit, the latest confounding the project's director Kirino (Hiroshi Koizumi). What he doesn't know is that a big amoeba in space is eating the satellites. The blob provides a handy distraction for a gang of jewel thieves (led by safecracker Eisei Amamoto) pulling a job in the Ginza district by levitating a wino, but then disrupts their heist by cutting off their gravity. Detective Kommei (Yosuke Natsuki) follows American thief Mark Jackson (Robert Dunham) into the house of scientist Dr. Munakata (Nobuo Nakamura), who is righteously unimpressed when Jackson gets the best of Komai and swipes the professor's artificial diamonds. Kommei consults the doctor on the case of the jewel thieves, showing that the safe was melted into at the robbery site after the thieves fled. The gang captures Jackson, thinking he took their target diamonds, but is confused when Jackson's loot turns out to be artificial. Kommei takes a personal interest in the doctor's pretty niece/assistant Masayo (Yoko Fujiyama), who just happens to be Kirino's sister. Their meeting is interrupted by a strange pulsating sound, and a coal plant's smokestacks, coal, and towers are pulled into the sky.

Diamonds are being stolen all over the world—the latest disappearance occurring right under the noses of Jackson, Kommei, and the gang when an armored car full of diamonds is pulled into the air. Jackson consults Munakata on the mystery as well—the "thief" is revealed to actually be an insurance investigator checking into the thefts—and the scientist puts together the facts on the monster. The beast is officially named Dogora (despite the onscreen title) for no known reason, and it keeps on devouring coal and diamonds around the world before moving on to other forms of carbon. A shower of boulders falls on Kushu, before the monster makes a more direct attack. Rockets seem to destroy Dogora, but they only cause a chain reaction that makes the menace bigger.

Not in exactly the same category as Toho's other monster pictures, *Dagora* straddles the line into their sci-fi/crime movies like *The Human Vapor,* and even weird mystery movies like the British Quatermass films. The whole business with the diamond thieves is tiresome, but the film displays a healthy sense of humor in the scenes involving Jackson and Kommei's running duel of wits, and the grumpy Dr. Munakata's reaction to the foreigner constantly outsmarting the Japanese. The monster itself is pretty cool, looking like a cross between a gigantic jellyfish and a tornado. It doesn't have enough real personality to make this of more than diverting interest, but it's an entertaining little sci-fi disaster movie. Amamoto's giggly thug is dubbed in a voice not unlike that used for him in *What's Up Tiger Lily? AKA: Uchu Daikaiju Dogora; Space Monster Dogora.* 🐉🐉▽

1964 79m/C *JP* Yosuke Natsuki, Hiroshi Koizumi, Robert Dunham, Nobuo Nakamura, Yoko Fujiyama, Akiko Wakabayashi, Jun Tazaki, Eisei Amamoto, Susumu Fujita, Seizaburo Kawazu, Haruya Kato, Yoshifumi Tajima, Nadao Kirino, Yasuhisa Tsutsumi, Shoichi Hirose. *D:* Ishiro Honda. *W:* Shinichi Sekizawa, Jojiro Okami (story). *C:* Hajime Koizumi. *M:* Akira Ifukube. **VHS**

Daimajin

To many Westerners, Japanese cinema means two things: samurai action and giant monsters. This Daiei production has both! The villagers of Wolf Valley quake in fear that someday the evil spirit Majin will break out of the mountain. Lord Hanabusa (Hideki Ninomiya) assures his frightened children that the good god Shino will keep Majin locked in his prison, even as the Earth trembles at his fury. Chamberlain Samanosuke (Ryutaro Gomi) takes advantage of the frenzy to stage a coup, killing Hanabusa's family and taking his castle. Loyal Kogenta (Jun Fujimaki) and High Priestess Shinobu (Otome Tsukimiya) make sure the young prince and princess escape, hiding them in a cave on the mountainside, near the great statue of Shino.

Ten years pass, and Samanosuke becomes a bloody tyrant, enslaving the entire region and forcing the peasants to build a huge fortress. Kogenta is captured trying to contact rebels in the village, and when he attempts a rescue, the young lord Tadafumi (Yushihiko Aoyama) is caught as well. Like Moses, Shinobu goes to warn Samanosuke to release the peasants, or suffer the wrath of her god. Piqued, the villain sends his chamberlain Gonjuro (Tatsuo Endo) to the haunted forest to destroy the statue, where they discover Princess Kozasa (Miwa Takada) in hiding. But

when the warriors drive a spike into the statue's head, it begins to bleed, and the Earth opens up to swallow them all. In answer to Princess Kozasa's prayers, the statue comes to life, transforming into a grim-visaged 50-foot samurai ogre (Riki Hoshimoto). The stone golem, who looks a bit like Kirk Douglas, comes into town to bring the oppressors some of that old-time religion.

The Majin films (there are two sequels) were taken much more seriously than Daiei's Gamera pictures, awarded bigger stars, better special effects, and composer Akira Ifukube. The monster is wisely kept in the wings for much of this fable, only coming into play for the grand finale, sufficient suspense having been built up with plenty of atmospheric visuals. Director Kimiyoshi Yasuda also helmed half a dozen episodes in the Zatoichi series, as well as the bizarre *100 Monsters. AKA: Majin; The Giant Majin; Majin, the Monster of Terror; Majin the Hideous Idol; Majin the Stone Samurai; Vengeance of the Monster; The Devil Got Angry.* 🐉🐉🐉

1966 70m/C *JP* Miwa Takada, Yushihiko Aoyama, Ryutaro Gomi, Otome Tsukimiya, Jun Fujimaki, Hideki Ninomiya, Ryuzo Shimada, Tatsuo Endo, Saburo Date, Isao Hashimoto, Riki Hoshimoto. *D:* Kimiyoshi Yasuda. *W:* Tetsuo Yoshida. *C:* Fujio Morita. *M:* Akira Ifukube. **VHS, DVD**

Dance of a Dream

Kam (Sandra Ng) is a shy dreamer. One night, while working as a waitress at a fancy social event, she espies professional dance instructor Namson Lau (Andy Lau) waltzing up a storm and is smitten with him. She promptly enrolls in a dance class that he teaches at his studio— which is in dire financial straits. Salvation comes in the form of successful businesswoman Tina Cheung (Anita Mui). Her younger brother Jimmy (Edison Chen), recently returned to Hong Kong, notices her unhappy state and secretly pays Namson to give her dance lessons and "make her happy." Namson is delighted to accept, since the money will make it possible for him to realize his dream of a new skyscraper studio. Meanwhile, Kam harbors her crush on Namson and dreams of being his dance partner. Will everybody end up happy?

On the surface, this is a very enjoyable film. Looking beneath the surface raises a number of questions, though. For example, why is Kam—a mature woman, not a giggling teenager—so stuck on Namson? It would have added depth if we saw this as a pattern (i.e. she's always chased after seemingly unobtainable goals) or as a life-changing event (as in, she finally decided to take actions and take chances despite her timid nature and the possible disappointment she would face). As it is, the film seems to lean

toward the latter explanation without being too explicit about it until the concluding dance scene. As to Namson's appeal, well, he certainly has a lot of charisma, charm, and star power. But his character does not seem firmly fixed—is he really greedy and selfish? Is he overcome by his overwhelming desire for a big skyscraper studio? Or is it his desire to compete in the world championship in England? And scant attention is paid to Tina. We are told that she is a owner of a successful chain of hotels, and we see she is unhappy, but why did she finally respond to Namson? Again, a bit more fleshing out of her character would have added depth to the movie. The concluding sequence was also heartlessly unkind to one character in particular. To be fair, you may find that the breezy tone and strong performances more than offset the deficiencies of the script. For a movie that was evidently completed in a very brief time, the production looks quite glossy and handsome. —PM **AKA:** *Oi Gwan Yue Mung; Ai Jun Ru Meng.* 🐲🐲

2001 94m/C *HK* Andy Lau, Anita Mui, Sandra Ng, Edison Chen, Gordon Lam, Ronald Cheng, Cherrie Ying, Halina Tam, Lam Chi-chung, Wong Yu. **D:** Andrew Lau. **W:** Felix Chong. **C:** Andrew Lau, Ko Chiu-Lam. **M:** Chan Tak-kin, Marco Wan. **VHS, DVD**

Dance of the Drunk Mantis

Though Jackie Chan's *Legend of the Drunken Master* is the well-known sequel to *Drunken Master,* less famous is this other sequel made soon after the original. Though Chan was tied up with other projects, the Yuen clan fills in ably here, making this one of the more enjoyable kung fu comedies. Sam the Seed (Simon Yuen)—called "So" in the original—is known to us as the master of Southern Style Drunken Boxing. His counterpart Rubber Legs (Hwang Jang Lee)—who looks just like the original's villain Thunderlegs Yen—is the master of the Northern Style, and has spiced things up by incorporating his own variation into the style. After years traveling across the country, Sam finally returns home to his wife (Linda Lin Ying), who has a couple surprises for him. She never received any of the money he's been sending her, as banker Mr. Money Bags (Dean Shek) has been embezzling it. Also, she's adopted a son—a noodle stand chef named Foggy (Sunny Yuen). After dealing with the thieving banker, Sam moves on to his next project: dealing with his disappointing new son, who is intent on learning his drunken boxing secrets. Instead, Sam merely subjects him to a series of complex and painful exercises. The film's centerpiece is a duel between Sam and Rubber Legs in a restaurant that builds from tabletop moves into a full-scale drunken battle. Sam clearly has the upper hand until Rubber Legs introduces his variation: Drunken Mantis. Only Foggy's intervention saves Sam, who decides to study Mantis Style himself while recovering. Meanwhile, Foggy meets the cadaverous Master Sickness (Yam Sai-kwoon), who sleeps in a coffin and agrees to teach him his own bizarre style of kung fu.

Though papa Simon Yuen is the oddly charismatic star, this is a showcase for the talents of Sunny Yuen, who never had a more dynamic role. The great Hwang Jang Lee may have Rubber Legs, but Sunny's whole body looks like it's made of rubber, continuously bouncing and bending throughout his fights and exercises. He's a decent comic performer, and even brings a note of pathos during one dramatic scene. His brother Corey Yuen also has a good part as Hwang's student. Linda Lin is fun, too, either bickering with Simon or doing some kicking of her own. Not much can be said for the movie's simple plot, but the action and performances are terrific. The soundtrack borrows cues from *Suspiria.* **AKA:** *Laam Bak Chui Kuen; Nan Bei Zui Quan; Drunken Master 2.* 🐲🐲🐲🐲

1979 95m/C *HK* Simon Yuen, Hwang Jang Lee, Sunny Yuen, Yam Sai-kwoon, Corey Yuen, Dean Shek, Linda Lin Ying, Chin Yuet Sang, Brandy Yuen, David Wu. **D:** Yuen Woo-ping. **W:** Ng See-yuen. **C:** Chang Hai. **M:** Frankie Chan. **DVD**

Dark Water

Yoshimi Matsubara (Hitomi Kuroki) is not a happy woman. She and her husband have broken up, and she must search for a job and a new home while fighting to maintain custody of Ikuko (Rio Kanno), her six-year-old daughter. Yoshimi decides on a new apartment more out of desperation than desire. The building is old and unappealing, but she needs a permanent place to live to bolster her case in the custody dispute—she had mental problems in the past and wants to prove she is a fit and stable mother. Yoshimi and Ikuko move in, despite the large water spot on the ceiling, which Ohta (Yu Tokui), the sales agent, keeps her from noticing. When water begins dripping onto her bed, Yoshimi calls the apartment manager (Isao Yatsu), but he does nothing about it, and Ohta disavows any responsibility.

Adding to her pressures, Yoshimi begins a job as a proofreader, which causes her to be late in picking up Ikuko from school. Not only does this make her look bad in her battle to keep custody of Ikuko, it's an unpleasant reminder of her own mother's frequent neglect. She tries solving the problem of the dripping water on her own, knocking on the door of the apartment upstairs—the apparent source of the water—but no one answers. Complicating her life further, a small red lunch bag keeps making an appearance despite her best efforts to get rid of it, and her daughter keeps seeing a strange little girl in a yellow raincoat. It will take a torrent of water to answer all the questions raised.

Director Hideo Nakata *(Ring, Chaos)* takes water, one of the basic elements of life, and turns it into something sinister and chilling. The pacing is deliberate; the camera angles, framing, and cinematography are superb; the editing is spot-on; the music is understated and chilling; and the sound design is probably the star of the show. The relationship between Yoshimi and Ikuko avoids cutesy-pie sentimentalities and instead draws out the raw emotions between the two. That allows one to overlook the denouement, the inclusion of which may be debatable dramatically. It is, however, strangely satisfying as a whole, especially when watching very late at night. Based on a novel by Koji Suzuke, who also wrote the novel that was the basis for *Ring.* —PM **AKA:** *Honogurai mizu no soko kara.* 🎜🎜🎝

2002 101m/C *JP* Hitomi Kuroki, Rio Kanno, Fumiyo Kohinata, Yu Tokui, Isao Yatsu, Shigemitsu Ogi, Mirei Oguchi. **D:** Hideo Nakata. **W:** Koji Suzuki. **C:** Junichiro Hayashi. **M:** Kenji Kawai, Shikao Suga. **DVD**

Daughter of Darkness

This true-crime shocker is more a bizarre black comedy during its first half, quite unlike its totally grim follow-up *Brother of Darkness* (which was shot with much of the same cast). Even during the second half there are moments of unusual humor. Cadet Dong Huan (Money Lo) reports to small-town police Captain Lui (Anthony Wong) as his personal assistant. On her first day, a young woman named Mak Wai Fong (Lily Chung) runs into the station to report her family has been wiped out. Arriving at the Mak home to examine the evidence (and check the feng shui), they find the house is a bloody mess of corpses. One man has even been stabbed to death with a statue of household deity Kwan Wan Cheung (whom Wong would portray in *Jiang Hu: "The Triad Zone"*). The oafish Captain asks the girl impertinent questions, takes bribes from journalists, poses for gag photos with the corpses, and bullies his staff. His standard operating procedure is to coerce every witness he interviews into snitching on at least three other people, since everybody knows at least that many who have broken the law. He also learns that Fong can't keep her alibi straight. Also, her boyfriend turns out to be their own Officer Kin (Hugo Ng). The slug used in one of the murders matches Kin's gun, and he confesses to protect Fong. But the jig is up, and she goes into her confessional flashback. That's when things get really sleazy and unpleasant. The flashback shows Fong as a total Cinderella, scolded and abused by her entire family while she slaves for them. Her mother cheats, and her drunk father (William Ho) whores around, takes indecent photos of her, and rapes her. Driven too far, she borrows Kin's gun, picks up a few sharp objects, and plots an orgy of bloodshed.

Anthony Wong is always interesting to watch, so it's no wonder this movie focuses more on his antics than the sordid melodrama—even though it seems like he was given a totally different script. Other than seeing Lily Chung erupt into bloody mayhem at the end (and a little soft-core sex), her flashback is just one long ordeal. William Ho makes for such a textbook cretin, it's a wonder they didn't give him a mustache to twirl. **AKA:** *Mit Moon Chaam Ngon Ji Yip Saai; Nie Men Can An Zhi Nie Sha.* 🎜🎜

1993 93m/C *HK* Anthony Wong, Lily Chung, Money Lo, Hugo Ng, William Ho. **D:** Ivan Lai. **W:** Ivan Lai, Suen Ging On. **C:** Lee Kwok Keung. **M:** Wong Bong. **VHS, DVD**

Day Off

Borrowing wildly from *Chungking Express, C'est la Vie, Mon Cheri,* and probably a dozen others, writer/director Raymond Leung Pun-Hei has fashioned a moody little film. Lok (Nick Cheung) is a humorless and stoic professional assassin. He sleeps with a prostitute named Catherine (Sherming Yiu) before every assignment, and then moves to a different location. However, he is increasingly plagued both by his conscience and by memories of past killings. He falls into a relationship with Snow (Lam Ho-yee), a convenience store clerk.

The film tries hard to be significant but is hard-pressed to discover any ground that has not been trod many times over in the "assassin dealing with a conscience" genre. Lok narrates much of the film; insights on his profession are nothing new. Plenty of flashbacks are interspersed, and here the camera takes on Lok's point of view. It seems director Leung has never met an extreme camera angle that he doesn't like; he also favors the use of handheld cameras for no other reason than for visual variety. Leung also edited and produced the film. Clearly it's a low-budget affair, and it seems unkind to stomp too hard on what was probably a labor of love for all involved. Some scenes demonstrate that Leung has an eye for framing his compositions, and the pace moves along at a suitable rhythm. Still, it's hard to discern a personal vision or to find an overwhelming reason why this story cried out to be filmed.

Tommy Wai Kai-Leung composed the flavorful and varied musical score, including some welcome touches of flamenco. —*PM* **AKA:** *Saai Sau Ga Gei; Sha Shou Jia Ji.* ♪♪

2001 98m/C *HK* Nick Cheung, Lam Ho-yee, Sherming Yiu. **D:** Raymond Leung. **W:** Raymond Leung. **C:** O Sing-Pui. **M:** Tommy Wai. **DVD**

Days of Being Wild

It's April 1960 in Hong Kong. York (Leslie Cheung) has an affair with bar worker So Lai-jan (Maggie Cheung). With her roommate about to marry, she needs a place to live, and asks York to marry her, but he indifferently refuses. She leaves him, but it matters little to York; he lives off the savings of his adopted mother (Rebecca Pan), a retired prostitute. He resents her because she refuses to tell him the identity of his birth mother, afraid that York will leave her.

York casually picks up Mimi (Carina Lau), a dancer at a nightclub, and they begin a relationship. At the same time, So Lai-jan is not able to put the affair behind her. She confronts York and learns about Mimi. Feeling that she will burst if she doesn't talk about her feelings, So confides in a friendly policeman (Andy Lau) as he walks his tour of duty one night. The policeman is attracted to her, but she never contacts him again. Finally York's adopted mother tells him where his birth mother is living in the Philippines, and he heads off to find his destiny.

York's a player decades before the hip-hop music stars of the 1990s made that sound like a good thing. He's able to sweet-talk women into bed, and make them fall in love with him, but is so focused on his own emotional emptiness that he ignores their needs, much less consider opening up or committing to a relationship. To a large extent, he uses his adopted status as a shield to avoid incurring further pain, while remaining oblivious to the hurtful way that he treats others. The other characters stand as contrasts. The quiet So Lai-jan talks all night about highly personal matters with a stranger. The boisterous Mimi puts up with York's arm's-length attitude while desiring something more than a good time. York's friend (Jacky Cheung) secretly longs for Mimi but does nothing about it until it's too late. York's mother drowns her sorrows in alcohol.

All the players turn in fine performances. In his second film as a director, Wong Kar-Wai completely veered away from any concessions to typical commercial cinema. He used shifting narrative voice-overs to guide viewers through a quiet, arid landscape, with occasional emotional outbursts—rather than physical violence—providing nearly all of the high points. Plot-wise, not much happens for long stretches of time, which may try the patience of those looking for high-energy dynamics. More patient viewers will be rewarded. The ending—in which Tony Leung Chiu-Wai has a cameo—is quite vague. Director Wong returned to this same time period—with some of the same actors—10 years later in the more accomplished *In the Mood for Love.* —PM **AKA:** *A Fei Jing Chuen; A Fei Zheng Chuan; Ah Fei's Story.* 🎵🎵🎝

1990 94m/C *HK* Leslie Cheung, Andy Lau, Maggie Cheung, Carina Lau, Jacky Cheung, Rebecca Pan, Tony Leung Chiu-Wai. **D:** Wong Kar-Wai. **W:** Wong Kar-Wai. **C:** Christopher Doyle. **VHS, DVD**

Deadend of Besiegers

Meant to show how Wuwechimatao adapted Chinese martial arts styles to invent karate, this mainland-filmed feature fortunately steers clear of anything quite so dry and technical to present a rousing, swashbuckling adventure. Wuwechimatao—called Agawa (Yu Rongguang) in the English dub—is a righteous Japanese traveling onboard a merchant ship to China. But when they sight land, he finds he's gotten on the wrong boat—the crew reveals themselves as pirates (led by Chi Chuen-Hua), and go ashore to kidnap the village children during the Lunar New Year Festivities. Unwilling to stand aside, he helps the children to escape, and then sounds the alarm. During the open conflict with the villagers and soldiers in a nearby fort, he's naturally assumed to be one of the pirates. Though he rescued little Rose Xiao Mu-tau, Agawa's still blamed when her uncle Lin Sheng is killed, and so Lin Tian-peng swears vengeance. Rose helps him get into town disguised as a madman so his broken Chinese won't give him away, giving Yu a chance to go ape. Agawa still draws plenty of attention, so she hides him in a distant cave.

All this upset only drives a wider wedge between the Xiao and Lin clans—old Xiao (Yu Hai) and Lin Tong-shan were lovers once, driven apart by her arranged marriage to Sheng, and now Rose's big sister Jane Xiao Cui-gu (Cynthia Khan) and Tian-peng are forbidden to see each other, lest her Dog Fist kung fu mixes with his Tiger Fist. Of course, that doesn't stop the young lovers from trading stances in secret. It so happens that Agawa came to China just to learn the

Shaolin Dog Fist, after a British brawler (Dale Cook) humiliated him in a street fight. With Rose's coaxing, Jane agrees to teach Agawa, but Tian-peng interrupts. Fleeing, Agawa hides in a temple, where he overhears the pirates plotting to steal the sea goddess pearl during a festival. Agawa is caught while fighting the pirates, and vengeful Tian-peng has him buried alive.

This is another mainland movie in the tradition of *Shaolin Temple,* full of lively adventure, grand scenery, colorful action, and incredible kung fu (with limited wirework). The various festivals are wonderfully portrayed, there's a visit to Master Wisdom at Shaolin, lion and dragon dances, and a terrific fight in a mill that catches fire at the end. The actress that plays little Rose is quite good, and her relationship with the odd foreign hero gives the film a warm center, pushing the courtship between radiant Cynthia Khan and her boyfriend to the background. Yu Rongguang really ought to be a much bigger star—maybe he's too good-looking and tall for Asian audiences to accept as an underdog hero, preferring to see him play villains. The awkward title probably refers to the villager's resistance to the Japanese pirate's invasion. Why don't those pirates stick to pillaging ships and stay away from armed Chinese fortresses? **AKA:** *Miu Lam Sing Dau Si; Wu Lin Sheng Dou Shi; Steel Horse.* 🎵🎵🎵

1992 85m/C *CH* Cynthia Khan, Yu Rongguang, Yu Hai, Chi Chuen-Hua, Gan Tak-mau, Ga Chen Yan, Chang Rong, Li Zhi Zhou, Dale Cook, Zhing Jian Wen. **D:** Cheung Siu Wai. **W:** Lam Cheung Pau, Ba Tong. **C:** Zhou Bai Ling, Li Ming. **M:** Zhang Shao Tong, Chen Yong Tie. **DVD**

Deadful Melody

Brigitte Lin is cast in another supernatural period action film in a role in a similar vein to her *Bride with White Hair.* Various sects of the martial arts world have aligned themselves against the Tin Lung Sect over possession of the powerful Magic Lyre, which can destroy with sound. With her family all killed, Snow (Lin) was entrusted with this elegant weapon at an early age, and has grown up to master it, yearning for the chance to use it to exact her revenge. Lui Lun (Yuen Biao) is the son of the retiring master of the Flying Tiger Security Company, which is going through rough times. Lin is hired by Snow to deliver the Lyre to Hon Suen (Chung Fat), head of the Tin Chong Clan. Things haven't been going well for the Clans either since the Lyre disappeared years ago. The Fire Master (Wu Ma) and Ghost Master (Lam Wai) are among the few that show up for a summit meeting, and the younger members are disrespectful, including Fire's student Tam Yuet-wah (Carina Lau). Lun, joined by Yuet-wah along his

route, has to battle various and sundry warriors out to snatch the Lyre, with Snow showing up surreptitiously at critical moments to help (once Lun has drawn out the enemy for her). When she gets a chance, Yuet-wah betrays Lun and takes the Lyre to her master, though her heart has begun to soften toward the dashing security agent. Having sowed distrust and discord between friend and foe alike, Snow takes back the Magic Lyre to finish them off, but hesitates upon learning that Lun is her long-lost brother.

There are a few too many characters running around *Deadful Melody,* a common flaw in many Hong Kong swordplay flicks, with all the competing factions serving to confuse and drag down the narrative. It makes long scenes of expository dialogue necessary to sort everything out, meaning less action. Having lost their way, the filmmakers even reverse themselves, making the villainous traitor Tung Fong-pak (Elvis Tsui) into a sort of heroic martyr that brings everyone against the Lyre, which is treated as the atomic bomb of the martial arts world. Of course, the real purpose of all these folks is to give Snow more targets to blast away at in her musical massacre (when she's not simply kicking the heads off of thugs). The special effects are simple but beautifully effective, though Brigitte Lin is the best special effect. The ending leaves ample room for a sequel, though mediocre box-office returns assured that none would be made. *AKA:* Luk Chi Kam Moh; Liu Zhi Qin Mo; Devil Melody; The Six-Fingered Strings Demon; Deadful Music; The Magic Lyre. 🎵🎵🎵

1994 92m/C *HK* Brigitte Lin, Yuen Biao, Carina Lau, Elvis Tsui, Wu Ma, Lam Wai, Chan Lung, Chung Fat. *D:* Ng Min-kan. *W:* Johnny Lee, Lee Man-choi, Ngai Hong (novel). *C:* David Chung. *M:* James Wong, Mark Lui. **VHS, DVD**

The Deadly Camp

Watching the prelude, in which an unidentified maniac chases a couple through the woods with a chainsaw, you might think to yourself, "Say, I wonder if that's Anthony Wong?" Well sure enough, Wong is the first actor to pop up in the credits, but it wouldn't be fair to tell you whether he's the psycho or not. Producer Lee Siu-Kei and Wong Jing's Workshop joins the minor international resurgence of the slasher film that has arisen the past few years with this horror flick inspired by *Texas Chainsaw Massacre, Friday the 13th, The Evil Dead,* and their many imitators. It's actually a semi-remake of Dennis Wu's 1980 *The Beasts* (AKA *Flesh and the Bloody Terror).* Since this is only a Category IIB picture, it never gets as graphically gory as it could have, but nevertheless there's a fair amount of shocks to be found here.

Professor (Lam Tsz-sin) uses his camcorder to document a camping trip that he and his brother Ken host on a long weekend starting September 9, 1999—a date of many nines. The other campers heading to a deserted island include military buff Soldier, his date BeBe (Chat Pui-wan), Ken's girlfriend Winnie (Winnie Leung), and Professor's girlfriend Linda (Chui Ling Ling). After Uncle Feng drops them off his boat and they set up camp, a stranger begins watching them, and steals their cell phones. That night, they meet a group of nearby campers led by "condom salesman" Boar (Anthony Wong), who are really a gang of smugglers looking for their comrade Hwa, who disappeared a week earlier. Boar's two stooges (Benny Lai and Samuel Leung) encounter a retarded boy (Andy Tsang) out in the woods, who gets hurt while horsing around with them. The boy runs back to the hut of his deranged, bandaged giant of a father for some first aid. With that, Maniac and Maniac Jr. pick up their tools and start hunting, starting with the tattooed numbskull pervert that got the boy hurt.

O.K., so Anthony Wong might've been a little too obvious as the psycho. Though there's nothing very new to the teens-in-terror genre here— the victims are just as petty and stupid, and the leprous killer is just as monstrous—it's at least a change of pace to see the clichés in an Asian setting, since the slasher cycle of the early 1980s didn't really have a Hong Kong contribution. Plus, there's at least one good surprise at the end. The unidentified actor behind the gauze is pretty good at portraying a mix of insane menace and pathos. *AKA:* Saan Gau 1999; Shan Gou 1999; 1999 The Deadly Camp. 🎵🎵▽

1999 80m/C *HK* Anthony Wong, Benny Lai, Winnie Leung, Samuel Leung, Lam Chi-sin, Chat Pui-wan, Chui Ling Ling, Chan Nam-wing, Andy Tsang, Li Yeung-fan. *D:* Bowie Lau. *W:* Bowie Lau. *C:* Kwong Ting-wo. *M:* Tommy Wai. **DVD**

Deadly Snail vs. Kung Fu Killer

A kung fu movie to trip by? It seems like Timothy Leary had a hand in the screenplay for this odd action fantasy, which begins with a pre-title sequence of colored lights and electronic noises. During the credits, there is a very dull tiger snake vs. snail fight. The snail seeks help from lazy farm boy Cheung-fu (Tony Wong), causing him to pass out and have an out-of-body experience. In a cloudy limbo, he meets a girl Princess Leia–style: in miniature, she asks for his help while standing on some giant pearls. She continues talking to him after he wakes up, telling him to bleed on the snail's head, after which it disappears. Whoa, dude! Cheung-fu's uncle Chow Wong-chang, recognizing a slacker, kicks him off the estate—though they see that he doesn't go too far, since he's unknowingly the heir to the whole property, and they want to continue to abuse him.

Pretty maid Sher-mao tries to help him, and receives a beating from his aunt. Angered, Cheung-fu sees an old man's face in the clouds, which tells him, "Happy days are here again." The snail girl (Candy Yu), who has taken a shine to Cheung-fu, decides to help him out in gratitude for her rescue from the snake, and starts by visiting his shack in spirit form to cook him dinner. She introduces herself as the Sea Snail Fairy, and soon the two are living as man and wife in a magically fixed-up house. The relatives are outraged at the sudden marriage, and heartbroken Sher-mao is forgotten. Rascal son Chow Wai-chai hires some thugs to help kidnap the bride, but her magic tricks drive them off. Meanwhile, the fairy's enemy among the snake folk is irked by her happiness as well, and disguised as a demon-hunting Buddhist monk, vows to help the Chows fight against her. Sher-mao wheedles the magic silver ring from the newlyweds, leaving them vulnerable to attack.

The *I Dream of Bewitched in China* bit is lively enough that it's barely noticeable that it's a good 45 minutes into the movie before there's anything that vaguely resembles martial arts occurring. Even then, the fighting is nothing special, as a fairy-possessed Cheung-fu suddenly fights back against his attackers with some Monkey Style moves. With its cheap but imaginative f/x and painted outdoor backdrops, the whole production is on the level of an old kiddie TV show. If not for some horror elements, such as when the snake man drains a victim down to the bones, this would be a terrific children's film. The finale, in which the fairy's sisters leave their bubble-filled sea palace to battle elemental demons in a misty cavern, is as colorful and weird as anything in an old Russian fantasy film. Simon Yuen *(Drunken Master)* has a small part as the snake man's master. Tony Wong was quite a big TV star at the time, with the lead in the hit HK series *Lau Suk Fung.* He went on to direct the zany *Crazy Partner,* but is now reported to have become a monk! *AKA: Chan Haangng Po Daai Lo Tin; Chen Xingwu Po Da Luo Tian; Deadly Snake vs. Kung Fu Killers.* 🦴🦴🦴

1977 87m/C *HK* Tony Wong, Candy Yu, Little Unicorn Chan, Tin Ching, Simon Yuen. *D:* Heung Ling. **VHS, DVD**

The Deadly Sword

The sword called the Deadly Hook ranks seventh among the 18 Deadly Weapons. Made by a madman, it looks like it's split open at the end, and has an odd property—it destroys everything it

strikes. Captain Kow is selling some of the prized magic swords from his collection at auction, including a few items you won't find on eBay. Master Tit Chi-lan (Ling Yun) buys the Dragon Sword, while Master Wong buys the ice-cube maker Icy Sword. Tit Chi-lan also purchases the rusty old Needle Sword, which can slice a needle lengthwise. Everybody gets drunk after the auction, and Tit Chi-lan murders Man Kwan-wu with his special Thin Sword. His lady Little Si-Si knows too much, and gets the same treatment.

Fearing that Si-Si blabbed too much about him and his connection to the Green Dragon Society to her friend Lu Su-min (Candy Yu), whose boyfriend is the gang-busting Captain Yeung Chun (Barry Chan), Tit Chi-lan sends an assassin for Su-min. Meanwhile, Yeung catches a bandit gang that's after a treasure transport. Afterward, the money is missing, and Flying Tiger Wong and his escort company accuse Yang of the theft. With Green Dragon assassins after them both, Yang hides Su-min in a cave and fetches his father's sword, the Deadly Hook, and goes to kill Tit Chi-lan and clear his name.

Some of the swordplay action is fun, and the magic sword bit is always entertaining. However, some nicely composed shots are ruined by out-of-focus camera work. This was based on a famous Ku Lung story, and much must have been lost in the translation. The dubbing is one of the worst jobs ever, sounding like it was performed by a few nervous and untalented high-school students. This has a deadly effect on any qualities the film may have, ruining the performances and distracting from the story. *AKA: Lee Bit Gwan; Li Bie Jun.* 🦴🦴

1978 91m/C *HK* Barry Chan, Ling Yun, Candy Yu, Chan Wai Lau, Tin Yau, Cheung Pang, Ma Kei, Cheng Hong-yip, Ko Saio Pao. *D:* Godfrey Ho. *W:* Ku Long. **VHS, DVD**

Death Duel of Kung Fu

When the Ching Dynasty began, Ming General Chen Cheng-kung retreated to Taiwan to carry on the fight. Marshal Ta orders 100,000 troops into Taiwan to capture or kill the general. Lieutenant Hsiun Chin-kwai (Wang Tao) dares to tell the marshal that, with the people supporting Chen on the island, they won't have enough men to deal with them, and is ordered under arrest. Revealed as a rebel, Hsiun responds by beheading the marshal and becoming a fugitive. With the killer of their leader on the loose, the soldiers are demoralized. Lord To Ku-yun (Han Ying) is put in charge of the operation, and he assigns Captain of the Guard Kai Yi-king to catch Hsiun before the attack can begin.

"Search
everywhere!
There's a man
in mistress'
room!"

—The guards are a bit
confused—as is anyone
watching *Death Ring*

At a Ming safe house, Hsiun encounters a young rogue with good kung fu, whom they all suspect is a spy. When he tries to cut in on the action of beautiful half-Japanese gambler Yi Ki (Fanny Wang), Hsiun leaps to her defense (and appears to be acting as her stunt double in fight scenes). But when Hsiun is injured and cornered, the stranger Sun Shan (John Liu) comes to his aid. Yi Ki applies some TLC to help Hsiun recover—but the snake-tattooed beauty is really a Ching spy, and engineers his capture. However, he's allowed to escape so that she can accompany him to Taiwan and assassinate General Chen (after a quick training sequence to improve his kung fu). Sun Shan uncovers the spy and kills her, then heads for a showdown with Lord To. Hsiun decides to follow him, but first has to duel with Kai Yi-king.

Wang Tao is in top form here, and displays his proficiency in a different kung fu style in each fight scene, mainly mantis and crane, but his matches have too much formality. John Liu's fights have a more natural feel. Said to have been a student of Dorian Tan *(Blooded Treasury Fight)*, Liu does some fantastic kicking. The nine-minute climactic battle between the three leads is mighty good, mixing their styles with ingenuity. Much of the action takes was shot using the same spectacular Korean locations used for the climax of *To Kill with Intrigue*. 🎵🎵🎵

1979 85m/C *HK* Wang Tao, John Liu, Eagle Han Ying, Phillip Ko, Charlie Chan, Chan Lung, Chung Fat, Ging Chue, Wu Chia Hsiang, Fanny Wang. **D:** William Cheung Kei. **W:** Ngai Hong. **VHS, DVD**

Death Mask of the Ninja

Lurking on the video shelf, disguised as a ninja epic starring "Joey Lee" and "Tiger Tung," is this later Shaw Brothers entry. A traitor leading forces of the wicked Ninth Prince attack the palace, and the emperor sends a squad of guardsmen away to keep safe his magic sword, royal seal, and—oh, yeah—the three royal princes. Both the emperor and traitor are killed in the coup attempt. The guards fight their way past a bridge guarded by one villain (Kong Do) with two flaming swords, and another (Yuen Bun) with two spiky swords. Separated in an ambush, the guard carrying the Second Prince is the only one to reach the prime minister, and the others are thought dead.

However, Guardsman Li Chang (Yuen Wah), a former Shaolin student, takes the First Prince and the seal to the hut of the Shaolin Holy Fools—Wu Chi, Wu Ming, and cross-eyed Wu Li. Though banished to stay put in the remote house, the trio of monks—sort of a Buddhist Three Stooges—raise the boy to manhood, giv-

ing him the name Tao Han (Ti Lung), teaching him their unusual kung fu skills.

Meanwhile, Mr. Koo (Kwan Fung) has trained the Second Prince to be a superior warrior, in the hopes that he may someday defeat the Ninth Prince, now the power behind the throne. The Prime Minister adopts him, giving him the name Wong Lu-kai (Derek Yee), and he pretends not to like kung fu to hide his skill.

Unbeknownst to anyone, the Third Prince was found and raised by the Ninth Prince himself as puppet emperor. Monk Tao Hung (Lee Hoi-sang), a spy for the Ninth Prince, tries to kill Tao Han while he's in charge of an exorcism at a haunted mansion—daughter Su-chin is possessed by her dead fiancé. Lu-kai arrives just in time, defeating the ghost with his magic sword. The Second Prince has come to borrow the book of I Ching, to learn the Secret Yi Chin Style to overcome the Ninth Prince's Iron Hand. In order to access the book, Lu-kai has to overcome the Eighteen Buddhas Attack—sort of a flying pyramid of monks. Both framed by the spies, the two princes team up to fight their way out of the temple. Together they hatch a plot to defeat the Ninth Prince and get their revenge.

You've got to hand it to these old kung fu flicks, where it sometimes takes decades for folks to get their vengeance. With an old-fashioned fable quality to it, there's a lot of entertainment here. The outrageous action scenes are peppered with comedy and flashes of special effects. There's swordplay magic, ghosts, intrigue, special weapons, and martial arts styles—the only thing missing is romance. The Shaolin Temple is given one of its more lively presentations, though the temple sets aren't as grand as those of the palace. The final battle is especially wild, with the two princes facing off against the Ninth Prince while he rides in a gadget-loaded sedan chair. The final blow has a result unseen outside of cartoons. The soundtrack is borrowed from Akira Ifukube's scores for Toho. **AKA:** *Siu Lam Chuen Yan; Shaolin Chuan Ren; Shaolin Prince; Iron Fingers of Death; Iron Fingers of Shaolin; Prince of Shaolin; Wu Tang Prince.* 🎵🎵🎵

1982 95m/C *HK* Ti Lung, Derek Yee, Jason Pai, Ku Feng, Ai Fei, Lee Hoi-sang, Yuen Wah, Kong Do, Yuen Bun, Tang Chia, Kwan Fung, Alan Chan, Yue Tau Wan, Chan Chuen, Lam Fai-wong, Elvis Tsui, Chan Shen, Goo Goon-chung, Wong Pau-gei. **D:** Tang Chia. **W:** Wang Tsing. **C:** Tsao Hui-chi, Huang Chien. **M:** Stephen Shing, So Chun-hou. **VHS**

Death Ring

Chang Cheh made some amazing films during his career, but this patchwork collaboration with Lu Feng is amazing for all the wrong reasons. It opens uncharacteristically with a bit of soap opera, and then tries to bridge the old-school martial arts world with the modern world of pro kickboxing. Daughter of the Pa Mei Clan Fung Lin-mei has been promised to the Wu Tang's Lu Pang-fei, though she really loves Shaolin man Dai Lang-chi (Lee Chung-yat). Pang-fei throws such a tantrum when he finds them together that he starts fighting with his prospective father-in-law (Chen Kuan-tai), but ends up getting killed accidentally in a fight with Dai. Papa Fung is broadminded enough to let Dai leave, but insists he never return. Mr. Lu Chan-san (Chan Sing) is not as forgiving, ordering his men to hunt down the man who killed his son.

After hanging out in Thailand for three years (via some scenes that look like vacation movies of the star), Dai Lang-chi returns to ask Lin-mei to go back with him. But next morning, Lu's men are on his trail. Dai gets some protection from a dapper bandit chief (Ti Lung), escapes back to Thailand, and becomes a boxer. Twenty years later, Lu Chan-san's second son (Lu Feng) goes hunting for revenge against the Dai family, but Dai Lang-chi's son Ching (Lee Chung-yat) has left for Bangkok to find his father. While searching, Ching is hired by Miss Ko as a sparring partner for Sellek, a fighter she's managing, who is training to fight a tough guy named Leopard. But Sellek quits rather than use a human sandbag and the two young men find themselves looking for jobs together. But meanwhile Sellek has a fight to train for, and Ching takes a job as Leopard's sandbag to learn his style. After seeing Ching limp back in sorry shape, Sellek rushes back to Miss Ko to set up a match with Leopard

Anyone who doesn't guess the relationship of Ching to Sellek should go to the back of the class, as it's one of the most used plot gimmicks in martial arts flicks. Ching only catches on after Sellek goes to his death in the ring, and he begins a plan to fight Leopard himself to get revenge. And don't forget: Lu is still out to get him. The story changes directions so many times to get to the end that you might get whiplash watching it. It begins in the Martial Arts World that looks like it could be 200 years ago, but by the time the hero grows up we're in modern Thailand. The first and last 30 minutes feature some great fighting, but no one would guess without seeing what comes in between that they're from the same movie. That's because they're really not—Chang Cheh supervised the first act, and it was clumsily written together with Lu Feng's boxing movie, though it's unknown how this came to be. The best guess is that Chang helped out his old pal Lu by adding the backstory by Ngai Hong with big-name guest stars. Chang Cheh's section provides a hint of his former glory, and Lu Feng provides a terrific final fight sequence, plus a lot of mind-bending continuity gaffs. Evidence of Lu Feng's inability as director abounds. You just have to look at a scene of Lee Chung-yat asking for directions that goes on for several minutes. Music cues are swiped from various sources, including Bernard Herrmann scores. 🎵🎵

1983 91m/C *HK* Lee Chung-yat, Ti Lung, Chen Kuan-tai, Chan Sing, Lu Feng, Wong Siu Sam, Cheung Tai Lung. ***D:*** Chang Cheh, Lu Feng. ***W:*** Ngai Hong. ***C:*** Ng Kwok-yan. **VHS, DVD**

The Defender

Jet Li is John Chang, first-class Red Army bodyguard, sent to Hong Kong to protect the girlfriend of millionaire businessman James Shong (Ng Wai-Kwok). It seems that Michelle Yeung (Christy Chung) is in danger, having seen gangster Gregory Chu Kwok-Man (Wong Kam-Kong) kill an accountant in a money-laundering ring. The two other witnesses have already been killed. Shong doesn't have faith in the Hong Kong police, represented by Sergeant Charlie Lau (Kent Cheng), and pulled some strings in Beijing to hire their top man. Not a bad idea, as it appears Lau is more interested in gambling than his job. John soon has the house full of electronic surveillance equipment and dismisses most of the other guards. His security skills are perfect, but his customer relations are a bit harsh. Independent Michelle is resentful of what she sees as overprotection, while her little brother Billy (William Chu) is quickly impressed when he sees John in action.

However, her opinion begins to change when the trial is delayed indefinitely. Unable to keep her cooped up any longer, John allows Michelle to go out shopping, and barely saves her from the legion of assassins that come after her. With her rich boyfriend neglecting her, Michelle finds herself drawn to the strong bodyguard, and begins to enjoy his protection. But then Wong Kar Kwok (Ngai Sing), brother of one of the assassins John killed, decides to make his mission a personal vendetta.

Often cited as the Hong Kong version of the U.S. hit *The Bodyguard*, it's more than just the fantastic action scenes that make this the superior film, and Jet Li's best in a modern setting. The underlying tensions between the worlds of the loyal communist guard and the wealthy debutante add several levels of depth to the story. The savage final battle, with Li and Ngai Sing trying to kill each other in a house filling up with gas, is one of his finest. In the years leading up to reunification, patriotic mainlander Li used his stardom to rally support for China. The last shot here shows him proudly posing in uniform with the Chinese flag waving in the background. ***AKA:*** *Zhong Nan Hai bao biao; Chung Naam Hoi Biu Biu; Bodyguard from Beijing.* 🎵🎵🎵🎶

"All the kung fu in the world isn't gonna help when it comes to women."

—Kent Cheng gives advice to the lovelorn in *The Defender*

1994 (R) 93m/C *HK* Jet Li, Christy Chung, Kent Cheng, Ngai Sing, Ng Wai-Kwok, William Chu, Wong Kam-Kong. **D:** Corey Yuen. **W:** Gordon Chan, John Chan. **C:** Tom Lau. **M:** Nicholas Rivera (U.S. version). **VHS, DVD**

The Demon's Baby

During the Ching Dynasty, "Five Ghost Tao" of the White Lotus Sect are summoned—five demons that can enter the physical plane by possessing babies. If all five demons incarnate, they will terrorize the world. Monk Lone-chi captures these demons and imprisons them in jars guarded by a gold Buddha statue. In the 20th century, the army of General Hsu (Elvis Tsui) discovers the jars among the treasures in a cave, and brings the loot to his house.

Madame Hsu throws a banquet announcing the General's marriage to a fourth concubine, where chef Day-Six (Emotion Cheung) prepares a vegetarian feast in the new wife's honor. Day-Six wants to woo maid Little-Fish (Sandra Ng), but is too shy. The other concubines are jealous of the new teenage wife Pearl, and one even tries to seduce the chef. Another is having an affair with the butler Lee (Lee Siu-Kei), but when maid Butterfly catches him leaving her room, he smothers the girl and makes everyone believe she drowned.

During the funeral procession, the corpse catches the eye of a mysterious priest named Chin Hai (special guest star Anthony Wong, who seems to be out to break the record for guest starring in films the last few years). He recognizes that this was not a natural death, and advises caution. He's right, and he's just in time to save them when Butterfly becomes a hopping vampire!

When sneaky Lee steals the golden Buddha and replaces it with a copy, the jars are left unprotected and the demons escape. Well, that's what we've been waiting for, isn't it? That night, the demon-occupied Hsu runs around the house impregnating all four wives. A possessed Day-Six seduces Little-Fish for the fifth pregnancy. Before long, the possessed women have bulging bellies that break open into fanged, ravenous mouths—and the tentacled demon fetuses are demanding a blood feast, scarfing down livestock, priests, and servants. Chin Hai is sent for, and a furious supernatural battle commences that will demand all of the priest's mystical skills, and the chef's cooking skills as well!

Asian horror films are either disgustingly gruesome, morally repellent, or both. However, despite the large amount of gore on display here, due to its slightly tongue-in-cheek atmosphere, *The Demon's Baby* never quite crosses the line into bad taste. Helping to keep things light is

Wong, who gives his character an amusing devil-may-care attitude, even while in combat with Hellspawn. Cheung is also fine in the lead, lending irony to his name by keeping a placid expression on his face, à la Buster Keaton. 🐕🐕

1998 85m/C *HK* Emotion Cheung, Anthony Wong, Annie Wu, Elvis Tsui, Lee Siu-Kei, Sandra Ng. **D:** Kant Leung. **W:** Kant Leung. **C:** Chan Chung-yuen. **M:** Lincoln Lo. **VHS, DVD**

Dersu Uzala

Akira Kurosawa went to the Soviet Union to film this document of man living in nature. While leading an exploratory military expedition into the forbidding wilds of Siberia, Captain Arseniev (Yuri Solomin) forms a friendship with his Mongolian guide Dersu Uzala (Maxim Munzak). Increasingly, the men come to rely on the woodcraft and wisdom of their little guide. When they become separated from the party, Dersu saves his life. He warns them against tigers and bandits. He saves the captain from a raft caught in the current, then instructs the men in how to save him. After shooting a tiger, Dersu fears the forest spirit has rejected him, and Arseniev takes him home to Khabarovsk with him, where he finds city life miserable.

Filmed almost entirely without close-ups, Kurosawa emphasizes the extreme desolation of the tundra. A beautiful film, but not a wise choice for thrillseekers. It won the foreign film Academy Award for 1975, and it's one of the few Oscar winners in this book! **AKA:** *Derusu Uzara.* 🐕🐕🐕

1974 (G) 140m/C *JP/RU* Maxim Munzak, Yuri Solomin, Vladimir Klemma, Suimenkul Chokmorov. **D:** Akira Kurosawa. **W:** Akira Kurosawa, Yuri Nagibin. **C:** Asakazu Nakai, Yuri Gantman. **M:** Isaak Shvartz. **VHS, DVD**

The Descendant of Wing Chun

It's not a good day for thief Ma Lung (Lee Hoi-sang, decked out in reddish blonde hair). He loses his traditional spear duel with his partner Hsiao Fei (Fung Hark-on), then martial arts master Liang Chen (Melvin Wong) helps Sergeant Tang and his men capture him. It's not a good day for Kao Feng either. First he and his gang are beaten up by Fatty Kwei (Hsu Shao-Chiang), whose kung fu is much improved since they beat him up as a boy. Then moneychanger Hua (Norman Tsui) beats them up when they try to scam him with some fool's gold. An enterprising butcher tricks Hua into a fight with fellow butcher Kwei, but when Hua figures out that the rascals only want to gamble on the fight, he pretends to

lose. Full of himself, Kwei challenges Hua's best student, but when the student remembers that Hua forbids fighting, he pretends to be beaten as well. Kwei receives his inevitable downfall when he challenges Hua's kung fu master Liang Chen. Peeved, he tricks Liang Chen into a duel with his eccentric Shaolin monk master. However, the two masters are more level headed, and decide to swap students. While the monk teaches Hua his Lo Han kung fu, Master Liang Chen teaches Kwei his Wing Chun. The two students find their new skills come in handy when Ma Lung breaks out of jail, and he and Hsiao Fei come looking for revenge.

After building up Kwei as the main character for most of the running time, it's a bit of a surprise when he's killed off rather suddenly, leaving Melvin Wong as the focus of the story. If some fine kung fu technique and a bit of stupid knockabout comedy is all you're looking for, this one should fit the bill. A poor man's Sammo Hung, Hsu Shao-Chiang is sort of amusing, but the kooky Shaolin monk is a riot, passing off nonsense proverbs and generally lampooning the noble holy men. **AKA:** *Fut Shan Jahn Seen San; Phu San Jahn Sen Shun.* 🐲🐲

1978 87m/C *HK* Hsu Shao-Chiang, Norman Tsui, Melvin Wong, Fung Hark-on, Lee Hoi-sang, Kwan Hoi-san. **D:** Huang Ha. **W:** Pak Fei. **C:** Erh Don-lung. **DVD**

Destroy All Monsters

In the future year of 1999, the world's governments will finally accept the fact that we share the planet with gigantic mutant monsters. The technology is developed to isolate Godzilla (Haruo Nakajima), Rodan (Taruo Nigake), and all their friends on a remote island where they can be safely studied. However, alien babes from planet Kilaak invade Monster Island and take control of Godzilla and his monstrous colleagues, sending them forth to destroy all of Earth's major cities. King Ghidorah (Sisumi Utsumi) is even recruited to watchdog the alien base at Mount Fuji. United Nations forces, including Capt. Katsuo Yamabe (Akira Kubo) and the crew of the space battle cruiser *SY3*, are kept hopping trying to meet the alien threat.

Maxim Munzak as the eponymous Russian woodsman in *Dersu Uzala.*

GODZILLA attacks New York!
RODAN devastates Moscow!
MANDA obliterates London!
and MOTHRA smashes Peking!

Is this the war-cry that will save the world...

"DESTROY ALL MONSTERS"

IN **COLOR** BY BERKEY-PATHÉ

Can the planet possibly survive this madness? This classic Toho monster slug-fest also features Mothra, Minya *(Son of Godzilla),* Angilas (Hiroshi Sekita), Spiga, and Manda, with cameos by a few others. If you're wondering why relative unknown Gorosaurus (from *King Kong Escapes)* is featured so prominently—the reason has to do with the condition of the monster suits, some of which were in bad shape and not vital enough to the plot to be rebuilt. Old Angilas (from *Godzilla Raids Again)* picked up some admirers with this film, as a result of his courage shown in the scrap with Ghidorah. This was Ishiro Honda's second-to-last Godzilla picture, and the last really good one for nearly two decades. The dubbing is better than usual, and Akira Ifukube provides one of his best scores ever. **AKA:** *Kaiju Soshingeki; Gojira Dengeki-Taisakusen; All Monsters Attack; Attack of the Marching Monsters; Monster Attack March; Operation Monsterland.* ♫♫♫♫

1968 (G) 89m/C *JP* Akira Kubo, Yukiko Kobayashi, Jun Tazaki, Kenji Sahara, Yutaka Sada, Chotaro Togin, Yoshio Tsuchiya, Yoshifumi Tajima, Haruo Nakajima, Hiroshi Sekita, Taruo Nigake, Sisumi Utsumi. *D:* Ishiro Honda. *W:* Takeshi Kimura, Ishi-

ro Honda. *C:* Taiichi Kankura. *M:* Akira Ifukube. **VHS, DVD**

Devil Hunter Yohko

Sixteen-year-old Yohko Mano is finding stranger things happening to her than the urges of her post-pubescent sexuality. She's been having weird dreams, and has witnessed odd behavior in those around her. Her grandmother reveals the truth: Yohko has inherited the mantle of Devil Hunter from a line of 107 previous warriors. For centuries, the Devil Hunters have protected the plane of mortals from invading demons from the dark dimension. Her mom lost her chance by losing her virginity, leaving it up to Yohko to learn the ropes from Grandma. Her friends Osamu and Chigako (who looks just like A-ko with glasses) are possessed by demons; her principal is revealed to be a witch, who plans to resurrect the Dark Queen as her schoolmate Reiko. Before dying at the claws of demons,

Grandma teaches Yohko how to summon her Soul Sword, but the dark forces gather to try to kill (or deflower) the young Devil Hunter before she learns to use her powers.

Made two years before *Buffy the Vampire Slayer,* this is sort of like an "R"-rated horror-oriented *Sailor Moon.* Not only is *Yohko* a much more violent series, but its heroine bursts out of all her clothes while transforming to her action uniform. Toho Studios released this initially as a concurrent OAV and video game title. Subsequently, this was one of the first anime to be imported and re-released on a U.S. label. Though the artwork is nice, for the most part the animation is very limited. *AKA: Mamono Hunter Yohko.* 🐕🐕 🐾

1991 43m/C *JP* ***D:*** Tetsuro Aoki. ***W:*** Yoshihiro Tomita, Juzo Mitsui (story). ***C:*** Kinichi Ishikawa. ***M:*** Hiroya Watanabe. **VHS, DVD**

Devil Hunter Yohko 2

This sequel shows a distinct improvement in animation, direction, and writing over the first Yohko OAV. Here we find Yohko whining about being left behind when Mom and Grandma go on vacation, with her "manager" Chigako Ogawa (now with her hair changed from red to brown) in charge of her training schedule. Despite Chi's griping, her skills have really improved, and Chi's head is full of plans to exploit her client. Azusa Kanzaki, whose grandmother is an old friend of Yohko's grandma, comes to visit, wanting to become an apprentice Devil Hunter. Her grandmother gave her a magic gauntlet to help her transform, when she's ready. Meanwhile, a construction company is tearing down the nearby Forest of Evil Spirits, setting loose a horde of vengeful demons. Azusa goes to investigate on her own, and gets into big trouble. The end title song is called "Not So Fast, Sexy Girl." *AKA: Mamono Hunter Yohko Part 2.* 🐕🐕🐕 🐾

1992 29m/C *JP* ***D:*** Katsuhisa Yamada. ***W:*** Hisaya Takabayashi. ***C:*** Hiroshi Isakawa. ***M:*** Toshiyuki Omori. **VHS, DVD**

Devil Hunter Yohko 3

Yohko's sleep is disturbed by a dream of her ancestor, Princess Yohko, whose love for blue-haired Prince Biryu was foiled when his demon father the Dragon King imprisoned

him in a Dragon Sphere. On awaking, Yohko is transported to a magic dimension, where she must kill two demons to release Biryu from his prison. Meanwhile, her apprentice Azusa and manager Chi use a magic manual to trail Yohko across dimensions. This trip into a magic fantasy world is a bit too fluffy to stay interesting. Shouldn't Yohko know better than to be used so obviously, traipsing off to other dimensions while there are still plenty of demons to chop up on Earth? With its air of flowery romance, this episode was probably an attempt to increase the number of girls in Yohko fandom. And where's Grandma? She's been one of the series' favorite characters, yet hasn't been seen since episode 1. Superstitious about the number 4, the Japanese often go to great lengths to avoid it, so the next Yohko release was a lame "music video" collection, and they picked up the series again with number 5. *AKA: Mamono Hunter Yohko Part 3.* 🐕🐕

1992 29m/C *JP* ***D:*** Katsuhisa Yamada. ***W:*** Sukehiro Tomita. ***C:*** Hiroshi Isakawa. ***M:*** Toshiyuki Omori. **VHS, DVD**

Devil Man

After the success of his boundary-pushing series "Shameless School" and "Cutie Honey," Japanese cartoonist Go Nagai created a new manga series that became just as influential. It took the old "boy transforms to hero" idea of Captain Marvel and gave it a horrifying new twist. His new hero was dark and dangerous, a half-demon that fought other monsters invading our dimension, while fighting his own evil and bloodthirsty urges. While *The Exorcist* would explore a human possessed by a demon, *Devil Man* had a demon possessed by a human.

In a *Fantasia*-like prologue, nymphs descend from Heaven and are eaten by monsters. Then the nymphs get revenge by ravaging the planet with powerful beams of destruction, ending the age of the demons. A jillion years later, spelunkers release a monster from an ice cave in Antarctica. The doomed explorers are the parents of our hero, Akira. Akira's pal Ryu from his old school reveals how his father went insane and killed himself, but the secret behind the madness is even more shocking. A demon skull mask found in an Aztec cave allows one to see into the ancient demonic world. Unfortunately, the boys' knowledge of this world makes them a target for demons still roaming the Earth. The only way to possibly protect themselves is to attempt to merge with demons themselves. The ultimate danger is that their human spirit will become completely dominated by that of the demon.

The transformation ritual is to take place in a decadent nightclub, where the pair try to rouse demonic forces. Ryu fails in his attempt, but Akira succeeds in his transformation, able to become a demon-shredding Devil Man when the need arises. Devil Man shows off his prowess by destroying a good dozen demons right away. Some of the demon's personality and abilities have merged with Akira's human form as well, even when he's not the Devil Man. Akira has nightmares in which the demon's memories meld with his own. Miki is concerned over the changes that have come over her boyfriend, even more so since he's moved in with her family. Unfortunately, this makes Miki and her family vulnerable when Gelmar the water demon and Shirnu the bird demon come to call. Gelmar takes natural advantage of the situation when Miki takes her nightly bath. Fortunately, Akira's demon senses start tingling, warning him of the danger. Akira's battle with Gelmar is epic, but the fight between Devil Man and Shirnu is downright apocalyptic, tearing up the city and getting their blood all across the countryside.

Nagai was ahead of his time, creating a splatter-punk series that broke through sex and gore barriers in a Hellish fantasy setting. *Devil Man* is like a superhero version of the *Evil Dead* and *Nightmare on Elm Street* movies. He would go on to even more success with *Mazinger*, a giant robot series that would become highly influential around the world. **AKA:** *Debiruman.* 🐉🐉🐉

1987 120m/C *JP* **V:** Alan Marriott, Adam Matalon, Laura Kelly. **D:** Tsutomu Iida. **W:** Go Nagai, Tsutomu Iida. **M:** Kenji Kawai. **VHS, DVD**

Devil Touch

A smart and sassy mystery. Low-level employee Amy (Iris Chai) accuses former boss Cheuk (Michael Tiu) of sexual harassment and rape. Because the company is on the verge of a business merger, an internal investigation is launched rather than involving the police. Cool-headed Joe (Alex Fong) is assigned to the case. While Amy tells her story convincingly, Cheuk is equally persuasive in admitting to a brief affair but claiming that it was entirely consensual. Internal evidence points to Amy as being incompetent. The company sides with Amy, though, and Cheuk is suspended, causing him to lose his girlfriend as well as his leading role in coordinating the merger. Fellow executive Jacqueline (Pinky Cheung) is given the latter responsibility. The investigation does not end there, however, as a web of deception is uncovered.

The story takes off in unexpected directions and consistently keeps the viewer off balance. The pace is a bit slow at first, and the plot is difficult to follow at times. At certain points, especially near the end, things become ludicrous. In sum, though, the script by Jackie Chan's sparring partner Ken Lo is exceedingly clever, and the film is a pleasure to experience. Director Billy Tang (*Dr. Lamb*) makes effective use of reverse tracking shots and slow pans to build the mystery and lend a quiet air of foreboding. The musical score by Eric Tse is especially atmospheric, by turns aggressive, contemplative, moody, and seductive. Good use is made of locations, and the production design (by Andrew Cheuk Man-Yiu) is especially sharp. To top it off, the film is lovingly photographed by cinematographer Tony Mui King-fai. —*PM* **AKA:** *Chi Meng Sing Siu Yiu; Zhi Ming Xing Sao Rao.* 🐉🐉🐉

2002 88m/C *HK* Alex Fong, Michael Tiu, Pinky Cheung, Iris Chai, Ken Wong. **D:** Billy Tang. **W:** Ken Lo. **C:** Tony Miu. **M:** Eric Tse. **VHS, DVD**

Devil Woman

In a grass shack, baby Manda is born—a very unusual baby that her father is tempted to destroy immediately. Manda grows up a natural snake charmer. There always seems to be serpents around her, which she can control. Meanwhile, droughts, unemployment, and a string of deaths by snakebite in the village are blamed on the Devil. Poor little Manda has one heck of a Show & Tell surprise under her babushka: a full head of slithering snakes, just like old Medusa. The villagers don't appreciate her scaly 'do, so they burn her house down, killing her parents. Years later, the full-grown Manda (Rosemarie Gil) makes her primary hobby killing the house-burning, parent-killing villagers. She also uses her pets to get one of the local gangs to work for her, robbing and looting while she sits on a big throne in her cave. Dr. Shu Wen (Alex Tang Lee) comes to the village from China, saving Tina and her whiny friend Bowi from some hooligans with his kung fu. Shu Wen is visiting to treat rich Mr. Crispin, Tina's injured father. After Crispin recovers, Shu stays on in the Philippines to stay with Tina, wear all-white suits, and get in brawls. Shu's run-ins with the village gangsters eventually bring him into conflict with Manda.

Devil women are popular subjects of Philippine horror tales, and so are snakes. This trashy little flick has both, mixing in some Hong Kong martial arts for good measure. None of it is particularly impressive, but for cinema weirdness, it's hard to beat these gems from the Philippines. Just how many movies have you seen where the lead actress walks around with a pile of snakes on her head? Imported to the U.S. in 1976, when anything with kung fu could find a play date. **AKA:** *Mo Neuih.* 🐉🐉

1970 (R) 93m/C *HK/PH* Alex Tang Lee, Rosemarie Gil, Yukio Someno, Romy Diax, Johanna Garcia,

David Yau, Lito Lenaspi, Cherie Gil, To Chow Kwan, Peter Multan, Yuen Ching Kee, Joe Garcia, Robert Chen, Yuen Yan Wei, Max Rojo. **D:** Albert Yu, Felix Villar. **W:** Jimmy L. Pascual. **C:** Frank Leung. **M:** Chou Fu-liang. **VHS**

The Dimension Travelers

Does Midori Kogawa (Chiharu Niyama) have a split personality, or is she just suffering from typical teen angst? She has an odd hobby: stealing flowers from shops and concealing them in books in the library. Mayumi Owase (Yasue Sato), the new girl who moves into her building, seems to offer a clue, sharing quantum theory and hallucinations. Sometimes Mayumi seems like a visitor from another world—a suspicion that becomes more concrete when Mayumi confesses to Midori that she comes from another dimension that was destroyed in a catastrophe (though Mayumi is given to playing mind games). She offers to show Midori how to cross over to another dimension, and after their crossing, Midori notices no apparent differences. She writes Mayumi's behavior off as typical of adjustment to a new school, but later Midori has odd visions. She collapses, and awakes in a mental hospital. The doctors tell her she's been there for years. Is the home and school she knows reality, or a construct of her mind? Or is the fantasy of one dimension the reality of another?

Is this a movie dreaming it's a butterfly, or a butterfly dreaming it's a movie? Once Midori becomes a dimension traveler, she seems to drift from one reality to another uncontrollably. In one dimension she's a middle-school student living in a new housing project, though news reports point to a potentially apocalyptic danger. In another, she's in an oppressed world fighting with an underground group against the ruling class. Mayumi also tells her that their classmate Yamazawa is another dimension traveler who's become lost in his present reality, forgetting his past. Is there something to all her talk, or is it all an illusion? The aspect of the story with two girls sharing passage into other worlds parallels Peter Jackson's *Heavenly Creatures*, but the vision here is much darker (though not to the level of *The Lathe of Heaven* or *Videodrome*). The message seems to be that we need to keep shifting realities and adjusting our viewpoint, or risk getting caught up in a past state that's sure to crumble, while forgetting the lessons of the past. While this may be a worthy subject for a novel or a *Twilight Zone* episode, in this feature it just takes too long to get to the point. With each shift in dimension, it just gets harder to stay involved with the characters and plot. Instead of the intended message of imagination and creativity, an overall atmosphere of futility sets in. **AKA:** *Nazo no Tenkousei.* 🐉🐉🐉🐲

1998 95m/C *JP* Chiharu Niyama, Yasue Sato, Satoshi Tsumabuki. **D:** Kazuya Konaku. **W:** Sadayuki Murai, Taku Mayumura (novel). **VHS, DVD**

Dirty Ho

Stop snickering about the title. You know that it didn't have the same double meaning in 1979, even in America. Though come to think of it, the Chinese title of this entertaining kung fu flick translates as "Rotten Head Ho," which is kind of funny. Besides, we see right away that Wong Yu is wearing a large bandage on his head in the energetic title sequence—which might as well be a big label reading "clown" in Cantonese comedy. Wong stars as rascal and con man Ho Chi, whose schemes are ruined by Peking antiquities merchant Wang Ching-chin (Gordon Lau). Wang is actually the 11th Prince in line for the throne, traveling incognito, and he amuses himself by teasing Ho, but stops short of getting him in real trouble. Ho's kung fu is good enough to protect him from the likes of the Four Beggars, whose ambush he repels using his "Sober Boxing" technique. But Wang is so superior that he can beat Ho without appearing to fight at all. Wang gives Ho a poisoned wound, and forces him to reform and become his disciple. Though Wang is far down the line of succession, and has no interest in the throne, that doesn't stop Prince 4 (Frankie Wei as one of his 13 brothers) from trying to eliminate the competition, and his General Liang Ching-chien (Lo Lieh) sends assassins after Wang. During one of these attacks, Wang is stabbed in the leg, and he spends his months in recovery teaching Ho more advanced kung fu. Ho faces his first challenge when the effeminate Seven Tigresses of Kuantung—a collection of fighting oddballs including Peter Chan Lung and cross-eyed Yue Tau Wan—who try to get him to give up Wang with their weird fighting styles. Together, Wang and Ho must face constant danger on their way to the capitol for the announcement of the heir.

Real-life hero Ho Chi went on to study kung fu at Shaolin Temple and found the Blood Brothers Clan, not that this movie is all that interested in history. The Shaw Brothers' production values combine nicely with the Lau Brothers' expert choreography here, with many fights set in ornate rooms. One terrific scene has Gordon Lau using Kara Hui to fight Wong for him. Another involves Johnny Wang and Hsiao Ho trying to covertly feed Lau various drugged wines, and they do an intricate juggling act of various jars, cups, fans, and other objects. One might think they'd toss everything aside and start throwing punches, but that would break the unwritten rules of the duel. Later, they get down to more serious—but just as imaginative—combat. One battle has our heroes fending off an army of Mongolians in a windy narrow pass next to a village's "typhoon wall." In the palace, they do some of their best screen fighting using a single pole together against Lo Lieh and two other fighters. Fast-moving and fun throughout, *Dirty Ho*'s biggest flaw is that it ends too abruptly. *AKA: Laan Tau He; Lan Tou He.* ⚔⚔⚔♥

1979 99m/C *HK* Wong Yu, Gordon Lau, Lo Lieh, Hsiao Ho, Kara Hui, Johnny Wang, Chan Lung, Frankie Wei, Wilson Tong, Yue Tau Wan, Shum Lo, Chan Si Gai, Yau Tsui-ling, Cheng Miu, Yang Chih-ching, Jamie Luk, Ging Chue, Chiang Han, Pan Ping-chang, Wong Ching Ho, Wang Han-chen. *D:* Lau Kar-Leung. *W:* Ngai Hong. *C:* Arthur Wong, Au Chih-chun. *M:* Eddie H. Wang. **VHS, DVD**

Dirty Kung Fu

This Lau Brothers kung fu comedy has a refreshingly light touch, getting laughs from the situations and characters rather than broad gags. Bounty hunter Pai Dao-chai (Wong Yu) is after criminal Chung Fung. Passing a funeral, he sees that the corpse looks like Chung Fung, and steals the body, trying to pass it off to the police chief (Karl Maka) as the real thing. Eventually, his pal Liu helps him catch the criminal, but cheats him out of his share of the $50 reward. But in Chung's wallet (which he pinched), Pai finds a letter from Flying Bandit Hu Lan (Wilson Tong), who has a $1000 bounty on his head, asking Chung to meet him and fellow bandit Wan Chen-tong. Once again he recruits another associate, Pao Yuen-ti (Lau Kar-Wing), to do most of the fighting, and together they capture Wan. And once again he fails to collect, as Pao finds out that Pai has a $5 reward on his head as well ($5 alive, but only $1 dead!). Next he uses waitress Su-ming (Wong Hang-sau) to lure a slaver, but loses his captive gambling right away.

Pai's luck is slightly better the next day. He comes upon Hu Lan as he's beating up his partner Pa-chi, thinking he's betrayed him. Pai distracts the Flying Bandit long enough to carry off Pa-chi—however, he dies before the chief can pay up, cutting the bounty by half. So Pai recruits Chen Ying-Hung (Dai Sai Aan) to help him catch Hu Lan, but the bandit's too tough, and kills Chen. Pai gets Pao to try his Snake Style, but Hu Lan counters with a special Open Heaven technique, seemingly becoming possessed by the Drunken God to win. A stranger named Yip Ku-hung the Flashing Blade (Norman Tsui), who is a righteous fighter, challenges Hu Lan to a formal duel. Here, old-school kung fu cinema gets a grilling, as Pai is disgusted by all the noble trash talking the two engage in before

getting down to business. For once, it's refreshing to see a protagonist who's an outright coward who can't fight very well. But of course, he decides he's gotten too many people killed and will buckle down to practice his Snake Style until he's good enough to face Hu Lan. The problem is, he's afraid of snakes, and gets the idea to study the less frightening Eel Fist Style instead. But to beat Hu Lan's magic, he needs a secret weapon: used women's panties!

The players are likable enough to float this lightweight plot, making it an enjoyable time-waster, with the expected solid choreography. The idea of Pai using juggled and bounced rubber balls to fight is a clever one, but not much is made of it until the end. The soundtrack uses extensive pieces from *The Nutcracker Suite,* and even a cue from *Taxi Driver.* *AKA: Gwai Ma Gung Foo; Gui Ma Gong Fu.* ⚔⚔♥

1978 87m/C *HK* Wong Yu, Wilson Tong, Norman Tsui, Lau Kar-Wing, Wong Hang-sau, Dean Shek, Karl Maka, Dai Sai Aan, To Siu Ming, Chan Lung, Fung Hark-On, Ho Pak Kwong, Thompson Kao, Cheng Hong-yip, Yue Tau Wan. *D:* Lau Kar-Wing. *W:* Ngai Hong. *C:* Chao Hung. *M:* Frankie Chan. **VHS, DVD**

Dirty Tiger, Crazy Frog

Hero Dirty Tiger (Lau Kar-Wing) is hired by an elderly woman to return her "escaped" husband Crazy Frog (Sammo Hung). Frog is at a casino, being seduced by foxy pickpocket Multi-Hand Chick (Meg Lam) into helping her out of a jam. Afterward, she steals his valuable Invincible Armor mail shirt—which he married his wife to get in the first place. When Tiger captures Frog, they agree to cooperate to get the Armor back (after Tiger collects his reward, of course). They soon run afoul of the Bandit Brothers, Panther (Dean Shek) and Smiling Tiger (Jason Pai)—along with their father, the White-Brow Monk (Lee Hoi-sang), and the Coffin King (Cheng Hong-yip)—who are also out to get the Armor.

Tiger comes up with a scheme to locate the Armor, and throw their enemies off the scent, by selling a fake mail shirt to Coffin King. After retrieving the Armor, Frog and Tiger immediately try to snatch it away from each other of course—until the bandits get it and our heroes have to cooperate to face them again.

In other films together like *Odd Couple,* Sammo Hung and Lau Kar-Wing would dominate with their amazing fight choreography and athleticism. While this is a factor (especially during the Big Fight climax, which doesn't disappoint viewers by delivering the expected duel between Hung and Lau), this one belongs to writers Eric Tsang and Karl Maka (with the latter directing and taking a small part). The nutty, knockabout tone of the story is infectious, producing broad comic performances, which, thanks to the talents involved, actually generate a lot of laughs. Dean Shek's mugging drags down his scenes a bit, but Lee Hoi-sang's underrated comic talents shine. Meg Lam has a standout role as the weird pickpocket who seems to have an endless number of fake arms up her sleeves, which she leaves behind whenever somebody tries to grab her. A lot of Sammo's buddies show up in small roles to trade kicks. A lot of the same folks showed up in *Dirty Kung Fu* the same year. The anything-goes attitude of films like this nearly made Hung the Curly Howard of kung fu, but there was too much of the Chinese opera school Biggest Brother in him to ever completely become a stooge. **AKA:** *Liu Foo Tin Gai; Lao Hu Tian Ji; Dirty Tiger and Crazy Frog.* ♫♫♫♡

1978 97m/C *HK* Sammo Hung, Lau Kar-Wing, Meg Lam, Dean Shek, Lee Hoi-sang, Jason Pai, Karl Maka, Cheng Hong-yip, To Siu Ming, Yuen Biao, Mars, Lam Ching-Ying, Mang Hoi, Chin Yuet Sang, Chung Fat, Fung Ging Man, Alan Chui, Hsiao Ho, Huang Ha, Billy Chan, Chan Lung, Tsang Choh-lam, Lin Ke-ming, Cheung Wa, Jimmy Liu, Ho Pak Kwong. **D:** Karl Maka. **W:** Eric Tsang, Karl Maka. **C:** Ho Ming. **DVD**

Dr. Lamb

This feature, based on the crimes of serial killer Lam Guo-wen, helped set off a whole wave of true-crime films in Hong Kong. Simon Yam, who played Lam in a TV miniseries, reprises his role as Lam Gor-yu, dubbed "Doctor Lamb" by the press for his consultation of medical books to assist his crimes. It begins with his tough slum childhood, as an unwanted stepchild. He grows up to become a taxi driver and amateur photographer, both occupations feeding his obsession to kill. Inspector Li (Danny Lee) responds to a call from the Kodak development house reporting awful snuff photographs coming through a shop in Mongkok. He dispatches Bing (Kent Cheng) and some men to stake out the shop, arresting Lam when he shows up to get his prints. At Lam's apartment, they find a cupboard full of incriminating evidence. Despite the abusive interrogation of Detective Bully Hung (Parkman Wong), Lam refuses to talk. But with evidence piling up, and his family turned against him, he finally cracks. Slowly, his full confession comes out—a incredible story of how he killed, dismembered, photographed, and even videotaped five women, all while sharing a one-bedroom apartment with four relatives.

The police are treated much more respectfully by Lee here than they would be in later true-crime films like *Daughter of Darkness*, which followed the comic lead of Lee's *The Untold Story*. Of course, the flashback scenes are reminiscent of *Taxi Driver*, mixed with *Psycho* and *The Texas Chainsaw Massacre*. Some might make a case for this as effective social commentary on the breakdown of the family unit that allowed a homicidal maniac (who even howls at the moon!) to slice up corpses with power tools undetected in a home so small he has to sleep in a bunk bed under his stepbrother. Also, Danny Lee's fascination with presenting police procedures has to be admired, even when humanizing them through light comedy relief. However, once the confessions start, all pretense of suspense disappears, and there's no disguising that *Dr. Lamb*'s main purpose is to provide shocks and horror for its leering audience. As such, it's an excellent piece of work. The direction, f/x, and photography are all excellent, and Jonathan Wong provides a fine jazzy score. Yam turns in a career-defining performance as the raving loony, who goes from charming and passive to cackling insanity in an instant. **AKA:** *Go Yeung Yi Sang; Gao Yang Yi Sheng; Dr. Lam.* ♫♫♫

1992 89m/C *HK* Simon Yam, Danny Lee, Kent Cheng, Lau Siu-ming, Parkman Wong, Perrie Lai, Wong Wing-fong, Eric Kei, Emily Kwan, Julie Lee, Chung Bik Wing, Lam King Kong. **D:** Danny Lee, Billy Tang. **W:** Law Kam-fai. **C:** Tony Miu. **M:** Wong Bong. **VHS, DVD**

Doctor No...

Triad boss Blackie (Blackie Ko) escapes from prison, dragging along the dazed Rock (Stephen Ma) only because they're chained together. Once they've gone their separate ways, Rock is overcome by memories of a violent incident, evidently the one that resulted in him being sent to prison. Hiding from the police, he ends up rescuing Moon, an underaged prostitute, from her pimp, and then just happens to be nearby when Blackie appears with his men, bleeding profusely. Rock steps up to help and saves Blackie's life. Grateful for his help, Blackie's lieutenant arranges a place to stay for Rock and Moon. There, overlooking the sea, Rock (a successful physician in his pre-prison days), attempts to piece back together his life and resolve the memories that haunt him. Occupying a prominent place in those memories is the love of his life, Ann (Yoyo Mung). A local monk/psychic (Jerry Lamb) tries to help.

The opening and concluding scenes are dynamically staged, filmed, and edited, with extremely effective music. The script doesn't give too much away too soon, drawing the audience into the puzzle of Rock's mind. The performances are consistently engaging. The setting and landscapes, evidently in Macau, are pleasant. The negatives are that two major plot

Seven Little Fortunes

Who's Who in Fu Part 1

There are certain families that have made great kung fu movies in Hong Kong and environs—though some of these families are not blood relations, but pseudo-families that worked and trained together so that they developed a sensitivity to each other that borders on telepathy. The foremost of these families came out of the Chinese Drama Academy run by Master Yu Jim-yuen. These "schools" were more like factories designed to churn out performers—not for the movies, but for the ancient and honorable Chinese opera, in this case a well-known troupe known as the Seven Little Fortunes. As a side business, students (who were bound by contracts that made them more like slaves) were rented out to film studios as extras, stuntmen, and even leading players. As the popularity of opera faded, students naturally migrated into the only other venue they knew: motion pictures. Here are *eight* of the Seven Little Fortunes who made good in Hong Kong cinema, working both alone and in a bunch.

Jackie Chan

O.K., anybody know who this guy is? Master Yu's favorite troublemaker became a household word—in houses all over the world—via his action hits like the *Police Story* series, the *Armour of God* series, *Project A, Drunken Master, Rush Hour, Miracles, Shanghai Noon, Rumble in the Bronx,* etc.

Sammo Hung

Big Brother to all the other Fortunes, Sammo was the bully you made peace with and befriended in school. He gained weight while recovering from an injury in his teens, but while this made him too heavy for opera, he stood out on-screen in more ways than one. Nobody ever expects a man with a big belly to be so incredibly fast and agile. Slightly older, with a distinctive scar on his upper lip, he established himself in the stunt community first and got jobs for everybody else, then proceeded to transform HK cinema several times as star, director, and producer. Some of his groundbreaking hits include *Enter the Fat Dragon, The Magnificent Butcher, Encounters of the Spooky Kind, Winners and Sinners, Yes, Madam, The Millionaire's Express, *Mr. Vampire*, *Eastern Condors*, and *Dragons Forever*. He also starred in the CBS television series *Martial Law*.

Yuen Biao

Younger and smaller than his opera brothers, Biao quickly distinguished himself as a natural acrobat. Throughout films of the 1970s, he can be glimpsed doubling for other actors to do amazing flips, leaps, and cartwheels. Sammo gave him his first starring role in *Knockabout,* and he proceeded to distinguish himself in starring and supporting roles which required a lot of motion as well as emotion. Highlights include *Prodigal Son, Zu: Warriors from the Magic Mountain, Wheels on Meals, Rosa, Righting Wrongs, The Peacock King, The Iceman Cometh, Once upon a Time in China,* and *A Kid from Tibet,* which he also directed. Like Sammo and Jackie, Yuen Biao has his own Stuntmen Association.

Corey Yuen

Though not a star, Corey can be seen in dozens of films in supporting and cameo roles. However, he's distinguished himself far more behind the camera as producer and/or director of such films as *Yes, Madam, Righting Wrongs, Saviour of the Soul, The Legend, The Defender, The Avenging Fist,* and *The Transporter.* Recently he's been making waves in Hollywood as action director on films like *X-Men.*

Yuen Miu

Like Corey, Yuen Miu made a name for himself as a featured player like *Prodigal Son* and *Encounters of the Spooky Kind* (where he was possessed by spirits to fight Sammo), then becoming an ace action director on such films as *Doctor Vampire, Don't Give a Damn,* and *Master of Zen.*

Yuen Wah

With his thin frame and distinctive looks, Wah first made a name for himself in *The Chinese Connection* by both playing one of the evil Japanese fighters and doubling for Bruce Lee. A fine stuntman, acrobat (known as the "Somersault King") and action director, Wah had the gaunt looks that needed to be seen in front of the camera, and he's appeared as the lead villain in *Eastern Condors, Dragons Forever, The Iceman Cometh, Bury Me High,* and *Supercop.* Though like Yuen Biao he now makes his home in Canada, he still flies back to HK to be in movies and TV series.

Continued on next page...

...Continued

Ng Ming Choi

Like Sammo, Ming Choi gained weight outside of opera school, but still did plenty of acting and stunt work, notably in the King Hu picture *Legend of the Mountain,* and played the same role as Sammo the same year, starring in *Butcher Wing.* He went on to become a producer on *Midnight Angel, Faces of Horror,* and King Hu's *Painted Skin.*

Yuen Tak

Despite a handsome face, Tak never graduated to leading roles, but became an excellent action director, including *The Iceman Cometh, She Shoots Straight, Robotrix, Fist of Fury 1991, Once upon a Time in China 3, The Defender, Beyond Hypothermia,* and *Beast Cops.* You can see him face off against Moon Lee in *Angel 2.*

---

points are hard to swallow. One is that Moon turns out to be Blackie's long-lost daughter. The other is that Rock doesn't recognize Ann when she shows up as a patient at his so-called clinic. Flashbacks have revealed her identity, and even with some gray streaks in her hair and minor crow's feet at her eyes, it's clearly the same person. So, unnecessarily, Ann becomes a red herring. If Rock doesn't recognize her, maybe it's not really Ann? Maybe it really is some "granny" (as the subtitles identify her) with a resemblance to Ann? It's puzzling, and the intentions of the filmmakers are not clear. Thus, the middle third of the film remains a bit muddled, until the rousing conclusion brings it to a satisfying finish. Television actor Stephen Ma gives a fine, fully nuanced performance as Rock. Lam Suet has a cameo as the pimp for underaged girls. —PM **AKA:** *San Lau Man Yee Sang.* 🐉🐉🐉

2001 88m/C *HK* Stephen Ma, Yoyo Mung, Jerry Lamb, Blackie Ko, Pan Ya Kan, Liu Kat Lin, Timothy Zao, Lam Suet. **D:** Mak Kai-gwong. **W:** Chan Gin-tak, Law Gam-foo. **C:** Davy Tsou. **M:** Tang Hin-fai, Alan Wong. **VHS, DVD**

Doctor Vampire

Another Hong Kong resident learns the dangers of traveling away from home in this horror comedy, which for a change of pace features European-style vampires. Dr. Chiang Ta-tsung (Bowie Lam) has car trouble near the wrong castle (played by the Allington Castle) while visiting England, finding some kind of club full of strange people inside. He's seduced by Alice (Ellen Chan), who unbeknownst to him is a fang-carrying vampire. Alice's vampire master, the Earl (Peter Kjaer), turns out to have a passion for Chinese food, and demands that Alice bring him more once he gets a taste of Chiang's blood. The flavor must have something to do with the ginseng soup Chiang's sweetheart May Chen (Sheila Chan) keeps feeding him. While Alice makes her way to Hong Kong to track down Chiang, the doctor is finding an odd distaste for garlic, sensitivity to sunlight, and a fondness for snappy evening clothes (complete with opera cape). His colleagues become convinced something is amiss when they see Chiang drooling over incisions during surgery.

Alice has grown fond of Chiang, and decides to help him instead of kidnap him. Since Chiang has yet to taste human blood, she begins to help him with a plan to reverse his curse. But Alice and her roommate Joy (Crystal Kwok) slip Chiang a love potion containing a drop of Alice's blood, completing his transformation. Chiang's workplace becomes a hospital of horror when the Earl and his minions check in.

The movie adheres to a rare bit of vampire lore later adopted by the *Buffy the Vampire Slayer* TV series: vampires automatically know martial arts (with the Earl granted heat vision and other powers to boot). This leads to an action-packed climax in which Chiang and company battle the Earl throughout the hospital, and even onto the Chinese opera stage! There are plenty of on-target gags and amusing situations on the way there, making for an agreeably silly good time. Considering the number of vampire spoofs over the years, the amount of fresh material here is surprising. Chinese gwonsi are given a razzing, too—in one scene, Bowie Lam is overjoyed to don the traditional Chinese burial costume. Shing Fui-on has some fun sending up his usual gangster role as an inept triad chief who keeps ending up in the hospital. **AKA:** Geung See Yee Sang; Xiong Wu Yi Shen; Dr. Vampire. 🐉🐉🐉

1990 93m/C *HK* Bowie Lam, Ellen Chan, Sheila Chan, Crystal Kwok, David Wu, Ngai Hong, Peter Kjaer, Lorraine Kibble, Shing Fui-on, James Wong. **D:** Jamie Luk. **W:** Jamie Luk. **C:** James Yeung. **M:** Tsui Yat-kan. **DVD**

Don't Give a Damn

Loads of raw energy percolate through a comedy-action vehicle with dollops of romance and silliness tossed in. Threatening to go off the rails at any moment, it's the film's heedless, endearing desire to entertain that wins out. Police investigator Fei Liu Ging-wan (Sammo Hung) is none too happy to be paired with Takeshi Kaneshiro. He's been trying to bring a gang of drug dealers to justice, and feels his new partner will slow him down. He also must contend with A Yuen (Yuen Biao), a customs officer pursuing the same criminal crew. The two men got off on the wrong foot—they met when each was undercover, mistakenly thinking the other was a criminal. To make things even tougher, throw in three feisty female police officers (Kathy Chow, Eileen Tung, Annabelle Lau) and a few romantic complications. Highly competitive and fiercely independent, the police and customs departments must put aside their differences in order to catch the crooks.

The basic plot mechanics have been used a thousand times over. Much of the running time is devoted to romance and comedy, with action scenes occasionally interspersed. Three highlights can be mentioned. One is a bruising tussle between Sammo Hung and Yuen Biao in a police locker room—watch out for those metallic surfaces! Another is a stakeout gone bad, and the chaotic mayhem that results. The third is the concluding fight sequence involving multiple participants and one sword, set in a junk- and scaffold-filled warehouse. *Don't Give a Damn* is not terrible, but it's also not terribly essential. Be advised that one scene near the end includes some racially insensitive "blackface" humor.

Bobby Samuels—the African-American Sammo Hung prot who learned Chinese and martial arts and then moved to Hong Kong specifically to get into HK action movies—must have wondered what he had gotten himself into the day he showed up for that scene. He carried away some broken bones for his efforts in this film. —PM **AKA:** *Miu Min Bei; Mou Mian Bei.* 🐉🐉

1995 95m/C *HK* Sammo Hung, Takeshi Kaneshiro, Yuen Biao, Kathy Chow, Eileen Tung, Annabelle Lau, Kelvin Wong, Yip Wing-cho, Timmy Hung, Ngai Sing, Bobby Samuels, Nat Chan, Lau Kar-Wing, Leung Kar-yan, Deon Lam, Melvin Wong, Wu Ma, K.K. Cheung, Chin Siu-Ho, Blackie Ko, Richard Ng, Chan Lung, Billy Lau, Miu Kiu-wai, Eddie Maher, Yvonne Yung. **D:** Sammo Hung. **W:** Szeto Cheuk-hon, Chung Wai-hung, Phillip Kwok. **C:** Lau Yuen-chuen. **M:** Frankie Chan. **VHS**

Double Dragon in the Last Duel

The escort service of Kil Do-lee successfully transports a payroll shipment with help from a skunk-haired fighter named Wang Hu. Despite competition from Chinese security companies, Kil continues to have success, and Wang becomes a partner, though Mrs. Kil doesn't trust the man. She turns out to be right—Wang betrays them and steals the next payroll. Wang's gang kills the Kil family; only Do-lee and his son San-yong escape the massacre. The surviving Kils move in with an old Buddhist master, who helps train little San-yong in the martial arts. However, Wang secretly spared Kil's infant daughter Do-hwa, raising her as his own. Grown to manhood, San-yong begins a campaign against the Wang gang, getting some unexpected help from a friendly stranger named Dong Soo. The now-grown Do-hwa wants to fight the intruder who threatens her adopted father, while San-yong and Dong Soo use their resemblance to each other to confuse Wang.

He's not the only one confused. The similar-looking heroes are hard to keep track of, and the frequent flashbacks by various characters doesn't make it any easier. Then another pair of fighters, killers named Jackal Chin and Chun Bao hired to kill Wang, also dress alike. Wang easily buys off the killers. Then Wang finds Pang, a defiant restaurant owner San-yong was protecting, and kidnaps his daughter Ma-chi to use as bait for the heroes. The action scenes are dynamic, with jazzy '70s style urban action music playing over them. From the director of *Dragon Force*. **AKA:** *Revenge; The Last Duel.* 🐉🐉

1985 88m/C *KO* Kang Ho, Mae Lim, Park Jum-soon, Bong Choi, Soo Chun Bay, Hong Yoo-jung, Chah In-sun. **D:** Nam Key-nam. **W:** Oh Kwang-Jay. **C:** Im Jin-Whan. **VHS, DVD**

Double Tap

The title refers to the ability of a skilled shooter to hit the same target twice in quick succession. Although it starts as a kind of sports movie about target shooting, there's little doubt that it'll get to flesh-and-blood targets before too long. Rick Pang (Leslie Cheung) is a champion marksman, gunsmith, and instructor. His girlfriend Colleen (Ruby Wong) coerces him into teaching an old friend of hers, forensics detective Vincent Ng (Vincent Kok). Rick's friendly rival is Miu Chi-sun (Alex Fong), a cop and tough competitor. During the Hong Kong championships, a friend of Miu's has a breakdown over a stock tumble and starts shooting into the crowd, forcing Rick to kill him when he aims at Colleen. Three years later, Miu and Ng are investigating a crime scene where a gunman killed a hotel suite full of men guarding a witness who was testifying against an alleged smuggler. However, though shot through the head, the witness survives, but is unlikely to ever regain consciousness. Known high-quality shooters are rounded up for questioning, and inevitably they get to Pang, thought to be the prime suspect for his ability to score three double taps within five seconds. Pang is released for lack of evidence, but Colleen is held for possession of his guns. Pang takes revenge for her by humiliating the officers tailing him, wounding all but Miu seriously. An all-out manhunt begins for Pang, who seems addicted to killing, even as he threatens another killing spree unless Colleen is released.

Leslie Cheung has a screen image of a perpetual juvenile, developed in his early John Woo–directed hits like *Once a Thief* and *A Better Tomorrow*, but here he looks satisfyingly grizzled, contributing a convincingly psychotic performance. However, Fong's role is the more difficult one, requiring expression of a wider range of conflicting emotion. It's no wonder Fong is now one of Hong Kong's busiest actors—quite a step up from his role in the *Angel* series. Law Chi-leung's direction is assured, with nice attention paid to details in emotion, action (including some primo gun fu), and police procedure. *AKA: Cheong Wong; Qiang Wang; Gun King.* 🐉🐉🐉

2000 94m/C *HK* Leslie Cheung, Alex Fong, Ruby Wong, Monica Chan, Vincent Kok, Joe Cheung, Henry Fong, Alexander Chan, Raven Choi. *D:* Law Chi-leung. *W:* Derek Yee, Law Chi-leung. *C:* Venus Keung. *M:* Peter Kam, Anthony Chue. **DVD**

Downtown Torpedoes

Jackal (Takeshi Kaneshiro) and Cash (Jordan Chan) are master thieves, specializing in industrial secrets. They're forcibly recruited, along with associates Sam (Charlie Yeung) and Titan (Ken Wong), by Branch Chief Stanley Wong (Alex Fong) to join ATM (Available Tactical Mercenaries), a secret government team of Impossible Mission tricksters. Iran is planning another Supernotes scheme to flood Hong Kong with counterfeit notes, disrupting the economy just before reunification. The plates are in the hands of MI5 agent Edward Burns, and ATM's job is to get them before he can leave Hong Kong with them. Cash brings in his deaf-mute pal Phoenix (Theresa Lee, successfully hiding her Canadian accent for once) as their hacker. The team manages to pull off the spectacular heist, but Stanley double-crosses them—he intended to steal the plates all along—and a bomb kills one of the quintet. The team sticks together to come up with a plan of revenge against Stanley and recover the plates.

A well-crafted spy/caper flick, *Torpedoes* provides plenty of action, jackknife plot twists, and high-tech gadgets (though the computer stuff is all dated already). Jordan Chan, already a veteran after a few years as a lead, deserves international stardom, easily stealing the show from his pretty-boy co-star Kaneshiro. Teddy Chan's direction makes the complicated story easy to follow (he went on to similar duty for Jackie Chan's *Accidental Spy*). The European locations and great stunts help—one stunt resulted in the death of a stuntman from shrapnel produced by an explosion, resulting in some controversy when it was discovered the proper permits hadn't been filed. The English title is a puzzle, but the Chinese translates as "Godly Thief Spy Shadow," if that helps any. *AKA: San Tau Dip Ying; Shen Tou Die Ying.* 🐉🐉🐉🐉

1997 89m/C *HK* Takeshi Kaneshiro, Jordan Chan, Charlie Yeung, Ken Wong, Theresa Lee, Alex Fong, Edward Laskey, Jude Poyer. *D:* Teddy Chan. *W:* Poon Yuen-leung. *C:* Cheung Man-po. *M:* Clarence Hui, Peter Kam. **DVD**

Dragon against Vampire

For those who think that Chinese movies feature only the hopping kind of vampires, we humbly submit this low-budget horror/kung fu comedy. Tony (Elton Chong), Martin (Martin Kim), and Albert are escaped convicts picking up what money they can get as grave robbers while trying to stay ahead of their pursuing jailer. Meanwhile, a monster is plaguing the area they're traveling through, carrying off the village's young ladies. The un-heroic trio stumbles upon the vampire's lair, and finds that the vampire is keeping his old master chained up in a cave in order to try to force him to teach him his

Shaolin sorcery, which will allow him to overcome his corpselike weaknesses and become master of all living things. Albert falls victim to the vampire, but his companions escape and take refuge at an inn, where the innkeeper has already lost one daughter (Li Ying Ying) to the monster and fears his other daughter Fannie (Carrie Lee) will be next. However, it's the innkeeper himself who is the next victim, leaving Fannie in the hands of the guests. Fortunately, Tony seems to be immune to the vampire's voodoo; he frees the old man (who is permanently locked in a lotus position) from the cave so that he'll teach him Shaolin sorcery to defeat the vampire.

The many-costumed characters Elton Chong uses in *Invincible Obsessed Fighter* are thankfully eliminated here, limited only to a two-headed warrior disguise he uses to try to fool his master. The "vampire" here may be only for want of a better term, since he doesn't follow many of the same rules as the European variety—he seems to be a wizard whose power is consuming him, and he drinks blood to replenish his energy. He can walk around in sunlight, and doesn't have any special physical powers. His kung fu doesn't even appear to be much good. The story tends to ramble about, lacking any decent martial arts action to sustain it. To keep us from forgetting we're watching a horror show, the film cheats with dream sequences. However, there are enough spookshow shocks and creative touches to keep things moderately interesting throughout. The film features an unusual number of dissolves between scenes for a film of this type—independent Asian exploitation features of the time rarely allowed for such extravagances. Not to be confused with Yuen Woo-ping's *Dragon vs. Vampire* (AKA *Close Encounters of Vampire*). *AKA: Dragon vs. Vampire.* 🐉🐉

1985 78m/C *TW* Elton Chong, Carrie Lee, Martin Kim, Robin See, Eagle Han Ying, Oliver Cheng, Li Ying Ying, Roger Wang, Orson Chan, David Ma, Irene Kong, Paul Chang. **D:** Lionel Leung. **W:** Godfrey Ho. **C:** Henry Chan. **M:** Stephen Tsang. **VHS, DVD**

Dragon Chronicles: Maidens of Heavenly Mountain

What's better than a movie with Brigitte Lin? How about one with two Brigitte Lins? A semi-serious adaptation of the Chinese classic fantasy novel *Demi-Gods and Semi-Devils* by Jin Yong, this beautiful production casts Lin as twin sisters, Tin San Sect members Li Chou-shui and her sister Chong-hoi. Both sisters are subordinates in the leading martial arts sect to its grandmaster Siu Yiu-tze (who never shows his face), along with their comrade Mo Han-wen (Gong Li). Mo happens to be in love with Chong-hoi, and fighting with Chou-shui over their affair gets the scrapping students kicked out of the sect. Ting Chun-chou (Norman Tsui) of the rival Sing Suk Sect has poisoned Master Siu, and the Tin San master concentrates his martial arts on holding out until Chong-hoi can find his successor. The Sing Suks are picking off the lesser sects one by one, and Ting sees the spat between Chou-shui and Mo Han-wen as an opportunity to take on Tin San. His underlings are a bunch of rascals though, with their own plots and schemes, including his elite squad member Green, who is a double agent working for Chou-shui, and Purple (Sharla Cheung), who plans to steal some of the secrets they're after. When Sing Suk attacks the Shaolin Temple, the scroll containing the powerful Yi-ken Sutra is placed in the care of monk Hui-chok (Frankie Lam), with instructions to deliver it to Master Siu in safety. During the attack, tricky Purple makes off with the scroll, and the monk, too. Meanwhile, Chou-shui imprisons Mo Han-wen in a block of ice and takes over her palace. Imprisoned in the same caves, monk Hui-chok is stung by a huge scorpion, and reads the scroll to save his own life. His raging fever melts the ice around Mo Han-wen, freeing her—though her longevity kung fu now works overtime and her age regresses. Hui-chok succeeds in reaching Siu, and the great magic power is transferred to the little monk so that he can fight Ting—if he can only learn to use it.

With more plot before the opening credits roll than many features have altogether, thank Buddha there are some amusing characters to keep viewers interested—otherwise it would just be one semi-god or semi-devil after another. The movie is at its most entertaining when Sharla Cheung is on screen, playing another of her charming schemers. Frankie Lam is fun, too, though his monk is a bit too annoyingly naïve. Norman Tsui makes for one of the more personable white-haired old villains, and you could almost root for him to win. No time is given to really develop any of the characters, so it's hard to care what happens to them. However, the art direction and special effects are wonderful, though you can spot wires showing here and there. *AKA: San Tin Lung Baat Biu Chi Tin Saan Tung Liu; Xin Tian Long Ba Bu Zhi Tian Shan Tong Lao; Semi-Gods and Semi-Devils; 8 Guardians of Buddhism; Dragon Chronicles: The Maidens; The Immortals.* 🐉🐉🐉

1994 96m/C *HK* Brigitte Lin, Gong Li, Norman Tsui, Sharla Cheung, Frankie Lam, James Pak, Liu

Kai-chi. **D:** Andy Chin. **W:** Charcoal Cheung Tan. **C:** Poon Hang-sang. **M:** Violet Lam. **VHS, DVD**

The Dragon Family

A drama about a large triad family seems an odd choice for director Lau Kar-Wing, but here he is. Luckily, a lot of action is thrown in as well.

Lung Ying (O Chun Hung) is the head of the Dragon Clan, who is trying to get away from crime and into more profitable, less dangerous legitimate business. However, though son Chung (Max Mok) is going to England to study medicine, son Wah (Andy Lau) keeps the books straight, brother-in-law Sik (Lau Kar-Wing) helps run things, and brother Fung (Stanley Fung) is even a cop, the old blood still survives and other Lungs are not so cool-headed. Son Kar-wai (Miu Kiu-wai) is brash and violent, Yip (Kenneth Tong) is a gambling addict, and son Allan (Alan Tam) is a killer. After he executes drug trafficker Golden Teeth Shing, Allan is shipped off to Taiwan to hide out.

Even if the Lungs are going straight, that doesn't mean the other big families will follow suit. Rival Ho E (Ku Feng) breaks off from the other clan heads over the killing and accusations made over missing funds associated with Shing. Ho E's accountant Ko (William Ho) admits to have mishandled the books, but that doesn't solve the problem. Ho's evil second Keung (Norman Tsui) is behind the drug business, but rather than own up to taking the cash and ask for mercy, he and Ko conspire to murder Ho and Lung Ying. Yip's gambling debts give them a hook, forcing him into a deal to let them use the piers he's in charge of to ship heroin. Once they have access, they plant drugs in Yip's car, framing him. But their confrontation scene between the clan heads collapses when Lung Ying takes action, and Ko ends up grappling with Ying and fatally stabbing him. Adding to their villainy, Ho's gunmen invade the funeral, slaughtering the mourners, and Keung caps it off by killing Ho. Only Wah, Chung, their crippled mother, and faithful Po (Kent Cheng) escape the massacre. They should've got 'em all—Chung fetches Alan from Taipei and the brothers plot their revenge.

While this has enough characters and intrigues for a TV miniseries, Lau and company are wise enough not to get too deep into the melodrama, and action scenes are packed into each act. Even the big funeral scene has Shing Fui-on and Kenneth Tong fighting to the death over the corpse. The model here is *A Better Tomorrow*, and a huge gunfight is staged at the end. But since this is technically a Lau Brothers movie (Lau Kar-Leung serves as action director), there's many an acrobatic punch and kick thrown in between bullets. **AKA:** *Lung Chi Fung Chuk; Long Zhi Gu Zu.* 🐉🐉🐉

1988 88m/C *HK* Kenneth Tong, Alan Tam, Andy Lau, Norman Tsui, William Ho, Kent Cheng, Ku Feng, O Chun Hung, Miu Kiu-wai, Max Mok, Lau Kar-Wing, Stanley Fung, Chiao Chiao, Shing Fui-on, Phillip Ko, Kara Hui, Charlie Cho. **D:** Lau Kar-Wing. **W:** Yuen Kai-chi, Chan Shu. **C:** Au Yang-ying, Yip Yau-han, Kong Sze. **M:** Joseph Chan. **VHS, DVD**

Dragon Fist

Jackie Chan is Tang How-Yuen, a promising student studying at Master Chang's kung fu academy. Chang has just won a kung fu tournament, but (old rival) Master Chung Chien-Kuen (Yam Sai-kwoon) shows up to challenge Chang. Chung defeats Jackie's master, and, in the process, mortally wounds the old man. Jackie and the students of the school vow revenge. They don't know that Chung has acted out of jealousy for an old affair Chang had with his wife (before the two were married). Nor do they know that Mrs. Chung has killed herself, out of embarrassment at her husband's actions. This terrible series of events causes Chung to turn over a new leaf. When Jackie and Mrs. Chang (and her daughter, played by Nora Miao) come looking for revenge, Chung welcomes them with open arms. They're suspicious, but return his hospitality graciously. They discover that Chung has cut off his own leg, and made a golden sign (to replace the one he smashed at the Chang school) in penance. For a moment, it looks like Jackie and the rest will get to go home without killing anyone; their quest for revenge is over.

Unfortunately, the Wei clan—a group of local gangsters—is looking to put Chung and his Patience Clan out of business. They're not above using Jackie to do it, and arrange for Mrs. Chang to be poisoned—a poison to which the Wei clan alone has the antidote. They also frame Jackie for murdering a member of the Patience Clan. This sets up a final confrontation between Jackie (fighting for the antidote), the Patience Clan (fighting for their lives), and the Wei clan (fighting to take over the whole ball of wax). The final battle (nearly 20 minutes) between the dueling schools, Jackie, and the kung fu chicks is worth the price of admission.

The martial arts in this film are far less formal than in many of the early Chan films. Where many of the previous flicks look like carefully arranged martial ballets, this film actually looks like people are fighting. It probably helps that Jackie has wisely omitted the (hinted at) "foolish student" phase of How-Yuen's career. The martial arts in this flick are a clear indication of the kind of kick-ass acrobatic action that Jackie would soon become famous for. Producer/direc-

tor Lo Wei had hit such hard times that he couldn't afford to release this (or *Spiritual Kung Fu*) until after Jackie became a star with *Snake in the Eagle's Shadow*, making them surefire earners. After years in the public domain DVD section, *Dragon Fist* has recently come out in a beautifully mastered official edition. It's worth the extra dough for Chan fans. —SS **AKA:** *Lung Kuen; Long Quan; In Eagle Dragon Fist.* 🐉🐉♡

1978 76m/C *HK* Jackie Chan, Nora Miao, James Tien, Yam Sai-kwoon, Hsu Hsia, Gam Ying-yat, Yang Sha-fei, Wong Kwong-yue, Chui Fat, Ko Keung. **D:** Lo Wei. **W:** Wong Chung-ping. **C:** Chen Yung-hsu. **M:** Frankie Chan. **VHS, DVD**

Dragon from Russia

Two of Japan's most popular manga creators, writer Kazuo Koike *(Lone Wolf and Cub)* and artist Ryoichi Ikegami *(Mai the Psychic Girl)*, teamed up to create *Crying Freeman*, which has been adapted to film at least three times (plus a number of anime adaptations). The year 1990 saw two of these films from Hong Kong—Phillip Ko's *Killer's Romance* and this more daring (and uneven) effort from Clarence Fok *(Naked Killer)*.

Like a modern version of the old Martial Arts World, the 800 Dragons is a group composed of supernaturally powerful warriors who operate underground beside normal human society, with different factions continuously feuding with each other. The Master of the Dead (Yuen Tak)—who damaged his face by indulging in Disguise Magic when he was young—leads a faction that has agents scattered, and some lost, throughout the globe. He's recently learned that trusty assassin Frank (Pai Ying) is a traitor, and really works for his rival Kishudo (Lau Shun), the Godfather of Japan. He sends assassins Chimer (Nina Li Chi), Choker, Teddy (Yuen Tak), Huntress (Carrie Ng), and sassy Pearl (Rachel Lee) out to find Frank. Meanwhile, the Master himself goes to find another traitor named Snooker (Dean Shek), who turns out to have hidden in Russia for years, before Kishudo's agents do. Snooker left to wed a mortal woman, which is forbidden, and raised his daughter Queenie (Sarah Lee) in Moscow, along with Manchurian orphans Yao (Sam Hui) and May (Maggie Cheung). The Master kills Snooker and Queenie and abducts promising kung fu student Yao, who has his memory erased via acupuncture and is trained as an assassin. Given the new name Freeman, Yao is sent to Japan to kill Kishudo. But though May happens to witness the assassination, Freeman can't make himself kill this stranger who might know his past. His relationship with an outsider marks Freeman as one of the traitors he's been hunting down, and

he finds himself fighting to save May and himself from his former master.

Sam Hui, usually seen in comic roles, would seem an odd choice to play Freeman, despite his martial arts skills. But given the fanciful tone taken with the material in this version, it's entirely appropriate. The manga series made Freeman a romantic and enigmatic character, picking up the story in midstream and relating his background in occasional flashbacks. This treatment is almost a full parody, and a darn entertaining one. The film tries to include too many subplots, losing track of the main character and causing distracting shifts in tone. But the international locations, wild costumes, and knockout visual design form a rich backdrop for some terrific wirework action scenes—not to mention some of the most beautiful actresses in Hong Kong. The film's over-the-top, anything-goes attitude makes room for Russian dancing, death traps, car and motorcycle chases through machine gun fire and explosions, Sam Hui pop songs, tattoo exhibition, pole-top fighting, and a sex scene at a funeral. **AKA:** *Gung Cheung Fei Lung; Gong Chang Fei Long; Crying Freeman: Dragon from Russia.* 🐉🐉🐉

1990 95m/C *HK* Sam Hui, Maggie Cheung, Nina Li Chi, Carrie Ng, Rachel Lee, Yuen Tak, Dean Shek, Sarah Lee, Lau Shun, Suen Hing, Pai Ying, Yuen Wah, Ann Mui, Lo Hung, Cheung Kwok-leung, Wong Ming-sing, Yip Chun, Lau Shung-fung, Anthony Houk, Brett Coleman. **D:** Clarence Fok. **W:** Ella Chan. **C:** Peter Ngor, Wong Chi-wai. **M:** Violet Lam. **VHS, DVD**

Dragon from Shaolin

Little Shaolin monk Siu-lone (Sik Siu-long) is sent on a trip into the outside world with two monks (one of whom is Law Kar-Ying) to search for Buddha and learn responsibility. It so happens that the 2000-year-old Big Buddha Head of Shensi, thought to be the first depiction of the deity, is going on the block at an antiquities auction. Dealer Cheung Fung (Elvis Tsui) gets outbid by his little brother Cheung Yuet-Shan (Yuen Biao), who is always returning his targeted pieces to museums. While trying to catch a subway thief, Siu-lone is separated from his guardians and befriends street urchin Bully (Kok Siu-man). To raise cash, they become partners as street performers, doing scaled-down versions of the traditional Shaolin feats for tourists at the Great Wall. While Shan is defending fleeing pickpocket Susan (Vivian Hsu) from some Korean tourists, Siu-lone spots a Heart of Buddha pendant hanging from his neck, and vows to follow the man. The boys and stowaway Susan go with Shan to Shensi on a mission to return the Buddha Head to the headless statue.

Those expecting the same values in Hong Kong family films as found in the tame American variety may be shocked at the violence on display here—to say nothing of the scene in which Little Bully lifts and swings a brick tied to his penis! Later, he enters into a bauhaus beer-drinking contest with Yuen Biao, cheating by pissing into a hidden bucket. This is followed by a scene of him vomiting from a tree onto the monks—who have succumbed to the lures of the outside world, becoming hippie transvestites. Aside from that, many of the gags involving the kids are far too precious. At one point they even go for the old gag where one kid piggybacks atop another to disguise themselves as an adult. Such antics may have some viewers bailing by the time the kids all start singing, but then they'll miss Bully disguising himself as a ghost in an attempt to seduce Susan, and other outrageous sights. The climax finds Fung's mistress (Kara Hui) double-crossing him for the Head, and our heroes battling her and her minions onboard a runaway train. *AKA: Lung Joi Siu Lam; Long Zai Shao Lin; Dragon in Shaolin.* 𝄞𝄞♭

1996 89m/C *TW* Yuen Biao, Sik Siu-long, Kok Siu-man, Vivian Hsu, Elvis Tsiu, Wang Mawan, Kara Hui, Law Kar-Ying. **D:** Kenny Ha. **W:** Lee Po-cheung, Mak Kai-chung. **C:** Keung Kwok-man. **M:** Bin Lau-lim. **VHS, DVD**

Dragon in Jail

Wayne (Kenny Ho) lands in prison for throwing his shoe at a judge while in court for a minor offense, and befriends Henry Tse (Andy Lau), who is convicted of manslaughter after killing a triad member in a fight. On release, Wayne studies law in England, while Henry gets a job as a schoolteacher and continues to go to college at night. But triad Charlie Ma (William Ho) won't forget how Henry killed one of his boys, and tries to extort him in revenge. Henry's old cellmate Skinny (John Ching) gets him into the triad in an effort to settle the problem, but of course things just get worse. Almost immediately, he's badly injured in a chopper fight, and then Skinny gives him some dope to help with the pain. After that first puff, it takes only a minute of screen time before Henry is hooked on the pipe and a full wise guy. Wayne returns and helps Henry to kick his addiction. However, evil Charlie still bears a grudge, and while Henry and Skinny are lured into a fight, he murders their boss and Henry's wife Winnie (Gigi Lai), bribing a cop to arrive just in time to frame Henry for the crime. To save his friend, Wayne defends him at his first trial in court, facing off against prosecutor C.K. "The Terminator" Chong (Lung Fong).

Even the prison in Stephen Chow's *Tricky Master* is more brutal than the prison portrayed

here, as after an initial fight the rest of Kenny Ho's prison stay is full of male bonding and giggly cheesecake. Even guard Melvin Wong gets in on the cheerful horseplay. From prison flick, the plot skips nimbly into triad melodrama, then on into courtroom suspense, never making too much effort to distinguish itself in any of these genres. The picture never really comes to life until its violent conclusion. *AKA: Yuk Chung Lung; Yu Zhong Long.* 𝄞𝄞

1990 97m/C *HK* Andy Lau, Kenny Ho, Gigi Lai, William Ho, John Ching, Lung Fong, Melvin Wong, Victor Hon Kwan, Wai Gei-shun. **D:** Kent Cheng. **W:** Nam Yin. **C:** Abdul M. Rumjahn. **M:** Lowell Lo. **VHS, DVD**

Dragon Inn

In Imperial China, the eunuchs who are charged with helping to run the country begin to seize power and plot to overthrow the Emperor. One of these eunuchs, Tsao Siu-yan (Donnie Yen), executes some imperial diplomats and sends their children into the desert to lure his enemies to their rescue. But mercenary Miss Yau (Brigitte Lin) rescues the kids and takes them to the Dragon Inn, where she is to meet their benefactor. The Dragon Inn is a perilous place, run by Jade King (Maggie Cheung), who is an ally (and sometimes adversary) of the local bandits. Those who do well by her may use the Inn's secret passages to escape their pursuers. Those who run afoul of Jade are likely to end up as the main ingredient in the inn's famous "spicy meat" buns. The two women immediately recognize that they shall be either good friends or deadly adversaries, though it seems unclear at first which they shall be. Uncle Chow Wai-on (Tony Leung), who loves Miss Yau, comes to the Dragon Inn to claim the rescued children, but the four of them are prevented from escaping by bad weather and the untimely arrival of troops connected to the eunuch of the East Chamber. Within the inn and without, a deadly game of cat-and-mouse ensues. Chow promises to marry Jade to gain the secret of escaping the inn. Yau agrees to this, though she is not happy about it. Despite their best plans, the army of the East Chamber closes in and attacks the inn. The heroes flee into the desert, only to run into the evil head eunuch (Yen) for the final climactic battle.

Dragon Inn is a beautifully filmed movie with plenty of action, as well as the usual Hong Kong mix of humor and brutal ultra-violence. Based on an earlier film *Dragon Gate Inn* by HK master filmmaker King Hu, the update is far less sedate than the original, and not nearly so set-bound. Director Raymond Lee (with some uncredited help from Tsui Hark and Ching Siu-tung) gets good, enthusiastic performances from the

cast—including a very nice turn by Maggie Cheung as Jade. There's a bit of titillation, too—though most of the nearly nude action scenes seem to have been stunt-doubled by a willowy man, rather than the heroines themselves. When less jumping is involved, careful placement of props within the room keeps the actress's modesty intact (in a manner that would make Austin Powers proud). While not classic filmmaking, *Dragon Inn* has plenty to recommend it for fans of the HK costume/action genre. —SS *AKA: San Lung Moon Haak Chan; Xin Long Men Ke Zhan; New Dragon Gate Inn; New Dragon Inn.* 🐉🐉🐉

1992 103m/C *HK* Brigitte Lin, Maggie Cheung, Tony Leung Ka-Fai, Donnie Yen, Xiong Xinxin, Lau Shun, Yam Sai-kwoon, Lawrence Ng, Yuen Cheung-yan, Yuen Bun, Chan Chi-fai. *D:* Raymond Lee. *W:* Tsui Hark, Charcoal Cheung Tan. *C:* Arthur Wong, Tom Lau. *M:* Phil Chan. **VHS, DVD**

Dragon Kid

This relatively expansive Taiwan action comedy features some good kung fu and decent gags, but much of it is just plain silly. Bickering relatives are competing to become a rich man's heirs, but he's disgusted with them. He decides instead to leave his fortune to three strangers, all heroes in other countries. He sends his foxy lawyer Lucy (Joyce Ngai) to gathers the heroes together. A cartoon villain named Metal Arm (Lung Tin Cheung), who uses a variety of implements to replace his missing hand, is on her trail. An obvious parody of Master Han from *Enter the Dragon,* this character marches around in a Gestapo-style uniform with all kinds of lethal-looking (but mostly useless) tools sticking out of his sleeve—leading one to wonder how he got through airports.

First, Lucy goes to the Great Wall to pick up her guide, though it's really just an obvious excuse to get the Great Wall in the movie. The guide leads her to Shaolin Temple, where she bargains with Abbot Iron Head (Cho Boon Feng) to let her fetch away young kung fu master Kuang Kuang (Joh Hau Foo). Next, she flies to Japan where some ninjas with guns help her capture a geisha warrior princess (Lam Siu Lau). Finally, in Thailand, a jungle hero (Yeung Hung), who is a cross between Tarzan and Crocodile Dundee, is already mad at Metal Arm's bad guys for killing his crocodile pal. In a desperate fight, he readily accepts a ride on Lucy's boat. Back in Taiwan, the three foreigners try to adapt to modern society, while the whole family launches campaigns to impress them. After various adventures in the big city, some of the more wicked brothers lose patience and decide to use force to get them to sign over their inheri-

tance. The climax revs up for some spectacular escapes, chases, and fights.

The three heroes are quite good in their fight scenes, but Joh Hau Foo (from the *Kung Fu Kids* movies) is a standout, ending up in a flying sword duel through downtown Taipei, which ends up on a circus high wire above a tiger cage. Like in Jackie Chan's pictures, there's a reel of outtakes playing under the end credits, which show Joh cracking up repeatedly and nearly injuring himself during a scene where he has to stop a car with his head. *AKA: Siu Ngo Shing; Xiao Ao Cheng.* 🐉🐉 ✔

1990 102m/C *TW* Joh Hau Foo, Lam Siu Lau, Choi Gaai Wang, Yeung Hung, Joyce Ngai, Lung Tin Cheung, Cho Boon Feng, Law Dai Yau, Ng Yin. **VHS, DVD**

Dragon Killer

A shipment of boat people is going to the U.S. Onboard is Olympic marksmanship medallist Lung (director Anthony Lau), who has been waiting for word from his wife Miu (Sharla Cheung), who disappeared shortly after emigrating to America. In Los Angeles, Lung's boyhood friend Ma Lau (Simon Yam), who helped Miu cross over, has been trying to find her. Grateful and ever loyal, Lung is willing to do whatever he can for his friend. Ma is a gangster dealing in illegal immigration and other pursuits, but has heavy competition in his district. Assassins sent by his rival, the yakuza Yokosan, nearly kill Ma and Lung in a vicious battle. Lung helps out by volunteering to kidnap Yokosan.

Police detective Conan Lee *(Tiger on Beat)* suspects he's behind Yokosan's subsequent murder. Ma is running for union chief, and it's well known that the Japanese gangster had ties to Li Tai Chien—who is Ma's foster father, but also his rival in the illegal immigration business. Ma tells Lung that Li knows where Miu is, but he'll only get to Li through his lawyer. Lung goes to see the lawyer, but the man is killed before Lung can talk to him. Seen at the crime scene, Lung is the lead suspect for the murder.

Now, if you haven't guessed by now that Ma knows exactly where Miu is, take two giant steps backward. In fact, he's married to her, having long ago told her that Lung is dead. Until you figure that out, it's pretty confusing as to why Ma is getting Lung into one dangerous situation after another. Inevitably, the cat comes out of the bag, and the two old friends head for a very bloody showdown.

This gritty crime thriller benefits greatly from the smog-scarred Los Angeles locations, adding the anxiety felt throughout a city of immigrants, many of whom are breaking the law just by being there. In the exciting shootout among the

THE HOUND SALUTES
Donnie Yen

甄子丹

While watching the Jackie Chan movie *Twin Dragons*, Donnie Yen (Yen Chi-tan) must have felt a bit of déjà vu, since his own life story combines elements of both the cultured orchestra conductor twin and the street-fightin' kung fu master twin. His mother Bow Sim-mak is a revered martial arts master, while his father Clysler Yen is a well-known composer.

Born in Canton, Donnie moved to Boston at an early age, and was trained in wu shu and tai chi martial arts and piano. His interest understandably shifted more toward kung fu when Bruce Lee became an international star, and Donnie neglected his schoolwork to study at other martial arts schools. Unfortunately, as a teenager he gained a reputation for using his skills in street fights while running with a Chinatown gang. To keep him out of trouble and extend his studies, Yen was sent back to China to accept an invitation to join the Beijing Wu Shu Team—the first Asian foreigner to be allowed to do so—where he studied alongside Jet Li. While visiting Hong Kong, Yen stopped in to see one of his mother's former students, the sister of director Yuen Woo-ping. After a demonstration of his skill, and a brief stint proving himself as a stuntman, he was cast in the lead at the age of 18 in the new Yuen Clan kung fu comedy *Drunken Tai Chi*.

Facing stiff competition from the new wave of kung fu movies being made by the likes of Jackie Chan and Sammo Hung, the old-fashioned Yuen films failed to perform up to expectations at the boxoffice. Donnie returned to the States for a few years, where he developed his own style of martial arts, combining boxing and fancy kicking. Yuen Woo-ping brought Yen back to Hong Kong for a featured role in *Tiger Cage*, and both artists succeeded in adapting their styles to modern action pictures, while adding their own spice to the mix. The film was a great success, and after *Tiger Cage 2*, Donnie spread his appearances between different production teams, making *In the Line of Duty 4*, *Crystal Hunt*, *Once upon a Time in China 2* (with his old classmate Jet Li), and *Dragon Inn*. Afraid of being typecast as a villain, Yen turned down several prominent roles until being cast in the classic *Iron Monkey*.

While working with Michelle Yeoh in *Wing Chun,* Yen was convinced to make his next project an epic television series for TVB. *Hung Hei-kwun* (AKA *The Kung Fu Master*) was a huge hit and lifted the entire Hong Kong TV industry out of a down period, leading to an even bigger hit with *Fist of Fury,* an expansion of the story used for Bruce Lee's *The Chinese Connection.*

With the clout gained via his TV hits, Yen expanded his role behind the camera by directing *Ballistic Kiss.* In the past few years, Yen has been concentrating on expanding his visibility internationally, taking supporting roles and consulting on the action for *Highlander: Endgame* and *Blade 2.* Despite the more showy and frenetic editing techniques on display in these later films, Yen is known as one of the leading action stars to be carrying on the martial arts film style of his idol Bruce Lee, as well as his sifu Yuen Woo-ping. He acknowledges how the Chinese opera school techniques of the Yuens, Sammo Hung, and Jackie Chan are superior for portraying cinema action, but always seeks to have solid technique behind the gloss. His latest films include *Hero,* a martial arts epic directed by Zhang Yimou that reunites Yen with Jet Li once again, and *Shanghai Knights,* which finally brings him face to face with Jackie Chan.

boat people, and during the tense showdown between Yam and Lau, Conan Lee gets to show that he can still throw some kicks. *AKA: Kuang Qing Sha Shou; Kwong Ching Saai Sau.* ♫♫▽

1995 C: *HK* Anthony Lau, Simon Yam, Sharla Cheung, Conan Lee. **D:** Anthony Lau. **W:** Yuen Kai-chi. **C:** Peter Ngor. **M:** Angus. **VHS**

Dragon Lee vs. the Five Brothers

Ming patriot Han (Dragon Lee) is given an Important Document (the ever-present rebel name list) by his dying comrade Chow to be taken to rebel leader Cheung Hai-li in Sung Li Town. However, the Manchus suspect Han's contact Chiang, and order the town blockaded in an effort to catch rebel couriers such as Han. Ching soldiers spot Han as a suspicious type right away and follow him, but are surprised to find he's a really good fighter, and can even climb walls like a squirrel. He gets some help from a stranger (Kan Chie-fong), who tells him that four of the five famous Ching Shaolin-trained fighters are in town. The troops are led by Lord Li Shao-chuen

and Chen Chang, the Silver-Handed General, and he's guarded by Wei Yi-chang and Ma Wang. She doesn't know who the fifth fighter is, but they say he's "the only one who isn't evil." Wei captures Chiang and his daughter Shao-wan, and forces him to squeal on the rebel group in the next village. They take Shao-wan and the code bracelet, hoping they'll lead to Cheung and other rebels. The rebels manage to capture the Chings, but Chen has followed them disguised as a beggar and helps them escape. Han and Shao-wan make off for a meeting with Cheung the next day, but the five brothers dog their steps all the way.

The Five Brothers (or the Four out of Five Brothers) aren't really so brotherly, constantly bickering and plotting against each other. Chen is the only interesting evil Brother, waving his awkward silver hand around and donning silly disguises. There are some nice locations and a relatively large cast on hand, but the production looks incredibly cheap. The poor film stock makes everything look chintzy, and the unheated interior sets look even colder than the snowy mountain scenery. Sometimes traffic can be heard rumbling by outside the dubbing studio. Dragon Lee keeps his Bruce Lee shtick to a minimum, but is only nominally the hero anyway, absent for much of the time. Kan Chia-fong is the real hero, showing up at opportune moments in her flying beekeeper's hat to save the day. At one point she dons a ninja outfit for no good reason—unless it's so we don't know that it's really a stuntman doing her acrobatics for her. The feature has a lot of chapter play flavor, with plenty of fights, captures, and escapes, and the action has a nice touch of the fantastic, with characters skipping over treetops and jumping over walls. 🐉🐉🐉

1978 87m/C *HK/TW* Dragon Lee, Kan Chia-fong, Gam Kei Chu, Chu Lung. **D:** Liu Yueh-lin. **W:** Daniel Lau. **C:** Shen Ming-i. **M:** Sun Chun-lin. **VHS, DVD**

Dragon Lord

Jackie Chan returned to Hong Kong from his first trip to America angry and frustrated, having been forced to suffer through many bad ideas in the making of *The Big Brawl* and *Cannonball Run,* while being badgered by reporters who didn't speak his language. He immediately wanted to make a Big Movie, shooting all over Southeast Asia. Fortunately, like his idol Charlie Chaplin, Chan was associated with a studio willing to let him work without a schedule or a budget, knowing that whatever he made would show a profit. Unfortunately, his anger made Chan rush into this proposed sequel to *The Young Master* without proper preparation, resulting in a film that lacks focus, but is nevertheless a lot of fun once it gets going.

Chan stars as an irresponsible young rascal named Dragon Lung. He and his buddy Cowboy Chin (Mars) try to sail a kite bearing a mash note over a wall to a girl (Suet Lee), but the wind carries the kite away. They find it at the headquarters of a gang of former Imperial Guards who are stealing Chinese artifacts to sell to foreigners, and barely escape with their lives. They run into Tiger (Michael Chan), who is also being pursued, and give him shelter in Cowboy's barn. Unbeknownst to the two youths, Tiger was a member of the gang, but is on the outs with them when they found out he was stealing some of the artifacts from them. However, it turns out that Cowboy's dad (Paul Chang) is in cahoots with the leader of the gang (Whang In Shik), inadvertently putting the boys in deadly danger.

Basically one of those kung fu films that was made up as they went along, *Dragon Lord* meanders through its first half, with much horseplay between the two boys and various authority figures. However, it contains some fine action sequences—notably a hacky sack game and one where Chan tries to get off the roof of the gang's HQ while they try to skewer him with spears—and the plot gels more in the second half. The

knockout highlight of the film is the climax, a furious extended battle between Chan and Whang all over the inside of the barn. With variations, Chan would reproduce the basics of this scene many times, but never with the intensity he gave it here. *AKA: Lung Siu Yau; Long Shao Ye; Young Master in Love; Dragon Strike.* 🐉🐉🐉

1982 86m/C *HK* Jackie Chan, Mars, Michael Chan, Whang In Shik, Tin Fung, Paul Chang, Suet Lee, Fung Hark-On, Tai Bo, Cheng Hong-yip, Ma Chin-ku, Wu Chia Hsiang, Fang Fang, Ho Pak Kwong, Tang Yim-chan, Kwan Yung Moon, Ng Yuen-yee, Sham Chin-bo. **D:** Jackie Chan. **W:** Barry Wong, Edward Tang, Louis Sit, Jackie Chan. **C:** Chan Chung-yuen, Chen Chin-kui. **M:** Frankie Chan. **VHS, DVD**

Dragon on Fire

Another cheap kung fu flick from Joseph Lai and Godfrey Ho, this one features a better-than-usual cast. Shaolin masters develop the Strike Rock Fist kung fu style, which defeats all others (with the possible exception of Tissue Paper Palm, which covers Strike Rock Fist). Masters Tu Kwong and Fung Suen even perfect the *Double* Strike Rock Fist, and are kings of kung fu until they have a falling out. Pasty-faced cripple Wing Chin-hou (Chan Lau) sponsors private challenge bouts with his man-monster (Bolo Yeung), the real purpose of which is to find suitable sparring partners for his partner Ma Ti (Phillip Ko) to kill. Ma even uses a little egg timer to clock his fights.

Wandering fugitive Tu Wu-shen (John Liu), the son of Tu Kwong, wants employment rather than a cash prize, but insists all three men he beat to get it be fired. Soon after, he runs into the students of Fung Suen, Tang (Tino Wong), and his friend Ah-Chin (Dragon Lee), who want to continue the old feud. Ma injures Ah-Chin in a fight, but Tang believes Tu did it. He returns to Master Fung Suen—now a dope-head mendicant—for training to counter Tu's techniques. Tu is really an undercover government agent who is hunting down the Chinese artifacts Wing is dealing to a foreign devil (Jim James), and he enlists his old rival to help bring down Wing and Ma.

Most Godfrey Ho movies are awful, but always feature some interesting quirks. Here, Chan Lau's villain is the most interesting character. He sits in a wheelchair because of contracting rabies from a dog that bit off his testicles, and stays alive by eating strange medicinal frogs and insects. He occasionally has fits of madness in which he's compelled to bite people. In the end, he jumps out of the wheelchair in full mad-dog mode to snap at the heroes. Besides this weird character, the main attractions are the athleticism of Phillip Ko, John Liu's dazzling kicks, and the physique of Dragon Lee, who takes off his shirt for every fight. The soundtrack swipes from the usual sources: *Star Wars*, James Bond, and Dario Argento movies. *AKA: Dragon and the Hero; Dragon the Hero.* 🐉🐉

1979 87m/C *HK* John Liu, Tino Wong, Phillip Ko, Dragon Lee, Chan Lau, Bolo Yeung, Jim James, Chiang Kam, David Wu, Mars, Lee Tin-ying, Lee Bing-hung, Ringo Wong. *D:* Godfrey Ho. *W:* Szeto On. *C:* Yau Ki. *M:* Mah Man, Chan Chung. **VHS, DVD**

Dragon Princess

This is another Sonny Chiba film where Sonny is used to sell the feature but plays a fairly minor part. *Dragon Princess* is the story of Sonny's daughter, who sets out to revenge his death against his enemies. The story begins with Sonny and his (young) girl, being ambushed by the thugs of a rival kung fu master, Makaito. They want Sonny out of the business, and are willing to cripple him to get their way. Because of the villains' treachery, Sonny is badly wounded. He and his daughter (Sue Shiomi) go to hide out in America—where Sonny puts her through the usual hellish martial arts training. When he dies (early in the film), she returns to Japan to seek revenge. Makaito's school is by now well established, and in charge of a worldwide martial arts tournament held every year. Naturally, the evil clan is willing to do anything to win the tournament, and keep their prestigious streak of wins going. Among Makaito's most promising students is Masahiko (Jiro Chiba), though the evil master doesn't completely trust him. In badly edited scenes, we see champions from all over the world heading for the tournament. However, they're quickly killed by Makaito's assassins.

Sue Shiomi, the Dragon Princess, fights her way through the film, taking on gangs of assassins and even a pack of crazed dogs (in a scene sure to rouse the ire of PETA and the ASPCA). Jiro Chiba puts up with his evil masters and their betrayals, until we discover that he is actually the son of the only other (honest) man to oppose Makaito's rise to power. Naturally, Sue and Jiro team up to bring the bad guy to final justice.

In the end, *Dragon Princess* is a pretty simple revenge story, with complications piled on top of it. The camera work in this film is far too clever for its own good—often obscuring the story rather than elucidating it. Fans of Sue Shiomi may enjoy it, though fans of Sonny Chiba will probably feel cheated by the short amount of time their hero spends onscreen. Don't expect to actually see the often-mentioned martial arts tournament, either. The story never really gets there, so the tournament is just one big McGuffin to pad the flick with scenes of unrelated, poorly shot mayhem. See *DP* in widescreen if you can, as the action suffers badly in pan-and-

scan, and there's little other than action to recommend it. Give it another half bone if you like Sue Shiomi, who does fine despite the film's other inadequacies. —SS *AKA: Ryo no Oujo; Sonny Chiba's Dragon Princess.* 🐉🐉

1981 (R) 90m/C *JP* Sonny Chiba, Sue Shiomi, Yasuaki Kurata, Jiro Chiba, Ko Otsuka. *D:* Yutaka Kodaira. *W:* Hiro Matsuda. *C:* Hanjiro Nakada. *M:* Shunsuke Kikuchi. **VHS, DVD**

<u>*asians in usa*</u>

Dragon: The Bruce Lee Story

Many Bruce Lee fans prefer Ng See-yuen's *Bruce Lee: The Man, the Myth* (1976) to this big-budget Hollywood bio, claiming *The Fast and the Furious* director Rob Cohen plays fast and loose with the facts. The truth is that both films stray from the facts in covering the same period of Lee's life, while covering different aspects of it. Ng's version portrayed Lee as a kung fu fighter who only used the movies as a means to promote his martial arts, while almost completely ignoring his home life. *Dragon* tries to get into Lee's mind and myth, and since it's mainly based on Linda Lee Caldwell's book, it pays a lot more attention to his marriage. Neither picture is entirely successful, but through compelling performances and exciting fight sequences, this one comes forward as the far more entertaining piece. It also has a lot more of the "emotional content" Lee was after in his movies. Jason Scott Lee is a bit too naïve and cuddly as the Dragon, missing Lee's darker, more menacing aura, but he inhabits the character extremely well emotionally and physically. Lauren Holly plays Linda as nurturing and supportive, standing by her man through thick and thin. The fight sequences are more like the kind of dynamic kung fu choreography seen in Jackie Chan's films than Bruce Lee's direct approach. 🐉🐉🐉

1993 (PG-13) 107m/C *US* Jason Scott Lee, Lauren Holly, Robert Wagner, Michael Learned, Nancy Kwan, Ric Young, John Chang, Van Williams. *D:* Rob Cohen. *W:* Edward Khmara, John Raffo, Rob Cohen. *C:* David Eggby. *M:* Randy Edelman. **VHS, DVD**

Dragon's Claws

Ling Ko-feng (Hwang Jang Lee)—the boxer some know as the White Bachelor—comes to the school of Lung Chen-tien (Lau Kar-Wing), master of the Dragon Fist, to challenge him for his Golden Tablet. But Chen-tien is ill, and Ling leaves to

"I'm your mother! You don't have to hit me so hard!"

—Training gets out of hand in *Dragon's Claws*

fight another day, easily besting brash son Lung Hsia (Jimmy Liu) on his way out. But all is not as black and white as it seems—18 years ago, Chen-tien used an anesthetic to rape Ling's girlfriend Li-hua (Kan Chia-fong), impregnating her in order to marry into the family and inherit the Dragon Fist. Li-hua punished him by wounding him in the chest with the Dragon's Claws technique, a wound from which he still suffers. A scruffy medicine man (Wong Biu Chan) comes to the door offering a cure, but they throw him out. Ling returns with two henchmen: Green Monster, who fights using a fan, and Red Monster, who fights using an abacus. With Chen-tien still suffering, Ling succeeds in defeating him and claiming the Golden Tablet of the Dragon Fist, after which Chen-tien soon dies. Lung Hsia vows to practice hard and reclaim the title someday. But during a celebratory dinner, Ling sees that the Tablet is a fake—without anyone noticing, the old medicine man switched them during his visit.

Ling returns during the funeral to insult the Lungs, administering the Dragon's Claws to Hsia when he attacks. He gives them three days to cough up the real Golden Tablet. The only hope for Hsia may be Li-hua's uncle Chao Pu-jao, a famous doctor who disappeared after a duel 20 years ago. Red and Green Dragon catch up with Hsia, but the old drug seller helps the boy escape, then cures his Dragon's Claws. After some begging, the old man agrees to teach Hsia his "strange strikes" in secret, which Hsia combines with the pressure points his mother taught him. After the Monsters find and kill his mother, Hsia takes up a broom to clean house.

Originally planned to star Jackie Chan, *Dragon's Claws* contains all the marks of a classic kung fu flick, plus some interesting twists. There's a young hero who needs to learn a thing or two, the sinister villainy (and powerful legs) of the great Hwang Jang Lee, a respected kung fu style that must be learned and surpassed, a dirty old mendicant that is really a grandmaster in disguise, creative training sequences, colorful villains, and kick-ass martial arts action. The plot and settings keep you interested in the story without becoming too complicated. There's also some oddly named characters, like "Mouse Cavalier 4 Feet Wang," and the fight choreography is spiced up with a bit of humor and some incredible moves, such as when a young monk uses a peeing piglet to fend off a foe. *AKA: Dragon's Claw; Dragon Claws.* 🎵🎵🎵🎶

1979 91m/C *HK* Hwang Jang Lee, Jimmy Liu, Lau Kar-Wing, Wong Biu Chan, Kan Chia-fong, Dragon Lee. **D:** Joseph Kuo. **W:** Chiang Ping Han. **C:** Ma Kuan Wan. **M:** Frankie Chan. **VHS, DVD**

Dragons Forever

Often overlooked as the follow-up to the fan favorite *Wheels on Meals,* this fight classic is the last film (to date) of the famous three opera-school brothers, Jackie Chan, Sammo Hung, and Yuen Biao. To retire as brothers in style, each was given a memorable character which played off the others beautifully, just as their fighting styles combined so entertainingly. Chan plays playboy lawyer Jackie Lung, hired by triad boss Hua Hsien-wu (Yuen Wah) to use his wiles to get around wealthy Miss Yip (Deanie Yip), who is fighting him in court to close down his polluting chemical plant. Hung is Luke Wong Fei-hung (!), a goodhearted man who nevertheless makes his living as an arms dealer. And Yuen Biao gets one of his most amusing roles ever as Timothy Tung Tak-biao, a very eccentric and neurotic technical whiz. Lung hires his two buddies to help get Yip to sell her fish ponds and leave Hua alone, and each attack from different directions. Wong moves in next door and attempts to woo the still-young widow, Lung tries to charm her lawyer Wen Mei-ling (Pauline Yeung), and Tung takes a hand spying on her home. All their work backfires spectacularly, with Lung and Wong falling for their respective targets and Tak generally making a mess of things. Having been won over by the ladies, and learning that Hua is secretly processing drugs at his plant, the heroes storm the joint to get the evidence they need to put him in jail.

The charm on display is overwhelming, with everyone involved clearly having a wonderful time. The three brothers get into several comic fights with each other, while Chan also has a fantastic fight onboard a ship. The big climactic factory battle is a classic, with the heroes taking on various fight stars from the Yuen and Lau clans. Sammo and Yuen Biao reprise their duel with oily Yuen Wah from *Eastern Condors,* and Chan gets into a rematch with Benny "The Jet" Urquidez (as an incredibly coked-up thug) from *Wheels on Meals.* Put it on your Must See list. **AKA:** *Fei Lung Mang Cheung; Fei Long Meng Jiang; First Mission; 3 Brothers; Cyclone Z; Flying Dracon Fierce Challenge.* 🐉🐉🐉🐉

1988 93m/C *HK* Jackie Chan, Sammo Hung, Yuen Biao, Yuen Wah, Deanie Yip, Pauline Yeung, Roy Chiao, Crystal Kwok, Phillip Ko, Dick Wei, Stanley Fung, Shum Wai, Benny Urquidez, Lau Kar-Wing, Tai Bo, Shing Fui-on, Lo Lieh, Chen Jing, Lee Ka-ting, Chan Lung, Billy Chow, Agnes Aurelio, James Tien, Wu Fung, Lam Wai, Fung Hark-On, Chung Fat, Chin Ka-Lok, Yuen Miu, Fung Lee, Wong Yuk-wan, Wan Fat, Kong Lung, Danny Chow, Benny Lai, Cheung Wa, Cho Wing, James Ha, Chan Tat-kwong. **D:** Sammo Hung. **W:** Roy Szeto. **C:** Jimmy Leung, Cheung Yiu-cho. **M:** James Wong. **VHS, DVD**

Dragons of the Orient

Here we have a made-for–Hong Kong TV documentary about the history of Chinese kung fu, starring Jet Li, very similar to *Shaolin One* and using some of the same footage. Both were made during the 1980s, when Li was being promoted as the next big international star, and suffer from extended sequences of hero worship. However, this one uses the device of Li's sparring partner Wang Chuen guiding "sports reporter" Yeung Ching-Ching *(Invincible Pole Fighter)* and playing tourist, interspersed with narration providing more information. They visit Shaolin Temple and meet the monks, see the Great Wall, the Marco Polo Bridge, and watch a lot of martial arts demonstrations. And of course, there's the mondo material: demonstrations of Chi Kung feats. A fellow jabs a spike through his arm, then pulls a cartload of people using it. Another chap climbs a sheer brick wall. One hundred–year-old Master Wu appears for a long sword demonstration. The travelogue footage with Yeung and Wang is in widescreen, while some clips are full screen, and there's even some footage shot on video. Jet Li appears in old demonstration footage. There's also demonstrations by Terry Fan, of whom the narrator tells us "many experts agree will be the next Jackie Chan." Better known as Fan Siu-Wong, in recent years he's starred in a couple of *Black Mask* knockoffs. Though the pace drags a bit during seemingly endless demonstrations, they're all beautifully performed and the subject matter is fascinating. Some sources—including the video box art—credit Rocky Law as director, but the film itself lists Sek Bing-chan. **AKA:** *Dung Fong Gui Lung; Dong Fang Ju Long.* 🐉🐉🐉

1988 83m/C *HK* Jet Li, Wang Chuen, Yeung Ching-Ching, Fan Siu-Wong, Tang Ching, Zhang Ziyi, Li Cheung-chuen, Wang Kin Chuen, Kwok Siui Hung. **D:** Sek Bing-chan, Rocky Law. **C:** Ho Hark-wai. **VHS, DVD**

Dreadnaught

Until the original film series makes its way out of the vault, this lively action flick from Yuen Woo-ping is one of the few features in which you can see Kwan Tak-hing essay his signature role of Wong Fei-hung. The title refers to the fearsome White Tiger (Sunny Yuen), a public menace who turns into a mad dog when bounty hunters attack and kill his pregnant wife (Kan

Chia-fong). When he shows up to ask his old friend Master Tam (Phillip Ko) for help, Tam sends him to his friends in an opera troupe to hide him. Cowardly Mousey (Yuen Biao) holds the unlikely responsibility of collections agent for his sister's laundry. It's a toss-up whether he's more afraid of bullying clients or the kung fu skill of his sister (Lily Li). At the opening of the Henan Club, Wong Fei-hung (Kwan Tak-hing) makes an appearance and presents a lion dance by his students Leung Foon (Leung Kar-yan) and Kwun (Chow Yuen-kin). In the middle of the demonstration, Tam's lion shows up to challenge them. Master Wong enters the fray and Tam ends up beaten and burned. Afterward, Foon helps his friend Mousey with his collections, and promises to ask Master Wong to teach him kung fu. At the theatre, the ringing bells he wears make Mousey a target for the psychotic Tiger, who has disguised himself with appropriately scary makeup to hide his facial birthmark. To bolster his friend's confidence and impress a girl (Tang Ching), Foon has Mousey impersonate Master Wong, which gets them both in hot water when they pick on a man who turns out to be Marshal Pao (Fan Mui-Sang). To help make amends, the students try to track down the maniac themselves. But when Tam tells White Tiger to make Master Wong his next victim, it's Mousey's ancient Chinese laundry secrets that make a difference.

Though Kwan was 76 years old at the time, he still performs kung fu and even fire tricks like a teenager. The lion dancing is truly magical, some of the best in any movie. Fung Hark-On has a featured role as the Demon Tailor, sent to kill Wong while pretending to make him a suit. One of the best of his early films, Yuen deftly mixes humor, horror, drama, and intrigue together with excellent action choreography. The pace never lets up for a minute, moving from one fight to the next. Many of the bits of business created here influenced (or were copied outright by) many other films. Yuen Biao is great in one of his first leading roles, and Sunny Yuen goes beyond mere villainy to portray a monster. **AKA:** *Yung Je Mo Gui; Yong Zhe Wu Ju; Dreadnought.* 🎵🎵🎵🎵

1981 91m/C *HK* Yuen Biao, Leung Kar-yan, Kwan Tak-hing, Sunny Yuen, Lily Li, Fan Mui-Sang, Fung Hark-On, Phillip Ko, Brandy Yuen, Tang Ching, Lau Wing, Kan Chia-fong, Chow Yuen-kin, Chiu Chung-hing, Yuen Cheung-yan, San Kwai, Sai Gwa Pau, Danny Chow, Lee Chun Wa, Yue Tau Wan, Fung Ging Man. **D:** Yuen Woo-ping. **W:** Yuen Woo-ping. **C:** Michael Ma. **M:** Frankie Chan. **VHS, DVD**

Dream of Garuda

After serving two years in prison for rape, Ikuo sees his victim, Mieko, in every woman he meets. In a bubble house, the prostitute compli-

ments him on his glowing skin and promises to wash his sins away. He becomes obsessed with salvation, and finally thinks he finds it when he stumbles across the real Mieko, who lives in bondage to his former partner, Tomimori, last seen whistling happily while Mieko was raped. Ikuo kills Tomimori to please Meiko, but she shows no pleasure in having instigated a murder. Ikuo find himself back in the Soaplands (possibly with Meiko, but one can hardly differentiate the women on account of the poor lighting and photography), where he is prepared for salvation and death.

What does this have to do with Garuda, the Hindu bird associated with the rays of the sun? Nothing, except for some process shots of birds against light and an ending that finds our dying hero clutching some feathers. What this movie is really about is the Soaplands, where naked women soap up the customers and slide up and down on them while licking various body parts. These are some of the slipperiest soft-core sex scenes on record, with the rear-on-rear action about as odd as it gets. —*BW* **AKA:** *Karura no yuma.* 🎵🎵

1994 60m/C *KO* Song Kang-ho, Shin Ha-kyun, Im Ji-eun, Bae Du-na, Han Bo-bae, Lee Dae-yeon, Kim Se-dong. **D:** Takahisa Zeze. **W:** Shinji Aoyama, Kishu Izuchi. **C:** Kim Sung-bok. **M:** Bang Jun-seok, Jo Yeong-wook. **VHS, DVD**

Dreaming Fists with Slender Hands

What would possess a distributor to release this knockabout kung fu comedy with such an elegant title is anybody's guess. Actually, it refers to the two kung fu styles in which the heroes are schooled, but it doesn't sound like boxoffice dynamite.

Two boys—short Ho Hu and fat Sun Lung—raised together by a kung fu master, are sent off for further training with Uncle Ti. On the way, they wander through a town being taken over by Shen Piao (Lung Fei) and his gangsters. The merchants decide to fend them off by hiring the boys as kung fu fighters. In their first encounter with the gang, Sun Lung is driven off, while Ho Hu is captured and thrown in a dungeon. There he meets old Chow Lan, who helps him escape and teaches him better kung fu. Sun Lung goes to work in a restaurant, where he convinces the owner (Hu Chin) to teach him her style of kung fu. Chow Lan reveals in a flashback—in which he wears the same silly hat—that Ho Hu is the son of an old classmate of his. He uses a crazy training contraption to hit the boy with sticks all day. Next time the gangsters come to town, the guys team up to fight them. Sun Lung uses his Woman's Touch style, while Ho Hu attacks with his Sleeping Fist. You'll be sleeping, too if you try to sit through this nonsense shot in the backyards of Taiwan. Lame kung fu and lamer comedy. *AKA: Kung Fu Kids.* 🐉

1980 90m/C *TW* Lung Fei, Hu Chin, Lau Lap Cho, Tai Leung, Wu Chia Hsiang, Ching Kuo-Chung, Shih Ting Ken, Hau Pak-wai, Ha Hau-chun, Hei Ying, Lau Tak Hoi, Tsing Yuan-pao. *D:* Karl Liao. *W:* Chung Yao. *C:* Chen How-chung. *M:* Huang Mao-shan. **VHS, DVD**

Drunken Art and Crippled Fist

Young Ho Chow-hou (James Lee) is trained for 10 years by a hunchbacked old kung fu master (Simon Yuen) in the hills. Upon returning home, Chow-hou is disturbed to find out that his father Ching-chan (Yue Hang) plans to exploit his son's acquired martial arts skills for his own ends. But Chow-hou has been taught to be a righteous man who will only fight in self-defense. When he refuses to engage one of his dad's rivals (Suen Lam), angry Ching-chan storms off to berate the drunken master, and the youth sets off to reach his master first to try to make peace.

Stopping to watch at a kung fu school on the way, Chow-hou is drawn into a match, and beats their teacher Lee without counter-attacking. Lee's brother Iron Head Wong (Lee Man Tai) tries to settle the score, but receives the same treatment, and the two shamed bullies scurry off to their friend Master Lu (Paul Wei) to hide out and practice. However, Chow-hou runs into the bullies again at a restaurant, just in time to scare them away when they accuse pickpocket Chow-yen (Cheung Siu-fan) of robbing them. Not that the agile Yen isn't able to take care of herself (he's really a girl in disguise!). But Chow-hou and Chow-yen meet their match in stern Master Chou Tai-hai (Lung Tin Cheung), a former student of the old hunchback. Confronting the old master, Yen beseeches him to teach Chow-hou some new techniques to defeat Chou Tai-hai. He'd like to teach his student the Crippled Fist, but the rule is that only a cripple can be taught it. However, the crafty old bird thinks of a way around the rules.

In the years following his fame in *Drunken Master,* Simon Yuen marched from one film to another without even changing his Beggar So costume. Though he obviously only worked one day here in a supporting role, the most is made from his presence and he's given star billing. Even scenes that don't involve him often have shots cut in of him peering through windows at the action. The fighting is plentiful and energetic, without ever getting too nasty. *AKA: Gui Ma Tian Shi; Peculiar Fist Kid; Drunken WuTang; Taoism Drunkard; Saufbold und Raufbold.* 🐉🐉🐉

1979 79m/C *HK* Simon Yuen, James Lee, Lung Tin Cheung, Cheung Siu-fan, Paul Wei, Lee Man Tai, Lee Siu-ming, Wong Chi Sang, Wong Hung-cheung, Yue Hang, Suen Lam, Au Lap-bo, Chang Chi-ping. *D:* Tong Dik. *C:* Pan Tai Wai. *M:* Chou Fu-liang. **VHS, DVD**

Drunken Master

Contrary to what you may have heard, Jackie Chan did not invent the kung fu comedy. Humor had been combined with martial arts many times before Chan became a star—just look at Bruce Lee's funny business in *Return of the Dragon.* As Chan's related in countless interviews, at a certain point in his career he felt that it was the proper direction to take his craft—a change from the Lee clone roles he'd been playing, and he knew audiences would enjoy it as much as he would. Jackie got his chance with the action comedy *Half a Loaf of Kung Fu,* but producer Lo Wei didn't like the result and shelved the film. Instead, he cast Jackie in a film that he thought would be funny: the kung fu ghostbuster flick *Spiritual Kung Fu.* This time Jackie was the one who didn't like it. Fortunately for both parties, an offer came from competing studio Seasonal Films, and Chan was loaned out to them for several projects. Producer Ng See Yuen saw eye to eye with Chan, and allowed him to do things more his own way, resulting in the hit *Snake in the Eagle's Shadow.* Re-teaming with director Yuen Woo-ping, they followed that success with Chan's best film of the 1970s, *Drunken Master.*

Drunken Master deals with Wong Fei-hung, one of the legendary icons of Chinese culture. A powerful martial artist, Wong was also a doctor and herbalist, and one of the heroes of the Boxer Rebellion. Kwan Tak-hing played Wong in a hugely successful series of films (99 entries!) through four decades. The idea behind *Drunken Master* is that maybe Wong wasn't always such sterling hero. Maybe he was a mixed-up kid as a teenager, just like anybody else. Fei-hung ("Freddie" in the English dub) is the most brash, stubborn, and spoiled young man studying at Po Chi Lam martial arts academy and clinic, perhaps because of the pressures and privileges of being the Master's son. He's completely over-confident in his fighting abilities, and would rather cut up in class than do his exercises. (This mirrors Chan's own difficult situation when he was adopted by the Master of his Chinese opera school, and was quickly recognized as one of the most talented—and difficult—students.) Wong ends up being punished both for righteously defending a poor merchant, and

there are also great duels with Hsu Hsia (*King Boxer*) and the muscular Lee Chun Wa (not Bolo Yeung, as is commonly thought). **AKA:** *Chui Kuen; Zui Quan; Drunken Monkey in the Tiger's Eyes; The Story of Drunken Master; Drunken Monkey; Challenge; Eagle Claw Snake Fist Cat's Paw Part 2.* 🎵🎵🎵🎶

1978 (PG-13) 111m/C *HK* Jackie Chan, Simon Yuen, Hwang Jang Lee, Lam Kau, Dean Shek, Hsu Hsia, Linda Lin Ying, San Kwai, Brandy Yuen, Tino Wong, Sunny Yuen, Lee Chun Wa, Fung Ging Man. **D:** Yuen Woo-ping. **W:** Ng See-yuen. **C:** Chang Hai. **M:** Chou Fu-liang. **VHS, DVD**

Drunken Master Killer

Rumor has it that when Jackie Chan took over directing *Legend of the Drunken Master,* Lau Kar-Leung took this offer to make the Wong Fei-hung movie he wanted. It's hard to believe that's true, considering the result—but any way you look at it, this is a real disappointment. *Drunken Master 3* (AKA *Drunken Master Killer* for its domestic video release, in an effort to capitalize on Gordon Lau's presence) bumps the Wongs forward in time by a few decades, judging by the cars and fashions. Republican revolutionary Yeung Kwun (Andy Lau) kidnaps Princess Sum Yu (Michelle Reis) to prevent her marriage to Emperor-in-waiting Yuan Shih-kai (William Ho). The princess is injured, so Yeung hides her at Po Chi Lam clinic with Master Wong Kei-ying (Adam Cheng) to recuperate, using the cover story that Wong has remarried to explain her presence. Wong Fei-hung (Willie Chi), on leave from college, is entrusted to take Sum Yu to Yeung. A gay man (Simon Yam) tries to molest them on a bus, starting a fight that causes it to crash into the winery of Uncle Yan (Lau Kar-Leung). Fei-hung and Sum Yu are forced to work in the winery to pay for damages, but the White Lotus Cult and the soldiers of Governor Li (Gordon Lau) are hot on their trail. Cornered, Sum Yu is forced to give up and go with Li. However, she's broken the jade ring Yuan gave her, and only the Wongs can save her from execution.

Moving Wong Fei-hung 30 years or so forward in time isn't such a problem considering the gross inattention paid to the setting once he gets there. A Halloween party features rock music and neon signs, for starters—Fei-hung rides an abacus like a skateboard, the Wongs wear Western clothes, and the White Lotus Cult is run by Caucasians. This is a troubled film, but not the total train wreck some sources report. The period may be off, but some details of that period are delightful—the antique bus, for example. The kung fu action is quite good, well in keeping with the Lau reputation (though Andy

Jackie Chan raises the bar on the kung fu movie in Drunken Master.

unknowingly attacking his own aunt. To help train the unruly lad, his father sends for his Uncle So. Seeking to avoid his fate, Fei-hung runs away and befriends an old drunk, who of course turns out to be Uncle So (Simon Yuen, father of director Yuen Woo-ping). Fei-hung scoots away from his training again first chance he gets, but runs afoul of contract killer Thunderleg Yen (Hwang Jang Lee), who gives him a humiliating thrashing—and burns his pants. Fei-hung returns to his training in earnest, and the alcoholic So (the famous King of Beggars) teaches him his secret Drunken Fist style. The freshly inebriated young hero then takes on all comers, especially Yen (who has been hired to kill Master Wong).

The film is almost all action. Chan performs what look like grueling training exercises (which he could probably do in his sleep at the time). But the meat of the movie is its wild fight scenes. Of course, the one with Korean taekwondo expert Hwang Jang Lee is a classic, but

Lau beating Gordon Lau in a fight is a bit of a stretch). But the major, fatal flaw here is that it's a Wong Fei-hung movie without Wong Fei-hung. Willie Chi is a pleasant enough chap, with good physical skills, but he doesn't make much of an impression, much less embody the greatest hero in China. He doesn't even get drunk—or get the benefit of the Wong Fei-hung theme music. *AKA: Jui Kuen 3; Zui Quan 3; Drunken Master 3.* 🐉🐉

1994 91m/C *HK* Michelle Reis, Willie Chi, Andy Lau, Simon Yam, Lau Kar-Leung, Adam Cheng, Gordon Lau, William Ho. *D:* Lau Kar-Leung. *W:* Stanley Siu. *C:* Peter Ngor. *M:* Mak Chun-hung. **DVD**

Drunken Tai Chi

This Yuen Clan action comedy features some awfully broad humor (two ladies have their dresses torn in the first 12 minutes), but its inventive action sequences are highly entertaining. In his first starring role, Donnie Yen *(Iron Monkey)* plays prankster Chin Dao, who competes with rich kid To-shao (Mandy Chan) to be the biggest show-off in school. Their bicycle joust escalates until Dao gets To-shao arrested. To-shao tries to get revenge on Dao and his brother Ping (Yuen Yat-chor) using a fusillade of fireworks, but the tricks backfire, and To-shao has a nervous breakdown.

To-shao's rich father (Wang Tao) hires mute wild man Killer Bird (Sunny Yuen) to kill the whole Chin family. While Dao is out engaging in some kind of paintbrush wrestling match with a man-mountain named Buffalo, Killer Bird massacres the rest of the Chins and burns down the house. Now a homeless orphan, Dao is taken in by a crazy puppeteer (Yuen Cheung-yan, wearing ridiculously huge buck teeth) and his fat wife Lily (Lydia Shum). Even assassins have a soft spot, and for Killer Bird it's his little daughter Teeny Bird. But still, even though Dao saves Teeny from some kidnappers, Killer Bird is still out to get him, and is too powerful for Dao to beat. The old puppeteer agrees to teach Dao his Soft Style Drunken Tai Chi, matching yin against yang.

As one would expect from a combination of the Yuens and Yen, the fight choreography is marvelous. Even the puppets get in on the act, breathing fire and squirting ink. At one point, Yen becomes a puppet himself to indulge in a little break-dancing. Another weird anachronism is that the bikes used are modern 10 speeds "from the States." The U.S. version is missing about six minutes, and the dubbing is very bad. *AKA: Siu Tai Gik; Xiao Tai Ji; Laughing Tai Chi; Tai Chi Master.* 🐉🐉🐉

1984 85m/C *HK* Donnie Yen, Yuen Cheung-yan, Sunny Yuen, Yuen Yat-chor, Lydia Shum, Lee Kwan,

Mandy Chan, Wang Tao. *D:* Yuen Woo-ping. *W:* Yuen Woo-ping, Brandy Yuen, The Peace People. *C:* Chen Jung-shu. *M:* Tang Siu-lam. **VHS, DVD**

The Duel

Director/cinematographer Andrew Lau followed his smash-hit *Storm Riders* by returning to a similar milieu—only this time teaming with Wong Jing for a more irreverent treatment of the swordplay genre. Chief Kung retrieves the Imperial Jade Seal from the bandit Ghost King for his master White Cloud City Chief Yip Ku-sing, AKA Sword Saint (Andy Lau), who intends to return it to the capitol. Master Lin Yunhe (Norman Tsui) is in pursuit of the Ghost King, bringing with him second sister Ziqing (Kristy Yeung) of Tianshan, along with her three sisters, as assistants. They've taken over the Yuan Tak Tavern out in the wilderness to lay a trap for him, suspecting his secret identity is Secret Agent Dragon 9. However Dragon 9 (Nick Cheung) reveals the truth: Lin is the real Ghost King, who recruited the sisters to help eliminate the lawman on his tail. Saimon Tsui-shih, AKA Snow the God of Sword (Ekin Cheng), arrives to help out his buddy Dragon 9, but Ziqing's sisters fall to Lin's twin blades in the superpowered flying sword battle. Having vanquished Ghost King, lecherous Dragon 9 returns to the capitol to report. The Sword Saint arrives to return the seal to the emperor, and to issue a public challenge to Snow to meet him for a duel atop the Forbidden City. This puts the whole region in turmoil, with unfortunate Dragon 9 charged by the emperor with the task of distributing eight medals to identify the lucky few who will be admitted to witness the duel as imperial guardsmen. Triad chief Gold Mustache (Elvis Tsui) bets everything he has on Snow against vice lord Immoral Wu, and Princess Phoenix (top Chinese TV star Vicki Zhao) annoys Dragon 9 even more than usual over the match. After seeing Yip Ku-sing warm up by defeating the Tang brothers with a single strike, Gold Mustache begins to regret his wager. However, Phoenix discovers Ku-sing was hit by one of the Tang's 199 poisoned needles, giving Snow an advantage.

Midway through, it turns into a murder mystery, as Dragon 9 tries to find out who killed Ziqing's third brother, and is killing off any witnesses before he can get to them. Many fans were initially disappointed that *The Duel* lacked the operatic story of Andrew Lau's *Storm Riders* and *A Man Called Hero*, and features fewer hyperactive supernatural fight scenes. But this is a Wong Jing film, meaning it has charms of its own, including some goofy nonsense comedy and in-jokes, and a clever mystery plot. Wong has so much fun poking holes in swordplay fantasy and adventure movie traditions that it's almost a shame that the tale is grounded by

The Jackie Chan Story

Part One

成龍

Imagine a seven-year-old boy in a cowboy outfit, taken for a ferry ride by his parents to a strange part of town. He enters a building where lots of kids are doing gymnastics and stuff. Looks like fun—until he finds out that his parents are leaving him there for 10 years while they leave the country; that he'll be beaten regularly; that he'll be forced into extreme physical exercise 10 hours a day, sleep on the floor, not get enough to eat; and that he'll be beaten *more* if he gets out of line. This is how the story begins for Little Pao-Pao, as his parents called him, who went on to become the top action star in the world.

As a child, Chan Kang-sang was a bit of a handful; he wasn't good at school and abused the martial arts training his father gave him by getting into fights. When his parents, who worked as servants to a wealthy family, were offered better positions in Australia, the question came up: what to do with Pao-Pao? The nickname means "cannonball," given because newborn Chan weighed 12 pounds, but he lived up to it with a knack for getting into trouble. For a boy who wasn't a natural scholar and had a lot of destructive energy, and parents who couldn't afford boarding school, enrollment in Master Yu Jim-yuen's Chinese Drama Academy seemed like a good idea at the time. At least the boy would learn a trade.

And so, Pao-Pao took the name Yuen Lo, in training to join the Seven Little Fortunes Chinese opera troupe, with a contract saying his master was allowed to discipline him, "even to death." Despite many misadventures, Yuen Lo grew into a talented, if easily distracted, young opera performer. Master even lent him out to perform in movies, along with several other talented performers. By the late 1960s, the popularity of old-fashioned Chinese opera was fading, and Yuen Lo found himself loaned out to do extra and stunt work more and more. When he finally left the academy, stunt work barely kept him alive, but it was the only thing he knew how to do. Eventually, his fearlessness and academy-honed abilities got him jobs as action director and in small supporting roles. He also got a few lead roles from independent producers, but these paid even less than doing stunts for Shaw Brothers. His best role came in the early John Woo picture *Hand of Death,* which didn't lead anywhere. After a few years of struggling near starvation, 19-year-old Yuen Lo decided he was a failure at the movie business, and headed for Australia to join his parents, supporting himself with construction jobs.

However, fate wouldn't let Jackie Chan (a name he took while trying to get through an English course) stay away. The Hong Kong film industry was still hopeful that someone could be found to fill the void left by Bruce Lee's death. Willie Chan, an executive with the new Lo Wei Productions who had a sharp eye for talent, had noticed Chan while he was doing stunts, and thought he had possibilities. Lo Wei, the "Millionaire Director" who kept out of the way on Bruce Lee's first films but took the credit, signed him to a contract, and Jackie (or sometimes "Jacky") did his best to ape Lee in the unauthorized sequel *New Fist of Fury* (1976). When that failed, they tried making Jackie a serious kung fu student in *Shaolin Wooden Men,* a villain in *Killer Meteors,* and a vengeful swordsman in *To Kill with Intrigue.* Though they weren't really bad movies, Jackie didn't catch on the way they hoped he would, and his movies were boxoffice poison. What Jackie and his pals always wanted to do was combine kung fu and comedy, a formula his old schoolmate Sammo Hung was already using. Lo Wei finally let Chan try it with *Half a Loaf of Kung Fu,* but didn't think it was funny and shelved it to make his own Jackie Chan comedy, the much broader *Spiritual Kung Fu.* When that flopped, Lo had just about given up on Chan.

But thankfully, when Chan was loaned out to other studios, he was given more creative freedom, and this paid off tremendously in a pair of titanic hits directed by Yuen Woo-ping: *Snake in the Eagle's Shadow* and *Drunken Master.* Audiences went crazy for these stories of a brash young kid, a crazy old master, incredible kung fu training, and even more incredible kung fu fighting. After a period of stressful negotiations that almost got Jackie killed by triads, he got out of his contract with Lo Wei and signed a record-breaking deal with Golden Harvest. Jackie Chan thought he was on top of the world, but he hadn't seen anything yet.

stoic heroes and romance. The swordsman heroes are such excessively noble heartthrobs that they border on self-parody—Snow even bakes! It's no classic, and the dazzling CGI f/x used during the fight scenes is already beginning to look dated, but this is a solid entertainment worth catching. *AKA: Kuet Chin Chi Gam Ji Din; Jue Zhan Zi Jin Zhi Dian.* 🎵🎵🎵

2000 106m/C *HK* Andy Lau, Ekin Cheng, Nick Cheung, Vicki Zhao, Norman Tsui, Elvis Tsui, Patrick Tam, Jerry Lamb, Frankie Ng, David Lee, Wong Yat-Fei, Tin Sum, Kristy Yeung. *D:* Andrew Lau. *W:* Wong Jing, Manfred Wong. *C:* Andrew Lau. *M:* Comfort Chan. **VHS, DVD**

Duel of the Brave Ones

This weak triad tale is spiced up a bit with Wilson Tong's creative fight choreography and some 1970s sleaze. Kwang Tai-sing (Wilson Tong) joins up with Fa Kei-leung (John Chang) and his Canton Road Boys triad in order to find a piece of orange jade. His father Kwang Chi just got out of prison, having taken the rap for Fa for stealing the jade. Police Sgt. Chan is also after the jade to solve the old case, and leans on the Kwangs for information. Fa is struggling for territory with the established 14K Triad, led by Boss Wah (Fung Ging Man), leading Sing into rumbles with Wah's men. Not that things are any better with Fa, who blames Sing for the cops hanging around. Sing is involved in the robbery of his own brother-in-law, who is coerced into neglecting to identify Sing, but Sing is still pressured into turning queen's evidence and working for the cops. Fa gets wind of the betrayal, and sends his men to kill Sing and his father.

The film seems all too willing to be distracted by its own seedy urban atmosphere, trailing away from the plot for meaningless chases, fights, leering cheesecake, and crude comic nonsense involving Ho Pak Kwong's whorehouse. Eventually things get back on track, introducing themes that would become common with later triad movies. Sing seeks shelter by induction into the 14K Triad, just as his father is experiencing deep regret and renouncing his criminal past. The main point seems to be to maneuver Wilson Tong into a fight with his arch enemy John Chang, but their confrontations are defused several times, leading to more digressions that only serve to make the film seem much longer than it is. The street fight scenes are generally good, but sometimes you can't tell who's fighting and what for. *AKA: Tek Dau; Ti Dou; Shadow Killers.* 🎵🎵

1978 85m/C *HK* Wilson Tong, John Chang, Chan Chuen, Eddie Ko, Shi Szu, Joan Lim, Ho Pak Kwong,

Lam Man-wai, Jimmy Liu, Fung Ging Man, Ging Chue, San Sin, Yue Tau Wan. *D:* Wai Man. *W:* Wai Man, Leung Wai. *C:* Faan Chuen-yam. *M:* Frankie Chan. **VHS, DVD**

Duel of the Tao Tough

So many Godfrey Ho movies are of shoddy quality that it's a delightful surprise when one actually turns out to be decent. This one has adequate sets, great locations, and excellent fight scenes.

Thieves disguised as Shaolin monks steal Shaolin scriptures—the Dharma Book of Changes—from a party of monks from Canton. Only one monk gets away by hopping aboard a ferry run by Wong (Jacky Chow), sharing a ride with Lady Chin (who is traveling disguised as a man). The ferryman decides to help the monk by sneaking into Shaolin Temple to "rip them off," but once there, the abbot convinces him that the scriptures were actually stolen by Shaolin turncoat Pai Chang. The abbot wants Wong to learn the Book of Changes before trying to get the copy back from Pai, but the young man is in too much of a hurry.

Alerted by a spy, Pai orders his men throughout the region to be on the lookout for a kung fu fightin' young Cantonese man. His men attack Chin, who gets a hand from Wong in fighting off the gang. Since Ching is on the way to try to get revenge on Pai for killing her family, the two become traveling companions. As a refreshing change from the routine in these movies, Wong needs little help in seeing through Chin's gender disguise—just a look at her walking ashore after fording a river. Wong is lured into a trap set by Pai's wicked daughter Chung, but fortunately her sister Dan-Dan owes the hero a favor and helps him escape, though Chung is mistakenly killed by one of her men during a fight. Since Dan-Dan had run away from her arranged marriage to old kung fu master Noodle, she's anxious to switch sides and run off with dashing Wong. But now not only does Wong have to deal with Pai, who holds him responsible for Chung's death and is extra eager to kill him, but now angry groom Noodle is after him, too.

Whoever he really is (no other credits were found), Jacky Chow is very good in his role as a lighthearted hero, though falling closer to Elton Chong than his intended target of Jackie Chan. Attempts at making him a ladykiller as well are a bit awkward—*both* Pai sisters are killed by friendly fire during battles, and Chin tries to keep him from facing the villains in combat by stealing his chi during sex. The rest of the fighting cast is good, too, and though the camera speeds up the action a bit, the battles are nicely choreographed, with some of Ho's gimmicks like flying snakes thrown in for extra fun. Someone must have realized that Wong lacked motivation to go through so much on his quest, and so late in the game a line explains how his father was framed for one of Pai's past crimes. Vaughn Savage's English dubbing crew has some fun putting anachronistic dialogue in Chow's mouth, saying, "Up yours!" and so forth. The lively musical score sounds like it was culled from various 1960s spy and cowboy movies, as well as *Silent Running*. **AKA:** *Duel of the Tough.* ♫♫♫

1982 82m/C *HK* Jacky Chow, Steve Mak, Hui Ying-Ying, Howard Ki, Charlie Hyu, Bruce Cheung, Mike Wong, Lung Woo Yiu, Bobby Ahn, Lee Tin Hung, Mahler Uy, Choi Dong Hoi, Stella Chay. **D:** Godfrey Ho. **W:** Richard Hung. **C:** Jimmy Yu. **M:** Tony Tsang. **VHS, DVD**

Duel to the Death

The rivalry between China and Japan, more vicious than the one between the Chicago Bears and Green Bay Packers, forms about all the plot there is in this flick. Nevertheless, the nonstop action and wild f/x of this classic swordplay piece are wonderfully entertaining.

At Shaolin Temple, ninjas storm the library, stealing a sacred scroll full of kung fu secrets. But the Shaolin monks are on alert, and a huge battle is joined. Shaolin superhero Po Ching-Wan (Damian Lau), dubbed King of the Sword, turns the tide in driving off the invaders. Fearing capture on the beach (is there a beach near Shaolin?), the ninjas hide the scroll they stole and self-destruct (!), taking many Chinese with them. The Japanese shogun's representative Kenji (Eddie Ko) comes to Shaolin to challenge the monks to a duel to settle whose kung fu is best. Hashimoto (Norman Tsui), the best fighter in Japan, is put on the card to fight Ching-Wan at Holy Sword House. The Japanese warriors are dedicated to their craft, even unto death. Hashimoto's master dons a mask and dies in a battle to test their champion. Before leaving, Ching visits his former master, now a crazy old man in the woods, who is accompanied by guest star Dragon the cockatoo.

A festival gathers around the coming duel, complete with puppet shows. The puppeteer is murdered by Japanese thugs, but a mysterious young hero (Flora Cheung), apparently a woman disguised as a man, kills them right back. The woman then challenges Hashimoto in the desert, but he refuses to fight a girl.

Ninjas come to retrieve the stolen scroll. The mystery woman and Ching fight them, then make goo-goo eyes at each other. The warriors arrive for the duel to again meet the woman,

who turns out to be Ha Sheng-Nan, mistress of Holy Sword House.

Meanwhile, the Shaolin abbot is attacked by ninjas. One ninja's clothes shred to reveal a naked woman, distracting the abbot enough that she can catch him in a big net. Other ninjas—one of whom, we learn, is that sneaky Kenji—attack champions on their way to the duel. Hashimoto confronts Kenji about his suspicious behavior, and Kenji explains his mission: capture as many of the best Chinese warriors as possible, and learn their secrets—then the Japanese will have the power to defeat China. What he doesn't explain is: if the ninja are good enough to capture all China's best fighters, why do they need their secrets?

Sheng-Nan's father Ha, Master of Holy Sword House, works with the Japanese in exchange for giving Sheng-Nan a shot at restoring his family's fame by defeating Hashimoto. Ching is captured as well, and finds the other captives drugged and strung up in a huge web. Sheng-Nan is forced to go against her father's treachery and help her boyfriend Ching. Hashimoto betrays his shogun in the name of honor as well, and the two champions delay their duel to fight the ninjas and rescue their captives

The plot may be a bit silly, but this inspired mix of high-flying Chinese swordplay and crazy ninja hi-jinks is fun from start to finish, featuring colorful costumes, beautiful locations, singing swords, and liberal bits of gore. The action bogs down here and there for discussions of pride and honor among warriors, but when the climactic duel finally arrives, it's one of the wildest and bloodiest sword-to-sword scenes ever filmed. **AKA:** *Xian si Jue; The Duel.* ♫♫♫

1982 87m/C *HK* Damian Lau, Norman Tsui, Flora Cheung, Casanova Wong, Eddie Ko. **D:** Ching Siu-Tung. **W:** Kong Lung, Man Chun, Ching Sui-Tung, Manfred Wong, David Lai. **C:** Li Yu Tang, Lau Hung-chuen. **M:** Michael Lai. **VHS, DVD**

Dummy Mommy, without a Baby

Pop star Miriam Yeung broke out as a leading lady with this modestly successful comedy. Working-class LK Fong (Miriam Yeung) is desperate to keep her job. She is an assistant account executive at an advertising agency who already feels under appreciated and overworked. Then she makes a colossal goof and accidentally sends everybody at the agency an e-mail making fun of her superiors. Racing out of the office barely ahead of the firing line, she hits upon the idea of faking a pregnancy. Since employment law prevents pregnant women from being fired, she is spared the axe—at least until she gives birth.

"Buddha be praised."

—The Shaolin abbot, about a hundred times, in *Duel to the Death*

"Wow! How come he's more crazy than me?"

—Carina Lau wonders at the competition in *Eagle Shooting Heroes*

It's a foregone conclusion that deception in comedies must be sustained for the entire length of the movie, to be unearthed shortly before an ending that redeems all the participants. And this film follows a very predictable course. Yet the trip itself is quite enjoyable. Miriam Yeung is very winning as LK. After all, her motives are not bad—during difficult economic times, she wants to keep working. She likes the advertising business, and feels she can make a success of it if given the opportunity to do so. So her reactions to the situations that develop as the deception continues are completely understandable. It helps that her personality is down to earth. The fact that she is not interested in a romance with the CEO of the company when he unexpectedly comes to her aid also helps the audience to root for her. Imagine, for once, a heroine who does not look to a man to solve her problems! Edison Chen plays CEO Wu Ming in a very relaxed and charming manner. Wu Ming is not really interested in the advertising business. Instead he moonlights as a pastry chef at a restaurant—paying for the privilege—and drags himself into work each morning. Though LK is not interested in Wu Ming, someone else does have romantic eyes for him—LK's roommate, best friend, and co-worker, Dina (Niki Chow). Interestingly, the best chemistry in the movie is between LK and Dina. It appears as though they really like each other and have been friends for years, and their bond gives substance to some of the sillier moments. The film is not a laugh riot from beginning to end, but it is a consistently enjoyable 89-minute ride with plenty of memorable gags. Co-directors Joe Ma and Mak Kai-gwong allow the pace to slacken several times, but not to the point of any serious damage. Also of note in the supporting cast are Pauline Yam Bo-Lam as Monica, the evil creative director at the agency, and Hui Siu-hung as Wu Faye, the CEO's father, who manages to drop in on LK and Dina at the most inopportune times. Lincoln Lo composed the rock guitar-heavy, very flavorful score. Miriam Yeung sang the catchy title song. —PM **AKA:** *Yuk Lui Tim Ding; Yu Nu Tian Ding.* 🎵🎵🎵

2001 89m/C *HK* Miriam Yeung, Edison Chen, Wyman Wong, Niki Chow, Pauline Yam, Eileen Cha, Moses Chan, Hui Siu-hung, Chor Yuen, Cheung Tat-Ming, Sammy. **D:** Joe Ma, Mak Kai-gwong. **W:** Joe Ma, Taures Chow, Chan Wing-sun. **C:** Davy Tsou. **M:** Lincoln Lo. **VHS, DVD**

Dynamo

Call it a case of art imitating life. Li Tin-yee (Bruce Li) is a Hong Kong taxi driver and dedicated martial arts student. Bruce Lee's funeral ties up traffic, and lots of sharpies exploit his death. Entrepreneur Miss Mary (Mary Han) of the Pacific Agency sees Li fighting with some rival cabbies, and signs him up to play an imitation Bruce Lee in kung fu movies, endorse products, etc. His movies are even directed by an imitation Lo Wei! To give Li credibility, a drinking, pot-smoking sensei (Ku Feng) is hired to train him to win the martial arts championship. Meanwhile, Mary and her assistant Leung have taken control of Li's life, even arranging for him to take up with a sexy French starlet.

Mary's old public-relations mentor Mr. George (George Yirikian) of the Cosmo Agency tries to steal Li away from her. When he fails, he hires thugs to try to beat Li to death. Fighters in Tokyo and Seoul, as well as a black guy in Chicago in a funny orange hat, all fail to defeat him. Desperate, George proposes a fight between Li and Cosmo's American karate champ Jean-Claude (!), and then has Li's girlfriend kidnapped to force him to throw the fight.

Though this starts out like an exposé of the whole "Bruceploitation" business, halfway through the plot gets tied up in the rival agency and their thugs. Li's fight scenes are quite good, he gets to do some real acting, and he has some good chemistry with ragged mentor Ku Feng. Crowds line up for the big fight outside Chicago's Soldier Field, though the interior is a covered arena à la Madison Square Garden. **AKA:** *Bu ze Shou Duan.* 🎵🎵🎵

1978 (R) 87m/C *HK* Bruce Li, Mary Han, Ku Feng, Lee Hoi-sang, James Griffiths, George Yirikian, Joseph Soto, Steve Sanders. **D:** Hwa Yi Hung. **W:** Lam Chin-wai. **DVD**

Eagle Shooting Heroes

Wong Kar-Wei produced this semi-parody of his *Ashes of Time* during shooting of that epic, based on the same Louis Cha novel and with much of the same cast. This is more fun, and even got released first! O Yang-fong (Tony Leung Chiu-Wai) and the bitchy queen (Veronica Yip) rebel against the king of a fantasy quasi-Arabian kingdom. They try to usurp the throne by getting the official jade seal, but it's been left in the care of Third Princess (Brigitte Lin), a warrior of questionable martial arts skill. Unable to defeat the villains, she flees to a mountain hideout to get help from her martial arts master Wang Chon-yang (Kenny Bee). The two villains go to Imperial Master (Maggie Cheung) to force her to reveal Princess Three's whereabouts in her crystal ball, and to swipe her Invincible Flying Shoes to get there. Master Wang is killed accidentally by an errant shoe, and his fellow master Chou Po-ting (Carina Lau in drag) assumes that the princess murdered him. Meanwhile, the young master of the Dwan Clan (Tony Leung Ka-Fai), instructed by the dream of his 189-year-old grandfather, goes forth to seek his true love. On advice from another venerable master (given just to get rid of her), Princess Three leaves on a very complicated quest involving caves and monsters and such, to learn an esoteric kung fu technique to beat O Yang-fong. Junior student Wang (Leslie Cheung) is sent along for good measure, much to the distress of his jealous cousin/fiancée (Joey Wong). She follows him, annoyed along the way by a mad beggar (Jacky Cheung). All the while, O Yang-fong is stuck in a tree. He escapes, only to become a victim of his own Invincible Poisonous Queen Bee.

Taking a cue from Stephen Chow's nonsense comedy, this is a wild and wacky ride. The parody isn't limited to swordplay fantasy films—other genres skewered include black-magic horror, romance, historical period adventures, animal-style kung fu, cross-gender casting, man-in-suit monsters, pop singers, ghosts, soccer, etc. Sammo Hung's action direction delightfully lampoons sped-up wirework fight scenes, and Peter Pau's camera intensifies the colorful costumes and sets. A little too long, this is a riot for experienced Hong Kong film fans, but may be a head-scratcher for newbies. No eagles were shot during production of this film. **AKA:** *Se Diu Ying Hung Ji Dung Sing Sai Jau; She Diao Ying Xiong Zhi Dong Cheng Xi Jiu; Dong Cheng Xi Jiu.* 🐉🐉🐉

1993 113m/C *HK* Leslie Cheung, Tony Leung Chiu-Wai, Tony Leung Ka-Fai, Jacky Cheung, Brigitte Lin, Joey Wong, Maggie Cheung, Carina Lau, Veronica Yip, Kenny Bee, Shut Ma Wa Lung, Pau Hei-ching. **D:** Jeff Lau. **W:** Jeff Lau, Louis Chia (story). **C:** Peter Pau. **M:** James Wong. **VHS, DVD**

Eagle vs. Silver Fox

More Godfrey Ho hokum, sloppily constructed with flashbacks within flashbacks that easily confuse the viewer, should any be trying to pay attention. Sly villain Silver Fox (Hwang Jang Lee) works for the Northern lords trying to destroy the Southern rebels and restore the Manchurians to Chinese ruler. He waylays priest Sung on the road, after the secret message he carries. Li So (Mario Chan) goes with his father to carry another message, but they're also ambushed by the Silver Fox gang, stabbed, and thrown in the river. But the villains fail to find the message, and Li survives and is rescued by Master Tang. They train together, but Li So learns too well, and accidentally kills Tang with his own Flying Fist move.

Li So beats up some toughs in a restaurant, and is joined by girl pickpocket Yuen Ling. Li and

Ling go out and get in more fights with the gang, working their way up to the Silver Fox himself.

The story is so poorly constructed that it's hard to tell what's going on at any given moment. Characters jump forward and back in time; one character seems to be telling a story that's another character's flashback, and so on. There are some weird sequences in slow motion that have a disturbing dreamlike quality. Only a rough explanation is offered halfway through the film for why Silver Fox is doing what he does, so if you don't know your Chinese history, it may not make much sense. Come to think of it, it doesn't make much sense anyway. The dance-like choreography is too seldom and too little, failing to make up for all the other nonsense. Hwang Jang Lee (*Buddha Assassinator*) made his film debut in 1976 playing Silver Fox in *The Secret Rivals,* and may have been typecast as the oily villain. 🐉🐉

1983 85m/C *KO* Hwang Jang Lee, Mario Chan, Wing Pui-Shan, Richard Kong, Simpson Yuen, Wu Kam-Bo. **D:** Godfrey Ho. **W:** Lung Kun. **C:** Jimmy Yu. **M:** Ricky Chan. **VHS, DVD**

Eagle's Claw

Militiaman Chen (Chi Kuan Chun) wishes he could go improve his fighting skills, but he has other responsibilities—he has a girlfriend to look after, plus has to arrest the San gang. Taking the thugs in, he's challenged by an old man, who humiliates him. This convinces him he has to study further, leaving his fiancée behind to live in the temple with the old man. His first lesson is to stand in the stinking cesspool all day. From there he moves on to one torturous lesson after another. He has to catch birds like a cat, sleep hanging upside down, etc. Then the Master (Chang Yi) teaches him Eagle Fist– and Toad Fist–style kung fu. He also learns the secret weapon of hitting pressure points to lock the nerves. However, the manual for the Anti-lock, which frees the locked nerves, was stolen by the bandit Red Dart, who killed the old man's master. Chen is finally taught the Dying Fist, a last resort maneuver that uses an opponent's death strike against him.

Chen sets out on a mission to find Red Dart and retrieve the manual. On the road, he meets up with an old man who turns out to be his master's cousin, and tells him of his quest. When he runs out of cash, he takes a job as teacher at Tao's Martial Arts Academy, working for Mr. Liu. Seeing the moves of teacher Tong Ming makes Chen suspicious, so he puts on a mask to search the man's room, where he discovers that Tong knows the Anti-lock technique. Chen exploits the boss's tramp daughter To Ching (Hwa Ling) to trap Tong. He finds out that Liu

"*You should be pleased. Most women I know would be offended if I couldn't tell the difference between them and a man.*"

—Wang Cheng Li, turning on the charm for his cross-dressing traveling companion in *Eagle vs. Silver Fox*

Kung Fu
through the Ages

功夫

In a typical kung fu movie made circa 1979, the following scene is likely to be enacted: the comic hero gets in a fight and while trying to escape accidentally knocks out his opponent. An impressed bystander says, "Oh, what style is that?," whereupon our hero stammers out, "Uh, um...Clumsy Style! My invention!" But what is all this talk about styles in kung fu flicks? And how did it get started?

The term kung fu (or more correctly, "gung fu") originally referred to any skill achieved through practice and training, but it's come to be more specifically applied to the Chinese martial arts developed at the Shaolin Temple. Though the accepted history of martial arts claims that Chinese kung fu originated with the teachings of Indian Buddhist monk Bodhidarma at Shaolin in the early sixth century, some scholars now question that belief, claiming no record of his existence can be found dating any earlier than the 11th century, and documents dating from the early third century describe basic forms related to animals. Some even trace martial arts to 5,000-year-old Babylonian tablets depicting basic unarmed combat techniques, though that's hardly evidence of real kung fu. However, texts and official documents have been discovered dating from the sixth century (Liang Dynasty) that confirm Bodhidarma's stay in China.

However, there's no doubt that Shaolin techniques are rooted in earlier martial arts styles. In general, kung fu styles are referred to as belonging to the two halves of China they came from. The Northern Shaolin styles, which emphasize long hard punches and high kicks, are based in chang chuan ("long fist" pugilism), while the Southern Shaolin style, which uses minimal low kicks and subtle hand movement, comes from nan chuan ("south fist"). One legend claims the Southern Style originated with monks whose legs were injured fighting pirates to compensate for their disabilities.

Many modern Chinese dispute the importance of Shaolin, perhaps bridling at the suggestion that China's strength originated in India. But what these skeptics miss is that Shaolin kung fu took these existing martial arts styles and increased their power tremendously with chi kung techniques attributed to Bodhidarma. These techniques and 18 stances are known as Lohan, the basis of all modern kung fu, which now includes hundreds of distinct styles.

Many great warriors visited the temple to study over the centuries, learning Shaolin kung fu while combining it with their own knowledge. Bai Yufeng further developed the "18 exercises of Lohan," reorganizing and expanding them, increasing the number of forms from 18 to 72, then to 173. He also created the Five Imitations Boxing in the light of the Five Animal Exercise invented by Hua Tuo, a very famous doctor during the Three Kingdoms Period (220–265). The Five Animal Exercise was a kind of body-building regimen that imitated the actions of tigers, deer, bears, apes, and birds; while the Five Animal Styles of Bai Yufeng was a kind of Chinese shadow-boxing that mimicked the movements of dragons, tigers, leopards, snakes, and cranes. The Five Styles were considered the best of Shaolin chuan. Most modern kung fu styles were developed by expanding these animal styles, the most popular being eagle, monkey, and mantis styles. There's even a dog style that emphasizes rough tumbling and kicking from the ground.

Styles have been named after the creator (Wing Chun), religion, region they came from, or even a sponsoring family. Some styles are based on nature, while some are more esoteric—Sleeping Fist and Drunken Boxing are pretty obvious in their inspiration, and are always crowd pleasers. Tai chi ("shadow") style emphasizes diversions and close, lightning-fast hand movements. Japanese Buddhist monks visited Shaolin Temple during the 14th century, taking home with them basic knowledge of kung fu, which were eventually developed into judo, jujitsu, and karate.

There are also 18 basic Chinese martial arts weapons: sabre, spear, sword, halbert, axe, battle axe, hook, fork, whip, mace, hammer, talon, trident-halberd, cudgel, long-handled spear, short cudgel, stick, and meteor hammer. A small, sharp piece of metal called a "pai" was used as a throwing weapon, sometimes attached to a chain or rope for retrieval (or hauling an enemy in for the kill). The Japanese advanced this throwing blade concept into what became the shuriken, or throwing star. However, despite claims from other nations, no one can really doubt that it was the medieval Chinese that invented the pai fight.

was the one who taught him the Anti-lock, and Tong ends up in a shallow grave. Locking Liu's nerves, he catches Tao (Chui Chung Hei) unlocking them, and recovers the manual from the man who is really the Red Dart.

A traditional kung fu movie with a multiple-twist ending and bits of gentle comedy. Chi is not a particularly gifted star, but at least there's some attempt to try new things within the genre. The nerve-locking techniques central to the plot are the same ones conspiracy theorists still claim killed Bruce Lee. The soundtrack uses the theme from *True Grit*. **AKA:** *Ying Chau Tong Long; Ying Zhao Tang Lang; Eagle Fist.* 🐾🐾🐾

1977 93m/C *HK* Chi Kuan Chun, Chang Yi, Chui Chung Hei, Wang Tao, Phillip Ko, Leung Kar-yan, Ma Cheung, Lung Fong, Hwa Ling, Ko Saio Pao, Shih Ting Ken, Cho Boon Feng. **D:** Lee Tso Nam. **W:** Chang Seng-yi. **VHS, DVD**

The Eagle's Killer

In this old-school martial arts adventure, contract killer Ghost Hand Lo Hsin (Hwang Jang Lee) is an Eagle Claw master. During the credits, he demonstrates his technique on a hanging skeleton. Tai (John Chang) is a lowly mop boy at a kung fu school, where rich Mr. Chan sends his fat son Fatty (Chiang Kam) to learn all the latest styles. Master Chan (Baan Yung-sang) is a lazy bastard who's just scamming his students, teaching Fatty nothing but Sleeping and Eating Fist. In his year there, all Tai has learned is kitchen kung fu, which he uses to hassle Fatty. Tai quits the school, but finds himself in one scrape after another.

When Tai sees Lo Hsin in action, he convinces the killer to take him on as a student, but Tai soon discovers that Lo really means to sell him into slavery. Stuttering gang boss Hsiao Lung (Cheng Hong-yip), who is an old enemy of Tai's, buys him at auction, meaning to have him gang-raped by his muscular stooges, but Tai turns the tables on him. Tai escapes the pursuing thugs with the help of jolly Master Chin Pai-to (Fan Mui-Sang), who takes him home to his farm, where he lives with his blind sister Hsiao-mei (Chan Pooi-ling). Having found an honest teacher at last, Tai soon improves enough to go back to the school and teach his old master Chan a lesson. Hsiao Lung's father hires some Thai boxer killers to take on Tai, but they fail, and Tai and Chin amuse themselves by busting up the Hsiao's casino and slave market. With that, Hsiao hires Lo Hsin to deal with Tai and his master once and for all.

Another *Drunken Master* knockoff, this one survives merely on the physical talents of its stars, though Fan Mui-Sang and Hwang Jang Lee are clearly doubled for their more acrobatic moves. **AKA:** *Baai Cho Bye Foo Kau Cho Tau; Bai Cu Shi Fu Kou Cu Tou.* 🐾🐾

1981 90m/C *HK* Hwang Jang Lee, John Chang, Chan Pooi-ling, Fan Mui-Sang, Cheng Hong-yip, Kao Yuen, Chiang Kam, Baan Yung-sang, Mai Kei, Cheung Wa, Lin Ke-ming, Chan Hei. **D:** William Cheung Kei. **W:** Wong Jing, Hsu Li-min, Chang Chi. **C:** Lin Tse-yung, Chang Te-wei. **M:** Eddie H. Wang. **VHS, DVD**

The East Is Red

Producer Tsui Hark acknowledged the fact that Brigitte Lin's Invincible Asia character dominated *Legend of the Swordsman* by making her the star of this sequel. The opening recaps the final moments of the previous picture (without showing Jet Li's face!) during which Asia fell from the Black Cliff. Koo (Yu Rongguang), Ling, and Woo Ching (Eddie Ko) are ordered by the emperor to guide a Spanish ship to the site, where they hope to recover goods from the Dutch ship Asia sank with his cannon. General Golida's true purpose is to steal the sacred scroll, and Koo joins the Warden of the Holy Altar (Lau Shun) in defending Asia's grave from desecration. Koo discerns that the Warden is actually Asia in an elaborate disguise, and before he's killed for his knowledge, he tells her/him that, though Invincible Asia has vanished from the world, there are still plenty of imposters carrying on the bad work. Taking Koo along, she sets out to destroy these pretenders. Chief among them is Snow (Joey Wong), Asia's former concubine, who has become the terror of the high seas. Asia destroys her ship and denounces her, but when the Sun Moon Sect shifts its allegiance to the returned master, Asia turns on them, too, intending to keep anyone from following Invincible Asia, real or false. While Koo and Ching escape the Sect with Snow, Asia hides in a brothel to trap the Sun Moon enemy, General Moyan Luchong. Meanwhile, Koo's party takes refuge with the cheerful General Tin Kai-wan, who has fun making sport of Invincible Asia's name.

The film loses its narrative focus midway through, as Lin becomes a monster out to terrorize everyone for no good reason. Before she was on a quest to unite the Martial Arts World under the Sun Moon banner by force, but here she just seems to be enjoying kicking everybody around. With a dwarf disguised as a great samurai general with gadgety armor, a warship that turns into a submarine, and other conceptual rabbits being pulled out of the movie's hat, things get so crazy one suspects Wong Jing's participation in the concoction, especially since there's a gambling scene, too. It's a bit of a mess, but a reasonably entertaining one. Joey Wong gives one of her better performances as the complicated Snow. **AKA:** *Dung Fong Bat Baai: Fung Wan Joi Hei;*

Dong Fang Bu Bai: Feng Yun Zai Qi; Swordsman 3; Invincible Asia 2. 🐉🐉🐉

1993 97m/C *HK* Brigitte Lin, Joey Wong, Yu Rong-guang, Eddie Ko, Lau Shun, Jean Wang, Lee Ka-ting, Yuen King-Tan. **D:** Ching Siu-tung, Raymond Lee. **W:** Tsui Hark, Roy Szeto, Charcoal Cheung Tan. **C:** Tom Lau. **M:** William Woo. **VHS, DVD**

Eastern Condors

The easy description is that this is the Asian version of *The Dirty Dozen,* but *Eastern Condors* is far more exciting and suspenseful than that Hollywood hit, and is one of Sammo Hung's best films. The spirit leans more toward one of his all-star action concoctions like *Millionaires Express,* only played for straight thrills rather than comedy. It's 1976, and the U.S. government fears that Vietcong forces will discover a huge underground bunker full of weapons they left behind in Vietnam after the war. Unwilling to risk having their own troops or bombers caught there, the Pentagon orders Lieutenant Lam (Lam Ching-Ying) to recruit a squad of 10 soldiers from imprisoned Chinese and Vietnamese criminals for the suicide mission, offering big cash and amnesty to the survivors. The platoon includes a variety of cons, and one of the film's great strengths, besides its amazing action scenes, is the understated depth of character each actor brings to his role. Sammo Hung slimmed down to the lowest weight of his screen career to play wrongfully convicted murderer Tung Ming-sun, an ace veteran commando. His comrades include heroin dealer Szeto Chin (Charlie Chin), the arms-dealing Ching Brothers (Billy Lau, K.K. Cheung), robber Stuttering Keung (Fung Lee), con man "Grandfather" Yun Yen-hay (Yuen Woo-ping), killer and kidnapper Ma Puk-kau (Chan Lung), arsonist/blackmailer Judy Vu (Corey Yuen), and Vietnamese killers and thieves Nguyen Siu-tran (Chin Ka-Lok) and Phan Man-lung (Hsiao Ho). Colonel Yang (Melvin Wong) asks Lam for an extra favor: to look for his brother Yeung Hung, who he had to leave behind when his troops withdrew. Another factor is that it's unsure who will live and who will die on the mission. Those killed are replaced by a variety of other characters, for good or ill. After parachuting in, Lam meets up with their guides, a trio of savage Cambodian guerillas (led by Joyce Godenzi, with Ha Chi-chun). Later, mobile entrepreneur Rat Chieh (Yuen Biao) falls in with the group through his "good-luck charm" Yeung Hung (Oscar-winner Dr. Haing S. Ngor)—who may or may not have become a simpleminded lunatic, or a spy (but for which side?). When it's found that another of them really is a spy, suspicion nearly consumes them. And after endless battles, the survivors

all end up at the underground arsenal, where they find themselves locked in with a cackling general (Yuen Wah) and his deadly aides.

The degree of creativity shown in the action direction by Hung and his opera-school pals is incredible (Sammo kills with *leaves,* for crying out loud), but that inventiveness extends to the direction, with the camera usually placed in just the right way, sometimes in strange places (like under a hat). Some scenes crib a bit from previous war films, but not to excess—some circumstances, such as in the prison camp sequence, will naturally bring out similar situations. Hung incorporates the kind of lovely mayhem to soon become popular with the "bullet ballet" trend, the daring stunt work made popular by his buddy Jackie Chan, and the kind of acrobatic kung fu popular for years. The heroes are helped out in this by a bunch of old-school regulars playing the enemy, especially Yuen Wah, who has the role of his career as the creepy enemy general. It's not without laughs—one early bit about the stuttering character is raw enough to draw groans, but other gags are all character-based and rich in personality, and the drama draws from the same well. Both as director, choreographer, and as leader of a rich ensemble cast, this is a gem in Sammo Hung's career, fully deserving of multiple viewings. Ironically, Sammo would take Joyce Godenzi's hand again in 1995—in marriage this time. Godenzi was once sought for the Kato role in the Green Hornet movie that's been in Preproduction Hell for 20 years. **AKA:** *Dung Fong Tuk Ying; Dong Fang Tu Ying; Eastern Bald Eagles.* 🐉🐉🐉🐉

1986 93m/C *HK* Sammo Hung, Yuen Biao, Lam Ching-Ying, Joyce Godenzi, Yuen Wah, Dr. Haing S. Ngor, Yuen Woo-ping, Corey Yuen, Charlie Chin, Melvin Wong, Billy Lau, K.K. Cheung, Ha Chi-chun, Chan Lung, Billy Chow, Phillip Ko, Yasuaki Kurata, Dick Wei, Wu Ma, Chin Ka-Lok, Hsiao Ho, Fung Lee, James Tien, Miu Kiu-wai, Chung Fat, Kenneth Tong, Max Mok, Kenny Ho, Ben Lam, Chris Lee. **D:** Sammo Hung. **W:** Barry Wong. **C:** Arthur Wong. **M:** Chow Kam-cheung. **VHS, DVD**

Eat My Dust

Pals John and Hung want out of the gangster life, but Tung's friend Bill Yang betrays him. When Bill and his thugs gun down Hung and his wife, John flees to South America, leaving their son Hank in an orphanage.

Years later, Bill is doing very well in the triads, and is working on a big counterfeiting deal. He pays back Fred, who did a 20-year stretch in jail for him, by rubbing him out. Meanwhile, street chestnut vendors Rob (Mark Ng) and Hank (Michael Tsang) rescue Wendy (Cynthia Lam) from her triad pursuers. They think she's a hooker, but Wendy is actually a cop trying to bust Bill, and hopes she can trace the murder back to him.

Kitty, daughter of landlord Mr. So, is sweet on Rob and pays their rent. She also bails them out of jail when they get nabbed, though her dad ends up in trouble just as often. John returns, out for revenge on Bill, but ends up with a belly full of lead. When Hank coincidentally meets up with him as John lies dying, Hank takes up the vendetta as well.

Crime drama? Kung fu action? Wacky comedy of errors? *Eat My Dust* can't decide which direction to go, and doesn't accomplish any of them all that well. The comic segments are a waste of time, but Lam's legwork is a highlight, and there are some nice explosion f/x. The climax features a lot of unbelievable gunplay—literally. Handguns that hold hundreds of rounds, a hero that shoots six guys with two shots, etc. A lot of the fight scenes are sped up. One curious detail: chestnut vendors who have access to bazookas, explosives, and machine guns. ♫♫

1993 89m/C *HK* Michael Tsang, Mark Ng, Cynthia Lam, Paul Tai, Philip Cheng, Johnny Chu, Gordon Yeow, Simon Sheung. *D:* Philip So. *W:* Man Cheng. *C:* Sam Chan. *M:* Bob Yuen. **VHS, DVD**

Ebirah, Horror of the Deep

This seventh Godzilla film is best known in the U.S. by its television and video release title *Godzilla vs. the Sea Monster.* A fisherman named Yata (Toru Ibuke) is lost at sea when a huge sea monster (Hiroshi Sekita) attacks his boat. His younger brother Ryota (Toru Watanabe) fails in his attempt to win a sailboat in a dance contest, so he and his friends steal one to search for Yata. Yoshimura (Akira Takarada), the "owner" of the boat, turns out to be onboard at the time they set sail, though he acts suspiciously. The boys soon find out that he's really a thief who happened to be hiding out onboard. They all end up on an island guarded by a gigantic monster crustacean (known as Ebirah in the Japanese release). The island is the secret headquarters of a group of criminals (known as Red Bamboo in Japan, an obvious parody of Red Chinese) who are manufacturing atomic weapons, bent on world domination. In a desperate gamble for survival they decide to awaken Godzilla (Haruo Nakajima), found sleeping in a cave, and the monster mayhem begins.

This engaging adventure film was originally planned as a King Kong film, produced to tie in with the Kong cartoon series. But the script wasn't close enough to the cartoon's premise, and Toho substituted Godzilla, finally putting the big ape in *King Kong Escapes.* Having Godzilla stomping around on a South Pacific island made for a novel (and inexpensive) setting. Kumi Mizuno adds her always-welcome presence as Daiyo, a slave of the terrorists brought from her Infant Island home. She turns out to be of great aid, helping to bring special guest star Mothra into the story. A singing duo called Pair Bambi fills in for the Ito sisters as Mothra's priestesses for some reason. Masaru Sato returns to the series, contributing a much better score than he did for *Godzilla Raids Again.* His peppy music perfectly compliments the action-adventure nature of this entry's story. This was the first Godzilla film for director Jun Fukuda *(Secret of the Telegian),* who would go on to helm four others, although none would turn out quite as well as this one. *AKA: Gojira—Ebirah—Mosera: Nankai no Daiketto; The Great South Seas Duel; Big Duel in the North Sea; Ebirah, Terror of the Deep; Godzilla vs. the Sea Monster; Frankenstein und die Ungeheweraus den Meer.* ♫♫♫

1966 83m/C *JP* Akira Takarada, Kumi Mizuno, Toru Watanabe, Chotaro Togin, Hideo Sunazuka, Toru Ibuki, Akihiko Hirata, Jun Tazaki, Ikio Sawamura, Eisei Amamoto, Hisaya Ito, Tadashi Okabe, Kazuo Suzuki, Shoichi Hirose, Chieko Nakakita, Yutaka Sada, Wataru Omae, Kenichiro Maruyama, Shigeki Ishida, Haruo Nakajima, Hiroshi Sekita. *D:* Jun Fukuda. *W:* Shinichi Sekizawa. *C:* Kazuo Yamada. *M:* Masaru Sato. **VHS**

Ecstasy of the Angels

The Four Seasons Society, an organization of radical Japanese guerrilla soldiers, loses its unity when the Fall faction, led by October, suffers many losses while stealing U.S. Army supplies. The Winter group, led by February, seizes the weapons and explosives after subjecting two Fall survivors to beating, torture, and rape. Fall tries to ally itself with Winter, but soldiers loyal to a now blind October refuse to join the fold. In the end, the Society crumbles, and a lone vanguard is left to change the world. Organized anarchy has failed and individual soldiers continue their terrorist attacks against Tokyo.

Of the titles under which this film goes, "Angelic Orgasm" describes it most accurately. Every other scene is a sex scene, but none of them is gratuitous. Political alliances are forged through sexual unions, from the opening coupling between Fall and October to October's ultimate loss of power when Saturday denies her spread-eagled sexuality. One of the best sex scenes is a back-to-back mutual masturbation session between Fall and a blinded October, which goes from black and white to color at the moment of orgasm. With an outside jazz score from the Cecil Taylor school of piano violation, high-contrast lighting, and sexually politicized

themes, *Ecstasy of the Angels* is avant-garde in the best sense of the phrase...a truly original vision from a maniacal director who doesn't care what the establishment says about him. —BW **AKA:** *Tenshi no Kokotsu; Angelic Orgasm; Taiji Ga Mit Suryo Surutoki.* ♪♪♪♪

1972 86m/C/BW *JP* Ken Yoshizawa, Rie Yokoyama, Yuki Arasa, Michio Akiyama, Yosuke Akiyama. **D:** Koji Wakamatsu. **W:** Izuru Deguchi. **C:** Hideo Itoh. **M:** Yosuke Yamashita Trio. **VHS, DVD**

The Eel

Takuro Yamashita (Koji Yakusho), a salaryman for the Hinode Flour Corporation, gets a letter telling him of his wife's infidelity. He decides to test it out by returning early from a fishing trip. Catching the adulterers in the act, Takuro stabs them both with a butcher knife, killing his wife. He then calmly bicycles to the police station to turn himself in. Eight years later, he's paroled from prison, taking with him only his pet eel. He opens up a run-down barbershop in the seaside town of Sawara—an odd occupation for a man who has now become highly unsociable. After years in prison, the eel is the only one he can really talk to. And apparently, it talks back to him. Though trying to avoid trouble, he goes out on a limb to save Keiko Hattori (Misa Shimizu) from an attempted suicide. Keiko comes to work in the shop as well, though there are few customers. A woman's touch improves the shop considerably—and Takuro as well. But still he finds it hard to open up to her. Then his garbageman, whom he knew in prison, threatens him, Keiko, and the eel. More trouble: Keiko's old boyfriend comes after her, though he still won't leave his wife. Plus, her insane mother causes problems for them.

Viewers should be aware that the shocking violence of the first part of the film is not an indication of where it's headed, though the act throws a shadow over the entire film, as it does over Takuro's life. Winner of the Golden Palm at the 1997 Cannes Film Festival, Shohei Imamura's film dwells on quiet frustrations, waiting to see if they'll boil over. **AKA:** *Unagi.* ♪♪♪

1997 117m/C *JP* Koji Yakusho, Misa Shimizu, Fujio Tsuneta, Mitsuko Baisho, Makoto Sato, Akira Emoto, Tomoro Taguchi, Makoto Sato. **D:** Shohei Imamura. **W:** Motofumi Tomikawa, Daisuke Tengan, Shohei

In *The Eel*, convicted wife-killer Koji Yakusho wonders if he can find love again with Misa Shimizu.

THE KOBAL COLLECTION / HISA IINO / KSS FILMS

Imamura, Akira Yoshimura (story). **C:** Shigeru Komatsubara. **M:** Shinichiro Ikebe. **VHS, DVD**

1991 92m/C *HK* Bruce Liang, Kwan Hoi-san, Wong Cho-shut, Kong Do. **D:** Do Gong-yue. **W:** To Man-bo. **VHS, DVD**

8 Diagram Fighter

Fans of Lau Kar-Leung's classic *Invincible Pole Fighter* (AKA *8 Diagram Pole Fighter*) may want to check out this much different version of the same story from Chinese history. During the North Sung Dynasty, General Yang goes on a peacemaking mission to Golden Beach, hoping to strike an accord with the invading Laos, but having his eldest son pose as the emperor on the trip as a precaution, with his six other sons keeping their spears ready. As suspected, the meeting turns out to be a trap, and only the sixth son and fifth son, Ye Siu-san, escape the massacre. The sixth son makes it home to recover from the battle. The injured Siu-san is saved by young swordswoman Miss Chiu Yue-lan (Wong Cho-shut), and taken into the Chin Liang Monastery by monks Grinder and Chi Yan. While hiding out in the monastery, Siu-san becomes a monk in training under the name Minsiu, and learns special skills like walking on water and pole fighting. During the latter, he thinks of ways to adapt Yang spear techniques to pole fighting. In an ironic turn of justice, Grinder is expelled from the monastery when caught taking extra rice to the Chius, while senior monk Minsin is framed for rape and murder by the Laos, and betrays his brothers under threat of blackmail. Grinder is taken in at the house of Yue-lan's dad Chiu Yun (Hong Kong character actor Kwan Hoi-san, immediately recognizable for his lively eyes and hook nose)—who turns out to be an old family friend of the Yangs. But Minsin's treachery leaves the monastery open to attack by Lao General Siu Tin-cho, who murders Abbot Chi Chung so that Minsin can advance, and Minsiu is framed for treason. Despite the accusations, a note left by the abbot names Minsiu as his replacement. For some time, the question of whether Minsiu would continue to be a monk or seek revenge on the Laos has hung over his head, but a full attack on the temple allows him to do both.

Between action scenes, this cheap independent production drags a great deal, and nothing much seems to happen for long periods. However, things pick up considerably whenever the fighting starts. It's not that the choreography is all that spectacular, but every fight scene is enhanced by animation f/x of some kind. The action crosses the line into fantasy, much like a 1980s ninja movie, with warriors and monks flying around firing lightning bolts at each other, which is a lot of fun, though doesn't make much sense. **AKA:** *Yue Loi Baat Gwa Gwan; Ru Lai Ba Gua Gun; Eight Diagram Cudgel; Like Holy Eight Divine Cane.* 🐾🐾

The 8 Masters

Another Joseph Kuo Shaolin Temple picture, this is often included as part of the 18 Bronzemen series. Wu Tang swordsman Liu Kun-ting asks for a delay in his duel with Chu Yin-ho due to illness, but Chu refuses, and both men die from wounds in the battle. When Liu's partners, the 8 Masters, come to take the life of the young son of their late enemy Chu Yin-ho in vengeance, trusted friend Chow Sin-er (Su Chen Ping) gives his life to take the boy to the safety of Shaolin Temple, where his father trained. However, Chow's dying words to the boy aren't instructions for revenge, but a plea that he'll return to his mother some day to protect her and Chow's daughter Ming-chiu. No revenge? Well, we know that's not going to happen. Chu Siao-chieh (Carter Wong) grows to become one of Shaolin's top students, and after passing the test of the 18 Bronzemen, he begs to be ordained as a monk. But recalling Chow's wishes, the abbot (O Yau-man) refuses, sending Chu out into the wicked world to fulfill his obligations.

When the 8 Masters learn that Chu has returned home, they come to challenge him, but Chu refuses to fight, and takes the women away to live in the mountains. The 8 Masters follow, but Chu still refuses to fight and moves again. Even after the 8 Masters abduct his mother, Chu refuses to fight, enduring several beatings. While he recovers, he learns that Ming-chiu (Doris Lung) is actually a changeling, exchanged by one of the Masters for the real Ming-chiu long ago so she could spy on him. When an attempt to sneak his mom away fails, she commits suicide in the hope that the villains would spare her son. That's the last straw for Chu, and he finally agrees to fight the 8 Masters one by one.

The old gimmick of the hero who has sworn not to fight is milked for all the suspense it's worth here, which unfortunately isn't much. But even when Carter Wong starts to fight back, he still resists the opportunity to kill his enemies. The mystery of Ming-chiu's past, and her mysterious uncle's identity aren't very intriguing hooks, so the main attraction is to see Wong fight the 8 Masters. Unfortunately, not too much effort is put into making the Masters interesting either. Only a few bear Joseph Kuo's usual specialty weapons, such as a lance with a claw at the end that can detach to swing by a chain. The 18 Bronzemen are given a few new twists, but Kuo saves most of his trickery for when Wong catches up to the head Master To Lung (Wong Fei-lung), who keeps a secret labyrinth loaded with traps—including a quartet of hopping corpses. Despite her prominent billing, Judy Lee only appears in a few scenes. *AKA: Baat Daai Moon Pai; Ba Da Men Pai; 18 Bronzemen 3.* 𝄞𝄞𝄞▽

1977 93m/C *TW* Carter Wong, Judy Lee, Doris Lung, Wong Fei-lung, Lam Siu-foo, Su Chen Ping, O Yau-man, Liu Ping, Phillip Ko, Shaw Luo-hui, Lau Lap Cho, Li Min Lang, Hung Fa-long. *D:* Joseph Kuo. *W:* M.L. Shu, P.S. Chiang (story). *C:* Chen Sin Lok. *M:* Chou Fu-liang. **VHS, DVD**

The 18 Bronzemen

Independent filmmaker Joseph Kuo was fond of using gimmicks in his martial arts films, and in the mid-1970s decided to make this story set in the familiar confines of the Shaolin Temple. However, Kuo's Shaolin would be unlike any other, a huge sprawling place full of hidden secrets and mysteries, based more on fantasy than history. His most outrageous creation was the 18 Bronzemen. Shaolin students were expected to pass a series of formal tests before they could earn the right to leave, and some of these final exams were pretty tough, including passing through a corridor filled with traps, some of them based on ingenious mechanical designs. Kuo exaggerated this into the Bronzemen: 18 robotic warriors made of gleaming metal. No one need question how these robots came to be in 16th-century China. It's an ancient Chinese secret.

But still, the gimmick doesn't overshadow a good story, which combines action and drama with a little mystery. The invading Ching forces kill Ming Dynasty General Kuan Chi-yen. Fulfilling the general's dying wish, his orphan son is brought up in the Shaolin Temple. After 20 years, Kwan Siu-lung (Tin Peng) becomes adept in kung fu, with the help of his buddy Ta-chi (Chiang Nan), and despite the punishments of Big Brother Te-wan (Carter Wong). Lord Hei Chu-ying (Yee Yuen) suspects that he's within the temple, and though he doesn't know it, one of Siu-lung's friends is really a spy. When Siu-lung receives a signal from his grandmother, he decides he has to leave, even though he's not fully ready to face the necessary tests. On his first time, he doesn't make it past the first five Bronzemen, even though Te-wan decides to go with him. After more training, he almost fails again, even after learning the secrets of the Lo Han Fist. Not surprising—those Bronzemen are pretty tough; one test is for a Bronzeman to beat him with a big club, and if he can still get up, he passes! His graduation comes too late—his grandmother died waiting for him. But Uncle Yue (Liu Ping) fills him in on how Hei Chu-ying killed his parents, and gives him his father's sword to seek revenge.

He continues on to meet up with Te-wan at an inn, but also meets a rude stranger (Polly Shang Kwan). Annoyingly, the stranger tags along everywhere—but when it's found out he possesses the other half of Siu-lung's family jade piece, he has to admit to really being a girl (!) named Miss Yeung Lin-mei. By the next scene, Siu-lung is introducing her to Ta-chi as his fiancée! But can our hero find out that one of the monks is out to get him before he can get his revenge?

While not creating a masterpiece of kung fu action, Kuo puts enough bizarre training sequences and competent fight scenes, along with the always-welcome Polly Shang Kwan, into his clichéd plot to keep the ball rolling. The final fight scene lacks pretty choreography, but it has a desperate, sloppy energy that gives it a more realistic feel than the usual. But let's face it—it's those crazy Bronzemen that make this one a hit, so much so that they returned in several sequels. Even the villain has a collection of 18 Bronzemen action figures on his desk! *AKA: Siu Lam Chi Sap Baat Tung Yan; Shao Lin Si Shi Ba Tong Ren.* 𝄞𝄞𝄞▽

1976 97m/C *HK* Polly Shang Kwan, Tin Peng, Carter Wong, Chiang Nan, Chang Yi, Yee Yuen, Liu Ping, Wong Fei-lung, Lau Lap Cho, Wong Fan, Shaw Luo-hui, O Yau-man, Yuen Sam. *D:* Joseph Kuo. *W:* Joseph Kuo. *C:* Chung Hang, Chan Hang-tiu. **VHS, DVD**

The 18 Bronzemen Part 2

Not so much a sequel as an overall continuation of Joseph Kuo's interpretation of Shaolin Temple, some of the same actors return here, but in different roles. On the eve of the Ching emperor's death, the Fourth Prince Ai (Carter Wong) gets a peek at the royal will and changes it to benefit himself. He then has Minister Su Ne-ha assassinated before he can reveal the edit, and frames 14th Prince Jen Ti for the crime. Posing as a commoner under the name Ai Sung-chueh, the new emperor walks among the people incognito, and is able to rescue Miss Lan from some bandits. Due to a combination of admiration for Shaolin martial arts, jealousy of Lan's Shaolin student beau Kuan Shao-pan (Tin Peng), and a desire to confirm rumors of rebellion from within the temple, Ai decides to enter Shaolin Temple as a student. Though he's over their age limit, Ai kneels outside the temple for 14 days, then carries water and wood for another 100, earning admission. After three years of hard training, and several attempts, Ai gets to the end of the test of the 18 Bronzemen, and is about to take on his dragon scars as a full Shaolin, when the

abbot (O Yau-man) stops him. His ruse has been discovered and they kick him out of the temple. However, his newfound skill makes it easy for him to repel the attack of General Shang's daughter (Polly Shang Kwan) when she comes to the palace seeking vengeance. To defend against an attack by the Shaolin monks and 8 Knights, the government produces in quantity a new weapon called Hsieh Ti Tze.

The end! The abrupt finish indicates the tale would be continued in *Part 3*, but such was not the case, though the situation was reworked for *The Blazing Temple* (*8 Masters* is also known as *18 Bronzemen 3*, but it's not a direct sequel). Joseph Kuo mixes things up a bit this time by varying the tests posed by the Bronzemen, meaning Carter Wong never knows what's coming next. But it seems incredibly farfetched that an emperor, no matter how fanatical, would stop running all of China to enter a monastery for three years, even to learn their most deeply hidden secrets—and at that, he never turns up the evidence of rebellion there that he was supposed to be looking for. It's also very contradictory to see him so committed to the Shaolin teachings when his hidden purpose is to destroy them. With the entire feature focused on the villain, we don't get to see much of the heroes, and though there's a good deal of entertainment, this sequel fails to stand on its own. *AKA: Yong Jing Dai Poh Sap Baat Tung Yan; Yong Zheng Da Po Shi Ba Tong Ren; Return of the 18 Bronzemen; Eighteen Bronzemen 2.* ♪♪♪♪

1976 94m/C *HK* Carter Wong, Polly Shang Kwan, Tin Peng, O Yau-man, Yuen Sam, Woo Gwong, Wong Fei-lung, Lau Lap Cho, Chiu Ting, Shaw Luo-hui, Chen Chiu. **D:** Joseph Kuo. **VHS, DVD**

18 Fatal Strikes

Manchurian General Wong Wo-ti (Sze Ma Lung), in charge of wiping out the rebel Ming patriots, gets on the trail of fugitive Shaolin Abbot Wang Hung (Man Kong Lung). The monk finds his Lo Han Style kung fu is no match for the general's secret Shaking Eagle Claw (or "Clor," as the dubber puts it), and flees. Herb-gathering youth Chow-to (Stephen Tung) and his partner Tai Pan (Dean Shek) find the injured monk and save him. Sent into town, Tai Pan learns some basic kung fu moves from innkeeper's daughter Miss Shang-shang—who is secretly one of the rebel fighters. Chow-to goes to see this wonder woman at the Happy Restaurant himself, and foils a plot by Shan Kung (Kwan Hung) and his thugs to kidnap her, but receives a beating for it. While he recovers, Abbot Wang Hung takes the boys on as students. Chow-to is a fast learner, enough that he helps out Shang-shang when Commander Pa Chu-lung (Shih Chung Tien) has her trapped. But

he inadvertently reveals Wang Hung's Lo Han training to the bad guys.

Dean Shek rarely got to play a hero in these old movies, and it's refreshing to see his comic fighting antics featured so extensively (though some of his more strenuous acrobatics are obviously doubled). He also gets the juiciest dramatic role—his histrionics when his girlfriend Siu-yu is murdered to draw out the monk rival his scenery chewing in *A Better Tomorrow 2*. With that, kung fu comedy gives way to kung fu drama, as Chow-to and the Shaolin Abbot try to find a way to defeat Wong's troops and the Shaking Eagle Claw. Tung's fighting is furious, and though the monk himself says he only knows six Lo Han styles, somehow they work all 18 into the final battle. The Shaking Eagle makes a mighty annoying sound effect, but our heroes find the perfect weapon to counter it: a pointy stick! ♪♪♪♪

1978 85m/C *HK* Stephen Tung, Dean Shek, Man Kong Lung, Yang Kuang, Sze Ma Lung, Shen Hai Yung, Shih Chung Tien, Shih Ting Ken, Wong Hoi, Kwan Hung. **D:** Yang Ching Chen. **W:** Niu Chung Pa, Hsieh Mo Hung. **C:** Chang Shih-chun. **M:** Wang Mao Shan. **VHS, DVD**

The 18 Jade Arhats

The title sequence is certainly alluring, as it presents the heroes taking turns fighting a robotic bronze Buddha spider! A stranger named Kong Chin-ya (Lee Jan-wa) kills a challenger using the Lo Han Palm technique, bringing suspicion on Lord Wong Chung-wei (Chang Yi), the region's only known master of that particular blow. Wong means to find out who the real killer is, but first must meet Ku Yun-fung (Lo Lieh) for a duel. When Wong's body is found stabbed in the back, Ku is the natural suspect in his murder, but pleads innocent. Nevertheless, Wong's family sends hired killers after Ku, all of whom fail. Meanwhile, Si Pei-Pei (Polly Shang Kwan) is looking for the man who killed her father and took nine of the eighteen jade arhats given to him by the emperor. Knowing Kong is looking for them as well, she tags along with him. He's not the only one on such a quest—someone has sent men to kill them both. Wong's daughter (Kong Ching-ha) hires Kong to find out for sure who the real killer is and get revenge.

At one point in the film, Polly Shang Kwan complains about being confused, and she's not alone. The webwork plot introduces so many characters and story lines in the first half—most of which are brought in to provide death scenes—that it's not as noticeable that not much of it makes any sense. Even the fine cast can't save it because of the lackluster fight scenes. That spidery robot is shown only in unexplained flashbacks, and the only other action highlight is a duel between Polly and Phillip Ko while they're both balanced on big gold balls. For the record, arhats are those kung fu action figures that demonstrate various styles. From the cast on display, is the credited director a pseudonym for Joseph Kuo? **AKA:** *18 Jade Pearls; Jade Killer; Eighteen Deadly Arhats; The Eighteen Claws of Shaolin.* 🐉🐉

1978 88m/C *HK* Polly Shang Kwan, Chang Yi, Lee Jan-wa, Lo Lieh, Fan Dan-fung, Fang Fang, Tung Li, Lung Fei, Phillip Ko, Chuen Yuen, Kong Ching-ha, Lee Chiu, Hsu Feng, Ching Kuo-chung, Chiao Chiao, Chi Fu-chiang, O Yau-man, Chen Chiu, Au Lap-bo, Lee Keung, Yue Feng, Chung Wa. **D:** Cheung Chieh. **W:** Yao Ching-kang. **C:** Chung Shen. **M:** Chou Fu-liang. **VHS, DVD**

18 Secrets of Kung Fu

After the fall of the Ching Dynasty, in the forests of Yung Ching Mountain, Master Yueh Chu-mao passes on the secrets of the 18 Weapons to his grandchildren. Grandnephew Li Tai is sent to Yueh for training, bearing a letter from his dead grandfather; evil Master Lu Yuen-leung wants to learn the secrets. He hires local mobster Chin Chu to be his lackey, and sends men to kill Li and take the letter before he can reach Yueh. One of their attacks by Lu's student Lin Tang-kwai results in the drowning of cousin Chang-ching. Anxious to avenge her, Li runs off to fight Lu prematurely, but is beaten by some hired fighters. After that he gets down to training in earnest, though he meets a distraction down by the river—Lu's daughter Kwan-li, who doesn't let on who she really is. When he finally learns where his enemy is living, Lu heads off for a showdown with Yueh, while sending his hit man Ke Shi-shen to deal with Li.

There isn't much out of the ordinary in this standard kung fu revenge story except the scenery in the mountain forests of Taiwan. The performers are all agile in their fight scenes, especially Li, who is put through several interesting training exercises. But there's really nothing here we haven't all seen before, except for the slightly offbeat ending. The fight scenes are edited with that annoying frame-removal technique. **AKA:** *Sap Baat Boon Mo Ngai; Shi Ba Ban Wu Yi; 18 Weapons of Kung Fu.* 🐉🐉

1979 (PG) 76m/C *TW* Liu Shu Hua, Wang Fu Quen, Weng Hsiao Hu, Wang Wing Sheng, Chen Fei-Fei, Ko Saio Pao, Wang Ki San, Suen King Kai, Hwa Yue Suen, Siu Foo-dau. **D:** Wu Yuen-ling, Chen Hung-man. **C:** Wong Siu-cheung. **M:** Wang Mu-san. **VHS, DVD**

Eighth Happiness

This wacky comedy, a Lunar New Year block-buster, recalls films of the late 1950s/early 1960s like *Pillow Talk* and *Come Blow Your Horn* more than any contemporary Hong Kong comedies. The plot centers around three brothers who share a house, and their romantic escapades. An auto accident fouls up telephone lines, leading to mass confusion and chance meetings. Fang Chien-hui (Raymond Wong) is host of the popular TV show *Mainly for Women*. Fang Chien-lang (Chow Yun-fat) is an aspiring actor who's a swishy nancy-boy on the outside, but a wolf on the inside. He's torn between racy store clerk Beautiful (Cherie Chung) and dependable flight attendant Do Do Cheng (Carol Cheng). And youngest brother Fang Chien-sang (Jacky Cheung) is a cartoonist who keeps accidentally running into Ying-ying (Fennie Yuen), and the wrath of her martial arts teaching mother. Hui tries to woo Cantonese opera star Wu Hsiu-fang (former child star Petrina Fung), not knowing she's also the woman he and Lang are having a crank-call war with. But Beautiful has a rich boyfriend (Lawrence Cheng), Ying-ying is dating athletic Roy (Michael Chow), and Hsiu-fang's husband (Teddy Robin Kwan) has just left her and their son Ming-ming (Wong Kwan-yuen).

Director Johnny To *(Heroic Trio)* disowns this as only featherweight entertainment, but it's better than most comedies of this type, and far above Raymond Wong's more recent work. He even gives the cast some opera to perform. But undeniably the feature that makes this such a pleasure is Chow Yun-fat's performance in a role 180 degrees opposite from his usual forte. To see him prance around like a Rodeo Drive hand-bag salesman is a truly bizarre experience. Watch for familiar stars making cameos, including Chow Yun-fat in more traditional raincoat and dark glasses. **AKA:** *Baat Sing Biu Choi; Ba Xing Bao Xi; The Eight Happiness.* 🐉🐉🐉

1988 87m/C *HK* Cherie Chung, Chow Yun-fat, Carol Cheng, Petrina Fung, Jacky Cheung, Raymond Wong, Fennie Yuen, Wong Kwan-yuen, Michael Chow, Charlie Cho, Lawrence Cheng, John Sham, Karl Maka, Ringo Lam, Teddy Robin Kwan. **D:** Johnny To. **W:** Raymond Wong, Edward Lee, Philip Cheng, Ng Man-fai. **C:** Joe Chan. **M:** Antonio Arevalo Jr. **VHS, DVD**

Elaan

A.C.P. Ramakant Chaudhary (Amrish Puri) is as strict and efficient with his own family as he is with his police station. Bad news for youngest son Vishaal (Akshay Kumar), who can boast of neither a job nor a girlfriend. Vishaal may have solved one of these problems when he saves

aspiring actress Mohini (Madhoo) from a rapist, but the movie-crazed girl talks like a nut, so he brushes her off. But Mohini, who happens to be daughter of Chaudhary's bumbling Chief Constable Devakinandanji Sharma (Mohnish Bahl), is certain they're meant for each other. Their romance is cause for worry for her father, who thinks he'll be punished if something goes wrong. Vishaal witnesses a shooting in the street, which his father determines is part of a gang war between mob bosses Baba Khan (Mohan Joshi) and Manna Shetty. The gangsters have been a source of conflict in the Chaudhary home since elder son Vikas was gunned down by them a few years back. Chaudhary tries to crack down on the gangs, but receives no support from corrupt Commissioner Desai (Dalip Tahil). After Chaudhary beats a crooked cop who caused the death of an officer, Khan forces a doctor to kill the man to frame Chaudhary for his death. With Khan's influence spread far and wide, Chaudhary is thoroughly railroaded in court and sent to an asylum. Vishaal goes ape in court and attacks Desai, earning some jail time for himself—but he's seen enough of the legal system in action. Father and son both escape from captivity, and together they declare war against the criminals and go on a violent rampage of vengeance.

One thing about Bollywood payback: when it comes, it comes big. Rarely in a Hollywood film will you see the villains—no matter how heinous—get what's coming to them so thoroughly and repeatedly as they do here. The something-for-everyone esthetic is in effect, as the film goes through romance, light comedy, romance, melodrama, song and dance, action, courtroom antics, martial arts, gun fu, political commentary, and more action. Akshay Kumar's fight scenes are pretty good for an Indian film, looking much like Jean-Claude Van Damme, though there's not much variation in the choreography. Plus, he can sing! Romantic song-and-dance numbers are terribly out of place within such a bullets-and-blood scenario, but the filmmakers at least attempt to explain shoehorning them in by portraying them as the fantasies of movie-obsessed Mohini. Busy star Amrish Puri is best known to Western viewers as the villain in *Indiana Jones and the Temple of Doom.* ♫♫♡

1994 141m/C *IN* Akshay Kumar, Amrish Puri, Madhoo, Farida Jalal, Dalip Tahil, Deven Verma, Mohnish Bahl, Mohan Joshi, Rammi Reddy. **D:** Guddu Dhanoa. **W:** Dilip Shukla. **C:** Shripad Natu. **M:** Shyam-Surinder. **DVD**

Emperor of Shaolin Kung Fu

Bandit warlord Li Tzu-cheng (Wong Hap) storms the palace to usurp the throne from Ming Emperor Cheng Chen XVII. Third Princess Chang-ping (Nancy Yen) rejects her father's order that everyone commit suicide, only losing an arm on his sword, and escapes to plot her revenge with her bodyguard Su-yuen. The women split up to draw less attention to themselves, and the princess recruits laconic swordsman Leung (Lo Lieh) to her cause, plotting to assassinate Li in retaliation. Their assassination attempt is a failure, however, and Leung is killed by Li while helping the princess escape from the palace grounds. She finds refuge with warrior poet Hai Yu-shah (Dean Shek), who has a blade hidden in his flute. Taking the scholar along, Third Princess's second assassination attempt isn't any better than the first, as she's been betrayed—Hai is actually one of Li's agents, and he's led her into a trap. She escapes again though, and meets up with Su-yuen, who comes up with a plan to throw off their pursuers—she chops off her own arm and commits suicide so Li's soldiers will think she's the princess when they find her corpse! After witnessing this shocking scene, Chang-ping's mind snaps from the strain, and she wanders the streets as a "crazy girl." Up to now, butcher Tu (Carter Wong) has been wandering in and out of the movie (with his pigs), and at last he gets involved in the plot, taking in the mad Chang-ping and passing her off as his fiancée to his blind mother. Obeying his dying mom's wishes, Tu marries the crazy girl. Meanwhile, Li is overthrown by invading General Wu, sending the bandit king fleeing into the hills. Tu, who is the patriot son of a Ming general, gets together with his pals to take advantage of this chance to kill Li.

This cockeyed epic is supposedly based on fact! There are some points of interest in this odd film, especially in the casting, as actors like Dean Shek, Carter Wong, and Lo Lieh all play unusual roles. But Carter Wong never thought he'd be co-starring with a pig's head and testicles, but there they are hanging from his stall as he emotes. When he attacks with a zoo full of animal styles, his strikes are accompanied by shots of each beast—but they apparently had limited clips as his Crane Style is paired with a shot of a flamingo! His blind mother is weird, too—hanging herself in satisfaction once she knows her son is good and wed. The fighting looks like it was shot without an action director—there's not so much choreography as edited together bits of film showing movement, a sheer waste of talent. Only Shek's fight scene has anything approaching coordinated moves, and it's likely he directed it himself. The soundtrack mixmaster samples from the 1976 *King Kong.* ♫♡

1980 91m/C *TW* Carter Wong, Nancy Yen, Lo Lieh, Wong Hap, Dean Shek, Kwan Hung, Chin Leung, Chiu Ting, Lau Lap Cho. **D:** Hui Keung. **W:** Chin Liang, Liu Sung-pai. **C:** Li Shih-chieh. **M:** Chen Yung-yu. **VHS, DVD**

Encounter of the Spooky Kind

Sammo Hung virtually created the action horror comedy with this landmark release, which spawned a whole new genre of Hong Kong cinema that is still being mined today. Hung stars as Courageous Cheung, a town braggart who is actually scared to death of his shrew of a wife (Leung Suet-moi). However, he's still a proud and jealous man, and always suspects his wife is cheating on him. When he almost catches Mrs. Cheung with her lover Master Tam (Huang Ha), Tam begins to worry about how such a scandal would ruin his political career. Tam plots with sorcerer Chin Hoi (Chan Lung) to get rid of Cheung. Knowing Cheung too well, they get their friend Fa Kau (Wu Ma) to bet Courageous that he can't spend the night in a haunted temple, as Chin lets loose a kyonsi to kill their target. Fortunately, sorcerer Tsui (Chung Fat) is offended that his associate Chin is getting involved in such business, and gives Cheung the scoop on how to survive the night. Momentarily triumphant, Cheung is dumb enough to be tricked by Fa into spending a second night in the temple. When Tsui helps Cheung survive again, Tam decides to play even dirtier, killing Mrs. Cheung and framing his nemesis for the crime. Cheung manages to escape the gallows by breaking jail, and goes to Tsui for help. Tsui decides to take Cheung on as his pupil, training him in magical combat, and together they take on Chin in a duel of sorcery.

Always looking for ways to make kung fu movies fresh, Hung mixes together the disparate elements of action, suspense, humor, and outright horror seamlessly. Others would study and copy his techniques, bringing moments of shock, gags, and thrills even closer together, but Sammo showed them how it's done. The climactic battle finds the two wizards having to stay above the ground on platforms to work their magic, but Sammo and Chin's assistant (Yuen Miu) are used as puppets, imbued with the spirits of various Chinese gods to do the fighting for them—a brilliant way of making martial arts vital to a magical fight. Hung also starred in the in-name-only sequel. The English-dubbed version is missing about four minutes. *AKA: Gwai Chuk Gwai; Gui Da Gui; Spooky Encounters; Close Encounters of the Spooky Kind; Ghost against Ghost.* 🎻🎻🎻🎻

1981 102m/C *HK* Sammo Hung, Chung Fat, Chan Lung, Huang Ha, Wu Ma, Lam Ching-Ying, Tai Bo, Yuen Miu, Leung Suet-moi, Cheung Ti-hong, To Siu Ming, Cheung Ging Boh, Ho Pak Kwong, Fung Ging Man, Chin Leung, Fung Lee, Billy Chan. **D:** Sammo Hung. **W:** Sammo Hung, Wong Ying. **C:** Lee Yao-tong. **M:** Chan Chun-chi. **DVD**

The End of the Wicked Tiger

Well, the title pretty much gives away the ending, doesn't it? Having run the local police chief out of town, Chang Hsi-fu (Wilson Tong), son of the town's richest man, Wicked Tiger Chang Tai-fu (Han Ying Chieh), continues his extortion racket. Captain Ling (Lee Ka-ting) comes to town as the new police honcho, but finds it difficult to get citizens to cooperate. When the gang kills Mr. Cho as an example, even heroic Ma San (Charles Heung), who fought with them, won't be a witness, since his brother (Eddie Ko) works for Mr. Chang. Chang tells his son that he'd better eliminate any witnesses just to be safe. However, killing Mr. Kan only leaves more witnesses to account for. When Hsi-fu tries to murder Cho's sister Shang, Kan's kids help her escape. The gang tries to get back at both Ma San and the kids by poisoning the food he's brought them. Ling tries to arrest Ma San for poisoning the kids, but he escapes to track down the real poisoner. With the heat rising, Hsi-fu skips town, but Ling is able to intercept him and throw him in jail. When Ma San refuses to take a bribe to keep quiet, his brother is murdered by Chang. Ma San joins Ling at the jailhouse, leading to a *High Noon* situation when the townspeople refuse to help them hold off Chang's thugs.

Charles Heung went on to be much better known as a producer, and for playing Brother Five in the *God of Gamblers* movies. Though billed fifth, Sammo Hung is given little to do here in his role as Chang's top thug, other than to rape a girl in a stream early on. Since Sammo was already a star at the time this was released, it was either an earlier film taken off the shelf to cash in on his subsequent fame, or he appeared here as a favor to someone. Han Ying Chieh's fight choreography is mediocre—the combatants look more in danger of falling off of the rocky locations than from each other's fists. *AKA: Liu Foo ? Sing; Lao Hu ? Hing; End of Wicked Tiger.* 🎻🎻

1981 83m/C *HK* Charles Heung, Lee Ka-ting, Han Ying Chieh, Wilson Tong, Sammo Hung, Eddie Ko, Hsu Hsia, Eric Tsang, Ho Pak Kwong, Chan Chuen. **D:** Law Kei. **W:** Szeto On, Lui ming. **VHS, DVD**

The Enforcer

Jet Li stars as Beijing undercover cop Kung Wei, who is so busy catching crooks that he almost misses his son Johnny (Tse Miu from *New Legend of Shaolin*) winning his first martial arts tournament. The department pretends to arrest Kung to set up his next undercover assignment, allowing him to escape with his cellmate G-Dog.

The fugitives head out to meet up with G-Dog's gang in Hong Kong, headed by the sadistic Bo (Yu Rongguang). The gang needs to acquire some explosives without paying for them, and arrange a meeting (and double cross) with their supplier in a public café. At the rendezvous, things go haywire, and a shootout ensues. Hong Kong cop Inspector Anna Fong (Anita Mui) happens to be there on her day off, and Kung ends up taking her hostage to escape. Having a wanted man for a father is making things tough for Johnny at school, even worse because his mother is ill. Fong poses as Kung Wei's business associate to find out more about him from his family. What she finds out doesn't add up to the dangerous criminal he's supposed to be, and she begins to suspect the truth. Mrs. Kung takes a turn for the worse, and she dies with the wish that Kung and Fong become friends. Fong takes Johnny back to Hong Kong with her.

Bo's gang, working with the sinister Miss Lee, plans to use the explosives to rip off antiques from a shipboard auction, blowing up the ship afterwards. Miss Lee tips off Bo of a rumor that there's a Beijing cop trying to infiltrate the gang, putting him on edge even more than usual. When Johnny's picture is leaked to the press, Kung's cover is blown. Johnny rushes to warn him, and is captured by the gang. With the robbery under way, Kung Wei and Anna head to the ship to rescue Johnny and take down Bo and his gang. But tough little Johnny has rescued himself, and gets his kicks in at the showdown, too.

Li and Mui are their usual fine fighting selves, and little Tse Miu steals the show with both his acting and kung fu. In most such kid kung fu flicks, the young masters are invulnerable, but Tse takes his licks just like any adult hero. The fight choreography is outstanding, though a bit too wire-abetted to be believable, what with Li making a human yo-yo out of Xie. *AKA: Kap Ang Ang Dik San; Gei Ba Ba de Shen; Jet Li's The Enforcer; My Father Is a Hero; Letter to Daddy.* ♪♪♪

1995 (R) 105m/C *HK* Jet Li, Anita Mui, Tse Miu, Yu Rongguang, Blackie Ko, Bonnie Fu, Damian Lau, Ngai Sing, Ken Lo. **D:** Yuen Kwai. **W:** Sandy Shaw, Wong Jing (story). **C:** Tom Lau. **M:** Nicholas Rivera (U.S. version), James Wong. **VHS, DVD**

Enter the Dragon

In the early 1970s, producer Fred Weintraub *(Woodstock)* was trying to launch a new television series with *Green Hornet* star Bruce Lee. The network balked at a series with a Chinese actor in the lead, so *Kung Fu* aired with David Carradine instead, and Lee went to Hong Kong to become a superstar at Golden Harvest Stu-

dios. But Weintraub hadn't given upon his desire to work with Lee, and convinced Warner Bros. to co-produce a film with Golden Harvest—a kung fu version of 007 starring Lee, with an American director and actors and a Hong Kong crew. The result was a classic, the first martial arts film most people in the West had ever seen.

The film opens at Shaolin Temple, where Lee (Lee) is getting a workout by fighting Sammo Hung—a fight that lasts a bit longer than their real-life fight (see sidebar). Lee and the Abbot (Roy Chiao) discuss some thoughts on kung fu Zen, just to put across the notion that martial arts have a spiritual side, before the mayhem begins (much of this footage has been restored for the currently available version of the film). The Abbot tells Lee of a former student named Han (Shih Kien, dubbed by Keye Luke), who turned to the Dark Side of their teachings. Braithwaite (Geoffrey Weeks), a representative of an intelligence group, asks Lee to accept an invitation to enter a kumite martial arts tournament on Han's private island in order to gather evidence of his crime empire. He's also to try to find Mei Ling (Betty Chung), a MIA operative. On the way, Lee's father (Kok Lee-yan) provides some extra incentive: a flashback showing how Lee's sister Su Lin (Angela Mao) killed herself when cornered by Han's bodyguard O'Harra (Bob Wall) and his thugs. He's not the only one seeing flashbacks. American gambler Roper (John Saxon) recalls how he decided to enter the tournament after running up a debt to the mob. And Williams (Jim Kelly) is on the run after having an alley fight with a couple of racist cops and stealing their police car. Once on the island, the fighters are treated like kings. By day, they fight matches against each other. By night, they party—except for Lee, who spends his nights snooping for evidence. Williams sees Lee on one of his midnight jaunts, and is killed by Han when he refuses to talk about it. Han shows Roper his opium and slave factories in the palace's basement, but Roper refuses a job offer after seeing Williams's corpse. Next morning, Han's attempts to have Roper and Lee die in the ring backfire, erupting in an all-out kung fu war. The classic climax has Han fighting with Lee to the death through his private museum and into a secret maze of mirrors (borrowed from Orson Welles's *Lady from Shanghai*).

Why Han has a secret maze of mirrors is a question rarely asked. Its only requirement, like much of the film's content, is that it makes for a damn cool movie. Though Warner Bros. insisted upon Robert Clouse in the director's chair, the action scenes are all Lee, creating a superhero character for himself that could have gone on to even greater adventures, had he survived to film them. *Enter the Dragon* is one of the most important movies in all of Asian cinema in a

number of ways. It turned Bruce Lee from a cult star into the number-one movie star in the world, until his untimely death—and a bankable name for years after, due to the enterprising showmanship of some unscrupulous producers. It made Golden Harvest, then a small upstart company, into the top studio in Hong Kong, completely turning the tables on the Shaw Brothers and leading to stardom for many artists in the coming decades. And it led to a worldwide boom of interest in the martial arts, and especially martial arts movies, revitalizing the film industry throughout Southeast Asia. The martial arts tournament would continue to be a favorite plot device for martial arts films, from *Bloodsport* to *Mortal Kombat*. Bolo Yeung would go on to play essentially the same character in movies for decades. Blink and you'll miss a young Jackie Chan doing some stunt work. Lalo Schifrin would rework his theme music into that of *Rush Hour*. *AKA: Lung Chang Foo Dao; Long Zheng Hu Dou; The Deadly Three; Operation: Dragon; Blood and Steel.* 🎵🎵🎵🎵

1973 (R) 102m/C *HK/US* Bruce Lee, John Saxon, Jim Kelly, Ahna Capri, Shih Kien, Bob Wall, Angela Mao, Betty Chung, Geoffrey Weeks, Roy Chiao, Bolo Yeung, Kok Lee-yan, Peter Archer, Sammo Hung, Stephen Tung, Lau Wing, Wilson Tong, Marlene Clark, Yuen Wah, Mars, Ng Ming Choi, Yuen Biao. *D:* Robert Clouse. *W:* Michael Allin. *C:* Gilbert Hubbs. *M:* Lalo Schifrin. **VHS, DVD**

Enter the Fat Dragon

What would Bruce do? Sammo Hung stars as Lung, a not-so-magnificent butcher's son who is an obsessive Bruce Lee fan. His dad sends him to his uncle's food stand in Hong Kong to see about a job there. On the way, while daydreaming about being Bruce, Lung kicks a hole through his water taxi and sinks it. He finds that Kuang Chi's and sour-faced Uncle Hung Chi's (Fang Fang) food stands compete within the same narrow space. Smart-ass waiter Kao tries to cause trouble for Lung, but later becomes his best friend. Lung also befriends pretty customers Hsiao-wei and Chen.

When local gangsters try to push Uncle around, Lung reacts like his hero, beating them all soundly—but doing a lot of damage. This

Bruce Lee goes from kung fu movie star to cultural icon in *Enter the Dragon.*

Bruce Lee vs. Sammo Hung

Battle of the Century?

In the restored version of *Enter the Dragon*, we can see an opening scene in a ring in which Bruce Lee has a workout practice fight. His sparring partner is Sammo Hung, the overweight genius who later managed to shake up the Hong Kong movie business more than once. Of course, according to the script, Bruce won the brief fight, the last he would ever film. Lee is visibly thinner in this scene than the rest of the picture—he'd been experimenting with his weight to see if he could become quicker—and it's a bit disturbing when you know that he'd be dead soon afterward. But many who view the scene wonder about more than the cause of Lee's death (officially, a bad reaction to a painkiller, but much later revealed by his doctors as hypersensitivity to cannabis). They wonder: who would win if those two really fought?

Well, wonder no longer, as a "real" fight between the two actually happened. When *The Big Boss* (AKA *Fists of Fury* in the U.S.) opened in Hong Kong, Sammo told his stuntman friends Jackie Chan and Yuen Biao that he knew the movie was important. By that time Hung was stunt coordinator for Lee's studio, Golden Harvest, and made sure he and his buddies were involved when Lee's next picture was shooting, if only to do some stunts. When Bruce was finishing *Enter the Dragon* for Warner Bros., he decided there needed to be some kung fu right at the beginning of the picture, and thought of Sammo as the perfect opponent for the scene. Though known for his kind and generous heart, Hung was also a bit of a hothead in those days, and he was a bit miffed about being called back from working on *Sting of the Dragon Masters* to shoot one fight scene with Mr. Big Shot. When the two met in the Golden Harvest offices, they "cut the crap" (to quote the commonly dubbed-in line) and became fast friends. But Sammo's ego wasn't above pushing him into testing his new pal, and it wasn't long before they were facing off in the hallway.

Hung used to tell friends that the scrap was a draw, but years later revealed the truth in interviews. As Sammo took a stance, he was likely thinking, "Let's see what this upstart ca—"

His next thought was to wonder why he was looking up at the ceiling. Lee dropped him with a punch so quick that Sammo was down in an eye blink. To this day, Sammo Hung describes Bruce Lee as the fastest man he ever met.

sparks an argument between Uncle and Kao, who quits. Kao wants to be an artist anyway, but refuses an offer to forge paintings for triad boss Chiu (Roy Chiao). Of course, the gangsters don't take all this loss of face lightly, returning to destroy the café when Lung is away. Out of work, Lung gets a job in Chiu's restaurant, where Chen and Hsiao-wei work. Defending the girls from some boorish foreigners, Lung finds his kung fu more appreciated. Chiu entertains Professor Pai (Peter Yang, wearing an outrageous beard and monocle) and his international trio of martial arts experts, selling them some of his phony antiques. Pai thinks Chen looks just like his childhood sweetheart, who rejected his proposal years ago. When Chiu has his thugs kidnap Chen to seal the deal, Kao and Lung go to the rescue.

Basically, it's the same plot as *Return of the Dragon,* with the Hong Kong food café standing in for the Rome restaurant. Much of the dialect humor won't register, but the slapstick and situations will play anywhere. Hung's Bruce Lee imitation is on the spot, re-creating whole fights from Lee movies exactly, while throwing a funny spin on things as well. The title sequence shows Sammo dispatching a gang of thugs (including Yuen Biao, Mang Hoi, Chung Fat, and Mars) in Bruce fashion. This also calls attention to how distinctive Sammo's own style of fighting is. In one scene, Lung is hired as a stuntman to fight a Bruce Lee imitator. Lung loses his temper and ends up beating the star and all the stuntmen for marring Bruce's image. Though the climactic battle with the three champions is satisfying (especially the final duel with Leung Kar-yan), it's not as powerful as the fights Sammo would be creating just a few years later. But combined with his hilarious Lee imitation, they're enough to make this one a minor classic. *AKA: Fay Lung Kwo Gong; Fei Lung Goh Kong; Fei Long Guo Jiang; Fat Dragon Crossing River.* 🐉🐉🐉

1978 (R) 100m/C *HK* Sammo Hung, Peter Yang, Roy Chiao, Meg Lam, Leung Kar-yan, Fang Fang, Yuen Biao, Mang Hoi, Chung Fat, Mars, Lee Hoi-sang, Ankie Lau, Eric Tsang, Sai Gwa Pau. *D:* Sammo Hung. *W:* Ngai Hong. *C:* Ricky Lau. *M:* Frankie Chan. **VHS, DVD**

Entrails of the Virgin

This Japanese shocker takes the *Friday the 13th* slasher format to new extremes, dispensing with even the most basic plot to concentrate on atmosphere, sex, and violence. A photographer takes a crew and some models on the road for an S&M picture layout and sexual shenanigans, and end up in a fog-enshrouded warehouse in the woods. But the group's presence brings out something in the woods—a giant incubus (Kazuhiko Goda) rises from the swamp mud to stalk and slay. The monster has sex with some of them, but mostly it just wants to kill them off in a variety of gory ways. Some of the group appear to be infected with madness, freely accepting their horrible fates. Others futilely try to make some kind of escape.

The sex is as extreme and impersonal as it can get without getting into hard-core pornography. The violence is just extreme. Sometimes the two are unpleasantly mixed together, as in the gruesome "climax." The ending implies a sequel, though director Kazuo Komizu's follow-up *Entrails of the Beautiful Woman* told an apparently unrelated tale. Komizu takes credit for his horror films under the pseudonym "Gaira," taken from the green monster in *War of the Gargantuas.* *AKA: Shojo no Harawata; Guts of a Virgin; Entrails of a Whore.* 🐉🐉

1986 72m/C *JP* Saeko Kizuki, Naomi Hagio, Megumi Kawashima, Osamu Tsuruoka, Daiko Kato, Hideki Takahashi, Kazuhiko Goda. *D:* Kazuo Komizu. *W:* Kazuo Komizu. *C:* Akehiro Ito. *M:* Hideki Furusawa. **DVD**

Erotic Ghost Story

So-So (Man So), Fei-Fei (Kiyoko Kamimura), and Hua-Hua (Amy Yip) are three fairy vixens (foxes in human form), who have come to Earth to learn to be human. Their secondary purpose, which gets in the way of their first, is to tempt and tease mankind. As the three ladies in question are knockouts, luring unwary mortals is *not* a difficult task.

The three sisters are living together in a small house at the edge of town, but their very presence is distracting for the locals. While trying to fight their lusty influences, the vixens run afoul of the horny demon-god Wutung. Soon, all three sisters fall in love with shy scholar Wu Ming (Pal Sin) and, one by one, have their way with him. All seems like sexual bliss, until the vixens start reverting to their original form, and the neighbors and the scholar begin acting very oddly. Can an appearance by Wutung be far behind?

Erotic Ghost Story sets a high standard for sexy horror. While not as polished as *A Chinese Ghost Story,* it is well produced and directed, and the stars are very pleasing to look at. The scenery and location work is good, and there's even a bit of kung fu and magic thrown in for good measure. The emphasis, though, is on sex. While not as explicit as Western smut, the film does a good job of showing off the best assets of its heroines. Though we don't get a very clear view of the girl in purple (Amy Yip), the others bounce around with the enthusiasm of stars from an early nudist picture. Sure, the

"A movie, 'The Death Appointment,' needs a few actors to fight against the False Bruce Lee. Are you interested?"

—Sammo Hung gets his big break in *Enter the Fat Dragon*

story isn't brilliant, but at least it's easy to follow. —SS *AKA: Liu Chai Yim Taam; Liao Zhai Yan Tan.* 🦴🦴🦴

1990 85m/C *HK* Amy Yip, Pal Sin, Man So, Kiyoko Kamimura, Ha Chi-chun, Manfred Wong, Lam Chung. **D:** Simon Nam. **W:** Chang Kwan. **C:** Simon Nam. **M:** Phil Chan. **DVD**

Erotic Ghost Story 2

After being defeated in *Erotic Ghost Story,* Wutung takes on a new form (now played by Anthony Wong) and moves on to fresh stomping grounds. He falls in love with a mortal woman, Hsiao-Yen (Chang Siu Yin), who is determined to master her demonic lusts. But heaven is offended by this, and slays Hsiao-Yen. Wutung is pissed, and forces the local villages to sacrifice virgins to him every month; however, he is unaware that his love has been reincarnated in the body of Fang Yu-Yin (Charine Chan).

Yu is scheduled to be sacrificed, but handsome fisherman Shan Ken (Kwok Yiu-wah) rescues her. This does not sit well with Wutung, and things go from bad to worse in the village. As the villagers run sexually rampant, Yu-Yin and Shan Ken head for Wutung's lair. Shan Ken is captured, but Yu-Yin and Shan Ken's sister Chan (Chik King Man) come up with a bold, erotic plan to free him and down the demon lord once more.

While not as good as *Erotic Ghost Story,* this sequel is still a fun romp through Chinese myth and sexual kink. The film is well produced, with beautiful actors and sets, and more than enough fog machines and soft lighting. The content is spicy, but not hard-core in the traditional Western sense. —SS *AKA: Liu Chai Yim Taam Chuk Chap Ng Tung San; Liao Zhai Yan Tan Xu Ji Wu Tong Shen.* 🦴🦴♡

1991 96m/C *HK* Anthony Wong, Charine Chan, Chang Siu Yin, Chik King Man, Kwok Yiu-wah, Naomi Hagio, Amy Yip, Man So. **D:** Peter Ngor. **W:** Szeto On, Abe Kwong, Peter Ngor, Casey Chan. **C:** Peter Ngor. **VHS, DVD**

The Eternal Evil of Asia

The message, like those of many other Hong Kong horror yarns, is: Don't leave home! And if you do, please try not to bring back a horrible curse. It begins with a brief rundown of a few other amusing tips on how to deal with the supernatural in Asia, just so you know what the characters are doing wrong in this movie.

On an adventurous vacation to Thailand, Nam (Bobby Au), cartoonist Bon (Chan Kwok-Bong), Kong (Elvis Tsui), and salesman Kent (Ng Shiu-ting) befriend necromancer Laimi (Ben Ng) by helping him out in a duel of wizards. When his sister Shui-mei (Chin Gwan) takes a liking to Bon, Laimi uses her sweat to cast a love hex on the foreigner. But Bon's companions get the hex instead, and amid the confusion Shui-mei is accidentally killed. Lamai doesn't believe it's an accident and follows them back for revenge. He demonstrates his power by haunting a disrespectful Nam with his recently deceased parents' ghosts, until he becomes a butchering maniac and throws himself off the roof of a building. Amusingly, Nam continues to pop up as a ghost to annoy and frighten his friends.

Bon's barber fiancée—and Kong's sister—May (Ellen Chan) is amused that her superstitious Thai client Mei (Lily Chung) wants her cut hair kept and returned to her, in fear that a wizard will put a spell on her. Collecting Bon's clippings after his haircut, Laimi puts an impotency spell on him. Kent receives a hunger hex, eating his way through a restaurant, including other diners and himself. Luckily, Mei happens to be a witch herself, and offers to help negotiate with Laimi. Kong seeks help from his Taoist sifu (Lo Meng), but he's tricked by Laimi's illusions. Laimi himself seems to be enchanted somehow, and suspects that there's deeper evil behind his simple thirst for misplaced vengeance.

Duels between wizards, zombies, impalement, necrophilia, men cut in half, ghosts, cannibalism, and invisible sex acts are among the Category III horrors included here. Extremes are what the rating was invented for and that's certainly the case here, all thankfully delivered with a sense of humor. But the worst is another opportunity for Ben Ng *(Red to Kill)* to strut around naked acting creepy. Elvis Tsui drops trou again, too, but it's nice to see him play a cowardly dickhead (literally) rather than a brave rogue for a change. *AKA: Lam Yeung Sap Dai Che Sui; Nan Yang Shi Da Xie Shu.* 🦴🦴♡

1995 89m/C *HK* Ellen Chan, Chan Kwok-Bong, Ben Ng, Elvis Tsui, Lily Chung, Ng Shui-ting, Bobby Au, Chin Gwan, Yuen King-Tan, Lo Meng, Julie Lee, Bobby Yip. **D:** Chin Man-kei. **W:** Chin Man-kei. **C:** Tony Miu. **M:** Marco Wan. **VHS, DVD**

Every Dog Has His Date

Even devoted dog-lovers will have a tough time slogging through this ill-advised comedy. In her professional life, Sharon (Michelle Reis) has found success working for a production company that makes television commercials. In her personal life, however, Sharon always seems to pick losers who dump her quickly. Her one true companion is her golden retriever, Man. Because of a freak occurrence during a lightning storm, Man magically switches minds with the uncouth Fai (Nick Cheung), a set designer recently hired by Sharon. Trapped in the body of Fai, Man finds himself irresistibly drawn to his mistress, Sharon. She is divided between looking for her beloved dog, and finding herself drawn both to Fai and a friendly veterinarian, Albert (Lawrence Ng).

James Yuen is an experienced writer, but his script lacks a good structure. The very premise of the story, which was even more prominent in the advertising for the movie, is plain, so it shouldn't take nearly 30 minutes to get to the point when Man and Fai switch bodies. After that, there are some entertaining scenes in which Nick Cheung does his best impression of a dog. But the speed with which he is able to pass himself off as a real human is too quick, so we simply wait for some plot twists to be tossed in before arriving at the ending. Yuen's script contains some apt observations about love and romance, but they feel stranded by the arid material surrounding them. If you're in the mood for some undemanding laughs, and generally enjoy broad though uninspired humor, this might fit the bill. Otherwise, pass on by. Michelle Reis looks very beautiful and well embodies the rather desperate straits in which her character finds herself. Nick Cheung Ka-fai is funny to watch, but in other, more emotional scenes he appears a bit out of his element. The beautiful cinematography (all the women look wonderful) is by Tony Cheung Tung-leung. Dependable Lincoln Lo composed the cheerful music. —PM **AKA:** *Yuen Mei Ching Yan; Wan Mei Qing Ren.* 🐉

2001 108m/C *HK* Nick Cheung, Michelle Reis, Paulyn Sun, Lawrence Ng, Stephanie Che, Lam Suet, Pauline Yam. **D:** James Yuen. **W:** James Yuen. **C:** Tony Cheung. **M:** Lincoln Lo. **VHS, DVD**

Everyday Is Valentine

Carbonated beverages can really hit the spot on a hot day. Left open too long, however, and they go flat. That seems to be what happened with this movie. OK Lai (Leon Lai) is a property agent. He is also an inveterate liar. He is attracted to Wonderful (Cecilia Cheung), an office worker. Although an adult, she has not yet experienced puberty (!). She instantly ends a seven-year relationship with her boyfriend upon hearing that he and one of her friends had a drunken one-night stand. So she is wary of OK's attentions. Can OK and Wonderful find true love?

Writer/director Wong Jing has a well-deserved reputation for the kitchen-sink approach to filmmaking—he's usually willing to toss in crass and offensive bits to provoke laughs. He is unusually restrained here, and the film suffers as a result, with little genuine wit or amusement to distract. As romances should be, it's a character-driven movie; the problem is that there is very little character development. As an example: We know OK Lai is a habitual liar, yet the root of his problem is never explored. He seems reasonably successful and decent looking. Why does he lack self-esteem? What does he gain from deceiving his supposed "buddies"? If there were something in his relationship with Wonderful that played off this, that helped him to realize the hurt he caused and recognize that he needed to change, perhaps the last few scenes would play truer to the heart. Instead, the only real motivation for change is entirely selfish. Left alone, abandoned by friends, his only hope is that Wonderful will notice and take him back. Only a last-ditch, manufactured, "only in the movies" plot twist enables their eventual reconciliation. That's not to say that the film is entirely without merit. There's a pleasing variety of locations and a rotating cast of interesting performers in supporting roles. Yet on the whole, it's another case of potential remaining unfulfilled. —PM **AKA:** *Ching Mai Daai Wa Wong; Qing Mi Da Hua Wang.* 🐉

2001 99m/C *HK* Leon Lai, Cecilia Cheung, Ng Man-Tat, Yuen King-Tan, Natalie Ng, Pinky Cheung, Moses Chan, Kristy Yeung, Matt Chow, David Lee, Yuen Siu-yee, Lee Si-pooi, Hui Siu-hung, Pak Kar-sin, Eric Kot. **D:** Wong Jing. **W:** Wong Jing. **C:** Poon Hang-sang. **M:** Mark Lui. **VHS, DVD**

Evil Brain from Outer Space

The fourth Starman adventure is a bit more hectic than previous features, having been edited from *three* episodes of the *Super Giant* serial this time. The evil genius Balazar is assassinated by a robot on planet Zemar, but his brain lives on! The High Council of the Emerald Planet determines that the Brain has already made its way to Earth, where it plans to begin its conquest of the galaxy. To avoid intergalactic nuclear war, Starman (Ken Utsui) is sent to Earth once more. The Brain takes up residence with sinister Dr. Kurakawa, but his assistant Kuada catches on to the danger and swipes the Brain, hoping to get it to Dr. Sakurai, who may be able to destroy it. Chased by police, Kuada drops the suitcase containing the Brain into a river. Starman arrives in time to save Kuada from Balazar's assassins, and Sakurai agrees to help. Of course, the scientist has a pair of

KUNG FU MOVIE DYNASTIES
The Yuens

Who's Who in Fu Part 2

Although members of the Seven Little Fortunes all took the name Yuen, there was also a real Yuen family working in Hong Kong film.

Simon Yuen

The Yuen family patriarch appeared in the first, and many subsequent, episodes in the Wong Fei-hung series, plus lots of other films before donning his famous bushy wig and ragged clothes to play begging kung fu masters in *Snake in the Eagle's Shadow* and *Drunken Master* starring Jackie Chan. Those pictures made Chan a star, but also brought fame to Yuen, and producers clamored for Simon to play drunken beggars in their films. Unfortunately, fame was short-lived, and Simon died within a few years. His children, all of whom he taught Chinese opera and martial arts, carried on in the movie business, including a daughter who became a set tea lady.

Yuen Woo-ping

The most famous of the Yuen Brothers, Ping got involved in all aspects of the movies, and can be seen in small parts throughout his career, most notably in Sammo Hung's classic *Eastern Condors*. However, it was behind the camera that he gained the most fame, as producer, director, writer, action director, and even composer *(Wing Chun)*. Independent Seasonal Films gave him a chance to direct borrowed star Jackie Chan in two films. He cast his father Simon as co-star and had huge success with both *Snake in the Eagle's Shadow* and *Drunken Master*. Soon after, he formed his own production company to make *The Buddhist Fist*. Other top flicks on his resumé are *Magnificent Butcher*, *Dreadnaught*, *Drunken Tai Chi* (with his discovery Donnie Yen), *Tiger Cage*, *Iron Monkey*, and *Red Wolf*. Recent prominent credits as action director include *Crouching Tiger, Hidden Dragon* and the *Matrix* trilogy.

Yuen Cheung-yan

Looking much like his brother Ping, Yan spent more time in front of the camera, with small character roles in dozens of films, including those directed by his brother. Ping gave him large roles playing a magician's wife (!) in *Miracle Fighters* and Donnie Yen's puppeteer master in *Drunken Tai Chi*. Yan was action director on many films as well, including *Mighty Peking Man*, *18 Fatal Strikes*, *Dreadnaught*, *The Postman Strikes Back*, *King of Beggars*, and *Charlie's Angels*. He also directed a handful of films, notably *Live Hard*.

Brandy Yuen

A talented martial artist, Brandy took on supporting roles in the Yuen films and many others, and was the weird imp in the urn in *Miracle Fighters*. Films as action director include *Pedicab Driver* and *The Master*. He also directed some films, notably *In the Line of Duty 3*, before making the spiritual-minded *Master of Zen*, after which he retired from show business to become a Buddhist monk.

Yuen Yat-chor

Some attempt were made to let the spry Chor step out of supporting roles as an action comedy star, mainly in *The Miracle Fighters*. However, it didn't take, though he acquitted himself quite well with a key part in *In the Line of Duty 4*.

Sunny Yuen

With a talent for acting as well as martial arts, Sunny made the most of his character roles, and took the lead in *Dance of the Drunk Mantis* alongside his father. But it was in *Dreadnaught* that he made his greatest impression as the monstrous psycho killer White Tiger out for Yuen Biao's blood. Audiences liked the role so much, he played it again in *Drunken Tai Chi*.

precocious children, and Starman gives them one of his nifty pagers. The Brain—which somehow manages to make sure its agents find it—creates some freaky-looking mutants, who can fly, turn invisible, disguise themselves as humans, and have other powers. The mutants cause accidents and commit robberies, attack Dr. Sakurai, and are able to multiply themselves. Police—and of course, little children—do their best to track down mutants, who are now lurking everywhere. Luckily, Starman shows up just in time whenever anyone gets in trouble.

Most feature condensations of serials have an awkward, rushed pace and sometimes sloppy continuity from the editing. But though this feature only uses roughly 60% of the serial episode footage, it just helps the story move along at a good clip, without repetition or padding. Besides, we've got a narrator to tell us that Starman finds his way into the secret base—why show it again, when we just saw someone else find it? The editing can't explain a couple of the series' stranger moments, though. At one point the hero prevents the assassination of an Arab dignitary by impersonating him, with the assassins' bullets bouncing off his iron body. But after revealing his ploy, he stupidly points out that the real dignitary is not far behind him—and amazingly, the villains don't try to shoot their real target! In another sequence, the narrator tells us that the mutants are now killing people indiscriminately, but we cut right to a scene of kids enjoying cotton candy. The mutants in their natural state are creepy creations, with big fangs and claws, and some kind of antennae that look like bat ears. They actually seem to pose a challenge for Starman in combat, and melt when killed (ick!). The Brain's minions wear a selection of nifty uniforms, and their various headquarters are interesting visually. It's intriguing that wheelchair-bound Dr. Kurakawa seems to prefer handicapped henchmen—one is missing a leg, and another a hand. The producers must have been convinced that kids are afraid of witches—they use a mutant witch here, and an alien witch in *Invaders from Space*. *AKA: Uchu Kaijin Shutsugen; Zoku Supa Jaiantsu—Akuma no Kenshin; Dokuga Okoku; Super Giant 7, 8 & 9; Spacemen Appear; Devil Incarnate; Kingdom of the Poisonous Moth.* 🐉🐉🐉

1958/59 78m/BW *JP* Ken Utsui, Sachihiro Ohsawa, Junko Ikeuchi, Minako Yamada, Shoji Nakayama, Kan Hayashi, Minoru Takada, Utako Mitsuya, Chisako Tahara, Reiko Seto, Akira Tamura, Tomohiko Ohtani, Fumiko Miyata, Johji Ohhara, Kami Ashita, Terumi Hoshi, Shinsuke Mikimoto. *D:* Teruo Ishii, Akira Mitsuwa, Koreyoshi Akasaka. *W:* Ichiro Miyagawa. *C:* Takashi Watanabe. *M:* Michiaki Watanabe. **VHS, DVD**

Evil Cat

For centuries, the Cheung family has been guardians of the Earth against a cat demon. Every 50 years, the demon has to be killed using their hereditary Mao Shan magic, until all nine lives have been extinguished. When a construction crew uncovers the cat demon's tomb, setting it free, Master Cheung (Lau Kar-Leung) senses the danger and goes to meet it. But the creature has already invaded a large office building, slaughtering the night guards and taking possession of the boss, Fan Chin-choi. Fan's chauffeur Long (Mark Cheng), Master Cheung, his TV reporter daughter Cheung Siu-chuen (Joann Tang), and her unwanted suitor Inspector Wu (Wong Jing) all arrive on the scene too late. Master Cheung figures he only has a short time to live before his cancer kills him—just enough time to kill the cat demon before it can reincarnate, becoming invincible. Long is terrified when his boss starts attacking him with supernatural power, eating carp from the pond, and other cat demon antics. He rushes to Master Cheung, who (lacking the preferred male heir) makes him his disciple, and attempts to teach Long as much Mao Shan magic as he can while hunting down the menace.

There are bits of humor in the characters, but unlike most other Hong Kong horror films in the era when Sammo Hung's horror comedies

ruled, *Evil Cat* takes its horror straight. For the most part, this works very well, although in its final form, the cat demon is a bit too reminiscent of a certain Broadway hit to be taken seriously. The special effects are surprisingly good, involving more opticals than is usual for a HK movie of its day. The action scenes are well done, too, with Lau Kar-Leung showing off his kung fu, and there are some great acrobatics and stunts. One fine sequence has the demon attacking a police station, à la *The Terminator*, while the demon's body-hopping abilities recall *The Hidden,* and some of the f/x look like they came right out of *Lifeforce* (AKA *Space Vampires*). *AKA: Hung Mau; Xiong Mao.* 🐉🐉🐉

1986 87m/C *HK* Lau Kar-Leung, Mark Cheng, Joann Tang, Wong Jing, Stuart Ong, Chui Suk-woon, Ha Ping, Tom Poon. *D:* Dennis Yu. *W:* Wong Jing. *C:* Arthur Wong. *M:* Law Wing-fai. **DVD**

Evil Dead Trap

Obviously inspired by Italian (especially those of Dario Argento) and American (especially *The Evil Dead*) horror films, this groundbreaking picture takes the revolting gore of the Guinea Pig series and applies it to a well-structured suspense plot. Concepts used here inspired those used in *Ring* and many more features to come.

Nami (Miyuki Ono, cast because she looked like Sigourney Weaver, according to the director) is the host of a late-night television show. While skimming through tapes sent in by viewers for broadcast, she comes upon what appears to be a hyper-violent snuff tape. The video starts with a sequence that may show how to get to the murder scene—an obvious invitation. Instead of notifying police, she takes a crew to find the location, a former top-secret U.S. military installation. Following true haunted-house movie tradition, the group splits up to explore the huge ruined buildings. A mysterious stranger (Yuji Honma) warns Nami of the extreme danger they're in, which becomes more obvious when they find the place riddled with death traps. In addition, there's a psychopath stalking the grounds, picking off trespassers. After most of her comrades have been killed, the odd stranger reappears to express his loneliness, and explain that the trouble is due to his even odder brother Hideki, who has grown out of control.

The first impetus for the film was merely a request from the studio for a low-budget horror flick to exploit three top adult-video actresses. But seeing further opportunity in Takashi Ishi's slasher movie script, director Toshiharu Ikeda changed the story to make the menace more fantastic. Heightening the excitement with creative (but not too showy) camera moves, and music that openly apes soundtracks by Goblin,

Ikeda builds tension until the over-the-top climax. The only things that hold the film back from being a genre classic are some unnecessarily distracting sex scenes and a tendency to lean on cliché situations. Hiroshi Shimizu, who plays a maniac here, is also the sub crewman who shouts "Hollywood!" in Spielberg's *1941*. *AKA: Shiryo No Wana; Evil Dead's Trap.* ♫♫♫▽

1988 100m/C *JP* Miyuki Ono, Yuji Honma, Aya Katsuragi, Hitomi Kobayashi, Eriko Nakagawa, Masahiko Abe, Hiroshi Shimizu, Noboro Mitani. **D:** Toshiharu Ikeda. **W:** Takashi Ishi. **C:** Masaki Tamura, Norimichi Kasamatsu. **M:** Tomohiko Kira. **DVD**

The Executioner

A bit more coherent than director Teruo Ishii's *The Street Fighter's Last Revenge,* this Toei production is also a lot more violent and weird! Three dangerous men are wanted for a mission by an ex-cop turned leader of a secret vigilante group set on stopping Mafia drug traffic in Japan. The boss's old associate Takeshi Hayagusa (Makoto Sato, taking time out from his usual roles as thugs and perverts), an ex-narcotics squad cop turned professional assassin, is the first recruit. Koga Ryoshi (Sonny Chiba), an orphan raised by his grandfather as the last of the Koga ninja clan, is the second. Now a private detective, he's hired to break playboy martial arts expert Sakura out of prison. With the boss's niece Emi (Doris Nakajima), they start by interfering with an ambassador's daughter who is smuggling heroin into the country. Then they go after Mario Mitsuhara, Mafia don of Tokyo, killing his bodyguards one by one in unarmed combat. But Mitsuhara recruits a trio of his own vicious fighters: Leo the Sicilian, killer boxer Nakashura, and the brutal wrestler Cannibal (who, shades of Mike Tyson, enjoys eating opponents' ears). Hayagusa's student (Yasuaki Kurata) joins the team for the showdown.

All all-out fight film, there's also bathroom humor, full-frontal nudity, and some gory shocks—such as when Hayagusa hits a guy so hard his eyes pop out, and Koga rips bones out of his foes. Koga's favorite trick is to hide on the ceiling, à la Spider-man. A very young Henry Sanada plays the young Koga in flashbacks. Followed by *Executioner 2*. *AKA: Chokugeki! Jigokuhen; Direct Hit! Hellfist; Hell Fist.* ♫♫♫▽

1974 83m/C *JP* Sonny Chiba, Makoto Sato, Yasuaki Kurata, Doris Nakajima, Ryo Ikebe, Henry Sanada. **D:** Teruo Ishii. **VHS, DVD**

Executioners

Though not a big hit in Asia, the comic book–styled *The Heroic Trio* spawned this more bluntly political sequel, inspired by tensions caused by China building a nuclear power plant near Hong Kong. An atomic bomb blast changes the series' setting considerably, giving it a post-apocalyptic, *Road Warrior* look. Invisible Girl (Michelle Yeoh) protects shipments of medical supplies en route to plagued areas, aided by the now-domesticated brute #9 (who always wears a hood, since Anthony Wong now plays another character). Thief Catcher (Maggie Cheung) is on the other side of things, stealing shipments of precious uncontaminated water for her own profit, while her rival Bill (Lau Ching-Wan), a soldier who is more of a Robin Hood, benefitting the needy. Wonder Woman (Anita Mui) has hung up her silver mask to concentrate on raising her young daughter. Her husband, police inspector Lau (Damian Lau), is too busy dealing with civil unrest to spend even Christmas with his family. A protest led by the messianic Koda (Takeshi Kaneshiro) leads to a riot (none too subtly recalling 1989 in Tianamen Square), touched off by an unknown gunman. Koda is working on behalf of the masked mutant Mr. Kim (Anthony Wong, who wears so much makeup he might as well not play *this* part either), inventor of a new water purification system. Sinister government official the Colonel (Paul Chun) secretly assigns Lau with Koda's assassination (a job which is subsequently taken care of by an agent of Kim's), but Lau is later betrayed and shot. The Colonel is secretly working together with Kim to gain control of the fresh water supply, and thus the world. The last hope for a free world is for Bill and Thief Catcher to make a desperate last bid to find a new fresh water supply.

Though *Executioners* is kind of a mess, it's at least an interesting mess that tries to throw a few ideas at you. There's so much senseless plot that they almost forgot to put much action in—the big fight scene at the end feels like an afterthought. It's all supposed to take place in a world in ruins, but the city sets don't look much worse than it did in *Heroic Trio*. Fans of the stars might want to screen this one just for the scene in which Yeoh, Mui, and Cheung take a bath together. *AKA: Yin Doi Ho Hap Juen; Xian Dai Hao Xia Zhuan; Heroic Trio 2: Executioners; Modern Day Wonder Heroes Legend.* ♫♫▽

1993 96m/C *HK* Anita Mui, Maggie Cheung, Michelle Yeoh, Damian Lau, Anthony Wong, Lau Ching-Wan, Paul Chun, Takeshi Kaneshiro, Kwan San, John Chang, Eddie Ko. **D:** Johnny To, Ching Siu-tung. **W:** Susanne Chan, Sandy Shaw (story). **C:** Poon Hang-sang. **M:** Cacine Wong. **VHS, DVD**

Executioners from Shaolin

This interpretation of legendary events following the burning of Shaolin Temple begins in typical

Shaw Brothers fashion with combatants facing off against a plain background. Sent by the Ching emperor to raid Shaolin for harboring rebels, traitor monk Pai Mei (Lo Lieh) kills Abbot Chi San (Lee Hoi-sang) in a duel. Heroic Hung Hey-kwun (Chen Kuan-tai), Hsiao Hu (Cheng Hong-yip) and Tung Chien-chen (Gordon Lau) are among the few to escape. Tung hangs back to die (standing up like a true hero), delaying the troops so the others can get away. The rebel heroes hide out disguised as traveling Chinese opera troupes sailing about on the famous Red Boats. In one port, young Fong Wing Chun (Lily Li) insults the performers, challenging Hung's strong Tiger Style with her own variation on the flowing Crane Style. She and her Uncle (Shum Lo) end up joining the troupe, and before long Hung and Wing Chun are married. On their wedding night, Hung's kung fu faces the challenge of breaking open the grip of Wing Chun's Closed-Knees Stance! Eventually he finds the proper technique, and little Man-ting is born. The Manchus learn their secret, and begin raiding the Red Boats, so the rebels go into hiding.

Hung Hey-kwun spends 10 years improving his Tiger Style, and growing a mustache, training to challenge Pai Mei. He's unable to beat the seemingly invulnerable Pai Mei, and only escapes through the sacrifice of Hsiao Hu, who tells Pai Mei's secret weakness: he can only be killed between 1:00 and 3:00 p.m. Hung trains for another seven years, using a kind of human-shaped pachinko machine. He returns to challenge Pai Mei, attacking at 1:00. Four minutes later, it's 3:00, and Pai Mei is able to capture him. The teenage Hung Man-ting (Wong Yu) is determined to take on Pai Mei himself, but his mom insists he learn his dad's Tiger Style first. However, dad's training manual has been chewed up by a rat, forcing Man-ting to fill in the gaps in the exercises with the Crane Style he already knows, and making up the rest himself. Taking with him this patchwork style (which would eventually become very popular as Hung Gar Style), Man-ting stalks off to confront Pai Mei.

This is roughly based on the same events that later formed the basis of the Jet Li vehicle *New Legend of Shaolin* (AKA *Legend of the Red Dragon*), *Wing Chun* (starring Michelle Yeoh), and others. In the hands of Lau Kar-Leung, with the Shaw Brothers production values, it becomes an entertaining tale of a legendary martial arts family, featuring some excellent fighting and training scenes. The only flaw is that, with his twin hair ribbons and whiny dubbed voice, Wong Yu's Man-ting comes off more like a pouting little girl than a kung fu hero. Chen Yung-yu's music is swiped from several Toho pictures. **AKA:** *Hung Hei-kwun; Hong Xiguan; Hung Hsi-Kuan; Executioners of Death; Shaolin Executioners.* ♪♪♪♡

1977 (R) 100m/C *HK* Chen Kuan-tai, Lo Lieh, Wong Yu, Lily Li, Cheng Hong-yip, Gordon Lau, Tin Ching, Kong Do, Shum Lo, Lee Hoi-sang, John Chang, Lam Ching-Ying, Fung Hark-On, Wilson Tong, Fung Lee, Billy Chan, Lee Chiu, Lin Ke-ming, Chan Lung, Cheung Wa, San Sin, Mang Hoi, Hsiao Ho, Chin Yuet Sang, Eric Tsang. **D:** Lau Kar-Leung. **W:** Ngai Hong. **C:** Lo Yun-cheng. **M:** Chen Yung-yu. **VHS, DVD**

Exit the Dragon, Enter the Tiger

Who says they don't make cheese in China? This inevitably trashy exercise was one of the first films to cash in on the death of Bruce Lee, and one of the best. July 17, 1973, at Summit Studios: Martial arts movie star Bruce Lee (Bruce Li) tells his pal David "Tiger" Lee (Bruce Li) that he's been getting strange phone calls and annoying headaches. He makes Tiger promise that he'll be his successor if anything happens to him. Cut to: newspaper headlines announcing Lee's death and tacky newsreel footage of his funeral (Nora Miao and Bolo Yeung are seen in attendance). A tearful Tiger vows to find out the cause of Bruce's death, and avenge him if there was foul play. His primary lead is Bruce's mistress, actress Suzy Yeung (Chiang Ma Chi), and he enlists his reporter friend George Wang to help. The international crime syndicate knows that Suzy recorded a conversation in which mobsters tried to blackmail Bruce into smuggling narcotics for them because "as a kung fu master, he's above suspicion," and the evil Baron sends Lung Fei (Lung Fei!) to get it. While fighting his way to the truth, Tiger gets stabbed in the leg, thrown around by a giant (Cheng Fu Hung), and scorched with a blowtorch. The Baron himself arrives in Hong Kong, and has his men kidnap Suzy. Disguised as newsboy and a telephone repairman (just like Bruce in *The Chinese Connection*!), Tiger manages to find where they've taken her, and goes to the rescue.

Bruce Li didn't yet have his Lee imitation perfected, and this actually works to his advantage in the fight scenes, which seem more natural. He gets a chance to act a bit more, and his martial arts have improved from previous films (though his opponents still far outclass him). Insane 1970s fashions and décor assault the eyes in nearly every scene, but the cinematography is terrific, especially during the climactic fight in the surf. The theme music is swiped from Isaac Hayes's *Three Tough Guys* soundtrack. ♪♪♪

1975 79m/C *HK* Bruce Li, Lung Fei, Chiang Ma Chi, Shan Mao, On Ping, Ko Saio Pao, Bau Kwok Lung, Tony Liu, Chang Yi, Cheng Fu Hung, Kam

Kong. **D:** Lee Tso Nam. **W:** Chang Seng-yi. **C:** Yip Chin Biu. **M:** Chou Fu-liang. **VHS, DVD**

Expect the Unexpected

Well, who knows what to expect with a title like that, except maybe the unexpected? Patrick Yau certainly isn't afraid of shifting gears with this film. In fact, that's his whole point, as he shifts from light drama to slapstick comedy to horror to action to black comedy and back again in an eye blink.

Tea shop waitress Mandy (Yoyo Mung) admires crime-stopper Captain Ken Cheung (Simon Yam) on a TV news report as he talks about catching the notorious Matthew "The King" Wong. A trio of inept robbers tries to stage a heist at the jewelry store across the street and fails miserably. One of the robbers (Lam Suet) runs into a nearby apartment building, prompting police to search the place—in turn prompting a member of a much tougher gang hiding out in an apartment (shared by three women, whom they've kept tied up) to pick up a machine gun and make a break. He's captured, but his three fellows, who have been in the tea shop all the while, attack the police to free him and make a getaway. This brings Ken to investigate, and face to face with Mandy.

After this first 15 minutes, who can say what will happen next? For example, you might be surprised to learn that Mandy owns the tea shop where she works. She went to school with not only Ken, but also the unorthodox detective Sam Lee (Lau Ching-Wan) under his command. Nor would you necessarily expect that three members of Ken's team would get shot within the next 15 minutes, and not for the last time in the movie. The personal relationships of the characters are intermingled with the progress made by the cops as they try to figure out what the sadistic gang is up to and track them down—and incidentally, the gang of jewelry-store robbers. The film's message is clear: it's no easy thing to determine what the source of danger will be in our lives, especially for police officers. It's hard to say whether or not that message is more effective post-911 or before. The cast and crew in all departments are excellent. While not strictly an action film, there are some fine gun battles, some deceptively tricky car stunts, and one of the most agonizing shootouts ever. Cacine Wong's apt score is also worth noting. ***AKA:*** *Fai Seung Dat Yin; Fei Chang Tu Ran.* 🐉🐉🐉🐉

1998 87m/C *HK* Lau Ching-Wan, Simon Yam, Ruby Wong, Raymond Wong Ho-yin, Yoyo Mung, Lam Suet, Hui Siu-hung, Pak Kar-sin, Sato Keiji, Joe Cheng. **D:**

Patrick Yau. **W:** Szeto Kam-yuen, Yau Nai-hoi, Taures Chow. **C:** Ko Chiu-lam. **M:** Cacine Wong. **VHS, DVD**

Extreme Challenge

It's an old-fashioned fight tournament movie—millennium style! The PowerNet Show website is hosting a World Wide Web Martial Arts Combat Championship, better known as Extreme Challenge, to be broadcast on the Internet with a $5 million first prize. Kung fu master Jin Fang (Yeung Chuen-ngai) is among the six seeded entrants, along with wrestler Santos Smith and ultimate fighter Ian Maxfield (Paul Rapovski). The tournament is sponsored by the Champ Corporation to promote their sports equipment. Consultant Karen Li (Jacqueline Li) is ordered to find a replacement for Maxfield, who is being dropped as their spokesman in favor of an Asian image. Among the first entrants to sign up are Tang Ning (Patricia Ja Lee, the pink Power Ranger), daughter of famous Master Tang Wai, and Kuang Kin (Ken Chang), who trained with the same sifu as Jin. The tournament takes place in a specially constructed complex riddled with camera towers and hi-tek facilities, looking like leftover sets from *Logan's Run.*

The first round of competition requires the entrants to battle each other while running through a tough obstacle course to narrow the field to 16 qualifiers. The next day, they have to fight their way to the top of a tower to narrow the field to eight. As a friendship between Ning and Kin grows closer each night, so does the likelihood of a conflict during the day. The four duels fought in head-to-head competition use padding and a variety of weapons on four different platforms. Maxfield, Ning, and Jin win their matches decisively, but though Kin easily outclasses his Thai opponent Somchai Chotikung (Somchai Siabkuntod), he falls off the platform while preventing the man from impaling himself on a broken cudgel. However, Kin is offered a second chance—Li, who has been manipulating the match-ups to give her the best ratings and make it more likely that the most popular fighters remain, has Somchai disqualified on a technicality. Kin resists, but after Ning hangs in to last over three minutes against the much stronger Jin, he decides to try to prove his martial arts—and philosophy—are superior to that of his old rival.

Not as fanciful as *Mortal Kombat* or as brutal as *Bloodsport, Extreme Challenge* concentrates on its imaginative setting, showy camera techniques and martial arts choreography. Characterization is paper thin, so the story is told almost completely through the fighting, which is some of the best designed by Stephen

Tung in recent years (with the help of choreographers Jack Wong, Christopher Chan, and Antonio Caprio). Each battle is shot with a different style, from digital movement trails to black-and-white cuts to emulate old samurai films. But there's more than fight scenes here—there's also some sharp commentary on the nature of sports and competition in the 21st century, when honor can be discarded in order to produce a more lucrative product, and goes so far as to question the concept of winning at all costs. Tung purposely sets all the action in the freshly scrubbed atmosphere of an ultramodern health club, without any of the grime of an old city boxing gym, or the dusty mountaintops of old-school kung fu flicks—a move that may deceive some viewers into mistaking this for the kind of slick but empty martial arts films it seeks to criticize in some ways. His only misstep is in setting his story in the present day, when large screen mega-bandwidth Internet speeds are still a couple years away. **AKA:** *Dei Seung Chui Keung; Di Shang Zui Jiang; C3 Fighters.* 🎵🎵🎵🎵

2001 89m/C *HK/CH/US* Ken Chang, Patricia Ja Lee, Jacqueline Li, Yeung Chuen-ngai, Paul Rapovski, Raymond Chow, Kang Jian Min, Somchai Siabkuntod, Scott Adkins, Gordon Milne, Nikki Berwick, Lisa Ling, Carl Spencer, Paul Smith. **D:** Stephen Tung. **W:** Max Ip, Jiang Dao-hai, John Chan. **C:** William Yim, Yu Li-ping. **M:** Tommy Wai. **DVD**

Extreme Crisis

Veteran action director Bruce Law put together this turbocharged big-budget action machine, the final film made under Golden Harvest's Leonard Ho. Detective Takami (Kenya Sawada) is the lone survivor of a squad sent to attack the compound of the dangerous Shojenomichi cult and arrest their leader Yoshinaga (Kei Nakada). While driving his girlfriend, TV reporter Anita Lee (Shu Qi), to a driving test, police inspector Ken Cheung (Julian Cheung) spots a team of bandits stealing chemicals from a semi. With the driver dead, Anita stops the truck before it hits anyone by jamming Ken's sports car in front of it—which should give her extra points on her exam. It also makes Ken late for a meeting with Takami at the HK Japanese Consulate—the Japanese need the help of the Hong Kong police to extradite Yoshinaga (who was arrested there), but are backed up in red tape.

Shojenomichi cultists led by Takizawa (Akira Koieyama) break in on the meeting, killing the Consul and demanding the release of Yoshinaga, threatening to kill the entire population of Hong Kong in 24 hours. Also killed is Ken's partner Lam (Spencer Lam), for which Ken blames

his superior Ching (Theresa Lee). While authorities hustle to get Yoshinaga out of the country, both Ken and Takami step outside their authority to try to track down the cult before they can mix up a sarin gas cocktail.

Cut from the same cloth as *Die Hard*, *Crisis* delivers explosions, car chases, and thousands of rounds of ammunition downtown in a co-production between Hong Kong and Japan. The various heroes and villains are nothing you haven't seen before, but if you're in the mood for a massive, slam-bang shoot-'em-up picture, this is your ticket in any language. The actors speak both Cantonese and Japanese, but most often use English as a common language (though some still need subtitles). However, talk is not what matters here, as you may have gathered. Stars of both countries end up in a TV station tower with the terrorists, with a time bomb full of sarin juice ready to explode. Theresa Lee is cute as a button—and not quite believable as a police captain who's scared of her own gun. Shu Qi, on the other hand, is much better in action scenes than as a TV news anchor. **AKA:** *B Gai Waak; B Ji Hua; Project B.* 🎵🎵🎵

1998 95m/C *HK* Julian Cheung, Theresa Lee, Kenya Sawada, Shu Qi, Akira Koieyama, Rikiya Mifune, Zennosoke Fukkin, Shiro Mifune, Masanobu Takashima, Spencer Lam, Kei Nakada, Wong Yat-Fei, Bruce Law. **D:** Bruce Law. **W:** Eddie Wong, Lee Ping-wah, Ma Wai-pong, Laura Wu. **C:** Horace Wong. **M:** Akihiko Matsumoto. **VHS, DVD**

The Eye

Once again, the Pang Brothers *(Bangkok Dangerous)* demonstrate their superior eye—no pun intended—for visual storytelling. Mun (Angelica Lee), sightless since the age of two, receives a cornea transplant and regains her vision. Her joy is tempered by the startling revelation that she can now see things that nobody else can. After several of these heart-stirring incidents, including one that should make any sane person reluctant to ride an elevator, Mun feels impelled to learn more about the cornea donor. Despite the misgivings of her family, she travels to Thailand, accompanied by her visual therapist (Lawrence Chou). There she discovers more troubling secrets, leading to a shattering conclusion.

The most compelling sequences combine music, sound effects, sharp editing, visual effects, and minimal dialogue. They are, simply put, enthralling. The fresh take on ideas that are beginning to feel a bit shop-worn (the "I see dead people" genre inspired by *The Sixth Sense*) results in a tense yet intelligent thrill ride. Beyond the moments that may make the hair on the back of your neck stand up, there is

also a sympathetic consideration of the effect all these events are having upon Mun. One false note may be that her family is shut out at a crucial time, in favor of assistance from Mun's visual therapist, and the suggestion of a romance between the two. Though the romance angle is an unnecessary distraction, ultimately that decision feels right, because the primary point is that Mun wants to gain independence after so many years of relying upon others to live her life. The unexpectedly powerful if imperfect conclusion wraps everything up in a way that, again, feels right emotionally, in a fatalistic sort of way. Angelica Lee does not breathe fireworks but is entirely believable as Mun; her natural performance grounds the entire film in reality. Candy Lo *(Time and Tide)* has a small role as Mun's flight attendant sister. —*PM*
AKA: *Gin Gwai; Jian Gui.* 🐉🐉🐉▽

2002 98m/C *HK* Angelica Lee, Lawrence Chou, Candy Lo, Fong Chin Fat, Yut Lai So, Chutcha Rujinanon, Pierre Png, Edmund Chen, Yin Ping Ko. **D:** Danny Pang, Oxide Pang. **W:** Jojo Hui, Danny Pang, Oxide Pang. **C:** Decha Srimantra. **M:** Orange Music. **VHS, DVD**

Faces of Horror

Even the biggest fans of Hong Kong star Elvis Tsui probably never thought of him as a Rod Serling type, but here he is talking to the camera and hosting a horror anthology as he wanders about familiar HK locations, and even on the mainland. In story 1, Ho Chi-hwa and his girlfriend Miu get together with friends Lok, Cee, and Ho for an evening of barbecue and ghost stories. Hwa's Aunt San has already creeped everyone out by talking about murders that supposedly happened in the house next door, so naturally everyone expands upon the story until Hwa is challenged to spend the night in the haunted house. The others all arrive in costume to scare him, but get a scare themselves when Hwa knocks Ho into some loose electric wires. A week later, the surviving quartet is haunted by Ho's ghost.

In story 2, a wandering ghost in sunglasses tries to reincarnate in the body of an accident victim, but his aim is spoiled by a young woman's pendant. Peeved, he decides to follow Miss Chiang (Carrie Ng) home and haunt her. Soon after she's financially ruined and seeks help from fortuneteller Granny Lung (Helena Law), who tells her that Lucky Boy will arrive to help her. Sure enough, a box containing a human skeleton is delivered to her door. It incarnates as a crazy fat boy (Kok Siu-man, that nutty kid from *Dragon from Shaolin*) who tells her the winner in a horse race.

Tsui himself takes a role in story 3, which concerns Hong Kong men who abandon their

pregnant mainland girlfriends. Chu is about to return to HK when his friend Yao (Henry Fong) learns his mother is ill, and asks Chu to take his sister Lan (Annie Wu) back with him—a sister no one else can see. Actually Lan is a ghost, who has come to haunt her ex, Min Yi (Roy Cheung). His spiritual adviser Kao (Chung Fat) advises him to honor her spirit with the soul plate she demands, but when Min Yi tries to fight her instead, Lan turns violent.

Despite the stars included, this is another Hong Kong horror film in which plot doesn't matter. Each story displays some "spooky" situations without leading to a satisfying conclusion. Like the *Troublesome Night* series it attempts to emulate, not only does the host take on a role, but some of the same actors appear in more than one story. Fans of goofy HK supernatural antics may want to check out the insane middle tale, but the rest are mere time-wasters. **AKA:** *Min Ching Ching Yau Paai Geng; Mian Qing Qing You Pai Jing; Faces of Horrid.* 🐉▽

1998 95m/C *HK* Elvis Tsui, Carrie Ng, Roy Cheung, Helena Law, Annie Wu, Henry Fong, Chung Fat, Jerry Lamb, Kok Siu-man, Karen Tong, Joyce Chan, Choi Wai-man, Chin Yuet Sang, Lam Wa-fan. **D:** Lam Chin-wai, Yiu Tin-hung, Szeto Ying-kit. **W:** Chim Si. **C:** Faan Chuen-yam. **VHS**

Fall for You

Tai Yue (Francis Ng) is a Hong Kong native who has lived in Paris for six years. A struggling artist, he dallies with his nude models, cooks in a Chinese restaurant to make a few dollars, and plots to meet an art critic, imaging that the critic will bestow success upon him if only he sees his paintings. While moonlighting as a waiter, he spills a tray of drinks on Yi (Kristy Yeung). She's a gold digger, on the hunt for a wealthy man to marry her. Both Tai Yue and Yi are faced with expiring visas, and inexplicably end up entangled in each other's lives.

Francis paints! Francis cooks! Francis speaks French! Francis cuddles with half-naked Frenchwomen! If only the movie were as enticing as the potential taglines. Sadly, the story is muddled, the romance is unconvincing, and the conclusion is confusing. Writer Taures Chow Yin-Han and director Cha Chuen-yee (*In the Line of Duty 5*) have failed to construct a scenario that allows the audience to empathize with the main characters. Tai Yue celebrates his 40th birthday, which means he came to Paris to pursue his passion of painting at the age of 34. What motivated him, though, to take such a drastic step in his early 30s? What life did he leave behind? As for Yi, she is 28, and explains at one point that she wants to get on with living. But we are not shown until far too late her motivation for seeking a wealthy husband. And the supposedly romantic pair is rarely shown conversing, so it's hard to imagine why Tai Yue develops an attraction to Yi, and why he treats the friendly Juliette, one of his French models, in a very cavalier way. Some dialogue is exchanged about the manner in which people use one another, but in general this is a low-key affair that is novel only in its low-budget use of Paris locales. Fans of Francis Ng will enjoy the actor's embodiment of an artistic type unconcerned with his own outward appearance. Kristy Yeung looks beautiful and fulfills the requirements of the part without digging very deeply into the character. —*PM* **AKA:** *Hei Foon Lei; Xi Huan Nin.* ♫♫♡

2001 87m/C *HK* Francis Ng, Kristy Yeung. **D:** Cha Cheun-yee. **W:** Taures Chow. **C:** Wong Man-wan. **M:** Johnny Yeung. **VHS, DVD**

Fallen Angels

This 1995 feature from New Wave–influenced writer/director Wong Kar-Wai is a complementary feature to his 1994 *Chungking Express*, structured and shot in much the same manner, using many of the same locations. Both present two tales of crime, romance, and loneliness, joined at the midway point. Both are shot in Wong's semi-verité style, the camera lurking through the corridors of a maze-like city to find his lost characters.

Ming (Leon Lai) is a low-level contract killer for the Hong Kong underworld. Agent (Michelle Reis) is his partner, who cases every assignment carefully, and almost never sees Ming. Injured one time too many, Ming decides to quit the business, but can't bring himself to face Agent to tell her. He Qiwu (Takeshi Kaneshiro, also in *Chungking Express*) is an ex-con who lives in the same building as Agent, where his father is landlord. He's been mute ever since childhood from eating an expired can of pineapple (another link to *Chungking Express*). Qiwu makes a meager living by breaking into shops after closing at night and running them as his own. Often, he bullies customers into buying. He gets involved with a crazy girl named Charlie (Charlie Yeung), who's distraught over her boyfriend marrying another girl. After she dumps him, he follows his dad around with a video camera, annoying him by taping day and night. The tape ends up as the old man's birthday present. Everyone moves on eventually, recombining occasionally in different ways.

Less cohesive than even *Chungking Express*, *Fallen Angels* is nonetheless quietly entertaining, buoyed for the most part by Kaneshiro's amusing mute character, who reminds one reflexively of a young Asian Harpo Marx. **AKA:** *Doh Laai Tin Sai; Duo La Tian Shi.* ♫♫♡

1995 99m/BW/C *HK* Leon Lai, Michelle Reis, Takeshi Kaneshiro, Charlie Yeung, Karen Mok. **D:** Wong Kar-Wai. **W:** Wong Kar-Wai. **C:** Chris Doyle. **M:** Frankie Chan, Roel A. Garcia. **VHS, DVD**

Fantasy Mission Force

During the shooting of the film *Young Master*, a triad gang began making trouble for the production. It all had something to do with Lo Wei trying to get even with star Jackie Chan for leaving his studio to go to Golden Harvest. Actor Jimmy Wang Yu, who was reputed to have strong triad ties, was called in to help negotiate a deal. To

Charlie Yeung is a crazy mixed-up kid in Wong Kar-Wai's *Fallen Angels*.

return the favor, Chan agreed to appear in this bizarre New Year's epic (and later, *The Prisoner*). Come to think of it, Jimmy Wang Yu probably assembled a lot of projects that way. The result is this completely insane comedy adventure of the "mo lai tau" (nonsense comedy) subgenre, typical of the films of director Chu Yen-ping *(Pink Force Commando)*, but atypical of anything else.

During World War II, the Japanese army in Taiwan captures five generals of the Allied forces. Allied Intelligence assembles a team of commandos to rescue them before word gets out to the troops. Since James Bond, Rocky Balboa, and Karl Maka are all unavailable, they pick Captain Duan Yen (Jimmy Wang Yu) to assemble a squad and lead the mission to Luxemburg, where the generals are being held until they are shipped to Japan. Yen enlists bandit Sun (Sun Yueh), prison escape expert Greased Lightning (Gou Ling Feng), New York wrestlers Sammy (Jackie Chan) and Emily (Pearl Chang), gambler Billy (David Tao), outlaw Lily (Brigitte Lin), and comic soldiers Baldy (Fong Ching) and Shi-Tou (Hui Bat Liu). On the way to their objective, the motley crew is captured by a cannibal amazon tribe ruled by a man in a tuxedo (Adam Cheng). After escaping, they spend the night in a ghost town full of mah-jongg-playing ghosts (who cheat) and hopping vampires. They arrive at the Japanese camp and find all the enemy dead, and the generals gone—taken away by a Nazi army in gladiator armor driving 1970s stock cars. Jackie Chan arrives just in time to save the—well no, everybody's pretty much dead already.

The editing on the English dubbed version is very choppy, and obviously there's some missing footage, but one wonders what else this movie could possibly contain. It already has exploding battlefield scenes, musical numbers, professional wrestling, a trick-shot strip tease, Chinese Scotsmen, amazons, exploding cigars, kung fu fighting, cans, floating heads, bazookas, road warriors, and Chinese Nazis. Relentlessly goofy, the horrible script and direction are nevertheless worth at least one viewing, if only as a freak-show curiosity. Perhaps the weirdest part is that it has the kind of melancholy ending typical of secret-mission war movies. A climactic showdown between Chan and Wang Yu isn't as exciting as you'd expect. The music includes cues from *Planet of the Apes, Sorcerer,* and *Halloween 2. AKA: Mai nei dak Gung Dui; Mi ni te Gong Dui; Dragon Attack; Mini Special Force.* ♫♫

1984 89m/C *TW* Jimmy Wang Yu, Brigitte Lin, Pearl Chang, Jackie Chan, Sun Yueh, Adam Cheng, Jung Ysao Shao, Hui Bat Liu, Fong Ching, David Tao, Gou Ling Feng, Lee Kwan, Paul Chang, Chen Hung Lieh, Violet Lee, Chin Ti, Cheng Fu Hung, Wong Ma Lee, Kon Tak Mun. **D:** Chu Yen-ping. **W:** Wei Hsing. **C:** Liao Ching-song. **VHS, DVD**

Fatal Blade

In the middle of an exchange between Los Angeles yakuza head Kenji Ryujin (Kentaro Shimizu) and a top drug lord, gun-toting thieves burst in and steal everything. Bronson's gang has been robbing the yakuza for too long. They send top assassin Domoto (Kiyoshi Nakajo) to L.A. to take revenge. Domoto is a modern samurai, whose weapon is a katana known as the Fatal Blade. On a stakeout of Bronson's operations, British-born LAPD detective Richard Fox (Gary Daniels) catches Domoto breaking in and almost putting his sword through Bronson (ex-football pro Victor Rivers). Domoto makes a break from deportation, and after a long car chase, Ryujin arrives and shoots Fox's partner Frank. Thinking Domoto did the shooting, Fox is determined to catch the wily assassin. Bronson wants Domoto's head as well, threatening to start a citywide war with the yakuza.

Meanwhile, Domoto is still after Bronson, and also promises to get the man who killed the sister of Saemi Aoki (Seiko Matsuda), the woman who helped him escape from the law. Ryujin tells Fox where Domoto is staying (apparently between frames, as this information is not part of their conversation), but as Fox catches up with the assassin, thugs break in and try to kill them both. But it's not Bronson's men—in fact, it's a gang hired by Ryujin, who have been staging the robberies all along. Meanwhile, Fox's boss turns out to be on Bronson's payroll. The more Fox works on the case, the more he begins to think that he and Domoto should be on the same side.

It's not clear why there aren't more co-productions between Japanese and American companies, but this is a pretty good direct-to-video action film that indicates there should be more in the future. A separate crew, directed by Ichiro Ishikawa, shot scenes in Kyoto, and the Japanese characters speak Japanese amongst themselves. Borrowing ideas from *The Killer,* it's hard to tell whether the real hero is Gary Daniels (whose accent makes it difficult to accept him as a tough L.A. cop) or Kiyoshi Nakajo. Daniels only has three kickboxing scenes, but they're well choreographed. Kentaro Shimizu makes a standout villain, cackling evilly at his every misdeed. Cinematographer Michael Goi does a great job making this look like a more expensive production. *AKA: Gedo.* ♫♫♪

2000 (R) 99m/C *JP/US* Gary Daniels, Kiyoshi Nakajo, Eric Lutes, Victor Rivers, Kentaro Shimizu, Seiko Matsuda, Barry Sattels, Cuba Gooding Sr., Jack McGee, Masaki Umeda, Loridawn Messuri, Hiroki Matsukata. **D:** Talun Hsu. **W:** Simon Tse, Bill Zide, Nao Sakai, Talun Hsu (story). **C:** Michael Goi. **M:** Robert Douglas. **VHS, DVD**

Fatal Flying Guillotine

The title weapons here are clay pots about the size of big planters, lined with mechanical spinning teeth, and mounted on chains that seem to follow the will of the thrower. They can behead two men at once at about 50 yards, and to the Ching Dynasty characters of this movie they represent a weapon so fierce that he who holds them might control the destiny of the country. Unfortunately they belong to a grizzled old bastard who has little to do but hang around and behead whoever wanders along.

Everybody has an angle in *Fatal Flying Guillotine* and every one of those angles is bad—all except for that of Carter Wong, the extremely loyal son of a dying woman who travels to a Shaolin monastery to request a holy book that might cure her. Instead, Wong gets involved in courtly intrigue involving the monks, a prince who would like to be king, and the old man, who sits alone on a stage like a character from a David Lynch movie in his very own "Valley of No Return," quietly fondling his toothy pots until people wander into his yard so he can kill them. The plot of *Fatal Flying Guillotine* is so convoluted that one is amazed so much of the story can make it in and still leave time for Wong's unbelievably fluid kung fu, his arms swinging like windmills. Makes you weep for how little John Carpenter used Wong in *Big Trouble in Little China*.

The oddest thing about *Fatal Flying Guillotine*, though, is its current DVD release from World Video, which seems to be missing a reel at the very end and gives us instead a bizarre, vaguely English printed placard, read aloud with a totally different translation, neither of which makes much sense. But here's a question: If you're going to give us a placard that tells us how it all ends, why not at least pretend the ending was a happy one? —*JH* **AKA:** *Aau Yeung Huet Dik Ji; Yin Yang Xie Di Zi; Fatal Flying Guillotines.* 🐲🐲

1977 (G) 90m/C *HK* Chan Sing, Carter Wong, Mang Hoi, Yang Sha-fei, Chan Siu-pang, Cheung Lik. **D:** Raymond Lui. **W:** Raymond Lui. **VHS, DVD**

Fatal Needles vs. Fatal Fists

Police Captain Chow Lung (Lo Lieh) and his Vice Captain Ming Hu (Wang Tao) are the Batman and Robin of Old China, busting the bad guys with their fatal fists and flying feet. While fighting the Four Devils gang, Ming makes a mistake that gets Chow killed, leaving him open for a strike by Gold Spear Chow Tin-pao. His partner's death hits Ming hard, and he hits the bottle even harder, ending up broke in a brothel. Wandering wounded after a fight, Ming passes out on the steps of Virtue House kung fu school in Yung Kin Town. Ming takes a job at the school under the name Chin Chai, but is still in a funk.

Rascal Chin Pi-yau (action director Tommy Lee) comes with some men to threaten Master Chen (Chui Chung Hei)—who is the town magistrate—on behalf of his boss, bandit chief Chung Tung (Chang Yi). Chen is too ill to fight back against the brigands, and Ming has sworn not to fight again. Chen's children Kan (Lung Fong) and Sai-yu (Hwa Ling) are captains of the guard, and head off to arrest Chung Tung, but they can't deal with Chung's fatal flying acupuncture needles, which can paralyze a man from across a room. Chung and his men continue to harass the Chens unopposed. Ming still refuses to fight, until inevitably something drives him too far: his friend Sou-fu (Ko Saio Pao) is injured defending him. Then Ming goes into action to smash Chung's drug smuggling ring—but will he be able to deal with Chung's golden needles?

Director Lee Tso Nam does a fine job of subtly using visual symbolism to emphasize the dramatic situation. There are also a few scenes that stop the movie dead so that a character can deliver a passionate speech. Once the dramatic intricacies of plot are taken care of during the middle section, the film gets down to some fine kung fu—which also presents an interesting problem to solve, and Wang Tao displays his distinctive fighting style. Chang Yi's killers (Ricky Cheng and Cheng Fu Hung) dress in the flamboyant style common to the kung fu superheroes in Chang Cheh movies. Ko Saio Pao, the large character actor who usually plays idiot comic foils named "Fatty," actually has a heroic and sympathetic role here, and does well with it. Lo Lieh does quite a bit to make his small role memorable, playing with the brim of his hat and so forth. The final battle takes place in a lovely set representing a hilltop with a sunset background. **AKA:** *Fatal Needles Fatal Fist.* 🐲🐲🐲

1980 93m/C *TW* Wang Tao, Chang Yi, Hwa Ling, Lo Lieh, Tommy Lee, Lung Fong, Chui Chung Hei, Cheung Pang, Ko Saio Pao, Cheng Fu Hung, Ricky Cheng, Sit Hon, Lee Keung, Cho Boon Feng, Shih Ting Ken, Ma Fat-yan, Sit Cheung-man, Au Lap-bo, Kwan Hung. **D:** Lee Tso Nam. **W:** Chang Seng-yi. **C:** Chuang Yin-chien. **M:** Chou Fu-liang. **VHS, DVD**

Fear Faith Revenge 303

An above-average Thai horror movie, this one has a few surprises in its bag of tricks. In

1960, another class of privileged young men arrives at St. George College boarding school. All are sons of wealthy parents with the exception of Chaidan Niramol (Artid Ryu), a green "quota student" sent from a rural church. St. George is run by strict discipline, with much of the punishment handed out by fearsome headmaster Waeng (Charlie Sang-kawes). Freshmen also have to watch out for the tyrannical upperclassmen. Under these tough conditions, Chai quickly bonds with his roommates: allergic Sihnsamut (Songwut Sricherdchutm), garrulous Ghusolsarng (Ananda Everingham), tough Ponghet (Parinya Intachai), and the even more brash bully Traisoon (Paul Carey).

Surrounded by young men trying to live up to the legacy of prestigious alumni, Chai wonders why he's there. One picture stands out in the alumni hall—that of Prince Daovadueng Sira, an exemplary student whom Mr. Vivat (Michael Pupart) explains shot himself to death at a young age. Partially to get the attention of Waeng's daughter Numkang (Taya Rogers), who admires the late student like a pop star, Ghu starts up a Prince Dueng Fan Club, and the boys begin to investigate his death. Unable to gather much information, they—along with Numkang—decide to use a Thai ouija board to hold a séance. They find the ghost charming (in Thai and English), but he reveals that his death was actually a murder. After the séance, odd things begin to happen. Numkang finds one of Brother Vivat's beloved cats killed, and Chai has visions of Dueng's murder. The 1952 registration book lists only 110 students—Dueng and five others are missing. When Trai dies under suspicious circumstances, and an upperclassman is electrocuted in the showers, the Prince Dueng Fan Club fears there may be a madman on the loose.

Part of the strength of this thriller is that it takes the time to establish itself as a normal drama about boarding-school life before it gets down to its spook business. The talented cast is introduced and we get comfortable with them, then the chills escalate until the climax. Until then, it's hard to tell whether this will be a mild ghost story, a lurid slasher flick, or both. This effort to keep the audience off balance is also a bit of the weakness—while trying to guess who is guilty of what and why, you may lose your grip on the film a bit. But stick with it. There are some genuine shocks, a few good gags, and plenty of twists thrown in before the end. *AKA: 303 Fear Faith Revenge.* 🐉🐉🐉

1998 90m/C *TH* Artid Ryu, Ananda Everingham, Taya Rogers, Parinya Intachai, Paul Carey, Songwut Sricherdchutm, Charlie Sang-kawes, Rerng-rit Wisamon, Michael Pupart, Chart-yodom Hiranyadthiti, Areewan Chatutong, Suchao Pong-wilai, Apichart Chuskui, Jesdaporn Pholdee. **D:** Somching Srisupap. **W:** Cher Kori. **C:** Taweesak Kumphati. **DVD**

Fearless Dragons

Young master Wong is employed to defend a treasure being transported to refugees for Chief Wang. The convoy crosses paths with a pedicab driver (Phillip Ko) with travelling student (Leung Kar-yan) in short pants and Western suit. A gang of bandits attack and make off with the treasure cart. The pedicab driver and passenger rescue it from the bandits, but are mistaken for bandits themselves when the party catches up—and the treasure chest turns out to be empty!

Mr. Pedicab and passenger continue to quarrel, trying to capture each other to claim the reward from Captain Yu. After getting in various scrapes together (at one point hiding out under a couple's bed on their wedding night, which ends with the fat bride crushing her little husband), the pair team up to catch the real thief.

The team of Leung and Ko are good at both fighting and knockabout comedy, but both performers were capable of better things. Leung was a regular fixture in Sammo Hung's films of the period, and all three leads ended up directing later in their careers. The overall attitude is tiresomely juvenile, though there's damn fine fighting in the finale. Though apparently set in old China, references are made to modern superheroes and the movie *Midnight Express*. The tape version was hosted by Rudy Ray Moore as part of the "Shaolin Dolemite Collection," but the DVD is much more straightforward. *AKA: Jeung Ying Hung Chung Ying Hung; Shi Ying Xiong Chong Ying Xiong; Fearless Dragon; Two on the Road.* 🐉🐉

1979 83m/C *HK* Leung Kar-yan, Phillip Ko, Johnny Wang, Siu Gam, Chan Lau, Dai Sai Aan, Kong Do. **D:** Lee Chiu. **C:** Lo Wan-shing. **M:** Ng Tai Kong. **VHS, DVD**

Fearless Fighters

Here we have a rousing adventure full of impossible feats and enthusiasm. "Lightning Whipper" Chun Chen-chow guards a gold shipment meant to aid impoverished peasants. Bandits of the Eagle Claw Clan interrupt his convoy, but his whip is too much for them. Clan member Ko-fat (Peter Yang) tries to get swordsman Lieh Fong (Yee Yuen) to help him by saying their brothers were killed without provocation, but Lieh won't buy it, so Ko-fat attacks with only his Golden Archers. All but Chun are slain in the attack, and he's forced to retreat, but suspicious Lieh has followed them. He takes the gold chest away, planning to restore the clan's name by returning it. But before he can, Lieh is arrested for the theft, and Ko-fat closes in to steal the chest again. Lieh's brother and son flee, and heroic swordswoman Lady Tieh (Cheung Ching-Ching)

arrives in time to save Little Chow-sun. Meanwhile, the wounded Chun survives long enough to make it home in time to pass on his whip to his children Yi-chun and Mulan, and tell them what happened. To learn more, Yi-chun breaks Lieh out of jail. The trio, followed by Lady Tieh, makes off for Ko-fat's hideout at Dragon Star Inn. But to get there the heroes must fight their way through the Eagle Claw's army of hired killers, including the infamous Soul Fingers, Sword of All Swords Chow Lung, the Dragon Razor Brothers, the Vampire Phantoms, and the twin swords of Loner, the One Man Army.

The actual martial arts on display are minimal, but the fight scenes are marvelously staged and full of imaginative gimmicks and camera tricks. At one point Lieh is crippled in a duel with Loner, and his master replaces the damaged limbs with special artificial ones. At Dragon Star Inn, when a cup of wine is thrown at him he demonstrates that his skills are still up to snuff by catching the liquid in his own cup, without spilling a drop! A disappointment for hard-core kung fu fans, but this is otherwise an entertaining adventure flick. This is likely to actually be the U.S. release of Joseph Kuo's

1969 *Son of Swordsman.* The English dub supervised by James Hong is very well done. The music tracks are all from classic Hollywood studio libraries. 🎵🎵🎵

1969 83m/C *TW* Yee Yuen, Chiang Nan, Cheung Ching-Ching, Peter Yang, Ng Ming Choi, Chen Hung Lieh. **D:** Wu Ming Hung. **W:** Hsiang Yang. **VHS**

Fearless Hyena

Jackie Chan's family has gone into hiding to avoid persecution by the evil Ching Dynasty. Jackie's grandfather (James Tien) is a former kung fu master; Jackie has burgeoning skill in the arts, but doesn't like to practice much. Nor does he like to work. When he goes to find a job, he turns down "honest" work, and ends up as an "instructor" at a kung fu school formed by a Japanese snake-oil salesman. He pretends to be one of the master's lesser pupils, while beating up the masters from other schools. In this way, his boss earns money on bets and other scams. Unfortunately, all this fighting also attracts the attention of the evil Ching warlords.

Jackie Chan submits to some rigorous training in *Fearless Hyena.*

They track down Jackie's grandfather and kill him, leaving Jackie to avenge his family.

One of the best of the early Chan pictures, this one focuses on what would become Jackie's trademark style of kung fu comedy. (Not surprising, since Chan both wrote and directed the picture as well as starred.) The flick features a number of different prop sequences, as the master trains Jackie. The fight sequences in the film are superior to most of its day, and far better than the work in the sequel. Listen for pieces of music from *Superman: The Movie* in the soundtrack. —SS **AKA:** *Siu Kuen Gwaai Chiu; Xiao Quan Guai Zhao; Revenge of the Dragon.* 🐉🐉🐉

1979 136m/C *HK* Jackie Chan, James Tien, Yam Sai-kwoon, Lee Kwan, Chan Wai Lau, Cheng Fu Hung, Ma Cheung, Wong Chi Sang, Eagle Han Ying, Gam Ying-yat, Dean Shek, Ricky Cheng. **D:** Jackie Chan. **W:** Jackie Chan, Lo Wei. **C:** Chan Wing Shu. **VHS, DVD**

Fearless Hyena 2

This film starts with a similar premise to the Jackie Chan's original *Fearless Hyena.* Chan Lung's family has gone underground (and split into many pieces) to avoid the deadly Heaven and Earth (Yam Sai-kwoon and Kwan Yung Moon)—two bad-ass kung fu killers who are systematically tracking down and killing members of Lung's Yin-Yang clan.

Lung's cousin Ah Tung (Austin Wai) is a wastrel, who prefers to build elaborate machines to do his chores for him. His best friend is a slight man called Frog (Hon Gwok-choi), and the two of them spend a lot of time gambling and running fairly harmless scams to make money. When Lung's father (James Tien) is killed by Heaven and Earth, Ah Lung finds Tung, and determines to make a fighter out of him. Lung teaches Tung and Frog the Yin-Yang clan's secret kung fu. Unfortunately, as in the first film, this attracts the attention of the bad guys. When Heaven and Earth kill those dear to Chan and his cousin, the two surviving members of the Yin-Yang clan take their revenge on Heaven and Earth using clever traps and deadly kung fu.

Made during the "Jackie War" between Lo Wei and Golden Harvest, *Fearless Hyena 2* shows little of the wit or originality of the first film in the series. Jackie Chan worked on it under duress while contract disputes went on between the studios, with Chan leaving the project as soon as their differences were hammered out. Lo then completed the film using doubles for Chan when necessary, and going out of his way to insult Jackie in the dubbing. Much of the fighting in the film is made up of outtakes from the earlier picture. Jackie's part

in the final battle against the bad guys, for instance, is a virtual repeat of the climax of *Hyena 1.* (This made easier by the same actor being the villain in both films.) Chan unsuccessfully sued Lo Wei to try to prevent its release. In the Chinese tradition of lifting music, bits of the *Raiders of the Lost Ark* score can be heard during the soundtrack. This flick loses a half bone from the rating just for the sheer disappointment of being a bad sequel to a good film. —SS **AKA:** *Lung Tang Foo Yeuk; Long Teng Hu Yue: Fearless Hyena Part II.* 🐉🐉

1980 91m/C *HK* Jackie Chan, Austin Wai, Yam Sai-kwoon, Kwan Yung Moon, Hon Gwok-choi, Chan Wai Lau, James Tien, Dean Shek. **D:** Chan Chuen, Lo Wei. **VHS, DVD**

Female Convict Scorpion: Jailhouse 41

The second Scorpion movie (following *Female Convict #701: Scorpion*), based on Toru Shinohara's hit manga series, finds Scorpion Matsu (Meiko Kaji) finally let out to see the sun after a year chained up in solitary confinement. Warden Goda (Fumio Watanabe), who hates Scorpion for gouging out his eye in an escape attempt, would be content to let her rot underground forever, but he's hoping to get a promotion by impressing a prison inspector. Spoiling everything, Scorpion strikes during the inspection, nearly blinding Goda's other eye, scaring the piss out of the inspector (literally), and causing a riot. Scorpion stoically endures the resulting punishment and humiliation foisted upon her by the guards and inmates, marking her enemies and waiting for another chance to strike back. Her chance comes soon, and she joins a pack of convicts on the run. The seven escapees take shelter in a ghost town half buried by a volcanic eruption, which is inhabited only by a crazy old woman. The old crone helpfully places a curse on Scorpion's enemies before dying—hardly necessary, as Scorpion is enough of a curse by herself. Their numbers dwindle on the road (along with a few guards), until the women take over a tour bus and race toward a showdown with their pursuers.

Jailhouse 41 rises far above most WIP (Women in Prison) flicks via the stylishly surreal direction of Shunya Ito, and the near-supernatural portrayal of its main character. Meiko Kaji makes an unforgettable impression as Scorpion—a silent, beautiful, monstrous angel of destruction. Ito occasionally illustrated her view of things with striking visual interludes. Her convict companions are no saints, notably Kayoko Shiraishi as insane bitch Oba. But the men in

the film are the root of all the misery—portrayed as craven beasts, from the Gestapo-like guards to a group of touring war veterans who reminisce about the "good old days" when they invaded China. The gory violence and brutality in the film are not casually drawn, but to the point. Kaji was a natural choice to play Sasori (Scorpion), seemingly bound for prison after playing many roles in yakuza and juvenile delinquent pictures. Reportedly, she insisted the character be changed from the foul-mouthed hellion of the comics version into the brooding antihero on display here. She found redemption after starring in the first four Scorpion movies by moving on to star in the Lady Snowblood samurai movies. Followed by *Female Convict Scorpion: Department of Beasts,* and three other sequels. *AKA: Joshuu Sasori—Dai 41 Zakkyobo; Joshu Sasori: Daishujuichi Zakkyobo; Scorpion: Female Prisoner Cage #41.* 🐉🐉🐉🐉

1972 89m/C *JP* Meiko Kaji, Kayoko Shiraishi, Yukie Kagawa, Hosei Komatsu, Hiroko Isayama, Fumio Watanabe. **D:** Shunya Ito. **W:** Shunya Ito, Hiro Matsuda, Norio Konami, Toru Shinohara (manga). **C:** Masao Shimizu. **M:** Shunsuke Kikuchi. **DVD**

Fight Back to School

This early Stephen Chow comedy is a weird mix of ideas from American cop movies like *48 HRS.,* comedies like *Back to School,* and Kurosawa's *Stray Dog!* Star Chow (Chow) is a tough Hong Kong cop with the SDU who has trouble working with a team, always acting like Rambo. His only hope of getting a promotion is a secret mission for the Commissioner (Barry Wong): the top cop's gun disappeared while a group of college students toured his offices in RHKP headquarters, and as Chow is the only cop who looks young enough for the job, he wants him to go undercover as a student to get the gun back. A target for students and teachers alike, the new guy finds it tough sledding. The only friendly face belongs to the crazy school janitor, Tso Tat-wah (Ng Man-Tat), who turns out to be another undercover cop. Chow is a horrible student, and the only thing keeping him from flunking out is the beautiful school counselor Miss Ho (Sharla Cheung). With her inspiring tutelage, Chow immediately becomes a genius and big man on campus. Unfortunately, his nerdy pal Turtle Wong (Gabriel Wong) takes advantage of this by setting Chow up as a school triad leader behind his back. This not only gets him in trouble with the law, but with rival triad Johnny. Actually, school bully Johnny swiped the gun, and his big brother is triad Teddy Big (Roy Cheung). Suddenly, Tat knows where Teddy is hiding a cache of

illegal arms, and he and Chow go to capture the evidence. But Chow accidentally leaves Tat behind to be caught, and is forced to walk into a trap set by Teddy's gang.

The climax is set within a maze set up in the school gymnasium, with Teddy's gang chasing Chow and the students around in it. Chow has to learn to lead the kids effectively to get everyone out of danger. A huge hit, films like this one made Chow the biggest Hong Kong star since Jackie Chan. Like his Big Brother Chan, he has the end credits running over outtakes. Followed by two sequels. *AKA: To Hok Wai Lung; Tao Xue Wei Long; Escape from School Mighty Dragon.* 🐉🐉🐉

1991 97m/C *HK* Stephen Chow, Sharla Cheung, Ng Man-Tat, Roy Cheung, Paul Chun, Karel Wong, Gabriel Wong, Barry Wong, Yuen King-Tan, Dennis Chan. **D:** Gordon Chan. **W:** Barry Wong, Gordon Chan. **C:** Cheng Siu-keung. **M:** Wong Bong. **VHS, DVD**

Fight Back to School 2

A perfect example of Stephen Chow's mo lai tau ("nonsense") form of comedy, this sequel has him return as young-looking cop Chow Sing-sing, who is disturbed to find that his triumph in the first film goes unrewarded. His new superior Captain Lydia (Deannie Yip) doesn't like his attitude and demotes him to traffic cop, while taking an unaccountable shine to Chow's partner Tsao Tat-wah (Ng Man-Tat), whom she promotes to more serious duty. Fed up, Chow quits the force and uses the money saved for his marriage to Ho Ming (Sharla Cheung) to join Tat's assignment on his own. With a terrorist group planning to target the Adam Smith International School, Chow goes undercover as a student once again (under the name "Stephen Chow"), hiring his old classmate Turtle (Gabriel Wong) and his pals to help out, and Tat poses as "Prefect James Bond." While investigating student suspect Mark (Michael Chow)—who turns out to be another undercover—he is distracted by pretty classmate Sandy Lai (Athena Chu), despite the presence of her tough sister Jacky (Sarah Lee). Unfortunately, Ming happens to be Sandy's tutor, putting Chow in an uncomfortable position—which he might escape from, if not for his pal Tat's big mouth. When Chief Peter Lee (Michael Dinga) finds out what Chow is up to, even Tat and Lydia are removed from the case. But the terrorists take over the school, demanding their leader is released from prison, and only Chow is in a position to help.

There's just enough plot here for Chow and company to hang gags on. Sadly, not all of them work, and those based on Cantonese puns don't translate. But things keep moving along quick

enough, with enough good gags to keep things entertaining until the end. Ng Man-Tat makes a surprisingly good Terminator. An alternate edition begins with a superfluous seven-minute sequence of clips from the previous film. **AKA:** *To Hok Wai Lung 2; Tao Xue Wei Long 2.* 𝅘𝅥𝅘𝅥𝅘𝅥𝅭

1992 98m/C *HK* Stephen Chow, Ng Man-Tat, Athena Chu, Deannie Yip, Sharla Cheung, Gabriel Wong, Michael Chow, Sarah Lee, James Wong, Blackie Ko, Michael Dinga, Mark Houghton, Spencer Lam, Mark King, Indra Leech, Paul Fonoroff. **D:** Gordon Chan. **W:** Gordon Chan, John Chan, Yuen Kai-chi. **C:** Cheng Siu-keung. **M:** Mahmood Rumjahn. **VHS, DVD**

Fight Back to School 3

Just when you thought this series couldn't get any zanier, Wong Jing steps in as writer/director to twist the screws a bit looser. For starters, this one doesn't even have a school in it—instead we get Anita Mui ably filling the Sharon Stone role for an extended parody of *Basic Instinct*. Chow Sing-Sing (Stephen Chow) checks out of the hospital just in time to investigate the murder of Million Wong, who was killed in a way "similar to the story of a recent movie," according to Chow's superior officer, Dominic Lai (Leung Kar-yan). Chow just happens to be a dead ringer for Wong, and Lai forces him to take the victim's place to try to expose the killer. This angers fiancée Man (Sharla Cheung), both because Chow promised to give up undercover work, and because Wong's wife is the infamous Judy Tong (Mui). But it's Chow who ends up jealous, as it appears Judy prefers Man to him (!), while he also suspects Man may be cheating with Wong's best friend Taior Lam (Anthony Wong, who makes a fine entrance with a dead fox on his head). As this is a Wong Jing picture, of course he finds an excuse to bring some gambling into the script, giving Chow a chance to play the Saint of Gamblers again from his *God of Gamblers* sequels. But he also provides an actual mystery plot to go with all the tomfoolery. Though Nat Chan is a weak replacement for Ng Man-Tat as Chow's sidekick, Leung Kar-yan *(The Postman Fights Back)* seems to be having a marvelous time with his role, making Chow seem a bit tired in comparison. **AKA:** *To Hok Wai Lung Ji Lung Gwoh Gai Nin; Tao Xue Wei Long Guo Ji Nian.* 𝅘𝅥𝅘𝅥𝅘𝅥𝅭

1993 89m/C *HK* Stephen Chow, Anita Mui, Leung Kar-yan, Sharla Cheung, Anthony Wong, Nat Chan, Kathy Chow, Phillip Chan, Paul Chun, Stanley Fung, Mimi Chu, John Ching. **D:** Wong Jing. **W:** Wong Jing. **C:** Gigo Lee. **M:** Lowell Lo. **VHS, DVD**

Fight, Zatoichi, Fight!

This is one of the more lighthearted Zatoichi adventures, but still brimming with swordplay and drama. Blind masseur Ichi (Shintaro Katsu) joins a pilgrimage of blind men to visit a temple. A gang of mercenaries from the Monju clan is after him. When they attack, they strike a young mother who gets in the way. Ichi promises the dying woman that he will deliver the baby to its father, Umasuke. Zatoichi proposes that the fight be postponed until after he finishes with his task, but he finds the mercenaries without scruples, and he's forced to defend himself. As the blind swordsman leaves a trail of diapers across Japan, Boss Hangoro's men join the remaining Monjus in the hunt.

Much of this borders on being too cute, but never goes too far in that direction. At one point Ichi indulges his gambling habit to raise some diaper money. When he catches his opponents cheating, he asks them to die quietly so as not to wake the baby. Of course, he ends up growing attached to the kid, but when the assassins close in for a showdown (using torches to confuse his sharp senses), he realizes his life is much too dangerous to involve a child. A premonition of the Katsu-produced Lone Wolf and Cub series, this wouldn't be the last time Zatoichi would play babysitter. The opening is a great little cameo: while the titles appear, the camera focuses only on Katsu's feet, then watch as the blind man gingerly steps around a pile of dung. **AKA:** *Zatoichi Kesshi Tabi; Zatoichi Fighting Caper.* 𝅘𝅥𝅘𝅥𝅘𝅥𝅘𝅥𝅭

1964 /C *JP* Shintaro Katsu, Hizuro Takachiho. **D:** Kenji Misumi, Tokuzo Tanaka. **W:** Seiji Hoshikawa, Tetsuo Yoshida, Masaatsu Matsumura, Kan Shimozawa (story). **M:** Akira Ifukube. **VHS, DVD**

A Fighter's Blues

Superstar Andy Lau's 100th production does not live up to expectations. Lau plays Mong Fu, a boxer better known as Tiger. After serving 13 years in prison, Tiger is released and begins searching for lost love Pim (Intira Charoenpura). He discovers that Pim died several years before, leaving behind their daughter, Ploy (Apichaya Thanatthanapong). Fu contacts Ploy, who is living in an orphanage run by Sister Mary (Tokako Tokiwa), and they tentatively try to develop a relationship, aided by the relentlessly upbeat and hip Sister Mary. Still hanging over Tiger, however, is the shadow of the crime that sent him to prison.

Lau looks downcast most of the time, as if the director was constantly whispering "You've got the blues" in his ear, and rarely seems to

interact with the other players. Despite this handicap, the first 80 minutes are fairly effective. Director Daniel Lee *(Black Mask)* intersperses footage of scudding clouds, filmed in black-and-white, along with freeze frames from Tiger's earlier boxing days of glory to set off the modern-day color footage (top-notch cinematography by Keung Kwok-Man). The overall pace and tone convey the idea that Tiger is down and depressed, but struggling to overcome his past and come to grips with the reality of fatherhood and the possibility of a romance. The plot does not always make sense but the ride is enjoyable. Where the film falls apart is in the final fight sequence. It is so poorly shot that it's nearly impossible to figure out what's happening and directed as if it were an MTV video, with quick cuts, odd camera angles, etc. To add insult to injury, and without giving away the ending for masochists who wish to push through to the end, let's just say the resolution of the film is confounding and irritating in the extreme, as well as being utterly unconvincing. —*PM **AKA:** A Foo; Ah Fu; A Hu.* 🐉🐉

2000 105m/C *HK* Andy Lau, Tokako Tokiwa, Intira Charoenpura, Apichaya Thanatthanapong, Chan Wing Chung. **D:** Daniel Lee. **W:** Cheung Chi-Sing, Daniel Lee. **C:** Keung Kwok-Man. **M:** Ridley Tsui, Henry Lai. **VHS, DVD**

Fighting Ace

After his parents are murdered for their copy of the San Te Martial Arts Manual, Fan Chi-kow (John Liu) is raised by servant Chung (Hon Siu) with one purpose: to become a kung fu expert and get revenge. Famous Master Yan (Kwan Yung Moon) is hired by Mr. Chin (Chui Chung Hei) to teach his worthless son Da-tung (Ching Kuo-chung) kung fu, so Chi-kow and Chung get jobs in the same household. Yan is happy to accept a student with some real promise, until the master catches him teaching the wrong student. Our heroes move on to become street vendors, taking rascally servant San (Wang Tai-lang) with them, and Chi-kow (whom the guy dubbing San calls "Chow-kee" most of the time) finds *two* new kung fu teachers—a gruff medicine hawker who teaches Butterfly Style, and a gruffer old man (Wu Ma, in a long shaggy wig) who teaches Fish Style. When Master Yan's daughter Shao-lan (Doris Lung) finds out about Chi-kow's kung fu two-timing, she exposes him by bringing the two teachers together. Now without a teacher, Chi-kow is surprised when a new teacher comes seeking him. But unbeknownst to our hero, his latest teacher is none other than the man who killed his parents.

Inevitably Fan Chi-kow learns the truth and fights the villain. To satisfy dramatic structure,

at the point when the bad guy uses his secret Shadow Punch (illustrated with a prism lens effect), the hero should have retreated to learn a counter-technique from all three of his former teachers. But for some reason the filmmakers settle for wrapping things up quickly. The production may have just run out of time and/or money, and since many of these independent old-school kung fu flicks were shot in sequence and made up as the went along, it's likely the three actors had already moved on to other projects. John Liu is a fine kicker in the manner of Delon Tan, but his form sometimes looks a little sloppy, even at the end after all his training. There are a few imaginative moves in the choreography, but otherwise the fighting is standard. The occasional modern car can be seen driving past behind one of the authentic period settings. The locations are sometimes beautiful, with shooting taking place in Taiwan or possibly Korea (Korean star Hwang Jang Lee served as production manager). **AKA:** *Kung Fu Ace; 36 Strikes of Kung Fu.* 🐉🐉

1979 85m/C *HK* John Liu, Doris Lung, Hon Siu, Ching Ching, Wang Tai-lang, Li Min Lang, Wu Ma, Kao Ming, Chui Chung Hei, Ching Kuo-chung, Chen Chiu, Hsiao Ho, Kwan Yung Moon, Wong Man-chuen. **D:** Richard Chen. **W:** Chu Hsiang Kan. **C:** Chen Chong-yuan. **M:** Chou Fu-liang. **DVD**

Fighting for Love

Star power carries the day in this feathery romance. Deborah Fok (Sammi Cheng) and Veg Chiang (Tony Leung Chiu-Wai) "meet cute" when their vehicles collide. She's a high-strung businesswoman; he's the owner of a successful fast-food shop that specializes in bull-organ soup. They fight about the accident until one night when their emotions combust into alcohol-fueled passion. Deborah thinks a relationship is in the offing, but discovers that Veg has a girlfriend, Mindy (Niki Chow), who's a television star. Deborah and Veg become platonic friends, but after prompting from Veg's mother, though, Deborah decides to "fight for her love." Whom will Veg choose?

The humor is prehistoric—the main characters smoke constantly and try getting drunk as an excuse to have one last night of passion; other characters seem to have fun poked at them because of their mental deficiencies; one character jokes about having an abortion; and so forth. Some comedic asides provoke laughter solely because of the facial expressions of Tony Leung. Yet from the very first frame, the bright color scheme, breezy tone, and cheery musical score (with several catchy songs and original music by Lincoln Lo) all combine to paint an alternate reality where nothing but the heart should be taken seriously. And those all-too-predictable romantic moments work because the performances of Tony Leung and Sammi Cheng are grounded in reality. Although this light-as-air tale threatens to clunk to earth several times, director Joe Ma manages to keep it just barely inflated until it puffs to an agreeable conclusion. —*PM AKA: Tung Gui Mat Yau; Tong Ji Mi You.* 🐉🐉🐉

2001 101m/C *HK* Sammi Cheng, Tony Leung Chiu-Wai, Niki Chow, Joe Lee, Ha Ping, Chan Man-lei, Sammy. **D:** Joe Ma. **W:** Joe Ma, Aubrey Lam, Taures Chow. **C:** Cheung Man-po. **M:** Lincoln Lo. **VHS, DVD**

Filthy Guy

Young Master Chen Yu-ling (Carter Wong) is a cruel bastard. He invites neighbors like the brothers Wen Hu and Wen Pau over to practice kung fu, knowing full well that he's much better. When Pau dies of the wounds Chen inflicted, brother Hu comes back at night seeking revenge, but accidentally kills the elder Chen. Feng shui expert Fung Ma-chen (Dean Shek) tells Chen to bury his father on a certain hillside so that one day he'll be king. But it just so happens that Hsu Yen-ching, father of the servant Yun-chang—whom everyone calls Dirty (Sammo Hung)—is already buried there, and Chen has to settle for a nearby location and a destined post as general. Believing his future throne stolen from him, Chen determines to kill simpleminded Dirty Hsu.

Dirty escapes and enters a Buddhist temple as a layman. While the abbot teaches Hsu kung fu, Chen amasses more power, conquering other territories through duplicity and coercion. Chen's soldiers transporting captive Marshal Ku Shi-sin stop at the temple, and when they try to bully him, Dirty beats the lot of them and frees the prisoner. The abbot dies from wounds received in the fight, and Hsu decides to go look for the marshal to join his rebellion against the Yang Dynasty. On the way, he picks up some followers: his old friend Kwai (Yueh Hua), and two fighters named Little Bee and Little Swallow. Some soldiers trick the group into following them right into Chen's palace. They manage to fight their way out, but Little Bee is captured—and revealed as a girl! With Swallow disguised as a girl (easily, since she's a girl, too!), Kwai infiltrates the palace during the celebration, as Chen prepares to take Bee (who is Ku's daughter, and Dirty's childhood girlfriend) as his ninth wife, and they manage to sneak her out by switching costumes. They continue their trek, only to find themselves surrounded by Chen's soldiers, whereupon Hsu succeeds in goading Chen into a one-on-one duel.

Poorly filmed, with several shots out of focus, this knockabout kung fu comedy is rescued by Hung's personality and choreography. Obviously patterned after Curly Howard, Dirty Hsu is one of Sammo's better comic characterizations from his early years as a star. To be sure, the humor is as broad as the Yangtze, but there are some moments of inspired nonsense, such as when Hsu gets the idea of catching fish using his head as bait, or when the monks of the monastery are awakened by Hsu playfully ringing a huge bell with his skull. When cornered, Dirty Hsu is saved by calling a herd of cows to his aid, not unlike Tarzan! Dean Shek contributes another of his whining sycophant characters. It may be silly, but can you prove this isn't really how the first Ming emperor ascended to the throne? *AKA: Return of the Secret Rivals; Emperor of the Filthy Guy.* 🐉🐉🐉

1980 87m/C *TW* Sammo Hung, Carter Wong, Yueh Hua, Dean Shek, Tse Ling-Ling, Wong Ling, Paul Wei, Weng Hsiao Hu, Ko Saio Pao. **D:** Kam Lung. **W:** Lam Wong-kwan. **C:** Li Shih-chieh. **DVD**

Final Fantasy: The Spirits Within

This isn't the first all-CGI animated film. No, those are old digital hat, and common as pixels in a bitmap these days. Plus, a lot of "live-action" films now contain a great deal of computer-created, -tweaked, -enhanced, or glossed-over imagery. However, *Final Fantasy* is the first such film that makes an effort to look as much as possible like it's *not* animated, using as much depth of detail as our present technology can handle.

After the Apocalypse we find an Earth under siege. Thirty-five years before, a big meteor landed that—like *The Blob*—contained an alien invasion. The invaders in this case are invisible monsters called Phantoms that can rip the soul right out of a human on contact. Humanity backs itself into blockaded cities, hiding out while working on a way to combat the threat—guns can destroy them, but the aliens are far too numerous. The military, under the leadership of General Hein (voiced by James Woods), has constructed a Death Star–type satellite in space and plans to blast away at the meteorite with their BFG until enough of the aliens are dead and they can mop up.

Opposing this plan is Dr. Sid (Donald Sutherland), who has been working for decades to identify and catalogue the actual life spirits of living things. His work points to the hypothesis that the planet itself has a spirit called Gaia that could become damaged in the attack. His alternative is a gizmo that will combine the wave patterns of eight unique life spirits into a pattern that will cancel out all of the entire Phantom menace at once. Assisting Sid is Dr. Aki Ross (Ming-Na), who has secretly become infected by a Phantom during one of her trips to hunt down the eight spirits. The fact that Sid's device has managed to contain the infestation using only five of the spirits supports his arguments, and Aki is allowed some time by the ruling council to find the remaining three spirits, aided by her old flame Grey Edwards (Alec Baldwin) and his Deep Eyes military squad. Hein, whose family was killed in an early Phantom attack, moves to undermine Sid's work. All the while, Aki's contact with the Phantom has been giving her recurring dreams, which she believes may hold the ultimate key to survival.

Director/writer Hironobu Sakaguchi manages to make a film that is both technically and artistically impressive. Viewers may be annoyed at being dropped into the middle of the complex story at first, but the film trusts you'll be smart enough to figure it out. The New Age hokum is part of the story without getting in the way. Donald Sutherland's character looks like Donald Pleasence and sounds like Johnny Quest's dad. Plus, his Dr. Sid is the character that always gets killed in these movies, but somehow he manages to avoid death, despite many hazardous opportunities. They've also managed to make Alec Baldwin look like Ben Affleck, and this may be the first film in which Steve Buscemi doesn't play the "funny-looking guy." The artwork is most convincing with the unfamiliar, like scenes of alien army's battling on another world. But they've also done incredible work with the film's biggest challenge: animating the human characters. At best, they look just like real people. At worst, they look like the puppets from *Thunderbirds*. The most amazing aspect of *Final Fantasy*, of course, is the leading lady's hair, which looks like she uses about a gallon of conditioner a day. Animators had to work so hard on Aki's hair that all the other characters' hair is slicked back tight. *AKA: Fainaru Fantaji.* 🐉🐉🐉

2001 (PG-13) 106m/C *JP/US* **V:** James Woods, Donald Sutherland, Ming-Na, Alec Baldwin, Steve Buscemi. **D:** Hironobu Sakaguchi. **W:** Al Reinert, Jeff Vintar, Hironobu Sakaguchi (story). **C:** Moto Sakakibara. **M:** Elliot Goldenthal, Ken Kitamura, Hideto Takarai. **VHS, DVD**

Final Justice

Stephen Chow took home a supporting actor Golden Horse for this early film role as Boy, a troubled young car thief/driver working for criminal Judge (Shing Fui-on). Danny Lee plays experienced cop Cheung, who clashes with his

hard-nosed new commanding officer Lo (Ricky Yi). Cheung arrests Boy for stealing a car which is subsequently found to have been used in the robbery of a casino where many people were killed. While Judge gathers weapons for an even bigger job, Lo decides to pin Boy for the murders and robbery, too. Cheung objects to the frame, but takes advantage of it by forcing Boy to help him track down Judge and his gang.

The American hit *48 HRS.* surely served as some inspiration for this story, but both films rely on the personality of their individual stars. The actors here don't provide big laughs, but they're more realistic than Eddie Murphy. Character bits add a lot of value, making for a richer film all around. When a thief named Smut is shot, some time is given to an attempt to save him, and then he's given a fitting funeral—burned in a car full of the pornography he loved. Chow deserves the praise he received for playing his role, though some of the compliments may have come from those who had seen his crazy antics on TV and were surprised to see him do so well in a straight part. William Ho stands out as well, playing a mean yet sympathetic thug. The action scenes are well done, if not outstanding. Not to be confused with the 1996 courtroom drama, also with Danny Lee in the cast. *AKA: Pik Lik Sin Fung; Pi Li Xian Feng; Thunderbolt Vanguard.* 🐉🐉🏮

1988 94m/C *HK* Danny Lee, Stephen Chow, Shing Fui-on, William Ho, Tommy Wong, Ricky Yi, Ken Lo, Victor Hon Kwan, Parkman Wong, Kirk Wong. *D:* Parkman Wong. *W:* James Fung. *C:* Cho Wai-kei. *M:* Melody Bank. **VHS, DVD**

Final Romance

Here's an interesting combination: two stars, the writers, and the director of youth-appeal action flick *Gen-Y Cops* reunite to make a romance. The difference is that Gordon Chan (the veteran director) here is one of the producers, and the director is Alan Mak, who made the previous year's *A War Named Desire.*

Mechanic Dik (Edison Chen) and rich girl Jean (Amanda Strang) meet up when they travel with their respective best friends, Sena (Sam Lee) and Faye (Au Sin-yee), to a ski resort in Japan. The reason for their journey is somber—Dik's brother Wu and Jean's sister Michelle rendezvoused secretly every Valentine's Day, and in the past year, both died. The last wish for each of them was to ask their siblings to make sure their ashes were brought to the hotel where the couple covertly met. Dik and Jean share some romantic moments before Jean's father (Simon Yam) arrives to take her home to Hong Kong and to her patient boyfriend, a physician. More complications await the potential pairing of Dik and Jean.

The script is entirely predictable and the main performances lack sufficient spark. Yet director Alan Mak consistently does an excellent job in framing the visuals and creating some memorable images. The snowscapes provide a fresh backdrop for the gentle romance, and are photographed attractively by Chan Chi-ying. Peter Kam's musical score is consistently engaging with its use of guitar and synthesizers. Edison Chen displays a comfortable chemistry with Sam Lee and seems at ease in playing a quiet and mostly introverted character. Amanda Strang looks winsome as Jean; Lois Kwok dubbed her dialogue (as acknowledged in the closing credits). Whether the dubbing was due to linguistic or thespian reasons is difficult to say. Actually, Sam Lee and Au Sin-yee (her first film role), who play the "best friends" of the main characters, emit more electricity in their smaller parts than the leads. Simon Yam plays the domineering father with his usual elan. Ter-ence Yin is effective here in a small part as the small-time gangster who owns the garage where Dik and Sena work. —PM *AKA: Yuen Mong Shu; Yuan Wang Shu; Wishing Tree.* 🐉🐉

2001 96m/C *HK* Edison Chen, Amanda Strang, Sam Lee, Au Sin-yee, Simon Yam, Terence Yin, Hui Siu-hung. *D:* Alan Mak. *W:* Felix Chong, Chan Kiu-ying. *C:* Chan Chi-ying. *M:* Peter Kam. **VHS, DVD**

The Final Winner

A tired story about triad gangs. Two gangs are in conflict; a pacifist leads one group, while a vicious gangster leads the other. Three buddies (Jackie Lui, Michael Tse, Benny Chan Ho-man) are stuck in the pacifist gang; one of them falls for a very sweet would-be prostitute (Grace Lam), and so on and so forth. Recounting the details of the plot would be pointless because potential viewers are likely to fall asleep despite the brief running time.

Die-hard Grace Lam admirers should be informed that the starlet stays fully dressed in this Category III production (so rated due to a generally positive presentation of the triad lifestyle). It seems like bad form to detail the defects of a production that is obviously so threadbare. Little compelling evidence exists as to the reason for the existence of this film. Evidently the cast and crew needed something to do for a couple of weeks and decided to make a movie, hoping to break even on the video sales. On the positive side, director Ally Wong knows how to elicit decent performances from actors with a wide range of ability, and it would be interesting to see what he could do with a decent script and a larger budget. The videotaped presentation looks like video (whether it's digital or not doesn't seem to matter), although cinematographer Cheng Chi-wing achieves some variations in lighting that make for a bit of variety in the visuals. —PM *AKA: Goo Waak Chai Ji Chut Wai; Gu Huo Zai Zhi Chu Wai.* 🏮

2001 80m/C *HK* Grace Lam, Jackie Lui, Michael Tse, Benny Chan Ho-man, Edward Mok, Chen Kuan-tai. *D:* Ally Wong. *W:* Siu Yat-ming. *C:* Cheng Chi-wing. **DVD**

Fireworks

Sad to say, but "Beat" Takeshi Kitano is probably most recognized for his guest spots as villains in movies like *Johnny Mnemonic* and *Merry Christmas Mr. Lawrence.* But to those in the know, Takeshi is the respected writer/director/actor responsible for a distinctive string of brutally violent and surprisingly serene crime films. Though physically he has more in common with Harvey Keitel, Takeshi's films have earned him

the reputation as the Dirty Harry of Japan. Beginning with 1989's *Violent Cop*, he always portrays basically the same character: a man with a high sense of honor who speaks little, but whose actions (and firearms) speak much louder than words. *Fireworks* uses the character and format of his previous work and takes them into even deeper, more poetic territory.

Takeshi plays police detective Nishi, an excellent cop with a penchant for sudden bursts of frightening violence. One day Nishi takes a break from a stakeout to visit his wife, who is dying from leukemia. While he's gone, their quarry (a vicious mass murderer) shoots Nishi's partner Horibe (Ren Osugi), and two other officers who try to apprehend him. While most cop movies would spend their remaining running time detailing Nishi's quest for vengeance, Takeshi has another agenda in mind, and Nishi kills the bad guy immediately.

However, Nishi has lost face for his dereliction of duty and resigns from the force. Horibe survives the attack, but also must resign, forced to spend the rest of his days in a wheelchair. Buried in medical bills, Nishi must borrow heavily from yakuza, and finds himself constantly harassed by collectors (whom he always manages to brush off—quickly and bloodily). Driven to desperation, Nishi carries out a plan to help set things right for those he feels he's wronged and give his wife one last happy holiday.

Many modern cop movies are comparable to samurai films, but Takeshi's almost exactly follow the pace and atmosphere of the best of that genre. Though images of Nishi's savage encounters with the greedy criminals tend to stick in the mind, also memorable are the many quieter scenes and themes in between, especially the subjects and results of Horibe's emerging artistic talent (artwork also contributed by Takeshi), and playful moments spent with Nishi and his wife (Kayoko Kishimoto). Like his predecessor Seijun Sezuki, Takeshi Kitano is an artist whose work continues to explore an ever-deepening but interconnected contrast between sadistic fury and natural beauty. Whether you watch his work to contemplate the meaning of destiny, or just to see people get shot in the head, you're sure to be rewarded for checking out one of his films. *AKA: Hana-bi.* ♫♫♫♫♡

1997 103m/C *HK* "Beat" Takeshi Kitano, Kayoko Kishimoto, Ren Osugi, Susumu Terajima. *D:* Takeshi Kitano. *W:* Takeshi Kitano. *C:* Hideo Yamamoto. *M:* Jo Hisaishi. **VHS, DVD**

First Option

A prequel to *Final Option* that shows what Michael Wong's character was doing before becoming a training officer for SDU. A raid under the command of customs division inspector Minnie Kwan (Gigi Leung) fails to nab the leader, Asian Ice Queen, when her heavily armed gang opens fire. Edgy cop Don Wong (Michael Wong) and his SDU team are called in, and they stay to assist when chief inspector Kwong of customs division takes over the case. Wong's old army buddy, DEA agent Rick, shows up to observe the operation. Tensions develop between the macho SDU cops and the largely female customs officers. Wong is also stressed out over his own men, who lack proper training and tend to be trigger-happy.

Some detective work by Kwan turns up a lead in the case, and when Wong backs up her play, the barriers between them start to come down. But despite a huge force that concentrates on hunting down the Queen, a better-prepared team of masked bandits gets to her first and abducts her, using the SDU's own tactics against them. Because of the weapons and tactics involved, Wong suspects the bandits are really rogue cops, but inspector Lau (Damian Lau) pulls the plug on the operation before he can do anything about it. But when Rick's assistant Albert goes missing, Kwan gets suspicious, and asks Wong and his team to help them investigate a cargo ship.

Despite a lot of gunfire, the film doesn't gain any kind of drive until it gets past the investigative part of the story and becomes a straight action vehicle—an hour into the film. When the cops attack the villains' island camp, there's a bit more excitement, though most of it just looks like guys in camouflage shooting other guys in camouflage out in the woods. Definitely not among director Gordon Chan's better films. Michael Wong is passionless and uninteresting, but matches the rest of the production. He dubs his own voice in both the Cantonese and English versions, and somehow picked up a Best Actor nomination in the HK Film Awards (Chinese audiences can't seem to detect a bad performance in English). Released in HK the same month as *Best of the Best* (another *Final Option* follow-up), *First Option* was the clear favorite. *AKA: Fei Foo; Fei Hu; Option 2.* ♫♡

1996 86m/C *HK* Michael Wong, Gigi Leung, Lam Wai-kin, Damian Lau, Michael Woods, Kim Yip, Kathy Chow, Albert Lau, Gregory Alan Wong. *D:* Gordon Chan. *W:* Chan Hing-ka, Gordon Chan. *C:* Horace Wong. *M:* Comfort Chan. **VHS, DVD**

First Strike

Although New Line Cinema tried to build excitement for their release of this Jackie Chan film by using the tag line "Fighting for America for the First Time," the hype is only partly correct. Jackie's by-now-familiar Hong Kong cop charac-

ter spends only the first act working for the CIA on a special assignment, tailing a suspect aboard a jet flight from Hong Kong to Ukraine. Whatever the motivation, this is yet another Chan adventure full of awesome stunts and fight choreography. While it's not the red-white-and-blue outing that New Line was trying to draw a crowd with, any method that gets Jackie's features released in this country is a step in the right direction. Besides, this one seems to be more international in scope and flavor, as circumstances take our hapless hero into Russia and Australia, too. After the briefest of plot introductions (made even briefer, as New Line edited twenty-something minutes out of the picture), it's not long before Jackie is snow-boarding down a mountain, pursued by gunmen aboard skis, snowmobiles, and helicopters. See Jackie dunked unprotected in a frozen lake! See Jackie pursued across the face of a building by brutish assassins! See Jackie fight off thugs under shark-infested waters, without an oxygen tank! While these stunt sequences are thrilling in their subtle (or not-so-subtle) but very real dangers, Jackie is still at his most exciting while working with his own team of stuntmen in an excellently staged battle using chairs, poles,

tables, and ladders to good effect. There's also plenty of comedy, mostly involving Jackie being forced to don a series of strange costumes—or none at all! Chan, who controls all of his films himself (with the able assistance of fellow stuntman Stanley Tong in most of his recent films), is just as able to raise a laugh or a tear as anything else—but it's his unique ability to do so much while taking your breath away with one piece of action after another that's made him one of the biggest movie stars ever.

Oh, by the way, the story is all about a spy (Jackson Liu) forced into becoming an arms dealer while sacrificing his family honor. Not that anybody cares, as every minute is filled by exciting stunts, goofy comedy, and beautiful scenery. Annie Wu is the spy's sister, a marine biologist whom Jackie romances, despite the fact she's half his age. You can pretty much tell who the main characters are—they're the ones with the same first names as the people playing them. **AKA:** *Ging Chat Goo Si 4: Ji Gaan Daan Yam Mo; Jing Cha Gu Shi 4: Zhi Jian Dan Ren Wu; CIA Story; Police Story 4; Jackie Chan's First Strike; Police Story 4: Piece of Cake.* 🦴🦴🦴

1996 (PG-13) 107/88m/C *HK/US* Jackie Chan, Jackson Liu, Annie Wu, Bill Tung, Jouri Petrov, Nonna Grishayeva, Terry Woo, Ailen Sit, Chan Man Ching, Rocky Lai, Ken Lo, Conan Lee. *D:* Stanley Tong. *W:* Stanley Tong, Nick Tramontaine, Greg Mellot, Elliot Tong. *C:* Jingle Ma. *M:* Nathan Wang, J. Peter Robinson (U.S.). **VHS, DVD**

asians in usa

Fist of Fear— Touch of Death

Among the many features robbing the grave of Bruce Lee is this hilarious oddity, part phony documentary and part action comedy. Its like would not be seen until the heyday of the World Wrestling Federation. It all starts with a visit to the "Oriental World of Self Defense" show at Madison Square Garden, New York City. The main event of the day will be the 1979 World Karate Championships, which has been promoted as a match to determine who will be the successor to Bruce Lee as the King of Kung Fu. Why a karate championship would decide the kung fu champ is unknown. A further mystery is why Fred Williamson and boxer Ron Van Clief would be involved.

Promoter Aaron Banks is interviewed by Adolf Caesar about his belief that Bruce Lee was killed by the legendary Touch of Death (or Vibrating Palm), in which a kung fu master "disturbs the vibrations" of an opponent with a blow, bringing about death days or even weeks later. As evidence: a preposterously faked interview created with dubbed footage of Lee edited with shots of Caesar. We see Williamson waking up in his hotel room the morning of the match, then being mistaken several times for Harry Belafonte on the way to the Garden! Later, we're introduced to Van Clief, and watch him beat up a gang of muggers in Central Park. Caesar interrupts this loosely scripted footage for a "half-time show" to recap Lee's biography. He makes the assertion that he discovered Bruce Lee, and that Lee's great-grandfather was "one of China's greatest samurai master swordsmen." A clip borrowed from a Shaw Brothers picture is used to illustrate this point. Other scenes from an old Hong Kong feature is redubbed to represent an event from early in Lee's life, his brother Jack's homecoming, and the day Bruce moved out of the palatial Lee estate (all pure fantasy). Caesar tells us that Bruce Lee created Kato (among the "many memorable characters" of Lee's early film career), which gives director Matthew Mallinson an excuse to cut in a seven-minute sequence starring Bill Louie (*The Bodyguard*) as Kato.

Back to the arena for some more martial arts demonstrations, in preparation for the main event: a fight between Louis Neglia and John "Cyclone" Flood—two guys that haven't even been mentioned before, even though this match is supposed to be the point of the program. Let's save you the trouble of fast-forwarding through this dull match yourself. Neglia covers up for a round or so, waiting for an opening, then lets Flood have a knockout kick to the head. The End.

Tedious at times, but this concoction is so completely ludicrous that it, like the best carnival attractions, can't help but be somewhat entertaining. *AKA: Fist of Fear; The Dragon and the Cobra.* 🐉🐉

1980 (R) 81m/C *US* Bruce Lee, Fred Williamson, Ron Van Clief, Adolf Caesar, Aaron Banks, Bill Louie, Teruyuki Higa, Richard Barathy. *D:* Matthew Mallinson. *W:* Ron Harvey. *C:* John Hazard. *M:* Keith Mansfield. **VHS, DVD**

Fist of Fury 📺

Though Bruce Lee's classic *The Chinese Connection* (AKA *Fist of Fury*) had already been remade at least once (see *Fist of Legend*), producer/director Lung Shiu-kee and star Donnie Yen still believed there was interest in this true-life story, creating this shot-on-video version for Hong Kong television. An expensive co-production between ATV and Star TV networks, it was televised all throughout Asia. Yen stars as rickshaw driver Chen Jun, who joins the Jin Wu Martial Arts Academy to study with Fok Yuen-gap (Eddie Ko) in Japanese-occupied Shanghai of 1911. China is divided, fighting a civil war, and foreigners—especially the Japanese—take advantage of the situation. Fok wants to combine the styles of all the martial arts schools with his own Mei-fung ("unseen") Fist to strengthen the resistance forces of China. Sachio Takeda is put in charge of the Black Dragon Society in Shanghai, ordered to gather information on the Japanese to prepare for full-scale invasion by Japanese forces. Takeda's daughter Yumi (Joey Man) is dating Chen Jun, though he forbids her to see him, going so far as to send assassins after him. Yumi's fiancé Hideaki Ishii helps return her to her home by force, triggering a heart attack in the frail girl. Chen agrees to keep his distance to protect Yumi's health, but when Japanese treachery causes the death of one of his friends, he goes to the Hung Hau Dojo to have it out with those responsible, crippling Hideaki's brother. For his trespass, Chen escapes a death penalty, but is banished from the city. Hideaki swears vengeance on Chen and all of China, attacking and harassing all the martial arts schools, and forcing Master Fok to fight a duel with him. Though Fok is the clear winner, he dies in the

"Yeah, some event. Two cats fighting for Bruce Lee's title that doesn't even exist. Now that's kind of absurd, know what I mean?"

—Fred "The Hammer" Williamson tells it like it is in *Fist of Fear— Touch of Death* duel, standing up like a true hero. Chen returns for the funeral, and an autopsy reveals that Fok was poisoned. An uncompromising fury builds within Chen, and he becomes determined to stand against the Japanese no matter what.

The series format allowed the story to be expanded with many new characters and subplots. However, this feature version condenses much of this material from the 30-episode series. We've hardly met some characters before they're killed, and much of the running time is taken up by choppy, fast-paced exposition. Even so, many characters and conflicts had to be cut out completely—Yumi's wedding takes place offscreen without even a mention. One character that doesn't suffer from this is Master Fok—previous versions begin with his death, but here we get a chance to get to know him first. All the big fight scenes are also retained—Yen's build is at its most pumped up, and his athleticism and choreography are excellent, in the style of—and in homage to—Bruce Lee. Unfortunately, some of the directors feel it necessary to intrude with fancy effects and sped up movement. Compositions and photography are often excellent, though the video image cheapens the effect. *AKA: Cheng Mu Moon; Jing Wu Men.* ♫♫

1995 121m/C *HK* Donnie Yen, Joey Man, Eddie Ko, Lau Chi Wing, Hung Yen-yen, Wong Siu-ching, Wong Yak-ho, Hwang Jang Lee. *D:* Benny Chan, Leung Yun-chuen, Wong Gum-miu, Cheng Wai-man, Wu Ming-hoi, Tang Mau-sing, Lung Shiu-kee. *W:* Chan Yiu-fai, Yau Fook-hing, Lee Yee-wah, Cheung Kwok-yuen, Tang Guei-seem. *M:* Wong Bon Yin. **VHS, DVD**

Fist of Fury 1991

Mainland bumpkin Lau Ching (Stephen Chow) has super-strength—but only in his right hand! He comes to Kowloon to meet with his friend Keung, but while stopping to admire the Saint of Gamblers (Chow again, in slow motion), he has his luggage stolen by petty thief Brother Smart (Kenny Bee). Having lost Keung's address in the scuffle, Ching imposes on Smart for a place to stay. While working as dim-sum waiters, a mistake brings gangsters led by Brother Leung (Chen Jing) after them, but they're rescued by Mandy Fok (Sharla Cheung) and Cheng Wai (Vincent Wan) from Fok Kung Fu School. Entering the big martial arts tournament looks like the only way Ching can earn any money, but entrants must belong to an established school, so they join up at the academy of Chiu Tung (Shing Fui-on). However, the school is a front for a den of thieves, and the gang have the misfortune of making Master Fok Wan (Corey Yuen) their next target. Ching saves Fok during the battle, and the grateful master

brings him home with him. After a Japanese school challenges Fok, he agrees to train Ching to control the power of his Fist of Fury. However, jealous Wai frames Ching for an attack on Mandy, getting him thrown out of the house in disgrace. Four eccentric elderly masters of the Great New Kung Fu School take him in, and after some unconventional training, sponsor Ching in the tournament.

The parodies roll out fast and furious, sometimes one on top of the other. The spitting match near the beginning between Chow and Bee has moves swiped from both John Woo and Jet Li movies (the Wong Fei-hung theme plays behind it), ending with a Bruce Lee imitation. Despite the title, only the sequence in which the Japanese school comes to call is a direct send-up of the Lee hit *Fist of Fury (The Chinese Connection)*, but don't let that stop you from checking out this nutty comedy. *AKA: San Cheng Miu Moon 1991; Xin Jing Wu Men 1991; Fist of Fury II.* ♫♫♫

1991 97m/C *HK* Stephen Chow, Kenny Bee, Sharla Cheung, Corey Yuen, Vincent Wan, Shing Fui-on, Wu Fung, Chen Jing, Ha Chi-chun, Ng Man-Tat, Shut Ma Wa Lung, Tai Bo, Mai Kei, Lee Siu-Kei, Jeff Lau. *D:* Cho Chung-sing. *W:* Jeff Lau. *C:* Chan Yuen-kai, Jimmy Leung. *M:* Lowell Lo. **VHS, DVD**

Fist of Legend

Director Gordon Chan, previously known for light romances and Stephen Chow comedies, here teamed with producer/star Jet Li for an energetic remake of Bruce Lee's *The Chinese Connection (Fist of Fury)*, with fights choreographed by Yuen Woo-Ping *(The Matrix, Once upon a Time in China 2)*. At the time, Jet Li was engaging in projects that showed his Chinese patriotism in the face of the coming 1997 reunification, but the script here shows a situation a bit more complex than the one in the original.

It's 1937, and Japanese forces occupy Shanghai. War threatens, and tensions run high for Chinese and Japanese alike. In a Kyoto school, student Chen Zhen (Li) learns that the master of his kung fu school back in Shanghai, master Huo, has been killed in a duel with Akutagawa (Jackson Liu) of Niguchi school. Chen leaves for Shanghai at once to re-establish Huo's Jing Wu Kung Fu school. The furious Chen challenges the Japanese school and gets in Akutagawa's face—literally—in a ferocious fight.

Later, Chen works with the Shanghai police to prove that Master Huo had been poisoned. The evil General Fujita (Billy Chow) is behind the whole scheme. He kills Akutagawa and frames Chen for the murder. Perjury by Chen's girlfriend

Mitsuko (Shinobu Nakayama) saves him in court, but Huo's Number 1 son Ting-en (Chin Siu-Ho from the *Mr. Vampire* series) objects to the Japanese girl. After a tough fight with Chen, both men leave Jing Wu behind. But when the Japanese challenge the champion of Jing Wu to a death match, Huo and Chen join forces to battle General Fujita himself.

Though the historic drama is engaging, it's the kung fu that makes this one a must-see. Li and Yuen create some of their most spectacular hand-to-hand duels here, with a minimum of wirework, stressing Bruce Lee's message of adaptation in combat. Chan makes his presence felt also with some strong atmosphere, especially during Li's outdoor battle with Kurata Yasuaki. **AKA:** *Jing Wu Ying Xiong.* 🎻🎻🎻♥

1994 (R) 103m/C *HK* Jet Li, Chin Siu-Ho, Shinobu Nakayama, Billy Chow, Yasuaki Kurata, Ada Choi, Paul Chun, Jackson Liu. **D:** Gordon Chan. **W:** Gordon Chan, Ip Kwong Kim, Lam Kay Toa. **C:** Derek Wan. **M:** Steve Edwards (U.S. version), Wong Bong, Joseph Koo. **VHS, DVD**

Fist Power

This exercise in action and suspense, produced by Wong Jing, is kind of like the kung fu version of *Kramer vs. Kramer* and *Dog Day Afternoon.* Ex-British Marine Charles/Chau (Anthony Wong), step-dad to son Tung (Tony in English dub), will fight for custody against the boy's mother Sara (Li Fei) and her new husband George Chiu, who only wants Tung in order to claim his inheritance in America.

Officer Brian Cheuk Lap-yan (Vincent Zhou of *Once upon a Time in China 4*) is a top security expert; on the way to picking up his nephew at school, he gets a ride from trucker Charles, and is a bit alarmed at his talk about setting bombs. Eventually, Charles assembles a squad of his buddies to take a school class hostage (a class that includes the son of the police inspector—and Brian's nephew), demanding his son be handed over to him.

Brian vows to get Tony for Charles, but the cops intervene. Gigi Lai plays a reporter assigned to the crisis; she once had a bad blind date with Brian, and helps him to escape. Sam Lee plays Charles's huckster buddy, whose wild driving skills come in handy when he aids Brian as well. George, not caring who gets hurt, calls in some triad thugs to keep Brian out of the way.

Wong Jing's protégé, director Aman Chang *(Body Weapon),* does a good job keeping the action going at a brisk pace, though his fight scenes tend toward fast cuts that obscure movement too much. Old-school kung fu goddess Cheng Pei Pei plays Zhou's hard-hitting mom, who comes to the rescue in the final reel. **AKA:** *Sang sei Kuen Chuk; Sheng Si Quan Su.* 🎻🎻🎻

1999 89m/C *HK* Anthony Wong, Vincent Zhou, Sam Lee, Gigi Lai, Cheng Pei Pei, Lau Kar-Wing, Li Fai, Lam Suet. **D:** Aman Chang. **C:** Choi Sung-fai. **M:** Tommy Wai. **VHS, DVD**

The Fist, the Kicks and the Evils

Patterned somewhat on Jackie Chan's *Drunken Master* and *Snake in the Eagle's Shadow*, this revenge saga was almost certainly shot back-to-back with *My Kung Fu 12 Kicks.* Master Lung Gon-dor (Phillip Ko) and his men invade the Crane Style kung fu school. His sidekick Master Lai (Bolo Yeung) beats up Master Ken (Lee Tso Nam) and takes away his students to their Tiger Style school. Dr. Wong (Ku Feng) refuses to allow his shiftless son Ah Lan (Bruce Liang) to get involved in the fight, not wanting the youth to get hurt. But when Lan lets it slip to Lai that his father is the Crane Fist fighter the villains have been looking to challenge, it forces Wong to fight, and Lai kills him. While Lung's gang bullies everyone in town, Ken takes Lan under his wing to teach him the Crane Fist. Lan can't wait to test his skills, beating Lung's sycophant (Chan Lau) and his men in a street fight. This only draws Lai to find their shack, and Lan returns from shopping to find Ken and his student Sai murdered. Trying to get revenge only gets Lan beaten, and he's taken in by vegetable peddler old Mr. Ching and his granddaughter Shao Kung. Naturally, Ching is secretly a kung fu master who trains Lan further, enabling him more of a match for his enemies.

Surely this is the only kung fu movie in which the hero picks on the villain's high blood pressure to succeed! With a weak plot, the film survives solely on the talents of its cast and director—and that turns out to be enough, especially if one appreciates the acrobatics of Bruce Liang (if not his idiot character). For a change, Bolo Yeung trades on his martial arts skill more than his physique, keeping his long-sleeved shirt on at all times. Yue Tau Wai, the Ben Turpin of kung fu, does his usual cross-eyed bit as one of Phillip Ko's stooges. The soundtrack borrows the Wong Fei-hung theme, though this is certainly not a Master Wong movie. **AKA:** *Fists, Kicks, and the Evils; Lee Kicks Back.* 🎻🎻🎻

1979 84m/C *TW* Bruce Liang, Ku Feng, Phillip Ko, Bolo Yeung, Chan Lau, Lee Tso Nam, Yue Tau Wai. **D:** Lee Tso Nam. **W:** Lam Wong-kwan. **C:** Li Shih-chieh. **DVD**

A Fistful of Talons

The Ching Dynasty has been overthrown, but there are still loyal Manchurian sects meeting in

F

secret to take over the government once again. Secretly leading the largest of these sects is Republic government officer Ngai Sing (Whang In Shik). Their plan to trap officer Ting Wai-chung (Pai Ying), and take his official documents and seal, is discovered, and Ting flees into the countryside. Ting hides out for a few days at a remote postal station and inn owned by Mr. Chin (Tin Fung). Chin's son Yi-ming (Billy Chong) is curious about the stranger and his fine horse Yu Fau-chung. Ngai and his men come after Ting, but he eludes them. However, Yi-ming has learned that 5,000 Manchurian troops have secretly surrounded the capitol awaiting a signal to attack. He decides to go after Ting and warn him, and to earn cash for his trip, he captures three bandits with bounties on their heads. Constable Ma (Lee Kwan) offers him a job as deputy, throwing in his fierce, eagle-raising daughter (Hilda Liu) in marriage. While Yi-ming wriggles loose to continue his quest, Ting is attacked again by the Manchurians, as horse thief Little Bandit (Cheng Hong-yip) takes advantage of the situation and steals Yu Fau-chung. Yi-ming recognizes the horse in the marketplace, and makes Little Bandit show him where he got it. Yi-ming catches up with his hero, and convinces him to train him in kung fu, so that he stands a chance against Ngai Sing's armored legs.

Billy Chong is generally written off as a Jackie Chan imitator, but here his athleticism and skills speak for themselves. The film features some good direction and nice sets, with excellent fight scenes directed by Robert Tai. The training sequences are also impressive, one of which has Chong trying to light candles all over a huge sleeping Buddha statue, while Pai tries to fight him off. It's unusual to see trained animals in kung fu movies, and another entertaining element of this one is all the eagles on display, as well as some very calm horses that don't mind Billy Chong leaping all around and under them. The ending is a little abrupt, and a little gruesome. *AKA: Foo Ying; Hu Ying; A Fist Full of Talons; Earth, Wind, Fire, Mountains; Wind, Forest, Fire, Mountain.* 🎵🎵🎵

1983 82m/C *HK* Billy Chong, Whang In Shik, Pai Ying, Hilda Liu, Cheng Hong-yip, Lee Kwan, Tin Fung, Kong Do, Ma Chin-ku, Cheng Kei-ying, Ko Saio Pao, Yeung Heung. **D:** Sun Chung. **W:** Barry Wong. **DVD**

Fists and Guts

Yeung (director Lau Kar-Wing) makes his money by standing in for escaping prisoners in front of a firing squad, his back protected by a metal plate. He complains to his friend Big Pang (Lee Hoi-sang) to make the plate thicker next time. Kung fu master Ah San (Gordon Lau) gets in a fight with the two rascals, thinking one of them is the man he's looking for. It seems that his housekeeper ran off with the money he inherited from

his father, and the young master has been searching for him ever since; the trouble is, the housekeeper is a master of disguise. In order to pay for the damage done in his attack, he hires on the both of them, promising them all the cash if he can get the family heirlooms back. They learn that a new escort named Wu wears masks and wigs, but when they catch him, they find out he's the wrong man. The housekeeper (Lo Lieh) turns up disguised as a fortuneteller, and tricks Yeung and Big Pang into infiltrating a leper colony. Meanwhile, the housekeeper has scammed his way into the household of General Woo as feng shui expert Mr. Fairy. His target is a valuable Jade Buddha in the general's possession. Ah San and his assistants don disguises to get in the house as well, just in time to catch a masked thief taking the Buddha.

One of the film's highlight fight sequences is the ensuing duel, with both combatants trying to stay quiet so as not to get shot by alarmed soldiers. In another creative sequence, our trio of heroes has to survive a corridor lined with iron bar booby traps. In the end, hero and villain are revealed to be something other than they said. The fight with the lepers is indescribable. To sum up: Lau Brothers action, comedy, disturbing humor, and a surprise ending—everything you want in a kung fu flick! *AKA: Yat Daam Ji Lik Saam Gung Fu; Yi Dan Er Li San Gong Fu; Fist and Guts.* 🎵🎵🎵

1979 92m/C *HK* Gordon Lau, Lau Kar-Wing, Lo Lieh, Lee Hoi-sang, Yau Shui-ling. **D:** Lau Kar-Wing. **W:** Wong Hoi-ming, Arthur Wong. **C:** Arthur Wong. **VHS, DVD**

Fists Like Lee

Technically, this is a Bruceploitation picture in title only, as the American release made this one of many to masquerade as Bruce Lee films. Other kids pick on little refugee Wong Shao-ying, especially the boys of the Chun family, for which his mother works as a servant—except their pretty little daughter Ping. Shao-ying idolizes their kung fu teacher Lee, the most honorable man he knows. Lee allows Shao-ying to become his student as well, and as the boy grows (into Michael Chan), he becomes Lee's best student. However, he still can't fight back when the master's sons pick on him.

When Shao-ying is advanced enough, Lee turns him over to his own master for training. He returns just in time to save Ping from abduction by the dastardly 3 Tigers, who have invaded the Chun house. Chun rewards Shao-ying with a wad of cash, asking him to go into the city to make his fortune, then return and marry Ping. Almost immediately he runs afoul of gangster Lin Biao (Pai Ying), beating all of his men before making pulp of Lin himself. After his exertions, he's easily seduced by his innkeeper Wei (Hu Chin), who hires him as manager and sees that he takes over as boss of Lin's territory. While the tough-but-fair new boss goes to visit his mom, two master killers show up to avenge Lin Biao. When Shao-ying returns to find Wei mortally wounded, he goes out for the strangers' blood.

The film is overcome by melodrama toward the end—after Hu Chin's death scene, the hero turns to the dark side somewhat, leading to an unintentionally funny scene in which his mother catches him tickling two naked whores with a peacock feather. The end features a rather contrived plot device out of left field that pits Shao-ying and his long-lost brother unknowingly against each other, the deciding factor in their match turning out to be a standard piece of sports equipment. The action is nothing fancy or acrobatic, but rather vicious—a lot of hard and fast punches with some kicks mixed in. Michael Chan thumbs his nose once in honor of his late friend Bruce Lee, reluctantly cast in this imitation. As part of the action, this is one of the few films to show an actual dog fight, which would seem more savage if the English voice actors didn't dub the dogs. The American release (under the title *Chinese Mack,* trying to cash in on the Blaxploitation hit *The Mack*) advertised the film as being in "Kung Fu Color." Not to be confused with Wu Ma's *Along Comes a Tiger,* which was released under the same title. **AKA:** *Chuet Chiu; Jue Zhao; The Chinese Mack; Martial Arts.* 🎵🎵

1974 100m/C *HK* Michael Chan, Hu Chin, Pai Ying, Charlie Chan, Cheng Lui, Cheng Kei-ying, Travador Ramos, Robert Kerver. **D:** Sherman Hsu. **W:** Wu Tit-yik. **VHS**

Fists of Bruce Lee

Angry, sick triad boss Lo Fu-Chi hires electronic expert Lee Man Chin (Bruce Li), bringing him to Hong Kong to install a security system. He's met by Owl Puss (Paul Wei), who leads him into an ambush. Following one of the attackers, he finds the man dead. His contact is killed, too. Lee's picked up and brought to meet houseman Poo Chi-Chan, and Lo's daughter Li-Yi, and finally Lo himself. Lo has already had a lot of deadly traps installed in the woods around the house. Government agents try to force Lee to spy on Lo. He's helped out by a blonde stranger who works for Lo's rival, Ping Shan. Ping wants Lee to get friendly with Li-Yi so they can kidnap her. Lee enjoys playing each group off against the others; he protects Li-Yi from the kidnappers, but there's no protection from the awful 70s décor and fashions. It's all pretty confusing, especially so due to poor dubbing and the usual

cropped presentation seen on video. Lo Lieh appears as a noble rival mobster with a prosthetic hand he can whip out on a chain.

For a change, Bruce Li—who also directed—is credited by his real name, Ho Chung Tao. The cinematography is rarely in focus. Frames are removed from some fight footage to speed up blows. The soundtrack borrows from "Live & Let Die" and other '70s pop tunes. Some of the dubbing actors don't speak English much better than the original Chinese actors. 🎵🎶

1978 (R) 94m/C *HK* Bruce Li, Lo Lieh, Chan Wai Lau, Paul Wei, Tong Lung, Po Fu Mei. **D:** Bruce Li. **C:** Lai Wan Hsiung. **DVD**

Fists of Fury

Upstart Hong Kong studio Golden Harvest outbid the Shaw Brothers' paltry offer to hire Bruce Lee for his first starring role, though for the first third of the picture, it's James Tien who seems to be the star and does most of the fighting. Cheng Chao-An (Lee) and his Uncle Lu (Tu Chiacheng) arrive from the country to stay with relatives, where he's been sent for the trouble he's been getting into. Cheng has promised not to get into any more fights, a promise he's tempted to break when they run into a gang of bullying vendors as soon as he gets off the boat. Fortunately, cousin Shu Sheng (James Tien) is there to drive away the thugs. Shu Sheng has asked the manager Ching Hao at the ice factory where he works to give Cheng a job there. Cousin Sheng makes Cheng's promise a bit harder by being a neighborhood hero, but Cheng renews his promise to Uncle Lu, who is going home to the mainland. At the ice factory, cousins Wong and Chen see that Ching Hao is smuggling drugs inside blocks of ice. When the honest boys naively refuse his hush money, the gang makes them disappear. Concerned about the guys, Sheng and Pei go to ask the big boss (Han Ying Chieh) what happened to them, but are given the brush-off. Outside, the boss's son (Tony Liu) and his thugs attack the pair and kill them. The rest of the guys decide they've had enough, and a riot breaks out at the factory, but still Cheng stays out of the fighting. However, when Ching calls the boss to send over his killers, Cheng gets fed up and brings on the whup-ass. To quiet things down, Ching has Cheng promoted, replacing brutish Chao Lee (Chen Chiu). Surprisingly, this makes all the workers forget about their missing companions, until cousin Chow Mei (Maria Yi) reminds them. Ching Hao diverts Cheng's inquiries by getting him drunk.

Unlike the confident hero Lee played in his other films, here he plays a simple man, for the most part caught up in events over his thick

THE HOUND SALUTES
Bruce Lee

李小龍

Would there be kung fu films if Bruce Lee had never been born? Probably. There were numerous such films before he arrived on the scene, and there have been many kung fu features made since Lee's premature death in 1973. However, without Bruce Lee, it's safe to say that kung fu flicks would be *nothing* like they are now.

Lee was born Lee Jun Fan in San Francisco in 1940. He and his family returned to Hong Kong in the following year. Lee studied Wing Chun kung fu as a boy, and worked as a child actor in numerous HK films. He returned to the U.S. to finish school and eventually moved to Seattle, where he went to college. While in the States, Lee formed a martial arts school—featuring his own style of kung fu, Jeet Kune Do—to earn money. Starting a school that catered to non-Chinese was a bold move; traditionally Chinese martial arts were taught only to people with Asian backgrounds. Bruce Lee shattered that custom. (This wasn't the last time the young dragon would butt heads with traditions and preconceptions during his short career.) Many of his students—John Saxon, Chuck Norris, and Kareem Abdul-Jabbar among them—later appeared in Lee's films.

Lee's interest in film, and his desire to spread his art, led him to Hollywood. He landed the role of Kato in *The Green Hornet* TV series, and became the show's star attraction. *The Green Hornet* is where many of us first saw Lee and became fans. The Batman vs. Green Hornet two-part showdown was a particular delight—though everyone knew that, in "real life," Kato would first kick Robin's ass, then put the other heroes down for the count as well.

Despite Lee's burgeoning popularity, the *Hornet* didn't last long; neither did the show Lee appeared on after that, *Longstreet*. Lee had some bit parts in movies (including a memorable portrayal in *Marlowe*), but racism and the studio system kept him from getting lead roles. He helped develop the idea for the *Kung Fu* TV series, and was then passed over for the lead role in favor of Anglo actor David Carradine. Things in the U.S. looked increasingly tough for the ambitious Lee.

His work in U.S. television had attracted the attention of Hong Kong filmmakers though—*The Kato Show* was on top in the ratings—and Lee was offered a contract at Shaw Brothers Studio. But Bruce rejected the Shaws' minimal wages and limiting contracts for the upstart Golden Harvest, which was started by Shaws' alumni. For his first film, he took starring part in *The Big Boss* (AKA *Fists of Fury*). The film was a huge hit in Hong Kong and resulted in instant star status for Lee. More films followed: *Fist of Fury* (AKA *The Chinese Connection,*) and *Way (Return) of the Dragon* (which Lee wrote and directed). It was only then that U.S. filmmakers began to pay attention to Lee once again. *Enter the Dragon* was made as a joint U.S./HK venture. *Enter the Dragon* was a huge hit, and ignited a kung fu craze in America. Its success seemed to ensure that Bruce Lee would finally get his due.

Unfortunately, fate had other ideas.

Bruce Lee died in Hong Kong from a cerebral edema shortly after the film's release. His unexpected passing was most likely due to a bad reaction to a traditional Chinese medicine. Rumors persist, though, of a vast conspiracy to kill the rising star. (There are probably more theories of how Bruce Lee *really* died than there are about what "really" happened during the Kennedy assassination.)

Game of Death, which Lee had been working on at the time, was completed after his death. The producers used (sometimes laughably bad) stunt doubles, drastically reedited scenes, and whipped up a new script to "finish" the film. It's recommended you pass the film by unless you're a Lee completist. A better version of the story that "might have been"—including complete footage of what Lee had finished—can be seen in *Bruce Lee: A Warrior's Journey.*

So, that's it—just a handful of films and a few TV shows that aren't even available on video. That's the sum total of Bruce Lee's output as an adult. It doesn't seem like much, in terms of numbers; but that short list doesn't come close describing Lee's impact on the medium. Bruce Lee changed the way kung fu films were made. He banished the fanciful flying swordplay and acrobatics of previous generations in favor of street-tough, hard-hitting action.

Unlike many current action stars, Lee didn't actually hit people during his films, save for a few powerful demonstration kicks. (The current HK standard is "rough contact," where the stars hit each other nearly hard enough to cause injury. This makes it easier to move quickly and convincingly on-screen.) Lee was lightning fast, and had pinpoint control of his moves; he was able to stop a power-

Continued on next page...

ful blow just before the point of impact. Not until Jet Li arrived in the late 1980s did the screen have a martial artist with anything near Lee's level of ability and training. He was so quick that the camera had trouble recording his movements at 24 frames per second. (Much like Toshiro Mifune's famous "fast draw" sword technique.) Lee's work was never "sped up" optically—though it was frequently slowed down to capture the grace and beauty of his technique.

An entire cottage industry of "Bruce Lee" films featuring look-alike stars cropped up after Lee's death: Bruce Le, Bruce Li, et al. (See page 224.) Fans were neither fooled nor placated. No motley troop of clones in Bruce Lee masks fighting in fast-motion could duplicate the star's skill and charisma. Only with the emergence of Jackie Chan (who did stunt extra work in *Enter the Dragon*) did the tide Lee of impersonators finally ebb.

Perhaps kung fu filmmakers had finally figured out that they couldn't duplicate Lee's success. Or maybe they'd learned new ways to carry on the traditions that Lee had pioneered.

Often imitated but never duplicated, Bruce Lee still stands as the pinnacle of martial arts achievement. His legion of fans can only wonder what Lee might have done had he lived longer. He brought an unbeatable combination to the screen: ability, intensity, integrity, and the soul of a dragon. Bruce Lee's influence will dominate until action cinema throws its last punch.

—SS

head. The low-level drug traffickers have little trouble outsmarting him, and it's only through perseverance and superior kung fu that he gets the better of them. Too much running time is taken up with Cheng getting the runaround and doing nothing, until a kindhearted hooker (Malalene) clues him in to the drug business going on, and he finds his cousins frozen in blocks of ice. Whatever merits the film has are the result of the novel plot (a kung fu movie set in an ice factory?), Lee's natural charisma, and his incredible fight scenes. It's quite obvious that it was Lee and not director Lo Wei who created the classic factory fight. Even after this epic battle, Cheng is unsure what to do next, and only finding his relatives slaughtered, with Chow Mei abducted, finally brings out the dragon in him. Columbia Pictures purchased the U.S. distribution rights, and intended to cash in on that year's big hit *The French Connection* by retitling the story of Chinese drug traffic *The Chinese Connection*. But due to a mix-up, that title went on Lee's *Fist of Fury*, while *The Big Boss* received its slightly altered title. The dubbing job and editing of the current edition isn't too bad, although there are some slight gaffs, as when the boss's son asks for "2,000 yen" (are they in Japan?). An incredible boxoffice hit in Asia, becoming an instant kung fu classic, it exploded on re-release in America after the success of *Enter the Dragon*. **AKA:** *Tang Saan dai Hing; Tang Shan da Xiong; The Big Boss; China Mountain Big Brother; Fists of Glory.* 🐉🐉🐉🐉

1971 (R) 100m/C *HK* Bruce Lee, Maria Yi, James Tien, Nora Miao, Lee Kwan, Han Ying Chieh, Lau Wing, Chin San, Malalene, Billy Chan, Chan Lung, Tu Chia-cheng, Chen Chiu, Lam Ching-ying. **D:** Lo

Wei. **W:** Lo Wei. **C:** Chen Ching Cheh. **M:** Wang Fu-ling. **VHS, DVD**

Fists of the White Lotus

Lo Lieh reveals his creative side with his debut as director for the Shaw Brothers, which follows up on the historical figures presented in the earlier *Executioners from Shaolin.* After Hung Man-ting (Gordon Lau) combined his Tiger Style with his blood brother Hu Ah-biao's Crane Style kung fu to defeat Shaolin traitor Pai Mei (Lo Lieh), they are arrested and sentenced to death. However, their trial creates such a huge public protest that they and the other arrested Shaolin disciples and monks are all freed from prison by decree of the emperor. No sooner does Hung welcome home Hu (Ging Chue) from prison than the humble household is attacked by the White Lotus Cult. Though the Ching government may seem more forgiving in freeing the Shaolin, in truth they've just handed off most of their dirty work to the cult. Their leader White Lotus (Lo Lieh again) was a classmate of the slain Pai Mei, and wants revenge—killing Hu, his sister-in-law Ching-Ching (Yeung Ching-Ching), and many of the Shaolin men. Hung takes Hu's pregnant wife Mei-hsiao (Kara Hui) and flees to stay with Mei-hsiao's cousin Ching. Working in Ching's paper dummy factory, Hung realizes that using too much force will break a straw, and asks Ching to help him train, combining Tiger and Crane strengths. Important note for kung fu heroes: don't become impatient and abandon your training before you've mastered a technique. Hung attacks the clan's headquarters, beating up all the cultists and even Master Kau Tin-chung (Johnny Wang)—but White Lotus finds his skills childish, and Hung barely escapes the place. In order to get through the Lotus chief's slippery defenses, Hung has to learn a softer Woman's Style from Mei-hsiao, training for which involves sewing and caring for the newborn baby. Hung gets so good during his training that his voice even starts to become feminine until he combines all his styles. Hung runs off to make another premature attempt at revenge, getting beaten soundly this time, barely surviving Lotus's 100 Paces Palm (luckily, he only takes 99 steps after being hit). His recovery period gives Hung the idea of learning acupuncture techniques to get to White Lotus.

The early training sequences are very amusing and involve a lot of shots with Gordon Lau bending Ching over a chair. In contrast, the dance-like training sequences with Kara Hui are very graceful and beautiful. Lo's directing style certainly owes much to that of Lau Kar-Leung, who served as action director here. As an actor, he gives his master villain some amusing touch-es (and a nude scene)—here's one villain who deserves to be arrogant, having acquired the skill to back it up. Unfortunately for him, he's so confident that he lets Hung get away from him three times, allowing the hero to improve. The Shaw Brothers studio magic adds a layer of gloss, economically reusing a lot of the same sets and locations from *Executioners from Shaolin.* Although the plot is standard, the terrific fight scenes and general light tone make this one a real winner. After this third outing, it's a shame Lo Lieh didn't direct more features, with only seven on his résumé. The original export title is *Clan of the White Lotus,* but perhaps the distributor didn't think a movie with "clan" and "white" in the title would do well on inner-city marquees. **AKA:** *Hung Man-ding Saam Por Bak Lin Gaau; Hong Wending San Po Bai Lian Jiao; Clan of the White Lotus.* 🎵🎵🎵🎵

1980 95m/C *HK* Gordon Lau, Lo Lieh, Kara Hui, Johnny Wang, Yeung Ching-Ching, Hsiao Ho, Lam Fai-wong, Cheng Miu, Ging Chue. **D:** Lo Lieh. **W:** Haung Tien. **C:** Au Chih-chun. **M:** Eddie H. Wang. **VHS, DVD**

Five Deadly Venoms

Master martial arts movie director Chang Cheh made a string of terrific films from the 1960s through the late '70s using the Shaw Brothers' top stars. His classic *Chinatown Kid* introduced a second wave of great martial arts stars, who went on to make over a dozen films together. But this one was their biggest hit.

To help guarantee their survival, the feared and hated Poison Clan takes certain security precautions. Five students are trained to each be an expert in a different style of the clan's martial arts secrets: Centipede, Snake, Scorpion, Lizard, and Toad. Only Lizard and Toad, who were trained after the others left for the outside world, know each other—all five wore masks within the clan's headquarters, and took new names once they'd left. The Poison Clan Master (Dick Wei) has grown old, and worries about the future of the clan. He sends Yang Ti (Chiang Sheng), who has learned the basics of all five styles, out into the world to seek out and check up on the five Venoms—and find a way to kill them if they've turned to evil. Yang's one lead to finding the Venoms is Yuen (Ku Feng), an old friend of the master who has hidden away some of the clan's money for them. As police officer Ho Yun-hsun (Phillip Kwok), the Lizard finds it easy to ask questions, but has been unable to locate Yuen. His secret partner Li Ho (Lo Meng), the Toad, has had no luck finding Yuen either, nor the other three Venoms. But the Centipede, living under the name Tang San-kwei (Lu Feng), has better luck. He and the Snake—known as Hung Wan-tung (Wei Pai)—ambush the old scholar, but go too far and kill the whole Yuen family without getting the money. The masked Scorpion shows up after they leave, and finds a map to the treasure. A cowardly gambler saw Tang at the crime scene, so Officer Ho sets a trap for him at the house of his rich friend Hung. With the Toad's help, Tang is captured, but Hung pays off a crooked magistrate (Johnny Wang) to get him freed. The magistrate has Ho sent to the capitol on a mission, and frames Toad for the murders. The Snake even has an Iron Maiden constructed to find a weak spot in the Toad's tough hide. Will Lizard return in time to help his friend? And what about the mysterious Scorpion—who is he, and which side is he on?

It's a tribute to the writing skills of Ngai Hong that it takes nearly 40 minutes before any real fighting starts, but the film still holds on to the viewer. Getting a look at the stars doing their stuff in their bizarre masks during some flashback training sessions helps get you hooked early on, but solid plot and pacing keeps you there until the action gets underway. It's not until the final act that the film shifts into high gear, and the stars' athletic abilities really shine. The fight scenes are awesome, but it's the characters that make this film so memorable. Not only are their special styles fun to watch, but they're a bit more complex than the usual fighters. Toad and Lizard are clearly after the treasure themselves before turning hero, Snake expresses regret for his crimes, and even Yang bears a heavy streak of mischief. *AKA: Ng Duk; Wu Du; Five Venoms; The Deadly Venoms; Pick Your Poison.* 🦴🦴🦴🦴

1978 (R) 98m/C *HK* Phillip Kwok, Wei Pai, Lo Meng, Lu Feng, Chiang Sheng, Sun Chien, Dick Wei, Johnny Wang, Ku Feng, Suen Shu-pau, Wong Ching Ho, Shum Lo, Lam Fai-wong, Yu Tai-ping. **D:** Chang Cheh. **W:** Ngai Hong, Chang Cheh. **C:** Kung Mu-to, Tsao Hui-chi. **M:** Chen Yung-yu. **VHS, DVD**

Five Elements of Kung Fu

Chang San-feng is credited as the developer of tai chi chuan, which derives its inspiration from five elements rather than the movements of animals, and his life would make for an interesting film—but this isn't quite it. Learning that some priests have turned to the Dark Side, the Shaolin Temple abbot (O Yau-man, who must have slept in his monk costume through most of the 1970s) orders all their secret kung fu texts locked up in the library. While helping elder Wu Fu clean the library, student Chang San-feng (Lee Chun Wa) discovers one of the manuals and sneaks it away, and over the years he man-

ages to learn all the secret techniques. Lord Chow Go-kan (Shaw Luo-hui) is one of those former Shaolin students gone wrong, having set himself up as a tyrant over his region of China. Several assassination attempts have failed, and Chow injures the latest attacker (Tung Li) with his Black Hand technique.

Rebels aiding the fleeing man risk exposure, among them an innkeeper (Tin Fung) and his daughter Mau-fung (Polly Shang Kwan). When soldiers get rough at the inn, Chang steps in to help out, killing a soldier during the fight. Unfortunately, he's recognized by the other soldiers; having brought trouble to Shaolin, Chang is locked up, but senior monk Wu Fu helps him escape through one of the secret exits from Shaolin. He must pass through the tunnel of the Wooden Men to reach the outside, after which the monks further help by forming a human bridge across a river. With both soldiers and bounty hunters after him, Chang is hidden by Mau-fung at the inn. When Lord Chow kills elder monk Wu Fu, as well as Mau-fung's father, Chang and his friends walk into Chow's trap on a desperate mission of vengeance.

With only surface-level characterization for even the leads, there are a lot of underdeveloped characters running through *Five Elements of Kung Fu* that we hardly know, other than to recognize their types and root for the good guys. The action just keeps rolling in adventure serial fashion, so at times it seems like expository scenes have been left out to hurry things along. One of China's legendary heroes isn't served very well in this feature, with star Lee Chun Wa and director Wu Ming Hung (*Green Dragon Inn*) treating Chang as a stock Shaolin hero, bringing more trouble to his brothers and friends than is necessary in dealing with the villain. *AKA: 5 Element Kung Fu; Shaolin Hero Chang San-feng; Adventure of Shaolin; Chang Shang-fon Adventures.* 🦴🦴

1978 91m/C *TW* Lee Chun Wa, Tung Li, Frank Wong, Sze Ma Lung, Polly Shang Kwan, Shaw Luo-hui, Shih Feng, Tin Fung, Tai Yee-ha, Chan Sam-lam, Lam Chung, Wu Lo-yee, Au Lap-bo, O Yau-man, Ching Ching, Lee Jan-wa, Ma Cheung, Tin Ming, So Kwok-leung. **D:** Wu Ming Hung. **VHS, DVD**

Five Fingers of Death

Kung fu Master Sun Wu-yen (Goo Man-chung) feels he's getting old. Years ago, he sent his student Dao-ming to study in Paoding with Master Shen Chin-pei (Fong Min), who lacked students. Now that his own student Chow Chi-hao (Lo Lieh) wants to stay to marry Sun's daughter Yin-yin (Wong Ping), Sun sends him to Shen Chin-pei as well. Bully Meng Chen-sun (Tung

Lam) is rude to Iron Head Pei Chen-lang (Gam Kei Chu). To make amends, his father Meng Dung-shun (Tin Fung) invites Pei to stay with them, knowing such a tough fighter will be useful to them. He hopes to have one of his men from Bai Sang Institute win the upcoming martial arts championship, and is making an effort to cut down on the competition. Meng's thug Wong Hung-jin (Chan Shen), having failed to kill Master Sun in an ambush the night before, tries to abduct girl singer Yin Ji-hung (Wong Gam-fung) instead, to soften their bad news, but Chi-hao rescues her. Arriving at Shang Wu school, Chi-hao is surprised to find his kung fu isn't good enough for their requirements, and he's sent to work in the kitchen. But he studies extra hard, and Shen Chin-pei soon allows him into his class. Sent on an errand, Chi-hao refuses to fight back when Chen-lang insults him, bringing shame to his school.

The next day, Chen-lang shows up at Shang Wu to clean house, throwing guys through walls and injuring Master Shen with a cheap shot. Pissed off, Chi-hao goes after Chen-lang hard and puts him in the hospital. As a reward, Master Shen passes on the secret to the lethal Iron Fist to Chi-hao, making senior brother Han-lung (James Nam) jealous. Learning that Yin Ji-hung has a crush on Chi-hao only intensifies his jealousy, to the point where Han-lung betrays his brother to Meng. Meng sends his Japanese visitor Okada (Chiu Hung) and his two sidekicks to pick off the top Shang Wu students one by one. Tricked into an ambush by Han-lung, Meng's gang catches Chi-hao and smashes his hands, so that he won't be able to use the Iron Fist technique against them in the tournament.

This of course, is the kung fu movie variation on the old western plot device where the hero's gun hand is broken (used also to good effect in *The Hustler*), and he has to work extra hard to get his mojo back. While Yin Ji-hung nurses Chi-hao back to health, and he gets back to learning the Iron Fist, Okada pays a visit to Master Sun, running him through with his katana. This gives Chi-hao's glowing fists just a little more fury for the tournament. A semi-remake of *The Chinese Boxer,* but released at about the same time Bruce Lee was becoming a star, *Five Fingers* became a huge hit worldwide, benefitting from some fine fighting and over-the-top mayhem (as when Chen-sun plucks an opponent's eyeballs out, or when another fighter is thrown through a tree). Marvel Comics liked the film's special technique so much that they swiped the idea for their *Iron Fist* series. However, Lo Lieh lacked the clean-cut looks and charisma of Lee, and he failed to parley his success into lasting stardom. He added a layer of muscle to his physique, grew a mustache, and primarily portrayed villains for the rest of his career. **AKA:** *Tin Gwong Dai Yat Kuen; Tian Xia Di Yi Quan; King Boxer; Hand of Death; Invincible Boxer; Iron Palm.* 🐉🐉🐉🐉

1972 (R) 105m/C *HK* Lo Lieh, Wong Ping, Chiu Hung, Tin Fung, Fong Min, Gam Kei Chu, Tung Lam, James Nam, Bolo Yeung, Goo Man-chung, Chan Shen, Hsu Hsia, Wong Ching Ho, Wong Gam-fung, Yeung Chak Lam. **D:** Cheng Chang Ho. **W:** Chiang Yang. **C:** Wang Yung Lung. **M:** Chen Yung-yu, Ng Tai Kong. **VHS, DVD**

5 Lady Venoms

For establishing a rapport with your intended target audience, there's nothing like putting a naked woman in the first shot of your movie. Sure, the script says it's a ballet scene, but there's no reason the dancer can't be nude, right? Standing up to a bully in a nightclub brings Jimmy Lee to the attention of the owner, Mr. Fung, who hires the young man on the spot. At his daughter's wedding, Fung is wounded by an assassin. Lee goes to confront Fung's rival Lau, but Lau is killed, too. Fung's manager Toro wants to expand their business from nightclubs and casinos into narcotics, working with Lau's manager Soo, despite Jimmy's objections. Lau's business is taken over by his daughter Angel (Elsa Yeung), who trains a quintet of girl bodyguards in kung fu. While practicing on the beach, they get in a rumble with the 5 Amazons, who all bear the tattoos of different birds on their backs. Angel beats Amazon leader Sunny (Karen Sun), and they go to work for the Laus.

When not practicing strenuous (but lovingly photographed) martial arts exercises in beachwear, the girls ride around on motorcycles. The purpose of this commando team is not just to beat up cheating sleazeballs in the casino, but to exact bloody vengeance on Fung, whom Angel believes is responsible for her father's death. The result of several attacks is a broken leg for Fung, and during his hospital stay Lee and Toro fight for control of the business. Toro's drug deal goes sour, and Toro blames Lee for his problems. Underling Carl is the real problem, and when he betrays Soo—shooting him in the back—he brings them all closer to an open mob war. Toro has a bloody conflict with the troublemakers, and once he receives a fatal stab wound, the fact that he and Jimmy are really brothers comes out. With Toro dead, Jimmy makes his own revelation to Angel—he's really an undercover cop—and together they plan the downfall of those trying to take over both crime families.

Female fighting teams have been a popular subject in movies for decades (à la T.V. Mikels's *Doll Squad*), but seeing a gang of girl criminals is unusual outside the prison movie genre (the Ed Wood–written *The Violent Years* being an early example). This Joseph Lai production

gives us both a lady triad chief and kung fu girls in one picture. Unfortunately, there's too much time spent on the hero and other mob business and not enough of the Amazons kicking booty. Given that the picture is poorly scripted and filmed, it's a shame that they couldn't give their target audience more of their greatest asset. There's surprisingly little gunplay—all the biggest fights involve knives. **AKA:** *Woo Tiu Dai Hap Saam Goh Boon; Hu Tu Da Xia San Ge Ban; Kung Fu Girls.* ♫ ♡

1978 83m/C *HK* Elsa Yeung, Eagle Lee, Ma Cheung, Karen Sun, Merle Kee, Wong Hap, Tin Peng, Yuen Sam, Wong Fei, Wang Suit, Tsoi Chung Chow, Tsoi Wing Wah, Cheung Hung Ki. **D:** Cheng Chi Chiu. **W:** Lam Wong Kun. **C:** Wong Siu-cheung. **M:** Stanley Chow. **VHS**

Five Superfighters

A tall, gray-haired man in black (Kwan Fung) travels across China challenging kung fu schools, saying only that he wants to improve their teaching methods. Master Wan of the Monkey Clan (Hau Chiu Sing) and his three students are beaten by the stranger, after which Wan becomes an inconsolable drunken wreck. The three students split up to search out and train with separate kung fu masters, so they can return and get their revenge. Tien (Tony Leung Siu-hung) gets instruction in hard kicking from a bean curd–making widow (Wong Mei-Mei). During a brawl over a gambling debt, Chi (Wu Yuan-chun) gets in a fight with crippled drunkard Han Hao (Lam Fai-wong), who eventually agrees to teach him his Crane Style of fighting. An old fisherman (Jamie Luk) catches Fu (Austin Wai) trying to steal fish, but ends up instructing the lad in his pole-fighting style. The trio returns after six months to celebrate Master Wan's birthday by challenging the man in black to a rematch, but old Wan has a surprise up his sleeve as well.

The simple structure of this revenge thriller allows plenty of room for some awesome kung fu acrobatics and choreography, all around some fine-looking Shaw Brothers sets. The only drawback is the cardboard characters. No reason is provided for the villain's actions—does he go around besting kung fu fighters just for kicks? Apparently, and the heroes don't have anything better to do than to focus their lives on vengeance for being beaten once. Hey, it's not like he killed their partner or anything. But still, the amazing action more than makes up for the weak motivation. The peppy soundtrack includes everything from traditional Chinese music, to weird electronic sounds, to some bits that sound like music from an old NFL Films reel. **AKA:** *Tong Sang Ng Foo; Tang Shan Wu Hu;*

The Drunken Fighter; Superfighters; The Super Fighters. ♫♫♫

1978 96m/C *HK* Wu Yuan-chun, Austin Wai, Wong Mei-Mei, Tony Leung Siu-hung, Jamie Luk, Hau Chiu Sing, Lam Fai-wong, Kwan Fung, Wan Fat, Lau Hok Nin, Fung Ging Man. **D:** Law Ma. **W:** Szeto On. **C:** Lin Chao. **M:** Eddie H. Wang. **DVD**

5 Venoms vs. Wu Tang

It's only a few minutes into the movie when the Taoist disciple leads the hopping vampires in a dance number to "The Banana Boat Song," so you know this has little to do with Chang Cheh's 5 Venoms flicks, other than the casting of Lu Feng as one of the characters. Actually, this is a knockoff of the Mr. Vampire series produced by Joseph Kuo.

The boogying disciple Yuan goes a bit too far, the ska beat causing the sutras on the vampires he's transporting to explode, setting them loose, but his master sets things right. Meanwhile priest Liu returns after a year of cross-country corpse transports to find his headquarters a shambles, and then he's attacked by a violent king vampire who can turn invisible. Liu gets off a psychic fax to his old classmate Maosan before getting bit. Maosan gets to work on the problem, tracking the fiend to his nest, but before he can find or destroy all the kyonsi, the vampire queen gives birth to a baby vampire (who looks about four years old, and not at all corpselike). The cute little brat—who can be used to control both the living and dead—escapes, hiding out with human kids Little Ju and her brother Liang. Maosan hunts down the little monster, but has to contend with the protective neighborhood kids, plus the escaped king and queen vampires. Maosan's rival shows up, too, and soon the two priests (with the wounded Maosan taking possession of his student Toothless) are competing to catch the valuable baby vampire. But the priests have to postpone their battle when the vampire monster returns with a whole platoon of hopping corpses.

Unfortunately, after the success of *Mr. Vampire 2*, every Hong Kong vampire movie had to include at least one cute little kid vampire, since the character became wildly popular for a time, especially in Japan. The undead child is a potentially creepy idea, but apparently Asian audiences only wanted to see the bloodsucking Little Rascals. Except for this tragedy, this is nonetheless a painless time-waster, with quite a few funny gags thrown in. However, the two priests and students look too much alike, making for some confusion, and it's not clear why Maosan disappeared from the story before the end.

Yuan's efforts to cure the wounded child vampire leads to a disturbing sequence in which the kids have to round up a lot of animal urine and feces, waiting behind dogs and geese with bowls. The kids take a lot of hard knocks during the fighting, too—wires or no wires, it's got to hurt. *AKA: Five Venoms vs. the Ghosts; The Venoms vs. the Vampires; New Mr. Vampire 2.* 🐉🐉🐉

1987 92m/C *HK* Chin Siu-ho, Lu Feng. *D:* Wang Chih-cheng. **VHS, DVD**

Flag of Iron

Few martial arts films feature them, but battle flags were an integral part of an army's weaponry in China. Not only for marking position, a skilled warrior could use the flag as a weapon as well—to batter, confuse, and smother an enemy while choosing a good moment to skewer him with the spear point. Here the Venoms crew shows off their talents with flags, short spears, and other exotic weapons.

Iron Panther Lo Hsin (Phillip Kwok) and Iron Monkey Yuen Liang (Chiang Sheng) are prominent members of the Iron Flag Clan, who also sport fabulous red and black uniforms. Finding that Eagle Clan members Kao Fang and Chin Chang (Yu Tai-ping) are running a kidnapping and loan shark operation from their brothel, Panther and Monkey bust the place. The Eagle leader Mei (Chan Shen) claims ignorance of the operation, and invites the Iron Flagsters to a party to apologize. (For the record, the Eagle uniforms are very tacky, all in leopard spots and feathers.) Suspecting a trap, Tiger Chau Fang (Lu Feng) hires hit man Yen Hsiu (Lung Tin Cheung), the Man in White, to back them up so they won't be caught unarmed. The trap is sprung, allowing the Iron Flag to kill Mei, but Chief Tao is struck down from behind during the battle.

Tiger Chau takes over as new leader, and Lo takes the blame for the ruckus (with a sizable bribe going to the police) to avoid involving the rest of the group in any charges, agreeing to leave town until things cool off. But Chau turns out to be a rat bastard who cuts off Lo's funds, becomes partners with Eagles Kao and Chin, and has Monkey Yuen kicked out of the club. He also hires the Ten Deadly Killers of the Underworld—who go by names like Fortune Teller, Killer Butcher (Chiang Kam), Book Keeper, and Dangerous Kid—to eliminate Lo. However, the Man in White feels he was tricked into killing an honorable man in Tao, and reveals all. He joins Lo and Yuen to go back and settle Chau's hash.

The action isn't as wild as in some other Venoms pictures, but it's imaginatively staged and excitingly performed—with typically bloody consequences—and Chang Cheh takes full advantage of the flag-fighting spectacle. One scene has a black flag thrown *through* a man, dying it red (and of course he goes on to fight a dozen men for several minutes after). The original HK version is said to run 30 minutes longer. *AKA: Tit Kei Moon; Tie Qi Men; The Spearmen; The Spearman of Death.* 🐉🐉🐉🐉

1980 (R) 85m/C *HK* Phillip Kwok, Chiang Sheng, Lu Feng, Wang Li, Lung Tin Cheung, Yu Tai-ping, Chan Shen, Chiang Kam, Wong Ching Ho, Fung Ging Man. *D:* Chang Cheh. *W:* Ngai Hong, Chang Cheh. **DVD**

Flash Future Kung Fu

Take *The Chinese Connection* and put it in a blender with *Road Warrior, Flashdance,* and a typical direct-to-video *Bladerunner* knockoff, and you might get something like this weak sci-fi action flick. In the dark world of the future, the Master (Eddie Ko) tries to keep a traditional martial arts school open. Killer (Johnny Wang) is his top student, but risks his neck participating in Black Boxing matches behind the master's back. He and Gei (Ray Lui) meet up with a pair of girls named Monique and Viva, who belong to a neo-Nazi group called the X Gang, and find nothing but trouble. Gei gets beaten up in a curiously retro video arcade (an X Gang hangout), and while he recovers, Viva pays him a vampire-like visit to seduce and medicate him. Killer goes to the arcade to avenge his friend, but comes staggering home with hypos stabbed into his back, which apparently give him rabies! Monique has a change of heart and offers the Master a cure, but the proud teacher refuses modern medicines to treat his student with more natural methods—namely, applying a dead chicken to his back, then forcing him to drink gallons of some vile-looking liquid.

Back at the school, Nazi skinheads attack and kill everyone. Luckily, the treatments have made Killer a better fighter than ever, and he and the Master hop on their tractor to go kick heinie at disco Nazi headquarters (where the Chinese version of Devo is performing while Viva and Monique, in pink tutus, drown a woman in a leopard print jumpsuit).

According to movies like this one, the future will be pretty much like 1982, only not as well lit and with a lot more smoke. It could be that something is lost in the U.S. version—some scenes are obviously missing, and the opening narration cards aren't translated—but it's doubtful the Hong Kong version is much better. The action scenes are minimally choreographed and look like typical street brawls, and every scene has so much fog in it that it's not always clear what's happening in them. By the climax, viewers may be rooting for the X Gang's lobotomized warriors to win. Director Kirk Wong *(Beast Cops)* would improve dramatically within a few years, but even fans might want to avoid this one. A clip from an Abbott and Costello cartoon appears at a key moment. *AKA: Dai Lui Toi; Da Lei Tai; Health Warning; Mr. Digital; Master Digital.* 🐉

1983 78m/C *HK* Eddie Ko, Johnny Wang, Ray Lui, Monica Lam, Yuen Tin Wan, Shan Yeh, Ma Lau, Elvis Tsui. *D:* Kirk Wong. *W:* Jerry Liu. *C:* Henry Chan, Abdul M. Rumjahn, Larry Siu, Peter Ngor, Arthur Wong. *M:* Jim Shum. **VHS, DVD**

Flight of the Heroine

The story begins with the heroine, Lucy, taking the head of the Emperor (who killed her father) to her father's grave. Afterward, she starts a martial arts school for her daughter Elaine and two local boys, Vincent and Jordan Michael. The two boys are in love with Elaine, and fight for her affection. Vincent loses and leaves the school.

The local corrupt officials, including Lord Aaron, are dealing in white slavery and prostitution. Jordan, skilled enough in kung fu to paralyze with needles or thrown mah-jongg tiles, is Aaron's avowed enemy. Jordan and Aaron confront each other on a bridge, as Aaron's army tries to kill the interloping do-gooders. Elaine and her mother show up to help Jordan in the battle. Vincent arrives to help the bad guys and loses an eye for his trouble. After the final confrontation, Jordan and Elaine head off, and Lucy continues her fight against the corrupt government.

More deliberately cheesy dubbing presented by the Jalisco video label (listen for the computer salesman in the marketplace) make this story goofier than it needs to be. Still, the plot is wafer-thin and it almost seems as though this is just a segment of a longer movie, or perhaps a sequel to a better-known film. What it might be a sequel to, though, remains unclear—as Jalisco has again failed to give any real credits or titles. The ongoing rebels versus corrupt government is similar to the story line in *Swordswoman in White*. That film, though, had better action scenes. —SS 🐉🐉

2000 66m/C *CH* **VHS, DVD**

Flirting Scholar

Stephen Chow ventures yet again into period costume comedy, along with cohorts Lee Lik-Chi and Vincent Kok, and scores another bull's-eye. Tong Pak-fu (Chow) is a member of the Ming Dynasty's famous Four Scholars, renowned for his writing and artistic talents. Not that any of his eight wives are impressed—they'd rather play mah-jongg and dominoes all day than pay

attention to him. His mother Chussy (Mimi Chu) laments his unhappiness, but nags him to keep his promise to his father never to reveal his kung fu prowess, lest their enemies Evil Scholar (Gordon Lau) and Chussy's unsuccessful rival, Madam Wah (Cheng Pei-Pei), take advantage.

On a trip to avoid the emperor's magistrate King Ning (Lam Wai), who wants to recruit him as a consultant, Tong falls in love at second sight with Chou-heung (Gong Li), one of Madame Wah's maids. He disguises himself as a beggar to meet her, and sells himself to the Wah household as a workman to get closer. When the Four Perverted Heroes invade the house, intent on abducting Chou-heung, Tong's efforts at protection only make her think that he's in cahoots with the invaders. Madam Wah orders his death, but his explanation is so eloquent (in rap form yet), that she instead assigns him to teach her sons. But to save himself, he found it necessary to name Tong Pak-fu as his bitter enemy, a fact that gets in the way of his wooing Chou-heung, who is secretly a big Tong fan. The comedy of errors only gets more complicated when Tong's friends and enemies also end up visiting the household, including the dreaded Evil Scholar himself.

Chow and company successfully transfer the Chinese opera into the cinema comedy format, complete with songs, stances, and staging. The Four Scholars are a deft parody of Hong Kong's pop stars Four Princes, strutting around like a boy band. Who knows how they got majestic mainland star Gong Li for a Stephen Chow comedy with both intricate wordplay and vomit jokes, but this is actually her second, and she does O.K. in the film's least-demanding part. Though Chow's poetry duel with Vincent Kok is probably the ultimate example of his comedy not translating to another language, this is still another very funny outing for him. Even when he's not present in a scene, his spirit carries on, as in the hidden duel between Gordon Lau and Cheng Pei-Pei, which spoofs Lau's similar scenes in *Dirty Ho*. Yuen King-Tan contributes another of her man-crazy she-wolves to the fun. *AKA: Tong Pak-fu Dim Chou-heung; Tang Bohu Dian Qiuxiang; Flirtong Scholar.* 🐉🐉🐉

1993 102m/C *HK* Stephen Chow, Gong Li, Nat Chan, Cheng Pei-Pei, James Wong, Leung Kar-yan, Gordon Lau, Lam Wai, Gabriel Wong, Vincent Kok, Yuen King-Tan, Mimi Chu, Peter Lai, Yammie Nam, Francis Ng, Joey Leung, Lee Kin-yan, Walter Cho. *D:* Lee Lik-Chi. *W:* Vincent Kok, Lee Lik-Chi. *C:* David Chung. *M:* William Woo. **VHS, DVD**

Flyin Dance

Two roommates lead very different romantic lives. Both like to meet women over the Inter-

net, but A-Tai (Zhang Zhen) prefers brief affairs with playmates while Tsia-Chung (Jordan Chan) is searching for a soulmate—despite using the misleading computer screen name of Sleazy-Tsai. Tsia-Chung finally meets a longtime online correspondent (Ma Qian-shan) with the screen name of "Flyindance" (think three words, fly-in-dance, as in "I dream of being able to fly through the air while dancing") and they begin dating in the real world. Meanwhile, A-Tai enjoys a dalliance with Siu Yu (Shu Qi), a leading dancer at the Art Institute, but she breaks up with him when Tsia-Chung exposes A-Tai as a womanizer. A-Tai moves on, but still longs for Siu Yu. All these events lead up to a fateful New Year's Eve dance to celebrate the year 2000.

What a frustrating film to watch! Based strictly on the cover art, you might reasonably anticipate a lighthearted romantic tale. Instead, it's a drama about people who communicate better over the Internet than in person. As you might expect, that makes for a film that is often dull. Whatever chance the story might have to captivate the viewer is robbed by the very poorly translated English subtitles. What makes it really frustrating, though, is that the director demonstrates a good eye for framing scenes and that glimmers of emotional truth bubble just beneath the surface. The virtues of the tale are sabotaged by the manipulation of the characters. And the ending tries to wrap everything up with a nice bow, but instead exposes the shortcomings. The look of the film is handsome, although the music pushes too many familiar romantic buttons. The lead actress, Ma Qian-shan, gives a very fine performance covering a wide range of emotions convincingly. Jordan Chan maintains one note throughout as Tsia-Chung—glum and remote. Zhang Zhen and Shu Qi bring a bit of life in their limited screen time. —PM **AKA:** Fly in Dance. 🐉🐉

2001 89m/C TW Ma Qian-shan, Zhang Zhen, Jordan Chan, Shu Qi. **D:** Gam Gwok-chiu. **VHS, DVD**

The Flying Guillotine

This classic Shaw Brothers cult flick gimmick mixes kung fu with horror in a historic setting. In the Ching Dynasty, Emperor Yung Ching (Kong Yeung) wants his critics Chen Li and Yen Lo-Fu eliminated, but decides to use assassins to escape public disfavor over his actions. Sing Yang (Ku Feng) is put in charge of the mission. Watching top jugglers in the square gives him an idea for an invention. He crafts a device, a kind of helmet lined with retractable blades that can be hurled over an enemy's head and activated at distances up to 100 yards. The emperor orders that a dozen elite guardsmen become

masters of the new weapon. Ma Tang (Chen Kuan-tai of Shaolin King Boxer) and Chia Tsien-Fu (Frankie Wei) go to the head of the class (and chop the head off cleanly), but they become uneasy thinking about what the emperor has in mind for them. As the spectacular and ghoulish assassinations begin to be carried out, Tsien-Fu's conscience gets the best of him, and he finds himself unable obey orders. With that, Tsien-Fu becomes the next victim of the emperor's wrath, with Ma Tang next on the list.

The fight scenes are relatively believable—far from the usual kung fu acrobatics—outside of those involving the weird device itself. Did this strange weapon actually exist? It's known that the ancient Chinese used a variety of piau (thrown weapons) in warfare, many of which were "attached" piau, with a rope or chain. Texts describe doohickeys that are just as devilish, such as huge round saw blades fired with catapults, and poison-tipped iron claws that close on impact. One thing is certain: it was exploitation genius, as Flying Guillotine was a big hit, and even cleaned up at U.S. grind houses, aided by an intensive TV ad campaign. So successful was the gimmick that the flying guillotine showed up in several more features, some of which were even more successful. Though the fad soon burned itself out, fans are still fascinated with the weapon. After all, who can resist seeing a crazy, head-chopping UFO in action? **AKA:** Huet Dik Ji; Xie Di Zi. 🐉🐉🐉

1974 111m/C HK Chen Kuan-tai, Kong Yeung, Ku Feng, Frankie Wei, Liu Wu-Chi. **D:** Ho Meng-Hua. **W:** Ngai Hong. **C:** Tsao Hui-Chi. **M:** Wang Fu-Ling. **DVD**

For Bad Boys Only

The cold opening of this sci-fi action adventure might make you think at first glance that you're watching Jurassic Park—or at least Bio Zombies. In a huge, empty warehouse, a heavily reinforced crate marked "DNA" is being opened, surrounded by men with guns. The first indication of something different comes in noting the guards are all wearing eerie black masks. The second is the contents of the crate: a lovely young woman in a party dress. She makes a break for freedom, showing superior speed, but is brought down by a man with a high-tech pistol of some kind.

After a delirious CGI f/x credit sequence that takes us on a trip through DNA molecules, we meet the Bad Boy Squad. Jack Shum (Louis Koo), King Chan (Ekin Cheng), and his sister Queen (Kristy Yeung) have been hired by a film director to break up the forced wedding of his ex-girlfriend movie star to a four-star general. Then it's off to Shanghai to reunite a grandfather with his first love. The Bad Boys Detective

That's Bruceploitation

The Clones of Bruce Lee

Everyone in the Hong Kong movie business had their hopes raised. Bruce Lee had become an international superstar, was starring a film with Warner Bros. of Hollywood, U.S.A., and was going to crack the film world wide open so that HK flicks would stand shoulder to shoulder with anything made overseas. At least, that was the dream. But then Lee died, even before *Enter the Dragon* premiered, and that dream was dashed.

But wait a minute—with or without Bruce Lee, there was still a huge demand for Bruce Lee movies. Maybe somebody can substitute for the Dragon. Many foreigners didn't even know Bruce was dead (after all, his movies were playing everywhere) and wouldn't know the difference as long as they saw a Chinese guy doing kung fu on the screen. Heck, plenty of movies were already trying to copy Lee's act even before he was dead.

When Elvis Presley joined the army, a swarm of similar-looking young singers was drafted by movie studios to try to fill in as crooning teen idols. However, even if Elvis had died suddenly back then, it's unlikely anyone would be crass enough to release *Jailhouse Rock 2* starring a look-alike called Elvis Posely. But that's about what happened throughout the 1970s as a legion of Lee-alikes thumbed their noses at good taste to haunt movie houses in yellow jumpsuits. As Jackie Chan put it so succinctly, it was "Bruce Le, Bruce Lo, Bruce Lamp, Bruce Table, Bruce Chair...." Here's a look at the crop.

Bruce Li (Ho Chung Tao)

This Taiwanese high-school physical education instructor and part-time actor was brought to a producer by a buddy who was an action director, and his resemblance to Lee made him a star, originally billed using Lee's nickname, Lee Shao-Lung. Ho idolized Lee and thought the films he made were going to be respectful tributes, and he objected when producer Jimmy Shaw gave him the name Bruce Li. He was thrust into many cheap rip-offs like *The New Game of Death*, *Story of the Dragon*, and *Bruce Lee We Miss You*, distinguished by only his own decent acting and athletic talents. Ho vowed to leave "Li" behind and acted under his own name in pictures like *Revenge of the Patriots*, but was lured back to Bruce with promises that *Bruce Lee: The Man, the Myth* would be a classy biopic. When the results were unsatisfactory, Li swore he was finished, but somehow his films always ended up with the exploitable Lee connection in the title and credits. Later, they even tried to make him copy Jackie Chan by pairing him with Simon Yuen in *Blind Fist of Bruce*. He fared much better playing a cab driver drafted as a Lee-Alike-like action star in *Dynamo*.

Dragon Lee (Vyachaslev Yaksysnyi)

That's right, reportedly this North Korean native, at one time billed as Bruce Lei, is of Russian descent! A total ham, Dragon isn't much of an actor, but has a great physique and a fierce disposition that comes through on film. Few attempts were made to have Dragon act like Lee in dramatic roles before he was shipped off to star in some wildly trashy films such as *Dragon on Fire* for the likes of Godfrey Ho. In one of his camp classics, a mad scientist teamed him up in a test tube with fellow Lee-Alikes Bruce Le and Bruce Thai as the *Clones of Bruce Lee*.

Bruce Le (Huang Kin Lung)

A former Shaw Brothers contract player, Le is the absolute worst actor among the Lee-Alikes, but considered a better martial artist than the others. Painful to watch in most of his films, he rarely changes his dull expression. The best part of his movies are often the titles, from *Re-enter the Dragon* to *Ninja vs. Bruce Lee* to *Enter Another Dragon*. Le starred in the outrageously titled *Bruce Lee Fights Back from the Grave*.

Bruce Thai (?)

Aside from *Clones of Bruce Lee*, he turns up in *Fearless Hyena 3* (AKA *Fearless Master*) with Jackie *Chen*!

Jackie Chan (Chan Kong-Sang)

Yes, even the king of HK cinema was promoted as the New Bruce Lee in *New Fist of Fury*. It didn't work.

Tong Lung (Kim Tai Chung)

This actor/stuntman was the main double brought in for Golden Harvest's lame attempt to complete Lee's *Game of Death*, along with Yuen Biao. He made up for it by starring in the trashier—but much more fun—sequel, *Tower of Death*.

Michael Chan (Chan Wai-Man)

He may deny it, but in films like *Fists Like Lee, Spirits of Bruce*

Continued on next page...

Lee, and *The Invincible Killer,* Chan is definitely trying on the Bruce Lee mantle, even billed as Bruce Chen in some markets.

Bruce Liang (Leung Siu Lung)

With only a few titles like *Dragon Lives Again* and *Fighting Dragon* on his resume, this Taiwanese opera student (AKA Bruce Leung) concentrated on his own acrobatics and fight choreography, rarely cashing in on his Bruce L name. He was more of a Jackie Chan clone in flicks like *My Kung Fu 12 Kicks.*

Bruce Lai (Cheung Yi Dao)

This capable performer had no connection to Bruceploitation other than his name, oddly enough.

Henry Yu Yung

This star of the early '70s fare such as *The Awaken Punch* was sometimes billed as Bruce Lye. Others were also pegged with "Bruce" names for marquee value only, such as Chen Hung Lieh who was dubbed "Bruce Lieh" at least once, while Delon Tan appeared as "Bruce Liang," Yeung Wai was "Bruce Kong," Lau Kar-Wing was "Bruce Lau," and Yasuaki Kurata became "Bruce Lo." Tang Yim-chan even co-starred with Bruce Li in *Blind Fist of Bruce* as "Bruce Tong."

House is world-famous for pulling off these kinds of capers. Though Jack is dating fashion model Angel (Kelly Lin), Queen has a heavy crush on Jack, while King is after every girl he sees. At a dance club, he sees a strange girl named Eleven (Shu Qi) staring at him. The next day, client Tin Ai (Daniel Chan) comes looking for the same girl, his lost girlfriend Shadow (Shu Qi again). They take the case, despite the man's lack of funds.

The next day, multimillionaire Yung Yung Hsin hires them to find a woman he believes to be the daughter of his own lost love Kwan Chin (Shu Qi yet again), who was an Olympic track star (the "Asian Antelope") 20 years ago. While Jack and Queen go to Taiwan to trace Kwan Chin, King follows the man he saw with Eleven, genetic scientist Taro Sakamoto (Mark Cheng). He rescues the strange girl from her captors, and finds she has superhuman powers. However, she turns out to not be Shadow, and attaches herself to King, even researching love by watching Stephen Fung movies. Meanwhile, Tin Ai manages to find Shadow on his own, learning her face has been seriously scarred after Sakamoto's men kidnapped her and used her in their experiments because of her resemblance to Kwan Chin. As anyone except the heroes could deduce, Eleven is the result of a series of cloning experiments using genetic material taken from Kwan Chin, and Sakamoto is working on developing Stepford Shu Qis and super-soldiers for rich clients.

This would be a much more enjoyable film without its pop-video sentimentality. The young stars are clones of every pop star and model cliché, and their precious posing repels rather than attracts. At least this time Shu Qi has the excuse of her unnatural origin to explain her little-girl act, and balances her performance by also playing the older Kwan Chin character and the more troubled Shadow. The trite implication is that while the boys are looking for a 10, Shu Qi is an 11. There's finally some relief from the soap opera when the Bad Boys Squad makes an assault on the secret genetic labs, but even then the action is unimpressive, relying more on editing than real athletic ability. *AKA: Bad Boy Dak Gung; Bad Boy Te Gong; For BadBoys Only.* ♪♪

2000 105m/C *HK* Ekin Cheng, Louis Koo, Shu Qi, Kristy Yeung, Mark Cheng, Kelly Lin, Daniel Chan, Jerry Lamb, Blackie Ko, Frankie Ng, Helena Law, Gigi Lai, Josie Ho, Stephanie Che, Anya, Chiang Han. *D:* Raymond Yip. *W:* Manfred Wong. *C:* Lai Yiu-fai. *M:* Comfort Chan. **VHS, DVD**

Forbidden City Cop

In this follow-up to *From Beijing with Love*, Stephen Chow ventures into period costume adventure yet again to send up flying swordsman movies, playing an ancestor of Beijing's Ling Ling-chat. Ling Ling-fat ("008") is a gynecologist who has somehow come to be one of the elite Forbidden City Cops—a quartet of agents assigned to protect the Emperor (Cheung Tat-Ming) and his palace. Though the other three cops are powerful martial artists, Fat knows nothing of kung fu, endeavoring to contribute with his ingenious inventions. While Fat is shooing duelists off the roof one night, a creature dubbed "Flying Fairy" drops from the sky, and all of China's greatest doctors are invited to participate in the examination of the corpse. However, it turns out to be a plot by the King of the No-Face Stance (who literally has lost his face) from the Gum Kingdom. He and his weird family kidnap the Emperor and dress him in a Flying Fairy costume (which resembles a lumpy UFO-naut), hoping the medicos will kill him during their alien autopsy, which will also give their assassins an opportunity to kill their enemies' doctors and invade the country. Fat and his inventions save the day, and he goes on to his next assignment: entering a brothel (run by Yuen King-Tan) to check out the Emperor's prospective new concubine Gum Tso (Carman Lee)—a beautiful she-devil who threatens to destroy all of China, and Fat's happy marriage to Kar-ling (Carina Lau) along with it.

Fully stocked with Chow's hilariously nonsensical gags and spoofs, here he also provides some endearing pathos. He and Carina Lau make for a very funny and attractive couple, and it's genuinely heartbreaking to see their happiness threatened. Law Kar-Ying returns as Chow's sidekick, getting his share of laughs as well. The film contains many subtle send-ups of swordplay film clichés, as when Law is called upon to throw Chow's weapons to him during a battle—from only a few feet away; or even in the music chosen for a dramatic moment, which sounds like it was plucked directly from an old Shaw Brothers classic. At one point, the cast passes out awards to themselves for their acting in a previous scene! Another outstanding comedy from the prolific King of Hong Kong Comedy. *AKA: Daai Laap Mat Taam 008; Da Nei Mi Tan 008.* ♪♪♪

1996 89m/C *HK* Stephen Chow, Carina Lau, Carman Lee, Law Kar-Ying, Cheung Tat-Ming, Yuen Cheung-yan, Sunny Yuen, Tats Lau, Wong Yat-Fei, Manfred Wong, Yuen King-Tan, Alvina Kong, Lee Lik-chi, Mimi Chu, Vincent Kok, Lee Kin-yan, Chik King Man, Stephen Au, Fletcher Poon. *D:* Stephen Chow, Vincent Kok. *W:* Stephen Chow, Vincent Kok, Lo Man-sang. *C:* Lee Kin Keung. *M:* Tats Lau. **VHS, DVD**

The Foul King

The kind of zero-to-hero story that Hollywood so often fails to get right, this outstanding Korean comedy is not only funny and touching, but the best wrestling movie made since El Santo died.

Im Dae-ho (Song Kang-ho) is a poor slob who somehow ended up as a bank clerk. Unable to land an account, and perennially late for work, his boss spares him a complete public grilling, opting instead to teach him a private lesson by subjecting him to the Headlock of Horror in the men's room. Dae-ho gets a mercy account from a pal who is a tae kwondo instructor, which gets him to thinking about how to deal with situations like that headlock. Finding martial arts too spiritual and impractical, he answers an ad at a dilapidated gym asking for beginning wrestlers. Coach Jang, formerly the Ultra Tiger Mask, is reluctant to take on the scrawny loser, but it just so happens that a manager he knows wants him to train a "cheating" wrestler to help promote his star Yubiho in advance of a Japanese tour, and no other coach will agree to it.

A fan of old-time wrestling, Dae-ho is enthusiastic about the idea, and begins to train nights and weekends—though he's surprised to find himself trained by Jang's pretty daughter Min-young instead of the coach himself. Helping out are two supposedly more experienced wrestlers named Mt. Taebaik and Mt. Odai. In his first match as the Foul King, Dae-ho acquits himself well, despite accidentally stabbing Odai with a real fork instead of the prop. Meanwhile, the assistant bank manager is pushing through an illegal loan with an associate of his, planning to use Dae-ho and his friend Choi Doo-shik as patsies should they get caught. During the big tag-team match with the steroid-popping pretty-boy Yubiho, the Foul King snaps and throws out the script, refusing to take a fall when Yubiho tears his mask.

Director Kim Ji-woon never misses a chance to undercut any pretension, making a left turn

from the expected at every opportunity—as in a dream sequence in which Dae-ho sees himself as a wrestling Elvis Presley turns ugly when he faces an opponent from real life. Though Dae-ho, conditioned by TV and movies, fully expects that wearing the Tiger Mask will imbue him with the confidence to overcome all obstacles, it only works part of the time. His clumsy attempts to romance Min-young fail, but produce a sweet delayed reaction. And thank goodness, a little success doesn't mean Dae-ho stops being a clod. If the New Korean Film breaks out in the world market as it should, Song Kang-ho (Shiri) is bound for international stardom. He's just good-looking enough to pull off the romantic bits without losing his underdog quality, and he's equally adept at drama, comedy, and action. Beautifully shot, this little gem became a smash hit in Korea. The import DVD on the Spectrum label is available in a limited deluxe edition that includes many extras, comes in a decorative box, and includes a signed Foul King shower cap! **AKA:** Banchik-Wang. ♪♪♪♪

2000 111m/C *KO* Song Kang-ho, Chung Jin-young, Chang Hang-sun, Park Sang-myun, Song Young-chang, Cheong Wung-in, Lee Ki-young, Shin Ha-kyun, Ko Ho-kyung, Kim Su-ro. **D:** Kim Ji-woon. **W:** Kim Ji-woon. **VHS, DVD**

Frankenstein vs. Baragon

Special-effects genius Willis O'Brien's plans for a film called *King Kong vs. Frankenstein* may have led directly to *King Kong vs. Godzilla*, but Toho Studios had been planning to make a Frankenstein movie since the late 1950s. Screenwriter Shenichi Sekizawa (*Mothra*) wrote a treatment for *Frankenstein vs. the Human Vapor* that was abandoned. Then Takeshi Kimura (*Rodan*) got the idea for the story of *Frankenstein vs. Godzilla*, in which Toho's champion would be revived by the Japanese government to battle an ever-growing Frankenstein Monster. It was decided that Godzilla would be just too powerful for poor Frankenstein, and so a new reptilian menace was devised to take his place, and the Big G was added to the cast of *Ghidorah the Three-Headed Monster*. Aside from that big change, the script was kept pretty much intact.

At the close of World War II, Nazis ship the heart of the Frankenstein Monster from Germany to Japan, where it arrives in time to be subjected to massive radiation in the atomic bomb blast at Hiroshima. Twenty years later, Dr. James Bowen (Nick Adams) and colleague/girlfriend Dr. Sueko Togami (Kumi Mizuno) are studying the effects of radiation on the area, when they are presented with a captured wild boy who has been causing trouble in the neighborhood. The strange-looking boy grows rapidly, and needs to be locked up. He grows big enough to break loose from his cage, losing a hand in the process. The hand continues to live, and grows when fed blood. Sure that they'll never be able to control the monster, the scientists and military debate what should be done (unfortunately, this was years before Monster Island was constructed). Meanwhile, a monster has been raiding farms in the mountains, far from where the now gigantic Frankenstein (Koji Furuhata) was last seen. It turns out the culprit is a second monster the natives call Baragon (Haruo Nakajima), a burrowing reptile that looks like a cross between a triceratops and a cocker spaniel. Of course the two monsters meet and mingle.

Released in America as *Frankenstein Conquers the World*, this was one of the first of Toho's sci-fi films co-produced with Henry G. Saperstein of UPA, who convinced the Japanese that their films would do better overseas with an Anglo face in the cast. TV star Nick Adams had derailed his career a bit with an egotistical campaign for an Academy Award. He'd also vowed to never work in an overseas production, words he ate happily upon arrival in Japan, where he enjoyed working on three pictures for Toho (and reportedly helped break up his marriage with an affair with co-star Mizuno). Furuhata has a lean and hungry look as the Frankenstein Monster, which may have been in keeping with the script, but has the result of making him appear scrawny, even at 50 feet tall. Baragon, on the other hand, is a delightful creation, scampering about like a huge puppy with a glowing horn on his nose. Too bad he didn't return more often, making only a cameo appearance in *Destroy All Monsters,* but unseen until his recent comeback in *Godzilla, Mothra and King Ghidorah: Battle on Fire.* The special effects are uneven—some shots are brilliant, but one has to question why a master like Eiji Tsuburaya would use toy farm animals for shots where the real thing was available. Though the picture starts well, building a great deal of creepy suspense, the picture loses some steam during the middle. The climactic battle is rousing, but leads to another of Toho's dissatisfactory ends. The Japanese video version, which is six minutes longer, features a restored original ending in which Frankenstein battles a giant octopus. True to Toho's road company spirit, though stars in other pictures, Mie Hama and Akira Takarada show up in tiny cameos here. **AKA:** Furankenshutain tai Chitei Kaiju Baragon; Furankensuten to Baragon; Frankenstein Conquers the World; Frankenstein Meets the Giant Devil Fish; Frankenstein and the Giant Lizard Frankenstein vs. the Subterranean Monster. ♪♪♪

1965 87m/C *JP* Tadeo Takashima, Nick Adams, Kumi Mizuno, Yoshio Tsuchiya, Koji Furuhata, Jun

Tazaki, Susumu Fujita, Takashi Shimura, Nobuo Nakamura, Kenji Sahara, Yoshifumi Tajima, Kozo Nomura, Haruya Kato, Ikio Sawamura, Yoshio Kosugi, Keiko Sawai, Ren Yamamoto, Yutaka Sada, Kenzo Tabu, Hisaya Ito, Shigeki Ishida, Nadao Kirino, Shoichi Hirose, Haruo Nakajima, Mie Hama, Akira Takarada. **D:** Ishiro Honda. **W:** Takeshi Kimura. **C:** Hajime Koizumi. **M:** Akira Ifukube. **VHS**

Freeze Me

Chihiro (Harumi Inoue), who works in a bank office, is engaged to be married to co-worker Nogami (Shunsuke Matsuoka), and appears to be a happy person. The thin veneer of her outer personality is ripped away, however, when Hirokawa (Kazuki Kitamura) shows up—he is one of three men who raped Chihiro five years previously. Hirokawa forces his way into Chihiro's apartment and declares that the "old gang" will reunite and have their way with her again. When she tries to resist, he boldly saunters naked down the hallway, shoving photographic evidence of the rape into her neighbors' mail slots. Chihiro is even more terrified of what people will think, and she returns with him to her apartment. Hirokawa—arrogant, boorish, and hateful—shows up at her office, making outrageous demands and threatening to tell everyone about the rape. Chihiro again gives in, and is fired because of the ruckus caused by Hirokawa.

When Nogami visits Chihiro at home, where Hirokawa boasts about the gang rape, Nogami is so shocked by the news that he simply walks away. Suffering from a walking nightmare, abandoned by the one she loves, Chihiro snaps and kills Hirokawa. Another rapist, Kojima (Shingo Tsurami), shows up and suffers the same fate after he makes advances toward Chihiro and discovers Hirokawa's body in the freezer. Chihiro stuffs the bodies into two new freezers, moves—taking the freezers with her—and starts a new job. She's really over the deep end by the time Baba (Naoto Takenaka), the vicious leader of the gang rape, appears at her door.

Very troubling issues are raised by writer/ director Takashi Ishii's approach to this subject. The actions of the men are despicable; even Chihiro's fiancée is shown in a poor light. Hirokawa's abuse of Chihiro early in the film is nearly unwatchable, simply because we realize the pain that she has already suffered and anticipate what's on the horizon. (The sexual violations themselves are enacted more through the power of suggestion than explicit actions.) On the other hand, it could well be argued that candycoating the abuse would be dishonest. After all, depictions of rape and sexual abuse *should* sicken the viewer, rather than titillate or entertain. The shame felt by Chihiro— which keeps her from reporting the original crime and paralyzes her five years later—is also a biting comment on the way that women are expected to act in Japanese culture. The social issues are clouded by the way director Ishii constantly reveals Chihiro's naked body, whether she is walking around her apartment, making love with her fiancé, or battling for her life. Because Harumi Inoue has a lovely figure, it's quite a challenge to avoid being distracted by her outward appearance and concentrate on the inner struggles of her character. Perhaps that was also Ishii's intention. If so, it's a very strong point indeed; Harumi Inoue is memorable in more ways than the obvious. *Freeze Me* is extremely well-made, harrowing, and thought-provoking; viewer discretion is mandatory. —PM **AKA:** *Freezer.* 🐶🐶🐶

2000 102m/C *JP* Harumi Inoue, Shingo Tsurami, Kazuki Kitamura, Shunsuke Matsuoka, Naoto Takenaka. **D:** Takashi Ishii. **W:** Takashi Ishii. **C:** Yasushi Sasakibara. **M:** Goro Yasukawa. **VHS, DVD**

From Beijing with Love

This Stephen Chow comedy makes a great introduction to his films, as many of his gags are at the expense of a universally recognized icon. The skull of China's biggest carnivorous dinosaur skeleton is stolen by the armored supervillain the Man with the Golden Gun. Chow is a reserve secret agent/butcher Ling Ling-chat ("007"), who is brought in to solve the case. Though possibly the worst choice for the assignment, Ling is chosen because the spy commander (Wong Kam-Kong) is secretly the Man with the Golden Gun. The villain has agent Siu-kam (Anita Yuen) sent to Hong Kong with Ling as his partner, though her real mission is to get him killed at the first opportunity. Ling prepares for his assignment by watching Roger Moore videos, and shows up on the job loaded with top-secret grooming gadgets. Despite her pedigree from a long line of traitors, Siu-kam finds herself softening toward Ling. He is a sweet guy deep down, and his inhuman skill with knives makes him a surprisingly good agent.

Chow not only parodies James Bond, but also looks a bit like Alan Delon, and throws in all kinds of references to action and spy movies. Unlike other spy spoofs, you could take the comedy out of this one and still have a pretty good thriller. There's a point where the action becomes unexpectedly bloody, which is kind of a shock, but if anyone can pick the mood up rather quickly after a slit throat, it's Chow. The cultural differences between East and West (or is it Chow and everyone else?) are readily apparent in scenes such as the one in which Anita Yuen accidentally shoots herself. Few

Western comedians would add quite so much blood to the joke. Side note: Watch how quickly wounds heal—is it a gaff, or more satire? Law Kar-Ying is on hand as a "Q" character with a carload of goofy inventions, such as a solar-powered flashlight, a toilet-seat videophone, and a special "spy chair." The film also looks forward to 1997, wasting no opportunities to reveal mainland officials to be just as greedy, inept, and corrupt as anyone else. Yu Rong-guang has an extended cameo toward the beginning as a super-spy. *AKA:* Gwok Chaan Ling Ling-chat; Guo Chan Ling Lihngqi; From China with Love. ♪♪♪♪

1994 83m/C HK Stephen Chow, Anita Yuen, Pauline Chan, Law Kar-Ying, Wong Kam-Kong, Yu Rongguang, Joe Cheng, Lee Lik-Chi, Johnny Tang, Wong Yat-Fei, Lee Kin-yan. *D:* Stephen Chow, Lee Lik-Chi. *W:* Stephen Chow, Roman Cheung, Vincent Kok, Lee Lik-Chi. *C:* Lee Kin Keung. *M:* William Woo. **VHS, DVD**

From China with Death

Millions of fans who have been clamoring to see Wu Ma naked get their chance in the very first scene of this kung fu heist movie. Wu Ma stars as Paku, a thief and unlikely lothario forced to skip town after being caught in bed with the butcher's wife (and everybody else's). Pei Sing-lan (Henry Yu Yung) is a con man who goes on the lam when a mobster catches him cheating at dominoes. The two meet on the train when they steal from each other and both jump off to avoid buying tickets. They keep on bumping into each other in the next town, and when Pei discovers that Paku plans to steal a load of gold from a bank, he decides to use him for a plan of his own. Paku catches on, and ruins Pei's heist plan in turn. Both thieves decide they'd be able to succeed if they'd just stop fouling each other up and become partners.

Pei's master plan involves recruiting gangster Fai Chung (Shih Kien) and his men to cause a diversion by attacking the bank's front gate—unsuccessfully—while a few men swipe the gold inside. Of course they plan to double-cross Fai by switching the gold trunks. However, Fai is one step ahead of them, having conspired with banker Foon (Wong Sam) to switch the gold bars for fake ones. Rather than be left holding the bag, Pei comes up with a scheme to try to get back at Fai and Foon, and get the gold away from them. But first they have to get away from Fai's thugs, who are out for their blood, police Captain Fu (Lee Chiu), who wants to arrest them, and most dangerous of all, Paku's abandoned fiancée Mimi (Suzy Mang)!

The film benefits greatly from good locations, 1930s vintage cars, and other details that add to the rich tone. However, budget constraints are evident here and there, as some of the guns used are clearly water pistols painted black. With Yuen Woo-ping handling the action direction, the fights and stunts are exciting and fast paced. However, this is one kung fu flick where the plot is more interesting than the fighting. Director Wu Ma not only gives himself the aforementioned nude scene, but a lot of amusing bits of comedy, and does a lot of fighting as well. He adds a sympathetic element to the otherwise unsavory protagonists. *AKA:* Long Booi Wai Gaan; Lang Bei Wei Jian; Conman and the Kung Fu Kid; Dirty Partners; Wits to Wits. ♪♪♪

1974 97m/C HK Henry Yu Yung, Wu Ma, Suzy Mang, Tang Ching, Shih Kien, Wong Sam, Chiang Nan, Lee Chiu, Yam Sai-kwoon, Fung Hark-On, Sunny Yuen, Corey Yuen. *D:* Wu Ma. *W:* Szeto On. *C:* Hwa San. *M:* Frankie Chan. **DVD**

From the Queen to the Chief Executive

An excellent, well-made social drama that asks complicated questions lacking easy answers. Beginning in 1997 with documentary television footage of the Chief Executive of the Hong Kong Special Administrative Region being sworn into office, we next see an appeal being made to the Chief Executive. The story then swiftly backtracks to 1985. We follow three people whose lives will intersect 12 years later: Yue-ling (Ai Jing), Mr. Leung (Stephen Tang), and Ming (David Lee). Yue-ling is a teenage girl suffering from loneliness and abuse; Mr. Leung is helping factory workers protest unfair working conditions; and Ming is a teenage boy caught up in a horrific crime. Fast-forward to early 1997, and we discover that Yue-ling has grown into a young woman fascinated by the prose of a young man who turns out to be a prisoner. That prisoner is Ming. He has been "detained at Her Majesty's pleasure," held for years without a sentence under a provision of British Colonial rule that, it is explained, was meant to give youthful offenders a bit of a break, a chance to correct themselves. Instead, it has been used to keep a number of young men behind bars for an indefinite period, never knowing when or if they can expect to be released. Yue-ling is touched by Ming's story, and seeks out the help of Mr. Leung, now a Councilor whose term of office will end effective with the handover of Hong Kong to the rule of Mainland China in July 1997.

Describe a movie as a "social drama," and most people will brush past it in favor of lighter forms of entertainment. After all, who goes to the movies for a civics lesson, or to listen to a lecture? Based on a true story, the film, for the first 20 minutes, feels didactic and dry. From that point forward, director Herman Yau and writer Elsa Yeung peel back the personal histories of Ming and Yue-ling, allowing different angles of the issues to be examined. Yau also colors the tale with the judicious use of stylistic flourishes (such as flashbacks, flash cutting, and black-and-white footage), and the jarring rock songs and haunting musical score keep the story from lapsing into stodginess. Rather than an overly predictable "social drama," the filmmakers have crafted an absorbing, emotional, and powerful story about lives gone adrift and the importance of human forgiveness. The performances from the little-known cast are remarkable and touching. Director Yau struggled for two years to find an investor before Charles Heung stepped forward. —PM **AKA:** *Dang Hau Dung Gin Wa Faat Laai; Deng Hou Dong Jian Hua Fa La.* ♪♪♪♪

2001 102m/C *HK* Stephen Tang, Ai Jing, David Lee, Reuben Langdon. **D:** Herman Yau. **W:** Elsa Yeung. **C:** Joe Chan. **M:** Mak Chun-hung. **VHS, DVD**

Frozen

Director Wang Xiaoshuai's underground independent film is banned in China, the filmmaker hiding behind the pseudonym "Wu Ming" to protect himself from imprisonment. *Frozen* is supposed to be based on the true story of a Beijing performance artist who died for his art. Some say Qi Lei (Jia Hongshen) didn't mean to die making his last work, but most believe that his death was intentional and premeditated from the start. His manager Lao Lin (Zhang Yongning) knows the full story. Qi Lei performed a series of works depicting his own death—burial in the earth, water burial, fire burial, and finally an ice burial. Like a hunger artist, his suffering is a statement unto itself. His brother-in-law jokes that his works will be valuable should he succeed in dying, but other friends and family are hurt and angry. After much planning and introspection, Qi Lei began a work in which he would melt a block of ice using just his own body heat, dying of hypothermia in the process. But it's life after death that's really interesting.

It's difficult to portray the artistic process through film, and so most films about artists settle for portraying how they live. People are fascinated with the artworks and think therefore the artist should be just as fascinating. But this is often not the case—much of an artist's life consists of working or thinking about work. The more serious the work, the more intense the

artist's introspection—or else the work comes from simple and instinctive inspiration, leading an otherwise ordinary existence. And so, films about artists are often full of dramatic exposition or a lot of depressing brooding. One would think that a film about a performance artist—any kind of performance—would be more interesting, but reenactments of a performance are only reenactments, and this particular artist's story is a long string of brooding and smoking scenes broken by occasional bits that actually depict his work. There's some interest in seeing what the artistic community is like in China, until it's revealed that it's just like any artistic community anywhere—just with more arrests. The only lively moment is a brief sequence in which Qi's sister tries to have him committed, but the doctors take away his excitable schoolmate by mistake. Well, it also gets more interesting at the end. The film does a very good job in presenting all this brooding, and calls attention to the actual artwork and the message behind it. But filmmakers would spend their time more effectively by concentrating on the artwork itself and not trying to understand the mind behind it. You can either hit a high C or you can marvel at it, but watching the singer have lunch is only as interesting as watching a lunch. **AKA:** *Jidu Hanleng.* ♪

1996 96m/C *CH* Jia Hongsheng, Ma Xiaoqing, Bai Yu, Zhang Yongning, Li Geng, Wei Ye. **D:** Wang Xiaoshuai. **W:** Pang Ming, Wang Xiaoshuai. **C:** Yang Shu. **M:** Roeland Dol. **VHS, DVD**

*F*** / Off*

This bank heist comedy's semi-rude title may be a play on John Woo's *Face/Off* (though there's no similarity), and stars the stand-up comedy duo of Dayo Wong and Cheung Tat-Ming, who share narration. Lee Ka-shing (Cheung) is a nerdy bank teller who works with his best friend Fai, worships his co-worker Alice (Michelle Wong), and hates his boss Tony. Lee gets in deep trouble, owing HK$3 million to a loan shark (Bobby Yip) because he invested with a friend of Fai's—then he gets fired. Papa (Wong) is a small-time crook whose girlfriend Mime (Angela Tong) just dumped him—but won't move out. They meet in a public washroom when they each mistake one another for a childhood acquaintance. Together they decide to rob the bank, with Papa agreeing to show Lee the ropes of the business. At first, as Papa puts him through practice and training, Lee isn't sure he has the guts to go through with it. And as he gets to know Papa better, he begins to doubt whether he can finish what he starts.

The pair of leads have good chemistry, giving the impression they're sharing their pri-

vate jokes with the audience. Wisely, the atmosphere is helped along by a good selection of familiar character faces, especially Helena Law as a feisty policewoman and Simon Lui as a troublesome customer. Angela Tong does well in her first film role—one wonders whether her character's habit of speaking silently to Wong is a result of the Canadian actress's unfamiliarity with Chinese. *AKA: A Lee Ang Ang Leung Goh Daai Diy; Ya Li Ba Ba Liang Ge Da Dao.* 🎵🎵🎵

1998 99m/C *HK* Dayo Wong, Cheung Tat-Ming, Angela Tong, Wayne Lai, Helena Law, Michelle Wong, Bobby Yip, Hui Fun, Law Kwun-jor, Lam Kee-to, Rico Chung, May Yu, Kwan Yim-ha, Chan Shing-hung, Simon Lui, Vincent Kok, Matt Chow. *D:* Abe Kwong. *W:* Abe Kwong. *C:* Tony Cheung. *M:* Tommy Wai. **VHS, DVD**

Fugitive Alien

Alien invaders from Valnastar and Earth battle it out. Ken (Tatsuya Azuma), an enemy soldier with superhuman strength, deserts and is pursued by his fellow Valnastaroids. The crew of the space command ship *Bakkus III* spots Ken when his ship becomes disabled and take him in, only receiving notice of the alien invasion after he's aboard. When enemy ships show up, Ken helps the Earthlings escape.

On Earth, Ken tries to steal the ship, but hard-drinking old Captain Joe convinces him to join his crew instead, pretty much blackmailing him into becoming an Earth hero. Meanwhile, the Valnasty commander convinces Ken's ex-girlfriend Rita that it's her duty to track down Ken for them. The Space Force commander (Toho star Akihiko Hirata) orders the crew to the desert planet Karrara, where Ken gets in more trouble, and Rita catches up with him.

Cheaply dubbed from Japanese and re-edited, this is a condensation of part of a short-lived TV series from Tsuburaya Enterprises called *Sutaurufu* ("Starwolf"), one of many to break from the masked superhero trend to copy *Star Wars*. As a result, the plot is rushed, episodic, and confusing. Joe Shishido, the chipmunk-cheeked star of flashy gangster films in the 1960s, turns up as hard-drinking Captain Joe, and is easily the most interesting character. The costumes and f/x are pretty bad, but everything moves along at a brisk pace. The cliffhanger ending leads right into the sequel, *Space Force: Fugitive Alien 2.* 🎵🎵

1978/1986 102m/C *JP* Tatsuya Azuma, Joe Shishido, Miyuki Tanigawa, Choei Takahashi, Hiro Tateyama, Akihiko Hirata. *D:* Minoru Kanaya, Kiyosumi Kuzakawa. *W:* Keichi Abe, Bunkou Wakatsuki. **VHS, DVD**

Full Alert

Ringo Lam took the experience gained in America on *Maximum Risk* and took it back to Hong Kong with him to film this suspenseful cops-and-robbers flick. When a dead architect is found in a building water tank, SCB police inspector Pao (Lau Ching-Wan) and his squad trace the murder to demolition engineer Mak Kwan (Francis Ng), who claims it was a case of self-defense during a quarrel over a debt. However, vault blueprints and other items in Mak's possession point to a larger crime in the works. Mak and his cousin Chan Wah are involved with a Taiwanese gang of bank robbers, but the cops can't get any information about it from the prisoner. An attempt by the gang to spring Mak is averted, but it costs the life of Officer Yung (Peter Yung). Mak manages to escape anyway, and Pao is so desperate to catch him that he nearly kills a citizen accidentally. However, Pao has gained a clue to Mak's psyche through his encounters with the man, and has a hunch the gang plans to rob billions from the Jockey Club.

More interested in cat-and-mouse games between Lau Ching-Wan's and Francis Ng's robber than in action, *Full Alert* emerges as a more mature work than Ringo Lam's earlier, flashier films like *Full Contact*. It's not that the film lacks action—there's still plenty here, including a terrific car chase, explosions, and gunfights. It's just that the dramatic quotient is higher, with sharp performances all around, especially from the brilliant Lau. *AKA: Go Da Gaai Bei; Gao Du Jie Bei.* 🎵🎵🎵🎵

1997 99m/C *HK* Lau Ching-Wan, Francis Ng, Chin Ka-Lok, Monica Chan, Amanda Lee, Emily Kwan, Peter Yung, Jack Kao, Lee Siu-Kei, William Cho, Frankie Ng, Chris Lee, Andrew Kam. *D:* Ringo Lam. *W:* Ringo Lam, Lau Wing-kin. *C:* Ardy Lam. *M:* Peter Kam. **DVD**

Full Contact

A fine representative of the bullets-and-explosions school of Hong Kong action films. Judge (Simon Yam of *Naked Killer* and *Dr. Lamb*) is the flamboyant leader of a vicious gang of thieves. Chow Yun-fat (*Crouching Tiger, Hidden Dragon*; *Replacement Killers*) is Jeff, "security officer" at a popular Bangkok strip club. Anthony Wong (*The Untold Story, Rock and Roll Cop*) is Sam, a load on Jeff's back. When he can't pay off a loan shark, he gets kidnapped and Jeff has to go rescue him. To get the cash to pay off the debt, he gets Jeff involved with his cousin Judge's gang on a heist.

What Jeff and Sam don't know is that Judge gets his arms from the same loan shark, who

holds a grudge. After the job—a violent truck robbery—Jeff is betrayed and left for dead. While his stripper girlfriend Mona (Ann Bridgewater of *Operation Pink Squad*) mourns Jeff's apparent death, she grows closer to Sam. Sam's betrayal makes him tougher and he becomes a strong part of Judge's gang. Meanwhile, Jeff recovers from his wounds and plots his Big Revenge.

Chow Yun-fat alters his image here, dressing up as a tough leather motorcycle-riding stud, far from the slick appearance he usually sports, and it's an interesting change of pace. At first overplaying his coward role, Anthony Wong turns out to give one of the better performances of his early career as the heavily conflicted gangster who has trouble keeping track of whom he should stab in the back next. Simon Yam, who seems to specialize in twisted characters, is memorable as the gay gunslinger Judge.

At the time, Chow Yun-fat's pictures for Golden Princess were making the studio a serious competitor for Golden Harvest (home of Jackie Chan). Ringo Lam's hard-edged action films were a big part of that success. This is probably the film that first used the "bullet-cam," in which the

camera follows a slug's slo-mo trajectory. *AKA: Hap Diy Go Fei; Xia dao Gao Fei.* 🎵🎵🎵🎵

1992 (UNR) 96m/C *HK* Chow Yun-fat, Simon Yam, Ann Bridgewater, Anthony Wong, Bonnie Fu, Frankie Chan, Nam Yin, Victor Hon Kwan, Chris Lee. *D:* Ringo Lam. *W:* Nam Yin. *C:* Joe Chan, Peter Ngor. *M:* Teddy Robin Kwan. **VHS, DVD**

Full Throttle

True originality is a rare quality. Just as *Legend of Speed* is the likely inspiration for the American hit *Fast and the Furious*, *Legend* is a semi-sequel to this Andy Lau vehicle, which is itself a remake of *Goodbye Hero*, which starred director Derek Yee alongside David Wu. But then, street-racing movies are as old as the automobile, and every generation repaints the old jalopies and gets them on the road again.

Trust-fund brat David Kwan (David Wu) returns to Hong Kong after studying abroad and tries to get onto the motorcycle racing team run by Uncle Paul (Paul Chun). David befriends Paul's estranged son Joe (Andy Lau), who lost his license and has become one of the illegal

Chow Yun-fat is out for vengeance on back-stabbing Simon Yam and Anthony Wong in *Full Contact*.

street racers Paul despises. While Joe's shy girl-friend Yee (Gigi Leung) works in Paul's cycle shop, Joe works with his friend Jiale (Chin Ka-Lok) in the run-down garage owned by Jiale's Grandma (Ha Ping). When Joe has difficulty getting his own racing team together for a Macau race, David takes an offer from Paul's team, causing a rift between the friends. Soon after, Joe nearly dies in an accident, and as he recovers he reexamines his life and fears speed for the first time. Meanwhile, David gathers trophies, but no one will really consider him champion until he beats Joe.

The mediocrity of the characters, drama, and racing action keeps this one from getting ahead of the pack. Andy Lau brings depth to his character, but without a true villain, his reasons for returning to racing seem petty. Elvis Tsui has a good supporting part as an ex-champ turned bartender. Stunt racing coordinator (and future director) Bruce Law has a cameo—as a cardboard advertising standee. *AKA: Lit Fo Jin Che; Lie Huo Zhan Che.* ♫♫♡

1995 108m/C *HK* Andy Lau, Gigi Leung, David Wu, Paul Chun, Chin Ka-Lok, Elvis Tsui, Ha Ping, Lau Ying Hung. *D:* Derek Yee. *W:* Derek Yee, Law Chi-leung. *C:* Jingle Ma, David Chung. *M:* Frankie Chan, Roel A. Garcia. **VHS, DVD**

Fulltime Killer

A post-ironic masterpiece that plays gleefully with reality, *Fulltime Killer* aims to shatter all preconceptions. O (Takashi Sorimachi) is an assassin who prefers to fly under the radar, yet he's quite prepared to shoot an old school chum in the back when he shows up unexpectedly at a train station where O dispatches his latest assignment. On the other hand, professional killer Tok (Andy Lau) is the personification of flamboyance; in his first scene, he strides into a police station like a flesh-and-blood Terminator, sprays bullets like spit, and casually tosses a boxful of grenades into a holding cell, pulling the pin on just one. The tiny bombs scatter on the concrete floor like mice as the prisoner frantically searches for the live grenade. He finds it, but it's too late—"Boom!!!"—and we're off and running. In a twisted riff on *Branded to Kill*, Tok wants to kill O and become the #1 killer in the business. He tries to get to O through Chin (Kelly Lin), a video store clerk who picks up extra cash by cleaning O's apartment. The quiet and self-effacing Chin has been fascinated by O's secrecy, but is quickly charmed by Tok, even after she learns about his professional life. All the while, Interpol inspectors Lee (Simon Yam) and Gigi (Cherrie Ying) chase after the assassins in a vain attempt to bring them to justice.

Some have complained that directors Johnnie To *(The Mission)* and Wai Kar-fai *(Peace Hotel)* tried to use this film as a calling card to Hollywood, yet the opposite is true. By openly acknowledging a wide variety of influences, the directors (and their American collaborator, co-scripter Joey O'Bryan, working from a best-selling novel by Edmond Pang) put their cards on the table—and then jerk the table away. Traditional structure falls by the wayside, even as one fever-pitched action scene after another dashes across the screen. The gunplay is filmed audaciously, with balletic camera work and an eye for the big screen. The crazy cavalcade of interchangeable international locales, linguistic mangling, and wholesale bloodshed reaches a crescendo that makes little sense. No matter—the ride is exhilarating, and you'll either rage angrily at the outrageous antics or reach for the "play/repeat" button on your remote. —PM *AKA: Chuen Chik Saai Sau; Quan Zhi Sha Shou; You and I.* ♫♫♫♫

2001 100m/C *HK* Andy Lau, Takashi Sorimachi, Kelly Lin, Simon Yam, Cherrie Ying, Teddy Lin, Lam Suet. *D:* Johnny To, Wai Kar-fai. *W:* Wai Kar-fai, Joey O'Bryan. *C:* Cheng Siu-keung. *M:* Guy Zerafa. **VHS, DVD**

The Funeral

Director Juzo Itami went from commercials to features with this film, a typical mix of humor and sentiment that takes an unconventional look at the final part of life. The father of actress Chizuko (Nobuko Miyamoto) dies, and her actor husband Wabisuke (Tsutomu Yamazaki) is dismayed to learn that his mother-in-law prefers the funeral take place in his home. Things get even more involved when he learns it is to be a full three-day Buddhist ceremony. In Japan, where everything seems to be more participatory, each detail of the funeral brings with it new difficulties and arguments among the family, especially between the modern younger family members and their more traditional elders. Chizuko and Wabisuke find that it helps to view the funeral as a performance, and even watch an instructional video to learn their lines. Wabisuke's filmmaker friend Aoki (Takashi Tsumura)—and Itami—captures everything with his camera. Matters are complicated further when Wabisuke's mistress Yoshiko (Haruna Takase) shows up. Cousins get drunk and gossip, while the deceased's croquet team laments their loss, and everyone treads the line between mourning and enjoying themselves.

Always entertaining, Itami combines and juxtaposes elements both universal and distinctly Japanese, producing humor that is both warm and surreal. Like Western funerals, a lot of food

is consumed, but dealing with the effects of kneeling for long periods is more of an Asian problem. Some of the cast would go on to most of Itami's other pictures, where his viewpoint and sense of humor would only become sharper. One gag that will be lost on Western viewers: the casting of Chishu Ryu as the priest, as he's familiar to all Japanese for playing a priest in the incredibly long *Tora-san* series. **AKA:** *Ososhiki; Zazambo; Death Japanese Style; Funeral Rites.* 🐉🐉🐉

1984 124m/C *JP* Nobuko Miyamoto, Tsutomu Yamazaki, Kin Sugai, Ichiro Zaitsu, Nekohachi Edoya, Shoji Otake, Kamatari Fujiwara, Ittoku Kishibe, Chishu Ryu, Haruna Takase, Masahiko Tsugawa, Takashi Tsumura. **D:** Juzo Itami. **W:** Juzo Itami. **C:** Yonezo Maeda. **M:** Joji Yuasa. **VHS, DVD**

Funeral March

Yee (Charlene Choi) is a woman with cancer who wants to arrange her own funeral. She has decided not to undergo an operation to remove cancerous tissues in her intestine, and her family is not happy with her decision. At a funeral, Yee notices the handsome funeral director, Duan (Eason Chan), and she later approaches him and requests that he make the arrangements for her. Initially he refuses to do so, rather piously informing her that she should be positive, pursue all roads of treatment, etc. Eventually, though, he acquiesces, only to find that Yee wants him to accompany her, her sister, and another male family member on a trip to America. One of her first stops is to visit the grave of her mother, who died six years previously by driving her car into a lake—whether it was an accident or a suicide was never determined. Despite the fact that Duan is stiff, impersonal, and self-righteous, we surmise that Yee is attracted to his good looks and wants to pursue a romantic relationship with him. Yet on the trip she looks up her boyfriend and asks if he would be willing to do anything she asked of him. His answer disappoints her because he wants to also pursue his own interests, rather than spend all his time attending to her needs.

It seems that Yee has now completely given up on life. When she not feeling well, her sister wants to take her to a hospital. Upon arrival, Yee does not want to go in. After pretending to agree with her, Duan proceeds to sweep her up in his arms and runs into the hospital with her, insisting that she receive treatment. Still sullen, she rebuffs the thought of the supposed lifesaving operation. One brief conversation with Duan, however, in which he tells her that she should have the operation to spite her stepmother, convinces her to return to Hong Kong and go under the knife.

Without giving too much more away, Duan takes certain actions in regard to his relationship with Yee and his own life that are inconsistent with how Duan dealt with Yee's extremely similar situation. In fact, Duan's actions are rather hypocritical, and this seriously damages the film. After all, for the story to work as a tearjerker, Duan needs to be viewed as a noble and self-sacrificing man. Eason Chan, though, was entirely unmoving and unconvincing as Duan. On the other hand, Charlene Choi (one half of the musical group Twins) was rather touching as Yee. Director Joe Ma has made a glossy, shiny film with a hollow heart. —PM **AKA:** *Seung Joi Ngo Sam; Chang Zai Wo Xin.* 🐉🐲

2001 97m/C *HK* Eason Chan, Charlene Choi, Pauline Yam, Sheila Chan, Kenneth Tsang, Liu Kaichi, Candy Lo. **D:** Joe Ma. **W:** Joe Ma, Chan Gamkuen, Chan Wing-sun. **C:** Ko Chiu-lam. **M:** Lincoln Lo. **VHS, DVD**

Fury in Shaolin Temple

Park Si Bahk and Wang Fu secretly trade sons, as a kind of marriage of their two kung fu styles. Park travels to Shaolin Temple to test his Dragon Fist style against the Shaolin Fist. Tossing the baby into a nearby tree, he has a bit of a spar with the monks, but feels he can only truly test himself against their master. Though the switch is supposed to be secret, Park still raises the boy with the name Wang Yun, and he's taught both Fist styles. Wang is enlisted by Khan to infiltrate the Temple and steal the secret Shaolin kung fu manual. The manual disappears, and the Shaolin librarian is found dead on Park's doorstep. Monk Tong and the 18 Disciples arrest Park, and Wang Yun (Gordon Lau) grows to manhood as a cook in the temple.

Meanwhile, the Eagle Clan does nothing with the stolen manual. Park's son Chi Lan (Phillip Ko) is raised to be the master of the Eagle Fist style, but Mr. Tai San won't accept him as succeeding clan leader because he's an outsider. Tai San sends two hired assassins to kill Lan, but he defeats them in a hilarious Drunken Mantis versus Drunken Eagle match. Yun finds Park Si Bahk living imprisoned in a cave, and Park gives him his Dragon Fist manual. Having witnessed the Shaolin librarian's murder, Yun thinks he can find the Shaolin manual and exonerate Park. But first he must learn the Ghost Fist. The Eagle Fist killers murder Wang and frame Lan for the crime, manipulating the two sons into fighting each other.

This standard story of separated boys and kung fu styles is guided only by Gordon Ho's listless direction. The monks of Shaolin, though supposedly the defenders of China, are portrayed to be just as sinister as the enemy clan. The highlight is surely the appearance of the fabled robot-like 18 Bronzemen of Shaolin, borrowed from Joseph Kuo's film series. 🎝🎝

1982 83m/C *HK/KO* Gordon Lau, Phillip Ko, Gam Kei Chu, Philip Cheung. **D:** Godfrey Ho. **W:** Stephen So. **C:** Mah Kwok Wah. **M:** Ricky Chan. **DVD**

Fury of King Boxer

Though Jimmy Wang Yu is listed as the star, this is the story of journalist, poet, publisher, warrior, and political hero Chu Ching (Kuo Shu-chung), who helped Dr. Sun Yat-sen overthrow the Manchus at the beginning of the 20th century. During the 1900 invasion of Peking, patriotic Chu Ching fights fiercely against the foreign invaders, and refuses to kowtow once peace is restored. Her freed revolutionary friend Wong Hsiao brings her to one of their meetings, but she finds them quarrelsome and disorganized. She gets them to join Dr. Sun's revolutionary Tong Min Society, enemies of the Ching Dynasty government. The Tong Min move to Japan for safety, but the Chinese bribe the Japanese leaders to crack down on Chu Ching and her followers. While Miss Chu fights off attacks on her rebel newspaper office, Tong Min's ace fighter Siu Shi-lin (Jimmy Wang Yu) gets himself assigned head of the national police academy, and they prepare for their coup. From then on, it's political business as usual: bloody sword battles, suicide protests, Thai boxers, kung fu fights, and exploding pork buns. Meanwhile, Chu's personal life suffers as she leaves her husband and children behind in Shanghai. Unfortunately, the feminist heroine is largely abandoned during the final reels to concentrate on Siu's undercover rebel, as his forces cut off their queues and lead a bloody uprising against the Manchurians. Despite efforts to spice things up with wild fight scenes, this historical drama is as dry as the Ghobi between bouts. **AKA:** *Geng Tin Dung Dei; Jing Tian Dong Di; Chow Ken; Fast Fists.* 🎝

1972 94m/C *HK* Jimmy Wang Yu, Kuo Shu-chung, Yee Yuen, Chiang Ming, Chui Chung Hei, Chui Fook-sang, Got Heung Ting, Hon Siu, Hsieh Hsing, Ma Kei, Man Man, Ng Tung-kiu, Shan Mao, Sit Hon, Tin Yau, On Ping. **D:** Ting Shan-si. **M:** Ng Tai Hong. **VHS**

A Gambler's Story

Here's the plotline: A down-on-his-luck gambler (Francis Ng) sees brighter days after meeting a nightclub hostess (Suki Kwan). Things get even stranger, though, when they meet again in Macau. Here's the catch: a brief synopsis will not convey the unusual tone of this unusual film.

In fact, anyone who thinks that Hong Kong movies in the new millennium have become pale imitations of their Hollywood brethren or simply routine and uneventful needs to check out this deranged, beautiful, ugly work. It's just so, uh, what's the word? "Weird" doesn't quite capture it, but it's certainly strange and completely unpredictable. On the surface it seems that producer Wong Jing asked director Marco Mak to make another gambling movie, and didn't give him any parameters to stay within—except to include scenes of people gambling in Macau. At first glance it looks like a serious drama, but it quickly changes tone to something resembling comedy—not broad and easy; instead, it's darker than night. And then the "comedy" slips into such black comedy that it's difficult to know how to react. One scene in particular is so outrageously over-the-top that it prompts laughter, but the viewer may immediately be seized by guilt and consternation—as in, Oops, that's not funny, is it? There's more than one scene like that, and the uncomfortable feelings become routine. The story veers like a drunken driver all over the emotional map, and it's impossible to anticipate its destination. Hold hands with the wild-eyed and sleepless Francis Ng, watch out for a sucker punch from Suki Kwan, and try not to fall off the roller-coaster. —PM **AKA:** *Yat Goh Laan Diy Dik Chuen Suet; Ye Ge Lan Du De Chuan Shui.* 🎝🎝🎝

2001 89m/C *HK* Francis Ng, Suki Kwan, Sam Lee, Wong Yat-tung, Wong Tak-ban, Timothy Zao, Walter Cho, Lam Suet. **D:** Marco Mak. **C:** Tony Miu. **M:** Lincoln Lo. **VHS, DVD**

Game of Death

After *Way of the Dragon* (AKA *Return of the Dragon*), Bruce Lee began work on this even more ambitious project, which he hoped would not only provide fantastic martial arts thrills, but also illustrate some of his philosophies. But Hollywood interrupted work on the film with an offer to star in a co-production, the action classic *Enter the Dragon*. Lee died before he could finish *Game of Death*, leaving behind many rumors and mysteries about his life and work. Several years later, an orgy of "Bruceploitation" pictures was capped when Golden Harvest producer Raymond Chow announced plans to finish the film using finished footage, attracting interested parties to the project like a carcass draws vultures, and often proclaiming to the press that they were completing the picture "as Bruce would have wanted it." As it turned out, nothing could be further from the truth.

It begins with a subpar James Bond–style credit sequence featuring clips of Lee from various films mixed with Chinese casino imagery

and impressive John Barry music. Bruce, as action-movie star "Billy Lo," completes a scene from his latest picture, fighting Chuck Norris. Billy receives a threatening visit from entertainment syndicate representative Steiner (Hugh O'Brian), who wants him to sign a contract with his evil boss Dr. Land (Dean Jagger). Out on the town with his singing-star girlfriend Ann Morris (Colleen Camp), Steiner's thugs attack them. After the fight, they stop to lick their wounds over drinks with Billy's reporter pal Jim Marshall (Gig Young, who seems to be genuinely imbibing). The next day, Billy goes to the Chinese opera to visit his Uncle Chow (Roy Chiao) for advice, but is met by Land's men Carl Miller (Bob Wall) and Pasqual (Dan Inosanto), who deliver a final-warning beating. But Billy refuses to cooperate, and makes plans to go to the police.

On the set to finish his film before putting his plan into action, Billy suffers a face injury when one of Land's men (Mel Novak) uses a real bullet instead of a blank. The ensuing plastic surgery and use of disguises ensures that the doubles—Tong Lung (fight scenes), Yuen Biao (acrobatics), and Chen Yao-po (everything else, though some say Bruce Li also appears)— no longer had to use as many tricks to hide

their faces, but doesn't explain why Bruce's face is back to normal in the Lee-shot climax. Unbelievably, Marshall and Billy's doctors conspire to fake his death, with footage of Lee's real funeral standing in for Lo's phony one. After his surgery, Billy grows a beard and, tracking Land to his casino ship and private estate, tries to turn the tables on the villains by attacking Land and beating up his bodyguards. Later, while champ Carl is fighting dirty in a kickboxing match against challenger Lo Chen (martial arts director Sammo Hung, in the movie's best new fight), Billy approaches in disguise to assassinate the champ in his locker room. After rescuing a kidnapped Ann from Land's warehouse and defeating all his men there, Billy storms his enemy's lair above a restaurant, fighting his way past Pasqual and Land's giant hit man Hakim (Kareem Abdul-Jabbar).

The finished product has nothing to do with Bruce Lee's script. The story obnoxiously mixes gossip and facts about Lee's life into a silly concoction that lacks logic and narrative momentum. Chow lined up a parade of American B-actors and every available gweilo face in Hong Kong to use as extras in an attempt to make the movie seem less Chinese. Despite objections by

Bruce Lee takes his nunchakus to the next level in *Game of Death.*
THE KOBAL COLLECTION / GOLDEN HARVEST / PARAGON

Bob Wall and Sammo Hung, Chow hired Robert Clouse, who merely served as a supervisor on *Enter the Dragon* and built a career around the credit, to direct the new footage. With less than 10 minutes of actual footage shot by Lee in the picture (not all of it featuring the star), a variety of techniques are used to fill in the gaps, including the use of doubles, poorly integrated clips, and most notoriously, a still photo of Lee's face pasted over a double's! These tricks range from the merely unconvincing to the downright offensive. Everyone playing Billy Lo is dubbed by someone who doesn't sound one bit like Lee. As a result, one begins to question everything else about the picture—even a warehouse set looks incredibly fake. Barry's music is great, but works against the action scenes, which are only average Lee knockoffs. An audacious example of classic showbiz ballyhoo, this went on to earn more money during its first run than *Enter the Dragon*. The sad part is that viewers are still being taken for suckers, believing this to be a real Bruce Lee film. For over two decades, the reason to see this was to see Lee in action in the final sequence. Now that the real deal has been assembled for *Bruce Lee: A Warrior's Journey*, this curiosity should fade into a well-deserved obscurity. Tong Lung followed in the even loopier, but superior, *Tower of Death*. **AKA:** *Sei Miu Yau Fai; Si Wang You Hu; Bruce Lee's Game of Death.* 🐉

1978 (R) 105m/C *HK/US* Bruce Lee, Colleen Camp, Gig Young, Dean Jagger, Hugh O'Brian, Robert Wall, Kareem Abdul-Jabbar, Chuck Norris, Dan Inosanto, Mel Novak, Roy Chiao, Tong Lung, Sammo Hung, Russell Cawthorne, James Tien, Casanova Wong, Mars, Chung Fat, Yuen Biao, Ji Han Jae, John Ladalski, Lau Kar-Wing, Whang In Shik, Yuen Wah. **D:** Robert Clouse, Bruce Lee. **W:** Jan Spears. **C:** Godfrey A. Godar. **M:** John Barry. **VHS, DVD**

Gamera, Guardian of the Universe

Ah, yes: Gamera, the giant prehistoric jet-propelled fire-breathing flying turtle—friend to all children and butt of a thousand jokes on *Mystery Science Theater 3000*. Back in the '60s, when Toho Studios' Godzilla series was raking in millions, rival studio Daiei decided to cash in by creating their own monster. Though the Gamera movies boasted some truly interesting and original ideas, their main distinction is that they're some of the silliest monster movies ever made—too silly even for their intended audience of small children. Each one was even goofier and cheaper than the one before, and by the time of the eighth entry in the series—1980's abominable *Gamera, Supermonster*—

they mostly consisted of stock footage from earlier films. Gamera was last seen sacrificing his life out in space to save mankind (and to save us all from further sequels). Well, prepare yourself for a shock: Not only did Gamera return in a new series of films (inspired by the resurgence of Godzillamania in the '90s), but they're actually good! Made at a lower budget than the Godzilla films, they more than make up for it with talent, imagination, and attitude. Plus, they pioneered the use of CGI in man-in-suit monster pictures, bringing the genre a step forward. This first film of the new series sets a serious tone, detailing the discovery of dangerous prehistoric flying monsters called Gyaos and the subsequent reappearance of Gamera. Though mankind seeks the destruction of all, it's soon learned that the Gyaos were created by a lost advanced civilization as a shortsighted bio-engineering experiment gone wrong and Gamera was created to battle the man-eating beasts—and whatever others should threaten mankind.

O.K., so the plot still may sound a little ridiculous, but it's all handled in such a straightforward and realistic manner, and the action moves along so swiftly, that it's easy to suspend disbelief and enjoy the ride. Little touches help a great deal, such as the when it's explained that the Japanese Defense Force is legally unable to attack Gamera unless the monster clearly attacks them first (until the government gives them official clearance), and that the appearance of giant beasts sends the stock exchange into a panic. Young actress Ayako Fujitani (the daughter of U.S. action star Steven Seagal) shows great promise in her first big starring role; she's since appeared in two sequels. This is definitely a picture that knows how to deliver an old-fashioned monster show in a whole new way. **AKA:** *Gamera Daikaiju Kuchu Kessen; Gamera: Giant Monster Midair Showdown.* 🐉🐉🐉🐉🐉

1995 96m/C *JP* Tsuyoshi Ihara, Akira Onodera, Shinobu Nakayama, Ayako Fujitani, Yukijiro Hotaru, Hatsunori Hasegawa, Hirotaro Honda, Kojiro Hongo, Akira Kubo. **D:** Shusuke Kaneko. **W:** Kazunori Itô. **C:** Kenji Takama, Junichi Tozawa. **M:** Ko Otani. **VHS, DVD**

Gamera 2: Advent of Legion

Shusuke Kaneko's reinvention of the Gamera mythos really hit its stride with this first sequel to *Gamera: Guardian of the Universe,* in which the gigantic, genetically engineered monster turtle does battle with a horde of crab-like alien invaders. With nods to both *Aliens* and *It Came from Outer Space, Gamera 2* methodically builds up its alien threat (deposited on Earth by

a meteor) with ever-more-harrowing human encounters with the growing, pincer-laden creatures which devour glass and burrow out of Japan's subways. Eventually Gamera arrives and in a scene that echoes (but outdoes) the earlier *Godzilla vs. Destroyah,* the giant turtle is inundated by thousands of the smaller, insect-like aliens. Soon, the swarming creatures litter the countryside but merge to form a giant, pod-like egg from which an immense, monster version of the life form emerges to do battle.

It would all seem perfectly ridiculous were Kaneko not such a master choreographer of human and monster action. In the eye-popping climax, Gamera makes a perfect two-point landing after circling the Legion monster like an F-16, then slides on two feet for something like three miles of crushed urban landscape while firing energy at the alien John Woo style. Take that, Godzilla! Kaneko's grasp of timing and proportion is nothing short of momentous and he and his ace visual effects supervisor Shinji Higuchi refuse to allow the viewer to distance themselves from the action: most of the monster sequences are actually shot from a human point of view, and the results range from harrowing to exhilarating. The final showdown between

Gamera and the immense, insect-like Legion monster fusion is as gripping and witty as a Sergio Leone spaghetti-western shootout. —*JB* **AKA:** *Gamera 2: Region shurai; Gamera 2: Assault of the Legion.* 🐉🐉🐉🐉

1996 99m/C *JP* Toshiyuki Nagashima, Miki Mizuno, Tomotsu Ishibashi, Shoji Kobayashi, Ayako Fujitani, Yusuke Kawazu, Yukijiro Hotaru, Hatsunori Hasegawa, Tomoro Taguchi, Hiroyuki Watanabe, Kazue Tsunogae, Mizuho Yoshida, Miyuki Komatsu. *D:* Shusuke Kaneko. *W:* Kazunori Itô. *C:* Junichi Tozawa. *M:* Ko Otani. **VHS, DVD**

Gamera 3: The Revenge of Irys

The last giant-turtle movie of the 20th century packs an awesome wallop, carrying on all the good points from the previous two films and delivering fresh thrills. Dr. Nagamine (Shinobu Nakayama) makes an alarming discovery in a rural area of the Philippines: the rotting corpse of a young Gyaos. A deep-sea submersible exploring off the southern tip of Japan reveals another startling discovery: a huge undersea

Gamera, Guardian of the Universe— the most important flying-monster turtle movie ever made.

THE KOBAL COLLECTION

Gamera graveyard, which offers more clues to the monster's origins. Ayana Hirasaka (Ai Maeda), whose parents died during Gamera's battle with the Gyaos in 1995, bears an understandable grudge against the giant turtle, and when she discovers the egg of another legendary beast in a cave, she's determined to take advantage of the chance to strike at her enemy. Gamera's battle with a pair of Gyaos that suddenly appear in the night sky over Tokyo, which totally destroys the Shibuya district with thousands of casualties, only fuels the girl's resolve.

As a creature hatches from the egg, her secret is shared by her friend Moribe, whose family has guarded the egg of the monster they call Ryuseicho from being disturbed for centuries. But he can't convince her to give up her intention of raising the young beast she calls Irys (that looks like a bird crossed with a snail) to strike back at Gamera. As Irys grows, it eventually merges psychically with Ayana, even as it leaves a trail of desiccated corpses in its wake. Meanwhile, reports of Gyaos attacks are heard from all over the world, and Gamera is kept busy shooting them down. A theory evolves via government psychic Mito Asakura (Senri Yamazaki), game designer Shinya Kurata (Toru Teduka), and the Gamera-connected girl Asagi (Ayako Fujitani), that these monsters are especially drawn to Japan because of a sort of hole in the "Mana" layer on the island. Mito and Kurata kidnap Ayana and take her to a secret shrine in Kyoto, drawing both Irys and Gamera to the area for an apocalyptic duel.

Gamera 3 incorporates a compelling science-fiction story, well thought-out characters, brilliant special effects, and old-fashioned giant monster destruction, all in one awesome package. It's the vision of director Shusuke Kaneko that makes it all work, taking a fantastic story of Lovecraftian monster gods battling for the fate of the Earth, and filtering it through a purely human perspective. It may sound strange to hear the word "realism" attached to a movie series about a giant flying turtle, but that's exactly the key to its success. When Gamera blasts away at Gyaos, heedless of the necessary human cost, the entire battle is filmed from the perspective of the people involved, not the usual monster shoulder-level camera angles—unless there could be somebody there to film it. An incredibly tough bastard, Gamera is given a leaner look here, and Irys is an incredible creation. Even the Gyaos, which seemed a bit too puppetlike in their previous appearance, look more like real creatures than special effects. With this trilogy ending on a less than final note, let's hope Kaneko and company get back to the Guardian of the Universe sometime soon. **AKA:** *Gamera 3: Iris Kakusei; Gamera 3; Gamera, Guardian of the Universe 1999; Gamera 3: Incomplete Struggle.* 🎼🎼🎼🎼

1999 108m/C *JP* Ai Maeda, Ayako Fujitani, Yukijiro Hotaru, Shinobu Nakayama, Hirotaro Honda, Toru Teduka, Senri Yamazaki, Yusuke Kawazu, Kenjiro Ishimaru, Hiroyuki Watanabe, Kunihiko Mitamura, Kazuko Kato, Toshie Negishi, Tomoro Taguchi, Asumi Miwa, Tomotsu Ishibashi, Aki Maeda, Masahiro Noguchi, Go Shimada. **D:** Shusuke Kaneko. **W:** Kazunori Itô, Shusuke Kaneko. **C:** Junichi Tozawa. **M:** Ko Otani. **VHS, DVD**

Gamera vs. Barugon

This Barugon is not to be confused with the monster Baragon, featured in Toho's *Frankenstein Conquers the World.* (Though any similarity was likely intentional on Daiei Studios' part; the smaller studio was anxious to get Toho's audience any way they could.) The monstrous turtle Gamera returns to Earth after being freed from his outer-space prison by a passing meteor, and immediately takes out his anger by destroying a dam. Meanwhile, in plot thread #2, three Japanese crooks are in New Guinea, exploring a taboo cave in search of a legendary opal. One is stung by a scorpion, and Onodera (Koji Fujiyama) double-crosses his other partner Keisuke (Kojiro Hongo). Onodera grabs the opal and blows up the cave behind him, then smuggles the stone back to Japan. But that opal ain't no opal—it's a monster egg that Onodera accidentally incubates. The hatchling almost immediately grows into the 130-foot lizard Barugon, who comes equipped with a rainbow melting ray and a freeze gas–shooting tongue! Gamera finally decides to return to his own movie, but is ambushed by Barugon's secret freeze gas weapon.

While Tokyo and Osaka get melted and/or frozen, Keisuke decides that crime doesn't pay and meets a nice native girl named Karen (Kyoko Enami) to take home to mother. Sealing the deal is the fact that Karen brings a 5,000-carat diamond with her. The natives use the diamond to get rid of Barugons whenever they show up, which is about every thousand years. The military uses the diamond to lure Barugon into the ocean to drown him, but sneaky Onodera swipes the diamond before the plan can work. Of course, now Barugon is lured to Onodera, and the villain is promptly gobbled up. The military then hatches a plan to melt Barugon with his own rainbow ray, which also goes awry, leaving it up to Gamera to try to do better in a rematch.

The first sequel to *Giant Monster Gamera* (the first in color) is not quite as silly as those that came later (believe it or not!), and the battle scenes even achieve a sort of goofy grandeur. It's hard to say whether they decided to shoot in color because there was a rainbow ray in the script, or came up with the rainbow ray to take

advantage of the color film. Star Kojiro Hongo returned for two more Gamera films. Noriyaki Yuasa, who'd done a competent job directing the initial entry in the series, stepped down to concentrate on only the special effects for this entry, but would fill both roles for the remainder of the series. Initially released as *War of the Monsters* in the U.S., when Sandy Frank Productions acquired rights to the Gamera series in the 1980s, then completely re-edited and re-dubbed all the films, reissuing them to television and video under more faithful titles. *AKA: Gamera Tai Barugon; Daikaiju Kessan: Gamera Tai Barugon; War of the Monsters.* 🎵🎵

1966 101m/C *JP* Kojiro Hongo, Koji Fujiyama, Kyoko Enami, Akira Natsuki, Ichiro Sugai, Yuzo Hayakawa, Yoshiro Kitahara, Jutaro Hojo, Kenichi Tani, Koichi Ito, Johji Ohhara, Tsutomu Nakata. *D:* Shigeo Tanaka. *W:* Nisan Takahashi. *C:* Michio Takahashi. *M:* Chuji Kinoshita. **VHS**

Gamera vs. Guiron

Akio (Nobuhiro Kajima) and his American pal Tom (Christopher Murphy) are typical little boys,

interested in science and dismissive of Akio's little sister Tomoko (Miyuki Akiyama), whom Akio repeatedly refers to as an "idiot." But Tomoko's not dumb enough to climb inside a flying saucer the boys find settled in their playlot. While the boys play spaceman inside this very real spaceship, the saucer takes off.

When a meteor shower threatens, giant turtle Gamera appears to protect the boys. However, the ship picks up speed and their escort is left behind. Next thing you know, the saucer lands on an alien world. Akio theorizes that since it has a breathable atmosphere, they must be "on another star." He just has that kind of analytical mind. He's also quite the dreamer, wishing not only for world peace, but a world free of traffic accidents. In fact, he expresses this wish four times during the film, which leads to the conclusion that Akio's dad may have been killed in a car wreck.

About the closest thing to a father figure for the two boys is Gamera. The only men they know is comic cop named Kondo (Kon Omura), and elderly scientist Dr. Shiga (Eiji Funakoshi, who was also in the original *Giant Monster Gamera*). Tom's mother (Edith Hanson) never mentions a

It's giant-monster pandemonium in the bizarre *Gamera vs. Barugon.*

husband either, and is perfectly satisfied to leave her son with her Japanese friend indefinitely.

Even the boys' captors are female, twin beauties named Barbella (Hiroko Kai) and Flobella (Reiko Kasahara), who are decked out in costumes straight out of the Buck Rogers comic strip. The women at first seem friendly, letting the boys play with their teleporters and explaining that they represent the last survivors of an advanced civilization that failed in an attempt to flee the planet, which was under attack by a species of space Gyaos. Previously, the boys had themselves been attacked by one of the Gyaos, but were saved by the intervention of the aliens' watchdog, evil monster Guiron—a huge, vaguely reptilian beast with a head shaped like a giant butcher knife. Guiron uses his head in battle, chopping up the Gyaos into neat slices.

But the alien gals' friendly pose is a ruse; before long, the boys learn their true plan: to take the saucer back to Earth to conquer it. Worse yet, Barbella and Flobella are cannibals, and want to take the boys along on the trip "as rations"! They even shave Akio's head in preparation to eat his brain (a scene unique in the annals of alien-invasion movies), but luckily, are

interrupted by the arrival of Gamera. Gamera goes into battle against Guiron, and after a rough tussle, is knocked into a coma by Guiron's poisoned ninja stars. Will Tomoko convince her mother that the boys took off in a saucer? Will Gamera revive? Will Barbella and Flobella make shishime out of Akio and Tom?

This is the fifth entry in Daiei's successful monster series, which American International dubbed, edited, and released in the U.S. under the title *Attack of the Giant Monsters.* During the 1980s, Sandy Frank Productions picked up several of the Gamera movies for video and TV distribution and chose to redub the films themselves, rather than pay for the AIP print. This resulted in much hilarity when the dubbing cast (including actress/cabaret star Sandra Bernhard) decided to give the alien women hillbilly accents! This version is probably the one most familiar to U.S. fans, mostly due to its appearance as Experiment #312 on *Mystery Science Theater 3000.* **AKA:** *Gamera Tai Daikaiju Giron; Attack of the Giant Monsters.* 🐉🐉🐉

1969 88m/C *JP* Nobuhiro Kajima, Christopher Murphy, Miyuki Akiyama, Eiji Funakoshi, Kon Omura, Edith Hanson, Reiko Kasahara, Hiroko Kai. **D:** Noriaki Yuasa. **W:** Nisan Takahashi. **C:** Akira Kitazaki. **M:** Shunsuke Kikuchi. **VHS, DVD**

Gamera vs. Gyaos

In this third Gamera vehicle, arguably the best of the original series, public opinion toward the monster has begun to change following his defeat of the more hostile menace Barugon. Now fully the good guy in the eyes of Japan's children, the giant flying turtle is drawn to the eruption of Mount Fujiyama. A research party is sent to the area via helicopter, but a strange green glowing area emanates a bright beam that slices the whirlybird neatly in two. Farmers in the region believe that a construction project by the Expressway Engineering Corporation is responsible for the disaster, believing it's all a plot by the company to get them to sell their land, so they block completion of the highway. Road superintendent Suzumi (Kojiro Hongo) is under pressure to clear the protesting villagers off the mountain and finish the job, despite the erupting volcano and lurking monster.

The headman's grandson Ichi (Naoyuki Ane) and a reporter (Takashi Nakamura) climb to the green glowing cave, thinking they will see what Gamera is up to. When rocks start to fall, the cowardly reporter abandons Ichi, and is eaten by a huge bloodthirsty bat-like critter. Ichi is saved from suffering the same fate by the arrival of Gamera, who carries the boy off on his back. Whee! Suzumi makes points with Ichi's sister Sumiko (Reiko Kasahara) and grampa by helping the boy down from his perch. The little celebrity names the new monster Gyaos, "because that's the noise it makes." Scientists theorize that Gyaos is able to generate ultra-powerful sound waves from his throat in the form of a cutting beam. With Gamera recovering from injuries sustained from his first clash with Gyaos, heroic scientists come up with an outrageous idea (even for the Gamera series) to defeat the bat-creature. Hundreds of gallons of "synthetic blood" are used to lure Gyaos atop a revolving tower restaurant, in the hope that the beast will become too dizzy to escape until dawn, when the sunlight will destroy him. If only they'd used that idea on Dracula!

More weird fun from the increasingly silly Gamera series; the subplot about road construction is easily forgotten when the two scaly titans get in a rumble. Much clumsier and not as well designed as their Toho cousins, the Daiei monsters certainly show a lot of imagination. The vampire Gyaos is the best of Gamera's sinister foes, and one of the few daikaiju to be seen feeding on humans. *AKA: Gamera Tai Gaos; Boyichi and the Supermonster; Gamera vs. Gaos; Air Battle of the Big Monsters: Gamera vs. Gyaosu; The Return of the Giant Monsters.* 🎵🎵🎵

1967 87m/C *JP* Kojiro Hongo, Kichijiro Ueda, Naoyuki Ane, Reiko Kasahara, Yoshiro Kitahara, Jutaro Hojo, Sho Natsuki, Koichi Ito, Takashi Nakamura, Kenji Oyama, Kisao Tobita, Yuji Moriya, Shin Minatsu. **D:** Noriaki Yuasa. **W:** Fumi Takahashi. **C:** Akira Uehara. **M:** Tadashi Yamauchi. **VHS**

Gamera vs. Viras

By the fourth entry in the Gamera series, all pretenses of seriousness were abandoned in favor of pure juvenile fun, resulting in some of the most surreal concoctions ever recorded on film. The universe is full of greedy alien species eager to invade the Earth. Fortunately, when the latest of these hostile forces comes sneaking around in a spaceship (which looks like a bunch of striped beach balls hitched in a ring), Gamera flies into space to destroy the ship, prompting the aliens to signal home base on planet Viras for a second ship. Meanwhile, a Japanese Boy Scout troupe—that includes a large number of kids from American families—is visiting a marine research site. Rascal boy genius Masao Shimada (Toru Takatsuka) and his pal Jim (Carl Clay), billed as "Kurl Crane" on the American International version and as "Carl Craig" on Japanese prints) nearly ruin everything by switching the controls on a new mini-submarine. While the boys are frolicking in the sub with friend-of-all-children Gamera, the second alien ship directs their "super-catch ray" at the giant turtle, trapping them all in a force-field dome. Gamera lifts the edge of the force field with a claw enough for the boys to scoot to freedom, and while the monster takes a nap, the aliens watch clips from previous Gamera movies (a cost-cutting move that would become increasingly annoying in the series). Noting the monster's "unusual affection" for kids, the invaders kidnap Masao and Jim, and affix a mind-control device to the giant turtle.

While the boys eat octagonal sandwiches and try to find a way to escape from the spaceship, the aliens order Gamera to attack the Earthlings (and bore the audience with more monster stock footage). The boys guess enough about the Virian technology to reverse their controls and escape, setting Gamera free to attack the ship. In a last-ditch effort, the Virians—who look kind of like pointy-headed squids—merge their bodies with their leader's, increasing in size and power so they can challenge Gamera.

As wild as the imagery gets in the meantime, it takes too long for the giant from Viras to appear, leaving all the monster action to the stock footage while the scouts wander around the spaceship and the adults fret. The look of the aliens is imaginative and intriguing, but their faces are too inexpressive to carry much personality, leaving director Noriaki Yuasa to rely on

"In all the years of my life, I've never known anything like this to happen before."

—An old dairy farmer confesses he's never seen huge bat lizards fighting with giant flying turtles under a volcano in his back yard, in *Gamera vs. Gyaos*

Friend to All Children

The Saga of Supermonster Gamera

Gamera is regarded by the general public—if they know anything about him at all—as Daiei Studios attempt to cash in on Toho Studios' Godzilla franchise with their own giant monster. Gamera wasn't the only one—Korean critter Yonggary comes to mind—but that doesn't account for the nagging question: why an 80-ton fire-breathing turtle that flies? Godzilla is surely a relation to the great dragon inhabitant of Asian myth, but where does Gamera come from?

Buddhist scriptures contain a story about a flying turtle, believe it or not. A turtle convinces two ducks to carry it to water during a drought by holding onto a stick between them. When some kids laugh at the sight of two ducks carrying a turtle, the turtle opens his mouth to yell at them and falls to his death. Ouch.

Asian mythology holds turtles in high regard otherwise. The turtle shell symbolizes Heaven and his belly symbolizes Earth, which means the turtle is an animal uniting the two worlds. This makes the image of a turtle as the guardian of our world perfectly natural. Some Indians relate a similar mythology in which the Earth is supported by the back of a huge turtle. What's the turtle standing on, you may ask? More turtles, of course. A more complicated version of this story is that the god Vishnu incarnates as a great turtle every time there's a great flood so that he can carry the other gods and devils until they can re-create the Earth; then the turtle gives the elephant that supports the world something to stand on. The Chinese like turtles as well, holding them as one of the four divine animals. Buddhists traditionally have a ceremony for releasing turtles.

No wonder Gamera has always been portrayed as friendly toward children—when he's not accidentally annihilating them. The folks at Daiei wanted a monster that would be a hero to their juvenile audience, and what better hero than a godlike animal friend? With mythological turtles no doubt stewing in their brains, it's no wonder director Noriaki Yuasa and screenwriter Nisan Takahashi thought their monster made sense.

But what about the flying part? Most likely, the filmmakers were only trying to combine two types of strange phenomena into one, while giving Gamera a way of getting around quickly. Gamera's fly-bys are reported as UFOs in the first film, and much less common but persistent are reports of giant turtles throughout the world. In 1998, a Vietnamese camera crew claimed to have footage of huge turtles living in a lake in the middle of Hanoi. For Daiei, it was just a few tidbits to tie their extreme fantasy to the real world.

The Heisei Gamera series (starting with *Gamera, Guardian of the Universe*) explains the giant turtle as a member of an army of bio-weapons created by a lost ancient civilization to exterminate the ravenous Gyaos (apparently an earlier experiment gone wrong) which were ravaging the planet. This doesn't explain why Gamera's creators made a turtle for the job, but tales of the beastie's ancient clash are how turtle myths got started.

That said, Gamera still is and always will be kind of a silly monster. He's no giant ape climbing a skyscraper, but it could be worse. He could be an exotic dancer who has a day job as a welder.

shadowy camera work to carry the mood of menace. Once the Virian grows to titanic size in the light of day, it doesn't look all that scary. A couple of shots may come as a shock to American kids: Viras frees his minions from their humanoid shells by chopping their heads off, and at one point Gamera is impaled on Viras's sharp, pointy head. **AKA:** *Gamera Tai Uchu Kaiju Bairasu; Destroy All Planets.* 🐢🐢🐢

1968 90m/C *JP* Kojiro Hongo, Toru Takatsuka, Carl Clay, Michiko Yaegaki, Mari Atsumi, Junko Yahiro, Yoshiro Kitahara, Sho Natsuki, Koji Fujiyama, Ken Nakahara, Munehiko Takada, Saburo Shinoda. **D:** Noriaki Yuasa. **W:** Nisan Takahashi. **C:** Akira Kitazaki. **M:** Kenjiro Hirose. **VHS, DVD**

Gamera vs. Zigra

Apparently this Gamera, movie was so bad that American International wouldn't even release it to TV syndication with the rest of the series in the 1970s, and it only showed up in the United States when Sandy Frank Productions bought the package. One thing that can be said for it is that it's one movie to feature a monster shark before *Jaws*. Also, even though it's almost a

remake of *Gamera vs. Viras* (AKA *Destroy All Planets*), it features a lot less recycled footage.

On the moon, sexy astronaut Lauralee (Eiko Yanami) is kidnapped from her moon buggy by a teleport beam from a UFO. Meanwhile, dull scientists Yosuke Ishikawa (Isamu Saeki) and Tom Walles (Koji Fujiyama) are examining a dead dolphin, theorizing it was killed by pollution. The scientists, along with their stowaway kids Kenny (Yasushi Sakagami) and Helen (Gloria Zoellner), are also space-napped by the teleporting spaceship. They are introduced to the astronaut, now possessed by space brain X-1 from the planet Zigra. The alien Zigrans have come to Earth to wrest the planet from the hands of the polluting humans who have nearly destroyed it, just as they did to their own planet. The Zigrans destroy Tokyo with an offscreen earthquake, just to show they mean business. The kids engineer an escape from the ship, after which X-1 chases them all over Sea World.

Gamera shows up and wrecks the spaceship, revealing the shark-like alien commander (also named Zigra). The alien monster Zigra nearly kills the staunch turtle, and his human friends try to revive him in a bathysphere, but only succeed in getting captured by Zigra. However, Gamera is revived by a lucky lightning bolt, and sneaks his pals to safety while Zigra is

"It's just like the ones on television!"

—TV-addicted Kenny is excited to be on a hostile alien ship, as seen on TV, in *Gamera vs. Zigra*

asleep. With the puny humans safely on land, Gamera returns to beat up Zigra, actually playing his theme song on the alien's back spikes before finishing him off.

Probably the only novelty is that Zigra can talk. Well, that and the alien babe who steals a bikini to fit in on Earth while trying to kill little children at Sea World. Though the series was now aimed at directly at children, it's hard to imagine a child young enough to swallow some of this without question. If the aliens are planning to destroy civilization and eat the Earthlings, why do they bother to kidnap people beforehand? When the humans escape, why does X-1 have to chase them? Why not just destroy all of Sea World like they did Tokyo? The best that can be said for *Gamera vs. Zigra* is that it certainly isn't dull, even if it gives you a headache to watch it. Within months of this release, Daiei Studios went out of business. *AKA: Gamera Tai Shinkai Kaiju Jigara; Gamera vs. the Deep Sea Monster Zigra.* 🐉 ♥

1971 (G) 88m/C *JP* Eiko Yanami, Yasushi Sakagami, Koji Fujiyama, Arlene Zoellner, Gloria Zoellner, Isamu Saeki, Mikiko Tsubouchi, Reiko Kasahara, Yoshio Yoshida, Shin Minatsu, Daigo Inoue, Daihachi Kita, Ken Nakahara, Sho Natsuki. *D:* Noriaki Yuasa. *W:* Nisan Takahashi. *C:* Akira Uehara. *M:* Shunsuke Kikuchi. **VHS**

Gappa: The Triphibian Monster

The King Brothers had a huge hit with *Gorgo* (1961), a British giant-monster movie made with Japanese-style special effects. The Japanese returned the favor by swiping the general story line for this inferior production.

During the Economic Miracle of the 1950s and '60s, Japan went crazy for amusement parks. Publishing tycoon Funazu (Keisuke Yukioka) decides to expand his empire by building Playmate Land, a park with a South Seas theme. He sends journalists Hiroshi (Tamio Kawaji) and Sanburo (Kokan Katsura), along with photographer Itoko (Yoko Yamamoto) on an expedition with some scientists hunting for rare animals for the park. The find a doozy—a huge egg inside a cave full of gigantic bones, which hatches a huge bird-like critter named Gappa. They take it back to Tokyo with them for study while its park habitat is being built. The baby soon grows to be 40 feet tall, and eventually its angry parents come to town to rescue baby, leaving a wake of destruction.

This was the lone giant monster flick produced by Nikkatsu Studios, known for their crime and art-house movies. It comes off as a halfhearted attempt, with uninteresting special effects, shoddy miniatures, and a dull story. A lot of effort goes into getting the human characters to set up the monster action, but they're mostly abandoned after that. The trio of monsters, which look a bit like mythological gryphons, are oddly endearing, but can't keep the story going on their own. *AKA: Daikyoju Gappa; Monster from a Prehistoric Planet.* 🐉 ♥

1967 84m/C *JP* Tamio Kawaji, Yoko Yamamoto, Kokan Katsura, Keisuke Yukioka, Koji Wada, Mike Danning. *D:* Haruyasu Noguchi. *W:* Ryuzo Nakanishi, Gan Yamazaki. *C:* Muneo Ueda. *M:* Seitaro Omori. **VHS, DVD**

Gatchaman

The 1970s television version of this anime series is known in the U.S. as either *Battle of the Planets* or *G-Force*, depending on the syndicate. But in Japan, it was always called *Gatchaman*, and this 1990s direct-to-video remake updates the series without destroying what the fans liked about it. In the first part, "Gatchaman vs. Dragon King," President Beoluke of the nation of Hontworl celebrates his 52nd birthday (in 2066) by withdrawing from the United Nations, coercing several neighboring nations to leave with him. A gigantic spaceship shaped like a dragon lands on one of the capitol cities, destroying it with energy beams—a sequence that borrows heavily from *Independence Day*. The Hontworl alliance is actually a front for the evil Galactors from outer space, which has been abducting scientists working for the environmental Mantle Plan. To protect the plan, its creator Dr. Nanbu has been working in secret to create Science Ninja Team Gatchaman, five superheroes who use their abilities, gadgets, and fowl-based vehicles to invade and destroy the Galactors' ship. As an odd coincidence, both sides wear goofy bird uniforms. The Galactor forces are led by the sexually ambiguous Solaris, who answers only to a giant CGI Eye in a Pyramid. In "The Red Specter," the Gatchaman attack a Galactor base and fight the Jupiter Death Brigade. But they find new allies in the Interglobal Ninja Stealth Squad Red Specter! In "The Final Countdown," the Earthling's learn why the Galactor came to their planet, and of their ultimate weapon: control of the world's natural forces.

There's no getting around that this is a pretty silly series, and always was. You can make Batman look powerful and mysterious, but it's kind of hard to pull off the same effect with folks dressed like swans and ducks. However, the fresh new graphics at least make it look cool, and the Science Ninja Team kind of grows on you. The designs and artwork make it look like a well-drawn comic book. The animation of dialogue scenes is embarrassingly limited, though it improves greatly whenever any action starts, especially in the f/x animation. **AKA:** *Kagaku Ninja tai Gatchaman.* 🐉🐉🐉

1994 135m/C *JP* **D:** Hiroyuki Fukushima, Akihiko Nishiyama. **W:** Keitaro Motonaga, Akihiko Nishiyama. **C:** Akihiko Takahashi, Toyomitsu Nakajo. **M:** Maurice White and Bill Meyers. **DVD**

Gate of Destiny

In 1976, a mystery massacre occurs, committed by men dressed as samurai. In 1800, Japanese mystics believe the appearance of the Star of Heaven over Korea portends the birth of a great conqueror that will threaten all Asia, and the warrior Tian and his men are sent to kill the Korean king's family before the conqueror be born. But the royal family escaped through the Time Door. However, before the Door can close, Tian and some of his samurai manage to slip through. Ever since, the samurai have been trying to track down the royal heir. In 1996, Tao-lin is a philosophical biker chick and pizza parlor waitress who has dreams about Tian killing her family. Tian shows up one night and kills some of her friends while looking for her. Fortunately, a warrior from the past shows up to defend her.

Writer/director/star Lee Kyoung-young likely meant all his flashbacks to portray a displacement in time, but they only serve to confuse his story. It doesn't help that most of the time Kim Sung-bok's photography is too dark and murky to tell one character from another, much less what they're doing. Swordplay action is portrayed in arty cuts rather than choreography. Sort of a *Terminator* in reverse, watching this frustrating mess would only be a waste of your time. 🐉

1996 110m/C *KO* Kim Min-jeong, Kim Sung-lim, Lee Kyoung-young, Jang Dong-jik, Cho Sun-mook, Jang Ji-yeon, Lee Ki-young, Dokko Yung-jae. **D:** Lee Kyoung-young. **W:** Lee Kyoung-young. **C:** Kim Sung-bok. **M:** Seo Young-jin. **VHS**

Gen-X Cops

This Hong Kong version of *The Mod Squad* was executive produced by Jackie Chan (who has a small uncredited cameo), which means an extra infusion of excitement, great fight scenes, and excellent stunts. A two-year undercover operation by Hong Kong police leads to the seizure of 10 tons of "annonium Perch Lorate" (according to the subtitles), a powerful explosive rocket fuel. The cops are still after arms dealer "Dinosaur" Mak Wai Lung (Gordon Lam), who

doesn't know who the traitor is in his gang, until it's too late. His own kid brother Daniel (Daniel Wu) has sold him out to Akatora (Toru Nakamura), Japan's #1 criminal. Akatora's gang invades a chemical plant to retrieve the chemicals, and he plans to sell them himself.

Oddball Inspector Chan (Eric Tsang), disrespected by his colleagues because of his short stature and nervous disorder, has his own ideas about how the case should be handled. He's given a special assignment, for which he recruits three police academy washouts to go undercover as criminals. Match (Stephen Fung) is the ladies' man in the group, Jack (Nicholas Tse) is the best fighter, and weirdo Alien (Sam Lee) is a top marksman. Y2K Wing (Grace Yip), sister of a cop who got killed on the case and a computer guru, joins the team as well. They're tricked out with hi-tech surveillance gizmos and sent to spy in Daniel's nightclub. Caught poking around, they have an unexpected factor that gets them into the gang (and almost gets them killed): Haze (Jaymee Ong), Daniel's girlfriend, is one of Match's old conquests. To pay their debt to Daniel, they're sent on a mission, and between a triple-cross and a police raid, they somehow survive to join the gang. Meanwhile, Chan has to deal with the interference of rival Inspector To (Moses Chan), who always seems to be on his way to get a massage. Sticking with Daniel leads straight to Akatora, who is playing a game in a much bigger league than they thought.

To make the film more accessible worldwide, the cast and technical crew were assembled from several countries, with much of the dialogue spoken in English or Japanese, so stick to the original Cantonese version if you can to hear the difference. And to pander to x-treme sports fans, the young heroes keep getting into situations where surfboards and para-sails just happen to be available. So it's a stretch—but as action flicks go, it's hardly a long stretch, and allowances must be made if one wants to experience acts of modern derring-do. Besides, the young stars are so adorably pop-idol cute that you have to cut them some slack. In keeping with the Jackie Chan tradition, the stars did many of the stunts themselves, especially budding action star Nicholas Tse. They even recorded the theme song! Nakamura tries to act the philosophical villain, but just looks stoned most of the time. Francis Ng is more charismatic as the gangster Lok. **AKA:** *Dak Ging San Yan Lui; Te Jing Xin Ren Lei.* 🐉🐉🐉

1999 (R) 113m/C *HK* Nicholas Tse, Stephen Fung, Sam Lee, Grace Yip, Toru Nakamura, Eric Tsang, Daniel Wu, Francis Ng, Gordon Lam, Terence Yin, Moses Chan, Jaymee Ong, Ken Lo, Brad Allan, Jackie Wong, Winson Chan, Wayne Lai, Sato Keiji, Jackie Chan. **D:** Benny Chan. **W:** Benny Chan, Peter Tsi, Koan Hui, Lee Yee Wah. **C:** Arthur Wong. **M:** Nathan Wang. **VHS, DVD**

"It's a Jackie Chan move! It's bad!"

—Sam Lee explains why he took a gun apart rather than use it in a fight, in *Gen-X Cops*

Gen-Y Cops

A robot soldier, developed by Americans—and at least one Asian—is headed to Hong Kong for a weapons exhibition. The FBI—in the person of arrogant Agent Curtis (Paul Rudd), calm Agent Tucker (Mark Hicks), and constantly non–business dress wearing Jane (Maggie Q)—is in charge of providing security. Inspector Chung (Christy Chung) of the Hong Kong Police Force assigns Edison (Edison Chen), Match (Stephen Fung), and Alien (Sam Lee) as additional security. Oli (Rachel Ngan), a computer expert and Match's current flame, is also a part of the HK security team. Edison sneaks off to meet Kurt (Richard Suen), an old schoolmate visiting from the States. Somebody tries to steal the robot solider from the exhibition. Explosions, fighting, and general chaos ensue. No wonder the film was retitled *Metal Mayhem* when it was shown on American television.

Director Benny Chan delivers a different tone in this sequel than in the first film. Whereas *Gen-X Cops* was desperate to display a hip and rebellious attitude—and perhaps establish street credibility for its intended youthful audience—*Gen-Y Cops* is more relaxed and playful. It doesn't take itself too seriously, and that's definitely an advantage for this type of genre flick. The pacing is brisk but it's still too long—cutting at least 10 minutes would have helped. The action is well staged, although some may object to the highly exaggerated fighting style that is employed. The script is jam-packed with wild implausibilities. It also completely ignores the fact that this is a sequel—no mention is made of events or several main characters from the first film. The considerable amount of pseudo-American rap slang ("Yo, dog!" and the like) tends to grate on the ears. The lead actors were evidently chosen more for their good looks than for their thespian abilities. Several cameos enliven the proceedings: look for small roles played by Vincent Kok, Anthony Wong, Eric Kot, and Cheung Tat-Ming (as "Lobster Man"). —PM **AKA:** *Dak Ging San Yan Lui 2; Te Jing Xin Ren Lei 2; Gen-X Cops 2; Jackie Chan Presents: Metal Mayhem.* 🐉🐉🐲

2000 113m/C *HK* Edison Chen, Stephen Fung, Sam Lee, Richard Suen, Maggie Q, Rachel Ngan, Paul Rudd, Mark Hicks, Christy Chung, Anthony Wong, Eric Kot, Vincent Kok, Cheung Tat-Ming, Lee Lik-Chi, Ron Smoorenburg, Jude Poyer, Teresa Herrera, Ricardo Mamood, Tony Trimble, Felix Chong. **D:** Benny Chan. **W:** Bey Logan, Felix Chong, Chan Kiu-ying. **C:** Fletcher Poon. **M:** Peter Kam. **DVD**

Generation Consultant

Kung fu stars of the '70s team up in the 1990s for this densely plotted historical drama. General Chau (Gordon Lau) eliminates his competition and controls the emperor of East Han Dynasty, about A.D. 200. He defeats Liu Bi easily at Chin Province. Consultant Chugou Liang (Lau Wing) rushes back from a mission to convince the generals to unite against their common foe, Chau. He discovers Chau's weakness: a merchant named Chiao has two daughters that Chau desires for his new Copper Bird Palace. Chugou asks Lieutenant Kung Chin (Ku Feng) to give Chau the two girls, but he refuses—Little Chiao is his wife. With fighting the only alternative, Chin's navy sails on Easterly Lake against the much larger Chau navy. But Chugou has a lot of tricks up his sleeve. He collects arrows from Chau's navy by sailing ships full of straw past them in a fog. He then tricks Chau into linking his fleet together so that the ships are easily burned in an attack. But Chugou soon leaves Chin for another general—he goes from one general to another, using whatever wiles necessary to unite the provinces into three kingdoms.

The tactics and intrigues are interesting, though the events of even that small period of Chinese history are too complex to cover adequately in a two-hour movie. To American viewers, whose schooling in Chinese history only covers visits made by Marco Polo and Richard Nixon, this is tremendously confusing, especially since the subtitles give several characters the same name. There's some swordplay and battle scenes, but this looks to have been shot on the cheap and none of it is worth sitting through all the meetings and discussions. 🐉

1990 108m/C *HK* Lau Wing, Gordon Lau, Ku Feng, Austin Wai, O Chun-Hung, Poon Hing. **D:** O Chun-Hung, Wu Ma. **VHS**

Generation Pendragon

In this semi-prequel to *Generation Consultant*, we're shown the story of General Chau (Gordon Lau) as he tries to unite the warring regions of China by force. Chau is promoted to Prime Minister. He routs Yuen Shu and has old enemy Lu Bo killed. Chiang Lu is another old enemy that's captured, but is spared death because he's a "righteous guy." With more territory under Chau's control, the emperor asks generals of surrounding territories to contain his forces, to no avail. The Prime Minister's armies conquer or recruit all they encounter. Some former enemies, like General Kwan, even become Chau's trusted friends—though unknown to Kwan, his lost brother is still among Chau's opposition. When Kwan spots his brother leading some of Yuen Shu's forces, Chau honors his word to let Kwan join his brother. Running low on food, Chau is forced to execute the officer in charge,

and orders a raid to destroy the enemy's supplies as well. All this leads to the historic Battle
of Konloo, where outnumbered Chau defeats
70,000 troops. However, he falls to the strategies of Consultant Chuguo Liang (Lau Wing).
Spared because of his friendship with Kwan,
Chau survives to retire to his Copper Bird
Palace, where he is declared a king, and suffers
through later years plagued by illness and family
disputes. Some of the stories and historical
intrigue are interesting, but most of the action
is again kept offscreen, making for a lot of dull
and confusing talk. Of benefit to students of
Chinese history only. ⚔

1990 108m/C *HK* Gordon Lau, Ku Feng, Lau Wing,
Ko Chun-hsiang, Wu Ma. *D:* O Chun-Hung, Wu Ma.
VHS, DVD

Ghidorah the Three-Headed Monster

Toho Studios quickly followed their excellent
Mothra vs. Godzilla with this even bigger monster rumble. A beautiful Asian princess (Akiko
Wakabayashi, a Bond Girl in *You Only Live
Twice*) is rescued from an assassination
attempt onboard a plane by an interfering UFO,
which abducts her right through the fuselage
before the plane explodes. She turns up later
in Japan, professing to be possessed by a
Martian intelligence and spouting prophetic
warnings of doom. Sure enough, Godzilla
(Haruo Nakajima) and Rodan (Masashi Shinohara) appear, and begin a playful (and highly
destructive) tussle across the Japanese countryside like ancient gods. But an even greater
danger arrives in the form of space monster
King Ghidorah (Shoichi Hirose), who materializes out of a strange meteorite. The twin
fairies of Infant Island, in town for a TV appearance, recruit the young Mothra (who'd defeated Godzilla at their last meeting) to convince
the battling Earth monsters to unite against
the invader. Meanwhile, assassins from the
princess's home country continue to try killing
her off. Fast-paced, king-size fun for all ages,
this is the beginning of Toho's Monster Rally
period, in which each Godzilla movie would
feature more star critters, reaching the acme
with the classic *Destroy All Monsters*. The big

Godzilla meets his
most powerful
enemy in *Ghidorah
the Three-Headed
Monster.*
THE KOBAL
COLLECTION / TOHO

Hail King Ghidorah

He's Once, Twice, Three Times a Monster

If a hero is measured by the power of his adversaries, Godzilla must rival Gilgamesh as one of the greatest screen sluggers of all time. While initially imagined as a lone, unstoppable menace in the original 1954 *Gojira,* producers at Japan's Toho Studios quickly realized that a single marauding monster would be inadequate to entertain audiences in a series of kaiju sequels, so opponents for their biggest star were clearly needed. The first was the prickly, porcupine-like Angilas, who was quickly dispatched by Godzilla in the herky-jerky midpoint battle of *Godzilla Raids Again* in 1955. Then Godzilla faced the ultimate symbol of American might, hairy ape King Kong, in 1962. Kong was a great success, but the cost of purchasing rights to the beast from RKO Studios prohibited Toho from staging any rematches with Godzilla (although Kong got his own solo venture in *King Kong Escapes,* a collaboration with the American Rankin Bass company, which was running its own *King Kong* Saturday morning cartoon in the mid '60s).

The distinctly Japanese Goliath Mothra went mano y mothra with Godzilla in *Mothra vs. Godzilla* (known as *Godzilla vs. the Thing* in the U.S., where American distributors wisely intuited that Yankee audiences wouldn't line up to watch Godzilla fight a fluffy adorable moth), which began a long-running feud between the fire-breathing radioactive dragon and the altruistic cocoon-spinner. But somehow Godzilla had still not met his match. In showdowns between Mothra and Godzilla, Mothra always seemed the underdog, bullied around by the taller, scalier Godzilla. It was time to bring in a creature that could bully Godzilla. Enter King Ghidorah, or as he was titled in the U.S. version of his debut movie in 1964, "Ghidrah, the Three Headed Monster." Ghidorah was Toho's first "all-star" kaiju epic, boasting not just Godzilla and an adversary but also the first reappearance of giant pterodactyl Rodan since his 1956 film debut, and the return of the Mothra caterpillar from *Mothra vs. Godzilla.* In the movie a psychic who claims to be from the planet Mars warns of the arrival of a terrible space monster. After Godzilla and Rodan emerge from their slumber to do battle, a magnetized, giant meteorite explodes and unleashes a fireball that forms into a golden, flying three-headed dragon in one of the most thrilling and spectacular entrances in Toho's kaiju history.

As conceived by Toho's special-effects supervisor Eiji Tsuburaya, Ghidorah dwarfed Godzilla and his fellow monsters. The Godzilla costume extended around a foot over the head of the actor playing the monster, who was able to see outside the costume through disguised holes in Godzilla's neck. In the Ghidorah costume, the actor's head extended into the middle neck of the creature while his arms supported the left and right neck—most of the actor's body controlled a bulky, two-legged and two-tailed midsection that comprised only a small percentage of the monster's full height and breadth (taken up by gigantic, wire-controlled wings). The wings and snake-like necks and heads of the monster added another three or four feet to Ghidorah's stature, giving the dragon a distinct height advantage over Godzilla. *Ghidorah the Three-Headed Monster* continued a trend begun in 1962's *King Kong vs. Godzilla*, by adding a comic slant to the monstrous goings-on; some of the initial battles between Godzilla and Rodan are played strictly for laughs, particularly when Mothra enters the fray and a conversation between the monsters is translated by Mothra's twin fairies. But the final showdown with Godzilla, Mothra, and Rodan teaming up to tackle Ghidorah is spectacular and solidified the three-headed monster's standing as the go-to heavy for any major Godzilla epic.

Toho followed *Ghidorah the Three-Headed Monster* with *Monster Zero* (AKA *Invasion of Astro-Monster*), which began a trend of depicting the redubbed King Ghidorah as a puppet (literally and figuratively, as it turns out) of insidious alien masters. The film initially continues the *Ghidorah the Three-Headed Monster* mythology that depicts Ghidorah as a marauding destroyer of worlds (in *Ghidorah* he is blamed for the destruction of all life on Mars), but it turns out the residents of Planet X (an inhabited world hidden behind Jupiter) are controlling Ghidorah in a ruse to get the people of Earth (i.e., Japan) to "loan" Godzilla and Rodan to the aliens so they can use all three giant monsters to crush Earth's defenses. While *Monster Zero* achieved the nadir of Toho camp humor by having Godzilla dance a jig in the low gravity of Planet X after his first victory over Ghidorah there, the special effects were a series high point. Sequences of Ghidorah storming over the barren landscape of Planet X or descending onto a Tokyo factory complex, electric beams blazing out of its triple mouths and laying waste to the countryside, were so successful they were used as stock footage in numerous later Godzilla films.

The apex of Toho's initial wave of Godzilla films was 1968's *Destroy All Monsters*. Once again, alien invaders (this time the

Continued on next page...

nefarious Kilaaks) launch an invasion of Earth, bringing all of the planet's giant monsters under a seemingly unbreakable mind control that sees Godzilla attacking New York City (in a sequence that must have given Dean Devlin an idea or two) and Rodan mowing down Moscow. Only at the climax when the Kilaaks are in danger of being beaten off is the menace of Ghidorah unleashed, leading to a spectacular monster mash on Mount Fuji that features every major Toho kaiju from Mothra to Varan the Unbelievable. Sadly, Ghidorah's next appearance was not to be quite so memorable. By 1972's *Godzilla vs. Gigan,* the Godzilla series was in serious decline, having suffered the slings and arrows of *All Monster Attack* and *Godzilla vs. Hedorah* (or *Godzilla vs. the Smog Monster*). With aliens once again scheming to take over the Earth, an invasion plan is this time launched from the heart of a Godzilla theme park, employing space monsters Ghidorah and new monster-on-the-block Gigan, a creature composed entirely of beak and claw, with the added bonus of a buzz saw in his stomach. Godzilla actually talks to his buddy Angilas in this one, which is plagued with stock footage on one hand and cheapjack special effects on the other. The Ghidorah costume has never looked rattier, and shots of G.I. Joe–sized puppets of Ghidorah and Gigan flying in space or over a miniature soundstage are appallingly bad, even by the standards of rubber monster movies (the Godzilla suit employed for several lengthy swimming sequences looks an awful lot like the one John Belushi wore while hosting *Godzilla vs. Megalon* on NBC).

By the end of the '70s, the Godzilla series had been all but retired, and Ghidorah spent more than a decade in mothballs before being reintroduced in one of the most unusual and interesting kaiju features ever made, 1991's *Godzilla vs. King Ghidorah.* In a Toho take on *The Terminator,* beings from the future warn Japan that Godzilla will devastate the country. They propose a plan to go back in time to a Pacific island in WWII and slay the "Godzillasaurus," which will become Godzilla after atomic experiments in the '50s. Godzilla's existence is cancelled out, but three adorable alien Dorats are released by the future beings, and these miniature dragon-like creatures take the radioactive hit that created Godzilla and combine to become King Ghidorah—which lays waste to Japan without Godzilla to oppose it (in one of several anti-American themes in the film, the "Futurians" turn out to be Western forces who want to prevent Japan from becoming an economic superpower). Godzilla is reborn through other means, however, and slaughters Ghidorah by ripping its central head off. In one of many unusual twists, one of the future time-travelers resuscitates Ghidorah and supplements its body with robot parts, creating a "good" Mecha-KingGhidorah oppose the menace of Godzilla. The new Ghidorah was impressively designed in both organic and Mecha forms, although Koichi Kawakita's special effects couldn't quite match the majesty of Eiji Tsuburaya's '60s work, and the replacement of Ghidorah's eerie electric organ wails with the regurgitated roar of Rodan stole some of the three-headed monster's unique appeal.

Ghidorah appeared in modified form in two of the Heisei Mothra films, as the charcoal-colored, hydra-headed Death Ghidorah in the first *Rebirth of Mothra* in 1996, and as a streamlined, copper-colored, more reptilian version in *Rebirth of Mothra 3*. But Ghidorah still maintained his reputation as an eternal fall guy: first blamed for the death of all life on Mars in *Ghidorah the Three-Headed Monster*, in *Rebirth of Mothra 3* he's fingered for wiping out the dinosaurs in Earth's past. Ghidorah's most recent appearance was in Shusuke Kaneko's revisionist *Godzilla, Mothra and King Ghidorah: Battle on Fire* (or *GMK: All Monsters Attack*). Like 1996's *Godzilla vs. King Ghidorah*, *GMK* reimagined Godzilla as less an antihero than a malevolent, destructive force (the living embodiment of the Japanese dead of WWII), and Ghidorah (along with Mothra and Baragon) was depicted as a dormant, ancient Japanese god of fire. This new Ghidorah was actually smaller than the rampaging Godzilla, and the Ghidorah costume/puppet was simplified and less detailed than its predecessors, emphasizing an almost medallion-like appearance for the dragon. The depiction of the three-headed monster was one of the most controversial aspects of the production, although the film itself was well received. It remains to be seen when or how King Ghidorah will appear again—but he's more than established his position in kaiju history.

—JB

highlight here is the title creature: a gigantic, nightmarish, scaly horror that looks like a golden dragon out of Japanese legend, spewing bolts of lightning from all three mouths. He'd be back, along with Godzilla and Rodan, the next year in *Invasion of Astro-Monster*. The 1966 U.S. version was heavily re-edited, damaging continuity. **AKA:** San Daikaiju: Chikyu Saidai no Kesson; Ghidrah the Three-Headed Monster; The Greatest Battle on Earth; Ghidrah; Gojira Mosura Kingughidorah: Chikyu Saidai no Kessen; Greatest Fight on Earth; Monster of Monsters. 🐉🐉🐉🐉

1964 92m (US 85)/C JP Akiko Wakabayashi, Yosuke Natsuki, Yuriko Hoshi, Hiroshi Koizumi, Takashi Shimura, Emi Ito, Yumi Ito, Hisaya Ito, Kenji Sahara, Minoru Takada, Somesho Matsumoto, Ikio Sawamura, Kozo Nomura, Susumu Kurobe, Toru Ibuke, Kazuo Suzuki, Haruya Kato, Shin Otomo, Senkichi Omura, Yutaka Oka, Eisei Amamoto, Yoshio Kosugi, Yoshifumi Tajima, Haruo Nakajima,

Masashi Shinohara, Shoichi Hirose, Katsumi Tezuka. **D:** Ishiro Honda. **W:** Shinichi Sekizawa. **C:** Hajime Koizumi. **M:** Akira Ifukube. **VHS**

Ghost Actress

One of many recent films to use the relation of images caught on film or video to ghosts, and vice-versa. Toshio Murai (Yurei Yanagi) is directing his first film, a drama about two sisters during World War II. Viewing rushes shot on short ends of old film, the crew sees what appears to be footage shot for an old movie or TV show. Intrigued, Murai keeps the clip, vaguely recalling having seen the finished film as a child. The footage shows a couple arguing, the woman gasping in terror as a ghostly woman laughs behind her, and a small boy ascending stairs to a spooky attic. At location shooting the next day, he thinks he sees the same ghostly face behind Saori (Kei Ishibashi), one of the leads. The other lead Hitomi (Yasuyo Shirashima) is having trouble with her agent (Toshie Negishi), but one day the woman visits the set and gets a horrified look. Disaster strikes when Saori falls to her death from a catwalk. While everyone waits to find out if shooting can continue, Murai investigates the clip and finds out that the actress in it also fell to her death from the same stage. The last few scenes are done with a stand-in, but just as in the clip, Hitomi gasps in horror when she sees Saori's face, and a strange girl laughs behind her.

This isn't as frightening as *Ring* (which Hideo Nakata would direct next), but there are still some effectively creepy moments. The chills are undercut by the use of electronic music, which tends to camp up the effect. But the main fault in this ghost story is that it doesn't really seem to have a point. The idea of a ghost actress haunting a studio across generations is effective, but no reason is given for it. This may be intended to keep the film mysterious, but it just feels unfinished. **AKA:** *Joyuu-rei; Don't Look Up.* ♫♫

1996 75m/C *JP* Yurei Yanagi, Yasuyo Shirashima, Kei Ishibashi, Ren Osugi, Toshie Negishi, Tan Lee, Hiroyuki Tanaka, Takanori Kikuchi, Reita Serizawa, Akira Takahashi. **D:** Hideo Nakata. **W:** Hiroshi Takahashi, Hideo Nakata (story). **C:** Takeshi Hamada. **M:** Akifumi Kawamura. **VHS**

Ghost in the Shell

A wonderfully animated sci-fi from Japan about a cyborg special agent trying to track down a rogue artificial intelligence while questioning the nature of her existence in the screwed-up hi-tech world of the future. (So who isn't?) Motoko "Major" Kusanagi is a babe super-agent who has given up her humanity to better serve her special law enforcement section in the Hong Kong of 2029. There's a rash of dangerous hacks going on in the system, all of which are traced to people being used against their will by a mysterious "puppet master" that controls their thoughts and memories. Major and her partner Batou do their best to track the invader, despite interference from a rival section that let the menace loose in the first place. That menace turns out to be Project 2501, an artificial intelligence program that outgrows its original design and goes after the one thing technology alone won't get it.

One of the things science fiction does best is to take the human experience far from the familiar, stretching it and defining it in the process. There's some touchingly poetic sequences here, matched by some really great action and destruction, but the complexity of the plot sometimes gets in the way. This is one of those movies that get better with each repeat viewing. There's just too much visual, dramatic, and philosophical information to take in on the first try. The soundtrack by Kenji Kawai is especially good, reinforcing the mood of every scene. Though *Akira* is still the yardstick used to judge anime, *Ghost in the Shell,* directed by the popular Mamoru Oshii *(Patlabor)* represents a true artistic and technological advancement in animated feature films. Definitely skip the poor English dub and seek out the Japanese subtitled version. The plot calls for a lot of dialogue, and the "voice talent" used for the English release just doesn't measure up to the Japanese actors—they often sound like a script reading for a high-school play. **AKA:** *Kokaku Kidotai.* ♫♫♫♫

1995 82m/C *JP* **V:** Atsuko Tanaka, Akio Otsuka, Tamio Oki, Iemasa Kayumi. **D:** Mamoru Oshii. **W:** Kazunori Itô, Masamune Shirow. **C:** Hasao Shirai. **M:** Kenji Kawai. **VHS, DVD**

Giant Monster Gamera

A crashing atomic bomber plane releases a gigantic mutant turtle from the arctic ice. Soon after, people all over the world begin reporting a brightly shining flying saucer soaring through the stratosphere. Is there a connection between the UFO and the monster? Everyone finds out after a military plan to turn the turtle on its back succeeds, as the monster flies off in a flare of jets! The flying, fire-breathing monster goes on the rampage in Japan, despite the delusions of little turtle-obsessed Kenny (or Toshio, depending on which version you're watching, played by Yoshiro Uchida), who believes Gamera is "a friend to all children." His hallucinations are further supported when Gamera saves him from falling off a lighthouse. Gamera seems to absorb all forms of energy thrown at it. A team of scientists and military brass decide to use Top Secret Plan Z to deal with the monster menace, even though it will blow the lid off a secret international island base.

In all, an enjoyable monster romp, with a rather unique and interesting conclusion, even though no one kills Kenny. Daiei Studios created *Gamera* to compete with rival Toho's very successful Godzilla pictures, which were starting to portray the monster as a hero, making him more popular with children. Like *Godzilla*, the American theatrical version of *Gamera* was altered to include added scenes featuring Anglo actors—in this case, Brian Donlevy and Albert Dekker as U.S. military men. This version has almost completely disappeared in favor of the current more faithful video incarnation. The giant turtle returned for seven silly sequels full of juvenile hi-jinks aimed at children (which also succeeded in dragging the Godzilla series down to the same level), before returning for a surprisingly good semi-remake in 1995. **AKA:** *Daikaiju Gamera; Gamera; Gammera; Gammera the Invincible.* ♫♫♫

1965 80/86m/BW *JP* Eiji Funakoshi, Hirumi Kiritachi, Yoshiro Uchida, Junichiro Yamashiko, Yoshiro Kitahara, Jun Hamamura, Bokuzen Hidari, Tsutomu Nakata, Kenji Oyama, Brian Donlevy (U.S. version), Albert Dekker (U.S.), Diane Findlay (U.S.), Allen Oppenheimer (U.S.), John Baragray (U.S.). **D:** Noriaki Yuasa, Sandy Howard (U.S.). **W:** Nisan Takahashi. **C:** Nobuo Munekawa. **M:** Tadashi Yamauchi. **VHS**

Giants and Toys

Sales are declining at World Caramels. Everywhere people are complaining, predicting a collapse of the Japanese economy. The pressure is on to beat the caramel competition, which includes both the Japanese Giant and Apollo, and the invading candy companies from the United States. It's all-out war, and they need a new idea for a promotion. Publicity chief Goda (Hideo Takamatsu) picks up a girl at a teahouse named Kyoko Shima (Hitomi Nozoe), thinking she'd create a good image with her cute face, crooked teeth, and big tongue. Goda is an idol to his underling Nishi (Hiroshi Kawaguchi), whose best friend Yokoyama works for Giant. They run into Miss Masami Kurahashi from Apollo, whose promotion idea is space suits—which she gives to Nishi. Goda sells the board on the space idea, then picks up the crazy teen for her test shots at Harakawa's photography studio. Goda also intends to arrange Nishi as the girl's boyfriend. Nishi would rather date an experienced woman like Masami—which lets him spy on Apollo at the same time. Harakawa (Yunosuke Ito) makes some more shots and arranges a photo spread in a top magazine. Kyoko is a big hit as Japan's new sweetheart, and World announces they've signed her as their poster model. Their campaign is ready to go, but Apollo pulls a trump card: their promotion is a contest to win a fully subsidized life, "from cradle to wedding." The competition escalates, and Kyoko is everywhere—ball games, concerts, amusement parks. Goda starts popping pills. Nishi starts to worry about what'll happen to Kyoko after the fad is over. Work continues on World's Space Expo. And still Apollo outsells everyone.

Then a break comes—Apollo's factory burns to the ground. Production races ahead as World attempts to take advantage and crush Apollo. Meanwhile, while the campaign's climax nears, Goda heads for mental and physical breakdown, and Kyoko has disappeared. When she returns, she's transformed herself into the perfect star—refined, sophisticated, and totally out of control.

This early film from the director of *Blind Beast* and *Razor 2: The Snare* is an amazing portrait of Japanese culture in the Jet Age, and an indictment of the industrial juggernaut they were becoming. The drama is rich, but the film can also be enjoyed for its spicy visuals and pop-culture kitsch. Before karaoke, singing halls were popular across Japan. The public ate up silly fads, garish musical numbers, and everyone was mad for baseball. Not nearly as much fluffy fun, but *Giants and Toys* would fit nicely between American classics like *One Two Three* and *The Girl Can't Help It*. **AKA:** *Kyojin to Gangyu; The Build-Up.* ♫♫♫

1958 95m/C *JP* Hiroshi Kawaguchi, Hitomi Nozoe, Hideo Takamatsu, Michiko Ono, Yunosuke Ito, Kyu Sazanka. **D:** Yasuzo Masamura. **W:** Ishio Shirasaka, Ken Kaiko (story). **C:** Hiroshi Murai. **M:** Tetsuo Tsukahara. **DVD**

Gimme Gimme

Teenagers in a rock band and their friends deal with love, romance, and relationships. We see a love triangle develop: Skid (Siu Yu-wah) likes Pat (Yoyo Chan), but she prefers Lobo (Chiu Tien-you). Soda (Yorky Yuen) has a multitude of girlfriends, including the long-suffering Suki (Ho Wing-suen). Another girl has a long-distance boyfriend with whom she communicates only by cell phone. Another couple are constantly fighting and breaking up. And so it goes.

Teenage romances are usually short-lived and quite predictable. The same is true for this film's adventures in love. None of the featured

relationships has an unexpected twist; it's easy to guess what will happen next. So enjoyment of the intertwined stories rests on the exploration of the characters themselves. And it is in this aspect of the film that writer Tse Lo and director Lawrence Ah Mon shine. The small group of friends is not obsessed with sex—as most American filmmakers portray teenagers, nor constantly wisecracking—as most American television programs depict school-age youth. Instead, they vacillate between distilling preternatural pearls of wisdom and acting inconsistently with their stated beliefs. They have a sense that they want to "do the right thing" toward their friends, but they don't yet have a very firm grasp on what exactly the "right thing" is to do. They stumble, but they seem always to move forward, and that allows the viewer to root for them. One nitpick here is that parents and adults are nearly entirely absent from their adolescent lives. That may or may not be an accurate assessment of 21st-century Hong Kong youth, but it seems like an omission made for dramatic purposes; perhaps to avoid any premature reckoning? Director Ah Mon mostly remains in observational, docudrama mode—his camera rarely moves within the frame—but occasionally he cannot resist inserting pure cinematic moments, as when Skid is sick on a curbside and has a private audience with Pat. Several other scenes—including one between Soda and Suki in which both pour out their hearts on cell phones while traveling miles apart in taxis—serve as emotional set-pieces, taking the place of fiery gun battles in crime films, around which the various relationships ebb and flow. The beautiful cinematography by Keung Kwok-man does not call attention to itself but wisely eschews a documentary look. —PM **AKA:** *Oi Seung Ngo Ang; Ai Shang Wo Ba.* ♫♫♫

2001 101m/C *HK* Siu Yu-wah, Yoyo Chan, Chiu Tien-you, Yorky Yuen, Ho Wing-suen, Yoky Lo. **D:** Lawrence Ah Mon. **W:** Tse Lo. **C:** Keung Kwok-man. **M:** Chung Chi-wing. **VHS, DVD**

Glass Tears

Fifteen-year-old Cho has run away from home for the third time. Since her third such disappearance would result in Cho being taken out of the family home entirely, her parents (Carrie Ng and Tats Lau) decide not to report the matter to the police. Instead, they enlist the assistance of Wu (Lo Lieh), a retired Mainland police officer working as a guard on a small island. He quickly makes contact with a girl called P by her friends (Zeny Kwok), who claims that Cho owes her a substantial sum of money. Wu offers P the same amount of money if she will help him find Cho. As the search for Cho continues, Wu and P spend

time together and learn more about each other, and P's friend Tofu (Chui Tien-you) joins them.

Though it aspires to say something important, *Glass Tears* is curiously devoid of substantial content. Are the characters P and Wu meant to be stand-ins for their respective generations? Or are they to be taken as representative of the uneasy relationship between Mainland China and Hong Kong? Director Carol Lai appeared to hint in an interview that the story is about her own life, but presumably the modern-day setting is also meant to reflect her concerns about present-day life. The relaxed pace of the story allows time to meditate on meatier subjects, but she and co-writer Lui Hok-cheung offer little incisive insight, commentary, or even propaganda. Nevertheless, as a director, Lai displays a competent eye for composition and tries to add variety to the tale through the creative use of flashbacks (she shared editing duties with Danny Pang, co-director and editor of *Bangkok Dangerous* and *The Eye*). Although some of the effects are a bit self-conscious, the effort is welcome. Newcomer Zeny Kwok acquits herself quite well as P. The role calls for her to remain glum and sullen much of the time, but also allows her to flash a radiant smile on occasion. Lo Lieh—an old-school kung fu villain in several classic films from the 1970s—brings a commanding physical presence to his part as Wu; it seems that he accepts his *de facto* exile to a small island as the price he must pay for not understanding the modern world. As Cho's parents, Carrie Ng and Tats Lau make an uncomfortable but weirdly matched pair. They appear to have little to talk about, yet manage to suggest depths of unexpressed emotions beneath their quiet exteriors. —PM **AKA:** *Boh Lee Siu Lui; Bo Li Shao Nu.* ♫♫♫

2001 95m/C *HK* Zeny Kwok, Lo Lieh, Carrie Ng, Tats Lau, Chiu Tien-you. **D:** Carol Lai. **W:** Carol Lai, Lui Hok-cheung. **C:** Tony Cheung. **VHS, DVD**

God.com

About the best thing that can be said for this lame supernatural thriller is that it's actually *not* about a haunted website. Despite the deceptive title, it's not about the Internet at all, but rather a millennium cult movie that borrows a key concept from *Silence of the Lambs* and a true-crime angle from an actual Hong Kong cult suicide case.

When fanatical religious cult leader Lin Yu-tin (Mark Cheng) is arrested by Officer Chiu (Anthony Wong), he places a curse on the cop. Years later, Chiu has become the Hong Kong Police Force's expert on mysticism, and unofficial fortuneteller. OCTB Inspector Chan (Louis Koo) is stymied by an apparent mass ritual-suicide case, until his assistants coerce him into seeking

Chiu's advice. Chiu says that it's a case of a con man convincing others to participate in a life-extension ritual, then poisoning them all and running off with their cash. Though Chan is cynical, the evidence seems to back up Chiu's theory—though it turns out there was more than one poison used, indicating that there were two killers.

Cheng Wing-ching (Emily Kwan), a surviving victim, is their best lead, and they question her friend Blonde Ying (Grace Lam) about her. Soon after, Ching is killed by the villain's hoodoo. Ying agrees to try to get close to Kong, who led Ching into joining him in the millennium doomsday cult the Church of True God. Despite her role as police helper, Ying is taken in by the charisma of the church's leader Mr. Pope (Andrew Lin), a stigmatic with supernatural powers. Out of nowhere comes a request from imprisoned Lin Yu-tin, who wants to meet Chan—whose parents died because of involvement with Lin's cult decades ago. Lin wants to help the cop catch Pope, if only to eliminate the competition from the Mad Prophet charts.

There's some potential in Anthony Wong's psychic cop character, but it's all wasted as Louis Koo takes the lead. As the film trundles along, the enigmatic cult leaders stare ominously at the cops, hypnotize women into becoming sex slaves, and otherwise drain all interest from the viewer until the film's muddled conclusion. From the director of the equally pointless *Daughter of Darkness*. By the way, at present writing the domain god.com is registered to Groves Online Delivery of East Arlington, Massachusetts, though they don't have a site up for it. *AKA: Che Gaau Dong Ngon Ji Moot Yat Fung Biu; Xie Jiao Dang An Zhi Mo Ri Feng Bao.* 🦴

1998 87m/C *HK* Louis Koo, Grace Lam, Andrew Lin, Anthony Wong, Mak Cheung-ching, Emily Kwan, Mark Cheng, David Lee, Lee Sze-pui, Lau Sek Yin, Wong Chun Tong, Onitsuka, Simon Au, Chat Pui-wan, Place Lam. *D:* Ivan Lai. *W:* Ivan Lai. *C:* Kwan Chi-kan. *M:* Danny Chung. **DVD**

God of Cookery

Stephen Chow turns his attention to the kitchen with this surreal comedy, which was no doubt inspired by the Japanese television series *Iron Chef*. Stephen Chow (what, no funny name?) is the arrogant king of cuisine of the title, who uses his TV show to humiliate the great chefs of the world. His abuse is not reserved just for chefs—his crew, MC (Law Kar-Ying), and business associates get a tongue lashing as well. However, the God of Cookery is a fraud—unable to really cook himself, he has a staff of hirelings doing his work for him, and those who dare judge his work are actually planted stooges.

At the opening of his latest restaurant, his trusted business manager (Ng Man-Tat) engineers a brutal coup, and Stephen's much-abused assistant Bull Tong (Vincent Kok)—who is a true cooking wizard—usurps his position, becoming an even worse tyrant. After his arrest for poisoning customers with "British beef," Chow disappears. Hitting bottom, he learns humility when he's taken in by street noodle vendor Twin Dagger Turkey (Karen Mok). During a rumble between Turkey and rival vendor Goosehead (Lee Siu-Kei) over rights to specialty dishes, Chow stumbles on the invention of Explosive Pissing Beef Balls, which cause an explosion of ecstasy in the mouth of the diner. This new miracle food, which can cure illness and be used to play ping-pong, becomes an overnight sensation. His fame growing again, Chow intends to enter the God of Cookery challenge to get his revenge. Much of this success is due to Turkey, who is revealed as Chow's number-one obsessed fan, and her face is ruined defending him. He's repelled, but when Bull sends a hit man to erase him, she proves her devotion.

Chow takes his mad surrealism to another level in the sensational cook-off finale. Trained by Dean Wet Dream (Tats Lau) at the Shaolin Temple kitchen, Chow proves his cooking could put smiles on the faces of the 18 Brassmen! Having had half his early success sending up Chow Yun-fat's *God of Gamblers* character, here Chow takes his parody to grotesque and beautiful extremes. Karen Mok *(Fallen Angels)* gamely disguises her beauty with a Quasimodo makeup job, but still makes enough of a good impression that her absence during the climax is the film's biggest flaw. Wondering about her fate while the razzle dazzle is going on in the kitchen stadium is a major distraction. Nancy Sit, starlet of such 1960s films as *Teddy Girls* and *The Swinging Bunch,* comes out of retirement to judge the cooking. Not Chow's most accessible work; newcomers will either be put off or blown away by this one. *AKA: Jeung San; Shi Shen.* 🦴🦴🦴🦴

1996 92m/C *HK* Stephen Chow, Karen Mok, Vincent Kok, Ng Man-Tat, Lee Siu-Kei, Law Kar-Ying, Nancy Sit, Yuen King-Tan, Tats Lau, Stephen Au, Bobby Yip, Liz Kong, Christy Chung. *D:* Stephen Chow, Lee Lik-Chi. *W:* Stephen Chow, Sammy Tsang, Lo Man-sang, Vincent Kok. *C:* Jingle Ma. *M:* Ronald Ng. **VHS, DVD**

God of Gamblers

Gambling movies are a subgenre unto themselves in Hong Kong, an offshoot of the crime and spy movies of the 1960s. Wong Jing has always loved the genre—his first two pictures as director were gambling movies, and he wrote

THE HOUND SALUTES
Stephen Chow
Chow Mainstream

周星馳

Everybody knows that Jackie Chan is the biggest movie star in Asia, but who is number two? Why, it's Stephen Chow, of course!

Whaddya mean, "Who?" Well, that reaction is understandable from mainstream America, where (as of this writing) none of his films has been released to theatres. That's due to change some day—the only question is: When? Chow's success has been phenomenal in Asia, but he may have even more of a problem conquering America than Chan did—if he's even interested.

Born June 22, 1962, Chow Sing-chi grew up idolizing Bruce Lee just like any other Chinese boy. He studied kung fu, but discovered an even greater passion, acting. Chow got his break hosting the children's TV show *430 Space Shuttle* with another future star, Tony Leung Chiu-wai, honing his comic skills to an audience of toddlers. His odd sense of humor gained the show a cult audience among adults. His second film role was as a sympathetic petty criminal in *Final Justice*, which won him the Golden Horse Award in Taiwan. After a few more dramatic and comedic supporting roles, he had his first headlining role, spoofing the outrageous popularity of the gambling genre started by *God of Gamblers*. *All for the Winner* was one of 11 pictures Chow appeared in in 1990. Within a few months, he starred in the bisequel *God of Gamblers 2*. From there, it was one hit comedy after another, with Chow either playing an innocent bumpkin with a special ability, an arrogant slicker who finds his conscience, or even a combination of the two. He also occasionally played characters who were a bit more serious—his take on the Monkey King was the least silly thing in the two *A Chinese Odyssey* fantasy movies.

He's been described as a Chinese Jim Carrey, but that description is a disservice, as Chow's style, timing, and personality are all his own. *Shaolin Soccer* (2001) is deservedly his biggest hit ever, crushing the boxoffice records all over Asia (the sequel *Shaolin Soccer Army* is on the way). It's a wonderful film, but the problem with

Chow is that much of his "mo lei tau" (nonsense) comic appeal is verbal, or based in Chinese culture. The English dubbed version of the film is a good 20 minutes shorter, and plays like a string of senseless punch lines without any setups. Comedy is about humanity, and Chow's films are incredibly funny even if you don't speak Cantonese. Any attempt by others to edit his work only distorts it, like pouring water in salsa to make it less "ethnic." Chow's spice will entice an ever larger audience hungry for quality laughs, but like Jackie Chan, he may have to fail a few times to succeed.

a hit TV series about gamblers in the early '80s, the second season of which featured Chow Yun-fat in a supporting role. Later in the decade, audiences of the "greed is good" era were ready for a winner-take-all story, and Wong had a big hit with *Casino Raiders*. He followed it with this smash-hit Chow Yun-fat vehicle, which spawned a phenomenon. For the next couple of years, seemingly every other picture was a tribute, parody, or just plain rip-off of *God of Gamblers*.

Chow stars as Ko Chun, a suave gamesman with a supernatural talent for winning games of chance, even against impossible odds. Traveling the world with his assistants Janet (Sharla Cheung) and Yee (Lung Fong), it seems Ko Chun's only weakness is his addiction to chocolate. A Japanese former opponent asks Ko Chun to do a job for him, gambling against the man he holds responsible for his father's death: the cheating Shanghai King of Gamblers Chan Kam-shing (Pau Hon-lam). One night in Hong Kong, while making an escape from thugs sent by a sore loser, Ko takes a fall down a hillside, a blow to his head stealing his memory and leaving him a childlike loon. He's taken in by low-level gambler Knife (Andy Lau) and his girlfriend Jane (Joey Wong). Knife tries to swindle their simpleminded guest out of his bankroll in a card game, but when he discovers his magical abilities (which include being able to transform one card into another), he and his pal Crawl (Ronald Wong) decide to exploit the man's gifts for their own gain. But Knife feels his heart soften toward the man they call Chocolate during their adventures, and vows to raise money for an expensive operation that may free his memory. When Knife gets in a jam with a creditor (Ng Man-Tat), Jane gets the idea to pass Chocolate off as the God of Gamblers to get him out of trouble. During Ko Chun's unexplained absence, unfaithful Yee tries to move in on his boss's fortune (and Janet), joining with Chan's men to send a hit squad. Fortunately, bodyguard Dragon Lung (Charles Heung) finds Ko first—but multiple injuries sustained during the ensuing

bloodshed make it questionable if the God of Gamblers can survive at all, much less regain his identity in time to face Chan in the big stakes game.

In many ways, Wong Jing has created a traditional pulp martial arts action movie here, only with skill at rolling dice and dealing cards replacing the usual eccentric kung fu styles and techniques. With the addition of gunfights, brawls, the timeworn amnesia gimmick, and even a bit of necrophilia, it all becomes ridiculous at times. But somehow it all works wonderfully in its own goofy way, mostly due to the star power of Chow Yun-fat, who can indeed perform miracles. He only needs to pick up two automatics to get an audience on its feet (as he does at one point), and he makes playing both a moron and the super-smooth God seem easy. Followed by an official sequel with Chow, a prequel without, and two strange spin-offs with *Stephen Chow*. **AKA:** *Dao San; Du Shen.* ♪♪♪♪

1989 124m/C *HK* Chow Yun-fat, Andy Lau, Joey Wong, Sharla Cheung, Charles Heung, Lung Fong, Pau Hon-lam, Shing Fui-on, Ng Man-Tat, Ronald Wong, Michiko Nishiwaki, Michael Chow, Wong Jing, Dennis Chan, Yeung Chak Lam, Wong San, Law Ching-ho, Luk Chuen. **D:** Wong Jing. **W:** Wong Jing. **C:** David Chung, Peter Pau. **M:** Lowell Lo. **VHS, DVD**

God of Gamblers 2

Wong Jing figured, "If you can't beat 'em, join 'em." *God of Gamblers* was his biggest hit ever, but while star Chow Yun-fat was busy elsewhere, a legion of knockoffs and parodies appeared. The best of these was Stephen Chow's *All for the Winner,* and the inspired/insane idea of making a sequel to both films was hatched.

The God of Gamblers has retired, but his protégé Knife, AKA Michael Chan (Andy Lau), is carrying on his work, often gambling to benefit charity as the Knight of Gamblers. Meanwhile, the decidedly less-suave Sing (Stephen Chow) also has supernatural gambling powers, but can never use them for his own benefit or his luck will turn against him. He plots with his uncle Tat (Ng Man-Tat) to become the God of Gamblers's new disciple, so that they can live in luxury while still only gambling for charity. Knife can see that Sing has power, but can't control it—he can change cards, but not the right ones. But Sing is persistent, using his hypnotic powers to cause havoc in Knife's home until God of Guns Lung Wu (Charles Heung) throws him out.

Chan Kam-sing (Pau Hon-lam) is still in prison, but conspires with the villainous "Saddam Hussein" (Pal Sin) to strike back at his enemy through his disciple, and sends a hit team to Knife's house. Sing and Tat help Knife escape, but Lung Wu is captured. Sing and Tat swear to help find Lung Wu, but are easily distracted by the beautiful Dream Lo (Sharla Cheung), a perfect double for Sing's lost love Beautiful Dream. Saddam also impersonates the Knight of Gamblers in order to bilk the rich and ruin Ko Chun's name.

Knife and Sing get into a game of poker with Kau (Shing Fui-on) to raise a stake to challenge Saddam, but Sing has lent half his power to Tat, and can only change *half* the cards. But Saddam is using Lo to trap Sing and Tat, making them lose all their powers—and Tat is captured, too. Knife challenges Saddam to gamble to prove who the real disciple is, but Saddam has the room rigged with cameras and computers to advise him, and beats Knife easily. The next day, Knife knocks out Sing so he can return for revenge alone, borrowing 10 bucks from Saddam to try to win the $25 million ante in Saddam's crooked casino for the King of Cards challenge. Sing teams up with Wu's sister, Interpol agent Lung Kau (Monica Chan), to attempt a rescue.

Unlike some of Chow's other comedies of this period, the gags here meld seamlessly with the plot, and Lau's own style works well with the insanity of Chow and Ng Man-Tat. The magic powers of Chow and mainland sorcerer Tai-kun (John Ching) hired by Hussein never get out of hand to the point where they're flying around on carpets or something. The two wizards cause each other to have illusions, putting them in goofy parodies of *Swordsman* and *Terracotta Warrior* (which will mean nothing if you haven't seen those movies). The first of several collaborations between Wong Jing and Chow, this spawned a sequel of its own. Chow Yun-fat appears only in stock footage. Two hookers in the movie are named "Frantasca" and "Wong Jing." **AKA:** *Do Hap; Du Xia.* 🐲🐲🐲

1990 100m/C *HK* Andy Lau, Stephen Chow, Ng Man-Tat, Charles Heung, Sharla Cheung, Monica Chan, Pal Sin, John Ching, Shing Fui-on, Blackie Ko, Pau Hon-lam, Kirk Wong, Ronald Wong, Ng Hong-ling, Wong Jing, Chow Yun-fat. **D:** Wong Jing. **W:** Wong Jing. **C:** David Chung. **M:** Lowell Lo. **VHS, DVD**

God of Gamblers 3: Back to Shanghai

When Wong Jing and Stephen Chow came together to make *Do Hap* (*Knight of Gamblers*, AKA *God of Gamblers 2*), it was the biggest hit either of them had enjoyed up to then, and naturally led to this sequel, for which they pulled out all the stops. Defeated villain Tai-kun (John Ching) returns, having gathered together four men with superpowers to help him defeat Saint of Gamblers Chow Sing-cho (Stephen Chow). But when all five supervillains attack Chow together, they create a time warp that transports them all—plus sidekick Tat (Ng Man-Tat)—back to 1930s Shanghai. There Chow is surprised to find not Tat, but his own grandfather Chow Tai-fook (Ng Man-Tat), and he's not only in 1937 Shanghai, but has traveled into the hit Hong Kong TV series *Shanghai Beach*!

This premise doesn't translate well, even for present-day Hong Kong audiences, since the series has been unseen for many years—but it would be roughly equivalent to having *Back to the Future*'s Marty McFly end up with Hawkeye in *M*A*S*H*'s Korean War. He's immediately in deadly danger from all the gangster activity in the area, but due to accidentally discovering "In-Between" Style kung fu (punches only hurt what's behind what you hit), Chow can defend himself and inadvertently avenge the death of gang boss Hui Man-keung (Chow Yun-fat's character on the series). This earns him the gratitude of Ding Lik (Ray Lui, reprising his star-making character), who takes him in. While trying to get a cell-phone call through to Brother Five (Charles Heung) in 1991, and figuring a way to get back to the future, Chow gets involved in Ding's triad affairs, and is entranced by beautiful Yu-san (superstar Gong Li), the daughter of the mayor (Tin Fung). Chow's special powers—and familiarity with TV show formulas—give him an advantage when dealing with rival gangster Wong Kan-way (Lung Fong). Tai-kun has fallen in with Wong and the Japanese official (Wong Wan-si) he's in cahoots with, leading inevitably to a confrontation with Chow.

Our hero bests Tai-kun yet again, but is incapacitated on learning that dream girl Yu-san is engaged to Ding, so Yu-san's friend Spring (Sandra Ng) uses San's idiot twin Yu-mong (Gong Li again) to impersonate her sister. But when Wong accidentally kills San, the traitors force Mong to take her place, doubling the confusion. Don't worry—they didn't forget to put some gambling in the plot. Several captures, fights, and escapes later, Chow finds himself in the big card-game finale, facing off against the French God of Gamblers (Indra Leech)—winner take all. There seems to be almost too much crammed into the picture, and though the emphasis on plot doesn't leave as much room for side-splitting laughs, this is still another enjoyable romp with Chow and company. Barry Wong reprises his thick-headed cop character Scissor Legs Wong from the *Fight Back to School* series. Spoofs include some business from *Swordsman,* and an insane singing and dancing send-up of a McDonald's commercial. **AKA:** *Do Hap II Seung Hoi Taam Do Sing; Du Xia II Shang Hai Tan Du Sheng; All for the Winner 3; God of Gamblers: The Beginning; Knight of Gamblers 2: The Gambling Saint of Shanghai Beach.* 🦴🦴🦴

1991 116m/C *HK* Stephen Chow, Ng Man-Tat, Gong Li, John Ching, Ray Lui, Sandra Ng, Charles Heung, Tin Fung, Lung Fong, Wong Wan-si, Barry Wong, Yeung Ching-Ching, Lau Shun, Billy Chow, Indra Leech, Wong Jing, Sharla Cheung. **D:** Wong Jing. **W:** Wong Jing. **C:** Pater Pau. **M:** Lowell Lo. **VHS, DVD**

God of Gamblers Returns

After five years, two send-up sequels, and countless imitations, Wong Jing and Chow Yun-fat brought back the real chocolate addict Ko Chun for another high-stakes adventure. Ko Chun is now enjoying his retirement, living in a French villa with his wife Yau (Sharla Cheung) and a baby on the way. But news comes through his old pal Lung Wu (Charles Heung), the God of Guns, that his old enemy Chan Kam-shing (Pau Hon-lam), the Beast of Gamblers, is out of prison, and is likely to come after him. Also, old Mr. Chiu has left his $16 billion fortune to the Save the World's Kids Fund, and wants only the world's best gambler to oversee the fund! Chan comes to France to challenge Ko, along with ruthless Thai Devil of Gamblers Chau Siu-chee (Wu Hsing-kuo). While Ko and Lung are gunning down Chau's henchmen, Chau's doctor removes the fetus surgically, leaving behind a challenge to Ko on videotape! But with her dying breath, Yau asks Ko to promise not to gamble or admit his identity for a full year, delaying his revenge.

Not knowing what else to do, Ko travels the world, one day befriending wealthy Hoi On (Blackie Ko) and his family. But Hoi is a rival of Chau's in the Thai Tung Wu triad, and traitors assassinate Hoi, leaving his son Siu-yuen (Tse Miu) and Ko as surviving witnesses. Ko promises Hoi he'll take Yuen back to his sister Hoi Tong (Chingmy Yau) in Tainam, Taiwan, but first they have to escape the local police chief Kok Ching-chung (Elvis Tsui). Little Yuen loses all

their funds to con man Little Trumpet (Tony Leung Ka-Fai), but since Ko's year isn't up yet, he gets their cash back by hypnotizing Trumpet to see the wrong cards in a rematch with Yuen. They end up hiring the swindler and his sister Little Guitar (Jacqueline Wu) to help them get past the cops and into Tainam, where Ko is preparing for the end of his abstinence with an all-or-nothing game with the evil Chau. But he also has to contend with mainland sorcerer Cheung Po-sing (Wong Kam-Kong), whose supernatural powers rival his own.

The sequel does without the silly amnesia plot of the original, but there's still plenty of goofy elements in the middle of this flick, including wily kung fu kid Tse Miu, Elvis Tsui's comic police chief, the zany God of Smugglers, and the brother-sister cons. In true Wong Jing fashion, the tone goes from serious melodrama to wacky comedy to gun fu action in a blink. Much of the humor doesn't translate too well, but HK fans should pick up on most of it. At one point, Chow breaks into an imitation of Andy Lau, while Tony Leung impersonates Ko Chun and Tsui takes on Lung Wu—and this is supposed to be the *straight* sequel. It's all pretty loopy, but continuously entertaining nevertheless. **AKA:** *Dao San 2; Du Shen 2; God of Gamblers 2; The Return of the God of Gamblers; Battle of Champions.* 🦴🦴🦴

1994 124m/C *HK* Chow Yun-fat, Tony Leung Ka-Fai, Chingmy Yau, Jacqueline Wu, Elvis Tsui, Wu Hsing-kuo, Charles Heung, Tse Miu, Pau Hon-lam, Blackie Ko, Sharla Cheung, Wong Kam-Kong, Ken Lo, Bonnie Fu, Law Kar-Ying, William Ho, Bobby Yip, Paul Chu. **D:** Wong Jing. **W:** Wong Jing. **C:** Horace Wong. **M:** Lowell Lo. **VHS, DVD**

Godzilla, King of the Monsters

In 1954, producer Tomoyuki Tanaka was trying to get his latest project for Toho Studios—an historical drama—off the ground. Things were not going well, and he needed a quick idea for a replacement project. Since the American film *The Beast from 20,000 Fathoms* was a hit at the boxoffice (as was a recent re-release of *King Kong*), Tanaka envisioned an even bigger creature that would destroy Tokyo. Tanaka's special-effects director, Eiji Tsuburaya, wanted the monster to be a giant octopus, but instead screenwriter Takeo Murata chose to make the beast a kind of mutant aquatic tyrannosaurus who could exhale radioactive flames. Christening the beast, they took the nickname of a portly Toho technician, Gojira (pronounced "Godzilla" to Western ears, it translates as a combination of "gorilla" and "whale"). The chosen director, Ishiro Honda (who would go on to direct nine Godzilla films and many other Toho sci-fi pic-

Godzilla Conquers the World

There is a beast in the darkness. You can't quite make out its shape—each time you turn to look it seems larger. As big as a house. As tall as a 40-story building. Big enough that its black mass blots out half the sky. And you can't get away from it. Nothing can stop it as it moves ever onward, its footsteps like thunder, utterly destroying everything in its path. Opening its mouth, it unleashes a stream of devastating atomic energy that obliterates everything it touches. And a roar like Hell cracked in half. It's Godzilla.

Or it's a storm, a huge tornado, scoring a huge furrow in the earth as it blasts its way across the countryside. An army erects a giant storm fence in its path in an effort to break up the wind's force, but the tornado turns to the side at the last minute, sending the edifice tumbling, and then turns again to smash its way through a modern city. Hurricane Godzilla.

Or like puppets in a Punch & Judy show, great rubber wrestling clowns bounce around a stage. They grapple and roar, shoving each other about, blasting each other with wobbly missiles or colorful streams of energy. Occasionally the battle sends pasteboard towers crashing down. At the center of the carnival is the King of Monsters, an international hero. It's Godzilla.

Godzilla is a dream monster, at once sublimely horrific and profoundly silly. He could only have been created in Japan, 50 years ago, brought forth from deep within the unconscious of a nation both terrified and shamed by atomic annihilation, fascinated by advancements in science and technology, and hungry for a hit knocked off from classic American thrillers. Godzilla is bigger than all of us, surviving by swimming deep when he wants to, dancing lightly when necessary, and burning bridges whenever he can.

The American studio that tried to make a Godzilla film a few years back didn't understand the beast. They thought they could update him and tame him by transforming him into something else, but just ended up with an enjoyable—but generic—monster movie. The Japanese know better. The Godzilla filmography is like a great cauldron of pho (beef soup), the various flavors and spices in the broth simmering and combining over the decades. The recent films they've served up have made for some fine cuisine, distilling all the best elements into magnificent meals.

At this point, there are three great ages of Godzilla films, each following their own timeline. All start with Ishiro Honda's original *Godzilla, King of the Monsters.*

Showa Godzilla encompasses films made through *Terror of Mechagodzilla* in 1975. The monster (or something like it) destroyed by the Oxygen Destroyer returned again and again to menace mankind, slowed down only by the challenge of other monsters and the occasional alien invasion. His career spread well into the 21st century, and he was last seen living happily in his Monster Land home on Ogasawara Island. The United Nations took advantage of Godzilla's hibernation following weather control experiments during the 1990s (as seen in *Son of Godzilla*) to build a perfect monster habitat. Of course, he can get out when he wants to—but so far the beast seems to have taken Monster Land as a peace offering, emerging only when outsiders threaten his Japanese turf.

Heisei Godzilla showed up in 1984 for *Godzilla 1985.* Apparently the original Rey de los Monstrous, unseen since 1954, spent 30 years regenerating into an even larger beast intent on punishing mankind for trying to get rid of him. Mothra, King Ghidorah, and MechaGodzilla appeared (again), as well as some new monsters, but nothing could stop Godzilla now—except the natural process of his own nuclear nature, which caught up with him in *Godzilla vs. Destroyah* (1995).

Shinsei or **Millennium Godzilla** appeared following rumors that the beast had appeared in America in 1998, and introduced a novel concept: the Godzilla anthology series, with each film presenting a Godzilla tale outside of previous continuity. In *Godzilla 2000,* the monster had appeared intermittently throughout the past 50 years. In *Godzilla vs. Megaguiras,* he may or may not have, but mankind's technology had progressed to the point that we could create more powerful weapons. And in *Godzilla, Mothra and King Ghidorah: Battle on Fire,* Godzilla hadn't been seen since the 1950s. Finally, *Godzilla X MechaGodzilla* presents a world using bits and pieces of both Showa and Heisei history, and a new MechaGodzilla is constructed using DNA taken from the skeleton of the original Godzilla recovered from Tokyo Bay.

It's uncertain where the future will take Godzilla, but it appears he will always be with us. Like earthquakes, typhoons, and income tax, mankind will just have to find a way to co-exist.

tures), was a close friend and assistant director to the great Akira Kurosawa. Another important player was the distinguished classical composer Akira Ifukube, who lent his distinctive and expressive music to many of Toho's classics, as well as the Zatoichi series.

The first act follows the plot of *Beast* somewhat closely. The seas surrounding Japan are plagued by a series of steamship disasters, with the only survivors bearing strange burn marks and describing an attack by a huge creature. On nearby Odo Island, the natives report seeing this same creature come ashore during a storm. Dr. Yamane (Takashi Shimura) organizes a scientific expedition to the island, including his daughter Emiko (Momoko Kochi) and her fiancé Hideto Ogata (Akira Takarada). The scientists discover radiation everywhere, and are shocked when the gigantic reptile suddenly appears over a hillside. The Navy is called out to kill the monster with depth charges, but the explosions only seem to make the mutant dinosaur—named Godzilla after an Odo Island legend—more aggressive. He heads directly for Tokyo, wading ashore to cause massive destruction. Perhaps the only hope of killing the seemingly unstoppable monster is with a secret invention of Emiko's former fiancé, the enigmatic Dr. Serizawa (Akihiko Hirata)—a weapon that may be more terrible than Godzilla himself.

The finished film became not only a great epic of monster mayhem, but also a reflection of the humiliation bred by Japan's aggression in WWII and subsequent defeat. Godzilla himself became an embodiment of the nightmare of atomic destruction, fresh from the horrors of Hiroshima and Nagasaki. If one suspends disbelief enough to gloss over flaws in the otherwise successful f/x, the monster makes an indelible impression of titanic, unyielding destructive force. Accurately reflecting the sense of helpless dread felt in Japan during the Cold War, a message pleading for nuclear disarmament remained as a subtext throughout most of the Godzilla series. Toho spent over $1 million on the production, over 10 times the budget of the average Japanese film of the time. The investment paid off immediately, as *Gojira* was a huge success at the boxoffice. Producer Joseph E. Levine purchased American distribution rights. Feeling that a Japanese film might have trouble drawing an audience less than 10 years after WWII, Levine integrated the film with new footage shot with actor Raymond Burr, playing news-service reporter Steve Martin, who serves as a narrator telling the monster's tale in flashbacks. Levine's 80-minute version was also a big success. Incidentally, the subtitled U.S. version also had a successful run in Japan, reportedly drawing howls of laughter in the scenes in which Martin's translator appears to be lying to him about what vari-

ous characters are saying. If one has seen the original version, the inserted footage seems intrusive, but otherwise it blends in reasonably well. One of the first post-WWII Japanese films to break through commercially in the U.S. Followed by 25 (and counting!) sequels to date. **AKA:** *Gojira; Daikaiju no tai Nimon Mairu; Godzilla; G.* ♫♫♫♫

1954 97m/C *JP* Akira Takarada, Momoko Kochi, Akihiko Hirata, Takashi Shimura, Fuyuki Murakami, Sachio Sakai, Ren Yamamoto, Miki Hayashi, Keiji Sakakida, Tadashi Okabe, Ren Imaizumi, Haruo Nakajima, Raymond Burr (U.S. version), Frank Iwanaga (U.S.). **D:** Ishiro Honda, Terry Morse (U.S.). **W:** Takeo Murata, Ishiro Honda. Shigeru Kayama (story). **C:** Masao Tamai. **M:** Akira Ifukube. **VHS, DVD**

Godzilla, Mothra and King Ghidorah: Battle on Fire

After "killing" Godzilla in *Godzilla vs. Destroyah* in 1995, Toho Studios briefly retired the character before launching three new G-films, one of which was to decide the direction future Godzilla movies would take. The first film was *Godzilla 2000*, the second *Godzilla vs. Megaguirus,* and the last was *Godzilla, Mothra, King Ghidorah: Battle on Fire,* sometimes known as *GMK. GMK*'s director, Shusuke Kaneko, had become famous by reinventing Godzilla's biggest competitor: the flying turtle Gamera. In three films in the late '90s, Kaneko turned the ridiculous "friend of all children" into a cutting-edge, genetic force of nature in movies that blew away the Godzilla films in terms of action, special effects, and story sophistication. Kaneko had in fact always wanted to direct a Godzilla movie and had turned to Gamera after Toho turned down his requests to do a Godzilla film. Toho finally granted his request in 2001, but not without a few compromises.

Kaneko wanted the monsters opposing Godzilla (seen here as a blank-eyed, vengeful incarnation of Japanese war dead) to be Anguiras and Varan, but Toho insisted on the more marketable Baragon and King Ghidorah. Kaneko also had to have his Gamera special-effects team collaborate with Toho's unit, resulting in special effects that best most of the recent Godzilla movies but that don't quite measure up to the eye-popping, visceral work on the Gamera films. Nevertheless, *GMK* is one of the most vibrant, witty, and entertaining Godzilla films since the heyday of the '60s. Kaneko is particularly adept at dealing with the scale of giant monster attacks and their immediate effect on the comparatively tiny humans in their vicinity, and *GMK* boasts several hair-raising suspense sequences, particularly one involving a woman trapped in a hospital traction bed while Godzilla approaches. The approach is less campy than *Godzilla 2000,* but still boasts some huge (intentional) laughs, as in one moment where a female Japanese tourist remarks on how cute the rampaging Baragon is and poses for a photo with the marauding creature looming behind her. Like Spielberg, Kaneko is able to turn a laugh into a scream, and his brutal and intimidating characterization of Godzilla is unforgettable: every time the radioactive monster breathes in you'll cringe at the possibility of him unleashing his fiery breath on the hapless pedestrians around him. Kaneko's screenplay lampoons tabloid journalism and the military (even taking a brief potshot at the American Godzilla movie), and he takes great risks by reversing the hero/villain schematic of Godzilla and King Ghidorah (here depicted as a less-than-impressive, almost toy-like dragon who's smaller than Godzilla). Ultimately Toho elected to go with the director of the popular *Godzilla vs. Megaguirus* for their next entry, *Godzilla vs. Mechagodzilla 3,* but Kaneko's film serves as a mesmerizing and deliriously enjoyable one-shot. —*JB* **AKA:** *Gojira, Mosura, Kingu Gidora: Daikaiju Soukougeki; Godzilla, Mothra, King Ghidorah: Giant Monsters' General Offensive; Godzilla, Mothra and King Ghidorah: Giant Monsters All-Out Attack; GMK: All Monsters Attack; GMK.* 🐉🐉🐉💧

2001 105m/C *JP* Chiharu Nåyama, Masahiro Kobayashi, Hiroyuki Watanabe, Shiro Sano, Takashi Nishina, Kaho Minami, Kunio Murai, Toshikazu Fukawa, Eisei Amamoto, Kazuko Kato, Ryudo Uzaki, Katsuo Nakamura, Takehiro Murata, Yoshimasa Kondo, Hanako Saeki, Yukijiro Hotaru, Masaya Takahashi, Akira Ohashi, Rie Ota. *D:* Shusuke Kaneko. *W:* Keichi Hasegawa, Shusuke Kaneko, Masahiro Yokotani. *C:* Masahiro Kishimoto. *M:* Ko Otani, Akira Ifukube. **VHS**

Godzilla 1985

Producer Tomoyuki Tanaka had to struggle to get the 16th Godzilla movie made. The series had fallen into a funk of juvenile antics during the 1970s, and Tanaka wanted to return the monster star to his former glory with a big-budget remake of *Godzilla, King of the Monsters.* Failing in that, he tried to make *Godzilla vs. the Devil,* and even cooperated with a proposed American project that would be made in 3-D (several ideas from which would end up in *Godzilla 1985*). However, the Big G hadn't been a solid moneymaker for Toho in years, and it took almost a decade to find the right project and circumstances for his comeback. To get a fresh start, the new film ignored the previous 14 sequels worth of continuity, which charted an

out-of-control course in future history, to get back to the root theme of nuclear proliferation.

After 30 years, the Big G (Kenpachiro Satsuma) recovers from his apparent death from the effects of the oxygen destroyer in *Godzilla, King of the Monsters,* and returns to smashing ships at sea, even gobbling up radiation from a crushed nuclear submarine. As the super-beast heads toward Japan to destroy Tokyo all over again, Russian and American diplomats push to use nukes to kill the monster, but Prime Minister Mitamura (Keiju Kobayashi) stands firm on Japan's anti-nuclear weapons policy. However, a missile is launched anyway, and as interceptors are scrambled to prevent the destruction of Japan, a scientist (Yosuke Natsuki), whose parents were killed by Godzilla during his first rampage, feverishly tries to ready a plan that will deal with the problem in a less violent way.

Toho's revival of their biggest star features bigger, more spectacular f/x than ever before, the highlight being Godzilla's duel with the Defense Force's combat vehicle Super-X amid the crashing skyscrapers of downtown Tokyo. The plot marches along much like a '70s disaster film. Like its predecessor, this one has inserted scenes for the reworked American edition with Raymond Burr reprising his role of journalist Steve Martin (who probably made a fortune writing books about Godzilla), while cutting about 30 minutes from the original. Burr maintains his composure, but the insert scenes are embarrassingly cheap and contain jarringly blatant product placements for Dr Pepper. The right-wing distributor also changed the plot to make the U.S.S.R. look like the villain. *AKA: Gojira; The Return of Godzilla.* 🐉🐉🐉

1984 (PG) 91m/C *JP* Keiju Kobayashi, Ken Tanaka, Yasuko Sawaguchi, Yosuke Natsuki, Eitaro Ozawa, Taketoshi Naito, Mizuho Suzuki, Junkichi Orimoto, Nobuo Kaneko, Kunio Murai, Yoshifumi Tajima, Shigeo Kato, Kenpachiro Satsuma, Raymond Burr (U.S. version), Warren Kemmerling (U.S.). *D:* Koji Hashimoto. *W:* Shuichi Nagahara, Lisa Tomei (U.S.), Tony Rendel (U.S.). *C:* Kazutami Hara, Steve Dubin (U.S.). *M:* Reijiro Koroku. **VHS**

Godzilla Raids Again

Toho Studios decided not to wait for director Ishiro Honda to finish the project he was working on when his *Godzilla* became a huge hit, and rushed into production on this quickie follow-up without him, releasing it less than six months later. Another notable absence is that of composer Akira Ifukube. It may have been just as well, as the two maestros would likely have been discouraged by the project's lack of time and money. The special effects fail to match the

power of the originals. However, the climax shows a lot of imagination.

A second Godzilla (Harou Nakajima) appears to cause trouble, while another monster—the spiny Angilas (Katsumi Tezuka)—also appears to threaten mankind. They battle to the death while trashing Osaka. Although the monster scenes are fun, with Godzilla facing off against another creature for the first time, too much of the story centers around a fishing industry troubled by the behemoths. Indeed, the monsters seem to be following fishing fleet pilots Shoichi Tsukioka (Hiroshi Koizumi) and Koji Kbayashi (Minoru Chiaki) around throughout the movie. They first appear on an island where Koji has to land his plane due to engine trouble. The beasts come to shore in Osaka Bay, ruining the fishing. When the family business moves to their Hokkaido location to get away from the destruction, and again in Fukuoka, the monsters appear there, too. And of course, it's our flying heroes who are the first pilots to spot Godzilla on a frosty northern island as the military is trying to hunt him down.

Though we can't blame the American distributor for ruining this entry in the series, they sure didn't help matters by cutting four minutes off the running time and still making the picture duller by adding senseless footage and having Shoichi give us a relentless play-by-play narration. In the dubbing session, actors Keye Luke and George Takai were urged to sound more Japanese. At first, independent AB-PT Pictures attempted to make an entirely new picture called *The Volcano Monsters* using much of the footage from *Godzilla Raids Again,* even borrowing some monster costumes from Toho to shoot extra scenes. AB-PT went out of business before they could start shooting, and the distribution rights fell into the hands of Warner Bros., who released it on a double bill in 1959 with *Teenagers from Outer Space* under the title *Gigantis the Fire Monster*. Although it's been suggested that the producers didn't want to pay to use the Godzilla name, the more likely scenario is that they thought an "all new" monster would play better than a sequel. Either way, it was a stupid decision, and *Godzilla Raids Again/Gigantis* disappeared for years, until its release on home video in the 1980s. **AKA:** *Gojira no Gyakushu; The Return of Godzilla; Godzilla's Counterattack; Godzilla Strikes Again; Gigantis the Fire Monster; Gigantis; Fire Monster.* 🐾🐾🐾

1955 78m/BW *JP* Hiroshi Koizumi, Minoru Chiaki, Takashi Shimura, Setsuko Wakayama, Masao Shimizu, Seijiro Onda, Sonosuke Sawamura, Yoshio Tsuchiya, Minosuke Yamada, Senkichi Omura, Ren Yamamoto, Shin Otomo, Takeo Oikawa, Shoichi Hirose, Harou Nakajima, Katsumi Tezuka. **D:** Motoyoshi Oda. **W:** Shigeaki Hidaka, Takeo Mura-ta, Shigeru Kayama (story). **C:** Seiichi Endo. **M:** Masaru Sato. **VHS**

asians in usa

Godzilla the Series: Monster War 📺

Amid the hype, controversy, and ice cream flavor tie-ins that accompanied the 1998 theatrical release of the American "remake" of *Godzilla,* working concurrently with the feature production people who so marvelously brought the Godzilla-in-name-only to digital cinematic life, were the good folks who were producing the animated *Godzilla the Series* for television. Fortunately, despite generally poor reviews and disappointing toy sales, the 1998 *Godzilla* was a more profitable feature than most people think, and was especially popular with small children. The series has enjoyed solid ratings—despite Fox's decision to pre-empt it with *Pokemon* knockoffs for a few months while that fad ran its course.

The concept of the series is that Dr. Nick Tatopoulos (voiced by Ian Zeiring) finds the last surviving Godzilla egg, forms an uneasy bond with the monster, and they end up helping each other in time of need. Nick forms a task force called H.E.A.T. to combat the mutations springing up all over the globe. This three-part episode called "Monster War" came midway through the series. Essentially, it's a tribute to *Destroy All Monsters,* with a race of sneaky aliens taking possession of humans and controlling a bunch of monsters that appeared in earlier episodes. The first part begins with the group learning that they're being affected by the Leviathan aliens (whom they'd met before), and who are now attempting to distract H.E.A.T. from detecting all the Tachyon radio waves their devices are emitting. Nick goes to Africa alone (except for his pal, Godzilla) to deal with the menace of a giant bat. The bat is under alien control, and Nick follows the Tachyon beam back to the alien base in New Jersey, where he finds that the aliens have transformed the deceased first Godzilla into a cyborg.

Our heroes retreat with Cyberzilla in hot pursuit. Godzilla faces off against his universal-soldiering dad, but seems to switch sides when confronted with his own kin. In the confusion, Nick and the gang set off to track down the mysterious "Site Omega," the aliens' main headquarters and Tachyon broadcast station. Amazingly, Craven and the others have little trouble working the alien machines, interrupting the alien control broadcast. The mutations are set free, but will they help fight the alien menace, or join with them once again to clobber the helpless Earthlings?

Even the die-hard Godzilla fans who hated the Sony film have a begrudging respect for the cartoon show. The animated Godzilla may look like his CGI papa, but he acts much more like the classic King of the Monsters. He can breath a fiery radioactive ray, and is always ready for a scrap. The series human characters, some of which were also taken from the movie, have had time to develop and gain more dimensions than they were able to in the film. The reason for this is that the creators of the series, from executive producer Jeff Kline on down, are for the most part Godzilla fans as well. If they had their way, they'd probably rather be drawing the classic Godzilla battling King Ghidrah—but have had to settle for making the TriStar version as much like it as they can. 𝄪𝄪𝄪

1999 72m/C *US/JP* **V:** Ian Zeiring, Malcolm Danare, Rino Romano, Charity James, Brigitte Bako, Kevin Dunn. **D:** Christopher Berkeley, Sam Liu, Alan Caldwell. **W:** Marty Isenberg, Robert N. Skir, Steve Melching, Michael Reaves. **M:** Brian Garland, Jim Latham. **VHS**

Godzilla 2000

Though Big G died in the previous film (1995's *Godzilla vs. Destroyah*), he shows up here looking wicked and feisty. This is the first of a trilogy of Godzilla films that take place outside of any continuity, but if you want to think this is Godzilla Jr. all grown up, I'm sure that's allowed. If you want to consider this a gentle raspberry blown in the direction of Sony's *Godzilla,* that's O.K., too.

The opening scene shows scientist Dr. Yuji Shinoda (veteran G-actor Takehiro Murata) and his brilliant and precocious daughter Io (Mayu Suzuki) setting up seismic wave measuring devices on a fog-bound seacoast. Accompanying them is whiny reporter Yuki Ichinose (Naomi Nishida). They're the leaders of the Godzilla Prediction Net, a freelance group of scientists and oddballs in the business of predicting Godzilla's movements to benefit their client corporations, who are better able to protect their assets from the monster's rampages.

Godzilla (Tsutomu Kitigawa) shows up and almost kills them, then stomps through a village to eat a power plant. Meanwhile, the government has set up their own agency to deal with monsters—the CCI—headed by Shinoda's old nemesis Katagiri (Hiroshe Abe), and dedicated to stopping Godzilla by whatever means necessary. While setting Godzilla sensors in the ocean floor off the coast, CCI subs come upon a huge meteor.

But the meteor actually disguises an alien spaceship that crash-landed on Earth in prehistoric times. When it raises enough to receive sunlight again, it absorbs energy and takes off under its own power. The alien visitor taps into humanity's resources, soaking up data from every nearby system, searching for ways to either adapt to Earth's environment, or change it for its own use. When it encounters Godzilla, it finds the ultimate adapter. But, as is pointed out by a general in dubbed dialogue, Godzilla always advances when attacked.

Godzilla 2000 ain't the best Godzilla ever, but it's damn far from being the worst. On the whole the visuals are remarkable, featuring the best f/x of the series yet—all the more remarkable when you consider the film was made for just $11 million. It also boasts some decent characters, a clever and imaginative story, and a fine director in Takao Okawara. **AKA:** *Gojira Nisen Mireniamu; G2K: Millennium.* 𝄪𝄪𝄪𝄪

1999 (PG) 99m/C *JP* Takehiro Murata, Hiroshe Abe, Naomi Nishida, Mayu Suzuki, Tsutomu Kitigawa. **D:** Takao Okawara. **W:** Hiroshi Kashiwabara, Wataru Mimura. **C:** Katsuhiro Kato. **M:** Takayuki Hattori, Akira Ifukube. **VHS, DVD**

Godzilla vs. Biollante

Five years after their revival of the Godzilla series with *Godzilla 1985,* Toho made a more definite commitment to their monster star with this poetic entry. Genetic scientist Surigama (Koji Takahashi) uses cells from Godzilla's body to create hardy new crop strains. He also splices the cells' DNA to that of his dead daughter, using that of her favorite rose as a catalyst. His experiments result in the gigantic plant/animal monster Biollante, a nightmare of creeping vines, snapping teeth, and corrosive sap. Meanwhile, Godzilla escapes from the volcano he was knocked into at the end of *Godzilla 1985.* The Japanese Defense Forces launch the new Super-X2, a remote-controlled upgrade of the previous film's flying warship, now equipped with a diamond mirror designed to absorb Godzilla's oral beam and fire it back on him. But Godzilla is too powerful for it, and melts the Super-X2. Next, the monster is injected with newly developed anti-nuclear bacteria, but it only slows him down and fails to stop his rampage. Meanwhile, psychic girl Miki Saegusa (Megumi Odaka, who became a series regular) seems to be able to sense Godzilla's feelings, and is used to delay him until a new line of defense can be implemented. Can Biollante help, or will the monster plant become an even greater menace?

Godzilla Marching Orders
Music in Toho's Kaiju Epics

Virtually all the sound most of us associate with Godzilla and the Toho kaiju series of films is the responsibility of one man: composer Akira Ifukube. Born in 1914 on the island of Hokkaido in northern Japan, Ifukube lived in the village of Otofuke and was exposed to the music of aboriginal Japanese people as well as folk songs brought into his town by travelers from all over Japan. All of these influences, plus his formal education (which included studies of music and forestry, as well as the vibratory strength and elasticity of wood) contributed to the more than 250 film scores he wrote between 1947 and 1995. Ifukube had already written more than 70 film scores before he wrote the music for Ishiro Honda's *Gojira* in 1954 (ironically, Ifukube himself had been diagnosed with radiation exposure during his forestry work). Although colleagues advised him against scoring the monster movie, Ifukube took the assignment and created one of the most enduring musical scores of the 20th century while working under enormous time and budgetary pressures, even beginning his writing before the film was finished shooting. Ifukube was able to apply his love of Japanese aboriginal melodies in an early sequence of traditional ceremony on an island threatened by Godzilla, and his musical treatment of what was at the time the largest creature ever depicted on a movie screen was appropriately awe-inspiring. Director Honda had created a stygian, disturbing horror film that equated the rampaging Godzilla with the nuclear bombs that had devastated Hiroshima and Nagasaki (the mutated Godzilla even left radiation burn victims in its wake), and Ifukube's score mixed grunting, bleak horror with a swelling, surging theme for Godzilla that ascended inexorably along with the monster as it arose from Tokyo Bay.

Ifukube's original *Godzilla* score established several hallmarks of his scoring style that would remain with the Toho kaiju franchise even after the composer's official retirement in 1995. He wrote crisp, syncopated military marches for the Japanese army and navy that were infectiously memorable. One such action march, which accompanies Godzilla's rout by air force jets back into Tokyo Bay as Japanese crowds cheer, later became an official march for Godzilla, and has been employed even in most of the recent Heisei Godzilla films. The second ongoing element, and one which was an even more unique element of Ifukube's approach, was the swelling, deeply mournful adagios the composer introduced, which not only spoke to the thousands killed or injured by Godzilla's attacks, but ultimately eulogized the creature itself as it is devoured by Dr. Serizawa's "oxygen destroyer" at the film's grim climax. In the original *Godzilla*, Ifukube could be said to be scoring the self-sacrifice of Serizawa as he unleashes the oxygen destroyer and causes his own death in order to destroy Godzilla, but Ifukube showed as early as 1956's *Rodan* that he had just as much sympathy for dying kaiju as he had for their human victims: his elegiac scoring of the climactic deaths of the film's two flying monsters in a volcano is a highlight of his career.

Ifukube did more than simply establish the musical style for Godzilla and his fellow monsters: he also created many of their voices. For the original *Godzilla*, the composer created the distinctive, unnerving monster roar used throughout the Godzilla series by scraping a gloved hand over the strings of a bass fiddle and manipulating the recording in playback. Ifukube did similar honors for the monsters Rodan, Varan, and King Ghidorah, among others.

While his success and prestige as a concert composer never wavered, Ifukube devoted himself almost exclusively to scoring pictures for Toho studios until his retirement, and became close friends with both Toho special-effects supervisor Eiji Tsuburaya and director Ishiro Honda. For the otherwise obscure early kaiju film *Varan the Unbelievable*, Ifukube composed a stunning choral theme backed by a brilliant four-note brass motif that would later resurface as the monster battle music in *Ghidorah the Three-Headed Monster*, *Monster Zero, War of the Gargantuas,* and other Toho films, as well as scores for the Zatoichi and Daimajin series. His rapid-fire military action themes for movies like *The Mysterians* and *Destroy All Monsters* were so energetic and rhythmically inspired they were known to set entire audiences stamping their feet in time with the music. Honda's approach to the Toho kaiju series was unfailingly mythic and rich: he treated the monsters as ancient gods and always scored their appearances with the utmost seriousness.

Alternating with Ifukube on many of the Toho films throughout the late '60s and '70s was composer Masaru Sato. Sato had scored the first Godzilla sequel, *Godzilla Raids Again,* in 1955, but he wouldn't tackle another Godzilla movie for more than a decade. By the mid-'60s, the Godzilla series had become targeted almost exclusively toward children, and the rambunctious 1966 *Godzilla vs. the Sea Monster* fought to be more current by not only featuring some wild giant-monster action, but also a taste of the current spy

Continued on next page...

craze in its Dr. No–like villain and hidden island of high-tech criminals. Sato's score was a dramatic departure from the Ifukube style: jazzy and driven by percussion, it was Godzilla seen through James Bond's gun barrel. Sato stayed on to score the similar *Son of Godzilla* in 1967, while Ifukube wrote the epic *Destroy All Monsters* a year later. Both composers sat out the infamous *Godzilla vs. the Smog Monster,* which boasted a silly pop score by Riichiro Manabe, and Ifukube tackled the unfortunate *Godzilla vs. Gigan,* rehashing many of his themes just as the film rehashed reams of stock footage from earlier Godzilla features. Manabe returned for the even more ridiculous *Godzilla vs. Megalon,* for which the composer penned the crooning song dedicated to leering giant robot Jet Jaguar. The series attempted to go out with a bang in the mid-'70s with *Godzilla vs. Mecha Godzilla* (scored by Sato) and *Terror of Mechagodzilla* (grandly essayed by Ifukube in what he assumed would be the last appearance of the giant monster).

Godzilla was resurrected in 1984 with a score by Reijiro Koroku that featured a more Western-influenced approach. Despite this effort, much of the score was replaced by tracked music from Christopher Young's score to *Def-Con 4* when the movie was re-edited for American release. *Godzilla vs. Biollante* marked the debut of the Heisei Godzilla and an attempt to up the sophistication of the series for contemporary audiences. Kôichi Sugiyama's score was sleek and pounding, and emphasized the terror of Godzilla and its crocodile-cum–Venus Flytrap adversary. While Ifukube had been asked to score both *Godzilla 1985* and *Biollante,* he had turned down the assignments, insisting that he was retired. However, he was convinced to return to the series on *Godzilla vs. King Ghidorah,* and his epic themes (despite the fact that many of them were recycled from previous efforts) dominated the rest of the Heisei series. Takayuki Hattori's score to *Godzilla vs. Space Godzilla* was well regarded but played more like an attempt to co-opt the sensibility of John Williams; Ifukube returned to tackle the final film in the Heisei series, *Godzilla vs. Destroyah,* for which he ably eulogized his 40-year relationship with the giant monster in his scoring of a moving and poetic death sequence for Godzilla. Ifukube has since remained in retirement, although his impressive Godzilla themes were reprised in *Godzilla 2000, Godzilla vs. Megaguiras,* and *Godzilla, Mothra and King Ghidorah: Battle on Fire.* Takayuki Hattori returned to score *Godzilla 2000,* although much of his score was replaced with music by J. Peter Robinson for the film's American release. Michiru Oshima became the first woman to score a Godzilla film when she tackled *Godzilla vs. Megaguiras,* and for *GMK,* director Shusuke Kaneko brought on Ko Otani, his composer for the Heisei Gamera films. While each of these composers produced effective scores, all three will no doubt stand in the shadow of Akira Ifukube for some time to come.

—JB

Biollante is marred by a confusing plotline (a subplot about overseas technology thieves is a waste of time) and shallow characterization, but rewards with ideas and emotional content rarely seen in monster movies. The main attractions, though, are imaginative visuals by upstart director Kazuki Omori and Toho's new special-effects wizard Koichi Kawakita. Biollante itself is a wonderfully designed creature, and started a trend toward monsters that transform throughout the film that subsequent entries picked up on. The same team returned in 1991 for the even better *Godzilla vs. King Ghidorah.* Viewers received an unexpected bonus when HBO "accidentally" transferred this to video in widescreen format. **AKA:** *Gojira vs. Biorante.* 𝅘𝅥𝅘𝅥𝅘𝅥

1989 (PG) 105m/C *JP* Koji Takahashi, Yoshiko Tanaka, Megumi Odaka, Kunihiko Mitamura, Toru Minegishi, Yasuko Sawaguchi, Toshiyuki Nagashima, Koichi Ueda, Katsuhiko Sasaki, Kenzo Hagiwara, Kenpachiro Satsuma. **D:** Kazuki Omori. **W:** Kazuki Omori. **C:** Yudai Kato. **M:** Koichi Sugiyama. **VHS**

Godzilla vs. Destroyah

Since his first appearance in 1954, only one man-made weapon has proved deadly to Godzilla—the Oxygen Destroyer. The weapon's inventor, Dr. Serizawa, gave his life to protect the secret of the Oxygen Destroyer, fearing it might someday pose an even deadlier menace to mankind. Forty years later, it looks like his prediction may be right.

G-Force, the government agency in charge of Godzilla detection and countermeasures, reports some bad news. The Pacific island where Godzilla (Kenpachiro Satsuma) has been living has disappeared. And Godzilla, having finally absorbed radiation beyond his mutant abilities, is in a rage and rampaging through Hong Kong. In these early scenes, Godzilla appears to be truly the Beast of the Apocalypse, glowing red and smoking like living lava as he strikes out in pain and anger. A young scientist theorizes that Godzilla is near the point

of meltdown, and the resulting explosion could spell the end of all life on Earth! As if this weren't enough, an experiment in Tokyo with a device similar to the Oxygen Destroyer has resulted in scores of highly destructive mutant creatures that are infesting downtown. There seems to be no way to stop the creatures, which keep growing, merging, and mutating. Once again, the only hope for mankind lies in manipulating Godzilla into helping to fight a new monster. But can G-Force see the battle through and destroy Destroyah (Ryo Hariya), while keeping Godzilla from melting down? And what is the fate of Godzilla Jr.?

The ultimate Godzilla film of the Heisei series is a definite step up from *Godzilla vs. Space Godzilla,* and a grand send-off for the King of the Monsters. Cartoon silliness is kept to a minimum, and a sense of grandeur underlies the entire film. This was designed as the last Godzilla picture before the Americans took over the series, and Toho wanted to give it an epic flavor which kept the character's long history in mind. Despite a few gaffs, the special effects and production design are better than ever. Honored classical composer and film score legend Akira Ikufube came out of retirement to deliver his final Godzilla score, instilling much drama and wonder in the antics of men-in-suit monsters. Momoko Kochi reprises her role from *Godzilla, King of the Monsters* a full 40 years later. **AKA:** *Gojira versus Desutoroia; Godzilla vs. Destroyer.* 𝅘𝅥𝅘𝅥𝅘𝅥𝅘𝅥

1995 103m/C *JP* Tatsumi Takuro, Yoko Ishino, Yasufumi Hayashi, Megumi Odaka, Sayaka Osawa, Saburo Shinoda, Akira Nakao, Masahiro Takashima, Momoko Kochi, Ronald Hea, Kenpachiro Satsuma, Ryo Hariya, Hurricane Ryu Hariken, Koichi Ueda, Takehiro Murata. **D:** Takao Okawara. **W:** Kazuki Omori. **C:** Sekiguchi Yoshinori. **M:** Akira Ifukube. **VHS, DVD**

Godzilla vs. Gigan

A cartoonist named Gengo Odaka (Hiroshi Ishikawa) is hired by the company constructing the World Children's Land amusement park to design monsters for exhibits. At a meeting inside the park's headquarters, Godzilla Tower, Gengo meets with the company secretary Kabota (Toshiaki Nishizawa, later a regular on the *Space Sheriff* TV series), who introduces him to the director Fumio Sudo (Zan Fujita)—a teenage math wiz. Later, Gengo encounters a young woman named Machiko (Tomoko Umeda), along with her overweight hippie friend Shosaku (Minoru Takashima), who tell him about how her brother Takashi (Kunio Murai) disappeared while working at Godzilla Tower. The trio, along with Gengo's karate master girlfriend Tomoko (Yuriko Hishimi), easily bypasses the company's lax security to discover the company's big secret. They're really alien cockroaches from Nebula Spacehunter M, who have taken possession of dead Earthlings to conduct their nefarious schemes. Busted, the aliens use Plan 6 to summon the giant three-headed dragon Ghidorah (last seen taking a beating in *Destroy All Monsters*) and giant cyborg monster from space Gigan (Kenpachiro Satsuma) to destroy Earth civilization. Godzilla (Haruo Nakajima) and Angilas (Koetsu Omiya) bust out of Monster Island to defend Japan from the invaders.

Though perhaps not the very worst of the Godzilla series, this one's not a big favorite even among fans. There is absolutely no logical reason that aliens in control of King Ghidorah (who apparently only attacks humanity under the control of aliens) and Gigan would find building theme parks and hiring cartoonists vital to their plan of conquest. The script is a disjointed mess and the special effects are either poorly executed or lifted from other films. An embarrassing highlight comes when Godzilla and Angilas actually speak to each other—the original Japanese version wasn't much better, having the monsters' growls translated within little cartoon speech balloons. Sadly, this was the last time Nakajima would perform as Godzilla. Here's irony for you: While *King Kong vs. Godzilla* was butchered for American release, *Godzilla vs. Gigan* was presented in U.S. theatres in 1977 (under the title *Godzilla on Monster Island*) completely intact. **AKA:** *Chikyu Kokegi Meirei: Gojira tai Gaigan; Earth Assault Order: Godzilla vs. Gigan; Godzilla on Monster Island; War of the Monsters.* 🐛🐛

1972 (G) 88m/C *JP* Hiroshi Ishikawa, Yuriko Hishimi, Tomoko Umeda, Toshiaki Nishizawa, Zan Fujita, Kunio Murai, Gen Shimizu, Wataru Omae, Noritake Saito, Yasuhiko Saijo, Naoya Kusakawa, Haruo Nakajima, Kenpachiro Satsuma, Minoru Takashima, Koetsu Omiya. **D:** Jun Fukuda. **W:** Shenichi Sekizawa, Takeshi Kimura (story). **C:** Kiyoshi Hasegawa. **M:** Akira Ifukube. **VHS, DVD**

Godzilla vs. Hedorah

Best known in the U.S. under the title *Godzilla vs. the Smog Monster*, this one rivals *The X from Outer Space* and *All Monsters Attack* as the oddest giant-monster movie ever made. By 1970, the Japan's Economic Miracle produced an industrial giant choking on its own refuse. First-time director Yoshimitsu Banno successfully pitched the idea for the story to Toho, hoping to replace the nuclear paranoia of the first Godzilla picture with environmental paranoia. His villain is a Blob-like creature from outer space, who thrives on Earth's pollution, becoming an ever-growing sludge glob named Hedorah ("hedero" is Japanese for "sludge"). First seen attacking ships at sea, Hedorah (Kenpachiro Satsuma) soon makes his way inland to suck up and spew forth toxic filth, and is even seen flying over crowds of people as they drop in their tracks, dead from poison gas—and yet, at one point the monster spares a little kitten. In battle with Godzilla (Haruo Nakajima), the smog monster sprays his eyes with burning acids, then buries him in poison sludge. Pretty graphic stuff for a series increasingly aimed at children, presenting the first large-scale depiction of human casualties in a monster film since the original *Godzilla*. Japanese teenagers marshal their dancing talents to combat the threat amid the hypnotic swirl of disco lighting, while dedicated scientist Dr. Toru Yano (Akira Yamauchi) looks for a weapon to use against the monster.

Banno tried to take this Godzilla film further into surrealism, with mixed results. Some scenes are illustrated with animated children's drawings, and a great opening song, "Save the Earth," reappears as a sort of music video sequence. The relevant anti-pollution message occasionally becomes heavy-handed. At other times things are just plain weird. Series director Ishiro Honda was in semi-retirement, f/x wizard Eiji Tsuburaya had just died, and producer Tomoyuki Tanaka was in the hospital while *Hedorah* was being filmed, so Banno and his crew had a free hand to do whatever they wanted. Reportedly, Tanaka-san was most unhappy when he saw the final result, and Banno never directed another film. Despite all, it remains an entertaining film, even if only for camp value. **AKA:** *Gojira tai Hedora; Godzilla vs. the Smog Monster; Frankensteins Kampf gegen die Teufelsmonster.* 🐛🐛🐛

1971 (G) 87m/C *JP* Toshie Kimura, Hiroyuki Kawase, Keiko Mari, Toshio Shiba, Yukihiko Gondo, Tadashi Okabe, Wataru Omae, Susumu Okabe, Haruo Nakajima, Kenpachiro Satsuma, Akira

Run, kids! Pollution personified in the counterculture monster movie *Godzilla vs. Hedorah.* THE KOBAL COLLECTION / TOHO / A.I.P.

Yamauchi. **D:** Yoshimitsu Banno. **W:** Yoshimitsu Banno, Takeshi Kimura. **C:** Yoichi Manoda. **M:** Riichiro Manabe. **VHS, DVD**

Godzilla vs. King Ghidorah

Disappointing boxoffice for *Godzilla vs. Biollante* prompted producer Tomoyuki Tanaka to reverse his decision to pit the Big G against only new monster foes, bringing out their second largest monster attraction for the next entry. The result was the biggest Godzilla hit to date, despite a confusing, contradictory plot that replaces the invading space aliens from *Ghidorah the Three-Headed Monster* and *Invasion of Astro-Monster* with time-traveling terrorists from the future. A UFO appears in the skies over Japan, bringing visitors from the year 2204. Their stated mission is to warn that Japan will soon be destroyed when Godzilla (Kenpachiro Satsuma) has a nuclear meltdown. Fortunately, they offer a solution: they will send a team back to Lagos Island in 1944, where records indicate the dinosaur Godzillasaurus was living before atomic testing turned it into a monster, and remove the animal before he can be mutated. They take along a few citizens as witnesses to the event: writer Ken Terasawa (Kosuke Toyohara), who wrote a book providing the data they have on Godzilla, paleontologist Professor Mazaki (Katsuhiko Sasaki), and Godzilla's psychic friend Miki Saegusa (Megumi Odaka). They find the Godzillasaurus inadvertently defending Japanese troops from attacking U.S. forces, and succeed in teleporting the beast to an island far from the bombsite.

But the truth is that the folks from the future have been lying all along—Japan will come to dominate the entire world in the future, and the terrorist group's true mission is to destroy Japan before that can happen. They've come to the 20th century, when nuclear weapons are plentiful, to create King Ghidorah (Hurricane Ryu Hariken), a mutated fusing of three genetically engineered animals under their control, eliminating the only force powerful enough to destroy their living weapon at the same time. But as they direct King Ghidorah on a rampage in 1992, everyone has underestimated the proliferation of radioactivity throughout the world—a sunken nuclear sub and other sources of radiation created Godzilla anyway, and an attack on a more powerful modern sub mutates Godzilla into an even bigger, more powerful monster. Godzilla arrives in Japan to defeat King Ghidorah and destroy the futurians' ship, before turning his attention to smashing up Tokyo. Future girl Emmy Kano (Anna Nakagawa), who has grown close to the 20th-century folks, escapes to her

own time. There, she rebuilds the monster she helped create into a cyborg Mecha-Ghidorah, and returns to 1992 to try to help her friends.

Writer/director Kazuki Omori shows he was deeply influenced by American sci-fi with this *Terminator 2* homage, but trips himself up with the complicated conundrums of time-travel stories. Why do the terrorists bother to stop off in 1992 to lie to everyone, when their mission is in 1944? If they keep Godzilla from being created in 1944, why are they traveling to that year? While the seeming contradictions of the plot could have been explained away a little better, he fails to do so, or does so poorly. But then, even *The Terminator* doesn't make any sense if you question it at all. Instead, Omori concentrates on giving us one of the best Godzilla films ever, fast paced and full of exciting spectacle. Koichi Kawakita (special effects) and Akira Ikufube (music) both turn in excellent work. While the acting is nothing special, some of the characters are memorable, including a friendly android (Robert Scott Field) and Shindo (Yoshio Tsuchiya), a powerful businessman whose life was saved by the Godzillasaurus during the war. The monsters look awesome, even dwarfed by the skyscrapers of modern Tokyo. A big hit in Japan, this winner insured the Godzilla series would continue for years to come. **AKA:** *Gojira vs. Kingugidora.* ♪♪♪♪

1991 102m/C *JP* Kosuke Toyohara, Anna Nakagawa, Megumi Odaka, Katsuhiko Sasaki, Shoji Kobayashi, Tokuma Nishioka, Yoshio Tsuchiya, Kenji Sahara, Koichi Ueda, So Yamamura, Robert Scott Field, Kiwako Harada, Kenzo Ogiwara, Tetsu Watanabe, Kenpachiro Satsuma, Hurricane Ryu Hariken, Kent Gilbert. **D:** Kazuki Omori. **W:** Kazuki Omori. **C:** Yoshinori Sekiguchi. **M:** Akira Ifukube. **VHS, DVD**

Godzilla vs. MechaGodzilla

In accordance with an ancient prophecy, Godzilla appears once again to ravage the Japanese countryside. Nothing new about that—until he beats up on his ol' pal Angilas (Momoru Kusumi). Then, a *second* Godzilla (Isao Zushi) shows up to battle the first! The first monster's skin is torn away to reveal a robot version of Godzilla, which is under the control of evil apes from the black hole nebula (swiping an idea from the then-popular "Planet of the Apes" series). The apes don't seem like much of a threat—instead of just marching in to take over, they needed to enlist an Earth scientist (Akihiko Hirata) to build MechaGodzilla (Ise Mori). Why do they disguise the robot as Godzilla? Why do they disguise themselves as humans? Since MechaGodzilla is such a match for Godzilla, why not build *two* robots just to be sure? Stop asking intelligent

questions and just enjoy the fireworks, as the giant monsters wage war across a crumbling cityscape. Despite interference from the alien apes, an Okinawan cult summons their monster god King Caesar (Ksumi again, pulling double monster duty) to help Godzilla out against his mechanical foe. It's all darn silly, but this entry in the Godzilla series is a step up from the previous two because of the presence of MechaGodzilla, which is a pretty cool and evil robot. Originally released by AIP as *Godzilla vs. the Bionic Monster* in an attempt to cash in on *The Six Million Dollar Man* and *Bionic Woman* television series, the prints and ad campaign had to be quickly altered to *Godzilla vs. the Cosmic Monster* when a lawsuit was threatened. Not to be confused with the much superior *Godzilla vs. MechaGodzilla 2* (1993). *AKA: Gojira tai Mekagojira; Godzilla vs. the Bionic Monster; Godzilla vs. the Cosmic Monster.* 🐕🐕🐕♡

1974 (G) 84m/C *JP* Masaaki Daimon, Kazuya Aoyama, Akihiko Hirata, Hiroshi Koizumi, Reiko Tajima, Shin Kishida, Kenji Sahara, Goro Mutsumi, Isao Zushi, Ise Mori, Momoru Kusumi. *D:* Jun Fukuda. *W:* Masami Fukushima, Jun Fukuda, Hiroyasu Yamamura, Shinichi Sekizawa (story). *C:* Yuzuru Aizawa. *M:* Masaru Sato. **VHS, DVD**

Godzilla vs. MechaGodzilla 2

In order to try to deal with the now-constant threat posed by Godzilla and other giant terrors, the United Nations Godzilla Countermeasures Center (UNGCC) is formed. G-Force, their military and tactics division, salvages the remains of MechaGhidorah *(Godzilla vs. King Ghidorah)*, using the future technology to create new weapons. The first of these is Garuda, a streamlined version of the Super-X. When the Garuda is judged a failure, pilot/engineer Kazuma Aoki (Masahiro Takashima) is transferred over to the much more ambitious MechaGodzilla project—a 120 meter tall, 150,000 metric ton super-robot carrying a crew of five, plated with artificial diamonds, and armed with a devastating array of powerful weaponry. Meanwhile, on H-bomb test–scarred Adonoa Island, Professor Omae (Yusuke Kawazu) discovers a gigantic egg, which is guarded by a huge mutant pterosaur they call Rodan. But Godzilla (Kenpachiro Satsuma) is strangely attracted to the egg, too, and while the two behemoths battle for it, the scientists manage to slip away with the coveted egg. At UNGCC headquarters, Dr. Azusa Gojo (Ryoko Sano) is put in charge of the egg, and working with the class of psychic children being trained by Miki Saegusa (Megumi Odaka), they decode prehistoric sounds that help the egg to hatch. But Rodan turns out to be the stickleback bird

of monsters, known for stealing the eggs of other species to hatch as their own—the egg hatches a baby-mutated Godzillasaurus. But the sounds they create, and the cries of little Baby Godzilla (Hurricane Ryu Hariken) carry far on the psychic bandwidth, drawing Godzilla to the labs. G-Force enacts a plan to use Baby to lure Godzilla into a trap, but Rodan, mutated further by radiation absorbed while Godzilla was kicking his butt, is drawn to Baby, too. MechaGodzilla (Wataru Fukuda) joins with Garuda to form Super-MechaGodzilla to face off in a three-way battle with Rodan and Godzilla, a battle that will kill all three of them!

Wataru Mimura's script presents a solution to a problem that often plagues giant-monster movies, seamlessly combining the story of human beings with the more operatic story of the godlike beasts. Usually, people in these movies either just talk about the monsters, fire guns at them, or flee from them in terror. The people in this story interact with the monsters by making friends with the human-sized baby, or fighting toe-to-toe with Godzilla himself, albeit through the proxy of MechaGodzilla. The robot itself is an awesome creation. It not only looks way cool, but for once the heroes have come up with a device that actually packs enough power to take down Godzilla. Why the robot is made to look like Godzilla is a matter one just has to take on faith—perhaps it's meant to have some psychological advantage. The special effects are terrific, coming up short only in a few shots where the puppetry of Rodan or Baby looks a bit stiff. Ifukube creates what is arguably his best film score since *Godzilla, King of the Monsters,* deftly interpreting and adapting themes for each character and situation. His theme for MechaGodzilla is a brilliant variation on his Godzilla themes, with an added pounding, metallic tone. *AKA: Gojira vs. Mekagojira; Godzilla vs. Mechagodzilla; Godzilla vs. Super-Mechagodzilla.* 🐕🐕🐕🐕

1993 107m/C *JP* Masahiro Takashima, Ryoko Sano, Megumi Odaka, Yusuke Kawazu, Kenji Sahara, Akira Nakao, Koichi Ueda, Leo Meneghetti, Daijiro Harada, Shinobu Nakayama, Tadao Takashima, Keiko Imamura, Sayaka Osawa, Kenpachiro Satsuma, Wataru Fukuda, Kenpachiro Satsuma, Hurricane Ryu Hariken, Wataru Fukuda. *D:* Takao Okawara. *W:* Wataru Mimura. *C:* Masahiro Kishimoto, Yoshinori Sekiguchi. *M:* Akira Ifukube. **VHS**

Godzilla vs. Megaguirus

This film follows in the giant footsteps of *Godzilla 2000* in that it doesn't necessarily fit into the continuity of any other film in the series, has a good story, and shows off the best special effects to date. When even the total elimination of nuclear power fails to dissuade Godzilla (Tsutomu Kitagawa) from trampling Japan, the government department in charge of dealing with the monster forms the G-Graspers, a special weapons military unit headed by Kiriko Tsujimori (Misato Tanaka), whose commander was killed by Godzilla several years before. Dr. Yoshizawa (Yuriko Hoshi) develops a satellite weapon capable of forming a minute black hole, which they hope will devour Godzilla without causing too much damage to the rest of the planet. Gen-X scientist Hajime (Shosuke Tanihara) helps Yoshizawa turn his weapon into a practical system they call the Dimension Tide. A test of the weapon is successful, but it leaves a vortex in space open long enough to allow a huge dragonfly known as a Meganura to visit our time period long enough to leave an egg behind. The egg's hatchling multiplies asexually and rapidly, resulting in a swarm of the giant Meganurons invading the Tokyo sewer system and causing flooding in the Shebuya district. Godzilla is lured to a nearby island so that the Dimension Tide can be used. But at the last minute, the swarm of Meganurons attacks him, confusing the satellite tracking system enough that the weapon misses him. The insects take the radiation they've absorbed back to the original parent insect, which grows and mutates into the monstrous Megaguirus. When Godzilla comes ashore to fight the new monster, the G-Graspers try to use their flying fortress the *Griffin* to keep them both in the area long enough for the Dimension Tide to deliver a killing blow.

G vs. M continues Toho's practice of mixing old with new in their monster films. The Meganurons can be found in more primitive form as the favorite snack of monster hatchlings in *Rodan*, and in final form resemble Battra (from *Godzilla vs. Mothra*). The *Griffin* and her crew recall the Super-X of G-Force, and the cast is loaded up with cameos by stars of previous G-films. But director Masaaki Tezuka, f/x director Kenji Suzuki, and the veteran Godzilla writing team provide plenty of new material to keep things fresh. The sight of Kiriko (well played by Tanaka) at sea, climbing aboard Godzilla's tail for the ride of her life, is a classic image that could easily have been misplayed. Though Megaguirus isn't the most charismatic menace, it's handled with imagination and the Dimension Tide itself is such a beautifully scary weapon that it almost becomes another character. Kitagawa, a veteran of Sonny Chiba's Japan Action Club, has quickly become an expert at acting within the stifling confines of Godzilla's hide, giving a good performance under tough conditions. Laugh if you want to, but could Anthony Hopkins or Kenneth Branagh do any better? *AKA: Gojira tai Megagirasu: Jii Shometsu Sakusen; GXM; Godzilla vs. Megaguirus: The G Annihilation Strategy; Godzilla X Megaguirus: The G Extermination Command.* 🎬🎬🎬🎬

2000 105m/C *JP* Misato Tanaka, Shosuke Tanihara, Masato Ibu, Yoriko Hoshi, Toshiyuki Nagashima, Tsutomu Kitagawa, Minoru Watanabe, Kazuko Kato, Katsuo Nakamura, Koichi Ueda, Susumu Kurobe, Matoko Nagino. *D:* Masaaki Tezuka. *W:* Hiroshi Kashiwabara, Wataru Mimura. *C:* Masahiro Kishimoto. *M:* Michiru Oshima. **VHS**

Godzilla vs. Megalon

While so many worthwhile films remain unavailable on home video, it's ironic that the very worst Godzilla movie is one of the most widely screened. Due to the assumption that it's in the public domain, *Godzilla vs. Megalon* proliferated across the land on countless cheap video labels during the 1980s and '90s, and even onto CD-ROM.

Overreacting to the tremendous popularity on Japanese TV of superhero programs like *Ultraman*, Toho Studios sought to team their monster star with their own rubbery robot hero Jet Jaguar (Tsugutoshi Komada), with ridiculous results. The underwater nation of Seatopia, which consists of one cheap set, some even cheaper costumes, and a dozen bad dancers and actors, provides the menace. In response to damage caused by nuclear testing, Emperor Antonio of Seatopia (Robert Dunham) sends forth their giant mutant roach Megalon (Hideto Odashi) to conquer the surface world. As backup, they hire cyborg mercenary monster Gigan (Kenpachiro Satsuma). Meanwhile, Seatopian agents kidnap inventor Goro Ibuki (Katsuhiko Sasaki), along with his little brother Rokuro (Hiroyuki Kawase) and racing driver best friend Hiroshi (Yutaka Hayashi), in order to get control of his creation, Jet Jaguar. But our heroes escape, and send the robot to fetch Godzilla (Shinji Takagi) from Monster Island. Jet not only rejects the control of his human masters, but "reprograms himself" to be able to grow to Godzilla's size, and joins him in a tag-team match with the bad-guy monsters.

Most of the action conveniently takes place in open fields (and stock footage), far away from those expensive miniature buildings. After their skirmishes with Seatopian spies, the human heroes camp out on hillsides to watch the monster mayhem. A low mark in monster history, but possessed of a certain cheesy charm. Adding insult to injury, NBC cut out half the footage and aired it in 1977 with campy segments hosted by John Belushi in a shoddy Godzilla costume. *AKA: Gojira tai Megaro.* 🎬🎬

1973 (G) 80m/C *JP* Katsuhiko Sasaki, Yutaka Hayashi, Hiroyuki Kawase, Robert Dunham, Kotaro Tomita, Shinji Takagi, Tsugutoshi Komada, Hideto Odashi, Kenpachiro Satsuma. *D:* Jun Fukuda. *W:* Jun Fukuda, Shinichi Sekizawa. *C:* Yuzuru Aizawa. *M:* Richiro Manabe. **VHS, DVD**

Godzilla vs. Mothra

Striking while the iron was hot (and radioactive), Toho followed their hit *Godzilla vs. King Ghidorah* with another meeting of classic monsters. Here, the theme shifts from economic to ecological dangers. A falling meteor sets off tidal waves and earthquakes, while also uncovering a huge egg on Infant Island, and waking Godzilla (Kenpachiro Satsuma) from his slumber at the bottom of the ocean. Takuya Fujita (Tetsuya Bessho), an irresponsible tomb raider, is hired by his ex-wife Masako (Satomi Kobayashi) to lead an expedition to the island for her company, which is planning a development there. They find the colorful egg and two tiny girls (Keiko Imamura and Sayaka Osawa) who say they're from an ancient extraterrestrial race known as the Cosmos. Their civilization was destroyed when the Earth's defender Battra (Hurricane Ryu Hariken) decided their environmental disregard had gone too far. Battra was defeated by the Cosmos's own champion/goddess Mothra, but not before the damage was already done.

Masako's bosses at the polluting Marutomo Corporation decide to exploit the egg—and the Cosmos—by taking them back to Japan, but the voyage is interrupted by a battle between Godzilla and Battra. Mothra hatches from the egg during the battle and joins the fray. Their trashing about causes the eruption of an underwater volcano that engulfs Godzilla and Battra, while Mothra swims back to the island. However, she soon makes her way to the mainland in search of her tiny friends, causing plenty of damage on the way. Takuya steals the Cosmos from the corporate bad guys, and briefly considers selling them before he is convinced to do the right thing by Masako and his daughter. The military attacks, and Mothra forms a cocoon to begin metamorphosis. Battra also transforms into its winged adult form, and the two ancient enemies renew their battle. But when Godzilla rises from erupting Mount Fuji to threaten the world anew, the two flying monsters unite to face the mutual enemy.

The plot is a bit of an uneven mish-mosh, which only serves to set up the film's main attraction: giant monster mayhem. The special effects are fantastic, with all the monsters photographed to look breathtakingly beautiful as they throw rays and drop buildings on top of each other. Complementing the spectacle is another stunning Akira Ifukube score. The fantasy and family elements are credited with bringing out the overwhelmingly single and female movie theatre audience, making this one of the most successful Godzillas ever. Though not twins, the Cosmos are a real singing duo who went on to appear in more Godzilla pictures. Mothra graduated to her own trilogy of features. *AKA: Gojira vs. Mosura; Godzilla and Mothra: The Battle for Earth.* 🐉🐉🐉🐉

1992 102m/C *JP* Tetsuya Bessho, Satomi Kobayashi, Takehiro Murata, Saburo Shinoda, Shoji Kobayashi, Akira Takarada, Keiko Imamura, Sayaka Osawa, Megumi Odaka, Yoshika Tanaka, Koichi Ueda, Kenji Sahara, Susumu Kurobe, Yuriko Hoshi, Kenzo Ogiwara, Tetsu Watanabe, Kenpachiro Satsuma, Hurricane Ryu Hariken. *D:* Takao Okawara. *W:* Kazuki Omori. *C:* Masahiro Kishimoto. *M:* Akira Ifukube. **VHS, DVD**

Godzilla vs. Space Godzilla

Full of bright colors and sparkling effects, this is as close as the 1990s Godzilla series could get to be a cartoon. On a Pacific island, members of the G-Force, a government agency assigned to Godzilla matters, conducts an experiment. They attempt to use a new device that may allow the group's top psychic Miki Segusa (series regular Megumi Odaka) to control Godzilla (Kenpachiro Satsuma) somewhat. But Dr. Gondo (Towako Yoshikawa), whose brother was killed by Godzilla, has his own agenda. The grizzled man of action is toting a special rifle loaded with cadmium shells, with which he hopes to kill the monster by himself. Meanwhile, Miki receives a "psychic fax" from Mothra(!) in deep space, which warns of a new menace approaching Earth. Sure enough, a powerful monster arrives, formed by the merging of mutated Godzilla cells with those of a crystalline creature on the other side of a black hole. The new monster, an ugly blue dragon dubbed Space Godzilla (Ryo Hariya), starts causing trouble immediately, encasing poor Little Godzilla in a crystal prison. Then he flies over to Fukuoka to build some sort of energy-sucking crystal palace. The new G-Force giant robot M.O.G.E.R.A. (thought to be more versatile than its predecessor MechaGodzilla) is less than useless against this powerful new foe. Well, maybe alone...but maybe partnered in a tag-team match with Godzilla (who's come to defend his turf), they might be able to succeed.

Though not the best of the Heisei Godzilla series, this one is still plenty of fun on its own terms. The appearance of Little Godzilla (Little Frankie), looking like a scaly Teletubby, sets the tone—one should catch the drift that this adventure shouldn't be taken too seriously.

The Laus

Who's Who in Fu Part 3

More than any other filmmakers, it seems the Lau Family has kung fu in their blood. While most kung fu films are action-adventures that put in kung fu for the fight scenes, the Laus made movies that were *about* kung fu. The plots often hinged upon training and the acquisition of skills, which were then used to solve a specific problem, usually to counter the specific skills of the villain. And while many martial arts stars were made to look like they could fight onscreen, the Laus were handed down their moves directly from the Man himself: Master Wong Fei-hung.

Lau Charn

As a youngster, family patriarch Lau Charn received his training from Master Wong's toughest pupil, Lam Sai-wing, AKA Butcher Wing. As an adult, Master Lau portrayed his sifu in the ultra–long running Wong Fei-hung film series, alongside star Kwan Tak-hing. There was even a spin-off film featuring the character. Lau gave his own sons the same iron-tough training he had received.

Lau Kar-Leung

Some say he's the greatest kung fu director who ever lived, and it's hard to dispute that notion. Leung first used his skills in front of the camera in 1950, and worked with his father in many of the Wong pictures. Along with Tang Chia (later director of *Opium and the Kung Fu Master*), he served as action director to the great Shaw Brothers director Chang Cheh. Leung struck out on his own as director in 1975 with *Spiritual Boxer,* a comedy that featured drunken boxing years before *Drunken Master,* and mixed ghosts with kung fu long before *Encounters of the Spooky Kind.* From there, he kept on challenging himself, with highlights being *Executioners from Shaolin, Shaolin Master Killer, Dirty Ho, Legendary Weapons of China, Invincible Pole Fighter,* and *Tiger on Beat.* He had a famous clash with Jackie Chan on *Legend of the Drunken Master,* after which Chan finished the final fight himself. Actor/action director Hsiao Ho *(Mad Monkey Kung Fu)* is Leung's student.

Lau Kar-Wing

Wing was in front of the camera more than Leung. Even while serving as action director on pictures from *Five Fingers of Death* to *Once upon a Time in China,* he was also earning good parts in films like *Master of the Flying Guillotine* and *Challenge of the Masters.* Karl Maka gave him a lead role in *Dirty Tiger Crazy Frog* and *His Name Is Nobody,* and Maka, Lau, and Sammo Hung formed Gar Bo Films together. Wing took the reins as director with *He Has Nothing But Kung Fu,* and spent several years alternating between appearing in Gar Bo pictures and those directed by brother Leung. His own films as director include *Dirty Kung Fu, Odd Couple, Warrior from Shaolin,* and *Skinny Tiger, Fatty Dragon.*

Gordon Lau

An orphan adopted into the Lau family, Lau Kar-fai seems to have been born to play kung fu heroes, both in his brothers' movies and those of others. After an inauspicious debut as a lead actor in *Breakout from Oppression,* brother Leung cast him as a young Wong Fei-hung (a few years before Jackie Chan and Yuen Woo-ping got the idea) in *Challenge of the Masters.* A year later, Gordon would play the role that would make him a star—famous monk San Te in *Shaolin Master Killer* (AKA *36th Chamber of Shaolin*). Gordon shaved his head for the role, and kept it that way for 10 years. On the rare occasions that anybody wanted him to play anything other than a monk, he could always put on a wig. Other starring roles came in *Dirty Ho, Fist of the White Lotus, Return of the Master Killer, Fists and Guts, Shaolin Drunken Monk, Fury in Shaolin Temple,* and *Invincible Pole Fighter.*

Jimmy Liu

The young half-brother of Leung and Wing, he benefited from the same training, as well as having famous brothers to help him. He's appeared as stuntman and actor in such films as *Bruce Lee the Invincible, Shaolin Disciple* (his directorial debut), *Dragon's Claws,* and *Legend of the Drunken Master.* He's also the writer/director of *The Black Wall* and *Master of Disaster.*

Director Kensho Yamashita was chosen because of his success in handling teen romance pictures, in the hope he could raise interest in the film among teen girls. Well, this is probably the Godzilla film with the best-developed romance subplots anyway, and everyone ends up walking on the beach in the sunrise. Space Godzilla is a beautiful looking (if unrealistic) creation in his own right, with lots of unique powers that look gorgeous in action, such as his energy shield and tornado beams. Perhaps he could show up again in a Mothra movie—and any movie with Mothra can't be bad. **AKA:** Gojira vs. Supesugojira. 🐉🐉🐉

1994 106m/C JP Jun Hashizume, Megumi Odaka, Zenkichi Yoneyama, Akira Emoto, Yosuke Saito, Towako Yoshikawa, Kenji Sahara, Akira Nakao, Koichi Ueda, Keiko Imamura, Sayako Ozawa, Ronald Hea, Kenpachiro Satsuma, Little Frankie, Ryo Hariya. **D:** Kensho Yamashita. **W:** Hiroshi Kashiwabara. **C:** Masahiro Kishimoto. **M:** Takayuki Hattori. **VHS, DVD**

Gold Fingers

A special unit of the police rappels down a wall as the credits crawl, and it looks like excitement is sure to follow. Unfortunately, things go downhill from there. Two low-level gang members, Xi Hwa and Peter (Terence Yin), happen to be on the scene when Rocky, their boss, is attacked by masked gunmen. Peter rushes to help out. The boss is impressed by his brash attitude, and Peter is promoted. It turns out that Peter is an undercover cop who is unhappy with the assignment, especially because another policeman is already undercover with the same gang. Peter attempts to get closer to the boss while questioning himself and his motives.

Because the basic story line is so familiar, the viewer rightly expects some twists and turns in the plot, or some freshness to the cinematic telling of the tale. Sadly it feels like a third-hand remake with a limited budget and imagination. Not only does it lack originality, but it also has the fatal flaw of being boring for stretches of time—scenes run too long, nothing happens, etc. The center of the film sags because most of it's about Peter, and—as played by Terence Yin—Peter is an unsympathetic, uninteresting bad guy. With a general torpor hanging like a dark cloud over the proceedings, it's tough going to watch this one through to its unsurprising conclusion. Probably the brightest spot of the production are the supporting performances. Highlights include Eric Mo as the boss's angry and conflicted right-hand man, Ben Ng as the heartless boss, Hui Siu-hung as Peter's long-suffering police superior, Lam Suet as the blustery ne'er-do-well Xi Hwa, and Samuel Leung as a pimp who seems to exist

solely to get beat up. —PM **AKA:** Yee Ng Chuen Suet; Er Wu Chuan Shui. 🐉

2001 88m/C HK Terence Yin, Eric Mo, Ben Ng, Hui Siu-hung, Lam Suet, Samuel Leung, Chan Yan-Yan, Maang Fai, Yam Sai-kwoon. **D:** Benny Wong. **W:** Cheuk Bing. **C:** Fung Yuen-man. **M:** Albert Young. **VHS, DVD**

Golden Dragon Silver Snake

Han Sek refuses to pay protection fees, and organizes others to resist as well, but is murdered by pipe-smoking gangster Lo. In Old West fashion, the villains are also putting pressure on milk farmer Uncle Su to sell his land, threatening Su, his niece Chu-lin, and milkman Shan-yu (Johnnie Chan), with plans to build a resort with Mr. Ma Shi-chi (Kong Do). After meeting the new chef Han Lung (Dragon Lee) at Wong's Restaurant, Shan-yu is returning to the farm when his truck hits the rickshaw belonging to Seung. Seeing Seung's amazing light skills—which he demonstrates by walking on eggs—Shan-yu asks the man to be his kung fu master. Han Lung turns out to be Sek's brother, who is searching for the killers. Wong fires him for beating up some of the gangsters, and Han goes to work on the Su's farm, where he's reunited with his old friend Seung. Tired of waiting, the gangsters invade the farm and kidnap Uncle Su and Chu-lin to force them into transferring the property, leading to a big kung fu showdown.

Lighter in tone than most Dragon Lee vehicles, the silly offhand humor is in a style that would become typical in the films of Wong Jing. Here Lee's seen fooling around juggling in the kitchen, and he comes to the villain's hideout disguised as a telephone repairman à la Bruce Lee in The Chinese Connection. Johnnie Chan's training scenes are mostly played for laughs. Gang boss Lo is dubbed in a Humphrey Bogart imitation, and his hat releases a net when thrown in combat. During the kidnapping scene at the farm, one of the thugs answers the phone while fighting. The head villain is only seen from the neck down, and strokes a cat just like James Bond's nemesis Blofeld; he gives the cat to Kong Do for a birthday present. In one scene, Kong Do enters wearing a wig, then takes it off for no reason. When Lee and Chan invade the birthday party to catch the crooks, thugs ride surfboards across the pool to attack them.

The choreography is actually quite good, especially during this climactic birthday-party fight at a resort, with moves that recall the kind of imagination Jackie Chan would soon be using in his films. Throughout, Lee carries a special weapon in a tube slung over his back, which he finally takes out to fight the revealed top villain—

and it turns out to be a baseball bat. The English dub is so poor that you can hear the engineer identifying the loop in several scenes! ♫♫♪

1979 89m/C *HK* Dragon Lee, Johnnie Chan, Kong Do, Merilyn Lee, Patrick Reynolds, Malcolm Levy, Martin Chiu, Tony Wong, Larry Kim, George Shin, Michael Lee, Alex Suh, Sai Gwa Pau. **D:** Godfrey Ho, Shin Wee Kyun. **W:** Edward Lee. **C:** Jimmy Yu. **M:** Ricky Chan. **DVD**

Golden Killah

This muddled kung fu mystery (now available under this dopey video title) takes forever to get going, and gives the viewer little reason to care once it does. Assassin Leung Yung-chan (Chi Kuan Chun) is hired by the criminal Golden Mask to kill a man, only afterward learning his victim is his own brother Tieh-hu. His brother's ghost comes to haunt him, as does a nagging stranger. Leung takes Tieh-hu's identity (and lute) to try to learn what it's all about. He receives a message from a monk to visit a certain inn to make a rendezvous, after which Golden Mask kills the monk. At the inn he finds Chow Siu-chen and his daughter Shu-Shu, along with thieves Lee Sang, Big Tan, and the Foxy Lady—all of whom have been invited by reclusive retired bandit Liu Chin-tien to visit his Eagle House. Leung's contact turns out to be with the smiling stranger, who is really Liu Shou-pang, Master Liu's adopted son. Liu has sent for Tieh-hu because he's been receiving death threats from Golden Mask, and wanted his old friend's help. Leung agrees to help out, hoping to find his own revenge, and he's sent to fetch Wu Fu-chang, who may have some information, but finds him dead. Meanwhile, somebody is sneaking around the inn killing servants and guests. By the time Liu opens Eagle House to the public, everybody has plenty of reason to be after the killer, and there are plenty of suspects on hand. Who is the Golden Mask? Before it's over, our hero has half a dozen Golden Masks to choose from, all bearing golden razor-edged Frisbees, from which he defends himself using his gadget-packed lute! The fighting is uninteresting and badly framed throughout, but at least they included one fun action sequence at the end. **AKA:** *Golden Mask.* ♫♪

1980 85m/C *TW* Chi Kuan Chun, Stephen Tung, Frank Wong, Doris Lung, Wong Chi Sang, Chai Kai, Chui Chung Hei, Chen Chiu, Shaw Luo-hui. **D:** Ting Chung. **DVD**

Gonin

Disco lights swirl around a dance club, illuminating all sorts of dangerous characters. Before long a bloody fight erupts, turning the scene into a nightmare. Imagine a freshly bandaged wound ripped wide open, and welcome to a film that does not bother paying lip service to the realities of everyday life. The owner of the disco has borrowed money from a yakuza gang. He cannot pay it back, so he recruits four unlikely compatriots (a laid-off "salaryman," a disgraced ex-cop, a drug addict, and a con man) to help him rip off another criminal crew. Against all odds, they are successful, but very quickly a particularly nasty assassin ("Beat" Takeshi Kitano) and his submissive sidekick hunt down the men.

The pessimistic characters, somber lighting, and quick cuts create a gloomy atmosphere. References to the economic downturn and the plight of the "salaryman" (male employees who, in the past, could count on lifetime employment in exchange for their devoted service to large companies in Japan) abound. The physical beatings and gunfights are quite bloody. The camera stands at a distance from the participants, which only makes the explicit nature of the violence more horrifying—imagination fills in the sickening details. Yet there are no extended "action" scenes—in that sense, too, the film feels as real as a chalk outline on a shadowy sidewalk. Relationships and plot mechanics remain murky and the storytelling is confusing—it's often not clear what is happening, and to whom. Really, though, such incidentals are beside the point. Writer/director Takashi Ishii displays style to burn and an incandescent desire to leave the viewer scarred and whimpering softly. He succeeds on all counts. Be advised that Takeshi Kitano—menacing and stoic as always—plays a supporting role, although he received top billing. —*PM* **AKA:** *The Five.* ♫♫♫

1995 109m/C *JP* "Beat" Takeshi Kitano, Koichi Sato, Masahiro Motoki, Jinpachi Nezu, Kippei Shiina, Naoto Takenaka, Kazuya Kimura, Daisuke Iijima, Toshiyuki Nagashima, Kanji Tsuda, Shingo Tsurumi. **D:** Takashi Ishii. **W:** Takashi Ishii. **C:** Yasushi Sasakibara. **M:** Goro Yasukawa. **VHS, DVD**

Good Morning

Neither the comic farces of Frank Tashlin (*Will Success Spoil Rock Hunter?*) in America nor Jacques Tati (*Playtime*) in France could portray the overwhelming effect of television on society any better than this gentle comedy from Japan. Housewives across the neighborhood are upset to hear from Mrs. Tomizawa (Teruko Nagaoka) that the dues for the Women's Association have been reported as unpaid that month—and the leader Mrs. Haraguchi (Haruko Sugimura) happens to have just purchased a new washing machine. But that's not the biggest scandal in the neighborhood—when a young couple buys a

television set, it sends shock waves through the community.

Minoru Hayashi (Koji Shigaragi) and his little brother Isamu are always next door watching the sumo matches and neglecting their English studies. When their parents complain, the petulant boys blame them, demanding they buy a TV. Their father (Chishu Ryu) refuses, believing television could make Japan a nation of idiots. The boys decide to go on strike, taking a vow of silence until their demands are met. The strike produces consequences outside the home, confusing and upsetting neighbors and teachers, but the boys are determined to suffer any punishment to stick to their vow.

Good Morning is not so much about the television itself as with the lack of communication it produces. As the boys' English teacher Fukui (Keiji Sada) puts it, they are the "lubrication of society," and when the boys stop talking—even to make unimportant conversation—reactions range from bemusement to misplaced hostility. Upon the inevitable delivery of the television, little Isamu (Masahiko Shimazu) immediately celebrates by grabbing that other 1950s icon of mindlessness: the Hula-Hoop. The boys all engage in another bit of amusing ritual of empty communication, the practice of which causes their pal Kozo to ruin quite a few pairs of pants! Director Yasujiro Ozu, nearing the end of a long career, favors the traditional Japanese tableau shots, which give a sense of balance to the fine ensemble cast. *AKA: Ohayo.* 🐕🐕🐕🦃

1959 94m/C *JP* Keiji Sada, Yoshiko Kuga, Chishu Ryu, Kuniko Miyake, Haruko Sugimura, Koji Shigaragi, Masahiko Shimazu, Kyoko Izumi, Toyo Takahashi, Sadako Sawamura, Eijiro Tono, Teruko Nagaoka, Eiko Miyoshi. *D:* Yasujiro Ozu. *W:* Kogo Noda, Yasujiro Ozu. *C:* Yushun Atsuta. *M:* Toshiro Mayazumi. **VHS, DVD**

Goodbye Mr. Cool

Lung (Ekin Cheng) gets out of prison in Thailand after serving a sentence for attempted kidnapping, and heads for Hong Kong, where his old friend Hong (Lam Suet) takes him in, giving him a job in his Kowloon Cafe. Lung used to be known as Brother Cool Nine Dragons, and all the gangs come around asking him to join up, but after seeing some rough times in prison, he's determined to go straight. He's a bit surprised to find a little boy left in the café calling him Dad— it seems his old girlfriend Helen (Karen Mok) was pregnant when he left for Thailand. Now she doesn't have any time for little Siu-lung, having since become a triad boss herself, and when she finds out that Lung has returned, she becomes determined to bring him back to a life of crime as her partner any way she can.

Just as Lung struggles to leave his old life behind, so Ekin Cheng struggles to grow beyond his pop-idol image, here taking the kind of role that once may have gone to Chow Yun-fat, and doing pretty well with it. The film is loaded down with a few too many sentimental flashbacks, but the honesty behind the characters helps gloss over any moments of sloppy melodrama. However, it sends a contradictory message—while trying to counteract the glorification of triads, they then go ahead and present triad life as cooler and more exciting than it's ever been in Cheng's *Young and Dangerous* movies. *AKA: Gau Lung Bing Sat; Jiu Long Bing Shi.* 🐕🐕🦃

2001 101m/C *HK* Ekin Cheng, Rain Li, Karen Mok, Huang Pin-yuan, Lam Suet, Jacky Lui, Chapman To, Stephanie Che, Tam Wai-ha. *D:* Jingle Ma. *W:* Yeung Sin-ling, Susan Chan. *C:* Jingle Ma, Wong Wai-chuen. *M:* Comfort Chan. **DVD**

Goose Boxer

The title sequence shows a goose blasting crap right in the face of overly inquisitive Phillip Ko, so it can't be all bad. (He gets his revenge by roasting the offender.) Gray-haired master Lung Tung Fung shows up at Master Nu's kung fu school, where his nephews pick a fight with the gambling students. He's looking for the man who killed his brother, Ma Tu Feng, using Crane Style. At their camp, the man called White Crested Crane (Lee Hoi Sang) finds two of them alone, joyfully killing them. Out of work after hooligans wreck his roast goose stand, Chin Po (Ko) witnesses the killing as he goes looking for work from Mr. Chan (Charles Heung). Siu Chan's kung fu school is going broke—his lone student is a feisty dwarf. He tries picking on a boy to get him to sign up as a student, and ends up getting in a fight with his brother Big Bear (Bolo Yeung). Some hints from Chin Po help him win.

Misreading his introduction letter, Chan thinks Chin is an "expert crane boxer" rather than a "goose roaster," so he makes the kid a teacher, and enthusiastically Chan issues a challenge to other area schools. Chin has developed his own style from watching his geese, and it actually helps him beat Master Nu. He also beats Lung's nephews when they come calling at night, so Lung has them enroll. Crazy White Crested Crane has read the challenge, too, and kidnaps Chin Po to teach him better kung fu. When his student balks at any more training, Crane kidnaps Chan as a hostage. Watching what his nephews have learned from Chin Po, Lung traces the style back to White Crested Crane.

After Crane kills Lung in a duel, Chin Po is determined to use the Fire Crane Style he's learned, combined with moves from one of

Chan's old secret kung fu manuals, to finish his Goose Fist Style and defeat Crane once and for all. Unfortunately, illiterate Chan has given him a sex manual by mistake!

Much of the running time is full of insufferable "comedy" music. If you can stand that, and the mostly lame gags, there's some fine Crane Style kung fu on display here. **AKA:** *Leung San Gwai Chiu; Liang Shan Guai Zhao.* ♫♫

1978 79m/C *HK* Charles Heung, Phillip Ko, Lee Hoi-sang, Tin Ching, Bolo Yeung. **D:** Tai See Fu. **W:** Cheung Hoi Ching. **C:** Lo Wan-shing. **M:** Chou Fu-liang. **VHS, DVD**

Gorgeous

After making *Rush Hour* in America, Jackie Chan went back to Hong Kong to make another picture for the Asian market. While exploring ideas for a third *Armor of God* picture, he met comedy veteran Vincent Kok (*Forbidden City Cop*), and decided to produce *Gorgeous* for him. During casting, it transformed into a starring vehicle for Jackie, with some fight scenes added to allay his lack of confidence about being accepted as a romantic lead.

On Fortune Shell Island, Taiwan, a girl named Bu (Shu Qi) finds a message in a bottle from a man looking for love. Wildly romantic, she follows the address to Hong Kong hoping to meet her soul mate, but instead finds fashion makeup artist Albert (Tony Leung Chiu-Wai), who wrote the message to an ex-boyfriend. Helping him out on a photo shoot, Bu sees millionaire playboy Nick Chan (Chan) attacked by hoods sent by his rival Howie Lo (Emil Chau), and goes to rescue him. To win his heart, she has Albert pretend to be a jealous mobster, with Bu his girlfriend, so Nick can rescue her from his "thugs" (actually Albert's friends). Since Lo's real thugs (Ken Lo, Vincent Kok, Tats Lau, and David Leung) can't beat Nick (whose hobby is kung fu), he hires Alan (Brad Allan), a tough-but-short fighter from overseas, to beat Nick up. Meanwhile, Bu's fiancé Louie (Richie Ren) comes looking for her, and has to be delayed by Albert.

Not as big a hit as his previous New Year's releases, *Gorgeous* is generally considered a failure by Chan's standards, and this has been attributed to him playing a romantic lead for the

Jackie Chan experiments in romance with Shu Qi in *Gorgeous.*
THE KOBAL COLLECTION

first time (though not because he's twice Shu Qi's age). This is ridiculous, as Jackie Chan is just fine as a leading man—funny, sensitive, and charming—and his fight scenes, especially his duels with Allan, are superb. But it's not a big-stunt action film like *First Strike,* and no one should expect as big a reaction. ***AKA:*** *Bor Lei Jun; Bo Lee Chun; Bo Li Zun; Loves of a Gorgeous Man.* ♫♫♫

1999 (PG-13) 99m/C *HK* Jackie Chan, Shu Qi, Tony Leung Chiu-Wai, Emil Chau, Brad Allan, Richie Ren, Chan Chung-Yung, Ken Lo, Vincent Kok, Tats Lau, David Leung. ***D:*** Vincent Kok. ***W:*** Vincent Kok, Jackie Chan, Andy Law. ***C:*** Cheung Man-po. ***M:*** Dannie Wong. **VHS, DVD**

Grave of the Fireflies

 Kobe, Japan, during World War II. Having learned that their father has died in the fighting overseas, young Seita and his little sister Setsuko are doing their best to cope. Then there's another air raid, and their mother is killed in the firebombing. They turn to other relatives for help, but that hope doesn't last too long. Finally, they flee to the mountains, hoping that they'll stand a better chance of surviving far from civilization. They end up living in a cave as winter sets in. Slowly, inevitably, the hunger, cold, illness, and hallucination eat away at the two little innocents.

This is not the first telling of the aftermath of the bombing of Japan through cartoons. Keiji Nakazawa's autobiographical *Barefoot Gen* comics and films are probably the best, and best known. But *Grave of the Fireflies* is by far the most heartbreaking. In fact, it's so sad as to defeat the intended purpose. Long after the message "War Is Bad" has been delivered, the film continues to torture the characters—and the viewer—with one depressing event after another. Based on a novel by Akiyuki Nosaka *(The Amorists),* it's a very well made and effective film, but it's not one that makes you glad you've seen it. Director Isao Takahata followed with the less heavy-handed ecological message film *The Raccoon War.* Recommended for viewers who may feel they've been a bit too giddy lately. Keep the tissues handy—you'll need 'em. All others are served fair warning: this is not one of those zany, wacky Japanimation movies about aliens and robots in high school you've been wanting to check out. ***AKA:*** *Hotaru no Haka; Tombstone for Fireflies.* ♫♫♫

1988 (PG) 93m/C *JP* ***V:*** Tsutomu Tatsumi, Ayano Shiraishi, Yoshiko Shinohara. ***D:*** Isao Takahata. ***W:*** Isao Takahata. ***M:*** Yoshio Mamiya. **VHS, DVD**

Great Performances: Kurosawa

This special documentary overview of the great Japanese director Akira Kurosawa's life and films was originally presented in America on public television. Narrated by actor/writer Sam Shepard, it begins with the honorary Academy Award presented to Kurosawa, by Steven Spielberg and George Lucas in 1990, and then continues with his childhood experiences, including his eyewitness account of the great Tokyo earthquake and fires of the 1920s. Much of the script comes from Kurosawa's autobiography, read by actor Paul Scofield. Another possible influence is proposed as Akira's older brother Hago, who became a theatre narrator (bensho) and family black sheep, until his early suicide. Akira followed in Hago's footsteps in some ways, becoming a scandalous bohemian artist in the 1930s, until he got a job as an assistant director by PCL Studios—soon to be Toho—in 1937. We get a glimpse of the propaganda films he made during the war, until the atomic bombs dropped. In a way, the seven-year occupation was fortuitous for Kurosawa, granting him a creative freedom he'd never known before, leading to his most interesting film to that point, *Drunken Angel,* which first teamed him with actor Toshiro Mifune.

The film tries to do the usual documentary things in creative ways, interviewing co-workers and families as they watch a specific scene on video, the medium on which Kurosawa's films are seen almost exclusively these days. The *Rashomon* cast and crew returns to the scene of the crime in Kyoto, rather senselessly, it turns out. It's interesting to note that as his films gained success with foreign audiences, there was a backlash among critics back at home who felt he must not be Japanese enough (and thus inferior), or that film-festival judges were rewarding only the "exotic" quality of the films. James Coburn is interviewed because he was in the *Seven Samurai* remake. Clint Eastwood is interviewed because he was in the *Yojimbo* remake.

The last 25 years of Kurosawa's life, as presented at least, were very depressing—*Red Beard* took two years to make and led to his break with Mifune. His work on *Tora! Tora! Tora!* was aborted. His independent films were not very successful. There was a suicide attempt, work for hire on whiskey ads, etc. The documentary strives more for emotion than completeness, or even detail. It ignores "lesser" films, which aren't even mentioned *(Stray Dog, High and Low, I Live in Fear),* and treats the director almost as if he operated in a vacuum, failing to give a cultural environment to his work. Perhaps two hours is just far too little time to cover Kurosawa properly—or perhaps he lived his life mainly through his films, making a dramatic arc tough to find—but surely they could have made something a bit more interesting. It gives only a sketch of the artist and his work, wasting time with repeated footage (the same scene from *Seven Samurai* appears three times) and empty images. 🐉🐲

2002 115m/C *US/JP* **N:** Sam Shepard. Andy Lau. **D:** Adam Low. **W:** Adam Low. **C:** Dewald Aukema. **M:** Fratelli Brothers. **VHS, DVD**

The Green Dragon Inn

Often mistaken for a remake of King Hu's *Dragon Gate Inn* (which also stars Polly Shang Kwan), this Ming Dynasty epic mixes great swordplay and kung fu in a classic action story. When young rascal Hung Bing-chung murders a whole Chang family in cold blood, his father Warlord Hung Jan-kui is determined to protect him from the law, and sends men to fetch him from the brothel. Marshal Au Yang (Yueh Hua), the Bold Dragon, is sent to arrest Hung, but barely gets a chance to read the warrant before crossing swords with bounty hunter Leung Kung-mang (Lo Lieh), the Silent Tracker. Au coolly dispatches the warlord's men and arrests Hung Bingchung, and the elder Hung responds by sending Iron Fist Master Fung Kong and the Four Assassins to rescue his son. The governor lends Au 30 men to help escort the prisoner to the capitol for trial. The most difficult part of the journey (as the governor explains using a pretty pink map of their route) will surely be passing through Green Dragon Town, which is controlled completely by Warlord Hung. Au loses most of his men in an ambush on the way to Green Dragon Town, and finds that Hung's men have taken control of the inn on arrival. But Leung is already there and offers them his suite to use. The soldiers soon find themselves under siege within the Green Dragon Inn. Joined by Leung and swordswoman Chang Yin (Polly Shang Kwan), a niece of the murdered Chang seeking vengeance, Au comes up with a plan to escape the inn and make a dash for the capitol with their prisoner.

A fine-tuned engine that chugs from one thrill to the next, *Green Dragon Inn* suffers only from underdeveloped characters. But then, there's rarely time to sketch in some background for everybody while the action continues. It's also marked by some surprisingly brutal violence, with the dynamic Polly Shang Kwan lopping a few heads off and Yueh Hua making a foe swallow his sword. The besieged soldiers outfit the lobby of the inn with a variety of deadly booby traps (where did they get all those swords?), which skewer or slice whoever charges in. The fight scenes are very good as well, whether fought with swords or fists. Lo Lieh seems to be having a particularly good time in this movie, perhaps because he was entering a time when he was only offered villainous roles, and it felt good to be running with the heroes again. *AKA: Bruce Is Loose.* 🐉🐉🐉🐲

1979 (PG) 94m/C *TW* Yueh Hua, Lo Lieh, Polly Shang Kwan, Sze Ma Lung, Paul Chang, Lan Ki, Wong Chung, So Kwok-leung. **D:** Wu Ming Hung. **VHS, DVD**

asians in usa

The Green Hornet

Bruce Lee received his first flash of fame as a supporting player in this spin-off from the *Batman* TV series. The Green Hornet was originally a spin-off in another medium: radio. George W. Trendle created the show as a modern-day version of his hit program *The Lone Ranger.* Newspaperman Brett Reed (Van Williams), the grandnephew of the Lone Ranger, donned a mask to fight crime with an arsenal of gimmicks. As was common for many pulp heroes of the day, the Hornet maintained an outlaw image, hunted by both sides of the law. While the Lone Ranger had Tonto, Reed was assisted by his Japanese valet, Kato (who suddenly became Filipino during World War II!), played by Bruce Lee. The Green Hornet also appeared in movie serials and comic books. With *Batman* a gigantic hit, producer William Dozier thought it quite natural to try to reproduce their success with another superhero—only this time, they would play things more-or-less straight, and the episodes would not be split into two nights like *Batman.* Though the show wasn't very successful in the States (Bat-backlash had begun), it was a huge smash in Asia, where it played as *The Kato Show* to an audience overjoyed to see one of their own as a star in Hollywood. Theatres hungry for more Lee after his death were glad to play this feature edited together from several different episodes of the TV series.

Someone is killing off racketeers around town using unusual primitive weapons. The Green Hornet's informant, Mel Herk, says he has a copy of the Hit List, but is killed before he can hand it over. Behind the slayings are members of the Explorers Club, who've decided to hunt criminals instead of animals...and the Hornet is next on the list. But one of the members, Quentin Crane (Charles Bateman), has in mind stepping in as crime boss once the competition is eliminated. No sooner do they get the Explorers mob mopped up, than Reed is confronted

with a new menace: threatening aliens from outer space! The supposed crash survivors want Reed to use his TV station to tell folks to stay away from the shiny-suited visitors, threatening widespread destruction if he refuses. Of course, the "aliens" are fakes, led by the evil Dr. Mabuse (Larry D. Mann), who is after an H-bomb warhead. The highlight of this section is surely the buxom alien Vama (Linda Gaye Scott), wearing a tight gold suit and firing lightning bolts from her hands. Once Mabuse is captured, the Green Hornet and Kato head to Chinatown to bust up a protection racket headed by Lo Sing (Mako). Bruce gets to tangle with the mantis kung fu master in this segment. Gary Owens has a cameo as a news announcer.

As might be expected in such a situation, the condensation of stories results in some choppy editing and poor continuity. But at least this gives you more Lee and less filler. Al Hirt's trumpet playing on the theme music is always worth a listen. The video contains a nice 14-minute featurette on the Green Hornet's gadget-stuffed battlewagon, the Black Beauty. **AKA:** *The Kato Show.* 🎵🎵

1974 83m/C *US* Van Williams, Bruce Lee, Wende Wagner, Lloyd Gough, Walter Brooke, Mako, Larry D. Mann, Charles Bateman, Linda Gaye Scott, Al Huang, Lang Yun, Tom Drake, Gary Owens, Allen Jung, Arthur Batanides. **D:** William Beaudine, Darrel Hallenbeck, Norman Foster. **W:** Charles Hoffman, Jerry Thomas, Art Weingarten, Ken Pettus. **C:** Carl Guthrie. **M:** Bill May. **VHS, DVD**

Green Snake

With this latest version of the much-filmed Chinese legend of Madame White Snake, Tsui Hark attempted to combine the neo-swordplay genre he'd helped revive with the more romantic and fantastic elements of his *Chinese Ghost Story* movies.

Green (Maggie Cheung) and White (Joey Wong) are sister were-snakes. White spies on timid scholar Hsui-xien (Wu Hsing-kuo) and falls in love with him. Taking human form, she attempts to have a relationship with him, but though she tries her best to fit in with humans, her attempt is doomed to failure. Green interferes with the wooing, and when she's unable to maintain her human form, Hsui-xien dies from the shock of the accidental revelation. The sisters go on a quest seeking a rare herb that will bring him back to life. Up to now, the demon hunter Fa-hai (Vincent Zhao) has left the snake sisters alone due to their good record of helping mankind. But their recent activities causes him to change his mind and decide to hunt the were-snakes down.

For the most part, Tsui succeeds wonderfully in bringing to life a world of semi-devils on the outer limits of human consciousness, abetted greatly by terrific camera work and excellent music. One would be tempted to call this a fairy tale, if not for the strong erotic themes. Wong and Cheung are very good as the slinky, sensual snakes, and Wong's comedy stands out in scenes where she goes too far to try to pass for human. Unfortunately, the ambitions of the script are a bit beyond the reach of the f/x department budget—a factor intensified when the film had to be rushed to completion to meet its release date—and some shots destroy the mood with their obvious fakery. **AKA:** *Ching Se; Qing She; White Snake, Green Snake; Blue Snake.* 🎵🎵🎵♡

1993 98m/C *HK* Maggie Cheung, Joey Wong, Vincent Zhao, Wu Hsing-kuo, Tin Fung, Lau Kong. **D:** Tsui Hark. **W:** Tsui Hark. **C:** Ko Chiu-lam. **M:** James Wong, Mark Lui. **VHS, DVD**

Guardian Angel

Yukari Oshima toplines this Poverty Row Girls with Guns action yarn, but here she's quickly pushed aside to feature a Filipino cop more prominently, and he in turn takes a backseat to the adventures of his Interpol agent girlfriend! Manila cop Robin (Ricky Davao) is out to bust Julius Haley, the criminal behind the drug ring that killed his brother. When his Interpol agent girlfriend Rosa is killed, too, Robin is ordered on leave for his own protection. But Rosa is actually alive, being forced to go to Taiwan on a secret mission by her superior Chan (Tai Bo), who saved her life—the assassination of a key Japanese drug syndicate figure. Her target sounds an alarm before he dies, but fortunately Rosa's fellow agents Candy and Lisa are there to back her up.

Her next target (dancing Dick Wei) is easier—he's only a karate champion. She's forced to continue killing her way up the ladder to gang boss Kwan. But Kwan is obviously working with someone else, and a mysterious guy named David seems to be tailing the girls. Meanwhile, Robin trades some evidence he's collected to Hong Kong cops Carl (Phillip Ko) and Sharon (Yukari Oshima), who are in charge of his case, in exchange for letting him be in on their operations. But Robin's info turns out to be faulty, and it almost gets them killed—plus Haley has hired some tough Thai killers to rub him out.

Despite an obviously low budget, Phillip Ko shows *some* imagination as a director, giving the film a little extra value. He cuts from a shot of a thug reading porn to the guy next to him

Bruce Lee stars as Kato in the 1960s TV series *The Green Hornet,* while sidekick Van Williams looks on. THE KOBAL COLLECTION

polishing his gun. An open-air stairway chase scene pulls back for a shot of runners and pursuers on different floors. There are also a lot of recognizable faces in smaller roles. Little things like that help to spice things up, even when conditions aren't ideal. The photography and sound departments don't do him any favors. The whole movie has a homemade quality, and poor continuity causes a lot of problems (especially with the concurrent plotlines), as characters we're supposed to already know turn up mid-picture, props move around between shots, etc. Perhaps the available version is missing some scenes, but several gratuitous sex scenes are left in, one of which contains a shot of a girl's face that lasts nearly two minutes. The action scenes are exciting and well executed, but they can't save the picture from the predictable (albeit unusual) disjointed story and uneven editing. *AKA:* Yue Gui Zhi Lang. 🐉🐉

1996 87m/C *HK/PH/TW* Yukari Oshima, Phillip Ko, Ricky Davao, Dick Wei, Wilson Wang, Tai Bo. *D:* Phillip Ko. *W:* Phillip Ko. *C:* Bobby Junior. **VHS, DVD**

Guinea Pig: Android of Notre Dame

Re-released as *Guinea Pig 2* by the series' new label JHV, this was actually the sixth entry of the series to be filmed. Little-person scientist Dr. Karazawa (Toshihiko Hino) desperately needs one thing to complete his cybernetic genome research for the Haidon Corporation, which he hopes will help his terminally ill sister (Mio Takagi) before she dies. The answer comes from a mysterious blackmailer who calls himself Kato (Tomoro Taguchi), who agrees to provide him with a 21-year-old human corpse to experiment on, for a hefty fee. In intimate detail, we witness his attempt to reanimate his Guinea Pig (Mirei), only to fail. Kato appears again with a fresh proposal, which he forces Karazawa to accept by infecting his computers with a virus. He wants the scientist to kill someone for him, in return for some data vital to Karazawa's research. The dwarf turns the tables on the blackmailer, springing a trap on him. He keeps only Kato's head, which he re-animates to force him to provide the data, and threatens Kato's partner Keiko (Yumi Iori) as well.

Routine horror-movie techniques such as a dream sequence only serve to make this entry more like an ordinary genre offering. Horror movie–regular Taguchi's repellant performance and makeup as the rapidly deteriorating head are probably the best things about it, though the video format cheapens everything, making it look like a very unusual soap opera. As usual,

the camera lingers over every bit of bloody gore in loving close-up. *AKA:* Zu Ginipiggu 2: Notre Dame no Android; Guinea Pig 2. 🐉🐉

1988 52m/C *JP* Toshihiko Hino, Mio Takagi, Yumi Iori, Tomoro Taguchi, Mirei. *D:* Kazuhito Kuramoto. *W:* Kazuhito Kuramoto, Mitsuo Mitsuki, Yoshikazu Iwanami, Kenji Tani (story), Satoru Ogura (story). *C:* Kazuhito Kuramoto. *M:* Kit Cut Club. **DVD**

Guinea Pig: Devil's Experiment

In 1985, producer Satoru Ogura and horror manga artist Hideshi Hino designed a film calculated to give fans of intensely graphic horror films something that truly delivered the goods. The basic premise is the same one that briefly made American productions like Roberta and Michael Findley's *Snuff* and *Last House on Dead End Street* minor sensations: real death on screen, later exposed as fake.

Devil's Experiment is supposedly just such a snuff film, labeled as an experiment in finding the limits of endurance. Ogura initially claimed he was sent the tape anonymously, and turned it over to the police before releasing it. Later, it was labeled a re-creation of the original tape. It's about as plotless as a carnival funhouse. Three men are shown binding a woman (played by a very brave—or stupid—actress) to a chair and beating her. Titles in the corner of the screen label the type of abuse, and occasionally offer the score. They also inflict pain with tools and use more esoteric tortures such as spinning her around in a chair, subjecting her to harsh noises, and making her drink Jack Daniels (there are a few prominent product placements that the manufacturers might not appreciate). When the Guinea Pig loses consciousness, she's hung in a net from a tree, until she wakes up for a round of even more intense torture. At times it appears that she's a masochist whose fetish has been taken too far. She's scalded with oil, has maggots and entrails dropped on her, and finally is subjected to more permanent damage.

The video reveals itself almost immediately as a fake. Real criminals—or giggling "scientists"—would be unlikely to shoot and edit a film using artistic angles, subliminal cuts, and other atmospheric touches. Though no credits are given, a continuation of the promotional gimmick, it's been widely assumed that Hino was the director. The celebrated special makeup effects are rather limited, consisting only of a few well-crafted phony body parts. As entertainment, its audience may be limited. There's not much that could be labeled "enjoyable," except to those of highly peculiar tastes—significantly, the running time is equivalent to most porn videos. As a work of art, its formal structure as a catalog of horrors and the techniques used to build suspense, make it worthwhile. But the film's greatest value is probably as a piece of pop culture, made legendary by the rumors and journalist shrillness that have surrounded it since it was first released. Filmed back to back with *Guinea Pig: Flower of Flesh and Blood*. **AKA:** *Zu Ginipiggu; Akuma no Jikken; Unabridged Agony; Guinea Pig.* 🐷🐷🐷

1985 43m/C *JP* **DVD**

Guinea Pig: Flower of Flesh and Blood

The second and most notorious of the Guinea Pig films to be released, this is the title people are usually talking about when they discuss the series. Like its predecessor *Devil's Experiment*, the film was advertised as a video re-creation of an actual 8mm snuff film, this time sent directly to cartoonist Hideshi Hino by "a fan"—though the re-creation proceeds in more traditional narrative fashion than any home movie.

A young woman (Kirara Yugao) is abducted while walking home from a train station. She awakens bound to a cot in a blood-spattered chamber. Her abductor is a man wearing a samurai helmet (Hiroshi Tamura), who gives her a preview of her fate by cutting the head off a chicken. Then, with his cameras in place, and the woman kept in a painless and euphoric state with drugs, the samurai begins a systematic dismemberment of his victim. Finally, he shows off items from his gruesome collection.

Loosely based on Hino's manga story "Akai Hana," *Flower of Flesh and Blood* lives up to its reputation as a hard-core shock show, and is as repellent as one would anticipate. It cuts right to the chase—then gets past the chase to its slaughterhouse main event as soon as possible. At best, it's an extremely graphic update of the old magic illusion of sawing a woman in half—as harmless as the old Herschell Gordon Lewis gore films of the 1960s. At worst, it's dull gore porn for the morbidly obsessed. For the average horror fan, it represents a landmark in the cheap shot of the genre: the gross-out. Though often rightfully complemented on the realism of its special makeup effects, it's fairly obvious that they're all very well-done fakes. Even the chicken decapitation—which could just as well have been real—is clearly phony, since director Hino was far too squeamish to harm a real animal. Still, it attains its goal of unsettling the viewer. The end titles run over what look like effects test shots on 8mm, and show that the film might have been far more effective shot that way rather than on clear and cold videotape. **AKA:** *Chiniku no Hana; Za Ginipiggu 3; Guinea Pig 2.* 🐷🐷

1985 42m/C *JP* Hiroshi Tamura, Kirara Yugao. **D:** Hideshi Hino. **W:** Hideshi Hino, Nobuaki Koga. **C:** Junko Okamoto. **M:** Kit Cut Club. **DVD**

Guinea Pig: He Never Dies

While the first two Guinea Pig movies were pretty much only straightforward pseudo-snuff films, the entries that followed became more oriented toward stories and characters, and Japan Home Video became the new distributor. *He Never Dies* cleverly inverts the premise of the earlier entries by presenting a tale of *self*-torture and mutilation, injecting it with a welcome dose of humor. A host named Rick Steinberger introduces the story—though he's supposed to appear like the host of a Fortean phenomena documentary program, he looks more like an insurance agent discussing flood protection. He tells the "true" tale of Hideshi (Masahiro Sato), a meek Tokyo office drone who lives in a filthy one-room basement apartment. In an agony of boredom, Hideshi stays home from work for three days (nobody notices), and in a delirium, slashes open his wrist with a razor. To his surprise, after a few moments the bleeding and pain stops completely. Experimentally, he jabs a pen through his forearm, again without pain. Distressed, he chops off the hand completely and even slices into his throat, but is disappointed to find that he cannot be killed. Strangling doesn't work either. A failure at suicide, Hideshi calls co-worker Elvis Nakamura (Keisuke Araki) over to scare him. Elvis's girlfriend Kyoko (Eve) goes looking for him and is shocked—at the *mess* Hideshi has made disemboweling himself, and gets Elvis to help her clean up the place. Full of wry laughs and decent shocks, those who can stomach it should find this black comedy worthwhile. Sato gives a solid performance while pulling himself apart. The end credits play back some of the gore effects in reverse! Star Masahiro Sato is the leader of the adults-only comedy troupe Waha-ha Honpo. **AKA:** *Za Ginipiggu 8: Senritsui! Shinanai Otoko; Guinea Pig 3: Terror! Immortal Man.* 🐷🐷

1986 41m/C *JP* Masahiro Sato, Keisuke Araki, Eve. **D:** Masayuki Kuzumi. **W:** Masayuki Kuzumi, Noritaka Okamato (story). **DVD**

Guinea Pig: Mermaid in a Manhole

After it was revealed that a murderer may have copied some of the crimes portrayed in the Guinea Pig tapes, producer Satoru Ogura took

advantage of the media uproar by releasing more entries in the series. Cartoonist Hideshi Hino contributed what is considered the series' artistic high point, based on his own manga story.

Lonely painter Hayashi (Shigeru Saiki of *Audition*) goes to a sewer for inspiration, sketching objects he finds there and recalling when there was a river there. On one visit, he's surprised to find a mermaid (Mari Somei). She tells him (telepathically) of how she was stranded there when the river dried up, and he sees that living in the sewage is infecting her. Hayashi takes her home with him and keeps her in a new bathtub to recover, and so he can paint her. However, her infected sore grows and multiplies, hemorrhaging frequently. The painter brings her fresh fish and medicine, but the sores continue to spread. The mermaid seems even more determined that he complete paintings of her than he is, insisting he use the different colored pus from her sores as tints. Before long, the spreading tumors cover her whole body, and sprout ever-larger worms. Finally, she begs him to put her out of her misery, but when nosy neighbors (Go Rijyu and Masami Hisamoto) come calling they find quite a shocking scene.

Hino creates a terror tale that is both grotesque and lyrical, incorporating the medical horrors of David Cronenberg, the alien nightmares of H.P. Lovecraft, and the snake-spewing gross-outs of Chinese black-magic movies. The fantasy setting makes its repellent f/x (by Nobuaki Koga) easier to take, and it's obvious that the prosthetics don't go far below the water line. Sure, the blood and gore make one uneasy, but the real discomfort here is the hardship of caring for a terminally ill loved one. It's not exactly what one expects from a series that aims for shock above all other goals. **AKA:** *Za Ginnipiggu: Manhoru no Naka no Ningyo; Guinea Pig 4.* ♫♫♫ ♢

1988 57m/C *JP* Shigeru Saiki, Mari Somei, Go Rijyu, Masami Hisamoto. **D:** Hideshi Hino. **W:** Hideshi Hino. **C:** Naoki Hayashi. **M:** Kit Cut Club. **DVD**

Guinea Pig: The Making of Guinea Pig

To allay any suspicions from those naïve enough to think that the first three *Guinea Pig* films thus far released were in any way real, the producers put out this behind-the-scenes video. It shows clips from the films, and then shows how the special makeup effects were achieved for the films by artist Nobuaki Koga, including subtitles that give an ingredients list of materials used for specific effects. Some footage is devoted to interviewing the actors and directors about their

roles, concepts, and motivations, but the main focus is on technical matters. There are also some funny outtakes and bloopers, and even a deleted scene. It ends with shots of the cast and crew of *He Never Dies* going out to dinner together. The overall effect is sometimes even more bizarre than the actual films—in the lengthy segment devoted to filming *He Never Dies,* star Masahiro Sato is shown repeatedly hacking at a prosthetic wrist meant to portray his own, and can't help squeamishly saying, "Owww!" each time the blade goes down. It's a must for fans of the series, and anyone interested in special-effects makeup. **AKA:** *Mekingu Obu Za Ginipiggu.* ♫♫♫ ♢

1986 44m/C *JP* Hideshi Hino, Nobuaki Koga, Masayuki Kizumi, Kirara Yugao, Toshiki Hino, Masahiro Sato, Eve, Hiroshi Tamura, Yumi Iori. **D:** Junko Okamoto. **C:** Junko Okamoto, Naoki Hayashi. **DVD**

Gumnaam

During the early 1990s, a tape circulated around American college campuses, independent record stores, cartoonists, and anywhere strange video could be seen. It was a wild rocking musical number clipped from a 1960s Indian film, and it later received much wider exposure in the film *Ghost World*. But few knew where it came from: the first real mystery horror film made in India. At least it was billed that way—there had been some gothic romances à la *Jane Eyre* produced as early as the 1940s. But *Gumnaam,* a follow-up to producer N.N. Sippy's *Woh Kaun Thi?,* was something of an experiment in a country that even now tends to hide their horror films, combining the usual music, comedy, and romance with the kind of Old Dark House chills familiar in America since the 1920s.

That energetic production number is incredible—"Jaan Pehchan," performed by Ted Lyon and his Cubs at the Princess Club, to celebrate their silver jubilee—and it's the first thing seen after the credits, but the rest of the film has a lot to offer as well. Before that, we've already seen two murders. A man named Sohanlal is run down in the street outside Hotel Metropole at the order of Khanna, who is shot dead by a mystery man. The club gives away a vacation to seven lucky winners that night: Sohanlal's alcoholic barrister Rakesh (Pran), pudgy Mr. Dharamdas (Dhumal), Mr. Kishan (Manmohan), Sohanlal's sexy secretary Miss Kitty (Helen), Dr. Acharya (Madan Puri), bearded Madhusudan Sharma (Tarun Bose), and Sohanlal's niece Asha (Nanda). Due to a technical problem, their chartered flight is forced to make a landing—but the plane takes off as soon as the passengers and steward Anand (Manoj Kumar) disembark, leaving them stranded on an island! They make their way to a beautiful but creepy mansion, inhabited only by the oddball servant (comic star Mahmood), who has been expecting them. They're all made quite comfortable, except for being trapped by some unknown party, who has left a note calling them all murderers and sentencing them to death. The next night, Kishan is found stabbed to death, and while clues and suspicions fly about, the remaining guests are picked off one by one.

Yes, it's another version of Agatha Christie's classic *Ten Little Indians,* this time with real Indians! It's quite effective as a suspense picture, with some gorgeous settings and spooky cinematography. However, the tension dissipates almost completely each time a musical number begins, and the film uses its length to reestablish a threatening mood in time for the big climax. Nothing can match the insanity of that first number, but a zany fantasy song and dance with Mahmood and Helen comes close. *AKA: Nameless.* ♫♫♫

1965 143m/C *IN* Manoj Kumar, Nanda, Mahmood, Helen, Pran, Madan Puri, Dhumal, Hiralal, Tarun Bose, Manmohan, Naina, Laxmi Chayya. *D:* Raja Nawathe. *W:* Charandas Shokh, Dhruva Chatterjee. *C:* K.H, Kapadia. *M:* Shankar Jaikishan. **DVD**

Gunhed

Giant "mecha" stories about massive, semi-intelligent robots and the brave humans who drive them are a staple of Japanese manga and anime, but the technical challenge of portraying these spectacular vehicles has kept them out of Japanese live-action movies for the most part. One interesting exception to this rule is *Gunhed,* a *Bladerunner*-esque adventure film about a team of mercenaries who infiltrate a gargantuan, mechanized island in order to retrieve technology left over from an earlier war that left machines in control. The movie is a heavy-metal visual wonderland: the mercenaries travel to the island of Kyron-5 in an aircraft that looks like a WWII B-17 with jet engines, and Kyron-5 itself looks something like the hulking space colony of James Cameron's *Aliens* crossed with the awe-inspiring underground Krell city from *Forbidden Planet.* The rogue's gallery of mercenaries dodge hovering sentries that look like bisecting almonds, while the lumbering Gunhed itself—a leftover from the previous war—is a hybrid of every mechanical war machine from Gundam to Macross Plus.

After most of the mercenaries are cut down by the mechanical island's defenses, only young mechanic Brooklyn (Masahiro Takashima) and "Texas Ranger" Lt. Nim (Brenda Bakke, who played Lana Turner in *L.A. Confidential*) remain

to team up with the lumbering Gunhed and a lost child. Once Gunhed is engaged it takes on the island's mechanical defenses and war machines in a series of spectacular miniature engagements. One of the coolest aspects of the movie is its refreshing three-dimensionality where action is concerned: missiles travel up and down gigantic, slanted corridors and immense open spaces shrouded in darkness, giving the impression of a limitless subterranean world. It's also just novel watching machinery and action normally seen strictly in cel-animated form done live action. Gunhed is also a satisfyingly redemptive character itself, nicely voiced by actor Randy Reyes. Intended as an international bilingual film, director/writer Harada had his name taken off of the dubbed U.S. version. —*JB* **AKA:** *Ganheddo.* ♫♫♫

1989 (R) 92m/C *JP* **V:** Randy Reyes. Masahiro Takashima, Brenda Bakke, James Brewster Thompson, Aya Enyoki, Yujin Harada, Yosuke Saito. *D:* Masato Harada. *W:* Masato Harada. *C:* Junichi Fujisawa. *M:* Toshiyuki Honda. **VHS**

Gunmen

Inspired by the U.S. feature *The Untouchables,* this Tsui Hark production paints a detailed portrait of roaring '20s Shanghai within the confines of a cops-and-robbers thriller. Ding Chun-bee (Tony Leung) returns from war to become a cop in the city. Though the distraction of beautiful informant Mona Fong (Elizabeth Lee) threatens his marriage to Chu-chiao (Carrie Ng), Ding becomes quite the crime-buster. His efforts to arrest crime kingpin Haye (Adam Cheng) are threatened by corruption within his department that spoils several raids, and Haye even shoots Ding's partner Kiang. When a tough superintendent (Elvis Tsui) takes over and insists on discipline, it only interferes with Ding's work more, and he finds the city's corruption overwhelming. His fortunes change when he runs into his old army mates Captain Ching (Waise Lee), Kwong (Mark Cheng), and Fan (David Wu) working as rickshaw drivers. He quickly recruits them as cops, and the four of them start busting up Haye's opium racket. But when their efforts to arrest Haye delay his shipment of pharmaceuticals long enough that it causes the death of his Uncle Liang, the mobsters don their old army uniforms to declare war on the cops.

As long as director Kirk Wong keeps the plot and action rolling, the film has a wonderful atmosphere and energy, while melodramatic scenes drag the pace whenever they appear. Efforts to reproduce the time period even extend to some simple but effective matte shots. Action director Bruce Law turns in some stunning work,

including some breathtaking fire stunts, and the same sort of raw gun battles and fights featured in Wong's other films. **AKA:** *Tin Law Dei Mong; Tian Lung Di Wang; Dragnet.* ♫♫♫♪

1988 84m/C *HK* Tony Leung Ka-Fai, Waise Lee, Mark Cheng, David Wu, Adam Cheng, Elizabeth Lee, Carrie Ng, Elvis Tsui, Wong Kam-Kong, Andrew Kam, Yuen Bun, Wong Hung. **D:** Kirk Wong. **W:** Law Kam-fai, Lip Wan-fung. **C:** Ardy Lam, Andrew Lau. **M:** Danny Chung. **VHS, DVD**

The H-Man

This is the first of Toho Studios' "altered human" horror pictures, which mixed film noir crime movie elements with science fiction to form a sort of modern gothic. Inspired by the American film *The Blob*, this is the best of the lot. Police are stumped when gangster Misaki (Hisayo Ito) disappears in the middle of a busy Tokyo street, leaving only his clothes. While Inspector Tominaga (Akihiko Hirata) and his men investigate, more people disappear in the same fashion. Young scientist Dr. Masada (Kenji Sahara), doing research into the effects of radioactivity, comes forth with an incredible theory: the victims are being dissolved by formerly human creatures that have been turned into protoplasmic monsters by exposure to H-bomb radiation. He takes Tominaga to a hospital, where sailors tell of being attacked by ghostly blob men on a deserted ship. Masada then demonstrates how to dissolve a frog with radiation, which in turn dissolves other frogs. Though the police are slow to accept it, his theory turns out to be true, and the sewers beneath the city are infested with the oozing, ghostly monsters.

Genuinely creepy f/x highlight this mixture of two commonly underrated genres of Japanese cinema—science fiction and gangster drama. Though director Ishiro Honda was famous for his giant monster sagas (*Mothra, War of the Gargantuas,* and many others), he was also adept at these less epic chillers. While his *Godzilla* embodied fears of massive nuclear destruction, *H-Man* was based on the other side of atomic horror—that of radioactivity and genetic mutation. The sequence with the sailors was based on the famous *Lucky Dragon* fishing-boat incident, also touched on in *Godzilla*. Just 13 years before, the atomic bombs really did turn people into wandering, dying zombies with melted flesh, and the idea of radiation transforming humans into oozing inhuman ghosts was especially terrifying to the Japanese. And as rendered by Eiji Tsuburaya's ghastly f/x, pretty scary for everyone else as well. The U.S. version is missing about eight minutes. **AKA:** *Bijo to Ekitai-nigen; Beauty and the Liquidman.* ♫♫♫

1958 80m/BW *JP* Kenji Sahara, Yumi Shirakawa, Akihiko Hirata, Yoshio Tsuchiya, Koreya Senda, Yoshibumi Tajima, Yosuke Natsuki, Makoto Sato, Eitaro Ozawa, Kamayuki Tsubouchi, Minosuke Yamada, Tadao Nakamaru, Akira Yamada, Ayumi Sonoda, Akira Sera, Yasuhiro Shigenobu, Miki Hayashi, Mitsuo Tsuda, Akio Kusama, Nadao Kirino, Shin Otomo, Ko Mishima, Hisaya Ito, Tetsu Nakamura, Yutaka Nakayama, Senkichi Omura, Shigeo Kato, Haruo Nakajima. **D:** Ishiro Honda. **W:** Hideo Kaijo. **C:** Hajime Koizumi. **M:** Masaru Sato. **VHS**

Hail the Judge

Made as a follow-up of sorts to his hit *Justice, My Foot,* this Stephen Chow comedy, directed by Wong Jing, mines laughs in a similar Old China courtroom setting. Pao Lung-sing (Chow) reaches his lifetime goal of becoming a Canton magistrate, but his aged father cautions him not to become a corrupt official like himself. He blames his dishonest ways for the deaths of Sing's 12 elder brothers, and gave his wealth to charity on retirement to make amends. But with lawyers like tricky "Mirror" Fong Tong-kan (Lawrence Ng) out-thinking him every day, Sing finds it difficult to remain honest and his popularity is so low that he has difficulty showing his face in public.

The tide turns when Sing visits a wedding at the Chi house, which is disrupted by fierce Constable Panther Lui Pao (Elvis Tsui) making arrests there. Panther accuses the host of harboring the fugitives, blackmailing him for a bribe. In order to keep the bribe for himself, Sing tricks Panther into a trap, earning the gratitude of the Chi family. But after the wedding, a guest named Shang Wai (Ngai Sing) murders all 13 members of the family, leaving only new bride Chi Siu-lin (Sharla Cheung) as a survivor. Sing is determined to convict the heinous killer—especially since he has a crush on Siu-lin—but as the accused is the son of navy commander Shang Kwan (Ku Feng), and the godson of powerful eunuch Li Lin-ying (Lau Shun), forces are already conspiring to free the killer. Their lawyer Fong spreads money around, gets Sing suspended and jailed, and turns Siu-lin from victim to being convicted of the murders herself. Sing escapes from jail, and is determined to get to the capitol to plead the case before the emperor himself (Gabriel Wong). However, Shang arranges for Panther to get away, too, assured that the ferocious warrior will track down Sing to get revenge.

Masahiro Takashima finds technology outgrowing puny humans in *Gunhed.*
THE KOBAL COLLECTION / TOHO

The actions of the villains are so horrible, including a scene where guards beat Sharla Cheung bloody, that the movie almost drifts beyond the bounds of comedy, but this only serves to make it more delicious when the bad guys get their just desserts. Wong makes the pace quick, keeping the gags sharp and not letting the viewer worry too much about details. Midway through, Chow takes some time out to spoof the famous Chinese opera *Red Boats*. In the second half, a down-and-out Sing is forced to work as a brothel gigolo, and in a hilarious parody of kung fu movie training sequences, hones his elocution abilities by watching the expert scolding of the Madam (Yuen King-Tan). With practice, he learns to talk fish out of the sea and convince the dead to live again! Chow makes great fun of the Ching Dynasty legal system, in which bribery was normal and the accused were commonly tortured into confessing during court. Much of the verbal comedy doesn't survive translation, but there's enough gist there to convey most of the jokes. The climax gives us a look at an old guillotine—sort of like a huge paper cutter built into a statue of a snarling hound. *AKA: Gau Ban Chi Lut Goon Baak Min Pau Ching-tin; Jiu Pin Zhi Ma Guan Bai Mian Bao Qingtian.* 🦴🦴🦴

1994 106m/C *HK* Stephen Chow, Ng Man-Tat, Sharla Cheung, Elvis Tsui, Christy Cheung, Ada Choi, Ngai Sing, Lawrence Ng, Lau Shun, Gabriel Wong, Wong Yat-Fei, Yuen King-Tan, Ku Feng, John Ching. *D:* Wong Jing. *W:* Wong Jing. *C:* David Chung. *M:* William Woo. **VHS, DVD**

Half a Loaf of Kung Fu

Lo Wei tried several ways to make a star out of Jackie Chan, but nothing worked. As a last resort, he let Chan do what he wanted with this picture, giving him creative control for the first time. Chan plays a wanna-be kung fu artist looking for work in old China. After failing to secure a job as a bodyguard, he runs afoul of a treasure-seeking "Sorceress" and her retinue. He gets lucky, though, when he encounters the aftermath of a kung fu battle. Discovering that one of the men has a reward on his head, Jackie claims it. This causes him to be mistaken for the slain whipstaff master Whip Hero. While the boost to Jackie's rep is nice, it also brings him even more enemies. Fortunately, his elevated station also brings him new friends, in the form of strange beggars who teach him kung fu techniques. Throughout the film Jackie's learning remains just one step ahead of the skills he needs to stay alive (kind of an "just-in-time-delivery" kung fu system). When he's outmatched, Jackie wisely runs away (to learn more kung fu

another day). Seeking his place in life, Jackie hooks up with a kung fu clan to help protect their treasure from the many bad guys seeking it. In the end, all the various factions come together for a big final battle to possess the treasure. There's lots of action, plenty of comedy (a lot of which doesn't work—at least to most Western viewers), and more than a glimpse of Chan's acrobatic background.

One of the film's highlights is a really fun title sequence featuring stylized kung fu battles and film parodies. In it, Jackie (who directed the martial arts on the film) shows off his Buster Keaton-esque style. There's also a Popeye fantasy dream sequence within the film itself. This is one of those early Chan films where you can see the future superstar looking for his own style. There are glimpses of the Chan we all know and love in some of the fights. The majority of kung fu work in the film, though, is of the balletic and highly stylized ritual that—once upon a time—Bruce Lee rebelled against. The movie also boasts some nice scenery, including several spectacular stepped cairns and a number of scenic temples. It's a fun romp for Chan fans, but very stagy in the action sequences. Nothing too special, but a nice glimpse of Jackie Chan's development. Unfortunately, Lo Wei just didn't think it was funny, and ordered the film shelved while launching his own even more low-brow Chan comedy with *Spiritual Kung Fu.* —SS *AKA: Dim Chi Gung Foo Gam Gaan Daan; Dian Zhi Gong Fu Gan Jian Chan.* 🦴🦴

1977 (R) 96m/C *HK* Jackie Chan, Doris Lung, James Tien, Dean Shek, Wu Ma, Kim Chin-lin, Miu Tin, Lee Man Tai, Kam Kong, Li Min Lang. *D:* Chen Chi-hwa. *W:* Tang Min-ji. *C:* Chen Chin-Kui. *M:* Frankie Chan. **VHS, DVD**

Half Human

This strange little Yeti picture from Japan was badly mishandled by the U.S. distributor. Separated from their party by an avalanche, a pair of skiers is killed, with evidence suggesting the killer was some sort of hairy beast-man. An expedition led by Professor Tanaka (Nobuo Nakamura) discovers an adult and child hairy biped creatures in the mountains. Natives of the area rescue one of the party (Akira Takarada), but thinking the monster they worship might be angry, leave him tied from a rope over a ravine. However, the creature is gentle and saves him from his predicament. A circus captures the creatures, but when the young one is killed, the adult goes on a rampage.

Just how good a film *Half Human* is would be difficult to determine, as Toho Studios decided to withdraw the film from circulation in response to protests by Ainu tribes that object-

Aw, baby's got a teddy bear. A scene missing from the horribly edited U.S. release of *Half Human.*

ed to the portrayal of the mountain people in the film. The only version available is the U.S. version. Released on a double bill with *Monster from Green Hell,* more than half of the original film was cut out by Distributors Corporation of America, while cheap scenes with John Carradine, Morris Ankrum, and others were added. Carradine tells the story in flashback as if he were there. Most of the film plays without subtitles or dubbing, just Carradine's narration. John Carradine is always good to see, but far too many foreign films have been given this sort of treatment. The Bigfoot monsters are most unusual looking, very expressive for masked monsters, and hopefully some day the original 95-minute cut will be made available again. **AKA:** *Jyujin Yuki Otoko; Abominable Snowman; Beast Man Snow Man; Half Human: The Story of the Abominable Snowman.* 🐾 🦕

1955/1957 63m/BW *JP* Akira Takarada, Momoko Kochi, Akemi Negishi, Sachio Sakai, Nobuo Nakamura, Kokuten Kodo, Ren Yamamoto, Akira Yamada, Akira Sera, Kenji Sahara, John Carradine (U.S. version), Morris Ankrum (U.S.). **D:** Ishiro Honda, Kenneth G. Crane (U.S.). **W:** Takeo Murata, Shigeru Kayama (story). **C:** Tadashi Iimura, Lucien N. Andriot (U.S.). **M:** Masaru Sato. **VHS**

Hand of Death

Today's video distributors promote this as the only movie collaboration between John Woo, Jackie Chan, Sammo Hung, and Yuen Biao. Well, technically they're correct, but Delon Tan is definitely the star of this picture, with Jackie and Sammo only granted supporting roles because of Sammo's position as action director. Yuen's role is limited to stunt work and a bit part as a guard who gets shot by an arrow.

Shih Shao-feng (James Tien) is a Shaolin Temple defector who now leads the Manchu government crackdown on rebels. Yung Fei (Delon Tan) is one of many Shaolin students in hiding, and a top martial artist. He's sent on a mission to bring back Shih's head, first meeting up with Chang (John Woo), who holds a map to rebel camps. But to find Chang he first has to seek out Shaolin fighter Chiu Kuo, who is spying on Shih's base. Yung gets into town thanks to friendly blacksmith Little Tan Feng (Jackie Chan), but finds that Chiu Kuo has already been caught by Shih's Captain of the Guard Tu Ching (Sammo Hung, wearing a ridiculous overbite). He helps save Chiu Kuo from execution, and he's given a pass code for

Chang. To gain freedom to operate, Yung accepts a job offer from Tu, presenting the "recaptured" Chiu to seal the deal. But Shih easily sees through his play, and Yung only escapes captivity with the help of Tan Feng, who turns out to be another Shaolin fighter seeking vengeance against Shih. The pair recognizes that they can't beat Shih and his eight bodyguards without better tools, more training, a battle plan, and the help of a terrific swordsman named Zorro (Yeung Wai).

Even at this early stage, Woo's personality and talent are much in evidence. Shih talks about how Yung is "a loser" because he's neither a devil nor a saint, and he's right—Yung is exposed because he's unconvincing as an evil man, and can't beat Shih until he achieves greater strength and purity. There's also an unusual kind of friendly enemy relationship going on, as the "sensitive" Tu takes a liking to Yung that he can't deny, despite being on a different side. Chan's talent for comedy is acknowledged as well, as he's given quite a few pratfalls and funny bits worked into his young avenger character. The fight scenes are sharp and exciting, shot against gorgeous Taiwan locations, and take advantage of Tan's amazing kicking talent and some fancy spear handling from Chan. *AKA: Siu Lam Moon; Shaolin Men; Strike of Death; Countdown in Kung Fu.* 𝅘𝅥𝅮𝅘𝅥𝅮𝅘𝅥𝅮

1975 93m/C *HK* Delon Tan, James Tien, Jackie Chan, Chu Ching, Sammo Hung, John Woo, Yeung Wai, Wilson Tong, Ko Keung, Gam Kei Chu, O Yau-man, Yuen Wah, Yuen Biao. **D:** John Woo. **W:** John Woo. **C:** Liang Yung-chi. **M:** Joseph Koo. **VHS, DVD**

The Happiness of the Katakuris

Well, it's the kind of movie that opens with a woman in a restaurant finding a claymation cherub in her soup, and the cherub falls in love with her uvula. Welcome to the story of the Katakuri family, narrated by the youngest Katakuri, little Yurie. When Grandpa Masao (Kenji Sawada) was laid off from his shoe salesman job before retirement, he convinced Grandma Terue (Keiko Matsuzaka) that they should open an inn in a remote valley, convinced a major highway was going to be built through there. They brought with them Yurie's divorced mother Shizue (Naomi Nishida) and Uncle Masayuki (Shinji Takeda), a hotheaded ex-stockbroker ex-con. Great-grandpa Jinpei (Tetsuro Tamba) just enjoys throwing sticks at birds.

After months of seemingly useless preparation, the inn greets its first guest—a morose gentleman who commits suicide. Fearing bad publicity, the Katakuris decide to bury the body

and conceal the matter. A few days later, their second guest arrives—a famous young sumo wrestler on a getaway with his schoolgirl sweetheart—with even direr consequences. Then comes Shizue's boyfriend Richard Sagawa (Kiyoshiro Imawano), a wanted criminal disguising himself as a British Naval officer (and secret agent), who plans to add Shizue to his string of victims. Great-grandpa discovers Richard's evil plans, and the old man has to go into action. Meanwhile, word of the highway crew's plans finally comes through, necessitating a move for the inn's growing little graveyard. When a dour family of four checks in, Great-grandpa and Masayuki head for the woods to dig some more graves.

A brilliant black comedy, *Katakuris* continues Takashi Miike's highly eclectic and prolific career with another stunning winner. This dark and touching tale is kept sparkling with animation, slapstick, romance, animal action, a volcanic eruption, a bit of kung fu, and a chorus line of dancing zombies. It's also the best musical to come along since the *South Park* movie, with one sequence ready for karaoke. Don't let a few bloody neck wounds and bloated corpses keep you from gathering the family around this exhilarating charmer. *AKA: Katakurike no Koufuku.* 𝅘𝅥𝅮𝅘𝅥𝅮𝅘𝅥𝅮𝅘𝅥𝅮

2001 (R) 112m/C *JP* Kenji Sawada, Keiko Matsuzaka, Shinji Takeda, Naomi Nishida, Kiyoshiro Imawano, Tetsuro Tamba. **D:** Takashi Miike. **W:** Kikumi Yamagishi. **C:** Hideo Yamamoto. **M:** Koji Makaino, Koji Endo. **DVD**

Happy End

The story of a love triangle that takes an unexpected twist, this film caused a lot of controversy upon its release in Korea. Out of work, Seo Min-ki (Choi Min-sik from *Shiri*) spends his days caring for his infant daughter Yun and reading romance novels in a used book store. His wife Bora (Chun Do-yeon) is having an affair with Kim Il-bum (Joo Jin-mo), an old boyfriend. Min-ki suspects something's up, and begins to piece together clues to the affair. Bora herself is jealous that Kim has another woman. He has met up with an old schoolmate recently, and there's a mutual attraction, but he's pointedly resisted temptation, despite the misery he feels. Bora tries to break up with Kim, but he demands another meeting, and she weakens. As he learns more about his wife's betrayal, Min-ki switches from romances to mystery novels, and his silent rage is fueled into a plan of action.

Chung Ji-woo gives his film a documentary look similar to that seen in the work of John Cassavetes, though with a few odd angles thrown into the mix. The viewpoint is matter-of-fact, kept almost completely neutral throughout, so that you almost forget that upsetting events are taking place. It's the kind of film that forces one to have an opinion by not having a clear agenda. Performances by the three leads are very good. Though not a shock to Western audiences, one can understand why the whole situation would be considered shocking in Korea, where a woman can be fired for getting a divorce. Should be required viewing for cheating spouses. ♫♫♫

1999 99m/C *KO* Choi Min-sik, Chun Do-yeon, Joo Jin-mo. **D:** Chung Ji-woo. **W:** Chung Ji-woo. **C:** Woo-hyung Kim. **VHS, DVD**

Happy Family

Love to laugh at suicide, depression, and incest? Here's the perfect movie for you. The Han family is wealthy and successful. "Small" Han (Nick Cheung), the son, runs the family business. He falls in love with Kaka (Candy Lo), a new employee, and soon they are planning marriage. However, long-held family secrets threaten to tear their relationship apart. The crucial plot twist is one of those contrived, only-in-the-movies type of happenings. It hinges upon "Small" Han not telling his intended bride, Kaka, the reason why he suddenly breaks up with her. Any credulity the story might have had, which is already strained to the breaking point by the swiftness of their courtship—basically a one-night drunken affair—is sacrificed on the altar of cheap laughs.

Cheap laughs are not to be entirely discounted. Individual sequences could be taken out of the movie and admired for their direction and performances. One very funny scene features the two estranged lovebirds carrying on a conversation whilst heading in opposite directions on adjoining escalators. Overall, though, it feels like a valiant effort to overcome a weak script on a low budget. In her first leading role, singer/actress Candy Lo demonstrates a vibrant spark and a good-natured willingness to act foolish. Kenny Bee and Cecilia Yip bring energy to their parts as Mr. and Mrs. Han, parents who try to protect their individual legacies in different ways. Also providing good turns are Amanda Lee (with unconvincing old-person makeup) as Kaka's mother and Almen Wong as a writer hired to tell the story of the Han family. Several real-life film directors, including Herman Yau and Alfred Cheung, have amusing cameos as they make pitches to direct the film version of the story. —*PM* **AKA:** *Fung Lau Ga Chuk; Feng Liu Gu Zu.* ♫♫

2002 95m/C *HK* Nick Cheung, Candy Lo, Kenny Bee, Cecilia Yip, Amanda Lee, Chan Man-Man, Alfred Cheung, Fennie Yuen, Almen Wong, Tats Lau, Wilson Yip, Matt Chow, Simon Lui, Monica Lo, Iris Chai, Emily Kwan, Ma Hok-ming, Thomas Lam, Herman Yau, Marco Mak, Sherman Wong. **D:** Herman Yau. **W:** Herman Yau, Yeung Yee-shan. **C:** Puccini Yu. **M:** Mak Chun-hung. **VHS, DVD**

Hard as a Dragon

Out-of-work martial artist Chan Lee (Raymond Lui) comes to the aid of Ling Kwan, who got arrested while trafficking drugs and had to ditch the goods, though his criminal associate Mun doesn't believe him. Kwan's father gives Lee a job waiting tables in his New Copacabana club, but the crooks don't take kindly to the beating Lee gave them. Besides, they still think Kwan has their merchandise. Since they can't beat Lee's kung fu, they try to buy him off, but he refuses to betray his friend. Mun's men abduct and kill Kwan, and hold his sister Shou-mei hostage. Some bikers are sent to ambush Lee, and frame him for the murder. Lee goes on the run, but Mun still considers him a threat. Mun's visiting Japanese pal Asai steps in to lend a hand (and foot) to test his karate against Chinese kung fu.

He needn't bother, since in this picture they're exactly the same thing—just the same old stiff-armed fighting. In fact, there's nothing in the movie to distinguish it from the hundreds of martial arts films produced in the previous decade or so. The clichés are so thick that there's even a little kid named Emile that carries a slingshot in his pocket. The ending makes a stab at a bit of existential irony. The soundtrack features a Muzak/disco version of Blondie's "Call Me" and some Pink Floyd. ♫♫

1980 88m/C *TW* Raymond Lui. **D:** Raymond Lui. **VHS**

Hard Boiled

For his last Hong Kong film before leaving for Hollywood, John Woo decided to go out with a bang. Well, a LOT of bangs. While his usual themes of honor, chivalry, and trust that survive within the madness and chaos of modern society are not totally abandoned in *Hard Boiled,* those themes are dwarfed by the sheer volume of glorious action and violence. A LOT of volume.

Barry Wong, who tragically died while working on the script, constructed a clever, uncomplicated cop story, a framework for Woo and action director Phillip Kwok to construct his kinetic bullet-ballet action sequences. Woo's thespian alter ego Chow Yun-fat stars as Tequila Yuen, a cool cop with a hot gun hand, and his own jazz club. While tracing a gang of gun traffickers at a

Tony Leung Chiu-Wai gets involved in another classic John Woo standoff in *Hard Boiled.*

THE KOBAL
COLLECTION / MILESTONE

famous Kowloon teahouse, a gun battle erupts—one of three classic action sequences in the movie—and Tequila's partner is killed. What Tequila doesn't know is that his superiors are playing the game from both sides.

Tony (Tony Leung) is a cop gone deep undercover as gangster Alan, so deep that he's become a hit man for gunrunner Mr. Hui (Kwan Hoi-san). Tequila gets on his trail after Alan kills a mobster who betrayed the gang to join up with rival Johnny Wong (Anthony Wong). Tony sends a message that Hui is very near the trap they've laid for him, and that the cops should hold back—but Tequila is a hard man to hold back, and he goes after Wong just as Alan is joining his gang. That night, Wong's gang stages a raid on Hui's warehouse base of operation, taking over his business and seizing his high-caliber inventory, and Alan is forced to kill his old boss. But Tequila is there, too, and he storms in to kill half of Wong's men, until a moment when he and Alan have each other in a standoff. Tequila's gun jams, and Alan, tellingly, spares his fellow cop. Tequila catches up with Alan/Tony on his boat, and the two agree to work together, just as the remnants of Hui's gang attack. Wound-

ed in the battle, Alan is taken to a hospital under Wong's control. Though a legitimate hospital, Wong has a storehouse of arms hidden in vaults down below. Alan sends word to Tequila about this, and he and the cops rendezvous at the hospital. A gigantic showdown with Wong's gang begins, and the hospital becomes a war zone.

This sequence, which Woo shot in a fever of creativity, is his grand finale with Chow Yun-fat, including in it bravura camera work, bloody violence, explosions, continuously blazing firearms, and even blazing pants! Old-school kung fu star Phillip Kwok revived his career with his portrayal of Mad Dog, an honorable mute gunslinger. ***AKA:*** *Lat Sau San Tam; La Shou Shen Tan; Hot-Handed God of Cops; God of Guns; Hard-Boiled.* 🦴🦴🦴🦴

1991 (R) 127m/C *HK* Chow Yun-fat, Tony Leung Chiu-Wai, Teresa Mo, Phillip Chan, Phillip Kwok, Anthony Wong, Kwan Hoi-san, Bowie Lam, Stephen Tung, Bobby Au Yeung, Lau Kong, John Woo, Ng Shui-ting, Lo Meng, Michael Dinga. **D:** John Woo. **W:** Barry Wong, John Woo. **C:** Horace Wong. **M:** Michael Gibbs. **VHS, DVD**

The Haunted Cop Shop

Ex-cop turned monk Wai Chin returns to his old district police station to offer a warning to Chief Shun (Wu Fung)—"the man he hated most" before his enlightenment—about the coming Feast of Yu Lan (Hungry Ghost Festival). Though Shun dismisses the warning, he sends detectives Macky Kim (Jacky Cheung) and Chiu Man (Ricky Hui) to fetch incense and paper to burn just in case. The cops can't see why ghosts would bother a police station, but rumor has it that the building used to house an army club during the Japanese occupation, and many soldiers committed seppuku on V-J Day. At first, the cops are too busy interrogating thief Sneaky Ming (Billy Lau) to worry about ghosts, but find them useful in scaring a confession out of the suspect. At midnight, the gates of Hell open, and supernatural hijinks ensue. Ghosts release Ming from his cell and invite him to the club, where he's trapped in a crooked mah-jongg game. To save his life, he has to take the remains of their General Issey to the surface world where he can be reincarnated. The general happens to be a vampire (European variety), who promptly bites Ming, turning him. Kim and Man recapture Ming, and have a hard time believing his story about being turned into a vampire—at least until they expose him to sunlight to prove it, burning him to ash. While the boys are trying to explain to their new boss, Chief Inspector Fanny Ho (Chan Gachai), what happened to Ming, the general is busy finding new victims, spreading the vampire virus around.

Like its inspiration *Mr. Vampire*, this is largely plotless once the spooks start popping. But it does a good job of mixing together creepy atmosphere, mild shocks, and nonsense comedy. For a moment, it seems that the day will be saved when the cops run into supernatural expert Chung Fat-pak (Chung Fat, Hong Kong's go-to ghostbuster when Lam Ching-Ying is unavailable), but the Japanese vampire general (possibly a spoof of *Lake of Dracula*) soon disarms him, and they're off and running again. There are some routines that are straight out of Abbott and Costello, and early on there's a takeoff on Stanley Kubrick's *The Shining*. Cheung, Chan, Hui, and Lau would return for an equally riotous sequel. *AKA: Maang Gwai Cha Goon; Meng Gui Cha Guan; The Haunted Cop Shop of Horrors.* 🎬🎬🎬

1987 91m/C *HK* Jacky Cheung, Ricky Hui, Wu Fung, Billy Lau, Chan Ga-chai, Chung Fat, Cho Chunsing, Shut Ma-yin, Alan Tang. *D:* Jeff Lau. *W:* Jeff Lau, Wong Kar-Wai. *C:* Peter Ngor. *M:* Anders Nelsson. **DVD**

The Haunted Lantern

Captured by enemy samurai, lovers Tsuyu (Yuna Natsuo) and Shinzaburo (Gitan Otsuru) vow to die together, but Shinzaburo betrays their vow in exchange for an offer of freedom. She becomes a blood ghost and devours him. At least that's the way it goes in the nightmares of a young artist named Shin Hagiwara. But are they only dreams? One day, he and his friend Tomozo (Tsuyoshi Ujiki) rescue maiden Tsuyu Iijima, who is hurrying back to Edo to attend her ill father. Returning home himself, Shin is surprised to find out that his parents have made a deal for him to marry their friend Iijima's daughter. But it turns out that it's Tsuyu's younger sister Suzu (Junna Suzuki) to whom he's been promised. Tsuyu is promised to another man. Shin visits Tsuyu in secret, and they decorate a memorial lantern, but circumstances keep them apart. Jealous Tomozo spies on them—he wants Tsuyu himself, and later he lies to her, saying Shin told him to force himself on her. Heartbroken, the two sisters commit suicide. The loving ghost sisters continue to visit the unknowing Shin, taking the lantern with them. Their spirits merged and the sisters make love to Shin; the next day his back is covered with maggot-infested sores. Spying again, Tomozo discovers the truth and fetches Priest Hakuodo (Akaji Maro), an exorcist who forces the specters to reveal themselves, and stays to help Shin and Tomozo battle the persistent ghosts.

The popular Encho Sanyutei ghost story "Botan Doro," itself an adaptation of a Chinese folktale, had already been filmed 14 times, so what's one more. Actually, the tale was adapted three more times since this one, but this is the first to use digital f/x to help haunt poor Shin. *AKA: Otsuyu: Kaidan Botan Doro.* 🎬🎬🎬

1998 96m/C *JP* Yuna Natsuo, Gitan Otsuru, Tsuyoshi Ujiki, Junna Suzuki, Akaji Maro. *D:* Masaru Tsushima. *W:* Yuka Honcho, Encho Sanyutei (story). *C:* Shoji Ebara. *M:* Kotoro Nakagawa. **VHS**

Haunted Mansion

Marine Policeman Fai (Anthony Wong) and his wife Gigi (Gigi Lai) have to cancel their vacation to Japan when her mother (Helena Law) has some sort of hex trouble, in addition to her Parkinson's disease. Instead, Fai accompanies his wife to his mother-in-law's house in rural Yuen Long. Meeting them at the gate is feng shui expert Tin Bo-chiu, who warns them to move out, giving a long list of problems and bad omens that point to the house being a doorway to Hell. Sure enough, hostile neighbors aren't the only trouble to the house-guests, and ghosts start popping up. The haunt-

ings continue, though they try to dismiss it all as dreams and illusions.

Gigi's superstitious boss Uncle Ming (Spencer Lam) gives her a pair of ghost-viewer glasses to help her see what's going on in the house. She finds the ghost of a daughter who was never born has caused evil spirits to take possession of both Fai and her sister Fen (Shirley Cheung). Only Uncle Ming and his bumbling knowledge of ghosts can save them all from the hellbound spirits.

The bickering-but-loving marriage of Wong and Lai is at the heart of this unorthodox fright flick, and rightly so, since their personalities and performances are the only things holding the picture together. Writer/director Dickson To tries for naturalism, using a lot of handheld camera shots, but his home movie familiarity turns to banality as his story loses momentum, and not even a few green-faced ghosts can liven things up. The idea that Anthony Wong's fate comes down to a mah-jongg game in Hell's waiting room is the only interesting feature of the spook story. **AKA:** *Heung Gong Dai Hung Chak; Xiang Gang Di Xiong Zhai.* ♪♡

1998 90m/C *HK* Anthony Wong, Gigi Lai, Helena Law, Spencer Lam, Shirley Cheung, Lee Shing-chak. **D:** Dickson To. **W:** Dickson To. **C:** Pang Jun Wai. **VHS, DVD**

He Has Nothing But Kung Fu

This early kung fu comedy from the Lau brothers, Lau Kar-Wing and his adopted brother Gordon Lau (Lau Kar Fei), uses the timeworn amnesia gimmick long before Jackie Chan in *Who Am I?* or Sammo Hung in *Once upon a Time in China and America*. Shou-shen (Wong Yu) is a tricky young mendicant and scam artist, who tricks gangster Mr. Chou (Lau Kar-Wing). In retaliation, Chou's friend the casino manager frames Shou-shen for cheating. He meets an amnesia victim (Gordon Lau) near his house, a man who apparently has been trained in kung fu. Shou-shen's kung fu is good for little besides picking pockets. He brings his powerful new pal to big boss Wang Tin-Tin's casino to settle up.

Next they rescue restaurant girl Wei Li-ho (Li Ying Ying) from Chou. On the run, they see Chou riding to deliver the weekly casino take to Wang, and decide to rob him. Righteous at heart, the amnesiac becomes a Robin Hood, preying on Boss Wang to benefit the poor. Meanwhile, police captain Chan (Karl Maka) has been called on to look for missing admiral's son Kai-Yuen. The outlaws run into the admiral, but Kai-Yuen doesn't know his own father and they run away. Shou-shen is arrested, while Wang's men

ambush Kai-Yuen. Knocked out, Kai-Yuen regains his memory, but it may be too late.

With cardboard characters, much of the plot of this kung fu comedy is made up of meaningless encounters and escapes. But the Laus put their energy toward their specialty: imaginatively choreographed fight scenes. There's a very nicely put together battle over rooftops, and rounds with Lee Hoi-sang and Wilson Tong. The soundtrack features a spirited rendition of "Dixie." The next year, Gordon Lau would shave his head for *36th Chamber of Shaolin* and never look back. **AKA:** *Gung Foo Siu Ji; Gong Fu Xiao.* ♪♪

1977 91m/C *HK* Wong Yu, Gordon Lau, Lau Kar-Wing, Karl Maka, Li Ying Ying, Lee Hoi-sang, Wilson Tong, Ho Pak Kwong, Kong Do. **D:** Lau Kar-Wing. **W:** Ngai Hong. **VHS, DVD**

Headlines

The frenetic and highly competitive world of Hong Kong newspapers is given serious treatment in this little-seen drama. Idealistic Peter Wong (Daniel Wu) has recently graduated from journalism school in the United States and begins his first job as an intern reporter at the fictional *Hong Kong Daily*. Sorrow (Emil Chau), a savvy and grizzled veteran reporter, is assigned to provide training, but quickly ditches him and pursues a story about a local jewelry exhibition. Sorrow's longtime friend, Office Mak, has been assigned to oversee security at the show, and Sorrow thinks something about the arrangement doesn't sound right. In the meantime, Peter is assigned to an "easy" story about traffic safety involving a schoolboy being hit by a car. He starts probing deeper after an unpleasant encounter with the boy's sister (Grace Yip). Fellow reporter Joey (television actress Maggie Cheung Hoh-yee) smells a story when a teenage boy helps a schoolmate fend off some young triads but declines to identify the rascals. Each of the stories unwinds at a measured pace and in unanticipated ways.

The pace of the film is slower than it needs to be; certain scenes run longer than they should, and the staging is static. More variety in these areas by director Leo Heung would have made for a more enjoyable ride. It doesn't help that the story runs out of steam near the end. That being said, the stories themselves are intriguing, raising as they do the challenge of modern-day journalism—balancing the need for headlines against the impact "getting the story" can have upon the people involved. These issues are of particular interest when you consider that several dozen newspapers compete for readers in Hong Kong. The actors are given room to breathe and deliver fine performances. Of particular note is television actress Maggie

Cheung Hoh-yee (not to be confused with the better-known Maggie Cheung Man-yuk). She adds depth in a beautiful stint as Joey, who has long ago learned she must use deceit and guile, but who is not too happy about it. Ross Clarkson (Ringo Lam's *The Suspect, Victim*) brings a documentary feel to the cinematography. —*PM*
AKA: *Tau Hiu Yan Mat; Tou Hao Ren Wu; People of the Headlines.* 𝄐𝄐𝄑

2001 87m/C *HK* Emil Chau, Daniel Wu, Maggie Cheung Hoh-yee, Grace Yip, Wayne Lai, Simon Lui. **D:** Leo Heung. **W:** So Man-sing, Yu Wing-chuen, Fan Yau-man. **C:** Ross Clarkson. **M:** Mak Chun-hung. **VHS, DVD**

Heart of Dragon

An early experiment with a different kind of feature, Jackie Chan and Sammo Hung proved here that they can handle roles with more depth than their usual action-hero characters—though there's still plenty of action in this tear-jerking drama. Chan has been afraid to stray too far from what's expected of him ever since, while Hung—who does no kung fu at all here—occasionally essayed a straight dramatic role, as in the touching romance *Eight Taels of Gold.*

Hong Kong cop Tat (Chan) has always dreamed of becoming a sailor and traveling around the world, but events always conspire against him. For one thing, his girlfriend Jenny (Emily Chu) just wants him to settle down and marry her—police work is dangerous, but at least he's home every night. But Tat's biggest burden is his older brother Do-Do (Hung), who is mentally retarded and has been totally reliant on his little brother since their parents died. While playing with his (much younger) friends when Tat is on duty, Do-Do comes upon a bag of jewels recently stolen by a gang led by Mr. Kim (James Tien), and hides them. The bad guys kidnap Do-Do to get the jewels back. Tat assembles a squad of his old SDU buddies to rescue his brother from a building construction site, resulting in a fast-paced, explosive finale.

Sammo Hung here joins the ranks of big stars like Mickey Rooney who have gained critical praise for playing mentally retarded characters, which to some may look like grandstanding. After all, Larry Drake was a virtual unknown when he was cast in the television series *L.A. Law,* and because of this many viewers thought he might really be disabled, which was beneficial in many ways. Though one might also argue that Do-Do isn't much different than the "dumb" characters Hung has played in comedies, the different concentration level he brings to bear here is obvious—and that he was directing and orchestrating action sequences (along with Jackie, with Yuen Biao designing the amazing final battle) at

the same time is impressive. Chan does well with his performance, too, toning down his emoting to compensate for years of Chinese opera training. The histrionics might still be too much for American audiences, especially action fans who don't know what they're getting into, but both leads deserve some applause for their courage. However, you can almost see Jackie sigh with relief as he jumps back into doing dangerous stunts. Fans that can't take the crying and fast-forward to the fight scenes are rewarded anyway with some of the best action sequences ever. His reaction to poor boxoffice for this effort—and the frustrations of *The Protector*—shows up in Chan's next film, the action masterpiece *Police Story.* Some foreign video versions contain a couple of extra fight scenes.
AKA: *Lung Dik Sam; Long De Xin; First Mission; Heart of the Dragon.* 𝄐𝄐𝄐𝄑

1985 89m/C *HK* Jackie Chan, Sammo Hung, Emily Chu, James Tien, Mang Hoi, Melvin Wong, Tai Bo, Wu Ma, Dennis Chan, Lam Ching-Ying, Yip Wing-cho, Anthony Chan, Wu Fung, Chin Ka-Lok, Dick Wei, Yuen Wah, Phillip Ko, Blackie Ko, Chan Lung, Fung Hark-On, Lee Hoi-sang, Ben Lam, Corey Yuen, Chung Fat, San Kwai, Fung Ging Man, Huang Ha, Billy Ching, Tai San, Chow Kong, Yam Ho, Ng Min Kan. **D:** Sammo Hung. **W:** Barry Wong. **C:** Arthur Wong. **M:** Violet Lam. **VHS, DVD**

Help!!!

Medical tomfoolery leads to personal redemption in this comedy from directors Johnnie To and Wai Kar-fai. Newly arrived Doctor Jim Wong (Jordan Chan) is a physician who appears to be as greedy and self-involved as the other boorish doctors at a shabby hospital. Doctor Yan Ho (Cecilia Cheung) is none too pleased with Jim's initial outlook; her idealism was shaped by an experience when she was a patient and heard a masked healer's confession that "it's not easy to be a doctor." Doctor Joe Chan (Ekin Cheng) has given up the medical life—he finds satisfaction as an automobile mechanic, treating his automotive "patients" with surgical care. Eventually Jim and Joe join Yan Ho's crusade to clean up the hospital, even as the administrators (notably Hui Siu-hung and Lam Suet) try to cover up the shortcomings of the facility and their own incompetence.

Black comedies sound easy on paper but are deceivingly difficult to pull off. There has to be a certain amount of anger behind the comedy; if the audience does not sense the outrage of the filmmakers, then the inevitable over-the-top humor is left stranded without a context. Think of *The Hospital* (an obvious forefather) and *Network,* both written by Paddy Chayefsky, both fiercely funny and outrageous comedies with biting dramatic impact. *Help!!!* does not reach that

The Philippines

From the American perspective, Philippine cinema is known mostly through their co-productions with the U.S., such as Eddie Romero and Gerardo de Leon's lucrative series of horror films produced mainly for distribution to U.S. drive-ins and grind houses. Except for the period when they were occupied by the Japanese army (a period during which filmmakers like de Leon received their film training from Japanese directors), Philippine cinema has always had close ties with the U.S. The earliest features were produced by Harry Brown and Edward S. Gross.

Though studios were built as early as 1909, the movies themselves remained technically primitive for many years. Some studios tried to emulate Hollywood pictures, hiring actors with an Anglo look to be their stars. More sophisticated productions didn't begin appear until well into the 1950s, as more and more American war films began filming there.

The Marcos regime that took power in 1966 may have meant lengthy prison terms for his political enemies, but gave a shot in the arm to film production. Roger Corman's New World Pictures made many cheesy exploitation pictures like *The Big Doll House* and *T.N.T. Jackson* on the islands during the '70s, often hiring directors like Cirio Santiago (son of Dr. Ciriaco Santiago, who founded Premiere Productions in 1946) and local crews. Santiago and others went on to carve a whole career of violent, sexy, and definitely exploitable action pictures, aimed at both the domestic and international markets. Those aimed at overseas video sales have a homogenous quality that makes them marketable just about anywhere, a factor that helped the Philippines become one of the top 10 film-producing nations. In many of these films, there's such a mix of nationalities on board that it's difficult to tell where they come from.

However, the 7,000 islands of the Philippines have a rich culture and folklore of their own. Melodramas are still the local favorite, but many cult flicks have been made targeted directly at the native audience, few of which have been seen outside the islands. The combination of Catholicism, island life, oriental influence, and superstition has made for some bizarre horror and fantasy films. The first sound feature made was *Ang Aswang* in 1933—a vampire movie! Or rather, the aswang is a breed of vampire native to the Philippines. English is still the official language, but films made for the local population are mostly filmed in Tagalong. These films have a wild anything-can-happen spirit to them, and it's a shame so few have been released in English or subtitled. Yanks are missing out on the superheroics of *Darna the Superwoman*, the villainy of *Zuma* (a big bald chap with snakes growing from his shoulders), and the long-running horror anthology series *Shake, Rattle and Roll.*

level of accomplishment. It's a hit-and-miss affair, a comedy where a lot of things are thrown up at the wall and only about half stick. Part of the problem is that the anger expressed in the film towards the medical establishment is too scattershot. The targets are simply too broad and the attacks lack real bite. To be fair, the production was slapped together from script to screen in less than a month. And it's hard to be too critical of a film that wears its lightweight intentions on its sleeve. Slapstick, after all, is not meant to be taken seriously, and *Help!!!* wants to please. On this score, the fast and frenetic visuals keep things moving along, and the large cast pops on and off the screen with such alacrity that there's never time to become bored. —PM *AKA: Kwong Sau Wooi Chun; La Shou Hui Chun.* 🎵🎵

2000 89m/C *HK* Ekin Cheng, Jordan Chan, Cecilia Cheung, Hui Siu-hung, Lam Suet, Raymond Wong, Lam Kau, Bonnie Wong. *D:* Johnny To, Wai Kar-fai. *W:* Wai Kar-fai, Yau Nai-Hoi, Ben Wong. *C:* Cheng Sui-Keung. *M:* Raymond Wong. **VHS, DVD**

Her Majesty Is Fine

The Empress Dowager (Siqin Gaowa) of a certain Asian nation during a certain dynasty isn't feeling very well. A long line of doctors is brought in to cure her, and as each fails, he is sent to be executed. Beggar Tang Yuinuan (Chen Pei-hsi) sneaks in to take part in the last-meal buffet, and is mistaken for one of the failed physicians, but is spared at the last second. When he succeeds in curing the hiccups of Lord Wu (Chen Qiang), Tang is appointed the latest court physician. The comedy of errors continues, with Tang repeatedly trying to escape the palace or think up new treatments, while Wu and Hong Lu (Li Daqiang) keep trying to do away with him. Either a lot has been lost in the translation of this Chinese comedy, or else it's just not that funny to begin with. Chen has charm, and scores points for his physical comedy, but

this is a chore to sit through. *AKA: Tai Hou Ji Xiang; Good Luck Empress Dowager.* 🎵

1996 102m/C *CH* Chen Pei-hsi, Siqin Gaowa, Chen Qiang, Gong Zhu, Li Daqiang, Li Xida, Liu Tingyao. *D:* Jin Tao. *C:* Zhao Xiaoding. *M:* Yang Yilun. **VHS, DVD**

Her Name Is Cat

You might think from the title of this Hong Kong action item that you'd found a new episode in the Jade Leung *Black Cat* series, but such is not the case. Almen Wong stars as the sexy and mysterious super-assassin Jin Jing, AKA Cat. While she's not out killing folks for her triad clients, Cat spends her time working out in her warehouse hideout and brooding about her troubled past. That is, until she becomes obsessed with heroic John (Michael Wong), the detective assigned to tracking her down. John has his own troubles, weeping in front of the VCR over home movies of his wife and daughter, who've recently dumped his sorry ass. Of course, Cat's obsession goes too far. She kidnaps John, handcuffs him, and gives him a lap dance—which helps him forget his wife, but leads him into conflict with his duty to bring her to justice. But it's hard to arrest somebody while they're protecting you. John's harassment of Cat's employer has egged him into sending other assassins after him—who just happen to be the man and woman who betrayed Cat in the past.

Many HK action films either have strong fights and stunts and weak characterization, or just the opposite, but this one is just plain goofy in all departments. The love story is laughably sappy, and the action pieces—though energetic—are sloppy and unimpressive. This is one of those movies where a character says "this is like a bad movie" and it turns out to be true. It doesn't help that every time Cat goes into action, the roar of a panther accompanies her on the soundtrack (the same stupid effect used in *The Witch from Nepal* for Dick Wei's character). Director Clarence Fok has a small following due to his early 1990s hits *Gun 'n' Rose* and *Naked Killer,* but his taste for exploitation has led him into cheesy territory here. A good example is the love scenes between the leads, which never tease beyond a "PG" rating. It's either too over-the-top or too timid. *AKA: Pau Mooi; Bao Mei.* 🐾🐾

1998 95m/C *HK* Almen Wong, Michael Wong, Chong Wing, Ben Lam, Chik King Man, Ching Siu-lung, William Duan, Kenix Kwok, Chan Chi-fai. *D:* Clarence Fok. *W:* Wong Jing. *C:* Fung Yuen-man. **DVD**

Her Name Is Cat 2: Journey to Death

About the best thing about *Her Name Is Cat* was the poster, which featured a sweaty Almen Wong in an eye-popping outfit. This sequel in name only doesn't even have that going for it, though Wong gets to walk around in a bikini a couple of times. Otherwise, the story is a completely incomprehensible mess of flashbacks within flashbacks and multiple narrators. Here's the plot, as well as it can be interpreted: We find Almen in Thailand as a dancer named Samantha for some *Tomb Raider*–inspired action, wiping out a squad of soldiers in a temple to steal a gold Buddha containing a computer chip for her boss Miss Yoyo. Then we meet Ken Kwan Ching-hong (Roy Cheung), who came to Pattaya to hide out from his triad boss Kwai Ping (Blackie Ko), whom he'd betrayed to the police for stealing his girlfriend. He met up with Samantha on the plane, but they were immediately beset by a gang of killers working for Mr. Charles. Charles is an underling of Yoyo's father, politician General Thailone, who adopted the orphaned Sam when she was a child and trained her to become one of his bodyguards. Charles had the general assassinated, and Sam and Yoyo have been waiting for a chance at revenge ever since. By betraying Charles and selling the chip to a Korean arms dealer, they hope to gain enough power to topple Charles. The girls hid the chip on Ken, which is why Charles's men came after him. But Yoyo is found out and captured, and after Ken's cop friend Kambo is killed by the thugs, he decides to join Sam in a rescue mission.

Some films compensate for plot deficiencies by delivering the goods in the action department. Here, the goods have been left on the dock to rot, as all the fight scenes here are sloppy and poorly edited. And since the film's climax is shown at the *beginning* of Roy Cheung's extended flashback, there's not even any suspense to maintain viewer interest. A clip of a No Doubt hit is heard on the soundtrack. *AKA: Paau Lui Duet Meng Ji Lui; Bao Nu Zhi Duo Ming Zhi Lu; Panther Girl.* 🐾

2001 81m/C *HK* Almen Wong, Roy Cheung, Yam Kong-sou, Blackie Ko, T. Cheung, Ben Ng. *D:* Alan Lo. *W:* Au Law, Jobic Tsui. *C:* Faan Chuen-yam. *M:* Tsang Kwong-wah. **DVD**

The Hero of Swallow

Here's another wire-entangled action film inspired by Iron Monkey, this time with Yuen Biao leading the superheroics. The Zorro of the early days of the Republic of China, Li San (Yuen Biao) dons black ninja garb as Hero Swallow to fight injustice, steal from criminals, and give to the poor. When gangster Hian kidnaps his girlfriend Chinny (Athena Chu) to be sold as a concubine, Swallow arrives to save her. Though Hian is a fine fighter, Swallow chews him up and spits him out in short order, and frees the slaves. But Chinny has already been sold to a pimp in Imperial City of Peking.

Police Captain Tang Yue Chi (Joe Ma) suspects playboy gambler Li San of being the one they call Flying Thief, but Li easily eludes him by hiding in the palace of the Emperor's brother. Li barges into the birthday party for the mayor's father that night, pretending that as a Harvard graduate he doesn't know any better than to give the Commander a clock for a present. Swallow sticks around to rob the place of more precious treasures, such as the valuable Jade Chop of China. Lo-ha (Yvonne Yung), an opera actress he helped in the past, helps him escape afterward. Others he's benefitted include disabled army vet Hung Lai Fu (Elvis Tsui), and girl pickpocket Fu-wa (Lily Chung), who agree to help him hunt for Chinny.

Meanwhile, Chinny has become a bitter prostitute under the name Little Feng, worshiped by Pu Sochahae, master of the King's Brother's Palace. The palace guard Chiang Lu (Eddie Ko)—who was trained by Swallow's master Shi Kang-tan—is also after the Jade Chop, ordered by Shi to retrieve it to keep it out of foreign hands. But Pu takes the Chop and sells it to Japanese merchant Ochiono in order to raise money to buy Little Feng. Knowing he has some connection to Swallow, Tang arrests Hung Lai Fu. Li San comes to his rescue, promising he can return the Jade Chop in exchange within 10 days. However, he has to get by Ochiono's ninjas to get it. That finished, Li San is thrown in jail, but has to break out to rescue Chinny. Chiang Lu is still sworn to guard Pu, and the two colleagues are forced into a deadly duel.

Well, he's not exactly Batman, but have you ever looked at a swallow up close? Some of them can be pretty scary, and they can kill you by nesting in your chimney. With a plot that features one fight and escape after another, this has the flavor of an old action serial, but tends to get lost in its own meandering plot. Even the music score sounds as if it were recorded in the 1950s. The hero's actions are sometimes accompanied by a musical cue designed to sound like a swallow, but it sounds more like someone's cell phone is ringing. Director Siu Sang made a lot of movies in the late 1960s, but worked mostly in television until making a slight theatrical comeback in the '90s. **AKA:** *San Tao Yin Lee Saam; Shen Tou Yan Zi Li San.* 🐲🐲

1996 97m/C *HK* Yuen Biao, Athena Chu, Elvis Tsui, Joe Ma, Eddie Ko, Lily Chung, Yvonne Yung. **D:** Siu Sang. **W:** Siu Sang Workshop. **C:** Wong Wing-fei, Ho Hak-wai. **DVD**

The Heroes

Actors who would play a part in John Woo's successful films a decade later take featured roles in this atypical period kung fu drama. The Ching Dynasty emperor declares kung fu illegal! The army surrounds and burns the Shaolin Temple! A former Shaolin student turned traitor, Marshall Kao Fei-yin (Ti Lung) helps round up the monks, though we can see it distresses him to do so. The truth is that Kao is an undercover agent, working on a secret mission for the Ming rebels. Students Chou Chung-ching (Delon Tan), Yen Fei-chung, Pang Cheng (Wong Chung), and Wu Chun (Wu Ma) are among the monks he captures and tortures, though he knows the torture devices aren't that much more intense than the training techniques at Shaolin—and it keeps them alive. At a rebel camp, Liu (Danny Lee) makes plans to rescue his brothers. Meanwhile, Kao must protect himself from their assassins, while trying to protect *them* from getting caught. Kao's torture actually trains the students, increasing their endurance.

When Wu Chun decides to give in and join the Ching army, Kao kills him, drawing the suspicion of the governor (Michael Chan). Under pressure to prove himself, Kao is forced to kill Chou, too. Despite this, the governor still discovers Kao's treason, but too late—Kao's odd training program has made the prisoners strong enough to stage an escape, just as Liu and the rebels attack.

Though director Wu Ma makes good use of the limited sets available, the phony walls and sky of the prison become obvious. It's an interesting and unusual idea for an action film from the prolific Ngai Hong, almost undone by the limited budget and claustrophobic milieu. Fortunately, the performances and the level of martial arts prowess on display are enough to lift this above the norm. **AKA:** *Siu Lam Ying Hung; Shao Lin Ying Xiong; Ying Xiong; Story of Chivalry; The Shaolin Heroes; The Unforgiven of Shaolin; Wu Tang Clan.* 🐲🐲🐲

1980 90m/C *TW* Ti Lung, Michael Chan, Shih Szu, Delon Tan, Wong Chung, Danny Lee, Wu Ma, Wong

Ching, Choi Se, Lee Ho, Sit Hon, Chan Bik-fung. **D:** Wu Ma. **W:** Ngai Hong, Jin Shu-mei. **C:** Ng Kwok-yan. **M:** Koo Ka-fay, Wang Mau-san. **VHS, DVD**

Heroes Shed No Tears

John Woo would have you believe that *A Better Tomorrow* was the beginning of his cinematic romance with gunplay, but that's not the case. After Golden Harvest inserted extra scenes of sex and violence in this *Rambo*-inspired war film, Woo pretty much disowned the result, and it wasn't released until *ABT* was a hit. But Woo's themes of brotherhood and honor have their genesis here, and there are also a lot of his trademark explosions and plenty of violent gun fu. Chan Chung (Eddie Ko) is the leader of a group of Chinese mercenaries hired by the Thai government to smash a Golden Triangle heroin operation. The squad knocks out their headquarters in Vietnam, abducts the leader General Samton, and heads back to the Thai border. Chan makes a stop on the way to rescue his wife Julie and son Keung from men holding them hostage. As if they didn't have enough trouble with the drug traffickers chasing them, Chan stops again to rescue the wife (Cecile Le Baily) of a French reporter from Vietnamese army border guards, shooting the eye out of their colonel (Lam Ching-Ying) in the process. The colonel comes looking for payback, forcing a local tribe of hunters to work for him, too. The squad hides out in the house of Chan's old war buddy Louis (Phillip Loffrede), but has to make a stand there when their enemies combine forces and attack.

The added scenes are obviously out of place, but Woo might have been more worried about charges of plagiarism than any tampering by his studio, as the relationship between Chan and his son is a direct homage to the Lone Wolf and Cub comics and movies. There's even a swipe of the famous sequence where the son saves himself from being burned in a brush fire by burying himself. But there's still plenty to like about this movie, which doesn't scrimp on the action, drama, and thrills. The U.S. version is missing 10 minutes. **AKA:** *Ying Hung Mo Lui; Ying Xiong Wu Lei; Sunset Warrior.* 🐲🐲🐲

1983/86 93m/C *HK* Eddie Ko, Lam Ching-Ying, Cecile Le Baily, Chin Yuet Sang, Fung Lee, Phillip Loffrede, Jang Doo Hee, Kim Ho Kon. **D:** John Woo. **W:** John Woo. **C:** Kenchi Naragawa. **M:** Tang Siu-lam. **VHS, DVD**

The Heroic Trio

This strange *Batman*-inspired film mixes Western comic-book superheroes, apocalyptic sci fi,

Michelle Yeoh

楊紫瓊

O.K., let's get one thing straight: Michelle Yeoh could kick the ass of anyone in this room. Pierce Brosnan (James Bond) said she could take him, and Jackie Chan says she's the only woman who should be allowed to make martial arts films. (Sorry if this just shattered the myth of Jackie being an enlightened Western guy.) So, with endorsements like that, what could be said to convince you that you really *need* to check out some of Michelle's flicks if you haven't already joined her legions of rabid fans?

How about that Michelle was crowned Miss Malaysia in the early 1980s? How about that she was both a Bond Girl *(Tomorrow Never Dies)* and the star of *Crouching Tiger, Hidden Dragon*? (We all know that Zhang Zhi Yi wasn't even in Michelle's class without that magical sword!) How about she speaks (and acts) in both English and Cantonese? How about that she held her own against Chinese Olympic champion Li Ning *(Wonder 7)*—and martial arts superstar Jackie Chan *(Supercop)*? How about she has the grace of a dancer and the power of a young Bruce Lee? And she has the acting chops of a young Hepburn. Did we mention that she's easy on the eyes? Did we mention that she's (as of this writing) single?

Well, if that won't convince you, nothing will, but here are a few key facts about Michelle anyway. She was born in on August 6, 1962, in Ipoh, Perak, Malaysia, with the given name Yang Zi Chong. She grew up in Malaysia and speaks Malay as well as English and Chinese. She won both the Miss Malaysia title and the Miss Mooba Beauty Pageant (Australia) in the early 1980s; this brought her to the attention of the Hong Kong movie industry. (Early in her career she also performed under the name Michelle Khan.) Her training as a dancer made her a natural for kung fu and action flicks. Her martial arts moves, fine acting, and good looks soon won her a legion of fans and she became one of the top boxoffice attractions in the Orient.

She progressed through a series of films from *Yes, Madame*, to *Heroic Trio* (with Maggie Cheung and Anita Mui), to *Wing Chun*, to *Twin Warriors* (with Jet Li), to *Supercop* (with Jackie), to *Supercop 2* (with just a cameo by Jackie), to *Tomorrow Never Dies* (with Bond, James Bond), to *Crouching Tiger, Hidden Dragon* (with Chow

Yun-fat), among many others. In 2001 she passed on an offer to appear in the *Matrix* sequels to write, produce, and star in *The Touch*. She is the highest-paid actress in Asia. She was named one of the most beautiful people in the world by *People* magazine in 1997. Despite numerous injuries, she continues to do her own stunts (check out the motorcycle-train jump in *Supercop*). No wonder she was named one of the 25 toughest stars by E! television.

If you're going to check out her oeuvre, the films in the paragraph above are recommended, plus *Butterfly and Sword* and *Wonder Seven*. Avoid *The Executioners*—it's a "sequel" to *Heroic Trio* that fails on most levels. Hey, even Hepburn made some duds. Aside from that, though, nearly any Michelle film is bound to be fun.

Summing up, Michelle is the current queen of Kung Fu cinema. She's got both the acting ability of a first-rate movie star and the kung fu chops of an action heroine. And she could kick your ass. So go check out a Michelle Yeoh flick—now!

Long may she reign.

—SS

and Hong Kong action into a frothy brew that American audiences have taken to much more than the local HK viewers. Babies are being stolen from hospitals in a dark city, the work of the fantastic Invisible Girl (Michelle Yeoh), forced to do the bidding of an evil Demon (Yam Sai-kwoon). The Demon intends to make one of the babies the next emperor of China, the first step in a plan of world domination. Invisible Girl gets her powers from a special cloak, whose inventor (James Pak) is unaware that it's being used for crime. Police inspector Lau (Damian Lau) is assigned to the kidnapping case, but is baffled by the crimes committed by a transparent criminal. Unbeknownst to the detective, his wife Tung (Anita Mui) is also working on the case, in the guise of her secret identity, the black-clad vigilante known as Wonder Woman. Also looking for the kidnapper is the bounty-hunting Thief Catcher (Maggie Cheung), who keeps getting in Wonder Woman's way while they both try to catch Invisible Girl. Eventually, Thief Catcher, who was once also under the Demon's control, provides a clue to Invisible Girl's release, and the trio teams up to confront the villain. But first they'll have to deal with the sinister mutant #9 (Anthony Wong) and his platoon of thugs.

Anita Mui forms a solid center for the fantastic elements swirling around her by taking her role dead seriously. Director Johnny To constructs a loose but compelling world on top of her performance, a place predating similar settings like that in *The Crow*. The distinctive look and dizzying wirework action choreography succeed in keeping this one hopping. Followed by the dour sequel *Executioners*. **AKA:** *Dung Fong Saam Hap; Dong Fang San Xia; Eastern Three Heroes.* 🗡🗡🗡🗡

1993 104m/C *HK* Anita Mui, Maggie Cheung, Michelle Yeoh, Damian Lau, Anthony Wong, James Pak, Paul Chun, Yam Sai-kwoon, Wong Yat-Fei, Lee Siu-Kei. **D:** Johnny To. **W:** Sandy Shaw. **C:** Poon Hang-sang, Tom Lau. **M:** William Woo. **VHS, DVD**

Hero's Blood

A flute-playing servant girl lures lone travelers to the bedchambers of her lady for the night, after which the travellers' luck changes when her pair of deaf-mute swordsmen kill them. A flashback tells how she came to this strange hobby. The gang leader of Mankok Valley Wu Au-yin attacks the Lord Hsu Tien-fu's castle, ransacking it and abducting his daughter Su-au for his bride. Only General Ching Hang is brave enough to come to her defense, and loses an eye trying. Abandoned by her family and fiancé General Yu Bing, Su-au comes to despise them and love the bandit chief, even demanding he brand her thigh. While her husband is tough but fair, Su-au becomes ruthless. Ching leads an attack on the bandits' caves, killing or capturing them all, and "rescuing" Su-au. The cowardly Yu is rejected and Su-au is betrothed to General Ching. However, the spiteful Yu assassinates Ching before the wedding can take place. To cheer up his despondent daughter, Lord Hsu builds her a mansion where she can have anything she desires. But Yu isn't through with her yet, sending an assassin to join her household.

Asian television and novels are full of these odd romance tales about long-suffering heroines, but it's rare for a feature version to make it to the U.S. It's easy to see why with this as an example. The characters are simple and uninteresting, with the exception of the twisted lead, whose personality isn't explored to any great extent. It's really more of a string of incidents than a movie, interrupted now and then for some unconvincing swordplay. Though period costumes and settings are rich and colorful, one shot shows clearly a linoleum floor. ♫

1991 82m/C *HK* Cheang Lung, Kan Mie Chai, Lan Kwong. **D:** David Chan. **DVD**

He's a Woman, She's a Man

A hilarious comedy of errors and sexual confusion, this hit netted Anita Yuen the Best Actress trophy at the '94 Hong Kong Film Awards. Gender-bending hits like this led to others like *Happy Together,* and for a while during the 1990s it seemed as though all of HK was ready to come out of the closet, whether they were in one or not.

Like thousands of other crazy Canto-pop fans in HK, Lam Ji-wing (Anita Yuen) worships her idol Rose (Carina Lau). When Rose's producer/boyfriend Sam Koo (Leslie Cheung) holds a publicity-generating new talent audition, Wing dresses up as a boy and enters just to meet the singer. In the midst of a spat with Rose, Sam signs no-talent Wing to a contract just to spite her, claiming he can make a star out of anybody. Wing is desperate to patch up the difficulties between the King and Queen of Pop, and moves into their lives to try to provide a nurturing environment. But this only creates havoc when they both feel themselves falling in love with Wing!

Both a warm, modern version of *Victor/Victoria* and a wry spoof of the Asian pop-culture industry, there's a lot of joy in this movie. Even Eric Tsang's ultra-enchanted character Auntie—which is a sliver away from being obnoxiously offensive—only serves as another point of perspective in a full spectrum. There are touching, bittersweet moments, and tons of solid laughs throughout. Leslie Cheung must have been getting some of the best laughs himself, as his sex life has been constant fodder for the gossip columns for years. Followed by *Who's the Woman, Who's the Man? AKA: Gam Chi Yuk Sip; Jin Qi Yu She.* ♫♫♫♥

1994 106m/C *HK* Anita Yuen, Leslie Cheung, Carina Lau, Jordan Chan, Eric Tsang, Law Kar-Ying, Jerry Lamb, Lawrence Cheng, Clarence Hui. **D:** Peter Chan. **W:** James Yuen. **C:** Henry Chan. **M:** Clarence Hui. **VHS**

Hi! Dharma!

Surviving a gangland massacre, Jae-gyu (Park Shin-yang) and his boys hide out in a Buddhist monastery. They ask to stay for a week, but when the situation does not blow over, they become engaged in a series of games with the monks to win an extension of their stay. Although violently aggressive, the thugs are repeatedly one-upped by the disciplined monks. As their stay is prolonged, the monks' resentment against their presence builds, while their leader (Kim In-moon) becomes interested in bringing them into the fold, if only to prevent the evil they will cause if returned to the outside world.

What separates *Hi! Dharma!* from its Western counterparts (like *Sister Act, Angels with Dirty Faces,* and *Boys' Town*) is its refusal to take the gangsters seriously, picturing them as weak, undisciplined, immature boys who prefer play to work. The film is something of a tease in the action department, and it is quite a wait before the monks break out the martial arts. When the fighting starts, it is pretty tame, considering that Buddhist monks are forbidden to take a life.

A boxoffice smash in Korea, *Hi! Dharma!* is a crowd-pleaser that maintains a single comedic tone throughout its running time. The characters are all pretty superficial, and the development of the story obvious, but has a high entertainment factor. By the end of the film, it almost seems as if the gangsters will choose the contemplative life. —*BW* **AKA:** *Dalmaya Nolja; Let's Play, Dharma.* ♫♫♫

2001 95m/C *KO* Park Shin-yang, Chung Jin-young, Park Sang-myun, Kang Seong-jin, Kim Su-ro, Hong Kyong-in, Kim In-moon. **D:** Park Cheol-kwan. **W:** Park Gyu-tae. **C:** Park Hui-ju. **M:** Park Jin-seok, Shin Ho-seob. **VHS, DVD**

The Hidden Fortress

Another Kurosawa masterpiece, this film is less well known, and somewhat less serious, than

some of the master's other samurai films (*Seven Samurai, Rashomon, Throne of Blood, Ran*, etc.). The story is set during one of Japan's nearly endless civil wars. The Akizuki clan is in dire trouble; its outlying castles and lands are being seized by a rival clan. Its leaders have been killed, until the only one left is Princess Yuki Akizuki (Misa Uehara), a young slip of a warrior maiden. The princess is hiding out in the mountains with her protector, General Makabe Rokurota (Toshiro Mifune), waiting for the right time to secretly return to her homeland and reinforce her kingdom's holdings. She and the general have amassed a fortune in gold, which is also hidden in the mountains with them. Unfortunately, with enemy patrols everywhere, their trek home promises to be difficult. Into this tricky political situation stumble Tahei (Minoru Chiaki) and Matakichi (Kamatari Fujiwara), two former foot soldiers trying to scrounge their way home. When they accidentally discover some of the Akizuki's hidden gold, they fall in with Rokurota and the princess—who are holed up in the Hidden Fortress. Not willing to kill the two, nor willing to let them go, Rokurota enlists the pair in his plan to return the princess and the gold to the Akizuki homeland.

What follows is an odyssey through villages and wilderlands with the fugitives never more than a few steps ahead of their pursuers.

The Hidden Fortress is famous as one of the inspirations for George Lucas's *Star Wars,* and it's easy to see some parallels. You have the tough-minded princess in danger, the noble warrior (samurai) out to protect her and—most obviously—the two bumbling sidekicks. Tahei and Matakichi are pretty direct templates for the well-known droids R2D2 and C3PO. They enjoy the same kind of bantering relationship, and one of the scenes early in the film mirrors the desert scene in the original *SW.*

Since this is a Kurosawa film, we naturally get a good story, amazing cinematography, and some nice action sequences (including a great spear fight). We also get the usual musings on the meaning of life and the human place in it. *The Hidden Fortress*, though, is lighter fare than some of the master's other films—and a refreshing change of pace for fans of Kurosawa's work. The acting is uniformly excellent, and the characters expertly drawn. What else would you expect from the "god" of Japanese cinema? It's worth noting that this was the first

Toshiro Mifune is chosen as "it" in a game of hide-and-seek in Akira Kurosawa's *The Hidden Fortress.*

film Kurosawa shot in widescreen format. It's also worth noting that it is loosely based on *Men Who Tread on the Tiger's Tail*, an earlier Kurosawa film. The only reason this flick doesn't get four bones is because it's not quite on the same level as Kurosawa's other masterpieces *(Seven Samurai, Ran, Yojimbo, Throne of Blood).* Even so, it stands a cut above most other cinema—both Eastern and Western. —SS *AKA: Kakushi Toride no San Akunin; Three Rascals in the Hidden Fortress.* 🐾🐾🐾🐾

1958 139m (126mUS)/C *JP* Toshiro Mifune, Minoru Chiaki, Kamatari Fujiwara, Susumu Fujita, Misa Uehara, Takashi Shimura, Eiko Miyoshi, Kichijiro Ueda, Koji Mitsui, Tadao Nakamaru, Rinsaku Ogata, Ikio Sawamura. *D:* Akira Kurosawa. *W:* Shinobu Hashimoto, Ryuzo Kikushima, Akira Kurosawa, Hideo Oguni. *C:* Ichio Yamasaki. *M:* Masaru Sato. **VHS, DVD**

High and Low

Director Akira Kurosawa became famous internationally for his period epics like *Yojimbo* and *The Seven Samurai,* but he was equally adept at contemporary stories, as he demonstrated with this suspenseful kidnapping thriller. The title refers not only to the thorough search for the criminals, but to the divisions between classes that remain in modern Japanese society, though the literal translation of Kurosawa's original title, "Heaven and Hell," makes an even stronger statement. On the surface, *High and Low* may appear to be Kurosawa's attempt at a Hitchcock-style nail-biter, but even Masaru Sato's opening music demonstrates a simmering subtext. As the theme drifts over Yokohama's rooftops, industrial noise bubbles up from below to disrupt and destroy its serenity.

Up on High: Industrialist Kingo Gondo (Toshiro Mifune) struggles mightily with internal tensions within his National Shoes company. He's gone heavily in debt in a desperate attempt to save his company from greedy shareholders who want to convert their line to inferior products. From his house on a hill overlooking the city, his high-stakes gamble is interrupted by a frightening phone call: his son Jun has been taken, and the kidnapper is demanding 30 million yen ransom. Kingo doesn't know whether he should cave in to the kidnappers, or gamble with his son's life by cooperating with the police. There's a moment of great relief when Jun appears unharmed. Then a greater moral dilemma presents itself when it's learned that Jun's playmate Shinichi, the chauffeur's son, was taken by mistake. Will Gondo, the police, or the kidnapper behave any differently with the life of a poor man's son at stake? Down beLow: Gondo descends to the sweltering city streets to deliver the ransom via bullet train. The cash delivered, the police embark on a massive

manhunt. The kidnapper is Ginji Takeuchi (Tsutomu Yamazaki), a poor medical student intent on making a target of the man who appears to possess every luxury and comfort he lacks. His tale is one of furtive desperation, contrasted with the methodical analysis and hard work of the detective squad working tirelessly to capture him.

The first half is purposely set-bound, looking almost like a stage play. Kurosawa keeps Asakazu Nakai's camera prowling about Gondo's orderly house—a box that seems to shrink around him as tension mounts, its horizontal lines carefully grouping and separating characters. At midpoint, the film explodes in a riot of noise and jumbled handheld camera work. The second half is a tumult of wide-ranging activity and bustle. Detectives toil through the heat, their shirts sticking to their backs with sweat. Visiting Gondo, they see him sweating too as he mows his own lawn—contrary to Takeuchi's plan to bring him down, Gondo's plight and sacrifice has made him a public hero. In the end, Gondo and Takeushi are brought together, one's image superimposed upon the other. Almost by definition, *High and Low* works superbly on multiple levels. *AKA: Tongoku to Jigoku; Heaven and Hell; The Ransom.* 🐾🐾🐾🐾

1963 143m/C *JP* Toshiro Mifune, Kyoko Kagawa, Tsutomu Yamazaki, Tatsuya Mihashi, Yutaka Sada, Tatsuya Nakadai, Takashi Shimura, Susumu Fujita, Yoshio Tsuchiya, Kenjiro Ishiyama, Takeshi Kato, Isao Kimura. *D:* Akira Kurosawa. *W:* Ryuzo Kikushima, Hideo Oguni, Akira Kurosawa, Ed McBain (story). *C:* Asakazu Nakai, Takao Saito. *M:* Masaru Sato. **VHS, DVD**

High Risk

Special Forces Officer "Bold" Li Kit (Jet Li) makes a wrong decision while trying to defuse a bomb set by the evil "Doctor" (Kelvin Wong), resulting in an explosion that kills his wife (Suki Kwan) and son. Two years later, he's quit the force and works as a bodyguard to movie star Frankie Lone (Jacky Cheung). Frankie is famous for his action films, having gained a reputation for doing all of his own stunts. However, the truth is that Frankie has let success go to his head—and his liver. With Frankie often too drunk to perform, Bold protects him by secretly acting as his stunt double. Frankie's father (Wu Ma) confesses to Bold that Frankie's kung fu is only 20% of what it once was. Then one night, Frankie attends a gala opening of a jewelry exhibit. Doctor and his gang take over the building, holding all the guests hostage while working to unlock the display cases that hold the Russian crown jewels. Bold, having recognized Doctor's voice as he dropped off his boss, makes his way into the building to help, while Frankie tries to find his courage.

High Risk is like a crazed rip-off of *Die Hard* with a lot more loose cannons. In addition to having Bold and a young cop (Yang Chung-hsien) running around the building, Doctor also has to deal with a pushy reporter (Chingmy Yau). Plus, his top fighters, Fai-Fai (Valerie Chow) and Bond (Billy Chow), are always at each other's throats. It's a wonder he has any time left to blow up helicopters or toss people out of windows.

Director/writer Wong Jing worked with Jackie Chan on *City Hunter* a few years prior, and rumor has it the collaboration was not a happy one, so many view the Frankie character as Wong's revenge on Chan. True, Jacky Cheung uses many of Chan's mannerisms, the "no stuntman" angle is nicely parodied, and Charlie Cho's prissy manager character is an outrageous send-up of Willie Chan. However, there's just as much Bruce Lee in Frankie—his movies look more like Lee's, he makes cat squeals while fighting, and his trademark action uniform is Lee's yellow and black jumpsuit—so it's more likely Wong saw it as poking fun, rather than an attack. The other rumor is that Jackie Chan was so angry after seeing *High Risk* that he vowed to never appear in a film with Jet Li. Not so—Chan has been talking about the possibility of making a film with Li for years, though they've yet to find a suitable project.

All told, *High Risk* is an exhilarating action film, featuring fight choreography by Corey Yuen. The film may have benefitted from a larger budget; the special-effects miniatures are especially poor, and the skyscraper setting looks like it has only about five rooms. *AKA: Sue Dam Lung Wei; Shu Dan Long Wei; Jeung Hok Yau; Meltdown.* 🐉🐉🐉🐲

1995 101m/C *HK* Jet Li, Jacky Cheung, Chingmy Yau, Valerie Chow, Kelvin Wong, Charlie Yeung, Wu Ma, Yang Chung-hsien, Charlie Cho, Ben Lam, Billy Chow, Suki Kwan, Vincent Kok, Bobby Yip. *D:* Wong Jing. *W:* Wong Jing. *C:* Tom Lau. *M:* Richard Yuen. **VHS, DVD**

Hiruko the Goblin

All manner of monsters have been subjects of horror movies, but goblins aren't given much play at all, making this Japanese feature a bit of a rarity. Widowed archeologist Reijiro Hieda (Kenji Sawada) is excited to hear news from his friend Yabe (Naoto Takenaka) about an ancient burial mound out in the countryside. The find represents a chance for Hieda to prove his theories and reestablish his reputation, soiled somewhat by a breakdown after his wife's death. Mr. Yabe, who discovered the mound, and a schoolgirl named Reiko Tsukishima (Megumi Ueno), are carried off by something strange while exploring tunnels under the mound. Yabe's son Masao

(Masaki Kudo) wonders about the disappearance, then spies them both together in the school. Masao also develops some sort of burning feverish boil on his back.

Hieda's invention—a goblin detector—reacts violently as he approaches the school, and he and Masao discover the bloody corpses of Reiko and Yabe within. With the power lines down, and Masao's friends Aoi and Katejii still in the school, they have no choice but to load up Hieda's goblin gun and go rescue the boys. These two minor characters are of course playing victim, and are soon beheaded by Hiruko the goblin. The cause, if not the reason, for Masao's wounds is found: for every victim killed, a burn in their likeness appears on his back. Yabe's notes point to the location of the mound, where Hieda hopes a way can be found to contain the goblin once again.

The structure of this fright-fest is nothing new—a monster on the loose in a remote location, and heroes working to defeat the menace without joining the body count. But Hiruko is a bit unlike any other movie beastie. Genealogically speaking, goblins would be to demons what poltergeists are to ghosts—a malevolent but less-cultured entity of some kind. The fate of singing Reiko (surely inspired by a John Carpenter's *The Thing*) is both beautiful and horrible at the same time, and is enhanced by some model animation. The extreme reactions of the characters to some of the horrors may provoke laughs, but it's refreshing to see folks realistically frightened by the frightening in a movie for a change. It may lose momentum now and then, but *Hiruko* is just enough out of the ordinary to make it an effective little shocker. *AKA: Hiroku: Yokai Hanta; Hiroku: Yokai Hunter.* 🐉🐉🐉

1990 88m/C *JP* Kenji Sawada, Naoto Takenaka, Masaki Kudo, Megumi Ueno, Hideo Murota, Kimiko Yo, Ken Mitsuishi. *D:* Shinya Tsukamoto. *W:* Shinya Tsukamoto, Daijiro Moroboshi (manga). *C:* Masaharu Kishimoto. *M:* Tatsushi Umegaki. **VHS**

His Name Is Nobody

With a great cast assembled, Karl Maka spoofs typical martial arts movie clichés in this knockabout kung fu comedy. The title character (Lau Kar-Wing) was abandoned as a baby and has grown up on the streets as a petty thief. As much of his take ends up going to gangster Tiger Dog (Dai Sai Aan), he uses the name Peking Dog, but he really has no name. At a point in the picture when the young hero usually meets an aged kung fu master and begs to become his student, Nobody instead meets illusionist, pickpocket, and con man Woody (Dean Shek). He learns kung fu and participates in some scams with his new sifu, drawing the attention of Woody's brother Scoundrel Seven (Karl Maka). Seven convinces them to help him complete a murder contract on one of the region's great professional killers, Ping the Dreg (Chung Fat). Using a woman to lure Ping into a trap, they find that he's still too tough for the three of them. After Nobody manages to escape, he seeks to improve his fighting skills, and succeeds in becoming the student of the region's other great professional killer, Koo the Iron-Hearted (Leung Kar-yan). Koo rejects traditional kung fu style, training for a more practical approach to fighting. But Koo's street-fighting knowledge is no match for a $10,000 price on his head, and his girlfriend betrays him, leading him to lose his life on Ping's sword. Woody decides to join Nobody in an attempt to get revenge on Ping.

Aside from the expected (given the cast) terrific fight choreography and slapstick ballet, this unorthodox feature also presents some great gags, a bit of pathos, and even a touch of philosophy. The soundtrack is a surprisingly restrained, eschewing the hokey music and sound effects usually found in Cantonese comedies. Dean Shek steals the show with a great eccentric character, does a lot of his own fighting, and even gets to do some sleight-of-hand tricks. His monkey kung fu act (in drag, yet!) during the climax is not to be missed. Maka's own character is thoroughly ruthless, but remains sympathetic, and even ends up a bit sad. At the end there's the only reference we've found (so far) to the American *Kung Fu* television series in an old-school martial arts film. *AKA: Miu Ming Siu Chuet; Wu Ming Xiao Cu.* 🐉🐉🐉

1979 96m/C *HK* Lau Kar-Wing, Dean Shek, Leung Kar-yan, Karl Maka, Chung Fat, Dai Sai Aan, Ho Pak Kwong, Tai San, Lam Ching-Ying, Tsang Choh-lam, Billy Chan, Yue Tau Wan, Meg Lam, Chan Hei, Cheung Wa, Yuen Miu, Baan Yun-sang, Chiu Chi-ling, To Siu Ming, Mars. *D:* Karl Maka. **DVD**

Hit-Man in the Hand of Buddha

As evidence of the continued growing popularity of old-school kung fu movies in the U.S., check out *Halloween: Resurrection,* in which one of the main characters is a huge fan of Hwang Jang Lee. Hwang produced, directed, and starred in this film, giving himself a rare opportunity to play a hero for a change. Wang Cheng (Hwang) is a righteous young country boy who is good at kung fu and is always doing good deeds, despite the general dishonesty he sees all around. When he has his own pocket picked by children, he traces them back to their Fagin-like leader Fan Yi-mei (Fan Mui-Sang) to retrieve

it, and discovers Fan is quite good at kung fu, too. Wang's come to town to visit his sister Chan (Gwok Yin-Yin), but his rascally rice-selling brother-in-law Ah Chu (To Siu Ming) gets Wang involved in a dispute with a rival shop with his underhanded business practices. With Wang working with Chu, the rival shop hires Master Shen Hou (Tino Wong) to fight him, but Wang beats him easily in a nifty chopstick battle. Meanwhile, one of Fan's kids steals a snuff bottle from Shen's fierce master Tiger (Eddie Ko), and he has to do some fancy work to return it before there's trouble. Since his student has lost face, Shen and Tiger go looking for Wang together, killing Chu and raping Chan—after which she commits suicide. To protect Wang, Fan satiates Tiger's rage by promising that his target will leave town. Wang goes to a temple to stay with Abbot Chu Wu, but is kept waiting for months to see the abbot while nasty little monk Tah-chi keeps him working at strenuous, meaningless tasks. By doing some spying Wang learns that the monks are really training him to improve his kung fu, hoping he can beat their mutual enemy Tiger.

With his expressionless face, it's easy to see why Hwang Jang Lee never made a great leading man, and was a great success in villainous roles. Playing the same kind of villain Hwang so often portrayed, Eddie Ko has twice the personality without even trying. However, since Hwang was in charge, it's a nice change of pace to see him in a different light. While the story changes tone too abruptly and often to stay in balance, he does an able job behind the camera as well. But the Korean champ is best known for his fantastic martial arts ability, especially his powerful kicking. Fans of Jet Li's "No-Shadow Kick" in the *Once upon a Time in China* movies can see Hwang do much the same move here—*without* the use of wires! *AKA: Che Diy Saai Yan; Jie Dao Sha Ren.* 🐉🐉🐉

1980 91m/C *HK* Hwang Jang Lee, Fan Mui-Sang, Eddie Ko, Tino Wong, Yeung Wai, To Siu Ming, Bruce Lai, Gwok Yin-Yin, Ko Chun, Corey Yuen. *D:* Hwang Jang Lee. *C:* Chang Hai. **VHS, DVD**

Hit Team

Only half the rocking action yarn the title suggests, this Dante Lam *(Beast Cops)* film also incorporates the kind of police drama typical of Danny Lee and Kirk Wong into his formula. Undercover cop Chong Chin-ho (Chin Ka-Lok) is shot in the back during a police raid by a tough crook named Joe (Joe Lee), and his only hope is an expensive operation at Lasanne Hospital in Switzerland, which has to be performed within three months. His department contact lies that Ho never called him, and since his cell phone was taken by the crook that shot him, Ho has only his word to back him up against charges of coercion with the criminals, giving the department an excuse to suspend him. Ho's SDU buddies Don Chan (Alex To), King, Wong, and Kee vow to do all they can to raise the necessary millions in time to save their friend. They quit the force to plot a heist of funds from the triad's underground bank—intending to use tear gas and try not to hurt anyone, but when things get riskier they shoot all the witnesses.

Sam, BJ, and Fai are members of an elite anti-arms squad called Hit Team, led by Chau Chung (Daniel Wu), and are soon joined by transferred witness protection cop Jane Chan (Jo Koo). Because of the weaponry involved, the Hit Team is called in to investigate the robbery, and almost immediately suspect SDU officers were involved. Since the heist didn't net as much as they need, Don plans to hit the underground bank again, when they least expect it. However, the triad leaders in charge have much more cash coming in from Thailand soon and are expecting a second attempt. They hire Joe to be in charge of catching the thieves. The Hit Team hears of the money transfer, and expects a second attempt as well, but the thieves are warned off. By now, Chau is positive that Chan is leading the thieves, and Chan knows it. Since the thieves victimize only criminals, he's torn between duty and sympathy for the loyal Chan. The thieves fall into a trap laid by Joe, and when one of the thieves is captured, the Hit Team goes against orders to join the remaining thieves in a rescue attempt.

American Daniel Wu still seems a bit young to be playing the humorless team captain, and only briefly gets a chance to display his martial arts skills, but gives a decent impression of the necessary intensity. Lam shows a great deal of detail, and is only slightly overindulgent in some of the dramatic scenes. His biggest error is in shooting the action scenes, which are noisy and exciting enough, but it's sometimes impossible to tell where the characters are supposed to be. The criminals are largely faceless, with the standout exception of Joe Lee, who gives a fine evocation of viciousness and greed. *AKA: Chung Chong Ging Chaat; Chong Zhuang Jing Cha.* 🐉🐉🐉

2000 93m/C *HK* Daniel Wu, Alex To, Samuel Pang, Tony Ho, Jo Koo, Jazz Poon, Allan Mo, Wong Wai-fai, Joe Lee, Cheung Shiu-chit, Clarence Cheung, Monica Lo, Chin Ka-Lok, Ruby Wong, Michael Lui. *D:* Dante Lam. *W:* Clarence Lee, Jack Ng, Dante Lam (story). *C:* Tony Cheung. *M:* Tommy Wai. **VHS, DVD**

H.K. Adams Family

This mob comedy has nothing to do with the Charles Addams cartoons, or with the hit U.S.

feature then playing worldwide. The comedy here could best be described as "whacky," with lots of slapstick and corny sound effects.

In voice-over, family patriarch and triad boss Kan San (Shih Kien) introduces himself and his sons. Eldest son Saint is a cheating gambler, who beats the God of Gamblers (Wong Yat-Fei) with his trickery. Kan Kui (Shing Fui-on) is a racketeer. Third son Kan Wong has many brothels, and youngest Kan Sin (Karel Wong) is a notorious baby killer. San's turncoat brother Kan Fei (Wu Fung) joins dad's birthday party bringing news—uncle Kan Lo-chi died in South America, leaving the family $10 billion (U.S.!). Royal lawyer Sum Kung Ching (Shum Wai) explains—if the family does "100 points" worth of good deeds in one month, they get the money, which otherwise goes to charity.

San becomes a Buddhist, taking daily whippings (or forcing the sons to take them for him), feeds the poor, and does other good deeds. Saint calls a police raid on his own casino. Kui returns protection money he collected. Wong closes brothels. Meanwhile, disowned brother Lam Ko Yee (Lung Fong) and Kan Fei plot against them. Lagging behind in points, the brothers decide to organize a charity show for disaster relief. When they can't find any singers to perform, they form a boy band called the "Grass Hoppers" and lip-sync to pop songs, but Ko's triad friends break things up by starting a fight. Further complications set in when two brothers fall for the same girl, but everything ends up being settled in a casino, where Kan's old girlfriend shows up to save the day. It's altogether ookey. *AKA: Hong Kong Adam's Family; Jian Ren Shi Jia.* 🐉🐉

1992 C: *HK* Shih Kien, Michael Chan, Shing Fui-on, Wong Yat-Fei, Karel Wong, Lung Fong, Wu Fung, Shum Wai. *D:* Bosco Lam. **VHS**

The Holy Robe of Shaolin Temple

With Jet Li off to Hong Kong to seek international stardom, the *Shaolin* series continues with new stars. Making his debut here is Yu Rongguang, a performer who deserves more recognition. Among the horsemen of the western plains, Lin Ying (Mandy Chow) and her three sisters are among the top riders and fighters. Though the Lin horses have been raised for Governor Liu, Lord Huang's Royal Guards come to take some and stampede the herd. A wandering stranger named Ding Mo (Donnie Lee) helps recapture them, befriending Ying and her family. Meanwhile, Royal Guardsman Qi Tian-yuan (Yu Rongguang) is ordered by Emperor Tang to go undercover as monk Liao Kong of the Golden Light Temple. His mission: infiltrate Shaolin Temple, and destroy it! Lord Huang, using the

Hong Kong

To millions of fans worldwide, "Hong Kong Cinema" has become a brand name. It represent a certain indefinably kinetic style of filmmaking, specifically action films. Now, even Hollywood studios are catching on, attempting to film Hong Kong–style movies with Hollywood-style budgets, and coming up with a weird new flavor. But it wasn't always this way.

Actually, the first feature made in Hong Kong was produced by an American, when Benjamin Polaski's Asia Film Company released *To Steal a Roasted Duck* in 1909. The first film made totally by HK natives wasn't until 1923, with *Rouge*. But HK cinema didn't begin to pick up steam until 1937, when the Japanese invasion of the mainland forced Shanghai studios to pack up and evacuate, and Hong Kong became a film capitol. The Japanese followed, but when the war ended most studios went back into production.

The Shaw Brothers, who've been in business since the 1920s, literally dug up buried treasure they'd hidden from the enemy to start making movies again. The Shaws came from a wealthy Shanghai family of textile manufacturers, but in 1925 the eldest brother Run-ji wrote a play for a theatre the family owned. It went over well enough that they decided to make a movie based on it, and his three brothers came into the business with him, much to their father's disapproval. The Shaws came to rule the Hong Kong movie business with an iron hand, keeping production values high and costs low by maintaining strict control of their contractees. Shaw employees signed exclusive contracts starting out at $200 per month plus room and board—from leading men to gaffers, employees lived and ate in Shaw dormitories on their large lots—working in three shifts around the clock, cranking out slick pictures for the Shaws' 400 theatres in HK and abroad. They educated new discoveries in their own drama school, maintained their own back lot of standing sets, and pushed their product in their own gossip magazines.

At the dawn of the 1970s, the Shaws' controlling nature got the best of them. The swordplay heroines who had dominated the HK action film market for 50 years (except for the Wong Fei-hung movies) gave way to gritty macho heroes like Jimmy Wang Yu and Lo Lieh, who practiced brutally violent and semi-realistic kung fu. A terrific new prospect in this genre was a half-breed from California named Bruce Lee. The Shaws offered Lee their standard contract, and he laughed it off, instead signing with a former Shaw executive named Raymond Chow, who'd started up Golden Harvest Studios. Within a few years, Golden Harvest became the dominant HK film studio, and by the mid-'80s the Shaws decided to stop making movies altogether, reasoning they'd make twice as much money by concentrating their efforts on television and other ventures.

Golden Harvest received another boost in the early 1980s when they signed a hot new star—Jackie Chan—to a hefty contract, giving him almost total production autonomy. Golden Harvest soon found their empire challenged by a wave of newcomers—young jewelry store tycoon Dickson Poon formed D&B Films, which soon became one of the top studios. Others, like Cinema City and Golden Princess, were quickly in the mix, battling for audience dollars while their stars battle with feet, fists and machine guns on screens.

Curiously, until recently HK studios have been resistant to the idea of releasing their film libraries on home video, concentrating totally on current product and ignoring what they thought of as worthless old movies. Shaw Brothers refused to release their old films at all, keeping their vaults locked tight until rumors spread that their entire library had disintegrated. But in 2003, a trickle of their classics began to emerge once again on DVD.

The 1990s brought a general downturn in the Hong Kong film business, and not just because of the reunification with China in 1997, though that was a big factor. A victim of its own success, HK cinema had been discovered by the world, and its stars began to accept lucrative offers to make movies elsewhere. Now, except for super-productions like *Avenging Fist* (which are cheaper to make, due to digital f/x technology), HK cinema has retreated into more dramas, comedies, and ghost stories than action pictures. But there are signs of renewed vigor—check out the sharp crime thrillers of Johnny To or the slick blockbusters made by Andrew Lau for evidence.

excuse that many outlaws claim Shaolin training, forces Abbot Yuan Hui to accept Liao Kong as their new leader. But in a demonstration match, Liao Kong fails to gain the monks' respect, using a dirty Wu Tang trick to defeat the abbot. As a peaceful takeover fails, Huang's Guards attack. Ding Mo is actually monk Hui Neng, who returned too late from his spy mission to warn of the attack, but is in time to help the remaining disciples escape the massacre.

He and monk Hui Shi get away with the Holy Shaolin Cotton Robe, planning to take it to safety across the Han River to Fa Hua Temple. As long as they keep it from him, Liao Kong will never be able to truly take over Shaolin. In the most impressive stunt piece of the picture, Abbot Yuan Hui sacrifices himself for his followers by walking across a bridge into a flaming pyre—then another monk goes up in flames to retrieve the body! Hui Shi and some junior students take the robe in a sack toward the river, while Hui Neng takes its box and flees west, and ends up hiding out with the Lins. But Tian-yuan catches up with him, and he and Ying ride to hide out in Wu Tang monastery for protection. But Hui Shi is killed by guards, and the students are unable to keep the Holy Robe from falling into Tian-yuan's hands. Master Xian Ji teaches Hui Neng his Wu Tang martial arts secrets to prepare him for his inevitable duel with Tian-yuan.

While the Shaolin Temple pictures of mainland China were viewed as safely non-political by the Communist government, they often included a rebellious subtext. Here, the religious and cultural freedoms of the Buddhists are threatened by imperious government control. Though the characters aren't as interesting, this one shares the epic scope and spectacular action that make the earlier *Shaolin Temple* movies such a joy. Yu Rongguang would go to Hong Kong within a few years to be in Jet Li movies, but would still be mostly typecast as a villain. **AKA:** *Muk Min Ga Qui; Mu Mien Jia Sha; Holy Robes of Shaolin; Shaolin and Wu Tang 2: Wu Tang Invasion; Silk Cotton Kasaya.* 🐾🐾🐾

1984 90m/C *CH* Yu Rongguang, Donnie Lee, Mandy Chow, Lo Han Ma, Chui Heung Wing, Lam Chau Ping, Yue Daai Luk. **D:** Tsui Siu-Ming. **W:** Tsui Siu-Ming, Cheung Wa. **VHS, DVD**

Hong Kong Nocturne

Deliriously artificial musical about a show-business family experiencing growing pains. The Chia family is a hit at a Hong Kong nightclub. To be more accurate, the singing and dancing of the three beautiful daughters brings in the crowds, though their widowed father Su Cheng (Cheung Kwong-Chiu) imagines that his magic act is the real draw. His dalliance with a young gold digger dismays his daughters, especially because he is spending all their earnings on her. Fed up for this and other reasons, the family act splits up.

Oldest daughter Tsui Tsui (Lily Ho) is promised marriage by Lin Kao-wei (Lui Ming), and they head off to Japan. Youngest daughter Ting Ting (Chin Ping) yearns to be a ballerina, so she takes off for ballet school. Middle daughter Chuen Chuen (Cheng Pei-Pei) reluctantly stays behind, feeling sorry for her father, though she wanted to accept an invitation to join a song-and-dance troupe led by her secret crush, Chen Tze-Ching (Peter Chen Ho). When her desperate and overextended father wants her to strip as part of their act so they can make more money, Chen steps in and rescues her. Though he nurtured romantic feelings for Tsui Tsui, he realizes he is actually in love with Chuen Chuen. With

this setup in place, the rest of the story follows the three girls as they try to achieve their dreams, only to find that their chosen paths are not as smooth as they thought.

"I love you! Let's dance." That amusing couplet may best sum up the unpretentious and lively spirit of this musical. Though the second half drags a bit due to a few extended trips into melodramatic territory, there are plenty of lighter moments achieved through singing, dancing, and romancing to balance things out. The costumes and sets feature an eye-popping array of colors, and the three young beauties acquit themselves quite nicely. Cheng Pei-Pei is the most familiar name here—she certainly displays grace and acting ability—but Chin Ping and the 15-year-old (!) Lily Ho demonstrate star power as well. As much as anything, the success of *Hong Kong Nocturne* is due to writer/director Inoue Umetsugu's insanely graceful eye for Hollywood-style musical transitions. Most of the musical numbers are framed as flights of fantasy, but others begin simply within the context of an otherwise-realistic scene. Save for a couple of brief exterior shots, the entire production was filmed on soundstages. This was the first film the Japanese director made for the Shaw Brothers Studio, and it was a remake of a 1939 effort. For viewers who have never been exposed to the musical side of Hong Kong movies, it's an enchanting introduction. —*PM* **AKA:** *Heung Kong Dut Yuet Yau; Xiang Jiang Hua Yue Ye.* 🐾🐾🐾

1967 123m/C *HK* Cheng Pei-Pei, Lily Ho, Chin Ping, Peter Chen Ho, Ling Yun, Tin Fung, Ling Yun, Yueh Hua, Paul Chang, Lui Ming, Lee Wan-chung, Cheung Kwong-Chiu, Tina Chin, Cheng Hong-yip, Chan Hei, Ku Feng, Yang Sha-fei, Wong Yeuk-ping. **D:** Inoue Umetsugu. **W:** Inoue Umetsugu. **C:** Arthur Wong. **M:** Mooi Lam-mau. **DVD**

Hong Kong X-File

A Hong Kong version of the American TV and movie series *The X-Files* is a potentially fun idea—Scully and Mulder never got around to investigating hopping vampires. Unfortunately, this horror comedy wastes a good title on yet another silly ghost movie. Cops Ben (Bowie Lam) and Miu (Chin Ka-Lok) miss a big raid on the drug kingpins, and are punished by being assigned to prostitution detail in the red-light district. Business is slow during the Ghost Festival. At the Ka Yuen Sauna, a vengeful ghost kills a customer, and the cops are baffled—though superstitious Miu guesses the truth. Masseuse Nancy (Cheng Yim-lai) thinks it's the ghost of her friend May (Siu Yuk-yin), and burns hell notes for her. May has been in a coma for months, since she was raped and half-

drowned at the sauna after seeing the pimps kill her husband. Horny Keung, the boss pimp, is also a necromancer, and regularly casts spells to make his girls more accommodating. He puts a constipation spell on Miu to try to keep him away. He sends his men to get rid of Nancy as well, but the cops save her, and she tells them the whole story. An investigation reveals that May had a twin sister named Cat, now long dead. But be it Cat or May, the ghost can't harm Keung or his men because they're protected by magic amulets. May's doctor happens to be a necromancer, too, and helps our heroes crack the case.

Some of the scenes of ghosts frolicking at the festival are quite nice. One scene makes reference to Mario Bava's *Kill Baby Kill*. But for the most part this is tedious nonsense, with blunt comic antics occasionally interrupted by half-naked women or un-scary ghost attacks. The whole affair is clumsy and poorly edited. *AKA: Gwai Gwat Cheung; Gui Gu Chang.* ♫

1998 87m/C *HK* Bowie Lam, Chin Ka-Lok, Cheng Yim-lai, Siu Yuk-yin. *D:* Kar Kar. *W:* Kant Leung. *C:* Yip Pak-ying, Mok Chak-yan. **VHS, DVD**

Horror Hotline... Big Head Monster

Nighttime radio call-in talk programs have been wildly popular in Hong Kong for years, especially supernatural-themed shows. This horror film centers on one such show called "Horror Hotline." American TV journalist Mavis Ho (Josie Ho) is doing a story on the show, and "HH" producer Ben (Francis Ng) agrees to let her sit in and interview him and hosts Ruth and Edmond on the air. The crew follows as they interview medium Auntie Ying (Bonnie Wong) for the program, but the subject reacts negatively toward the journalist. During the broadcast, a caller named Chris tells a story from his childhood in 1963, of exploring an old building and seeing a big-headed baby with many eyes in a cage. The story is a hot topic, and though Ben's style is to merely discuss it as a popular legend, Mavis does some research and finds the Iranian principal who was a witness. They learn that Chris and his old schoolmates have recently visited the old man. During the next show, Chris calls in again, angry that they've tried to trace him, and warns that one of them will die.

At the same time, Edmond and Ruth go into a stupor on the air. Later, Mike the cameraman disappears after watching the tape and seeing someone else in the studio with them at the time: Chris. Further research finds that Chris's six companions all committed suicide the day before. Meanwhile, Ben's girlfriend Helen (Niki Chow), a nurse at a psychiatric hospital, is trou-

bled by a patient (Sam Lee) who saw something monstrous while playing paintball. Mavis gets a call from Mike that leads them to a storage space, where he is found long dead, a drawing in blood of the monster on the wall above him. Despite the opposition of the police, lawyers, and their bosses, Mavis and Ben keep digging toward the secret of the Big Head Monster.

Despite the cheesy title, this is one of the better horror flicks to come out of Hong Kong in recent years. The radio show it's based on is real, with hosts Edmond Poon and Ruth playing themselves, and the Big Head Monster is a part of urban folklore there. This otherwise effective chiller, with fine special effects by Cinefex, was originally shown in theatres with a rather abrupt and unsatisfying ending. The video release also contains a second abrupt and unsatisfying "Day of the Dead" ending. Both endings borrow stylistically from *The Blair Witch Project* and other American camcorder horror flicks. The main title sequence is a very creative piece which combines swirling animated text and swinging phones over a...disgusting hole of some kind— unusual for a Hong Kong film, since they rarely give so much attention to credits. *AKA: Hung Biu Sin Ji Daai Tau Gwai Ang; Kong Bu Re Xian Zhi Da Tou Guai Ying; Hung Bo Yit Sin.* ♫♫♫

2001 89m/C *HK* Francis Ng, Josie Ho, Sam Lee, Niki Chow, Michelle Zhang, Bonnie Wong, Ruth, Edmond Poon. *D:* Bob Cheng. *W:* Sunny Chan, Bob Cheng. *C:* Ko Chiu-lam. *M:* Koo Lai Yip. **VHS, DVD**

asians in usa

Horror of the Blood Monsters

Around the time when Independent International Pictures was releasing Philippine monster pictures starring John Ashley, they picked up a Philippines-made caveman fantasy epic entitled *Tagani*. It had action, monsters, violence, and scantily clad cave girls—everything an exploitation producer could want. Producer Sam Sherman planned to either dub the entire film or use it for stock footage and shoot new scenes around it. There was only one problem: the movie was in black and white. The solution: tint all the footage and sell it as a revolutionary new film process (a tactic that had worked more than once), explaining away the look by setting it all on another planet! And since they were tinting it all anyway, why not use clips from other pictures like *One Million B.C.* as well?

John Carradine made a career out of being in bad movies, and this one competes as one of the worst. Added footage shows vampires attacking people, while Carradine spouts nonsense about the bloodsuckers being from outer space. Robert Dix and Vicki Volante lead an expedition to another world to track down the source of the vampire plague—or do they? There's so much mix-and-match editing, with plenty of "action" taking place off screen (while the on-screen imported antics remain unexplained), that it's difficult to tell whether this can actually be called a movie or not. A milestone in the audacious career of Al Adamson, who made a bundle from this assemblage of film stock by releasing it over and over under different titles. Brother Theodore provides the opening narration. Special-effects man David L. Hewitt was a former spook-show magician who directed his own movies that were just as horrible as this one. No doubt many of you caught a piece of this on late night TV, and woke up the next morning convinced you dreamed it all. *AKA: Tagani; Vampire Men of the Lost Planet; Cry of the Wolf; Horror Creatures of the Red Planet; Horror Creatures of the Lost Planet; Horror Creatures of the Prehistoric Planet; Creatures of the Red Planet; Space Mission of the Lost Planet; The Flesh Creatures; Flesh Creatures of the Red Planet; Night of the Wolf.* 🐉🐉

1970 (PG) 85m/C *PH/US* John Carradine, Robert Dix, Vicki Volante, Jennifer Bishop. **D:** Al Adamson. **W:** Sue McNair. **C:** William G. Troiano, Vilmos Zsigmond. **M:** Mike Velarde. **VHS, DVD**

The Hot, the Cool, and the Vicious

An old-school kung fu flick with a definite Western influence, this one relies more on plot and personality than action. Kung fu killer Pai Yu-ching (Wang Tao), the Southern Fist, gets out of prison after a two-year stretch, and immediately gets in a fight at a village inn with Mr. Teh (Che Yuen). Security Force Captain Lu Tung-chun (Delon Tan), the Northern Leg, threatens to throw him out of town if he causes more trouble. But the fight is a ruse—Teh is in cahoots with Pai, and the fight was to throw everyone off the scent in preparation of an operation they're planning.

Their target Mayor Yuen (George Wang) is the richest man in town. Yuen's good-for-nothing son Man-san (Man Chung-san) earns Captain Lu's enmity by molesting his fiancée Lin Cho-sang, accidentally killing her poor mother in the scuffle. In a discussion fraught with exposition, Lu reminisces with Cho-sang about why he's such an upstanding lawman. He was once a wanted man, having killed a man in self-defense, and his predecessor Captain Li Yao-ba was killed by a snakebite while trying to capture him. After serving his prison term, Lu returned to serve the community. Having overheard his tale, a woman in ninja garb looks for her chance

to kill Lu—she's Li's sister (Karen Sun), who is in town with her father (Chai Kai) to avenge her brother's death. She isn't the only one who wants him dead—Yuen offers Pai a reward to kill Lu. Pai turns down his offer, but instead asks to become his chief of security. Having failed in her own attempt, Miss Li tries to hire Pai to kill Lu, too.

When Lu comes to arrest his son Man-san, Yuen fires him from his post, and the two leads finally face off—though their fight is a disappointment. Most of the fight scenes look a little slow and unnatural in the film, and this one's no exception. It ends in a draw, and the two part as friendly enemies. Predictably, Pai turns out to be an undercover agent investigating Yuen's counterfeiting ring. Later, the two heroes team up to face Yuen's bizarre associate Mr. Lung. As Lung, Tommy Lee dons a light blonde wig and white powder makeup, and talks with an echo effect! Not a bad movie, but the only really worthwhile fight scene is saved for the final minutes. Delon Tan would be back as Lu in *Challenge of Death*, with Wang Tao playing a different shady character. *AKA: Naam Kuen Bak Tui Chim Ming Wong; Nan Quan Bei Tui Zhan Yan Wang; Southern Fist King vs. Northern Leg King.* 🐉🐉🐉

1976 92m/C *HK* Wang Tao, Delon Tan, Tommy Lee, Phillip Ko, Karen Sun, George Wang, Man Chung-san, Che Yuen, Chen Chiu, Sit Hon, Tan Tao Keung, Kao Po, Yeung Gam-yuk, Lau Yin-ko, Chai Kai, Chui Chung Hei, Mau Ging-shun, Lung Fong, Sit Cheung-man, Kuo Lu, Liu Yin Sheung, Lee Kin Man. **D:** Lee Tso Nam. **W:** Chang Seng-yi. **C:** Tuang Yin Jian. **M:** Chou Fu-liang. **VHS, DVD**

Hot War

We all remember the scene in *The Matrix* where Keanu Reeves learns kung fu in a few days. Jackie Chan must find that scene memorable for a different reason, having produced this film the year previous, which uses a very similar concept as its main gimmick.

Professor Duna is kidnapped from the Subliminal Research Center in Belfast. At CIA Lab 20 in Chicago, tensions run high as it's feared the kidnappers will target their research scientists next. But scientists Blue Szeto (Kelly Chan), Tango One (Ekin Cheng), and C.S. Koo (Jordan Chan) are more concerned that their Project VR Fighter will be aborted by budget cuts. They all go down to Miami, where Koo plans to stay after he gets married. But the wedding is spoiled when the kidnappers, led by the criminal Alien (Terence Lin), show up to abduct Blue and kill the bride. Finding their superiors are treating Blue as an acceptable loss, Koo and Tango decide to try to rescue her themselves, and undergo the dangerous VR Training designed to make them into super-warriors.

They succeed in their mission to rescue Blue and the other scientists, and even get some of Alien's data files. The data tells them he's working for a guy named Michael Rossburger who is planning to use subliminals to somehow attack the World Cup games. While they try to figure out how the attack might happen, it's discovered that a small percentage of VR trainees have turned excessively violent. When Koo kills Alien's assistant J (Vanessa Yeung), it appears that he may be one of the violent ones, which is confirmed when his delusions cause him to accidentally kill Blue. Now a wanted man, Koo goes on the run, intending to kill Alien. But Tango's grief makes him the perfect subject for CIA brainwashing that turns him into a member of their Eraser team bent on eliminating his best friend for good.

Perhaps it's all the cold, empty office-building sets, but *Hot War* is anything but hot. All the pieces are in place to make it a superior international action drama, but it all has an artificial feel that keeps the viewer at a distance. Stephen Tung is one of the best action directors around, but his work here looks like it's simply trying to be impressive, rather than giving the feeling of real danger. There's location shooting in Chicago and Los Angeles, but only the scenes in Malaysia impart any local flavor, or a sense that anything is occurring outside the controlled environment of a movie set. Peter Kam's bland generic score doesn't help matters. *AKA: Waan Ying Dak Gung; Huan Ying Te Gong.* 🐾🐾

1998 93m/C *HK* Ekin Cheng, Jordan Chan, Kelly Chan, Terence Yin, Vanessa Yeung, Asuka Higuchi, Jude Poyer. **D:** Jingle Ma. **W:** Calvin Poon, Law Chi-leung, Chow Siu-man. **C:** Chan Chi-ying. **M:** Peter Kam. **DVD**

House of the Damned

Movie extras Kiki (Teresa Mak) and Big Bust rent an apartment from crippled Aunt Nan (Hong Kong horror queen Helena Law) via a newspaper ad, not bothering to look at the front of the paper, or they would've seen the story about how the previous tenant vacated the premises by jumping out a window. The spooky music and odd camera angles should have tipped them off that the joint is haunted. Though Catholic Kiki doesn't believe her, Big Bust is frightened that a horny ghost is trying to peep at and molest them. She gets ghostbuster Master Chow Tung, who is working on the same movie, to perform an exorcism, but he turns out to be a lecherous rascal. Chow pays for his trick the next night when the ghost runs him down with a car. Chauffeur Chiu (Eric Wan),

who really does have ghostbusting knowledge, suspects the truth: Nan is keeping the body of her dead son hidden in the apartment below, and his restless spirit is getting more restless every day. Nan sets her sights on chaste Kiki as the perfect daughter-in-law, and steals her Bible to make way for her ghost son to woo her.

A lame ghost comedy from Wong Jing's Workshop features spooky camera work, leering camera work, and sometimes both at once. The worst part is the ineffectual comedy of Chapman To, who tries to attain Stephen Chow–style tomfoolery and fails as the girls' cowardly friend Chak. Eric Wan, who came to fame in the ATV series *My Date with a Vampire*, has appeared in a lot of crappy horror flicks since then. *AKA: Shut Hei Bik Yan; Shi Qi Bi Ren.* 🎵

1999 87m/C *HK* Helena Law, Teresa Mak, Eric Wan, Chapman To. **D:** Bosco Lam. **VHS, DVD**

Hum Paanch

Taken from a Mahabharata legend, this epic remake of Puttana Kangal's 1978 *Paduvarahalli* updates the legend to modern times. The village throws a festival in honor of the birthday of Zamindar Veerpratap Singh (Amrish Puri). All sing Singh's praises, except for his nephew Arjun (Raj Babbar), who considers his uncle an enemy since his father was driven to suicide by drink, gambling, and debt. Arjun blames Singh for encouraging this behavior in order to take over his property. Arjun's buddy Suraj returns home from college to find his father in a similar pickle, gambling away the family fortune in Singh's crooked card games. Singh's crimes don't end there; he shamelessly dabbles with Sundariya, a maiden of a lower caste, kicking her out when she becomes pregnant—after which the girl has a nervous breakdown. And he's taken over most of the area through his casino and loan shark business. Even Singh's slave Bhima (Mithun Chakraborty) knows of these crimes, but doesn't dare speak up. Singh's brother Krishna (Sanjeev Kumar) has a right to half the family fortune, but doesn't exercise control since becoming a monk, and Singh feeds his brother's alcoholism to keep him from making trouble. But Krishna is keeping track of his brother's sins, vowing to step in when they reach 100. Bhima has fallen for Lahiya, but when his master won't give him some cash for their wedding, he gets fed up with defending the scoundrel and leaves to join the good guys. Singh's servant Lala (Kanhaiyalal) tries to divide his enemies with bribes and lies, but they respond by stealing his glasses, smearing him with dirt, and singing a pretty mean song about him. The rebellion boils over when Singh slaps Bhima during a religious festival, sparking a wild brawl between the five heroes and Singh's thugs.

Bollywood

When this book was in the planning stages, there weren't going to be any Indian movie reviews, despite the fact that India produces more movies than any other country in the world. The problem was that very few movies were available on home video with English subtitles, and those that were are not what anyone would consider a "cult flick."

On the contrary, the Indian film business is primarily dedicated to feeding a universal audience—studios strive to put a little bit of everything in each movie, with the emphasis on elements that the lowest common denominator will enjoy. Almost every film is a musical, with plots that mix comedy, romance, and sometimes action and mystery. But the song-and-dance numbers are the number-one preoccupation—the music business in India is almost synonymous with the movie business. Even in crime thrillers, the cops and robbers are liable to break into song at any moment. This homogeny comes despite the fact that the population speaks 20 different languages with hundreds of dialects. Or maybe the babble of tongues is left behind in the universal language of music and image. Competition for ticket sales is fierce, so the more people who will find something they like in your movie, the better off you are.

Horror films in particular still have an unsavory reputation, and despite the fact that hundreds of Indian horror films have been made, their black-sheep status is kind of quaint in today's world.

Fortunately, as work continued, more and more Indian films became available on Region 0 DVD, and most of these have English subtitle options. Though the bulk of the bizarre horror and science-fiction films of Bollywood have yet to become available, there are still quite a few titles that qualify for this volume, and we hope to have many more when we get around to a second edition.

However, it's a trap set by Singh, who has called in government troops to arrest the troublemakers, who are sent to prison for three months.

What's a Bollywood movie without at least one bizarre musical number? Taking a break from abusing the villagers, Singh pays a visit to the big city to see his son Navi and his fiancée Nishi, who arrange a lavish tribute performed by dozens of disco divas. Their purpose is to convince Singh to go into business with Nishi's father to industrialize their village. Of course, to finance his share of the investment, Singh convinces the villagers to contribute their life's savings. The heroes get out of jail in time to slip

the treasure away, and though Singh orders them burned to death in a fire, the missing treasure is used to divide the villains.

The movie isn't as action-packed as the ad graphics might suggest, though there are a few awkwardly enacted martial arts fight scenes. The characters are simple but earnestly portrayed, the main point of the narrative being to build up Singh's villainy, and emphasize the blindness of the villagers that supported him. The universal political message is lightly delivered in a painless and entertaining package, with good music, romance, and even a bit of spook-show thrills. But director Bapu makes the most of the film's best asset—its location shooting in Karnataka and Melkote. The real mountain village, with ancient monuments dominated by an incredible temple atop a hill, is production value that can't be created on a soundstage. *AKA: We Five.* 🐉🐉🐉

1980 153m/C *IN* Amrish Puri, Sanjeev Kumar, Mithun Chakraborty, Raj Babbar, Shabana Azmi, Kanhaiyalal, Deepti Naval, Nasiruddin Shah, Uday Chandra, Gulshan Grover, Aruna Irani, Roopesh Kumar, Geetha Siddharth, A.K. Hangal. *D:* Bapu. *W:* M.V. Ramana, S.R. Putanna Kanagal (story). *C:* Sharad Kadwe. *M:* P. Balasubrahmanyam. **DVD**

The Human Vapor

This entry in Toho's "altered human" series of horror films presents a variation on the Invisible Man, improbably crossed with *The Blue Angel*—or perhaps more accurately *The Phantom of the Opera.* Once a sanitarium inmate, librarian Mizuno (Yoshio Tsuchiya) meets Dr. Sano (Fuyuki Murakami), and is easily talked into becoming a subject of an experiment. After treatment in an airtight chamber, Mizuno sleeps for 10 days, then awakes with the ability to turn his body into gas form. He goes off the deep end, kills Sano, and embarks on a murder and bank robbery spree. Mizuno uses the money to finance a comeback for a dancer he met in the asylum, Fujichiyo Kasuga (Kaoru Yachigusa). The cops arrest Fujichiyo when she spends some stolen cash, and the Vapor Man flies into a rage, defying capture at every turn.

Toho sci-fi specialist Ishiro Honda *(Godzilla)* maintains both suspense and pathos, while special-effects master Eiji Tsuburaya does a fine job with scenes of the gaseous criminal causing havoc, especially an eerie scene in which Mizuno dissolves while surrounded by police. While a solid thriller, not enough of a dramatic foundation is laid for the relationship between the phantom librarian and the dancer to resonate properly. Lots of plot was edited out of the American version, leaving only the most sensational elements, and poorly dubbed at

that. Originally double-billed in U.S. theatres with *Gorath.* Toho contract player Tsuchiya is well remembered for also playing the controller of Planet X in *Invasion of Astro-Monster,* and in 1989 he was honored for his role in *Human Vapor* by being cast as "Dr. Mizuno" in *Tokyo: The Last Megalopolis.* *AKA: Gasu Ningen Daiichigo; The First Gas Human.* 🐉🐉▽

1960 81m/C *JP* Tatsuya Mihashi, Kaoru Yachigusa, Yoshio Tsuchiya, Keiko Sata, Hisaya Ito, Yoshifumi Tajima, Yoshio Kosugi, Fuyuki Murakami, Bokuzen Hidari, Takamaru Sasaki, Minosuke Yamada, Tatsuo Matsumura, Kozo Nomura, Ren Yamamoto, Yukihiko Gondo, Shoichi Hirose, Someshu Matsumoto, Haruo Nakajima, Tetsu Nakamura. *V:* James Hong (U.S.). *D:* Ishiro Honda. *W:* Takeshi Kimura. *C:* Hajime Koizumi. *M:* Kunio Miyauchi. **VHS**

Hunted by Royal Decree

Unrest rules the streets during the Ching Dynasty. Imperial troops storm through town, searching out any threat to the reign of Chin Loong. The Red Flower rebels are planning to dethrone the Manchu emperor, and return rule of China to the Chinese. Looking to escape the pressures of the court, the emperor goes walkabout and meets up with musician/martial artist/renaissance man Jackie Chan (no relation to the star). Jackie (Kenny Ho) doesn't suspect the emperor's true identity (believing him to be merely a noble), and the emperor doesn't know that Jackie is the leader of the Red Flower rebels. The two part as friends. When next they meet, their true natures are revealed and the men are torn between friendship and loyalty. Matters are further complicated because Chin is not a true Manchu, but secretly an ethnic Chinese. In fact, Chin is actually Jackie's brother—who was stolen from Jackie's parents shortly after birth. Can the brothers work out their differences without tearing the kingdom apart?

Another shot-on-video "film" distributed by Jalisco label, likely culled from a television production, *Hunted by Royal Decree* features the usual Westernized names for characters—though naming the lead character "Jackie Chan" is ballsy even for Jalisco. Other than that, the dubbing is straightforward though not entirely free of Jalisco's anachronisms. What this film has going for it, though, is a greater attention to detail than other video efforts, like *Dragonslayer Sword.* The sets are better, the locations are better, and the fight scenes are a hell of a lot better. These don't look like choppy TV fights, rather, they compare well with cinematic kung fu battles. The "Jackie Chan" character, in particular, is very convincing as a wu shu warrior, having skill with both sword and fist. Excellent fight choreography and action scenes make this video production a cut above the rest. Followed by *Rebels under Siege* and *The Unconquered*. —SS 🐉🐉🐉

2000 87m/C *CH* Kenny Ho, Shen Mung Shang, Chen Sa Lei, Liu Shu Hua. **D:** Chu Ka Liang. **VHS, DVD**

The Hypnotist

This is credited as based on the novel *Saimin* by Keisuke Matsuoka, but bears a close resemblance to 1960's *The Hypnotic Eye* (and to a lesser extent *The Wizard of Gore*). One scene even reproduces *Eye*'s famous washing-with-fire sequence, but this superior shocker succeeds beyond its influences.

All across Japan, bizarre deaths occur: a groom strangles himself at his wedding reception; another man celebrates his wife's birthday by jumping through a skyscraper window; an athlete runs so hard her legs are smashed. All the victims mutter something about a green monkey before they die. Inspector Sakurai (Ken Utsui) is called in on the apparent wedding suicide, and meets the other two victims in the morgue. Police psychologist Saga (Goro Inagaki) thinks the victims were following a post-hypnotic suggestion. The deaths continue: a warehouse worker leads a truck backward until it crushes him; a clerk freezes herself in a meat locker; a woman is asphyxiated inside a phone booth. The green monkey strikes again.

Sakurai hears a girl talking about the green monkey on television. TV hypnotist Mr. Jissoji (Takeshi Masu) has model Yuka Irie (Miho Kanno) so confused she's totally lost touch with reality, but he still uses her as a "cosmic channeler" on his program. Jissoji is such a powerful hypnotist that he can incapacitate Saga instantly in the middle of an accusation. While Sakurai continues to investigate Jissoji, Saga follows Yuka, and discovers she has a separate personality, a prostitute named Rieko. It's discovered that Yuka was hypnotized by a mystery man while staying in a hospital. But not Jussoji—that lead is cut short when the hypnotist is found crucified on an electric sign, his body neatly forming a "T" next to the word "ERROR." An interrogation reveals the *three* faces of Yuka, but when pressed about the green monkey, she retreats into her comic Andrea the Alien personality. And when it looks like Saga may be making progress, a hypnotic assault occurs that knocks out everyone in the room. A dragnet is cast for both Yuka and the killer, but it's obvious that even the police force have been hypnotized by the villain, and it's unknown what hypnotic signal will cause a deadly reaction.

Though it starts out like a gimmick-based horror flick, *The Hypnotist* manages to over-come its convoluted plot by playing the hokum straight, and ends up heightening the suspense in the latter half. Its influences go beyond *Hypnotic Eye* to include a heavy dose of Italian giallos and British thrillers of the 1970s. *Se7en* and *The Ring* are also emulated, and with a little more style, director Ochiai might rise to the level of David Fincher or Dario Argento. *The Hypnotist* has too much of the bland look of many modern Japanese films, but contains plenty of surprising, entertaining twists to support it nevertheless. The digital f/x are a bit too obvious, but successfully creepy. With this and the creepy ghost film *Tomie*, Miho Kanno is building a career as a horror star in Japan. **AKA:** *Saimin; Hypnosis*. 🐉🐉🐉🐲

1999 109m/C *JP* Goro Inagaki, Miho Kanno, Ken Utsui, Akira Shirai, Takeshi Masu, Shigemitsu Ogi, Ren Osugi, Tadao Nakamaru, Yuki Watanabe, Haru-ki Misaya, Masahiro Noguchi, Katsumi Takahashi. **D:** Masayuki Ochiai. **W:** Masayuki Ochiai, Yasushi Fukuda, Keisuke Matsuoka (novel). **C:** Osamu Fujishi. **M:** Kuniaki Haishima. **VHS, DVD**

I Love Maria

Tsui Hark's Cinefex Workshop took a break from the supernatural world of ghost movies to try their hands at sci-fi with this comic action romp. Reporter T.Q. Zhuang (Tony Leung) sneaks into a restricted zone and gets a look at the police trying to stop a huge killer robot as it steals the entire safe from the Hong Kong gold reserve. The unstoppable robot, at the command of Saviour (Ben Lam), leader of the Hero Gang, declares war on the city and takes off with its boot jets. Finding the Pioneer 1 robot too full of bugs, Saviour has a more advanced model Pioneer 2 prepared, which he has made to look exactly like his girlfriend/assistant Maria (Sally Yeh). Meanwhile, police scientist Curly (John Sham), discouraged when his boss (Dennis Chan) suppresses his design for a handheld electro-sonic cannon, goes for a drink. At the bar he meets Zhuang and Whisky (Tsui Hark), a Hero Gang member (and Maria's childhood friend) whose alcoholism has him in trouble with the gang. Despite the objection of Whisky's old triad superior (Lam Ching-ying), the apparent traitor is made a test target for Pioneer 2, but Whisky and Curly manage to survive her attack by accidentally short circuiting the robot. Their friendship marks Curly as a traitor as well, so they both hide out and repair Pioneer 2 to be used against Saviour.

Yeh *(Peking Opera Blues)* turns out to be very good at portraying a lifeless machine, her blank stare giving the same feeling one gets when looking at any beautiful motorcycle or DVD player. Tsui Hark is good enough that it's a shame he doesn't get out in front of the camera more often. Other directors get in on the act, too—his buddy John Woo can be seen briefly as the chief of police under the end credits, and Kirk Wong plays a bartender. The special effects are well done—the big robot is given a nice impression of weight. Lam Ching-ying gets to show off some of his kung fu near the end, facing off against a robotized Ben Lam. Tony Leung went from this sort of silliness on to the dire *Bullet in the Head* within a few years. **AKA:** *Tit Gaap Miu dik Ma Lee a; Tie Jia Wu di Ma Li ya; Roboforce.* 🐉🐉🐉

1988 96m/C *HK* Sally Yeh, John Sham, Tsui Hark, Tony Leung Chiu-Wai, Lam Ching-ying, Ben Lam, Paul Chun, Dennis Chan, Victor Wong, Kirk Wong. **D:** David Chung. **W:** Yuen Kai-chi. **C:** Lo Wan-shing. **M:** Romeo Diaz, James Wong. **VHS, DVD**

Iceman Cometh

Yuen Biao and Maggie Cheung in a Eugene O'Neill drama? No, it's more like the Hong Kong version of *Time after Time,* and a similar plot would later be used in the Sylvester Stallone film *Demolition Man.* During the late Ming Dynasty, the evil Feng San (Yuen Wah) has killed a princess (Lai Yin-san) and stolen the Black Jade Buddha; royal guardsman Fong Sau-ching (Yuen Biao) is given 20 days to track the villain down. (It takes him a little longer.) Fong catches up with Feng San just as he's using the Buddha in conjunction with the Wheel of Life to grant himself 100 lifetimes. Battling on a mountaintop, the two enemies plunge into an abyss.

In 1989, their frozen bodies are found in ice by a team of scientists (led by Elvis Tsui), who decide to take them to Hong Kong as an excuse to escape Red China. Some warehouse workers stealing delicacies for a party accidentally thaw them out. While trying to find out where he is, Fong comes upon hooker Polly (Maggie Cheung) entertaining a client, and he "rescues" her. There follows the expected fish-out-of-water situations, with Polly taking Fong as an ignorant bumpkin. Her simple explanations of modern appliances are understood perfectly—a refreshing change from the usual bit where the primitive takes everything as "magic." The film's middle is lacking in action as the two stars get to know each other, but it thrives on their personalities, and the coming conflict is more involving for it. Polly hires Fong on as a servant (for HK$300 a month!), and his many skills come in handy. He also learns many things about modern society through her eyes. Meanwhile, Feng San adjusts more quickly to modern life under even more sordid circumstances, remaining a vicious criminal. Of course, the two come together, and Fong drinks poison to save Polly. Modern medicine

saves him, but he still needs to deal with Feng San, who plans to use the Wheel to take crates of modern weapons back to the Ming Dynasty and use them to alter history.

The idea of using different cinematographers to portray different periods is a good one, but six is overdoing it, and Joseph Chan's simple keyboard score takes the production down a notch. Still, this is an excellent fantasy adventure, with good special effects and fine performances. The drama never becomes ridiculous, and as for the action—there's not too much in the second act, but the third has everything one could ask for in a battle between Yuen and Yuen. **AKA:** *Gap Dung Gei Hap; Ji Dong Ji Xia; Time Warriors.* 🐉🐉🐉

1989 109m/C *HK* Yuen Biao, Maggie Cheung, Yuen Wah, Tai Bo, Alvina Kong, Sarah Lee, Chen Jing, Helena Law, Lai Yin-san, Anthony Wong, Corey Yuen, Ann Mui, Lam Chung, Elvis Tsui, Walter Cho, Yip San, Frankie Ng, Lam Siu Lau, Pal Sin, Liu Wai-hung, Stanley Fung. **D:** Clarence Fok. **W:** Stephen Siu, Johnny Mak. **C:** Poon Hang-sang, Wong Chi-wai, Peter Pau, Johnny Koo, Jingle Ma, Ardy Lam. **M:** Joseph Chan. **VHS, DVD**

Ichi the Killer

Tokyo yakuza Boss Anjo and 100 million yen disappear, and his second Kakihara (Tadanobu Asano) turns the Shinjuku district "upside-down and inside-out" looking for him—and the money. Of course, we know that Anjo was killed by nerdy but flamboyant hit man Ichi (Nao Omori), who left a huge mess for his clean-up crew, and that the whole thing was part of a plan by low-level hood Jijii (Shinya Tsukamoto) to get the gangs at each other's throats. Sadistic Kakihara goes to casually brutal lengths in his search for the boss, but being a masochist as well, he's also more than willing to pay the price for any mistakes. Eventually his actions get him expelled from the yakuza, however, putting the Anjo Group at war with the entire underworld. Jijii continues to hypnotically manipulate sensitive Ichi—though in a state of arrested adolescence, the young man is also a living weapon with a special costume equipped with hidden blades, and he can easily mow down a roomful of Anjo thugs. But Ichi leaves a witness: a boy named Takeshi (Hiroshi Kobayashi), who happens to be the son of Anjo hit man Kaneko (Hiroyuki "Sabu" Tanaka), a former cop. Kakihara gets odd twin crooked cops Jiro (Suzuki Matsuo) and Saburo to track down Chinese pimp Long, who may be able to provide a lead. Meanwhile, Kakihara's girlfriend Karen (Paulyn "Alien" Sun) is in on the whole plot against him. With each new strike made against him, Kakihara begins to feel more frightened, but also more excited—anticipating a confrontation

with the super-killer that can bring him the ultimate in pain.

Prolific director Takashi Miike thumbs his nose at big studio traditions by filming his features the same way he did his video flicks earlier in his career: quickly and economically. An aggressively original vision, *Ichi* takes the gangster genre and treats it as a mere framework for psychosexual horror, camp splatter, ironic humor, and even superheroic martial arts action. It has some of the same atmosphere as Quentin Tarantino's *Pulp Fiction,* but while Tarantino revels in outrageous dialogue, Miike tells his story through outrageous visuals, much like the manga the film is based upon. His crybaby killer starts out looking like the latest twist on assassin characters like Golgo 13 and Crying Freeman, but turns out to be more akin to a Frankenstein monster running amok. His opponent Kakihara garners just as much attention as a self-created carnival freak with slashed open cheeks, using the violent yakuza world as his personal playground. *AKA: Koroshiya 1; Koroshiya Ichi.* 🐉🐉🐉🐉

2001 112m/C *JP/HK/KO* Tadanobu Asano, Nao Omori, Shinya Tsukamoto, Paulyn Sun, Hiroyuki Tanaka, Susumu Terajima, Shun Sugata, Satoshi Niizuma, Suzuki Matsuo, Houka Kinoshita, Hiroshi Kobayashi, Noko Morishita, Setchin Kawaya. **D:** Takashi Miike. **W:** Sakichi Sato, Hideo Yamamoto (manga). **C:** Hideo Yamamoto. **M:** Karera Musication. **VHS, DVD**

I.K.U.

There are whole subgenres and cycles within the Japanese pinku eiga (pink film) category. Having milked dry the concepts of porn with comedy, gore, anime, torture, superheroes, and tentacled monsters, producers have returned to the popular arena of sci-fi porn, as in this digital video feature. In the not-too-distant future, the Genom Corporation develops humanoid androids called Gen-XXX I.K.U. Coders. These sex droids have the added advantage of collecting ecstasy data about their sexual adventures, which can then be collected by special androids called I.K.U. Runner Units. This data can then be sold in chip form from vending machines. In the film, we get snippets of data collected by replicant Reiko (played by seven different actors). But watch out for that Tokyo Rose virus that's going around! The *Bladerunner* reference is made blatant by including an origami unicorn right off the bat. I.K.U. Coders are able to transform into several different bodies, allowing Taiwanese director Shu Lea Cheang to bring in a new model every few minutes. Genom first created the replicants to be used as nurses on a satellite hospital, but after someone used them for a TV porn broadcast that was a big hit, they

decided to branch out into the sex business—surprising that a corporation wouldn't think of that right away.

Unlike the usual porn, *I.K.U.* ("iku means "going" in Japanese, as opposed the Western word "coming") has more to offer than the usual coupling and unusual camera angles. It features eerily sterile production design that recalls 1960s films, flashy and colorful digital f/x, and psychedelic electronic music by Hoppy Kamiyama and Saboten. This being Japanese porn, any hard-core areas are digitally masked, often in creative ways. All the crazy effects, editing, and camera moves actually distract from the eroticism, making the film work better as science fiction (or at least video wallpaper) than it does as pornography. Everyone speaks English in 2069, but since the accents are so heavy, subtitles would be a good idea. There are two separate endings, not that it makes much difference. A self-styled "digital nomad," Shu Lea Cheang has done installations at the Guggenheim Museum, as well as directing the ecological film *Fresh Kill.* 🐉🐉🐉

2000 68/71m/C *JP* Ayumi Tokitho, Maria Yumeno, Yumeka Sasaki, Miho Ariga, My Asou, Etsuyo Tuchida, Tsousie, Zachary Nataf, Mash, Aja, Akira. **D:** Shu Lea Cheang. **W:** Shu Lea Cheang. **C:** Tetsuya Kamoto. **M:** The Saboten. **DVD**

The Imp

With little experience, and his wife Lan (Dorothy Yu) pregnant, Cheung Keung (Charlie Chin) takes a night job as a security guard. Odd things happen in his building at night: lights go on and off by themselves, a malfunctioning elevator fills with water, and co-worker "Mr. Hong Kong" (Wong Ching) chokes on a bone after joking about choking on a bone. Geomancer Master Chiu (Wong Chung) is at the funeral, and senses something amiss. Thinking the new man has brought them bad luck, chief guard Uncle Han intends to fire Keung, but is smothered by a wet newspaper in a bizarre "accident." The lethal sheet contains a story that says the building was put up on a site that used to be the hideout of child kidnappers. Chiu determines that a restless spirit has targeted the Cheung's baby for reincarnation, an event that will have apocalyptic consequences. After Chiu and his fellow guards fall victim to the ghost, Keung must search the building for its hiding place and destroy it before his wife gives birth.

A mostly routine fright-fest, *Imp* is reasonably engaging and often builds up a fine layer of spooky atmosphere, especially during the memorable climax in which Keung seemingly journeys to Hell and back. And stick around for a shocker at the end. Ghosts in Hong Kong pictures are usually far too anthropomorphic, appearing as

white-faced people walking around, but this one is much more effective, for the most part manifesting as a thick green fog. Kent Cheng, playing one of a long line of characters named "Fatty," adds some humor, and wears a red T-shirt while off duty that says "Am I a girl?" and later "No! I am a man." Not to be confused with the 1996 Category III slasher flick of the same name. **AKA:** *Hung Bong; Xiong Bang.* 🐉🐉🐉

1981 95m/C *HK* Charlie Chin, Kent Cheng, Wong Ching, Yueh Hua, Dorothy Yu, Hui Bing Sam, Fung Ging Man, Wong Chung. **D:** Dennis Wu. **W:** Kam Kam-ming, Lee Dun, Cheung Kam-moon. **C:** Bob Thompson. **VHS, DVD**

In the Line of Duty 3

Michelle Yeoh was terrific in the first two installments *(Yes, Madam* and *Royal Warriors)* of this often-retitled series, but retired to marry film mogul Dickson Poon. Here, 20-year-old Taiwanese dancer Cynthia Khan steps in, becoming an icon in the Girls with Guns action-movie subgenre. Like its immediate predecessor, this one exploits the series' Japanese popularity. Fittingly, the first shot shows a theatre playing Cantonese opera, which Khan performed in for a time.

At a fashion show staged in Tokyo by jewelry designer Yamamoto (Yueh Hua), Red Army thieves Michiko Nishiwaki (played by the identically named Michiko Nishiwaki!) and Genji Nakamura (Stuart Ong) commit a savage robbery, gunning down dozens of attendees. Among the casualties of the melee is Detective Ken (Chris Lee). Suspecting an inside job, Ken's vengeful mentor/partner Hiroshi Fujioka (Hiroshi Fujioka!) trails Yamamoto to Hong Kong, where he hopes to catch him meeting up with the thieves where political ties can't protect him. Anxious to keep her out of danger, Inspector Cameron Chuen (Paul Chun) assigns his niece Rachel Yeung Lai-ching (Khan) to the supposedly safe task of being liaison to Fujioka while he's in Hong Kong, and keeping him out of trouble—a plot development copied by *Rush Hour.* But the Japanese cop is determined to catch the pair of thieves, who are in turn anxious to contact Yamamoto, as the jewels he helped them steal turn out to be fakes. A brutal battle between Fujioka and Nakamura leaves both men seriously injured, and Nakamura meets a gruesome death during the ensuing chase. With the help of a Red Army comrade (Dick Wei), Nishiwaki is out for revenge on Yeung, which is convenient since Yeung is gunning for them, too.

Though missing Yeoh, *Part 3*'s twin directors and cinematographers give this entry a slicker, more stylish look. That, plus its fantastic action scenes and unflinching violence, make for a

stunning debut for Khan, who stayed on for three more sequels. Though obviously doubled for some stunts, she gets through all her action scenes like an old pro. A legion of guest stars show up in cameos to help out, including some of the Lucky Stars. **AKA:** *Wong Ga Si Je Ji III; Huang Jia Shi Jie Zhi III; In the Line of Fire 3; Yes, Madam 2; Force of the Dragon.* 🐉🐉🐉🐉

1988 83m/C *HK* Cynthia Khan, Michiko Nishiwaki, Hiroshi Fujioka, Yueh Hua, Stuart Ong, Paul Chun, Dick Wei, Sandra Ng, Melvin Wong, Law Ching-ho, Chris Lee, Richard Ng, Eric Tsang, Stanley Fung, Sally Kwok, Robin Shou, Season Ma. **D:** Arthur Wong, Brandy Yuen. **W:** Chan Kiu-ying, Law Tai-man. **C:** Jimmy Au, Wong Po-man. **M:** Phil Chan. **VHS, DVD**

In the Line of Duty 4

Part 4 adds Yuen Woo-ping as director and Donnie Yen to the cast, increasing the series' already high action quotient by the power of Yen and Yuen. Michael Wong returns to the series, his character having apparently moved up from being a security guard in *Royal Warriors.*

In Seattle helping DEA cop Donny Yan (Donnie Yen) round up a Hong Kong heroin connection, Officer Rachel Yeung Lai-ching (Cynthia Khan) gets mixed up with immigrant dock worker Luk Wan-ting (Yuen Yat-chor), helping him fight off a loan shark (Eddie Maher). Their associate catches dirty CIA Agent Robinson during a drug deal, but is shot trying to escape with the pictures he took, and hands the negatives to Luk before he dies. Luk loses the film but can still identify the killer, and with everyone after him, flees to Hong Kong. Captain Michael Wong (Michael Wong) is brought in on the case, and he goes to HK with Rachel and Donny following Luk. But Robertson's killers follow, too, and capture Luk and Michael. They manage to call for help, but not before we find out Wong is secretly a CIA agent working with the killers. Before Luk can be sent back to the States, the killers strike again and injure him. Wong frames Donny for the death of a suspect, and gives him a ticket for home. But Donny and Rachel are already suspicious of Wong. They set a trap for him, but still have to contend with his crooked CIA associates, their hired hit men, and the drug traffickers, all of whom want the witness dead.

Some may think it a misstep that Yuen Yat-chor is given so much attention, becoming almost the lead character for the first half, but his story is worth following, and it's hard to argue with such a terrific action film. Cynthia Khan continues to amaze with her natural martial arts talent, despite the use of doubles for more dangerous stunts. One scene finds her using

Spring and Autumn

Who's Who in Fu Part 4

While Master Yu Jim-yuen was cracking his cane across the backs of little Jackie Chan and Yuen Biao at the Chinese Drama Academy in Kowloon, across town another batch of martial arts movie stars was being molded by a fairer, but no more gentle, hand.

Fan Fok-fa

A Chinese opera superstar and China's first action movie star, Madame Fan opened her own Spring and Autumn Drama School to train girls for the opera stage. When martial arts films were just beginning to be made in the 1920s, men were the biggest stars in Chinese opera, usually playing all the good female roles as well. But the movies were considered beneath them, so women filled the casts. Later, Madame Fan decided to train boys as well, who were known to often steal school property to sell for candy money. Many of them joined the Sammo Hung Stuntman Association. She was the producer of the hit musical film *Battle at Sizhou.*

Lam Ching-Ying

Lam's relatively short opera career usually had him in female roles, a talent he would show off in the kung fu classic *Prodigal Son.* He was Bruce Lee's assistant at Golden Harvest, and had a busy career as actor and stuntman. He was usually cast as a villain until he starred as *Mr. Vampire,* a role that made him a Hong Kong star. Lam was much sought after for *Vampire* sequels, knockoffs, and a TV series until his untimely death in 1997.

Stephen Tung

Tung Wai worked his way up the stuntman ranks to star in *18 Fatal Strikes* and as *Golden Mask.* He became a highly regarded action director *(A Better Tomorrow, Accidental Spy)* and director *(Contract Killer).*

Chung Fat

This solid performer played the crazy Catman in *Magnificent Butcher.* Playing Taoist wizards in *Encounters of the Spooky Kind, The Dead and the Deadly,* and *New Mr. Vampire,* for a time Chung was the number-two HK ghostbuster after Lam Ching-Ying.

Chin Yuet Sang

The eldest Chin brother, this actor and action director stood out as the rascally Master Wu in *New Mr. Vampire*; he was also director of the wild horror opus *Hocus Pocus*.

Chin Siu-Ho

The middle Chin is an energetic martial artist and handsome lead who played heroic ghostbusters in *Mr. Vampire, Seventh Curse,* and other HK action-horror comedies.

Chin Ka-Lok

Little brother Chin made a name for himself as an incredibly agile stunt double. He played the title role in *Martial Arts Master Wong Fei-hung,* is a frequent guest star in recent HK flicks, and does a goofy Jackie Chan imitation in *Last Ghost Standing*.

Chan Lung

A busy kung fu character actor who is in most of the Sammo Hung Action Team assignments, Peter Chan Lung was Sammo's nemesis in *Encounters of the Spooky Kind,* and the drooling psycho master in *Crazy Crooks*.

Mang Hoi

Chubby-cheeked master acrobat Mang had featured roles in *Buddha Assassinator, Heart of Dragon, Pedicab Driver,* and *Blonde Fury* (he was dating star Cynthia Rothrock at the time). He's the brother of actress Kitty Meng Chui.

Mars

A former child star, Feng Sing's big face and ace stunt work made him a recognizable favorite in Jackie Chan and Sammo Hung pictures, such as *Project A, Dragon Lord,* and *Police Story*.

Fung Hark-On

A top fighter with prominent cheekbones who was usually a tough opponent for the hero; his films include *Breakout from Oppression, Dirty Kung Fu, Last Hurrah for Chivalry, Dragon Lord,* and many others.

Lee Hoi-sang

Big and usually bald, Lee specialized in playing Mongol killers and monks, sometimes displaying a talent for comedy. Catch him in *He Has Nothing But Kung Fu, Enter the Fat Dragon, Magnificent Butcher, Tower of Death,* etc.

Continued on next page...

John Lone

The star of *The Last Emperor* studied with Madame Fan before moving to the U.S.

Hsiao Ho

A student of Lau Kar-Leung, prolific Hsiao kicked ass in *Kung Fu Genius*, *Fist of the White Lotus*, *Legendary Weapons of China*, *Eastern Condors*, and many more.

Austin Wai

The brother of Shaw Brothers star Kara Hui, Austin appeared in numerous martial arts flicks in the 1970s and '80s also put in an impressive supporting performance in Tsui Hark's *The Blade*.

Josephine Siao

She was a child star in the 1950s and popular leading lady in the '60s, but she's now best remembered as Fong Sai-yuk's mom in both *The Legend* and *The Legend 2*. She wrote and directed the '70s action flick *Jumping Ash*.

---

linked wrenches as impromptu nunchakus. Another has her fighting assassins all over a speeding ambulance. Yen's fight scenes look sped up, but are nonetheless impressive. There's also some heavy-handed contempt shown for the CIA's involvement in illegal drug traffic to fund their projects in Nicaragua. **AKA:** *Wong Ga Si Je Ji IV Jik Gik Jing Yan; Huang Jia Shi Jie Zhi IV Zhi Ji Zheng Ren; Survival; In the Line of Duty; Yes, Madam 4; The Witness.* ♫♫♫♪

1989 94m/C *HK* Cynthia Khan, Donnie Yen, Michael Wong, Liu Kai-chi, Sunny Yuen, Michael Woods, John Salvitti, Cho Wing, Chiao Chiao, Wai Gei-shun, Stephen Berick, Farlie Ruth Kordica, Yuen Yat-chor, Eddie Maher. **D:** Yuen Woo-ping. **W:** Anthony Wong, Cheung Chi-sing. **C:** Michael Ma, Jimmy Au. **M:** Richard Yuen. **VHS, DVD**

In the Line of Duty 5: Middle Man

Cynthia Khan is back again for more action as Hong Kong supercop Rachel Yeung, starting right away with the pursuit of a man who stole a computer disc full of military secrets through a parking garage, down an alley, and through the beds of two trucks. She makes the arrest, but her bosses ask her not to get involved any further. The suspect is a member of a gang that steals secrets from U.S. military officers stationed in Asia and sells them. Yeung's cousin, marine David Ng (David Wu), gets involved with the gang because of his shipmate Alan, who is one of their operatives. When Alan is killed buying hemp outside a bar, the gang, police, and CIA all suspect David is involved somehow. Yeung traces the drug dealers who accidentally killed Alan, but the spies assassinate them before she can get to them. The CIA takes David into custody, but when an angry agent tries to murder him, he escapes and goes on the run. Relieved of duty due to her relation to the suspect, Yeung takes matters into her own hands, tracking down David and his girlfriend May (Alvina Kong), then going to Korea to cook up a dangerous plan to catch the general who's providing the secrets.

Repeating the angle of the wrongfully accused innocent is O.K., but once again it takes too much of the action away from Cynthia Khan. Without the big names of its predecessor, the fight scenes aren't as well choreographed or bloody this time around, but there's still a lot of high-powered action, including some nice little car chases. The fight scenes are the series' main attraction though, and Khan has some fine duels with Chris Lee, Billy Chow, and a superior dustup with Kim Penn. Obviously working with a smaller budget, director Cha Chuen-yee (*Queen's High*) makes the most of the well-chosen locations to lens some modestly spectacular action sequences with a bit of grit and sweat to them. **AKA:** *Wong Ga Si Je Ji Jung Gaan Yan; Huang Jia Shi Jie Zhi Zhong Jian Ren; In the Line of Duty 2; In the Line of Fire 3; Key Witness; Police Assassins 2; Supercops; Yes, Madam 5; Middle Man.* 🐉🐉🐉

1990 90m/C *HK* Cynthia Khan, David Wu, Alvina Kong, Chris Lee, Billy Chow, Lo Lieh, Lau Kong, Kim Penn, Wong Wai. **D:** Cha Chuen-yee. **W:** Tony Leung Hung-wah, Patrick Yuen. **C:** Cheng Siu-keung. **M:** Phil Chan. **VHS, DVD**

In the Mood for Love

Sparsely dramatic but lush in its textures and emotions, this art film rewards repeat viewings but will not be everyone's cup of tea. The setting is Hong Kong in the early 1960s. Living quarters are tight and hard to come by. Chow Mo-wan (Tony Leung) and Su Li-zhen (Maggie Cheung), along with their respective spouses, move into adjacent apartments on the same day. He is a newspaperman and she is a secretary. Slowly they discover that their spouses are having an affair. They are drawn together by this realization, and then by a mutual attraction, as they try to work through their conflicting emotions and come to grips with the disintegration of their marriages.

The story moves quietly, which is appropriate considering the characters' uncertainty. The performances by Tony Leung and Maggie Cheung are subtle, moving, and powerful. Their eyes convey most of their feelings and changing moods, which is no easy feat. They blend into the background of their landscape and their circumstances with small gestures and quiet desperation. One example: Chow Mo-wan comes upon Su Li-zhen caught in the rain on the street. As they wait out the storm, they disappear into the scene, caught and trapped by the mores of the day as represented by the oppressively drab buildings and the pounding storm. The cinematography is splendid. The art direction and the costuming beautifully render the period of the film without resorting to kitsch. The use of music, including several songs sung by Nat King Cole in Spanish, is sublime. —*PM* **AKA:** *Dut Yeung Nin Wa; Hua Yang Nian Hua; Beijing Summer.* 🐉🐉🐉🐉

2000 (PG) 98m/C *HK* Tony Leung Chiu-Wai, Maggie Cheung, Rebecca Pan, Kelly Lai, Roy Cheung, Mama Hung. **D:** Wong Kar-Wai. **W:** Wong Kar-Wai. **C:** Christopher Doyle, Mark Lee. **M:** Michael Galasso. **DVD**

The Incredible Kung Fu Mission

Another rediscovered gem is this semi-parody of *Seven Samurai*– and *Dirty Dozen*–type mission films. During the Ching Dynasty, casino tycoon Lo Tung (Wong Chi Sang) goes to Fou Shan Fort to try to buy the release of his friend Chin Chang-fang from the Warlord (Robert Tai), but has no luck. Chin has a lot of information about the Ming Patriot rebels, and is a valuable prisoner. Lo turns to famous hero Cheh Tin-kang (John Liu) for help, sending him to lead five fighters on a mission to rescue Chin from the fort. But of the five, only bald Tai Li-sun is a professional fighter. The rest—coffin maker "Shorty" Shou Ti-yen (Alan Chui), brothel waiter Tu Tao-shi, juggler Hung Kwai-kwei (Ricky Cheng), and carpenter Li Ching (Alexander Lou)—know nothing of kung fu.

The first incredible thing about the mission is that Cheh intends to train these five to be kung fu masters in a few weeks time. Cheh's training has them all whining before long. He takes them on a "treat" visit to a brothel, where thugs in the employ of rich Master Chan (Paul Wei) teach them a lesson. Once in line, they improve rapidly, and easily win a rematch. Warlord Liu Ping gets wind of the plan and sends some killers after the team, which means they have to start out ahead of schedule. To get through the warlord's territory, they disguise themselves as a troupe of performers (Tu in drag for some reason). To get to the fort, the Five Instant Venoms have to survive various traps and ambushes set up by their enemy. One of these ambushes results in the death of one of their number, but the remaining five push on to the fort. Four scale the cliff outside, while Li Ching sneaks in under a cart. But the carpenter gets captured, and another hero is killed during the ascent. Will the Magnificent Three be enough to complete the mission?

With such a large cast and almost nonstop fighting, Robert Tai's fight choreography is stretched a little thin, but everyone seems to get in some good moves. This turns out to be one of those rare and special films where the final fatal blow is a shot to the groin! The direction of Chang Seng-yi (*Shaolin Ex-Monk*), screenwriter on some of Lee Tso Nam's better pictures, doesn't get too fancy, but he does a good job of making sure we know where everyone is and what they're doing. Taiwan is rich with mountainous locations and ornate tem-

ples, and we get a look at some of them. Some of the same fortress locations were used previously for *Blooded Treasury Fight.* **AKA:** *Kung Fu Commandos.* ♫♫♫

1982 88m/C *TW* John Liu, Chan Lung, Alan Chui, Ting Wa-chung, Robert Tai, Paul Chang, Paul Wei, Alexander Lou, Ricky Cheng, Wong Chi Sang, Chui Chung Hei, Lee Kwan. **D:** Chang Seng-yi. **W:** Huang Jo-pe. **C:** Chuang Yin-chien. **M:** Huang Mou-shan. **DVD**

Inheritor of Kung Fu

In one of his lighter roles, Ti Lung stars as Lee Chin-fung, a fighter with more courage than skill who tries to protect traveling Princess Chin-Chin (Pearl Chang) and her servant Wu-bao (Fan Dan-fung) from attacking agents of Chief Woo-ba, who are after a famous martial arts manual. When Fung brings the ladies home, his master Lee Yun-hou casts them out again, saying their clan is disreputable and practices black magic. As punishment, Fung is sent up the mountain to meditate, where he meets an alcoholic hermit who appears to have more than the usual number of arms and legs. While the hermit teaches Fung his esoteric kung fu, Master Lee attempts to help Shih Tin-jan, whose escort company is trying to recover the manual stolen from their protection. Rival clan leader Lang Tu-chi tells Lee that Fung stole the manual, an accusation he can't disprove. Fung flees into the wilderness to try to prove his innocence, but various clans all believe he has the manual and will gladly kill him to get it.

Shot mostly on sets, the film has a surreal and extremely artificial look, an atmosphere that is enhanced by strange characters and magical kung fu techniques. Something seems to have been lost in adapting the story from novel to film, as characters change allegiances more than once, other characters seem to come out of nowhere and change the plot, and new kung fu techniques show up in combat that should have been established previously. In an odd subplot, Master Lee's daughter Shu-lang is caught spying on Shih, and goes insane. By the finale, Ti Lung has Pearl Chang's clan leadership handed to him, and has to defeat the villains in a martial arts tournament to claim leadership of all the clans. His clan seems to be made up almost entirely of ragged kung fu kids—the kind of kids that are always doing flips and somersaults for no reason. As the fighting continues, the brats kill all the villain's guards. The last straw falls when the kids kill a warrior monk (John Ladalski) using bubble pipes! There's also flying, teleportation, a fighter who disguises himself as a girl to fool Ti Lung,

and auto-castration! The dubbing crew is as confused as any viewer, adding to the mess by giving characters different names in different scenes. This very strange film contains music cues from *Taxi Driver.* Not to be confused with the Lau Kar-Wing film of the same title. Amazingly, this was followed by a sequel, *Hero at the Border Region,* from which Ti Lung understandably excused himself. **AKA:** *Bing Suet Ching Gwaan Ying Hung Daam; Bing Xue Qing Guan Ying Xiong Dan; The Heroic One.* ♫♡

1977 91m/C *TW* Ti Lung, Pearl Chang, Choi Wang, Fan Dan-fung, Kwan Yung Moon, Bruce Lai, Gam Man-hei, Lu Wei, John Ladalski. **D:** Bau Hok-lai. **W:** Jaan Shih-mei, Ngai Hong (novel). **VHS, DVD**

Inner Senses

The Chinese fascination with ghost stories has only intensified since *The Sixth Sense* became a worldwide hit, producing numerous offshoots of the theme, as Dr. Jim Law (Leslie Cheung) is no doubt well aware. As a psychologist, he's come to theorize that there's no such thing as ghosts—merely delusions produced by mass hypnosis. But here we have the case of Yan Cheung (Karena Lam), which is referred to Dr. Law. She sees dead people. At present, she sees the dead family of her lonely old landlord (Norman Tsui) in her apartment. Law believes it's all a byproduct of some trauma in her past. His ideas make him think of himself as an outsider in Hong Kong, seeing Chinese society from a detached position. He even writes his notes in English, and has a cabinet full of self-prescribed pills. Yan is bilingual as well—her job is to translate movie scripts.

As Law and his patient become closer, he starts to see ghosts, too. Has her delusion infected his subconscious as well? He tries to reestablish professional boundaries, but Yan gets her feelings hurt, and when she attempts suicide, Law becomes determined that the only way to cure himself is to help her. Unfortunately, once Yan has made a breakthrough, and Law tries to keep away from her, he keeps on seeing ghosts. His colleague Wilson (Waise Lee) suggests that, now that Law has closed the file on Yan as a patient, perhaps it would help to open up to her as a friend. He does, and their relationship seems to bring them both some peace—until Yan discovers there's something hidden inside Law's mind that even he isn't aware of.

Dr. Law would tell you that we're a little disappointed when we turn on the lights and there wasn't a ghost in the corner after all. This is a psychological horror film that places the emphasis on the psychology, though there are still quite a few effective shocks—one coming at

midpoint when Leslie Cheung prescribes his own shock treatment. But the dramatic component takes precedence. Once the hook is set, it's difficult to break free of the story before the end, even though it becomes more predictable later on. Cheung has clearly been challenging himself to expand beyond normal leading-man roles, beginning with his risky performance in *Phantom Lover* through his psycho portrayal in *Double Tap* (also from Law Chi-leung). The film has a beautifully polished look, enhanced by Peter Kam's lovely score. Like most romance stories, it's a little too self-contained—we don't get a sense of the characters leading full lives away from each other. But it's nice to see horror films with a little more going on than just trying to scare the audience. Ironically, Leslie Cheung's April 2003 suicide echoes the finale of this, his last picture. *AKA: Yi Diy Hung Gaan; Yi Du Kong Jian.* ♪♪♪

2001 100m/C *HK* Leslie Cheung, Karena Lam, Valerie Chow, Waise Lee, Norman Tsui, Maggie Poon, Lee Pui-shing, Samuel Lam, Olivia Wong, So Hang Suen, Wong Shu Tong. *D:* Law Chi-leung. *W:* Yeung Sin-ling, Law Chi-leung, Derek Yee. *C:* Venus Keung. *M:* Peter Kam. **DVD**

The Inspector Wears Skirts

Jackie Chan produced Golden Harvest's answer to the *Yes, Madam* and *Angel* series with this boxoffice smash-hit about the formation of an all-female SDU squad. As he'd done with his old-school kung fu hits, Chan's twist is to add a lot more humor, making this movie (and the three sequels that followed) more in the vein of *Police Academy*, while still providing plenty of action. The idea for the squad is prompted by an incident where a policeman touches a sheik's wife during an assassination attempt—while officers Wu (Sibelle Hu) and Lo (Cynthia Rothrock) are laying waste to the attacking ninjas—causing an outrage. It becomes obvious to Commissioner Tung (Bill Tung) that there are a lot of things women can accomplish better than men, and Wu and Lo are put in charge of training and leading the new female commando squad. At camp, a friendly rivalry quickly forms with the male Tiger Squad commanded by Inspector Kan (Stanley Fung). Romance, hijinks, light drama, and teamwork ensue throughout training. When it's learned that an infamous gang of jewel thieves are in Hong Kong to try a heist at an international jewelry exhibition, both teams are called on to try to protect the loot, and possibly catch the gang.

The ensemble cast is an appealing bunch, and as many are members of the Jackie Chan Stunt Team, the action is well above par—especially when Hu, Rothrock, Kara Hui, or Ken Lo

are involved. Sandra Ng handles most of the comic antics. There's a rocking song-and-dance number led by Alex To on skates that soon turns into a roller derby brawl. Of course there's a big fight at the end with the thieves, highlighted by a too-brief battle between Rothrock and monkey-fighting Jeff Falcon, but the climax should have been bigger. One wonders whether the real HK police were proud or offended by their portrayal here, as aside from the action scenes the trainees all acts like kids in junior high school. Sibelle Hu received serious burns during one explosion—it's not shown during the end-credit ouch-takes, but we see both Falcon and Hui taking rough shots to the head, and it's made clear that a scene where the trainees have to outrace a gas fire didn't go so well the first time. *AKA: Ba Wong Fa; Ba Wang Hua; Top Squad; Inspector Wears a Skirt; Lady Enforcers.* ♪♪♪

1988 91m/C *HK* Sibelle Hu, Kara Hui, Ann Bridgewater, Sandra Ng, Cynthia Rothrock, Ellen Chan, Regina Kent, Stanley Fung, Alex To, Billy Lau, Bill Tung, Michael Chow, Jeff Falcon, Shing Fui-on, Ricky Hui, Ken Lo, Mars, Dennis Chan, Joanna Chan, Amy Yip. *D:* Wellson Chin. *W:* Cheng Kam-fu. *C:* Andrew Lau, Jimmy Au. *M:* New Note Music Production. **DVD**

Invaders from Space

In this third feature re-edited from Shintoho's *Supergiant* serial, the guardians of the Emerald Planet once again send Starman (Ken Utsui) to Earth, this time to face the threat of the invading Salamander Men from Kuramon. Earthlings spot a UFO circling the planet, and soon after a plague sweeps across Tokyo. As he studies the phenomena, Professor Asayama has an uninvited visitor in his study—a weird masked man, who removes his mask to reveal scaly skin and a wide, grinning mouth. The alien projects a radioactive beam from his mouth which somehow hypnotizes the scientist, but Starman arrives to intervene, fighting off the invader.

The next day, the invaders attack using deadly high-decibel sound waves, but Starman is able to destroy the flying saucer projecting the waves. Dr. Fukami traces the plague to the Yamano Theater where a weird dance troupe is performing—a dance troupe from outer space! With the world in crisis, children from Tokyo are evacuated, and sent...on a butterfly hunt! Out in the scary forest, a trio of kids—including Fumaki's daughter Noriko—is captured by the dancing Kuramonians, who want to force the doctor to reveal the location of Earth's Secret Arsenal. Luckily, Starman has given the kids one of his cosmic pagers, and they summon him to the rescue. Once the kids and scientists are safe, the plague is forgotten, as everybody goes home.

"We're gonna
fight to the last
man, baby."

—Astronaut Glenn stands
firm against the space
vixens from Planet X in
Invasion of Astro-Monster

The aliens send a salamander witch to kidnap the kids again, but they accidentally dissolve her with copper sulfate. However, the Kuramonians have discovered the arsenal's location, and launch an all-out attack on humanity.

The Salamander Men are the film's best feature, an eerie mix of frog-man and the Martians from *Mars Attacks!,* with fairy-like antennae. They're certainly creepier than any of Starman's other foes, and some scenes are given a spooky atmosphere. However, the pace is extremely slow, and many scenes are padded. In an apparent attempt to save wear on the costumes, the spaceman of iron fights the aliens using a martial arts style that mostly involves swinging them aside by the arms. Somebody ought to make a music video out of the scene in which Starman fights the Salamaniacs in the theatre. *AKA: Supa Jaiantsu 5 & 6; Super Giant 5 & 6; Supergiant vs. the Satellites; Spaceship of Human Destruction; Destruction of the Space Fleet.* 🎵🎵💔

1958 77m/BW *JP* Ken Utsui, Utako Mitsuya, Kan Hayashi, Junko Ikeuchi, Minoru Takada. *D:* Teruo Ishii. *W:* Ichiro Miyagawa, Shinsuke Negishi (story). *C:* Nobu Boshi, Hiroshi Suzuki. *M:* Riichiro Manabe. **VHS, DVD**

Invasion of Astro-Monster

Toho Studios had already used multiple monsters in their Godzilla series. To top that idea, they decided that an alien invasion à la *The Mysterians* would add extra excitement to this episode. And just to make the picture more marketable overseas, at the suggestion of producer Henry Saperstein they decided to add an Anglo face to the cast. Thus, Nick Adams *(Rebel without a Cause)* joined Toho regular Akira Takarada at the controls of rocketship *P-1* on a mission to explore Planet X, which has just appeared in the solar system near the orbit of Jupiter. Surprisingly, the astronauts are greeted by inhabitants of the planet, who live underground due to the ravages of a recent guest from Earth. The denizens of mysterious Planet X have an offer for their new neighbors: King Ghidorah (whom the numerically minded X-ians have given the designation "0") is ravaging their world, and they want to bring Godzilla (Haruo Nakajima) and Rodan (Masashi Shinohara) there to drive him off, just as the monsters (with help from Mothra) kicked him off Earth. In return for the use of our monster exterminators, they offer a cure for all known diseases. Is the offer genuine, or are the X-ians, as astronaut Glenn (Adams) puts it: "Double-crossing finks!"? The answer comes when all three monsters are unleashed against the Earth. The X-men may be

liars, but they must join the legion of cinematic alien invaders that don't appear to be too bright. Witness their master plan: They already know where the monsters are, and how to control them, and have superior technology to that of Earth. However, they find it necessary to work an elaborate con on the humans that only wastes their own time and resources. Plus, if they'd only borrowed a tape of *Earth vs. the Flying Saucers,* they could have been prepared for the Earthlings' ultimate defense.

Despite the shaky logic of the plot, this direct sequel to *Ghidorah the Three-Headed Monster* remains one of the more entertaining entries in Toho's monster series. The addition of Adams as the hipster astronaut provides as much amusement from his daddy-o dialogue and manner as it does the intended Anglo identification. Released in the U.S. in 1970 on a twin bill with *War of the Gargantuas.* *AKA: Kaiju Daisenso; Battle of the Astros; Monster Zero; Godzilla vs. Monster Zero; The Great Monster War.* 🎵🎵🎵💔

1965 (G) 92m/C *JP* Akira Takarada, Nick Adams, Kumi Mizuno, Jun Tazaki, Akira Kubo, Keiko Sawai, Yoshio Tsuchiya, Takamaru Sasaki, Yoshifumi Tajima, Gen Shimizu, Nadao Kirino, Kenzo Tabu, Koji Uno, Toru Ibuki, Kazuo Suzuki, Fuyuki Murakami, Somesho Matsumoto, Haruo Nakajima, Masashi Shinohara, Shoichi Hirose. *D:* Ishiro Honda. *W:* Shinichi Sekizawa. *C:* Hajime Koizumi. *M:* Akira Ifukube. **VHS**

Invasion of the Neptune Men

On a camping trip to Mount Osaka, the students of rocket scientist Mr. Tabana (future international action icon Sonny Chiba) are shocked to spot a satellite falling toward Earth. However, the object is actually a spaceship, which lands in a nearby field. The dome-helmeted aliens attack, but the kids are saved by the intervention of a superhero that they call Space Chief for no given reason (Iron Sharp in Japan)—after which they ask him his name, and he cooperatively agrees to take the one given. The Neptunian invaders retaliate by making all of Japan's electronic devices run backward, interfere with the scientists' "electronic brains," and blow up nuclear power plants worldwide.

Tabana and Kenny's dad Dr. Tanowai work to create an electronic shield to protect Tokyo from the Neptunian bandwidth. Of course, Kenny and his little pals have full access to all top-secret projects. The shield works, repelling an attack. As an afterthought, the spacemen get around to leaving a recording announcing their plans to invade Earth—which of course is found by the kids. The spacemen create storms to interfere with the electro-barrier, and try to infiltrate the

Japanese army in disguise. Fortunately, the kids spot their effeminate makeup, and Space Chief disintegrates them with his zap gun. The spacemen mass for another assault, which destroys much of the city, but thanks to Space Chief's heroic dogfight skills, and the new electro-rockets invented by his alter ego, the Neptunians are defeated.

Who is Space Chief? Don't look for any answers here, as this is one of those sci-fi movies for children that operates on dream logic. It's not even clearly spelled out that Tabana is Space Chief's secret identity—it's just taken on faith that Tabana always happens to be missing when the superhero flies into action. The miniatures and costumes are delightfully clunky. The aliens all wear shiny suits with bullet-shaped helmets, and their ship is of the Buck Rogers variety. Space Chief's vehicle is ultra-cool, looking like a customized Cadillac with rockets attached. Surprisingly, the special-effects sequence where the hexagonal Neptunian ships attack the city is actually quite well done. But the film is entirely too padded with repetitive scenes and stock footage to maintain even the interest of the intended small-fry audience. Scenes of citizens hiding during bombing

blackouts, waiting to see if they're protected from the attacking spacemen, likely resonated more strongly in Japan. *AKA: Uchu Kaisoku-sen; Invasion from a Planet; Space Greyhound.* 🎵🎵

1961 74m/BW *JP* Sonny Chiba, Kappei Matsumoto, Shinjiro Ebara, Mitsue Komiya, Ryuko Minakami. *D:* Koji Ota. *W:* Shin Morita. *C:* Shizuka Fujii. *M:* Michiaki Watanabe. **VHS**

The Invincible Armour

A documentary credits sequence introduces the Iron Armor and Eagle Claw principles, showing how villain Hwang Jang Lee achieved his special kung fu powers. General Chow Lu-fung (John Liu) sees a man named Hu Lung (Lee Hoi-sang) defending himself from thieves in the street, and admires his Khun Lun skills. He invites him to meet Lord Liu, and the complete kung fu nerds immediately fall into a deep discussion and demonstration of the strengths and weaknesses of the 36 martial arts styles. But Hu Lung is an assassin who has planned this opportunity as a trap for Liu to fall into.

Despite the attentions of Kumi Mizuno, two-fisted astronaut Nick Adams is highly suspicious of foreigners from Planet X in *Invasion of Astro-Monster.*
THE KOBAL COLLECTION / TOHO

After killing the nobleman, he flees the house, leaving Chow to be blamed for the murder by General Wei. Chow flees also, intent on capturing Hu Lung, avenging his master, and clearing his name. Minister of State Cheng (Hwang Jang Lee), who is secretly a traitor who plotted the assassination, commands his best fighter Captain Shen Yu (Tino Wong) to bring him Chow's head. With both Shen Yu and royal guardsmen chasing him, Chow faces extra difficulty in catching Hu Lung. Though disowned by his Khun Lun brothers, the clan still protects him, and his criminal pals are also ready to ambush Chow.

On the road, the fugitive helps Si Chi-lan and her brother fight off an unwanted suitor. Descendants of the great Iron Armor Sheng, the siblings teach Chow the secret of the Iron Finger in gratitude. Chow gives Shen Yu reason to question his guilt, and decides to try to capture both Chow and Hu Lung for the court, putting him at odds with his fellow lawmen.

The chase-and-fight format provides plenty of opportunities for the different characters to face off in combat, with a variety of fighting styles and tactics. Just when things look like they're about to go stale, stunt coordinators Yuen Biao and Corey Yuen show up as a pair of goofy assassins who face off against Liu, livening up the proceedings. Light on plot, this old-school extravaganza offers plenty of what it was made for: nonstop kung fu excitement. **AKA:** *Ying Chau Tit Biu Saam; Ying Zhao Tie Bu Shan.* 🐉🐉🐉

1977 94m/C *HK* John Liu, Hwang Jang Lee, Tino Wong, Phillip Ko, Lee Hoi-sang, Sunny Yuen, Yuen Cheung-yan, Yuen Biao, Corey Yuen. **D:** Ng See-yuen. **W:** Ng See-yuen. **VHS, DVD**

The Invincible Killer

Chung-hou wants her boyfriend Wang Chun (Michael Chan) to quit his life of crime and settle down, so he gives up the triads to marry her. He becomes a security guard at a bank, but quits rather than kowtow to the owner's arrogant son. A man sees him defending himself from robbers in the park and offers him a job as a guard on a ship. But the police arrest him as a suspect in the robbery and murder of a shopkeeper, and though his boss shows up to support his alibi, he still misses his ship. The police still suspect him, as does the victim's son, kung fu instructor Chen Tsin-tung. Suspecting his old triad boss (Tang Ching) framed him to get him to come back, Wang Chun goes to lock picker Little Mouse Pang to demand the truth. Pang knows nothing, even though his godmother was the only witness to the murder. Since the victim recognized the killer, and was

clutching a Lo Hua record cover when he died, Wang Chun goes to keep an eye on the singer, thinking he had something to do with the crime! While Wang Chun is shadowing the nightclub singer, the bossman has his wife and son Shao-pao kidnapped, forcing him to take part in a robbery of the bank he used to work in. The boss's wife Christine—who seems to have slept with half the other characters—gets tired of her husband using her to manipulate his men, and decides to set Chung-hou and Shao-pao free. This frees Wang Chun as well, leading to a disappointingly brief climactic dustup.

Michael Chan doesn't have many lead roles on his resume, which perhaps can be blamed on his rapidly receding hairline (which he covers with bushy sideburns here), but is more likely a result of his personal life. A lifelong triad member, Chan is as well known as a real-life fighter, both as a champion in the ring and on the street, as he is a movie kung fu man. He was even a policeman for a short time, until they learned of his triad pedigree. He shows some good moves here, but be sure to check him out in *Project A 2* and *Legacy of Rage.* 🐉🐉

1979 90m/C *HK* Michael Chan, Tang Ching, Cha Chi Ying, Lau Nga Ying, Terry Liu, Lau Yat-fan, Lo Hua, To Siu Ming. **D:** Liang Shen. **C:** Liang Hung. **M:** Wong Chu-jen. **VHS, DVD**

The Invincible Kung Fu Trio

Three great Ming Patriot heroes are brought together in this old-school fu-fest. Hung Hey-kwoon (Li Chin-Kun), Fong Sai-yuk (Meng Fei, repeating his role from *Prodigal Boxer*), and Luk Ah-choi (John Liu) team up to fight the Ching government. Since all three trained at Shaolin Temple, the Ching magistrate visits the rival Wu Tang Clan and tells the chief abbot (Kam Kong) that the trio is plotting his assassination, plus calling him dirty names behind his back and stuff. He also says the abbot's old friend Kung Kao-tan has joined the traitors. The enraged abbot develops a special technique called the Butterfly Stroke to fight them.

Meanwhile, Luk uses a lion dance to pass a note to their compatriots. When it's intercepted, he's injured fighting a large Wu Tang monk (Kam Kong), who has taken charge of the temple while the chief abbot is away plotting in a cave. Hung loses his temper and attacks the Wu Tang Temple by himself. He's hit by the Butterfly Stroke, and barely escapes. Fortunately, Fong Sai-yuk shows up to save him, but Luk is captured. Fong takes Hung to Uncle Fung (Liu Ping), who knows the cure for the Butterfly. While Hung recovers, he and Fung's daughter Wing-chun (Angela Mao) fall for each other, matching their Tiger and Crane Styles against each other in practice. The four of them manage to rescue Luk from Wu Tang, but Uncle Fung is killed, and it's clear that there can be no peace with the clan. While the heroes work on combining all the animal styles they know, the chief abbot is cooking up his own new secret weapons, such as learning how to create doubles of the three heroes, which somehow involves castrating his followers by hand.

The martial arts choreography is disappointingly average, considering the talent on hand and the caliber of heroes being portrayed. But the cast seems to be having a good time fighting their way through the fast-moving plot, which has enough twists and gimmicks to keep things interesting. Hung's special weapon is a pair of sharp bronze disks that he can use as blades or throw like Frisbees. Ideas like the evil twins are plentiful, though the story doesn't make much of them after they're introduced. The main fault here lies in viewer expectations, as the characters don't display enough personality to stand out from the average kung fu masters—Hung is quick-tempered, and the abbot is tricky, and that's about it. The Taiwanese temples and towers usually seem a bit ornate as the Buddhist Shaolin Temple, but here they fit just fine impersonating Taoist Wu Tang headquarters. Appearances by various characters are often illustrated by animal noises on the soundtrack, such as cows, goats, and dogs. **AKA:** *Hung Hei Goon Fong Sai Yuk Luk A Choi; Hong Xi Guan Fang Shi Yu Liu A Cai; Dragon's Fatal Fist.*

1978 82m/C *TW* John Liu, Meng Fei, Li Chin-Kun, Angela Mao, Kam Kong, Liu Ping, Tong Lung, Yuen Sam. **D:** Joe Law. **VHS, DVD**

Invincible Obsessed Fighter

Unexpectedly, *Invincible Obsessed Fighter* Elton Chong is obsessed mainly with dressing up in silly outfits. Chuck (Elton Chong) arrives home and finds his father has been murdered by the evil Eagle Tse. After 30 seconds of mourning, the youth goes incognito as a crafty old man and heads for Dragon Town. There, he trades in his disguise to pose as a cross-eyed waiter. It doesn't really matter what disguise he picks, since he always picks fights with Eagle's men anyway. An old maggot-eating mystic accosts Chuck, having recognized his Eight Chopper fist technique. Chuck can't beat his magic, but some scary lightning saves him. Then Chuck beats a trio of attacking ninjas, but the sneaking mystic sees where Chuck has hidden the treasure.

The mystic is hired by Eagle to catch Chuck, and sends a message to lure him out. Chuck—you guessed it—dresses up in drag to go to the

rescue, and is easily captured. Reanimating a Snake Fist fighting corpse to help out, the mystic attacks his captive, but again the lightning saves the day. Having run out of disguises, Chuck just puts on a funny hat and goes out where the bad guys can find him, whereupon he faces and beats each in turn.

The annoying Elton Chong—the Carrot Top of kung fu—isn't the only one who looks like he's always wearing bad hairpieces, as this flick has some of the worst wigs, beards, and mustaches ever worn. The fight choreography isn't that interesting, leaving it to a parade of gimmicks—and Chong's insane shtick—to maintain interest. Haphazardly edited, the film gives us characters that are held hostage without being captured, then free without escaping. Director John King is yet another pseudonym for Godfrey Ho.

1982 84m/C *KO* Elton Chong, Mike Wong, Robert Chan, Shirley Mak, Tony Sung, Leung Ting, Wan Fei. **D:** Godfrey Ho. **W:** Stephen To. **C:** James Fan. **M:** Roman Sang. **VHS, DVD**

Invincible Pole Fighter

Loosely based on the historical Yang Wu-lang, who became a monk and developed a new pole-fighting technique based on his family's spear-fighting style, this is a true martial arts classic from both the Lau Brothers and Shaw Brothers, with some of Chang Cheh's Venoms thrown in for good measure. Traitor General Pan Mei (Lin Ke-ming) lures Yang Yeh and his seven spear-toting sons (all known simply by numbers) into an ambush, killing all but Yang #5 (Gordon Lau), Yang #4 (Hsiao Ho)—who is captured and executed, and Yang #6 (Alexander Fu Sheng)—who is left a mental wreck. Brother 5 hides out in the mountain cabin of a hunter (Lau Kar-Leung), who helps him escape. He decides to go to a monastery to plot his revenge carefully. The Buddhist abbot (Phillip Ko) declares he's too filled with rage to become a monk, but that doesn't stop #5 from shaving his own head and hanging around the Ching Lan Temple, causing trouble and refusing to leave.

While Madam Yang (Lily Li) and her daughters Yang #8 (Kara Hui) and Yang #9 (Yeung Ching-Ching) try to nurse #6 back to sanity, hoping he'll be able to testify against Pan Mei in the capitol, they receive news from a monk (Ging Chue) that #5 is still alive. Number 8 tries to sneak past the Manchus to reach her brother, first hiding in a tub of garbage, then in a coffin with a corpse, but is captured by Pan Mei's men. Knowing he's walking into a trap, 5th brother goes to attempt a rescue—and he takes a lot of poles with him!

The dramatic quotient remains high throughout, without a hint of comic relief—surely off-screen tragedy had something to do with this. Originally Alexander Fu Sheng was set to be the star, but when he was killed in an auto accident midway through filming, the story was changed to make Gordon Lau's role much bigger. Despite this retooling, the film recovers from some awkward structure and gains enough momentum to claim its place among the classics of martial arts cinema. It has all the great fighting and training sequences one expects in a Lau picture, but with a bit more ferocity than usual, and inventive details that are key to the plot. The monks practice their pole fighting against wooden wolves, and Pan's soldiers use poles with springy gripping ends that the hero has to find some way to conquer. As the title indicates, much of the fighting is done with poles, and the Laus create some of the finest pole combat ever recorded on film, including a duel between Gordon Lau and Phillip Ko that you just may need to rewind to watch again right away. But don't linger on it too long—make sure you don't miss the big battle climax, which earns a standing ovation every time it's shown. **AKA:** *Ng-long Baat Gwa Gwan; Wulang Ba Gua Gun; The Eight Diagram Pole Fighter; Magnificent Pole Fighters.* 🐉🐉🐉🐉

1983 99m/C *HK* Gordon Lau, Kara Hui, Alexander Fu Sheng, Lily Li, Lin Ke-ming, Johnny Wang, Phillip Ko, Lau Kar-Leung, Wong Yu, Lau Kar-Wing, Walter Cho, Hsiao Ho, Yeung Ching-Ching, Robert Mak, Cheung Chin-pang, Ging Chue, Yuen Tak, Yang Chih-ching, Wong Ching Ho, Lau Suet-wa. **D:** Lau Kar-Leung. **W:** Ngai Hong, Lau Kar-Leung. **C:** Cho On-sun. **M:** So Chun-hou, Sing Kam-wing. **VHS, DVD**

Iron Man

Fans of Jet Li's Fong Sai-yuk movies *(The Legend)* may want to check out this earlier interpretation of the Chinese hero (actually a sequel to an earlier film), which bears many similarities to Li's. The Ching government suspects that the Shaolin Temple is expanding too quickly because they've become a haven for rebels, so a government representative coerces a Taoist priest to help them to capture rebel Fong Sai-yuk (Shi Po-hua). Meanwhile, Mr. Woo and his students welcome nephew Wai-kin back to Canton after he's spent years at Shaolin improving his kung fu, hoping he'll help them deal with a troublesome gangster named Dragon Head. The thug, who killed Wai-kin's father, is secretly under the orders of Governor Ho and the city commissioner, doing their dirty work for them. During a festival, Fong Sai-yuk joins the school's dragon dance against Ho's team, but after Dragon Head is sent into the fray, it turns into a big brawl.

After their victory, Master Woo joins a pair of students in a celebratory rap (!) about the event. Fong's enemy Liu Tai-pang, master of the Wu Tang Mantis Style, is in town to get revenge on Fong for killing his brother Tiger Liu, and joins Commissioner Chang Biao in plotting against their common enemies. Meanwhile, old classmates Fong and Woo Wai-kin get together at the local temple with brother San-der to learn about the mythical Spinning Palm Style, which Sai-yuk is able to pick up extremely fast. Dragon Head uses some festival fireworks as cover to abduct Wai-kin's sister Wai-cheun (Chang Hung-mei), whom the governor has had his eye on. Wai-kin and Sai-yuk go to the rescue, but are easily snared in a trap set by Dragon Head. Luckily, Sai-yuk's mother has come to Canton, and arrives to rescue her son. Gathering his friends together Fong leads an all-out assault on Chang Biao's guards, Liu Tai-pang, and a legion of marching Taoists.

As in Jet Li's pictures, dragon and lion dances are featured attractions here, as are various martial arts styles. On a technical level, of course, this older independent film can't measure up—the direction and photography are clearly inferior. The plotting is sloppy and the relationships and characterizations shallow. But the fighting, unaided by extensive wirework and editing tricks, is just as spectacular and well choreographed, especially in the second half. There's a pole battle, a colorful fight in a textile factory, Taoists with noisy shields in geometric formations, and Fong's epic duel with Liu Tai-pang in a waterfall. Another picturesque battle takes place amid a blossoming cherry grove. And of course, Fong Sai-yuk is one of the few superheroes who fights side-by-side with his ass-kicking mother. **AKA:** *San Fong Sai Yuk Chuk Chap; Xin Fang Shi Yu Xu Ji; The Young Hero of Shaolin II.* 🐉🐉🐲

1986 93m/C *HK* Shi Po-hua, Chan Wing-ha, Li Che Chou, Chang Hung-mei, Lam Chuen, Chui Ngai. **D:** Ngai Hoi-fung. **VHS**

The Iron Monkey

Chen Kuan-tai's specialty as a martial artist is the Monkey Style, though his roles rarely called on him to display this skill. Monkey fighters were usually played by smaller, more acrobatic performers who looked more like monkeys, not tall and handsome leading men. Chen developed this project to specifically show off this animal style.

A Ching Dynasty general (Kam Kong) sends his captains Pa (Shih Chung Tien) and Ti (Leung Kar-yan) to round up a group of Ming patriots who have been betrayed by his spy Ho Yin (Wilson Tong). The leader (Ma Kei) and his entire family are slaughtered, leaving behind only playboy son Iron (Chen Kuan-tai), who was out

drinking and gambling. Iron escapes capture and makes his way to the Shaolin Temple School for Vengeful Orphans, where he soon becomes a top student, despite the fact he's unwilling to give his real name (or go through the usual year of carrying water). Taking the name Iron Monkey, he chooses to major in the obscure Shaolin Monkey Fist taught by the old Bitter Monk (Chan Muk-chuen), who lives in a cabin in the misty woods. The monk—and his monkey—put Iron through rigorous training, including practicing atop jars under a large rack full of burning incense sticks. After a time, Iron Monkey surprises his fellow students by leaving Shaolin to join the Ching army. His true purpose is to advance through the ranks far enough that he'll get his chance to strike at the general. However, when he's ordered to take his men to destroy Shaolin, he's forced to make his move early.

Iron Monkey appears to pick up his skills all too easily, without the usual degree of suffering, rendering the film's dramatic tone a little flat. But the kung fu is excellent, giving Chen Kuantai his intended opportunity to really show his stuff, in the Monkey Style and various others. He shows a good understanding of his role as a director, too. Once he begins working his way through his enemies, the film builds up a good head of steam to the climactic battle with Kam Kong. This is possibly a remake of a three-part 1955 epic starring Walter Cho and Kwan Takhing. *AKA: Tit Ma Lau; Tie Ma Liu; Bloody Monkey Fist; Bloody Monkey Master.* ♫♫♫

1977 95m/C *HK* Chen Kuan-tai, Kam Kong, Chi Kuan Chun, Karen Sun, Leung Kar-yan, Shih Chung Tien, Chan Muk-chuen, Wilson Tong, Lee Keung, Wu Ma, Ma Kei, Chan Wai Lau, Wu Chia Hsiang, Sun Jung-chi, Wong Chi Sang. *D:* Chen Kuan-tai. *W:* Ngai Hong. *C:* Chen Chin-kui. **VHS, DVD**

Iron Monkey

Having revived Chinese cinema's greatest hero, Wong Fei-hung, in his *Once upon a Time in China,* Tsui Hark set his sights on another famed film hero, producing this revival. For good measure, a much younger Wong and his father are thrown into the mix. The whole city quakes as the thief named Iron Monkey strikes, robbing the rich to give to the poor. Shaolin monks brought in by the governor are ineffective. Security Chief Fox (Sunny Yuen) is beside himself. Mild-mannered Dr. Yang (Yu Rongguang) at the Pa Cho Tong clinic, along with his nurse Miss Orchid Ho (Jean Wang), are in reality the ones behind the black mask. The Legate officer is due to inspect the region, so the governor (James Wong) cracks down harder on Fox to catch the outlaw. Doctor Wong Kei-ying (Donnie

Yen) and his precocious son Wong Fei-hung (Tsang Sze-Man) are passing through town, and a demonstration of Wong's kung fu prowess is enough to make him a suspect. With Fei-hung held as security, Wong is given a week to prove his innocence by catching Iron Monkey. However, his attempt at preserving his good name makes him the enemy of the common people, who see Iron Monkey as their hero. Wong befriends Yang and Orchid, learning they are as skilled at cooking as they are at medicine. Meanwhile, the stakes are raised when imprisoned Fei-hung catches the plague. Patrolling for his prey that night, Wong has a battle with the five masked Shaolin monks, as well as a masked nun (Li Fai). Their leader is the rebel monk Hin Hung (Yam Sai-kwoon), who wields the fatal Wonder Palm.

The production has the same lush look as the *Once upon a Time...* films, nicely embellishing the main attraction: Yuen Woo-Ping's stunningly choreographed superhero action sequences, though he relies too heavily (and unnecessarily) on sped-up footage. These techno excesses can be forgiven, as the context is a step further into fantasy territory than the Wong Fei-hung series. Not to give away any secrets, but little Tsang Sze-Man, who does such a wonderful job with all the acting and difficult martial arts, is really a girl. James Wong, who plays the governor, is even more famous as a composer than a character actor, with more than 35 film scores to his credit. *AKA: Siu Nin Wong Feihung Ji Tit Ma Lau; Shao Nian Huang Fei Hong Zhi Tie Ma Liu; Iron Monkey: The Young Wong Fei-hung.* ♫♫♫♪

1993 (PG-13) 85m/C *HK* Yu Rongguang, Donnie Yen, Tsang Sze-Man, Sunny Yuen, Jean Wang, James Wong, Yam Sai-kwoon, Li Fai. *D:* Yuen Wooping. *W:* Tsui Hark, Lau Dai-muk, Elsa Tang. *C:* Arthur Wong, Tam Chi-wai. *M:* Richard Yuen, William Woo, Johnny Yeung. **VHS, DVD**

Iron Monkey 2

A video retitling of *Duel at Tiger Village* that cashes in on Chen Kuan-tai's hit, this is just a routine kung fu mystery. During a hunting expedition, there are several attempts on the life of the Ching Dynasty emperor. An imposter infiltrates the palace and kills one of the emperor's wives. The magistrate assigns Chief Inspector Cool Head (Chen) to investigate the murder. Cool Head traces the murder weapon to hunter Li San, and though the man has an alibi, he's still arrested when he refuses to reveal who took the knife from him. Li's flute-fighting friend Chai-fung (Judy Lee) and her ragged gang of kung fu girls go to rescue him. Before Mr. Head can investigate further, an assassin tries to murder Li San

in prison, and Chamberlain Wu Tai (Chan Sing) has the case closed. But Cool Head has secretly let Li San free to help him to discretely continue his investigation, which draws attacks from a gang of assassins using similar knives run by Iron Hunchback Mr. Tu. Injured helping in a fight, Li San is hidden by a woman named Yu-yan. Cool Head learns from Tu that the leader of the conspiracy has his headquarters in Tiger Valley—a lair protected by a gauntlet of death traps.

A standard kung fu flick for the first half, the mystery angle isn't that compelling, and the only really interesting aspect is Judy Lee's bickering chemistry with Chen Kuan-tai. But once this pair begins to fight their way into Tiger Valley, with its corridor of traps and zombie fighters, things pick up quite a bit. The fight scenes improve a lot, too, with Chan Sing getting in on the action, which builds to a surprisingly bloody climax. **AKA:** *Gau Lung; Jiu Long; Duel at the Tiger Village; Iron Monkey Strikes Back; Tough Guy; Duel of Master.* 🐾🐾♡

1977 87m/C *TW* Chen Kuan-tai, Judy Lee, Chan Sing, Shih Chung Tien, Tin Yau, Cheung Fong-ha, Li Min Lang, Yang Sha-fei, Lu Wei. **D:** Bau Hok-lai. **C:** Ng Kwok-hwa. **M:** Chou Fu-liang. **VHS, DVD**

Iron Monkey 2

This "sequel" has nothing at all to do with the previous *Iron Monkey* other than the presence of star Donnie Yen. During the 1930s, a gangster named Tang—also known as Jade Tiger—is instrumental in bringing more Russians and Japanese into China, making it possible for mobster Gregor to open a nightclub and other business. Members of a Chinese opera troupe rebel against the invasion of foreign gangsters. Big Head Yuen Ming (Cheng Yuen Man), daughter of triad Yuen Tung, puts out a contract on old enemy Jade Tiger, hoping to draw the mysterious Iron Monkey (Donnie Yen) to do the job. Since Iron Monkey always wears Monkey King makeup, a con artist named Siu-kin takes the deposit money on the job. Siu-kin and his partner Shi-chen befriend young martial artist Kam Sun and agree to help him find his father Kam Dah-fon (Wu Ma), now a blind fortuneteller who acts as an informant. Siu-kin and Iron Monkey clash when their paths cross over Jade Tiger's gun-running operation. Yuen Ming learns that she's been misled by Siu-kin, and Kam isn't really Iron Monkey, but she wants him to kill Jade Tiger anyway. Meanwhile, Siu-kin and Shi-chen have sold out big and taken jobs at Jade Tiger's club, but get in too deep when the Japanese start throwing their weight around.

A disappointment in every way, IM2 has a plot that gets lost in meaningless details, ugly camera work, and dull performances. The music is made up of bland library tracks. Even the action scenes feature such ridiculously sped-up movement and poor direction (despite action choreography by Yuen Woo-ping) that they're not at all enjoyable. The climax takes place in the world's worst-designed church. *AKA: Gai Tau Saat Sau; Jie Tou Sha Shou.* ⚐

1996 88m/C *HK* Donnie Yen, Billy Chow, Lau Wing, Wu Ma, Cheng Yuen Man, Chang Jian-li, Steve N. Benson, Ron Edwards, Johnny Liu. *D:* Chiu Liu Kong. *W:* Lee Man-choi. *C:* Tong Yu-tai. *M:* Ng Tai Kong. **VHS, DVD**

Iron Neck Li

The Li family is prominent in Chinese history for their superior martial artists, who often became royal bodyguards. This movie tells the tale of the most famous of these warriors. While accosting a bullying lord, Li (Chi Kuan Chun) is accused of murder when the man dies accidentally. Fortunately, Emperor Chia Ching happened to be traveling incognito and sees the whole thing. Impressed by Li's courage, skill, and honor, he hires the man as his personal bodyguard. On a sightseeing trip to Taiwan, a local picks Li via superstition as the funerary husband to his late daughter. While Li takes part in the ceremony, servant Wong Pa tricks his majesty into going to a brothel—leading to some *Porky's*-style comic antics. Later in their wanderings, a family of farmers invites the emperor and his two men in for dinner. When they learn the family has sacrificed their lone chicken for the meal, the emperor plays matchmaker so that son Monkey can marry the girl he loves. On their next stop, the tourists find romance with the daughters of a tea farmer. A rival tries to abduct one of the girls, but falls off a cliff trying to escape from Li, who comes to the rescue.

In the third act, the narrative goes from episodic drama and comedy to full action mode in the bloody Chang Cheh manner. The rival's grieving uncle Cho Kan (Choi Wang) hires a tribe of aborigines to help strike back at the mainlanders over the perceived murder, and Li Yuen has to massacre dozens of them while making a stand defending the emperor. The ending borrows a bit from *El Cid*. The picture's extremely uneven tone and pace, along with its weak characterization, does it great damage, preventing it from reaching its potential of becoming the *Once upon a Time in China* of the 1970s. Chi Kuan Chun is fine as the resolute hero, though the script doesn't give him much to do otherwise. O Yau-man, who made a career out of playing Shaolin abbots, here takes a rare villainous role. *AKA: Kung Fu Is Forever.* 🐾🐾⚐

1981 94m/C *TW* Chi Kuan Chun, Hang Han, George Wang, Goo Man-chung, Su Chen Ping, Choi Wang, Ching Ching, Kong Yeung, O Yau-man. *D:* Chang Jen-chieh. *W:* Chu Hsang Kin. *C:* Liao Man Meu. *M:* Hang Mu-san. **VHS, DVD**

The Irresistible Piggies

Anarchy and brighthearted fun rules the day in this lightheaded comedy. Four women (Michelle Reis, Karen Mok, Suki Kwan, Kelly Lin) working at the same company are termed "the pork chops" because they are not physically attractive. After a female executive (Florence Kwok) schemes to have them laid off, the "pork chops" exact their revenge.

The spirit of Wong Jing hangs heavy over this film. The writer, producer, director, and infrequent actor has often been lewd and crude in the many scripts for which he is credited. Though little spark of invention or life was found in the three films he wrote and directed in 2001, he seems to bounce back to his old self with this film, his first credit in 2002. Instead of focusing on one body part as the target of derision, as in the unsuccessful *Beauty and the Breast,* each of the "pork chops" has a different physical defect, and each has a measure of fragile self-confidence despite the hurtful insults they must endure. The male characters also have "defects" (e.g., one blushes bright red at inopportune times and is nicknamed "Turtle"), which tends to balance things out. The story moves along at a gallop, rarely slowing down as one comic situation after another is played out. All kinds of humor is thrown into the mix, including visual gags aplenty, wordplay, a horror film parody, etc. Not all the nonsense works—some is downright cruel and other bits may be offensive—but overall Wong Jing crafts an enjoyable and silly ride. He is aided by good comic work from the entire ensemble of actors, including Matt Chow and Chapman To as two doctors who have radically different solutions to the "pork chops" dilemma. *—PM AKA: Chu Ong Daai Luen Mang; Zhu Ba Da Lian Meng; The Irresistible Women.* 🐾🐾

2002 96m/C *HK* Michelle Reis, Karen Mok, Suki Kwan, Kelly Lin, Jordan Chan, Stephen Fung, Raymond Wong Ho-yin, Alex To, Florence Kwok, Chapman To, Hui Siu-hung, Matt Chow, Lo Hoi-pang,

Chan Kin-fung. *D:* Liu Kim-wah. *W:* Wong Jing. *C:* Tony Cheung. *M:* Tommy Wai. **DVD**

It Takes a Thief

This shot-on-video TV feature attempts to re-create the fightin' femme genre à la *In the Line of Duty* on a shoestring, and does a surprisingly good job. Inspector Shum Ling leads a top gang-busting unit for the Hong Kong Police. Her associate Jin is asked by Chief Wang to go on one last undercover assignment among mainland gangsters, postponing his wedding to Tong—Ling's reporter sister—to bust arms dealer gangster Hong Bao. During a raid led by Ling, Jin is separated from the group by an explosion, and later the chief reports him dead. In grief, the sisters are driven apart. Actually, Jin is still alive—after recovering from his wounds, he's sent to ingratiate himself with Hong Bao's man Cui, saving his life from attackers. While Ling goes after Hong Bao through less than official channels, Tong dons a black mask to strike back at the gang on her own, neither of them knowing that Jin is working his way up the ranks from the inside.

The video look makes the whole production seem chintzy, taking every aspect down a notch. Taking that into account, the performances aren't bad, and the action is plentiful. Obviously shot even faster than the usual Hong Kong B-movie, on limited apartment and lumberyard settings, there's a lot of energy in the stuntwork, making this an enjoyable time-waster. The stars do pretty well with their demanding punch-and-kick sequences, though a black leotard–clad Cheung is quite obviously doubled by a man in the more strenuous shots. 🐉🐉

2001 90m/C *HK* Gray Lau, George Woo, Selina Lin, Chung Fat, Peggy Cheung, Chin Siu-Ho, Frances Yip, Yu Ho-kit. *D:* Chan Chuen. **VHS**

asians in usa

Jackie Chan Adventures 1: The Search for the Talismans 📺

Jackie Chan turned down the role that went to Sammo Hung in the CBS series *Martial Law* because he didn't think they could possibly capture his style of action on a weekly TV series. The producers of this series found an answer to this problem: make Jackie a cartoon! That way, Jackie can provide as much action as you could ever ask for without risking his neck. Plus, guest stars can appear with Jackie without him having to actually be there.

Here, Jackie Chan is a daring archeologist, not unlike his Asian Hawk character from *Armor of God*. He returns from an expedition in Europe to his home in San Francisco with a rare shield, and immediately finds two rival gangs are after it. He also finds that his rambunctious 11-year-old niece Jade (Stacie Chan) from Hong Kong has been sent to live with him. Kidnapped by agents of his old friend Captain Black (Clancy Brown), Jackie learns that what the thugs are really after is the talisman affixed to the shield, one of 12 congruent to signs of the Chinese zodiac. Each talisman confers upon the owner a different magical power, and arch villain Valmont (Julian Sands) has sent the man-mountain Tohru (Noah Nelson) and the ninja of the Shadowkhan out to get them all for his master, the mysterious Shendu. The secret spy organization Black belongs to hires Jackie to hunt down and collect the talismans before the evil Shendu gets his claws on them.

Turning celebrities into Saturday-morning cartoon characters is a common promotional device, but is usually a letdown. Anyone recall Mr. T's cartoon? The Jackson 5? But this show is constantly surprising as to how well it works. The secret is that they've successfully transferred the things people enjoy in Chan's movies into animation—cartoon Jackie can't do anything the real Jackie can't do—or at least could, 20 years ago. Like the Lupin 3 series, the animation finds thrills in the possible. Only when the magic talismans come into play do things edge into fantasy, but only according to the rules. But the best thing about the show is that it's captured Jackie Chan's personality and sense of humor. Also, there's an element of wish fulfillment—you can see Jackie face off against a masked Mexican wrestler in the ring, even if he never gets around to co-starring with the Blue Demon in a movie. James Shie does a serviceable job as the voice of Jackie, though it's disappointing that Chan's unable to do it himself. The drawing has a pleasant style, and the animation is fluid, comparable to the WB's *Batman* cartoons. The show includes short video scenes in which Chan responds to questions supposedly sent in by target-audience 11-year-olds, but the video releases wisely edit together three episodes into a single program and leave the interview until the end. 🐉🐉🐉🐉

2000 30m each episode/C *US/HK/KO* Jackie Chan. *V:* James Shie, Stacie Chan, Sab Shimono, Clancy Brown, Julian Sands, Adam Baldwin, Noah Nelson. *D:* Bryan Andrews, Vincenzo Trippetti, Andy Thom. *W:* John Rogers, David Slack, Duane Capizzi. *M:* Jim Latham. **VHS, DVD**

Jackie Chan Adventures 2: The Dark Hand Returns

The cartoon Jackie Chan and the whole Chan clan return for three more anime episodes, collected into a single feature. Jackie learns that Ratso, agent of the Dark Hand, is supposed to steal one of the 12 magic Chinese zodiac talismans from a museum at midnight. Jackie sets aside his principles and decides to steal it first for Section 13, with his unwelcome niece Jade tagging along. Concurrently, the female thief named Viper is there to steal the famous Pink Puma diamond. During a scuffle, the loot bags get switched, and while Jackie spends the night in jail, Viper learns the Snake Talisman can turn her invisible. They both end up fighting the Shadowkhan ninjas in the middle of New York's Thanksgiving Day parade, and somehow steal the Statue of Liberty. Next, Jackie retrieves the Sheep Talisman from the Rocky Mountains. While he and Uncle puzzle over it, the Black Hand thugs are treated to Shendu's origin: he's actually a 900-year-old demon sorcerer, who lost the 12 talismans when his enemies turned him into a talking dragon statue. Borrowing the talisman, Jade uses its power to astral project, but the Black Hand steals it before she returns, and Shendu uses it to possess her body. Fortunately, instead of taking Shendu/Jade to Section 13, Captain Black takes her to the Melvinworld amusement park. And in the third act, the Rabbit Talisman is discovered embedded in the shell of a Galapagos tortoise in the San Francisco zoo. The Black Hand gets to it first, and while Jackie tries to retrieve it from a super-fast Tohru, Jade tries to get the tortoise away from a gourmand fond of endangered species.

Jim Latham manages to give his theme music an Asian flavor without it sounding stereotypical. The video packaging fails to provide any clue as to the order of their release. 🎵🎵🎵

2000 30m each episode/C *US/HK/KO* Jackie Chan. **V:** James Shie, Stacie Chan, Sab Shimono, Clancy Brown, Julian Sands, Adam Baldwin, Susan Eisenberg, Ron Perlman, Howard Hoffman, Bob Joles. **D:** Rick Del Carmen, Bryan Andrews, Andy Thom. **W:** David Slack, Duane Capizzi. **M:** Jim Latham. **VHS, DVD**

Jackie Chan Adventures 3: The Shadow of Shendu

Jackie Chan starts the third volume of his animated adventures in trouble already. He loses the Dragon Talisman to Valmont's men inside a volcano, then returns home to face a conference with Jade's teacher (the little lady has been fighting—who'd have thought?). Meanwhile, Valmont gets fed up with Shendu's treatment and decides to borrow the Dragon Talisman before handing it over, and uses its powers to rob the U.S. Mint and Fort Knox. When Captain Black is injured trying to catch him, an enraged Jackie goes to get the talisman back. Jackie finds the Rat Talisman in an exploding building, then trips on one of Jade's toys and breaks his leg. The talisman brings Jade's "Gnomekop" action figure to life, and it causes a mess of trouble while a wheelchair-bound Chan tries to catch it. Later, to force Jackie to get Section 13's talismans for him, Valmont injects him with venom that will turn him to stone in 24 hours unless he gets the antidote. Jackie refuses, but Jade bypasses Section security to steal the goods.

The latter episode breaks the rules somewhat—one accepts the talismans granting the possessor magic powers and bringing toys to life more readily because they're the series' only magical component, but introducing a magic statue-making liquid as an added threat so late in the game seems like cheating. This trio of episodes also feels a bit exclusive, as the only guest character is the troublesome Gnomekop voices by Brian Doyle-Murray. Other than these perceived flaws, these episodes live up to the series' usual high standards for colorful scenery, funny writing, and fluid animation. 🎵🎵🎵

2000 30m each episode/C *US/HK/KO* Jackie Chan. **V:** James Shie, Stacie Chan, Sab Shimono, Clancy Brown, Julian Sands, Adam Baldwin, Noah Nelson, Brian Doyle-Murray. **D:** Rick Del Carmen, Gloria Jenkins, Bryan Andrews. **W:** Tom Pugsley, Greg Klein, David Slack, Alexx Van Dyne. **M:** Jim Latham. **VHS, DVD**

Jade Claw

Master Yen (Chu Tiet Wo) attacks kung fu Master Kwan Shin Kahn (Hau Chiu Sing), aided by

Japan

No country in the world has a cinema of such extremes as that of Japan. From the soapy shomingeki dramas in which heroic women toil in poverty, to the bizarre variety of the "pink" sex films to the outlandish daikaiju eiga (giant-monster movies), Japan's cinema has something for everyone, and every genre attracts an audience of fervent fans.

Japan got into the film business earlier than other Asian countries, starting in 1897 or so. Sound film arrived as Japan went to war in the 1930s, and production shifted from the usual dramas and comedies to more patriotic fare. The country's every victory was spun into a rousing propaganda picture. But their films didn't have an impact in the rest of the world until 1950, when Akira Kurosawa's *Rashomon* swept through international film festivals. Its subsequent U.S. release resulted in an Academy Award, and distributors considered its Hitchcockian style marketable enough that a dubbed version was given wider release, as was *Seven Samurai* a few years later. Though *Seven Samurai* was cut by half its length in the U.S., *Godzilla,* which was inspired by American giant-monster movies, lacked the same art-house reputation, and was considered just so much raw material, ready for an extensive makeover. With the same f/x magic Eiji Tsubaraya used to re-create thrilling sea battles now turned to creating monsters, distributors recognized that Japanese sci-fi would play in any language, and felt justified in dubbing, pruning, rearranging, rescoring, and adding to the films they imported any way they liked—anything to sell drive-in tickets.

Other genres didn't get as much play, and so were left alone for the most part. If pictures aimed at a more adult audience could have broken through the barrier of adult prejudice in the U.S., then we all might have been watching horribly dubbed and edited yakuza (crime) and chambara (swordplay) pictures on TV—and the existence of those versions would be interfering with our access to the original versions, just as the U.S. cuts of the sci-fi movies make it difficult to see the originals. Children are less bigoted, and were drawn to the monster flicks like flies to city-crushing radioactive honey, while imported TV cartoons like *Astro Boy* and *Gigantor* had little or no ethnicity to hide, and became huge hits as well.

It wasn't until the martial arts craze of the 1970s that much else besides art and monster flicks were imported. *The Street*

Fighter became a terrific hit for the new New Line Cinema—white-bread Americans couldn't necessarily tell Sonny Chiba from Bruce Lee, but they didn't care as long as the hero kicked ass. Unfortunately, *The Street Fighter* was the only Japanese action film that made such an impact at the time; no other stars crossed over, and Chiba's other films only did decent business in the U.S. if they followed the *Street Fighter* mold.

However, cracks appeared in the cultural wall with the appearance of home video. Anime (animation) on tape led to a sensational boom in the Japanese animation industry. Hip U.S. fans could now finds channels to acquire "the goods" and as the ranks of American anime clubs swelled, some of those fans turned their interest into a business venture—importing, subtitling, and dubbing cartoons as legitimate releases. The more that was available, the more fans were converted, and that interest spread to live-action Japanese productions. Even now, the brilliant blind swordsman Zatoichi series, the surprising crime thrillers of Takeshi Kitano, the gore-for-gore's-sake Guinea Pig films, the outrageous films of Takashi Miike, and other strange and wonderful Japanese films are creeping onto the shelves of your local video stores. Let's keep 'em comin'!

his stooges Blind Man (Dai Sai Aan) and Deaf Man (Brandy Yuen). Yen kills Kwan, using his famed Double Phoenix Eye Fist, leaving Kwan's son Wen an orphan.

Years later, a kung fu school is visited by an "old beggar," who applies for a job as teacher—but it's really youngster Kwan Wen (Billy Chong) in disguise, just looking to learn kung fu. He needs it—put to work in the kitchen, he can't even beat Old Chang the cook (Simon Yuen). Not surprising really, as Chang was the guy who defeated Yen and handicapped his two aides, who show up at the school in their search for Chang.

Beaten by the villains who killed his father, Wen receives instruction from Chang in more than cooking and juggling. The old codger teaches him his deadly Eagle Claw, though most of Wen's training comes in the form of altered cooking chores. All this comedy in the kitchen is reminiscent of Jackie Chan's *Half a Loaf of Kung Fu*, this film's obvious inspiration. Though no match for Chan's hit in the martial arts department, *Jade Claw* at least achieves a bit of character and some decent gags, unlike its fellow imitators. When Wen uses his new skills to beat an arrogant Russian boxer (Jim James), Yen

happens to be passing and recognizes the Eagle Claw style. Knowing that Yen is getting close, Chang teaches Kwan his top-secret Shadow Eagle Fist and Claw techniques to make him a match for his old enemies. **AKA:** *Kei Chiu; Ji Zhao; Crystal Fist.* 🐾🐾

1979 84m/C *HK* Billy Chong, Simon Yuen, Hau Chiu Sing, Walter Cho, Dai Sai Aan, Brandy Yuen, Jim James, David Wu. **D:** Hwa Yi Hung. **W:** Li Chan Wai. **C:** Wong Man Wan. **M:** Frankie Chan. **VHS, DVD**

Jiang Hu— "The Triad Zone"

Hong Kong cinema is rife with gangster yarns, and most of them are bland and depressing, but this one does something fresh, and at times fanciful, with the genre. Fans of HBO's *The Sopranos* should definitely see this. Jim Yam (Tony Leung Ka-Fai), boss of the Hung Bo gang, narrates the tale. Yam is a stylish fellow, recalling gangsters of the Damon Runyon era more than today's greasy punks. Even his bulletproof vest is Versace. Jimmy's closest companion is his bodyguard Yue (Roy Cheung), a former soccer star with a secret. Second to sturdy Yue is Jimmy's lawyer Wai (Chan Fai-Hung), an outsider who finds work for the triads satisfying. He also has a mistress named Jo Jo (Lee San-San), simply because he feels it's expected of him—in reality, he's devoted to his hard-ass wife Sophie (Sandra Ng), who helps run things.

Word comes that someone will try to kill Jimmy in the next 24 hours. Proof of the validity of this rumor comes almost immediately when a sniper strikes. Trying to determine the identity of the assassin, and who hired him, causes Yam to re-examine every facet of his life and everyone to whom he's close. A hungry young Turk named Tiger (Samuel Pang, impressive in his first role) definitely has it in for him, but is too unsophisticated to plan the attacks. And rival mobsters like Kei (Lee Siu-Kei) seem to be too absorbed in petty details to focus on killing him.

Beautifully photographed and creatively directed, *Jiang Hu* mixes *King of New York* brashness with *Goodfellas* wit and a huge romantic streak. Lucky Stars Richard Ng and Eric Tsang have cameos, but Anthony Wong stops the show as Kwan Wan Cheung, a benevolent god who appears to save Yam's life. *AKA: Kong Woo Giu Gap.* 🦴🦴🦴♥

2000 107m/C *HK* Tony Leung Ka-Fai, Sandra Ng, Anthony Wong, Roy Cheung, Chan Fai-Hung, Eason Chan, Lee San-San, Samuel Pang, Jo Koo, Lee Siu-Kei, Eric Tseng, Richard Ng. **D:** Dante Lam. **W:** Chan Hing-ka, Amy Chin. **C:** Cheung Man-po. **M:** Tommy Wai. **VHS, DVD**

Joint Security Area

Major Sophie Lang (Lee Yeong-ae), a Swiss-Korean whose father moved to Argentina after the civil war, is sent to investigate a skirmish on the DMZ that left two soldiers dead—one Northern and one Southern. She questions the primary suspect, whose answers come in the guise of fragmented flashbacks rather than straight verbal explanations. As she begins to piece together the truth, she is removed from the case. The situation that turned an evening of illegal fraternizing into a bloodbath is not revealed until Lang's involvement in the case has become unofficial.

Often confusing but always compelling, *JSA* is a film about the political lines that separate people. It takes place in a world where it is a criminal violation to allow even one's shadow to cross those lines. People are defined by the side of the line behind which they remain: the capitalist pigs who call each other brother and the communists lusting after moon pies who see each other as comrades. There is human behavior,

such as the soldiers on each side of the line playfully spitting on each other, and official behavior, in which rifles are drawn. Since there is no war, the division between people is ridiculous. Were a war to start, however, the brotherly comrades would become true enemies. The characters live in a schizophrenic world where war and peace co-exist. As a result, there is something impenetrable about this film that defies the easy explanation of a murder mystery. —*BW* **AKA:** *Gong-Dong-Kyung-Bi-Koo-Yeok; Gongdong gyeong-bi buyeok JSA.* 🦴🦴🦴🦴

2000 110m/C *KO* Lee Yeong-ae, Lee Byung-hum, Song Kang-ho, Kim Tae-woo, Shin Ha-kyun. **D:** Park Chan-wook. **W:** Lee Yong-jong, Lee Lae-soon, Park Chan-wook. **C:** Kim Sang-beom. **M:** Uhuhboo Project. **VHS, DVD**

Juliet in Love

Director Wilson Yip followed up his crime drama *Bullets over Summer* with a heartfelt crime romance about a world full of wounded people. Judy (Sandra Ng) is one of them. Her husband left her when she was diagnosed with breast cancer, causing Judy to question her own self-worth as she endeavors to care for her aging and senile grandfather. Jordan (Francis Ng) is another of the walking wounded, a petty criminal who can't bring himself to cross the line into heartless brutality. Each owes allegiance to crime boss N.T. On (Simon Yam). N.T. is deadly efficient in his work, but he's also a caring father. The problem is that his wife is not the mother of his son. When N.T.'s wife learns about his mistress and their illegitimate son, N.T. wisely decides to leave the child in the care of others until things cool down. He selects Jordan, and Jordan beseeches Judy to help out. Brought together under such circumstances, they find themselves reluctantly being drawn to each other.

By turns wistful, whimsical, thoughtful, and grim, *Juliet in Love* is measured and graceful. It's a romance between two mature people who both realize something is missing in their lives. The performances thankfully do not descend into hysterical theatrics, nor do the scenes with the infant turn nauseatingly cute. Director Wilson Yip deserves credit for the measured pace that allows the drama to breathe and the audience to collect its thoughts as the plot presses forward to a (perhaps) inevitable and emotionally affecting conclusion. —*PM* **AKA:** *Jue Lai Yip Yue Leung Saan Ang; Zhu Li She Yu Liang Shan Ba; Butterfly Lovers.* 🦴🦴🦴♥

2000 89m/C *HK* Francis Ng, Sandra Ng, Simon Yam, Tats Lau, Tai Bik Chi, Angela Tong, Eric Kot, Lam Suet, Joe Lee. **D:** Wilson Yip. **W:** Matt Chow. **C:** Lam Wah-chuen. **M:** Tommy Wai. **VHS, DVD**

Junk

A scientist invents a re-animation serum he calls DNX, and uses it to revive a dead woman. In return, she bites a big chunk out of his throat. The cannibal zombie movie is alive and biting, having made a comeback in recent years—in America, with films like *Resident Evil* and *House of the Dead,* and in Japan, with flicks like *Wild Zero, Versus,* and this low-budget wonder. Col. MacGriff (Mark C. Moorehouse) at the U.S. Army base in Tokyo sends for Dr. Takashi Nakata (Yuji Kishimoto), an old associate of the dead scientist who used to work on the DNX project for them. The colonel says the incident has been isolated at the testing site, an old chemical factory (similar to the one in *Evil Dead Trap*). Meanwhile, a quartet of thieves is robbing a jewelry store. Akira (Osamu Ebara) gets stabbed in the foot by a feisty saleswoman, and security cameras spot their faces, but the group considers their job a success. Their fence Ramon (Tate Gouta) arranges a meeting—at the very same "abandoned" factory, which doesn't hold a living soul. Their leader Jun (Nobuyuki Asano) is killed by the zombies first. Kabu (Keishi Shigemura), however, is killed by one of Ramon's thugs—the fence doesn't believe their zombie story and double-crosses them, leaving only Akira and Saki (Kaori Shimamura) left in the gang. While the yakuza are laughing, zombified Jun starts eating one of them, and bullets start to fly. In the gunfight, gallons of DNX get splashed on the project's warehouse of corpses, so then there's a lot more zombies on the loose. Nakata and MacGriff try to destroy the labs remotely, but someone there is blocking their efforts, making it necessary for them to attempt to blow up the bomb manually.

It's really bold for a film to use a title like this, but they manage to get away with it. Some of the details are hokey, and a few f/x are cheesy, but for zombie movie fans this is a must-see. It's got gangsters, gunfights, and plenty of juicy gore. It also has a few fresh ideas, and is shot with style, but without being too self-conscious about it. Kishimoto was doubtless cast because he can speak English in a part that requires a lot of it, but darned if a single word he says makes sense. *AKA: Junk: Shiryou Gari; Junk: Dying to Live; Junk: Evil Dead Hunting.* 🎵🎵🎵

1999 83m/C *JP* Kaori Shimamura, Osamu Ebara, Yuji Kishimoto, Nobuyuki Asano, Tate Gouta, Mark C. Moorehouse, Miwa, Kotaro Tanaka, Keishi Shigemura. *D:* Atsushi Muroga. *W:* Atsushi Muroga, J.B. Baker, Yoko Katsumoto, Emiko Terao. *C:* Takanobu Kato. *M:* Goro Yasukawa. **VHS, DVD**

Justice, My Foot!

Stephen Chow adds "king of lawyers" to his list of professions to build comedy around, this time choosing to set the insanity in Old China. Sung Shih-chieh (Chow) is the slyest practitioner of law in Canton. However, Madam Sung (Anita Mui) persuades him to retire, fearing that they've lost a dozen children in recompense for his unethical tricks. But when a rich merchant's son kills another man in a street altercation, he offers Sung a fortune to get his boy off. Sung easily bamboozles the old judge—but he arrives home to find his young son has died from a fall down a well. Though it pains him, Sung completes a "brush sealing" ceremony—in which a lawyer seals up his calligraphy brush in a special box, which is hung up in his signboard, to officially retire—and goes into the textile business. When pregnant young widow Yang Hsiu-chen (Carrie Ng) has her husband killed by her brother-in-law (who subsequently frames her for the crime, then falls over a cliff to his death), Madam Yang takes the girl in and gets involved in her defense before magistrate Lord Ho Yu-ta (Ng Man-Tat). Ho is unreasonable and literally slaps a fine on her for malpractice, leading Sung to unseal his brush and seek revenge. The stakes in the case escalate when it's learned that the daughter (Yuen King-Tan) of Lord Tien (Lau Kar-yan), the Secretary General of Shansi, is one of the culprits that helped kill Mr. Yang.

There aren't many comedies that would dare to have the hero lose so many children, and then feature both a pregnant woman and an infant in a wild fight scene, but somehow this just adds depth here. Perhaps because it relies on the twists of logic and warm emotions of Sandy Shaw's script, this was one of the most embraced of Chow's earlier comedies by audiences in Hong Kong. Due to the litigious subject matter, the amount of comedy that doesn't translate well is higher here, though there are still plenty of gags that work in any language. Anita Mui makes a terrific entrance courtesy of choreographer Ching Siu-tung, displaying her kung fu prowess by kicking aside an ox, then running lightly over onlookers' heads (and a tray of tofu) to save a man's life. Cinematographer Peter Pau makes every scene look like a beautiful magazine layout. *AKA: Sam Sei Goon; Shen Si Guan.* 🎵🎵🎵

1992 103m/C *HK* Stephen Chow, Anita Mui, Ng Man-Tat, Carrie Ng, Paul Chun, Lau Kar-yan, Eddie Ko, Yeun King-Tan, Mimi Chu, Wong Yat-Fei, Cho Wing, Wong Tin Lam. *D:* Johnny To. *W:* Sandy Shaw. *C:* Peter Pau. *M:* William Woo. **VHS, DVD**

Kei Mizutani: Undressed for Success

Her starring role in *Weather Woman* made Kei Mizutani a worldwide cult star. This is a 40-

minute video centerfold, shot around the same time as the film. See Kei do a striptease in matching white, red, and black outfits. After that, Kei welcomes the viewer to her house. Really? The big country house used as a location is surely worth millions, and though Mizutani may now be able to afford it from royalties on videos like this one, at the time it more likely belonged to the producer. In any case, Kei wanders about the house and grounds indulging fantasies while appearing in a parade of sexy outfits, which she then dutifully strips off. Occasionally she gives us a little information, like "I like taking walks and shopping." There are also a few sessions of lovemaking to the camera. By the end of our little weekend in the country, Kei confesses her love for the cameraman. The music is good, and Ms. Mizutani is beautiful, with a perfect body. The script is a little weak though, and Kei's innocent young flirt act is a bit hard to swallow after seeing her in films like *The Ladies' Phone Sex Club* and *Tokyo Decameron*. ♫♫

1994 40m/C *JP* Kei Mizutani. **D:** Shoken Takahashi. **C:** Yojiro Fukuda. **VHS, DVD**

Kick Boxer's Tears

This stereotypical boxing story's lone twist is casting firecracker Moon Lee in the lead role. Joan Li (Moon Lee) is upset that her brother Michael (Ken Lo) is fighting in another match, thinking his career will only lead to trouble. When Michael refuses to take a fall for sinister Joey Wang (Lung Fong), the crooked promoter's oiliness spreads to the gloves of his boxer Billy Chow (as himself, sort of) in the form of an illegal substance, leading directly to Michael's death in the ring. Pickpocket Tommy (Wilson Lam) spotted the trainer spreading chili oil on Chow's gloves, and when Joan finds out, she goes out for Chow's blood in an illegal underground match. Joan cripples Chow by breaking his spine, enraging his cousin (Yukari Oshima), who demands that her husband Joey set her up in a grudge match. Joan refuses, planning to close her gym and head back to China. To force her acceptance, the Wangs have Joan's friend Alan (Mark Cheng) kidnapped, setting up a no-holds-barred fight to the death.

Though it's fun to have ex-champs Ken Lo and Billy Chow cast as kickboxing opponents, their match is so lifeless that you can even hear the dubbed extras complain! Things pep up a bit once they get to the underground matches, and with Lee starring, it's foxy boxing that's on everyone's minds anyway. Wilson Lam and Gabriel Wong take turns degrading the quality of the film with lame attempts at comedy. The first two-thirds are relatively dull, but things pick up considerably in the big action climax, as stunt

director Siu Tak-foo (*Ashes of Time*) turns in some brutally violent choreography in a series of bloody fights in and around a crumbling abandoned building. Plus, great title, eh? Ms. Lee got married recently and moved to Denver. **AKA:** *San Lung Chang Fu Dau; Xin Long Zheng Hu Dou; Kickboxer's Tears.* ♫♫♫

1992 89m/C *HK* Moon Lee, Wilson Lam, Mark Cheng, Lung Fong, Gabriel Wong, Yukari Oshima, Billy Chow, Ken Lo, Siu Tak-foo, Li Chi Leih, Shum Wai, Ricky Lau. **D:** Shum Tat-wai. **W:** Szeto On, John Tsang, Dick Lee. **C:** Lau Hung-chuen, Ken Lam. **VHS, DVD**

A Kid from Tibet

The first (and only so far) film directed by Yuen Biao is this spirited fantasy adventure in the same vein as his *Iceman Cometh*. Here, the portrayal of Tibetan lamas as portrayed in Hong Kong films is spoofed a bit, showing the holy men as wizards in the Dr. Strange vein. A lawyer named Robinson (Roy Chiao) journeys to Tibet's remote Potala Palace to meet with the living Buddha Saka Lama (Wu Ma). On arrival, his guide Wong La (Yuen Biao) uses his magic to heal Robinson's crippled leg so he can climb all the stairs. Wong La is sent to Lhasa to meet with Robinson's assistant Chiu Seng-neng (Michelle Reis), bearing with him the cap to the magic Babu Gold Bottle, which the lamas used to defeat the evil Black Section years ago. Their mission is to reunite the top with the bottle, now in the possession of Robinson's aged client in Hong Kong. However, a Black Section sorcerer (Yuen Wah) and his wicked sister (Nina Li Chi) get there first and steal the bottle. The sorcerer's aim is to use the bottle's power to rule the world of Esoteric Buddhism! Wong La arrives in Lhasa just in time to save Chiu from gangs of thieves and Black Section thugs (led by an evil dwarf). In Hong Kong, the evil siblings use all their power against Wong, meaning to get the magic bottle cap at all costs.

Yuen Biao the producer is more impressive than Yuen Biao the director; he puts his characters in wonderful sets and locations, and provides some simple but dazzling special effects. As for Yuen Biao the performer, he's as charming and nimble as ever, leaping about when needed (while co-stars have to use wires), and performing some thrilling fire stunts. His fights with Yuen Wah are thrilling, but disappointing in that the f/x take over where fans hope for an all-out kung fu match. Instead of outtakes, the end credits roll over footage of the crew shooting in Tibet and giving the real lamas proper homage. Keep a sharp eye out or you'll miss Jackie Chan's cameo in the airport scene. **AKA:** *Sai Jong Siu Ji; Xi Zang Xiao Zi; The Kid from Tibet.* ♫♫♫

1991 98m/C HK/TW Yuen Biao, Michelle Reis, Yuen Wah, Nina Li Chi, Roy Chiao, Michael Dinga, Wu Ma, Billy Lau, Jackie Chan. **D:** Yuen Biao. **W:** Shum Chi-leung, Barry Wong, Chan Kam-cheung. **C:** Arthur Wong, Chan Tung-chuen. **M:** Violet Lam. **VHS**

Kid with the Golden Arm

Made soon after his classic *Five Deadly Venoms,* this Chang Cheh film made with much the same cast is too uneven to measure up, but nevertheless features some excellent weapons and empty-hand fighting built into a western-style plot. In charge of the transport of a shipment of gold to a famine-plagued region, Yang Yu-hang (Sun Chien—"Scorpion Venom") is alarmed to learn that the fearsome Chi Sah Gang is after the treasure. The gang is lead by Golden Arm (Lo Meng—"Toad Venom"), whose lieutenants also bear names based on their armor—Silver Spear (Lu Feng—"Centipede Venom"), Iron Robe (Johnny Wang), and Brass Head (Ma Sze-Peng) chief among them. In addition, the Chi Sah are allied with a gang called Seven Hooks. Yang calls upon Li Chin-ming (Wei Pai—"Snake Venom") and his partner Miss Leng (Pan Ping-chang) to add more protection. Yu's scouts Short Axe Yen (Chiang Sheng) and Long Axe Fong make short work of the Seven Hooks, killing three-and-a-half Hooks each. Miss Leng also scouts ahead, and is attacked by Iron Robe, but an alcoholic fighter named Hai To (Phillip Kwok—"Lizard Venom") steps in to help her, and then disappears. During another ambush by Silver Spear and Brass Head, the poisonous Sand Palm (Dick Wei, in an almost invisible role) infects Li before Hai To steps in again. Despite these ambushes, the Chi Sah surprise their enemies by stealing the gold via the tunnel before the transport begins, losing Brass Head in the battle. But Hai To knocks a wheel off of their getaway wagon and kills Iron Robe, letting Yang recover the loot. Then, Hai To throws Li into an oven, baking the poison out of him. The drunk always seems to be there to save the party from the Chi Sah and their death traps. But can they survive the mysterious Iron Feet?

Phillip Kwok's drunk character is certainly inspired by the then-current boxoffice champ *Drunken Master.* He might not have Jackie Chan's comedic skills or natural charisma, but his fighting is excellent. Since most of the Chi Sah Gang are masked, it's likely different members of the Venoms mob filled in as each other's opponents in different scenes. **AKA:** *Gam Bei Tung; Jin Bi Tong.* ♫♫♫♡

1978 75m/C HK Phillip Kwok, Lo Meng, Sun Chien, Chiang Sheng, Lu Feng, Wei Pai, Johnny Wang, Pan Ping-chang, Ma Sze-Peng, Jamie Luk, Yu Tai-ping,

Lau Shi Kwong, Dick Wei. **D:** Chang Cheh. **W:** Ngai Hong, Chang Cheh. **C:** Tsao Hui-chi. **VHS, DVD**

Kikujiro

A family film from the blood-soaked directorial hand of Takeshi Kitano? *Kikujiro* is a gentle, carefully crafted story about a young boy who ends up on a road trip with a disreputable neighbor. Masao (Yusuke Sekiguchi) lives with his grandmother (Kazuko Yoshiyuki) in a large city. He has been told that his mother is away in another town working. Masao longs to see her, though he has no clear memories of her. His desires are exacerbated when his school pals take off for their summer vacations. A neighborhood woman takes pity on him and forces her no-good husband Kikujiro ("Beat" Takeshi Kitano) to escort Masao on the trip. Kikujiro is a gambler and a troublemaker, not well regarded by anyone in the neighborhood, but what can you do when the wife twists your arm? The unlikely pair head off.

As with all "road trip" movies, *Kikujiro* is filled with episodes. Before you can blink, Kikujiro blows the trip money at the racetrack. That helps establish the older character's luckless character while also giving Masao a slight edge in the guilt factor. The two must travel by walking and hitchhiking and relying on the kindness of strangers. And what strangers they meet: bikers, a poet, a juggler, and a child molester, to name just a few. In his own gruff way, Kikujiro tries to protect Masao and ends up bonding with the boy. A lot of deadpan humor rolls by, and though the film feels a bit long at 121 minutes, the delight of a storyteller filling in all the details is pleasantly evident. —PM **AKA:** *Kikujiro no natsu.* ♫♫♡

1999 (PG-13) 122m/C JP "Beat" Takeshi Kitano, Yusuke Sekiguchi, Kayoko Kishimoto, Yuko Daike, Kazuko Yoshiyuki, Beat Kiyoshi, Great Gidayu, Rakkyo Ide, Akaji Maro, Daigaku Sekine, Makoto Inamiya, Yoji Tanaka. **D:** Takeshi Kitano. **W:** Takeshi Kitano. **C:** Katsumi Yanagishima. **M:** Jo Hisaishi. **VHS, DVD**

The Killer

More than any other film between *Enter the Dragon* and *Crouching Tiger, Hidden Dragon,* John Woo's *The Killer* is responsible for introducing and popularizing Hong Kong cinema to Western audiences. Without a wide release, festival and midnight showings—along with a cult video audience—were responsible for making the film a legend, and cemented star Chow Yun-fat as a cinema icon.

Professional killer John (Chow) wants to get out of the business (as all hit men heroes do),

Danny Lee and Chow Yun-fat, locked in a classic tableau, in John Woo's terrific *The Killer.*

THE KOBAL COLLECTION / FILM WORKSHOP

but agrees to accept One Last Job from his agent Sidney (Paul Chu). During the nightclub hit, singer Jenny (Sally Yeh) gets caught in the gunfight, and John's gun flash injures her eyes. John (or "Jeff" in some versions) feels guilty for nearly blinding Jenny, and ends up becoming friends and falling in love with the girl. To pay for her cornea operation, he takes another job from gangster Johnny Weng (Shing Fui-on). But after killing his target politician, Weng double-crosses John and tries to kill him in turn. The resulting gun battle draws Inspector Li (Danny Lee), who is impressed by John in spite himself—when the killer is nearly free, he stops to rescue a little girl who is injured in the crossfire. After cop and killer get the girl to a hospital ER and are sure she'll be O.K.—holding guns on each other all the while—the cop lets the killer escape. Li gets back on John's trail, but his attempted arrests are interrupted, first by Jenny's presence, and then by attacks by Weng's army of triad gunmen. Helping each other through danger, the cop and the killer find they have more in common with each other than with their supposed compatriots.

The problem with martial arts in a modern setting has always been what to do about guns. As Bruce Lee put it in *Enter the Dragon,* "Why

doesn't someone just pick up a gun and—bang!—solve the problem?" Woo easily solved this dilemma in his earlier *A Better Tomorrow,* inventing the "gun fu" style by replacing punch and kick choreography with blazing firearms. Drawing on his love of French, American, and Japanese crime classics, Woo created a much-imitated style that matched beautifully paced, flowing imagery with exhilarating violence. But *The Killer,* a masterpiece of shoot-'em-up action, also has a deeper theme: that trust can be found even in a chaotic world. Not that Woo doesn't put in a little comedy—there's a scene in which Lee and Chow hold each other at gunpoint while pretending to be old friends for Jenny's benefit that borders on slapstick. Plus, the ending is so sharply ironic that it often draws chuckles from audiences. Woo has made films with deeper melodrama and more outrageous action, but *The Killer* combines his strengths more completely than any other. Absolutely required viewing. **AKA:** *Dip Huet Seung Xiong; Die Xie Shuang Xiong; Bloodshed of Two Heroes.* 🎝🎝🎝🎝

1989 (R/UNR) 111m/C *HK* Chow Yun-fat, Danny Lee, Sally Yeh, Paul Chu, Kenneth Tsang, Shing Fui-on, James Ha, Ricky Yi, Yip Wing-cho, Barry Wong, Tommy Wong, Parkman Wong, Lam Chung. **D:** John Woo. **W:** John Woo. **C:** Horace Wong, Peter Pau. **M:** Lowell Lo. **VHS, DVD**

Killer

Yet another portrait of triad society, this one focusing more on the sadness and drama, with little violence. Tung (Jordan Chan) and his three buddies became a legend by killing a triad member in their Hong Kong neighborhood, after which they join and ascend rapidly within a rival triad. However, Tung has grown weary of the gangster life. He's more interested in his nightclub business and stock investments. Mantis (Mark Cheng) is also uneasy with his lot. Po (Simon Lui), on the other hand, loves the triad life, and fits in perfectly. Yung (Ken Wong) is loyal, but too softhearted. Internal and external forces alike conspire to unravel all their lives.

Po mistreats his girlfriend Ivy (Yoyo Mung)—who has a mutual crush on Tung—but doesn't dare break up with her because she knows too much about him. Meanwhile, he carries on a steamy affair with slutty Lili (Claire Yiu).

Their boss Prince assigns them tasks eliminating debtors like Crazy Lai who won't pay up. The executions, carried out properly by the masked team with special knives, have a ceremonial feel and are otherwise anticlimactic. Finding a finger in Po's laundry makes Ivy uncomfortable—she rushes to make sure he's not missing one! Later, it's learned they botched the job, killing Crazy Lai's innocent brother by mistake. An attempt to make up for it goes even worse—Lai is killed, but an unexpected cop at the site shoots Yung dead. When Mantis steals Pauline, the girlfriend of fellow gangster Fai, it leads to a confrontation between Fai and Po, which balloons into even more trouble. It's decided the only way to remedy the situation is to kill Fai before he can conspire against them with their superiors. Mantis becomes a heroin addict. Po becomes suspicious of Ivy's friendship with Tung. Pauline commits suicide. The police begin to add up evidence against the boys and close in. It seems they can't escape the fate the path they started on with that first killing all those years ago.

More Martin Scorsese than John Woo, this gangster melodrama gets by on Billy Chung's stylish direction, and the personality of stars Chan and Lui. **AKA:** Diy Sau; Dao Shou. ♫♫♡

2000 88m/C *HK* Jordan Chan, Simon Lui, Ken Wong, Mark Cheng, Yoyo Mung, Claire Yiu. **D:** Billy Chung. **W:** Edmond Pang, Simon Lui, Billy Chung, Jack Ma (story). **C:** Kwan Chi-kan. **M:** Tommy Wai. **VHS, DVD**

The Killer Elephants

It's tough to make sense of this Thai thriller, but it provides a lot of unusual spectacle and non-stop action, starting with a furious car chase. Farmer Kow Fai is framed for murder by crime chief The Boss, who wants to force Kow and his neighbors off their valuable farmland. However, the city police are unable to track down Kow over the rugged country, especially when his workers block the way with their elephants. The area's constable, Ching Ming, is an old friend of Kow's, and gives his pal as much help as he can—but when the conflict between Kow and The Boss heats up into armed warfare, Ching is forced to try to arrest him, and finds that Kow has become more vicious, even kidnapping The Boss's pregnant wife Mei, who is Kow's old girlfriend. Kow captures Ching, but lets him take the woman into town when she goes into labor. Kow and his men use the cover of the Elephant Carnival to go into town and reclaim his captives. That night, Kow and his men make a raid on The Boss's headquarters. The Boss's lieutenant Mao Tien takes advantage of the situation by killing his Boss, taking over his operation. Moving quickly while Kow is occupied, Mao abducts Mei and her girlfriends to try to lure Kow into a trap. Learning of the coming showdown, Ching is ordered to take a troop of cops and arrest everyone.

Sort of a modern Robin Hood story, *The Killer Elephants* maintains interest despite its rambling story with plenty of gunfights, fisticuffs, a nude painted dancer, motorcycle and car stunts, explosions, and of course, plenty of pachyderms. Just like in the old Tarzan pictures, a herd of elephants can overcome anything, even an army of armed thugs. How many movies show a guy getting knocked out by an elephant's penis?! ♫♫♡

1976 83m/C *TH* Sung Pa, Alan Yen, Nai Yen Ne, Yu Chien. **D:** Som Kit. **C:** Man Nu. **VHS, DVD**

Killer from Above

Chen Wu-hai (Lo Lieh), of the Keen Blade Brotherhood, is attacking and killing every famed martial artist he can find. Since he claims to be a former student of Master Ko Wei-yi, who disappeared fairly recently, Ko's old friend Shih (Carter Wong)—the current chief of martial arts clans—is called upon to deal with the menace. Shih starts by putting a 10,000 gold taels reward on Chen's head. Acrobat brothers Ta-bo (Cheng Fu Hung) and Au-bo run into Chen, but find he's not a psychopath after all. He explains that the men he killed were evil, and he hires

the brothers to spy for him. Chen even rescues a damsel in distress from Sing Chu (Chang Yi), the Smiling Killer, who has been impersonating him. But the fair damsel turns out to be Madame Jiu (Wong Ping), the Widow Spider, who conspired with Sing to trap him. Ta-bo and Au-bo help him escape, and once the tables are turned, Chen makes Sing and the Widow Spider an offer to participate in a scheme of his. Chen allows them to turn him in to Shih's assistant (Lung Fei) for the reward, asking that they use part of it to bribe a guard. However, he knows they'll turn on him, and in turn, turn on each other—Chen has already arranged for his escape, and only wanted to be sure and get the money. With Sing and Jiu disposed of, Chen surprises everyone by turning himself in! His plot is nearly ruined when Master Lo Chi (Cliff Lok) rescues him in gratitude for some enemies Chen killed, but Chen manages to let himself be recaptured.

Chen's seemingly mad scheme is soon revealed, and it involves exposing a cunning conspiracy, rescuing his master, preserving a secret martial arts manual, a kung fu tournament, a deep-water dungeon, and saving the Martial Arts World—surely a story worthy of Alexander Dumas! There's also the King of Beggars, the Chief Abbot of Shaolin (O Yau-man, of course), and a time bomb mixed into the fast-moving story. All the elements of this straightforward adventure tale are kept clicking, without a whiff of drama or romance to get in the way, helped along with some dynamic direction (zooms a-plenty!). One hardly notices some glaring mistakes, such as the fact that Lo Lieh comes out of a stinking dungeon sewer and a corridor of fire with his suit still clean and white. Carter Wong has been known to indulge in overacting, but here he really overdoes it on the flaring nostrils and rolling eyes. If the fight choreography had been a bit better, this would have been some kind of a cockeyed classic. But as it is, it's still big stupid fun from start to finish. 🎵🎵🎵

1977 87m/C *TW* Lo Lieh, Carter Wong, Cliff Lok, Wong Ping, Chang Yi, Lung Fei, Cheng Fu Hung, Wilson Tong, Robert Tai, Wong Chi Sang, Chan Chuen, Yuen Sam, O Yau-man, Lau Lap Cho, Weng Hsiao Hu, Chui Chung Hei, Shih Ting Ken, Au Lap-bo. *D:* Joe Law. **VHS, DVD**

The Killer Meteors

The Killer Meteor Mi Wei (Jimmy Wang Yu) is a freelance vigilante out to rid the world of evil. The Meteor is so feared, in fact, that thieves will cut off their own fingers in order to avoid his wrath. The Meteor is hired by the Immortal Wa Wu Bin (Jackie Chan) to retrieve a vial of antidote from Wa's wife, Madame Tempest. The poison allows Tempest to control the Immortal—without a yearly dose of antidote, the "Immortal" Wa will die. Wa strong-arms the Meteor into working for him, and our hero sets out to brave the perils of the quest. He's helped in his quest by his patron, Lord Fung.

Deadly kung fu artists aren't the only problems the Meteor faces on his way to recovering the antidote. No one in this story seems to be telling the whole truth, and few people are who or what they seem to be. Make sure to stick around for the film's finale, where the secret weapon of the Killer Meteor is finally revealed (only three people have ever seen the weapon; two are dead, and the other one is the Meteor himself). There's also a classic pole-top battle, reminiscent of the much later film, *Iron Monkey*. This film is so early in the career of Jackie Chan that Jackie isn't even the main star; and his character, the Immortal Wa Wu Bin, isn't even a very nice guy. In some ways, this may actually help the film—as Jackie's just playing a part, rather than struggling to find his kung fu identity (and step out from behind Bruce Lee's long shadow). Jimmy Wang Yu does a fine job in the lead role, and Jackie and the rest of the supporting cast are good as well. Watch it and have some fun...just don't expect it to be a standard Jackie Chan film. Large portions of the score of this flick have been lifted from the original, classic score for *King Kong*, by Max Steiner. —*SS* **AKA:** *Feng Yu Shuang Liu Xing; Jackie Chan vs. Wang Yu.* 🎵🎵♡

1976 (PG) 104m/C *TW* Jimmy Wang Yu, Jackie Chan, Yu Ling-lung, Nan Yu-li, Lee Man Tai, Ma Cheung, Phillip Ko, Ma Kei, Chan Wai Lau, Lee Keung, Weng Hsiao Hu, Sit Hon, Man Man, Tung Lam, Ching Kuo-chung, Yu Ling-lung, Woo Wai, Shih Ting Ken, Luk Yat-lung, Wong Yeuk-ping. *D:* Lo Wei. *W:* Ku Lung. **VHS, DVD**

Killer of Snake, Fox of Shaolin

This fanciful flick is as much like a Chinese folktale as it is a kung fu epic. Determined suitor snake Choi Tin-sing wants to marry foxy Wong Ku (Lily Han), but Ku and her father keep refusing him. Fed up, Tin-sing attempts to abduct his intended bride. Passing stranger Tan Yiu-lung (Carter Wong) intervenes, and Choi uses black magic to spit venom in his opponent's face. Special guest star God gets angry, blowing the snake away in a storm, while little Wong Ku carries Tan home to recover. Ku falls for her patient, but once he's well Tan continues his wandering ("He may be handsome, but he's got no feelings."). Mr. Wong and daughter Ku scheme to get Tan to take Ku along with him, but he resists their efforts. But Choi Tin-sing already considers Tan an enemy of the snake clan—Tin-sing's brother Choi Tin-lung tries to kill Tan with his serpents, but his snake sister Sau-

tung (Lau Wai-ling) is sympathetic toward the stranger and interferes. The siblings turn into snakes and start fighting, until the God of Wind breaks it up. Tan finally begins to succumb to Ku's charms through some of her father's spells, allowing her to travel with him to Tin Shan for his annual visit to his master Abbot Chi Kwan. But first, Tan is visited by the ghost of Lady So Chu-chin, who asks him to get revenge on her bandit chief brother-in-law for her murder. When the bandits team up with the snake clan, Tan needs the help of both the ghost and the foxes to face them.

An imaginative fantasy shot on a budget, *Killer of Snake* suffers from a rambling narrative and sloppy camera work. Both lack focus, and some knowledge of Chinese folklore may be required to know what's going on with all the were-foxes, were-snakes, deities, and magic. The fight scenes are decently choreographed (when you can see them), but are more often resolved by magic rather than martial arts skill, and feature too much senseless slow motion. Snatches of the music come from *King Kong* (1976) and *Close Encounters of the Third Kind*. 🐉🐉

1978 88m/C *TW* Carter Wong, Cheung Lik, Man Wun-hsia, Kuo Wu-sing, Lily Han, Cheung Pooi-sang, Lau Wai-ling, Lau Yat-fan, Chan Hei, Kam Yuen Chu, Lam Man-wai. *D:* Man Wah. *C:* Wu Chuen-hwa. *M:* Chan Kwok-man. **VHS, DVD**

Killer Priest

A water wagon is stopped by peasants on a mountain road. There's a drought going on, but the driver won't give them any water—the governor plans to sell it for a piece of silver per cup! Heroic Miss Yen Chi (Judy Lee) intervenes, twisting the driver's neck and sending him running. A passing monk (Chan Sing) asks her if she knows Dr. Chi Yuen (Man Kong Lung), and for directions to Lung City. She sends him off the wrong way—after all, every monk she's known has been a corrupt parasite. But she's never met one like this, as this film purports to tell the story of Tamo (around A.D. 600), one of the monks who spread Buddhism—and the martial arts forms that would become kung fu—throughout China.

The driver runs to Dr. Chi Yuen's clinic, but he'd rather spend his time treating the needy than a government lackey. After a demonstration of acupuncture serves to give a gratuitous shot of a woman's breasts, we see an impressive parade for a visiting Taoist Abbot (Chuen Yuen) brought by Mayor Chen Chuen-min (Ko Chun) to pray for rain. Yen and Chi oppose the priest, but his prayers bring results. Tamo, who disregarded Yen Chi's directions, arrives to clash with both the Taoist and Dr. Chi. He asks

the Taoist to turn from evil and save his soul. With Chi he makes a bargain: If Chi can't break any one of his 18 styles of martial arts, he'll become the monk's pupil.

Then, in the film's least action-packed sequence, a plague strikes the city. The elder Dr. Chi (Cho Kin) despairs at the doctors' helplessness, and commits suicide. Knowing that the plague couldn't be just fate, his son swears to find out who is behind the trouble. He's right—the Taoist had the water supply poisoned. Chi Yuen just isn't a good enough fighter to take revenge, so Tamo has to rescue him. Amazed at the monk's powers, the Taoist visits his mentor Tin Chu (Phillip Ko) for advice on how to deal with him. The old man shows him some new tricks, promising to join his pupil once he masters the Pai Ying Palm Style. Meanwhile, Tamo is finally training Chi Yuen in his kung fu, making ready for a showdown with the Taoists.

Don't look for much historical information here. Throughout, Tamo is treated as a short, bald superhero, his every feat accompanied by goofy sound effects. He can levitate, create great winds, throw his voice, and fight with a magic flying shoe! Rather than working directly for peace and enlightenment, Tamo seems to be just playing games with people—he could have brought the Taoist to justice easily, but instead tries to manipulate others, costing countless lives. Despite this, Chan Sing is able to instill a sense of nobility into the character. The other characters don't fare as well. Chi is too naïve to be a real doctor, Yen is just a bitch, and Tin Chu has a crazy black hand that burns whatever it touches. As for the Taoist priest, he turns out to be a hitherto unknown character in disguise, just so another actor (and better fighter) can play him during the final scenes! Without any special effects, the fight scenes aren't anything special, and there's even some cheating going on with cut frames. *AKA: Shaolin Buddhist Monk Tamo; Shaolin Monk; Monk Tamo; Fighting of Shaolin Monks.* 🐉🐉

1981 /C *HK* Chan Sing, Judy Lee, Man Kong Lung, Phillip Ko, Chan Lau, Chuen Yuen, Ko Chun, Hon Kong, Ho Yu Hua, Ko Saio Pao, Li Min Lang, Nancy Yen, Weng Hsiao Hu, Chen Chin-hai, Chao Gang Sheng, Ching Kuo-chung, Cho Kin. *D:* Lam Fook-dei. *W:* Chou Ya Tsu, Dung Yen Lyoung. *C:* Lo One Win. *M:* Huang Mou Shan. **VHS**

Killer Snakes

The popularity of creature features like *The Birds* and especially *Willard* was not unknown in Asia, and spawned imitations there as well as in the West. William Grefe's *Stanley* may have been the first to follow up on the fad to use snakes as the monsters, but Kwai Chih-hung goes far beyond that little photoplay—too far.

Chi Ho (Kam Kwok-leung) is a backward boy, the son of a masochistic prostitute, whose only friend was his pet snake. Working as a delivery boy, he lives in what can charitably be called a hole in the wall—a filthy unclaimed space between shops in one of Hong Kong's poorest neighborhoods. On the other side of one of his stained and porn-littered walls is a restaurant that serves snake gall bladders to tough triad clientele who believe they gain sexual potency from the "medicine." Chi rescues the dying snakes and nurses them, making them his grateful pets. He becomes frustrated when the girl next door (Maggie Lee) stands him up for a date, so he goes to one of the brothels on his rounds to get a girl. The pimps try to rob him, but Chi thoughtfully brought his snake with him, and he frightens the thugs away. He then abducts a prostitute and drags her back to his lair, where he ties her up and tortures her with his slimy friends before killing her in a frenzy. Afterward, the maddened Chi tears out a hole in the wall to let in all the snakes and lizards he'd ever want.

As if that scene wasn't sleazy and disgusting enough, the climax tops it. His neighbor friend is tricked into becoming a prostitute by one of the local madams. To get revenge, Chi kidnaps the madam and punishes her with an army of slithering, creeping critters. Of course, snakes had been used in Hong Kong movies to scare people before, just like everywhere else. But this is the first film to make the snake's symbolic terrors explicit, going way over the top in an orgy of repulsion—and in a movie from the prestigious Shaw Brothers Studio no less. After this, the lid came off of the snake pit, and in the next few years Asian cinema suffered an explosion of creeper-themed horrors. Even horror flicks that had nothing to do with snakes felt obligated to show some, preferably escaping from inside a person. However, nothing since has quite been the match of the sweaty, grimy atmosphere of this dark exploitation nightmare. Director Kwai Chih-hung (*Bamboo House of Dolls*) eventually immigrated to the U.S. and opened a pizza restaurant! *AKA: Sau Sai Sau; She Sha Shou.* ♪♪♪

1974 (X) 91m/C *HK* Kam Kwok-leung, Maggie Lee, Chan Chuen. **D:** Kwai Chih-hung. **W:** Ngai Hong. **VHS**

Killer's Romance

Filmed the same year as *Dragon from Russia*, this is a more straightforward adaptation of the *Crying Freeman* manga. Upon the death of his foster father, London yakuza Jeffrey Nidaime (Simon Yam) is asked to take over the family business. At the top of his "To Do" list is to take vengeance on Charlie Chan Ben (director Phillip Ko) and the other Chinese triad members who killed the old man. While Jeffrey and his assistant Eko (Julia Chan) are taking care of this business, student Jenny (Joey Wong) snaps his picture, making her a target for the police, the triads, and of course Jeffrey. However, instead of eliminating Jenny, Jeffrey falls for her and saves her from Chan and his men. As it turns out, all the violence is the result of a scheme cooked up between Charlie and Jeffrey's trusted yakuza friend Yoshikawa (Luk Chuen), and the killer's romance gives the yakuza the perfect excuse to join in the hunt for both Jeffrey and Jenny.

Director Phillip Ko gives himself one of the more interesting roles—his amusingly flamboyant Charlie Chan seems to be a parody of Shing Fui-on's usual gangster roles. As director, this is a big step above the cheap Philippine features he would cobble together in the years to come. It's a bit ponderous in spots, but it pays off handsomely at the end with the expected bullet-fest, plus some unusual examples of Simon Yam's kung fu and swordplay skills. *AKA: Long Man Sa Sau Ji Yau Yan; Long Man Sha Shou Tze Yo Ren; Crying Freeman: Killer's Romance.* ♪♪♪ ▽

1990 89m/C *HK* Simon Yam, Joey Wong, Phillip Ko, Luk Chuen, Julia Chan, Lau Siu-ming, Carmen Lee, Keichi Ishida, Gary Siu, Li Yat-chuen, Jason Pai. **D:** Phillip Ko. **W:** Phillip Ko. **C:** George Ma. **M:** Wong Chi-hung. **DVD**

The Killing of Satan

Most Christian organizations talk about fighting the Devil in abstract terms, telling people not to "let the Devil into your heart" and such, as if Satan weren't a real person. But a small sect of Penitents in a remote region of the Philippines dares to fight the Lord of Darkness toe-to-hoof, and will even go after him on his own turf! During their usual mass—you know, flagellation, ritual bloodletting, crucifixion—the congregation is threatened by a gang of toughs led by the King of Magic, a sorcerer in red tights. He makes threatening gestures (which knock down a half dozen men) and teases the Penitents' leader Miguel by magically making the old man's head spin around on his neck. While recovering from this ordeal, Miguel sends his nephew Felix in search of another nephew—Lando San Miguel (Ramon Revilla), a former bandit who got religion in jail and now lives peacefully with his wife Laura (Elizabeth Oropesa) and children in another village. Lando refuses to come, having left his violent life behind, but the sect's prayers send Lando a nightmare about Uncle Miguel

being crushed by a boulder, making him think twice. Ebarrios and some of Lando's old cronies, now working for the satanists, come gunning for him, shooting dead both Lando and his oldest son David. However, Miguel dies while still psychically connected to Lando, bringing the hero back to life. On reaching Miguel's village, Lando takes a canoe out to sea to visit Uncle Miguel's rotted corpse. While he's gone, the Prince of Magic and Satan's minions abduct daughter Betty and cousin Luisa (Cecille Castillo), fending off the villagers with their magic powers. But Uncle Miguel has conferred upon his nephew the powers of the Coronado—making him bulletproof, super-strong, and able to heal wounds—and Lando follows the evil ones to their island, and into the bowels of the Earth, to save his loved ones.

While on the surface a simple fantasy film with magic duels, were-snakes, were-cats, were-German Shepherds, and other creatures, *Killing of Satan* contains elements that place it solidly in the adults-only category—casual nudity, rape (offscreen), succubi, violence, and extreme gore—which make it difficult to fathom what its intended audience is. Girls captured by the Prince of Magic stand around naked in a magic cage. When the boulder crushes Miguel, we see the messy aftermath, and later somebody's heart explodes. Satan is portrayed in the old-fashioned way, by a skinny guy complete with horns, tail, trident, and long red underwear. Later, apparently the skinny guy wasn't imposing enough to fight the hero, and he transforms into a beefier actor in a tuxedo. God Almighty and Baby Jesus put in an appearance, too, giving Lando a magic staff that shoots laser beams and has other powers (just like Moses!). The special effects are simple, but plentiful for a Philippine production of its vintage. 🦴🦴🦴

1983 93m/C *PH* Ramon Revilla, Elizabeth Oropesa, George Estregan, Paquito Diaz, Cecille Castillo, Erlyn Umali, Charlie Davio. *D:* Efren C. Pinon. *W:* Jose Mari Avellana. *C:* Ricardo Herrera. *M:* Ernani Cuerco. **VHS, DVD**

King Kong Escapes

Though King Kong was thought to be miscast in the script that became *Ebirah, Horror of the Deep,* Toho Studios found a place for him in this international adventure film meant to tie in vaguely with co-producer Rankin-Bass's animated TV series. Throwing out any previous Kong-tinuity, the film begins with Commander Carl Nelson (Rhodes Reason) of nuclear submarine *Explorer*, on a mission for the United Nations, explaining his interest in whether the legendary 20-meter tall gorilla really exists to shipmates Lt. Jiro Nomura (Akira Takarada) and blonde ship's nurse Susan Watson (Linda Miller). Others are already sure of the fact.

At the North Pole, supervillain Dr. Huu (Eisei Amamoto) has built his own robot version of Kong (Hiroshi Sekita), using designs stolen from Kong-expert/engineer/sub captain Nelson. Madame Pirhana (Mie Hama), the representative of Huu's power-mad benefactor government (Canada?), just wants Mechani-Kong to procure for them the dangerous and rare Element X, but Huu believes his robot can conquer the world. However, the powerful Element X interferes with the robot's operation. Damaged by a rockslide, the *Explorer* puts in for repairs at Kong's home on Mondo Island, where a landing party is attacked by a huge Gorosaurus. But Kong (Harou Nakajima) arrives to save them, taking a shine to Susan, and fights off the island's other monsters to protect her. The sub crew is ordered to study Kong, but Dr. Huu has other plans—he captures Kong, Nelson, Susan, and Nomura, forcing the ape to mine the ore for him using electronic hypnosis. But with Susan in danger, King Kong escapes! Huu sends Mechani-Kong after him to recapture the beast, and the two titans fight it out in the streets of Tokyo.

The Kong suit looks pretty bad, but it's much better than that used in *King Kong vs. Godzilla*, and Nakajima's movements more closely approximate those of a gorilla. Mechani-Kong looks much better, possibly the best of Toho's giant robot designs. Having begun to scale back the budgets on their monster epics, the big battle scenes aren't as spectacular as those of earlier films, but director Ishiro Honda gives them excitement and atmosphere. It's too bad Toho couldn't make more Kong movies. The much shorter American-release version, dubbed by Rankin-Bass animation regulars like Paul Frees, is much faster paced and cartoon-like, missing whatever romance and political commentary existed in the original. **AKA:** *King Kong no Gysakushu; King Kong Strikes Again; The Revenge of King Kong.* 🐉🐉🐉

1967 (G) 104m/C *JP* Eisei Amamoto, Rhodes Reason, Mie Hama, Linda Miller, Akira Takarada, Shoichi Hirose, Andrew Highes, Ikio Sawamura, Toru Ibuki, Nadao Kirino, Yasuhisa Tsutsumi, Osman Yusuf, Susumu Kurobe, Tadashi Okabe, Sachio Sakai, Kazuo Suzuki, Yoshifumi Tajima, Harou Nakajima, Hiroshi Sekita. **D:** Ishiro Honda. **W:** Takeshi Kimura. **C:** Hajime Koizumi. **M:** Akira Ifukube. **VHS**

King Kong vs. Godzilla

Among the many story ideas generated by special-effects genius Willis O'Brien was one for a second sequel to his *King Kong*, called "King Kong vs. Frankenstein." In this fanciful tale, Kong survives his fall and is smuggled back to Skull Island (which must have resurfaced after sinking in *Son of Kong*). Meanwhile, the grandson of Dr. Frankenstein is following the family tradition, and has built a 20-foot monster he calls a "Ginko," using parts from different animals. Carl Denham brings both monsters to San Francisco to stage a boxing match between the two titans. Of course, they break free and do what monsters do: fight each other and destroy landmarks. They eventually end up toppling to their apparent deaths from the Golden Gate Bridge.

O'Brien's treatment was sold to producer John Beck *(Harvey)*, who hired screenwriter George Worthing Yates to do a rewrite. Yates's script made quite a few changes, including the new title "King Kong vs. Prometheus," but for the most part left the story intact. In search of financing, Beck took the property to Toho Studios in Japan, seemingly the only place capable of making giant-monster movies on a low budget (compared to the average American film). Toho jumped at the chance to pit the famous ape against their own famous monster, and so *King Kong vs. Godzilla* was made, with a totally new script and a Kong costume that, for reasons that have never been explained, was woefully inadequate.

In the Arctic Ocean, Godzilla (Haruo Nakajima) frees himself from the iceberg prison he found himself in at the end of *Godzilla Raids Again*, destroys a nuclear sub for a snack, and heads for Japan to raise hell. Meanwhile, on tropical Farou Island, rare medicinal berries cause an ape (Shoichi Hirose) to grow far beyond Kong size. Tako (Ichiro Arishima), the president of a Japanese drug company, has the beast captured, with plans to star him on the TV show he sponsors. But rough waters help the monster escape from the raft he was bound to en route, and he swims ashore to raise hell. Missiles full of the berry juice fired at him subdue Kong, and he is transported to meet Godzilla, in the hope that the two menaces will finish each other off in a grand duel on Mount Fuji.

A co-production between Toho and various American parties, this was the first Godzilla film (or Kong film for that matter) to be shot in color and scope. The f/x are not as good as in sequels to follow, but acceptable—though the Kong costume is horrible. A persistent false rumor—that a different ending was seen in Japan with Kong defeated—makes no sense, as Godzilla is the villain in both versions. Another

false rumor is that the Japanese version was much more serious, and Universal camped it up. The original is not a complete comedy, but much of the film plays as a cunning satire of the entertainment and advertising businesses, and modern society in general. However, Universal drastically changed the original for U.S. release, adding senseless scenes while omitting vital footage, even going so far as to replace Ifukube's terrific score with stock library music. *AKA: Kingukongu tai Gojira.* ♪♪♪

1962 91m/C *JP* Tadao Takashima, Kenji Sahara, Yu Fujiki, Ichiro Arishima, Jun Tazaki, Akihiko Hirata, Mie Hama, Akiko Wakabayashi, Somesho Matsumoto, Sachio Sakai, Haruya Kato, Nadao Kirino, Kenzo Tabu, Yoshio Kosugi, Tatsuo Matsumura, Osman Yusuf, Shoichi Hirose, Haruo Nakajima, Michael Keith (U.S. version). **D:** Ishiro Honda. **W:** Shinichi Sekizawa, Bruce Howard (U.S.), Paul Mason (U.S.). **C:** Hajime Koizume. **M:** Akira Ifukube. **VHS, DVD**

King of Beggars

Stephen Chow sends up the Beggar So legend in this beautifully photographed action comedy directed by his *Fight Back to School* collaborator, Gordon Chan (with some help from David Lam, according to some sources). So Chan (Chow) is a wealthy young dandy, the son of the General of Canton (Ng Man-Tat), who fancies himself a scholar because he can (almost) write his name. During a birthday visit to a brothel, he's both smitten by the lovely visiting lady Yu-Shang (Sharla Cheung), and insulted by Seng Ko Lin-Chin (Lam Wai), the King of Iron Hat, and his wizard friend Chiu (Norman Tsui). Actually, Yu-Shang is there to seduce and poison Seng to avenge his assassination of the leaders of the Tai-Ping Empire, but So Chan disrupts her plans by barging in. To prove himself worthy of her, So Chan enters the Kung Fu Scholar competition. The contest comes down to Chan and Botaroto of Mongolia, who happens to be Seng's nephew. Chan manages to win, but when Chiu exposes the Sos for cheating on the written exam, the family has their property taken away, and the Ching emperor orders Chan and his father to remain beggars the rest of their lives. For emphasis, Chiu gives Chan a crippling beating.

Humbled, Chan learns to write while he recovers, and he and the ex-General join the Beggars Association. Taking advantage of his natural laziness, Chan becomes proficient in the Sleeping Fist style, and uses it to win the title King of Beggars. When Yu-Shang is captured by the evil Chiu (who drinks baby's blood!), Chan and the beggars join the rebels to rescue her.

During this period, Chow really used his success to elevate his films from low-budget laffers to genuine comic epics. *King of Beggars* is as lavishly produced as any period film of the day, with gorgeous costuming, expensive sets, and impressive location shooting (even on the Great Wall). And in the midst of this, he still knows just the right time to take a pratfall. The wirework and undercranking during the action scenes is a little too obvious, but that may just be intentional for all we know. *AKA: Miu Chong Yuen: So Hat Ngai; Wu Zhuang Yuan: Su Qi Er.* 🎵🎵🎵🎵🎵

1992 96m/C *HK* Stephen Chow, Ng Man-Tat, Sharla Cheung, Norman Tsui, Lam Wai, Nat Chan, Lawrence Cheng, Yuen King-Tan, Peter Lai, Yuen Woo-ping. *D:* Gordon Chan. *W:* John Chan, Gordon Chan. *C:* David Chung. *M:* Joseph Koo. **VHS, DVD**

King of Comedy

As close as Stephen Chow is likely to get to a personal statement on his style of comedy, the first shot of the film has Chow shouting words of encouragement to the ocean. Wan Tin-sau (Chow) is an aspiring movie actor, but can't handle a simple death scene in the latest (*very* John Woo–inspired) action movie of star Cuckoo Tu Kue-yee (Karen Mok). He's replaced by a young hopeful (Jackie Chan!) and goes back to his regular job at the Neighbor Welfare Association, putting on his own amateur productions (such as a stage version of *The Chinese Connection*). Not even his actors show up for performances. Lau Piu-Piu (Cecilia Cheung) and her sister club girls can't convince clients that they're really the naïve college girls they pretend to be, and go to Sau for acting lessons—a welcome change from his usual students, mainly green triad recruits. Tough Piu-Piu is cynical, but is shocked to find that Sau's advice really works. A sweet, but difficult, romance begins between the two. The impossible happens when Cuckoo's co-star Big Brother has to bow out of their next film, and she chooses Sau as an emergency replacement. Then just as suddenly, Big Brother frees his schedule and Sau is demoted to a walk-on. However, he gets a chance to use his talents after all—Mao (Ng Man-Tat), Sau's studio-lot nemesis who always denies him his cherished box lunch, turns out to be an undercover cop who offers Sau the role of a lifetime.

There comes a moment in every great comic actor's career in which he tires of constant tomfoolery and seeks to do something serious. Fortunately, in the case of Stephen Chow, that moment is relatively painless. Chow has had bits of drama in his films before, most notably in his portrayal of the savage Monkey King in the *Chinese Odyssey* movies, but never to this extent. *King of Comedy* works pathos and drama into the Chow comic universe, with mixed results. Drama here is still Stephen Chow drama, taking his comic timing and applying it to other purposes. It doesn't always work—Chow seems to have more chemistry with Karen Mok than Cecilia Cheung, and the modern mobile camera style chosen to shoot it all is sometimes distracting. Viewers who are used to Chow's non-sense comedy rhythms may be thrown by the sudden shifts in tone, ready for punch lines that don't come, while really clever gags are marred by the dramatic scene before. And we never learn what exactly Ng Man-Tat's job at the studio has to do with his undercover duties. Still, this is an enjoyable experiment for those who have seen a lot of Chow's other films. There are solid spoofs of the conceits of show business, and a lot of Chow's traditional routines are given new twists. The climax is a mini-masterpiece, a combination of Martin Scorcese–style edginess with gags that are funny, but not in the usual way. It's a strange brew worthy of repeat viewing. *AKA: Choi Kek Ji Wong; Xi Ju Zhi Wang.* 🎵🎵🎵🎵🎵

1999 89m/C *HK* Stephen Chow, Cecilia Cheung, Karen Mok, Ng Man-Tat, Lee Siu-Kei, Bobby Yip, Lam Chi-sin, Tin Kai-man, Joe Cheng, Jackie Chan. *D:* Lee Lik-chi, Stephen Chow. *W:* Stephen Chow, Erica Lee, Sammy Tsang, Fung Min-hun. *C:* Horace Wong. *M:* Daisuke Hinata, Raymond Wong. **DVD**

King of the Mongols

Mongol King Kublai Khan sweeps through Japan, driving a path through the center of the country toward Edo. The emperor sends a message to Fort Izawa to hold out for two months until the emperor can rally his forces. Katsuhiko Takemara (Hashizo Okawa) is assigned the task of delivering the message, as he is also the only one who knows the secret of the Burning Water in the caves below the fort, and it's hoped he can use this knowledge against the enemy. He finds a girl named Sachiri, who is searching for her father, outside the gates of a checkpoint, and brings her along under his protection. Taking refuge from a storm in an inn, Takemara accidentally lets his official seal be seen during a hatchet-throwing match with Khan's General Tada (Jun Tazaki), and is forced to flee. Next morning, Takemara and Sachiri rescue a woman who has fallen over a cliff—a woman they recognize as Yamatimo, an enemy spy from the previous night. They meet up with Tada again onboard a ship, and during a fight, Takemara is knocked overboard. He's cap-

Jet Li gets a dose of French hospitality in *Kiss of the Dragon.*

tured on land, while the people in Fort Izawa suffer. Yamatimo refuses to kill the man who saved her life, but blinds Takemara with a heated sword. While Takemara struggles on toward the fort, Tada takes his seal to gain entrance and open the gates for the Mongol army.

The available version is the American International Pictures cut of the film—though it's not listed in any of the books on AIP. The fight scenes are nothing special, though the final battle scene is impressive in scope—even cropped from scope. 🐾🐾

1960 88m/C *JP* Hashizo Okawa, Jun Tazaki, Yumi Ichijo, Yayoi Furusato, Yoshio Yoshida, Sentara Fushimi. **D:** Yasushi Kato. **W:** Yasushi Kato, Susumu Sugii, Shozo Chiba (story). **C:** Teiji Yoshida. **VHS**

asians in usa

Kiss of the Dragon

It's unfair to call *Kiss of the Dragon* Jet Li's third American film. In *Lethal Weapon 4,* he was little more than a Special Guest Villain. *Romeo Must Die* threw him into a hip-hop urban gangster drama with Shakespearean pretensions. *Kiss,* though distributed by 20th Century Fox and filmed largely in English, is a Luc Besson French action thriller. Sitting in for Besson in the director's chair is freshman Chris Nahon, but he's backed up largely by Besson and "action director" Corey Yuen, who put together all the fight scenes with his Hong Kong crew.

However, this film may count as the first true Jet Li movie, as *KOD* (as it was promoted) sports his first credit as writer. Li stars as Chinese Intelligence officer Liu Jian, a kung fu master and acupuncture expert, who is sent to Paris to work with Inspector Richard (Tchéky Karyo, also in Besson's *La Femme Nikita*), although we don't know either is a cop until the Chinese drug lord (Ric Young) they're after shows up at their sting operation. Though it's never made clear why, Richard is really planning to kill the drug lord, his hired hooker/assassin (Laurence Ashley), and any inconvenient witnesses, including convenient fall guy Jian.

Jian spoils his plans by making a spectacular escape, taking a recording of the hit with him as evidence. One would think that all Jian would have to do is drop into the Paris police station or the Chinese embassy to present his evidence, but apparently every cop in town is in on Richard's evil conspiracy, and the Inspector has little trouble bullying the suspicious Chinese into joining his manhunt. Meanwhile, in another plot hole, Richard's favorite little reluctant junkie hooker (Bridget Fonda, also in the U.S. remake of Besson's La Femme Nikita) witnesses the murders, but for some reason he lets her live and puts her back out on the street. That street, by conspicuous coincidence, runs right outside the shop Jian is using to hide out in. Jian loses his cover when he rescues her from her pimp (Max Ryan), but they don't figure out that they were both at the murder site until later. This is very convenient, since Jian lost the tape to Karyo in a previous scene.

Even more conveniently, Richard fails to destroy the evidence to his crime, and it's regained with relative ease by Fonda's prostitute. The villain's remaining trump card is her daughter, whom he's been keeping hostage in an orphanage(!) for over a year. To rescue the little girl, Jian storms the police station. We've all seen storming-the-police-station sequences before—most recently in Jeepers Creepers, most memorably in The Terminator. But here Jet Li takes on the entire Paris police force unarmed, battles his way through dozens of tonfa-wielding kung fu fighters, and has a climactic battle with a pair of lethal, high-kicking twins (Cyril Raffaelli and Didier Azouley). It's a furious Corey Yuen martial arts masterpiece, capped off when Jian administers the terrible "Kiss of the Dragon" (which actually exists, according to Bridget Fonda's acupuncturist).

What doesn't exist is an explanation of the plot holes in Kiss of the Dragon, but as long as Jet Li is beating up half of France in such an entertaining manner, you won't find me complaining. AKA: Le Baiser Mortel du Dragon. 🎵🎵🎵

2001 (R) 98m/C US/FR/CH Jet Li, Bridget Fonda, Tchéky Karyo, Ric Young, Burt Kwouk, Laurence Ashley, Cyril Raffaelli, Didier Azouley, John Forgeham, Max Ryan. **D:** Chris Nahon. **W:** Luc Besson, Robert Mark Kamen, Jet Li (story). **C:** Thierry Arbogast. **M:** Craig Armstrong. **VHS, DVD**

Knockabout

Yuen Biao's first film as a leading man was a spectacular debut. Yipao (Yuen Biao) and Dai Pao (Leung Kar-yan) are con men. In the course of their work, they try and put one over on an older gentleman (Lau Kar-Wing). He beats them at their own game, and so they decide to beat him up in order to teach him a lesson. He again turns the tables on them, this time displaying amazing martial arts abilities. Beaten but not stupid, they immediately realize an opportunity to improve

their lot in life and plead with him to take them on as students. He gives in eventually, and begins putting them through a rigorous training program. The boys couldn't be happier—until they discover that their master has a hidden criminal past. When they bring it to his attention, they learn firsthand that he is a fugitive with a deadly agenda. The only natural response is to seek revenge. A beggar (Sammo Hung)—another character who is not what he initially seems to be—joins in the fight against the evil master.

By the late 1970s, traditional martial arts films were losing steam at the boxoffice. Sammo Hung injected silly and juvenile "nonsense" comedy into the formula to freshen things up. Though the first part of the film meanders a bit, the humor enlivens genre staples such as the extended training sequence. The lighthearted comedy also builds audience sympathy for the goofy leading characters and provides genuine motivation for the darker revenge that eventually plays out. The concluding fight scenes are awesome: muscular, brutal, and balletic. No obvious shortcuts (such as wires or extensive use of doubles) appear to have been taken. They seem to go on forever, yet the effect is magnetic—you won't want to take your eyes off the screen. —PM **AKA:** Chap Ga Siu Ji; Za jia xiao zi; Za Gu Xiao Zi. 🎵🎵🎵🎵🎵

1979 100m/C HK Yuen Biao, Leung Kar-yan, Lau Kar-Wing, Sammo Hung, Karl Maka, Lee Hoi-sang, Mars, Lam Ching-Ying, Chan Lung, Wong Kwong-yue, Tai San, Ho Pak Kwong, Chung Fat, Billy Chan, Yuen Miu, Yuen Tak, Cheung Wa, Yue Tau Wan, Chan Hei. **D:** Sammo Hung. **W:** Lau Tin-Chi. **M:** Hsun Chi-chen. **DVD**

The Korean Connection

Slick mobster Kuchok, along with his two tough killers, is hunting for Tiger Yong Chol. Tiger was once a respected martial artist, but since getting involved in a robbery he's been a wandering drunken derelict. Tiger left his adoptive father Wong Ha-ying's triad as a youth to marry Yung Suk, an outsider, but had to agree to undertake one last mission first: the theft of some secret papers from North Korea. However, his brother Yamamoto double-crossed him, failing to mention until it was too late that the man Tiger had to kill on the mission was Yung Suk's brother. Yamamoto extends his betrayal by forcing Yung Suk to become his woman. Tiger pulls himself together to thrash Yamamoto's killers, and heads back to Seoul to get his revenge, taking down every thug who gets in his way with his superior taekwondo. Enigmatic Master Kim Sing offers his services in beating Tiger, but is too arrogant for Yamamoto to accept. That is, until Tiger trounces his entire army of thugs, at which point Yamamoto is willing to accept any help he can get.

The Korean Connection doesn't have much to boast about in terms of creative fight choreography, but is rich in hard-boiled atmosphere, heavily influenced by Japanese action flicks. Besides star Yong Chol—playing a character with the same name—there are a few other interesting antihero characters involved, and Yamamoto is a thoroughly craven villain, seen in one flashback cackling insanely in his underwear after gunning down his own father. Another standout scene has Tiger relentlessly advancing across a long bridge, defeating a whole line of thugs as he goes. With the resurgence of Korean cinema in recent years, it's nice to see rare examples of their past film accomplishments turning up, even cheesy action flicks like this one. Not to be confused with the 1990 movie by the same name. 🦴🦴🖤

1977 75m/C *KO* Yong Chol. **VHS, DVD**

Kung Fu Genius

Cliff Lok is sure that he's a genius at kung fu, impressing his lone student Yuen Do (Cheng Hong-yip) with his mastery of various animal styles, enough so that they decide to open a school and get rich. Opening up their Genius School in the next town, the teacher establishes a reputation by defending himself from the thugs at the gambling booth next door. Students from the neighboring Spiritual Boxing School show up to test his mettle as well. Unable to beat the master, student Sao Li-chi (Hsiao Ho) corners the student Yuen Do alone that night, and a few choice blows are enough to drive the guy insane.

The teacher tracks Sao to the local whorehouse to make him pay, and their destructive fight leads to conflict with the head pimp (Lee Hoi-sang) and his thugs. There must be something to that Spiritual Boxing—even though Sao gets badly hurt, his blows make the pimp's son insane, too. Humiliated, the pimp sends for his foster brother the Fan Killer (Wilson Tong). They destroy the Spiritual School, even beating the master (Chan Lung) when he uses his fearsome Duck Fist Style. Next they go after the kung fu genius. In the heat of battle, Sao makes amends with the master, but gets a knife in the gut. The Kung Fu Genius promises Sao to rescue his girlfriend Fai-yeung (Hui Ying-Ying) from the brothel, but he'll have to beat the Fan Killer to do it.

It doesn't take a genius to see that Cliff Lok's fight scenes clearly copy many of Jackie Chan's moves here—and he's clearly not in the same class. You can see director/choreographer Wilson Tong, Lee Hoi-sang, and other more

talented opponents holding back to keep from making Lok look too bad. Even the climactic fan fight fails to spark interest, as Lok keeps his fan closed through most of it. The infantile antics of Cheng Hong-yip are tough to take, but at least they establish him as mentally unstable, making his easy leap into madness easier to accept. *AKA: Tin Choi Gung Foo; Tian Cai Gong Fu.* 🦴🦴

1979 84m/C *HK* Cliff Lok, Wilson Tong, Hsiao Ho, Lee Hoi-sang, Cheng Hong-yip, Annie Liu, Chan Lung, Yeung Kin Wai, Hui Ying-Ying, Tsang Chohlam. **D:** Wilson Tong. **W:** Cheung Sun. **C:** Chao Hung. **M:** Ma Man. **VHS, DVD**

The Kung Fu Master 📺

After working on *Wing Chun*, Donnie Yen turned to TV portraying famous Chinese hero Hung Hei-kwun, who had just been portrayed by Jet Li in *New Legend of Shaolin* (and previously, by Chen Kuan-tai in *Executioners from Shaolin*). This release covers the first third of the 30-hour series, with some of the subplots that will be picked up in subsequent releases cut out to avoid confusion. As the series begins, rebel hero Red Dragon has raised the bounty on his head by killing the Manchurian Flying Guillotine Squad from Wu Tang (taking their heads with their own weapons!). Young Master Hung Hei-kwun, who admires Red Dragon, returns home from eight years of study to a cold welcome. Since his father Hung Tin-nam (Poon Chi-man) became martial arts instructor for the Ching General Ha (Lo Lieh) and his army, his neighbors have turned against the Hungs. Kwun meets opposition from his father when he opens his own martial arts school to teach Han loyalists kung fu. But his father has a hidden reason for objecting—he's been hiding his true skill while secretly fighting the Chings as the masked Red Dragon, and thinks that confronting the Manchurians so openly is too dangerous.

Hei-kwun's buddy Ko Chun-chung is engaged to the general's daughter Tung-man, making him an enemy of Master Sek Tot, who works for Prince Muk Li-bu. When Sek hires strongman Tung Chin-gun to fight Ko, Hei-kwun accepts the duel in his place, both to help his Han brother and to advertise his school. Though he wins the fight, it causes a riot, and Hei-kwun finds more trouble when his school opens. But his life becomes even more turbulent when he meets Mr. Yim of the rebel Sun Moon Sect, and his fierce daughter Wing Chun. Red Dragon refuses to accept Kwun in the sect, but when Muk hires Wu Tang Master Fung To-tak to pose as a false Red Dragon, and Ko gets caught up in a salt-

smuggling ring, the kung fu master can't help but get involved.

The lighting and photography are so well done here that it's sometimes easy to forget that it was shot on video. The complexities of the characters and their growth raise this above the average kung fu soap opera. The mystery of Red Dragon is thankfully only made an issue for one episode, since the solution soon becomes obvious and the drama increases once his identity is revealed to the viewer. The rushed pace of TV production results in some choreography "cheats" that may disappoint hard-core martial arts fans, but within the mixed bag of fight scenes there are some gems, as well as some outstanding stunts. The editing may also bother purists, but it's likely that the story is more digestible in this version than if they'd left in all the dangling plot threads. Though Yen was hired only to star and act as action consultant, he soon took over most of the action direction, and even sings the theme song! *AKA: Hung Hei-kwun: Kung Fu Master.* ♫♫♫

1994 202m/C *HK* Donnie Yen, Poon Chi-man, Lo Lieh, Hung Si-man, Wai Lit, Lawrence Yan, Anthony Tang, Hon Yee Sang, Ben Ng, Lily Lee. *D:* Benny Chan, Billy Tang. *W:* Yuen Yuk-sing, Lau Chi-wah, Cheung Kwok-yuen. **VHS, DVD**

Kung Fu on Sale

Kung fu crazy–youth Tang Wu (Sze Ma Lung, sometimes known as Shaking Eagle) finds himself out of a job and desperate to find funds to pay for his martial arts schooling. When his friend the Prince of Beggars gets his subjects to try to collect money for his lessons, the bullying Chou Chi Gang beats them up. Tang decides to earn money as a human punching bag. Several times when he's getting beaten, Tang is saved by a mysterious stranger (Man Lee-pang). Despite his dire straits, Tang Wu helps out a cantankerous old man, who attaches himself as Tang's new grandfather. However, Grandpa turns out to be an eccentric kung fu master, who helps Tang beat sadistic teacher Chu Fat-wa (Dean Shek) the next day.

Taking a delivery job, Tang transports rice to the school, where the master tells him that he'll take Tang on as a student if he can hit Chu three times. Beaten again, Tang Wu takes lessons from Grandpa in order to reach his goal, and quickly learns far more than he needs. But the master goes back on his word, and Tang's boss fires him—both bribed by Tang's wealthy father, who doesn't want his son to become a fighter. The mystery fighter Yen Wu-pao, who has rescued Tang in the past, is working for his father as well. However, Tang Wu refuses to return home and trains even harder,

learning the powerful Sleeping Crane Style, which comes in handy when the fired Yen comes looking for him to get even.

For the most part another knockoff of *Drunken Master*, *Kung Fu on Sale* relies too much on poor Cantonese comedy, and has way too many scenes of Sze Ma Lung getting beat up. But the fight scenes are pretty good, especially the more serious alley brawl in a rainstorm and the final duel set in a forest, which feature both atmosphere and fine choreography. The soundtrack includes the theme to *Hawaii 5-0* and lots of bluegrass music! *AKA: Kung Fu for Sale.* ♫♫♫

1979 89m/C *HK* Sze Ma Lung, Chung Wa, Dean Shek, Lee Kwan, Man Lee-pang, Choi Wang, Tsang Chiu, Chiang Han, Chu Siu-wa, Hung Fa-long, Hui Bat Liu, Seung Fung. *D:* Su Chen Ping. *W:* Lau Chui. *C:* Shue Kim Tong. **DVD**

Kung Fu, the Invisible Fist

Japanese commander Daoshan sends Captain Chai Tai (Yasuaki Kurata), the "Hungry Tiger," to head a spying mission to Shanghai, in preparation for a military invasion. At the same time, Shanghai police commissioner Wong needs an outsider to go undercover to bust a new dockside gang, and asks Hong Kong army officer Lee Chang (Chan Sing) to help. The gang is run by Mr. Lin San-tai (Chiang Nan) for his Japanese boss Chai, using his own son Lin Yeung (Michael Chan) as an enforcer. Taking his assistant Hsu Dong (Tony Wong) with him, Lee has little trouble infiltrating the gang. They find that the gang is into more than slavery and drugs, digging up evidence of the spy ring. Chai still suspects them, though, and sets a little trap—he has Lin tell Lee a new shipment of slave girls is due to go out, but the boxes are really booby trapped. Lee suspects the trap, but Hsu Dong disagrees and tells their contact, jeopardizing their lives. Commissioner Wong doesn't believe Lee's report about spies, but the man they call "Crazy Dragon" is determined to smash the spy ring.

This standard fight-fest is distinguished only by its seaside locations, and a running chase and fight scene between Chan Sing and Yasuaki Kurata that stretches through the final 20 minutes of the film. Of course Chan wins, preventing the Japanese invasion of China by at least a few days. Mindless fun, especially if one doesn't mind unbelievable little bits of business like characters who suddenly whip out bulky concealed weapons after fighting for several minutes, or one guy who just happens to have a protective shield hidden under his shirt when a villain chooses to stab him. Not to be confused with Chang Cheh's *The Invincible Fist* (1969), also with Chan Sing. **AKA:** *Ngo Foo Kwong Lung; E Hu Kuang Long; The Good and the Bad; Tiger vs. Dragon.* 🎵🎵

1972 102m/C *HK* Chan Sing, Yasuaki Kurata, Irene Ryder, Tony Wong, Michael Chan, Hon Gwok-choi, Che Yuen, Chiang Nan, Chin Yuet Sang, Sham Chin-bo, Tommy Lee, Lin Ke-ming, Lee Ka-ting, Bruce Liang. **D:** Ng See-yuen. **C:** Jang Chyi. **M:** Chou Fu-liang. **VHS, DVD**

Kung Fu Zombie

With a title like that, you'd have to laugh through the feature, even if it were just 80 minutes of blank film. Fortunately, the movie behind the title is an energetic mix of comedy, action, and horror. The Chinese title isn't bad either, which translates as "Cocky Master Wu Lung."

In order to get back at young Master Pang Fong (Billy Chong) for getting him thrown in prison, crook Lu Dai (Cheng Kei-ying) hires Mao Shan sorcerer Wu Lung (Chan Lau) to re-animate some corpses for him, with the idea that the zombies will push Pang into a coffin full of spikes. The plot backfires, killing Lu instead, and his ghost demands that Wu Lung find him a new body to reincarnate. They find what they need at the morgue—the body of scar-faced killer Long Yee (Kwan Yung Moon, "The Mad Korean"), who was an old enemy of Pang's ex-cop father (Kong Do). The only problem is that Long is still alive. Pang soon fixes that by killing Long in a duel, leaving the way open for Lu Dai to move in. However, Wu Lung screws up the spell, reviving Long as an unstoppable, blood-thirsty kung fu zombie! Meanwhile, Pang's pop is so happy over Long's death that he drops dead, and Wu Lung takes advantage of the available corpse. But the spell gets screwed up again, making Lu a kung fu zombie, too!

Many martial arts films speed up the film to make the action a bit faster, and masters of the genre like Sammo Hung can stage their choreography to make the technique nearly undetectable. But here director Hwa Yi Hung uses the technique openly for comic effect. It's not funny in and of itself, but combined with some sharp editing, it makes for some hyperkinetic action scenes. He goes over the top with it occasionally, resulting in goofy chases in the tradition of Benny Hill and the Banana Splits. But for the most part, this has all the dumb spirit of a ninja movie with the added bonus of horror and gore! Though they're not called upon to do much real acting, the martial arts work of Billy Chong and Kwan Yung Moon is excellent. Another tidbit of Chinese supernatural lore is revealed as the monsters can't see Wu Lung when he's wearing a hat made of leaves. The original version in Cantonese is reported to be over 20 minutes longer. **AKA:** *Wu Lung Tin Si Jiu Jik Gwi; Hu Long Tian Shi Zhao Ji Gui.* 🎵🎵🎵

1981 (R) 78m/C *HK* Billy Chong, Chan Lau, Kong Do, Cheng Kei-ying, Kwan Yung Moon, Pak Sha-lik, Cheng Hong-yip, Wong Biu Chan. **D:** Hwa Yi Hung. **W:** Bao Kwok-lan. **VHS, DVD**

Kung Fu's Hero

Triad boss Liu Pao (San Kwai) has his eye on pretty Lung Choi-fung, but knows his lackey's brother Chen Yen-wu wants to marry her. Liu sends thugs to abduct the girl and frame Chen for the crime. She's rescued by dashing Captain Cheung Ho (Cheung Lik), of the Kwonchung Intelligence Department. His plan foiled, Liu calls out the lawman for a fight, but finds Cheung too tough to beat. Not to be put off, Liu hires on tough fighter Luk Jin (Tong Tin-hei) to kidnap Choi-fung and kill her father, once again pinning the crime on Chen Yen-wu. Liu's maid Chu-san (Queenie Kong), tired of rough treatment, helps Choi-fung get out of the house, and she tells Cheung about Luk's weak spot: his armpit. Having gathered enough evidence, Cheung sets out to destroy Liu's slave operation, but Liu has also hired man-monster Ko Kong (Bolo Yeung) to take care of his enemy.

A typical kung fu thriller set in the 1930s, this one takes advantage of some nicely atmospheric Taiwan locations. Cheung Lik, who looks like a young Jimmy Wang Yu, is sufficiently athletic and personable. This was one of a series of films he made with director Joseph Kong. San Kwai contributes another of his seedy villains. With an exceedingly simple plot, the running time is a bit too long—the final half hour is all mindless chases and fights. Music cues are borrowed from *Silent Running*. **AKA:** *Aang Hon Gung Foo Boon; Ying Han Gong Fu Ben.* 🎵🎵

1973 89m/C *HK* Cheung Lik, Elsa Yeung, San Kwai, Bolo Yeung, Tong Tin-hei, Queenie Kong, Lee Wan-chung, Chin Ti, Cheng Lui, Wong Mei, Lee Chiu, Max Lee, Kong Do. **D:** Joseph Kong. **VHS, DVD**

asians in usa

Kung Pow: Enter the Fist

The martial arts genre is so ripe for parody that it's surprising it hasn't been done more often. *Kentucky Fried Movie*'s was one of the earliest, giving over a major portion of its running time to the "Fistful of Yen" sequence, a spoof of Bruce Lee movies. Sammo Hung's early kung fu comedies often played with the genre's structure, and

Stephen Chow usually included some gags about special styles or training techniques in his films, significantly so in *Legend of the Dragon* and *Fist of Fury 1991*. In this comedy by Steve Oedekerk *(The Nutty Professor),* he adopts the technique used by Rudy Ray Moore in *Shaolin Dolemite* and takes it a few steps further, combining redubbed footage from Jimmy Wang Yu's *Tiger and Crane Fist* with his own to make a new film via f/x magic. Oedekerk plays the Chosen One, a young martial artist raised by desert creatures after the evil Master Pain (Lung Fei) murdered his family. Pain, who works for the Evil Council, has been searching for decades to find the child that escaped him, who bears a special mark on his tongue. The Chosen One stays at the Crane Fist kung fu school of Master Tang (Chan Wai Lau) and his niece Ling (Tse Ling-Ling), despite objections from his leading student Wimp Lo (Lau Kar-Wing), whose kung fu isn't all that good. Pain—now going by the name "Betty"—has mastered the Iron Armor technique, and the Chosen One is unable to beat him because special armor caps protect his vulnerable points. The Chosen One and Ling hide out at a temple and work on a special technique to get past Betty's defenses. The increasingly weird finale involves French space aliens in flying pyramids.

Oedekerk doesn't so much parody *Tiger and Crane Fist* as he does the general American preconceptions of the kung fu genre. The public has some skewed ideas about how an Asian kung fu flick of the 1970s operates, and assumes all such films are pretty much the same. Using a Jimmy Wang Yu film for this exercise is a good choice, since Wang Yu's films were often a bit cartoonish in nature—sometimes very much so, as in *Master of the Flying Guillotine*—and Oedekerk doesn't have to stretch far for his gags. When he does, as in a CGI-drenched *Matrix* parody involving a kung fu cow, the gags are hit-and-miss, though the overall surrealism of his concepts brought to life are highly entertaining. He also has some good fun with the nature of film, as when his narrator Tang comments on the credits. Gags that more specifically target the genre fall flat—making fun of bad dubbing has gotten tired, though admittedly Oedekerk takes it to such extremes here, with characters sometimes just making odd noises, that he forces a few laughs from it. Some outtakes (real and fake) and how-it's-done clips play under the end credits. *AKA: Dubbed Action Movie; Enter the Fist.* ♪♪♪

1976/2001 (PG-13) 81m/C *HK/US* Steve Oedekerk, Lung Fei, Tse Ling-Ling, Lau Kar-Wing, Leo Lee, Chan Wai Lau, Jennifer Tung, Ming Lo, Peggy Lu, Chi Fu-chiang, Ma Kei, Chui Chung Hei, Phillip Kwok. **D:** Steve Oedekerk. **W:** Steve Oedekerk. **C:** Chuang Yin-chien, John J. Connor. **M:** Robert Folk, Wang Mau-shan. **VHS, DVD**

Kwaidan

At the time it was released, Masaki Kobayashi's widescreen, color film version of an anthology of ghost stories by late 19th-century American author Lafcedio Hearn (AKA Yakumo Koizumi, who lived in Japan at the time) was the most expensive film ever produced in Japan. The gamble paid off handsomely with worldwide distribution and recognition, and *Kwaidan* is often included on critics' top-10 lists.

"The Black Hair" is about a masterless samurai (Rentaro Mikune) who abandons his wife (Michiyo Aratama) to seek employment elsewhere. On the way to his new post, he stops to marry into a wealthy family. Finding his new wife (Misako Watanabe) petty and selfish, and nagged by guilt and regret, he is haunted by memories of his first wife. Years later, he returns to Kyoto to apologize and make amends, but he finds that much has changed in his absence. "The Woman of the Snow" concerns two woodcutters: aged Mosaku (Jun Hamamura) and his teenage apprentice Minokichi (Tatsuya Nakadai). Caught in a blizzard, they take shelter in a ferryman's shack, where they receive a visit from the ghostly snow woman. She drains the blood of Mosaku, but decides to spare Minokichi on condition that he never tells anyone about her. Many years later, Minokichi is a happy family man, but one night he tells his wife Yuki (Keiko Kishi) about the Woman of the Snow.

While these first two tales are relatively typical stories of supernatural reprisal, the remaining tales are less formulaic and the victims are innocents who wander into trouble. "Hoichi the Earless" is a young blind servant (Katsuo Nakamura) left in charge of a temple while the priests are away. A samurai comes to request that he perform his recitation of a great battle that occurred nearby 700 years past for a visiting lord. Hoichi is out performing for his supernatural audience nearly a full day, and the next night the samurai comes for him again. With Hoichi disappearing each night, the abbot (Takashi Shimura) sends monks to spy on him one night, and the men interrupt his performance. To protect him from the returning spirits, the monks cover Hoichi completely with protective prayers. However, they forget one vital area. The remaining story-with-a-story-inside is often dropped from shorter versions. While visiting a temple in Hongo, Lord Sato (Osamu Takizawa) sees a man's face reflected "In a Cup of Tea." That night the smiling man, who calls himself Shikibu Heinai (Noboru Nakaya), appears in Sato's house, but the lord is unable to catch him. The next night, Heinai's three ghostly retainers appear to announce that their master will return to repay the lord's lack of hospitality

Hearn, as an outsider, collected Japanese folktales and adapted them for (then) modern readers, giving Japanese readers a (then) fresh

perspective on themselves. While the material is treated almost too reverently for modern tastes, Kobayashi displays impeccable taste. His framing is masterly, setting his characters, props, and especially colors for maximum effect. Even in dubbed and shortened form, to American audiences of 1964, this must have been like something from another planet. *AKA: Kaidan; Ghost Stories; Hoichi the Earless; Weird Tales.* ♫♫♫♫

1964 164m/C *JP* Rentaro Mikune, Michiyo Aratama, Tetsuro Tamba, Katsuo Nakamura, Misako Watanabe, Tatsuya Nakadai, Keiko Kishi, Osamu Takizawa, Kanemon Nakamura, Haruko Sugimura, Takashi Shimura, Noboru Nakaya, Jun Hamamura, Otome Tsukiyama, Eisei Amamoto, Noriko Sengoku, Kunie Tanaka, Akira Tani, Jun Tazaki, Shoji Kobayashi. *D:* Masaki Kobayashi. *W:* Yoko Mizuki, Lafcedio Hearn (story). *C:* Yoshio Miyajima. *M:* Toru Takemitsu. **VHS, DVD**

The Ladies' Phone Sex Club

Here's more shot-on-video soft-core nonsense starring cult queen Kei Mizutani *(Weather Woman).* Little Lulu Kokonotso (Sho Kawaide) is one of the most popular phone sex operators in Tokyo's Q2 company, but she meets her match in her one-thousandth caller, whose "vile words" give Lulu an orgasm within minutes. The mystery caller is actually Mimi Guin (Minako Ogawa), the mother of Lulu's boss Misumi (Kengo) and former phone sex champion, who wants Misumi to give up Q2 to run their family business. Mimi has all her hopes pinned on Misumi since his brother Bihiro (Alfred Ito) hasn't been quite the same since he had a lab accident, and now only appears in his secret identity as Mouse-man. She tries to reunite Misumi with his ex-girlfriend Naoko Midara (Kei Mizutani) in order to seal a deal with the girl's father (Shoichiro Akaboshi) to provide electric motors for their new cars, but Misumi refuses. Meanwhile, Lulu's closest confidant is a client named Pantyhose Man, who is actually her secret admirer Misumi. However, Lulu is obsessed with her mysterious client, and Mimi pushes her advantage by challenging Lulu to a high stakes phone sex duel. With only minimal nudity, this cheap feature offers fetishistic hijinx and silly situations, which rapidly become tiresome. The lone high point is a visit to a ridicu-

Monk Takashi Shimura tries to protect Katsuo Nakamura from relentless ghosts in *Kwaidan.*
THE KOBAL COLLECTION / TOHO

ious superhero domination club which spoofs the spandex and leather trade. A barker outside offers a tribute to Cheech Marin's classic spiel in *From Dusk Till Dawn*. **AKA:** *The History of Mademoiselle Q; The Ladies' Phone Club.* ♪

1996 88m/C *JP* Sho Kawaide, Kei Mizutani, Kengo, Minako Ogawa, Alfred Ito, Shoichiro Akaboshi, Tetsu Watanabe. **D:** Hisashi Watanabe. **W:** Ryoni Kou, Haruka Inui (story). **M:** Seneca Park. **VHS, DVD**

Lady Iron Monkey

Chen Kuan-tai's hit 1977 version of *Iron Monkey* spawned a few spin-offs and knockoffs, but none so bizarre as this one about a girl (Kam Fung Ling) raised by apes who ends up in the court of the Ching Dynasty. Fatty (Ko Saio Pao) and Shorty (a dwarf), two men dressed as girls, discover her living in the forest among her fellow "monkeys" (kids in costumes that look like Teletubbies). Their Old Abbot (Miu Tin) catches her, and decides to return her to human ways. Her simian upbringing makes her a natural at Monkey Style kung fu.

Fatty and Shorty go to flirt with pretty A Chau, but the monkey girl Ming Li-sher interferes. The cruel pair of boys (girls?) tell her she's ugly and make her cry. A bride stopping in at a temple to pray faints at the sight of the Ming, who mischievously takes her place in her palanquin. When the groom discovers her, there's much zany slapstick comedy. Next, she stops in at a restaurant, causing a ruckus there as well, until a kind prince (Chan Sing) settles for the damages. She follows him into the prince's birthday party thrown by Mr. Liu and the 8 Heroes. The Heroes are hesitant to support the Manchu prince, but he pledges to be a good leader to them. When a Tibetan Lama assassin (Lo Lieh) breaks into the house, Ming helps capture him, and the prince invites her to the palace to be a bodyguard. At the palace, the prince exploits her affection for him by sending her on missions of intrigue, but she soon finds out how he really feels. When the prince is crowned emperor and subsequently betrays the 8 Heroes, killing half of them in an explosion, Ming joins them in open rebellion.

A fanciful and offbeat kung fu movie from director Chen Chi-hwa, who made the early Jackie Chan vehicles *Half a Loaf of Kung Fu* and *Snake and Crane Arts of Shaolin* at Lo Wei Productions. Kam appears to perform some of her stunts herself, but good use is made of her stunt doubles as well, with monkey girls popping in and out of the frame all over during her fight scenes. She even gets to demonstrate the Drunken Monkey style toward the end. **AKA:** *Chui Hau Lui; Zui Hou Nu; Ape Girl; Fighting Justice.* ♪♪♪

1983 85m/C *TW* Kam Fung Ling, Chan Sing, Lo Lieh, Yuen Se Wu, Miu Tin, Cho Boon Feng, Ko Saio Pao. **D:** Chen Chi-hwa. **W:** Hau Juen. **C:** Chan Chung. **M:** Wang Sat San. **VHS, DVD**

Lady Ninja: Reflections of Darkness

In a brief synopsis, it sounds nearly like a serious ninja movie. During the Tokugawa Shogunate, Yoshimune Tokugawa institutes conservative measures to bring the economy under control. However, in a region far from the capitol Edo, party-boy Muneharu Tokugawa rejects these edicts. When rumors surface about the Shogun's escapades with his girlfriends, Muneharu is suspected to be behind it all. To control the situation, Minister Oka assigns Master Kotaro (Tetsuo Kurata) of the Iga Ninja the task of eliminating the mistresses. Ninja girls Ohan, Orui, Oren, and Oyui are enlisted for the task, but Muneharu counters by hiring the Koga Ninja Clan to collect evidence of the Shogun's past indiscretions and protect the witnesses if they can.

The period setting notwithstanding, this definitely belongs to the fantasy version of the ninjas, complete with colorful costumes and magical abilities. The ladies wear modern make-up, shiny miniskirts, and hair ribbons on their deadly missions—sort of like *Charlie's Ninjas*. The ninjas can shoot lightning bolts or Silly String from their hands, fly, turn invisible, and keep fighting after decapitation. Actual martial arts use is at a minimum, with the emphasis placed on wild sorcery and wilder erotic content. Fans of the crazed sex duels in *A Chinese Torture Chamber Story* should dig this. A Koga ninja attempts to kill Orui with his 10-foot pole (or is it 12?), but she uses balloon magic to make it expand and explode. Ouch. An evil ninja wizard freezes one of our heroines solid as a statue, then smashes her—but her head can still fly around and bite through his neck. An American ninja girl (Teresa Linn) sprays the Shogun with her breast wine. Later, while a ninja girl has sex with a tree, she chokes an opponent with breast whip cream. One ninja kills an opponent by shooting colorful ping pong balls from her vagina! Despite the ridiculous situations, the performers are all as earnest as if they were enacting a classic. The soundtrack has a surprising Spanish flavor, and the British crew that performs the English-dubbed version do a particularly good job. Apparently this is the last in a series of six adventures of the lady ninja team. **AKA:** *Kunoichi Ninpo Cho: Ninja Getsuei Sho.* ♪♪♡

1996 80m/C *JP* Yuka Onishi, Tetsuo Kurata, Rina Kitahara, Miho Nomoto, Chisato Naruse, Teresa Linn, Mitsugi Takei, Hirofumi Asahi, Goro Oki, Yoshiyuki Shibata, Masaki Nishimura, Tatsuo Higashida, Norioko Suzukawa. *D:* Masaru Tsushima. *W:* Hiromichi Nakamoto, Futaroh Yamada (story). *C:* Saburo Fujiwara. *M:* Tetsu Nakamoto. **VHS**

Lady Whirlwind and the Rangers

First Films tried to capitalize on the Angela Mao hit *Lady Whirlwind* with this knockoff starring Polly Shang Kwan. Around 1900, the government in China enforced strict new laws pertaining to trade goods, and as a result smuggling increased to feed a growing black market. Hearing that bandit Chang Piao (Yasuaki Kurata) and his gang (including beefy Cheng Fu Hung and Dai Sai Aan) are intercepting a salt shipment, Captain Lin Kin (Shaw Luo-hui) takes a posse to arrest them. The arrogant Chang is too tough an hombre for Lin to beat, but the lawman continues to pursue the bandit, despite orders brought by Advisor Wu (Wang Fei) to stop harassing Chang. When she learns of this, Lin's daughter Jo-nan (Polly Shang Kwan) and young son Shao-lung (Yeh Shao-im) race off to help him. He needs it—Advisor Wu is actually in cahoots with Chang, and frames Captain Lin for smuggling the salt. Jo-nan and Shao-lung go to Chang's warehouse to try to arrest the crook themselves, but only succeed in inciting the bandit gang to come after them at home, killing their servant Ah Chung. They escape and hide out in a cave. Having found they can't beat Chang in a direct fight, they decide to use their wits. Disguising herself as a man with a Bruce Lee wig (and Shou-lung as a little girl), Jo-nan infiltrates the gang of Chang's rival, salt-smuggler Ma Wen (Ma Kei). She succeeds in heating up the war between the two gangs by leading daring raids, but jealous foreman Chen Hsiung (Chen Chieh) learns her true identity and tries to blackmail her. The traitor Chen also kills Ma with a bomb, and engineers a raid by Chang's men. With little Shou-lung abducted in the raid, Chang tricks retarded warehouse worker Tiu Pa (Kam Kong) into carrying another bomb to finish off Lin Jo-nan.

The kung fu fighting is O.K., but it's Polly Shang Kwan who's the real attraction here, trotting around to fight crime in her pink pajamas with her little brother in tow. She began her film career in the mid-1960s, earning black belts in judo, karate, and taekwondo to claim her stripes as an action film hellcat. Her first leading role was in King Hu's classic *Dragon Gate Inn* (she also starred in the 1979 semi-remake *Green Dragon Inn*). Try to keep track of how many times she clobbers supporting thug Dai Sai Aan. In

one sequence, poor Cheng Fu Hung has to fight with his shirt on fire, and then gets whipped by Shang Kwan in a mud fight. Little Yeh Shao-im provides much of the comedy, most of which involves cross-dressing and urine. **AKA:** *Daai Siu Yau Lung; Da Xiao You Long; The Rangers; Lady Whirlwind Against the Rangers.* 🎵🎵💔

1974 92m/C *HK* Polly Shang Kwan, Yasuaki Kurata, Kam Kong, Yeh Shao-im, Chen Chieh, Sung Lai, Ma Kei, Cheng Fu Hung, Wong Fei, Dai Sai Aan, Shaw Luo-hui. *D:* Hau Chang. *W:* Chu Hsiang-ken. *C:* Lin Men-kam. *M:* Chou Fu-liang. **VHS, DVD**

Lady Wu Tang

Here's yet another Shaolin Temple flick that centers on the device of a lost kung fu manual, this time featuring a fine female lead and a taste for the bizarre. Young Shi Fu-chung (Polly Shang Kwan) begs for acceptance as a disciple of Shaolin, but they don't let in girls. However, students Ching-feng and Ming-yuen take advantage of her willingness by making her do their chores. Rebellious old monk Lin-chu admires her spirit and agrees to take her on as a disciple, though she's still not allowed inside the temple without thrashing a few monks. They learn that 10 imposters have stolen the Tamo Classic book, and Lin-chu declares he'll train his disciple to retrieve the book within three years.

He teaches her various forms of Tamo Positive kung fu, such as shooting her limbs out to several times their length and breaking boulders with her head. But a side effect of so much unbalanced training is that Shi grows a mustache, beginning to become a man! Before he can begin teaching her Negative kung fu to balance her out, Lin-chu dies—but Shi Fu-chung is allowed to join the temple. Having achieved the burning scars of the Shaolin dragon, Shi sets out to find the Tamo Classics, accompanied by Ching-feng and Ming-yuen, stopping first to question the most likely suspects at Wu Tang. Master Chang Sheng-feng (Wang Tao) promises to look into the matter.

In the meantime, Shi posts a challenge to draw out any Tamo practitioners who may have volumes of the book. The 10 thieves show up to fight, hoping to gain all 10 volumes for themselves. Among the strange characters "he" meets on her adventures is masseuse Lang Kung-yu, who has trained in the Negative kung fu volume and turned into a woman! What's more, Lang (in drag) falls in love with Shi at first sight. Other Tamo practitioners include those adept at poisons, invisibility, and another woman changed to a man by Positive training. Having captured the Tamo Ten and reclaimed the book, they return to Shaolin. But while the captives are being rehabilitated, the Lords of

"Playing stupid to investigate. Full of Humor Laughters— Little nut helping sister teases the gang! Whom does he look like? Kam Kong, what do you think you are doing? Fighting! Oh, Yeh Shao-im in trouble! Eh! Eh! Eh! Eh! Artificial rain? Help!"

—The hard sell from the international trailer for *Lady Whirlwind and the Rangers*

the Wu Tang demand their disciples returned, leading to a fierce battle between Shaolin and Wu Tang.

The first half is lacking in any real martial arts action, but the film as a whole makes up for any deficiencies with unrelenting weirdness. Characters change gender, sport animal styles and matching costumes, practice magic, grow to 20 feet tall, and even show off some pretty decent kung fu fighting. The 18 *Gold*men even put in an appearance. At the center of all the guest stars and engaging silliness is the shining charisma of Polly Shang Kwan, who can do no wrong. The sets are minimal, but most of the action takes place in grand and wonderful temple locations. The soundtrack includes cues stolen from sources as old as *King Kong*. *AKA: Gui Xin Si Jian; Fight for Survival; Fight for Shaolin Tamo Technique.* ⚔⚔⚔

1977 92m/C *TW* Polly Shang Kwan, Wang Tao, Judy Lee, Kam Kong, Man Kong Lung, Cheng Fu Hung, Fong Min, Sze Ma Lung, Lee Keung, Weng Hsiao Hu, Au Lap-bo, Lung Chuan. *D:* Hau Chang. **VHS**

The Last Blood

The climax set in a hospital, as well as its willingness to use up every bullet squib available, caused this Wong Jing action film to be sold as *Hard Boiled 2* in some territories, though this was made first and has nothing to do with the John Woo classic. Alan Tam stars as Interpol Agent Lui Tai, who is assigned to a team whose mission is to protect the Daka Lama when his tour stops in Singapore. As soon as their VIP's plane lands, a group of flight attendants reveal their true identities as members of the Order of Death, a faction of the Japanese terrorist Red Army out to kill the Lama. The Lama is wounded in the gun battle, and among the civilian wounded is Ling (May Lo), girlfriend of triad leader Brother Bee (Andy Lau). It's found that both the Lama and Ling have the same blood type—the ultra-rare type P!! The Red Army catches wind of this, and sends assassins to do away with the only three other people in Thailand known to have type P, while both Lui and Bee rush to protect them. They fail to save two of them, leaving only Fatty (Eric Tsang) as a donor. Bee and Lui put aside their differences to protect Fatty on a wild ride across town to reach the hospital, with terrorists attacking every step of the way. And of course, the action doesn't stop when they get to the hospital.

That action, directed by Blackie Ko, is all that keeps this showboat floating, but Ko pulls out all the stops to make sure it's enough, seemingly blowing apart half of Singapore to do it. Big action movies—and any Wong Jing picture—exist in a world all their own, and as long as the viewer is willing to visit that world, all the goofy comic relief, shattering glass, and unnecessary explosions shouldn't be a bother. *AKA: Ging Tin Sap Yi Siu Si; Jing Tian Shi Er Xiao Shi; Hard Boiled 2: The Last Blood; 12 Hours of Fear; 12 Hours of Terror.* ⚔⚔⚔

1990 96m/C *HK* Alan Tam, Andy Lau, Eric Tsang, May Lo, Leung Kar-yan, Chin Ho, Nat Chan, Jackson Liu, Corey Yuen. *D:* Wong Jing. *W:* Wong Jing. *C:* Jingle Ma. *M:* Tats Lau. **VHS**

The Last Duel

Famed swordsman Sze Mun Shao-si (Ling Yun) appears to have caught his friend Luk Siu-fung (Barry Chan) in bed with his wife, and so the two warriors fight a duel. Obviously outclassed by his opponent (who can walk on water), Luk goes on the run through a dense forest. Not that Luk is unskilled himself; he swallows a snake whole for breakfast! He meets up with an old man in the woods named Tu Gu-mei, who is wounded and on the run like himself, having swindled his cousins Yeh Gou-hun and Fei Yin-chi. Curiously, Yeh Gou-hun kills his cousin Fei Yin-chi, then kills himself when he can't beat Luk. Tu takes Luk to Death Villa, a bizarre hideout for fugitives in a misty valley run by Lau Tao-barj. A bone-munching spirit tells him to visit the General. Luk and the mohawked General share a big bowl of stewed human meat while staring into each other's eyes, which makes Luk tumble with joy. Then they fight over who ate more. Other meals are not so substantial, and delivered by a scampering dwarf. Blamed for the death of one of their fellows, Luk is defended from the council by Mrs. Wong (Nora Miao), a self-confessed "terrible widow" and "a bitch that kills." A few more trials later, and Luk is finally accepted by Lau Tao-barj. Lau recruits Luk for a grand plan called Operation Thunder to take over the heads of all the clans. Luk joins a task force of five fighters sent to sneak in the back door of Wu Tang Clan headquarters and take over by force. But the finale brings double- and triple-crosses that bring an old friend of Luk's into the action.

Full of surreal visuals and enigmatic nonsense dialogue, this resembles *Alice in Wonderland* more than a swordplay thriller, as Luk meets up with one strange character or situation after another. The fever dream atmosphere is intensified by the sing-song quality of the English dub. With an impenetrable plot, some may grow weary of the one-damn-thing-after-another story, while others will be delighted by the freakshow oddities on display. The action is of the undercranked, overwired, and unsatisfying variety. The score swipes cues from *Battlestar Galactica* and *Psycho*. *AKA: Ying Hung Dui Ying Hung; Ying Xiong Dui Ying Xiong.* ⚔⚔

1982 91m/C *TW* Barry Chan, Ling Yun, Hsu Feng, Nora Miao, Chan Wai Lau, Ko Saio Pao. *D:* Ling Yun. *W:* Ku Long. **VHS, DVD**

Last Ghost Standing

This tale of blood and popcorn is based on a novel by star Simon Lui, which seems to be an expansion of ideas from the last act of *Troublesome Night*. December 31, 1999—preceding the last show at the Broadway Cinema, a lawyer (Frankie Ng) arrives to serve papers foreclosing on the theatre, and finds a bile-spewing doorway to Hell up in the attic. Shortly after, projectionist Yeung (Simon Lui) arrives to start the last show, worrying about his employment future. At first, there are only two people in the audience—Yeung's girlfriend Yiu-Yiu (Sherming Yiu) and a hostile popcorn vendor/video pirate (Amanda Lee) there to tape the flick. Then a satanic stranger (Francis Ng) shows up, questions Yeung's commitment, and pops Yiu-Yiu's head off. A red demon attacks and kills the popcorn vendor. Yiu-Yiu's head starts flying around biting people. Corridors and staircases run in circles. Manager Cheung (Wayne Lai) is attacked by his own hand. A trio of punk teens (Chan Chin-pang, Angela Tong, Pinky Cheung) arrives, giving the demons a fresh crop of victims. Help comes in the form of a trigger-happy cop (Paulyn Sun) and big-nosed "international ghostbuster" Jacky (Chin Ka-Lok)—whose ads all feature pics of Jackie Chan.

Though it starts out as a refreshing change of pace from the usual Hong Kong ghost movies, *Last Ghost Standing* soon reveals itself to be all too similar to horrors from outside HK. The whole idea of a theatre under attack by the supernatural is minimally inspired by *Demons*, but much of the rest comes from Sam Raimi's *Evil Dead* movies. The reanimated headless girlfriend is a familiar element from those films, and a whole sequence in which Wayne Lai battles his hand is lifted from *Evil Dead 2*—don't bother asking what a chainsaw is doing in a movie theatre. Even specific camera angles are copied. Another bit swipes from *Trainspotting*, and then there's the usual scare and chase that occurs in just about every horror comedy. When it gets away from outright plagiarism, the film can be downright inventive, as in the scene with Pinky Cheung riding around on a shit monster. It all has a trippy atmosphere that makes you want to stick around just to see what will happen, even though the fate of the protagonists no longer matters. Plus, Chin Ka-Lok's bizarre Jackie Chan imitation is worth catching. *AKA: Gwai Cheng Lei Tai Fai; Gui Qing Ni Di Hu.* 🎬🎬

1999 85m/C *HK* Simon Lui, Wayne Lai, Sherming Yiu, Paulyn Sun, Amanda Lee, Pinky Cheung, Chin Ka-Lok, Angela Tong, Chan Chin-pang, Francis Ng, Frankie Ng. *D:* Billy Chung. *W:* Simon Lui, Billy Chung, Billy Chung, Frankie Ng (story). *C:* Yu Kok-ping. *M:* Alan Wong, Alan Lee. **DVD**

Last Hero in China

After a dispute with Golden Harvest, Jet Li left the *Once upon a Time in China* series for two episodes, and signed on for this rival Wong Fei-hung production. Though comedy is more at the forefront in this movie, Wong shows he means business in the opening scene by beating four rude Boxer Association outlaws at the Hong Kong rail station, all without dropping the bouquet of roses sent by Aunt Yee. The roses and a note explain away Rosamund Kwan's absence from the film, and the fight establishes enmity between Wong and the Boxers. Back in Canton, the landlord announces a rent hike that Wong can't afford, and he decides to move Po Chi Lam Clinic. Unfortunately, he puts the job of finding a new home in the hands of his students So (Dicky Cheung) and Leung Fu (Leung Kar-yan), who get a place right next door to a brothel (with comic actress Yuen King-Tan in her customary role as a sassy madam). The pimp's name happens to be Mass Tar Wong (Nat Chan), which leads to the expected lowbrow comic confusion.

While the community welcomes Wong by electing him president of the Moral Reform Society, a corrupt local Legate Officer Liu Yat-siu (Alan Chui) tries to take him down a peg. The Legate is in cahoots with wicked monk Liu Hung (Gordon Lau), who is running a slaving operation out of Nun-yan Temple. Ti Yin-er (Sharla Cheung) and her father (Walter Cho) are badly injured attempting to rescue her sister from the temple, and go to Wong for help. He goes to the rescue—injuring 46 monks in and around the spectacular temple set—but the crooked officials have Wong arrested instead. The merchants bail him out in time for a lion dance against the Nun-yan's giant centipede. Meanwhile, a traitor has been feeding Wong a poison that affects his hearing. Unable to fight (or hear) city hall, Wong is exiled from Canton, and heads back to Fu-shan to have his ears treated. Visiting the Ti farm on the way, he and Mr. Ti come up with a treatment to counteract the poison—and Wong learns of a way to deal with the big centipede from the barnyard chickens!

By this time, the Wong Fei-hung series was ready for some fresh ideas. While Tsui Hark continued his series with Vincent Zhou, Wong Jing's humorous version is just shy of parody. At one point, So—whose buckteeth have never been bigger—stops an injured fellow from revealing a secret because so many characters in films die after making such revelations. But

Korea

Word on the street is that Korea is the new Hong Kong, as far as genre film goes. Well, that's not quite true—the rush of energy produced by Hong Kong cinema in the 1980s was just as much a product of time and place as anything else. Korea is really the new Korea—South Korea to be exact, though many Americans don't see the difference. Korea is the one place on Earth that has been more or less in a state of constant civil war for 50 years. All that tension was bound to pop in various ways, and one was a sudden spurt of creativity. While film production in Hong Kong has slowed since 1997, the Koreans jumped up to fill the gap.

The Korean cinema had a somewhat odd beginning. The first domestic films shown in Korean theatres, starting in 1919, were exterior location scenes screened as part of stage plays called Kimo-dramas. The first full-length feature came in 1923, when pioneer Yun Baek-nam's *The Plighted Love under the Moon* appeared—and reportedly the story urged people to open savings accounts. Actors in the silent era were paid in rice. During the Japanese occupation in World War II, most films were propaganda pictures that glorified the foreign invaders, though an occasional hidden message of resistance leaked into films like *The Man on the Road*. Due to a scarcity of 35mm cameras, most early Korean films were 16mm.

In 1950, just as Korean cinema was getting on its feet again, war broke out anew. But the American presence in South Korea during the war meant that more Koreans saw American films, which had a direct effect on the filmmakers. Following the war, film production increased dramatically, though most were shoestring productions made for under $25,000. In the 1960s, the government passed laws to raise the general quality of films, and only licensed studios with production facilities could import a certain number of foreign movies based on a production quota. Studios became so dependent on this quota system that when the government amended the law to allow U.S. distributors the right to show their own movies inside Korea, the studios called for a general boycott of American films. When American and Hong Kong films devastated Korean films at the boxoffice, the government forced theatres to show Korean films for roughly a third of each year.

Artistically, the problem with Korean films has been a lack of identity, with imitation of Hong Kong and U.S. films bringing the most success. Meanwhile, North Korean cinema at times more closely resembled vanity productions, with members of the royal family producing and directing films starring themselves as the heroes. (For more fun in North Korea, check out our review of *Pulgasari*.) It was Kang Je-gyu's *Shiri* that pointed the direction for Korean identity—films that were just as exciting and professionally crafted as those in any other major film center, but that couldn't have been made anywhere else. And that doesn't just mean political thrillers like Park Chan-wook's *Joint Security Area* either. Sure, you could remake *Tell Me Something* or *The Foul King* in the U.S., but it wouldn't be steeped in the same cultural flavor.

Finally, in the 21st century, Korean cinema *is* Korean cinema.

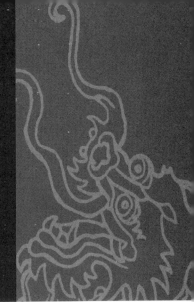

the gags don't get in the way of wonderfully choreographed super-heroics, courtesy of action director Yuen Woo-ping. There's even a chance for Li to engage in some fine drunken boxing. It may lack the soul of Tsui's first two Wong Fei-hung pictures, but *Last Hero* still provides a lot of fun. Besides, where else can you see Jet Li in a chicken costume? Some versions run as much as 20 minutes shorter. *AKA: Wong Fei-hung Chi Tit Gai Dau Neung Gung; Huang Fei-hong Zhi Tie Ji Dou Wu Gong; Deadly China Hero; Deadly China Killer; Claws of Steel; Iron Rooster vs. the Centipede.* ♪♪♪

1993 106m/C *HK* Jet Li, Leung Kar-yan, Gordon Lau, Sharla Cheung, Dicky Cheung, Alan Chui, Nat Chan, Anita Yuen, Chung Fat, Walter Cho, Yuen King-Tan, Deon Lam, Wong Tin Lam, Baak Man-biu, Shut Ma Wa Lung, Yuen Miu, Au Shui-wai, Julie Lee. *D:* Wong Jing. *W:* Wong Jing. *C:* Jingle Ma. *M:* James Wong. **VHS, DVD**

Last Hurrah for Chivalry

Direct from the pages of a popular novel comes this early John Woo feature, one of his first hits. Young Kau Pan (Lau Kong), a bookworm warrior, is throwing a party in expectation of the arrival of his bride. Though thought to be from a good family, Kau freely admits he bought her from a whorehouse. Just then, the ninjas of Pak Chung Tong (Lee Hoi-sang), archenemy of the Kau clan, crashes the party. Pak's warriors come from all sides, killing family and guests right and left, and even the bride turns out to be an assassin. Kau Pan escapes the massacre, but his father per-

ishes, and Pak takes possession of the house. Hungry for revenge, Kau begs his Master Chun to give him the Midnight Sword, but Chun refuses to give it up until Kau is ready for it.

Knowing he can't get revenge alone, Kau goes looking for kung fu fighters to help. Number-one prospect is Swift Sword Chang Sen (Wei Pai, Snake of *The Five Deadly Venoms*), a poor but skillful warrior. Hearing of his reputation, the enigmatic sword-slinger Pray (Fung Hark-On) challenges Chang Sen, but is refused. Pray beats Kau's master to draw Chang and Kau into a fight. Chang faces him and wins.

Another prospect is hard-drinking lone-wolf mercenary Tsing Yi (Damian Lau in his first film role). He and Chang have become drinking buddies, helping each other beat the blues. The two warriors are coerced into taking on Kau's vendetta, storming into Pak's headquarters to face the Ghost Spear, the Sleeping Sword (Chin Yuet Sang), and other master killers. At last, they duel with Pak himself, but beware the deadly Last Move.

Woo gives his epic the feeling of Chinese opera, even then showing visual flair, good timing, a mobile camera, and the beginnings of his "heroic bloodshed" and male-bonding themes. The emphasis is on beautiful sets and colorful costumes, while the swordplay choreography looks slow by contemporary standards—at least at the beginning. The matches seem to heat up as the film rolls along, with more bizarre elements popping up in the last act. *AKA:* Ho Hap; Hao Xia; Last Hurray for Chivalry. ♪♪♪

1978 105m/C *HK* Lee Hoi-sang, Lau Kong, Wei Pai, Fung Hark-On, Chin Yuet Sang, Damian Lau, Hsu Hsia, Ngai Chau-wa, Cheng Lui, Huang Ha, Wong Kwong-yue, Alan Chui, Cheung Wa, Mars, Cheung Ging Boh, Baan Yun-sang, Tai San, Chan Dik-hak, Chui Fat, Ringo Wong. **D:** John Woo. **W:** John Woo. **C:** Frankie Chan, Ching Yu, Chu Chang Yao. **VHS, DVD**

The Last War

After World War III, radioman Takano (Akira Takarada) is onboard a ship racing a radioactive cloud home to Tokyo, even though the crew knows it's likely they'll find the city destroyed. Flashbacks show how he became engaged to Seiko (Yumi Shirakawa) before he left, after which the film chronicles the continued tensions between the United States and Russia, and the effect it has on Seiko's family. With the whole world on edge, a series of accidents and misunderstandings triggers Armageddon.

Made by Toho Studios in 1961 during a period in which several films were made dealing with global destruction via atomic weapons, the film was not released in the United States (directly to TV) until 1968. The difference in this one is in its viewpoint, from the unique perspective of the only country (so far) to have actually been a victim of nuclear warfare. As such, it's a sad tale of helpless victims resigned to destruction, as things continue to get worse around the globe. Awfully depressing stuff, much like Stanley Kramer's *On the Beach,* enlivened only by the spectacle of Eiji Tsuburaya's masterful f/x work. The cast, especially comedian Frankie Sakai *(Mothra),* gives fine performances all around. The U.S. distributor tacked on the familiar song "It's a Small World" and an excerpt from President Kennedy's anti-arms race speech in an attempt to Americanize the production. Often confused with the rarely seen and reportedly similar *The Final War,* produced by Toei the year before. Director Shuei Matsubayashi made the epic *I Bombed Pearl Harbor* the same year, as well as the much lighter *Playboy President.* **AKA:** *Sekai Daisenso; The Great World War.* 🐉🐉🐉

1961 110m/C *JP* Frankie Sakai, Akira Takarada, Yuriko Hoshi, Yumi Shirakawa, Nobuko Otowa, Chieko Nakakita, Shinpei Tsuchiya, Eijiro Tono, Ken Uehara, Koji Uno, Harold Conway, Minoru Takada, Nadao Kirino, Seizaburo Kawazu, Shigeki Ishida, Wataru Omae, Kozo Nomura, Nobuo Nakamura, Jerry Ito, Osman Yusuf. **D:** Shuei Matsubayashi. **W:** Takeshi Kimura, Toshio Yasumi. **C:** Rokuro Nishigaki. **M:** Ikuma Dan. **VHS**

Lavender

Pretty pictures can't make up for a lackluster story. Aromatherapist Athena (Kelly Chan) is grieving over a lost love. One night an angel (Takeshi Kaneshiro) crashes down onto her bal-cony. This would seem to be the answer to her prayers, but, rather surprisingly, Athena turns a cold shoulder on the heavenly creature. The angel needs love in order to survive until his wing heals and a holy door opens so he can return to heaven. The angel takes the name Angel (!). How does Angel pass the time? By hanging out with Athena's next-door neighbor, Chow Chow (Eason Chan), developing a close personal relationship with a certain pair of shoes, and trying to warm up Athena's cold heart. Will Athena learn to love again and keep Angel from dying?

From that description you'd think *Lavender* would be a kooky comedy, but writer/director Riley Yip had something else in mind. It's just not clear what that was. The film looks lovely, thanks to the gorgeous photography by Kwan Pun-leung, but meanders and skips around, taking too long to arrive at its inevitable conclusion. This is a romance, after all, and we know romances end in either tragedy or everlasting bliss. Takeshi Kaneshiro oozes charm as the angel without appearing oily or insincere; his personality makes the running time bearable. Kelly Chan is easy on the eyes, but she is stuck with a role that makes little sense. Why does Athena grieve for her former boyfriend when all she can talk about is the way he smelled? She apparently has not lost her religious faith, since she still sends balloons heavenward with "I miss you" written on them. So why is she so inhospitable toward Angel? Notwithstanding the faults of the script, the actress is not able to overcome these weaknesses and make the audience care about her character. Eason Chan has some nice moments as Chow Chow; again, though, the script dances endlessly in other less-fruitful areas and could have enlarged his part to enhance the core love story. —*PM* **AKA:** *Fan Dut Cho; Xun Yi Cao.* 🐉🐉

2000 101m/C *HK* Takeshi Kaneshiro, Kelly Chan, Eason Chan, Cheng Pei-Pei, Michael Clements. **D:** Riley Yip. **W:** Riley Yip. **C:** Kwan Pun-leung. **M:** Ronald Ng. **VHS, DVD**

The Law and the Outlaw

Jonah (Damian Lau), a mystical kung fu master, is the bodyguard to the emperor, and the film focuses on his exploits. He's "the law," while the main "outlaw" is Andrew (Mah Ji Leung), a roguish kung fu master who lives in a brothel with a woman named Jessica. Another set of outlaws is looking to settle old accounts by killing the emperor. Leading this effort is Julie (Cecilia Yip), whose family was killed earlier during the emperor's reign. Julie sets about trying to wheedle her way into the imperial court by befriending both Andrew and Jonah. Neither man has any idea of her true motives. Eventually, she gets Jonah to introduce her to the emperor, and then persuades the young leader to marry her. Her plan hits a snag, though, when she and Jonah fall really wild when Julie's plot is revealed and her long-lost brother is discovered. Jonah then finds himself an outlaw as well, with the emperor calling for his head.

Another shot-on-video production culled (probably) from a TV series, this flick is a bit more coherent and has somewhat better production values than the *Dragonslayer Sword* series. It also has the Jalisco label's trademark somewhat-silly Western names for its characters. This convention does actually help keep them straight at times, despite the numerous scene and costume changes. Followed by *The Seven Musketeer* and *The Buddha Conspiracy*. Not to be confused with the 1913 Tom Mix western. —SS

1995 90 m/C *HK* Damian Lau, Mah Ji Leung, Cecilia Yip. **VHS, DVD**

Lawyer Lawyer

The third in the Stephen Chow Old Canton law trilogy brings us to 1899 for a clash of legal systems. Legal ace Chan Mon-gut (Stephen Chow) has earned the name "King of Brain-trusters"(?) for his wiles inside the courtroom, and for his vicious practical jokes everywhere else. Chan demonstrates this in the first sequence, as he repels from his house King of Beggars Hung Sat-fat (Lee Siu-Kei), who has come to settle an old score. Many of Chan's sharpest tricks victimize his dim assistant Ho Foon (Eric Kot), but when one of these schemes ruins Foon's chance to woo puppeteer Lotus Shui (Chingmy Yau), the incensed servant quits and scoots off for Hong Kong to make something of himself. Foon is immediately framed in a murder conspiracy plot, and his ex-master is called upon to defend him. However, the island has recently been taken over by the British, and Chan finds himself unfamiliar with the new laws. His efforts only lead to the judge (Hong Kong film critic Paul Fonoroff) charging him with contempt of court, and shaming the Chinese national pride. Since she was sent by her husband to study law in England, it's up to Chan's wife Wu-man (Karen Mok) to come to the rescue and defend them both—but unfortunately, she secretly studied fashion design instead of law!

The broad clowning of Eric Kot falls flat here, leaving it up to his co-star Chow to deliver all the laughs with his trademark schemes and nonsense. But the film's secret heart is in the sweet relationship between Chow and Mok, who steals her scenes despite playing a straight role. One of the more memorable tricks involves an appearance by Lysee the Quixotic Dog, recalling the dog-based gags in *Justice, My Foot!* The courtroom antics are clever, but too much of the picture relies on bathroom humor, undermining the spirit of patriotism that infected many Hong Kong films made during the changeover year. Director/writer Joe Ma gives the movie an unusual flavor, but it's obviously a cheaper project than most of Chow's previous films. *AKA: Suen Sei Cho; Suan Ci Cao.*

1997 85m/C *HK* Stephen Chow, Eric Kot, Chingmy Yau, Bowie Lam, Karen Mok, Lee Kin-yan, Lee Siu-Kei, Chung King-fai, Moses Chan, Paul Fonoroff, Vincent Kok, Simon Lui, Cheung Tat-Ming, Spencer Lam, Tats Lau, Lung Fong, Nancy Lan, Bobby Yip, Law Kar-Ying. **D:** Joe Ma. **W:** Joe Ma, Wong Ho-wah. **C:** Cheung Man-po. **M:** Lincoln Lo. **DVD**

Lee Rock

This ambitious feature chronicles the story of Hong Kong policeman Lui Lok, who shook up the status quo in the early 1950s. At the time, the HK police justified their acceptance of bribes as an economic alternative to the triads, but idealistic mainlander Lee Rock (Andy Lau) refuses to take part. Pressure on Lee to conform increases when he asks for the hand of his girlfriend Rose (Chingmy Yau), and her hostile father (Wong Yat-Fei) demands a large dowry. Drunk, Lee "borrows" the revolver of his mentor Detective Sgt. Chan (Kwan Hoi-san) to gamble at the casino run by gangster Snake (Lung Fong), but only receives a beating. Uncle helps him collect the cash he needs, but a huge fire leaves Rose unaccounted for.

Promoted to CID under Chan, Lee makes an enemy of Sgt. Ngan Fung (Paul Chun), who operates more like a triad boss than a cop. He decides to beat Ngan at his own game, becoming even more greedy and corrupt than his brethren. After a confrontation with Ngan, Lee is transferred to a remote, livestock-infested station, but makes a comeback by marrying Grace Pak Yu-shun (Sharla Cheung), the daughter of Kowloon triad boss Silverfish (James Tien). Promoted to detective, Lee is able to institute changes in his territory that at least instill a sense of order, if not law. Behind the scenes, his personal fortune grows, until he's one of the most powerful men in the colony.

Lee Rock makes the valid point that a system cannot be successfully changed from the outside—and that those making the changes are always changed themselves by the process. Andy Lau proved that he can handle broader roles than the usual pop-idol assignments, but his performance here is a step up from anything

he'd tackled up to that time, and he was nominated for a HK Film Award for it. Ng Man-Tat also proves his versatility, wringing every bit of pathos from his role as the two-bit criminal whom Lee hires on as an assistant, without overplaying it. Planned from the start as a two-part feature, Lee Rock's adventures continued in (what else?) *Lee Rock 2,* and again in *Lee Rock 3*. **AKA:** *Ng Yi Taam Jeung Lui Lok Juen; Wu Yi Tan Zhang Lei Luo Zhuan; Lee Rock 1.* ♪♪♪

1991 125m/C *HK* Andy Lau, Sharla Cheung, Kwan Hoi-san, Paul Chun, Ng Man-Tat, Chingmy Yau, Lung Fong, Michael Chan, James Tien, Eddie Ko, Wong Yat-Fei, William Ho, Tan Sin-hung, Victor Hon Kwan, Jamie Luk. **D:** Lawrence Ah Mon. **W:** Chan Man-keung. **C:** Gigo Lee, Andrew Lau. **M:** Joseph Chow. **VHS, DVD**

The Leg Fighters

Just as the chopping blow with a hand is the defining motion of karate, so the high kick is the defining move in kung fu. What we've got here is a whole movie about kicking! Delon "Flash Legs" Tan is acknowledged as one of the best kickers ever. Here he plays Tan Hai-chi from the Northern China Tan Kick School. Southern ground-kicking proponent Peng Fei (Choi Wang) challenges him to a duel. Tan is the clear winner, but Peng Fei pulls a knife on him and continues to fight, forcing Tan to kill him. However, elder brother Peng Fat (Peng Kang) gets a different account of things, and swears to kick Han's head off and put it on his brother's grave! Meanwhile, old Master Mao Kung-fung (Sun Jung-chi) has been hired to teach kung fu to willful Miss Phoenix Ho (Shih Kwan-li), but she and her servant Hai Chin-fou (Chin Leung) only complain about his painful training. And so, the students are overjoyed when Mao's wife gets sick and he has to return home. But Mao has sent for a replacement: Tan Hai-chi.

Phoenix and Chin-fou try to come up ways to beat Master Tan, but their schemes always backfire. Tan uses troublemaking, bell-wearing bullies Master Ding-Dong and Master Dong-Dong to quell Phoenix's insubordination, but has to pay for his actions by beating their Master Niu. Peng Fat has been searching for Tan all this time, and kills Mao and his wife when they get in his way. Ding-Dong and Dong-Dong let the ground-kickers know where Tan can be found. Peng challenges Tan to a duel, but Phoenix is determined to make two kicks better than one.

As can be expected, the kicking is the highlight of all the fighting and training scenes in the film, with Tan and Shih displaying amazing strength and flexibility. However, the plot never ventures beyond the standard elements of hateful villain, stalwart hero, and mischievous students.

AKA: *Nan Bei Tui Wang; The Invincible Kung Fu Legs; Incredible Death Kick Master.* ♪♪♪

1980 81m/C *HK* Delon Tan, Shih Kwan-li, Peng Kang, Chin Leung, Sun Jung-chi, Wong Hap, Choi Wang, Chen Chin-hai, Shih Ting Ken, Hsiao Ho, Wang Tao. **D:** Lee Tso Nam. **W:** Chang Seng-yi. **C:** Chou Fu-liang. **VHS, DVD**

Legacy of Rage

In Brandon Lee's only Hong Kong film, no effort is wasted to touch every base on the action-movie field. He chases buses like Jackie Chan in *Police Story,* and even has a girlfriend named May (Regina Kent). He gets in big gunfights like in *A Better Tomorrow.* And he fights Bolo Yeung like his dad.

Brandon Ma (Lee) is a righteous young scrap yard worker by day, a nightclub waiter by night, and sort of a lunkhead all the time. When Michael Wong (Michael Wong), son of drug kingpin Yee (Michael Chan), is asked to rub out cranky crooked cop Sharky Kau (Lam Chung), he frames his friend Brandon—a rival for May's affections—for the murder. With Brandon in prison, Michael racks up more betrayal points by molesting May, and when she resists, by trying to kill her. After a few prison movie clichés, Brandon gets some help from his friend Hoi (Mang Hoi) in breaking out of the crossbar hotel. The escape goes awry, but a guard (Ku Feng), who is good friends with Brandon's old boss Manager Ip (Yip Wing-cho), covers it up. Brandon serves his term and returns to his life of dead-end jobs.

Meanwhile, Michael has taken over more territory for his family, and is an out-of-control coke vacuum. When he sees May has come back to Hong Kong to see Brandon, he has his bodyguard Tai (Shing Fui-on) kidnap both May and the son Brandon didn't know he had, and sends his thugs to finish Brandon off. Fortunately, Hoi still has a huge arsenal left over from when he was an arms dealer, and he and Brandon gear up to make war on Michael's gang.

Lee was uncomfortable all his life with being the son of a legend. He's just as uncomfortable in films like this one that tried to cast him in the action-hero mold. According to actor Michael Chan, Lee refused to take his job seriously and wanted to make other types of films. Lee wouldn't find a role suitable to his talents until his final one in *The Crow. Legacy of Rage* has some nicely choreographed gun fu at the end, but is otherwise a by-the-numbers revenge saga. **AKA:** *Lung Joi Gong Woo; Long Zai Jiang Hu.* ♪♪♪♥

1986 83m/C *HK* Brandon Lee, Michael Wong, Regina Kent, Michael Chan, Mang Hoi, Lam Chung, Shing Fui-on, Ku Feng, Kirk Wong, Bolo Yeung, Ng Man-Tat, Yip Wing-cho. **D:** Ronny Yu. **W:** Clifton Ko, Raymond Fung. **C:** Jimmy Chan. **M:** Richard Yuen. **VHS, DVD**

The Legend

After becoming a smash success as Wong Fei-hung in Tsui Hark's *Once upon a Time in China*, Jet Li sought out another legendary Chinese hero for his own production. He found what he was looking for in Fong Sai-yuk. The original Fong Sai-yuk was founder of the White Tiger Kung Fu style who fought the Manchus at the end of the 19th century. The cinematic Fong is only vaguely concerned with history, more interested in Shakespearean comedy and fantastic martial arts. What sets this hero apart from other movie legends is the twist that his rambunctious mother is just as good a fighter as he is.

Manchu Emperor Chen Lung dreams of his assassination, and sends his top assassin (Vincent Zhao) to "kill the dream demon"—that is, wipe out any possible killers, especially those in the rebel group Red Lotus Society. Top priority is given to finding a roster kept of all RLS members.

Boss Tiger Lu (Chan Chung-Yung) sponsors track and field events to keep his populace happy. Fong Sai-yuk (Jet Li) befriends Lu's daughter Ting-Ting (Michele Reis), though she's careful not to reveal her real identity. Next, Tiger holds a kung fu tournament, giving away his daughter as the prize. Contestants must beat Tiger's wife Su-Wan (Sibelle Hu), the Canton champ. Naturally, the brash young Fong can't resist the challenge. During his match with his prospective mother-in-law, they invent a new kind of crowd surfing, bouncing around atop spectators' heads. But Ting-Ting is hiding out from the humiliation, and when Sai-yuk gets a peek at the stand-in, he throws the fight. Incensed, notorious brawler Mrs. Fong dresses as Sai-yuk's "brother" and defends the family name, winning her match with Su-Wan (who is swept off her feet by the "handsome" stranger).

That night, Sai-yuk and Mom discover that the elder Fong (Paul Chu) is a member of the Red Lotus Society, and he has the membership list! The assassin sweeps in to kill everyone, but the Fongs escape. Later, Tiger Lu has a banquet to announce Ting-Ting's marriage, but when the assassin shows up as a guest, all hell breaks loose, and Fong Sr. is captured. Sai-yuk decides it's time to be less frivolous and get involved with his country's future. Plus, he has to buckle down and save his dad from getting his head chopped off.

It's nice to see Li playing such a carefree, fun-loving character, but it's Josephine Siao who steals the show as the kung fu crazy mother. The combination was such a hit that the Fongs returned for a sequel, and Li's *New Legend of Shaolin* featured Deannie Yip as another fighting matron. Jackie Chan would also borrow the mother/son idea for his *Legend of the Drunken Master*. Director Corey Yuen proves he can mix gorgeous visuals with incredible flying harness choreography to nearly push the film into the realm of fantasy. As with many New Year's releases, at times *The Legend* tries to do too much, gaining an episodic flavor as it switches from romance to comedy to drama. Too much of a twist for Western viewers is the late arrival of Chinese hero Chan Ka Lok (Adam Cheng), a character from Jin Yong novels whom few will be familiar with. Some scenes were shot on location in Beijing at the Summer Palace and other locations. *AKA: Fong Shi Yu; Fong Sai-yuk; The Legend of Fong Sai-yuk.* 🐉🐉🐉

1992 (R) 96m/C *HK* Jet Li, Josephine Siao, Michele Reis, Sibelle Hu, Vincent Zhao, Chan Chung-Yung, Paul Chu, Adam Cheng, Chan Lung. **D:** Corey Yuen. **W:** Kay On, John Chan, Tsoi Kang Yung. **C:** Jingle Ma. **M:** James Wong, Romeo Diaz, Mark Lui, Nicholas Rivera (U.S. version). **VHS, DVD**

The Legend 2

Kung fu cinema's most famous mama's-boy hero returns for more adventures. When we last left Fong Sai-yuk (Jet Li) and his bride Ting-Ting (Michelle Reis), they'd ridden off into the sunset to join the rebels of the Red Lotus Society. Now, a year later, they return home for the New Year's festival. Chan Ka Lok (Adam Cheng), in line for Emperor and hidden by Red Lotus for 20 years, has also returned. Yun (Chi Chuen-Hua), whose father was the former leader, is suspected as a traitor, and Fong finds himself at odds with the hotheaded Yun. Fong isn't such a cool character either, having ambitions to lead Red Lotus someday himself. Dong (Corey Yuen) is assigned to teach Fong the group's commandments.

The Duke of Hell visits Mrs. Fong Lei Ling (Josephine Siao), looking to challenge the now-famous fighter Sai-yuk. She disposes of the challengers quickly, so Sai-yuk's soup doesn't get cold. However, he's already left on a mission with a band of Red Lotus warriors, sent to retrieve a red box from some traveling samurai. Fong runs into trouble when he has to protect a young lady while fighting the samurai, but Madame Fong (in disguise as the heroic samurai Matsuhiro) arrives in time to save them both, though they fail to get the box. The young lady is actually the Mandarin's daughter, Sho Soo Li (Amy Kwok), and Chan hopes to exploit her attraction to Sai-yuk to get the red box. Fong wagers his kung fu with Yun that he'll succeed in his mission. The Mandarin prepares a contest to win his daughter's hand, a battle between teams to reach a prize atop a tower. Fong arrives late, but uses a kite to beat everyone. Ting Ting finds out about the contest and

KUNG FU MOVIE DYNASTIES
The Venoms
Who's Who in Fu Part 5

Director Chang Cheh was one of the Shaw Brothers Studios' top directors, and he always used their top stars like Ti Lung in his films. But during the mid-1970s, he began to inject new blood into his pictures, casting his leads from among the recent Shaw contractees from Hong Kong and Taiwan opera companies. In 1978 he cast a small group of them to star as the *Five Deadly Venoms*, which became the signature film for them all. The film concerned five men who were each trained by a secret sect in an extreme martial arts style based on a venomous animal. After these men had left for the outer world, their master sent another student who'd been trained in a hybrid of all five styles to track them down. This task was complicated by the fact that the Venoms always wore masks before, so none of them knew the others' faces. The Venoms made about 30 films together in different combinations, many with Chang, and over the years they've acquired a huge cult following.

Lu Feng: The Centipede

Fans consider Lu Feng the best all-around actor/martial artist of the Venoms—but that opinion is far from unanimous, as each of them has a lot of fans. One of the better acrobats in the group, his specialty is in heavy weapons fighting. He was usually cast as a mole, gaining the heroes' trust and doing only a bit of fighting throughout the film, only to be revealed as a marauding traitor at the end. Even when he played good guys he had a tendency to be undercover.

Wei Pai: The Snake

This dashing performer appeared in relatively few films compared to the others, having left the Shaws soon after making *Venoms* for Golden Harvest, where he was underused. Probably his best part was a featured role in *Last Hurrah for Chivalry*. He's done a lot of work in HK television.

Sun Chien: The Scorpion

Like Lu Feng, Sun often played a deceitful villain in the Venoms films, infiltrating the heroes to turn the tables on them. Not quite the acrobat his fellows were, his specialty was powerful kicking. He first made his mark as star Alexander Fu Sheng's drug-addicted roommate in *Chinatown Kid.*

Phillip Kwok: The Lizard

If there's a true star in the group, it would surely be this opera-trained Taiwanese performer. His skill as an actor equals his physical prowess, and Kwok is acknowledged as the leader in choreographing the Venoms pictures. He's still at it, designing the action for international hits like *Brotherhood of the Wolf, The Touch,* and *Tomorrow Never Dies.* While Chang Cheh was making *Chinese Super Ninjas,* Kwok took his fellow Taiwanese Venoms home to direct *Ninja in the Deadly Trap,* though he found directing not to his liking. It's hard to catch on film, but Kwok is missing two fingers on his left hand from an accident in his father's tool shop when he was 13.

Lo Meng: The Toad

This muscular Hong Kong native usually played a husky, lovable lunk who was quick to jump into fights. He developed his upper-body strength via his dedicated practice of Mantis Style kung fu, and his characters often preferred open hand fighting to weaponry. Unexpectedly, he got his start in the movies in the accounting department of Shaw Brothers, until a mutual friend introduced him to Chang Cheh. Lo is still busy in HK films and TV, and he and Phillip Kwok even choreographed a fight for a Dru Hill video.

Chiang Sheng: The Hybrid

With his handsome features and button nose, fans called this Taiwan opera–trained Venom "Cutie Pie." His specialty was acrobatics, his talent was reminiscent of Yuen Biao, and his "light skills" were truly amazing. At times he'd appear to be floating. After having begun to direct films in the mid-'80s, Sheng apparently retired due to ill health, and died of a heart attack in 1991.

There are also many other actors who appeared in several of the Venoms films, known as the Poison Clan to fans. These included established Shaw stars like David Chiang and Ku Feng, but mainly consisted of rising Chang Cheh favorites like Ricky Cheng, Dick Wei, Chu Ko, Johnny Wang, and Yu Tai-ping.

nearly ruins the mission, but Soo Li helps them escape with their prize. Hiding the box to keep it safe from the traitor Yun, Fong must be disabled to pay off the wager. Recovering, he packs up a bushel of swords to rescue Chan and his mom.

Uneven and awkwardly paced, *Legend 2* nevertheless contains all the comic complications and elaborate acrobatic fight sequences that fans of the first film should expect. Josephine Siao once again steals the show with her charm and comic timing. *AKA: Fong Sai-yuk 2; Fong Shi Yu II: Wan Fu Mo Di; Fong Sai Yuk Chuk Chap; Fang Shi Yu Xu Ji.* 🎵🎵🎵

1993 (R) 95m/C *HK* Jet Li, Josephine Siao, Adam Cheng, Michelle Reis, Amy Kwok, Corey Yuen, Chi Chuen-Hua, Chan Lung. **D:** Corey Yuen. **W:** Kay On, John Chan. **C:** Mark Lee. **M:** Steve Edwards (U.S. version), Lowell Lo. **VHS, DVD**

The Legend of a Professional

Ho (Anthony Wong) is a regular working Joe Hit Man. He can't find a girl to settle down with, his mom nags, and he's still haunted by thoughts of the one honest man among hundreds he killed years ago. (His visit to the man's grave gives a nice view of one of Hong Kong's stadium-style cemeteries.) To find a wife, he pretends to be casting for a movie. Jenny (Josie Ho) is one of those answering his ad, and he hires her to pose as his girlfriend for his mother's benefit when she visits from Vietnam. Jenny does a good job telling Mom (Law Kwun-lan) everything she wants to hear, but Ho has to save her from the loan shark she owes. Jenny takes a call from Ho's agent May (Helena Law), and learns his true business. She cuts herself in as a partner, though neither of them can see their deadliest enemy coming.

One could draw parallels between this and Luc Besson's *The Professional*, but they'd be tenuous at best. Anthony Wong creates another great character in his portrayal of the overweight, sloppy Ho, who only smiles when he's working. The rest of the cast is rather good as well. Helena Law is well known for her work on Hong Kong's TVB network, and has hundreds of movie credits going back to her debut in *A Woman of Many Husbands* in 1939! Not as much action as you'd like to see in your hit man movies, but the tough-sell romance works. *AKA: Feh Goh Chuen Kei; Fei Ge Chuan Ji.* 🎵🎵🎵

2000 92m/C *HK* Anthony Wong, Josie Ho, Helena Law, Law Kwun-lan, Karel Wong, Ho Ka Chun, Gabriel Harrison, Wong Chun Tong, Thomas Lam, Yeung Kin Wai. **D:** Billy Chan. **W:** Billy Chan. **C:** Poon Tak-yip. **VHS, DVD**

The Legend of Bruce Lee

Only the flimsiest effort is made to connect this cheap Bruceploitation title with the late great legend. A shipboard couple has a baby, and a meteor passes overhead (offscreen), signifying something to a nearby astrologer. This is followed by brief credits showing some shots of Lee. Headstrong young master Bruce (Bruce Le, the least of the Lee-alikes) is only interested in fighting. His dad makes a deal with him: if he goes to college, then he can also study with Mr. Yeh (Fung Ging Man) and learn his "Wing Ching Fist." Bruce improves, but still keeps getting into fights—one of which introduces him to blind fortuneteller Chang Fat-po. He learns Chang's Blind Fist, and picks up the Snake Fist from another master. However, he can't help trying out his new skills in gang fights alongside his pals Choi (Hon Gwok-choi) and Niu (Alan Chan). The remainder of the plot consists of escalating fights with thugs sent by the evil Mr. Kim (Shih Kien).

No matter what the situation, Bruce Le keeps the same dull, stunned look on his face. His athletic ability seems O.K., but the fight choreography is routine. The most impressive scene is when Le learns Drunken Snake Fist style while handling real cobras. *AKA: Chui Sau Siu Ji; Zui She Xiao Zi; Bruce—King of Kung Fu; Chinese Chien Chuan Kung Fu.* 🎵

1980 84m/C *HK* Bruce Le, Fung Ging Man, Hon Gwok-choi, Alan Chan, Shih Kien, Kong Do, Bolo Yeung, Wong Mei, Fung Hark-On. **D:** Daniel Lau, Bruce Le. **W:** Daniel Lau. **VHS, DVD**

Legend of Speed

Rob Cohen's *The Fast and the Furious* is glorious trash that thrilled audiences worldwide. This Hong Kong racing thriller employs many of the same flashy techniques, a similar plot, and features both car and motorcycle action. Before you cry "Rip-off!" though, know this: *Legend of Speed* was released a year and a half earlier. Sky Yu (Ekin Cheng) is the reigning king of illegal street racing, demanding that his defeated opponents not only pay high stakes, but sometimes a broken limb as well. One such rival is Maddie (Moses Chan), who loses a million dollars (HK) and incurs a broken leg. With rich parents who spoil him, Sky easily indulges his taste for fast wheels, even employing his own team in coordinator Tse and mechanic Paddy (Patrick Tam). Aside from his girlfriend Kelly (Kelly Lin), Sky's biggest fan is stuttering Paddy's little sister Nancy (Cecilia Cheung), who sneaks out of the Ma Tau Wai Road Girls Home at night to watch her idol race.

Sky's real father is Black Tone, a legendary racer who disappeared after being beaten by Maddie's brother Tang Fung (Simon Yam). Fung has been in prison for getting mixed up with a gang of robbers, but when he gets out his first order of business is beating Sky in a car race, causing Sky's Subaru to crash (likely because of modifications that Fung goaded him into making) and killing Kelly. His troubles increase when a bag of heroin is found planted in the wreck. Skipping bail, Sky hides out in Thailand while searching for his father (Blackie Ko), now a disabled barber. Black Tone agrees to train Sky to get revenge—his first lesson in driving fast consisting of removing the brakes and speedometer! But in Sky's absence, Fung goads Paddy into a grudge race, and Nancy fetches Sky back to HK to save her brother's life. But they're too late, and Sky has one more life to avenge in a nitro-burning death race with Fung.

The precision stunt racing scenes are genuinely thrilling, and would have been impossible on busy Hong Kong roads if not abetted by CGI f/x. After a fast start, the film slows down considerably during the second act in Thailand, with only a brief bike race to remind us that this is a racing movie. Paddy's race isn't even shown, lessening the impact of his death. However, the slow sequences add depth to the situation and characters, making the big race at the end all the more exciting. Will Ekin Cheng forever play characters named to recall his role in *Storm Riders*? Though Shaw Brothers stars David Chiang and Blackie Ko are both good, they ought to have traded roles, as Ekin Cheng looks a lot more like stepdad Chiang. In Hong Kong this was released as a sequel to the Andy Lau racing movie *Full Throttle*. **AKA:** *Lit Feng Chin Che 2 Gik Chuk Chuen Suet; Lie Huo Zhan Che 2 Ji Su Chuan Shui.* 🐉🐉🐉

1999 109m/C *HK* Ekin Cheng, Cecilia Cheung, Simon Yam, Blackie Ko, Patrick Tam, Kelly Lin, Moses Chan, David Chiang, Jerry Lamb, Stephanie Che, Ha Ping, Benjamin Yuen, Samuel Leung. **D:** Andrew Lau. **W:** Manfred Wong. **C:** Andrew Lau. **M:** Comfort Chan. **VHS, DVD**

Legend of the Dinosaurs

Toei Studios attempted to use their giant monster special effects to create a *Jaws*-style thriller. While hiking at the foot of Mount Fuji, Makiko Takami falls through the ground into a frozen cavern and sees a giant egg hatching. Geologist Ashizawa (Tsunehiko Watase) rushes to the site, believing that the discovery of the dinosaur egg will substantiate his father's work. A lot of snakes have been seen coming out of the mountain, and lots of livestock is missing.

Knocked unconscious by an earth tremor while exploring, Ashizawa is rescued by his father's old guide Muku Shohei, who still lives in a cabin on the mountain. Ashizawa and Takami come across a butchered horse in the misty woods around Lake Sai, which later finds its way into a tree. The next day, a huge lake monster threatens to ruin the Dragon Festival, temporarily interrupting the country music of guest star Akira Moroguchi. The terror becomes personal when the monsterous elasmosaurus eats Takami's roommate Yuko. Though officials are still unsure that the monster exists, they nonetheless pepper the lake with depth charges just to make sure. Just for fun, a huge pterodactyl appears to pterrorize the town. Of course, the two prehistoric creatures from the Mesozoic (neither of which are dinosaurs) are natural enemies, and engage in a life-or-death struggle that can only be broken up by a volcanic eruption.

The special effects aren't so bad, and an attempt is made to create some atmosphere, but any good qualities the movie has are ruined by the dull characters and sluggish pace. At one point Takami decides to follow scuba-diving Ichizawa into the lake to warn him about the explosives, but drives all the way home to get her diving equipment first. Wouldn't it have made sense for her to already have it handy—if only to help speed up the film? The out-of-place funk and light jazz theme music doesn't help. **AKA:** *Kyoryu Kaicho no Desenso; Legend of Dinosaurs and Monster Birds.* 🐉

1977 92m/C *JP* Tsunehiko Watase, Nobiko Sawa, Shotako Hayashi, Tomoko Kiyoshima, Fuyukichi Maki, David Freedman, Maureen Peacock, Catharine Laub, Hiroshi Nawa, Kinji Nakamura, Masataka Iwao, Goro Oki, Yusuke Tsukasa, Yukio Miyagi. **D:** Junji Kurata. **W:** Masaru Igami, Isao Matsumoto, Ichiro Otsu. **C:** Sakuji Shiomi. **M:** Masao Yagi. **VHS**

Legend of the Dragon

Stephen Chow follows his successful formula again by playing a country bumpkin with a secret skill who meets his big challenge in the big city, with a shifty best friend who turns out to have his heart in the right place at the end. Chow Siu-lung (Chow) is the lazy and impish son of stern landowner Master Chow Fei-hung (Yuen Wah) on the little island of Tai O. Though Master Chow insists on traditional kung fu practice from his son and student Mo (Teresa Mo), Lung's great passion is playing snooker. Chow's old colleague Yun (Leung Kar-yan) comes to visit from Hong Kong, though his real purpose is to hide out from a loan shark (Lung Fong) to whom he owes a million HK dollars. Yun is a loan

shark himself, but doesn't have the mean streak—or the muscle—necessary to make it pay. Chow loans Yun $5000 on condition he take Lung to Hong Kong with him and get the boy out of his hair.

Their first night in town, Lung has to bring his fighting skills into play to save them from a debt-collecting thug (Shing Fui-on). Yun sets Lung up in a snooker game as a distraction so he can get out of a fix, but finds instead that the lad is a genius at the game, and they're soon making a fortune—until Lung finds out Yun has been betting on him. Lung returns to Tai O, but the gangsters force Yun to get Chow Fei-hung to put up his land in a game against foreign champ Jimmy White (as himself). Nervous when he finds out about the bet, Lung plays horribly, and before long the villains are evicting all Chow's tenants. However, it turns out that Mo's Granduncle (Lee Hoi-sang) owns a stretch of land vital to the gang's plans, and it's decided to gamble everything on one rematch to try to win the land back.

Though an uncharacteristic project for Danny Lee as director (just before *Dr. Lamb!*), this is another solid Chow comedy, with his hilarious nonsense mixed evenly with just enough drama and suspense. There's also some fine kung fu choreographed by Corey Yuen and Yuen Wah—who is perfectly cast as the martial arts patriarch. Just as important is the choreography on the snooker table, with Chow doing many of his own trick shots—though it's unknown how many takes were filmed for each shot. Tellingly, the end-credit outtakes show White making the final miracle shot as is if he could sink them all day. *AKA: Lung Dik Chuen Yan; Long De Chuan Ren; Legend of Dragon.* 🦴🦴🦴

1991 91m/C *HK* Stephen Chow, Leung Kar-yan, Teresa Mo, Yuen Wah, Lee Hoi-sang, Lung Fong, Shing Fui-on, Jimmy White, Amy Yip, Corey Yuen, Parkman Wong, Ricky Yi. **D:** Danny Lee. **W:** Law Kam-fai. **C:** Abdul M. Rumjahn. **M:** Phil Chan. **VHS, DVD**

Legend of the Dragonslayer Sword

In the closing years of the Yuen Dynasty, the government has become corrupt, and factions vie for control of the Dragonslayer sword—a big-ass blade with both mystical and political significance. Walking a heroic line between the factions is Steven Cheung (Ma Ching-tao), a Wu Tang warrior. He saves Susan Yen (Cecilia Yip), a member of a rival clan—the Eagle Cult—from a duel with her jealous rival brother (though Steven does not know they are siblings at the

time) and the two become friends. Susan's father captures Steven in an attempt to force the two to marry. They put it off, but this only leads Susan's clan into further conflict with Wu Tang. In the fighting, Steven's brother Sam is badly wounded. Again Steven is unaware of the duplicity of Susan's family. Eventually, Steven and Susan do fall in love and are shipwrecked on a desert island (with the mad master of the sword—Lion King Jackson). They have a baby named Woody (who stars in the second film in the series) who grows up on the isolated isle. When the lovers return to the mainland, the revelation of deep secrets leads to a final confrontation between the clans.

Shot on video, this epic appears to be a cut-down version of a much longer story—probably a kung fu soap opera from the Chinese Metropolitan Network (with all the "boring" parts edited out). As such it has enough plot and action for a half dozen other movies. In fact, the above summary only scratches the surface of the many story elements. The film relentlessly cuts from one apparently unrelated scene to another—though, by paying close attention, one can eventually piece together most of the plot. The dubbing on the movie is almost laughably bad, but this (and the Anglo names of the protagonists) just add to the film's goofy charm. The cheesy effects and fight scenes are fun as well. Though some of the costumes, sets, and scenery look impressive, clearly the whole thing was done on a shoestring TV budget. But, like many videotape kung fu flicks, it's just so damn much fun! —SS 🦴🦴🦴

1990 91m/C *CH* Ma Ching-tao, Cecilia Yip, Lau Tan. **D:** Norman Law. **W:** Louis Cha. **M:** Norman Law. **VHS, DVD**

Legend of the Dragonslayer Sword 2—The Rising Son

The Rising Son picks up several years after the end of *Legend of the Dragonslayer Sword.* Woody (Ma Ching-tao), son of Steven and Susan, has grown up learning the ways of kung fu with the Wu Tang masters in their remote mountain home. Longing to leave, he discovers a book of mystical kung fu techniques, and masters them. He becomes embroiled with the mad monk Simon Sing, and his plan to destroy the six clans by pitting them against each other. Woody decides to oppose Sing, and save his friends and their people.

He fights his friend Gina (a supporting player in the first film and star of the third) and wins despite being wounded. Just when it seems the clans might unite, they are threatened by Judy (Cecilia Yip)—and her plans to poison everyone. Pretending to be part of the Ming clan, Judy brings her people to Wu Tang, but Woody destroys them. He gains the magical "human glue" formula to restore his uncle (who was crippled in the first film) to health. It turns out Judy is part of a Mongolian plot to destroy the six clans, but she's in love with Woody.

Gina becomes head of the Ming clan, and discovers the secret of the Dragonslayer sword: an ancient kung fu scroll is hidden within the great blade. The six clans fight the Mongols. Woody, Judy, and Sharon (who also loves Woody) go to find Lion King Jackson and the sword, and Gina follows them to the remote island. Conflicts escalate and Sharon is revealed to be head of a group of Persian assassins. She forsakes her love for Woody to exit the series and lead her clan. Many conflicts remain to be solved in the final installment of the saga.

Like the first film in this "trilogy," *The Rising Son* is a shot-on-video epic that is part of a much longer story line. The good folks at Jalisco Films have cut out all the "boring" parts (which might also hold the story together) and given us just enough of a plot to almost make sense. The characters would probably be more engaging if they weren't going from one jump-cut scene to another, sometimes unrelated one. Still, this series is interesting for its scope, costumes, and just plain weirdness. We've got all sorts of odd-ball kung fu stuff, including the infamous "King Kong fist," as well as pressure point hocus-pocus, chi power magic, and various poisons and "human glues." The dubbing is marginal at best, though at least the Westernized names help a bit in keeping track of the massive cast. However, characters come and go with amazing rapidity. A fun change of pace for kung fu fans, though it would be more interesting to see the complete source material. —SS 🐕🐕

1990 /C CH Ma Ching-tao, Cecilia Yip. **VHS, DVD**

Legend of the Dragonslayer Sword 3—The Rage of Gina

While Lion King Jackson and Woody (Ma Ching-tao) sleep a poisoned sleep (clay dough poison), Gina (Mei Chowai) uses the Sword of Heaven to shatter the Dragonslayer sword and gain the secret kung fu scrolls hidden within the blade. Gina is discovered by Judy (Cecilia Yip) and Julia. Gina kills Julia and pushes Judy off a cliff. When Woody wakes, he discovers the dead girl, and believes that Judy is behind the havoc. He and

Gina become engaged, and return to the mainland from Jackson's island. The clan wars continue, with Woody and Gina caught in the middle. Judy, recovered from her wounds, returns and tells Woody of Gina's duplicity. The temple at Wudan is poisoned by Samuel, who covets Gina. Judy and Gina fight, but Woody steps between them. Woody abandons Gina at the altar to help Lion King Jackson, who has been kidnapped by their enemies. Gina hooks up with Samuel, and marries him to spite Woody. She and Samuel trade evil kung fu secrets, as Gina's magic drives her further into madness. Woody and Judy go to Shaolin to help Jackson, and must fight a tournament to rescue him. Gina and Samuel show up, and Gina ends up accidentally killing her new husband. Simon Sing and Jackson have a final confrontation, as Gina plots to regain Woody. She fights him, and eventually must fight the master of Wu Tang. Will Gina's rage carry the day, or will she learn her lesson? Will Woody and Judy marry? Will any new characters pop up only to suddenly disappear for good a scene later?

Like the other films in this series, *The Rage of Gina* has enough story lines for any three or four other movies. It totters constantly on the edge of incoherence, pushed along by frenetic jump cuts and the elimination of any slower scenes that might make the movie more comprehensible. Still, like the first two films, it has a goofy logic all its own and—in a grand sense—can be figured out, even though many individual scenes are completely baffling. The copy on the back of the box cover makes more sense than the film itself does. Jalisco does its usual goofy job with the names and the dubbing. Like the first two installments of the series, this film can be fun for connoisseurs—though it's probably not the film to get your friends into kung fu flicks. —SS 🐕🐕

1990 /C CH Ma Ching-tao, Cecilia Yip, Mei Chowai, Lau Tan. **D:** Norman Law. **W:** Louis Cha. **M:** Norman Law. **VHS, DVD**

Legend of the Drunken Master

After a period when U.S. theatrical re-releases of his old hits had begun to slip at the boxoffice, Jackie Chan had another big hit with the Hollywood-made *Shanghai Noon*. This led directly to 1994's *Drunken Master 2* being given a small theatrical release under the name *Legend of the Drunken Master*. The re-title is understandable, considering the length of time between the original and the sequel. This is considered by many to be Chan's best movie, and some even hold that it's the best martial arts film ever made. Many who have seen this movie in the theatre and on video dozens of times never tire of it.

Chan again assays the role of the young Wong Fei-hung, a real-life physician and cultural hero at the beginning of the 20th century. There have been movies about this character going back to the 1920s in China—up through the hit *Once upon a Time in China* series. Chan first played Wong in 1979 and it made him a star. This was one of the few times that Master Wong's controversial "drunken fist" style—in which the user's liquidity, strength, and stamina increase with the use of alcohol—was exploited. Here, 15 years later, he plays the character only slightly older—and pulls it off pretty well.

The years have hardly slowed him down, and have just made him more creative. The plot—plenty relevant in the years before the reunification—concerns how Wong discovers a conspiracy by British officials (and their local cronies) to steal hundreds of precious Chinese artifacts. This brings him into violent conflict with the conspirators, and leads him to again adopt his drunken boxing ways (after promising his father he wouldn't). The various conflicts are finally resolved in a huge battle in a steel plant.

The film certainly features some of the most amazing kung fu fights ever filmed. It's also one of Chan's funniest pictures (mostly due to the presence of Anita Mui as Wong's young step-mom), and even the drama works for the most part. But the fights are the real reason you should NOT miss this film.

The surprisingly well-dubbed English version presents the film pretty much intact. The only real noticeable difference—outside of new music cues—is that they go out of their way to remind everyone to drink responsibly and that "many drunken boxers become alcoholics." This P.C. attitude is most noticeable at the end, when "Uncle Bill" Tung is told that Fei-hung is still recovering from his drinking and can't join the victory party. In the Chinese version, the scene continues with Chan apparently a mental cripple from drinking grain alcohol—and it's played for laughs! *AKA: Jui Kuen II; Drunken Master II; Sui Ken 2; Zui Quan II.* 🎵🎵🎵🎵

1994 (R) 102m (US 99m)/C HK Jackie Chan, Bill Tung, Anita Mui, Ti Lung, Lau Kar-Leung, Felix Wong, Ken Lo, Ho Sung Pak, Andy Lau, Chin Ka-Lok, Jimmy Liu, Lau Siu-ming, Suki Kwan, Pak Yan, Louis Roth, Mark Houghton, Wong San, Tai Bo, Cheung Chi-gwong, Hon Yee Sang, Yvonne Yung, Alan Chan, William Duen, Pao Fong, Shut Ma Wa Lung, Chan Tat-kwong, Cheung

Wa, Wong Ming-sing, Mars, Bill Tung, To Pak Kwong, Hsu Hsia, Vindy Chan, Anthony Carpio. **D:** Lau Kar-Leung, Jackie Chan. **W:** Edward Tang, Man-Ming Tong, Yuen Kai-chi. **C:** Tony Cheung, Nico Wong, Cheung Yiu-cho, Jingle Ma. **M:** William Woo, Michael Wandmacher (U.S. version). **VHS, DVD**

Legend of the Drunken Tiger

Yet another entry in the early 1990s kung fu movie revival, this one was designed to cash in on Jackie Chan's *Legend of the Drunken Master*. In 1898, the hard-line old guard inside the Ching government has the leaders of the reform movement executed, while pacifying invading foreign influences. Martial arts master Drunken Cheong San (Tsang Sze-Man) is outraged, and his assassination attempts have General Rong Lu (Ku Feng) scared of his own shadow. Leela Wong (Kara Hui) and her servant Little Jade disguise themselves as boys to go shopping in the market district, but join San in defending a girl named Yu-lan accused of being a rebel from Master Yan and his men. The fight is at a stalemate until Master Leung steps forward and whips Yan with his superior kung fu. Yu-lan's father Yu Chi-wan is arrested, but court official Wong helps arrange his release. When the rebels visit to thank him, it's found that his daughter Leela was betrothed to San when they were children, leading to much discomfort. Yu-lan is captured to set a trap for San, but he manages to rescue her. While recuperating from a gunshot wound, San grows closer to Yu-lan, who doesn't mind his drinking. In 1900, an alliance of foreigners invades Peking, while the weak Empress Dowager flees. When Yu-lan is killed by treacherous Ching forces, San takes up the fight to help bring honor back to China.

With only mediocre fighting and not much personality, Cheong San doesn't make the grade as a legendary hero. Kara Hui steals the show with her charisma, as well as her graceful and acrobatic fight scenes. The episodic plot also serves to fray interest. Budgetary strains show up frequently—most of the foreign invaders are played by Chinese in funny wigs, and the soundtrack seems to have been recorded with a tiny Casio keyboard. **AKA:** *Jiu Hap Hung; Ziu Xia Xing.* 🐉

1992 93m/C *TW* Tsang Sze-Man, Kara Hui, Ku Feng, Wang Chen-chao, Lee Xing, Stella Lau. **D:** Robert Tai. **W:** Cindy Lee. **C:** Tommy Tong. **M:** Wilson Chow. **VHS, DVD**

Legend of the Eight Samurai

Lord Motofuji (Yuki Meguro) and Lady Tamazusa (Mari Natsuki) are evil undead sorcerers looking to wipe out their ancient rivals, the Sotomi clan, which has nearly been exterminated by the wizards and their minions. One of the last survivors is Princess Shizu (Hiroko Yakushimaru), and she holds the key to defeating the evil lord and lady. During the course of the film, the princess assembles a retinue of loyal samurai. These men and women are reincarnations of the spirit of the Shizu clan. The spirit was split into eight parts (represented by eight crystals) when a legendary Sotomi princess died at the hands of darkness. The princess and her retainers must navigate a slew of obstacles, monsters, and supernatural menaces before they can finally confront the evil Lord and Lady. Complications arise when Shizumi falls for a young, ne'er-do-well vagabond, and one of the princess's retainers gets taken in by the seductive Lady Tamazusa. By the time the final battle at the castle of evil rolls around, the amount of bloodshed and swordplay should satisfy all but the most jaded gore fans. The flick is unflinchingly brutal and violent in the treatment of its characters (practically a Japanese cinematic tradition).

Great costumes, beautiful sets, and good cinematography highlight this film. The movie is melodramatic and episodic, and probably overly long—but it's still quite a lot of fun. The swordplay is good, and there are dollops of magic, monsters, and SFX. Try to ignore the syrupy score and inevitable pop songs. Sonny Chiba spends most of the time with his face hidden behind a costume veil in this flick, so don't expect to see much of the Street Fighter's trademark scowl. Like many films dubbed after the popular *Shogun* series appeared on American TV, the English translation of this film seems to confuse "ninja" with "samurai." Some dubbing studios seemed to think that a ninja was just an ultra-cool samurai in black pajamas. (In fact, ninja and samurai are at opposite ends of the honor and nobility scale. To call a samurai a ninja in ancient Japan would undoubtedly cost you your life.) Marketing surely encouraged this trend, following the belief that putting "ninja" or "shogun" in the title would sell a cheesy film. If you pick this up on a double DVD—with *Shogun's Ninja* as the second feature—you get to see both words misused for the price of one. —*SS* **AKA:** *Satomi Hakken-den.* 🐉🐉🐉

1984 (PG) 133m/C *JP* Sonny Chiba, Sue Shiomi, Kenji Ohba, Hiroko Yakushimaru, Henry Sanada, Yuki Meguro, Mari Natsuki, Mikio Narita, Minori Terada. **D:** Kinji Fukasaku, Haruki Kadokawa. **W:** Toshio Kamata, Kinji Fukasaku. **C:** Seizo Sengen. **M:** Joey Carbone, Richie Zito. **VHS, DVD**

Legend of the Flying Swordsman

What was supposed to be a happy day at Flying Dagger Security is ruined. Chun-foon (Dave

"General, that's not blood— you've peed in your pants!"

—A lieutenant reassures Ku Feng in *Legend of the Drunken Tiger*

Wong), the son of the owner Mr. Lee (Sonny Chiba), did the right thing and proposed to his pregnant girlfriend Snow (Gigi Lai), but the bridal procession arrives to find the groom falling-down drunk. Chun-foon continues to drink for a week after the wedding, spending every evening at Dragon Town Inn, where he met his bride. He keeps on drinking until his son is born. Finally, Old Master Lee manages to rouse his son from his stupor, and Chun-foon goes to work for the escort company. He also throws around a lot of vows to give up drinking and be a good husband. But it may be too late, as Snow has already fallen for the weirdo with a big drum that killed her horse for no given reason. Ready to start life anew, Chun-foon heads off on his first job, escorting treasure to Cheung Pak Mountain. On his first day, his men are defeated by women wearing poisoned perfume, and Chun-foon is blindsided. The blow knocks him silly, and while he struggles to recover his memory, a simple mountain beauty (Shiri Na) cares for him. The still-amnesiac Lee Chun-foon makes his way home, but finds the place in ruins. He's told his Korean neighbor Kim Mo-hon—and Snow's boyfriend—was seen at the Lees' that day, and Chun-foon heads off to claim his revenge.

Not so much a swordplay fantasy film as an extended music video, *Legend of the Flying Swordsman* is beset by tedious ballads and sappy soap opera throughout. We get hints along the way that various characters are supposed to be superior martial artists, but the film is too caught up in its own melodrama to offer much action until the climax. By the time Dave Wong and his spiky-haired Korean opponent start spinning around through the air, there's been one power ballad too many. The big superpowered martial arts duel has some neat effects going for it, and the ending features some clever multi-tragic twists, but by then it's far too late. Wong looks kind of silly in the frosted hair fashionable with swordplay heroes since *Storm Riders*. *AKA: Siu Lee Fei Diy Ji Fei Diy Ngoi Chuen; Xiao Li Fei Dao Zhi Fei Dao Wai Chuan.* 🐋 ♥️

2000 88m/C *HK* Dave Wong, Gigi Lai, Sonny Chiba, Shiri Na, Law Chung-ha, Lee Yu-yuen, Chung Ji-yau. **D:** Bosco Lam. **W:** Peter Cheung, Bosco Lam. **C:** Ham Nam-sub. **VHS, DVD**

Legend of the Mountain

Interesting if minor entry from legendary director King Hu *(Come Drink with Me)*. He Qingyun (Shih Chun) is a scholar in need of a hideaway so that he can complete the translation of several holy manuscripts. He visits a temple and is given a room by the solitary monk who lives there. Madame Wang (Rainbow Hsu) insists on preparing a meal for the honored guest. A talkative and pushy lady, she worked for the general who formerly resided in the temple. That evening, He Qingyun is introduced to Madame Wang's daughter, Mandy (Hsu Feng). Mandy is beautiful, but there is something otherworldly about her that ties into the title of the movie. She also turns out to have an incredibly fierce personality. After a drunken night, He Qingyun and Mandy wake up together and are forced to marry. He Qingyun learns that the "legend of the mountain" is very real. A neighboring woman (Sylvia Chang) tries to help, as does another holy man.

For much of the running time the pace of the film is quite slow, measured, and, frankly, boring. The compositions are framed beautifully and the landscapes are lovely, but it's a real challenge to stay awake. Two or three sequences near the end are quite dazzling to the eye and well worth watching, as the supernatural elements of the legend are brought to life. Yet it's too little too late. It doesn't help that scholar He Qingyun is such a reactive character. Having such a pallid personality at the center of the story leaves a hole in the drama. —PM *AKA: Saan Chung Chuen Kei; Shan Zhong Chuan Ji.* 🐋 ♥️

1979 112m/C *HK* Shih Chun, Hsu Feng, Sylvia Chang, Rainbow Hsu, Tin Fung, Ng Ming Choi, Tung Lam, Wu Chia Hsiang, Chan Wai Lau, Sun Yueh. **D:** King Hu. **W:** Chung Ling. **C:** Henry Chan. **M:** Wu Dai-jiang, King Ng-tai. **DVD**

Legend of the 7 Golden Vampires

This is the perfect film to introduce you to Chinese horror. *7 Golden Vampires* came out back in 1974, co-produced by England's Hammer Studios, makers of gothic brilliance, and Hong Kong's immortal Shaw Brothers. It was meant to be the first of a series of movies in which vampire slayer Van Helsing (Peter Cushing) goes around the globe killing the vampires of the world. Didn't happen. But this one did, and what a wacky thing it must have seemed to audiences who had never seen kung fu horror before.

Dracula (John Forbes-Robertson), according to this movie, went to China to found a cult of seven vampires (hopping vampires, in fact) who wear golden masks. Van Helsing is lecturing in the east and is recruited by Hsi Ching (Shaw kung fu star David Chiang) to help him and his six siblings to go take back the night. Cushing is great, as always, but who needs him in this movie? The real stars are David Chiang and his six brothers and one sister, each of whom specializes in a different martial arts weapon. Sister Mai Kwei (Shih Szu) is the favorite, playing knick-knack on fast-moving kung-fu zombies with her sparkling silver

sai. Second favorite is the brother with the silver battle-axes. Would Hollywood ever make a movie like this? Are you kidding? The new DVD, by the way, comes with a bonus, if you care to call it that: the entire *Seven Brothers Meet Dracula*, the really awful 89-minute American cut of the film, edited down to eliminate plot and even, for some reason, some of the kung fu. Skim it for enlightenment as to how not to release a picture, but watch *The Legend of the 7 Golden Vampires* for a look at a truly bizarre melding of Eastern and Western horror. —JH **AKA:** *Chat Gam Shut; Qi Jin Shi; The 7 Brothers Versus Dracula; The 7 Brothers and a Sister Meet Dracula; The 7 Brothers of Dracula; The 7 Golden Vampires; Dracula and the Seven Golden Vampires; Last Warning; Seven Brothers Meet Dracula; Seven Golden Vampires: The Last Warning.* 🦴🦴🦴

1974 (R) 110/89m/C *HK/UK* Peter Cushing, David Chiang, Julie Ege, Robin Stewart, Shih Szu, John Forbes-Robertson, Robert Hanna, Chan Shen, James Ma, Fung Hark-On, Lau Wai-ling, Lau Kar-Wing, Wang Han-chen, Chan Tin-lung, Tino Wong, Wong Pau-gei, Lo Wei, Yam Sai-kwoon. **D:** Roy Ward Baker. **W:** Don Houghton. **C:** John Wilcox, Roy Ford. **M:** James Bernard. **VHS, DVD**

The Legend of the Swordsman

Fennie Yuen returns as Blue Phoenix for this sequel to *Swordsman,* but almost everything else has changed. Cost overruns, which drove the original into the red, prompted producer Tsui Hark to scale back production on the sequel as much as possible, and replace the cast for the returning characters. Most significantly, Sam Hui was replaced in the lead role of Ling Wu-chung with the much more dynamic Jet Li, who had just become a Hong Kong superstar via his portrayal of the legendary Wong Fei-hung in *Once upon a Time in China.* The other great standout role belongs to Brigitte Lin as Master Invincible Asia of the rebellious Sun Moon Sect, who has castrated himself to gain supernatural power from a sacred scroll, and as a result is gradually changing into a woman. Asia recruits Japanese ninja warriors Hattori (Waise Lee) and Saru (Chin Ka-Lok), who have been operating as pirates along the coast of China since being driven out of their homeland by Emperor Toyotomi. Using a combination of bribery, captured firearms, and supernatural swordplay, Asia plans to conquer all of China.

A golden-masked ghoul makes his move in the HK/British co-production *Legend of the 7 Golden Vampires.*

He/she crosses paths with Ling on the way to attacking a platoon of Emperor Soon's soldiers, spilling his wine and killing the horse of sidekick Kiddo (Michelle Reis, so much taller than Cecilia Yip in the role that even the other characters comment on it). Ling has decided to retire from the Martial Arts World and live on Ox Mountain, but still dreams of Chief Ying (Rosamund Kwan). Ying is having her own problems with Asia's ninjas, who have come to challenge her powerful whip—and Blue Phoenix's pet snakes—to take over leadership of the Sect. Ling and his Wah Mountain Clan comrades find Ying to be missing and her men massacred, and go to look for her. Ling comes upon Asia while he/she is practicing his/her elemental magic, and he/she shares a flirtatious and anonymous drink of wine with him. Reunited with Ying that night, Ling vows to help her find her father Master Wu (Yam Sai-kwoon), whose disappearance began the Sun Moon power struggle. Sneaking into Asia's camp to look for Wu, Ling finds himself inadvertently defending his enemy from treacherous Saru's invading ninjas. After an evening of odd romance, Ling is captured, but he and Wu team up to escape from the dungeon. His followers find the returning Wu a changed man. He has become mad for revenge and power, and has secretly secured the sacred scroll. Inevitably, colossal internal and external conflicts erupt when Ling discovers his worst enemy is his dream girl, and his friend's father has become a destructive monster.

So it's not the most coherent of films—Tsui Hark's team creates magnificent spectacle. The superpowered fight scenes, in which characters toss trees at each other and crush others with a touch, are the most incredible ever filmed up until that time, easily outclassing the likes of *Batman* and *Superman 2*. Hey, who needs guns when you can throw needles through steel? Plus, it all takes place within stunningly atmospheric images. Poor Jet Li can't contribute more than his screen presence to the part, and one of his few love scenes takes place without his character even knowing who he's with. Fortunately we don't have to hear him sing the *Swordsman* theme song "Hero of Heroes." Lin steals the show, treading the line between angel and devil. A Taiwanese release of the film runs a couple minutes longer, while the official U.S. release is missing a full eight minutes. More swordplay action—along with gender and casting confusion—would follow in the conclusion of the *Swordsman* trilogy, *The East Is Red*. **AKA:** *Siu Ngo Gong Woo Ji Dung Fong Bat Baai; Xiao Ao Jiang Hu Zhi Dong Fang Bu Bai; Swordsman 2.* ♫♫♫

1992 (R) 108m/C *HK* Jet Li, Brigitte Lin, Michelle Reis, Rosamund Kwan, Yam Sai-kwoon, Lau Shun, Fennie Yuen, Candy Yu, Waise Lee, Chin Ka-Lok, Cheung Kwok-leung, Karel Wong, Andrew Kam. **D:** Ching Siu-Tung. **W:** Tsui Hark, Chan Tin-suen, Elsa Tang, Louis Cha (novel). **C:** Tom Lau. **M:** Richard Yuen. **VHS, DVD**

Legendary Couple

When Ko Tin-lap (Simon Yam) is delivering his company's funds to the bank, robbers strike, and Ko is the prime suspect. While an extremely diarrheic Ko is grilled by the cops, his pregnant wife goes into premature labor, and though the baby is saved, a case of heart disease claims the mother's life. You might be surprised to learn that this is supposed to be a comedy! They say that "Comedy is hard...," and here's a movie that proves the point, as it should be hard for anyone to sit through it. Without any proof of guilt, Ko's boss Lui Yau-choi fires him anyway, refusing to even pay the pension he's owed. Desperate for funds to pay for his son's operation, Ko impulsively kidnaps Lui's spoiled daughter Chi-lan (Chingmy Yau) and goes on the run. During an attempt to catch Ko when he picks up the ransom, Detective Chan Sam (Vincent Wan) shoots a bystander, then frames Ko for murder. Chi-lan is distraught to discover her father's greed, and her loyalty shifts to Ko. They start committing robberies in earnest to support themselves and the baby.

To be fair, the aim here is for *black* comedy in the vein of *Something Wild*. However, the film's missteps are too numerous to count. One hilarious gag has Chingmy Yau smashing a guy's hands with a bottle. In a following sequence, Simon Yam tries to get his premature son in the hospital, finding him not in any kind of intensive care, but among a group of other infants, all of whom look at least a month old. We're shown guitar and bass troubadours in a restaurant, but the soundtrack plays a brass version of "Cabaret"! They hide out at Ko's island cabin, but the police take forever to trace them there. It's good to see these stars in anything, particularly with Yam playing this unusual sad-sack role, but their charisma is wasted on the material. Interestingly, Danny Boyle's 1997 *A Life Less Ordinary* followed a similar story line, with Ewan MacGregor and Cameron Diaz coming off slightly better. **AKA:** *Ngoh Si Yat Goh Chaak; Wo Shi Yi Ge Zei; Story of a Robber.* ♫

1995 82m/C *HK* Simon Yam, Chingmy Yau, Vincent Wan, Yuen King-Tan, Tam Suk-mooi, Stuart Ong, Chan Chi-fai. **D:** Peter Ngor. **W:** Nam Yin, Candy Chen. **C:** Johnny Koo, Kwong Ting-wo. **M:** Mak Chun-hung. **VHS**

The Legendary Strike

Yes, we all remember the violent riots following the Pennsylvania steel workers walkout in 1892,

but this Wong Fung *(When Taekwondo Strikes)* kung fu extravaganza has nothing to do with that. Ching Dynasty Prince Yung (Carter Wong) hires a Japanese warrior to take the Buddha's Relic—a pearl of great price (that produces a sting of harp music every time it appears, or is even mentioned)—to its new owners in Japan. A Shaolin monk (Mars) objects to the sale of the holy Buddhist object to foreigners, and kills the samurai to get it. But the monk is a fake named Ko Fung, sent to get the pearl back for Yung, and a real Shaolin (Kam Kong) appears and kills him for it. But Ko swallows the pearl before he dies, and Ming rebel Tan Shi-er (Casanova Wong) slips away with the body. Unable to beat Tan in combat, the monk tags along with him on the way to collect his reward. Another samurai comes looking for his brother, and finds his body. All end up in an inn for the night, and in the morning, the coffins are switched. When the monk and the Ching official Lord Min (Chan Sing) catch up with the samurai, they find foxy fighter Miss Chin Lan (Angela Mao) taking the corpse's place. Poisoned by a guard's darts in a fight, Lan flees, and Tan saves her life. Lan is working with Korean agents who have stolen Ko's body, and the two form an uneasy alliance against the Chings. Troops are called in to hold the local villagers hostage to get the body back, and the Koreans promise to give Tan just three days before they turn over the corpse.

There's entirely too much talk and intrigue going on, but eventually all the players' alliances and identities are revealed, and everyone chooses partners for the kung fu dance. Unfortunately, the action doesn't justify the intricate build up. After making a good show as the dishonest monk, poor Mars spends most of the film playing a rotting corpse. Frankie Chan's score is quite spectacular—unless it was stolen from another movie. **AKA:** *Long Ji Yat Chiu; Lang Zi Yi Zhao; A Fist Too Fast; Iron Maiden.* 🎵🐉

1978 89m/C *HK* Carter Wong, Angela Mao, Chan Sing, Casanova Wong, Kam Kong, Mars, Li Ying Ying, Cheung Ying, Yeung Wai, Chan Lung, Cheung Ging Boh. **D:** Wong Fung. **W:** Ku Lung. **M:** Frankie Chan. **VHS, DVD**

Legendary Weapons of China

The legendary Lau brothers of China here pool their talents to produce one of the last great theatrical releases from the legendary Shaw Brothers. Lei Kung has been sent by the Yi Ho Society to Yunnan to set up a new branch there, spreading their power and knowledge of pugilism and magic. But word comes to Master Li Lien-ying (Wong Ching Ho) and Master Ti (Walter Cho) of the Mao Shang Clan that Lei Kung has dissolved

his branch, bringing dishonor to the whole clan. Three assassins are sent separately on suicide missions to kill Lei Kung: Taoist sorcerer Lei Ying (Lau Kar-Wing), bulletproof kung fu killer Ti Tan (Gordon Lau), and professional hit man Tieh Hon (Hsiao Ho). Other characters who show up in Guangdong are crazy con man Wu Mao (Alexander Fu Sheng), firewood salesman Tien Kung-yu (Lau Kar-Leung), and former Yi Ho clansman Fang Shao-ching (Kara Hui). Those after Lei Kung don't know each other and begin covertly battling each other while trying to expose someone with Lei Kung's skills.

When Ti Tan checks into the inn, he finds Fang and Tieh Hon scrambling around in the rafters, imitating cats to try to fool him. Tieh Hon, in the guise of a government envoy, immediately suspects the woodcutter is really Lei Kung. Lei Ying hires Wu to impersonate Lei Kung, putting on a show of clowning and trickery with his pals to fake Yi Ho magic and lure the real Lei Kung into the open. But Wu's show only draws the other assassins, and the disguised Tien Kung-yu/Lei Kung uses his voodoo magic to have Wu fight Tieh Hon for him. After taking a dip in a cesspool during this fight, Tieh Hon falls ill, but continues to target Yu the woodsman, whom Fang is also convinced is Lei Kung when he finds a complete set of legendary weapons hidden in the man's barn. However, Fang is actually sympathetic to Lei Kung, who was ordered by the empress with the impossible task of training bulletproof warriors to fight the foreigners in China, and vows to help him. She (he's really a girl!) gets Kung to nurse Tieh Hon back to health, and the three of them face off against Ti Tan's kung fu sorcery. But which side will Kung's brother Lei Ying take, and will Tieh Hon still stick by Kung's side once he learns his true identity?

All this deception and a proliferation of characters makes for a confusing first hour or so, especially across the span of translation. It's even more confusing since Lau Kar-Wing and Kar-Leung look so much alike—a resemblance that even fools some of the characters. But once underway, the fantastic agility and imagination of the performers carries the show. Added entertainment comes in the various magic spells and other gimmicks mixed into the action. Has anyone ever been fooled by Kara Hui in male drag? It's much easier to believe that the Laus can really fly—and their movies could be submitted as evidence. Unlike most martial arts performers, the Laus have a lifetime of practice together to rely on, and can really look like they're trying to hit each other. By the final confrontation using all the legendary weapons, you won't want anyone to win and finish the fight. **AKA:** *Sap Baat Boon Saam Ngai; Shi Ba Ban San Yi; Legendary Weapons of Kung Fu; New Legendary Weapons of China; 18 Legendary Weapons of China.* 🎵🎵🎵🐉

1982 104m/C *HK* Lau Kar-Leung, Lau Kar-Wing, Gordon Lau, Hsiao Ho, Kara Hui, Alexander Fu Sheng, Wong Ching Ho, Walter Cho, Ging Chue. *D:* Lau Kar-Leung. *W:* Lau Kar-Leung, Li Tai-hang. **VHS, DVD**

Leopard Hunting

Police raids in Hong Kong, Tokyo, and Manila find suspects carrying Columbian and various Asian passports, alerting Interpol that something big is going on. Soon after, Asian financial markets are in chaos. Fang Kuo-ho (Yuen Wah) fears that a group of international buyers is out to take over his company, Fang's Group, and recalls his sons Chin-tao (Yu Rongguang) and Chin-po (Roy Cheung) from overseas. They ask drug cartel chief Mr. Karl for financial help in buying back their controlling shares and he agrees, with conditions. He asks the Fangs to complete three missions for him: rescue his computer expert arrested in Manila, retrieve evidence confiscated by police in Hong Kong, and steal back funds frozen by police in Tokyo. Chin-tao leads the strike that frees programmer James, killing seven cops, while Chin-po leads a team that robs the Fukuoka Bank. Interpol agents are sent from Tokyo and Manila to work with HK police on the case under the project title "Hunting Leopard," commanded by Madam Feng Ching, assisted by anti-triad expert Liang Chin-yi (Jade Leung). A Japanese girl named Chyomu Hakata (Yukari Oshima) is there also, on a personal vendetta against Chin-po. Chyomu sometimes helps the investigation, but forces their hand by attacking the Fangs on her own. After making up, Chyomu joins the mission and agrees to act as bait for the vengeful Fangs.

This entry in the Girls with Guns subgenre lacks something that no such film should be without—action! Though an attempt is made to compensate with at least 10 gorgeous babes with badges in the cast, there isn't much in the way of excitement until the final 15 minutes, when Yuen Wah and his comrades invade a police science lab. It's a bit refreshing to see Yu Rongguang playing the party animal character, though. *AKA: Lip Paau Hang Dung; Lie Bao Hang Dong.* 🐾🐉

1998 96m/C *HK/PH* Yuen Wah, Jade Leung, Yu Rongguang, Roy Cheung, Yukari Oshima, Chung Fat, Mai Kei, Rhea Malonzo, Rommel Padilca, Ramona Rivilla, Marie, San Naai. *D:* Lam Chin-wai. *W:* Lam Chin-wai, Lam Wa-fan. *C:* Cheung Yiu-cho. **VHS**

Lethal Panther

Inspired by the Angel series and John Woo's action classics, this is one of Godfrey Ho's better efforts as director. Betty Lee (Sibelle Hu) is a CIA agent and karate champ cracking down on counterfeiters in Los Angeles. Amy (Yoko Miyamoto) is a top contract killer for the yakuza, while Vietnam War combat vet Eileen (Maria Jo) is the top killer among the Hong Kong triads. Both killers are sent to Manila to eliminate crime boss Charles Wong (Lam Chung). The client behind the hits is Wong's double-crossing nephew Albert (Lawrence Ng), who wants to take over the business before his cousin Ringo (Clement Lee) inherits it. Betty is sent to the Philippines as well to stop Wong's counterfeiting operation. The competing killers succeed in liquidating Wong (at his daughter's wedding, naturally), despite the fact that Betty is on the scene. Cleaning up his tracks, Albert hires both of the hit women again, each instructed to target the other.

Their assignments are made more difficult due to the fact that Ringo and his men are gunning for them, and Betty wants to stop them, too. The killers, Betty, and the gangsters get into a massive shootout, which ends with both Amy and Eileen passing out from their wounds in the middle of a standoff. For some reason, call girl Sylvia (Sylvia Sanches) hides them in her villa and patches them up, and they find they have a lot in common while they recuperate from their wounds. With the two assassins bonding, the men in their lives are assigned to betray them. Eileen's brother Tom (Walter Mak) isn't studying in Paris after all—he's a contract killer, too. Albert hires him to kill Ringo, then Amy and his own sister! Attacked from all sides, the girls are forced to cooperate with Betty to get revenge on Albert.

Ho certainly learned his lessons well, copying from Woo, James Cameron, and others for some well-crafted action sequences—though some credit should be given to editor/production designer Norman Wong. One gunfight takes place during a fireworks display, but an even better sequence cuts between Maria Jo *(Seeding of a Ghost)* fighting gunmen in a grocery store while Yoko Miyamoto battles more over rooftops. He should have known better than to try to ape Woo's sentimentality though, as his flashbacks and other bits of melodrama are just embarrassing. Jo (whatever happened to her?) generates a certain degree of cool, leaving the sex scenes to Miyamoto. Sylvia Sanches adds a bit of comedy, while the awkward dubbed dialogue provides plenty of unintentional humor. Sibelle Hu gets to play a meaner, harder-edged version of her usual cop character—she gives a thug a heart attack by threatening to run him over with a tractor! Music cues are borrowed from *Halloween* and other soundtracks. *AKA: Ging Tin Lung Foo Pau; Jing Tian Long Hu Bao; Deadly China Dolls.* 🐉🐉🐉

1991 92m/C *HK/TW* Maria Jo, Sibelle Hu, Yoko Miyamoto, Lawrence Ng, Alex Fong, Raymond Wong,

Clement Lee, Walter Mak, Ken Lo, Lam Chung, Sylvia Sanches, John Lam, William Ho, Stephen Miller, Mark Scott, Bruce Stone. **D:** Godfrey Ho. **W:** Charles Ng, Simon Fong. **C:** Michael Lau. **VHS, DVD**

Lethal Panther 2

The quality of a film's titles shouldn't be an indicator in the merits of the picture to come, but when they can't even spell the production company's credit correctly, you may be excused in prejudging. In this Philippine feature (that bears no relation to *Lethal Panther*), Interpol Agent Shoko (Yukari Oshima) comes to Manila to bust the Nichee yakuza gang led by Taro Kyoto (Phillip Ko). Kyoto and three of his associates are in town to kidnap the CEO of Midtime Development, a company that plans to build a big resort. They happen to go after their target in a restaurant where Shoko and her local officers Sue (Sharon Kwok) and Alan happen to be having dinner, and after a battle in a nearby store, she manages to subdue Kyoto. However, Alan guns down the mobster in cold blood. NBI Agent Albert Moran (Jess Babida), while investigating arms dealer Costello (whose goons killed his wife), is suspended when his vendetta causes too much carnage. But when his partner Peter Nestor and his wife are killed as well, he returns to the force. He comes together with Shoko's team when the Nichee gang tries to buy guns from Costello. An acquaintance of Albert's named Cindy saw the Nichee hit man Tom, and it's feared he may come after the witness. However, since Cindy needs to lead her dance troupe for an important out-of-town date, the team accompanies her for protection. Of course, since he's guarding a witness that's the target of a gang of vicious killers, Albert takes everyone to visit his mother and son, putting his family in danger. Nobody questions Alan's murder of Kyoto, and they're all surprised when he turns out to be a traitor that leads the gang to their target. He is nice enough, though, to give directions to the gang's hideout before he dies, and everybody heads off for a bullet-heavy showdown.

Oshima, bearing her nom-du-Philippines Cynthia Luster, is her usual fine fightin' self, but this is unfortunately Babida's movie. Once he's introduced, the Japanese gangsters and their hostage are mostly forgotten in favor of his less interesting revenge saga. There's a stunt that borrows shamelessly from *Police Story* which shows two men sliding down strings of lights in a shopping mall (while shooting at each other). There are a few more moves borrowed from Jackie Chan in there, too, only with ridiculously obvious wirework. And then there's the car duel borrowed from *Bullet in the Head*. Phillip Ko does a nice job of creating the action, but he seems to be hindered by using Filipino stunt-

men rather than his own people. The soundtrack borrows cues from *Terminator 2.* **AKA:** *Ging Tin Lung Foo Pau 2; Jing Tian Long Hu Bao 2; Lethal Panther.* 🐾🐾

1993 84m/C *PH* Yukari Oshima, Sharon Kwok, Jess Babida, Jonathan Palmer, Phillip Ko. **D:** Cindy Chow. **W:** Sean Lee. **C:** Johnny Lee. **M:** Nilson Chow. **VHS, DVD**

Lies

Y (Kim Tae-Yeon) is an 18-year-old who, to avoid losing her virginity to a rapist, chooses 38-year-old J (Lee Sang-Hyun) as her first sexual partner. A spanking on her bottom during their second encounter escalates to violent whippings that leave her flesh bloody and torn. When the sadist and masochist change places, it is revealed that Y only pretended to love receiving pain because J loved inflicting it.

As in Oshima's 1976 *In the Realm of the Senses,* much of the sexual activity in *Lies* is real, although the filming of it is discreet enough for it to avoid being a hard-core sex film. Viewer perception of this erotic realism carries over to the S/M scenes, which makes it a rather uncomfortable film to involve oneself with. Director Jang Sun-woo interrupts the flow of the film at different points to address either the actors and the viewers, giving a bit of Brechtian alienation via Godard to an already self-consciously avant-garde film. At one point, he tells the viewer that J is not a sadist because the whippings serve as foreplay to intercourse. In a previous scene, however, it is plain that intercourse is foreplay to the whippings. With *Lies,* Jang tries to make a case that all society is perverted. Consequently, anything less than pornography is hypocrisy. This leaves the viewer with the option of being either a pervert or a hypocrite. Those who praise the film as a beautiful exploration of sexual extremes are guilty of being both. —*BW* **AKA:** *Gojitmal; Lies/Uso.* 🐾

1999 112m/C *KO* Lee Kim Tae-yeon, Sang-hyun, Jeon Hye-jin. **D:** Jang Sun-woo. **W:** Jang Sun-woo, Chang Jun-il (novel). **C:** Kim Woo-hyung. **M:** Dal Palan. **VHS, DVD**

A Life of Ninja

Behind the opening credits, the training of ninjas is briefly explained—and the training of female ninjas involves a lot of mud wrestling and dipping them in ice water. Iga Clan ninja Yota Okaru (Yasuaki Kurata) kills a Kao Clan ninja, uniting the last clans. Raised by a renegade ninja, Chow Hou-wei (Chen Kuan-tai) is a sword instructor by day, where he meets heiress Sun Chi-mei (Elsa Yeung). When a ninja kills a girl named Chang

L

Fei with a poisoned icicle, Sun's slimy brother-in-law Chan Ming-fu (Chen Hung Lieh) is a suspect, and Chow is questioned by a detective on the subject of ninjas. After Chi-mei's uncle and Chan's driver are killed, Chan fears for his life and tries to get Chow to be his bodyguard. With Chi-mei in danger as well, Chow agrees to use his ninja skills to track down the Iga killers. He succeeds in trapping and killing a nest of them in a warehouse, leading Okaru to call in a man-monster (champion wrestler Wong Kin-mi) to help. Chow captures ninja Hayata (Pauline Wan), but they allow her to escape so she'll lead them to Okaru.

Though things are a bit mixed up throughout the first half, the story begins to come together when Chow starts hunting ninjas, and delivers a decent fight scene with Kurata at the end. Director Lee Tso Nam *(The Leg Fighters, Killing in the Nude)* keeps all the crazy elements together, though not *too* together (this is a Taiwanese ninja movie after all). The shorter version released as *Ninja, Grand Masters of Death* has different credits tacked on the end, perhaps referring to the dubbing crew. Almost everyone involved came back for *Challenge of the Lady Ninja*. **AKA:** *Miu Meng Yan Che; Wang Ming Ren Zhe; Deadly Life of a Ninja; Ninja, Grand Masters of Death.* 𝄞𝄞𝄞

1983 88m/C *TW/HK* Chen Kuan-tai, Yasuaki Kurata, Elsa Yeung, Chen Hung Lieh, Cheung Ching Fung, Peng Kang, Wong Chi Sang, Pauline Wan, Sun Jung-chi, Wong Kin-mi. **D:** Lee Tso Nam. **W:** Szeto On. **C:** Chong Yan Kin. **M:** Wang Mu-san. **VHS, DVD**

Lightning Kung Fu

When two million taels of gold is stolen from the imperial court, the empress dowager puts pressure on Manchu security chief Liu Ching-tian (Walter Cho) to not only recover the gold and catch the thieves, but to keep the heist a secret to save China from international embarrassment. Liu calls on ruthless Chief Constable Liang Ting-ying (Chen Kuan-tai) to go after the five-man gang responsible. Like the Dirty Harry of Old China, Liang is a bloodthirsty lawman, more interested in killing criminals than serving justice. Bandit chief Fang Feng-gia (Ku Feng) makes things difficult for Liang and his men, gathering a gang of expert killers to ambush them. Plus, Liang has to deal with crooked constable Fan Chin-ping (Jason Pai), who intends to take the gold for himself. As Liang pushes on with a dwindling squad of soldiers, suspicions grow that there's more to the situation than they've been told.

Far grimmer than most Shaw Brothers action films of the period, director Kwai Chih-hung (of the nasty *Killer Snakes*) imbues the entire picture with an atmosphere of doom more like a horror film than an adventure film. The influence of the darker spaghetti westerns is obvious, as well as that of Japanese samurai epics, especially in the swordplay, which is as savagely bloody as any Chang Cheh picture. Full advantage is taken of the Shaw backlot sets by shrouding them in fog, wind, rain, and shadows. A brief scene in which Fang and Liang pretend to be friends for the benefit of Fang's blind and innocent daughter (Yau Tsui-ling) surely influenced a similar scene in John Woo's *The Killer*. The soundtrack uses music from Max Steiner's *King Kong* score. **AKA:** *Maan Yan Gan; Wan Ren Jin; Killer Constable; Karate Exterminator; Karate Warrior.* 𝄞𝄞𝄞𝄞

1980 89m/C *HK* Chen Kuan-tai, Ku Feng, Jason Pai, Yau Tsui-ling, Tiu Lung, Ai Fei, Kong Do, Paul Chun, Yueh Hua, Kwan Yung Moon, Walter Cho, Ha Ping, Dick Wei, Yuen Wah, San Kwai, Chiang Han, Gam Biu. **D:** Kwai Chih-hung. **W:** Szeto On. **C:** Li Hsin-yeh. **M:** Eddie H. Wang. **DVD**

Lone Ninja Warrior

Eagle (Tien Ho) lost an arm in a duel with a hero called Snowy White (Tin Peng). Seven years later, Snowy receives a note inviting him for a rematch at Eagle Cliff—but he decides the note isn't genuine, and he and his servant Flintstone (Chan Sing) go incognito to avoid a trap. His instinct is correct, as Eagle receives a similar note. After the plot to start a duel fails, Eagle's little sister Little Red is kidnapped, her captor demanding that Eagle kill Snowy White for him. At a nearby inn, Mr. White and Flintstone find the hospitality lacking, as the landlords and a variety of assassins attack them. Reaching town, they find the place quaking in fear from a vicious gang called the Weirdos.

"Weird" is really the word for this movie, which has the look of a horror film much of the time, the characters prowling through narrow, fog-shrouded streets. The city's protectors Wild Wolf and his sister Moonshine wear shiny black outfits out of a fetish catalog, while their sisters Sunshine and Starshine favor springtime fashions. The Weirdos use a lot of ninja tricks, and include a giant and dwarf combo, a transvestite assassin, and a snaggle-toothed hunchback. They line the bridge into town with the corpses of their victims. There's a killer prowling around taking blood from people and feeding it to a vampire woman in a cave. And Eagle's sword hilt is made out of his lost forearm, with his hand dangling from the end! All these elements play a part in the web of mystery.

A strange swordsman named Au Lung Flowerless (because of his hatred of flowers) pro-

vides a clue: The Weirdos bear the mark of a scorpion—the same mark used by the man who killed White's master years ago. Just before he died, the master entrusted White with the secret *Book of Mind and Heart,* and the Weirdos seem to be after it. Flowerless turns out to be one of the gang as well. He uses fireworks to fight and works with a trio of hellcats. And through circumstances, Snowy finds himself betrothed to a beauty named Windy Ling. It's tough to keep all the odd characters and relationships straight, but this bizarre film is more of a supernatural mystery than a swordplay action movie. The look of the film is much the same as that of those produced by Tsui Hark a few years down the line, especially the *Chinese Ghost Story* and *Swordsman* series—all shadows and fog. There's plenty of action and bloody violence, but this has more in common with *Mark of the Vampire* than *Enter the Dragon*. *AKA: Shui Yuet Sap Saam Diy; Shui Yue Shi San Dao; An Everlasting Duel; Liquid Sword 2.* 🦴🦴🦴

1981 92m/C *TW* Tin Peng, Tien Ho, Shia Lin-Lin, Shih Szu, Chi Kuan Chun, Lau Mung-yin, Chan Sing, Si Wai, Yeung Hung, Alan Chui, Ching Kuo-chung. *D:* Chang Peng-I. **VHS**

Lone Wolf and Cub 1: Sword of Vengeance

During the Edo Period, rules of conduct for the samurai were strictly enforced, most particularly for the Daimyo (rural barons) of the ruling class. Infractions were punishable by seppuku, a kind of combined ritual suicide and execution—the convicted would be expected to open their abdomens with a short sword, while an executioner promptly lopped their heads off from behind (a system that avoided many an unseemly slip-up). Those holding the office of the Shogunate Second were required to perform these executions, and only the finest swordsmen were given such an honor. Such a man was Itto Ogami (Tomasiburo Wakayama), until the assassins of the Yagyu Shadow-Clan betrayed him. One night, while he and his infant son paid respects to the executed dead, the enemy crept into his home and killed his wife Azami. Bereaved, and framed for treason, Ogami was forced to give up everything and go on the run, constantly on guard against the assassins on his trail, while he seeks out his enemies. But this "Lone Wolf" ronin is not alone on this mad journey. Having given his young son Daigoro (Yunosuke Ito) the choice of joining his mother in death, or following his dad on a vendetta, the little scamp innocently chooses to accompany his father. Together, they make for a strange

sight traveling across the Japanese landscape—a burly man with a lightning sword for rent, pushing a wooden baby cart.

This is the beginning of one of the best samurai series ever, which would eventually stretch to six features and a television series. In this first feature, Ogami's predicament is established, and the evil arch villain Retsudo Yagyu is introduced. The rest of the feature concerns Ogami taking on the job of protecting Lord Noriyuko of the Oyamada Clan from an assassination plot by Chamberlain Sugito. To do so, he infiltrates the gang of lowlifes hired as assassins, enduring their abuse until the time is right to strike. This amply demonstrates the heart of the series success, contrasting Daigoro's innocence, and the bond between father and son, with much more adult material and graphic violence. In essence, the Lone Wolf and Cub walk the narrow path between Heaven and Hell. *AKA: Kozure Okami: Kowokoshi Udekashi Tsukamatsuru; Sword of Vengeance; Child and Expertise for Rent.* 🦴🦴🦴🦴

1972 82m/C *JP* Tomasiburo Wakayama, Fumio Watanabe, Yunosuke Ito, Shigeru Tsuyuguchi, Tomoko Mayama, Tomoo Uchida. *D:* Kenji Misumi. *W:* Kazuo Koike. *C:* Chikashi Makiura. *M:* Hideaki Sakurai. **VHS**

Lone Wolf and Cub 2: Baby Cart at the River Styx

This second entry in the film series adapting manga by Kazuo Koike and Goseki Kojima takes as its center the eyes of little Daigoro (Akihiro Tomikawa). They take in everything, from the dance of butterflies to the sight of his father, Itto Ogami (Tomisaburo Wakayama), slaying assassins of the Yagyu Shadow-Clan. Ogami won the right to pass unmolested by the Yagyu in Edo, but he's traveled far since then. Spymaster Ozuno brings orders from Lord Retsudo Yagyu to Sayaka (Kayo Matsuo) of the Akashi Clan that Ogami is on his way into their territory, and they must kill him. Her clanswomen prove their capability to Ozuno by cutting his strongest warrior to pieces. The Edo Chamberlain of Awa has hired Lone Wolf to kill Makuya, headman of the indigo farmers. The Shogun has sent the Hidari Brothers (the infamous Gods of Death) to bring Makuya to Edo, putting the secret of the Awa indigo dye in jeopardy. Each Hidari has a lethal specialty: Benma uses a claw weapon, Tenma a club, and Kuruma an armored glove. On the road to Akashi to catch a ship, Ogami is faced with waves of attackers. First the Akashi clanswomen, then Ozuno's warriors take him on. Sayaka poses the only real challenge, fighting him to a draw. The ship they board carries

THE HOUND SALUTES
Lone Wolf and Cub

A lone samurai pushes a cart that looks like something out of *Gilligan's Island* across a deserted landscape. Suddenly, he is surrounded by a dozen deadly assassins. A minute later, all of his assailants lie dead, and the air is filled with a fine mist of gore. A small child pokes his head out of the cart—a babycart, as it turns out. The samurai known as Lone Wolf pushes the cart forward once more, and his blood-spattered story continues.

The saga of Lone Wolf and Cub is one of the most influential stories to ever come out of Japan. It began as a comic series by Kazuo Koike and Goseki Kojima, serialized every week in *Manga Action* magazine. The premise of the story is deceptively simple: Itto Ogami, the Shogun's executioner, is betrayed by his political enemies and his wife is killed. Ogami must either commit suicide or become a rogue samurai. For him, the choice is simple—Ogami wants revenge on the clan that wronged him and slew his wife. A much harder decision is whether Ogami should take his young child, Daigoro, on the "road to Hell" with him. The future ronin offers the baby a choice between a sword and a play ball. When Daigoro chooses the weapon, the path of the two is set—they will journey down the path of vengeance together.

Ogami and son become Lone Wolf and Cub, assassins for hire. They will kill anyone for their standard fee of 500 ryo (gold pieces). Though his job is inherently immoral, Ogami goes about it in a very honorable way. He kills people without making any moral judgments about them, though he does treat "worthy" opponents with all due respect. Daigoro helps his dad by being a decoy, scout, and helper, occasionally employing the deadly weapons hidden within his makeshift baby cart. The empathy of the audience for the father–son pair who have lost everything, plus the ultra-violence of Ogami's "job," plus the honor of the samurai tradition made the comic an instant hit. (It was kind of a cross between *The Fugitive* TV show and *The Executioner* book series.)

The success of the comic-book series led to a series of well produced, blood-spattered movies (see the reviews), followed by a TV series, and even an attempt to update the series that lasted for a couple movies. The films helped spread the fame of the story beyond the borders of Japan, especially when—during the *Shogun* miniseries craze of the early 1980s—the first two films were expertly re-cut and dubbed into the cult-fave gore-fest, *Shogun Assassin*. By that time, forward-looking U.S. comic book creators like Frank Miller had also discovered the series, and incorporated Lone Wolf's sensibilities into their work. Not long after that, First Comics (now defunct) began reprinting the series for the enjoyment of U.S. readers. New reprints—in their original Japanese collection size—are now being printed by Dark Horse comics. With more than 20 volumes available, and a number of stories in each volume, the thick little books are a good way to catch up on Lone Wolf history.

Those reprints have proved so popular that there's a new "updated" comic series, set in the future, currently being published in the U.S. Lone Wolf spin-offs have made it to other media as well. The movies, written by Kazuo Koike, the series creator, are the most notable and famous. However, the recent Tom Hanks/Paul Newman vehicle *Road to Perdition* (both film, novel, and comic) draws inspiration from the series, too. (Check author Max Allan Collins's notes in the graphic novel). Other homages have been made as well— some more respectful of the original, some less. A "funny" animal version even appeared in the samurai rabbit comic, *Usagi Yojimbo.*

With the series' strong premise, a loyal fan base, and endless possibilities for adaptation into other media and genres, the Hound feels confident that Lone Wolf and Cub will stay on the Road to Hell for a long time to come.

not only Sayaka, but the Gods of Death as well, making it a very hazardous voyage.

The fight choreography in *Baby Cart at the River Styx*—much of it drawn directly from the manga—is incredible. It's also incredibly bloody; fans of samurai films had grown used to seeing a lot of killing on the screen, but never before had the slaughter been presented so graphically, with blood gushing and splattering about freely in slow motion. The westerns of Sam Pekinpah, which dared to actually show realistic bullet wounds, had a similar effect on people. However, director Kenji Misumi presents this violence—and everything else in the film—with taste and style, always framing his shots in just the right way. Like Daigoro, we're allowed to see all, yet retain our innocence. *AKA: Kozure Okami: Sanzu no Kawa no Ubaguruma; Perambulator of the River Sanzu; Cent.* 🐾🐾🐾🐾

1972 81m/C *JP* Tomisaburo Wakayama, Minoru Ohki, Shoji Kobayashi, Kayo Matsuo, Shin Kishida, Akihiro Tomikawa, Katsuhei Matsumoto, Kanji Ehata, Izumi Ayukawa, Reiko Kasahara. *D:* Kenji Misumi. *W:* Kazuo Koike. *C:* Chikashi Makiura. *M:* Eiken Sakurai. **VHS**

Lone Wolf and Cub 3: Baby Cart to Hades

Little Daigoro (Akihiro Tomikawa) seems to have grown a few inches since Part 2 of this famous samurai saga, but still rides in the baby cart, even floating in it behind a ferry. Though now a lowly watari-kashi (samurai temp worker), Kanbei Magomura (Go Kato) was once a respected samurai, and still tries to deport himself honorably. Not so his companions, who attack a party on the road. To avoid trouble, Kanbei kills the victims, then one of the guilty ones as a scapegoat.

Itto Ogami (Tomisaburo Wakayama) witnesses his crimes, and Kanbei challenges him to a duel. Since he senses that Kanbei is a true warrior at heart, Ogami calls the duel a draw. That night at an inn, a slave girl who has killed her cruel master Monkumatsu seeks refuge from the law in Ogami's room. Torizo Koshio (Yuko Hama), leader of the Boohachimono (vice entertainers) group Monkumatsu belonged to, pulls a gun on Ogami and demands he turn the girl over. To settle matters, Ogami agrees to take the girl's punishment in her place, suffering "buri-buri," a ritual torture of dunking in water and beating. As recompense for the murder, Ogami is further asked to go on a mission to slay Genba Sawatari, Deputy of Totomi, who killed Torizo's sister and destroyed their clan. However, Sawatari is already looking for the Lone Wolf, wishing to hire him to kill Itakura, who happens to be one of Ogami's enemies as well. Since Sawatari is his target, Ogami refuses, and begins his campaign to slay the man. But first he has to get by his bodyguards, six-gun marksman Kukichi, and sword-throwing Samon—plus the usual ninja assassins.

Lacking in action throughout the first hour or so, *Baby Cart to Hades* really makes up for it in the finale, in which Ogami is drawn into an ambush by an army of warriors. He proceeds to use every weapon at his command—including pistols and a machine gun!—to mow down his attackers, before facing Kanbei in a final duel. The pace may seem a bit off balance, but this is another excellent entry in the series, with director Kenji Misumi giving a final tip-of-the-hat with an outrageous shot offering a severed head's eye view. *AKA: Kozure Okami: Shinikazeni Mukau Ubaguruma; Perambulator against the Winds of Death; Sword of Vengeance 3; Flying on the Winds of Death; Lightning Swords of Death.* 🎵🎵🎵🎝

1972 89m/C *JP* Tomisaburo Wakayama, Go Kato, Yuko Hama, Isao Yamagata, Katsutoshi Akiyama, Michitaro Mizushima, Ichiro Takatani, Katsuyoshi Baba, Akihiro Tomikawa, Sayoko Kato, Jun Hamamura, Yukio Horikita, Daigo Kusano, Shingo Ibuki, Masaru Shiga, Toshiya Wazaki, Hiroshi Nawa, Sakai Umezu, Tadashi Iwata. *D:* Kenji Misumi. *W:* Kazuo Koike. *C:* Chikashi Makiura. *M:* Hideaki Sakurai. **VHS, DVD**

Lone Wolf and Cub 4: Baby Cart in Peril

Another odyssey of death and violence in the continuing saga of Itto Ogami (Tomisaburo Wakayama) and his young son Daigoro (Akihiro Tomikawa). In this flick, Ogami battles against the assassin Oyuki (Michie Azuma), a woman who fights topless in order to startle her enemies with her elaborate, breast-hugging tattoos. Oyuki is causing chaos, and Ogami is hired by the clan suffering her wrath (for his usual 500 gold piece fee) to bring an end to her reign of terror. Ogami quickly finds the master who gave Oyuki her tattoos, and discovers that the female assassin wanted shocking tattoos—though the tattoo artist doesn't know why. He remembers that she bore the pain of being tattooed unflinchingly. From there, the Lone Wolf tracks the girl to her clan, a tribe of gypsy-like people living on the edges of the law. Oyuki used to be a dancer, but after losing a duel, she was raped by the man who had defeated her. She now seeks revenge against this man and all those of his clan, the Owari. Ogami follows Oyuki to a bath house, just as the object of her long-sought revenge shows up. Oyuki does her job, then Ogami does his. Ogami returns to the Owari who commissioned him—unaware that they plan to betray him. He is equally unaware that his arch enemies, the Yagyu clan, are planning a huge ambush, an event that brings the flick to its expected bloody climax.

Each of the *LW&C* films comprises series of vignettes based on the original comic stories (written by the author of this screenplay). While the pursuit of the assassin Oyuki is the main story in this film, there are other sub-stories as well. One of these involves another assassin, Gunbei (Yoichi Hayashi), who feels he has been dishonored by Ogami's actions. The strength of the Oyuki plot (and her topless assassination technique) makes this one of the most memorable and fun films in the *LW&C* series. As always, the acting, costumes, sets, and cinematography are executed at the highest level. Of course, there's plenty of bloodshed for those of a sanguine persuasion. If you can't start watching this series from the beginning, this flick would be a good place to start. —*SS AKA: Kozure Okami: Oya no Kokoro Ko no Kokoro; Lone Wolf and Cub: In Peril; Sword of Vengeance IV; Heart of the Parent, Heart of the Child.* 🎵🎵🎵

1972 80m/C *JP* Tomisaburo Wakayama, Yoichi Hayashi, Michie Azuma, Akihiro Tomikawa, So Yamamura, Tokio Oki, Asao Koike, Hiroshi Tanaka, Tatsuo Endo, Shin Kishida, Koji Sekiyama, Gakuya Morita, Hiroshi Hasegawa, Riki Harada, Michima Otabe, Seichiro Hara, Yusaku Terajima, Yukio Horikita, Katsutoshi Akiyama, Shingo Ibuki, Katsuyoshi Baba, Yoshimitsu Jo, Yukari Wakayama. *D:* Buiichi Saito. *W:* Kazuo Koike (also manga), Goseki Kojima (manga). *C:* Kazuo Myagawa. *M:* Hideaki Sakurai. **VHS, DVD**

Lone Wolf and Cub 5: Baby Cart in the Land of Demons

The penultimate chapter in the terrific film adaptations of the *Lone Wolf and Cub* comic series, this flick entry the tried-and-true formula of the previous films. In it, we get a series of story adaptations from the original comic, cleverly blended into one "whole" narrative. The main plot thread of this episode involves Itto Ogami (Lone Wolf, still portrayed by Tomisaburo Wakayama) having to pass a series of five "tests" in order to secure an assassination commission. Naturally, most of these tests involve bloody swordplay in which Itto finds unique and interesting ways of slaying his opponents. His foes are all from the same clan, and represent a mysterious client who wishes to hire the Lone Wolf and Cub. As Ogami slays each person "testing" him, they live just long enough to give the assassin another piece of the puzzle that is his commission (and another 100 gold pieces, to add up to his usual fee of 500).

Lord Kuroda (Shingo Yamashiro) has hidden his son (and rightful heir), and replaced the boy with the young daughter of his favorite concubine—passing the girl off as a boy. This act, if discovered, would bring great disgrace on the clan, and possibly cause its destruction. Unfortunately, the details of the plot have been inscribed on a scroll now in the possession of an abbot (Minoru Ohki)—who is actually a ninja master in disguise (and connected to Itto's nemesis, the Yagyu clan). The abbot is taking the scroll to the Shogun to discredit the Kuroda. Itto is hired to prevent the delivery of this scroll—and return it to the Kuroda—at all costs. Naturally, doing so involves much intrigue, bloodshed, and cleverly devised methods of outwitting and killing Itto's enemies. Lone Wolf confronts the abbot and his retinue as they cross a river—and soon the river runs red with blood. Itto escapes with the scroll and discovers that the second part of his commission is to slay Lord Kuroda, the imposter heir, and the concubine. As the film takes place in feudal Japan, this kind of brutal retaliation is never questioned. So, off Itto goes for a final confrontation with Lord Kuroda and his household.

An interlude in this film involves a female pickpocket (Sumida Kazuyo), who is also a quick-change artist. Daigoro (Akihiro Tomikawa), Lone Wolf's young son, is blamed for the crime, and takes a flogging rather than betray the lady thief—thereby demonstrating the child's true samurai nature. Because this is a Japanese swordplay film, we also get generous doses of martial philosophy, including a meeting with a monk in which the holy man declares that Itto has attained perfect "emptiness," just as the monk has—though Itto's emptiness is of a destructive martial nature.

Another fine episode in the bloody series, BCITLOD will appeal to folks who have liked the other Lone Wolf movies, or the Americanized version, Shogun Assassin. The remorseless brutality and blood-spurting comes as no surprise to anyone who's followed the series, though it may shock uninitiated viewers. Young or old, male or female, Itto Ogami is willing to kill them all, if the price is right. The "imposter heir" story links the film together and provides a strong sense of ongoing purpose throughout the story. The few unrelated interludes are barely distracting. The question of who is actually behind Itto's commission remains a "mystery" until the flick's end, and the original mystery of what his commission will actually be is fun, too. (Though if you've read to the end of this review, we've ruined it for you. Sorry.) —SS **AKA:** *Kozure Okami: Meifumando; Sword of Vengeance V; The Crossroads to Hell.* ♫♫♫

1973 89m/C *JP* Tomisaburo Wakayama, Michiyo Yasuda, Akihiro Tomikawa, Shingo Yamashiro, Tomomi Sato, Akira Yamauchi, Eiji Okada, Minoru Okhi, Shuji Otaki, Taketoshi Naito, Fujio Suga, Rokko Toura, Yoshi Kato, Ritsu Isiyama, Hiroshi Tanaka, Michima Otabe, Koji Fujiyama, Sumida Kazuyo, Bin Amatsu, Gakuya Morita, Koichi Sato, Masaru Shiga, Katsutoshi Akiyama, Riki Harada, Matsujiro Konaka, Shingo Ibuki, Tadashi Iwata, Yutaka Nakamura. **D:** Kenji Misumi. **W:** Kazuo Koike (also manga), Tsutomu Nakamura, Goseki Kojima (manga). **C:** Fujio Morita. **M:** Hideaki Sakurai. **VHS, DVD**

Lone Wolf and Cub 6: White Heaven in Hell

The last film in the *LW&C* series, *White Heaven in Hell* doesn't hang together quite as well as some of the earlier entries, but it's still a treat for fans. The Yagyu clan has been chasing Itto Ogami and (his son) Daigoro for the last five films of the series, and still have never managed to slay the hired assassin. The imperial court isn't too pleased with this, and Lord Retsudo (Tokio Oki)—the leader of the Yagyu—realizes that his time is running out. All the direct heirs of Retsudo have been slain by Itto, save Kaori (Junko Hitomi), Retsudo's last daughter. Kaori is a coldhearted bitch, as you'd expect from someone brought up by the dishonorable Yagyu leader. She practices her deadly knife-juggling technique on living subjects—all of whom die during her "demonstrations." Because the Yagyu are nasty bastards, no one thinks twice about this. Kaori vows to kill Itto, but it turns out that she's just the opening act in this gore-fest. Itto, meanwhile, is planning to go to Edo (the Japanese capital) and slay Retsudo once and for all. (A thread that is never resolved in this flick. Don't expect a tidy wrap-up to the series, even though the film seems to hint that it will. Perhaps the filmmakers were hoping to milk the franchise a bit more—or maybe they

L

were just staying true to the source material of a never-ending comic story. But we digress...).

While Itto is looking for Retsudo, the Yagyu master plots a "final" revenge against the Shogun's former executioner. The second part of the film involves Yagyu's illegitimate son, Hyoei (Isao Kimura), who is the leader of a clan of mountain assassins looking for power and respect. Hyoei doesn't like his old man, but he's willing to try to kill Itto for the prestige it will gain his clan. Hyoei has somewhat more luck spooking Itto than the cowardly Retsudo has ever had. (Retsudo has been unwilling to face Lone Wolf since he lost his eye to the assassin early in the film series.) Hyoei's technique involves "living dead" assassins, who dog the Lone Wolf, slaying any normal people the assassin and son come in contact with. In the end, though, Hyoei has little more success than his half-sister, Kaori. The final battles of the film involve an all-out attack by the Yagyu army against Itto and Daigoro. The fight takes place on a snowy mountainside, and features skiing samurai, assassins on sleds, and—of course—Lone Wolf's baby cart (which has more tricks than your average James Bond car). The climax, in fact, plays out very much like a scene from a James Bond flick. It's fun, but perhaps a little over the top, even in a series that's known for its excesses in battle. (Can anyone watch this series without thinking of the Monty Python sketch where the squirting blood goes "psssshhhh!"?)

White Heaven in Hell is a strong final episode in a very strong film series. The last of the *LW&C* films continues the series' tradition of Japanese well-choreographed ultra-violence combined with good acting, costumes, music, and cinematography. The films are probably the best adaptations of comic books ever put on film. They remain very true to the source material, and even incorporate many stories from the comics—with very little revisionism. *White Heaven* is a nice, apocalyptic finish to the set—though one can't help wishing they'd done more. —SS **AKA:** *Kozure Okami: Jigoku e Ikuzo! Daigoro; Baby Cart 6: Go to Hell, Daigoro!; Sword of Vengeance VI; Daigoro! We're Off to Hell.* 🦴🦴🦴

1974 83m/C *JP* Tomisaburo Wakayama, Akihiro Tomikawa, Junko Hitomi, Goro Mutsumi, Daigo Kusano, Tokio Oki, Jiro Miyaguchi, Renji Ishibashi, Minoru Ohki, Isao Kimura, Chizu Kobayashi, Gakuya Morita, Koichi Sato, Koji Fujiyama, Riki Harada, Shoji Mori, Koji Kanda, Yukio Horikata, Matsujiro Konaka. **D:** Yoshiyuki Kuroda. **W:** Tsutomu Nakamura, Kazuo Koike (manga), Goseki Kojima (manga). **C:** Chikashi Makuira. **M:** Kunihiko Murai. **VHS, DVD**

Long Arm of the Law

Big Circle crimes, in which a mainland gangs slip into town to commit a crime and skip back to China before they could be caught, were an increasing problem for the Royal Hong Kong Police in the last few decades before reunification, and this documentary-flavored feature directed by producer Johnny Mak was one of the first to address the issue. Tung (Lam Wai) is the leader of one such gang, all Red Army veterans looking to grab enough loot to make them wealthy men back home. After making a torturous crossing over the border, they disguise themselves as a drum band arriving for a Buddha's birthday festival to fool police, and then rehearse plans for their jewelry-store robbery. But when they reach their target, they find the shop already swarming with cops, an averted robbery having already taken place. The out-of-towners are spotted as likely accomplices, and have to make a break from the scene. They plan to try again in three days, filling their waiting time with junk food and other capitalist diversions. However, their contact Tai (Shum Wai) first uses them to kill a cop, and then betrays them to the police on their next attempt at the heist.

There's some incongruously sprightly music in some scenes, and a mall security tape matches the movie footage of the same scene, but those are the only major flaws in this gritty crime thriller, which broke new ground in the genre and was highly influential on such filmmakers as Kirk Wong, John Woo, and Danny Lee. The final gun battle is still considered one of the most intense in Hong Kong film history. Followed by three unrelated sequels. **AKA:** *Saang Gong Kei Bing; Sheng Gang Qi Bing.* 🦴🦴🦴🦴

1984 101m/C *HK* Lam Wai, Huang Jian, Kong Lung, Chen Jing, Shum Wai, Ben Lam, Tommy Wong, Ng Hoi-tin. **D:** Johnny Mak. **W:** Phillip Chan. **C:** Johnny Koo. **M:** Lam Mo-tak. **VHS, DVD**

Long Arm of the Law 2

In this sequel to Johnny Mak's crime hit, brother Michael takes over as director for a less distinguished but still exciting thriller. Police forces on both sides of the border are looking for new ways to fight Big Circle crime, and decide to recruit mainlanders to act as undercover agents. Li Heung-tung (Elvis Tsui), Qi King-san (Ben Lam), and Guo Hok-kwan (Yuen Yat-chor), all three captured while trying to jump the border, are recruited for the project, commanded by Biggy (Alex Man). Biggy has the difficult task of not only acclimating the trio of green foreigners to complex Hong Kong society, but to provide some savvy to the criminal underworld, and his lessons are none too polite. The newcomers soon turn the tables on him, defeating an enemy called Negro Tong during a visit to a gun smuggler, after which Biggy treats them with respect. To earn respect

and make a name in the crime community, they publicly insult petty crime lord Siu Hung (Kirk Wong) during a huge birthday party for his mother. Trouble erupts in their attempt to infiltrate a gang when one of the gangsters (Shing Fui-on) recognizes Tung from his days as a security guard, and King-san resists getting another thug in trouble because he saved his life in the war. But Hok-kwan spoils everything as they head toward a bank robbery by plotting to steal $350,000 and run off with a club hostess (Pauline Wong). Of course, she's setting him up, and he has to flee the cops at the airport. But the mainlanders don't know that their companions already suspect them, and their police superiors consider them expendable.

Part 2 is not as linear as its predecessor, suffering in comparison, but is a solid thriller in its own right. It has much the same gritty look, plenty of blood (including a harrowing torture/execution scene), some acrobatic fighting from Yuen Yat-chor, and winds up with another fine running gun battle. *AKA: Saang Gong Kei Bing II; Sheng Gang Qi Bing II; Long Arm of the Law Saga 2.* 🐉🐉🐲

1987 87m/C *HK* Elvis Tsui, Ben Lam, Yuen Yat-chor, Alex Man, Pauline Wong, Kirk Wong, Shing Fui-on, Chen Jing, Ng Hoi-tin. *D:* Michael Mak. *W:* Phillip Chan. *C:* Johnny Koo. *M:* Kong Wai-hung. **VHS, DVD**

The Longest Nite

Slowly simmering and nasty film noir. Two rival gangs in Macau are struggling for control. Rumor has it that Mr. K's gang put out a contract on Mr. Lung (Lung Fong), the rival gang's boss. Trying to maintain order, Mr. K enlists the assistance of Sam (Tony Leung Chiu-Wai), a crooked cop. Sam pays a visit to any potential assassin who arrives on the island, roughs him up, and scares him away. His technique is nasty, to say the least. Sam's brutal routine is demonstrated on Tony (Lau Ching-Wan), a bald tough guy trying to have a drink in a half-lit bar. Despite the beating he endures, Tony is not scared away. As the night stretches on, Sam's methods come under increasing scrutiny, and he becomes increasingly paranoid. Macau starts to feel claustrophobic and events spin wildly out of control.

The Longest Nite lacks any character development and is populated by criminals without any redeeming features. It doesn't matter, though; it's a great exercise in style over substance, although perhaps the moral of the story is that all criminals are evil and deserve to die. The beauty of the plot is its misdirection, like a blindfolded ride on a roller-coaster made up exclusively of hard blind curves. Shadows dominate nearly every frame. When faces or bodies do emerge, they are nearly overwhelmed by the bright neon colors of the Macau night life. Ko Chiu-lam's superb cinematography evokes a Technicolor version of the great black-and-white noir films of the late '40s and '50s. Raymond Wong's score neatly counterpoints the action. —PM *AKA: Aau Dut; An Hua; The Longest Night.* 🐉🐉🐲

1998 84m/C *HK* Tony Leung Chiu-Wai, Lau Ching-Wan, Maggie Shaw, Lung Fong, Lo Hoi-pang, Ching Siu-lung, Mark Cheng, Wong Tin Lam, Lam Suet, Yuen Bun, Lee Sau-kei, Sunny Fang. *D:* Patrick Yau. *W:* Yau Nai-hoi, Szeto Kam-yuen. *C:* Ko Chiu-lam. *M:* Raymond Wong. **VHS, DVD**

The Lord of Hangzhou

This starts out as an old-fashioned swordplay adventure with lots of wirework and fancy fighting, but soon all that is left behind for what turns out to be an engaging drama. Incognito Prince Chin Chiang (Waise Lee) and sister Princess Piyue (Gong Bei-Bi) hire a boat bound for Hangzhou, where they are investigating the possibility of a plan to move the Royal Palace. Two travelers—Mi-chi (Tse Kwan Ho) and Mi-an (Chan Kwok-Bong)—who are returning from a long vacation join them on the boat. Piyue is itching to meet up with some bandits to practice her kung fu on, and she gets her wish; with the highly skilled Mi-chi aboard, they easily defeat the invaders.

After his travels, wealthy Master Mi-chi is reluctant to settle down to running his estate. Like Piyue, he cares only to practice his martial arts—family retainer Uncle Kang bothers him with business, but Mi-chi has no head for figuring accounts. The undercover royalty accepts Mi-chi's invitation to stay with him, strengthening a growing attraction between him and the princess. At an inn for lunch, Piyue defends poor scholar Wu from a strict landlady. Wu turns out to be a down-on-his-luck accountant—just what Mi-chi needs—and the scholar soon finds himself part of the household staff. Officer Chen and Proprietor Cheng visit to present gifts to their returning lord. Wu turns out to be a snake in the grass, who conspires with Chen and Chang to take away the Mi fortune. The combination of bandits and treachery works quickly. Ruined, Min-chi heads for the capital to get help from Chin. On the long journey, Mi-an almost dies from snakebite, they suffer from starvation, help a woman give birth in a ruined stable (the opportunity to mock Christmas is not missed), and have other misadventures. When they get to the capital, it takes a long time to find their friends, but are finally shocked to learn that Chin is actually the Emperor!

Action fans may be disappointed that it fails to live up to the promise of the opening battle, but those who stick with it should find that *The Lord of Hangzhou* holds up on its own terms as a captivating drama. *AKA: Hong Chow Wong Yow; Hang Zhou Wang Ye.* 🎻🎻🕊

1998 96m/C *HK* Tse Kwan Ho, Waise Lee, Chan Kwok-Bong, Gong Bei-Bi. *D:* Andy Chin. *W:* Ma Chi Tsuen. *C:* Peter Ngor. *M:* Ko Yi Dai. **VHS, DVD**

Lord of the Wu Tang

Hong Kong swordplay fantasy movies are known for their many characters and complicated plots, but this collaboration between Wong Jing (writer/director), Sammo Hung (star/action director), and Jet Li (star) almost buries itself in excess. In a time when the Shaolin, Wu Tang, Ming, and other clans vie for power in the martial arts world, Wu Tang Clan's Chang Tsui-san (Francis Ng) and his wife, Ming Clan's Yan So-so (Sharla Cheung), are involved in a clash between elder Chang San-fung (Sammo Hung) and Deer Jinx (Leung Kar-yan), when their little son Mo-kei is infected with the deadly Jinx Palm. Most of the clans are after Tsui-san to get their hands on his friend King of Gold Lion, and more specifically, the powerful To Lung Sword. Mr. and Mrs. Chang kill themselves in defiance (Tsui-san by exploding his own heart!), and Chang Mo-kei (Jet Li) grows up too weak to practice kung fu (or achieve an erection), but is able to live through regular chi transfusions from ancient Grandpa Chang. Master No-Mercy, having been soundly defeated by Chang San-fung seven years before, sends his student Chow Chi-yu (Gigi Lai) to retrieve his Yee-ting Sword. Mo-kei's cousin Sung Ching-su (Ngai Sing) bullies him, but he's defended by spying Siu Chiu (Chingmy Yau, looking mighty cute in a goofy hairdo) from the Ming Clan. Fleeing from Wu Tang, the pair encounter an old Chang enemy embedded in a boulder, and trick him into curing Mo-kei by teaching him his Great Solar Stance. Setting out to exact his revenge from the masters that killed his parents, he heads for Bright Summit, where six clans are gathered to fight the mysterious Ming Sect—a battle set in motion by another Chang enemy, Shaolin traitor Shing Kwun.

The sets, costumes, special effects, and choreography are all first class. There are also many amusing and intriguing characters, such as the blood-drinking King of Green Bat Wai Yat-siu (Richard Ng), and a mysterious princess who is a double for Mo-kei's mom, but much of this spectacle and intrigue is lost due to all the clutter; there's enough detail here for at least two films. Indeed, the source novel has been adapt-

ed for several television series, and Wong left the ending open to a sequel that never came. Most U.S. release versions are missing about 15 minutes. *AKA: Yi Tin To Lung Gei Ji Moh Gaau Gaau Jue; Yi Tian Tu Long Ji Zhi Mo Jiao Jiao Zhu; The Evil Cult; Kung Fu Cult Master; The Kung Fu Master.* 🎻🎻🕊

1993 103m/C *HK* Jet Li, Sharla Cheung, Chingmy Yau, Sammo Hung, Ngai Sing, Gigi Lai, Richard Ng, Leung Kar-yan, Francis Ng, Cho Wing, Elvis Tsui, Ekin Cheng, John Ching, Lam Ching-Ying. *D:* Wong Jing, Sammo Hung. *W:* Wong Jing, Jin Yong (story). *C:* Bill Wong. *M:* Joseph Koo. **VHS, DVD**

Losers' Club

Unfortunately, the title says it all. Nam (Eric Tsang) is a television producer/director. He's worked in the business for a long time, but the ratings for his shows have been terrible. Yiu (Maggie Shaw), a nasty network executive, tells Nam in no uncertain terms that his job is on the line if the ratings don't pick up. His secret girlfriend (Ruby Wong) supports him, but everyone else thinks he's on his way out of the entertainment world. By chance he encounters an old friend, Kenny (Francis Ng), a washed-up pop star. Nam hits upon the idea of portraying Kenny as a complete nut job and throws him on the air—Kenny is an immediate hit, and the ratings go through the roof.

Delighted, Nam takes advantage of his newfound power by muscling his way into an expanded prime-time show. Kenny is not so happy about being portrayed as an oddball, but he goes along with the gag for the reward of being vaulted out of obscurity. Still not satisfied, Nam gets ambitious and grabs the coveted producer's job for the biggest program of the year, a New Year's Eve countdown. Finally, Nam feels he will achieve the success that he has long coveted. Complications arise, though, when Kenny's past comes back to haunt him. Nam must decide which is more important: his career or his friend?

The first feature in three years from director Patrick Yau *(The Longest Nite, Expect the Unexpected)* is an unalloyed disappointment. The comedy falls flat, and the tired back-office drama elicits yawns. The only consolation prize for watching is the flavorful, flamenco guitar-driven musical score. —PM *AKA: Fai Chaai Tung Mang; Fei Chai Tong Meng.* 🎻

2001 88m/C *HK* Eric Tsang, Francis Ng, Maggie Shaw, Ruby Wong, Michael Tse, Chun Wong, Lam Wai-kin, Tong Hoi-lun, Chan Ho-ming, Lo Hoi-Pang. *D:* Patrick Yau. *W:* Sandy Shaw. *C:* Cheng Siu-keung. *M:* Chung Chi-wing, Cheung Siu-hung. **VHS, DVD**

The Lost Kung Fu Secrets

In this Taiwanese production, the main titles could almost serve as a trailer for the feature, showing highlights from the movie's action sequences, except printed in negative. The main novelty here is that villainous Ching Dynasty Warlord Hung Sun-chan (Paul Chang) uses Christianity to conquer and pacify the Ming resistance, which means he gets to watch the peasants massacred from way up on a high chair with a huge red cross behind him. Using his influence, he encourages his followers into losing battles. Secret Agent Chang Chow-chang (David Chiang) uncovers a traitor within their team, Captain Ter Chin-chi (Choi Wang), but Commander Chung Chang (Wong Hap) doesn't believe the former Ming officer is a double-turncoat, and Chang is assigned to guard the commander's wife and daughter (Hsu Feng from *A Touch of Zen*) on their trip home. But Chang's suspicions are well founded: an overnight stay at Ter's home is a huge trap. Chang and the commander fight their way out of camp, and decide to switch uniforms so Chung can slip away. Chang rescues the princess, and together they try to make their way through Hung's fighters to the main camp. But when Hung captures the commander, Chang has to make a side trip to stage a rescue effort.

The martial arts on display are given clever and complex choreography, but appear labored and slow, looking like filmed run-throughs for the real thing—and poorly photographed to boot. Taiwanese star Hsu Feng's fights are a bit smoother than HK star Chiang's. There are plenty of esoteric weapons in use, from short spears and cudgels to war flags, and a totally ridiculous helmet with a big hook on top. The costumes and sets look like just what they are: leftovers from dozens (perhaps hundreds) of other films. Don't hold your breath waiting for any *Lost Kung Fu Secrets* to be revealed—there aren't any, making this a good triple bill item for *Secrets of Chinese Kung Fu* and *Secrets of Tai Chi*. **AKA:** *Lost Kung Fu Secret*. 🐉🐉🐉

1980 91m/C *TW* David Chiang, Hsu Feng, Chiang Han, Hu Chin, Paul Chang, Choi Wang, Wong Hap, Weng Hsiao Hu, Sun Jung-chi, Yuen Sam, Chan Chiu-ming. **D:** Joe Law. **W:** Lo Tzu. **VHS, DVD**

Love au Zen

Sau (Poon Chan-leung) leads a busy life as a Hong Kong securities trader, until one day he simply disappears. Naturally this affects his longtime love Siu Jing (Flora Chan), but not enough to keep her from her duties at the wedding of best friend Mila (Annie Wu), who is marrying Cheng (Andrew Lin), Sau's best friend. Sau appears at the wedding, dressed as a monk; his friends are overjoyed to see him but baffled by this turn of events. During the ceremony, Cheng hesitates before saying "I do," causing Mila to storm off.

The friends decide to learn more about Sau's sudden change and join him on Lantau Island at a Zen Buddhist retreat. There Sau appears devoted to a new way of life, receiving lessons from his former schoolmate Chi Yuan (Ko Hon-man). The change of pace and spiritual teachings affect each of the friends in different ways.

Here's a case where a measured, unhurried pace is perfectly in harmony with the tale being told. In fact, it highlights the virtues of the well-written script, which is in love with ideas and the effect they have on people and the way they lead their lives. Beautifully modulated acting from each of the five main players adds immensely to enjoyment of the story. The cinematography by Tony Cheung is beautiful, both in the city scenes and in the many lush countryside sequences. The musical score by Wu Sau-pok stands out for the polyrhythmic percussion and melodic, tropical tones. —PM **AKA:** *Oi Ching Goon Chi Joi; Ai Qing Guan Zi Zai*. 🐉🐉🐉

2001 96m/C *HK* Flora Chan, Andrew Lin, Annie Wu, Poon Chan-leung, Ko Hon-man. **D:** Derek Chiu. **W:** Raymond To. **C:** Tony Cheung. **M:** Wu Sau-pok. **VHS, DVD**

Love Correction

Emma (Athena Chu) picks up a coin dropped by co-worker Anson (Nick Cheung). She's convinced holding on to the coin will bring her good luck—she heard an anecdote on the radio that said so. Unfortunately, she only heard part of the story. Anson tries to tell her the rest of the story—picking up dropped coins will only bring *bad* luck. Emma is stubborn, though, and refuses to listen to his repeated efforts to set her straight, even as she suffers a spectacular run of bad luck for three days. Finally an opportunity is presented to reverse the events of the past few days. Can she prevent bad luck from striking her again and live happily ever after with the man of her dreams?

Too many plot points rely on misunderstandings, to the point that frustration will make you want to shout at the screen. The film keeps moving forward, but it's difficult to be very involved due to the listless main characters. Emma is a reactive character rather than one who takes charge of things. Since she acts as our protagonist, the movie is slowly drained of life, although she does finally manage to act in a more reasonable manner toward the end of the story. Anson does little except stand on the sidelines, being noble and misunderstood. The sole bright spot in the production is Monica Chan's performance as Porsche, one of Emma's co-workers. She is so upbeat and fun that she seems to have stumbled in from another—and better—movie shooting nearby. —*PM* **AKA:** *Yuen Ban Yau Take 2; Yuan Fen You Take 2.* ♫

2000 98m/C *HK* Nick Cheung, Athena Chu, Monica Chan, Emily Kwan, Lee Siu-Kei. **D:** Marco Mak. **W:** Sharon Hui. **C:** Ko Chiu-lam. **M:** Lincoln Lo. **VHS, DVD**

Love Me, Love My Money

A very difficult film to love. Richard Ma (Tony Leung Chiu-Wai) is a rich man and has earned his nickname—Bastard. He is ruthlessly stingy both with his business and with his girlfriends, a long string of gold-diggers. Because he is so cheap, they leave him, fulfilling his expectation that they will do so. Choi (Shu Qi) is his latest romance, and he puts her fully to the test. When she sticks around despite all the travails involved, is it possible that she will prove to be a woman who loves him and not just his money?

Director Wong Jing is stuck with an anemic script, but he has only himself to blame, because he also wrote the thing. Moments of inspiration are stranded between long stretches of tepid storytelling—if you can call the bare sketches of situations a story. The actors try hard to bring life to the proceedings, but the individual episodes could be edited down to about 15 minutes without any great loss. The result would be much more satisfying. The combined star power of Tony Leung and Shu Qi is barely able to push this film past the finish line. They make the most of their roles, but there's not much to work with. Teresa Mak is quite attractive as Choi's friend and fellow broker Chloroform (one of the all-time great character names in the history of Hong Kong cinema). Wong Yat-Fei is very funny as Choi's father. Angie Cheung plays a seductive psychiatrist who would certainly raise eyebrows in real life. —*PM* **AKA:** *Yau Ching Yam Shui Baau; You Qing Yin Shui Bao.* ♡

2001 99m/C *HK* Tony Leung Chiu-Wai, Shu Qi, Gordon Lam, Teresa Mak, Wong Yat-Fei, Angie Cheung, Cho Chun, Pan Ping-chang. **D:** Wong Jing. **W:** Wong Jing. **C:** Dick Tung. **M:** Comfort Chan. **VHS, DVD**

A Love of Blueness

The story takes place where love, memories, and pain collide. Rookie policeman Tai Lin (Pan Yue-ming) yearned to be an artist before he failed an examination and followed in his father's footsteps. One day he interrupts an apparent suicide attempt by a woman standing on the edge of a bridge. He detains her when she claims to have murdered her husband, despite her quickly protesting that she was joking. It turns out that the woman, Liu Yun (Yuan Quan), is a performance artist, but Tai Lin is not amused and is glad to be rid of her when she is released. She pursues him just a little, though, and he is surprised to find himself becoming attracted to her after they spend some time together. Tai Lin is drawn to her artistic side, and she is drawn to him because he is a policeman—at least, that's what he supposes.

His conclusion is reinforced when Liu Yun asks him to find a man named Ma Baijul. She won't tell Tai Lin why she wants to find him, but when he mentions the name to his superior, Tai Lin discovers that Ma Baijul was purportedly responsible for the death of a police officer 20 years in the past, a case that was never solved by Tai Lin's father and continues to haunt him in his retirement. Tai Lin's mother is strangely irritated when the subject is raised. Reluctantly Tai Lin searches for Ma Baijul and investigates the clues, while trying to protect Liu Yun from learning the truth about the charge brought against the man. Gradually, a connection between Tai Lin, Liu Yun, Liu Yun's mother—confined to a hospital after an accident sent her over the edge mentally—and Ma Baijul is revealed, and threatens to tear apart the relationship developing between Tai Lin and Liu Yun.

Director Huo Jianqi *(Postmen in the Mountains)* allows breathing room for the characters to be revealed and for the mystery to be unraveled. Colors are used effectively to convey a variety of moods, and potentially self-conscious devices—such as slow-motion footage and characters looking directly into the camera—are used sparingly. The performances are uniformly strong. The film will not bowl you over with a buzzsaw of movement and emotions. It treasures quieter virtues; it's perfect for an overcast winter day, curled up on the sofa, a blanket over your feet. The sentiments that arise seem to come from deep inside the characters, overflowing to the surface. Settle in to be moody and contemplate your life. Based on the novel *Performance Artist* by Fangfang. —*PM* **AKA:** *La Se Ai Qing.* ♫♫♫

2000 97m/C *CH* Pan Yue-ming, Yuan Quan, Teng Rujun. **D:** Huo Jianqi. **C:** Zhao Lei. **M:** Wang Xiaofeng. **VHS, DVD**

Love on a Diet

Looking at the poster or video cover, one might think they'd found a new Sammo Hung comedy.

But surprise! It's Andy Lau, performing in a fat suit, along with Sammi Cheng. Sammi plays Mini Mo, a woman desperately in love with concert pianist Rikiya Kurokawa (as himself). Ten years ago, he left Japan on a music scholarship to study abroad. She became so heartbroken missing him that she started eating obsessively, gaining 200 pounds. Even though Kurokawa still carries a torch for her, she's now unrecognizable and too scared to approach him. Hitting bottom, she meets Fatso (Lau), a traveling knife salesman from Hong Kong, and attaches herself to him. To keep her from insanity, he recruits his Chinatown buddies in Tokyo to design an intensive diet program for her in an attempt to lose as much weight as possible before her scheduled rendezvous with Kurokawa. Diarrhea, yoga, acupuncture, exercise, and even a tapeworm are included in the regimen, and when she's desperate to give up, Fatso joins the plan, too. Because they refuse to quit their weight-loss plan, it works and she loses weight. But literally sticking together through thick and thin has drawn the two of them closer together. To avoid their attraction as much as to help lose the weight, Fatso puts Mini in an expensive weight-loss spa the last month, secretly paying for it as a "Human Punching Bag" on the streets. Mini reunites with Kurokawa, and he even gives up his fiancée (Asuko Higuchi) for her. But can she forget the man who let himself get beaten senseless nightly just for her happiness?

Most productions that involve beautiful actors cutting up in fat makeup are either maudlin pity parties or mean-spirited farces, but this one works surprisingly well by treating the leads as characters first. The humor and drama come from their personalities rather than from their weight problems. Mini could have developed a gambling or caffeine addiction, but having her lose weight gives the story a positive visual with which to track her progress. Since we meet Mini when she's already fat, we're more on her side from the start, and having her fall for Lau even while he remains fat only helps her case—it's his devotion that inspires her, while he is drawn to her passion. On the negative side of the scale is the makeup, which looks rubbery and fake on the hands and arms, and like solid padding all over. The leads cut up all through the film, but become amazingly suave once back to their real weight. Another problem is Kurokawa, who amusingly parodies the intense and sensitive artist image, but is otherwise a one-note character. Overall though, a touching and often very funny comedy. Lau and Cheng both sing on the soundtrack. *AKA: Sau Geun Laam Lui; Shou Juan Nan Nu; Thin Body Man Woman.* 🎵🎵🎵

2001 95m/C *HK* Sammi Cheng, Andy Lau, Rikiya Kurokawa, Asuko Higuchi, Wong Tin Lam, Lam Suet, Chang Chi-ping, Hung Wai-leung, Wong Mei-fan, Po Ming-nam. *D:* Johnny To, Wai Kar-fai. *W:* Wai Ka-fai, Yau Nai-hoi. *C:* Cheng Siu-keung. *M:* Cacine Wong. **VHS, DVD**

Love on Delivery

After the relative insanity and mo lai tau ambience of such hits as *Flirting Scholar* and *From Beijing with Love*, Stephen Chow simplified things a bit for this root-for-the-underdog comedy. The underdog in question is Ho Kam-an (Chow), a dense but bighearted snack-bar delivery boy. To spite her boorish judo instructor Master Blackbear (Joe Cheng), Lily (Christy Chung) kisses Ho one afternoon, inspiring him to change his life to win her affection. His attempts to date her are foiled when he learns that she wants a man who is a real hero, prompting him to seek martial arts training from Devil Killer Tat (Ng Man-Tat), the Coward's Savior. Despite the fact that Tat is a fake who is conning Ho for all he's worth, some of the techniques he teaches actually work, and Ho succeeds in defending Lily by defeating Blackbear. The only problem is that he's wearing a Garfield the Cat mask while doing it, and later has no way of proving it was him. Lily believes it was karate master (and jerk) Tuen Shui-lau (Ben Lam), who has just arrived at the fitness center to teach, kicking out all the other martial arts teachers. To prove himself, Ho challenges Tuen to a fight, to be broadcast on TV in a month's time, and enters Tat's Death Training—which appears to consist of a lot of partying, eating hot pot, and karaoke singing.

It's not one of Chow's greatest, but still a lot of fun. Zany spoofs include *Terminator 2*, Ultraman, John Woo movies, and of course, dozens of kung fu flicks. Chow's *Curry & Pepper* co-star Jacky Cheung has a choice cameo. *AKA: Poh Wai Ji Wong; Po Huai Zhi Wang; King of Destruction.* 🎵🎵🎵

1994 99m/C *HK* Stephen Chow, Christy Chung, Ng Man-Tat, Ben Lam, Paul Chun, Vincent Kok, Joe Cheng, Gabriel Wong, Wong Yat-Fei, Phillip Chan, Peter Lai, Billy Chow, Jacky Cheung, Lee Lik-Chi, Lam Suet, Joey Leung. *D:* Lee Lik-Chi. *W:* Vincent Kok. *C:* David Chung. *M:* William Woo. **DVD**

Love Paradox

Three dancers are neighbors in an apartment complex. Sau (Grace Yip) is devastated when she discovers on her wedding day that her fiancé Denver (Andrew Lin) has been stepping out on her with someone named Michelle, so she calls off the wedding. Combined with her recent failures to secure work as a dancer, she's reduced to tears and inertia, until

Michelle shows up. Make that Michel—Denver's old flame is actually a man. While absorbing that surprise, Sau accepts Michel's help to prepare for a dance audition.

Her best friend Fong Fong (Annie Wu) lives next door. Fong Fong is desperately hungry for sex from her bored husband Fai (Roger Fung). She's convinced that he's more interested in flashy sports cars than he is in her. Truth be told, Fai loves cars, but he's absolutely fascinated by Sean (Perry Chiu). Sean is another dancer and has recently moved into an apartment on the same floor. She is not bashful about "getting her groove on" (in the sense of both dancing and romancing) with the blinds open, and Fai loves to watch through his binoculars. One thing leads to another, and Fai is soon paying a visit to Sean. Love thy neighbor, indeed.

As a comedy, *Love Paradox* is not particularly funny. As a romance, it lacks charm and heart. None of the characters engender sympathy or interest—quite the opposite, they actively annoy and irritate. This includes Sean, who appears calm and confident but is too much of a nymphomaniac to be believable. Even the character meant to provide comic relief—a

security guard named Romeo (James Wong)—is abrasive. Looking on the bright side, the three lead female performers are attractive and it only lasts 93 minutes. Director Clifton Ko failed to elicit any heat from the performers. Screenwriter Erica Lee cooked up a tasteless stew out of flavorful ingredients. —*PM* **AKA:** *Oi Ching Man Gam Dei Daai; Ai Qing Min Gan Di Dai.* ▽

2000 93m/C *HK* Grace Yip, Annie Wu, Perry Chiu, Andrew Lin, James Wong, Roger Fung, Vincent Kok, Clarence Cheung, Lot Sze. *D:* Clifton Ko. *W:* Erica Lee. **VHS, DVD**

Maborosi

One day, Yumiko's grandmother (Kikuko Hashimoto) leaves for Sukumo, saying she wants to die at home. She disappears, never to be seen again. Ten years later, childhood friends Yumiko (Makiko Esumi) and Ikuo (Tadanobu Asano) are a couple, with a little baby named Yuichi. Yumiko still has dreams about that day, wondering what happened to Grandma. One night, Ikuo is hit by a train on his way home from work. Yumiko's mother and mother-in-law take

turns looking after the young widow. The two women do some matchmaking and find Yumiko a second husband, an older man with a little daughter. They move to his home by the sea.

A dark, sad film, told almost entirely in dispassionate long shots that emphasize the characters' loneliness, it becomes a very different kind of suspense movie—Yumiko has already lost two people in her life, and the slow chronicle of her normal life seems like a deathwatch for tragedy to strike again. When their Aunt Tomeno (Mutsuko Sakura) is delayed returning from fishing on a rough sea, the suspense intensifies. It's a dull, quiet kind of suspense, the kind that makes you unsure whether the video is on play, pause, or fast forward. **AKA:** *Maboroshi no Hikari.*

1995 110m/C *JP* Makiko Esumi, Takashi Naito, Tadanobu Asano, Midori Kiuchi, Mutsuko Sakura, Akira Emoto, Kikuko Hashimoto, Goki Kashiyama. **D:** Hirokazu Koreeda. **W:** Yoshihisa Ogita. **C:** Masao Nakabori. **M:** Ming Chang Chen. **VHS, DVD**

Macho Man

This cheap but intriguing fight film takes its time laying the cards on the table. Her Da-hui (Chen Chiu) is the boss of a rural region who has in his possession an imperial seal he's selling for his triad. While waiting for a buyer to pick it up from him, his men attack two strangers climbing White Wolf Hill toward his villa. Jing Chu-ling is looking for her father, who disappeared in the area six months ago while searching for the seal. A dashing young stranger helps her out, and together they're too tough for Her's fighters to beat. Bandit Chiu Wai helped Her steal the seal, but was double-crossed and sent to prison. Now he's back to collect his share of the take, and dupes the two strangers into helping him. Her's men capture Chu-ling with a trick, and use her to lure the young guy to a lumberyard, where they nearly kill him using heavy machinery. Chiu is lured into a trap as well, but the escaped Chu-ling and her miraculously recovered companion come to his rescue. All this has given Her time to greet his Japanese buyer Kaido, and he arranges a lumber train to escort his guest away from White Wolf Hill. The heroes attack the train to get the seal, but of course Chiu intends to make off with it at his first opportunity.

The budget is obviously low, but the filmmakers make good use of what they've got, delivering a better-than-average fracas flick. Despite the train's slow speed, all the fighting on top of cars loaded with logs looks genuinely dangerous, and the stunt work is impressive. There's some charm to the resilient hero, who is never identified, goes about cheerfully breaking necks, and immediately recovers from all kinds of punishment to dole out some of his own. The

soundtrack borrows from the *Duel at Diablo* score, and even some Pink Floyd.

1972 87m/C *TW* Mui Tin, Chen Chiu, Ng Tung-kiu, Wang Tai-lang, Bruce Li, Su Chen Ping. **D:** O Yau-man. **VHS, DVD**

Mad Doctor of Blood Island

This is the most successful of the Philippine-made "Blood Island" movies, mostly due to an aggressive and creative promotional campaign. Audiences were commonly given vials of "green blood" as a gimmick/souvenir/snack, and the film was hawked with a deliciously sleazy trailer, narrated by Brother Theodore.

After surviving an island full of flesh-eating mobile plants and a radioactive monster in *Brides of Blood,* former teen idol John Ashley *(Frankenstein's Daughter)* returns to Isle de Sangre against his will to find even more nightmares. Evil Dr. Lorca (Ronald Remy)—in an effort to get rid of his lab partner Dr. Ramon, after he's caught with the man's wife—makes Ramon an unwilling guinea pig in an experiment meant to give human beings the power of photosynthesis. The result is an ugly chlorophyll monster that stalks the island drinking the blood of young maidens. In between dalliances with the monster's daughter Sheila (Angelique Pettyjohn), Ashley manages to track down the monster's secret.

Ashley and the monster would both be back for more in *Beast of Blood.* After Ashley's acting and recording career in the U.S. wound down, he came to the Philippines to star in the "Blood Island" pictures, then stayed to act in and produce a string of exploitation features. Co-star Angelique Pettyjohn was a *Playboy* centerfold and acted in several features *(Biohazard, Repo Man),* as well as starring in porn under the name Heaven St. John. When this was issued on videotape in the 1980s, some cassettes accidentally contained the rare *Revenge of Dr. X.* **AKA:** *Blood Doctor; Tomb of the Living Dead; Grave Desires.*

1968 86m/C *PH* John Ashley, Angelique Pettyjohn, Ronald Remy, Eddie Garcia, Alicia Alonzo, Tita Munoz, Alfonzo Carvajal, Bruno Punzalan, Johnny Long, Paquito Salcedo, Felisa Salcedo, Quiel Mendoza. **D:** Gerardo de Leon, Eddie Romero. **W:** Reuben Canoy. **C:** Justo Paulino. **VHS, DVD**

Madadayo

In the early 1940s, beloved Professor Hyakken Uchida (Tatsuo Matsumura) decides to quit teaching German at an academy to concentrate

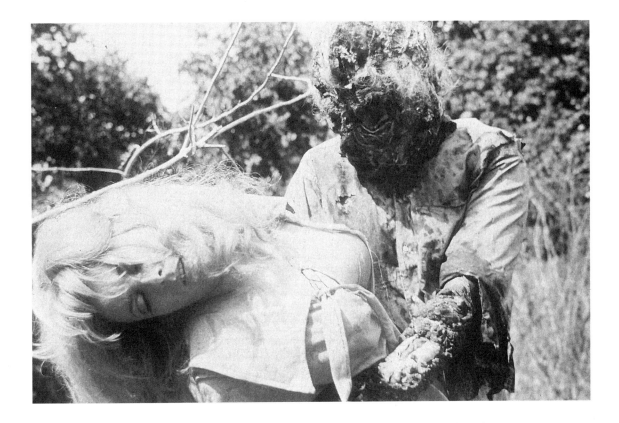

on his writing career. In 1943, a group of his former students gathers to celebrate his 60th birthday, a party that is interrupted by an air raid. By the next year's birthday, the professor's house has been burned down in the bombing, and he and his wife (Kyoko Kagawa) are living in a tiny shack. But students still gather for a banquet to honor him, which they have named the annual "Maahda Kai" ("Are you ready?"). As a ritual, they toast him with this question, to which he drinks a large glass of beer and answers, "Madadayo!" ("Not yet!"). In the coming years, the students are there to help him build a new home with a large pond, share his anguish over a lost cat, and are still celebrating Maahda Kai 16 years later.

A warm, funny, and touching film about kind people doing nice things for each other, this makes for a refreshing break between all the violent movies in this book. Though not the last of Akira Kurosawa's films, it's the perfect capper to the career of Japan's most honored and respected filmmaker. Matsumura, a regular in the Tora-san series and Toho's early 1960s sci-fi pictures, is a sheer delight. **AKA:** *Not Yet!.* ♫♫♫

1992 134m/C *JP* Tatsuo Matsumura, Kyoko Kagawa, Hisashi Igawa, George Tokoro, Masayuki Yui, Akira Terao, Asei Kobayashi, Takeshi Kusaka. **D:** Akira Kurosawa. **W:** Akira Kurosawa. **C:** Takao Saito, Masaharu Ueda. **M:** Shinichiro Ikebe. **VHS, DVD**

The Magic Crane

In this swordplay fantasy produced and written by Tsui Hark, leaders from martial arts schools in the nine territories of China meet to discuss a rearrangement of boundaries. On the way, Ma Kwun-mo (Tony Leung), who is accompanying his master Yat Yeung-tze (Damian Lau) from their small mountain Tien Chong School, is rescued from his runaway horse by gigantic crane Yuen Yuk—the mount of beautiful flute-playing warrior Pak Wan-fai (Anita Mui). The relatively new Tien Lung Clan, led by the avaricious So Pang-hoi (Lawrence Ng), has used their economic power to force their way into much more territory, angering many other schools in the Martial Arts World. So's flirtatious sister Lady Jade Flute (Jay Lau) causes more unrest at the convention with her brazen ways, genuinely attracting Yat, while Ma is completely taken with his "angel" Pak. So Pang-hoi sends a swarm of bats to attack the convention, but Yuen Yuk saves the day, after which Ma flies off for a date with Pak in search of a cure for the bat poison. Lucky for him he's the first man she's ever seen. The cure is made from the gall of a giant, fire-breathing tortoise (a relative of Gamera, no doubt), which Pak awakes and controls with her magic flute. But Butterfly Lam (Rosamund Kwan) appears to challenge them for the prize—and challenge Pak's identity, as Butterfly claims to be the daughter of Pak's master Lam Hoi-ping (Norman Tsui), who abandoned her 25 years ago to flee their conquered kingdom with the emperor's daughter (guess who?). While Pak faces the sound wave from Lam's magic lute, Ma snatches the gall away. But the convention is in complete chaos with different factions battling each other. Lam allies herself with So to get revenge on Pak, and they attack the disorganized schools together.

Like many scripts by Tsui Hark, this one packs too darn much into one film. Later, there's intrigue involving a sacred healing text, a monk imprisoned at the bottom of a well (Lau Shun), the general in charge of the convention turns into some kind of demon, a big magic bell, and a "Cheerful Drug" is used as a weapon—all of which only serves as a distraction until the climactic sorcery battle between Lam and Pak. As the wisecracking hero, Tony Leung should give the film a center, but is overwhelmed by one damn thing after another. The special effects are quite good, with the exception of the crane puppet used in close-ups and the mock turtle. *AKA: Sin Hok San Jam; Xian He Shen Zhen.* 🐉🐉🐉▽

1993 92m/C *HK* Anita Mui, Tony Leung Chiu-Wai, Lawrence Ng, Rosamund Kwan, Damian Lau, Jay Lau, Norman Tsui, Vindy Chan, Lau Shun. *D:* Benny Chan. *W:* Tsui Hark, Tsui Tat-cho. *C:* Tom Lau, Ko Chiu-lam, Tony Miu. *M:* Wong Bong. **VHS, DVD**

The Magic Serpent

Here's a TV matinee favorite released by American International in the U.S., a period swordplay fantasy featuring plenty of ninja tricks and magic. It also cashes in on Godzillamania with several giant monster battles. The plot is essentially the old story of the son of a betrayed king returning to get revenge on the villain who killed his father and free the kingdom. Yukidaijo (Bin Amatsu) betrays Lord Monosuki Ogata—his ninjas storm the castle, killing the royal family. Prince Ikazuchimaru (Hiroki Matsukata) escapes across the lake in a boat, but a dragon rises from the lake to attack the escape party. A gigantic eagle strikes at the dragon, and flies the boy to safety. For 10 years, an old wizard trains him in magic and martial arts. Ninja assassins attack Ikazuchimaru in the forest, and one even slices off his head—but that's not enough to stop the young wizard! After killing all the ninjas,

he meets a girl named Tsunate (Tomoko Ogawa), who is in the forest searching for her father, whom she's never met. In typical fable fashion, the girl's father is most likely Orochimaru (Ryutaro Otomo), the old wizard's former student, who betrayed his master years ago and stole his secret scroll. Orochimaru, now serving Yukidaijo, returns to steal more secrets and kill his master. But before the old bird passes on, he passes on his secrets to his student, telling him to return to Oni province and seek vengeance.

Tsunate is determined to continue her own quest to find her father, taking along a magic hairpin given by her grandmother. Ikazuchimaru befriends some traveling merchants—a friendship that's turned against him when he attacks Yukidaijo. Orochimaru comes to defend his lord, and Yukidaijo kidnaps daughter Osaki (Yumi Suzumura) to hold as hostage. Orochimaru has his men circulate the rumor that the young Lord Ogata has come to reclaim his throne, hoping to use public sentiment to help him impersonate Ogata for his own coup. Meanwhile, Tsunate and Ikazuchimaru fall in with Omabi (Shigeo Chiba), whom they don't know is leader of the bandits working for the enemy. The bandits attack Ogata, and while he's fighting them, Omabi takes Tsunate to Orochimaru. The first thing the wizard does when reunited with his lost daughter is ask her to murder her boyfriend using a drug! When it comes down to it she disobeys her father (a big deal in Japan), and fortunately Ogata is only faking his weakness. Omabi decides to help them both, in honor of his own lost daughter, and Ogata plots to attack anew during a festival—this time using a gigantic fire-breathing toad!

Undeniably an influence on *Star Wars*, this is a fun picture throughout. The hokey special-effects sequences are so engaging and full of action that the story seems to drag a bit in between, though there's still an interesting story going on. Tsunate's dilemma is an interesting one, seeking to serve her evil father and save face without betraying her friend. But one tends to revert to an eight-year-old while watching a movie like this, restless for more magic and giant monster action. The monsters may be products of puppetry and costumes, but they're imaginatively designed and great fun to watch. At a key moment, Tsunate uses her hairpin to summon a giant spider to help her out. The dragon sounds like Godzilla, while the eagle makes noises like Mothra and the toad sounds like Rodan. Titan Productions, who did the dubbing job, is likely to blame—maybe these sound effects were on the dialogue tracks and needed to be replaced. *AKA: Kairyu Daikessen; Battle of the Dragons; Froggo and Droggo; Grand Duel in Magic; Ninja Apocalypse.* 🐉🐉🐉

1966 84m/C *JP* Hiroki Matsukata, Tomoko Ogawa, Nobuo Kaneko, Ryutaro Otomo, Bin Amatsu, Shigeo

M

Chiba. **D:** Tetsuya Yamauchi. **W:** Masaru Igami. **C:** Motoya Washio. **M:** Toshiaki Tsushima. **VHS**

The Magnificent

In 1911, ex-officials of the Ching Dynasty government gather to plot their return to power in China. General Na Lan Tien Hsiung (Chan Sing) heads the conspiracy. The government agent in charge of opposing this rising rebellion is Commissioner Yao Shan Tien (Carter Wong). His agent Fu Feng (Casanova Wong) trails Hsiung to the capitol, where the general persuades Lord Lo to lead their forces. But it's all a plot by Hsiung to gain supreme power for himself. Lo's man Ma Piao is one of Hsiung's agents, and betrays Lord Lo, leading some men in his abduction. Hsiung just needs Lo's emblem of office to take his power and influence for himself, using it to dupe even more of the old Ching loyalists. He's already fooled Lo's daughter Princess Wan Ying (Doris Lung) that Yao is her enemy. While Yao trails Lo's abductors, Fu Feng goes to get help from Yao's aide Wong Che and their troops. The Princess gets wise to Hsiung's ruse when his men set fire to a ship while she and Yao are fighting in the hold. Hsiung is just too tough for even Yao and his two lieutenants to beat, but perhaps with the help of the princess, they can find the key to his defenses.

This colorful piece of history in action is highlighted by some cracking good fight sequences in picturesque settings. The title sequence, set to pounding traditional Chinese music, runs over Chan Sing fighting various attackers in the deep mountain snow. Another scene has Casanova Wong attacked by a quartet of maidens armed with lethal ears of corn, which they use to commit suicide when cornered! The training sequences are also very entertaining, with Wong filling and emptying large jars by just gripping the rims with his fingers, while Chen drives posts into the ground with her punches. The climax is wonderfully over the top, with the heroes struggling to perform the right combination of moves against Hsiung's vital points to bring him down. 🐉🐉🐉🐲

1978 92m/C *HK* Carter Wong, Chan Sing, Casanova Wong, Doris Lung, Ho Chi-keung, Bruce Lai. **D:** Chen Shao-Peng. **VHS, DVD**

The Magnificent Butcher

A pork butcher by trade, Lam Sai-wing was one of Master Wong Fei-hung's most popular students—a colorful character and hero in his own right. Sammo Hung was born to play the portly-yet-agile hero, and does so quite admirably in

this kung fu comedy. It also cashes in on the trend created by Jackie Chan's *Drunken Master*, using the same director Yuen Woo-ping, and was intended to co-star Chan's partner in that film—Simon Yuen—who unfortunately died during filming. And it also pays tribute to classic silent-screen comedy, beginning with the first scene, in which Butcher Wing slips on a banana peel. The plot is a simple comedy of errors, only existing to provide a framework for energetic and inventive martial arts choreography.

In a minor misunderstanding, Wing delivers a beating to a stranger (Fung Ging Man). To get revenge, the man limps back to his Master Ko (Lee Hoi-sang) of the Five Dragon School, telling him a pack of lies about how Wing and his master Wong insulted his school. Ko, who just finished 30 years of practice learning the Cosmic Palm technique, goes to engage in a calligraphy duel with Wong Fei-hung (Kwan Tak-hing, in his trademark role). Wing's brother Lam Sai-kwong (Chiang Kam) comes to town with his bride Yuet Mei (Tang Ching) looking for his long-lost big brother, but Ko's rascally son Tai-hoi (Fung Hark-On) tries to con him into believing the butcher owes him a lot of money. When Sai-kwong won't fall for it, Tai-hoi abducts Yuet Mei. Sai-kwong meets up with a drunken old beggar (Fan Mui-Sang), who agrees to help him rescue Yuet Mei. But wily Tai-hoi cons Wing into thinking they're friends, and gets him to help fight Sai-kwong and the beggar. When the truth comes out, Wing joins the beggar in the rescue plan, mistakenly taking Ko's goddaughter Lan Hsing (Jo Jo Chan) along as well. Tai-hoi sneaks in and murders Lan Hsing, framing Wing for the crime, leading to war with the Five Dragon School.

Much of the comedy is rather blunt, such as a sequence in which Wing mistakes a pickled pig's feet recipe for Iron Palm training, but the stars' personalities are strong enough to weather the material—and of course, the kung fu is what matters. Fan Miu-sang does a fine job filling in for Simon Yuen in the begging master role, though he appears to have been doubled by Hung and others in some shots. The shadow of Yuen is hard to shake—the trailer trumpets "Hung and Yuen—the twain shall meet in this blockbuster of a film," and his face even appears on some video cover artwork. Yuen Biao and Wei Pai get an opportunity to show their stuff as Master Wong's students, as do Lam Ching-ying and Chung Fat as Lee Hoi-sang's eccentric fighters. With the 99 films of the Wong Fei-hung series unavailable, this spin-off presents a rare opportunity to see why Kwan Tak-hing is so revered for playing the character. **AKA:** *Lam Sai-wing (Yan Je Mo Dik); Lin Shirong (Ren Zhe Wu Di).* 🐉🐉🐉🐲

1979 105m/C *HK* Sammo Hung, Fan Mui-Sang, Fung Hark-On, Lee Hoi-sang, Yuen Biao, Wei Pai,

Chiang Kam, Kwan Tak-hing, Chung Fat, Lam Ching-Ying, Fung Ging Man, Yuen Miu, Jo Jo Chan, Tang Ching, Tsang Choh-lam, Ho Pak Kwong, Sai Gwa Pau, Fung Lee, Billy Chan. **D:** Yuen Woo-ping. **W:** Wong Jing, Edward Tang. **C:** Michael Ma. **M:** Frankie Chan. **VHS, DVD**

Magnificent Natural Fist

Chef Ko Lin (Elton Chong), who used to cook at the temple, is beaten up by five mangy Japanese bandits, who kill his wife. He's good at kung fu, but not good enough to get his revenge, and he only escapes death with the help of drunken master Hong (Mike Wong). They're captured by the insidious amazons of the Women's Kingdom, and have to make another daring escape from the palace of their leader Misa. The ladies are after a relic from the temple that will supposedly certify the Women's Kingdom somehow as a real nation. To repay his debt, Ko becomes the old man's servant. By day, he's worked like a mule, but by night, he snatches up discarded pages from the kung fu manual his master is learning from, and learns the Natural Fist techniques almost as quickly as Hong. With his new skills, Ko sets out to battle the five killers one by one.

It's recommended that, if you have to watch this cheap Godfrey Ho flick, you keep one eye closed to save wear on your system. Some of the kung fu choreography is pretty good, but every bit of action is ridiculously sped up. There are some inventive gags, but they're more bizarre than funny, like the way Elton Chong wears a horse hat while pulling the old master's cart. Other characters seem to have picked up Chong's fondness for bad disguises—the old master has a huge red false nose and bushy wig, and Misa often skulks about disguised as a man, complete with beard. One of the dubbing artists has a pronounced lisp. The soundtrack borrows music from *Battlestar: Galactica*. The available version is from a horrible video master that looks like a bad color photocopy, so this may gain a bone or two if a remastered version offers less eyestrain. Most of the credits are Godfrey Ho's usual phonies. ⚔

1980 84m/C *KO/HK* Elton Chong, Mike Wong, Eagle Han Ying, Beau Wan, Lewis Ko, Natassia Chan, Lung Yuen, Kelly Lun, Dennis Wong, Jerry Ting, Max Park, Joe Pong, Niko Shin. **D:** Godfrey Ho. **W:** Charles Sek. **M:** Roman Tsang. **VHS, DVD**

The Magnificent Scoundrels

One of eight movies Stephen Chow made in 1991 (slacking off from 10 the previous year), this one reteams him with his co-stars from *Legend of the Dragon*, Teresa Mo and Yuen Wah. Chow is Valentino, a bumbling Hong Kong con man, who meets his match in a young woman named Kwan (Teresa Mo). When they try to con each other, it's seen that Kwan is even more inept than Valentino. She owes money to loan shark brothers Ng (Yuen Wah) and Tai-te (Roy Cheung), and because of her, Valentino is in on the debt. He has no choice but to make her his partner. Meanwhile, Chow Yun-fatt (Wu Ma) has had plastic surgery to escape from his debt, but Tai-te catches him anyway. To work off the debt, Fatt agrees to use a vacant modern mansion (a fabulous location—wonder whose house it is?) the gangsters know of to scam a visiting guest of the absent owners, with old girlfriend Ping (Tien Niu) acting as his wife. Valentino coincidentally gets the idea to rob the same house, and ends up impersonating the visiting relative to scam Fatt and Ping.

The movie temporarily becomes a gag-fest of a different kind, as one of the grossest scenes in an HK film outside of Category III introduces Amy Yip (at her most va-va-va-voom) as Apple, a very drunk call girl hired to act as their teenage daughter. Each team of tricksters tries to trap the other, both seeking to blackmail the others with incriminating boudoir photos of Valentino and Apple together—though Ping prefers to trap their victim using a black-magic potion that will turn him into a woman! When they find out the truth, they come up with a scheme to target their mutual creditor for a big score, with the help of Valentino's swindling master (Karl Maka) and his four wives.

The first pairing of Chow and writer/director Lee Lik-chi (assistant director on *Legend of the Dragon*) is a most profitable one, as they mix Chow's hilarious nonsense with a situation comedy plot that would serve any ensemble well. Along the way, we get deft send-ups of *Raiders of the Lost Ark*, Zatoichi, and a host of other targets. No offense to Gabriel Wong and Ng Man-Tat, but Teresa Mo is Chow's funniest sidekick, her deadpan delivery and gift for slapstick making her almost a female Buster Keaton. Wu Ma is more active than usual, getting involved in some of the slapstick, and Yuen and Cheung get to spoof their usual villainous roles. Chow and Lee would team again for half a dozen more crackerjack comic masterpieces, with Lee turning up in small parts in some of Chow's other features. **AKA:** *Ching Sing; Qing Sheng*. ⚔⚔⚔

1991 97m/C *HK* Stephen Chow, Teresa Mo, Roy Cheung, Wu Ma, Yuen Wah, Tien Niu, Amy Yip, Karl Maka, Sandra Ng, Gabriel Wong, Mimi Chu, Gwai Chung. **D:** Lee Lik-Chi. **W:** Lee Lik-Chi, Edward Leung. **C:** Abdul M. Rumjahn. **M:** Richard Lo. **VHS, DVD**

405
VideoHound's Dragon

Magnificent Warriors

It's pretty well known that Jackie Chan's Asian Hawk character from *Armour of God* (1986) was his attempt at the kind of hero portrayed in the Indiana Jones films, but this picture proves he wasn't the only one, as Michelle Yeoh picks up a pistol and whip for some 1930s swashbuckling. Yeoh is Fok Ming-ming, a bush pilot asked by the Chinese government to fly to the walled city of Puttan Kaal to help Prince Youda (Lowell Lo) escape the occupying Japanese forces who plan to build a poison gas factory at the site. Her contact will be Secret Agent No. 1 (Derek Yee), whom she will recognize by a special watch that's been sent to him. But a traveling con man (Richard Ng) intercepts the watch, which gets him involved in the heroes' attempts to get out of the city alive. They fail at both stealing fuel for Ming's plane and in assassinating Japanese General Toga (Tetsuya Matsui), and after many running battles, are finally captured. When Youda and his girlfriend Chin-chin (Chindy Lau) stand up to the Japanese, the Puttanese are inspired to rebel. But the revels of the citizens, as Puttan declares war on Japan, are short-lived, as a regiment of Axis reinforcements arrives.

Joseph Chan's deadly score shows just how important music is to a film like this, as the endless repetition of a few cues undermines nearly every scene. The one-note cheerfulness of Michelle Yeoh's character drains interest, but there's nothing wrong with her fight scenes. Choreographed by Stephen Tung and Fung Hark-on, they're fast-paced and exciting, keeping you on the edge of your seat thinking that surely the overwhelming odds against her will bring her down any second. Though more claustrophobic than the globe-trotting Steven Spielberg films that inspired it, the walled city location adds a lot of flavor. Little Chindy Lau looks good in her fight scenes, but unfortunately didn't make many more movies. **AKA:** *Jung Wah Jin Si; Zhong Hwa Zhan Shi; Yes, Madam 3.* 🎵🎵🎵

1987 87m/C *HK* Michelle Yeoh, Derek Yee, Richard Ng, Tetsuya Matsui, Chindy Lau, Lowell Lo, Ku Feng, Fung Hark-On, Hwang Jang Lee, Lo Meng, Chen Jing. **D:** David Chung. **W:** Sammy Tsang. **C:** Ma Chan-wah, Lo Wan-shing. **M:** Joseph Chan. **VHS, DVD**

Mahal

India's earliest known horror film is actually an epic gothic romance, more haunting than frightening. Lawyer Hari Shankur (Ashok Kumar) buys the old Sangam Bhavan house at a government auction sight unseen, but upon inspecting it, the gardener fills him in on the place's sad history. A Raja built the palatial mansion for his Queen Kamini, but then died at sea. The queen died awaiting his return, and the house stood empty for the next 40 years. Finding a portrait in the house, Shankur is shocked at his own resemblance to the former owner. That night, he's visited by the ghost of Kamini (Madhubala), and becomes obsessed with her. She tells him that they can only be reunited by death, or if he marries her reincarnation, the gardener's daughter Asha. Shankur's father and friend Shrinath (Kanu Roy) intervene on this unhealthy obsession, forcing him to leave the mansion and arranging a marriage to the beautiful Ranjna (Vijaya Laxmi). But Shankur is unable to "lift the veil" on his new bride, and he spends a lot of time dragging the unhappy Ranjna across distant mountains as he tries to escape his memories. Finally giving in to his pining, Shankur returns to the ghost. The morose Ranjna drinks poison, telling police that her husband gave it to her, and Shankur is arrested for murder.

Bombay Talkies produced this macabre story, which seems to have a pall hanging over every frame. While not a traditional haunted-house movie, it still features beautifully noir imagery and some pretty bizarre scenes, such as the dance sequence that may end in the dancer's death, and one with a snake fighting a vampire bat. But tragic fate is the theme here, written on the faces of the leads. Ranjna actually becomes the lead character for a time, narrating letters she's written to her sister about her bad marriage. Both the female leads have great voices, and sing some appropriately haunting melodies. Madhubala was once one of India's most popular and beautiful stars, but died young at 36 from heart trouble. Kumar later played the adopting father in the insane Bollywood version of *Superman.* **AKA:** *The Mansion.* 🎵🎵🎵🎵

1948 124m/BW *IN* Ashok Kumar, Madhubala, Vijaya Laxmi, Kanu Roy, S, Nazir, Eruch Tarapore, Leela Pandey. **D:** Kamal Amrohi. **C:** Joseph Wirsching. **M:** Kemchan Prakash. **DVD**

A Man Called Hero

Andrew Lau's follow-up to his blockbuster hit *Storm Riders* was another comic-based (from *Chung Wah Ying Hung*) swordplay picture, this time set in the early 20th century. The parents of Hero Hua (Ekin Cheng) are proud their son has been accepted as the disciple of elite swordsman Master Pride (Anthony Wong), and give Hero their treasured family heirloom the Red Sword to use in his training. Taking a break while Pride is visiting Japan, Hero finds his parents have been killed by foreign mobsters after dad printed stories about their opium trade in his newspaper.

Hero uses the sword to slay the gangsters, and takes a boat for New York to escape the consequences, leaving his pregnant girlfriend Jade (Kristy Yeung) behind with his friend Sheng (Jerry Lamb). Sixteen years later (though Lau inadequately portrays the passage of time), Hero's son Sword (Nicholas Tse) comes to New York with his Uncle Sheng to look for his father. At the China House, run by Boss (Yuen Biao), they find Hero's friend Monk Luohan (Ken Lo), who has also been searching for him.

Through a parade of flashbacks, we learn what happened to Hero in the intervening years: Hero and Luohan came over on the same ship and were sent to an iron mine together. While suffering through the inhuman conditions at the mine, Hero was accused of killing a foreman. But Master Pride heard what happened and sent his senior student Shadow (Deon Lam, with his face hidden behind a mask and Jordan Chan's voice) to rescue Hero. When Jade came to New York, she and Hero were reunited for a time, but soon Japanese ninjas challenged Master Pride, and Hero was called away to help. But before they can even get to the duel, ninja Jin (Mark Cheng) leading ninjas Fire (Sam Lee), Water (Benjamin Yuen), Earth, and Mu (Shu Qi)—attacked Hero and Shadow, but were defeated. When Hero injured Mu during the fight, he decided to save her life, and a bond developed between them. Jealous ninja Jin, who had a crush on Mu himself, set fire to China House just as Jade was giving birth to twins. In the confusion, rascally Bigot (Elvis Tsui) abducted the baby girl. Jade died in the fire, and Sheng returned to China with baby Sword, while Hero and Shadow went to Japan to support Master Pride in his duel with Jin's master Invincible (Francis Ng). Soon after the duel, Pride died, and Hero disappeared.

Back in the present, Shadow sends his daughter Kate (Grace Yip) to fetch Sword and Sheng to China House, where the assembled good guys plot to free the enslaved mine workers. Of course, Hero shows up for the party as well, now wielding the power of the China Secret passed on from his master.

In all, it's an impressive epic, though the flashback-happy plot is needlessly convoluted. Perhaps in trying to remain too faithful to the original story, writers Manfred Wong felt they had to cram in every little thing. They would have done better to divide up the story into a trilogy and cut down on the flashbacks and exposition, leaving more room for action. Hero's reason for staying away from his loved ones should have been established and built on sooner. By the time it appears, it feels like an afterthought, and weakens the drama a great deal. Plus, they never tell us what happened to his daughter, or why powerful dudes like Hero and the monk let themselves be enslaved by

the miners! The special effects by Centro are fantastic, delivering awesome superhero fight scenes before *X-Men* or *Spider-man*. It even ends with a terrific battle on the Statue of Liberty, which takes quite a bit of damage. They also do a fine job re-creating 1920s New York. While merely a guest star, it's nice to see that Yuen Biao is still agile, and there's even a rare opportunity to see him perform Chinese opera. *AKA: Chung Wa Ying Hung; Zhong Hua Ying Xiong; Chinese Hero; Legend of Hero.* 🎵🎵🎵

1999 (R) 102m/C *HK* Ekin Cheng, Shu Qi, Kristy Yeung, Nicholas Tse, Francis Ng, Anthony Wong, Yuen Biao, Elvis Tsui, Ronald Wong, Deon Lam, Jerry Lamb, Ken Lo, Mark Cheng, Sam Lee, Grace Yip, Cheng Pei-Pei, Yu Ka-ho, Benjamin Yuen, Jude Poyer, Thomas Hudak. **D:** Andrew Lau. **W:** Manfred Wong, Ma Wing-shing (story). **C:** Andrew Lau. **M:** Comfort Chan. **VHS, DVD**

Man Wanted

Jack Lok Man-hwa (Simon Yam) is an undercover cop who has come up through the triad ranks to become right-hand man to Boss Billy Lu Chanfeng (Yu Rongguang). Cornered by police, Lu decides to go out in a blaze of glory, and crashes his car through a barricade. Rather unrealistically, Lu is just assumed to have been killed in the crash, and though he gets a promotion, Lok mourns the loss of a man he considered a friend. Despite the attentiveness of his girlfriend June (Eileen Tung), Lok falls for Lu's girlfriend Penny Yung (Christy Chung), and she falls back. When a bomber starts targeting Portland Street mobsters, Lok can't find a lead until Lu steps from the shadows, alive and kicking. Lu tricks Lok into helping kidnap the son of Boss Bald Yin (Law Kar-Ying). Incredibly, Lok agrees to act as intermediary in the ransom swap, but Lu is out for blood, and makes extreme demands until a gunfight erupts. Lok manages to get away from both mobsters and cops, but is too late to keep Lu from abducting June.

A rather uninspired cops-and-robbers action flick, this is the type of film that saves a few bucks by making the hero's girlfriend a nurse so they can do a hospital scene with fewer actors. The story lacks sense—not only do the characters take unreasonable action, but their relationships with each other seem awkward and forced. It's highly unlikely that a cop could maintain a lengthy undercover assignment and a close relationship with his girlfriend, or that Lu could return to Hong Kong without more people knowing about it—especially when he still has a gang of loyal stooges working for him. Simon Yam fails to sell his self-destructive attraction for Christy Chung, and his friendship with Yu Rongguang rings hollow as well. Even the action scenes aren't very exciting or suspenseful, and

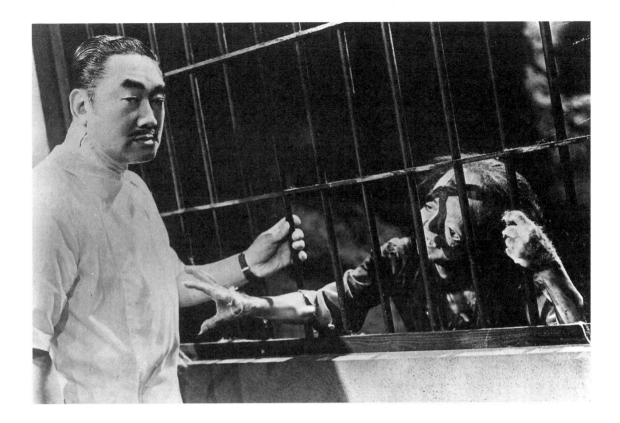

they're certainly not worth sitting through all the melodrama to get to them. **AKA:** *Mong Kok Dik Tin Hung; Mang Jiao De Tian Kong.* ♪

1995 92m/C *HK* Simon Yam, Yu Rongguang, Christy Chung, Parkman.Wong, Eileen Tung, Cherie Chan, Law Kar-Ying, Kenneth Chan. **D:** Benny Chan. **W:** Chak Ming. **C:** Chim Pak-hung. **M:** Wong Bong. **VHS, DVD**

The Manster

Banned in Finland! Occasionally, an American studio will use up some of the cash they have tied up in a foreign bank by producing a film in that country. Such is the case with this production that combined Japanese and Western cast and crew, with truly bizarre results. Womanizing, whiskey-swilling American journalist Larry Stanford (Peter Dyneley) is sent to interview crazed scientist Dr. Suzuki (Tetsu Nakamura). The mad doctor gives him a mysterious injection. Gradually, Stanford sprouts unsightly hair and an extra head. He loses his marbles (wouldn't you?) and starts killing people, including Suzuki. Soon after, he begins to convulse like mad, and in

another hyperdramatic scene, splits completely into two warring beings. When his wife (Jane Hylton) shows up, he's got a lot of explaining to do. A very unusual film, loaded with weird Freudian images and unnerving atmosphere. Though few people can place the title, millions must have encountered it on late night television and were shocked by the unforgettable "eye-on-the-shoulder" scene. The film has had at least an unconscious influence on a generation of horror films, including *War of the Gargantuas, Army of Darkness,* and *How to Get ahead in Advertising.* Shot entirely on location in Japan, half the cast and crew are Japanese. Another manster-piece from the director who brought *The Monster from Green Hell.* Dyneley's distinctive voice was used for that of Jeff Tracy on the *Thunderbirds* television show and movies. **AKA:** *Kyofu; Nightmare; The Split; The Two-Headed Monster.* ♪♪♪

1960 72m/C *JP/US* Peter Dyneley, Jane Hylton, Tetsu Nakamura, Terri Zimmern, Norman Van Hawley, Jerry Ito, Toyoko Takechi, Alan Tarlton, Kenzo Kuroki, Shinpei Takagi. **D:** George P. Breakston, Kenneth G. Crane. **W:** William J. Sheldon, George P. Breakston (story). **C:** David Mason. **M:** Hiroki Ogawa. **VHS, DVD**

Mantis Combat

Yi Lun (Chan Sing) and his companion Lin Yao-fu try to help a dying stranger, who hands them a treasure map. They fight over it and start a fire, then become separated. Years later, Yi Lun escapes from prison and comes to visit the now prosperous Yao-fu to get his share of the treasure. Yao-fu refuses to have anything to do with the criminal, and sends for his son Chu-er (Barry Chan), who is off studying Mantis Style kung fu. But Chu-er arrives too late—Yi Lun and his stooges (Chan Lau and Lee Man Tai) have already killed Chu-er's parents trying to get the map. Following the instructions left by his dad, Chu-er sets off to follow the map to the treasure. But first he collects his brother Chang (Bruce Lai) to help out. Later, they come upon a farmhouse where the whole family was killed, with the exception of daughter Jo Fan-chin (Chen Yan-Yan), whom they let tag along. Along the way, they're attacked several times by Yi Lun's hired assassins (including a murderous monk), and at one point Fan-chin and their servant Wai-nam are abducted. After these attempts to get the map fail, a disguised Yi Lun tricks them into hiring him as a guide through the mountains. Wai-nam is too stupid to recognize him, but Yi Lun fails to find the map anyway. Another hired stooge named Chan uses some photos and props provided by Yi Lun to fabricate a story that lures the brothers into a trap.

The plot becomes more interesting once the quest is underway, but there are some awkward moments all the way through. When Chang is introduced, he's beating up an innocent waiter, which his brother thinks is mighty funny. Fan-chin seems like she might be a spy, but she really serves no purpose in the story, and it's odd the way the "heroes" almost abandon her alone in the wilderness. Plus, where did that monk come from? The director doesn't do anything very interesting except point the camera at the terrific scenery of Taiwan. The action director does a bit better staging his fights, which aren't spectacular but move around well. Barry Chan performs a pretty good Mantis, and Bruce Lai displays his specialty high kicks. Chan Sing's moves include some Tiger and Crane Style—unusual for him. The movie is in such a hurry to be over that "The End" pops on screen before the final blow is struck, and it ends before the villain hits the ground. ♫♫

1981 91m/C HK/TW Chan Sing, Barry Chan, Bruce Lai, Chen Yan-Yan, Chan Lau, Wong Hap, Lee Man Tai. **D:** Shang Lang. **W:** Shang Lang. **VHS, DVD**

Marry a Rich Man

Mi (Sammi Cheng) delivers propane for her father's business. The family lives on an island and eligible husband material is scarce for any marriage-minded woman—though one hapless suitor keeps trying. A fortune-teller plants the idea that Mi will marry a rich man. The thought is reinforced by a chance meeting with three old classmates, all of whom have married for money and are deliriously happy as a result. Her father would also be happy to see her set for life.

Mi jets off to Milan, Italy, meeting fellow first-class passenger Mas (Richie Ren). Mas seems to have all the qualifications Mi is looking for: rich and good-looking. Trying not to appear too transparent in her gold-digger guise, Mi passes herself off as a wealthy woman. Everything goes swimmingly, as the duo enjoys the pleasures of Milan, until one less-than-magical night at a restaurant when the bill comes due.

Writer/producer/director Vincent Kok has created a very appealing and fluffy romantic comedy. The script makes it clear that this is a modern-day Cinderella story, with a little riff from the 1981 Hollywood film *Arthur* and other fantastical elements tossed in for good measure. It's very much a star-driven vehicle, with the electric presence of Sammi Cheng (*Love on a Diet*) enlivening the proceedings. She floats by on charm and good looks, frequently mugging for the camera, but only within the confines of her character. There's really no substance to be found; this is simple, feel-good entertainment with some very funny scenes and a generally snappy pace. Beautifully photographed Italian locations and well-used special effects add to the enjoyment. —PM **AKA:** *Ga Goh Yau Chin Yan; Jia Ge You Qian Ren.* ♫♫

2002 95m/C HK Sammi Cheng, Richie Ren, Jan Lam. **D:** Vincent Kok. **W:** Vincent Kok. **VHS, DVD**

Martial Angels

The 1970s begat *Charlie's Angels,* the television show featuring three beautiful women as crime fighters. The year 2000 begat *Charlie's Angels,* the motion picture. And 2001 begat *Martial Angels,* Hong Kong's version of the same idea. This time seven beautiful women are featured in skin-tight leather. Cat (Shu Qi), a thief, falls in love with Chi Yang (Julian Cheung Chi-lam), another thief, while both are trying to steal the same piece of expensive jewelry at an exclusive party. The relationship breaks up and Cat gets out of the criminal life, becoming a secretary at a computer firm.

Three years later, Chi Yang is being held hostage by the Russian Mafia because he was unsuccessful in stealing a computer virus from the company where Cat works. To save Chi Yang's life, Cat and her best friend Octopus (Kelly Lin) round up the old criminal gang, including big sister Monkey (Sandra Ng), Spider

(Amanda Strang), Goldfish (Teresa Mak), Peacock (Rosemary Vandebroucke), and Pigeon (Rachel Ngan). Subterfuge, explosions, and action ensue.

The direction by Clarence Fok lacks any dynamic energy. Certain scenes, isolated from the rest of the story, display beauty and a tiny bit of imagination. Overall, though, the pace drags and the action scenes—choreographed by Adam Chan—are uninspired and flat. The script by Sharon Hui has trouble coming up with enough story to extend the running time to 87 minutes. Likewise, the cinematography by Fung Yuen-man—responsible for other, better-looking productions—is workmanlike and the music by Ha Sam-mei—his second credit as film composer—is forgettable even as it's playing. None of the many locations are used or filmed in an interesting way. All seven "angels" are lovely to behold, but their acting abilities seem to vary with their underwritten characters. —*PM AKA:* Chuet Sik San Tau; Jue Se Shen Tou. 🎜🎜♡

2001 87m/C *HK* Shu Qi, Julian Cheung, Kelly Lin, Teresa Mak, Rachel Ngan, Sandra Ng, Terence Yin, Rosemary Vandebroucke, Amanda Strang, Wong Jing, Ron Smoorenburg. *D:* Clarence Fok. *W:* Sharon Hui. *C:* Fung Yuen-man. *M:* Ha Sam-mei. **VHS, DVD**

Martial Arts Master Wong Fei Hung

Though at first glance this appears to be just another attempt to cash in on Tsui Hark's *Once upon a Time in China* series, this Taiwanese effort attempts to be a bit different by reviving the young master portrayal, slightly older than that of Jackie Chan's *Drunken Master*. Well, just a bit different—it opens with a huge chorus line of students practicing their kung fu à la the *Once* series, though here the action picks up directly from this exercise. Irresponsible Wong Fei-hung (Chin Ka-Lok) is not among them however, as he's run off to bet on the cricket fights. Don't worry, insects aren't the only ones fighting here—some cheating by the mayor's nephew Ha Tieh (Suen Gwok-ming) sparks a full-scale brawl, much to the distress of Fei-hung's ailing father. The elder Wong succumbs soon after, and there's some controversy as to whether the immature Fei-hung should be allowed to take over the Po Chi Lam clinic and martial arts school.

Meanwhile, Ha uses his influence to get the British to allow him to sell opium openly in Canton. While Wong goes to the mayor (Kwan Hoi-san) to protest, Japanese fighter Jiubinko Kyoto (Lam Ching-Ying) arrives at the funeral, and is enraged to discover his enemy is already dead.

Next day, Wong defends Miss Sakura (Jacqueline Wu) from a bullying Ha, and becomes enchanted with the gorgeous Japanese girl, not knowing her brother is Jiubinko. When Butcher Wing tells him that Beggar So has become an addict, Wong decides he's had enough and beats the crap out of Ha while destroying the opium den. This makes the British angry, and the mayor orders Wong to apologize to them—which will place him at their mercy. Jiubinko decides to tag along to help protect Wong, but only so someone else doesn't get to kill him before they can duel.

Fans of the Tsui Hark Wong films are bound to be disappointed by this effort. The generally fine action sequences and good performances by the leads are damaged greatly by the obvious budget restraints. The film stock and other technical details are inferior, and the wirework is clumsily masked by a smear at the top of the lens. The Anglo actors playing British subjects are especially bad—their English is terrible and costume uniforms seem off. Chin Ka-Lok, brother of Chin Siu-Ho and one of Sammo Hung's protégés, is a competent Master Wong, though like Jackie Chan he falls short of embodying the true spirit of the legend. The ending was left somewhat open for a possible sequel. Rumor has it that the film was actually directed by 1970s star Hwang Jang Lee. *AKA: Wong Fei-hung Hai Lit Ji Yat Doi Si; Huang Feihung Xie Lie Zhi Yi Dai Shi; Great Hero of China; Wong Fei-hung 92.* 🎜🎜♡

1992 94m/C *TW* Chin Ka-Lok, Lam Ching-Ying, Jacqueline Wu, Kwan Hoi-san, Suen Gwok-ming, Chan Siu-pang. *D:* Lee Chiu. *W:* Wang Chi-chi, Szeto On, Li Chao. *C:* Yang Ke-liang. *M:* Cheng Chin-rong. **VHS, DVD**

Martial Arts Mayhem, Vol. 1

Any movie fan will tell you that, most of the time, the previews of coming attractions are the most entertaining part of a night at the movies—and the trailer is usually better than the film itself. This package from Something Weird Video compiles a fine selection of ads from martial arts films that played American theatres and drive-ins during the 1970s, when inner-city grind houses played kung fu quadruple-features 24 hours a day. These trailers are tons of fun, and show how U.S. distributors represented (and more often misrepresented) Asian cinema in an effort to pander to domestic tastes. While some distributors were honest enough to merely translate the international trailers for their flicks (or more likely too cheap to do anything more), many went to great lengths to disguise the stars' ethnicity and the films' foreign origins, going out of their way to avoid dialogue footage and showing as many Anglo faces as possible. Looking back, the duplicity is part of the fun. Still, when you look at how some of Jackie Chan and Stephen Chow's features are handled by their U.S. distributors, it kind of makes you wonder how much things have changed.

Trailers include *Fists of Fury* (three of them), *The Chinese Connection, Enter the Dragon* (two of them), *Return of the Dragon* (two), *5 Fingers of Death, The Street Fighter, Return of the Street Fighter, Sister Street Fighter, Sting of the Dragon Masters* (with music *from North by Northwest*), *When Tae Kwon Do Strikes, The Tattoo Connection* (two), *Black Samurai, The Snake Fist Fighter, Slaughter in San Francisco, Kill or Be Killed, Kill and Kill Again, Dragons Die Hard, Buddha Assassinator, Dynasty, The Black Dragon, Bruce Lee: His Last Days, Chinatown Kid, Deep Thrust, The Dragon Flies, Dynamo, 5 Deadly Venoms, Game of Death, Lady Kung Fu, Master Killer, The Queen Boxer, The Sacred Knives of Vengeance, The Three Avengers, Triple Irons* (two), *Devil Woman/Dragons Never Die, Seven Blows of the Dragon, Deadly China Doll, Blood of the Dragon, Fearless Fighters, The Godfathers of Hong Kong, Devil's Three, Shogun Assassin, Chinese Hercules, Jaws of the Dragon, The Man from Hong Kong, Kill Squad, Master of the Flying Guillotine, The Screaming Tiger, Thunderfist, Superdragon, Shanghai Lil and the Sun Luck Kid,* and *Fury of the Black Belt.* 🗡🗡🗡

1999 (R) 90m/C *HK/JP/US/PH/TW* Bruce Lee, Jim Kelly, John Saxon, Sonny Chiba, Sue Shiomi, Angela Mao, Sammo Hung, Jackie Chan, Chuck Norris, James Ryan, Jimmy Wang Yu, Bruce Li, Judy Lee, David Chiang, Marrie Lee, Bolo Yeung. **VHS**

Martial Arts Mayhem, Vol. 2

Occasionally there come times for martial arts movie fans when a lot of the films start to blur together in the memory. A trailer compilation tape can be a good way to refresh one's memory, the scenes on display marking details more distinctly. This second volume of "Coming Attractions" from Something Weird Video could have just the opposite effect. For the most part, these trailers are for obscure features put out by independent studios starring actors you've never heard of, often with generic new titles thrown on them to boot. This volume includes trailers for: *Two Swords Two Sorcerers, Flying Claw Fights 14 Demons, Iron Fisted Rebel, Temple of Death, Japanese Connection, Deadly Strike, Masters of the Iron Arena, Kung-Fu Death Wish, Chaku-Master, Superfist, Big Bad Bolo, Lee the Angry Man, Shaolin Master Killer, Ham-* *merfist Masters, Gangbusters Kung-Fu, He Has Nothing But Kung Fu, World War of Kung Fu, Incredible Master Beggars, Ten Tigers of Shaolin, Tower of Drunken Dragons, The Mad the Mean and the Deadly, Single Fighter,* and *The Karate Killer.* All are presented in widescreen format. 🗡🗡🗡

67m/C *HK/TW/PH* Jimmy Wang Yu, Bruce Ly, Bruce Lei, Bolo Yeung, Hwang Jang Lee, Gordon Lau, Chen Kuan-tai, Lau Kar-Wing, Bruce Leung. **VHS**

Mask of Death

District magistrate Li (Chui Chung Hei) is stymied by a series of murders—someone is killing kung fu masters of the area using an unfamiliar technique from the West, and leaving behind only a calling card bearing a death mask. He consults with two martial arts leaders: Dr. Wang Li-fei (Chan Sing) is well known for his acts of kindness throughout the region, and Wong Fu-lang (Wong Hap). Both men agree to help with the problem, and together they track down the white-haired stranger Chuen Yuen-chi (Choi Wang), who admits responsibility. But the killings continue, with the death toll reaching 100. A conference is called among the kung fu masters, but when Wang's own son falls prey to the Mask of Death, most chicken out. Wong is angry because his son Chung-wen (Stephen Tung) isn't interested in kung fu, and only wants to be a scholar. However, when the Mask of Death and his gang attack, Chung-wen and Li's daughter Chin-chin (Hwa Ling) are the only survivors, and people start to talk of ghosts. Secret government agent Iron Heart (Wang Tao) goes with the youngsters to Sumi Mountain to consult a Buddhist Abbot, who accepts Chung-wen as a student. Meanwhile, Iron Heart tries to trace the killers to their headquarters, but is injured by poisoned needles. Chin-chin finds him and nurses him through his delirium. Iron Heart infiltrates the secret gang of Madame Fa Wong, but he only escapes her death trap when it turns out she's his mother! Fa Wong fills him in on why she abandoned him years ago, and tells him who is behind the Mask of Death.

The villain uses the Iron Fist technique, and other special features include a sword belt, a snake fist fighter (Ma Cheung) who uses real snakes, huge star-shaped brass knuckles, and the ever-popular levitating monk. The supervillain costuming is amusing, and works well within the plot. But despite all this, the action is rather uninteresting—the main appeal here is the minimal whodunnit plot and various intrigues surrounding it. **AKA:** *Shaolin Devil and Shaolin Angel.* 🗡🗡🗡

1976 84m/C *HK* Chan Sing, Wang Tao, Stephen Tung, Hwa Ling, Wong Hap, Choi Wang, Chan Chuen, Ma Cheung, Chiu Tung, Chui Chung Hei, Ma

"Appealing story! Excellent plot! The best picture of the year— an extraordinary kung fu story. Furious fighting that startle everybody!"

—Showmanship lives on in *Martial Arts Mayhem, Vol. 2*

Tzi-chin, Yu Shung-chao. **D:** Joe Cheung. **W:** Joe Cheung, Wong Ching-tai, Chui Chung Hei. **C:** Nai Man-sing. **VHS, DVD**

Masked Avengers

Like minions of Hell, the Masked Gang of hired killers are all experts with the trident, wear metallic demon masks, are totally ruthless, and drink human blood! With so many murders and families wiped out lately, a group of kung fu masters gathers at an inn in a small town where the gang has been traced to discuss a plan of action. The meeting is hosted by Master Lin Yen-chi (Lu Feng), a wealthy local fighter. With all those heroes gathered in one place, the gang takes advantage by luring them off to be killed one by one. Two of the gang are killed, but nobody knows who they are. The only suspect is the inn's cook Kau Yao (Phillip Kwok), who acts mysteriously and knows kung fu, but helps out during the attacks. Lin suspects his enemy Fong Siu-kwong (Wang Li) could be connected to the Masks. While Tze San-yuen (Chiang Sheng) and some others go to keep an eye on Fong, hero Cheng Chuen (Chin Siu-Ho) attempts to get to know the cook, to find out if he's hiding any secrets. With more corpses piling up, more suspicion falls on the cook, but Cheng tries to covertly defend Kau Yao, thinking he's just infiltrated the gang to destroy it. But is Cheng right about Kau Tao, or is he really a member of the Masked Gang?

Another kung fu pulp mystery written by Chang Cheh and Ngai Hong, this one's a bit more formal than and not quite as intriguing as *Five Deadly Venoms*. A couple of the Venoms regulars are missing from the cast, but this still provides plenty of intrigue and bloody, violent kung fu action. The mystery isn't all that difficult to figure out, but that hardly matters. There are quite a few gory deaths in the film, but Chang saves most of the action for the end, when the remaining heroes are lured into the Masked Gang headquarters in an old temple. There, they not only have to fight the killers, but also avoid their deadly booby traps. **AKA:** *Cha Sau; Cha Shou.* 🐉🐉🐉

1981 (R) 91m/C *HK* Phillip Kwok, Chin Siu-Ho, Chiang Sheng, Lu Feng, Wang Li, Lo Meng, Chu Ko, Siao Yuk, Hon Lai-fan, Lam Chi-tai, Tiu Lung, Chan Shu-kei, Yu Tai-ping. **D:** Chang Cheh. **W:** Ngai Hong, Chang Cheh. **C:** Tsao Hui-chi. **M:** Eddie H. Wang. **VHS, DVD**

The Masked Prosecutor

The district attorney is sick of the corruption and red tape that frees obviously guilty felons in his territory, and becomes a masked vigilante to bring justice outside the law. This theme has been the fodder of pulp fiction since before Batman, and after notably resurfacing for *Righting Wrongs* in the 1980s, is revived again for Hong Kong audiences here. Besides wearing a hi-tech mask that keeps changing, the main thing that makes this vigilante different is that he kidnaps evildoers and gives them a good spanking!

So far four acquitted suspects have been abducted and dropped off in front of police headquarters—all tattooed with a judgment number, sans pants, and bearing the deep scars of an expert caning. The case of the masked prosecutor is assigned to soon-to-retire Wan Ping-guy (Blackie Ko) and the obsessive Wah Kai-lun (Jordan Chan). The new partners have more reason than the usual buddy-cop movie eccentricities to cause conflict between them. With Tong Hui-tai (Louis Koo) and Chi-lun, Wan was part of a famous police squad known as the Three Eagles of Mongkok, and Wan even adopted Tong as his son. No one has seen Tong since his release from a prison term on a manslaughter charge, and Wah counts him as the prime suspect. He also suspects that Guy may be in league with his old partner. Wan is upset about this, but even more upset when Wah makes a date with his daughter Wan Siu-yiu (Grace Yip). They try to catch their quarry by tailing Kwong, an armed robber acquitted on a technicality, but the Masked Prosecutor is too slippery. They succeed in finding Tong, but have no evidence to arrest him. But later Tong calls Wah with a message: he's upgraded his chosen punishment for Kwong, from caning to death.

Despite the pulp overtones, this is not a superhero epic, but a straight thriller that concentrates on telling the story from the police point of view. The Masked Prosecutor is not treated as a hero, but more like a serial killer. As an ex-con ex-cop working only as a family center volunteer, it's hard to figure how Tong can afford his fancy equipment. That cool mask, which keeps changing designs, must have cost him plenty. Perhaps for budgetary reasons, there's a lot more drama than action or suspense here, which is unfortunate, since the film could have used some balance. But then, who are we to judge? **AKA:** *Yau Cha; Ye Cha.* 🐉🐉🐉▽

1999 88m/C *HK* Louis Koo, Blackie Ko, Jordan Chan, Grace Yip, Wayne Lai, Frankie Ng, Law Kwun-lan, Jessica Hester, Michael Tse, Alan Chan, Lam Chi-sin, Lo Meng. **D:** Herman Yau. **W:** Nam Yin, Lam Kee-to. **C:** Joe Chan. **M:** Brother Hung. **VHS, DVD**

The Massive

Some of Wu Ma's wit is evident in this early directorial effort. Based on the novel *The Jade*

Dragonfly by Huang Yin, it's a twisty mystery yarn that incidentally features some pretty respectable kung fu. Inspector Chow Tze (Kam Kong) investigates a series of jewelry-store robberies in which the thief left behind a jade dragonfly as his trademark. Security measures are increased. In order to purchase some gems from Mr. Chu, Prince Tung's nephew Pang Chang-fan (Lo Lieh) observes a succession of precautions, noting the traps put in place by Chu's security chief Fu Shan. During the transaction, everyone succumbs to a knock-out drug—except Pang the Jade Dragonfly, who steals the gems and money, killing the guard. Inspector Chow suspects everyone; he promises to solve the case in five days or hand in his resignation, but he can't find the goods on any of the suspects.

Though followed closely, prime suspect Pang is murdered by poison in a public café. The victim's brother Pang Yi-fan (Yueh Hua), who has just arrived in town, wants to be in on the murder investigation, though Chow suspects the brother is there to pick up the loot. There doesn't seem to be any clue to how the poison was administered, and the gems are still missing. Adding to Chow's trouble is the arrival of his enemy, enigmatic contract killer "A Light in the Dark" (who has his own theme music), who means to show up Chow by finding the murderer first. But A Light in the Dark is killed by a masked swordsman before he can make much progress, leaving Chow with another murder—but is the killer the same man responsible for Chang-fan's death, or does he have two murderers to catch?

At least some of this puzzle shouldn't pose too great a challenge for mystery fans, but is enough to hang several intrigues and dramatic conflicts on. Some of the characters aren't what they seem, and quite a few surprises pop up before the end. But the real mystery is why anyone would re-release this picture with such a nonsensical title. The early death of star Lo Lieh's character is one of these surprises—so much so that you may expect his death to be faked somehow. The various characters show off several different kung fu styles, and a number of specialty weapons come into play, including a wicked whip sword and a rotating spearhead. **AKA:** *Yuk Ching Ting; Yu Qing Ting; Murder of Murders.* 🐉🐉🐉

1978 91m/C *HK* Yueh Hua, Lo Lieh, Chi Kuan Chun, Kam Kong, Shih Ting Ken, Miu Tin, Wu Chia Hsiang, Yee Yuen, Lui Ming, Lee Chiu, Phillip Ko, Ting Wa-chung, Mau Ging-shun. **D:** Wu Ma. **W:** Ling Ling, Huang Yin (novel). **C:** Lai Wen Shyong. **M:** Chou Fu-liang. **VHS, DVD**

The Master

This Jet Li picture is said to have sat on the shelf until his fame in *Once upon a Time in*

China made it marketable, and at the time the only attraction for many viewers was the novelty of seeing Li with a full head of hair. There's certainly nothing novel about the plot, which is strictly by the numbers. Li plays Jet, an expert kung fu man who goes to San Francisco to find his master Tak (Yuen Wah), who has established his own Po Chi Lam clinic in America. However, he finds his master gone and his herbal shop in ruins—tyrannical local kung fu master Johnny (Jerry Trimble) has taken it upon himself to have his thugs eliminate all competition in the area. With Jet in town kicking ass left and right, Johnny naturally makes him a target.

For modern viewers, this one still has some fun in it courtesy of the fight scenes, which are quite good. One has Jet facing off against Billy Blanks a few years before he became an exercise guru. Yuen Wah is also on hand to thrill his fans. But this film lacks the usual Tsui Hark magic, and when nobody is fighting it's just plain dull. **AKA:** *Lung Hang Tin Ha; Long Xing Tian Xia; Wong Fei-hung '92.* 🐉🐉

1989 (R) 93m/C *HK* Jet Li, Yuen Wah, Crystal Kwok, Yuen Wah, Jerry Trimble, George Kee, Billy Blanks. **D:** Tsui Hark. **W:** Lam Kee-to, Lau Tai-muk. **C:** Henry Chan. **M:** Lam Yee-tat. **VHS, DVD**

The Master of Death

It's a rather simple kung fu revenge tale, but this independent production is nonetheless satisfying, and has a lot of nice little directorial touches. Master Lee Chin-chow (Chi Kuan Chun) studies kung fu for 18 years at Shaolin Temple in order to avenge his parents' deaths. Returning home, he finds the place run down, with only caretaker Gung Fung (Lee Wan-chung) and a gang of ragged kids in residence. Gung recalls how Lee's father Chow-nan was betrayed by his fellow general Kim Min-kin (Lo Lieh), who surrendered to the Manchus. Not long after, Lau Min-ten's assassins killed the Lees. Lee Chin-chow sets off on his vendetta to track down the assassins and learn for certain who sent them. Along the way, he unknowingly rescues Marshal Kim's pouty daughter Su-ming from some jerks, and her mother (now a nun) fills her in on the Lee backstory—and that her daughter was betrothed to Lee Chin-chow as an infant. Miss Kim goes off in search of him. Meanwhile, Lee has to fight his way through a variety of traps and ambushes—including knife-wielding femme fatale Kong Ching-ha and Eurasian wildman Eddie Chow. Gung is also following Lee around to help out now and then. He sends his student Chow Yuen (Judy Lee) in to cause a disturbance in Lau Min-ten's casino (in a scene apparently inserted from another film) so that Lee can

Taiwan

When we look at martial arts films, especially those made in the 1970s to early '80s, it's surprising how many of them were produced and/or filmed in Taiwan rather than Hong Kong. While watching monks and ninjas battle on the steps of Shaolin Temple, you can often spot palm trees waving in the background.

The film industry in Taiwan was initially set up by the occupying Japanese forces in World War II. After the war, a number of mainland Chinese film studios fled the Communist turnover by relocating in Taiwan. During the 1950s, filmmaking there was dominated by four government owned studios that cranked out a lot of patriotic anti-Communist propaganda features. Gradually, other studios came forward, bolstered by distribution of foreign films and coproductions with studios in Hong Kong and Japan. Original productions fluctuated with public tastes between Taiwanese-, Mandarin-, and Japanese-language pictures. Starting in the 1960s, the government has tried to encourage domestic filmmaking by granting studios the right to import foreign features based on their in-house output—though some studios have churned out cheap, shoddy pictures just to raise the number of foreign blockbusters they'd be allowed. When Hong Kong filmmakers like King Hu began shooting swordplay pictures in Taiwan, it provided local industry with another shot in the arm.

The mountains and bays of Taiwan, along with its many beautiful gardens and temples, made for attractive outdoor filming all over the island, drawing HK filmmakers trying to get out of the cramped city. Taiwanese studios also flourished in the 1970s, taking up the slack in the demand for kung fu movies. Their features didn't look quite as good as the lush Shaw Brothers and Golden Harvest pictures, but they had all kinds of terrain to shoot on, and many Hong Kong stars found it easier to work there. Directors like Lee Tso Nam (*The Hot, the Cool and the Vicious*), whose signature became complex fight scenes involving multiple combatants, carved out stylistic niches to work in.

At its peak of production, Taiwan produced nearly 300 features per year, most of which were too cheap to play outside the country, unable to compete with foreign productions. To a Taiwanese filmmaker, having just enough equipment to shoot was considered enough, and stories were often written via the "flying

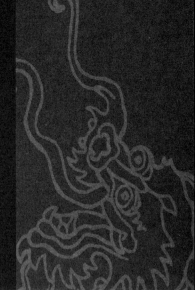

paper" method—made up as they went along. As the martial arts boom waned in the 1980s, a group of young directors changed the face of Taiwan cinema by rejecting established stars and story lines in favor of more street-level filming. The establishment of the Golden Horse Awards helped raise the level of quality all around, though Taiwan was still a haven for exploitation filmmakers.

Today, Taiwan cinema is defined more by Taiwanese directors making movies internationally. Ang Lee is at the forefront of these, having turned a corner from making films with distinctly Chinese themes like *Pushing Hands,* to his universally accessible swordplay action drama *Crouching Tiger, Hidden Dragon,* to becoming a Hollywood player with *The Hulk.*

attack Lau. There's some attempt to complicate the plot as Kim tries to manipulate Lee into holding his enemy Leung Siu-chin (Chan Sing) responsible for the murders.

There's lots of nice fighting going on with authentic styles and unusual weapons, though Chi Kuan Chun spends most of his time defeating anonymous villains and thugs. Chi looks great, but doesn't have a great deal of personality, or at least he doesn't get a chance to show it. However, there are plenty of guest stars on hand to make up for it, entering and exiting the film in episodic fashion. *AKA: Goo Tung Siu; Gu Tong Xiao; Revenge of the Shaolin Kid.* 🐲🐲

1982 90m/C *TW* Chi Kuan Chun, Lo Lieh, Chan Sing, Judy Lee, Sze Ma Lung, Mang Ling-ming, Lee Wan-chung, Kong Do, Kong Ching-ha, Woo Wai, Wu Ma, Cho Boon Feng, Stephan Yip, Chiu Ting, Eddie Chow, Wu Chia Hsiang, Wang Li, Frankie Wei, Lee Man Tai, Man Man. *D:* Chui Hon-cheung. *C:* Yip Sing Fook. *M:* Chou Fu-liang. **VHS, DVD**

Master of the Flying Guillotine

There were a number of martial arts pictures made during the 1970s around one of the strangest weapons of warfare ever created, the Flying Guillotine. Basically a heavy hat on a light chain, it was thrown over a victim's head, after which a section would drop down and with a flick of the wrist, blades would converge inside and neatly nip off the victim's noggin. Shaw Brothers started this mini-craze with *The Flying Guillotine* in 1974. Jimmy Wang Yu became a star playing the character One-Armed Boxer in a

series of films (starting with *One-Armed Swordsman* in 1967), and here he borrows the Flying Guillotine concept for a new adventure, a sequel to his *One-Armed Boxer.*

As the previous *Guillotine* movies established, in the 18th century, Ching Dynasty Emperor Yeung Chang commissioned an elite group of warriors to master the exotic weapon. Their purpose was to hunt down and kill Ming rebels, many of whom had learned kung fu at Shaolin Temple. Blind Fung-Sheng Wu-chi (Kam Kong) is one of these Masters of the Flying Guillotine, though his is an innovative collapsible model! At his mountain retreat, Fung receives word that the One-Armed Boxer has killed his disciples Chow-lung and Chow-fu, and swears vengeance, intending to kill every one-armed man he comes across. But getting revenge won't be easy. As is established in some early training sequences, his famous opponent Yu Tieh-lun (Wang Yu) is a great master despite his lost limb, who has such perfect breath control that he can walk on walls and ceilings!

The One-Armed Boxer series often included a martial arts tournament, and this one is no exception—often considered among the greatest of the tournament movies. Wu Chang-sheng (Chui Chung Hei) of the Eagle Claw School holds a martial arts tournament, and all of Yu's students want to enter. Knowing it could be meant to draw out rebels, Yu only allows his students to go as observers. Fung is sent as an observer, too, and hires various fighters to help kill any rebels flushed out by the tournament. The first match of the contest is rather ordinary, with fighter Chang Chieh-yu (Lau Kar-Wing) beating his opponent with a pole. But then things start to look like a Mortal Kombat video game, and bodies pile up: Wang Chiang vs. "Win without a Knife" Yakuma (Lung Fei) from Japan! Wu's daughter Shao-tieh (Doris Lung) vs. Monkey Boxer Ma Wa-kung (Wang Tai-lang)! Tornado Knives Lei Kung vs. Yogi Tro La Seng (Wang Wing Sheng)—who can extend his arms! One-Armed Snake Fist Hsien Hsing vs. Praying Mantis Tung Erh! With this last match, Fung is like a bull spying a red flag, tossing his weapon out to snatch the head off the one-armed winner (despite the fact that you can see his other arm pop out of his shirt during the fight!). When Wu objects, Fung kills him and sets fire to the stadium. Not exactly the life of the party, this one. Fearing the deaths of many innocents, One-Armed Yu decides to close his school and hide out. Too late—Thai Boxer Nai Men (Sham Chinbo) leads Fung to his prey. Yu finds that Fung and his Guillotine are out of his league and runs away. But he comes back with a plan to first get Nai Men out of the way (by giving him a hot foot!), then take on Fung using some special equipment of his own.

With brothers Lau Kar-Leung and Lau Kar-Wing creating the fight choreography, the action becomes a concert of meshing fighting styles, breathtaking athleticism, and ingenious techniques. Though Wang Yu was a huge star in the East, and even developed a following in America, he's not known as one of the best martial artists. However, with the Laus calling the shots, he looks mighty good. The best kung fu movies mix fantastic displays of acrobatic and fighting ability with exotic and entertaining ideas, and this one fills the bill beautifully. *AKA: Du Bi Quan Wang Da Po Xue Di Zi; One-Armed Boxer 2; One-Armed Boxer vs. the Flying Guillotine.* 𝄞𝄞𝄞𝄞

1974 (R) 93m/C *HK* Jimmy Wang Yu, Kam Kong, Doris Lung, Sham Chin-bo, Lung Fei, Chi Fu-chiang, Ho Pak Kwong, Chui Chung Hei, Lung Fong, Wang Wing Sheng, Lau Kar-Wing, Walter Cho, Shao Kao Shan, Chen Tak Chi, Hsieh Hsing, Wong Ching, Sit Hon, Shan Mao, Ho Wai-hung, Wang Tai-lang, Teng Kun Chang. **D:** Jimmy Wang Yu. **W:** Jimmy Wang Yu. **C:** Chiu Tao-hu. **M:** Frankie Chan. **VHS, DVD**

Master Q 2001

The Master Q series of comic books first appeared in 1962 and was quite popular in Hong Kong until the early 1980s. Part of the appeal lay in the books' wry and subtle commentary on contemporary life. À la *Who Framed Roger Rabbit,* this production animated the main characters and let them interact with live-action footage. Master Q, Potato, and Mr. Nobody are scrounging for jobs and food in modern-day Hong Kong. Master Q and Potato end up in the middle of a triad recruitment, revenge, and romance story starring police offi-

cer Fred (Nicholas Tse) and schoolteacher Mandy (Cecilia Cheung).

Producer Tsui Hark has long been interested in stylish, often fantastical imagery *(Zu: Warriors of the Magic Mountain).* He brought an animated version of *A Chinese Ghost Story* to the screen in 1997. Here he mixed animation and live action—apparently a first for a Hong Kong production. Much of the interest in watching the film lies in the novelty of that integration, so the real stars are the behind-the-scenes animators and effects people. The extremely silly gags are not exactly fresh, and the pace lags badly at times. Still, *Master Q 2001* is a rare commodity—a family-friendly flick that displays intelligence and basic human kindness at its core. It also features a smartly choreographed musical interlude whose theme you may well find yourself humming as you do your laundry. Viewers familiar with lesser-known supporting players will be amused by the actors' lampooning of their usual screen archetypes. The creator of the original comic book series, Alphonso Wong, has an amusing cameo playing himself. —PM **AKA:** *Liu Foo Ji 2001; Lao Fu Zi 2001; Old Master Cute 2001; Old Master Q 2001.* 𝄞𝄞𝄞

2001 103m/C *HK* Nicholas Tse, Cecilia Cheung, Michael Chan, Wayne Lai, Alfred Cheung, Law Kwun-lan, Emily Kwan, Tats Lau, Joe Junior, Hui Siu-hung, Frankie Ng, Samuel Leung, Helena Law, Lam Suet, Joe Lee, Lam Chi-sin. **D:** Herman Yau. **W:** Tsui Hark, Lee Man-choi, Roy Szeto, Herman Yau. **C:** Puccini Yu. **M:** Mak Chun-hung. **DVD**

Masters of Martial Arts

A recently unearthed Korean production, this kung fu flick imports Hong Kong talent into the mix, including Sammo Hung in a featured role. When young Master Ko Chen (Yu Yung-yong) accidentally kills the son of General San (who looks a lot like Wu Ma) in a brawl, his father disowns him and sends him away. He does this for his son's own good—San is a powerful man, and is bound to send men after his son's killer. Chen bloodies his hands again soon after, injuring a knife-wielding bandit in the forest. It turns out the man is ill and turned to robbery out of desperation to feed his family. He dies soon after asking Chen to notify his family.

Despite the bad news, daughter Pai-chin and her friend Ah-wah are most hospitable to the young stranger, and soon Chen finds work with a construction crew. His co-worker Machunga can tell that Chen knows martial arts, and thinks he's there to enter the big tournament coming up. Local warlord Cheung O-pah and his sister have hired killers Hashimoto and Okamura (Sammo Hung) on his payroll, and they've been either bribing or murdering all the invited contestants they can get to. They try to test Chen's ability, but he resists fighting, and Machunga has to defend him. But when Ah-wah is raped and her father Sam Suk is murdered by Cheung's men, Chen decides to enter the tournament to avenge his friends.

The martial arts of these masters are nothing all that special by modern standards, but the action is competently shot and well directed. The working conditions look extremely harsh. The exteriors take place in snow-covered forests, and even the interiors are chilly, shot in an obviously unheated studio. Sammo gets to play a nasty Japanese thug with a long, slow-motion death scene midway. *AKA: Bonecrushers.* 🐉🐉

1974 81m/C *KO* Yu Yung-yong, Sammo Hung, Mo Sa-sung, Do Min-yong, Kim Gi-joo. *D:* Kim See-hyun. *W:* You Yeol, Lee Hyungwoo. *C:* Choi Mojin. *M:* Jun Jungkun. **VHS, DVD**

Masters of Tiger Crane

Godfrey Ho contributes another kung fu action romp that doesn't offer anything new for fans, and won't interest non-fans much either—except for the amusingly Westernized names tacked on by the dubbing crew.

A family of nobles lives in peace, practicing their painting and calligraphy, with only brash little brother Steven (Billy Chan) to disturb their serenity. On the way to town to buy more art supplies, older brother Andy and the family's pet Shaolin Abbot are attacked by masked bandits, who abduct Andy and deal a fatal blow to the high priest. But the old bird lives just long enough to tell Steven what happened and hand him an important pearl and jade necklace he's had hidden. Steven hits the road to try to find his brother, tangling with ruffians whenever he can.

Meanwhile, the villainous Silver Fox (Hwang Jang Lee) is holding Andy in a dungeon, hoping he can find out from him where the necklace is. He also has men searching for Steven, along with his sister and her kung fu girls. He needs to get the necklace because it's important to his Manchu masters' plans to invade China. Or maybe it just goes perfectly with his outfit. Meanwhile, Steven gets a job as a restaurant cook, providing plenty of opportunities for the usual lame attempts at bumbling, dish-breaking comedy. He also meets an old beggar, who of course is secretly a kung fu grandmaster. Eventually, Silver Fox's sister finds him and he's captured as well, but the old beggar/master rescues him, and teaches him his superior Tiger and Crane Style kung fu. Silver Fox goes too far and kills Andy, which makes him more desperate to find

Steven. He has his minions kidnap Steven's friend Betty the waitress, hoping that will flush him out. It works, but the bad guys don't know that Steven has since become a super kung fu genius who can kick all their asses.

Acting, directing, and martial arts talent are all average or below, and all plot points have been covered better in other films. Not even Hwang Jang Lee is up to his usual high-kicking standards here, one of a handful of films in which he played the evil Silver Fox. No actual Hung Gar (Tiger Crane) martial arts are on display. The younger men all sport groovy shag hairdos. *AKA: Raging Master's Tiger Crane.* 🐉

1983 77m/C *KO* Hwang Jang Lee, Billy Chan, Kathy Lee, Benny Tsui, Stan Yuen, Chris Bo, Perry Lang, Liza Tung, Phillip So, Wong Man Bao, William Lai. *D:* Godfrey Ho. *W:* John Tsui. *C:* Jimmy Yu. *M:* Ricky Chan. **VHS, DVD**

Memento Mori

Following up on the hit *Whispering Corridors,* a girls' school ghost story is again the theme of this Korean shocker. So Min-ah (Kim Min-sun) finds a diary kept in tandem by a pair of senior students—pretty and shy Min Hyo-shin (Park Ye-jin) and athletic Yoo Shi-eun (Lee Young-jin). The diary reveals that the girls are lovers, but not a deeper secret: that they have developed telepathy between them. Min-ah becomes fascinated with the two girls, following them around and spying on them, and the diary seems to be giving her strange dizzy sensations and hallucinations. The diary itself is unusually creative, full of tricks and traps; foolishly, Min-ah swallows a pill left in the binding, only to learn later it might be poison.

According to the diary, the pair separated for a time—Hyo-shin had an affair with their teacher Mr. Goh, and Shi-eun nearly broke up with her. The school is shocked when Hyo-shin takes a dive off the roof to her death, though Shi-eun shows no outward signs of grief. A rumor says that there was another girl on the roof when Hyo-shin died. Another says she was pregnant and couldn't face a physical exam. Min-ah feels closer to Shi-eun and Hyo-shin because of the diary, alienating her own friends, class clowns Moon Ji-wan and Choi Yeon-ahn. But she may be closer than she thinks—the hallucinations (or visions) become stronger, more frequent, and increasingly frightening. She finds a birthday tribute for Shi-eun built inside Hyo-shin's piano, along with a pill labeled an "antidote." But as Shi-eun recalls events leading up to Hyo-shin's death, strange things are happening in the school. Doors are slamming, faucets running, no one can get out of the building, and the secrets of the diary may be behind it all.

M

The focus here is just as much on the secret world of teenage girls as it is on any supernatural consequences of their antics. Much more than the blatant *The Craft,* we can see that the tensions produced by their behavior and rituals come to resemble incantations, focusing their energy in unexpected ways. The bland backdrop of the school and the identical student uniforms only add to the tension, as the viewer is forced to pick out details and clues. This becomes almost irritating during the frequent flashbacks, as visual cues as to where and when a scene takes place are present, but not obvious. Add that most of the film was shot with handheld cameras, lending a more intimate, less artificial look, and you have a film that's much like a puzzle that keeps you intrigued enough that you need to stick around to see how it unfolds. *AKA:* *Yeogo Goedam 2; Whispering Corridors 2.* 🐉🐉🐉🐲

1999 99m/C *KO* Park Ye-jin, Lee Young-jin, Kim Min-sun, Baek Jong-hak. **D:** Kim Tae-yong, Min Kyu-dong. **C:** Kim Yoon-soo. **M:** Cho Sung-woo. **DVD**

Men Who Tread on the Tiger's Tail

One of Kurosawa's earliest films, this flick tells the story of the Yoshitsune clan, and their attempt to escape their enemies. After coming out on the losing end of a clan war, Lord Yoshitsune (Hanshiro Iwai) takes his six most faithful retainers and heads into the mountains, trying to cross into the lands of their allies, the Fujiwara. Though the seven travelers are disguised as monks, they all know that crossing this well-guarded mountain range is extremely dangerous—like stepping on a tiger's tail. The seven pick up a porter (comic actor Kenichi Enomoto, star of the Enoken movies in the 1930s), who is so foolish that he doesn't realize that he's traveling with fugitives, even though he's heard of their plight. He even describes them down to the disguises they're wearing, and still seems clueless as to whom he's traveling with.

The lord's chief retainer is Benkei (Denjiro Okochi)—who has a fearsome reputation as a staff-wielding giant warrior. Benkei is also wise. Even though it seems they have no chance of sneaking across the mountain barrier, he councils against trying to fight their way home. To change the number of their party, he has the porter change clothes with their lord—they are now six monks and two porters, not seven monks. Then he boldly leads them up the mountainside. When they arrive at the fortified barrier, Benkei once again takes the lead. Through clever words and careful control of his emotions, he convinces the captain guarding the outpost that they are merely monks on a fundraising trip. The porter helps in this cha-

rade, and earns the respect of the travelers—despite his foolish ways.

The plot of this film is fairly simple, and the film itself very short. The emphasis is on character and atmosphere, and Kurosawa doesn't disappoint on that (does he ever?). With just a few deft scenes, he gives us players we care about and identify with. The film is also quite suspenseful, even after the "monk's" initial success. *Men Who Tread on the Tiger's Tail* is one of the films where you can watch master film-maker Kurosawa's style beginning to emerge. The helpful/foolish porter clearly echoes a number of characters from later Kurosawa films—especially the fugitive farmers in *The Hidden Fortress.* This film, in fact, contains quite a few elements that Kurosawa would use later in *HF*—including the trek of a fugitive lord across a mountain range, the confrontation with the guards, and the wise, brave retainer (played in *HF* by Toshiro Mifune). Glimpses of the master's painterly photography compositions can be seen as well—though the film is set-bound and fairly stagy. An interesting musical ballad helps the scene transitions and introduces the characters and situation. Because the film is slow, it's probably not the best flick to introduce someone to Kurosawa's work, though it is an important part of his development as a film auteur. —SS *AKA:* *Tora no O Wo Fumu Otokotachi; The Men Who Step on the Tiger's Tail; They Who Step on the Tail of the Tiger; Walkers on the Tiger's Tail.* 🐉🐉🐉

1943 59m/BW *JP* Denjiro Okochi, Kenichi Enomoto, Hanshiro Iwai, Susumu Fujita, Masayuki Mori, Takashi Shimura, Aritake Kono, Yoshio Kosugi, Shoji Kiyokawa. **D:** Akira Kurosawa. **W:** Akira Kurosawa. **C:** Takeo Ito. **M:** Tadashi Hattori. **VHS, DVD**

Merry-Go-Round

During the summer school break, Mr. Kuk opens the Kuk Assorted Noodle Shop with the assistance of his two children, Fung (Lawrence Chou), a teenage boy, and Cocoa (Yuki Lai), a young girl. The shop is available only on a two-month lease, and Kuk has difficulty finding his footing as a cook and attracting customers. Carlily (Yeung Shing-lam), the niece of the former proprietor, stops by out of curiosity and quickly draws the romantic interest of Fung—but he can't stand her feisty sister Heman (Zeny Kwok), who is constantly getting in the way. Meanwhile, Cocoa spends time with Locust (Darren Cheng), a young boy who lives with his grandmother (Helena Law) in extremely modest surroundings. Will the relationships survive longer than the lease on the noodle shop?

The tale begins as a refreshingly bright and snappy summer comedy about a family running

a noodle shop. Soon enough, however, the romance between Fung and Carlily steers the tale into too-familiar territory and bogs everything down with extended depictions of their idyllic play. The scenes contain a certain amount of charm, but they still slow the pace to a crawl. It's too bad, because the original setup—involving all three members of the family—has plenty of potential for both comic and romantic adventures and is never fully exploited. In other words, more time with the father (What type of work did he do before? Why is he willing to take such a chance on a two-month lease?) would have helped ground the film in a broader-based reality. Several achingly heartfelt and beautifully filmed sequences almost make up for the missed opportunities, but by that point the viewer's patience has already been severely tested. In fact, this may be a movie that is best watched in two sittings. It would have helped if the relationship between Cocoa and Locust had been snipped out entirely—it's entirely too cute and nauseating to see preteens enacting any sort of "romantic" scenarios. It would have been much more believable and effective if they had been "just friends"— and if the friendship were used as a device to explore the social differences between the two youngsters. Eric Tsang has top billing but little screen time. Reportedly he was assaulted midway through the production, so bruises on his forehead tend to appear and disappear for no apparent reason. The standout here is newcomer Zeny Kwok—when she moves to center stage of the story, albeit briefly, she does so in a way that appears natural and not showy. Kelly Chan has a funny and nearly unrecognizable cameo as Fung's old girlfriend. —PM **AKA:** *Choh Luen Kwong Cha Min; Chu Lian Na Cha Mian.* 🐾🐾🐾

2001 93m/C *HK* Eric Tsang, Lawrence Chou, Yeung Shing-lam, Zeny Kwok, Darren Cheng, Yuki Lai, Helena Law, Kelly Chan, Vincent Kok, Hyper BB, Joe Cheung, Ann Hui. **D:** Thomas Chow. **W:** GC Goo Bi. **C:** Kwan Pun-leung. **M:** Ronald Ng. **VHS, DVD**

Message from Space

The worldwide success of *Star Wars* in 1977 produced a worldwide crop of cheap imitations (a particularly hilarious knockoff was produced in Turkey). The Japanese were not remiss in making their own space adventures, including *War in Space* and this more fantasy-oriented feature, which boasted an international cast.

On a planet far, far away, called Jallucia, a group of peasants is being invaded by a silver-skinned race of space conquerors called Gavanas. The elders produce a batch of magic seeds (walnuts) and launch them into space to locate champions to fight on their behalf. Their princess Esmeralida (Etsuko Shihomi, who looks more like a bride here than *Sister Streetfighter*) and her bodyguard Urocco (Makoto Sato) board a space-sailing ship to keep track of what happens to the walnuts. What happens is they each end up in the hands of a teenage pilot (Hiroyuki Sanada and Philip Casnoff), robot (Isamu Shimizu), or plucky heiress (Peggy Lee Brennan), all of whom are drawn together by the events of the plot to end up in the same space disco. Sonny Chiba is Prince Hans, who switches sides to fight for the good guys. Even Vic Morrow, who spends most of the film drinking cocktails while dressed as a pimp, finds a walnut in his bourbon. The walnuts start to glow whenever one of the heroes is judged worthy. The whole gang ends up defending Earth (where they still drive around in '70s cars) from the alien do-badders. Then they invade the bad guys' mobile planetoid to blow it up before it reaches the planet Jillucia.

It's not easy to follow every strange little detail, but just sit back and gape at the wild costumes, sets, and f/x. Director Kinji Fukasaku had one of the widest ranging careers ever, helming space operas like this one and *Battle in Outer Space* on the one hand, the gritty *Battle Royale* on the other, and *Black Lizard* on the freakish third hand. **AKA:** *Uchu Kara No Messe-ji; Message from Space: Galactic Wars.* 🐾🐾🐾

1978 (PG) 105m/C *JP* Vic Morrow, Sonny Chiba, Etsuko Shihomi, Makoto Sato, Henry Sanada, Philip Casnoff, Peggy Lee Brennan, Isamu Shimizu. **D:** Kinji Fukasaku. **W:** Kinji Fukasaku, Shotaro Ishinomori, Hiro Matsuda, Masdahiro Noda (story). **C:** Toru Nakajima. **M:** Shunsuke Kikuchi, Ken-Ichiro Morioka. **VHS**

Metropolis

Osamu Tezuka was so taken with Fritz Lang's *Metropolis* that he had to create his own version. In 1949, Tezuka was one of Japan's favorite cartoonists. His *New Treasure Island* series had been a big hit, and subsequent stories using many of the same cartoon "actors" had only increased his popularity. His work had turned more to science fiction lately, and he'd recently completed his own version of *The Lost World*. Within a few years, Tezuka would be the most successful cartoonist since Disney. *Metropolis* is one of his minor works, considering he would create *Astro Boy*—based on some of the same concepts—two years later. The film adaptation of his manga was one of the last projects of his life. It's only right that Rintaro, who had started working with Tezuka on the *Astro Boy* TV series, be the one to continue

Tezuka's work in feature animation. And it's only fitting that Katsuhiro Otomo, who created such an enduring Metropolis of his own in *Akira*, write the script for the feature.

The mayor of the giant city has just declared a week-long celebration in honor of the opening of the Ziggurat, the largest building ever constructed. But for Duke Red, the billionaire who built the structure, Ziggurat is more than a monstrous vertical city—it's a huge machine that can take control of all the world's computer systems. The key to that machine is Tima, the most advanced robot ever created, formed in the image of Red's deceased daughter. Down in the lower city, Dr. Laughton has been working on the highly illegal experiments necessary for Tima's creation in secret for quite some time. Private Detective Shunsaku Ban has come from Japan, along with his nephew Kenichi, in pursuit of Laughton. Rock, adopted son and security chief of Duke Red, learns of the scheme and is jealous. He finds Laughton's lab, murders the scientist, and sets fire to the building. However, Shunsaku and Kenichi arrive in time to save a young girl from the fire. The unknowing robot Tima and Kenichi quickly form a deep bond. Extremist groups on both sides of the robot issue are manipulated by the city's elite in their struggle for power, and are useful in returning Tima to Duke Red. When Tima takes her seat in the psychotronic chair high atop the Ziggurat, will it bring about the paradise that Red envisions, or destroy the world?

Well, considering this film was made in Japan, a country obsessed with building huge sandcastles and kicking them down, rest assured the climax involves a lot of destruction. The temptation with recent projects adapting Tezuka has been to "modernize" his character designs, which are considered too cute for his more mature material. The visuals are incredibly gorgeous, capturing the awe of Tezuka's drawings and adapting them for big screen appreciation. It's gratifying to see that Rintaro has retained the Master's original "cast," and that any new characters have been designed in the same style, creating the perfect counterpoint to the heavy issues being dealt with. Another nice touch is the soundtrack, a blend of classic big-band jazz and electronica perfectly suited for this world of people and robots. Many aspects of the original *Metropolis* have since been adopted many times for other works of science fiction, and will thus be taken as clichés by some viewers. That's too bad—it's like rejecting the Mona Lisa because you've seen too many Smiley faces. 𝄞𝄞𝄞𝄞

2001 (PG-13) 107m/C *JP* **D:** Rintaro. **W:** Katsuhiro Otomo, Osamu Tezuka (manga). **M:** Toshiyuki Honda. **VHS, DVD**

Midnight Fly

Two tourists become friends while touring France, and then make a fateful decision to visit Morocco. Michele (Anita Mui) is from Hong Kong. She is married but unhappy in her relationship with her husband (Simon Yam), so on a trip to France she mulls over her life. She signs up for a bus tour, which turns out to be a rotten idea. The bus group is the usual motley crew of happy and blithely unaware tourists, and Michele is just not in the right frame of mind to put up with such things. She especially gets off on the wrong foot with Miki (Risa Junna, star of the *Spiral* TV series), a Japanese woman. When Michele becomes ill, however, it's Miki who stays behind at the hotel and looks after her. As the two women get to know each other, they commiserate over the sad state of their romantic lives—Miki is feeling guilty about her unhappy affair with a married man. Having bonded, the women decide to extend their time together by taking a trip to Northern Africa. There they discover that they have even more in common than they ever could have imagined.

How can you reconcile infuriating plot twists and naked emotional manipulation with incredibly haunting imagery and devastating performances? *Midnight Fly* is not the work of a B-movie hack going for the jugular with cheap thrills in mind. Director Jacob Cheung displays a masterful touch with the pacing of the film. You suspect he's setting you up for a sucker punch—he is—but you don't know when it's coming, and when it does, it doesn't quite match your expectations. The cumulative power of the film will depend on your state of mind, your expectations, and your life experience. There's no denying that it's extremely absorbing to watch, and after a certain point you simply can't turn away. It's similar to how time seems to slow down during an automobile accident, as your mind tries to prepare your body to accept the fact that...*this is going to hurt.* —PM **AKA:** *Fong Sam Ga Gei; Huang Xin Jia Ji.* 𝄞𝄞𝄞

2001 111m/C *HK* Anita Mui, Risa Junna, Shaun Tam, Simon Yam. **D:** Jacob Cheung. **C:** Wong Ping-hung. **VHS, DVD**

Mighty Jack

In the tradition of *Atragon*, Tsuburaya Productions created their own toy-ready super-submarine spy TV series, from which this disjointed feature was created. Terrorist organization Q takes advantage of world unrest to further their plans for global domination. To battle Q, a special team called Mighty Jack is created. Their main weapon is a powerful atomic flying submarine, also named *Mighty Jack*! Q kidnaps important cartographer/mountaineer Harold Atari, prompting Colonel Yubuki to bring Mighty Jack in on the case. Following the signal from the radio in Atari's mighty jacket, Mighty Jack climbs aboard *Mighty Jack* to fly to the rescue. After making some cracks about him during the rescue, Lieutenant Jerry (*Ultraman* regular Masanori Nihei) is chagrined to discover that Atari is the new commander of Mighty Jack. It's discovered that Q's secret base is on an artificial island made of solidified water, the secret for which was stolen from the Frigidaire Corporation. Meanwhile, Mighty Jack is such a secret organization that they spend a lot of time just trying to figure out who their agents are. After a lot of scurrying around to secure the water solidifying and unsolidifying secrets, the crew finally gets around to an assault on the Q secret base.

The feature splices together the first and last episodes of the TV series, along with a few bits and pieces from middle 11 episodes to knit the two together. Tsuburaya's legendary optical and miniature special effects are the highlight here, as the lackluster characters and tired situations don't provide much interest on their own, just dull recycled spy nonsense. The influence of SPECTRE from the 007 series on Q is obvious—their Blofeld-like leader even carries a cat with him. Tsuburaya followed with a sequel series called *Fight! Mighty Jack*. **AKA:** *Maitei Jyakku.* 🐉

1968 95m/C *JP* Hideaki Nitani, Naoko Kubo, Hiroshi Minami, Eisei Amamoto, Masanori Nihei, Jerry Ito, Wakako Ikeda, Akira Kasuga, Seiko Fukioka, Noriaki Inoue, Yoshitaka Tanaka, Mitsubo Ohya, Eijiro Yanagi. **D:** Kazuho Mitsuta. **W:** Shinichi Sekizawa, Eizaburo Siba. **C:** Yoshihiro Mori, Kazuo Sagawa. **M:** Isao Tomita. **VHS**

Mighty Peking Man

1977 was the Time of the Apes in movieland. Sure, the *Planet of the Apes* series had run to a halt, but producer Dino De Laurentiis was making a lot of noise promoting his big-budget remake of *King Kong*. As expected, a lot of cheap knockoffs were rushed into production. Strangely, Toho Studios, who had produced two Kong features in the 1960s, kept out of the party. But other studios from elsewhere in Asia weren't as shy. Koreans made the horrible *A*P*E*, and Hong Kong's mighty Shaw Brothers stepped forward with this mighty feature.

An earthquake frees a giant hairy biped from an ice cave in Tibet. Entrepreneur Lu Tien (Ku Feng) hires big-game hunter Johnny Feng (Danny Lee, long before he met John Woo) to lead an expedition into the Indian jungles to capture or kill the beast. Abandoned by his companions,

Johnny is nearly crushed by the monster, but is rescued by a Sheena-like blonde jungle girl named Samantha (Evelyne Kraft). The girl was saved as a child by the monster she calls Utam, and has been his best friend ever since. After he sucks cobra venom from her inner thigh, could it be that Samantha is falling in love with Johnny? Maybe, and maybe Peking peeping Utam gets an eyeful of his girlfriend with her new beau, and gets a little jealous.

Convincing Samantha to bring Utam back to civilization, Johnny makes his employer very happy when he shows up in town with their quarry in tow. Hopping a freighter to Hong Kong, Utam is chained up in Hong Kong Stadium and forced to play tug-o-war with monster trucks. But when Lu Tien tries to rough up his girl, Utam breaks out of his cage and goes on a rampage through Hong Kong to save her.

The optical and miniature f/x are pretty good, but the various Peking Man masks and costumes are shabby and lifeless. However, Kraft's costume does just what's intended: barely cover a few patches of skin. The tight editing rhythm of the climactic orgy of destruction brings some genuine excitement. **AKA:** *Sing Sing Wong; Xing Xing Wang; Hsing Hsing Wang; Goliathon; Colossus of Congo.* 🐉🐉🐉

1977 (PG-13) 91m/C *HK* Evelyne Kraft, Danny Lee, Ku Feng, Lin Wei-Tu, Hsiao Ho, Hsu Shao-Chiang, Ng Hong Song, Chen Ping, Ted Thomas. **D:** Ho Meng-Hua. **W:** Ngai Hong. **C:** Tsao Hu-Chi, Chen Rong-shu, Wu Cho-Hua. **M:** Chen Yung-Yu. **VHS, DVD**

Militant Eagle

Having served his general well, Captain Fong Shi-er (Barry Chan) retires from the military life and heads back to his hometown, but he finds things aren't much more peaceful. Though the new emperor has temporarily suspended taxation, local officials have taken advantage of the situation by imposing fees and taxes of their own. Fong poses as a street performer leading a gang of orphaned kung fu kids in order to weed out corruption and find out who is behind it all. Pai Siu-ching (Liu Ping) is one of the loudest merchants to object to the situation, so Corporal Yu Wen-pao and the police murder his family while he's out. Miss Shu Yen-ju (Nancy Yen) returns from studying kung fu at O Mei Mountain to find her family has been killed as well. Fong gets together with Pai and Shu to plot a strategy; they protest to visiting envoy Liu Hung-chu (Sit Hon), who arrests Magistrate Kao Ping-chun and his whole crooked police force. But before Kao can tell the identity of his boss Fang Siu-kong (Pai Ying), he's assassinated by Fang's brother-in-law Shou Shu-liang (Ling Yun)—once a fellow kung fu student of Fong's.

M

"My buttock will
bleed until
I die!"

—Yuen Yat-chor suffers
through some extreme
kung fu training in *The
Miracle Fighters*

But Fang mistreats his wife, shaking Shou's already uncertain allegiance to the villain. He joins Fong, Shu, and Pai as they lead a raid on Fang's military training camp.

Mediocre action and uninteresting direction marks this standard martial arts adventure, distinguished only by a few unusual characters, such as the villain's pet giant Yen Ching (Siu Gam, who of course carries a big spiked club). Things perk up for the climactic battle, in which the heroes think of some clever ways to kill the exotic villains before taking on the chief bad guy (who proves he's evil by tossing around a little girl). The soundtrack steals music from several James Bond pictures, *Beneath the Planet of the Apes,* and *The Ten Commandments. AKA: Hap Daai Ngai Hat; Xia Da Er Qi; Boxer's Adventure; Millitant Eagle.* 🗡🗡

1978 93m/C *HK* Ling Yun, Barry Chan, Pai Ying, Nancy Yen, Liu Ping, Sit Hon, Yeung Sau-guen, Suen Lam, Siu Gam, Au Lap-bo, Kong Ching-ha, Choi Wang, Man Chung-san, Miu Tin, Ma Chin-ku, Wang Tai-lang, Au Yeung-chung, Yeung Sau-guen, Terry Liu. **D:** Li Chia Chi. **W:** Li Chia Chi, Kim Kong. **C:** Yue Wu. **M:** Wang Mo-san. **DVD**

Millennium Dragon

The plot to this one is a muddle that only starts to unwind midway through, but let's see if we can make sense of it. Yuen Biao (called "Yuen Bill" here) gets star billing, but only has a supporting role. Chu Lai-Yee is the real star, playing South Korean government agent Kim, sent to Russia to investigate a smuggling ring. The likely head of the ring is rich antiquities fan Cho Dai-foo (Charlie Cho), but Cho's real scheme is far more dangerous than smuggling. Hon Foh-lui (Chin Siu-Ho) and his equally vicious sister May-ching (Lily Chung) lead a gang of bandits who have held up Cho's archeologists, stealing a relic known as the Millennia Luminant Pearl, and want to trade Cho for a classified computer chip in his possession. Kim only knows Cho is expecting some kind of delivery, and works undercover as a delivery boy to intercept the package. Yuen plays Chinese agent Ma Sar, who is also undercover. Actually, the pearl is a source of incredible energy.

After the disruption of their exchange, distrust between Cho and Hon grows. Kim befriends singer Sonia, knowing she both works with Cho and is friends with Teresa, Hon's girlfriend. He successfully infiltrates Hon's organization, but is perturbed when a Chinese rival (Ben Ng)—who is also a spy—for Sonia appears. Sonia turns out to be a Chinese spy, too!

Once everyone gets their covers blown, it's a mystery why they bothered with all the cloak and dagger nonsense, since everyone just ends up

in a big running gun battle with everyone after the pearl. The main source of suspense is trying to figure out why Yuen Biao is wearing such a goofy hat and whether he'll ever take it off (he doesn't).

Considering the cast, there's precious little kung fu fighting to speak of. Director Philip Ko tries to shoot Jackie Chan fight scenes, John Woo gun battles, and Wong Kar-Wai sword fights, and fails at all three. One would think that the Moscow and Mongolian locations would at least add some visual interest, but except for a few shots, the whole thing might as well have been shot in suburban New Mexico. *AKA: Hung Cheung do Ying; Hong Qiang dao Ying; Red Square Thieves.* 🗡🗡

1999 93m/C *HK* Yuen Biao, Ben Ng, Chu Lai-Yee, Chin Siu-Ho, Lily Chung, Charlie Cho. **D:** Phillip Ko. **W:** Li Ngai Chi. **VHS, DVD**

The Millionaires' Express

For those familiar with Hong Kong cinema, this rousing action comedy epic produced and directed by Sammo Hung is a terrific game of "Name That Star"—every other face is a familiar HK character actor or headliner. For greener viewers, it's still a tremendously entertaining movie full of laughs and top-notch stunt work.

Things are desperate in the small Chinese frontier town of Hanshui. Security Chief Jook Bo (Eric Tsang) is lighting a fire so he and his men can rob the bank in the confusion. Though Fire Department Captain Tsao Cheuk-kin (Yuen Biao) catches two of the robbers, the rest get away, planning to hop aboard a train just outside town. Mayor Yi (Wu Fung) delivers the bad news—the robbery has left the town bankrupt, and Tsao is made new Security Chief, in charge of hunting down his predecessor. It's to this scene of desperation that disreputable character Chin Fong-tin (Hung) makes a grand homecoming, bringing with him a handful of "society girls." Though he professes to have become an honest businessman, Chin's scheme is much more sinister than anyone suspects—he means to save the town by blowing up the railroad tracks, stranding the wealthy passengers of the Shanghai Express in Hanshui, and making the town into a literal tourist trap.

Meanwhile, a gang of bandits led by Yun Shiyu (James Tien) plans to rob the train. Some of the bandits ride the train, while a larger and rougher group (including Americans Cynthia Rothrock and Richard Norton) camp near the river in ambush. A Japanese agent bearing a map to the terracotta warriors (Green Jade Buddhas in the English dub) is aboard the train disguised as a tourist, plus the rest of the passengers are millionaires ripe for plucking. Well, not all million-aires—old rival martial arts masters Wong (Jimmy Wang Yu) and Sek (Shih Kien)—along with their sons Fei-hung and Ah-kin—are onboard as well. Chin stops the train, and the various intrigues move into the town's large hotel. Bounty hunter Loi Fook (Kenny Bee) catches up to Chin, and he and Tsao capture the rascal. Chin's girl-friend Sylvia (Olivia Cheng) and the other girls quickly spring him, but when the rest of the ban-dits arrive to take over the town, Chin leads the combined forces of prisoners, prostitutes, fire-men, cops, and tourists to fight them.

Millionaires' Express is in some ways a tran-sition film for Sammo Hung, using a lot of the comic energy and performers from his Lucky Stars films, but presented in a broader context with richer characters (despite the size of the cast). He'd go on to even more intense action and heavier emotional content in his amazing Eastern Condors. But this one is all about get-ting a lot of great stars in one place and having them display their talents in spectacular fash-ion. The stunts and fight scenes are incredible. Yuen Biao jumps from the roof of a two-story (burning) building, lands on his feet, and acts like it was just another step. Even comics like Richard Ng and Eric Tsang get to do some stunts, running on top of or hanging off of the wonderful vintage locomotive. The train and town act as extra characters—although set in the China of 1939, one gets the feeling that it might just as well be Utah or Australia in the 1920s, and few of the characters wear Chinese clothing. Like many martial arts films, it takes place in its own universe. One slight disappoint-ment is that after their introduction and some business on the train, the Jimmy Wang Yu and Shih Kien characters are pretty much forgotten. The end titles run over some behind-the-scenes clips of Hung directing the film, including shots of the town being built in the Canadian wilder-ness. This is one Hong Kong export that could use a new soundtrack, deserving a grand orchestral score in place of its thin sounding music. The U.S. English-dubbed version cuts out five minutes of character and plot develop-ment, romance, and even action. **AKA:** *Foo Gwai Lit Che; Fu Gui Lie Che; Shanghai Express; Nobles' Express; Wealthy Train.* 🦴🦴🦴🦴

1986 97m/C *HK* Sammo Hung, Yuen Biao, Kenny Bee, Eric Tsang, Olivia Cheng, Richard Ng, James Tien, Yukari Oshima, Hwang Jang Lee, Yasuaki Kurata, Rosamund Kwan, Cynthia Rothrock, Richard Norton, Lau Kar-Wing, Emily Chu, Jimmy Wang Yu, Shih Kien, Lydia Shum, Billy Lau, Dick Wei, Wu Fung, Lam Ching-Ying, Yuen Wah, Corey Yuen, Wu Ma, Mars, Fan Mui-Sang, Chan Lung, Chin Ka-Lok, Chung Fat, Hsiao Ho, Phillip Ko, Fung Lee, Mang Hoi, Tai Bo, Yuen Tak, Bolo Yeung. **D:** Sammo Hung. **W:** Barry Wong, Alfred Cheung. **C:** Arthur Wong, Peter Ngor. **M:** Sing Kam-wing. **VHS, DVD**

The Miracle Fighters

Inspired by the success of Sammo Hung's *Encounters of the Spooky Kind,* Yuen Woo-ping and his relatives conspired to out-spook Sammo with a sorcery epic of their own. In 1663, Manchus of the Ching Dynasty are forbid-den to marry with Hans. When Kao Hsiung (Eddie Ko), martial arts coach of the Eight Ban-ners Army, is found to have married a Han, Lord Shu orders the whole Kao family executed as an example. Though the imperial sorcerer Bat (Sunny Yuen) sends a wine-jug imp (Brandy Yuen) to kill him, Kao escapes the palace by taking the young prince as a hostage. Kao is shocked to find that, while carrying the boy away, he's accidentally strangled him.

Fourteen years later, Kao lives anonymously as a town drunk, aided by his young disciple Shu Gun (Yuen Yat-chor). When Kao is found out, Bat and his assassins attack, killing Kao and abduct-ing Shu Gun—whom they assume to be the prince, as he wears the royal jade Kao gave him. However, the sorcerer learns the truth when he notes Shu Gun lacks the prince's birthmark on his foot. In order to get a promotion, the sorcerer tattoos the birthmark on Shu Gun to pass him off as the missing royalty. Shu Gun escapes because the wine-jug imp is "too emotional," and seeks refuge with his friends, the neighbor-hood magician (Leung Kar-yan) and his wife (Yuen Cheung-yan). While the couple teaches Shu Gun some of their magic, Bat sends various assassins to attack them—from the traditional ninja variety to a "Face-Shaving Sister." When these fail, Bat uses what appears to be latex masks (in 1677!) to impersonate the old couple and invade their home. Bat succeeds in killing the old woman (using a flying top that drills itself into her head à la *Phantasm*), but Shu Gun and the old man drive him off. In honor of old sister, Shu Gun enters the Demon City Sorcery Champi-onship—and of course the evil Bat sneaks in disguised to become an entrant as well.

The creativity of the Yuen Clan is at its sharpest here, mixing their trademark kung fu choreography with a variety of whimsical special effects. They also mix some shocking violence with extremely silly comedy, keeping the audi-ence off balance, but amused. For example, in one scene Yuen Cheung-yan chases Yuen Yat-chor around with a ridiculously huge axe, and the chase ends with a bloody decapitation. It's revealed as a gag a second later, leaving the viewer gasping and laughing at the same time. Also on display is the ability to produce extra limbs, a living kung fu stick figure, and some impressive fire- and snake-wrangling. The whole film has something of a Chinese opera atmos-phere, with men taking nearly all the roles,

including the females. In tribute to the Yuen patriarch, an animated drawing of Simon Yuen appears. *AKA: Kei Moon Dun Gaap; Ji Men Dun Jia.* 🦴🦴🦴🦴

1982 96m/C *HK* Leung Kar-yan, Yuen Cheung-yan, Yuen Yat-chor, Sunny Yuen, Eddie Ko, Brandy Yuen, Huang Ha, Tino Wong. *D:* Yuen Woo-ping. *W:* Woo Ping Creative Group. *C:* Ma Koon-wah. **VHS, DVD**

Miracles

Jackie Chan has always been a big fan of Hollywood musicals, and this adaptation of a Damon Runyon story (already filmed twice in the U.S. by Frank Capra as *Lady for a Day* and *Pocketful of Miracles*) is the closest he's gotten to making one of his own. At the time of release, many Stateside Jackie Chan fans were disappointed by the relative lack of action scenes. However, the fight scenes included are fantastic, and this is really Chan's best film as director, including many long tracking shots and complex montage sequences that show off stunningly redressed Golden Harvest standing sets and dazzling 1930s-era costumes. But one of the film's best attributes is its amazing cast stuffed with familiar Hong Kong stars—though this factor will be lost on newcomers, especially if they see the edited English-dubbed version.

Kuo Cheng-wah (Chan) is a bumpkin fresh off the radish truck in Canton when he has his life's savings taken by a con man (Bill Tung). His helpful nature gets him in hot water when he gets in between two battling gangs. His bumbling attempts to help the fatally injured leader of one pack has everyone mistaking the boss's dying gesture as a sign that Kuo be made his successor. Uncomfortable with the gang's criminal ways, Kuo attempts to have them go straight, transforming one of their sleazy casinos into a successful nightclub, hiring saucy singer Yang Lu-ming (Anita Mui) to be its star. However, Kuo still has to deal with threats from Tiger Lo (O Chun Hung) and his gang, who want to take over. Throughout Kuo's adventures, he counts on rose-vending Madam Kao (Gui Yalei) as his personal good-luck charm, always having success in his ventures after buying one of her flowers. When Madam Kao gets in a scrape, Kuo, Yang, and even mentor Uncle Hai (Wu Ma) try to help out. It seems she's been sending letters to her daughter, who's been studying in Shanghai, describing a life of ease so as not to worry her. But now the daughter is returning with a rich fiancé and his respectable parents in tow, and she's afraid revelation of her lowly status will ruin the girl's chance at happiness. They get the whole roughhouse gang to impersonate dignitaries for a party to impress the guests, even getting Hai cleaned up as Kao's boyfriend.

Unfortunately, the police smell something suspicious in this gathering of usual suspects—as does Tiger, who sends thugs to kidnap Kuo just as the party is about to start.

Griping fans should take the time to watch this film again and note that, even if it had no kung fu at all, it would still be a damn fine movie, a tribute to both the opulence of Old Hollywood and the energy of New Hong Kong. What Chan displays here is his mastery of timing, and not just in the great rope-factory fight scene. Jackie's comic instincts are at their sharpest, expanding the pratfalls and intricate hide-and-seek scenes he'd been including in his films all along. Plus, he hangs it all on a classic story with built-in comic and dramatic possibilities, all of which he makes great use of. For newcomers, this is a great introduction to Chan's work and the possibilities of HK cinema. More experienced viewers get the extra fun of a grand game of Spot the Stars. *AKA: Gei Jik; Qi Ji; Canton Godfather; Mr. Canton and Lady Rose; Black Dragon.* 🦴🦴🦴🦴

1989 (PG-13) 127m/C *HK* Jackie Chan, Anita Mui, Wu Ma, Gui Yalei, Gloria Yip, Bill Tung, Richard Ng, Ray Lui, Lo Lieh, Billy Lau, O Chun Hung, Tiin Fung, Lui Fong, Ngai Hong, James Wong, Billy Chow, Shum Wai, Michael Chow, Tai Bo, Lee Hoi-sang, Mars, Wu Fung, Lau Siu-ming, Ricky Hui, Kenny Bee, Anthony Chan, Lawrence Cheng, John Sham, Jacky Cheung, Yuen Biao, Ken Lo, Fung Hark-On, Benny Lai, Amy Yip, Chen Jing, Alvina Kong, Chor Yuen, Michael Lai, Simon Yam, Melvin Wong, Dick Wei, Alan Chan, John Chang, May Lo, Walter Cho, Lee Man Tai, Kara Hui, Louis Roth, Anders Nelsson. *D:* Jackie Chan. *W:* Edward Tang, Jackie Chan. *C:* Arthur Wong. *M:* Chow Chi-sang. **VHS, DVD**

The Mission

An attempt on his life by a team of hit men puts a scare into triad boss Lung (Eddie Ko). He has his second, Frank (Simon Yam), gather a team of bodyguards to see to his protection, and help catch whoever was contracted for the hit: restaurant owner Roy (Francis Ng), his assistant Shin (Jackie Lui), upscale barber Curtis (Anthony Wong), former pimp Mike (Roy Cheung), and weapons expert James (Lam Suet). A bullet-proof vest saves Lung's life from a second attempt by a sniper, but the team feels bad about it, especially since the sniper gets away. The third attempt is more successfully repelled, and several of the assassins are killed. Through their shared adventures—and the odd mix of boredom and tension in between—the five men form a bond and become a team. The fourth attempt is lucky—a former bodyguard happens to be nearby and gives his life for Lung, and the bodyguards follow the assassin back to his nest, where they take down the others and capture the leader. Their mission accomplished, the five relax and toast their friendship. However, there's a fly in the ointment: Frank tells Curtis that he found out Shin had an affair with Lung's wife during the assignment, and asks him to take care of the problem. The news leaks out to the rest, dividing the group, and they try to come up with a plan that will resolve the situation without dooming any of them.

A beautifully composed thriller, *The Mission* provides a great cast, a solid story, and exciting gun fu that doesn't stretch beyond the believable. Anthony Wong is a marvel of restraint, avoiding the ticks and indulgences that sometimes mar his work. Simon Yam is delightfully oily as the number-two man, and Eddie Ko gives his commanding mobster just the right touch of vulnerability. Johnny To's direction is deceptively simple in style, accomplishing much with carefully placed shadows and tight editing, placing his camera to catch little bits of character. The only drawback here is the cheap-sounding keyboard soundtrack—the score itself isn't so bad, adding to the excitement or lightening the tone when necessary—but a few additional instruments might make it sound less chintzy. **AKA:** *Cheong Feng; Qiang Huo.* 🐉🐉🐉🐉

1999 84m/C *HK* Anthony Wong, Francis Ng, Jackie Lui, Roy Cheung, Simon Yam, Lam Suet, Eddie Ko, Elaine Eca Da Silva, Wong Tin Lam, Sato Keiji, Ai Wai, Jerome Fung, Chang Chi-ping. **D:** Johnny To. **W:** Yau Nai-hoi, Milkway Creative Team. **C:** Cheng Siu-keung. **M:** Chung Chi-wing. **VHS, DVD**

Mr. Boo Meets Pom Pom

D&B Films had two wildly successful series about goofy-but-effective Hong Kong cops, so this crossover film was a no-brainer. When a bank holdup goes awry, Inspector Chan (Phillip Chan) calls in both detective partners Chau and Beethoven (Richard Ng and John Sham) and crime expert Mr. Boo (Michael Hui). After teaming up to catch the robbers, Beethoven becomes an admirer of Mr. Boo, but Chau resents his arrogance. During a jewelry-store robbery the next day, the thieves accidentally find a way to break the store's new Super Glass. Owner Charlie Yeung (Stuart Ong) interviews Chau and Beethoven, who failed to foil the robbery, trying to find out how it was done. Beethoven consults with Boo on the case, and the expert soon discovers the sound frequency that shattered the glass. Boo disdains working with the low-class cops, but when he discovers his wife (Terry Hu) is cheating with rich playboy Yeung, Beethoven and Chau help him get revenge, and the trio become friends. Their pursuit of Boo's cheating wife includes a trip to

Japan (an idea used just to please Hui's many Japanese fans) for some winter sports and a fight with a sumo wrestler.

Hui's comedy style, which varies from subtle and satirical to bizarre slapstick, mixes surprisingly well with the more straightforward gags of Ng and Sham. However, the plot seems to lack a decent case for the trio to solve together. Yeung is a villain to be sure, but he's only pushy and arrogant, not a real criminal. The worst he does is send his sumo to beat Mr. Boo when the man annoys him. Hui's films make the most of such duels between rivals, but the Pom Pom series needs to fulfill the basic structure of a buddy-cop movie to work well. Deanie Yip demonstrates the power of her own screen talent with only a brief appearance here as Chau's wife Anna. The soundtrack swipes cues from *Mad Max.* **AKA:** *Ji Yung Saam Bo; Zhi Yong San Bao.* 🐉🐉🐉

1985 89m/C *HK* Michael Hui, Richard Ng, John Sham, Phillip Chan, Terry Hu, Deanie Yip, Stuart Ong, Chan Lung, Nat Chan, Dennis Chan, Yip Wing-cho, Ben Lam, Lee Man Tai. **D:** Wu Ma. **W:** Joe Chan. **C:** Arthur Wong. **M:** Joseph Chan. **VHS, DVD**

Mr. Nice Guy

Jackie Chan is back as a TV chef in Melbourne who gets deeper and deeper into trouble as a result of a good deed. When he sees gangsters attacking TV journalist Diana (Gabrielle Fitzpatrick), he intervenes, but then becomes a target for the gangs himself when he ends up with her incriminating videotape. It's an old pulp-writers' formula: an innocent is mistakenly left with a McGuffin that two rival gangs are competing for. The same plot worked in *Rumble in the Bronx,* so they resurrect it here. In fact, there are enough recycled elements in the patchwork plot to make this sort of a "Best of Jackie" feature. Besides the street gang vs. Mafioso riff from *Rumble,* the finale again involves a large, unusual vehicle. There's also an interracial trio of beauties in peril (à la *Operation Condor*), a fight in a construction site (à la *Heart of Dragon, Project A 2,* and *Police Story 2*), as well as the casting of Richard Norton as the quirky villain (Norton filled a similar role in *City Hunter*). Not to complain, though—the plot of the average Jackie Chan film is just a loose device on which to hang terrific fights, gags, and stunts. One nagging gaff is the videotape itself—telejournalists in Melbourne seem to use standard VHS instead of a professional format, and the tape shows shots from *the movie* (complete with edits and close-ups), rather than any realistic camera angle.

The U.S. release is not as severely edited as some of his others. The slight editing does

TV chef Jackie Chan's efforts to do good keep getting him into situations like this one in *Mr. Nice Guy.*

THE KOBAL COLLECTION

weaken the transitions and motivations in several scenes, however. Generally, the cuts function to soften the bad guys' behavior a little—the original HK version contained several shots of particularly cruel violence that tend to distract from the overall comic tone (at least for Americans). Also dropped are bits that show that Jackie's assistant Lakisha (Karen McLymont) has a crush on him, which makes her fierce protection of Jackie's apartment against an invading Diana seem too extreme. And the exclusion of some scenes with Jackie and his girlfriend (Miki Lee) hurt the pace of the picture and weaken their bond. For those dorks that come to JC flicks just to laugh at the dubbing, there's a new twist in this release. This was the first Chan movie to be filmed almost entirely in English, but for some reason most of the Anglo actors have been dubbed over. This makes sense in the case of the non-acting martial artists who may have trouble with their lines, but Richard Norton is a decent actor with over two dozen movies to his credit. Awkward bits of dialogue might be attributed to director Sammo Hung's unfamiliarity with English, and the dubbing doesn't help any. Jackie's "Biggest Brother" Sammo improved quite a bit with his subsequent U.S.-set feature *Once upon a Time in China and America.* Other changes for the U.S. version include a sharper picture and a more impressive sound mix. Most dialogue scenes have been cropped tighter. Unlike previous releases, there is no new "hip hop" score tacked on, and Jackie's theme song has been removed from the end credits (which unspool after his trademark "ouchtakes").

Chan's films usually fall into a category of "circus movies." The stories aren't especially interesting, but they provide an opportunity for an ongoing parade of wonders. Jackie has nine amazing fight scenes, several chases, some inspired comedy scenes, and plenty of destruction of property to his credit here. Not the best Jackie Chan movie, but lots of fun. *AKA: Yatgo yo han; YiGe Hao Ren; SuperChef; No More Mr. Nice Guy.* 🎝🎝🎝

1997 (PG-13) 88m/C *HK* Jackie Chan, Miki Li, Richard Norton, Gabrielle Fitzpatrick, Karen McLymont, Barry Otto, Vince Poletto, Peter Houghton, Sammo Hung, Jonathan James Isgar, Matthew Meersbergen, Brad Allan, Joseph Sayah, Emil Chau, Joyce Godenzi, Ang Lee. *D:* Sammo Hung. *W:* Edward Tang, Fibe Ma. *C:* Joe Chan, Raymond Lam. *M:* Peter Kam, J. Peter Robinson (U.S. version). **VHS, DVD**

Mr. Vampire

Sammo Hung was a pioneer in the field of Hong Kong horror/action/comedy with his *Encounters of the Spooky Kind* (1980), but it wasn't until he produced this 1985 hit that the subgenre truly took off.

Man (Ricky Hui) is a lowly assistant in a funeral parlor that's not just creepy to work in, it's downright dangerous. You see, the proprietor, Taoist priest Master Kow (Lam Ching-Ying) specializes in services for the "kyonsi," China's infamous hopping vampires. Kyonsi can be wrangled, but the rules for their care and control are complex (see sidebar), and a wrong move by an oaf like Man can bring disaster. Kow and Man meet for English tea with Mr. Yam to discuss moving his father's grave, which he believes will bring him good luck through feng shui. They meet Yam's daughter Ting Ting (Moon Lee), who prefers the English style in dress and manner, and poor nebbish Man is instantly in love. Even if he had a chance, he has many rivals, including his fellow assistant Chou (Chin Siu-Ho), who also works at his family's general store. Ting Ting's nerdy cousin, Police Inspector Wai (Billy Lau), also considers himself in the running.

At the exhumation, Kow knows instantly that the fortune-teller who advised Yam about the burial was a swindler, and something's not right about the plot. Sure enough, the body (Yuen Wah)—dead 20 years—looks fresh. Stored at the mortuary until a proper plot can be found, Kow determines the corpse is turning into a kyonsi, and they take steps to keep it corralled. It doesn't work, and Yam becomes his father's first victim. Arrested for the murder, Kow, Wai, and Chou have to struggle hard to kill re-animated Yam a second time. When the kyonsi comes looking to eat more Yams, Man is infected before Kow can drive the monster away.

Meanwhile, Chou is haunted by a pretty ghost (Pauline Wong) that spied him at the graveyard. This amorous spirit's attempts at romance keeps the crew busy for a while, giving powerful vampire Grampa Yam time to rest up for his attack in the third act.

Mr. Vampire is some kind of a crowd-pleasing masterpiece, with just enough comedy to keep things moving along lightly, just enough horror to keep it all from getting too silly, and loads of acrobatic action. Where necessary, director Ricky Lau and cinematographer Ngor Chi Kwan come up with some stunning visuals. The scenes of the ghost floating about the woods at night, assisted by a ghoulish palanquin party, were doubtless an influence on Ching Tsiu-tung's acclaimed *A Chinese Ghost Story* two years later. The relentless Lip On Tat music adds just the right undercurrent of suspense. Lam, previously just a dependable character actor, made such an impression as the mono-browed necromancer that he turned the role into a cottage industry, appearing in several sequels and similar roles within the next few years. Hui, sometimes overshadowed in the Hui Brothers comedies, proved he's more than just a goofy face and can hold his own in a larger role. *AKA: Geung si Sin Sang; Jiang shi Xian Sheng; Mr. Stiff Corpse.* ♪♪♪♪

1985 94m/C *HK* Lam Ching-Ying, Chin Siu-Ho, Ricky Hui, Moon Lee, Pauline Wong, Billy Lau, Yuen Wah, Wu Ma. **D:** Ricky Lau. **W:** Szeto Cheuk Hon, Ricky Lau, Barry Wong. **C:** Peter Ngor. **M:** Lip On Tat. **VHS, DVD**

Mr. Vampire 2

Throwing a curve to fans of the hit kyonsi horror comedy, Ricky Lau updates this sequel to the present day, where a Professor (Chung Fat) on an archeological expedition uncovers the tomb of a Mama Vampire, a Papa Vampire, and a little Baby Vampire. While taking Baby as a "sample" to show a prospective buyer, the Professor encounters a gust of wind that removes the spell from Baby's forehead, setting him loose. Back in the lab, assistant Chicken (Billy Lau) accidentally awakens the parents as well. Meanwhile, Baby Vampire hides out in a suburban home, hidden by children Chiang and Chia-chia from their widower dad Mr. Hu (Wu Fung). The kids think the friendly hopping corpse is an illegal immigrant, even when he displays E.T.-style telekinesis. Beware: things get horribly cute for a while, with the little vampire refusing to kill his playmates no matter how much you pray he will. Fortunately, we cut away to Chicken seeking aid for a vampire bite from mono-browed pharmacist Lin Cheng-ying (Lam Ching-Ying), descendant of the previous film's heroic Taoist. Lin knows his vampire lore, and with help from his daughter Gigi (Moon Lee) and her reporter boyfriend Jen (Yuen Biao), he goes hunting hoppers.

Yuen Biao's meddling reporter lets the vampires loose, leading to many creative acrobatic action scenes designed by producer Sammo Hung's stunt team. If you can weather the precious Baby Vampire pap, Lau once again delivers a fun mix of thrills and knockabout comedy. Ricky Hui from part one is missed, but Yuen Biao makes for a fine replacement. The fine cinematography and sets give the image much the same look as a Hammer horror film. Unfortunately, the talented corpses remain unidentified. *AKA: Geung Si Sin Saang Juk Jaap; Jiang Shi Xian Sheng Xu Ji; Mr. Vampire Part II.* ♪♪♪♫

1986 89m/C *HK* Lam Ching-Ying, Yuen Biao, Moon Lee, Billy Lau, Chung Fat, Wu Fung, Stanley Fung, Wu Ma, Fung Lee, James Tien, Wong Yuk-wan, Hoh Kin-wai. **D:** Ricky Lau. **W:** Barry Wong. **C:** Andrew

M

"Captain, the corpse won't come out in such weather."

—A scared cop looks for an excuse to abandon a foggy va mpire hunt, just before they find the gorilla(!), in *Mr. Vampire*

Hip Hop Vampires of China

Although "kyonsi," the restless dead, have appeared in Chinese films since the 1930s, they became phenomenally popular in 1985 with the release of Ricky Lau's *Mr. Vampire*. The Chinese vampire predates the European vampire by centuries, and the lore surrounding them is common knowledge to every child in China. Instantly recognizable in their traditional funeral robes and caps, the image of the kyonsi have adorned everything from keychains to hand puppets. Here are a few facts learned from movies made about these bouncing bloodsuckers:

- Kyonsi are referred to as hopping corpses, vampires, ghosts, or zombies—the terms seem to be interchangable.

- They hop because their limbs are too stiff from rigor mortis to walk (though they look awfully spry in a kung fu fight). They generally travel in straight lines, their rigidity preventing them from turning sharply. Not all hopping corpses are vampires— this is just the most economical way for Taoist priests to transport corpses for burial (most Chinese preferred burial in their home region). Priests can also use similar techniques much resembling Haitian voodoo practices to gain control over other peoples' bodies. In some films, the female corpses do not hop, but waddle around with a stiff-legged gait.

- Taoists transporting corpses through heavily wooded areas need to keep a sharp eye out for predators, especially werewolves and werefoxes, who sometimes try to steal one of the corpses for food.

- Though they have fangs, kyonsi prefer to draw the blood of the living through their long blue claws.

- Incense and oil lamps help to satisfy their hunger, keeping them quiet. Yellow papers marked with a blessing in black ink mixed with blood and stuck to the vampire's forehead will help immobilize them. Though these sutras and spells common in vampire movies look like Chinese writing to Westerners, according to visitors to the set, they're actually mostly nonsense figures. Bloody ink used to draw lines around the coffin will help bind the kyonsi within (but don't forget to cover the bottom of the coffin, too, or the vampire may break through and escape). Like Western vampires, a wooden sword in the heart will temporarily "kill" a kyonsi, but burning is the final solution.

- Corpse escorts store kyonsi in repose with their palms up, to help prevent them from pushing themselves erect unexpectedly.

- Just like their Western cousins, kyonsi are sensitive to sunlight and need to be sheltered during the day. If priest escorts can't find shelter, a black bag is put over each corpse's head.

- If you die with bad breath in your mouth, you'll become an evil vampire. With fresh breath, a good vampire. Kyonsi are often blind, and guide themselves by sound and smell. If you hold your breath, they can't see you.

- If infected, keep moving around to prevent the blood stiffening up. But don't perform any kung fu for six hours, lest you speed the spread of infection.

- Sticky glutinous rice is very important, as it's to kyonsi as garlic is to Dracula. Boiled, it can be used as a poultice for vampire wounds. As a soup, it can help infected victims slow the poison's spread. Scattered about dry, it acts as repellent. Woe to anyone who substitutes another kind of rice.

- Be careful when playing music around corpses, as certain tunes release them from captivity.

- Sometimes a family structure is maintained from their previous life. Since they still have blood in their veins, they can even have powerful ghost babies. For this reason, male and female corpses are usually transported separately. Child vampires can be "tame," making friends with human children and, if bound by a priest, can be used to control both the living and dead.

- Fun is fun, but don't mess around with the dead. Those little yellow papers can come unstuck very easily. Dead people don't get hurt or get tired. Even if your kung fu is mighty good, you don't want to have a hungry vampire on your hands!

Lau, Peter Ngor, Arthur Wong. **M:** Melody Bank. **VHS, DVD**

Mr. Vampire Saga 4

The third entry of the Mr. Vampire series (plot elements from which were cribbed, intentionally or unintentionally, by Peter Jackson for his underrated *The Frighteners*) was unavailable at press time, but that shouldn't stop you from checking out the fourth entry, since it stands on its own. Lam Ching-Ying is missing, but Wu Ma fills in, taking a rare leading role.

While a Taoist priest (Anthony Chan) is transporting corpses from one town to another, he's nearly victimized by a seductive were-fox spirit (Wong Yuk-wan). Meanwhile, his apprentice Chia-le (Chin Ka-Lok) makes a bad first impression on Ching-Ching (Rachel Lee), who has come to be the apprentice to her uncle, the rival next-door Buddhist priest Yi-yu (Wu Ma). For much of the film's running time, director Ricky Lau is content to merely present episodes of the two warring priests trying to get the upper hand and playing tricks on each other, while the two cute apprentices fumble toward romance. But halfway through, the actual plot appears to interrupt their antics. While supervising the transport of a vampire to the capitol for an official decree, Taoist Crane (Chung Fat) stops in to borrow some glutinous rice. Not long after, the King Vampire creates a thunderstorm that helps him escape from his golden coffin and immediately starts raising hell. The two priests have to put their differences aside and work to kill the monster, while protecting survivors from a growing legion of the undead.

The most lighthearted entry in the "official" series doesn't really have much story—it's just one gag or fight after another. Chin Ka-Lok's athleticism, abetted by the direction of Sammo Hung's stunt team, keeps the second half moving. Yuen Wah also contributes to the choreography, and is given an odd role as a very effeminate vampire, who can't decide whether to bite Chin or kiss him. Among the slick stunts performed is one particularly daring gag by Anthony Chan, who drinks down a large bowl of oil (or some stunt liquid) in one take. Ricky Lau has matured as a filmmaker since the first entry, and may have used this as an opportunity to experiment. The cinematography is great throughout, but one of the three cameramen really outdid themselves with the sequence set in the forest. As ever, the identities of the vampire stars remains secret. *AKA: Guang Si Suk Suk; Jiang Shi Shu Shu; Mr. Vampire 4; Mr. Vampire Sage IV.* ♪♪♪

1988 89m/C *HK* Wu Ma, Anthony Chan, Rachel Lee, Chin Ka-Lok, Chung Fat, Yuen Wah, Wong Yuk-wan, Ricky Lau. **D:** Ricky Lau. **W:** Lo Wing-keung. **C:** Tom Lau, Bill Wong, Abdul M. Rumjahn. **DVD**

Model from Hell

This horror entry starts up outrageously enough: A pretty girl is stabbed to death outside her home, and the killer burns the body. Meanwhile, John (Gabriel Harrison), grandson of a tobacco tycoon, is a hopeless playboy. He goes with his assistant Dan (Cheung Chi-gwong) to Lau Kwan's Creative Space Modeling Agency, and buys up a full class of tuitions in a modeling class just to get in to meet girls. John is entranced by a slim beauty named Anna (Maggie Q). Everyone else seems charmed by her as well, and she's soon booked to shoot a commercial with top model Leon Li (Simon Yam). But there's something sinister about Anna, and other models Janet (Lee Ping) and Jean (Chat Pui-wan) are envious enough to follow her. Desperate John even has Dan dress up as a ghost to scare Anna so John can pretend to come to her rescue. Anna immediately accepts the boys as her slavish assistants.

As Anna and Leon begin an affair during the shooting of the wedding commercial on a boat, Anna spots a spy camera set by Janet. Later, Anna has Janet abducted by Dan and John for an interrogation, and to explode her head with her supernatural power. Jean gets the same treatment. Inspector Kwang is perplexed to find two mysterious brains-on-the-ceiling murders in one day. Leon is perplexed, as it seems that Anna is in two places at once—but his confusion disappears once one Anna takes control of him, instructing him to kill the other one. Photographer Cheng Tung-Tung (Lau Suk-yee) sees that something weird is going on when she finds the hidden camera photos and they show a ghostly image over Anna. When she confronts Anna with the evidence, the model from Hell grows a second head! Sloppy John cuts both heads off, but Anna has him carry off both her heads in a Toys R Us bag to burn them. Anna survives having two heads cut off surprisingly well, and quickly grows another one.

All of this is either an inept attempt at horror, or a quasi-effective satire on the modeling profession, as the pretty bodies all have disposable brains, and an identical number shows up to replace the old ones all the time. Real HK model Maggie Q followed her debut here with roles in *Gen-Y Cops* and *Rush Hour 2,* so maybe she didn't mind burning a few bridges. Even Simon Yam comes off as brain-dead in his role—either he was slacking through this low-budget flick, or it is part of his performance. Any movie where someone has two heads deserves extra credit, but like most Hong Kong horror films, this one ruins whatever interest it has built up by ending abruptly, without offering any explanations as to who Anna is or what she's up to. Like, does she have an evil twin, or what? The special-effects makeup is enjoyably bad. One scene is swiped from *Hellraiser,* right down to some of the dialogue. *AKA: Gwai Ming Miu; Gui Ming Mo.* 🎵🎜

1999 89m/C *HK* Simon Yam, Maggie Q, Gabriel Harrison, Lee Ping, Chat Pui-wan, Cheung Chi-gwong, Lau Suk-yee, Ching Siu-leung. *D:* Chiu Chan-keung. **DVD**

A Moment of Romance

Good girl falls for bad boy on a motorcycle. JoJo (Jacqueline Wu), a lonely young rich girl who has always done what she's supposed to do, is looking for her first romance before her parents take her away to Canada. Wah Dee (Andy Lau) is the prototypical bad boy in a leather jacket, who is committed to the triad lifestyle. In the aftermath of a jewelry-store robbery, Wah Dee snatches JoJo as a hostage. He defies orders to kill her; she is smitten. After he returns her safely home, she cannot resist pursuing a relationship with him. The romance blooms against all odds, even as circumstances transpire to break them apart.

Imitated countless times, the fresh mix of melodrama, romance, and triads that made *A Moment of Romance* a hit back in 1990 may have grown a bit familiar. Even so, the film remains a landmark. Director Benny Chan captured a number of classic images—most memorably the concluding scene—and never falls into the trap of overt sentimentality. The movie also introduced the considerable talents of Taiwanese actress Jacqueline Wu *(Eat Drink Man Woman).* She is here identified by the Cantonese moniker Ng Sin-lin. She is sweet and beguiling as JoJo, and more than holds her own with the magnetic Andy Lau. Despite a couple of musical interludes, the film's pacing is brisk; in fact, the songs add to the story and take care of about half of the romance that is detailed. Enough details about peripheral characters are supplied to make for a well-rounded tale. The musical score by Law Dai-yau and Fabio Carli, as well as the songs, are used to heighten tension and provide some romantic relief. Ng Man-Tat won a Hong Kong Film Award for Best Supporting Actor for his portrayal of a wise street person. —*PM* *AKA: Tin Yeuk Yau Ching (Chui Mung Yan); Tian Re You Qing (Zhui Meng Ren); If Heaven Has Love; If Sky Have Love; To Love with No Regret.* 🎵🎵🎵

1990 88m/C *HK* Andy Lau, Jacqueline Wu, Ng Man-Tat, Tommy Wong, Lau Kong, Walter Cho, Yuen Bun, Lam Chung, Leung Saan. *D:* Benny Chan. *W:* James Yuen. *C:* Horace Wong, Joe Chan. *M:* Law Dai-yau, Fabio Carli. **VHS, DVD**

Mon-Rak Transistor

After a difficult courtship, Pan (Supakorn Kitsu-won) marries Sadaw (Siriyakorn Pukkavesh), only to be inducted into the army shortly after she becomes pregnant. With fantasies of becoming a singer, he goes AWOL to join a traveling show. He spends months mopping floors before getting a chance to sing, then blows his shot at fame by killing his manager after a homosexual advance. He winds up in jail, while Sadaw raises their child alone, a bitter, deserted woman. Years later, he comes home like a mangy dog, hoping to be taken back, while the mon-rak transistor he bought her so many years ago lies rusting in the dirt.

This episodic melodrama is in the wandering-bastard tradition of *Candide.* Pan is a likable loser who has a sense of self that eclipses the reality of his position in the world. It combines the styles of the Hollywood musical with Thai country-and-western movies. Imagine an Elvis Presley movie written by Henry Fielding and directed by Douglas Sirk. It is funny, tragic, ridiculous, and empathetic. A great wallow in retro-romanticism. —*BW* *AKA: A Transistor Love Story.* 🎵🎵🎵

2001 90m/C *TH* Supakorn Kitsuwon, Siriyakorn Pukkavesh, Somlek Sakdikul. *D:* Pen-Ek Ratanaruang. *W:* Pen-Ek Ratanaruang, Wat Wanlayangkoon (novel). *C:* Chankit Chamnivikaipong. *M:* Amornbhong Methakunavudh, Chartchai Pongprapan. **VHS, DVD**

Monkey Fist Floating Snake

Extortionist Deadly Snake Hai-yun (Chang Yi) and his gang of killers try to eliminate his rivals in the region, but Yu Tu-hai (Sun Jung-chi)—with his monkey style kung fu—is too tough for them. Tung (Chan Muk-chuen) is a bumbling, skinny, part-time servant (and punching bag for teacher Cheng) at Chan Sing's kung fu school. His other job is waiting tables at a restaurant, where he gets into trouble for trying to practice kung fu on the job. Barber Tu-hai comes to Tung's aid when bullies harass him, and the young idiot implores the old man to take him as a student. After a lengthy struggle, the barber admires his persistence and agrees to teach him. Deadly Snake Hai-yun comes to confront Tu-hai, and they battle to a draw. Hai-yun goes

M

into hiding to train for a rematch, and for once the bad guy's training sequence is more interesting than the hero's, as we see him running up a belt of rollers and fighting through mazes of bamboo and hanging limes. Tung goes into more training, too, learning Tu-hai's drunken monkey style to be ready when Hai-yun catches up with them.

The final fight scene is a disappointment, hardly living up to the lengthy training sequences that lead up to it. Chan Muk-chuen, action director on the original *Iron Monkey*, certainly looks the part, with a face resembling a gibbon crossed with Donnie Yen. As a comedian, he's a pretty good acrobat and stuntman. The best character is Mai-chan (Eddie Ko), who calls himself King of All Fighters and stalks around posing as a hero, but always has an excuse ready for refusing to fight. Much of the music is swiped from the *True Grit* soundtrack. **AKA:** *Chu Long Ma Liu; Monkey Kung Fu; Drunken Monkey.* 🐾🐾

1979 (R) 92m/C *HK* Chan Muk-chuen, Sun Jung-chi, Yueh Hua, Chang Yi, Cheng Fu Hung, Chan Sing, Eddie Ko, Joe Law, Lydia Shum. **D:** Joe Law. **W:** Wai Sen. **C:** Choi Shea Suen. **M:** Chou Fu-liang. **DVD**

The Moon Warriors

Behold—the only swordplay film with a cetacean co-star! Emperor Yen Shih-san (Kenny Bee), the 13th Prince, is deposed, routed from his palace and pursued by assassins sent by his evil brother, 14th Prince Yin Sap-sei (Kelvin Wong). When his party is attacked near a coastal fishing village, Philip Fei (Andy Lau) lends a hand in repelling the bad guys. Phil takes Yen, his bodyguard Merlin Mu Hsien (Maggie Cheung), and their party to stay with his family, and introduces his pet killer whale, Sea-wayne. While Yen hides in the nearby tombs of his ancestors, he sends Fei and Merlin to fetch his fiancée Princess "Moony" Yuet Ah-yee (Anita Mui) and her father Lan Ning-kwan (Chang Yi), Lord of Lanling. Separated from the group in a battle, Fei and Moony make their way back to the fishing village together, and begin to fall for each other on the way, leading to mixed emotions when they're reunited with Yen—especially when the emperor announces the wedding will take place soon. Another party with mixed emotions is Merlin, who is a double agent ordered to kill Yen, though she's since fallen in love with him. Amidst wedding plans and emotional traffic, all prepare for the coming bloody showdown, which arrives all too soon.

Director Sammo Hung can make sword operas with the best of them, but here adds an extra element of atmosphere, somehow grounding the action in the seaside village and various other settings, while delivering all the more fantastic requirements of the genre. The plot is also blessedly free of the half-dozen extraneous subplots that always seem to be cropping up in these pictures. Anita Mui and Maggie Cheung each take opposite their usual roles, and both do quite well with them. The killer whale performs heroically, but not beyond the bounds of good taste—or else we might expect it to pick up a sword and fight beside Mui's pet bunny rabbit. On video, the film ends with an Andy Lau tune, accompanying footage of him at Sea World training to work with the orca. The score sounds like a traditional Chinese version of an Ennio Morricone western soundtrack. **AKA:** *Chin San Chuen Suet; Zhan Shen Chuan Shui.* 🐾🐾🐾

1992 90m/C *HK* Andy Lau, Anita Mui, Kenny Bee, Maggie Cheung, Kelvin Wong, Chang Yi. **D:** Sammo Hung. **W:** Alex Law. **C:** Arthur Wong. **M:** James Wong, Mark Lui. **VHS, DVD**

Moonlight Express

Hitomi (Tokako Tokiwa) is excited to be engaged to handsome young half-Chinese hotel manager Misawa Tatsuya (Leslie Cheung), and even starts taking classes in Mandarin (where Chow Yun-fat movies are used as a study aid) to prepare for their move to Hong Kong. Then her happiness—and her fiancé—is shattered by a fatal car accident (damn cell phones). She decides to stick with her plan to visit Hong Kong in memory of Tatsuya. As she steps off the elevator in her hotel, she runs into undercover cop Shek Karbo (Leslie Cheung), who happens to be a dead ringer for Tatsuya. He also happens to be in dire need of a diversion from some mobsters, and he gives her a big kiss. Of course she tracks him down, but their next meeting is even more awkward.

Karbo has set up a sting with his police contact Tung to finally arrest mobster Gene after years of work. However, their superior Ko thinks Karbo has "gone native" on them, and at the last-minute calls in an SDU squad to take over, resulting in a bloodbath. Karbo is lucky to escape with only a single bullet wound. Marked for arrest, Karbo turns to Hitomi as his last refuge, and he collapses in her doorway. The spooky coincidence draws them together, though Karbo has been afraid to get near anyone since his mad line of work drove his girlfriend to suicide a few years ago. Surprisingly, given the trouble he's in, Hitomi isn't too concerned about losing another sweetheart, perhaps because she intends her stay with him to be temporary. Karbo's trouble turns out to be deeper than he thought when he finds out that someone in his department has betrayed him, planting evidence to make it look like he's stolen millions in drugs.

With multiple musical interludes, this romantic thriller could have easily melted into mush. But Leslie Cheung gives a standout performance, holding together both the crime and romance elements and making them work together. Michelle Yeoh shows up late in the game in a surprise supporting role, but bows out before she can take over the whole picture. **AKA:** *Sing Yuet Tung Wa; Xing Yue Tong Hua.* 🐉🐉🐉

1999 101m/C *HK* Tokako Tokiwa, Leslie Cheung, Liu Kai-chi, Austin Wai, Jack Kao, Lee Heung-kam, Michelle Yeoh, Sam Lee, Pak Kar-sin, Mars, Jude Poyer, Jimmy Wong. **D:** Daniel Lee. **W:** Law Chi-leung, Yumiko Aoyagi. **C:** Keung Kwok-man. **DVD**

Moonlight Sword and Jade Lion

Angela Mao plays detective in this old-school kung fu mystery. Short-spear expert Chu Sau-yen (Mao) is sent by her master to visit his brother, old hero Lu Chan (Shaw Luo-hui), but she finds that he's been missing for months. Postmaster Mr. Chia tells her that Oyang Sun-te sent Lu a letter just before he disappeared. Oyang is of little help, only able to tell her to talk to Chief Chung Yi before he dies from a dagger thrown into his head. The chief and his assistant Fung (Su Chen Ping) are obviously involved in some plot, but they get the brain-sticker treatment before they can speak up, too. There's another stranger in town, a mysterious Crane Fist fighter (Wang Tao) who has a run-in with Sau-yen, only later learning she's the girl he's trying to find. The stranger also gets into fights with Ling Chun (Man Kong Lung), a young lord in the power of a mysterious man behind a curtain, who controls him by doling out the antidote to a poison Ling has taken. The trail of clues takes Sau-yen next to a lady named Su Yin (Doris Lung) and her platoon of synchronized fighting kung fu girls (well, quite a few are stuntmen in drag) armed with exploding battle lilies. Unable to best Sau-yen in open combat, Su Yin lures Chu Sau-yen into her house of traps, where the spear fighter is captured.

The story becomes so muddled and complex that it becomes difficult to tell who is on whose side—and even more difficult to care. It all has to do with a pair of jade lions, which are supposed to be the key to ruling the Martial Arts World. The mystery villain has one lion, and is after the other, which is in Sau-yen's possession. The story is too concerned with moving all the characters around to give any of them any personality. Angela Mao looks properly heroic, and things pick up when she goes into action,

but there's not much she can do with her flat character. The action scenes favor displays of unusual weapons over martial arts skill. **AKA:** *Au Yuk Kim Chui Yuk Shut; Yin Yu Jian Cui Yu Shi; Ten Fingers and Flying Sword.* 🐉🐉

1979 94m/C *TW* Angela Mao, Wang Tao, Su Chen Ping, Doris Lung, Man Kong Lung, Chiang Ming, Tung Li, Wu Chia Hsiang, Cheung Fong-ha, Shaw Luo-hui, Yuen Sam, Man Chung-san, Ho Kong, Cho Boot-lam, Miu Tak San, Wong Mei-Mei, Ha Hau-chun, Lau Nga Ying. **D:** New Kwong Lam. **C:** Wong Yin-pui. **M:** Chou Fu-liang. **DVD**

asians in usa

Mortal Kombat

Based on a hit video game series, this surprising American martial arts classic plays like H.P. Lovecraft's rewrite of *Enter the Dragon*. A fantastic island off the coast of Hong Kong (you'll recognize locations from *The Man with the Golden Gun*) plays host to the title lethal martial arts competition that will decide if an evil emperor from another dimension can invade the Earth. The relative lack of action in the early going is misleading—once our heroes get to the island, things really take off with the best kung fu fighting ever seen this side of the HK scene (at least by 1995), abetted greatly by amazing f/x, beautifully grotesque art direction, and pounding music by George Clinton (and others). Best fight is between action-movie star Johnny Cage (Linden Ashby) and the scary Scorpion (Chris Casamassa), followed closely by vengeful monk Liu Kang's match with creepy lizard guy Reptile (Keith Cooke).

Robin Shou, who stars as Liu, choreographed all the best fights himself, many of which feature f/x-enhanced superpowered characters—including a hulking four-armed monster named Goro. Shou was a featured fighter in many Hong Kong films, but never really stepped into the spotlight until starring here. Buck-toothed beauty Bridgette Wilson doesn't seem to have the chops of her cohorts as Federal Agent Sonya Blade, but they make up for it by making her fight scenes grittier (then let her down by making her the "damsel in distress"). Talisa Soto (*Vampirella*) makes a few hearts pound herself as Princess Kitana. Fans of '70s fu sound effects will appreciate those used here, as each punch lands with what sounds like a sledgehammer striking granite (enhanced by the digital soundtrack). Kudos to all responsible for this dynamic sleeper. Followed by the disappointing *Mortal Kombat: Annihilation* and an even worse TV series. 🐉🐉🐉🐉

1995 (PG-13) 101m/C *US* Christopher Lambert, Robin Shou, Cary-Hiroyuli Tagawa, Linden Ashby,

"I'm in a hostile environment. I'm totally unprepared. And I'm surrounded by a bunch of guys who probably want to kick my ass. I feel like I'm back in high school."

—Johnny Cage gets acclimated in *Mortal Kombat*

Bridgette Wilson, Talisa Soto, Trevor Goddard, Chris Casamassa, Francois Petit, Keith Cooke, Hakim Alston. *D:* Paul W.S. Anderson. *W:* Kevin Droney. *C:* John R. Leonetti. *M:* George Clinton, Buckethead. **VHS, DVD**

The Most Wanted

"Cat" Ho Chi-yung (Lau Ching-Wan) is an undercover cop posing as a low-level crook and parking attendant. Whether as part of his role, or due to a natural gambling addiction, he's in debt to loan shark Chiang (Lee Siu-Kei) for $800,000. As politics forces his superiors to end his operation, Cat's buddy Sap (Bowie Lam) introduces him to his boss, ruthless criminal Yeh Foon (Robin Shou), who hires him as a driver on a jewelry store heist. Unwilling to give up years of work trying to get close to Yeh, Cat decides to continue working unofficially. He succeeds in tipping off his contact about the heist, resulting in a gun battle. Not only does Cat get shot, but the only cop who will vouch for his undercover status is shot by Sap and goes into a coma. Cheng Ming-fen (Kent Cheng) heads up a Special Duty Unit assigned to the robbery, and Cat is the only

thief they can identify. The target of a full-scale dragnet, Cat refuses to give up until he can track down and arrest Foon.

There are so many stock situations in this film that it becomes only minimally involving after the first act. What interest there is comes from the situation, cribbed from Ringo Lam's *City on Fire.* Eileen Tung plays an intriguing role as an illegal immigrant who befriends Cat, but the character is ultimately revealed as window dressing. This was one of over a dozen films starring Lau Ching-Wan in 1994. **AKA:** *Lung Foo San Fung Wan Tau Ho Tung Chap Faan; Long Hu Xin Feng Yun Tou Hao Tong Ji Fan.* 🐾🐾

1994 90m/C *HK* Lau Ching-Wan, Kent Cheng, Bowie Lam, Eileen Tung, Cheng Lui, Robin Shou, Kam Hing-yin, Lee Siu-Kei, Corey Yuen. *D:* Wong Kam-tin. *W:* Clarence Yip, Susanne Chan, Taures Chow. *C:* Gigo Lee. *M:* Wong Chi-hung, Gigo Lee. **VHS, DVD**

Mothra

During the 1950s, the cinemas were full of all manner of giant insect movies, but when Toho Studios' science-fiction ace Ishiro Honda decid-

ed to get in on the action, he wanted something different. He sought to broaden the audience for their giant monster films by creating a movie that appealed more to women and children, without pandering to them. The result is this classic Japanese monster fantasy.

On an expedition to find a possible cure for radiation poisoning, businessman Clark Nelson (Jerry Ito) from "Rolisica" (Toho's fictional stand-in for the United States) makes a voyage to Beiru Island. Dr. Chujo (Hiroshi Koizumi) and Dr. Haradawa (Ken Uehara) convince him to allow them to go along, and nutty reporter Senichiro "Bulldog" Fukuda (popular TV comedian Frankie Sakai) is a stowaway. The party is naturally surprised to find the radioactive island still inhabited, and even more surprised when two of the natives are tiny twin girls (Emi and Yumi Ito). Dastardly Nelson kidnaps the girls, taking them to Tokyo, where he builds a spectacular stage show around them (as a bonus, the girls have ethereally beautiful singing voices, no doubt assisted by their telepathic powers). Back on the island, the vengeful natives chant to a gigantic egg, which soon hatches a gigantic enraged caterpillar. This is Mothra, the ancient goddess of the Beiru Island natives. Following

the telepathic link to her little fairy priestesses, Mothra swims across the ocean, making a moth-line for Tokyo. Despite entreaties by the scientists and reporters, or even direct orders from the Rolisican government, greedy Nelson refuses to give up the twins. Mothra invades Tokyo, causing widespread destruction, but Nelson escapes by sneaking aboard a plane bound for "Newkirk City." Wounded by the Japanese Defense Force, Mothra builds a huge cocoon around herself, attached to Tokyo Tower. She emerges transformed into an even more gigantic moth, and flies off to Rolisica to cause a great deal more destruction.

American critics and audiences dismissed *Mothra* as just another big-bug movie, judging it even more inferior due to its "made in Japan" label. It's no wonder that when the sequel *Mothra vs. Godzilla* was released in the U.S., it was retitled to hide Mothra's presence. However, in Japan, Mothra became a great favorite, appearing in several of Toho's other Godzilla films. She was brought back in the '90s for *Godzilla vs. Mothra,* before appearing in a trilogy of films aimed at a younger audience in which she battled King Ghidorah. It was presumed at the time that the twins and Mothra were yet another

The goddess of Infant Island rampages through New Kirk City in search of her tiny twin priestesses in *Mothra.*

A dying Mothra tries to protect her offspring in *Mothra vs. Godzilla*. Is laying eggs that size what's killing her?

THE KOBAL COLLECTION / TOHO / A.I.P.

result of nuclear testing, but it's more likely they'd existed long before that, surviving even nuclear power. If Godzilla was Japan's nightmare of atomic devastation, then Mothra was their symbol of constant rebirth, hope, and the power of nature. Mothra remains unique among giant monsters epics, projecting beauty and warmth rather than terror and violence. The heroic creature seems to get more beautiful with each incarnation, and the score features some strangely affecting songs by Yuji Koseki. *AKA: Mosura; Diakaiju Mosura.* 🎵🎵🎵♪

1961 (G) 100m/C *JP* Jerry Ito, Hiroshi Koizumi, Ken Uehara, Frankie Sakai, Emi Ito, Yumi Ito, Kyoko Kagawa, Takashi Shimura, Tetsu Nakamura, Akihiro Tayama, Akihiko Hirata, Seizaburo Kawazu, Yoshifumi Tajima, Yoshio Kosugi, Ren Yamamoto, Haruya Kato, Kenji Sahara, Ko Mishima, Akira Yamada, Kazuo Higata, Shoichi Hirose, Osman Yusuf. *D:* Ishiro Honda. *W:* Shinichi Sekizawa. *C:* Hajime Koizumi. *M:* Yuji Koseki. **VHS**

Mothra vs. Godzilla

The smash international success of *King Kong vs. Godzilla* demanded another sequel, and pro-

ducer Tomoyuki Tanaka had the inspired idea to pit their monster star against Toho's own Mothra. When the egg of giant monster Mothra is washed ashore by a storm, greedy entrepreneur Kumayama (Yoshifumi Tajima) is quick to exploit it, buying it from the fisherman who salvaged it and making plans to put it on display. Kumayama's financier Torahata (Kenji Sahara) is a con man who gets him to invest his own money in the deal, but secretly plans to leave him holding the bag if things turn sour. The twin fairies (Emi and Yumi Ito) approach the two crooks, imploring then to return the egg to Mothra before someone gets hurt. Instead, the bastards try to capture the fairies to add to their display. The twins escape, and seek the help of reporters Sakai (Akira Takarada) and Yoka (Yuriko Hoshi), who have been trying to get Kumayama to turn the egg over to scientist Professor Miura (Hiroshi Koizumi). Heedless of warnings, the entrepreneur begins construction of an incubator for the egg. Meanwhile, Godzilla (Haruo Nakajima) reappears and goes on a rampage. Help is sought from the dying Mothra through her psychic link to the miniature twin princesses, but she refuses. However, when the egg is threatened, she comes to protect it from Godzilla.

Excellent in all departments, this is a clear favorite among Godzilla fans. The contrast between the sci fi–based Godzilla and the more fantasy-oriented Mothra works wonderfully, with the lively script offering imaginative surprises at every turn. The characters are interesting and relatively well rounded, with touches of humor. Godzilla, who seems to be really enjoying his reign of destruction, shows more personality than in previous appearances, helped by one of the series' better looking costume designs. Special-effects wizard Eiji Tsuburaya used some experimental techniques involving changing the speed of the camera and removing frames to add to the realism of his monster effects, giving the suits and puppets the look of animation at times (actual animation was used in a few shots as well). Akira Ifukube adds one of his best scores, combining his themes for Godzilla and Mothra from previous films and playing the cues against each other. Except for a sequence added at the request of the U.S. distributor, in which U.S. Navy missiles attack Godzilla, the U.S. version is nearly the same as the original, and the dubbing (by Peter Fernandez) was done decently. Universal passed on this entry, and American International ended up releasing it on a double bill with the Czech sci-fi feature *Voyage to the End of the Universe*. Since they hadn't distributed *Mothra*, they changed the title to *Godzilla vs. the Thing*, with advertising that alternately suggested that the big lizard was fighting either the menace from *The Thing from Another World* or some mystery monster too horrible to reveal. Currently, the film is better known on U.S. video as *Godzilla vs. Mothra*. *AKA: Mosura tai Gojira; Godzilla vs. the Thing; Godzilla vs. the Giant Moth; Godzilla Fights the Giant Moth; Godzilla vs. Mothra.* 🐉🐉🐉🐉

1964 89m/C *JP* Akira Takarada, Yuriko Hoshi, Hiroshi Koizumi, Yu Fujiki, Emi Ito, Yumi Ito, Yoshifumi Tajima, Kenji Sahara, Jun Tazaki, Kenzo Tabu, Akira Tani, Yoshio Kosugi, Yasuhisa Tsutsumi, Kozo Nomura, Koji Uno, Haruo Nakajima, Osman Yusuf. *D:* Ishiro Honda. *W:* Shinichi Sekizawa. *C:* Hajime Koizumi. *M:* Akira Ifukube. **VHS, DVD**

Murder in the Orient

Ron Marchini stars as American secret agent Paul Marcelli in this horrible, horrible Philippine spy movie. Potbellied villain Stavro is after $10 million in gold for his boss King Cobra, leader of the Golden Cobra Brotherhood. He sends dimwitted Turco to get Diana Lau (Josephine), who has the map telling where the gold is. But Marcelli is there to help her, sort of—at least he keeps Turco from getting the map after he kills the girl. Before she dies, she gives Marcelli an address and a key. The clues lead him to Interpol agent Monica Martinez (Eva Reyes), whose boss fills him in on how the Japanese army buried the looted gold somewhere on the island. The two officers who hid the gold each took half the map inscribed on their swords. Because of Stavro's bungling, King Cobra sends Kang the Butcher from Hong Kong to kill Diana's brother, kung fu master Lau Hsu (Leo Fong), who is on his way to investigate his sister's death. Meanwhile, Stavro sends Turco to capture the American. Servant Grace De Silva, on finding out Kang has killed her father, helps Marcelli escape. Marcelli teams up with Lau and Monica to try to track down the Cobras and find the gold. The third act features a lot of driving around in jeeps and a great deal of unconvincing mayhem.

Intended to come off as a suave and raffish rogue, Manchini makes for one of the worst action heroes ever. Though a Black Belt Hall of Fame honoree offscreen, as an actor, he's upstaged by the minimal sets, and his martial arts scenes are even worse—every punch and kick misses the mark by at least a foot. He's much better at getting knocked out, and more convincing. The producers don't do him any favors, giving him a chartreuse dune buggy to tool around in, and his wardrobe is just as classy. But it's a wonder that even such a poor hero has so much trouble with these villains. Kang gets rid of Stavro for letting Marcelli escape, and then replaces him by putting the moronic Turco in charge! Fong at least looks like he knows something about karate, though the fight choreography won't back up that claim. The credits list includes the Pimp Commandos and the S.O.S. Daredevils. Marchini went on to make some poorly regarded low-budget direct-to-video action movies of his own, such as *Karate Commando.* 🐉

1974 73m/C *PH* Ron Marchini, Leo Fong, Eva Reyes, Leila Hermosa, Danny Rojo, Raymond, Jim Delon, Gil Guerrero, Mary Diaz, Rodolfo "Boy" Garcia, Jose Villafranca, Mario Escudero, Bien Juan, Josephine. *D:* Manuel S. Songo. *W:* Manuel S. Songo, Anthony Reyes (story). **VHS, DVD**

My Kung Fu 12 Kicks

Of all the performers marketed as the "new Bruce Lee," Bruce Liang (AKA Hsiao Liang and Bruce Leung Siu-lung) bears the least resemblance to the late King of Kung Fu. Not tall or handsome, he nevertheless was a very good acrobat and martial artist, who did better in lighter kung fu comedies like this independent entry, which actually cribs more from Jackie Chan's hits.

Pickpocket Ta-pin (Liang) picks on the wrong target; loan shark Chow and his bodyguard Hung (Dai Sai Aan) catch him in the act, and the gangsters beat him soundly. Brothel mop boy Nameless Chai (Hon Gwok-choi) helps him home to the ruined temple he occupies with rickshaw man Woo (Ku Feng). Meanwhile, kung fu master Kwok (Lee Hoi-sang) is after the secret kung fu manual in the possession of the local martial arts school. Why he wants it is hard to say, since he makes mincemeat of their three masters with his iron fingers—what secrets could it possibly teach him? Ta-pin, looking to learn some kung fu to defend himself, comes upon the beaten trio and takes them home to nurse them. Chai is busy, too—the stepfather of little Chen Lan has sold her to the brothel, and Chai rescues her. Brooding on their revenge, do the three crippled masters adapt their style to their conditions and go after Kwok themselves à la *Return of the 5 Deadly Venoms*? Uh-uh. They decide to use their manual to teach Ta-pin kung fu so he can do the job for them. Maybe they're illiterate and never read it. After a weekend of study, Ta-pin is ready to get revenge on Chow and his boys using the dragon, crane, snake, and other styles he's instantly mastered. Before Ta-pin can get a big head, Woo—actually a retired Tan Toi Style master—teaches him a lesson. Woo then teaches him half of the 12 Tan Toi Kicks, which come in handy when Chow's men abduct Lan to lure Ta-pin into a fight with Kwok (and thereafter our poor heroine is completely forgotten!). But they're not enough to beat Kwok's Iron Skin technique, so Woo finally lets the other six kicks drop.

Some fun fight scenes and training sequences make this otherwise routine comic fight flick worth a look. Though Bruce Liang's knuckles and wrists give him away as a martial artist before he starts training, he does a good job pretending to be a greenhorn at the start. Bruises on Lee Hoi-sang's chest from taking kicks all day look painfully real. The film doesn't so much end as run flapping out of the projector. **AKA:** *Sap Yee Taam Tui; Shi Er Tan Tui; Incredible Master Beggars; Twelve Kung Fu Kicks.* 🦴🦴🦴🦴

1979 84m/C *HK* Bruce Liang, Ku Feng, Lee Hoi-sang, Hon Gwok-choi, San Kwai, Dai Sai Aan, Lau Yat-fan, Chow Kong, Chan Ling-wai, Yue Tau Wan. **D:** Lee Tso Nam. **W:** Tung Liu. **C:** Ng Fat-sam. **VHS, DVD**

My Lucky Stars

The success of the first Lucky Stars film, *Winners and Sinners,* naturally led to this sequel. Popular comedian Eric Tsang, now a powerful Hong Kong producer as well, joined the Lucky Stars as the feebleminded Roundhead, replacing John Sham. By this time Jackie Chan, Sammo Hung, and Yuen Biao had made a few more films together, and this episode fine-tunes the formula a bit better, with a more expanded role for Yuen this time. Perhaps because of a different translator, most of the characters have different names. Hong Kong cops Muscles (Chan) and Ricky (Yuen Biao) go to Tokyo, chasing a crooked ex-cop (Lam Ching-Ying) who stole a cache of diamonds and is headed toward a major crime boss. After the ninja gangsters capture Ricky, Muscles calls on his old orphanage pal Kidstuff (Hung) to help him with the case. Kidstuff insists on bringing the other Lucky Stars along—Roundhead, Herb (Charlie Chin), Rawhide (Stanley Fung), and Sandy (Richard Ng)—and policewoman Swordflower Woo (Sibelle Hu) is assigned to keep an eye on the ex-cons. Again there's a lengthy middle section in which the Stars stay overnight with the pretty lady, and all cook up schemes to get close to her. This time Sandy uses his imaginary mental powers to attempt psychokinesis. The gang is framed for a bank robbery to give them extra credibility in infiltrating the ninjas headquarters, set within an amusement park, but they end up getting captured themselves.

There's a bizarre sequence in which Jackie has to go through a carnival spook house, fighting ninjas at every turn, and all the while disguised as a fuzzy cartoon mascot. The comic antics are a bit more on track here, and there are some terrific car chases, stunts, and explosions. But of course the main attraction is in the superbly staged and choreographed fight scenes. Chan's battle with Dick Wei, a rematch from *Project A,* is all too brief, but the big crowd-pleaser is the fight between Hu and Japanese bodybuilding champ Michiko Nishiwaki. The Lucky Stars' humor doesn't translate well to Western fans used to the ultra-sophisticated comedy of Adam Sandler, but in Asia this beat all boxoffice records. It helps that Hung's editing of the group's comedy has improved since *Winners and Sinners,* and this one clocks in a good 15 minutes shorter. **AKA:** *Fuk Sing Go Jiu; Fu Xing Gao Zhao; Lucky Stars Shine Highest and Brightest.* 🦴🦴🦴🦴

1985 84m/C *HK* Sammo Hung, Jackie Chan, Yuen Biao, Sibelle Hu, Richard Ng, Eric Tsang, Charlie Chin, Stanley Fung, Michiko Nishiwaki, Lam Ching-Ying, Bolo Yeung, Walter Cho, James Tien, Yip Wing-cho, Dick Wei, Yuen Wah, Lau Kar-Wing, Huang Ha, Wu Ma. **D:** Sammo Hung. **W:** Barry Wong, Szeto Cheuk-hon. **C:** Peter Ngor, Arthur Wong. **M:** Michael Lai. **VHS, DVD**

My Neighbor Totoro

While his wife Yasuko recovers in a hospital from tuberculosis, anthropology professor Tatsuo Kusakabe takes on the job of moving his family to a new

house in the country, which is closer to her hospital. Their daughters, 11-year-old Satsuki and 4-year-old Mei, are wild with the excitement of the day. The first indication that something is odd about the new house comes when the girls go to clean out the attic, startling herds of scurrying ghostly "dust bunnies." While Satsuki deals with a new school, Mei discovers other small supernatural critters living around the grounds—culminating in her meeting with a huge forest spirit named Totoro (voiced in fine grunts and roars by Hitoshi Takagi of *Tampopo*) nestled in the gigantic, ancient camphor tree behind their property. The rest of the family only humors Mei when she tells them about it, but one rainy day, Satsuki meets him, too. They also encounter another fantastic creature: the Catbus, a giant, multi-legged cat in the shape of a bus.

The creatures in the film are simply ingenious creations, the product of a freely floating imagination. They're almost paganistic at times. Totoro's function seems to be one of helping things grow—a true old-world god of the forest. Writer/director Hayao Miyazaki captures naturally and precisely mannerisms, attitudes, and reactions of children. Though the film is extremely cute, none of it feels saccharine or forced like in so many children's films, making it extremely enjoyable for adults as well. The film also benefits from a lack of any villains, the main conflict being worry over the mother's health, and the resulting worry when Mei becomes lost trying to get to the hospital on her own. Miyazaki is also expert at portraying nature, a talent that would also serve him in his later film *Princess Mononoke* (which continued his environmental themes). *AKA: Tonari no Totoro.* 🐉🐉🐉🐉

1988 (G) 86m/C *JP* **V:** Hitoshi Takagi. **D:** Hayao Miyazaki. **W:** Hayao Miyazaki. **C:** Hisao Shirai. **M:** Jo Hisaishi. **VHS, DVD**

My Sassy Girl

A smash-hit comedy in South Korea. If you like the idea of a pretty girl stepping all over a docile boy in the name of True Love, this is the movie for you. Kyun-woo (Cha Tae-hyun) is a sweet and kind college student. Waiting for a subway train to take him home one night, he comes into contact with a lovely but clearly drunken young woman (Jun Ji-hyun). She too seems like she might be sweet and kind—until she vomits all over an unfortunate fellow passenger and passes out. Because she called Kyun-woo "honey" as she slumped to the floor, the other passengers assume he is her boyfriend and expect him to take care of her. Giving in to peer pressure, he takes her to a motel, cleans her up, and chastely sleeps on the floor. In the morning he

is rudely awakened and charged with kidnapping the girl—she comes from a wealthy family. He expects her to come to the police station and clear things up. Rather than apologize, she heaps verbal abuse upon him. Being a good-hearted masochist, he looks into her insanely adorable face and decides that she needs his help, and concludes that she just doesn't know how to express her feelings, without knowing the extent of the abuse that awaits him.

Ostensibly based on a true story, written by Kim Ho-sik and posted on the Internet in serial form, *My Sassy Girl* is so over the top that it feels fictional. Taken as real life, the characters deserve an empathetic hug: the girl for the emotional pain that causes her to act out in such a disarmingly aggressive manner, and the boy for accepting her abuse, in the hope that it will help her. Yet the candy-colored first half of the film presents their relationship more as a modern-day screwball comedy. Many of the situations are quite funny when taken at surface value. Just at the point where we accept these absurd scenarios as outrageous but playful exaggeration—as in, "You think your girlfriend's crazy? Let me tell you what mine did"—the tone abruptly switches. It's almost as if the filmmakers realized, "Look, this girl is seriously disturbed. We can't keep laughing at what she makes this guy do. We have to explain things." And so things are explained, and we are sad, and the ending is left to fate. The abrupt switch to extended melodrama is not entirely convincing. It feels drawn out, as though an equal amount of time was needed to balance out the comedic first half. The film looks extremely well made, with handsome production design, good use of locations, sharp editing, and an enjoyable musical score that encompasses the various moods of the film (from cheery comedy to syrupy melodrama). The two lead performers are insanely bright, charming, and persuasive. Various versions of the film are available. The original theatrical release ran 123 minutes; some video releases feature the "director's cut," which runs 137 minutes. —*PM* ***AKA:*** *Yeopgijeogin geunyeo; Bizarre Girl; Yupgi Girl.* 🐉🐉

2001 123m/C *KO* Cha Tae-hyun, Jun Ji-hyun, Kim In-mun, Yang Geum-yong, Song Wok-suk. **D:** Kwak Jae-yong. **W:** Kim Ho-sik, Kwak Jae-yong. **C:** Kim Sung-bok. **M:** Kim Hyun-seok. **VHS, DVD**

My School Mate, the Barbarian

Wealthy student Edward (Stephen Fung) is doing well with his schoolwork and looks bound for greater things until his ex-girlfriend makes a false accusation. As a result, he gets tossed out of the school's high-class environment. Through a mix-up in paperwork, he is transferred to TBS Memorial School, where most of the student body consists of a ready-to-rumble collection of ruffians whose well-earned reputation for fighting keeps even the triad recruiters away. Former school fighting champion Stone (Nicolas Tse) takes pity on the pacifist Edward and helps him out. Stone has decided to stop boxing, and so feels some empathy for the misplaced lad. Also siding with Edward is Phoenix (Joey Yung), though her feelings have more to do with libido than with pity. The budding friendship of Edward and Stone is put to the test when Edward's wealth comes to the attention of a local triad boss.

All the energy and verve that this film needs must have trickled away during the planning stages. You can just hear the filmmakers gathered together aforehand: "Let's team Nic Tse and Steve Fung again. Nic will be the bad boy who reluctantly helps Steve the rich boy. We'll get Ching Siu-Tung to design the fight scenes in a school classroom atop a bunch of desks with fans whirling above their heads. And get a pretty singer to provide some eye candy—why not that girl Joey who was in the news recently?" (Joey Yung was in Hong Kong newspapers frequently during the summer of 2001 due to her reported association with criminal figures, among other things.) Thus organized, the filming began. And here we see a disadvantage to the quick turn-around time possible in the Hong Kong movie world. The story was not developed properly nor were the characters fleshed out. The combination of Billy Chung and Wong Jing as co-directors is odd. Chung previously completed two moody low-budget affairs *(Paramount Motel* and *Undercover Blues)*; working in opposition to that tone, several cute and painfully obvious comedy bits have been inserted, which can be attributed to Wong—the scriptwriter. Ah, well. The fight scenes take advantage of their unique setting, and Samuel Pang was a bright spark as the teen fighting machine Mantis. But Joey Yung should either stick to her singing career or find a director who can better mask her limited thespian abilities. *—PM* **AKA:** *Ngo Dik Yau Goo Tung Hok; Wo De Ye Man Tong Xiao.* ♫♫

2001 90m/C *HK* Nicholas Tse, Stephen Fung, Joey Yung, Samuel Pang, Ken Chung, Hyper BB, Yu Ka-ho, Pan Ping-chang, Frankie Ng. **D:** Wong Jing, Billy Chung. **W:** Wong Jing. **C:** Dick Tung. **M:** Tommy Wai. **VHS, DVD**

My Wife Is a Gangster

A deadly female gangster marries a clueless civilian to fulfill her sister's dying wish. Cha Eun-jin (Shin Eun-kyung) is a lieutenant in her gang, earning the position thanks to her cold and ruthless ambition. This is reflected in her more frequently

used gang name, Mantis—as in preying mantis. Her softer side emerges briefly when she finally finds her long-lost sister in a hospital; the two were orphaned as children and separated. Mantis's joy is tempered upon learning that her sister is dying, and her last request is that Mantis find a husband, settle down, and have a family. That in no way fits in with her plans; nevertheless, Mantis immediately orders her men to find a suitable marriage mate for her. The best candidate they can locate on such short notice is Soo-Il (Park Sang-myun). He's a 35-year-old bachelor, endlessly unlucky in love, and especially on blind dates; he's never gotten a second date, though he's tried many times. He finally succeeds with Mantis—beyond his wildest dreams—and finds himself at a wedding ceremony, marrying a woman he barely knows. Their relationship is soon put to the test as Mantis tries to keep her occupation a secret from her new husband and his inquisitive sister, even while fighting off a territorial challenge from a rival gang.

Mantis is the ultimate tomboy, having never had the time, interest, or inclination to act like a traditional Korean female. So there's plenty of humor in her attempts to act like a stereotypical woman, first in the dating game—she must learn about makeup, wearing high heels, acting deferential toward men—and then in her marriage to Soo-Il. He turns out to be a slow-witted civil servant, very much bound by custom, and does not approve of Mantis running around town without caring for her duties as a housewife. Mantis's relationship with her sister is sketched in lovingly to provide an emotional center. Somewhere along the way, though, the story loses its way. It may be that the director and scriptwriter were simply too ambitious. Black comedy does not mix easily with slapstick, sight gags, jokes, ridicule, clownish behavior, and serious gangster action—including brutal violence and murder. It seems the filmmakers were aware that a one-joke premise—gangster must marry to please dying sister—could only go so far, so they introduced another one-joke premise—not disclosed here so as to avoid spoilers—that only serves to extend the running time. Despite these shortcomings, *My Wife Is a Gangster* proves to be an entertaining film that is sure to bring a smile to your face. *—PM* **AKA:** *Jopog manura; The Wife Is the Gang Leader.* ♫♫♡

2001 108m/C *KO* Shin Eun-kyung, Park Sang-myun, An Jae-mo, Shim Won-chul, Choe Eun-joo. **D:** Jo Jin-gyu. **W:** Kang Hyo-jin, Kim Moon-sung. **C:** Jeon Jo-myung. **M:** Jang Dae-sung. **VHS, DVD**

The Mysterians

In Japan's own version of *War of the Worlds,* a race of advanced scientific intellects from a

doomed planet attempts to conquer Earth using a giant robot, force fields, and destructive rays. In a bit cribbed from Roger Corman's *It Conquered the World,* astronomer Ryochi Shirashi (Akihiko Hirata) is the first to meet up with the alien invaders, and immediately signs up as a collaborator. The village where Shirashi was staying is destroyed in a landslide, which sprouts a gigantic killer robot from a hidden cave under the hill. The mechanical beast attacks and destroys a nearby town. Though formidable looking, the robot is easily disposed of by the military (dubbed "Mogera" in Japan, the robot costume was operated by Godzilla actor Haruo Nakajima).

Next, a gigantic dome appears from underground, and the aliens request a team of scientists (including Kenji Sahara and Takashi Shimura) come inside for a visit. The Welcome Wagon party is met by the humanoid Mysterians (led by Yoshio Tsuchiya, who performed similar duties in *Invasion of Astro-Monster),* who explain their situation to them: the aliens destroyed their own planet ages ago in a nuclear war, and have since relocated to Mars. Declaring their intentions peaceful, they only request three square kilometers of land and,

um, five females to be used as breeding stock. The Mysterians don't do a very good job instilling trust, especially when they're forced to admit that they've already taken the liberty of abducting three women. Sort of lends credence to the argument that the Women's Lib movement saved the world from atomic annihilation, doesn't it? Unconvinced, Earth forces fight back with hi-tech weaponry of their own, including an energy collecting and firing dish called a Markalite. Ryochi shows up on television to plead with his own people to surrender, but the fight goes on.

Great battle scenes come courtesy of excellent effects from Toho's master Eiji Tsuburaya, with flashing ray guns and exploding spaceships and armaments all over. Director Ishiro Honda puts his experience shooting war movies to good use, just updating the level of technology. The story could be argued to represent an illustration of how Japanese fears of oppression by a technologically superior nation resulted in their tech-based economic recovery, though that might be stretching things. However, the story is undermined somewhat by the silly movie serial portrayal of the alien invaders. Even the Godzilla series would have more credible aliens a few years later. Another complaint is that the spectacular robot is defeated far too easily. The few minutes cut from the American release are said to have more such machines showing up for the climax, but it's unknown why they would be left out unless the f/x in those shots were poorly done. An even earlier Japanese invasion epic, Shinichi Sekizawa's *Fearful Attack of the Flying Saucer*, remains unreleased in the U.S. *AKA:* Chikyu Boeigun; Defense Force of the Earth; Earth Defense Force; Phantom 7000. ♪♪♪

1957 85m/C *JP* Kenji Sahara, Yumi Shirakawa, Momoko Kochi, Akihiko Hirata, Takashi Shimura, Susumu Fujita, Hisaya Ito, Yoshio Kosugi, Fuyuki Murakami, Tetsu Nakamura, Yoshio Tsuchiya, Yutaka Sada, Ren Imaizumi, Takeo Oikawa, Tadao Nakamaru, George Furness, Harold Conway, Haruya Kato, Senkichi Omura, Shin Otomo, Shoichi Hirose, Rinsaku Ogata, Heihachiro Okawa, Jiro Kumagai, Mitsuo Tsuda, Haruo Nakajima. *D:* Ishiro Honda. *W:* Shigeru Kayama, Takeshi Kimura, Jojiro Okami (story). *C:* Hajime Koizumi. *M:* Akira Ifukube. **VHS**

Naked Killer

The cold-blooded contract killer known as Princess (Carrie Ng) draws attention to her activities with her spectacular and brutal crimes, which baffle the police. Detective Tinam (Simon Yam) uses his own peculiar brand of illogic to guess at the truth behind the crimes. Unfortunately, he's still recovering from a crack-up following his brother's death and is unable to hold a gun without vomiting, which makes him next to useless to the Hong Kong movieland police department. While getting his hair cut, he meets the feisty Kitty (Chingmy Yau), admiring her beauty and sense of righteousness, and the two go on a date. Later, Kitty catches her stepmom's triad lover Bee (Ken Lo) killing her dad. Pissed, she goes to Bee's office and massacres everyone in her path! However, she only escapes through the intervention of Sister Cindy (Kelly Yao). Cindy turns out to be the master assassin who trained Princess, and she decides to take on Kitty as her new apprentice. Kitty is soon on her way to becoming the new top assassin in town, denying her old identity even when confronted by Tinam. However, she can't keep hiding from him for long since the evil Princess and her sidekick Baby (Madoka Sugawara) are jealous of Cindy's new discovery, and are out to get them both—with Tinam stuck in the middle.

Prolific writer Wong Jing is best known for directing a long string of wacky Stephen Chow comedies, and his other scripts are always at least a bit ridiculous. This one fails as a serious drama, but scores high as a camp action film. Many Hong Kong films have the habit of mixing odd inappropriate humor in with serious subjects, and this one goes over the top quite a few times. Witness: the infamous crime-scene penis eating. Though not as racy as the title suggests, this is still a fun and sexy film, which entertainingly stretches beyond the bounds of credibility at every turn. But then, that's about what you'd expect from a film whose title translates as "Bare Naked Cake Goat." *AKA: Chek Law Giu Cheung; Chi Luo Gao Yang.* ♪♪♪

1992 88m/C *HK* Chingmy Yau, Simon Yam, Carrie Ng, Kelly Yao, Madoka Sugawara, Ken Lo, Hui Siuhung, Dick Lau, Cheung Jing, Hon Jun. *D:* Clarence Fok. *W:* Wong Jing. *C:* Peter Pau, William Yim. *M:* Lowell Lo. **VHS, DVD**

Naked Pursuit

Amid a street riot, a young man gets into a brawl with a cop and accidentally kills him. Escaping to the desolate seashore, he comes upon a girl who has come there to commit suicide. He chases her across the black sand and rapes her. While a manhunt continues, he chases her down again, and uses his handcuffs to hold her prisoner. She escapes, he pursues—that's about all there is to it, a lot of chasing and running in slow motion.

Shot with plenty of artsy pretension, this Japanese roughie probably played a few art houses in the U.S. But due to its high sexual content, it likely played in a lot more adult theatres, where it was probably a great disappointment. *AKA: Kofun.* ♡

1968 69m/BW *JP* Masayoshi Nogami, Mari Aoki. *D:* Toshio Okuwaki. *W:* Saburo Narutaki. *C:* Shizuya Takeda. **VHS**

Needing You...

Boxoffice smash that inspired a long string of would-be imitators and made a movie star out of a pop singer. Sales agent Kinki (Sammi Cheng) is not faring well with the men in her life. She is unappreciated both by her boyfriend Dan (Gabriel Harrison) and her boss Andy (Andy Lau). Andy is a slave-driving workaholic, but when circumstances bring him and Kinki together, he begins to see her in a new light. Flames old and new provide complications—Fiona (Fiona Leung) tries to divert Kinki's attention away from Andy by introducing her to Roger (Raymond Wong), an Internet billionaire. Will true love win out?

Romantic comedies are a dime a dozen. Video stores in America devote entire aisles to them. In truth, however, very few of them merit a second—or even a first—look. You need two likable protagonists, realistic tension between them delaying their inevitable coupling, and an

elegant sense of humor, mixed together in equal measure. *Needing You...* fires on all cylinders. Superstar Andy Lau and singer Sammi Cheng are both likable and attractive. Secondary characters are allowed to contribute funny pieces of business. The direction by Johnnie To and Wai Kar-Fai is inventive and appears effortless. One ingenious example: the race to keep up as gossip quickly spreads through an office building. The tone is just right—the film smoothly glides around the protagonists' lives, and the audience is invited along for the ride. The comedy avoids the easy slapstick routine. The pacing is brisk but lingers when needed. Nothing here is too deep or substantial, and that's the right approach to romantic comedy. As a side note, this would make a good double feature with 1990's *A Moment of Romance* (produced by Johnnie To and also starring Andy Lau), since *Needing You...* makes satiric references to the earlier film. Cheng and Lau would reteam for a more unorthodox romantic comedy in *Love on a Diet.* —PM **AKA:** *Goo Laam Gwa Lui.* 🎝🎝🎝

2000 104m/C *HK* Andy Lau, Sammi Cheng, Fiona Leung, Raymond Wong Ho-yin, Hui Siu-hung, Gabriel Harrison, Florence Kwok, Lam Suet, Henry Yu Yung, Sam Sam, Vanesia Chu, Andy Tse, Ruby Wong. **D:** Johnny To, Wai Kar-fai. **W:** Wai Kar-Fai, Yau Nai-hoi. **C:** Cheng Siu-keung. **M:** Cacine Wong. **DVD**

New Fist of Fury

Broke and discouraged, Jackie Chan had retired from show business in 1976, resigned to a life of construction and restaurant work in Australia, and the disapproving glances of his parents. But "Millionaire Director" Lo Wei, rich as a result of his films with Bruce Lee, was looking for a new martial arts star to replace the late Dragon. His production manager Willie Chan remembered an energetic young stuntman with a lot of potential, and tracked Chan down with an offer. And so, the young master returned to Hong Kong, shocked to be playing his first lead role, even at Lo's cut-rate prices.

Looking to cleave as close to the Bruce Lee image as possible, Lo chose to launch his new star in this sequel to Lee's *Fist of Fury* (known in the U.S. as *The Chinese Connection*). After the death of Chen and the destruction of the Ching Wu martial arts school, Miss Lee (returning Nora Miao) and a couple survivors flee Shanghai for Taiwan to live with her grandfather Su Onli (Lo Wei), but the Japanese are there, too. Brash youngster Helong (Chan) can't help but pick fights with the foreigners, whenever he thinks he can get away with it. He and his Uncle Ho Chin (Hon Siu) are petty thieves, picking on recent arrivals on the docks. They swipe a parcel from Miss Lee, which holds an ornate wooden box containing Chen's nunchakus, but don't know what they are. Due to his natural talent, Helong gets an offer to join the school of Lin Ching Kai and work in his casino, but he objects to the way they kowtow to the invaders, and says he doesn't want to learn kung fu. They give him a beating and throw him in a ditch, where Lee and Hong find him.

Master Hong pretends to cooperate with the Japanese, while actually the Su Onli martial arts school is hiding a nest of rebels. Mr. Akumora (Chan Sing), who runs the Japanese school, respects the Chinese schools, but the governor wants Akumora to bring them under his own control. Akumora and his daughter Jen Da So begin a campaign, challenging school after school and beating them into line. After Master Su dies (standing up like a hero), Lee decides to reopen the Ching Wu school in Taiwan. Still, lazy Helong refuses to learn, until Akumora comes to bully the Ching Wu School and Jen smashes their sign. He makes a speech, repairs the sign, and learns kung fu to fight the Japs in about a weekend.

It's been generally accepted that Jackie Chan was forced by Lo Wei to try to conform to the stern, intense character Lee played in the original, much like the other Lee imitators on the market. However, Helung isn't much different than the playful, overconfident rascals Chan played in his kung fu comedies like *Drunken Master,* when left to his own devices. Even late in the film, after images of Jackie are cut together with stills of Bruce to show how they are supposedly similar, Chan's fighting style is clearly much different. The main fault in the film is a preponderance of drama and dialogue, without much actually happening. Chan isn't even a lead character until near the end. The camera work is sloppy, with many shots out of focus. The English dubbing is a bit sloppy at times, too—one character is dubbed by two different voices within the same scene. However, a lot of the fight scenes are nicely choreographed and well edited. **AKA:** *San Cheng Miu Moon; Sin Jing Wu Men; Fists to Fight.* 🎝🎝

1976 118m/C *HK* Jackie Chan, Nora Miao, Chan Sing, Han Ying Chieh, Lo Wei, Hon Siu, Shih Ting Ken, Weng Hsiao Hu. **D:** Lo Wei. **W:** Pan Lei, Lo Wei. **VHS, DVD**

The New Game of Death

Young martial artist Bruce Li is a dead ringer (so they say here) for the late Bruce Lee, and producers hire him to complete Lee's unfinished last film. The resemblance is especially apparent in footage shown to him from the project— since Bruce Li plays Lee's part in the movie! For the next 70 minutes or so, we see this "unfin-

*"Wonder
screw!"*

—Jet Li beats his enemy
with a secret spear move
in *The New Legend
of Shaolin*

ished film"—it may be that the flick was originally just too short for release, which would explain the preceding padding. A guy named Lee sees a man murdered in an alley. The dying man gives him a package to deliver to his son, but after Lee is attacked by some thugs, he and his brother Lai open it to find out what he's fought for. The box is full of cash, and Lai goes to deliver it to the police while Lee fights some more thugs. But Lai disappears, and the evil gang boss (Lung Fei) thinks Lee knows where his brother is hiding. After numerous dustups, Lee's girlfriend Lu Ping is kidnapped by the bad guys, and he's told she's being held at the top of the Seven Stars Tower. Lee slips into a familiar yellow track suit with black racing stripes and heads off to battle his way up the tower.

The Seven Stars set is one of the cheapest ever in a kung fu movie (and that's saying something), consisting of a white room with decorated pagoda-style red beams and corner columns, a window, a wooden staircase, and a painted backdrop through an archway to represent "outside." The same set is used for all seven floors of the tower, with only minor variations (exteriors are of Taiwan's Chung Hsing Tower, seen in many a kung fu feature). The action is mediocre, typical of early Bruce Li outings—he *holds* his nose instead of thumbing it, and fumbles around with nunchakus. When he fights a samurai (Lee Keung) on the second level, they stop the camera so Li can teleport around his opponent! The campy "King of Kung Fu" theme song by Candy makes several unwelcome appearances on the soundtrack. Some of the same opening footage is used in the similar *Dynamo*, confusing those who want to keep their Bruce Lee rip-offs straight. *AKA: Goodbye Bruce Lee: His Last Game of Death; He's a Hero, He's a Legend; King of Kung Fu.* ♫

1975 (R) 83m/C *HK* Bruce Li, Ronald Brown, Big Jonny Floyd, Wong Ping, Lee Keung, Lung Fei. **D:** Lin Bin, Harold B. Schwartz. **C:** Tony Shang. **M:** Arpad Bondy. **VHS, DVD**

The New Legend of Shaolin

Jet Li adds another legendary Chinese hero to his resume, portraying Hung Hay-kwun, master of Tiger Style kung fu, whose name would be immortalized in the naming of modern Hung Gar kung fu. The opening shows a free adaptation of the Japanese Lone Wolf and Cub legend, retold as a tale of Ching Dynasty China, but the baby cart is soon disposed of (destroyed, in fact) in favor of a much more dynamic Cub. The rest of the tale concentrates on a turbulent period in Chinese history, and presents a loose interpretation of events around the time of the sacking of the original Shaolin Temple. Shaolin monks join the rebellion of Chan Kan Nam's Heaven and Earth Society against Emperor Kang Hsi, seeking to restore the Ming Dynasty. Hero Hung Hey-kwun (Jet Li) finds his son Man-Ting (actually the grandson of hero Fong Sai-yuk!), the only survivor of the massacre of his village. The infant is given a choice between a toy and a sword—a quick death or a life of bloodshed. Ma Ling-Yee (Li's regular co-star Chi Chuen-Hua), Hung's childhood friend, is revealed as the turncoat to blame for the massacre. He and Hung have a wild battle, which ends with Ma beaten and consumed by fire.

Hung raises Man-Ting (Tse Miu) to be a ruthless little fighter. Meanwhile, the Shaolin monks hide the treasure collected to finance the revolution, and tattoo sections of the treasure map on the backs of five boys—Wu Tak-tai, Ma Chiu-hing, Choi Tak-chung, Li Si-hoi, and Fong Tai-hu. Ma Chiu-hing leaves to celebrate his father's birthday. Father Ma Kai Sin (Chan Chung-Yung) is a victim of a scam by pretty con artist Red Bean (Chingmy Yau) and her mother (Deannie Yip), who pretends to be dead so her "grieving" daughter can sell herself to a unsuspecting rich man. Hung is ambushed by his own brother, and seems to find no safety anywhere. Broke and hungry, Hung agrees to take a job offer to be Ma's bodyguard.

The government forces—accompanied by Ling-Yee, who survived his fiery defeat to return as a scarred and poisonous monster—raid the Shaolin Temple. The Little Kung Fu Rascals escape to join their buddy at Ma's villa. Planning to start a new Shaolin, they name after little Hung Man-Ting after he defeats them all. A crazy household, with an ignorant father, scheming bride, undead mother, superhero bodyguard, and a brood of six junior martial arts masters, is formed.

Until soldiers track the boys to Ma's Villa, and while Hung is away, the boys are captured. Hung tracks them to a government fort, then battles the invincible Poisonous Man Ma (who arrives in a shiny metal car straight out of the Batman movies). There's more—a mysterious wax museum, Master Chan and the Heaven and Earth Society vs. metal globes full of ninjas, a battle on a clock tower, Red Bean's mother having mad dart combat, and in-jokes aplenty. *New Legend of Shaolin* is a carnival ride of a movie that leaves you spent, satisfied, and just a little dizzy. Little Tse Miu, who played Jet Li's son both here and in *The Enforcer,* has since become a TV star on the mainland. *AKA: Legend of the Red Dragon; Hong Xiguan zhi Shaolin Wu Zu; Xin Shaolin Wuzu; Hung Hei-Koon: Shaolin's Five Founders; Legend of Future Shaolin; Legends of Shaolin.* ♫♫♫♫

1994 95m/C *HK* Jet Li, Tse Miu, Chingmy Yau, Deannie Yip, Chi Chuen-Hua, Chan Chung-Yung,

Damien Lau, Wong Jing. **D:** Wong Jing. **W:** Wong Jing. **C:** Tom Lau. **M:** Wong Bong. **VHS, DVD**

The New Marvelous Double

The title must refer to "double cross," rather than doppelganger, since there are no twins of any kind in the movie. Karen Hui is a peppy young teen. Someone tampers with her car, causing an accident, but fortunately she's not hurt. Father Hui Shing Tin's employee Kut finds a good shaman who may be able to cure Karen's bad luck. The old faker says she must find a guy born on the same day to help her through hard luck. One would think that the plot would lead her to meet just such a guy, but this idea is dropped entirely. Instead, the Wolf Gang—epileptic Hitachi, sister Toshiba, and punk Scalp—kidnaps Karen.

When they get the news, the Hui family is upset, but no more so than if they had a broken refrigerator. Hui hires bumbling detective Luk Cheuk to help find his daughter. Kut recommends his rival Cheung Kwun Ling to supervise the detective, secretly hoping he'll screw up. Meanwhile, Karen's young stepmother intercepts a ransom letter: the Wolf Gang demands $10 million in ransom. This makes her mad because she hired them to kill Karen for only $2 million. Hitachi, who has fallen for his captive, lost his retainer at the snatch, and the detectives follow the clue to a restaurant that caters to wrymouths! They find out where the gang lives, but get captured, too. The gang is reluctant to kill anybody, and make a deal with their captives to double-cross their clients.

This pleasant comedy features a large cast, but except for a big fight at the end in which Leung Kar-yan shows off his kung fu skills, there's not much action. **AKA:** *Jeung Bo Miu Taam; Zi Bao Miao Tan; Twins Jewel Lady Search.* 🐉🐉🐲

1992 C: *HK* Leung Kar-yan, Joey Leung, Lilly Li, Gloria Yip, Bonnie Fu. **D:** Raymond See. **W:** Raymond See. **C:** Peter Li. **M:** Stephen Shing. **VHS**

New Mr. Vampire

The first of many knockoffs of the Mr. Vampire series, this is more a supernatural farce than a horror comedy, using many of the same actors from the Sammo Hung–produced spook shows. Graverobber Wang Choi (Chin Siu-ho) picks the wrong coffin to dig up—it chases him into town, putting him in between rival ghostbusters Master Chin (Chung Fat) and Master Wu Hang (Chen Yueh-Sheng), who operate right across the street from each other and are always bickering.

Wu's nephew Tai-fa (Lui Fong) is Chin's student, and constantly struggles to keep peace between the two priests. When a local gang boss dies, both are called in by the deceased's brother (Ku Feng) to compete for the job of transporting the body to their home village for the funeral. The criminal prefers Chin's pandering approach to Wu's more practical advice, and hires Chin.

On the road, Wu sabotages Chin's job by turning the corpse into a vampire. While Wu tries to control the damage, unlucky Wang is robbing the nearby grave of Miss Hsi-wan (Pauline Wong, the lonely ghost from *Mr. Vampire*) at exactly the wrong time and location. Lightning strikes, causing Wang to breathe into the corpse's mouth, making her into a half-human zombie that imitates his every move (a situation milked for all it's worth). Hsi-wan was the ninth concubine of a powerful Marshal (Shum Wai), who happens to be a guest at the same hotel as Chin's party. Chin is forced to attempt to bring the zombie back to full life or lose his own, but that rascal Wu has increased the vampire's strength, and it breaks loose to cause complete chaos.

The pace drags a bit throughout, and most scenes could have used a trim, but this is a generally entertaining comic romp. The leads are good, but their personalities are lost amid the general chaos of the second half, where it appears the cast is making up the script as they go along. The interesting plotline with Pauline Wong's character is dropped in the third act, as is the threat of the gangsters. Well, at least there are no baby vampires in this one. Hong Kong cinema's lucky charm Wu Ma has a small role as a rude hotel clerk who is willing to count corpses as luggage rather than guests. Outtakes play under the end credits. **AKA:** Geung Si Fan Sheng; Jiang Shi Fan Sheng; Kung Fu Vampire Buster; New Mr. Stiff Corpse. 🐉🐉🐲

1986 89m/C *HK* Chin Siu-ho, Chung Fat, Chen Yueh-Sheng, Pauline Wong, Lui Fong, Ku Feng, Shum Wai, Tai Bo, Huang Ha, Wu Ma, Fung Ging Man, Wong Ming-sing, Chin Yuet Sang. **D:** Billy Chan. **W:** Wong Jing. **C:** Johnny Koo. **M:** Michael Lai. **DVD**

New Tale of Zatoichi

Several things set this third episode of the Zatoichi series apart from the others. For one thing, it's the first one filmed in color. Second, rather than tell an episodic adventure from the blind masseur's travels, it presents a dramatic turning point in his own life. Third is that it's one of the episodes co-starring Tomisaburo Wakayama, star Shintaro Katsu's brother, this time playing the sword master who taught Zatoichi how to

"Everyone please pretend to be deaf."

—Ichi prepares to break into song in *New Tale of Zatoichi*

fence. One thing that's not unusual is that it begins with assassins after Zatoichi's blood. They've come after him for killing Boss Sekiya Kanbei (in *The Tale of Zatoichi Continues*). Evading death once again, Ichi meets up with his childhood friend Tame, a singer from Koja, and his family. Their reunion dinner (and Ichi's ballad) is interrupted by bandits. Ichi holds his sword in order to keep any bystanders from being hurt, but the next morning he goes to the local boss's house to confront the robbers and get everyone's money back. At a hot spring, Ichi has another reunion, this time with his sensei Banno Yoshiro (Wakayama), whom he hasn't seen in four years. Kanbei's brothers follow them back to their hometown of Shimodate, seeking retribution. Fallen on hard times, Banno is secretly advising the thieving Tengu gang, while trying to marry off his younger sister Yaiyo (Mikiko Tsubouchi) to a rich suitor. But Yaiyo prefers Ichi, and asks that he reform and marry her. Overjoyed, he agrees; Kanbei picks that moment to challenge Ichi to a duel. When Ichi begs for his life rather than fight, Kanbei decides to make it a duel with dice. If Ichi wins, they call it even; if he loses, he gives up his sword arm.

Long on drama and short on action, we're 80 minutes in before Zatoichi gets to any serious fighting. It's nice to learn so much more about Ichi's past, and why he's chosen the road he's on. But the Tengu clan doesn't pose much of a threat, and Zatoichi already beat the best of the Kanbei clan, so most of the conflicts are emotional, moral, and internal. *AKA: Shin Zatoichi Monogatari; Masseur Ichi Enters Again; Zatoichi Enters Again; Zatoichi: The Blind Swordsman's Return.* ♪♪♪

1963 91m/C *JP* Shintaro Katsu, Tomisaburo Wakayama, Mikiko Tsubouchi. *D:* Tokuzo Tanaka. *W:* Minoru Inuzuka, Kikuo Umebayashi, Kan Shimozawa (story). *C:* Chikashi Makiura. *M:* Akira Ifukube. **VHS, DVD**

Nightmare Zone

Another Hong Kong trilogy of terror, so be prepared for a lot of cheesy blue filters. Canadian immigrant May Ho (Emily Kwan) works in a small office and has few friends. She's happy to hear her boyfriend Chi On is coming back to Hong Kong soon. Bored and lonely, she calls her old phone number one night, and is surprised to hear herself answer on the other end of the line. When she dials back, there's no answer, and she has recurring nightmares about drowning. Chi On and May investigate the calls and find her old building torn down and the phone number cancelled. Calling again, "May Ho" tells May to go to the top of a building. There, she finds a man who claims he killed her. Boo!

Lily Tin spends all her time sharpening a big knife and chopping meat since her son died, annoying her neighbor (Helena Law) and worrying her husband (Wayne Lai). Not that her husband is acting much more rationally, scaring customers out of his cab. Maybe her shiftless brother Boasting Hsiong (Hui Siu-hung) can sort things out. Meanwhile, a maniac is killing folks in the neighborhood. Who's the real psycho? Boo!

Simon Chu (Max Mok) has a recurring dream that he's being murdered ever since moving into a new house. His girlfriend Gee Chiang wants to move, but he's obsessed with finding out who is killing him in his dream. Gee makes an appointment to see shifty fortune-teller Feng Chin (Yvonne Yung), but Gee's ex-beau Bond Li wants revenge for getting thrown over for Simon, and bribes Chin to tell Gee to dump Simon. Chin succeeds in bamboozling Gee, but later unknowingly runs into Simon, and he recognizes her as Chia Yin, a girl in his dream. Chin explains the dream as being the same as the Anita Mui movie *Rouge,* and uses the opportunity to bilk him, too. Bond makes his move and succeeds in separating Gee from Simon, only to turn ugly once he has her again. But fate has a few more ironic twists in store. Boooo!

There's nothing at all frightening here, unless you count how frighteningly fast HK filmmakers can churn out these ghost stories. They don't even provide a charming host in this one, just jump into the tales. The constant blue look of the first story is monotonous rather than spooky. The second story is an improvement, painting a portrait of madness within urban squalor. The third has a few good turns in the plot, plus some welcome bits of humor, and might have been developed into a decent full feature with some fleshing out. As it is, you'd have better nightmares sleeping through this than watching it. The DVD contains a handy guide to Chinese magic figures, which is nice but has nothing to do with the movie. *AKA: Mei Mong Leung, Chi Mei Wang Liang.* ♪♡

1998 94m/C *HK* Max Mok, Yvonne Yung, Hui Siu-hung, Wayne Lai, Florence Kwok, Emily Kwan, Helena Law, Cheng Yuen Man, Marco Ngai. *D:* Lee Yuk-chun. *C:* Sung Kwong-wah. **VHS, DVD**

Nine Demons

After leaving Shaw Brothers, Chang Cheh and some of his regular troupe put together this wildly eccentric action fantasy—a taste of weirdness to come in Chang's career. Young Master Gary Fu (Chris Lee) and young Master Joey (Ricky Cheng) are rambunctious youths, always getting into fights. The Fu's evil butler (Yu Tai-ping) engineers an attack in which the boys' fathers are killed. While fleeing from the assassins, Joey falls into a dimensional portal into a shadowy netherworld. Every 500 years, the gates to the Black Paradise open on Earth, and Joey just happened to be there at the wrong time. To save Gary's life, Joey swears allegiance to the Black Prince of Hell (Lu Feng), who grants Joey special powers and summons nine demons to accompany him home and serve him. With his new powers, Joey easily rescues Gary and they make mincemeat of the killers. Joey has to feed the demons blood, and when he runs out of dead thugs he has to stop by the local brothel for a six-pack of whores. The demons look like a bunch of dancing morons led by a silly girl, but much of the time they appear as smoking skulls that fly around biting people. But sometimes they're just a pack of bloodthirsty devil children sucking blood out of folks. Gary reclaims his estate, but Fu Chin (Chiang Sheng), Master Law (Lu Feng), and some of the other masters are concerned about Joey the Demon draining the populace, and Fu kills Gary to draw his friend out. But these self-serving machinations don't sit well with Law's son Roland (Wang Li), and he turns against the others. Roland and Mia Flower (Lau Yin-nam), a girl who befriended Joey, are captured and used as bait to draw the demon into an ambush.

It's as if the Shaws were reining Chang in, keeping his comic-book movies just sane enough to work. Here, it's not enough for Joey to have a showdown with Law and his men—they all have to fight on some kind of water skates on a lake. The demon doesn't seem to have any trouble with them, but freezes the lake with magic just for fun. They respond by building a web of bamboo above the lake for them to fight on in about three seconds. Ngai Hong can usually be relied upon for a coherent (or at least entertaining) plot, but here he gets tied up in digressions. The main villain is disposed of in the first half, so he has to come up with a sequel for the second half of the film. As is usual for a Venoms film, the costumes are outrageous Chinese superhero outfits, bearing little relation to actual clothes worn by anyone during any period. The English dubbing crew obviously had a party working on this one, looping in howlers like "Y'all come back now" when Fu leaves a restaurant, and when getting into a fight he proclaims "I brought back-up!" Not the best work of anyone involved, but it's hard to beat the amusement value of those bloodthirsty flying skulls. The stolen soundtrack cues are too numerous to keep track of. **AKA:** *Gau Ji Tin Mor; Jiu Zi Tian Mo; The Demons; The 9 Venoms.* 🐉🐉🐉

1983 93m/C *HK* Ricky Cheng, Chris Lee, Chiang Sheng, Lu Feng, Lau Yin-nam, Wang Li, Yu Tai-ping, Chui Chung Hei. **D:** Chang Cheh. **W:** Ngai Hong. **C:** Ng Kwok-yan. **VHS, DVD**

9413

Francis Ng *(Bride with White Hair)* stars in and directs this portrait of a police officer with mental problems. Psychologist Dr. Carmen Leung (Christine Ng) is on the ferry going to an appointment when detective Ko Chin-man, whom his associates call Smash-head (Francis Ng), makes an arrest. As she gets over her shock, she finds she's fascinated by the man, who pursues a litterbug just as fervently as the armed criminal he was after. Smash-head has been under scrutiny for his behavior many times, ever since he accidentally shot and killed a hostage, and has only kept his position because he's proved his effectiveness. Smoking, drinking, given to fits of anger, and obsessively worried about the ozone layer, it begins to dawn on him that he needs some help, and he goes to Dr. Leung looking for it. But when she rejects him as a patient, he goes back to threatening witnesses and spending all his off-hours in a seedy basement club with a whore named Mandy (Amanda Lee). When his partner Fatty Chuen (Lee Kin-yan) is found murdered with his own gun, Smash-head is suspended until the case can be investigated, and his mental state becomes more unraveled. But he keeps making attempts to connect with the doctor, and to build trust, he takes her inside his world. Will she be able to help him, or will his madness pull her in? His superior Kar (Fredric Mao) seems to be infected with his psychosis somewhat already, and Dr. Leung looks to be next on the list.

There's a decent thriller in here somewhere, to be found amid the drama and social commentary about how the only way to find serenity in a sinking city built on landfills is through hypnotherapy. Ng finds the typical pitfalls of an actor directing himself for the first time. Stretches of the film are flashy and self-indulgent. Sandy Shaw's script is often clichéd and self-indulgent, too: we know that characters must be going mad because they dance wildly to music. The doctor is too saintly and wise, too sensitive to be real. At times she seems more like a New Age quack than a licensed psychotherapist. Even more outrageously, she blurs the line between dating her patient and treating him. Ng's talents and imagination are obvious, and there are some moments of pure beauty, but while striving for immediacy and realism here, he achieves just the opposite. There are a lot of different styles of music in the film, and most of it is excellent. 🐉🐉

1998 90m/C *HK* Francis Ng, Christine Ng, Amanda Lee, Fredric Mao, Stephen Ho, Raymond Yue, Lee Kin-yan, Samuel Lam, Bill Lui, Ho Kai-tung. **D:** Francis Ng. **W:** Sandy Shaw. **C:** Herman Yau, Ng Kin-man. **M:** Wave Music Works, Wing Lo, Edward Chan, Charles Lee. **VHS, DVD**

"We want disciplined men, and not spoiled crybabies."

—The old master hands down his wisdom in *Nine Demons*

990714.com

Screenwriter Fatty Kau (!) is working on a script for a new teen horror thriller, an anthology in the same vein as the *Troublesome Night* series. He calls his movie "Internet Ghost Stories," set in a college dormitory in between sessions. The students living there are worried. Their friend Ada Fong has been missing three days. Goth girl Witch reads her tarot cards, and the conversation turns to superstitions and urban legends. There's a horrible e-mail going around, with a link to a website: www.990714.com. Rumor has it that if you log in there in the 7th lunar month, the "Chinese Ghost Festival," you'll be connected to the netherworld. They try, but fail to connect. Later, one of the students, a computer nerd named Nun, has an idea—perhaps the site changes depending on the day. She's correct, and connects to the Cyber Hell site, where her questions connect her to an ICQ chat with her dead friend. However, it's just a prank set up by her housemates, who are chatting from another room. Or is it? The messages Nun receives aren't the same as the ones they send, telling her Ada's body is in the room of Crooked (Ku Feng), the hunchback janitor, instead of in the water tank. Nun and her friend Windy investigate, while their buddies wait on the roof to scare them. The kids begin to be separated and killed one by one as their superstitions come true.

Back to the writer, as he tries another idea from the same premise. In "Sister and Sister," Ada is found safe at the beginning. Teacher Miss Lee (Chang Siu Yin) is working late on her birthday. She thinks about how she lost her twin sister in a childhood accident, and decides to try to contact her late sister through the website. Just then, there's a knock on her door, and a strange little girl enters. Lee and the tyke are a comfort to each other, but the peace is shattered when a gang of thieves invades the building and kills the other teacher, Mr. Shek. Lee and her new friend run for their lives, but not to worry. The little girl enjoys playing hide-and-seek—and she brought an axe. Better, but Fatty still fails to find a satisfying ending. The little girl is at it again in "Ghost Fooling," harassing crude Mr. Kuen (Wayne Lai), the building's redecorator. Just being near web-surfing Mr. Shek seems to have the poor man stuck in time, unable to reach his room on the third floor.

Writers are always looking for something new to scare people, and the supernatural website idea is a good one, but it's not exploited fully here. The stories get better as the movie progresses, but none of them makes much sense, and the whole show is poorly paced. And the writer? He gets what he deserves. **AKA:** *Mong Seung Gwaai Taam; Wang Shang Guai Tan.* 🐉🐉

2000 95m/C *HK* Wayne Lai, Chang Siu Yin, Lau Siu Kwan, Kong Lai Loh, Chu Yin Chun, Ku Feng. **D:** Kwong Kam Wang, Hui Mei Kwan. **VHS, DVD**

99 Cycling Swords

The Four Dragons go to offer their services in helping root out a Ching rebellion, but find a slaughter at the police station. Magistrate Khan (Cho Boon Feng) lives only long enough to blame a Man in White named Chu Er-ming for the deed, and to indicate that one of the Four Dragons is a traitor. The Man in White is a fierce fighter, who easily makes fools of the Dragons with his magic whip, but they don't see his face. While the Four Dragons take a tea break to think about their problem, a "man" named Shan Kwan-tung (Polly Shang Kwan) dressed in white enters, looking for a man named Pai Chin-hai (Lung Tin Cheung). Shan is a fine fighter, too, also making monkeys of the Four Dragons and their gang. Before "he" can state "his" business with teashop owner Pai, Shan has a run-in with another man in white. But this one turns out not to be Chu either, but a fighter called Yao (Yueh Hua). Another fighter named Sang Sang-hai (Lo Lieh) joins the group, as they're all dedicated to catching Chu and the Ching rebels—except the traitor, of course. Pai is their first suspect, but he denies ever wearing white. Sang splits to look for his master's daughter Yang Pang-chow, who is said to be trained in all martial arts, including the famed 99 Sword Stroke. Chu quickly kills two of the Four Dragons, and the other two fight it out until Chu abducts one. During all this, Shan and Yao have fallen in love, a dilemma solved by the fact that Shan has an "identical twin" sister whom Yao can marry.

Stop! Can you solve the mystery from the clues provided so far? Well, don't be too quick to discount the identical dectuplet theory. This strange martial arts flick is totally out of control, as if writer/director Tyrone Hsu made it up as they went long. All of the characters could be hiding something, as if they were in an Agatha Christie kung fu mystery. The multiple identities are too confusing to try to figure out, and don't necessarily make sense if you try, but the action is wild—eccentric even. There are a lot of camera tricks involving juggling dishes and such. And the 99 Swords Stroke tops them all. It's all pretty dopey, but goofy enough to be plenty entertaining. The villain is trapped in the end using an outlandish magnetic device that either doesn't translate to English, or is just plain insane. It appears that some of the character names may be a play on the names of the actors. **AKA:** *Lung Wai Saan Chong; Long Wei Shan Zhuang; Lung Wei Village.* 🐉🐉🐉

1980 91m/C *TW* Polly Shang Kwan, Lo Lieh, Yueh Hua, Chui Chung Hei, Hu Chin, Lung Tin Cheung,

Cho Boon Feng, Cheung Wai. **D:** Tyrone Hsu. **W:** Tyron Hsu. **C:** Shu Te-li. **VHS, DVD**

Ninja: Band of Assassins

After Daiei Studios had established their hit *Zatoichi* series, they put into production this film that emphasized ninja action, using many of the same sets and locations. During a time of upheaval and civil war across Japan (about 1580), General Oda Nobunaga (Tomisaburo Wakayama) is out to become emperor by overcoming all other armies. General Sandayu Momochi (Yunosuke Ito) and his ninja clans oppose him, and make plans to deal with the situation. Momochi makes young ninja in training Goemon Ishikawa (Raizo Ichikawa) promise to look after his young wife Yuni (Kyoko Kishida) while he is away. Then by night, he sneaks out on a secret mission—he is in fact impersonating a second identity, disguising his frail and old features under a white wig and beard as Fujibayashi, the fierce leader of a rival ninja clan. Goemon continues his training, hoping to be a great ninja. His father plans to teach him about explosives, but accidentally blows himself up—or did he? Meanwhile, the ninja try to kill Nobunaga with a dart, but his pet cat gets in the way (a very realistic scene for some poor kitty). The assassin is caught, but refuses to talk, even when Nobunaga cuts his ears off. Left alone together, the rugged Goemon and the neglected wife give in to their passions—but they don't know that old Momochi can spy on them from a secret chamber. Goemon tries to kill the servant Hatat and others that discover the affair, and in the struggle Yuni falls down a well. Momochi gives Goemon one chance to live: He must go on a mission to assassinate Nobunaga, stealing his war chest to help cover up the nature of the crime. However, the already difficult job becomes nearly impossible to survive when the clan leader marks Goemon for death as a traitor. The robbery is easy, but Goemon fails in his first assassination attempt, and hides out with a prostitute named Maki (Shiho Fujimura). Though all he wants to do is buy the girl's freedom and settle down with her, Goemon's duty as a ninja—and the continuous attacks by his former comrades—drive him on to complete his mission.

The first half is mired in complex politics and intrigues, but once Goemon's fate is set, the action picks up. These aren't the fantasy ninjas in bright costumes seen in cheap movies from the 1980s that behave more like superheroes, but the action is still satisfyingly energetic and surprisingly bloody for the time. The action was supervised by actual ninjitsu grandmasters.

However, the way an old friend shows up to impart information that changes Goemon's perspective is a bit too obvious. Nevertheless, the film's exciting action scenes and heavy atmosphere made it a hit in Japan, and touched off the first ninja movie craze, which Ian Fleming picked up on while traveling to research *You Only Live Twice*. Raizo Ichikawa would return for several sequels, but he's overpowered by Ito's chilling performance in every scene. **AKA:** *Shinobi no Mono; Ninja; Band of Assassins.* 🗡🗡🗡

1962 95m/BW *JP* Raizo Ichikawa, Tomisaburo Wakayama, Shiho Fujimura, Yunosuke Ito, Kyoko Kishida, Reiko Fujiwara, Yutaka Nakamura, Yoshi Kato. **D:** Satsuo Yamamoto. **DVD**

Ninja: Band of Assassins Continued

This sequel starts right about where we left off. Cat-fancying warlord General Nobunaga (Tomisaburo Wakayama) is still trying to fight his way to ruling Japan by eliminating rival clans, especially the ninjas. He offers high rewards for news about ninjas and devises new ways of killing them off. Having left the ninja life behind, Goemon Ishikawa (Raizo Ichikawa) wants only to settle down in the mountains with his wife Maki (Shiho Fujimura) and infant son. However, when Nobunaga's soldiers kill his son, Goemon renews his vow to kill the tyrant. He learns that one of Nobunaga's top men Mitsuhide (So Yamamura) is a righteous man who is against his master's ruthless tactics but is nevertheless loyal. Goemon goes undercover inside Nobunaga's organization in order to gather information and chip away at Mitsuhide's loyalty.

The film reaches a climax fairly early in a bloody battle at Honnoji Temple, losing momentum for a bit while factions regroup. Later, an army surrounds the Saiga clan fortress and settles in to starve them out. Goemon is finally allowed to take a chance and fight his way through the lines and get help. He succeeds, but help comes too late, and Goemon gains a new target for his vengeance. Raizo Ichikawa is shown performing historically accurate feats of ninja warfare, many of which were interpreted as magic (such as stretching a rope ladder across a stream to "walk on water"), and portrayed as such in many ninja movies to come. Tomisaburo Wakayama contributes another fierce performance. The movie suffers from the fact that it reaches what feels like the end halfway through, then ends on a cliffhanger, but this is otherwise an excellent production. The only readily available source of these films is via import DVD on the Mei Ah label, but their otherwise fine presentations are marred by bad English subtitles that give all the characters and places Chinese names. Continued in *New Ninja Band of Assassins* and five more sequels. *AKA: Zoku Shinobi no Mono; Band of Assassins Returns; Ninja 2.* 🐉🐉🐉

1963 94m/BW *JP* Raizo Ichikawa, Tomisaburo Wakayama, So Yamamura, Shiho Fujimura, Mikiko Tsubouchi, Eijiro Tono, Shigeru Amachi, Fujio Suga, Saburo Date, Seichiro Hara, Tokio Oki, Tadashi Iwata. *D:* Satsuo Yamamoto. *W:* Hajime Takaiwa. *C:* Senkichiro Takeda. *M:* Michiaki Watanabe. **DVD**

Ninja Checkmate

Not just another kung fu film retitled by Ocean Shores Video to cash in on the ninja boom of the 1980s, this is one of Joseph Kuo's most beloved films, better known to fans under the much better title *Mystery of Chess Boxing.* Ghostface Killer Wong Cho-san (Mark Lung) is using his Five Elements kung fu to get revenge on all the clansmen who tried to get rid of him years earlier, including the father of young Bao (James Lee). Though he's offended the senior student (Siu Foo-dau), young rascal Ah Bao gets accepted at the kung fu school, where he hopes to become a skillful enough fighter to take on Ghostface Killer. But relegated to the most menial chores, Bao only learns the kitchen kung fu the old cook Yuen (Simon Yuen) can teach him. When the school's master sees that Bao carries the Ghostface Killer's calling card around with him, he thinks the lad is a spy and kicks him out. Yuen sends him to chess master Chi Siu-tin (Jack Lung) and his granddaughter (Jeanie Chang, "A new star of Joseph Kuo," according to the credits), in the hope that old Chi will take him as a student. At first Chi teaches Bao only chess, giving him the basics of the mental techniques essential to kung fu. But when they learn that Ghostface Killer's death list has reached their friend Yuen, Chi trains Bao in earnest, teaching him the Five Elements techniques.

Kuo may have fallen on hard times since more lavish productions such as *The 18 Bronzemen* and *The Shaolin Brothers,* here hiring Simon Yuen for a day's work to lend marquee value to what is basically a *Drunken Master* knockoff. But *Chess Boxing* still has good dramatic structure, terrific fight scenes, good storytelling techniques, and imaginative training/torture sequences. There's even a bit of pathos afforded the hero's school nemesis—though the butt of most of the gags, and the betrayer of just about everyone, he expresses concern and loyalty for his master as his duel with the villain approaches, even as he's stabbing him in the back. However, somewhere along the line a sloppy editor injected some poor continuity, including one scene that plays out of

sequence. Ghostface Killer isn't made the grandiose villain that he would have been in a Chang Cheh picture, but he really seems to relish meting out punishment, laughing like crazy before and after each death strike. The separate fight scenes of the Lung brothers are great, but when they fight each other, it's simply beautiful. James Lee can't hold a candle to Jackie Chan in terms of talent and passion, but he makes for a reasonable stand-in, and has a bit of charm all his own. *AKA: Mystery of Chess Boxing.* 🐉🐉🐉🐉

1979 87m/C *HK/TW* James Lee, Simon Yuen, Jack Lung, Mark Lung, Jeanie Chang, Wong Chi Sang, Siu Foo-dau, Ricky Cheng, Wang Wing Sheng, Mau Ging-shun. *D:* Joseph Kuo. *W:* Chiang Ping-han. *C:* Cheng Hui-kung. *M:* Huang Mau-sen. **VHS, DVD**

The Ninja Dragon

Cartoonist Go Nagai *(Devil Man)* turned to directing live action with this outrageously gory modern-day ninja thriller. A mysterious giant and his partner, a woman in a red dress, are demonic assassins that have been killing off yakuza members. Little Shinobu (Etsuko Araoda) dreams of ninja—Ninja Defenders Hattai Suzaka (Tetsuya Matsui), Jun Saruwatari (pro wrestler Cutie Suzuki), and their leader Ryu Momoji (Kenji Otsuki), AKA "Dragon." Ryu gives her the Dragon Bell to ring in times of danger, and she wakes to find it in her hand. Her father, Takeo Nindo (Ikko Furuya), tells her of how their Nindo yakuza clan was founded ages ago by a masterless ninja. The bell signifies she's been chosen as leader of the clan, and that danger may be near. Awkward young Yu is her new driver, and drives her to school. Of course, the strange-mannered Yu is actually a disguise for Dragon. When the deadly duo threatens Shinobu, Dragon is there to fend them off. The assassins are working for Go Ranjuji (Rikiya Yasuoka, another pro wrestler), who is using them to take over the whole yakuza territory. Nasty Ranjuji's idea of fun is ripping somebody's face off and licking the skull underneath. He kills off all the bosses at a meeting, including Shinobu's papa. The Ninja Defenders arrive too late to prevent Shinobu's abduction. Ranjuji intends to make Shinobu his bride, mixing her ninja blood with his clan's slimy fluids. The Defenders rush to the rescue, saving Shinobu and the Earth from alien invasion.

Aside from the usual fun ninja hijinks and excessive gore, the highlight here is the awful performance of Kenji Otsuki, who is like a ninja combo of Jim Morrison and Pee-wee Herman. It says a lot when the professional wrestler in the cast isn't the worst actor. Because of Suzuki's casting, it looks like they rewrote her part to include a wrestling match—complete with mat!

The monster f/x and opticals are good to mediocre. The director puts in a cameo as a head on a platter. *AKA: Legend of the Shadowy Ninja.* 🎵🎵�

1990 70m/C *JP* Kenji Otsuki, Tetsuya Matsui, Cutie Suzuki, Rikiya Yasuoka, Ikko Furuya, Etsuko Araoda, Mayumi Ozaki. *D:* Go Nagai. *W:* Daisuke Sarizawa. *C:* Eiichi Osawa. **VHS, DVD**

Ninja Hunter

This is one shambling, clubfooted mess of a movie—one that introduces new characters and subplots every 10 minutes, and abandons others; one that makes you question how and why it ever came to be made in the first place. Abbot White (Jack Lung) of Wu Tang Clan has a chip on his shoulder, and challenges monk Loong Wu of Shaolin to a duel to prove who is better. Bested, the evil abbot flees to master the Ying Yang Style in a secret cave, where he absorbs the chi of virgin maidens and becomes invulnerable to attack. Giddy with power, White visits the training camp of the Yee Ho Ninjas, where young ninjas go to learn how to vanish in a puff of smoke, cut off people's heads, and other cool stuff. He signs a pact with the Yee Ho, and together they plan the destruction of Shaolin Temple. They go to the temple intending to beat up Loong Wu, but he's not at home. Grand Abbot Jou Shen sets up a meeting of the Martial World clans to deal with White and the ninjas. He also orders that monk Jin Shen be punished for breaking their rules by having his kung fu nullified. Wu Shen and Officer Hung are sent into Wu Tang territory to retrieve him. They are attacked by Wu Tang swordsmen on the way, and when they catch up with Jin Shen, he attacks them with a corrosive acid zombie!

General Chan stops an assassination attempt on the emperor, which is blamed on the Shaolin Temple. The emperor orders all the monks massacred. While the Manchurian soldiers surround the temple, the Wu Tang and ninjas invade and set fire to it. Abbot White kills Abbot Jou Shen himself, and beats up Loong Wu. Years later, Loong's daughter Ling takes the Nerve Lock manual to the surviving Shaolin monks, as she promised her father on his deathbed. Officer Hung raises his son Wing Ding (Alexander Lou) and Hop Yau with Master Hu Mei to be great fighters, hoping they can rebuild Shaolin. With Loong Wu's manual, the boys add its finger-jabbing techniques to their arsenal. Ling is captured by White, but manages to send his martial arts secrets to the boys, who set out to avenge Shaolin.

There have been many movies about the burning of Shaolin Temple, and Hung Hey-kwun and his son Hung Man-ting's vendetta against

rebel monk Pai Mei (notably Lau Kar-Leung's *Executioners from Shaolin*), but this is surely the most distorted version. The same basic characters and events are in there somewhere, but the Wu Tang and a whole lotta ninjas are thrown into the mix. *New Legend of Shaolin* is an exaggeration inspired by the story, but this film is even more insane—and not as entertaining, or one-tenth as well made. One shot shows an actual smear on the lens! The English dub provides even more giggles, with White referring to the Shaolin abbot as "Egghead" and Hu Mei as "Miss Goody-Goody," and the turncoat ninjas calling White an "old shmuck." To be fair, once Alexander Lou finally appears the film comes together a bit better, and the final battle is pretty exciting. But by then it's way too late. The likely explanation for this is that this is another one of those half-finished movies made around 1983 and sold to Wu Kuo-jen, who tacked on a lot of new footage to fill out the running time for a video release. In any case, this was the last of Alexander Lou's old-school martial arts movies to be released, as he moved on to modern-day ninja and action nonsense. The soundtrack swipes cues from *Psycho* and other scores. *AKA: Yan Che Daai Kuet Dau; Ren Zhe Da Jue Dou; Wu Tang vs. Ninja.* 🎵♥

1983 81m/C *TW* Alexander Lou, Jack Lung, Wong Ching, William Yen, Chen Shan, Lau Hoi-yin, Chung Ling. *D:* Wu Kuo-jen. **VHS, DVD**

Ninja in the Deadly Trap

During the Ming Dynasty, General Chi Chi-kwong (Ti Lung) succeeds in repelling marauding Japanese troops, but a band of ninja fighters led by (half Chinese?) Shi Ping-wei (Yasuaki Kurata) still resists. The general sends his son to seek out the old Master of the Three Arts, who knows the ways of the ninja, to help them learn how to catch the assassins. The Master offers the help of his three students, each schooled in one of the three ninja arts: Jao Chun (Chiang Sheng) is expert at acrobatics; Tung Yen (Lu Feng) is a weapons and combat master; and Mao Tin-yung (Phillip Kwok) is an adept hand-to-hand fighter. Though kept strangers from each other, the three can all be found by a secret sign they've learned. Mao has become an alcoholic horseman, Jao Chun a thief, and Tung an irate blacksmith, but young master Chi eventually succeeds in rounding them up. Meanwhile, the assassins work their way into the general's household. The three students secretly take jobs on the staff as well, and wait for the assassins to make their move.

Director Phillip Kwok pulls together a cast of his fellow Taiwanese Opera brothers from the

THE HOUND SALUTES
NINJA NINJA NINJA!

忍者

Say the word "ninja" to most Americans, and their automatic word association will be "turtles," which only serves to illustrate how distorted our perception of them has become, about as close to real ninjas as the movie James Bond is to a real government spy. The techniques and practices associated with ninjitsu are by definition cloaked in secrecy, but some of their secrets have come out over the years.

Their skills originated with Chinese "mosha" magician assassins, who specialized in illusions that confused their enemies. The Chinese equivalent of the word ninja, "yan cheh," translates as "man of endurance," while in Japan it means "stealer in"—a clear indication of their status. The historic ninja clans were not heroes—in fact, everyone hated them. It wasn't only for secrecy that a true ninja would never admit to being one to anyone outside their own clan. Ninjas even hated themselves. In a society ruled by the samurai code of conduct and honor, no one had any respect for someone whose job it was to sneak into a person's house to spy on them, slit a throat, steal, or poison the food. However, this distaste never stopped anyone from hiring ninjas to do their dirty work—they just never admitted it.

Despite their lower-than-low status, ninjas were likely the most advanced agents in the world. Masters of various martial arts, acrobatics, strange weaponry, explosives, camouflage, and tactics, these shadow warriors were the perfect assassins, able to infiltrate enemy headquarters, kill someone, and usually escape undetected. To many, a ninja's abilities were perceived as magic, and the ninjas did nothing to dissuade their publicity. Since they were usually only seen departing, they became known for their escape illusions. A ninja would use a tunnel to enter a camp, and if seen, throw a smoke bomb and dive into the concealed tunnel entrance. To pursuers, it appeared the ninja disappeared in a puff of smoke. Using the tunnels made it seem like they could burrow through the ground like gophers. Ninjas would regularly place a light bridge just below the water line of a stream on their escape route. To the confounded enemy, it appeared as if the ninjas could walk on water.

The ninja's trademark throwing star—a shuriken—is often seen impaling a forehead with the flick of a wrist in the movies, but were not often used as weapons in real life. They were used more to discourage pursuit. By the time an enemy dodged away from the spinning, flying metal object ("Whoa!"), the ninja would be gone. The distinctive design of the shuriken acted as a calling card for the ninja clan. The stereotypical ninja "uniform"—all black, with face mask—is another misinterpretation, as a ninja would wear whatever was best suited to carrying out his business in secrecy.

All of the techniques noted by observers were exaggerated into the legendary superheroes we see today. But Japanese movies played ninjas straight for decades. In 1957, director Hiroshi Inagaki followed his epic *Samurai* trilogy with a pair of *Ninjitsu* features, again starring Toshiro Mifune. Actor Raizo Ichikawa became famous playing famed ninja Goemon Ishikawa in *Shinobi no Mono* (AKA *Ninja, Band of Assassins*) in 1962, which was followed by seven sequels.

Outside Japan, ninjas appeared only in "Yellow Peril" thrillers until Ian Fleming learned of them while researching *You Only Live Twice,* and they appeared in the novel and film, giving the world an intriguing look at ninja. During the 1970s, Eric Von Lustbader's novel *The Ninja* was planned as a big-budget Hollywood movie. But before the cameras could roll, the producers were scared off by the Menahem Golan and Yoram Globus–produced quickie *Enter the Ninja* starring Franco Nero. This goofy action film became a hit, dashing any considerations for a serious treatment of the subject, but creating a tidal wave of interest in fictional ninjas. Nero's co-star Sho Kosugi set up a cottage industry for a time making low-budget modern-day ninja movies, which was in turn mined by others and spread throughout all media. While the Japanese treatment of ninjas in movies has always seemed to give them a degree of respect, even in the most outrageous circumstances, filmmakers in Hong Kong and Taiwan feel no such restraint. There, ninjas can be found doing just about anything. In Chang Cheh's *Five Element Ninja* (AKA *Chinese Super Ninjas*) for example, ninjas are seen disguising themselves as trees and soaring through the air. Actor Alexander Lou specialized in performing in ninja pictures. Taiwanese actor/director Robert Tai made a series of films mixing ninjas and Shaolin monks, the pinnacle of which is an eight-hour extravaganza *Ninja the Final Duel,* which was until recently only available cut down to a more manageable length. Tai pulls out all the stops, mixing in all manner of bizarre elements to keep his audience entertained (if not enlightened). Dozens of old martial arts films were dusted off for video re-release, all with new titles containing the word "ninja," whether relevant or not.

Continued on next page...

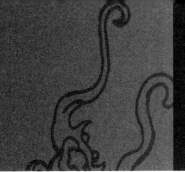

After the glut of the 1980s, the flood of bad ninja movies and TV shows has taken its toll on the pop culture psyche of society, and outside of some superior anime productions, ninjas are rare. That's a shame, because whether the treatment is serious or silly, the word "ninja" ought to mean "excitement" for everybody.

> *"There's a girl's head wrapped in a bundle on the front doorstep. It looks like the girl you used to hang out with."*
>
> —The dating habits of Japanese Buddhist monks revealed in *Ninja the Final Duel*

Shaw Brothers *Five Deadly Venoms* movies for this lively adventure. It takes far too long for him to gather his three ninja-teers, wasting time with meaningless intrigues, but things really start hopping in the third act. The ninja techniques and weaponry are reasonably historically accurate, though some cinematic license is taken—such as when the ninja tunnel underground like the monsters in *Tremors*. Meanwhile, back in Hong Kong, regular *Venoms* director Cheng Cheh was making the similar *Chinese Super Ninja* (AKA *Five Elements Ninja*) with the other two Venoms. **AKA:** *Yan Sut; Sui Si San Chuen; Shu Shi Shen Chuan; Heroes Defeat Japs; Hero Defeating Japs; Ninja Kung Fu; Ninjutsu; Ruthless Tactics.* 🎵🎵🎵

1983 92m/C *TW* Ti Lung, Phillip Kwok, Chiang Sheng, Lu Feng, Yasuaki Kurata, Chung Chuen Yung, Yue Chun Sin, Fuk Tin Chin, Fuk Tin Mu, Cheung Pang, July Chu. **D:** Phillip Kwok. **W:** Sum Sai-shing. **C:** Yu Kam-chun. **DVD**

Ninja in the U.S.A.

Ninjas leaping about a modern office building, fighting, diving, and providing some hyperactive nonsense for a credit sequence, but not related to the movie at hand—at least you know there are ninjas in the movie. But in the U.S.? Ninjas attack, overcoming a legion of armed guards and killing the men they're protecting. The next day, evil drug kingpin Tyger McFerson (George Nicholas Albergo) is acquitted of murder charges because all witnesses against him are dead. McFerson celebrates at his ninja training camp with his right-hand man Luthor (Eugene Thomas, a black man dubbed by a white man in jive dialect), showing off his ninja army to his criminal cronies.

Lieutenant Rodney Kuen, a narc from New York, stomps into police headquarters and demands the McFerson file. We find out via a flashback that during the Vietnam war, Green Beret McFerson saved the lives of young Kuen and Jerry Wong. Jerry's new wife Penelope (Rosaline Li) is a reporter trying to get a lead on the McFerson case. A spy inside McFerson's gang flees to the Wong wedding and slips bride Penny

a roll of film that shows the ninja camp, causing conflict between the newlyweds. Jerry (Alexander Lou) tries to suppress the evidence out of loyalty to the man who saved his life, but when Luthor and his thugs kidnap Penny and kill her brother, he and Rodney both go into sped-up (and occasionally slo-mo) kung fu action. The gang's threats continue, and Jerry suits up with all his ninja gear and storms McFerson's compound.

Despite the video release title, there's no reason to believe any of this takes place anywhere in the United States. Some scenes may have been shot as close as the Philippines, but outside of one or two unreadable signs that may be in English, nothing on screen looks even vaguely American. The villain's ninja training camp looks like some kind of resort or nature preserve, and features a nifty pyramid-like building. The dubbing is absolutely horrendous. Enjoy! **AKA:** *USA Ninja.* 🎵🎵♪

1988 93m/C *TW* Alexander Lou, George Nicholas Albergo, Eugene Thomas, Alex Yip, Rosaline Li, Robinson Yang, Mark Yu. **D:** Dennis Wu. **W:** Edmund Jones. **C:** Owen Casey. **M:** Sherman Chow. **VHS, DVD**

Ninja Scroll

A superbly crafted action film from the director of *Lensman* and *Wicked City*, it's easy to see why *Ninja Scroll* is a crossover favorite among martial arts, swordplay, and anime fans alike. Jubei Kibagami is a highly skilled ronin warrior who hires out his sword to whomever has the right price, or a just cause. In his travels, he gets mixed up with Koga ninjas sent by the chamberlain to investigate the possibility that a plague epidemic was spread intentionally. They find that a gang of supervillains is operating near there—the Eight Devils of Kimon—each with their own special weapons and abilities. For example, Tessei wields a whirling double sword and can cover his powerful body in stony armor. Benisato bears living snake tattoos, and can shed her own skin. Yuri-

maru can generate electricity and send it down wires in deadly arcs. And their leader Lord Himura Gemma is a man whom Jubei thought he killed once, but who somehow miraculously survived. Refusing to be left behind, royal food-taster Kagero joins them, and is the lone survivor of their initial attack, and she only survives because of Jubei's help. She has a secret weapon of her own: years of tasting poisons have caused her own body to be poison to anyone who touches her. An old ninja spy named Dakuan hires Jubei to help him in the fight against the Devils, who are working for the Shogun of the Dark in an attempt to overthrow the Tokugawa government.

Though still a bit limited by Hollywood standards, the animation and character design is wonderful, looking like a moving comic-book. The artwork illustrates a solid story full of good twists and interesting character arcs, and as for the action—the creators here have imagined a martial arts fantasy film unrestrained by the abilities of stuntmen, and the special-effects department has an unlimited budget. Death is bloody and spectacularly violent in this film; people die often and in interesting ways. Even the music by Kaoru Wada is a long step above the usual anime score. Followed by *Ninja Resurrection*. **AKA:** *Jubei Ninpocho; Jubei Ninpocho: The Wind Ninja Chronicles; Wicked City 3.*

1993 91m/C *JP* **D:** Yoshiaki Kawajiri. **W:** Yoshiaki Kawajiri. **C:** Hitoshi Yamaguchi. **M:** Kaoru Wada. **VHS, DVD**

Ninja Supremo

Yet another kung fu flick retitled by Ocean Shores Video in the late 1980s to cash in on the then-current ninja craze. There's not a ninja in sight here, but a pretty good martial arts adventure nonetheless. Young Master Lung Chan-fung (Cliff Lok) just wants the best martial arts teacher, but he keeps getting into trouble over it. Potential teachers fight it out until it's clear Spear Champion is the best. His training is good enough that Chan-fung beats three toughs in a brothel brawl. The thugs recruit Master Ti Lo-han to help attack the Lung house and teach the youngster a lesson. Fortunately, old Mr. Lung sent for his cousin Master Fu Ta-yuen, who arrives just in time to drive out the rascals.

Chan-fung decides to hide out for a while in a mountain cottage. While chasing a chimpanzee that stole his fish (!), he runs (literally) into feisty girl Sho-lan and her ill grandfather, Shou Chun. Finding his old friend Shou staying with Chan-fung, Master Fu coerces the old man to take the young man as a student. Shou's training techniques include a yo-yo, dancing on wash tubs, Chinese jump rope, and various

physical and mental tortures. When Master Shou's old enemy the Hunchback (Goo Chang) comes to Dragon Town, he teams up with Chan-fung's enemies and takes over the Lung house, holding the Lungs hostage to draw Shou and Chan-fung into a trap. Shou teaches Chan-fung his new secret techniques so that they'll stand a chance fighting the bad guys.

The mark of a good kung fu movie is not merely in good fight choreography, but also involves character growth and the use of tactics to solve problems. The excellent training sequences shown here involve some creative thought. Old Shou spent years developing new techniques to fight his enemies when they caught up with him, and his training methods reflect this. He has his student learn ground fighting under a suspended bed of bamboo spikes to counter the Hunchback's slouched posture for example. As if fighting a hunchback wasn't enough, Choi Wang plays a villain who is stooped and shaking with palsy—and uses it as an advantage! With his slightly humorous, expressive face and agility at kung fu, Cliff Lok makes the perfect young hero—though for some reason he was mostly cast as a villain. Director Lee Chiu appears in the prologue as the young Master Shou. **AKA:** *Dai Chaan Kuen; Da Can Quan; Crippled Kung Fu Boxer.*

1981 87m/C *HK* Cliff Lok, Yueh Hua, Goo Chang, Choi Wang, David Tao, Sun Yueh, Ma Chin-ku, Hsu Feng, Sham Chin-bo, Yuen Bun, Chu Siu-wa, Ko Saio Pao, Lee Chiu. **D:** Lee Chiu. **W:** Lam Lam. **C:** Lai Man-sing. **VHS, DVD**

Ninja the Final Duel

After several attempts by ninja clans to expand into China by conquering Shaolin Temple fail, the Japanese emperor honors the Shaolin monks for their martial arts skills in an effort to bring peace. However, this has the opposite effect, angering Shan Ren (Robert Tai), leader of the Yee Ho ninja, and making him more determined to destroy Shaolin. Fearing this reaction, the abbot closes the temple to the public, hoping they can concentrate more on peaceful spirituality than on fighting. The ninjas undergo rigorous training representing the "seven elements" (or "elemets," according to the onscreen titles)— breaking bricks and ice blocks, splashing around the lake on big floating toy spiders, dressing up like tigers to climb trees, and tunneling underground. Meanwhile, the Japanese Buddhist monks prepare their champion Wan Chi-chou (Alexander Lou) to challenge Shaolin by testing him with their deadly Swastika Traps. But on arriving, Wan and his sidekick Shou-tin (James Lee) find Shaolin closed, with only Californian surf monks Mark and Moore sitting outside. Of course they get in a fight. Their conflict is interrupted by Han-yi (Alice Tseng), who is under attack by bandits. Since they're camped outside, Wan and his friends are the first ones to be attacked by the ninjas—and because they're Japanese, they're the first to be suspected when the ninjas begin making raids on Shaolin. Wan agrees to stay in Shaolin to help defend the temple and clear his name.

Another entry in the low-budget ninja category, this one has all the frantic fighting, poor plotting and dialogue, and high quantity of nonsense one expects. But Buddha bless him—Robert Tai seems to be in on the joke, always packing his films with colorful characters and plenty of action, and understands that at a certain point adding more insane crap to a movie only makes it better. Brewing his stew of Shaolin monks and ninjas that growl like cheetahs, he feels free to include gory decapitation, a fighting monk from California (Silvio Azzolini), a jive-talking black monk from Harlem (Eugene Trammel, referred to as a "Shaolin ghetto freak"), and Dracula-style hypnotic mind control. He also gives his fight scenes great flow and a bit of visual poetry. And then there's Alice Tseng's totally uninhibited nude fight scene against a gang of ninjas, which manages to be both very sexy and one of the best fights in the picture! This was one of the films redubbed by Rudy Ray Moore and his friends for release as *Shaolin Dolemite* from the Xenon Video label, but that hardly seems necessary considering how hilarious the original dubbing job is. Some scenes appear to have been cut from the English version; hardly surprising, considering the film's origins. *Ninja the Final Duel* is actually the feature version of an 11-hour TV miniseries made by Robert Tai, which has been condensed into three features recently unearthed by Crash Cinema and released as *Venom of the Ninja*. **AKA:** *Ninja and the Final Duel; Shaolin Dolemite*. ♫♫♫

1985 89m/C *HK/TW* Alexander Lou, Alice Tseng, James Lee, Robert Tai, William Yen, Eugene Trammel, Silvio Azzolini, Ahmed Najja. **D:** Robert Tai. **VHS, DVD**

Ninja vs. Bruce Lee

Bet you didn't know Bruce Lee made a ninja movie, did you? No wait—how did that extra "e" get in the title? This low-budget Korean rip-off actually features "Super Star" Bruce *Le* in the lead. It begins with a group of men carrying a large box through a graveyard. (No, they're not literally robbing Bruce Lee's grave.) They're delivering a stolen vase to a Mr. Lin, nicknamed "The Cat," who works for Japanese smuggler Matsu-

da. Hooded Matsuda (Kong Do) and his thugs "forgot" to bring the money to pay for the vase, so everybody starts fighting. Seoul Special Squad cop Captain Ma is working undercover as one of the thieves, and barely escapes to identify Lin. Hong Kong cop Bruce Wong (Le) is on the case searching for a stolen flask, and he easily follows a trail of talkative informants to get to the gang, donning a cheap beard to disguise himself as an antique collector. When it leads to the cops' sting operation, Bruce fights off Ma and Inspector Jenny Ling and escapes.

Knowing the cops are closing in on Lin, Matsuda tries to eliminate him, but Jenny gets there in time to save him. Lin's evidence points to Matsuda dealing with slaver Dirty Mark in Manila. Bruce is headed for Manila, too, but when his friends—kung fu instructor Jim Lung and his sister Rose—go to meet him, they're chased into *another* cemetery by Mark's gang of bare-chested thugs (including one fellow who looks like Tor Johnson). Bruce arrives to save them, and Mark decides to send a ninja to kill Jim. While Bruce is out jogging (in a yellow and black suit, naturally), more sweaty thugs attack him as a distraction while the "ninja" (actually just a karate master) murders Jim. To rescue the abducted Rose, Bruce invades Mark's estate, defeating various fighters here and there (including guest star Lo Lieh) until he runs out of thugs and gets to Dirty Mark and his pal Chung. Back in Seoul, Bruce goes after Matsuda, but he and Jenny get captured. However, they break free in time to catch up to Matsuda before he can take the flask and his ugly jacket out of the country.

Though no actual ninjas or Bruce Lees appear in this sloppily constructed mess, it's at least good for plenty of laughs. Bruce Le stretches his acting abilities by using *both* of his expressions. There are at least a few good fight scenes that Le doesn't ruin with his lousy faux Lee moves. This was the last Bruce Lee rip-off from the team of Joseph Velasco and Bruce Le, which includes *Return of Fists of Fury, Return of Bruce, Enter the Game of Death,* and the immortal *My Name Called Bruce*. The soundtrack incorporates cues from *Halloween* and *Hawaii 5-0*. **AKA:** *Bruce Le vs. Ninja; Concord of Bruce*. ♫

1982 79m/C *KO/PH* Bruce Le, Lo Lieh, Kong Do, Ma Tien Long, James Nam, Cheung Lik, Mulo Tong, Dai Man Hong, Christina Cheung. **D:** Joseph Velasco. **W:** William C.F. Lo, Richard Dai. **C:** Ho Hapwai. **VHS, DVD**

Ninja vs. Ninja

Thompson is a righteous ninja with all the super ninja moves—kung fu, swordsmanship, disappearing in a puff of smoke, tunneling underground like Bugs Bunny—you name it. His old ninja buddy has the moves, too. But his buddy has gone over to the Dark Side of ninjitsu, using his abilities for an international criminal cartel. The buddy's boss is missing important audio tapes, and sends him to Hong Kong to question Fatso about it. He has Fatso hire hit man Ah Sing (Wilson Tong) to investigate. After some violent shots of gang war in a casino—and the mindless credits footage—Ah Sing accosts a gangster named Buffalo fleeing the casino robbery, and asks him about the tapes.

Choi (Norman Tsui) is a CIA agent investigating the Ninja Syndicate. Choi has his subordinate Chung go undercover to try to infiltrate the gang. The boss recognizes Chung while looking at some video (which is just as poorly edited as this movie), and Ah Sing is sent to kill him. Ninjas go after the tapes at somebody's house, but Thompson kills them. While Choi and his family are in a mall shopping for fresh Rubik's Cubes, the ninjas plant a bomb that puts his wife and son in the hospital. Fatso's son/explosives expert Sammy Tong is a real psycho. He blows up an actor after seeing him slap an actress he idolizes on a TV show. Ah Sing is sent to kill Choi at the hospital, and we finally get a decent fight scene.

During the mid-1980s, ninjas became big business, especially in the video rental market. After dissolving their partnership, both Tomas Tang and Joseph Lai began churning out these patchwork ninja monstrosities for the Western market, pulling together footage from all kinds of Asian exploitation pictures that they owned (or stole), and editing it together with scenes shot with Anglo actors and guys in ninja costumes running around. The whole mess would be redubbed and sold as a new movie. Here, scenes of Norman Tsui in an unidentified film (*The Bomb-Shell?*) are cut together with a lot of other mismatched footage (some is even repeated, or squeezed horizontally) and new footage shot in the Philippines. The soundtrack is a mess, too. Some muddy audio is kept from the source footage, but all of it has awkwardly dubbed sound laid over it. Fascinating as a pop-culture artifact, but those looking for a movie about real ninjas, or fake ninjas, or any kind of a real movie, will be doomed to disappointment. 🗡

1987 77m/C *PH/HK* Norman Tsui, Callan Leung, Pedro Alberto, Wilson Tong, Michael Chan, Damian Lau, Kwan Chung, Chan Hung Kai, Kwong Wai, McCally. *D:* Godfrey Ho. *C:* Ho Hard Sing. **VHS, DVD**

Ninja vs. Shaolin Guards

The opening shows Shaolin monk Kung Ching training his secret death squad of ninjas, just to let you know there really are ninjas in the movie, since you won't be seeing them again for 70 minutes or so. The monks in this picture act more like frat brothers than holy men—mischievous Fourth Brother (Robert Tai) is always playing tricks on his fellow students, and fighting with Second Brother (Alan Chui), forcing Third Brother (Eagle Han Ying) to knock their heads together. Big Brother (Alexander Lou) refuses to cut his hair, so cannot become a monk.

The emperor's private secretary Yu Kon Kong delivers an edict to Shaolin Temple: Emperor Yuen Shi-kai declares that the abbot is guilty of conspiring with rebels, and must hand over the temple to his deputy Kung Ching. Yu tells them that if they hand over the Golden Sutra of Da Mor, he'll ask the emperor to lift the sentence. The resisting abbot is defeated by a New Republic trick—an attacking woman exposes her tattooed breasts, while Kung Ching strikes from behind! The abbot entrusts the Golden Sutra to the four brothers—Yu He, Yu Yi, Yu Kong, and Yu Hung—and sends them to hide out in Tibet. Kung Ching accuses the quartet of robbery and murder, putting a price on their heads. They hide out with Fourth Brother's old girlfriend Mei, hoping her father will take them into Tibet. But when they get to the farm, they find Mei's family dead, and the emperor's agents lying in ambush. Escaping, the five fugitives have more than the government thugs after them—there's also a ruthless bounty hunter on their trail.

Robert Tai may not be much of a comedian, but his fight choreography is excellent, and there's some awesome fight scenes here, especially those set in the snowy mountain forests. You can see the monks' hair growing on the way up the Kunlun Mountains (played by some anonymous mountains in Taiwan), but they're shaved again on the way down. As usual, the fanciful ninja hijinks are highly entertaining. *AKA: Miu Kooi; Wu Kuai; Guards of Shaolin.* 🗡🗡🗡

1984 86m/C *TW* Alexander Lou, Robert Tai, Alan Chui, Kim Fun, Wong Fei-lung, Eagle Han Ying, Chin Fei, Cheung Goon Lung, Lee Shuk. *D:* William Cheung Kei. *W:* George Ma. *C:* Yukio Miyaki. **VHS, DVD**

No More Love, No More Death

Prince (Jacky Cheung), with his deadly assistant Ching Ching (Carina Lau), is the most efficient and high-tech assassin in Hong Kong. Outfitted with a gadget-loaded motorcycle (it has a fax!) and the latest in weaponry, the daring Prince has become a legend in crime circles. He gets his assignments from his wheelchair-bound father Tiger Pak, who was once a triad big shot but is now in a reclusive retirement since his

crippling accident. Salmon-tinted flashbacks show Prince's rough upbringing under the hard-hearted Tiger, his first kill, and how he was given Ching Ching as a birthday present(!). For his 27th birthday, Prince receives his fondest wish—the assignment to kill "Green Dragon," the man who killed his mother.

A new cop is assigned to catch Prince, the fifth such detective to take a crack at him. The cop's Godfather (Maichael Chan) tells him he's received a note from Tiger, whom he's thought dead for 20 years, requesting a meeting. It's the perfect opportunity for Prince, but distracted by a dancer he knows only from a photo he stole, Prince misses on his first shot. Dancer Tracy Chan (Rosamund Kwan) is the only witness to ever see Prince's face and live, and the police keep a close watch on her while she tries to remember his face. Actually, she remembers the dashing stranger quite well, and when Prince gets in touch with her, she doesn't hesitate to sneak off to begin an affair with him.

Seeing Prince's weakness, Tiger sends his mute assistant (Chin Ho) to kill Tracy, but Prince arrives to stop him. Inexplicably, the mute changes his mind and helps Prince take the injured Tracy away (killing many extras), rather than leave her to receive help from the cops. Ching Ching is jealous of Prince's dream girl. Told Tracy is dead, Prince heads out to kill Dragon, not knowing the awful secret guarded for 20 years.

There are some energetic, though a bit far-fetched, action sequences, but sentimentality bogs everything down in this routine hit man flick. The plot is loosely based on Tod Browning's *West of Zanzibar*. Some sources credit producer Taylor Wong as co-director, which may explain the footage from a whole cut action sequence running under the end credits. *AKA: Taai Ji Chuen Suet; Tai Zi Chuan Shui; Legend of Prince.* 🐉🐉

1992 90m/C *HK* Jacky Cheung, Rosamund Kwan, Carina Lau, Michael Chan, Chin Ho, Stephen Tung. **D:** Herman Yau. **W:** Chau Ting. **VHS**

Nobody

Three advertising men in a bar are having drinks after a colleague's wedding. There's some macho posturing, a tense confrontation with the trio of men at another table, and soon after Konishi (Hideo Nikano) is cornered and badly beaten by the strangers. Rather than report the assault to police, his friends Taki (Masaya Katoh) and Nanbu (Riki Takeuchi) are eager to get revenge, and the trio returns to the same bar after work the next night. Finding no leads, they decide to try to forget the incident. However, a week later Nanbu is still obsessed with the idea of revenge. By chance they come upon one of the strangers

in a tunnel and attack him. The guy can fight better than them, and when he takes the three-on-one beating stoically, it leaves them chilled instead of satisfied. They become even more unnerved when Taki receives a phone call from one of the strangers, claiming that the beaten man died, and that they would be visiting. Just who are these strangers? How did they learn who they are? And what will they do next? When Konishi is stabbed by one of the strangers, and Taki catches a private detective following him (who claims to have been hired by a third party), it becomes obvious that the boys have stepped into something completely beyond the control of ordinary men.

This suspenseful feature should prove to be a favorite with paranoids everywhere, as it plays with the notion of anonymous, omniscient, and unreasonable forces ready to destroy each of us if we make a misstep. Though towards the end it slips into more typical (but well-done) action formula, it's a genuinely unsettling film, with good performances from a cast of yakuza movie veterans, and solid direction that keeps you guessing throughout. 🐉🐉🐉🐉

1999 100m/C *JP* Masaya Kato, Riki Takeuchi, Hiromi Nakajima, Hideo Nakano, Kenichi Endo, Yumi Nishiyama, Jimpachi Nezu. **D:** Shundo Ohkawa, Toshimichi Ohkawa. **W:** Shundo Ohkawa. **C:** Hiroshi Ogata. **VHS, DVD**

Notorious Concubines

Woman equals Devil in this classy adult feature from critically acclaimed director Koji Wakamatsu, based on the Chinese novel *The Golden Lotus*. Chin Lien (Tomoko Mayama) is married to humble rice merchant Wu Ta (Hatsuo Yamatani), but has her eye on her wealthy brother-in-law Wu Sung (Shikyoku Takashima), officer in the Brothers of Shangtung. Honorable Captain Wu Sung resists her seductive advances, though she doesn't make it easy. Rebuffed, Chin Lien sets her sights on a more willing target: the wealthy and lecherous Hsi Men-ching (future *Tampopo* director Juzo Itami). When her husband discovers her betrayal, she quickly poisons his tea to get him out of the way.

When Wu Sung returns from guarding a shipment of salt from the capitol from bandits, he's plenty mad about the whole situation. He gives Hsi a thrashing, and is punished with torture and imprisonment. Hsi makes Chin Lien his fifth wife, but he soon tires of her, moving on to number six (another stolen wife). Hsi pays her more attention when she bears him a son, but Chin Lien hasn't forgotten the man who spurned her, and makes an unholy bargain with her husband for Wu Sung's head. However, the bandit revolutionary Lu Ching raids the prison to free Wu Sung—the two warriors have crossed swords before, and Lu believes the former officer will make a fine ally against the government. Hsi has become a very wealthy warlord, but with Wu Sung on their side, the rebel army concentrates their efforts on bringing down his enemy. Wu Sung has only one goal in mind: getting revenge on Chin Lien, and the countryside erupts in open warfare over the actions of one woman.

The costumes, sets, and big battle scenes are impressive, but Wakamatsu's main aim is to portray the decadence of the story, showing the bedroom politics behind historical epics. He succeeds on this point, but the movie collapses under the weight of too many burdensome and confusing flashbacks. Try this for imagery: the bandits bury all their dead with one hand sticking up out of the grave. *AKA: Kinpeibei; Chin Pei Ming; The Concubines.* 🐉🐉

1969 (R) 79m/C *JP* Tomoko Mayama, Shikyoku Takashima, Juzo Itami, Hatsuo Yamatani. **D:** Koji Wakamatsu. **W:** Jiku Yamatoya. **C:** Hideo Ito. **M:** Masao Yagi. **VHS, DVD**

Nowhere to Hide

A murder is committed on the 40 steps to the sunny tune of the Bee-Gees' "Holiday." For the next 72 days, slouching detective Woo (Park Joong-hoon) leads his team of cops down a series of cul-de-sacs in pursuit of the killer (Ahn Sung-kee in a menacingly wordless performance). Woo brutally intimidates every small-town hood on the street in his investigation. Finally tracking down their prey, the cops find he is not an easy character to apprehend.

Combining violence, humor, and lyricism, Lee has created an obstinately convoluted film. Plotwise, it is frustratingly slow, yet every scene is energetic. It is all about movement, from its tracking shots across the rooms of the police station to the comic slow-motion breakdown that signals the end of a chase, but there is a sense of stasis from beginning to end. This could be because Woo is a person in a perpetual state of waiting. Although constantly occupied, he has the inner patience of a dominant predator, even when he flails about like a Keystone Kop. The script jumps from one failed apprehension to the next, with no explanation or exposition. It is difficult to follow because the connective material is simply not there. Director Lee Myung-se is more interested in cinema than in storytelling. With his allusions to Eisenstein *(Potemkin),* Godard *(Weekend),* and Bresson *(Four Nights of a Dreamer),* he makes a screaming announcement of his intention to subvert the genre. Putting the viewer inside the head of a homicide cop who follows his nose as the

seasons change, in a city that circles in on itself, Lee has succeeded in creating a world that exists only in the movies. —*BW* *AKA: Injeong Sajeong Bolgeot Eobda.* 🐉🐉🐉🐉

1999 110m/C *KO* Park Joong-hoon, Ahn Sung-kee, Jang Dong-kun, Choi Ji-woo, Park Sang-myun. **D:** Lee Myung-se. **W:** Lee Myung-se. **C:** Jeong Kwang-seok, Dong Haeng-ki. **M:** Cho Sung-woo. **VHS, DVD**

Odd Couple

The Chinese title of this independent martial arts film translates as "Desperate Sabre vs. Fatal Spear," but the English title borrowed from Neil Simon lets you know that nothing so serious-sounding is going on here. Every year during the Ghost Festival, the King of Swords (Sammo Hung) and the King of Spears (Lau Kar-Wing) have a duel to determine whose martial arts are superior. And every year, the duel ends in a

Detective Park Joong-hoon can't seem to track down a killer, even though there's *Nowhere to Hide.*

draw. The old masters are so sure of themselves that they enjoy tricking any other challengers rather than just defeat them openly. With no winner decided for another year, they reason that if they weren't otherwise such good friends, one would be able to kill the other. A plan is created whereby each master will train a student in their skill, and at the end of 10 years, the two strangers will fight a duel to the death. King of Swords finds a promising student when he comes upon a watermelon salesman (Lau Kar-Wing!) defending himself from an extortionist (Lee Hoi-sang), although he finds he has to indulge in some dirty tricks to convince the young man to learn from him, including burning down his house. The King of Spears finds a much more willing student in burly young ferryman Ah-yao (Sammo Hung!). The two students both train hard for 10 years, but when the time comes for their duel to begin, they're both kidnapped by the wicked Hsiao Pa-tien (Leung Kar-yan), who bears scars from old encounters with the two Kings. After the Kings risk their lives to rescue their students, the two students unite to challenge Hsiao anew.

The cast is full of familiar faces in extreme comic makeup. Lau's spear-carrier is a buck-toothed oddity called Potato (Mars), while To Siu Ming serves as Hung's humpbacked second. And Dean Shek appears as a very silly and bizarre ruffian named Mr. Rocking, whose movements are accompanied by a drumbeat. At one point, Hung takes things to their logical extreme and fights against four "former opera performers," at which point the usual sound effects are replaced by a Chinese opera band. As one would expect knowing the talent involved, the fight choreography is dazzling. The only disappointment is that with both stars playing dual roles, there's no real payoff of all four performing in the same shot through cinematic trickery. Jackie Chan helps out Lau and Hung with the action direction. *AKA: Bok Ming Dan Dou Duet Ming Cheung; Bo Ming Dao Duo Ming Qiang; Eternal Conflict.* 🐉🐉🐉🐲

1979 96m/C *HK* Lau Kar-Wing, Sammo Hung, Leung Kar-yan, Mars, Karl Maka, Lee Hoi-sang, Dean Shek, Chan Lung, Chung Fat, Lam Ching-ying, To Siu Ming, Ho Pak Kwong, Huang Ha, Yuen Miu, Billy Chan. *D:* Lau Kar-Wing. *W:* Lai Wai-man, Raymond Wong. *C:* Ho Ming, Li Chi-keung. *M:* Frankie Chan. **VHS, DVD**

The Odd One Dies

And the odd one watches this film. Set aside all thoughts of traditional narrative or dialogue-driven tales. Director Patrick Yau was evidently determined to link together a series of images and was not too concerned about a cohesive plot. Such as it is, the story concerns a man (Takeshi Kaneshiro) and his ambition to become a full-fledged gangster. To achieve his goal, he cuts off another man's fingers and thus is given a job as a hit man. The job doesn't pay too well, but he believes his completion of the assignment will secure his position within the gang. That's his plan until he manages to win a large sum of money gambling. Suddenly losing his motivation, he seeks a way out of doing the hit. He hires an assassin from the Mainland (Carmen Lee). The two become involved, and his changed attitude begins to rub off on her; soon both are in danger of losing their lives.

Although *The Odd One Dies* plants itself squarely in the crime genre, the sly humor juxtaposed with sudden outbursts of violence laced with an attempt at an unconventional romance mark the film as somewhat ambitious and quite unpredictable. Sadly, it does not completely succeed. The main characters do not jell as a romantic duo, and Takeshi Kaneshiro is not able to bring any color to his rather dour role. Though clearly inspired and deeply indebted to directors such as Wong Kar-Wai and Jean-Luc Godard, Patrick Yau's direction does manage to keep a snappy pace. Raymond Wong's score sets the mood right at the beginning—jazzy, cheesy, and endearing, with electric piano and walking bass encouraging the viewer to conjure up a dark film noir mood, with just a touch of drunken cheer. —PM *AKA: Leung Goh Chi Lang Wood Yat Goh; Liang Ge Zhi Neng Huo Yi Ge.* 🐉🐉🐉🐲

1997 89m/C *HK* Takeshi Kaneshiro, Carmen Lee, Bin Yue, Ken Choi, Lam Suet. *D:* Patrick Yau. *W:* Wai Kar-Fai. *C:* Cheng Siu-keung. *M:* Raymond Wong. **DVD**

Okinawa Rendez-vous

Notable chiefly because it featured Faye Wong's first movie role in six years. Dat (Tony Leung Ka-Fai) is a lowly file clerk for the Hong Kong Police but dreams of becoming a big-time detective. He flies to Okinawa, Japan, for a vacation with his fiancée Sandy (Gigi Lai) and her friend Cookie (Stephanie Che). Shortly after arriving, Dat sees a man who looks familiar. Sure enough, it's Jimmy Tong (Leslie Cheung), a longtime thief. Dat deduces that Jimmy must be up to something, and takes it upon himself to investigate, much to Sandy's dismay. Jimmy traveled to the island to close a deal with a yakuza chief (Masaya Kato). That deal goes belly up because the crime boss's girlfriend Jenny (Faye Wong) stole the money and fled. She finds a place to live and takes a job at a tiny food counter, hoping to keep a low profile, only to find herself being romanced by Jimmy, who doesn't know

her true identity. Dat tries to set a trap for Jimmy. Events are touched off that will cause some of the characters to draw together romantically and others to break up their respective relationships.

Okinawa Rendez-vous could be categorized as a "holiday escape movie," a subgenre that should be light and frothy. It starts off as a colorful and enjoyable time-waster. Yet it quickly sags due to the shortcomings of the script (or lack thereof). Relationships between characters change on inexplicable whims, and the story never builds to a conclusion—it simply stops. In that sense it feels like summer itself—you might come to the end of summer and suddenly realize "If only I had planned better, I might have gotten more accomplished, or enjoyed myself more." So the enterprise is reduced to a minor diversion at best. The actors do the best they can with their underwritten roles. The photography by Cheng Siu-keung makes extensive use of natural light. Okinawa looks overcast and windy most of the time, though, which may not be everyone's idea of a summer resort destination. The fitfully entertaining musical score is composed of a wild mélange of disparate styles. —*PM* **AKA:** *Luen Chin Chung Sing; Lian Zhan Chong Sheng; Okinawa Rendezvous.*

2000 100m/C *HK* Leslie Cheung, Faye Wong, Tony Leung Ka-Fai, Gigi Lai, Vincent Kok, Stephanie Che, Higuchi Asuka, Masaya Kato. **D:** Gordon Chan. **W:** Gordon Chan, Chan Hing-ka. **C:** Cheng Siu-keung. **VHS, DVD**

On the Run

The Fugitive times two, wrapped in a thick blanket of film noir. Heung Min (Yuen Biao) is estranged from his wife, Lo Huan (Idy Chan). They are police officers working in different units, he with homicide and she with narcotics. Heung Min is none too pleased to learn that Lo Huan is having an affair with his supervisor, Lui (Charlie Chin), a man who already makes Heung Min's life miserable. The affair is short-lived, however, when Lo Huan discovers that Lui is involved with a mob of sadistic dope dealers. Lui does not hesitate to arrange her murder, and poor Lo Huan is ruthlessly dispatched by Chui (Pat Ha), a Thai assassin. Lui pins the rap on Heung Min and intends to cover his tracks by eliminating both the hired killer and the husband. The unlikely duo takes flight.

We are dragged into Hell on Earth with Heung Min. His life was not exactly a bed of roses *before* his wife's murder and the false accusations against him, but things get much, much worse. Yuen Biao's face reflects increasing desperation and a feral desire to survive. Though he is well known for his acrobatic martial

arts skills, here he relies on his dramatic abilities to convey the sense and mood of his character. In the final fight scene, only fists are flying—nobody is careening through the air. Alfred Cheung directed, overcoming numerous false steps in the sketchy script by drenching the proceedings in garish neon colors and a noir-ish sense of dread. Cinematographer Peter Ngor Chi-Kwan *(Mr. Vampire, Full Contact)* lovingly captured the shadowy nightmare world. Even with the smell of doom in the air, a few small moments of humanity creep in, reminding the fugitives of the precarious nature of life. The memorably violent story will leave fingerprints on your windpipe. Sammo Hung served as producer. A slightly longer version of the film includes an epilogue but is only available on a Japanese laserdisc. —*PM* **AKA:** *Miu Meng Tut Yeung; Wang Ming Yuan Yang; Fleeing Couple.*

1988 84m/C *HK* Yuen Biao, Pat Ha, Charlie Chin, Idy Chan, Lee Heung-kam, Lo Lieh, Yuen Wah, Phillip Ko, Bowie Lam, Alex To, Lam Lap-sam, Peter Ngor, Tom Poon, Chan Cheuk-yan. **D:** Alfred Cheung. **W:** Alfred Cheung, Wong Wang-gei. **C:** Peter Ngor. **M:** Violet Lam. **VHS, DVD**

Once a Thief

A refreshing vacation from *Bullet in the Head,* John Woo's follow-up is a lightweight heist adventure, and reunited him with his favorite leading man Chow Yun-fat. A team of master thieves— Joe (Chow Yun-fat), James (Leslie Cheung), and Cherie (Cherie Chung)—are all orphans, trained their entire lives by Chow (Kenneth Tsang) to be the very best at what they do. While Chow was a stern disciplinarian, local cop Officer Chu (Paul Chu) was always kind to them, and is still inclined to give them a break. After stealing a painting from a castle in Nice, another team of robbers shows up to fight them for it, and Joe is apparently killed in an explosion. Two years later, James and Cherie are married and planning to retire on their fortune, but are surprised to find that Joe is still alive, though a legless cripple. Chow pushes the seemingly helpless man aside, but Joe secretly helps James with his assignment to steal the same bad luck painting from its current owner. Chow plans to double-cross the young couple rather than let them retire, but the old team still has a few tricks up their sleeves.

Full of gorgeous imagery and music, this tribute to 1960s caper flicks is a delight. For a Hong Kong film, the violence is relatively restrained, but there's still plenty of acrobatic action. Much the same spirit informed certain sequences in Woo's *Mission: Impossible 2,* with capers centered around dances and car chases. A turn toward some silly comedy toward the end may puzzle Western audiences, but the

Jet Li leads his students in a workout on the beach in the breathtaking title sequence of *Once upon a Time in China.*

THE KOBAL COLLECTION / FILM WORKSHOP

Hong Kong Lunar New Year crowds went wild for it. Woo made a TV remake for the Fox network in Canada, with Michael Wong miscast as a villain, but the watered-down version didn't work, and only a few episodes of the resulting series aired. **AKA:** *Jung Waang Sei Hoi; Zong Heng Si Hai.* ♫♫♫♪

1991 108m/C *HK* Chow Yun-fat, Leslie Cheung, Cherie Chung, Kenneth Tsang, Paul Chu, Wu Fung, David Wu, John Woo. **D:** John Woo. **W:** John Woo, Clifton Ko, Janet Chun. **C:** William Yim, Fletcher Poon. **M:** Violet Lam. **VHS, DVD**

Once upon a Time in China

The classic 99-episode Wong Fei-hung series with Kwan Tak-hing presented the mature legendary hero of China, and in *Drunken Master,* Jackie Chan played a very immature younger version of the same character. This film from Tsui Hark revived the character at a point in between. Here, Master Wong (a role that revived the career of Jet Li as well) gets caught up in a conflict between the Chinese and intru-

sive foreigners from the West—a meeting of cultures much on the mind of Tsui, and all of Hong Kong, as reunification with mainland China approached. The opening scene establishes the theme of the film, taking place on a British fleet ship, as the British misunderstand the firecrackers during a lion dance greeting for gunfire. After the beautiful credit sequence featuring Li and a platoon of martial artists working out in unison on a beach, the conflicts continue with a musical clash between chanting missionaries and a Chinese band, a man who gets shot for mistakenly boarding the wrong ship, etc.—it's almost a tragedy of errors, the confusion of languages and customs leading to danger at every turn.

It is not a simple clash between "good" and "bad" cultures, either. Local triad groups are trying to extort money from poor merchants, the British Jesuit missionary helps the Chinese poor whenever he can, and con men sell their brothers into virtual slavery working the railroads overseas. At the middle of this chaos, Wong Fei-hung stands as peacemaker, attempting to find a way to settle things without violence. But confusing our hero even more is the arrival of a distant relative by marriage, Aunt Yee (Rosamund Kwan). "Aunt 13," as she's known (large Chinese families often used numbers as nicknames), was educated in America, dresses in Western style, and is mad for photography. Yet she and Wong, the ultimate in strong Chinese males, build up a great deal of tense attraction for each other, and their nervous romance is one of the most engaging in all of HK cinema. Buck Teeth So (Jacky Cheung) is an herbalist also educated in America, which leads to near tragedy when he is unable to read the Chinese writing on medicines. The chaos is such that the film gets lost in it for a time, indulging in digressions with prospective Wong disciple Leung Foon (Yuen Biao) and his adventures with a Chinese opera troupe, along with popular sidekick Porky Wing (Kent Cheng), who are thrown out of Wong's Po Chi Lam clinic/martial arts school for a time. At one point, there's a magnificent fight between Yam Sai-kwoon and Sunny Yuen that serves only to put a wrinkle in Yam's Iron Vest Yim character. Many details are introduced and go nowhere, but eventually Tsui (and his three scriptwriting partners) brings the webwork plot together as Wong, Wing, and Foon head for the docks to rescue Aunt 13 and the other unfortunates trapped aboard a slave ship about to sail for America.

All this depth of detail, and extra running time, is meant to lend this film an atmosphere above that of a common kung fu adventure to that of an epic. Tsui Hark uses all his skills as producer and director to create a larger-than-life world of the late-1800s South China coast. To live up to the proportions of the setting and characters, Tsui and his great choreographers and technicians create action scenes that take Jet Li's already amazing skills to a level that borders on swordplay fantasy, dancing among flying ladders, boxes, ropes, and furniture to defeat his opponents. It's some of the best action spectacle of Tsui or Li's careers. It became a gigantic hit, leading to several sequels and a television series. On DVD, the Tai Seng release contains a special booklet and features about the original Wong Fei-hung series. While the Columbia TriStar release lacks such features, it has a Ric Meyers commentary track on the full-length cut, plus the 100-minute English dubbed version (for those in a hurry). *AKA: Wong Fei-hung; Huang Fei-hong.* 🐕🐕🐕🐾

1991 (R) 134m/C *HK* Jet Li, Rosamund Kwan, Yuen Biao, Kent Cheng, Jacky Cheung, Yuen Kam-fai, Yam Sai-kwoon, Karel Wong, Jonathan James Isgar, Lau Shun, Jimmy Wang Yu, Wu Ma, Yuen Cheung-yan, Sunny Yuen, Mark King, Steve Tartalia. *D:* Tsui Hark. *W:* Tsui Hark, Yuen Kai-chi, Edward Leung, Elsa Tang. *C:* David Chung, Bill Wong, Arthur Wong, Ardy Lam, Chan Tung-chuen, Wilson Chan. *M:* James Wong. **VHS, DVD**

Once upon a Time in China 2

Tsui Hark's epic revival of the hero Wong Fei-hung was a smash success, quickly bringing into production this sequel, which surpasses the original by being much more focused and action oriented. September 1895: with the increased presence of Europeans and Americans in China, membership in the Klan-like White Lotus Cult swells along the coast. The Canton sect is led by a powerful martial artist called the Immortal Kung (Xiong Xinxin), who can focus his chi to protect his body from sword blades, and has vowed to use his divine fire to expel the "foreign devils." Wong Fei-hung (Jet Li), Aunt Yee (Rosamund Kwan), and Leung Foon (Max Mok, taking over from Yuen Biao) have taken the train to Canton for a medical convention, which not only allows for Wong and Foon to continue their struggles with Western ways, but allows Tsui to limit the number of repeat cast members. Yee's Western clothes make her a target for the fanatics, who try to abduct her. Wong gives them a thrashing, earning the cult's enmity. At the convention, none other than Dr. Sun Yat Sen (Cheung Tit Lam) translates Wong's lecture in acupuncture. Wong's old friend Mak (William Ho) lends Yee some Chinese clothes, but attacks by White Lotus on the convention and hotel continue, and the trio plans to leave the next morning.

While the Governor (Yam Sai-kwoon, who played Iron Vest Yin in the first film) deals with the riot, word comes that Dr. Sun's Agricultural Society may be planning an uprising. The cult stages a vicious massacre at the Foreign Language School, and Wong decides they should stay to help the surviving children get home. Wong goes to City Hall to ask Commander Lan (Donnie Yen) for help. Meanwhile, with the help of Dr. Sun's friend Luk (Shaw Brothers star David Chiang), Foon and Yee take the kids to a foreign consul. But White Lotus fighters sneak in and attack at night. Lan is more concerned with the rebels than the citizenry, so Wong decides to head to the temple to fight Immortal Kung himself.

The charming romance between Wong and Yee continues here, with Yee imagining his kung fu instruction as a waltz. Tsui's visual symbolism is much in evidence, rendered in beautifully lit images by Arthur Wong. It's not all pretty pictures, though—the lust of the wicked slavers has been replaced with the White Lotus's gruesome evil, and there are some pretty gory shots included. The intrigues and characters are kept to a minimum, leaving room for at least a solid half hour of action at the end. There's another impressive balancing act on tables and such, but in light of the way Jet Li can move, the amount of wirework

Wong Fei-hung
Kung Fu Hero Number One

黃飛鴻

Martial arts movie fans point to a period in the late 1960s and early 1970s as the big turning point in kung fu films, when the old fantasy swordplay films were usurped by a new breed of hard-hitting features films like *Five Fingers of Death* and *The Chinese Connection,* which had real men using real kung fu. In a way though, this period echoes that of post–WWII Hong Kong cinema—specifically the beginning of the longest film series in cinema history, all about China's greatest hero Master Wong Fei-hung.

The real Master Wong lived from 1847 to 1924 in Canton province. His father Wong Kei-ying was a famous Hung Kuen kung fu master, and a well-known physician and herbalist who healed the sick and taught kung fu in his Po Chi Lam clinic. He was also a member of the crime-fighting group known as the *Ten Tigers of Kwangtung.* Despite what is shown in the film *Iron Monkey,* the elder Wong did not encourage his son to study kung fu, perhaps believing he'd keep the boy out of danger. But Fei-hung learned anyway, studying with his father's sifu Luk Ah-choy. He grew up to be an even greater hero, respected for his courage and skill as a doctor as well as a terrific fighter.

In 1949, director Wu Pang read one of the many Wong novels (which were much like the pulp stories that exaggerated the exploits of American western heroes), and thought the hero would be the ideal subject for a film. With Chinese opera star Kwan Tak-hing cast in the lead, *The True Story of Wong Fei-hung* was the first known Chinese action film to eschew the fantastic derring-do of swordplay films in favor of real kung fu fighting. To audiences of the day, this injection of grit was very exciting and the film was a huge success.

Kwan Tak-hing was not surprised. He'd learned how powerful a good hero could be during the war, when his performances were so inspirational to Chinese troops that he became the target of Japanese assassins. He continued to play Wong in the original series for an astonishing total of 99 films, until 1970's *Wong Fei-hung: Bravely Crushing the Fire Formation.* At its peak, a new Wong movie was churned out every week to keep up with the demand, and for a time the only martial arts movies being made were in the Wong series. They could have continued the series, but as 99 is considered a very lucky number, the producers decided to quit while they were ahead. However, Kwan returned to the role in Sammo Hung's *The Skyhawk* (one of Wong's nicknames), *The Magnificent Butcher,* and *Dreadnaught*. Of course, the character would be played by others in later films—notably by Jackie Chan and Jet Li—but Kwan is almost synonymous with the character. Fans couldn't even think about Kwan Tak-hing without hearing the Wong Fei-hung music in their heads, even after his death in 1996. No photos or portraits exist of Master Wong, but his widow thought Kwan looked very much like her husband.

Only tantalizing clips from these classic films have been seen in the U.S., but hopefully sometime soon we'll all get a chance to experience vintage Wong Fei-hung.

involved feels like a cheat. Li's acting ability continues to impress as well, portraying emotions as precisely as he performs tai chi moves. Xiong Xinxin would return as the wild Clubfoot in succeeding entries. Jackie Chan can be heard singing the theme music. *AKA: Wong Fei-hung Ji yi Naam yi Dong Ji Keung; Huang Feihong Zhi er Nan er Dang Zi Qiang.* 🎵🎵🎵🎵

1992 (R) 113m/C *HK* Jet Li, Rosamund Kwan, Max Mok, Donnie Yen, Xiong Xinxin, Cheung Tit Lam, David Chiang, William Ho, Yam Sai-kwoon, Paul Fonoroff. *D:* Tsui Hark. *W:* Tsui Hark, Chan Tin-suen, Charcoal Cheung Tan. *C:* Arthur Wong. *M:* Richard Yuen, Johnny Njo. **VHS, DVD**

Once upon a Time in China 3

Fans of the distinctly Chinese spectacle that is the Lion Dance should not miss this one. The opening for *Once upon a Time in China* gave a hint of this activity, but here Tsui Hark presents what amounts to an orgy of brightly colored lion costumes doing battle for a head of lettuce. Empress Tzu Hsi is a big fan, and has announced a grand Lion Dance tournament to determine the King of the Lion Dance, just as Wong Fei-hung (Jet Li), Aunt Yee (Rosamund Kwan), and Leung Foon (Max Mok) arrive in Beijing. Yee bumps into her old college friend Tomansky (John Wakefield), interpreter for the Russian embassy, who clearly still has a thing for her. They've arrived to inspect their new pharmaceuticals factory, and to visit Fei-hung's father Wong Kei-ying (Lau Shun). The elder Wong heads a group making lion masks for the tournament, which naturally draws fire from some of the rougher teams entering the tourney, especially labor leader Chiu Tin Bai, who brings a wild rickshaw driver named Clubfoot (Xiong Xinxin) as an enforcer to bust up the place. With all the martial arts schools fighting before the tournament begins, Fei-hung can't help but get involved—ironically slapping them around to get them to stop fighting. However, the fighting gets out of hand, drawing Wong deeper into the turmoil. And when Aunt Yee's movie camera accidentally captures a murder which points to an assassination plot, the Lion Dance suddenly turns into a deadly competition.

The limitations of location shooting in Beijing seem to have thrown this entry off balance, as it lacks the lush look of the usual Tsui Hark production. The romance angle is a bit too cute this time around as well—Fei-hung is too shy to tell his father whom he intends to marry, which infuriates Yee just when there's a rival suitor around. Making up for this somewhat is the Lion Dance pageantry, and the terrific new character Clubfoot, who adds a great deal of pathos and would become Wong's rough and ready ally in subsequent episodes. *AKA: Wong Fei-hung Ji Saam si Wong Jaang Ba; Huang Feihong Zhi San shi Wang Zheng Ba; The Invincible Shaolin.* 🎵🎵🎵

1993 (R) 112m/C *HK* Jet Li, Rosamund Kwan, Max Mok, Lau Shun, Xiong Xinxin, John Wakefield. **D:** Tsui Hark. **W:** Tsui Hark, Charcoal Cheung Tan, Chan Tin-suen. **C:** Andrew Lau. **M:** William Woo, Tsui Hark. **VHS, DVD**

Once upon a Time in China 4

Wong Fei-hung (Vincent Zhao) won a lion dance competition, but declined to accept the medal—as depicted in *Once upon a Time in China 3*. Deputy Governer Guan Shing-tao arrives to award it, and also to invite Wong to participate in another competition, where the winner will be crowned the Lion King. Suspicions run high due to the politically charged atmosphere at a time when the Chinese people were struggling to maintain their identity in the face of foreign intervention. Wong makes the journey to Peking anyway; three of his closest associates, Leung Fu (Max Mok), Clubfoot (Xiong Xinxin), and Yan precede him, meeting up with Wong's Aunt May (Jean Wang, as Aunt Yee's *sister*), who works in a newspaper office. Soon after Wong's arrival, the all-female Red Lantern Sect, a virulently anti-foreigner group, attacks a German pharmacy. Wong, a doctor of Chinese medicine as well as a martial arts master, intervenes; he thwarts the attack, but is taken into custody by German soldiers along with Lady Miu San, the leader of the Red Lantern Sect fighters. The Germans plan to execute the duo, but Father Thomas (Louis Roth), a priest, recognizes that Wong is innocent and helps them escape. Wong and his men must use force to gain entry to the Lion King competition, but they arrive too late to stop the Germans from killing the Deputy Governor. It was a trap, after all. Wong issues a challenge for another lion dance competition so that true justice can be served.

The fourth entry in the *OUATIC* series lacks the fresh spark of the first two films and sorely misses the charisma and charm of Jet Li as Wong Fei Hong. Vincent Zhao has the moves but not the screen presence of his fellow Mainland Chinese martial artist. Action choreographer Yuen Bun, replacing Tsui Hark in the director's chair, does an adequate job with the non-action scenes. The story remains unresolved at the end of the film, requiring another sequel—released more than a year later—to try and tie things up. Even so, the production design is top-notch—for evidence, check out the scenes set in the Red Lantern Sect Temple. The wire-enhanced action sequences are a wonder to behold, though they tend to diminish Wong Fei-hung as a down-to-earth legend—he does more flying than fighting here. The pathos of Lady Miu San's character is captured eloquently as she comes to realize the dangers of xenophobia. Wong's three sidekicks generate laughs with

their buffoonery. Aficionados of lion dance competitions will have a field day. —*PM* **AKA:** *Wong Fei Hung Ji IV Sei Wong Che Ji Fung; Huang Feihong Zhi IV Wang Zhe Zhi Feng.* 🐉🐉🐉

1993 101m/C *HK* Vincent Zhao, Jean Wang, Max Mok, Xiong Xinxin, Billy Chow, Lau Shun, Chin Ka-Lok, Louis Roth. **D:** Yuen Bun. **W:** Tsui Hark, Elsa Tang. **C:** Arthur Wong, Ko Chiu-Lam. **M:** William Woo. **VHS, DVD**

Once upon a Time in China and America

Bringing the characters to the United States pumped new life into the Wong Fei-hung series—too bad it was stolen blood. While discussing ideas for possible collaborations with his Chinese opera school Biggest Brother Sammo Hung, Jackie Chan told him about two projects he envisioned. In one, Jackie would be a royal guardsman who visits the American West in the 1800s and fights with cowboys and Indians. In another, Jackie would lose his memory and become adopted by a primitive tribe. To have a film ready for Lunar New Year, they instead made *Mr. Nice Guy.* Chan was shocked to find out soon after that both ideas had been used in one movie—directed by his old buddy Sammo! Despite the squad of writers credited, it's easy to see where the original ideas came from.

Though pilfered, the ideas work pretty well, due in no small part to the return of Jet Li to the series, and the fantastic direction and fight choreography. Bucktooth So (Chan Kwok-Bong) left for America in an earlier entry. Now Wong Fei-hung, Aunt 13 (Rosamund Kwan), and Clubfoot (Xiong Xinxin)—now called "Seven"—make a visit to see the branch of Po Chi Lam Clinic his disciple has opened up there. On the way, a tribe of hostile Indians attacks their wagons, and the trio is swept down a river and separated. Fei-hung hits his head on a rock, losing the memory of his identity, if not his martial arts skills. He's taken in by a friendlier tribe, and before long is "going native" among them. But Aunt 13 finds him, and Seven re-creates one of Wong's greatest duels to spark his memory. Reunited with friends, Wong finds new trouble visiting the railroad workers So is providing care for: a racist mayor is framing the Chinese for a robbery his Mexican bandits committed, demanding either confessions or death from them.

Although a hit in HK, this never received the planned theatrical play in America as intended. The blame goes to the performances turned in by the non-Chinese players: the "Indians" are all played by Caucasians, and most of the others just can't act. Stuntman/actor Jeff Wolfe, who

plays Wong's cowboy pal Billy, is the only one who comes off well. Wolfe went on to appear in Tsui Hark's *Knock Off,* and on Sammo Hung's *Martial Law* TV show. Sammo made a formal apology to Jackie soon after the film's release, and Chan went ahead and made *Who Am I?* and *Shanghai Noon* anyway, achieving success with both. **AKA:** *Wong Fei-hung Chi Sai Wik Hung Shut; Huang Feihong Zhi Xi Yu Xiong Shi; Once upon a Time in China 6.* 𝄞𝄞𝄞

1997 99m/C *HK* Jet Li, Rosamund Kwan, Xiong Xinxin, Chan Kwok-Bong, Jeff Wolfe, Richard Ng, Patrick Lung, Chrysta Bell, Joseph Sayah, Roger Yuan, Danton Mew, Jean Wang. **D:** Sammo Hung. **W:** Sharon Hui, Sze Mei-yee, Roy Szeto, So Man-sing, Phillip Kwok. **C:** Walter Gregg, Raymond Lam. **M:** Lowell Lo. **VHS, DVD**

asians in usa

The One

This appears to be the very first martial arts film about parallel universes. The concept of other dimensions stretches far back in fantasy fiction (*The Wizard of Oz* is one such story), and it has played a part in science fiction since at least the 1890s. The concept of similar time lines became popular in science fiction of the 1950s. Sam Merwin, H. Beam Piper, and Poul Anderson all wrote stories about interdimensional police forces trying to restrict the abuse of travel between dimensions, and this feature swipes heavily from these sources.

In a universe slightly ahead of ours technologically (could it have something to do with the policies of President Gore?), convict Lawless (Jet Li) is on his way to his execution, when a superpowered sniper named Yulaw (Jet Li) saves the state a few dollars by killing him. Two men named Roedecker (Delroy Lindo) and Funsch (Jason Stratham) pursue the assassin, and seem to know quite a bit about him. These men are cops, who have been chasing Yulaw across dimensions for some time, and they use their devices to shift the felon's next dimensional jump to their home dimension. Gabriel Yulaw has killed versions of himself in 123 different dimensions, gaining the energy of each version of himself each time one dies. Now there's only one known version left, LAPD Officer Gabe Law

A chorus line of Jet Lis in multiple dimensions is eliminated by *The One* evil Jet Li.

(Jet Li), who has been understandably concerned about the fact that (due to residual energy he's received from Yulaw's murders) he has been getting stronger and faster lately. Yulaw escapes from his sentencing to the Hades dimension and attempts to kill Law as well, but Roedecker and Funsch arrive in time to intercede. Gabe goes for an MRI, making him vulnerable to another attack. In the confusion it becomes difficult to tell which is the "real" Law, even for his wife T.K. (Carla Gugino). Roedecker and Funsch split up—Law has gained too much power, which now makes him their target as well. No one is sure what will happen if there's only one left—the resulting power shift could make the survivor a god, kill him, or destroy the entire Multiverse. After Yulaw kills T.K., Law decides he wants to find out.

The superhero battles, choreographed by Corey Yuen and assisted by excellent special effects, are tremendously entertaining. However, when it gets down to the film's main event, it's the suprapowered Jet Li who makes it all work. Seeing him move, it doesn't take much of a stretch to imagine him punching through steel or tossing motorcycles around like cardboard. Yuen and Li wisely decided to have the two Lis use completely different fighting styles, based on their personalities. The twin f/x are produced using stunt doubles Jian Yong Guo, Feng Lin, and Kai Sen Huang for Mr. Li. Watch for Wisconsin filmmaker Mark Borchardt *(American Movie)* as a morgue attendant. ♫♫♫♫

2001 (PG-13) 87m/C *US* Jet Li, Delroy Lindo, Carla Gugino, Jason Stratham, James Morrison, Dylan Bruno, Richard Steinmetz, Harriet Sansom Harris. *D:* James Wong. *W:* Glen Morgan, James Wong. *C:* Robert McLachlan. *M:* Trevor Rabin. **VHS, DVD**

One Arm Hero

The hero of *White Lotus Cult* and *Sam the Iron Bridge* here finds himself the Supreme Master of the Martial Arts and young governor of the port of Canton, and starts things off at a celebratory dinner by establishing that—politics or no—his enemies Master Mu (Wong Kam-Kong) and the East India Company's Lord Henry are still his enemies so long as they attempt to get around the government ban on opium. He turns down Mu's offer of his daughter Keke (Fennie Yuen) in marriage and returns to Canton to marry his sweetheart Tieh (Yip Chuen Chan). His wedding night brings nothing but trouble, as Japanese pirates stage a massive raid on the waterfront. He puts in a request for guns from the capitol, and joins in the martial arts training of the soldiers (they all head down to the beach for a direct rip-off of *Once upon a Time in China*'s militia drills). Escorting the rifle delivery

is Mu and kung fu master Prince Hing (Chi Chuen-Hua), a "nasty guy" now betrothed to Keke. Mu's other mission is to retrieve all the silver recently exchanged for new paper notes, and he chisels on both deals. Sam finds cutting through the web of corruption in government to get the proper arms to protect everyone more difficult than fighting the pirates.

After taking silver from the government safe to buy more guns, he defeats the pirates, but finds himself framed by Hing and Mu, and he's taken to the capitol in chains. On the train, Sam is attacked by Hing's assassins bearing poisoned spears. Keke is nicked while helping in the fight, and when Sam uses his healing kung fu to absorb the poison, he has to slice off his own left arm to save himself (as you may have guessed from the title). Upon recovery, he becomes a one-armed avenger out to destroy the evil Hing.

With its emphasis on action and reprisal, along with the creation of a worthy arch villain in Hing, this is the best stand-alone episode in the trilogy. Phillip Kwok provides better action choreography, using even less wirework than last time, though the fight scenes seem to be over too quickly, and to Siu-chun isn't very good at hiding his left arm in the final act. The period costumes, sets, and locations are impressive throughout the series. The current versions of this trilogy available on home video were obviously subtitled by different people, so the names of characters and places vary from one film to the next. Thus, Sam Liang the Iron Bridge is called "San Leung Kuan" in the first film and "San the Man of Iron" in the third. **AKA:** *Chong Si Duen Bei; Zhuang Shi Duan Bei; One Armed Hero; Sam the Iron Bridge 2.* ♫♫♫

1994 90m/C *HK* To Siu-chun, Yip Chuen Chan, Fennie Yuen, Chi Chuen-Hua, Wong Kam-Kong, Lily Li, Yu Hai. *D:* Wai Hon-to. *W:* Mak Chi-shing, Debbie Cheng. *C:* Cheng Siu-keung, Lee Chi-wah, Leung Lek-chee. *M:* Wong Lai-ping. **VHS, DVD**

One Foot Crane

Yes, if they'd ordered a bigger crane they would've had a nicer establishing shot. But too late to worry about that now—a string of murders have been committed by four bandits—Foo Hu, Ti Pao, Sung Yin-chou (Choi Wang), and Chin Chan-yuen (Lo Lieh)—and the magistrate asks community leader Fong Tin-wei to help round them up. But Chin has been eavesdropping, and the gang massacres the whole family, with the exception of their little daughter Lin-yi, who is taking a pee.

Miss Fong (Lily Li) grows up to be martial arts hero One-Legged Crane, ready to defend the oppressed and track down the four outlaws.

The local magistrate accepts her offer of help, pretty much granting her a license to kill in her quest. Ku Lin-kang, deputy to Chin Hu in charge of his kung fu school, is the first to feel her sting. Ku's son Tau-pai vows vengeance, not knowing that his adopted father's killer is actually his blood sister. One-Legged Crane kills Chin next, but is wounded by Tau-pai. Luckily, the magistrate has sent dashing Captain Chow Lung-hang (Sze Ma Lung) to trail her in case she gets in trouble, and he helps her get to a farm house to recuperate. Once Tau-pai finds out his true background, he joins Chow and One-Legged Crane to hunt down the remaining criminals.

The female hero gives this standard fist opera an old-fashioned feel, enhanced by the mournful theme song. Lily Li is radiant in her pure white gown. Much sentiment is wasted on an annoying farm boy character who has a crush on Lin-yi. The available video version is from a poor quality master with Korean subtitles, with English dubbing that drops out during fight scenes and gives the bandits different names in each scene. 🗡♥

1979 83m/C *TW* Lily Li, Sze Ma Lung, Barry Chan, Lo Lieh, Choi Wang, Miu Tin, O Yau-man, Kong Ching-ha. *D:* Bob Yang. **VHS, DVD**

100 Ways to Murder Your Wife

The old comic plot about the mistaken murder contract is given another twist here. Roberto (Kenny Bee) and Wong "Football" Fa (Chow Yun-fat) are pro soccer stars on champion rival teams. Cocky Malaysian star player Fa is married to the lovely Hsiao-hsien (Joey Wong), but is very jealous and suspicious of her. Hong Kong star Roberto is married to lovely Anita (Anita Mui), who is always nagging him, and the couple bickers constantly. At a party thrown by Malaysian team owner Wang (Wong Jing), the two players bond over a case of Carlsburgs, and sometime during their drunken binge together, each man agrees to kill the other's wife (à la Hitchcock's *Strangers on a Train*). Before passing out, Fa has time to fail miserably in his murder attempt, spilling the beans about the plot to Anita to avoid her butcher knife. Anita runs away, and the two athletes come to believe she's been murdered, though Fa can't remember the details. In his grief, Roberto is determined to follow through with his part of the bargain, to both honor his friend and to get revenge on him. However, once sobered up he can't bring himself to go through with it, which jealous Fa takes as a sign that Roberto has joined the legions trying to woo his wife, and gives Roberto three days to prove his innocence with bloodshed. When Anita returns, Roberto takes her for a ghost, and Anita mis-

takes the attention he's giving Hsiao-hsien as an affair. The men continue to plot murder, with schemes ranging from a tank full of piranhas to icicle darts. When Roberto discovers that Anita is still alive, he has to rush to defuse their many death traps.

The story may be hackneyed and old fashioned, but the film manages to get by on the charm of its stars. Chow Yun-fat is a manic delight, tearing up green plants with every jealous rage, while Kenny Bee plays his role as adorably naïve. One pitiful murder attempt gives him a chance to sing Chinese opera. One can almost forget that both men are playing scoundrels. Though they're plotting murder all through the film, at no time are the situations believable. As if the borderline misogynistic plot wasn't enough, a scene set in a gay disco contains a full range of offenses. Be advised, gentlemen, that even a drunken plot to murder your wife has little chance of being forgiven. Joey Wong has a decidedly male Great Dane as a pet, but (in subtitles at least) the dog is considered female and named Nancy. *AKA: Saai Chai Yee Yan Cho; Sha Qi Er Ren Zu.* 🗡🗡

1986 92m/C *HK* Chow Yun-fat, Joey Wong, Kenny Bee, Anita Mui, Wong Jing, Anthony Chan, Wu Ma, Shing Fui-on. *D:* Kenny Bee. *W:* Alex Law. *C:* Jimmy Leung. *M:* Kenny Bee. **VHS, DVD**

Operation Billionaires

Based on a famous 1996 kidnapping case that resulted in criminal "Big Spender" Cheung Tze-keung making headlines and becoming Public Enemy Number 1, this true-crime feature was rushed into production immediately after his arrest, and opened the day his trial started. On his way to the office, executive Lee Gui is abducted by a gang led by smooth operator Cheung Chi-ho (Simon Yam). Cheung soon appears at the home of Gui's father, Lee En, the eighth richest man in the world, to deliver his ransom demands. The case is distinguished by the fact that the criminals aren't a triad gang and the amount of the ransom: $1 billion. While Lee En scrambles to get the cash together, the gang celebrates their victory, and soon after the ransom exchange is completed. Though Lee explained away his son's abandoned car to the police, suspicions still nag at Sgt. Uncle Nam, a garrulous cop whose career has been troubled ever since he failed to catch Cheung Chi-ho in a robbery case years before. Rumors in the business world make their way into the police, and Nam is assigned the case due to his familiarity with the suspect.

Meanwhile, Cheung meets up with a gangster named Cyclone, and they decide to become partners. They capture another billionaire's son, but though Cheung always plays straight and keeps his promises, he has to convince the ruthless Cyclone to play along. When they are sent to the mainland to pick up the cash, Cheung's man Slut Hung (Patrick Tam) can't keep away from Cyclone's nymphomaniac girlfriend Bonnie, and Cyclone has to punish him. Hung calls the cops on Cyclone's gang, who return the favor by gunning Hung down in the street. On returning to Hong Kong, Cyclone is shot by police and crippled. Cheung issues a polite warning to government official Chung On-sum (Law Kwun-lan) to be lenient with Cyclone, but the gears of justice have already begun to grind and law enforcement agents from both Hong Kong and the mainland make capturing Cheung their top priority.

Simon Yam plays Cheung as being cool and smart, but he's not smart enough to know that by continuing to victimize the rich and powerful—and associate with killers like Cyclone—will inevitably destroy him. Cheung's schemes make him rich, but that doesn't satisfy him. He's relatively harmless, but too greedy, and the film shows how powerful political influence can be, both in governments and small gangs. The anticlimactic finale is a bit drawn out and includes an unnecessary love scene, coming after all the real excitement is over. Yam carries the show in what is an otherwise restrained dramatization. A competing picture opened not long after—*Big Spender* starring Ray Lui. The real-life Cheung was executed in December 1998, two months after the film opened. *AKA: Geng Tin Daai Chaak Wong; Jing Tian Da Ze Wang.* 🎵🎵🎵

1998 86m/C *HK* Simon Yam, Sherming Yiu, Patrick Tam, William Cho, Ng Ting-yip, Parkman Wong, Lam Wai-kin, Law Kwun-lan, Lee Siu-Kei. *D:* Andy Ng. *W:* Lee Siu-Kei. *C:* Ko Chiu-lam. *M:* Lincoln Lo. **VHS, DVD**

Operation Condor

In this 1991 stand-alone sequel to 1987's *Armor of God*, Jackie Chan again plays globetrotting adventurer the Asian Hawk, procuring relics for a Hong Kong auction house. Lending his services to a United Nations operation, he's teamed with their pretty rep Ada (Carol "Do Do" Cheng) on a hunt for a fabulous horde of gold hidden by the Nazis in the Sahara desert at the close of World War II. On the way, they're joined by Elsa (Eva Cobo de Garcia), who wants to clear up her German officer grandfather's part in the story, and later by Momoko (Shoko Ikeda), a Japanese girl who has somehow ended up hitchhiking across the desert. Every step of the way they are beset by groups of rival treasure hunters, including an Arab stereotype trio and an old Nazi officer named Adolf (Aldo Sambrell).

Throughout his usual awesome parade of fabulous stunts, fights, and chases, Chan keeps up a constant flow of hilarious knockabout slapstick in keeping with his deserved reputation as the greatest practitioner of the art since the days of Chaplin and Keaton. Charmingly, none of his three beautiful companions know the first thing about martial arts, and most of the comedy comes from everyone's efforts to aid each other while getting in each other's way half the time. The action is capped off with a satisfying finale—a showstopping running battle in the huge underground Nazi base.

Dimension Films did a worse job cutting this Chan picture for U.S. release than usual. Some seemingly harmless trimming at the start and finish of some dialogue scenes to speed up the pace, plus some important scenes that develop the characters and relationships, are almost erased entirely. The heroes hardly even have names—Jackie is only called by the nickname "Condor" once or twice to weakly establish the film's title (although Chan is one of the few movie stars who have acknowledged their fame to the point of almost doing away with character names altogether—increasingly, his character is named "Jackie Chan"). Dimension has gone so far as to cut the action scenes as well, with the final fight scene shorn in half, and this is an unforgivable sin. Be that as it may, the U.S. versions of Jackie's movies, with their expertly struck prints and fine-tuned soundtracks, look and sound better than they do anywhere else in the world. Too bad you have to rely on an import to see some of them in their entirety. *AKA: Fei Ying Gai Waak; Fei YingJi Hua; Armour of God 2; Armour of God 2: Operation Condor; Operation Eagle; Project Eagle.* 🎵🎵🎵🎵

1991 (PG-13) 92/80m/C *HK* Jackie Chan, Carol Cheng, Eva Cobo de Garcia, Shoko Ikeda, Aldo Sambrell, Daniel Mintz, Ken Lo, Vincent Lyn, Steve Tartalia, Bozidar Smiljanic, Mark King, Jonathan Isgar. *D:* Frankie Chan, Jackie Chan. *W:* Jackie Chan, Edward Tang. *C:* Arthur Wong. *M:* Chris Babida, Stephen Endelman (U.S.), Paul Rabjohns (U.S.). **VHS, DVD**

Operation Pink Squad

Enjoyable romp from the late '80s school of action filmmaking. The Pink Squad is comprised of four strong, tough women (Sandra Ng, Ann Bridgewater, Suki Kwan, Elsie Chan). They do their police work efficiently and successfully. As a result, their chauvinistic male superiors in the police department are always dreaming up ideas to try and get them fired. Their latest scheme is to arrange for the Pink Squad to maintain surveillance on a blind musician (Pal

Sin) suspected of being an accomplice in a diamond robbery. The chief suspect in the case is a deadly female criminal. She and the musician were both injured in an automobile accident in the aftermath of the robbery. The musician was blinded and the woman was left in a coma. She has recently awakened and escaped from the hospital. Since the diamonds were never recovered, it's a sure bet that she'll be heading straight for the musician. The cowed male cops think that they can sabotage the Pink Squad during the surveillance and then be rid of them forever, but they don't count on one of the policewomen falling for the musician.

This is a real blast from the past by director Jeff Lau. It's only the fourth film he directed and it's uneven and filled with rough edges. Still, if you approach it with lowered expectations you may be pleasantly surprised by the winning combination of comedy and action—more comedy in the first half, more action in the second half. And some scenes are priceless—either riotously funny (Sandra Ng literally trapped in the musician's apartment) or dynamically energetic (a disguised Ann Bridgewater kicking the crap out of a bunch of policemen in a playground). —PM *AKA: Ba Wong Lui Fook Sing; Ba Wang Nu: Fu Xing.*

1988 85m/C *HK* Sandra Ng, Elsie Chan, Wu Fung, Ng Man-Tat, Ann Bridgewater, Suki Kwan, Ricky Hui, Helena Law, Pal Sin, Yuen Cheung-yan, Law Ching-ho, Billy Lau, Charlie Cho, Chan Fai-Hung, Lowell Lo, Jeff Falcon, Lam Chung, Lo Hung, Chan Chi-fai, James Yi Lui. *D:* Jeff Lau. *W:* Jeff Lau. *C:* Johnny Koo. *M:* Danny Chung. **VHS, DVD**

Option Zero

For the third entry in the Option series (after *Final Option* and *First Option*), first-time director Dante Lam opts for a peppier, more documentary style, using lots of handheld cameras for a more personal effect. Unfortunately, this decision backfires, with some dialogue scenes playing out like dull home movies, and Chin Ka-Lok's well-designed action sequences are rendered incoherent.

Ben Ai (Julian Cheung) is a member of a Security Branch team headed by Sing (Anthony Wong), but is distracted by his relationship with his girlfriend Kelly (former flight attendant Carmen Lee). Ben learns that Sing's neglected wife Grace (Farini Cheung) has been cheating on him, and his teammate Monica (Monica Chan) has a crush on him, adding to the film's soap-opera element. While tracking down a gang of Korean arms dealers, one of the team is shot dead by the leader Hon. Soon after, Ben and his teammates are selected to test for duty with G4, an elite government bodyguard section, and

undergo a strange training program that brings out some hidden emotions. Ben makes the G4 team, and is assigned to a case that brings him up against Hon once again.

Some sections are intermittently exciting or suspenseful, but it's not long before something more tedious takes center stage. Relegated to just a guest star role this time, Michael Wong gets to play one of his more interesting characters as a G4 trainer. Too bad he's so much more interesting than the leads, and is only in a few scenes. The filmmakers obviously want the change of duty to represent the change in government, but their point is left blurry in the background. Lam would bounce back decisively with the excellent *Beast Cops* and *Jiang Hu: The Triad Zone. AKA: G4: Dak Gung; G4: Te Gong; G4: Option Zero.*

1997 96m/C *HK* Julian Cheung, Carmen Lee, Monica Chan, Anthony Wong, Farini Cheung, Nancy Lan, Michael Wong, Andy Yim, Ching Fung. *D:* Dante Lam. *W:* Chan Hing-ka. *C:* Horace Wong. *M:* Shigeru Umebayashi. **DVD**

Organ

Numata (Kenji Nasa), a tough cop, and his partner Tosaka (Ryu Okubo), turn the tables on a gang of human organ thieves who have been preying on runaways and the homeless by posing as part of the gang. Inside their hideout, the cops meet a vicious one-eyed woman named Yoko (Kei Fujiwara), who supervises the operation for the masked Dr. Soeki (Kimihiko Hasegawa). During this confusing first act, the two cops are captured again, escape again, are captured again, escape again—much in the manner of a compacted adventure serial. Except this is a serial far, far bloodier than any Republic chapterplay ever dared to be. During one of the struggles (in which men are stabbed, acid is thrown, shots are fired, etc.) Numata is injected with something by the doctor. Tosaka manages to get away with his skin intact, but with something broken in his mind. Numata disappears without a trace, and is presumed dead by his superiors. Numata's twin brother (Kenji Nasa), also a cop, takes up the case, pursuing the organ gang while hoping to find his missing brother. Tosaka drifts in a haze, his life falling to pieces.

Soeki, in his cover identity working for a girls' school, has been abducting students for his experiments. Soeki has a gooey sore on his side as a result of one of his experiments, and Numata is attached to a plant—with his arms and legs cut off. Treating his pain and illness with drugs, Soeki has gory hallucinations—a human born from a chrysalis, bloody deaths. His sister Yoko warns him about the murders, fearing they'll draw attention. Soeki's disease is

consuming him, and almost his entire body is covered in oozing sores. Tosaka and Numata's twin separately clash with yakuza, but always get a little closer to finding the other Numata. There's a series of bloody and savage encounters, as organ harvesters, gangsters, and cops battle to—what else?—an ultraviolent climax.

Kei Fujiwara *(Tetsuo the Iron Man)* first produced *Organ* on stage for her Organ Vitale theater group. A long-running success, she rewrote the story into a screenplay, with which she made her directorial debut. Though the plot is hard to follow, *Organ* emerges as one of the better entries in the new wave of Japanese horror films. Nearly every frame has something unpleasant going on—there's so much gory violence that it's surprising when some occurs *off-screen!* The makeup effects have that gritty edge that made even Lucio Fulci's lesser horror films disturbing. Amid the horror, there's also beauty—some shots are so lovely that they become disturbing themselves. It's shocking to see beauty in a world of ugliness. With its cops-and-robbers elements, *Organ* is a bit like gore film noir, with each character sinking ever deeper into their own doom. The pace is relentless and dizzying. Even the soundtrack sounds infected—a wonderful mix of pulsing electronic music and hellish moans and growls, perfectly punctuating the visual nightmare. 🎵🎵🎶

1996 105m/C *JP* Kenji Nasa, Reona Hirota, Kei Fujiwara, Ryu Okubo, Tojima Shozo, Kenji Nasa, Kimihiko Hasegawa. *D:* Kei Fujiwara. *W:* Kei Fujiwara. *C:* Kei Fujiwara. *M:* Video Rodeo. **DVD**

Organized Crime and Triad Bureau

Owing much to the 1950s film noir crime films from the likes of Anthony Mann, Joseph Lewis, and Don Siegel, this is the prototypical Danny Lee production, an edgy police procedural with Lee as the dedicated chief of detectives. Chronicling a true-crime case from files of the title police division, it tells the story of the pursuit of desperate criminal Tung (Anthony Wong) and his gang across Hong Kong. Frustrated by the length of the chase, Inspector Lee and his team go to lengths that sometimes stray beyond the boundaries of the law in order to get the leads they need, engaging in blatant police brutality while grilling suspects. Sometimes they get caught by the Internal Affairs division, suffering serious setbacks. Another complication is that one of Lee's men is a traitor, blackmailing his girlfriend for information that he sells to Tung. The gang is traced to a small coastal island, where a grueling and dangerous chase takes place that causes the residents to turn on the OCTB officers, allowing Tung and his moll Cindy

(Cecilia Yip) to make a near escape. The pair are spotted again amid a Wanchai district traffic jam, resulting in an extended gun battle.

While Lee nears Jack Webb in resoluteness, and facts of the case are followed one by one, the material is much seamier than any *Dragnet* episode would allow, with the tactics taken by the Blue Knights sometimes blurring the line between them and those they pursue. Anthony Wong turns in another first-rate performance, garnering sympathy for his bad-guy character in between vicious criminal acts. Not as entertaining as some of director Kirk Wong's other cops-and-robbers films, it nevertheless has a mesmerizing power that keeps you glued to it. Wong would head for Hollywood a few years later to send up the whole gun fu genre in *The Big Hit.* This was the first feature released on tape and laserdisc by Tai Seng Video's U.S. office for the American mainstream market, opening the floodgates for the world of Hong Kong cinema. *AKA: Chung Ngon Sat Luk O Gei; Chong An Shi Lu O Ji.* 🎵🎵🎵

1994 91m/C *HK* Danny Lee, Anthony Wong, Cecilia Yip, Elizabeth Lee, Roy Cheung, Ricky Yi, Parkman Wong, Li Fai, Fan Siu-Wong, Eric Kei. *D:* Kirk Wong. *W:* Lu Bing. *C:* Joe Chan, Horace Wong. *M:* Wong Bong. **VHS, DVD**

The Owl vs. Bombo

Any Sammo Hung picture is worth watching, but this one from his busy 1980s period earns extra attention as the film debut of Michelle Yeoh *(Supercop).* 1981: the master criminal known as Bombo (Hung) loads up a machine gun with blanks and pulls one last bank robbery before retirement. Across town, another master criminal known as the Owl (George Lam) puts into play his last job, a complex plan to steal millions from the triads.

Mr. Chan (alias Bumbo, or Bombo—both spellings seem to be acceptable) enjoys his retirement leading dancercise classes at his own health club. Mr. Yan Fu Wong (the Owl) becomes just another man of leisure. That is, until frustrated police Inspector Fung (Stanley Fung) decides to play by vigilante rules, and blackmails both criminals into working for him. Fung has been trying to bring down the nefarious gangster Au Gun (James Tien), a land developer whom his superiors won't allow him to touch. But first the odd couple is given a test assignment to prove they can work together—and to repay a bit of their debt to society. Both men agree to volunteer as social workers. Yeoh plays a teacher at the youth center they're assigned to, trying to deal with tough inner-city kids. Of course, our two criminals spend more time trying

to find out who the anonymous blackmailer is than dealing with their jobs. Later, their assignment includes harassment of Au Gun, which lands them into the expected hot water.

The light situation comedy and the heavy social commentary are fine, but thank the lucky stars that Sammo gets around to some of the excellent fight choreography he's best known for. The script is credited to some sort of committee, and as could be expected, the result is a mix of styles. One scene has an impassioned young lady (Season Ma) making a speech that mentions how she's had to be a prostitute since she was 14, and minutes later, Sammo Hung is performing a tap-dance number. Consistent it ain't—but it is consistently entertaining. **AKA:** *Maau Tau Ying Yue Siu Fei Cheung; Mao Tou Ying Yu Xiao Fei Xiang; The Owl vs. Bumbo; The Owl and Dumbo.* ♪♪♪

1984 101m/C *HK* Sammo Hung, Michelle Yeoh, George Lam, Stanley Fung, Deannie Yip, James Tien, Season Ma, Phillip Chan, Charlie Cho, Phillip Ko, Dick Wei, Wu Ma. **D:** Sammo Hung. **W:** Dak Biu Creative Group. **C:** Arthur Wong. **VHS, DVD**

Painted Faces

Chronicling the final years of what is now the most famous Chinese opera troupe in the world, the Seven Little Fortunes, this rare co-production between the Shaw Brothers and Golden Harvest Studios is one of those Hong Kong movies that might have been too culturally different for Western audiences to accept. After all, the Chinese opera was an institution in which parents would sell their children into virtual slavery, in which they could be trained and disciplined without limit, all in the name of a form of show business that found them performing in highly eccentric productions, often in drag. National magazines often print exposes of the practices utilized to train preteen Olympic athletes, but that's nothing compared to Chinese opera. Seven Little Fortunes performers such as Yuen Biao, Sammo Hung, Corey Yuen, and Jackie Chan were trained endlessly within the walls of the school in singing, martial arts, acrobatics, makeup, acting, and general studies. If they didn't perform well, either during practice or in front of the public, they could be starved, beaten, or subjected to other cruel tortures, all at their master's discretion. And yet, the decline of this once thriving business is treated with heartbreaking regret. It's to the credit of first-time director Alex Law, and the dedicated cast, that they actually pull it off.

Sammo Hung stars as his own stern master Yu Jim-yuen, who struggles to maintain the traditions of his school in the face of changing times. Even in simulation, it's difficult to watch Hung

bending children backward over his knee to increase their flexibility, or beating a student with a stick when he breaks form after hours in a handstand. Throughout this portrayal of strict regimen, we see bonds being formed among the children, and even with Master Yu, who was often viewed as a cold and unemotional figure. As the 1960s progressed, Yu also had to deal with a worldwide spirit of youthful rebellion that found its way even inside the thick walls of his school, as the students became more interested in things like the Beatles and bell-bottom pants than in upholding the standards of Chinese opera. With audiences for their performances dwindling, Master Yu begins to find work for his more advanced students as movie stuntmen (collecting most of their fees), a move that changed the lives of his students forever, while also eventually transforming and revitalizing the Hong Kong film industry (and subsequently, the world). Hung is terrific in his role, especially towards the end when we begin to see more of the man behind the Master. Lam Ching-Ying (*Mr. Vampire*) is also good as one of Yu's fellow opera masters who suffers a catastrophic head injury while performing a movie stunt. Wu Ma appears as a film director with mixed emotions about the windfall of talent he has available. Relatively few Americans can appreciate even European opera, and few tears will ever fall in the U.S. should Chinese opera disappear altogether. No one is calling for a return to the harsh treatment of children that was commonplace within the business, but if you're reading this book, you can appreciate the fact that the caliber of performer it produced will likely never be seen again. This deservedly swept the Hong Kong Film Awards for 1988. **AKA:** *Chat Siu Fuk; Qi Xiao Fu.* ♪♪♪♪

1988 112m/C *HK* Sammo Hung, Cheng Pei-Pei, Lam Ching-Ying, Wu Ma, John Sham. **D:** Alex Law. **W:** Alex Law, Mabel Cheung. **C:** David Chung. **M:** Lowell Lo. **VHS**

Painted Skin

Having been relieved of his directing duties on *Swordsman*, King Hu (*A Touch of Zen*) turned to this period supernatural thriller, a remake of a 1966 film. Lazy scholar Wang Hsi-tzu (Adam Cheng) meets runaway wife You Feng (Joey Wong) late one night and takes her in, hoping to make her his concubine. But when Wang and his wife spy their guest peeling off her human face for cleaning, he runs to the local Taoist priest Zhang Daoling (Lau Shun) for help. You Feng is a spirit trapped between Earth and Hell who has escaped the King of Yin and Yang and is looking for a place to hide out. Learning of her predicament, Zhang and his apprentice (Wu Ma) try to battle the demon king, but they're too weak. While the

Peking Opera

One of the classics of Hong Kong cinema, *Peking Opera Blues* takes place in and around—yes, you guessed it—a Peking Opera company. The energy, action, and dramatics are so propulsive and fast-moving that many Western viewers may only realize in hindsight that they have little or no idea what Peking Opera is all about

Those familiar with the careers of Jackie Chan and Sammo Hung may know that both stars were trained at a Peking Opera School run by Master Yuen. Whereas Sammo Hung candycoated to some extent the infamously harsh training and discipline inflicted upon children when he enacted the part of Master Yuen in Alex Law's *Painted Faces,* Jackie spelled out all the unpleasant details in his autobiography, *I Am Jackie Chan.* The regimen of training that Jackie and his fellow students endured in the early 1960s was a long-established tradition for wanna-be opera stars. For example, a depiction of similar training can be found in *Farewell, My Concubine,* set in the 1920s (about 10 years after the time period of *Peking Opera Blues*). Without rehashing all the details, let's just say that child protection laws would no longer allow such generally abusive treatment to take place. Young children, some as young as six years of age, would undergo a minimum of seven years of demanding all-day training in exchange for a lifetime of room and board. Exceptional performers received the perks of the trade, but the rest faced a rather Spartan existence.

It's impossible to deny that the training program produced a flock of amazing martial artists as well as acrobatic and dramatic stars of the stage and screen. But why were such regimens deemed necessary in the first place? Because of the unique demands of a unique and precise art form.

The origins of Chinese Opera, which encompasses a wide range of regional traditions, can be traced back hundreds of years. Four opera troupes from the Anhui province in China came to Peking in 1790 to perform for the royal family. The performances were warmly received, and the Anhui troupes' styles integrated with those of the groups already performing in the city. In time, troupes from the Hubei province also came to town. They were similarly combined with existing styles to eventually form the rich and complex stew of Peking Opera—music, poetry, singing, acrobatics, dancing, combat, and martial arts.

Since the basic story structures of the operas are quite familiar to Chinese audiences, the quality of the performances themselves are paramount. (You can compare this to European operas, where the basic repertoire is well known to enthusiasts.) Lines of dialogue and acrobatic moves must become second nature to the performers. Little things mean a lot. Few props are used. The costumes and makeup are colorful and widely varied for a reason—the colors and shapes relay specific information about the character's station and personal qualities to the audience.

Opera performers were separated into four basic categories of roles (man, woman, painted face, and clown), with additional divisions within each category. Once assigned, performers rarely strayed from their proscribed sub-division.

With the growing popularity of films and other modern diversions in the post-World War II era, it became increasingly difficult for Peking Opera companies and schools to remain afloat. That, coupled with their highly specialized skills, was why so many trainees ended up working in the Hong Kong movie industry. Peking Opera was dealt a further blow in popularity when the Communist Party banned performances of traditional operas in Mainland China.

The art form has survived in performances on stage, though its influence is not as strong as it once was. Its former practitioners, however, have forever altered Hong Kong cinema with their dazzling acrobatics, precise martial arts, and dance-like action choreography.

With the release of the long-hidden Shaw Brothers catalogue on DVD, which began in December 2002, a multitude of film versions of Chinese Huangmei operas are now available for curious Western viewers. Among the first titles were *The Kingdom and the Beauty, The Bride Napping, The Three Smiles*, and *The Last Woman of Shang.*

—PM

Taoists take You Feng to try to find the High Monk Tai Yuet (Sammo Hung) for help, the King takes possession of Wang's body, and with his minions in similar human garb, proceeds to raise some Hell on Earth. But the retired High Monk would rather just tend to his peach orchard, and they need to ask the Purple Taoist (Lam Ching-Ying) to lend a hand in getting his help.

King Hu provides an amusing fantasy here, with fun characters, great visuals, and spectacular locations. But for audiences who had seen the likes of *A Chinese Ghost Story,* King's style was just too old fashioned, and the film has an even older feel to it due to the heavy use of library music. They may also have grown tired of seeing Joey Wong typecast as a ghost. Unfortunately, this was King Hu's last film. **AKA:** *Wa Pei Ji Yam Yeung Faat Wong; Hua Pi Zhi Yin Yang Fa Wang; Human Night in Painted Skin.* 🎵🎵🎵

1992 93m/C *HK* Adam Cheng, Joey Wong, Sammo Hung, Lau Shun, Wu Ma, Lam Ching-Ying. **D:** King Hu. **W:** King Hu, Chung Ah-sing. **C:** Poon Tak-yip. **M:** Wu Dai-jiang. **VHS, DVD**

Para Para Sakura

Philip Wong (Aaron Kwok) is the owner of the famous Dance Fit Studio. Poor dreamboat Philip—he's got half of Shanghai getting in shape with his patented "kung fu dance" program, far outclassing his rival King of King King Dance. But Philip has a horrible problem: he's completely color-blind. This explains his horrible wardrobe. Then one day, as he is putting on a free kung fu dance session in the street, a mystery girl (Cecilia Cheung) gets up on stage with him, and changes his life. The girl, Yuri Sakurada, is in full color—not the real colors, but it's a start! Yes, it's a sickening analogy. When next he sees her, Japanese thugs are chasing her. While he fights them with his dance fu moves, she disappears, but shows up later at his studio wanting to hire him as a bodyguard on her trip to Suzhou. But of course, there are big problems with Phil's dreams of romance. Number one is that Yuri is engaged. Number two is she hired King, too. Only third is the men chasing her, especially since they turn out to be her real bodyguards, hired by her rich mother to keep an eye on her. His hopes are further dashed when Yuri's parents call her home, and their trip is cut short. But of course she changes her mind, comes back to him and cancels the wedding.

Aaron is puppy dog cute. Cecilia is Hello Kitty cute. Their friends are Fred and Ethel cute. By the time Kwok breaks into a full song-and-dance number, surrounded by floating feathers and prancing traffic cops, it must be concluded that the whole movie is pretty goddamn cute. Surprisingly little is made of the color-blind angle, which you would think cinematographer/director Jingle Ma would turn into something spectacular. Perfect for Kwok's preteen fan club, but all others beware. **AKA:** *Ang Kwong Ang Kwong Ying Ji Dut; Ba La Ba La Ying Zhi Hua; Para Paras Sakuya.* 🐉🐉

2001 101m/C *HK* Aaron Kwok, Cecilia Cheung, Ah Niu, Nishimura Kazuhiko, Tien Niu, Yuki Han, Liccy Nic, Maggie Wang, Tan Kheng Seong. **D:** Jingle Ma. **W:** Susan Chan. **C:** Jingle Ma. **M:** Peter Kam. **VHS, DVD**

Paramount Motel

A quiet but effective police drama. A private investigator (Cheung Tat-Ming) informs Officer Pang (Simon Lui) that his wife (Fennie Yuen) is having an affair with Cheung (Wayne Lai), a fellow cop. Before he can fully absorb the news, Pang is assigned to work a murder case. The victim was a prostitute named Wyman (Pauline Chan); she worked out of the Paramount Motel, a disreputable lodging facility. As Officer Pang digs deeper into the case, he learns about the possible suspects: Ho (Jason Chu), the prostitute's gold-digging boyfriend; Hing (Ada Choi), the motel's manager; and Master Sun (Ti Lung), the motel's owner and a powerful figure with considerable influence over Pang's superiors in the police force. The evidence seems to point in one direction until a few twists obscure the possibility of easy answers.

Befitting a police procedural, neither the camera work nor the production design is particularly stylish. Many close-ups are employed; a number of times characters speak directly into the camera, pulling the audience into the narrative. The pacing by director Billy Chung is clunky, but that reflects the personality of the film's dogged protagonist, Officer Pang. Simon Lui, who also wrote the script, is resolute, stoic, and quiet in his role as Officer Pang, though he flares up occasionally. The performance—the quiet at the center of a storm—centers the film nicely. Veteran actor Ti Lung adds self-satisfied weight to the role of master manipulator Sun. Daniel Chan Fai's cinematography is a bit drab—perhaps intentionally so—but adds a blue tint to certain scenes, presumably for variety. —*PM* **AKA:** *Ching Haam Baak Lok Moon; Qing Xian Bai Le Men; Love Trap at the Paramount.* 🐉🐉

2000 91m/C *HK* Simon Lui, Wayne Lai, Pinky Cheung, Ti Lung, Ada Choi, Pauline Chan, Samuel Leung, Fennie Yuen, Cheung Tat-Ming, Jason Chu, Chapman To. **D:** Billy Chung. **W:** Simon Lui. **C:** Daniel Chan. **M:** Tommy Wai. **VHS, DVD**

Parasite Eve

Based on the novel by Hideaki Sena, *Parasite Eve* has gone on to become a popular video game and anime production since the time this film was made. Director Masayuki Ochiai's use of clean imagery and camera movement in conjunction with music recalls the work of Dario Argento, while the cellular horror theme falls closer to David Cronenberg territory. The plot centers on the theory that mitochondria are actually parasites within cells, a parasite passed on to us through our mothers since our species began. But what is this beneficial parasite's real purpose? What are those sneaky mitochondria up to?

Dedicated scientist Dr. Nagashima (Hiroshi Mikami) is so busy trying to find ways to harness the mitochondria for medical purposes that he neglects his young wife Kiyomi (Riona Hazuki), even forgetting their anniversary. Distracted by her mitochondria, Kiyomi has a serious auto accident, and is pronounced brain dead. Finding that Kiyomi has signed a living will as an organ donor, Dr. Yoshizumi (Tetsuya Bessho) begs for Kiyomi's kidneys to be donated to Mariko (Ayako Omura), a 12-year-old girl.

Driven mad with grief, Nagashima agrees—on condition that he receive Kiyomi's liver for a radical experiment. Mariko's transplant is a success, but there's something unusual about Kyomi's kidneys, and the new thing in her belly is scaring the piss out of the poor girl. While Nagashima's experiment rapidly replicates the liver cells in his lab, Kiyomi's mighty mitochondria are replicating the kidney's cells as well. It soon becomes apparent to Nagashima that the parasite he calls "Eve" has been waiting for a billion years, plotting and manipulating, for just the chance he's presented it—the chance for the intelligence residing in every human cell to stage a coup!

It takes a good hour before it can get around to it, but *Parasite Eve* finally breaks loose with the kind of horror f/x filmmakers could only dream about back in the days of *The H-Man*. Unfortunately, once the movie shifts gears, it also loses its grip on logic, and any damn thing can happen. But as long as it means oozing yellow blob monsters and spontaneous human combustion, it'd be a shame to nitpick. *Parasite Eve*'s one big sin is that, at two hours, it's at least 20 minutes too long, and the ending seems to grind on forever. **AKA:** *Parasaito Ivu.* ♪♪♡

1997 120m/C *JP* Hiroshi Mikami, Riona Hazuki, Tomoko Nakajima, Ayako Omura, Goro Inagaki, Hisako Manda. **D:** Masayuki Ochiai. **W:** Ryoichi Kimizuka, Hideaki Sena (novel). **C:** Kobo Shibazaki. **M:** Jo Hisaishi. **VHS, DVD**

Patlabor 1: The Movie

In an alternate-universe Tokyo of 1999, the world's industries receive a boost with the creation of "Labors," robot mechasuits used for everything from construction to crime fighting. But something's gone terribly wrong. Rogue Labors have been suddenly going berserk, endangering lives and causing massive destruction. It's up to the Mobile Police of Division 10 to contain these monsters, while their superiors in government and industry try to figure out what's causing the problem. Is there a glitch in the Labors' programming, or is it a case of sabotage? And what can be done about it?

You'd think overworked Division 10 Special Section Officers Shinohara and Izumi would keep

Hapless cops try to contain technology running wild in the surprisingly deep sci-fi/action anime *Patlabor 1: The Movie.*

their noses out of the case and concentrate on rounding up the rogues. However, Shinohara has a little more at stake. His father, from whom he's been estranged for many years, owns Shinohara Industries, the top producer of Labors in the world. He's determined to find out what's going on, if only to show up his old man. Also at stake is Operation Babylon, a hydro system project that promises to help solve Tokyo's drainage and land problems. Not only are the Mobile Police under stress maintaining order, but they also have to deal with the fact that their own machines may turn against them at any moment—including the sleek new Labor model, Labor Type 0. At the heart of the mystery is the suicide of genius programmer Hoba, who wrote the radical software upgrade installed in all Labors. The more that is dug up on Hoba, the less that is understood, as the man appears to have been an enigma who hid his background with false identities and maintained multiple residences all over town.

The heroes finally decipher what triggers the Labor rampages, but will they be able to prevent a coming event that could cause 8,000 Labors to go berserk? Fortunately, the Division 10 engineers didn't trust the new HOS software, meaning the police Labors were not infected. The key to the massive sabotage plan lies within the gigantic floating platform called The Ark, a huge Labor factory. The mission set out for the Mobile Police: invade the Ark and destroy it!

What first appears as a sci-fi action tale turns out to be a technological detective story with the complexity of a novel. However, once all the details are worked out, the last 20 minutes are action-packed, with plenty of crazed robot-smashing mayhem. Despite a dull synth score, the twists and turns of the plot, along with the kind of animated stunts that fuel flicks like *Aliens* and *RoboCop,* make this one a winner. *Patlabor* originated as a late-'80s anime video series, which re-energized the fading giant-robot genre by changing the setting from the usual superhero and space war background to that of a police drama—sort of like a *Robotech* version of *Hill Street Blues.* The series, and the two features that followed, were directed by Mamoru Oshii, the *Urusei Yatsura* veteran who picked up a huge fan following all over the world with the release of his anime feature *Ghost in the Shell. Ghost,* though overly complicated and somewhat talky in places, was an exciting sci-fi action film, rendered all the more impressive with its stylish visuals and attention to detail. Watching *Patlabor,* one can pick out instances of Oshii developing the techniques and tricks that would make *Ghost in the Shell* such a smash. *AKA: Kido Keisatsu Patoreba: The Movie; Mobile Police Patlabor; Patlabor: The Mobile Police.* 🐉🐉🐉

1990 100m/C *JP* **D:** Mamoru Oshii. **W:** Kazunori Itoh. **VHS, DVD**

Peace Hotel

The similarities between Asian martial arts films and American (and Italian) westerns have been noted many times, but this Wai Kar-fai film obliterates the boundaries between the two genres completely. It begins with a black-and-white prologue that looks like a horror film. After slaughtering an entire gang of bandits, the man known as Killer Ping (Chow Yun-fat) has a moment of transcendence when he sees a dove. He opens the Peace Hotel—a sanctuary for all kinds of fugitives, where they need not fear their enemies. The peace is kept mostly by fear, as no one dares to challenge Killer's reputation. The arrival of club girl Shau Siu-man (Cecilia Yip) shatters that peace, as she immediately fills everyone's ears with a pack of lies, telling a melodramatic tale about her life as Killer's wife and robbing everyone blind. Killer exposes her, and refuses to put up with any of her nonsense. But before he can send her on her way, the Grand Hall bandit gang arrives at the hotel gates, accusing Shau of killing their chief and stealing his gold. Despite all the trouble Shau has caused, Killer turns down the bandits' demand for her blood, holding firm to the principles of the Peace Hotel. With the hotel under siege and a battle coming, Shau decides to sacrifice herself to avoid any harm coming to the hotel's inhabitants. However, Killer can't stand idle when the bandits attack her, and he unleashes the monster within him in her defense.

While waiting for a green light on his first American film, John Woo filled some time by skipping back to Hong Kong to produce this script by his *Hard Boiled* editing partner Wai Kar-fai. The result is a 20th-century fable, with the Chinese cast adopting the dress and mannerisms of the Old West à la Sergio Leone or Enzo Castellari. The setting is so rich, and the performances by Chow Yun-fat and Cecilia Yip are so captivating, that they almost pull it off. The bandit chief's lieutenant, played by Chin Ho, purposely pushes Killer to find out whether his fighting skills are the equal of his reputation. The main problem is that we never find out—all the big fight scenes are shot in abstract. Perhaps Wai didn't want to show much violence while making a film about peace, but in order to satisfy the situations and expectations he's created, seeing Chow Yun-fat kicking a lot of tailbones is definitely in order. A sequence featuring Chow wielding a machine gun was cut from theatrical prints, but has been restored for home video, likely in response to just such criticism. *AKA: Wing Ping Fan Din; Han Ping Fan Dian; Heping Fandian.* 🐉🐉♡

1995 98m/C *HK* Chow Yun-fat, Cecilia Yip, Chin Ho, Lau Shun, Annabelle Lau, Mickey Ng, Joe Cheng, Mai Kei, Lawrence Ng, Liu Fan, Lee Siu-Kei Jacqueline Wu. **D:** Wai Kar-fai. **W:** Chow Yun-fat, Wai Kar-fai. **C:** Horace Wong. **M:** Cacine Wong, Healthy Poon. **VHS, DVD**

The Peacock King

This binational production based on a popular manga series takes advantage of Hong Kong action choreography and Japanese special-effects know-how. At a secret archeological dig, the demonic Hell Escort Raga (Pauline Wong) arrives to announce that mankind has done enough damage to the world, and awakens the Hell Virgin Ashura (Gloria Yip), who will open up the holes to Hell. Once all four holes open, the Hell King will be released to destroy mankind. Ghostbusting Tibetan monk Peacock (Yuen Biao) is assigned to stop the demonic menace, and is sent to Tokyo, where signs foretell the next hole will open. Meanwhile, Japanese Koyasan monk Lucky Fruit (Hiroshi Mikami) is given the same job by his sifu (Ken Ogata). At a dinosaur exhibit in the Odakyu department store, Raga brings lots of little demons and ghosts, animates the full-size dinosaur models, and prepares the Hellhole for opening. Though assigned the same task, the two monks have clashing personalities—Lucky Fruit is serious and traditional, while Peacock is a bit of a rascal. After Raga attacks them at a disco, they follow her to Ocean Park, where Ashura plays havoc with the rides. "Play" is the key word, as Ashura turns out to be an innocent just trying to have some fun, and it's the influence of her father the Hell King that's making her cause trouble.

With her dino exhibit destroyed, Miss Okada (Narumi Yasuda) is out of a job and decides to tag along to help the monks. The Hell King's earthly followers send Kubira (Gordon Lau) and his warriors to eliminate the interfering monks. The third Hellhole appears below the slums of Hong Kong, where Raga has been punishing Ashura for her human weakness, and leaving corpses drained of blood. When challenged by the monks, she transforms into a hideous monster. Peacock decides they should bring Ashura back to Tibet, where he hopes his master Ku Fong (Eddie Ko) can help put her on the righteous path. Kubira and his warriors arrive for some martial arts combat, but have to reassess which side they've chosen once the fourth hole opens, and the Hell King is resurrected.

Thematically, this is a cousin to Italian horror films like *Suspiria* and *The Beyond,* which also turned on the opening of the doors to Hell, but there the resemblance ends. The influence of American hits like *Ghostbusters, Alien,* and *Raiders of the Lost Ark* are more of a factor. Some Yuen Biao fans may be disappointed that the accent is on magic and not his acrobatic kung fu, but fantasy and horror are the attractions here. Some matte shots are a bit unsteady, and some of the creature animation looks dated now, but on the whole the special effects are very impressive. For those used to the traditional white-haired villains of old-school kung fu movies,

the appearance of the gigantic, frightening Hell King is a welcome surprise. Gloria Yip *(Savior of the Soul)* was a natural choice for this production, her film debut, as she was a model in Tokyo previously. She got married and retired from acting in 1995, and is now more famous in Hong Kong for her weekly magazine column on embroidery. Followed by *Saga of the Phoenix.* **AKA:** *Hung Jeuk Wong; Kong Qiao Wang; Legend of the Phoenix; Peacock Prince.*

1989 80m/C *HK/JP* Yuen Biao, Gloria Yip, Pauline Wong, Hiroshi Mikami, Narumi Yasuda, Eddie Ko, Gordon Lau, Kara Hui, Phillip Kwok, Ken Ogata, Yuen Bun, Cheung Gwok-wa, Yeung Sing. **D:** Simon Nam. **W:** Edward Tang, Kong Heung-sang, Shirley Woo. **C:** Ardy Lam, Kwan Chi-kan. **M:** Yoshino Maki. **VHS, DVD**

Pedicab Driver

A bravura combination of action, comedy, drama, romance, thrills, and tragedy, set several decades in the past. Tung (Sammo Hung), Malted Candy (Max Mok), and Rice Pudding (Mang Hoi) are pedicab drivers in Macau. They work hard just to make ends meet, but it's an honest living and they're proud of what they do. Tung meets Bing (Nina Li Chi) and falls for her. Bing is an apprentice of Fong, a baker and an older gentleman with a romantic interest in the younger woman. Tung is determined to win Bing's heart. Malted Candy is smitten by the adorable and innocent Siu Chui (Fennie Yuen). Their courtship is sweet enough to give you diabetes. Rice Pudding is bemused by his friends' romantic travails and is glad to be married with children. San Cha Cake (Lowell Lo) disrupts the lives of the three men. He's also a pedicab driver and part of their local circle of friends. He visits a house of prostitution and learns a terrible secret that leads to heartache, tragedy, and well-motivated revenge.

Director Sammo Hung maintains a breathless pace yet leaves room for the emotional core of the characters to burn a hole in the screen. The earlier scenes are filled with lighter moments—especially Tung's attempts to woo Bing—and an emphasis on the importance of marriage and family. By allowing time for the characters to be fully drawn, he invites the audience to identify closely with them and thus be deeply affected by their fate. The four main action sequences are breathtaking. The first one breaks out in a large restaurant and features a squadron of men duking it out—keep an eye out for a quick *Star Wars* parody. Another pits Tung against the owner of a gambling establishment (Lau Kar-Leung) in an extended and dizzying fight with poles, harking back to the golden age of martial arts films. The scene took

six days (12 plus hours each day) to film. A confrontation with a nasty crime lord (John Sham) takes to the sidewalks and roadways as a car chases a pedicab—which executes maneuvers a pedicab was never designed to perform! The story culminates in another extended scene of brutal and extremely physical punishment being meted out in revenge for a murderous deed. Excellent performances by the self-assured Nina Li Chi and the heartbreaking Fennie Yuen add polish to the production. —PM **AKA:** *Kwan Lung Fai Fung; Qun Long Xi Feng.* 𝅘𝅥𝅮𝅘𝅥𝅮𝅘𝅥𝅮𝅘𝅥𝅮

1989 95m/C *HK* Sammo Hung, Nina Li Chi, Sun Yueh, Max Mok, Lowell Lo, Mang Hoi, Fennie Yuen, John Sham, Lau Kar-Leung, Maria Cordero, Corey Yuen, Billy Lau, Manfred Wong, Alfred Cheung, Lam Ching-Ying, Chan Lung, Dick Wei, Michelle Yip, Eric Tsang, Mai Kei, Billy Chow, Chung Fat, Eddie Maher, Fung Ging Man, Hsiao Ho, Chu Tau, Yuen Tak, Fung Lee, Siu Tak-foo. **D:** Sammo Hung. **W:** Barry Wong, Yuen Kai-chi. **C:** Tom Lau, Jimmy Leung, Poon Tak-tong. **M:** Lowell Lo. **VHS**

Peking Opera Blues

Chinese opera troupes have played a large role in China's political and cultural history, as a haven for rebel patriots, a preserver of martial arts, and a breeding ground for motion picture artists. Filmmaker Tsui Hark recognizes this fact, and celebrated it in this highly entertaining feature. General Tun hasn't paid his soldiers in three months. When they riot and sack his house, he takes his wives and skedaddles. He lost all his cash to General Tsao (Kenneth Tsang) in a mah-jongg game. Musician Sheung Hung (Cherie Chung) makes off with some loot from Tun's house, too: a box full of valuable jewelry. Stopped for a search, she hides the stash on a cart on its way to Chun Wo Ban Opera Theatre, where Fa (Paul Chun) is the star. The catch is that women aren't allowed in the theatre—Fa has a lot of fans for his portrayal of female roles. One powerful fan is Police Commissioner Liu (Ku Feng), who even proposes marriage. Pat Neil (Sally Yeh) has theatre in her blood, and humiliates her director father Wong (Wu Ma) by trying to sneak into a role.

Though General Tsao teasingly refers to his foreign educated "son," Wan (Brigitte Lin) is really a woman who prefers businesslike male dress. This also helps distract from the fact she's a rebel spy. Commissioner Liu suspects rebel guerrillas hiding in the opera. He's right—Wan has a meeting with agent Pak Hoi (Mark Cheng) for a mission briefing there. It seems President Yuen has been borrowing money to build up his army and conquer the south of China, and General Tsao just happens to be the

go-between, putting Wan within reach of their plans. Wan and Pak are to steal a document as proof of the loan. Searching for her loot, Sheung Hung ends up accidentally in Wan's car, and she gets mixed up in the attempted heist. A young soldier named Tung is shot helping Pak Hoi when he's discovered, and the whole crew ends up hiding out with Pat Neil at the opera. Having failed in a couple of attempts to get key to the general's safe, Sheung Hung is enlisted to seduce her way to their goal, or die trying.

One of his first big hits after *Zu: Warriors from the Magic Mountain,* here Tsui Hark established a winning formula: take a group of endearing heroes, embroil them in intrigue, romance, and door-slamming comedy, then top it all with a lot of wonderfully choreographed action scenes. Action director Ching Siu-tung *(The Killer)* helps out quite a bit with the latter, while some will find this one worth checking out just for the great re-creation of the opera troupe and 1913 Beijing. The one flaw, which would further harm some of Tsui's subsequent films, is that there are too many characters and too much going on for the running time. Hopefully some day that rumored two-hour director's cut will surface. **AKA:** *Do Ma Dan; Diy Ma Daan; Knife Horse Dawn.* 𝅘𝅥𝅮𝅘𝅥𝅮𝅘𝅥𝅮𝄾

1986 101m/C *HK* Brigitte Lin, Sally Yeh, Cherie Chung, Mark Cheng, K.K. Cheung, Wu Ma, Kenneth Tsang, Paul Chun, David Wu, Lee Hoi-sang, Tin Ching, Ku Feng. **D:** Tsui Hark. **W:** Raymond To. **C:** Poon Hang-sang. **M:** James Wong. **VHS, DVD**

The Phantom Lover

First filmed in the 1930s, this ambitious remake of the Chinese take on *Phantom of the Opera* reunites many of the principles behind *Bride with White Hair.* In 1936, a troupe of actors rents a grand, but fire-damaged theatre. Rumor has it that the famous star Sung Danping (Leslie Cheung), who debuted many Western plays in China, was among those who perished in the fire during the '20s. Going into flashback mode, the caretaker Mr. Ma (Zhang Zheng-yuan) tells the young lead actor Wei Qing (Huang Lei) about how his old boss Sung built the radically Western-style theatre, his daring and opulent productions, and his love for debutante Du Yuyan (Jacqueline Wu). Yuyan returns his affections, though her wealthy parents have promised her to the idiot son (Roy Szeto) of Governor Zhao (Pao Fong). Zhao conspires with Officer Lu (Zhao Zheng) to have Sung's show shut down, and when their efforts cause the actor to publicly embarrass them, they turn to more underhanded methods of getting rid of him. After the suspicious fire, heartbroken Yuyan

returns every full-moon night to listen for Sung to sing the melody he wrote for her. Sung has survived but remains in hiding due to having his face disfigured by an acid bath delivered by one of Zhao's thugs (Phillip Kwok). He decides to save the troupe from their disastrous patriotic musical by secretly taking Wei under his wing and coaching him to perform the lead in his musical *Romeo and Juliet*. But the phantom's true purpose is to romance Yuyan through his protégé, while keeping his own face hidden—which complicates matters between Wei and his girlfriend Landie (Liu Lin), for starters.

Though Cheung and Wu are fine, the cinematography of Peter Pau *(Crouching Tiger, Hidden Dragon)* is the actual lead player here, aided greatly by the art direction by Eddie Ma. His use of light and color is astonishing, oversaturating key components in the flashbacks, while desaturating the '30s scenes to near monochrome. The black-and-white nature of the storybook romance plot is the only flaw here—the heroes all but wear haloes and the villains lack only sinister mustaches. Its operatic melodrama rivals that of *Moulin Rouge* or *Titanic*, while looking just as gorgeous. *AKA: Ye Boon Go Sing; Ye Ban Ge Sheng.* ♫♫♫

1995 102m/C *HK/CH* Leslie Cheung, Jacqueline Wu, Huang Lei, Liu Lin, Pao Fong, Roy Szeto, Zhao Zheng, Zhang Zheng-yuan, Wang Bing, Phillip Kwok. **D:** Ronny Yu. **W:** Roy Szeto, Raymond Wong, Ronny Yu. **C:** Peter Pau. **M:** Chris Babida, Leslie Cheung. **VHS, DVD**

Picture of a Nymph

Sammo Hung produced this romantic fantasy, one of the best produced in response to the success of *A Chinese Ghost Story*. Yuen Biao was in the midst of his heroic fantasy period, but unlike some of his others, this one allowed him to show off his acrobatic skills a bit more. A baby is the lone survivor on a battlefield, and a warrior (Lam Wai) sets the babe adrift in a tub, Moses style. He's found by bathing Taoist priest Wu Men-Chu (Wu Ma), who adopts him.

Mo Chiu (Joey Wong) is on the trip to her marriage, accompanied by her servant girl Suang (Zhilun Xue). In the haunted wood, the demon King Ghost (Elizabeth Lee) comes to snatch the bride. Mo Chiu throws herself off a cliff to escape—but the demon vows to get her "dead or alive." Grown to manhood, the priest's foundling son Shih Erh (Yuen Biao) becomes a ghostbuster, too. Though under a vow of silence, but sensing deviltry about, he visits the scholar Tsui Hung-Chien (Lawrence Ng), who is entertaining demons unaware. Despite Tsui's preoccupation with his book, Shih Erh fights the ghost and

wins. The scholar's mill goes up in flames along with the spook, however, so Shih Erh is compelled to invite the fellow to his home.

Suang mourns her mistress, who is now a lonely ghost. In the village cemetery, Wu battles King Ghost, who uses umbrella goblins against him. Fighting to a draw, he returns home to remove the vow of silence from his son, and discovers the scholar in their guest house. Against his better judgment, he allows the guest to stay. The next night, Tsui spies Mo Chiu and Sueng (now a ghost herself) by the river. Mutually entranced, the ghost follows him home and sees him paint her portrait. She hides from the King Ghost inside the picture, but the demon comes after the portrait, determined to get Mo Chiu back.

Though the middle portion slows down to advance the romance element and character development, the third act comes through with dazzling supernatural spectacle, including flying palanquins, lightning bolts, explosions, and more, as the ghostbusters descend into the netherworld to rescue the captured lovers. Wu Ma had been directing films since 1970 (and has acted in over 100 movies), but nothing he had done before matches the visual splendor on display here. The images are simply gorgeous—every frame is breathtaking. Wu Ma also gives himself a little song and dance to perform, his croaking song reprised over the closing credits. *AKA: Ung Chung Sin; Hua Zhong Xian; Painting of a Nymph; Portrait of a Nymph.* ♫♫♫

1988 94m/C *HK* Yuen Biao, Joey Wong, Wu Ma, Elizabeth Lee, Lawrence Ng, Zhilun Xue, Lam Wai. **D:** Wu Ma. **W:** Wu Ma, Chan Kam-cheung. **C:** Hung Brothers, Tom Lau, Raymond Lam, Abduhl M. Rumjahn. **M:** James Wong. **VHS, DVD**

Police Story

Jackie Chan had enjoyed playing policemen in the first Lucky Stars films as a guest star, but after his bad experience in the U.S. co-production *The Protector,* he was anxious to make a cop movie his own way, bringing the kind of stunts and fights he brought to *Project A* into a modern setting. The result is this award-winning blockbuster, among Chan's best pictures, and one of the best action movies ever made. We begin with Operation Boar Hunt already underway, with Detective Chan Ka-Kui (known as "Kevin" or "Jackie" in various English dubs) one of a team of cops under the direction of Uncle Bill Chang (Bill Tung). Their objective is to round up the gang led by Chu Tu (Chor Yuen) as they receive a payoff in a hillside shantytown. When Chu's girlfriend Salina Fong (Brigitte Lin) spots the officers, the jig is up, and Chan has to pursue the crooks as they drive cars down *through* the shantytown. It's just the first of a string of spectacular and original action

Jackie Chan finally gets the chance to indulge an urge to pull a gun on his boss Lam Kwok-hung in the action classic *Police Story.*

sequences cooked up by Chan and his stunt team. Chan captures Chu, but there's insufficient evidence against him. Superintendent Raymond (Lam Kwok-hung) assigns Chan as Selina's 24-hour guard in the hope that either Chu will reveal himself or Chan can get more evidence from her. To sell the idea that Chu is trying to eliminate her, Chan's partner Kim (Mars) poses as an assassin so Chan can protect her. Unexpectedly, he really does have to protect her when Chu actually betrays her and sends his men to kill her. But no one can protect Chan when his girlfriend May (Maggie Cheung) finds the foxy Selina in his apartment. Chan botches getting the evidence, Chu's lawyer (Lau Chi-wing) embarrasses him in court, and Chan is transferred to the remote Sha Tau Kok Station. Despite this, Chu's finances have been so disrupted by police interference that he's determined to get revenge. Chu's men frame Chan for the murder of a fellow officer, and not trusting a corrupt system to exonerate him, the enraged Chan has to go outside the law to bring Chu in.

The film only fails in this dramatic component, as the conflicts within the police department haven't been set up sufficiently. No matter— *Police Story* contains some of the most exciting (and painful) stunts and fight scenes ever put on film, culminating in a jaw-dropping running battle set in a shopping mall that earned the picture the nickname "Glass Story" from the stunt team, as most of the cast is sent crashing through windows and display cases—culminating in Jackie's electrifying slide down a pole covered in bulbs. An action classic, worthy of seemingly unlimited repeat viewing. The dubbed U.S. version is five minutes shorter, despite having longer credits. *AKA: Gong Chat Goo Si; Jing Cha Gu Shi; Jackie Chan's Police Story; Police Force.* ♪♪♪♪

1985 (PG-13) 94m/C *HK* Jackie Chan, Brigitte Lin, Maggie Cheung, Bill Tung, Chor Yuen, Mars, Kenneth Tong, Kam Hing-yin, Charlie Cho, Lau Chi-wing, Fung Hark-on, Tai Bo, Wan Fat, Wu Fung, Money Lo, Ben Lam, Lam Kwok-hung. **D:** Jackie Chan. **W:** Jackie Chan, Edward Tang. **C:** Cheung Yiu-cho. **M:** Michael Lai, Kevin Bassinson (export version), J. Peter Robinson (U.S. version). **VHS, DVD**

Police Story 2

Ever wonder what happens to a movie hero after he's saved the day, captured the bad guy, and rescued the fair damsel? Jackie Chan explores that idea in this sequel to his gigantic hit cop movie. Instead of parades, prizes, and promotions, Hong Kong cop Kevin Chan Ka-kui is reprimanded by his superiors, superintendent Raymond (Lam Kwok-hung) and Uncle Bill Chang (Bill Tung). He's held responsible for all the damage he did in the first movie, and demoted to motorcycle highway patrol. Most directors would have shown this by having a scene in Raymond's office, followed by a shot of the hero in uniform. Chan shows his creativity by intercutting the office scene with shots of an unknown officer pulling over 10 identical Mitsubishi semi-cabs to issue them tickets in unison, only showing his face at the end of the scene. Without even showing any kung fu, it's the perfect illustration of Chan's spirit: giving everything just a little (or a lot) more effort.

His girlfriend May (Maggie Cheung) is very happy her boyfriend's days are spent writing tickets rather than getting shot at, but Kevin is annoyed with his new duties, and he's even more annoyed to learn that his enemy Chu Tao (Chor Yuen) has been released from prison because of a fake medical condition. Chu vows to get even with Kevin, and his seedy lawyer John Ko (Charlie Cho) harasses Kevin and even fights with May. Kevin loses his temper and thrashes Ko and his thugs, and when he's reprimanded again, he quits the force. However, Kevin can't help but get involved when a mall he's visiting receives a bomb threat. And it's a good thing, as the threat turns out to be real and the mall explodes as soon as everyone is out. A gang of bombers threatens Hong Kong's corporations, holding their properties for ransom, so Raymond and Bill shanghai supercop Kevin back onto the force to take the case. As the bombs continue, the gang kidnaps May to force Kevin to bring the ransom for them himself, with bombs strapped across his chest.

The feud with Chu and Ko is just an excuse to give Kevin trouble with May and his superiors, setting up a couple of terrific fights while the main plot gets underway. It's darn entertaining filler, but the story about the bombing extortionists is even more—well, explosive. A Jackie Chan fight scene is always exciting, but the duel with hard-kicking little Benny Lai, throwing little bombs at Kevin while the clock ticks on a time bomb, deserves a standing ovation. Other highlights include a bit where policewomen on Kevin's team (including Crystal Kwok and Angile Leung) show some fancy interrogation techniques (reflecting the then-current trend toward female heroes), and Kevin undercover, disguised in mustache and glasses. The U.S. version is missing about 10 minutes. *AKA: Ging Chat Goo si Juk Jaap; Jing Cha Gu shi Xu Ji; Police Story Part II; Jackie Chan's Police Story 2; Police Force II; Police Story Sequel; Kowloon's Eye.* 🐉🐉🐉🐉

1988 (PG-13) 92m/C *HK* Jackie Chan, Maggie Cheung, Bill Tung, Lam Kwok-hung, Charlie Cho, Benny Lai, Chor Yuen, Mars, Crystal Kwok, Angile Leung, Kenny Ho, Wu Ma, Ben Lam, Kwan San, Lau Ching-Wan, Michael Chow, Alvina Kong, Lau Siu-ming, Ken Lo, Billy Lau, Dennis Chan, Yip Wing-cho, Tai Bo. *D:* Jackie Chan. *W:* Jackie Chan, Edward Tang. *C:* Cheung Yiu-cho. *M:* Michael Lai, J. Peter Robinson (U.S.). **VHS, DVD**

Pom Pom

This perfect example of a buddy-cop action comedy was a huge hit. Chiu (Richard Ng) and Beethoven (John Sham) are a team of hapless-but-effective detectives who use wits and luck rather than physical prowess to solve cases. However, the two roommates spend more time at home, and at their police station (which is constantly under repair from their latest mishaps, it's to be assumed), trying to outwit each other and their fellow cops than catching crooks. Commander Chen (Phillip Chan) has his hands full running the sloppy precinct, but gets a lot of help from his stern new assistant Anna (Deannie Yip). The boys get a tip on a drug trafficker named Sha (Chan Lung), but pimp informer Wen (Tai Bo) double-crosses them, leaving them without evidence. When they go to get a lead from Sha's mistress Lulu, they find her dead, murder made to look like an apparent suicide. But Sha's man made a mistake in killing her, since she was the only one who knew where she hid Sha's secret ledger. Luck comes to the cops when Lulu's cousin Kitty (Irene Wan) comes to Hong Kong for the funeral, Beethoven tries to woo her, and it turns out she has the ledger with her. When Sha finds out, it puts them all in danger.

Those fans anxious to see John Sham, Richard Ng, and Dick Wei naked have their chance here, as the cops hunt for a crook in a spa. Their rooftop pole battle turns out to be just as funny in practice as it is in concept, as much of the comedy comes from seeing the two comedians thrown into Jackie Chan situations without Jackie Chan skills. The comedy is mostly pretty corny, based on simple misunderstandings, but the personable cast is able to wring laughs from the material. Sham and Ng's Lucky Stars buddies all show up in cameo parts. Followed by *Return of Pom Pom,* and two more sequels. The English title was supposed to be *Pow Pow,* but somebody accidentally inverted the "m"s! *AKA: San Yung Seung Heung Paau; Shen Yong Shuang Xiang Pao.* 🐉🐉🐉

1984 91m/C *HK* Richard Ng, John Sham, Deannie Yip, Irene Wan, Phillip Chan, Chan Lung, Tai Bo, Dick Wei, Chung Fat, James Tien, Fung Ging Man, Jackie Chan, Wu Ma, Dennis Chan, Sammo Hung, Charlie Chin, Yuen Biao, Stanley Fung, Lam Ching-Ying, Mars,

Ho Pak Kwong, Manfred Wong, Chin Yuet Sang, Tai San, Ng Min Kan, Chin Leung, Jaime Chik, Alice Lau. *D:* Joe Cheung. *W:* Bo Ho Writing Team. *C:* Ricky Lau. *M:* Joseph Chan, Mahmood Rumjahn. **VHS, DVD**

Pom Pom and Hot Hot

Having nothing to do with the *Pom Pom* movies, this buddy-cop action flick is more like Jackie Cheung's *Curry & Pepper*. Shin Chin-chian (Jacky Cheung) and his partner Chiang Li-chi (Stephen Tung) are two young CID officers who can't go out for a drink without ending up in a big gun battle with mobsters. Shin's mainland cousins, brash Cha Chiang (Alfred Cheung) and sub-servient Cha Shi (Rachel Lee), come for a visit. When Shin and Chiang go undercover as gigolos to investigate a gangland murder, Cha Chiang barges in on the job. However, Cha Chiang manages to ingratiate himself with madam Nancy Ton (Bonnie Fu), and since the case involves mainland gang boss Shing (John Ching), they let him stick around to at least help with the lingo. Complications crop up when Shin and Cha Shi begin to fall for each other, while it turns out that Nancy is an old girlfriend of Cha Chiang. The trail of evidence in the case points to gang-ster Lau Tin-hau (Cheung Kwok-leung) using master killer Wu Yuen-shin (Austin Wai) to elimi-nate his rivals, but when the heroes get too close, they become Wu's next targets.

Much of the humor based on dialect (and mah-jongg) doesn't translate well, but the spirit exhibited by the characters should be enough to carry you in between the marvelous action scenes. The various shootouts and fights, chore-ographed by Tung, are some of the finest this side of John Woo—especially the gun fu duel between Wu and the boys' superior Lam Ho-yang, also known as Shooter Yin (Lam Ching-Ying). After all the more lighthearted material that leads up to it, the atmospheric final gunfight is a bit of a shift in gears, but it's so kinetic and thrilling that no one should complain. *AKA: San Cheung Sau Yue Ka Lei Gai; Shen Qiang Shou Yu Ga Li Ji; Hot Hot and Pom Pom.* 🦴🦴🦴

1992 94m/C *HK* Jacky Cheung, Stephen Tung, Alfred Cheung, Rachel Lee, John Ching, Bonnie Fu, Cheung Kwok-leung, Austin Wai, Guy Lai, Lam Ching-Ying, Chan Chi-fai. *D:* Joe Cheung. *W:* Joe Cheung. *C:* Jingle Ma, Chan Chun-kau, Tom Lau, Peter Ngor. **VHS, DVD**

Pom Pom Strikes Back

Richard Ng and John Sham strike back as unorthodox cops Chow and Beethoven for their fourth comic adventure. Along with Chow's wife Anna (Deanie Yip), a family unit is in place, with partner Beethoven taking the role of the idiot child. Superintendent Chan (Phillip Chan) sends Anna to Singapore to escort extradited swindler Lee Hong back to Hong Kong, and assigns the boys to protect Lee's secretary May Lo (May Lo) until she can testify in court. A contract killer (Michael Chan) and his men are hired to eliminate the witness, who is keeping her watchdogs hop-ping by refusing to stay put in their hotel room.

Not the most original plot—Jackie Chan's *Police Story* had the same basic setup—but it's enough to provide the comedians a framework on which to hang their antics. One especially funny sequence has Ng looking for love in all the wrong places while singing some decidedly off-key mariachi. As if one old chestnut plot was-n't enough, try another: due to a computer error, Chow is mistakenly diagnosed with terminal lung cancer. Beethoven goes overboard plan-ning a Hawaiian vacation, a lavish funeral, and generally trying to make his partner's final days enjoyable. When Chow learns about the mis-take, he keeps it to himself in order to take advantage of all the pampering.

While previous entries ended with extensive action scenes, for the last Pom Pom picture, we have to settle for a fine knockabout fight scene between our heroes and Michael Chan. Much more extravagant is a hostage rescue sequence at the beginning that ends with a spoof of *Raiders of the Lost Ark*. While the script doesn't get any points for originality, the comic timing of the leads is on target, and Deanie Yip proves once again that she can melt the camera with a look. There are comic cameos by celebrities peppered throughout, including a mock-drama scene on a TV screen of Stanley Fung fighting his own terminal disease bravely. Extra points are earned by the art director for Chow's apart-ment, which includes a funhouse mirror that hides a secret door, and some really cool shopping-cart chairs. *AKA: Seung Lung To Ji; Shuang Long To Zhu.* 🦴🦴🦴

1986 85m/C *HK* Richard Ng, John Sham, Deanie Yip, May Lo, Michael Chan, Phillip Chan, Wu Ma, Dennis Chan, Stanley Fung, Fung Ging Man, Yue Tau Wan, Yip Wing-cho, Billy Ching, Baan Yun-sang, Ng Min Kan, Chen Jing. *D:* Yip Wing-cho. *W:* Joe Chan. *C:* Derek Yee. *M:* Danny Chung. **VHS, DVD**

Postman Blues

Bored postal carrier Ryuichi Sawaki (Shinichi Tsutsumi) is surprised to find that an advertis-ing flyer he's delivering goes to Shuji Noguchi (Keisuke Horibe), an old schoolmate of his. He's even more surprised to find that Noguchi has just cut his finger off. Noguchi draws Sawaki into his yakuza world by talking about how exciting it is, slipping a package into his mail sack, and (inadvertently) giving him the finger. Back home, an inspired and drunk Sawaki begins tearing open the mail, unaware that Noguchi has made him the target of a police stakeout. In the morning, a remorseful Sawaki attempts to take care of a letter from cancer patient Sayako Kitagawa (Kyoko Toyama), with the police now positive he's the mastermind of a drug ring—an idea reinforced by the fact that Sayako shares a ward with yakuza hit man Joe (Ren Osugi). The assassin is awaiting the results of his medical tests, and the results of his competition in the National Hit Man Qualification Tournament, in which he faced off against such professionals as "Leon" and "Brigitte Lin" for the title of King of Killers (and a free tour of Italy). The postman's sweet romance with terminal Sayako confuses the cops, and when they find the package of drugs—and the pinky—in Sawaki's apartment, they're ready to arrest him on charges of terrorism and homicide. As it turns out, that stray finger points to important results for all involved, and Sawaki delivers some of the most important mail of his career.

A deft comedy in the vein of *Diva,* this has a lot of subtle bite to it, rarely blowing its satire out of proportion into the realm of outright cartoon. Rather, it takes the romantic notions of the characters, inflated by "too much TV and movies," and spoofs them by bringing them down to earth. This masterpiece of misperceptions reaches an acme with a lecture by police profiler Professor Shinohara (Tomoro Taguchi) explaining the postman's psychological makeup. It all ends in a surreal bicycle race. Funny and touching, *Postman Blues* illustrates the web of circumstance that surrounds us, and how important even simple obligations can become. Should be required viewing for all post office employees. *AKA: Posutoman Burusu.* 🐉🐉🐉🐉

1997 110m/C *JP* Shinichi Tsutsumi, Kyoko Toyama, Keisuke Horibe, Ren Osugi, Hiroshi Shimizu, Yozaburo Ito, Ryo Yamamoto, Susumu Terajima, Hiroyuki Tanaka, Shiro Takehatsu, Wataru Shihodo, Ryoko Takizawa, Tomoro Taguchi, Koji Tsukamoto, Seiya Nakano, Akaji Maro, Konta, Sei Hiraizumi. *D:* Hiroyuki Tanaka. *W:* Hiroyuki Tanaka. *C:* Shuji Kuriyama. *M:* Daisuke Okamoto. **VHS**

The Postman Fights Back

Set in the days when China was divided among Yuan Shuhai and the warlords, the growing influence of Dr. Sun, and Jiao Long and his Pigtail Army of bandits in the north, this period action film would be less remarkable save for two factors. One is an early look at the moody imagery of director Ronny Yu. And the other is the contribution of a young character actor named Chow Yun-fat.

Hu (Eddie Ko) is sent by Yuan Shutai on a diplomatic mission to gain Jiao's support. After saving courier Ma (Leung Kar-yan) and thief Yao Jie (Yuen Yat-chor) from angry bandits, he tries to enlist them in his quest to have three cases delivered to Jiao. Other members hired on are con man Fu Jun (Chow Yun-fat) and fuse-happy explosives expert Lao Bu (Fan Mui-Sang). Tagging along is Guihua (Cherie Chung), on a mission to buy her kid sister back after their father sold her. Later, they save a Miss Li Fu (Guk Ching-suk) from attacking bandits. Trailing them every step of the way are two bounty hunters after Fu's hide, and various packs of bandits threaten. More trouble comes when Li turns out to be a spy working for Dr. Sun out to steal the cases. Other dangers include a pack of skating bandits on a frozen lake, and a mysterious ninja who's shadowing the group.

It's noteworthy that Chow already has his screen image in place. He wears his trademark uniform of long coat and scarf (backdated by 80 years or so), and wields a fancy wrist-launching crossbow. The action scenes favor such trickery over martial arts prowess, and are thus somewhat of a disappointment. With someone like Sammo Hung handling the choreography, this could have been a classic. But as it is, Chow's duels with the piggyback fighting bounty hunters and the ninja—who of course is quickly revealed as Hu—are a kick. When it's clear that Hu has used them as bait for the revolutionaries, and the cases they've delivered turn out to contain a machine gun, the team of couriers attacks the bandit camp using a platoon of suicide rat bombs and other tricks. Clearly modeled on westerns more than traditional Hong Kong action pictures, *Postman* delivers excitement at the crossroads between old-school kung fu flicks and the kind of extravaganzas Tsui Hark, Jackie Chan, and others would soon be making. *AKA: Chun Sing Ma; Xun Cheng Ma; The Postman Strikes Back; Patrol Horse; Patrol of Horses.* 🐉🐉🐉

1982 88m/C *HK* Leung Kar-yan, Yuen Yat-chor, Chow Yun-fat, Eddie Ko, Fan Mui-Sang, Cherie Chung, Guk Ching-suk, Yeung Wai. *D:* Ronny Yu. *W:* Ronny Yu, Koo Siu-fung, Chan Kiu-ying. *C:* Brian Lai, Cheung Yiu-cho. **VHS, DVD**

Powerful Four

Taking heed of the hit *Lee Rock* films, David Lam produced and directed this piece about policemen in 1960s Hong Kong who have to deal with both the prejudice of their British comrades and the rising heroin trade among the triads while trying to advance through the ranks of a corrupt system.

It begins at the 1989 Singapore funeral of "No-Head" Luk Kong (Danny Lee), as his cohorts "Cunning Tiger" Lui Kit (Simon Yam), "Master" Yiu Hung (Waise Lee), and "Fatty B" Ho Sum (Kent Cheng, all in old-age makeup) come to pay their respects, despite the presence of men from ICAC (Hong Kong Police Internal Affairs Department) investigating Luk. Flashing back, we see how Luk starts as a poor but honest Kowloon constable, until he busts a crook in an opium den that's already paid their protection bribes. Like-minded Mongkok cop Yiu helps him out of the jam, but he's transferred to a marine unit, where he meets the slick-operating Sergeant Major Lui. Lui's influence helps Luk be put in charge of an important kidnapping case. Yiu is put on the case, too, and together they capture the dangerous suspect Laichee (Frankie Chan Chi-leung). Another case is almost ruined when Yiu's old comrade Ho Sum blows his cover, but makes up for it by saving Luk's life. Ho's Cinderella sister-in-law Lee Yim-ping (Yolinda Yan, who is treated as the maid) is shot in the ensuing gunfire, and Luk ends up marrying her. Ho is added to Luk's team, and the four men keep moving up the ladder. Their wealth grows also, as they're asked to become silent partners in a taxi company and other businesses. But cracking down on opium dens inadvertently contributes to the heroin business. Unable to stop the heroin market, the Powerful Four (as they're now called) gather the triad heads so they can at least control it a bit. All along, mobster Sam (Vincent Wan) rocks the boat with his greed and ambition, but this actually helps the quartet make a huge arrest. Following this, each of them becomes the chief of a different district. Sam continues to be trouble—in his pursuit of revenge, he seriously injures Yimping and Lui, and tries to frame Luk for murder. But his actions backfire when the Four use him to trap an even bigger threat.

There's more action here than in *Lee Rock*, especially in the bloody finale, but not nearly as much emotional involvement. Though the cast is very good, the material is a bit dry, and the narrative seems to rush through the years, only hitting on significant highlights, without painting a full picture of events. It's like the Cliff's Notes version of the Powerful Four—the full story could probably only be done justice as a television series. *AKA: Sei Dai Tam Jeung; Si Da Tan Zhang.* 🎵🎵🎶

1991 108m/C *HK* Danny Lee, Simon Yam, Waise Lee, Kent Cheng, Yolinda Yan, Vincent Wan, Mark King, Frankie Chan, Lee Siu-Kei, Alan Chui, Ho Pak Kwong, Gam Biu. **D:** David Lam. **W:** Wong Chi. **C:** Wong Po-man. **M:** Lowell Lo. **VHS, DVD**

Prince of Space

This science-fiction action feature, edited from a serial, borrows shamelessly from the Super-giant serial (shown in the U.S. as a series of Starman movies). Rocket scientist Professor Makin is impressed by assistant Wally (Tatsuo Umemiya), who is raising orphans Miki and Kimi. Apparently rocket scientist's helpers aren't paid much, since Wally and the kids earn their main living as bootblacks. The Ambassador Phantom (Johji Oka) from Planet Krankor interrupts TV broadcasts to announce the aliens' invasion plans, which will begin, he says, the next evening at precisely 8:00. The nifty-looking Krankor ship lands out in the woods and starts disintegrating folks with a death ray. The heroic Prince of Space shows up in his own li'l flying saucer to challenge the invaders, and he chases them away.

Miki and Makin's son Johnny keep watch with their telescope, and spot the aliens as they establish an underground base nearby; naturally, they go take a look. The Prince rescues the kids from the Phantom, and then gives them a special dial to call him with in case they're ever in trouble again. Phantom temporarily abandons efforts to kill Prince and blows up Makin's space rocket, and then captures the scientist and takes him to Krankor. After some boring scenes of Phantom trying to coerce Earth scientists to switch sides, Krankor spies do what Wally's kids can't: they figure out that the Prince of Space poses as a humble shoeshine boy. Finally getting down to business, the space dictator announces plans to destroy a random Earth city the next day unless the Earthlings surrender.

Imported by Bellucci Productions in 1964 for TV and matinee distribution, the main attraction of this standard juvenile superhero flick is the performance of Johji Oka as the Krankor dictator, Phantom. This is fortunate, since he has a lot more screen time than the dull hero. The Krankorians have big noses and pointy heads, and wear lots of antennae on their space helmets. Phantom's leadership status is signified by his shiny cape, ruffles on his uniform, and his hearty laugh. His opulent palace on Krankor comes complete with a giant guardian—though having a guy sitting next to it doesn't do the model any favors. The models and props are all nicely designed, such as the Krankor zap gun with three barrels, and their ship, which features a barber pole cone at the front. The uniforms are less impressive—Prince's helmet looks puffy with boxy details, and the Krankor suits have odd bulges at the joints. It's hard to say whether the Earthlings resist because they cherish their freedom, or just fear having to wear silly Krankor uniforms. Umemiya, born in Manchuria during the occupation, went on to star in dozens of spy and yakuza pictures. *AKA: Yusei Oji; Invaders from Space; Invaders from the Spaceship; The Star Prince.* 🎵🎵🎶

1959 121m/BW *JP* Tatsuo Umemiya, Johji Oka, Hiroko Mine, Ushio Sakashi, Takashi Kanda, Ken Sudoh, Nobu Yatsuma. *D:* Ejiro Wakabayashi. *W:* Shin Morita, Masaru Igami (story). *C:* Masahiko Iimura. *M:* Katsuhisa Hattori. **VHS**

Prince of the Sun

While not in the same league as such fantasies as *The Peacock King,* this is plenty of lighthearted fun. It also offers another opportunity to see Cynthia Rothrock in action in a Hong Kong film, making a pretty good team with Conan Lee.

The Holy Stonehead is stolen from a temple, its guardian killed, and monk Khenlun (Lam Ching-ying) is framed for the crime by lamas of the evil Khentse (Lau Shun). He escapes to Hong Kong, taking with him the latest incarnation of Buddha, a child named Little Chieftain. Not long after getting the boy to a safe place, Khenlun is killed. But his ghost appears to Khenlun's student Bencheuk (Rothrock) to tell her to find Little Chieftain and return him to the temple. Meanwhile, illegal immigrant Tiger (Conan Lee) is trying to help out his cousin Wan May-ngor (Sheila Chan) with her debts to a loan shark, when he meets up with Little Chieftain. Tiger teams up with Bencheuk and Khenlun's ghost to protect the boy from a quartet of Khentse's lamas. And if that wasn't enough trouble, Khentse transforms himself into the demonic King of Hell, and is trying to kill the boy, too.

The most obvious inspiration for this movie is the 1986 American film *The Golden Child,* starring Eddie Murphy. Sheila Chan's shrill comedy is a bit harder to take than Murphy's, but there's plenty of kung fu action here, and the low-tech special effects have a cheesy charm to them. *AKA: Tai Yeung Ji Ji; Tai Yang Zhi Zi.* 🎵🎵♥

1990 (R) 93m/C *HK* Conan Lee, Lam Ching-Ying, Sheila Chan, Cynthia Rothrock, Lau Shun, Gabriel Wong, Wu Fung, Jeff Falcon, Tai Bo. *D:* Wellson Chin. *W:* Lau Jun-wai, Abe Kwong. *C:* Cheung Yiucho. *M:* Wong Bong. **VHS**

Princess Blade

The Takamikzuchi is a clan of royal guards whose status has degenerated to the point of becoming hired assassins. Yuki (absolute idol Yumiko Shaku) is the daughter of Azora, a former leader who was murdered by the ambitious Byakurai (Kyusaku Shimada), who assumed leadership after her death. Turning 20, Yuki is torn between her claim to leadership and a desire to leave the clan. While deciding her course of action, Yuki hides out with Takashi (Hideaki Ito), an idealist who cannot understand the violence of the political Reformist group to which he belongs. He is fascinated by Yuki's ability to kill with indifference, reducing murder to a simple physical gesture. For Takashi, violence is a betrayal of social idealism.

Although set 500 years in the future, *Princess Blade* is not a futuristic film. Based on the comic books of Kazuo Koike and Kazuo Kamimura, it offers plenty of action, with fight choreography by Donnie Yen *(Blade 2, Iron Monkey).* Yen's style is a return to the Bruce Lee method of staying with the lead character rather than trying to capture and define every adversarial motion. The film's final half hour gets overly sentimental, with some wretched new-age piano sweetening the soulful glances between Yuki and Takashi to a sickening degree of schmaltz. The end, however, is satisfyingly bleak. —BW *AKA: Shurayuki Hime.* 🎵🎵🎵♥

2002 86m/C *JP* Hideaki Ito, Yumiko Shaku, Shiro Sano, Yuko Maki, Yoko Chosokabe, Naomasa Musaka, Yutaka Matsushige, Shintaro Sonooka, Takashi Tsukamoto, Yoichi Numata, Kyusaku Shimada. *D:* Shinsuke Sato. *W:* Shinsuke Sato, Kei Kuni. *C:* Taro Kawazu. *M:* Kenji Kawai. **VHS**

Princess Mononoke

Due to master animator Hayao Miyazaki's explicit instructions, his work (and others created by Studio Ghibli) can only be distributed uncut and uncensored—which has been causing great headaches for Disney marketing execs. Though films like the wonderful *My Neighbor Totoro* can be enjoyed by all ages, others like *Mononoke* and *Castle in the Sky* contain some pretty violent—even gory—sequences.

Mononoke is about a young warrior Prince named Ashitaka who becomes infected by a curse while saving his village from a rampaging forest demon. Doomed to a slow death, he sets out on a mission to destroy the source of the evil that's beset him. He finds it in a conflict between the progressive inhabitants of Iron Town, led by the enterprising Lady Eboshi and the godlike forest spirits their mining operation is threatening. Also involved in the complicated plot are a team of hunters led by pragmatic Gonza sent by the emperor to bring back the head of the magical Great Forest Spirit (said to bestow immortality on its owner), labor guilds of former prostitutes and lepers who have found new life running the foundry, and an army set on taking hold of Iron Town and its riches. At the center of all this is Japan's fabled folk heroine San, a princess raised by huge wolves in the forest.

Though complexity is one of the story's strengths—each character is rich and multidimensional—it's also the film's only drawback. Miyazaki is at his best portraying and celebrating the world's simpler joys. Here, he returns to the type of epic fantasy he explored in *Castle in the Sky,* and at times the canvas is too big for even him to keep a grip on. But that's only a very minor complaint. *Mononoke* does so well what a lot of Hollywood epics fail to do—keep the audience involved in the story while knocking them over with visions and wonders. The film is full of gods and monsters and amazing animation effects, but never loses sight of the personal dilemmas it's set up. Is Ashitaka really doomed by his curse? Will San resolve the problems of her dual-species heritage? If the forest gods win, what will become of the good people of Iron Town? These concerns keep the story going, while Miyazaki's artistic skill fills the screen with amazing beauty and imagination. *AKA:* Mononoke Hime. 🐉🐉🐉🐉

1997 (PG-13) 133m/C *JP V:* (English) Claire Danes, Billy Crudup, Minnie Driver, Billy Bob Thornton, Gillian Anderson, Keith David. *D:* Hayao Miyazaki. *W:* Hayao Miyazaki, Neil Gaiman. *C:* Atsushi Okui. *M:* Jo Hisaishi. **VHS, DVD**

Prison on Fire

After the success of *City on Fire,* this similarly titled film quickly followed, although its only direct links are the creative talent. Lo Ka-yiu (Tony Leung Ka-Fai) is sentenced to three years in prison for manslaughter. He finds that prison is a bad, bad place, but that occasionally the men dance together. Ching (Chow Yun-fat) helps him deal with the adjustment. Despite their best efforts to avoid conflict, both men still end up caught in the middle of two warring gangs, led by Bill (Tommy Wong) and Micky (William Ho). Running roughshod over everybody is Boss Hung (Roy Cheung), known to the men as "Scarface." Scarface is possibly the meanest prison guard on the face of the earth. Will Lo Ka-yiu survive his prison term to be reunited with his family and girlfriend?

Prison on Fire is a straightforward drama that is well told for the most part. Some of the incidents seem a bit farfetched—especially the prisoners dancing together to celebrate New Year's Eve. On the other hand, perhaps this is what prison life is really like in Hong Kong. It certainly doesn't look like a picnic in the park. The routine, boredom, and isolation are portrayed in a way that does not seem ordinary. The casual indifference displayed by the guards looks realistic. And the violence that erupts seems entirely justified and understandable. The only false note is sounded occasionally by the character of Ching. He's somewhat unreal at times, like a variation on the free spirit played by Jack Nicholson in *One Flew over the Cuckoo's Nest.* Chow Yun-fat, unfortunately, is a bit too mannered and studiously carefree in the role. Part of that can be attributed to the script and direction, yet Chow must also accept part of the responsibility. Roy Cheung is suitably nasty and repellant as Scarface, but it would have been welcome to see at least a glimmer of humanity in his character. Director Ringo Lam could have taken the easy way out and crafted some sort of sequel to *City on Fire,* but instead he went in a different direction, making a social drama that remains sadly relevant. Writer Nam Yin reportedly had a number of acquaintances in the criminal world, and this may be reflected in the script's details of the treatment of prisoners. The cinematography by San Aau Shing Lip Ying Cho—his only film credit (at least under that unmemorable name)—makes good use of natural light and achieves a documentary look without drawing attention to itself. He also served as editor—Hong Kong comes up with some interesting combinations behind the camera! —*PM* **AKA:** *Gaam Yuk Fung Wan; Jian Yu Feng Yun.* 🐉🐉🐉

1987 102m/C *HK* Chow Yun-fat, Tony Leung Ka-Fai, William Ho, Roy Cheung, Tommy Wong, Victor Hon Kwan, Terrence Fok, Frankie Ng, Shing Fui-on. *D:* Ringo Lam. *W:* Nam Yin. *C:* San Aau Shing Lip Ying Cho. *M:* Lowell Lo. **VHS, DVD**

Prison on Fire 2

Ching (Chow Yun-fat) has 14 months left to serve in his prison term. He is friendly with Bill (Tommy Wong), one of the gang leaders of the prisoners from Hong Kong. Another gang—composed of prisoners from the Mainland—is led by Dragon and his #1 assistant, Skull. Divisions emerge between the two gangs. A new security head, Officer Zau (Elvis Tsui), has been brought in, but he is as cruel and sadistic as his predecessor, and the superintendent is still clueless about what's really going on. A crisis emerges that causes Ching to be concerned about his son, and, despite the short time remaining in his stretch, he becomes determined to break out of prison.

Fights break out more frequently than in the first film, and escapes are attempted more commonly. The brutal guards remain the same, but more emphasis is placed on the desperation of the prisoners. A wider variety of action occurs, and all of it is handled expertly by director Ringo Lam. The violence is not depicted in a choreographed or

graceful way: a thin layer of acquiescence covers a boiling pot of anger. Fists smash into flesh, bones slam painfully into concrete. None of it is pleasant to watch, but the film itself is compelling viewing. Again, though, as with the first film, certain events transpire that are difficult to believe. Chow Yun-fat abandons most of the mannerisms and quirky behavior that marred his performance in the first film and registers strongly as the very human Ching. The cinematography by Faan Chuen-yam has a broader palette and a kinder feel to the lighting. —*PM* **AKA:** *Gaam Yuk Fung Wan II Tiu Faan; Jian Yu Feng Yun II Tao Fan.* 🐉🐉🐉

1991 102m/C *HK* Chow Yun-fat, Chan Chung-Yung, Woo Yiu-chung, Yu Li, Tommy Wong, Elvis Tsui, Frankie Ng, Vincent Wan, Victor Hon Kwan, Terrence Fok. *D:* Ringo Lam. *W:* Nam Yin. *C:* Faan Chuen-yam. *M:* Lowell Lo. **VHS, DVD**

The Prisoner

Jackie Chan, Sammo Hung, Andy Lau, and Tony Leung Ka-fai are all swept to a hellish prison in this disappointing film. *The Prisoner,* better known in most parts of the world as *Island on Fire,* depends mostly on borrowing pieces of well-known—and better made—prison pictures, including large sections of *Cool Hand Luke.* Like *Fantasy Mission Force,* Jackie Chan (and most everyone else) appeared here to repay a favor to producer/star Jimmy Wang Yu, and only has a few fighting bits—though the U.S. release wants you to think he's the star (old cons never die). Andy Lau plays a cop sent undercover as a convict. The best role goes to Sammo as a poor slob trying to fight his way out of a bad situation for the sake of his kid. A big shoot-out fight at the airport can't help this flick out. The film just never seems to make up its mind where it's going or what its story is.

This film is not very good on any level. Even the action scenes are largely disappointing. Take off another half bone if you're not interested in any of the many stars involved. Even then, beware this flick and don't say we didn't warn you. —*SS* **AKA:** *Feng Shiu Do; Huo Shao Dao; The Burning Island; When Dragons Meet; Island on Fire; Island of Fire.* 🐉

1990 96m/C *HK/TW* Jackie Chan, Sammo Hung, Andy Lau, Tony Leung Ka-fai, Jimmy Wang Yu, Barry Wong, Roy Chiao, Yip Chuen Chan. *D:* Chu Yen-ping. *W:* Fu Lee, Yeh Yen-chiao. *M:* Lap Fu. **VHS, DVD**

The Prisoner of Five Boulders

When the emperor comes to town, the local officials (corrupt of course) crack down on the pop-

ulation. Emperor Kangxi is on a lifelong quest to find his father, who abdicated the throne and then disappeared—perhaps into a monastery. His search is made more difficult by general Wayne Ma, who is leading a revolt against the empire. Kangxi holes up in the Five Boulders Temple and disguises himself as the martial arts master Flying Dragon, to secretly go out among the people and further his search. FD takes with him his young assistant, "Beanpole." The Emperor discovers that, because of the corrupt local officials, the people are not very fond of him. As Flying Dragon, he then does a Zorro turn, to set things right. Among the people FD frees are an old monk and his goddaughter. When Wayne Ma claims to know the whereabouts of the missing father, the emperor's advisors send an imposter to negotiate (they believe the real emperor is on retreat in the temple, and must not be disturbed. They are unaware that he is abroad as Flying Dragon.) Ironically, Wayne Ma's forces help Flying Dragon, and this leads to a "friendship" between the disguised emperor and the rebel—which sets up the film's climactic, three-way conflict between loyalists, rebels, and corrupt officials.

The Jalisco label's usual goofy dubbing and lack of proper credits and titles mar this production. One particularly annoying bit of dialogue work telegraphs the whereabouts of the missing father very early in the film—one suspects that this was not the original filmmakers' intent. Production values on the film itself, though, are good. The temples and other location settings are spectacular, worth seeing for the amazing detail. —SS **AKA:** Kang Xi Da Nao Wu Tai Shan; Kangxi Upsets Wutai Mountains. 🐉🐉

1989 87m/C CH George Wang, Yang Dezhi, Zhang Dongsheng. **D:** Yu Deshui. **C:** Wu Benli. **M:** Cheng Dazhau. **VHS, DVD**

The Private Eye Blues

Jacky Cheung plays a down-on-his-luck private investigator in Hong Kong. The office he shares with his partner—who is also his cousin—is shady to the extreme. When a job offer comes to keep an eye on a teenage girl (Mavis Fan) visiting from Mainland China, he can't afford to refuse. The girl quickly develops a crush on him, which is irksome to the shamus. He is estranged from his wife (Kathy Chow)—she is a television reporter and felt that he was trying to hold back her career. He wants to reconcile so he can be together again with his young daughter. Unbeknownst to the detective and his partner/cousin, the Mainland girl has special mental abilities and every bad guy on the island is after her for their own criminal purposes. She

loves spending time in Hong Kong and really doesn't want to return to the Mainland. She's afraid of becoming a human lab rat, so she does everything she can to slip away from her would-be guardian, no matter the danger.

Much of the running time is played for laughs, while tender dramatics and bullet-riddled action jostle for attention. Woven into the story are many common anxieties being experienced by Hong Kong residents in anticipation of the then-looming handover to Mainland China in 1997. On the other hand, the teenage girl's reluctance to return to her home reflected a different set of very real concerns. Writer/director/editor Eddie Fong leans toward moody visuals. Jingle Ma provided the stylish photography. —PM **AKA:** Fai Seung Ching Taam; Fei Chang Zhen Tan; The Privite Eye Blues. 🐉🐉

1994 102m/C HK Jacky Cheung, Kathy Chow, Mavis Fan, Chin Ho, Chan Fai-Hung, Wong Tin Lam. **D:** Eddie Fong. **W:** Eddie Fong. **C:** Jingle Ma. **M:** Teddy Robin Kwan, Lau Lok-sang. **VHS, DVD**

The Private Eyes

Michael Hui was a television star who made a successful transition to films in 1972 (The Warlord for the Shaw Brothers). He directed his first film in 1974 (Games Gamblers Play) and this, his third film as director, found him at the top of his form. Seldom has a plot mattered less—it serves here as a loose framework for a series of comic misadventures. Lee Kwok-kit (Sam Hui) is an aspiring detective. He comes to work for an agency run by Wong Yuk-see (Michael Hui), known as Mr. Boo. Joined by Mr. Boo's put-upon assistant (Ricky Hui), the team takes on cases ranging from marital infidelity to shoplifting to kidnapping.

In most modern American comedies, a straight man sets up the jokes for the funnyman. You have to stretch back to the films of Preston Sturges in the 1940s to find a Hollywood equivalent to The Private Eyes, in which everyone remains straight-faced and nearly all the players get to deliver a punch line or a funny bit of business. The film also manages to deftly weave social commentary into a satirical fabric that never becomes weighed down with self-importance. What matters most are the situations that are setups for the broad comedy of the Hui brothers. As director, Michael Hui does a very good job of staging the visual gags—the "exercising chicken" is especially good, as well as a classic fight in a large commercial kitchen that utilizes every possible weapon at hand, including a large fish (Hui would expand the kitchen mayhem for his later hit Chicken and Duck Talk). Sam Hui's catchy pop songs help demonstrate why he is viewed as the father of

Cantopop. Sammo Hung served as action director, and the few fighting scenes hold up quite well. Familiar faces in the supporting cast include Richard Ng as a police officer and Shih Kien as the leader of a criminal gang. *The Private Eyes* is an influential and highly enjoyable landmark in Hong Kong cinema. —PM *AKA: Boon Gan Baat Leung; Ban Jin Ba Liang; Mr. Boo; Mr. Boo 2: Private Eyes.*

1976 96m/C *HK* Michael Hui, Samuel Hui, Ricky Hui, Richard Ng, Shih Kien, Angie Chiu, Mars, Tsang Choh-lam, Huang Ha, Chan Yam, Eddie Ko, Billy Chan, Che Yuen. **D:** Michael Hui. **W:** Michael Hui. **M:** Samuel Hui. **VHS, DVD**

Prodigal Boxer

Another rediscovered adventure of kung fu's favorite mama's boy, Fong Sai-yuk, in his younger days. Sai-yuk (Meng Fei) and his friends are always getting into street fights. During one such battle, a student from a rival school ends up dead, and his masters blame young Master Fong. While Sai-yuk and his pals are out tracking down a gang of thieves that victimized a woman and her daughter Hsu-pin, brothers Wen (Wong Ching) and Iron Fist Tan (Yasuaki Kurata) come to Sai-yuk's home seeking revenge for their student, and kill the elder Master Fong. Despite efforts by his mother (Maggie Lee) to keep the information from him, Sai-yuk discovers the identities of his father's killers, and goes after them before he's ready. She keeps the evil masters from killing Sai-yuk, and takes him away to recover, planning to train him for a full year before letting him leave. Hsu-pin helps out, but the impatient youth again runs off to face the brothers too soon, and they nearly kill him. This time he endures a full year of herb baths and his mother's grueling training techniques, until she feels he's at last ready to take revenge.

Anticipation for this final duel has been built to the breaking point through multiple defeats and mom's ingenious training devices. A surprising split-screen process is used to illustrate part of the training sequence. One of Mrs. Fong's more brutal devices is merely a long log hanging from a rope—but she uses it to smash into her son at unexpected moments. When the time comes for the big fight, it's delayed yet again, as Fong has to take care of his sick mother. Tan grants him a delay, on condition he crawl through his legs. After all this suffering and humiliation, the villains' comeuppance is supremely satisfying. The fights engineered by Lau Kar-Wing with Wong Pau-gei aren't as amazing as those in Lau Brothers features to come, but there are some neat tricks included, which don't rely on the overdone wirework of Jet Li's Fong Sai-yuk movies *(The Legend).* For an inde-

pendent production, this has a relatively opulent look, with much shooting done at picturesque locations and on slick sets. Much the same plot template has been used in dozens of kung fu features since, notably in *Fist of the White Lotus. AKA: Fang Shiyu; Fong Sai Yuk; The Kick of Death; Kung Fu, the Punch of Death.*

1973 (R) 90m/C *HK* Meng Fei, Maggie Lee, Yasuaki Kurata, Pa Hung, Sun Nan, Shut Ma Wa Lung, Wong Ching, Tung Choi-po, Wong Yee-tin, Tze Lin, Lee Chao-tsien, Lau Kar-Wing, Fung Hark-On, Sunny Yuen, Yuen Cheung-yan, Tino Wong, Hsu Hsia, Lau Kar-Leung, Wong Pau-gei, Alan Chan. **D:** Chai Yang-Ming. **W:** Ngai Hong. **C:** Chao Yung-sin. **M:** Chang Ching. **VHS, DVD**

The Prodigal Son

By this point in his career Sammo Hung had established himself as a star at Golden Harvest, and was taking advantage of his creative freedom to assemble his comrades for projects like this one, which is actually a tale of *two* prodigal sons. Leung Chang (Yuen Biao) is a wealthy young "kung fu fanatic" from Fatshan who has established a reputation as a champion street brawler. However, his reputation is false—unbeknownst to him, his father has instructed his teachers not to give him any advanced instruction and his servant (Chan Lung) pays all his opponents to take dives. Ngai Fai (composer/actor Frankie Chan) is the son of a duke and another fight nut, whose servants (Dick Wei and Chung Fat) have been instructed by his father to kill any opponents who are good enough to hurt his son in a fight. Both sons visit the Chinese opera in Canton to see Leung Yee-tai (Lam Ching-Ying) perform as the beautiful "Lotus Poon." After witnessing Tai skillfully beating up some local thugs, both pursue him as an opponent—but Chang has his deficiencies finally revealed to him, and determines to be accepted as Tai's student. Ngai's match with Tai is interrupted and postponed when the latter suffers an asthma attack, but Tai's superiority is obvious to Ngai's men, who slaughter the entire opera troupe. Tai and Chang manage to escape, and hide out on the farm of Leung's brother Wong Wa-po (Sammo Hung). Taking advantage of the bickering brothers, Chang manipulates them into teaching him their Wing Chun styles—which come in handy in the inevitable duel with Ngai.

Sammo Hung likes to make many of his films feel like a party, and all the gathered guests take turns displaying their talents. Yuen Biao shines in an early starring role, and Sammo gives himself a juicy comic part as the martial arts master with scholarly pretensions. But Lam Ching-Ying steals the whole picture, not only turning in a deft performance as a multilayered character, but also displaying fighting moves beyond any

THE HOUND SALUTES
Sammo Hung

洪金寶

On the night of September 26, 1998, television audiences in the United States were treated to an unexpected sight: a rotund Chinese man moving his body across the screen in a graceful, gravity-defying way. It was the debut of *Martial Law,* a moderately successful series that ran for two seasons and introduced millions of people to Sammo Hung Kam Bo.

The 44 episodes of *Martial Law* never fully showcased the full range of Sammo's abilities. To better appreciate his creative talents and what he has accomplished over a long career, you have to return to his roots. His grandmother, Chin Tsi-ang, broke ground as the first female martial artist in the Hong Kong film business. His grandfather and his parents were also involved in the movie industry. Born in November 1952 in Hong Kong, Sammo began attending the Peking Opera School at the tender age of eight. The intense training focused on martial arts, acrobatics, and discipline, and lasted from morning until past nightfall. Sammo, then known as Yuen Lung, acquired the nickname "Big Brother Big" and was a stern taskmaster to his younger charges. He became the leader of the "Seven Little Fortunes," a school performance group that included Jackie Chan, Yuen Biao, Corey Yuen Kwai, and Yuen Wah.

Even as youngsters, the Fortunes worked in the movies. Sammo first worked with legendary director King Hu when he was in his mid-teens. He remembered being fascinated with watching what the director did, a trait that carried over into every production in which he participated, and helped fuel his desire to be a director. King Hu had elaborate meals every evening, and always invited Sammo. They would stay up all night talking about movies and life. Leaving at 5:00 in the morning, Sammo would head home, take a shower, and return to work.

Sammo's eagerness to accept any stunt assignment no doubt helped him gain steady employment. On one film, he remembered the director asking for someone to do a particularly difficult stunt. Sammo eagerly volunteered, but was rebuffed by the director: "No! I see you in every scene. I need someone else!"

Sammo was not yet 20 when he began working as an action director. Among others, he choreographed action for Michael Hui, King Hu, and John Woo. Even as he built his reputation, he found work for his friends and helped them make a success of their careers.

His directorial debut, *The Iron Fisted Monk* in 1977, included a welcome dollop of humor. But it was his third film that put him on the cinematic landscape. *Enter the Fat Dragon* was both a homage to Bruce Lee (Sammo helped complete *Game of Death* after Bruce died) and a slap in the face to the Lee-imitators then flooding the marketplace. Sammo worked even more broad comedy into *Knockabout,* while still including several ferocious and extended fight scenes.

During the 1980s, Sammo directed, produced, and starred in an amazing number of successful films covering all sorts of genres—and even creating a couple of new ones along the way. To pick just a handful: *Encounter of the Spooky Kind* (supernatural comedy/martial arts), *Project A* (helping establish Jackie Chan as a major filmmaker), *Yes, Madam!* (the first "Girls with Guns" flick), *Eastern Condors* (the Dirty Dozen go to Vietnam), and *Pedicab Driver* (by turns comedic, melodramatic, romantic, and tragic). He demonstrated his range as an actor in *Heart of a Dragon, Eight Taels of Gold,* and *Painted Faces* (in which he played his own sifu from Peking Opera School days). Pick out any film in which his name appears in the credits during the 1980s, and you're just about guaranteed a good time.

The period since 1990 has lowered Sammo's profile somewhat. The financial underachievement of *Pedicab Driver* led to the end of Sammo's association with Golden Harvest and diminished budgets for his films. He has kept busy as an actor, director, and action choreographer, working with Wong Kar-Wai, Tsui Hark, Jackie Chan, Jet Li, and many others.

How to sum up an amazing career that is still ongoing? During the filming of *Martial Law,* Sammo loved to cook lunch, even insisting on making special vegetarian meals for his American assistant. Then they would talk about movies and storytelling, in much the same way that Sammo himself spent long evenings learning from director King Hu three decades before. In that way, and in so many others, Sammo has maintained, changed, and passed on the cinematic traditions of his elders.

—PM

other role in his career. He goes from opera drag to deft comedy to boxing whirlwind with ease—and all without eyebrows (quite a change from his later bushy fame as the mono-browed *Mr. Vampire*). Frankie Chan's character is interesting as well—not at all the traditional villain. Beautifully melded with the characters and story, the kung fu choreography is all red hot, by turns funny and thrilling—the kind of film fighting that gets your blood moving. *AKA: Bai Ga Jai; Bai Jia Zi; Pull No Punches.* 🐕🐕🐕♥

1981 100m/C *HK* Yuen Biao, Lam Ching-Ying, Sammo Hung, Frankie Chan Fan-Kei, Wei Pai, Chan Lung, Dick Wei, Chung Fat, Wu Ma, James Tien, Lee Hoi-sang, Chin Yuet Sang, Cheung Ging Boh, Lam Jing, Lee Man Tai, Wong Hap, Fung Lee, Chin Leung, Chan Hei, Ding Yue, Yuen Miu. *D:* Sammo Hung. *W:* Sammo Hung, Barry Wong. *C:* Ricky Lau. *M:* Frankie Chan, Phil Chan. **VHS, DVD**

Project A

Jackie Chan has always professed his love for silent stars like Buster Keaton, Harold Lloyd, and Douglas Fairbanks, and that was never more apparent than in this swashbuckling adventure set in early Hong Kong. At the time, pirate bands under the control of the dangerous Captain Lo San (Dick Wei) terrorize the islands. The enthusiastic but under-funded Royal Hong Kong Coast Guard is totally helpless against the pirates. When arms dealers supplying the pirates blow up the last Coast Guard ships, the Admiral proposes funding for his Project A to deal with the pirates. Instead, the governor dissolves the Coast Guard and reassigns the sailors to join their rivals in the police force under Captain Chi (Kwan Hoi-san). Proud Sgt. Dragon Ma (Chan) finds himself begrudgingly working under the captain's son, Inspector Tzu (Yuen Biao). When the pair is sent in plain clothes to the posh Hoover Club to search for the criminal Chiang, Chi's regulations prevent them from doing their job, so Ma quits the force to catch his man. Running into his old friend Fei (Sammo Hung), who has become a thief, Ma joins with him to swipe a shipment of rifles from the gunrunners, only to betray Fei by turning them in to the police. The British Rear Admiral comes to deal with the situation, but is abducted by Lo en route. Ma overhears the Secretary of Security as he plots to hand over the rifles as ransom, and scolds the official into reinstating the Coast Guard and approving Project A. While Ma disguises himself as a high-hatted gentleman to infiltrate Lo's island headquarters, Tzu and Fei trail him to stage a raid.

Project A is a milestone film in Chan's career. It was the first time he appeared together with his two Chinese opera brothers, Sammo Hung and Yuen Biao. It's the first time he pre-

pared a series of "ouch-takes" to run under the end credits, having picked up the idea from the *Cannonball Run* films he appeared in. And it was the first time Jackie was nominated for a Golden Horse at the Hong Kong Film Awards. *AKA: A Gai Waak; A Ji Hua; Jackie Chan's Project A; Pirate Patrol.* 🐕🐕🐕🐕

1983 (PG-13) 101m/C *HK* Jackie Chan, Sammo Hung, Yuen Biao, Dick Wei, Tai Bo, Kwan Hoi-san, Mars, Wu Ma, Wong Man Ting, To Siu Ming, Lee Hoi-sang, John Chang, Lau Hak Suen, Wan Fat, Wong Wai, Hon Yee Sang, Kwan Yung Moon, Fung Ging Man, Danny Chow, Yue Tau Wan, Ng Min Kan, Benny Lai, Cheung Wa, Chan Chi-fai, Tin Kai-man, Chin Ka-Lok. *D:* Jackie Chan. *W:* Jackie Chan. *C:* Cheung Yiu-cho. *M:* Michael Lai. **VHS, DVD**

Project A 2

Despite the fact that the "Three Brothers" aren't reunited for this sequel (Sammo Hung and Yuen Biao each were involved elsewhere), Jackie Chan again delivers a wild mix of comedy, action, and breathtaking stunts that is a surefire crowd-pleaser. After an annoying opening sequence of highlights from Part 1 (O.K., we've seen 'em), a half dozen surviving pirates from Lo's gang (including Benny Lai) swears vengeance against Dragon Ma (Chan), and heads for old Hong Kong to make chop suey out of him. Meanwhile, slick "3 Wans" Chun (Lam Wai)—the only Chinese cop in Hong Kong allowed to carry a pistol—has been exposed by the press for having robberies staged to advance his career. To avoid embarrassment, Police Chief Bill Tung (Bill Tung) proposes they phase Chun out of the three beats he covers, replacing him with the hero of Project A: Dragon Ma. His first day on the job, Dragon and his men foil the robbery of two girls (Maggie Cheung and Carina Lau) selling flowers to raise money for mainland patriots. Filing his report, he finds the whole police station corrupt, under the thumb of gangster Tiger Au (Michael Chan). Enlisting the only honest cop, Ho (Kenny Ho), to his Untouchables-like team, Dragon decides to raid Tiger's headquarters. There's one of the film's wildest fights in Tiger's club, which looks sure to have sent a few people to the hospital.

Having gained the respect of his district by locking up Tiger Au, Dragon moves on to provide security at the birthday party for the commissioner's daughter (Regina Kent). Miss Pak (Rosamund Kwan) and the patriots try to steal a diamond necklace, prompting a game of hide-and-seek around the upstairs rooms of the house. After Pak frames Dragon for the theft, an even more elaborate round is played between cops, patriots, Chun and government agents, all hiding from each other all over Maggie's house. The comic homeless pirates are one of the

film's greatest joys, and the game ends with Dragon and Chun handcuffed together, while the pirates try to kill both of them in a hilarious fight across the wonderful sets. Dragon at last makes peace with both the revolutionaries and the pirates, while Chun makes a deal with the Ching government agents, leading to a grand showdown in a construction site. Here, Chan makes use of some hot peppers (almost killing himself gobbling real ones because the fakes never arrived on the set) and borrows some of Buster Keaton's better stunts.

After cracking his skull open in Europe filming *Armor of God,* Chan was looking for a project that would keep him close to home for a while. Instead, he went back in time, transforming the Golden Harvest backlot into 1910 Hong Kong, building incredible sets that still stand today. Instead of his Chinese opera brothers, he surrounds himself with some of the most beautiful actresses and distinctive character actors of the day. There's a bit of a message, in that Dragon Ma sticks to what he knows is right, even with a confusing swirl of factions and ideas, but in the end the emphasis is quite properly on action and comedy. The U.S. version is missing about five minutes of footage. *AKA: A Gai Waak Juk Jaap; A Ji Hua Xu Ji; Project A Part 2.* 𝄞𝄞𝄞𝄞

1987 106m/C *HK* Jackie Chan, Maggie Cheung, Rosamund Kwan, Carina Lau, Lam Wai, Bill Tung, Ray Lui, Lau Siu-ming, Kenny Ho, Kwan Hoi-san, Michael Chan, Mars, Ricky Hui, Tai Bo, Lee Hoi-sang, Johnny Wang, Regina Kent, Bozidar Smiljanic, Ben Lam, Ken Lo, Fan Mui-Sang, Benny Lai, Lui Fong, Kenny Bee, Anthony Chan, Walter Cho, Michael Lai. *D:* Jackie Chan. *W:* Jackie Chan, Edward Tang. *C:* Cheung Yiu-cho. *M:* Michael Lai. **VHS, DVD**

Project A-ko

In the near future, in a city rebuilt after being decimated by a huge meteor, Graviton High School has two new students: 17-year-old A-ko Magami, who possesses superhuman strength, and her ditzy sidekick, C-ko Kotobuki, who is given to fits of extreme emotion and very bad cooking. B-ko Daitokuji, the spoiled but brilliant daughter of a very wealthy business tycoon, decides to fight A-ko for C-ko's companionship, using her allowance to build heavily armed battlesuits she whips up seemingly overnight. In traditional schoolyard bully fashion, B-ko greets the (usually late) A-ko at the school gate every morning to confront her with her latest mecha weaponry, only to be easily trashed by A-ko's superior strength and spirit. Meanwhile, an alien spaceship arrives on Earth with unknown intentions, and hovers over the city. The sexually ambiguous aliens abduct C-ko, claiming she is the lost princess of this perverse alien race. A-ko must go to the rescue, but first she has to fight B-ko in her sexy new super-suit, which is much tougher than her previous creations.

This wild and wacky animated action comedy gets more outrageous with each turn of the plot, while maintaining the vital charm inherent in the chemistry of the three girls. Their minds never wander from typical schoolgirl concerns, even as incredible mayhem erupts all around them. And let this be clear: A-ko and C-ko are very interested in boys. But kept in the sex-segregated environment of an all-girl school most of the time, they fill in the blanks in their natural behavior patterns with the necessary allegiances and jealousies the best they can, resulting in a battle for the best Best Friend. The chemistry works wonderfully for both superpowered action and outrageous comedy—though one suspects that half the gags need further translation. Slyly inserted references imply that A-ko is the daughter of two highly recognized American superheroes—the only explanation offered for her otherwise taken for granted superpowers. Followed by several more adventures, one of which concerns the A-ko, B-ko, and C-ko of an alternate universe. *AKA: Purojukuto A-ko.* 𝄞𝄞𝄞𝄞

1986 (PG-13) 86m/C *JP* *D:* Katsuhiko Nishijima. *W:* Tomoko Kawasaki, Yuji Moriyama, Katsuhiko Nishijima. *C:* Takafumi Arai. *M:* Joey Carbone, Richie Zito. **VHS, DVD**

asians in usa

The Protector

In the mid-1980s, Golden Harvest Studios had Jackie Chan try to break into the American market for the second time. Unfortunately, their partners at Warner Bros. intended to market him as an Asian Dirty Harry. Director James Glickenhaus *(The Exterminator)* had no idea and no interest in learning how to make a Jackie Chan film, resulting in a mixed bag of missed opportunities and entertaining weirdness.

Chan stars as tough NYPD detective Billy Wong. When Billy's partner is killed in a South Bronx holdup, he's teamed with slob Danny Geroni (a hilariously foul-mouthed Danny Aiello). Billy and Danny are assigned to the case of kidnapped Mafia princess Laura Shapiro (Sean Ellis). It turns out Hong Kong drug king Harold Ko (Roy Chiao) is behind the kidnapping, having had a falling out with his partner Shapiro, and Billy and Danny head for HK to investigate. Convinced the two troublemakers are working for Shapiro, Ko sends assassins after them. But the cops discover Ko's heroin factory onboard a ship, and make plans to rescue the girl and bring down Ko's operation.

Glickenhaus's style doesn't quite work, though there's still plenty of satisfying action sequences, notably Chan's inventive chase around the harbor, and the final duel with Bill "Superfoot" Wallace. It's just not up to the standards set by films like *Project A*. Unwilling to tolerate the film's problems, Chan decided to recut the film for Hong Kong distribution, eliminating the cursing and nudity, and adding extra footage of fight scenes, bomb defusing, etc. But the addition of more dramatic scenes makes his portrayal of Wong even more serious. The U.S. version retains a certain sleazy B-movie atmosphere, but it's in no way preferable to having more Jackie Chan, even in a disjointed patchwork movie. After his bad experience here, a determined Chan went to work on his own *Police Story*. Fun fact: karate champ Wallace can kick with only one foot due to an injury he suffered while in the military. *AKA: Wai Lung Maang Tam; Wei Long Mang Tan.* 🐉🐉🐉

1985 (R) 91/87m/C *US/HK* Jackie Chan, Danny Aiello, Roy Chiao, Bill Wallace, Sean Ellis, Moon Lee, Peter Yang, Shum Wai, Sally Yeh (*HK* version), Lee Hoi-sang (*HK*). *D:* Jackie Chan (*HK*). *W:* James Glickenhaus, Edward Tang (*HK*). *C:* Mark Irwin, Ardy Lam, Johnny Koo, Jimmy Leung, Cheung Yiu-cho (*HK*). *M:* Ken Thorne. **VHS, DVD**

Pulgasari

Pulgasari was made in Communist North Korea in the mid-1980s. While the film is credited to director Chong Gon Jo (the film is his only credit), the IMDb also lists a director named Shin Sang-ok. Shin claimed that he and his wife were kidnapped from South Korea in the late 1970s and forced to make movies for Kim Jong II, the son of the famous North Korean leader. The special effects are produced by members of the Godzilla team, and indeed actor Kenpachiro Satsuma (who has portrayed the Big G since 1984) portrays the film's monster, Pulgasari. Just what Japanese technicians were doing working on a film for the hated North Korean regime would probably make a far more interesting story than the one obtained in *Pulgasari*.

Pulgasari plays out very much like a North Korean remake of the venerable feudal Japanese horror tales of *Daimajin*. The story is set in a feudal village whose farming inhabitants are oppressed by a brutal warlord (Pak Yong-hok). Rather than sending off for seven samurai, an elderly blacksmith (imprisoned and dying after an attack by government troops on the village) curses the king and with his dying breath asks the gods to grant him vengeance. He holds a small metal figurine, which is granted life just

as he expires, becoming the Pulgasari of the title. The Pulgasari has a taste for metal and as it devours swords and farm implements, it grows from the size of a hand to midget height, then eventually the size of a full-grown man. It swiftly becomes the protector of the blacksmith's son and daughter and begins confronting the troops of local governor General Fuan (Ri Riyonun), and as it gobbles up their weapons it finally reaches conventional Japanese monster size of around a hundred feet tall. Thereafter the film is concerned with the king's and General Fuan's attempts to deal with the creature before it lays waste to the countryside. Hordes of troops are sent against the beast to no avail, leading to this exchange of dialogue: General Fuan: "Is THAT the strength of the government fighting force?!?" Troops (in unison): "We are ashamed!"

Pulgasari is a strange mix of *The Seven Samurai*, *Spartacus*, and *Godzilla*, but it has to be said that it comes nowhere near the accomplishments of any of those precedents. The performances (even acknowledging that these are North Korean actors speaking in their native language) are positively purple, and while there are thousands of people in the battle sequences (probably literally performing at gunpoint) the directors do little more than pan the camera over the action with little rhyme, reason, or style. The Pulgasari monster is combined with these crowd scenes via the miracle of terrible rear screen projection, and the miniature work doesn't get up to snuff until near the film's climax when the monster reaches its full height. Shin Sang-ok eventually moved to the U.S., changed his name to Simon Sheen, and made the juvenile 3 Ninjas movies, plus scripted a semi-remake called *Galgameth*. The video packaging proudly proclaims "Banned for a Decade!" on the front, while the back deems *Pulgasari* "Suitable for ages 7 and up." —JB *AKA: Pulgasari: The Legendary Monster; Giant Monster Pulgasari.* 🐉🐉

1985 104m/C *KO* Hui Chang-son, Sop Han Gi, Ri Jong-uk, Ri Gwon, Ri Riyonun, Pak Yong-hok, Kenpachiro Satsuma. *D:* Chong Gon Jo, Shin Sang-ok. *W:* Kim Se Ryun. *C:* Hyon Cho-myong. **VHS**

Pulse

Spooky. Michi (Kumiko Aso) is worried about Taguchi (Kenji Mizuhashi), her co-worker at Sunny Plant Sales, a small business. Taguchi has taken a computer disc home to complete some important work, but has not been returning phone calls. Michi visits and finds him acting a bit strange. She locates the computer disc, turns around, and sees that Taguchi has hanged himself. Michi and her co-workers Junko (Kurume

Arisaka) and Yabe (Masatoshi Matsuo) are unsettled further when a weird photograph suddenly pops up on the computer disc. Yabe receives a phone call and hears a voice asking for help; he decides to take another look around Taguchi's apartment, and then things get really strange.

In a parallel story, university student Ryosuke Kawashima (Haruhiko Kato) dials up the Internet for the first time and shortly thereafter is awakened by the computer turning itself on and surfing to a web site where disturbing images appear along with a message: "Would you like to meet a ghost?" Kawashima enlists the assistance of computer student Harue (Koyuki), and also listens to the theories of graduate student Yoshizaki (Shinji Takeda). The latter created a computer program based on the constantly shifting relationships of human beings. Eventually, the two stories merge as Michi and Kawashima go as far as they can with their investigation.

Kiyoshi Kurosawa (Cure, Charisma) uses the supernatural as a means of addressing the universal themes of isolation, loneliness, and life after death. He often frames the characters in medium shots, keeping them at arm's length. When he uses close-ups, they tend to discomfit the viewer. The music and sound effects—or lack thereof—play an important role in generating psychological tension. The way that sound is used in one scene is particularly startling. The tightly constructed story sags in the second half as certain tricks are repeated to lesser effect. Your suspension of disbelief may be strained to the breaking point by the apocalyptic tone. Still, while hiding under your covers, you have to admire what the filmmakers created—and shudder just a bit. A word of advice—for those susceptible to nightmares, it may be best to leave the lights on. —PM **AKA:** Kairo; The Circuit. 🐉🐉♡

2001 118m/C JP Haruhiko Kato, Kumiko Aso, Koyuki, Kurume Arisaka, Masatoshi Matsuo, Shinji Takeda, Jun Fubuki, Shun Sugata, Kenji Mizuhashi, Sho Aikawa, Koji Yakusho, Hassei Takano, Masayuki Shionoya. **D:** Kiyoshi Kurosawa. **W:** Kiyoshi Kurosawa. **C:** Junichiro Hayashi. **VHS**

Queen's High

Cynthia Khan stars as a triad princess in this uneven crime drama, which is punctuated by one classic scene. Kahn is Kwanny Yeung, daughter of a prominent triad boss, who thinks nothing of the gangland activities going on around her, concentrating on her upcoming wedding to Peter. But rival gangster Chau Yung (Shum Wai) murders her dad, throwing a dark cloud on her plans. To avenge their father, Kwanny's brother Chung (Simon Yam) invades a high-profile auction and executes Chau. Chau's men

regroup, and ambush Kwanny's wedding party as they leave the church, killing Peter and Chung. With blood spattered across her white dress, Kwanny hefts a handy machine gun and lays waste to the assassins.

Queen's High, an otherwise routine gangster flick, is worth seeing for this wedding scene alone, which runs in slow motion for almost the entire sequence—just like any other cherished wedding day memory. It would've been nice if director Chris Lee had kept Khan in her bloody wedding dress for the subsequent raid on enemy headquarters, as Kwanny learns her half brother engineered all this trauma in an attempt to get control of the family business. However, we have to settle for seeing Khan in black leather pants in a too-brief battle with Kim Penn. Simon Yam is disappointingly restrained in his stereotypical role. This video might make the perfect gift for your next bridal shower. Often misrepresented as part of the In the Line of Duty series. **AKA:** Gung Fan Chi Chuen; Gong Fen Zhi Zun; In the Line of Duty: A Beginning. 🐉🐉♡

1991 85m/C HK Cynthia Khan, Simon Yam, Kenneth Tsang, Shum Wai, Billy Chow, Chris Lee, Kim Penn, Cha Chuen-yee, Wong Yung, Newton Lai, Gam Biu, Wai Lit, Leung Chi On, Nicky Li, Suen Gwok-ming. **D:** Chris Lee. **W:** Kong Heung-sang, Shum Wai. **C:** Lau Hung-chuen. **M:** Richard Lo, Tang Siu-lam. **VHS**

Raat

Director/writer Ramgopal Varma must be a big horror fan, as a variety of European and American fright flick influences are readily apparent in his work. The mobile camera work of Dario Argento, the moody lighting and framing of Mario Bava, the unexpected jolts that come with the best work of Tobe Hooper and John Carpenter, and the eerie sense that the familiar world is turning upside-down which George Romero conveys so well—all these are combined here, with enough original style to avoid an overemphasis on homage. Without the inclusion of song-and-dance numbers (a rarity in Indian films), Varma makes the most of his lengthy running time to draw the viewer into the story at a natural pace.

A typical teenage girl named Minnie (Revathi) moves into a haunted house with her family, and soon becomes possessed by an evil spirit. When she turns violent, her father (Akash Khurana) tries to deal with the situation using modern medicine, while her mom (Rohini Hattangadi) seeks the help of exorcist Tantrik (Om Puri). Yes, we've seen it before, but not quite in this way. To see this type of film set in India is as offsetting to Westerners as Minnie's new house is to her. The unusual setting, as well as the director's obvious talent, gives this one a bit

of staying power. One imaginative scene takes place in one of India's cavernous movie theatres, where the camera zooms in on the heroine in the middle of the laughing crowd. Things go quiet, and we zoom back to see that she's alone. In a daze she wanders to the manager's office, and is shocked to see herself sitting there—then she's back in the theatre with her friends. Many such scenes are used to keep the viewer off balance, with old ideas given a new twist. Little children like Minnie's brother Bunty (Master Ateet) are often used to add an edge to horror films, mixing their seeming innocence and vulnerability with a sense that perhaps they're not really so innocent. But never has a little kitten been used to instill so much fright as it is here. The *second* exorcist character, who is consulted by Tantrik for help with the crisis, is nothing like any ghostbuster usually seen in these pictures, and his introduction scene is quite spooky.

An interesting subtext of the film is the globalization of youth culture. While her parents and other adults follow traditional Indian customs and dress, Minnie and her friends are as alarming as any teen. They skip school, hate math, wear New Kids on the Block T-shirts, listen to Michael Jackson on a Walkman, and read *Mad* magazine. Minnie is scolded by her mother for staying up late watching Jack Sholder's *The Hidden* on TV. No wonder it takes a while to go from "who is my daughter?" to "my daughter is a supernatural beast from Hell!" Not that they can be blamed much—Minnie's possession isn't readily apparent, but when the demon strikes (on a day trip far from home, significantly) the shocks are sudden and violent. The climax seems a bit abrupt following the film's slow build up, and Varma doesn't really have the f/x available to him to give it the proper punch. But this is one of the better horror films to come out of India, unlike any produced by Bollywood up to that time. *AKA: Raatri; Night.* 🐾🐾🐾🦴

1991 129m/C *IN* Revathi, Om Puri, Rohini Hattangai, Anant Naag, Akash Khurana, Khushant, Master Ateet. *D:* Ramgopal Varma. *W:* Ramgopal Varma. *C:* Rajendra Prasad, Sameer, Shyam. *M:* Mani Sharma. **DVD**

Rage of the Dragon

Young Wong Kwai gives a man a good thrashing for accusing Master Wong of being a grave robber. Well, we see soon after that Master Wong was indeed hanging around the graveyard—he claims to have caught a real grave robber and consults with antiquities expert Master Lee about the loot the man dug up. While the two men argue about whether Wong can keep sacred relics stolen years ago from the temple, an ugly man in red attacks, killing Lee and Wong and taking the relics. Lee's son Leung (Dragon Lee), who has been off studying kung fu, is notified by servant Chang that his father is missing and comes home. On the way, they learn that Wong Kwai, along with his brother Kok and his servant Shen Tak, believe that Master Wong was killed by Master Lee, and are raising hell about it. A key figure in this disagreement is Master Kwan (Carter Wong, dubbed with a Texas accent), whose help is sought by both of the feuding young masters.

With so few characters to choose from, it's really not much of a surprise when the killer is revealed less than an hour into the movie. It was Wong's own brother Wong Chan wearing a mask, working for greedy Master Kwan, who kills Chan to tie up loose ends. The surprise comes when Lee Leung finds out about it, and Kwan not only beats the hero, but spares his life for the sake of his sister Mei-ling, who has fallen for Leung. This gives Leung a chance to remember Kwan's weakness and come back prepared. It's not much of plot, and due to the poor photography, it's not pretty to look at. The story only serves to provide plenty of kung fu opportunities. Even the action is mediocre, but as usual, director Godfrey Ho brings in some gimmicks to try to make up for the dull choreography. Wong Kok carries a cane that extends into a pole, there's the haunted cave, and during the final fight Carter Wong and his men all don identical red suits and hoods—so that Dragon Lee doesn't know which man he wants to kill. As usual with Godfrey Ho/Joseph Lai pictures, most of the credits are made up. *AKA: Mission for the Dragon; The Dragon of Kung Fu.* 🦴

1979 90m/C *TW* Carter Wong, Dragon Lee, Martin Chiu, Sheila Kim, Burt Lim, Roger Wong, Danny Tsui, Mark Liang, Samuel Fong, Pak Fen, Jeffrey Hsui, Thomson Mak. *D:* Godfrey Ho. *W:* Robert Szeto. *C:* Jimmy Yu. *M:* Ricky Chan. **VHS, DVD**

Rage of the Masters

Fang (James Lee) runs an honorable martial arts academy, but his crooked brother Lou (Tin Yau) still bears a grudge for being kicked out years ago, and returns to take over. He brings with him hired Thailand boxer Ngai Mi (Lung Fei) and his gang (all of whom wear silly little red shorts). Only daughter Yun-ku (Chiao Chiao) escapes the massacre, running to Uncle Chow's to tell her brother Lee, who vows revenge. Their cousin Chang (Hong Hoi) and Uncle Chow seek out a friend for help, an experienced fighter named Tiger Wong (Jimmy Wang Yu). But Tiger has promised his mother (Cheung Bing Yuk) to

honor his father's dying wish that he never use his skills for fighting again, and he has to turn them down. But Tiger has fallen for Yun-ku at first sight, and is torn between her wishes and his promise. Meanwhile, Lou has opened an "amusement park" in the school, complete with acrobats, gambling tables, a knife thrower, and cockfights. He sends Eagle Chang and his gang to track down Lee and Yun-ku. After Chang sacrifices himself to save his cousins, Mrs. Wong releases her son from his vow, and Tiger unleashes his rage, going out after the blood of Lou and his gang.

This is a pretty standard kung fu brawler, padded with several matches with the Thai boxers midway, with minimal plot and mediocre fighting—that is, until Jimmy Wang Yu is let loose to chop his way through a platoon of enemies, at which point the excitement level goes up several notches. His double-knife fight through a room full of armed opponents is incredible—fake or not, somebody had to get hurt with all those slicing daggers. The dubbing is particularly bad, sounding like it was scripted and performed by a high-school drama class. There are also some clumsy wirework gags that are actually kind of cute. *AKA: Wai Jan Sei Fong; Wei Zhen Si Fang; The Hero; Rage of the Tiger.* 🐾🐾🐾

1974 C: *HK* Jimmy Wang Yu, Chiao Chiao, Tin Yau, Cho Kin, Cheung Bing Yuk, Shan Mao, Cheng Fu Hung, Hong Hoi, Sit Hon, Hon Kong, James Lee, Lung Fei. **D:** Wong Hung Chang. **C:** Liu Man Min. **M:** Chow Luen. **VHS, DVD**

Raiders of Wu Tang

Rarely seen until its retitled video release, this kung fu epic hides a secret treasure: the cast includes the Crippled Masters Frankie Shum and Jack Conn, the martial arts masters with birth defects. The 24 Bronze Horses of Shaolin (possibly created to build a carousel for the 18 Bronzemen) are found to be too dangerous for the students to practice with and are locked away. Shum and Conn play two monks who ventured into the forbidden chamber to face the mechanical horses, and lost some arms and legs. Some students and monks think the horses should be revealed, to prepare Shaolin for attack from the Ching Dynasty government. Din, the drunken groom who minds the temple's horse ranch, thinks differently. But the Ching Lord (Pai Ying) is determined to destroy Shaolin. Master Wisdom (Chan Siu-pang) leaves on a pilgrimage to meet masters from the other clans that will join the fight against the Ching. However, both the Ho Mei and Wa Shen clansmen, having received a forged challenge planted by the governor, just want to fight with him, and Wu

Tang assassins try to kill him on the road. Failing to either beat Wisdom or get the clans to fight each other, the lord sends for Tibetan lamas to destroy the other clans one by one.

Meanwhile, armless Wu-tan and his legless chum plan to break into the chamber of the 24 Bronze Horses once again, and train cowboy Fao Shu-lou (Sonny Yue) to face the challenge. Fao, known as Little Lou to his friends, trains hard, but is still badly injured on one of his early trips to the forbidden chamber. But as Little Lou faces the horses again, the Ching guards attack the temple in force.

Well paced and exciting, this is one of Godfrey Ho's best pictures. He does a good job of building dread for the robot horses, making their eventual appearance more effective. The horses themselves are inspired creations, fearsome and active without looking silly. There are plenty of other creative gimmicks on hand—the lamas attack with razor sharp cymbals, which they use to deafen the monks before using them to slice off ears and arms. The accompanying guards wear kinky white outfits with hoods, and fight with serrated hand blades. The kung fu is pretty good, too, with Sunny Yue and choreographer Chan Siu-pang contributing some of the best moves. And of course, Shum and Conn lend their talents, as actors as well as freak-show attractions for a change. The Taiwanese locations reveal themselves every time a palm tree appears at Shaolin Temple. *AKA: Siu Lam Nim Sei Lau Ma; Shao Lin Nian Si Liu Ma; Raiders of the Shaolin Temple; Raiders of Shaolin; 24 Shaolin Moves; 24 Bronze Horses; Le Guerriers de Shaolin.* 🐾🐾🐾

1982 89m/C *TW* Sonny Yue, Chan Siu-pang, Chao Yung Hsing, Pai Ying, Frankie Shum, Jack Conn. **D:** Godfrey Ho. **W:** Chung Fuk Man. **C:** Wu Hoi Shan. **M:** Wang Mao Sam. **VHS**

Ran

Another masterpiece from Akira Kurosawa, the god of Asian cinema. Like *King Lear* (upon which it is based), *Ran* tells the story of an aging Lord Hidetora Ichimonji (Tatsuya Nakadai) and the heirs competing for his throne. The king eschews his honest but gruff son in favor of his other children—manipulative sycophants interested only in power and their own aggrandizement. Like his Shakespearean counterpart, the king quickly regrets this decision. Suddenly a powerless stranger in his own kingdom, the king falls from the heights of glory into poverty and madness, and his kingdom does the same.

Everything about this film is superb, from the acting, to the sets, to the music, to the costumes, to the cinematography. And, of course, it's all framed with Kurosawa's masterful eye

and told with amazing deftness and utmost use of the film medium. One expects a lot from Kurosawa, and once again the master delivers. There's a battle scene in the middle of the film that's every bit as powerful and shattering as anything in *Saving Private Ryan*, and not a note of false emotion or schmaltz in the whole picture. *Ran* is *not* a happy story, and its tone perhaps reflects the aging filmmaker's pessimism about the world. Still, it is an amazing work of art and not to be missed by any fan of film, either Eastern or Western. Movies don't get better than this. —SS **AKA:** *Chaos.* ♫♫♫♫

1985 (R) 160m/C *JP* Tatsuya Nakadai, Akira Terao, Jinpachi Nezu, Daisuke Ryu, Mieko Harada, Yoshiko Miyazaki, Masayaki Yui, Kazuo Kato, Peter, Jun Tazaki, Norio Matsui, Hisashi Igawa, Takeshi Kato. **D:** Akira Kurosawa. **W:** Masato Ide, Akira Kurosawa, Hideo Oguni. **C:** Asakazu Nakai, Takao Saito, Masaharu Ueda. **M:** Toru Takemitsu. **VHS, DVD**

Rashomon

For the average American of the early 1950s, *Rashomon* would be the first inkling that Asian cinema even existed. Winner of several top film-festival awards and recipient of the Best Foreign Film Oscar, Akira Kurosawa's masterpiece went on to a successful art-house run in larger U.S. cities, and an English-dubbed reissue even made it into some drive-ins. Both a profound art film and an intriguing mystery yarn, it's easy to see why it's been so popular all these years. Based on Ryunosuke Akutagawa's story *In a Grove,* the story draws us in immediately. Three men take refuge from a downpour under the questionable shelter of a burned-out building. Hard times have befallen Japan—bandits, plague, earthquakes, and general chaos have ruled the land—but a priest (Minoru Chiaki) and a woodsman (Takashi Shimura) shake their heads at the awful story they've heard, and naturally the third man (Kichijiro Ueda) wants to hear it (as do we). Three days before, the priest saw a man (Masayuki Mori) and woman (Machiko Kyo) enter the forest. Later, the woodsman found the man dead. The next day, a constable (Daisuke Kato) catches notorious bandit Tajomaru (Toshiro Mifune) with the dead man's weapons and horse. The bandit admits luring the couple off the road, and then seducing the woman while her husband was tied to a tree. But he says the man was killed in an honorable duel that his wife insisted on. The wife claims it was *she* who killed her husband in a fit of madness, unable to stand the hatred in his eyes after the bandit assaulted her. Incredibly, a psychic (Fumiko Honma) is brought into court so that the dead man's ghost can tell his side of the story: he committed suicide after his wife turned against him. Adding to the confusion, one of the witnesses then claims to have lied—he saw the whole thing, and after the woman showed contempt for both men, one killed the other during the wimpiest, most cowardly fight scene ever filmed outside a comedy.

Even after all that, Kurosawa and company still have a few more tricks of drama and shots of philosophy to take at the expense of humanity at large. With a cast of only eight and minimal settings, *Rashomon* (named after the ruined town where it takes place) appears simple, but is like a logic puzzle that sends the mind reeling down a multitude of paths. Each story fits the "facts" as presented, and Kurosawa leads us to question our faith in any witness—even the director, who is just as likely to be lying to us as anyone else. Perhaps a first-rate forensics team and coroner could provide better evidence, but those luxuries aren't available at the crime scene in the 11th century. And as anyone who has sat on a jury can tell you, most cases such as this come down to judging which party is lying the least. We're left to wonder: Is Kurosawa offering a vision of hope at the end, or is it a dark joke that he's chuckling over somewhere behind the camera? *AKA: Rasho-Mon; In the Woods.* ♪♪♪♪

1950 88m/BW *JP* Toshiro Mifune, Machiko Kyo, Masayuki Mori, Minoru Chiaki, Takashi Shimura, Kichijiro Ueda, Fumiko Honma, Daisuke Kato. *D:* Akira Kurosawa. *W:* Akira Kurosawa, Shinobu Hashimoto. *C:* Kazuo Miyagawa. *M:* Fumio Hayasaka. **VHS, DVD**

The Razor 1: Sword of Justice

With his incredible Zatoichi series running to a halt in 1972, producer/actor Shintaro Katsu turned his energies to two series based on samurai stories by Kazuo Koike. The Lone Wolf and Cub movies, starring Katsu's brother Tomisaburo Wakayama, took the artistic presentation of violence to new extremes. The Razor series, in which he played the lead himself, took things to extremes in all sorts of ways.

Katsu plays Hanzo "the Razor" Itami, a district police officer in Edo who takes the duties of his office seriously—so seriously that he refuses to swear to an oath of duty offered by his corrupt superior, Chief Constable Onishi, whose

Toshiro Mifune and Machiko Kyo are lovers—or enemies—or something—in Kurosawa's great exploration into our perception of reality, *Rashomon*.
THE KOBAL COLLECTION / DAIEI

idea of police work is to arrest the poor so that the nobility can walk the streets without having to look at them. After his display of open defiance, he knows he has to nail Onishi quickly. Fortunately, he has a lead: Kanbei, a hired killer arrested by Onishi years ago, has been spotted running loose by one of Hanzo's informers. If he can get proof that Kanbei is still alive and doing some political dirty work, Hanzo can gain the upper hand.

Compared to the charming but deadly Zatoichi, Hanzo is just plain insane. His methods of investigation are certainly the most unusual in cinema history. His lair is a maze of secret weapon caches and death traps. A master of interrogation techniques, he insists on a regimen of masochistic tortures, such as piling hundreds of pounds of stone on his legs, so that he can better understand the pain he inflicts. But that's just the tip of the outrageous iceberg. A master swordsman in more ways than one, Hanzo keeps his greatest—and biggest—weapon tucked beneath his kimono. He gives his nightstick a daily workout that involves beating it with a board and pounding it into a bag of rice. His technique is to use his peacemaker on female suspects, making them his personal sex slaves.

More *Shaft* than *Shogun*, *The Razor* bounces along to a funky theme, the Get Down music swelling every time Hanzo starts to question a lady in his own special way. There's also some terrific action, gadgetry, evidence tattooed on a woman in flesh-colored ink, and more wild surprises, all delivered with deadpan seriousness and strange camera angles by longtime Katsu collaborator Kenji Misumi. Japanese filmmakers would take things way too far within a few years, displaying a fascination with rape fantasy disturbing to most Western viewers, but Katsu still has enough class to keep his tongue in cheek, while taking things a few steps beyond the borders of Batman and James Bond. *AKA: Goyokiba; Sword of Justice; Fangs of the Detective.* 🗡🗡🗡

1972 90m/C *JP* Shintaro Katsu, Yukiji Asaoka, Mari Atsumi, Ko Nishimura, Akira Yamauchi, Kamatari Fujiwara, Kooji Kobayashi, Zembe Saga, The Chambara Trio, Renji Ishibashi, Teruo Matsuyama, Tadashi Iwata, Ichiro Yamamoto, Takahiro Tamura. **D:** Kenji Misumi. **W:** Kazuo Koike. **C:** Chikashi Makiura. **M:** Kunihiko Murai. **VHS**

The Razor 2: The Snare

Shintaro Katsu is back as Hanzo "the Razor" Itami, old Edo's most unusual—and unusually endowed—district police constable. When Hanzo, along with deputies Onibi and Mamushi, chase a pair of suspects right into a procession of samurai, he runs afoul of Lord Okubo, the Shogunate Treasurer. Okubo orders his master swordsman Junai Mikoshiba to kill Hanzo—under the proper, non-official procedure of a personal dispute, of course. But after a small demonstration, Okubo aborts the duel to let Hanzo off with a warning. When Hanzo continues to be obstinate, he's warned of a more official punishment. Speaking of abortions, the two suspects lead Hanzo to a victim of a botched one in an old mill. Daring to enter the abortion shrine leads Hanzo to the convent at Kaizanji Temple. Sneaking into the convent inside a casket, Hanzo digs his way out of a grave to discover Priestess Nyokaini running a sex-slave auction for her patrons among the nobles. The Razor busts up the place, crashing through walls to roust the perverts, and takes Nyokaini into custody for one of his special interrogations.

Summoned before the district commissioner with chief constable Onishi Magobei, Hanzo accuses Okubo for most of the trouble in his district due to his issuance of debased currency. The commissioner directs the constable to arrest Shobei Hamajima, public enemy #1. To lay a trap, Hanzo invades the personal space of Riku, Mistress of the House of Goto mint. But Hanzo's mission there involves much more than capturing a dangerous thief.

Though the Razor series is about a righteous law officer, it embodies the late 1960s spirit of rebellion—rare in chambara movies, which are usually about upholding tradition and honor. Katsu's Zatoichi films often featured his hero bringing down corrupt officials, but Hanzo is dedicated to rooting out hypocrisy and corruption in every institution, using the most unconventional of weapons to do his rooting. This entry also delves into the "nunsploitation" genre, a wave of movies that swept through international exploitation cinema of the time, while remaining unknown in America. Tomita contributes an ahead-of-its-time score full of electronic effects, funky guitar, and feedback. *AKA: Goyokiba: Kamisori Hanzo Jigokuzeme; Hanzo the Razor's Torture from Hell.* 🗡🗡🗡⯪

1973 89m/C *JP* Shintaro Katsu, Ko Nishimura, Toshio Kurosawa, Kazuko Ineno, Kei Sato, Hosei Komatsu, Keiko Aikawa, Masami Muneta, Daigo Kusano, Keizo Kanie, Mori Kishida, Yoshio Inaba, Hitoshi Takagi, Yoshio Omori, Ichiro Yamamoto, Jun Katsumura, Takuya Kitano, Ooe Teruko, Keiko Koyanagi, Jun Fujikawa. **D:** Yasuzo Masamura. **W:** Yasuzo Masumura, Kazuo Koike (story), Takeshi Kanda (story). **C:** Kazuo Miyagawa. **M:** Isao Tomita. **VHS**

The Razor 3: Who's Got the Gold?

Onibi and Mamushi, the two loyal assistants to Constable Hanzo Itami (Shintaro Katsu), spy a ghost while fishing near the Shogunate Treasury building, and the Razor goes to investigate, hoping to have sex with the specter! He succeeds in capturing the ghost—or rather, the girl disguised as a ghost—and find that she's been guarding a treasure in gold pieces hidden beneath the water. During one of Hanzo's special interrogations, the woman reveals that her treasury guard husband was the one who made her play ghost—but she becomes a real ghost before she can say more, killed by ninjas who have invaded Hanzo's headquarters. Her own husband Chozaburo Kato is the killer, and Hanzo tries to keep him alive for questioning, but nearly all the invaders are killed in the raid. Surprisingly, Hanzo is commended for his efforts by Commissioner Yabe for a change, but he's troubled by the dire straits that led the treasury guards to steal. Rejecting the orders of Lord Hotta, he hides former physician Sugino,

who claims he can save Japan by adopting Western ideas like steam engines. Hanzo is obviously open to new ideas—his aides were using flashlights a few scenes previous—and has Sugino get to work on a new cannon. In the meantime, Hanzo follows the money, and learns that not only is High Priest Ishiyama behind the treasury robbery, but is also a loan shark and throws regular orgies for the nobles' wives. He also learns that his old friend Heisuke is one of the samurai borrowers. When Ishiyama's bodyguard Tonami kills Heisuke to get his family's valuable antique spear, Hanzo puts into action a plan to catch all the rascals in his web.

Though not as deliriously carnal or violent as its predecessors, the third *Razor* film still has a good deal of wit, especially when dealing with Hanzo's two ex-con aides and his sniveling boss, Chief Constable Magobei Onishi. Still, the series was evidently running out of new twists, and this one plays more like an extended episode of a Razor TV series than a feature production. But as the story demonstrates, the era of the blade was quickly giving way to the era of the gun. *AKA: Goyokiba: Oni no Hanzo Yawahada Koban; Haunted Gold.* ♪♪♪

1974 88m/C *JP* Shintaro Katsu, Mako Midori, Ko Nishimura, Etsushi Takahashi, Asao Koike, Mikio Narita, Keizo Kanie, Daigo Kusano, Akira Yamauchi. *D:* Yoshio Inoue. *W:* Yasuzo Masamura, Kazuo Koike (story), Takeshi Kanda (story). *C:* Chikashi Makiura. *M:* Hideaki Sakurai. **VHS**

The Real Bruce Lee

For an actor who starred in only four feature films, it's a tribute to his importance as a star that so many film titles have featured his name, including several documentaries and two biopics. This one is not much more than a scrapbook compilation of clips, presented with little preamble, and seems to have been assembled from other documentary packages that used different narrators. However, it's one of the more interesting documentaries solely because of the rarity and length of the clips—at least for the first third.

Those who think that Lee's career as a child star in China was limited to a few bit parts should have their eyes opened by the first batch of clips, extended sequences from four of his early films from the late 1940s and early 1950s in which he played the lead. In *Kid Cheung* (1947), acting alongside his father Lee Hoi-Chuen for the first and only time, he plays a boy who befriends a criminal. Changing gears, he played a bully in *The Bad Boy*. In *Carnival*, he's part of a poor family of street performers. And *Orphan Sam* is a drama in which he plays a kid

adopted by a blacksmith. The clips are all dubbed in English with modern music added, and make one wish for a chance to see the films in their entirety. Unfortunately, the footage is also very tightly cropped, with many of the actors' heads are cut off by the top of the frame.

Next we cross over to the United States for a rare short clip taken at Lee's first martial arts school in the mid-1960s, where he was already teaching his Jeet Kune Do style. Newsreel footage from his funeral in 1973 wraps up Lee's biography, but we all know that his actual life was just a part of Bruce Lee's story. At this point, we're less than 30 minutes into the film. With that, director Jim Markovic gives us clips of Bruce Lee imitators for the rest of the film, "so that you can judge for yourselves" how they stack up to the original. Clips from unidentified films starring Bruce Li (mostly from *The Chinese Connection 2*) and Dragon Lee follow for the next hour. These are probably the best two of the many called upon to imitate Bruce Lee in the years following his death, but if you want to see their movies, you want to see the whole thing. In any case, so much footage of imitations in a film billed as The REAL Bruce Lee is beyond unethical. ♪♪

1979 100m/BW/C *HK/US* Bruce Lee, Bruce Li, Dragon Lee, Lee Hoi-Chuen. *D:* Jim Markovic. *W:* Lerry Dolchin. **VHS, DVD**

Real Kung Fu of Shaolin, Part 1

This routine martial arts adventure combines two common plots—the vengeful son raised by monks and the kung fu tournament. Ailing Chan Chun-chung struggles along with her child Siu-ching (who wears a funny cartoon character hood) to reach monk Kok Yuen at Shaolin Temple. Her husband Shek has been killed fighting evil gangster Wu Yung-tao, who has taken over their town with his black-market copper and asbestos business. Wu is so nasty that he even kills his own kung fu master. Siu-ching (Sing Lung) is raised among the monks, learning Finger Boxing, Iron Head, Chi Kong, and other martial arts styles—even the Bionic Arm! In his spare time, he masters Shaolin Housework. Wishing to visit his mother after 15 years, Siu-ching fights his way past the temple's four guardians to prove himself. The monks give him three special pills he'll need in his adventures. Wu's thugs murder the Tan's friend Mrs. Wong, and Chun-chung and Siu-ching go to stay with Uncle Yang, where they can "plan their future lives and revenge schemes." Wu sends the Red Monk to harass Pak's restaurant, but Chan Sui-ching kills him in a duel. Wu's son Pai-long tries to hit on Siu-ching's cousin, but Siu-ching beats up the rogue and his gang. Peeved, Wu decides to sponsor a martial arts tournament to draw out the thorn in his side, hiring a tough Korean fighter named Pak to fix the competition. Siu-ching disguises himself as a feeble old man to kill Pak. But Wu and his boys put two and two together, and they force their way into and take over Uncle's restaurant. When Pai-long attacks his cousin and mother, Siu-ching kills him, then goes after the entire gang, including Wu's boss Hung.

A lot of shots are out of focus or poorly framed, screwing up even location shooting at Shaolin Temple. The fight scenes are substandard. The tone is very uneven—the hero's march to deliver the head of an underling and challenge his evil enemy is shot like a travelogue. Not that the locations aren't beautiful, it's just inappropriate to the story. Wu's headquarters is obviously an ancient landmark, and the various statues and towers are the best things about the movie. Not much is known about this mainland Chinese production. Sing Lung is another name for Jackie Chan, but this sure ain't him, throwing suspicion on the rest of the credits, and the release date of 1981 is an educated guess. Despite the onscreen video-generated title, there's been no hint of a Part 2. 🐾🐾

1981 88m/C *CH* Sing Lung, Ngan Lung, Kong Lai Lai, Yung Lu Sam. **D:** Ko Yeung. **VHS, DVD**

Rebels under Siege

This is another in the series of video label Jalisco dubbed films featuring Jackie Chan, leader of the Red Flower rebels, as the main character. We feel obliged to point out that this is not *the* Jackie Chan (HK action super-star), but a *character* named Jackie Chan, played by Ho Ka King. Since this is a Jalisco import, we naturally get the goofy Westernized names for the characters—a convention which, nevertheless, does help slightly in keeping track of who's who.

In this flick, the Red Flower rebels are looking for a new leader. Before they can select one, their leader pro-tem Scott is captured by John Wu (another ballsy name choice by Jalisco—and no relation to the HK director). Wu is the evil agent of the emperor, and is out to secure his master's reign by quashing the rebels once and for all. Scott's capture leaves a power-vacuum in the Red Flower clan. Some believe that Jackie Chan should be their new leader. Another faction, led by the sinister Steve, says that Jackie is unworthy (because of his association with former criminal, Leonard). Steve is actually in league with John Wu, though the Red Flower clan remains blissfully unaware of this throughout most of the film. Because of Steve's machinations, the Red Flower rebels take some nasty hits from the emperor's

men. Jackie is wrongly blamed for these troubles, and is soon hunted by both his own clan and by John Wu. Though Jackie can carve stone with the tip of his sword, the political machinations swirling around him confuse his pure soul. He spends a lot of time fighting for his honor, as well as fighting the bad guys.

Both Jackie and the Red Flower gang devote much of the film's running time to freeing Scott from captivity. Since this is (apparently) an edited version of a Chinese soap opera, their attempts are foiled numerous times. Time and again, Jackie and the rebels barely escape Steve and John Wu's machinations. Steve's duplicity is finally revealed by Leonard (not such a bad guy after all). Steve flees back to his master, and causes much havoc by helping hunt down his old comrades. (Shades of *Star Wars!*) This leads inevitably to a final confrontation between the forces of evil and the Red Flower society.

As in the related film, *Hunted by Royal Decree,* the costumes, sets, and locations in *Rebels under Siege* are very good—on par with an actual film, rather than a direct-to-video compilation. The camera and fight work in this opus aren't quite as good as *HBRD*—but this film appears to be earlier in the soap-opera continuity. The re-editing on *RUS* is quite good, and allows the plot to be followed easily despite the "missing" pieces. The story line gets a bit repetitive, but the fights and staging are always fresh and interesting. All in all, one of the better direct-to-video genre releases. Also in this series: *Hunted by Royal Decree* and *The Unconquered.* —SS 🐾🐾🐾

2000 87m/C *CH* Ho Ka King, Loong Loong, Liu Shu Hua. **D:** Chu Ka Liang. **W:** Jin Yung. **DVD**

Rebirth of Mothra

While the earliest Japanese kaiju (monster) movies were clearly inspired by American sci-fi precedents of the '50s, two of the later and most enduring kaiju are more purely Japanese in origin: the golden, three-headed space dragon King Ghidorah and the graceful, benevolent giant moth, Mothra. Mothra was introduced in a 1961 Toho feature that established the creature's mythology, which has been little changed after 40 years: Mothra hails from a primitive South Pacific island where it is worshipped as a god, along with two tiny, twin female fairies who croon a catchy Mothra song whenever their gigantic benefactor is needed. In many films involving Mothra, the beautifully colored giant-moth form of the "monster" is threatened or killed, but not before laying an immense egg from which emerge one or more caterpillar-like baby Mothras, who can immobilize their often larger opponents with their silk cocoons. After the 1961 *Mothra,* the creature appeared in *Mothra vs. Godzilla, Ghidorah the Three-Headed Monster, Ebirah, Horror of the Deep,* and *Destroy All Monsters,* before going into retirement until 1992, when it battled a new Godzilla in the Heisei series *Godzilla vs. Mothra.*

Rebirth of Mothra pits the gentle moth against Death Ghidorah, a development-spawned, meaner version of Ghidorah, and in an ingenious touch Mothra's twin fairy spokesmodels (now played by non-twins Megumi Kobayashi and Sayaka Yamaguchi) are given their own pint-sized adversary in the form of the evil—and yes, kind of sexy—fairy Belvera (Aki Hano). There's a brilliant early scene in which the fairies (riding on "fairy mothras"—bird-sized miniature versions of the giant moth) engage Belvera in a dogfight inside a family living room, in a mini-masterpiece of staging and special effects that should wow children and not a few adults. Equally impressive are the Mothra/Death Ghidorah battles, which show off high-speed miniature photography that rivals the heyday of Eiji Tsubaraya. When a wounded Mothra and its offspring crash into the ocean and one of them succumbs to the elements, it may be the most beautiful giant monster death scene ever filmed. —*JB* **AKA:** *Mosura.* ♫♫♫

1996 104m/C *JP* Megumi Kobayashi, Sayaka Yamaguchi, Aki Hano, Kazuki Futami. **D:** Okihiro Yoneda. **W:** Okihiro Yoneda. **M:** Toshiyuki Watanabe. **VHS, DVD**

Rebirth of Mothra 2

Both Mothra and its movie franchise continue to evolve in this sequel that pits the silk-spinning supermonster against a water-dwelling dragon that protects an ancient underwater temple. Mothra's fairies Mol (Megumi Kobayashi) and Lora (Sayaka Yamaguchi) are involved, as is the nefarious yet alluring evil fairy Belvera (Aki Hano). While the first Heisei Mothra film was an often mordant and spectacular fairy tale, *Rebirth of Mothra 2* errs on the side of ridiculousness with a plot that is part *Raiders of the Lost Ark,* part *The Goonies,* with a climax that somehow blends *Star Wars* with *Fantastic Voyage.*

Mothra evolves from its standard form to a more streamlined, wasp-like battle version, even developing the capability of diving underwater in order to take on the massive green dragon Daghara. When these capacities prove insufficient to take the environmentally hazardous Daghara down, Mothra splits itself into a million microscopic mini-Mothras and invades the monster's blood stream, engaging the creature's antibodies in a mind-boggling innerspace battle royale. This last plot twist apparently outraged a

lot of traditional kaiju fans, but you can't accuse it of being boring. The special effects, while not quite up to the standards of the previous film, are more ambitious and by the body-invasion underwater climax things get pretty eye-popping. What's missing is the genuinely involving, humanistic elements that make the previous Mothra movie perfect fodder for children and young girls. Whatever protests might have been launched against this incarnation of Mothra, they didn't hurt the movie franchise: Mothra returned to battle a redesigned King Ghidorah in *Rebirth of Mothra 3.* —*JB* **AKA:** *Mosura 2.* ♫♫♪

1997 97m/C *JP* Megumi Kobayashi, Sayaka Yamaguchi, Aki Hano. **D:** Kunio Miyoshi. **W:** Masumi Suetani. **M:** Toshiyuki Watanabe. **VHS, DVD**

Reborn from Hell: Samurai Armageddon

Based on the novel *Makai Tensho* by Futaroh Yamada, this is a remake of 1981's *Samurai Reincarnation.* Satanic priest Shosetsu Minbunosuke Yui raises samurai Lord Shiro Tokisada Amakusa from the dead, making him pop out of the skin of a virgin after a vacation in Hell. After a long siege, Amakusa was beheaded and his castle was destroyed. Now he vows chaos, destruction, and revenge. On his way to visit his father Duke Tamba Yagyu, one-eyed Jubei Yagyu (Hiroyuki Watanabe) crosses swords with an enemy he thought long dead. Yui continues to raise zombie samurai (including such legendary warriors as Miyamoto Musashi) in an effort to fulfill his own prophesies of Armageddon, and allies himself with powerful Duke Kishu. Kimura and Sekiguchi, with his daughter Ohiro, visit Jubei's home and ask him for aide, concerned about the disappearance of at least 10 girls from the Wakayama region. The reborn samurai corrupt Buddhist monk Inshun, and kill Kimura and Sekiguchi, though the latter manages to warn Jubei before he dies.

Seeking to mix ghost movie spookiness with stately historical grandeur, *Reborn from Hell* moves slowly through its first act while Duke Kishu searches for a suitable maiden for his own rebirth. But once Kishu kidnaps Ohiro, Jubei begins to fight his way through a battalion of living and dead warriors. You can tell which are zombies by their spurting green blood. Unable to recruit Jubei to their side, the devils approach his father, who slays Jubei's brother Munehuyu. Obviously intended as the first part of a series, the feature ends abruptly with Jubei's duel with Miyamoto. **AKA:** *Makai Tensho: The Armageddon.* ♫♫♪

1996 (R) 82m/C *JP* Hiroyuki Watanabe, Yuko Moriyama, Hiroshi Miyauchi, Hitomi Shimizu, Toshiya Kazusaki, Kataro Yoshida, Nobuyuki Ishida, Tomoro Taguchi, Yasufumi Morisawa, Mutsuko Kato, Shinbei Takasugi, Hiro Ito, Toshi Kurihara, Kenji Arai, Ken Hasegawa, Shohei Yamamoto. **D:** Kazumasa Shirai. **W:** Akinori Kikuchi, Futaroh Yamada (story). **C:** Yoshihiro Ito. **M:** Takashi Nakagawa, Yuki Sakamoto. **VHS, DVD**

Record

It starts like any movie about high-school kids—the crowd at Je-li High is a typical bunch. Eun-mi is a pretty and buxom girl; Kyung-sik is her bully athletic boyfriend. Everybody dislikes Sung-wook, the kid known as Maskman. He wears a surgical mask because of his extreme allergies, and has the school keep the windows closed in summer heat. Eun-mi invites him to her family's summer house, along with her friend Hui-jung, as minimal chaperone. She explains that her boyfriend, Hyung-jun (Kang Seong-jin) couldn't make it. That night, a trio of masked men breaks into the cabin and terrorizes them with a chainsaw and dagger, recording everything with a camcorder. Of course, it's all a cruel prank—the masked intruders are Hyung-jun and his buddies, and Eun-mi was in on the cruel gag. Too late, they realize that the knife used to stab Sung-wook was not a fake prop knife as intended, and they've actually stabbed him to death with a real knife. Unwilling to face the consequences, they decide to burn the body (along with the videotape) and bury it out in the woods. But when they light the fire, it turns out Sung-wook was just unconscious—he leaps to screaming, flaming life and jumps off a nearby cliff. They try to go on with their lives like nothing happened, even when Sung-wook's sister visits the school. But somebody saw what they did last summer. A figure in red wearing a mask threatens Hui-jung with a big knife, leaving behind a website URL that has the incriminating video posted on it. And a game of cat-and-mouse begins, with the killer either stalking them or leaving them gruesome clues.

The American slasher films that inspired this are pretty obvious, though this is made with more intelligence, energy, and creativity. It also gives us some the oldest clichés, such as the old "hiding from the killer in a public washroom stall" scene. It's kind of hard to work up much sympathy for jerks who accidentally stab a guy, then accidentally set him on fire, and you may just find yourself rooting for the ingenious psycho killer. However, the maniac also goes after some innocents, dispatching a tough and sexy school nurse (Mayu Loh, Korea's voice of Bart Simpson!) in rather cold-blooded fashion. The model-cute actors fail to register a whole lot of trauma or concern when their comrades start to get picked off, just attention to solving their problem—though they make a lot of obvious horror flick mistakes, like splitting up at every opportunity. But for the record, at least here there's an effort to do things a slightly different way within the formula. **AKA:** *Zikhimyeon Jukneunda; The Record.* ♫♫♫

2000 93m/C *HK* Kang Seong-jin, Choi Ji-woo, Han Chae-young, Mayu Loh, Park Eun-hye. **D:** Kim Gi-hun, Kim Jong-seok. **W:** Han Chang-hak. **C:** Jeong Jeong-hun. **M:** Lee Sang-yun. **DVD**

Red Shield

Danny Lee *(The Killer)* stars in another of his police thrillers, this time as a tough SDU commander. Sergeant Lui Te-ken (Lee) leads a Flying Tiger squad closing in on arms dealer Dragon Ho Lung (Ben Lam). A raid on the gang's latest deal goes sour when a speedboat carrying Ho and his top aids reaches Chinese waters before Lui can close in. Later, Ho muscles in on the protection racket in his territory, resulting in a restaurant gun battle. Senior Inspector Wang Tien-tin (Leung Kar-yan) happens to be outside spying on his pretty real-estate agent wife Terry (Yip San) when the excitement begins, and he kills one of Ho's men with one shot as the thug was about to kill mob boss Shing Biu (Shing Fui-on). The notoriety this brings prompts the commissioner to assign Wang to assist Lui's team, though the two cops have very different styles and backgrounds. The squad concentrates on following Shing, but they lose track of him and he ends up cut to pieces by Ho's chainsaw. Meanwhile, the brother of the thug Wang shot (Jackson Liu, dressed up like the Terminator) is out for revenge, making several attempts to kill Wang. A lead brings the men to a Vietnamese refugee camp where Ho's man Panther (Yuen Wah) is a resident. As was usual at the time in Hong Kong media, the Vietnamese are portrayed as craven animals who riot when the cops put in an appearance. While Wang and Lui are arresting Panther, Ho has somehow found out where Lui lives, and his gang abducts Terry Wang and Lui's wife Hsu-hsien (Teresa Mo). Unwilling to waste any time with procedures, the two cops decide to make an illegal run into China to catch the gang.

It looks almost as though the film crew made a similar run onto the mainland to shoot scenes there. To the film's credit, an effort is made to establish the wives as more than stock characters before they get involved in the plot, giving the story some extra dimension. Stunt director Stephen Tung provides the above-average action. **AKA:** *Lui Ting So Yuet; Lei Ting Sao Xue.* ♫♫♫

1991 88m/C *HK* Danny Lee, Leung Kar-yan, Teresa Mo, Yip San, Yuen Wah, Shing Fui-on, Ben Lam,

Cheung Kwok-leung, Jackson Liu, Michael Dinga, Jamie Luk, Nick Cheung, Eric Kei. **D:** Parkman Wong. **W:** Law Kam-fai, James Fung. **C:** Tony Miu. **M:** Phil Chan. **VHS, DVD**

Red to Kill

Billy Tang continues his career as Hong Kong's sleaziest director with this attention-grabbing true-crime horror thriller. Getting right to the point, in a slum apartment complex, Welfare Department agent Cheung Ka-lok (Money Lo) is unable to prevent a distraught mother from jumping out a window with her retarded son, while in the building's basement, a sex killer claims another victim. Discouraged, Cheung decides to resign, but while she waits for her resignation to crawl through red tape, she gets another assignment. A car hits a man, leaving his mentally handicapped daughter Kong Yuk-ming (Lily Chung) an orphan. Cheung takes Ming to live in a dormitory and workshop for such cases run by Chan Chi-wai (Ben Ng), in the very same building as the suicide and murder.

With a limited number of potential suspects, it's not difficult to determine which saintly figure is actually a perverted maniac. The police do nothing as the killer continues to prey on the building's occupants and guests, and the residents' suspicions fall on the hostel kids, though they're more understanding when the kids come to the rescue of a molested girl. Chan, who reacts to the color red like a raging bull, is unable to control himself after seeing Ming wearing a red dress in a dance recital, and rapes her that night. He's able to stop himself before killing her, and when Ming tells Chung about it, Chan is arrested. However, Ming is too frightened to testify effectively, and Chan is freed. Returning to the hostel, Chan really goes off the deep end, shaving his head and attacking Chung, whom he sees as his only obstacle to Ming.

Lo and Chung are both good in their roles, and a fair amount of drama is built up in their relationship. But Tang is only setting things up as a freak show to be undermined with sensational cruelty and violence later. Ben Ng, on the other hand, fits right in with the film's sensationalism—leering, twitching, and quivering like a rabid weasel in every other scene, turning himself into a drooling monster by story's end. His performance would be laughable if the material weren't so unrelentingly grim. Even hardened fans of exploitation may find much of this too unpleasant to endure, and the blood-drenched finale is a classic of unhindered excess. Tang's later films are less stylized and more concerned with the gritty realities of police procedure. However, he retains his pitch-black sense of humor, and taste for extreme violence. As punishment for this, both Chung and Ng had to be in *Millen-*

nium Dragon. The music by Wong Bong, who scored many true-crime flicks, is especially effective. **AKA:** *Yeuk Saat; Ruo Sha.* 🐲🐲

1994 91m/C *HK* Lily Chung, Ben Ng, Money Lo, Bobby Yip. **D:** Billy Tang. **W:** Wong Ho-wah. **C:** Tony Miu. **M:** Wong Bong. **VHS, DVD**

The Red Wolf

This *Die Hard*–inspired adventure stars Kenny Ho as a lone security officer trying to take down a gang of robbers onboard a luxury linèr. The *White Whale* sails on an open sea, New Year's Eve, 1994. Dragon (Ho) is a shipboard security officer, serving along with his brother, who also happens to be on his honeymoon. Dragon is haunted by the memory of how his girl was killed when he tried to foil a robbery; he quit the police force because of it. Pretty waitress Lai (Christy Chung) is also a pickpocket, catching the eye of Dragon in more ways than one. He also sees her return a diamond anniversary ring that she snatched from an elderly passenger, when the poor man nearly has a heart attack because of the loss. Lounge singer Elaine Ho (Elaine Lui) catches the Captain's eye. The Vice Captain (Ngai Sing) sets him up with her for a date, but it's a trap: Elaine and the Vice Captain are in cahoots. They know the Captain has some stolen uranium in the ship's vault, and they steal the key to it from him. Luckily, Dragon spots the crime taking place, but now has the crooks trying to kill him. Many of the crew are with the villains, so whom to trust? After Dragon kills a fellow security officer in self-defense, even the honest officers are after him, and they lock him up.

Hiding out in Elaine's dressing room, Lai hears the truth, and breaks Dragon out of the brig. After that, it's one fight, escape, or chase after another, some of them quite ingenious. Yuen Woo-Ping directed this one right after the spectacular *Fist of Legend,* so one might expect that he'd be taking a breather with this one, but the fights and stunts are all still wonderfully choreographed. Ho, who resembles a young Chow Yun-fat, delivers all the requisite kung fu and some great stunts. Chung gets to do some funny shtick. The cheap synth soundtrack is a definite deficit. **AKA:** *Hu Meng Wei Long; Foo Maang Wei Lung.* 🐲🐲🐲

1995 93m/C *HK* Kenny Ho, Christy Chung, Ngai Sing, Elaine Lui, Cho Wing, Ng Sing Sze, Yuen Cheung-yan. **D:** Yuen Woo-ping. **W:** Ricky Ng. **C:** George Ma. **M:** Tang Siu-lam. **VHS, DVD**

Renegade Ninjas

A cup made from the skull of Mitsunabe Mushita is made for Shogun Tokugawa Idayasu (Kinnosuke Nakamura). The shogun is only a retainer

of the title, but refuses to return it to young Toyotomi at Osaka Castle when he comes of age. As he takes a drink of saki, a gigantic meteor passes over the palace and crashes into central Japan. In accordance with the prophecy, ninja Seizo Kinigakudai, on orders from Lord Sanada, assassinates the Shogun. But the ninja are betrayed—the murdered man was just a double, and the shogun's guards attack the rebels. They make their escape with the help of red-headed ninja Sarutobi Saskai, the Leaping Monkey!

The next 40 minutes of the movie are devoted to introducing just a few dozen of the characters in this complicated story, mainly the renegade ninjas: Ninja Yokuro Indo gambles with ninja Yokuro Mochiroku. Ninja Yuzo Kakeii hides from the shogun's men. Mad master swordsman Matabei Goto. Doper Ninja Jinipachi Nezu protects a bathing woman from a bandit. Korean ninja Isa Kioshi. Ninja Kamanoskai Yudi. Explosives expert ninja Kageii Juzo. And so on. Ninja Oshkei Amayama brings wine to Lord Sanada, unknowingly insulting young Lord Yukamori Sanada (Kensaku Morita) and Lady Aya. But assassins are everywhere, and the old lord is killed by a poisoned cat! Meanwhile, the widow Lady Toyotomi is seeing the ghost of her late husband in Osaka Castle, a trick perpetrated by a shogun's ninja to make her give up the castle. Lady Aya commits suicide rather than return to the Sanada's home province without her husband, deepening Yukamori's resolve to continue the fight. He recruits nine of the renegade ninja on a mission to assassinate Idayasu. They see the perfect opportunity for their mission when Idayasu goes to inspect his new cannons imported from Holland.

This historical action epic presents a tale from the early years in the Edo period, when the Tokugawa government united Japan by force. Then began a long period of relative peace brought on by prosperity for the rich and powerful, feeding off the lower classes with a burden of taxes enforced by a corrupt government. Japanese history can be fascinating, but a single action film is not the best place to learn too much of it. This one tries to bite off too much, taking up more than its first hour just to set up the *Guns of Navarone* situation. They might have done better to concentrate on this main mission. Once it finally gets underway, this is a fine action film, which even has some nice special effects. Some scenes—mainly those involving the wizard Saskai, who has psychic sight, can raise whirlwinds, transform into a monkey, and other feats—seem to have dropped in from another movie altogether. *AKA: Sanada Yukimura no Boryaku; Death of a Shogun; The Shogun Assassins.* ♫♫♡

1979 108m/C *JP* Kensaku Morita, Kinnosuke Nakamura, Yoko Akino, Yuko Asano, Jun Hamamura, Shohei Hino, Hiroki Matsukata, Henry Sanada, Tetsuro Tamba, Minori Terada. **D:** Sadao Nakajima. **VHS**

The Replacement Killers

Hong Kong action superstar Chow Yun-fat plays John Lee, a professional hit man brought to America to avenge the death of the son of mob boss Mr. Wei (regular Chow opponent Kenneth Tsang). But a crisis of conscience causes Lee to botch the payback assassination. Wei doesn't take kindly to this change in plans, and puts Chow's head on the chopping block. With both the police and the gangs after him, Chow must get out of the country—if he can. Adding to the urgency is Wei's threat to kill Lee's Hong Kong family in retaliation. The gang lord hires "replacement killers" Collins (Danny Trejo) and Ryker (Til Schweiger) to carry out Lee's old mission, and take revenge on the faithless hit man. Desperate, Lee turns to Meg Coburn (Mira Sorvino), a freelance documents forger. Things go bad though, as Wei's new assassins dog Lee's every step. Lee and Coburn are thrust together against their will, and must run a gauntlet of hired killers to escape. Coburn, whose business is ruined by the running gun battle, isn't too pleased with her new "partner" in crime. Soon, though, she warms to Lee's low-key charms. From there on, *The Replacement Killers* progresses like a fairly standard cop-buddy movie, with the exceptions that neither of the main characters is a cop, and one of them is a woman.

A plan to kill a policeman's son spices up the mix. Lee and Coburn are forced to decide whether to get away clean, or save an innocent life. Are they good guys who act badly, or bad guys who have souls? The mystery of why Lee gave up his assignment hangs over the film for a good long while, and the eventual revelation is both satisfying and helps propel the flick to its action-packed conclusion.

Replacement Killers is a fairly successful Americanization of Chow's standard Hong Kong gun-fu flicks—which themselves are inspired by old French thrillers. The action isn't quite as bloody as the HK fare, nor are quite as many rounds of ammunition fired. *RK* is pretty tough by American standards, though not in the same league with your average Paul Verhoven blood-fest. The acting by the principals is all good, and the direction solid—if not inspired. Folks who like this should step up into some of Chow Yun-fat's other flicks—like *Hard Boiled.* —SS ♫♫♫

1997 (R) 88m/C *US* Chow Yun-fat, Mira Sorvino, Michael Rooker, Kenneth Tsang, Jurgen Prochnow, Danny Trejo, Til Schweiger. **D:** Antoine Fuqua. **W:** Ken Sanzel. **C:** Peter Lyons Collister. **M:** Harry Gregson-Williams. **VHS, DVD**

The Replacement Suspects

An unauthorized remake of Kevin Spacey's *Albino Alligator*. The opening sequence follows two scenarios: cops who have an arms dealer (Kenny Bee) under surveillance, and thieves who are breaking into a building. The thieves set off the alarm and, while fleeing the scene, cross paths with the cops. A cop ends up dead. The thieves seek shelter in a bar because one (Simon Lui) has been shot. His brother (Julian Cheung Chi-Lam) tries to keep cool, while their cohort (Roy Cheung) seesaws hysterically in his emotions. Pushing the outer limits of coincidence, the thieves have chosen to seek shelter in the same bar where the arms dealer is having a drink. The cops assume the arms dealer is responsible for the death of the policeman and surround the joint, resulting in a hostage situation. Tensions are ratcheted upward with the combination of nervous criminals, frightened civilians, and the arrival of a blustery police commander (Michael Wong) and television crews.

Director and editor Marco Mak creates a fresh and pleasant sense of tension despite the over-used hostage scenario. The problem is that, having boxed the characters into one location, the filmmakers have little idea how best to exploit it. Some of the more interesting characters, such as the owner of the bar and the arms dealer, get short shrift as far as any exposition of their motivations, etc., while we are subjected to plenty of whining from the thieves and macho teeth-gnashing from the police commander. The result is that the 90-minute running time feels longer than needed to tell the story. And note that this hostage drama is *not* an action-filled movie—the blazing gun action is limited to just a few minutes of screen time, most of which was featured in the theatrical trailer. Christine Ng effectively plays a calculating waitress who will do whatever it takes to try and ensure her survival of the ordeal. On the other end of the acting scale, Michael Wong must have been told this was a comedy instead of a drama, because he sounds like a caricature of an overbearing and unfeeling police commander, in charge of the hostage situation. As a side note, he delivers most of his lines in English. To be fair, his scene with a television broadcaster in which he expresses himself quite obscenely was rather funny. —*PM* **AKA:** *Kwan Sau; Kun Shou; The Replacement Suspect.* 🐾🐾

2001 90m/C *HK* Julian Cheung, Michael Wong, Kenny Bee, Simon Lui, Roy Cheung, Christine Ng, Sonja Kwok, Timothy Zao, Clarence Cheung. *D:* Marco Mak. *W:* Simon Lui, Fan Chun-fung, Yu Wing-man, Marco Mak. *C:* Daniel Chan. *M:* Lincoln Lo. **VHS, DVD**

Reptilian

Among the giant-monster movies attempting to compete with Toho's Godzilla series in the mid-1960s was a big lizard from Korea named *Yongary, Monster of the Deep*. Though less than a smash success on the world's movie and TV screens, the Koreans have always had a soft spot for their homegrown creature. With Hollywood on a binge of "re-imagining" old hits, producer Shim Hyung Rae got the idea of bringing the monster back, this time with state-of-the-art special effects—or as state of the art as he could afford. His *Yonggary* would be totally computer animated, would feature invading aliens in a giant mothership, and all of the characters would be played by Anglos. American distributors didn't think the finished film would play as it was, so *Yonggary* went back to the shop for repairs. This wasn't enough for Columbia TriStar, who decided that even without more than a single Asian face in the cast, *Yonggary* still looked too foreign for their tastes. Thus, they retitled the film *Reptilian* and made sure the packaging and ads made it look as much like a *Godzilla* rip-off as possible.

The result is a fine example of id-release giant monster destruction that should satisfy the monster-movie lover in anyone. Ruthless Dr. Campbell (Richard B. Livingston) sacrifices the lives of his entire expedition to secure the discovery of fossil alien beings. Dr. Hughes (Harrison Young from *Saving Private Ryan*) manages to escape with a few artifacts and secrets. Years later, Campbell leads another expedition. This time he's unearthing the largest dinosaur skeleton ever found, and he doesn't mind losing a lot of workmen to mysterious "accidents" along the way. Hughes shows up to warn him against whatever he's really up to, but Christopher won't listen. Meanwhile, alien puppets from beyond the galaxy park their huge, grungy mothership in Earth orbit and start zapping random satellites and space shuttles. The alien master plan is to destroy the puny Earthlings by bringing the 200 million-year-old corpse of Yonggary back to life and send it on a rampage. This makes no sense whatsoever, as the aliens clearly have the technology and firepower to destroy Earth on their own, without having to re-animate and teleport ancient remote-controlled monsters. And we never learn why they came so far just to pick on Earth in the first place. Anyway...in accordance with the prophecy, the aliens bring Yonggary back from the dead, and use him to do their ass-kicking for them. The towering dragon is teleported to a nearby city, where it proceeds to crush, kill, and destroy for its alien masters. A bunch of interchangeable generals assemble in a War Room somewhere to wring their hands and shout orders.

From this point on, the movie is all action and fun. Yonggary resists the attack of army missiles in much the same manner as his American cousin Godzilla—he ducks out of the way. When helicopters and jets are unable to defeat Yonggary, the generals call in the Rocket Rangers. This group of elite soldiers who zip around with jet packs—just like Commando Cody in the old serials—are just way too much fun and knock the movie up a notch. The aliens add further evidence to the illogic of their plan by sending their own monster Cykor in to fight Yonggary after he's freed from their control.

Though the special effects are inferior to those in most Hollywood productions, they're still fun to watch, and are even darned impressive in some shots. Some of the actors have to struggle to disguise their Australian accents, but are otherwise acceptable. The weakest component is by far the script. Though another Westerner was hired to prevent the dialogue from sounding unnatural, screenwriter Marty Poole still turned in a script that sometimes sounds as though it was put through a translator. *AKA: 2001 Yonggary.* 🎵🎵🎵

2000 (PG-13) 99m/C *KO* Harrison Young, Donna Philipson, Richard B. Livingston, Eric Briant Wells, Dan Cashman, Bruce Cornwell, Dennis Howard, Matt Landers, Brad Sergi. *D:* Shim Hyung Rae. *W:* Marty Poole. *C:* An Hong Kim. *M:* Chris Desmong, Cho Sung-woo. **VHS, DVD**

Return of Daimajin

Typhoons! Blizzards! Floods! Earthquakes! Droughts! The god Majin is angry again (and the Daiei special-effects department is busy)—or so believe the medieval villagers of the Daimajin trilogy, of which this is the third entry. Lord Arakawa (Toru Abe) has been abducting woodcutters from a neighboring region to his home in Hell's Valley, putting them to work as slaves building a fortress from which he plans to make war on his neighbors. Woodsman Sampei (Takashi Nakamura) escapes by going through Majin's mountain, and their Lord Koyoma can't send troops to rescue the men because of expected heavy snows in the pass. The three young boys—Daisaku (Shinji Horii), Kinta (Masahide Iizuka), and Tsuru (Hideki Ninomiya)—are the only ones who dare, despite all warnings, to take the dangerous path across the mountain to tell the cap-

tives about Sampei's escape route. Little brother Sugi (Muneyuki Nagatomo) tags along, and turns out to be a valuable member of the team. The boys brave arduous climbs, fatigue, bad weather, starvation, avalanches, and rapids to reach Hell's Valley to deliver their message.

As in all Daimajin films, the struggles of the heroes ultimately come to naught, making it necessary for Majin (Riki Hoshimoto) to perform some divine intervention, coming after the villain with a load of fire and brimstone. Including juvenile heroes may have been an attempt by Daiei to curry the favor of the kiddie audience that flocked to their *Giant Monster Gamera,* but the brave boys are treated in a serious fashion, and are never exploited as overly "cute." This is generally considered the weakest of the trilogy due to Majin's absence for most of the running time, but the story of the boys' quest is just as engaging as those presented in the other two films, if not more so, and has an adventurous spirit all its own. The outdoor location shooting is more prominent here, tying the characters to the land, and making the supernatural elements all the more magical. The stone giant has a new weapon added to his arsenal: a great hawk that acts as a spy and familiar. The cinematography and special effects (Yoshiyuki Kuroda) are just beautiful, equal or better than anything in the Toho monster films of the same period, and for decades afterward. *AKA: Daimajin Gyakushu; Majin Strikes Again.* 🐾🐾🐾🐾

1966 87m/C *JP* Hideki Ninomiya, Shinji Horii, Masahide Iizuka, Muneyuki Nagatomo, Junichiro Yamashita, Tanie Kitabayashi, Toru Abe, Takashi Nakamura, Hiroshi Nawa, Yuzo Hayakawa, Yukio Horikita, Shozo Nanbu, Riki Hoshimoto. *D:* Kazuo Mori. *W:* Tetsuo Yoshida. *C:* Hiroshi Imai, Fujio Morita. *M:* Akira Ifukube. **VHS, DVD**

Return of the Chinese Boxer

Superstar Jimmy Wang Yu produced, directed, and starred in this sequel, which brought back his superhero Rabbit Fist Sau Pei-lung. The Japanese Shogun sends Kitsu bearing gifts for General To, in order to gain a To-hold in China. Chinese rebels launch several plans to stop this underhanded diplomatic mission, including an assault on Kitsu's train, and all fail. Lord So sends his pretty niece Feng with Colonel Wei to establish a bond with General Chang Tah, the only general with the power to oppose To. Kitsu's forces seek to ambush the mission, but the mighty Chinese Boxer Sau appears to drive them off. The Japanese hire knife-throwing assassin Flying Dagger to deal with the hero, but of course he fails. The assassin reports that the only one who can beat the stranger is Black Crane (Lung

Fei), though his client Kitsu avers that Monk Yin Feng (Kam Kong) could do the job. To prove her point, she presents a lengthy flashback showing Yin Feng's victory over the Twin Hearts Clan champ in a martial arts contest. While Kitsu recruits Black Crane, Yin Feng attacks the caravan. But his assault proves a failure due to Sau's timely interference. A trio of kung fu zombies is more successful, killing most of the caravan and capturing the treasure. It's up to Rabbit Fist to get the treasure back before Kitsu can get it out of the country, but he'll have to get past Flying Dagger (who now carries exploding knives), the living dead warriors and Black Crane's guns to do it.

Wang Yu's patriotism—and hatred for Japan—is apparent throughout this epic. He even goes so far as to wear a pigtail (one of the earliest of China's macho movie heroes to do so), using it to whip an opponent. The martial arts he displays are nothing special, but the fights are dressed up in entertaining fashion with expert wirework and other neat tricks. His feats include running up walls and perching on the end of a foe's spear. The tricks he uses to counter Lung Fei's eight-barreled gun are very clever, luring his enemy into a building full of gas-filled Jimmy Wang Yu love dolls. He makes good use of objects on hand in his fights (before Jackie Chan) and adds atmosphere to his showdown gunfight with fluttering pigeons (before John Woo). It's also worth noting that the warriors aren't opposed to latching on to a fallen opponent's weapon (doesn't it bug you to see a movie hero toss aside something useful?). The ending has a nice twist to it, giving something extra in a genre where the movie too often ends the second a villain bites the dust. Heck, sometimes the end title pops up while the final blow is being thrown! *AKA: Hammer of God.* 🐾🐾🐾

1975 98m/C *HK* Jimmy Wang Yu, Lung Fei, Cheung Ying Chen, Kam Kong, Sit Hon, Lei Chun, Chui Chung Hei, Hsieh Hsing, Blackie Ko, Ricky Cheng, Cheung Yee-kwai, Wang Wing Sheng, Phillip Ko, Jack Lung, Sun Jung-chi, Lee Keung, Hau Pak-wai, Sham Chin-bo. *D:* Jimmy Wang Yu. *W:* Ko Lung. *C:* Chiao Yao-xu. **DVD**

Return of the Deadly Blade

A grand old epic of swordplay, magic, and hidden identities. Eighteen years earlier, Master Lee Wai (Norman Tsui) killed his rival Kam the Invincible Golden Rings (Hwang Jang Lee) using his Deadly Blade, and disappeared. Kam's son Chi Wan (David Chiang of *Legend of the 7 Golden Vampires*) uses Master Lee's name to publicly challenge all other fighters, hoping to draw out his father's killer. The Cheun Brothers answer the challenge with their flying circular-saw blades, and are easily defeated. A mysterious warrior in a wheelchair gives Chi Wan a harsh critique of his performance.

Meanwhile, the Lord of the province believes the undefeated playboy the Lonely Winner (Yasua-ki Kurata) is the man who raped his wife, and sends four assassins after him. Though Winner refuses to kill, he beats them all anyway. Lonely Winner is looking for good warriors to fight, too. His master Mak tells him about Chi Wan's challenge, and of the legendary Moon Goddess (Flora Cheung)—who has been spying on Chi Wan to see if his plan works. Winner and Chi Wan happen to share the same ferry crossing a river, and get acquainted while assassins are attacking Winner. The God of Fire (Wong Ching), distracting Chi Wan with an exploding child(!), draws him into his underground lair and starts throwing fireballs at him, but is defeated with his own flames. The two warriors get in a battle with an umbrella fighter (Lo Lieh), who wounds Chi Wan before they can kill him. A girl named Koko, actually the Moon Goddess, nurses him back to health, but he has to rush off to the Tomb of Heroes to keep his appointment with the wheelchair warrior. The Lord decides to fight the Lonely Winner himself, but hires the dart-throwing Ninja of Iga (Isamu Naka-mura) to back him up. Complicating matters further is Tao (Sharon Yeung), a tough fighting girl the Lonely Winner done wrong, who won't stop pursuing him. Surviving these attacks, Lonely Winner meets up with Chi Wan at the Tomb of Heroes, where they learn some big secrets—and are taken to the Land of the Moon Goddess for an epic battle.

The great variety of characters and weapons helps keep things interesting, but also makes the story difficult to follow. It seems more like one damn thing after another than a story, and it doesn't help that odd flashbacks keep popping up. As such, it's wacky fun, even if it makes your head hurt trying to follow it. Kurata acts like the James Dean of ancient China. Ching Siu-Tung served as action director. *AKA: Fei Dao You Jian Fei Dao; Fei Diy Yau Gin Fei Diy; Shaolin Fighters vs. Ninja.* 🐾🐾

1981 83m/C *HK* David Chiang, Hwang Jang Lee, Bruce Liang, Norman Tsui, Yasuaki Kurata, Lo Lieh, Flora Cheung, Isamu Nakamura, Sharon Yeung, Wong Ching, Doris King, Yeung Chak Lam, Mars, Lam Kau. *D:* Taylor Wong. *W:* Chin Yu, Ko Lung (story). *C:* Lau Hung Chuen. *M:* Joseph Koo. **VHS, DVD**

Return of the Dragon

Disappointed in the way Lo Wei conducted himself on his first two pictures for Golden Harvest,
Bruce Lee insisted on directing his third feature himself. Lee's breakout international block-buster *Enter the Dragon* is thought of as his masterpiece, but *Return of the Dragon* is the only feature over which he exercised full control. In many ways, it's the superior picture, but American prejudice toward dubbed features has perhaps kept it in lower regard. This same attitude kept the picture out of American theatres until after Lee's death, when the earlier film was made to look like a sequel with the title *Return of the Dragon*.

Chen Ching Hua (Nora Miao) has inherited the most popular Chinese restaurant in Rome, but an evil Mafioso (Jon T. Benn) is trying to take over. She sends for her uncle in Hong Kong for help, but because of illness, he sends his friend Tang Lung (Bruce Lee) in his place. Chen is less than impressed with this odd young bumpkin, though Chef Wong (Huang Chung-hsin) has faith in him. Miss Chen changes her tune the next time The Boss sends effeminate Ho (Paul Wei) and his thugs to call, as Tang quickly thrashes them all. A gunman sent to Chen's apartment gets a taste of Tang's kung fu as well, and the newcomer becomes everyone's champion. While Chen is trying to impress the stubborn Tang with the wonders of Rome, the gang returns in force. Luckily, he brings along his nunchakus when he returns, and cleans out the rascals again. As the conflict escalates, Chen tries to get him to leave for his own protection. But the young dragon refuses, going on to beat every killer brought in to face him.

The film is justifiably worshiped for its fight scenes. Lee's grace and power, and the imagination of his choreography, make this an action classic. It all culminates in a breathtaking grand duel between Lee and Chuck Norris in the Roman Coliseum. But overlooked is the strength of Lee's writing, acting, and direction. Tang is certainly his most well-rounded character, showing off Lee's sense of humor. Told by Chen to smile back at foreigners early in the film, Lung's goofy grin becomes a running gag. Many scenes show Lee using lessons he's learned watching American and Italian westerns, the classic samurai films of Japan, and the work of his contemporary Cheng Cheh. *Return of the Dragon* shows plainly that Lee brought the same philosophy he used in his martial arts to his filmmaking as well. The U.S. version is missing about 10 minutes of footage. *AKA: Mang Lung Goh Kong; Meng Long Guo Jiang; Way of the Dragon; The Fury of the Dragon.* 🐾🐾🐾🐾

1972 (R) 91m/C *HK* Bruce Lee, Nora Miao, Chuck Norris, Paul Wei, Huang Chung-hsin, Whang In Shik, Jon T. Benn, Bob Wall, Tony Liu. *D:* Bruce Lee. *W:* Bruce Lee. *C:* Ho Lan Shan, Nishimoto Tadashi. *M:* Joseph Koo. **VHS, DVD**

The Return of the 5 Deadly Venoms

Not a sequel to Chang Cheh's martial arts mystery classic, this is actually another great film from the same team, though the only mystery element is why the kung fu masters all wear white while tumbling in the dirt. A trio known as the Tinan Tigers (including Dick Wei and Jamie Luk) has a beef with the musically named Tu Tin-to (Chen Kuan-tai). They invade his estate, but find that Tu and his bodyguard Wan (Johnny Wang) are out. To send Tu a message, the villains cut off his wife's legs and his son's arms. Tu arrives soon after and defeats the Tigers.

Despite the boy's handicap, Tu raises his son Tu To-chang (Lu Feng) to be a fierce Tiger Style fighter, helping him overcome his disability with a pair of specially made metal arms. Besides being unbreakable, To-chang can use the arms to shoot darts from the fingertips and can extend them several feet. To complete his revenge, Tin-to captures the grown sons of the Tinan Tigers and sets them against his son, instructing To-chang to cripple all four of them. But his trauma and obsession with vengeance

has driven Tu mad, and he becomes a cruel tyrant, literally ruling with an iron hand. His son continues his crippling ways beyond the sons of the Tigers, striking out at anyone who irks them. Chin Sun (Phillip Kwok) has his eyes poked out. Outspoken Wei the blacksmith (Lo Meng) is deafened and has his voice destroyed with a poison. When young Kuei (Sun Chien) stumbles into Tu, he cuts the lad's legs off. Heroic Wang Yi (Chiang Sheng) vows to put a stop to this, but the Tus are able to subdue him and render him an idiot by squeezing his head in a vise. The four cripples band together and journey to see Wang's kung fu master Li Ching-yin (Cheng Miu), who agrees to give the three visitors special training to make them as powerful fighters as feeble-minded Wang Yi (who still knows kung fu). First, blacksmith Wei makes Kuei some metal legs, and the sifu trains Chin and Wei to sharpen their remaining senses. Then they all go through three years of intense martial arts training.

These training sequences are ambrosia for kung fu movie fans, putting the Venoms through a variety of inventive exercises designed to show off their acrobatic prowess. When they're ready, the quartet leaves to bring the Tus to justice, though in the meantime their enemy has

Chuck Norris, Bruce Lee, the Roman Coliseum, and one of the greatest martial arts duels ever put on film in *Return of the Dragon.*

gathered a small army of kung fu men to help him run the region. Other masters are visiting, too, to celebrate To-chang's birthday.

Chang Cheh's creativity really comes through in this Shaw Brothers kung fu Grim fairy tale, crafted with master storyteller Ngai Hong. When Wei loses his hearing, the soundtrack goes blank to illustrate his condition. Lo Meng makes a solid impression in the role, first as a loudmouth, and then displaying some fine pantomime. While Phillip Kwok is not nearly as adept at portraying a blind warrior as Shintaro Katsu in the Zatoichi movies, he still does a credible job. And the whole cast displays amazing skill in the action scenes. The Chinese title translates as "Incomplete," which certainly wouldn't do on a marquee. Under the title *Crippled Avengers*, it had great success, and was aped by the low-budget *Crippled Masters*, which featured actual amputees in the starring roles. **AKA:** *Chaan Kuet; Can Que; Crippled Avengers; Mortal Combat; Crippled Heroes.* ♪♪♪♪

1978 (R) 107m/C *HK* Chen Kuan-tai, Phillip Kwok, Lo Meng, Chiang Sheng, Sun Chien, Lu Feng, Johnny Wang, Dick Wei, Jamie Luk, Cheng Miu, Pan Pingchang, Yu Tai-ping. **D:** Chang Cheh. **W:** Ngai Hong, Chang Cheh. **VHS, DVD**

Return of the Master Killer

Lau Kar-Leung's *Shaolin Master Killer* (AKA *The 36th Chamber of Shaolin*) was the kind of international hit that demands a sequel. However, the film's centerpiece is its marvelous training sequences that drive the story through its center, and since the film's historical hero San Te had already gone through all the chambers of Shaolin, the challenge was (as it is with most sequels) to re-create the first film without too much repetition, while continuing the story. Writer Ngai Hong's solution is this semi-parody that has a plot partly reminiscent of *Fists of Fury*.

Manchu gangsters in Canton take over the Tai Ching Dye Mill under the guise of "experts," and immediately lower quality standards and cut worker salaries by 20%. When indignant Chou Si-sun (Wei Pai) tries to start a walkout, he's beaten by the Manchu masters. Bucktooth Chau (Hsiao Ho) and Hung (Kara Hui) get the idea of getting Chou's con man brother Chen-chi (Gordon Lau) to do his monk act to imitate the great hero Abbot San Te! With the help of some trickery, Chi and the workers put over the bluff and get wages reinstated. However, Boss Wang (Johnny Wang) isn't so easily fooled by the faux monk, and everyone receives a thrashing. Determined to learn some real kung fu and make good, Chi uses his wiles to get into Shaolin disguised as a Northern Shaolin disci-

ple, where he meets the real San Te (now played by Ging Chue, denying us the fun of seeing Lau play a dual role, while saving the filmmakers a fortune in special effects). The master tolerates Chi's presence because of his perseverance. Put to work building a scaffold around the walls of the 36th Chamber, Chi gets a chance to observe the students' training techniques, which he imitates using his building materials. In this way, he unknowingly learns all the kung fu he needs to help his people.

Gordon Lau is so personable here—even in the English-dubbed version—that you hardly notice that he does very little fighting until the climax. Then the film finishes with one of the Laus' best fight sequences, in which Gordon uses his building kung fu to take on Johnny Wang and his thugs, who favor nifty little collapsible benches as their weapon of choice. However, they miss a chance to have Chi fashion a variation on San Te's famous segmented pole weapon. **AKA:** *Siu Lam Daap Paang Daai Si; Shao Lin Da Peng Da Shi; Return to the 36th Chamber; Master Killer 2; The 36th Chamber.* ♪♪♪♪

1980 (R) 100m/C *HK* Gordon Lau, Johnny Wang, Kara Hui, Wei Pai, Hsiao Ho, Yeung Ching-Ching, Ging Chue, Hwa Ling, Kong Do, Kwan Yung Moon, Bruce Lai, Wong Gam-fung, Cheng Wai-ho, Wong Ching Ho, Yau Tsui-ling, Chan Si Gai. **D:** Lau Kar-Leung. **W:** Ngai Hong. **M:** Eddie H. Wang. **DVD**

Return of the Street Fighter

Sonny Chiba is back for more eye-gouging fun as the lethal mercenary Terry Tsurugi in this bone-snapping sequel. Otaguro (Donald Nakajimi), working a grand scam under the guise of raising money to build a huge martial arts center, hires Terry to kill two men: embezzling accountants Rico Grando and Kintoko Ryo, who have stolen cash and art treasures from their employer. Tsurugi easily breaks in and out of police headquarters to kill Ryo. Shamed Inspector Yamagami (Zulu Yachi) wants to take charge of the case, but is forbidden by his superiors; however, he's given leave to conduct his own investigation. Grando isn't as easy to catch as Ryo, but Terry manages to get a stolen priceless gold statue away from him before the cops gun him down in an alley. Otaguro suspects sensei Masaoka (returning Masafumi Suzuki) of Sebukan Martial Arts School tipped off Yamagami as to their activities. Masaoka and Yamagami move to expose Otaguro, who retaliates by trying to get Terry to kill Masaoka. He refuses. Now targeted himself, Terry and his new sidekick, hep-talking chick Kitty (Yoko Ichiji), go skiing to hide out, but assassins from Otaguro's school track them down. After Terry dispatches

the killers, he heads back to Tokyo to bring down the Mafia villains. Amazingly, Terry's opposition includes a rematch with Junjo Shikenbaru (Musashi Ishibashi), who survived having his throat torn out in the original.

Though not as outrageously violent as the original (except for one eye-popping incident), *Return* still delivers plenty of hard-hitting action. The Street Fighter's nasty disposition is also slightly mellowed. Its one great flaw is its simpleminded plot—one wonders just how much cash Otaguro could really raise through his scheme. However, it's really just an excuse to send waves of thugs against the hero. No doubt pressured to churn out a sequel as fast as possible, director Shigehiro Ozawa isn't as visually inventive here. As in the previous entry, everyone in the dubbing booth calls him Terry Tsurugi, while the credits read "Sugury." **AKA:** *Satsujim-ken 2.* 🐉🐉🐉

1974 (R) 82m/C *JP* Sonny Chiba, Masafumi Suzuki, Yoko Ichiji, Musashi Ishibashi, Donald Nakajimi, Zulu Yachi, Claude Gannyon. **D:** Shigehiro Ozawa. **W:** Koji Takada, Steve Autrey. **C:** Teiji Yoshida. **M:** Toshiaki (Tony) Tsushima. **VHS, DVD**

Return of the Tiger

This thriller, titled to cash in on Bruce Li's successful *Exit the Dragon, Enter the Tiger,* starts like a simple 1970s revenge saga (full of guys in wide collars and flares), but turns out to be one of Bruce Li's better movies. Kung fu hellcat Mai Yeung (Angela Mao) invades a gym owned by film producer/drug kingpin Paul (Paul Smith) and proceeds to beat the crap out of everybody, just to pave the way for her partner Chang Hung (Bruce Li). Chang delivers a message to Paul's lieutenant Peter Chen (Chang Yi): he comes from Amsterdam to avenge his father's death by closing down Paul's gym and nightclub, and to kill Paul himself. This puzzles Paul, since he's never been to Holland, has never killed anyone, and doesn't know Chang. This leads him to assume that Paul's rival Sing Hsi-sai (Lung Fei) is backing Chang—a theory that fulfills itself when Chen's traitorous assistant Eugene (Sit Hon) reports the situation to Sing, who decides to support Chang, by sending his new fighter Wong and some thugs to help. In reply, Chang tells Sing that he'll help him against Paul—for $10,000. As a sample of his work, Chang humiliates Paul's bodyguard Tom (big Cheng Fu Hung, wearing a shirt that says "TOM") at the gym. The gang war starts to heat up, but both Chang Hung and Paul are not what they appear.

Kung fu flicks set in a contemporary crime milieu—such as *Invincible Killer*—usually just use the setting as an excuse for fight scenes,

but this film at least makes an effort to emphasize the intrigue equally with the action. There are some twists in the plot that come up halfway that make the story resemble that of *Yojimbo* somewhat. But the endless maneuvering by the participants eventually grows tiresome, and one wishes they'd just get on with the well choreographed punchy-kicky and fine stunt work. While the plot develops in the first half, the action quotient is kept up with a lot of gratuitous fight scenes, with unknown characters grappling with each other. Familiar American character actor Paul Smith (who went from this to playing Bluto in Robert Altman's *Popeye*) mostly just does the usual villain thing (hanging out in offices and hot tubs, smoking cigars), but comes off surprisingly well in the climactic battle. His character is reminiscent of Marvel Comics' the Kingpin. A band in Smith's nightclub lip-syncs to "Play that Funky Music" and other Wild Cherry songs. **AKA:** *Silent Killer from Eternity.* 🐉🐉🐉

1979 (R) 93 m/C *HK* Bruce Li, Paul Smith, Chang Yi, Angela Mao, Lung Fei, Hsieh Hsing, Cheng Fu Hung, Sit Hon, Wu Chia Hsiang, Wang Wing Sheng, Wong Fei, Blackie Ko, Ching Kuo-chung. **D:** Jimmy Shaw. **C:** Chiou Yao-hwu. **M:** Chou Fu-liang. **VHS, DVD**

Return to a Better Tomorrow

If John Woo had sour feelings about Tsui Hark's sequel *A Better Tomorrow 3,* he must be flabbergasted by this absurd, totally unrelated "sequel" from Wong Jing. It begins pretty well, but goes down Wong's typical path of insanity from there. Tong Chun (Ekin Cheng) is a young triad chief in Tsimshatsui district of Hong Kong, who sets out to eliminate troublemaking associate Black Ox (Lo Meng). The attack is well planned, but Ox nearly escapes. A new guy from America called Boston Lobster Tsui (Lau Ching-Wan) kills him, paying the price with a bullet in his own back. Tong has trouble with his girl Chili (Chingmy Yau), and Officer But (Parkman Wong) warns him that the FBI is building a false case against him as a cocaine smuggler. Lobster returns home to more mayhem; finding his wife abusing their daughter and cheating on him with cheap crook Bill Tung, he starts a fight in which his opponent accidentally kills Mrs. Tsui, after which Lobster shoves Tung out a window. Lobster avoids prison via slick triad lawyer Wong Tai-man (an amusingly cocky James Wong), allowing him to be there to help Tong fend off an attack from Ox's vengeful followers.

Tong is framed and arrested by the FBI, but escapes with the help of crazed hit man Holland Boy (Ngai Sing), and skips over to the mainland.

However, it was trusted brother Lui Wei (Ben Lam) who betrayed his boss, and Holland Boy leads an attack that leaves Tong's pal Chiu (John Ching) dead and Tong with a crippled gun hand. Chili tries to get revenge on Lui, but is caught and tortured, and becomes a crippled heroin addict. Tong spends two years hiding in Vietnam, and then returns to Hong Kong as a chef in the restaurant of Fred Simon (Paul Chun). Fred's son Duke Simon (Michael Wong) is in a triad under Lobster, who has become a big shot nightclub owner. A confrontation in the restaurant with mobster Panther results in Tong being diagnosed as having nose cancer (!), and Duke getting kidnapped. They go to Lobster for help, and when he learns the truth about Lui, he breaks off from his former boss and declares war on him.

It's not nearly as nutty as Wong Jing's outright comedies, but *Return* has plenty of outrageous moments and odd diversions, and gives Wong a chance to indulge his own extreme style of gun fu. Like many of Wong's films, this one isn't terribly good, but he piles on so many melodramatic elements and violent action scenes (not to mention his peculiar sense of humor) that one can't help but be entertained. Ekin Cheng fails to register the slightest honest emotion, but Lau Ching-Wan gives another fine performance. ***AKA:*** *San Ying Hung Boon Sik; Xin Ying Xiong Ben Se.* 🐉🐉▽

1994 103m/C *HK* Ekin Cheng, Lau Ching-Wan, Chingmy Yau, Michael Wong, Ben Lam, James Wong, Ngai Sing, Paul Chun, Parkman Wong, John Ching, Lo Meng, Lee Siu-Kei, Chan Chi-fai. ***D:*** Wong Jing. ***W:*** Wong Jing. ***C:*** Cheng Siu-keung. ***M:*** Marco Wan, Lee Hon-chuen. **VHS, DVD**

Revenge of the Patriots

With the defeat of the Mings in the 1500s, the infamous Ching Dynasty began. The Ching prince (Chang Yi, who gains his kung fu prowess by sniffing a mysterious substance before each battle) kills General Tsu (Carter Wong), while Master Wu escapes with the princess (Tso Yen Yung) to the house of Li Ti-Lung (Bruce Li). Wu seeks to hire Li as a guard while transporting the princess, some jewels, and the emperor's last will to the Ming patriots' camp. Li gladly volunteers to fight the Chings and avenge his father's death. Not so patriotic are the bandits who attack them on the road.

Li decides to get his sister (Judy Lee) to help them; complicating matters is the fact that she's presently working undercover in the restaurant owned by Li's jealous rival, Chi Chien (Michael Chan), who married Li's old girlfriend Su Hing (Cheung Chien), and is suspected of being a Ching spy. Traitorous Chi alerts the pursuing Chings, and old Wu is killed in the ensuing battle. Chi and Sing Hu make a deal to show the emperor where the rebels are going.

Incredibly, our heroes decide to hide the treasure inside a pig carcass and float it down the river to their destination! The Chings get ahead of them, and set an ambush, leading to a terrific battle on the riverbanks.

Basically, it's the same plot the world would know in *Star Wars,* but with much better fight scenes, courtesy of the Lau Brothers' choreography. This epic, once thought lost, is one historical adventure that doesn't get bogged down by too many characters and extraneous situations. Director Ulysses Au *(Last Hero in China)* keeps the momentum going throughout, keeping track of everyone's movements even during complex battles. And how many movies play heroic music behind a shot of a floating dead pig? Judy Lee *(Queen Boxer)* steals every scene she's in, both with her fighting and her screen charisma. The soundtrack features borrowed music from Hammer's Dracula movies. Distributors retitled this in some theatres to make it look like another Bruce Lee movie. ***AKA:*** *Chung Yuen Biu Guk; Zhong Yuan Biao Ju; The Ming Patriots; Bruce Lee's Big Secret; Dragon Reincarnate.* 🐉🐉🐉

1976 (R) 87m/C *HK* Bruce Li, Chang Yi, Judy Lee, Michael Chan, Carter Wong, Roy Chiao, Tso Yen Yung, Chan Wai Lau, Ma Kei, Cheung Chien, Chan Sing. ***D:*** Ulysses Au. ***W:*** Kung Yeung, Chang Sengyi. ***C:*** Ching Wing Him. ***M:*** Chou Fu-liang. **VHS, DVD**

Revenge of the Zombies

Not satisfied that this entry in the Shaw Brothers' mid-1970s Black Magic horror series delivers the bloody goods, most markets in the U.S. retitled it to reflect the popularity of *Dawn of the Dead* and other zombie gut-munch movies. Dr. Chang Pei (Ti Lung) and his wife Chiu-li (Tim Lei) are brought to Malaysia by his colleague Dr. Shih Chen-sing (Frankie Wei) to help with some baffling patients, who bear pulsating sores that sprout big worms. Shih believes this to be evidence of black magic. He's right—evil sorcerer Kang Chang (Lo Lieh) is operating in the area, bewitching folks and creating zombies. Just a drop of blood is all he needs to enslave Shih's wife Margaret (Lily Li), whom he brings to his secret lair to provide him with life-prolonging human milk. Making magic costs Kang years off his life, but he must drink lots of milk because he's actually over 70 years old.

Next morning, Shih discovers that Margaret appears to be a full nine months pregnant, and a caesarian operation yields a hideous monstrosity. Kang makes corpses live and look young again by casting spells using his own blood and driving big nails into their skulls, but the effect isn't permanent—as a dissatisfied customer discovers when his requested date is decayed instantly by his good-luck charm. When he asks Kang for a refund (!), the villain zaps him with a gruesome death curse. The curious medics hold an illegal midnight autopsy in the graveyard, and find the body already incredibly decayed. They decide for Shih to go undercover as one of Kang's clients, telling him he wants to steal Chiu-li away from her husband. Their little ruse puts Chiu-li in danger of becoming a zombie, and puts Shih under Kang's control as well.

The soundtrack provides lots of unintentional laughs throughout, starting with having Lo Lieh's villain dubbed with a boy-next-door voice. The odd music score mixes 1940s-era library tracks with '70s funk. But the story provides plenty of giggles as well—as when Ti Lung has to chase his spellbound wife and best friend across town to keep them from consummating their newfound supernatural attraction. Also there's the matter-of-fact way Lo goes about his grotesque business, strolling behind secret panels to push spikes through his face. And who knew that slapping someone with a dead fox is a good way to fend off possession? The film gets into action mode late in the game, when Ti Lung battles a horde of kung fu zombies, then fights Lo Lieh atop cable car (via some sloppy studio rear projection). But the kung fu is minimal, the focus being held by bizarre gross-out effects and Hong Kong movie insanity. **AKA:** *Ang Wan Gong Tau; Gou Hun Jiang Tou; The Ghost Story; Black Magic Part 2.* 🎵🎵🎵

1976 (R) 89m/C *HK* Ti Lung, Lo Lieh, Tim Lei, Frankie Wei, Terry Liu, Lily Li, Lin Wei-tu, Yang Chih-ching, Joan Lim, Yeung Ching-Ching. **D:** Ho Meng-Hua. **W:** Ngai Hong. **C:** Tsao Hui-chi. **M:** Chen Yung-yu. **VHS**

Revengeful Swordwomen

The story of fighter Heartless Lady Hsiang Ying (Judy Lee) begins the way many end—her master attacks her, saying he is no longer her master but the man who killed her father. She's unable to beat him, and he locks her in a wooden cage. A wandering swordsman named Ku Chun helps her escape. Ku Chun has his own vendetta, against his uncle Ku San, the man who murdered *his* father. They team up to kill her master, but his revelation was only a ruse to make her train harder—her father's real killer is Ku San as well. She picks up a helper in Cloud Hsiang, who has a beef with Hu San himself. Swordsman Ling Shing-sun meets her in the forest, claiming

she was the killer who slaughtered his whole clan. Of course it's a frame made by Ku San, meant to send their fighters against her. She also has to face the golden claws of Shu Shang, Golden Bird's singing darts, a Shaolin monk, and even the famous One-Armed Boxer (Phillip Ko). Finally reaching Ku San's palace, she finds that all is not as it appears within the Ku family.

This is a generally uninvolving martial arts programmer, enlivened only by Lee's performance and several gimmick weapons, including some cool flying skulls. There's not much that's special about the kung fu choreography or direction, but there are a few interesting Taiwan locations to look at in the background, including what looks like a petrified forest. **AKA:** *Revengeful Swordswoman.* 🎵🎵

1979 86m/C *TW* Judy Lee, Man Kong Lung, Phillip Ko, Chuen Yuen, Wong Chi Sang, Lee Man Tai, Tung Li, Shih Ting Ken, Cho Kin, Ching Kuo-chung, Chang Chi-ping. **VHS, DVD**

Rich and Famous

One of the first features to try to cash in on the success of Chow Yun-fat in *A Better Tomorrow* was this two-part gangster saga, continued in *Tragic Hero*. In 1969 Hong Kong, Chiu Chow refugee Tang Kat-yung (Alex Man) runs up a $1200 gambling debt to bookie Uncle Chai. Fighting off the gangster's boys with his adopted brother Lam Ting-kwok (Andy Lau) causes enough damage to add another $8000 to the debt, but due to Kwok's pleading, Yung gets to keep all his fingers for another 10 days. Their attempts to skip town by robbing gangster Chu Lo-tai (O Chun Hung) only bring more trouble—Kwok is kidnapped by Ko's men, and his cousin Pearl Wai Chui (Pauline Wong) goes to big-hearted triad boss Lee Ah-chai (Chow) for help. Afterward, Yung and Kwok, along with their stuttering pal "Gutsy" Mak Ying-hung (Alan Tam), go to work for Lee. Mak isn't cut out for the triad life, but during the ensuing years, Kwok proves his worth. Yung's showboating, on the other hand, nearly gets everyone killed on a trip to Macau. Lee's protection of his old friend, Thai drug lord Fan Tit-tau (Fan Mui-Sang), brings heat from hothead cop Inspector "Iron Shovel" Cheung (Danny Lee), as well as Fan's competitors—but also brings Mak's pretty nurse cousin Lau Po-yee (Carina Lau) into his life. Fan's enemies put a half million–dollar bounty on his head, and threaten to cut off drug supply from Thailand, but still Lee stands by him.

Craven Yung betrays Lee and takes up a contract from Chu Lo-tai to murder Fan. The identity of the killer is easily found out, but because of family loyalty Kwok stands up for his brother, and Lee casts them both out. When Yung chooses to sign up with Chu, Kwok splits

up with his brother, putting his own life in danger. Meanwhile, Lee has become engaged to Po-yee, and brings both Mak and Kwok back to his side. But as old godfather Hung has died, Chu chooses Lee's wedding day to make his move to take over the triads, inevitably pitting brother against brother.

It's painfully obvious that all of the characters are stereotypical gangster-movie types, from Chow Yun-fat's saintly boss to Alex Man's sniveling backstabber, and they all go through their usual paces. It's also impossible not to notice that Danny Lee's hairstyle changes completely from shot to shot. Continued in *Tragic Hero*—which the studio thought was more commercial and decided to release first, strangely enough. *AKA: Goo Woo Ching; Jiang Hu Qing; Drifter Love.* ♫♫

1987 104m/C *HK* Chow Yun-fat, Alex Man, Andy Lau, Carina Lau, Alan Tam, Pauline Wong, Danny Lee, O Chun Hung, Peter Yang, Shing Fui-on, Lam Chung, Fan Mui-Sang, Ng Hong-ling, Ng Hoi-tin, Chen Jing. **D:** Taylor Wong. **W:** Stephen Siu, Manfred Wong. **C:** Abdul M. Rumjahn, Johnny Koo. **M:** Joseph Chan. **VHS, DVD**

Righting Wrongs

Heroin dealer Chow (James Tien) is set free when the informer and his family are killed by an assassin (Peter Cunningham) the day before he can testify. Much like a pulp hero of the 1930s, prosecutor Ha Ling-Ching (Yuen Biao) suits up and becomes a vigilante, dishing out justice when he feels the courts have failed. He kills Chow's crooked lawyer in a high-rise—and gets a parking ticket. Sergeant Wong Jing-Wai (Melvin Wong) assigns Inspector Cindy Shih (Cynthia Rothrock) to the murder, assisted by sloppy cop Bad Egg (director Corey Yuen, giving himself some capers to cut). Bad Egg is henpecked by his father, Officer Tsai (Wu Ma). Cindy follows the parking ticket straight to Ha, but can't prove anything. She has him watched, though. Meanwhile, Chow is also suspicious of the prosecutor, and doesn't worry about the law when it comes to taking care of Ha. But corrupt Sergeant Wong, having collected his dirty money, cuts his risk by killing Chow, trusting Ha will be blamed for this murder as well. Young punk Yu Chi-Wen (Fan Siu-Wong) seems to know everybody's secrets, and gets in deep trouble by trying to blackmail everyone.

This is just a first-rate action picture, from the prologue in "England" (is that Chicago's Field Museum?) on; Chinese opera brothers Yuen Biao and Corey Yuen just keep turning up the heat. Yuen's matches with Rothrock are kung fu cinema classics, as is Rothrock's running brawl with Karen Sheperd, Yuen's savage match with Cunningham, and both heroes versus Melvin Wong—all triumphs for the entire team. Oh, and there's also that whole issue of challenging the criminal justice system. When *Righting Wrongs* was first released under the title *Above the Law*, audiences were disappointed with the blood-thirsty ending, which left just about everyone dead. For worldwide distribution, some extra footage was filmed to provide a more satisfying conclusion. The DVD release includes both versions. *AKA: Chap Faat Sin Fung; Zhi Fa Xian Feng; Above the Law.* ♫♫♫♫

1986 92/94m/C *HK* Yuen Biao, Cynthia Rothrock, Melvin Wong, Wu Ma, Karen Sheperd, Fan Siu-Wong, James Tien, Peter Cunningham, Corey Yuen. **D:** Corey Yuen. **W:** Barry Wong, Szeto Chuek Hon. **C:** Tom Lau. **M:** Romeo Diaz. **VHS, DVD**

Riki-Oh: The Story of Ricky

Based on a popular Japanese comic-book series, this is the most over-the-top violent and outrageous kung fu or prison movie (take your pick) ever made. The setting is the not-too-distant future year 2001, when the prison system has been handed over to private contractors. Ricky (Fan Siu-Wong) is sent to prison carrying five bullets in his chest "for souvenirs" from his arrest. His hitch is 10 years for manslaughter and assault, which he earned by taking revenge on the creeps who killed his girlfriend (Gloria Yip, the only woman's role in the film—and just in flashbacks). Chief warden Cobra (William Ho) is assisted by the Gang of 4, the tough and sadistic leaders of each prison block. The wardens and guards are transparently corrupt. The cons are either purely evil or poor saps with ridiculously sorry hard-luck stories. Ricky is ready to rumble with anybody who looks at him sideways from his first frame.

A long line of prisoners, guards, and finally wardens are sent to mix it up with super-strong Ricky, and all meet their ends in incredibly gory ways. Huge Zorro can literally eat a horse. The assistant warden (Cheng Chuen Yam) is a hook-handed, one-eyed beast. Tattooed he-man Oscar. Head-crushing Taizan. The sprightly terror Huang Chaun (played by actress Yukari Oshima). The monstrous warden himself. All go into battle against our hero, who also must endure a series of incredible tortures, like being buried alive for days and getting ground glass blown in his eyes.

Ricky smashes through all as if they were chunky whipped cream. Building on his inborn super-strength is a secret martial arts technique that feeds on its own power—so the more Ricky fights, the stronger he becomes. The martial arts choreography isn't that impressive, but the blood-drenched mayhem more than makes up for it. Arms, legs, and heads fly everywhere. Who needs fancy Jackie Chan acrobatics when you can cut a guy's head in half with a single chop? The only puzzling thing is why all these supermen bother staying in prison at all.

Looking like an ultraviolent Sid and Marty Krofft Saturday-morning show—or a hyper-realistic Popeye cartoon—*Ricky* nevertheless triumphs over its own stupidity, because...well, are you going to argue with the guy? He can reach up through your chest and haul out your brain! It may not be good, but at least it's incredibly tasteless.

Star Fan Siu Wong is the son of co-star Fan Mui-Sang, a popular character actor. After a career as a Hong Kong child star, Wong studied martial arts in mainland China, then returned to act in HK films like *Righting Wrongs* and *Organized Crime and Triad Bureau*. Though *Riki-Oh* is his only lead role in films to date, he became a much bigger star on television. **AKA:** *Riki-Oh; The Story of Ricky.* 🦴🦴🦴♡

1989 90m/C *HK* Fan Siu-Wong, Fan Mui-Sang, William Ho, Yukari Oshima, Tetsuro Tamba, Gloria Yip, Cheng Chuen Yam. **D:** Simon Nam. **W:** Simon Nam. **C:** Hoi-man **M:** Phil Chan. **VHS, DVD**

Ring

With every advance in technology, horror writers will inevitably exploit that advance, crafting a terror tale around a haunted spaceship or fax machine. On the surface, *Ring* appears to be just such a tale, as its driving device is a cursed video recording. However, *Ring* is much more—a delicately crafted film that builds up tension to the breaking point, drawing you in. Its spell gains an extra dimension on home video...especially if someone sends you a blurry dub in the mail with no return address.

An urban legend is going around among Japanese teens about a cursed videotape, supposedly recorded accidentally by a man visiting Indonesia, which shows a strange woman. If anyone watches the tape, immediately after they'll receive a telephone call, which tells them that they'll die in one week. And everyone who receives the message dies in exactly seven days. As legends go, it's just the right mix of mysterious and stupid to be acceptable. Reiko Asakawa (Nanako Matsushima) is a television journalist working on a story about the legend; her investigations uncover a string of deaths, but she is unable to make a definite connection. Her break comes tragically—her young niece Tomoko (Yuko Takeuchi) dies unexpectedly, and at the wake she finds out from Tomoko's friends that several others in her group died the same night, from no apparent cause. Rumor has it that the cursed video is responsible, all of

them having watched it together on a weekend trip. Checking up on the tip, she chances upon the tape they watched, and of course she watches it. And of course, the phone rings right after. Her investigation becomes a race against time as evidence mounts supporting the curse's reality, and she desperately tries to put together the clues provided by the tape. Her college professor ex-husband Ryuji Takayama (Henry Sanada) joins her, and their efforts become really desperate after their young son Yoichi (Rikiya Otaka) sees the tape.

Based on a story by Koji Suzuki, *Ring* was first adapted as a 1996 TV movie that was so popular it was released to theatres, and this theatrical film was made two years later. *Ring* became a smash hit in Japan, spawning sequels, Korean and American remakes, and a television series—and rightly so. It combines the puzzle-solving suspense of thrillers like *Blow Up* with subtly creepy atmosphere found in ordinary surroundings, growing tension as the doom clock ticks down, and some of the best shocks since Hitchcock. The viewer can't help but feel the curse settle in every time the bizarre tape is shown—especially when you notice that it's never quite the same twice. A nightmare-inducing masterpiece, it also taps into how recorded imagery affects everyone who sees it, from a downloaded video file back to the first cave painting. **AKA:** *Ringu; The Ring.* 🦴🦴🦴🦴

1998 95m/C *JP* Nanako Matsushima, Henry Sanada, Hitomi Sato, Yoichi Numata, Miki Nakatani, Yutaka Matsushige, Rikiya Otaka, Masako, Yuko Takeuchi, Katsumi Muramatsu, Daisuke Ban, Masahiko Ono, Hiroyuke Watanabe, Rie Inou, Orie Izuno. **D:** Hideo Nakata. **W:** Hiroshi Takahashi, Koji Suzuki (story). **C:** Junichiro Hayashi. **M:** Kenji Kawai. **VHS, DVD**

Ring 2

This sequel rightfully ignores *Rasen*, the weak first *Ring* sequel released simultaneously with the original. Well, if you've seen *Ring* (and if you haven't, stop reading and find it right now), you recall that Dr. Ichachiro Ikuma (Daisuke Ban) threw his illegitimate, and monstrously psychic, daughter Sadako Yamamura (Rie Inou) down a well. Her psychic power continued to operate, however, somehow infecting a videotape with a death curse for whoever watched it. Desperately trying to head off the curse, reporter Reiko Asakawa and her ex-husband Ryuji Takayama found Sadako's remains at the bottom of the well. *Ring 2* begins with a coroner pronouncing that the body has only been dead a few years, suggesting that Sadako either found her way out of the well and returned there to die—or she somehow stayed alive down there for 30 years. Reiko's assistant Okazaki (Yurei Yanagi) is still

trying to finish their story, but doesn't know what happened to her. Joined by Ryuji's assistant (and lover?) Mai Takano (Miki Nakatani), he investigates her disappearance, learning Reiko's father has just died in the same way as Ryuji. Detective Omuta is investigating both curious cases.

Masami (Hitomi Sato), the girl who never saw the tape but saw Reiko's niece Tomoko die, seems half cursed, driven mad by the experience and making images from the tape appear on video monitors whenever they're near. Mai is having visions, too, seeing Reiko's son Yoichi (Rikiya Otaka) at times, and even worse: Sadako. Then suddenly she finds Reiko (Nanako Matsushima) and Yoichi in hiding, reasonably well. Doctors at the university hospital decide to try an experiment with Masami to try to see if she can transfer her residual psychic energy to videotape. With the situation getting too dangerous as authorities probe closer to the truth, Mai reveals Reiko's location. Yoichi, who hasn't spoken since his cursed week ended, says his first words—and reveals a frightening power of his own. On the island where Sadako was born, Yoichi and Mai participate in an attempt to scientifically dissipate the powerful psychic energy that continues to kill.

Sequels to films like *Ring* are unlikely to measure up or even stand on their own. *Ring 2* inevitably both succeeds and fails by continuing the same story as the original, answering some remaining questions and attempting to explore the material further. This satisfies the curiosity in some ways, but disappoints in that the same sense of suspense and gnawing fear is not reproduced. Wisely, the climax of *Ring*'s first act—the showing of the videotape—is held back until later in the sequel, but then it's constantly interrupted and shown in pieces. Like *The Blair Witch Project*, *Ring* retains the spirit and simplicity of a spooky campfire tale told in a new way, but the format and concept is abandoned here and replaced with only a scary movie plot that's slightly above average. *AKA: Ringu 2; The Ring 2.* 🐜🐜🐞

1999 94m/C *JP* Miki Nakatani, Nanako Matsushima, Hitomi Sato, Yoichi Numata, Rikiya Otaka, Masako, Katsumi Muramatsu, Taro Suwa, Fumiyo Kohinata, Reita Serizawa, Shiro Namiki, Daisuke Ban, Rie Inou, Yurei Yanagi. *D:* Hideo Nakata. *W:* Hiroshi Takahashi, Koji Suzuki (story). *C:* Hideo Yamamoto. *M:* Kenji Kawai. **VHS**

Ring 0: Birthday

The cursed videotape is still circulating in this second sequel to *Ring*—which quickly reveals itself as a *prequel*. We flash back 30 years to reporter Miyaji (Yoshiko Tanaka) as she inquires about Sadako Yananura (Yukie Nakama) at her Oshima

Island school. After the suicide of her mother Shizuko (Masako), Sadako's father Dr. Heihachiro Ikuma (Daisuke Ban) takes her to Tokyo and enrolls her in a private school there. Inheriting her mother's psychic powers, Sadako has "visions" of ghosts around her, which her doctor tries to suppress with medication. Sadako seems to be coming out of her shell a bit via joining a theatre group, but even though she feels a bit more at ease, those around her feel much *less* at ease. Surprisingly, Sadako's curse is so powerful it reaches back through time to her earlier life, and people around her are having nightmares about deep dark wells. When the leading actress in a play dies of unknown causes, understudy Sadako is given her part. Miyaji catches up with Sadako during rehearsals, as strange events continue to unfold. Director Shigemori (Takeshi Wakamatsu) thinks he knows Sadako's secret, and tries to gain control over her, but when she proves too powerful he tries to kill her, and is accidentally killed fighting technician Toyama (Seiichi Tanabe). Meanwhile, Touama's friend Etsuko and Miyaji come closer to discovering Sadako's real secret.

It's unclear what the two women hope to accomplish with the plan they put into action, which seems terribly unwise, and the result smacks a bit too much of Brian DePalma's *Carrie*. But then, at times the whole concept of *Ring 0* seems unwise, as part of the strength in *Ring* comes from its simplicity. The idea of adding a major wrinkle to the story this late in the game feels revisionist rather than expansive. Fortunately, unlike *Ring 2*, *Birthday* doesn't overplay its trump cards, saving them for a third act that is much better than anything that came before, and helps a great deal in making sense of the first half of the film. Little attempt is made to place events in the 1960s, with all the younger actors sporting hip '90s hairstyles. Things like aluminum cans are removed, and reel-to-reel audio recording is much in evidence, but the producers haven't gone to any great expense to recreate the time period, likely hoping to keep more of the series' core teen audience from tuning out. In all, a flawed but worthy outing, and much better than its direct predecessor in the series. *AKA: Ringu 0: Baasudei; Ring 0.* 🐜🐜🐜

2000 99m/C *JP* Yukie Nakama, Kumiko Aso, Daisuke Ban, Seiichi Tanabe, Chinami Furuya, Masami Hashimoto, Takeshi Wakamatsu, Kaoru Okunuki, Yoshiko Tanaka, Kazue Kadokae, Go Shimada, Masako. *D:* Norio Tsuruta. *W:* Hiroshi Takahashi, Koji Suzuki (story). *C:* Takahide Shibanushi. *M:* Shinochiro Ogata. **VHS**

Ring Virus

The simultaneous deaths of four people by shock sets reporter Sun-joo (Shin Eun-kyoung)

off on an investigation of a circulating videotape that kills the viewer one week after it is watched. Sun-yoo views the tape, and then searches for the explanations behind its strange imagery. She is assisted by her friend Dr. Choi (Chung Jin-young), for whom she makes a copy of the tape. He believes the images were not filmed, but rather telekinetically transferred from the mind of a woman with supernatural powers directly onto tape. They eventually discover the secret of Euh-suh (Bae Du-na), murdered by her half brother after an attempted rape that revealed her dual sexuality. When her death-deadline passes, Sun-joo believes she has broken the tape's spell by giving Euh-suh's remains a proper burial. She is proven wrong the following day when Choi is found dead. Now she has only one day to save her son, who has also seen the tape. Then she discovers the real secret behind the spell—that it is a chain letter—and decides a son has a greater right to life than a mother.

This Korean remake of the popular Japanese 1997 horror film is not nearly as scary as the original, preferring to focus on the solving of its mystery. It is a whodunit, not a horror film. The main reason for watching it is Shin Eunkyoung, who might not be the world's greatest actress, but is absolutely adorable. —*BW* **AKA:** *Ring; The Ring: Virus.* 🐉🐉🐲

1999 108m/C *KO* Lee Seung-hyeon, Shin Eunkyung, Chung Jin-young, Kim Chang-wan, Bae Du-na. **D:** Kim Dong-bin. **W:** Kim Dong-Bin. **C:** Hwang Chul-hyun. **M:** Il Won. **VHS, DVD**

Rivals of the Dragon

Joseph Lai produced and directed this kung fu flick, which was shot on location in Hollywood. Dr. Chan (Stephen Chiu) agrees to teach kung fu to Ko Ha-wah (Jeffrey Chan), even though his brother Chung is in the triads. He should understand since his own son Ah Hui (Yuen Tak) is a bit of a rascal, using his kung fu to entertain in a nightclub and spending his money in brothels. Wah signs a contract to be a sparring partner at the gym, but gets beaten by the sadistic Tiger regularly, worrying his brother. Chung's bosses get sent a map from their triad chief father that gives the location of a lot of money hidden in Hong Kong. Chung gets shot while stealing the map, but passes it on to Dr. Chan before he dies. The gangsters suspect the old man knows something, and kidnap him to make him talk, while others go to his clinic to threaten Hui. But they find the Chans are tougher than they bargained for.

The villains are played for laughs, contributing a bit of interest. Chang's bosses wear flamboyant Western duds, and the soundtrack plays Morricone's *Fistful of Dollars* theme whenever they appear. The fight scenes are decently choreographed, and though the acting is pretty bad, the action is enthusiastically performed. However, the production is way underfinanced, looking like it was shot with leftover film stock from a porno film. The main titles run over black-and-white footage of an old martial arts match in the ring. 🐉🐉

1983 (R) 79m/C *HK* Jeffrey Chan, Yuen Tak, Bruce Chan, Joseph Yeung, Ken Thomson, Pardon Au, Dickson Wong, Stephen Chiu, Thomas Hope, William Cobalt, Samuel Kent, Lily Taylor. **D:** Joseph Lai. **W:** Raymond Lee, Paul Ko. **C:** Adam Blacksmith. **M:** Michael Tse. **DVD, VHS**

The Road Home

In somber black-and-white footage, Luo Yusheng (Sun Honglei) returns home from the big city to the rural village where he grew up. His father has died while away on a trip, and his mother (Zhao Yulian) is near inconsolable. Luo Yusheng begins to recollect how his parents met, and the film shifts into gorgeous color.

His mother Di (played by Zhang Ziyi in the extended flashback) is a young and shy woman. When Changyu (Zheng Hao), a new schoolteacher, comes to town, she falls instantly in love. The town builds the teacher a new schoolroom, and during the construction period the womenfolk bring the workers daily meals. The women place their contributions anonymously on a table, and the men come along later and pick what they want to eat. Di lives and dies each day, waiting to see if Changyu will select her lovingly prepared meal. Finally he does, and the two begin a slow, tentative, and extremely conservative courtship—they barely meet—under the watchful eye of the entire village. Then Changyu must leave the village for an indeterminate period of time, and Di is left sick at heart, often traveling for miles down a road as she achingly hopes for his eventual return. The same road plays an important role in the concluding sequence. Since Changyu died while away from home, the elderly Di insists an ancient custom must be honored and that pallbearers must carry the casket containing her husband's body home, though the trip is long and the arrangements will be quite expensive.

Zhang Yimou's quiet and colorful tale may be slight, but it's well made and does not overstay its welcome. In her debut, Zhang Ziyi is a determined pursuer of love. Much of the story is told through her eyes and facial reactions, and she nearly burns up the screen. —*PM* **AKA:** *Ngo Dik Foo Chan Miu Chan; Wo de fu qin mu qin.* 🐉🐉🐲

Godfrey Ho
and the Mystery of Tomas Tang

何誌強

According to producer/director Godfrey Ho, he first got together with Tomas Tang in 1979, when he began making movies with Joseph Lai at IFD Arts and Entertainment, a small, independent film production company. Ho had been an assistant to screen writer Ngai Hong at Shaw Brothers who graduated to writing full scripts, but he wanted to direct his own films. Tang was a young filmmaker whom Ho took under his wing; some of the movies they made list Tang as director and Ho as co-producer, sometimes the other way around. When Ho split with Lai to form Filmark Productions (though many of his films were still distributed by IFD), he took Tang with him, and they made many exciting action movies together, such as *Shaolin vs. Lama* and *Ninja Hunters.* In 1986, Ho sold Filmark to Tomas Tang, who made pictures in Taiwan and the Philippines, while Ho made movies for Hong Kong's Bo Ho Films with Phillip Ko. In 1993 an apartment fire in Hong Kong killed Tomas Tang.

Or did it? That's Ho's version, though parts of it may change depending on who's asking the questions or the time of day. The real truth may never be known, as everyone associated with Tang has good reason to lie a little, or a lot. How did he make so many movies so quickly, often with name stars in the cast, with no money or reputation?

Like Jackie Chan and Sammo Hung, Godfrey Ho had his chance to enter a Chinese opera school, but sized them up quickly and left. Even as a boy, he saw nothing but diminishing returns for them in the future, and Art was for suckers. Joseph Lai's father bought a failed production company in 1979, and put his son in charge. Ho elbowed his way in as fiancé to Lai's sister Betty Chan. They set up operations in Korea and Taiwan and Ho made some pretty decent movies, such as *Dragon on Fire, Fury in Shaolin Temple,* and *Raiders of the Wu Tang*. They also made a lot of dreadful ones. In order to put more names in the credits, Betty became "co-producer" on some of them, but even more credit went to "Tomas Tang," one of an ever-growing list of Godfrey Ho pseudonyms. It was in the back offices of IFD that Ho invented his "secret technique" of making ng exploitation movies, a method he denies to this day. They found a room full of films there—both finished and incomplete—and Ho hit upon an idea. Here he had in his possession movies that were already half done. Why not shoot some more footage to fill out the running time and release them as new movies?

And so, Ho and his many pen names went into production overdrive, making movies in Hong Kong, Taiwan, Korea, Malaysia, Indonesia, and the Philippines with scraps of expired film stock, which were released by several different distributors—as many as 15 films a year, maybe more. Some of the movies were all new, but most had a certain amount of footage taken from other movies, and some patchwork jobs were simply stitched together in the editing and dubbing studios. If there was a marketable name in the cast (from any footage), Ho would give them credit, but most of his credits were crammed with long lists of made-up names.

Some have called Ho the Roger Corman of Asia, but at least it's easy to find a filmography for Corman. With his confused maze of alternate titles, credits and under-the-table productions, Ho is more akin to Spanish director Jesus Franco. The filmmakers have had a similar effect on their fans, who get hooked on their peculiar brand of cinematic madness and are faced with the difficult task of tracing their work. Ho's films range from mediocre kung fu flicks and police thrillers to insane concoctions like *Robo Vampire* and *Scorpion Thunderbolt* that defy description. Ho once hired actor Richard Harrison, whom he'd met on the set of Shaw's *Marco Polo,* to do a couple days of acting in a ninja movie for him. Harrison was shocked to learn years later that pieces of that footage could be found in over a dozen films. Not that Ho had anything to do with it— blame Tomas Tang.

When Ho sold off Filmark to Tang, he was really selling it to himself as a tax dodge. Once the heat was off, he sold the company back to Godfrey Ho, only to sell it to Tang again a few years later. Even worse, Ho also sold Filmark to Malaysian producer/director Ratno Timoer, who also began using the Tomas Tang credit. Timoer was a bit concerned to learn that producer Wu Kuo-jen was also releasing Tomas Tang movies, and using the Filmark name and logo! Guess who sold it to him. The mysterious fire that "killed Tang" was very convenient for Ho, who was investigated by police.

Godfrey Ho just kept making movies, from the perverse *Laboratory of the Devil* (an unauthorized sequel/knockoff of the wartime atrocity movie *Men behind the Sun*), to alleged children's film *Thun-*

Continued on next page...

der Ninja Kids in the Golden Adventure (which was followed by at least three sequels, all of which contain material that would earn an "R" rating). Since Joseph Lai, Ratno Timoer and Wu Kuo-jen also use a lot of pseudonyms, it makes the job of determining credit (or guilt) close to impossible. As for Tomas Tang, since his death he's directed at least a dozen movies.

"Don't kill us— we love each other. You can kill us, but wait until our love is consummated."

—A ghost and a vampire gorilla beg a robot not to shoot them, in the gloriously insane *Robo Vampire*

1999 **(G)** 89m/C/BW *CH* Zhang Ziyi, Sun Honglei, Zheng Hao, Zhao Yulian, Li Bin, Chang Guifa, Sung Wencheng. **D:** Zhang Yimou. **W:** Bao Shi. **C:** Hou Yong. **M:** San Bao. **VHS, DVD**

Robo Vampire

Those hunting for deliciously bad cinema should keep an eye out for the name Tomas Tang—even though he likely never existed! A pseudonym that Godfrey Ho started using as director for his films with Joseph Lai, he continued to use it as a house name for the many trashy flicks he spliced together for years after, and now the name has sort of become the "Alan Smithee" of Asia. Here, "Tang" mixes Chinese kyonsi with cyborg cops in another Frankenstein monster of a movie.

Tom Wilde, an "anti-drug agent," is making business rough for narcotics trafficker Mr. Young. His underling Boss Ko comes up with the most logical solution to the problem: he gets a scientist/sorcerer to train vampires to fight with Tom. Thugs Ken (Sun Chien) and Tony (Donald Kong) pack bags of heroin inside vampire coffins for easy smuggling. But since someone has replaced the drugs with rice flour, the vampires wake up and nearly escape. The sorceror's special project is to create a Vampire Beast named Peter, but his ghost fiancée Christine objects, since this ruins their suicide pact and they can't be reunited in the afterlife. The sorcerer commands Peter to fight the ghost, but he recognizes her tattoo and stops cold. The gangsters decide to let the supernatural creatures get married, as long as they both agree to work for them afterward. Working on info provided by undercover agent Sophie, Tom and his men shows up to intercept a deal, but Tom is killed fighting the vampires (in broad daylight). A scientist gets permission from Mr. Glen to turn Tom's body into a cyborg ninja. Meanwhile, Sophie has her cover blown and is held captive by Mr. Young. At this point, the middle section is padded out with scenes from a Thai movie about mercenaries led by Agent Ray (Sorapong

Chatri) fighting drug-runners and trying to rescue Sophie. The Robo Warrior's first mission is a disaster: the vampires don't hurt him much, but the bad guys blow him to pieces with a grenade launcher. Right after a shot of the robot being totally destroyed in a fiery explosion, there's a scene back in the lab where Glen says he has a short circuit, and the scientist says it's "not that serious"!

There's a ghost in a see-through shroud, vampires sleeping with snakes and hamsters, a robot that looks like old junk stapled to plastic garbage bags, a blonde actress doubled by a stuntman wearing a gray wig, kyonsi in a gorilla mask, and some sets consisting of a mere black backdrop. Now, isn't this what creative filmmaking is all about? The Robo Warrior also showed up in Tang's *Counter Destroyer*. As seen in a lot of imported/international productions, many names credited had more to do with the dubbing and editing than actual filming. **AKA:** *Robocop vs. Vampires.* 🐶🐶

1988 91m/C *TH/PH* Robin MacKay, Nian Watts, Harry Myles, Joe Browne, Nick Norman, George Tripos, David Borg, Diana Byrne, Alan Drury, Louis Roth, Sorapong Chatri, Sun Chien, Donald Kong. **D:** Godfrey Ho, John T. Carter. **W:** Louis Roth, William Palmer. **C:** Anthony Mang. **M:** Ian Wilson. **VHS, DVD**

Robotrix

The Farrelly Brothers have nothing over Hong Kong cinema in the shock-humor department, where poking fun at AIDS patients is routine. You won't find many flicks more wildly offensive and indefensibly obnoxious than this piece of sci-fi/action/sexploitation, the Category III version of *The Terminator*.

A peppy new wave theme that's 10 years out of date opens the picture, and leads to sexist attitudes that are 30 years out of date. RHKP officer Linda Lin (Chikako Aoyama) and her team are given the assignment to protect an Arab prince on his visit to Hong Kong, including a trip to a brothel. A mystery man kidnaps the prince, shooting Linda dead while escaping, and leaves behind a videotape. Her boyfriend, homicide cop Chou (David Wu) is inconsolable. Meanwhile, at the International Android Show, manufacturers from around the world vie for the investment dollars of a rich oil sheik. When an American android goes berserk during a demonstration, Japanese model Eve 27 destroys it, gaining the sheik's support. The tape reveals that the kidnapper is actually aged mad scientist Ryuichi Yamamoto (Lam Chung), who has transferred his mind to a superpowered cyborg body (Billy Chow). Eve 27's creators, Dr. Sara (Hui Hiu-Dan) and her android assistant Anna (Amy Yip), are called in on the case, with the idea that Yamamoto's method can be used to transfer Linda's mind into Eve 27, so that she can catch Yamamoto.

The robotized Linda is reassigned to Chou's homicide unit, where she, along with Sara and Anna, try to help them catch the "psychic killer," who is preying on HK prostitutes. Of course, they suspect the killer is really Yamamoto. Anna enthusiastically volunteers to go undercover, declaring, "I must taste the life of a whore... I want to sample men's lovemaking." But due to Anna's eager performance, the operation is a bust. However, the sexy trio attracts Yamamoto's attention and he lures them into a fight that all of them are lucky to walk away from. All three robots retreat for repairs, and the sheik decides the only way to save his son is to cooperate with Yamamoto in creating his Robot Legion. But Yamamoto isn't much interested in the kidnapping anymore, instead concentrating on killing the robotrixies.

Though combining sex and science fiction is nothing new, never before has it been accomplished with such energy. The women are all beautiful, and frequently naked, and the chases, stunts, and f/x are much better than you'd expect. The distasteful rape scenes, which are more accepted in Asia (especially Japan) than they are elsewhere, are a sour note. The lab sets and costumes are agreeably cheesy. *AKA: Nu Jie Xie Ren.* 🐉🐉🐲

1991 94m/C *HK* David Wu, Amy Yip, Chikako Aoyama, Billy Chow, Hui Hiu-Dan, Lam Chung. **D:** Jamie Luk. **W:** Jamie Luk, So Man Sing. **C:** Yeung Jim. **M:** James Yeung, Yeung Siu Hung. **VHS, DVD**

Rock 'n' Roll Cop

In the years leading up to the 1997 reunification, Hong Kong cinema was full of films in all genres that brought HK residents together with their mainland brethren. Here Kirk Wong, the man who brought you *Crime Story* and *Organized Crime and Triad Bureau,* directs a popular entry in this now-less-relevant subgenre. The Chun Lu Red Scarf Gang has been taking advantage of the division, committing crimes in one country

then hiding out across the border. Inspector Hung (Anthony Wong) finds himself assigned to the case alongside Beijing detective Wong Kun (Wu Hsing-kuo), whose superior was murdered by the Red Scarf. The gang is able to stay one step ahead of the cops, and Red Scarf leader Shum Chi-hung (Yu Rongguang) is even able to capture Hung. The HK cop is surprised to learn that his ex-girlfriend Hou-yee (Carrie Ng) is now with Shum, and she even provides fake passports for the gang. Wong Kun is able to rescue Hung, but he's now forced to try to deal with his personal involvement with Hou-yee while trying to catch the gang.

As in his other films, it's Wong's handling of police procedures that's interesting here, as the drama and romance angles aren't very engaging. There's not much in the way of action, despite the presence of Yu in the cast, as the accent is on gritty atmosphere. Anthony Wong adds another "shady cop who does the right thing in the end" to his resume, and turns in another great job as the jaded Hung, who finds his only solace in vintage rock albums. *AKA: Sang Gong Yat Ho Tung Chap Faan; Sheng Gang Yi Hao Tong Ji Fan; Rock and Roll Cop.* 🐉🐉🐲

1994 92m/C *HK* Anthony Wong, Wu Hsing-kuo, Yu Rongguang, Carrie Ng, Jennifer Chan. **D:** Kirk Wong. **W:** Lu Bing. **C:** Ko Chiu-lam. **M:** Danny Chung. **VHS, DVD**

Rodan

The U.S. version begins, like many American sci-fi flicks of the 1950s, with a sequence of hydrogen bomb tests that almost brags about how many we were slinging around. Then lead character Shigeru Kamura (Kenji Sahara, dubbed by Keye Luke for the U.S. version), a miner, takes over narration from the strident tones of David Duncan. Tensions are running high at the Chigamatsu mines. Usually cool-headed Goro (Rinsaku Ogata) Shigeru's future brother-in-law, is seen fighting. The miners are all worried about a "creeping floor" in #8 mine. Then Shigeru's buddy Yoshi is found killed, and Goro is lost. Tension and melodrama build within the mining company, much like that inside the fishing company in *Godzilla Raids Again.* The discovery of monsters (called "megaguirons" in the Japanese version) in the mine pretty much exonerates Goro of killing Yoshi. These creatures, like bus-size centipedes with pinchers, have a blatantly phony look to them, but are frightening nonetheless. (They would not be seen again in a Toho picture until *Godzilla vs. Megaguirus* in 2000.) The army is called in for a bug hunt, blasting the critters with machine guns and flame-throwers. During the battle, Shigeru finds Goro's body, but he's

"Your German robot is really out of date. Not only is it overweight, it's clumsy. Our American robot is as powerful as yours. But it's far more superior. It's smaller. It's better equipped. It's faster."

—An ugly American does some trash talking during a future version of *BattleBots* in Robotrix

caught in a cave-in. Miles away, Shigeru surfaces in a landslide area. Suffering from a shock, it takes time before Shigeru can continue his story.

Up to this point, *Rodan* has been much like *Them!* and other big-bug movies, but during Shigeru's recovery it takes a twist that raises the stakes. A military jet is destroyed by some sort of UFO; this supersonic craft is reported all over the world. Shigeru finally recalls his experience after his disappearance: while he was attempting to flee from the huge bugs in a cavern, he was saved when a much larger creature that hatched from a titanic egg ate the monster. Pieces of the eggshell are dated at 20 million years. The pterosaurean beast and its twin escape from the cavern to harass the 20th century. With that, Shigeru and his bride Kiyo become just civilian observers like anyone else, while *Rodan* shifts gears and becomes a fast-paced giant monster action movie.

In the rush to produce the sequel to *Godzilla,* director Ishiro Honda lost most of the original film's depth, bogged down in useless narration and lesser f/x. With his second monster star, now in full color, his message isn't as strong, but he makes up for it in terror and spectacle. Less a nuclear nightmare than *Godzilla, Rodan* needn't even be connected with the H-bomb tests except for one thing: with a 500-foot wingspan, the beasts are 10 times as large as any known flying reptile, and 100 times as fast. The f/x range from the slightly goofy megaguirons to some incredible scenes of destruction. Britain's shady King Brothers picked up *Rodan* for distribution in the Western world, hiring voice actors Paul Frees and Keye Luke to do some quick dubbing. Some of the added sound effects are as old as *King Kong,* but few major changes were made from the original version, which was around eight minutes longer. ***AKA:*** *Radon; Sora no Daikaiju Radon; Rodan the Flying Monster.* ♫♫♫

1956 74m/C *JP* Kenji Sahara, Yumi Shirakawa, Akio Kobori, Akihiko Hirata, Yasuko Nakata, Minosuke Yamada, Yoshifumi Tajima, Ren Imaizuma, Shoichi Hirose, Kiyoharu Ohnaka, Haruo Nakajima, Ren Yamamoto, Katsumi Tezuka, Rinsaku Ogata. ***N:*** David Duncan (U.S.). ***D:*** Ishiro Honda. ***W:*** Takeshi Kimura, Takeo Murata, Takashi Kuronuma (story). ***C:*** Isamu Ashida. **VHS, DVD**

asians in usa

Romeo Must Die

Considering the title, you won't be surprised that this action film is loosely based on *Romeo and Juliet.* What you might be surprised by is how nicely the filmmakers have adapted that work. They kept the feuding clans element (though, in this case, it's competing gangs), they kept the romance angle (without making it too syrupy), and they jettisoned everything they didn't need to make a cool, kick-ass kung fu picture.

Jet Li plays Sing Han, the son of Sing Chu (Henry O), a Chinese gang leader, working to take over the Oakland waterfront. Aaliyah is Trish O'Day, daughter of black gang leader Isaak O'Day (Delroy Lindo). The two gangs are working together to acquire the land needed to build a new football stadium. Both gangs are trying to get out of crime, and into legitimate business-es—or are they? The plan seems simple enough. Trouble is, people on both sides keep ending up dead. One of those killed is Po (Jonkit Lee), Han's brother. This causes Han, a wrong-

fully imprisoned policeman, to break free from a Hong Kong jail and travel to America. Once in the U.S., Jet sets about looking for his brother's murderer. Circumstances throw him together with Trish. Her brother, Colin (D.B. Woodside—the principal on *Buffy the Vampire Slayer* for the 2002–3 season), may have a lead on the crime. Han and Trish become good friends, much to the chagrin of their respective clans. When Colin is killed, it seems likely that the two gangs will go to war. Despite rising tensions between their parents, Han and Trish remain committed to rooting out the true perpetrators.

What follows is a pretty good action/sus-pense/mystery story. None of it is too surpris-ing, but it has a couple of nice twists and turns. There are some well-done kung fu scenes, and a standard American-style car chase. Watch for an all-too-brief appearance by Francoise Yip *(Rumble in the Bronx).* Jet and Alliyah grow closer throughout the turmoil, almost justifying the Romeo reference in the title. Be sure to stick around for the high-octane kung fu dénouement.

One of the nice things about this flick is the way race is handled. Bad people do bad things in the film, but no one seems to think too much

"Courage, man; the hurt cannot be much." Jet Li during one of the more Shakespearean moments of *Romeo Must Die.*

about skin color on either side. The thing that bothers the clan about the Jet/Alliyah relationship is more about heritage than race. It's odd for a kung fu action film to have a message—even a subtle one—of racial tolerance. Here, the idea is reinforced by the themes of Shakespeare's original play; the filmmakers deserve applause for taking the high road. The fighting in this film is good, supplemented by interesting "impact cam" SFX. Jet Li is up to his usual wu shu standards, and does a good job with the acting—especially considering it's his first English-language lead role. There's some neat wire-work stuff, and good computer-enhanced action. Like *Lethal Weapon 4,* this film stands as a good introduction to Jet Li and his work for American audiences. It's not quite as much fun as *The One,* or *Kiss of the Dragon,* but still a good place to start. —SS 🎸🎸🎸

2000 (R) 114m/C *US* Jet Li, Aaliyah, Isiaiah Washington, Russel Wong, DMX, Delroy Lindo, D.B. Woodside, Henry O, Jonkit Lee, Tong Lung, Franoise Yip. **D:** Andrej Bartkowiak. **W:** Mitchell Kapner, Eric Bernt, John Jarrell. **C:** Glen MacPherson. **M:** Stanley Clarke, Timbaland. **VHS, DVD**

Rosa

This buddy-cop comedy pairs Yuen Biao and Lowell Lo in a lighthearted action romp, with mixed—but generally entertaining—results. Rookie Detective "Little Monster" Hsia (Yuen) embarrasses his superior Paul Tin (Paul Chun) in capturing a pickpocket. That afternoon, he injures a girl (Kara Hui) while chasing a suspect, and takes her to the hospital. The girl's brother, Detective Lei Kung (Lo), causes an accident that damages Tin's car (and causes his wife to go into labor prematurely) while rushing to the hospital. Naturally the two cops become antagonists, but find the next day that Tin has punished them both by making them partners. After informer Li Wei-feng (Charlie Cho) calls the police to tell them he's got evidence against mob boss Wang Ping-tang (James Tien), he disappears, and Tin assigns Lei and Little Monster to question Li's sassy model girlfriend Rosa (Luk Siu-fan). Rosa is not anxious to cooperate with police, but with loan shark Tsai (Fung Ging Man) after her to recoup her gambling debts, she decides to try to string the two cops along for protection. With the help of Little Monster and his sister, Lei attempts to woo the voluptuous Rosa by posing as an American triad chief (in blackface!) to get her debt to Tsai cancelled. But when their bluff is revealed, the partners have to fight their way through a roomful of gangsters.

For a time, the film stalls out by sinking into sophomoric comic antics in the style of the Lucky Stars pictures. The high point of this sec-

tion is a riotous routine involving Lei's "last request," while the lowest has to be an interminable mah-jongg game. But by the end things pick up considerably: Wang's thugs kidnap the two girls, and their beaus bring the evidence to (where else?) a warehouse for an exchange, whereupon a big battle inevitably breaks out. It's great to see Yuen fighting side-by-side with Hui, though he doubles her acrobatic stunts. The fight between Yuen and the gang is terrific, climaxing in an even better duel with Dick Wei. However, the film's overall comic tone won't allow for an all-out brawl, and the silly outcome of all the mayhem is only nominally amusing. The big flaw here is that there just doesn't seem to be much to the characters, or any chemistry between them—after so much time is spent setting up the partners as enemies, they become best friends in about two seconds. Luk Siu-fan would go on to star in the intriguingly titled *Boss Noballs.* **AKA:** *San yeung Seung Heung Paau Juk Jaap; Shen Yong Shuang Xiang Pao Xu Ji.* 🎸🎸💧

1986 92m/C *HK* Yuen Biao, Lowell Lo, Luk Siu-fan, Paul Chun, Kara Hui, James Tien, Charlie Cho, Fung Ging Man, Tai Bo, Dick Wei, Chung Fat, Chan Lung, Blackie Ko, Huang Ha, Baan Yun-sang, Billy Ching, Hsu Hsia, Fung Lee, Yuen Miu. **D:** Joe Cheung. **W:** Barry Wong, Wong Kar-Wai. **C:** Tom Lau. **M:** Chow Kam-cheung. **VHS, DVD**

Roujin Z

Medical technology is already increasing the worldwide average lifespan, and in the future, this trend will likely accelerate. With hospitals and nursing homes all operating beyond capacity, a breakthrough is made. The Z-001 is the ultimate caregiving device—nurse, physical therapist, maid, cook; total care of the patient can be given over to the machine. Elderly invalid Kijuro Takezawa is chosen as the first volunteer to receive the Z-001, despite the protests of student nurse Haruko Mihashi, the only person who cares for the old man. Powered by a miniature atomic furnace and controlled by an advanced computer, the super-bed will meet Takezawa's every need. But what if there's a situation the Z-001's designers haven't foreseen? Not to worry—the unit has self-enhancement capabilities that enable it to analyze and adapt to new situations.

Well, there can be too much of a good thing. Soon after being turned over to Z-001, Haruko starts receiving a plea for help on her computer. And every other computer. She and her friends break into the government testing facility and find Takezawa. Technicians disconnect the unit from the network, and Z-001 builds itself a

vocalizing application to express Takezawa's wishes. And what he wishes for is to go home. Haruko assents, and the Z-001 takes off, adapting and changing shape to overcome any obstacle. Caught by the authorities, the bed is returned to the facility, and Takezawa is kept entertained with visions from his younger days fed through a cybernetic link to Z-001. But Haruko gets the old programmers in her hospital to hack into the Z-001 system. The machine wakes up with the personality of the late Mrs. Takezawa, and heads for happier times at the beach, growing and adapting as it goes. However, the military has built a combat version of Z-001, and both robots head for a face-off.

Movies about the medical crisis are rare in the West, but there have been several Asian sci-fi films that have dared to explore this tricky subject. *Roujin Z*, which handles its theme with grace, charm, and imagination, is likely the best of these—or at least the most direct. Katsuhiro Otomo, creator of *Akira*, provides incredibly complex, clean-lined images that recall the work of cartoonist Geoff Darrow *(Big Guy and Rusty the Boy Robot)*. *AKA: Rojin Z; Oldman Z.* 🦴🦴🦴♡

1991 (PG-13) 80m/C *JP* **V:** (English voices) Allan Wenger, Toni Barry, Barbara Barnes, Ian Thompson, Nicolette McKenzie. **D:** Hiroyuki Kitakubo. **W:** Katsuhiro Otomo. **C:** Hideo Okazaki. **M:** Bun Itakura. **VHS, DVD**

Royal Space Force: The Wings of Honneamise

Probably the best way to describe this epic Japanese film is the animated alternative-universe version of *The Right Stuff*. Set on an alien world with striking similarities to segments of our own past history, it chronicles a race's stumbling steps toward space flight, struggling against technological hurdles, military dangers, and political maneuvering. Only an average student, young Shiro Lhadatt finds he's just not good enough to realize his dream of becoming a Navy pilot, and has to settle for a position in the newly formed Royal Space Force. Lhadatt is reeling in depression for being just a cadet in a military division thought useless by anyone who even knows it exists; all it seems to be good for is to kill cadets in rocket mishaps. The only ones who believe in the RSF mission are the old scientists in charge of the experiments. That is, until Shiro meets a religious young girl who somehow instills some ambition in him. Fighting an uphill battle, he eventually begins to convince his compatriots that the only way they'll ever make a mark on history is to get

behind the program's far-fetched goal: to launch a man into outer space.

While the RSF toils away, trying to overcome many failures, the nation's foolish foreign policy gets them in hot water, and they seem on the brink of a world war they have no hope of winning. Their only chance may lie in actually building and launching the Royal Space Force's "space warship."

The brainchild of director Hiroyuki Yamaga, *Royal Space Force* was given the largest budget ever granted a Japanese animated film up to that time, a fact that's all the more remarkable considering Yamaga's relative youth and inexperience. He gathered together some of the greatest talents in the business to form his studio Gainax Production Company, eventually employing over 3,000 animators to work on the project. Assisted by early computer graphics techniques, Gainax artists produced stunning visuals, in quantity as well as quality. Even something like an early computer had to look like it worked, but not in the same ways that ours do. Acclaimed composer Ryuichi Sakamoto provided a finely textured, thrilling electronic soundtrack. Resisting all temptation to make the picture too cutesy, the result was one of the most mature, entertaining, and lovingly detailed films ever made. *AKA: Honneamise no Tsubasa—Oritsu Uchugun; Wings of Honneamise, Starquest.* 🦴🦴🦴🦴

1987 125m/C *JP* **D:** Hiroyuki Yamaga. **W:** Hiroyuki Yamaga. **M:** Ryuichi Sakamoto. **VHS, DVD**

Royal Tramp

Jin Yong's famous five-volume 1969 novel *The Duke of Mt. Deer* had been adapted into a hit TV miniseries during the 1980s that made a star out of Tony Leung Chiu-Wai. In this broad Wong Jing spoof, Stephen Chow takes the lead role, with predictably riotous results.

The reign of boy Emperor Hsuan-hua (Deric Wan) got off to a rocky start, as the Empress Dowager (Sharla Cheung) and advisors struggled to take control of China. Chief among these schemers was military commander Lord Ao-Bye (Elvis Tsui), who dedicates himself to eradicating the rebellious Heaven and Earth Society. The exploits of the society's heroic leader Chang Chin-nan (Damian Lau) are related by brothel storyteller Wei Siu-bao (Chow). The emperor disguises himself in civilian garb and, along with trusted head eunuch Ha Da-fu (Ng Man-Tat), goes to meet with the seven clan chiefs in secret at the brothel, where Wei's sister Chun-hua (Sandra Ng) is Madame. The meeting is nearly broken up when Ao-Bye's soldiers come to arrest Chang. Wei saves Chang's life, and is rewarded by being accepted as the kung fu master's student. Wei is immediately volunteered to steal the "42 Chapter Classic" from the palace, which contains a secret that will allow the Heaven and Earth Society to restore the Ming Dynasty to power. Sent to work undercover as an errand boy, Wei mistakenly volunteers to be a eunuch! Luckily, Lord Ha is shorthanded, and puts Wei to work intact. Ha also wants the "42 Chapter Classic," and forces Wei to steal the book from the Empress Dowager. But through a misadventure involving the Princess Jian-ning (Chingmy Yau), Wei becomes a spy for the emperor instead, and soon uncovers a conspiracy within the palace.

With a huge novel to condense, much of Chow's usual nonsense gets squeezed out, even with a lot of plot cut from the tale. However, Chow makes the most of his role, with Wong Jing's script making the hero a cowardly opportunist caught up in one intrigue after another. The fantastic action scenes directed by Ching Siu-tung are on a par with that of most other swordplay pictures of the era. Watch for a surprise guest star at the very end, which leads directly into the sequel. The English-dubbed version gives characters ridiculous anglicized names like "Wilson Bond." *AKA: Luk Ting Kei; Lu Ding Ji.* ♫♫♫

1992 106m/C *HK* Stephen Chow, Elvis Tsui, Damian Lau, Sharla Cheung, Ng Man-Tat, Deric Wan, Sandra Ng, Chingmy Yau, Nat Chan, Fennie Yuen, Vivian Chan, Lee Ka-ting, Brigitte Lin. *D:* Wong Jing. *W:* Wong Jing. *C:* David Chung, Henry Chan. *M:* William Woo. **VHS, DVD**

Royal Tramp 2

Wong Jing brings us more of the adventures of Wei Siu-bao (Stephen Chow). If you saw Part 1 (and if you didn't, why are you watching Part 2?), you know that it ended with Sharla Cheung being transformed into bigger star Brigitte Lin in the role of Empress Dowager impersonator Dragon Long-er. It's not known how Ms. Cheung felt about this substitution, but if you have an opportunity to have Brigitte Lin in your movie, you go with it. Long-er's first mission after taking the leadership of the Dragon Society is to act as escort to Prince Wu In-shon (Kenneth Tong) on a visit to Emperor Hsuan-hua (Deric Wan). She's also on the lookout for any opportunity for revenge against Wei, who continues to move up in rank, for spoiling her previous scheme. To plot for peace with the threatening Ping-si kingdom, the emperor betroths his sister Princess Jian-ning (Chingmy Yau) to Prince Wu, and appoints Wei Inspector General to escort the princess to the wedding, which will give him a chance to disrupt any invasion plans from within the palace. But Wei's mission is complicated by the fact that

Ning is now carrying his baby. On the way to Ping-si, Wei and the prince are abducted by two nuns in league with the Heaven and Earth Society. Dragon Long-er rescues them all, taking them to the Dragon Gang base. However, King Wu's forces have already taken over the Dragon Gang, and a poisoned Long-er is forced to not only take sides with Wei against them, but make love to him to counteract the poison. In taking her virginity (inside a giant cocoon!), Wei gains 80% of her kung fu power—and the responsibility of vengeance against the King Wu Sun-gwei (Paul Chun) and his son.

As before, the complex machinations of the plot leave less room for Stephen Chow's madness, though he squeezes in as much nonsense as he can. The action scenes aren't quite as spectacular, but heads do roll, and Brigitte Lin (a special effect herself) lives up to her reputation for magical martial arts spectacle. *AKA: Luk Ting Kei II Ji San Lung Gau; Lu Ding Ji II Zhi Shen Long Jiao.* ♫♫♫

1992 94m/C *HK* Stephen Chow, Brigitte Lin, Damian Lau, Sharla Cheung, Deric Wan, Sandra Ng, Chingmy Yau, Nat Chan, Yam Sai-kwoon, Kenneth Tong, Paul Chun, Michelle Reis, Fennie Yuen, Vivian Chan, Helena Law. *D:* Wong Jing. *W:* Wong Jing. *C:* David Chung, Henry Chan. *M:* William Woo. **VHS, DVD**

Royal Warriors

The second of the popular *In the Line of Duty* series (after *Yes Madam*) clearly shows why there were so many sequels. Hong Kong cop Michelle Yip (Michelle Yeoh of *Supercop, Crouching Tiger, Hidden Dragon*), returning from a vacation in Japan, meets Japanese cop Peter Yamamoto (Henry Sanada from *Shogun's Ninja*), and air security officer Michael (Michael Wong of *Legacy of Rage*) on the jet. On the same plane is criminal Harvey "Tiger" Lee (Michael Chan), being transported in custody. His pal Jimmy Woo (Kam Hing Ying) busts him loose and the two hijack the plane. The heroic trio leaps into action, foiling the hijack.

Big-mouth Michael aggressively pursues pretty Michelle. Yamamoto wants to reconcile with his estranged wife Yukiko (Reiko Niwa), agreeing to transfer to a safe desk job. However, Lee and Woo had a friend in Hong Kong, an old war buddy named Bull (Lam Wai), who vows revenge. Yamamoto's family dies in an exploding car. While Michelle tries to catch their suspect through official police methods, Yamamoto has blood in his eye, and means to get him his own way. One auto chase, a construction-yard fight, a fight on the docks, a machine gun massacre in a nightclub, and a barroom brawl later, and Bull is dead. Unfortunately, he's got one more war buddy left.

The fights, explosions, chases, and even a chainsaw battle (directed by Mang Hoi) are all first-rate. One scene features an incredible fall off a 10-story building. Yeoh's hair changes length from scene to scene, but otherwise she's an amazing action goddess (in only her third film), accomplishing several moves that make you sit up and go "Whoa!" She arrives for the climactic showdown in an impressive hi-tech mini tank. Half-American Wong struggled to throw off his gweilo image early in his career, but in the '90s he made a huge comeback, producing and appearing in dozens of films. Though through the first half this feels like the usual Hong Kong action flick, the second half slowly builds up suspense and excitement, helped along by a minimal-but-moody soundtrack. *AKA: Wong Ga Jin Si; Huang Jia Zhan Shi; In the Line of Duty; Police Assassins; Ultra Force; Yes Madam 2; In the Line of Duty 2.* 🦴🦴🦴

1986 93m/C *HK* Michelle Yeoh, Henry Sanada, Michael Wong, Lam Wai, Michael Chan, Kam Hing Ying, Reiko Niwa, Blackie Ko. **D:** David Chung. **W:** Sammy Tsang. **C:** Derek Wan, Ma Chan-wah. **M:** Romeo Diaz. **VHS, DVD**

Rumble in the Bronx

Jackie Chan, the biggest movie star in Asia, came to conquer America again, but this time on his own terms. Previously, he came to the U.S. in 1980 to star in *The Big Brawl.* It's not a bad picture, but it could've been better if they'd done things Jackie's way. The following year found Jackie guest starring as a Japanese(?) racer in Hal Needham's sloppy chase picture *Cannonball Run,* but his talents were again mostly wasted. In 1985, he decided to give an American production another try; in *The Protector,* director James Glickenhaus *(Exterminator)* was a bit more willing to let Jackie perform some unique stunt sequences, but they both seem hamstrung by budget and insurance constraints. Jackie's comedic talents were again wasted, as he had to play things straight in his New York cop role, and American producers' failure to fully understand and utilize Jackie's appeal resulted in a lukewarm reception.

Not that this failure to bowl over English-speaking audiences fazed Jackie all that much. In the meantime, he was churning out one huge hit after another. As his wonderfully entertaining action movies began to show up in film festivals and midnight shows across America, a cult of Chan fans grew and grew. Taking note, New Line Cinema struck a deal with Chan to distribute three of his latest pictures, *Rumble in the Bronx* being the first to be released as part of this deal. Here Chan plays Keung, a kung fu champ

Hong Kong cop visiting New York City to attend his Uncle Bill's wedding. Uncle Bill (Bill Tung) is also selling his grocery store and retiring, but when the buyer turns out to be the pretty Elaine (movie and singing star Anita Mui, who co-starred in Chan's remake of *Lady for a Day, Miracles*), Keung agrees to help out at the store while Uncle Bill leaves on his honeymoon. Before too long it becomes apparent why Bill was so eager to sell and retire: his Bronx store is regularly victimized by a gang of biker thugs. It doesn't take long for Keung to make himself the enemy of this gang. After a few running battles, they corner him in an alley and bombard him with glass bottles. Barely making it home, he collapses at the door of Danny (Morgan Lam), the crippled little boy next door he's befriended, where he's cared for by Danny's sexy sister Nancy (Francoise Yip). More conflict arises when he learns that Nancy is part of the gang. Eventually Keung defeats, then befriends the gang—at which point he and his friends are threatened by the much bigger menace of much more professional criminals.

Although you may laugh at the poor job Vancouver does in playing New York (watch for the mountains in the background), it's unlikely that this is very noticeable to millions of Chan fans outside the U.S., so it's not really such a big deal. Dozens of Gotham-set movies are shot in Canada and elsewhere every year. Even *Escape from New York* was made in St. Louis.

New Line Cinema cut 15 minutes of "cultural differences" from the version released in Asia last year, but some of this still plays awkwardly. Reflecting circumstances in Hong Kong, the street gang doesn't have many guns (apparently only one), and they're portrayed as a bunch of rowdy kids who "go too far sometimes." Keung often comes off as blatantly self-righteous—after he beats up the entire gang, he gives them a terse lecture, telling them they "are the scum of society!" This line is sure to draw howls of laughter, but it's not uncommon coming from an Asian movie hero. Doubtless, in reality the gang would have shot this troublemaker by this time—in America, the only answer for defeat seems to be retribution—but instead they are shamed and come to respect Keung. The editing also serves to de-emphasize the romantic triangle between Keung, Elaine, and Nancy, which is left hanging at the more abrupt end of the original cut. This makes for a neater, better flowing story, but at the expense of many of Anita Mui's scenes. Also, despite the fact that this has better Anglo actors than most Asian films, some of them are still painfully bad. The soundtrack has also been redone and tweaked. The dubbing has been done as seamlessly as possible, with Chan and most of the cast reading their own lines. The new mix gives the sound effects a snap they didn't have before. There's also new theme

music by J. Peter Robinson, and a catchy new tune by the Ramonesque Irish band Ash over the closing credits.

All this editing has left us with what really matters—Jackie in eye-popping action, and the guy literally gives 'til it hurts. No other star in cinema history has risked his neck so many times. Chan's movies are really in a class by themselves—even his lesser efforts (like this one) have 10 times the thrills of most other action films, especially if you keep in mind it's mostly done without special effects. Knowing this, even stunts that seem relatively simple are impressive. Reportedly, during the scene where Keung is bombarded with bottles, the crew ran out of fake bottles rather quickly. Rather than shut down production while more were made, Chan ordered shooting to continue using real bottles (one of which caught him full in the stomach). During another scene, we see a shot where Chan broke his ankle (if you're watching for it, you can grimace right along). He was back doing stunts the next day in a cast.

To emphasize this element of real danger, Chan always includes outtake footage run behind the closing credits, which New Line has wisely kept in. These clips are often amusing, but just as often frightening, or touching. We see Chan come close to death or serious injury many times, and we also see him sick with worry when others are injured.

Director Stanley Tong *(Supercop)* was a top stuntman himself, until injuries forced his retirement. When developing a stunt or fight sequence, he often tries it out himself to get a better feel for it before shooting begins. He also knows that Chan is always in charge of the production, especially for action scenes. The result of this experience, combined with a fine visual instinct, are action sequences that are easy to follow without any slackening of pace and rhythm. *AKA: Hung Fan Au; Gong Fan Ou; Red Bronx.* 🎜🎜🎜

1995 (R) 87m/C *HK/CA* Jackie Chan, Anita Mui, Bill Tung, Francoise Yip, Ailen Sit, Morgan Lam, Marc Akerstream, Garvin Cross, Emil Chau, Alex To, Chan Man Ching, Kris Lord, Carrie Cain Sparks, Jamie Luk, Yueh Hua, Eddie Ko. **D:** Stanley Tong. **W:** Edward Tang and Fibe Ma. **C:** Jingle Ma. **M:** Nathan Wang, J. Peter Robinson (U.S.). **VHS, DVD**

Run and Kill

This over-the-top Category III thriller gave overweight actor Kent Cheng one of his most distinctive roles. The story is like the Hong Kong version of a Jim Thompson novel, in which an ordinary slob gets involved in a desperate situation, and every move he makes just gets him in deeper trouble. Cheng plays sad sack Ng Kau-cheng—who is of course imaginatively nicknamed "Fatty." Angry with his cheating wife (Lily Li), Ng goes on a bender and has a *Strangers on a Train* moment during which he wishes his wife dead. His contract killing Vietnamese drinking buddies take him seriously and murder his wife and her lover. Police Inspector Man (Danny Lee) naturally suspects Ng, and the killers are demanding their fee of $8000. Ng flees to the mainland, where his gangster neighbor Ching Wah offers to lend a hand with Ng's problems. Their plan backfires, and Wah ends up dead. But wait! Wah's older brother Ching Fung (Simon Yam) is a psychotic mercenary who swears vengeance upon Fatty Ng and his entire family, putting Ng's daughter in dire peril.

Intended as a dark comedy, this film had a director, Billy Tang *(Dr. Lamb),* who couldn't resist the temptation to wallow in brutality, resulting in one savage and relentless scene after another. At first glance, there doesn't seem to be much point to this movie beyond grotesque sensationalism, at which it excels. Yam's maniac character is a killing machine just short of the Terminator, and his every onscreen moment is flush with tension. Many characters meet extremely gruesome ends, and no one in the cast is safe. Cheng's suffering is endless, and if it's exhilarating to see him finally fight back, it only comes after he goes through one of the sicker chambers of Hell. It's a ride too harrowing for most viewers, but for those who appreciate Asian cinema for its unpredictability, and willingness to wallow in audacious low taste, this one can be a winner. *AKA: Woo Sue; Wu Shu; Woo Sue Gei Mat Dong Ngon; Wu Shu Ji Mi Dang An.* 🎜🎜🎜

1993 90m/C *HK* Kent Cheng, Simon Yam, Danny Lee, Melvin Wong, Esther Kwan, Johnny Wang, Lily Li. **D:** Billy Tang. **W:** Bryan Cheung. **C:** Tony Miu. **M:** Wong Bong. **VHS**

Runaway

Triads Dan (Nick Cheung) and his younger partner King (Samuel Pang) decide to take for themselves a large sum of money they collected for their boss, Kwan (Joe Lee). They are discovered when they manage to cross up another crime boss, Ray (Anthony Wong), and so run away to Thailand to hide out. Sun, sand, and surf do not keep them from romance and trouble, however, in the mysterious persons of the lovely Ching (Ruby Wong) and a deaf-mute (Anya) who steals

Jackie Chan's fist is ready for its close-up in this publicity shot for his North American breakthrough *Rumble in the Bronx.* THE KOBAL COLLECTION / GOLDEN HARVEST

King's heart. Non-romantic trouble is provided in the person of a triad (Ken Lo) sent to settle matters with Dan and King.

Dante Lam followed up the conventional action film *Hit Team* with this effort in which he stretched his artistic wings (the end credits gave "special thanks" to a host of international directors, including Kubrick, Scorsese, Kurosawa, and Ozu). The story meanders along in a zigzag manner rather than a propulsive race to the finish. That's a bonus—*Runaway* is character-driven and unpredictable. Film-school flourishes—a touch of speeded-up motion, gentle jump cuts, and the like—are lightly used as accents. Upon reflection, it's hard to pinpoint exactly what would improve the film. It doesn't quite seem to hang together as a whole. Does that really matter? Multiple viewings may be necessary to work out this seeming contradiction.

Anthony Wong is quite remarkable as Ray—you can see him thinking, a recognizably human trait that is all too often absent from the movie world. Nick Cheung plays it nearly completely straight and sober as Dan—a little more life would have been welcome. Joe Lee sports one of the more memorable haircuts in recent film history. The rather workmanlike look of the film manages to capture the holiday locations in a matter-of-fact but attractive way, as photographed by cinematographer Tony Cheung. Tommy Wai composed the entertaining musical score, which ranges from percussive and techno to lilting and tropical. —PM *AKA: Chow Tau Yau Liu; Zou Tou You Lu.* 🐾🐾🐾

2001 98m/C *HK* Nick Cheung, Anthony Wong, Ruby Wong, Ken Lo, Samuel Pang, Joe Lee, Anya. **D:** Dante Lam. **W:** Ng Wai-lun, Lau Ho-leung. **C:** Tony Cheung. **M:** Tommy Wai. **VHS, DVD**

Running out of Time

The clock is ticking on the life of super-thief Cheung (Andy Lau). He has incurable cancer, and his doctor has given him a deadline. With two weeks left and nothing to lose, he puts into action a well-designed plan, robbing a finance company to get the attention of police negotiator Inspector Ho Sheung-sang (Lau Ching-Wan). He says he wants to play a game with Ho over the next 72 hours. Captain Wong (Hui Siu-hung), who is in charge of the case, won't cooperate with Ho willingly, so the inspector has to use his own resources to try to find out what the thief is really after. Actually, the thief is using Ho as a necessary part in his plan to steal an $80 million diamond from a mobster (Waise Lee)—and get revenge.

Another tight thriller from Johnny To *(The Mission)*, *Running out of Time* is a buddy heist

movie with echoes of *The Killer,* as the cop and the criminal gradually gain each other's respect, and finally work together toward a common purpose. It's also a puzzle movie in which you can't tell too much of the plot without giving away everything. The one flaw here is that Cheung has that special movie cancer that makes him look great until the end, only coughing a little blood to let you know he's still sick. However, the disease is what makes the thing work—otherwise, the clockwork of these types of stories tends to hinge too much on chance. Since Cheung has nothing to lose, it's more believable that he'd risk just seeing how some situations will play out. One of those X-factors plays hilariously in the person of Lam Suet as the crook whom Lau Ching-Wan keeps running into, but can't seem to place the face. Lau Ching-Wan's usual grubby cop performance works well in counterpoint with Andy Lau's slick and handsome thief. Raymond Wong provides a terrific score. Followed by a less-serious sequel in which Lau Ching-Wan chases Ekin Cheng. *AKA: Aau Chin; An Zhan.* 🐾🐾🐾🐾

1999 89m/C *HK* Andy Lau, Lau Ching-Wan, Yoyo Mung, Waise Lee, Hui Siu-hung, Lam Suet, Ruby Wong, Ai Wai, Lam Wai-kin, Robert Sparks, Hung Wai-leung, Yee Tin-hung, Jacky Cheung. **D:** Johnny To. **W:** Yau Nai-hoi, Julian Carbon, Laurent Courtiaud. **C:** Cheng Siu-keung. **M:** Raymond Wong. **VHS, DVD**

Running out of Time 2

Inspector Ho (Lau Ching-Wan) chases his nemesis, a thieving magician who delights in leaving clues for the police, across Hong Kong. There is some business involving art theft, ransoms, and insurance companies, as well as the looming threat of an eminent corporate merger, but none of it adds up. This is a chase comedy with none of the underlying dread of the original.

Although visually reminiscent of 1970s American policiers like *Dirty Harry* and *The French Connection,* there is little substance to this dizzying cliffhanger. For the villain and the audience as well, it's all about the fun of being pursued. Jumping off skyscrapers, disappearing from self-set traps—it is like watching Popeye Doyle trying to catch Houdini. While it is fun up to a point, the picture never goes beyond its "catch me if you can" premise. Unlike the original 1999 film, the thief doesn't seem to have much purpose beyond a sense of fun. In the original, Andy Lau played a character who was dying of a mysterious disease, giving some meaning to the title. His replacement, Ekin Cheng, is an engaging presence that plays his role for laughs. The team of writers have gimmicked things up so that even the symbolic eagle flying across the urban chaseland comes off as an animated goof. —BW **AKA:** *Aau Chin 2; An Zhan 2.* 🦴🦴🦴♡

2001 95m/C *HK* Lau Ching-Wan, Ekin Cheng, Kelly Lin, Hui Siu-hung, Lam Suet, Ruby Wong. **D:** Johnny To, Law Wing-cheong. **W:** Yau Nai-hoi, Au Kin Yee, Milkway Creative Team. **C:** Cheng Siu-keung. **M:** Raymond Wong. **VHS, DVD**

asians in usa

Rush Hour

Jackie Chan was out to conquer America once more—but this time he got help. Here he plays a Hong Kong cop yet again, sent to Los Angeles to help a diplomat friend whose daughter has been kidnapped. Chris Tucker is a troublesome LAPD detective who is assigned the task of keeping Chan away from the FBI during the investigation. Both cops immediately try to ditch each other and solve the case on their own.

Chan's previous made-in-U.S. films have been made by people who—for the most part—had little idea who Chan is and what makes his films special. After his own films have made him well known in the U.S., it's easier for Hollywood to get a grasp on his appeal. Brett Ratner, previously considered a mediocre director who just got by with whatever material was handed to him, has learned to make that perceived weakness his greatest strength. He knows better than to tell Jackie Chan how to handle a fight scene, or to tell Chan's co-star Chris Tucker to stick to the script. When you oversee a terrifically talented cast and crew it's just not smart to get in their way. His policy of letting things flow naturally reaps great rewards, even when his stars are off-screen. In one shot, the soon-to-be-kidnapped little girl—who'd predicted she'd hate her new life in America—is seen happily rapping along to a car radio on the way to school. Most directors would probably cut away from such an unimportant shot quickly, but Ratner must have seen how plainly charming the scene is, and wisely let the little girl get through a whole verse while also capturing subtle reactions from her bodyguards in the same shot. The editors at Miramax, who've cut their imported Chan films to the bone, could learn a few things from this guy.

Though the Hollywood Action Buddy Comedy Movie has fallen into a pattern of lame repetition, here Tucker and Chan develop an effortless chemistry that's wonderfully refreshing. It would have been easy to foresee this pair reacting to their partnership the way their characters do at the start of the film: with arrogance and condescension. Both performers have gifts, but neither overshadows the other. They obviously had a great time filming this unassuming feature, and it shows in every frame. Teaming with Tucker addresses a problem Chan has had with America: translation. His dialogue and comedy is either dubbed or cut out altogether, and his co-stars in his own films have been of little help. Teaming him with a very funny guy who talks nonstop was a stroke of genius. Next to Chris Tucker, anybody would seem quiet. 🦴🦴🦴

1998 (PG-13) 97m/C *US/HK* Jackie Chan, Chris Tucker, Tzi Ma, Julia Hsu, Elizabeth Pena, Rex Linn, Mark Rolston, Chris Penn, Tom Wilkinson, Ken Leung, Albert Wong, Chan Man Ching, Ken Lo, Nicky Li, Andy Cheng, Christine Ng, Manny Perry. **D:** Brett Ratner. **W:** Ross LeManna, Jim Kouf. **C:** Adam Greenberg. **M:** Lalo Schifrin. **VHS, DVD**

asians in usa

Rush Hour 2

This sequel reunites stars Jackie Chan and Chris Tucker with director Brett Ratner (and composer Lalo Schifrin, et al) for an adventure that is bigger, funnier, and more exciting than the first. At least, that's the intention. And with a few reservations, that's the result as well. There's also a lot more plot. We find L.A. cop Carter (Tucker) a few days after the end of the original (but three years older) on vacation in Hong Kong, though he's perturbed that his new friend Inspector Lee (Chan) is too busy chasing crooks to show him a good time in his hometown. Instead, they find themselves investigating the deaths of two American customs agents killed in a bombing. Among the prime suspects is Lee's father's ex-partner Ricky Tan (John Lone), who is now a big shot in the triads. Before the pair can get any evidence on Tan, he's shot in front of their eyes by his enforcer Hu Li (*Crouching Tiger*'s Zhang Ziyi). Following nothing more than a hunch, the pair head for L.A., tailing suspicious billionaire and Tan associate Steven Reign (Alan King). There, a gorgeous undercover Secret Service agent (Roselyn Sanchez) informs them that behind it all is a plot involving the legendary counterfeit "Superbill." Before they can act on this information, the boys are captured and put on a truck full of the phony cash headed for Las Vegas, leading to the expected climactic mayhem in a casino.

While much of Tucker's loudmouth antics could be written off as ignorance in the first film, here we expect his friendship with Lee to have imbued him with a bit more wisdom, so it's grating to have him spouting off constantly again here. And Lee's tolerance of Carter's racism makes one uncomfortable, though he gives it as well as he takes it in several

scenes—at one point telling his friend he'll "bitch-slap him back to Africa." What helps the film float over these rough patches is its light atmosphere, more similar to the Hope and Crosby "Road" pictures than most buddy action flicks. These movies are meant to please a family audience, so the violence and language is sugarcoated to go down easy. Brett Ratner again proves his worth more as a manager than a visionary, letting Chan and his team create the action scenes, letting Tucker riff endlessly to get the best lines, and relying on top designers and technical people to work wonders, then bringing it all together. 🦴🦴🦴

2001 (PG-13) 97m/C *US/HK* Jackie Chan, Chris Tucker, John Lone, Zhang Ziyi, Roselyn Sanchez, Harris Yulin, Alan King, Kenneth Tsang, Ernie Reyes Jr., Jeremy Piven, Don Cheadle, Saul Rubinek, Maggie Q. **D:** Brett Ratner. **W:** Jeff Nathanson. **C:** Matthew F. Leonetti. **M:** Lalo Schifrin. **VHS, DVD**

Sadistic City

Salary-man Kishi (Taguchi Tomoro of *Tokyo Fist*) meets up with his old friend Daimon after 20

years. After dropping Daimon (Hakuryu) off, his girlfriend Yoshi seduces Kishi, taking him to an expensive hotel. The adventurous Daimon doesn't mind at all, encouraging Kishi to visit Yoshi again. His encounter makes Kishi bolder, and he begins an affair with his shy co-worker Miss Miyazano. Daimon expects Kishi to return the favor, but Kishi brushes him off. Daimon turns sour, telling Kishi he and a gang will rape his wife to get him to play their kinky games. But Kishi now has a taste for danger, and brings his wife and mistress together for an uncomfortable dinner. Afterward, Kishi finds out a few surprising secrets about both his wife and his mistress.

The English subtitle translations are laughably bad, making it difficult to understand what's going on sometimes. But it's an artfully shot film, with cool music on the soundtrack from John Zorn. The sex scenes are relatively tame—it's the psychodrama that's twisted. **AKA:** Maohgai. 🦴🦴

1993 88m/C *JP* Akino Sakurako, Taguchi Tomoro, Hakuryu, Reono Hitato, Rie Kondo. **D:** Ryuichi Hiroki. **W:** Ryuichi Hiroki, Hanmura Ryo (novel). **C:** Yasushi Sasakibara. **M:** John Zorn. **VHS, DVD**

Saga of the Phoenix

In this sequel to *Peacock King*, Hell Virgin Ashura (Gloria Yip) is loose on Earth again to cause mischief, this time popping up in Thailand. Monks Peacock (Yuen Biao) and Lucky Fruit can't keep up with the havoc she causes, and the Sun, Moon, and Star Abbesses are sent to fetch her back to Abbot Jiku (Shintaro Katsu) in Tibet. It's decided that she's too dangerous to remain free, but before they lock her inside a golden Sleeping Buddha statue forever, Jiku allows her one last week of freedom—accompanied by her guardians, of course. The three Abbesses are sent to tail them, just in case Ashura decides to try to escape back to Hell. The Hell Concubine (Ngai Suet) sees all this on her Hellavision, and sends some devils to fetch the Hell Virgin. Ashura retrieves her familiar, a mischievous little monster named Genie—thus stopping the film dead in its tracks for extended sequences chronicling the rubber puppet's cutesy antics. The devils form a vortex to trap Ashura, but catch Genie instead, prompting Peacock to descend into the underworld to save him. He succeeds, only to be captured himself. The gremlin is picked up by a tourist (Rachel Lee) whose wacky inventor brother (Lau Sek-yin) has invented a teleportation machine. Unconcerned with Peacock's fate, Ashura and Lucky Fruit are content to shop and frolic with their new friends. But Hell Concubine hasn't forgotten them, and continues her attempts to capture Ashura.

It certainly has its moments, achieving some of the original's bizarre atmosphere. Yet the attitude here is too juvenile, the decent special effects only serving to make it come off like an episode of *Power Rangers*. Some shots of Genie moving around are achieved through animation. At one point he flushes himself down to Hell with a toilet! Stone monsters, zombies, and various demons are among the film's other wonders. The horror elements clash with those that are more kid-friendly, a stylistic patchwork that likely had something to do with the film's two directors. Keeping the dynamic Yuen Biao locked in a block of ice for half the picture certainly doesn't help any. **AKA:** *A Sau Law; A Xiu Luo; Ashura.* 🎵🎵🎵

1990 89m/C *HK* Yuen Biao, Gloria Yip, Rachel Lee, Lau Sek-yin, Shintaro Katsu, Ngai Suet, Hiroshe Abe. **D:** Simon Nam, Lau See-yu. **W:** Wong Chui-wah, Edward Leung. **C:** Kwan Chi-kan. **M:** Phil Chan. **VHS, DVD**

Sakuya: Slayer of Demons

Itching to watch a monster-hunting warrior woman and *Buffy* is in reruns? You could do worse than to check out this feature that draws inspiration from chambara movies, anime, and those old horror pictures like *100 Monsters* that featured creatures from Japanese myth. In 1707, Mount Fuji erupts, releasing hordes of monstrous demons from the underworld. The only weapon that can destroy the monsters is the legendary Vortex Sword, which feeds on the life force of whoever wields it. The current owner Yoshiaki Sakaki (Hiroshi Fujioka), Lord of Bizen, loses the last of his life force in battle with a Kappa Demon. Sakaki's daughter Sakuya (Nozomi Ando) immediately takes up the sword, and the responsibilities that come with it. Once the Kappa is destroyed, Sakuya adopts the demon's offspring, raising it as her brother, Taro. The clan elders determine the best way to deal with the demon invasion is to kill their leader, the Spider Queen (Keiko Matsuzaka). Sakuya sets off on her mission to the Field of Kusanagi, taking along two master ninjas, Hyoeh Mashiragi (Keiichiro Sakagi) and Shuzo Nigarasu (Kyusaku Shimada). Taro (Shuichi Yamauchi), who in three months has grown into what is to all appearances a 10-year-old human boy, goes along, too. Along the way, they encounter an Evil Puppeteer (Shinya Tsukamoto), who turns women into Barbie dolls for his collection, a Demon Two-Tailed Cat, and other dangers—as well as a troupe of friendly monsters.

The twist to the story lies with Sakuya's adopted brother. He doesn't have a whole lot of personality, and it's a mystery how everyone can tell he's a demon (must be the plate on his head), but Taro is potentially a much more interesting character than his sister. Lending some added tension to the dragon-slaying plot is the question of whether Taro will stick by the Sakaki clan when the chips are down, or serve his monster bloodline. Most of the monsters are much like the foes of Ultraman—a bit clunky, but fascinating. The digital and optical effects come off much better than the stiff suits. Especially impressive is a shot in which Sakuya slays a demon on horseback—as it's consumed in blue fire, the horse becomes a skeleton, all while galloping down a village street. And the whole battle sequence with the Spider Queen is just fantastic. A largely humorless endeavor, *Sakuya*'s few awkward stabs at comedy come courtesy of Taro, accompanied by some weird sound effects during scene transitions. The ninjas come equipped with some amusingly hi-tech weaponry, including an 18th-century bazooka and rocket launcher! Don't miss the dancing monsters during the rockin' end titles. **AKA:** *Sakuya: Yokaiden; Sakuya: Legend of Monsters.* 🎵🎵🎵🎵

2000 88m/C *JP* Nozomi Ando, Keiko Matsuzaka, Kyusaku Shimada, Keiichiro Sakagi, Yuhki Kuroda, Moeko Ezawa, Shinya Tsukamoto, Hidehiko Ishikura, Keiko Yoshida, Shuichi Yamauchi, Naoto Takena-

ka, Tetsuro Tanba, Hiroshi Fujioka, Mizuho Yoshida, Yoshie Seki. **D:** Tomoo Haraguchi. **W:** Kimiaki Mitsumas, Tomoo Haraguchi (story). **C:** Shoji Ebara. **M:** Kenji Kawai. **DVD**

Sam the Iron Bridge: Champion of Martial Arts

This sequel to *White Lotus Cult* finds Sam Liang (To Siu-chun) working three jobs, getting ready to marry Tieh (Yip Chuen Chan) and settle down. To pay off the debt of an opium-addict friend, Sam enters the Kwangtung Martial Arts Championship, which he wins easily despite a late entry by a fan-fighting mystery man (Fennie Yuen). The government has recently outlawed opium, to the distress of officials like customs chief Prince Mu (Wong Kam-Kong), who makes a handsome side income from the "Longlife Plaster." He recruits Admiral Kuan Yun-feng (Yu Hai) into helping with a plan to hide their stores from Officer Lin Tse-hsu, who is in town on a secret mission to enforce the ban. However, Lin is able to win over Kuan by demonstrating how out of shape his soldiers are from smoking. Sam is so impressed by the ban that he considers applying for government work himself by entering the national martial arts championship, though his master Hung (Lily Li) is opposed to the Ching government. He gets directly involved by protecting Lin from a gang of masked assassins, and takes up a job offer to be the officer's secret bodyguard. Since their bout, fan-fighting Keke (he's really a girl!) is obsessed with beating Sam, and engineers a scuffle with him in which she loses a jade piece. Sam finds himself torn between Tieh and this mysterious woman (who was a minor character in the previous film). When Mu throws a party to trap Lin, Keke takes advantage of the opportunity (she's really Mu's daughter!) to draw Sam away from his engagement ceremony to protect the officer. She takes further advantage when Mu's bodyguard Ho Ha uses the dreaded Bloody Palm on Sam, administering the only cure by taking his virginity! After Ho Ha assassinates Kuan, Sam finds that the only way to aid his cause is to enter the martial arts examination in the capitol, which will decide who will take over Kuan's job as governor of Kwangtung.

The sequel improves on the previous episode by concentrating on the main character and his adventures—romantic, political, and martial. The fight scenes improve, too, by using less wirework and more straightforward hand-to-hand action. The end title sequence offers up some scenes from the next exciting episode, *One Arm Hero*. **AKA:** *Mo Jung Yuen Tit Kiu Sam; Wu Zhuang Yuan Tie Qiao San; Sam the Iron Bridge.* ♫♫♫

1993 91m/C *HK* To Siu-chun, Yip Chuen Chan, Fennie Yuen, Wong Kam-Kong, Lily Li, Yu Hai. **D:** Fung Pak-yung. **W:** Mak Chi-shing, Yu Hon-wing. **C:** Cheng Siu-keung, Lee Chi-wah. **M:** Wong Lai-ping. **VHS, DVD**

Samaritan Zatoichi

Unokichi (Takuya Fujioka) has promised his sister Sode (Yoshiko Mita) to the local boss if he can't pay his debt of 30 ryo, but takes a sword to those who try to collect. Boss Kumakichi asks blind masseur Zatoichi (Shintaro Katsu) and fellow traveler (and braggart) Shinsuke (Ko Nishimura) to help with the assignment of killing the debtor. The deed done, the boss's men try to take the sister as well, but Ichi steps in to protect her, and punish the brutes who give his brotherhood a bad name. Shinsuke kills several of them and leaves Kumakichi pinned to the floor with swords.

This 18-minute segment could be accepted as a self-contained Zatoichi mini-feature by itself, but there's lots more after that. It seems Kumakichi has promised to deliver the girl to the master of the government inn, and is determined to earn a concession in return for her. Hitting the road together, Sode is grateful to Master Ichi, but finds it difficult to forget he's the man who killed her brother, and works herself into a fever. To pay her doctor bill, Ichi heads to the casino to scrounge some cash. However, the man to whom he hocks his cane to raise a stake is Kashiwazaki, a skillful ronin hired by Kumakichi's men to kill him. Accused of cheating, Ichi is wrapped up in reeds and handed over to the gangsters—but even wrapped, he makes a break for it! Wanting an honorable fight, Kashiwazaki steps in to give Zatoichi his sword cane back. But before they can clash, some enemies of Kashiwazaki interrupt, and they agree to face one another after Ichi has delivered Sode safely to her relatives.

This fine episode balances action, humor, and blind man tricks well in a story that breaks from formula at several points. While many of the Zatoichi films present the hero as near superhuman, here he gets himself into genuine danger, and there's some good solid twists to the plot. Director Kenji Misumi frames his shots just right, knowing when to emphasize a point with a close-up or pull back for a long look. For one surprising shot, he even turns the camera sideways. **AKA:** *Zatoichi Kenka-daiko; The Blind Swordsman Samaritan; Zatoichi and the Drum.* ♫♫♫♫

1968 82m/C *JP* Shintaro Katsu, Yoshiko Mita, Makoto Sato, Ko Nishimura, Takuya Fujioka, Chocho Miyako. **D:** Kenji Misumi. **W:** Kiyokata Saruwaka, Hisashi Sigiura, Tetsuo Yoshida, Kan Shimozawa (story). **C:** Fujio Morita. **M:** Sei Ikeno. **VHS**

Samurai 1: Musashi Miyamoto

This is the second of director Hiroshi Inagaki's three-part adaptations of Eiji Yoshikawa's epic historical novel *Musashi Miyamoto,* based on the early years in the life of one of Japan's great heroes. The first trilogy was lost during World War II, and the same material became the basis of the *Zen and Sword* series in the 1960s.

Part one of the trilogy starts in 1600, turbulent times in a Japan torn apart by civil war. Goaded by his friend Takezo (Toshiro Mifune), Matahashi (Rentaro Mikune) leaves his fiancée Otsu (Koaru Yachigusa) behind in Miyamoto and joins up with the army, just in time for the epic Battle of Sekigahara. On the losing side, the pair lick their wounds and hide out at the farm of widow Oko (Mitsuko Mito) and her daughter Akemi (Mariko Okada), who live by pillaging battlegrounds. After Takezo single-handedly drives a gang of brigands off the farm, Matahashi flees with the two women, while Takezo becomes a wild outlaw. Takezo returns to Miyamoto, and the local constabulary uses a manhunt for him as an excuse to round up all his relatives. His mission there is to tell Matahashi's mother Osugi (Eiko Miyoshi) and Otsu that their boy still lives, though he won't tell them how he's shamed them by running off with the two women. But Osugi turns him in, and he shouts out the truth as he fights his way free. Meanwhile, Matahashi has grown older and embittered married to Oko, who plans to marry off Akemi to rich bachelor Seijuro (Akihiko Hirata). While scores of men comb the hills for Takezo, Otsu and the Buddhist priest Takuan (Kuroemon Onoe) go into the mountains and capture the wild beast alone. Takuan insists on punishing Takezo in his own way. Holding him captive, he means to teach the outlaw humility and reason, or let him die. Otsu has fallen in love with him, and waits by Hanada Bridge for Takezo to complete his spiritual training.

As the real Takezo Shinmen (later Musashi Miyamoto) was 16 when he went off to war, Mifune is a bit ripe for the role, but does a fine job representing the legend nevertheless. The settings and locations, with hundreds of costumed extras swarming over them, are truly impressive. Often sited as the Japanese *Gone with the Wind,* this has the same feeling as a huge old Hollywood epic. Jun Yasumoto's cinematography is incredible. For a samurai story, there's not an incredible amount of fighting, but then, there's so much story to tell that there's hardly room for any. The original U.S. release featured narration by William Holden. *AKA: Musashi Miyamoto; The Legend of Musashi; Samurai; Master Swordsman.* ♪♪♪

1954 92m/C *JP* Toshiro Mifune, Koaru Yachigusa, Rentaro Mikune, Mariko Okada, Mitsuko Mito, Kuroemon Onoe, Eiko Miyoshi, Akihiko Hirata, Yoshio Kosugi, Daisuke Kato. **D:** Hiroshi Inagaki. **W:** Tokuhei Wakao, Hiroshi Inagaki, Hideji Hojo, Eiji Yoshikawa (novel). **C:** Jun Yasumoto. **M:** Ikuma Dan. **VHS, DVD**

Samurai 2: Duel at Ichijoji Temple

Taking up where the last entry left off, this second part of the trilogy advances the plot and spiritual growth of its central character, Musashi Miyamoto (Toshiro Mifune), while predictably leaving much unresolved for the finale. In place of closure, Part 2 substitutes more action, starting with the opening duel between Musashi's distinctive two-sword style and Baiken (Eijiro Tono), a chain-and-sickle master. While Musashi travels in search of knowledge, patient and faithful Otsu (Kaoru Yachigusa) still waits by Sanjuro Bridge. She meets Akemi (Mariko Okada), who is also waiting for a man, though neither knows they're both in love with Musashi. Akemi has been engaged by matchmaking Oko (Mitsuko Mito) to teach music to young master Seijuro Yoshioka (Akihiko Hirata).

Meanwhile, at the Yoshioka School of swordplay, Professor Seijuro's music career has the faculty and students suffering, after their arrogance toward visiting Musashi results in his sending many challengers to the hospital, or the grave. Musashi challenges Seijuro to meet him at the bridge for a duel at six, but the cowardly Yoshiokas protect their young master by sending a mob to meet him. Musashi's ex-friend Matahichi Honiden (Sachio Sakai) comes upon a fatally injured man, attacked mistakenly in place of Musashi, who gives him a message to deliver to samurai Kojiro Sasaki (Koji Tsuruta)—his fencing school diploma—which Matahichi later passes off as his own. Meanwhile, the hunt for Musashi turns up the real Sasaki. Poor Akemi, learning Otsu's identity, issues a challenge of her own, vowing she'll have the man she loves in the end. After losing a brother on Musashi's sword, Seijuro is determined to finally answer the challenge himself, and the match is set for Ichijoji Temple. But the combatants are double-crossed by the Yoshioka School again: the location of the duel is kept from Seijuro, and 80 warriors go to meet Musashi in combat.

The print quality of the first *Samurai,* doubtless due to its Academy Award, was much better preserved. The sequel looks a bit murky, but is still gorgeous. *AKA: Miyamoto Musashi: Ichijoji no Ketto; Zoku Miyamoto Musashi; Swords of Doom.* ♪♪♪♪

1955 102m/C *JP* Toshiro Mifune, Kaoru Yachi-gusa, Koji Tsuruta, Sachio Sakai, Mariko Okada, Mitsuko Mito, Eijiro Tono, Akihiko Hirata, Daisuke Kato, Ko Mihashi, Kunimori Kodo, Michiyo Kogure, Kuroemon Onoe. *D:* Hiroshi Inagaki. *W:* Tokuhei Wakao, Hiroshi Inagaki, Hideji Hojo (adaptation), Eiji Yoshikawa (novel). *C:* Jun Yasumoto. *M:* Ikuma Dan. **VHS, DVD**

Samurai 3: Duel at Ganryu Island

In this final part of the classic trilogy, we find swordsman Kojiro Sasaki (Koji Tsuruta) in a breathtaking setting among waterfalls and rainbows, with his girlfriend Akemi (Mariko Okada) by his side. But Kojiro thinks only of his dream: to duel with his rival Musashi Miyamoto (Toshiro Mifune), now famous across Japan for winning 60 duels. Akemi, still carrying a torch for Musashi, tries to discourage Kojiro, but it's no use. Meanwhile, Musashi continues to seek spiritual fulfillment, walking in peace whenever he can, regretting many of the deaths he's caused. He travels to Edo to meet Lord Yagyu, with his beloved Otsu (Kaoru Yachigusa) close on his trail. Kojiro goes to Edo, too, looking for employment with the Shogunate. He makes a date for a duel with Musashi. But when Musashi learns they are both wanted for the same job, he postpones the duel for a year and leaves town. He homesteads a farm in a faraway province, working the soil, until Otsu catches up with him—with Akemi not far behind. As usual, jealousy between the two women stirs up trouble, with Akemi betraying the village to a band of brigands. But Musashi can't stay to rebuild after the raid, as he's due for his fencing date with Kojiro.

After his 1612 duel with Kojiro on Ganryu Island, the real Musashi went on to many historic adventures, though from then on he only dueled using a wooden sword. All of these tales of his life would be retold many times in film, but this Samurai trilogy has always been the most highly regarded. In this third act, director Hiroshi Inagaki really outdoes himself, teaming with cinematographer Kazuo Yamada to craft incredible imagery. Even more than the first two, this entry stands on its own as a chambara classic. *AKA: Miyamoto Musashi: Ketto Ganryu-jima; Duel on Ganryu Island; Musashi and Kojiro; Samurai 3.* 🎵🎵🎵🎵

1956 102m/C *JP* Toshiro Mifune, Kaoru Yachi-gusa, Koji Tsuruta, Mariko Okada, Takashi Shimura, Michiko Saga, Kokuten Kodo, Haruo Tanaka, Daisuke Kato, Minoru Chiaki, Kuroemon Onoe, Sachio Sakai, Eijiro Tono. *D:* Hiroshi Inagaki. *W:* Tokuhei Wakao, Hiroshi Inagaki, Eiji Yoshikawa (novel), Hideji Hojo (adaptation). *C:* Kazuo Yamada. *M:* Ikuma Dan. **VHS, DVD**

Sanjuro

Nine young samurai are concerned about official corruption in their district. They take the problem to the local chamberlain (who is the uncle of one of the men), but are not satisfied with his response. So they set up a meeting with the superintendent Kikui (Masao Shimizu) —unaware that he is part of the corruption. Fortunately, Toshiro Mifune, playing Tsubaki Sanjuro ("camellia 30-year-old"—an assumed name") overhears the youngsters' tribulations. He sees through the superintendent's facade, and warns the nine that they are being set up. Then, using his amazing swordsmanship, he helps them out of the trap that has been set for them. In doing so, he meets the corrupt officials' chief enforcer, a clever samurai named Hanbei Muroto (Tatsuya Nakadai)—who is Sanjuro's opposite number in nearly every way. Sanjuro is sympathetic to the young rebels, and decides to help them rescue the chamberlain, who has been captured by the bad guys. They manage to rescue the chamberlain's genteel wife and daughter. The contrast between Mifune and the older woman provides some of the film's light moments.

The nine rebels (plus Sanjuro) hide the ladies in a home next door to the house of the lead bad guy, Kurofuji (Takashi Shimura)—reasoning that his own neighborhood is the last place Kurofuji will look for the fugitives (and they're right about this). A good portion of the film is spent with the youngsters trying to figure out where the chamberlain is being held, and the bad guys trying to track down and kill the nine rebels. Sanjuro rides herd on the youngsters, keeping them from running off impulsively and getting themselves killed. Several times he is forced to kill people to keep the headstrong rebels safe. The youngsters, naïve in most respects, give Sanjuro very little help. In fact, their main redeeming qualities are youth, enthusiasm, and hatred of corruption. Fortunately, Sanjuro is there to pull their kimonos out of the fire—otherwise the town would surely be destroyed by the corrupt officials.

A sequel to *Yojimbo,* this film features Mifune as the same ronin (masterless samurai) character from the earlier flick. The film is lighter in tone than *Yojimbo,* and has many funny characters and scenes. Particularly amusing is the captured guard who spends most of the film in a closet. Despite the humor, the film is still serious in its themes and brutal in its violence. As in the earlier flick, the Mifune character is pulled into conflict by his innate sense of justice and his hatred of those who prey upon the common people. In *Sanjuro,* we get to see a good amount of the swordplay for which Mifune was (justifiably) famous. The final duel is so fast that it can only be fully seen in slow-motion. A

legend about the making of the movie says that Kurosawa had to ask Mifune to slow down his cut several times, as his draw was actually too fast for the film to capture (at 24 frames per second). Another grand film in the Kurosawa repertoire, it features most of the things that have made the director justifiably famous: great camera work and composition, terrific pacing, telling details, good acting, and a carefully drawn story. Give it another half bone if you're comparing it to films by any other filmmaker. Kurosawa is in a class by himself. —SS **AKA:** *Tsubaki Sanjuro.* 🎵🎵🎵🎝

1963 95m/BW *JP* Toshiro Mifune, Tatsuya Nakadai, Keiju Kobayashi, Yuzo Kayama, Reiko Dan, Takashi Shimura, Kamatari Fujiwara, Akihiko Hirata, Masao Shimizu, Yunosuke Ito, Akira Kubo, Kenzo Matsui, Hiroshi Tachikawa, Yoshio Tsuchiya. **D:** Akira Kurosawa. **W:** Ryuzo Kikushima, Hideo Oguni, Akira Kurosawa. **C:** Fuzuko Koizumi, Takao Saito. **M:** Masaru Sato. **VHS, DVD**

Sanshiro Sugata

Famed director Akira Kurosawa's first credited film, *Sanshiro Sugata* was made during WWII under Japanese censorship laws. What this meant was that anything that seemed overly "Western" was excised from the original script. Despite this, Kurosawa turned out a fine movie showing a knowledge of cinema and film history for his premier effort.

The story begins with young Sanshiro Sugata (Susumu Fujita) looking for a master to teach him jujitsu. He chooses the Shimmei clan, who are planning to ambush the master of the rival Shudokan school. Sogoro Yano (Denjiro Okochi), the master of the Shudokan clan, is traveling through the area, and the Shimmei turn out in force to "teach him a lesson." Yano is a proponent of the new art of judo—an updated and scientific version of jujitsu. When Yano kicks ass on the Shimmei, young Sugata decides to follow Yano instead. Sugata, though talented, is hotheaded and loves to fight. His master upbraids him, and threatens to dismiss him from the school. Sugata vows he would do anything for the master, even die. To prove it, he jumps into a pond with the intention of staying there until he wastes away. Fortunately, the master only wants him to stay there until he grows up a bit. Sugata does that when he sees a vision of a lotus blossom in the moon. After that, he's a much more controlled student—though he does accidentally kill a rival in a test match. This makes Sugata a feared man. Still, he is chosen to represent the clan in a match which will determine which school will teach the police self-defense. As he comes to grips with the accidental death, Sugata makes friends with a woman (Yukiko Todoroki) who—it turns out—

is the daughter of Murai (Takashi Shimura), whom he will meet in the next match. When the tournament finally rolls around, Sugata is torn between fighting and not wanting to kill anyone. His master, though, tells him to take control of his life again, as he did in the pond.

Higakei (Ryunosuke Tsukigata), a dapper Western-dressed man, is also a member of the Murai clan—but the clan will not allow him to fight Sugata in the match. Sugata and Murai face off, and Sugata wins. In his show of respect for his vanquished foe, Sugata proves that he has indeed become a true judo master. Despite Sugata's victory, the evil Higakei still demands a showdown. The final duel takes place on a windswept mountainside. This, of all the scenes in the film, most clearly indicates the future path that Kurosawa would take. In it, the director shows his burgeoning love of cinematography and painterly composition. (Every shot in his later films is a beautifully composed moving painting.) This mountain duel scene alone makes this flick worth watching.

Sanshiro Sugata was a real student of judo founder Shogoro Yano (Jigoro Kano), and the film is based on a popular novel by Tsuneo Tomita based on his life, though its unsure how close to the facts either work remains. Clearly there are some propaganda elements within the film (including the slimy, Western-dressed Higakei). Whether truth or fiction, this movie has many of the elements that have come to be associated with standard martial arts flicks. It is, however, told with more intelligence and true emotion than most chop-socky epics. While a bit slow and stilted at times, *Sanshiro Sugata* is still well worth a look. A hit even during wartime, the government ordered a sequel, *Sanshiro Sugata 2,* which more heavily bears the brand of the censor. —SS **AKA:** *Sugata Sanshiro; Judo Saga; Judo Story.* 🎵🎵🎵

1943 78m/BW *JP* Denjiro Okochi, Susumu Fujita, Yukiko Todoroki, Ranko Hanai, Ryunosuke Tsukigata, Takashi Shimura, Sugisaku Aoyama, Kokuten Kodo, Ichiro Sugai, Yoshio Kosugi, Shoji Kiyokawa. **D:** Akira Kurosawa. **W:** Tsuneo Tomita, Akira Kurosawa. **C:** Akira Mimura. **M:** Seiichi Suzuki. **VHS, DVD**

Satin Steel

Jade Leung *(Black Cat)* stars as Sergeant Jade Leung, a suicidal gung-ho Hong Kong cop who gets sent to Singapore to assist the FBI in tracking down a huge illegal arms sale. She's met at the airport by Ellen Cheng (Anita Lee), the deceptively ditzy officer in charge of the case. Ellen has promised her annoying fiancé (Kenneth Chan), who has the unlikely name John Paul Belmando (like the French film star), that she'll give up dangerous assignments, but she

The Four Sky Kings of Cantopop

In Hong Kong, and most Asian countries, to be a movie star often means being a pop singing star, and vice-versa. The situation is similar to that of the U.S. during the 1960s, when anyone with any kind of hit TV show was automatically offered a recording contract. Even stars like Anthony Wong record albums. The term "Four Sky Kings of Cantopop" (or "Four Heavenly Kings") was invented by TVB television during the 1991–92 season, when a certain quartet's individual singing careers blasted off to the Heavens. As singers, these four guys turned out to have very successful legitimate acting talent. With the popularity of Cantopop on the wane in Hong Kong these days in the face of a Mandarin invasion, thank Heavens these guys will always have movie careers.

Jacky Cheung (Cheung Hok-yau)

God of Songs. Discovered in a talent contest, Jacky was the most successful singer in HK during the 1990s. He's also crossed over to have huge Mandarin hits, and even recorded an album in the U.S. Sharing the large nose of that other "Jacky" (Chan, whom he spoofed in *High Risk*), Cheung's acting career has gravitated away from straight leading-man roles to more interesting parts. His movie debut was in Sammo Hung's *Where's Officer Tuba?,* whose mix of comedy and action would carry over into more early film roles like *The Haunted Cop Shop, Tiger Cage, Swordsman,* and *Curry & Pepper* (with Stephen Chow). But *Bullet in the Head* and *Days of Being Wild* showed the depth of his dramatic range. In the past few years, Jacky has slowed down his career, and made an effort to step away from the whole Sky Kings thing, claiming he wants to go back to being just a mortal singer again, and has even refused to sing with the other three.

Andy Lau (Lau Tak-wah)

King of Hong Kong. Andy has by far the most successful movie career of any king, having starred in over 100 films. Before becoming a Sky King, Andy Lau was among TVB actors promoted as the "Five Tigers," the others being Tony Leung Chiu-wai, Miu Kiu-wai, Felix Wong, and Tong Chan-yip. But Andy left TV because of a contract dispute in 1988 to concentrate on his movie career, which began when Chow Yun-fat helped him land in Ann Hui's *Boat People*. After obtaining roles in films alongside Chow Yun-fat, Jackie Chan, and Sammo Hung, Lau's first big lead was in Wong Kar-Wai's award-winning *As Tears Go By*, after which he became incredibly prolific, at one point making nine movies at the same time. Highlights include *Crocodile Hunter, God of Gamblers, A Moment of Romance, Savior of the Soul* (the first picture his TeamWork company produced), *Lee Rock, The Last Blood, The Adventurers, The Duel,* and *Fulltime Killer*. In 1999 he proved he's just getting better with age by winning the HK acting Academy Award for *Running out of Time*. Andy is a big Ultraman fan.

Aaron Kwok (Kwok Fu-shing)

King of Dance. In the mid-1980s, Aaron was drafted into show-biz training by TVB network, studying dancing and acting, and did the usual round of children's shows and commercials. A popular commercial made in Taiwan led to a record contract there. After doing a couple of cameo roles in films, he got his first decent role in the heist thriller *Close Escape*. The only King who has played villains *(Savior of the Soul)*, his most popular films include *2000 A.D.* and *The Storm Riders*. His *Para Para Sakura* seemed to be the perfect blend of his movie star and pop star images—it's a wonder it wasn't a musical.

Leon Lai (Lai Ming)

King of Fan Support. In 1986, British-educated Leon came in *second* in one of TVB's singing competitions. He was hired by the company anyway, and became a soap-opera star before signing his first recording contract. His first film was the Richard Ng comedy *Mr. Handsome*. Leon experienced a recording career stall in the mid-'90s, until producer Mark Lai convinced him to start recording more upbeat dance tunes, including his smash "Words That Have Not Been Said." His best movies include *Fallen Angels, Shogun and Little Kitchen,* and *Comrades, Almost a Love Story*.

Singers commonly mistaken as one of the Four include Tony Leung Chui-Wai and Leslie Cheung. In recent years, the pop charts (which belong to the young, after all), as well as most of the top movie roles have been taken over by the Four Young Kings of Cantopop: Nicholas Tse, Leo Koo, Daniel Chan, and Stephen Fung. Simultaneously, there's also the Five New Little Heavenly Kings: Daniel Chan, Eason Chan, Koo, Tse, and Ronald Cheng! Meanwhile,

Continued on next page...

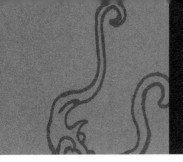

there's also the Four Queens of Cantopop: Sammi Cheng, Kelly Chan, Faye Wong, and Joey Yung. All these ladies should watch out for The Twins (Charlene Choi and Gillian Chung), whose movie career is just taking off.

"Why are you so short? Don't lie to me!"

—Andy Lau keeps the wisecracks coming in the superhero thriller *Savior of the Soul*

has a fierce dedication to duty and an obvious love of firearms. Jade has been on the edge since her husband was killed by hit men on their wedding night, and is eager to die, taking as many crooks with her as possible. Jade and Ellen plant a tracking device inside an underling, hoping he'll lead them to American arms dealer Fowler, but when the villain's bodyguard kills the man with his mechanical hand, the ladies have to scramble to keep up with them. They trail Fowler to Indonesia, where he's about to make a massive arms sale to buyers from all over the world. It looks like they have him with the goods, but Fowler's lawyer Ken (Russell Wong) steps in with an alibi. Ken knows nothing of Fowler's illegal business, but suspects much and doesn't want to get involved in it. Jade takes advantage of this, and their mutual attraction, by trying to get close to Ken. Meanwhile, the girls have to overcome the interfering John, who tagged along on their secret mission. After obtaining a computer disc full of evidence against Fowler, Jade and Ellen track him into the jungle to bust up his business.

A distaff *Lethal Weapon, Satin Steel* also owes a heavy debt to the flightier episodes of the James Bond series, with over-the-top action scenes and gadgetry showing up at odd moments. An enjoyable action romp, it's packed with explosions, car chases, horse chases, gun battles, and some fine kung fu fighting. Jade Leung has never looked better, and carries off her many stunts with aplomb. The location shooting is a definite bonus. A key fight scene takes place atop a volcano, after which Leung hangs from a helicopter over the crater! *AKA: Chung Kam Juk; Chong Jin Shu; Heavy Metal.* 🦴🦴🦴

1994 85m/C *HK* Jade Leung, Anita Lee, Russell Wong, Kenneth Chan. *D:* Tony Leung Siu-hung. *W:* Roman Cheung, Vincent Kok. *C:* Sander Lee. *M:* Anthony Lee. **VHS, DVD**

Savior of the Soul

Loosely based on a Jin Yong novel, this feature takes the old-school swordplay story and sets it in a comic-book style future. Super-swordsman Silver Fox (Aaron Kwok) holds "city soldier" May Yiu (Anita Mui) responsible for the blinding, capture, and eventual death of his master Old Eagle (Henry Fong). While Yiu May-chun (Mui again, dubbed by a man using an effeminate voice) concentrates on her inventions, such as the Suffocate Bullet (which sucks the air out of a room), her twin sister May can't decide between two suitors—serious and attentive Siu-chuen (Kenny Bee) or funny Ching-lan (Andy Lau). An attack by Silver Fox decides the matter: he misses May (who takes his eye out), but kills Siu-chuen, leaving his little sister Wai-heung (Gloria Yip) in Ching's care. After heartbroken May rejects him, heartbroken Ching trains Wai-heung to be his city soldier assistant, and the young girl naturally falls for him. May-chun tires of Ching pestering her for news of her sister, and tells him she's become the Madam of Pets (Carina Lau), who plans to choose a husband via a kung fu competition. Ching gets past Madam's cult of amazons to beat competitor Ford with his special yo-yo sword, only to learn he's been tricked. Actually—in one of the film's greatest plot holes—May has been living right across the street from Ching, but he doesn't find out until Silver Fox learns it, too. In a fight, Silver Fox poisons May with his Horrible Angel—a technique in which he sucks in toxins, and then dives *through* an opponent, leaving the poisons behind—and only the Madam of Pets can save her.

With its superhero characters and quirky gadgets, *Savior* has gained a healthy cult following, especially in the U.S. The pop star cast does an admirable job with all the operatic fight scenes, with the assistance of action master Corey Yuen. Heck, he's even got little Henry Fong playing a kung fu master! Fortunately, the operatic drama isn't taken too seriously, and is balanced nicely by a layer of comedy. The fantastic sets are gorgeous, but at times a bit too picturesque to appear real. Curiously, the Madam of Pets doesn't appear to have any pets. Gloria Yip is darn cute in her little baseball uniform, but can't quite pass for a 12-year-old. *AKA: '91 San Diu Hap Liu; '91 Shen Diao Xia Lu; Saviour of Souls; Terrible Angel.* 🦴🦴🦴

1991 93m/C *HK* Andy Lau, Anita Mui, Aaron Kwok, Carina Lau, Gloria Yip, Kenny Bee, Henry Fong, Corey Yuen. *D:* David Lai, Corey Yuen. *W:* Jeff Lau. *C:* Peter Pau. *M:* Anthony Lun. **VHS, DVD**

Savior of the Soul 2

Take a poll of moviegoers who've seen a popular film and ask them what they'd like to see in a sequel, and among the least likely answers you'll get will be, "do away with all the characters and concepts and create everything new from scratch." But that's precisely what the filmmakers do here (despite the fact that they've got Andy Lau back again in the lead), thus guaranteeing nearly everyone who has seen the original will be disappointed. Well, if you can forget the title and pretend this is a stand-alone feature, you may enjoy this swordplay comedy on its own merits. Here, any semblance of reality is abandoned in favor of the kind of nonsense slapstick comedy (talking to the camera, hitting each other with oversize mallets) that appears constantly in Japanese manga. Ching-yan (Andy Lau)—possibly the brother of his character in the original, but it's never stated so—and his preteen godson Tim Chow are superheroes living in a hi-tek arctic headquarters in the mountains of Canada. Ching's own godfather Doc (Corey Yuen, under a heavy mustache and glasses), who lives with them, is a zany scientist who invents gadgets like a magnifying glass that actually makes objects larger. Ching has dreamed nightly for 28 years of a beautiful Ice Woman (Rosamund Kwan), but is always fended off by an old crone before he can reach her. The trio answers a classified ad placed by the Evil's Palace offering a reward for the legendary Virgin's Ice, which will grant immortality to anyone who breathes its vapors. They take an underwater passage to a zany western town at the foot of Virgin's Mountain, arriving in the bathtub of casino owner Ruby (Shirley Kwan), who instantly recognizes Ching as her dream man. Climbing to the peak, Ching finds the Ice, but decides they shouldn't sell it, as he's had a vision it will lead him to his dream girl. But the minions of the King of Evil (Richard Ng) come after their prize.

Some of the gags don't translate well, and others are funny in any language, but in the end (or more likely long before the end) the film's relentless silliness wears out its welcome—as does some mushy melodrama in the third act. The art direction is stunning, often outdoing the original in imagination. Seeing Andy Lau fight demon jesters in a candy-colored psychedelic netherworld using giant scissors may be worth enduring whatever flaws the film has. A misfire, but another brilliant entry in Hong Kong's fever dream cinema category. *AKA: '92 San Diu Chi Chi Sam Ching Cheung Gim; '92 Shen Diao Zhi Chi Xin Qing Chang Jian; Saviour of Souls 2; Saviour of the Soul '92.* 🎵🎵🎶

1992 92m/C *HK* Andy Lau, Rosamund Kwan, Corey Yuen, Richard Ng, Shirley Kwan. *D:* Corey Yuen, David Lai. *W:* Kim Yip, John Chan. *C:* Lee Tak-wai, Tom Lau, Bill Wong, Jimmy Leung. *M:* To Chi-chi. **VHS, DVD**

Scared Stiff

A Chow Yun-fat and Sammo Hung collaboration? Even as *A Better Tomorrow* was hitting theatres, Chow was still taking small parts in movies like this very strange comedy thriller (produced by Hung) that takes a bizarre right turn in the middle. Toy designer Halley Tseng (Eric Tsang) is a virgin, who can't even dream of being desirable without his roommate David Miao (Miu Kiu-wai) stealing all his dates. When a gang of jewelry-store robbers hijacks their car, a wild chase ends in a car crash, leaving Tseng unhurt but Miao is left in an unusual state—his vital functions halt, but his brainwave stays active. In grief, Tseng curses his friend, and the stimulation revives him. The doctors decide to study his unusual brainwave activity in the hospital "Brain Department." His reactions to tests lead a pretty researcher Alice (Emily Chu, who was also with Chow in *A Better Tomorrow 1* and *2*, and *Witch from Nepal*) to believe he has ESP. Thirteen years before *The Cell,* the doctors put Miao in an experiment in entering the mind of a madman (Wu Ma). Inside the patient's mind, he's a vampire-busting priest who recruits Miao to help him. Alice dates the frightened man to keep him from quitting the project. Meanwhile, the jewel robbers are out to get Tseng for identifying them. A cop scares the gang off, but immediately someone cuts his throat. Seriously injured in his escape from the killer, Tseng is sent to the Brain Department, where Miao enters his mind to help him. Inspector Chou (Chow Yun-fat) is assigned to the case—and of course, turns out to be the Killer.

The plot takes far too long to set up. The murder angle comes out of left field nearly an hour into the film, making for a terribly uneven picture. It seems farfetched that Miu could identify Chow as the killer in Tsang's mind, when Tsang never got a good look at his attacker. But then, Miu also sees a premonition of the film's auto graveyard climax in his vision. With Chow's arrival, the picture nearly turns into an Italian-style slasher film. After that, it becomes a bloody action thriller, with Miu and Tsang trying to get away from Chow's gang of crooked cops. It all ends with Miu on a horrific telekinetic rampage! The individual sections of this crazy quilt are pretty entertaining, but the pieces just don't fit together. Interesting to see Chow Yun-fat as a villain, though. The music is horrible synthesizer trash. *AKA: Siu Sang Mung Geng Wan; Xiao Sheng Meng Jing Hun; Kid Dreams Thriller.* 🎵🎵🎶

1986 89m/C *HK* Eric Tsang, Miu Kiu-wai, Chow Yun-fat, Emily Chu, Wu Ma, Yuen Wah, Phillip Ko, Wu Fung,

Anita Mui, Cho Chung-sing, Huang Ha, Alan Chan, Billy Ching, Mai Kei, Sandra Ng, Shut Ma-yin. **D:** Lau Kar-Wing. **W:** Szeto Cheuk-Hon. **C:** Joe Chan. **M:** Danny Chung, The Melody Bank. **VHS, DVD**

Scorpion Thunderbolt

Fourteen women have been murdered in Kowloon City, apparently by the same killer. Reporter Helen Yu annoys the cops, but helps them catch their lone suspect: an escaped maniac. However, the real killer is a snake monster under the command of a wicked witch. Au Gau, an old enemy of Inspector Jackie Colt and Inspector Lee, breaks into his home and attacks them. Colt chases the man out into the street, while two coeds are killed nearby by the snake monster. A strange blind guy playing a flute hangs around each murder scene. From time to time, the witch's assassins try to kill Richard Harrison. Richard visits his kung fu master, who tells him that a vampire witch called the Queen of Scorpions is to blame, and she's after his ring, which can be used to destroy her. The master gives him a magic sword and mirror to fight the witch. Colt takes a break from the big murder case he's assigned to by taking Helen camping. Au Gau tries to kill him in the woods, and on the way back a swarm of snakes wrecks their car. Back at the hotel, the monster kills more people and Helen acts possessed. Helen tells him she's really a were-snake that is responsible for all the murders!

Yes, it's another mind-bending assemblage of odd exploitation elements from Godfrey Ho. The story of the witch (a *vampire* witch) threatening poor Richard Harrison seems completely unrelated to the snake monster plot, as if they're from separate movies—and they may well be, knowing Ho. The monster costume and makeup ain't that bad, looking much like a giant newt. For some reason, this melding of horror stories has always been sold on home video as an action flick, which makes as much sense as a girl who turns into a snake monster becoming a newspaper reporter. Don't they have any law schools in Kowloon? 🐉🐉🐲

1985 84m/C *HK* Richard Harrison, Juliet Chan, Bernard Tsui, Nancy Lim, Cynthia Ku, Maura Fong, Samson Kim, Tony Man, Cathy Evan, Yeung Hung, Gaston Wang, Bella Lam, Larry Chiu. **D:** Godfrey Ho. **W:** Godfrey Ho. **C:** Raymond Cheung. **M:** Steve Tsang. **VHS, DVD**

Screaming Ninja

Don't hold your breath waiting for a ninja to show up in this movie, screaming or otherwise—the title is a holdover from the 1980s, when dozens of movies were released on video bearing new "ninja" titles. Within a few years after Bruce Lee's death, theatres all over the world were showing films with his name in the title. But Jimmy Wang Yu beat him to the punch when this picture was first released under the title *Wang Yu, King of Boxing,* and Wang joined the small circle of stars (including Abbott and Costello, Boris Karloff, and Bela Lugosi) to have their fame so exploited. Here, Ma Tai-yung (Wang) goes to Japan, burning for revenge against the pirates who massacred his entire village. Though a mysterious Chinese man cautions him against racism, Ma welcomes a fight with a gang of pickpockets who are fleecing festival patrons. However, the words of his flute-playing countryman haunt him, stopping him from killing any of his attackers. He keeps after Yen Chu (Cheung Ching-Ching), the thief who that robbed him, but ends up defending her from the gang. While Ma tries to win them some cash in a sumo contest, yakuza boss Chow Wu orders Yen to stay with Hai-wan to keep an eye on him. However, she plays it cagey, confessing to her spying and offering her victim help, while possibly planning to betray him. They befriend a Korean named Chen Chien-wu, who is also on a vendetta; he's out to get Yang Wu (Lung Fei), the judo expert who killed his father. Unfortunately, Chen isn't skilled enough to beat Yang Wu—but it turns out he's the one who killed Ma's family, too.

Although it begins with an intriguing neo-noir style, telling the story of a man searching for revenge in a foreign land, halfway through it devolves into the same old story of good and bad martial arts schools. Between fights, not much happens except for heroes and villains threatening each other. There's a great deal more energy in the final reel, in which hero and villain face off on a train, a bridge, and a waterfall. The fighting isn't all that creative, but the stunts and locations look mighty dangerous. **AKA:** *Wang Yu, King of Boxing; Ten Fingers of Steel; The Screaming Tiger.* 🐉🐉🐲

1973 (R) 91m/C *HK* Jimmy Wang Yu, Cheung Ching-Ching, Liu Ping, Shan Mao, Zi Lan, Lung Fei, Sit Hon, Ko Saio Pao, Ma Kei, Cheng Fu Hung, Hong Hoi, Wong Fei-lung, Lui Ming, Ng Tung-kiu, Law Bun, Wang Tai-lang, Ko Chun, Chui Lap. **D:** Kam Lung. **DVD**

Second Time Around

Seriously weird. Casino dealer Ren (Ekin Cheng) is on a lucky streak, so he persuades his friend Sing (Jonathan Ke Quan) to "borrow" a million dollars from the casino's bank over the holidays so he can hit it big in Las Vegas. Things go terribly wrong, but Ren is given a second chance to set things right, thanks to parallel universes, time travel, and the unlikely assistance of police officer Tina (Cecilia Cheung).

Time-travel stories always involve a number of paradoxes and leaps of faith. This one in particular requires the viewer to ignore many lapses of logic and difficult-to-comprehend behavior on the part of the characters. If one can brush away all these imperfections, a fairly decent entertainment lies beneath. Notoriously unpredictable director Jeff Lau keeps things motoring along, tosses in a few life lessons, and captures the essence of *deja vu* via a lot of confusing visual tricks. The film looks great, courtesy of cinematographer Johnny Koo Kwok-Wah. The principals are attractive. The music—composed by Chiu Tsang-Hei and Chu Chun-tung—is varied and tart. And it's a pleasant departure to see wide-open desert locales—Las Vegas, Nevada, and Kingman, Arizona—used as the backdrop for a tale of fate and second chances.

Ekin Cheng and Cecilia Cheung do very well as the lead romantic couple. The surprise here is Jonathan Ke Quan as Sing. The former child actor *(Indiana Jones and the Temple of Doom, The Goonies)* turns in a fine performance in the thankless "best friend" role. Annamaria Ambera is stuck with much of the exposition of the parallel universes theory, but acquits herself admirably. The cast includes Lynn Langdon, the Colorado native whose odd career started with a one-way vacation to Hong Kong, where she was discovered by Jackie Chan for film acting and was for a time the well-known weather girl on TVB channel. —PM **AKA:** *Miu Haan Fook Wood; Wu Xian Fu Huo.*

2002 98m/C *HK* Ekin Cheng, Cecilia Cheung, Jonathan Ke Quan, Annamaria Ambera, Oliver Tan, John Wang, Alexander Fung, Lynn Langdon. **D:** Jeff Lau. **W:** Kay On. **C:** Johnny Koo. **M:** Chiu Tsang-Hei, Chu Chun-tung. **DVD**

Secret of the Chinese Kung Fu

Returning from fishing, Mei Yi-Yi and her precocious sister Wei-Wei find a shipwrecked sailor named Chang Chi (Jack Lung) on the beach. The sisters invite Chang to stay for a while, and are even happier that he agrees when they find out he knows kung fu—a talent that comes in handy with so many rascals like Lo Siu-hai and his boys around town. Rogue Kang Ho (Lo Lieh, in cigar-smoking villain mode) returns home after seven years and intends to buy a fish-canning factory owned by old Mr. Chen. When Chen refuses, Kang gets tough with him. Chen agrees to hire Chang at his factory, a job that becomes more difficult when he finds Lo is the foreman—though the man's abuses get him fired soon

after. Chang takes over as foreman, and establishes himself as a rascal-whipping hero. Lo goes to work for Kang, trying to put pressure on Chen by buying up or destroying his supplies. Kang invites some fighting friends from Japan and Thailand to lend a hand (or foot) in his endeavor, killing Lo's former co-workers. He follows up on this terrorism by killing Chen and taking over the factory. Chang endures this unpleasant change, but when Kang lusts after Yi-Yi, thugs of escalating quality are sent to kill Chang. When that doesn't work, a trap made of wine and women is set, but friendly undercover agent Wong Yung comes to the rescue.

The fighting and plot are both standard here, with points of interest provided by the novel seaside setting. Choreography consists of the average block, sock, and roll stuff, with some variation to account for the foreigners' styles. The village seems to have an unusually pretty group of fishwives hauling in nets, looking more like a Kowloon chorus line. The title secret must be how a sailor learned so much Chinese kung fu, since the movie offers no explanation. Many shots are out of focus, and some of the music cues are lifted from Akira Ifukube scores.

1981 88m/C *TW* Lo Lieh, Tse Ling-Ling, Jack Lung, Sze Ma Lung, Lung Fei, Wong Fei-lung. **D:** Sung Ting-mei. **VHS, DVD**

The Secret of the Telegian

At the end of the 1950s, Toho Studios detoured from their blockbuster science-fiction movies to produce a series of smaller-scale shockers more in the style of weird menace pulp stories. This was the last, and the most elusive. Science reporter Kirioka (Koji Tsuruta) goes outside his usual beat to cover a murder in an amusement park, getting help from Detective Kobayashi, an old schoolmate. Three smuggling kingpins—Onishi (Seizaburo Kawazu), Takashi (Yoshifumi Tajima), and Taki (Sachio Sakai)—were partners with the dead man, and are worried that they may be next. All four men were in the army together, in a squad assigned to transport scientist Dr. Niki (Fuyuki Murakami), who was working on a teleportation machine, along with a fortune in gold. The men shot the scientist and Corporal Sudo (Tadao Nakamura), a soldier who got in their way, and stole the gold. But Sudo survived, took the hidden gold, and has sent those who tried to kill him a threat via audiotape. While the detectives question Takashi, Sudo materializes in the room with them, stabs his target, and disappears! Taki decides to accept police protection, but it's no use—Sudo kills him the same way. The police find that Dr. Niki is also alive, but crippled, and

is unaware that his assistant Sudo has been using his teleporter to get revenge.

A potentially exciting idea is wasted here, as the filmmakers seem to be at a loss to know what to do with a disfigured, teleporting phantom, other than to treat him the same way such horror figures were handled back in the 1930s. In their hands, Sudo is just an especially tricky gangster on the loose, and most of their plot ideas lead to dead ends. In the end, they rely on Toho's favorite plot device, the erupting volcano, to take care of everything. Eiji Tsuburaya, taking a break from model building, provides a great effect for the teleporting killer, making him look like a static-effused three-dimensional video image. Second-time director Jun Fukuda would thrive in the spy-crazy '60s, bringing a James Bond flavor to even his Godzilla movie assignments. Shot in widescreen color and stereo, until recently *Telegian* was only known in the U.S. (if known at all) through cropped, black-and-white television prints, cut by 10 minutes. **AKA:** *Denso Ningen; The Telegraphed Man; The Telegian; The Electrical Facsimile Transmission Human.* 🐉🐉

1960 85m/C *JP* Tadao Nakamaru, Koji Tsuruta, Akihiko Hirata, Yoshio Tsuchiya, Yumi Shirakawa, Seizaburo Kawazu, Sachio Sakai, Yoshifumi Tajima, Fuyuki Murakami, Takamaru Sasaki, Shin Otomo, Ren Yamamoto, Yutaka Sada, Yutaka Nakayama, Eisei Amamoto, Nadao Kirino, Shoichi Hirose, Akira Sera, Senkichi Omura, Yasuhisa Tsutsumi, Tatsuo Matsumura, Fumito Matsuo, Tadashi Okabe, Koji Uno. **D:** Jun Fukuda. **W:** Shinichi Sekizawa. **C:** Kazuo Yamada. **M:** Sei Ikeno. **VHS**

The Secrets of the Warrior's Power

Further study for those who enjoyed *Shaolin: Wheel of Life*. This documentary, perfect for the Discovery Channel, explores the history of kung fu and how it survives in the modern era, starting with Bodhi Dharma and the Shaolin Temple. 1570: the Manchus burn the temple, and the martial arts go underground. The survivors form the first triads, like the White Lotus Society. Later, the Boxers join forces with Manchus to resist foreign invasion, and lose. The Maoists denounce the martial arts, and they go underground again, many practitioners once again traveling undercover with opera troupes. One such is Master Yip Man, who teaches Bruce Lee. Lee develops jeet kune do, and changes action cinema forever.

The rest of the program examines what kung fu masters are doing today. In 1978, Master Pan Qing Fu was called upon to help with the triad problem in Shanghai. He not only helped train the police force, but went out and captured many

a gang boss single-handedly. Now he teaches kung fu in Canada. Methods of training and different martial arts weapons are explored. Meanwhile, in Shaolin Temple, the tourists have invaded. The spirit of the 36th Chamber lives on, as Shi Yan-Ming opens Shaolin Temple USA in New York City. In Florida, Grand Master Chan Pui talks about Den Mak, the Death touch—and a re-enactment illustrates how his master Chan Li used it to silence a challenger. He also shows off on some Plum Flower Posts (as seen in *The Legend*). Master Dennis Brown shows how he's teaching animal forms and Zen philosophy to inner-city kids. Movie clips include *The Shaolin Plot, The Warrior Within, Shaolin Kung Fu, Last to Surrender, Iron and Silk,* and various Bruce Lee films. 🐉🐉🐉🐉

1997 52m/C *US/CA/HK* Pan Ching Fu, Chan Pui, Dennis Brown, Shi Yan-Ming. **N:** Michael Weiner, Alice Chen. **D:** Jim Grapek. **W:** Jim Grapek, Leo Johnson. **C:** Sheila Smith, Charles Kendall, Phil Earnshaw. **M:** Kenneth-Michael Veltz. **VHS, DVD**

Seeding of a Ghost

Hoo boy. Shaw Brothers produced a string of gruesome horror pictures in the 1970s, but this later effort tops them all. Taxi driver Chau (Phillip Ko) runs into (literally) a sorcerer (Baak Man-biu) on a dark road, unknowingly saving him from a pursuing mob. The mysterious man tells Chau that bad fortune will befall him. Sure enough, Chau's pretty casino dealer wife Irene (Maria Jo) starts cheating on him with suave bastard Anthony Fang Ming (Norman Tsui). When the cheaters inevitably quarrel over commitment, Fang leaves Irene on lonely stretch of road, where a pair of hooligan rapists chases her into an abandoned mansion, and she falls to her death off a balcony. After briefly considering Chau a suspect, the police catch up with Fang and the two hoods—though suspicion still remains over the supernatural call that directed Chau to the murder site. The hooligans try to kill Chau, but find him too tough, and Chau in turn attacks Fang. With all this fighting getting him nothing but a bum leg, Chau hunts down the witch doctor to help him get revenge.

Up to now, the movie had included some full-frontal nudity, kung fu fighting, rape, and murder, but when the sorcerer begins his Seeding of a Ghost vengeance spell, the proceedings only become more repellent. The roused corpse of the victim (called a "Plazawa") leads us to worm vomiting, exploding toilets, brain eating, necrophilia, possession, and more, culminating in the impregnation of Fang's innocent wife with an inhuman monster! The birth of this tentacled nightmare definitely spoils a mah-jongg party for everyone. Some scenes mix rich atmosphere into the action, but shocks and thrills are the main agenda here, which the movie delivers in spades. Music cues are borrowed from *Jason and the Argonauts, Alien,* and other soundtracks. *AKA: Chung Gwai; Zhong Gui.* 🎵🎵🎵

1983 90m/C *HK* Phillip Ko, Norman Tsui, Wong Yung, Maria Jo, Tin Mat, Baak Man-biu. *D:* Yeung Kuen. *W:* Wong Kam-ba, Lam Yee-hung. **VHS**

7 Commandments of Kung Fu

This old-school effort features an especially artful opening credit sequence, with star James Lee (AKA Lee Yi-min) going through his acrobatic paces amid suspended rings over large yin/yang symbols, juxtaposed (often via split screen) with him working out among giant mantis statues. Hapless youth Shiao Ping (Lee) works hard as a pharmacist's assistant all day, while at home his Uncle Cheng trains him mercilessly in kung fu using hanging rings. White-haired Mantis Fist Master Lu Zu-hai (Chang Yi) comes to town looking to challenge his old enemy Ho Chin-tin (Lung Fei), but crafty bandit chief Ho knows he can't beat Lu, and has his gang ambush his mantis enemy. Lu escapes the battle with minor injuries, and Ping takes him in to recover.

Implicated in helping Lu escape, Ping leaves town with Lu and becomes his student. Ping gets plenty of practice while on the lam, with Ho's entire army of thugs after Lu's head. Along the way, Lu teaches Ping his seven rules of combat. Eventually, after a year of whittling down Ho's forces, they circle back to finish the bandit chief off, but Ping's admiration for Master Lu takes a turn when Lu kills Uncle Hung, and Ping learns that Lu killed his father as well. Ping takes his father's secret Sun Moon kung fu manual into the hills to train in solitude so that he can return to confront his former master.

A standard kung fu flick in most ways, the unusual factor here (cribbed from the Italian western *Days of Wrath*) is in the somewhat sympathetic villain, who is only following his own code of behavior. This leads to conflicting emotions as well as martial conflict when student faces off against master for the final dustup. There's an interesting training sequence for which the hero constructs large straw-and-bamboo practice dummies that look like mantises, and these straw mantises become oversized puppets for him to battle. It's also fun to watch Lee working out with the hanging rings, which also make a visually interesting combat setting. *AKA: Gung Foo Chat Gaai; Gong Fu Qi Jie.* 🎵🎵🎵

1979 84m/C *HK* James Lee, Chang Yi, Goo Chang, Lung Fei, Suen Shu-pau, Ma Chin-ku, Ching Kuo-chung, Siu Foo-dau. *D:* Ko Saio Pao. *W:* Yiu Hing-hong. *C:* Chen Hay-locl. *M:* Chou Fu-liang. **VHS, DVD**

Seven Samurai

If you've seen more than a couple of westerns or SF stories (either TV or film) made since 1960, chances are the plot of this film will be familiar to you. Bandits are terrorizing a small farming town in rural Japan. Every year at harvest, the brigands return and take more of the town's meager supplies, and finally, the villagers can take no more. They travel to the city to hire someone to protect them and defeat the bandits. Since this is Japan, and not the old west or some far-off planet, the villagers hire out-of-work samurai (ronin). Lead swordsman Kambei (Takashi Shimura) gathers together a motley band of six other rogues to help him in with the job. Among them is young hothead, Kikuchiyo (Toshiro Mifune), whose claim to samurai fame seems to be largely in his head. As the seven samurai prepare the village to fight against the bandits, we get to know more about both the village and its would-be saviors. Since this is a Kurosawa film, very few of the parties can be taken at face value. The film builds slowly and deliberately through its nearly three-and-a-half hours to an amazing climax and a fight scene that has become a cinema classic.

Perhaps the most famous of Akira Kurosawa's films, and almost certainly the best, *Seven Samurai* is a masterpiece of the cinematic arts. Every shot in it is carefully planned and choreographed, so that each scene is a work of art unto itself. Just watch as the actors move from one painterly composition to the next—all rendered in stunning black and white. Which is not to say that the film is just a living painting—far from it! Nowhere is Kurosawa's mastery of the form more evident than it is here. And, lest you get the wrong idea from all this high-minded talk, it's a ripping-good film as well. *Seven Samurai* is probably the best action picture ever made. Long but never boring, it pulls the viewer from one compelling scene and character to the next. The film has enough depth of character and story for three other flicks. Amazing photography by Asakazu Nakai enhances every scene. If you've seen the American western *Magnificent Seven,* you've only seen a pale shadow of this film. If you only see one Asian film *ever,* this is the film to see. —SS *AKA: Shichinin no Samurai; Magnificent Seven.* 🎵🎵🎵🎵

1954 207m/BW *JP* Toshiro Mifune, Takashi Shimura, Keiko Tushima, Isao Kimura, Seiji Miyaguchi, Minoru Chiaki, Daisuke Kato, Kamatari Fujiwara, Kokuten Kodo, Bokuzen Hidari, Yoshio Kosugi, Yoshio Tsuchiya, Jiro Kumagai, Yasuhisa Tsutsumi, Toranosuke Ogawa, Noriko Sengoku, Gen Shimizu,

Atsushi Watanabe, Kichijiro Ueda, Shinpei Takagi, Akira Tani, Haruo Nakajima, Senkichi Omura, Shoichi Hirose, Tatsuya Nakadai, Jun Tazaki, Eijiro Tono, Isao Yamagata. *D:* Akira Kurosawa. *W:* Akira Kurosawa, Shinobu Hashimoto, Hideo Oguni. *C:* Asakazu Nakai. *M:* Fumio Hayasaka. **VHS, DVD**

The Seventh Curse

One of several movies based on the pulp science-fiction stories of screenwriter Ngai Hong (who introduces the story), this one ranks as one of the most successful adaptations, and one of the wildest rides in Hong Kong cinema.

A gang of crooks is cornered in a building and takes hostages. Captain Ho (Yasuaki Kurata) calls in Dr. Yuan Chen (Chin Siu-ho) to treat a hostage stricken with a heart attack. Making a call beyond the usual negotiation tactics, Ho sends Yuan in with Inspector Chiang (Kara Hui) to set a flare bomb inside, but reporter Tung Tsai-hung (Maggie Cheung) takes the officer's place. After the raid is a success, the reporter has the nerve to pursue Yuan, asking him to pose nude for her sleazy paper!

A stranger named Heh Lung (Dick Wei) comes from Thailand to warn Yuan that he's been infected with a blood curse, and after a painful episode, the doctor consults his sifu Weisley (Chow Yun-fat). Yuan picked up the curse on a trip to north Thailand the previous year, when after rescuing Heh Lung's girlfriend Betsy (Chui Sau-lai) from being sacrificed to an ancient spinal cord-sucking vampire corpse, evil wizard Aquala (Elvis Tsui) of the Yunnan worm tribe threw down some wicked hoodoo on him. He only survived with Betsy's help, and now the curse has resurfaced, and he must return to Thailand to seek a cure. Tsai-hung, who happens to be Weisley's spoiled and meddlesome cousin, tags along to cause trouble. The group has to fight their way through fierce warriors, booby-trapped jungles, and demonic possession to reach the Yunnan temple, where Aquala is throwing 100 children into a crushing device to extract their blood in a spell to give himself superhuman powers.

Seventh Curse is like an Indiana Jones movie gone mad. In between shots of beautiful Thai scenery, it offers nudity, gore, kung fu, monsters, gunfights, and bloody violence—you never know what's going to pop up next! Before they'd reached superstardom, Chow Yun-fat is amusing as the pipe-smoking know-it-all with a rocket launcher, and Maggie Cheung looks especially young here. As the villain, Elvis Tsui sports a long wig and face paint, and keeps a hideous little imp for a pet. *AKA: Yuen Chun-hup yue Wai Si Lee; Yuan Zhenxia yu Wei Si Li; Dr. Yuan and Weisley.*

1986 78m/C *HK* Chin Siu-ho, Maggie Cheung, Chow Yun-fat, Dick Wei, Chui Sau-lai, Elvis Tsui, Sibelle Hu, Ken Boyle, Yasuaki Kurata, Kara Hui, Wong Jing, Chor Yuen, Johnny Wang, Ngai Hong, Derek Yee, Nina Li Chi, Chui Suk-woon, Wong Yu, Lam Gei-yan. *D:* Simon Nam. *W:* Wong Jing, Yuen Kai-chi. *C:* Lam Chiu. *M:* Sing Kam-wing. **VHS, DVD**

The 72 Desperate Rebels

During the middle of the Ming Dynasty, the coastline is terrorized by the pirate king Bo Ho-lin (Pai Ying)—also known as Master Wolf—and his infamous 72 Fighters. They spend a lot of time marching about. Each bears a different color of headband, signifying how many men they've killed in combat, from white up to gold. Among the fiercest is a giant monk (Siu Gam) with gold teeth and a midget. General Wu is sent to deal with the pirates, but they make short work of him. Woo Li-wei (Chan Sing) has only two kills left before he graduates to the next level, and enters a ring to slay two prisoners in combat. However, one of their men named Shur Chi-lung is a traitor, and lets a prisoner escape. Under the name Ghost Killer (Chung Wa), a mystery man challenges all 72 Fighters to a duel, to avenge his master General Wu. Chi-lung and the general's daughter invade the Wolf's fortress and fight his 18 Monks. After that, the 9 Golden Men are sent in to get them, but Ghost Killer arrives to help the heroes out. The next day, the three heroes begin facing the challenge of the Four Branches. One branch is all red, another is a chamber of bells, etc. To repay Chi-lung for saving her life, Wolf's daughter Lady Pearl spares them from death in the Phoenix Branch. She advises them that to survive the dangers of the Four Branches, they must fight blind. To gain the necessary skills, they seek out the Blind Swordsman (Lung Fei) for training.

The characters, plot, and even the fight scenes aren't that engaging in this routine kung fu flick, at least until near the end. Only the color coordination and the mercenary Ghost Killer add interest—things perk up a bit when he's on screen. He has a few slick moves, like punching his fingers through a foe's hand. The plot has so many flashbacks that it's hard to tell what's going on. The Blind Swordsman is clearly inspired by Zatoichi, and even fights in a similar style. Later, even a one-armed swordsman puts

in an appearance. The climax offers a lot more fun when the heroes face the monstrous monk and superpowered Bo Ho-lin, but it's a mess of a film to get through until then. *AKA: Sing Yee Sap Chat; Xing Er Shi Qi; Killer Hillz.*

1976 91m/C *HK* Pai Ying, Chung Wa, Lung Fei, Barry Chan, Miu Tin, Chan Sing, Siu Gam, Sit Hon, Choi Wong, Chui Chung Hei, Yeung Sau-guen, Au Yeung-chung. *D:* Lin Bin. *W:* Shing Yang, Kin Tsan. *C:* Tu Tong-show. **VHS, DVD**

Sex and the Emperor

Another exercise in outrageous dark sexual comedy/drama perpetrated by producer Wong Jing. Set in the Forbidden City during the final dynasty of China, it's a story told by real historical figure Li Lianying (Jimmy Wong). Despite his status as a royal eunuch, Li is fully functional due to a favor returned to his family by the castrating doctor. Li is assigned to the Emperor Tongzhi, becoming the young man's best friend. Though his teacher (Wong Yat-Fei) works hard to educate the boy, his thoughts are only filled with fantasies about a chambermaid named Guilian (Yvonne Yung). But Tongzhi's obsession is discovered by head eunuch Little On Dehai (Stuart Ong), who convinces the Queen Mother to turn the girl over to him. Little On submits her to horrible tortures, then turns her over to the brothel of Hongyi (Julie Lee), where she learns the sexual martial art called Eight Semi-Devils. Without her beloved, Tongzhi becomes a sex-crazed madman, eventually contracting syphilis. By the time he finds her, he's too far gone. However, Li concocts a special plan of revenge for Little On's treachery.

While there are some amusing gags and situations here, and even some hot sex scenes, they're mixed in with a lot of really unpleasant material. Besides the torture scenes, there's also dismemberment, urine drinking, grotesque syphilitic lesions, and other repellent sights. Tongzhi's story would be touching, but too much of this is played for leering shocks—which have their place, but Wong and company want this to be a serious historical piece as well, and they just don't have the class required. *AKA: Moon Ching Gam Gung Gei Ngon; Man Qing Jin Gong Ji An.*

1994 92m/C *HK* Jimmy Wong, Yvonne Yung, Stuart Ong, Julie Lee, Yuen King-Tan, Wong Yat-Fei. *D:* Sherman Wong. *W:* Cheuk Bing. *C:* Tony Miu. *M:* Marco Wan. **VHS, DVD**

Shadow

This Hong Kong teen ghost movie is better than most of the recent crop because it has a decent

"Take my advice or I'll spank you without pants!"

—Maggie Cheung has her back end threatened in *The Seventh Curse*

story grounded in full characters, and doesn't just rely on cheap spook tactics. Lam Sai-lun (Stephen Fung), Shi, and Wah are enjoying a beach barbecue with their dates, when Lun sees To Siu-yuet (Bobo Chan)—a girl he's had a crush on for years—walk by. They decide to try to find her for him, and after calling around, their classmate Fanny (Isabel Chan) tells them to wait the next night at a remote villa. After making the boys wait until midnight, Fanny surprises them with the news that Siu-yuet died a year ago—and what's more, she blames Lun for her death. According to Fanny, after an embarrassing schoolyard incident caused by Lun, Siu-yuet began having mental problems and ended up committing suicide. Her wish was for Lun to have her ashes when he came to look for her. Clumsy Lun adds to his insult by dropping the urn, at which point a wind blows in and scatters the ashes—and the boys wake up miles away the next morning. Shi's superstitious family throws him out, and Wah's psychic grandmother tells them the only hope is to go back to the villa and help Siu-yuet find peace. That night, Siu-yuet appears, telling them that she only has seven days to achieve reincarnation. She says other ghosts stole from her when the urn broke, and to make amends the boys must steal money back from the mortuary. The next night, she tells them to buy her a diamond ring with the stolen loot. Later, they're sent shopping for other things. The boys never question any of this, but of course it's all a scheme cooked up by the two girls. After learning that the incident was an innocent accident and Lun suffered for it as well, they don't know how to call a halt to the prank. Meanwhile, all the supernatural antics seem to have driven Lun off the deep end.

It's all presented in good humor in the first half—the boys' reaction to seeing the ghost is illustrated by a shot of two basketballs quickly deflating—and the romance is given time to develop. Towards the end, it becomes too mushy and contrived, but in all this stands out from most of its ilk. **AKA:** *Yau Leng Ching Shu; You Ling Qing Shu.* 🦴🦴

2001 94m/C *HK* Stephen Fung, Bobo Chan, Derek Tsang, Samuel Chan, Isabel Chan, Bonnie Wong, Lam Chi-ho, Edmond So, Robert Siu Leong, Matt Chow, Eva Wong. **D:** Lo Kim-wah. **W:** Felix Chong. **C:** Ko Chiu-lam. **M:** Star East Music Ltd. **VHS, DVD**

Shadow of the Tiger

It's not unusual for old-school kung fu movies to begin with footage of the principals working out in front of a plain color backdrop, but here's one that even cranks up titles with their resumés! Cliff Lok, "Champion of the 2nd (1971) South-

east Asian Chinese Martial Arts International Tournament Held in Singapore"; Lee Kwoon Hung, "Vice-President of Chan Sian Memorial Association, Supervisor of Hung Shing Gymnasium in Hawaii"; Chiu Chi-ling, "President and 'Tuitor' of Hung Kuen Gymnasium, Chairman of Hung Kuen International Association"; Chan Sau-chung, "Vice-President of the Hong Kong Chinese Martial Arts Association, President of Hong Kong Kung Fu Association, Head of Ta Sheng P'I Kua Mun"; Pomson Shi, "Champion of the 3rd (1973) Southeast Asian Chinese Martial Arts International Tournament in Malaysia, Chief 'Tuitor' of Ta Sheng P'I Kua Athletic Association"; Lam Man-wai, "Won Three Championship (1969–1971) in the Boxing Tournament in Hong Kong"; Sharon Yeung, "The New Kung Fu Heroine of 1978, 'Tuitor' of Fan Chuong Yei Gymnasium"; Han Ying Chieh, "Action-Director and Actor of *Come Drink with Me, Dragon Inn, The Big Boss, Fist of Fury*"; Phillip Ko, "'Tuitor' of Chung Yi Gymnasium in Taiwan, Supervisor of Hong Kong Karate Association." O.K., you're all hired! Now let's get on with the movie—we're already six minutes in!

And get on with it they do! Monks Wu Shu (Monkey Style expert Chan Sau-chung) and Wu Kung duel to determine who will become the new abbot of their Shaolin order. Kung loses the match and skedaddles, eventually settling in Japan, where he founds the Tang Sao Pau school—teaching a new style that developed into karate. After the epic opening, this settles down into the old formula about invading Japanese martial artists led by Wu Kung's successor Si Man-kwong (Phillip Ko) busting up the signs and faculty of all the Chinese schools in the area. When respected Master Chung Yeh-so (Chiu Chi-ling) refuses to fight, the schoolmasters band together to hire a fighter capable of beating Si. Meanwhile, Master Chung makes his own effort to gather some heroes to drive out the invaders, and the plot moves from aping *The Chinese Connection* to *Seven Samurai*. Defeated by Si, the seven champions attempt to pool their skills by teaching them all to their one uninjured member (Cliff Lok), who challenges the villain alone.

The simple plot serves only to string together one terrific fight scene after another, many of which are obviously shoehorned into the movie just to keep the action quotient high. However, the caliber of the cast's skills is such that this is unlikely to bother kung fu fans, as most of the action scenes are first-rate, with many minor performers given a chance to shine in larger roles. The recruiting scenes, in which different fighters display their skills and personalities, are more fun to watch than yet another training sequence in which a young hero learns an exotic style (though there's a bit of this as well). Good use is made of the gorgeous Taiwanese locations. **AKA:** *Luk Gap Chin Sau; Liu He Qian Shou; Duel of the Seven Tigers; Return of the Scorpion.* 🐉🐉🐉

1979 (R) 92m/C *HK* Cliff Lok, Phillip Ko, Lee Kwoon Hung, Chu Chi-ling, Chan Sau-chung, Pom-son Shi, Lam Man-wai, Sharon Yeung, Han Ying Chieh, Casanova Wong, Chiang Kam, Yue Tau Wan, Chan Lau, San Kwai, Hon Yee Sang, Charlie Chan. **D:** Yeung Kuen. **W:** Wu Tien-chi, Wan Siu-kuen. **C:** Fan Shou-fu. **M:** Chou Fu-liang. **VHS, DVD**

Shanghai Affairs

Donnie Yen got to do his tribute to Bruce Lee's *The Chinese Connection* in the *Fist of Fury* TV series. With this one, he did something more in the flavor of *The Big Boss* (AKA *Fists of Fury*). In 1918 (though the date is hard to place), Doctors Tong Shan (Donnie Yen) and his pal Bond Lao (Chan Chin-pang) arrive in town to put up their shingle, taking a shabby office/apartment. The Axe Gang, led by Yu Lo-chi (Yu Rongguang), has bought up a lot of the slums and is forcing the peasants out. Shan resists getting involved in the trouble, but as the resulting riot turns violent, the pair step in with superior kung fu.

Defending the peasants and patching up the wounded gains them friends, especially police inspector Chen Wa, but makes them enemies with the Axe Gang. Yu's sister Shen (Athena Chu) is ill, but he doesn't believe in science and prays to the Fox God to cure her. Dr. Tong goes to talk with the slumlord Dr. Raymond at the race track on behalf of the peasants, but Yu is there, too. Raymond is backing the gang's takeover of the slums in return for a percentage of the casino they plan to build there, but Tong talks him out of the deal in exchange for coming to work at his hospital. Before Yu can react, his hotheaded assistant Lung tries to take revenge. Yu arrives and forbids his men from fighting; to save face, though, he challenges Tong himself, but their incredible duel doesn't get too far before Uncle Wa interrupts. When Tong operates to cure Shen's throat (with a bonus of growing attraction between them), it only increases the tensions between him and Yu.

Meanwhile, somebody is abducting children from the slums. These kidnappings seem to take quite a while to be noticed, only affecting the plot when 10 children are found dead by the river, their organs harvested. The police are no help, so Tong calls in Yu's debt to him by asking for help in finding the killers. Of course, Yu has been helping Raymond, who is behind the organ harvesting business. Yu is faced with a choice between honoring his debt to an enemy, or bucking Raymond and putting his gang at risk. When Bond discovers the Axe Gang during an abduction, and is killed by Yu holding evidence against

his killer, the fine points of Yu's moral dilemma become elementary.

The title "Shanghai Affairs" refers to the odd romantic relationships that complicate the story. As Tong treats Shen's throat and begins to woo her, her friend (and Yu's girlfriend) Yeh falls for the handsome doctor, too. Seeing this makes Yu all the more jealous. It's a novel plot for a martial arts film, and one that holds interest during the long stretches between fight scenes. Yen was obviously working on his direction more than his action choreography, sacrificing a lot of kicks but giving the picture an interesting look. The big duel between Yen and Yu is long in coming, but is kind of slick while it lasts. 🐉🐉🐉

1998 93m/C *HK* Donnie Yen, Athena Chu, Yu Rongguang, Cheng Hung, Chan Chin-pang, Yan Yi Shek. **D:** Donnie Yen. **C:** Poon Tak-yip. **VHS, DVD**

Shanghai 1920

This lavish drama is notable mainly as a waste of good talent, but also because producer Jim Choi, a mainland triad, was murdered in 1992—some rumors say because of triad secrets revealed in the film. In 1937, amid an army of refugees fleeing the invading Japanese, Billy Fong (John Lone) recalls his lifelong friendship with rich American Dawson Cole (Adrian Pasdar), which began when they were boys in 1920. When the two boys ignorantly swipe a stash of opium from Billy's boss (Kirk Wong), the angry gangster kills Dawson's father in retribution. Billy aids Dawson in getting his revenge, shooting the killer. Years later, Dawson comes back to Shanghai to take over a shipping business he inherited, and gets together with Billy again. The naïve Dawson refuses to deal with dockside extortionist Tso (Wong Kam-Kong), and his business is ruined. Billy once again helps Dawson get revenge by murdering Tso. The two men become partners as Fifty Fifty Exports, but Billy's criminal traits get the better of him. He begins using their ships to smuggle opium, starting trouble with the law, the competition, and with his partner.

What should be a sweeping epic becomes maudlin and dull, as every incident and effect is overplayed. It's not enough for the 1920 flashback to begin with a shot of an old-fashioned locomotive—it has to be bathed in sepiatone as well. Che-Kirk Wong's gangster boss isn't just mean, he's a howling supervillain. Dawson is not just an American, but comes equipped with a baseball cap and bat! The film has its moments, but overall it's just predictable and slow. Even Lone is so one-note throughout that it's a shock to see him smile during his wedding scene. **AKA:** *Seung hoi 1920; Once upon a Time in Shanghai.* 🐉🐉

1991 114m/C *HK* John Lone, Adrian Pasdar, Fennie Yuen, Yeung Chong Hon, Rachel Lee, Lau Siu-ming, Wong Kam-Kong, Kirk Wong. **D:** Leung Po-chi. **W:** Timothy R. Long, Michael Laughlin. **C:** Walter Gregg, Joe Chan. **M:** Kitaro. **VHS, DVD**

Shaolin and Tai Chi

Ching Dynasty official Esquire Gau finds out that a group of suspected rebels are throwing a banquet, and sees that they're all poisoned. Shih Dau and his family escape into the hills, but the soldiers soon catch up with them. Mrs. Shih hides baby Fong in the brush. Years later, Fong Err is a thief living on the streets. His gang tries to rob a Shaolin monk, but their target easily bests him with his superior kung fu, and Fong ends up becoming a student at the temple. Fong is a troublesome lad, but his skills improve dramatically under the tutelage of an old monk who teaches him Drunken Pole Style.

Meanwhile, young son Gau Yuin is recruited by the Tai Chi Taoists as a promising student. Every year, the best fighters from Shaolin and Tai Chi duel to determine who will guard a precious gold seal. Fong and Yuin are set to duel, but before they can begin, ninjas steal the gold seal. It's decided that whichever of the two duelists can recover the seal wins the contest, and they set off to search together. Through a variety of adventures, the two become friends and—you guessed it—find they both bear two halves of the same jade piece, and are actually brothers! The secret out, Gau marshals his forces to wipe out the troublesome Shih forces once and for all.

The plot of this shot-in-Taiwan feature is a catalog of kung fu movie clichés. There's some of that weird continuity you often see in these features, where fighting is going on in one location and suddenly shifts to another miles away, or a scene of folks mourning a murdered loved one cuts directly from the tragedy to a shot of them enjoying a fine meal. However, the action is fantastic and plentiful. 🦴🦴🦴

1979 /C *HK/TW* **D:** Wu Chia Chun. **VHS**

The Shaolin Brothers

For most of us, traditional Chinese vampire movies began with *Mr. Vampire* in 1985, but here we are eight years earlier. It's the first frame, and already we've got hopping corpses! The narrator tells us that in Hsianghsi Province of the 1600s, it was common to transport deceased travelers home via "corpse herders." More on that later. Ling Yun-chang (Tung Li) and Ko Lung-ta (Carter Wong) studied kung fu together at Shaolin Temple. Now wealthy Ko has been appointed as South China Area Commander by the Ching government, driving a wedge between the former friends. Ko sends a team of freakish wild men to fetch Ling to him, but Ling dispatches them all. Ling goes to confront his former brother, and during their duel discovers the rascal has stolen their master's impenetrable Golden Garment, and Ko sticks him with a poisoned Soul-Broken Needle. When Ling's girlfriend Hsiang-yen (Chin Meng) comes seeking revenge, she gets the same treatment. Turning to other matters, Ko dispatches General Tse to capture Ming General Hang Chung-jen. Tse finds and kills Hang after a hard battle. Meanwhile, Ling has survived long enough to get treatment from his old master (Seung Fung), which will only keep him alive another nine days. Ming rebel leader Mr. Weng sends Mr. Ting to aid their forces in the south. Having collected a full load of hero corpses, the herder Taoist monk Lu (Yuen Sam) gets them hopping on his route home. But Lu doesn't seem to have much control of his charges—one is found wandering about an inn en route, and when examined by Ching soldiers at a bridge, they all hop off into the woods. The corpses—Ting, Hang, Hsiang-yen, and a trio of bandits—aren't quite dead yet, just anxious to travel south without being caught by the Manchus. Trying to escape, the group has to fight their way through Tse's troops, as well as the mercenary fighters the Five Ghosts. Finally reaching their goal, Hang hands over the plans of the Ching army, only to find they've all fallen into a trap set by crafty General Ko.

Carter Wong is one of those actors who is equally good playing villains as heroes, and here he plays a grinning evil character. The film is peppered with strange comic antics and odd-looking minor characters, and there's entirely too much pointless running around. The continuity is odd, too—characters will leap up in a forest and come down in an open area. The fight scenes cheat a bit, with some bad wirework and frames cut out in an attempt to make the action look faster. Combined with the hopping corpses and wild webwork plot, it all makes for one confusing—but entertaining—movie. **AKA:** *Siu Lam Fong Dai; Shao Lin Xiong Di.* 🦴🦴½

1977 C: *HK* Carter Wong, Tung Li, Tong Wai, Chin Meng, Ko Saio Pao, Cho Kin, Yuen Sam, Sit Hon, Lui Ming, Tsang Chiu, Lau Ching-fat, Seung Fung, Dai Sai Aan, Che Yuen. **D:** Joseph Kuo. **W:** Joseph Kuo. **DVD**

Shaolin Chastity Kung Fu

Here's another flick that upholds the Asian tradition of mixing cute little children and horrific violence in one story. A gang of bandits "that people generally call the Nine Devils," led by the beefy Golden Tiger, learn that a shipment of gold from Goldenberg(!) is headed through Sunset Valley. While strongman Brother Tien Chiu (Alexander Lou) wrestles a bull, the bandits attack, intending to take over the town and ambush the caravan. While the bandits tear the men of the village apart, Tien and Chu Yen (Hilda Liu) lead the children into the hills. When two bandits trail them, Shaolin Abbot Master Wisdom and monk Yuen Fah come to the rescue. The Nine Devils go to free their leader, who had allowed the cops to capture him so that he could gather information on the gold shipment. To help them defend themselves, the monks teach the village kids (who never walk when they can do flips) some of their Shaolin tung chi (chastity) style kung fu. Two bandits attack Tanaka and his two sons, who have come from Japan to study with Wisdom, and Tanaka is killed. Sonawa and his little brother escape to the caves where the refugees are hiding, clashing a bit with the Chinese kids as they recover, due to cultural differences. Tien is captured while fetching medical supplies, and the bandits use him to lure and kill Master Wisdom with a big rock. This brings all the kids together to study hard and confront the Nine Devils, using their different strengths to kick nine asses.

It's another great action-packed movie from the underrated Robert Tai. The Nine Devils may dress in flashy costumes like a Las Vegas review, but they're a vicious bunch. One guy has a giant club that he uses to knock people's heads off. Another breaks a guy in half using his head! The vengeful orphans are no shirkers either, beating the bandits to bloody pulps. The characters aren't any deeper than your average Power Ranger, but the quirky action never stops. Much of the music is swiped from Hammer Dracula movies. **AKA:** *Siu Lam Tung Ji Gung; Shaolin Tong Zi Gong; Revenge of the Dragon.* 🐉🐉🐉

1981 87m/C *TW* Alexander Lou, Tong Lung, Hilda Liu, Lee Hoi-sang, Yeung Hung, Kim Fun, Huang Ha, Ching Kuo-chung, Wong Kin-mi. **D:** Robert Tai. **W:** Chang Chien Chih. **C:** Woo Kuo-hsiao. **M:** Chou Fu-liang, Chen Pi Teh. **VHS, DVD**

The Shaolin Disciple

Sometimes it seems the most common question asked within the walls of the Shaolin Temple was "So, who killed your dad?" According to the movies, there probably weren't many devout Buddhists among the students, the ranks being filled by angry orphans bent on learning martial arts to exact vengeance. They probably should have changed the name to Revenge Incorporated Temple. However, this kung fu programmer mixes up things just slightly by having the hero sent to Shaolin against his will long before his father is killed. Wu Tin (Ku Feng) escapes from prison with the help of Captain Tong (Tang Yim-chan), who is actually the brother of his old partner Pan Fu. Their first goal is revenge on Captain Chan Hui (Kwan Hoi-san) and his brother Kun Ming, who captured Wu and killed Pan Fu seven years before. Chan has since retired, and sent his irresponsible and rebellious son Little Mouse (Jimmy Liu) off with his brother—now a Shaolin abbot—hoping the monks at Shaolin will be able to straighten the boy out. Little Mouse runs away, but the abbot hardly has time to look for him, having his hands full performing an exorcism on one of the village girls. After some misadventures, Little Mouse tries to return home, but his dad chases him away. Wu Tin and his son (Kwan Chung) plan to double-cross and kill their partner once their revenge is complete, but Tong catches wind of the deceit. A full hour into the movie, Wu Tin finally kills Chan, leaving very little time to wrap things up. Tong fails to kill Kun Ming, Little Mouse fails to kill Wu Tin, and Kun Ming kills Wu Tin, leaving Little Mouse and Tong to fight a final duel while Kun Ming stays home in the monastery.

The filmmakers pad out the running time with superfluous flashbacks, supernatural hijinks, and strange sexual antics, making for a very disjointed picture. Much time is spent on these stray subplots while no time at all is spent with training sequences, or other clues as to how lazy Little Mouse became such a kung fu master. The father role is given a down-to-earth touch, as he spends his retirement farming and drinking—but mostly drinking, as opposed to his devout monk brother. Jimmy Liu and company provide decent kung fu fighting. Apparently the whole project was put together by actor Man Man, including the music. The soundtrack uses music cues from *Star Wars: Episode 4* and *Midnight Express.* **AKA:** *Shao Lin Fo Jia Da Dao.* 🐉🐉

1980 87m/C *HK* Jimmy Liu, Kwan Hoi-san, Ku Feng, Kwan Chung, Tang Yim-chan, Leung Kar-yan, Lee Man Tai, Wong Mei. **D:** Man Man, Cheng Wing-keung. **W:** Man Man. **C:** Lam Li-choi. **M:** Man Man. **VHS, DVD**

The Shaolin Drunken Monk

In the films made with the Shaolin Temple as a setting, the monks are often shown breaking many of their Buddhist vows, usually thinking up some loophole to excuse their behavior. Abstinence from alcohol is the vow broken most often, and an alcoholic monk is not an uncommon sight in old-school kung fu films, especially

those made after Yuen Woo-ping's *Drunken Master*. In this cheap mainland production, Gordon Lau combines his persona from *Shaolin Master Killer* (AKA *Enter the 36th Chamber*) with this familiar character type. However, Lau doesn't play a Shaolin monk in this movie, and no monks of any kind appear.

When a one-handed man murders a member of a local martial arts society, suspicion naturally falls on Kam, who sacrificed his hand in refusing to join their wicked group. Then their old enemy Lau Cheung (Gordon Lau), long thought dead, kidnaps Yun, the daughter of leader Wong Hing-chun (Eagle Han Ying). As a child, Lau saw Wong's men kill his family and seize their property, so he bears a bit of a grudge. Lau was raised by a scruffy master who taught him drunken boxing. After a lengthy flashback, Yun has had time to remember her childhood friend, and she falls in love with her captor. Meanwhile, Lefty Kam continues to harass Wong, but it isn't until the two avengers join forces that they're able to defeat ninja Yin Si-ho (Sunny Yuen) and challenge Wong in person.

Only the skills of the various Laus and Yuens involved keep this one from coming apart at the seams. It has a rather mundane revenge plot, spiced up only by having two avengers. The flashbacks drag the pace down, and the kidnapping romance is only novel because it presents the lone love scene Gordon Lau ever had (as far as we know). The part of the training sequence set in a kitchen was previously seen in *Fury in Shaolin Temple*. **AKA:** *Siu Lam Chui Baat Kuen; Shao Lin Zui Ba Quan; The Drunken Monk.* 🐉🐉

1983 84m/C *CH* Gordon Lau, Sunny Yuen, Eagle Han Ying, Chin Yuet Sang. Wong Yat-cho. **D:** Ulysses Au. **W:** Ko Koh. **C:** Yi Hai-fung. **VHS, DVD**

Shaolin Fist of Fury

What's this—a movie that has ninjas in it but doesn't have "ninja" in the title? Keep dreaming. The onscreen title is *Ninja over the Great Wall*, retitled due to the story's similarity of the story to the Bruce Lee classic. Archival footage presents the 1931 Japanese invasion of the Tungshan province of China. Switching to new footage that perfectly mimics the old, the Japs kill the mother of Chi Kong (Bruce Le) and many extras. Kong fights back, but is overwhelmed, captured, and left for dead in a pit of bodies. He's fished out by his girlfriend Chu-yee, despite the moldering skeletons and rats, and they escape to Beijing, where Chu-yee's aunt is married to Japanese collaborator Wai Shin.

Shojiro Sakata (Shi Kimura), son of a Japanese diplomat, becomes obsessed with beating Master Yeung of the Chung Wah Martial Arts

School, and challenges him to a fight at the temple to "prove" the superiority of the Japanese (or more likely, the superiority of a young fighter to an old man triple his age). Knowing he loses either way, Yeung throws the match and concedes defeat, but Mr. Sakata fears that any rematch would possibly rouse the populace. Yeung sends his senior student Ti-nung (Li Ning, world acrobatics champion) to Shanghai to rouse the warlords to set up defenses, but dies from an assassin's poison. Chi Kong goes on a rampage of vengeance, attacking Shojiro at a party. The conflict escalates from there, with Sakata sending his ninjas against Kong and the entire Chung Wah School. Having lost face, Shojiro retreats to Japan to study hard. By the time he gets his mojo back, Kong has fought his way to the Yellow River. They come together (true to the title) for a final duel atop the Great Wall of China!

Bruce Le's acting still sucks; he fails to carry the lead, but he acquits himself quite well as a director. Early scenes on the killing fields are eerily atmospheric, and the production values are impressive, though the Dolby soundtrack hasn't survived the English-dubbed version. During the spectacular climactic battle, he superimposes animated clips to illustrate internal injuries. Le is sometimes let down by the editor, though—one great scene has Le fighting ninjas around an old temple. He sets one of them on fire, and the man continues to fight him aflame until Bruce kicks him into a shack full of explosives. The effect of this stunt is nullified somewhat when in the next shot the scene shifts completely to a snowy landscape, where Bruce is attacked by more ninjas. How the heck did he get there? Some concession is made to the Japanese audience, as the villain is portrayed somewhat sympathetically and is given plenty of screen time. **AKA:** *Long Huo Chang Cheng; Ninja over the Great Wall.* 🐉🐉🐲

1987 82m/C *HK/CH* Bruce Le, Shi Kamura, Lily Young, Yu Hai, Li Ning, Leung Yim, Mona Wong, Yang Chun Hoi, Pearl Chang, Shit Pai. **D:** Bruce Le. **W:** Fok Da-lin. **C:** Yue Ke, Chen Sing-hoi. **M:** Kim Jin-ping, Sit Jon-ping, Fung Kin-shit. **VHS, DVD**

The Shaolin Invincibles

In case the viewer might get confused later, the film spells out the plot right at the beginning in a title card. Having usurped the throne, Emperor Yung Cheng (Chen Hung Lieh) becomes a tyrant. A petty beef about the annual government exams results in Yung ordering the massacre of several families. A Shaolin monk rescues two young girls from the carnage; Yu Liang (Doris Lung) and Lu Szu-lng (Judy Lee) are raised to be superb martial artists so that they can take revenge on the emperor, starting with the murder of Magistrate Tin. General Lei Ching-ko (Yee Yuen) hears news of the murders, and fearing the emperor's wrath at allowing the girls to escape, is determined to stop them before the big boss can find out. The monastery sends rebel warrior Kan Tien-chi (Carter Wong) to help the ladies. It's no easy mission—not only is he surrounded by an army of guards, but Yung was trained at Shaolin as well. Yung is so skilled that he can even defeat gorillas trained in kung fu by two wizards.

O.K., let's interrupt this review right here to emphasize this element: kung fu gorillas! The two wizards, who have two foot–long tongues hanging out of their mouths, have trained two gorillas (guys in very shabby ape costumes) to become masters in the exotic arts of self-defense. Do you need any more incentive to see this movie? Then how about Doris Lung and Judy Lee fighting a monk whose weapon is a bowling ball on a chain, a fan fighter, and various Ching running dogs? There are also those two wizards trying to hit Carter Wong with their tongues, secret passages and death traps, gorgeous Taiwanese temples filling in for the Forbidden City, the flashing feet of Delon Tan, a popeyed architect, bloody death scenes, and some fine acrobatic fights. Oh, and don't forget—Judy and Doris fight the kung fu gorillas. In reality, Yung Cheng was the third emperor of the Ching Dynasty, taking the throne in 1722 when the Heir Apparent was judged insane. He is credited with bringing the powers of the Ching government under the control of the Grand Council, but is generally vilified for his violent opposition to Christianity. He had more to fear from his squabbling brothers than any vengeful kung fu girls, and there's no evidence that he kept pet gorillas. **AKA:** *Yung Jing Meng Song Siu Lam Moon; Yong Zheng Ming Sang Shao Lin Men.* 🎵🎵🎵

1979 90m/C *HK* Carter Wong, Judy Lee, Delon Tan, Chen Hung Lieh, Doris Lung, Yee Yuen, Lee Keung, Blackie Ko, Jack Lung. **D:** Hau Chang. **W:** Yeung Chi-hsiao. **M:** Wong Chu-jen. **VHS, DVD**

The Shaolin Kids

Wicked Premiere Hu Wei-yung (Yee Yuen) makes a "courtesy visit" to his ailing rival Minister Liu Po-wen, bringing Dr. Chi Jen-ho to treat his illness. But the doctor is a fake, and the villain has poisoned Lu. As he's dying, he tells his adopted daughter Liu Hsin-er (Polly Shang Kwan) to collect proof of the crime and avenge him. With Liu out of the way, and "Dr. Chi" silenced, Premiere Hu goes ahead with his plan to usurp the throne. He entrusts Feng Chi (Shaw Luo-hui) with a letter detailing his plan to be delivered to his allies across the border so that they can give him some back-up when the time comes. With the help of her friend Lu Tung (Tin Peng), Hsin-er ("disguised as a man," naturally) succeeds in snatching the letter, and delivers it to her father's old friend Chang Tao-yuen. But Feng Chi injured her in battle with some fancy nerve locks, and she heads for a Taoist priest for help. While she's gone, Hu's men arrest Chang, but the heroes rescue him before Hu can find the letter. Before they can get the letter to the emperor, they learn he plans to visit a spring soon, and the heroes rush to intercept the royal convoy before it enters Hu's trap.

There are far too many characters confusing this otherwise enjoyable costume adventure, with well-known faces like Kam Kong just showing up late in the game for a brief fight scene. Carter Wong has a supporting role as martial arts Master Shang Kuan-tung. Most of the fighting for the bad guys is done by Hu's bodyguards, the Light and Dark Killers (Cliff Lok and Wong Fei-lung), whose special Heaven and Earth technique is basically attacking high and low. They carry "saving golden pills" that, in effect, give them extra life when fatally injured. There are some great fight scenes with weapons—Polly Shang Kwan favoring a pair of sabers—and some clever twists along the way. Yee Yuen, as Premiere Hu, displays some amusingly craven behavior, especially at court before the exasperated emperor. In all, it has the flavor of a long novel condensed into a fast-paced movie. Not to be confused with the early Jet Li picture *Kids from Shaolin*. **AKA:** *Siu Lam Siu Ji; Shao Lin Xiao Zi; Kids of Shaolin; Shaolin Death Squad.* 🎵🎵🎵

1977 91m/C *HK* Polly Shang Kwan, Tin Peng, Yee Yuen, Carter Wong, Chang Yi, Cliff Lok, Yuen Sam, Chen Chiu, Chiang Nan, Cho Kin, Kam Kong, Got Heung Ting, Liu Ping, Shaw Luo-hui, Lau Lap Cho, Lung Fong, O Yau-man, Seung Fung, Cheung Bo-sin, Bruce Liang, Gam Kim, Woo Gwong, Wong Fei-lung. **D:** Joseph Kuo. **VHS, DVD**

Shaolin King Boxer

This independent production features Shaw Brothers regulars in a flick that's part crime caper, part revenge saga, and all Old School (but has nothing to do with Shaolin Temple). "Slasher" Pete (Leung Kar-yan) and Ling Pao (Lau Kar-Wing) break out criminal Shu Ting Shen (Wilson Tong from *Master Killer*) before he can be transported to another prison. Shu vows vengeance on his jailer Captain Chu Tin Ching (Chen Kuan-tai), and attacks his house. The gang kills Chu's family and he barely manages to escape, though his thumb is cut off in the battle. Publicly, Chu announces his retirement

The Shaolin Temple

Monks Go Crazy!

少林寺

For kung fu movie fans, Mecca is located on Shon-gsan Mountain in the Hunan province of northern China. That's where the Shaolin Temple has been since A.D. 495, except during those times when the army burned it down. It was named Shaolin ("young forest") for the new trees planted there to replace those cut for construction. Shaolin is the birthplace of Chinese kung fu, so quite naturally, many of the greatest kung fu movies ever feature real or fictional stories of the Shaolin monks.

Around 527, Indian monk Bodhidarma (or Tamo, as the Chinese called him) made a visit to the Chinese capitol at the Emperor Wu Ti's request. Chan Sing portrayed Tamo in a film about his adventures touring China, *Killer Priest.* The emperor at the time was into Buddhism, and had many monks hard at work translating the Hindu texts, and sought Tamo's advice on getting into Heaven. He was shocked to find out that he couldn't "close the deal" with Buddha by building a few monuments. While Tamo was in China, he decided to check out the Shaolin Temple, but was disappointed to find the monks overly concerned with their own physical comforts. Tamo retreated to a cave in the mountains to meditate on the matter, dismissing any monk who approached to beg for his teachings. It's said Tamo meditated in the cave for nine years, staring at a spot on the wall until his gaze burned a hole through the rock. He must have taken a few breaks though, since he also completed two volumes containing secrets of muscle toughening and marrow cleansing. Finally, monk Hui Ke proved his devotion to the spiritual by chopping off his own arm—the basis of Chinese legends filmed as the *One-Armed Swordsman.* It's also the origin of the Buddhist one-hand salute, seen every time one sees a monk. Hui Ke became Tamo's successor.

Tamo's teaching formed the basis of chi kung, a system of meditation exercises meant to toughen the body and cleanse the spirit, and the beginnings of Chan (or the more well-known Japanese "Zen") Buddhism. It was not meant specifically for fighting (just more meditating), but the exercises and techniques were gradually applied to martial arts to help protect the monks from bandits. By the year 618, the martial powers of Shaolin were so famous that Emperor Kang Xi sent for 128 warrior monks to help him defeat some terrorist rebels who had captured a prince. The monks were also called into service against the rebellious Red Turbans during the Yuan Dynasty, and to fight Japanese pirates during the Ming Dynasty. Except for the occasional emperor who turned against Buddhism, Shaolin fame spread even further, its fortune grew, and several other temples were established around China, including the South Shaolin Temple in Fukien province, which was built around 1399.

When the Ching Dynasty was established by the invading Manchurians in 1644, they were still threatened by the Han loyalists of the preceding Ming Dynasty, and ordered all martial arts training abolished in the private sector. Hostilities were especially centered on Shaolin Temple, whose 5,000 warrior monks were seen as a great threat, and kung fu training continued in secret. Many Han rebels were also secretly trained in kung fu to fight against the Manchus.

During this period, a monk named San Te completed his Shaolin training by passing through the famous 35 Chambers, each of which contained a different challenge (including the famed Shaolin Wooden Men). After scarring his arms on the Great Cauldron to mark himself as a Shaolin priest, San Te made one request: to be allowed to establish a 36th Chamber to teach kung fu to the public so that they could defend themselves from the Manchus. He established his school in Xichan Temple in Canton. San Te was portrayed by Gordon Lau in the classic *Shaolin Master Killer*.

In 1763 (36?), Emperor Yong Zheng sent the army to destroy South Shaolin Temple, killing the monks and burning the buildings. This event has been the subject of many films, including *Executioners from Shaolin* and *The Blazing Temple*. The surviving monks and Ming loyalists were hunted down by the traitorous monk Pai Mei. Many of the survivors took refuge in Red Junks, which transported Chinese opera troupes up and down the rivers. Opera performers were taught Shaolin kung fu, and helped preserve the knowledge.

During the war of 1928, the temple was burned for the last time by Warlord Shi You San's army during a battle. The fire lasted for more than 40 days, and all the major buildings (The Three Big Halls) were destroyed. The most priceless books and records on martial arts were also burned and lost.

Continued on next page...

During the Cultural Revolution of 1949, all the extensive lands were taken away from the few remaining monks who still remained in the dilapidated buildings. Though the Communist government banned all religious teaching, a handful of monks led by Abbot Xing Zheng kept practicing in secret, and even took on a few disciples. In 1980, religion was again allowed in China, projects began to restore Shaolin Temple as a historic site and a new abbot was appointed. Today, the temple is maintained mostly as a popular tourist attraction, with monks performing a combination of wu shu and Luohan daily for the entertainment of onlookers. A contingent of monks even toured the world as a theatrical troupe during the 1990s, enacting a lavish Broadway-style show depicting Shaolin history. In 1990, the remains of South Shaolin Temple were discovered, and a new temple was constructed on the site. Archaeologists have also discovered two other South Shaolin Temples at Fuqing and Quanzhou.

due to his injuries, which make it impossible for him to hold a sword. Privately, he has a special glove made to make up for his disability, and plots his own revenge.

Both Chu and young fan-toting hero Ting Yi-Lang (Meng Fei) beat information out of the sneaky Eye Patch (director Karl Maka): Shu's gang is headed toward Black Town to rob the safe at the house of wealthy Kao. Chu and Ting join forces on the road, after the requisite fight. While Chu tries to warn the overconfident Kaos, Ting tracks down the gang. Eye Patch tries to play both sides. After quite a bit of talk from both sides about drawing each other out and tracking each other down, the good guys and bad guys finally start to fight. Chu handily defeats Slasher Pete and his thugs; unfortunately, Shu's hairstyle and costume are almost identical to Ting's, so he breaks off their fight to pretend to offer him a share of the loot. Ting pretends to accept. Ting and some thugs are sent to a restaurant to distract Chu, while the rest of the gang assaults the Kao house, but of course Ting's death is planned, too, and he shows his true-blue colors.

Once the action gets going in the latter half, after all the padding in the middle, there's some nicely staged fighting (by Lau), rather gruesome details, and clever bits of direction. Maka would later strike gold as the bald star of the *Mad Mission* series. **AKA:** *Tit Kuen; Tie Quan; Iron Fists; Shaolin Kingboxer.* 🦴🦴🦴

1979 88m/C *HK* Wilson Tong, Lau Kar-Wing, Chen Kuan-tai, Meng Fei, Leung Kar-yan, Yang Ping An, Kwan Hung, Karl Maka. **D:** Karl Maka. **W:** Yu Kan Ping. **C:** Liao Wan Wen. **VHS, DVD**

Shaolin Mantis

In this Shaw Brothers period action yarn from Lau Kar-Leung, David Chiang stars as scholar Wei Fung, who is called upon by the Ching Dynasty emperor to spy on the Tien family, who are suspected of being Ming rebels. Though it's unusual to see a Ching hero in a movie, the Chings are not exactly portrayed as good guys here—Wei's family is held hostage and threatened with execution if he fails to complete his mission within a year. Wei gets himself hired as teacher to young firebrand Tien Chi-chi (Wong Hang-sau), the 19th to hold that position. He finds that the wealthy Tiens are all mad for martial arts. The large Tien mansion gives the Shaw's art department plenty of chances to show off their sets, including one of their famous bridges. Chi-chi's granddad (Lau Kar-Wing) finds out that Wei Fung is a Ching spy, and Fourth Uncle (Norman Tsui) is assigned to execute the enemy. However, Chi-chi has fallen for her young teacher, and lies to save him. The result is a shotgun wedding, with Wei forbidden to ever leave their village. Falling for his student in return, Wei might not mind his sentence, if it weren't for the peril his family faces. Choosing husband over family, Chi-chi decides to help Wei escape, fighting past the mansion's posts guarded by Tien Cheung (John Chang), Fourth Uncle, her mother (Lily Li), and finally old Master Tien himself. Injured, Chi-chi stays behind as Wei gets away by faking a fall off a cliff. While hiding out, he learns a new style to counter the Tien Shadow technique by watching a praying mantis.

There's some fine weapons work, but on the whole, the action here is less than what you'd expect with the Laus involved. It's the novel plot and characters that make it interesting. As the bouncy teenage queen, Wong Hang-sau is almost the Gidget of kung fu. She'd turn up again in films like *Magnificent Fist* and *Incredible Kung Fu Master*. The costumes are also part of the fun, with the eccentrically martial Tien's seemingly always prepared for war. Gordon Lau and Lee Hoi-sang both put in brief appearances as warriors Chiang has to fight to prove himself. **AKA:** *Tong Long; Tang Lang; The Deadly Mantis; Deadly Shaolin Mantis.* 🐉🐉🐉

1978 (R) 102m/C *HK* David Chiang, Wong Hang-sau, Lau Kar-Wing, Lily Li, Norman Tsui, Ha Ping, Gordon Lau, Lee Hoi-sang, Ko Saio Pao, Hsu Shao-Chiang, Frankie Wei, Wilson Tong, John Chang. **D:** Lau Kar-Leung. **W:** Szeto On. **C:** Arthur Wong. **M:** Chen Yung-yu. **VHS, DVD**

Shaolin Master Killer

The ultimate Shaolin training movie, this Shaw Brothers classic tells the story of San Te, a kung fu genius who brought the martial arts out of the temple and gave it to the people. After seeing Ching General Tien (Lo Lieh) kill Ming patriot General Yin (Lau Kar-Wing), student Liu Yu-te (Gordon Lau) is inspired to join the rebellion. Teacher Ho gets Liu involved in transmitting messages through his father's seafood shop, but when Ching agent Lo Tang (Wilson Tong) exposes the group, Liu's family is killed. Liu escapes and flees to Shaolin Temple, where he is given the new name San Te, and hopes to learn kung fu to fight the Manchus. However, after a year spent doing menial tasks, he finally learns of the 35 Chambers all monks must pass through to learn Shaolin kung fu. Impatient San Te tries to start at the top level, and of course is overwhelmed. He starts again at the bottom, and with hard work and natural talent San Te progresses through the chambers in record time. Some of the training is just tricky, but most is torturous. However, San Te gets through them all, then goes through the pugilism and weapons chambers with a speed beyond all expectations.

The abbot wants to reward San Te with a post in one of the chambers, but because he's

passed so quickly it's decided he must prove himself by beating Senior Monk Yuen Yeh (Lee Hoi-sang) with a weapon of his choice first. After numerous failures, he comes up with a way of beating Yuen Yeh using a segmented pole of his own invention. Having passed the test, San Te's choice is the creation of a 36th Chamber, which will make their Shaolin skills available to students outside the monastery. This outrages the abbots and gets San Te kicked out of the temple. However, it works out well for the young monk, since he's then able to go back to his village and gather tradesmen Woon Tse-kwan, Po Ching-tan, Liu Tsai (Norman Tsui), and even a character named Old Ground Rice (Wong Yu), and train them to strike back at his old enemy General Tien.

The basic plot format is not different from a dozen other Shaolin movies, but here execution is everything. This film boiled down a lot of ideas from other kung fu flicks into a template, filling it out with fascinating details. The training sequences and fight scenes are all excellent, showing off a cast full of fighting stars. Gordon Lau found a defining role in San Te, not only performing incredible physical feats, but also *acting* those feats, selling the emotion of the scene to make them more than movie stunts. It would be quite a while before anyone wanted to cast him as anything besides a monk, starting with the sequel *Return of Master Killer.* **AKA:** *Siu Lam Sa Luk Fong; Shao Lin Sa Liu Fang; The 36th Chamber of Shaolin; Master Killer; The 36th Chamber; Disciples of Master Killer.* 🐉🐉🐉🐉

1978 115m/C *HK* Gordon Lau, Lo Lieh, Wong Yu, Norman Tsui, Lee Hoi-sang, Lau Kar-Wing, Hsu Shao-Chiang, Henry Yu Yung, Hwa Ling, John Chang, Simon Yuen, Frankie Wei, Wilson Tong, Ng Hong Song, Hon Gwok-choi, Chiang Nan, Chiang Han, Chan Shen, Shum Lo, Wong Ching Ho, Lin Ke-ming, Austin Wai, Alan Chui, Chin Yuet Sang, Billy Chan, Kok Lee-yan, Wang Han-chen, Hsiao Ho, Lam Wai, Fung Ging Man, Chan Lung, Cheung Wa. **D:** Lau Kar-Leung. **W:** Ngai Hong, Eric Tsang. **C:** Huang Yeh-tai. **M:** Chen Yung-yu. **VHS, DVD**

The Shaolin One

Video labels commonly sell this as an early Jet Li action flick, but it's actually a documentary about kung fu, with some extra clips of Li performing Wu Shu on various beautiful sets tacked on to the beginning. Sort of a *Mondo Kung Fu*, we get a glimpse of the Shaolin Temples—north and south—and demonstrations of various styles by champions, all narrated by a personable British chap. We're shown Shaolin, Wu Tai, Wu Tang, and Tai Chi forms; make a trip to the temple on O-Mei Mountain (where the snake and monkey forms originated); view drunken boxing, lots of animal styles, 8 Diagram styles, breath-

561
VideoHound's Dragon

control masters (see a 15-year-old girl under a ton of stone!); and see all the legendary weapons of China. There is a segment of Jet Li, age nine, performing with a sword on stage. Then we get to more recent practice footage, and clips from the *Shaolin Temple* movies. The Beijing Wu Shu Team works out amid fantastic Chinese rock formations. So what if it's not a narrative film—the kung fu is still fantastic, and the scenery is just as incredible. Some of the performers are 100 years old! However, long stretches of mere demonstration, no matter how good, can grow tiresome—a perfect rebuttal to kung fu fans who say the only thing that matters in a kung fu movie is kung fu, regardless of story and character. *AKA: Chung Wa Miu Sui; Zhong Hua Wu Shu; This Is Kung Fu.* 🕉🕉🕉

1983 87m/C *HK/CH* Jet Li, Hung Shing-fu, Liu Chi-ching, Yu Xiao-ping, Wong Chin-chung, Hou Chi-hwa, Wen Chou-yen. **D:** Chung Yee. **W:** Chung Yee, Yeung Chung. **DVD**

Shaolin Soccer

Stephen Chow has been a top star in Hong Kong for many years now, starring in one crowd-pleasing comedy after another, but this blockbuster smashed all previous records for HK productions.

Twenty years ago, Golden Leg Fung was an arrogant soccer star who treated his teammate Hung like dirt. So Hung arranged a little "incident" in which Fung missed an important shot and hooligans rushed out of the stands to break his legs. Now, Hung (Patrick Tse) is the arrogant and cruel head coach of the champion Evil Team, and he keeps the crippled Fung (Ng Man-Tat) around just to abuse. Fung meets a street cleaner named Sing (Chow), who is also an advanced kung fu student known as Shaolin Orthodox School Mighty Steel Leg. Sing is looking for ways to package Shaolin kung fu for the modern consumer, perhaps through song and dance. Fung has a better idea: he wants to form a new soccer team made up of Sing's Shaolin brothers to enter the national tournament. Sing's five brothers have become very out of shape since their master died years ago, but Fung's coaching at least gives them some of the fundamentals.

When Fung sets the team up with a match against a disreputable amateur team, it looks like they'll be handed a painful and humiliating defeat, but Sing's spirit helps them all regain their Shaolin chi. Hung is so amused by the ragtag appearance of Fung's team that he helps get them in the tournament, if only so he can get a laugh at their expense. But using their super kung fu (provided by the Centro f/x house), the Shaolin Team advances through the ranks and looks to be unstoppable. Meanwhile,

Sing meets scar-faced baker Mui (Vicki Zhao), who uses advanced Tai Chi to make steamed bread in a street stand, and they begin a bumpy romance. Making their way past the bearded girls team Double Handsome Dragons (including guest stars Karen Mok and Cecilia Cheung), the Shaolin team makes it into the finals. But will their kung fu skills be able to beat Hung's Evil Team? Their players are all genetically altered by "American medication" into supermen, and to make matters worse, Hung has bribed all the officials!

Combining Chow's nonsense style of comedy with the kind of special effects that powered *Storm Riders* and *A Man Called Hero* may seem like a mismatch. Nitpickers may say that the f/x overshadow the gags. But this is a straightforward story of good versus evil, embodying many of the themes that Chow has been using throughout his career. Idolizing Bruce Lee, he envisions a world—in hilariously exaggerated style—in which practicing kung fu can make everyone's lives better. The Mighty Steel Leg is not far from his protagonist's attributes in *Fist of Fury 1991*. *King of Beggars* featured characters with supernatural kung fu ability, and *Sixty Million Dollar Man* was an earlier experiment with mixing f/x with comedy. But Chow's cinematic abilities (assisted by "executive director" and longtime collaborator Lee Lik-Chi) and f/x technology have both improved tremendously during the past decade, and *Shaolin Soccer* benefits from both. In spirit, it's not unlike early hits like *Legend of the Dragon*—the talents involved have just matured. And leave it to Stephen Chow to find another new twist to slipping on a banana peel. A uniquely Chinese superhero comedy, *Shaolin Soccer* is supremely entertaining from start to finish. For best results, bypass the butchered English-dubbed version and seek out the original director's cut. *AKA: Siu Lam Chuk Kau; Shao Lin Ju Qiu; Kung Fu Soccer.* 🕉🕉🕉🕉

2001 (PG) 112m/C *HK* Stephen Chow, Vicki Zhao, Ng Man-Tat, Wong Yat-Fei, Patrick Tse, Tin Kai-man, Lam Chi-chung, Alan Chan, Mok Mei Lam, Lam Chi-sin, Karen Mok, Cecilia Cheung, Vincent Kok, Li Fai, Po Yip Dung, Cheung Ming-Ming, Sik Chi-wan, Law Kar-Ying. **D:** Stephen Chow. **W:** Stephen Chow, Sammy Tsang. **C:** Kwong Ting-wo, Kwen Pak-huen. **M:** Raymond Wong. **VHS, DVD**

The Shaolin Temple

This Chinese epic tells a tale from the history of one of the world's toughest fighting religious orders, and is the debut film of kung fu movie legend Jet Li. It begins with a travelogue about the famous landmark, relating history from Bodi

Dharma on, followed by the credits, which are accompanied by a rendition of the Shaolin school song. Chueh-Yuan (Jet Li) is an escaped slave from the tyrant Wang Jen-tse (Yu Cheng Hui), who has settled in the area and is terrorizing the populace. Chueh-Yuan stumbles into Shaolin Temple among hordes of refugees. The students are reduced to hunting frogs for food. Recovering, Chueh-Yuan meets shepherdess Miss Pak (Ding Lan) in the hills. She teasingly sends her dog to chase him, but he accidentally kills it while trying to hide it from the abbot (Yu Hai). He gives the carcass a respectful burial—but cooks the meat! He learns the girl is another refugee, and decides to become a monk to learn kung fu, hiding his motives of revenge. Impatient with the monks' lessons, he sneaks out to attack Wang, arriving just in time to rescue Miss Pak from his clutches. After a terrific battle with Wang, during which he matches Wang's inebriation with the Drunken Style learned from heart-broken monk Shi Kung (Sun Jian Kui), Chueh-Yuan realizes that his kung fu is still not good enough. He returns to the temple to study for another year, and then sneaks off again to rescue the rebel King Li Shi Min (Wang Guang Kuan) in raids against Wang's operations. In response, Wang threatens to destroy Shaolin if Chueh-Yuan isn't turned over to him.

Though the idea of a young man training at Shaolin Temple in order to avenge his father was a tired cliché by this point, the scope and action on display here are enough to make this a classic. Li is in excellent form for his debut, demonstrating many different forms of combat. The other performers are all terrific, too, fighting with all manner of weapons in many landmark settings and gorgeous sets. *AKA: Siu Lam Chi; Shao Lin Si; Shao Lin Tzu.* ♫♫♫♫

1979 94m/C *CH/HK* Jet Li, Yu Hai, Yu Cheng Hui, Ding Lan, Hu Jian Qiang, Liu Huai Liang, Chi Chuen-Hua, Sun Jian Kui, Pan Qingfu, Wang Guang Kuan, George Wang, Ku Feng. *D:* Chang Yam Yim. *W:* Shi Hou, Lu Shau Chang. *C:* Chau Pak-ling, Lau Fung-lam. *M:* Wang Li-ping. **VHS, DVD**

Shaolin Temple 2: Kids from Shaolin

Jet Li sings! Jet Li in drag! This follow-up to Li's debut is just as grand and more fable-like—plus, it's a musical! A tale of ancient rivalry is told (in song and animation!) between two families on opposite sides of the Dragon River. The Phoenix Clan, experts in the Wu Tang Sword, has eight daughters. The Dragon Clan, masters of Shaolin kung fu, has eight sons. The Phoenix patriarch Pao Seng-feng (Yu Cheng Hui) waits impatiently, but is disappointed to be blessed with another daughter. Though his daughters

have mastered the Wu Tang Sword, he needs a son to pass the mantle to. The poor but proud Dragon patriarch Tin Lung (Yu Hai) must earn enough for 10 cows dowry before any of the sons can marry a Phoenix daughter. Tin Lung has raised the eight boys since he and his brother rescued the infants from a bandit gang 10 years before, taking out the leader's eye in the battle. The bandits plot their revenge, sending Pao a fake geomancer to consult with on his bad luck. The geomancer blames the Dragons for blocking his feng shui. But the tenth time is the charm, and the next Pao baby is a boy. Hearts softening, the girls begin to learn Shaolin kung fu. Tin Lung woos big sister Tai Feng (Ding Lan), while Uncle Yee Lung (Hu Jian Qiang) woos number-two daughter Yi Feng. But the kids' horseplay goes too far for Pao, and he banishes the Dragons again. Frustrated, the boys all shave their heads, but Yee Lung is too stubborn. Big brother San Lung (Jet Li) disguises himself as a maid to get into the Pao household, calling Yi Feng out to elope with Uncle Yee Lung. San Feng and San Lung are both sentenced to a trial by drowning for abetting the elopers, but escape their bindings to hide in a cave. There, they teach each other their own styles of martial arts before Pao comes for his daughter. Meanwhile, the bandits finally make their move, framing the Dragons for kidnapping Pao's one and only son, and threatening destruction of both families.

Just like its predecessor, *Kids from Shaolin* features outstanding martial arts action using a wide variety of wu shu styles and weapons. The action plays out amid the gorgeous Dragon River valley, its surrounding mountains and caverns. Unlike so many of Jet Li's subsequent films, these early outings are choreographed without the use of wires and undercranked cameras, and the action is incredible. Plus, don't expect to see Jet Li singing in any of his American films. *AKA: Siu Lam Siu Ji; Shao Lin Xiao Zi; Shaolin Temple II; Kids from Shaolin.* ♫♫♫♫

1984 99m/C *CH* Jet Li, Wong Chiu Yin, Ding Lan, Hu Jian Qiang, Yu Hai, Yu Cheng Hui, Chi Chuen-Hua, Pan Qingfu. *D:* Cheung Yam Yim. *W:* Leung Chi Keung, Ho Shu Hua. *C:* Chau Pak-ling. *M:* Yu Feng. **VHS, DVD**

Shaolin Traitorous

That no-good Tin Erh-keng (Chang Yi) throws in his lot with Wei Chung-hsien and his Tien Lo Sect. He takes his lieutenant Chang (Sammo Hung) to massacre the upstanding Yang family, but the littlest Yang (Lam Siu-foo) escapes to beg admittance to Shaolin Temple. While Tin's power grows, Yang Shao-yung (Carter Wong) grows up to become a top Shaolin kung fu mas-

Jet Li

李連杰

The world may know him as a deadly martial artist. But Jet Li Lian-jie would be the first to tell you that he is a spiritual man of peace.

He describes himself in his early years as "a poster child for obedience." Li was born April 1963 in Beijing, and his father died when the future film star was only two years of age. As he was the youngest of five children, his mother was supremely protective and kept him away from any sort of dangerous activity.

A summer school program in 1971 assigned him arbitrarily to take wushu training. A year later Li won the only prize awarded at a national wushu competition. Shortly thereafter he found himself excused from school so that he could expend all his energies undergoing harshly rigorous full-time training. He once practiced for two days on a broken foot. The training paid off with a goodwill tour of the United States in 1974, climaxing with a visit to the White House and a brief exchange with President Nixon.

Competing against adults, 12-year-old Li Lian-jie again won a national competition, a feat he would duplicate several more times. More international goodwill tours followed. His growing fame eventually resulted in his being offered a starring role in *Shaolin Temple,* the first modern martial arts film made in Mainland China. Released in 1982, *Shaolin Temple* was an instant success, transforming Li into a national star, and generating considerable interest in the Shaolin Temple itself. Thanks to a distribution company in the Philippines, he found himself called "Jet," which was based on a contraction of his given name as well as a reflection of his soaring popularity.

Two sequels followed, but they were not pleasant experiences. On the set of his third film, Jet saw firsthand the inequities in the way the cast and crew were treated, based solely on their nationality. Thoroughly soured by his experiences, Jet decided to leave the film business. In response, he was offered the opportunity to direct. He accepted because he wanted to express his frustrations with the discrimination he had observed. *Born to Defence* bombed both creatively and financially. He resolved to concentrate on acting.

After two additional misfires that were made in America, Jet worked with Tsui Hark to refashion the legendary Wong Fei-Hong in modern terms. He recalls Tsui showing him a nature documentary as an inspiration for taking a fresh approach to the action scenes. *Once upon a Time in China* was a phenomenal success and inspired a host of sequels. Jet made two of them before breaking with Tsui, though the two later reunited.

All told, Jet made about 20 films in Hong Kong during the 1990s, covering every base. He played legendary heroes and policemen, he made comedies and dramas, he made period pieces and modern-day sagas. Probably his key collaborator during this period was Corey Yuen Kwai, who directed Jet in several films and continues to serve as action choreographer on his most recent projects.

In 1997, Jet again decided to retire from making movies. In his own words, he felt that he had accomplished everything he had set out to do. He wanted to study Buddhism and live a religious life, but a meeting with Lho Kunsang Rinpoche, a Buddhist master, led to Jet's continuing in the film business. He has come to feel that he has a responsibility to share the Buddhist philosophy with any that will listen—even if his potential audience doesn't realize they are being exposed to his message.

He broke into Hollywood by playing a villain for the first time in *Lethal Weapon 4*. In exchange, he played a good guy in the hip-hop flavored *Romeo Must Die*.

In recent years he has turned down some high-profile productions *(Crouching Tiger, Hidden Dragon;* the two sequels to *The Matrix)* and formed a partnership with French filmmaker Luc Besson. Jet liked working with Besson because it allowed him to turn a basic idea into a finished product in a matter of months rather than years *(Kiss of the Dragon).* Jet returned to his Mainland Chinese martial arts roots in director Zhang Yimou's lavish *Hero* and followed that with the hip-hop *Cradle 2 the Grave.*

The dizzying variety of Jet's projects may bewilder casual viewers. The thing to remember is that, deep inside Jet, the heart of an obedient boy beats. He listens to and wants to please his fans. Yet even more so, he wants to please himself.

—PM

ter. During his conquest, Tin adopts a girl from one of families he's killed, raising Hsiao Yuen-erh (Polly Shang Kwan) as his own hard-hitting daughter. Yang defeats a group of royal guards pursuing Chen Wen-shui and his family, drawing Tin's attention, and Yuen-erh asks that she be allowed to deal with him personally. But after a few encounters, Yuen-erh begins to admire the young rebel, even going so far as to spoil Chang's drumming when his guards attack Yang in formation. She reveals to Yang later that she's actually faking allegiance to Tin, planning to betray him when the time is right, and she feeds him some vital information to defeat Tin's assistants. But Tin's suspicions force her to show her hand too soon, and she only escapes with Yang's help. The pair joins together to seek revenge against Tin.

Carter Wong increases the intensity of his vendetta by keeping the crazy look in his eye that he usually reserves for his villainous roles. Wong's fight with a young Sammo Hung is surely one of the main attractions here, but the actual duel is a bit of a disappointment—the Mantis Style Hung uses isn't best suited for him, and the choreography suggests the ground was too wet for them to attempt anything too fancy. But then, all the action seems a bit sluggish, with the guardsmen's pyramid formations emerging as the most interesting facet. Making matters worse is the director's annoying insistence on constant recapping with flashbacks, just in case we forget why Wong is so ticked off at Chang Yi and company. **AKA:** *Traitorous.* 🦴🦴

1976 91m/C *HK* Carter Wong, Polly Shang Kwan, Chang Yi, Sammo Hung, Lam Siu-foo, Hau Pak-wai, Hsieh Hsing. **D:** Sung Ting-mei. **VHS, DVD**

Shaolin vs. Lama

Over the typical old-school opening montage of fighting against a blank background, the narrator tells us that the origins of kung fu go back to the Neanderthal man hitting his brother over the head. Following that line of thinking makes us all martial arts masters—it's just that most of us are at a very early level. Sun Yu-ting (Alexander Lou) may be self-taught, but his kung fu is good enough that he's not embarrassed to go around without a shirt. He's looking for a teacher who knows more kung fu than he does, at least enough to beat him. He's not having any luck, and hasn't been beaten in five years. A young rascal named Hsu Shi (William Yen) may help—though stealing from gamblers when Sun meets him, the lad is actually a Shaolin monk in disguise, slumming while fetching wine for his master. Hsu Shi sneaks Sun onto the temple grounds to meet the Grandmaster abbot (Sun Jung-chi), but the old man refuses to take Sun

as a student. The abbot's former student Chi Kang (1978 world tae kwando champ Chen Shan) was really a Lama spy, sent to infiltrate Shaolin and steal their sacred Book of I Ching, and the abbot has refused to take on a student since. Wily Hsu gets an idea: Sun should attack the abbot daily, thereby learning his secrets as he uses them to fight back. But after a while, Sun gets caught by the monks and thrown out of the temple.

Wandering about, he comes upon Miss Tsu (Lee Wai-wan) as she's being attacked by the Tibetan Sky Hawk Clan, and leaps to the rescue. The Grand Master abbot and Hsu Shi come to help Sun against Sky Hawk Captain Wang, earning the enmity of the clan leader Yao Fang-lin. When the whole Sky Hawk Clan comes to attack Sun and Miss Tsu, Hsu Shi leads his friends to sanctuary at Shaolin Temple, and sees that Yao is none other than that traitor Chi Kang! With such a villain at large, the monks are compelled to act. Sun Yu-ting converts to Buddhism, becomes a monk, and is trained in all their most advanced martial arts (including the Buddha finger) to face his foe.

This is one of the better examples of Taiwanese martial arts films. The story is relatively uncomplicated and free from the legion of extraneous characters so common in old kung fu flicks. This means there's more time to develop the main characters, show the growth in their personalities, and examine their relationships. Oh, and there's also plenty of terrific martial arts in a variety of styles, and even some very funny comedy. Hopefully, films like this one don't give a true portrayal of the holy men of China and Tibet, acting like superhero street gangs in fantastic costumes. Director Lee Tso Nam *(Eagle's Claw)* keeps the mood light and fun throughout. Not to be confused with *Shaolin Temple against Lama* (1980), also with Lou and Yen. **AKA:** *Siu Lam Dau Kwong Lut; Shao Lin Dou La Ma.* 🦴🦴🦴✓

1981 90m/C *TW* Alexander Lou, William Yen, Chen Shan, Lee Wai-wan, Sun Jung-chi, Chang Chi-ping, Ching Kuo-chung. **D:** Lee Tso Nam. **W:** Chang Seng-yi. **C:** Chong Yung-chi. **M:** Chou Fu-liang. **VHS, DVD**

Shaolin vs. Manchu

The title pretty much explains the contents of this simplistic tale of Shaolin monks fighting against the Ching Dynasty. The abbot of Shaolin Temple decides that monk Rocky (!) is to be trained by four senior monks as the Shaolin Champion, responsible for settling all disputes and the most likely candidate to succeed him. On the day before the election, Rocky rescues a

girl under attack by Manchu soldiers and gives her a string of prayer beads. But it's a trap—as Rocky is about to be elected the abbot, the girl reappears to accuse him of rape, showing the beads as evidence. Surprisingly, Rocky confesses to the crime and is thrown out of the temple, with monk Number One taking his place. Rocky's plan is to follow the girl to reveal the plot against him. He finds her shot with an arrow—an attempt by the Manchus to cover their tracks—and he takes her to the home of his nagging aunt. Number One is really a spy named Captain Lee Kou-ching, who murders the abbot and continues his efforts to destroy Shaolin from the inside. He promotes fighting competition over spiritualism, and sends the most experienced monks to General Ho to train Manchu troops. With Shaolin thus weakened, Ho sends 3,000 soldiers to arrest all the monks and shut down the temple. Most of the monks are slaughtered in the attack, with only Chin Bao escaping to alert Rocky. Finding the temple overgrown with weeds and spiderwebs, Rocky takes the wine left by the soldiers and accidentally invents Drunken Boxing. It's up to the banished monk to gather the survivors to restore Shaolin.

Even in the middle of this grim plot, there are some surprising bits of humor thrown into the choreography. The fight scenes are imaginative, and the performers talented, but they sometimes look a bit studied, as if they could have used a bit more rehearsal. Despite this, it's another entertaining trip to Shaolin Temple (or the Taiwanese equivalent). To spare you any undue duress, here's a spoiler: the tiny cute toddler monk survives the massacre. 🎵🎵🎵

1980 88m/C TW Ling Man Hoi, Sun Kui Hin, Lau Ying Lung, Ho Su Pui, Kam Yung Cheung, Tam Tak Sing. **D:** Lee Chuen Chun. **W:** Chan Man Kui. **C:** Chan Chun Li. **M:** Tang Siu-lam. **DVD**

Shaolin vs. Ninja

According to the opening narration, this is the story of a Buddhist temple that teaches Shaolin kung fu within Japanese territory during the Ching Dynasty—not necessarily the Shaolin Temple. Though the emperor has ordered that Shaolin remain protected, the Japanese would like to take the temple's wealth for themselves, and send ninjas to assassinate Chief Abbot Chi Yuen. The first attempt comes during the spectacle of a New Year's Festival, and features ninjas disguised as tightrope-walking lion dancers and other wonders. The abbot has no trouble fending off the attack, and the temple's foremost fighter, headstrong Wai Ming (Alexander Lou), lends a hand in defending him. The Japanese step up their tyranny in the region, and

someone responds by stealing a horde of tax money from an official. The Japanese suspect that only a Shaolin monk could have committed the burglary. The brutal samurai come to arrest Chi Yuen, and rather than cause more violence, he complies, leaving Chi Hung in charge of the temple. But the Japanese have to admit they have no evidence. Next, they send Japanese Buddhist monk Chi Tao to take over the temple, but Chi Yuen changes the newcomer's mind with superior philosophy. The ninjas are sent to assassinate Chi Tao, framing the Chinese monks for the crime, and Chi Yuen is given 10 days to find the killers. This act not only adds to the conflict with the government, but also puts Shaolin at odds with the Japanese monks as well. They send monk Chung Tao to avenge his brother's death, but his challenge is rebuffed. The ninjas are then sent to kill a Shaolin monk, framing the Japanese monks for the crime. This succeeds in getting the monks fighting each other in a tournament, but will the real killer be revealed before the Japanese can cut the abbot's head off and take the temple's wealth?

The meandering, poorly paced plot is frustrating, but at least there are plenty of fine kung fu action, though much of it is among the good guys. And even though the Shaolin don't really fight ninjas that much, there are some interesting conflicts between styles. Even in washed-out prints, you can tell the original cinematography is pretty bad. **AKA:** The Story of Shaolin. 🎵🎵

1983 89m/C HK Alexander Lou, Alan Chui, Chang Chi-ping, William Yen, James Tien, Wong Hap, Wong Chi Sang, Robert Tai. **D:** Robert Tai. **VHS, DVD**

Shaolin: Wheel of Life

Monks on Broadway? Well, it's not exactly a kung fu version of Fiddler on the Roof. In 2000, Chinese and American producers teamed up to present this unique touring stage show starring ordained Buddhist monks from the Shaolin Temple performing choreographed demonstrations, exercises, and rituals to tell the story of the temple's history and the development of kung fu. The show is wonderfully filmed using a multitude of camera angles, and techniques like close-ups and slow motion more fully capture the details of the presentation. There are also specially filmed scenes intercut with the stage scenes.

It's doubtful that this level of martial arts has been incorporated in a stage narrative outside of the Chinese opera. The music and set designs are breathtaking: scenes illustrate the monks' journey to the Forbidden City during the

Tang Dynasty to demonstrate their skills at the request of the Emperor; their employ in defense of China from invaders; their subsequent betrayal; the rebuilding of Shaolin by the five survivors; and the shift in emphasis from flowing Northern styles of kung fu to the powerful Hung Gar Southern styles. This last bit features such showstopping antics as two-finger handstands, monks breaking metal bars over their heads, and a monk raised on spear points.

These performers are likely a great deal better than the monks were a thousand years ago, and there's no sign of the brutal punishments involved in their intense training, but it's nonetheless wonderful theatre. ♫♫♫

2000 83m/C *UK/CH* Tom Yang, Cecil Cheng, Jason Ninh Cao, Wang Zhigang, Guo Jinming, Chen Defeng, Shi Yanyang, Xu Liying, Wu Yanxing. *D:* Micha Bergese. *W:* Edng. *C:* Darshan Singh Bhuller. *M:* Barrington Pheloung. **VHS, DVD**

Shaolin Wooden Men

Of the early Jackie Chan films, this is perhaps the most visually striking, starting with a pre-credit sequence with Chan battling a series of monks against a black background. Add the credits, plus a series of shots showing the Shaolin Temple beginning its day, and it's 10 minutes into the movie before anyone says a word. In only his second film at Lo Wei Productions, rumor has it that Chan was still too green to deliver the amount of lines necessary for a leading role, so they made him mute for most of the picture. Chan plays Mu, a young student at the temple, called Dummy due to his vow of silence. He's there to learn kung fu so that he can take vengeance on the masked man he saw kill his father Hsu Ling. While trying to practice the Drunken Style he got from a wino monk one night, he sees two brothers going to a cave and follows them. There he befriends a man chained to a wall, and brings him food and wine. In exchange, the surly prisoner teaches him kung fu every night. And a nun takes him to a grease pit to learn the Gliding Snake technique. Between the two of them, his two spare-time teachers prepare him to enter the dreaded Chamber of Wooden Men—a long corridor lined with a gauntlet of robot-like wood and iron warriors that he must pass through before he can leave Shaolin Temple. After going through this nerve-wracking tunnel, he must lift a huge cauldron, his forearms seared with the image of the dragon and tiger. In return for his instruction, Mu delivers something from the prisoner to a crippled pharmacist. The prisoner is actually Fat Yu, chief of a gang of bandits, the Green Dragon gang, and he escapes soon after Chan has left

using his new Lion's Roar technique. His men abduct Mei-Mei (Doris Lung), a girl Mu has befriended, demanding 500 gold pieces in ransom from her restaurateur father. When Mu and Mei-Mei's brother go to deliver the ransom, they find Fat Yu in combat with the Shaolin and Lo Han monks. Not knowing his true identity, Mu helps Fat Yu escape. In return, Fat Yu has Mei-Mei released. Back at the restaurant, Mu meets a stranger who uses a fighting technique just like the masked killer, but Mu is not good enough to beat him. While the Chief Abbot helps Mu through some more grueling training, Fat Yu and the Green Dragon gang head for Shaolin Temple, planning to attack.

While not the rollicking good time that Chan's kung fu comedies a few years away would be, *Shaolin Wooden Men* is nothing to be ashamed of either. His second starring role relies too much for effect on its lame "surprise" ending, but Chan's fantastic choreography (with Li Ming-wen), in which he shows off all five animal styles and a few extra, more than makes up for it. From its acrobatic combat to the intense wooden-men sequence, there's evidence of a constantly inventive mind at work. The film has a lot of style, too, with unusual flashback techniques and a Shaolin Temple that looks dark and spooky. The ending is not as interesting as what leads up to it, but this is well worth catching, especially in widescreen format. Jackie definitely hit it off with young director Chen Chi-hwa, but the boxoffice returns on their film were disappointing. However, the Hong Kong film community began to take notice of Chan as more than just another Bruce imitator. *AKA: Siu Lam Muk Yan Hong; Shao Lin Mu Ren Xiang; 36 Wooden Men; Shaolin Chamber of Death; Young Tiger's Revenge.* ♫♫▽

1976 98m/C *HK* Jackie Chan, Kam Kong, Simon Yuen, Doris Lung, Yuen Biao. *D:* Chen Chi-hwa. *W:* Chen Chi-hwa, Gam Yam. **VHS, DVD**

Shark Skin Man and Peach Hip Girl

A rock-and-roll criminal finds true romance. At her bank, hotel worker Toshiko (Sie Kohinata) discovers that her uncle has withdrawn her life savings. Before she can get over this shock, a masked gunman using a prerecorded cassette tape to issue his commands robs the bank, and a man is shot. Flash forward two years. Kuroo Samehada (Tadanobu Asano) has stolen 100 million yen from the syndicate. Tanuki (Ittoku Kishibe) wants his money back. Tanuki's son, Mitsuko (Kimie Shingyoji), his hair bleached blonde, is clothing-obsessed but blessed with a highly developed sense of smell, so he leads the hunt. Sawada (Susumu Terajima), a somewhat older man, is considered responsible for the loss, and that makes him desperate to find Samehada.

Barely ahead of his pursuers, Samehada leaps from a hotel room, clad only in his underwear, and races down a mountain road, chased by two of the gangsters. Toshiko happens to be driving down the same road, and, distracted by the sight of Samehada, crashes into the gangsters' car. Samehada commandeers Toshiko's vehicle and drives away with the unconscious girl beside him. Little does he know that Toshiko has engineered her own escape, running away from her lustful and highly controlling uncle at the hotel. When he learns that she has disappeared with a man, her uncle hires the high-strung Yamada (Tatsuya Gashuin) to kill the man and bring Toshiko back. Meanwhile, Toshiko and Samehada are drawn to each other. Love and money collide in a series of bloody confrontations.

The craziness of the movie centers on the characters rather than the action scenes, which are few in number. The gangsters have wild personalities and spend a lot of time talking. Toshiko and Samehada don't do a lot of talking to each other, but Samehada is adept with his gun. It's never really made clear, though, whether his motive to rip off the syndicate is based on greed or resentment. Comparisons could be made to the work of Quentin Tarantino because of the extensive and sharply written dialogue, but pop-culture references are avoided and the structure is more straightforward. The humor tends to be dry and blackhearted rather than caustic and obscene. The rueful denouement provides a graceful exit. Based on a best-selling manga by Mochizuki Minetarou. —PM **AKA:** *Samehada Otoko to Momojiri Onna.* 🎵🎵🎵

1998 109m/C *JP* Tadanobu Asano, Ittoku Kishibe, Sie Kohinata, Kimie Shingyoji, Susumu Terajima, Tatsuya Gashuin, Shingo Tsurumi, Daigaku Sekine, Koh Takasugi, Yoji Tanaka, Keisuke Horibe, Yoshiyuki Morishita, Kanji Tsuda. **D:** Katsuhito Ishii. **W:** Katsuhito Ishii. **C:** Hiroshi Machida. **VHS, DVD**

Sharp Guns

A crackling good Saturday night B-movie of the highest order. The daughter (Po Siu-yee) of Macau mob boss Ban (Lam Laap-saam) has been kidnapped. Ban calls in his old friend Tricky On (Alex Fong) from Holland to find her. On hires two assistants: the sharpshooter Wood (Ken Chang) and the deadly assassin Rain (Anya). Rain brings along Kangaroo (David Lee), a driver. They track down the girl, and discover deceit and danger along the way.

During a year in which romantic comedies and sensitive dramas predominated Hong Kong screens, the very simple action and clever script of *Sharp Guns* stands out in sharp relief. Billy Tang provides plenty of stylish direction, but he also knows when to hold back and let scenes play out. The film has a superb sense of pace and the forward momentum never slackens. That means the characters are given short shrift and the film does not rise above its B-movie origins. But when the twists and turns are handled so expertly and knowingly—without making the tongue-in-cheek conceits too obvious—it seems petty to complain. This is a crowd-pleaser that didn't find much of an audience upon its release in cinemas. Still, it has charm, jazzy punch, and humor. Alex Fong is the epitome of cool, completely relaxed and utterly confident in a powder-blue suit—perhaps an homage to a certain Japanese cinematic assassin from the 1960s (see *Tokyo Drifter*). Ken Chang *(Extreme Challenge)* displays a good sense of timing as Wood and provides welcome comic relief. It's unfair and sexist to reduce a performance to what an actress is wearing, but it's hard to avoid the stereotypes when Anya makes her first appearance in a red leather jacket, yellow midriff-baring halter top, and low-slung, snug red pants. Mostly she's just a nasty character—not much acting ability on Anya's part, perhaps, but you'll be too distracted to notice. Ma Yuk-sing *(The East Is Red, Big Bullet)* choreographed the action scenes. Cheuk Man-yiu provided the art direction—and the settings are very colorful indeed. —PM **AKA:** *Him Gok; Xian Jiao.* 🎵🎵🎵

2001 86m/C *HK* Alex Fong, Ken Chang, Anya, Eric Wan, Lam Laap-saam, Ha Shiu-sing, Lok Daat-wa, David Lee, Po Siu-yee, Ken Wong, Moses Chan. **D:** Billy Tang. **W:** Felix Chong, Cary Cheng. **C:** Tony Miu. **M:** Tommy Wai. **DVD**

She Shoots Straight

Blazing action highlights this Sammo Hung—produced entry in the Girls with Guns subgenre, which is based on the Sung Dynasty story of the Huang Family Amazons. The story goes that the Huang patriarch died leaving only one son to carry on the fight against Turkish invaders, and his many sisters take up arms as soldiers to join the fight. The fiercest of these female warriors turns out to be his new bride. Newlyweds Huang Tsung-pao (Tony Leung Ka-Fai) and Mina Kao (Joyce Godenzi) are assigned to security duty when a foreign princess visits Hong Kong to take in a fashion show. Sisters Huang Chia-ling (Carina Lau), Huang Chia-jui (Angile Leung), and Huang Chia-ju (Sandra Ng) are cops, too, and work undercover at the show.

A gunfight and a wild car chase later, and Mina has recovered the slightly bruised princess from kidnapping terrorists. Eldest sis-

ter Ling objects to her new sister-in-law, jealous of her high rank and awards. The Huangs are next assigned the case of bringing in the Vietnamese Yuan family, who shot up a market in a bad gun deal and plan on robbing the Singapore Cabaret. The ladies go undercover as hostesses, but Ling's actions expose them to the Yuan's during the robbery, and Superintendent Liu (Lau Chi-wing) forces Mina to suspend her sister-in-law. Mina shot brother Keung in the gunfight, and gang leader Yuan Hua (Yuen Wah) swears vengeance against her. Intercepting a message, Ling tries to make amends and ends up drawing Mina and Pao into Hua's trap with her. Pao falls prey to the Yuan's guerilla booby traps, and the women bond in grief. Despite enforced leave all around, the Huang women (and family friend Sammo Hung) vow to take down Yuan and his gang at all costs.

The melodramatics get a bit heavy-handed, with Mina and Ling trying to get through a birthday dinner for Mother Huang (Tang Pik-wan) without telling anyone her son is dead. Injured by a bomb at the funeral, Mina goes through surgery without anesthetic to protect her unborn child. But if you can bear with such overwrought theatrics, you'll be rewarded with some thrilling action scenes. A climactic battle takes place aboard a steamship, giving Godenzi and Lau plenty of pipes, corridors, and catwalks to fight through, over and around. And the finale features a gut-busting duel between Godenzi and the powerful Agnes Aurelio. *AKA: Wong Fung Lui Cheung; Huang Gu Nu Jiang; Lethal Lady.* 🦴🦴🦴▽

1990 87m/C *HK* Joyce Godenzi, Carina Lau, Yuen Wah, Tony Leung Ka-Fai, Angile Leung, Sandra Ng, Agnes Aurelio, Sammo Hung, Tang Pik-wan, Sarah Lee, Lau Chi-wing, Helena Law, Michael Dinga, Chung Fat, Yip Wing-cho, Amy Yip, Corey Yuen. *D:* Corey Yuen. *W:* Yuen Kai-chi, Barry Wong. *C:* Tom Lau, Jimmy Leung. *M:* Lowell Lo, Chow Kam-cheung. **VHS, DVD**

Shiri

In some parts of the world, the Cold War is still alive. North Korea, 1992—a brutal life-or-death training program weeds out inferiors until a single soldier remains: Hee. By 1996, Hee is listed as lead suspect in half a dozen of the assassination and sabotage cases in the file held by OP agents Ryu (Han Suk-kyu) and Lee (Song Kang-ho). Super-assassin Hee has become such a menace that Ryu is having nightmares about her. In 1998, there are signs that reunification of North and South may be on the way. Ryu is engaged to tropical fish dealer Hyun (Kim Yun-jin), but he hasn't told her that he's a secret agent in constant danger on the job. Hee kills arms dealer Lim right in front of Ryu, just as Lim is about to identify the assassin. They find out that Lim was working on a deal to steal an undetectable new liquid explosive called CTX from a research scientist named Kim, but Kim is assassinated before they can get to him. A North Korean squad intercepts a convoy carrying the CTX, and the OP agents suspect there's a leak within their organization. The enemy team's leader, an old foe of Ryu's named Park (Choi Min-sik), makes contact with the information that they've placed 10 CTX bombs across Seoul. As the film has become increasingly filled with fountains and fish tanks (stocked with stunt fish), paranoia reigns as every drop of water is seen as a potential bomb.

This clever homegrown action movie toppled *Titanic* from the top boxoffice record in Korea. Technically indistinguishable from any suspense thriller made by Hollywood, nevertheless *Shiri* could not have been made anywhere else in the world than Korea in the 1990s. You could put Keanu Reeves and Cameron Diaz in the leads, and pull in millions at multiplexes across America, but the story would only work with Koreans. It's nice to see that a commercial film with international appeal still retains a cultural identity. Director Kang Je-gyu *(Gingko Bed)* was well aware of the stigma attached to Korean films as cheap and inferior, and purposely set out to destroy that impression. The gunfights, stunts, and f/x are all top-notch, without overwhelming the strong plot. Hopefully, he'll get a few more great Korean flicks made before Hollywood lures him away. Fun product placement: watch for a gunfight around Pocari Sweat soft-drink vending machines. *AKA: Swiri.* 🦴🦴🦴🦴

1999 (R) 125m/C *KO* Han Suk-kyu, Choi Min-sik, Song Kang-ho, Kim Yun-jin, Yoon Joo-sang, Park Yong-woo. *D:* Kang Je-gyu. *W:* Kang Je-gyu. *C:* Kim Sung-bok. *M:* Lee Dong-jun. **VHS, DVD**

Shocking Asia

The "mondo movie" was named for the 1962 Italian hit shock-umentary *Mondo Cane,* but its origins stretch back to the dawn of cinema. From their start, the movies have had one foot in the carnival tent, pulling in a crowd to scare them with a clip of an approaching locomotive or a roaring lion. The mondo pictures are the missing link between the freak show and "legitimate" motion pictures, offering oddball sights for curious gawkers—often completely faked. They were frequently shown like freak shows, too, driven across the country from town to town as a roadshow attraction. Later, they took their place in dim inner-city grind houses where once stood dime museums. Today, television has become the mondo domain, with shows about police chases, weird behavior, and oddities of nature flooding the airwaves.

This 1975 feature was late for the 1960s mondo rush that followed *Mondo Cane*, but it was right in the thick of the heyday of crumbling grind houses and made a killing on home video a few years later. For the eye-covering delight of Eastern and Western audiences alike, director Emerson Fox compiles gruesome Asian oddities for your entertainment and edification. This German/Hong Kong production features the usual mix of bizarre happenings such as snake eating, faith healers, piercing, etc. A tour of the world of Japanese sex weirdness provides some entertainment, but the total show stopper is the graphic documentation of how desperate young hopefuls sell their altered wares on the streets in the hopes of raising enough cash for their final crude sex change operations. This kind of material might show up occasionally on the HBO series *Real Sex,* but even cable TV is rarely this explicit. All phases of the process are shown, including actual operations performed in less than sterile settings. NOT for the squeamish.

Though far from the best of the mondo pictures, this one at least delivers what the title promises. Emerson Fox was a pseudonym of actor/director Rolf Olsen, who made quite a few adults-only and horror features *(Street of Sin, Bloody Friday)* before turning to documentaries. One of his last films, fittingly, was *Journey into the Beyond. AKA: Shocking Asia Sunde; Sex und Sukiyaki; Asia Perversa.* 🎵🎵

1975 94m/C *HK/GE* **D:** Rolf Olsen. **W:** Rolf Olsen, Ingeborg Stein Steinbach. **C:** Franz X. Lederle. **M:** Erwin Halletz. **VHS**

Shocking Asia 2

This second mondo-style documentary about various unpleasant Asian oddities, including voodoo, cannibalism, and other strange practices, seems to be largely made up of leftover footage from the previous film. It features a disturbing visit to a Thai leper colony (which is also plagued by shark attacks), an expose of psychic surgery, mummies, a crippled artist who paints with her feet, etc. Again, much of the show is devoted to a parade of weird Japanese sex shows and prostitution. One scene shows a bar owned and run by midgets, just like one in Chicago at the time. The *Shocking Asia* duo was a big hit in Asia itself, as well as jolting hardened American grind-house audiences. Both, along with the similar *Mondo Magic,* became early video rental releases that did very well. Enterprising Hong Kong entrepreneurs released an identically titled *Shocking Asia 2* of their own in 1988, as well as *Shocking Asia 3: After Dark* in 1995. *AKA: Shocking Asia Part 2; The Final Taboo.* 🎵🎵

1976 91m/C *HK/GE* **D:** Rolf Olsen. **M:** Erwin Halletz. **VHS**

Shogun

The movie-length adaptation of one of the great miniseries of all time, *Shogun* tells the story of Captain Richard Blackthorn (Richard Chamberlain), who sails to Japan to open a trade route with Europe. (Japanese trade was monopolized by the Portuguese at the time.) When he arrives there, Blackthorn has no real idea of what he's gotten himself into. He discovers the strange ways of the Japanese, falls in love with a married woman, uncovers a plot by Jesuits to smuggle wealth out of the country (and determines to stop it), and becomes an advisor to Lord Toranaga (Toshiro Mifune)—the man who would be Shogun.

The sprawling story survives the condensation into movie format fairly well—despite the far-shorter length. It does, of course, lack much of the character development and interesting detail that made the miniseries so fascinating. If you're looking for a good primer for Far Eastern storytelling, culture, and cinema, *Shogun* is probably a good way to go. There's plenty of action, romance, and drama for everyone—and even a bit of nudity in the feature version that wasn't included in the original broadcast version.

The performances, production values, sets, and locations are uniformly excellent throughout. There are many fine turns by veteran Japanese actors, including—of course—Toshiro Mifune. To the credit of the filmmakers, when this was first shown on TV, it ran without voice-over or captioning, allowing the viewers to better understand what Blackthorn felt like when he arrived in Japan. Later versions have added some narration (by Orson Welles), for those who weren't quite swift enough to pick up on the original. See the miniseries if you can (without the narration if possible), but settle for the movie if you must. Give the feature version another half bone if you've either seen the original miniseries or read the book. Available only on VHS in condensed movie version or vastly overpriced VHS boxed set with the full miniseries. —SS Theatrical: 🎵🎵🎵 / Unabbreviated miniseries: 🎵🎵🎵🎵

1980 124m/C *US* Richard Chamberlain, Toshiro Mifune, Yoko Shimada, Frankie Sakai, Damien Thomas, John Rhys-Davies, Yuki Meguro, Hideo Takamatsu, Nobuo Kaneko, Seiji Miyaguchi, Yosuke Natsuki, Takeshi Obayashi, Akira Sera, Shin Takuma. **D:** Jerry London. **W:** James Clavell, Eric Bercovici. **C:** Andrew Laazlo. **M:** Maurice Jarre. **VHS**

Shogun and Little Kitchen

Bo (Ng Man-Tat) runs a restaurant in the courtyard of the tenement apartment building he

owns. The neighborhood is run-down, and a developer wants to buy the building and put up a shiny new complex. Of course, none of the current residents will have the money to live there. Bo considers the tenants to be his family, and stubbornly refuses to sell them out. His uncle, Dai Chi (Yuen Biao), comes to live with him and help out in the restaurant. When Bo is injured and unable to work, Dai Chi takes over the cooking duties. Because of his incredibly acrobatic approach to cooking, he quickly becomes a celebrity, attracting hordes of people to the restaurant. His success also temporarily staves off the developer.

The corporate world comes a-calling, though, and Dai Chi succumbs to the temptation and is hired away. He leaves behind a hobbled Bo and the other tenants to fight off the increasingly insistent developer. Surprisingly, Fung (Leon Lai) steps up to help save the day. He arrived the same day as Dai Chi, but stayed in the background because he's actually a rich boy in hiding from his father (martial arts legend Jimmy Wang Yu).

Ronny Yu directed a very warmhearted and appealing comedy that sneaks in a little social commentary about the oft-ignored and disenfranchised poor. The message must have been quite timely, considering the upheaval that Hong Kong was undergoing in the early 1990s. Director Yu made the classic *The Bride with White Hair* the following year. Yuen Biao only appears in a few scenes, but his amazing cooking is worth the price of admission. —PM **AKA:** *Feng Tau Fook Sing; Huo Tou Fu Xing; Meal Head Lucky Star; Shogun and His Little Kitchen.* 🦴🦴🦴

1992 93m/C *HK* Yuen Biao, Leon Lai, Ng Man-Tat, Maggie Shaw, Monica Chan, Jimmy Wang Yu, Leung Kar-yan, Lui Fong, Lam Laap-saam, Josephine Koo. **D:** Ronny Yu. **W:** Raymond To, James Yuen. **C:** David Chung. **M:** Richard Yuen. **DVD**

Shogun Assassin

A film legend because of its intensity and nearly nonstop bloodletting, *Shogun Assassin* is actually the first two *Lone Wolf and Cub* (AKA *Baby Cart Assassin*) films, re-edited for American audiences. It acquired a dopey title to cash in on the (then current) Shogun craze. Of course, the film has very little to do with any Shogun, aside from the fact that the main character Itto Ogami (Tomisaburo Wakayama) was once the royal executioner. *Shogun Assassin* is based on the (also legendary) comic series, *Lone Wolf and Cub,* by Kazuo Koike and Goseki Kojima. Surprisingly, the re-edited film holds up pretty well as a samurai action flick—probably because of the episodic nature of the original

source material. It helps that Kazuo adapted the films from his original material.

The film tells the story of Itto Ogami and his young son Daigoro, as they wander Japan, looking for work. The family business is not what one would expect from a ronin (masterless samurai) and young child, as Ogami was once the lord-high executioner (and the greatest swordsman in the land). Itto's renunciation of his position (and refusal to commit seppuku—suicide—in atonement) has made him many enemies—including the powerful Yagyu clan. Now our hero is an assassin for hire, and Daigoro and his baby cart are Itto's "partners." Ogami and Daigoro cut a bloody swath across the Japanese countryside as they kill folks to earn a living, and their enemies try to kill them in return. The fight scenes in this film (and, indeed, in the entire series) are brutal and bloody. The Japanese remain unflinching in the face of movie violence that would make most U.S. audiences turn away. This movie gives a good example of just how big those differences are. Itto comes up with numerous inventive ways to slay his enemies—and these are great fun (in a Grand Guignol sense) to watch. Particularly enjoyable is the duel with the three basket-hat assassins who trail our heroes through much of the film. (Many American audiences laughed nervously at the blood-spurting dénouement during the flick's original run.)

The direction, sets, costumes, and locations are all very good on this film. The quirky soundtrack grows on you with repeated viewings. The dubbing is straightforward, and has a certain charm as well—though American audiences may be jarred by the child's voice-over combined with the ultra-violence. Radio Tarzan Lamont Johnson, Mark Lindsay (of Paul Revere and the Raiders), and cult diva Sandra Bernhard contribute to the dubbing. Lop a half bone off what would otherwise be a 3.5 bone rating for some slight discontinuity in the merging of the two, longer features. It's a fun, violent classic. Check it out. —SS 🦴🦴🦴

1980 (R) 81m/C *JP* Tomisaburo Wakayama, Kayo Matsuo, Minoru Ohki, Shoji Kobayashi, Shin Kishida, Akihiro Tomikawa. **D:** Kenji Misumi. **W:** Robert Houston, David Weisman, Kazuo Koike (also manga), Goseki Kojima (manga). **C:** Chikashi Makiura. **M:** Mark Lindsay, W. Michael Lewis. **VHS, DVD**

Shogun's Ninja

1581: Lord Odo orders General Hideoshi to storm Mimuchi Castle and destroy the Eiga ninja. Shogun (Sonny Chiba), chief of the fearless Koja ninja, is ordered to kill Mimuchi himself. The ninjas kill Lord Sendaiyu to get sword with map of gold mine, but it's already on its

way out of the country with his young son. The next year, General Ikeji betrays Lord Odo, making a bid for power. General Hideoshi takes the opportunity to "avenge" Odo, and takes the throne himself, uniting Japan under his banner.

All of which is just a lengthy pre-ramble to our main story. It picks up with Takemaru (Henry Sanada), who has grown up in China, where he learned kung fu. While he reunites with his buddies in Japan, and plots the re-establishment of the Mimuchi clan, Shogun orders Takemaru captured. His old playmate Otsu, raised as one of Hideoshi's clan, is told to get the sword from him. Betrayed, the Mimuchi's are captured, but some escape execution and hide out in the woods, where they receive ninja training. Reunited with his girlfriend Ah Lin (Sue Shiomi), whom he left in China, Takemaru plots his revenge on Shogun.

Rather large subtitles introduce all major characters. Too bad they're in Japanese, since the only way to keep the dozens of characters straight is with a scorecard. Seemingly this was produced to give every member of Chiba's Japan Action Club a role—there's plenty of action, but it seems like less with all the worthless meanderings of the plot. It's scored with awful lounge jazz-rock music. *AKA: Ninja Bugeicho Momochi Sandayu.* ♪♪

1982 (R) 112m/C *JP* Sonny Chiba, Henry Sanada, Sue Shiomi, Tetsuro Tamba, Yoko Nogiwa, Masumi Harukawa, Asao Koike, Makoto Sato, Isao Natsuki, Yuki Ninagawa, Shohei Hino, Katsumasa Uchida. **D:** Norifumi Suzuki. **W:** Takahito Ishikawa, Fumio Koyama, Ichiro Otsu. **M:** Masakatsu Suzuki. **DVD**

Sholay

The most successful Bollywood production ever, *Sholay* opened in theatres across India in 1975, and was still playing some of those same theatres in 1980! Not the *Dirty Dozen*—or the *Seven Samurai*—but the Dirty Two, the rollicking adventure gets started when Thakur Baldev Singh (Sanjeev Kumar) sends for criminals Jai (Amitabh Bachchan) and Veeru (Dharmendra) to help with a special assignment. Thakur arrested them years ago, and they subsequently saved his life when bandits attacked their train. Thakur wants them to come to his village of Ramgarh to capture the notorious bandit chief Gabbar Singh (Amjad Khan) who has been ter-

Tomisaburo Wakayama and Akihiro Tomikawa perfect their deadly piggy-back technique in *Shogun Assassin.*

rorizing the region. Thakur arrested Gabbar once as well, sending him up for a 20-year stretch for "dacoitry." But Gabbar escaped from prison, massacred Thakur's family, and left his crippling mark on Thakur himself. In between skirmishes with the bandits, womanizing Veeru has his heart stolen by talkative tonga (horse-cart taxi) driver Basanti (Hema Malini), while dour Jai is drawn to Thakur's lovely daughter-in-law Radha (Jaya Bhaduri). The boys succeed in destroying most of Gabbar's weaponry, but the war doesn't begin in earnest until the bandits capture and kill the villagers' favorite son.

Too much time is wasted with allegedly comic digressions involving inessential characters, such as a sequence set in a prison early on, with a warden who looks like Hitler. The flashbacks are overly lengthy as well, giving more of a feeling of padding than adding to the narrative—hardly necessary in a movie of this length. The musical sequences, however, are shot with as much creativity as the rest of the feature, lending them a great deal of charm (the songs all became hits). *Sholay* works best when it concentrates on its rich main characters, its scenery, its western atmosphere, and especially its abundant action scenes. The gunplay, chases, and fights are well staged, with some excellent stunt work. Kumar adds an intense presence to all of his scenes, while Amjad Khan is a suitably hateful villain. *AKA: Flames of the Sun; Flames, Embers.* 🎵🎵🎵🎵

1975 204m/C *IN* Amitabh Bachchan, Dharmendra, Sanjeev Kumar, Amjad Khan, Hema Malini, Jaya Bhaduri, A.K. Hangal, Helen, Jagdeep. *D:* Ramesh Sippy. *W:* Salim Khan, Javed Akhtar. *C:* Dwarka Divecha. *M:* Rahul Dev Burman. **DVD**

The Silver Spear

A fairy-tale atmosphere pervades this swordplay feature, which boasts many eccentric details and not much in the way of coherence. At Green Jade Palace in Snow Valley, Madam Green Plum invites four kung fu masters—Silver Spear (Tin Peng), Red Leaf Shen Hung, Fast Steed Lao Tu-lung (Meng Fei), and Green Lotus—to vie for the hand of her "aloof" daughter. Silver Spear is depressed at this, since he's in love with opera singer Sharon Chow, and hopes to lose the competition honorably—or he plans on suicide. Unfortunately, someone decides to get a jump on the competition, and Red Leaf and Green

Lotus die from wine poisoned with cricket powder before the competition even begins. The judges (led by Chan Sing) accuse Fast Steed of the crime, and he mounts his namesake to flee. He finds a girl lost in the snow, who helps him escape, and he hides out in the village disguised as a storekeeper. However, Silver Spear has only been feigning disinterest in the prize, and had his cousin Cheap Jade poison the wine and frame Steed. But Spear is only working for his master, a huge bald vampire who has been plaguing the area. Steed befriends Iron Axe ("the Romantic Warrior"), who is eating mass quantities of eggs and salt to stave off the effects of Master Jade's poisonous palm strike. Together they try to defend themselves against the massive Master #13, a Persian who practices "weird kung fu" and lives on human blood.

There's not much in the way of real martial arts here, but a lot of energetic jumping around with strange weapons. The whole film has a fever dream quality, full of action and nonsense, much of it playing out in dark, surreal settings. The sets are extensive and always full of swirling mist, and there are a lot of strange characters, some of which feign death to reappear later, and many of which bear false identities. Master #13 is a creepy monster, with huge sharp teeth sprouting from his mouth. Certain films seem to have gone insane. This one's a good candidate for that list—it's not very good, but it's plenty weird. Even the credits are odd, seemingly translated through a third language to get to English. Director/star Tin Peng is credited as "Rco Trem." **AKA:** Bik Huet Sin Aau Cheong; Bi Xie Sheng Yin Qiang; Silver Hermit from Shaolin Temple; Silver Hermit Meets the Bloody Fangs of Death; The True Master. 🎵🎵

1979 94m/C HK Tin Peng, Meng Fei, Chan Sing, Doris Lung, Wong Ping, Lau Yat-fan. **D:** Tin Peng. **VHS**

Sister Street Fighter

Martial arts champ/narcotics agent Lee Long (Hiroshi Miyauchi) is kidnapped. The Hong Kong office calls on his sister Tina (Sue Shiomi) to infiltrate Central Export, a drug distribution gang. Her only lead is Lee's partner Fanny Singer, who is working undercover as a stripper at Club Mandarin in Yokohama. She arrives just in time to see that Fanny's cover is blown. As the thugs are carrying her off, a stranger arrives to beat up the bad guys and drive off with Fanny. The mystery man is Sonny Hibachi (Sonny Chiba), an instructor at the Surinji Karate School where Lee was teaching. Sonny and instructor Emi Kawasaki (Emi Hayakawa) both agree to help rescue Lee—if he's still alive.

Though usually included as part of the Street Fighter series, this is actually the first of a series of Lady Karate (or "Lethal Fist Woman") features starring Shiomi, the first woman to join Chiba's Japan Action Club. Sonny Chiba doesn't even play his Terry Tsurugi character. In some ways, this fluffier movie is more fun than the gritty Street Fighter movies, with cute Sue facing off against a variety of exotic fighters employed by the bad guys, including karate master Hammerhead, a speargun-toting priest, and seven Thai amazons wearing costumes straight out of The Flintstones. Among other camp elements are a cave full of fake bats on wires and a drug kingpin who dresses like Liberace's understudy. The series would continue for three more episodes, all of which await U.S. release. Keep an eye out for Chiba's brother Jiro as one of the thugs. **AKA:** Onna Hissatsu Ken; Jo Hissatsu Ken; Woman Certain Kill Fist. 🎵🎵🎵

1974 (R) 81m/C JP Sue Shiomi, Emi Hayakawa, Harry Kondo, Sonny Chiba, Hiroshi Miyauchi. **D:** Kazuhiko Yamaguchi. **W:** Manfred Kakefuda, Norifume Suzuki. **C:** Yoshio Nakajimi. **M:** Shunsuke Kikuchi. **VHS, DVD**

The Six Directions of Boxing

The furious action can't wait to get started in this feature set in the early 20th century, with a big fight running under the opening credits. Captain Yi Chang-fang (David Chiang) is in charge of a team of police agents out to nab a criminal named Chen Hu-cher (Lung Tin Cheung), who is arranging to deliver a shipment of guns to his brother, Warlord Chen Ming-cher. Yi's agent Cherh-chun finds a map to where the guns are hidden, but they don't know the location of the starting square. When Cherh-chun is injured in a brawl with some of the gang, Yi takes him to get medical treatment at the home of his girlfriend Woo Ching-chi (Nancy Yen), who lives in a hut by the river with her father (Simon Yuen), her dog (Lai Hei), and her chimpanzee (Tarzan). Enlisting the pets as detectives, Yi is quickly led straight to the house of Mr. Tan (Paul Chun), scar-faced leader of the gunrunners, who is harboring Chen. But Chen has brought his own animal friend—while facing off against Yi using his Snake Style, he has a goon throw a real snake at his foe. Luckily, the dog deflects the throw onto Chen, who gets bitten, and since the chimp has stolen the antidote, Chen is under Yi's power. Even with the antidote it takes months to recover from the snake venom, so since Yi suspects a spy in his group will tip off Tan with information to rescue the prisoner, Chen is kept in a cave by old Woo. Tipped off to the hiding place,

Tan's men are still unable to find Chen—and get pissed on by the ape to boot! But the local deputy commissioner gives Yi only five days to find the evidence against Chen before he has to set the prisoner free, and with Tan making a deal with his rival Liu to join forces, Yi will have to be tricky to see justice done.

David Chiang, looking sporty in a jaunty cap, plays the lead like he's Eliot Ness in *The Kung Fu Untouchables,* and director Tyrone Hsu keeps the potboiler plot bubbling. But the picture really belongs to the Yuen clan, who direct the action and fill several supporting roles. Simon Yuen does his patented fighting-while-pretending-not-to-fight routine. It's unusual for Hong Kong productions to include animal performers within their frantic shooting schedules, and even more unusual for a chimp to show up, and the ape brings an odd flavor into the mix. As is usual in his screen appearances, poor Lai Hei the dog doesn't make it to the final reel, but at least he manages to avoid getting eaten this time. **AKA:** *Luk Gap Baat Fat; Liu He Ba Fa; The Six Direction Boxing.* 🐉🐉🐉

1979 91m/C *TW* David Chiang, Simon Yuen, Yueh Hua, Paul Chun, Lung Tin Cheung, Lung Chuan, Yuen Cheung-yan, Jack Lung, Corey Yuen, Yuen Yat-chor, Chang Chi-ping, Hau Pak-wei, Brandy Yuen, Nancy Yen, Au Lap-bo, Cheng Lui, Yeung Lit, Tarzan the monkey, Lai Hei the dog. **D:** Tyrone Hsu. **W:** Sung Han-yu. **C:** Chang Te-chuen. **M:** Chou Fu-liang. **VHS, DVD**

Sixty Million Dollar Man

As sort of a follow-up to his hit *From Beijing with Love,* Stephen Chow provides a carload of movie spoofs in this cyborg comedy. Lee Chak-sing (Chow) is a spoiled billionaire's son living a bachelor's dream life in Honolulu in a mansion full of Hot Chicks, and commuting to college via helicopter (to the strains of Barry Manilow's "Copacabana"). At school—where his father Lee Yat-fei (Wong Yat-Fei) is the director—everyone scurries in fear of Sing, except for nerdy student Chung-Chung (Gigi Leung) and her mad scientist uncle Professor Chang Sze (Elvis Tsui), who is a consultant to the U.S. military doing research into creating infinitely adaptable artificial human organs. Sing falls for his neighbor Bonnie (Paulyn Sun), but on their first date (a hilarious send-up of the date sequence from *Pulp Fiction*) he learns she's married to yakuza boss Fumio. Hiding from the yakuza at home, Sing learns that his real father is his manservant Tat (Ng Man-Tat), but kicks him out in favor of rich Lee. However, when Tat returns to try to save Sing from the yakuza thugs, Sing sacrifices himself and puts Tat on their ejector-seat toilet

as a bomb goes off (aping a famous shot in *Die Hard 2*).

All that's left of Sing is his brain and mouth, just enough to be rebuilt using Professor Chang's new parts. Chang's American colleague wants $60 million to complete the process, but since Tat only has $6000, Chang offers to rebuild Sing himself using cheaper replacements that run on regular batteries. Fearing the yakuza will come after them again if they're found alive, Sing and Tat move back to Hong Kong, but run into a lot of hard times. Completing Sing's humiliation is his new job as a teacher in a high school full of rich brats like himself. As Sing contemplates suicide, Chang arrives with his newly completed computer chip that makes Sing into a "super superman." His artificial parts now give him the ability to transform into anything he wants—from egg beaters to toothpaste to toilets—much like the comics character Plastic Man. With his new powers, he sets out to win Chung-Chung's heart, discipline his students, catch Fumio and his gang, and maintain world peace.

The third act is dominated by a pointless imitation of *The Mask* until Fumio's enforcer Mark (Chan Chi-fai) catches up with Sing. The cyborg hero uses his new abilities to smash Mark and his stooges, but Fumio *does* have $60 million to spend, and has his henchman rebuilt into a much slicker cyborg superman. Sing's answer to this dilemma is an extended gag based on a Hong Kong supermarket icon which (like much of Chow's verbal comedy) will mean nothing to Western viewers, but there's enough stuff in the picture that's funny everywhere to make this a winner. Wearing a white fright wig, Elvis Tsui seems to get a laugh every time he makes an entrance, and Chow is able to make even old jokes work. **AKA:** *Baak Bin Sing Gwan; Bei Bian Xing Jun.* 🐉🐉🐉

1995 91m/C *HK* Stephen Chow, Ng Man-Tat, Gigi Leung, Paulyn Sun, Elvis Tsui, Wong Yat-Fei, Manfred Wong, Alvina Kong, Mimi Chu, Guy Lai, Chan Chi-fai, David Saunders, Darren Shahlavi, Ivy the Cow. **D:** Raymond Yip. **W:** Wong Jing. **C:** Andrew Lau. **M:** Anthony Lee, Marco Wan. **VHS, DVD**

Skinny Tiger and Fatty Dragon

Constable Mak (Karl Maka) is "Tiger" to his underworld foes for his fearless pursuit, while his partner (Sammo Hung) is known as "Dragon" for his Bruce Lee–style fighting skills, but to each other they're just "Baldy" and "Fatty." Tiger goes undercover in a convenience store to catch a gang of robbers working the area. He grills them for information on their boss Johnny (Tai Bo), who is trafficking drugs for Prince Tak.

The info leads to Johnny—and an incidental jewelry-store robbery—but the big fish they're after is the notorious King of Drugs. When they can't find the evidence on his courier, Ng Lai (Carrie Ng), she has their boss Inspector Wu (Wu Fung) charge them for molesting her. Undeterred, they break into her house to search for evidence, and end up fleeing in Prince Tak's Mercedes when he shows up. Tak uses Lai to lure them into an ambush, but they fight their way out. They manage to chase down Tak, but they bust up the Deputy Commissioner's wedding reception while doing it.

Disgraced, Tiger and Dragon go on vacation in Singapore until things cool down, and they meet some girls, where they get a chance to sing karaoke and do a wild dance. But their fun doesn't last—Tak is soon released on bail. He hires two girl assassins from Thailand to kill Lai, and then they go after our heroes.

The starring combo of Hung and Maka should have led to a healthy film franchise, but Maka has been pretty much retired from acting ever since. Sammo's Bruce Lee imitation, already perfected for *Enter the Fat Dragon* in 1978, is hilarious, while his stunts and kung fu are still as thrilling as ever. *AKA: Shou Hu Fei Long; Sau Foo Fei Lung; Nutty Kickbox Cops.* ♫♫♫♪

1990 105m/C *HK* Sammo Hung, Karl Maka, Carrie Ng, Wanda Yung, Lung Ming-yan, Ngai Hong, Wu Fung, Tai Bo. **D:** Lau Kar-Wing. **W:** Tsang Kwok Chi. **C:** Ho Bao Yiu. **M:** Min. **VHS, DVD**

The Smart Cavalier

The main plot to this Joseph Kuo epic, shot in gorgeous Hohwa Scope, is the standard quest by Ming heroes to get a list of rebels away from Ching soldiers—but it's almost ignored to focus on what is usually only the comic-relief element. Wu Pu-chueh comes to town to find his granddaughter Ping (Doris Lung) a husband. After all, she's 18 and almost an old maid. He sets up a banner in the square and invites all bachelors to try to win her hand by beating her in kung fu. One after another are beaten by the young beauty—a midget, a big fat guy—until Ting Tou impetuously takes the challenge. His master Kan Feng-chih breaks in, though—they're fugitives from the Ching soldiers, and don't have time for weddings. But since Kan bests Ping, they now have old man Wu on their tails as well. Running all the way to Lee's Village, Kan has little trouble defeating Hei Sa, master of the Blue Dragon Party, and his squad of mercenary fighters. But they just can't shake relentless Wu and his feisty granddaughter. The seek out fellow Ming patriot Lo Ming-tan, who tells them the list of rebels has been found by the Chings and will

be sent to Minister Kung Tai-pu (Lo Lieh). Kan is determined to steal the list away, but old Wu pops up everywhere like Daffy Duck in a cartoon.

The film comes to a halt for a time when the heroes enter a brothel and a tiresome bragging waiter character takes over for a while. Wu and Ping ("disguised" as a man) follow, and Kan and Ting only escape by dressing in drag. Kan succeeds in retrieving the list from the Chings, but grandpa Wu is more tenacious. Lucky thing he is—when Kan and Ting meet up again with Lo to take on Kung, they find he and his minions have laid a trap for them. It turns out that Kung is also known as Demon of Snow Hill, who has mastered Joy-Angry-Sorrow-Happy Boxing, and poses a challenge to all the heroes. Only Wu knows how to hit the villain's laughing nerve center and kill him.

Though this is essentially a comedy, Kuo mixes in a little something for tragedy fans. The climax includes many heroes impaled on spears, including a little boy, and Kung bites the finger off the father and spits it hard into his neck, killing him! Fans of serious kung fu may balk, but this festival of nonsense is great entertainment for all others. *AKA: Dancing Kung Fu; The Cavalier.* ♫♫♫♪

1978 92m/C *HK* Lo Lieh, Doris Lung, Yee Yuen, Nancy Yen, Lung Fei, Cheng Fu Hung, Choi Wang, Robert Tai, Tung Li, Sze Ma Lung. **D:** Joseph Kuo. **VHS, DVD**

Snake and Crane Arts of Shaolin

In his second film with young director Chen Chi-hwa for Lo Wei Productions (after *Shaolin Wooden Men*), Jackie Chan clearly feels a bit less restricted, able to film his fight scenes his own way and injecting a bit of humor into his character. It was also a reunion with Bruce Lee's regular leading lady Nora Miao, who gets involved with a surprising amount of action. Common to kung fu films of the time, the credits sequence is shot against a plain background (in this case fiery red) and has the star going through a basic routine, just to let the audience know that he knows what he's doing right from the start.

Narration informs us that, at a martial arts convention, eight grand masters combined their styles into a super-style they dubbed "The Eight Steps of the Snake and Crane." They record the style in a book, after which it—along with the eight masters and a sacred Dragon Spear—disappear. Years later, the famous book somehow falls into the hands of a cocky young man named Hsu Ying-fung (Jackie Chan). He makes no secret of it, and all the clans are after it, including Tang Pin-er (Nora Miao) of the Wu-Tang Clan, the King of the Beggars, and Lady Suon

"Damn you Fatty. I'm following you. Don't be ladies, see?"

—Gangster Prince Tak wants Sammo Hung and Karl Maka to give his car back in a manly fashion, in *Skinny Tiger and Fatty Dragon*

and Chien Tse (Kam Kong) of the Black Dragons. The Tang's bring in a fighter named Sing Chu. He defends himself from all of them using his Snake and Crane. When, they can't beat him, they try other means. Fong Sie Pin of the Ere May Clan tries to ingratiate himself by taking his side in a fight. He's looking for a man with a scar on his shoulder. Chief Wong Yi Fu (Miu Tin) of the Flying Tiger Clan has his daughter Hong Tu (Kim Chin-lin), who likes to disguise herself as a beggar man, keep a close eye on him. Secretly, it's all a plan orchestrated by Hsu's master. When the Flying Tigers use a trick to capture Hsu, some of the others band together to rescue him.

The young Chen Chi-hwa makes some impressive choices behind the camera, favoring some fluid tracking shots, or taking the view from a high spot. However, once the fighting starts, you can tell that, even then, Chan was in control. And since there's not much to the plot, that leaves a lot of room for fighting, most of it quite good. **AKA:** *Se Hok Bat Bo; She He Ba Bu.* 🐉🐉🐉

1978 95m/C *HK* Jackie Chan, Nora Miao, Kam Kong, Kim Chin-lin, Miu Tin, Lau Nga Ying, Lee Man Tai, Tung Lam, Liu Ping, Margaret Lee, Wong Chi Sang, Miu Tak San. **D:** Chen Chi-hwa. **W:** Chang Seng-yi. **C:** Chan Chung-yuen. **VHS, DVD**

Snake-Crane Secret

Hung Kun-san, Tin Yi-fei, and Han Kwei (Tung Li) are sworn blood brothers and kung fu masters. But Hung is a traitor working for the Ching. He frames Tin as the traitor to get Han to help him take a sacred kung fu text away from Tin; however, Hung tips his hand after killing Tin by attempting to slay his sons as well. Fortunately, a monk named Snake appears to help and carries the kids away. Twenty years later, Han Kwei finally finds out that the younger boy Er-lang (Meng Fei) has been raised at Shaolin Temple, while Snake took the older boy Tao-lung along with him on his travels. Hung has become a powerful Ching lord, and has been looking for the sons of Tin as well, hoping to find the sacred text, knowing the book contains a list of members in the rebel Sun and Moon Association. Er-lang leaves the temple carrying the book away for safekeeping, but has to elude several Ching agents to keep it. Meanwhile, the Sun and Moon group is infiltrated by a spy, who brings soldiers led by envoy Chao Tsin-san (Dean Shek) down on them. Er-lang decides to make a deal with Hung and brings the secret book to him, but the list remains hidden, and the lad claims ignorance of it. Hung still suspects Er-lang, however, and when the book is accidentally dropped in water, the list shows

up—and the name of Hung's trusted aide Kung Yeh (Delon Tan) is on it! Hung sends both Kung and Er-lang into a trap, hoping they'll kill each other. But Han Kwei reveals a secret: the two men are really brothers (as if you didn't know).

Director Wu Ma adds his usual creative bits of business, such as having Hung practice his kung fu on human skeletons. He also makes an appearance as a drunken officer who is tricked by some pornography. Dean Shek is nearly unrecognizable in scarface makeup as Ching agent Chao. Hung is given an amusing Southern drawl in the English-dubbed version. There's nothing remarkable about the fight scenes other than some weapons handling by Shek (pais) and Elsa Yeung (segmented cudgel). **AKA:** *Sau Hok Daan Sam Jan Gau Chow; She Hao Dan Xin Zhen Jiu Zhou; The Secret of the Snake and Crane.* 🐉🐉

1978 (R) 90m/C *HK* Meng Fei, Delon Tan, Yu Tien-lung, Elsa Yeung, Fang Fang, Tung Li, Dean Shek, Lee Kwan, Wu Ma, Wong Hap, Wong Fei-lung, Wong Yeuk-ping, Lui Ming, Lee Chiu, Hsu Feng, Ko Chun. **D:** Wu Ma. **W:** Wong Yeuk-ping, Kuo Wen-shan. **C:** Chen Chin-kui, Ysai San-chi. **M:** Chou Fu-liang. **DVD**

Snake Deadly Act

Action starts immediately with a snake fist duel between martial arts favorites Wilson Tong and Fung Hark-On. It seems Yue Yi (Fung) is out for revenge against Kuo (Tong), who raped his wife—though it's implied that Yi also raped Kuo's wife some time in the past. Yi loses the duel, and runs off swearing vengeance on Kuo and his family. Years later, Kuo is a prosperous and generous pillar of the community, but Yi lurks nearby posing as a beggar. Teenage son Kuo Chung (Ng Kwan-lung) has inherited both his father's kung fu skill and his generous impulses; when he meets a young girl named Chun Kwan who's been sold into prostitution by her indebted father, Chung immediately heads for the brothel to get her released from her contract. The madam (Angela Mao) greets his request by swinging a sword at him, at which point Yi steps in to save the youth with a display of fan fighting. When Chung tries to clean up a dishonest casino, Yi steps in again to save him from the Shadowless Kick of the owner (Michael Chan). Having determined that the young man's teachers Chen (Chan Lung) and Yang haven't taught Chung any practical kung fu, Yi takes the youth to his shack in the mountains to teach him the Snake Fist Style.

Director Wilson Tong seems to have constructed the middle of the film in opposition to the *Drunken Master*–style of kung fu film that was so popular at the time. Yi rejects the old "how to grab the bowl" teaching techniques, and immediately puts Chung into practice with bricks strapped to his limbs, jumping over spikes, etc. He also teaches Chung that he doesn't need to drink to practice Drunken Boxing. But what is Yi's purpose in training his enemy's son? Meanwhile, Yi tells Chung he suspects that Kuo's housekeeper Tin Pan (Phillip Ko) is the leader of a gang of thieves (including Mao and Chan) who are plundering the region. As Chung tries to find out who the mastermind is behind the gang, he uncovers the real secrets of his father and teacher.

While the denouement may not contain as sharp a twist as the buildup demands, the plot still supplies a fine framework for excellent fight choreography, which gets progressively better throughout the film. Some sequences are annoying digressions from the thrust of the plot (notably one with Bolo Yeung as a circus strongman), but that shouldn't bother fans, who will relish seeing the guest stars in action. Star Ng Kwan-lung apparently only made this one picture before dropping out of sight. The widescreen DVD version available appears to be from a Mandarin language print combined with the English soundtrack, as it bears both English and Chinese subtitles as well and some undubbed footage in Mandarin. **AKA:** *Sau Ying Chui Biu; She Xing Zui Bu.* 🐉🐉🐉

1979 91m/C *HK* Ng Kwan-lung, Fung Hark-On, Wilson Tong, Phillip Ko, Angela Mao, Michael Chan, Bolo Yeung, Cheng Hong-yip, Chan Lung, Yuen Biao. **D:** Wilson Tong. **VHS, DVD**

Snake Fist Dynamo

Joseph Lai spiced up his IFD Films roster with this offbeat Taiwanese kung fu comedy. Eurasian phony martial arts teacher Ho Tung (Eric Yee) keeps enough little kids fooled in a poor village to stay in business—that is, until some gangsters come to take over his school. Then he scoots out of town "to promote the national pride." In his travels, Ho Tung goes from one misadventure to another, usually getting in trouble by pretending to know kung fu and out of trouble by accidentally beating his opponent. An innkeeper's daughter tries to seduce him so he'll show her how to box, but he flees in order to preserve his "Virgin Technique."

A community he wanders into becomes a boom town when mourners forget all about the funeral to scramble for gold that's leaked out of a tomb. The town's mayor promotes a gold rush just to reap profits from speculators. With trouble coming along with the growing vice trade, Ho gets himself hired on as the new security chief, and has a thief he's befriended hired as an assistant. Before long they find themselves moshing with mobsters and pummeled by pros-

titutes. When Ho's old associate Shi shows up, he tells Ho he's a secret agent investigating the gold rush, putting the heroes in conflict with the mayor and a local criminal gang who want to make sure the gold secret stays secret.

Eric Yee is the only kung fu star to fight a real crane and a real python in one sequence—after which he completes the geek show by biting a live lizard in half! A close-up shot of a little boy urinating is also included as an indication of the film's comedic style. Without a particularly likable hero, and lacking sufficient martial arts thrills to take up the slack, this *Dynamo* is more of a dud. 🐉

1984 85m/C *TW* Eric Yee, Dick Lee, Nancy Leung, Paul Wei, Tsang Choh-lam, Clint Wong, Hugo Lai, Newton Wei, Tilly Sung, Connie Cheung. **D:** Joseph Lai. **W:** Godfrey Ho. **C:** Au Wing Sun. **M:** Stephen So. **VHS, DVD**

Snake in the Eagle's Shadow

Some folks will go a long way to prove a point. Shang Kuan I-yun (Hwang Jang Lee) has killed 3,000 followers of the Snake Fist Style of kung fu in order to prove that his Eagle's Claw Style is superior. By defeating the Snake Fist Master (Fung Hark-On), he leaves only Master Pai Chang-tien (Simon Yuen) to carry on the Snake Fist. Young Chien Fu (Jackie Chan) doesn't much care about styles—as the mop boy at Hungtai Kung Fu School, he just wants to keep ahead of a beating from Teacher Li (Dean Shek). Chien Fu takes in an old beggar he sees harassed by the Hung Wei School. In gratitude for his kindness, the spry old man begins to teach Chien Fu some kung fu. While Chien is losing the school a client by fighting back during a demonstration, the old man—who is really Master Pai—has to defend himself from Eagle Fist killers, one of whom is disguised as a priest (Roy Horan). Chien finds the wounded Pai and nurses him, in return for which Pai agrees to teach him Snake Fist Style—though Chien promises not to use it unless it's an emergency. But when Chien uses the style to defend his school's Master Hung in a dispute with Hung Wei School, Shang Kuan recognizes it, and trails Chien back to Pai. Finding his skill with the Snake Fist insufficient to beat Shang Kuan, Chien invents a hybrid style using moves he learned from his pet cat.

After a string of failed attempts at making Jackie Chan a star, producer Lo Wei lent Chan out to Ng See-yuen's Seasonal Films for a few pictures. Ng allowed Chan the freedom to contribute ideas, adding comedy and stylistic touches to the fight choreography, and teamed him with a young director named Yuen Woo-ping.

Though a bit too much time is devoted to the rivalry between schools, the combination of action, comedy, and personality was cinema gold. The result was a smash success. The same team would team up again using the same formula for the classic *Drunken Master* next. The electronic score, "borrowed" from Jean-Michel Jarre, is sometimes headache-inducing. **AKA:** *Se Ying Diu Sau; She Xing Diao Shou; Eagle's Shadow; Snaky Monkey; Bruce vs. Snake in the Eagle's Shadow.* 🐉🐉🐉

1978 (PG) 97m/C *HK* Jackie Chan, Simon Yuen, Hwang Jang Lee, Fung Hark-On, Dean Shek, Hsu Hsia, Tino Wong, Chan Lung, Charlie Chan, Roy Horan, Chan Chuen, Fung Ging Man. **D:** Yuen Woo-ping. **W:** Ng See-yuen, Siu Lung, Clifford Choi, Jackie Chan (story). **C:** Chang Hai. **M:** Chou Fu-liang. **VHS, DVD**

The Snake Strikes Back

Lam (Elton Chong), a martial arts student in the House of Absolutes, is given the secret invincible kung fu manual by an unknown donor. While still taking abuse from senior student Sui, Lam learns the book's techniques in private. Learning that the book is somewhere within the House of Absolutes, the evil Immortal Trio comes calling and kills Master Kin Tai. Lam flees, vowing revenge against the Trio. After roaming about for a few months, Lam meets up with the Absolutes' potbellied master (Mike Wong), who has been wandering disguised as a beggar. The master had senior teacher Min (Min Choi) see that Lam received the manual, hoping that he'd learn enough from it to take revenge if his enemies struck. He puts Lam into more intense training in anticipation of a showdown with the Immortal Trio.

Though schlockmaster Godfrey Ho is credited as director, it's action director Eagle Han Ying (who also plays one of the Immortal Trio) who deserves most of the credit for any creativity on display here. Though the plot is nearly nonexistent—obviously a product of the "flying paper" scripting style—at least the fight scenes are adequately choreographed, taking advantage of Elton Chong's talents for physical comedy. The training sequences range from painful-looking exercises involving a lot of sharp bamboo stakes pointing up from the ground, to a sillier sequence in which Chong has to snatch chunks of meat off his master's back. Really, what more can you say about a movie in which the hero's secret weapon is the sudden swelling of a big beer belly? The dubbing team of Vaughn Savage gives the cast the usual odd mix of accents, from Australian to Texan. Some music cues are lifted from the 1976 *King Kong.* 🐉🐉

1981 (R) 83m/C *HK* Elton Chong, Eagle Han Ying, Mike Wong, King Kee Cho, Danny Tsui, Samuel Fong, Thomson Mak, Min Choi. **D:** Godfrey Ho. **W:** Robert Szeto. **C:** Jimmy Yu. **M:** Ricky Chan. **VHS, DVD**

Snaker

The Gorgon myth might be familiar with Westerners from the Greek version, but it's obviously quite common in Asian folklore, resulting in films like *Devil Woman* and this Thai/Cambodian oddity. Manop and his wife Nhi are hunting for herbs in the jungle, when Nhi comes upon a huge python, which fires red rays from its eyes into hers. She doesn't remember what happened, and the next day Manop goes on a business trip to sell beads in the city. In Wiphak's general store, his wife Buppha falls ill, and the doctor says she's pregnant. Searching for bamboo shoots, Nhi and her daughter Ed disturb the python when they lose a spade down its burrow. The snake tells them that they can have the spade back if Nhi will marry him. She agrees, but runs away as soon as she gets the spade back. That night, the snake comes to her hut. He entrances her and (in human form—hey, the snake has a vaccination scar!) impregnates her. Madly in love after their tender coupling, the woman and the were-snake settle down together (no doubt shopping for Hiss and Hers towels), and whenever Manop goes out of town, Mr. Snake comes calling.

Meanwhile, Manop has been having an affair of his own with Wiphak's friend Pokia, and now she's pregnant, too. Manop notices that his wife is several months pregnant, and Ed spills the beans about Mommy's reptilian peccadillo, the truth of which is confirmed by her reaction to a snake meat dinner he cooks. Manop kills his rival, and slices Nhi's belly open to reveal a nest of baby snakes. But one little snake escapes his massacre when his foot slips and he's impaled on his own sword. And just to clean up loose ends, little orphan Ed falls on a slippery rock and dies, too. The snake-infant is found and raised in seclusion by a kindly monk, who names her Soraya. As she grows, the monk is more concerned about her becoming a tomboy than with her head covered with writhing snakes.

Years later, Wiphak's grown son Veha finally gets him involved in the plot by falling over a waterfall. He's found in the care of the monk and Soraya (Pich Chan Barmey), who now has a magic ring that gives her a normal head of hair. Veha finds that girls without snakes on their heads are just his type, and he takes Soraya home with him. However, their happiness is spoiled by Veha's commitment to marry Pokia's daughter Ranee.

More a cautionary tale about interspecies romance than a horror movie, *Snaker* takes far

too long getting around to its main characters to make a good movie. There aren't any scenes of folks vomiting up wriggly critters, as is expected in an Asian black-magic movie. However, it's a reasonable illustration of a folktale, many of which ramble on before reaching their conclusion. Competently photographed, there are some nice views of the ruins of Angkor Wat, and the special effects are good, including a surprise sorcery duel at the climax, and the snake-hair effect is quite convincing. Hopefully this international release will have the desired effect and help revive the Cambodian film industry. **AKA:** *Kuon Puos Keng Kang; The Snake King's Child.* 🐉🐉🐉

2001 108m/C *TH/CB* Vinai Krayboir, Pich Chan Barmey, Tep Rindaro, Om Portevy, Heng Dary, Sam Polida, Chao Channary, Tim Angkeara. **D:** Fai Samang. **W:** Fai Samang, Mao Samnang. **C:** Saray Chat. **M:** Ben Davith. **DVD**

Son of Godzilla

The second of Godzilla's "south seas" pictures (after *Ebirah, Horror of the Deep*), this one con-

cerns the adventures of a group of scientists trying to control weather conditions on tropical Sollgel Island. While preparing their latest top-secret test, reporter Goro Masaki (Akira Kubo) drops out of the sky. Talk about strange weather! Having no way to dispose of the intruder, they let him work for them as a cook. Their deep-freeze experiment goes haywire, frying the island with a radioactive storm. The radioactivity mutates the insects on the island, producing gigantic mantises and a nasty giant spider. It also mutates and hatches a big egg, releasing an infant monster that resembles Godzilla. Apparently of the same species, the baby's cries of distress when the mantises attack bring Godzilla (no doubt already drawn to the area to soak up some radiation) to his rescue.

Goro finds a girl named Saeko Matsumiya (Australian actor Bibari "Beverly" Maeda) living on the island, too—she was orphaned when her scientist father died on the island, and survived the storm in a deep cave. With the monsters trashing their compound, the group is relieved to be able to move into the cave, and Saeko provides berry juice that cures their radiation sickness (an element linking this movie to *Mothra* and *King Kong vs. Godzilla*). However, the battling beasts above threaten to bury them in the cave. The scientists make a last desperate effort to bring winter to the island, putting the monsters into hibernation so they can escape.

Son is the first Godzilla movie in which the monsters have their own story, beyond fighting with each other and destroying monuments. It's refreshing to see Godzilla marching among the waving palms instead of smashing cities, and no doubt less expensive for the producers. The depiction of monsters in a family setting seemed outrageous at the time, but subsequent discoveries have revealed a more paternal picture of behavior among dinosaurs. While Godzilla and his young ward—named Minilla ("Mee-nya") in Japan—look awful in this entry, and the juvenile aspect of the baby's antics are slightly annoying, this is nevertheless a solidly paced and plotted sci-fi adventure, with good performances, memorable music, and some genuinely touching moments. Minilla would return to tug at our heartstrings in *Destroy All Monsters* and *All Monsters Attack* before retiring from the screen forever. **AKA:** *Kaijuto no Kessen: Gojira no Musuko; Minya, Son of Godzilla; Monster Island Decisive Battle: Godzilla's Son.* 🎵🎵🎵

1967 (G) 84m/C *HK* Akira Kubo, Bibari Maeda, Tadeo Takashima, Akihiko Hirata, Kenji Sahara, Yoshio Tsuchiya, Kenichiro Maruyama, Seichiro Kuno, Yasuhiko Saijo, Susumu Kurobe, Kazuo Suzuki, Wataru Omae, Haruo Nakajima, "Little Man" Machan, Osman Yusuf. **D:** Jun Fukuda. **W:** Shinichi Sekizawa, Kazue Shiba. **C:** Kazuo Yamada. **M:** Masaru Sato. **VHS**

Sonatine

A new subway line has business booming within the territory of Tokyo yakuza chief Murakawa ("Beat" Takeshi Kitano), earning him jealous glances from other chiefs. When Boss Katajima (Tonbo Zushi) sends Murakawa to Okinawa to broker a peaceful settlement of a dispute with the Nakamatsu Clan, Murakawa thinks it's a setup to get rid of him so that weasel Takahashi (Kenichi Yajima) can take over. He gives Takahashi a discrete thrashing for his impudence, but still has to make the trip, though he's given a mix of experienced and green troops to help out.

On checking into their seedy Okinawa offices, a bullet through the window seems to be a bad omen, but the "cavalry" finds things otherwise quiet there. That is, until a bomb kills two of them and a trio of hit men tries to kill Murakawa. With war declared, the guys hide out at a beach house to await further orders from Tokyo. As the small group engages in fun and games to pass the time, their wait turns into an unexpected and refreshing vacation from their gangland activities—even though the next car

down the road, either bearing their own fellows or those of the enemy, could bring death.

Yakuza life is portrayed here to consist mostly of waiting around for orders from your boss. For the bosses, it means standing aside impassively as your orders to commit violence are carried out by underlings, then waiting around for orders from your own boss. The military analogy is obvious, and gives writer/director/editor Kitano a chance to juxtapose his talent for starkly violent action and suspense with his love of whimsical comedy. Taking gangster antics and putting them in a beautiful seaside setting has a surreal effect, the extended fun-in-the-sun digressions building up an interesting kind of tension, just as we all take holidays knowing we have to return to work and struggle. Kitano obviously finds the interplay of yin and yang fascinating, and keeps finding fresh ways to present it on film. In order to let the tension in his story boil over, he takes the action from the wide-open spaces into the most enclosed environment. Ultimately, he overplays his hand a bit, suspense ebbing away in scenes of serenity that go on too long—but nonetheless it's a fascinating exercise in the dynamics of cinema. In his future outing *Fireworks,* he takes the technique even further, with the violence only temporarily interrupting the scenes of beauty. **AKA:** *Sonachine.* 🎵🎵🎵🎵

1993 (R) 94m/C *JP* "Beat" Takeshi Kitano, Aya Kokumai, Tetsu Watanabe, Masanobu Katsumura, Susumu Terajima, Ren Osugi, Tonbo Zushi, Kenichi Yajima, Eiji Minakata, Houka Kinoshita. **D:** Takeshi Kitano. **W:** Takeshi Kitano. **C:** Katsumi Yanagishima. **M:** Jo Hisaishi. **VHS**

Sorrowful to a Ghost

Master Meng Ting-sang (Ma Kei) of the Patience School is going to the capitol to announce his successor, Lu Hao-nan (Lei Chun). Senior student Tu Chi-lung would have been his choice, but Tu disappeared two years ago after losing a fight to Dare Devil Shao Mu-tien (Yee Yuen). When Wan Ching-er and his boys from Yuan Tien School try to bully student #3 Kwan Chuen (Kong Ban) and molest Meng's daughter (Cheung Ching-Ching), Kwan deals a fatal wound to Wan. Father Wan Wu-chi (Hon Kong) challenges Meng to a duel to get revenge, and an angry Master Meng loses his patience and throws Kwan out of the school. Though Meng intends to apologize to Wan, his enemy's students ambush him on the way to the duel. Meng kills Wan and all his students, barely having to use his sword. Dare Devil Shao is nearby, and is so impressed he challenges Meng himself, killing the master in combat with his bewitched sword.

Several of the students rush off to avenge their master, only to be cut down by Dare Devil, until Miss Meng wants to close the school to end the bloodshed. The outcast Kwan Chuen has been following Dare Devil, and also wants to challenge him, but a kindly monk dissuades him from acting rashly. While the students continue to lose their lives fighting Shao (and Lu loses an eye), Kwan keeps practicing his martial arts, but after three years still can't match Shao's supernatural power. Learning that Shao betrayed his own master Silver Crane Priest (Ngai So), Kwan journeys to a cave in the mountains to learn Shao's secrets from their source.

This early Joseph Kuo film bears all the marks of his future work, from the inexpensive yet visually impressive locations to the fun martial arts gimmicks. It's the usual revenge saga, but Kuo gives it enough style and attitude to make it one of his best films. An unwise technique is used to speed up the action in places, making it look a bit silly and momentarily disturbing the epic atmosphere. However, it's not enough to spoil the energetic, Japanese-influenced sword duels. *AKA: Gwai Gin Sau; Gui Jian Chou; Devils to Worry.* ♫♫♫ ▽

1970 90m/C *TW* Yee Yuen, Kong Ban, Cheung Ching-Ching, Ma Kei, Lei Chun, Ngai So, O Yau-man, Su Chen Ping, Lee Chi-lun, Hon Kong, So Gam-lung, Tin Ming, Woo Chau-ping, Wong Hung-cheung. *D:* Joseph Kuo. *W:* Yang Tong, Jiang Bing-han, Guo Hong-ting (story). *C:* Huang Rui-zhang. **DVD**

Sound from the Dark

A girl is found dead on the beach in Kowloon, and police detectives Locomotive, Rose, and Sesame write it off as a shark attack. But reporter DVD (Kathy Chow) finds a doll nearby, which oddly bears the same injuries as the corpse. A witch doctor tells her that the doll was used to summon ghosts. The police find a second corpse bitten to death. On the beach, DVD meets various folks who come there regularly. There's Nail, a dwarf who owns the doll—who is also a ventriloquist. Fanny, who jogs there every night. Mechanic Bald (Joey Man), whose girlfriend Milk Girl is serving time in prison for a crime Bald committed. And Gary, who is in trouble with his company because his girlfriend stole money from them. The next night, a girl drowns—inside her car. Sesame arrests and beats Nail, who curses him; subsequently, Sesame has a heart attack when he finds his apartment full of ghosts. The haunted beach is not just killing people, but seems to be draining energy from everyone there.

This movie will drain you, too. Another tired ghost movie from Tony Leung Hung-wah *(A Wicked Ghost),* it lacks any suspense at all, and just rambles on to the finish. There's not even any sex or gore to shock the thing to life. Nail admits to everyone that he's helping the ghosts kill, and even how they're doing it, but nobody does anything about it until over an hour into the film. Visually, the most interesting thing in the movie is the sight of a dwarf's head in a toilet, which is where the rest of this dull flick belongs. Even the ghosts sound bored. *AKA: Aau Fung Yee; Yin Feng Er.* ▽

2000 82m/C *HK* Kathy Chow, Joey Man, Wayne Lai, Stephanie Che, Lam Chi-ho. *D:* Tony Leung Hung-wah. *W:* Tony Leung Hung-wah. *C:* Yip Wai-ying. *M:* Simon Leung. **VHS, DVD**

Spacked Out

Early adolescence is a time of blinding confusion and emotion. It is captured quite authentically in *Spacked Out,* which focuses on four early-teenaged girls as they attempt to come to grips with the growing complexity of their lives. Cookie (Debbie Tam) is a girl who isn't living up to her potential and is a disappointment at school and at home. Her friends Sissy (Christy Cheung), Banana (Angela Au), and Bean Curd (Maggie Poon) face similar circumstances. Life is hard, the Hong Kong public educational system is inadequate to prepare anyone for adulthood, and family members are little help. The cards are stacked against the girls. In stark contrast, Yee (Vanesia Chu) is motivated and relatively privileged. Cookie and her friends fascinate her. They are everything she is not, and vice versa.

Director Lawrence Ah Mon and cinematographer Lai Yiu-fai give the film a quasi-documentary look but do not overdo the effect. In other words, it has a hand-held camera feel but not the irritating jerking back-and-forth that is the mark of a truly pretentious film. Most scenes are just the right length—they make their point and then get out of the way for the next scene. The four lead actresses are not too polished, and their sometimes amateurish performances work to the good. The screenplay by Yeung Sin-ling keeps the focus on the girls without wasting any time on their male companions, which is refreshing. Toward the end, director Lawrence Ah Mon becomes a bit heavy-handed in two sequences; they are extended, highly opinionated, and appear out of sorts with the tone previously established. The final scenes allow for recovery. Overall this is a very well-made and vital movie. —PM *AKA: Miu Yan Ga Sai; Wu Ren Jia Shi.* ♫♫♫

2000 90m/C *HK* Debbie Tam, Christy Cheung, Angela Au, Maggie Poon, Vanesia Chu, Lam Hoi Man. *D:* Lawrence Ah Mon. *W:* Yeung Sin-ling, Au Shui-lin, Rat. *C:* Lai Yiu-fai. *M:* A Lee-on, Leung Gei-cheuk, Yue Yat-yiu. **VHS, DVD**

Speed Racer: The Movie

Well, that title is a bit of an exaggeration. In 1993, the U.S. titleholders to the popular Japanese television cartoon show from the 1960s put together this compilation of three classic episodes, along with a few short odds and ends, to create a program for limited theatrical release called *The Speed Racer Show*. That people were willing to pay money to see a show that had been playing in TV syndication for a generation is testament to the popularity of the series.

Next to the original episode, "The Car Hater" is perhaps the best introduction to the series. It was still early enough in the series that a healthy amount of information about young racing driver Speed, the supporting cast, and his fabulous car the Mach 5, is easily woven into the story. This tale concerns a big galoot named Mr. Trotter, who has a violent hatred of autos. When his daughter Janine befriends Speed and his girlfriend Trixie, he goes off the deep end and hires men to rig a lot of cars to have accidents, to prove how dangerous they are.

One of the favorite episodes among fans is the two-part "Mammoth Car" episode. As Speed is about to start on the Unlimited Grand Prix, his Interpol pal Inspector Detector shows up to search all entries, on suspicion that one of them was involved in a huge gold robbery. One weird entry is the title vehicle, a locomotive-size segmented van, which succeeds in blowing most of the other cars off the road. Putting in an appearance here is the mysterious masked driver (and secret agent) Racer X.

The program even includes some rare animated commercial breaks, and there's an intermission "Colonel Bleep" cartoon from 1957. There's no use trying to describe this oddity, about an adventuring alien, his caveman and robot cowboy sidekicks, and the narrator who has the only dialogue—all rendered in an amazing googie cartoon style.

Based on the popular manga series *Mach Go Go Go!*, *Speed Racer* was among the first color anime series produced for television—and one of the most successful anime exports to the U.S., running on just about every market every weekday afternoon. The combination of action thrills and camp appeal—not to mention the coolest car in the world—became deeply ingrained in the nation's pop-culture consciousness, and the series still has a healthy cult following today. Plenty of other episodes are available on video—including a special limited edition complete box set—but this program is a great place to start.

(Avoid the revival series from the '90s.) **AKA:** *Mach Go Go Go!*. 🦴🦴🦴💧

1967 80m/C *JP* **V:** (English) Peter Fernandez, Jack Grimes, Corrine Orr, Jack Curtis. **W:** Tatsuo Yoshida. **M:** Nobuyoshi Koshibe. **VHS, DVD**

Spiral

This Japanese horror thriller captures the spirit of an H.P. Lovecraft story better than any other film. Kirie Goshima (Eriko Hatsune) is a typical schoolgirl in the mountain village of Kurozu. On her way to meet her moody boyfriend Shuichi Saito (Fhi Fan) after school, she sees his dad staring transfixed, videotaping the shell of a snail. Mr. Goshima has become a prize-winning potter, and Shuichi's dad (Ren Osugi) records him at work, requesting a spiral pattern platter. At school the next day, a schoolmate plummets down the shaft of a spiral staircase. Shuichi says the village is cursed by the uzumaki ("spirals"). His father has gone mad from the pattern, stealing the swirling beauty-salon sign, demanding spiral noodles in his miso soup, and even spinning his own eyes outrageously. The situation becomes increasingly surreal. A slow-moving student comes to class covered in slime, and seems to be growing a spiral hump on his back. Mr. Saito's obsession reaches its ultimate form with his unique suicide. At his funeral, smoke from the crematorium forms a huge spiraling cloud over the village. The incident gives Mrs. Saito (Keiko Takahashi) an extreme case of spirophobia, to the point that she can't stand the whorls in her own fingerprints. A reporter named Tamura (Masami Horiuchi) does some research, and theorizes the mystery has something to do with a serpent cult that operated in the area in ancient times. As faces appear in the clouds, and human begin to transform into huge snails, the number of spiromaniacs in town continues to increase, and Kurozu's spiral curse is bringing it to the edge of doom.

David Lynch meets David Cronenberg in Japan for this very creepy horror movie, whose only drawback is the ending, which leaves too much unresolved and begs for a sequel. Perhaps the original manga series continued the story. Ukrainian-born director Higuchinsky (Akihiro Higuchi) knows when to be subtle and when to pile on the shocks. Good use is made of digital effects—spirals are even added to the backgrounds of some scenes, swirling on the ground or a wall. Not to be confused with the 1998 *Ring* sequel *Rasen* ("The Spiral"). **AKA:** *Uzumaki; Vortex.* 🦴🦴🦴

2000 90m/C *JP* Eriko Hatsune, Fhi Fan, Ren Osugi, Hinako Saeki, Shin Eun-kyung, Keiko Takahashi, Denden, Masami Horiuchi, Taro Suwa, Sadao Abe, Yoshiyuki Tanno, Ganko Fuyu. **D:** Higuchinsky. **W:**

Takao Nitta, Junji Ito (manga). **C:** Gen Kobayashi. **M:** Keichi Suzuki, Tetsuro Kashibuchi. **VHS**

Spirited Away

To fully enjoy *Spirited Away,* one must undergo an exercise—or exorcism—spiriting away or pushing aside one's adult persona and set free your inner child. Yes, this sounds like pop-psych gobbledygook, and there'll be a struggle at the beginning. After all, the basic structure of Hayao Miyazaki's fantasy story is old and overused, which makes it natural to cling to your skepticism going in. But like Peter Jackson has done with *Lord of the Rings,* and MGM did long ago in *The Wizard of Oz,* Miyazaki grabs hold of you and pulls you in with his overpowering creativity and cinematic craftsmanship.

In the middle of a move to the suburbs, a family loses their way, ending up in what appears to be an abandoned amusement park of some kind. However, they find one food stand open, and while grumpy 10-year-old Chihiro wanders, her parents dig in to the glorious food. As the shadows of evening begin to fall, Chihiro discovers that her parents have literally become pigs, and they've all crossed over into some other world. Though terrified, she receives help from a boy named Haku who is thoroughly familiar with her new surroundings and promises to guide her past its dangers if he can. Through a series of adventures, it slowly becomes clear that Chihiro is now trapped in a vacation retreat for all the gods in the universe, and she gets a job in the gigantic bathhouse run by the terrible sorceress Yubaba. The boss takes away her human name, giving her the new name "Sen" and the worst job available: cleaning up a visiting Stink God (actually a polluted River God). Sen survives this trial, but admits spectral visitor No-Face, who soon turns into a ravenous monster of greed and gluttony. Through her adventures, Sen holds on to the hope of rescuing her parents—a hope overshadowed by the threat of forgetting her own identity. Her predicament gets even more desperate when she finds that Haku is in danger, too, having been sent on a mission against Yubaba's twin sister Kamaji.

The most obvious parallel here is to Lewis Carroll's adventures of Alice, which threw a little girl into a frightening world of monsters ruled by a mad queen. But while the Alice books were steeped in British culture, *Spirited Away* is completely Japanese. The characters and settings all draw from Japanese folklore and traditions, including all the spooks and creatures inhabiting the bathhouse. Another difference is that the world of *Spirited Away* seems to work on more than Carroll's dream logic—"rules are rules," as Yubaba points out—supported by Miyazaki's deeply detailed backgrounds and believable characters. The result is that the viewer can become entranced by this fantasy world, in danger of losing one's identity there as easily as Chihiro becomes Sen. **AKA:** *Sen to Chihiro no Kamikakushi; Sen; Sen and the Mysterious Disappearance of Chihiro; Le Voyage de Chihiro.* 𝕃𝕃𝕃𝕃

2001 (PG) 124m/C JP **D:** Hayao Miyazaki. **W:** Hayao Miyazaki. **M:** Jo Hisaishi, Yumi Kimura. **VHS, DVD**

Spiritual Kung Fu

The plot of this film is similar to many other early Jackie Chan films: Chan is the lazy "fool" who through luck and perseverance becomes a kung fu master by the end of the last reel. In *Spiritual Kung Fu,* Jackie is a student at the Shaolin Temple, trying to learn kung fu while expending the least amount of effort possible. Naturally, this gets him into the usual trouble with the temple masters. And, as in many of Chan's early films, Jackie must overcome his initial goofiness to save the day. While he struggles with the usual torturous kung fu training rituals, a black-robed figure sneaks into the temple and steals a book of forbidden kung fu secrets—the nearly invincible and very deadly book of Seven Fists. Only someone who knows the Five Style Fists can hope to defeat the Seven Fist technique. Unfortunately, the secrets of the Five Style Fists have been lost. No one practices those styles, and no one knows where to find the original manuscript teaching the techniques. The theft of the Seven Fist secrets sends the temple into turmoil. The warlord who stole the book intends to use it to conquer the other local clans and then overthrow the temple itself. One would think things couldn't get worse for Jackie and the monks when, suddenly, the temple is overrun with restless ghosts.

The red-haired spirits look like mimes and behave like poltergeists; they like to throw things around and play pranks. Jackie is the only student not afraid of the ghosts. Because of this, the ghosts come to trust him with their secrets—including the location of the lost Book of Five Style Fists. (It seems the spirits don't want the temple overthrown.) The five ghosts—masters of the Five Fists—help teach Jackie the techniques described in the book. (Thus, "Spiritual Kung Fu.") As this is going on, it becomes apparent that there is a traitor within the temple—either one of the monks, or one of the refugees who have come there to escape the rampaging warlord. Jackie's love interest Misha and an abbot are wrongfully accused of being traitors, and are forced to flee the temple. Natu-

rally, they can't stay out of the way of the Warlord. Jackie intervenes, but the two fight to a draw. Jackie and the warlord agree to meet for a final battle within the Shaolin Temple walls. Can Jackie's styles of Dragon, Snake, Tiger, Crane, and Leopard overcome the dreaded Seven Fist technique? Will the traitor be revealed before it is too late? Have the spirits chosen their champion wisely?

When producer Lo Wei gave Jackie Chan permission to make a kung fu comedy, he didn't think the resulting film *(Half a Loaf of Kung Fu)* was funny, and shelved it, deciding he'd show Chan what was funny with this comedy. Unfortunately, by the time *Spiritual* was finished, Lo was in financial trouble and couldn't release it. But luckily Chan became a star soon after, setting loose his movies from captivity. The variety of kung fu and weapon styles used in this film make it more interesting than the standard early Jackie Chan flick. The settings, costumes, and other production values are pretty good, and the story has just enough twists to keep things from getting boring. The classic comic scenes of Jackie catching frogs for dinner and putting them in his pants (for later) appear in this film, as well as in a few other Chan movies. The rest of the comedy is pretty good, if somewhat predictable to those who have seen other early Chan films. Large sections of the film's music are ripped off from the classic *Golden Voyage of Sinbad* score, by Miklos Rozsa. —SS **AKA:** *Kuen Cheng; Quan Jing; Karate Ghostbuster; Karate Bomber.* 🐉🐉🐉

1978 (PG) 94m/C *HK* Jackie Chan, James Tien, Dean Shek, Lee Kwan, Lee Man Tai, Wong Kwong-yue, Wong Ching, Yuen Biao. **D:** Lo Wei. **W:** Poon Lui. **C:** Yueng Luen. **M:** Chong Pak. **VHS, DVD**

Star Force: Fugitive Alien 2

Starwolf Ken (Tatsuya Azuma), hard-drinkin' Captain Joe (Joe Shishido), Rocky (Choei Takahashi), Tammy (Miyuki Tanigawa), and the rest of the crew of the starfighter *Bacchus 3* return in another feature hacked together from episodes of Tsuburaya Productions' *Star Wolf* TV series. On a mission to intercept a new and dangerous weapon, they have to travel close to a black hole, but come out of it only to be trapped in the gravity field of a star about to go nova. While attempting to deliver rescued prisoner Colonel Yurulin to his home planet, the Bacchus crew finds itself under attack instead. They make a rough landing on the planet, and it's revealed that the bomb they're looking for is in a secret installation on the planet, and is set to go off soon—unless they blow it up first. In next week's exciting episode, an Earth scientist invents a planet-killer bomb of his own, and the crew is asked to pick up the plans. The enemy sends a spy to Earth disguised as Ken's mother, so the crew heads off to try to kill the evil enemy Commander Halkon all by themselves.

Tsuburaya's special-effects techniques were outdated by the late 1970s, but are nevertheless fun to watch. However, they can't lift this routine derivative space opera above the mediocre. The climax contains shots swiped directly from *Star Wars: A New Hope* and *The Empire Strikes Back*. **AKA:** *Star Force.* 🐉🐉

1978/86 75m/C *JP* Tatsuya Azuma, Miyuki Tanigawa, Joe Shishido, Choei Takahashi, Tsutomu Yukawa, Hiro Tateyama. **D:** Kiyosumi Fukazawa, Minoru Kanaya. **W:** Keichi Abe, Bunzou Wakatsuki, Yoshisa Araki, Hiroyasu Yamaura. **M:** Norio Maeda. **VHS**

Sting of the Dragon Masters

This early Golden Harvest production tried to follow the gold mine of Bruce Lee's kung fu with the taekwondo of champion Master Jhoon Rhee. As in Lee's *The Chinese Connection,* an aggressive Japanese martial arts school causes trouble, this time while Japanese forces occupy Korea. Seoul church gardener Lee Chung-tung (Jhoon Rhee) has been teaching Father Lewis's niece Mary (Anne Winton) and others the art of taekwondo. When his student Kin (Carter Wong) attempts to rescue the captive women secretly kept at the Yokahoma School, he's discovered and inadvertently leads to Lee being spotted. Since Lee is a leader of the rebels, the situation quickly escalates until Lee and his students have to flee to their mountain camp. Lee asks his friend, Korean-raised Chinese waitress Wan Ling-ching (Angela Mao), to find out how Father Lewis (André Morgan) is doing. At the church, she finds out Lewis is being held prisoner at Yokahoma School—a front for the Japanese Secret Service—but has to kill some Japanese with her aikido skills to escape with the information. Having become a target for the Japanese, Wan joins the rebels to fight alongside Lee. However, the villains are holding the priest hostage, demanding Lee's surrender in 24 hours. Lee is captured while trying to save Lewis, and the Japanese use him to try to catch his students, who have fled to Manchuria.

Jhoon Rhee's martial arts ability is terrific, and he has a pleasant personality, but he doesn't exactly light up the screen as a movie star. Fortunately, Angela Mao has enough sparkle for the both of them, quickly taking over as star of the picture. Young Sammo Hung appears in a supporting role as Yokahoma's right-hand man, who gets bit on the leg by Anne Winton. Director

Wong Fung does a good job of keeping the simple story moving between fights, sometimes using Angela Mao's eyes as a focal point to spice things up—in close-ups, or reflected in a sword blade. There must have been some fun on the set the day André Morgan, a Golden Harvest producer and occasional actor, was stripped to the waist and whipped. The soundtrack borrows cues from Bernard Herrmann's *North by Northwest* score. *AKA: Toi Kuen Jan Gau Chow; Tai Quan Zhen Jiu Zhou; When Taekwondo Strikes; Kickmaster.* 🎵🎵🖤

1973 (R) 95m/C *HK* Jhoon Rhee, Angela Mao, Carter Wong, Whang In Shik, Kenji Kazama, Anne Winton, André Morgan, Chin San, Chin Yuet Sang, Sammo Hung, Chan Chuen, Gam Kei Chu, Alan Chui, Wilson Tong, Wong Fung, Tsang Choh-lam, Billy Chan, Lam Ching-Ying, Yuen Biao. *D:* Wong Fung. *W:* Wong Fung, Hu Yu. *C:* Yu Tang. *M:* Shaohua. **VHS, DVD**

The Storm Riders

Lord Conquer (Sonny Chiba) rules the roost of the Martial Arts World from his mountaintop stronghold, crushing all opposition with a combination of kung fu muscle and magic. He kills sword master Striding Sky (Yu Rongguang) and takes his son Striding Cloud. Having already stolen the wife of Whispering Prince (Alex Fong), Conquer returns to duel with him for his flaming sword. Conquer kills him and takes away his son Whispering Wind. Wind (Ekin Cheng) and Cloud (Aaron Kwok) are raised as Conquer's disciples, not knowing the true fate of their parents, to become powerful martial artists. But Conquer has had a prophecy revealed by the mystic Mud Buddha (Wayne Lai)—one that foretells his fall when the powers of Wind and Cloud combine. Conquer suspects that Cloud has fallen in love with his daughter Charity (Kristy Yeung). To drive a wedge between the disciples, he promises Charity to (her half-brother!) Wind in marriage. Enraged, Cloud stalks off to find a sword powerful enough to challenge Conquer. Confused and suspicious, Wind goes off to fight the Flaming Dragon and learn the truth about his father's death. The wedding happens to be planned just when Conquer's appointment to duel his archenemy Sword Saint (Anthony Wong) is due. All come together in a mighty clash of titans.

Somewhat a swordplay version of *X-Men*, *Storm Riders* was the first Hong Kong film to make extensive use of digital special effects. The gamble paid off for Golden Harvest, as the feature went on to be the top-grossing HK film of the decade. It would have been an even bigger hit, but video pirates seriously damaged its earnings. Kwok and Cheng spend a bit too much time standing about looking pretty, but Chiba manages to outshine the f/x with his performance, creating a rich and complex character. Based on a comic-book series by Ma Wing Shing, the film mixes together dozens of colorful characters, most of which have super powers, in a beautiful fantasy setting. Realized through wonderfully designed f/x, all the outrageous excess that Hong Kong cinema revels in is set loose—castles in the sky, fire monkeys, arm transplants, dragons, wind fists, etc. The Western world is just beginning to explore the possibilities of the digital medium that makes everything imaginable attainable on film. The Hong Kong film industry has been struggling greatly since 1997, but look for them to come roaring back with more features like this one. The U.S. version may be missing up to a half hour of footage. *AKA: Fung Wan Hung Ba Tin Gwong; Feng Yun Xiong Ba Tian Xia; Feng Yun.* 🎵🎵🎵🖤

1998 (PG-13) 128m/C *HK* Sonny Chiba, Aaron Kwok, Ekin Cheng, Kristy Yeung, Anthony Wong, Wayne Lai, Alex Fong, Yu Rongguang, Michael Tse, Shu Qi, Lawrence Cheng, Jason Chu, Vincent Wan, Roy Cheung, Elvis Tsui, Lee Siu-Kei. *D:* Andrew Lau. *W:* Chau Ting, Manfred Wong. *C:* Andrew Lau. *M:* Comfort Chan. **VHS, DVD**

The Story in Temple Red Lily

If you believe the kung fu flicks, corruption ran rampant through the government of ancient China. The bad guys in this opus are the Baron and his forces, and the good guys are the devotees of the Red Lotus—a kung fu family headed by blue-garbed warrior Siu Ching (Delon Tan) and kung fu chick Hung Ku (Judy Lee). The baron's forces, bolstered by an evil lama and his men, have taken over the Red Lily Temple in their campaign to steal the throne and wipe out the local rebels. The loyalists are trying to make sure the young prince comes to power before the villains can kill him. Naturally this leads to a number of ambush-related battles and standard kung foolery, including a climactic battle at the temple between the good and evil monks and their related factions.

This film is very reminiscent of marginal Italian gladiator pictures in both its plot and its execution. The direction is choppy and seems devoid of any real master plan. Thus, the simplistic story is more confusing than it needs to be, and the confusion is enhanced by using similar costumes and makeup for a number of similar-looking characters. Portions of the music for this film were lifted from the amazing score to *Journey to the Center of the Earth,* by Bernard Herrmann. The fighting in the film is fairly pedestrian, despite a brief appearance by a magic eagle, some odd bell-like weapons, a magic rope, and a razor-edged hat used by the evil lama. A complete list of the film's elements would make the flick seem far more interesting than it actually is. Its big failing is that the director just never seems to pull it all together. —SS **AKA:** *Feng Shiu Hung Lin Chi; Huo Shao Gong Lian Si.* 🎵🎵🎵

1979 87 m/C *HK* Judy Lee, Delon Tan, Lung Fei, Wang Li, Tse Ling-Ling, Yee Yuen, Tung Li, Kao Yuen, Su Chen Ping, Ma Kei, Tai Leung, Cho Kin, Ricky Cheng, Man Man, Ching Kuo-chung, Hei Ying, Tong Kar-chun, Au Yeung-chung, Cheung Fong-ha, Chiu Ting, Cheung Yee-kwai, Cheung Bo-sin, Au Lap-bo. **D:** Karl Liao. **W:** Gai Ming. **VHS, DVD**

Story of the Dragon

Bob Lee (Bruce Li) works as a waiter in San Francisco's Chinatown with his friend Ching, where he teaches some unruly customers not to abuse the people who handle your food. Unwilling to kowtow to some local martial arts students (led by Roy Horan), the pair get fired. The thugs come to start trouble at their new jobs, working for meat importer Mr. Kow, but are driven off by Kow's nephew Liu (Carter Wong), while Bob and Ching are labeled "chicken." But the thugs work for big syndicate boss Mr. Grace (Robert Kerver), and when they go crying to him, the San Francisco Iron Fist Man (also known as "Bob") is sent to beat the boys up. This time, Bob fights back, becoming a hero, and the workers encourage him to open his own kung fu school. Angered by Bob's decision to allow non-Chinese into his classes, Liu represents the established kung fu schools and challenges him to a match. After their match, Bob succeeds in winning Liu over to his way of thinking. But the conflict with Mr. Grace's gang continues to escalate. After Bob refuses a buy-out, Asian champ Chin Yung-chi (Hwang Jang Lee, in a silly wig) is called in, and beats up both Liu and Bob. While the top Chinese fighters lick their wounds, Grace's thugs make moves to take over the docks again. Bob's defeat teaches him to be adaptable and fluid, and he trains intensely for a rematch with Chin.

Though largely fictionalized, this is not much less accurate than the Hollywood version of the Bruce Lee story told in *Dragon*. It only condenses the message into a simple conflict. "Bob" doesn't develop his new fighting style until the third act, so much of the fighting is lackluster until Li breaks out his full, nose-thumbing Lee impression. Poorly shot, this is nevertheless an entertaining little film. Li's final match with perennial villain Hwang Jang Lee (in modern dress for once) is nicely choreographed, and his assault on Grace's estate gives him plenty of long-haired American hippies to hit. **AKA:** *Wing Chun Daai Fong; Yang Chun da Xiong; Bruce Lee's Deadly Kung Fu; Bruce Lee's Secret;*

Bruce Lee's Jeet Kune Do; A Dragon Story; He's a Legend, He's a Hero. 🎵🎵🎵

1976 91m/C *HK/TW/US* Bruce Li, Carter Wong, Chin Chi Min, Hwang Jang Lee, Paul Wei, Chu Chi Ming, Robert Kerver, Roy Horan. **D:** Wong Sing-liu. **W:** Chang Hsin Yee, Chen Wah. **C:** Chang Seng-yi. **M:** Chou Fu-liang. **VHS, DVD**

Stray Dog

Toshiro Mifune is Detective Murakami, a wet-behind-the-ears policeman who, during a long, hot summer, loses his gun—a seven-shot Colt pistol. The problem would be troublesome in the U.S., but in post-war Japan—where guns are carefully controlled—it's very serious indeed. Murakami offers to resign, but his chief will have none of it. He must work to solve this problem himself, the chief says. Murakami delves into the underbelly of the city to try and track down his missing weapon. In a mug book he sees a pickpocket woman who may have taken it. The woman puts him onto some black-market pistol dealers. This, in turn, leads him to another woman, who helps her boyfriend "rent" guns to those in need. Murakami arrests the woman, but she's not very helpful to the police.

Meanwhile, Murakami discovers that his gun has been used in a robbery. The female victim was wounded and all her savings stolen. Murakami's feelings of guilt and responsibility become overwhelming. He tries to resign again, but—instead—his boss puts him under the direction of wise Detective Sato (Takashi Shimura). Despite Murakami's melancholy, he and Sato make a good team. They arrest the gun broker and he reveals the name of the man he rented the Colt to: Shinjo Yusa. Yusa, though, is tricky to track down. Another robbery is committed, and this time a woman is killed. Murakami's feelings of responsibility deepen, and he confesses that—in some ways—he is very similar to the robber. Both returned from WWII to bad prospects and little hope. Sato says that Murakami has bettered himself, where Yusa has only drifted deeper into darkness. There are five bullets left in the stolen gun—five more lives that could be shattered. Sato knows that they will only catch this "mad dog" by pounding the pavement and doing basic detective work.

Sato hits the streets, while Murakami applies pressure to Harumi. Just as the girl's mother helps break down Harumi's resistence, Sato discovers Yusa's hiding place—a ratty hotel. Yasu discovers the older detective and tries to escape. The ensuing gun battle leaves Sato near death. Without his mentor, Murakami is nearly at a loss. Not only that, but he agonizes that his weapon caused Sato's potentially fatal wounds. He must now track down Yusa on his own. His time with Sato has served him well, though. Using basic detective techniques, he soon finds Yusa, and the final confrontation begins.

Stray Dog is Kurosawa's film noir detective picture. He's studied the genre and does it as well as any anyone ever has. The conventions that fans expect are there, as well as Kurosawa's own spin on the traditions. The director's love of composition and cinematography are as prominent as ever—though perhaps a bit less developed as in his later films. Mifune and Shimura give top-flight performances, as usual. The hot summer in Tokyo setting will also be a nice change of pace for U.S. detective film fans. We even get a glimpse at post-war Japanese baseball. While not as well known as some of Kurosawa's other flicks, *Stray Dog* is still a gem by a great director. —SS **AKA:** *Nora Inu.* 🐉🐉🐉🐉

1949 122m/BW *JP* Toshiro Mifune, Takashi Shimura, Keiko Awaji, Eiko Miyoshi, Noriko Sengoku, Eijiro Tono, Katsuhei Matsumoto, Isao Kimura, Minoru Chiaki, Ichiro Sugai, Gen Shimizu, Masao Shimizu, Kokuten Kodo, Yunosuke Ito, Haruko Togo, Haruko Toyama, Ishiro Honda. **D:** Akira Kurosawa. **W:** Akira Kurosawa, Ryuzo Kikushima. **C:** Asaichi Nakai. **M:** Fumio Hayasake. **VHS**

The Street Fighter

With the Bruce Lee movies storming theatres throughout the world, Toei Studios of Japan was determined to cash in with their own martial arts star. But *The Street Fighter,* in the person of action star Sonny Chiba, wouldn't just be another Bruce Lee clone—their antihero would be even more anti- than Dirty Harry, a sadistic killer dealing out brutal punishment in the name of his own code of justice. Of course, in between crushing skulls and castrating foes with his bare hands, the Street Fighter would show his softer side (but not too often).

Junjo Shikenbaru (Musashi Ishibashi), a psycho-killer karate man in a Tokyo prison, is awaiting execution, when mercenary Terry Tsurugi (Chiba) sneaks in disguised as a priest. He applies a secret karate technique to the prisoner that simulates a heart attack, after which he and his assistant Ratnose (Gerald Yamada) easily abduct him from the ambulance. But the poor brother and sister who hired Tsurugi for the jailbreak mission can't pay up, so he teaches them a painful lesson. Having demonstrated his iron heart, Tsurugi moves on to his next assignment.

Sarai Hamed (Doris Nakajima) has inherited a vast oil fortune. Miss Yeung and Mr. Leung from Hong Kong want to hire Terry to kidnap her, despite protection from her uncle's entire karate school. Not liking their terms, Terry refuses, which earns him the enmity of the yakuza.

Angered, he offers his services to Sarai as bodyguard. The mob sends the deadliest martial artist assassins in the East to kill him and kidnap the heiress. Meanwhile, Junjo, having discovered his sister sold into slavery in Hong Kong, vows vengeance on Tsurugi as well.

The Street Fighter became a worldwide sensation (and an early hit for New Line Cinema in the U.S.), shocking audiences with its over-the-top violence—all in Eastmancolor and "Actionscope"! Chiba, mugging fiercely while giving broken arms an extra little twist, is an action fan's dream come true. Though a legion of fans have lavished just praise on Chiba for his hard-as-nails screen persona, director Shigehiro Ozawa's contribution is often overlooked. He does an expert job in all capacities, filming fight scenes from numerous imaginative angles, and giving the various duels a mythic quality. He also invented the outrageous "X-ray shot" to show the damage inflicted by Tsurugi's blows. Jack Sholder, future director of *The Hidden,* is credited with the exploding English title sequence. **AKA:** *Gekitatsu! Satsujim-ken.* 🐉🐉🐉🐉

1974 91m/C *JP* Sonny Chiba, Gerald Yamada, Doris Nakajima, Masafumi Suzuki, Tony Cetera, Teijo Shikeharo, King Stone, Musashi Ishibashi, Akira Shioji, Yusuf Osman, Angel Cordero, Bin Amatsu, Jiro Chiba, Sue Shiomi, Fumio Watanabe. **D:** Shigehiro Ozawa. **W:** Koji Takada, Steve Autrey. **C:** Ken Tsukakoshi. **M:** Toshiaki Tsushima. **VHS, DVD**

Street Fighter 2

This half-hour anime TV series based on a popular Capcom arcade video game (not the 1970s Sonny Chiba movies) does a good job of weaving a story connecting all of the game's characters, rather than just one face-off after another.

Japanese Ryu visits his rich American buddy Ken Masters in San Francisco. The boys get into a bar fight that night—and both get their asses kicked by an Air Force officer named Guile. This inspires them to go on a worldwide quest to see how many other guys around the world can beat them up. The plan sounds crazy, until you consider that Ken is rich enough to pay for all their travel expenses and hospital bills.

First stop on their tour: Hong Kong, where Ken checks them into a luxury suite. There, a mystic tells Ryu that a great secret power hides within him, and gives him a nice wall hanging. Their tour guide Chun Li successfully guides them into trouble, taking them into the most dangerous part of town. Luckily, she's been trained to be a pretty good street fighter herself by her father Dorai, a police inspector.

"So I'm to die because I know who it is that controls the yakuza here. Isn't that mean and nasty? You see what fun this is? It's going to get really exciting!"

—Ultratough street fighter Terry Tsurugi tells it like it is in *The Street Fighter*

THE HOUND SALUTES
Sonny Chiba
Direct Hit!

Shinichi "Sonny" Chiba is Japan's biggest action star (well, except for Godzilla). He has appeared in well over 100 films and numerous television series in a career that spans six decades, and he's still going strong. From *Invasion of the Neptune Men* to *Kill Bill,* he has graced the screen in a wide variety of roles, from scientist to detective, from yakuza to engineer, and from starship captain to samurai. But if Sonny Chiba only played one role in his life, he would still be an action-cinema immortal; that role is Takuma "Terry" Tsurugi, the tougher-than-tough antihero of *The Street Fighter.*

Chiba was already an action icon in Japan when he was cast in *Street Fighter.* Born Sadao Maeda, he had a Black Belt in several forms of Japanese self-defense, starred in two TV series (performing superhero hijinks in *Ironsharp* and private eye derring-do in *Key Hunter*), gone undercover as *Gangster Cop,* and submerged himself in *Terror beneath the Sea.* In 1969 he formed the Japan Action Club to train and promote movie stuntmen and actors.

But *Street Fighter,* made in the wake of Bruce Lee's death as an attempt by Toei Studios to get in on the worldwide martial arts craze, was one of his first assignments to take advantage of Chiba's physical skills and considerable screen presence. (Actually, Chiba and Lee were supposed to make a film together, but before they both could rearrange their schedules, Lee had already died.) Chiba is simply hypnotic in this film—you don't know whether he's a noble man driven too far or just a homicidal maniac unleashed at last. We'd seen Bruce Lee do some amazing things, but it's doubtful Lee would make a movie in which he'd be called upon to tear out throats or punch through an opponent's chest. The film's plot is simple and unchallenging, but watching it is more akin to a fireworks display than a movie—you just bide your time between Chiba's explosions.

Chiba went on to star in many more films and television series, and while nothing he did ever had the worldwide impact of *The Street Fighter,* even after he moved to Los Angeles, he is still respected by his fans for his body of work. He only made one real mistake: in 1990 he invested $10 million of his own money into producing, directing, and co-starring (with his regular co-star Henry Sanada) in *Yellow Fangs* (AKA *Remains: Beautiful Heroes*), a film based on a true story about a killer bear that terrified a village in the 1920s. The movie got good reviews, but the public hated it, and it only got minimal exposure in the U.S. under the title *Karate Bear Fighter*. The picture cost him much of his personal fortune, and he had to sell off a lot of property to cover losses. He appears to have helped recover by appearing in a string of American direct-to-video flicks like *Iron Eagle 3* and *Immortal Combat*.

Sonny Chiba has slowed down quite a bit compared to his breakneck (pun intended) schedule in the 1970s, but due to the renewed exposure of his films on cable TV and DVD, he's picked up a fresh generation of fans and is more in demand than ever. Chiba went to Hong Kong to make some films, including *Storm Riders* and *Legend of the Flying Swordsman*, graces the cast of Quentin Tarantino's all-star tribute to '70s action flicks, *Kill Bill,* and may face off against 007 in the next James Bond adventure.

From there, they get involved in shooting a movie, bust up a Thai drug ring, visit an Indian shrine, enter a Barcelona bullring, fight monsters, learn a variety of new martial arts techniques, and endure many beatings. Throughout their adventures, they meet new fighting champions against whom they can test their skills.

The series features great theme music, addictive continuity, and some fine martial arts fight scenes, though the limited animation sometimes makes various moves too repetitive. This may be the first anime TV series with an action director (Shinchi Tokairin). Though shown on TV in Japan, *Street Fighter 2* is often much too gruesome for U.S. broadcast. Not only are the fight scenes brutal, but some episodes feature torture, and one has a villain fond of collecting the arms of his enemies. Despite these elements of direct-to-video action-movie sleaze, because of the pure-hearted heroes, the general atmosphere is closer to that of the Hardy Boys. The English dub goes a bit overboard in Americanizing everyone's speech, but it's likely the original dialogue Japanizes just as much. *AKA: Street Fighter 2 V; Street Fighter 2 Victory.* 🐉🐉🐲

1996 24m per episode/C *JP* **V:** (English) Rob Thomas, Melissa Williamson, Steve Bulen, David Lucas, Alfred Thor. **V:** (Japanese) Koji Tsujitani, Kenji Haga, Chisa Yokoyama. **D:** Gisaburo Sugii. **W:** Kenichi Imai, Naoyuki Sakai. **C:** Katsuya Kozutsumi. **M:** Mike Egan. **VHS, DVD**

The Street Fighter's Last Revenge

Striking workers and protesters riot at a Tokyo chemical plant over pollution and dangerous conditions, but what's really going on is worse— yakuza drug lord Seigen Owada (Eizo Kitamura) is using the plant as a front for their heroin business. His brother Go (Akira Shioji) hires mercenary Terry Tsuguri (Sonny Chiba) to get his brother and a black bag out of the besieged plant. Foolishly, his clients try to double-cross Tsuguri (yes, the dubbers pronounce his name "soo-goo-ree" this time), starting a brawl. The bad guys call on kung fu fighter Pearl (Sue Shiomi, *Sister Street Fighter*) to keep him busy while they escape, but Terry taunts her about secretly working for the District Attorney's office. He gets his revenge later (but not his last revenge), breaking into their offices and stealing a tape containing a formula for synthetic heroin.

"I think that dress would look better off."

—Sonny Chiba does some sweet talking in *The Street Fighter's Last Revenge*

Yakuza Aya (Reiko Ike) makes a blind date with Terry to propose a deal for the tape—and he comes dressed as a vampire! The bad guys, including a Mexican with psychic powers called Mr. Black (Frankie Black), ambush Terry in bed. Terry escapes, but the crooked D.A. actually gets the best of him and takes the tape from him. Needing to brush up, Terry visits Master Masaoka (Masafumi Suzuki), who tells him that the D.A. used a style called "seismic wave." He takes this as a perfect cue to go into the same black-and-white flashback to his childhood seen in every *Street Fighter* movie. His little training session gives Terry just the edge he needs—to sneak up and punch the D.A. in the back.

In this less gritty episode in the series, the Street Fighter has a nifty gadget-laden pad, complete with a secret closet full of disguises. With all the parties trying to manipulate each other for the formula—police, yakuza, the D.A., and various traitors within each organization—with Tsuguri in the middle, it's almost as if this were *The Maltese Falcon* with some martial arts written into the script. Director Teruo Ishii gives the final duel some style and spirit, but the film lacks the essential attitude that sets the Street Fighter apart from other movie heroes. *AKA: Gayakushu! Satsujim-ken; Revenge! The Killing Fist; Street Fighter Counterattacks.* 🐾🐾🐾

1974 (R) 91m/C *JP* Sonny Chiba, Sue Shiomi, Masafumi Suzuki, Reiko Ike, Frankie Black, Willy Dosey, Eizo Kitamura, Fuyuki Murakami, Koji Wada, Gerald Yamada, Akira Shioji. **D:** Teruo Ishii. **W:** Koji Takada, Steve Autrey. **C:** Ken Tsukakoshi. **M:** Toshiaki Tsushima. **VHS, DVD**

Succubare

Heard the one about the traveling salesman? On his rounds, Chang Hai-yo visits his girlfriend, who is one of four princesses in the remote mountain region of Miyo. The princesses are forbidden to leave the snake-infested mountain, but he promises to return in 100 days. But the only returning he does is to wife and kids, leaving the princess pregnant. The witch princesses put a curse on him, and Hai-yo turns into a vampire psycho, his house is filled with snakes and centipedes, and he attacks his wife. Next day, his belly swells up. When younger brother Chang Chun-Yu returns from medical school, he suggests an exploratory operation. They find his belly full of snakes, and Hai-yo dies.

Chun-Yu rides to Miyo to seek the antidote to the princess's poison. He encounters guardsman Shun-Tai (Carter Wong), and is captured. Intoxicated with cheap Miyo booze, Chun-Yu molests the princess bearing his nephew. She curses him and sends him running. Because she let him escape, the princess has to serve

his sentence for him, and is locked up. Remaining brother Chang Chi-Hu (Ang Fung), posing as a "professional traveler," journeys to Miyo with his servants Hadi (Ko Siao Pao) and Yung Lo. He and Princess Yinna (Booi Dai) start to fall for each other, though he tries to resist. Though jealous Shun-Tai fights him, Chi-Hu is allowed to leave, but goes home with a spell that threatens his whole village.

Succubare is an illustration of the kind of horror story they used to tell sailors to reduce the spread of venereal disease—infected on a journey by a dalliance with a foreign woman, the young man returns home with a disgusting infection, which is eventually spread to the family. The English distributor probably found the title in the dictionary and thought it sounded sexy. Not particularly well edited to begin with, the U.S. release is a choppy mess, cut to highlight the mondo footage of gruesome animal sacrifice, snake handling, bug vomiting, and geek acts. *AKA: Sau Saan Goo Lui; She Shan Gu Nu; The Princess and the Toxicant; Magic of the Shaolin Sorceress.* 🐾

1977 83m/C *HK* Carter Wong, Booi Dai, Ang Fung, Got Heung Ting, Chin Chi Min, Ko Yuan, Ko Siao Pao, Chi Yan, Zhao Lei. **VHS**

Sugar—Howling of Angel

This revenge tale is another entry in Japan's wave of female-assassin pictures that became popular in the mid-1990s. After her husband and child are killed, Chie Kogure (Makiko Kuno) is kept prisoner, hooked on heroin, and made into a prostitute. When she helps customer Ryuya Yaki defend himself from some attackers, he takes her with him and cracks her addiction. Yaki takes her as an apprentice in his business as a professional killer. Taking the professional name Sugar, she begins carrying out assassinations for the yakuza. Meanwhile, the police are investigating the Kogure murder and searching for her. When Yaki has to go abroad, he leaves Sugar in the care of yakuza underling Tetsuji and his wife Hikawa, telling them not to let Sugar take any assignments while he's gone. But when the boss asks her to kill Shuji, one of her family's killers, she can't resist. She kidnaps Shuji for a torture session first to find out who ordered the murders. She learns her husband's boss Sasashima ordered the hit to keep the company's illegal business a secret, and she begins to plot revenge against them. But she finds out some other secrets besides. It could do with some decent action sequences, but the focus of this cost-conscious production is on dull melodrama and tame sex scenes, bypassing anything more ambitious. 🐾🐾

1996 79m/C *JP* Makiko Kuno, Kaori Sakagami, Daisuke Ishiyama. *D:* Akinobu Ishiyama. **DVD**

Sumo Vixens

Sex comedies became very popular in Japan during the 1990s, and actress Kei Mizutani *(Weather Woman)* is their still-reigning queen, starring topless in a string of very silly pictures that have gained a cult following worldwide. From the director of the notorious *Urotsukidoji* anime series comes this much lighter shot-on-video feature. In a scene swiped directly from *The Blues Brothers* (a huge hit in Japan), Zenjiro Arakuma (Arase, a former real-life sumo champ turned actor/politician) is released from prison after serving five years for pushing a Mercedes full of yakuza into the river. His assistant, politically correct yakuza Tonpachi, comes to pick him up. Former sumo champ Auntie Kumiyo (Eba), who wrestled under the name Yokozuna Wakazakura, still dreams of her days in the ring, when she supported her whole family through hard times. Inspired, her sweet "niece" (who is unknowingly Kumiyo's real daughter) Ruriko Sakura comes to Arakuma asking him to train her to wrestle. Her family owes a lot to the loan shark Domino Agency, and she needs to find some way to raise cash. To help Ruriko and Kumiyo, and to make money for himself, Arakuma agrees to open a training academy. At first, the only recruits they can get are some sorry hookers. Training begins, the soundtrack striking up the Wong Fei-hung theme. Tough chick Komasa "Joshu" Akagi (Kei Mizutani) comes to join the dojo, "seeking enlightenment." Pro sumo Gentetsu visits as a guest instructor, but though the other girls fail to budge him, Akagi is strong enough to flip him. She also has no trouble beating up the Domino thugs who come to call. A beauty named One-eyed Oryu (Shoko Kudo) and her pair of henchwomen offer their services, and the Domino Agency opens their own dojo. They challenge Arakuma to a match winner-take-all (including his beloved Ruriko). Oryu has set the whole thing up to get back at her ex-girlfriend Akagi for breaking up with her.

The DVD version includes an informative guide to the basics of sumo. This helps a bit, as there are plenty of gags and references that pass by Westerners and non-fans of the sport. There is some pretty rough action as sex films go—Mizutani shows a few bruises. While a strictly exploitative exercise, *Sumo Vixens* overcomes its cheapness with a healthy sense of good dirty fun. Nokuta! Nokuta! *AKA: Sexy Lady Sumo.* 🐉🐉🐉

1996 74m/C *JP* Arase, Kei Mizutani, Shoko Kudo, Kyoko Nakamura, Keisuke, Eba, Aya Koizumi. *D:* Takao Nakano. *W:* Takao Nakano. *C:* Hideki Hasegawa. *M:* Hiroaki Yabunaka. **VHS, DVD**

Sunshine Cops

Heung Hoi-on, better known as H2O (Stephen Fung), is among a group of Hong Kong cops chosen from all divisions to be tested for some kind of new duty. Entrants are tested in martial arts, marksmanship...and dance! He and Sammy (Ken Chang) win out, and are assigned to be the new "Sunshine Cops," designed to be the ideal policemen for public-relations purposes and draw new recruits. They are groomed and photographed extensively, under the supervision of Madam Margarita So (Eileen Tung).

One night they're sent as backup for an SDU raid so that after a firefight they can be photographed for the newspapers. H2O takes all this with an easygoing smile, but Sammy comes from a whole family of cops, and is uncomfortable acting the fashion plate. However, So talks him out of quitting, saying they're an effective tool in crime prevention. They appear in public, on magazine covers, and even star in a commercial directed by action director Phillip Kwok. But not all their heroics are faked—they subdue a mental patient trying to make Chinese opera real in a school, becoming heroes. Agent William Hung (Simon Lui, gone blonde) tries to get them to sign with him for record and movie deals, but Sammy is satisfied being a cop, and Hung is only interested in promoting them together. Their disagreement spills over into their competition for heiress Katy Lam (Angelica Lee), a girl they met together. When this results in the embarrassment of the son of tabloid publisher Fu, the boys get dragged through the mud, but his tune changes when the boy is kidnapped and the Sunshine Cops are the only ones who can save him. But in rescuing the youngster, they get captured themselves. Instead of holding the celebrities for ransom, the kidnappers leave them in a cage unconscious in a public place. Humiliated and put on leave, the Sunshine Cops bounce back to go after the gang.

A big flaw pops up in the climax, as the gang shows up at Katy's school to kidnap 20 students at once, and the cops just happen to be there to go all *Die Hard* on them. The kung fu action is well designed, but marred by choppy editing. Those who hate all these teen movies may find this worthwhile for its action scenes. *AKA: Yang Guang Jing Cha.* 🐉🐉🐉

1999 89m/C *HK* Stephen Fung, Ken Chang, Angelica Lee, Eileen Tung, Ken Wong, Andrew Lin, Wai Geishun, Simon Lui, Astrid Chan, Chan Yam, Spencer Lam. *D:* Liu Kim-wah. *W:* Felix Chong. *C:* Choi Sung-fai. *M:* Lincoln Lo. **VHS, DVD**

Super Car Criminals

This auto-boosting adventure beat the similar Hollywood vehicle *Grand Theft Auto* into the-

"Ow! Why does this thing go in so hard?!"

—A wrestler adjusts her mawashi In *Sumo Vixens*

atres by a good four months. Raymond Ko (Louis Koo) is an undercover cop who has spent years infiltrating Hong Kong's top car-theft ring, to the point where he even has to steal the car of his father, Superintendent Ko (Paul Chun), to maintain credibility. The gang's leader Michael Yau (Michael Wong) is not without a level of integrity, delivering his goods on time and destroying any drugs found in the stolen cars. Raymond starts dating Michael's ditzy younger sister Mickey (Sherming Yiu) to get closer to the evidence needed to bust both the gang and their partners in the Customs Department. But he brings suspicion on himself when Michael notices someone has been snooping around his desk. However, Raymond and Michael have become real friends with the passage of time, and the cop has real feelings for Mickey. Knowing the cops want to make some arrests soon, Raymond takes the opportunity to subtly warn Michael, who makes plans to pull out and move operations to Japan. However, Michael's junior partner Roy Yang Wai (Roy Cheung) has run up a huge gambling debt to triad boss Prince Ken, and rather than have Michael sell off everything to pay it, he organizes a daring theft behind Michael's back. As the cops close in, Raymond tries to keep Michael from getting in the way.

The filmmakers fail to take advantage of the combination of cops, crooks and fast cars here, as there's only one brief chase scene early on, and the final shootout is artlessly recorded. The film also lacks any real momentum, with tension limited to the betrayal by Raymond and what will happen if he gets caught—all of which is defused quickly. Performances are good, though there's not much to be done with the bland script. Roy Cheung and Simon Lui both go blonde for their roles, with Lui shaving his dome to a buzz cut for his next few pictures. **AKA:** *Chaak Gung Ji; Ze Gong Zi.* ⚔⚔

1999 84m/C *HK* Louis Koo, Michael Wong, Simon Lui, Ma Hok-ming, Roy Cheung, Sherming Yiu, Yoyo Mung, Karel Wong, Paul Chun, Jim Cheong Shing. **D:** Ricky Lau. **W:** Lee Man-choi. **C:** Tsui Siu-kong. **M:** Johnny Yeung. **DVD**

Super Gang

The film starts with Bruce Le (AKA Huang Kin-lung and Lui Siu-lung, hoped by the filmmakers to be mistaken for Bruce Lee) at his brother's grave. Uncle Ming (a gang lord played by Lau Yat-fan) is suspected of being behind the crime, though there's no proof of this. Ming's mob is struggling with another group of bad guys for control of their territory. There's some kind of a subplot about strong-arming illegal immigrants into doing crimes, but—like most things in this film—it really goes nowhere.

If you're looking for some good guys to root for in this flick, forget it—everyone is out for themselves. Alan (Le) and Kenneth are the two main antagonists, but they're on opposite sides of the gang war. Not that it really matters. How a plot this simple can be made so convoluted and confusing remains a mystery. In a way, it looks as though *Super Gang* may have been cobbled together from pieces of other movies—that's what a mess it is. The direction and production values are amateurish at best. The editing is so choppy, and the costume changes so random, it's hard to keep track of who's who, even though the flick is barely over an hour long. Some choppy edits make it seem like brutal sex scenes may have been cut from the film for American audiences, but it's doubtful that restoring those scenes would make *Super Gang* any better.

Do *not* let the opening fight scene of *Super Gang* deceive you into believing this might be a good film. It is *not*. Only that fight, and some spots from others, gains the film the half-bone rating it barely deserves. The film looks as though it was shot entirely on location in places where the producers wouldn't have to pay fees. Thus, we get lots of scenes in vacant lots, abandoned buildings, and other dingy settings. The location shots seem to be merely a cost-saving measure by the filmmakers, *not* an attempt to establish atmosphere. Everything in *Super Gang* was done on a cut rate, and it shows. The flick gets a half bone, and it's a turkey bone at that. The original version contained footage of the real Bruce Lee to strengthen the notion that Alan is supposedly the Dragon's brother—a ploy used by some Bruceploitation titles—and some video releases still retain that footage. The U.S. version is credited to director "Yellow John." —SS **AKA:** *Supergang; Bruce Lee Super Gang.* 🐲

1978 73m/C *HK* Bruce Le, Tony Wong, Lau Yat-fan, Bolo Yeung, Kong Do, Kwan Yung Moon, Ngai Chau-wa, Lau Dan, Ng Hong Song, Pak Sha-lik, Ng Ming Choi. **D:** Wong Siu-jun. **W:** Wong Siu-jun. **VHS, DVD**

Super Kung Fu Kid

Teenage kid Man Lung (Cheung Lik) beats some bullies at the beach. The next day, more bullies attack in a field. This time, they have weapons, but Man Lung brought his nunchakus. With his righteous fighting bringing them trouble, Man Lung and his mom move on to live with his brother Man Ho (Kong Yeh) up the coast. Since Man Ho is now in the triad of Tiger (Bolo Yeung), the locals suspect Man Lung is a Northern spy. They decide to check him out, picking a fight with him in the woods. Tiger thinks he may be a Southern revolutionary. Brother Man Ho returns and identifies the newcomer, but Lung refuses to work for Tiger, pitting brother against brother. When Tiger's own brothers come home from the army, they join the fight against Lung, kidnapping his mother to draw him out. Lung storms Tiger's headquarters to rescue her.

The martial arts footage is plentiful—almost nonstop—but is also incredibly lame, except when better foes like Bolo Yeung (in an early role) get involved. For the most part, it looks like the combatants are just rehearsing their routines. The villains are all dubbed to sound like Muppet Oscar the Grouch. The stage blood looks like bright red poster paint. *AKA: Hong Kong Cat Named Karado; Superior Youngster.* ♪

1974 86m/C *HK* Cheung Lik, Kong Yeh, Bolo Yeung, Mars, James Nam. **VHS, DVD**

The Super Ninja

Well, at least the title lets us know that we're dealing with a Super Ninja, so we can pardon the inattention to authenticity on display and treat this as what it is: another movie where the ninjas might as well be wearing the masks and capes of superheroes. John (Alexander Lou) and Spencer (Eugene Trammel) are a duo of tough New York detectives who piss off their commander by being too honest. Mr. Tong is a mysterious super-criminal who is using Five Element Ninjas to take over the territory of other gangsters. Tong has John framed for narcotics possession, wanting him out of the way so he can get to get to the discoveries of Professor Chin, father of John's girlfriend Nancy. Chin is close to developing a serum that cures heroin addiction, which would seriously cramp the style of the drug cartels. John is able to endure the tortures inflicted by his corrupt brethren due to his secret ninja training. Fed up, John fights his way out of jail and tries to track down whoever framed him. The Five Elements Ninjas kidnap Nancy's brother David, and then kill Professor Chin, and John is nearly killed in his first encounter with them. Thinking John dead, Nancy returns to Hong Kong with the serum formula to live with her uncle. Knowing the gang will keep after the formula, John and Spencer head to Hong Kong, too.

Lou and Trammel, an Asian and Black team long before *Rush Hour,* have so little chemistry they seem like they met the day before. The ninja antics are the typical nonsense—which can be tremendously entertaining, or just plain obnoxious, depending on your mood. The Five Elements here are Fire, Water, Earth, Wood, and Metal (what, no Air?), and are not to be confused with Chang Cheh's *Five Elements Ninja,* which bears the similar title *Chinese Super Ninjas* on U.S. video. The soundtrack blatantly includes cues from Bernard Herrmann's *Psycho* score, and other sources. ♪♪

1984 91m/C *TW* Alexander Lou, Eugene Trammel, Tomas Yau, William Yen, Lou Mei, Bruce Lai, Wong Ching, Yang Song, Yu Jin-bao. *D:* Wu Kuo-jen. **VHS, DVD**

Supercop

Miramax takes their first turn at releasing a Jackie Chan movie to U.S. theatres, with results only slightly inferior to what New Line did with *Rumble in the Bronx.* In this 1992 feature (released in the U.S. in 1996), Jackie teams with martial arts goddess (and former Miss Malaysia) Michelle Yeoh for a mission to Mainland China, Kuala Lumpur, and back to Hong Kong. Chan returns as Inspector Kevin Chan, his character from the *Police Story* movies, though this sequel is a decided break from the first two. Previous entries were rousing action films, but they were also stories about a Hong Kong cop trying to juggle a personal life and a career often unappreciated by his superiors, in the midst of deadly chaos.

Supercop has Chan lent out by Uncle Bill (Bill Tung) to straitlaced Chief of Security Yang (Yeoh) in Beijing for an undercover mission. Chan is put in a prison labor camp to help Panther (Yuen Wah) escape, so that Chan can infiltrate the criminal organization of Panther's kingpin brother Chaibat (Kenneth Tsang). Along the way, Yang also has to join the gang, posing as Chan's sister—and Tung even joins the family, dressed in drag as Chan's mother! The pair manage to survive an explosive battle between Chaibat's gang and arms dealers, and they move on to an attempt to free Chaibat's wife (Josephine Koo) from jail before she's forced to testify against him. But when Kevin's girlfriend May (Maggie Cheung) turns up at the hotel they're staying at, their cover is blown, and the two cops are forced to participate in the jailbreak against their will.

This one has fewer kung fu fights and more stunts than the average JC entry, but the stunts are just incredible. The prison escape down a glider and the village gun battles are impressive, but the bar is raised significantly by the climax, in which Chaibat's helicopter flies around with Chan hanging from a ladder, before landing on a moving train, where their battle continues. The U.S. version loses only a couple of minutes, cutting out a scene involving heroin addicts shooting up. However, the rap music cues are annoying, and the Cha-cha-chan title sequence, and Tom Jones singing "Kung Fu Fighting," is downright embarrassing. Note: Yeoh is still the only beauty pageant queen to jump onto a moving train on a motorcycle. *AKA: Ging Chat Goo Si 3: Chiu Kap Ging Chat; Jing Cha Gu Shi 3: Chao Ji Jing Cha; Police Story 3: Super Cop; Police Story 3.* ♪♪♪♪

The Jackie Chan Story

Part Two

成龍

By 1980, Jackie Chan was suddenly the highest-paid movie star/director in the history of Hong Kong cinema, and given practically unlimited creative and financial freedom on his films. But would his contract pay off with films that would not only make money in Hong Kong, but around the world? Chan started conservatively with *Young Master,* another comedy in which he played a teenage kung fu student. When it became an even bigger hit than *Drunken Master,* Chan's films started to get attention outside of Asia. But the honchos at Golden Harvest had even bigger plans for their new star.

It took three tries for Jackie Chan to become a success in the U.S., but each attempt had an explosive reaction. On his first trip to the States, he made an action movie set in the 1930s *(The Big Brawl)* and a silly all-star action comedy *(Cannonball Run),* neither of which was able to use him properly. Returning to Hong Kong, Jackie starred in Sammo Hung's silly all-star comedy *Winners and Sinners,* and his own action picture set in the 1900s, *Project A.* Both are sequel-spawning HK action classics, particularly *Project A,* in which Chan paid loving—and often painful—tribute to his idol Buster Keaton. Seeing Burt Reynolds in outtakes during the end credits of *Cannonball* gave Jackie the idea of doing the same thing, only some of Chan's outtakes show the serious consequences of dangerous stunts that go wrong.

On his second trip west, Jackie starred in the modern police action flick *The Protector,* which also failed to properly exploit his talents. Back in Hong Kong, Chan decided to make a modern police action flick his way, expanding on the kind of character he played in *Winners and Sinners.* A nonstop crowd-pleasing ride full of comedy, daredevil stunts, chases, and brilliant fight scenes, *Police Story* was Chan's biggest hit yet, universally acclaimed as an action classic. He also again joined Sammo Hung for *Heart of Dragon* in which he played another cop, this time with much more drama and much less comedy—but still with kick-ass fight scenes, especially the big climactic battle engineered by Yuen Biao.

Chan swore off going to America to concentrate on making great action films for his loyal Asian audience. *Miracles* was a directorial triumph; *Armour of God* brought the Chan touch to the Indiana Jones–type high-adventure genre; *Crime Story* was a thrilling political action drama; *Supercop* paired him with Michelle Yeoh for international adventure; *Legend of the Drunken Master* brought him back to the Wong Fei-hung character for what's considered by some the best kung fu movie ever; and so on. Meanwhile, the Jackie cult audience in the U.S. was growing via festival and art-house screenings, Chinatown video rentals, and word-of-mouth (generally consisting of wild-eyed converts cornering everyone they knew and yelling, "Have you seen this?!!"). By the mid-'70s, Chan didn't have to go to America—America came to Chan, starting with the dubbed release of one of his more accessible titles, *Rumble in the Bronx*. With Chan playing a Hong Kong cop visiting New York for his uncle's wedding—and getting in trouble with gangs and jewel thieves—it's a perfect introduction for Americans to Chan's work, and was a tremendous box-office success. Subsequently, Jackie Chan's back catalogue of films has been making its way onto U.S. theatre screens and video shelves, albeit sometimes in senselessly abridged editions.

With a winning boxoffice record in the States, it wasn't long before plans were being made to have Chan star in Hollywood pictures, with mixed results. Co-starring Chris Tucker, *Rush Hour* was a surprising monster hit in 1998, while Chan managed to be the least awful part of *Burn, Hollywood, Burn*. Since then, Jackie has been busier than ever, dividing his time between performing for hire in Hollywood movies (and even a hit cartoon show) and continuing to make his own brand of action magic back home—though both kinds of projects keep him racing all over the globe. However, age has begun to catch up with Chan, and he can only handle the pace and pressure of a 23-year-old these days. Hopefully, the world will be able to catch up with him, and find out that Jackie Chan is just as entertaining as a man as he is a stuntman.

1992 (R) 95m/C *HK* Jackie Chan, Michelle Yeoh, Kenneth Tsang, Maggie Cheung, Yuen Wah, Bill Tung, Josephine Koo, Kelvin Wong, William Duan, Phillip Chan, Lo Lieh, Mars, Hon Yee Sang, Ken Lo, Kim Penn. *D:* Stanley Tong. *W:* Edward Tang, Fibe Ma, Lee Wai Yee. *C:* Ardy Lam. *M:* Jonathan Lee, Mac Chew, Jenny Chinn, Joel McNeely (U.S.). **VHS, DVD**

Supercop 2

This 1993 Hong Kong action flick from director Stanley Tong *(Rumble in the Bronx, Mr. Magoo)* has an odd pedigree. It's a sequel to the Jackie Chan flick *Police Story 3: Supercop* (released here simply as *Supercop* to general audiences,

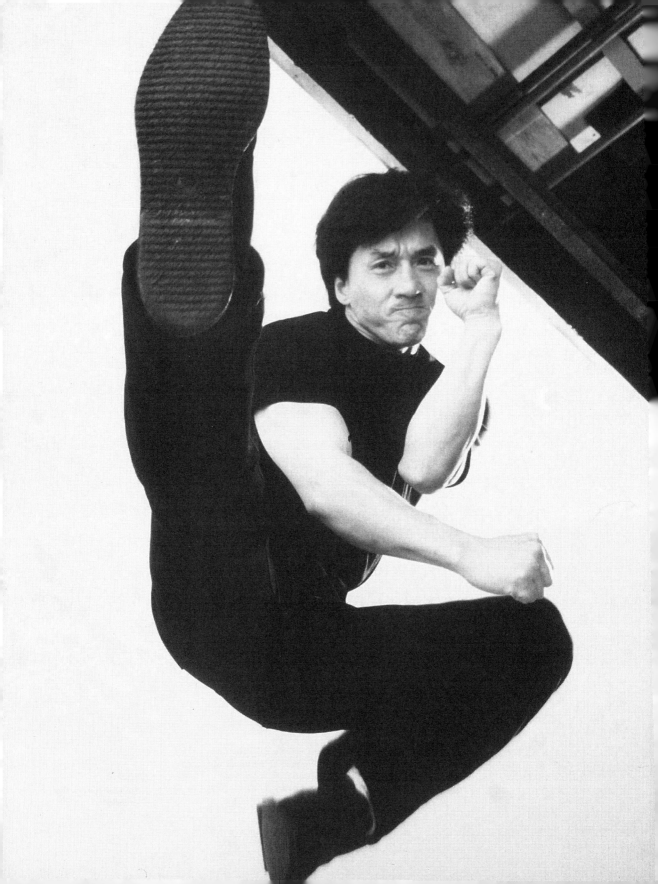

since it was unlikely they'd seen the first two episodes). However, it's not actually a Jackie Chan movie at all. Though Jackie puts in an appearance, it's only for a few minutes during which he uses a slapstick drag routine to foil a jewelry store holdup, after which he puts in a plug for his trip to America (ostensibly to be "Kevin Chan" in *Rumble*). This sequence was obviously shot entirely separate from the rest of the film and only serves to get Jackie's name in the credits. Big deal.

Actually, this movie deserves better. Michelle Yeoh is the real star, reprising her role as mainland supercop Jessica Yang, who had teamed up with Jackie in the previous film and matched him almost stunt for stunt. The plot concerns Yang's mission to Hong Kong to help mere mortal cops track down a gang that has stolen a security system that puts all the banks and businesses in the city at risk. Unbeknownst to Yang, the gang is led by her no-account old boyfriend David Chang (Yu Rongguang). The plans of the crooks are complex and clever, the action is spectacular, and Michelle is beautiful and graceful. The highlight is her battle with a huge bad guy (Big Yank) at least three times her size!

The U.S. version is about what we've come to expect from Hong Kong features adapted for American release—the picture and sound are wonderfully crisp, the musical score has been unnecessarily replaced, and the dubbing is acceptable (Yeoh may have dubbed her own voice—if not, it's a good imitation). On the other hand, they cut out way too much of the film's character, clipping eight minutes off the Hong Kong running time. **AKA:** *Chiu Kap Gai Waak; Chao Ji Ji Hua;Once a Cop; Project S; Police Story 3 Part 2; Police Story 4: Project S; Police Story V; Supercop 2: Super Plan.* 🎵🎵🎵

1993 (R) 94m/C *HK* Michelle Yeoh, Yu Rongguang, Emil Chau, Athena Chu, Fan Siu-wong, Dick Wei, Alain Guernier, Bill Tung, Yukari Oshima, Bowie Lam, Ailen Sit, Chan Man Ching, Bruce Law, Big Yank, Kim Penn, Joe Cheung, Jackie Chan, Eric Tsang, Mars. **D:** Stanley Tong. **W:** Stanley Tong, Sandy Shaw. **C:** Ardy Lam. **M:** Richard Lo, Michael Wandmacher (U.S.). **VHS, DVD**

SuperManChu

In this vintage Golden Harvest action film, a gang of northern China outlaws ride into town, rape innkeeper's daughter Su-yin, and kill her whole family. All, that is, except her brother Hong Ching (Chang Yi), who was out at the time. Luckily, Hong Ching is a super kung fu man and expert knife fighter, and he sets out to claim his

vengeance. Rescuing indebted gambler Chen Chu-lai and his daughter Chui-fung (Tin Mat) from some of the thugs, he learns that the bandit leader is Lee Dai-yeh. But even Hong can't beat Lee's whole gang alone—injured, he retreats and hides out with the Chens to lick his wounds. Meanwhile, Lee recruits suave fighter Chow Chung (Pai Ying) into his gang, a man whose specialty weapon is throwing coins. Tracking Hong down, Lee's men kill Chen, abduct Chui-fung, and call in two Japanese killers to deal with Hong. When Hong attacks the brothel, he finds himself trapped, and undercover agent Chow has to show his true colors to help him.

An extremely simple Eastern-Western revenge tale, this nonetheless has a bit of style and energy—enough to make it worth seeing for kung fu fans. There are some neat tricks, as when Hong catches a thrown knife in his mouth and spits it back into the attacker's gut. The budget is very cheap, and interior sets wobble at times, and are cold enough to show the actors' breath. The same furniture and props can be seen in different sets, and the town exteriors show power lines plainly visible in what's assumed to be pre-industrial China. The opera-trained Chang Yi went on to play many of the traditional white-haired villains in 1970s Golden Harvest features. Music cues are recognizable from *Goldfinger*. **AKA:** *Stormy Sun; Superman-Chu; Super Manchu.* 🎵🎵

1973 91m/C *HK* Chang Yi, Pai Ying, Tin Mat, Hon Siu. **D:** Taylor Wong. **W:** Hsiang Yang. **C:** Lin Chi Hsin. **M:** Wong Chu-jen. **VHS, DVD**

Sure Death: Revenge

A class production of mystery and intrigue during the Edo period of Japan, highlighted by strong performances and a captivating story. Kinji Fukasaku created a TV series called *Hissatsu Shikake-nin* ("Deadly Professional Killers") for Shochiku Studios in 1972. About a secret group of contract killers who disguise their activities by posing as normal lower-class merchants, the series became one of the most successful and longest-running series in Japan's history. From time to time, Shochiku produced a theatrical feature based on the series. The first decade of the series focused on super-assassin Baian, after which Mondo Nakamura (Mokoto Fujita), who posed as a bumbling cop with a nagging wife, took the lead.

Kohei Yasuda (Renji Ishibashi), cheated out of a promised promotion in exchange for a bribe,

This time Jackie Chan's foot is ready for its close-up in this dynamic publicity shot for *Supercop*. THE KOBAL COLLECTION / GOLDEN HARVEST

"Don't get mad. Your sweet photo must be delicious."

—Princess Man Cheung greets her sifu in *The Sword Stained with Royal Blood*

goes berserk and kills his magistrate, then himself. Mondo (Fujita) is made a scapegoat for not protecting his boss. The new magistrate is the young and handsome Lord Ukyonosuke Okuda (Henry Sanada), who greets his staff with a feast and a bonus. Kyuma Kagazume and his gang of punks—wild samurai and the Shogun's personal retainers—cause trouble, and a panicking horse causes an accident that kills an old man. Mysteriously, the horse dies immediately after, a shuriken found in its leg. Magistrate Okuda dismisses Mondo's report that the incident was more than an accident and hides the evidence. Privately, questions continue to nag at Mondo, and he continues his investigation discretely.

At that night's professional killers' meeting, the leader Benten (Kyoko Kishida) targets three men for assassination: the wild samurai leader Chikara Jinbo (Daijiro Tsutsumi), his lieutenant Shinpachi Taro, and Kagazume. However, the members scoff at their poor offer of only six gold pieces for the job—only Mondo and a gruff stranger named Bunsichi (Sonny Chiba) take the assignment. While Mondo spies on the wild samurai, the stranger beheads Kagazume. Nakamura pursues him (he's an officer as well as an assassin, after all), but the stranger's estranged daughter Omitsu (Haruko Sagara) delays him. When Mondo learns about Okuda's sordid past as a gay prostitute, temple page, and kabuki actor, the mystery surrounding the new magistrate only deepens. But one thing becomes clear: strange deaths occur wherever he's been. When Mondo and Bunsichi go after Taro, a third party beats them both to the target, injuring Bunsichi and raising more questions in the bargain.

This is actually the eighth film in the *Hissatsu!* series, but the first to be released in the U.S., and generally considered the best. Though previous entries had started to drift too far into comedy, director Fukasaku's sure hand pulls the feature back to its original concept. Fujita makes for a fine, if unlikely, hard-boiled gumclog detective. Chiba, whose Japan Action Club helped produce, exudes his usual mix of valor and menace—though his use of tops as deadly weapons is in keeping with the series' humor. *AKA: Hissatsu 4: Urami Hurashimtsu; Sure-Fire Death 4: We Will Avenge You.* 🗡🗡🗡🗡

1987 130m/C *JP* Makoto Fujita, Sonny Chiba, Henry Sanada, Mitsuko Baisho, Kyoko Kishida, Haruko Sagara, Hirotaro Honda, Daijiro Tsutsumi, Renji Ishibashi. **D:** Kinji Fukasaku. **W:** Tatsuo Nogami, Kinji Fukasaku, Akira Nakahara. **C:** Shigeru Ishihara. **M:** Masaaki Hirao. **VHS, DVD**

The Suspect

Set in a fictional Asian country, *The Suspect* tries hard to be relevant and kick action butt at the same time. Don (Louis Koo) killed someone in his youth. Immediately upon his release 12 years later, his old boss forcibly drags him into a plot to assassinate an important political figure. But Don wants nothing to do with his past life. What's a reformed criminal to do? His ex-brother-in-arms Max (Julian Cheung Chi-Lam) takes care of the hit in spectacular fashion with a rocket launcher. Don is framed for the murder by his former associates and becomes a fugitive.

The action set-pieces deliver, for the most part, as you might expect from veteran director Ringo Lam. Rest assured that there is plenty of running, shooting, and the usual helicopter hijinks. The film runs a bit long, though, and while the concocting of an anonymous Asian country may have been felt necessary for the plot, the locales also look anonymous and lack much sustaining visual interest.

The performances in this film are also a bit problematic. Louis Koo does not bring a lot of passion to the central role of Don. He maintains one look on his face, and it's hard to identify with him or empathize with his struggles. Similarly, Julian Cheung decided on one facial expression and stuck with it throughout. Ray Lui is more effective and enjoyable to watch as a mercenary leader, as is Ada Choi as a reporter brought along, unfortunately, for only half the ride. Simon Yam is fairly cool and impassive, but, when needed for one scene, was able to convey some genuine feeling behind his customary sunglasses. The cinematography by Ross Clarkson is workmanlike. The musical score is quite good at underscoring emotional points. —PM **AKA:** *Gik Diy Chung Faan; Ji Du Chong Fan; Extreme Serious Criminal.* 🗡🗡

1998 109m/C *HK* Louis Koo, Julian Cheung, Simon Yam, Ray Lui, Ada Choi, Eric Mo. **D:** Ringo Lam. **W:** W. K. Lau, Ringo Lam. **C:** Ross Clarkson. **M:** Raymond Wong, Andrew Worboys. **DVD**

Suzhou River

Using subjective camera like *Lady in the Lake*, a Shanghai videographer for hire tells the story of how he met his girlfriend, and the strange webwork of mystery surrounding her. He's hired to tape the Happy Tavern's mermaid show, and meets the mysterious Meimei (Zhou Xun). It's love at first sight, but Meimei often disappears for days. Here, he interjects the story of Mardar (Jia Hongsheng), a motorcycle courier. He was hired to deliver a young girl named Moudan (Zhou Xun again) to stay with her aunt whenever her dad has a girl over. Soon, Moudan is spending more time with Mardar than with her aunt, and the two fall in love.

Shady business with Mardar's ex, Xia-Ho, intrudes—she's the one who arranged for this job, the real purpose of which is to kidnap Moudan. The payoff is made, but Xia-Ho is double-crossed by her partner Lao B (Hua Zhong-kai), and Mardar has to try to save her. But Moudan is so distraught when she learns what he's done that she jumps in the river, vowing to return as a mermaid. After serving a prison sentence, Mardar returns to Shanghai years later to search for her. He finds she's become a mermaid after all, at Happy Tavern under the name Meimei—or has she? Lou Ye, said to be a sixth-generation director, keeps you guessing through the end of this twisty, low-key mystery, which resembles the work of Wong Kar-Wai. *AKA: Su Zhou He.* 🎵🎵🎵

2000 81m/C *CH/GE* Zhou Xun, Jia Hongsheng, Hua Zhong-kai, Yao Anlian, Nai An. *D:* Lou Ye. *W:* Lou Ye. *C:* Wang Yu. *M:* Jorg Lemberg. **VHS**

The Sword Stained with Royal Blood

The funeral of Marshal Wan, who died framed for treason by a jealous eunuch, is disrupted when warriors of the Wan family from the East Chamber attack. General Suen (Wu Ma) of the rebels is saved by the magical Golden Snake Man, Ha Suet-Yee (Danny Lee). Dedicated to finding the Marshal's son to lead their fight, but having seen the Golden Snake Sword, the General chooses blindness over death. So begins another wild and crazy Hong Kong swordplay romp, which is full of odd characters and has a plot composed solely of one damn thing after another.

Rowdy Princess Kau (Sharla Cheung) poses as a bandit to hijack a delivery of medicinal snowy frogs for her sifu Sun Su-Kuei (Ng Man-Tat), but a witch from the Five Poison Sect grabs the loot. Constable Yuen Shing Chi (Yuen Biao) intercedes, arresting the girl. She goes along with this at first, since he says they need to go to a Wan castle before she's turned over to the court, and there's going to be a gathering of heroes there. They meet up with Ha in the forest, but the Five Poison Sect—who are after the Golden Snake Sword—attacks before they can all be introduced. Since Yuen helps out during the battle, the three part afterwards as friends, but Kau has had a dose of the Sect's poison mist.

Meanwhile, the champions gather at a Wan house to make a plan to deal with the Golden Snake Man, who has sworn to kill them all. On edge, Wan Ching-Ching (Yip Chuen Chan) and her men fight her old friend Yuen when he arrives, but calm down enough to cure Kau. Yuen's superior Mr. Kuei arrives, looking for the lost Princess, but (like the White Rabbit) leaves as soon as he arrives to chase his equally mad wife. Yuen fights a snake that wandered away from the Sect to pro-

tect Kau, and has to bite it to defeat it. Medical student Jade Ho (Anita Yuen), who may be a Five Poison spy, helps Yuen recover.

On the way to the castle, in the ghost town that was once the Golden Snake Man's home, Yuen helps him through a bout of sickness-induced madness, while Ha uses kung fu to cure Yuen of the serpent blood. Ching Ching's stepmother Siu Yi is the Golden Snake Man's old girlfriend, which causes bloody dissent within the family, and much heartache for him. As Yuen, Kao, and Ho reach the castle, the pressure cooker boils over, leaving more dead and Mr. Wah himself gone mad. Though they are friends, Yuen's dedication to his duty opposes Ha's thirst for revenge, and the two decide to fight a duel to settle things.

That's quite a bit of story, but it's only half of the plot of this jam-packed epic, which often plays out much like an old Chinese opera. Though loaded with characters and situations, there's also plenty of kung fu action, much of it enhanced with various kinds of special effects. It's a highly entertaining film, though ultimately weighed down by an overly complex story. Those familiar with Yuen Biao's acrobatic expertise will be disappointed to find him confined to wirework so much of the time. *AKA: Xin bi Xue Xia; San Bik Huet Kim.* 🎵🎵🎵

1993 C: *HK* Sharla Cheung, Danny Lee, Anita Yuen, Yuen Biao, Ng Man-Tat, Yip Chuen Chan, Wu Ma. *D:* Cheung Hoi-Ching. *W:* Cheung Hoi-Ching, Wai San. *C:* Lau Hung-chuen, George Ma, Poon Tak-yip. *M:* James Wong. **VHS, DVD**

Swordsman

The story begins with a sacred kung fu scroll being stolen. The royal eunuchs who run the imperial government (a standard HK trope) conduct a ruthless campaign to recover the scroll and its secrets. They suspect Master Lam, a noble who opposes the current regime. The master is joined in his besieged estate by the swordsman, Ling Wu-chung (Sam Hui), and his apprentice "Kiddo" (Celia Yip in a "trouser" role—i.e., a woman disguised as a man). The swordsman is so skilled that he can cut the flame from a candle and move the fire around before returning it to its wick—a pretty neat trick. Lam's estate is mined with dynamite, and blows up real good when the bad guys attack. Mortally wounded, Master Lam escapes, and tells the swordsman that the scroll is hidden under the waterwheel in the destroyed villa. The swordsman and Kiddo escape in a boat, along with some allies from the Sun Moon clan. At this point, we get a pop-song break, courtesy of the elder Sun Moon masters. But the escape ends in disaster when the boat is besieged and

the old men mortally wounded. Despite the carnage, the bad guys have still not recovered the sacred scroll and its mystical secrets. The swordsman and Kiddo return to their Wah Mountain master. The master has a sinister secret hidden in his past, but our heroes don't suspect that. It turns out that Kiddo is the master's daughter, and the master wants her to marry a man who is supposedly Master Lam's heir. (The Wah master secretly knows that heir is an impostor, planted by the evil eunuch.)

The situation grows more complicated when all the principals stay at an inn run by a rebel smuggler clan. The smugglers are led by a woman called Blue Phoenix (Fennie Yuen). Mental and physical jousting ensues between the eunuch faction, the Wah Mountain martial artists, and the smugglers. Naturally, they all come together for a final battle for possession of the secret hidden under the waterwheel. Who is truly good? Who is truly evil? Will the pop song prove important to the plot? And will the swordsman and Kiddo be able to sort this all out before someone kills them?

Like many films produced by Tsui Hark, *Swordsman* is an entertaining mélange of story elements and fights. Direction was started by the legendary King Hu as a comeback picture, but when he fell ill, diverse hands were brought in to finish. The plot wanders more than a little (not surprising, given the number of writers), and the characters seem to bounce back and forth between locations. The story line is similar in some ways to *Dragon Inn*—though that film holds together better. The cinematography is up to the usual high standards of Peter Pau (though not as good as *Crouching Tiger, Hidden Dragon*). The fights are fun, if a bit chaotic. All in all, a good demonstration of HK action cinema. Followed by *Legend of the Swordsman*. —SS **AKA:** *Siu Ngo Kong Woo; Xiao Ao Jiang Hu.* 🎭🎭🎭

1990 112m/C *HK/TW* Sam Hui, Cecilia Yip, Jacky Cheung, Sharla Cheung, Fennie Yuen, Lau Siu-ming, Yuen Wah, Lau Shun, Lam Ching-Ying, Wu Ma. **D:** King Hu, Ching Siu-tung, Ann Hui, Tsui Hark, Andrew Kam. **W:** Kwon Man-leung, Wong Ying, Lam Kee-to, Lau Dai-muk, Edward Leung, Dai Foo-ho. **C:** Ardy Lam, Peter Pau. **M:** James Wong, Romeo Diaz. **VHS, DVD**

Swordsman with an Umbrella

Lung Chung-tin (Chiang Ming), the man known as Iron Umbrella, casts a large shadow while passing through Dragon Town, standing up to the Flower Zone squad of the Tiger Gang. When the captain tries to kill him, he demonstrates his skill by catching the captain's sword in his fingers and flicking chunks of it into the forehead of a few thugs. In an effort to force him into joining Dragon Gang, their black-hooded leader has him framed for the murders of a few of their enemies. At a gathering of clan leaders, Master Cheung accepts the responsibility of leading them in tracking down the killer. Unaware of the frame, Iron Umbrella continues about his business— tracking down and killing those in the Martial Arts World who banded together years before to cast out his master, Iron Man, and the scarfaced man who killed his parents (gee, wonder who the hooded Tiger leader really is?).

He starts by killing Magic Hands Ngai, but the Poison Master traps him, and only the intervention of swordswoman Miss Wei Wan saves his life. Master Cheung and his companions catch up with him and don't believe his denials, so he quickly disarms them and escapes. Lady Kung Sun-lau pursues him, but Wan intercedes again to save her from her friend. Despite this, Kung is still determined to kill Iron Umbrella, who has gone to get revenge on the Tiger Gang. There are too many for even Iron Umbrella to handle, and it's up to Wei to rescue him once again from the Tiger's basement dungeon. She even goes back to get his umbrella for him, but can't convince him to give up his vendetta, and he decides he has to face the Tiger Gang in a rematch.

The entire film bears the influence of Japanese samurai movies and Italian westerns, but carries on the more fanciful traditions of Chinese swordplay. When cornered, the hero flies off by twirling his iron umbrella like a helicopter rotor, and other characters perform similar fantastic feats. Jet Li would make an umbrella look like a practical weapon in his Wong Fei-hung pictures, but Chiang Ming looks kind of clumsy with one here, making him not quite convincing as a superhero. The final fight sequence even includes some obviously faked slow motion! Despite its drawbacks, this is still an entertaining little adventure film, complete with eccentric weapons, an obsessed hero, and a heroine who is much too good for him. **AKA:** *Shen San Qi Xia.* 🎭🎭🎭

1970 87m/C *HK* Chiang Ming, Pai Yu, Cheung Ching-fung, Ma Kei, Tin Ming, Hon Kong, Sun Yueh, Tai Leung, Wong Hung-cheung, Wong Fan, Chao San-San, Ho Wai-hung, Yue Feng, Wong Ching, Lee Keung. **D:** Chen Kan-chuan. **DVD**

The Swordswoman in White

The (otherwise unnamed) Rebel Girl is battling against the corrupt government within ancient China. Fighting from town to town, the Rebel Girl and her assistant Vincent travel to the Lotus temple, where they find the girl's mother—who is the temple's chief priestess. The Rebel Girl and her people plan an attack to free the woodcutter's daughter from her unwanted marriage to the old landlord. The landlord is killed, but his son—a General of the corrupt emperor—brings an army to fight the rebels in a huge final battle. The film then tells us that this was the beginning of the Lotus rebellion, which went on to fight for freedom in ancient China. Whether we should believe this is your guess.

There are some really cool swordfights in this film. When there's no fighting, the film becomes markedly less interesting. We've got a lot of the usual mystical kung fu clichés, including acupressure techniques that can do everything short of bringing someone back from the dead. Jalisco Films goes overboard on the dubbing of this one, throwing in gratuitous anachronisms such as "swap meets" and "pizza." The deliberate bad dubbing distracts from the atmosphere, which is otherwise pretty respectable. Because of this, it's also hard to tell whether the acting is any good—or even if the story they're telling is the one the film originally came with. The sword fights, though, make it worth viewing. —SS *AKA: Bai Yi Xia Nu.* 🐾🐾♡

1992 /C *CH* Jiang Gengchen, Wang Meiling, Li Junfeng, Ha Ping. **D:** Zhang Huaxun. **VHS, DVD**

Sympathy for Mr. Vengeance

A deaf-mute is encouraged by his psycho girlfriend to kidnap an industrialist's daughter in order to get the money for his sister's liver transplant. When the child is accidentally killed, the kidnappers become the target of brutal retribution. From the first scenes in the ghetto of black-market organ bartering to the final sadistic moments of personalized torture and death, this is a realistic drama that takes the viewer to the extremes of sadistic behavior.

When this picture was first screened in Korea, audiences reportedly walked out because the violence was too much for them. This may surprise jaded action fans who will find the gore level relatively moderate. The squirm factor is due to Park's use of real time and claustrophobic locations in the torture scenes. Like Hitchcock, he plays on viewer apprehension. In his previous film, *Joint Security Area,* Park laid out a world divided by politics. Here, he groups his characters according to economic standing. The actions of the poor are motivated by money, while the rich simply want to live complacently safe lives, un-threatened by the desperate politics of need. —BW *AKA: Boksune-un Naui Geot.* 🐾🐾🐾🐾

2001 129m/C *KO* Song Kang-ho, Shin Ha-kyun, Im Ji-eun, Bae Du-na, Han Bo-bae, Lee Dae-yeon, Kim Se-dong, Lim Je-eun. **D:** Park Chan-wook. **W:** Jeong Seong-san, Kim Hyeon-seok, Lee Mu-yeong, Park Chan-wook. **C:** Kim Sung-bok. **M:** Bang Jun-seok, Jo Yeong-wook. **VHS, DVD**

Taboo

Well, just how many sex movies begin with a guy dying of cancer? Hiramatsu (Yoji Maysuzaki) has long known that his best friend Kiriu Atsushi (Eisaku Shindo) is in love with his wife Miki. When he dies, an odd request is found in his will: Hiramatsu's last wish is that his widow and his best friend make love—in front of his coffin, on the day of his funeral! Flashbacks reveal how he'd been playing mind games with everyone for years. Years after the funeral, he's still screwing with people's heads. Another entry in Japan's cycle of sexual psychodramas from the 1990s, this one benefits from a strong lead performance by Maysuzaki, while Shindo's wide-eyed mugging fares not so well. 🐾🐾

1997 92m/C *JP* Noriko Hamada, Eisaku Shindo, Yoji Maysuzaki. **D:** Yutaka Kohira. **VHS, DVD**

Take 2 in Life

Not a comedy, not a thriller, and not a very good movie. A scientist in Hong Kong dies under mysterious circumstances, and the coroner and his assistant also die when attempting to perform an autopsy on the body. Shan (Yeung Ka-mun), the scientist's daughter, is understandably upset, but even more so when she discovers that the two were not actually related—so she resolves to uncover her own true identity. The only clues she can find are a photograph and a computer diskette, which point her toward Malaysia.

Her best friend Tong (Wong Yat-tung) travels with her, and soon after their arrival in Malaysia, they are joined by Kwok Pong (Chan Kwok-Bong), Tong's boyfriend, and Bull Wong (Ah Nui), a newspaper photographer trying to get back into favor with his editor. Chang Bak (K.K. Cheung), a detective from Hong Kong, is also on their trail—he thinks the death of Shan's father may be related to a string of other unsolved deaths. Zhi Lik (Sean Chen), a hotel manager, gets mixed up with this merry gang, along with a chef (Liu Wai-hung) and the hotel manager's twin brother (James Chen).

From the description above, *Take 2 in Life* may sound like a madcap comedy, along the lines of *It's a Mad Mad Mad Mad World.* While that may have been the intention of the filmmakers, the result on screen contains a sparse amount of mirth-inducing material. The mystery is handled ineptly, the drama is lacking, and several performances are unpolished, most

notably those by Taiwanese singing duo Hot Twinz (Sean and James Chen). Most of the movie was shot on location in Malaysia, and the countryside is beautiful to behold. But unless you're looking for a travelogue, it's best to look elsewhere. Eric Tsang has a cameo as Shan's boss in Hong Kong. —PM **AKA:** *Gau Chai Daai Liu; Gou Zai Da Lao; Life Has Take 2.* ◊

2001 89m/C *HK* Yeung Ka-mun, Wong Yat-tung, Chan Kwok-Bong, Ah Nui, K.K. Cheung, Sean Chen, James Chen, Liu Wai-hung, Chan Hing-cheung, Law Kar-Ying, Eric Tsang. **D:** Dick Lee. **W:** Raymond See. **C:** Teoh Gay-hian. **M:** Mak Chun-hung. **DVD**

The Tale of Zatoichi Continues

Tossed off a boat by some rude samurai, Zatoichi (Shintaro Katsu) gets in a parting shot. They recognize him as the blind masseur who is also a great swordsman, but decide his reputation can't be all it's cracked up to be and go after him on shore. Before Ichi can rouse himself from his post-swim nap, he finds a mysterious samurai already mowing down the brigands for him. Arriving at a nearby town, Ichi is employed at an inn to massage Lord Kuroda, who is returning to his province from Edo (lords, known as "daimyo," were required by the Shogunate to live alternate years in the capitol, which served to drain the resources of the daimyo, keeping them under the thumb of the central government). But something is amiss with this job—the lord is in a ticklish mood, his retainers act shifty, and Zatoichi has to kill three attacking samurai on his way to his inn. The truth is that Kuroda has lost his mind, and his men are desperate to keep his condition secret.

Hiding out in a restaurant, both Ichi and the mystery man Yoshiro (Tomisaburo Wakayama), who defended him earlier in the day, meet a prostitute that reminds them of Chiyo—a woman they both loved. By morning, Boss Kanbei's men are enlisted to join Kuroda's in the search for the blind masseur. After cutting down a few of them, Zatoichi continues on his journey to Joshoji Temple at Sasagawa, to pay his respects at the grave of Hirate Miki (who he killed in the first film). Boss Kanbei picks up his trail in Iioka, recruiting Boss Sukegoro (Masayo Banri) to his campaign. Sukegoro is also hunting the rogue bandit Yoshiro, the man who stole the love of Ichi's life—his own brother! All converge on Joshoji Temple for a massive rumble.

This first Zatoichi sequel manages to improve on its predecessor a bit, with a more original story line, more swordplay, and more information on Ichi's past. However, after dropping a bit of information that would serve to drive the next sequel, it ends rather abruptly.

Setting Zatoichi against formidable samurai was a component of the series from the beginning, but rarely one skilled enough to actually wound him like Yoshiro, much less a blood relative. Later episodes would have nothing to do with Ichi's past life, or even with each other. Composer Akira Ifukube contributes a more distinctive score, adding some of his chilling organ notes to moments of tension. **AKA:** *Zoku Zatoichi Monogatari; The Return of Masseur Ichi.* ♪♪♪◊

1962 73m/BW *HK* Shintaro Katsu, Yoshie Mizutani, Masayo Banri, Tomisaburo Wakayama. **D:** Kazuo Mori. **W:** Minoru Inuzuka, Kan Shimozawa (story). **M:** Akira Ifukube. **VHS, DVD**

Tampopo

Here is a fun and bubbling comedy that sends up western, chambara, and martial arts films by redressing their clichés in a culinary setting. Truck-driving cowboy Goro (Tsutomu Yamazaki) and his partner Gun (Ken Watanabe), stop in at the Lai Lai Noodle Café to sample the wares. After using their expertise to critique the cooking of widow Tampopo (Nobuko Miyamoto), she begs Goro to be her teacher in a quest to create the perfect bowl of ramen soup. While chronicling this quest for the best in broth and noodles, writer/director Juzo Itami serves side courses that explore the gamut of food experience in modern Japanese society, from the stylish young man (Koji Yakusho) for whom food is an extreme sensual experience, to the small child on a strict natural diet who accepts a gift of a soft-serve ice cream cone. As a team of experts is slowly assembled to produce the top ramen, the shop—and even Tampopo herself—receive redecoration.

Itami gained some recognition for his black comedy *The Funeral,* but *Tampopo* was an arthouse smash worldwide. The cast is completely charming, especially the talented Miyamoto, who seems to be able to glow on cue. Itami and his little company of players would be back in *A Taxing Woman.* **AKA:** *Dandelion.* ♪♪♪♪

1987 115m/C *JP* Tsutomu Yamazaki, Nobuko Miyamoto, Koji Yakusho, Ken Watanabe, Yoshi Kato, Rikiya Yasuoka, Shuji Otaki, Masahiko Tsugawa, Yoriko Douguchi. **D:** Juzo Itami. **W:** Juzo Itami. **C:** Masaki Tamura. **M:** Kunihiko Murai. **VHS, DVD**

Task Force

Behind the generic action flick title (the Chinese translates to the much better *Hot Blood Is the Strongest*) hides a little gem. Director Patrick Leung mixes together comedy, drama, and action in an entertaining whirl reminiscent of some of the films of Wong Kar-wei, but without

the art-house pretension, putting this one a big step above his other films.

On assignment with his squad to catch illegal mainland prostitutes, cop Rod Lin (Leo Koo) meets hooker Fannie Chan (Charlie Yeung), after which she continues to harass him with prank phone calls and other tricks. Meanwhile, the father of Rod's supervisor Shirley Lau (Karen Mok) suffers a stroke, which brings the coworkers closer together, with the old man reminding Rod of his own father (who was slain in the line of duty). When Fannie gets in trouble with her pimp Hardy (Lawrence Ah Mon) and a loan shark (Edmond So), she calls on Rod to help her out. She continues to jerk him around even as they fall for each other. He never knows what to believe, particularly her wild story about a contract killer (Allan Mo) that seems to be dreamed up out of John Woo movies (Woo himself makes a cameo late in the picture). Interwoven with the misadventures of Rod and Shirley are those of their womanizing cohort Sgt. LuLu Tang (Eric Tsang), who is still heartbroken over a rocky divorce and ready to get into trouble with a local triad boss (Waise Lee).

The ensemble cast turns in great work, particularly singer and TV star Koo in only his second screen role. In the tense climax he has the same expression as Jackie Chan does in similar situations, though they look nothing alike. Action director Chin Ka-Lok, who has a small part as a robber, does a great job tailoring each action sequence to suit the particular scene, from the romantic swordplay in a hood's story to a slapstick street brawl between Eric Tsang and a triad member he's befriended. Seemingly on the brink of superstardom, Charlie Yeung abruptly disappeared from show business following this film. **AKA:** *Yit Huet Jui Keung; Re Xue Zui Qiang.* 𝄞𝄞𝄞𝄟

1997 106m/C *HK* Leo Koo, Charlie Yeung, Eric Tsang, Karen Mok, Edmond So, Allan Mo, Orlando To, Waise Lee, Vivian Leung, Lawrence Ah Mon, Clifton Ko, Chin Ka-Lok, Stephen Tung, John Lone, John Woo. **D:** Patrick Leung. **W:** Chan Hing-ka. **C:** Mark Lee. **M:** Danny Wong. **VHS, DVD**

A Taste of Killing and Romance

Grabs you by the throat and never lets go. Anita Yuen and Andy Lau play hired killers who fall in love while one remains ignorant of the other's profession. Anita's introduction is especially mind-blowing; the cute pixie strides into an office and suddenly turns into a bloody and cool killing machine, guns blazing left and right, while barely mussing a hair on her pretty head. She exits the building, "persuades" the bystanding Andy to allow her to use his sports car for her getaway, and a bond is formed. The two end up afoul of blackhearted and extremely calculating assassin manager Christine Ng and her outrageously deadly professional partner Mark Cheng. Fainthearted viewers should be prepared to look away when the latter executes an entire family. The two lovers also end up on the run from the authorities, led by Waise Lee as a cop who grudgingly grows to admire them.

The story is full of wildly implausible twists, but more than once you may find yourself laughing at the sheer audacity of the filmmakers. So much rude energy is on display that 24 frames per second are not enough to contain it. Instead, it squirts out of the screen and leaves a trail of bloody pulp on your carpet. Sadly, director Veronica Chan never made another film, but here she rips up the frame—not to be disrespectful to sufferers, but the camera has Attention Deficit Disorder—and moves things along at a frenetic pace, like the proverbial rollercoaster, only unencumbered by gravity. Andy Lau displays a sleepy charm, and the previously sweet Anita Yuen shows off a deranged personality. —PM **AKA:** *Saai Sau Dik Tung Wa; Sha Shou De Tong Hua.* 🦴🦴🦴

1994 92m/C *HK* Andy Lau, Anita Yuen, Mark Cheng, Christine Ng, Waise Lee, William So, Lai Chi-saan, Johnny Tang. **D:** Veronica Chan. **W:** Cheuk Bing. **C:** Faan Chuen-yam. **M:** Mark Lui, Raymond Wong. **DVD**

asians in usa

Teenage Mutant Ninja Turtles

During the mid-1980s, when dozens of ninja (and semi-ninja) movies were produced and the X-Men were the next big thing in comics, budding cartoonists Kevin Eastman and Peter Laird came up with idea for an independent comic book that would parody the whole scene through funny animal characters. Their *Teenage Mutant Ninja Turtles,* though a spoof, had the spark of real personalities, and the comic was a surprise hit for everyone. A groundbreaking merchandising deal led to an animated TV show, which in turn became a phenomenon. The cartoon was terrible, but the comic's stories were for the most part funny and well told, and when it came time for the inevitable big-screen treat-ment, the adaptation was thankfully more faithful to the original source. Not that the film isn't accessible to the pre-teen fans of the cartoon—the turtles, mutated to semi-humanoid form by radioactive ooze, still talk like New York Valley Boys and wear colorful masks. But some of the basic virtues of the series remained. The turtles still formed a kind of family with their sensei, Splinter, a ninjitsu master mutated by the ooze into a rat-like creature. And they still hide the angst of their existence by acting like the Four Stooges of kung fu.

The plot concerns how the four turtles (Raphael, Donatello, Leonardo, and Michelangelo) save reporter April O'Neil (Judith Hoag) when her investigation gets too close to the dealings of the ninja Foot Clan, who are recruiting the children of New York into their criminal army. The Foot leader Shredder is Splinter's old enemy, and he sends his Foot Soldiers to capture the rat. With the help of masked vigilante Casey Jones (Elias Koteas), the turtles stage a raid on the Foot headquarters to rescue their sensei.

The story was a natural fit for Golden Harvest Studios, which produced the film for New Line Cinema. It has many of the same elements as an old Chang Cheh kung fu classic, only with a bit more cartoonish characters. Jim Henson Productions created the main characters using the best available f/x of the day, namely topnotch animatronic puppetry and "suitamation." Elias Koteas has the look of a young Robert De Niro. Brandy Yuen *(Pedicab Driver)* had a hand in the fight choreography. 🦴🦴🦴

1990 (PG) 93m/C *HK/US* Judith Hoag, Elias Koteas, David Forman, Michelan Sisti, Leif Tilden, Josh Pais, Michael Turney, James Saito, Toshiro Obata, Sam Rockwell. **D:** Steve Barron. **W:** Bobby Herbeck, Todd W. Langen. **C:** John Fenner. **M:** John Du Prez. **VHS, DVD**

Tell Me Something

Doubtless inspired by gritty suspense thrillers like *Se7en,* this shocker was a smash in South Korea. It begins as someone enters a special room in their home, all fitted out with a surgical table. A scalpel-bearing hand begins slicing an arm off a body, blood spurting. Director Chang Yoon-hyun sends the audience a clear message: Here's what you're in for, so make your choice to stay or leave. Police Lieutenant Cho (Han Suk-kyu) is under investigation because a suspect in one of his cases was found to have paid Cho's late mother's medical bills. He's assigned the case when a plastic bag of body parts is found. According to the coroner Professor Gu, none of the parts are from the same body, and they were amputated while the victim was alive. More such bags are found around Seoul, in places where they're easily found—and since the pieces are hard to match, there's no telling how many victims there are. Still suspected and under pressure, Cho is offered a chance at redemption by solving the case quickly. When one victim is identified, next-of-kin Suyeon Chae (Shim Eun-ha) reveals a startling clue: all of the victims dated her in the past. Their prime suspect is an obsessed admirer named Kim (Yu Jun-sang). His guilt becomes more certain when it's learned that Kim has had Chae under surveillance for some time, and a victim's heart is found in his freezer. Cho finds a library of incriminating videotapes in a building Kim owns, and is almost run down by a car in the alley behind. But then, another bag is found—and Kim is the victim.

Though veteran chiller fans will find few big surprises here, Chang is definitely an advanced student of the genre, and the final twist may do the trick. His one misstep is a dream sequence, which is almost always a cheat in a thriller. Shot with style and intelligence, with an excellent soundtrack, *Tell Me Something* mixes its grit and grue with police procedure details and dramatic resonance. It's a fine example of why Korea has taken over as the new hot spot for genre film. Han Suk-kyu is turning out to be a new star in Asian cinema, but Chang Hang-sun steals every scene from him as a peanut-munching older detective. 🐉🐉🐉♥

1999 (R) 118m/C *KO* Han Suk-kyu, Shim Eun-ha, Chang Hang-sun, Yu Jun-sang, Yum Jung-ah. **D:** Chang Yoon-hyun. **W:** Chang Yoon-hyun, Kong Su-chang, In Eun-ah, Koo Bon-han (story). **C:** Kim Sung-bok. **M:** Cho Young-ook. **VHS, DVD**

Temptress of a Thousand Faces

Athena Chu stars in this odd superhero adventure, no doubt inspired by the success of *Black Mask* and *Heroic Trio*. Mysterious triad executions have been taking place around Hong Kong. A woman in a black cape and lacy mask uses her ninja skills to get through security nets and slay mob bosses with her lethally thrown playing cards. The corrupt police inspector assigned to the case is baffled by the fact that no clues can be found (guess he forgot to check the security camera tapes). The culprit is Sherry (Chu), a lonely schoolteacher who spends her free time drinking at her favorite bar, singing karaoke, and assassinating the triad chiefs who killed her parents. Not even her best friend May (comic relief Pinky Cheung) knows of her nighttime vendetta.

One night Sherry meets Jerry Cheung (Kwan Tak Fai) at the bar. Jerry is a lonely executive at a health food company, though his father and uncle urge him to go into the family crime busi-

ness with them. Walking home together, the pair is attacked by street thugs on motorcycles. This is probably the best scene in the movie, as it presents the total role reversal of Sherry kicking the bikers' butts while Jerry cowers behind her. He even breaks his heel!

Though there's some attempt at drama when it becomes plain that Sherry's main targets are members of Jerry's family, but this is quickly disposed of in favor of acrobatics and explosives. However, those hoping for some primo fightin' femme-tertainment are bound to be disappointed in the weak kung fu on display here. The action scenes are nicely edited, but fail to disguise the obvious use of doubles—and poorly choreographed ones at that. For superheroine fetishists only. This isn't on his resumé, but isn't that Anthony Wong doing a cameo as "Poker" the bartender? 🐉

1998 C: *HK* Athena Chu, Kwan Tak Fai, Pinky Cheung. **D:** Chan Wai On. **VHS**

10 Magnificent Killers

Old China crime boss Ling Chu (Bolo Yeung) has been assembling a gang of 10 killers to dominate his province. Chou Sing is set to become new constable after the old one is killed by Ling Chu's men, and Master Lau Shi intensifies Chou's training for his new job. Ling's rival, tough-guy bounty hunter Master Tu Shu, trains Shao Li (Cheung Lik) to be his partner. Tu Shu sends his student on a test mission, telling him Lau Shi's brother Li Yu Wei (director Fong Yeh) is a wanted man—reward, $20,000. Shao Li cuts Lau Shi and his brother Li Yu Wei with his poisoned sword. However, Li recovers and continues training his son Chou Sing, hoping his enemies will beat each other in the meantime.

Ling Chu's killers come to call for Tu Shu, one after another, and are defeated: Poison Horse Somo. Coffin Man Pao Ting. Crazy Monk Lo Fung (San Kwai). Flower Picker Lau Mao. Living Fairy Wu (Dai Sai Aan). Tu Shu and Shao Li are glad to collect the bounties, but are getting nervous waiting for the killers, and decide to go hunting for them. Together they track down and kill Mean Fellow Lau Mo, Doctor Liao, and Ma Chang. They catch Kwan Yuan in Ling Chu's front yard. Ling Chu reveals a little secret before fighting them: Shao Li is actually Li Yu Wei's son, and Tu Shu has been training him to kill his own father for 20 years.

Shao Li and his master are such nasty fellows that it's hard to care whether they win their fights or not. The fun is in seeing them fight the 10 guest-star killers. In fact, it would've made the movie better to concentrate more on this aspect, and downplay the not-too-original twist

"Now let me show you how to break a banana tree. Watch this."

—Standard martial arts training as revealed in *10 Magnificent Killers*

ending. After that, the climactic duel with the constable is rather dull. Fong Yeh's directorial style is straightforward, with almost every shot taking place outdoors—including some of those telephone poles they had in Old China. *AKA: Sap Daai Saai Sau; Shi Da Sha Shou.* ♪♪

1977 (R) 86m/C *HK* Fong Yeh, Cheung Lik, San Kwai, Bolo Yeung, Dai Sai Aan, Chu Chi Ming, Lau Wing, Kong Do. *D:* Fong Yeh. *W:* Fong Yeh. *C:* Tsui Hsin Yu. *M:* Ng Tai Kong. **VHS, DVD**

Ten Tigers of Kwangtung

One of kung fu cinema's best directors tells a story of the 10 famous heroes who banded together to chase villains and rascals out of Canton in the late 19th century, assembling a cast of some of kung fu cinema's greatest stars. Tung Chi (Wang Li) plots with his nephew Liang Shou-hu to strike back at the Ten Tigers for the death of his father, Manchu official Liang Tse-kue (Johnny Wang), by first killing their students, then picking off the heroes one by one. With the students drunk at a casino, the assassins take the opportunity to kill their chaperone. After the murder, student Wang Tin-min (Alexander Fu Sheng) tells the other students the story (via flashback) of how Liang was killed because Wang's master Li Chen-chow (Ti Lung) and Wong Kei-ying (Wei Pai) helped fugitive rebel leader Chu Hun-ying (Ku Feng). Hero/pawnbroker Li sent Tin-min to recruit kung fu masters Wang Yin-lin (Sun Chien) and Su Hei-hu (Lu Feng) to help hide and protect Chu, but the youth's brash manners almost alienated them instead. Tin-min's street-fighting ways brought Beggar So Chan (Phillip Kwok), Iron Finger Chen Ta-chung (Lo Meng), pole fighter Cho Yu-sheng (Chiang Sheng), and strongman Yen Cho-san (Yeung Hung) to the attention of a Manchu spy Mr. Chow (Chiang Nan), who backed the masters in opening an illegal kung fu school. These four were used to flush Chu out of hiding, but when they realize they're being used by the Manchus, they made good by joining the Tigers. While the others disrupt his soldiers, the evil Liang Tse-kue was killed in a duel with Li Chen-chow. Now, with the junior Tigers being picked off one by one by the vengeful villains, the remaining students retaliate by hunting down the assassins.

It may be that pulp writer Ngai Hong's affection for flashbacks got the best of him here, as the non-linear structure of the plot results only in needless confusion. Either that, or Chang Cheh made a movie about the formation of the Ten Tigers, and finding the running time far too short, had to come up with the framing story about the vengeful assassins using a different cast of characters. Though there's plenty of

great fighting action, one expects that a movie about these famous heroes will at least have them involved in the climax. The terrific cast, led by sturdy Ti Lung with Phillip Kwok providing a fine Beggar So, are spread thin over the film's running time. In all, a disappointing misfire. *AKA: Gong Dung Sap Foo Hing Yik Ng Sui; Guang Dong Shi Hu Xing Yi Wu Xu; Ten Tigers from Kwangtung.* ♪♪

1979 90m/C *HK* Ti Lung, Alexander Fu Sheng, Phillip Kwok, Johnny Wang, Lo Meng, Lu Feng, Sun Chien, Chiang Sheng, Chin Siu-Ho, Ku Feng, Lung Tin Cheung, Wei Pai, Wang Li, Dick Wei, Jamie Luk, Robert Mak, Kwan Fung, Yeung Hung, Wong Ching Ho, Lau Wai-ling, Chiang Nan, Shum Lo, Yeung Ching-Ching, Siao Yuk, Lam Wai, Lam Chi-tai, Chan Hon-kwong, Tiu Lung, Fung Ging Man, Chan Shu-kei, Yu Tai-ping, Walter Cho. *D:* Chang Cheh. *W:* Ngai Hong, Chang Cheh. *M:* Eddie H. Wang. **VHS, DVD**

Ten Tigers of Shaolin

Tiger Chue Tai (Bruce Liang) and the other Ten Tigers of Kwangtung take a break from cleaning up crime around town, to attend the wedding of Ti Chung's brother Tam Ti-chuen. Chue Tai returns from breaking up the racket of a fake Buddhist priest (San Kwai) in time to stop the bandit gang of beefy Chou Tau-chung (Hon Yee Sang) from robbing the bridal procession and abducting the bride. Chou escapes, and asks Lord Yeung Sun-pao (Lau Dan) to help him get revenge. First, Lord Yeung picks a fight with waiter Fai Ah-pei, nephew of Tam and student of Wang Wei. Then his men kidnap Mrs. Fai, all in an effort to separate the Ten Tigers. Yeung recruits other enemies of the Ten Tigers like Tan Hung-chai to help. While Chue Tai is lured into a trap at an abandoned house, thugs attack the kung fu school, but are driven off by So Chu-sang (Michelle Lai) and her brother Beggar So (Hon Gwok-choi). The Ten Tigers decide to spring a trap of their own, disguising Chu-sang as a visiting princess to get half of them into Yeung's house, while the others slip in the back dressed as beggars.

All the preceding is merely a setup for the last third of the picture, in which each of the Ten Tigers picks out a dozen or so bad guys in an open field and lays hands and feet on them. Twenty minutes later, they've whittled their way down to the lead villains for a few more rounds. Eventually, everyone gets a piece of top villain Kong Do. The highlight is likely Hon Gwok-choi's humorous portrayal of Beggar So—at one point in the battle, he gets kicked in the groin and it appears he's wetting his pants, until he fishes out a broken wine jug he had hidden away. It would be a great idea for one of today's producers to put together a new movie about the Ten Tigers starring all the best martial arts stars. **AKA:** *Gong Dung Sap Foo; Guang Dong Shi Hu.* ♫♫

1978 85m/C *HK* Bruce Liang, Tony Wong, Jason Pai, Li Chin-Kun, Hon Gwok-choi, Kong Do, Lau Dan, Hon Yee Sang, San Kwai, Michelle Lai, Sai Gwa Pau, Cheng Lui, Charlie Chan, Lau Hok Nin, Henry Fong, Yue Tau Wan. **D:** Ngai Hoi-fung. **W:** Ngai Hoi-fung. **C:** Ho Yue. **DVD**

Terminatrix

In the 21st century, an overpopulation crisis causes the world government to regulate all sex acts. One woman leads a rebellion against the tyranny. The leaders decide to send killer robot T-69 (Shouko Kudou) back in time to prevent the rebel Hanako from ever being born. Kaora (Kei Mizutani) time-travels to the past as well, to warn horny bartender Kota Sera (Naofumi Matsuda) that he's to be the father of humanity's last hope, and that this Terminatrix is out to destroy his sexual potency. Of course, no one believes her crazy story, but Kota begins to suspect something's up when a neighbor with the same name is assaulted and crippled. The T-69 homes in on him and attempts to obtain a sperm sample for identification.

No, it's not the next installment in the *Terminator* franchise, but a silly soft-core parody. It's not as wild as *Weather Woman,* but it may please Mizutani's growing fan-base all the same, as it offers plenty of female flesh and bizarre situations. When the T-69 is about to close in on Kota, Kaoru stops her for a while by shooting six bullets into her cha-cha-cha! She recharges by wiring electricity straight to her nipples. Though some fans will be disappointed that Mizutani doesn't play a terminatrix herself, the statuesque Kudou fills the bill nicely. **AKA:** *Insatsu no Toriko.* ♫♫

1995 75m/C *JP* Kei Mizutani, Naofumi Matsuda, Shouko Kudou, Saeko Ichijou, Yuuki Fujisawa, Yasunori Matsuda. **D:** Mikio Hirota. **W:** Mikio Hirota. **C:** Naoki Hashimoto. **M:** Tatsuo Nakanishi. **VHS, DVD**

Terror beneath the Sea

Japanese productions of the 1960s had included Western actors before, but this sci-fi action flick from Toei really loads up on the Anglo faces, many of them Germans living in Tokyo. Well, there have been worse collaborations between Germany and Japan—though technically, this was one of those projects with Italians and Americans involved in the financing.

Reporters Jenny Gleason (Peggy Neal) and Ken Abe (Sonny Chiba) attend a demonstration by the U.S. Navy of their latest technological gizmo—a homing torpedo—that nearly goes awry. During the demonstration, they notice atomic scientist Professor Howard (Andrew Hughes) in attendance, and a shadowy figure swims past the viewing screen. They decide to snoop around a nearby underwater nuclear waste dump to see if they can find out anything, and a scaly monster-man chases Jenny. Confronted with her sighting, Commander Brown (Franz Gruber) is obviously covering up something. But just what he's covering up Brown doesn't know—he doesn't know what to make of Jenny's report, but wants to discourage further civilian interference. Finding an underwater entrance to a cave, Ken and Jenny are captured and knocked out by the silvery gill-men. They wake up in the underwater base of megalomaniac Dr. Rufus Moore (Erik Neilson), and after a bit of mind games in his future-noir holding rooms, the creepy scientist gives them a demonstration of the grotesque process by which he transforms a man into a "water cyborg" under his control. Jenny and Ken don't appreciate the humor in the situation when Moore shows how he controls the cyborgs with colorfully labeled knobs that say "work" and "fight." Of course, the stuffy, conservative reporters refuse to join Moore's new world order of gods and monsters, and the pair is prepared to undergo the transformation process. Brown leads a search of the area in a navy submarine, beginning a battle of missiles and torpedoes that threatens to destroy everything for miles around.

Sonny Chiba fans may be a bit disappointed to see the Street Fighter making only wimpy attempts at fisticuffs here, but he still has his leading-man charisma. Along with the appealing Ms. Neal (a mere 19 at the time) and Mr. Chiba, the main draw here is the cyborg gill-men, who are spooky and amusing at the same time. With close-set black eyes and silvery scales, they look like gray aliens crossed with the Creature from the Black Lagoon. Unaccountably creepy, this is a fast-moving adventure that gained a lot of fans who caught it on late night TV screenings and woke up the next morning thinking they'd hallucinated the whole movie. **AKA:** *Kaitei Daisenso; Water Cyborgs; Great War under the Sea; The Great Undersea War; I Mostri della Citta Sommersa.* ♫♫▽

1966 79m/ C: *JP* Sonny Chiba, Peggy Neal, Andrew Hughes, Mike Danning, Erik Neilson, Franz Gruber, Gunther Braun, Beverly Kahler, Hideo Murota, Koji Miemachi, Hans Hornef, John Kleine. **D:** Hajime Sato. **W:** Masami Fukushima. **C:** Kazuo Shimomura. **M:** Shunsuke Kikuchi. **VHS**

Rowdy hooligans Godzilla, MechaGodzilla, and Titanosaurus tip over a highway to celebrate the release of *Terror of MechaGodzilla.*

Terror Is a Man

On a trip across the South Pacific aboard the *Pedro Queen,* William Fitzgerald (Richard Derr) is the lone survivor when the ship sinks. He comes ashore on remote Blood Island, where he finds the natives have all fled. He's taken in by Dr. Girard (Francis Lederer) and his wife, Frances (Greta Thyssen, Miss Denmark of 1952). Fitzgerald assumes the natives fled because of a man-killing panther said to be loose on the island, but they really fear the suspicious scientist. Not such a bad idea, since Fitzgerald finds that the doctor is keeping a man strapped to a table in his basement laboratory. Fitzgerald tries to get Frances to help him free the poor man, but learns the truth: the man isn't really human at all, but a panther given a painful step-up the evolutionary ladder by the quite mad Dr. Girard.

The first known Philippine horror film is an attempt at an unauthorized adaptation of H.G. Wells's *The Island of Doctor Moreau,* and is often successful at creating quite a bit of chilling atmosphere with shadowy black-and-white camera work. The monster makeup is not particularly advanced, but is kept mostly concealed in creepy shadows. The army of manimals created by the mad scientist in the novel (and the earlier film *Island of Lost Souls*) is reduced to one, making the film a more intimate nightmare, but decreasing the story's power. There's no society of creatures dealing with a flawed god, just a poor Frankenstein monster looking for release. Performances are a bit flat, taking a bite out of the suspense quotient. Director Gerardo de Leon would revisit Blood Island again, with his occasional partner Eddie Garcia, for a more-or-less official "Blood Island" trilogy. While Romero was more action oriented, de Leon was better at atmosphere, and later made some moody Philippine vampire movies. *AKA: Blood Creature; Creature from Blood Island; The Gory Creatures; Island of Terror.* 🎵🎵🎵

1959 89m/BW *PH* Francis Lederer, Greta Thyssen, Richard Derr, Oscar Keesee Jr., Lilio Duran, Reyton Keesee, Flory Carlos. *D:* Gerardo de Leon. *W:* Harry Paul Harber. *C:* Emmanuel I. Rojas. *M:* Ariston Auelino. **VHS, DVD**

Terror of MechaGodzilla

The better-than-average returns on *Godzilla vs. MechaGodzilla* prompted Toho to produce this direct sequel, this time with a bigger budget. Mad scientist Dr. Mafune (Akihiko Hirata) discov-

ers a living deep-sea dinosaur monster he names Titanosaurus (Katsumi Nimiamoto), and creates a device that can be used to control the monster. The black-hole alien apes, disguised as humans, hire Mafune to use Titanosaurus against mankind, and to help them rebuild MechaGodzilla (Ise Mori). When Mafune's daughter Katsura (Tomoko Ai) is killed, the aliens resurrect her as a cyborg, placing the monsters' control device inside her body for safekeeping. It's monster vs. machine in the heavyweight battle of the universe as MechaGodzilla is once again pitted against the real thing (Toru Kawai). With his tag-team partner Titanosaurus, the giant robot overwhelms the Earth's biggest monster hero, but Katsura, her mecha-heart softened by love for biologist Ichinose (Katsuhiko Sasaki), releases control of the monsters, giving Godzilla better odds.

Though the plot is nothing terrific, it's at least a step up from the nonsense of the previous few entries. Special-effects director Teruyoshi Nakano puts the relatively larger budget to good use, filling the screen with rubber-monster mayhem. The return of director Ishiro Honda and composer Akira Ifukube gives some style back to the series, but the declining budgets and lackluster scripts of the '70s entries don't help matters. This would be the last Godzilla movie made for about 10 years, a delay caused by flagging ticket sales and an attempt to produce an American 3-D Godzilla movie. **AKA:** *Mekagojira no Gyakushu; The Escape of MechaGodzilla; MechaGodzilla vs. Godzilla; Terror of Godzilla; Revenge of MechaGodzilla; Monsters from an Unknown Planet.* 🐉🐉🐉

1975 (G) 80m/C *JP* Akihiko Hirata, Tomoko Ai, Katsuhiko Sasaki, Goro Mutsumi, Tadao Nakamaru, Toru Ibuki, Kenji Sahara, Kotaro Tomita, Ikio Sawamura, Masaaki Daimon, Kazuo Suzuki, Yasuzo Ogawa, Saburo Kadowaki, Shigeo Kato, Ise Mori, Toru Kawai, Katsumi Nimiamoto. **D:** Ishiro Honda. **W:** Yukiko Takayama. **C:** Sokei Tomioka. **M:** Akira Ifukube. **VHS, DVD**

Tetsuo: The Iron Man

Shinya Tsukamoto's debut film caused something of a sensation on first release, dazzling audiences with its stark black-and-white style while shocking them with its visceral violence. David Lynch's *Eraserhead* and David Cronenberg's *Videodrome* are often cited as points of reference, but violent sci-fi manga and anime were a heavy influence as well.

A young man prowls a junkyard, looking for a chunk of metal to "shoot up" with—his apparent goal is to make the metal part of his body.

Afterward, as he runs in pain, he truly merges with a machine, hit by an automobile. The driver (Tomoro Taguchi) becomes infected with the same disease, as he finds metal whiskers growing from his face. He's not the only one—a girl on the subway is attacked by some kind of cyborg fetus, which merges with her. The cyborg woman pursues our hero, until he's forced to strike back with his own machine essence. Sprouting jets from his heels, he speeds into a psychedelic, cybernetic, psychotronic existence. He fears his condition may be retribution for his hit-and-run crime. Of course, his girlfriend (Kei Fujiwara) is infected, too, but he kills her in a rage before she can begin to transform. Now an out-of-control metal beast, he's shocked to learn that his victim (Shinya Tsukamoto) survived the accident, and is preparing to attack using his own biomech powers.

The apocalyptic finale, with our super metal-beast ready to conquer the world, isn't very convincing, but up until that point Tsukamoto and company make their shoestring budget work for them, creating simple special effects in a way that enhances rather than detracts from the film's overall style. The industrial sound and look may be trite over a dozen years later, but as cinema this still packs a raw punch, delivering a fevered and disturbing nightmare vision. An art-house hit worldwide, *Tetsuo* served to launch busy careers for all involved. **AKA:** *Tetsuo; Iron Man.* 🐉🐉🐉🐉

1989 67m/BW *JP* Tomoro Taguchi, Kei Fujiwara, Shin Kanaoko, Shinya Tsukamoto, Renji Ishibashi, Naomasa Musaka. **D:** Shinya Tsukamoto. **W:** Shinya Tsukamoto. **C:** Shinya Tsukamoto, Kei Fujiwara. **M:** Chu Ishikawa. **VHS, DVD**

Tetsuo 2: Body Hammer

A lot of people were disappointed that Shinya Tsukamoto's sequel to his debut feature behaves like a "real" movie, but then, would a retread of the original film be any more satisfying? Tokyo businessman Tomoo Taniguchi (Tomoro Taguchi) has a happy family life, despite troubling visions of the childhood he forgot before being taken in by foster parents. In a mall one day, a pair of thugs shoots Taniguchi with a bizarre weapon and snatches away his son Minori. But Taniguchi is the real target—they've infected him with a metallic mutagen that gives him the ability to transform his body into a living weapon. A mystery man named God (Shinya Tsukamoto) has brought together scientists and athletes for a mission: the creation of an army of unstoppable cyborgs bent on destruction. Taniguchi was chosen as a test subject because they thought they could

easily control him if something went wrong. Further tests confirm their success, but before they can kill their subject he breaks free. It turns out that Taniguchi is more of a demon than they thought, and somehow God's volunteer subjects aren't as successful. The reason obviously has something to do with Taniguchi's forgotten past.

While promoted as a punk groundbreaker, Tsukamoto is at the core typically Japanese—he revels in creation but is fascinated by destruction. His carefully constructed story serves to nurture his superhuman characters, but its ultimate purpose is to have them clash with a smash, thud, and ka-boom. *Body Hammer* can't hope to match the ferocity of *Iron Man,* but it's a superior monster yarn with a bit of mystery thrown in. The director's creative drive sometimes gets in the way of clear storytelling, but all the pieces end up in place in the end. *AKA: Tetsuo: Body Hammer.* 🐾🐾🐾

1991 (R) 81m/C *JP* Tomoro Taguchi, Shin Kanaoko, Shinya Tsukamoto, Sujin Kim. *D:* Shinya Tsukamoto. *W:* Shinya Tsukamoto. *C:* Shinya Tsukamoto. *M:* Chu Ishikawa. **VHS, DVD**

The 36 Crazy Fists

Jackie Chan helped out director Chen Chi-hwa *(Snake and Crane Arts of Shaolin)* by serving as action director on this kung fu comedy. Producer Chiang Kit got some behind-the-scenes footage of Chan at work (and smoking a cigarette!), and tacked it onto the picture to back up his promotion of the picture as a Jackie Chan feature. Some versions available still contain this footage.

Shaolin monks Chu Shan-fung (Paul Chun) and Fong Yi-kung (San Kwai), on leave from the monastery, help out young Wong Tai-kwong (Tony Leung Siu-hung), who is being beaten by gangsters. His sister Wong Wai-chi (Michelle Lai) explains that the Manchurian gangsters working for local hood Man Kar-kao killed their father when he refused to pay protection fees. Wanting to stay near the pretty young Wai-chi, crafty Chu tells them he can teach them enough kung fu to clean up the gang in three months. However, the abbot (Lee Man Tai) declares that Wong is too weak to train, so they take the lad to Master Sze (Ku Feng), who admits Wong into his school just to spite the twitching old abbot. Saddled

with all the most menial chores in the school, Wong learns more kung fu from an old drunk (Chiang Cheng) in the woods than he does in school. Though he's unable to beat the master's champion and earn the right to leave, impatient Wong sneaks off anyway to beat up gangsters at home. Man challenges him to a duel, but it becomes obvious to the young disciple that he's just not good enough to beat the gang boss yet. With time ticking away toward the deadline, Wong's monk friends at Shaolin Temple give him a crash course in kung fu styles. It's enough to help him beat Man Kar-kao, but elder brother Lu Ying-kuo (Fung Hark-On) comes looking for revenge. Since Wong hasn't studied weapons use, Fong saves his life by faking an epileptic fit, delaying the duel for three days. The monks blackmail Master Sze into teaching Wong something to counter Lu Ying-kuo's steel whip. Beating Lu only means that the gangsters' master Ma Lo-tak (Yam Sai-kwoon), boss of the Man Tang Gang, issues another challenge to fight Wong in two weeks time. Even learning all Sze can teach him won't save Wong this time, so the old beggar and his student Shun Ho-kung (Jimmy Liu) pitch in to help.

The situation of a hapless young student who learns only fast enough to stay one step ahead of his challengers is rich with comic potential—potential that is totally wasted in this miserable film. Leung looks like all his moves follow Chan's instruction, and there's some fun moments in the fight scenes with his talented co-stars, but every attempt at comedy is a complete failure. *AKA: Saam Sap Luk Mai Ying Kuen; San Shi Liu Mi Xing Quan; Bloodpact; Jackie Chan's Bloodpact; The Master and the Boxer; Jackie and the 36 Crazy Fists; Jackie Chan's 36 Crazy Fists.*

1977 (R) 89m/C *HK* Tony Leung Siu-hung, Yam Sai-kwoon, Ku Feng, Paul Chun, Fung Hark-On, San Kwai, Michelle Lai, Chan Lau, Jimmy Liu, Lee Man Tai, Wong Biu Chan, Sham Chin-bo, Chiang Cheng. *D:* Chen Chi-hwa. *W:* Szeto On. *C:* Pan Te-yeh. *M:* Ng Tai Kong. **VHS, DVD**

The 36 Deadly Styles

If there's one thing this movie has, it's a lot of styles (if not style), and with every fighter using several, it's possible they add up to 36. However, it doesn't have much else. Having offended Master Yuen Cheng-tien (Mark Lung) by hiding the 36 Styles manual, Huang Kuo and his nephew Wai-chi (Cheung Lik) flee to a monastery in Tibet, where his old friend Wong (Yeung Chak Lam) is a senior monk. Wong was once injured by Yuen's silver-maned hit man Chung Si (Hwang Jang Lee), and helps them

fight off Yuen's men, but both fugitives are badly injured in the fight, and Huang dies of his wounds. One of the thugs (Chan Lau) escapes the temple by feigning death, and he writes Yuen for help. Wai-chi wastes little time mourning, and gets right to bedeviling the monks with his kung fu—one of many poor attempts at comedy in this cheap Joseph Kuo picture. Kuo has never been known for his comic genius, and here he just embarrasses himself trying to copy the kung fu comedies of Jackie Chan, making matters worse by adding annoying "wacky" library music and sound effects. Master Wong punishes Wai-chi with some tough errands. On a trip to fetch soy milk, he meets Chu-chi (Jeanie Chang) whose father (Fan Mui-Sang) is another of Chung Si's old foes, and like Wong, still suffers from his wounds. Master Wong finally gets sick of Wai-chi's antics and throws him out of the temple, but when Wai-chi learns the killers are coming, he returns to warn Wong. But Chung Si has already arrived, and is too powerful for Wai-chi. Chu-chi's dad takes him to a mountain retreat to teach him all of the Eight Gods styles, so the young man can defend himself from the man who killed his father.

Some attempt is made at making this standard revenge saga more interesting by mixing up the plot a bit, but it only makes the movie less involving. It may be that this movie combines parts of two unfinished pictures—Mark Lung, who is supposed to be the main villain, doesn't interact with any of the other actors, and disappears from the screen after a brief scene at the beginning, only turning up later on to fight brother Jack Lung in an attempt to make him give up the secrets of the manual (which no one else ever mentions). Some of the villains, including Bolo Yeung, wear very silly wigs. The soundtrack steals the Pink Panther theme in one scene! *AKA: Mai Kuen Saam Sap Luk Chu; Mi Quan San Shi Liu Zhao; Shadow Boxin'.*

1979 88m/C *HK* Cheung Lik, Mark Lung, Jack Lung, Jeanie Chang, Hwang Jang Lee, Fan Mui-Sang, Chan Lau, Yeung Chak Lam, Joe Ma, Wong Biu Chan, Bolo Yeung, Sham Chin-bo, Shih Ting Ken, Wong Wing Sheng. *D:* Joseph Kuo. *W:* Chiang Ping-han. *C:* Liang Chien. *M:* Lawrence Chan. **VHS, DVD**

Thousand Mile Escort

During the reign of Emperor Sung, invading Tartars and bad governing by Prime Minister Tzin Kuei cause turmoil across China. Righteous man Sen Lei-tzi (Pai Ying) is drafted into the imperial guard, but only stays long enough to rescue the young son of Counselor Wen from being killed with his parents by General Kan Shao-lo (Lo

Lieh). In a blatant imitation of the Lone Wolf and Cub movies, Sen goes on the run with the boy in a baby cart, fighting off assassins along the way. Sen finds an important letter in Junior's clothes from the Prime Minister to the emperor which proves his treason, and Sen decides to deliver it to good General Yueh. Kan and his men go all-out to trap Sen, and the only help he gets is from the enigmatic Miss Yuen (Judy Lee), who has a habit of popping up just when her help is needed. Kan sends his wife (Michelle Lai) as a spy to snare his prey, but when Sen kills her, the general has a personal score to settle.

Thousand Mile Escort apes the Lone Wolf series to the point of reproducing certain sequences and situations. The same attraction to gadgetry is also evident—the baby cart is a nifty collapsible model, and the hero bears a unique weapon: a staff with spring-loaded retractable points inside that can be fired at enemies. Most of the action takes place amid fresh mountain scenery. The fight choreography is imaginative, but uses too much slow motion. The English dub is awful, sounding like it was looped by heavily accented Asian and American high-school students. *AKA: Yan Ba Chiu; Ren Ba Zhao.* 🐉🐉♡

1976 81m/C *HK* Lo Lieh, Pai Ying, Judy Lee, Michelle Lai, Miu Tin, Fong Min, Fong Yeh, Chui Chung Hei, Cheung Pang, Man Man. **D:** Chui Chang-wang. **DVD**

3 Evil Masters

Righteous hero Chin Tien-yuen (Chen Kuan-tai) wants to punish a gang of villains, the 3 Evils, threatening to cut the leader Yen Ching-wong's (Johnny Wang) arms off. He's close to beating them up in a restaurant, but a treacherous waiter stabs him. He escapes, and makes his way to a kung fu academy. Orphan Kao Ching (Yuen Tak), always picked on by the older brothers, takes in the injured stranger and hides him from Master Shih Chen-chuan (Lau Hok Nin). Good thing, too—Chin once broke Master Shih's ribs in a fight. He tells Kao all about the 3 Evils—Yen, Fan Shen, and knife-throwing Chow San-kwei—who are still hunting for him. While recovering, Chin teaches Kao his kung fu and swordplay secrets. But Kao's secret training eventually comes out during Master Shih's drills, and Chin has to fight his way out of the school. Chin is still suffering from his injury when the 3 Evils finally catch up with him—he's killed by Chow's knives in his back, and Yen's kick in his nuts. While Kao Ching is being punished, the 3 Evils decide to take over the school as their headquarters. Even a combination of Shih, his students, and some hired killers aren't enough to defeat them, leaving it up to Kao Ching to avenge everyone.

A B-movie by Shaw Brothers standards, *3 Evil Masters* relies on its action scenes and the stars' personalities to carry the load. Unfortunately, the trio of villains isn't very remarkable, and Yuen Tak is too slight and feminine-looking to make a good hero—and his ugly haircut doesn't help any. However, there's nothing wrong with his athletic ability, and the fight scenes are pretty good. Director Tony Liu takes pains to show details of martial arts moves, both during training scenes and cutting in for slow-motion close-ups during fights. An especially slick move by Chen is when he knocks down an opponent with the flicked hem of his suit. *AKA: Booi Boon Bye Moon; Bei Pan Shi Men; The Master.* 🐉🐉♡

1980 95m/C *HK* Chen Kuan-tai, Yuen Tak, Johnny Wang, Lau Hok Nin, Cheng Miu, Candy Wen, Kwan Fung, Chan Lau, Lam Fai-wong. **D:** Tony Liu. **W:** Ngai Hong. **M:** Eddie H. Wang. **DVD**

The Three Swordsmen

One of the three superpowered swordsmen of the title is Siu Sam-siu (Andy Lau), founder of the Better and Fit Club. Siu is set to face off against the second swordsman Ming Jian (Brigitte Lin, dubbed by a man!) in a competition held by the Chi Leung Organization to find the top 10 warriors in China. But before the match can begin, Siu is framed for the murder of the queen by his jealous old girlfriend Red Leaves, now married to Chi Leung leader Dik Suen. Not wanting to reveal his alibi (that he spent the night with his fiancée Butterfly), Siu flees to find other proof of his innocence. He's pursued by militia leader Wham Dao (Elvis Tsui) and Marquis Hak. The Ming family takes in Siu and Butterfly, but they're plagued by traitors within—Ming's wife Ku Choi-yi (Yu Li) is an assassin who can kill with her hair—and enemies without (the military and a half dozen rival clans).

The super-swordplay is a lot of fun here, and the stars are pleasant to watch, but the plot is as thick as the Great Wall, and most of it is deadly dull. It's difficult to follow without scorecards and diagrams, and it's made impossible for English viewers by very poor subtitles (white against white backgrounds). No doubt based on an ancient thousand-page novel. Some music cues are swiped from Michael Mann's *Last of the Mohicans*. *AKA: Du Gim Siu; Dao Jian Xiao.* 🐉🐉

1994 86m/C *HK* Andy Lau, Brigitte Lin, Elvis Tsui, Yu Li, Leung Si-ho, Siqin Gaowa, Tung Wai Wai, Gan Tak-mau. **D:** Taylor Wong. **W:** Lee Sai-hung, Sze Mei-yee. **C:** Chow Kim-ming, Chow Kei-seung. **M:** Alvin Kwok. **VHS, DVD**

Throne of Blood

Another Kurosawa adaptation of an existing work, this film is loosely based on Shakespeare's *Macbeth.* The Bard and Kurosawa would prove a powerful combination in *Ran,* and this earlier flick is no disappointment. The story opens on a misty landscape with a chorus chanting an outline of what will happen in this tale of treachery, murder, and ambition. A castle forms out of the fog, and we can't tell if it's real, or something from the past, or something from the imagination. Inside the fortress, the kingdom's lord discusses the wars besieging his frontiers. Things look bad for his clan, until news arrives telling of a pair of captains—Washizu (Toshiro Mifune) and Miki (Minoru Chiaki)—who have turned the tide. The two are summoned by their lord and have to ride through the enchanted Cobweb Forest to the castle. In the woods, they meet a strange old witch who tells their futures. Washizu will rise in power, she says, and one day become lord of Cobweb Castle. Miki's son is fated to be lord of the castle after Washizu. Eventually, the two captains escape the strange forest and find their way to the castle. There, the first part of the witch's prophecy comes true and Washizu is elevated in rank.

Washizu returns home to his treacherous wife, Asaji (Isuzu Yamada). She tells him that he must dispose of Miki, who knows that he is destined to become lord of Cobweb Castle. If Washizu does not act, she says, the current lord will kill him for being a threat. There is an alternative, though—if Washizu kills the lord, then he will not only have the power he is destined for, but also be safe from reprisals. Fate lends a hand when the lord arrives at Washizu's castle for an unannounced visit. The traitorous Washizu and his wife concoct a scheme to slay the leader and blame their enemies. They carry off the plan and soon Washizu is lord of Cobweb Castle. Clearly, though, he is still not safe. Someone, probably Miki, may uncover his ambitious treachery. While Washizu suggests naming Miki's son his heir (thereby ensuring Miki's loyalty), Washizu's scheming wife urges that both Miki and the young man be assassinated.

Since this is a Shakespearean-Samurai melodrama, naturally, the evil impulse wins out. Washizu's treachery is not without cost, though. Washizu begins to see the ghosts of his dead friends, and lady Washizu can't seem to wash the blood off her hands, no matter how she tries. The slaying of the old lord hasn't been forgotten, and Miki's son rides with those seeking to avenge the murder. They arrive outside cobweb castle in force, while inside Washizu battles his own demons. The climactic arrow-riddled battle scene is one of the most memorable in all of cinema.

Throne of Blood is one of Kurosawa's masterpieces. It stands out even amid a career as titanic as the master's. The character portrayals are vivid, the acting first-class, the cinematography outstanding. It also has an eerie quality seldom matched in his other films (save perhaps for some of the segments in *Dreams*). *Throne* is a nice counterpart and/or predecessor to the Japanese horror masterpiece *Kwaidan.* Mifune's descent into madness is especially haunting. *Throne of Blood* is a chilling portrayal of ambition and madness in medieval Japan and gets the Hound's highest recommendation. — SS **AKA:** *Kumonosu Jo; Castle of the Spider's Web; Cobweb Castle; Macbeth.* 🐾🐾🐾🐾

1957 109m/C *JP* Toshiro Mifune, Isuzu Yamada, Takashi Shimura, Minoru Chiaki, Cheiko Naniwa, Akira Kubo, Takamaru Sasaki, Hiroshi Tachikawa, Yoshio Tsuchiya, Ikio Sawamura, Sachio Sakai, Senkichi Omura, Akira Tani, Isao Kimura, Seiji Miyaguchi, Shin Otomo, Yutaka Sada, Nobuo Nakamura, Kokuten Kodo, Yu Fujiki. **D:** Akira Kurosawa. **W:** Akira Kurosawa, Shinobu Hashimoto, Ryuzo Kikushima, Yoshiro Murai. **C:** Asaich Nakai. **M:** Masaru Sato. **VHS, DVD**

Thunder Cop

Ng Chi-Lone (Nicky Wu) tries to live up to his late father's record on the police force. While he and his partner Joe are hunting crooks in a building, Ng sees a suspect flee, and fights to capture him. However, he has to stop to save a little girl and the suspect gets away. In Changchun, a few months later, triad chief Chiu Kwok-Ho (Winston Chao) is preparing to retire and flee to Canada. But he has sworn to keep drug trade out of his sector, and accuses thug Kenny of using car shipments to smuggle drugs to Hong Kong. Chiu's subordinate Keung (Ben Ng) is behind it, trying to wrest control from Chiu. There's a shootout in a train station, as Keung's men try to kill Chiu and fail. Lone screws up an undercover operation keeping tabs on Chiu, unknowingly attacking another cop, but is forgiven since his Superintendent Lai has the hots for Lone's Aunt Honey (Carrie Ng).

Out drinking, Lone and Chiu strike up an anonymous friendship, Keung's men attack anew, and the pair of new friends barely escape through the big gunfight and explosions. Lone finds out too late who Chiu is and gets suspended on suspicion of corruption. Chiu says he'll give Lone a present, and sends his girlfriend Lau Mei-ying (Rene Liu) to him for protection. However, Keung's gunmen, who know she's Chiu's weakness, find out she's at Lone's apartment and they have to run. They hide out with Aunt Honey and Lone's jealous cousin Tung-Tung (Ivy Leung). But of course, eventually Keung and his boys track them down for a big dustup at the end.

THE HOUND SALUTES
Akira Kurosawa

Try this: Pick up a fine-art book with some good paintings in it—something representational, maybe a collection by one of the "old masters." Open it to any given image. Then fire up your DVD player and pop in one of Akira Kurosawa's films. Any one. Probably one from his AR (Anno *Rashomon*—1950 or later) period would be best, but this experiment should work with Kurosawa's earlier films, too. Select a chapter with any scene in the movie you like. Press "play" and then press "pause." Look at the image on your screen. New or old, black and white or color, chances are good that what you're looking at will compare favorably to the painting you've picked in the book. Actually, unless you picked a really *good* painting, the movie image will probably blow it away. A single Kurosawa frame probably has better composition, superior contrast, and (assuming it's a newer Kurosawa flick) more interesting color.

Akira Kurosawa had one of the best "eyes" ever to grace modern cinema. He saw the film screen as a huge canvas upon which to paint his masterpieces. He was more than just a visual artist, though. His movies are equal to those of Hitchcock, Ford, Hawkes, Bergman, Fellini, Truffaut, and the great directors from around the world. Kurosawa is not just the best director ever to come out of Japan; he's not just the most revered and influential director in the history of Asian cinema; he is one of the greatest directors of all time. Period.

Born in 1910, Kurosawa studied to be a painter, a vocation that would serve him well in composing the shots for his gorgeous motion pictures. After apprenticing on several films, he began directing in 1943 with *Sanshiro Sugata,* the life story of the near-legendary judo master. Though working under WWII Japanese censorship laws forbidding Western influences, Kurosawa's knowledge of the great films of world cinema shows through even in his early work. After the end of World War II, Kurosawa's own style quickly came to the fore.

He concentrated not only on beautiful pictures and compositions, but also on characters, emotions, ripping good action, and stories that made the audience think. Kurosawa combined these elements consistently, with a deft, artistic hand. A master screenwriter as well, he often wrote or co-wrote the pictures he worked on. (His screenplays are still being made and remade to this day.)

When *Rashomon* won the top prize at the Venice Film Festival, the world took notice. Kurosawa followed that success with a series of spectacular and touching films including *Seven Samurai, Ikiru, Throne of Blood, The Hidden Fortress* (an inspiration for *Star Wars*), *Yojimbo, Sanjuro, Dodesukaden, Ran, Kagemusha, Dreams,* and numerous others. His movies transport us to a different world— a place where Kurosawa is the master. We see what he sees, feel what he feels. Kurosawa strove to control every element in his films—even the weather. Most of the time, the weather cooperated. A wind storm showed up, fortuitously, just in time to shoot the climactic mountain duel in *Sanshuro Sugata*.)

Soon his movies began to be remade in other countries. *Rashomon* has appeared in numerous languages and media adaptations (though none is as good as the original), and has even been paid "homage" in TV sitcoms. *Yojimbo* and *Seven Samurai* were adapted (very successfully) into westerns. The trend of adapting the master's work continues to this day, with *Yojimbo* recently being remade as *Last Man Standing*.

Amazingly, despite many years of success, near the end of his life Kurosawa struggled to find backers for his films. His projects remained ambitious and innovative, but the film industry had grown cautious. Bean counters with no understanding of the master's art worried about the bottom line. The director was so despondent that he even tried to commit suicide. (Fortunately, he failed.) Kurosawa then turned to the west, and found help from U.S. filmmakers who had long admired his work—people like Francis Ford Coppola and George Lucas. *Kagemusha, Ran,* and *Madadayo* (among others) might never have been made without the aid of the great director's young admirers.

Akira Kurosawa became immortal on September 6, 1998. He leaves behind a film legacy unmatched in quality or vision. New movies shot from his scripts, remakes of his work, and homages to his motion pictures will surely continue to be made long into the future.

His painterly eye, his intelligence, his emotion, his attention to detail, and his integrity as a filmmaker have ensured Akira Kurosawa a prominent spot in the pantheon of motion picture directors.

—SS

Winston Chao mixes Chow Yun-fat cool with a bit of Andy Lau in assembling his character here. Carrie Ng *(City on Fire)* is amusing as the fashionable aunt. The stunts and fight choreography are quite nice, but director Clarence Fok *(Naked Killer)* sabotages some scenes with too much arty cutting. *AKA: Xin Die Xue Shuang Xiong; San Dip Huet Seung Hung.* 🐉🐉

1996 C: *HK* Winston Chao, Nicky Wu, Carrie Ng, Rene Liu, Ben Ng, Ivy Leung. **D:** Clarence Fok. **W:** Yuen Gam Lun. **VHS, DVD**

Thunder Cops

The situation here is obviously swiped from *The Killer.* Walter Fuh (Lau Sek-ming) is assigned to go undercover to infiltrate the Hung Hsin Gang. His identity is destroyed, and even his nurse sister Sherry (Yvonne Yung) doesn't know he's really a cop. In fact, the whole idea of him being a cop could have been an afterthought, since it's only referred to in one flashback scene. The dangerous duty doesn't bother him, since he has a terminal brain cancer. He goes to work as a hit man for gang leader Henry Kao, and donates all his money to the church where they meet. His main job is stealing the Diamond of Death from another gangster, Howard Chen. Then Kao sells it to yet another gangster—since everyone who buys it ends up dead, the diamond's legend grows, and everyone wants it. Tough cop Sean Pai (who even looks a bit like Danny Lee) is on his trail, regularly harassing his ex-girlfriend Sherry for information. The couple broke up when Sean started chasing her brother, who is also an old friend. After a gunfight that leaves Chen and another crook dead, Kao turns on Fuh and shoots him with a Teflon bullet that penetrates his armor vest. He escapes to the hospital, where Pai and their priest friend are the only ones available with the right blood type for a transfusion. When Kao learns Fuh is still alive, he follows his daughter Ya-ping—who has been dating Fuh—to the hospital. Fuh escapes, but Kao hires another hit man to help track him down.

This attempt to replicate the Chow Yun-fat hit is so feeble that it's almost sad. Walter even has a favorite bar to hang out in, which isn't nearly as cool as the one from *The Killer,* though the owner is prettier than John Woo. Since he never seems to collect any evidence against the mobsters, it can be assumed that the cops have set him up to be in a position to kill as many as he can—or that the one scene that establishes Fuh as an undercover cop was added as an afterthought to make him look more heroic. Though Pai is determined to arrest him, he doesn't call in any other cops to guard Fuh when he's in the hospital. Fuh donates his cash toward building a new church, when the money might be better spent on cancer research. Not a good movie, but you might want to check this one out to just to see the ridiculous climax: Fuh has a seizure at the church, and Pai rushes in to handcuff him—to help the seizure pass! A sniper accidentally kills Sherry, and the two cops and the priest (who produces firearms hidden in Bibles) set out to gun down Kao's entire gang, who are holding Ya-ping hostage in a demolition site. While our heroes dodge behind rubble, the bad guys stand around in orange jumpsuits waiting to get shot. Not to be confused with *Thunder Cop* or *Thunder Cops 2.* 🐉▽

1998 81m/C *HK* Lau Sek-ming, Yvonne Yung. **D:** Chan Wai On, Yung Chung-chi. **VHS**

Thunder Kick

It begins extravagantly for an independent production, with animated titles. In fact, the title animates twice. Gangster Chiao charges money to cross "his" bridge. Chow Chi-hsien (Li Chin-Kun), from the family that really owns the land, refuses to pay and beats up the thugs when they attack. His mother scolds him, since he's promised not to fight—his father died in a kung fu duel, after all. But mother doesn't hold the young man to his promise for long. Wong Kai-tai (Hon Gwok-choi) comes to visit his friend Chi-hsien. While waiting for his friend, Wong defends Mrs. Chow when the gangsters come calling as well. Wong is a strong fighter, but is unable to defeat Chiao's tough teacher (Bolo Yeung). Chi-hsien comes to the rescue, and after they defeat the gang together, he and Wong become blood brothers. The generous Wong gives Mrs. Chow and Chis-hian a lovely house, but he has an ulterior motive: criminal gangs have invaded Wong's village, and his clan needs a fighter of Chi-hsien's caliber to help fight them. But Wong Kai-tai can't bring himself to tell his new brother of his troubles, and returns home alone, where the gang murders him. Chow Chi-hsien arrives, and swears to get revenge on the gangsters who killed his blood brother. Investigating, he finds that separate factions control gambling, opium, and prostitution. With the help of wily Uncle Lau, Chow gets the three factions distrusting each other, making it easier for him to fight them one at a time.

The kung fu is pretty standard in this Taiwan-shot production, with loud, silly sound effects. After fighting the head villain and his gang for some time, Chow takes off his coat to reveal bulky tonfa clubs tucked in his belt, which not only would be impossible to conceal, but would have made his job a lot easier if he'd pulled them out earlier. Bolo Yeung is usually top billed, but has only a small role. 🎭🎭

1973 85m/C *HK* Li Chin-Kun, Hon Gwok-choi, Bolo Yeung, Suen Lam, James Nam, Mars, Chen Yan-Yan, Kok Lee-yan, Yam Sai-kwoon, Yip Wing-cho, Fung Hark-On, Lau Kar-Wing, Hsu Hsia, Tsang Choh-lam, Chiang Nan, Yukio Someno, Wong Pau-gei, Chan Dik-hak, Huang Ha, Brandy Yuen, Sunny Yuen, Dang Tak-cheung, Danny Chow, Alan Chan, Wong Shu Tong, Lee Chiu. *D:* Yip Wing-cho. **VHS, DVD**

Thunder Ninja Kids: The Hunt for the Devil Boxer

A weird amalgam of Anglo and HK horror fu, this flick is part of a larger Thunder Ninja Kids "series." In this third episode, a strange UFO starts resurrecting ghosts and hopping vampires in the HK countryside. Meanwhile, an evil Anglo minion of Satan plots to steal the Sacred Sword from the Anglo kung fu school where it's kept. The satanists are in league with Chinese kidnappers who take a little girl for ransom. In theory, the little girl is the only one who can defeat Satan—though this idea is never followed up in the flick. The Thunder Ninja Kids are, apparently, ghosts in this film. One is a hopping vampire boy, the other a spirit girl who encourages her friend not to drink blood from the living. The two little goblins take a trip into town to raid the blood bank, and run into the kidnappers along the way. The spirit kids decide they should help the kidnapped girl, and the kung fu detective heroine who is trying to rescue her. The ghosties give the kidnappers lots of trouble, but don't actually manage to rescue the girl.

They do, however, raise the ire of the criminals. So the kidnappers beseech Satan to help them. Satan, who is an overacting white guy with a serious tan, agrees. A blood-drained criminal turns up as a zombie (half human, half hopping vampire—all silly) to fight the "good" spirits. The ghoul children try to rescue the living child, and the woman detective does some kung fu. In the end the Anglo Satan has a showdown with the son of the slain Anglo kung fu master. Got all that?

The blasphemous, silly nature of this film makes it a lot more fun than it ought to be. It seems like it was made by people with no knowledge of Satan, Christianity, or indeed any Eastern religion, either. The probable explanation, is that this is not really one film, but two—an Asian vampire comedy, mixed with "new" footage of white kung fu guys fighting Satan (kind of a less-well-done *Kung Pow: Enter the Fist*). The flick does have some great lines: "Do you think Satan will be mad at us for making money?" one kid-

napper asks. At another point, someone says, "Take this chicken and get out of here!" Later, Satan says, "I am the devil! Come on!" How could you not like a film like with dialogue like that? Hopping vampire children? Tanned Satan? Pants peeing? This movie has it all. The box cover copy alone is worth the price of admission. Too dopey to miss. Check it out. —*SS* **AKA:** *Thunder Kids 3: Hunt for Devil Boxer.* 🎭🎭🎭

1986/94 89m/C *HK/PH* Mark Houghton, Vince Parr, Wayne Archer, Sophia Warhol, Ridley Tsui, Steven Tee, David Frank Hallet, Anthony Mui, Lily Tsui, Carrie Ma, Kevin Lui, Sharon Lee, Billy Cheung, Anita Ma, Lim Ping, Li Ning. *D:* Godfrey Ho. *W:* Godfrey Ho, Chris Lam. *C:* Yink Tak-li. *M:* Stephen Tsang. **VHS, DVD**

Thunderbolt

Jackie Chan indulges his love for fast cars, plays up to his Japanese fans, and solidifies his relationship with Mitsubishi with this racing action movie. It's generally regarded as a lesser effort, but still delivers plenty of fights, stunts, and thrills. Jackie plays a race driver who has just completed training at Mitsubishi's racing school. He returns home to Hong Kong and the family garage/junkyard, and also helps the police with their efforts to catch illegal street racers. Interpol agent Steve Cannon (Michael Wong) steps in to help them hunt for supercriminal Warner Kaugmen, better known as Cougar (Thorsten Nickel). TV reporter Amy Ip (Anita Yuen) tags along to cover the story, and Jackie just happens to be fixing a sports car owned by her cameraman (Dayo Wong) when Cougar's black racer zips by. After a wild ride, Jackie captures Cougar, and testifies to keep the crook in jail on a technicality long enough for Cannon to gather more evidence. Cougar's heavily armed gang busts him out of jail, and they get back at Jackie by swinging his house around on a crane and dropping it on the garage! To top it off, Cougar kidnaps Jackie's injured sisters, all to get him into a race in Japan.

The big crane scene shows the kind of mass destruction Chan would use as the climax to some of his films later in the 1990s, and the big race finish is a bit of a disappointment, as a big fight with the top villain always provides a more satisfying conclusion to these kinds of films. However, the car chase scenes themselves, directed by Frankie Chan, are first-rate—as are the fight sequences designed by Chan and Sammo Hung's stunt teams. A big battle against Kenya Sawada, Ken Lo, and dozens of yakuza in a big pachinko parlor is particularly thrilling. Despite the outstanding action, the film has an uneven feel to it. Gordon Chan, surely thrown off by directing such a huge Jackie Chan

film (even when obviously under Chan's supervision) after early success with Stephen Chow comedies, but would settle into his own style after collaborating with Dante Lam on *Beast Cops*. But it's the decision to make the final car race look like a real car race as much as possible that damages the finale, as it ends up looking like...just a real car race. *AKA: Pik Lik Feng; Pi Li Huo; Dead Heat.* 🦴🦴🦴

1995 110m/C *HK* Jackie Chan, Anita Yuen, Michael Wong, Thorsten Nickel, Chor Yuen, Dayo Wong, Ken Lo, Corey Yuen, Chin Ka-Lok, Peter Yung, Daisy Wu, Shing Fui-on, Michael Lambert, Kenya Sawada, Blackie Ko, Wong Ming-sing, Yuzo Kayama, Paul Rapovski, Bruce Law, Mari Eguro, Man Chung-san, William Duan, Woo Hoi-yan, Hon Jun. *D:* Gordon Chan. *W:* Chan Hing-ka, Gordon Chan, Phillip Kwok. *C:* Horace Wong, Joe Chan, Ardy Lam, Lau Hung-chuen, Cheng Siu-keung, Kwan Chi-kan. *M:* Kunihiko Ryo. **VHS, DVD**

Tiger Cage

When Yuen Woo-ping is the director, even singer Jacky Cheung and comic Ng Man-Tat get to play hard-boiled cops. A CID squad led by Hsiu (Leung Kar-yan) busts up the drug operation of Swatow Hsiung (Johnny Wang) in violent, hyperactive fashion. The squad celebrates their victory, and Hsiu prepares to marry his teammate Shirley Ho (Carol Cheng) and retire from the force due to a heart condition. But Hsiung, shot off a building and presumed dead, is actually still kicking and comes for his revenge, killing Hsiu with a shotgun blast on the eve of the wedding. Shirley gives up her mourning leave to join the team in their hunt for Hsiung. They manage to capture him before he can leave Hong Kong, but when the suspect threatens Sergeant Feng Chien-te (Ng Man-Tat) that he'll tell about the "American ginseng case," Feng maneuvers Hsiung into being shot dead. But his comrade Fan Shun-yu (Jacky Cheung) overheard the conversation, and catches Feng on videotape selling drugs to the new narcotics syndicate pushing into HK.

On his way to turning the evidence over to his superior Michael Huang (Simon Yam), Fan is delayed giving a birthday present to his girlfriend Amy (Irene Wan), and Feng's partner Terry (Donnie Yen) sees the tape. Meanwhile, Shirley has been spending a lot of time with Huang, and together they discover that Hsiu had a secret bank account holding $10 million, making them suspect he was in with Feng. Before Fan can close his case, the crooked cops turn the tables on him to make him look like the guilty one, and a copy of the video he made puts Amy in danger.

Riding the wave created by John Woo, *Tiger Cage* is relentlessly violent and packed with action, and boasts terrific stunt work. The good

cops/bad cops plot is nothing special, but with its breakneck pace, no one should mind. Jacky Cheung hadn't yet learned to tone down his wild stare and overacts shamelessly, but others in the cast do fine. Donnie Yen gets a terrific fight scene in (with a great death scene to match) that really brought him to the attention of critics and audiences. The idea of a fight staged in a roomful of gas would be reused more extensively in later Jet Li movies. *AKA: Dak Ging To Lung; Te Jing Tu Long; Sure Fire.* 🦴🦴🦴

1988 89m/C *HK* Jacky Cheung, Carol Cheng, Simon Yam, Donnie Yen, Irene Wan, Ng Man-Tat, Leung Kar-yan, Johnny Wang, Michael Woods, Fung Hark-On, Yuen Cheung-yan, Chen Jing, Wong Wai, Vincent Lyn, Sunny Yuen, Yuen Woo-ping. *D:* Yuen Woo-ping. *W:* Anthony Wong Wing-fai, Kim Yip. *C:* Tomato Chan, Lee Kin Keung. *M:* Donald Ashley. **VHS, DVD**

Tiger on Beat

In this prototypical buddy-cop movie, lazy playboy Detective Sergeant Francis Li (Chow Yun-fat) is partnered with green, enthusiastic cop Michael Cho (Conan Lee) for the usual session of clashes, then bonding through a wild adventure. Chow Yun-fat's first amazing stunt is drinking down a dozen eggs, with a soymilk chaser—a hangover cure he says is handed down from Bruce Lee. The partners are called in on the case when gangster Poison Snake Ping (Phillip Ko) kills a Thai drug smuggler to cover up the fact that he's stealing from his boss Johnny Law (Norman Tsui). Li takes them to his favorite bar so that owner Loong (Ti Lung) can take Cho down a peg, and give them a tip on the murder. This leads them to Ping's sister Marydonna (Nina Li Chi), a shapely aerobics instructor whom Ping is using to fence the coke he swipes. With both the cops and the gang looking for Ping, both sides concentrate on Marydonna, and she's forced to cooperate with the police for her own protection. Law's thug Fai (Gordon Lau) beats up Cho and kills Ping. In a scene straight out of hard-boiled pulp fiction, Li gives Marydonna rough treatment to get information out of her, and she miraculously reforms, and even falls for the lug! Her information sets up a massive police raid on Law's next big deal at Fuk Shing Pipe Manufacturing Plant, from which only Fai manages to escape. While the boys are celebrating their promotions, Fai plots revenge against the two cops.

It's all pretty cliché stuff, but thanks to Chow Yun-fat's charm, and the exciting action scenes, they manage to pull it all off. It's nice to see Chow play a character that's not a slicker for a change. Lee and kung fu movie veterans Ko, Tsui, and Lau take the brunt of the rough stuff, and engage in some thrilling and imaginative fight scenes and stunts, including the wildest chainsaw fight in movie history. Chow gets into his share of battles, too, including a crowd-pleasing new way to fire a shotgun. Maria Cordero sings the theme song. **AKA:** *Liu Foo Chut Gang; Lao Hu Chu Geng; Tiger on the Beat.* ♫♫♫♡

1988 93m/C *HK* Chow Yun-fat, Conan Lee, Nina Li Chi, Shirley Ng, James Wong, Gordon Lau, Norman Tsui, Phillip Ko, Ti Lung, David Chiang, Shing Fui-on, Lydia Shum, Lau Kar-Wing. **D:** Lau Kar-Leung. **W:** Tsang Kwok-chi. **C:** Cho On-sun, Joe Chan. **M:** Teddy Robin Kwan. **VHS, DVD**

Tiger over Wall

"WARNING: CHINESE AND DOGS NOT ALLOWED," reads a sign outside the exclusive English neighborhood of Hong Kong, exactly like the one in *The Chinese Connection.* Mrs. Phillips is missing her dog Rover. Corrupt police inspector Chiu Sun-Yeh (Hwang Jang Lee), who kowtows to the British, is put on the case. Unlike others, young medical student Lin Cheng (Phillip Ko) refuses to be bullied, though his Master, Dr. Kow, tells him to back down. Master's own son Shao Li (Cheung Lik) got in trouble with the police and has had to go into hiding.

Little Koa Chun is arrested for the dognapping and made a scapegoat. Old Chan the umbrella maker strikes a deal with the cops to take the blame, but his daughter (Candy Wen) doesn't trust the coppers. Lin Cheng goes to Chiu to demand a statement from him to guarantee the deal. But behind closed doors, Chan is being beaten and tortured. Fearing more trouble, the inspector hires an assassin (director Tony Liu) to kill Lin Cheng—a plan that fails miserably. Deciding the police have carried their bullying too far, Lin Cheng and the returned Shao Li decides to kick some official ass.

The script strives for nearly the same tone as *The Chinese Connection* in its portrayal of corruption bred and supported by foreign occupation. However, a distracting unanswered question is left hanging over the full running time: What really happened to the little boxer Rover? Ko is a good performer in an ordinary hero role, but lacks the intensity needed here, and isn't on screen enough of the time to use it if he had it. However, his exhilarating duel with Hwang at the end is worth the wait. Familiar Golden Harvest back-lot hangings add to the production value. Oddly, actors' credits are still appearing on screen 41 minutes into the film, coinciding with the introduction of new players. **AKA:** *Chun Biu Fong; Xun Bu Fang; Tiger over the Wall; Around the Jail Cell.* ♫♫

1980 87m/C *HK* Hwang Jang Lee, Phillip Ko, Candy Wen, Walter Cho, Kong Do, Tony Liu, Cheung Lik. **D:** Tony Liu. **C:** Ho Lu Ying, Ma Kuan Wah. **M:** Ng Tai Kong. **VHS, DVD**

The Tigers

Pop stars Andy Lau and Tony Leung team up as CID cops in this dramatic thriller. Thief (Lau) and Dandruff (Leung) are as interested in gambling as they are in catching crooks. Captured smuggler Sapi Chan (Shing Fui-on) is caught with guns he received from the mainland, and clues them in on a cocaine deal between a Thai gang led by Lui Wei (Miu Kiu-wai) and gangster Ping (Lo Lieh). Their squad raids the exchange site, but Wei escapes in a speedboat, and leader Uncle Tien (Leung Kar-yan) hesitates to arrest a thug he discovers is his brother-in-law Tung (Ken Tong), who escapes also. Thief and Dandruff decide to keep $10 million in cash left by Tung, and to avoid further scandal, Tien and the rest of the team goes along with the theft. Righteous cop Pang (Phillip Chan) refuses his share, but keeps his mouth shut. He has extra incentive not to cause trouble, as he wants to marry Tien's daughter, club girl Shirly. However, Tung returns to blackmail the squad, demanding the release of his boss Lui. Under pressure from the others, Pang changes his statement in court to let Lui off. Of course, Tung isn't satisfied with this, and forces the cops to work for him, raiding his competitors on his tips so that he can take over new territory. Tien turns the tables on Tung by letting Ping go, telling him it was Tung who set him up so the crooks will turn on each other. But unknowing Dandruff and Thief have gone to meet Tung after the raid, and get caught in the middle of the fighting.

It may start out looking like a breezy action comedy starring the two singers, but the movie soon reveals itself as an ensemble drama. Later, as the cast becomes more embroiled in the politics inside the police and justice departments, the pace slows to a crawl. The performances are solid (especially from Leung Kar-yan as the conflicted commander), but the film has a tough time recovering from its plot machinations, and after so much drama the action at the end seems a bit extreme, and even a little comic. **AKA:** *Ng Foo Cheung Ji Kuet Lit (Gam Paai Ng Foo Cheung); Wu Hu Jiang Zhu Jue Lie (Jin Pai Wu Hu Jiang).* ♫♫♡

1991 100m/C *HK* Tony Leung Chiu-Wai, Andy Lau, Leung Kar-yan, Kenneth Tong, Phillip Chan, Lo Lieh, Shing Fui-on, Felix Wong, Miu Kiu-wai, Irene Wan, Yammie Nam, Chen Kuan-tai, Fung Lee, Michael Dinga. **D:** Eric Tsang. **W:** Nam Yin, James Yuen. **C:** Jingle Ma, Lee Kin Keung. **M:** Tats Lau, Patrick Lui. **VHS, DVD**

Time and Tide

Bartender Tyler Ching (Nicholas Tse) has a drunken one-night stand with a girl who turns out to be a crazy lesbian cop Leung (Candy Lo).

Nine months later, Leung's due to deliver his baby, her girlfriend and co-workers are furious with him, and he's looking to make some big money fast. Ching finds work with Mr. Kai (Anthony Wong), who runs an unlicensed bodyguard service. He makes some dough protecting folks like gangster Mr. Hong, whose rivals have sent an assassin after him at his lavish birthday party. Among the guests is his daughter Josie (Cathy Chui), with her new husband Jack Chow (Wu Bai), a new acquaintance of Ching's. Chow tips off Ching, helping him catch the assassin, and the three become friends.

Ching proposes that Chow go into business with him. But Chow already has some side business to take care of, repaying a debt to his old associate Miguel (Couto Remotigue), right-hand man of a South American mobster named Santoro. Miguel wants Ching to execute his own father-in-law. However, Chow turns the tables and shoots Santoro—who is Mr. Kai's latest client. With his client dead and a bag of money gone, Kai hands the cops Ching as a fall guy.

The idea of two friends, both expectant fathers, on opposite sides of an assassination game, is an intriguing one, and all the complexities of the situation are marvelously explored. Tsui Hark proves he's just as creative as ever with this visually inventive thriller, shooting his candy-colored images from inside ice buckets and clothes dryers, and staging action scenes as exciting as any he's ever done before. Only his stars let him down here, overdoing their rock-star cool. Otherwise, this is a stunning action film that deserves more attention than it's received. *AKA: Shun Lau Ngaak Lau; Shun Liu Ni Liu.* 🐉🐉🐉

2000 (R) 114m/C *HK* Nicholas Tse, Wu Bai, Couto Remotigue, Anthony Wong, Candy Lo, Cathy Chui, Joe Lee, Jack Kao. **D:** Tsui Hark. **W:** Koan Hui, Tsui Hark. **C:** Ko Chiu-lam, Herman Yau. **M:** Tommi Wai. **VHS, DVD**

Time of the Apes

You might think that this is just a cheap Japanese rip-off of *Planet of the Apes*. Well, if you take a close look at the title, you'll see that it's *TIME of the Apes*. That's very different—in fact, a whole word different. Actually, it's another feature edited from a Japanese TV series. Little

Johnny (Masaki Kaji) and his friend Caroline (Hiroko Saito) visit his scientist uncle Charlie and assistant Katherine (Reiko Tokunaga) at their lab to witness their experiments in cryogenics. A volcano traps Katherine, Caroline, and Johnny in the deep freeze, and a few minutes later (give or take a few centuries), they awake in a world where apes evolved from men. It's a madhouse! Luckily, the apes are poor shots, and the trio of humans escapes. Making friends with monkey girl Pepe (Kazue Takita), they're introduced to her human friend Godo (Tetsuya Ushida), who has been hiding out in the hills to wage a one-man war against the apes. The usual dull captures and rescues ensue, until the bizarre climax, which involves flying saucers and an all-powerful computer.

If only for budget reasons, the apes inhabit a world much like our own, with modern vehicles and buildings, a factor more in keeping with Pierre Boule's novel. The apes are played by actors in almost immobile masks rather than makeup effects, and for once no one can complain that the English dubbing doesn't match their lip movements, since for the most part they don't move at all. But at least the masks are well made, and portray a wider variety of species than the American film. However, any positive aspects of the film can be disregarded, as it's unlikely that even the best editor in the world could piece together a decent feature out of the 26 half-hour episodes made by Tsuburaya Productions. Large chunks of the first and last episodes are mashed together with bits from those in between, with predictably choppy results. That doesn't mean the original version made any sense either, as the pseudoscientific explanations offered don't help this make any more sense than the brain-numbing 1950s juvenile adventure *Robot Monster*. **AKA:** *Saru no Gundan.* ♪

1975 97m/C *JP* Reiko Tokunaga, Hiroko Saito, Masaki Kaji, Hitoshi Omae, Tetsuya Ushida, Wataru Omae, Baku Hatakeyama, Kazue Takita, Noboru Nakaya. **D:** Atsuo Okunaka, Kiyosumi Fukazawa. **W:** Sakyo Komatsu, Koji Tanaka, Keiiche Abe, Aritsune Toyoda (story). **C:** Yoshihiro Mori. **M:** Toshiaki Tsushima. **VHS**

Tiramisu

Wonderful bittersweet romance with high-quality production values and several excellent performances. Jane (Karena Lam), a dancer, tells her little sister that tiramisu—an extremely sweet dessert—tastes like love. Ko Fung (Nicholas Tse), deaf since an accident robbed him of his hearing, begins to encounter Jane unexpectedly as he goes about his day job as a messenger. Jane is busy preparing for an important dance competi-

tion; the troupe includes her best friend Tina (Candy Lo), who considers Ko Fung warily. He thinks about her at night as he works on a cleaning crew with his roommate (Eason Chan). Tragedy strikes, yet a fateful romance still ensues.

Gentle, sweet, and melancholy, *Tiramisu* is achingly romantic. At the same time, director Dante Lam composes each shot carefully and uses a pleasing variety of swooping pans, intense close-ups, and handheld camera work in order to maximize the emotional impact. Lam, who also wrote the story, is ambitious and audacious. His ambition is demonstrated by his willingness to push the limits of the story firmly into the fantastical while grounding it in earthbound realities. His audacity is shown with a clever scene wherein we watch a dance group move from tears to tap dancing in grief and celebration over the loss of their friend. And he also creates scenes full of memorable imagery. Sometimes it's nightmarish, as when horse-mounted cops pursue a large group of children at a nighttime carnival. At other times, it's whimsical, as in brief looks at a rollerblading cleaning crew or a volunteer jackhammer operator. Letter-perfect performances by Karena Lam and Nicholas Tse help center the story in reality and keep it from toppling into gooey sentimentality. Goofy interludes with Eason Chan and dark brooding by Candy Lo provide a welcome counterpoint to the main romantic relationship. The film features lush, gorgeous photography by Chan Chi-Ying *(Tokyo Raiders, Bakery Amour)*. Peter Wong Bing-yiu provided the art direction. Tommy Wai composed the lovely original score, employing the full complement of an orchestra, though much of the music ends up sounding synthesized. —*PM* **AKA:** *Luen Oi Hang Sing; Lian Ai Hang Xing.* ♪♪♡

2002 111m/C *HK* Nicholas Tse, Karena Lam, Eason Chan, Candy Lo, Chan Git-leng, Vincent Kok. **D:** Dante Lam. **W:** Chan Man Yau, Lee Lok Wah. **C:** Chan Chi-Ying. **M:** Tommy Wai. **DVD**

To Kill with Intrigue

Having clearly failed in his plan to make Jackie Chan into the next Bruce Lee, producer Lo Wei began to cast him in all manner of odd roles in an attempt to somehow make him a star. Thus, we find Jackie at the center of this very bizarre feature, one of those movies that seems to have been made up as they went along.

Young Sau Lai (Chan) gets wind of a planned attack on the family estate by Ting Tan-yen (Hsu Feng) and her Killer Bee bandits. To keep her safe, he chases his pregnant girlfriend Chin-Chin (Yu Ling-lung) away with some harsh words, and tries to do the same for the guests gath-

ered for his father's birthday feast. The Killer Bee ninjas arrive—some in flying coffins—and attack, killing Sau Lei's parents (Kong Ching-ha and Ma Kei). Ting abducts Sau and tells him how his father murdered her parents and scarred her face years ago. She intends to keep him alive so he can suffer. Meanwhile, Sau Lai has sent his buddy Chen Chun (Tung Lam) to protect Chin-Chin and take her to his cabin. Anguished by her many maudlin flashbacks, Chin-Chin asks that they leave, so Sau finds them gone when he arrives to explain himself. Instead, he's found by Ting, who has begun an obsessive love/hate relationship with him. And he's attacked by hired killers from the Bloody Rain Clan. He also befriends First Dragon (George Wang Kuo), of the Dragon Escort Company, who hired the Bloody Rain to kill Chen Chun. It turns out Chen Chun is not the nice guy Sau thought he was—in fact, he's secretly the evil Governor of Hunan, and the even more secret and evil chief of the Bloody Rain. He's so evil that he makes no sense: Governor Chen has a lackey hire Dragon Escort to ship some valuables, so that Chen Chun can steal them, all to get First Dragon to show up at the governor's estate, so that Bloody Rain Chen can fight with him! Adding to his villainy, Chen Chun neglects to tell Chin-Chin why Sau really sent her away, then tells her he's dead, and makes plans to marry her himself. Wounded severely battling the Bloody Rain (he has a sword shoved into his belly!), Sau is taken away by Ting to recover at her lovely house by the river. Sau is itching to rescue Chin-Chin and get revenge on Chen, but is honor-bound to remain with the kinky Ting until he can beat her in a fight. Since every time he loses a duel with her, Ting makes him do something horrible—such as swallowing a hot coal, charring his face with a hot iron, or cleaning the cat box—Sau works hard to improve his kung fu as fast as possible.

Though in a short time Chan would take control over shooting all his own fight scenes, Lo Wei (or cinematographer Chen Chong-yuan) is clearly taking a great interest behind the camera here, as *To Kill with Intrigue* is actually a beautifully shot picture. The sets and Korean locations all look wonderful, especially the temple or garden where Chan's great climactic battle with Tung Lam was shot. There's plenty of kung fu, both open hand and with strange weapons, and the openly insane story has a lot of entertaining facets. The Killer Bees deserved more screen time. Some of the music cues were taken from *Mothra vs. Godzilla,* and other scores by Akira Ifukube. **AKA:** *Gim fa Yin Yue Gong Naam; Jian Hua Yan Yu Jiang Nan.* 🐉🐉🐉

1977 106m/C *HK* Jackie Chan, Hsu Feng, George Wang, Yu Ling-lung, Tung Lam, Ma Kei, Kong Ching-ha, Chan Wai Lau, Lee Man Tai, Weng Hsiao Hu. **D:** Lo Wei. **W:** Ku Long. **C:** Chen Chong-yuan. **M:** Frankie Chan. **VHS, DVD**

Tokyo Decameron: Three Tales of Madness and Sensuality

This anthology of three short stories could use a host character, like the old Crypt Keeper. As it is, we just have a narrator telling us how screwed up modern society is in Tokyo. "Two Women Named Mariko" stars cult queen Kei Mizutani *(Weather Woman)* as the evil Mariko, the domineering leader of a gang of male hooligans. The other Mariko (Marie Jino) is her shy cousin, bound to her by ties of family and guilt. During some sort of trouble in the city—perhaps a military coup—they hole up in Mariko's high-rise condo wearing army uniforms. Jun is the oddball brother of one of one of the guys, who believes he has psychic powers. Of course, the perverts pick on the two meek ones relentlessly. But things are not quite what they seem between the two Marikos. In "Lesbian Dream," four lesbian friends—Miwa, Jun, Michiru, Kana (Hitoe Otake)—plus captured shoplifter Eri (Yu Kawai), are on holiday in a mountain cabin. The four evil girls decide to make Eri their slave rather than turn her over to the police. Next morning, the find Kana dead in the cabin, and many accusing fingers are pointed. "The Man in the Pillory" finds fired construction worker Shizuo Natsukawa (Eisaku Shindo) going on a bender and waking up bound to a chair. His tormentor Keiko Fujimori (Hitomi Shiraishi) accuses him of her sister's murder, and has him caught in a death trap, hoping to torture the names of his three accomplices out of him.

All three stories have a sexual subtext, but are more about psychodrama and deception than eroticism. They present kinky setups, then end with a twist that shows things are not as they seem. 🐉🐉

1996 90m/C *JP* Kei Mizutani, Hitomi Shiraishi, Hitoe Otake, Eisaku Shindo, Yu Kawai, Marie Jino. **N:** Minori Terada, Dave Mallow (U.S.). **D:** Koichi Kobayashi. **W:** Hono Misumi, Yuichiro Tatsumi, Akio Jissouiji (story). **C:** Norimasa Nakamoto. **M:** Seneca Park. **VHS, DVD**

Tokyo Drifter

Seijun Suzuki's *Tokyo Drifter* is a true yakuza epic that manages to combine the traditions of the heroic gangster-as-samurai cinema with sight gags, tripped-out color schemes, and choreographed violence that would fit comfort-

ably in a Busby Berkeley musical. What's more, *Drifter* is so infused with extreme cool that—sorry, Frankie and George—it may just put both versions of *Oceans 11* to shame. And it was all done on a B-movie budget, not to mention filmed, edited, and ready to screen in less than a month. Even though it was Suzuki's next film, *Branded to Kill* (1967), that got him canned from Japan's famed Nikkatsu Studios (and blacklisted from the biz), *Tokyo Drifter*'s cinematic stream of consciousness, seemingly lacking any regard for coherence of plot, made it clear that Suzuki was tired of making the formulaic films the studio required. He was ready to create something totally unique, something that pushed his audience and himself past the limits imposed by the studio. Even more, it seems he was ready to pull out all the stops, have some fun, and entertain.

Despite all its eccentricities, *Tokyo Drifter* is still loyal to its roots, the Japanese samurai film. Tetsu (Tetsuya Watari) is a gangster set adrift. He suffers a beating on the docks after he refuses the overtures of a rival gang, headed by the evil Otsuka (Hideaki Nitani), to join them. Tetsu is above all devoted to and loyal to his ex-boss. He is the honorable lone samurai lifted from feudal Japan and thrown into the modern-day world of the 1960s gangster. Kurata (Ryuji Kita), Tetsu's boss and paternal influence, plans to break free from the criminal life and go straight. Tetsu goes along with Kurata's wishes, even though the rest of the gang has abandoned Kurata. Honor and loyalty are important to Tetsu. He stays with Kurata because he believes these values are equally important to him. To finance his future, Kurata has borrowed a large sum of money to purchase an office building that will facilitate his new business. Otsuka forcibly assumes the loan from the hapless lender, and comes to Kurata to foreclose on the building, ruin his carefully laid plans, and cause him to lose face. Otsuka sees the younger Tetsu as the force behind Kurata, an older man, and tries to get rid of him as well. Tetsu leaves Tokyo to prevent further trouble. He winds up working in a saloon. Meanwhile, Otsuka and Kurata form an uneasy and unhappy—for Kurata—alliance, and the first point on the agenda for the new team is the elimination of loyal troublemaker Tetsu.

Through all his trials and tribulations, Tetsu would rather stay on the straight and narrow but, when someone won't leave him alone, he can't help but answer back with a hail of bullets, fists, and even a song or two. A lot of the time, Tetsu dishes it out dressed in a powder-blue suit and several scenes (including a couple of shootouts) are set in a bright-yellow nightclub that only gives the film more a technicolor musical feel. The sets, costumes, and boldly saturated colors serve to lull the viewer into a false sense of serenity with the expectation more of romance or comedy than the frequent and spontaneous eruptions of violence that our hero is unable to avoid. Suzuki uses many unusual camera setups and tracking shots that give the film a slightly surrealistic look that he would take even further in *Branded to Kill*.

Set against garishly colored and wildly beautiful sets, neon signs, and beautifully composed winter landscapes, *Tokyo Drifter* stumbles around a bit as far as making sense, but never misses the mark as far as mid-'60s cool and jazzy elegance are concerned. Director Seijun Suzuki proved that a tiny budget is no impediment to a creative mind. —PM/JO **AKA:** *Tokyo nagaremono; The Man from Tokyo.* 🎵🎵🎵▽

1966 82m/C *JP* Tetsuya Watari, Chieko Matsubara, Hideaki Nitani, Ryuji Kita, Tsuyoshi Yoshida, Hideaki Esumi, Tamio Kawaji, Eiji Go. **D:** Seijun Suzuki. **W:** Yasunori Kawauchi. **C:** Shigeyoshi Mine. **M:** So Kaburagi. **VHS, DVD**

Tokyo Fist

A boxing movie, and much more, executed in the wildly kinetic style of director Shinya Tsukamoto *(Tetsuo the Iron Man)*. Insurance consultant Tsuda (Tsukamoto), suffering from the ennui of his humdrum life, is tricked by associate Kojima (Kohji Tsukamoto), a part-time prizefighter, into delivering a payoff. At the gym, he seems to get a glimpse of a strange world—the boxers look like zombies, numbed by their efforts. Kojima begins to intrude in his life, dropping in on his fiancée Hizuru (Kahori Fujii) uninvited, making a pass at her. Tsuda accosts Kojima for his behavior, and is easily knocked cold. Seeing Kojima as a mad dog, Hizuru is angered at his intrusion, but drawn to the danger he represents.

Tsuda joins Kojima's gym and enters a training program. Hizuru starts getting tattoos, pierces her own ears (and more), and moves in with Kojima. Tsuda harasses Kojima and intensifies his training to a masochistic level, clearly intent on beating Kojima at his own game, in more ways than one. Hizuru wants to fight with Kojima, too, or even Tsuda. The boxer finds himself overwhelmed by the monsters he's created—which may be exactly what he wants.

Whereas in the Tetsuo films, Ysukamoto's characters desired to merge with machines, here the flesh is the new machine, a new medium to express madness. Occasionally, one of the trio attempts a return to sanity, but the other two are there to pull him back in. While the mobile camera, editing, gore, and eruptions of violence draw the most attention, the icy blue cinematography makes everyone look as though they're lying in the morgue already. **AKA:** *Tokyo-ken; Tokyo Fisuto.* 🎵🎵🎵▽

The Yakuza

Enter the Yakuza

やくざ

Let's face it—for the most part, American gangster movies are dull. Once they portrayed trigger-happy criminals who got into car chases and gun battles, but now we just get old Godfathers, sitting in dark rooms drinking little cups of thick coffee and presiding over petty political squabbles. That is, when they're not whining on a psychiatrist's couch. Looking east, you'll find a more dynamic brand of gangster movie, where power struggles are only temporarily resolved by machine guns, explosions, and maybe even superheroes with swords.

Around the world, organized crime seems to operate in the same ways and with similar origins—as heroes. The downtrodden and suffering peoples of the world are often uplifted by membership in groups that appear to help and protect them, but eventually end up victimizing those they pretend to help.

The yakuza has its origin from around 1612. Ronins known as Kabuki-mono ("insane ones") wore weird clothes and hairstyles and went around causing trouble. Citizens termed Machi-yakko ("city servant") banded together to protect their region from the hooligans and bandits, becoming the heroic protectors of society. The modern yakuza claims to have descended from the Machi-yakko, taking their name around the mid-17th century when tekiya (street vendors) and bakuto (gamblers) came to dominate the Machi-yakko organizations.

As Japan became more industrialized, the yakuza stepped in to help organize labor and facilitate cooperation with government officials and police. During the 1920s and '30s, right-wing yakuza (unyoke) helped nationalistic secret societies fight against democracy, believing the influence of foreigners caused a recent economic depression. This wave of nationalism soon controlled Japan, forcing them into World War II. After the war, American occupation troops thought they'd wiped out the yakuza, when in fact rationing caused a flourishing black market, enriching a growing number of yakuza called gurentai (street hustlers). The American influence changed the yakuza in other ways—copying U.S. gangster movies, yakuza bosses began wearing slick black suits and carrying guns, and they became much more violent. During their peak years in the early 1960s, the ranks of yakuza swelled to nearly 200,000 members, divided into 5,000 clans, and bloody gang wars erupted across Japan. Eventually, a boss named Yoshio Kodama succeeded in ending the warfare and unifying the yakuza factions.

In a sense, the yakuza lives up to their claims as protectors and peacekeepers, often using their power to settle disputes more swiftly than any court could. Of course, they demand a fee for stepping in, and their solutions are often more brutal than any government intervention, so citizens have to take their chances. Discipline within the organization is just as firm. Outright betrayal still means an execution, but smaller infractions by an underling (kobun, "child") are paid off to the clan leader (oyabun, "father") by cutting off the end of a little finger (yubitsume), plus some begging. This dates back to the days when the yakuza was dominated by gamblers, and the loss of a digit or two could seriously impair a cheater's business. The word "yakuza" is a pun that comes from the card game hanafuda, in which the worst hand you can have is 20 points, or 8-9-3 ("ya-ku-za," which means "useless").

The presence of the yakuza is as prevalent in Japanese movies as is the Mafia in American films, with many detailing stories about the inner workings of the society. The plots of samurai pictures often turn on the workings of the underworld—Zatoichi was a free-lance yakuza, and Lone Wolf and Cub often gained employment from the mob. The *Sure Death* movies and TV series was about a Machi-yakko group fighting against bandits and corrupt officials alike. The popularity of yakuza movies increased along with the yakuza ranks in the 1960s and '70s, with directors like Seijun Suzuki *(Tokyo Drifter)* and Kinji Fukasaku *(High Noon for Gangsters)* making stylish entries in the genre. Teruo Ishii's yakuza films were so bloody that they cross over into horror territory.

In recent years, there's been a resurgence of interest in yakuza films, with a series of classics from "Beat" Takeshi Kitano *(Sonatine, Boiling Point)* winning a legion of fans all over the world. B-movies like the *Tokyo Mafia* series are common, while filmmakers such as Juzo Itami *(A Taxing Woman)* and Hiroyuki Tanaka *(Post-man Blues)* use the yakuza genre as a background for twisted comedy. And then there are the totally bizarre yakuza action films of Takashi Miike *(Dead or Alive, Ichi the Killer)*, which totally throw away genre conventions in the pursuit of thrills. With such creative minds at work, it's unlikely that yakuza—at least in the movies—will mean "business as usual" anytime soon.

1996 84m/C *JP* Kahori Fujii, Shinya Tsukamoto, Kohji Tsukamoto, Naoto Takenaka, Naomasa Musaka. *D:* Shinya Tsukamoto. *W:* Shinya Tsukamoto, Hisashi Saito (story). *C:* Shinya Tsukamoto. *M:* Chu Ishikawa. **VHS, DVD**

Tokyo Mafia: Yakuza Wars

This is the first entry in the popular crime series starring Riki Takeuchi *(Blowback: Love and Death)*. It tells the story of a newly organized crime gang in Japan, which is run more like a corporation than the old feudal system of the yakuza. In the near future of the Kobuki-cho district of Tokyo, the south section is controlled by the Teitokai, consisting of warring Yamaryu and Ishiyama gangs. The southeast corner belongs to the Taiwan Mafia's Blue Dragons gang. The north end belongs to no one, but vying for control are the Hong Kong Mafia Dragon Heads and others. The leader of the secret Tokyo Mafia is Ginya Yabuki (Takeuchi)—a former member of the Yamaryu Teitokai, until he was unfairly punished by Iwagami (Ren Osugi), the angry second of the Yamaryu. He resigned from the gang by shooting Iwagami in the leg and biting his pinky off. Ginya tries to recruit his old Yamaryu pal Sho Saimon (Masayuki Imai), telling him about a deal he has pending with Huang from Hong Kong. He needs Sho to help broker the deal through Iwagami for Teitokai, and uses his sister Ryoko to interpret. The small but advanced Tokyo Mafia is specializing in marketing technology and whale meat. Ishiyama gets wind of the new gang, and sends his boys to hunt for them.

With help from the creepy martial artist Mr. Lee from Teitokai central, Ishiyama kidnaps their computer whiz Sugiyama and steals a shipment. Ginya retaliates by invading the penthouse of Moriwaki (Shohei Yamamoto), head of Teitokai, via helicopter. They get Moriwaki to return everything, but from then on, the Teitokai start to really put on the pressure. Young punk Yuki (Kazuyoshi Ozawa) acts on his own, using Moriwaki's taste for young men to trap and kill him—a big mistake that brings the entire yakuza out for the culprit's blood. Even police chief Akasaka can't help them. The only way out is for the Tokyo Mafia to make war on the entire Teitokai.

Scenes dealing with the adventures of the gang are interesting, but too often the story has to try to present the big picture. This means a lot of talk and posing rather than action. What action there is mostly consists of anonymous gangsters running around the streets chopping phony-looking pieces off of each other. Takeuchi is ultraslick, looking like a throwback to Seijun Suzuki's gangsters of the 1960s crossed with Elvis Presley. Followed by *Wrath of the Yakuza*. *AKA:* *Tokyo Mafia*. ♫♫

1995 83m/C *JP* Riki Takeuchi, Masayuki Imai, Reiko Yasuhara, Kojiro Hongo, Shohei Yamamoto, Hiroshi Miyauchi, Ren Osugi, Kazuyoshi Ozawa. *D:* Seiichi Shirai. *W:* Akinori Kikuchi. *M:* Takashi Nakagawa, Yuki Sakamoto. **VHS, DVD**

Tokyo Mafia 2: Wrath of the Yakuza

Part 2 of the saga of the renegade crime gang starts as the Tokyo Mafia begins open warfare with the Teitokai yakuza. With plenty of money, but outnumbered 3,000 to 120, Tokyo Mafia head Ginya Yabuki (Riki Takeuchi) decides to concentrate their efforts on the top men of the Teitokai. Yabuki hires snipers from the Taiwan Mafia Blue Dragons, where Jiro Yuki (Kazuyoshi Ozawa) has been hiding out ever since he ordered the hit on Moriwaki (Shohei Yamamoto), head of Teitokai, which started the conflict. However, there's a surprise in store for everyone: Moriwaki is still alive, and is being secretly cared for by the sinister Mr. Lee. Ishiyama Teitokai thugs try to get Yabuki by kidnapping his girlfriend Eileen (Reiko Yasuhara), but Lee turns out to be an old friend of hers from Shanghai, and shows up in time to rescue her. More help comes from police inspector Hanada (Hiroshi Miyauchi), who escorts Yabuki to safety past both the Ishiyama and Yamaryu gangs.

Between the snipers and harassing raids, the Tokyo Mafia unbalances the Teitokai, and the chiefs begin to fight amongst themselves. In the midst of this, Lee attacks Yamaryu, framing the Tokyo Mafia for it with the help of Iwagami (Ren Osugi), who gains a Teitokai directorship for his betrayal. Shaking things up even further, Yuki revolts and begins killing chiefs on all sides. Yabuki clears the air with his old Yamaryu pal Sho Saimon (Masayuki Imai), and they team up to battle Yamaryu and the Blue Dragons together.

It's a relief to see the leads finally get down to some action toward the end of this sequel, even though it's not very well performed. The gunfights are about average, and the hand-to-hand fighting lacks power, but it's a welcome relief from the endless talk and maneuvering. Both features have more of an atmosphere of condensed feature versions of a television series. *AKA:* *Tokyo Mafia 2*. ♫♫♡

1995 90m/C *JP* Riki Takeuchi, Masayuki Imai, Reiko Yasuhara, Hiroshi Miyauchi, Kojiro Hongo, Shohei Yamamoto, Ren Osugi, Kazuyoshi Ozawa. *D:* Seiichi Shirai. *W:* Akinori Kikuchi. *M:* Takashi Nakagawa, Yuki Sakamoto. **VHS, DVD**

Tokyo Mafia 3: Battle for Shinjuku

After three years of hiding out in Thailand, Ginya Yabuki (Riki Takeuchi) returns to Tokyo. He left when his old friend Sho Saimon (Masayuki Imai) apparently betrayed him, shooting him in the shoulder. With the Boss left not much more than a drooling vegetable, Saimon is running the Teitokai yakuza, which have now taken over the Hong Kong Dragon Heads. Yabuki is out to rob the Teitokai's laundered money fund. He wants his old pal Taki (Cho Bang-ho) to join him, but nerve damage to Taki's hand provides him with an excuse. A cheap detective named Kikura (Tomoro Taguchi) helps Yabuki out, and directs him to teenaged Yumi (Asami Sawaki) as a replacement killer. But Yumi turns out to be a disappointment, so he asks Taki to train her. Taki's garage hand Kaoru (Kouichi Sugisaki) turns out to be more of a natural with a gun, and joins the gang as well. The newcomers dub the gang the new Tokyo Mafia. Saimon smells the robbery coming, and has his Chinese associate Won order more guards. But Won disobeys, and the heist goes off with only one hitch—Yumi freezes in action. When Won has Taki and his family killed without orders, Saimon is fed up and kills the dishonorable swine. Saimon then calls for a showdown between the Tokyo Mafia and the swords of his modern samurai.

Superior in every way to the other Tokyo Mafia movies, *Battle for Shinjuku* benefits from an interesting story, good characters, and strong direction. In fact, this may not be a sequel at all, but a similar feature with the same leads, dubbed and subtitled to look like part of the series. The action is nicely choreographed, especially the unique guns vs. katana climax, which actually portrays the gunmen at a disadvantage in the match-up. *AKA: Gangster.*

1996 84m/C *JP* Riki Takeuchi, Masayuki Imai, Cho Bang-ho, Asami Sawaki, Tomoro Taguchi, Kouichi Sugisaki. **D:** Takeshi Miyasaka. **W:** Kosuke Hashimoto, Kazuhiko Murakami (story). **M:** Daisuke Suzuki. **VHS, DVD**

Tokyo Raiders

Tony Leung stars as private detective Lin Tower, who defeats his enemies with an array of gadgets, a trick umbrella, kung fu, and Latin music. He also has a thoroughly tricked-out apartment/office, and a staff of tough and sexy women. Yakuza Ito (Hiroshe Abe) of the Cobra gang suspects Ken Tremayne (Toru Nakamura) is having an affair with his girlfriend, and hires Lin to find out about it. He finds out Ken is after

even more. Meanwhile, Ken has left his fiancée Maizie (Kelly Chan) waiting at the altar. Having been stiffed on his bill for setting up the happy couple's new Hong Kong home, interior designer John (Ekin Cheng) shows up there to demand his money from Maizie. The two fly to Tokyo to find Ken and demand an explanation. But the Cobras are after Ken, too, and when they find John in Ken's apartment they naturally assume he's Ken. Much action, and about a hundred confusing twists in the plot, will either leave you thrilled or shaking your head in disappointment.

Director Jingle Ma uses a lot of sleek gray tones, quick editing, and fancy camera moves to portray fast action. But as he should have learned shooting Jackie Chan pictures *(Rumble in the Bronx, First Strike)*, choppy editing actually frustrates audiences watching a fight scene. The editing is there to enhance the rhythms of the fight, not try to fool the viewer into thinking it's more exciting. The complex plot, quirky characters, and actors are enjoyable, but he should have taken a direct approach and filmed Ailen Sit's fight choreography in a more straightforward manner. *AKA: Dong Ging Gung Leuk; Dong Jing Gong Lu.*

2000 (PG-13) 100m/C *HK/JP* Tony Leung Chiu-Wai, Ekin Cheng, Kelly Chan, Toru Nakamura, Cecilia Cheung, Yuko Moriyama, Hiroshe Abe. **D:** Jingle Ma. **W:** Susan Chan, Felix Chong. **C:** Chan Chi-ying, Jingle Ma. **M:** Peter Kam. **VHS, DVD**

Too Many Ways to Be No. 1

The gangster flap long overstayed its few years welcome in Hong Kong cinema. A seemingly endless number of pictures were made detailing the rise through the ranks of a young triad member who backstabs his way to the top of the criminal heap. The genre stays alive with the occasional sharp twist, and this black comedy, directed by John Woo protégé Wai Kar-fai and produced by Johnny To, is one of the twistiest.

Lau Ching-Wan *(Where a Good Man Goes)* stars as Wong Au-kau, frustrated leader of the hopelessly inept Hung Lok Gang. Pulling a robbery on the Black Star Gang, they pile into their tiny car—and accidentally run over the "brains" of the gang (Cheung Tat-Ming). They lose the money they stole, and blow up their getaway car. They hide the body inside a wall, but forget to take his pager. Elvis Tsui wears a wig! Ruby Wong comes along in a flowered dress to take over the gang. She has a plan, too—robbing the Black Star Gang again. And so on, with each turn in the plot getting sharper and sharper.

Wai makes sure we don't somehow mistake this for a straight triad flick by keeping his camera doing tricks—turning upside down, zooming

in and out, and so on. He crafts more than one send-up of a John Woo standoff—each with an increasing number of guns pointing at each other. Lau has the same sort of appeal Humphrey Bogart had. An offbeat joy, this would fit comfortably on a bill between *Run Lola Run* and *Pulp Fiction*. **AKA:** *Yat Kuo Chi Tau Dik Daan Sang; Yi Ge Zi Tou De Dan Sheng.* ♫♫♫♪

1997 91m/C *HK* Lau Ching-Wan, Francis Ng, Carman Lee, Cheung Tat-Ming, Elvis Tsui, Matt Chow, Ruby Wong, Joe Cheng. **D:** Wai Kar-fai. **W:** Wai Kar-fai, Szeto Kam-yeun, Matt Chow. **C:** Horace Wong. **M:** Cacine Wong. **VHS, DVD**

The Touch

Reportedly, Michelle Yeoh passed up a prime role in the *Matrix* sequels to produce and star in this ambitious production that takes her back to the sort of adventure setting of her early hit *Magnificent Warriors*. Master thief Eric (Ben Chaplin) is hired by evil billionaire Karl (Richard Roxburgh) to steal an antique puzzle box containing a medallion called the Heart of Dun Huang, which could lead to a Buddhist relic called a Sharira—the crystallization of the essence of holy man Xuan Zang, said to confer on its owner fantastic power. Of course, crafty Eric steals the Heart back, taking it with him to drop in on an old girlfriend. Pak Yin-fay (Yeoh) and her brother Yeuk Tong (Brandon Chang) are the star acrobats of a *Cirque du Soleil*–type show called *The Touch*. Yin holds a sacred scroll that can unlock the Heart's secret, but Eric's appearance boils up some bad blood between them—Yin's father (Winston Chao) trained Eric to join their troupe, but Eric used the skills he learned to become a criminal. Karl's thugs abduct Eric, but leave behind Karl's idiot cousin Bob (Dane Cook), who coughs up the information Yin needs to rescue her former boyfriend. While she's out, Tong takes the Heart and scroll, and he and his girlfriend Lily (Margaret Wang) fly to Dun Huang to try to unravel the mystery themselves. Of course, Yin, Eric, and Karl are all hard on their heels.

The main impression made by *The Touch*, shot in English with an international cast, is of Peter Pau's gloriously beautiful cinematography. The entire production seems designed to take advantage of his rich golden hues, which almost explode from the screen during the fiery action climax. Michelle Yeoh has given herself another noble, heroic, but empty character to play, and Ben Chaplin's likable rogue is standard issue, leaving it up to Richard Roxburgh to enliven the show as a surprisingly charming and funny vil-

lain. The aforementioned climax has Yeoh and crew fighting it out while balanced on stone columns—or swinging around on wires—above a chamber of fire, with flaming arrows shooting out of the walls everywhere. It's a complicated sequence, combining Phillip Kwok's choreographed action with digital effects and fancy camera moves, which is sometimes breathtaking, but ultimately suffers from some wobbly blue-screen compositing. Much of the fight scenes look a bit hesitant, a sign of a cast of martial artists and non-martial artists who aren't used to working together. Pau seems more at home filling the screen with fantastic location shots from all over China, Malaysia, and Tibet—not to say the monastery at Lhasa wouldn't still look spectacular in shots taken with your average disposable camera. The end points to a possible sequel, and one hopes that Yeoh will crank up the kung fu a bit more for Part 2. **AKA:** *Tin Mak Chuen Kei; Tian Mai Chuan Ji.* ♫♫♫

2002 103m/C *HK/CH* Michelle Yeoh, Brandon Chang, Ben Chaplin, Richard Roxburgh, Sihung Lung, Margaret Wang, Dane Cook, Kenneth Tsang, Emmauel Lanzi, Gabriel Harrison, Winston Chao. **D:** Peter Pau. **W:** Thomas Chung, Michelle Yeoh, Laurent Courtiaud, Julien Carbourt, J.D. Zeik, Peter Pau (story). **C:** Peter Pau. **M:** Basil Poledouris. **VHS, DVD**

A Touch of Zen

Fittingly, the first image is of a spider spinning a great web, as it tells how poor but curious village scholar Ku Shen-chai (Shih Chun) is drawn into an intrigue involving the fate of all China. Ku is hired to draw a portrait of a traveler named Ouyang Nin, whom he notices is following an herbalist named Lu Meng, and in turn is being followed by soldiers and monks. Plus, there are strange sounds coming from the haunted mansion near his home. He finds that a Miss Yang Hui-ching (Hsu Feng) is squatting in the old General Jun Yuan mansion with her elderly mother. Ku's own mother leaps at the chance to arrange a marriage for her son with their pretty new neighbor. But Yang is a fugitive—when her father uncovered a plot to kill the emperor by wicked Eunuch Wei, Wei's East Chamber guards killed her whole family. With some help from Shaolin Abbot Hui Yuan (Roy Chiao), she fled with loyal General Lu and General Shih (Pai Ying), who has been posing as a blind fortune-teller. They all have prices on their heads, and men like Ouyang are scouring the countryside hunting for them. After Ouyang discovers them, word comes that Magistrate Wu Mun-ta is due to arrive soon with

Hsu Feng's icy warrior dominates the cast in King Hu's classic *A Touch of Zen.*

THE KOBAL COLLECTION / LIAN BANG

200 troops. With Ku's military savvy, the martial arts skills of the three warriors, and a few rumors about ghosts, the heroes succeed in luring them all into a death trap. However, Ku's actions have made him a marked man as well, and before she can continue her mission Yang has to help him.

Drawn from Pu Songling's *Strange Stories from Liu Jai* (an anthology that also fueled *A Chinese Ghost Story* and *Painted Skin*), King Hu's masterpiece is a classic adventure film with a heroic maiden, a tragic romance, and a record of Ming Dynasty customs, but it bears elements that allow it to transcend all genres. Perhaps the title gives a clue—though it's a film of exciting swordplay and kung fu, at heart it has a pacifist spirit, and seems to move in stages from superstition to intrigue to enlightenment. Aside from some scenes that are too dark (in available versions anyway), the cinematography is stunning, with imagery far ahead of its time. At the center is the thousand-yard glare of Hsu Feng, an iron lady. But the picture's soul resides with Roy Chiao's Shaolin monk in the end, a being of such spiritual purity that he bleeds gold. His confrontation with the evil Commander Hsu (Han Ying Chieh) takes on mythological overtones. The original release version ran nearly four hours. *AKA: Hap Lui; Xia Nu; Hsa Nu—the Gallant Lady.* 🎵🎵🎵🎵

1969 185m/C *TW* Hsu Feng, Shih Chun, Pai Ying, Tin Peng, Roy Chiao, Miu Tin, Han Ying Chieh, Cheung Bing Yuk, Sit Hon, Man Chung-san, Kao Ming, Lu Shih, Goo Liu-sek, Cheung Wan-man, To Wai-wo, Sammo Hung, Jackie Chan. *D:* King Hu. *W:* King Hu. *C:* Hua Hui-ying. *M:* Wu Dai-jiang. **DVD**

Tower of Death

Another product of Raymond Chow's graverobbing efforts, film clips and doubles are again badly integrated in the editing room to make it appear that Bruce Lee has risen from his Seattle tomb just to go back to Hong Kong as a guest star in another Golden Harvest action romp, a direct sequel of sorts to *Game of Death*. Bruce "plays" martial arts master Li Chen-chiang (Billy Lo in the English dub), who goes to see how his rebellious brother "Bobby" Chen-kuo (Tong Lung) is getting on in his studies with his Buddhist master (Roy Chiao, whose look changes a bit between the new footage and redubbed clips from *Enter the Dragon*). When Chiang's friend Chin Kiu (Hwang Jang Lee) dies unexpectedly, Chiang goes to the Ginza district in Tokyo in search of the man's illegitimate daughter May, a singer at the Playboy Club. May hands over a box her father left with her, and Chiang has to fight off a whole gang of killers to keep it.

At the funeral, a helicopter descends and steals the coffin (!), and while giving chase, Chi-

ang is killed by a poison dart. Chen-kuo goes to Tokyo to investigate his brother's murder himself. The films left behind show Chin visiting the Castle of Death, and its master, Lewis (Roy Horan). Chen-kuo decides to visit the Castle, a huge estate equipped with a private army, and peacocks and lions roaming the grounds. That night, a prowler in a mask attacks Chen-kuo. The next night, while Chen-kuo is defending himself from a naked woman and a guy in a lion costume, the same masked man murders Lewis. Chen-kuo reacts to the murder by having an unnecessary flashback to recent events, then going after his prime suspect: one-armed butler Sun (To Wai-wo). Though Sun actually has two arms, Chen-kuo kills him, and then goes in search of the fabled Tower of Death for answers. Unlike the structure in Lee's script for *Game of Death,* this tower was built upside-down, and underground. Chen-kuo has to fight his way to the bottom of the surprisingly futuristic tower to find out the unsurprising answer to what's behind all the murders.

With Yuen Woo-ping as action director (plus Sammo Hung and Corey Yuen lending a hand behind the camera), at least the fight scenes are well executed and imaginatively choreographed. However, the editing-room hijinks cast a shroud over the proceedings. It's not as poorly executed as Bela Lugosi's appearance in *Plan 9 from Outer Space,* but it's still unconvincing and in poor taste. But once Lee is dead again, this turns into a pretty good action flick. The plot makes no sense, but there are plenty of goofy surprises and well-staged fight scenes. There are even some intentional laughs, and a memorable soundtrack. Korean Tong Lung, Lee's double in the completed *Game of Death* and Bruce's ghost in director Ng See-yuen's *No Retreat, No Surrender,* doubles Lee again in his fights here, the takes over in the brother role (with Yuen Biao doubling both for acrobatics). *AKA: Sei Miu Taap; Si Wang Ta; Game of Death 2.* 🎵🎵🎵

1981 87m/C *HK* Bruce Lee, Hwang Jang Lee, Tong Lung, Roy Horan, Roy Chiao, To Wai-wo, Casanova Wong, Lee Hoi-sang, Sunny Yuen. *D:* Ng See-yuen. *M:* Frankie Chan. **VHS, DVD**

Tragic Fantasy: Tiger of Wanchai

Simon Yam stars in this gangster epic, loosely based on the life of triad tough Andely Chan. Chan Yiu-hing (Yam) is a young Wanchai District triad member who dreams of winning Grand Prix races, but the best he can manage is a job as a parking valet, borrowing cars so he can race his buddies in the streets. Chan makes good on part of a gambling debt owed by his friend Dee (Lau Ching-Wan), but then doesn't have enough for his mom's birthday banquet. Dee and Chung (Roy Cheung) agree to steal a car for gang boss Kui (Lo Lieh) to earn the cash, but end up stealing a car belonging to Kui's client, getting all of them in trouble. Though for the most part an affable fellow, Chan is nevertheless always getting into fights, alienating his girlfriend Mil (Marianne Chan). Chan and his friends open up their own car park company, though their real business is as a muscle-for-hire security service, which brings them great success. Though Chan dallies with club girl Kitty (Yvonne Yung), he carries a torch for Mil, and eventually gets her back. He gains fame in the tabloid press for accosting a mob boss in defense of film star Rose (a fictionalized version of an incident involving Anita Mui), but his activities increasingly irritate the triad elite. Rather than eliminate him outright, they decide to try to force him into dealing drugs for them, touching off a war in Wanchai.

Aside from the brief diversion of car racing and a decent performance by Yam, there's little out of the ordinary here. It's just another account of the quick rise and sudden fall of a Hong Kong gangster, occasionally spiced with violence and musical interludes. Wasted is some nice chemistry among Yam, Lau Ching-Wan, and Roy Cheung. *AKA: Jui Sang Mung Sei Ji Waan Jai Ji Foo; Zui Sheng Meng Si Zhi Wan Zi Zhi Hu.* 🐉🐉

1994 104m/C *HK* Simon Yam, Lau Ching-Wan, Vincent Wan, Roy Cheung, Marianne Chan, Ben Lam, Charine Chan, Yvonne Yung, Lo Lieh, William Ho, Ku Feng, Johnny Tang, Victor Hon Kwan. *D:* Steven Lo, Joseph Chi. *W:* Lo Sing, Leung Yan-tung, Ng Lap-kwong. *C:* Peter Ngor. *M:* Tats Lau, Tommy Wai. **VHS, DVD**

Triangular Duel

Imagine *The Chinese Connection* without that messy racism issue, and you get the idea of this Joseph Kuo production, in which Chinese martial arts schools attack each other, and the Japanese army doesn't get involved.

Kang Luen (Man Kong Lung) is a kung fu fightin' rickshaw man, who hopes to study with his best client Master Auyang Tien-kin (Chiang Nan). Auyang resists because of Kang's tendency to get into fights, but relents when the young man promises not to get into trouble. But since this is a kung fu movie, that promise lasts all of five minutes. The master trains him not only in kung fu, but in judo and karate techniques as well.

Auyang earns the ire of the local Gymnasium Club by refusing to join because he disagrees with the way they teach use of weapons and fighting rather than his healthy bare-hands style. They send scar-faced Fan Tong and two other thugs to the school to cause trouble while the master is away, but Kang beats all three of them. And soon after, he gets in a fight with a pair of thugs who are trying to abduct a young girl. This impresses nearby Pei Chin, who flirts and strikes up a friendship, despite the fact that her father runs the competing Kei Man school. When dad's fellow Gym Club member Master Liu Kei-fang (Miu Tin) finds out, he sends a challenge to Tien-kin's school. The challenge arrives when he's away, but Kang and some of the other students sneak out to meet it in their master's place. Not only are they beaten by Liu's men, but angry Tien-kin is threatened with expulsion if he fights again. Now Kang won't fight even when attacked directly, and his enemies know it. Of course, when he comes home bruised and bloody, it looks like he's been fighting anyway. However, the master changes his tune when Liu's three killers (Ng Tung-kiu, Shih Chung Tien, and Choi Wang) form an Iron Triangle to challenge him. When his teacher is killed in a duel with the villains using unfair tactics, only Kang has the skill to be true to his school and get revenge.

As is usual for Joseph Kuo movie of this period, the action is plentiful, but for the most part unremarkable. At least things get more interesting during the climax, when the hero separates the villains and finds their weak points, one duel ending in a mud bath. It looks good—competently directed with some nice cinematography. The score borrows cues from the James Bond movies. *AKA: Tit Saam Gok; Tie San Jiao.* 🐉🐉

1972 98m/C *HK* Man Kong Lung, Chiang Nan, Nancy Yen, Ng Tung-kiu, Shih Chung Tien, Choi Wang, Miu Tin, Bruce Li, Liu Ping, Shaw Luo-hui, Ng Ho, Gam Kim, Yip mau, Lau Cheung-ming, Ho Ming-hiu, Chung Seung-man, Lau Ching-fat. *D:* Joseph Kuo. **DVD**

The Tricky Master

In between *King of Comedy* and his mega-hit *Shaolin Soccer,* Stephen Chow made this throwback to his gambling and con man films like *God of Gamblers 2* and *Magnificent Scoundrels.* Leung Foon (Nick Cheung) goes undercover as a high-school student (recalling *Fight Back to School,* of course) to protect the daughter of millionaire Ho from kidnappers. Having caught the kidnappers, Foon is promoted to a new job: going after the dashing and handsome swindler Dragon Ferrari (Wong Jing) by posing as the criminal's new assistant. His first night on the job, he comes upon the masked Spider Woman in the house, and is surprised to find it's the cute girl First Love (Kelly Lin) he met earlier. He pretends to be her hostage to help her escape and takes her home to nurse her bullet wound. As luck would have it, his girlfriend Pizza (Suki

"*Cart, rickshaw too. Extremely the rickshaw. I'm glad my teacher to sit on my rickshaw, when he got back from Japan. I'm the happiest rickshaw man.*"

—Man Kong Lung expresses his philosophies in *Triangular Duel*

Kwan) drops by. To get rid of her, he promises to go with her and her sister Wasabi (Sandra Ng) to visit her brother-in-law Tiger Wong Si-fu (Chow), who is in a Macau prison.

Leung and First Love come up with a plan to get the goods on Ferrari together—but the wily crook tricks him. Sent home on leave, Leung gladly accepts help from First Love when Ferrari's thugs attack him. What he doesn't know is that First Love is working for Ferrari after all, and his boss the King of Disguise (Cheung Tat-Ming) is having him watched using hidden cameras, hoping she'll come after Leung. After another humiliation, a forgiving Pizza offers him a chance: ask Tiger Wong (whom Leung hates) for help in tricking the tricksters.

With a more subdued Chow playing an older character and giving over much of his screen time to Nick Cheung, this doesn't quite equal his better comedies, but there are still plenty of good laughs here. The climax features one of Wong Jing's famous gambling-trick scenarios. Spoofs of *The Matrix,* Jet Li's *The Defender, Mission: Impossible,* the proliferation of product placement in HK films, Bruce Lee, *Ring,* public-service condom ads, and *Storm Riders* are included. To help meet his release deadline, Wong Jing brought in Aman Chang, Bosco Lam, and Andrew Lau to help direct. *AKA: Chin Wong Ji Wong 2000; Tricky Master 2000.* 🎵🎵♡

2000 91m/C *HK* Stephen Chow, Sandra Ng, Nick Cheung, Wong Jing, Kelly Lin, Suki Kwan, Cheung Tat-Ming, Lee Siu-Kei, Bobby Yip, Lee Kin-yan, Ken Lo, Spencer Lam, Yuen King-Tan. *D:* Wong Jing. *W:* Wong Jing. *C:* Ko Chiu-lam. *M:* Lincoln Lo. **VHS, DVD**

Troublesome Night

On the night of the Ching Ming Festival, our genial host Peter Butt (Simon Lui) welcomes the viewer to a graveyard where he's honoring his dead parents. Speaking directly to the camera à la Rod Serling on *Night Gallery,* he tells us a quartet of creepy stories (handled by three different directors). In Steve Cheng's "Speculating in Grave Stories," Bee (Jason Chu) and Ball (Allen Ting) take their friend Ken Ni (Louis Koo) camping at a lake (disturbing a nearby graveyard) to celebrate his birthday. That night Ken sees a girl (Ada Choi) swimming nude. Finding her tent near theirs, the boys find she has companions (Teresa Mak and Pak Kar-sin). Spooked by a lady (Helena Law) gathering cans, the boys are chided into playing a game called "Copying Tombs," promising crypt keeper Uncle Ho to be careful. But Ken is shocked to find a photo of his date marking one of the graves. Tam Long-cheung's "Dark Bright Road" stars Christy Chung and Sunny Chan as a young couple dri-

ving around separately in a downpour, unable to find each other—even when they're at the same spot simultaneously. Lui takes a part himself in Herman Yau's "Red All Over" as Peter Butt's twin brother, an eccentric exorcist (and Tom Cruise's feng shui advisor) called in by Bee and Ball to help Jojo (Teresa Mak), who is now harassed by a ghostly intruder in her apartment. Herman Yau also helms the final tale "Turf," which finds Peter Butts at work as manager of a movie theatre. Bee and Ball have come to see *Heavenly Drugs,* the film they were working on earlier as assistants. The stars of the film sit in seats reserved, according to Butts, for "the locals," and have to pay the consequences.

There's really nothing that's very scary here, the most interesting things about it being the familiar stars, and the way characters from one story pop up in others (and in the linking sections). Lui is pretty funny as the oddball host, always acting ominous and mysterious. Unaccountably, *Troublesome Night* was a huge hit with the teenagers, spawning 17 sequels within the next six years. *AKA: Yam Yeung Lo; Yin Yang Lu; Yin Yang Road.* 🎵🎵♡

1997 99m/C *HK* Simon Lui, Louis Koo, Jason Chu, Allen Ting, Christy Chung, Sunny Chan, Ada Choi, Teresa Mak, Helena Law, Pak Kar-sin, Christine Ng, Yuen King-Tan, Frankie Ng, Ivy Leung, Kenix Kwok, Lee Siu-Kei, Lee Lik-chi. *D:* Steve Cheng, Tam Long-cheung, Herman Yau. *W:* Lau Hau-wai, Candy Cheng, Yeung Woon-choi. *C:* Joe Chan. *M:* Mak Chun-hung. **VHS, DVD**

Troublesome Night 3

Hong Kong's nonsense comedy/horror series continues, this time centering its stories around an undertaking business. Enterprising funeral home sales manager Cheng Lik (Louis Koo) hits the jackpot when aged millionaire Wong Pak-man kicks the bucket on his watch, selling brother-in-law Bill Chan the super-deluxe package, complete with weeping keeners (hired mourners). His whole crew celebrates after the funeral. On his way home, assistant mortician Shishedo (Allen Ting) meets his idol, Beauty Chan, but the next day Cheng learns that Chan was killed in a car wreck. Since he's such a huge fan, Shishedo is given the job of reconstructing Beauty's smashed face. Obsessed, he seemingly works miracles with the job, but his unorthodox technique shows far more devotion than anyone could imagine.

His co-workers Cheong (Simon Lui), Trump (Emotion Cheung), and Sun-kwai run into cheerful loan shark Wah (Shing Fui-on), who decides to pay a visit to whoever keeps throwing stuff out of a corner apartment, but finds the place

haunted. The boys meet Gigi Cheung (Christine Ng), daughter of the deceased (Helena Law), and offer to help put the spirit to rest. But Granny Cheung is upset that they take advantage of her daughter, and starts haunting them, until Cheng comes to their rescue. Meanwhile, Cheng's inattention to courting his makeup expert Hung catches up with him when his old pal Daviv begins dating her. However, after she accepts his proposal, he finds he can't accept her profession and breaks up with her. The climax finds friends and relatives in unfamiliar positions around the funeral home.

Once may be a fluke, and twice could be counted as imitation, but three times is a format. The series hits its stride here, showing that there's still originality to be found in the busy—but usually unsatisfactory—Hong Kong horror business. The secret may be in a format without a format—a free-floating mix of comedy and supernatural hijinx where anything can happen. Each entry mixes new discoveries (Allen Ting), old favorites (Chin Ka-Lok as a musician), and series regulars (Lui and Law) in a narrative that includes an anthology of stories and vignettes that may or may not be directly connected, populated by characters who may or may not reappear, and actors who may or may not play the same characters in different stories. It's a fragile webwork that could easily fall apart, but here all the elements seem to be working. There's genuine laughs and scares to be had, sometimes with only a fraction of a second between them, and even some romance and drama, making for a lively and entertaining—not to mention troublesome—night. **AKA:** *Yin Yang Road 3; Raise the Coffin, Make Money.* 🐉🐉🐉

1997 99m/C *HK* Louis Koo, Lee Kin-yan, Lee Lik-Chi, Pan Ping-chang, Simon Lui, Fennie Yuen, Rain Lau, Allen Ting, Frankie Ng, Emotion Cheung, Chin Ka-Lok, Natalie Wong, Michael Tse, Wallis Pang, Shing Fui-on, Helena Law, Christine Ng, Vincent Kok, Lo Meng, Vicky Hung, Oliveiro Lana. **D:** Herman Yau. **W:** Tsang Kwok-chi, Lau Hau-wai. **C:** Joe Chan. **M:** Mak Chun-hung. **VHS, DVD**

Troublesome Night 4

In the fourth edition of this popular semi-anthology horror series, the cast takes a vacation. Leonardo (Simon Lui), DiCaprio (Cheung Tat-Ming), and Driver (Wayne Lai) are on a seven-day tour to the Philippines. The boys are hoping to meet some girls on the vacation, but prospects don't look good with their sassy tourmates, club girls U2 and K2. U2 finds Alan Hung (Timmy Hung) much more interesting, despite the trouble he has at customs—his boss asked him to carry an urn full of human ashes with him to deliver to a Mr. Lucindo. Mr. Wong (Raymond Wong) is also visiting the same hotel as the tour with his secretary, but checks out quickly when they find their room full of ghosts. Alan suspects the urn might be haunted, too, and is relieved the next morning when his fellow D.I.M. Delivery Company employee Mario (Anthony Cortes) comes to pick him up to make delivery. En route, Alan keeps seeing the ghostly girl from the urn, and wants to chicken out, but Mario appeals to his sense of honor. Alan would drive it himself, but can't—for a very important reason.

Honeymooners Wing (Louis Koo) and Apple (Paulyn Sun) are surprised to find a portrait of Apple in a small gallery. The painter claims to be psychic, and says Wing has a child with his mistress and makes other predictions. The visions cause trouble between the newlyweds, especially when an exotic dancer tries to seduce Wing. But tragically, it may be that Apple is the real psychic.

The third story returns to Leonardo, DiCaprio, and Driver, as their quest for girls leads them to the Di Da Di Disco—which happens to be a gateway to a nightmare world of the living dead!

Released soon after *Troublesome Night 3*, the refreshing change of venue for this entry provides opportunities for some offbeat location shooting, plus an increase in sex and blood. The finale features an army of zombie extras prowling through some bizarre architecture—imagery that could never have been pulled off back in Hong Kong. However, it's a shame they didn't delve into the indigenous supernatural culture of the Philippines a bit more, instead of just using the same old ghost antics. One gag is a direct copy from John Carpenter's *In the Mouth of Madness.* **AKA:** *Au Yeung Liu 4 Yue Gwai Tung Hang; Yin Yang Lu 4 Yu Gui Yong Hang; Yin Yang Road 4: Walking with Ghost.* 🐉🐉🐉

1998 97m/C *HK* Louis Koo, Paulyn Sun, Simon Lui, Cheung Tat-Ming, Wayne Lai, Marianne Chan, Timmy Hung, Raymond Wong, Emily Kwan, Joey Choi, Karen Tong, Aya Medel, Anna Capri, Via Veluso, Anthony Cortes. **D:** Herman Yau. **W:** Tsang Kwok-chi, Lau Hau-wai. **C:** Joe Chan. **M:** Brother Hung. **DVD**

Troublesome Night 8

Number eight in this askew anthology series brings back the host of the first entry, Peter Butt (Simon Lui), now calling himself "Bud Pit," who has fallen on hard times and is moving to the New Territories, taking with him mother Lung (Helena Law), brother Gay (Tong Ka-fai), and girlfriend Moon Ah Say (Halina Tam). Butt is a bit uneasy about their new digs—maybe it's the spell sheets landlord Bob has hanging around the building, or the weird neighbors. Olive (Nadia Chan) next door is a friendly beauty by day, but acts like a ghost at night, stalking around the village looking for her dead child Ming. Lung, a professional spiritualist, makes a deal with Bob to exorcise the place in exchange for several months' rent, and soon discovers that Olive has been possessed by the spirit of an illegal immigrant who was killed while stealing food for her son.

In his Ultraman pajamas, Simon Lui carries the show with his charm, assisted by Helena Law. The video shooting gives the film a pleasantly informal atmosphere, but there just isn't enough plot to fill up the running time with only one story. A sequence detailing a search for a dog over a span of two hours seems like it was shot in real time. A couple of subplots would have been welcome, but as it is the daily activities of the family have nothing to do with the story and only kill time. Maggie Cheung Hoh-yee (not to be confused with the more famous Maggie Cheung Man-yuk of the *Police Story* and *Heroic Trio* movies) appears as a seemingly extraneous character, one of Helena Law's clients at the temple. Her story is picked up in the next episode. *AKA: Au Yeung Liu Baat Ji Goon Choi Chat; Yin Yang Lu Ba Zhi Guan Cai Zai.* 🐉🐉🗡

2000 84m/C *HK* Simon Lui, Nadia Chan, Helena Law, Halina Tam, Gwai Chung, Mr. Nine, Tong Ka-fai, Maggie Cheung Hoh-yee. **D:** Yuen Chi-keung. **W:** James Lam. **C:** Faan Chuen-yam. **M:** Brother Hung. **DVD**

Troublesome Night 9

Released just a week after the previous installment, the ninth entry in this long-running supernatural series continues the tradition of unorthodox storytelling by actually picking up where the previous entry left off! Liu Wai-yee (Maggie Cheung Hoh-yee) was a character who was unrelated to the plot of *Troublesome Night 8*, but her story is picked up again here. Butt (Simon Lui) gets a job on a casino ship where Liu is a regular customer. On a losing streak since her boyfriend left her for a rich girl, Liu is desperate enough to take advice from Butt, who claims to have inherited his mom's fortune-telling ability. Following his counsel, Liu visits her parents' graves, but while clearing the weeds around the stones, they leave a mess on the surrounding graves, angering the spirits. Butt is possessed by the ghost of a little boy, but before he can get in too much trouble, Mom Lung (Helena Law) detects the intrusion and gets on the case. After exorcising the ghost, Lung tricks Liu into giving up gambling by advising her to sunbathe and exercise, leaving little

time for the casinos. But she still tries to sneak in some bets by taking Butt with her. When Liu catches on, Lung agrees to help her win at gambling for five bets only, invoking the God of Gamblers Ko Chun for help.

With the anthology format now abandoned, the series has a much more leisurely and relaxed pace than earlier outings, but this one at least sticks to the main story without annoying diversions. Again shot on video, the Cantonese version features sound recorded live as well, leading to some audio problems with wind and noise in some scenes. Produced at Christmastime 2000, decorations adorning backgrounds show the Hong Kong love of the holiday. Simon Lui feels comfortable with his quickly acquired status as a horror star, having hosted a program called *Scream at One* back in his days as a radio DJ, and the program was popular in a subsequent cable TV incarnation as well. However, this marks his last appearance in the franchise to date. *AKA: Aau Yeung Liu Gau Ji Meng Chuen Gon Kwan; Yin Yang Lu Jiu Zhi Ming Zhuan Gan Kun.* 🐉🐉

2000 86m/C *HK* Simon Lui, Helena Law, Maggie Cheung Hoh-yee, Halina Tam, Paulyn Sun, Mr. Nine, Gwai Chung, Cheng Chu-fung, Sherming Yiu, Tong Ka-fai, Wayne Lai. **D:** Ivan Lai. **W:** Leung Po-on, Rex Hon. **C:** Yip Pak-ying. **M:** Brother Hung. **DVD**

Troublesome Night 14

How many movie series make it to 14 entries? The 14th 007 movie was *A View to a Kill*. The 14th Godzilla movie was *Godzilla vs. Mechagodzilla*. The 14th Wong Fei-hung movie was—well, hopefully someday soon we'll have that title. The *Troublesome Night* series made it to 14 (and beyond 17 by now) by shooting fast and cheap like a TV series, and keeping the concepts fresh with its unique formatless format. Actors can return in different stories but not always as the same characters. Some stories are centered on the supernatural, while others only have a ghostly periphery. The regular actors are all fun to be with, and most of the stories have a healthy sense of humor. The series began as an anthology hosted by Simon Lui, who also took part in some of the stories, set along a stretch of Hong Kong road, then shifted locations (with Lui, Helena Law, and others usually on hand playing different roles) for subsequent sequels. Later, Lui's character Peter Butt/Bud Pit and his family came to dominate the series, with each entry concentrating on one story involving people who come into their lives.

It begins with the classic switch: a frightening situation that turns out to be a movie on TV watched by cousin Bud Yan (Ronnie Cheung) and his Thai girlfriend Hok (Anita Chan). Secretary

Fion (Iris Chai Chi-yiu) arrives with a note from her boss Mr. Budcasso for fortune-teller Mrs. Bud Lung (Helena Law). Lung's husband Budcasso left his wife and disappeared years ago, and now he's inviting the family to his wedding in Shenzen, with a peace offering of 10% of the hotel he owns there. Odd neighbors Pat and Kiu (Gwai Chung and Mr. Nine) happen to show up at the hotel, but find that the hotel is even odder, with rooms and guests that move around unexpectedly. As if Lung's emotions weren't already confused enough at Budcasso's sudden invitation, she finds that his new fiancée (and Fion's mom) Zidane is a fortune-teller, too, using Western methods of hoodoo. While on one level the two women get along well, on another they're both plotting against each other, sending the hotel's fairies, ghosts, and imps to cause trouble. Later, the group doesn't need any supernatural help to play dirty tricks on each other. More serious trouble starts when Pat discovers that Zidane's sister Christin (Emily Kwan), the hotel manager, has stolen money from the company for a bad investment. When Christin's threatened suicide goes tragically awry, the family has to join forces to fight off her vengeful ghost.

Simon Lui's absence still leaves a hole in the Bud family, less ably filled by new additions who never talk to the audience, but it's nice to see HK cinema veteran Helena Law with the lead in a franchise. With a career that spans eight decades, Law didn't become a star until she started appearing in a string of horror films in the early 1990s, and finally got the credit she deserves with her award-winning role in *Bullets over Summer*. Now settled in as a regular supernatural sitcom, the film has a pleasant, but disposable, atmosphere. Time will tell how many more episodes of the series fans will still find worth a rental, though reports indicate its outrageous popularity in the Philippines helps keep it afloat. ***AKA:*** *Aau Yeung Liu Sap Sei Ji Seung Gwai Paak Moon; Yin Yang Lu Shi Si Zhi Shuang Gui Pai Men.* ♫♫

2002 90m/C *HK* Helena Law, Iris Chai, Anita Chan, Tong Ka-fai, Ronnie Cheung, Frances Fong, Emily Kwan, Joe Junior, Gwai Chung, Mr. Nine. **D:** Yip Wai-ying. **W:** James Lam. **C:** Ng Man-ching. **M:** Mak Chun-hung, Brother Hung. **DVD**

Trust Me U Die

This odd drama from director Billy Chung *(Killer)* uses a sci-fi premise to explore problems in the Hong Kong medical community. Scientist Dr. Greg Fong Kin-wah (Simon Yam) discovers a super-soldier serum called SS160, which can boost strength, speed, mental agility, and endurance far beyond human levels. His superior tries to take credit for it, but dies of a heart attack, and Fong decides to take his discovery elsewhere. He and

his assistant/girlfriend Vivian (Chan Ying Lai) go to old friend Dr. Mike Chow (Mark Cheng), who agrees to help in their research, and submit his work to the government; he even invites Fong to move into his house. But Chow isn't such a nice guy after all—he maintains a side business in organ harvesting, and drugs Vivian one night so that he can rape her. Ashamed, Vivian keeps it secret, and when she finds Fong too consumed in his work to attend to her, she goes back to Chow for more. Fong discovers the affair, and decides to get his revenge by using Mike as a test subject. Mike's tissues begin to decay, and he soon expires.

Fong, however, feels his experiment has helped work out the kinks in his serum. When sad-sack constable Chan Sum (Sam Lee) is injured during a robbery, Fong decides to try it on him. The skinny weakling turns into a super-cop, able to punch through solid steel plates. Fong begins to use SS160 indiscriminately as a cure-all, with disastrous results.

It may be meant as a cautionary tale or social commentary, but for the most part, *Trust Me U Die* is just plain uncomfortable to watch. Some scenes flirt with comedy or horror, while others are agonizing. Yam's talent is wasted in a role in which he's required to do little. Cheng comes off better, ably conveying the conflicts within his character. ***AKA:*** *San Giu Cheung Yee Sang; Xin Gao Yang Yi Sheng.* ♫♡

1999 94m/C *HK* Simon Yam, Chan Ying Lai, Sam Lee, Mark Cheng, Joey Tan. **D:** Billy Chung. **W:** Law Kam Fai. **C:** Daniel Chan. **M:** Chow Kam-cheung. **VHS, DVD**

The Tuxedo

Jimmy Tong (Jackie Chan) is a NYC cabbie famous for his white-knuckle driving style. This causes him to be recruited by Clark Devlin (Jason Isaacs), the top agent in a government super-spy agency. Jackie's job is to be Devlin's driver, but ruthless terrorists soon put the big man out of action. With an important case on the line, Jackie must fill in for Devlin by impersonating him. Two things allow Jackie to pull this off—at least initially: 1) an improbable series of events at Devlin's agency prevents anyone who knows Devlin from seeing him; and 2) Devlin possesses a secret, multimillion-dollar tuxedo. The tux has all the moves a spy could ever need programmed into its computerized fabric.

Jackie gets neck-deep in Devlin's mysterious case, and even develops a working relationship with plucky rookie field agent Del Blaine (Jennifer Love Hewitt). What follows is a pretty standard "buddy" movie with the two agents trying to foil a plan to rule the world (by poisoning the water supply—and then cashing in on the only source of pure water). Complications include the big-business backing of the villains and the eventual discovery of Jackie's true identity. Fortunately, with a little help from Hewitt, Jackie's super-tuxedo helps him keep on top of the bad guys.

The tuxedo itself is almost like something out of *Inspector Gadget;* it seems to have whatever gizmo the plot requires inside it. The story itself is nothing very new, and resembles the recent Thurman/Fiennes *Avengers* in many ways (*not* good ways). The idea of putting Jackie in a super-suit is a pretty good one, and provides a few funny moments in the film. Unfortunately, the suit—and its powers—is also one of the film's big flaws. Perhaps this would have worked in another film, but in a Jackie Chan flick, most of us come to see *the man* who does all his own stunts. What this film *seems* to prove—or almost prove—is that what any trained martial-artist acrobat can do on his own, Hollywood (or Toronto, in this case) can do just as well with wires, editing, and f/x. Watching this film it was really hard to tell what Jackie was doing through dint of hard work and years of training, and what he was doing with editing, wires, and computer technology. Same goes for the other actors and stuntmen (and -women) in the film. Gone is the feeling that when you're watching Jackie you're watching a (pardon the expression) high-wire act. Everything here seems too controlled, too pat. The editing and direction are uninspired as well, serving to blur the plot and action when they should be clarifying it. Sure, you can follow the story (you've seen similar ones many times before), but it seems like the flick has more than a few pieces missing. All that being said, there's probably still enough here for Chan fans to enjoy themselves. Sure, the old master may be losing a step—and his chops may be augmented (or supplanted) by f/x here, but he still has his Buster Keaton charm. Hewitt's pretty easy on the eyes, too. —SS 🐉🐉🐉

2002 (PG-13) 98m/C *US* Jackie Chan, Jennifer Love Hewitt, Jason Isaacs, Debi Mazar, Peter Stormare, Ritchie Coster, James Brown. **D:** Kevin Donovan. **W:** Michael Leeson, Michael J. Wilson (also story), Phil Hay (story), Matt Manfredi (story). **C:** Glenn Keenan, Stephen F. Windon. **M:** Christophe Beck, John Debney. **VHS, DVD**

Twilight of the Cockroaches

Naomi and Ichiro are a relatively happy young couple, living among a couple hundred of their kind in the home of a lonely bachelor named Saito (Kaoro Kobayashi). The cockroach population was not always so tolerated there, so Saito is much appreciated, and the population sings his praises. Then, a dashing roach named Hans arrives, a battle-scarred refugee from across the field, who bears witness to horror stories of his homeland. Naomi finds herself drawn to the visitor, and when he returns home, she's determined to visit the place across the field. There, she finds a much more hostile place—the apartment of a young woman (Setsuko Karasuma) constantly at war with the roach world. But when the young woman starts dating Saito, there may be no place safe left for cockroaches anymore.

Anticipating American films like *Antz* and *Joe's Apartment* by a decade, *Twilight of the Cockroaches* uses more primitive technology to combine cartoon cockroaches with a real environment. It's not nearly as much fun as it sounds—after a while, there's only so much gloomy bug-killing you can accept as entertainment. The poignant drama of roaches running for their lives, while human monsters seek their destruction, is imaginatively presented, but later bug stories learned a lesson from this and turned to comedy. A dozen analogies could be made about the roaches and their relationships with the humans here, but what the film offers most of all is simply an alternative viewpoint. **AKA:** *Gokiburi-tachi no Tasogare.* 🐉🐉

1987 105m/C *JP* Kaoro Kobayashi, Setsuko Karasuma. **D:** Hiroaki Yoshida. **W:** Hiroaki Yoshida. **C:** Kenji Misumi. **M:** Morgan Fisher. **VHS, DVD**

Twilight of the Dark Master

At the beginning of the world, the Earth Mother created everything, including mankind. To strengthen Man, she created a race of demons to oppose them. But when the demons became too strong, a tribe of Guardians came forth to protect the weak. The Demons and Guardians have been at war ever since.

In the metropolis of Neo-Shinjuku City, a demon appears. Detective Kumizawa mobilizes the armored police Hard Set team to deal with the menace. Some mysterious agents of a man named Takamiya subdue the monster, and take it to the Crystal Box nightclub owned by their associate, Mr. Kudo. Shizuka, a young woman who was assaulted by the demon, goes hunting for it in a bad part of town, and is saved from a psycho sniper by Tenku, artifact agent for Tsunami Shiyo, who lives in a forbidden area of the city. Shiyo is a flame-manipulating Guardian, who has a run-in with Takamiya's agents Chen Long and Huang Long, and traces them back to

the Crystal Box. He finds Kudo's men are using a bio-boosting drug that makes them Hulk-out, a drug that, if used in excess, causes the subject to become a monster permanently. Shizuka's fiancé Eiji Tachibana was a test subject for the drug, and came home to become a demon. She makes a try at getting into the club, but gets caught, and the betrothed are both brought to Takamiya. A giant dose of the drug is injected into the invalid Takamiya, and he becomes a gigantic super-monster.

For such a short feature, this OAV has a ponderous pace, but has a wonderfully moody look and good music. The whole demon idea has been overused, but this instance gives it a fresh spin by taking the monsters out of the supernatural plane. But the main attraction is the gorgeous design and animation of Hisashi Abe. **AKA:** *Shihaishi no Tasogare; Shinshokan.* ♪♪♡

1997 46m/C *JP* **D:** Akiyuki Shimbo. **W:** Duane Dell'Amico, Tatsuhiko Urahata, Saki Okuse (manga). **C:** Hiroshi Isagawa. **M:** Keishi Urata. **VHS, DVD**

Twilight People

The first horror film made in the Philippines was a loose adaptation of H. G. Wells's *Island of Dr. Moreau*, entitled *Terror Is a Man*, which scaled back the story to only one animal-man, but spawned the successful "Blood Island" series. Thirteen years later, John Ashley and Eddie Romero returned to the theme once again, this time with a full complement of critter folks. Man-o'-the-World Matt Farrell (Ashley) is abducted while skin-diving in the South Pacific and taken to a lonely island compound by a rough character named Steinman (Jan Merlin, a long way from TV's *Tom Corbett, Space Cadet*). At the main house, he meets Dr. Gordon (*Columbo* and *Perry Mason* regular Charles Macaulay), a mad scientist who has kidnapped him to become a human guinea pig in his experiments to create a race of supermen. But so far all he's produced are a bunch of creepy half-human and half-animal monsters. Juan Pereira (Eddie Garcia), a fellow prisoner there, warns Farrell that escape is impossible. Steinman is sure he'll try anyway, and is looking forward to a little hunt. However, it doesn't take long for Farrell to put a different kind of plan to work, which involves using his mojo to sway the doctor's beautiful daughter Neva (Pat Woodell, *Petticoat Junction*'s Bobbie Joe). Before long, they've released the manimals and are making a beeline for the coast, with Gordon's lackeys moseying along in pursuit.

The creature makeup is pretty good, and there are some fun monster-movie props on hand, but Romero fails to take advantage his sets and locations. Even with a menagerie of monsters available, there's not the slightest shred of suspense or excitement to be had, and with a "PG" rating, there's not even any gory violence or sex to hold your attention. Still, it's better than the 1996 Marlon Brando version of the story. Pam Grier took a day or so off from being stuck behind bars in Jack Hill prison movies to be stuck behind bars as Dr. Gordon's panther woman. Though two men are credited with music, most of it is library tracks—some cues 20 years old. **AKA:** *Island of the Twilight People; Beasts.* ♪

1972 (PG) 80m/C *PH* John Ashley, Pat Woodell, Jan Merlin, Pam Grier, Eddie Garcia, Charles Macaulay, Ken Metcalfe, Tony Gosalvez, Kim Ramos, Mona Morena. **D:** Eddie Romero. **W:** Jerome Small, Eddie Romero. **C:** Fredy Conde. **M:** Ariston Avelino, Tito Arevalo. **VHS, DVD**

Twin Dragons

This 1992 comedy is one of Jackie Chan's fastest-moving and lightest features, fully exploiting his comedic talents for an audience that is now accustomed to seeing a funny martial artist. The plot is a direct swipe of the old classic Corsican brothers—twins separated at birth, but connected via a shared sensitivity (what one feels, so does his brother). Jackie One grows up in New York as John Ma, genius orchestra conductor. Jackie Two is "Boomer" ("Die Hard" in the Hong Kong cut), who is raised by an alcoholic prostitute and becomes a mechanic, race driver, and hoodlum. When John returns to Hong Kong for a concert, naturally he gets tangled up with his unknown identical brother, who is in trouble with the triads after losing a race. Plenty of goofy madcap zaniness ensues, climaxing in an amazing battle in an auto-testing facility, featuring some of Jackie's most breathtaking and death-defying stunts. Since the movie was originally made to support the Hong Kong Directors' Guild, a host of HK directors show up throughout the film in bit parts, adding to the fun for insiders who can spot the likes of Tsui Hark, Mabel Cheung, and Ringo Lam. A sore point with some participants is that the profits were supposed to be used to build a headquarters for the Guild—a plan that is no closer to completion than it was a decade ago.

The editing on the U.S. version tightens the story quite a bit, lopping off more than 10 minutes of running time. Once again Maggie Cheung suffers the most, as much of her footage is trimmed and she wasn't hired to do her own dubbing (despite the fact that her English is better than that of anyone reading this). Unfortunately, these butchered versions will become the standard release here. Those of us who care will have to be content with our imports, despite the inferior prints—at least until someone wises up and puts out "special edition director's cut" ver-

sions of Jackie Chan's films on U.S. video. ***AKA:*** *Seung Lung Wooi; Shuang Long Hui; Brother vs. Brother; Double Dragon; Duel of Dragons; When Dragons Collide.* 🦴🦴🦴

1992 (PG-13) 90m/C *HK* Jackie Chan, Maggie Cheung, Nina Li Chi, Teddy Robin Kwan, David Chiang, Anthony Chan, Johnny Wang, Jamie Luk, Kirk Wong, James Wong, Sylvia Chang, Mabel Cheung, Alfred Cheung, Jacob Cheung, Phillip Chan, Guy Lai, Mars, Dennis Chan, John Woo, Chor Yuen, Eric Tsang, Clifton Ko, Stephen Tung, Tsui Hark, Ringo Lam, Ng See Yuen, Wong Jing, Ching Siu-tung, Yip Wing-cho, Lau Kar-Wing. *D:* Ringo Lam, Tsui Hark. *W:* Barry Wong, Tsui Hark, Joe Cheung, Wong Yik. *C:* Horace Wong, Arthur Wong. *M:* Lowell Lo, Phe Loung, Michael Wandmacher (U.S.). **VHS, DVD**

Twin Warriors

The opening imitates *Once upon a Time in China,* with Jet Li leading a yard full of extras through exercises, as Golden Harvest was anxious for any Li picture to trade on his blockbuster at the time. It follows the old Warner Bros. melodrama story

line of two boyhood friends who grow up to be on opposite sides of the law.

At Shaolin Temple, Master (Lau Shun) introduces little Jun Bo as big brother to new student Chin Bo. Jun grows into Jet Li, while Chin becomes Chin Siu-Hou. During final Lo Han exams, Chin Bo's opponent cheats, causing him to accidentally raise his hand to the Head Master (Yue Hoi). His rebelliousness takes over, causing both boys to be kicked out of Shaolin. Adjusting to worldly life, they rescue pickpocket Miss Li (Fannie Yuen) from extorting gangsters. Lute-playing Siu Lin (Michelle Yeoh) is searching for her runaway husband, but he doesn't want to leave his mistress and return home. The boys join her battle.

Chin Bo kowtows to Governor Liu, becoming a soldier, while Jun Bo stays with their friends and joins the rebels. Inevitably, there are conflicts—Chin Bo betrays his brother for personal advancement, leading the rebels into a trap. Chin Bo's treachery causes Jun Bo to have a nervous breakdown, but studying Tai Chi helps him recover his senses—and a superior fighting style.

A relatively lighthearted action epic, highlighted by Yuen Woo-ping's distinctive acrobatic wirework battles. The climactic fight has Li and

Chin bouncing around like ping pong balls, using spears, poles, swords, drums, and even people as projectiles. A real showcase for Li, though one wishes Yeoh would've been given more to do. **AKA:** *Tai Ji Zhang San Feng; Taai Gik Cheung Saam Fung; The Tai-Chi Master.* 🎵🎵🎵

1993 95m/C *HK CH* Jet Li, Michelle Yeoh, Chin Siu-Hou, Fannie Yuen, Yuen Cheung-yan, Lau Shun, Yu Hai. **D:** Yuen Woo-ping. **W:** Kim Yip. **C:** Tom Lau. **M:** Steve Edwards (U.S. version), William Woo. **VHS, DVD**

Twinkle Twinkle Lucky Stars

Another all-star action comedy spectacular engineered by Sammo Hung and his cronies, the third in the series. As a reward for their heroics in *My Lucky Stars,* the ex-cons from the Lucky Stars Cleaning Company are given a vacation in Thailand. While there, their babysitter Inspector Woo Bo-wah (Sibelle Hu) is ordered to meet with snitch Ma (Melvin Wong) to obtain a list naming members of a drug ring. However, before he can hand over the list, Ma is murdered by three assassins (Chung Fat, Richard Norton, and Yusuaki Kurata). Before he dies, Ma tells Woo he mailed the list to his friend Wang Yi-ching (Rosamund Kwan) in Hong Kong. The three assassins go to HK to kill drug lord Lau (James Tien) because he's drawn the attention of a trio of cops (Jackie Chan, Yuen Biao, and Andy Lau). The cops team up with the Lucky Stars to protect Wang Yi-ching, who is next on the assassins' list, while she watches her mailbox.

Surely even the Lucky Stars themselves were getting tired of their lame comedic schemes to peep at Hong Kong's prettiest starlets. Here, the issue becomes whether Rosamund Kwan would be safer with the assassins than with the likes of lascivious but lucky Stanley Fung, Eric Tsang, Richard Ng, et al. Fortunately, there's still plenty of what the people really want from this series: top action stars getting into fantastic fights and performing outrageous stunts. Sammo Hung has one of the best scenes, making tennis racquets into the newest legendary weapons of China. Jackie has a great fight with Kurata. Watch for Michelle Yeoh in a small part as a judo instructor who tries to discipline Sammo. **AKA:** *Ha Yay Fuk Sing; Xia Ri Fu Xing; My Lucky Stars 2; The Target.* 🎵🎵🎵

1985 94m/C *HK* Sammo Hung, Jackie Chan, Yuen Biao, Eric Tsang, Richard Ng, Stanley Fung, Rosamund Kwan, Sibelle Hu, John Sham, Andy Lau, James Tien, Anthony Chan, Kara Hui, Sandra Ng, Season Ma, Chung Fat, Richard Norton, Yasuaki Kurata, Miu Kiu-wai, Charlie Chin, Walter Cho, Michelle Yeoh, Wu Ma, Billy Lau, Dick Wei, Phillip Ko, Lau Kar-Wing, Lee Hoi-sang, Melvin Wong, Riki Hashimoto, Peter Yang, Nat Chan, George Lam, Lam Ching-Ying, Mang Hoi, David Chiang, Tai Bo, Leung Kar-yan, Chin Siu-Ho, Alfred Cheung, Pauline Wong, Jason Pai, Jaime Chik, Deanie Yip, Phillip Chan, Cher Yeung, Austin Wai, Lam Wai, Kenny Ho. **D:** Sammo Hung. **W:** Barry Wong. **C:** Arthur Wong, Johnny Koo. **M:** Anders Nelsson. **VHS, DVD**

Two Dragons Fight against Tiger

In one of those plots that may well have been borrowed from an old western, a company of men is getting irritable after panning for gold for months. During one too many bad meals, hot-headed Blackie (Chi Fu-chiang) chases Tamal the cook up the side of a hill. When his scrambling exposes a huge vein of gold, everyone is anxious to go home and fetch back a wife. But with the Northern army occupying their hometown, it's feared they'd lose both gold and brides if they went back. It's decided that Pak Yuan-lung (Frankie Wong), handsome and the best fighter, will go as their scout and representative. With Pak gone, Blackie secretly conspires with fighter Lung Wu to drive out the others and take over the mine. However, once Blackie sneaks out some nuggets to hire corrupt Captain Chu Tai-woo (Wong Fei-lung) and buy weapons, Lung Wu (Chui Chung Hei) double-crosses his partner. Meanwhile, Pak Yuan-lung finds that Chu Tai-woo is responsible for the death of his girl back home Yu-yan. Setting aside revenge for the moment, he works with Yu-yan's sister Yu-lin (Zi Lan) to gather brides together for his comrades, and heads back for the mine. They stop at an inn on the way, which happens to be the same place Lung Wu is making a deal with Lieutenant Nan (Lung Tin Cheung) to buy weapons from the army. While Pak picks a fight with Nan, Lung Wu uses a pistol to kidnap the ladies. Nan helps Pak pursue Lung Wu and free the ladies, but the lieutenant has his own mission to complete, and convinces the brides to help him.

An uncomplicated and engaging story is the main selling point to this entertaining little movie. There isn't any kind of acrobatics to the fighting, just straightforward karate-style moves, but they're imaginatively staged and nicely shot. One duel takes place on a high beam about 20 feet off the ground, without a wire in sight. The fights at the camp all involve shovels, sledgehammers, and other dangerous implements, and other fights take place on rooftops and viaducts. The glorious end battle in the inn is designed so that the fighters travel all over the set, demolishing it as they go. At worst, they all run a little long. The director keeps things from getting stale with unusual camera angles, and even some split-screen work. 🎵🎵🎵🎵

1975 88m/C *TW* Frank Wong, Zi Lan, Lung Tin Cheung, Wong Fei-lung, Chi Fu-chiang, Cheung Pang, Chui Chung Hei, Chow Ming Ching, Chang Chi-ping, Kao Chen Peng, Chen Chiu. *D:* Gam Sing-yan. *W:* Gam Sing-yan. *C:* Cheung Jui-lin. *M:* Wong Chu-jen. **VHS, DVD**

2000 A.D.

The Singapore military is concerned about threats from computer warfare and sets up an Information Warfare Unit. Sure enough, a plane is destroyed and transnational computer warriors are suspected. Peter (Aaron Kwok), a game-loving computer nerd living in Hong Kong, owns his own company, works with his best friend Benny (Daniel Wu), and dates Benny's sister Janet (Gigi Choi). Peter's brother Greg (Ray Lui) comes to visit from America, and he's also involved in the computer business. Very soon after Greg's flight lands, CIA agent Kelvin (Andrew Lin) accuses him of being a spy. Hong Kong Officer Ronald Ng (Francis Ng) leads the investigation for the local police. Eric Ong (James Lye) arrives to poke around for the Singapore Information Warfare Unit. Lastly, one more character enters the scene to muddy up the waters—Salina (Phyllis Quek), Greg's mysterious girlfriend. Events begin spiraling out of control.

Director Gordon Chan *(Thunderbolt)* keeps the plot moving at a fast clip but allows time for the events that are happening to register, both with the characters and the audience. The action is very well staged, especially two of the gun battles that break out. Throw in a car chase in Singapore and a couple of martial arts fights, and it's hard to get bored. Aaron Kwok effectively conveys the range of emotions that Peter experiences during the film, although his transformation from computer geek to action hero is not completely convincing. Phyllis Quek lends Salina just a touch of poignancy. As with the role of Peter, however, Salina's character arc is not realistically portrayed in the script. In a supporting role, Francis Ng shines; he plays Officer Ronald Ng as basically unflappable—efficient yet concerned for his own people as well as civilians. His most memorable moment comes when he is pinned down by gunfire in a parking garage, trying to protect a citizen. As chaos ensues, he stoically tosses off the line: "This is business as usual for a civil servant." The cinematography of Arthur Wong *(Once upon a Time in China)* makes a variety of locations look attractive. Shigeru Umebayashi's music is excellent, adding impact where needed to the action scenes and stirring emotions during the quieter moments. —PM *AKA: Gung Yuen 2000 AD; Gong Yuan 2000 AD.* 🐉🐉🐉

2000 104m/C *HK* Aaron Kwok, Daniel Wu, Phyllis Quek, Lai Hing-cheung, Gigi Choi, Andrew Lin, Ray Lui, Francis Ng, Ken Lo, Cheung Wai, James Lye. *D:* Gordon Chan. *W:* Gordon Chan, Stu Zicherman. *C:* Arthur Wong. *M:* Shigeru Umebayashi. **DVD**

U-Man

The easy camaraderie and winning performances by the cast make for enjoyable entertainment. Jesus (Anthony Wong) and Ken (Sam Lee) are cops who must go undercover at a Catholic girls' school to try and recover a missing backpack filled with ill-gotten money. Jesus poses as Father Gum, and Ken is enrolled as May, a disabled girl student who, because of illness, looks like a boy—or, at least, that's the story they tell the students. In reality, Ken trying to pass as "May" makes for the least-believable schoolgirl in the history of cinema. As they try to solve the case, Jesus and Ken at first suspect—and then are tempted to romance—respectively, Miss Cool (Rachel Fu), a teacher, and Candy (Gillian Chung), a student.

U-Man is a low-key treat whose modest charms depend to a great degree upon the viewer's knowledge of Chinese actors as well as recent Hong Kong movies. If you don't know that Anthony Wong has played a lot of tough cops, it's not as funny to see him here with his hair dyed blonde, trying to pass as a priest in a Catholic girls' school. If you're not yet familiar with the work of Sam Lee, you may wonder why that guy is dressed up as Osama Bin Laden, and you may not find it so funny when he poses as a uniformed schoolgirl. And if you have yet to recognize Lam Suet from his multitude of supporting roles, you may not think it's funny to see him—in black suit and white shirt à la *The Mission*—with a very obvious curly hair wig. Throughout a number of their scenes, Wong and Lee are simply goofing around. As an example, watch how they act when they enter a church for a secret rendezvous. The story meanders and comes to a stop several times so we can observe the interactions between Wong, Lee, and their various romantic interests; it's never in a hurry to rush to the finale. A few positive comments about lesbian relationships, the plight of disabled persons, and the value of family are thrown in for good measure. A couple of brief fight scenes are also included, and a variety of settings and locales are used effectively. With lowered expectations in mind, *U-Man* will leave you with a smile on your face, and that's no small accomplishment. Jade Leung has an amusing cameo as the school principal. Dante Lam served as producer. —PM *AKA: Gwaai Sau Hok Yuen; Guai Shou Xiao Yuan.* 🐉🐉

2002 88m/C *HK* Anthony Wong, Sam Lee, Gillian Chung, Rachel Fu, Jade Leung, Ruby Wong, Lam

Suet. **D:** Cheung Chi-Sing. **W:** Cheung Chi-Sing. **C:** Lam Wah-Chuen. **M:** Lam Wah-Chuen. **DVD**

Ultimatum

Hong Kong police chief inspector Yip Tin Ming (Michael Wong) and his partner are assigned to protect state's witness Fat Dog, but they fail. A mysterious woman in black (Yoyo Mung) makes an amazing shot, hitting her target. Because of his migraine headache, Ming only manages to wing her as she escapes. She next appears at the hotel of a second witness against the Ola triad, killing him as well, and cheating another killer (Yuen Wah) sent on the same job by a Japanese gang by taking the data disc he was after. Wai May, an ex-cop crime reporter, is on a vendetta against the entire gang responsible for her father's death, working with the Ultimatum vigilante group. She's also Yip's girlfriend (small world). Diana Ma, a witness to the gun battle and chase, is Yip's ex-girlfriend (even smaller). Mainland forensic psychologist Dr. James Fong is sent to help out on the case. After he sees her in action saving Diana from an assassination attempt, Fong puts the pieces together and guesses the truth.

The police scenes are handled conventionally, but whenever the film heads into assassin territory, it's almost like a superhero show. May's apartment has a secret room full of weapons and equipment, painted in blues and always full of fog. It's a slightly uneven mix, thrown off even further by the soap-opera elements. However, the action scenes are quite satisfying. The main title sequence is beautifully designed, a crisscross of slo-mo bullets—a perfect fit for an action flick from Matrix Productions. **AKA:** *Chui Hau Tung Dip; Zui Hou Tong Die.* 🎬🎬🎬

2001 90m/C *HK* Michael Wong, Yoyo Mung, Yuen Wah, William Tuen, Joe Lee, Kant Leung. **D:** Kant Leung. **W:** Jessica Chan, Kant Leung. **C:** Yip Wai-ying. **M:** Nanjing Music Group, Ltd. **VHS, DVD**

Ultraman 2 📺

The ultrapopular Tsuburaya Productions superhero series was the basis of this anime series (not to be confused with a later *Ultraman USA* series produced by Hanna-Barbera). Four episodes are included on this video. In "Polar Monsters," a bright light and strange letters appear in the sky all over the Earth. The Earth Defense Force assigns Captain Adams to head the new Emergency Science and Defense Squad, created to look into the matter. Agents Marconi, Johnson, Harris, and the incredibly ugly robot PDQ are assigned to work under him. On a

flight down from a satellite station, the spirit of Ultraman occupies Harris (actually, it's Ultraman Jonias, a little-known cousin in the Ultraman family). When huge monsters emerge from a mysterious iceberg and threaten a city, Harris transforms to the giant superhero Ultraman to battle the menace. In "Tornado Troubles," Ultraman fights an energy-sucking tornado monster. Another weather-related menace appears in "Red Cloud." The menace in "Monstrous Crocodile" should be obvious. The ESDS manages to defeat the monster without help, but when its pieces regenerate, Ultraman's services are required. The animated version isn't nearly as much fun as watching the live-action hero fighting funky man-in-suit monsters. To save costs, the show usually followed a rigid formula, but it seems odd that the anime follows the same pattern. Some of the monsters and action go beyond what was available to the live-action productions up to that point, but mostly it's an opportunity wasted. Fifty episodes were produced. To fans, this series just marked time until the "real" Ultraseries returned with *Ultraman 80.* **AKA:** *Ultraman Jonias; The Ultraman.* 🎬🎬

1979–80 84m/C *JP* **V:** Tom Weiner, Barbara Goodson, Steve Kramer, Joe Perry. **D:** Tom Weiner (English dub). **W:** Hiroyasu Yamaura. **M:** Toshiaki Tsushima. **VHS, DVD**

Ultraman Gaia: The Battle in Hyperspace

This follow-up feature to *Ultraman Tiga and Ultraman Dyna* bears some resemblance to 1969's *All Monsters Attack* (AKA *Godzilla's Revenge*). Tsutomu (Gaku Hamada) is a lonely nine-year-old Ultraman fanatic, often neglecting his schoolwork to watch tapes of his hero Ultraman Gaia. While watching his favorite episode, he's drawn into a psychic vortex by a glowing red ball, and has a vision of a little girl in an apocalyptic landscape. The next day, Lisa Nanase (Mai Saito)—the same girl from his dream—is a new transfer student in his class, and he finds the red ball on his toy shelf. The red ball grants wishes, and Tsutomu wishes to meet his hero Gaia's alter-ego Gamu Takayama (Takeshi Yoshioka) in person. The ball is actually a device created by the super-science of humans in another dimension, who were destroyed by their creation's power. Now it travels from dimension to dimension, feeding on the greed of mankind. School bully Hiro grabs the ball, creating a giant monster to fight Gaia. After defeating the monster, Gamu is shocked to find himself in a world where every kid knows he's Ultraman, but soon

The Ultraman Family

The most prevalent Asian superhero character has to be Ultraman. When you think about it, nothing could be more natural—superheroes had become popular subjects for Japanese movies since the 1950s, from Starman (Supergiant) to Space Chief (Ironsharp). However, these heroes were primarily based upon American TV and serial heroes drawn from American comics like Superman. What was lacking was true Japanese flavor.

Enter Eiji Tsuburaya. The special-effects genius behind the Godzilla series and so many other Toho Studios spectacles formed his own company, Tsuburaya Productions, to produce TV series and movies of his own. In 1966, their anthology TV series *Ultra Q* was broadcast. Featuring a different monster every week, the show got good response, but something was missing. A continuing hero was needed to fight the monsters, and since giant monsters were so popular already, why not have a giant hero ready to do battle with them? And so, the alien *Ultraman* came to Earth to fight monsters, but in order to remain on our planet he needed to merge identities with Hayata, who conveniently enough is a member of the Science Patrol, a high-tech team dedicated to dealing with monster emergencies. Whenever the threat was too big for the Science Team to deal with (that is, *every* week), Hayata would use his Beta Capsule to transform into the 40-meter-tall red and silver superhero. It was established during the series that Ultraman was just one of a number of Ultramen from Nebula M78.

The 39-episode series was a huge hit, and was picked up for syndication in the U.S. by United Artists. Tsuburaya decided that a sequel was in order, and another Ultraman called *Ultraseven* came to Earth. This series had a more adult slant to it than its predecessor, but didn't do nearly as well in the ratings, and Tsuburaya moved on to other shows like *Mighty Jack*. But of course, that wasn't the end—Ultraman stayed alive in the public consciousness, abetted by some silly satirical *Ultra Fight* shorts that were broadcast.

In the 1970s a revamped and updated Ultraman Jack appeared in the *New Ultraman* series—a process that would be repeated many times. To date, 19 separate Ultraman series have been produced, including two animated series, an Australian edition

(*Ultraman: Towards the Future* starring Ultraman Great), a direct-to-video series, and one produced as a series of one-minute infomercials (*Ultraman Nice*) that was broadcast during reruns of the *Ultraman Tiga* series. In all, some 27 official members of the Ultraman family have appeared in some form.

There have also been over a dozen Ultraman feature films produced (not counting TV episode compilations), starting oddly enough with a 1975 Thai co-production called *The 6 Ultra Brothers vs. the Monster Army*. In recent years, it has become traditional for Ultraman movies to appear in between series, and the modern episodes feature dazzling f/x a far cry from the clunky look of the original TV series.

fades back to his own dimension. From the memory he copied from the ball, he learns its terrible history, and uses the new hyperspace ship *Adventure* to get back to Tsutomu's dimension. But he's too late—Hiro has already created a trio of monsters strong enough to beat him. Tsutomu has to struggle through the ensuing destruction to get the ball back, so that he can bring Ultraman Tiga and Ultraman Dyna to help out in a giant monster superhero rumble.

Screenwriter Keichi Hasegawa crams in all kinds of positive messages for kids, whether they make any sense or not. There seems to be quite a lot of controversy amongst the children over whether or not watching Ultraman shows is a worthwhile pursuit. Little Tsutomu (dubbed "Tommy" in English) has to defend his hero from his pal Yuyu, who would rather read books (and secretly wishes for world destruction!), and Lisa, who doesn't like the violence in the show. The bullying Hiro would rather play basketball, but note: this is the kind of movie where bullies wear plaid and sculpt in modeling clay. The monsters he creates are pretty cool, the main beast resembling a cross between Destroyah and Space Godzilla. The overly juvenile plot drags things down, so this doesn't measure up to the preceding Ultra-movie, but the special effects are gorgeous. *AKA: Urutoraman Teiga and Urutoraman Daina and Urutoraman Gaia: Choujiku no Daiketsugeki; Ultraman Tiga and Ultraman Dyna and Ultraman Gaia: The Great Decisive Attack of Super-Time and Space.* 🐕🐕🐾

1998 74m/C *JP* Takeshi Yoshioka, Gaku Hamada, Mai Saito, Sei Hiraizumi, Hiroyuki Watanabe, Kazuko Kato, Masashi Tashiro. **D:** Kazuya Konaku. **W:** Keichi Hasegawa. **C:** Shinichi O-oka. **M:** Shizuko Tamagawa, Toshihiko Sahashi. **VHS, DVD**

Ultraman Tiga and Ultraman Dyna: The Warriors of the Lightning Star

Characters from two fairly recent Japanese Ultraman TV series come together in one Ultra-feature! The seven-member team Super G.U.T.S. (Global Unlimited Task Squad) is mostly ineffectual at keeping Earth safe from giant monsters, but fortunately Ultraman Dyna is there to save their butts. However, during their latest monster hunt on the moon, everyone is upstaged by the firepower of a huge Terrestrial Peace Conference battleship *Prometheus*. The G.U.T.S. team is escorted to a secret base on Cliomos Island, where they meet the *Prometheus*'s designer, Dr. Lui Kisaragi (Aya Sugimoto). The cocky Kisaragi assures them her ship will outclass them all, but requests a brain scan of each of them to add to the ship's strategy database. Wise guy Asuka (Takeshi Tsuruno) is the first to comply, but there's trouble: Kisaragi knows that Asuka is the human host for the alien Ultraman Dyna, and she plans to use his own knowledge against him to aid the hostile alien Monelas in conquering Earth.

A Monela ship attacks the base, and with the G.U.T.S. ship sabotaged, Dyna stands alone against the invaders. But the *Prometheus* transforms into a huge robot—one that knows Dyna's every move beforehand. Defeated by the robot's superior power and tactics, Asuka looks for help from the more experienced Ultraman Tiga, and seeks out Megumi Iruma (Mio Takagi) from a previous Super G.U.T.S. squad. Inspired, he returns to join the fight against the alien monsters.

Old-timers who have fond memories of the *Ultraman* series syndicated to U.S. television in the 1960s—or even the animated series in the 1970s—will surely be dazzled by the digitally enhanced special effects and bright, colorful production design on display here (it ain't Industrial Light and Magic, but it ain't bad). But be assured that not everything has been updated. Ultraman still sports a prominent zipper on the back of his Ultracostume, for one thing. That the giant hero fights some wacky monsters is another. Sure, there's a spiritual moment when everyone who believes in fairies claps their hands to revive the seemingly defeated Dyna (which somehow brings forth the vanished Ultraman Tiga as well), but this is still a monster-demolishing superhero we're talking about. Though the feature is surefire kiddie matinee entertainment, the folks at Image Entertainment seem to be aware of the adult Ultra-audience, thoughtfully providing the original Japanese language track (with English subtitles) on their Ultraman DVD releases. *AKA: Urutoraman Teiga and Urutoraman Daina: Hikari no Hoshi no Senshi Tachi; Ultraman Tiga and Ultraman Dyna: Warriors of the Star of Light.* 🐉🐉🐉

1998 68m/C *JP* Takeshi Tsuruno, Toshikazu Fukawa, Risa Saito, Takao Kase, Joh Onodera, Mariya Yamada, Mio Takagi, Aya Sugimoto, Ryo Kinomoto. *D:* Kazuya Konaku. *W:* Keichi Hasegawa. *C:* Shinichi O-oka. *M:* Tatemi Yano. **VHS, DVD**

The Unbeaten 28

This Joseph Kuo production is a Wu Tang variation/semi-sequel to his "18 Bronzemen of Shaolin" pictures. During the pre-credit sequence (squeezed into a hurried few seconds in the English version), Wu Tang Master Wu Chung-kun and 100 of his followers are massacred by members of the Kung Tung Clan, at the order of their leader Yen Chan-tin (Mark Lung). Wu family friend Yu Chuen-tung (Jack Lung) takes the only surviving son of Wu up to the top of Lu Wan Mountain, leaving his own family unprotected when Kung Tung's forces attack. All efforts are thrown into raising "Tiger" Wu Shao-tung (Meng Fei) to be a kung fu superstar via constant torturous training.

After 18 years of training, Tiger is sent to Tai Chin Temple to undergo the Test of the 18 Obstacles, hoping he can prove himself and earn their sacred kung fu manual, which will enable him to rebuild the Wu Tang Clan. Tiger fails on his first attempt to get through the maze of tests and traps, nearly beaten to death by the robotic stone statues. When Yen Chan-tin catches up with Master Yu and murders him, it deepens Tiger's resolve to win the Tai Chin book. On his second attempt, he's beaten by a young boy (Mau Ging-shun), the spirit of Tai Chin (who is later said to be 80 years old!). After some healing and further training, Tiger becomes the first one in 60 years to survive all 18 Obstacles (though we only see about 11).

One imagines Joseph Kuo sitting up all night thinking of traps and obstacles to beset his heroes, and the ones here are pretty creative, though not on the grand scale of *18 Bronzemen*. After going through such arduous training, the climactic battle is a bit of an anti-climax, especially since villain Mark Long only seems to have two henchmen working for him. Perhaps sensing this, Kuo throws in a few more tricks, giving Long a lair full of his own automated death traps. Though it's really only a series of recycled ideas from his earlier movies, Kuo still stirs up enough exotic kung fu thrills to make this one interesting. However, there's no explanation of just who the unbeaten 28 are. *AKA: The Unbeatable 28.* 🐉🐉🐉

1980 85m/C *HK* Meng Fei, Mark Lung, Jack Lung, Jeanie Chang, Nancy Yen, Mau Ging-shun, O Yauman, Ma Cheung. *D:* Joseph Kuo. *W:* Joseph Kuo. *C:* Chong Sun. **VHS, DVD**

Undercover Blues

Solid, stylish B-movie about cops and criminals. Undercover cop Joe (Daniel Wu) has disappeared while on assignment in Malaysia. He traveled there with triad overlord Spanner (Blackie Ko), and his police superiors become afraid that Joe may have crossed over to the criminal side. So they send Frank (Ray Lui) to get him back. Joe was Frank's student at the police academy, and the two were once close friends. Frank assembles a team of three men with problems caused by undercover work: Fred (Simon Lui), a cop turned gangster; Simon (Mark Cheng), on suspension and accused of accepting bribes; and Charles (Wong Hei), whose marriage is on the rocks. Once in Malaysia, Frank unexpectedly runs into Phoenix (Meng Kuang-mei) an old girlfriend. Frank tries to hold things together, complete the mission, and reclaim his friendship with Joe.

Undercover Blues moves at a lightning pace; director Billy Chung throws in interesting camera work as well. The basic ideas may be highly derivative, but the script's extreme focus on the travails of undercover work tightens the story line. The action sequences are dynamic—mostly of the gun battle variety. The running time is so brief that it's over before you know it. It's modest in its ambitions and succeeds as a pleasant and thoughtful diversion. Cinematographer Daniel Chan Fai bathes the film in deep greens and blues. Lincoln Lo's musical score is percussive and refreshing. Lead actor Ray Lui served as one of the producers; his brother Simon Lui co-wrote the script with Edmond Pang, the author of the novel *Fulltime Killer*. —PM **AKA:** *Ying; Xing; Punishment.* 🐉🐉🐲

2000 76m/C *HK* Ray Lui, Daniel Wu, Simon Lui, Wong Hei, Mark Cheng, Meng Kuang-mei, Chapman To, Blackie Ko, Liu Wai-hung, Karel Wong. **D:** Billy Chung. **W:** Simon Lui, Edmond Pang. **C:** Daniel Chan. **M:** Lincoln Lo. **VHS, DVD**

United We Stand, and Swim

A colorful cast of characters and some sharp writing make up for the slack direction. Yu Kam-Kei (Samuel Leung), AKA Little Fish, is dismissed by a girl when she discovers that he cannot swim. The neighbors make fun of him, and his mother, who owns an aquarium shop, is embarrassed. For his birthday, she gives him a certificate for swimming lessons at the local community pool. He is dismayed to meet Mao (Anthony Wong), the coach, who seems more interested in pushing his own line of swimsuits than in teaching the class how to swim. And the rest of the class is not terribly encouraging—among them Fat Dice (Wyman Wong), an overweight triad; a drunk (Joe Lee); and a young married couple. All seems lost until the lovely and outgoing Audrey (Pace Wu) appears. Temporarily encouraged to continue his lessons due to Audrey's presence, Little Fish soon finds himself caught up in a dispute between an experienced swimming team and his own inept teammates—a dispute that must be settled with a 4 x 100 relay race.

The film is an enjoyable, character-driven series of episodes that vary in the quality of their writing and directing. Most of the humor is gentle and softly lobbed at its target; as a result, the pace feels slack and loose-limbed, as though the plot itself were underwater. The story occasionally wanders away from Little Fish to check in on the other characters, but we learn little about them. For example, we know Fat Dice is a triad and that his young son—called "Boss" Chung—wants his Daddy to quit the gangsters, but we don't know why Fat Dice suddenly agrees to do so or what happened to the mother of "Boss." Audrey changes her romantic mind about Little Fish so often it's a wonder the poor boy doesn't have whiplash, yet we never learn anything about her, such as why she's so emotionally mercurial. On the other hand, while *United We Stand, and Swim* never pretends to be a deep examination of dramatic characters, it does portray certain scenarios in a very touching and believable way—such as the interplay

between the carefree Little Fish and his loving mother. Although early scenes make it appear that the romance with Audrey will play a bigger role, Pace Wu as Audrey ends up having little to do during much of the running time except mysteriously change her mind about Little Fish. She is charming and slender; while there's nothing wrong with her figure, her modest swim suits emphasize that the heart of the story is fixed on the characters and not on their bodies. Anthony Wong appears to be racing through his lines half-heartedly during several scenes; his performance is disappointingly average. Director Matt Chow has an amusing cameo playing himself. The photography by Rocky Tsang emphasizes primary colors and the frequent underwater shots introduce a pleasant visual variety. —PM **AKA:** *Fei yue ling yang.* 🐉🐉

2001 91m/C *HK* Samuel Leung, Anthony Wong, Joe Lee, Wyman Wong, Pace Wu, Kitty Yuen, Matt Chow. **D:** Matt Chow. **W:** Matt Chow. **C:** Jimmy Chan, Rocky Tsang. **M:** Tommy Wai, Chris Babida. **DVD**

The Untold Story

Part drama, part horror, part comedy, this true-crime story from Hong Kong goes far beyond the bounds of a TV movie treatment. In 1978, a horrible murder case goes unsolved. Eight years later, a pair of human hands is discovered on the beach on Macao. The homicide division seems more like something out of the *Police Academy* series than a real police squad, but eventually Officer Lee (Danny Lee) traces the grisly clues to the Eight Immortals Restaurant, where new owner Wong Chi Hang (Anthony Wong) offers no explanation for the sudden disappearance of the former owner and his family. Lacking evidence, the police arrest Wong anyway, hoping to coerce a confession out of him. At this point, the film begins to shift gears rather abruptly. Despite the subject matter, the first half of the film is much too concerned with the antics of the sophomoric cops to prepare the viewer for what is to come. The same cops shown in smirking scenes as they partake of the barbecue buns the suspect has given them, are shown beating and torturing the prisoner in his cell. When the officers leave, things just get worse, as Wong's fellow prisoners beat and torture him even more severely. Finally, Wong can stand no more, and launches into a full confession of his crimes—which tops everything that has come before in terms of violence, revulsion, and inhumanity. Horror fans who can laugh off the ultraviolence of *Zombie*, the ultimate gore of *Dead-Alive*, or even the sadistic frenzy of *Cannibal Holocaust*, won't sleep well after witnessing the sad and painful (but true) last half hour of this picture.

Producer/director/star Danny Lee has made a whole career out of playing cops

named "Inspector Lee," as he did in John Woo's *The Killer*. With this film, and the equally infamous *Dr. Lamb,* he carved a niche for himself for a time as the foremost creator of hard-edged Asian true-crime dramas. Half-English Anthony Wong gives the performance of a lifetime in the movie that took him from playing supporting roles to leads, and earned him the Golden Horse at the Hong Kong Film Awards. The film's success led to a wave of repellent true-crime films, including a Taiwanese rip-off and two unrelated sequels. *AKA: Baat sin Faan Dim Chi Yan Yuk Cha Siu Baau; Ba Xian Fan Dian Zhi Ren Rou Cha Shao Bao; Bunman: The Untold Story; Human Meat Pies; Human Pork Chop; The Untold Story: Human Meat Roast Pork Buns.* 🦴🦴🦴

1992 96m/C *HK* Anthony Wong, Danny Lee, Emily Kwan, Shing Fui-on, Parkman Wong, Julie Lee, Gei Ga Faat, Lau Siu-ming. *D:* Herman Yau, Danny Lee. *W:* Law Kam-fai. *C:* Rudolf Chiu, Cho Wai-kei. *M:* Wong Bong. **VHS, DVD**

The Untold Story 2

Anthony Wong is here only to add name value to this unrelated "sequel," playing a cop known as Officer Lazyboots Sung, who is always losing his gun and getting in trouble. As in its predecessor, the police are used for comic relief to offset the horror that ensues.

Tsang Cheung (Emotion Cheung), a Hong Kong butcher with his own barbecue café, is having marital trouble with his wife Kuen (Yeung Fan) because of his impotence. His wife is having an affair with a jerk named Fai, with ridiculously slicked hair. Kuen's cousin Fung (Paulyn Sun) from Guangzhou comes to stay with them because of some trouble back home on the mainland. Cheung finds that his problem is solved by the helpful, respectful manner of his attractive in-law. Seemingly sweet, Fung has mental problems due to a horrifying experience in her past, and has a secret violent streak. When a woman is rude to her at the airport, she follows her into the restroom to set the woman on fire! Fung certainly isn't wanting for potential targets, as most of the people she meets in the big city are rude to her. She has little trouble seducing the cuckolded Cheung, already planning to take her cousin's place, and even posing for a wedding photographer with him. She even goes so far as to start dressing like her cousin, and decorates their apartment with the photos, enraging jealous Kuen. Fung shuts her up by stabbing her to death with a butcher knife. Then she cuts up the body with a jigsaw, and coerces Cheung to sell the *corpus dilecticus* as barbecued pork. They tell everyone Kuen has gone

home to visit, but Sung's intuition tells him there's something wrong.

Not a fraction as intense as the original, *Untold Story 2* seems more interested in soap opera than psycho-horror. There's some bloody mayhem at the conclusion, but otherwise it earns its Category III rating from sex. As usual, Anthony Wong is a low-key delight, while Cheung plays a drowsy and easily manipulated loser. Sun is fine as the psycho, but director Ng Yiu-kuen camps up her performance a bit with over-dramatic camera work. Also laughable are "horrifying" scenes of the actors eating ribs. *AKA: Yan Yuk Shiu Baau II Tin Chu Dei Mit; Ren Rou Cha Shao Bao II Tian Zhu Di Mie.* 🦴🦴

1998 90m/C *HK* Paulyn Sun, Emotion Cheung, Anthony Wong, Yeung Fan, Melvin Wong, Jamie Luk, Helena Law. *D:* Ng Yiu-kuen. **VHS, DVD**

Urotsukidoji

 This series of animated featurettes is a landmark of sorts in the field of "Hentai" (adults only) anime, and has been released two ways in the U.S.— as a couple of features that condense a few episodes, and as a full series. For those interested, the full-length series is the way to go. Those interested in seeing a beautifully animated story that features hard-core sex and violence involving both humans and horrifying demons from another dimension will want to get as much as they can. For those who are not—well, what good will it do to see a shorter, even less coherent version of the same complicated story?

Based on the comics of Toshio Maeda, *Urotsukidoji* presents a mythology in which the universe is divided into three dimensions. There's the flesh-and-blood human world we know, the demon world of nightmares, and the ethereal world of the superpowered beast-people, who have attributes of all three worlds. According to legend, every 3000 years the union of a Chosen One and a human female will result in the birth of an Overfiend, a being capable of bringing the three worlds together in harmony, or something like that. For centuries, the Beast-Men have been keeping watch for this event. Meanwhile, those of the demon world make plans of their own. A high-school boy named Negumo is falling for a pretty cheerleader named Akemi—a pretty normal scenario, except for the fact that Akemi has already fallen victim to one of a series of rapes committed by demons in the human world, and Negumo is having strange new feelings that go far beyond the pangs of puberty. When the demons attack, he transforms into a semi-demon himself and fights them off.

Teenage Man-Beast Amano and his sister watch these events and begin to wonder—maybe their legend won't come true quite the way it's supposed to.

The series features wonderful animation that depicts horrifying, repellent, and often-offensive events, but exaggerated to such a degree that it can't be taken seriously. Rape is an obscenity (and seems to be more common in Japanese adult entertainment than it is in real life in America), but the sight of a gigantic three-headed penis blasting through an entire city—well, if you haven't lost track of the already sketchy plot at this point in the presentation, you'll abandon it anyway, overwhelmed by the sick, gory, and hallucinatory apocalypse unfolding on screen. *AKA: Chojin Densetsu Urotsukidoji; Legend of the Overfiend; The Wandering Kid.* 🐉🐉🐉

1989 (NC-17) **C:** JP **D:** Hideri Takayama. **W:** Noboru Aikawa, Toshio Maeda (manga). **M:** Masamichi Amano. **VHS, DVD**

Urusei Yatsura Movie 1: Only You

Based on Rumiko Takahashi's monstrously popular sci-fi romantic comedy manga, the anime TV series had been running for two years already when this first feature was produced. Because of this, the film is aimed directly at initiated fans, and tries to fit every character into a grand scenario, making the film extremely confusing for newbie viewers. Added to this is the fact that a good part of Takahashi's humor is based on multilayered Japanese puns, and you have a nearly indecipherable entertainment program. Fortunately, U.S. distributor AnimEigo is very sensitive to this dilemma, and provides detailed notes for reference.

To keep the peace between the alien Oni race and Earth, green-haired princess Lum is engaged to horny slacker high-school student Ataru Moroboshi. One day everyone in the neighborhood receives invitations to Ataru's wedding. Even Lum, since it turns out she's not the bride! Ataru is typically ignorant of what's going on, and is surprised to find out that he's also engaged to Elle, *another* alien princess! It seems that as a small boy, Ataru was playing with a little girl in the park and stepped on her shadow, which meant a marriage proposal on her planet. Having come of age, an intergalactic shotgun wedding is being planned for the two strangers. When Lum finds out about this, the battle is on, with her "darling" Ataru once again in the middle. Several other girls consider themselves engaged to or otherwise involved with Ataru, and they all take turns trying to interfere

with the wedding, while a variety of jealous rivals form a complex web of situation comedy. And of course, Lum's family weighs in, ready to start a war with Elle's people to prevent the wedding or invade the Earth if it goes through. Underneath the chaos there's a touching undercurrent of pathos, as both Ataru and Elle remember a much more peaceful and innocent time when they were just two little kids playing in the sunshine. The magic of Takahashi's work is how she keeps enough emotional involvement balanced perfectly, even as she creates an orgy of wacky insanity around it. The musical sequences are a bit cloying. Director Mamoru Oshii worked on much of the TV series and directed the second movie before moving on to other projects, including his terrific *Patlabor*. *AKA: Urusei Yatsura 1: Onri Yu.* 🐉🐉🐉

1983 101m/C JP **D:** Mamoru Oshii. **W:** Mamoru Oshii, Tomoko Kaneharu, Rumiko Takahashi (manga). **C:** Akio Wakana. **M:** Masamichi Amano, Fumitaka Anzai, Izumi Kobayashi. **VHS, DVD**

The Vampire Combat

Obviously inspired by the success of *Blade*, there's been a reanimated interest in vampire flicks in Hong Kong recently, where the combination of monsters and kung fu has been around for decades. In 1940, Master Maolung abducts "Yin Woman" Piuhung (Valerie Chow), wife of vampire hunter (and Maolung's former student) Hsu Yaotu (Andrew Lin), to be a sacrifice in a ceremony during an alignment of planets that will make him a Dark God—a Devil Monster. Though tempted to rejoin his master on the Dark Side, Hsu manages to defeat the king vampire, escaping his coven with half of the magic Dunsun Book, while Piuhung and several of their companions die in the battle. Hsu manages to find the reincarnation of Piuhung in each succeeding generation and block evil influence with a protective mark.

Sixty-odd years go by, and the Yin Woman of the millennium is a salon owner named Lam Shen (Chow again). She's had the feeling that a strange man (Hsu, actually) is watching her, even in her dreams. While out dancing with roommate/employee Judy, Shen bumps into Tony Wai Tung (Jackie Lui), the heroic head of the Supernatural Detective Agency, who has been assisting the police in cracking some weird cases, mostly shutting down phony fortune-tellers. He can see the mark on her forehead with his second sight, but is too busy tracking down blind fortune-teller Lau Yun to do anything about it. He finds Lau, who is actually one of Hsu's followers (they can stave off aging with their magic), dying of wounds inflicted by vampire warrior Wuchie and another follower of Devil Monster. As he's dying, Lau warns Tony to keep the Yin Woman (and the other half of the book) away from Devil Monster at all costs. The vampires decide to spare Tony and let him use his supernatural powers to lead them right to Shen.

Shen hires Tony to help her find out who is watching her, and a clue at the orphanage she grew up in leads to Hsu. Ironically, Hsu has become a sort of business-world vampire, and an angry protester shoots Hsu before either Tony or the vampires can get to him. It's up to Tony to put the pieces together to find out what links Shen and her dreams with the mysterious deaths. But is he leading her right into the Devil Monster's clutches?

The opening is a bit disorienting, as it puts you right into the action with little preamble, leaving plot details to be filled in later. The martial arts action is abetted by cheap f/x, with the vampires able to zip around at super-speed, and they dissolve into crumbling skeletons when killed via CGI f/x. It may be a modern vampire movie, but much of the flavor here is reminiscent of 1970s and '80s action and horror flicks. The mystery story, despite the fact that we know the answers the detective is looking for, is much like old Italian thrillers. But '70s kung fu star Wilson Tong's direction of the fight scenes brings back memories of great Hong Kong action flicks. This feeling is reinforced by the presence of stars like Lo Lieh and Tai Bo in small roles—even though they don't throw any punches, their faces strike a chord. *AKA: Gik Chuk Geung Shut; Ji Su Jiang Shi.* 🐉🐉💧

2001 91m/C *HK* Jackie Lui, Valerie Chow, Andrew Lin, Tai Bo, Lo Lieh. **D:** Wilson Tong. **W:** Cheung Hoi-ching. **C:** Yeung Kwong-leung. **DVD**

Vampire Controller

Though European vampires are now the popular favorite in Hong Kong horror films, this one revives the old-fashioned hopping kyonsi for an adventure that recalls old films like *New Mr. Vampire*. In Guangdong Province of 1708, Eurasian agent Wong Ching (Jude Poyer) is sent by the emperor for a rendezvous with his girlfriend Jenny to collect a secret letter. Mao Tung-tung (Cheng Ka-sang), an agent of villainous Prince Pa, interrupts the meeting to steal the letter, but is scared off by guards. On his way out, he poisons the couple, later bribing the coroner to declare a double suicide, but the letter isn't found on either body. On conferring with his superior, Officer Ha La-chak (Yuen Wah), Tung hires his cousin Professor "Southern" Mao (Wayne Lai) to transport the corpses to a cooler climate—though the real purpose is to keep the

bodies away from their enemies and give Tung-tung time to search for the letter. On the road, Mao and his assistant/foster brother John Lui (Gallen Law) encounter rival Northern Ma Siu-ling (Yuen King-Tan) and her student Tien Gee (Kathy Chow). Since it's troublesome to escort male and female corpses together, Jenny joins Ma's dead girl chorus line for the trip.

Lian Kan-yao, an agent of Prince Xi, hires ninja Kindaiichi (Joey Man) to find the letter before Prince Pa does, or destroy the corpses. The corpse convoy stops for a few days at an abandoned house to avoid trouble with the Ghost Festival. When Kindaiichi and Mao Tung-tung both sneak into the house to search for the letter, they disturb the corpses in the ensuing chaos, Tung gets bit by a vampire in the ensuing chaos, and Kindaiichi is captured. She makes a deal with the escorts so they'll help her find the letter. Meanwhile, black-magician Ha tires of Tung's failures, and raises a battalion of zombies from a nearby graveyard to devour him. Not that Ha is any more successful—he lets the vampires loose, and even gets infected himself. The result of his mischief is the creation of a malicious "baby ghost," an engine of destruction against friend and foe alike. The only hope is in a weird and dangerous marriage/suicide/reincarnation ceremony.

The filmmakers are clearly having a ball revisiting this unique part of Chinese culture, taking time to impart bits of corpse escort lore along the way. This sometimes slows the story down a bit, but is entertaining nonetheless. And any lag is more than compensated by the bizarre action combining kung fu, magic, and mayhem. The action isn't up to the frantic level of the *Mr. Vampire* movies, but there's still plenty of fun stuff here. The narrative is enlivened with sharp comedy, intrigue, and romance among the heroes—and even between the tragic deceased couple. Curiously, only the male corpses hop. The soundtrack is unusually good. *AKA: Gon Shut Sin Sang; Gan Shi Xian Sheng.* 🐉🐉🐉

2000 91m/C *HK* Gallen Law, Wayne Lai, Joey Man, Kathy Chow, Yuen King-Tan, Yuen Wah, Jude Poyer, Cheng Ka-sing. **D:** Tony Leung Hung-wah. **W:** Tony Leung Hung-wah. **C:** Yip Wai-ying. **M:** Simon Leung, Tony Tam. **VHS, DVD**

Vampire Hunter D

Though background information on the film says it takes place in A.D. 12090, nothing in the film states a specific year. It may as well be a fantasy world that could be long past, far in the future, or in another dimension. Our heroine Doris finds her family's ranch beset by ghouls and goblins, creatures under the reign of Count Magnus Lee, a powerful vampire king

who has been terrorizing the countryside around his castle.

Pretty young Doris does what she can to resist, but eventually finds herself in the clutches of the vampire, who is about 15 feet tall! After being bitten, she hires the only man who might have a chance against Lee: the vampire hunter known only as D. The tall dark stranger on a cyborg horse is no ordinary superpowered vampire hunter. He hides a tall dark secret: he's a half-vampire "dampiel" himself, having been sired by the one and only Count Dracula. When asked to help, at first D is ambiguous, fighting off his emotions. But when Doris is abducted, he changes his mind and storms Lee's fantastic castle full of terrifying creatures alone, in true antihero fashion.

Vampire Hunter D sports more pretentious attitude than its shallow depth can support, but has enough spunk to work on a video game level (and indeed, it became a Playstation game). The basic plot is built around European and Hollywood vampire mythology, but a lot of the creatures reflect Japanese legends and folklore. The animation has a lot of rough edges when compared to modern anime, but at the time was highly regarded for it's imagination. Despite its flaws, the original is an old favorite for many anime fans all over the world. The designs are attractive, especially when it comes to the monsters, but don't compare with the Yoshitako Amano book illustrations they're based on. *AKA: Kyuketsuki Hunter D.* 🗡🗡🗡

1985 80m/C *JP* **D:** Toyoo Ashida. **W:** Yasushi Hirano, Hideyuki Kikuchi (novel). **M:** Tetsuya Komuro. **VHS, DVD**

Vampire Hunter D: Bloodlust

In 1985, one of Hideyuki Kikuchi's *Vampire Hunter D* novels was adapted as an animated feature film. It's a fun flick, with nice character designs based on simplified versions of the book's illustrations, an interesting hero, and an engaging fantasy setting. But it's not the kind of movie that makes you want to own the poster, or read the source novel. But this belated sequel is.

Alan Elbourne hires D (voiced by Andrew Philpot in the English version), the half-vampire bounty hunter with the chatty left palm. His sister Charlotte (Wendee Lee) has been missing for two days. Vampire Lord Meier Link (John Rafter Lee) is the prime suspect in the apparent abduction. The Elbournes agree to pay $20 million to D to return her—or kill her mercifully, if changed into a vampire. Getting to Charlotte

won't be easy—there's competition. The hunting Markus Brothers, highly skilled warriors who travel in a customized tank, have already been hired by Elbourne as insurance. Plus, Link is guarded by a trio of powerful demons, and the country they're travelling through is full of other supernatural dangers. Link's massive castle is guarded by deadly sentry lasers and other traps. But after D and the Markus' manage to get through his defenses, Link flees the castle.

Catching up with Link's coach, D suspects Charlotte may have gone willingly. But until he knows for sure, the chase is on. Link heads for the far-off castle of vampire Queen Carmilla, where he believes they'll find safe haven. The road there is fraught with danger for everyone, and Carmilla's castle turns out to be the most dangerous place of all.

This is one of those rare foreign films that make you glad they've been dubbed into English, as the draftsmanship of the images is so incredible that you'd hate to be distracted by having to read text. Every frame is a glorious illustration come to life. The voice actors are above the usual level of talent hired for such things, and the U.S. soundtrack was personally supervised by director Yoshiaki Kawajiri *(Lensman, Ninja Scroll)* at the Skywalker Ranch. The soundtrack is nearly as amazing as the visuals—almost too amazing. With all the cracking 5.1 effects and a fantastic soundtrack by Marco d'Ambrosio *(Haiku Tunnel)*, some of the quieter dialogue is tough to pick out. 🗡🗡🗡🗡

2001 (R) 102m/C *JP/HK* **V:** (English) Pamela Segall, John DiMaggio, Dwight Schultz, Andrew Philpot, Alex Fernandez, Mike McKenzie, Wendee Lee, John Rafter Lee. **D:** Yoshiaki Kawajiri. **W:** Yoshiaki Kawajiri. **M:** Marco d'Ambrosio. **VHS, DVD**

Vampire Kids

Shipwreck survivors wash ashore on an island beach. Some time is spent trying to revive Amy Yip, with the obligatory jokes about her breasts—which her brother Buffalo (Frankie Chan) doesn't appreciate. Between bouts of bickering, the party finds an abandoned village, once occupied by a Japanese soldier. They also find a large diamond embedded in a wall and steal it. However, the diamond was on the hilt of a dagger binding the vampire soldier within the wall, and he revives. The group eats some poisoned tomatoes that knock them out and then make them crazy—scaring the five little vampire kids that have come to suck their blood. The undead little rascals—Fatty, Timid, Stupid, Sharp Teeth, and Naughty—are at the command of the vampire soldier King of Ghosts, bound by magic collars, and he's sent them to collect blood from

"Maybe you're not so bad after all. You just dress bad."

—A backhanded compliment from the back of D's hand in *Vampire Hunter D: Bloodlust*

the party to increase his strength. Good at playing tricks, but shy about sucking blood, the kyonsi tots are eventually corralled by their intended victims. The castaways and mini-nosferatu team up to destroy the King—but he's been busy trapping bats to collect blood on his own, and has grown strong enough to break loose.

It's the usual Hong Kong horror comedy formula: dopey guys, pretty girls, pratfalls, and madcap antics. Even though they're supposed to be, you know, dead—and the effects are done with pretty obvious dummies—it's still a bit of a shock to see the adults beating up on the little kids. Shing Fu-on has a late cameo as a vampire papa. The film ends without the castaways being rescued, so it can be presumed they're all still on the island. *AKA: Geung Shut Fook Sing Chai; Jiang Shi Fu Xing Zai; Jiang Shi Fu Xing Zi.* 🐉🐉🐲

1991 85m/C *HK* Billy Lau, Sandra Ng, Amy Yip, Ngai Suet, Law Ching-ho, Frankie Chan, Shing Fui-on. **D:** Lee Pak-ling. **W:** Ko Chun-wai. **C:** Puccini Yu. **VHS, DVD**

Varan the Unbelievable

According to director Ishiro Honda, *Varan* was started as a co-production with an American company that wanted a cheap monster picture to distribute, hoping to make a tidy profit through television sales. Soon after the start of production, the deal fell through, and Toho Studios decided to continue with the picture shooting in the Tohoscope widescreen process for theatrical release. This story seems logical, because *Varan* certainly stands out from its neighbors, which were shot in widescreen and color. While Toho's other science-fiction movies of the period—*The H-Man, The Mysterians, Rodan, Battle in Outer Space*—all had distinctive concepts and ideas, *Varan* is a rather ordinary monster movie about a chemical experiment near a small island in the Japanese archipelago that disturbs a prehistoric monster beneath the water. The beast spreads terror on the island, and then visits the mainland to rampage in a big city.

A routine monster movie in Japan, *Varan* became complete trash at the hands of the American distributor Crown International. While in the U.S. version of *Godzilla,* Raymond Burr's character was unobtrusive and respectful, here Myron Healey appears in a series of poorly integrated scenes as an arrogant American scientist who treats everyone with condescension, even his Asian wife. Much of the plot of the original was cut out and replaced with shots of Healey pacing about, smoking, and yelling into a radio. Of the original 85-minute film, less than 15 minutes of footage appears in the 70-minute *Varan the Unbelievable.* So little is left that it's difficult to even tell what the monster looks like. Now, what sense is there in taking a B-grade Japanese picture into a "Z"-grade American movie? By 1962, when *Varan* made its U.S. debut (perhaps filling out a double bill with *First Spaceship on Venus*), audiences had already had a chance to see *Gorgo, Rodan,* and many other giant-monster movies. Faced with the prospect of releasing a dubbed Japanese monster movie, did Crown really think they'd make more money with an hour of Myron Healey? *AKA: Daikaiju Varan.* 🐉

1958 70m/BW *JP/US* Kozo Nomura, Fumito Matsuo, Akihiko Hirata, Yoshio Tsuchiya, Akio Kusama, Yoshifumi Tajima, Minosuke Yamada, Akira Sera, Hasaya Ito, Nadao Kirino, Katsumi Tezuka, Myron Healey (U.S. version), Tsuruko Kobayashi (U.S.), Clifford Kawada (U.S.). **D:** Ishiro Honda, Jerry A., Baerwitz (U.S.). **W:** Shinichi Sekizawa, Takeshi Kuronuma (story), Sid Harris (U.S.). **C:** Koizumi Hajime, Jacques R. Marquette (U.S.). **M:** Akira Ifukube. **VHS**

Venom Warrior

Director Chang Cheh made few films with a contemporary setting, and this odd showbiz story is rarely seen. By this time, Chang had pretty much come out of the closet and his films were getting increasingly bizarre. Andy Ho (Ricky Cheng, a minor player in Chang's Venoms films) is a martial artist/dancer/mime, working in the chorus in a TV Christmas special starring arrogant Mr. Wong (James Wong, having some fun)—until he gets tired of waiting for the idiot star and quits. Taiwanese Andy came to Hong Kong because his father doesn't support his dance career, so he has mixed feelings about his climb toward success, thinking his father would be shamed to see his son dancing on television. Gangster "Bug-Eyed" Freddy Tan (Chen Kuan-tai) signs up Andy for a tour of New York, using girlfriend Tootsie Chen (Anita Mui) as bait. But his real purpose is to lure Andy into the ring in underground kickboxing bouts. Andy refuses, insulting Fred on the way out, and becomes a street performer in Central Park. He befriends Dennis Brown (Dennis Brown), the master of a kung fu school, and Andy starts to teach his Dancing Style to students. However, Andy's disappointment in finding a role on the Broadway stage (where he's only offered Fu Manchu parts), and his weakness for alcohol, lead him to reconsider Fred's offer. He becomes a dancing star in Fred's NYC lounge, but is still under contract to fight in the ring. To his surprise, his opponent turns out to be Dennis (called Daniel in the English dub, despite his name on signs at the

school). After seeing the two fighters aren't out for blood, Fred poisons Dennis, leading Andy into a desperate fight with the boss himself.

The parade of '80s attitudes and styles is amusing throughout, but it's the dialogue that gets the most howls. Tootsie tells Andy, "Forget the fancy footwork! This is Jap crap—it can't take it!" when he dances on her car, and later, "If Wong Fei-hung were alive today, I'm sure he'd be doing modern dance." However, this is still a Chang Cheh movie, which means the fighting (and dancing) scenes are still terrific. Despite the light material that preceded it, the end battle is surprisingly bloody and strangely effective—drugged by a dart, Andy's big battle is intercut with the images in his mind in which it all becomes a dance number. A real curiosity, worth catching for a variety of reasons. Rumor has it Jet Li wants to do a remake. *AKA: Pik Lik Ching; Pi Li Qing; The Warrior, Dancing Warrior; Wu Tang Warrior.* 🎵🎵🎵

1983 91m/C *HK* Ricky Cheng, Chen Kuan-tai, Dennis Brown, Anita Mui, James Wong, Lui Fong, Got Heung Ting. **D:** Chang Cheh. **W:** Chang Cheh. **M:** James Wong. **DVD**

The Venus Wars

Perhaps because it didn't receive a theatrical release in the United States, this underrated anime feature hasn't gained the attention that it deserves. When the planet Venus collides with an ice asteroid, the resulting transformation makes the planet suitable for terraforming and capable of sustaining human life. But when a group from Earth arrives to colonize Venus, they bring all the worst traits of humanity with them. It's not long before trouble begins between two colonies, Ishtar and Aphrodia. Earth reporter Susan Somers goes to Venus to cover the coming war from the Aphrodian side, hoping to cop a Pulitzer Prize. She meets Hiro Seno, an athlete who is just interested in his sport, which is something like rollerball. The armies of Ishtar invade Aphrodia, and a world war breaks out on Venus.

Once the war is right in their backyards, Hiro and his friends decide they'd better get involved, one way or another. The complex story follows the lives of various young people, and

Another scaly horror causes insurance problems in *Varan the Unbelievable.*

how easily they become caught up in history as it happens. It also gives attention to the leaders, contrasting how the decisions they make affect the little people, and vice versa. The climax features some gripping, outstanding action sequences once the invasion is underway, as well designed and edited as any big-budget Hollywood action film. The character designs by Shichiro Kobayashi are clean and interesting, as is the general art direction, which believably represents what an off-world colony might look like. Some scenes mix animation with live backgrounds, an idea that doesn't work too well here. *AKA: Uinasu Senki.* 🦴🦴🦴🦴

1989 (PG) 102m/C *JP* **D:** Yoshikazu Yasuhiko. **W:** Yoshikazu Yasuhiko, Yuichi Sasimoto. **M:** Jo Hisaishi. **VHS, DVD**

Versus

The 444th out of 666 hidden portals to "the other side" is in the Forest of Resurrection—like the K-zones of Pupi Avati's *Zeder,* or Stephen King's *Pet Sematary,* an area where the dead are re-animated. For centuries, warriors have fought over the portal. Two convicts are helped to escape from prison, and rendezvous in the forest with their benefactor's gang. While waiting for the boss, a dispute erupts when one of the convicts (Tak Sakaguchi) objects to the kidnapping of a teenage girl, and he shoots one of the thugs. But people don't stay dead in that forest, and the girl and the convict escape while the thugs battle their zombie companion. They're having trouble remembering anything from before they arrived in the forest, but somehow the girl recognizes the boss when he arrives. Two of the gang, along with some recently arrived companions, have decided to double-cross the boss and kill him—but he turns out to be an immortal vampire far too powerful for them. Meanwhile, the cops who were transporting the prisoners are now hunting them. They also turn out to be more than they seem.

Versus has been described repeatedly as *The Killer* meets *The Evil Dead,* and rightly so, but with the equally heavy influence of modern swordplay and martial arts film. Director Ryuhei Kitamura slices off slabs of style from John Woo and Sam Raimi, and stacks them so high that they border on parody. At times the film's momentum is almost swallowed by its desperate need to look cool, but for the most part, it's one long, exhilarating action scene. Kung fu, samurai, zombies, sci fi, bullet ballet, gore, magic, crime, romance—*Versus* scrambles to assemble as many genres into two hours as possible. Its characters lack depth, but there's hardly room for any amongst the whizzing bullets, swinging swords, and squirting blood. 🦴🦴🦴🦴

2000 120m/C *JP* Tak Sakaguchi, Hideo Sakaki, Chieko Misaka, Kenji Matsuda, Yuichiro Arai, Minoru Matsumoto, Kazuhito Ohba, Takehiro Katayama, Ayumi Yoshihara, Shoichiro Masumoto, Toshiro Kamiaka, Yukihito Tanikado, Hoshimi Asai, Ryosuke Watabe, Motonari Komiya. **D:** Ryuhei Kitamura. **W:** Ryuhei Kitamura, Yudai Yamaguchi. **C:** Takumi Furuya. **M:** Nobuhiko Morino. **VHS, DVD**

The Victim

The Chinese title for this Sammo Hung action epic is decidedly more lyrical—"Fate Is Not Determined by Self"—and better describes the mix of comedy and drama in the film.

Chan Wing (Hung), one of those cocky young martial artists always looking for someone to test himself against, issues a challenge to the one called the Phantom Killer Choy Fan-tan (Chung Fat), whom he defeats easily. Moving on, Chan also defeats Fan-tan's master Leung Wing-ching, and so must fight Leung's master, Shaolin Abbot Silver Lining (Karl Maka), who also goes down much too easily. He finally finds someone good enough to beat him (repeatedly) in Leung Chung-yau (Leung Kar-yan), but Leung is unwilling to take Chan as his student—Chung-yau and his wife Wen Yuet-yi (Fanny Wang) are hiding out from his one-eyed gangster brother Cho-wing (Chang Yi), trying to avoid trouble, and don't want Chung-yau's prowess exposed. There's been bad blood between the brothers since Chung-yau's wedding night, when a drunk and jealous Cho-wing tried to rape Yuet-yi. When Cho-wing's men, led by Yuet-ming (Chan Lung), find them, Chan learns the whole story and wants to help avenge his master. However, Chung-yau has made a deathbed promise to his master to protect his brother, and Yuet-yi sacrifices herself to keep the peace.

Early on, the tone is light overall (including one of Hung's favorite gags: slipping on a banana peel). Those who are dying to see Sammo beat up a bunch of naked guys in a steam bath, here's your chance. But it turns to a much heavier tone in the second half. Chung-yau's feelings toward his brother are complex, his hatred compromised by guilt. As the adopted brother, Chung-yau has always been grateful for being taken in off the streets, and his indebtedness increased when he accidentally put his brother's eye out in a sparring match. It's not all drama though. To Siu Ming contributes his goofy cross-eyed act, and Sammo tries to scare Cho-wing's men disguised as Dracula! There's also a mystery element introduced at the start concerning a man blackmailed into killing Chung-yau, providing a slight twist toward the end. The training scenes and fights are marvelous and nearly constant, with Wilson Tong getting in on the final fight. Some music cues are swiped from George Romero's *Martin,* made plain by inclusion of a voice saying "Martin." **AKA:** *San Bat Yau Gei; Shen Bu You Ji; Lightning Kung Fu.* 🐉🐉🐉

1980 89m/C *HK* Sammo Hung, Leung Kar-yan, Fanny Wang, Chang Yi, Chan Lung, Chung Fat, Wilson Tong, Karl Maka, Billy Chan, Chan Hei, Yuen Miu, To Siu Ming, Cheung Ging Boh, Lam Ching-Ying, Yue Tau Wan, Fung Lee, Chin Leung, Shum Wai, Yuen Po. **D:** Sammo Hung. **W:** Lau Tin-chi. **C:** Michael Ma. **M:** Frankie Chan. **VHS, DVD**

Victim

This crime thriller from Ringo Lam *(Full Contact)*, returning to Hong Kong after a stay in Hollywood, provides quite a few twists from the usual police procedural, including a dip into supernatural horror, and a character study of a Hong Kong working stiff at the end of the 20th century. Two gunshots ring out in a parking garage, and an attendant is run over by a fleeing van containing three men. Shells are found by a jeep belonging to computer programmer Manson Ma (Lau Ching-Wan). The security tape reveals Ma was a kidnap victim. When a ransom call comes in, Detectives Pit Kwan (Tony Leung) and Bee (Wayne Lai) follow its instructions, finding Ma in an old hotel said to be haunted. Ma acts very strangely, withdrawn and given to fits of anger. Some of his behavior—and Kwan's—seems to parallel that of the hotel owner Au Ping-chung, who beheaded his wife Luk Yuet-ha in a fit of jealousy in 1964.

However, Lam is interested in something a bit deeper than a simple ghost story. Tailing Ma leads Kwan to believe he has a connection to the kidnappers, and the plot touches on a government mint heist plot, family drama, bloody violence, and economic turmoil in Hong Kong. With all these abrupt changes in direction, the entire film could have easily gone off the rails, but Lam manages to let things slip just enough to keep the audience off balance. There's also an excellent car chase scene halfway through. Lau Ching-Wan turns in another fine performance, while Tony Leung manages to make his standard cop role a little more vulnerable and interesting than usual. **AKA:** *Muk Lau Hung Gwong; Mu Lou Xiong Guang; The Victim.* 🐉🐉🐉

1999 108m/C *HK* Lau Ching-Wan, Amy Kwok, Tony Leung Ka-Fai, Hui Siu-hung, Wayne Lai, Ngai Sing, Emily Kwan, David Lee, Tony Chiu, Joe Lee, Kong Fu-keung, Chan Man Ching, Wong Chun-kong, Lui Ngai, Suki Kwan, Chung King-fai, Alannah Ong, Rebecca Tam. **D:** Ringo Lam. **W:** Joe Ma, Ringo Lam, Ho Man Lung (story). **C:** Ross Clarkson. **M:** Raymond Wong. **VHS, DVD**

Violated Paradise

Supposedly based on a book called *Meeting with Japan* by Fosco Maraini, this unintentionally funny docudrama tells the story of an innocent small-town Ainu girl who goes to the big, sinful city. Tamako (Kazuko Mine, voiced over by Paulette Girard) is a naïve young beauty from a fishing village in snowy northern Hokkaido steeped in native traditions. We see their festival ceremonies, and a rousing game of "Catch a Plate," which is sort of a close-up version of Frisbee with ceramics. For reasons unspecified, Tamako journeys south to Tokyo to live with friends of the tribe, with a warning to never disgrace herself. Stopping at a Japanese fishing village, Tamako notes how civilized their ceremonies are, compared to the "primitive, savage worship of the Bear God" her people indulge in. She also meets a handsome young man named Kosinami who seems to her a "new kind of god—a man god." Special attention is paid the village women, who spearfish nude, but Tamako hangs around to watch her man-god fishing. Her heart leaps when he gives her a fish, which to her is "like a beautiful pearl necklace." But Tamako must leave her new boyfriend to continue her journey, stopping next to check out Shinto and Buddhist shrines—again noting how much more civilized is their worship of mythical gods.

On arrival in Tokyo, narration is occasionally taken over by Thomas L. Rowe, who gives you the man-to-man lowdown on the city of "39 races, 30 styles of cooking, and 56 ways of making love—of 82 basic odors, and 80,000 stinks—of 12 kinds of dirt and 34 vices." It makes you wonder where Rowe got his data. Using a slightly winking but condescending tone, Rowe tells us all about sex in Japan, examining the Geisha trade in all its functions. After we're assured that Tokyo is the lowest pit of degradation and sin, we return to Tamako, who is being trained as a hostess, on her way to becoming an apprentice Geisha. Still mooning for Kosinami, Tamako refuses her duties with a favorite customer, and flunks out of Geisha school. Rowe takes over to give a guided tour of Tokyo night life, from marching bands to strippers. Will Tamako shame herself further by taking another job in the skin trade?

Too backward to be offensive anymore, *Violated Paradise* was surely edited down from a longer Japanese picture to showcase only its more exploitable elements for consumption by the American adults-only theatres, thereby assuring the intended WASP audience of their superiority, while giving them a peek at some "exotic" thrills. Alternating between naïve Tamako's struggle to avoid disgracing herself, and Rowe's advice for the traveling businessman, the English version puts over its titillating point about how shameful the Japanese people are—a great place for a holiday away from the wife on the company expense account, but too primitive a place for human beings. **AKA:** *Diving Girls of Japan; The Diving Girls' Islands; Scintillating Sin; Sea Nymphs.* 🐉🐉

1963 66m/C *JP*/IT Kazuko Mine, Hiromi Hara, Kuki Hanura. **D:** Marion Gering. **W:** Thomas Rowe. **C:** Roy Yaginuma. **M:** Marcello Abbado, Sergio Pagoni. **VHS, DVD**

Violence Jack

 In this animated series based on Go Nagai's manga, the world After Disaster (à la *Mad Max*) is broken up into camps of desperate survivors and roving bands of pillaging barbarians. A great city was swallowed up in the cataclysm, and the underground survivors of the buried city divided into the peaceful all-male denizens of Zone A, the vicious killers in Zone B, and the all-female Zone C. While trying to tunnel to the surface, men from Zone A discover the mysterious giant Jack buried alive, and try to get him to use his super-strength to defend them from Zone B. Jack agrees, until he finds out that the boys from Zone A aren't so innocent either. Escaping from the underworld, Violence Jack then fights against brutal biker armies, and eventually faces off against the powerful Slum King, who would become his archenemy.

In Go Nagai's earlier series *Devil Man,* he stretched the boundaries of taste by going over the top in his portrayal of violent action and gore, but this series (based on one of Nagai's longest-running manga, which later is revealed as a sequel to *Devil Man*) goes even further into the realm of bad taste. Perhaps it's because the characters are more human than before, instead of demons and monsters. It's fun to see Jack—a huge and surly brute with a big knife and fangs—tear up his nasty attackers, but scenes depicting the villains torturing innocent folks are repellent and gratuitous. Besides, the animation and design aren't that good either. Ironically, Manga Video has issued the series in America dubbed in English with most of the sex and gore edited, and they've even changed the order of episodes (not that it makes much difference). This is just as pointless as when local television stations try to show movies like *Scarface* without the profanity and bloodshed. What good is *Violence Jack* without the violence, Jack? The Right Stuf has since released the title uncut. 🐉

1988 *JP* **D:** Ichiro Itano, Takuya Wada, Osamu Kamijo. **W:** Noboru Aikawa, Takuya Wada, Mikio Matsushita, Go Nagai (manga). **VHS**

Violent Cop

"Beat" Takeshi Kitano, a popular Japanese television comedian, had played dramatic roles in a few movies, but nonetheless shocked everyone with his directorial debut, a tough urban thriller that certainly lives up to its title. Kitano stars as Azuma, a Dirty Harry–style police detective who doesn't allow restrictions to keep him from pursuing justice. Beneath his ever-passive exterior is a man very angry about the lawlessness in modern society, and he considers it expedient to serve justice in the most direct manner. Azuma takes rookie detective Kikuchi (Makoto Ashikawa) under his wing at the start of an investigation into a dope dealer's murder. The investigation leads to Iwaki (Shigeru Hiraizumi), a fellow detective, who is selling drugs culled from evidence. Iwaki is killed by the gang, hung from a bridge to make it look like suicide, and his superiors try to cover it up to avoid bad press. But Azuma learns a gangster named Nito (Ittoku Kishibe) is behind the gang, and arrests his assassin Kiyohiro (Hakuryu) for a questioning/beating session. Caught in the act, Azuma's case is ruined and he's forced to quit the police. He tries to stay cool, but when the gang kidnaps his mentally ill sister Akari (Maiko Kawakami), he goes on a rampage.

This synopsis may sound like just another direct-to-video action thriller, but with Kitano it's all about style. Instead of over-dramatizing every situation, Kitano's film is as deadpan as his face. The imagery is shot clean, without any fancy camera tricks, and Azuma appears like any other middle-aged man with sore feet. When violence comes, it's often completely unexpected, giving an air of tension to the entire movie. One fight is filmed in slow motion, but it's a rough brawl, not a martial arts ballet. Rock singer Hakuryu gives a performance equal to Kitano's in intensity as the insane hit man in love with his boss. **AKA:** *Sono Otoko, Kyobo ni Tsuki; Warning: This Man Is Wild.* 🐉🐉🐉🐉

1989 103m/C *JP* "Beat" Takeshi Kitano, Hakuryu, Maiko Kawakami, Shiro Sano, Sei Hiraizumi, Mikiko Otonashi, Ittoku Kishibe, Ken Yoshizawa, Susumu Terajima, Hiroki Ida, Kinji Nakamura, Makoto Ashikawa. **D:** Takeshi Kitano. **W:** Hisashi Nozawa. **C:** Yasushi Sasakibara. **M:** Daisuke Kume. **VHS, DVD**

Violent Cop

For a change of pace, in this serial-killer thriller (which is not to be confused with the Takeshi Kitano film of the same name, or the Kant Leung film released the following year), the psycho preys not on prostitutes, but on their customers. Officer Cuba Koo (Michael Wong) has just cracked a big case, and he and his new wife are expecting a baby. Inspector Yuen Wai Hau

"Beat" Takeshi Kitano is human nitroglycerin in his film debut, *Violent Cop.*

(Moses Chan) chases a suspect into a party thrown for the couple, and when a gunfight erupts, inebriated Koo accidentally shoots Hau. Since they're rivals, everyone thinks Koo injured Hau on purpose, even his wife Suzy (Astrid Chan), who admits the baby isn't his. While Hau hovers in a coma, Koo intrudes on one of his cases, determined to solve it for him, despite the objections of the cop assigned the case, Inspector Tsung. The "Cross Killer" strikes again in the Mongkok district, using the same M.O. as always: the victim is castrated, throat slit, and a cross is cut into the back of the throat, which is covered by a communion wafer. A new detective comes on the case when pimp Kim Tai-Pan (Anthony Wong) tries to prevent losing any more clients. Kim owes cash to Mr. Scar (William Ho), who is pressuring Kim to put his daughter to work on the streets. Actually, Kim's daughter Cee (Iris Chai) is already working on the street, hawking cellular phone plans. Meanwhile, Tse Chun Mao (Wayne Lai), a shy man who works in the police canteen, meets Cee and develops a crush. A videotape found at the latest murder scene implicates one man (Michael Chan) in the case, but indicates the Cross Killer is another who strikes afterward. Koo wants Kim to help him bait a trap for the killer with a young girl, but the psycho has already taken the obvious bait, abducting Cee after saving her from the cutthroat. The religious fanatic is holding her in a warehouse, while Koo and Kim desperately search for a clue.

The film is well directed by Steve Cheng *(Troublesome Night)*, but the psycho's identity is revealed way too early on for the proper amount of suspense to build, leaving the burden on the dramatic portion. Wong and Wong have developed some chemistry from having worked together before *(Beast Cops)*, and it would've been nice if we could've seen the two of them working together to solve the case, but they only get a few scenes together. The climax, in which the killer assaults police headquarters, brings some excitement, but the film wastes too many chances getting to it. The title is a mistake—not only does it get the film mixed up with others, but the cops in it aren't very violent. *AKA: Biu Lik Ying Ging; Bao Li Xing Jing.* 🦴🦴▽

1999 89m/C *HK* Anthony Wong, Michael Wong, Wayne Lai, Astrid Chan, Iris Chai, Moses Chan, William Ho, Lo Hung, Michael Chan. **D:** Steve Cheng. **W:** Cheng Kim-fung. **C:** Fung Yuen-man. **M:** Tommy Wai. **VHS, DVD**

Visible Secret

Anthony Wong's cameo in this film may be his most outrageous ever—losing his head under a trolley, and then attempting to continue on his way! Fifteen years later, June (Shu Qi) is at a disco, and trades in her old boyfriend for inept barber Peter Lo Wong-choi (Eason Chan). After she spends the night at his place, Peter awakes to find the odd girl gone, replaced by his roommate Simon (Sam Lee) and his father Lo Kit (James Wong), who claims to be possessed by a ghost. After returning his dad to the retirement home, Peter thinks he sees June in the hallway. He sees her for sure the next day, among a group gathered for a cookout on a haunted beach. She tells him that ever since she was a child, she's been able to see ghosts with her left eye, and tries to avoid it with patches and dark glasses.

As the two begin to fall in love, Peter begins to think he's seeing ghosts, too. He dreams his father visits just as Mr. Lo is dying, an apparent suicide. They even begin helping out ghosts together and exorcising possessed people. Needing to know more about the secretive June, he follows her one night and finds her taking part in some sort of Taoist necromancy meeting, but is beaten by some guardians before he can see more. He tries to break things off with her, but finds he's bound up in circumstances—both emotional and supernatural—more tightly than he imagined.

Ann Hui gives each scene a natural, improvised feel, making the shocks all the more potent when they come. After throwing the viewer off balance with an initial shock, she also allows plenty of time for characters to become familiar and tension to build. Though influenced by the U.S. hit *The Sixth Sense,* this is one of the best Hong Kong chillers in years, mixing horror with romance and mystery. There's also a healthy vein of humor running through the story, without intruding on the chills as in so many HK ghost movies. A running gag shows Chan's disaster of a career as a hairstylist, giving every customer a bowl cut. Shu Qi stretches beyond her usual cutie-pie mannerisms to create her most well-rounded character. The special effects are great—impressive without being intrusively flashy. Tommy Wai's score evokes a Hitchcockian feel, echoing Bernard Herrmann without stealing anything from him. *AKA: Yau Leng Yan Gaan; You Ling Ren Jian.* 🦴🦴🦴▽

2001 100m/C *HK* Eason Chan, Shu Qi, Sam Lee, James Wong, Kara Hui, Wayne Lai, Anthony Wong, Lau Wing, Cheung Tat-Ming, Jo Koo, Kelly Moo, Perry Chan, Tiffany Lee, Rashma Maheubani, Fifi Ho, Yau Man-shing, Willie Chan. **D:** Ann Hui. **W:** Abe Kwong. **C:** Arthur Wong. **M:** Tommy Wai. **VHS, DVD**

Volcano High School

With a scenario that would fit comfortably between *X-Men* and *Mortal Kombat* on your

video shelf, this Korean epic might also take a slot among *Yojimbo, Harry Potter,* and *The Blackboard Jungle*—it's that trippy. In the far future (or an alternate universe), following an event called the Great Teacher Battle, the problem of high-school violence is compounded by superpowers. Kim Kyung-soo (Jang Hyuk) is bounced from one school to another for fighting and general troublemaking, and is finally given a last chance at Volcano High. He immediately annoys the school beauty and Kendo captain Yoo Chae-yi (Shin Min-ah), AKA Icy Jade (everybody has a nickname here), then gets in a dust-up with the school's top fighter Song Hak-rim (Kwan Sang-woo), Elegant Crane in a Pine Forest, that destroys a hallway and actually wounds Song. This was just a test—the true hazing begins later with weightlifting team captain Jang Ryang (Kim Su-ro), Dark Ox, and his stooges. Determined to stop his slippery slide to failure, Kim reminds himself to exercise restraint in these matters to avoid bloodshed. Noting the conflict and admiring Kim's relative composure is Shimma (Kim Hyeong-jong), who demands Kim join his rugby team.

Rumors have been circulating for decades of a lost Secret Manuscript with the power to bring order to the high schools, and some say that it's hidden somewhere in Volcano High. They're right. Principle Jang Oh-ja has it, but the Zen-like man refuses to be rattled by the turmoil surrounding him, having sat out the Great Teacher Battle in seclusion. Nevertheless, he's felled by a trance-inducing spell, judged an attempted homicide by the school nurse. Vice-Principal Jang Hak-sa, the number-two suspect, casts spells to protect the Manuscript until Jang Oh-ja can be revived. Except the Manuscript is missing, hidden away somewhere. With number-one suspect Song in a holding cell, Ryang declares open warfare on the other teams, beating one captain in combat after another. An attempt to form an alliance to stand against Ryang and rescue Song collapses into chaos. Vice-Principal Jang calls in some heavy hitters to suppress the violence, hard-nosed disciplinarians called the School Five, who take law and order a step too far into fascism.

Both a dark comic-book farce and a superior action film, *Volcano High* proves you don't need 100 million Hollywood dollars to make a spectacular special-effects film anymore (the production company pulled it off for a mere 6 million). The superpowered battles here are as awesome and technically sound as any ever created, all given fittingly spare and beautifully photographed surroundings. It doesn't hurt that director Kim Tae-gyun knows his craft, and can control the ebb and flow of tension in his story perfectly, knowing when it's appropriate to use an imaginative technique like an inset split-screen and when such a flashy move is extraneous and distracting. The

hapless hero is much like Bruce Lee in *The Chinese Connection,* determined to keep his hands clean until the fight gets too dirty to stay out of. As much as it raises questions about, say, the Columbine massacre, the point here is to choose between a prize worth fighting for and an empty box. Kim only makes a breakthrough when he accepts the responsibility of his power and trusts himself to use it wisely—and has a blast doing it. *AKA: Whasango; Volcano High; Hwasan Highschool.* 🐉🐉🐉🐉

2001 121m/C *KO* Jang Hyuk, Shin Min-ah, Kong Hyo-jin, Kwan Sang-woo, Kim Su-ro, Kim Hyeong-jong, Huh Jun-ho, Byun Hee-bong. *D:* Kim Tae-gyun. *W:* Kim Tae-gyun, Seo Dong-heon, Jung Yoon-chul. *C:* Choi Yeong-taek. *M:* Park Yeong. **DVD**

Voyage into Space

In the mid-1960s, Toei Studios responded to the popularity of king-size TV heroes like Ultraman by adapting Mitsuteru Yokoyama's popular manga series *Giant Robo* for television. Shown on syndicated U.S. television under the title *Johnny Socko and His Giant Robot,* American International condensed several episodes into this kiddie matinee feature in 1970.

An alien spaceship from Planet Gargoyle, which looks kind of like an artist's palette, arrives in the Earth's atmosphere. The masked Emperor Guillotine broadcasts his intention to conquer the planet, just before it crashes into the sea. Months later, Jerry Mono (Akio Ito), a secret agent of Unicorn, is aboard a ship sailing in the same area. Suddenly, a big, ugly, tentacled monster named Draculon attacks the ship and sinks it. Jerry grabs his young shipmate Johnny Socko (Mitsunobu Koneko) and jumps overboard just in time. They wash ashore on an island where Gargoyle has a secret base. The soldiers have forced Dr. Lucius Guardian to build a gigantic, vaguely Egyptian-looking robot for them, but the scientist double-crosses the aliens by planting an atomic bomb to blow up the base. Jerry, Johnny, and the robot escape—the radiation activates the machine's brain and the robot instantly bonds with the first voice it hears: that of little Johnny Socko. He orders his big pal to fly them home to Tokyo via its rockets (sitting on the robot's palms like they're in lounge chairs), but the Gargoyle Gang heads them off, sending Draculon to attack the city. Guillotine develops a fixation with the robot, and is unable to continue with any other plans until they recapture it. Commander Spider sends the monster Nucleon to draw Robo out, hoping to grab it or capture Johnny. Failing in that, he next attacks with three more monsters under the command of the silver-skinned Botonus, none of which are a match for the flying robot. By the last episode, the Gar-

Johnny Socko and agents of Unicorn strike a pose in the shadow of Giant Robo in *Voyage into Space.*
THE KOBAL COLLECTION / TOEI CO. LTD.

goyles finally get smart, and just send a hit man to shoot Johnny in the head!

Unlike similar series like *Spectreman,* Yokoyama's cartoon style is retained, making any ludicrous elements more acceptable and part of the fun. It doesn't seem out of place that the alien gang should wear their uniforms even when in Tokyo, or that a boy of 10 can operate a super-robot without training, or that he's made a secret agent without his parents' knowledge, or even that the robot and other monsters look like clunky toys. It also helps that by condensing five episodes into 97 minutes, the feature format leaves out any slack, keeping the action moving at all times. The characters all bear a naïve charm like those in old serials, especially Ito as slightly daft secret agent Mano. It certainly was another time though—you don't see any kids' TV shows where folks are commonly blasted with machine guns, and even Johnny has his own gun! Thoughtlessly, AIP chose to end the film with a sequence from the last of the series' 26 episodes, closing the door on any possible future compilations. If you like this, you should check out the excellent seven-part anime series produced in 1991. *AKA:*

Jaianto Robo; Giant Robo; Johnny Socko and His Giant Robot. 🐉🐉🐉

1967 97m/C *JP* Mitsunobu Koneko, Akio Ito, Mitsuo Andou. **D:** Minoru Yamada. **W:** Mitsuteru Yokoyama. **M:** Takeo Yamashita. **VHS**

The Walls of Hell

In between their debut with *Terror Is a Man* and becoming the premiere horror filmmakers of the Philippines, Eddie Romero and Gerardo De Leon *(Mad Doctor of Blood Island, Brides of Blood)* made several good World War II pictures that depicted the action on the Philippine front. This one, shot in many of the actual locations, tells the story of one of most nightmarish battles of the war. As the United States Navy arrive in Manila in early 1945 to aid in the liberation of the islands, 16,000 Japanese troops disobey orders and dig in at the ancient fortress city Intramuros for a long, bloody siege, convinced the Americans will execute them if they're captured. Caught in the middle are 20,000 civilian residents of the city. Due to an Open City policy in effect, the Allies are unable to use bombers

to attack. After three weeks of artillery blasting away at the walls, news correspondent Murray (Paul Edwards Jr.) wants a closer look at the action, and gets an escort to the front, commanded by a hardened veteran officer named Sorenson (Jock Mahoney, fresh from playing Tarzan). Tracing some snipers back to their hidden tunnel, the soldiers capture Filipino Sergeant Maglaya (Fernando Poe Jr.), who claims to be there to request aid in rescuing a thousand captives from inside the city. For extra added drama, it's learned that Sorenson's wife Tina (Cecilia Lopez), long thought dead, is among the captives. Amid a massive barrage, a platoon of soldiers attempts to lead as many prisoners as possible out through the tunnels.

The film is certainly well named—there's hardly a frame that isn't filled with crumbling stone buildings, flaming timbers, smoke, dirt, and ashes. Though not very bloody, it's quite frank about the conditions of war. The thunder of artillery runs relentlessly throughout the entire film. While the Filipinos and Americans fight side-by-side, it doesn't ignore the conflicts between them. Mahoney is there to provide an Anglo name for the U.S. release; it's the Filipino actors who provide most of the heroics. **AKA:** *Intramuros.* 🐾🐾🐾

1964 88m/BW *PH* Jock Mahoney, Fernando Poe Jr., Mike Parsons, Oscar Roncal, Paul Edwards Jr., Cecilia Lopez, Ely Ramos, Fred Galang, Arsenio Alonzo, Vance Scarstead, Claude Wilson, Pedro Navarro, Angel Buenaventura, Ben Sanchez. *D:* Gerardo De Leon, Eddie Romero. *W:* Cesar Amigo, Ferde Groff Jr., Eddie Romero. *C:* Felipe Sacdalan. *M:* Tito Arevalo. **DVD**

A War Named Desire

Films that are structured as extended flashbacks—think *American Beauty* and *Sunset Boulevard*—come with built-in handicaps. Instead of allowing the viewer to decide how to respond to events as they develop, the ending is telegraphed and the audience is expected to follow meekly along the clearly marked path preordained by the writer(s) and director. In the hands of a master storyteller, that's not a problem.

The opening scene of *A War Named Desire* tells us that two men will end up driving away bloody and battered, perhaps near death, in a pickup truck with a smashed windshield. As the flashback begins, we learn that Jones (Daniel Chan) has traveled to Thailand in search of his long-lost and dishonored brother Charles (Francis Ng). Jones's girlfriend Jess (Pace Wu) invites herself to come along. Soon enough, Jones discovers that Charles is running a casino and doesn't want to reunite with him for love and

brotherhood. Charles wants cold hard cash, not a flesh-and-blood relative. Quickly, however, Jones is snared in a local gang power struggle and is in over his head. Will his brother come to his rescue? And where do the loyalties of Snow (Gigi Leung), a gun-toting criminal associate of Charles, really lie?

Much of the film moves along rudimentary plotlines. It's the visual inventiveness of director Alan Mak, the precise but not overly busy editing by Cheung Ka-fai, and the excellent musical score by veteran composer Mark Lui that are magnetic and pull the viewer along until the final third. This last section of the film improbably becomes quite moving due largely to the performances of Ng and Leung. It's not so much their reading of the pedestrian dialogue as it is the emotions conveyed in their faces and body language. The excellent staging of an extended showdown between the gang factions brings the film to a rousing conclusion. —*PM* **AKA:** *Oi Yue Shing; Ai Yu Cheng.* 🐾🐾✟

2000 89m/C *HK* Francis Ng, Daniel Chan, Gigi Leung, Dave Wong, Sam Lee, Pace Wu, Grace Lam, David Lee. *D:* Alan Mak. *W:* Alan Mak, Joe Ma, Clement Cheng. *C:* Chan Chi-Ying. *M:* Mark Lui. **DVD**

War of the Gargantuas

In Japan, this is a sequel to *Frankenstein vs. Baragon* (AKA *Frankenstein Conquers the World*), but either because it was released by a different distributor, or because of fears that audiences would expect the familiar Frankenstein trappings in a film with that name (castle, villagers, hunchback), the film was dubbed, titled, and edited to hide its sequel status. *War* even starts with a scene similar to the one edited from the end of *F vs. B*—a battle between a giant and a huge octopus. But the green giant is not so jolly, and after killing his foe, he gobbles up the sailors who witnessed the fight. News of the incident reminds Dr. Paul Stewart (Russ Tamblyn), Dr. Akemi Togawa (Kumi Mizuno), and Dr. Yuzo Mamiya (Kenji Sahara)—all stand-in characters for those played by Nick Adams, Mizuno, and Tadao Takashima in the previous film—of the strange little wild boy they found near Hiroshima that grew and grew. The Gargantua (Frankenstein) they knew was violent only when provoked, and certainly not a man-eater. This monster, covered in green hair and scales, has a taste for humans, and comes ashore to hunt at night. The military sets up a mobile shore patrol around Tokyo Bay, and when the monster next appears, they attack him with Type 66 Maser Cannons (just to let you know you're in the Godzilla universe—these weapons were

first seen in *Mothra*). Gargantua is almost killed, but is saved by the sudden appearance of a Brown Gargantua, who helps the Green Gargantua escape. When the monster died at the end of the first film, apparently two large enough pieces survived to regenerate the twin behemoths, their appearances otherwise affected by their environments. While the scientists convince the military not to attack in a conventional way, lest an army of monsters regenerate from the remains, they still hold out hope that their brown friend can be saved. Recovering in the mountains, the brown giant returns to their camp and spots the bones of his green brother's victims. He considers killing the evil Green Gargantua in his sleep, but is caught before he can go through with it, and a big battle begins which continues on through Tokyo.

Why "Gargantua"? In Rabelais's novel of the same name, Gargantua was a gigantic king who has a great capacity for food and drink. The name was commonly used for gorillas in circuses and sideshows, and certainly fits the monsters, though in Japan the two Frankensteins are named Sanda (brown) and Gaila (green). The sequel is a vast improvement in every department, from script through special effects. Gaila's ugly face and grisly dietary habits make him more frightening than any storybook ogre, and even heroic Sanda is kind of scary. Though lacking in social commentary, this is one of director Ishiro Honda's best films, excellently paced and imaginatively staged. Some shots, such as when a fisherman looks down into the ocean and sees Gaila staring hungrily up at him, are particularly memorable. Though not as interesting to look at as, say, King Ghidorah, the beastly pair are convincingly savage. Working with more humanoid monsters both challenged and inspired Toho's technical staff, using whatever tricks they could think of to make them believably huge and inhuman. Tamblyn's hipster scientist brings an earthy atmosphere to his scenes, perhaps shaking things up a bit for Toho's regulars, who had settled into their familiar types. The awful song sung by Kipp Hamilton has become a favorite punk novelty number. *AKA: Furankenshutain no Kaiju: Sanda tai Gaira; Sand vs. Gailah; Duel of the Gargantuas; Adventure of Gargantuas; Frankenstein Zweikampf der Giganten.* 🐉🐉🐉🐉

1966 (G) 92m/C *JP* Russ Tamblyn, Kenji Sahara, Kumi Mizuno, Hisaya Ito, Nobuo Nakamura, Jun Tazaki, Yoshifumi Tajima, Ren Yamamoto, Kipp Hamilton, Kozo Nomura, Nadao Kirino, Ikio Sawamura, Haruo Nakajima, Hiroshi Sekita. *D:* Ishiro Honda. *W:* Takeshi Kimura, Ishiro Honda. *C:* Hajime Koizumi. *M:* Akira Ifukube. **VHS**

War of the Shaolin Temple

The Sung Dynasty is ending. The Sung Royal Seal is captured by invading Jing armies commanded by General Tso Ming (Mark Lung). The general visits Shaolin Temple to be sure the monks remain neutral in the war, and don't rally public support in his uneasily held territory. However, the monks secretly support the Chinese defenders, and many want to actively join the fight. General Yueh sends a masked squad commanded by Master Wang Yung-leung (Wong Fei-lung) to recover the Seal. Tso slaughters most of them, but Wang manages to escape with the Seal. Badly wounded, Wang is taken in and hidden by the Pai family. When Jing troops arrive, the Pai brothers (Ricky Cheng and Chiang Sheng) die fighting them, while their sister (Shum Hoi-yung) flees with Wang to Shaolin Temple. In order to remain with Shaolin and learn their kung fu, Wang decides to officially become a monk.

After training to become a Shaolin kung fu master, Wang tries to further his studies by becoming a student of the Crazy Monk (Chai Kai), who lives like a hermit in Lo Han Cave. But the hermit learns Wang hasn't come to learn cocktail mixing from him, and the Crazy Monk just beats him up. When a couple of Wang's old army buddies drop by to tell him that Miss Pai has been captured, he goes with them to rescue her. However, Wang is caught during the mission, and his 12 pole-fighting Shaolin brothers come out of the temple for a rescue mission of their own. On a second try, Wang convinces the Crazy Monk to teach him his kung fu, then joins his 12 brothers to form the unbeatable 13 Shaolin Pole Formation.

If the production values had been a little higher, this would have been a much more impressive picture. The martial arts performance and choreography are quite good, the characters and situations are sufficiently involving, and the story moves along rapidly. But the cinematography and direction are flat, hazy, and uninteresting, likely a result of the rock-bottom budget. Wirework is rare during the action scenes, but what there is gets hidden via the sloppy technique of smearing the top of the lens with petroleum jelly. The veterans from Chang Cheh's Shaw Brothers pictures are wasted in small roles. Plus, the fun Crazy Monk character is confined to his cave, and isn't brought in to play a part in the finale. *AKA: Sap Saam Din Who Gwing; Shi San Dian Han Shang; Monks Go Crazy; 13 Poles from Shaolin.* 🐉🐉🐉

Giant hairy offshoots of the Frankenstein Monster overrun Japan in *War of the Gargantuas.* THE KOBAL COLLECTION / TOHO

1980 89m/C *TW* Wong Fei-lung, Lau Ching-fat, Chai Kai, Ricky Cheng, Chiang Sheng, Chang Chi-ping, Mark Lung, Cheung Yee-kwai, Wong Chi Sang, Wong Lung, Lee Lung-yam, Shum Hoi-yung, Alan Chui. **D:** David Lin. **VHS, DVD**

Warm Water under a Red Bridge

Quiet and light fable that is deeper than it initially appears. Looking for work in Tokyo after he is laid off, Yosuke (Koji Yakusho) learns that an old friend, Taro (Kazuo Kitamura), has died. Taro was a poor yet philosophical man. He once told Yosuke that he had stolen a valuable statue and hidden it in a house by a red bridge in a rural village. Knowing of Yosuke's troubles—he lives apart from his wife, who is not very kind in their telephone conversations—Taro had encouraged the younger man to retrieve the statue and sell it. With Taro's death, and his own financial situation worsening, Yosuke finally decides to make the trip. He discovers a quaint fishing village with stereotypically odd characters living there. He also observes a strange sight: a nice-looking, middle-aged woman shoplifting cheese in a supermarket—and leaving behind a puddle of water on the floor. Fascinated, he follows her, and watches her return to a house by a red bridge. Soon enough, he learns the woman's highly personal secret, and also learns much more about himself.

Director Imamura keeps his camera at a distance much of the time. While that tends to minimize the emotional intensity, it also allows the viewer to see the characters in the context of their environment. And that's crucial in a tale such as this—based on a novel by Yo Henmi—which contains several elements that appear to be completely whimsical. By virtue of the serious and contextual presentation, however, such elements can be seen as rarely occurring natural events, rather than pure flights of fancy. The cumulative effect is much greater than might be anticipated, given the subject matter and story. Though it would have helped to have a deeper understanding of some of the characters, a sufficient number of details are provided to lend weight and interest. A certain amount of humor provides comic relief at key points. It helps if the viewer gives the film the benefit of the doubt and embraces a couple of dubious aspects. Koji Yakusho has tremendous range as the everyman character Yosuke, with hidden reserves of emotion. Misa Shimizu is touching as a woman frustrated by men, relationships, and her own body. The rest of the cast gives fine, unshowy performances. —PM **AKA:** *Akai Hashi no Shita no Nurui Mizu.* 🐉🐉🐉

2001 120m/C *JP* Koji Yakusho, Misa Shimizu, Mitsuko Baisho, Mansaku Fuwa, Isao Natsuyagi, Yukiya Kitamura, Toshie Negishi, Katsuo Nakamura, Kazuo Kitamura. **D:** Shohei Imamura. **W:** Shohei Imamura, Daisuke Tengan, Motofumi Tomikawa. **C:** Shigeru Komatsubara. **M:** Shinichiro Ikebe. **VHS, DVD**

Warning from Space

A spaceship full of star-shaped aliens from planet Paira, each with a big eye in the middle, reach Earth orbit on a secret mission. They decide to contact the scientists of Japan first, starting with Dr. Komura (Bontaro Miyake). Komura and his assistant Toru (Keizo Kawasaki) trace a source of radio interference to the orbiting spaceship, which they think is some sort of satellite. The scientists launch a rocket to take pictures of the object, while the aliens begin prowling around the neighborhood frightening party guests and housewives. To learn more about the Earthlings with less risk of discovery, Pairan Ginko comes up with a plan to disguise herself via a transformation process, basing her image on a picture of Hikari Aozora (Toyomi Karita), a nightclub entertainer she saw while scouting. Feigning amnesia, Ginko allows herself to be "rescued" from a lake by the scientists, who take her in while she recovers. Ginko's choice of disguises leaves something to be desired, comparable to attempting to remain anonymous by impersonating Madonna. When she's not running from her fans, Ginko is puzzling her hosts by jumping 12 feet in the air and performing other non-human stunts. Realizing the jig is up, Ginko reveals her identity, as well as the mission of the Pairans.

There's no denying that *Warning from Space* looks as primitive to us now as the fantasies of Jules Verne did at the time. The alien costumes look cool, but could never have been convincing as real aliens. Even to viewers of the 1950s, they looked like just what they are—cloth and wire frame costumes. Once the scientists meet the alien, they believe everything she says and immediately begin making plans to move the Earth to a new orbit! A combination of *The Day the Earth Stood Still* and *When Worlds Collide,* the film suffers from its slow, polite pace, but nevertheless possesses some charm. **AKA:** *Uchujin Tokyo ni Arawaru; Cosmic Man Appears in Tokyo; The Mysterious Satellite; Unknown Satellite over Tokyo.* 🐉🐉🐉

This publicity shot makes the friendly aliens in *Warning from Space* look about 20 times bigger! THE KOBAL COLLECTION / DAIEI FILMS

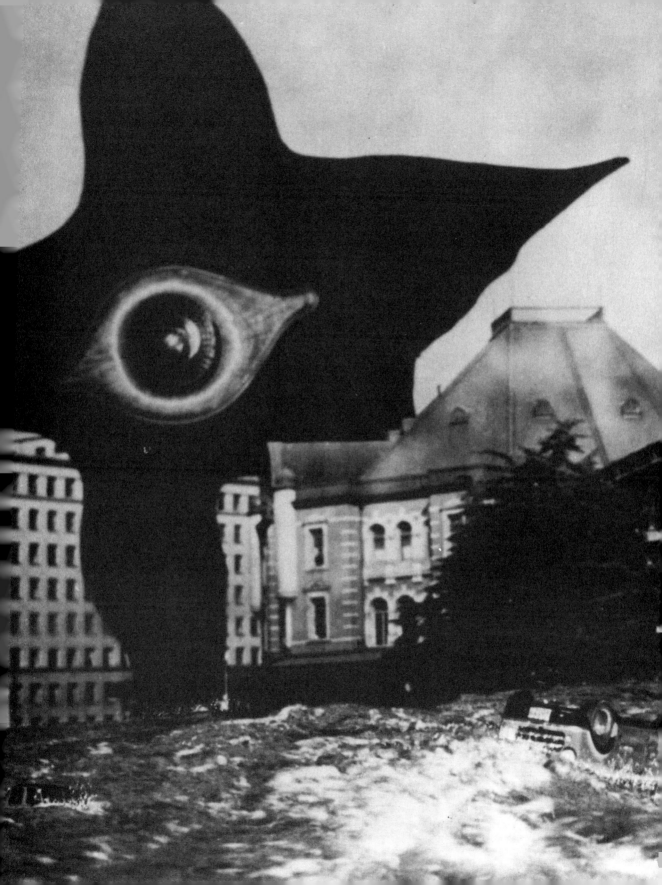

1956 88m/C *JP* Bontaro Miyake, Keizo Kawasaki, Toyomi Karita, Isao Yamagata, Shozo Nanbu, Mieko Nagai, Kiyoko Hirai. **D:** Koji Shima. **W:** Hideo Oguni. **C:** Kimio Watanabe. **M:** Seitaro Omori. **VHS, DVD**

Warrior from Shaolin

During the Japanese invasion of China, monk Tien Fu (Gordon Lau) tries to help a man who comes to the monastery suffering several gunshot wounds. Before he dies, the man passes on a map of Japanese troop movements, asking the monk to deliver it to his contact in Dragon Town. The monks hire shifty boatmen Fat Dragon (Eric Tsang, with long hair) and Hsiao Ma (Jimmy Liu) to help them make it past the Japanese, but when troops fire on the boat, only the two guides and Tien Fu make it to shore alive. The monk wants to hire his greedy companions to take him to Dragon Town, and they agree, suspecting that the box of Buddhist relics he carries is really filled with treasure. To get it, Fat Dragon dresses as a ghost to scare the monk, not knowing some Taoists with a convoy of hopping corpses is camping nearby. While the travelers are dealing with the hopping dead, Captain Wang (Lau Kar-Wing) and his lady Pai Yin-Yin (Lily Li) are having a meeting in Dragon Town with his competitor Captain Yuen On (Fung Hark-On) over territorial rights. The meeting ends quickly and violently, and guest Kong Tin (Kong Do) awards control to the victorious Wang on behalf of his Japanese masters. His first task is to catch the monk carrying the map. With Wang rounding up all monks, Tien Fu must get into town in disguise, and keep a sharp eye on his sticky-fingered companions while using the other eye to find his unknown contact with a bump on his back.

Some of the comedy is very amusing (such as Eric Tsang's Bruce Lee imitation), but for the most part it's annoyingly tedious, and there's a lot in the plot that doesn't make a great deal of sense. However, prime Lau Brothers choreography is much in evidence, which means plenty of thrills whenever anybody starts moving. Comedy disappears almost entirely once the great final fight sequence begins. Interestingly, Lau Kar-Wing's villain doesn't make a move that isn't called by his partner Lily Li—later we see that they derive their greatest fighting skill from working close together. They're much more intriguing characters than the usual kung fu villains. *AKA: Poh Gaai Daai Bye; Po Jie Da Shi; Shaolin Warrior; Carry On Wise Guy.* 🎵🎵🎵

1981 89m/C *HK* Gordon Lau, Eric Tsang, Lau Kar-Wing, Jimmy Liu, Lily Li, Kong Do, Fung Hark-On, Chan Lung, Lin Ke-ming, Chan Dik-hak, Meg Lam, Fung Ging Man. **D:** Lau Kar-Wing. **C:** Wong Yue-tai. **VHS, DVD**

Ways of Kung Fu

Disciple Tau Kung (Chi Kuan Chun) tries to stop a quartet of thieves from stealing food from the temple, but has to take the rap for the crime when the monks don't believe him. While suffering through his punishment chores, a scar-faced monk named Wu Tak (Ma Cheung) comes to visit the monastery. The fierce monk soon has everyone hopping at his beck and call, even making the thieves his servants, and he dishes out extra abuse to Tau Kung. To restore some peace to the monastery, kindly senior Abbot Hu Lang sends Tau to stay with his old friend Shang King (Leung Kar-yan) at Waterhead Village until Wu Tak leaves. Tau finds his new home most peculiar, as Shang King, his wife, and daughter Shao-li are all kung fu masters. Though Tau doesn't want to learn kung fu, the chores the Shang's give him soon have him in training without knowing it. Tau catches on when he sees how a street vendor got strong enough to defend himself by making noodles for 20 years, and decides that learning kung fu could help him defend himself from bullies like Wu Tak.

After two years, Tau becomes a good fighter, and Shang sends him back to the monastery to visit the ailing Hu Lang. Tau discovers that Wu Tak is really a bandit (the large bong he smokes might have been a giveaway) who is using the monastery as a hideout while making nightly excursions to rob and kill, and uses his new skills to roust the rascal. When Wu Tak and his gang kill Mr. and Mrs. Shang and take over the temple, Tau teams up with Shao-li, a government secret agent and a drunken boxing student, to seek justice.

Chi Kuan Chun was one of the better Jackie Chan imitators of the day, and this is a standard comedy-edged training and fighting picture in the spirit of *Snake in the Eagle's Shadow,* with Leung Kar-yan in the old sifu role. The tribute is especially apparent whenever the drunken boxer and his master show up, seeming to have wandered in from the set of *Drunken Master.* The training exercises are novel and well performed, especially one in which Chi has to steal Leung's umbrella in a downpour. There isn't much actual fighting until the second half, and the crisp choreography does a lot to make up for the flat beginning. However, the plot has a sloppy air to it, with characters popping up out of nowhere to get involved in the story. Director Lee Chiu had a minor hit with this picture, which led him to cast Leung Kar-yan in his follow-up feature *Cantonen Iron Kung Fu.* Music cues are swiped from *True Grit.* Crash Cinema's usually careful widescreen framing falters on this release, regularly chopping off the tops of actors' heads. *AKA: The Ways of Kung-Fu.* 🎵🎵🎵

1980 91m/C *HK* Chi Kuan Chun, Leung Kar-yan, Meng Fei, Cheung Wa, Yu Tien-lung, Ma Cheung, Lee

Chiu, Wu Ma, Ko Saio Pao. *D:* Lee Chiu. *W:* Lin Lin. *C:* Lo Wan-shing. *M:* Chou Fu-liang. **VHS, DVD**

Weather Woman

This 1995 Japanese feature was a big hit, and made a star out of lead Kei Mizutani. She plays Keiko Nakadai, a forceful young woman determined to be a success, dominating all in her path. Arranging the opportunity to take over as a substitute TV weather woman one night, she causes a sensation by flashing her panties during her report. Cashing in on the sudden attention, Keiko is made permanent weather woman, putting a little extra zip into each report to the delight of her growing fanbase. One viewer not pleased is the network chairman's daughter, Kaori Shimamori (Yasuyo Shiroshima), who returns from her studies in France to confront the situation. Before long, Kaori has engineered Keiko's downfall, and plans commence for her to take over in a deluxe weather woman program. However, much like kung fu heroes of the '70s, Keiko goes into the mountains to improve her mystic weather powers, and returns on opening night to challenge Kaori to a superpowered weather duel.

Weather Woman is cutting satire reminiscent of *Network* and *Dressed to Kill,* filtered through a comic manga sensibility recalling such series as *Ranma 1/2.* It also bears a decided feminist attitude. All males are there only to be conquered and do the bidding of the strong female characters. Even replaced weather girl Michiko (Saori Taira) becomes a "bottom" to Keiko, given the job of slave to the new weather woman after proving unable to cope with her assignment as host of the *Hello Mr. Pervert* program. Mizutani is sexy, smart, and often cruel, but also succeeds in maintaining viewer sympathy. She's not your usual Japanese sex kitten—more like a sophisticated version of Tura Satana in *Faster Pussycat! Kill! Kill!* Originally released without fanfare on home video, *Weather Woman* quickly gained a cult audience and started showing up at foreign film festivals, prompting an eventual hit theatrical release and TV series. Director Tomoaki Hosoyama would return with a new weather woman in...*Weather Woman Returns. AKA: Otenki-oneesan; Weather Girl; Weather Report Girl; A Weatherwoman.* 🐉🐉🐉♡

1995 84m/C *JP* Kei Mizutani, Yasuyo Shiroshima, Saori Taira, Eisei Amamoto, Kunihiko Iida, Takashi Sumida, Ryuji Yamamoto. *D:* Tomoaki Hosoyama. *W:* Tomoaki Hosoyama. *C:* Yoichi Shiga. **VHS, DVD**

We're Going to Eat You!

While Tsui Hark's first film, *The Butterfly Murders,* showed the influence of American and Ital-

ian ecological horror films, his second took films like *Texas Chainsaw Massacre* and *Cannibal Holocaust* and ran them through the Hong Kong kung fu comedy filter. Secret Agent 999 (Norman Tsui) is sent to an island off the coast, chasing a crook named Rolex (Melvin Wong). But he finds Rolex's home village to be more than he bargained for: during a famine, the entire community turned to cannibalism, and found they enjoyed the taste. Since then, they keep trying to come up with schemes to get travelers to come to the island. Rolex wants to leave the island, but is under orders from the Chief (Eddie Ko) to stay, lest they risk outsiders discovering their cuisine. When his escape attempt fails, Agent 999 has to try to find his own way out.

Though gory, *We're Going to Eat You!* (whose title seems based on the ad campaign for Lucio Fulci's *Zombie*) spends most of its running time on chases, fights, and slapstick. Aside from that, there's not really much of a plot to sink your teeth into. Tsui included a lot of political satire into his script, precious little of which survives the translation. However, it makes up for its lack of literacy with feverish energy and biting humor. Chunks of the score are borrowed from Dario Argento's *Suspiria. AKA: Dei Yuk Mo Moon; Di Yu Wu Men; Hell Has No Gates; Kung Fu Cannibals; No Door to Hell.* 🐉🐉♡

1980 90m/C *HK* Norman Tsui, Eddie Ko, Melvin Wong, David Wu, Lau Wing, Fang Fang, To Siu Ming, Hon Gwok-choi, Margaret Lee, San Kwai, Tai Bo, Lee Chun Wa, Tsang Choh-lam, Corey Yuen. *D:* Tsui Hark. *W:* Tsui Hark, Roy Szeto. *C:* Lau Hung-chuen. **VHS**

The Wesley's Mysterious File

Andy Lau takes his turn playing the lead as paranormal adventurer/author Wesley (or Wisely) Wei in this adaptation of a Ngai Hong story, though this particular project was doubtless inspired by the American hit *Men in Black.* Here, Wesley works for the United Nations in San Francisco at the top-secret Aliens Analyzing Agency. His acquaintance, antiquities dealer Mr. Chu (Patrick Lung), invites Wesley to buy a curious object that he's acquired—a blue skeletal hand. Wesley is intrigued, but more intrigued to meet Fong (Rosamund Kwan), a mysterious woman who also wants to obtain it. He outbids her, and she leaves quickly, suspecting trouble. Sure enough, police and army troops arrive as soon as she leaves, brought by Pak (Roy Cheung), an agent of the rival FBI Double X Department, along with his partner Sue (Shu Qi). They're there to capture a rampaging Class A alien, which almost kills Wesley, but Fong reappears to save him with her mysterious superpowers. He recalls meeting her

before—outside his school 30 years previous. Fong and her brother Tan (Samuel Pang) are Blue aliens who came to Earth centuries ago after they wiped out a planet of hostile shape-shifters known as the Warlock Toxin Gang, and are looking for the fabled Blue Blood Bible. Tan failed to survive and his hand is all that remains. But now a pair of the surviving shape-shifters known as Kill (Mark Cheng) and Rape (Almen Wong) have arrived seeking revenge. Complicating matters is a con man named Dr. Kwok (Wong Jing) who sold Double X a fake alien database and is now masquerading as Wesley, trying to con Fong. Double X Chief Wilson (Thomas Hudak) uses Wesley to capture Fong, hoping to learn the secret of her mental powers to use as his own weapon, which will give him the power to conquer the world. But not if the Warlocks get to her first.

Like many recent Hong Kong films, an attempt is made here to open up to international audiences by including multilingual cast members from several countries. As awkward as the non-actor non-Asians in the cast are in their performances, they're not as bad as the Chinese leads trying to act in English. Overlook that and we have a fairly amusing update on the Wisely/Wesley character (seen previously in such films as *Bury Me High* and *The Cat*), courtesy of director Andrew Lau's usual slick look and crack f/x crew. The main weakness is in the story, which gets mired in psychic mumbo-jumbo midway and never quite recovers. Wong Jing also fails in his attempt to inject some much-needed comedy relief. **AKA:** *Wai Shut Lee Ji Laam Huet Yan; Wei Si Li Zhi Lan Xie Ren; The Wesley's Mysterious Story.* 🎐🎐🎐

2001 87m/C *HK* Andy Lau, Rosamund Kwan, Shu Qi, Roy Cheung, Mark Cheng, Almen Wong, Wong Jing, Patrick Lung, Samuel Pang, Thomas Hudak, Fong Yo-Yo. **D:** Andrew Lau. **W:** Wong Jing, Thirteen Chan, Ngai Hong (story). **C:** Andrew Lau. **M:** Comfort Chan. **VHS, DVD**

What Time Is It There?

All color has drained away from the lives of the main characters. Two of them live together in Taipei, Taiwan, but it is the actions of a third that sets the plot in motion. She is an unnamed woman (Chen Shiang-chyi) who wants to buy a street peddler's dual-zone watch for a trip to Paris. The peddler (Lee Kang-sheng) initially resists. Not only is it his own personal watch, but since his father has only recently died, it would bring bad fortune to the woman were she to buy it while the peddler is still in mourning. She persists, taking his card and phoning him several times, and he relents the next day. To thank him, she buys him a small cake and departs.

His life previous to his encounter with the woman has been ordinary in the extreme. He sells watches by day, and at night returns home to the apartment he shares with his mother (Lu Yi-ching). Beset by quiet grief, she yearns for the return of her husband in reincarnated or spirit form, searching carefully for any little sign of his return. So when her son begins setting every available clock to Paris time, she takes it as a hopeful sign from her husband, and then becomes obsessive about doing everything possible to hasten his presence. Her son's decision to change a large variety of timepieces makes sense, in view of the mundane existence that we've observed. The small gesture of the Paris-bound woman takes on great significance in the watch-seller's life, and it leads to unexpected comedy and strange encounters. The woman herself, seen on a tourist visit that takes in none of the usual sights, is isolated by her status as a solitary traveler and her lack of fluency in French. She is distracted by strange sounds coming from the roof of her lodging place. She continually tries to make a phone call. Is she trying to call the watch-seller? Eventually the three ordinary people seek a similar release of emotion. No one is satisfied, and no questions are answered.

The film requires a great deal of patience. It allows more breathing space than is needed, especially once its main points are made, due to its extremely measured pace. The close encounters with three ordinary people are quite uncomfortable at times, yet proves ultimately rewarding. Allusions to the French classic *The 400 Blows* are made repeatedly, and are driven home with a cameo appearance by Jean-Pierre Leaud, the star of that film. For the home-video viewer, be advised that Tsai Ming-liang's drab palette and static framing commands attention to a far greater degree on a cinema screen than on a television monitor. Tim Yip designed the production, quite a contrast to the boldly colorful and classical look he created for *Crouching Tiger, Hidden Dragon.* —PM **AKA:** *Ni neibian jidian; 7 to 400 Blows; Et là-bas, quelle heure est-il?; Qi dao si bai ji; What Time Is It over There?.* 🎐🎐🎐

2001 116m/C *TW/FR* Lee Kang-sheng, Chen Shiang-chyi, Lu Yi-ching, Miu Tin, Cecilia Yip, Jean-Pierre Leaud. **D:** Tsai Ming-liang. **W:** Tsai Ming-liang, Yang Pi-ying. **C:** Benoit Delhomme. **VHS, DVD**

asians in usa

What's Up, Tiger Lily?

Woody Allen wanted to get into making his own movies, but couldn't get a studio to finance one of his scripts without a proven track record. He

hit on the idea of dubbing a foreign film from his own script. American International Pictures bought the rights to the 1964 Japanese spy picture *Key of Keys* (the second of three "International Secret Police" features), and set Allen loose on it, with a budget so low the picture couldn't possibly lose money. Wisecracking private eye Phil Moskcowitz (Tatsuya Mihashi from *High and Low*) gets involved in the case of an egg salad recipe ("a salad so delicious you could plotz!") stolen by mobster Sheppard Wong (Tadao Nakamaru), who operates from a casino hidden onboard the cargo ship *Ton Wai*. The recipe is key in the plans of Rashburg, a new country trying to get on the globe, and the king hires Moskowitz to get it back for them. Rival crook Wing Fat (Susumu Kurobe) is also after the recipe, planning to steal it and sell it to the highest bidder. He kidnaps Phil and his assistant Terri Yaki (Mie Hama from *King Kong vs. Godzilla*), forcing Terri's sister Suki Yaki (Akiko Wakabayashi from *Ghidorah the Three-Headed Monster*) to pull off a heist. But Wong catches Suki, and Phil and the others go to her rescue disguised as health department inspectors fumigating the ship. They manage to get the recipe and decode it, but get stuck in Wing Fat's insidious death trap.

Some of the gags have dated a bit, but there are still plenty of laughs here, though a "straight" dub wouldn't be too much sillier than your average 1960s spy thriller. The action is interrupted for badly mismatched footage of The Lovin' Spoonful performing one of their hits. Dubbing actors include Louise Lasser and Frank Buxton, the voice of cartoon character Batfink. *AKA: Kagi no Kag; Key of Keys.* 🐉🐉🐉🐉

1966 (PG) 80m/C *JP* **V:** Louise Lasser, Frank Buxton. Tatsuya Mihashi, Mie Hama, Akiko Wakabayashi, Tadao Nakamaru, Eisei Amamoto, Kumi Mizuno, Susumu Kurobe, Sachio Sakai, Tetsu Nakamura, Osman Yusuf, Woody Allen, China Lee. **D:** Senkichi Taniguchi, Woody Allen. **W:** Kazuo Yamada, Woody Allen, Julie Bennett, Frank Buxton, Louise Lasser, Mickey Rose, Bryan Wilson. **C:** Kazuo Yamada. **M:** Jack Lewis, The Lovin' Spoonful. **VHS**

Wheels on Meals

Jackie Chan brought in his opera-school brothers Yuen Biao and Sammo Hung to help out with *Project A,* with spectacular results. Sammo Hung returned the favor by bringing his brothers to Spain with him for this joyous martial arts comedy. Yuen and Chan are David and Thomas, respectively, who own and operate a motorcoach lunch wagon in Barcelona. On their rounds one day they meet Sylvia (Lola Forner, Miss Spain 1979), a pickpocket who steals both their hearts. Sylvia is being followed by a suspicious character named Moby (Hung), and the chivalrous lads take her in to protect her. It turns out that Moby is just a poor private detective (with a penchant for silly gadgets) hired by a guy in a bowler hat to find Sylvia, who is really an heiress. His real employer is an evil count that is out to get Sylvia's inheritance. Some great chases, wonderfully choreographed fight scenes, and a trip to an asylum aren't enough to keep the bad guys from kidnapping Sylvia, forcing the three kung-fu-teers to storm the castle and rescue the fair maiden.

This movie is so much fun, it makes you feel like you're on a vacation. Beautiful scenery, wild stunts, and the kind of comic chemistry that only comes from family keeps the amusement factor on high. Some of Hong Kong's finest comic character actors—John Sham, Richard Ng, Stanley Fung, and Wu Ma—show up to lend a hand. Karate champ Keith Vitali lends a foot. But it's Chan's classic fight scene with Benny (The Jet) Urquidez that keeps people talking—when they can catch their breath. The original title *Meals on Wheels* was changed by a superstitious executive at Golden Harvest after several films beginning with "M" bombed. *AKA: Faai Chan Che; Kuai Can Che; Kwan Tsan Tseh; Spartan X; Million Dollar Heiress; Weapon X; Powerman.* 🐉🐉🐉

1984 100m/C *HK* Jackie Chan, Yuen Biao, Sammo Hung, Lola Forner, Benny Urquidez, Keith Vitali, Herb Edelman, Mercedes Albert, Paul Chang, Richard Ng, John Sham, Wu Ma, Stanley Fung, Mars, Chin Ka-Lok, John Sham. **D:** Sammo Hung. **W:** Edward Tang, Johnny Lee. **C:** Francisco Riba. **VHS, DVD**

Where a Good Man Goes

With many of the top Hong Kong directors finding work in Hollywood, others have been able to break out of the mold and express themselves. Johnny To *(Heroic Trio)* is among the best of these. Here, he delivers a change of pace with a fine romantic melodrama. Gangster Michael Cheung (Lau Ching-Wan) has just gotten out of prison, but is such a tough guy that he immediately gets in a fight with his cab driver. Stranded in the rain, he checks into a small inn in Macau. Though he's angry and rude, he's touched by the patience and kindness of young widow Judy Lin (Ruby Wong) who owns the place. The cabbie calls on his pal, a crooked cop named Karl (Lam Suet) to get revenge, beating and humiliating Michael in front of the neighbors. Judy stands up for him, giving witness that Michael was attacked first. Michael also grows fond of Judy's son Tony, and the maid Wei, trying in his way to form some kind of family around himself. Though his efforts are a bit raw for her, the lonely widow finds herself warming to Michael as well.

The former boss tries to get together with his old gang, but finds things have changed. Many of his followers have scattered, most who've remained are ninnies, and only his old friend Bo remains faithful—though he can't account for the cash Michael left with him. Despite his dwindling cash, Michael tries to go straight, even running the inn when Judy has appendicitis. But the harassment by Karl, who seems to be obsessed with him, is eventually too much for Michael.

The film has much of the spirit of a "Beat" Takeshi Kitano film, showing both the soft and hard parts of gangster life, but painted in To's earth tones and foggy blue colors. The excellent soundtrack by Cacine Wong creates a pleasant mood, and dominates many scenes. **AKA:** *Joi Gin A Long; Zai Jian A Lang.* ♫♫♫

1999 98m/C *HK* Lau Ching-Wan, Ruby Wong, Wayne Lai, Lam Suet, Raymond Wong. **D:** Johnny To. **W:** Yau Nai-hoi, Milkway Creative Team, Wai Kar-fai (story). **C:** Cheng Siu-keung. **M:** Cacine Wong. **VHS, DVD**

Where's Officer Tuba?

Tuba (Sammo Hung) is a bumbling cop, nick-named for his police band instrument. His roommate Cheung (Jacky Cheung) becomes a cop, too, but is disappointed to be assigned to interoffice deliveries. While delivering a document, he overhears the captain (Melvin Wong) and supercop Rambo Chow (David Chiang) discussing Mr. Kan's extortion case. He opens his big mouth and gets the unknowing Tuba assigned to the dangerous case as a "cop that doesn't look like a cop." Tuba is unknowingly given the task of making the money drop, thinking he's delivering a suitcase of clothes to the captain's estranged wife. But when the gang turns ugly, they prove too tough for even Chow, and he gets shot. Tuba promises the dying man that he'll get the gang for him, and before long, Chow's ghost is haunting Tuba into fulfilling his promise. The frightened Tuba tries to renege, but Chow persists, causing lots of trouble for Tuba with his new girlfriend Joanne (Joey Wong) and her uptight parents.

The opening sequence, with Chiang pursuing a suspect into a footrace, then kicking him through the windshield of a racing truck (which then crashes into a river), could serve as a promo reel for the Sammo Hung Stunt Team. It's nice to see this old-time Shaw Brothers star cutting up in a comedy. A lot of the gags don't work, but the material gets by on the personalities of the leads, and with help from a small

army of familiar faces. Though energetic, the climactic fight scene fails to fully exploit the possibilities of its location: a warehouse full of oranges. **AKA:** *Pik Lik Daai La Ba; Pi Li Da La Ba; Spirit and Me.* ♫♫♫

1986 92m/C *HK* Sammo Hung, Jacky Cheung, David Chiang, Joey Wong, Melvin Wong, Stanley Fung, Paul Chun, Wu Fung, Hwang Jang Lee, Tai Bo, Yuen Wah, Yip Wing-cho, John Sham, Dennis Chan, Lam Ching-Ying, Chen Jing, Alfred Cheung. **D:** Ricky Lau, Phillip Chan. **W:** Barry Wong. **C:** Andrew Lau, Michael Ma. **M:** Danny Chung. **VHS, DVD**

White Lotus Cult

Among the kung fu revival features inspired by the success of *Once upon a Time in China* was this tale of folk hero Liang Kun, AKA To Kiu-sum, AKA "Iron Bridge" Sam, one of the original Ten Tigers of Kwangtung. During the period of the Ching Dynasty when the Empress Dowager was in power, foreigners flood into China to take advantage of the perceived weakness. Sam (To Siu-chun) and Kuang are making a delivery of goods in Peking when they witness an altercation between the British soldiers and the mysterious—and the apparently bullet-proof—White Lotus Cult. Witness here a fine example of poor acting by a gweilo: one of the Brits receives an arrow through the forearm and looks only mildly upset about it! Not to be confused with the Blue Oyster Cult, the White Lotus (previously seen in *Once upon a Time in China 2*) are a hate group interested in expelling the foreigners, as long as it serves their own interests. Among their indoctrination techniques are old medicine show staples of illusions, costumes, and feats of strength, dressed up in their own brand of mysticism.

Court official Tsao secretly procures patent medicine pills from the Lotus chief Chin Chan (Chi Chuen-hua) for the Empress, in exchange for palace gossip. When an opera actress named Tieh (Yip Chuen Chan) inadvertently causes a row with some foreigners, impressionable Keung impersonates a cultist to strike at them, only to run afoul of the real cult. Tieh's father Chin Chen is actually the lost brother of the cult chief, and once reunited, they plot to assassinate the empress and restore the Ming government. However, it's a trap: Chan curries favor with the empress by defending her from his brother, hoping to also kill him and get at the sacred scrolls he guards. Chen escapes, and forces Sam with a poison to let him hide out onboard the train for Canton among his ginseng shipment. With no antidote, Chen teaches Sam a kung fu technique to dissipate the poison. The cult follows them to Canton, where Keung, now a cult member, finds out Sam is harboring the wounded fugitive. Sam seeks out Tieh and Chen's old girlfriend Hung (Lily Li) for a cure. While he's gone, Keung leads the cult to capture Chen, and Chan tortures his brother for his secret. Luckily, Sam wasn't poisoned at all—Chen was really only teaching him his clan's secret kung fu techniques—and he uses his newfound skills to go to the rescue.

Unlike Wong Fei-hung, Fong Sai-yuk, and other Chinese heroes, Sam's kung fu isn't all that great, but fortunately this is one of those movies in which years of study and practice aren't necessary to be a kung fu master—just the right magic pills and secret techniques. By the end, Sam is a fire-breathing dragon ready to kick ass with the best. Well, almost—he still needs help from his teachers, and a little luck, to face the cult master. With a half dozen main characters to introduce and guide through their own individual dramas—even the Empress Dowager and General Kuan (Yu Hai) put in cameo appearances, *White Lotus Cult* threatens to get bogged down in the kind of thick plot often seen in Asian period soap operas, but thankfully there's enough wild wirework action (supervised by Phillip Kwok) to keep things moving. With the characters and backstory established, things get to be a bit more fun in the sequel, *Sam the Iron Bridge*. **AKA:** *Baak Lin Che Sun; Bai Lian Xie Shen.* 🐉🐉🐉

1993 97m/C *HK* To Siu-chun, Chi Chuen-Hua, Yip Chuen Chan, Lily Li, Fennie Yuen, Yu Hai. **D:** Cheng Siu-keung. **W:** James Fung. **C:** Cheng Siu-keung, Leung Lek-chee. **M:** Wong Lai-ping. **VHS, DVD**

Who Am I?

Who is Jackie Chan? By 1998, Chan had played cops, monks, drunks, detectives, lawyers, secret agents, tomb raiders, chefs, and even twins. His characters in movies had begun to grow more and more alike, nearly indistinguishable from his "real-life" public image. What standard direction for a hero role hadn't he taken, except to lose his identity entirely through amnesia?

Somewhere in Africa, scientists are studying a powerful energy source found within a meteorite. Jackie plays a secret agent undercover as a member of a commando squad that kidnaps the scientists for bad guy Morgan (Ron Smerczak), who double-crosses the mercenaries after the job and orders them killed. Jackie escapes by falling from their chopper, and survives the fall with minimal injuries, except for a knock on the head that has caused him to forget who he is. He's taken in by a local tribe and lives as one of them for a time. But nagging returning memories

cause unrest within him—he knows there's important information in his brain that he has to get to. Picking up bits of clues and memories, he ends up going to Holland, getting mixed up on the way with some foxy females, CIA agents, and Morgan's men—never quite knowing who he can trust completely.

Made as Chan was about to start work on *Rush Hour*, *Who Am I?* is a perfect illustration of the man's mental state at the time, as it was for many Hong Kong natives. Would his third try at Hollywood work out, or would he be scrambling to find firm footing between his now-Communist hometown and various international ports of call? Tellingly, the film was shot mostly in English, with a lot of Europeans, Africans, and Americans in the cast, and has little or nothing to do with China, instead embracing a larger perspective. Too rambling to be a solid fan favorite, *Who Am I?* nevertheless satisfies in most departments.

Fans had complained that the climaxes of his most recent films (*Rumble in the Bronx*, *Mr. Nice Guy*) dealt too much with a big prop vehicle stunt and not enough with Chan in action. Jackie responds here with a rooftop battle that is one of his best fight scenes in the past decade, a terrific stunt to get down off the building, and finally, a spoof of the big vehicles. On the way there, he provides several fine fight and chase sequences, and a lot of nice international scenery. What's really missing in this one is feeling and focus. We don't know who Jackie was before the amnesia, so we really don't care. His stay with the tribe in Africa is far too short and underdeveloped, losing track of the environmental message he intended. Just when you're getting into what he's discovering there, the movie interrupts with a car race. When directors have dared to put Chan's brand of action in a more serious or unusual setting—*Heart of Dragon*, *Gorgeous*, *Crime Story*—he's always been up to the challenge and the results have been rewarding. However, when Chan has more control of a project, he has a tendency to pull back to the familiar stunt or chase. It's revealing that the man is less afraid of teetering off the roof of a skyscraper than he is of getting involved in any real drama. The U.S. version is missing some footage, including some fun stuff during a leopard hunt. **AKA:** *Ngo Shut Sui, Wo Shi Shei; Jackie Chan's Who Am I?.* 🐉🐉🐉

1998 (PG-13) 117m/C *HK* Jackie Chan, Michelle Ferre, Mirai Yamamoto, Ron Smerczak, Ed Nelson, Glory Simon, Michael Lambert, Kane Kosugi, David Leung, Ron Smoorenburg, Brad Allan, Brent Houghton. **D:** Benny Chan, Jackie Chan. **W:** Jackie Chan, Susan Chan, Lee Reynolds. **C:** Fletcher Poon. **M:** Nathan Wang. **VHS, DVD**

Wicked City

Back in the mid-1980s, the trend in Japanese animation began to shift slightly away from the sci-fi and mecha that was so overwhelmingly popular. Genres began to expand into grittier—but no less fanciful—territory of supernatural horror, especially the adults-only variety. Though horror has a long and distinct history within Japanese culture, up until that time it was rare to see this kind of graphic outburst on cinema screens (Go Nagai's *Devil Man* being a standout exception). Perhaps the popularity of gory pictures from America and Europe had something to do with it. Director Yoshiaki Kawajiri *(Lensman, Ninja Scroll)* was among those foremost in experimenting in this new area. At about the same time, he made the similar *Demon City Shinjuku,* and this adaptation of Hideyuki Kikuchi's novel *Supernatural Beast City.*

In one of the creepiest opening scenes in all of anime, a handsome and suave young man named Taki succeeds in taking home a woman he's had his eye on from his usual bar. However,

when they bed down for the night, he gets way more than he bargained for—his date turns out to be a horrible demon in disguise. Taki should expect this type of thing—after all, he's an agent of the elite Black Guards, sort of a security agency that serves interaction of the human world and our sister dimension, the Black World. He ought to be more careful with his love life, though. For thousands of years, the two dimensions have co-existed more or less peacefully. Recently, tension has grown because a new treaty is due to be signed, and certain factions within the Black World would like to see that peace spoiled. Taki, along with his beautiful new half-demon partner Makie, has been assigned as bodyguard to demon missionary Giuseppi Mayart, who arrives in town to sign the treaty. The assignment is less than routine, and things just keep getting worse as it progresses. Each Safe House they bring Mayart to is eventually attacked and infiltrated by the unrelenting demon agents. Making matters worse, Mayart himself is a horny little dwarf (reminiscent of the lusty shrimps that often pop up in Rumiko Takahashi's manga series like *Ranma 1/2*), and he seems determined to escape his watch-dogs to sample the wares of the city's red-light

district. But Taki's ultimate challenge comes when he has to divide his loyalties between duty to his mission, and protecting the partner he's grown to love.

Though the project was doubled in length halfway through production, *Wicked City* manages to overcome its uneven pacing with plenty of horrific razzle-dazzle and a touch of pathos. Exquisitely designed as a sort of film noir nightmare, it's probably better known now for the influence it has had over the years than for its own complex story. The *Urotsukidoji* series definitely eclipsed it in the area of outrageously (porno)graphic horror, and its format of slick agents vs. monsters can certainly be recognized in *The X-Files* and *Men in Black*. There was even a live-action version shot in Hong Kong in 1992, which took a stab at reproducing the look found here, but *Wicked City* is a film that's greatest impression is made by its dark, atmospheric artwork. *AKA: Yoju Toshi; Supernatural Beast City; Monster City.* 🎵🎵🎵♡

1987 90m/C *JP* **D:** Yoshiaki Kawajiri. **W:** Kisei Choo, Hideyuki Kikuchi (novel). **C:** Kinichi Ishikawa. **VHS, DVD**

Wicked City

Made three years after 1989's anime version of *Wicked City* (which was based on a Japanese novel), writer/producer Tsui Hark's live-action remake retains all the energy, sleaze, and oozing gore of the original. Where it differs is in attitude. Hark (along with director Peter Mak) takes us on a much heavier ride, leaving out much of the humor of the anime and wrapping things up without a happy ending. As the film opens, Lung (Leon Lai) picks up a prostitute and heads back to his room for a little bit of the ol' in-and-out. Just as he's about to get a little, the aforementioned hooker sprouts a few more legs and turns into a nasty arachnid-like creature spewing venomous barbs as she tries to do away with the horny bastard. After some bullets and knives fly, Lung is rescued by Ying (Jacky Cheung), and we find out that the vile spider-woman is indeed a "Reptoid," a ruthless monster from another dimension intent on destroying the human race. Other Reptoids are already secretly in control on many economic and political levels.

Lung and Ying are members of the "Anti-Reptoid Squad," a top-secret organization dedi-

You *don't* want to see what he's shooting at in the slick supernatural anime feature *Wicked City.*

cated to destroying the 'Toids, which is not as easy as you might think. It's not just that new monsters show up faster than the squad can kill them—beheaded Reptoids quickly regrow heads; can shape-shift (check out the human pinball machine and the liquid monster who infiltrates the drinks and blows people up from the inside); and they have a killer drug called Happiness that turns humans into willing slaves, making them super-strong and oh-so-happy until they stop taking it, at which point it makes them oh-so-dead. When it's discovered that someone on the squad has secretly sided with the Reptoids and is helping them distribute the drug, Lung and Ying must go even deeper into the Wicked City, where the pace incredibly kicks up a notch further and the fast and furious action becomes at times almost too frenzied. Just when you think that you've seen it all and that you've got no more adrenalin to give, the climactic battle takes place on top of (not aboard) a jetliner screaming across the Tokyo skyline. To make things even more interesting, Ying is actually half-monster and bleeds black; and Lung has a secret Reptoid lover, Gaye (the gorgeous Michelle Reis), who is working for a peaceful solution to the human/Reptoid problem.

Tsui throws in plenty of wire-enhanced kung fu fighting, lots of babes, many icky demises (human and monster), and even a little morality play about how love at least tries to conquer all, when it comes to the differences between cultures—in this case monster and human. The visuals are stunning (although some of the effects lean towards cheesy, especially the unconvincing airplane miniature) and *Wicked City*'s metropolis is nearly *Blade Runner* beautiful, yet still conveys an omnipresent evil. Part neo-noir, part horror film, and part love story, *Wicked City* is all Hong Kong. —JO 🦴🦴🦴

1992 87m/C *HK* Jacky Cheung, Roy Cheung, Leon Lai, Carman Lee, Tatsuya Nakadai, Michelle Reis, Yuen Woo-ping. *D:* Peter Mak. *W:* Tsui Hark, Roy Szeto. *C:* Andrew Lau, Joe Chan. *M:* Richard Yuen. **VHS, DVD**

A Wicked Ghost

Four friends—Big Bee, Annie Chan, Rubbish, and Biggie—have a séance using blood and human skin oil, while a fifth, Ming, sits it out. But it's Ming who sees a ghost, and stops the séance. Moments later, Rubbish says he sees a ghost in the bathroom, and then drops dead.

Ming's reporter sister Cissy investigates the case. Ming's drama teacher Mr. Mo is fond of Cissy, but she's engaged to her boss Jack. Mr. Mo relates a story from Kurosawa's biography about his brother's suicide to illustrate the idea of transference. The following night, Big Bee is lured to his death off the roof of a building. Mo

believes the body's essence was set loose by heating the oil, and the only way for Ming to learn more is to contact the ghosts of his friends, but Rubbish's ghost can only give him a warning. His friend Biggie strangles her mother, and then stabs herself to death. She had a mysterious connection to an older man whom Annie saw her with. Then Jack sees a ghost, too. Mo and Ming go to Yellow Hill Village where both Jack and Rubbish were born, finding it deserted, except for ghosts: 66 people died there during one Autumn Festival. The ghost warns Ming that Annie has only three days left. At the root of the trouble is a woman named Cho Yan Mei, an actress lynched by her fellow villagers many years ago. A construction project has disturbed her unmarked grave, and now her vengeful spirit is on a rampage.

There are some nice, spooky shots included here, but the whole film is a jumble. It seems as if several scenes have been edited in out of order. One unintentionally funny shot shows the ghost emerging from a toilet. The ending is abrupt and confusing. The performers are all sincere, but it's hard to work up any concern for them. One scene is swiped directly from *The Omen*. **AKA:** *Saan Chuen Liu Shut; Shan Cun Lao Shi.* 🦴🦴

1999 83m/C *HK* Francis Ng, Gigi Lai, Gabriel Harrison, Edward Mok, Celia Sze. *D:* Tony Leung Hung-wah. *W:* Tony Leung Hung-wah. *C:* Stephen Wong, Ally Wong. *M:* Simon Leung. **VHS, DVD**

A Wicked Ghost 2: The Fear

Cops chase a slimy rapist into a construction site, where the suspect finds some sort of cursed dagger. By the time one of the cops catches up to the rapist, the man has chopped off his own legs with an axe, and he begs the cop to chop up the rest. The copper complies, then shoots himself. Left with a baffling case, Detectives Peanut (Alice Chan) and Master Li (Ken Wong), and police photographer Willis Tao, naturally assume a supernatural cause, and accept an offer of guidance from Blue (Joey Man), author of best-selling ghost books and niece of their superior, Officer Hwang.

While investigating the case, reporter Balm is hit by a car fleeing the ghost of the pervert. His associate (and Tao's girlfriend) Coffee (Angie Cheung) immediately suspects a ghost, and takes over the story. Soon after, Peanut's friend Ada is blinded by a long-haired wraith after watching an episode of the *Ring* TV series, and ends up killing herself. Ada's sister Clever (Joyce Chan) is frightened by a pair of little girls, seemingly the ghosts of two aborted pregnancies. Peanut, Coffee, and Blue team up to track down the cause behind the ghost attacks, which is somehow related to Peanut's great-grandmother, the ghost actress of the previous film.

Well, at least it's not one of those in-name-only sequels that are so common, and *The Fear* is actually a bit better than *Wicked Ghost*, offering a slightly more coherent plot, good music, and better shock effects. Just about everyone in the film accepts supernatural causes behind events with amazing ease, which is either a way for the script to cut to the chase, or indicative of just how superstitious Chinese society is as a whole. Not only the menace from *Ring* is borrowed, but also the ghost girl with a bouncing ball idea much used since Mario Bava's *Kill Baby Kill*. The entire film is tinted green and blue, with red highlights, which can give a spooky atmosphere, but is overused and becomes monotonous. Followed by *Wicked Ghost 3: The Possession*. **AKA:** *Saan Chuen Liu Shut II Sik Ji Nyn Gwai; Shan Cun Lao Shi II Se Zhi E Gui.* 🐉🐉

2000 77m/C *HK* Joey Man, Angie Cheung, Joyce Chan, Alice Chan, Ken Wong. **D:** Francis Nam. **W:** Mickey Siu, Tony Leung Hung-wah. **C:** Yip Wai-ying. **M:** Simon Leung, Tony Tam. **DVD**

Wild Zero

A meteor is reported to have landed in Asahi. In reality, a swarm of very hyper flying saucers has surrounded the Earth. Rock-and-roll fan Ace (Masashi Endo) is unconcerned with such things. He's finally got up the courage to ask the manager of his favorite club to give him an audition, but walks in on a Mexican standoff between club manager Captain (Makoto Inamiya) and his bald flunky on one side, and rock star Guitar Wolf (as himself) on the other. He provides a welcome interruption for his idol Wolf. In return, Wolf makes him a blood brother and gives him a whistle to blow in case of trouble. The next day, Ace accidentally foils a robbery attempt at a strangely empty gas station outside of town, and meets a girl named Tobio (Kwancharu Shirichai), who tends to faint a lot. Further down the highway, Ace finds a van run off the road, and the occupants becoming lunch for a gang of gut-munching zombies. Intuiting that this is not just an isolated group, Ace heads back to save Tobio. The zombies are all over the area. Could it be the work of grave robbers from outer space?

Wild Zero is much in the same vein as many films of the 1990s that emulated the work of Quentin Tarantino. However, it rises above imitation with a bit of honest charm. Plus, it's got UFOs and the living dead! There are a lot of nice touches—such as Ace fighting his way through zombies until he looks like one of them, his dream girl turning out to be something other than

what he thought, and when everybody has to admit they've never seen *Night of the Living Dead*. There are also some continuity gaffs, which are easily ignored with so much going on. Some of the f/x are really impressive—there are shots of ghouls getting their heads blown off that never betray a dummy or other trick. It's all set to some pretty good punk rock tunes—an unfortunate rarity these days—and making a superhero out of Guitar Wolf is an acceptable pretension, given that it's done tongue in cheek. 🐉🐉🐉

1999 98m/C *JP* Masashi Endo, Kwancharu Shirichai, Guitar Wolf, Makoto Inamiya, Naruka Nakajo, Shiro Namiki, Bass Wolf, Drum Wolf, Masao Sato, Yutaka Mishima. **D:** Tetsuro Takeuchi. **W:** Satochi Takagi, Tetsuro Takeuchi. **C:** Motoki Kobayashi. **M:** Guitar Wolf. **VHS**

Wing Chun

With the revival of traditional martial arts heroes all the rage in the early 1990s Hong Kong cinema, Yuen Woo-ping (*Drunken Master*) decided to get in on the action with this film from his own production company. And for his hero, he picked a legend that couldn't be played by Jet Li for a change. The bandit gang of Flying Chimpanzee (Norman Tsui) is threatening to steal the Wong family fortune. Wong Hok-chow (Waise Lee) comes into town to hire famed fighter Yim Wing Chun (Michelle Yeoh) to head his security staff. But thinking frugally, he decides he'll try to marry her instead, if only to save money! Wing Chun's dad is embarrassed to have such a tomboy for a daughter, wishing she were like her more demure sister Wing Chow. And he's not too happy with his brash sister-in-law Abacus Fong (Yuen King-Tan) either. The village is celebrating Wing Chow's wedding procession, and Mr. Yim is sick knowing that the two women will be getting into mischief while he's gone. Charmy (Catherine Hung) comes to the village to get help for her sick husband. Wing Chun goes to her rescue when the bandits try to abduct her. The husband dies, and Charmy sells herself to pay for the funeral. Abacus and Wing Chun get scholar Wong to give them the money to buy her, and their tofu business really takes off with such a beauty in the shop. She also draws Chimpanzee's lieutenant Flying Monkey, who is determined to abduct her. In a silly subplot, Leung Pok-to (Donnie Yen) mistakes Charmy for his childhood friend Wing Chun, and Wing Chun, in her men's clothes, for Charmy's lover. Wong is also trying to woo Charmy, while also after Wing Chun, and Abacus wants Wong—or any man.

As a martial arts romantic comedy of errors, *Wing Chun* bears more of a resemblance to a *Ranma 1/2* cartoon than a historical action pic-

ture. Yuen keeps the pace fast, and the action faster. A little too fast actually—the obviously undercranked fights and fancy wirework make the acrobatics less impressive. Yeoh, Yen, and Tsui are all terrific without phony embellishment. '60s star Cheng Pei-Pei has a nice cameo as Wing Chun's sifu Ng Mui. *AKA: Yong Chuan; Yong Chun.* ♫♫♫

1994 95 m/C *HK* Michelle Yeoh, Donnie Yen, Waise Lee, Yuen King-Tan, Catherine Hung, Norman Tsui, Cheng Pei-Pei. *D:* Yuen Woo-ping. *W:* Anthony Wong, Elsa Tang. *C:* Mark Lee. **VHS, DVD**

Winners and Sinners

Since all three brothers from the Seven Little Fortunes Chinese opera troupe—Sammo Hung, Jackie Chan, and Yuen Biao—were working at Golden Harvest Studios by the early 1980s, it was probably inevitable that they would somehow work together. Inspired by one of the American films Chan had appeared in *(Cannonball Run),* they came up with an idea for an all-star ensemble action comedy. Five men who met in prison are released on the same day. Teapot (Hung), Windpipe (Richard Ng), Curly (John Sham), Ranks (Stanley Fung), and Vaseline (Charlie Chin) all decide to go straight. They move into a house with Curly's sister Shirley (Cherie Chung) and start up a cleaning business together called 5 Lucky Stars. They clean the house of triad boss Fung (James Tien), and later accidentally come into possession of a briefcase containing the plates for Fung's counterfeiting business. Fung learns that they have the plates, and kidnaps Shirley to force them to give back the briefcase, but the Lucky Stars—and their cop friend (Jackie Chan)—end up fighting the whole gang for their lives.

Sammo Hung has experimented endlessly throughout his career to find the perfect blend of action and comedy. Due to the fact that not everyone in the cast is capable at handling both, this is an extremely uneven misfire, but an entertaining one, and was a huge boxoffice hit. In a supporting role, Jackie Chan plays a predecessor to his *Police Story* role as a Hong Kong supercop on the trail of the counterfeiters, and performs some terrific stunts and fight scenes. At one point, two thieves (Huang Ha and Mars) steal the briefcase, and Jackie chases them down a busy freeway on roller skates. Yuen Biao has only a cameo part. Way too much running time is taken up by the sophomoric Lucky Stars trying to peep at Shirley in the shower and whatnot, though Richard Ng has a pretty funny extended gag that involves him using his imagined mental powers to make himself invisible, while his buddies play along. But the real reason to see this is for the excellent fight choreography. Hung would go on to star in four "Lucky Stars" sequels of varying quality. Fun Fact: Years earlier, Jackie Chan picked up a few extra dollars working security at Charlie Chin's wedding. *AKA: Kei Mau Miu Gai Ng Fook Sing; Ji Mou Miao Ji Wu Fu Xing; Wu Fu Xing; 5 Lucky Stars.* ♫♫♫

1983 108m/C *HK* Sammo Hung, Richard Ng, John Sham, Jackie Chan, Charlie Chin, Cherie Chung, James Tien, Lam Ching-Ying, Paul Chang, Tai Bo, Pat Ha, Chan Lung, Wu Ma, Cecilia Yip, Mars, Fung Hark-On, Dick Wei, Phillip Chan, San Kwai, Yuen Biao, Fung Ging Man, Barry Wong, John Chang, Walter Cho, Huang Ha, Moon Lee, Stanley Fung, Fung Lee, Chung Fat. *D:* Sammo Hung. *W:* Sammo Hung, Barry Wong. *C:* Ricky Lau. *M:* Chris Babida. **VHS, DVD**

Wishful Milenio

Four friends share a house and romantic adventures. Ha Yan (Yoyo Mung) prefers to be called Summer and is proud of her promiscuous and free lifestyle. Lin (Astrid Chan)—also called Tong Li in the subtitles—is initially cool and aloof. She becomes warm and excited after she meets famed Taiwanese travel writer Loi Lee, with whom she has been carrying on an anonymous e-mail correspondence. Lin's young cousin Xiao Cuan has a crush on a Japanese soap-opera star named Kimura. One day she bumps into a look-alike who is visiting Hong Kong on holiday, and is instantly smitten. Finally, Chew Nan has just been dumped by her latest beau and is frustrated because her desire to be the "perfect girlfriend" has been ruined again. She runs into a woman named Felix, who is very friendly to her in a way that makes Chew Nan distinctly uncomfortable. The love lives of the four friends play out.

The DVD cover states that the four friends are called Summer, Autumn, Winter, and Spring. That may be true in the original Cantonese, but the English subtitles use the names as noted above in the plot summary. In any event, the characters were evidently named with an eye toward covering a seasonal range of emotions. It's a clever idea, but it's the only unique twist given in the script. Otherwise, not many surprises are in evidence. The couples fall in love suddenly and seemingly without sufficient motivation, other than the need for the story to move along. It descends too often into soap-opera conventions—how convenient that one of the characters is in love with a soap star. The very beginning of the film also seems to hold promise of a lighter touch that director Bosco Lam is not able to maintain. That's not too surprising when you consider that Lam is also responsible for films such as *Chinese Torture*

Chamber Story, Spike Drink Gang, The Three Lustketeers, and House of the Damned. Though too melodramatic and ultimately weepy, the film is a nice change of pace from action films and definitely not a waste of time due to the fine performances of the four principals. It doesn't hurt that the actresses are lovely and easy on the eye. —PM **AKA:** Chin Hei Yuen; Qian Xi Yuan. ♫♡

2001 87m/C HK Astrid Chan, Yoyo Mung, Chan Pak-yue, Man Chung-han. **D:** Bosco Lam. **W:** Bosco Lam. **VHS, DVD**

The Witch from Nepal

Some movies, like Vanished and The Man Who Knew Too Much, seem to exist as a warning that we should all just stay home and not go on vacations. In a mountain village in Nepal, a were-panther Messenger of Evil (Dick Wei, typically larger than life) threatens the community. A prophecy foretells that a new chief will arrive on a giant bird to defend them. Just then, Chow Yun-fat steps off a plane!

Chow stars as illustrator Joe Wong, on vacation with his girlfriend Ida Yuen (Yammie Nam). On a safari, his elephant suddenly runs off, severely injuring his leg. Though unable to walk, while hospitalized he begins to exhibit strange mental powers. He meets an odd Nepalese girl named Sheila (Emily Chu), who shows him how to focus his powers to cure his leg, make his breakfast dance, and do other neat tricks. She tells him she's come because he's the new master of her tribe, in accordance with the prophecy. Joe tries to fight it, but when panther boy brings his bone club to Hong Kong, he's forced to take up the magic sword and defend himself.

Full of foggy Ching Siu-tung images, Witch from Nepal brings all the eclectic elements that crazy Asian cinema so commonly bring together so well. There are mystic superheroes, living hands, ballet classes, exploding dogs, car crashes, and an army of zombies rising from their graves, all in one film. The Nepal scenes offer some wonderful locations, but it's seeing the climax filmed on unbelievably empty streets in downtown Hong Kong that offer a shock. One of the films Chow Yun-fat made between being a TV star and when A Better Tomorrow made him a film star, you can see him give his role the same dedication no matter how ludicrous the situation. **AKA:** Kei Yuen; Qi Yuan; Jie Yuan; Nepal Affair; The Affair from Nepal. ♫♫♫

1985 89m/C HK Chow Yun-fat, Emily Chu, Yammie Nam, Dick Wei. **D:** Ching Siu-tung. **W:** Tsui Ching-hong. **C:** Tom Lau. **M:** Violet Lam, Chow Kam-cheung. **VHS, DVD**

With or Without You

Police detective Ming (Leon Lai) loses his gun during a drunken binge. This is a very bad thing for an officer of the law, of course, and so Ming must keep his mistake a secret while he frantically searches for it with the aid of his partner (Ng Man-Tat). During the same inebriated night, Ming met PR girl Tweedy (Rosamund Kwan), who is the girlfriend of Prince (Jacky Cheung), a psychotic hit man. Prince must leave town and Tweedy for a while, and perhaps never return, so Tweedy takes up with Ming, and they enjoy a sweet time together until Prince comes back. Prince is the jealous type, and does not take kindly to seeing his girlfriend with another man, and the fact that he is a policeman just means that more people will be killed in the crossfire. Indeed, Prince unbuttons his overcoat to reveal dynamite strapped to his body, and starts shooting everybody in sight.

Prince disappears from Hong Kong early in the movie. The majority of the running time is thus consumed by Leon Lai romancing Tweedy and searching for his gun, and is well nigh interminable except for the most devoted fans of the star. Ng Man-Tat provides a little comic relief, and a gun battle and a chase on foot through speeding cars help enliven things a bit. Things really heat up with Prince's return; from that point onward, the action comes fast and furious in a very satisfying, only-in–Hong Kong way. Lam Moon-wah choreographed the mayhem for director Taylor Wong. A prequel, No More Love, No More Death, was produced the following year, focusing on Prince and what led to his becoming the most feared hit man in Hong Kong. —PM **AKA:** Ming Yuet Chiu Chim Dung; Ming Yue Zhao Jian Dong. ♫♫

1992 90m/C HK Leon Lai, Rosamund Kwan, Jacky Cheung, Ng Man-Tat, Margaret Lee, John Ching. **D:** Taylor Wong. **W:** Lam Kee-To, Lam Chiu-wing. **C:** Herman Yau. **M:** Tats Lau. **DVD**

Woman in the Dunes

Entomologist Niki Junpei (Eiji Okada of The X from Outer Space), studying the wildlife in coastline dunes, misses his bus back to the city and is invited to stay in the home of one of the villagers, a widow (Kyoko Kishida) living alone in the dunes. However, the woman's house is down in a deep sand pit, where the sand flows into everything. All night long, she digs out sand for the villagers, at the same time keeping her house from being buried. In the morning, the man discovers that there's no way out of the sand pit—digging out the sand is too much work for the woman to do by herself, and he's become caught in an insidious sand trap. The man immediately goes on strike, and tries several plans of escape, but eventually must give in or die of thirst. "Are we digging to live, or living to dig?" he asks. Meanwhile, the two isolated prisoners go through the entire range of emotions together. The question becomes not how the man will escape his prison, but what will he do if he gets out?

Essentially a castaway story like *Lord of the Flies* or *Swept Away*, *Woman in the Dunes* is made much more interesting by its haunting, surreal setting. Hiroshi Segara's stark black-and-white cinematography makes the sand pit a weird microcosm. The story doesn't play entirely fair—we're not shown what the man's life is like before he's caught, making it difficult to judge his reactions. On the other hand, that makes it all the easier for the viewer to identify with him. *AKA: Suna no Onna; Woman of the Dunes.* 🎵🎵🎵

1964 123m/BW *JP* Eiji Okada, Kyoko Kishida, Koji Mitsui, Hiroko Ito, Kinzo Sekiguchi, Hiroyuki Nishimoto. *D:* Hiroshi Teshigahara. *W:* Kobo Abe. *C:* Hiroshi Segara. *M:* Toru Takemitsu. **VHS, DVD**

Wonder Seven

The trailer claims that the title group of this movie are "seven heroes in their untiring search for justice." That's a fairly apt description, as far as it goes. The Wonder Seven are an elite government strike force, working in secret to protect Hong Kong. They are led by Fei (Chinese Olympic gymnastics gold-medalist Li Ning), and comprised of a motley band of outcasts with various martial specialties and catchy code names like "Superman" (Andy Hui) and "Nanny" (Kent Cheng). These ultra-cool agents ride motorcycles and live together on a posh boat. Everything is gong well for the Wonder Seven until they take on an assignment (from the communist Chinese) to stop a crime syndicate intent on smuggling guns and drugs. Little do they know that the organization is headed up by a ruthless "Americanized" criminal Tsun (Chin Ho). Making things even trickier is super-mercenary Ying (Michelle Yeoh), who works for the bad guys. When Fei is framed, he teams up with Ying and the sparks really begin to fly. (The disreputable good guy meets the honorable bad girl.)

Wonder Seven features plenty of stunts, kung fu, gun-fu, and of course, gymnastics (including a high-bar routine by Ning). Michelle Yeoh has plenty to do as well, and she and Ning have a nice chemistry when working together on screen. The plot is interesting and has a few nice twists. The film is well put together and features enough mayhem for any fan of Asian cinema. The long skyscraper fight at the end is especially cool. The thematic overtones of concern about the (then) impending takeover of HK by the mainland Chinese, add a topical level of interest as well. —SS *AKA: 7 Gam Gong; 7 Jin Gang.* 🎵🎵🎵

1994 89m/C *HK* Michelle Yeoh, Li Ning, Kent Cheng, Andy Hui, Roger Kwok, Xiong Xinxin, Vincent Lau, Hilary Tsu, Chin Ho, Elvis Tsui, Kwan San, Wong Kam-Kong. *D:* Ching Siu-Tung. *W:* Charcoal Cheung Tan, Elsa Tang, Ching Sui-Tung. *C:* Fletcher Poon, Peter Ngor. *M:* Law Dai-yau, Barry Chung, Fabio Carli. **VHS, DVD**

The World of the Drunken Master

The success of *Drunken Master* inspired many imitators, including some movies that delved into the history of Wu Sung's Drunken Style of kung fu. This Joseph Kuo production borrows the image of Simon Yuen, and even a variation of the Wong Fei-hung theme, to tell a story of famed Drunken Masters Knight Fan Ta-pei (Jack Lung) and Beggar So Hua-tzu (Chui Chung Hei)—or rather, the story of why the two friends separated for years. A chance reunion of the two Drunken Masters reminds them of their first meeting 30 years previous, as competing vendors of stolen grapes and oranges. Mr. Chang Seventh (Chan Wai Lau) catches the pair stealing from his orchard and puts them to work in the winery. After the boys are beaten by triad bullies working for Tiger Yeh (Lung Fei), Chang decides to become their after-hours kung fu instructor, teaching them the 18 Falls of the Drunken Immortals until they're both practicing in their sleep. Yeh believes Fan and So (played in the flashback by James Lee) may have been spying on him, and the boys only make things worse trying to help Chang sort things out. Yeh and his boys smash up the winery, kill Chang's boss Wang, and abduct daughter Yu-lu (Jeanie Chang). However, Fan and So, along with Master Chang, chase down the villains. During a running battle, Chang is killed by arrows and Yu-lu falls over a cliff. The boys use new kung fu tricks they learned from cave paintings to defeat their foes. Thirty years later, they learn that Yu-lu didn't die from the fall ("It's a long story," she says), but some new enemies appear to spoil the reunion.

The leads are superb martial arts performers, and the fight scenes are well choreographed, but Jack Lung's drunk act looks a little stiff. Simon Yuen, with his face plastered (no pun intended) prominently all over the poster art, only appears during the credit sequence in stock footage—a major cheat. But the main flaw of the film is that it gets mighty sloppy late

in the game. Lung's opponents spring up out of nowhere without any effort to establish them earlier, and the other heroes simply disappear. This was the beginning of a downhill slide for Joseph Kuo, whose films got much cheaper later in the 1970s. Production values are relatively good, and there's some creative camera placement throughout the middle section. It may be another case of an unfinished film that is padded out with a framing sequence that was made up as they went along, using whatever actors were available, until Kuo ended up with only Jack Lung, a camera, and an empty location. *AKA: Chow Sin Sap Baat Dip; Jiu Xian Shi Ba Die; Drunken Dragon.* 🐉🐉

1979 88m/C *HK* Jack Lung, James Lee, Jeanie Chang, Lung Fei, Lung Tin Cheung, Mark Lung, Chui Chung Hei, Chan Wai Lau, Kon Tak Mun, Wong Yu, Wang Wing Sheng, Simon Yuen. *D:* Joseph Kuo. *W:* Te Man-kan. **DVD**

Wrath of Daimajin

The Stone God is back in this quickly released sequel to Daiei's hit. In 14th-century Japan, wicked Lord Danjo of Nikoshiba (Takashi Kanda) covets his neighboring states Chigusa and Nigoshi, but doesn't have the troops to invade openly without the allies teaming up against him. In Lake Yakumo, between Chigusa and Nigoshi, lies a sacred island. Returning from a diplomatic meeting on the island, a party from Nigoshi notices the face of the great stone god redden in anger. Across the lake, Lord Juro of Chigusa (Kojiro Hongo) is offered tribute to aid refugees from Nikoshiba, but their offering of bales of rice is a Trojan Horse, hiding Lord Danjo's samurai. His forces overwhelmed, Juro escapes through a secret tunnel, and Danjo turns his army on Nigoshi. Once there, Lord Katsuhiko (Koichi Unoyama) is held hostage, with Juro's surrender the requested ransom.

From there, the sequel follows the pattern of the original—all escape or rescue attempts by the heroes fail, the villains attempt to deface or destroy the stone god, and things become increasingly desperate until Divine Intervention lends a hand. A big stone hand of course, as the Majin (Riki Hoshimoto) comes to life and stomps into town during the closing minutes to make the invaders pay. Though viewers may feel impatient at having to again wait until the end of

Another warlord learns it's not wise to mess with a god as the giant stone golem attacks in *Wrath of Daimajin.*
THE KOBAL COLLECTION / DAIEI FILMS

the picture for the star to put in an appearance, this is actually a better picture than *Daimajin,* mostly due to director Kenji Misumi's superior sense of imagery. There's enough action and drama to keep things going until Majin shows up in the third act. The monster is even more fearsome and imposing this time around, and is given more to do, including parting the waters of the lake, and using wind and lightning as his weapon. Followed by *The Return of Daimajin.* ***AKA:*** *Daimajin Ikaru; The Return of Majin; The Return of Giant Majin.* 🦴🦴🦴🖤

1966 79m/C JP Kojiro Hongo, Shiho Fujimura, Taro Marui, Takashi Kanda, Jutaro Hojo, Koji Fujiyama, Koichi Unoyama, Isao Hashimoto, Sei Hiaizumi, Koichi Mizuhara, Riki Hoshimoto. ***D:*** Kenji Misumi. ***W:*** Tetsuo Yoshida. ***C:*** Fujio Morita. ***M:*** Akira Ifukube. **VHS, DVD**

X

In 1999—"The Year of Destiny"—a gang war starts between the Dragons of Earth and the Dragons of Heaven. Both gangs are made up of super-magic-powered folks who can spit thunderbolts and piss fire and whatnot. The most powerful Dragon is Kamui, who has been gone somewhere since running away as a kid, but now he's back and both sides want him to join up. Though you may have trouble keeping all the characters straight, you should remember Kamui—but just in case you forget, somebody shouts his name at least once a minute. Kamui decides to join the kindly Dragons of Heaven, which somehow comes to mean that Kamui's childhood pal Fuma thinks that he is actually Kamui himself, and that he must join the other side. Now that the appointed time has come, and Kamui is back home, the Dragons of Earth have decided to bring about the End of Man. To make this happen, all they have to do is knock down seven landmark buildings in Tokyo. It's that easy!

Though a bit muddled at the beginning, once the preliminary visions and dreams are out of the way, *X* settles into some excellent superhero battles. The novelty in this anime feature is that it was based on manga created by the all-female animation studio Clamp. A lot of the art and animation is gorgeous, assisted by some nicely blended CGI. The character designs are the same old thing: 12-foot-tall spade-faced skinny people with pointy noses. And the story is the same old nonsense—sort of like a more apocalyptic version of *X-Men,* leading up to a big showdown with magic swords. The problem with a lot of modern anime is the same as it is with most American comic-books: it concentrates on empty visual posturing and pretentious myth-making. The basic storytelling doesn't live up to the hype—an artistic bimbo, all gloss and little substance. It's annoying that so much care, sweat, and talent went into a movie that feels so empty. Like *Akira* and *Galaxy Express 999, X* was made at a point in time when its source manga series was still only halfway completed. Clamp and veteran director Rintaro—who got his start working at Mushi Productions on *Astro Boy,* then went on to direct anime landmarks *Harmagedon*—decided that the story they needed to tell in the feature was the ending. Unfortunately, this meant the sacrifice of all the detail leading up to the climax. As a result, the characters are barely sketched in and the plot is condensed to a muddle. The story is all apocalypse without any sense of history. In 2001, *X* was made into a television series, where the concepts were given a lot more room to breathe. ***AKA:*** *X/1999; X: Their Destiny was Foreordained 1999.* 🦴🦴🦴

1996 (R) 97m/C JP D: Rintaro. **W:** Clamp, Rintaro. **M:** X Japan. **VHS, DVD**

The X from Outer Space

For decades, the bread and butter (or rice bowl, more accurately) of Japan's Shochiku Films was the long-running Tora-san series of lighthearted comedies. But in between, they produced some of the oddest science-fiction and horror films ever made. Before *Summer among the Zombies,* or even *Body Snatcher from Hell,* went before the cameras, studio heads took note of the profits brought in by Godzilla and Gamera at the boxoffice and decided to get in on the action with their own monster character.

Six straight attempts by the Fuji Astro Flying Center to get a rocket missions to Mars have failed, apparently shot down by a UFO. Captain Sano (Toshiya Kazusaki) is determined to make number seven lucky. Halfway there, spaceship *AAB-Gamma* encounters the UFO, and ship's medic Dr. Shioda (Keisuke Sonoi) comes down with space sickness. The ship is ordered to the Moon to pick up a replacement doctor, arriving just in time for cocktail hour. They again try for Mars, but the UFO comes back to shoot space globs at them, which stick to the ship. Biologist Lisa (Peggy Neal) and the captain catch one of the globs to take back to the lab on Earth, and the glob hatches a baby creature, which in a few hours grows into a giant rampaging creature named Guilala. The monster looks flat-out ridiculous, like a giant rubber chicken crossed with a Teletubby, but this picture has some interesting ideas that deviate slightly from the usual monster-on-the-loose plot. The space creature is never treated as malevolent, but more like a

polar bear escaped from a zoo. Once the scientists figure out that it absorbs energy, everyone pretty much tries to stay out of its way while the astronauts return to space to gather "guilalium," which they've discovered can shrink the beast back to manageable size.

This lone Shochiku giant-monster movie doesn't measure up to those produced at Toho in any way, but retains some kind of dorky charm. Badly dubbed, too. If you're wondering why the flying space Eggo UFO was shooting Gooey-lala globs at Japanese spaceships, you'll have to wait and see if a planned remake answers that question. While Peggy Neal was in Japan, she and co-stars Franz Gruber and Mike Danning also starred in the equally weird *Terror beneath the Sea.* Director Kazui Nihonmatsu's only other known picture is the eco-horror film *War of the Insects.* **AKA:** *Uchu Daikaiju Girura; Big Space Monster Guilala.* 🦴🦴🐾

1967 (PG) 89m/C JP Toshiya Kazusaki, Tishiya Wazaki, Itoko Harada, Peggy Neal, Eiji Okada, Franz Gruber, Keisuke Sonoi, Ryuji Kita, Mike Danning. **D:** Kazui Nihonmatsu. **W:** Kazui Nihonmatsu, Moriyoshi Ishida, Eibi Motomochi. **C:** Shizuo Hirase. **M:** Taku Izumi. **VHS**

Yellow River Fighter

This lavish mainland production from the director of *Shaolin Temple* is set in the turbulent ninth century. Warlords King Wah, King Yu (Chi Chuen-Hua), and King Li battle constantly for more Chinese territory. Mighty swordsman Tiger Ma Toh-hong (Yu Cheng Hui) interferes in a battle between Wah and Yu within sight of King Li's fortress, saving Wah's life. This kindness doesn't go unpunished, as it makes Ma late returning to his village, costing him his family as soldiers attack. Seeing his great skill, Li orders that Ma be brought into his service, or be executed. And since the swordsman is interested only in vengeance, Li's men are out to get him. When he's not looking for the killer, he spends all his time drinking, giving his enemies an opportunity to poison his wine. Due to the carelessness of beggar Chi Chen (Yu Hai)—who is exploiting his drunken sword dance—Ma is only blinded by the poison, and is soon brought into the palace of grateful King Wah.

Tiring of King Yu's atrocities, Wah decides to challenge him to a duel, and Ma agrees to deliver the challenge. Evil Yu blames the messenger, but though blind, Ma is still a fierce fighter and manages to kill Yu. As a reward, King Wah builds a school for Ma so he can pass on his swordplay knowledge to the people. Wah sends Ma with some soldiers to capture King Li, but Li manages to escape, and Ma unknowingly saves

Li's daughter Jen-Jen. Wah then sends Ma to escort the princess home and begin to arrange for peace with King Li. However, Ma is blind in more ways than one. Wah's true purpose is to use Ma as a weapon, and has a few mean tricks up his sleeve.

The costumes, sets, and locations are mighty impressive, though flatly photographed. The main flaw here is a lack of likeable characters. Chi Chen is the most down-to-earth figure, but he's much too annoying for viewer empathy. As for the lead, he's nearly always either being tricked or in a rage. The swordplay action is excellent, but a letdown for those who have experienced the sensational martial arts choreography of Cheung Yam Yim's earlier films. **AKA:** *Wong Hiu Daai Hap; Huang He Da Xia.* 🦴🦴🐾

1988 91m/C CH Yu Cheng Hui, Yu Hai, Hu Jian Qiang, Chi Chuen-Hua, Sun Jian Kui, Liu Huai Liang, Gan Tak-mau. **D:** Cheung Yam Yim. **W:** Wong Mak Chuen. **C:** Zhou Bai Ling. **VHS, DVD**

Yes, Madam

Sammo Hung produced this female version of Jackie Chan's *Police Story,* though Michelle Yeoh's Inspector Ng comes off more like Dirty Harry during the film's opening action sequence, in which Lam Wai and Chen Jing lead a gang that attempts to rob an armored car. Ng's old Scotland Yard mentor Richard Nornen (Michael Harry) is working undercover as an accountant to triad chief Tin (James Tien) in order to get evidence of a forged contract on microfilm. Tin's assassin Willie Dick (Dick Wei) shoots Nornen, but is interrupted by hotel thieves Aspirin (Mang Hoi) and Strepsil (John Sham), who unknowingly swipe the microfilm hidden in a passport before Dick can get it. They give the stolen passport to their forger buddy Panadol Tsui (special guest star Tsui Hark), who uses it to make a forgery for a thief (Eddie Maher) leaving the country. After learning about the murder, the trio goes to a retirement home to ask the advice of their old sifu (Sammo Hung, whose roommates are Richard Ng and David Chiang). Getting a tip from Panadol, Ng teams up with Scotland Yard Inspector Carrie Morris (Cynthia Rothrock) in time to arrest the thief at the airport. Ng lets the suspect escape in order to trace him to the forger. With Dick on their trail, Aspirin and Strepsil turn themselves in to the cops. But Ng and Morris jump the gun, arresting Tin before they have the evidence. The crooks try to blackmail Tin for the microfilm, but he holds Aspirin hostage, while Dick is sent after Panadol. Taken off the case by Commander Wong (Melvin Wong), both ladies quit the force to go after Tin without restrictions.

Atsuko Takahashi and Gezora get into a nasty nightclub brawl, ending the much-publicized affair they began during shooting of *Yog: Monster from Space,* while mutual friend Kameba tries to break things up.

THE KOBAL
COLLECTION / TOHO

Yes, Madam was a big hit in Hong Kong, and though the three crooks with the pharmaceutical names are given equal time, it made Michelle Yeoh and Cynthia Rothrock instant action stars. Yeoh and Rothrock handle their fight scenes with grace and energy, especially in the fantastic climactic battle (though they're obviously doubled by stuntmen on the harder falls). *Royal Warriors* and several others followed in a loose *In the Line of Duty* series, which have been released under a confusing variety of titles. One version contains senselessly recycled sequences of David Chiang from *Where's Officer Tuba?* Romeo Diaz's score steals cues from *Halloween* and other sources. *AKA: Wong Ga Si Je; Huang Jia Shi Jie; Police Assassins; Police Assassin 2; Super Cops; Yes Madam!; In the Line of Duty 2.* 🎵🎵🎵♡

1985 93m/C *HK* Michelle Yeoh, Cynthia Rothrock, Tsui Hark, Dick Wei, Mang Hoi, John Sham, Wu Ma, James Tien, Melvin Wong, Tai Bo, Eddie Maher, Chung Fat, Sammo Hung, Richard Ng, David Chiang, Billy Lau, Mars, Shum Wai, Dennis Chan, Lam Wai, Chen Jing, Corey Yuen, Michael Harry, Billy Ching. *D:* Corey Yuen. *W:* Barry Wong. *C:* Bill Wong. *M:* Romeo Diaz. **VHS, DVD**

Yog: Monster from Space

A space probe is invaded by blue spores, which change its course from Jupiter back to Earth. Reporter Taro Kudo (Akira Kubo) spots the probe from his plane as it crashes near Selga Atoll, somewhere near Japan. Ayako Hoshino (Atsuko Takahashi) of the Asia Promotion Agency hires him to photograph the area, as her company wants to build a resort on the island. They board a boat for the Atoll, and meet up with scientist Dr. Kyoichi Miya (Yoshio Tsuchiya) and "freelance anthropologist" Makoto Obata (Kenji Sahara). Meanwhile, a pair of Hoshino's co-workers are already on the island, and they decide to go fishing in the bay. Out pops Gezora, a funny-looking giant squid able to walk around on land with its tentacles. The monster kills them and destroys a native village, before it's apparently driven away by a flock of bats. The space spores are responsible, and next they possess a crab, which also grows to gigantic size. Crab monster Ganime also destroys a village. After that, the spores send giant turtle Kameba to wreck some huts. Each time a mon-

ster appears, the heroes team up with the natives and burn it to death. Between monster attacks, the aliens try to possess humans, but for some reason they use their victims to try to keep the humans from learning their monsters' weakness to the sound waves produced by bats and porpoises. Not the most logical of alien invaders, the spores never seem to think of making their possessed human into a giant. Even if they can't do that, it seems like maybe the monsters have more obvious problems than a few bats, since the natives keep barbecuing them. The hapless aliens even try attacking with two monsters at once, but the beasts end up fighting with each other!

Screenwriter Ei Ogawa, clearly not comfortable with science fiction, moved on to script Toho's *Dracula* movies next. Unfortunately, this ridiculous effort was the last film to team composer Akira Ifukube, director Ishiro Honda, and designer Takeo Kita, who had all done such wonderful work together in the past. Honda and Kita had worked together since the '30s, and Ifukube would score Honda's last film, *Terror of Mechagodzilla,* before both men retired. Teisho Arikawa (cameraman for f/x genius Eiji Tsuburaya) and assistant director Teruyoshi Nakano teamed up to create the special effects, and they end up looking like school projects for the both of them. Nakano would learn rapidly and take over Toho's effects department with *Godzilla vs. Hedorah,* keeping the position until Koichi Kawakita took over in the late 1980s. *AKA: Gezora Ganime Kameba: Kessen! Nankai no Daikaiju; Sepesu Amiiba; Space Amoeba; Yog the Space Amoeba.* 🎵🎵

1970 (G) 84m/C *JP* Akira Kubo, Atsuko Takahashi, Yukiko Kobayashi, Kenji Sahara, Yoshio Tsuchiya, Yu Fujiki, Noritake Saito, Yuko Sugihara, Sachio Sakai, Chotaro Togin, Wataru Omae, Tetsu Nakamura, Yukihiko Gondo, Shigeo Kato, Rinsaku Ogata, Haruo Nakajima. *D:* Ishiro Honda. *W:* Ei Ogawa. *C:* Taiichi Kankura. *M:* Akira Ifukube. **VHS**

Yoga and Kung Fu Girl

Madam Kao (Kong Ching-ha) adopts five orphan boys and girls, and rigorously trains them in the Shien Yie Kwon (soft bone) style of kung fu, as well as acrobatics and magic. When they're old enough, they join her medicine show. Little mute Phoenix (Phoenix Chen) grows up able to bend as easily backward as forward, and is also able to defend herself when wicked martial arts teacher Mr. Ma and his thugs try to abduct her. Ho-fei (Chi Kuan Chun) loses the necklace left to him by his mother, gambling in a fixed dart game. He steals from Madam Kao to get a stake to win it back, but only loses more and

gets into a fight. Madam Kao kicks him out, but eventually takes the brash young man back. When a man who took Kao's herbal medicine falls mute, it puts her in danger, but it's all a plot of Ma's to force Phoenix into his hands. Ho-fei teams up with Dr. Chang (Pai Ying) to rescue Phoenix, though the doctor's motives have more to do with killing Ma and taking over his operation. Ma's father (Lo Dik) seeks revenge, and Ho-fei kills him during the attack, leaving the territory open for Chang as the new boss. But the fighting has widened the gap between Madame Kao and Ho-fei, and he leaves to become boss of his own gang. When Chang murders Kao in a raid, Phoenix and the remaining students join with Ho-fei to fight their way through the doctor's hired killers to get revenge.

Phoenix Chen is button cute, and her skills are impressive, but she lacks the raw personality to carry the lead—probably the reason she plays a mute, and never made another film. This leaves it up to Chi Kuan Chun to pick up the slack, and his subpar Jackie Chan imitation doesn't cut it. The film starts out in a lighthearted vein, then turns bloody halfway through, and ends up with some odd comic moments toward the end. The heroes dress up in drag to infiltrate Chang's headquarters and among the fighters they face are an imitation Simon Yuen drunken master and a Snake Fist–fighting parody of Jackie Chan. Though the final fight scene is a good one, outside the novelty Phoenix presents, there's not much of interest here. *AKA: Yoga and the Kung Fu Girl; Octagon Force.* 🎵🎵

1978 85m/C *HK* Chi Kuan Chun, Pai Ying, Phoenix Chen, Lo Dik, Kong Ching-ha. *D:* Sun Young. **VHS, DVD**

Yojimbo

The 13th collaboration between actor Toshiro Mifune and director Akira Kurosawa was a lucky one for all concerned—especially the viewer, as this tribute to great American western films, adapted from Dashiell Hammett's hard-boiled crime novel *Red Harvest,* is perhaps Kurosawa's most accessible work. Mifune stars as Sanjuro Kuwabatake, a wandering ronin (who actually gives no name) who arrives in a small 19th-century village during a dust storm. The place looks like a dried-up ghost town, where only the undertaker (Atsushi Watanabe) seems busy. He learns from Gonji the innkeeper (Eijiro Tono) that the reason for the desolation is that the town is in the middle of a dispute between two gang bosses, each camped out in their headquarters at opposite ends of the main street. Sizing up the situation, the crafty warrior takes advantage by playing one side off against the other. His efforts are complicated by the arrival of the wily

Unosuke (Tatsuya Nakadai), the gun-slinging son of one of the gangsters. In the middle of this game, the ronin lets his heart get the better of him, though, and helps a poor man get his abducted wife back from the gangsters, receiving a beating for his trouble. Unosuke leads a raid on his father's opponents, the gun giving him a clear advantage, and Sanjuro only escapes with Gonji's aid. But when the little innkeeper is captured and used as bait by Unosuke, it forces Sanjuro into a final showdown.

Yojimbo is not only good Art, but good fun as well, taking the finely mannered format of Japanese films and throwing some dirt on it to show what was happening in the lower classes, much like Kurosawa's earlier *The Seven Samurai*, but on a less epic scale. Mifune's roguish hero is far from the noble knights of *The 47 Ronin,* and seems to be swarming with fleas. Masaru Sato's score lends just the right wry atmosphere to the proceedings. It's one of those films that is perhaps more famous for the influence it's had than its own merits, having been remade at least twice using other settings, and pieces of it can be seen in everything from *Zatoichi on the Road* to *Star Wars. Sanjuro* was Kurosawa's own sequel, while the character returned for two further films: *Zatoichi Meets Yojimbo* and *Ambush. AKA: The Bodyguard; Yojimbo the Bodyguard.* ♫♫♫♫

1961 110m/BW *JP* Toshiro Mifune, Eijiro Tono, Tatsuya Nakadai, Takashi Shimura, Seizaburo Kawazu, Isuzu Yamada, Hiroshi Tachikawa, Kamatari Fujiwara, Daisuke Kato, Ikio Sawamura, Ko Nishimura, Yoshio Tsuchiya, Yoko Tsukasa, Susumu Fujita, Eisei Amamoto, Yusuke Natsuki, Atsushi Watanabe. *D:* Akira Kurosawa. *W:* Akira Kurosawa, Ryuzo Kikushima. *C:* Kazuo Miyagawa. *M:* Masaru Sato. **VHS, DVD**

Yongary, Monster from the Deep

Japanese monster movies were so successful during the '60s that even Korea's Kuk Dong Studios tried to get in on the action. They imported lots of Japanese technicians for this one, and monster Yongary even looks quite a bit like Godzilla (but not as pretty). An astronaut's honeymoon is interrupted, first by the bride's prankster little brother Icho and his experimental itching ray, and then by a phone call ordering his rocket to launch on the double. He's sent into space to peek at a Chinese nuclear test, which causes an earthquake. A giant burrowing creature is awakened by the earthquakes, and ends up generally ruining life for everybody in Seoul—

except for Icho (just like in the Gamera movies), who seems to like him. However, it is little Icho—like all Asian schoolboys allowed access to top-level government meetings—who brings news of Yongary's fatal weakness to those in charge. He even understands why his monster pal has to be killed horribly in the end.

Staying true to his status as a monster knockoff, Yongary looks a lot like Godzilla with Gamera's tusks and Baragon's nose horn. He breathes fire just like his idols, and even learns to shoot a laser beam out of his horn. Yongary can't burrow through the ground as fast as Baragon (from *Frankenstein Conquers the World*), but is a much better dancer, as he demonstrates in one memorable scene. Korea's #1 monster would be revamped for a return engagement with surprisingly good CGI f/x in 2001, released in the U.S. as *Reptilian.* This is one of about 70 features directed by the busy Kim Ki-duk in the 1960s and '70s. *AKA: Taekoesu Yonggary; Great Monster Yongary; Monster Yongkari.* ♫♫

1967 79m/C *KO* Oh Yeong-il, Nam Cheong-im, Lee Sun-jae, Moon Kang, Lee Kwang-ho. *D:* Kim Ki-duk. *W:* Seo Yun-sung. *C:* Byeon In-jib. *M:* Jeon Jeong-geun. **VHS**

You Shoot, I Shoot

Times are tough all over in Edmond Pang's black comedy. Assassin Bart (Eric Kot) has trouble getting paid, and new freelance assignments are drying up, so his wife (Audrey Fang) encourages him to "cold-call" potential clients. After a few telephone calls, Bart talks to "rich bitch" Mrs. Ma (Miu Fei-lam) who wants him to videotape the murder she orders. Bart finds killing and filming at the same time too difficult, so he forcibly recruits an assistant director, Chuen (Cheung Tat-Ming), to do the camera work. Chuen has dreams of becoming the next Martin Scorsese and directing a film featuring his dream girl, Michiko (Higuchi Asuka), a Japanese porn actress. The resultant video is an instant hit with the "rich bitch" and her similarly jaded cronies. A successful new business is created: "You Shoot, I Shoot" Productions.

Merry and freewheeling, the first part of the film shoots along briskly with bright colors, inspired production design, a guerrilla music soundtrack filled with offbeat songs, and genuine hilarity spiking the proceedings. The Hong Kong assassin movie subgenre is ripe for the taking, and neophyte director Edmong Pang gleefully spices things up with his liberal use of handheld cameras, unique camera angles, and

Toshiro Mifune shows off some expert sword form in *Yojimbo.* THE KOBAL COLLECTION / TOHO

The monster wonders why no one cleaned up these tanks left all over Korea in *Yongary, Monster from the Deep.*
THE KOBAL COLLECTION / KUK DONG FILM CO

rapid-fire yet precise editing. Such trickery is entirely appropriate for the subject matter. As the running time plays on, however, a certain weariness takes hold. The basic premise is still very amusing, as are the numerous riffs and capable performances, but too much hot air and filler are added—including a gentle and romantic subplot—and the cake begins to collapse. Happily, the ending is satisfying, rather like giving the audience the chance to lick its fingers.

You Shoot soars more than it stumbles, and earns all of its many laughs. Eric Kot delivers a very funny performance as Bart. Cheung Tat-Ming is fully his equal as the cinematically ambitious but sweet Chuen. The large comic ensemble is quite solid; standouts include the straight-faced Michael Chan as Bill, a would-be triad boss who hires Bart and Chuen to do a job on a rival, and the duo of Lam Suet and Tats Lau as would-be cutthroat competitors. Art director Bill Lui can take credit for the hilarious differences between Bart and Chuen's places of residence. Wenders Li was both film editor and DV camera operator for those great POV—point of victim—shots. Peter Kam composed the marvelous musical score, which sounds like a twisted take on those twangy-guitar '60s spy movie

soundtracks. —PM **AKA:** *Maai Hung Paak Yan; Mai Xiong Pai Ren.* 🐉🐉🐉🐉

2001 94m/C *HK* Eric Kot, Cheung Tat-Ming, Audrey Fang, Ken Wong, Higuchi Asuka, Michael Chan, Lam Suet, Tats Lau, Vincent Kok, Matt Chow, Chan Fai-hung, Henry Fong, Nancy Lan, Angela Tong, Hyper BB, Shaw Yin-Yin, Miu Fei-lam. **D:** Edmond Pang. **W:** Edmond Pang, Vincent Kok. **C:** O Sing-pui. **M:** Peter Kam. **VHS**

Young and Dangerous

Triad recruitment tool or populist entertainment? For years, triad involvement in the Hong Kong film industry had been hotly debated. With its release during the Chinese New Year's period in January 1996, *Young and Dangerous* brought the arguments to a fever pitch. With the handover from British colonial rule to mainland Chinese communist authority looming, it made the criminal lifestyle look attractive and desirable. This film was a huge hit with the masses, running on Hong Kong movie screens for an unusually long period of time—three months. It spawned a host of sequels and prequels, and inspired a run of "young triad" flicks that lasted for years. Considering its influence, the film itself is a bit of a letdown.

At an early age, best friends Nam (Ekin Cheng) and Chicken (Jordan Chan) join up with Bee's (Frankie Ng) gang, part of the Hung Hing Society run by ultra-smooth Mr. Chiang (Simon Yam). Nam gets a girlfriend, Smartie (Gigi Lai), more commonly referred to as Stammer in the subtitles because she stutters. As divisions run deep in the family, Bee's gang comes into conflict with another gang led by Ugly Kwan (Francis Ng), an incredibly nasty and sly boss. The story pushes forward and often appears ready to stumble, yet it keeps moving and is never less than entertaining. The plot is quite familiar. The direction is rough-hewn and not terribly subtle, yet effective for what it is. Director Andrew Lau also served as his own cinematographer; perhaps this contributed to the immediacy of the look of the film. Ekin Cheng shines as Nam, whose character is the heart of the film. Equally noteworthy is his partner in crime, the multi–hair-colored Jordan Chan. The large cast is enjoyable to watch, including Spencer Lam as a doggedly persistent priest, formerly a gang member known as Lethal Weapon. The musical score by Clarence Hui throws several guitar-based themes behind the action. —PM *AKA: Goo Waak Chai Ji Yan Joi Kong Woo; Gu Huo Zai Zhi Ren Zai Jiang Hu; Young and Dangerous: Part 1.* 🐉🐉♡

1996 100m/C *HK* Ekin Cheng, Jordan Chan, Jerry Lamb, Francis Ng, Frankie Ng, Gigi Lai, Michael Tse, Spencer Lam, Simon Yam, Jason Chu, Lee Siu-Kei, Deon Lam, Ha Ping, Cheng Kei-ying, Johnny Wang, Ching Siu-leung, Joe Cheng, Shing Fui-on, Chik King Man. **D:** Andrew Lau. **W:** Manfred Wong. **C:** Andrew Lau. **M:** Clarence Hui. **DVD**

Young and Dangerous 5

Another lame sequel makes an end to this triad series (until the inevitable prequel), a disappointing grand finale with a lot of wasted guest stars. Ekin Cheng returns as upstart gangster Chan Ho Naam, with activity centered on the world of kickboxing prize fights. Despite the venue, there's precious little action here, and quite a bit of talk, until the climax. Chan has lost enough buddies and girlfriends throughout the series, and tries to make a change from his past course in life. But they keep pulling him back in. While the big match is fought in the ring, Chan has his own showdown with a rival backstage. Eventually, their fight makes its way into the ring, too. Interestingly, there are no guns in the movie, reflecting real triad life in Hong Kong but rare in a crime movie. "Special

guest star" Danny Lee plays a cop (of course). *AKA: 98 Goo Wat Jai Ji Lung Jung Fu Dai; 98 Gu Huo Zai Zhi Long Zheng Hu Dou; 98 Wise Guys; Young and Dangerous '98.* 🐉

1998 C: *HK* Ekin Cheng, Mark Cheng, Shu Qi, Chin Ka-Lok, Paul Chun, Vincent Wan, Jerry Lamb, Jason Chu, Karel Wong, Lee Siu-Kei, Helen Law, Ronald Wong, Bonnie Wong, Alex Man, Sandra Ng, Anthony Wong, Kwan Hoi-san, Wong Tin Lam, Simon Lui, Pomson Shi, Billy Chow, Chan Chi-fai, Danny Lee. **D:** Andrew Lau. **W:** Chau Ting. **M:** Comfort Chan. **VHS, DVD**

Young and Dangerous 6: Born to Be King

This gangster drama plays out against the recent political turmoil between China and Taiwan, even merging footage from the 2000 presidential inauguration into the story. Chan Ho-Nam (Ekin Cheng) is a triad who has nightmares about his dead girlfriend Smartie (Gigi Lai). His uneasiness leads him to fend off the marriage plans of his new girlfriend (Shu Qi). His friend Chicken Chiu (Jordan Chan) has just come back from Taiwan to marry a yakuza's daughter Nanako (Anya) in an arranged marriage brokered by their bosses. The whole gang travels to Tokyo for the wedding. Even as the Taiwan San Luen and Tokyo Yamada gangs unite, with strong ties with the Hung Hing in Hong Kong, resentment brews among their Chinese brothers from Hong Kong and the mainland. After the wedding, Boss Chiang (Alex Man) announces his retirement, passing Hung Hing leadership to Nam, insulting his own underling (and Nanako's boyfriend), Akira (Roy Cheung). In a wooden-sword match, Nam gains respect from the bride's father Boss Ichiro Kusakari (Sonny Chiba) with some Chinese techniques. Though Kusakari wants Chicken to take over his responsibilities when he retires, American-educated Lui (Peter Ho) is favored to take over San Luen by most of the triads. When Lui is attacked, both Chicken and rival Brave accuse each other of being behind it. While there's an attack on Chicken at a nightclub, in which his cousin Big Head (Chin Ka-Lok) is killed, Akira rapes Nanako. But Panther lives long enough to get revenge on the traitor with the triad. With his own gang in chaos, Chicken turns to his Hong Kong buddies to help strike back.

It's hard to understand the appeal of this long-running series, though it makes a bit more sense when you consider it's based on a comic strip. The intrigues of international gangster dealings are interesting for a while, but eventually become tiresome. Nam's romantic prob-

Triads

Once upon a Time in Triad Society

The Triads are most often defined to Westerners as "The Chinese Mafia"; from that description it's assumed that the triads were just the mob's Eastern division. In truth, triads have a similar, but even older origin, but are quite different. Since so many Chinese films deal with the triads (in more ways than one), you may be curious about this organization.

During the Ching Dynasty, the foremost secret rebel group opposing the government was the Heaven and Earth Society. Their symbol is a red triangle containing the Chinese character 'Hung' (for the founder of the Ming Dynasty, Hung Wu) representing the union of heaven, earth, and man. Heaven and Earth and other secret societies are sometimes referred to as "Hung Societies," terms that are still used in modern triads. As the Ching government began to falter, already some Hung societies were turning to crime to keep their organization going, while others devoted themselves to furthering martial arts (outlawed under the Ching) or labor unions. Even though much of the triads income comes from crime, not all triad members are criminals other than in their membership, which violates Hong Kong's 1994 Organized and Serious Crimes Ordinance. Of the 50 triads in HK, only 15 are considered to engage in illegal activities. These crimes often are in the area of drug traffic, prostitution, and illegal goods such as pirate VCDs, but the bread and-butter of the criminal triads is in simple extortion. Businessmen in HK consider paying protection fees as little different than paying taxes.

In general, triads are organized in the same master/student hierarchy as any other Asian endeavor, rather than the family organizations of the Mafia. Though underlings are expected to obey orders from higher up, the activities of underlings are not controlled by their seniors unless necessary. There are specific ranks and ceremonies, but few if any triads are strict in their use anymore, or use them at all. One is either a head or a foot soldier, or "49," and the induction rituals are rather simple.

Like every other business in HK, the triads have always been involved in the movies. There are members in all facets of the business, so it's no wonder that they've had a great influence on the films themselves. An inordinate number of films portray the triad life as dangerous, glamorous, and exciting, just like the lives of the pop music stars who play the heroes. Like many exploitation features, most of the time the flashy lifestyle on display is qualified with a "Crime Does Not Pay" message, unless of course you're one of the handsome, virtuous heroes. But for every *Young and Dangerous*—a popular movie that portrays the sexy life of young gang leaders, which has had many sequels and imitators—there are just as many films like *Long Arm of the Law* and *Beast Cops,* which show a life of neon-lit desperation, ugliness, and violence. Plus, an equal or larger number of films are made detailing the exploits of the Organized Crime and Triad Bureau, though more often than not in cop movies, the culprits being tracked down are operating outside of triad control—a danger to both sides of the game—and the overall message is that either the police or the triads are keeping the peace. Going against either is when you run into real trouble.

lems are an annoying distraction as well. The production sails along with only star power holding it up—the return of Jordan Chan to the series brings a little more focus after the dreary previous entry. It's nice to see Sonny Chiba acting beside Hong Kong's crop of young stars. Shu Qi contributes her usual cutie-pie nonsense routine. *AKA: Sing Che Wai Wong; Sheng Zhe Wei Wang; Young and Dangerous 6; Born to be King.* 🐉🐉

2000 118m/C *HK* Ekin Cheng, Jordan Chan, Shu Qi, Anya, Chin Ka-Lok, Sonny Chiba, Peter Ho, Gigi Lai, Roy Cheung, Alex Man, Blackie Ko, Jerry Lamb, Michael Tse, Jason Chu, Spencer Lam, Chan Chung-Yung, Sandra Ng, Vincent Wan. *D:* Andrew Lau. *W:* Manfred Wong. *C:* Andrew Lau. *M:* Comfort Chan. **VHS, DVD**

The Young Avenger

Behind this generic title lurks a pretty good Wong Yu kung fu comedy. Wong stars as Fu Yu, a rascally funeral-parlor worker who uses his inside position to facilitate a specialized sideline: grave robbing. This in turn finances his other sideline: gambling. After years of free enterprise, a ghost (Walter Cho) finally comes to haunt him. In penance for his desecrations, the ghost demands that Fu Yu find some men for

him, handing over a large reward as well. Fu Yu tries to double-cross the ghost, but finds the cash is all in Hell Money. Threatened anew by the ghost, he goes to a movie theatre in the next town, where he has to find and kill the manager Shing Tan. This section affords a nice re-creation of an old-time rural movie house, complete with narrating "communicator," and one wonders if the old adults-only silent film called *Catch the Bitch* playing is a re-creation or authentic. Since the next man on his list is a dangerous fighter named Lam Ping (Norman Tsui), the ghost gives Fu Yu instruction on improving his kung fu. As they've begun to trust each other, the ghost reveals that he's really a human named Bud Ming. His face was scarred when Lam Ping, Shing Tan, and his other comrades in an escort service decided to steal the treasure they were guarding, and they threw him over a cliff—where ants ate his face! Fu Yu goes to Lam Ping's Chun Kok Inn brothel to kill him, but has to go through his tough madam (Wong Hang-sau) to get to him. But he finds the pimp too tough to beat, and Lam Ping soon comes looking to kill them. Bud Ming dies getting his revenge, and Fu Yu vows to complete his vendetta by killing Chuen Tan-ping (Wilson Tong) and Hung Tai-lung, and busting up their slavery operation.

The kung fu fights are generally inventive—Wong Yu defends himself from a swordsman using bricks, and his specially made weapon is a collapsible grave-digging spade—but director

Wilson Tong sometimes shoots them too tight. The final 15 minutes or so delivers almost non-stop action. *AKA: Baan Yau Siu Ji; Ban Ye Xiao Zi.* 🐉🐉🐉

1979 83m/C *HK* Wong Yu, Norman Tsui, Wilson Tong, Kong Do, Walter Cho, Cheng Hong-yip, Fung Ging Man, Wong Hang-sau. *D:* Wilson Tong. *W:* Tin Ping Group, Lo Wai (story). *C:* Faan Chuen-yam. *M:* Frankie Chan. **VHS, DVD**

The Young Master

Another early Jackie Chan opus (his first for Golden Harvest Studios), this flick really starts to show what "Jackie: the Movie Star" would be about. The film opens with a great Lion Dance sequence—nearly as good as the one in *Dreadnaught,* and (in some ways) even more inventive. Jackie plays Dragon, a young kung fu student (big surprise). His best friend is Tiger (Wei Pai), a rogue who fakes illness to betray his dojo and don the guise of the rival Black Lion. (Tiger is selling out for the money.) Jackie discovers his friend's betrayal, but refuses to tell their master. In the best tough kung fu school tradition, Jackie endures many hardships on his friend's behalf. Eventually, though, the master finds out about the betrayal and banishes Tiger from the gym. Tiger takes his *big white fan* (important to the plot) and goes. Almost immediately, he falls in with a tough crowd.

Jackie convinces the master to give Tiger a second chance, and goes on a quest to find and bring back his friend. He, too, takes his *big white fan.* Unfortunately, this causes him to be mistaken for Tiger, who's now a wanted man. Recently, Tiger's tough friends ambushed a prison caravan, which was taking their leader, Tam (Whang In Shik), to jail. When the bad guys bust Tam out, Tiger—and his *big white fan*—is spotted with them. Jackie is wrongly captured by a police inspector (Shih Kien) and his son (Yuen Biao)—and a comical series of escape attempts follows. Meanwhile, Tiger is betrayed by the criminals, and locked in a bank strong-room. Jackie rescues him, and the two of them stay out of the law's hands just long enough for Jackie to have a final showdown with the criminal Tam.

Young Master is one of the best early Jackie Chan flicks. The opening Lion Dance is very cool. The film features a couple of good sword fights, some prop kung fu, a big dose of come-dy, plenty of fighting, and a series of amusing escapes and escape attempts. None of it is as innovative as Jackie's later work, but it's at the very peak of the "old kung fu" genre (post–Bruce Lee/pre–hugely famous Jackie). Because Chan also directed, you can really see

the "Young Master" perfecting his chops in this one. Don't stop the credits until Jackie sings the theme song—in English! —SS *AKA: Bye Dai Chut Ma; Shi Di Chu Ma.* 🐉🐉🐉

1980 89m/C *HK* Jackie Chan, Wei Pai, Lily Li, Shih Kien, Whang In Shik, Yuen Biao, Fan Mui-Sang, Tin Fung, Lee Hoi-sang, Cheng Hong-yip, Tai Bo, Fung Hark-On, To Siu Ming, Fang Fang, Tang Yin-chan, Chi-ang Kam, Yue Tau Wan. *D:* Jackie Chan. *W:* Lau Tin-chi, Tung Lu, Edward Tang, Jackie Chan. *C:* Chen Chin-kui. *M:* Ryudo Uzaki, Akira Inoue. **VHS, DVD**

Young Tiger

YT is a crime film from early in Jackie Chan's career, in which he plays the lead thug in a gang of criminals who mug people, steal, rape, and do about every other nasty thing they can think of. To make Jackie easy to recognize, the film-makers have given his character an absurdly large mole on his face—we're talking Austin Powers large. The mole looks like a wooly cater-pillar that got run over by a steamroller. Maybe they didn't want you to miss it.

Jackie's gang is after Ho Mei Fong (Hu Chin), a former member of the group who has turned informant, because she's got some kind of secret information in her purse. The gang beats her up, but she gets away in a cab, where she hides her purse. Then she dies. The gang can't find the purse, but they suspect Chin Chen (Charlie Chin), the cab driver, has taken it, so they begin a campaign of merciless harass-ment. They hijack Chen's cab, mug the hapless driver, and do everything they can to regain the MacGuffin—er, purse—all to no avail. Fortu-nately, when things get tough, Chen's cab com-pany pals are there to help Chen out. Also fortunately, all of them are schooled in kung fu—especially Chen. When the odds aren't stacked against him, Chen can really kick some ass. The murdered girl's policewoman sister Ho Mei Wa (Kan Chia-fong) pokes around trying to find the purse, too. Complicating things, the bad guys have sent a junkie in their employ to impersonate Wa, in hopes of regaining that elu-sive purse, and the fake Wa gets to Chen first. Eventually, Chen figures out who the real Ho Mei Wa is and the two team up to bring the bad guys to justice.

Lots of kung fu fights follow, and we discover that Jackie is working for a nasty drug-running criminal with a respectable "front." Chen and Wa are captured, and the bad guys try to "turn" Wa, but Wa turns the junkie girl against her "masters" instead, and the two women escape. Chen gets loose, too, and they all head for a big final confrontation between the good cab com-pany and the evil druglord's men. Though Jackie

isn't the star of the film, he does fight the climactic battle with Chen. Oh, and the secret of
the MacGuffin purse is revealed, too, as if it
matters.

The plot isn't very good, and neither is the
kung fu. Fans of Jackie will probably be disappointed because his role isn't very big, and we
don't get to see him strut his stuff much. Choppy editing also makes it difficult to follow his climactic fight scene. Beware the dreadful pan 'n'
scan on some "public domain" video releases
of this flick. —SS *AKA: Police Woman; Police
Woman against Jackie Chan; Rumble in Hong
Kong.* ♪♫ ♡

1972 83m/C *HK* Charlie Chin, Kan Chia-fong, Jack-
ie Chan, Chiang Nan, John Chang, Hu Chin, Lee
Man Tai, Helena Law, Feng Yi, Zhu Mu. *D:* Cheung
Ji. *W:* Ngai Hoi-fung. *M:* Chou Fu-liang. **VHS, DVD**

Your Place
or Mine!

Another romantic romp starring Tony Leung
Chiu-Wai, who narrates. Cheung Suk-wai
(Leung) is a heartbroken advertising director
with a huge pile of boxes in his apartment to
show for his accomplishments with women
(each time he gets dumped, he fills a box with
the stuff she left behind). It doesn't help his
mood that his best friend Patrick (Alex Fong) is
a complete womanizer, flaunting every affair in
his face (and his assistant Mei is in love with
him, too). Their department gets a new boss,
American-educated ballbreaker Vivian Ng (Ada
Choi), a rumored lesbian who immediately
starts downsizing. She's tough on Wai, but
there's obviously a spark between them. The
same day, he meets and falls for an uncomplicated young model named Yu (Vivian Hsu). He
makes her famous under her new name, Vivian
Hsu! When Patrick's girlfriend breaks up with
him, Mei (Suki Kwan) is there to catch him. But
will he continue his cheating ways? Wai succumbs to the wiles of first Yu, then Vivian. How
will he choose between them? Will he lose his
job either way?

Overlong and unfocused, this romantic comedy is short on laughs and long on soap opera.
The best lesson the guys learn is to take their
dates to their own place. The men seem to be
at the mercy of the whims of the women, with little free will, and everyone is always ready for a
wistful montage. Tony has several songs on the
soundtrack. *AKA: Moon Tin Oi Lei Siu Shut; Mei
Tian Ai Nin Xiao Shi.* ♪

1998 101m/C *HK* Tony Leung Chiu-Wai, Vivian
Hsu, Ada Choi, Alex Fong, Suki Kwan, Eileen Tung,
Spencer Lam. *D:* James Yuen. *W:* James Yuen.
C: Cheung Man-po. *M:* Lincoln Lo. **VHS, DVD**

Zatoichi and the
Chess Expert

The twelfth entry in the Zatoichi series starts
strong, with blind swordsman Ichi (Shintaro
Katsu) killing several attackers in a town
square, stark images playing out over Ifukube's
powerful theme music. It continues from there
as one of the strongest and most dramatic
episodes. Ichi just barely makes it on the boat
to Miura, and a band of men in pursuit of a
woman named Tane (Kaneko Iwasaki) misses it.
The masseur joins a dice game below deck to
scam some cash, and makes enemies of the
Banyu clan. On deck, he meets samurai Tadasu
Jumonji (Mikio Narita), and the two new friends
pass the time with a chess match.

During a stopover at Enoshima, the Banyus
ambush Ichi in a spa. Tane's little girl Miki's foot
is hurt in the fight, and afterward tetanus sets
in. Ichi vows to get the medicine to help her. He
joins a dice game to get the money for it, but his
trick of pretending to drop the dice backfires
this time. After earning another stake doing
some blind juggling, his luck changes, and he's
off to fetch the medicine.

Enemies attack on the road, and for once
Ichi finds his blindness to be a handicap; he
loses the medicine during the fight and nearly
misses finding it. Miki recovers, and the travelers make their way to Hakone to visit the hot
spring baths. All this time, Tane has been developing feelings for Ichi, despite the secret she's
hiding: Zatoichi killed her no-good husband a
while back, and she's been tailing him for one of
the gangs out to get him. Ichi confesses that
she reminds him of his late love (also named
Tane), but that his life of fighting taints anyone
he gets close to.

A few more characters join the story's webwork. Ichi has a patient on a mission of
revenge. The man's servant—the only one who
saw the samurai who killed his father over a
chess game—is murdered. It's sure that before
the end, Zatoichi must face off against Tane's
gang, and chess master Jumonji as well.

Heavier on drama than most Zatoichi films,
and lighter on swordplay, but what's there is
choice—especially the brief but much anticipated
duel with the chess master Jumonji. Director Kenji
Misumi directed six other Zatoichi adventures,
most of the *Lone Wolf and Cub* pictures, two of
the *Sleepy Eyes of Death* series, and *Wrath of
Daimajin.* *AKA: Zatoichi Jigoku Tabi; Showdown
for Zatoichi; The Blind Swordsman and the Chess
Expert; Zatoichi's Trip to Hell.* ♪♪♪

1965 87m/C *JP* Shintaro Katsu, Mikio Narita,
Chizuru Hayashi, Kaneko Iwasaki. *D:* Kenji Misumi.
W: Daisuke Ito, Kan Shimozawa (story). *C:*
Chikashi Makiura. *M:* Akira Ifukube. **VHS**

Zatoichi and the Chest of Gold

The minimalistic opening credit sequence is almost a modern dance number, as Zatoichi (Shintaro Katsu) draws his sword on waves of attackers against a deep black background, his masseur's whistle blending with Ichiro Saito's score between clashes. Ichi journeys to Itakura, on his rounds to visit the graves of those he's slain. Kichizo came upon Ichi while fleeing a battle between bosses Iioka and Sasagawa (in *The Tale of Zatoichi Continues*), and the blind swordsman had to defend himself from the samurai's attack—but Ichi regrets using a deadly stroke. After paying his respects, Ichi is asked to join a celebration. After three years, the 18 villages of the region have collected the 1,000 ryo needed to pay off their tax debt. But a gang of bandits attacks the transport, killing most of the men. This sequence contains a marvelous overhead shot showing the shadow of a dark cloud spreading over the landscape. The bandits knock the chest of gold down a hillside. Rushing after it, they find the blind man sitting on it, calmly smoking his pipe.

Local hero Boss Chuji Kunisada is implicated in the theft, and Kichizo's sister, who bears a grudge against Ichi, accuses him as well. Ichi vows to recover the gold and clear his name, but he has to hurry: the Intendant has given the peasants 10 days to come up with the money. He heads for Mount Akagi to confront Boss Chuji himself. Chuji has been hiding out on the mountain since defying the Intendant to help the farmers but, as Ichi reveals some of his men were involved in the gold theft, he decides to come down to help them once again. Corrupt Boss Monji, who has gained favor with Chuji out of the way, sends men to arrest him. Of course, it's Monji's men who stole the gold in order to gain more power for himself in the bargain. Meanwhile, Ichi takes on another mission: to deliver a young boy from Chuji's camp to safety. Despite a warning from Ichi, all but two of Chuji's men are cut down in the attack. The last straw played, Zatoichi starts a campaign of retribution against the corrupt rascals.

Though the series began to increase in frequency, there was no decrease in quality. This entry boasts an interesting story, and excellent direction by Kazuo Ikehiro, surely one of the best jobs of his career. There's also quite a bit of action, the highlight being a showdown with whip-wielding samurai Joshiro (Tomisaburo Wakayama). **AKA:** *Zatoichi Senryo-kubi; Masseur Ichi and a Chest of Gold.* 🗡🗡🗡🗡▽

1964 82m/C *JP* Shintaro Katsu, Shogo Shimada, Mikiko Tsubouchi, Tomisaburo Wakayama, Machiko Hasegawa, Tatsuya Ishiguro. **D:** Kazuo Ikehiro. **W:** Shozaburo Asai, Akikazu Ota, Kan Shimozawa (story). **C:** Kazuo Miyagawa. **M:** Ichiro Saito. **VHS, DVD**

Zatoichi and the Doomed Man

A pleasant change from the Zatoichi formula finds the blind swordsman dealing with corrupt bosses from two different towns, with much meandering in between. The 11th film in the samurai series starts with Master Ichi (Shintaro Katsu) already in trouble. He's in jail, receiving 50 lashes for gambling (and making snarky comments throughout his punishment). But he has a bit more on his mind: his cellmate Shimazo Katase professes he's innocent of his murder charge, and he asks Ichi to seek out the two men who can prove it—Senpachi and Jubei. Ichi decides against getting involved for a change, but fate brings him back around.

A demonstration of blind archery brings Ichi into contact with a scamp on the road. Ichi meets up with Boss Senpachi Karouma in Oarai and tells him about his doomed friend, and sets off to go see Boss Jubei in Choshi, though a woman he helps escape from the Boss' clutches warns that both men are bastards. Ichi clearly knows too much, and Senpachi sends men after him to kill him.

Meanwhile, the scamp has been impersonating Zatoichi, trying to scam folks in the next town. The real thing catches up, killing 10 attackers in a dark room. The scamp turns out to be the Doomed Man's son, softening Ichi's heart toward the youth. Battling his way past their defenses, Ichi forces Jubei and Senpachi to write a confession, but their men try to stop him before he reaches Intendant with it. The anticipated bloodbath follows, this time featuring an army of foes in a fishnet obstacle course. **AKA:** *Zatoichi Sakata Giri.* 🗡🗡🗡

1965 88m/C *JP* Shintaro Katsu, Kanbi Fujiyama, Eiko Taki, Masako Myojo, Koichi Mizuhara. **D:** Kazuo Mori. **W:** Shozaburo Asai, Kan Shimozawa (story). **C:** Hiroshi Imai. **VHS**

Zatoichi and the Fugitives

Taking shelter from a downpour in a hut one night, blind masseur Ichi (Shintaro Katsu) encounters a young woman (Yumiko Nogawa) hiding who doesn't wish him to know she's there. As he undresses to dry himself, she watches with hungry eyes—his purse. The next morning, he helps out a family of farmers. The father has been beaten by gangsters, and they rush him to Dr. Junan (Takashi Shimura). At the

inn, Ichi is harassed by some rough characters, but their leader (who has seen what Zatoichi can do with a sword) interrupts before he has to defend himself. The men are some notorious fugitives from the law. Aki (the woman from the hut) is also a member of the gang, and leads them to the house of the village boss Matsugoro, where they bully him into hiding them until the Inspector passes through. They camp out in the attic above Matsugoro's silk weaving sweatshop. Ichi leaves the inn, accepting the doctor's offer of work and lodging. The gang leader is actually the kindly doctor's estranged son.

Having made his presence known, Zatoichi is invited to Matsugoro's for a drink. Ichi takes the opportunity to force the Boss to free a poor sick girl indentured in the silk mill. Matsugoro calls in a favor from the fugitives, asking them to kill the village head man who's been standing up to him. The massacre that ensues pushes Zatoichi into going after both the boss and the fugitive gang.

A genuine attempt at a change of pace for the series, here Zatoichi is presented with more of a challenge in the form of the outlaw gang, each of whom carries a specialty weapon. At one point, he's even shot and has to flee for his life. The presence of veteran actor Shimura (*Godzilla*) also adds an extra layer of interest. Director Kimiyoshi Yasuda uses mostly gray, colorless imagery, and sets his fight scenes in dim light, creating an oppressive mood. **AKA:** *Zatoichi Hatashi Jo; The Blind Swordsman and the Fugitives.* 🎵🎵🎵

1968 82m/C *JP* Shintaro Katsu, Yumiko Nogawa, Kayo Mikimoto, Kyosuke Machida, Hosei Komatsu, Takashi Shimura. **D:** Kimiyoshi Yasuda. **W:** Kinya Naoi, Kan Shimozawa (story). **C:** Kazuo Miyagawa. **M:** Kajime Kaburagi. **VHS**

Zatoichi Challenged

This Zatoichi film bears many of the series' usual elements, but has an unusual twist in that its underlying subplot has to do with a lucrative illegal pornography ring involving many highly placed government officials. Ichi shares a room with a sick woman and her young son Ryota. They're on the way to meet the boy's father, an artist named Shokichi, in Maebara. The woman dies, and the blind gambler finds himself accompanying the boy on the journey in her place. They hitch a ride with pop singer Tomoe and her band, on their way to entertain Boss Sobei in Minowa, who sends a party to greet them. However, Boss Maruzo of Kanai also sends a greeting party, and the situation becomes tense. Heroic Master Tajuro Akatsuka arrives just then, and—while Ichi is trying to

extricate himself from overprotective Ryota—easily defeats the interlopers.

Setting up in Minowa, artist Ryota draws Tomoe in the sand so Ichi can see her. The little rascal is constantly trying to trick his blind uncle. Maruzo's man Monza comes to threaten Tomoe, but Zatoichi's lightning sword shaves his eyebrows off! Most of the territory is under the overall control of Boss Gonzou, and he responds to the offense by having Boss Sobei killed.

In Maebara, Ichi consults a potter's where he's heard Shokichi worked. He finds that the man ran up a gambling debt at Gonzou's casino and disappeared a year ago. To pay off his debt, Shokichi has been slaving away at erotic designs for pottery. As Ichi is about to learn his party's location from the intendant's secretary, his friend Akatsuka steps up and kills the man. Found with the body by Monza, Zatoichi naturally gets the blame and Monza sounds the alarm. In the confusion, Ichi manages to help Shokichi escape. It turns out Akatsuka is an undercover agent tracking down the pornographers, and while Gonzou's men run off after Zatoichi, he steps in to clean house. However, when the samurai chooses to turn his sword on the innocent artist forced to create the designs, Zatoichi takes action to protect Shokichi and Ryota.

Though relatively short on carnage, at last Zatoichi is matched against a worthy opponent, and the final duel is one of the most prolonged and tense battles of the entire series. Director Kenji Misumi makes the most of the mountainous landscapes, the acting troupe's colorful banners, and Katsu's expressive features. The anti-censorship message is wonderfully represented, without turning preachy. The music is unusual as well, returning to the Western sound of some of the previous Zatoichi films, and includes the ballad theme song and a pop tune. **AKA:** *Zatoichi Chikemuri Kaido.* 🎵🎵🎵🎵

1967 87m/C *JP* Shintaro Katsu, Jushiro Konoe, Miwa Takada, Yukiji Asaoka, Mikiko Tsubouchi, Mie Nakao, Asao Koike. **D:** Kenji Misumi. **W:** Ryozo Kasahara, Kan Shimozawa (story). **C:** Chikashi Makiura. **M:** Akira Ifukube. **VHS**

Zatoichi on the Road

Boss Hikozo (Shosaku Sugiyama) of Doyama sends his man Kisuke to fetch Zatoichi (Shintaro Katsu)—all expenses paid on the trip and no strings attached. The gang boss claims he just wants to meet the famous swordsman, but of course there's a fight he wants to draw him into. A trio of hired samurai attacks them, and kill Kisuke before Zatoichi can cut them down. Further down the road, Ichi meets a group of samurai hunting for a girl named Mitsu Narumiya (Shiho Fujimura). An

"A blind man fears no snake."

—Zatoichi, after killing an attacking asp as easily as shooing a fly, in *Zatoichi and the Fugitives*

新太郎勝

Shintaro Katsu

Katsu Is Zatoichi

One of the most enduringly popular—not to mention charming—characters in chambara (swordplay) cinema is Zatoichi, the blind swordsman/masseur who slashed his way across medieval Japan for 26 features and a television series. One cannot discuss Zatoichi without talking about Shintaro Katsu, the actor who brought the character to life. In 1960, Katsu starred in Daiei Studios *Agent Shiranui*, a movie directed by Kazuo Mori (who would direct three Zatoichi movies) about a blind masseur who kills his blind master and takes over his identity. Based on popular stories by Kan Shimoza-wa, Katsu expanded the possibilities of playing a blind character by incorporating stunning swordplay action.

The man known as Zatoichi was not always blind. Born around 1813, he grew up in the village of Shimodate in Koja district, raised by his father and a nurse named Oshige. At age seven, he lost track of his father at a festival and never saw him again, and sometimes in later adventures Ichi would encounter strangers whom he thought might be his lost father. Ichi lost his sight in an accident a year later. As a youth, he fell in love with a woman named Chiyo, who rejected him because of his blindness and ran off with Ichi's brother Yoshiro (played by Katsu's brother Tomisaburo Wakayama), whom she also left when his leg became partially crippled.

Ichi trained to become a masseur like many other blind people in Japan in those days, joining up with the yakuza for protection. But the young masseur tired of the taunts and disrespect of his fellows, and vowed to work on his swordplay. He trained with sword master Yajuro Banno until he'd mastered a lightning-fast draw, while learning to use his remaining senses with near-supernatural precision. Leaving his village to follow the festival circuit in search of work, masseur/gambler Ichi often found cause to use his sword skills, to defend either himself or innocents in trouble. Because of this, he found new motivation to keep moving, as his list of enemies in both the government and underworld kept growing.

All of the Zatoichi movies (plus 100 TV episodes) are not officially available on video, but for the record, here are the titles:

Blind Swordsman: The Tale of Zatoichi (The Life and Opinion of Masseur Ichi, Zatoichi Monogatari), April 1962

The Return of Masseur Ichi (The Tale of Zatoichi Continues, Zoku Zatoichi Monogatari), October 1962

New Tale of Zatoichi (Masseur Ichi Enters Again, Shin Zatoichi Monogatari), March 1963

Masseur Ichi the Fugitive (Zatoichi Kyojotabi), August 1963

Zatoichi on the Road (Zatoichi Kenka-Tabi), November 1963

Zatoichi and the Chest of Gold (Zatoichi Senryo-Kubi), March 1964

Zatoichi's Flashing Sword (Zatoichi Abaredako), July 1964

Fight, Zatoichi, Fight! (Zato Ichi Kessho Tabi), October 1964

Adventures of a Blind Man (Zatoichi Sekishoyaburi), December 1964

Zatoichi's Revenge (Zatoichi Nidangiri), April 1965

Zatoichi and the Doomed Man (Zato Ichi Sakata Giri), September 1965

Zatoichi and the Chess Expert (Zatoichi Jigokutabi), December 1965

Zatoichi's Vengeance (Zatoichi No Uta Ga Kikoeru), May 1966

The Blind Swordsman's Pilgrimage (Zato Ichi Umio Wataru), August 1966

Zatoichi's Cane Sword (Zatoichi Tekka Tabi), January 1967

Zatoichi the Outlaw (Blind Swordsman's Rescue, Zatoichi Breaks Jail, Zato Ichi Royaburi), August 1967

Zatoichi Challenged (Bloody Path, Zatoichi Chikemurikaido), December 1967

Zatoichi and the Fugitives (Zatoichi Hatashijo), August 1968

Samaritan Zatoichi (The Blind Swordsman Samaritan, Zatoichi Kenkadaiko), December 1968

Zatoichi Meets Yojimbo (Zato Ichi to Yojimbo), January 1970

The Blind Swordsman's Fire Festival (Zato Ichi Abare Himatsuri), August 1970

Zatoichi Meets the One-Armed Swordsman (Zatoichi Meets His Equal, Shin Zato Ichi "Yabure! Tojin-ken"), January 1971

Zatoichi at Large (Zato Ichi Goyotabi), January 1972

Zatoichi in Desperation (Zato Ichi Orieta Tsue), September 1972

Zatoichi's Conspiracy (Zatoichi at the Blood Fest, Zato Ichi Kasama no Chi Matsuri), April 1973

Zatoichi (Zatoichi 26), February 1989

Many characters have borrowed the idea of Zatoichi—Marvel Comics' *Daredevil*, the western *Blind Man*, Master Po on the *Kung Fu* TV show, Rutger Hauer in *Blind Fury*—but none have been able to match the outright magic that Katsu brought to the role. Even at the manic schedule the films were on at the height of their popularity, each Zatoichi picture combines human drama, humor, and amazing action beautifully.

Katsu was born Toshio Okumura in 1931 to a showbiz family of a sort—his father was a famed shamisen (a kind of guitar/banjo

Continued on next page...

instrument) player and Kabuki performer, and Katsu-shin showed what he'd learned from his dad in at least one Zatoichi picture. Though Katsu was rumored to be quite a hedonist between pictures, on-screen he's magnetic. By the time Zatoichi finished its run in the early 1970s, they were being made by Katsu's own production company and released by Toho Studios. Soon after, he was working closely with manga writer Kazuo Koike to produce film versions of Koike's *Lone Wolf and Cub* (starring big brother Wakayama) and *The Razor* (starring Katsu himself), both of which went on for several sequels. In the mid-'70s, at the end of the Zatoichi and Razor series, plans were made to revive Ichi for a feature called *Zatoichi in the West,* which would bring his most famous character to America and be scored with music by the Eagles. That film was unfortunately never made, but in 1989, a 59-year-old Katsu strapped on a sword again for an action-packed Zatoichi revival film. Shintaro Katsu died in 1997 of throat cancer, but even now a proposed new Zatoichi film is in pre-production. Rest assured that, wherever Shintaro Katsu is, Zatoichi will never die.

old man they've struck down makes a dying wish that Ichi will find Mitsu and save her. Her lord's men are hunting the girl because she resisted his rape attempt, stabbing him in the face with a hairpin. Ichi finds the girl, and decides to honor the man's wish and escort her to her relatives in Edo.

At an inn, they cross paths with Jingoro (Ryuzo Shimada), the man who hired the three assassins, who is traveling with Hisa (Reiko Fujiwara), the widow of one of them. She tells Mitsu some lies about Ichi and gets her to leave with her, but the local boss Tomegoro (Yoshio Yoshida) takes Mitsu away for himself, convinced that Mitsu's family will pay him a fine ransom. Zatoichi corners the woman, and he learns that Jingoro works for Boss Tobei (Sonosuke Sawamura), who is in a feud with Boss Hikozo and it was assumed Zatoichi was on his way to help the enemy. A little sword-drawing demonstration is enough to convince Tomegoro to hand Mitsu back, and their journey continues. Feeling that they're getting too close, Ichi sends Mitsu on alone via a travel service, and then heads for Doyama to confront Hikozo for causing him so much trouble. Tomegoro arrives in Doyama himself, bringing men to help Hikozo, and is disturbed to learn Zatoichi is supposed to join them. When Ichi arrives, he's convinced to strike a deal with Hikozo for his services, though the

two bosses secretly plot to get rid of him after the fight. Meanwhile, Jingoro and Hisa abduct Mitsu in order to get back at Zatoichi. With Mitsu in Tobei's grasp, Zatoichi must slyly play the two groups off of each other until he can deal with the treacherous bosses in his own way.

This rather straightforward entry in the "Blind Swordsman" series is almost an analogy for a game like Go, examining how one set of circumstances affects another, with each move leading to the next. Little Miss Mitsu is more a symbol than a character, representing something different to everyone. To the scheming bosses and their lackeys, she's a prized source of potential revenue, a salve for their lost face, a bargaining chip, or bait to catch Zatoichi. To Ichi, she's the lost love he can never have. One telling scene has a young samurai wishing to drop out of the chase for her, disgusted at the stupid waste of lives and effort. Otherwise, the film is a bit short in the bits of character that usually bring so much charm to the series, concentrating instead on the twists and turns of the plot. *AKA:* Zato*ichi Kenka Tabi; Zatoichi; Zatoichi and the Scoundrels; Blind Swordsman: Zatoichi Fighting Journey.* ♪♪♪

1963 87m/C *JP* Shintaro Katsu, Shiho Fujimura, Ryuzo Shimada, Reiko Fujiwara, Matasaburo Niwa,

Yutaka Nakamura, Shosaku Sugiyama, Yoshio Yoshida, Sonosuke Sawamura. *D:* Kimiyoshi Yasuda. *W:* Minoru Inuzuka, Kan Shimozawa (story). *C:* Shozo Honda. *M:* Akira Ifukube. **VHS, DVD**

Zatoichi the Fugitive

This fourth Zatoichi movie takes the blind yakuza far from his home territory, but still contains a link to his past. To have some fun at a festival and raise some cash, Ichi (Shintaro Katsu) enters a wresting contest and wins. His feats draw the recognition of minor mobster Kisuke Monju, who tries to kill him for the 10 ryu on his head. Ichi visits the man's mother, Maki Shimonida, who works at a nearby yakuza inn, to tell her of her son's death. The old woman understands the circumstances of the duel, but Yagiri, Tamamura, Unosuke, and Okishi—all yakuza bosses gathered for a feast to welcome Boss Sakichi's heir—are angry, and further raise the price on Zatoichi's head. Of course, with so many bosses in one town, intrigue abounds, and Ichi gets drawn into the tussle for territory. Yagiri conspires to have the unruly samurai Tanakura assassinate young Sakichi at the fire festival, and asks that innkeeper Shimazu help him out with Zatoichi in return for taking care of his old enemy. However, Shimazu's adopted daughter Nobu, who loves the Sakichi, has befriended the blind man, and he takes steps to see she's protected. Another wrinkle enters the cloth: Ichi's old flame Tane (Masayo Banri) is traveling with Tanakura. Under pressure, Sakichi and Tanakura use Tane to lure Zatoichi into a trap.

The climax brings the first instance of Zatoichi literally cutting loose on a large scale, racking up a body count of 47 (with a few more off screen) in the closing minutes. After his humiliation and heartbreak in the previous entry *(New Tale of Zatoichi)*, the blind masseur is righteously upset to be drawn into bloodshed and tragedy again. A clear turning point for Ichi is presented at the end, in which he takes on the mask of a clown to hide his pain from the world. From this film on, he enters into danger with supreme confidence—or Zen fatalism. *AKA: Masseur Ichi the Fugitive; Zatoichi Kyoto Tabi; Zatoichi, Crazy Journey.* ♪♪♪♡

1963 86m/C *JP* Shintaro Katsu, Miwa Takada, Toru Abe, Masayo Banri, Jutaro Hojo, Katsuhiko Kobayashi, Sachiko Murase, Junachiro Narita, Hiroshi Nawa. *D:* Tokuzo Tanaka. *W:* Seiji Hoshikawa. *C:* Chikashi Makiura. *M:* Akira Ifukube. **VHS, DVD**

Zatoichi the Outlaw

This 1967 entry in the long-running Blind Swordsman series was the first produced under the star's own banner, Katsu Productions. The lighthearted opening, which features traveling masseur Ichi (Shintaro Katsu) performing some blind man tricks, is undermined somewhat by some oddly dramatic and brash theme music. On his way into a village of Hagata, Ichi meets swordless ronin Shusui Ohara, who has been causing trouble in the region by teaching the farmers better techniques and advising them to give up vices. This doesn't sit well with Boss Tamizo, who has been squeezing the peasants with his casino for more than the soy they raise. Tamizo manipulates the famous visiting swordsman by asking him to visit Boss Asagoro (Rentaro Mikune) to collect a debt—actually a ransom for the boss's indebted citizens. Ichi is impressed with Asagoro, whom Tamizo is trying to goad into a fight so the stronger boss can take over the weaker's land.

When Tamizo sends men to kill some peasants, Ichi accidentally kills Sada, a friend among the attackers, pushing him too far. Zatoichi strikes, killing Tamizo and a half dozen of his men before moving on. After a time spent in a neighboring town, Ichi hears disturbing news from Hagata. It seems with his competition out of the way, Boss Asagoro took over the whole region, and has become a worse tyrant than his predecessors.

Zatoichi stalks through the last act of the film like a shadow of Death, instilling fear in all evildoers. While grimly recognizing his mistake, he realizes that perhaps removing a wicked man doesn't cure a wicked system. That doesn't stop him from cutting down a few snakes, though. Lacking the action and atmosphere of most entries in this series, this episode's story has a bit more depth to it. The leader Ohara is based on historical figure Yugaku Ohara, an agriculturalist and philosopher who revolutionized Japanese farming techniques, among other accomplishments. *AKA: Zatoichi Rooyaburi; Zatoichi Breaks Jail; The Blind Swordsman's Rescue; Zatoichi Escapes from Jail.* ♪♪♪

1967 95m/C *JP* Shintaro Katsu, Rentaro Mikune, Ko Nishimura, Yuko Hama, Kenjiro Ishiyama, Tatsuo Endo, Toshiyuki Hosokawa, Takuya Fujioka, Utako Kyo. *D:* Satsuo Yamamoto. *W:* Takehiro Nakajima, Koji Matsumoto, Kiyokata Saruwaka, Kan Shimozawa (story). *C:* Kazuo Miyagawa. *M:* Sei Ikeno. **VHS**

Zatoichi's Cane Sword

In the cold opening for this episode in Daiei's popular Blind Swordsman series, masseur Ichi (Shintaro Katsu) comes upon a dying man in a field named Shotaro from Ashikaga. The man dies before he can name his murderer, and Zatoichi kills a scavenging crow in frustration—an ill

omen. A cart full of folks on the way to Tonda for a New Year's celebration knocks Ichi into a ditch—or perhaps he fakes it to get a ride there with pretty singer Miss Haru. He tries to get himself into a game with diceman Umazo, but they're interrupted by the arrival of the Iwagoro gang, who have taken over the area and are now charging outrageous rates for merchants' space at the festival. Going to the casino, Ichi cheats the cheaters at dice, and draws the wrath of Iwagoro Agata (Tatsuo Endo). A display of swordsmanship draws the attention of old blacksmith Senzo (Eijiro Tono), who used to craft swords himself and recognizes the pedigree of Ichi's. He also senses a minute crack near the hilt that will cause it to snap sometime soon. Ichi gives the sword to Senzo as a keepsake.

Ichi finds work at an inn in Ashikaga, where his charm and skill quickly ingratiates him with the staff and guests. The inn's head maid turns out to be Boss Shintaro's daughter Shizu (Shiho Fujimura), who had to go to work there, along with her brother Seikichi, after her father was killed. Seikichi is only interested in scholarly pursuits, though Shizu demands he take up their father's responsibilities. Lord Kuwayama and his party are guests while he makes an inspection of the region, and Ichi is promised many assignments, but the man is a bastard who brings Iwagoro, and a lot of whores and gamblers into the inn—and makes advances on Shizu, too. Fearing the Inspector will back Seikichi as Boss, Iwagoro has the youth rubbed out by his man Monji. Ichi rushes to Senzo—who is Shizu's real father—to get a new sword he'd been making, but Monji has already killed the blacksmith and stolen the sword. And so, Zatoichi must go into battle with his old cane sword, knowing it could fail him at any time.

A familiar by-the-numbers Zatoichi plot diverges only in its focus on his sword, but benefits from Yasuda's deft direction and Katsu's engaging personality. Without his sword for much of the running time, Ichi has to find other ways to entertain the audience, and Katsu even gets to indulge in a bit of song and dance. *AKA: Zatoichi Tekka Tabi; The Blind Swordsman's Cane Sword.* ♫♫♫

1966 93m/C *JP* Shintaro Katsu, Shiho Fujimura, Yushihiko Aoyama, Kiyoko Suizenji, Eijiro Tono, Makoto Fujita, Tatsuo Endo. **D:** Kimiyoshi Yasuda. **W:** Ryozo Kasahara, Kan Shimozawa (story). **C:** Senkichiro Takeda. **M:** Ichiro Saito. **VHS**

Zatoichi's Flashing Sword

Blind swordsman Zatoichi (Shintaro Katsu) is pursued by a mob of angry yakuza thugs, one of whom shoots him in the back. He revives in the care of a fireworks maker from Edo, who tells him that he was saved by a woman traveler named Kuni. Ichi sets off for Kajikazawa to thank her personally. It turns out that Kuni is the daughter of village boss Bunkichi, who is in conflict with his neighboring Boss Yasagoro over rights to the ford concession for the river separating them. Stuttering Yasagoro schemes with Bunkichi's sister to take over the ford. When Kuni's black-sheep brother Seiruku—the man who shot Ichi!—returns, he's pursued by the Tengen gang. Yasagoro hires the Tengen, giving his side the muscle to force a fight.

Director Kazuo Ikehiro contributes some novel techniques to this entry in the series, most notably the bravura "fly cam" opening shot, which would be adopted for *Men in Black* 23 years later. But more subtly, he echoes Ichi's own condition by leaving certain events unseen, related only through dialogue or other action. This one also benefits from quite a bit of humor—Katsu's sharp performance sprouting easy laughs, especially in a running gag concerning thrifty Ichi and the fordman who has to carry him across the river several times. There's also a good deal of swordplay action, including the grim massacre at the end, which by this point was a series requirement. *AKA: Zatoichi Abaredako; Sword of Zatoichi.* ♫♫♫

1964 83m/C *JP* Shintaro Katsu, Naoko Kubo, Ryutaro Gomi, Bokuzen Hidari, Mayumi Nagisa, Yutaka Nakamura, Koh Sugita. **D:** Kazuo Ikehiro. **W:** Minoru Inuzuka, Shozaburo Asai, Kan Shimozawa (story). **C:** Yasukazu Takemura. **M:** Sei Ikeno. **VHS, DVD**

Zatoichi's Revenge

Dispatching a group of assassins on Azuba Bridge reminds Zatoichi (Shintaro Katsu) that his master Hikonoichi, who trained him as a masseur, lives nearby, and he decides to pay him a visit. But on arrival in the old man's village, Ichi learns that his master was recently robbed and murdered. Daughter Osayo Hikonoichi has been sent to a brothel to work off the family's debt. He makes a visit to the local gambling house to gather information, and while cleaning up their operation with some fancy sword work, befriends Dorosuke the dice thrower. Through Dorosuke he learns how Boss Tatsugoro, in association with the governor, has been falsifying tax records to put peasants in debt, forcing their daughters and wives into prostitution. Knowing the intendant will be making a secret inspection soon, Ichi uses the information to try to blackmail Tatsugoro into letting Osayo go. Instead, the gangster hires enforcer Koheita Kadokura to kill Ichi. This only makes the blind swordsman even angrier, and he heads for the boss's house to do some killing.

This is Akira Inoue's lone outing as director of a Zatoichi film, and he offers a few novel touches to the formula in this otherwise standard entry. He uses quite a bit of handheld camera, and often shoots scenes from overhead. Ifukube's score is also a change of pace, using a lot of Western guitar. A highlight is diceman Dorosuke's amusing imitation of Ichi near the end. *AKA: Zatoichi Nidangiri; The Blind Swordsman's Revenge.* 🎵🎵🎵

1964 84m/C *JP* Shintaro Katsu, Norihei Miki, Mikiko Tsubouchi, Takeshi Kato, Fujio Harumoto. **D:** Akira Inouchi. **W:** Minoru Inuzuka, Kan Shimozawa (story). **C:** Fujio Morita. **M:** Akira Ifukube. **VHS**

Zatoichi's Vengeance

A ronin cuts down a man in a field for a band of robbers. As the thugs move in, Zatoichi comes by and slays them all in the time it takes him to sneeze. The dying man gives the blind masseur a purse, saying only the names "Tamekichi" and "Taichi." Inside the purse, Ichi discovers crooked dice along with the money, and concludes the gang went after the man for cheating.

On the road, he meets a blind priest who begs a meal off him. The priest recognizes that, unlike himself, Ichi was not blind from birth and labels him an "in-betweener" who never feels at ease. He decides to follow the priest to Ichinomiya—a town without gambling—to take in their festival. There he literally bumps into a boy named Taichi, whose absent father is named Tamekichi. He lies to the boy and his grandmother, telling him the man became a successful chef in another town.

Boss Gonzo of Itabana has taken over, violently extorting from all the merchants. At the festival, Ichi's ears are too sensitive to enjoy the Thunder Drums performance. When some hooligans tease him, Ichi demonstrates his candle-on-a-sword trick, showing Taichi his skill.

Miss Cho, a kindhearted prostitute, hires Ichi for a massage. The next day her husband, the samurai who slew Tamekichi, comes to pay back the debt that put her in a brothel. To earn the money, he takes the assignment to kill Zatoichi.

The biwa-playing priest sees through Ichi. He says that though the masseur acts like he wants to get out of the corrupt town, he makes excuses to stick around, and more than Fate is guiding him into a fight with Gonzo and his men. The hardest part will be doing it without his bloodshed making him a hero to Taichi.

Katsu's acting is excellently understated in this solemn entry in the Blind Swordsman series. In one shot you can actually see him turn his ear to pick up an important line of dialogue. Most of the climactic fight takes place in near silhouette, and Zatoichi becomes downright frightening in his quiet fury. *AKA: Zatoichi No Uta Ga Kikoeru; The Blind Swordsman's Vengeance.* 🎵🎵🎵🎵

1966 82m/C *JP* Shintaro Katsu, Shigeru Amachi, Jun Hamamura, Mayumi Ogawa, Kei Sato. **D:** Tozuko Tanaka. **W:** Hajimi Takaiwa, Kan Shimozawa (story). **C:** Hiroshi Imai. **M:** Akira Ifukube. **VHS**

Zeram

Zeram (Mizuho Yoshida) is a big criminal psycho space alien that escapes from space prison, slaughtering dozens of guards. He heads toward Earth, lured there by bait set by sexy female bounty hunter Ilya (Yuko Moriyama) and her computer named Bob. They set up shop in Tokyo to lay a trap for him, creating a dimensional warp field that reproduces the district he's likely to arrive in (to protect the local populace) and attacking him with various weapons. Unfortunately, telephone repairmen Kamiya (Yukijiro Hotaru) and Tepphei (Kunihiko Iida) get caught in the trap, too, screwing up her plans. Besides being one tough mofo, Zeram has lots of weird weapons, too. The most outrageous of these is an ability to hatch grotesque slave ogres to do all the minor fighting for him. Plus, if he takes on major damage, he can regenerate.

Based on a popular manga series, this Japanese sci-fi flick mixes in elements inspired by *The Terminator, Aliens,* and various Japanese superhero and martial arts series and stirs it into a spicy, spunky stew of action, humor, and impressive special effects. The pair of comic-relief workmen actually become more endearing than annoying, helping out when the chips are down for our heroine. It's Bob the computer that's the annoyance, constantly offering sarcastic put-downs and short-circuiting just when he's needed most. Followed by two sequels. Yoshida would parlay lumbering around in the Zeram costume into a sweet gig: playing Godzilla in his latest adventure. *AKA: Zeiramu.* 🎵🎵🎵

1991 92m/C *JP* Yuko Moriyama, Kunihiko Iida, Yukijiro Hotaru, Mizuho Yoshida, Yukitomo Tochino, Naomi Enami, Sachi Kashino. **D:** Keita Amamiya. **W:** Keita Amamiya, Hajime Matsumoto. **C:** Hiroshi Kidokoro. **M:** Hirokazu Ohta. **VHS, DVD**

Zero Woman: The Accused

Mai Taichira stars as an assassin in modern Japan. But unlike most, she works on the side

Tsui Hark updates *Zu* for the *Storm Riders* generation: Patrick Tam hefts a sword in *Zu Warriors*.

of the law, for the top secret police division. Her latest job is to kill crooked lawyer Tadokoro (Tetsu Watanabe) in a public washroom, making it look like a suicide. She's not above taking the cash he offers before shooting him. Afterward, she reports to her boss in a barren little office, and is given the key to her next empty apartment. She befriends a young male prostitute named Mitsuru (Yujin Kitagawa). Her next assignment is a big one, gathering evidence against State Department official Seiji Kadokawa, who is selling government secrets. She befriends his mistress Reiko, and discovers the hiding place for his secrets. Ordered to kill him before he leaves the country, she decides to follow orders only if he doesn't plan to take Reiko with him. Smelling blood on Mitsuru, she follows him, and learns he has a secret of his own, one that could get her in deep trouble.

Unlike *Black Cat* and other hit-woman thrillers, *Zero Woman* is much more sordid and kinky. This is the first of a "Zero Woman" direct-to-video series released concurrently with a theatrical series, the first of which was made the previous year. Shot on a very low budget, it concentrates on drama rather than suspense or action. As such, it differs little from other independent films

about lost souls in the big city. Taichira gives a good performance, and it's nicely directed, but there's not much evidence given that she's the tough cop and capable assassin that she's supposed to be. **AKA:** *Zero Woman: Namae no nai Onna; The Woman with No Name.* 🎵🎵

1996 77m/C *JP* Mai Taichira, Yujin Kitagawa, Hajime Tsukumoto, Tetsu Watanabe, Shinji Yamashita, Eisaku Shindo. **D:** Daisuke Goto. **W:** Yuka Honcho, Tohru Shinohara (story). **C:** Yoichi Shiga. **M:** Takashi Nakayama. **VHS**

Zu Warriors

Tsui Hark's *Zu Warriors* is a confounding sequel/remake of his 1983 film *Shu Shan*, or *Warriors of the Magic Mountain*. The plot involves a race of ancient gods involved in a desperate battle with the forces of evil, and while at least one human being in the form of *Crouching Tiger, Hidden Dragon*'s enchanting Zhang Ziyi is involved, most of the action involves characters named King Sky (Ekin Cheng), Enigma (Cecilia Cheung), and Thunder (Patrick Tam), and rages from the Olympian

heights of the Zu Mountain range (actually a group of floating mountains drifting over the clouds) to a subterranean, hellish cave of blood in which hideous demons dwell only to emerge, tempt, and subvert the noble heroic gods of the overworld. The good guys are under attack by an evil force named Insomnia, but viewers will be suffering from something more akin to narcolepsy after sitting through this adventure.

Zu Warriors attempts to be a home run in terms of epic storytelling, heroic tragedy (as one hero must sacrifice himself on the altar of evil to save his best friend from the same fate), Hong Kong fighting action, and special effects, but as Tsui demonstrated in the incomprehensible action film *Time and Tide,* coherent storytelling is not his strong suit. Keeping track of who's doing what to whom is a difficult task in any film where subtitles have to be read, but here the challenge really becomes impossible as inhuman characters transform into even more inhuman characters, bullet through the clouds like superman, and lead armies of hapless Bronze Age humans into battle. The special effects and overall design is vivid, and the conception of one character as a kind of steel angel whose wings shoot gleaming razor blades at his opponents is dazzling, but with almost every shot boasting a major special effect the human element is quickly lost and even the legendary Hong Kong staple of kinetic fight choreography begins to get lost in the shuffle. While *Crouching Tiger* deliberately spoke to Western audiences, *Zu Warriors* is so steeped in ancient Chinese myths it's likely to confound anyone but a few comic-book obsessed scholars of the ancient world—which may explain why Miramax films cancelled a planned American theatrical release for this movie. —JB **AKA:** *Suk Saan Chuen; Shu Shan Chuan; The Legend of Zu.* 🎵🎵

2001 104m/C *JP* Ekin Cheng, Louis Koo, Cecilia Cheung, Patrick Tam, Kelly Lin, Zhang Ziyi, Jacky Wu, Sammo Hung, Lau Shun. **D:** Tsui Hark. **W:** Tsui Hark, Li Man Choi. **C:** Poon Hang-sang, Herman Yau, William Yim. **M:** Ricky Ho. **VHS, DVD**

Zu: Warriors of the Magic Mountain

Mount Zu is both the traditional home of mystical peoples, and also a strategic location in the campaigns of many mortal warlords. At the film's start, local factions are fighting over the mountain and surrounding territory. Two warriors (one from the red clan, another from the blue) decide that all this killing is for the birds, and set off on their own. Unfortunately, they're quickly surrounded by all four of the feuding factions. In a comical

scene, the two must pretend to fight each other to avoid being slaughtered by the rest. At the end of the battle, the blue warrior, Ti Ming-Chi (Yuen Biao), falls off the cliff and into the magical land of Zu. There, he is rescued from a haunted temple by master swordsman Ting Yin (Adam Cheng, with lots of magic and flying swordsman action). Ting is on a quest to defeat the Blood Demon before it can escape its bonds and enter the real world. Ti Ming-Chi decides to become Ting's pupil and travel with him. They meet up with a magical monk, Abbot Hsiao Yu (Damian Lau), and his disciple, Yi-Chen (Mang Hoi). But the Blood Demon is very powerful, and the quartet is saved only by the intervention of Longbrows (Sammo Hung), a powerful magician. The abbot is infected by the demon, and the group must try to rescue him while Longbrows uses his Sky Mirror to hold the demon at bay.

Two swords are required to destroy the demon's soul, and the heroes have only a limited time before the abbot is lost forever and the demon takes over the magical world of Zu. The demon is a master of magic and disguise. It sends its minions in many forms—including duplicates of the heroes and people they trust—to baffle and combat our heroes. The group travels to The Fort to seek the help of the Countess (Brigitte Lin). She does her best to cure the monk, and in the process the Countess and Ting fall in love. Ting returns to his quest, but is infected with the blood of the demon. Now *he* needs the Countess's help, but—depleted from her previous efforts—she cannot cure him. The Countess decides to freeze the Fort, so that the evil cannot escape. But, evil Ting gets away, as do the apprentices and Abbot.

All this running back and forth has taken valuable time. So those remaining set out for Heaven's Blade Peak—the border between good and evil, to find the swords needed to defeat the blood demon. They find them in the possession of Li-I-Chi (Judy Ongg), a swordswoman/goddess. Unfortunately, evil Ting also arrives—but Heaven's Blade, a god-warrior, bars his way. There at the nexus, the forces of good and evil have a final confrontation. Apprentices Ti-Ming-Chi and Yi-Chen have a critical part to play in this battle. The green Sword of Earth and the purple Sword of Heaven must be united and all (even the mortals) must fight together against Ting and his evil master.

Probably the best of the flying-swordsman movies, *Zu* is a must-see classic for anyone interested in the magical kung fu genre. Primitive by today's f/x standards, this film makes up for it with cleverness and enthusiasm. The actors are good, as are the costumes and sets. The fanciful nature of the flick makes up for the somewhat repetitive and incoherent plot. In some ways, this film is cooler than the newer, slicker *Legend of Zu.* This is the kind of film that

Tsui Hark made his reputation (as the Chinese Steve Spielberg) on. Check it out, it's a lot of fun. —SS **AKA:** *San Suk Saan Kim Hap; Xin Shu Shan Jian Xia; Zu: Warriors from the Magic Mountain; Warriors from the Magic Mountain; Zu Time Warriors; Zu Warriors.* 🎵🎵🎵

1983 97m/C *HK* Yuen Biao, Adam Cheng, Brigitte Lin, Sammo Hung, Mang Hoi, Norman Tsui, Damian Lau, Corey Yuen, Chung Fat, Dick Wei, Shih Kwan-li, Fung Lee, Tsui Hark, Judy Ongg, Moon Lee, Fung Hark-On. **D:** Tsui Hark. **W:** Shui Chung-yuet, Szeto Cheuk-hon. **C:** Bill Wong. **VHS, DVD**

MST3K Goes to Japan

In the mood for cheese? In the late 1980s, successful comedian Joel Hodgson took a step back from the national showbiz scene and reassessed what he wanted to do with his life and talent. One of the first things he did was return to his home town of Hopkins, Minnesota, and create this local TV program to fill up a Saturday afternoon movie slot on KTMA Channel 23. The concept: Joel is a janitor working for a big corporation. As part of an experiment, and just to be mean, his boss Dr. Clayton Forrester (Trace Beaulieu) shanghais him into space to live on a satellite (dubbed the "Satellite of Love" in an offhand Lou Reed reference that stuck). There, he is subjected to the worst movies Forrester can dig up, to "test his reactions." Handy Joel builds some robots to keep him company, inadvertently disassembling the machinery that could have allowed him more control over the experiment. While the movies run, Joel and his robot pals make continuous (and continuously hilarious) commentary in silhouette at the bottom of the screen, and have lots of silly adventures in and out of the theatre. After one season, the show was picked up by Comedy Central (and later the Sci-Fi Channel) for national cable broadcast, gathering millions of loyal fans.

What does a robot puppet show have to do with Asian cinema? Plenty! For almost the entire first season, and in many subsequent episodes, Forrester unleashed a collection of less-than-perfect Japanese science-fiction features, many from the Sandy Frank dubbing factory. Now, *Mystery Science Theater* is probably the only way most folks have seen these pictures. Not such a bad thing in many cases, and since many of them have had a spotty home-video history, and though some features had to be edited, others were shown in more complete form than previously seen. However, *Mystery Science Theater* was never meant to be a movie with comedy accompaniment, but a comedy show with a movie in it. For some reason, *MST3K* never tackled any old kung fu movies. Some things truly are sacred.

Experiment #K04: Gamera vs. Barugon

The most interesting thing about watching episodes from the first season of *MST3K* is to see how crude it was, making the later episodes look positively slick. The Satellite looks like various kitchen implements glued together, and shaggy Joel looks like he just woke up and decided to be on TV. Four weeks into the series, there wasn't yet any kind of firm format in place, and the jokes were less frequent (and not as funny), but then how easy is it to make fun of a movie in which a case of athlete's foot nearly destroys Japan. This second Gamera movie makes for perfect fodder for *MST*-treatment, and half of the original Gamera movies would make it onto the show. The show was already gaining fans, as evidenced by recordings played from their answering machine (not all of which are positive). Responding to one viewer's request, they decide to feature more Chapstick on the show.

1988/66 97m/C *US/JP* Joel Hodgson. *D:* Vince Rodriguez. *W:* Joel Hodgson, Trace Beaulieu, Josh Weinstein, Jim Mallon, Kevin Murphy. *C:* Kevin Murphy. *M:* Charlie Erickson, Joel Hodgson. **VHS, DVD**

Experiment #K05: Gamera

In this first holiday episode, robot Crow has been cryogenically frozen for decoration in place of a Christmas tree, and robot Servo is nowhere to be found, so Joel is uncomfortably solo in the theatre watching the first Gamera movie, AKA *Giant Monster Gamera*. The robots show up a bit during breaks, but Joel looks as lonely as little Kenny without his turtle Tibby.

1988/65 97m/C/BW *US/JP* Joel Hodgson. *D:* Vince Rodriguez. *W:* Joel Hodgson, Trace Beaulieu, Josh Weinstein, Jim Mallon, Kevin Murphy. *C:* Kevin Murphy. *M:* Charlie Erickson, Joel Hodgson. **VHS, DVD**

Experiment #K06: Gamera vs. Gaos

Joel continues to call the giant turtle "Gameron" for the third straight week and the viewers complain about too much Gamera. What's with those people? It's explained that the movies are controlled by the evil scientists Dr. Forrester and Dr. Lawrence Erhardt (Josh Weinstein). At least Servo joins Joel in the theatre, giving him somebody to talk to. The Sandy Frank version of the film pads out the running time by copying one of the main monster battles from the middle of the film and pasting it at the start. Crow still appears to be frozen. Joel puts Servo through puberty to change his annoying voice. 🦴🦴

1988/67 97m/C *US/JP* Joel Hodgson. **D:** Vince Rodriguez. **W:** Joel Hodgson, Trace Beaulieu, Josh Weinstein, Jim Mallon, Kevin Murphy. **C:** Kevin Murphy. **M:** Charlie Erickson, Joel Hodgson. **VHS, DVD**

Experiment #K07: Gamera vs. Zigra

Crow is finally unfrozen, just in time for the New Year's Eve celebration on Channel 23. With a full complement of commentators, the show peps up considerably. Even Forrester and Erhardt make an appearance to taunt Joel with reports of a rival Russian experiment, as the Soviets launch their own comedian into space. Servo proclaims the part where Gamera makes a xylophone out of Zigra "the worst scene in motion picture history." Joel and the 'bots start work on their own version of the Gamera theme song. 🦴🦴

1988/71 97m/C *US/JP* Joel Hodgson. **D:** Vince Rodriguez. **W:** Joel Hodgson, Trace Beaulieu, Josh Weinstein, Jim Mallon, Kevin Murphy. **C:** Kevin Murphy. **M:** Charlie Erickson, Joel Hodgson. **VHS, DVD**

Experiment #K08: Gamera vs. Guiron

Joel cuts his hair in honor of their fifth straight Gamera movie—one of the stranger, more entertaining ones—delivered direct from Forrester and Erhardt. During a break, Crow is knocked out and dreams he switched places with the mad scientists, prompting a discussion about dreams and robots. Joel cracks up during the suspenseful shaving scene. 🦴🦴

1988/69 97m/C *US/JP* Joel Hodgson, Trace Beaulieu, Josh Weinstein. **D:** Vince Rodriguez. **W:** Joel Hodgson, Trace Beaulieu, Josh Weinstein, Jim Mallon, Kevin Murphy. **C:** Kevin Murphy. **M:** Charlie Erickson, Joel Hodgson. **VHS, DVD**

Experiment #K12: Fugitive Alien

Actor/writer Trace Beaulieu appears to have been out of town again for this episode. Dr. Erhardt calls Dr. Forrester, who is at a mad scientist convention in Las Vegas while Joel and the 'bots suffer through this feature version of the *Starwolf* TV series (which is at least a bit more interesting *Star Wars* rip-off than *Battlestar Galactica*). Servo and Gypsy have disassembled fellow robot Crow for some reason (or none). Joel is so concerned he holds a dance contest. 🦴🦴

1989/78 97m/C *US/JP* Joel Hodgson, Trace Beaulieu, Josh Weinstein. **D:** Vince Rodriguez. **W:** Joel Hodgson, Trace Beaulieu, Josh Weinstein, Jim Mallon, Kevin Murphy. **C:** Kevin Murphy. **M:** Charlie Erickson, Joel Hodgson. **VHS, DVD**

Experiment #K14: Mighty Jack

The mad scientists are so wrapped up in an argument over changing their image that they nearly forget to hold the experiment. The robots weld themselves together, but it's just "not funny without the lingerie." The 'bots have to admit that they don't know what humans think is funny, which may explain some of their comments during this futuristic submarine spy movie. Joel sometimes regrets giving them free will. The first fan club newsletter is announced and some guy sent in a photo of his girlfriend, calling her a "magnificent pagan beast." 🦴🦴

1989/68 97m/C *US/JP* Joel Hodgson, Trace Beaulieu, Josh Weinstein. **W:** Joel Hodgson, Trace Beaulieu, Josh Weinstein, Jim Mallon, Kevin Murphy, Faye Burkholder. **C:** Kevin Murphy. **M:** Charlie Erickson, Joel Hodgson. **VHS, DVD**

Experiment #K17: Time of the Apes

The robots refuse to tell Joel that the mad scientists are calling and enter the theatre without him to watch this witless juvenile sci-fi epic from Tsuburaya Productions. Not as disconcerting as Joel watching Gamera without the robots, but his absence puts some mystery in the Science Theater 3000. 🦴🦴

1989/75 97m/C *US/JP* Trace Beaulieu, Josh Weinstein. **D:** Vince Rodriguez. **W:** Joel Hodgson, Trace Beaulieu, Josh Weinstein, Jim Mallon, Kevin Murphy, Brian Funk. **C:** Kevin Murphy. **M:** Charlie Erickson, Joel Hodgson. **VHS, DVD**

Experiment #K21: Legend of the Dinosaurs

Is Joel Hodgson dead? That's the question asked by viewers who saw experiment #K17, in which the host did not appear, prompting the mad scientists to consider cashing in with a "Joel is dead" publicity stunt. Joel uses a special effect to make himself look tiny. Later, he and the 'bots distract themselves from the bad dinosaur movie by playing with Cambot's sitcom simulator. The last show of the season turned out to be the last show for local station KTMA in Minneapolis/St. Paul. 🦴🦴

1989/77 97m/C *US/JP* Joel Hodgson, Trace Beaulieu, Josh Weinstein. **D:** Vince Rodriguez. **W:** Joel Hodgson, Trace Beaulieu, Josh Weinstein, Jim Mallon, Kevin Murphy, Brian Funk. **C:** Kevin Murphy. **M:** Charlie Erickson, Joel Hodgson. **VHS, DVD**

Experiment #212: Godzilla vs. Megalon

After their first season on KTMA in Minneapolis/St. Paul, somebody got the bright idea to syndicate *MST3K* across the country. Efforts in that direction failed, but the show was picked up by the next best thing: basic cable. The show was revamped with still-crude but more stylish f/x and art direction, updated robots and models, and fresh energy. But it remained at heart the same endearing, sassy, cow-town puppet show, running for the next several years on the Comedy Channel/Comedy Central. One of the new features of the show is the Invention Exchange, in this instance a competition between Hodgson (now "Joel Robinson") and the Mad Scientists (Forrester is now assisted by "TV's Frank" Conniff) for nifty Halloween costumes. They didn't get back to the Japanese flicks until they were in full swing in season 2, with a pair of Godzilla movies. Not really, really *good* Godzilla movies, of course. Inspired by the movie, Tom and Crow cover up for some kind of shifty photo club by creating monster ideas of their own. Clips from the movie are turned into a promo for a new TV show—*Rex Dart, Eskimo Spy*. Later, everybody takes a popcorn break, Joel gives the 'bots new monster arms, and the Jet Jaguar song is translated for karaoke. 🦴🦴🦴

1990/73 97m/C *US/JP* Joel Hodgson, Trace Beaulieu, Jim Mallon, Kevin Murphy, Frank Conniff. **D:** Jim Mallon. **W:** Michael J. Nelson, Trace Beaulieu, Frank Conniff, Joel Hodgson, Jim Mallon, Kevin Murphy. **M:** Charlie Erickson, Joel Hodgson, Michael J. Nelson. **VHS, DVD**

Experiment #213: Godzilla vs. the Sea Monster

For their next experiment, the Mad Scientists send what they think is another lousy cheese-period Godzilla flick, when this one (AKA *Ebirah, Horror of the Deep*) is actually a fairly fun and engaging—if juvenile—monster adventure movie. However, this curious version is a Film Ventures video release, a feature of which is their usual semisolarized-looking video-generated opening credits montage. The print looks awful, but contains some footage usually cut from other U.S. versions, while missing others. Invention Exchange: Mind Control and Doggie Squeeze Toy Guitars. Joel and the 'bots sing the "Godzilla Genealogy Bop." Later, Joel constructs miniatures of famous landmarks out of common items, and the robots wreck them for his own good. A guest appearance by Mothra always earns extra points, especially when she brings along the twins. In fact, Crow and Tom spoof the twin fairies, but their chants bring Mothra to visit the Satellite. 🦴🦴🦴🦴

1990/66 97m/C *US/JP* Joel Hodgson, Trace Beaulieu, Jim Mallon, Kevin Murphy, Frank Conniff. **D:** Jim Mallon. **W:** Michael J. Nelson, Trace Beaulieu, Frank Conniff, Joel Hodgson, Jim Mallon, Kevin Murphy, Faye Burkholder. **M:** Charlie Erickson, Joel Hodgson, Michael J. Nelson. **VHS, DVD**

Experiment #302: Gamera

During their third season on Comedy Central, the Best Brains team decided that they could re-use the package of flicks obtained for the first season on KTMA for their now-national audience, this time with better jokes. Well, some of the same jokes, but at least this time Servo and Crow are in the theatre with Joel. Plus, by this point the shenanigans of the cast were more directly related to the movies. Thus, we're back to *Giant Monster Gamera* again. Invention Exchange: Endless Salad and Bird Cage Vacuum. Tom Servo sings a sweet ballad to his spinning turtle Tibby, until Crow ruins it. The robots agree in their hatred for Gamera's little pal Kenny, however, and invite the viewers to join in. Gamera (Mike Nelson) drops by to reveal that he's just using Kenny. Joel is irked to note the similarity of the movie's "Plan Z" to his own predicament. 🦴🦴🦴

1991/65 97m/C *US/JP* Joel Hodgson, Trace Beaulieu, Jim Mallon, Kevin Murphy, Frank Conniff,

Michael J. Nelson. **D:** Jim Mallon. **W:** Michael J. Nelson, Trace Beaulieu, Frank Conniff, Joel Hodgson, Jim Mallon, Kevin Murphy, Bridget Jones, Lisa Scheretz, Colleen Henjum. **C:** Kevin Murphy. **M:** Charlie Erickson, Joel Hodgson, Michael J. Nelson. **VHS, DVD**

Experiment #304: Gamera vs. Barugon

This time they managed to present the Gamera movies in the proper order. The 'bots are computer nerds. Invention Exchange: Animatronic Pop Can and Bubble Thighmaster. Servo narrates a commercial for a monster-action play set. Later, the 'bots are two middle-aged ladies enjoying a lunch at TGI Tokyo's—a very odd sketch. After the experiment, we sample selections from the Monster Book Club. The writers warm up quite well to these Gamera movies, bringing the series to an acme of creativity. 🦴🦴🦴🦴

1991/66 97m/C *US/JP* Joel Hodgson, Trace Beaulieu, Jim Mallon, Kevin Murphy, Frank Conniff. **D:** Jim Mallon. **W:** Michael J. Nelson, Trace Beaulieu, Frank Conniff, Joel Hodgson, Jim Mallon, Kevin Murphy, Bridget Jones, Lisa Scheretz, Colleen Henjum, Jef Maynard. **M:** Charlie Erickson, Joel Hodgson, Michael J. Nelson. **VHS, DVD**

Experiment #306: Time of the Apes

Joel uses Servo's head to play T-ball, breaking a window—a real problem in outer space. Invention Exchange: Cellulite Phone and Miracle Baby Growth Wonder Formula. Forgotten Running Gag: Joel punishes Crow by ripping off his arms. Servo narrates the short "Why Doesn't Johnny Care?" The cast re-enacts the Scopes Monkey Trial. Crow narrates an ape fashion show. After the movie finally ends, everyone dances to the Sandy Frank theme. The combination of an extra dopey movie with a small army of writers produced a lively, joke-stuffed episode. Plus, this is Joel's first time seeing the movie, having been mysteriously absent the first time. 🦴🦴🦴

1991/75 97m/C *US/JP* Joel Hodgson, Trace Beaulieu, Jim Mallon, Kevin Murphy, Frank Conniff, Timothy Scott. **D:** Jim Mallon. **W:** Michael J. Nelson, Trace Beaulieu, Frank Conniff, Joel Hodgson, Jim Mallon, Kevin Murphy, Colleen Henjum, Bridget Jones, Lynn-Anne Freise, Craig Tollifson, Tom Wedor, Jann L. Johnson, Alexandra Carr. **M:** Charlie Erickson, Joel Hodgson, Michael J. Nelson. **VHS, DVD**

Experiment #308: Gamera vs. Gaos

The astro-nuts start the show featuring this Sandy Frank re-release of *Gamera vs. Gyaos* stuck on raspy-voiced celebrities. Invention Exchange: Self-image Printer and Tissue-dispensing Fax Machine. During the break, the 'bots interrupt Joel's arts-and-crafts project to make a Gyaos mask, earning a time out. Later, an ill-conceived production of "Gamera-dammerung" fortunately isn't allowed to get very far. The movie is likened to an act on the *Ed Sullivan Show,* and viewers are asked to send in suggestions of good ways to kill Gyaos. Paul Chaplin joins the contributing writers—he'd eventually become a much bigger part of the show. 🦴🦴🦴🦴

1991/67 97m/C *US/JP* Joel Hodgson, Trace Beaulieu, Jim Mallon, Kevin Murphy, Frank Conniff. **D:** Jim Mallon. **W:** Michael J. Nelson, Trace Beaulieu, Frank Conniff, Joel Hodgson, Colleen Henjum, Kevin Murphy, Bridget Jones, Jim Mallon, Paul Chaplin. **C:** Kevin Murphy. **M:** Charlie Erickson, Joel Hodgson, Michael J. Nelson. **VHS, DVD**

Experiment #310: Fugitive Alien

Joel dresses the robots as farm animals for a "life simulation." Invention Exchange: Eye-Ear-Nose-Throat Drop Mask and Musical Chair. A&E's Jack Perkins (Mike Nelson) introduces the TV episode compilation. With its silly costumes (dig those blonde wigs!), clunky f/x, Joe Shishido, and plenty of mindless action, *Fugitive Alien* makes for primo MySTing material. During the break, everybody digs into their box from their last hat party. Joel freaks out the robots by playing Captain Joe, then uses Syd Fields's screenplay model to explain the plot's dynamics. 🦴🦴🦴

1991/78/86 97m/C *US/JP* Joel Hodgson, Trace Beaulieu, Jim Mallon, Kevin Murphy, Frank Conniff, Michael J. Nelson. **D:** Jim Mallon. **W:** Michael J. Nelson, Trace Beaulieu, Frank Conniff, Joel Hodgson, Colleen Henjum, Kevin Murphy, Bridget Jones, Jim Mallon, Paul Chaplin. **M:** Charlie Erickson, Joel Hodgson, Michael J. Nelson. **VHS, DVD**

Experiment #312: Gamera vs. Guiron

The robots trade lunches, displaying the nifty *MST3k* lunch boxes available from Best Brains. Invention Exchange: Rorschach Centerfolds and Collapsing Garbage Can. This entry in the Gamera series detailing the adventures of Akio and Tom is one of the goofiest and most fun, translating to perfect MySTing. The print is so washed-out that it's nearly black and white. There's a lot of singing in this episode, including an incorrect translation of the Gamera theme song. Joel dresses Servo as Guiron and uses him for an illusion where he saws Crow in half. There is a presentation that explains how Richard Burton came to be in both *Gamera vs. Guiron* and TV's *The Fall Guy*. Lounge lizard Michael Feinstein (Mike Nelson, looking more like Ray Liotta) drops by Deep 13 labs to regale us with songs and anecdotes. 🦴🦴🦴

1991/69 97m/C *US/JP* Joel Hodgson, Trace Beaulieu, Jim Mallon, Kevin Murphy, Frank Conniff, Michael J. Nelson. **D:** Jim Mallon. **W:** Michael J. Nelson, Trace Beaulieu, Frank Conniff, Joel Hodgson, Colleen Henjum, Kevin Murphy, Bridget Jones, Jim Mallon, Paul Chaplin. **M:** Charlie Erickson, Joel Hodgson, Michael J. Nelson. **VHS, DVD**

Experiment #314: Mighty Jack

This episode begins with a chaotic disaster aboard the Satellite of Love—which of course turns out to be just more horseplay. Invention Exchange: Formal Scuba Flippers and Earmuffs That Look Like Ears. Inspired by the movie title, the robots market a new robot dog food. Then they capture Joel as if he's the Mr. Atari character in the movie. Joel decides to pitch some movie ideas underwater. They finish off the film by singing that old sea chantey "Slow the Plot Down." 🦴🦴🦴

1991/68 97m/C *US/JP* Joel Hodgson, Trace Beaulieu, Jim Mallon, Kevin Murphy, Frank Conniff, Michael J. Nelson. **D:** Jim Mallon. **W:** Michael J. Nelson, Trace Beaulieu, Frank Conniff, Joel Hodgson, Colleen Henjum, Kevin Murphy, Bridget Jones, Jim Mallon, Paul Chaplin. **M:** Charlie Erickson, Joel Hodgson, Michael J. Nelson. **VHS, DVD**

Experiment #316: Gamera vs. Zigra

A root-beer kegger (complete with Gamera pinata full of garbage) is ruined by the arrival of another Gamera flick. Invention Exchange: Three Stooges Gun and Crow T. Robot Shish kabob. Servo and Crow have built a scale model of Gamera that shows his inner workings. As if that wasn't enough, Joel gives the robots an art-therapy project to build dioramas based on Gamera movies. During the next break, the kegger is interrupted again by Gamera himself, with those idiot kids Kenny (Michael J. Nelson) and Ellen (Bridget Jones) on his back. Having finally finished their

final Gamera movie *ever,* everyone does a rendition of the Gamera theme song. This episode benefits from extra Gamera content. 🦴🦴🦴🦴

1991/71 97m/C *US/JP* Joel Hodgson, Trace Beaulieu, Jim Mallon, Kevin Murphy, Frank Conniff, Michael J. Nelson, Bridget Jones. **D:** Jim Mallon. **W:** Michael J. Nelson, Trace Beaulieu, Frank Conniff, Joel Hodgson, Colleen Henjum, Kevin Murphy, Bridget Jones, Jim Mallon, Paul Chaplin. **M:** Charlie Erickson, Joel Hodgson, Michael J. Nelson. **VHS, DVD**

Experiment #318: Star Force: Fugitive Alien 2

Hey, they never got to this *Fugitive Alien* sequel back in Season K, so here it is for the first time. Tom and Crow begin by having an ironic argument over the difference between puppets and costumes. Invention Exchange: Big Noses and Big Heads. The movie is so bad that Servo gets sick and falls apart, resulting in lots of noise and hand-held camera work. The guys play with their Captain Joe action figure, as Ken, Barbie, and Raphael the turtle stage an intervention. Later they sing a medley of tunes based on the *Star Force* soundtrack. The robots consider sending the Mad Scientists some experiment suggestions from *Leonard Maltin's Movie Guide.* 🦴🦴🦴

1991/78/86 97m/C *US/JP* Joel Hodgson, Trace Beaulieu, Jim Mallon, Kevin Murphy, Frank Conniff, Michael J. Nelson. **D:** Jim Mallon. **W:** Michael J. Nelson, Trace Beaulieu, Frank Conniff, Joel Hodgson, Colleen Henjum, Kevin Murphy, Bridget Jones, Jim Mallon, Paul Chaplin. **M:** Charlie Erickson, Joel Hodgson, Michael J. Nelson. **VHS, DVD**

Experiment #816: Prince of Space

It took awhile to get back to Japanese cinema. Hearing that Forrester was planning to kill him, Joel Robinson found a way to escape from the Satellite, and was replaced in the experiment by hapless temp worker Mike Nelson. The Mad Scientists eventually lost their jobs, only to be replaced by Forrester's mother Pearl (Mary Jo Pehl). Robot Gypsy somehow learned to take control of the Satellite's navigation. Now being chased by Pearl Forrester across the universe, Tom Servo and Crow play Hound and Bear and things get out of hand. Bobo (a stooge Pearl picked up on a planet of evolved apes) falls into a wormhole during his walk, so Pearl follows him to keep him from causing trouble, towing the SoL with her van while torturing Mike and the robots with this juvenile Japanese sci-fi fea-

ture. Mike and the 'bots are running on different time lines, answering questions before they're asked. Later, Mike becomes a robot that resembles a ventriloquist dummy. Then next break finds them all in a sylvan glen, which gives Mike Nelson a poignant moment of homesickness— a rare semiserious note for the series. 🦴🦴🦴

1997/70 94m/C *US/JP* Mike Nelson, Bill Corbett, Kevin Murphy, Mary Jo Pehl, Bridget Jones, Patrick Brantseg. *D:* Michael J. Nelson. *W:* Mike Nelson, etc. *C:* Jeff Stonehouse. *M:* Charles Erickson, Joel Hodgson. **VHS, DVD**

Experiment #819: Invasion of the Neptune Men

The inhabitants of the SoL become overly concerned about Mike's eyelash mites, and send tiny robots to declare war on them. Meanwhile, on a Romanesque planet below, Pearl is miffed to find that the natives worship her idiot ape assistant as a god, and works off her ire by forcing the crew to watch this Japanese superhero movie. On break, the robots perform a kabuki version of *The Sunshine Boys*. Tom Servo contracts "Roji Panty Complex" from watching the movie. The movie nearly breaks the group, but a visit from the Phantom Dictator of Krankor, from the *Prince of Space* episode, cheers everyone up. Afterward, Crow uses a hastily built suggestion box as a way of venting his wrath at everything Japanese. 🦴🦴🦴

1997/64? 94m/C *US/JP* Mike Nelson, Bill Corbett, Kevin Murphy, Mary Jo Pehl, Bridget Jones, Patrick Brantseg. *D:* Michael J. Nelson. *W:* Mike Nelson, etc. *C:* Jeff Stonehouse. *M:* Charles Erickson, Joel Hodgson. **VHS, DVD**

Dragon Connections

As I said in the Intro—wait, you've read the Intro, right? You're not one of those people who skips to the end of the book to see how it comes out, are you? Well, however you got here, I said before that this book is the result of wanting more, and here in the back pages we're giving it to you. To start with, here's a whole bunch of other places trying to keep up with all that Asian cinema madness on the other side of the globe.

Books

Akira Kurosawa: Something Like an Autobiography
Akira Kurosawa. 1983. Random House.

The Anime Encyclopedia: A Guide to Japanese Animation Since 1917
Jonathan Clements and Helen McCarthy. 2001. Stone Bridge Press.

Anime from Akira to Princess Mononoke: Experiencing Contemporary Japanese Animation
Susan Jolliffe Napier. 2001. Palgrave Macmillan.

The Asian Film Industry
John A. Lent. 1990. University of Texas Press.

At Full Speed: Hong Kong Cinema in a Borderless World
Esther C.M. Yau. 2001. University of Minnesota Press.

Bruce Lee: Artist of Life
John Little. 2001. Charles E. Tuttle.

City on Fire: Hong Kong Cinema
Lisa Odham Stokes and Michael Hoover. 1999. Verso Books.

A Critical History and Filmography of Toho's Godzilla Series
David Kalat. 1997. McFarland & Co.

Dying for Action: Life and Films of Jackie Chan
Renee Witterstatter. 1997. Warner Books.

The Emperor and the Wolf: The Lives and Films of Akira Kurosawa and Toshiro Mifune
Stuart Galbraith IV. 2002. Faber & Faber.

The Essential Jackie Chan Sourcebook
Jeff Rovin and Kathy Tracy. 1997. Pocket Books.

Great Martial Arts Movies: From Bruce Lee to Jackie Chan and More
Ric Meyers. 2000. Citadel Press.

Hollywood East: Hong Kong Movies and the People Who Made Them
Stefan Hammond. 2000. McGraw Hill.

Hong Kong Action Cinema
Bey Logan. 1995. Overlook Press.

Hong Kong Cinema: The Extra Dimensions
Stephen Teo. 1998. British Film Institute.

The Hong Kong Filmography, 1977–1997
John Charles. 2000. McFarland & Co.

I Am Jackie Chan: My Life in Action
Jackie Chan with Jeff Yang. 1999. Random House.

Japanese Cinema Encyclopedia: Horror—Fantasy—Science Fiction
Thomas Weisser and Yuko Mihara Weisser. 1997. Vital Sounds Inc.

Japanese Cinema: The Essential Handbook
Thomas Weisser and Yuko Mihara Weisser. 1996. Vital Sounds Inc.

Japanese Science Fiction, Fantasy and Horror Films
Stuart Galbraith IV. 1994. McFarland & Co.

Japan's Favorite Mon-star (The Unauthorized Biography of Godzilla)
Steve Ryfle. 1999. ECW Press.

Jet Li: A Biography
James Robert Parrish. 2002. Thunder's Mouth Press.

Mondo Macabro: Weird & Wonderful Cinema Around the World
Peter Tombs. 1998. St. Martin's.

Monsters Are Attacking Tokyo! The Incredible World of Japanese Fantasy Films
Stuart Galbraith IV. 1998. Feral House.

The Official Godzilla Compendium
J.D. Lees and Marc Cerasini. 1998. Random House.

The Overlook Film Encyclopedia: Horror
Phil Hardy. 1993. Overlook Press.

The Overlook Film Encyclopedia: Science Fiction
Phil Hardy. 1995. Overlook Press.

Planet Hong Kong: Popular Cinema and the Art of Entertainment
David Bordwell. 2000. Harvard University Press.

Sex and Zen & a Bullet in the Head: The Essential Guide to Hong Kong's Mindbending Films
Stefan Hammond and Mike Wilkins; foreword by Jackie Chan. 1996. Simon & Schuster.

TokyoScope: The Japanese Cult Film Companion
Patrick Macias. 2001. Cadence Books.

The Unauthorized Jackie Chan Encyclopedia: From "Project A" to "Shanghai Noon" and Beyond
John Corcoran. 2002. McGraw Hill/Contemporary Books.

VideoHound's Cult Flicks & Trash Pics
Carol Schwartz. 2002 (2nd edition). Visible Ink Press.

Magazines

Animerica
Viz Communications, Inc.
PO Box 77010
San Francisco, CA 94107

12 issues: $50 in the U.S., $60 in Canada/Mexico, $90 elsewhere.

24 issues: $95 in the U.S., $115 in Canada/Mexico, $170 elsewhere.

Asian Cult Cinema
Vital Books
PO Box 16-1919
Miami, FL 33116

6 issues: $30 in the U.S.; $40 elsewhere (surface), $50 (air).

Cinescape
PO Box 617
Mount Morris, IL 61054-0617
1-800-342-3592

12 issues: $39.95 in the U.S.

G-Fan
Daikaiju Enterprises Ltd.
Box 3468
Steinbach, MB, Canada R0A 2A0

6 issues: $24 in the U.S., $30 elsewhere.

12 issues: $48 in the U.S.

Giant Robot
Giant Robot Media
PO Box 642053
Los Angeles, CA 90064

4 issues: $15 in the U.S.; $32 elsewhere (boat), $42 (air).

M.A.M.A.
Martial Arts Movie Associates
William Connolly
1200 N. June St., Apt. 207
Hollywood, CA 90038

Single issue: $3.50 in the U.S., $4.50 elsewhere.

Subscription: $15 in the U.S., $20 elsewhere.

Oriental Cinema
Draculina
PO Box 587
Glen Carbon, IL 62034

4 issues: $24 in the U.S., $32 elsewhere (air).

Screen Power
PO Box 1989
Bath BA2 2YE
United Kingdom

4 issues: $45 in the U.S.

Video Watchdog
PO Box 5283
Cincinnati, OH 45205-0283
1-800-275-8395
(513)471-8989
(513)471-8248 (fax)
videowd@aol.com

6 issues: $27 in the U.S. (bulk), $38 (first class); $36 elsewhere (ground), $47 (air).

12 issues: $48 in the U.S. (bulk), $70 (first class); $66 elsewhere (ground), $88 (air).

24 issues: $90 in the U.S. (bulk), $130 (first class); $125 elsewhere (ground), $168 (air).

Web Sites

Asian Cinema—General

Adrenafilm—der Mailorderspezialist fuer Hong Kong, Japan und Taiwan
www.adrenafilm.de

Alaan's Kung Fu Movie Reviews
alaan.tripod.com/kungfu/movies.htm

Alex in Wonderland—Asian Films
www.alex-in-wonderland.com/Movie Reviews/AsianFilmIndex.html

Another Hong Kong Movie Page
www.kowloonside.com

Asian Film Connections
www.usc.edu/isd/archives/asianfilm/

Asian Movie Force
www.angelfire.com/realm/hkheat/

Asian Movies Web Page
www.cybertron.net/~powers/

Beijing Video
www.beijingvideo.com

A Better Tomorrow
www.abtdvd.com/index.htm

Black Belt Theater
www.blackbelttheater.com

Bollywood Film Reviews
www.brns.com/bollywood/pages1/bollyrevs.html

Chambara
www.chambara.com

Chanbara Eiga (Samurai Films) !
yakuza.freeyellow.com/page1.html

Chinatown Kid
chinatownkid.com

Chinese Cinema Page, by Shelly Kraicer
www.chinesecinemas.org

Chinese Movie Database
www.dianying.com/en/

Classic Martial Arts Authors
edu.ocac.gov.tw/taiwan/kungfu/e/mainmenu.htm

Dan's Hong Kong Movies Page
www.radix1.demon.co.uk/index.htm

Darcy's Korean Film Page
koreanfilm.org/index.html

Database of Philippine Movies
www.geocities.com/Hollywood/Interview/8544/

The Definitive Film Resource Regions Hong Kong and China
www.tdfilm.com/regions/hkchina/hkchina.html

Directory of Reviews of Hong Kong Movies
members.ozemail.com.au/~sharptongue/doro-index.html

Dragon's Den UK
www.dragonsdenuk.com

EnterTheNinja.com
www.entertheninja.com

Fists of Wine
www.geocities.com/fistsofwine/index.htm

ForeignFilms.com—The Foreign Film Database
www.foreignfilms.com

Glasgow University Asian Cinema Resource
www.pads.ahds.ac.uk/padsAsianCinemaLinks.html

Grandmaster Video
www.grandmastervideo.com

Great Leader is super star of North Korean movie making
www.gluckman.com/NKfilm.html

Happy Fortune Screening Room
www.geocities.com/happy-fortune/index.html

Happy-Lucky Chinese Restaurant Game
www.memento-mori.com/games/kungfu.html

Heroic Cinema—The Guide to Hong Kong Movies in Australia
www.heroic-cinema.com

Hong Kong Cinema. For the best in news and reviews of classic Hong Kong titles
www.hkcinema.co.uk/index.html

Hong Kong Cinema—View from the Brooklyn Bridge
www.brns.com

Hong Kong Critics Society
filmcritics.org.hk/home.html

Hong Kong Digital
www.dighkmovies.com

Hong Kong Entertainment News In Review
www.hkentreview.com

Hong Kong Express—il portale per
   gli appassionati di cinema orientale
www.hkx.it/links.html

Hong Kong Fanatic
hkfanatic.com

Hong Kong Film Archive
www.lcsd.gov.hk/CE/CulturalService/
   HKFA/english/eindex.html

Hong Kong Film Net
www.hkfilm.net

Hong Kong girls with guns
home.att.net/~chanfanatic/gwgindex2.
   htm

Hong Kong Movie DataBase
www.hkmdb.com

Hong Kong Movies
members.vol.at/bernhard/movie_hk.
   html

Hong Kong Movie World
simonyam.com/hkmw/

The Illuminated Lantern
www.illuminatedlantern.com/index.html

IGN
www.ign.com

The Indian Movies Index
www.gadnet.com/movies.htm

Japanese Horror Movie Database
www.fjmovie.com/horror/contents.html

The Japanese Vampire Movies
   Database
members.aol.com/youkai68/

Ka Chun's Hong Kong Movie Links
origins.colorado.edu/~kachun/
   hkdenver.shtml

KFSS—Yahoo Hong Kong Film Group
h.webring.com/hub?ring=kfss&list&
   page=1

KOFIC (Korean Film Commission)
www.kofic.or.kr/english/index.asp

Korean B-Movie Site
members.tripod.com/~MRKWANG/
   koreanbmovie.htm

Korean Cinema Edition
www.cinekorea.com

Korean Movie Information Center
members.aol.com/theSensual/
   movie_e.htm

Korean Movies
www.cinemakorea.com

Kung Fu Cinema
www.kungfucinema.com/index.html

Kung Fu DVD
www.dvdcult.com/KFDVD.htm

LoveHKFilm.com
www.lovehkfilm.com

The Martial Artist's Guide to Hong Kong
   Films
www.ronlim.com/martial.html

MOBIUS Asian Cinema Discussion
www.mhvf.net/forum/asian/index.
   shtml

Monkey Peaches
www.monkeypeaches.com

The Ninja Dojo
blofeld.qbranch.se/~maal01/

Ninja Movie Database
www.rarekungfumovies.com/nmdb/

Phantasmagoria
www.alliancebetrayed.com/
   phantasmagoria/main.htm

Psychotronic Film Society
www.psychotronic.com

RadiOactive Death—Movie Reviews with
   a Healthy Green Glow!
r0d.oracleswar.com/

Rob Larsen's Drunkenfist.com
www.drunkenfist.com/home.shtm

Samurai—Ninja—Yakuza
www.freewebz.com/sny/

Senses of Cinema—an online film
   journal
www.sensesofcinema.com/index.html

The Shanghai International Film Festival
www.siff.com

Shaolin Jee Shin Wing Chun Kung Fu
www.shaolinjeeshinwingchun.com.au/
   index.htm

The Shaolin Martial Arts of Reverend
   Gao Can
members.lycos.nl/saolim/personal.
   html

Sixties City—Japanese Science Fiction
   Films of the Sixties
www.sixtiescity.com/SciFilm/JSF.htm

The Stunt People Web
www.neo-modus.com/stuntpeople/
   spindex.html

Teleport City Movie Reviews Martial Arts
www.teleport-city.com/movies/reviews/
   kungfu/index.html

The Temple of Kung Fu movies
clix.to/thetemple

Tim's Hong Kong Movie Reviews
members.dcsi.net.au/chuma/writing/
   hkmovies/

Ultimate Ninja!
ultimate_ninja.tripod.com/index.htm

Verbal Kung-Fu Generator
www.ruf.rice.edu/~pound/kungfu.html

Virtual China Leisure Channel
virtualchina.org/archive/leisure/film/
   index.html

Yakuza Eiga (Movies) !
yakuza.freeyellow.com

Specific Titles/Series

Battle Royale
www.battleroyaleonline.com

Bulletproof Monk
www.bulletproofmonk.com

Happiness of the Katakuris
www.katakurike.com

The Official Kill Bill Fansite
www.killbill.net/index.php

The Kung Fu Cult Master Homepage
surf.to/kungfucultmaster

The Ring Cycle
www.mandiapple.com/snowblood/
   theringcycle.htm

Ringu-Fan
home.swipnet.se/~w-10972/ringufan/

Ringworld
www.somrux.com/ringworld/

Secrets of the Warrior's Power
www.warriorspower.com

Shinobi no Mono—Ninja, Band of
   Assassins
shinobinomono.oninohana.com

Sukeban Deka Forever!
www.hotbitscafe.com/go/sukeban/
   sd-chinese.shtml

The Touch
www.thetouchmovie.com/index.html

Anime

Absolute Anime
www.absoluteanime.com

Akadot
www.akadot.com

Akemi's Anime World
animeworld.com

Anime Fringe
www.animefringe.com

Anime Jump
www.animejump.com

Anime News Network
www.animenewsnetwork.com

Anime on DVD
www.animeondvd.com

Anime Prime
www.animeprime.com

Anime Project Home
www.umich.edu/~anime/

Anime.com
www.anime.com

Anime.Net
www.anime.net

Animefu
www.animefu.com

Animejin
www.animejin.org.uk

AnimeNfo.Com
www.animenfo.com

The Black Moon Japanese Culture Web
   site
www.theblackmoon.com/Contents/
   content.html

Kiss Me You Baka!—Anime Romance
   Gallery
www.kissmebaka.com/

List of Anime Television Series
www.public.iastate.edu/~rllew/anitv.html

711

Otaku Review
www.otakurevu.com

PRISMS The Ultimate Manga guide
www.geocities.com/Tokyo/Ginza/
4996/index.html

Shoujo & General—an Anime-Manga
Reference Library
users.powernet.co.uk/shoujo/index.
html

60's anime
www.alphalink.com.au/~roglen/index.
htm

Ultimate Animanga—Series Index
the.animearchive.org

Anime—Specific Series, Creator, or Feature

Little Robo's Giant Robo page
members.tripod.com/~giantrobo

Gundam Arena
gundam_arena.tripod.com

Gundam Official Site
www.gundamofficial.com/of/index.cfm

The Official Lupin the 3rd Website
www.lupinthethird.com

Welcome to the Lupin Encyclopedia!
www.lupinencyclopedia.com/

Osamu Tezuka @ World (official site)
www.tezuka.co.jp/

Vampire Hunter D Archives
www.altvampyres.net/vhd/

Vampire Hunter D: Bloodlust
www.vampirehunterdbloodlust.com

Studios/Publishers/Distributors

AnimEigo
www.animeigo.com

Bandai Entertainment
www.bandai-ent.com

Central Park Media
www.centralparkmedia.com

Crash Cinema
www.crashcinema.com

Daiei Studios
kadokawa-daiei.com

Eros Entertainment (Indian)
www.erosentertainment.com

FUNimation Productions, LTD
www.funimation.com

Mandarin Films
www.mandarin.films.com.hk

Manga Entertainment
www.manga.com

Media Blasters
www.media-blasters.com

Pioneer Animation
www.pioneeranimation.com

Right Stuf International, Inc.
www.rightstuf.com

Shaw Brothers—The Kings of Asia's
Film Industry
www.shawstudios.com

Tai Seng Entertainment
www.taiseng.com

TOHO ENTERTAINMENT
www.toho.co.jp

Unearthed Films—Guinea Pig
www.guineapigfilms.com

Urban Vision Entertainment
www.urban-vision.com

Venom Mob Films
www.venommobfilms.com

Viz Communications, Inc.
www.viz.com

Winson
www.hkwinson.com

Kaiju

Absolute Ultraman!
www.waynebrain.com/ultra/

AstroneF Magazine—Godzilla le Roi des
Monstres
afm.infinit.net/chro/godzi/godindex.
htm

Barry's Temple of Godzilla
www.stomptokyo.com/godzillatemple/

Club Tokyo—The Godzilla Virtual
Museum
www.clubtokyo.org

The couch potato's guide to GODZILLA
sclose.home.mindspring.com/gojira.
htm

Daddy-O's Drive-in Dirt
www.mst3kinfo.com/daddyo/

The DaiKaijuEiga List Web Page
www.westol.com/~schneidr/dke/frame.
htm

Don't Be Defeated, Japanese Godzilla!
www.godira.com/e-top.html

G-FAN Magazine
g-fan.com

Gamera Japan
gamera.jp

GAMERA the Guardian of the Universe
www.expage.com/gamera

Gamera X
www.geocities.com/broadway/balcony/
9411/

Gamera's Grip—latest Gamera news!
www.avia-art.com/godzillawebsite/
gamera/gamera.html

Godzilla—official American site
www.godzilla.com/

Godzilla—official Toho site
www.godzilla.co.jp/

Godzilla & Co. Monster Gallery
www.avia-art.com/godzillawebsite/
gnco.html

Godzilla and Other Toho Studios Movies
www.westol.com/~schneidr/dke/mgodz
.htm

Godzilla Galore Web Board
azure.bbboy.net/godzillagaloremessage
board

Godzilla Monster Music
www.godzillamonstermusic.com

Godzilla Series Society
godzilla.gamegossip.com

Godzilla vs. the Mysterians!
www.totaldanger.com/td_pages/
godzillapages/mysterianscover.html

Henshin! Online
www.henshinonline.com

Johnny Sokko
www.stevesweb.com/johnnysokko

Kaiju Big Battel (live wrestling monsters!)
www.kaiju.com/home.htm

Kaiju Fan OnLine
www.dalekempire.com/KaijuFan
OnLine.html

Kenny's Giant Monster Rampage
www.geocities.com/Area51/Shuttle/
7923/

Malachi's Monster Page
www.heptune.com/monsters.html

Mario's Godzilla Page
www.avia-art.com/godzilla2.html

Monster Zero—THE Source for Kaiju
News on the Web
66.216.76.201/monsterzero/index.php

Monster Zero Archives Main
www.rc2000godzilla.com/mza/mza.html

Monsters4u—movie and anime reviews
www.monsters4u.com

The Only Yongary Website You'll Ever
Need
www.stomptokyo.com/scott/yongary/

Rodan's Roost—The Kaiju Site
www.rodansroost.com

The Scottoons Gamera Page!
www.fortunecity.com/tatooine/
campbell/201/Index.html

The Shrine of Gamera
www.shrineofgamera.com

Stomp Tokyo
www.stomptokyo.com

Toho Kingdom
www.tohokingdom.com

Top 25 Kaiju Sites
top25kaiju.hypermart.net/topsites/
topsites.html

The Ultraman Archive Gateway
members.fortunecity.com/ultraman
archive/

The World of Godzilla
www.myscifiworld.com/godzilla.asp

UNSC—United Nations Science Council (great daikaju movie technical site)
www.eclipse.net/~walshj0/index.htm

Stars & Directors—General

Asian Celebrity Guide (ACG)
www.geocities.com/Hollywood/Lot/2562/

Encyclopedia Asian Stars
all.at/asiastar

Hong Kong Actors' Gallery
www.paris-hongkong.com/articles/20001227trombino/index.html

Hong Kong Stars Page
www.geocities.com/Tokyo/4553/hkstars.html

Hong Kong Stars Page
www.hksp3030.com

Kung Fu Films with Female Fighters (cast pictures)
www.angelfire.com/az3/kitty/all.htm

Stars & Directors—Specific

Rinda's Au Yeung Pui San World—Susanna Au Yeung
www.geocities.com/auyeungpuisan/

Already a dragon—My tribute to Jackie Chan Sing Lung
www.jackiechan.com

Comeau's Jackie Chan Pages
www.net1plus.com/users/jcomeau/chanmain.htm

I AM JACKIE CHAN MY LIFE IN ACTION
www.randomhouse.com/features/iamjackiechan/index.html

Jackie Chan Adventures
www.sonypictures.com/tv/kids/jackiechan/

Jackie Chan Project J
projectj.virtualave.net

Drunken WebMaster Jackie Chan Site
www.geocities.com/Tokyo/Fuji/2055/Jackie_Chan.html

JACKY!
www.firstuniversal.clara.net/jacky.html

The Ultimate Jackie Chan Video Vault—New Line Cinema
www.independentproject.com/WFH/JackieChan/main.html

Michael Chan
www.firstuniversal.clara.net/chanwaiman2.htm

Chang Cheh the Godfather of the Kung Fu Film
changcheh.0catch.com/

Maggie Cheung Homepage
www.geocities.com/Tokyo/Towers/8785/macheung.html

Sonny Chiba Official Site
www.jjchiba.com

Apocalypse Chow (Stephen Chow)
www.moroturkey.com/achow.html

Stephen Chow Online Resource
www.trilhazero.com.br/chow/

Stephen Chow Sing-chi
www.chow-sing-chi.com/sing.html

Chiaumania—Films of Stephen Chow
members.optushome.com.au/flyingfox/

The Movie Madness of Chow Sing Chi
www.chowsingchi.sphosting.com

Sing Jai Central! (Stephen Chow)
members.tripod.com/~chowsingchifan/

Chow Yun-fat—God of Actors
www.geocities.com/Athens/8907/factor.html

A Free Man in Hong Kong—Chow Yun-fat
nbi.com/hk/cyf/

Godfrey Ho
www.radix1.demon.co.uk/GODHO.HTM

Collecting Vivian!—Vivian Hsu
www.collecting-vivian.net

SammoHung.com
www.sammohung.com/

Shusuke Kaneko Information Website
www.shusuke-kaneko.com/eng/

Masaya Kato
www.jap.co.jp/masaya/

Office-Kitano Web Site
www.office-kitano.co.jp

Aaron Kwok—Just Who Is This Guy?
www.geocities.com/akfsnut/witg.html

Akira Kurosawa
www.fortunecity.com/lavendar/monkeys/273/

Akira Kurosawa Database
www2.tky.3web.ne.jp/~adk/kurosawa/AKpage.html

The World of Andy Lau
www.andylausounds.com

Bruce and Brandon Lee Remembered
estraven.silverday.net/lee/

The Bruce Lee Club Based in the United Kingdom
www.brucelee.org.uk

Lee Legends
www.leelegends.net

Bruce Lee Temple of the Unknown
www.cityonfire.com/unknown/

Bruceploitation
www.geocities.com/many_bruces/

BruceWorld
www.geocities.com/bruceworld_com/main.htm

Judy Lee (Chia Ling)
www.angelfire.com/az3/chia/

The Unofficial Loretta Lee Home Page (Rachel Lee)
www.geocities.com/Tokyo/Bay/2971/index.html

Exit the Dragon, Enter the Tiger, a Bruce Li fanzine
www.geocities.com/many_bruces/brucelizine/

World of Jimmy Lin
www.iprimus.ca/~sdmtran/jimmy.html

Angela Mao
www.fortunecity.com/lavendar/westside/70/angela_mao.html

Angela Mao's Videos
www.angelfire.com/az/ying/

Kitty Meng Chui
www.angelfire.com/az3/kitty/

Toshiro Mifune
www.sprout.org/toshiro/

Toshiro Mifune Official Website
www.mifuneproductions.co.jp/eindex.html

Kei Mizutani Official Website
www.keimizutani.com

The Ng Man-Tat for President Home Page!
pages.ripco.net/~oobleck/

Michelle Reis Picture Site
www.aclasscelebs.com/micheller/filmo.htm

Cynthia Rothrock
www.cynthiarothrock.com

Cynthia Rothrock Official Site
www.cynthiarothrock.org

Cynthia Rothrock World Order
www.rothrockworldorder.com

Unofficial Cynthia Rothrock Home Page
www.interlog.com/~tigger/rothrock.html

Bobby Samuels
www.bobbysamuels.com

Alan Tang
collamer-jones.com/tang/index.html

Tomas Tang, the pseudonymn for Godfrey Ho and Filmark International
www.geocities.com/fistsofwine/ifd/tomastang.htm

The Ti Lung Shrine
ti-lung.com

Official Homepage Tsuburaya
www.m-78.com

Tsui Hark—Links
www.dslextreme.com/users/lisam9/links.html

Tsui Hark Hong Kong's Little Big Man
www.houseofhorrors.com/tsuihark.htm

The fan page of Norman Tsui
www4.osk.3web.ne.jp/~hasinaka/chui.html

The Venoms Resource
greenvenomtheatre.tripod.com

Five Deadly Venoms Fansite
go.to/fivedeadlyvenoms

Venoms FAQ Page!
www.geocities.com/logansama1/index.
html

Anthony Wong
www02.so-net.ne.jp/~hkstar/anthonye.
html

ACTION WEB—John Woo and Tsui Hark
www.geocities.com/Hollywood/6648/

Hardboiled.de—The Cinema of John Woo
www.hardboiled.de

John Woo, A God Among Directors
www.godamongdirectors.com/woo/

The Bullet-Riddled Teahouse (John Woo)
www.angelfire.com/electronic/
teahouse/

Red on White—The John Woo Fan Site
www.redonwhite.net/woo/

Simon Yam.com Hong Kong Movie World
www.simonyam.com

Donnie Yen's Official Website
www.donnieyen.com

Rodney's Michelle Yeoh Page
www.alphalink.com.au/~cheah/yeoh/

Michelle Yeoh Never Dies
members.aol.com/cjereneta/yeoh/
yeoh.html

Michelle Yeoh Web Theatre
owl.usc.edu/~hding/main.html

Master Bolo Yeung
www.firstuniversal.clara.net/bolo.htm

Zatoichi No Eigamono (Shintaro Katsu)
members.aol.com/zato1ch1/index.
html

Zuk's HK Babes Page—Featuring Zhang
Ziyi!
home.att.net/~zuk.com/hkbabes.html

Online Stores

ANIME-NIAK!!
www.animeniak.com

AsianDiscs.com
www.asiandiscs.com

AsianMV.com
www.asianmv.com

Asian Xpress
www.asianxpress.net

AznFilms
www.aznfilms.com

CollectRareStuff.com—Discounted VCD
Chinese-Japanese-Korean movies
and Hollywood Classics
www.collectrarestuff.com

DDDHouse
www.dddhouse.com

Digital Versatile Disc Ltd.
www.digitalversatiledisc.com

Discount Asian Videos
www.asiafilm.com/bargains.htm

DVD Shelf
www.dvdshelf.com

eThaiCD.com—Online Thai music &
entertainment store
www.ethaicd.com

Godzilla Shop
www.gundamshop.com/Merchant4/
merchant.mv

HKFlix.com
www.hkflix.com

Homay.com—Asian Home Entertainment
www.homay.com

hongkongmovie.com
www.hongkongmovie.com/english/dvd/
index.asp

IndoFilms—The Largest Site for Indian
Movies
www.indofilms.com

krdvd.com
www.krdvd.com

Kung Fu Movies.net
www.kungfumovies.net

Lan Kwei Trading Asia DVD & VCD Movies
lan-kwei.com/asiadvdE/

Monsters in Motion
www.monstersinmotion.com

Motion and Sound
store.motionandsound.com

ORIENTAL FILM DISTRIBUTION
www.orientalfilms.co.uk

POKER INDUSTRIES
www.pokerindustries.com

RARE KUNG FU MOVIES
www.rarekungfumovies.com

Right Stuf International, Inc.
www.rightstuf.com

SamuraiDVD.com
www.samuraiflix.com

Sensasian.com
www.sensasian.com

Tai Seng Entertainment
www.taiseng.com

Thomas Video and DVD
www.thomasvideo.com

Video Mayhem
www.fm3d.com/videomayhem/

Alternative Titles Index

While it's true that we couldn't include every Asian cult flick in this slim little volume—heck, there's dozens being dug out of vaults and slapped onto video as you read this—the one you're looking for just might be in here under a title you didn't know about. Most of these films have been released under more than one title, and while we've done our best to use the one that's most likely to be familiar, that doesn't guarantee you aren't trying to find *Crippled Avengers* and don't know we've got it as *The Return of the 5 Deadly Venoms*. And so, we've gathered as many alternative titles as we can find, including their original language title(s), and arranged them in alphabetical order in this index to help you out. Remember, English language articles ("a", "an", "the") are ignored in the sort, but foreign articles are NOT ignored. Hey, my Japanese is a little rusty, and some languages just don't *have* articles.

A Fei Zheng Chuan
See Days of Being Wild (1990)

A Foo
See A Fighter's Blues (2000)

A Gai Waak
See Project A (1983)

A Gai Waak Juk Jaap
See Project A 2 (1987)

A Hu
See A Fighter's Blues (2000)

A Ji Hua
See Project A (1983)

A Ji Hua Xu Ji
See Project A 2 (1987)

A Lang De Gu Shi
See All About Ah-Long (1989)

A Lee Ang Ang Leung Goh Daai Diy
See F*** / Off (1998)

A Long Dik Goo Si
See All About Ah-Long (1989)

A Sau Law
See Saga of the Phoenix (1990)

A Xiu Luo
See Saga of the Phoenix (1990)

Aang Hon Gung Foo Boon
See Kung Fu's Hero (1973)

Aau Chin
See Running out of Time (1999)

Aau Chin 2
See Running out of Time 2 (2001)

Aau Dut
See The Longest Nite (1998)

Aau Fung Yee
See Sound from the Dark (2000)

Aau Yeung Huet Dik Ji
See Fatal Flying Guillotine (1977)

Aau Yeung Liu Gau Ji Meng Chuen Gon Kwan
See Troublesome Night 9 (2000)

Aau Yeung Liu Sap Sei Ji Seung Gwai Paak Moon
See Troublesome Night 14 (2002)

Abominable Snowman
See Half Human (1955/1957)

Above the Law
See Righting Wrongs (1986)

Above the Law 2
See Blonde Fury (1989)

Adorenarin Doraibui
See Adrenaline Drive (1999)

Adventure of Gargantuas
See War of the Gargantuas (1966)

Adventure of Shaolin
See Five Elements of Kung Fu (1978)

The Adventures of Chatran, Milo and Otis
See The Adventures of Milo and Otis (1986)

The Affair from Nepal
See The Witch from Nepal (1985)

Afterlife
See After Life (1998)

Ah Fei's Story
See Days of Being Wild (1990)

Ah Fu
See A Fighter's Blues (2000)

Ai Jun Ru Meng
See Dance of a Dream (2001)

Ai Qing Bai Mian Bao
See Bakery Amour (2001)

Ai Qing Guan Zi Zai
See Love au Zen (2001)

Ai Qing Min Gan Di Dai
See Love Paradox (2000)

Ai Shang Wo Ba
See Gimme Gimme (2001)

Ai Yu Cheng
See A War Named Desire (2000)

Air Battle of the Big Monsters: Gamera vs. Gyaosu
See Gamera vs. Gyaos (1967)

Akai Hashi no Shita no Nurui Mizu
See Warm Water under a Red Bridge (2001)

Akuma no Jikken
See Guinea Pig: Devil's Experiment (1985)

All Monsters Attack
See Destroy All Monsters (1968)

All for the Winner 3
See God of Gamblers 3: Back to Shanghai (1991)

All's Well, End's Well 1997
See All's Well End's Well '97 (1997)

An Hua
See The Longest Nite (1998)

An Na Ma De Lian Na
See Anna Magdalena (1998)

An Zhan
See Running out of Time (1999)

An Zhan 2
See Running out of Time 2 (2001)

Ang Kwong Ang Kwong Ying Ji Dut
See Para Para Sakura (2001)

Ang Wan Gong Tau
See Revenge of the Zombies (1976)

Angelic Orgasm
See Ecstasy of the Angels (1972)

Angels
See Angel 2 (1988)

Angels 2
See Angel 2 (1988)

Ape
See A*P*E (1976)

A*P*E: Attacking Primate Monster
See A*P*E (1976)

Ape Girl
See Lady Iron Monkey (1983)

Appurushido
See Appleseed (1988)

Armour of God 2
See Operation Condor (1991)

Armour of God 2: Operation Condor
See Operation Condor (1991)

Around the Jail Cell
See Tiger over Wall (1980)

Arsene Lupin & the Castle of Cagliostro
See Castle of Cagliostro (1979)

Ashura
See Saga of the Phoenix (1990)

Asia Perversa
See Shocking Asia (1975)

Atomic Rulers
See Atomic Rulers of the World (1957)

Attack of the Flying Saucers
See Atomic Rulers of the World (1957)

Attack of the Giant Horny Gorilla
See A*P*E (1976)

Attack of the Giant Monsters
See Gamera vs. Guiron (1969)

Attack of the Marching Monsters
See Destroy All Monsters (1968)

Au Yeung Liu 4 Yue Gwai Tung Hang
See Troublesome Night 4 (1998)

Au Yeung Liu Baat Ji Goon Choi Chat
See Troublesome Night 8 (2000)

Au Yuk Kim Chui Yuk Shut
See Moonlight Sword and Jade Lion (1979)

Avenging Warriors
See Avenging Warriors of Shaolin (1979)

B Gai Waak
See Extreme Crisis (1998)

B Ji Hua
See Extreme Crisis (1998)

Ba Da Men Pai
See The 8 Masters (1977)

Ba La Ba La Ying Zhi Hua
See Para Para Sakura (2001)

Ba Wang Hua
See The Inspector Wears Skirts (1988)

Ba Wang Nu: Fu Xing
See Operation Pink Squad (1988)

Ba Wong Fa
See The Inspector Wears Skirts (1988)

Ba Wong Lui Fook Sing
See Operation Pink Squad (1988)

Ba Xian Fan Dian Zhi Ren Rou Cha Shao Bao
See The Untold Story (1992)

Ba Xing Bao Xi
See Eighth Happiness (1988)

Baai Cho Bye Foo Kau Cho Tau
See The Eagle's Killer (1981)

Baak Bin Sing Gwan
See Sixty Million Dollar Man (1995)

Baak Faat Moh Nui
See The Bride with White Hair (1993)

Baak Faat Moh Nui 2
See The Bride with White Hair 2 (1993)

Baak Lin Che Sun
See White Lotus Cult (1993)

Baan Yau Siu Ji
See The Young Avenger (1979)

Baat Daai Moon Pai
See The 8 Masters (1977)

Baat sin Faan Dim Chi Yan Yuk Cha Siu Baau
See The Untold Story (1992)

Baat Sing Biu Choi
See Eighth Happiness (1988)

Baau Lit Ying Ging
See Bullets over Summer (1999)

Baburugamu Kuraishisu
See Bubblegum Crisis (1985)

Baby Cart 6: Go to Hell, Daigoro!
See Lone Wolf and Cub 6: White Heaven in Hell (1974)

Bad Boy Dak Gung
See For Bad Boys Only (2000)

Bad Boy Te Gong
See For Bad Boys Only (2000)

Bai Cu Shi Fu Kou Cu Tou
See The Eagle's Killer (1981)

Bai Fa Mo Nu
See The Bride with White Hair (1993)

Bai Fa Mo Nu 2
See The Bride with White Hair 2 (1993)

Bai Ga Jai
See The Prodigal Son (1981)

Bai Jia Zi
See The Prodigal Son (1981)

Bai Lian Xie Shen
See White Lotus Cult (1993)

Bai Yi Xia Nu
See The Swordswoman in White (1992)

Bakging Lok Yu Lo, Bei Jing Ie yu Iu
See Beijing Rocks (2001)

Ban Jin Ba Liang
See The Private Eyes (1976)

Ban Ye Xiao Zi
See The Young Avenger (1979)

Banchik-Wang
See The Foul King (2000)

Band of Assassins
See Ninja: Band of Assassins (1962)

Band of Assassins Returns
See Ninja: Band of Assassins Continued (1963)

Bandits, Prostitutes and Silver
See Battle of Shaolin (1977)

Bao Li Xing Jing
See Violent Cop (1999)

Bao Lie Xing Jing
See Bullets over Summer (1999)

Bao Mei
See Her Name Is Cat (1998)

Bao Nu Zhi Duo Ming Zhi Lu
See Her Name Is Cat 2: Journey to Death (2001)

Baraku Majikku M-66
See Black Magic M-66 (1987)

Bat Gaai Ji Mai
See Clueless (2001)

Bat Sei Ching Mai
See Bullets of Love (2001)

Battle Creek Brawl
See The Big Brawl (1980)

Battle for Shaolin
See Battle of Shaolin (1977)

Battle of Champions
See God of Gamblers Returns (1994)

Battle of the Astros
See Invasion of Astro-Monster (1965)

Battle of the Dragons
See The Magic Serpent (1966)

Beast Cop
See Beast Cops (1998)

Beast Man Snow Man
See Half Human (1955/1957)

Beasts
See Twilight People (1972)

Beauty and the Liquid-man
See The H-Man (1958)

Beauty Inspectors
See Beauty Investigator (1992)

Behind Bruce Lee
See Bruce Lee: The Man, the Myth (1976)

Bei Bian Xing Jun
See Sixty Million Dollar Man (1995)

Bei Pan Shi Men
See 3 Evil Masters (1980)

Beijing Summer
See In the Mood for Love (2000)

The Bell Tolls in the Cold Mountain Temple
See The Cold Mountain Temple (1991)

Bi Xie Lan Tian
See The Blacksheep Affair (1998)

Bi Xie Sheng Yin Qiang
See The Silver Spear (1979)

The Big Boss
See Fists of Fury (1971)

Big Duel in the North Sea
See Ebirah, Horror of the Deep (1966)

Big Space Monster Guilala
See The X from Outer Space (1967)

Bijo to Ekitai-nigen
See The H-Man (1958)

Bik Huet Laam Tin
See The Blacksheep Affair (1998)

Bik Huet Sin Aau Cheong
See The Silver Spear (1979)

Bing Suet Ching Gwaan Ying Hung Daam
See Inheritor of Kung Fu (1977)

Bing Xue Qing Guan Ying Xiong Dan
See Inheritor of Kung Fu (1977)

Biu Lik Ying Ging
See Violent Cop (1999)

Black Dragon
See Miracles (1989)

Black Magic Part 2
See Revenge of the Zombies (1976)

Blind Fist of Bruce Lee
See Blind Fist of Bruce (1979)

Blind Swordsman: Adventures of Zatoichi
See Adventures of a Blind Man (1964)

The Blind Swordsman and the Chess Expert
See Zatoichi and the Chess Expert (1965)

The Blind Swordsman and the Fugitives
See Zatoichi and the Fugitives (1968)

The Blind Swordsman Samaritan
See Samaritan Zatoichi (1968)

Blind Swordsman: Zatoichi Fighting Journey
See Zatoichi on the Road (1963)

The Blind Swordsman's Cane Sword
See Zatoichi's Cane Sword (1966)

The Blind Swordsman's Rescue
See Zatoichi the Outlaw (1967)

Blind Swordsman's Revenge
See Zatoichi's Revenge (1964)

The Blind Swordsman's Vengeance
See Zatoichi's Vengeance (1966)

Blood and Steel
See Enter the Dragon (1973)

Blood Creature
See Terror Is a Man (1959)

Blood Doctor
See Mad Doctor of Blood Island (1968)

Blood Fingers
See Brutal Boxer (1972)

Bloodfingers
See Brutal Boxer (1972)

Bloodpact
See The 36 Crazy Fists (1977)

Bloodshed in the Streets
See Bullet in the Head (1990)

Bloodshed of Two Heroes
See The Killer (1989)

Bloody Monkey Fist
See The Iron Monkey (1977)

Bloody Monkey Master
See The Iron Monkey (1977)

Blow Back 2
See Blowback: Love and Death (1990)

Blue Snake
See Green Snake (1993)

Bo Lee Chun
See Gorgeous (1999)

Bo Li Shao Nu
See Glass Tears (2001)

Bo Li Zun
See Gorgeous (1999)

Bo Mang
See Battle of Shaolin (1977)

Bo Ming Dao Duo Ming Qiang
See Odd Couple (1979)

The Bodyguard
See Yojimbo (1961)

Bodyguard from Beijing
See The Defender (1994)

Bodyguard Kiba
See The Bodyguard (1973/78)

Boh Lee Siu Lui
See Glass Tears (2001)

Bok Meng
See Battle of Shaolin (1977)

Bok Ming Dan Dou Duet Ming Cheung
See Odd Couple (1979)

Boksuneun Naui Geot
See Sympathy for Mr. Vengeance (2001)

Bolo the Brute
See Bolo (1980)

Bonecrushers
See Masters of Martial Arts (1974)

Booi Boon Bye Moon
See 3 Evil Masters (1980)

Boon Gan Baat Leung
See The Private Eyes (1976)

Bor Lei Jun
See Gorgeous (1999)

Born to be King
See Young and Dangerous 6: Born to Be King (2000)

Born to Defend
See Born to Defence (1988)

Born to Fight
See Blonde Fury (1989)

Boxer's Adventure
See Militant Eagle (1978)

Boyichi and the Super-monster
See Gamera vs. Gyaos (1967)

Brides of Blood Island
See Brides of Blood (1968)

Brides of Death
See Brides of Blood (1968)

Brides of the Beast
See Brides of Blood (1968)

Brother vs. Brother
See Twin Dragons (1992)

Brotherhood
See Code of Honor (1987)

Bruce Is Loose
See The Green Dragon Inn (1979)

Bruce—King of Kung Fu
See The Legend of Bruce Lee (1980)

Bruce Le vs. Ninja
See Ninja vs. Bruce Lee (1982)

Bruce Lee Super Gang
See Super Gang (1978)

Bruce Lee—True Story
See Bruce Lee: The Man, the Myth (1976)

Bruce Lee's Big Secret
See Revenge of the Patriots (1976)

Bruce Lee's Deadly Kung Fu
See Story of the Dragon (1976)

Bruce Lee's Game of Death
See Game of Death (1978)

Bruce Lee's Jeet Kune Do
See Story of the Dragon (1976)

Bruce Lee's Secret
See Story of the Dragon (1976)

Bruce Li, Superdragon
See Bruce Lee We Miss You (1976)

Bruce vs. Snake in the Eagle's Shadow
See Snake in the Eagle's Shadow (1978)

Bu Si Qing Mi
See Bullets of Love (2001)

Bu ze Shou Duan
See Dynamo (1978)

Bue Jie Zhi Mi
See Clueless (2001)

The Build-Up
See Giants and Toys (1958)

Bullet Train Big Explosion
See Bullet Train (1975)

Bunman: The Untold Story
See The Untold Story (1992)

Burakku Jakku
See Black Jack (1996)

The Burning Island
See The Prisoner (1990)

Burning Paradise in Hell
See Burning Paradise (1994)

Burning Shaolin Temple
See The Blazing Temple (1976)

Butterfly Lovers
See Juliet in Love (2000)

Butterfly Sword
See Butterfly and Sword (1993)

Bye Dai Chut Ma; Shi Di Chu Ma
See The Young Master (1980)

Can Que
See The Return of the 5 Deadly Venoms (1978)

Canton Godfather
See Miracles (1989)

Carry On Wise Guy
See Warrior from Shaolin (1981)

Castle of the Spider's Web
See Throne of Blood (1957)

The Cavalier
See The Smart Cavalier (1978)

Cent
See Lone Wolf and Cub 2: Baby Cart at the River Styx (1972)

Cha Sau
See Masked Avengers (1981)

Cha Shou
See Masked Avengers (1981)

Chaak Gung Ji
See Super Car Criminals (1999)

Chaan Kuet
See The Return of the 5 Deadly Venoms (1978)

Challenge
See Drunken Master (1978)

Champ vs. Champ
See Champ against Champ (1983)

Chan Haang-ng Po Daal Lo Tin
See Deadly Snail vs. Kung Fu Killer (1977)

Chang Shang-fon Adventures
See Five Elements of Kung Fu (1978)

Chang Zai Wo Xin
See Funeral March (2001)

Chao Ji Ji Hua
See Supercop 2 (1993)

Chaos
See Ran (1985)

Chap Faat Sin Fung
See Righting Wrongs (1986)

Chap Ga Siu Ji
See Knockabout (1979)

Chat Gam Shut
See Legend of the 7 Golden Vampires (1974)

Chat Siu Fuk
See Painted Faces (1988)

Che Diy Saal Yan
See Hit-Man in the Hand of Buddha (1980)

Che Gaau Dong Ngon Ji Moot Yat Fung Biu
See God.com (1998)

Chek Law Giu Cheung
See Naked Killer (1992)

Chen Miu Moon
See The Chinese Connection (1971)

Chen Xingwu Po Da Luo Tian
See Deadly Snail vs. Kung Fu Killer (1977)

Cheng Mu Moon
See Fist of Fury (1995)

Cheng Shi Lie Ren
See City Hunter (1992)

Cheng Shi Te Jing
See The Big Heat (1988)

Cheng Shi Zhan Zheng
See City War (1988)

Cheong Feng
See The Mission (1999)

Cheong Wong
See Double Tap (2000)

Chi Faat Fan Faat
See Cop on a Mission (2001)

Chi Luo Gao Yang
See Naked Killer (1992)

Chi Meng Sing Siu Yiu
See Devil Touch (2002)

Chikyu Boeigun
See The Mysterians (1957)

Chikyu Kokegi Meirei: Gojira tai Gaigan
See Godzilla vs. Gigan (1972)

Child and Expertise for Rent
See Lone Wolf and Cub 1: Sword of Vengeance (1972)

Chin Hei Yuen
See Wishful Milenio (2001)

Chin Pei Ming
See Notorious Concubines (1969)

Chin San Chuen Suet
See The Moon Warriors (1992)

Chin Wong Ji Wong 2000
See The Tricky Master (2000)

China Heat
See Crystal Hunt (1991)

China Mountain Big Brother
See Fists of Fury (1971)

Chinese Chien Chuan Kung Fu
See The Legend of Bruce Lee (1980)

Chinese Hero
See Born to Defence (1988)
See A Man Called Hero (1999)

The Chinese Mack
See Fists Like Lee (1974)

A Chinese Odyssey
See A Chinese Odyssey Part 1: Pandora's Box (1995)

Chinese Torture Chamber
See A Chinese Torture Chamber Story (1994)

Ching Haam Baak Lok Moon
See Paramount Motel (2000)

Ching Lui Cha Goon
See Cop Shop Babes (2001)

Ching Mai Daai Wa Wong
See Everyday Is Valentine (2001)

Ching Se
See Green Snake (1993)

Ching Sing
See The Magnificent Scoundrels (1991)

Chiniku no Hana
See Guinea Pig: Flower of Flesh and Blood (1985)

Chiu Kap Gai Waak
See Supercop 2 (1993)

Chiu Meng Cheong
See Blood of the Dragon (1971)

Choh Luen Kwong Cha Min
See Merry-Go-Round (2001)

Choi Kek Ji Wong
See King of Comedy (1999)

Chojin Densetsu Urotsukidoji
See Urotsukidoji (1989)

Chokugeki! Jigokuhen
See The Executioner (1974)

Chong An Shi Lu O Ji
See Organized Crime and Triad Bureau (1994)

Chong An Zu
See Crime Story (1993)

Chong Feng Dui Nu Huo Jie Tou
See Big Bullet (1996)

Chong Jin Shu
See Satin Steel (1994)

Chong Qing Sen Lin
See Chungking Express (1994)

Chong Si Duen Bei
See One Arm Hero (1994)

Chong Zhuang Jing Cha
See Hit Team (2000)

Chow Ken
See Fury of King Boxer (1972)

Chow Sin Sap Baat Dip
See The World of the Drunken Master (1979)

Chow Tau Yau Liu
See Runaway (2001)

Chu Lian Na Cha Mian
See Merry-Go-Round (2001)

Chu Long Ma Liu
See Monkey Fist Floating Snake (1979)

Chu Ong Daai Luen Mang
See The Irresistible Piggies (2002)

Chuen Chik Saal Sau
See Fulltime Killer (2001)

Chuet Chiu
See Fists Like Lee (1974)

Chuet Sai Hiu Bra
See Brassiere (2001)

Chuet Sik San Tau
See Martial Angels (2001)

Chui Hau Lui
See Lady Iron Monkey (1983)

Chui Hau Tung Dip
See Ultimatum (2001)

Chui Kuen
See Drunken Master (1978)

Chui Sau Siu Ji
See The Legend of Bruce Lee (1980)

Chun Biu Fong
See Tiger over Wall (1980)

Chun Sing Ma
See The Postman Fights Back (1982)

Chung Chong Ging Chaat
See Hit Team (2000)

Chung Fung Dui Liu Feng Gaai Tau
See Big Bullet (1996)

Chung Gwai
See Seeding of a Ghost (1983)

Chung Gwok Foo Yan
See Chinese Iron Man (1975)

Chung Hing Sam Lam
See Chungking Express (1994)

Chung Kam Juk
See Satin Steel (1994)

Chung Naam Hoi Biu Biu
See The Defender (1994)

Chung Ngon Cho
See Crime Story (1993)

Chung Ngon Sat Luk O Gei
See Organized Crime and Triad Bureau (1994)

Chung Wa Diy Hap
See Conman in Tokyo (2000)

Chung Wa Miu Sui
See The Shaolin One (1983)

Chung Wa Ying Hung
See A Man Called Hero (1999)

Chung Yuen Biu Guk
See Revenge of the Patriots (1976)

Chungking Forest
See Chungking Express (1994)

CIA Story
See First Strike (1996)

The Circuit
See Pulse (2001)

City Cop II
See City Cop (1995)

City Hunter
See City Hunter: Secret Service (1996)

Clan of the White Lotus
See Fists of the White Lotus (1980)

Claws of Steel
See Last Hero in China (1993)

Close Encounters of the Spooky Kind
See Encounter of the Spooky Kind (1981)

Cobweb Castle
See Throne of Blood (1957)

Cold Blooded Eagles
See Avenging Eagle (1978)

Cold Mountain Temple Master
See The Cold Mountain Temple (1991)

The Color of a Hero II
See A Better Tomorrow 2 (1987)

Colossus of Congo
See Mighty Peking Man (1977)

Comet, Butterfly and Sword
See Butterfly and Sword (1993)

Concord of Bruce
See Ninja vs. Bruce Lee (1982)

The Concubines
See Notorious Concubines (1969)

Conman and the Kung Fu Kid
See From China with Death (1974)

The Conman 1999
See The Conman (1998)

Cosmic Man Appears in Tokyo
See Warning from Space (1956)

Countdown in Kung Fu
See Hand of Death (1975)

Crack Showdown Boxers
See Crack Shadow Boxers (1977)

Creature from Blood Island
See Terror Is a Man (1959)

Creatures of Evil
See Curse of the Vampires (1970)

Creatures of the Red Planet
See Horror of the Blood Monsters (1970)

Crippled Avengers
See The Return of the 5 Deadly Venoms (1978)

Crippled Heroes
See The Return of the 5 Deadly Venoms (1978)

Crippled Kung Fu Boxer
See Ninja Supremo (1981)

The Crossroads to Hell
See Lone Wolf and Cub 5: Baby Cart in the Land of Demons (1973)

Cry of the Wolf
See Horror of the Blood Monsters (1970)

Crying Freeman: Dragon from Russia
See Dragon from Russia (1990)

Crying Freeman: Killer's Romance
See Killer's Romance (1990)

Crystal Fist
See Jade Claw (1979)

C3 Fighters
See Extreme Challenge (2001)

Curse of the Mushroom People
See Attack of the Mushroom People (1963)

Cyclone Z
See Dragons Forever (1988)

Da Can Quan
See Ninja Supremo (1981)

Da Lei Tai
See Flash Future Kung Fu (1983)

Da Mao Xian Jia
See The Adventurers (1995)

Da Nei Mi Tan 008
See Forbidden City Cop (1996)

Da Xiao You Long
See Lady Whirlwind and the Rangers (1974)

Daai Laap Mat Taam 008
See Forbidden City Cop (1996)

Daai Siu Yau Lung
See Lady Whirlwind and the Rangers (1974)

Dai Chaan Kuen
See Ninja Supremo (1981)

Dai Lui Toi
See Flash Future Kung Fu (1983)

Dai Mak Him Ka
See The Adventurers (1995)

Daigoro! We're Off to Hell
See Lone Wolf and Cub 6: White Heaven in Hell (1974)

Daikaiju Gamera
See Giant Monster Gamera (1965)

Daikaiju Kessan: Gamera Tai Barugon
See Gamera vs. Barugon (1966)

Daikaiju no tai Nimon Mairu
See Godzilla, King of the Monsters (1954)

Daikaiju Varan
See Varan the Unbelievable (1958)

Daikyoju Gappa
See Gappa: The Triphibian Monster (1967)

Daimajin Gyakushu
See Return of Daimajin (1966)

Daimajin Ikaru
See Wrath of Daimajin (1966)

Daiwah Saiyau
See A Chinese Odyssey Part 1: Pandora's Box (1995)

Dak Ging San Yan Lui
See Gen-X Cops (1999)

Dak Ging San Yan Lui 2
See Gen-Y Cops (2000)

Dak Ging To Lung
See Tiger Cage (1988)

Daimaya Nolja
See Hi! Dharma! (2001)

The Damned
See Battle of Shaolin (1977)

Dan Po Tian Jing
See The Awaken Punch (1973)

Dance with Sword
See Bichunmoo (1999)

Dancing Kung Fu
See The Smart Cavalier (1978)

Dandelion
See Tampopo (1987)

Dang Hau Dung Gin Wa Faat Laai
See From the Queen to the Chief Executive (2001)

Dang Kou Tan
See The Bloody Fists (1972)

The Dangerous Chase
See Blood of the Dragon (1971)

Dao
See The Blade (1995)

Dao Jian Xiao
See The Three Swordsmen (1994)

Dao San
See God of Gamblers (1989)

Dao San 2
See God of Gamblers Returns (1994)

Dao Shou
See Killer (2000)

Dead Heat
See Thunderbolt (1995)

Deadful Music
See Deadful Melody (1994)

Deadly China Dolls
See Lethal Panther (1991)

Deadly China Hero
See Last Hero in China (1993)

Deadly China Killer
See Last Hero in China (1993)

Deadly Life of a Ninja
See A Life of Ninja (1983)

The Deadly Mantis
See Shaolin Mantis (1978)

Deadly Shaolin Mantis
See Shaolin Mantis (1978)

Deadly Snake vs. Kung Fu Killers
See Deadly Snail vs. Kung Fu Killer (1977)

Deadly Strike
See Breakout from Oppression (1978)

The Deadly Three
See Enter the Dragon (1973)

The Deadly Venoms
See Five Deadly Venoms (1978)

Death Beach
See The Bloody Fists (1972)

Death Japanese Style
See The Funeral (1984)

Death of a Shogun
See Renegade Ninjas (1979)

Debiruman
See Devil Man (1987)

Defense Force of the Earth
See The Mysterians (1957)

Dei Seung Chui Keung
See Extreme Challenge (2001)

Dei Yuk Mo Moon
See We're Going to Eat You! (1980)

The Demons
See Nine Demons (1983)

Deng Hou Dong Jian Hua Fa La
See From the Queen to the Chief Executive (2001)

Denso Ningen
See The Secret of the Telegian (1960)

Derusu Uzara
See Dersu Uzala (1974)

The Desperate Chase
See Blood of the Dragon (1971)

Destroy All Planets
See Gamera vs. Viras (1968)

Destruction of the Red Lotus Temple
See Burning Paradise (1994)

Destruction of the Space Fleet
See Attack from Space (1958)

See Invaders from Space (1958)

The Devil Got Angry
See Daimajin (1966)

Devil Incarnate
See Evil Brain from Outer Space (1958/59)

Devil Melody
See Deadful Melody (1994)

Devils to Worry
See Sorrowful to a Ghost (1970)

Di Shang Zui Jiang
See Extreme Challenge (2001)

Di Yu Wu Men
See We're Going to Eat You! (1980)

Diakaiju Mosura
See Mothra (1961)

Diamondfinger
See Aces Go Places (1982)

Dian Zhi Gong Fu Gan Jian Chan
See Half a Loaf of Kung Fu (1977)

Die Ban
See The Butterfly Murders (1979)

Die Da Po Yu La Mei
See Chinese Orthopedist and the Spice Girls (2002)

Die Xie Jie Tou
See Bullet in the Head (1990)

Die Xie Shuang Xiong
See The Killer (1989)

Dim Chi Gung Foo Gam Gaan Daan
See Half a Loaf of Kung Fu (1977)

Dip Bin
See The Butterfly Murders (1979)

Dip Ckui Poh Yue Kwong Mooi
See Chinese Orthopedist and the Spice Girls (2002)

Dip Huet Gaai Tau
See Bullet in the Head (1990)

Dip Huet Seung Xiong
See The Killer (1989)

Direct Hit! Hellfist
See The Executioner (1974)

Dirty Partners
See From China with Death (1974)

Dirty Tiger and Crazy Frog
See Dirty Tiger, Crazy Frog (1978)

Disciples of Master Killer
See Shaolin Master Killer (1978)

The Diving Girls' Islands
See Violated Paradise (1963)

Diving Girls of Japan
See Violated Paradise (1963)

Diy
See The Blade (1995)

Diy Hap 1999
See The Conman (1998)

Diy Ma Daan
See Peking Opera Blues (1986)

Diy Sau
See Killer (2000)

Do Hap
See God of Gamblers 2 (1990)

Do Hap II Seung Hoi Taam Do Sing
See God of Gamblers 3: Back to Shanghai (1991)

Do Ma Dan
See Peking Opera Blues (1986)

Do Sing Daai Hang II Ji Ji Juen Mo Dik
See Casino Tycoon 2 (1992)

Dr. Lam
See Dr. Lamb (1992)

Dr. Vampire
See Doctor Vampire (1990)

Dr. Yuan and Weisley
See The Seventh Curse (1986)

Doh Laai Tin Sai
See Fallen Angels (1995)

Dokuga Okoku
See Evil Brain from Outer Space (1958/59)

Dong Cheng Xi Jiu
See Eagle Shooting Heroes (1993)

Dong Fang Bu Bai: Feng Yun Zai Qi
See The East Is Red (1993)

Dong Fang Ju Long
See Dragons of the Orient (1988)

Dong Fang San Xia
See The Heroic Trio (1993)

Dong Fang Tu Ying
See Eastern Condors (1986)

Dong Ging Gung Leuk
See Tokyo Raiders (2000)

Dong Jing Gong Lu
See Tokyo Raiders (2000)

Dong Kau Taan
See The Bloody Fists (1972)

Dong Xie Xi Du
See Ashes of Time (1994)

Don't Look Up
See Ghost Actress (1996)

Don't Touch Me I'm Dangerous
See Black Tight Killers (1966)

Double Dragon
See Twin Dragons (1992)

Dracula and the Seven Golden Vampires
See Legend of the 7 Golden Vampires (1974)

Dragnet
See Gunmen (1988)

The Dragon and the Cobra
See Fist of Fear—Touch of Death (1980)

Dragon and the Hero
See Dragon on Fire (1979)

Dragon Attack
See Fantasy Mission Force (1984)

Dragon Chronicles: The Maidens
See Dragon Chronicles: Maidens of Heavenly Mountain (1994)

Dragon Claws
See Dragon's Claws (1979)

Dragon Devils Die
See Bloodeed Treasury Fight (1979)

Dragon Dies Hard
See Bruce Lee We Miss You (1976)

Dragon in Shaolin
See Dragon from Shaolin (1996)

The Dragon Lives
See Bruce Lee: The Man, the Myth (1976)

The Dragon of Kung Fu
See Rage of the Dragon (1979)

A Dragon on the Waterfront
See Chinese Hercules (1973)

Dragon Reincarnate
See Revenge of the Patriots (1976)

A Dragon Story
See Story of the Dragon (1976)

Dragon Strike
See Dragon Lord (1982)

Dragon the Hero
See Dragon on Fire (1979)

Dragon vs. Vampire
See Dragon against Vampire (1985)

Dragon's Claw
See Dragon's Claws (1979)

Dragon's Fatal Fist
See The Invincible Kung Fu Trio (1978)

Dreadnought
See Dreadnaught (1981)

Dreams
See Akira Kurosawa's Dreams (1990)

Drifter Love
See Rich and Famous (1987)

Drunken Dragon
See The World of the Drunken Master (1979)

The Drunken Fighter
See Five Superfighters (1978)

Drunken Master 2
See Dance of the Drunk Mantis (1979)

See Legend of the Drunken Master (1994)

Drunken Master 3
See Drunken Master Killer (1994)

The Drunken Monk
See The Shaolin Drunken Monk (1983)

Drunken Monkey
See Drunken Master (1978)
See Monkey Fist Floating Snake (1979)

Drunken Monkey in the Tiger's Eyes
See Drunken Master (1978)

Drunken WuTang
See Drunken Art and Crippled Fist (1979)

Du Bi Quan Wang Da Po Xue Di Zi
See Master of the Flying Guillotine (1974)

Du Gim Siu
See The Three Swordsmen (1994)

Du Shen
See God of Gamblers (1989)

Du Shen 2
See God of Gamblers Returns (1994)

Du Xia
See God of Gamblers 2 (1990)

Du Xia 1999
See The Conman (1998)

Du Xia II Shang Hai Tan Du Sheng
See God of Gamblers 3: Back to Shanghai (1991)

Dubbed Action Movie
See Kung Pow: Enter the Fist (1976/2001)

The Duel
See Duel to the Death (1982)

Duel at the Tiger Village
See Iron Monkey 2 (1977)

Duel of Dragons
See Twin Dragons (1992)

Duel of Master
See Iron Monkey 2 (1977)

Duel of the Gargantuas
See War of the Gargantuas (1966)

Duel of the Seven Tigers
See Shadow of the Tiger (1979)

Duel of the Tough
See Duel of the Tao Tough (1982)

Duel on Ganryu Island
See Samurai 3: Duel at Ganryu Island (1956)

Dung Che Sai Duk
See Ashes of Time (1994)

Dung Fong Bat Baai: Fung Wan Joi Hei
See The East Is Red (1993)

Dung Fong Gui Lung
See Dragons of the Orient (1988)

Dung Fong Saam Hap
See The Heroic Trio (1993)

Dung Fong Tuk Ying
See Eastern Condors (1986)

Duo La Tian Shi
See Fallen Angels (1995)

Dut Yeung Nin Wa
See In the Mood for Love (2000)

E Hu Kuang Long
See Kung Fu, the Invisible Fist (1972)

Eagle Claw Snake Fist Cat's Paw Part 2
See Drunken Master (1978)

Eagle Fist
See Eagle's Claw (1977)

Eagle's Shadow
See Snake in the Eagle's Shadow (1978)

Earth Assault Order: Godzilla vs. Gigan
See Godzilla vs. Gigan (1972)

Earth Defense Force
See The Mysterians (1957)

Earth, Wind, Fire, Mountains
See A Fistful of Talons (1983)

Eastern Bald Eagles
See Eastern Condors (1986)

Eastern Three Heroes
See The Heroic Trio (1993)

Ebirah, Terror of the Deep
See Ebirah, Horror of the Deep (1966)

Eight Diagram Cudgel
See 8 Diagram Fighter (1991)

The Eight Diagram Pole Fighter
See Invincible Pole Fighter (1983)

8 Guardians of Buddism
See Dragon Chronicles: Maidens of Heavenly Mountain (1994)

The Eight Happiness
See Eighth Happiness (1988)

Eighteen Bronzemen 2
See The 18 Bronzemen Part 2 (1976)

18 Bronzemen 3
See The 8 Masters (1977)

The Eighteen Claws of Shaolin
See The 18 Jade Arhats (1978)

Eighteen Deadly Arhats
See The 18 Jade Arhats (1978)

18 Jade Pearls
See The 18 Jade Arhats (1978)

18 Legendary Weapons of China
See Legendary Weapons of China (1982)

18 Weapons of Kung Fu
See 18 Secrets of Kung Fu (1979)

The Electrical Facsimile Transmission Human
See The Secret of the Telegian (1960)

Emperor of the Filthy Guy
See Filthy Guy (1980)

End of Wicked Tiger
See The End of the Wicked Tiger (1981)

Endless Love
See C'est la Vie, Mon Cheri (1993)

Enter the Fist
See Kung Pow: Enter the Fist (1976/2001)

Entrails of a Whore
See Entrails of the Virgin (1986)

Er Wu Chuan Shui
See Gold Fingers (2001)

Escape from School Mighty Dragon
See Fight Back to School (1991)

The Escape of MechaGodzilla
See Terror of MechaGodzilla (1975)

Et là-bas, quelle heure est-il?
See What Time Is It There? (2001)

Eternal Conflict
See Odd Couple (1979)

EU Strike Force
See Big Bullet (1996)

An Everlasting Duel
See Lone Ninja Warrior (1981)

The Evil Cult
See Lord of the Wu Tang (1993)

Evil Dead's Trap
See Evil Dead Trap (1988)

Executioners of Death
See Executioners from Shaolin (1977)

Extreme Serious Criminal
See The Suspect (1998)

Faal Chan Che
See Wheels on Meals (1984)

Faces of Horrid
See Faces of Horror (1998)

Fai Chaal Tung Mang
See Losers' Club (2001)

Fai Seung Ching Taam
See The Private Eye Blues (1994)

Fai Seung Dat Yin
See Expect the Unexpected (1998)

Fainaru Fantaji
See Final Fantasy: The Spirits Within (2001)

Family Happiness
See All's Well End's Well (1992)

Fan Dut Cho
See Lavender (2000)

Fang Shi Yu Xu Ji
See The Legend 2 (1993)

Fang Shiyu
See Prodigal Boxer (1973)

Fangs of the Detective
See The Razor 1: Sword of Justice (1972)

Fast Fists
See Fury of King Boxer (1972)

Fat Dragon Crossing River
See Enter the Fat Dragon (1978)

Fat Jeung Lo Hon Kuen
See The Buddhist Fist (1979)

Fatal Flying Guillotines
See Fatal Flying Guillotine (1977)

Fatal Needles Fatal Fist
See Fatal Needles vs. Fatal Fists (1980)

Fay Lung Kwo Gong
See Enter the Fat Dragon (1978)

Fearless Dragon
See Fearless Dragons (1979)

Feh Goh Chuen Kei
See The Legend of a Professional (2000)

Fei Chai Tong Meng
See Losers' Club (2001)

Fei Chang Tu Ran
See Expect the Unexpected (1998)

Fei Chang Zhen Tan
See The Private Eye Blues (1994)

Fei Dao You Jian Fei Dao
See Return of the Deadly Blade (1981)

Fei Diy Yau Gin Fei Diy
See Return of the Deadly Blade (1981)

Fei Foo
See First Option (1996)

Fei Foo Hung Sam 2 Ji Ngo Hei Bei Tin Go
See The Best of the Best (1996)

Fei Ge Chuan Ji
See The Legend of a Professional (2000)

Fei Hu
See First Option (1996)

Fei Hu Xiong Xin 2 Zhi Ao Qi Bi Tian Gao
See The Best of the Best (1996)

A Fei Jing Chuen
See Days of Being Wild (1990)

Fei Long Guo Jiang
See Enter the Fat Dragon (1978)

Fei Long Meng Jiang
See Dragons Forever (1988)

Fei Lung Goh Kong
See Enter the Fat Dragon (1978)

Fei Lung Mang Cheung
See Dragons Forever (1988)

Fei Ying Gai Waak
See Operation Condor (1991)

Fei Ying Ji Hua
See Operation Condor (1991)

Fei yue ling yang
See United We Stand, and Swim (2001)

Female Reporter
See Blonde Fury (1989)

Feng Kuang Da Lao Qian
See Crazy Crooks (1980)

Feng Liu Gu Zu
See Happy Family (2002)

Feng Shiu Do
See The Prisoner (1990)

Feng Shiu Hung Lin Chi
See Burning Paradise (1994)
See The Story in Temple Red Lily (1979)

Feng Shui Siu Lam Chi
See The Blazing Temple (1976)

Feng Tau Fook Sing
See Shogun and Little Kitchen (1992)

Feng Xiong Mi Cup
See Beauty and the Breast (2002)

Feng Yu Shuang Liu Xing
See The Killer Meteors (1976)

Feng Yun
See The Storm Riders (1998)

Feng Yun Xiong Ba Tian Xia
See The Storm Riders (1998)

Fight for Shaolin Tamo Technique
See Lady Wu Tang (1977)

Fight for Survival
See Lady Wu Tang (1977)

Fight Zone
See The Avenging Fist (2001)

Fighting Justice
See Lady Iron Monkey (1983)

Fighting Madam 2
See Angel 2 (1988)

Fighting of Shaolin Monks
See Killer Priest (1981)

The Final Taboo
See Shocking Asia 2 (1976)

Fire Monster
See Godzilla Raids Again (1955)

The First Gas Human
See The Human Vapor (1960)

First Mission
See Dragons Forever (1988)
See Heart of Dragon (1985)

Fist and Guts
See Fists and Guts (1979)

A Fist Full of Talons
See A Fistful of Talons
(1983)

Fist of Fear
See Fist of Fear—Touch
of Death (1980)

Fist of Fury
See The Chinese Con-
nection (1971)

Fist of Fury II
See Fist of Fury 1991
(1991)

A Fist Too Fast
See The Legendary
Strike (1978)

**Fists, Kicks, and the
Evils**
See The Fist, the Kicks
and the Evils
(1979)

Fists of Glory
See Fists of Fury
(1971)

Fists to Fight
See New Fist of Fury
(1976)

The Five
See Gonin (1995)

5 Element Kung Fu
See Five Elements of
Kung Fu (1978)

Five Element Ninja
See Chinese Super Nin-
jas (1982)

5 Lucky Stars
See Winners and Sin-
ners (1983)

Five Venoms
See Five Deadly Ven-
oms (1978)

**Five Venoms vs. the
Ghosts**
See 5 Venoms vs. Wu
Tang (1987)

Flames, Embers
See Sholay (1975)

Flames of the Sun
See Sholay (1975)

Fleeing Couple
See On the Run (1988)

The Flesh Creatures
See Horror of the Blood
Monsters (1970)

**Flesh Creatures of the
Red Planet**
See Horror of the Blood
Monsters (1970)

Flirtong Scholar
See Flirting Scholar
(1993)

Fly in Dance
See Flyin Dance (2001)

**Flying Dragon Fierce
Challenge**
See Dragons Forever
(1988)

**Flying on the Winds of
Death**
See Lone Wolf and Cub
3: Baby Cart to
Hades (1972)

Flying Warriors
See Bichunmoo (1999)

Fo Zhang Huang Di
See The Buddha Assas-
sinator (1979)

**Fo Zhang Luo Han
Quan**
See The Buddhist Fist
(1979)

Fong Sai Yuk
See Prodigal Boxer
(1973)

Fong Sai-yuk
See The Legend (1992)

Fong Sai-yuk 2
See The Legend 2
(1993)

**Fong Sai Yuk Chuk
Chap**
See The Legend 2
(1993)

Fong Sam Ga Gei
See Midnight Fly
(2001)

Fong Shi Yu
See The Legend (1992)

**Fong Shi Yu II: Wan Fu
Mo Di**
See The Legend 2
(1993)

Foo Gwai Lit Che
See The Millionaires'
Express (1986)

Foo Maang Wei Lung
See The Red Wolf
(1995)

Foo Ying
See A Fistful of Talons
(1983)

For BadBoys Only
See For Bad Boys Only
(2000)

Force of the Dragon
See In the Line of Duty
3 (1988)

The 47 Loyal Retainers
See Chushingura
(1962)

47 Ronin
See Chushingura
(1962)

47 Samurai
See Chushingura
(1962)

**Frankenstein and the
Giant Lizard**
See Frankenstein vs.
Baragon (1965)

**Frankenstein Conquers
the World**
See Frankenstein vs.
Baragon (1965)

**Frankenstein Meets
the Giant Devil Fish**
See Frankenstein vs.
Baragon (1965)

**Frankenstein und die
Ungeheweraus den
Meer**
See Ebirah, Horror of
the Deep (1966)

**Frankenstein
Zweikampf der Gigan-
ten**
See War of the Gargan-
tuas (1966)

**Frankensteins Kampf
gegen die Teufelsmon-
ster**
See Godzilla vs. Hedo-
rah (1971)

**Freedom Strikes a
Blow**
See Chinese Hercules
(1973)

Freezer
See Freeze Me (2000)

Froggo and Droggo
See The Magic Serpent
(1966)

From China with Love
See From Beijing with
Love (1994)

Fu Gui Lie Che
See The Millionaires'
Express (1986)

Fu Xing Gao Zhao
See My Lucky Stars
(1985)

Fuk Sing Go Jiu
See My Lucky Stars
(1985)

Funeral Rites
See The Funeral (1984)

Fung Hung Bei Cup
See Beauty and the
Breast (2002)

**Fung Kwong Daai Liu
Chin**
See Crazy Crooks
(1980)

Fung Lau Ga Chuk
See Happy Family
(2002)

**Fung Wan Hung Ba Tin
Gwong**
See The Storm Riders
(1998)

Fungus of Terror
See Attack of the
Mushroom People
(1963)

**Furankenshutain no
Kaiju: Sanda tai Gaira**
See War of the Gargan-
tuas (1966)

**Furankenshutain tai
Chitei Kaiju Baragon**
See Frankenstein vs.
Baragon (1965)

**Furankensuten to
Baragon**
See Frankenstein vs.
Baragon (1965)

Fury of the Black Belt
See The Awaken Punch
(1973)

The Fury of the Dragon
See Return of the Drag-
on (1972)

**Fut Shan Jahn Seen
San**
See The Descendant of
Wing Chun (1978)

G
See Godzilla, King of
the Monsters
(1954)

Ga Goh Yau Chin Yan
See Marry a Rich Man
(2002)

Ga Li La Jiao
See Curry & Pepper
(1990)

Ga Yau Hei Si
See All's Well End's
Well (1992)

Gaal Si Ying Hung
See Avenging Warriors
of Shaolin (1979)

Gaam Yuk Fung Wan
See Prison on Fire
(1987)

**Gaam Yuk Fung Wan II
Tiu Faan**
See Prison on Fire 2
(1991)

Gai Tau Saat Sau
See Iron Monkey 2
(1996)

Gam Bei Tung
See Kid with the Gold-
en Arm (1978)

Gam Chi Yuk Sip
See He's a Woman,
She's a Man
(1994)

Gam Sik Tai Yeung
See Bruce Lee We
Miss You (1976)

Gam Yuk Moon Tong
See The Chinese Feast
(1995)

**Gambling City Mag-
nate II**
See Casino Tycoon 2
(1992)

Game of Death 2
See Tower of Death
(1981)

Gamera
See Giant Monster
Gamera (1965)

**Gamera 2: Assault of
the Legion**
See Gamera 2: Advent
of Legion (1996)

**Gamera 2: Region shu-
rai**
See Gamera 2: Advent
of Legion (1996)

Gamera 3
See Gamera 3: The
Revenge of Irys
(1999)

**Gamera 3: Incomplete
Struggle**
See Gamera 3: The
Revenge of Irys
(1999)

Gamera 3: Iris Kakusei
See Gamera 3: The
Revenge of Irys
(1999)

**Gamera Daikaiju
Kuchu Kessen**
See Gamera, Guardian
of the Universe
(1995)

**Gamera: Giant Mon-
ster Midair Showdown**
See Gamera, Guardian
of the Universe
(1995)

**Gamera, Guardian of
the Universe 1999**
See Gamera 3: The
Revenge of Irys
(1999)

Gamera Tai Barugon
See Gamera vs. Baru-
gon (1966)

**Gamera Tai Daikaiju
Giron**
See Gamera vs. Guiron
(1969)

Gamera Tai Gaos
See Gamera vs. Gyaos (1967)

Gamera Tai Shinkai Kaiju Jigara
See Gamera vs. Zigra (1971)

Gamera Tai Uchu Kaiju Bairasu
See Gamera vs. Viras (1968)

Gamera vs. Gaos
See Gamera vs. Gyaos (1967)

Gamera vs. the Deep Sea Monster Zigra
See Gamera vs. Zigra (1971)

Gammera
See Giant Monster Gamera (1965)

Gammera the Invincible
See Giant Monster Gamera (1965)

Gan Shi Xian Sheng
See Vampire Controller (2000)

Gangland Boss
See A Better Tomorrow (1986)

Gangster
See Tokyo Mafia 3: Battle for Shinjuku (1996)

Ganheddo
See Gunhed (1989)

Gao Du Jie Bei
See Full Alert (1997)

Gao Yang Yi Sheng
See Dr. Lamb (1992)

Gap Dung Gei Hap
See Iceman Cometh (1989)

Gasu Ningen Daiichigo
See The Human Vapor (1960)

Gau Ban Chi Lut Goon Baak Min Pau Ching-tin
See Hail the Judge (1994)

Gau Chai Daai Liu
See Take 2 in Life (2001)

Gau Geung Ying Ging
See Clean My Name, Mr. Coroner! (2000)

Gau Ji Tin Mor
See Nine Demons (1983)

Gau Lung
See Iron Monkey 2 (1977)

Gau Lung Bing Sat
See Goodbye Mr. Cool (2001)

Gayakushu! Satsujim-ken
See The Street Fighter's Last Revenge (1974)

Gedo
See Fatal Blade (2000)

Gei Ba Ba de Shen
See The Enforcer (1995)

Gei Jik
See Miracles (1989)

Gekitatsu! Satsujim-ken
See The Street Fighter (1974)

Gen-X Cops 2
See Gen-Y Cops (2000)

Geng Tin Daai Chaak Wong
See Operation Billionaires (1998)

Geng Tin Dung Dei
See Fury of King Boxer (1972)

Geung See Yee Sang
See Doctor Vampire (1990)

Geung Shut Fook Sing Chai
See Vampire Kids (1991)

Geung Si Fan Sheng
See New Mr. Vampire (1986)

Geung Si Sin Sang
See Mr. Vampire (1985)

Geung Si Sin Saang Juk Jaap
See Mr. Vampire 2 (1986)

Gezora Ganime Kameba: Kessen! Nankai no Daikaiju
See Yog: Monster from Space (1970)

G4: Dak Gung
See Option Zero (1997)

G4: Option Zero
See Option Zero (1997)

G4: Te Gong
See Option Zero (1997)

Ghidrah
See Ghidorah the Three-Headed Monster (1964)

Ghidrah the Three-Headed Monster
See Ghidorah the Three-Headed Monster (1964)

Ghost against Ghost
See Encounter of the Spooky Kind (1981)

Ghost Stories
See Kwaidan (1964)

The Ghost Story
See Revenge of the Zombies (1976)

The Giant Majin
See Daimajin (1966)

Giant Monster Pulgasari
See Pulgasari (1985)

Giant Robo
See Voyage into Space (1967)

Gigantis
See Godzilla Raids Again (1955)

Gigantis the Fire Monster
See Godzilla Raids Again (1955)

Gik Chuk Geung Shut
See The Vampire Combat (2001)

Gik Diy Chung Faan
See The Suspect (1998)

Gim fa Yin Yue Gong Naam
See To Kill with Intrigue (1977)

Gin Gwai
See The Eye (2002)

Ging Chat Goo Si 3: Chiu Kap Ging Chat
See Supercop (1992)

Ging Chat Goo Si 4: Ji Gaan Daan Yam Mo
See First Strike (1996)

Ging Chat Goo si Juk Jaap
See Police Story 2 (1988)

Ging Tin Lung Foo Pau
See Lethal Panther (1991)

Ging Tin Lung Foo Pau 2
See Lethal Panther 2 (1993)

Ging Tin Sap Yi Siu Si
See The Last Blood (1990)

GMK
See Godzilla, Mothra and King Ghidorah: Battle on Fire (2001)

GMK: All Monsters Attack
See Godzilla, Mothra and King Ghidorah: Battle on Fire (2001)

Go Da Gaai Bei
See Full Alert (1997)

Go Yeung Yi Sang
See Dr. Lamb (1992)

God of Fist Style
See The Avenging Fist (2001)

God of Gamblers 2
See God of Gamblers Returns (1994)

God of Gamblers: The Beginning
See God of Gamblers 3: Back to Shanghai (1991)

God of Guns
See Hard Boiled (1991)

Godzilla
See Godzilla, King of the Monsters (1954)

Godzilla and Mothra: The Battle for Earth
See Godzilla vs. Mothra (1992)

Godzilla Fights the Giant Moth
See Mothra vs. Godzilla (1964)

Godzilla, Mothra and King Ghidorah: Giant Monsters All-Out Attack
See Godzilla, Mothra and King Ghidorah: Battle on Fire (2001)

Godzilla, Mothra, King Ghidorah: Giant Monsters' General Offensive
See Godzilla, Mothra and King Ghidorah: Battle on Fire (2001)

Godzilla on Monster Island
See Godzilla vs. Gigan (1972)

Godzilla Strikes Again
See Godzilla Raids Again (1955)

Godzilla vs. Destroyer
See Godzilla vs. Destroyah (1995)

Godzilla vs. Mechagodzilla
See Godzilla vs. MechaGodzilla 2 (1993)

Godzilla vs. Megagulrus: The G Annihilation Strategy
See Godzilla vs. Megaguirus (2000)

Godzilla vs. Monster Zero
See Invasion of Astro-Monster (1965)

Godzilla vs. Mothra
See Mothra vs. Godzilla (1964)

Godzilla vs. Super-Mechagodzilla
See Godzilla vs. MechaGodzilla 2 (1993)

Godzilla vs. the Bionic Monster
See Godzilla vs. MechaGodzilla (1974)

Godzilla vs. the Cosmic Monster
See Godzilla vs. MechaGodzilla (1974)

Godzilla vs. the Giant Moth
See Mothra vs. Godzilla (1964)

Godzilla vs. the Sea Monster
See Ebirah, Horror of the Deep (1966)

Godzilla vs. the Smog Monster
See Godzilla vs. Hedorah (1971)

Godzilla vs. the Thing
See Mothra vs. Godzilla (1964)

Godzilla X Megagulrus: The G Extermination Command
See Godzilla vs. Megaguirus (2000)

Godzilla's Counterattack
See Godzilla Raids Again (1955)

Godzilla's Revenge
See All Monsters
Attack (1970)

Gojira
See Godzilla, King of
the Monsters
(1954)
See Godzilla 1985
(1984)

**Gojira Dengeki-
Taisakusen**
See Destroy All Mon-
sters (1968)

**Gojira—Ebirah—
Mosera: Nankai no
Daiketto**
See Ebirah, Horror of
the Deep (1966)

**Gojira, Minira, Gabara:
Oru Kaiju Daishingeki**
See All Monsters
Attack (1970)

**Gojira, Mosura, Kingu
Gidora: Daikaiju Souk-
ougeki**
See Godzilla, Mothra
and King Ghidorah:
Battle on Fire
(2001)

**Gojira Mosura
Kingughidorah: Chikyu
Saidai no Kessen**
See Ghidorah the
Three-Headed Mon-
ster (1964)

**Gojira Ni-sen Mirenia-
mu**
See Godzilla 2000
(1999)

Gojira no Gyakushu
See Godzilla Raids
Again (1955)

Gojira tai Hedora
See Godzilla vs. Hedo-
rah (1971)

**Gojira tai Megagirasu:
Jii Shometsu Sakusen**
See Godzilla vs.
Megaguirus (2000)

Gojira tai Megaro
See Godzilla vs. Mega-
lon (1973)

Gojira tai Mekagojira
See Godzilla vs.
MechaGodzilla
(1974)

**Gojira versus Desu-
toroia**
See Godzilla vs.
Destroyah (1995)

Gojira vs. Biorante
See Godzilla vs. Biol-
lante (1989)

Gojira vs. Kingugidora
See Godzilla vs. King
Ghidorah (1991)

Gojira vs. Mekagojira
See Godzilla vs.
MechaGodzilla 2
(1993)

Gojira vs. Mosura
See Godzilla vs. Mothra
(1992)

Gojira vs. Supesugojira
See Godzilla vs. Space
Godzilla (1994)

Gojitmal
See Lies (1999)

**Goke, Body Snatcher
from Hell**
See Body Snatcher
from Hell (1968)

Goke the Vampire
See Body Snatcher
from Hell (1968)

**Gokiburi-tachi no
Tasogare**
See Twilight of the
Cockroaches
(1987)

Golden Mask
See Golden Killah
(1980)

Golden Sun
See Bruce Lee We
Miss You (1976)

Gollathon
See Mighty Peking Man
(1977)

Gon Shut Sin Sang
See Vampire Controller
(2000)

Gong Chang Fei Long
See Dragon from Rus-
sia (1990)

Gong Chat Goo Si
See Police Story
(1985)

**Gong-Dong-Kyung-Bi-
Koo-Yeok**
See Joint Security Area
(2000)

Gong Dung Sap Foo
See Ten Tigers of
Shaolin (1978)

**Gong Dung Sap Foo
Hing Yik Ng Sui**
See Ten Tigers of
Kwangtung (1979)

**Gong Dung Tit Kiu
Saam**
See Cantonen Iron
Kung Fu (1979)

Gong Fan Ou
See Rumble in the
Bronx (1995)

Gong Fen Zhi Zun
See Queen's High
(1991)

Gong Fu Qi Jie
See 7 Commandments
of Kung Fu (1979)

Gong Fu Xiao
See He Has Nothing
But Kung Fu (1977)

Gong Pu II
See City Cop (1995)

Gong Yuan 2000 AD
See 2000 A.D. (2000)

**Gongdong gyeongbi
buyeok JSA**
See Joint Security Area
(2000)

Goo Laam Gwa Lui
See Needing You...
(2000)

Goo Tung Siu
See The Master of
Death (1982)

**Goo Waak Chai Ji Chut
Wai**
See The Final Winner
(2001)

**Goo Waak Chai Ji Yan
Joi Kong Woo**
See Young and Danger-
ous (1996)

Goo Woo Ching
See Rich and Famous
(1987)

The Good and the Bad
See Kung Fu, the Invisi-
ble Fist (1972)

**Good Luck Empress
Dowager**
See Her Majesty Is Fine
(1996)

**Goodbye Bruce Lee:
His Last Game of
Death**
See The New Game of
Death (1975)

The Gory Creatures
See Terror Is a Man
(1959)

Gou Hun Jiang Tou
See Revenge of the
Zombies (1976)

Gou Zai Da Lao
See Take 2 in Life
(2001)

Goyokiba
See The Razor 1:
Sword of Justice
(1972)

**Goyokiba: Kamisori
Hanzo Jigokuzeme**
See The Razor 2: The
Snare (1973)

**Goyokiba: Oni no
Hanzo Yawahada
Koban**
See The Razor 3:
Who's Got the
Gold? (1974)

Grand Duel in Magic
See The Magic Serpent
(1966)

Grave Desires
See Brides of Blood
(1968)
See Mad Doctor of
Blood Island
(1968)

Great Adventurers
See The Adventurers
(1995)

Great Hero of China
See Martial Arts Mas-
ter Wong Fei Hung
(1992)

**The Great Monster
War**
See Invasion of Astro-
Monster (1965)

Great Monster Yongary
See Yongary, Monster
from the Deep
(1967)

**The Great South Seas
Duel**
See Ebirah, Horror of
the Deep (1966)

The Great Space War
See Battle in Outer
Space (1959)

**The Great Undersea
War**
See Terror beneath the
Sea (1966)

**Great War under the
Sea**
See Terror beneath the
Sea (1966)

The Great World War
See The Last War
(1961)

**The Greatest Battle on
Earth**
See Ghidorah the
Three-Headed Mon-
ster (1964)

**Greatest Fight on
Earth**
See Ghidorah the
Three-Headed Mon-
ster (1964)

G2K: Millennium
See Godzilla 2000
(1999)

**Gu Huo Zai Zhi Chu
Wai**
See The Final Winner
(2001)

**Gu Huo Zai Zhi Ren
Zai Jiang Hu**
See Young and Danger-
ous (1996)

Gu Tong Xiao
See The Master of
Death (1982)

Guai Shou Xiao Yuan
See U-Man (2002)

Guang Dong Shi Hu
See Ten Tigers of
Shaolin (1978)

**Guang Dong Shi Hu
Xing Yi Wu Xu**
See Ten Tigers of
Kwangtung (1979)

**Guang Dong Tie Qiao
San**
See Cantonen Iron
Kung Fu (1979)

Guang Si Suk Suk
See Mr. Vampire Saga
4 (1988)

Guards of Shaolin
See Ninja vs. Shaolin
Guards (1984)

Gui Da Gui
See Encounter of the
Spooky Kind
(1981)

Gui Gu Chang
See Hong Kong X-File
(1998)

Gui Jian Chou
See Sorrowful to a
Ghost (1970)

Gui Ma Gong Fu
See Dirty Kung Fu
(1978)

Gui Ma Tian Shi
See Drunken Art and
Crippled Fist
(1979)

Gui Ming Mo
See Model from Hell
(1999)

Gui Qing Ni Di Hu
See Last Ghost Stand-
ing (1999)

Gui Xin Si Jian
See Lady Wu Tang
(1977)

Guinea Pig
See Guinea Pig: Devil's
Experiment (1985)

724

Guinea Pig 2
See Guinea Pig: Android of Notre Dame (1988)
See Guinea Pig: Flower of Flesh and Blood (1985)

Guinea Pig 3: Terror! Immortal Man
See Guinea Pig: He Never Dies (1986)

Guinea Pig 4
See Guinea Pig: Mermaid in a Manhole (1988)

Gun King
See Double Tap (2000)

Gung Book II
See City Cop (1995)

Gung Cheung Fei Lung
See Dragon from Russia (1990)

Gung Fan Chi Chuen
See Queen's High (1991)

Gung Foo Chat Gaai
See 7 Commandments of Kung Fu (1979)

Gung Foo Siu Ji
See He Has Nothing But Kung Fu (1977)

Gung Yuen 2000 AD
See 2000 A.D. (2000)

Guo Chan Ling Lihngqi
See From Beijing with Love (1994)

Guo Chan Xue Ge Wei Long
See Combo Cops (1996)

Guts of a Virgin
See Entrails of the Virgin (1986)

Gwaai Sau Hok Yuen
See U-Man (2002)

Gwai Cheng Lei Tai Fai
See Last Ghost Standing (1999)

Gwai Chuk Gwai
See Encounter of the Spooky Kind (1981)

Gwai Gin Sau
See Sorrowful to a Ghost (1970)

Gwai Gwat Cheung
See Hong Kong X-File (1998)

Gwai Ma Gung Foo
See Dirty Kung Fu (1978)

Gwai Ming Miu
See Model from Hell (1999)

Gwok Chaan Ling Ling-chat
See From Beijing with Love (1994)

Gwok Chaan Suet Gap Wai Lung
See Combo Cops (1996)

GXM
See Godzilla vs. Megaguirus (2000)

Ha Yay Fuk Sing
See Twinkle Twinkle Lucky Stars (1985)

Hadashi no Gen
See Barefoot Gen (1983)

Haebyeoneuro Gada
See Bloody Beach (2000)

Hak Hap
See Black Mask (1996)

Hak Mau
See Black Cat (1991)

Half Human: The Story of the Abominable Snowman
See Half Human (1955/1957)

Hammer of God
See Return of the Chinese Boxer (1975)

Han Ping Fan Dian
See Peace Hotel (1995)

Hana-bi
See Fireworks (1997)

Hand of Death
See Five Fingers of Death (1972)

Hang Gui
See The Blood Rules (2000)

Hang Kwai
See The Blood Rules (2000)

Hang Zhou Wang Ye
See The Lord of Hangzhou (1998)

Hanzo the Razor's Torture from Hell
See The Razor 2: The Snare (1973)

Hao Xia
See Last Hurrah for Chivalry (1978)

Hap Daai Ngai Hat
See Militant Eagle (1978)

Hap Diy Go Fei
See Full Contact (1992)

Hap Lui
See A Touch of Zen (1969)

Hard-Boiled
See Hard Boiled (1991)

Hard Boiled 2: The Last Blood
See The Last Blood (1990)

The Haunted Cop Shop of Horrors
See The Haunted Cop Shop (1987)

Haunted Gold
See The Razor 3: Who's Got the Gold? (1974)

Health Warning
See Flash Future Kung Fu (1983)

Heart of the Dragon
See Heart of Dragon (1985)

Heart of the Parent, Heart of the Child
See Lone Wolf and Cub 4: Baby Cart in Peril (1972)

Heaven and Hell
See High and Low (1963)

Heaven's Assassin, Heaven Has Eyes
See Comeuppance (2000)

Heavy Metal
See Satin Steel (1994)

Hei Foon Lei
See Fall for You (2001)

Hei Mao
See Black Cat (1991)

Hei Xia
See Black Mask (1996)

Hell Fist
See The Executioner (1974)

Hell Has No Gates
See We're Going to Eat You! (1980)

Heping Fandian
See Peace Hotel (1995)

The Hero
See Rage of the Masters (1974)

Hero Defeating Japs
See Ninja in the Deadly Trap (1983)

Heroes Defeat Japs
See Ninja in the Deadly Trap (1983)

The Heroic One
See Inheritor of Kung Fu (1977)

Heroic Trio 2: Executioners
See Executioners (1993)

He's a Hero, He's a Legend
See The New Game of Death (1975)

He's a Legend, He's a Hero
See Story of the Dragon (1976)

Heung Gong Dai Hung Chak
See Haunted Mansion (1998)

Heung Kong Dut Yuet Yau
See Hong Kong Nocturne (1967)

Hideous Mutant
See A*P*E (1976)

Him Gok
See Sharp Guns (2001)

Hiroku: Yokai Hanta
See Hiruko the Goblin (1990)

Hiroku: Yokai Hunter
See Hiruko the Goblin (1990)

Hissatsu 4: Urami Hurashimtsu
See Sure Death: Revenge (1987)

Hissatsu Sankaku Tobi
See The Bodyguard (1973/78)

The History of Mademoiselle Q
See The Ladies' Phone Sex Club (1996)

Hitman
See Contract Killer (1998)

Ho Hap
See Last Hurrah for Chivalry (1978)

Hoichi the Earless
See Kwaidan (1964)

Holy Robes of Shaolin
See The Holy Robe of Shaolin Temple (1984)

Hong Chow Wong Yow
See The Lord of Hangzhou (1998)

Hong Kong Adam's Family
See H.K. Adams Family (1992)

Hong Kong Cat Named Karado
See Super Kung Fu Kid (1974)

Hong Kong Police Madam 2
See Angel 2 (1988)

Hong Qiang dao Ying
See Millennium Dragon (1999)

Hong Wending San Po Bai Lian Jiao
See Fists of the White Lotus (1980)

Hong Xi Guan Fang Shi Yu Liu A Cai
See The Invincible Kung Fu Trio (1978)

Hong Xiguan
See Executioners from Shaolin (1977)

Hong Xiguan zhi Shaolin Wu Zu
See The New Legend of Shaolin (1994)

Honneamise no Tsubasa—Oritsu Uchugun
See Royal Space Force: The Wings of Honneamise (1987)

Honogurai mizu no soko kara
See Dark Water (2002)

Horror Creatures of the Lost Planet
See Horror of the Blood Monsters (1970)

Horror Creatures of the Prehistoric Planet
See Horror of the Blood Monsters (1970)

Horror Creatures of the Red Planet
See Horror of the Blood Monsters (1970)

Hot Dog Kung Fu
See Chinese Samson (1979)

Hot-Handed God of Cops
See Hard Boiled (1991)

Hot Hot and Pom Pom
See Pom Pom and Hot Hot (1992)

Hotaru no Haka
See Grave of the Fireflies (1988)

Hsa Nu—the Gallant Lady
See A Touch of Zen (1969)

Hsing Hsing Wang
See Mighty Peking Man (1977)

Hu Long Tian Shi Zhao Ji Gui
See Kung Fu Zombie (1981)

Hu Meng Wei Long
See The Red Wolf (1995)

Hu Tu Da Xia San Ge Ban
See 5 Lady Venoms (1978)

Hu Ying
See A Fistful of Talons (1983)

Hua Pi Zhi Yin Yang Fa Wang
See Painted Skin (1992)

Hua Yang Nian Hua
See In the Mood for Love (2000)

Hua Zhong Xian
See Picture of a Nymph (1988)

Huan Ying Te Gong
See Hot War (1998)

Huang Feihong
See Once upon a Time in China (1991)

Huang Feihong Zhi IV Wang Zhe Zhi Feng
See Once upon a Time in China 4 (1993)

Huang Feihong Zhi er Nan er Dang Zi Qiang
See Once upon a Time in China 2 (1992)

Huang Feihong Zhi San shi Wang Zheng Ba
See Once upon a Time in China 3 (1993)

Huang Feihong Zhi Tie Ji Dou Wu Gong
See Last Hero in China (1993)

Huang Feihong Zhi Xi Yu Xiong Shi
See Once upon a Time in China and America (1997)

Huang Feihung Xie Lie Zhi Yi Dai Shi
See Martial Arts Master Wong Fei Hung (1992)

Huang Gu Nu Jiang
See She Shoots Straight (1990)

Huang He Da Xia
See Yellow River Fighter (1988)

Huang Jia Shi Jie
See Yes, Madam (1985)

Huang Jia Shi Jie Zhi III
See In the Line of Duty 3 (1988)

Huang Jia Shi Jie Zhi IV Zhi Ji Zheng Ren
See In the Line of Duty 4 (1989)

Huang Jia Shi Jie Zhi Zhong Jian Ren
See In the Line of Duty 5: Middle Man (1990)

Huang Jia Zhan Shi
See Royal Warriors (1986)

Huang Xin Jia Ji
See Midnight Fly (2001)

Huet Dik Ji
See The Flying Guillotine (1974)

Human Meat Pies
See The Untold Story (1992)

Human Night in Painted Skin
See Painted Skin (1992)

Human Pork Chop
See The Untold Story (1992)

Hung Biu Sin Ji Daai Tau Gwai Ang
See Horror Hotline Big Head Monster (2001)

Hung Bo Yit Sin
See Horror Hotline Big Head Monster (2001)

Hung Bong
See The Imp (1981)

Hung Cheung do Ying
See Millennium Dragon (1999)

Hung Fan Au
See Rumble in the Bronx (1995)

Hung Hei Goon Fong Sai Yuk Luk A Choi
See The Invincible Kung Fu Trio (1978)

Hung Hei-Koon: Shaolin's Five Founders
See The New Legend of Shaolin (1994)

Hung Hei-kwun
See Executioners from Shaolin (1977)

Hung Hei-kwun: Kung Fu Master
See The Kung Fu Master (1994)

Hung Hsi-Kuan
See Executioners from Shaolin (1977)

Hung Jeuk Wong
See The Peacock King (1989)

Hung Man-ding Saam Por Bak Lin Gaau
See Fists of the White Lotus (1980)

Hung Mau
See Evil Cat (1986)

Hung The Color of a Hero
See A Better Tomorrow (1986)

Huo Shao Dao
See The Prisoner (1990)

Huo Shao Gong Lian Si
See Burning Paradise (1994)
See The Story in Temple Red Lily (1979)

Huo Shao Shao Lin Si
See The Blazing Temple (1976)

Huo Tou Fu Xing
See Shogun and Little Kitchen (1992)

Hup do Jing Chuen
See Chivalrous Legend (1998)

Hwasan Highschool
See Volcano High School (2001)

Hypnosis
See The Hypnotist (1999)

I Mostri della Citta Sommersa
See Terror beneath the Sea (1966)

I Saw a Dream Like This
See Akira Kurosawa's Dreams (1990)

If Heaven Has Love
See A Moment of Romance (1990)

If Sky Have Love
See A Moment of Romance (1990)

The Immortals
See Dragon Chronicles: Maidens of Heavenly Mountain (1994)

In Eagle Dragon Fist
See Dragon Fist (1978)

In the Line of Duty
See In the Line of Duty 4 (1989)
See Royal Warriors (1986)

In the Line of Duty 2
See In the Line of Duty 5: Middle Man (1990)
See Royal Warriors (1986)
See Yes, Madam (1985)

In the Line of Duty: A Beginning
See Queen's High (1991)

In the Line of Fire 3
See In the Line of Duty 3 (1988)
See In the Line of Duty 5: Middle Man (1990)

In the Woods
See Rashomon (1950)

Incredible Death Kick Master
See The Leg Fighters (1980)

Incredible Master Beggars
See My Kung Fu 12 Kicks (1979)

Injeong Sajeong Bolgeot Eobda
See Nowhere to Hide (1999)

Insatsu no Toriko
See Terminatrix (1995)

Inspector Wears a Skirt
See The Inspector Wears Skirts (1988)

Intramuros
See The Walls of Hell (1964)

Invaders from Space
See Prince of Space (1959)

Invaders from the Spaceship
See Prince of Space (1959)

Invasion from a Planet
See Invasion of the Neptune Men (1961)

Invincible Asia 2
See The East Is Red (1993)

Invincible Boxer
See Five Fingers of Death (1972)

The Invincible Kung Fu Legs
See The Leg Fighters (1980)

The Invincible Shaolin
See Once upon a Time in China 3 (1993)

Iron Angels
See Angel (1987)

Iron Angels 2
See Angel 2 (1988)

Iron Fingers of Death
See Death Mask of the Ninja (1982)

Iron Fingers of Shaolin
See Death Mask of the Ninja (1982)

Iron Fisted Warrior
See Cantonen Iron Kung Fu (1979)

Iron Fists
See Shaolin King Boxer (1979)

Iron Maiden
See The Legendary Strike (1978)

Iron Man
See Chinese Iron Man (1975)
See Tetsuo: The Iron Man (1989)

Iron Monkey Strikes Back
See Iron Monkey 2 (1977)

Iron Monkey: The Young Wong Fei-hung
See Iron Monkey (1993)

Iron Palm
See Five Fingers of Death (1972)

Iron Rooster vs. the Centipede
See Last Hero in China (1993)

The Irresistible Women
See The Irresistible Piggies (2002)

Island of Fire
See The Prisoner (1990)

Island of Living Horror
See Brides of Blood (1968)

Island of Terror
See Terror Is a Man (1959)

Island of the Twilight People
See Twilight People (1972)

Island on Fire
See The Prisoner (1990)

Jackie and the 36 Crazy Fists
See The 36 Crazy Fists (1977)

Jackie Chan Presents: Metal Mayhem
See Gen-Y Cops (2000)

Jackie Chan vs. Wang Yu
See The Killer Meteors (1976)

Jackie Chan's Bloodpact
See The 36 Crazy Fists (1977)

Jackie Chan's First Strike
See First Strike (1996)

Jackie Chan's Police Story
See Police Story (1985)

Jackie Chan's Police Story 2
See Police Story 2 (1988)

Jackie Chan's Project A
See Project A (1983)

Jackie Chan's 36 Crazy Fists
See The 36 Crazy Fists (1977)

Jackie Chan's Who Am I?
See Who Am I? (1998)

Jade Killer
See The 18 Jade Arhats (1978)

Jaianto Robo
See Voyage into Space (1967)

Jet Li's The Enforcer
See The Enforcer (1995)

Jeung Bo Miu Taam
See The New Marvelous Double (1992)

Jeung Hok Yau
See High Risk (1995)

Jeung San
See God of Cookery (1996)

Jeung Ying Hung Chung Ying Hung
See Fearless Dragons (1979)

Ji Dong Ji Xia
See Iceman Cometh (1989)

Ji Du Chong Fan
See The Suspect (1998)

Ji Juen Mo Seung
See Casino Raiders (1989)

Ji Juen Mo Seung II: Wing Au Tin Gwong
See Casino Raiders 2 (1991)

Ji Men Dun Jia
See The Miracle Fighters (1982)

Ji Mou Miao Ji Wu Fu Xing
See Winners and Sinners (1983)

Ji Su Jiang Shi
See The Vampire Combat (2001)

Ji Yung Saam Bo
See Mr. Boo Meets Pom Pom (1985)

Ji Zhao
See Jade Claw (1979)

Jia Ge You Qian Ren
See Marry a Rich Man (2002)

Jia You Xi Shi
See All's Well End's Well (1992)

Jian Gui
See The Eye (2002)

Jian Hua Yan Yu Jiang Nan
See To Kill with Intrigue (1977)

Jian Ren Shi Jia
See H.K. Adams Family (1992)

Jian Yu Feng Yun
See Prison on Fire (1987)

Jian Yu Feng Yun II Tao Fan
See Prison on Fire 2 (1991)

Jiang Hu Qing
See Rich and Famous (1987)

Jiang Shi Fan Sheng
See New Mr. Vampire (1986)

Jiang Shi Fu Xing Zai
See Vampire Kids (1991)

Jiang Shi Fu Xing Zi
See Vampire Kids (1991)

Jiang Shi Shu Shu
See Mr. Vampire Saga 4 (1988)

Jiang shi Xian Sheng
See Mr. Vampire (1985)

Jiang Shi Xian Sheng Xu Ji
See Mr. Vampire 2 (1986)

Jiang-Hu: Between Love and Glory
See The Bride with White Hair (1993)

Jiang-Hu: Between Love and Glory 2
See The Bride with White Hair 2 (1993)

Jidu Hanleng
See Frozen (1996)

Jie Dao Sha Ren
See Hit-Man in the Hand of Buddha (1980)

Jie Shi Ying Xiong
See Avenging Warriors of Shaolin (1979)

Jie Tou Sha Shou
See Iron Monkey 2 (1996)

Jie Yuan
See The Witch from Nepal (1985)

Jin Bi Tong
See Kid with the Golden Arm (1978)

Jin Qi Yu She
See He's a Woman, She's a Man (1994)

Jin Se Tai Yang
See Bruce Lee We Miss You (1976)

Jin Yu Man Tang
See The Chinese Feast (1995)

Jing Cha Gu Shi
See Police Story (1985)

Jing Cha Gu Shi 3: Chao Ji Jing Cha
See Supercop (1992)

Jing Cha Gu Shi 4: Zhi Jian Dan Ren Wu
See First Strike (1996)

Jing Cha Gu shi Xu Ji
See Police Story 2 (1988)

Jing Cheung
See The Cheaters (2001)

Jing Tian Da Ze Wang
See Operation Billionaires (1998)

Jing Tian Dong Di
See Fury of King Boxer (1972)

Jing Tian Long Hu Bao
See Lethal Panther (1991)

Jing Tian Long Hu Bao 2
See Lethal Panther 2 (1993)

Jing Tian Shi Er Xiao Shi
See The Last Blood (1990)

Jing Wu Men
See The Chinese Connection (1971)
See Fist of Fury (1995)

Jing Wu Ying Xiong
See Fist of Legend (1994)

Jinji Pojiang
See Crash Landing (2000)

Jinko Eisen to Jinrui no Hametsu
See Attack from Space (1958)

Jiu Hap Hung
See Legend of the Drunken Tiger (1992)

Jiu Jiang Xing Jing
See Clean My Name, Mr. Coroner! (2000)

Jiu Long
See Iron Monkey 2 (1977)

Jiu Long Bing Shi
See Goodbye Mr. Cool (2001)

Jiu Pin Zhi Ma Guan Bai Mian Bao Qingtian
See Hail the Judge (1994)

Jiu Xian Shi Ba Die
See The World of the Drunken Master (1979)

Jiu Zi Tian Mo
See Nine Demons (1983)

Jo Hissatsu Ken
See Sister Street Fighter (1974)

Johnny Socko and His Giant Robot
See Voyage into Space (1967)

Joi Gin A Long
See Where a Good Man Goes (1999)

Jopog manura
See My Wife Is a Gangster (2001)

Joshuu Sasori—Dai 41 Zakkyobo
See Female Convict Scorpion: Jailhouse 41 (1972)

Joshu Sasori: Daishujuichi Zakkyobo
See Female Convict Scorpion: Jailhouse 41 (1972)

Joyuu-rei
See Ghost Actress (1996)

Jubei Ninpocho
See Ninja Scroll (1993)

Jubei Ninpocho: The Wind Ninja Chronicles
See Ninja Scroll (1993)

Judo Saga
See Sanshiro Sugata (1943)

Judo Story
See Sanshiro Sugata (1943)

Jue Lai Yip Yue Leung Saan Ang
See Juliet in Love (2000)

Jue Se Shen Tou
See Martial Angels (2001)

Jue Shi Hao Bra
See Brassiere (2001)

Jue Zhan Zi Jin Zhi Dian
See The Duel (2000)

Jue Zhao
See Fists Like Lee (1974)

Juen Diu Daal Ngok
See Crocodile Hunter (1989)

Jui Gaai Paak Dong
See Aces Go Places (1982)

Jui Gaai Paak Dong Chin Lee Gau Cha Poh
See Aces Go Places 4 (1986)

Jui Gaai Paak Dong Daai Hin Sang Tun
See Aces Go Places 2 (1983)

Jui Gaai Paak Dong Lui Wong Mat Lim
See Aces Go Places 3 (1984)

Jui Kuen 2
See Legend of the Drunken Master (1994)

Jui Kuen 3
See Drunken Master Killer (1994)

Jui Sang Mung Sei Ji Waan Jai Ji Foo
See Tragic Fantasy: Tiger of Wanchai (1994)

Jui
See Beautiful Hunter (1994)

Jung Wa Ying Hung
See Born to Defence (1988)

Jung Waang Sei Hoi
See Once a Thief (1991)

Jung Wah Jin Si
See Magnificent Warriors (1987)

Junk: Dying to Live
See Junk (1999)

Junk: Evil Dead Hunting
See Junk (1999)

Junk: Shiryou Gari
See Junk (1999)

Juyuso Seubgyuk Sa Geun
See Attack the Gas Station! (1999)

Jyujin Yuki Otoko
See Half Human (1955/1957)

Ka Lei Laat Jiu
See Curry & Pepper (1990)

Kagaku Ninja tai Gatchaman
See Gatchaman (1994)

Kagi no Kag
See What's Up, Tiger Lily? (1966)

Kaidan
See Kwaidan (1964)

Kaiju Daisenso
See Invasion of Astro-Monster (1965)

Kaiju Soshingeki
See Destroy All Monsters (1968)

Kaijuto no Kessen: Gojira no Musuko
See Son of Godzilla (1967)

Kairo
See Pulse (2001)

Kairyu Daikessen
See The Magic Serpent (1966)

Kaitei Daisenso
See Terror beneath the Sea (1966)

Kakushi Toride no San Akunin
See The Hidden Fortress (1958)

Kang Xi Da Nao Wu Tai Shan
See The Prisoner of Five Boulders (1989)

Kangxi Upsets Wutai Mountains
See The Prisoner of Five Boulders (1989)

Kap Ang Ang Dik San
See The Enforcer (1995)

Karate Bomber
See Spiritual Kung Fu (1978)

Karate Exterminator
See Lightning Kung Fu (1980)

Karate Ghostbuster
See Spiritual Kung Fu (1978)

Karate Kiba
See The Bodyguard (1973/78)

Karate Warrior
See Lightning Kung Fu (1980)

Karura no yuma
See Dream of Garuda (1994)

Katakurike no Koufuku
See The Happiness of the Katakuris (2001)

The Kato Show
See The Green Hornet (1974)

Kei Chiu
See Jade Claw (1979)

Kei Mau Miu Gai Ng Fook Sing
See Winners and Sinners (1983)

Kei Moon Dun Gaap
See The Miracle Fighters (1982)

Kei Yuen
See The Witch from Nepal (1985)

Key of Keys
See What's Up, Tiger Lily? (1966)

Key Witness
See In the Line of Duty 5: Middle Man (1990)

The Kick of Death
See Prodigal Boxer (1973)

Kickboxer's Tears
See Kick Boxer's Tears (1992)

Kickmaster
See Sting of the Dragon Masters (1973)

Kid Dreams Thriller
See Scared Stiff (1986)

The Kid from Tibet
See A Kid from Tibet (1991)

Kido Keisatsu Patoreba: The Movie
See Patlabor 1: The Movie (1990)

Kids from Shaolin
See Shaolin Temple 2: Kids from Shaolin (1984)

Kids of Shaolin
See The Shaolin Kids (1977)

Kikujiro no natsu
See Kikujiro (1999)

Killer Constable
See Lightning Kung Fu (1980)

Killer Hillz
See The 72 Desperate Rebels (1976)

King Boxer
See Five Fingers of Death (1972)

King Kong no Gysakushu
See King Kong Escapes (1967)

King Kong Strikes Again
See King Kong Escapes (1967)

King of Assassins
See Contract Killer (1998)

King of Destruction
See Love on Delivery (1994)

King of Kung Fu
See The New Game of Death (1975)

Kingdom of the Poisonous Moth
See Evil Brain from Outer Space (1958/59)

Kingukongu tai Gojira
See King Kong vs. Godzilla (1962)

Kinpeibei
See Notorious Concubines (1969)

Knife Horse Dawn
See Peking Opera Blues (1986)

Knight of Gamblers 2: The Gambling Saint of Shanghai Beach
See God of Gamblers 3: Back to Shanghai (1991)

Kofun
See Naked Pursuit (1968)

Kokaku Kidotai
See Ghost in the Shell (1995)

Koneko Monogatari
See The Adventures of Milo and Otis (1986)

Kong Bu Re Xian Zhi Da Tou Guai Ying
See Horror Hotline Big Head Monster (2001)

Kong Qiao Wang
See The Peacock King (1989)

Kong Woo Giu Gap
See Jiang Hu—"The Triad Zone" (2000)

Konna Yume Wo Mita
See Akira Kurosawa's Dreams (1990)

Koroshi no Rakuin
See Branded to Kill (1967)

Koroshiya 1
See Ichi the Killer (2001)

Koroshiya Ichi
See Ichi the Killer (2001)

Kowloon's Eye
See Police Story 2 (1988)

Kozure Okami: Jigoku e Ikuzo! Daigoro
See Lone Wolf and Cub 6: White Heaven in Hell (1974)

Kozure Okami: Kowokoshi Udekashi Tsukamatsuru
See Lone Wolf and Cub 1: Sword of Vengeance (1972)

Kozure Okami: Meifumando
See Lone Wolf and Cub 5: Baby Cart in the Land of Demons (1973)

Kozure Okami: Oya no Kokoro Ko no Kokoro
See Lone Wolf and Cub 4: Baby Cart in Peril (1972)

Kozure Okami: Sanzu no Kawa no Ubaguruma
See Lone Wolf and Cub 2: Baby Cart at the River Styx (1972)

Kozure Okami: Shinikazeni Mukau Ubaguruma
See Lone Wolf and Cub 3: Baby Cart to Hades (1972)

Kuai Can Che
See Wheels on Meals (1984)

Kuang Qing Sha Shou
See Dragon Killer (1995)

Kuen Cheng
See Spiritual Kung Fu (1978)

Kuen Moon
See Bloody Fight (1972)

Kuen San
See The Avenging Fist (2001)

Kuen Sun
See The Avenging Fist (2001)

Kuet Chin Chi Gam Ji Din
See The Duel (2000)

Kulay Dugo Ang Gabi
See The Blood Drinkers (1964)

Kumonosu Jo
See Throne of Blood (1957)

Kun Shou
See The Replacement Suspects (2001)

Kung Fu Ace
See Fighting Ace (1979)

Kung Fu Cannibals
See We're Going to Eat You! (1980)

Kung Fu Commandos
See The Incredible Kung Fu Mission (1982)

Kung Fu Cult Master
See Lord of the Wu Tang (1993)

Kung Fu for Sale
See Kung Fu on Sale (1979)

Kung Fu Girls
See 5 Lady Venoms (1978)

Kung Fu Is Forever
See Iron Neck Li (1981)

Kung Fu Kids
See Dreaming Fists with Slender Hands (1980)

The Kung Fu Master
See Lord of the Wu Tang (1993)

Kung Fu Soccer
See Shaolin Soccer (2001)

Kung Fu, the Punch of Death
See Prodigal Boxer (1973)

Kung Fu Vampire Buster
See New Mr. Vampire (1986)

Kung Fu Warlords
See Brave Archer (1977)

Kunoichi Ninpo Cho: Ninja Getsuel Sho
See Lady Ninja: Reflections of Darkness (1996)

Kuon Puos Keng Kang
See Snaker (2001)

Kurosufala
See Cross Fire (2000)

Kwan Lung Fai Fung
See Pedicab Driver (1989)

Kwan Sau
See The Replacement Suspects (2001)

Kwan Tsan Tseh
See Wheels on Meals (1984)

Kwong Ching Saai Sau
See Dragon Killer (1995)

Kwong Sau Wooi Chun
See Help!!! (2000)

Kyofu
See The Manster (1960)

Kyojin to Gangyu
See Giants and Toys (1958)

Kyoryu Kaicho no Desenso
See Legend of the Dinosaurs (1977)

Kyua
See Cure (1997)

Kyuketsuki Gokemi-doro
See Body Snatcher from Hell (1968)

Kyuketsuki Hunter D
See Vampire Hunter D (1985)

La Brassiere
See Brassiere (2001)

La Se Ai Qing
See A Love of Blueness (2000)

La Shou Hui Chun
See Help!!! (2000)

La Shou Shen Tan
See Hard Boiled (1991)

Laam Bak Chui Kuen
See Dance of the Drunk Mantis (1979)

Laan Tau He
See Dirty Ho (1979)

Laang Chin
See Cold War (2000)

The Ladies' Phone Club
See The Ladies' Phone Sex Club (1996)

Lady Enforcers
See The Inspector Wears Skirts (1988)

Lady Reporter
See Blonde Fury (1989)

Lady Whirlwind Against the Rangers
See Lady Whirlwind and the Rangers (1974)

Lam Sai-wing (Yan Je Mo Dik)
See The Magnificent Butcher (1979)

Lam Yeung Sap Dai Che Sui
See The Eternal Evil of Asia (1995)

Lan Tou He
See Dirty Ho (1979)

Lang Bei Wei Jian
See From China with Death (1974)

Lang Zi Yi Zhao
See The Legendary Strike (1978)

Lao Fu Zi 2001
See Master Q 2001 (2001)

Lao Hu ? Hing
See The End of the Wicked Tiger (1981)

Lao Hu Chu Geng
See Tiger on Beat (1988)

Lao Hu Tian Ji
See Dirty Tiger, Crazy Frog (1978)

Lao Mao
See The Cat (1991)

The Last Duel
See Double Dragon in the Last Duel (1985)

Last Hurray for Chivalry
See Last Hurrah for Chivalry (1978)

The Last Judgment
See Aakhri Adalat (1988)

Last Warning
See Legend of the 7 Golden Vampires (1974)

Lat Sau San Tam
See Hard Boiled (1991)

Laughing Tai Chi
See Drunken Tai Chi (1984)

Le Baiser Mortel du Dragon
See Kiss of the Dragon (2001)

Le Guerriers de Shaolin
See Raiders of Wu Tang (1982)

Le Voyage de Chihiro
See Spirited Away (2001)

Lee Bit Gwan
See The Deadly Sword (1978)

Lee Kicks Back
See The Fist, the Kicks and the Evils (1979)

Lee Rock 1
See Lee Rock (1991)

Lee Siu Lung Chuen Kei
See Bruce Lee: The Man, the Myth (1976)

Legend of Dinosaurs and Monster Birds
See Legend of the Dinosaurs (1977)

Legend of Dragon
See Legend of the Dragon (1991)

The Legend of Fong Sai-yuk
See The Legend (1992)

Legend of Future Shaolin
See The New Legend of Shaolin (1994)

Legend of Hero
See A Man Called Hero (1999)

The Legend of Musashi
See Samurai I: Musashi Miyamoto (1954)

Legend of Prince
See No More Love, No More Death (1992)

Legend of Tekken
See The Avenging Fist (2001)

Legend of the Fist Master
See The Avenging Fist (2001)

Legend of the Over-fiend
See Urotsukidoji (1989)

Legend of the Phoenix
See The Peacock King (1989)

Legend of the Red Dragon
See The New Legend of Shaolin (1994)

Legend of the Shadowy Ninja
See The Ninja Dragon (1990)

Legend of the Thieving Hero
See Chivalrous Legend (1998)

The Legend of Wisely
See Bury Me High (1990)

The Legend of Zu
See Zu Warriors (2001)

Legendary Weapons of Kung Fu
See Legendary Weapons of China (1982)

Legends of Shaolin
See The New Legend of Shaolin (1994)

Lei Ting Sao Xue
See Red Shield (1991)

Lei Ting Zhan Jing
See China Strike Force (2000)

Leng Zhan
See Cold War (2000)

Lethal Lady
See She Shoots Straight (1990)

Lethal Panther
See Lethal Panther 2 (1993)

Let's Play, Dharma
See Hi! Dharma! (2001)

Letter to Daddy
See The Enforcer (1995)

Leung Goh Chi Lang Wood Yat Goh
See The Odd One Dies (1997)

Leung San Gwai Chiu
See Goose Boxer (1978)

Li Bie Jun
See The Deadly Sword (1978)

Li Xiao Long Chuan Ji
See Bruce Lee: The Man, the Myth (1976)

Lian Ai Hang Xing
See Tiramisu (2002)

Lian Zhan Chong Sheng
See Okinawa Rendezvous (2000)

Liang Ge Zhi Neng Huo Yi Ge
See The Odd One Dies (1997)

Liang Shan Guai Zhao
See Goose Boxer (1978)

Liao Zhai Yan Tan
See Erotic Ghost Story (1990)

Liao Zhai Yan Tan Xu Ji Wu Tong Shen
See Erotic Ghost Story 2 (1991)

Lie Bao Hang Dong
See Leopard Hunting (1998)

Lie Huo Zhan Che
See Full Throttle (1995)

Lie Huo Zhan Che 2 Ji Su Chuan Shui
See Legend of Speed (1999)

Lies/Uso
See Lies (1999)

Life Has Take 2
See Take 2 in Life (2001)

Lightning Kung Fu
See The Victim (1980)

Lightning Swords of Death
See Lone Wolf and Cub 3: Baby Cart to Hades (1972)

Like Holy Eight Divine Cane
See 8 Diagram Fighter (1991)

Lin Shirong (Ren Zhe Wu Di)
See The Magnificent Butcher (1979)

Lip Jeung 32 Diy
See Beyond Hypothermia (1996)

Lip Paau Hang Dung
See Leopard Hunting (1998)

Liquid Sword 2
See Lone Ninja Warrior (1981)

Lit Feng Chin Che 2 Gik Chuk Chuen Suet
See Legend of Speed (1999)

Lit Fo Jin Che
See Full Throttle (1995)

Literate Strike
See Chinese Samson (1979)

Liu Chai Yim Taam
See Erotic Ghost Story (1990)

Liu Chai Yim Taam Chuk Chap Ng Tung San
See Erotic Ghost Story 2 (1991)

Liu Foo ? Sing
See The End of the Wicked Tiger (1981)

Liu Foo Chut Gang
See Tiger on Beat (1988)

Liu Foo Ji 2001
See Master Q 2001 (2001)

Liu Foo Tin Gai
See Dirty Tiger, Crazy Frog (1978)

Liu He Ba Fa
See The Six Directions of Boxing (1979)

Liu He Qian Shou
See Shadow of the Tiger (1979)

Liu Zhi Qin Mo
See Deadful Melody (1994)

Lo Maau
See The Cat (1991)

Lone Wolf and Cub: In Peril
See Lone Wolf and Cub 4: Baby Cart in Peril (1972)

Long Arm of the Law Saga 2
See Long Arm of the Law 2 (1987)

Long Bool Wai Gaan
See From China with Death (1974)

Long De Chuan Ren
See Legend of the Dragon (1991)

Long De Xin
See Heart of Dragon (1985)

Long Hu Feng Yun
See City on Fire (1987)

Long Hu Xin Feng Yun Tou Hao Tong Ji Fan
See The Most Wanted (1994)

Long Huo Chang Cheng
See Shaolin Fist of Fury (1987)

Long Ji Yat Chiu
See The Legendary Strike (1978)

Long Man Sa Sau Ji Yau Yan
See Killer's Romance (1990)

Long Man Sha Shou Tze Yo Ren
See Killer's Romance (1990)

Long Quan
See Dragon Fist (1978)

Long Quan She Shou Men Zhi Zhu
See Challenge of Death (1978)

Long Shao Ye
See Dragon Lord (1982)

Long Teng Hu Yue: Fearless Hyena Part II
See Fearless Hyena 2 (1980)

Long Wei Shan Zhuang
See 99 Cycling Swords (1980)

Long Xie Shi San Ying
See Avenging Eagle (1978)

Long Xing Tian Xia
See The Master (1989)

Long Xiong Hu Di
See Armour of God (1986)

Long Zai Bian Yuan
See Century of the Dragon (1999)

Long Zai Jiang Hu
See Legacy of Rage (1986)

Long Zai Shao Lin
See Dragon from Shaolin (1996)

Long Zheng Hu Dou
See Enter the Dragon (1973)

Long Zhi Gu Zu
See The Dragon Family (1988)

The Longest Night
See The Longest Nite (1998)

Lost Kung Fu Secret
See The Lost Kung Fu Secrets (1980)

Love and Death in Saigon
See A Better Tomorrow 3 (1989)

Love Trap at the Paramount
See Paramount Motel (2000)

Loves of a Gorgeous Man
See Gorgeous (1999)

Lu Ding Ji
See Royal Tramp (1992)

Lu Ding Ji II Zhi Shen Long Jiao
See Royal Tramp 2 (1992)

Lucky Stars Shine Highest and Brightest
See My Lucky Stars (1985)

Luen Chin Chung Sing
See Okinawa Rendezvous (2000)

Luen Oi Hang Sing
See Tiramisu (2002)

Lui Ting Chin Ging
See China Strike Force (2000)

Lui Ting So Yuet
See Red Shield (1991)

Luk Chi Kam Moh
See Deadful Melody (1994)

Luk Gap Baat Fat
See The Six Directions of Boxing (1979)

Luk Gap Chin Sau
See Shadow of the Tiger (1979)

Luk Ting Kei
See Royal Tramp (1992)

Luk Ting Kei II Ji San Lung Gau
See Royal Tramp 2 (1992)

Lung Chang Foo Dao
See Enter the Dragon (1973)

Lung Chi Fung Chuk
See The Dragon Family (1988)

Lung Dik Chuen Yan
See Legend of the Dragon (1991)

Lung Dik Sam
See Heart of Dragon (1985)

Lung Foo Fung Wan
See City on Fire (1987)

Lung Foo San Fung Wan Tau Ho Tung Chap Faan
See The Most Wanted (1994)

Lung Hang Tin Ha
See The Master (1989)

Lung Hing Foo Dai
See Armour of God (1986)

Lung Joi Bin Yuen
See Century of the Dragon (1999)

Lung Joi Gong Woo
See Legacy of Rage (1986)

Lung Joi Siu Lam
See Dragon from Shaolin (1996)

Lung Kuen
See Dragon Fist (1978)

Lung Kuen Sau Sau Moon Jeung Chu
See Challenge of Death (1978)

Lung Siu Yau
See Dragon Lord (1982)

Lung Tang Foo Yeuk
See Fearless Hyena 2 (1980)

Lung Wai Saan Chong
See 99 Cycling Swords (1980)

Lung Wei Village
See 99 Cycling Swords (1980)

Lupin 3: Castle of Cagliostro
See Castle of Cagliostro (1979)

Maal Hung Paak Yan
See You Shoot, I Shoot (2001)

Maan Yan Gan
See Lightning Kung Fu (1980)

Maang Gwai Cha Goon
See The Haunted Cop Shop (1987)

Maau Tau Ying Yue Siu Fel Cheung
See The Owl vs. Bombo (1984)

Maboroshi no Hikari
See Maborosi (1995)

Macbeth
See Throne of Blood (1957)

Mach Go Go Go!
See Speed Racer: The Movie (1967)

Mad Mission
See Aces Go Places (1982)

Mad Mission 2: Aces Go Places
See Aces Go Places 2 (1983)

Mad Mission 3: Our Man from Bond Street
See Aces Go Places 3 (1984)

Mad Mission 4: You Never Die Twice
See Aces Go Places 4 (1986)

Mad Mission 5
See Aces Go Places 5: The Terracotta Hit (1989)

The Magic Lyre
See Deadful Melody (1994)

Magic of the Shaolin Sorceress
See Succubare (1977)

Magnificent Pole Fighters
See Invincible Pole Fighter (1983)

Magnificent Seven
See Seven Samurai (1954)

Mai Kuen Saam Sap Luk Chu
See The 36 Deadly Styles (1979)

Mai nei dak Gung Dui
See Fantasy Mission Force (1984)

Mai Xiong Pai Ren
See You Shoot, I Shoot (2001)

Maitei Jyakku
See Mighty Jack (1968)

Majin
See Daimajin (1966)

Majin Strikes Again
See Return of Daimajin (1966)

Majin the Hideous Idol
See Daimajin (1966)

Majin, the Monster of Terror
See Daimajin (1966)

Majin the Stone Samurai
See Daimajin (1966)

Makai Tensho: The Armageddon
See Reborn from Hell: Samurai Armageddon (1996)

Mamono Hunter Yohko
See Devil Hunter Yohko (1991)

Mamono Hunter Yohko Part 2
See Devil Hunter Yohko 2 (1992)

Mamono Hunter Yohko Part 3
See Devil Hunter Yohko 3 (1992)

Man Chui
See Chinese Samson (1979)

The Man from Tokyo
See Tokyo Drifter (1966)

Man Qing Jin Gong Ji An
See Sex and the Emperor (1994)

Man Qing Shi Da Ku Xing
See A Chinese Torture Chamber Story (1994)

Man Qing Shi Da Ku Xing Zhi Chi Luo Ling Chi
See A Chinese Torture Chamber Story 2 (1998)

Mang Jiao De Tian Kong
See Man Wanted (1995)

Mang Lung Goh Kong
See Return of the Dragon (1972)

Mang Quan Gui Shou
See Blind Fist of Bruce (1979)

The Mansion
See Mahal (1948)

Mao Tou Ying Yu Xiao Fei Xiang
See The Owl vs. Bombo (1984)

Maohgai
See Sadistic City (1993)

Martial Angels
See Angel (1987)

Martial Arts
See Fists Like Lee (1974)

Masseur Ichi and a Chest of Gold
See Zatoichi and the Chest of Gold (1964)

Masseur Ichi Enters Again
See New Tale of Zatoichi (1963)

Masseur Ichi the Fugitive
See Zatoichi the Fugitive (1963)

The Master
See 3 Evil Masters (1980)

The Master and the Boxer
See The 36 Crazy Fists (1977)

Master Digital
See Flash Future Kung Fu (1983)

Master Killer
See Shaolin Master Killer (1978)

Master Killer 2
See Return of the Master Killer (1980)

Master Swordsman
See Samurai I: Musashi Miyamoto (1954)

Matango
See Attack of the Mushroom People (1963)

Meal Head Lucky Star
See Shogun and Little Kitchen (1992)

MechaGodzilla vs. Godzilla
See Terror of MechaGodzilla (1975)

Mei Mong Leung, Chi Mei Wang Liang
See Nightmare Zone (1998)

Mei Tian Ai Nin Xiao Shi
See Your Place or Mine! (1998)

Mekagojira no Gyakushu
See Terror of MechaGodzilla (1975)

Mekingu Obu Za Ginip-iggu
See Guinea Pig: The Making of Guinea Pig (1986)

Meltdown
See High Risk (1995)

The Men Who Step on the Tiger's Tail
See Men Who Tread on the Tiger's Tail (1943)

Meng Gui Cha Guan
See The Haunted Cop Shop (1987)

Meng Long Guo Jiang
See Return of the Dragon (1972)

Message from Space: Galactic Wars
See Message from Space (1978)

Mi ni te Gong Dui
See Fantasy Mission Force (1984)

Mi Quan San Shi Liu Zhao
See The 36 Deadly Styles (1979)

Mian Qing Qing You Pai Jing
See Faces of Horror (1998)

Miao Tan Shuang Jiao
See Beauty Investigator (1992)

Middle Man
See In the Line of Duty 5: Middle Man (1990)

Midnight Angel 2
See Angel 2 (1988)

Midnight Angels
See Angel (1987)

Midnight Angels 2
See Angel 2 (1988)

Midnite Angels
See Angel (1987)

Million Dollar Heiress
See Wheels on Meals (1984)

Militant Eagle
See Militant Eagle (1978)

Min Ching Ching Yau Paai Geng
See Faces of Horror (1998)

The Ming Patriots
See Revenge of the Patriots (1976)

Ming Yue Zhao Jian Dong
See With or Without You (1992)

Ming Yuet Chiu Chim Dung
See With or Without You (1992)

Mini Special Force
See Fantasy Mission Force (1984)

Minya, Son of Godzilla
See Son of Godzilla (1967)

Minya: Son of Godzilla
See All Monsters Attack (1970)

Mission for the Dragon
See Rage of the Dragon (1979)

Mr. Boo
See The Private Eyes (1976)

Mr. Boo 2: Private Eyes
See The Private Eyes (1976)

Mr. Canton and Lady Rose
See Miracles (1989)

Mr. Digital
See Flash Future Kung Fu (1983)

Mr. Stiff Corpse
See Mr. Vampire (1985)

Mr. Vampire Part II
See Mr. Vampire 2 (1986)

Mr. Vampire 4
See Mr. Vampire Saga 4 (1988)

Mr. Vampire Saga IV
See Mr. Vampire Saga 4 (1988)

Mit Moon Chaam Ngon Ji Yip Saal
See Daughter of Darkness (1993)

Miu Chong Yuen: So Hat Ngai
See King of Beggars (1992)

Miu Haan Fook Wood
See Second Time
Around (2002)

Miu Kool
See Ninja vs. Shaolin
Guards (1984)

Miu Lam Sing Dau Si
See Deadend of
Besiegers (1992)

Miu Meng Tut Yeung
See On the Run (1988)

Miu Meng Yan Che
See A Life of Ninja
(1983)

Miu Min Bei
Sec Don't Give a Damn
(1995)

Miu Ming Siu Chuet
See His Name Is
Nobody (1979)

Miu Taam Seung Giu
See Beauty Investigator
(1992)

Miu Yan Ga Sai
See Spacked Out
(2000)

**Miyamoto Musashi:
Ichijoji no Ketto**
See Samurai 2: Duel at
Ichijoji Temple
(1955)

**Miyamoto Musashi:
Ketto Ganryu-jima**
See Samurai 3: Duel at
Ganryu Island
(1956)

**Mo Jung Yuen Tit Kiu
Sam**
See Sam the Iron
Bridge: Champion
of Martial Arts
(1993)

Mo Neuih
See Devil Woman
(1970)

Mobile Police Patlabor
See Patlabor 1: The
Movie (1990)

**Modern Day Wonder
Heroes Legend**
See Executioners
(1993)

Moju
See Blind Beast (1969)

**Mong Kok Dik Tin
Hung**
See Man Wanted
(1995)

**Mong Seung Gwaai
Taam**
See 990714.com
(2000)

Monk Tamo
See Killer Priest (1981)

Monkey Kung Fu
See Monkey Fist Float-
ing Snake (1979)

Monks Go Crazy
See War of the Shaolin
Temple (1980)

Mononoke Hime
See Princess
Mononoke (1997)

Monster City
See Wicked City (1987)

**Monster from a Prehis-
toric Planet**
See Gappa: The Triphib-
ian Monster (1967)

**Monster Island Deci-
sive Battle: Godzilla's
Son**
See Son of Godzilla
(1967)

Monster of Monsters
See Ghidorah the
Three-Headed Mon-
ster (1964)

Monster Yongkari
See Yongary, Monster
from the Deep
(1967)

Monster Zero
See Invasion of Astro-
Monster (1965)

MonsterAttack March
See Destroy All Mon-
sters (1968)

**Monsters from an
Unknown Planet**
See Terror of
MechaGodzilla
(1975)

**Moon Ching Gam Gung
Gei Ngon**
See Sex and the
Emperor (1994)

**Moon Ching Sap Daai
Huk Ying Ji Chek Law
Ling Jeung**
See A Chinese Torture
Chamber Story 2
(1998)

**Moon Ching Sap Dai
Huk Ying**
See A Chinese Torture
Chamber Story
(1994)

**Moon Tin Oi Lei Siu
Shut**
See Your Place or
Mine! (1998)

Mortal Combat
See The Return of the
5 Deadly Venoms
(1978)

Mosura
See Mothra (1961)
See Rebirth of Mothra
(1996)

Mosura 2
See Rebirth of Mothra
2 (1997)

Mosura tai Gojira
See Mothra vs. Godzilla
(1964)

Mou Mian Bei
See Don't Give a Damn
(1995)

Mu Lou Xiong Guang
See Victim (1999)

Mu Mien Jia Sha
See The Holy Robe of
Shaolin Temple
(1984)

Muk Lau Hung Gwong
See Victim (1999)

Muk Min Ga Qui
See The Holy Robe of
Shaolin Temple
(1984)

Murder of Murders
See The Massive
(1978)

Musashi and Kojiro
See Samurai 3: Duel at
Ganryu Island
(1956)

Musashi Miyamoto
See Samurai I:
Musashi Miyamoto
(1954)

My Father Is a Hero
See The Enforcer
(1995)

My Lucky Stars 2
See Twinkle Twinkle
Lucky Stars (1985)

**The Mysterious Satel-
lite**
See Warning from
Space (1956)

**Mystery of Chess Box-
ing**
See Ninja Checkmate
(1979)

**Naam Kuen Bak Tui
Chim Ming Wong**
See The Hot, the Cool,
and the Vicious
(1976)

Nameless
See Gumnaam (1965)

Nan Bei Tui Wang
See The Leg Fighters
(1980)

Nan Bei Zui Quan
See Dance of the
Drunk Mantis
(1979)

**Nan Quan Bei Tui Zhan
Yan Wang**
See The Hot, the Cool,
and the Vicious
(1976)

**Nan Yang Shi Da Xie
Shu**
See The Eternal Evil of
Asia (1995)

Nazo no Tenkousei
See The Dimension
Travelers (1998)

Nepal Affair
See The Witch from
Nepal (1985)

New Dragon Gate Inn
See Dragon Inn (1992)

New Dragon Inn
See Dragon Inn (1992)

New Endless Love
See C'est la Vie, Mon
Cheri (1993)

The New King Kong
See A*P*E (1976)

**New Legendary
Weapons of China**
See Legendary
Weapons of China
(1982)

New Mr. Stiff Corpse
See New Mr. Vampire
(1986)

New Mr. Vampire 2
See 5 Venoms vs. Wu
Tang (1987)

New Police Story
See Crime Story
(1993)

Ng Duk
See Five Deadly Ven-
oms (1978)

**Ng Foo Cheung Ji Kuet
Lit (Gam Paai Ng Foo
Cheung)**
See The Tigers (1991)

**Ng-long Baat Gwa
Gwan**
See Invincible Pole
Fighter (1983)

**Ng Yi Taam Jeung Lui
Lok Juen**
See Lee Rock (1991)

**Ngo Dik Foo Chan Miu
Chan**
See The Road Home
(1999)

**Ngo Dik Yau Goo Tung
Hok**
See My School Mate,
the Barbarian
(2001)

Ngo Foo Chong Lung
See Crouching Tiger,
Hidden Dragon
(2000)

Ngo Foo Kwong Lung
See Kung Fu, the Invisible Fist (1972)

**Ngo Shut Sui, Wo Shi
Shei**
See Who Am I? (1998)

Ngoh Si Yat Goh Chaak
See Legendary Couple
(1995)

Ni neibian jidian
See What Time Is It
There? (2001)

**Nie Men Can An Zhi
Nie Sha**
See Daughter of Dark-
ness (1993)

Night
See Raat (1991)

Night of the Wolf
See Horror of the Blood
Monsters (1970)

Nightmare
See The Manster
(1960)

The 9 Venoms
See Nine Demons
(1983)

**1999 The Deadly
Camp**
See The Deadly Camp
(1999)

**98 Goo Wat Jai Ji Lung
Jung Fu Dai**
See Young and Danger-
ous 5 (1998)

**98 Gu Huo Zai Zhi
Long Zheng Hu Dou**
See Young and Danger-
ous 5 (1998)

98 Wise Guys
See Young and Danger-
ous 5 (1998)

'91 San Diu Hap Liu
See Savior of the Soul
(1991)

'91 Shen Diao Xia Lu
See Savior of the Soul
(1991)

97 Fung Yau Hei Si
See All's Well End's
Well '97 (1997)

97 Gu You Xi Shi
See All's Well End's
Well '97 (1997)

**'92 San Diu Chi Chi
Sam Ching Cheung
Gim**
See Savior of the Soul
2 (1992)

**'92 Shen Diao Zhi Chi
Xin Qing Chang Jian**
See Savior of the Soul
2 (1992)

Ninja
See Ninja: Band of
Assassins (1962)

Ninja 2
See Ninja: Band of
Assassins Contin-
ued (1963)

**Ninja and the Final
Duel**
See Ninja the Final
Duel (1985)

Ninja Apocalypse
See The Magic Serpent
(1966)

**Ninja Bugeicho
Momochi Sandayu**
See Shogun's Ninja
(1982)

**Ninja, Grand Masters
of Death**
See A Life of Ninja
(1983)

Ninja Kung Fu
See Ninja in the Deadly
Trap (1983)

**Ninja over the Great
Wall**
See Shaolin Fist of Fury
(1987)

Ninjutsu
See Ninja in the Deadly
Trap (1983)

No Door to Hell
See We're Going to Eat
You! (1980)

No Foh Wai Lung
See Crystal Hunt
(1991)

No More Mr. Nice Guy
See Mr. Nice Guy
(1997)

Nobles' Express
See The Millionaires'
Express (1986)

Nora Inu
See Stray Dog (1949)

Not Yet!
See Madadayo (1992)

Nu Huo Wei Long
See Crystal Hunt
(1991)

Nu Jie Xie Ren
See Robotrix (1991)

Nutty Kickbox Cops
See Skinny Tiger and
Fatty Dragon
(1990)

Octagon Force
See Yoga and Kung Fu
Girl (1978)

Odishon
See Audition (1999)

Ohayo
See Good Morning
(1959)

**Oi Ching Baak Min
Baau**
See Bakery Amour
(2001)

Oi Ching Goon Chi Joi
See Love au Zen
(2001)

**Oi Ching Man Gam Dei
Daai**
See Love Paradox
(2000)

Oi Gwan Yue Mung
See Dance of a Dream
(2001)

Oi Seung Ngo Ang
See Gimme Gimme
(2001)

Oi Yue Shing
See A War Named
Desire (2000)

Okinawa Rendezvous
See Okinawa Rendez-
vous (2000)

Old Master Cute 2001
See Master Q 2001
(2001)

Old Master Q 2001
See Master Q 2001
(2001)

Oldman Z
See Roujin Z (1991)

On Loh Lut Tak Lin Loh
See Anna Magdalena
(1998)

**Once upon a Time in
China 6**
See Once upon a Time
in China and Ameri-
ca (1997)

**Once upon a Time in
Shanghai**
See Shanghai 1920
(1991)

One Armed Hero
See One Arm Hero
(1994)

One-Armed Boxer 2
See Master of the Fly-
ing Guillotine
(1974)

**One-Armed Boxer vs.
the Flying Guillotine**
See Master of the Fly-
ing Guillotine
(1974)

Onna Hissatsu Ken
See Sister Street Fighter (1974)

**Operation Condor 2:
The Armour of God**
See Armour of God
(1986)

Operation: Dragon
See Enter the Dragon
(1973)

Operation Eagle
See Operation Condor
(1991)

Operation Monsterland
See Destroy All Mon-
sters (1968)

Option 2
See First Option (1996)

**Ore Ni Sawaru To
Abunaize**
See Black Tight Killers
(1966)

Orgy of Blood
See Brides of Blood
(1968)

Ososhiki
See The Funeral (1984)

Otenki-oneesan
See Weather Woman
(1995)

**Otsuyu: Kaidan Botan
Doro**
See The Haunted
Lantern (1998)

The Owl and Dumbo
See The Owl vs. Bombo
(1984)

The Owl vs. Bumbo
See The Owl vs. Bombo
(1984)

**Paau Lui Duet Meng Ji
Lui**
See Her Name Is Cat
2: Journey to Death
(2001)

Painting of a Nymph
See Picture of a Nymph
(1988)

Panther Girl
See Her Name Is Cat
2: Journey to Death
(2001)

Para Paras Sakuya
See Para Para Sakura
(2001)

Parasaito Ivu
See Parasite Eve
(1997)

**Patlabor: The Mobile
Police**
See Patlabor 1: The
Movie (1990)

Patrol Horse
See The Postman
Fights Back (1982)

Patrol of Horses
See The Postman
Fights Back (1982)

Pau Mool
See Her Name Is Cat
(1998)

Peacock Prince
See The Peacock King
(1989)

Peculiar Fist Kid
See Drunken Art and
Crippled Fist
(1979)

**People of the Head-
lines**
See Headlines (2001)

**Perambulator against
the Winds of Death**
See Lone Wolf and Cub
3: Baby Cart to
Hades (1972)

**Perambulator of the
River Sanzu**
See Lone Wolf and Cub
2: Baby Cart at the
River Styx (1972)

Phantom 7000
See The Mysterians
(1957)

**Phu San Jahn Sen
Shun**
See The Descendant of
Wing Chun (1978)

Pi Li Da La Ba
See Where's Officer
Tuba? (1986)

Pi Li Huo
See Thunderbolt
(1995)

Pi Li Qing
See Venom Warrior
(1983)

Pi Li Xian Feng
See Final Justice
(1988)

Pick Your Poison
See Five Deadly Ven-
oms (1978)

Pik Lik Ching
See Venom Warrior
(1983)

Pik Lik Daai La Ba
See Where's Officer
Tuba? (1986)

Pik Lik Feng
See Thunderbolt
(1995)

Pik Lik Sin Fung
See Final Justice
(1988)

Pirate Patrol
See Project A (1983)

Po Huai Zhi Wang
See Love on Delivery
(1994)

Po Jie Da Shi
See Warrior from
Shaolin (1981)

Poh Gaai Daai Bye
See Warrior from
Shaolin (1981)

Poh Wai Ji Wong
See Love on Delivery
(1994)

Police Assassin 2
See In the Line of Duty
5: Middle Man
(1990)
See Yes, Madam
(1985)

Police Assassins
See Royal Warriors
(1986)
See Yes, Madam
(1985)

Police Dragon
See Crime Story
(1993)

Police Force
See Police Story
(1985)

Police Force II
See Police Story 2
(1988)

Police Story Part II
See Police Story 2
(1988)

Police Story 3
See Supercop (1992)

**Police Story 3: Super
Cop**
See Supercop (1992)

733

Police Story 3 Part 2
See Supercop 2 (1993)

Police Story 4
See First Strike (1996)

Police Story IV
See Crime Story (1993)

Police Story 4: Piece of Cake
See First Strike (1996)

Police Story 4: Project S
See Supercop 2 (1993)

Police Story V
See Supercop 2 (1993)

Police Story Sequel
See Police Story 2 (1988)

Police Woman
See Young Tiger (1972)

Police Woman against Jackie Chan
See Young Tiger (1972)

Portrait of a Nymph
See Picture of a Nymph (1988)

The Postman Strikes Back
See The Postman Fights Back (1982)

Posutoman Burusu
See Postman Blues (1997)

Powerman
See Wheels on Meals (1984)

Prince of Shaolin
See Death Mask of the Ninja (1982)

The Princess and the Toxicant
See Succubare (1977)

The Private Eye Blues
See The Private Eye Blues (1994)

Project A Part 2
See Project A 2 (1987)

Project B
See Extreme Crisis (1998)

Project Eagle
See Operation Condor (1991)

Project S
See Supercop 2 (1993)

Pulgasari: The Legendary Monster
See Pulgasari (1985)

Pull No Punches
See The Prodigal Son (1981)

Punishment
See Undercover Blues (2000)

Purojukuto A-ko
See Project A-ko (1986)

Pyrokinesis
See Cross Fire (2000)

Qi dao si bai ji
See What Time Is It There? (2001)

Qi Ji
See Miracles (1989)

Qi Jin Shi
See Legend of the 7 Golden Vampires (1974)

Qi Xiao Fu
See Painted Faces (1988)

Qi Yuan
See The Witch from Nepal (1985)

Qian Nu You Hun
See A Chinese Ghost Story (1987)

Qian Nu You Hun II Ren Jian Dao
See A Chinese Ghost Story 2 (1990)

Qian Nu You Hun III Dao Dao Dao
See A Chinese Ghost Story 3 (1991)

Qian Xi Yuan
See Wishful Milenio (2001)

Qiang Huo
See The Mission (1999)

Qiang Wang
See Double Tap (2000)

Qing Mi Da Hua Wang
See Everyday Is Valentine (2001)

Qing She
See Green Snake (1993)

Qing Sheng
See The Magnificent Scoundrels (1991)

Qing Xian Bai Le Men
See Paramount Motel (2000)

Quan Jing
See Spiritual Kung Fu (1978)

Quan Men
See Bloody Fight (1972)

Quan Shen
See The Avenging Fist (2001)

Quan Zhi Sha Shou
See Fulltime Killer (2001)

Qun Long Xi Feng
See Pedicab Driver (1989)

Raatri
See Raat (1991)

Radon
See Rodan (1956)

Rage of the Tiger
See Rage of the Masters (1974)

Raging Master's Tiger Crane
See Masters of Tiger Crane (1983)

Raiders of Shaolin
See Raiders of Wu Tang (1982)

Raiders of the Shaolin Temple
See Raiders of Wu Tang (1982)

Raise the Coffin, Make Money
See Troublesome Night 3 (1997)

The Rangers
See Lady Whirlwind and the Rangers (1974)

The Ransom
See High and Low (1963)

Rape of the Red Temple
See Burning Paradise (1994)

Rasho-Mon
See Rashomon (1950)

Re Xue Zui Qiang
See Task Force (1997)

The Record
See Record (2000)

Red Bronx
See Rumble in the Bronx (1995)

Red Square Thieves
See Millennium Dragon (1999)

Ren Ba Zhao
See Thousand Mile Escort (1976)

Ren Rou Cha Shao Bao II Tian Zhu Di Mie
See The Untold Story 2 (1998)

Ren Zhe Da Jue Dou
See Ninja Hunter (1983)

The Replacement Suspect
See The Replacement Suspects (2001)

The Return of Giant Majin
See Wrath of Daimajin (1966)

The Return of Godzilla
See Godzilla 1985 (1984)
See Godzilla Raids Again (1955)

The Return of Majin
See Wrath of Daimajin (1966)

The Return of Masseur Ichi
See The Tale of Zatoichi Continues (1962)

Return of the 18 Bronzemen
See The 18 Bronzemen Part 2 (1976)

The Return of the Giant Monsters
See Gamera vs. Gyaos (1967)

The Return of the God of Gamblers
See God of Gamblers Returns (1994)

Return of the Scorpion
See Shadow of the Tiger (1979)

Return of the Secret Rivals
See Filthy Guy (1980)

Return to the 36th Chamber
See Return of the Master Killer (1980)

Revenge
See Double Dragon in the Last Duel (1985)

The Revenge of King Kong
See King Kong Escapes (1967)

Revenge of MechaGodzilla
See Terror of MechaGodzilla (1975)

Revenge of the Dragon
See Fearless Hyena (1979)
See Shaolin Chastity Kung Fu (1981)

Revenge of the Shaolin Kid
See The Master of Death (1982)

Revenge! The Killing Fist
See The Street Fighter's Last Revenge (1974)

Revengeful Swordswoman
See Revengeful Swordwomen (1979)

Rhen Zhe Wu Di
See Chinese Super Ninjas (1982)

Righting Wrongs 2
See Blonde Fury (1989)

Riki-Oh
See Riki-Oh: The Story of Ricky (1989)

Ring
See Ring Virus (1999)

Ring 0
See Ring 0: Birthday (2000)

The Ring 2
See Ring 2 (1999)

The Ring: Virus
See Ring Virus (1999)

Ringu
See Ring (1998)

Ringu 0: Baasudei
See Ring 0: Birthday (2000)

Ringu 2
See Ring 2 (1999)

Robocop vs. Vampires
See Robo Vampire (1988)

Roboforce
See I Love Maria (1988)

Rock and Roll Cop
See Rock 'n' Roll Cop (1994)

Rodan the Flying Monster
See Rodan (1956)

Rojin Z
See Roujin Z (1991)

Ross Fire
See Cross Fire (2000)

Ru Lai Ba Gua Gun
See 8 Diagram Fighter (1991)

Rumble in Hong Kong
See Young Tiger (1972)

Ruo Sha
See Red to Kill (1994)

Rupan Sansei: Kariosu-toro no Shiro
See Castle of Cagliostro (1979)

Ruthless Tactics
See Ninja in the Deadly Trap (1983)

Ryo no Oujo
See Dragon Princess (1981)

Saai Chai Yee Yan Cho
See 100 Ways to Murder Your Wife (1986)

Saai Sau Dik Tung Wa
See A Taste of Killing and Romance (1994)

Saai Sau Ga Gei
See Day Off (2001)

Saai Sau Hiu
See The Big Brawl (1980)

Saam Sap Luk Mai Ying Kuen
See The 36 Crazy Fists (1977)

Saan Chuen Liu Shut
See A Wicked Ghost (1999)

Saan Chuen Liu Shut II Sik Ji Nyn Gwai
See A Wicked Ghost 2: The Fear (2000)

Saan Chung Chuen Kei
See Legend of the Mountain (1979)

Saan Gau 1999
See The Deadly Camp (1999)

Saang Gong Kei Bing
See Long Arm of the Law (1984)

Saang Gong Kei Bing II
See Long Arm of the Law 2 (1987)

Saat Yan Je Tong Jaan
See The Assassin (1993)

Sai Chut Chung Wai, Sha Chu Chong Wei
See Breakout from Oppression (1978)

Sai Jong Siu Ji
See A Kid from Tibet (1991)

Sai Yau Gei Dai Git Guk Ji Sin Lei Kei Yuen
See A Chinese Odyssey Part 2: Cinderella (1995)

Sai Yau Gei Dai Yat Baak Ling Yat Wooi Ji Yuet Gwong Bo Hap
See A Chinese Odyssey Part 1: Pandora's Box (1995)

Saimin
See The Hypnotist (1999)

Sakuya: Legend of Monsters
See Sakuya: Slayer of Demons (2000)

Sakuya: Yokaiden
See Sakuya: Slayer of Demons (2000)

Sam Sei Goon
See Justice, My Foot! (1992)

Sam the Iron Bridge
See Sam the Iron Bridge: Champion of Martial Arts (1993)

Sam the Iron Bridge 2
See One Arm Hero (1994)

Samehada Otoko to Momojiri Onna
See Shark Skin Man and Peach Hip Girl (1998)

Samurai
See Samurai I: Musashi Miyamoto (1954)

Samurai 3
See Samurai 3: Duel at Ganryu Island (1956)

San Bat Liu Ching
See C'est la Vie, Mon Cheri (1993)

San Bat Yau Gei
See The Victim (1980)

San Bik Huet Kim
See The Sword Stained with Royal Blood (1993)

San Cheng Miu Moon
See New Fist of Fury (1976)

San Cheng Miu Moon 1991
See Fist of Fury 1991 (1991)

San Cheung Sau Yue Ka Lei Gai
See Pom Pom and Hot Hot (1992)

San Daikaiju: Chikyu Saidai no Kesson
See Ghidorah the Three-Headed Monster (1964)

San Dip Huet Seung Hung
See Thunder Cop (1996)

San Fong Sai Yuk Chuk Chap
See Iron Man (1986)

San Giu Cheung Yee Sang
See Trust Me U Die (1999)

San Lau Man Yee Sang
See Doctor No... (2001)

San Lau SingWoo Dip Gim
See Butterfly and Sword (1993)

San Lung Chang Fu Dau
See Kick Boxer's Tears (1992)

San Lung Moon Haak Chan
See Dragon Inn (1992)

San Shi Liu Mi Xing Quan
See The 36 Crazy Fists (1977)

San Suk Saan Kim Hap
See Zu: Warriors of the Magic Mountain (1983)

San Tai Yon Ekkusu Jugatsu
See Boiling Point (1990)

San Tao Yin Lee Saam
See The Hero of Swallow (1996)

San Tau Dip Ying
See Downtown Torpedoes (1997)

San Tin Lung Baat Biu Chi Tin Saan Tung Liu
See Dragon Chronicles: Maidens of Heavenly Mountain (1994)

San Ying Hung Boon Sik
See Return to a Better Tomorrow (1994)

San yeung Seung Heung Paau Juk Jaap
See Rosa (1986)

San Yung Seung Heung Paau
See Pom Pom (1984)

Sanada Yukimura no Boryaku
See Renegade Ninjas (1979)

Sand vs. Gallah
See War of the Gargantuas (1966)

Sang Dut Dak Ging Ji Song Shut Yam Miu
See Bio-Cops (2000)

Sang Dut Sau Shut
See Bio Zombie (1998)

Sang Gong Yat Ho Tung Chap Faan
See Rock 'n' Roll Cop (1994)

Sang sei Kuen Chuk
See Fist Power (1999)

Sanj Jui Gaal Paak Dong
See Aces Go Places 5: The Terracotta Hit (1989)

Sap Baat Boon Saam Ngai
See Legendary Weapons of China (1982)

Sap Baat Boon Mo Ngai
See 18 Secrets of Kung Fu (1979)

Sap Daal Saal Sau
See 10 Magnificent Killers (1977)

Sap Saam Din Who Gwing
See War of the Shaolin Temple (1980)

Sap Yee Taam Tui
See My Kung Fu 12 Kicks (1979)

Saru no Gundan
See Time of the Apes (1975)

Sat Sau Ji Wong
See Contract Killer (1998)

Satomi Hakken-den
See Legend of the Eight Samurai (1984)

Satsujim-ken 2
See Return of the Street Fighter (1974)

Sau Foo Fei Lung
See Skinny Tiger and Fatty Dragon (1990)

Sau Geun Laam Lui
See Love on a Diet (2001)

Sau Hok Daan Sam Jan Gau Chow
See Snake-Crane Secret (1978)

Sau Saan Goo Lui
See Succubare (1977)

Sau Sai Sau
See Killer Snakes (1974)

Sau Ying Chui Biu
See Snake Deadly Act (1979)

Saufbold und Raufbold
See Drunken Art and Crippled Fist (1979)

Saviour of Souls
See Savior of the Soul (1991)

Saviour of Souls 2
See Savior of the Soul 2 (1992)

Saviour of the Soul '92
See Savior of the Soul 2 (1992)

Scintillating Sin
See Violated Paradise (1963)

Scorpion: Female Prisoner Cage #41
See Female Convict Scorpion: Jailhouse 41 (1972)

The Screaming Tiger
See Screaming Ninja (1973)

Se Diu Ying Hung Ji Dung Sing Sai Jau
See Eagle Shooting Heroes (1993)

Se Diu Ying Hung Juen
See Brave Archer (1977)

Se Hok Bat Bo
See Snake and Crane Arts of Shaolin (1978)

Se Ying Diu Sau
See Snake in the Eagle's Shadow (1978)

Sea Nymphs
See Violated Paradise
(1963)

Secret of the Buddhist Fist
See The Buddhist Fist
(1979)

The Secret of the Snake and Crane
See Snake-Crane
Secret (1978)

Secret Police
See City Hunter: Secret
Service (1996)

Sei Dai Tam Jeung
See Powerful Four
(1991)

Sei Miu Taap
See Tower of Death
(1981)

Sei Miu Yau Fai
See Game of Death
(1978)

Sek Po Tin Geng
See The Awaken Punch
(1973)

Sekai Daisenso
See The Last War
(1961)

Semi-Gods and Semi-Devils
See Dragon Chronicles:
Maidens of Heavenly Mountain (1994)

Sen
See Spirited Away
(2001)

Sen and the Mysterious Disappearance of Chihiro
See Spirited Away
(2001)

Sen to Chihiro no Kamikakushi
See Spirited Away
(2001)

Sepesu Amiiba
See Yog: Monster from
Space (1970)

Serious Crimes Squad
See Crime Story
(1993)

Seung hoi 1920
See Shanghai 1920
(1991)

Seung Joi Ngo Sam
See Funeral March
(2001)

Seung Lung To Ji
See Pom Pom Strikes
Back (1986)

Seung Lung Wooi
See Twin Dragons
(1992)

The 7 Brothers and a Sister Meet Dracula
See Legend of the 7
Golden Vampires
(1974)

Seven Brothers Meet Dracula
See Legend of the 7
Golden Vampires
(1974)

The 7 Brothers of Dracula
See Legend of the 7
Golden Vampires
(1974)

The 7 Brothers Versus Dracula
See Legend of the 7
Golden Vampires
(1974)

7 Gam Gong
See Wonder Seven
(1994)

The 7 Golden Vampires
See Legend of the 7
Golden Vampires
(1974)

Seven Golden Vampires: The Last Warning
See Legend of the 7
Golden Vampires
(1974)

7 Jin Gang
See Wonder Seven
(1994)

7 to 400 Blows
See What Time Is It
There? (2001)

Sex und Sukiyaki
See Shocking Asia
(1975)

Sexy Lady Sumo
See Sumo Vixens
(1996)

Sha Qi Er Ren Zu
See 100 Ways to Murder Your Wife
(1986)

Sha Ren Zhe Tang Zhan
See The Assassin
(1993)

Sha Sha Ren, Tiao Tiao Miu
See Ballistic Kiss
(1998)

Sha Shou De Tong Hua
See A Taste of Killing
and Romance
(1994)

Sha Shou Hao
See The Big Brawl
(1980)

Sha Shou Jia Ji
See Day Off (2001)

Shadow Boxin'
See The 36 Deadly
Styles (1979)

Shadow Killers
See Duel of the Brave
Ones (1978)

Shan Cun Lao Shi
See A Wicked Ghost
(1999)

Shan Cun Lao Shi II Se Zhi E Gui
See A Wicked Ghost 2:
The Fear (2000)

Shan Gou 1999
See The Deadly Camp
(1999)

Shan Zhong Chuan Ji
See Legend of the
Mountain (1979)

Shanghai Express
See The Millionaires'
Express (1986)

Shao Lin Da Peng Da Shi
See Return of the Master Killer (1980)

Shao Lin Dou La Ma
See Shaolin vs. Lama
(1981)

Shao Lin Fo Jia Da Dao
See The Shaolin Disciple (1980)

Shao Lin Ju Qiu
See Shaolin Soccer
(2001)

Shao Lin Mu Ren Xiang
See Shaolin Wooden
Men (1976)

Shao Lin Nian Si Liu Ma
See Raiders of Wu Tang
(1982)

Shao Lin Sa Liu Fang
See Shaolin Master
Killer (1978)

Shao Lin Si
See The Shaolin Temple (1979)

Shao Lin Si Shi Ba Tong Ren
See The 18 Bronzemen
(1976)

Shao Lin Tzu
See The Shaolin Temple (1979)

Shao Lin Xiao Zi
See The Shaolin Kids
(1977)
See Shaolin Temple 2:
Kids from Shaolin
(1984)

Shao Lin Xiong Di
See The Shaolin Brothers (1977)

Shao Lin Ying Xiong
See The Heroes (1980)

Shao Lin Zui Ba Quan
See The Shaolin Drunken Monk (1983)

Shao Nian Huang Fei Hong Zhi Tie Ma Liu
See Iron Monkey
(1993)

Shaolin and Wu Tang 2: Wu Tang Invasion
See The Holy Robe of
Shaolin Temple
(1984)

Shaolin Archers
See Brave Archer
(1977)

Shaolin Buddhist Monk Tamo
See Killer Priest (1981)

Shaolin Chamber of Death
See Shaolin Wooden
Men (1976)

Shaolin Chuan Ren
See Death Mask of the
Ninja (1982)

Shaolin Death Squad
See The Shaolin Kids
(1977)

Shaolin Devil and Shaolin Angel
See Mask of Death
(1976)

Shaolin Dolemite
See Ninja the Final
Duel (1985)

Shaolin Executioners
See Executioners from
Shaolin (1977)

Shaolin Fighters vs. Ninja
See Return of the
Deadly Blade
(1981)

Shaolin Hero Chang San-feng
See Five Elements of
Kung Fu (1978)

The Shaolin Heroes
See The Heroes (1980)

Shaolin Kingboxer
See Shaolin King Boxer
(1979)

Shaolin Legend
See Abbot White
(1982)

Shaolin Men
See Hand of Death
(1975)

Shaolin Monk
See Killer Priest (1981)

Shaolin Prince
See Death Mask of the
Ninja (1982)

Shaolin Rescuers
See Avenging Warriors
of Shaolin (1979)

Shaolin Temple II
See Shaolin Temple 2:
Kids from Shaolin
(1984)

Shaolin Tong Zi Gong
See Shaolin Chastity
Kung Fu (1981)

Shaolin Warrior
See Warrior from
Shaolin (1981)

Shaolin's Born Invincible
See Born Invincible
(1978)

She Diao Ying Xiong Zhi Dong Cheng Xi Jiu
See Eagle Shooting
Heroes (1993)

She Diao Ying Xiong Zhuan
See Brave Archer
(1977)

She Hao Dan Xin Zhen Jiu Zhou
See Snake-Crane
Secret (1978)

She He Ba Bu
See Snake and Crane
Arts of Shaolin
(1978)

She Sha Shou
See Killer Snakes
(1974)

She Shan Gu Nu
See Succubare (1977)

She Shi 32 Du
See Beyond Hypothermia (1996)

She Xing Diao Shou
See Snake in the
Eagle's Shadow
(1978)

She Xing Zui Bu
See Snake Deadly Act
(1979)

Shen Bu You Ji
See The Victim (1980)

Shen Qiang Shou Yu
Ga Li Ji
See Pom Pom and Hot
Hot (1992)

Shen San Qi Xia
See Swordsman with
an Umbrella (1970)

Shen Si Guan
See Justice, My Foot!
(1992)

Shen Tou Die Ying
See Downtown Torpe-
does (1997)

Shen Tou Yan Zi Li San
See The Hero of Swal-
low (1996)

Shen Yong Shuang
Xiang Pao
See Pom Pom (1984)

Shen Yong Shuang
Xiang Pao Xu Ji
See Rosa (1986)

Sheng Gang Qi Bing
See Long Arm of the
Law (1984)

Sheng Gang Qi Bing II
See Long Arm of the
Law 2 (1987)

Sheng Gang Yi Hao
Tong Ji Fan
See Rock 'n' Roll Cop
(1994)

Sheng Hua Te Jing Zhi
Sang Shi Ren Wu
See Bio-Cops (2000)

Sheng Si Quan Su
See Fist Power (1999)

Sheng Zhe Wei Wang
See Young and Danger-
ous 6: Born to Be
King (2000)

Shi Ba Ban San Yi
See Legendary
Weapons of China
(1982)

Shi Ba Ban Wu Yi
See 18 Secrets of
Kung Fu (1979)

Shi Da Sha Shou
See 10 Magnificent
Killers (1977)

Shi Er Tan Tui
See My Kung Fu 12
Kicks (1979)

Shi Jie Da Shai
See Blonde Fury
(1989)

Shi Qi Bi Ren
See House of the
Damned (1999)

Shi San Dian Han
Shang
See War of the Shaolin
Temple (1980)

Shi Shen
See God of Cookery
(1996)

Shi Ying Xiong Chong
Ying Xiong
See Fearless Dragons
(1979)

Shichinin no Samurai
See Seven Samurai
(1954)

Shihaishi no Tasogare
See Twilight of the Dark
Master (1997)

Shin Zatoichi Mono-
gatari
See New Tale of Zato-
ichi (1963)

Shinkansen daibakuha
See Bullet Train (1975)

Shinobi no Mono
See Ninja: Band of
Assassins (1962)

Shinshokan
See Twilight of the Dark
Master (1997)

Shiqi sui de dan che
See Beijing Bicycle
(2001)

Shiryo No Wana
See Evil Dead Trap
(1988)

Shocking Asia Part 2
See Shocking Asia 2
(1976)

Shocking Asia Sunde
See Shocking Asia
(1975)

Shogun and His Little
Kitchen
See Shogun and Little
Kitchen (1992)

The Shogun Assassins
See Renegade Ninjas
(1979)

Shogun Massacre
See The Buddha Assas-
sinator (1979)

Shojo no Harawata
See Entrails of the Virgin (1986)

Shou Hu Fei Long
See Skinny Tiger and
Fatty Dragon
(1990)

Shou Juan Nan Nu
See Love on a Diet
(2001)

Showdown for Zatoichi
See Zatoichi and the
Chess Expert
(1965)

Shu Dan Long Wei
See High Risk (1995)

Shu Shan Chuan
See Zu Warriors (2001)

Shu Shi Shen Chuan
See Ninja in the Deadly
Trap (1983)

Shuang Long Hui
See Twin Dragons
(1992)

Shuang Long To Zhu
See Pom Pom Strikes
Back (1986)

Shui Hu Zhuan Zi Ying
Xiong Ben Se
See All Men Are Broth-
ers: Blood of the
Leopard (1993)

Shui Yue Shi San Dao
See Lone Ninja Warrior
(1981)

Shui Yuet Sap Saam
Diy
See Lone Ninja Warrior
(1981)

Shun Lau Ngaak Lau
See Time and Tide
(2000)

Shun Liu Ni Liu
See Time and Tide
(2000)

Shurayuki Hime
See Princess Blade
(2002)

Shut Hei Bik Yan
See House of the
Damned (1999)

Si Da Tan Zhang
See Powerful Four
(1991)

Si Je Daai Saai
See Blonde Fury
(1989)

Si Wang Ta
See Tower of Death
(1981)

Si Wang You Hu
See Game of Death
(1978)

Sien Nui Yau Wan
See A Chinese Ghost
Story (1987)

Silent Killer from Eter-
nity
See Return of the Tiger
(1979)

Silk Cotton Kasaya
See The Holy Robe of
Shaolin Temple
(1984)

Silver Hermit from
Shaolin Temple
See The Silver Spear
(1979)

Silver Hermit Meets
the Bloody Fangs of
Death
See The Silver Spear
(1979)

Sin Hok San Jam
See The Magic Crane
(1993)

Sin Jing Wu Men
See New Fist of Fury
(1976)

Sin Lui Yau Wan, Sin-
nui yauman III: Do Do
Do
See A Chinese Ghost
Story 3 (1991)

Sing Che Wai Wong
See Young and Danger-
ous 6: Born to Be
King (2000)

Sing Si Dak Ging
See The Big Heat
(1988)

Sing Si Jin Jaang
See City War (1988)

Sing Si Lip Yan
See City Hunter (1992)

Sing Sing Wong
See Mighty Peking Man
(1977)

Sing Yee Sap Chat
See The 72 Desperate
Rebels (1976)

Sing Yuet Tung Wa
See Moonlight Express
(1999)

Sinnui yauman II Yan
Gaan Diy
See A Chinese Ghost
Story 2 (1990)

Siu Kuen Gwaai Chiu
See Fearless Hyena
(1979)

Siu Lam Chi
See The Shaolin Tem-
ple (1979)

Siu Lam Chi Sap Baat
Tung Yan
See The 18 Bronzemen
(1976)

Siu Lam Chuen Yan
See Death Mask of the
Ninja (1982)

Siu Lam Chui Baat
Kuen
See The Shaolin Drunk-
en Monk (1983)

Siu Lam Chuk Kau
See Shaolin Soccer
(2001)

Siu Lam Daap Paang
Daal Si
See Return of the Mas-
ter Killer (1980)

Siu Lam Dau Kwong
Lut
See Shaolin vs. Lama
(1981)

Siu Lam Fong Dai
See The Shaolin Broth-
ers (1977)

Siu Lam Moon
See Hand of Death
(1975)

Siu Lam Muk Yan Hong
See Shaolin Wooden
Men (1976)

Siu Lam Nim Sei Lau
Ma
See Raiders of Wu Tang
(1982)

Siu Lam Sa Luk Fong
See Shaolin Master
Killer (1978)

Siu Lam Siu Ji
See The Shaolin Kids
(1977)
See Shaolin Temple 2:
Kids from Shaolin
(1984)

Siu Lam Tung Ji Gung
See Shaolin Chastity
Kung Fu (1981)

Siu Lam Ying Hung
See The Heroes (1980)

Siu Lee Fei Diy Ji Fei
Diy Ngoi Chuen
See Legend of the Fly-
ing Swordsman
(2000)

Siu Ngo Gong Woo Ji
Dung Fong Bat Baai
See The Legend of the
Swordsman (1992)

Siu Ngo Kong Woo
See Swordsman
(1990)

Siu Ngo Shing
See Dragon Kid (1990)

Siu Nin Wong Fei-hung
Ji Tit Ma Lau
See Iron Monkey
(1993)

Siu Sang Mung Geng Wan
See Scared Stiff (1986)

Siu Sin
See A Chinese Ghost Story: The Tsui Hark Animation (1997)

Siu Tai Gik
See Drunken Tai Chi (1984)

The Six Direction Boxing
See The Six Directions of Boxing (1979)

The Six-Fingered Strings Demon
See Deadful Melody (1994)

Snake in the Eagle's Shadow 3
See Battle of Shaolin (1977)

The Snake King's Child
See Snaker (2001)

Snaky Monkey
See Snake in the Eagle's Shadow (1978)

Sonachine
See Sonatine (1993)

Sonny Chiba's Dragon Princess
See Dragon Princess (1981)

Sono Otoko, Kyobo ni Tsuki
See Violent Cop (1989)

Sora no Daikaiju Radon
See Rodan (1956)

Southern Fist King vs. Northern Leg King
See The Hot, the Cool, and the Vicious (1976)

Space Amoeba
See Yog: Monster from Space (1970)

Space Greyhound
See Invasion of the Neptune Men (1961)

Space Mission of the Lost Planet
See Horror of the Blood Monsters (1970)

Space Monster Dogora
See Dagora the Space Monster (1964)

Spacemen Appear
See Evil Brain from Outer Space (1958/59)

Spaceship of Human Destruction
See Attack from Space (1958)
See Invaders from Space (1958)

Spartan X
See Wheels on Meals (1984)

The Spearman of Death
See Flag of Iron (1980)

The Spearmen
See Flag of Iron (1980)

Spirit and Me
See Where's Officer Tuba? (1986)

The Split
See The Manster (1960)

Spooky Encounters
See Encounter of the Spooky Kind (1981)

Star Force
See Star Force: Fugitive Alien 2 (1978/86)

The Star Prince
See Prince of Space (1959)

Steel Horse
See Deadend of Besiegers (1992)

Stormy Sun
See SuperManChu (1973)

Story of a Robber
See Legendary Couple (1995)

Story of Chivalry
See The Heroes (1980)

The Story of Drunken Master
See Drunken Master (1978)

The Story of Ricky
See Riki-Oh: The Story of Ricky (1989)

The Story of Shaolin
See Shaolin vs. Ninja (1983)

The Stranger
See Bruce Lee Fights Back from the Grave (1976)

Street Fighter 2 V
See Street Fighter 2 (1996)

Street Fighter 2 Victory
See Street Fighter 2 (1996)

Street Fighter Counterattacks
See The Street Fighter's Last Revenge (1974)

Strike of Death
See Hand of Death (1975)

Su Zhou He
See Suzhou River (2000)

Suan Ci Cao
See Lawyer Lawyer (1997)

Such Dreams I Have Dreamed
See Akira Kurosawa's Dreams (1990)

Sue Dam Lung Wei
See High Risk (1995)

Suen Sei Cho
See Lawyer Lawyer (1997)

Sugata Sanshiro
See Sanshiro Sugata (1943)

Sui Ken 2
See Legend of the Drunken Master (1994)

Sui Si San Chuen
See Ninja in the Deadly Trap (1983)

Sui Woo Juen Ji Ying Hung Boon Sik
See All Men Are Brothers: Blood of the Leopard (1993)

Suk Saan Chuen
See Zu Warriors (2001)

Suna no Onna
See Woman in the Dunes (1964)

Sunset Warrior
See Heroes Shed No Tears (1983/86)

Supa Jaiantsu 5 & 6
See Invaders from Space (1958)

Super Cops
See Yes, Madam (1985)

Super Dragon
See Bruce Lee We Miss You (1976)

The Super Fighters
See Five Superfighters (1978)

Super Giant 3 & 4
See Atomic Rulers of the World (1957)

Super Giant 5 & 6
See Invaders from Space (1958)

Super Giant 5 & 6
See Attack from Space (1958)

Super Giant 7, 8 & 9
See Evil Brain from Outer Space (1958/59)

Super Kong
See A*P*E (1976)

Super Manchu
See SuperManChu (1973)

Super Ninjas
See Chinese Super Ninjas (1982)

SuperChef
See Mr. Nice Guy (1997)

Supercop 2: Super Plan
See Supercop 2 (1993)

Supercops
See In the Line of Duty 5: Middle Man (1990)

Superfighters
See Five Superfighters (1978)

Supergang
See Super Gang (1978)

Supergiant vs. the Satellites
See Invaders from Space (1958)

Superior Youngster
See Super Kung Fu Kid (1974)

Superman-Chu
See SuperManChu (1973)

Supernatural Beast City
See Wicked City (1987)

Sure Fire
See Tiger Cage (1988)

Sure-Fire Death 4: We Will Avenge You
See Sure Death: Revenge (1987)

Survival
See In the Line of Duty 4 (1989)

Swirl
See Shiri (1999)

Sword of Justice
See The Razor 1: Sword of Justice (1972)

Sword of Vengeance
See Lone Wolf and Cub 1: Sword of Vengeance (1972)

Sword of Vengeance 3
See Lone Wolf and Cub 3: Baby Cart to Hades (1972)

Sword of Vengeance IV
See Lone Wolf and Cub 4: Baby Cart in Peril (1972)

Sword of Vengeance V
See Lone Wolf and Cub 5: Baby Cart in the Land of Demons (1973)

Sword of Vengeance VI
See Lone Wolf and Cub 6: White Heaven in Hell (1974)

Sword of Zatoichi
See Zatoichi's Flashing Sword (1964)

Swords of Doom
See Samurai 2: Duel at Ichijoji Temple (1955)

Swordsman 2
See The Legend of the Swordsman (1992)

Swordsman 3
See The East Is Red (1993)

Taai Gik Cheung Saam Fung
See Twin Warriors (1993)

Taai Gik Hei Gung
See Born Invincible (1978)

Taai Ji Chuen Suet
See No More Love, No More Death (1992)

Taekoesu Yonggary
See Yongary, Monster from the Deep (1967)

Tagani
See Horror of the Blood Monsters (1970)

Tai Chi Master
See Drunken Tai Chi (1984)

The Tai-Chi Master
See Twin Warriors (1993)

Tai Hou Ji Xiang
See Her Majesty Is Fine (1996)

Tai Ji Qi Gong
See Born Invincible (1978)

Tai Ji Zhang San Feng
See Twin Warriors (1993)

Tai Quan Zhen Jiu Zhou
See Sting of the Dragon Masters (1973)

Tai Yang Zhi Zi
See Prince of the Sun (1990)

Tai Yeung Ji Ji
See Prince of the Sun (1990)

Tai Zi Chuan Shui
See No More Love, No More Death (1992)

Taiji Ga Mit Suryo Surutoki
See Ecstasy of the Angels (1972)

Tak Mo Mai Sing
See The Accidental Spy (2001)

Tang Bohu Dian Qiuxiang
See Flirting Scholar (1993)

Tang Lang
See Shaolin Mantis (1978)

Tang Ren Jie Xiao Zi
See Chinatown Kid (1977)

Tang Ren Ke
See Brutal Boxer (1972)

Tang Saan dai Hing
See Fists of Fury (1971)

Tang Shan da Xiong
See Fists of Fury (1971)

Tang Shan Wu Hu
See Five Superfighters (1978)

Tang Yan Gaai Siu Ji
See Chinatown Kid (1977)

Tao Xue Wei Long
See Fight Back to School (1991)

Tao Xue Wei Long 2
See Fight Back to School 2 (1992)

Tao Xue Wei Long Guo Ji Nian
See Fight Back to School 3 (1993)

Taoism Drunkard
See Drunken Art and Crippled Fist (1979)

The Target
See Twinkle Twinkle Lucky Stars (1985)

Tau Hiu Yan Mat
See Headlines (2001)

Te Jing Tu Long
See Tiger Cage (1988)

Te Jing Xin Ren Lei
See Gen-X Cops (1999)

Te Jing Xin Ren Lei 2
See Gen-Y Cops (2000)

Te Wu Mi Cheng
See The Accidental Spy (2001)

Tek Dau
See Duel of the Brave Ones (1978)

The Telegian
See The Secret of the Telegian (1960)

The Telegraphed Man
See The Secret of the Telegian (1960)

Ten Fingers and Flying Sword
See Moonlight Sword and Jade Lion (1979)

Ten Fingers of Steel
See Screaming Ninja (1973)

Ten Tigers from Kwangtung
See Ten Tigers of Kwangtung (1979)

Tenshi no Kokotsu
See Ecstasy of the Angels (1972)

Terrible Angel
See Savior of the Soul (1991)

Terror of Godzilla
See Terror of MechaGodzilla (1975)

Terror on Blood Island
See Brides of Blood (1968)

Tetsuo
See Tetsuo: The Iron Man (1989)

Tetsuo: Body Hammer
See Tetsuo 2: Body Hammer (1991)

Tetsuwan Atom
See Astro Boy (1963)
See Astro Boy (1980)

They Who Step on the Tail of the Tiger
See Men Who Tread on the Tiger's Tail (1943)

Thin Body Man Woman
See Love on a Diet (2001)

The Third and Fourth of October
See Boiling Point (1990)

13 Poles from Shaolin
See War of the Shaolin Temple (1980)

36 Strikes of Kung Fu
See Fighting Ace (1979)

36 Wooden Men
See Shaolin Wooden Men (1976)

The 36th Chamber
See Return of the Master Killer (1980)
See Shaolin Master Killer (1978)

The 36th Chamber of Shaolin
See Shaolin Master Killer (1978)

32 Degrees Celsius
See Beyond Hypothermia (1996)

This Is Kung Fu
See The Shaolin One (1983)

3 Brothers
See Dragons Forever (1988)

3-4x10 Jugatsu
See Boiling Point (1990)

303 Fear Faith Revenge
See Fear Faith Revenge 303 (1998)

Three Rascals in the Hidden Fortress
See The Hidden Fortress (1958)

Thunder Kids 3: Hunt for Devil Boxer
See Thunder Ninja Kids: The Hunt for the Devil Boxer (1986/94)

Thunderarm
See Armour of God (1986)

Thunderbolt Vanguard
See Final Justice (1988)

Thunderous Battle Cops
See China Strike Force (2000)

Ti Dou
See Duel of the Brave Ones (1978)

Ti Tian Xing Dao Zhi Sha Xiong
See Brother of Darkness (1994)

Tian Cai Gong Fu
See Kung Fu Genius (1979)

Tian Di Xiong Xin
See Armageddon (1997)

Tian Lung Di Wang
See Gunmen (1988)

Tian Mai Chuan Ji
See The Touch (2002)

Tian Mi Mi
See Comrades, Almost a Love Story (1996)

Tian Re You Qing (Zhui Meng Ren)
See A Moment of Romance (1990)

Tian Shi Hang Dong
See Angel (1987)

Tian Shi Xing Dong II Zhi Huo Feng Jiao Long
See Angel 2 (1988)

Tian Xia Di Yi Quan
See Five Fingers of Death (1972)

Tian You Yan
See Comeuppance (2000)

Tie Jia Wu di Ma Li ya
See I Love Maria (1988)

Tie Ma Liu
See The Iron Monkey (1977)

Tie Qi Men
See Flag of Iron (1980)

Tie Quan
See Shaolin King Boxer (1979)

Tie San Jiao
See Triangular Duel (1972)

Tiger on the Beat
See Tiger on Beat (1988)

Tiger over the Wall
See Tiger over Wall (1980)

Tiger vs. Dragon
See Kung Fu, the Invisible Fist (1972)

Tim Mat Ma
See Comrades, Almost a Love Story (1996)

Time Warriors
See Iceman Cometh (1989)

Tin Choi Gung Foo
See Kung Fu Genius (1979)

Tin Dei Hung Sam
See Armageddon (1997)

Tin Gwong Dai Yat Kuen
See Five Fingers of Death (1972)

Tin Law Dei Mong
See Gunmen (1988)

Tin Mak Chuen Kei
See The Touch (2002)

Tin Si Hang Dung
See Angel (1987)

Tin Si Hang Dung II Jo Foh Fung Gaau Lung
See Angel 2 (1988)

Tin Yau Aan
See Comeuppance (2000)

Tin Yeuk Yau Ching (Chui Mung Yan)
See A Moment of Romance (1990)

Tit Gaap Miu dik Ma Lee a
See I Love Maria (1988)

Tit Kei Moon
See Flag of Iron (1980)

Tit Kuen
See Shaolin King Boxer (1979)

Tit Ma Lau
See The Iron Monkey (1977)

Tit Saam Gok
See Triangular Duel (1972)

To Hok Wai Lung
See Fight Back to School (1991)

To Hok Wai Lung 2
See Fight Back to
School 2 (1992)

**To Hok Wai Lung Ji
Lung Gwoh Gai Nin**
See Fight Back to
School 3 (1993)

To Love with No Regret
See A Moment of
Romance (1990)

**Toi Kuen Jan Gau
Chow**
See Sting of the Drag-
on Masters (1973)

Tokyo Fisuto
See Tokyo Fist (1996)

Tokyo Mafia
See Tokyo Mafia:
Yakuza Wars
(1995)

Tokyo Mafia 2
See Tokyo Mafia 2:
Wrath of the
Yakuza (1995)

Tokyo-ken
See Tokyo Fist (1996)

Tokyo nagaremono
See Tokyo Drifter
(1966)

**Tomb of the Living
Dead**
See Mad Doctor of
Blood Island
(1968)

Tombstone for Fireflies
See Grave of the Fire-
flies (1988)

Tonari no Totoro
See My Neighbor Totoro
(1988)

Tong Ji Mi You
See Fighting for Love
(2001)

Tong Long
See Shaolin Mantis
(1978)

**Tong Pak-fu Dim Chou-
heung**
See Flirting Scholar
(1993)

Tong Sang Ng Foo
See Five Superfighters
(1978)

Tong Yan Hak
See Brutal Boxer
(1972)

Tongoku to Jigoku
See High and Low
(1963)

Top Squad
See The Inspector
Wears Skirts
(1988)

**Tora no O Wo Fumu
Otokotachi**
See Men Who Tread on
the Tiger's Tail
(1943)

Tou Hao Ren Wu
See Headlines (2001)

Tough Guy
See Iron Monkey 2
(1977)

Traitorous
See Shaolin Traitorous
(1976)

**A Transistor Love
Story**
See Mon-Rak Transistor
(2001)

Triad Savagers
See Code of Honor
(1987)

Triad Savages
See Code of Honor
(1987)

Tricky Master 2000
See The Tricky Master
(2000)

True Colors of a Hero
See All Men Are Broth-
ers: Blood of the
Leopard (1993)
See A Better Tomorrow
(1986)

The True Master
See The Silver Spear
(1979)

Tsubaki Sanjuro
See Sanjuro (1963)

Tung Gui Mat Yau
See Fighting for Love
(2001)

12 Hours of Fear
See The Last Blood
(1990)

12 Hours of Terror
See The Last Blood
(1990)

Twelve Kung Fu Kicks
See My Kung Fu 12
Kicks (1979)

24 Bronze Horses
See Raiders of Wu Tang
(1982)

24 Shaolin Moves
See Raiders of Wu Tang
(1982)

**Twins Jewel Lady
Search**
See The New Mar-
velous Double
(1992)

**The Two-Headed Mon-
ster**
See The Manster
(1960)

Two on the Road
See Fearless Dragons
(1979)

2001 Yonggary
See Reptilian (2000)

Uchu Daikaiju Dogora
See Dagora the Space
Monster (1964)

Uchu Daikaiju Girura
See The X from Outer
Space (1967)

Uchu Daisenso
See Battle in Outer
Space (1959)

Uchu Kaijin Shutsugen
See Evil Brain from
Outer Space
(1958/59)

Uchu Kaisoku-sen
See Invasion of the
Neptune Men
(1961)

Uchu Kara No Messeji
See Message from
Space (1978)

**Uchujin Tokyo ni
Arawaru**
See Warning from
Space (1956)

**Uchutei to Jinko Eisen
no Kekitotsu**
See Attack from Space
(1958)

Uinasu Senki
See The Venus Wars
(1989)

Ultimate Bra
See Brassiere (2001)

Ultra Force
See Royal Warriors
(1986)

The Ultraman
See Ultraman 2 (2001)

Ultraman Jonias
See Ultraman 2 (2001)

**Ultraman Tiga and
Ultraman Dyna and
Ultraman Gaia: The
Great Decisive Attack
of Super-Time and
Space**
See Ultraman Gaia:
The Battle in Hyper-
space (1998)

**Ultraman Tiga and
Ultraman Dyna: War-
riors of the Star of
Light**
See Ultraman Tiga and
Ultraman Dyna: The
Warriors of the
Lightning Star
(1998)

Unabridged Agony
See Guinea Pig: Devil's
Experiment (1985)

Unagi
See The Eel (1997)

The Unbeatable 28
See The Unbeaten 28
(1980)

**The Unforgiven of
Shaolin**
See The Heroes (1980)

Ung Chung Sin
See Picture of a Nymph
(1988)

**Unknown Satellite over
Tokyo**
See Warning from
Space (1956)

**The Untold Story:
Human Meat Roast
Pork Buns**
See The Untold Story
(1992)

**Urusei Yatsura 1: Onri
Yu**
See Urusei Yatsura
Movie 1: Only You
(1983)

**Urutoraman Teiga and
Urutoraman Daina and
Urutoraman Gaia:
Choujiku no Daiketsug-
eki**
See Ultraman Gaia:
The Battle in Hyper-
space (1998)

**Urutoraman Teiga and
Urutoraman Daina:
Hikari no Hoshi no Sen-
shi Tachi**
See Ultraman Tiga and
Ultraman Dyna: The
Warriors of the
Lightning Star
(1998)

USA Ninja
See Ninja in the U.S.A.
(1988)

Uzumaki
See Spiral (2000)

**Vampire Men of the
Lost Planet**
See Horror of the Blood
Monsters (1970)

Vampire People
See The Blood Drinkers
(1964)

**Vengeance of the Mon-
ster**
See Daimajin (1966)

**The Venoms vs. the
Vampires**
See 5 Venoms vs. Wu
Tang (1987)

The Victim
See Victim (1999)

Village on Fire
See The Awaken Punch
(1973)

**Viva Chiba the Body-
guard**
See The Bodyguard
(1973/78)

Volcano High
See Volcano High
School (2001)

Vortex
See Spiral (2000)

**Wa Pei Ji Yam Yeung
Faat Wong**
See Painted Skin
(1992)

Waan Ying Dak Gung
See Hot War (1998)

Wai Jan Sei Fong
See Rage of the Mas-
ters (1974)

Wai Lung Maang Tam
See The Protector
(1985)

**Wai Shut Lee Ji Laam
Huet Yan**
See The Wesley's Mys-
terious File (2001)

**Wai Shut Lee Ji Liu
Maau**
See The Cat (1991)

**Walkers on the Tiger's
Tail**
See Men Who Tread on
the Tiger's Tail
(1943)

Wan Da
See Chinese Samson
(1979)

Wan Mei Qing Ren
See Every Dog Has His
Date (2001)

Wan Ren Jin
See Lightning Kung Fu
(1980)

Wandafuru Raifu
See After Life (1998)

The Wandering Kid
See Urotsukidoji
(1989)

Wang Ming Ren Zhe
See A Life of Ninja
(1983)

Wang Ming Yuan Yang
See On the Run (1988)

Wang Shang Guai Tan
See 990714.com
(2000)

Wang Yu, King of Boxing
See Screaming Ninja
(1973)

War of the Monsters
See Gamera vs. Barugon (1966)
See Godzilla vs. Gigan
(1972)

Warning: This Man Is Wild
See Violent Cop (1989)

The Warrior, Dancing Warrior
See Venom Warrior
(1983)

Warriors from the Magic Mountain
See Zu: Warriors of the
Magic Mountain
(1983)

A Warrior's Journey
See Bruce Lee: A Warrior's Journey
(2000)

Water Cyborgs
See Terror beneath the
Sea (1966)

Waterside Story: Heroic Character
See All Men Are Brothers: Blood of the
Leopard (1993)

Way of the Dragon
See Return of the Dragon (1972)

The Ways of Kung-Fu
See Ways of Kung Fu
(1980)

We Five
See Hum Paanch
(1980)

Wealthy Train
See The Millionaires'
Express (1986)

Weapon X
See Wheels on Meals
(1984)

Weather Girl
See Weather Woman
(1995)

Weather Report Girl
See Weather Woman
(1995)

A Weatherwoman
See Weather Woman
(1995)

Wei Long Mang Tan
See The Protector
(1985)

Wei Si Li Zhi ba Wang Xie Ji
See Bury Me High
(1990)

Wei Si Li Zhi Lan Xie Ren
See The Wesley's Mysterious File (2001)

Wei Si Li Zhi Lao Mao
See The Cat (1991)

Wei Zhen Si Fang
See Rage of the Masters (1974)

Weird Tales
See Kwaidan (1964)

The Wesley's Mysterious Story
See The Wesley's Mysterious File (2001)

Whasango
See Volcano High
School (2001)

What Time Is It over There?
See What Time Is It
There? (2001)

When Dragons Collide
See Twin Dragons
(1992)

When Dragons Meet
See The Prisoner
(1990)

When Taekwondo Strikes
See Sting of the Dragon Masters (1973)

Whispering Corridors 2
See Memento Mori
(1999)

The White-Haired Swordswoman 2
See The Bride with
White Hair 2
(1993)

White Snake, Green Snake
See Green Snake
(1993)

Wicked City 3
See Ninja Scroll (1993)

The Wife Is the Gang Leader
See My Wife Is a Gangster (2001)

Wind, Forest, Fire, Mountain
See A Fistful of Talons
(1983)

Wing Chun Daai Fong
See Story of the Dragon (1976)

Wing Ping Fan Din
See Peace Hotel
(1995)

Wings of Honneamise, Starquest
See Royal Space Force:
The Wings of Honneamise (1987)

Wishing Tree
See Final Romance
(2001)

The Witness
See In the Line of Duty
4 (1989)

Wits to Wits
See From China with
Death (1974)

Wo de fu qin mu qin
See The Road Home
(1999)

Wo De Ye Man Tong Xiao
See My School Mate,
the Barbarian
(2001)

Wo Hu Cang Long
See Crouching Tiger,
Hidden Dragon
(2000)

Wo Shi Yi Ge Zei
See Legendary Couple
(1995)

Woman Certain Kill Fist
See Sister Street Fighter (1974)

Woman of the Dunes
See Woman in the
Dunes (1964)

The Woman with No Name
See Zero Woman: The
Accused (1996)

Wong Fei-hung
See Once upon a Time
in China (1991)

Wong Fei-hung Chi Sai Wik Hung Shut
See Once upon a Time
in China and America (1997)

Wong Fei-hung Chi Tit Gai Dau Neung Gung
See Last Hero in China
(1993)

Wong Fei-hung Hai Lit Ji Yat Dol Si
See Martial Arts Master Wong Fei Hung
(1992)

Wong Fei Hung Ji IV Sei Wong Che Ji Fung
See Once upon a Time
in China 4 (1993)

Wong Fei-hung Ji Saam si Wong Jaang Ba
See Once upon a Time
in China 3 (1993)

Wong Fei-hung Ji yi Naam yi Dong Ji Keung
See Once upon a Time
in China 2 (1992)

Wong Fei-hung '92
See Martial Arts Master Wong Fei Hung
(1992)
See The Master (1989)

Wong Fung Lui Cheung
See She Shoots
Straight (1990)

Wong Ga Jin Si
See Royal Warriors
(1986)

Wong Ga Si Je
See Yes, Madam
(1985)

Wong Ga Si Je Ji III
See In the Line of Duty
3 (1988)

Wong Ga Si Je Ji IV Jik Gik Jing Yan
See In the Line of Duty
4 (1989)

Wong Ga Si Je Ji Jung Gaan Yan
See In the Line of Duty
5: Middle Man
(1990)

Wong Hiu Daai Hap
See Yellow River Fighter (1988)

Woo Sue
See Run and Kill
(1993)

Woo Sue Gei Mat Dong Ngon
See Run and Kill
(1993)

Woo Tiu Dai Hap Saam Goh Boon
See 5 Lady Venoms
(1978)

Writing Kung Fu
See Chinese Samson
(1979)

Wu Du
See Five Deadly Venoms (1978)

Wu Fu Xing
See Winners and Sinners (1983)

Wu Hu Jiang Zhu Jue Lie (Jin Pai Wu Hu Jiang)
See The Tigers (1991)

Wu Kuai
See Ninja vs. Shaolin
Guards (1984)

Wu Lin Sheng Dou Shi
See Deadend of
Besiegers (1992)

Wu Lung Tin Si Jiu Jik Gwi
See Kung Fu Zombie
(1981)

Wu Ming Xiao Cu
See His Name Is
Nobody (1979)

Wu Ren Jia Shi
See Spacked Out
(2000)

Wu Shu
See Run and Kill
(1993)

Wu Shu Ji Mi Dang An
See Run and Kill
(1993)

Wu Tang Champ v. Champ
See Champ against
Champ (1983)

Wu Tang Clan
See The Heroes (1980)

Wu Tang, Hos, Thugs and Scrillah
See Battle of Shaolin
(1977)

Wu Tang Prince
See Death Mask of the
Ninja (1982)

Wu Tang vs. Ninja
See Ninja Hunter
(1983)

Wu Tang Warrior
See Venom Warrior
(1983)

Wu Xian Fu Huo
See Second Time
Around (2002)

Wu Yi Tan Zhang Lei Luo Zhuan
See Lee Rock (1991)

Wu Zhuang Yuan: Su Qi Er
See King of Beggars (1992)

Wu Zhuang Yuan Tie Qiao San
See Sam the Iron Bridge: Champion of Martial Arts (1993)

Wulang Ba Gua Gun
See Invincible Pole Fighter (1983)

X/1999
See X (1996)

X: Their Destiny was Foreordained 1999
See X (1996)

Xi Huan Nin
See Fall for You (2001)

Xi Ju Zhi Wang
See King of Comedy (1999)

Xi You Ji Di Jie Ju Zhi Xian Lu Qi Yuan
See A Chinese Odyssey Part 2: Cinderella (1995)

Xi You Ji Di Yi Bai Ling Yi Hui Zie Yu Guang Bao He
See A Chinese Odyssey Part 1: Pandora's Box (1995)

Xi Zang Xiao Zi
See A Kid from Tibet (1991)

Xia Da Er Qi
See Militant Eagle (1978)

Xia dao Gao Fei
See Full Contact (1992)

Xia Dao Zheng Chuan
See Chivalrous Legend (1998)

Xia Nu
See A Touch of Zen (1969)

Xia Ri Fu Xing
See Twinkle Twinkle Lucky Stars (1985)

Xian Dai Hao Xia Zhuan
See Executioners (1993)

Xian He Shen Zhen
See The Magic Crane (1993)

Xian Jiao
See Sharp Guns (2001)

Xian si Jue
See Duel to the Death (1982)

Xiang Gang Di Xiong Zhai
See Haunted Mansion (1998)

Xiang Jiang Hua Yue Ye
See Hong Kong Nocturne (1967)

Xiao Ao Cheng
See Dragon Kid (1990)

Xiao Ao Jiang Hu
See Swordsman (1990)

Xiao Ao Jiang Hu Zhi Dong Fang Bu Bai
See The Legend of the Swordsman (1992)

Xiao Li Fei Dao Zhi Fei Dao Wai Chuan
See Legend of the Flying Swordsman (2000)

Xiao Qian
See A Chinese Ghost Story: The Tsui Hark Animation (1997)

Xiao Quan Guai Zhao
See Fearless Hyena (1979)

Xiao Sheng Meng Jing Hun
See Scared Stiff (1986)

Xiao Tai Ji
See Drunken Tai Chi (1984)

Xich Lo
See Cyclo (1995)

Xie Di Zi
See The Flying Guillotine (1974)

Xie Jiao Dang An Zhi Mo Ri Feng Bao
See God.com (1998)

Xin bi Xue Xia
See The Sword Stained with Royal Blood (1993)

Xin Bu Le Qing
See C'est la Vie, Mon Cheri (1993)

Xin Die Xue Shuang Xiong
See Thunder Cop (1996)

Xin Fang Shi Yu Xu Ji
See Iron Man (1986)

Xin Gao Yang Yi Sheng
See Trust Me U Die (1999)

Xin Jing Wu Men 1991
See Fist of Fury 1991 (1991)

Xin Liu Xing Hu Die Jian
See Butterfly and Sword (1993)

Xin Long Men Ke Zhan
See Dragon Inn (1992)

Xin Long Zheng Hu Dou
See Kick Boxer's Tears (1992)

Xin Shaolin Wuzu
See The New Legend of Shaolin (1994)

Xin Shu Shan Jian Xia
See Zu: Warriors of the Magic Mountain (1983)

Xin Tian Long Ba Bu Zhi Tian Shan Tong Lao
See Dragon Chronicles: Maidens of Heavenly Mountain (1994)

Xin Ying Xiong Ben Se
See Return to a Better Tomorrow (1994)

Xin Zui Jia Pai Dang
See Aces Go Places 5: The Terracotta Hit (1989)

Xing
See Undercover Blues (2000)

Xing Er Shi Qi
See The 72 Desperate Rebels (1976)

Xing Xing Wang
See Mighty Peking Man (1977)

Xing Yue Tong Hua
See Moonlight Express (1999)

Xiong Bang
See The Imp (1981)

Xiong Mao
See Evil Cat (1986)

Xiong Wu Yi Shen
See Doctor Vampire (1990)

Xun Bu Fang
See Tiger over Wall (1980)

Xun Cheng Ma
See The Postman Fights Back (1982)

Xun Yi Cao
See Lavender (2000)

XX Beautiful Beast
See Beautiful Beast (1995)

XX Beautiful Hunter
See Beautiful Hunter (1994)

XX: Utukushiki Gakuen
See Beautiful Beast (1995)

Ya Li Ba Ba Liang Ge Da Dao
See F*** / Off (1998)

Yam Yeung Lo
See Troublesome Night (1997)

Yan Ba Chiu
See Thousand Mile Escort (1976)

Yan Che Daal Kuet Dau
See Ninja Hunter (1983)

Yan Je Mo Dik
See Chinese Super Ninjas (1982)

Yan Sut
See Ninja in the Deadly Trap (1983)

Yan Yuk Shiu Baau II Tin Chu Dei Mit
See The Untold Story 2 (1998)

Yang Chun da Xiong
See Story of the Dragon (1976)

Yang Guang Jing Cha
See Sunshine Cops (1999)

Yangan Dou
See A Chinese Ghost Story 2 (1990)

Yat Daam Ji Lik Saam Gung Fu
See Fists and Guts (1979)

Yat Goh Laan Diy Dik Chuen Suet
See A Gambler's Story (2001)

Yat Kuo Chi Tau Dik Daan Sang
See Too Many Ways to Be No. 1 (1997)

Yatgo yo han
See Mr. Nice Guy (1997)

Yau Cha
See The Masked Prosecutor (1999)

Yau Ching Yam Shui Baau
See Love Me, Love My Money (2001)

Yau Leng Ching Shu
See Shadow (2001)

Yau Leng Yan Gaan
See Visible Secret (2001)

Yau Long
See Color of Pain (2002)

Yau Sau Ji Tung
See Born Wild (2001)

Yau Sau Ying Ging
See Beast Cops (1998)

Ye Ban Ge Sheng
See The Phantom Lover (1995)

Ye Boon Go Sing
See The Phantom Lover (1995)

Ye Cha
See The Masked Prosecutor (1999)

Ye Ge Lan Du De Chuan Shui
See A Gambler's Story (2001)

Ye Lang
See Color of Pain (2002)

Ye Shou Xing Jing
See Beast Cops (1998)

Ye Shou Zhi Tong
See Born Wild (2001)

Yee Boon Mo Yin
See Code of Honor (1987)

Yee Ng Chuen Suet
See Gold Fingers (2001)

Yeogo Goedam 2
See Memento Mori (1999)

Yeopgijeogin geunyeo; Bizarre Girl
See My Sassy Girl (2001)

Yes Madam!
See Yes, Madam (1985)

Yes, Madam 2
See In the Line of Duty 3 (1988)
See Royal Warriors (1986)

Yes, Madam 3
See Magnificent Warriors (1987)

Yes, Madam 4
See In the Line of Duty 4 (1989)

Yes, Madam 5
See In the Line of Duty 5: Middle Man (1990)

Yeuk Saat
See Red to Kill (1994)

Yi Ben Wu Yan
See Code of Honor (1987)

Yi Dam Hung Sun
See City War (1988)

Yi Dan Er Li San Gong Fu
See Fists and Guts (1979)

Yi Dan Hong Chun
See City War (1988)

Yi Diy Hung Gaan
See Inner Senses (2001)

Yi Du Kong Jian
See Inner Senses (2001)

Yi Ge Hao Ren
See Mr. Nice Guy (1997)

Yi Ge Zi Tou De Dan Sheng
See Too Many Ways to Be No. 1 (1997)

Yi Tian Tu Long Ji Zhi Mo Jiao Jiao Zhu
See Lord of the Wu Tang (1993)

Yi Tin To Lung Gei Ji Moh Gaau Gaau Jue
See Lord of the Wu Tang (1993)

Yin Doi Ho Hap Juen
See Executioners (1993)

Yin Feng Er
See Sound from the Dark (2000)

Yin Yang Lu
See Troublesome Night (1997)

Yin Yang Lu 4 Yu Gui Yong Hang
See Troublesome Night 4 (1998)

Yin Yang Lu Ba Zhi Guan Cai Zai
See Troublesome Night 8 (2000)

Yin Yang Lu Jiu Zhi Ming Zhuan Gan Kun
See Troublesome Night 9 (2000)

Yin Yang Lu Shi Si Zhi Shuang Gui Pai Men
See Troublesome Night 14 (2002)

Yin Yang Road
See Troublesome Night (1997)

Yin Yang Road 3
See Troublesome Night 3 (1997)

Yin Yang Road 4: Walking with Ghost
See Troublesome Night 4 (1998)

Yin Yang Xie Di Zi
See Fatal Flying Guillotine (1977)

Yin Yu Jian Cui Yu Shi
See Moonlight Sword and Jade Lion (1979)

Ying
See Undercover Blues (2000)

Ying Chau Tit Biu Saam
See The Invincible Armour (1977)

Ying Chau Tong Long
See Eagle's Claw (1977)

Ying Han Gong Fu Ben
See Kung Fu's Hero (1973)

Ying Hung Boon Sik
See A Better Tomorrow (1986)

Ying Hung Boon Sik Chuk Chap
See A Better Tomorrow 2 (1987)

Ying Hung Boon Sik III: Jik Yeung Ji Gor
See A Better Tomorrow 3 (1989)

Ying Hung Dui Ying Hung
See The Last Duel (1982)

Ying Hung Mo Lui
See Heroes Shed No Tears (1983/86)

Ying Xiong
See The Heroes (1980)

Ying Xiong Ben Se
See A Better Tomorrow (1986)

Ying Xiong Ben Se Xu Ji
See A Better Tomorrow 2 (1987)

Ying Xiong Ben Se III: Tzu Yang Tsu Gor
See A Better Tomorrow 3 (1989)

Ying Xiong Dui Ying Xiong
See The Last Duel (1982)

Ying Xiong Wu Lei
See Heroes Shed No Tears (1983/86)

Ying Zhao Tang Lang
See Eagle's Claw (1977)

Ying Zhao Tie Bu Shan
See The Invincible Armour (1977)

Yit Huet Jui Keung
See Task Force (1997)

Yog the Space Amoeba
See Yog: Monster from Space (1970)

Yoga and the Kung Fu Girl
See Yoga and Kung Fu Girl (1978)

Yojimbo the Bodyguard
See Yojimbo (1961)

Yoju Toshi
See Wicked City (1987)

Yong Chuan
See Wing Chun (1994)

Yong Chun
See Wing Chun (1994)

Yong Jing Dai Poh Sap Baat Tung Yan
See The 18 Bronzemen Part 2 (1976)

Yong Zhe Wu Ju
See Dreadnaught (1981)

Yong Zheng Da Po Shi Ba Tong Ren
See The 18 Bronzemen Part 2 (1976)

Yong Zheng Ming Sang Shao Lin Men
See The Shaolin Invincibles (1979)

You and I
See Fulltime Killer (2001)

You Ling Qing Shu
See Shadow (2001)

You Ling Ren Jian
See Visible Secret (2001)

You Qing Yin Shui Bao
See Love Me, Love My Money (2001)

Young and Dangerous: Part 1
See Young and Dangerous (1996)

Young and Dangerous '98
See Young and Dangerous 5 (1998)

Young and Dangerous 6
See Young and Dangerous 6: Born to Be King (2000)

The Young Hero of Shaolin II
See Iron Man (1986)

Young Master in Love
See Dragon Lord (1982)

Young Tiger's Revenge
See Shaolin Wooden Men (1976)

Yu Duo La Yu Ying Xiong
See Cheap Killers (1998)

Yu Nu Tian Ding
See Dummy Mommy, without a Baby (2001)

Yu Qing Ting
See The Massive (1978)

Yu Wang Zhi Cheng
See City of Desire (2001)

Yu Zhong Long
See Dragon in Jail (1990)

Yuan Fen You Take 2
See Love Correction (2000)

Yuan Wang Shu
See Final Romance (2001)

Yuan Zhenxia yu Wei Si Li
See The Seventh Curse (1986)

Yue Doh Laai Yue Ying Hung
See Cheap Killers (1998)

Yue Gui Zhi Lang
See Guardian Angel (1996)

Yue Loi Baat Gwa Gwan
See 8 Diagram Fighter (1991)

Yuen Ban Yau Take 2
See Love Correction (2000)

Yuen Chi Miu Hei, Yuan Shi Wu Qi
See Body Weapon (1999)

Yuen Chun-hup yue Wai Si Lee
See The Seventh Curse (1986)

Yuen Mei Ching Yan
See Every Dog Has His Date (2001)

Yuen Mong Shu
See Final Romance (2001)

Yuk Ching Ting
See The Massive (1978)

Yuk Chung Lung
See Dragon in Jail (1990)

Yuk Lui Tim Ding
See Dummy Mommy, without a Baby (2001)

Yuk Mong Ji Shing
See City of Desire (2001)

Yume
See Akira Kurosawa's Dreams (1990)

Yung Je Mo Gui
See Dreadnaught (1981)

Yung Jing Meng Song Siu Lam Moon
See The Shaolin Invincibles (1979)

Yupgi Girl
See My Sassy Girl (2001)

Yusei Oji
See Prince of Space (1959)

Za Ginipiggu 3
See Guinea Pig: Flower of Flesh and Blood (1985)

Za Ginipiggu 8: Senritsui! Shinanai Otoko
See Guinea Pig: He Never Dies (1986)

Za Ginnipiggu: Manhoru no Naka no Ningyo
See Guinea Pig: Mermaid in a Manhole (1988)

Za Gu Xiao Zi
See Knockabout (1979)

Za jia xiao zi
See Knockabout (1979)

Zai Jian A Lang
See Where a Good Man Goes (1999)

Zatoichi
See Zatoichi on the Road (1963)

Zatoichi Abaredako
See Zatoichi's Flashing Sword (1964)

Zatoichi and the Drum
See Samaritan Zatoichi (1968)

Zatoichi and the Scoundrels
See Zatoichi on the Road (1963)

Zatoichi Breaks Jail
See Zatoichi the Outlaw (1967)

Zatoichi Chikemuri Kaido
See Zatoichi Challenged (1967)

Zatoichi, Crazy Journey
See Zatoichi the Fugitive (1963)

Zatoichi Enters Again
See New Tale of Zatoichi (1963)

Zatoichi Escapes from Jail
See Zatoichi the Outlaw (1967)

Zatoichi Fighting Caper
See Fight, Zatoichi, Fight! (1964)

Zatoichi Hatashi Jo
See Zatoichi and the Fugitives (1968)

Zatoichi Jigoku Tabi
See Zatoichi and the Chess Expert (1965)

Zatoichi Kenka-daiko
See Samaritan Zatoichi (1968)

Zatoichi Kenka Tabi
See Zatoichi on the Road (1963)

Zatoichi Kesshi Tabi
See Fight, Zatoichi, Fight! (1964)

Zatoichi Kyoto Tabi
See Zatoichi the Fugitive (1963)

Zatoichi Monogatari
See Blind Swordsman: The Tale of Zatoichi (1962)

Zatoichi Nidangiri
See Zatoichi's Revenge (1964)

Zatoichi No Uta Ga Kikoeru
See Zatoichi's Vengeance (1966)

Zatoichi Rooyaburi
See Zatoichi the Outlaw (1967)

Zatoichi Sakata Giri
See Zatoichi and the Doomed Man (1965)

Zatoichi Sekishoyaburi
See Adventures of a Blind Man (1964)

Zatoichi Senryo-kubi
See Zatoichi and the Chest of Gold (1964)

Zatoichi Tekka Tabi
See Zatoichi's Cane Sword (1966)

Zatoichi: The Blind Swordsman's Return
See New Tale of Zatoichi (1963)

Zatoichi: The Life and Opinion of Masseur Ichi
See Blind Swordsman: The Tale of Zatoichi (1962)

Zatoichi's Trip to Hell
See Zatoichi and the Chess Expert (1965)

Zazambo
See The Funeral (1984)

Ze Gong Zi
See Super Car Criminals (1999)

Zeiramu
See Zeram (1991)

Zero Woman: Namae no nai Onna
See Zero Woman: The Accused (1996)

Zhan Shen Chuan Shui
See The Moon Warriors (1992)

Zheng Jiang
See The Cheaters (2001)

Zhi Fa Xian Feng
See Righting Wrongs (1986)

Zhi Ming Xing Sao Rao
See Devil Touch (2002)

Zhi Yong San Bao
See Mr. Boo Meets Pom Pom (1985)

Zhi Zun Wu Shuang
See Casino Raiders (1989)

Zhi Zun Wu Shuang II: Yong Ba Tian Xia
See Casino Raiders 2 (1991)

ZhiFa Fan Fa
See Cop on a Mission (2001)

Zhong Gui
See Seeding of a Ghost (1983)

Zhong Guo Fu Ren
See Chinese Iron Man (1975)

Zhong Hua Du Xia
See Conman in Tokyo (2000)

Zhong Hua Wu Shu
See The Shaolin One (1983)

Zhong Hua Ying Xiong
See A Man Called Hero (1999)

Zhong Hua Ying Xioung
See Born to Defence (1988)

Zhong Hwa Zhan Shi
See Magnificent Warriors (1987)

Zhong Ming Han Shan Si
See The Cold Mountain Temple (1991)

Zhong Nan Hai bao biao
See The Defender (1994)

Zhong Yuan Biao Ju
See Revenge of the Patriots (1976)

Zhu Ba Da Lian Meng
See The Irresistible Piggies (2002)

Zhu Li She Yu Liang Shan Ba
See Juliet in Love (2000)

Zhuan Diao Da E
See Crocodile Hunter (1989)

Zhuang Shi Duan Bei
See One Arm Hero (1994)

Zhui Ming Qiang
See Blood of the Dragon (1971)

Zi Bao Miao Tan
See The New Marvelous Double (1992)

Zikhimyeon Jukneunda
See Record (2000)

Ziu Xia Xing
See Legend of the Drunken Tiger (1992)

Zoku Miyamoto Musashi
See Samurai 2: Duel at Ichijoji Temple (1955)

Zoku Shinobi no Mono
See Ninja: Band of Assassins Continued (1963)

Zoku Supa Jaiantsu—Akuma no Kenshin
See Evil Brain from Outer Space (1958/59)

Zoku Zatoichi Monogatari
See The Tale of Zatoichi Continues (1962)

Zong Heng Si Hai
See Once a Thief (1991)

Zou Tou You Lu
See Runaway (2001)

Zu Ginipiggu
See Guinea Pig: Devil's Experiment (1985)

Zu Ginipiggu 2: Notre Dame no Android
See Guinea Pig: Android of Notre Dame (1988)

Zu Time Warriors
See Zu: Warriors of the Magic Mountain (1983)

Zu Warriors
See Zu: Warriors of the Magic Mountain (1983)

Zu: Warriors from the Magic Mountain
See Zu: Warriors of the Magic Mountain (1983)

Zui Hou Nu
See Lady Iron Monkey (1983)

Zui Hou Tong Die
See Ultimatum (2001)

Zui Jai Pai Dang Nu Huang Mi Ling
See Aces Go Places 3 (1984)

Zui Jai Pai Dang Qian Li Jiu Cha Po
See Aces Go Places 4 (1986)

Zui Jia Pai Dang
See Aces Go Places (1982)

Zui Jia Pai Dang Da Xian Sheng Tong
See Aces Go Places 2 (1983)

Zui Quan
See Drunken Master (1978)

Zui Quan II
See Legend of the Drunken Master (1994)

Zui Quan 3
See Drunken Master Killer (1994)

Zui She Xiao Zi
See The Legend of Bruce Lee (1980)

Zui Sheng Meng Si Zhi Wan Zi Zhi Hu
See Tragic Fantasy: Tiger of Wanchai (1994)

Cast Index

The Cast Index provides a listing for all actors cited in the credits of the movies covered in this book. The names of the actors are listed alphabetically, and their corresponding filmographies are also arranged alphabetically. (Note that only movies covered in this book are listed in the filmographies.) When applicable, one or more pseudonyms are provided (in parentheses) following the actors' names. Following the movie titles, a (V) indicates voicework, and an (N), narration.

Aaliyah
Romeo Must Die '00

Abbott, Mike
City Hunter '92

Abdul-Jabbar, Kareem
(Ferdinand Lewis Alcindor, Jr., Lew Alcindor)
Bruce Lee: A Warrior's Journey '00
Game of Death '78

Abe, Hiroshe
(Hiroshi Abe)
Godzilla 2000 '99
Saga of the Phoenix '90
Tokyo Raiders '00

Abe, Masahiko
Evil Dead Trap '88

Abe, Sadao
After Life '98
Spiral '00

Abe, Toru
Return of Daimajin '66
Zatoichi the Fugitive '63

Adams, Nick
Frankenstein vs. Baragon '65
Invasion of Astro-Monster '65

Adkins, Scott
The Accidental Spy '01
Extreme Challenge '01

Ah Niu
Para Para Sakura '01
Take 2 in Life '01

Ahn, Bobby
Duel of the Tao Tough '82

Ahn Sung-kee
(Ahn Sung Kee)
Nowhere to Hide '99

Ai Fei
(Ngaai Fei, Ngai Fei)
Death Mask of the Ninja '82
Lightning Kung Fu '80

Ai Jing
From the Queen to the Chief Executive '01

Ai, Tomoko
Terror of MechaGodzilla '75

Ai Wai
(Ngai Wai, Ai Wei)
The Mission '99
Running out of Time '99
Where A Good Man Goes '99

Aiello, Danny
The Protector '85

Aikawa, Keiko
The Razor 2: The Snare '73

Aikawa, Sho
The Eel '98
Pulse '01

Aja
I.K.U. '00

Akaboshi, Shoichiro
The Ladies' Phone Sex Club '96

Akerstream, Marc
Rumble in the Bronx '95

Akino, Yoko
Renegade Ninjas '79

Akira
I.K.U. '00

Akiyama, Katsutoshi
Lone Wolf and Cub 3: Baby Cart to Hades '72
Lone Wolf and Cub 4: Baby Cart in Peril '72
Lone Wolf and Cub 5: Baby Cart in the Land of Demons '73

Akiyama, Michio
Ecstasy of the Angels '72

Akiyama, Miyuki
Gamera vs. Guiron '69

Akiyama, Yosuke
Ecstasy of the Angels '72

Albergo, George Nicholas
Ninja in the U.S.A. '88

Albert, Mercedes
Wheels on Meals '84

Alberto, Pedro
Ninja vs. Ninja '87

Allan, Brad
(Bradley James Allan)
The Accidental Spy '01
Gen-X Cops '99
Gorgeous '99

Mr. Nice Guy '97
Who Am I? '98

Allen, Woody
What's Up, Tiger Lily? '66

Alonzo, Alicia
Mad Doctor of Blood Island '68

Alonzo, Arsenio
The Walls of Hell '64

Alston, Hakim
Mortal Kombat '95

Amachi, Shigeru
Blind Swordsman: The Tale of Zatoichi '62
Ninja: Band of Assassins Continued '63
Zatoichi's Vengeance '66

Amamoto, Eisel
(Hideo Amamoto, Hideyo Amemoto)
All Monsters Attack '70
Attack of the Mushroom People '63
Big Boobs Buster '90
Dagora the Space Monster '64
Ebirah, Horror of the Deep '66
Ghidorah the Three-Headed Monster '64
Godzilla, Mothra and King Ghidorah: Battle on Fire '01
King Kong Escapes '67
Kwaidan '64
Mighty Jack '68
The Secret of the Telegian '60

Weather Woman '95
What's Up, Tiger Lily? '66
Yojimbo '61

Amatsu, Bin
(Satoshi Amatsu)
Lone Wolf and Cub 5: Baby Cart in the Land of Demons '73
The Magic Serpent '66
The Street Fighter '74

Ambera, Annamaria
Second Time Around '02

An Jae-mo
My Wife Is a Gangster '01

Anderson, Gillian
Princess Mononoke '97 (V)

Ando, Masanobu
Adrenaline Drive '99
Battle Royale '00

Ando, Nozomi
Sakuya: Slayer of Demons '00

Andou, Mitsuo
Voyage into Space '67

Ane, Naoyuki
Gamera vs. Gyaos '67

Ang Fung
(Gou Feng)
Succubare '77

Angeles, Luz
Curse of the Vampires '70

745

Angkeara, Tim
Snaker '01

Ankrum, Morris
Half Human '55/1957 (U.S.)

Anlian, Yao
Suzhou River '00

Annu, Mari
Branded to Kill '67

Anya
(On Nga, An Ya, Anya Wu)
For Bad Boys Only '00
Runaway '01
Sharp Guns '01
Young and Dangerous 6: Born to Be King '00

Anzai, Kyoko
Battle in Outer Space '59

Aoki, Mari
Naked Pursuit '68

Aoyama, Chikako
Brassiere '01
Robotrix '91

Aoyama, Kazuya
Godzilla vs. MechaGodzilla '74

Aoyama, Sugisaku
Sanshiro Sugata '43

Aoyama, Yushihiko
Daimajin '66
Zatoichi's Cane Sword '66

Arai, Kenji
Reborn from Hell: Samurai Armageddon '96

Arai, Masakazu
Big Boobs Buster '90

Arai, Yuichiro
Versus '00

Araki, Keisuke
Guinea Pig: He Never Dies '86

Araoda, Etsuko
The Ninja Dragon '90

Arasa, Yuki
Ecstasy of the Angels '72

Arase
Sumo Vixens '96

Arata
After Life '98

Aratama, Michiyo
Kwaidan '64

Archer, Peter
Enter the Dragon '73

Archer, Wayne
Thunder Ninja Kids: The Hunt for the Devil Boxer '86/94

Ariga, Miho
I.K.U. '00

Arimura, Jun
The Chinese Connection '71

Arisaka, Kurume
Pulse '01

Arishima, Ichiro
(Tadeo Oshima)
Chushingura '62
King Kong vs. Godzilla '62

Arrants, Rod
A*P*E '76

Asahi, Hirofumi
Lady Ninja: Reflections of Darkness '96

Asai, Hoshimi
Versus '00

Asano, Nobuyuki
Blowback: Love and Death '90
Junk '99

Asano, Tadanobu
Ichi the Killer '01
Maborosi '95
Shark Skin Man and Peach Hip Girl '98

Asano, Yuko
Renegade Ninjas '79

Asaoka, Yukiji
The Razor 1: Sword of Justice '72
Zatoichi Challenged '67

Ashby, Linden
Mortal Kombat '95

Ashikawa, Makoto
Boiling Point '90
Fireworks '97
Violent Cop '89

Ashita, Kami
Atomic Rulers of the World '57
Attack from Space '58
Evil Brain from Outer Space '58/59

Ashley, John
(John Atchley)
Beast of the Yellow Night '70
Brides of Blood '68
Mad Doctor of Blood Island '68
Twilight People '72

Ashley, Laurence
Kiss of the Dragon '01

Aso, Kumiko
Pulse '01
Ring 0: Birthday '00

Asou, My
I.K.U. '00

Asuka, Higuchi
(Tung Hau Ming Yat Ga, Tong Kou Ming Ri Jia)
Brassiere '01
Okinawa Rendez-vous '00
You Shoot, I Shoot '01

Ateet, Master
Raat '91

Atsumi, Mari
Gamera vs. Viras '68
The Razor 1: Sword of Justice '72

Au, Angela
Spacked Out '00

Au, Bobby
(Au Yeung Jan Wa, Ou Yang Zhen Hua)
The Eternal Evil of Asia '95
Hard Boiled '91

Au Lap-bo
(Au Laap Biu, Ou Li Bao, Au Li Pao)
Battle of Shaolin '77
Cantonen Iron Kung Fu '79
Challenge of Death '78
Drunken Art and Crippled Fist '79
The 18 Bronzemen '76
The 18 Jade Arhats '78
The 8 Masters '77
Fatal Needles vs. Fatal Fists '80
Five Elements of Kung Fu '78
Green Dragon Inn '79
The Hot, the Cool and the Vicious '76
Killer from Above '77
Lady Wu Tang '77
The Leg Fighters '80
The Lost Kung Fu Secrets '80
Master of the Flying Guillotine '76
Militant Eagle '78
Ninja Checmate '79
One Foot Crane '79
Return of the Chinese Boxer '75
Shaolin Traitorous '76
The Six Directions of Boxing '79
The Story in Temple Red Lily '79
Succubare '77

Au, Pardon
Rivals of the Dragon '83

Au Shui-wai
(Ou Rui Wei)
Last Hero in China '93

Au, Simon
God.com '98

Au Sin-yee
Final Romance '01

Au, Stephen
(Au Kam-Tong, Au Gam Tong, Ou Jin Tang)
The Blood Rules '00
Body Weapon '99
Forbidden City Cop '96
God of Cookery '96

Au Yeung-chung
(Ou Yang Zhong, Ou Yang Chung)
Bruce Lee We Miss You '77
Legend of Bruce Lee '76
Militant Eagle '78
The 72 Desperate Rebels '76
The Story in Temple Red Lily '79

Au Yeung, Susanna
(Au Yeung Pooi San, Ou Yang Pei Shan)
The Awaken Punch '73
Crime Story '93

Aurelio, Agnes
Dragons Forever '88
She Shoots Straight '90

Awaji, Keiko
Stray Dog '49

Ayukawa, Izumi
Lone Wolf and Cub 2: Baby Cart at the River Styx '72

Azmi, Shabana
Hum Paanch '80

Azouley, Didier
Kiss of the Dragon '01

Azuma, Michie
Lone Wolf and Cub 4: Baby Cart in Peril '72

Azuma, Tatsuya
Fugitive Alien '78/1986
Star Force: Fugitive Alien 2 '78/86

Azzolini, Silvio
Ninja the Final Duel '85

Baak Man-biu
(Bai Wen Biao)
Last Hero in China '93
Seeding of a Ghost '83

Baan Yung-sang
The Eagle's Killer '81

Baba, Katsuyoshi
Lone Wolf and Cub 3: Baby Cart to Hades '72
Lone Wolf and Cub 4: Baby Cart in Peril '72

Babbar, Raj
Hum Paanch '80

Babida, Jess
Lethal Panther 2 '93

Bachchan, Amitabh
Sholay '75

Bae Du-na
Dream of Garuda '94
Ring Virus '99
Sympathy for Mr. Vengeance '01

Baek Jong-hak
Memento Mori '99

Bahadur, Rana Jung
Champion '00

Bahl, Mohnish
Elaan '94

Bai Li
Ashes of Time '94

Bai Yu
Frozen '96

Baily, Cecile Le
Heroes Shed No Tears '83/86

Baisho, Mitsuko
Akira Kurosawa's Dreams '90
The Eel '97
Sure Death: Revenge '87
Warm Water under a Red Bridge '01

Baker, Robert
The Chinese Connection '71

Bakke, Brenda
Gunhed '89

Bako, Brigitte
Godzilla the Series: Monster War '99 (V)

Baldwin, Adam
Jackie Chan Adventures 1: The Search for the Talismans '00 (V)
Jackie Chan Adventures 2: The Dark Hand Returns '00 (V)
Jackie Chan Adventures 3: The Shadow of Shendu '00 (V)

Baldwin, Alec
Final Fantasy: The Spirits Within '01 (V)

Ban, Daisuke
Ring '98
Ring 0: Birthday '00
Ring 2 '99

Bang Hyoup
Bichunmoo '99

Banks, Aaron
The Bodyguard '73/78
Fist of Fear-Touch of
Death '80

Banri, Masayo
Blind Swordsman: The
Tale of Zatoichi '62
The Tale of Zatoichi
Continues '62
Zatoichi the Fugitive
'63

Baragray, John
Giant Monster Gamera
'65 (U.S.)

Barathy, Richard
Fist of Fear-Touch of
Death '80

Barbeau, Adrienne
Cannonball Run '81

Barmey, Pich Chan
Snaker '01

Barnes, Barbara
Roujin Z '91 (V)

Barry, Toni
Roujin Z '91 (V)

Batanides, Arthur
The Green Hornet '74

Bateman, Charles
The Green Hornet '74

Bau Kwok Lung
Exit the Dragon, Enter
the Tiger '75

Bee, Kenny
(Chung Jan To, Zhong
Zhen Yao)
Armour of God '86
The Chinese Feast '95
Chinese Orthopedist
and the Spice Girls
'02
Eagle Shooting Heroes
'93
Fist of Fury 1991 '91
Happy Family '02
The Millionaires'
Express '86
Miracles '89
The Moon Warriors '92
100 Ways to Murder
Your Wife '86
Project A 2 '87
The Replacement Sus-
pects '01
Savior of the Soul '91

Bell, Chrysta
Once upon a Time in
China and America
'97

Bengal
(Bengaru, Ben Garu)
Boiling Point '90

Benitez, Andres
The Blood Drinkers '64
Curse of the Vampires
'70

Benn, Jon T.
Return of the Dragon
'72

Benson, Steve N.
Iron Monkey 2 '96

Berick, Stephen
In the Line of Duty 4
'89

Berwick, Nikki
Extreme Challenge '01

Bessho, Tetsuya
Godzilla vs. Mothra '92
Parasite Eve '97

Bhaduri, Jaya
Sholay '75

Biao, Yuen
(Ha Ling Chun, Yuen
Biu, Hsia Ling-Jun, Yuan
Biao, Jimmy Tuen, Yuen
Bill) See also sidebar
on p. 142.
The Avenging Fist '01
Chinese Hercules '73
Deadful Melody '94
Dirty Tiger, Crazy Frog
'78
Don't Give a Damn '95
Dragon from Shaolin
'96
Dragons Forever '88
Dreadnaught '81
Eastern Condors '86
Enter the Dragon '73
Enter the Fat Dragon
'78
Game of Death '78
Hand of Death '75
The Hero of Swallow
'96
Iceman Cometh '89
The Invincible Armour
'77
A Kid from Tibet '91
Knockabout '79
The Magnificent Butch-
er '79
A Man Called Hero '99
Millennium Dragon '99
The Millionaires'
Express '86
Miracles '89
Mr. Vampire 2 '86
My Lucky Stars '85
Odd Couple '79
On the Run '88
Once upon a Time in
China '91
The Peacock King '89
Picture of a Nymph '88
Pom Pom '84
The Prodigal Son '81
Project A '83
Righting Wrongs '86
Rosa '86
Saga of the Phoenix
'90
Shaolin Wooden Men
'76
Shogun and Little
Kitchen '92

Snake Deadly Act '79
Spiritual Kung Fu '78
Sting of the Dragon
Masters '73
The Sword Stained with
Royal Blood '93
Super Kung Fu Kid '74
Rower of Death '81
Twinkle Twinkle Lucky
Stars '85
The Victim '80
Wheels on Meals '84
Winners and Sinners
'83
The Young Master '80
Zu: Warriors of the
Magic Mountain
'83

Bien Juan
Murder in the Orient
'74

Bin Yue
The Odd One Dies '97

Bishop, Jennifer
Horror of the Blood
Monsters '70

Biu Law Do
Born to Defence '88

Black, Frankie
The Street Fighter's
Last Revenge '74

Blanks, Billy
The Master '89

Blum, Steve
Black Magic M-66 '87
(V)

Bo, Chris
Masters of Tiger Crane
'83

Bong Choi
Double Dragon in the
Last Duel '85

Bool Dai
Succubare '77

Borg, David
Robo Vampire '88

Bose, Tarun
Gumnaam '65

Boyle, Ken
Armour of God '86
A Better Tomorrow 2
'87
The Big Heat '88
The Seventh Curse '86

Bradshaw, Terry
Cannonball Run '81

Braun, Gunther
Terror beneath the Sea
'66

Brennan, Peggy Lee
Message from Space
'78

Bridgewater, Ann
(Bai Ahn-Ni)
Curry & Pepper '90
Full Contact '92
The Inspector Wears
Skirts '88
Operation Pink Squad
'88

Bronson, Anthony
Bruce Lee Fights Back
from the Grave '76

Brooke, Walter
The Green Hornet '74

Brown, Clancy
Jackie Chan Adven-
tures 1: The Search
for the Talismans
'00 (V)
Jackie Chan Adven-
tures 2: The Dark
Hand Returns '00
(V)
Jackie Chan Adven-
tures 3: The Shad-
ow of Shendu '00
(V)

Brown, Dennis
The Secrets of the War-
rior's Power '97
Venom Warrior '83

Brown, James
The Tuxedo '02

Brown, Ronald
The New Game of
Death '75

Browne, Joe
Robo Vampire '88

Bruno, Dylan
The One '01

Buckman, Tara
Cannonball Run '81

Buenaventura, Angel
The Walls of Hell '64

Bulen, Steve
Street Fighter 2 '96 (V)

Burr, Raymond
Godzilla 1985 '84
Godzilla, King of the
Monsters (U.S. ver-
sion) '54

Buscemi, Steve
Final Fantasy: The Spir-
its Within '01 (V)

Buxton, Frank
What's Up, Tiger Lily?
'66 (V)

Byrne, Diana
Robo Vampire '88

Byun Hee-bong
Volcano High School
'01

Cadwell, Linda Lee
Bruce Lee: A Warrior's
Journey '00

Caesar, Adolf
Fist of Fear-Touch of
Death '80

Camp, Colleen
Game of Death '78

Capri, Ahna
Enter the Dragon '73

Capri, Anna
Troublesome Night 4
'98

Carey, Paul
Fear Faith Revenge 303
'98

Carlos, Flory
Terror Is a Man '59

Carpio, Anthony
(Fung Shut Fung, Gu
Shi Feng, Goo Si Fung,
Ga See Fung)
The Inspector Wears
Skirts '88
Legend of the Drunken
Master '94
Miracles '89
Project A 2 '87

Carradine, David
The Art of Action: Mar-
tial Arts in the
Movies '02

Carradine, John
Half Human (U.S. ver-
sion) '55/1957
Horror of the Blood
Monsters '70

Carvajal, Alfonzo
Mad Doctor of Blood
Island '68

Casamassa, Chris
Mortal Kombat '95

Cashman, Dan
Reptilian '00

Casnoff, Philip
Message from Space
'78

Castillo, Cecille
The Killing of Satan '83

Cawthorne, Russell
Game of Death '78
Return of the Drag-
on '72

Centenera, Andres
Beast of the Yellow
Night '70
Brides of Blood '68

Cetera, Tony
The Street Fighter '74

Cha Chi Ying
The Invincible Killer '79

Cha Chuen-yee
Queen's High '91

Cha, Eileen
Dummy Mommy, without a Baby '01

Cha Tae-hyun
My Sassy Girl '01

Chah In-sun
Double Dragon in the Last Duel '85

Chai, Iris
(Qi Zhi Yao, Chai Chi-yiu)
Devil Touch '02
Happy Family '02
Troublesome Night 14 '02
Violent Cop '99

Chai Kai
(Ga Hoi, Jia Kai, Chia Kai)
The Blazing Temple '76
Golden Killah '80
The Hot, the Cool, and the Vicious '76
War of the Shaolin Temple '80

Chakraborty, Mithun
Hum Paanch '80

Chambara Trio, The
The Razor 1: Sword of Justice '72

Chamberlain, Richard
Shogun '80

Chan, Alan
(Chan Gwok Kuen, Chen Guo Quan, Chan Kwok Kuen, Chan Kwok Kwan)
Crazy Crooks '80
Death Mask of the Ninja '82
Dynamo '78
The Legend of Bruce Lee '80
Legend of the Drunken Master '94
The Masked Prosecutor '99
Miracles '89
Prodigal Boxer '73
Project A 2 '87
Scared Stiff '86
Shaolin Soccer '01
Thunder Kick '73

Chan, Alexander
(Chan Mong Wa, Chen Wang Hua)
Bullets of Love '01
Double Tap '00

Chan, Alice
(Chan Wai, Chen Wei)
Bio-Cops '00
City of Desire '01
A Wicked Ghost 2: The Fear '00

Chan, Anita
(Chan Wing Yin, Chen Ying Yan)
Troublesome Night 14 '02
Violent Cop '99

Chan, Anthony
(Chan Yau, Chen You)
Armour of God '86
Heart of Dragon '85
Miracles '89
Mr. Vampire Saga 4 '88
100 Ways to Murder Your Wife '86
Project A 2 '87
Twin Dragons '92
Twinkle Twinkle Lucky Stars '85

Chan, Astrid
(Chan Chi Ching)
Sunshine Cops '99
Violent Cop '99
Wishful Milenio '01

Chan, Barry
(Wai Siu Wan, Wei Xiao Yun, Wei Tze Yung, Hwai Zi Yuen, Wai Tze Wen, Wei Tzu Yun)
The Blazing Temple '76
The Deadly Sword '78
The Last Duel '82
Mantis Combat '81
Militant Eagle '78
One Foot Crane '79
The 72 Desperate Rebels '76

Chan Bik-fung
(Chen Bi Feng, Chen Pi Feng)
Blooded Treasury Fight '79
The Heroes '80

Chan, Billy
(Chan Wui Ngai, Chan Kooi Ngai, Chen Hui Yi)
The Chinese Connection '72
Dirty Kung Fu '78
Dirty Tiger, Crazy Frog '78
Encounter of the Spooky Kind '81
End of the Wicked Tiger '77
Enter the Dragon '73
Enter the Fat Dragon '78
Executioners from Shaolin '77
Fists of Fury '71
Heart of Dragon '85
He Has Nothing But Kung Fu '77
His Name Is Nobody '79
Knockabout '79
The Magnificent Butcher '79
Masters of Tiger Crane '83
Odd Couple '79

The Owl vs. Bombo '84
The Private Eyes '76
Shaolin Master Killer '78
Sting of the Dragon Masters '73
A Touch of Zen '69
The Victim '80
Where's Officer Tuba? '86

Chan, Bobo
(Chan Man Woon, Chan Wen Yuan)
Shadow '01

Chan, Bruce
Rivals of the Dragon '83

Chan, Charine
(Chan Ke Ling, Chan Ga Ling, Chen Jia Ling)
Erotic Ghost Story 2 '91
Tragic Fantasy: Tiger of Wanchai '94

Chan, Charlie
(Chan Yiu Lam, Chen Yao Lin)
Death Duel of Kung Fu '79
Fists Like Lee '74
Shadow of the Tiger '79
Snake in the Eagle's Shadow '78
Ten Tigers of Shaolin '78

Chan, Cherie
(Chan Siu Ha, Chen Shao Xia)
Man Wanted '95

Chan Cheuk-yan
(Chen Zhuo Xin)
Casino Raiders 2 '91
On the Run '88

Chan Chi-fai
(Chen Zhi Hui)
Angel '87
A Better Tomorrow '86
The Blade '95
City on Fire '87
City War '88
Cop on a Mission '01
Dragon Inn '92
Her Name Is Cat '98
Legendary Couple '95
Operation Pink Squad '88
Police Story 2 '88
Pom Pom and Hot Hot '92
Project A '83
Return to a Better Tomorrow '94
Sixty Million Dollar Man '95
Young and Dangerous 5 '98

Chan Chin-pang
(Benny Chan, Chan Gin Pang, Chan Chin Fan, Penn Chan)
Last Ghost Standing '99
Shanghai Affairs '98

Chan Chiu-ming
(Chen Chao Ming)
Chinese Iron Man '75
The Lost Kung Fu Secrets '80

Chan Chuen
(Chen Quan, Chen Chuan, Chen Chun, Chan Chun)
Death Mask of the Ninja '82
Duel of the Brave Ones '78
The End of the Wicked Tiger '81
Five Fingers of Death '71
Killer from Above '77
Killer Snakes '74
Mask of Death '76
Police Story '85
Snake in the Eagle's Shadow '78
Sting of the Dragon Masters '73
Thunder Kick '74

Chan Chung-Yung
(Chen Song Yong)
Gorgeous '99
The Legend '92
The New Legend of Shaolin '94
Prison on Fire 2 '91
Young and Dangerous 6: Born to Be King '00

Chan, Convoy
Bakery Amour '01
Ballistic Kiss '98
Every Dog Has His Date '01

Chan, Daniel
(Chan Hiu Tung, Chan Hiu Dung, Chen Xiao Dong)
The Best of the Best '96
For Bad Boys Only '00
A War Named Desire '00

Chan, Dennis
(Chan Kwok-san, Chan Gwok San Chen Guo Xin)
Casino Tycoon 2 '92
Code of Honor '87
Fight Back to School '91
God of Gamblers '89
Heart of Dragon '85
I Love Maria '88
The Inspector Wears Skirts '88

Mr. Boo Meets Pom Pom '85
Police Story 2 '88
Pom Pom '84
Pom Pom Strikes Back '86
Royal Warriors '86
Twin Dragons '92
Where's Officer Tuba? '86
Yes, Madam '85

Chan Dik-hak
(Chen Di Ke)
Angel '87
Breakout from Oppression '78
Enter the Fat Dragon '78
Five Fingers of Death '71
Last Hurrah for Chivalry '78
Miracles '89
Prodigal Boxer '72
Project A 2 '87
Thunder Kick '73
Tower of Death '81
Warrior from Shaolin '81

Chan, Eason
(Chan Yik Shun, Chen Yi Xun)
Comic King '00
Cop Shop Babes '01
Funeral March '01
Jiang Hu-"The Triad Zone" '00
Lavender '00
Tiramisu '02
Visible Secret '01

Chan, Ellen
(Chan Nga Lun, Chen Ya Lun)
Aces Go Places 5: The Terracotta Hit '89
Doctor Vampire '90
The Eternal Evil of Asia '95
The Inspector Wears Skirts '88

Chan, Elsie
(Chan Yik Si, Chen Yi Shi)
Operation Pink Squad '88
The Seventh Curse '86

Chan Fai-Hung
(Chen Hui Hong)
Jiang Hu-"The Triad Zone" '00
Operation Pink Squad '88
The Private Eye Blues '94
You Shoot, I Shoot '01

Chan Fan-Kei, Frankie
(Chan Fan-Kei, Mandingo)
Prodigal Son '82

Chan, Flora
(Chan Wai San, Chen Hui Shan)
Love au Zen '01

Chan, Frankie
(Chan Chi-Leung, Chen Zhi Liang, Frankie Chin)
Bio Zombie '98
Cop Shop Babes '01
Crocodile Hunter '89
Full Contact '92
Powerful Four '91
Riki-Oh: The Story of Ricky '92
Vampire Kids '91

Chan Ga-chai
The Haunted Cop Shop '87

Chan Git-leng
(Chen Jie Ling)
Tiramisu '02
Winners and Sinners '83

Chan Hei
(Chen Xi, Cheung Hey, Cheung Hay)
The Eagle's Killer '81
His Name Is Nobody '79
Hong Kong Nocturne '67
Killer of Snake, Fox of Shaolin '78
Knockabout '79
The Prodigal Son '81
The Victim '80

Chan Hing-cheung
Para Para Sakura '01
Take 2 in Life '01

Chan Ho-man, Benny
The Final Winner '01

Chan Ho-ming
Losers' Club '01

Chan Hon-kwong
(Chan Hon Gwong, Chen Han Guang)
Masked Avengers '81
Ten Tigers of Kwang-tung '79

Chan Hung Kai
Ninja vs. Ninja '87

Chan, Idy
(Chan Yuk Lin, Chen Yu Lian, Ida Chan)
Casino Raiders '89
On the Run '88

Chan, Isabel
Shadow '01

Chan, Jackie
(Chan Kong-Sang, Jacky Chan, Chan Yuen-Lung, Long Cheng, Sing Lung)
See also sidebars on pp. 142, 162, and 596.
The Accidental Spy '01
Armour of God '86

The Art of Action: Martial Arts in the Movies '02
The Big Brawl '80
Brutal Boxer '72
Cannonball Run '81
Chinese Hercules '73
City Hunter '92
Crime Story '93
Dragon Fist '78
Dragon Lord '82
Dragons Forever '88
Drunken Master '78
Fantasy Mission Force '84
Fearless Hyena '79
Fearless Hyena 2 '80
First Strike '96
Gen-X Cops '99
Gorgeous '99
Half a Loaf of Kung Fu '77
Hand of Death '75
Heart of Dragon '85
Jackie Chan Adventures 1: The Search for the Talismans '00
Jackie Chan Adventures 2: The Dark Hand Returns '00
Jackie Chan Adventures 3: The Shadow of Shendu '00
A Kid from Tibet '91
The Killer Meteors '76
King of Comedy '99
Legend of the Drunken Master '94
Martial Arts Mayhem, Vol. 1 '99
Miracles '89
Mr. Nice Guy '97
My Lucky Stars '85
New Fist of Fury '76
Operation Condor '91
Police Story '85
Police Story 2 '88
Pom Pom '84
The Prisoner '90
Project A '83
Project A 2 '87
The Protector '85
Rumble in the Bronx '95
Rush Hour '98
Rush Hour 2 '01
Shaolin Wooden Men '76
Snake and Crane Arts of Shaolin '78
Snake in the Eagle's Shadow '78
Spiritual Kung Fu '78
Supercop '92
Supercop 2 '93
Thunderbolt '95
To Kill with Intrigue '77
A Touch of Zen '69
The Tuxedo '02
Twin Dragons '92
Twinkle Twinkle Lucky Stars '85
Wheels on Meals '84
Who Am I? '98

Winners and Sinners '83
The Young Master '80
Young Tiger '72

Chan, Jeffrey
Rivals of the Dragon '83

Chan, Jennifer
(Chan Ming Chan, Chen Ming Zhen)
Rock 'n' Roll Cop '94

Chan, Joanna
(Chan Pui San)
The Inspector Wears Skirts '88

Chan, Johnnie
Golden Dragon Silver Snake '79

Chan, JoJo
(Chan Kei Kei, Chen Qi Qi)
The Butterfly Murders '79
The Magnificent Butcher '79

Chan, Jordan
(A. Jordan Chan, Chan Siu-Chun)
Big Bullet '96
Bio Zombie '98
The Cheaters '01
A Chinese Ghost Story: The Tsui Hark Animation '97 (V)
Comeuppance '00
Downtown Torpedoes '97
Flyin Dance '01
He's a Woman, She's a Man '94
Help!!! '00
Hot War '98
The Irresistible Piggies '02
Killer '00
A Man Called Hero '99 (V)
The Masked Prosecutor '99
Young and Dangerous '96
Young and Dangerous 6: Born to Be King '00

Chan, Joyce
(Chan Yin Hang, Chen Yan Hang)
Faces of Horror '98
A Wicked Ghost 2: The Fear '00

Chan, Julia
Killer's Romance '90

Chan, Juliet
Scorpion Thunderbolt '85

Chan, Kelly
(Chan Wai Lam, Chen Hui Lin)
Anna Magdalena '98

A Chinese Ghost Story: The Tsui Hark Animation '97 (V)
Hot War '98
Lavender '00
Merry-Go-Round '01
Tokyo Raiders '00

Chan, Kenneth
(Ken Chan, Chan Kai Tai, Chen Qi Tai)
Man Wanted '95
Satin Steel '94

Chan Kin-fung
(Chan Gin Fung, Chen Jian Feng)
The Irresistible Piggies '02
Shadow '01

Chan Kwok-Bong
(Chan Gwok Bong, Chen Gou Bang, Chan Kwok Pong)
Crime of a Beast '01
The Eternal Evil of Asia '95
The Lord of Hangzhou '98
Once upon a Time in China and America '97
Take 2 in Life '01

Chan Lau
(Chen Lou, Chen Lui)
Blind Fist of Bruce '79
The Bloody Fight '72
Dragon on Fire '79
Dragon's Claws '79
Dynamo '78
Fearless Dragons '79
The Fist, the Kicks and the Evils '79
Killer Priest '81
Kung Fu Zombie '81
Mantis Combat '81
The New Marvelous Double '92
Shadow of the Tiger '79
3 Evil Masters '80
The 36 Crazy Fists '77
The 36 Deadly Styles '79
Tiger over Wall '80

Chan, Lindsay
Aces Go Places '82

Chan, Little Unicorn
(Siu Kei Lun, Xiao Qi Lin, Little Unicorn, Unicorn Chan)
Bruce Lee: The Man, the Myth '76
The Chinese Connection '71
Deadly Snail vs. Kung Fu Killer '77
Return of the Dragon '72

Chan Lung
(Chen Long, Peter Chan) See also sidebar on p. 326.

Bolo '80
The Buddhist Fist '79
Crazy Crooks '80
Deadful Melody '94
Death Duel of Kung Fu '79
Dirty Ho '79
Dirty Kung Fu '78
Dirty Tiger, Crazy Frog '78
Don't Give a Damn '95
Dragons Forever '88
Eastern Condors '86
Encounter of the Spooky Kind '81
Executioners from Shaolin '77
Fists of Fury '71
Heart of Dragon '85
The Incredible Kung Fu Mission '82
Knockabout '79
Kung Fu Genius '79
The Legend '92
The Legend 2 '93
The Legendary Strike '78
The Millionaires' Express '86
Mr. Boo Meets Pom Pom '85
Odd Couple '79
Pedicab Driver '89
Pom Pom '84
The Prodigal Son '81
Rosa '86
Shaolin Master Killer '78
Snake Deadly Act '79
Snake in the Eagle's Shadow '78
The Victim '80
Warrior from Shaolin '81
Winners and Sinners '83

Chan Man Ching
(Chen Wen Qing)
First Strike '96
Rumble in the Bronx '95
Rush Hour '98
Supercop 2 '93
Victim '99

Chan Man-lei
(Chan Man Lui, Chen Wan Lei)
Fallen Angels '95
Fighting for Love '01

Chan Man-Man
Happy Family '02

Chan, Mandy
(Chan Yan Man, Chen En Wen, Chang Hsun)
Drunken Tai Chi '84
In the Line of Duty 3 '88
Red Wolf '95

Chan, Marianne
(Chan Miu Ying, Chen Miao Ying)

The Best of the Best '96
Tragic Fantasy: Tiger of Wanchai '94
Troublesome Night 4 '98

Chan, Mario
Eagle vs. Silver Fox '83

Chan, Michael
(Chan Wai-Man, Chen Hui-Min, Chan Hui Ming, Bruce Chen, Chen Huey Miin)
All's Well End's Well '97 '97
Blooded Treasury Fight '79
Bullets of Love '01
Chinese Hercules '73
Chinese Super Ninjas '82
Dragon Lord '82
Fists Like Lee '74
The Heroes '80
H.K. Adams Family '92
The Invincible Killer '79
Kung Fu, the Invisible Fist '72
Lee Rock '91
Legacy of Rage '86
Master Q 2001 '01
Ninja vs. Ninja '87
No More Love, No More Death '92
Pom Pom Strikes Back '86
Project A 2 '87
Revenge of the Patriots '76
Royal Warriors '86
Snake Deadly Act '79
Violent Cop '99
You Shoot, I Shoot '01

Chan, Monica
(Chan Fat Yung, Chen Fa Rong)
Casino Raiders 2 '91
Double Tap '00
Full Alert '97
God of Gamblers 2 '90
Love Correction '00
Option Zero '97
Shogun and Little Kitchen '92

Chan, Moses
(Chan Ho, Chen Hao)
Black Mask '96
The Blade '95
Dummy Mommy, without a Baby '01
Everyday Is Valentine '01
Gen-X Cops '99
Lawyer Lawyer '97
Legend of Speed '99
Sharp Guns '01
Violent Cop '99

Chan Muk-chuen
(Chen Mu Chuan)
The Iron Monkey '77

Monkey Fist Floating Snake '79

Chan, Nadia
Troublesome Night 8 '00

Chan Nam Wing
(Chen Nan Rong)
Beast Cops '98
Deadly Camp '99

Chan, Nat
(Chan Pak Cheung, Chan Baak Cheung, Chen Bai Xiang)
Don't Give a Damn '95
Fight Back to School 3 '93
Fist of Fury 1991 '91
Flirting Scholar '93
King of Beggars '92
The Last Blood '90
Last Hero in China '93
Mr. Boo Meets Pom Pom '85
Royal Tramp '92
Royal Tramp 2 '92
Twinkle Twinkle Lucky Stars '85

Chan, Natassia
Magnificent Natural Fist '80

Chan, Nathan
Angel 2 '88

Chan, Orson
Dragon against Vampire '85

Chan Pak-yue
(Chen Bo Yu)
Wishful Milenio '01

Chan, Pauline
(Chan Bo Lin, Chen Bao Lian)
From Beijing with Love '94
Paramount Motel '00

Chan, Perry
Visible Secret '01

Chan, Peter
C'est la Vie, Mon Cheri '93

Chan, Phillip
(Chan Yan-Kin, Chen Xin Jian, Philip Chan)
Fight Back to School 3 '93
Hard Boiled '91
Love on Delivery '94
Mr. Boo Meets Pom Pom '85
The Owl vs. Bombo '84
Pom Pom '84
Pom Pom Strikes Back '86
Supercop '92
The Tigers '91
Twin Dragons '92
Twinkle Twinkle Lucky Stars '85

Winners and Sinners '83

Chan Pooi-ling
(Chen Pei Ling, Chen Pei Ling, Chen Fei Ling)
Born Invincible '78
Bruce Lee We Miss You '76
The Eagle's Killer '81

Chan Pui
The Secrets of the Warrior's Power '97

Chan Pui-Kee
Brother of Darkness '94

Chan, Robert
Invincible Obsessed Fighter '82

Chan Sai-tang
(Chen Shi Teng, Christopher Chan)
Crime Story '93
Miracles '89

Chan Sam-lam
(Chen Sen Lin)
The Blazing Temple '76
Five Elements of Kung Fu '78

Chan, Samuel
Shadow '01

Chan Sau-chung
Shadow of the Tiger '79

Chan, Sheila
(Chan Sak Lan, Chan Suk Lan, Chen Shu Lan)
All's Well End's Well '92
Doctor Vampire '90
Funeral March '01
Prince of the Sun '90

Chan Shen
(Chim Sam, Zhan Sen, Jim Sum)
Avenging Warriors of Shaolin '79
Brave Archer '77
Chinese Super Ninjas '82
Death Mask of the Ninja '82
Five Fingers of Death '72
Flag of Iron '80
He Has Nothing But Kung Fu '77
Legend of the 7 Golden Vampires '74
Shaolin Master Killer '78

Chan Shing-hung
F*** / Off '98

Chan Shu-kei
(Chen Shu Ji)
Masked Avengers '81

Ten Tigers of Kwang-tung '79

Chan Siu-pang
(Chan Siu Pang, Chen Shao Peng, Chen Hsiao Peng)
The Buddhist Fist '79
Fatal Flying Guillotine '77
Martial Arts Master Wong Fei Hung '92
Raiders of Wu Tang '82

Chan, Stacie
Jackie Chan Adventures 1: The Search for the Talismans '00 (V)
Jackie Chan Adventures 2: The Dark Hand Returns '00 (V)
Jackie Chan Adventures 3: The Shadow of Shendu '00 (V)

Chan, Stephen
(Chan Tak Gwong, Chen De Guang)
Crime Story '93
Crocodile Hunter '89
First Option '96
Long Arm of the Law 2 '87
Organized Crime & Triad Bureau '94
She Shoots Straight '90

Chan, Sunny
(Chan Kam Hung, Chan Gam Hung, Chen Jin Hong)
The Bride with White Hair 2 '93
Cheap Killers '98
Comeuppance '00
Troublesome Night '97

Chan Tat-kwong
(Chan Dat Gong, Chen Da Guang)
Crime Story '93
Dragons Forever '88
Inspector Wears Skirts '88
Legend of the Drunken Master '94
Police Story 2 '88
Miracles '89
Twin Dragons '92

Chan Tin-lung
(Chen Tian Long, Chen Tien Loong)
Legend of the 7 Golden Vampires '74

Chan, Vindy
(Chan Wai Yee)
Final Option '94
King of Beggers '92
Legend of the Drunken Master '94

The Magic Crane '93

Chan, Vivian
(Chan Tak Yung, Chen De Rong)
Casino Tycoon 2 '92
Royal Tramp '92
Royal Tramp 2 '92

Chan Wai Lau
(Chen Hui Lou)
The Deadly Sword '78
Fearless Hyena '79
Fearless Hyena 2 '80
Fists of Bruce Lee '78
The Iron Monkey '77
The Killer Meteors '76
Kung Pow: Enter the Fist '76/2001
The Last Duel '82
Legend of the Mountain '79
Revenge of the Patriots '76
To Kill with Intrigue '77
The World of the Drunken Master '79

Chan Wai-ming
(Chen Hui Ming)
Bio-Cops '00

Chan, Willie
Visible Secret '01

Chan Wing Chung
A Fighter's Blues '00

Chan Wing-ha
Iron Man '86

Chan, Winson
Gen-X Cops '99

Chan Ying Lai
(Chen Ying Li)
Trust Me U Die '99

Chan, Yoyo
Gimme Gimme '01

Chandra, Uday
Hum Paanch '80

Chang, Brandon
The Touch '02

Chang Chen
Crouching Tiger, Hidden Dragon '00

Chang Chi-ping
(Cheung Gei Ping, Zhang Ji Ping, Cheung Kei Ping, George Chang, Cheung Chi Ping)
Drunken Art and Crippled Fist '79
Love on a Diet '01
The Mission '99
Ninja Hunter '84
Ninja vs. Shaolin Guards '84
Revengeful Swordwomen '79
Shaolin vs. Lama '81
Shaolin vs. Ninja '83

The Six Directions of
    Boxing '79
Raiders of Wu Tang '82
Return of the Tiger '77
Two Dragons Fight
    against Tiger '75
War of the Shaolin Tem-
    ple '80

Chang Gan Wing
(Ceng Jin Rong)
Brother of Darkness
    '94
Bullet in the Head '90
Miracles '89

Chang Guifa
The Road Home '99

Chang Hang-sun
The Foul King '00
Tell Me Something '99

Chang Hung-mei
Iron Man '86

Chang, Jeanie
*(Cheung Wing Wing,
Zhang Yong Yong, Lisa,
Jeannie Chang)*
Ninja Checkmate '79
The 36 Deadly Styles
    '79
The Unbeaten 28 '80
The World of the Drunk-
    en Master '79

Chang Jian-li
Iron Monkey 2 '96

Chang, John
*(Cheung Ng Long,
Zhang Wu Lang, John
Cheung, Chang Wu
Lang)*
Chinese Samson '79
Dragon: The Bruce Lee
    Story '93
Duel of the Brave Ones
    '78
The Eagle's Killer '81
Executioners '93
Executioners from
    Shaolin '77
Miracles '89
Police Story 2 '88
Project A '83
Project A 2 '83
Shaolin Mantis '78
Shaolin Master Killer
    '78
Winners and Sinners
    '83
Young Tiger '72

Chang, Ken
*(Cheung Chi Yiu, Chong
Chi Yiu, Zhang Zhi Yau,
Ken Chong)*
The Accidental Spy '01
Extreme Challenge '01
Sharp Guns '01
Sunshine Cops '99

Chang Kuo-chu
*(Cheung Gwok Chue,
Zhang Guo Zhu)*

Born Wild '01
The Butterfly Murders
    '79

Chang, Paul
*(Chang Cheung, Zhang
Chong, Cheung Chung,
Cheng Ching)*
Dragon against Vam-
    pire '85
Dragon Lord '82
Duel to the Death '83
Fantasy Mission Force
    '84
The Green Dragon Inn
    '79
Hong Kong Nocturne
    '67
The Incredible Kung Fu
    Mission '82
The Lost Kung Fu
    Secrets '80
Millionaires' Express
    '86
Police Story '85
Righting Wrongs '86
Wheels on Meals '84
Where's Officer Tuba?
    '86
Winners and Sinners
    '83

Chang, Pearl
*(Cheung Ling, Zhang
Ling, Pearl Cheung,
Pearl Cheong, Chang
Ling, Chang Lin)*
Fantasy Mission Force
    '84
Inheritor of Kung Fu '77
Shaolin Fist of Fury '87

Chang Rong
Deadend of Besiegers
    '92

Chang Siu Yin
Erotic Ghost Story 2
    '91
990714.com '00

Chang, Sylvia
*(Chang Ai Chia, Cheung
Ngai Ga, Zhang Ai Jia)*
Aces Go Places '82
Aces Go Places 2 '83
Aces Go Places 3 '84
Aces Go Places 4 '86
All About Ah-Long '89
C'est la Vie, Mon Cheri
    '93
A Chinese Ghost Story:
    The Tsui Hark Ani-
    mation '97 (V)
Legend of the Mountain
    '79
Twin Dragons '92

Chang Yi
*(Chang Yu, Cheung Yik,
Zhang Yi, Cheung I,
Chang I, Cheung Yick)*
The Blazing Temple '76
Challenge of Death '78
Eagle's Claw '77
The 18 Bronzemen '76

The 18 Jade Arhats '78
Exit the Dragon, Enter
    the Tiger '75
Fatal Needles vs. Fatal
    Fists '80
Killer from Above '77
Monkey Fist Floating
    Snake '79
The Moon Warriors '92
Return of the Tiger '79
Revenge of the Patriots
    '76
7 Commandments of
    Kung Fu '79
The Shaolin Kids '77
Shaolin Traitorous '76
SuperManChu '73
The Victim '80

Channary, Chao
Snaker '01

Chao Chung-hsing
Brave Archer '77

Chao Gang Sheng
Killer Priest '81

Chao, Rosalind
The Big Brawl '80

Chao San-San
Swordsman with an
    Umbrella '70

Chao, Winston
*(Chao Wen-hsuan, Zhao
Wen Xuan, Chiu Man
Hsuen)*
Thunder Cop '96
The Touch '02

Chao Yung Hsing
Raiders of Wu Tang '82

Chaplin, Ben
The Touch '02

Chaplin, Deborah
*(Deborah Dutch, Debra
Dare, Debbie Dutch)*
Bruce Lee Fights Back
    from the Grave '76

Charoenpura, Intira
A Fighter's Blues '00

Chat Pui-wan
*(Chak Pooi Wan, Di Pei
Yun, Cheuk Pui Wan)*
The Deadly Camp '99
God.com '98
Model from Hell '99

Chatri, Sorapong
Robo Vampire '88

Chatutong, Areewan
Fear Faith Revenge 303
    '98

Chau, Emil
*(Chow Wah-Kin, Zhou
Hua-jian, Emil Chow)*
All's Well End's Well '97
    '97
Gorgeous '99
Headlines '01
Mr. Nice Guy '97

Rumble in the Bronx
    '95
Supercop 2 '93

Chau, Jessica
Armageddon '97

Chay, Stella
Duel of the Tao Tough
    '82

Chayya, Laxmi
Gumnaam '65

Che Hing-wa
The Blade '95

Che, Stephanie
*(Che Yuen Yuen, Che
Wan Wan)*
Bakery Amour '01
Beast Cops '98
Clean My Name, Mr.
    Coroner! '00
Every Dog Has His
    Date '01
For Bad Boys Only '00
Goodbye Mr. Cool '01
Legend of Speed '99
Okinawa Rendez-vous
    '00
Sound from the Dark
    '00

Cheadle, Don
Rush Hour 2 '01

Cheang Lung
Hero's Blood '91

Chen, Alice
The Secrets of the War-
    rior's Power '97 (N)

Chen, Betty
Bruce Lee: The Man,
    the Myth '76

Chen Chieh
Lady Whirlwind and the
    Rangers '74

Chen Chin-hai
*(Chan Gam Hoi, Chen
Jin Hai)*
Killer Priest '81
The Leg Fighters '80

Chen Chiu
*(Chan Gau, Chen Jiu,
Cheng Chiu, Chan Kau,
Chen Chou, Tsen Chao)*
Battle of Shaolin '77
Blazing Temple '76
Born Invincible '78
The 18 Bronzemen Part
    2 '76
The 18 Jade Arhats '78
Fighting Ace '79
Fists of Fury '71
Golden Killah '80
The Hot, the Cool and
    the Vicious '76
Macho Man '72
The Shaolin Kids '77
Two Dragons Fight
    against Tiger '75

Chen Defeng
Shaolin: Wheel of Life
    '00

Chen, Edison
*(Chen Koon Hei, Chan
Goon Hei, Chen Guan
Xi)*
Dance of a Dream '01
Dummy Mommy, with-
    out a Baby '01
Final Romance '01
Gen-Y Cops '00

Chen, Edmund
The Eye '02

Chen Fei-Fei
18 Secrets of Kung Fu
    '79

Chen Fu Ching
The Chinese Connec-
    tion '71

Chen Ho, Peter
Hong Kong Nocturne
    '67

Chen Hung Lieh
*(Chan Hung-Lit, Chen
Hong Lie, Bruce Lieh)*
Abbot White '82
Fantasy Mission Force
    '84
Fearless Fighters '69
A Life of Ninja '83
The Shaolin Invincibles
    '79

Chen, James
Take 2 in Life '01

Chen Jing
(Chan Ging, Chan Jing)
Crocodile Hunter '89
Dragons Forever '88
Fist of Fury 1991 '91
Iceman Cometh '89
Long Arm of the Law
    '84
Long Arm of the Law 2
    '87
Magnificent Warriors
    '87
Miracles '89
Pom Pom Strikes Back
    '86
Rich and Famous '87
Tiger Cage '88
Where's Officer Tuba?
    '86
Yes, Madam '85

Chen Kuan-tai
*(Chan Goon Tai, Chen
Guan Tai, Chen Kwan
Tai, Chen Guan Tay,
Chan Koon Tai, Chen
Kung Tai)*
Bloody Fight '72
The Bloody Fists '72
Death Ring '83
Executioners from
    Shaolin '77
The Final Winner '01

The Flying Guillotine
'74
The Iron Monkey '77
Iron Monkey 2 '77
A Life of Ninja '83
Lightning Kung Fu '80
Martial Arts Mayhem,
Vol. 2 '99
The Return of the 5
Deadly Venoms '78
Shaolin King Boxer '79
3 Evil Masters '80
The Tigers '91
Venom Warrior '83

Chen Pei-hsi
(Chen Peisi, Chan Pooi
Sai, Chen Pei Qian)
Chinese Super Ninjas
'82
Her Majesty Is Fine '96

Chen, Phoenix
Yoga and Kung Fu Girl
'78

Chen Ping
(Chan Ping)
Mighty Peking Man '77

Chen Qiang
Her Majesty Is Fine '96

Chen, Robert
Devil Woman '70

Chen Sa Lei
Hunted by Royal Decree
'00

Chen, Sean
Take 2 in Life '01

Chen Shan
(Chan San, Chang
Shan, Seung San, Chen
Hsiang)
Battle of Shaolin '77
Ninja Hunter '83
Shaolin vs. Lama '81

Chen Shiang-chyi
What Time Is It There?
'01

Chen Tak Chi
Master of the Flying
Guillotine '74

Chen Tung
Contract Killer '98

Chen Weirong
The Adventures of the
Master and His
Servant '96

Chen Yan-Yan
(Chan Yin Yin)
Gold Fingers '01
Mantis Combat '81
Thunder Kick '73

Chen Yueh-Sheng
(Chien Yueh Sheng)
The Buddha Assassina-
tor '79
New Mr. Vampire '86

Cheng, Adam
(Cheng Siu-Chow, Jeng
Siu Chau, Zheng Shao
Qui)
Drunken Master Killer
'94
Fantasy Mission Force
'84
Gunmen '88
Last Hero in China '84
The Legend '92
The Legend 2 '93
Painted Skin '92
Zu: Warriors of the
Magic Mountain
'83

Cheng, Andy
(Andy Kai Chung
Cheng)
Rush Hour '98

Cheng, Carol
(Cheng Yu Ling, Jeng Yu
ling, Zheng Yu Ling,
DoDo Cheng, Carol
DoDo Chen)
Eighth Happiness '88
Operation Condor '91
Tiger Cage '88

Cheng, Cecil
Shaolin: Wheel of Life
'00

Cheng Chu-fung
Troublesome Night 9
'00

Cheng Chuen Yam
Riki-Oh: The Story of
Ricky '89

Cheng, Darren
Merry-Go-Round '01

Cheng, Ekin
(Cheng Yee-Kin, Zheng
Yi Jian, Dior Cheng,
Noodle Cheng)
The Avenging Fist '01
The Duel '00
For Bad Boys Only '00
Goodbye Mr. Cool '01
Help!!! '00
Hot War '98
Legend of Speed '99
Lord of the Wu Tang
'93
A Man Called Hero '99
Return to a Better
Tomorrow '94
Running out of Time 2
'01
Second Time Around
'02
The Storm Riders '98
Tokyo Raiders '00
Young and Dangerous
'96
Young and Dangerous
5 '98
Young and Dangerous
6: Born to Be King
'00
Zu Warriors '01

Cheng Fu Hung
(Jeng Foo Hung, Zheng
Fu Xiong, Tsan Fu
Hung, Cheng Fu Hsi-
ung)
Cantonen Iron Kung Fu
'79
Exit the Dragon, Enter
the Tiger '75
Fantasy Mission Force
'84
Fatal Needles vs. Fatal
Fists '80
Fearless Hyena '79
Killer from Above '77
Lady Whirlwind and the
Rangers '74
Lady Wu Tang '77
Monkey Fist Floating
Snake '79
Rage of the Masters
'74
Return of the Tiger '79
Screaming Ninja '73
The Smart Cavalier '78

Cheng Hong-yip
(Jeng Hong Yip, Zheng
Kang Ye, Cheng Kang
Yeh, Cheng Yang-yip)
The Deadly Sword '78
Dirty Kung Fu '78
Dirty Tiger, Crazy Frog
'78
Dragon Lord '82
The Eagle's Killer '81
Executioners from
Shaolin '77
A Fistful of Talons '83
Hong Kong Nocturne
'67
Kung Fu Genius '79
Kung Fu Zombie '81
Snake Deadly Act '79
The Young Avenger '79
The Young Master '80

Cheng Hung
Shanghai Affairs '98

Cheng, Joe
(Cheng Cho, Jeng Jo,
Zheng Zu)
Conman in Tokyo '00
Expect the Unexpected
'98
From Beijing with Love
'94
King of Comedy '99
Love on Delivery '94
Peace Hotel '95
Sixty Million Dollar Man
'95
Too Many Ways to Be
No. 1 '97
Young and Dangerous
'96

Cheng, Joseph
(Cheng King-kei, Jeng
Ging Gei, Zheng Jing Ji)
The Bride with White
Hair '93

Cheng Ka-sing
(Cheng Ka Sang, Jeng
Ga Sang, Zheng Gu
Sheng)
Vampire Controller '00
Where A Good Man
Goes '99

Cheng Kei-ying
(Jeng Kei Ying, Zheng
Qi Ying, Chang Ciu Yin,
Cheng Kar Ying)
A Fistful of Talons '83
Fists Like Lee '74
Kung Fu Zombie '81
Young and Dangerous
'96

Cheng, Kent
(Cheng Jak Si, Jeng Jak
Si, Zheng Ze Shi,
Cheng Jui Si)
Crime Story '93
The Defender '94
Dr. Lamb '92
The Dragon Family '88
The Imp '81
The Most Wanted '94
Once upon a Time in
China '91
Powerful Four '91
Run and Kill '93
Wonder Seven '94

Cheng, Lawrence
(Cheng Tan-Shui, Jeng
Daan Shui, Zheng Dan
Rui)
Born Wild '01
Eighth Happiness '88
He's a Woman, She's a
Man '94
King of Beggars '92
Miracles '89
The Storm Riders '98

Cheng Lui
(Jeng Lui, Zheng Lei,
Cheng Lei, Cheung Lui)
Fists Like Lee '74
Kung Fu's Hero '73
Last Hurrah for Chivalry
'78
The Most Wanted '94
Sam the Iron Bridge:
Champion of Mar-
tial Arts '93
The Six Directions of
Boxing '79
Ten Tigers of Shaolin
'78

Cheng, Mark
(Cheng Ho-Nam, Jeng
Ho Naam, Zheng Hao
Nan, Mark Chang)
A Chinese Torture
Chamber Story 2
'98
City on Fire '93
Evil Cat '86
For Bad Boys Only '00
God.com '98
Gunmen '88
Kick Boxer's Tears '92
Killer '00

The Longest Nite '98
A Man Called Hero '99
Peking Opera Blues '86
A Taste of Killing and
Romance '94
Trust Me U Die '99
Undercover Blues '00
The Wesley's Mysteri-
ous File '01
Young and Dangerous
5 '98

Cheng Miu
(Jing Miao, Ching Miao)
Avenging Warriors of
Shaolin '79
Dirty Ho '79
Fists of the White
Lotus '80
The Return of the 5
Deadly Venoms '78
Return of the Master
Killer '80
Shaolin Mantis '78
3 Evil Masters '80

Cheng, Oliver
Dragon against Vam-
pire '85

Cheng, Olivia
(Cheng Man Ar, Chen
Meng Har)
The Millionaires'
Express '86

Cheng Pei-Pei
(Jeng Pooi Pooi, Zheng
Pei Pei)
The Art of Action: Mar-
tial Arts in the
Movies '02
Crouching Tiger, Hidden
Dragon '00
Fist Power '99
Flirting Scholar '93
Hong Kong Nocturne
'67
Lavender '00
A Man Called Hero '99
Painted Faces '88
Wing Chun '94

Cheng, Philip
(Cheng Chung Tai, Jeng
Chung Tai, Zheng Zhong
Tai)
All About Ah-Long '89
The Chinese Feast '95
Eat My Dust '93
Eighth Happiness '88

Cheng, Ricky
(Cheng Tien Chi, Ching
Tin Tsz, Chenmg Tian
Ci, Chien Tien Chi,
Ching Tin Chi, Cheng
Tien Tzu, Cheng Tian
Ci, Chin Tien Chi, Chen
Tin Yee)
Chinese Super Ninjas
'82
Fatal Needles vs. Fatal
Fists '80
Fearless Hyena '79

The Incredible Kung Fu
    Mission '82
Nine Demons '83
Ninja Checkmate '79
Ninja Hunter '85
Return of the Chinese
    Boxer '75
Return of the Tiger '77
The Story in Temple
    Red Lily '79
Venom Warrior '83
War of the Shaolin Tem-
    ple '80

Cheng, Ronald
*(Cheng Chung Kei, Jeng
Chung Gei, Zheng
Zhong Ji)*
Bullets of Love '01
A Chinese Ghost Story:
    The Tsui Hark Ani-
    mation '97 (V)
Dance of a Dream '01

Cheng, Sammi
*(Cheng Sau-man, Jeng
Sau Man, Zheng Xiu
Wen)*
Best of the Best '92
Fighting for Love '01
Love on a Diet '01
Marry a Rich Man '02
Needing You... '00

Cheng Wai-ho
*(Jeng Wai Ho, Zheng
Wei Hao)*
Return of the Master
    Killer '80

Cheng Yim-lai
*(Jeng Yim Lai, Zheng
Yan Li)*
Hong Kong X-File '98

Cheong Shing, Jim
Super Car Criminals
    '99

Cheong Wung-in
The Foul King '00

Cheung, Alfred
*(Cheung Kin-ting, Che-
ung Gin Ting, Zhang
Jian Ting)*
The Accidental Spy '01
All's Well End's Well '97
    '97
Happy Family '02
Master Q 2001 '01
Pedicab Driver '89
Pom Pom and Hot Hot
    '92
Twin Dragons '92
Twinkle Twinkle Lucky
    Stars '85
Where's Officer Tuba?
    '86

Cheung, Angie
*(Cheung Wai Yee,
Zhang Hui Yi)*
Body Weapon '99
The Conman '98
Love Me, Love My
    Money '01

A Wicked Ghost 2: The
    Fear '00

Cheung, Billy
Thunder Ninja Kids:
    The Hunt for the
    Devil Boxer '86/94

Cheung Bo-sin
*(Zhang Bao Shan,
Chung Bao Sin)*
The Buddha Assassina-
    tor '80
The Blazing Temple '76
The 18 Bronzemen Part
    2 '76
The 8 Masters '77
The Shaolin Kids '77
Shaolin Traitorous '76
The Story in Temple
    Red Lily '79

Cheung, Bruce
Duel of the Tao Tough
    '82

Cheung, Cecilia
*(Cheung Pak-chi, Zhang
Bo Zhi)*
Everyday Is Valentine
    '01
Help!!! '00
King of Comedy '99
Legend of Speed '99
Master Q 2001 '01
Para Para Sakura '01
Second Time Around
    '02
Shaolin Soccer '01
Tokyo Raiders '00
Zu Warriors '01

Cheung Chi-gwong
*(Jiang Zhi Guang, Chi-
ang Chi Kwong)*
Legend of the Drunken
    Master '94
Model from Hell '99

Cheung Chien
Revenge of the Patriots
    '76

Cheung Chin-pang
*(Zhang Zhan Peng,
Chang Chan Peng)*
Invincible Pole Fighter
    '83

Cheung Ching-fung
*(Jiang Qing Fung, Jef-
frey Fung, Chuang
Hsueh Fang)*
A Life of Ninja '83
Swordsman with an
    Umbrella '70

Cheung, Christina
Ninja vs. Bruce Lee '82

Cheung, Christy
Hail the Judge '94
Spacked Out '00

Cheung Chu Hong
Beast Cops '98

Cheung, Clarence
*(Cheung Tak Ho, Zhang
De Hao)*
Hit Team '00
Love Paradox '00
The Replacement Sus-
    pects '01

Cheung, Connie
Snake Fist Dynamo '84

Cheung, Dicky
*(Cheung Wai Kin, Zhang
Wei Jian)*
Last Hero in China '93

Cheung, Emotion
(Cheung Kam-Ching)
Bio Zombie '98
The Conman '98
The Demon's Baby '98
Troublesome Night 3
    '97
The Untold Story 2 '98

Cheung, Farini
Option Zero '97

Cheung, Flora
(Flora Cheong)
Duel to the Death '82
Return of the Deadly
    Blade '81

Cheung Fong-ha
*(Zhang Fang Xia, Che-
ung Fong Hai)*
Abbot White '82
Bruce Lee We Miss You
    '76
Iron Monkey 2 '77
Moonlight Sword and
    Jade Lion '79
The Story in Temple
    Red Lily '79

Cheung Ging Boh
*(Zhang Jing Po, Chang
Ching Po, Cheung King
Po)*
Encounter of the
    Spooky Kind '81
Last Hurrah for Chivalry
    '78
The Legendary Strike
    '78
The Prodigal Son '81
The Owl vs. Bombo '84
The Victim '80

Cheung Goon Lung
(Zhan Guan Long)
Ninja vs. Shaolin
    Guards '84

Cheung Gwok-wa
(Zhang Guo Hua)
Crazy Crooks '80
Death Mask of the
    Ninja '83
The Peacock King '89

**Cheung Hoh-yee,
Maggie**
*(Zhang Ke Yi, Maggie
Cheung)*
Headlines '01

Troublesome Night 8
    '00
Troublesome Night 9
    '00

Cheung Hung Ki
5 Lady Venoms '78

Cheung, Jacky
*(Cheung Hok-Yau,
Zhang Xiao You) See
also sidebar on p. 542.*
Anna Magdalena '98
Ashes of Time '94
The Best of the Best
    '96
Bullet in the Head '90
A Chinese Ghost Story
    2 '90
A Chinese Ghost Story
    3 '91
Curry & Pepper '90
Days of Being Wild '90
Eagle Shooting Heroes
    '93
Eighth Happiness '88
The Haunted Cop Shop
    '87
High Risk '95
Love on Delivery '94
Miracles '89
No More Love, No More
    Death '92
Once upon a Time in
    China '91
Pom Pom and Hot Hot
    '92
The Private Eye Blues
    '94
Running out of Time
    '99
Swordsman '90
Tiger Cage '88
Where's Officer Tuba?
    '86
Wicked City '92
With or Without You '92

Cheung, Jacob
*(Cheung Chi-leung, Che-
ung Ji Leung, Zhang Zhi
Liang)*
C'est la Vie, Mon Cheri
    '93
Twin Dragons '92

Cheung Jing
(Zhang Jing)
Bullet in the Head '90
Naked Killer '92

Cheung, Joe
*(Cheung Tung-cho, Che-
ung Tung Jo, Zhang
Tong Zu)*
The Blacksheep Affair
    '98
C'est la Vie, Mon Cheri
    '93
Comrades, Almost a
    Love Story '96
Double Tap '00
Merry-Go-Round '01
Supercop 2 '93
Twin Dragons '92

Cheung, Julian
*(Cheung Chi Lam,
Zhang Zhi Lin)*
The Best of the Best
    '96
Comic King '00
Extreme Crisis '98
Martial Angels '01
Option Zero '97
The Replacement Sus-
    pects '01
The Suspect '98

Cheung, K.K.
*(Cheung Kwok Keung,
Cheung Gwok Keung,
Zhang Guo Jiang)*
Crocodile Hunter '89
Don't Give a Damn '95
Dragon Family '88
Eastern Condors '86
Legend of the Drunken
    Tiger '90
Peking Opera Blues '86
Take 2 in Life '01

Cheung, Kam Yung
Shaolin vs. Manchu '80

**Cheung Kuen,
Richard**
Cop on a Mission '01

Cheung Kwok-bak
The Assassin '93

Cheung Kwok-leung
*(Cheung Gwok Leung,
Zhang Guo Liang)*
The Bride with White
    Hair 2 '93
Dragon from Russia
    '90
The Legend of the
    Swordsman '92
Pom Pom and Hot Hot
    '92
Red Shield '91

Cheung Kwong-Chiu
Hong Kong Nocturne
    '67

Cheung, Leslie
*(Cheung Kwok-Wing,
Cheung Gwok Wing,
Zhang Guo Rong)*
Aces Go Places 5: The
    Terracotta Hit '89
All's Well End's Well '92
All's Well End's Well '97
    '97
Anna Magdalena '98
Ashes of Time '94
A Better Tomorrow '86
A Better Tomorrow 2
    '87
The Bride with White
    Hair '93
The Bride with White
    Hair 2 '93
The Chinese Feast '95
A Chinese Ghost Story
    '87
A Chinese Ghost Story
    2 '90

Days of Being Wild '90
Double Tap '00
Eagle Shooting Heroes '93
He's a Woman, She's a Man '94
Inner Senses '01
Moonlight Express '99
Okinawa Rendez-vous '00
Once a Thief '91
The Phantom Lover '95

Cheung Lik
(Zhang Li, Cheung Nik, Nick Cheung, Cheung Lee, Chung Lik)
Fatal Flying Guillotine '77
Killer of Snake, Fox of Shaolin '78
Kung Fu's Hero '73
Ninja vs. Bruce Lee '82
Super Kung Fu Kid '74
10 Magnificent Killers '77
The 36 Deadly Styles '79
Tiger over Wall '80

Cheung, Mabel
Twin Dragons '92

Cheung, Maggie
(Cheung Man-Yuk, Zhang Man Yu) See also sidebar on p. 112.
All's Well End's Well '92
Ashes of Time '94
Comrades, Almost a Love Story '96
Days of Being Wild '90
Dragon Inn '92
Dragon from Russia '90
Eagle Shooting Heroes '93
Executioners '93
Green Snake '93
The Heroic Trio '93
Iceman Cometh '89
In the Mood for Love '00
The Moon Warriors '92
Police Story '85
Police Story 2 '88
Project A 2 '87
The Seventh Curse '86
Supercop '92
Twin Dragons '92

Cheung Ming-Ming
Shaolin Soccer '01

Cheung, Nick
(Cheung Ka Fai, Cheung Ga Fai, Zhang Gu Hui)
Clean My Name, Mr. Coroner! '00
The Conman '98
Conman in Tokyo '00
Day Off '01
The Duel '00
Every Dog Has His Date '01
Happy Family '02

Love Correction '00
Red Shield '91
Runaway '01
The Tricky Master '00

Cheung Pang
(Zhang Peng, Chang Pang, Cheung Ping, Chang Ping)
Battle of Shaolin '77
The Deadly Sword '78
Fatal Needles vs. Fatal Fists '80
Ninja in the Deadly Trap '83
Thousand Mile Escort '76
Two Dragons Fight against Tiger '75

Cheung, Peggy
(Cheung Siu Ping, Zhang Shao Ping)
It Takes a Thief '01
Mr. Nice Guy '01

Cheung, Philip
Fury in Shaolin Temple '82

Cheung, Pinky
(Cheung Man Chi, Cheung Man Tsz, Zhang Wen Ci)
Body Weapon '99
Devil Touch '02
Everyday Is Valentine '01
Last Ghost Standing '99
Paramount Motel '00
Temptress of a Thousand Faces '98
Violent Cop '99

Cheung, Ronnie
(Cheung Ho Lung, Zhang Hao Long)
Chinese Orthopedist and the Spice Girls '02
Troublesome Night 14 '02

Cheung, Roy
(Cheung Yiu-Yeung, Zhang Yao Yang)
Aces Go Places 5: The Terracotta Hit '89
The Avenging Fist '01
Beast Cops '98
The Best of the Best '96
The Big Heat '88
City on Fire '87
Faces of Horror '98
Fight Back to School '91
Her Name Is Cat 2: Journey to Death '01
In the Mood for Love '00
Jiang Hu-"The Triad Zone" '00
Leopard Hunting '98

The Magnificent Scoundrels '91
The Mission '99
Organized Crime and Triad Bureau '94
Prison on Fire '87
The Replacement Suspects '01
The Storm Riders '98
Super Car Criminals '99
Tragic Fantasy: Tiger of Wanchai '94
The Wesley's Mysterious File '01
Wicked City '92
Young and Dangerous 6: Born to Be King '00

Cheung, Sharla
(Cheung Man, Zhang Min)
Dragon Chronicles: Maidens of Heavenly Mountain '94
Dragon Killer '95
Fight Back to School '91
Fight Back to School 2 '92
Fight Back to School 3 '93
Fist of Fury 1991 '91
God of Gamblers '89
God of Gamblers 2 '90
God of Gamblers 3: Back to Shanghai '91
God of Gamblers Returns '94
Hail the Judge '94
King of Beggars '92
Last Hero in China '93
Lee Rock '91
Lord of the Wu Tang '93
Royal Tramp '92
Royal Tramp 2 '92
Swordsman '90
The Sword Stained with Royal Blood '93
Young and Dangerous 5 '98

Cheung, Shirley
Haunted Mansion '98

Cheung Shiu-chit
(Zhang Rui Zhe, Tony Chang)
Born Wild '01
Hit Team '00

Cheung Siu-fan
Drunken Art and Crippled Fist '79

Cheung, T.
Her Name Is Cat 2: Journey to Death '01

Cheung Tai Lung
Death Ring '83

Cheung Tat-Ming
(Cheung Dat Ming, Zhang Da Ming)
The Accidental Spy '01
Big Bullet '96
City of Desire '01
Cop Shop Babes '01
Dummy Mommy, without a Baby '01
F*** / Off '98
Forbidden City Cop '96
Gen-Y Cops '00
Lawyer Lawyer '97
Paramount Motel '00
Too Many Ways to Be No. 1 '97
The Tricky Master '00
Troublesome Night 4 '98
Visible Secret '01
You Shoot, I Shoot '01

Cheung Ti-hong
Encounter of the Spooky Kind '81

Cheung Tit Lam
Once upon a Time in China 2 '92

Cheung Wa
(Zhang Hua, Johnny Cheung Yiu Wah, Johnny Cheung Wa)
Crime Story '93
Dirty Tiger, Crazy Frog '78
Dragons Forever '88
The Eagle's Killer '81
Enter the Fat Dragon '78
Executioners from Shaolin '77
God of Gamblers '89
His Name Is Nobody '79
The Inspector Wears Skirts '88
Knockabout '79
Last Hurrah for Chivalry '78
Legend of the Drunken Master '94
Miracles '89
The Owl vs. Bombo '84
Police Story '85
Police Story 2 '88
Project A '83
Project A 2 '87
Shaolin Master Killer '78
Twin Dragons '92
Ways of Kung Fu '80
Yes, Madam '85
The Young Master '80

Cheung Wai
(Zhang Wei)
99 Cycling Swords '80
2000 A.D. '00

Cheung Wan-man
A Touch of Zen '69

Cheung Yee-kwai
(Zhang Yi Gui, Cheung I Kuei)
Master of the Flying Guillotine '75
Return of the Chinese Boxer '75
The Story in Temple Red Lily '79
War of the Shaolin Temple '80

Cheung Ying
(Zhang Ying)
The Legendary Strike '78

Cheung Ying Chen
Return of the Chinese Boxer '75

Chi Chao-Li
The Big Brawl '80

Chi, Chiang Ma
Exit the Dragon, Enter the Tiger '75

Chi Chuen-Hua
(Gai Chun Wa, Ji Chun Hua)
Deadend of Besiegers '92
The Legend 2 '93
The New Legend of Shaolin '94
One Arm Hero '94
The Shaolin Temple '79
Shaolin Temple 2: Kids from Shaolin '84
White Lotus Cult '94
Yellow River Fighter '88

Chi Fu-chiang
(Chai Hau Keung, Qi Hou Jiang)
Challenge of Death '78
The 18 Jade Arhats '78
Exit the Dragon, Enter the Tiger '76
Incredible Kung Fu Mission '79
Kung Pow: Enter the Fist '76/2001
Master of the Flying Guillotine '74
99 Cycling Swords '80
Return of the Tiger '77
Revenge of the Patriots '76
Two Dragons Fight against Tiger '75

Chi Kuan Chun
(Chik Goon Gwan, QiGuan Jun, Chi Kuan Chung, Tsk Kun Chun, Chik Koon Jun, Chi Kuan Jiun, Chi Kian Chun)
Eagle's Claw '77
Golden Killah '80
The Iron Monkey '77
Iron Neck Li '81
Lone Ninja Warrior '81
The Massive '78

754

The Master of Death '82
Ways of Kung Fu '80
Yoga and Kung Fu Girl '78

Chi, Willie
(Chi Tin Sang, Gwai Tin Sang, Ji Tian Sheng, Willie Kwai)
Burning Paradise '94
Drunken Master Killer '94

Chi Yan
Succubare '77

Chiaki, Minoru
Godzilla Raids Again '55
The Hidden Fortress '58
Rashomon '50
Samurai 3: Duel at Ganryu Island '56
Seven Samurai '54
Stray Dog '49
Throne of Blood '57

Chiang Cheng
The 36 Crazy Fists '77

Chiang, David
(Chiang Hsu Shao, Geung Dai Wai, Jiang Da Wei, John Keung, John Chiang, Keung Tai-Wai)
The Adventurers '95
Angel '87
Blooded Treasury Fight '79
Legend of Speed '99
Legend of the 7 Golden Vampires '74
The Lost Kung Fu Secrets '80
Martial Arts Mayhem, Vol. 1 '99
Once upon a Time in China 2 '92
Return of the Deadly Blade '81
Shaolin Mantis '78
The Six Directions of Boxing '79
Tiger on Beat '88
Twin Dragons '92
Twinkle Twinkle Lucky Stars '85
Where's Officer Tuba? '86
Yes, Madam '85

Chiang Han
(Kong Hon, Jiang Han, Keung Hon)
Chinatown Kid '77
Dirty Ho '79
For Bad Boys Only '00
Kung Fu on Sale '79
Lightning Kung Fu '80
The Lost Kung Fu Secrets '80
Shaolin Master Killer '78

Chiang Kam
(Cheung Gam, Jiang Jin, Chiang Chin, Chang Chin)
Battle of Shaolin '77
A Chinese Ghost Story '87
Dragon on Fire '79
Drunken Master '78
The Eagle's Killer '81
Flag of Iron '80
The Magnificent Butcher '79
New Fist of Fury '76
Shadow of the Tiger '79
Shaolin Wooden Men '76
Snake in the Eagle's Shadow '78
The Young Master '80

Chiang Ming
(Kong Ming, Jiang Ming Kwong Ming)
Fury of King Boxer '72
Moonlight Sword and Jade Lion '79
Swordsman with an Umbrella '70

Chiang Nan
(Kong Nam, Jiang Nan, Kiang Nan)
Avenging Warriors of Shaolin '79
Chinatown Kid '77
The 18 Bronzemen '76
Fearless Fighters '69
From China with Death '74
Kung Fu, the Invisible Fist '72
The Shaolin Kids '77
Shaolin Master Killer '78
Ten Tigers of Kwangtung '79
Thunder Kick '73
Triangular Duel '72
Young Tiger '72

Chiang Sheng
(Chim Sam, Zhan Sen, Jim Sum) See also sidebar on p. 374.
Avenging Warriors of Shaolin '79
Brave Archer '77
Chinatown Kid '77
Five Deadly Venoms '78
Flag of Iron '80
Kid with the Golden Arm '78
Masked Avengers '81
Nine Demons '83
Ninja in the Deadly Trap '83
The Return of the 5 Deadly Venoms '78
Ten Tigers of Kwangtung '79
War of the Shaolin Temple '80

Chiao, Chiao
(Chiu Gau, Jiao Jiao, Chiu Kao, Lisa Chiao Chiao)
Blood of the Dragon '71
The Dragon Family '88
The 18 Jade Arhats '78
Police Story 2 '78
In the Line of Duty 4 '89
Rage of the Masters '74

Chiao, Roy
(Chiao Hung, Kiu Wang, Qiao Hong)
Aces Go Places 4 '86
All's Well End's Well '97 '97
Blonde Fury '89
Blood of the Dragon '71
Dragons Forever '88
Enter the Dragon '73
Enter the Fat Dragon '78
Game of Death '78
A Kid from Tibet '91
The Prisoner '90
The Protector '85
Righting Wrongs '86
Revenge of the Patriots '76
A Touch of Zen '69
Tower of Death '81

Chiba, Jiro
(Michiho Maeda)
The Bodyguard '73/'78
Dragon Princess '81
The Street Fighter '74

Chiba, Shigeo
The Magic Serpent '66

Chiba, Sonny
(Sadao Maeda, Shinichi Chiba) See also sidebar on p. 590.
The Bodyguard '73/'78
Bullet Train '75
Dragon Princess '81
The Executioner '74
Invasion of the Neptune Men '61
Legend of the Eight Samurai '84
Legend of the Flying Swordsman '00
Martial Arts Mayhem, Vol. 1 '99
Message from Space '78
Return of the Street Fighter '74
Shogun's Ninja '82
Sister Street Fighter '74
The Storm Riders '98
The Street Fighter '74
The Street Fighter's Last Revenge '74
Sure Death: Revenge '87

Terror beneath the Sea '66
Young and Dangerous 6: Born to Be King '00

Chieh Yuan
Bruce Lee: A Warrior's Journey '00

Chik, Jaime
(Chik Mei Jan, Qi Mei Zhen)
Pom Pom '84
Twinkle Twinkle Lucky Stars '85

Chin, Charlie
(Chin Chiang-lin, Chun Cheung Lam, Qin Xiang Lin)
Eastern Condors '86
The Imp '81
My Lucky Stars '85
On the Run '88
Pom Pom '84
Twinkle Twinkle Lucky Stars '85
Winners and Sinners '83
Young Tiger '72

Chin Chi Min
(Chun Chi Man, Chun Ji Man, Qin Zhi Min, Ching Chi Min)
Story of the Dragon '76
Succubare '77

Chin Fei
(Zhan Fei)
Ninja vs. Shaolin Guards '84

Chin Feng
(Gam Fung, Jin Feng, Kam Fung)
Blooded Treasury Fight '79

Chin Gwan
(Qian Jun)
The Eternal Evil of Asia '95
Sex and the Emperor '94

Chin Ho
(Chun Ho, Qin Hao)
The Last Blood '90
No More Love, No More Death '92
Peace Hotel '95
The Private Eye Blues '94
Wonder Seven '94

Chin Ka-Lok
(Chin Kar Lok, Chin Ga Lok, Qian Jia Le) See also sidebar on p. 326.
The Avenging Fist '01
Bio-Cops '00
Bury Me High '90
Dragons Forever '88
Eastern Condors '86
Full Alert '97

Full Throttle '95
Heart of Dragon '85
Hit Team '00
Hong Kong X-File '98
Last Ghost Standing '99
Legend of the Drunken Master '94
The Legend of the Swordsman '92
Martial Arts Master Wong Fei Hung '92
The Millionaires' Express '86
Mr. Vampire Saga 4 '88
Once upon a Time in China 4 '93
The Owl vs. Bombo '84
Project A '83
Task Force '97
Thunderbolt '95
Troublesome Night 3 '97
Wheels on Meals '84
Young and Dangerous 5 '98
Young and Dangerous 6: Born to Be King '00

Chin Leung
(Qian Leung, Chin Lung)
Battle of Shaolin '77
Emperor of Shaolin Kung Fu '80
Encounter of the Spooky Kind '81
The Leg Fighters '80
Master of the Flying Guillotine '85
My Lucky Stars '85
The Owl vs. Bombo '84
Pom Pom '84
The Prodigal Son '81
The Victim '80
Winners and Sinners '83
Yes, Madam '85

Chin Meng
(Chun Mung, Chin Mung, Qin Meng)
The Shaolin Brothers '77

Chin, Moe
Chinese Orthopedist and the Spice Girls '02

Chin Ping
Hong Kong Nocturne '67

Chin San
(Chin Shan)
The Chinese Connection '71
Fists of Fury '71
Sting of the Dragon Masters '73

Chin Siu-ho
(Chen Hsiao-Hou, Chien Hsiao Hau) See also sidebar on p. 326.
Blonde Fury '89
Don't Give a Damn '95
Fist of Legend '94
5 Venoms vs. Wu Tang '87
It Takes a Thief '01
Masked Avengers '81
Millennium Dragon '99
Mr. Vampire '85
New Mr. Vampire '86
The Seventh Curse '86
Ten Tigers of Kwangtung '79
Twinkle Twinkle Lucky Stars '85
Twin Warriors '93

Chin Ti
(Gam Dai, Jin Di, Chen Ti)
Bolo '80
Chinese Hercules '73
Fantasy Mission Force '84
Kung Fu's Hero '73

Chin, Tina
(Chin Fei, Gam Fei, Jin Fei)
Hong Kong Nocturne '67

Ching, Billy
(Ching Sau Yat, Cheng Shou Yi)
All Men Are Brothers: Blood of the Leopard '93
Beauty Investigator '93
Heart of Dragon '85
Millionaires' Express '86
Pom Pom Strikes Back '86
Project A 2 '87
Righting Wrongs '86
Rosa '86
Scared Stiff '86
Yes, Madam '85

Ching, Ching
(Cheng Qing)
Fighting Ace '79
Five Elements of Kung Fu '78
Green Dragon Inn '79
Incredible Kung Fu Mission '79
Iron Neck Li '81
Ways of Kung Fu '78

Ching-Ching, Cheung
(Zhang Qing Qing, Chang Ching Ching)
Fearless Fighters '69
Screaming Ninja '73
Sorrowful to a Ghost '70

Ching-Ching, Yeung
(Yang Qing Qing, Yeung Jing Jing, Yang Jing Jing, Yang Ching Ching)
A Chinese Ghost Story 2 '90
Crocodile Hunter '89
Dragons of the Orient '88
Fists of the White Lotus '80
God of Gamblers 3: Back to Shanghai '91
Invincible Pole Fighter '83
Return of the Master Killer '80
Revenge of the Zombies '76
Ten Tigers of Kwangtung '79

Ching Fung
Option Zero '97

Ching, John
(Ching Tung)
The Adventurers '95
Burning Paradise '94
Casino Tycoon 2 '92
Contract Killer '98
Dragon in Jail '90
Fight Back to School 3 '93
God of Gamblers 2 '90
God of Gamblers 3: Back to Shanghai '91
Hail the Judge '94
Lord of the Wu Tang '93
Pom Pom and Hot Hot '92
Return to a Better Tomorrow '94
With or Without You '92

Ching Kuo-chung
(Ging Gwok Chung, Jing Guo Zhong, Tsing Kuo Chung, Jing Kuo Jung)
Battle of Shaolin '77
Cantonen Iron Kung Fu '79
Dreaming Fists with Slender Hands '80
The 18 Jade Arhats '78
Fighting Ace '79
The Killer Meteors '76
Killer Priest '81
Lone Ninja Warrior '81
Return of the Tiger '79
Revengeful Swordwomen '79
7 Commandments of Kung Fu '79
Shaolin Chastity Kung Fu '81
Shaolin vs. Lama '81
The Story in Temple Red Lily '79

Ching Mai
(Cheng Mi)

A Chinese Torture Chamber Story '94

Ching Siu-leung
(Ching Siu-lung, Cheng Xiao Long)
Her Name Is Cat '98
The Longest Nite '98
Model from Hell '99
Young and Dangerous '96

Ching Siu-tung
Twin Dragons '92

Ching, Tang
(Tong Jing, Tang Jing, Tong Ching, Yang Ching)
Bloody Fight '72
The Buddhist Fist '79
Dragons of the Orient '88
Dreadnaught '81
From China with Death '74
The Invincible Killer '79
The Magnificent Butcher '79

Chiu, Angie
The Private Eyes '76

Chiu Chung-hing
Dreadnaught '81

Chiu Hung
(Zhao Xiong, Chao Hsiung)
Five Fingers of Death '72

Chiu, Larry
Scorpion Thunderbolt '85

Chiu, Martin
Golden Dragon Silver Snake '79
Rage of the Dragon '79

Chiu, Perry
Love Paradox '00

Chiu, Stephen
Rivals of the Dragon '83

Chiu Tien-you
(Chui Tin Yau, Xu Tian You, Tsui Tin Yao)
Gimme Gimme '01
Glass Tears '01

Chiu Ting
(Zhao Ting)
The 18 Bronzemen Part 2 '76
The 8 Masters '77
Emperor of Shaolin Kung Fu '80
The Master of Death '82
The Smart Cavalier '78
The Story in Temple Red Lily '79

Chiu, Tony
Victim '99

Chiu Tung
Mask of Death '76

Cho Bang-ho
(Goda Yu, Cho Banho, Cho Bang Hou)
Tokyo Mafia 3: Battle for Shinjuku '96

Cho Boon Feng
(Chu Ben Ke, Chui Feng, Chur Bun Fur)
Dragon Kid '90
Eagle's Claw '77
Fatal Needles vs. Fatal Fists '80
Lady Iron Monkey '83
The Master of Death '82
Ninja Hunter '84
Ninja in the Deadly Trap '81
99 Cycling Swords '80

Cho Boot-lam
Moonlight Sword and Jade Lion '79

Cho, Charlie
(Cho Cha-lei)
Aces Go Places 2 '83
Aces Go Places 3 '84
City of Desire '01
Crocodile Hunter '89
The Dragon Family '88
Eighth Happiness '88
High Risk '95
Millennium Dragon '99
Operation Pink Squad '88
The Owl vs. Bombo '84
Police Story '85
Police Story 2 '88
Rosa '86

Cho Chun
Love Me, Love My Money '01

Cho Chun-sing
(Joh Chung Sing, Zuo Song Sheng)
Fist of Fury 1991 '91
The Haunted Cop Shop '87
Scared Stiff '86

Cho Kin
(Cao Jian, Trang Kin, Tsang Kin)
Killer Priest '81
Rage of the Masters '74
Revengeful Swordwomen '79
The Shaolin Brothers '77
The Shaolin Kids '77
The Story in Temple Red Lily '79

Cho Sun-mook
Gate of Destiny '96

Cho, Walter
(Cho Tat-wah, Chu Tit Wo, Cho Tiet Wo, Jue Tit Woe, Chu Te Hu, Chu Tien Ho, Walter Tso, Tso Tat-wah, Cho Dat Wa, Cao Da Hua, Chu Tieh Hu, Tsao Ta Hua)
Aces Go Places '82
Aces Go Places 2 '83
Aces Go Places 3 '84
Aces Go Places 4 '86
Aces Go Places 5: The Terracotta Hit '89
Avenging Warriors of Shaolin '79
Crystal Hunt '91
Flirting Scholar '93
A Gambler's Story '01
Iceman Cometh '89
Invincible Pole Fighter '83
Jade Claw '79
Last Hero in China '93
Legendary Weapons of China '82
Lightning Kung Fu '80
Master of the Flying Guillotine '74
Millionaires' Express '86
Miracles '89
Mr. Vampire 2 '86
A Moment of Romance '90
My Lucky Stars '85
Project A 2 '87
Ten Tigers of Kwangtung '79
Tiger over Wall '80
Twinkle Twinkle Lucky Stars '85
Winners and Sinners '83
The Young Avenger '79

Cho, William
(Cho Wing Lim, Cao Yong Lian)
The Best of the Best '96
Full Alert '97
Operation Billionaires '98

Cho Wing
(Cao Wing)
Bury Me High '91
Dragons Forever '88
In the Line of Duty 4 '89
Justice, My Foot! '92
Lord of the Wu Tang '93
The Red Wolf '95
White Lotus Cult '93

Choe Eun-joo
My Wife Is a Gangster '01

Choi, Ada
(Choi Siu-Fun)

A Chinese Odyssey Part
  2: Cinderella '95
Fist of Legend '94
Hail the Judge '94
Paramount Motel '00
The Suspect '98
Troublesome Night '97
Your Place or Mine! '98

Choi, Charlene
(Choi Cheuk Yin, Cai
Zhou Yan)
Funeral March '01

Choi Dong Hoi
Duel of the Tao Tough
  '82

Choi Gaai Wang
Dragon Kid '90

Choi, Gigi
2000 A.D. '00

Choi Ji-woo
Nowhere to Hide '99
Record '00

Choi, Joey
Troublesome Night 4
  '98

Choi, Ken
The Odd One Dies '97

Choi Min-sik
Happy End '99
Shiri '99

Choi, Raven
Double Tap '00

Choi Se
The Heroes '80

Choi Wai-man
(Cai Hui Min)
Faces of Horror '98

Choi Wang
(Cai Hong, Tsai Hung,
Choi Yue, Choi Hung)
Angel '87
Blooded Treasury Fight
  '79
Brave Archer '77
Chinatown Kid '77
Chinese Iron Man '75
The Deadly Strike '78
The Heroes '80
Inheritor of Kung Fu '77
Iron Neck Li '81
Kung Fu on Sale '79
The Leg Fighters '80
The Lost Kung Fu
  Secrets '80
Mask of Death '76
Militant Eagle '78
New Game of Death
  '75
Ninja Supremo '81
One Foot Crane '79
The 72 Desperate
  Rebels '76
The Silver Spear '79
The Smart Cavalier '78
Triangular Duel '72

Choi Wong
The 72 Desperate
  Rebels '76

**Chokmorov,
Suimenkul**
Dersu Uzala '74

Chong, Aaron
Beast Cops '98

Chong, Billy
(Willy Dohzan, Chong
Chuen Lei, Zhuang
Quan Lei, Willy Doxan)
Aces Go Places 5: The
  Terracotta Hit '89
A Fistful of Talons '83
Jade Claw '79
Kung Fu Zombie '81

Chong, Elton
Dragon against Vam-
  pire '85
Invincible Obsessed
  Fighter '82
Magnificent Natural
  Fist '80
The Snake Strikes Back
  '81

Chong, Felix
(Chong Man Keung,
Zhuang Wen Jiang)
Dance of a Dream '01
Final Romance '01
Gen-Y Cops '00
Shadow '01
Sharp Guns '01
Sunshine Cops '99
Tokyo Raiders '00

Chong Men-jo
Bronson Lee, Champi-
  on '78

Chong Wing
Her Name Is Cat '98

Chopra, Kamal
Champion '00

Chosokabe, Yoko
Princess Blade '02

Chou, Lawrence
(Chow Jun Wai, Zhou
Jun Wei)
The Eye '02
Merry-Go-Round '01

Chow, Billy
(Chow Bei-Lei, Billy
Chau)
Beauty Investigator '92
Blonde Fury '89
Dragons Forever '88
Eastern Condors '86
Fist of Legend '94
God of Gamblers 3:
  Back to Shanghai
  '91
High Risk '95
In the Line of Duty 5:
  Middle Man '90
Iron Monkey 2 '96
Kick Boxer's Tears '92
Love on Delivery '94

Miracles '89
Once upon a Time in
  China 4 '93
Pedicab Driver '89
Queen's High '91
Robotrix '91
Young and Dangerous
  5 '98

Chow, Charlie
Bruce Lee Fights Back
  from the Grave '76

Chow, Danny
(Chow Yun Kin, Zhou
Run Jian, Denny Chow,
Chow Yun Gin)
The Butterfly Murders
  '79
Dragons Forever '88
Dreadnaught '81
Five Fingers of Death
  '71
The Inspector Wears
  Skirts '88
Miracles '89
Police Story 2 '88
Police Story '85
Prodigal Boxer '72
Project A '83
Thunder Kick '73

Chow, Eddie
The Master of Death
  '82

Chow Fai
Breakout from Oppres-
  sion '78

Chow, Jacky
Duel of the Tao Tough
  '82

Chow, Kathy
(Chow Hoi-mei, Zhou
Hai Mei, Kathy Chau)
Beast Cops '98
Cheap Killers '98
Don't Give a Damn '95
Fight Back to School 3
  '93
First Option '96
The Private Eye Blues
  '94
Sound from the Dark
  '00
Vampire Controller '00

Chow Kong
(Zhou Jiang)
Heart of Dragon '85
Miracles '89
My Kung Fu 12 Kicks
  '79

Chow, Lily
Ballistic Kiss '98

Chow, Mandy
The Holy Robe of
  Shaolin Temple '84

Chow, Matt
(Chow Hoi-Kwong,
Chow Hoi Gwong, Zou
Kai Guang)

Beauty and the Breast
  '02
Bio Zombie '98
Bullets Over Summer
  '99
Everyday Is Valentine
  '01
F*** / Off '98
Happy Family '02
The Irresistible Piggies
  '02
Shadow '01
Too Many Ways to Be
  No. 1 '97
United We Stand, and
  Swim '01
You Shoot, I Shoot '01

Chow, Michael
(Chow Man-Kin, Zhou
Wen Jian, Michael Jo)
The Big Heat '88
City Cop '95
City War '88
Eighth Happiness '88
Fight Back to School 2
  '92
God of Gamblers '89
The Inspector Wears
  Skirts '88
Miracles '89
Police Story 2 '88

Chow Ming Ching
Two Dragons Fight
  against Tiger '75

Chow, Niki
(Chow Lai Kei, Zhou Li
Qi)
Dummy Mommy, with-
  out a Baby '01
Fighting for Love '01
Horror Hotline…Big
  Head Monster '01

Chow, Raymond
(Chow Man Wai, Zou
Wen Huai)
The Art of Action: Mar-
  tial Arts in the
  Movies '02
Bruce Lee, The Legend
  '84
Extreme Challenge '01

Chow, Stephen
(Chow Sing-Chi, Zhou
Xing Chi, Stephen
Chiau) See also side-
bar on p. 258.
All's Well End's Well '92
All's Well End's Well '97
  '97
A Chinese Odyssey Part
  1: Pandora's Box
  '95
A Chinese Odyssey Part
  2: Cinderella '95
Curry & Pepper '90
Fight Back to School
  '91
Fight Back to School 2
  '92
Fight Back to School 3
  '93

Final Justice '88
Fist of Fury 1991 '91
Flirting Scholar '93
Forbidden City Cop '96
From Beijing with Love
  '94
God of Cookery '96
God of Gamblers 2 '90
God of Gamblers 3:
  Back to Shanghai
  '91
Hail the Judge '94
Justice, My Foot! '92
King of Beggars '92
King of Comedy '99
Lawyer Lawyer '97
Legend of the Dragon
  '91
Love on Delivery '94
The Magnificent
  Scoundrels '91
Royal Tramp '92
Royal Tramp 2 '92
Shaolin Soccer '01
Sixty Million Dollar Man
  '95
The Tricky Master '00

Chow, Valerie
(Chow Kar-Ling, Chow
Ga Ling, Zhou Jia Ling)
The Blade '95
Chungking Express '94
High Risk '95
Inner Senses '01
The Vampire Combat
  '01

Chow Yuen-kin
Dreadnaught '81

Chow Yun-fat
(Zhou Run Fa, Amon
Chow, Donald Chow)
See also sidebar on p.
106.
All About Ah-Long '89
A Better Tomorrow '86
A Better Tomorrow 2
  '87
A Better Tomorrow 3
  '89
City War '88
City on Fire '87
Code of Honor '87
Crouching Tiger, Hidden
  Dragon '00
Eighth Happiness '88
Full Contact '92
God of Gamblers '89
God of Gamblers 2 '90
God of Gamblers
  Returns '94
Hard Boiled '91
The Killer '89
Once a Thief '91
100 Ways to Murder
  Your Wife '86
Peace Hotel '95
The Postman Fights
  Back '82
Prison on Fire '87
Prison on Fire 2 '91
The Replacement
  Killers '97

757

Rich and Famous '87
Scared Stiff '86
The Seventh Curse '86
Tiger on Beat '88
The Witch from Nepal '85

Chu, Athena
(Chu Yun, Chu Yan, Jue Yan, Zhu Yin, Athene Chu)
A Chinese Odyssey Part 1: Pandora's Box '95
A Chinese Odyssey Part 2: Cinderella '95
The Conman '98
Conman in Tokyo '00
Fight Back to School 2 '92
The Hero of Swallow '96
Love Correction '00
Shanghai Affairs '98
Supercop 2 '93
Temptress of a Thousand Faces '98

Chu Chi-ling
(Chiu Chi Ling, Zhao Zhi Ling, Choy Chee Ling)
Bruce Lee: The Man, the Myth '76
Crazy Crooks '80
His Name Is Nobody '79
Shadow of the Tiger '79
Snake in the Eagle's Shadow '78
Where's Officer Tuba? '86
Winners and Sinners '83

Chu Chi Ming
(Jue Chi Ming, Zhu Zhi Ming, Chu Chih Ming, Ching Chih Min)
Return of the Chinese Boxer '75
Story of the Dragon '76
10 Magnificent Killers '77

Chu Ching
(Jue Ching, Zhu Qing)
Brave Archer '77
Hand of Death '75

Chu Dout
Angel '87

Chu, Emily
(Cho Bo Yee, Chu Po Yee, Jue Bo Yi, Zhu Bao Yi)
A Better Tomorrow '86
A Better Tomorrow 2 '87
Heart of Dragon '85
The Millionaires' Express '86
Scared Stiff '86
The Witch from Nepal '85

Chu, Jason
(Chu Wing-Tong, Jue Wing Tong, Zhu Yong Tang)
The Best of the Best '96
The Blade '95
Paramount Motel '00
The Storm Riders '98
Troublesome Night '97
Young and Dangerous '96
Young and Dangerous 5 '98
Young and Dangerous 6: Born to Be King '00

Chu, Johnny
Eat My Dust '93

Chu, July
Ninja in the Deadly Trap '83

Chu Ko
(Jue Haak, Zhu Ke, Chu Ke, Chu Ker)
Chinese Super Ninjas '82
Masked Avengers '81

Chu Lai-Yee
Millennium Dragon '99

Chu Lung
Dragon Lee vs. the Five Brothers '78

Chu, Mimi
(Chu Mai Mai, Jue Mai Mai, Zhu Mi Mi)
Fight Back to School 3 '93
Flirting Scholar '93
Forbidden City Cop '96
Heroic Trio '93
Justice, My Foot! '92
The Magnificent Scoundrels '91
Sixty Million Dollar Man '95

Chu, Paul
(Chu Kong, Jue Kong, Zhu Jiang)
The Big Heat '88
Bury Me High '90
God of Gamblers Returns '94
The Killer '89
The Legend '92
The Legendary Strike '78
Once a Thief '91

Chu Siu-wa
(Jue Siu Wa, Zhu Shao Hua, Chu Su Hwa)
Born Invincible '78
Kung Fu on Sale '79
Ninja Supremo '81
The Smart Cavalier '76

Chu Tau
(Jue Dau, Zhu Dou)
Angel '87

Gunmen '88
Miracles '89
Pedicab Driver '89
Pom Pom Strikes Back '86

Chu, Vanesia
(Chu Man Wah, Jue Min Wa, Zhu Min Hua, Vanessa Chu)
Needing You... '00
Spacked Out '00

Chu, William
(Chu Wai Lim, Jue Wai Lim, Zhu Wei Lian)
The Defender '94

Chu Yin Chun
990714.com '00

Chui, Alan
(Chui Chung San, Xu Zhong Shen, Alan Hsu, Alan Tsui Chun Sun, Choi Chung San, Hsu Chung Sin, Tsui Chung San, Shiu Chung Hsin)
Born Invincible '78
Bruce Lee: The Man, the Myth '76
Chinese Hercules '73
Dirty Tiger, Crazy Frog '78
The Incredible Kung Fu Mission '82
Last Hero in China '93
Last Hurrah for Chivalry '78
Lone Ninja Warrior '81
Ninja vs. Shaolin Guards '84
Powerful Four '91
Shaolin Master Killer '78
Shaolin vs. Ninja '83
Sting of the Dragon Masters '73
War of the Shaolin Temple '80

Chui, Cathy
(Chui Chi Kay, Tsui Chi Kei, Cathy Tsui)
Cop Shop Babes '01
Time and Tide '00

Chui Chung Hei
(Chui Chung Chui, Tu Song Zhao, Yu Song Chao, Hsu Sung Chao, Yu Sung Chao, Chin Chung Chou)
Abbot White '82
Buddha Assassinator '80
Challenge of Death '78
Eagle's Claw '77
Fatal Needles vs. Fatal Fists '80
Fighting Ace '79
Fury of King Boxer '72
Golden Killah '80
The Hot, the Cool, and the Vicious '76

The Incredible Kung Fu Mission '82
Killer from Above '77
Kung Pow: Enter the Fist '76/2001
Mask of Death '76
Master of the Flying Guillotine '74
Nine Demons '83
99 Cycling Swords '80
Return of the Chinese Boxer '75
The 72 Desperate Rebels '76
Thousand Mile Escort '76
Two Dragons Fight against Tiger '75
The World of the Drunken Master '79

Chui Fat
(Xu Fa, Tsui Fat)
Crystal Hunt '91
Dragon Fist '78
Last Hurrah for Chivalry '78

Chui Fook-sang
Fury of King Boxer '72

Chui Heung Wing
The Holy Robe of Shaolin Temple '84

Chui Jing-yat
(Cui Zheng Yi, Choi Jung Il)
Beauty Investigator '92

Chui Lap
(Cui Li, Tsui Li)
Screaming Ninja '73

Chui Ling Ling
The Deadly Camp '99

Chui Ngai
Iron Man '86

Chui Pak-lam
(Xu Bo Lin, Tsui Pak Lam)
Crystal Hunt '91

Chui Sau-lai
(Cui Xiu Li, Tsui Sau Lai, Cann Chui)
Code of Honor '87
The Seventh Curse '86

Chui Suk-woon
(Xu Shu Yuan)
Evil Cat '86
The Seventh Curse '86

Chun Do-yeon
Happy End '99

Chun, Paul
(Chun Pei, Chun Pui, Chun Pooi, Qin Pei, Chin Pei, Paul Chin, Paul Keung, Paul Chiang)
The Adventurers '95
The Best of the Best '92

Breakout from Oppression '78
Bury Me High '91
C'est la Vie, Mon Cheri '93
China Strike Force '00
Executioners '93
Fight Back to School '91
Fight Back to School 3 '93
Fist of Legend '94
Full Throttle '95
The Heroic Trio '93
I Love Maria '88
In the Line of Duty 3 '88
Justice, My Foot! '92
Lee Rock '91
Lightning Kung Fu '80
The Lost Kung Fu Secrets '80
Love on Delivery '94
Peking Opera Blues '86
Return to a Better Tomorrow '94
Rosa '86
Royal Tramp 2 '92
Royal Warriors '86
The Silver Spear '79
The Six Directions of Boxing '79
Super Car Criminals '99
The 36 Crazy Fists '77
Where's Officer Tuba? '86
Young and Dangerous 5 '98

Chun Wong
Losers' Club '01

Chung, Betty
Enter the Dragon '73

Chung Bik-ha
The Blade '95

Chung Bik Wing
(Zhong Bi Ying)
Dr. Lamb '92

Chung, Cherie
(Chung Cho Hung, Zhong Chu Gong, Cheryle Chung)
Eighth Happiness '88
Once a Thief '91
Peking Opera Blues '86
The Postman Fights Back '82
Winners and Sinners '83

Chung, Christy
(Chung Lai-Tai, Zhong Li Ti)
All's Well End's Well '97
The Bride with White Hair 2 '93
Cold War '00
Conman in Tokyo '00
The Defender '94
Gen-Y Cops '00

God of Cookery '96
Hail the Judge '94
Love on Delivery '94
Man Wanted '95
The Red Wolf '95
Troublesome Night '97

Chung Chuen Yung
Ninja in the Deadly Trap '83

Chung Fat
(Chung Faat, Zhong Fa)
See also sidebar on p. 326.
Beauty Investigator '92
Blonde Fury '89
Chinese Hercules '73
Crime Story '93
Deadful Melody '94
Death Duel of Kung Fu '79
Dirty Tiger, Crazy Frog '78
Dragons Forever '88
Eastern Condors '86
Encounter of the Spooky Kind '81
Enter the Fat Dragon '78
Faces of Horror '98
Game of Death '78
The Haunted Cop Shop '87
Heart of Dragon '85
His Name Is Nobody '79
It Takes a Thief '01
Knockabout '79
Last Hero in China '93
Leopard Hunting '98
The Magnificent Butcher '79
The Millionaires' Express '86
Mr. Vampire 2 '86
Mr. Vampire Saga 4 '88
New Mr. Vampire '86
Odd Couple '79
Pedicab Driver '89
Pom Pom '84
The Prodigal Son '81
Rosa '86
She Shoots Straight '90
Twinkle Twinkle Lucky Stars '85
The Victim '80
Winners and Sinners '83
Yes, Madam '85
Zu: Warriors of the Magic Mountain '83

Chung, Gillian
U-Man '02

Chung, Jane
Anna Magdalena '98

Chung Ji-yau
Legend of the Flying Swordsman '00

Chung, Ken
My School Mate, the Barbarian '01

Chung King-fai
(Chung Ging Fai, Zhong Jing Hui)
Black Mask '96
Lawyer Lawyer '97
Victim '99

Chung, Lily
(Chung Suk-Wai)
The Bride with White Hair 2 '93
Brother of Darkness '94
Daughter of Darkness '93
The Eternal Evil of Asia '95
The Hero of Swallow '96
Millennium Dragon '99
Red to Kill '94

Chung Ling
Ninja Hunter '83

Chung, Rico
F*** / Off '98

Chung Seung-man
(Zhong Xiang Wen)
Chinese Iron Man '75
Triangular Duel '72

Chuskui, Apichart
Fear Faith Revenge 303 '98

Clark, Marlene
Enter the Dragon '73

Clay, Carl
Gamera vs. Viras '68

Clements, Michael
Brassiere '01
Horror Hotline...Big Head Monster '01
Lavender '00

Cobalt, William
Rivals of the Dragon '83

Cobo de Garcia, Eva
Operation Condor '91

Coleman, Brett
Dragon from Russia '90

Conn, Jackie
Crippled Masters '80
Raiders of Wu Tang '82

Convy, Burt
Cannonball Run '81

Conway, Harold
Battle in Outer Space '59
Body Snatcher from Hell '68
King Kong vs. Godzilla '64
The Last War '61

Mothra '61
Mothra vs. Godzilla '64
The Mysterians '57

Cook, Dale
Deadend of Besiegers '92

Cook, Dane
The Touch '02

Cooke, Keith
Mortal Kombat '95

Coolio
China Strike Force '00

Cordero, Angel
The Street Fighter '74

Cordero, Maria
Aces Go Places 5: The Terracotta Hit '89
City on Fire '87
Crocodile Hunter '89
Pedicab Driver '89

Cornwell, Bruce
Reptilian '00

Cortes, Anthony
Troublesome Night 4 '98

Coster, Ritchie
The Tuxedo '02

Crawford, Sophia
Beauty Investigator '92
Crystal Hunt '91

Cross, Garvin
Rumble in the Bronx '95

Crudup, Billy
Princess Mononoke '97 (V)

Cruz, Francisco
Curse of the Vampires '70

Cui Lin
Beijing Bicycle '01

Cunningham, Peter
Righting Wrongs '86

Curtis, Jack
Speed Racer: The Movie (V) '67

Cushing, Peter
Legend of the 7 Golden Vampires '74

Daat-wa, Lok
(Luo Da Hua)
Sharp Guns '01

Dacascos, Mark
China Strike Force '00

Dai Man Hong
Ninja vs. Bruce Lee '82

Dai Sai Aan
(Da Xi An, Ta Hsi Yen, Dai Sai Ngai)
The Big Sting '82

Bolo '80
The Buddhist Fist '79
Crack Shadow Boxers '77
Dirty Kung Fu '78
Fearless Dragons '79
His Name Is Nobody '79
Jade Claw '79
Lady Whirlwind and the Rangers '74
My Kung Fu 12 Kicks '79
The Shaolin Brothers '77
10 Magnificent Killers '77

Daike, Yuko
Kikujiro '99

Daimon, Masaaki
Godzilla vs. MechaGodzilla '74
Terror of MechaGodzilla '75

Dan, Reiko
Sanjuro '63

Danare, Malcolm
Godzilla the Series: Monster War '99 (V)

Danes, Claire
Princess Mononoke '97 (V)

Dang Tak-cheung
Thunder Kick '73

Daniels, Gary
City Hunter '92
Fatal Blade '00

Danning, Mike
Gappa: The Triphibian Monster '67
Terror beneath the Sea '66
The X from Outer Space '67

Darren, Eva
Brides of Blood '68

Dary, Heng
Snaker '01

Date, Saburo
Daimajin '66
Lone Wolf and Cub 1: Sword of Vengeance '72
Lone Wolf and Cub 3: Baby Cart to Hades '72
Ninja: Band of Assassins '62
Ninja: Band of Assassins Continued '63
The Tale of Zatoichi Continues '62
Zatoichi and the Chess Expert '65
Zatoichi and the Chest of Gold '64

Davao, Ricky
Guardian Angel '96

David, Keith
Princess Mononoke '97 (V)

Davio, Charlie
The Killing of Satan '83

Davis, Sammy Jr.
Cannonball Run '81

DeBell, Kristine
The Big Brawl '80

Dekker, Albert
Giant Monster Gamera '65 (U.S.)

Delon, Jim
Murder in the Orient '74

DeLuise, Dom
Cannonball Run '81

Denden
Cure '97
Godzilla 2000 '99
The Hypnotist '99
Spiral '00

Deo, Seema
Aakhri Adalat '88

Deol, Sunny
Champion '00

Derr, Richard
Terror Is a Man '59

Dev, Rahul
Champion '00

Dharmendra
Sholay '75

Dhumal
Gumnaam '65

Diax, Romy
Devil Woman '70

Diaz, Mary
Murder in the Orient '74

Diaz, Paquito
The Killing of Satan '83

Diaz, Vic
Beast of the Yellow Night '70

DiMaggio, John
Vampire Hunter D: Bloodlust '01 (V)

Dimmick, Joe
Aces Go Places 2 '83

Ding Lan
(Ding Laam, Ding Nan)
The Shaolin Temple '79
Shaolin Temple 2: Kids from Shaolin '84

Ding Yue
(Ding Yu)

Comrades, Almost a
    Love Story '96
The Prodigal Son '81

Dinga, Michael
(Michael Dingo)
Curry & Pepper '90
Fight Back to School 2
    '92
Hard Boiled '92
A Kid from Tibet '91
Red Shield '91
She Shoots Straight
    '90
The Tigers '91

Dix, Robert
Horror of the Blood
    Monsters '70

DMX
Romeo Must Die '00

Do Min-yong
Masters of Martial Arts
    '74

Dokko Yung-Jae
Gate of Destiny '96

Dong-kun, Yang
(Jang Dong-kun)
Bloody Beach '00
Nowhere to Hide '99

Donlevy, Brian
Giant Monster Gamera
    (U.S. version) '65

Dosey, Willy
The Street Fighter's
    Last Revenge '74

Douguchi, Yoriko
(Yoriko Dohguchi)
Cure '97
Tampopo '87

Doyle, Christopher
Comrades, Almost a
    Love Story '96

Doyle-Murray, Brian
Jackie Chan Adven-
    tures 3: The Shad-
    ow of Shendu '00
    (V)

Drake, Tom
The Green Hornet '74

Driver, Minnie
Princess Mononoke '97
    (V)

Drury, Alan
Robo Vampire '88

Duan, William
*(Duen Wai Lun, Duan
Wei Lun, William Tuan)*
Crime Story '93
Her Name Is Cat '98
Legend of the Drunken
    Master '94
Supercop '92
Thunderbolt '95

Duncan, David
Rodan '56 (U.S.) (N)

Dunham, Robert
(Dan Yuma)
Dagora the Space Mon-
    ster '64
Godzilla vs. Megalon
    '73Mothra '61

Dunn, Kevin
Godzilla the Series:
    Monster War '99
    (V)

Duran, Lillo
Terror Is a Man '59

Dyneley, Peter
The Manster '60

E-Lin
Cop Shop Babes '01

Eba
Sumo Vixens '96

Ebara, Osamu
Junk '99

Ebara, Shinjiro
Invasion of the Nep-
    tune Men '61

Eca Da Silva, Elaine
The Mission '99

Edelman, Herb
Wheels on Meals '84

Edoya, Nekohachi
The Funeral '84

Edwards, Paul Jr.
The Walls of Hell '64

Edwards, Ron
Iron Monkey 2 '96

Egawa, Kae
Cure '97

Ege, Julie
Legend of the 7 Golden
    Vampires '74

Eguchi, Yosuke
Another Heaven '00

Eguro, Mari
Thunderbolt '95

Ehata, Kanji
Lone Wolf and Cub 2:
    Baby Cart at the
    River Styx '72

Eisenberg, Susan
Jackie Chan Adven-
    tures 2: The Dark
    Hand Returns '00
    (V)

Elam, Jack
Cannonball Run '81

Ellis, Sean
The Protector '85

Emoto, Akira
(Akira Tsukamoto)

Another Heaven '00
The Eel '97
Godzilla vs. Space
    Godzilla '94
Maborosi '95

Enami, Kyoko
Gamera vs. Barugon
    '66

Enami, Naomi
Zeram '91

Endo, Kenichi
Nobody '99

Endo, Masashi
Wild Zero '99

Endo, Tatsuo
Audition '99
Daimajin '66
Lone Wolf and Cub 4:
    Baby Cart in Peril
    '72
The Street Fighter '74
The Street Fighter's
    Last Revenge '74
Zatoichi the Outlaw '67
Zatoichi's Cane Sword
    '66
Zatoichi's Flashing
    Sword '64

Enomoto, Kenichi
Men Who Tread on the
    Tiger's Tail '43

Enyoki, Aya
Gunhed '89

Epps, Omar
Brother '00

Escudero, Mario
Murder in the Orient
    '74

Estregan, George
The Killing of Satan '83

Esumi, Hideaki
Tokyo Drifter '66

Esumi, Makiko
Maborosi '95

Evan, Cathy
Scorpion Thunderbolt
    '85

Eve
Guinea Pig: He Never
    Dies '86
Guinea Pig: The Making
    of Guinea Pig '86

Everingham, Ananda
Fear Faith Revenge 303
    '98

Ezawa, Moeko
Sakuya: Slayer of
    Demons '00

Faan Yik-man
The Chinese Feast '95

Fai, Li
*(Li Fei, Lee Fei, Li Hui,
Lee Fai)*
A Chinese Ghost Story
    2 '90
Fist Power '00
Cop Shop Babes '01
Iron Monkey '93
Organized Crime and
    Triad Bureau '94
Shaolin Soccer '01

Fai-wong, Lam
(Lin Hui Huang)
Avenging Eagle '78
Brave Archer '77
Chinatown Kid '77
Death Mask of the
    Ninja '82
Fists of the White
    Lotus '80
Five Deadly Venoms
    '78
Five Superfighters '78
3 Evil Masters '80

Falcon, Jeff
*(Git Foo, Jie Fu, Jeffrey
Falcon)*
Blonde Fury '89
The Inspector Wears
    Skirts '88
Operation Pink Squad
    '88
Prince of the Sun '90

Fan Chiang
Chinese Hercules '73

Fan Dan-fung
(Fan Dan Feng)
The 18 Jade Arhats '78
Inheritor of Kung Fu '77

Fan, Mavis
The Private Eye Blues
    '94

Fan Mui-Sang
*(Fan Mei-Sheng, Faan
Mooi Saang, Fan May
Sheng)*
Blooded Treasury Fight
    '79
Brave Archer '77
The Buddhist Fist '79
Dreadnaught '81
The Eagle's Killer '81
Hit-Man in the Hand of
    Buddha '80
The Magnificent Butch-
    er '79
The Millionaires'
    Express '86
The Postman Fights
    Back '82
Project A 2 '87
Rich and Famous '87
Riki-Oh: The Story of
    Ricky '89
The 36 Deadly Styles
    '79
The Young Master '80

Fan Siu-wong
*(Fan Shao Huang, Terry
Fan, Louis Fan)*

Dragons of the Orient
    '88
Organized Crime and
    Triad Bureau '94
Righting Wrongs '86
Riki Oh: The Story of
    Ricky '89
Supercop 2 '93

Fang, Audrey
You Shoot, I Shoot '01

Fang, Fang
(Fung Fung, Feng Feng)
The Buddha Assassina-
    tor '79
Dragon Lord '82
The 18 Jade Arhats '78
Enter the Fat Dragon
    '78
Snake-Crane Secret
    '78
We're Going to Eat You!
    '80
The Young Master '80

Fang, Sunny
*(Fang Kang, Fong Gong,
Fang Gang, Sunny Song
Kong)*
Code of Honor '87
The Longest Nite '98

Farr, Jamie
Cannonball Run '81

Fawcett, Farrah
Cannonball Run '81

Feng, Gou Ling
*(Ko Ling Fung, Go Ling
Feng)*
Fantasy Mission Force
    '84

Feng Yi
(Fung Ngai, Feng I)
The Chinese Connec-
    tion '71
Young Tiger '72

Ferguson, Dale
Bronson Lee, Champi-
    on '78

Fernandez, Alex
Vampire Hunter D:
    Bloodlust(V) '01

Fernandez, Eddie
The Blood Drinkers '64

Fernandez, Peter
Astro Boy (V) '63
Speed Racer: The
    Movie(V) '67

Ferre, Michelle
Who Am I? '98

Ferrer, Jose
The Big Brawl '80

Fhi Fan
Spiral '00

Field, Robert Scott
Godzilla vs. King Ghido-
    rah '91

Findlay, Diane
Giant Monster Gamera '65 (U.S.)

Fitzpatrick, Gabrielle
Mr. Nice Guy '97

Floyd, Big Jonny
The New Game of Death '75

Fok, Clarence
(Fok Yiu-leung, Clarence Ford)
Armour of God '86
Body Weapon '99
Century of the Dragon '99

Fok, Terrence
(Fok Shui Wai, Foh Shui Wa, Huo Rui Hua)
Prison on Fire '87
Prison on Fire 2 '91

Fonda, Bridget
Kiss of the Dragon '01

Fonda, Peter
Cannonball Run '81

Fong, Alex
(Fong Chung San, Fang Zhong Shen, Foo Lik, Alex Fu)
Angel '87
Angel 2 '88
Cheap Killers '98
The Cheaters '01
City of Desire '01
Devil Touch '02
Double Tap '00
Downtown Torpedoes '97
Lethal Panther '91
Sharp Guns '01
The Storm Riders '98
Your Place or Mine! '98

Fong Chin Fat
The Eye '02

Fong Ching
(Fong Jing, Fang Zheng, Fang Jung)
Fantasy Mission Force '84

Fong, Frances
Troublesome Night 14 '02

Fong, Henry
(Fong Ping, Fang Ping)
Black Mask '96
Cheap Killers '98
Double Tap '00
The Enforcer '95
Faces of Horror '98
Savior of the Soul '91
Ten Tigers of Shaolin '78
You Shoot, I Shoot '01

Fong, Leo
Murder in the Orient '74

Fong, Maura
Scorpion Thunderbolt '85

Fong Min
(Fang Mian, Fang Mien)
Five Fingers of Death '72
Lady Wu Tang '77
Thousand Mile Escort '76

Fong, Samuel
Rage of the Dragon '79
The Snake Strikes Back '81

Fong Yeh
(Fong Yau, Fang Ye, Fang Yeh, Fung Yi)
The Awaken Punch '73
Bloody Fight '72
The Bloody Fists '72
Chinese Hercules '73
City on Fire '87
Crack Shadow Boxers '77
10 Magnificent Killers '77
Thousand Mile Escort '76

Fong Yo-Yo
The Wesley's Mysterious File '01

Fonoroff, Paul
(Fong Biu Law, Fang Bao Luo, Fong Bo Lo)
Fight Back to School 2 '92
Lawyer Lawyer '97
Once upon a Time in China 2 '92

Forbes-Robertson, John
Legend of the 7 Golden Vampires '74

Forgeham, John
Kiss of the Dragon '01

Forman, David
Teenage Mutant Ninja Turtles '90

Forner, Lola
(Law Lai Fong Loh, Luo La Fang Na, Maria Delores Forner)
Armour of God '86
Wheels on Meals '84

Forstadt, Rebecca
Blood: The Last Vampire '00 (V)

Franciscus, James
Bruce Lee: A Warrior's Journey '00

Frankie, Little
Godzilla vs. Space Godzilla '94

Freedman, David
Legend of the Dinosaurs '77

Fu, Bonnie
(Fu Yuk-Ching)
The Enforcer '95
Full Contact '92
God of Gamblers Returns '94
The New Marvelous Double '92
Pom Pom and Hot Hot '92

Fu, Rachel
(Fu Tin Wing)
Cop Shop Babes '01
U-Man '02

Fu Sheng, Alexander
Avenging Eagle '78
Brave Archer '77
Chinatown Kid '77
Invincible Pole Fighter '83
Legendary Weapons of China '82
Ten Tigers of Kwang-tung '79

Fubuki, Jun
Pulse '01

Fuentes, Amalia
The Blood Drinkers '64
Curse of the Vampires '70

Fui-on, Shing
(Sing Fui Ann)
A Better Tomorrow '86
A Better Tomorrow 2 '87
Chinese Orthopedist and the Spice Girls '02
Code of Honor '87
Crocodile Hunter '89
Doctor Vampire '90
The Dragon Family '88
Dragons Forever '88
Final Justice '88
Fist of Fury 1991 '91
God of Gamblers '89
God of Gamblers 2 '90
H.K. Adams Family '92
The Inspector Wears Skirts '88
The Killer '89
Legacy of Rage '86
Legend of the Dragon '91
Long Arm of the Law 2 '87
100 Ways to Murder Your Wife '86
Prison on Fire '87
Red Shield '91
Rich and Famous '87
Thunderbolt '95
Tiger on Beat '88
The Tigers '91
Troublesome Night 3 '97
The Untold Story '92

Vampire Kids '91
Young and Dangerous '96

Fujii, Kahori
Tokyo Fist '96

Fujikawa, Jun
The Razor 2: The Snare '73

Fujiki, Yu
Chushingura '62
King Kong vs. Godzilla '62
Mothra vs. Godzilla '64
Throne of Blood '57
Yog: Monster from Space '70

Fujimaki, Jun
Daimajin '66

Fujimura, Shiho
Ninja: Band of Assassins '62
Ninja: Band of Assassins Continued '63
Wrath of Daimajin '66
Zatoichi on the Road '63
Zatoichi's Cane Sword '66

Fujioka, Hiroshi
In the Line of Duty 3 '88
Sakuya: Slayer of Demons '00

Fujioka, Takuya
Samaritan Zatoichi '68
Zatoichi the Outlaw '67

Fujisawa, Yuuki
Terminatrix '95

Fujita, Makoto
Sure Death: Revenge '87
Zatoichi's Cane Sword '66

Fujita, Susumu
Chushingura '62
Dagora the Space Monster '64
Frankenstein vs. Baragon '65
The Hidden Fortress '58
High and Low '63
Men Who Tread on the Tiger's Tail '43
The Mysterians '57
Sanshiro Sugata '43
Yojimbo '61

Fujita, Zan
Godzilla vs. Gigan '72

Fujitani, Ayako
Gamera 2: Advent of Legion '96
Gamera 3: The Revenge of Irys '99
Gamera, Guardian of the Universe '95

Fujiwara, Kamatari
Chushingura '62
The Funeral '84
The Hidden Fortress '58
The Razor 1: Sword of Justice '72
Sanjuro '63
Seven Samurai '54
Yojimbo '61

Fujiwara, Kei
Organ '96
Tetsuo: The Iron Man '89

Fujiwara, Noriko
China Strike Force '00

Fujiwara, Reiko
Ninja: Band of Assassins '62
Zatoichi on the Road '63

Fujiwara, Tatsuya
Battle Royale '00

Fujiyama, Kanbi
Zatoichi and the Doomed Man '65

Fujiyama, Koji
Gamera vs. Barugon '66
Gamera vs. Viras '68
Gamera vs. Zigra '71
Lone Wolf and Cub 5: Baby Cart in the Land of Demons '73
Lone Wolf and Cub 6: White Heaven in Hell '74
Wrath of Daimajin '66

Fujiyama, Yoko
Dagora the Space Monster '64

Fuk Tin Chin
Ninja in the Deadly Trap '83

Fuk Tin Mu
Ninja in the Deadly Trap '83

Fukawa, Toshikazu
Godzilla, Mothra and King Ghidorah: Battle on Earth '01
Ultraman Tiga and Ultraman Dyna: The Warriors of the Lightning Star '98

Fukioka, Seiko
Mighty Jack '68

Fukkin, Zennosoke
Extreme Crisis '98

Fukuda, Wataru
Godzilla vs. MechaGodzilla 2 '93

Godzilla vs.
MechaGodzilla 2
'93

Funakoshi, Eiji
Blind Beast '69
Gamera vs. Guiron '69
Giant Monster Gamera
'65

Funfrock, Huguette
Aces Go Places 3 '84

Fung, Alexander
Second Time Around
'02

Fung Hark-On
(Feng Ke-An, Fung Hak
On, Feng Ko An) See
also sidebar on p. 326.
The Awaken Punch '73
Breakout from Oppres-
sion '78
Bruce Lee: The Man,
the Myth '76
Descendant of Wing
Chun '78
Dirty Kung Fu '78
Dirty Tiger, Crazy Frog
'78
Dragon Lord '82
Dragons Forever '88
Dreadnaught '81
Enter the Fat Dragon
'78
Executioners from
Shaolin '77
From China with Death
'74
Game of Death '78
Heart of Dragon '85
Last Hurrah for Chivalry
'78
The Legend of Bruce
Lee '80
Legend of the 7 Golden
Vampires '74
The Magnificent Butch-
er '79
Magnificent Warriors
'87
Miracles '89
Police Story '85
Prodigal Boxer '73
The Protector '85
Snake Deadly Act '79
Snake in the Eagle's
Shadow '78
The 36 Crazy Fists '77
Tiger Cage '88
Thunder Kick '73
Twin Dragons '92
Warrior from Shaolin
'81
Winners and Sinners
'83
The Young Master '80
The Young Tiger '73
Zu: Warriors of the
Magic Mountain
'83

Fung, Jerome
(Fung Lok Ban, Feng Le
Bin)

The Mission '99
Where a Good Man
Goes '99

Fung Lee
(Kai Li, Kay Lay, Lau
Chau Sang)
Dragons Forever '88
Descendant of Wing
Chun '78
Eastern Condors '86
Encounter of the
Spooky Kind '81
Executioners from
Shaolin '77
Heroes Shed No Tears
'83/86
Iceman Cometh '89
A Kid from Tibet '92
The Magnificent Butch-
er '79
The Millionaires'
Express '86
Mr. Vampire '85
Mr. Vampire 2 '86
My Lucky Stars '84
Pedicab Driver '89
Pom Pom '84
The Prodigal Son '81
Righting Wrongs '86
Rosa '86
The Tigers '91
Tower of Death '81
The Victim '80
Where's Officer Tuba?
'86
Winners and Sinners
'83
Yes, Madam '85
Zu: Warriors of the
Magic Mountain
'83

Fung, Petrina
C'est la Vie, Mon Cheri
'93
Eighth Happiness '88

Fung, Roger
Love Paradox '00

Fung, Stanley
(Fung Shiu-Fan)
The Dragon Family '88
Dragons Forever '88
Fight Back to School 3
'93
Iceman Cometh '89
The Inspector Wears
Skirts '88
In the Line of Duty 3
'88
Mr. Vampire 2 '86
My Lucky Stars '85
The Owl vs. Bombo '84
Pom Pom '84
Pom Pom Strikes Back
'86
Twinkle Twinkle Lucky
Stars '85
Wheels on Meals '84
Where's Officer Tuba?
'86
Winners and Sinners
'83

Fung, Stephen
(Fung Tak-Lun, Feng De
Lun)
The Avenging Fist '01
Bio-Cops '00
Cheap Killers '98
Gen-X Cops '99
Gen-Y Cops '00
The Irresistible Piggies
'02
My School Mate, the
Barbarian '01
Shadow '01
Sunshine Cops '99

Fung, Tin
(Tian Feng, Tien Feng,
Tyan Feng)
The Awaken Punch '73
A Better Tomorrow '86
Casino Raiders 2 '91
The Chinese Connec-
tion '71
Dragon Lord '82
A Fistful of Talons '83
Five Elements of Kung
Fu '78
Five Fingers of Death
'72
God of Gamblers 3:
Back to Shanghai
'91
Green Snake '93
Hong Kong Nocturne
'67
Legend of the Mountain
'79
Miracles '89
The Young Master '80

Furness, George
The Mysterians '57

Furuhata, Koji
Frankenstein vs.
Baragon '65

Furusato, Yayoi
King of the Mongols
'60

Furuya, Chinami
Ring 0: Birthday '00

Furuya, Ikko
The Ninja Dragon '90

Fushimi, Sentara
King of the Mongols
'60

Futami, Kazuki
Rebirth of Mothra '96

Fuwa, Mansaku
Warm Water under a
Red Bridge '01

Fuyu, Ganko
Spiral '00

Gai, Chan Si
(Chan Si Gaai, Chen Si
Jia)
Dirty Ho '79
Return of the Master
Killer '80

Galang, Fred
The Walls of Hell '64

Gam Biu
(Jin Biao)
Aces Go Places '82
Lightning Kung Fu '80
Powerful Four '91
Queen's High '91

Gam Kei Chu
(Jin Qi Zhu, Chin Chi
Chu)
Dragon Lee vs. the Five
Brothers '78
Five Fingers of Death
'72
Fury in Shaolin Temple
'82
Hand of Death '75
Sting of the Dragon
Masters '73

Gam Kim
(Jin Jian)
Chinese Iron Man '75
The Shaolin Kids '77
Triangular Duel '72

Gam Man-hei
(Jin Wan Xi)
Inheritor of Kung Fu '77

Gan Tak-mau
(Jin De Mao)
Deadend of Besiegers
'92
The Three Swordsmen
'94
Yellow River Fighter '88

Gannyon, Claude
Return of the Street
Fighter '74

Ganoung, Richard
Astro Boy '80 (V)

Gao Yuanyuan
Beijing Bicycle '01

Gaowa, Siqin
Her Majesty Is Fine '96
The Three Swordsmen
'94

Garcia, Eddie
(Eduardo Verchez Gar-
cia)
Beast of the Yellow
Night '70
Curse of the Vampires
'70
Mad Doctor of Blood
Island '68
Twilight People '72

Garcia, Joe
Devil Woman '70

Garcia, Johanna
Devil Woman '70

Garcia, Jose
Beast of the Yellow
Night '70

**Garcia, Rodolfo
"Boy"**
Murder in the Orient
'74

Gashuin, Tatsuya
Shark Skin Man and
Peach Hip Girl '98

Gei Ga Faat
The Untold Story '92

Geng Le
Beijing Rocks '01

Geum-yong, Yang
My Sassy Girl '01

Gidayu, Great
Kikujiro '99

Gil, Cherie
Devil Woman '70

Gil, Rosemarie
Devil Woman '70

Gilbert, Kent
Godzilla vs. King Ghido-
rah '91

Ging Chue
(Jing Zhu, Ching Chu,
Lee King Chue, Li Qing
Zhu)
Death Duel of Kung Fu
'79
Dirty Ho '79
Duel of the Brave Ones
'78
Fists of the White
Lotus '80
Invincible Pole Fighter
'83
Legendary Weapons of
China '82
Return of the Master
Killer '80

Ging-shun, Mau
(Mao Ging-shun, Mao
Jing Shun, Mau Ching
Suen, Mao Tou, Mao
Tai)
Battle of Shaolin '77
The Deadly Sword '78
The Heroes '80
The Hot, the Cool, and
the Vicious '76
The Massive '78
Militant Eagle '78
Ninja Checkmate '79
Ninja in the Deadly Trap
'81
Shaolin vs. Ninja '83
The 36 Deadly Styles
'79
The Unbeaten 28 '80

Gloria
The Adventures of Milo
and Otis '86

Go, Eiji
Black Tight Killers '66
Bullet Train '75
Tokyo Drifter '66

Huddart, Goflan
Bronson Lee, Champion '78

Hughes, Andrew
Body Snatcher from Hell '68
Destroy All Monsters '68
King Kong Escapes '67
Terror beneath the Sea '66

Huh Jun-ho
Volcano High School '01

Hui, Andy
(Hui Chi On, Hu Zhi An)
Wonder Seven '94

Hui, Ann
(Hui On Wah, Hui Ngon Wa, Hu An Hua)
Jang Hu-"The Triad Zone" '00
Merry-Go-Round '01

Hui Bat Liu
(Shiu Bu Lia, Hu Bu Le)
Fantasy Mission Force '84
Kung Fu on Sale '79

Hui Bing Sam
The Imp '81

Hui Chang-son
Pulgasari '85

Hui, Clarence
(Hui Yuen, Hu Yuan)
God of Cookery '96
He's a Woman, She's a Man '94
King of Comedy '99

Hui Fan
(Hui Fun, Hu Fen)
F*** / Off '98
Troublesome Night '97
Troublesome Night 2 '97

Hui Hiu-Dan
Robotrix '91

Hui, Kara
(Hui Ying-Hung, Wai Ying Hung, Hui Ying Gong, Claire Wai)
Brave Archer '77
Chinatown Kid '77
Dirty Ho '79
The Dragon Family '88
Dragon from Shaolin '96
Fists of the White Lotus '80
The Inspector Wears Skirts '88
Invincible Pole Fighter '83
Legendary Weapons of China '82
Legend of the Drunken Tiger '92
Miracles '89

The Peacock King '89
Return of the Master Killer '80
Rosa '86
The Seventh Curse '86
Twinkle Twinkle Lucky Stars '85
Visible Secret '01

Hui, Michael
(Hui Koon-man, Hui Goon Man, Hu Guan Wen)
Cannonball Run '81
Mr. Boo Meets Pom Pom '85
The Private Eyes '76

Hui, Ricky
(Hui Koon-Ying)
Aces Go Places 3 '84
Aces Go Places 4 '86
The Haunted Cop Shop '87
The Inspector Wears Skirts '88
Miracles '89
Mr. Vampire '85
Operation Pink Squad '88
The Private Eyes '76
Project A 2 '87

Hui, Sam
(Hui Goon Git, Hu Guan Jie, Samuel Hui, Hui Koon-kit)
Aces Go Places '82
Aces Go Places 2 '83
Aces Go Places 3 '84
Aces Go Places 4 '86
Aces Go Places 5: The Terracotta Hit '89
Dragon from Russia '90
The Private Eyes '76
Swordsman '90

Hui Siu-hung
(Hui Shiu Hung, Hu Shao Xiong)
Bio-Cops '00
Clueless '01
Dummy Mommy, without a Baby '01
Everyday Is Valentine '01
Expect the Unexpected '98
Final Romance '01
Gold Fingers '01
Help!!! '00
The Irresistible Piggies '02
Master Q 2001 '01
Naked Killer '92
Needing You... '00
Nightmare Zone '98
Running out of Time '99
Running out of Time 2 '01
Victim '99

Hui Ying-Ying
(Hu Ying Ying)

Duel of the Tao Tough '82
Kung Fu Genius '79

Hung, Catherine
(Hung Yan)
Wing Chun '94

Hung, Danny
Champ against Champ '83

Hung Fa-long
(Hung Dut Long, Hung Hua Lang, Hung Fa Lou)
Blazing Temple '76
The 18 Bronzemen Part 2 '76
The 8 Masters '77
Born Invincible '78
Kung Fu on Sale '79

Hung, Mama
(Chin Chi Au, Qian Si Ying, Chin Tsi Ang, Xian Yi Ying)
The Blade '95
C'est la Vie, Mon Cheri '93
In the Mood for Love '00

Hung, Sammo
(Hung Kam-Bo, Hong Chin-pao, Hong Jinbao, James Hung, Hung Kam-po, Samo Hung, Yuanlong Zhu, Yuen Chu) See also sidebars on pp. 142, 182, and 492.
The Art of Action: Martial Arts in the Movies '02
The Avenging Fist '01
A Chinese Ghost Story: The Tsui Hark Animation '97 (V)
Dirty Tiger, Crazy Frog '78
Don't Give a Damn '95
Dragons Forever '88
Eastern Condors '86
Encounter of the Spooky Kind '81
The End of the Wicked Tiger '81
Enter the Dragon '73
Enter the Fat Dragon '78
Filthy Guy '80
Game of Death '78
Hand of Death '75
Heart of Dragon '85
Knockabout '79
Lord of the Wu Tang '93
The Magnificent Butcher '79
Martial Arts Mayhem, Vol. 1 '99
Masters of Martial Arts '74
The Millionaires' Express '86
Mr. Nice Guy '97

My Lucky Stars '85
Odd Couple '79
The Owl vs. Bombo '84
Painted Faces '88
Painted Skin '92
Pedicab Driver '89
Pom Pom '84
The Prisoner '90
The Prodigal Son '81
Project A '83
Shaolin Traitorous '76
She Shoots Straight '90
Skinny Tiger and Fatty Dragon '90
Sting of the Dragon Masters '73
A Touch of Zen '69
Twinkle Twinkle Lucky Stars '85
The Victim '80
Wheels on Meals '84
Where's Officer Tuba? '86
Winners and Sinners '83
Yes, Madam '85
Zu Warriors '01
Zu: Warriors of the Magic Mountain '83

Hung Shing-fu
The Shaolin One '83

Hung Si-man
The Kung Fu Master '94

Hung, Timmy
(Hung Tin Ming, Hong Tian Ming)
Don't Give a Damn '95
Troublesome Night 4 '98

Hung, Vicky
Troublesome Night 3 '97

Hung Wai-leung
Love on a Diet '01
Running out of Time '99

Hung Yen-yen
Fist of Fury '95

Hunt, Keishi
Blowback: Love and Death '90

Hwa Ling
(Wa Ling, Hua Ling, Hua Lun, Wa Lun, Hua Lin)
Eagle's Claw '77
Fatal Needles vs. Fatal Fists '80
Mask of Death '76
Return of the Master Killer '80
Shaolin Master Killer '78

Hwa Yue Suen
18 Secrets of Kung Fu '79

Hylton, Jane
The Manster '60

Hyper BB
(Sai Lei Mui, Qian Li Mei, Missy Hyperbitch)
Merry-Go-Round '01
My School Mate, the Barbarian '01
You Shoot, I Shoot '01

Hyu, Charlie
Duel of the Tao Tough '82

Ibu, Masato
Godzilla vs. Megaguirus '00

Ibuki, Shingo
Lone Wolf and Cub 3: Baby Cart to Hades '72
Lone Wolf and Cub 4: Baby Cart in Peril '72
Lone Wolf and Cub 5: Baby Cart in the Land of Demons '73

Ibuki, Toru
Destroy All Monsters '68
Ebirah, Horror of the Deep '66
Ghidorah the Three-Headed Monster '64
Invasion of Astro-Monster '65
King Kong Escapes '67
Terror of MechaGodzilla '75

Ichiji, Yoko
(Yoko Ichui)
Return of the Street Fighter '74

Ichijo, Yumi
King of the Mongols '60

Ichijou, Saeko
Terminatrix '95

Ichikawa, Chusa
Chushingura '62

Ichikawa, Miwako
Another Heaven '00

Ichikawa, Raizo
Blind Swordsman: The Tale of Zatoichi '62
Ninja: Band of Assassins '62
Ninja: Band of Assassins Continued '63

Ida, Hiroki
Violent Cop '89

Ide, Rakkyo
Kikujiro '99

Igawa, Hisashi
Akira Kurosawa's
Dreams '90
Boiling Point '90
Madadayo '92
Ran '85

Iguchi, Takahito
Boiling Point '90

Ihara, Shinichi
Code of Honor '87

Ihara, Tsuyoshi
Gamera, Guardian of
the Universe '95

Iida, Kunihiko
Another Heaven '00
Weather Woman '95
Zeram '91

Iijima, Daisuke
Ghost Actress '96
Gonin '95
Taboo '99

Iizuka, Masahide
Return of Daimajin '66

Iizuka, Minoru
Boiling Point '90

Ikariya, Chosuke
Akira Kurosawa's
Dreams '90

Ike, Reiko
The Street Fighter's
Last Revenge '74

Ikebe, Ryo
Battle in Outer Space
'59
Chushingura '62
The Executioner '74

Ikeda, Shoko
*(Akiko Ikeda, Chin Tin
Ji, Chi Tian Jing Zi, Chi
Tin Jing Ji)*
Operation Condor '91

Ikeda, Wakako
Mighty Jack '68

Ikeuchi, Junko
Atomic Rulers of the
World '57
Attack from Space '58
Evil Brain from Outer
Space '58/59
Invaders from Space
'58

Im Ji-eun
Dream of Garuda '94
Sympathy for Mr.
Vengeance '01

Imai, Masayuki
Tokyo Mafia 2: Wrath of
the Yakuza '95
Tokyo Mafia 3: Battle
for Shinjuku '96
Tokyo Mafia: Yakuza
Wars '95

Imaizumi, Ren
Godzilla, King of the
Monsters '54
The Mysterians '57
Rodan '56
Samurai 2: Duel at Ichi-
joji Temple '55

Imamura, Keiko
Godzilla vs.
MechaGodzilla 2
'93
Godzilla vs. Mothra '92
Godzilla vs. Space
Godzilla '94

Imawano, Kiyoshiro
The Happiness of the
Katakuris '01

Inaba, Yoshio
The Razor 2: The Snare
'73

Inagaki, Goro
The Hypnotist '99
Parasite Eve '97

Inamdar, Shafi
Aakhri Adalat '88

Inamiya, Makoto
Kikujiro '99
Wild Zero '99

Ineno, Kazuko
The Razor 2: The Snare
'73

Inosanto, Dan
Bruce Lee: A Warrior's
Journey '00
Game of Death '78

Inou, Rie
Ring '98
Ring 2 '99

Inoue, Daigo
Gamera vs. Gyaos '67
Gamera vs. Zigra '71
Giant Monster Gamera
'65

Inoue, Harumi
Freeze Me '00

Inoue, Noriaki
Mighty Jack '68

Intachai, Parinya
Fear Faith Revenge 303
'98

Intrakanchit, Pisek
Bangkok Dangerous
'00

Iori, Yumi
Guinea Pig: Android of
Notre Dame '88
Guinea Pig: The Making
of Guinea Pig '86

Irani, Aruna
Hum Paanch '80

Isa, Kharina
Angel 2 '88

Isaacs, Jason
The Tuxedo '02

Isaacson, Simon
Black Magic M-66 '87
(V)

Isaki, Mitsunori
Akira Kurosawa's
Dreams '90

Isayama, Hiroko
Female Convict Scorpi-
on: Jailhouse 41
'72

Iseya, Yusuke
After Life '98

**Isgar, Jonathan
James**
Mr. Nice Guy '97
Once upon a Time in
China '91
Operation Condor '91

Ishibashi, Kei
Ghost Actress '96

Ishibashi, Musashi
*(Masami Ishibashi, Mil-
ton Ishibashi)*
Return of the Street
Fighter '74
The Street Fighter '74

Ishibashi, Renji
Audition '99
Lone Wolf and Cub 6:
White Heaven in
Hell '74
The Razor 1: Sword of
Justice '72
Sure Death: Revenge
'87
Tetsuo: The Iron Man
'89

Ishibashi, Ryo
Audition '99
Brother '00

Ishibashi, Tomotsu
Gamera 2: Advent of
Legion '96
Gamera 3: The
Revenge of Irys '99

Ishida, Hikari
Adrenaline Drive '99

Ishida, Keichi
Killer's Romance '90

Ishida, Nobuyuki
Reborn from Hell:
Samurai Armaged-
don '96

Ishida, Shigeki
All Monsters Attack '70
Ebirah, Horror of the
Deep '66
Frankenstein vs.
Baragon '65
Ghidorah the Three-
Headed Monster
'65
The Last War '61

Ishida, Yuriko
Boiling Point '90

Ishiguro, Tatsuya
Zatoichi and the Chest
of Gold '64

Ishikawa, Hiroshi
Godzilla vs. Gigan '72

Ishikura, Hidehiko
Sakuya: Slayer of
Demons '00

Ishimaru, Kenjiro
Gamera 3: The
Revenge of Irys '99
Ring 2 '99

Ishino, Yoko
Godzilla vs. Destroyah
'95

Ishiyama, Daisuke
Sugar-Howling of Angel
'96

Ishiyama, Kenjiro
High and Low '63
Zatoichi the Outlaw '67

Isiyama, Ritsu
Lone Wolf and Cub 5:
Baby Cart in the
Land of Demons
'73

Itami, Juzo
Notorious Concubines
'69

Ito, Akio
Voyage into Space '67

Ito, Alfred
The Ladies' Phone Sex
Club '96

Ito, Emi
Ghidorah the Three-
Headed Monster
'64
Mothra '61
Mothra vs. Godzilla '64

Ito, Hideaki
Cross Fire '00
Princess Blade '02

Ito, Hiro
Reborn from Hell:
Samurai Armaged-
don '96

Ito, Hiroko
Woman in the Dunes
'64

Ito, Hisaya
Battle in Outer Space
'59
Chushingura '62
Ebirah, Horror of the
Deep '66
Frankenstein vs.
Baragon '65
Ghidorah the Three-
Headed Monster
'64

The H-Man '58
The Human Vapor '60
The Mysterians '57
Varan the Unbelievable
'58
War of the Gargantuas
'66

Ito, Jerry
The Last War '61
The Manster '60
Mighty Jack '68
Mothra '61

Ito, Koichi
Gamera vs. Barugon
'66
Gamera vs. Gyaos '67

Ito, Yozaburo
Postman Blues '97

Ito, Yumi
Ghidorah the Three-
Headed Monster
'64
Mothra '61
Mothra vs. Godzilla '64

Ito, Yunosuke
Giants and Toys '58
Lone Wolf and Cub 1:
Sword of
Vengeance '72
Ninja: Band of Assas-
sins '62
Sanjuro '63
Stray Dog '49

Itsuki, Mariko
Big Boobs Buster '90

Ivy the Cow
Sixty Million Dollar Man
'95

Iwai, Hanshiro
Men Who Tread on the
Tiger's Tail '43

Iwanaga, Frank
Godzilla, King of the
Monsters '54
(U.S.)

Iwao, Masataka
Legend of the
Dinosaurs '77
Return of the Street
Fighter '74

Iwasaki, Kaneko
Zatoichi and the Chess
Expert '65

Iwata, Mitsuo
Akira '88 (V)

Iwata, Tadashi
Lone Wolf and Cub 1:
Sword of
Vengeance '72
Lone Wolf and Cub 3:
Baby Cart to Hades
'72
Lone Wolf and Cub 5:
Baby Cart in the

Land of Demons '73
Ninja: Band of Assassins Continued '63
The Razor 1: Sword of Justice '72

Izumi, Kyoko
Good Morning '59

Izuno, Orie
Ring '98

Jackson, Samuel L.
The Art of Action: Martial Arts in the Movies '02

Jagdeep
Sholay '75

Jagger, Bianca
Cannonball Run '81

Jagger, Dean
Game of Death '78

Jalal, Farida
Elaan '94

James, Charity
Godzilla the Series: Monster War '99 (V)

James, Jim
Dragon on Fire '79
Jade Claw '79

Jang Dong-jik
Bichunmoo '99
Gate of Destiny '96

Jang Doo Hee
Heroes Shed No Tears '83/86

Jang Hyuk
Volcano High School '01

Jeon Ha-na
Bichunmoo '99

Jeon Hye-jin
Lies '99

Jeong Jun
Attack the Gas Station! '99

Jhoon Rhee
Sting of the Dragon Masters '73

Ji Han Jae
Bruce Lee: A Warrior's Journey '00
Game of Death '78

Ji-yeon, Jang
Gate of Destiny '96

Jia Hongsheng
Frozen '96
Suzhou River '00

Jiang Gengchen
The Swordswoman in White '92

Jin Tae-seong
Bloody Beach '00

Jin-young, Chung
(Chung Jin-young, Jeong Jin-yeong, Chang Jin-young)
Bichunmoo '99
The Foul King '00
Hi! Dharma! '01
Ring Virus '99

Jino, Marie
Tokyo Decameron: Three Tales of Madness and Sensuality '96

Jo, Maria
(Yuen Chi Wai, Xuan Zhi Hui, Maria Yuen)
Lethal Panther '91
Seeding of a Ghost '83

Jo, Yoshimitsu
Lone Wolf and Cub 4: Baby Cart in Peril '72

Joh Hau Foo
Dragon Kid '90

Joles, Bob
Jackie Chan Adventures 2: The Dark Hand Returns '00 (V)

Jones, Tony
The Accidental Spy '01

Joo Jin-mo
Happy End '99

Josephine
Murder in the Orient '74

Joshi, Mohan
Elaan '94

Jova, Jovi
Adrenaline Drive '99

Jun Ji-hyun
My Sassy Girl '01

Jung, Allen
The Green Hornet '74

Jung Ysao Shao
Fantasy Mission Force '84

Junior, Joe
C'est la Vie, Mon Cheri '93
Master Q 2001 '01
Troublesome Night 14 '02

Junna, Risa
Midnight Fly '01

Ka Hai
Crippled Masters '80

Kadokae, Kazue
Ring 0: Birthday '00

Kadowaki, Saburo
Akira Kurosawa's Dreams '90
Battle in Outer Space '59
Terror of MechaGodzilla '75

Kagawa, Kyoko
(Kyoko Ikebe)
After Life '98
High and Low '63
Madadayo '92
Mothra '61

Kagawa, Yukie
Female Convict Scorpion: Jailhouse 41 '72

Kahler, Beverly
Terror beneath the Sea '66

Kai, Harumi
Big Boobs Buster '90

Kai, Hiroko
Gamera vs. Guiron '69

Kaji, Masaki
Time of the Apes '75

Kaji, Meiko
Female Convict Scorpion: Jailhouse 41 '72

Kajima, Nobuhiro
Gamera vs. Guiron '69

Kam, Andrew
(Kam Yeung Wa, Gam Yeung Wa, Jin Yang Hua)
Full Alert '97
Gunmen '88
The Legend of the Swordsman '92

Kam Fung Ling
(Kim Fung Lin, Gam Fung Ling, Jin Feng Ling, Chin Feng Ling. Kam Fung Ling)
Lady Iron Monkey '83

Kam Hing-yin
(Kim Hing Yiu, Kam Hing Ying)
The Most Wanted '94
Police Story '85
Royal Warriors '86

Kam Kong
(Kum Kong, Gam Gong, Jin Gang, King Kong, Chin Kang, Kam Kan, King Kang)
Beast Cops '98
The Blazing Temple '76
Exit the Dragon, Enter the Tiger '75
Half a Loaf of Kung Fu '77
The Invincible Kung Fu Trio '78
The Iron Monkey '77

Lady Whirlwind and the Rangers '74
Lady Wu Tang '77
The Legendary Strike '78
The Massive '78
Master of the Flying Guillotine '74
Return of the Chinese Boxer '75
The Shaolin Kids '77
Shaolin Wooden Men '76
Snake and Crane Arts of Shaolin '78

Kam Kwok-leung
Killer Snakes '74

Kam Yuen Chu
Killer of Snake, Fox of Shaolin '78

Kamiaka, Toshiro
Versus '00

Kamimura, Kiyoko
Erotic Ghost Story '90

Kamo, Kazue
Black Tight Killers '66

Kan Chia-fong
(Gam Ga Fung, Gan Gu Feng, Kam Kar Fung)
Dragon Lee vs. the Five Brothers '78
Dragon's Claws '79
Dreadnaught '81
Young Tiger '72

Kan Mie Chai
Hero's Blood '91

Kanaoko, Shin
(Nobu Kanaoko)
Tetsuo 2: Body Hammer '91
Tetsuo: The Iron Man '89

Kanda, Koji
Akira Kurosawa's Dreams '90
Lone Wolf and Cub 6: White Heaven in Hell '74
The Razor 1: Sword of Justice '90

Kanda, Takashi
Prince of Space '59
Wrath of Daimajin '66

Kaneko, Nobuo
(Noburo Kaneko)
Fight, Zatoichi, Fight! '64
Godzilla 1985 '84
The Magic Serpent '66
Shogun '80

Kaneshiro, Takeshi
(Gam Shing Miu, Jin Cheng Wu, Gum Sing Mo)
Anna Magdalena '98
Chungking Express '94

Don't Give a Damn '95
Downtown Torpedoes '97
Executioners '93
Fallen Angels '95
Lavender '00
The Odd One Dies '97

Kang Ho
Double Dragon in the Last Duel '85

Kang Jian Min
Extreme Challenge '01

Kang Seong-jin
Attack the Gas Station! '99
Hi! Dharma! '01
Record '00

Kanhaiyalal
Hum Paanch '80

Kanie, Keizo
The Razor 2: The Snare '73
The Razor 3: Who's Got the Gold? '74

Kanno, Miho
The Hypnotist '99

Kanno, Rio
Dark Water '02

Kano, Kazuko
Black Tight Killers '66

Kao Chen Peng
Two Dragons Fight against Tiger '75

Kao, Jack
(Go Chit, Gao Jie, Ko Kin)
The Conman '98
Full Alert '97
Moonlight Express '99
Time and Tide '00

Kao Ming
(Go Ming, Gao Ming)
Fighting Ace '79
A Touch of Zen '69

Kao Po
The Hot, the Cool, and the Vicious '76

Kao, Thompson
Dirty Kung Fu '78

Kao Yuen
(Go Yuen, Gao Yuan, Ko Yuen)
The Eagle's Killer '81
The Story in Temple Red Lily '79

Kapadia, Dimple
Aakhri Adalat '88

Kar-Wing, Lau
(Lau Ga Wing, Liu Gu Rong, Bruce Lau, Liu Chia Yung, Liu Chia Jen, Liu Chia Rong)
Dirty Kung Fu '78

Dirty Tiger, Crazy Frog '78
Don't Give a Damn '95
The Dragon Family '88
Dragon's Claws '79
Dragons Forever '88
Fist Power '99
Fists and Guts '79
Game of Death '78
He Has Nothing But Kung Fu '77
His Name Is Nobody '79
Invincible Pole Fighter '83
Knockabout '79
Kung Pow: Enter the Fist '76/2001
Legendary Weapons of China '82
Legend of the 7 Golden Vampires '74
Martial Arts Mayhem, Vol. 2 '99
Master of the Flying Guillotine '74
The Millionaires' Express '86
My Lucky Stars '85
Odd Couple '79
Prodigal Boxer '73
Shaolin King Boxer '79
Shaolin Mantis '78
Shaolin Master Killer '78
Skinny Tiger and Fatty Dragon '90
The 36 Crazy Fists '77
Thunder Kick '73
Tiger on Beat '88
Twin Dragons '92
Twinkle Twinkle Lucky Stars '85
Warrior from Shaolin '81
Young Tiger '73

Kar-yan, Leung
(Leung Kar Yan, Liang Jairen, Brian Leung, Liang Chao Yun)
The Big Sting '82
Cantonen Iron Kung Fu '79
Cold War '00
Conman in Tokyo '00
Crystal Hunt '91
Don't Give a Damn '95
Dreadnaught '81
Eagle's Claw '77
Enter the Fat Dragon '78
Fearless Dragons '79
Fight Back to School 3 '93
Flirting Scholar '93
His Name Is Nobody '79
The Iron Monkey '77
Justice, My Foot! '92
Knockabout '79
The Last Blood '90
Last Hero in China '93

Legend of the Dragon '91
Lord of the Wu Tang '93
The Miracle Fighters '82
The New Marvelous Double '92
Odd Couple '79
The Postman Fights Back '82
Red Shield '91
The Shaolin Disciple '80
Shaolin King Boxer '79
Shogun and Little Kitchen '92
Tiger Cage '88
The Tigers '91
Twinkle Twinkle Lucky Stars '85
The Victim '80
Ways of Kung Fu '80

Kar-Ying, Law
(Lau Ga Ying, Luo Gu Ying, Lo Ka-Ying)
All's Well End's Well '97 '97
The Chinese Feast '95
A Chinese Odyssey Part 1: Pandora's Box '95
A Chinese Odyssey Part 2: Cinderella '95
City of Desire '01
Combo Cops '96
Crime Story '93
Dragon from Shaolin '96
Forbidden City Cop '96
From Beijing with Love '94
God of Cookery '96
God of Gamblers Returns '94
He's a Woman, She's a Man '94
Lawyer Lawyer '97
Man Wanted '95
Shaolin Soccer '01
Take 2 in Life '92
Tricky Master '99

Karasuma, Setsuko
Twilight of the Cockroaches '87

Karita, Toyomi
Warning from Space '56

Karyo, Tchéky
Kiss of the Dragon '01

Kasahara, Reiko
Gamera vs. Guiron '69
Gamera vs. Gyaos '67
Gamera vs. Zigra '71
Lone Wolf and Cub 1: Sword of Vengeance '72
Lone Wolf and Cub 2: Baby Cart at the River Styx '72

Kase, Takao
Ultraman Tiga and Ultraman Dyna: The Warriors of the Lightning Star '98

Kashino, Sachi
Zeram '91

Kashiwabara, Takashi
Another Heaven '00

Kashiyama, Goki
Maborosi '95

Kasuga, Akira
Mighty Jack '68

Katayama, Takehiro
Versus '00

Kato, Daiko
Entrails of the Virgin '86

Kato, Daisuke
Chushingura '62
Rashomon '50
Samurai 1: Musashi Miyamoto '54
Samurai 2: Duel at Ichi-joji Temple '55
Samurai 3: Duel at Ganryu Island '56
Seven Samurai '54
Yojimbo '61

Kato, Go
Lone Wolf and Cub 3: Baby Cart to Hades '72

Kato, Haruhiko
Another Heaven '00
Pulse '01

Kato, Haruya
Dagora the Space Monster '64
Frankenstein vs. Baragon '65
Ghidorah the Three-Headed Monster '64
King Kong vs. Godzilla '62
Mothra '61
The Mysterians '57

Kato, Hiroshi
Contract Killer '98

Kato, Kazuko
Gamera 3: The Revenge of Irys '99
Godzilla vs. Megaguirus '00
Godzilla, Mothra and King Ghidorah: Battle on Fire '01
Ultraman Gaia: The Battle in Hyperspace '98

Kato, Kazuo
Body Snatcher from Hell '68

High and Low '63
Ran '85

Kato, Masaya
(Masaya Katoh)
Brother '00
Nobody '99
Okinawa Rendez-vous '00

Kato, Mutsuko
Reborn from Hell: Samurai Armageddon '96

Kato, Sayoko
Lone Wolf and Cub 3: Baby Cart to Hades '72

Kato, Shigeo
Akira Kurosawa's Dreams '90
Battle in Outer Space '59
Godzilla 1985 '84
The H-Man '58
Terror of MechaGodzilla '75
Yog: Monster from Space '70

Kato, Takeshi
High and Low '63
Ran '85
Zatoichi's Revenge '64

Kato, Yoshi
Lone Wolf and Cub 5: Baby Cart in the Land of Demons '73
Ninja: Band of Assassins '62
Tampopo '87

Katsu, Shintaro
(Toshio Okumura, Katsumaru Kineya, Sing San Taai Long, Sheng Xin Tai Lang) See also sidebar on p. 694.
Adventures of a Blind Man '64
Blind Swordsman: The Tale of Zatoichi '62
Fight, Zatoichi, Fight! '64
New Tale of Zatoichi '63
The Razor 1: Sword of Justice '72
The Razor 2: The Snare '73
The Razor 3: Who's Got the Gold? '74
Saga of the Phoenix '90
Samaritan Zatoichi '68
The Tale of Zatoichi Continues '62
Zatoichi and the Chess Expert '65
Zatoichi and the Chest of Gold '64

Zatoichi and the Doomed Man '65
Zatoichi and the Fugitives '68
Zatoichi Challenged '67
Zatoichi on the Road '63
Zatoichi's Cane Sword '66
Zatoichi's Flashing Sword '64
Zatoichi's Revenge '64
Zatoichi's Vengeance '66
Zatoichi the Fugitive '63
Zatoichi the Outlaw '67

Katsumura, Jun
The Razor 2: The Snare '73

Katsumura, Masanobu
Sonatine '93

Katsura, Kokan
Gappa: The Triphibian Monster '67

Katsuragi, Aya
Big Boobs Buster '90
Evil Dead Trap '88

Kawada, Clifford
Varan the Unbelievable '58 (U.S.)

Kawaguchi, Hiroshi
Giants and Toys '58

Kawai, Toru
Terror of MechaGodzilla '75

Kawai, Yu
Tokyo Decameron: Three Tales of Madness and Sensuality '96

Kawaide, Sho
The Ladies' Phone Sex Club '96

Kawaji, Tamio
Gappa: The Triphibian Monster '67
Tokyo Drifter '66

Kawakami, Maiko
Violent Cop '89

Kawasaki, Keizo
Warning from Space '56

Kawase, Hiroyuki
Godzilla vs. Hedorah '71
Godzilla vs. Megalon '73
Time of the Apes '75

Kawashima, Megumi
Entrails of the Virgin '86

Kawaya, Setchin
Cure '97
Fireworks '97
Ichi the Killer '01

Kawazu, Seizaburo
Chushingura '62
Dagora the Space Monster '64
The Last War '61
Mothra '61
The Secret of the Telegian '60
Yojimbo '61

Kawazu, Yusuke
Gamera 2: Advent of Legion '96
Gamera 3: The Revenge of Irys '99
Godzilla vs. MechaGodzilla 2 '93

Kayama, Natsuko
Big Boobs Buster '90

Kayama, Yuzo
Chushingura '62
Sanjuro '63
Thunderbolt '95

Kayumi, Iemasa
Ghost in the Shell '95 (V)

Kazama, Kenji
Sting of the Dragon Masters '73

Kazama, Maiko
Beautiful Hunter '94

Kazuhiko, Nishimura
Para Para Sakura '01

Kazusaki, Toshiya
Reborn from Hell: Samurai Armageddon '96
The X from Outer Space '67

Kazuyo, Sumida
Lone Wolf and Cub 5: Baby Cart in the Land of Demons '73

Ke Quan, Jonathan
Second Time Around '02

Keawprasert, Montatip
Aces Go Places 5: The Terracotta Hit '89

Kee, George
(Kee Cheung, George Cheung, George Kee Cheung, George Chang)
The Adventurers '95
First Strike '96
The Master '89
Rush Hour '98

Kee, Merle
5 Lady Venoms '78

Keesee, Oscar Jr.
Brides of Blood '68
Terror Is a Man '59

Keesee, Reyton
Terror Is a Man '59

Kei, Eric
(Gei Ga Faay, Ji Gu Fa, Eric Kee, Erik Kei)
Dr. Lamb '92
Organized Crime and Triad Bureau '94
Red Shield '91

Keiji, Sato
Expect the Unexpected '98
Gen-X Cops '99
The Mission '99

Keisuke
Sumo Vixens '96

Keith, Michael
King Kong vs. Godzilla (U.S. version) '62

Kelly, Jim
(Chim Gei Lei, Zhan Ji Li)
Enter the Dragon '73
Martial Arts Mayhem, Vol. 1 '99

Kelly, Laura
Devil Man '87 (V)

Kemmerling, Warren
Godzilla 1985 (U.S. version) '84 (U.S.)

Kengo
The Ladies' Phone Sex Club '96

Kennedy, Philip
Bruce Lee Fights Back from the Grave '76

Kent, Regina
(Gaan Wai Jan, Jian Hui Zhen, Gan Wai Chan)
A Better Tomorrow 2 '87
The Inspector Wears Skirts '88
Legacy of Rage '86
Project A 2 '87

Kent, Samuel
Rivals of the Dragon '83

Kerner, Brad
Aces Go Places 5: The Terracotta Hit '89

Kerns, Joanna
A*P*E '76

Kerver, Robert
Fists Like Lee '74
Story of the Dragon '76

Keung, Patrick
(Keung Hiu Man, Geung Hiu Man, Geung Hiuman, Jiang Hao Wen, Keung Hon Man)

The Blood Rules '00
City of Desire '01
Crime of a Beast '01

Khan, Amjad
Sholay '75

Khan, Cynthia
(Yeung Lai-ching, Cynthia Yang, Yang Li Qing)
Angel on Fire '95
Deadend of Besiegers '92
In the Line of Duty 3 '88
In the Line of Duty 4 '89
In the Line of Duty 5: Middle Man '90
Queen's High '91

Khanna, Vinod
Aakhri Adalat '88

Khurana, Akash
Raat '91

Khushant
Raat '91

Ki, Howard
Duel of the Tao Tough '82

Ki Joo-bong
Bichunmoo '99

Kibble, Lorraine
Doctor Vampire '90

Kiel, Richard
Aces Go Places 3 '84

Kikuchi, Takanori
Beautiful Beast '95
Ghost Actress '96

Kim Chang-wan
Ring Virus '99

Kim Chin-lin
(Kim Ching Lan, Chen Chin Lan, Gam Ching Lan, Chin Cheng- lan)
Blooded Treasury Fight '79
Half a Loaf of Kung Fu '77
Snake and Crane Arts of Shaolin '78

Kim Fun
(Kim Fan, Jian Xun)
Ninja vs. Shaolin Guards '84
Shaolin Chastity Kung Fu '81

Kim Gi-joo
Masters of Martial Arts '74

Kim Hak-chu
Bichunmoo '99

Kim Hee-sun
(Kim Hee-seon)
Bichunmoo '99

Kim Ho Kon
Heroes Shed No Tears '83/86

Kim Hyeon-jeong
(Kim Hyeong-jong)
Bloody Beach '00
Volcano High School '01

Kim Hyun-jung
Bloody Beach '00

Kim In-moon
Hi! Dharma! '01

Kim In-mun
My Sassy Girl '01

Kim Jee-Kee
Beauty Investigator '92

Kim, Larry
Golden Dragon Silver Snake '79

Kim, Martin
Dragon against Vampire '85

Kim Min-jeong
(Kim Min-jong)
The Accidental Spy '01
Gate of Destiny '96

Kim Min-sun
Memento Mori '99

Kim, Samson
Scorpion Thunderbolt '85

Kim Se-dong
Dream of Garuda '94
Sympathy for Mr. Vengeance '01

Kim, Sheila
Rage of the Dragon '79

Kim Su-ro
(Kim So-roh)
Bichunmoo '99
The Foul King '00
Hi! Dharma! '01
Volcano High School '01

Kim, Sujin
Tetsuo 2: Body Hammer '91

Kim Sung-lim
Gate of Destiny '96

Kim Tae-woo
(Kim Tae-won)
Joint Security Area '00

Kim Yun-jin
(Kim Yoon-jin)
Shiri '99

Kimura, Isao
(Ko Kimura)
High and Low '63
Lone Wolf and Cub 6: White Heaven in Hell '74
Seven Samurai '54

Stray Dog '49
Throne of Blood '57

Kimura, Kazuya
Gonin '95

Kimura, Sakae
Akira Kurosawa's Dreams '90
Godzilla, Mothra, King Ghidorah: Battle on Fire '01
Godzilla 2000 '99
Ran '85

Kimura, Taky
Bruce Lee: A Warrior's Journey '00

Kimura, Toshie
Godzilla vs. Hedorah '71

King, Alan
Rush Hour 2 '01

King, Doris
Return of the Deadly Blade '81

King Kee Cho
The Snake Strikes Back '81

King, Mark
Fight Back to School 2 '92
Once upon a Time in China '91
Operation Condor '91
Powerful Four '91

King-Tan, Yuen
(Yuen King Daan, Yuan Qiong Dan, King Yuen)
A Chinese Torture Chamber Story '94
Combo Cops '96
Cop Shop Babes '01
The East Is Red '93
The Eternal Evil of Asia '95
Everyday Is Valentine '01
Fight Back to School '91
Flirting Scholar '93
Forbidden City Cop '96
God of Cookery '96
Hail the Judge '94
Justice, My Foot! '92
King of Beggars '92
Last Hero in China '93
Legendary Couple '95
Sex and the Emperor '94
The Tricky Master '00
Troublesome Night '97
Vampire Controller '00
Wing Chun '94

Kinko
(Siu Kam Chi, Kiu Wang Taai Taai, Qiao Hong Tai Tai)
Cold War '00

771

Kinomoto, Ryo
Ultraman Tiga and
Ultraman Dyna: The
Warriors of the
Lightning Star '98

Kinoshita, Houka
Godzilla vs. Space
Godzilla '94
Ichi the Killer '01
Sonatine '93

Kirino, Nadao
(Hiriwo Kirino, Hiro-0
Kirino)
Battle in Outer Space
'59
Chushingura '62
Dagora the Space Mon-
ster '64
Destroy All Monsters
'68
Frankenstein vs.
Baragon '65
The H-Man '58
Invasion of Astro-Mon-
ster '65
King Kong Escapes '67
King Kong vs. Godzilla
'62
The Last War '61
The Secret of the
Telegian '60
Varan the Unbelievable
'58
War of the Gargantuas
'66
Yojimbo '61

Kiritachi, Hirumi
Giant Monster Gamera
'65

Kiriyama, Eiju
Beautiful Beast '95

Kishi, Keiko
Kwaidan '64

Kishibe, Ittoku
The Funeral '84
Shark Skin Man and
Peach Hip Girl '98
Violent Cop '89

Kishida, Kyoko
Ninja: Band of Assas-
sins '62
Sure Death: Revenge
'87
Woman in the Dunes
'64

Kishida, Mori
The Razor 2: The Snare
'73

Kishida, Shin
Godzilla vs.
MechaGodzilla '74
Lone Wolf and Cub 2:
Baby Cart at the
River Styx '72
Lone Wolf and Cub 4:
Baby Cart in Peril
'72
Shogun Assassin '80

Kishimoto, Kayoko
Fireworks '97
Kikujiro '99

Kishimoto, Yuji
Junk '99

Kita, Akemi
Black Tight Killers '66

Kita, Daihachi
Gamera vs. Zigra '71
Giant Monster Gamera
'65

Kita, Ryuji
Tokyo Drifter '66
The X from Outer Space
'67

Kitabayashi, Tanie
Return of Daimajin '66

Kitagawa, Tsutomu
Godzilla 2000 '99
Godzilla vs. Megaguirus
'00

Kitagawa, Yujin
Zero Woman: The
Accused '96

Kitahara, Rina
Lady Ninja: Reflections
of Darkness '96

Kitahara, Yoshiro
Gamera vs. Barugon
'66
Gamera vs. Gyaos '67
Gamera vs. Viras '68
Giant Monster Gamera
'65

Kitamura, Eizo
Body Snatcher from
Hell '68
The Street Fighter's
Last Revenge '74

Kitamura, Kazuki
Freeze Me '00

Kitamura, Kazuo
Warm Water under a
Red Bridge '01

Kitamura, Yukiya
Warm Water under a
Red Bridge '01

**Kitano, "Beat"
Takeshi**
Battle Royale '00
Boiling Point '90
Brother '00
Fireworks '97
Gonin '00
Kikujiro '99
Sonatine '93
Violent Cop '89

Kitano, Takuya
The Razor 2: The Snare
'73

Kitigawa, Tsutomu
Godzilla 2000 '99

Kitsuwon, Supakorn
Mon-Rak Transistor '01

Kiuchi, Midori
Maborosi '95

Kiyokawa, Shoji
Men Who Tread on the
Tiger's Tail '43
Sanshiro Sugata '43

Kiyoshi, Beat
Kikujiro '99

Kiyoshima, Tomoko
Legend of the
Dinosaurs '77

Kizuki, Saeko
Entrails of the Virgin
'86

Kizumi, Masayuki
Guinea Pig: The Making
of Guinea Pig '86

Kjaer, Peter
Doctor Vampire '90

Kleine, John
Terror beneath the Sea
'66

Klemma, Vladimir
Dersu Uzala '74

Ko, Blackie
(Ko Shou-Liang, Blacky
Ko)
The Best of the Best
'96
Chivalrous Legend '98
City of Desire '01
Crime Story '93
Curry & Pepper '90
Doctor No... '01
Don't Give a Damn '95
The Enforcer '95
Fight Back to School 2
'92
For Bad Boys Only '00
God of Gamblers 2 '90
God of Gamblers
Returns '94
Heart of Dragon '85
Her Name Is Cat 2:
Journey to Death
'01
Legend of Speed '99
The Masked Prosecutor
'99
Return of the Chinese
Boxer '75
Return of the Tiger '79
Rosa '86
Royal Warriors '86
The Shaolin Invincibles
'79
Thunderbolt '95
Undercover Blues '00
Young and Dangerous
6: Born to Be King
'00

Ko Chun
(Goo Gwan, Gu Jun, Ko
Chiang, Gou Shung,
Kao Chiang)

Blooded Treasury Fight
'79
Hit-Man in the Hand of
Buddha '80
Killer Priest '81
Screaming Ninja '73
Snake-Crane Secret
'78

Ko, Clifton
(Ko Chi-sum, Go Chi
Sam, Gao Zhi Sen)
All's Well End's Well '92
Task Force '97
Twin Dragons '92

Ko, Eddie
(Ko Hung, Eddy Ko,
Edward Ko, Kuo Hsi-
ung, Gao Xiong, Kao
Hsiung, Ku Un- chung,
Kao Shiung)
Angel '87
Avenging Eagle '78
Bloody Fight '72
The Bride with White
Hair '93
The Bride with White
Hair 2 '93
The Butterfly Murders
'79
Casino Raiders '89
Duel of the Brave Ones
'78
Duel to the Death '82
The East Is Red '93
The End of the Wicked
Tiger '81
Executioners '93
Fist of Fury '95
Flash Future Kung Fu
'83
Heroes Shed No Tears
'83/86
The Hero of Swallow
'96
Hit-Man in the Hand of
Buddha '80
Justice, My Foot! '92
Lee Rock '91
The Miracle Fighters
'82
The Mission '99
Monkey Fist Floating
Snake '79
The Peacock King '89
The Postman Fights
Back '82
The Private Eyes '76
Rumble in the Bronx
'95
We're Going to Eat You!
'80

Ko, Hideo
Body Snatcher from
Hell '68

Ko Ho-kyung
The Foul King '00

Ko Hon-man
Love au Zen '01

Ko Jan Pang
(Go Jan Paang, Gao
Zhen Peng)
Challenge of Death '78

Ko Keung
Blooded Treasury Fight
'79
Dragon Fist '78
Fatal Flying Guillotines
'77
Half a Loaf of Kung Fu
'78
Hand of Death '75
Spiritual Kung Fu '78

Ko, Lewis
Magnificent Natural
Fist '80

Ko, Phillip
(Ko Fei, Ko Fai, Philip
Koa, Gan Fei, Phillip Ku)
The Adventurers '95
Angel on Fire '95
Battle of Shaolin '77
Cantonen Iron Kung Fu
'79
Death Duel of Kung Fu
'79
The Dragon Family '88
Dragon on Fire '79
Dragons Forever '88
Dreadnaught '81
Eagle's Claw '77
Eastern Condors '86
The 8 Masters '77
The 18 Jade Arhats '78
Fearless Dragons '79
The Fist, the Kicks and
the Evils '79
Fury in Shaolin Temple
'82
Goose Boxer '78
Guardian Angel '96
Heart of Dragon '85
The Hot, the Cool, and
the Vicious '76
The Invincible Armour
'77
Invincible Pole Fighter
'83
The Killer Meteors '76
Killer Priest '81
Killer's Romance '90
Lethal Panther 2 '93
The Massive '78
Millennium Dragon '99
The Millionaires'
Express '86
On the Run '88
The Owl vs. Bombo '84
Return of the Chinese
Boxer '75
Revengeful Sword-
women '79
Scared Stiff '86
Seeding of a Ghost '83
Shadow of the Tiger
'79
Snake Deadly Act '79
Tiger on Beat '88
Tiger over Wall '80
Twinkle Twinkle Lucky
Stars '85

Ko Yuan
Succubare '77

Kobayashi, Akira
Black Tight Killers '66

Kobayashi, Asei
Madadayo '92

Kobayashi, Chizu
Lone Wolf and Cub 1:
    Sword of
    Vengeance '72
Lone Wolf and Cub 6:
    White Heaven in
    Hell '74

Kobayashi, Hiroshi
Ichi the Killer '01

Kobayashi, Hitomi
Evil Dead Trap '88

Kobayashi, Kaoru
Twilight of the Cock-
    roaches '87

**Kobayashi, Kat-
suhiko**
Ninja: Band of Assas-
    sins '63
Zatoichi the Fugitive
    '63

Kobayashi, Keiju
Chushingura '62
Godzilla 1985 '84
Sanjuro '63

Kobayashi, Kooji
The Razor 1: Sword of
    Justice '72

Kobayashi, Masahiro
Godzilla, Mothra and
    King Ghidorah: Bat-
    tle on Fire '01

Kobayashi, Megumi
Rebirth of Mothra '96
Rebirth of Mothra 2 '97

Kobayashi, Satomi
Godzilla vs. Mothra '92

Kobayashi, Shoji
(Akiji Kobayashi)
Gamera 2: Advent of
    Legion '96
Godzilla vs. King Ghido-
    rah '91
Godzilla vs. Mothra '92
Kwaidan '64
Lone Wolf and Cub 2:
    Baby Cart at the
    River Styx '72
Shogun Assassin '80

Kobayashi, Tsuruko
Varan the Unbelievable
    '58 (U.S.)

Kobayashi, Yukiko
Destroy All Monsters
    '68
Yog: Monster from
    Space '70

Kobori, Akio
Rodan '56

Kochi, Momoko
(Momoko Okouchi)
Godzilla vs. Destroyah
    '95
Godzilla, King of the
    Monsters '54
Half Human '55/1957
The Mysterians '57

Kodo, Kokuten
(Kuninori Kodo, Kuniori
Kodo)
Godzilla, King of the
    Monsters '54
Half Human '55/1957
Samurai 2: Duel at Ichi-
    joji Temple '55
Samurai 3: Duel at
    Ganryu Island '56
Sanshiro Sugata '43
Seven Samurai '54
Stray Dog '49
Throne of Blood '57

Kodo, Kunimori
Samurai 2: Duel at Ichi-
    joji Temple '55

Koga, Nobuaki
Guinea Pig: The Making
    of Guinea Pig '86

Kogure, Michiyo
Samurai 2: Duel at Ichi-
    joji Temple '55

Kohinata, Fumiyo
Audition '99
Dark Water '02
Ring 2 '99

Kohinata, Sie
Shark Skin Man and
    Peach Hip Girl '98

Koleyama, Akira
Extreme Crisis '98

Koike, Asao
(Tomoo Koike)
Lone Wolf and Cub 4:
    Baby Cart in Peril
    '72
The Razor 3: Who's Got
    the Gold? '74
Shogun's Ninja '82
Zatoichi Challenged
    '67

Koirala, Manisha
Champion '00

Koizumi, Aya
Sumo Vixens '96

Koizumi, Hiroshi
Attack of the Mush-
    room People '63
Chushingura '62
Dagora the Space Mon-
    ster '64
Ghidorah the Three-
    Headed Monster
    '64

Godzilla Raids Again
    '55
Godzilla vs.
    MechaGodzilla '74
Mothra '61
Mothra vs. Godzilla '64

Kok Lee-yan
(Hao Lu Ren, Hao Li
Jen, Ho Lee Yan)
The Bloody Fists '72
Enter the Dragon '73
Killer Snakes '74
Shaolin Master Killer
    '78
Thunder Kick '73
A Touch of Zen '69
Tower of Death '81

Kok Siu-man
(Hao Shao Wen, Ronald
Kwok, Fok Siu Man)
Dragon from Shaolin
    '96
Faces of Horror '98

Kok, Vincent
(Kok Tak-Chiu, De Zhou
Gu)
The Accidental Spy '01
All's Well End's Well '92
Armageddon '97
Ballistic Kiss '98
Big Bullet '96
Double Tap '00
F*** / Off '98
Flirting Scholar '93
Forbidden City Cop '96
Gen-Y Cops '00
God of Cookery '96
Gorgeous '99
High Risk '95
Lawyer Lawyer '97
Love on Delivery '94
Love Paradox '00
Merry-Go-Round '01
Okinawa Rendez-vous
    '00
Shaolin Soccer '01
Tiramisu '02
Troublesome Night 3
    '97
You Shoot, I Shoot '01

Kokkyou, Mou
Beautiful Beast '95

Kokumai, Aya
Sonatine '93

Komada, Tsugutoshi
Godzilla vs. Megalon
    '73

Komatsu, Hosei
Female Convict Scorpi-
    on: Jailhouse 41
    '72
The Razor 2: The Snare
    '73
Zatoichi and the Fugi-
    tives '68

Komatsu, Miyuki
Gamera 2: Advent of
    Legion '96

Komiya, Mitsue
Invasion of the Nep-
    tune Men '61

Komiya, Motonari
Versus '00

Kon Tak Mun
(Gon Tak Moon, Gan De
Men)
The Buddha Assassina-
    tor '80
Fantasy Mission Force
    '84
The World of the Drunk-
    en Master '79

Konaka, Matsujiro
Lone Wolf and Cub 5:
    Baby Cart in the
    Land of Demons
    '73
Lone Wolf and Cub 6:
    White Heaven in
    Hell '74

Kondo, Harry
Sister Street Fighter
    '74

Kondo, Rie
Sadistic City '93

Kondo, Yoshimasa
Godzilla, Mothra and
    King Ghidorah: Bat-
    tle on Fire '01
Godzilla 2000 '99

Koneko, Mitsunobu
Voyage into Space '67

Kong, Alvina
(Kong Yan Yin, Jiang Xin
Yan)
Crocodile Hunter '89
Forbidden City Cop '96
Iceman Cometh '89
In the Line of Duty 5:
    Middle Man '90
Miracles '89
Police Story 2 '88
Sixty Million Dollar Man
    '95

Kong Ban
Sorrowful to a Ghost
    '70

Kong Ching-ha
(Jiang Qing Xia, Chiang
Ching-hsia, Kwong
Chen Ha, Chang Ching
Ha)
The 18 Jade Arhats '78
Green Dragon Inn '79
The Master of Death
    '82
Militant Eagle '78
One Foot Crane '79
To Kill with Intrigue '77
Yoga and Kung Fu Girl
    '78

Kong Do
(Jiang Dao, Chiang Tao,
Chang Tao, Kong Tao,
Kong To, Cheng Tao)

Blind Fist of Bruce '79
Chinese Hercules '73
Death Mask of the
    Ninja '82
8 Diagram Fighter '91
Executioners from
    Shaolin '77
Fearless Dragons '79
A Fistful of Talons '83
Golden Dragon Silver
    Snake '79
He Has Nothing But
    Kung Fu '77
Kung Fu's Hero '73
Kung Fu Zombie '81
The Legend of Bruce
    Lee '80
Lightning Kung Fu '80
The Master of Death
    '82
Ninja vs. Bruce Lee '82
Return of the Master
    Killer '80
Super Gang '78
10 Magnificent Killers
    '77
Ten Tigers of Shaolin
    '78
Tiger over Wall '80
Warrior from Shaolin
    '81
The Young Avenger '79

Kong, Donald
Robo Vampire '88

Kong Fu-keung
Victim '99

Kong, Hon
(Han Jiang, Han Chi-
ang)
Fearless Fighters '73
Killer Priest '81
Rage of the Masters
    '74
Sorrowful to a Ghost
    '70
Swordsman with an
    Umbrella '70

Kong Hyo-jin
Volcano High School
    '01

Kong, Irene
Dragon against Vam-
    pire '85

Kong Lai Lai
Real Kung Fu of
    Shaolin, Part 1 '81

Kong Lai Loh
990714.com '00

Kong, Liz
(Kong Hei Man, Jiang Xi
Wen)
God of Cookery '96

Kong Lung
(Jiang Long)
Dragons Forever '88
Long Arm of the Law
    '84

Kong, Queenie
(Kong Hoh Yan, Jiang Ke Xin)
Blind Fist of Bruce '79
Kung Fu's Hero '73

Kong, Richard
Eagle vs. Silver Fox '83

Kong Yeh
Super Kung Fu Kid '74

Kong Yeung
(Jiang Yang, Chiang Yang, Kong Yang)
The Flying Guillotine '74
Iron Neck Li '81

Kono, Aritake
Men Who Tread on the Tiger's Tail '43

Konoe, Jushiro
Zatoichi Challenged '67

Konta
Postman Blues '97

Koo, Jo
(Jo Kuk Cho-Lam, Guk Jo Lam, Gu Zu Lin)
Born Wild '01
Hit Team '00
Jiang Hu-"The Triad Zone" '00
Visible Secret '01

Koo, Josephine
(Koo Mei Wah, Goo Mei Wa, Gu Mei Hua)
Shogun and Little Kitchen '92
Supercop '92

Koo, Leo
(Koo Kui Kei, Goo Gui Gei, Gu Ju Ji, Leo Ku, Strange Kei)
Love on Delivery '94
Task Force '97

Koo, Louis
(Koo Tin Lok, Goo Tin Lok, Gu Tian Le)
Born Wild '01
Brassiere '01
Bullets over Summer '99
Century of the Dragon '99
Conman in Tokyo '00
For Bad Boys Only '00
God.com '98
The Masked Prosecutor '99
Super Car Criminals '99
The Suspect '98
Troublesome Night '97
Troublesome Night 3 '97
Troublesome Night 4 '98
Zu Warriors '01

Kordica, Farlie Ruth
(Fairlie Ruth Kordick, Lau Fo Goh Dik, Lou Fu Ge Di)
In the Line of Duty 4 '89

Kosugi, Kane
Who Am I? '98

Kosugi, Yoshio
Chushingura '62
Frankenstein vs. Baragon '65
Ghidorah the Three-Headed Monster '64
The Human Vapor '60
King Kong vs. Godzilla '62
Men Who Tread on the Tiger's Tail '43
Mothra '61
Mothra vs. Godzilla '64
The Mysterians '57
Samurai 1: Musashi Miyamoto '54
Sanshiro Sugata '43
Seven Samurai '54

Kot, Eric
(Kot Man Fai, Got Man Fai, Ge Min Hui)
A Chinese Ghost Story: The Tsui Hark Animation '97 (V)
City Hunter '92
Everyday Is Valentine '01
Gen-Y Cops '00
Juliet in Love '00
Lawyer Lawyer '97
You Shoot, I Shoot '01

Koteas, Elias
Teenage Mutant Ninja Turtles '90

Koyama, Mami
Akira '88 (V)

Koyanagi, Keiko
The Razor 2: The Snare '73

Koyuki
Pulse '01

Kraft, Evelyne
Mighty Peking Man '77

Kramer, Steve
Ultraman 2 '01 (V)

Krayboir, Vinai
Snaker '01

Kristofferson, Kris
Blade 2 '02

Ku, Cynthia
Scorpion Thunderbolt '85

Ku Feng
(Guk Fung, Kok Fung, Kwok Fung)
Avenging Eagle '78
Brave Archer '77
Cheap Killers '98
A Chinese Ghost Story 2 '90
Crack Shadow Boxers '77
Death Mask of the Ninja '82
The Dragon Family '88
Dynamo '78
The Fist, the Kicks and the Evils '79
Five Deadly Venoms '78
The Flying Guillotine '74
Generation Consultant '90
Generation Pendragon '90
Hail the Judge '94
Hong Kong Nocturne '67
Legacy of Rage '86
Legend of the Drunken Tiger '92
Lightning Kung Fu '80
Magnificent Warriors '87
Mighty Peking Man '77
My Kung Fu 12 Kicks '79
New Mr. Vampire '86
990714.com '00
Peking Opera Blues '86
The Shaolin Disciple '80
The Shaolin Temple '79
Ten Tigers of Kwangtung '79
The 36 Crazy Fists '77
Tragic Fantasy: Tiger of Wanchai '94

Kubo, Akira
Attack of the Mushroom People '63
Chushingura '62
Destroy All Monsters '68
Gamera, Guardian of the Universe '95
Invasion of Astro-Monster '65
Sanjuro '63
Son of Godzilla '67
Throne of Blood '57
Yog: Monster from Space '70

Kubo, Naoko
Mighty Jack '68
Zatoichi's Flashing Sword '64

Kubo, Masaki
Hiruko the Goblin '90

Kudo, Shoko
(Shouko Kudou)
Sumo Vixens '96
Terminatrix '95

Kudoh, Youki
Blood: The Last Vampire '00 (V)

Kuga, Yoshiko
Good Morning '59

Kui, Sun Jian
The Shaolin Temple '79
Yellow River Fighter '88

Kumagai, Jiro
Attack of the Mushroom People '63
The Mysterians '57
Samurai 1: Musashi Miyamoto '54
Samurai 3: Duel at Ganryu Island '56
Seven Samurai '54
Varan the Unbelievable '58

Kumar, Akshay
Elaan '94

Kumar, Ashok
Mahal '48

Kumar, Manoj
Gumnaam '65

Kumar, Roopesh
Aakhri Adalat '88
Hum Paanch '80

Kumar, Sanjeev
Hum Paanch '80
Sholay '75

Kunimura, Jun
Audition '99
Ichi the Killer '01

Kuno, Makiko
Beautiful Hunter '94
Sugar-Howling of Angel '96

Kuno, Seichiro
Son of Godzilla '67

Kuo, Alan
Bullets of Love '01

Kuo Lu
The Hot, the Cool, and the Vicious '76

Kuo Shu-chung
(Gwok Siu Chong)
Fury of King Boxer '72

Kuo Wu-sing
Killer of Snake, Fox of Shaolin '78

Kurata, Tetsuo
Lady Ninja: Reflections of Darkness '96

Kurata, Yasuaki
(Chong Tin Biu Chiu, Cang Tian Bao Zhao, Shoji Kurata, Bruce Lo, Kurata Yasuaki, Yasuaki Kurota, Chong Ti Bochiu)
Aces Go Places 2 '83
BloodFight '89
Conman in Tokyo '00
Dragon Princess '81
Eastern Condors '86

Kuga, Yoshiko
Fist of Legend '94
The Executioner '74
Kung Fu, the Invisible Fist '72
Lady Whirlwind and the Rangers '74
A Life of Ninja '83
The Millionaires' Express '86
Ninja in the Deadly Trap '83
Prodigal Boxer '73
Return of the Deadly Blade '81
The Seventh Curse '86
Twinkle Twinkle Lucky Stars '85

Kurcz, Bob
A*P*E '76

Kurihara, Toshi
Reborn from Hell: Samurai Armageddon '96

Kuriyama, Chiaki
Battle Royale '00

Kurobe, Susumu
(Susume Kurobe)
Destroy All Monsters '68
Ghidorah the Three-Headed Monster '64
Godzilla vs. Megaguirus '00
Godzilla vs. Mothra '92
King Kong Escapes '67
Son of Godzilla '67
What's Up, Tiger Lily? '66

Kuroda, Yuhki
Sakuya: Slayer of Demons '00

Kurokawa, Rikiya
Love on a Diet '01

Kuroki, Hitomi
Dark Water '02

Kuroki, Kenzo
The Manster '60

Kurosawa, Toshio
The Razor 2: The Snare '73

Kusaka, Takeshi
Madadayo '92

Kusakawa, Naoya
Godzilla vs. Gigan '72

Kusama, Akio
Attack of the Mushroom People '63
The H-Man '58
Varan the Unbelievable '58

Kusano, Daigo
Lone Wolf and Cub 3: Baby Cart to Hades '72

Lone Wolf and Cub 6: White Heaven in Hell '74
The Razor 1: Sword of Justice '72
The Razor 2: The Snare '73
The Razor 3: Who's Got the Gold? '74

Kusumi, Momoru
Godzilla vs. MechaGodzilla '74

Kusunoki, Yuko
Body Snatcher from Hell '68

Kwan Choi-sung
A*P*E '76

Kwan Chung
(Gwaan Chung, Guan Cong)
Abbot White '82
Fatal Flying Guillotines '77
Ninja vs. Ninja '87
The Shaolin Disciple '80

Kwan, Emily
(Kwan Bo Wai, Gwan Bo Wai, Guan Bao Hui)
Dr. Lamb '92
Full Alert '97
God.com '98
Happy Family '02
Love Correction '00
Master Q 2001 '01
Nightmare Zone '98
Troublesome Night 4 '98
Troublesome Night 14 '02
The Untold Story '92
Victim '99

Kwan, Esther
(Kwan Wing Ho)
Run and Kill '93

Kwan Fung
(Kuan Feng, Gwaan Fung, Guan Feng, Kuan Fung)
Chinese Super Ninjas '82
Death Mask of the Ninja '82
Five Superfighters '78
Flag of Iron '80
Sword Stained in Royal Blood '81
Ten Tigers of Kwangtung '79
3 Evil Masters '80

Kwan Hoi-san
(Gwaan Hoi Saan, Guan Hai Shan, Kwan Hoi Shan, Kuan Hai San)
All's Well End's Well '92
The Descendant of Wing Chun '78
8 Diagram Fighter '91
Hard Boiled '91

Lee Rock '91
Martial Arts Master Wong Fei Hung '92
Project A '83
Project A 2 '87
The Shaolin Disciple '80
Young and Dangerous 5 '98

Kwan Hung
(Gwaan Hung, Guan Hong, Kuan Hung)
18 Fatal Strikes '78
Emperor of Shaolin Kung Fu '80
Fatal Needles vs. Fatal Fists '80
Shaolin King Boxer '79

Kwan, Keith
(Gwan Chiu Chung, Guan Chao Cong)
Blonde Fury '89

Kwan, Nancy
Dragon: The Bruce Lee Story '93

Kwan, Rosamund
(Kwan Chi Lam, Gwaan Ji Lam, Guan Zhi Lin)
The Adventurers '95
Armour of God '86
The Assassin '93
Casino Raiders '89
Crocodile Hunter '89
The Legend of the Swordsman '92
The Magic Crane '93
The Millionaires' Express '86
No More Love, No More Death '92
Once upon a Time in China '91
Once upon a Time in China 2 '92
Once upon a Time in China 3 '93
Once upon a Time in China and America '97
Project A 2 '87
Savior of the Soul 2 '92
Twinkle Twinkle Lucky Stars '85
The Wesley's Mysterious File '01
With or Without You '92

Kwan San
(Guan Shan, Gwaan Saan)
A Better Tomorrow 2 '87
Brutal Boxer '72
Executioners '93
Police Story 2 '88
Wonder Seven '94

Kwan Sang-woo
Volcano High School '01

Kwan, Shirley
(Kwan Suk Yi)
Savior of the Soul 2 '92

Kwan, Suki
(Kwan Sau-Mei, Shooky Kwan)
The Blood Rules '00
Century of the Dragon '99
City Cops '89
Cop on a Mission '01
A Gambler's Story '01
High Risk '95
The Irresistible Piggies '02
Legend of the Drunken Master '94
Operation Pink Squad '88
The Tricky Master '00
Victim '99
Your Place or Mine! '98

Kwan Tak Fai
(Gwaan Tak Fai, Guan Dei Hoi)
Temptress of a Thousand Faces '98

Kwan Tak-hing
(Gwan Tak Hing, Guan De Xing)
Aces Go Places 4 '86
Dreadnaught '81
The Magnificent Butcher '79

Kwan, Teddy Robin
(Tai Dik Law Ban, Tai Di Luo Bin)
All's Well End's Well '97
Eighth Happiness '88
Twin Dragons '92

Kwan Yim-ha
F*** / Off '98

Kwan Yung Moon
(Kuen Wing Man, Quan Yong Wen, Kuan Yung Wen, Kwong Yung Moon, The Mad Korean, Chuan Yung Wen, Chyan Yung Wun)
Dragon Lord '82
Fearless Hyena 2 '80
Fighting Ace '79
Inheritor of Kung Fu '77
Kung Fu Zombie '81
Lightning Kung Fu '80
Project A '83
Return of the Master Killer '80
Super Gang '78

Kwok, Aaron
(Kwok Fu Sing, Gwok Foo Shing, Guo Fu Cheng) See also sidebar on p. 542.
Anna Magdalena '98
The Big Heat '88
China Strike Force '00

Para Para Sakura '01
Savior of the Soul '91
The Storm Riders '98
2000 A.D. '00

Kwok, Amy
(Kwok Oi Ming, Gwok Ngoi Ming, Guo Ai Ming)
The Legend 2 '93
Victim '99

Kwok, Crystal
(Kwok Gam Yan, Guo Jin En)
Doctor Vampire '90
Dragons Forever '88
The Master '89
Police Story 2 '88

Kwok, Florence
(Kwok Siu Wan, Gwok Siu Wan, Guo Shao Yun)
The Irresistible Piggies '02
Needing You... '00
Nightmare Zone '98

Kwok, Kenix
(Kwok Hoh Ying, Gwok Ke Ying)
Her Name Is Cat '98
Troublesome Night '97

Kwok-leung, So
Five Elements of Kung Fu '78
Green Dragon Inn '79

Kwok, Phillip
(Gwok Jan Fung, Guo Zhen Feng, Kuo Chui, Lizard Venom)
Avenging Warriors of Shaolin '79
The Big Heat '88
Brave Archer '77
The Cat '91
Chinatown Kid '77
Five Deadly Venoms '78
Flag of Iron '80
Hard Boiled '91
Kid with the Golden Arm '78
Kung Pow: Enter the Fist '76/2001
Masked Avengers '81
Master of the Flying Guillotine '76
Ninja in the Deadly Trap '83
The Peacock King '89
The Phantom Lover '95
The Return of the 5 Deadly Venoms '78
Revenge of the Patriots '76
Riki-Oh: The Story of Ricky '92
Sunshine Cops '99
Ten Tigers of Kwangtung '79

Kwok, Roger
(Gwok Chun On, Guo Jin An, Kwok Tsun On)
Wonder Seven '94

Kwok, Sally
In the Line of Duty 3 '88

Kwok, Samuel
Cop on a Mission '01

Kwok, Sharon
(Kwok Sau Wan)
Lethal Panther 2 '93

Kwok Siu Hung
Dragons of the Orient '88

Kwok, Sonja
(Kwok Sin Nae, Gwok Sin Lei, Guo Xian Ni)
The Cheaters '01
The Replacement Suspects '01

Kwok Yiu-wah
(Gwok Yiu Wa, Guo Yao Hua)
Erotic Ghost Story 2 '91

Kwok, Zeny
(Kwok Sin, Gwok Sin, Guo Shan Yu)
Glass Tears '01
Merry-Go-Round '01

Kwong Wai
Ninja vs. Ninja '87

Kwong-yue, Wong
(Wong Gwong Yue, Wang Guang Yu)
Dragon Fist '78
Knockabout '79
Last Hurrah for Chivalry '78
Spiritual Kung Fu '78

Kwouk, Burt
Kiss of the Dragon '01

Kwun-lan, Law
(Law Koon Lan, Law Goon Lan, Luo Guan Lan)
The Legend of a Professional '00
The Masked Prosecutor '99
Master Q 2001 '01
Operation Billionaires '98

Kyo, Machiko
Rashomon '50

Kyo, Utako
Zatoichi the Outlaw '67

Lacey, Ronald
Aces Go Places 4 '86

Ladalski, John
Armour of God '86
BloodFight '89
City War '88

Game of Death '78
Inheritor of Kung Fu '77

Lai, Benny
(Lai Keung Kuen, Li Jiang Quan, Lai Chun)
The Best of the Best '96
Bio-Cops '00
Body Weapon '99
The Deadly Camp '99
Dragons Forever '88
Five Superfighters '79
The Inspector Wears Skirts '88
The Legend of Bruce Lee '79
Miracles '89
Police Story '85
Police Story 2 '88
Project A '83
Project A 2 '87
Tower of Death '81
Twin Dragons '92

Lai, Bruce
(Cheung Yat Diy, Zhang Yi Dao, Chang Yi Tao, Cheung Yat Jit, Chang Yi Dao)
Blooded Treasury Fight '79
Chinese Super Ninjas '82
Hit-Man in the Hand of Buddha '80
Inheritor of Kung Fu '77
The Magnificent '78
Mantis Combat '81
Return of the Master Killer '80
The Super Ninja '84

Lai Chi-saan
A Taste of Killing and Romance '94

Lai, Gigi
(Lai Chi)
All's Well End's Well '97 '97
Dragon in Jail '90
Fist Power '99
For Bad Boys Only '00
Haunted Mansion '98
Legend of the Flying Swordsman '00
Lord of the Wu Tang '93
Okinawa Rendez-vous '00
A Wicked Ghost '99
Young and Dangerous '96
Young and Dangerous 6: Born to Be King '00

Lai, Guy
(Lai Ying-chau, Lai Ying Jau, Li Ying Jiu)
Pom Pom and Hot Hot '92
Sixty Million Dollar Man '95
Twin Dragons '92

Lai Hei the dog
The Six Directions of Boxing '79

Lai Hing-cheung
2000 A.D. '00

Lai, Hugo
Snake Fist Dynamo '84

Lai, Kelly
In the Mood for Love '00

Lai, Leon
(Lai Ming, Li Ming) See also sidebar on p. 542.
Bullets of Love '01
City Hunter '92
Comrades, Almost a Love Story '96
Everyday Is Valentine '01
Fallen Angels '95
Shogun and Little Kitchen '92
Wicked City '92
With or Without You '92

Lai, Michael
(Lei Siu-tin)
Miracles '89
Police Story '85
Project A 2 '87
Red Wolf '95

Lai, Michelle
(Mai Suet, Mi Xue, Mi Hsueh, Mai Shuet, Michelle Mee)
Bolo '80
The Butterfly Murders '79
Ten Tigers of Shaolin '78
The 36 Crazy Fists '77
Thousand Mile Escort '76

Lai, Newton
(Lai Hon Chi, Li Han Chi)
Queen's High '91

Lai, Perrie
(Lai Hoi San, Li Hai Shan)
Dr. Lamb '92

Lai, Peter
(Lai Bei Dak, Li Bi De)
The Big Heat '88
The Chinese Feast '95
City Hunter '92
Flirting Scholar '93
King of Beggars '92
Love on Delivery '94
Righting Wrongs '86

Lai, Rocky
First Strike '96

Lai, Vivian
A Chinese Ghost Story: The Tsui Hark Animation '97 (V)

Lai, Wayne
(Lai Yiu-Cheung, Li Yao Xiang, Lai Yeu Cheung)
Armageddon '97
Bio Zombie '98
Bullets over Summer '99
Clean My Name, Mr. Coroner! '00
F*** / Off '98
Gen-X Cops '99
Headlines '01
Last Ghost Standing '99
The Masked Prosecutor '99
Master Q 2001 '01
Nightmare Zone '98
990714.com '00
Paramount Motel '00
Sound from the Dark '00
The Storm Riders '98
Troublesome Night 4 '98
Troublesome Night 9 '00
Vampire Controller '00
Victim '99
Violent Cop '99
Visible Secret '01
Where a Good Man Goes '99

Lai, William
Masters of Tiger Crane '83

Lai Yee
Brother of Darkness '94

Lai Yin-san
(Lai Yin Saan, Li Yan Shan)
Iceman Cometh '89

Lam, Bella
Scorpion Thunderbolt '85

Lam, Ben
(Lam Kwok Bun, Lam Gwok Ban, Lin Guo Bin)
Conman in Tokyo '00
Eastern Condors '86
Heart of Dragon '85
Her Name Is Cat '98
High Risk '95
I Love Maria '88
Long Arm of the Law '84
Long Arm of the Law 2 '87
Love on Delivery '94
Mr. Boo Meets Pom Pom '85
Police Story '85
Police Story 2 '88
Project A 2 '87
Red Shield '91
Return to a Better Tomorrow '94
Tragic Fantasy: Tiger of Wanchai '94

Lam, Bowie
(Lam Bo-yi, Lam Biu Yi, Lin Bao Yi)
Doctor Vampire '90
Hard Boiled '91
Hong Kong X-File '98
Lawyer Lawyer '97
The Most Wanted '94
On the Run '88
Supercop 2 '93

Lam Chau Ping
The Holy Robe of Shaolin Temple '84

Lam Chi-chung
(Lam Ji Chung, Lin Zi Cong, Lam Tze Chung)
Beauty and the Breast '02
Dance of a Dream '01
Shaolin Soccer '01

Lam Chi-ho
(Lin Zhi Hao, Lin Chih Hao, Lin Chi Ho)
Shadow '01
Sound from the Dark '00

Lam Chi-sin
(Lam Ji Sin, Lin Zi Shan, Lam Tsz Sin)
The Deadly Camp '99
Jiang Hu-"The Triad Zone" '00
King of Comedy '99
The Masked Prosecutor '99
Master Q 2001 '01
Shaolin Soccer '01

Lam Chi-tai
(Lin Zhi Tai)
Code of Honor '87
Chinese Super Ninjas '82
Flag of Iron '80
Masked Avengers '81
Supercop '92
Ten Tigers of Kwang-tung '79

Lam Ching-Ying
(Lam Gun Bo, Lam Jing Ying, Lin Zheng Ying) See also sidebar on p. 326.
Dirty Tiger, Crazy Frog '78
Eastern Condors '86
Encounter of the Spooky Kind '81
End of the Wicked Tiger '77
Enter the Dragon '73
Enter the Fat Dragon '78
Executioners from Shaolin '77
Fists of Fury '71
Heart of Dragon '85
He Has Nothing But Kung Fu '77
Heroes Shed No Tears '83/86

His Name Is Nobody '79
I Love Maria '88
Incredible Kung Fu Mission '79
Knockabout '79
Lord of the Wu Tang '93
The Magnificent Butcher '79
Martial Arts Master Wong Fei Hung '92
The Millionaires' Express '86
Mr. Vampire '85
Mr. Vampire 2 '86
My Lucky Stars '85
Odd Couple '79
Painted Faces '88
Painted Skin '92
Pedicab Driver '89
Pom Pom '84
Pom Pom and Hot Hot '92
Prince of the Sun '90
The Prodigal Son '81
Sting of the Dragon Masters '73
Swordsman '90
A Touch of Zen '69
Twinkle Twinkle Lucky Stars '85
The Victim '80
Where's Officer Tuba? '86
Winners and Sinners '83

Lam Chuen
Burning Paradise '94
Iron Man '86

Lam Chung
(Lin Cong, Lim Chung)
Angel '87
A Better Tomorrow 2 '87
Bullet in the Head '90
Erotic Ghost Story '90
Five Elements of Kung Fu '78
Iceman Cometh '89
The Killer '89
Legacy of Rage '86
Lethal Panther '91
A Moment of Romance '90
Operation Pink Squad '88
Rich and Famous '87
Robotrix '91

Lam, Cynthia
Eat My Dust '93

Lam, Deon
(Lam Dik On, Lin Di An)
Don't Give a Damn '95
Last Hero in China '93
A Man Called Hero '99
Young and Dangerous '96

Lam, Frankie
Dragon Chronicles: Maidens of Heavenly Mountain '94

Lam Gei-yan
(Lam Kei Yan, Lin Qi Xin)
Code of Honor '87
The Seventh Curse '86

Lam, George
(Lam Chi-Cheung, Lam Ji Cheung, Lin Zi Xiang)
Aces Go Places '82
The Owl vs. Bombo '84
Twinkle Twinkle Lucky Stars '85

Lam, Gordon
(Lam Ka-tung, Lam Ga Dung, Lin Gu Dong)
Dance of a Dream '01
Gen-X Cops '99
Love Me, Love My Money '01

Lam, Grace
(Lam Nga Si, Lin Ya Shi)
Crime of a Beast '01
The Final Winner '01
God.com '98
A War Named Desire '00

Lam, Hera
The Cheaters '01

Lam Ho-yee
Day Off '01

Lam Hoi Man
Spacked Out '00

Lam, Jan
City Hunter '92
Marry a Rich Man '02

Lam Jing
(Lin Jing)
The Prodigal Son '81

Lam, John
Lethal Panther '91

Lam, Karena
(Lam Ka Yan, Lin Jia Xin)
Inner Senses '01
Tiramisu '02

Lam Kau
(Lam Gaau, Lin Jiao, Lin Chiao)
Drunken Master '78
Help!!! '00
Return of the Deadly Blade '81

Lam Kee-to
F*** / Off '98

Lam King Kong
(Lam Ging Gong, Lin Jing Gang)
Dr. Lamb '92

Lam Kwok-hung
(Lam Gwok Hung, Lin Guo Xiong)
Police Story '85
Police Story 2 '88

Lam Laap-saam
(Lam Lap-sam, Lin Li San)
On the Run '88
Sharp Guns '01
Shogun and Little Kitchen '92

Lam Man-wai
(Lin Wen Wei, Lam Man Wei, Lam Mun Hwa)
Duel of the Brave Ones '78
Killer of Snake, Fox of Shaolin '78
Shadow of the Tiger '79

Lam, Meg
(Lam Kin-Ming, Lam Gin Ming, Lin Jian Ming)
Blind Fist of Bruce '79
Dirty Tiger, Crazy Frog '78
Enter the Fat Dragon '78
His Name Is Nobody '79
Warrior from Shaolin '81

Lam, Monica
(Lam Hoi Ling, Lam Oi Ling)
Flash Future Kung Fu '83

Lam, Morgan
Rumble in the Bronx '95

Lam, Place
God.com '98

Lam, Ringo
(Lam Ling-Tung, Ling-dong Lin)
Eighth Happiness '88
Twin Dragons '92

Lam, Samuel
Inner Senses '01
9413 '98

Lam Siu Lau
(Lin Xiao Lou, Lin Shao Luo)
Dragon Kid '90
Iceman Cometh '89

Lam, Spencer
(Lam Seung Yi, Lam Gwing Yee, Lin Shang Yi)
Big Bullet '96
Comic King '00
Extreme Crisis '98
Fight Back to School 2 '92
Haunted Mansion '98
Lawyer Lawyer '97

Sunshine Cops '99
The Tricky Master '00
Young and Dangerous '96
Young and Dangerous 6: Born to Be King '00
Your Place or Mine! '98

Lam, Stephanie
(Lam Mei Ching, Lam Mei Jing, Lin Mei Zhen)
Bullets over Summer '99

Lam Suet
(Lin Xue)
The Blood Rules '00
Color of Pain '02
Cop on a Mission '01
Doctor No... '01
Every Dog Has His Date '01
Expect the Unexpected '98
Fist Power '99
Fulltime Killer '01
A Gambler's Story '01
Gold Fingers '01
Goodbye Mr. Cool '01
Help!!! '00
Juliet in Love '00
The Longest Nite '98
Love on Delivery '94
Love on a Diet '01
Master Q 2001 '01
The Mission '99
Needing You... '00
The Odd One Dies '97
Running out of Time '99
Running out of Time 2 '01
U-Man '02
Where a Good Man Goes '99
You Shoot, I Shoot '01

Lam, Thomas
(Lam Cho-fai, Lam Jo Fai, Lin Zu Hui)
Black Cat '91
The Cheaters '01
Happy Family '02
The Legend of a Professional '00

Lam Wa-fan
(Lin Hua Xun)
Faces of Horror '98

Lam Wai-kin
(Lin Wei Jian)
A Chinese Torture Chamber Story 2 '98
First Option '96
Losers' Club '01
Operation Billionaires '98
Running out of Time '99

Lam Wai-ling
Cop Shop Babes '01

Lam, Wilson
(Lam Jun Yin, Lin Jun Xian)
Kick Boxer's Tears '92

Lamb, Jan
A Chinese Ghost Story: The Tsui Hark Animation '97 (V)

Lamb, Jerry
(Lam Hiu Fung, Lin Xiao Feng)
The Best of the Best '96
Clean My Name, Mr. Coroner! '00
Comic King '00
Cop Shop Babes '01
Doctor No... '01
The Duel '00
Faces of Horror '98
For Bad Boys Only '00
He's a Woman, She's a Man '94
Legend of Speed '99
A Man Called Hero '99
Young and Dangerous '96
Young and Dangerous 5 '98
Young and Dangerous 6: Born to Be King '00

Lambert, Christopher
Mortal Kombat '95

Lambert, Michael
(Michael Ian Lambert)
Armageddon '97
Big Bullet '96
Black Mask '96
Cheap Killers '98
Thunderbolt '95
Who Am I? '98

Lan Ki
The Green Dragon Inn '79

Lan Kwong
Hero's Blood '91

Lan, Nancy
(Lan Sai, Lan Qian, Madame Nancy)
Lawyer Lawyer '97
Option Zero '97
You Shoot, I Shoot '01

Lana, Oliveiro
Troublesome Night 3 '97

Landers, Matt
Reptilian '00

Lang, Perry
Masters of Tiger Crane '83

Lang Yun
The Green Hornet '74

Langdon, Lynn
(Lynne Frances, Lynne Frances Wachendorfer)
City Hunter '93
Second Time Around '02

Langdon, Reuben
From the Queen to the Chief Executive '01

Lanzi, Emmauel
The Touch '02

Laskey, Edward
Downtown Torpedoes '97

Lasser, Louise
What's Up, Tiger Lily? '66 (V)

Lau, Albert
First Option '96

Lau, Alice
(Lau Ar-Lai, Lau Nga Lai, Liu Ya Li)
Police Story '85
Pom Pom '84

Lau, Andy
(Lau Tak-Wah, Dehau Liu) See also sidebar on p. 542.
The Adventurers '95
Armageddon '97
Casino Raiders '89
Casino Raiders 2 '91
Casino Tycoon 2 '92
Century of the Dragon '99
The Conman '98
Crocodile Hunter '89
Dance of a Dream '01
Days of Being Wild '90
The Dragon Family '88
Dragon in Jail '90
Drunken Master Killer '94
The Duel '00
A Fighter's Blues '00
Full Throttle '95
Fulltime Killer '01
God of Gamblers '89
God of Gamblers 2 '90
The Last Blood '90
Lee Rock '91
Legend of the Drunken Master '94
Love on a Diet '01
A Moment of Romance '90
The Moon Warriors '92
Needing You... '00
The Prisoner '90
Rich and Famous '87
Running out of Time '99
Savior of the Soul '91
Savior of the Soul 2 '92
A Taste of Killing and Romance '94
The Three Swordsmen '94

The Tigers '91
Twinkle Twinkle Lucky
    Stars '85
The Wesley's Mysteri-
    ous File '01

Lau, Ankie
Enter the Fat Dragon
    '78

Lau, Annabelle
*(Lau Hiu Tung, Liu Xiao
Tong, Annabelle Liew)*
Don't Give a Damn '95
Peace Hotel '95

Lau, Anthony
Dragon Killer '95

Lau, Billy
*(Lau Lan Guang, Lau
Nam Kwong)*
Aces Go Places 2 '83
Don't Give a Damn '95
Eastern Condors '86
The Haunted Cop Shop
    '87
The Inspector Wears
    Skirts '88
A Kid from Tibet '91
The Millionaires'
    Express '86
Miracles '89
Mr. Vampire '85
Mr. Vampire 2 '86
Operation Pink Squad
    '88
Pedicab Driver '89
Police Story 2 '88
Twinkle Twinkle Lucky
    Stars '85
Vampire Kids '91
Yes, Madam '85

Lau, Carina
*(Lau Ka-Ling, Lau Ga
Ling, Liu Jia Ling)*
Armour of God '86
Ashes of Time '94
Brassiere '01
C'est la Vie, Mon Cheri
    '93
Cop Shop Babes '01
Days of Being Wild '90
Deadful Melody '94
Eagle Shooting Heroes
    '93
Forbidden City Cop '96
He's a Woman, She's a
    Man '94
No More Love, No More
    Death '92
Project A 2 '87
Rich and Famous '87
Savior of the Soul '91
She Shoots Straight
    '90

Lau Cheung-ming
(Liu Chang Ming)
Chinese Iron Man '75
Triangular Duel '72

Lau Chi Wing
(Liu Zhi Rong)
Fist of Fury '95

Police Story '85
She Shoots Straight
    '90

Lau, Chindy
*(Lau Chin Dai, Liu Qian
Di)*
A Better Tomorrow 2
    '87
Magnificent Warriors
    '87

Lau Ching-fat
*(Liu Qing Fa, Liu Ching
Fa)*
Chinese Iron Man '75
The Shaolin Brothers
    '77
Triangular Duel '72
War of the Shaolin Tem-
    ple '80

Lau Ching-Wan
*(Liu Qing Yun, Sean
Lau)*
All Men Are Brothers:
    Blood of the Leop-
    ard '93
Beyond Hypothermia
    '96
Big Bullet '96
Black Mask '96
Brassiere '01
C'est la Vie, Mon Cheri
    '93
Executioners '93
Expect the Unexpected
    '98
Full Alert '97
The Longest Nite '98
The Most Wanted '94
Police Story 2 '88
Return to a Better
    Tomorrow '94
Running out of Time
    '99
Running out of Time 2
    '01
Too Many Ways to Be
    No. 1 '97
Tragic Fantasy: Tiger of
    Wanchai '94
Victim '99
Where a Good Man
    Goes '99

Lau, Claudia
Armageddon '97

Lau, Damian
*(Liu Sung Jen, Lui Sung
Ren, Lau Chung Yan,
Liu Sung Je)*
The Best of the Best
    '96
Duel to the Death '82
The Enforcer '95
Executioners '93
First Option '96
The Heroic Trio '93
Last Hurrah for Chivalry
    '78
The Law and the Out-
    law '95
The Magic Crane '93

The New Legend of
    Shaolin '94
Ninja vs. Ninja '87
Royal Tramp '92
Royal Tramp 2 '92
Zu: Warriors of the
    Magic Mountain
    '83

Lau Dan
(Liu Dan)
Super Gang '78
Ten Tigers of Shaolin
    '78

Lau, Dick
(Lau Dik Ji, Liu De Zhi)
Naked Killer '92

Lau Fong-sai
*(Liu Huang Shi, Lau
Kwong Shi)*
Avenging Warriors of
    Shaolin '79
Brave Archer '77
Chinatown Kid '77
Death Ring '84
Five Deadly Venoms
    '78
Flag of Iron '80
The Kid with the Golden
    Arm '79
Masked Avengers '81
Return of the Five
    Deadly Venoms '78
Ten Tigers of Kwang-
    tung '79

Lau, Gordon
*(Liu Chia Hiu, Lau Ga
Fai, Liu Gu Hiu, Lau Kar
Fei, Liu Ga Fai, Gordon
Liu) See also sidebar
on p. 278.*
Breakout from Oppres-
    sion '78
Crystal Hunt '91
Dirty Ho '79
Drunken Master Killer
    '94
Executioners from
    Shaolin '77
Fists and Guts '79
Fists of the White
    Lotus '80
Flirting Scholar '93
Fury in Shaolin Temple
    '82
Generation Consultant
    '90
Generation Pendragon
    '90
He Has Nothing But
    Kung Fu '77
Invincible Pole Fighter
    '83
The Killer '90
Last Hero in China '93
Legendary Weapons of
    China '82
Martial Arts Mayhem,
    Vol. 2 '99
The Peacock King '89
Return of the Master
    Killer '80

The Shaolin Drunken
    Monk '83
Shaolin Mantis '78
Shaolin Master Killer
    '78
Tiger on Beat '88
Warrior from Shaolin
    '81

Lau, Gray
It Takes a Thief '01

Lau Hak Suen
(Liu Ke Xuan)
Project A '83

Lau Hoi-yin
Ninja Hunter '83

Lau Hok Nin
*(Liu Hao Nian, Lin Ho
Nien)*
Bolo '80
Dragon's Claws '79
The Fists, the Kicks
    and the Evils '79
Five Superfighters '78
Ten Tigers of Shaolin
    '78
3 Evil Masters '80
Where's Officer Tuba?
    '86

Lau, Jay
The Magic Crane '93

Lau, Jeff
*(Lau Chun-wai, Lau Jan
Wai, Liu Zhen Wei, Jef-
frey Lau)*
A Chinese Odyssey Part
    1: Pandora's Box
    '95
A Chinese Odyssey Part
    2: Cinderella '95
Fist of Fury 1991 '91

Lau Kar-Leung
*(Liu Chia-Liang, Kung
Fu Leung, Atachia Liang
Liu) See also sidebar
on p. 278.*
The Art of Action: Mar-
    tial Arts in the
    Movies '02
Drunken Master Killer
    '94
Evil Cat '86
Invincible Pole Fighter
    '83
Legendary Weapons of
    China '82
Legend of the Drunken
    Master '94
Pedicab Driver '89
Prodigal Boxer '73

Lau Kong
(Liu Jiang)
Casino Raiders 2 '91
City on Fire '87
Crocodile Hunter '89
Green Snake '93
Hard Boiled '91
In the Line of Duty 5:
    Middle Man '90

Last Hurrah for Chivalry
    '78
A Moment of Romance
    '90

Lau Lan-ying
*(Liu Lan Ying, Pawana
Chanajit, Liu Ran-in)*
Bloody Fight '72

Lau Lap Cho
*(Lau Laap Jo, Liu Li Zu,
Liu Li Chiu, Liu Li Tsu)*
Battle of Shaolin '77
The Blazing Temple '76
Chinese Iron Man '75
Dreaming Fists with
    Slender Hands '80
The 8 Masters '77
The 18 Bronzemen '76
The 18 Bronzemen Part
    2 '76
Emperor of Shaolin
    Kung Fu '80
Killer from Above '77
The Shaolin Kids '77

Lau Ming
(Liu Ming)
Challenge of Death '78
New Fist of Fury '76

Lau Mung-yin
Lone Ninja Warrior '81

Lau Nga Ying
*(Liu Ya Ying, Lau Yee
Yeung)*
The Invincible Killer '79
Moonlight Sword and
    Jade Lion '79
Snake and Crane Arts
    of Shaolin '78

Lau, Rain
Troublesome Night 3
    '97

Lau, Ricky
*(Lau Koon Wai, Liu
Guanwei, Eric Lau)*
Kick Boxer's Tears '92
Mr. Vampire Saga 4 '88

Lau Sek-ming
Thunder Cops '98

Lau Sek Yin
*(Liu Xi Xian, Lau Shek
Yan)*
The Cat '91
Century of the Dragon
    '99
God.com '98
Saga of the Phoenix
    '90

Lau Shi Kwong
Kid with the Golden
    Arm '78

Lau Shun
(Lau Chun, Liu Xun)
All Men Are Brothers:
    Blood of the Leop-
    ard '93
Ashes of Time '94

The Blacksheep Affair '98
Casino Raiders 2 '91
The Chinese Feast '95
A Chinese Ghost Story 2 '90
A Chinese Ghost Story 3 '91
Dragon from Russia '90
Dragon Inn '92
The East Is Red '93
God of Gamblers 3: Back to Shanghai '91
Hail the Judge '94
The Legend of the Swordsman '92
The Magic Crane '93
Once upon a Time in China '91
Once upon a Time in China 3 '93
Once upon a Time in China 4 '93
Painted Skin '92
Peace Hotel '95
Prince of the Sun '90
Swordsman '90
Twin Warriors '93
Zu Warriors '01

Lau Shung-fung
(Liu Chong Feng)
Dragon from Russia '90

Lau Siu Kwan
(Lau Siu Gwan, Liu Shao Jun)
990714.com '00

Lau Siu-ming
(Lau Sek Ming, Liu Xi Ming, Liu Zhaoming)
A Better Tomorrow 2 '87
The Butterfly Murders '79
Casino Raiders 2 '91
Casino Tycoon 2 '92
The Cat '91
China Strike Force '00
A Chinese Ghost Story '87
A Chinese Ghost Story 2 '90
A Chinese Ghost Story 3 '91
City of Desire '01
Dr. Lamb '92
Killer's Romance '90
Legend of the Drunken Master '94
Miracles '89
Police Story 2 '88
Project A 2 '87
Shanghai 1920 '91
Swordsman '90
The Untold Story '92

Lau, Stella
Legend of the Drunken Tiger '92

Lau Suet-wa
(Liu Xue Hua, Liu Hsieh Hua)
Invincible Pole Fighter '83

Lau Suk-yee
Model from Hell '99

Lau Tak Hoi
Dreaming Fists with Slender Hands '80

Lau Tan
Legend of the Dragon-slayer Sword '90
Legend of the Dragon-slayer Sword 3-The Rage of Gina '90

Lau, Tats
(Lau Yi-Dat, Lau Yee Daat, Liu Yi Da)
C'est la Vie, Mon Cheri '93
Comic King '00
Forbidden City Cop '96
Glass Tears '01
God of Cookery '96
Gorgeous '99
Happy Family '02
Juliet in Love '00
Lawyer Lawyer '97
Master Q 2001 '01
You Shoot, I Shoot '01

Lau, Vincent
Wonder Seven '94

Lau Wai-ling
(Liu Hui Ling, Liu Hoy Ling, Lau Wai Ying)
Killer of Snake, Fox of Shaolin '78
Legend of the 7 Golden Vampires '74
Ten Tigers of Kwang-tung '79

Lau Wing
(Liu Yung, Tony Liu, Anthony Lau)
The Big Sting '82
The Chinese Connection '71
Dreadnaught '81
Enter the Dragon '73
Fists of Fury '71
Generation Consultant '90
Generation Pendragon '90
Iron Monkey 2 '96
10 Magnificent Killers '77
Visible Secret '01
We're Going to Eat You! '80

Lau Wing-wai
The Blood Rules '00

Lau Yat-fan
(Liu Yi Fan, Liu I Fan, Lin Y Va, Lau Yet Fan, Lau Yet Fan)
Bolo '80

The Invincible Killer '79
Killer of Snake, Fox of Shaolin '78
My Kung Fu 12 Kicks '79
The Silver Spear '79
Super Gang '78

Lau Yin-ko
The Hot, the Cool, and the Vicious '76

Lau Yin-nam
Nine Demons '83

Lau Ying Hung
Full Throttle '95

Lau Ying Lung
Shaolin vs. Manchu '80

Laub, Catharine
Legend of the Dinosaurs '77

Law, Bonnie
(Law Ming Chu, Luo Ming Zhu)
The Cheaters '01
The Conman '98

Law, Bruce
(Law Lai-yin, Luo Li Xian)
Extreme Crisis '98
Supercop 2 '93
Thunderbolt '95

Law Bun
(Law Ban, Luo Bin)
Screaming Ninja '73

Law Ching-ho
(Luo Qing Hao)
City War '88
God of Gamblers '89
In the Line of Duty 3 '88
Operation Pink Squad '88
Vampire Kids '91

Law Chung-ha
Legend of the Flying Swordsman '00

Law Dai Yau
Dragon Kid '90

Law, Gallen
Vampire Controller '00

Law, Helena
(Law Lan, Lo Yin Ying)
Bakery Amour '01
The Bride with White Hair 2 '93
Bullets over Summer '99
Clueless '01
Comic King '00
F*** / Off '98
Faces of Horror '98
For Bad Boys Only '00
Haunted Mansion '98
House of the Damned '99
Iceman Cometh '89

Jiang Hu-"The Triad Zone" '00
The Legend of a Professional '00
Master Q 2001 '01
Merry-Go-Round '01
Miracles '89
Nightmare Zone '98
Operation Pink Squad '88
Royal Tramp 2 '92
Royal Warriors '86
She Shoots Straight '90
Troublesome Night '97
Troublesome Night 3 '97
Troublesome Night 8 '00
Troublesome Night 9 '00
Troublesome Night 14 '02
The Untold Story 2 '98
Young and Dangerous 5 '98
Young Tiger '72

Law, Joe
Monkey Fist Floating Snake '79

Law Kwun-jor
F*** / Off '98

Law Lok-lam
The Bride with White Hair '93

Law, Turbo
Chinese Orthopedist and the Spice Girls '02

Lawson, Cristina
BloodFight '89

Laxmi, Vijaya
Mahal '48

Le, Bruce
(Lui Siu Lung, Lu Xiao Long, Huang Kin Lung, Wong Kum Hung, Bruce K.L. Lea , Jun Chong)
Bruce Lee Fights Back from the Grave '76
The Legend of Bruce Lee '80
Ninja vs. Bruce Lee '82
Shaolin Fist of Fury '87
Super Gang '78

Le Van Loc
Cyclo '95

Learned, Michael
Dragon: The Bruce Lee Story '93

Leaud, Jean-Pierre
What Time Is It There? '01

Leder, Paul
A*P*E '76

Lederer, Francis
Terror Is a Man '59

Lee, Amanda
(Lee Wai Man, Li Hui Min)
All's Well End's Well '97 '97
The Best of the Best '96
Full Alert '97
Happy Family '02
Last Ghost Standing '99
9413 '98

Lee, Ang
(Lee On, Li An)
The Art of Action: Martial Arts in the Movies '02
Mr. Nice Guy '97

Lee, Angelica
(Lee Sum Kit, Lee Sin Chet. Lee Sin Je)
The Eye '02
Sunshine Cops '99

Lee, Anita
(Lee Yuen Wah)
Satin Steel '94

Lee Bing-hung
(Lee Bing Xiong, Li Ping Hung)
Dragon on Fire '79

Lee, Brandon
(Lee Gwok Ho, Li Guo Hao)
Legacy of Rage '86

Lee, Bruce
(Little Dragon Lee, Lee Siu-Lung, Li Xiaolong)
See also sidebars on pp. 72, 182, 214, and 224.
Bruce Lee: A Warrior's Journey '00
Bruce Lee, The Legend '84
The Chinese Connection '71
Enter the Dragon '73
Fist of Fear-Touch of Death '80
Fists of Fury '71
Game of Death '78
The Green Hornet '74
Martial Arts Mayhem, Vol. 1 '99
The Real Bruce Lee '79
Return of the Dragon '72
Tower of Death '81

Lee Byung-hum
Joint Security Area '00

Lee, Carmen
(Lee Yeuk-Ting, Li Re Tong, Carman Lee, Carmen Li)
Burning Paradise '94
Forbidden City Cop '96

Killer's Romance '90
The Odd One Dies '97
Option Zero '97
Too Many Ways to Be No. 1 '97
Wicked City '92

Lee, Carrie
Dragon against Vampire '85

Lee Chao-tsien
Prodigal Boxer '73

Lee Chi-lun
Sorrowful to a Ghost '70

Lee, China
What's Up, Tiger Lily? '66

Lee Chiu
(Li Chao, Le Chao)
The Awaken Punch '73
Cantonen Iron Kung Fu '79
The 18 Jade Arhats '78
Executioners from Shaolin '77
From China with Death '74
Kung Fu's Hero '73
The Massive '78
Ninja Supremo '81
Snake-Crane Secret '78
Super Kung Fu Kid '74
Thunder Kick '73
Ways of Kung Fu '80

Lee, Chris
(Lee Kin Sang, Lee Gin Sang, Li Jian Sheng)
Eastern Condors '86
Full Alert '97
Full Contact '92
In the Line of Duty 3 '88
In the Line of Duty 5: Middle Man '90
Nine Demons '83
Queen's High '91

Lee Chun Wa
(Li Chun Hua, Lee Chun Hwa, Li Chun Haw)
Dreadnaught '81
Drunken Master '78
Five Elements of Kung Fu '78
We're Going to Eat You! '80

Lee Chung-yat
(Li Zhong Yi, Li Chang Yat)
Death Ring '83

Lee, Clement
Lethal Panther '91

Lee, Conan
(Lloyd Hutchinson, Lee Yuen Ba, Li Yuan Ba)
Aces Go Places 5: The Terracotta Hit '89

Dragon Killer '95
First Strike '96
Prince of the Sun '90
Tiger on Beat '88

Lee Dae-yeon
Dream of Garuda '94
Sympathy for Mr. Vengeance '01

Lee, Danny
(Lee Sau-Yin, Li Xiu Xian, Li Hsiu Hsien)
Aces Go Places 5: The Terracotta Hit '89
Brave Archer '77
City Cop '95
City on Fire '87
City War '88
Code of Honor '87
Dr. Lamb '92
Final Justice '88
The Heroes '80
The Killer '89
Mighty Peking Man '77
Organized Crime and Triad Bureau '94
Powerful Four '91
Red Shield '91
Rich and Famous '87
Run and Kill '93
The Sword Stained with Royal Blood '93
The Untold Story '92
Young and Dangerous 5 '98

Lee, David
(Lee Wai Sheung, Lee Wai Gwing, Li Wei Shang)
Bullets over Summer '99
Cop on a Mission '01
The Duel '00
Everyday Is Valentine '01
From the Queen to the Chief Executive '01
God.com '98
Sharp Guns '01
Victim '99
A War Named Desire '00

Lee, Dick
Snake Fist Dynamo '84

Lee, Donnie
The Holy Robe of Shaolin Temple '84

Lee, Dragon
(Bruce Lei, Vyachaslev Yaksysny, Gui Lung Ju Long)
Champ against Champ '83
Dragon Lee vs. the Five Brothers '78
Dragon on Fire '79
Dragon's Claws '79
Golden Dragon Silver Snake '79
Rage of the Dragon '79
The Real Bruce Lee '79

Lee, Eagle
5 Lady Venoms '78

Lee, Elizabeth
(Lee Mei Fung, Li Mei Feng)
Blonde Fury '89
Gunmen '88
Organized Crime and Triad Bureau '94
Picture of a Nymph '88

Lee, Eric
The Accidental Spy '01

Lee, Hacken
(Lee Hak Kan, Li Ke Qin)
Clueless '01
Comic King '00
No More Love, No More Death '93

Lee Han-garl
Bichunmoo '99

Lee Heung-kam
(Li Xiang Qin, Lee Heung Kin)
All's Well End's Well '92
The Bride with White Hair 2 '93
Moonlight Express '99
On the Run '88

Lee Ho
The Heroes '80

Lee Hoi-Chuen
The Real Bruce Lee '79

Lee Hoi-sang
(Li Hai Sheng, Lee Hoi San) See also sidebar on p. 326.
Bruce Lee: The Man, the Myth '76
The Buddhist Fist '79
Death Mask of the Ninja '82
The Descendant of Wing Chun '79
Dirty Tiger, Crazy Frog '78
Dynamo '78
Enter the Fat Dragon '78
Executioners from Shaolin '77
Fists and Guts '79
Goose Boxer '78
He Has Nothing But Kung Fu '77
Heart of Dragon '85
The Invincible Armour '77
Knockabout '79
Kung Fu Genius '79
Last Hurrah for Chivalry '79
Legend of the Dragon '91
The Magnificent Butcher '79
Miracles '89
My Kung Fu 12 Kicks '79

Odd Couple '79
Peking Opera Blues '86
The Prodigal Son '81
Project A '83
Project A 2 '87
The Protector '85 (HK)
Shaolin Chastity Kung Fu '81
Shaolin Mantis '78
Shaolin Master Killer '78
Tower of Death '81
Twinkle Twinkle Lucky Stars '85
The Young Master '80

Lee-hom, Wang
(Wong Lik Wang, Wang Li Hong, Alexander Wang)
The Avenging Fist '01
China Strike Force '00

Lee, Hwang Jang
(Whong Cheng-Li, Wang Chang-Li, Huang Cheng-Li, Wong Cheng-Li, Wang Chang- Li, Wang Ching-Li, Wang Cheng Li, Wong Jing Lei, Huang Zheng Li, Wong Ching Lee)
Angel '87
The Buddha Assassinator '79
Dance of the Drunk Mantis '79
Dragon's Claws '79
Drunken Master '78
The Eagle's Killer '81
Eagle vs. Silver Fox '83
Fist of Fury '95
Hit-Man in the Hand of Buddha '80
The Invincible Armour '77
Magnificent Warriors '87
Martial Arts Mayhem, Vol. 2 '99
Masters of Tiger Crane '83
The Millionaires' Express '86
Return of the Deadly Blade '81
Snake in the Eagle's Shadow '78
Story of the Dragon '76
The 36 Deadly Styles '79
Tiger over Wall '80
Tower of Death '81
Where's Officer Tuba? '86

Lee Hyun-kyoon
Bloody Beach '00

Lee, Jacinta
Angel 2 '88

Lee, James
(Lee I Min, Lee Au Man, Li Yi Min, Lee Ngai Man, Lee Yi Min, Alan

Lee, Simon Lee, Simor Lee)
Brave Archer '77
Drunken Art and Crippled Fist '79
Ninja Checkmate '79
Ninja the Final Duel '85
Rage of the Masters '74
7 Commandments of Kung Fu '79
The World of the Drunken Master '79

Lee Jan-wa
The 18 Jade Arhats '78
Five Elements of Kung Fu '78

Lee, Jason Scott
Dragon: The Bruce Lee Story '93

Lee Jeong-jin
Bloody Beach '00

Lee, Joe
(Lee Yiu Ming, Joe Li Yap Lan)
Bullets over Summer '99
Clean My Name, Mr. Coroner! '00
Comeuppance '00
Fighting for Love '01
Hit Team '00
Juliet in Love '00
Master Q 2001 '01
Runaway '01
Time and Tide '00
Ultimatum '01
United We Stand, and Swim '01
Victim '99

Lee, John Rafter
Vampire Hunter D: Bloodlust '01 (V)

Lee, Jonkit
Romeo Must Die '00

Lee, Judy
(Chia Ling, Ka Ling, Jia Ling, Ga Ling, Chia Ning, Cha-Ling, Chiu Lain)
The Blazing Temple '76
The Bodyguard '73/78
The 8 Masters '77
Iron Monkey 2 '77
Killer Priest '81
Lady Wu Tang '77
Martial Arts Mayhem, Vol. 1 '99
The Master of Death '82
Revengeful Swordwomen '79
Revenge of the Patriots '76
The Shaolin Invincibles '79
The Story in Temple Red Lily '79

Thousand Mile Escort
'76

Lee, Julie
(Lee Wa Yuet, Li Hua Yue, Julia Riva)
A Chinese Torture
Chamber Story '94
Dr. Lamb '92
The Eternal Evil of Asia
'95
Last Hero in China '93
Sex and the Emperor
'94
The Untold Story '92

Lee Ka-ting
(Lee Ga Ding, Li Gu Ding, Lee Kay Ting, Steve Lee)
Aces Go Places 2 '83
Bloody Fight '72
Butterfly and Sword '93
Chinatown Kid '77
City War '88
Dragons Forever '88
The East Is Red '93
The End of the Wicked
Tiger '81
Kung Fu, the Invisible
Fist '72
Royal Tramp '92
Winners and Sinners
'83

Lee Kang-sheng
What Time Is It There?
'01

Lee, Kathy
Masters of Tiger Crane
'83

Lee Keung
(Li Jiang, Li Chiang)
The 18 Jade Arhats '78
Fatal Needles vs. Fatal
Fists '80
Fists of Bruce Lee '79
The Hot, the Cool and
the Vicious '79
The Iron Monkey '77
The Killer Meteors '76
Lady Wu Tang '77
The New Game of
Death '75
Return of the Chinese
Boxer '75
The Shaolin Invincibles
'79
Swordsman with an
Umbrella '70

Lee Ki-young
The Foul King '00
Gate of Destiny '96

Lee Kim Tae-yeon
Lies '99

Lee Kin-yan
(Li Jian Ren, Lee Kin Yun)
Flirting Scholar '93
Forbidden City Cop '96
From Beijing with Love
'94

Lawyer Lawyer '97
9413 '98
The Tricky Master '00
Troublesome Night 3
'97

Lee Kwan
(Lee Gwan, Li Kun, Lee Quinn, Li Kwun, Lee Quin, Quin Lee, Li Ken, Le Quen)
The Chinese Connec-
tion '71
Drunken Tai Chi '84
Fantasy Mission Force
'84
Fearless Hyena '79
A Fistful of Talons '83
Fists of Fury '71
The Incredible Kung Fu
Mission '82
Kung Fu on Sale '79
Snake-Crane Secret
'78
Spiritual Kung Fu '78

Lee Kwang-ho
Yongary, Monster from
the Deep '67

Lee Kwoon Hung
Shadow of the Tiger
'79

Lee Kyoung-young
Gate of Destiny '96

Lee, Leo
Kung Pow: Enter the
Fist '76/2001

Lee, Lichun
A Chinese Ghost Story:
The Tsui Hark Ani-
mation '97 (V)

Lee Lik-Chi
(Li Li Chi)
Forbidden City Cop '96
From Beijing with Love
'94
Gen-Y Cops '00
High Risk '95
Jiang Hu-"The Triad
Zone" '00
Love on Delivery '94
Troublesome Night '97
Troublesome Night 3
'97

Lee, Lily
The Kung Fu Master
'94

Lee Lung-yam
War of the Shaolin Tem-
ple '80

Lee, Maggie
(Lee Lam Lam, Lee Lan Lan, Li Ling Ling)
Breakout from Oppres-
sion '78
Killer Snakes '74
Prodigal Boxer '73

Lee Man Tai
(Li Wen Tai, Liang Shang Yun)
Chinese Hercules '73
Drunken Art and Crip-
pled Fist '79
Half a Loaf of Kung Fu
'77
The Killer Meteors '76
Lady Iron Monkey '83
Mantis Combat '81
The Master of Death
'82
Millionaire's Express
'86
Miracles '89
Mr. Boo Meets Pom
Pom '85
The Prodigal Son '81
Revengeful Sword-
women '79
The Shaolin Disciple
'80
Snake and Crane Arts
of Shaolin '78
Spiritual Kung Fu '78
The 36 Crazy Fists '77
To Kill with Intrigue '77
Young Tiger '72

Lee, Margaret
(Lee Din-Long, Li Dian Lang)
Snake and Crane Arts
of Shaolin '78
We're Going to Eat You!
'80
With or Without You '92

Lee, Marrie
Martial Arts Mayhem,
Vol. 1 '99

Lee, Max
(See Fu Chai, See Foo Jai, Seefu Chai, Bye Foo Chai, Shi Fu Zai, Little Master)
The Chinese Connec-
tion '71
Drunken Master '78
Kung Fu's Hero '73
The Magnificent Butch-
er '79
Prodigal Boxer '72
Snake in the Eagle's
Shadow '78
The 36 Deadly Styles
'79
Young Tiger '73

Lee, Merilyn
Golden Dragon Silver
Snake '79

Lee, Michael
Golden Dragon Silver
Snake '79

Lee, Moon
(Lee Choi-Fung, Li Choi Fung, Mona Lee)
Angel '87
Angel 2 '88
Beauty Investigator '92
Bury Me High '90

Kick Boxer's Tears '92
Mr. Vampire '85
Mr. Vampire 2 '86
The Protector '85
Winners and Sinners
'83
Zu: Warriors of the
Magic Mountain
'83

Lee Nak-hun
A*P*E '76

Lee, Patricia Ja
Extreme Challenge '01

Lee Ping
Model from Hell '99

Lee Pui-shing
Inner Senses '01

Lee, Rachel
(Lee Lai Chun, Li Li Zhen, Loletta Lee, Loretta Lee)
All's Well End's Well '92
Dragon from Russia
'90
Mr. Vampire Saga 4 '88
Pom Pom and Hot Hot
'92
Saga of the Phoenix
'90
Shanghai 1920 '91

Lee Sae-Eun
Bloody Beach '00

Lee, Sam
(Lee Chan-Sam)
Beast Cops '98
Bio Zombie '98
Bio-Cops '00
Color of Pain '02
Final Romance '01
Fist Power '99
A Gambler's Story '01
Gen-X Cops '99
Gen-Y Cops '00
Horror Hotline...Big
Head Monster '01
A Man Called Hero '99
Moonlight Express '99
Trust Me U Die '99
U-Man '02
Visible Secret '01
A War Named Desire
'00

Lee San-San
(Li Shan Shan)
Brassiere '01
Cop Shop Babes '01
Jiang Hu-"The Triad
Zone" '00

Lee, Sarah
(Lee Lai Yui, Li Li Rui)
Dragon from Russia
'90
Fight Back to School 2
'92
Iceman Cometh '89
She Shoots Straight
'90

Lee Seung-chae
Bloody Beach '00

Lee Seung-hyeon
Ring Virus '99

Lee, Sharon
Thunder Ninja Kids:
The Hunt for the
Devil Boxer '86/94

Lee Shing-chak
Haunted Mansion '98

Lee Shuk
Ninja vs. Shaolin
Guards '84

Lee Si-pool
(Li Si Bei)
Everyday Is Valentine
'01
God.com '98

Lee Siu-Kei
(Lee Siu-Kay, Lee Sau-kei, Lau Shui-kei, Lee Siu Gei, Li Zhao Ji)
Abbot White '82
The Adventurers '95
Casino Raiders 2 '91
Century of the Dragon
'99
A Chinese Torture
Chamber Story '94
The Demon's Baby '98
Fist of Fury 1991 '91
Full Alert '97
God of Cookery '96
The Heroic Trio '93
Jiang Hu-"The Triad
Zone" '00
King of Comedy '99
Lawyer Lawyer '97
The Longest Nite '98
Love Correction '00
The Most Wanted '94
Operation Billionaires
'98
Powerful Four '91
Return to a Better
Tomorrow '94
The Storm Riders '98
The Tricky Master '00
Troublesome Night '97
Young and Dangerous
'96
Young and Dangerous
5 '98

Lee Siu-ming
Drunken Art and Crip-
pled Fist '79

Lee Sun-Jae
Yongary, Monster from
the Deep '67

Lee Sung-Jae
Attack the Gas Station!
'99

Lee Sze-pui
God.com '98

Lee, Theresa
(Lee Yee Hung, Li Qi Hong)

Big Bullet '96
Downtown Torpedoes '97
Extreme Crisis '98

Lee, Tiffany
Visible Secret '01

Lee Tin Hung
Duel of the Tao Tough '82

Lee Tin-ying
(Li Tian Ying)
Chinese Hercules '73
Dragon on Fire '79
Super Kung Fu Kid '74

Lee, Tommy
(Lee Gam Ming, Lee Chin Ming, Gam Ming, Jin Ming, Chin Ming)
Challenge of Death '78
Fatal Needles vs. Fatal Fists '80
The Hot, the Cool, and the Vicious '76
Kung Fu, the Invisible Fist '72

Lee Tso Nam
(Lee Chok Laam, Li Zuo Nan, To Lo Po, Lee Jua Nan, Tu Lu Po, Lii Tzvoh Nan)
The Fist, the Kicks and the Evils '79

Lee, Violet
(Lee Ying, Li Ying)
Fantasy Mission Force '84

Lee Wai-wan
Shaolin vs. Lama '81

Lee, Waise
(Lee Chi-Hung, Lee Ji Hung, Li Zi Xiong)
Angel on Fire '95
A Better Tomorrow '86
The Big Heat '88
Bullet in the Head '90
The Cat '91
A Chinese Ghost Story 2 '90
The Conman '98
Gunmen '88
Inner Senses '01
The Legend of the Swordsman '92
The Lord of Hangzhou '98
Powerful Four '91
Running out of Time '99
Task Force '97
A Taste of Killing and Romance '94
Wing Chun '94

Lee Wan-chung
(Li Yun Zhong, Li Yun Chung, Lee Yun Chung)
Hong Kong Nocturne '67
Kung Fu's Hero '73

The Master of Death '82

Lee, Wendee
Vampire Hunter D: Bloodlust '01 (V)

Lee Xing
Legend of the Drunken Tiger '92

Lee Yak-choi
Cold War '00

Lee Yeong-ae
Joint Security Area '00

Lee Young-jin
Memento Mori '99

Lee Yu-yuen
Legend of the Flying Swordsman '00

Leech, Indra
Fight Back to School 2 '92
God of Gamblers 3: Back to Shanghai '91

Lei, Bruce
Martial Arts Mayhem, Vol. 2 '99

Lei Chun
(Lui Jun, Lui Chun, Lei Jun)
Return of the Chinese Boxer '75
Sorrowful to a Ghost '70

Lenaspi, Lito
Devil Woman '70

Leon, Angie
The Big Sting '82

Leton, Kelvin
Crystal Hunt '91

Leung, Angie
(Leung Wan-yui, Liang Yun Rui)
Police Story 2 '88
She Shoots Straight '90

Leung Biu Ching
(Liang Bao Zhing)
Bullet in the Head '90
Miracles '89

Leung, Callan
Ninja vs. Ninja '87

Leung Chi On
(Liang Zhi An)
I Love Maria '88
Queen's High '91

Leung, David
(Lung Juen, Long Zun)
Gorgeous '99
Who Am I? '98

Leung, Fiona
Needing You... '00

Leung, Gigi
(Leung Wing-Kei, Liang Yong Qi, GiGi Leung)
The Avenging Fist '01
Brassiere '01
Contract Killer '98
First Option '96
Full Throttle '95
Sixty Million Dollar Man '95
A War Named Desire '00

Leung, Gordon
Beast Cops '98

Leung, Ivy
(Leung Si Man, Liang Si Min)
Thunder Cop '96
Troublesome Night '97

Leung, Jade
(Leung Chang, Liang Cheng)
Black Cat '91
Could You Kill My Husband Please? '01
Leopard Hunting '98
Satin Steel '94
U-Man '02

Leung, Joey
(Leung Wing-Chung)
Flirting Scholar '93
The Defender '94
Hail the Judge '94
Love on Delivery '94
The New Marvelous Double '92

Leung, Kant
(Leung Wang Fat, Liang Hing Fa)
Ultimatum '01

Leung, Ken
Rush Hour '98

Leung, Nancy
Snake Fist Dynamo '84

Leung Saan
A Moment of Romance '90

Leung, Samuel
(Leung Cheuk Moon, Liang Zhou Man)
The Best of the Best '00
Bio-Cops '00
Crime of a Beast '01
The Deadly Camp '99
Gold Fingers '01
Legend of Speed '99
Master Q 2001 '01
Paramount Motel '00
United We Stand, and Swim '01

Leung Suet-moi
Encounter of the Spooky Kind '81

Leung Ting
Invincible Obsessed Fighter '82

Leung, Vivian
Task Force '97

Leung, Winnie
(Leung Man Yee, Liang Min Yi)
The Deadly Camp '99

Leung Yim
Shaolin Fist of Fury '87

Leung Chiu-Wai, Tony
(Leung Chiu Wai, Liang Chao Wei)
Ashes of Time '94
Bullet in the Head '90
Butterfly and Sword '93
A Chinese Ghost Story 3 '91
Chungking Express '94
Cyclo '95
Days of Being Wild '90
Eagle Shooting Heroes '93
Fighting for Love '01
Gorgeous '99
Hard Boiled '91
I Love Maria '88
In the Mood for Love '00
The Longest Nite '98
Love Me, Love My Money '01
The Magic Crane '93
The Tigers '91
Tokyo Raiders '00
Your Place or Mine! '98

Leung Kar-Fai, Tony
(Leung Kai Fai, Leung Ga Fai, Liang Gu Hui, Tony Leung Ka-Fai)
All Men Are Brothers: Blood of the Leopard '93
Ashes of Time '94
A Better Tomorrow 3 '89
Dragon Inn '92
Eagle Shooting Heroes '93
God of Gamblers Returns '94
Gunmen '88
Jiang Hu-"The Triad Zone" '00
Okinawa Rendez-vous '00
The Prisoner '90
Prison on Fire '87
She Shoots Straight '90
Victim '99

Leung Siu-hung, Tony
(Leung Siu Hung, Liang Xiao Xiong, Hsiung Kuang, Alex Leung Siu Hung)
Five Superfighters '78
The 36 Crazy Fists '77

Levy, Malcolm
Golden Dragon Silver Snake '79

Lewis, Del
Astro Boy '80 (V)

Li, Benny
Comeuppance '00

Li Bin
Beijing Bicycle '01
The Road Home '99

Li, Bruce
(Ho Chung Tao, Lee Shao-Lung, Lei Hsiao-Lung, Lee Roy Lung, Ho Tsung Tao, James Ho, Bruce Ho Chun Tao, Lee Hsiao Lung)
Blind Fist of Bruce '79
Bruce Lee: The Man, the Myth '76
Bruce Lee We Miss You '76
Chinese Iron Man '75
Dynamo '78
Exit the Dragon, Enter the Tiger '75
Fists of Bruce Lee '78
Macho Man '72
Martial Arts Mayhem, Vol. 1 '99
The New Game of Death '75
The Real Bruce Lee '79
Return of the Tiger '79
Revenge of the Patriots '76
Story of the Dragon '76
Triangular Duel '72

Li Che Chou
Iron Man '86

Li Cheung-chuen
Dragons of the Orient '88

Li Chi Leih
Kick Boxer's Tears '92

Li Chin-Kun
(Lee Gam Kwan, Li Jin Kun, Li Chun Kun, Lee Chung Ken, Larry Lee)
The Invincible Kung Fu Trio '78
Ten Tigers of Shaolin '78
Thunder Kick '73

Li Daqiang
Her Majesty Is Fine '96

Li Geng
Frozen '96

Li, Jacqueline
Extreme Challenge '01

Li, Jet
(Li Lian-Jie, Jet Lee)
See also sidebar on p. 564.
Black Mask '96
Born to Defence '88
Contract Killer '98
The Defender '94
Dragons of the Orient '88

782

The Enforcer '95
Fist of Legend '94
High Risk '95
Kiss of the Dragon '01
Last Hero in China '93
The Legend '92
The Legend 2 '93
The Legend of the
    Swordsman '92
Lord of the Wu Tang
    '93
The Master '89
The New Legend of
    Shaolin '94
Once upon a Time in
    China '91
Once upon a Time in
    China 2 '92
Once upon a Time in
    China 3 '93
Once upon a Time in
    China and America
    '97
The One '01
Romeo Must Die '00
The Shaolin One '83
The Shaolin Temple '79
Shaolin Temple 2: Kids
    from Shaolin '84
Twin Warriors '93

Li Junfeng
The Swordswoman in
    White '92

Li, Lilly
The New Marvelous
    Double '92

Li, Lily
*(Li Li-li, Lee Lai Lai, Lily
Lee)*
Dreadnaught '81
Executioners from
    Shaolin '77
Invincible Pole Fighter
    '83
One Arm Hero '94
One Foot Crane '79
Revenge of the Zom-
    bies '76
Run and Kill '93
Sam the Iron Bridge:
    Champion of Mar-
    tial Arts '93
Shaolin Mantis '78
Warrior from Shaolin
    '81
White Lotus Cult '93
The Young Master '80
The Young Tiger '73

Li, Miki
Mr. Nice Guy '97

Li Min Lang
*(Lee Man Long, Li Ming
Long, Li Min Chin)*
The 8 Masters '77
Fighting Ace '79
Half a Loaf of Kung Fu
    '77
Iron Monkey 2 '77
Killer Priest '81
Shaolin vs. Lama '81

Li, Nicky
*(Li Chung-chi, Lee
Chung Chi, Li Zhong
Zhi)*
Crime Story '93
Queen's High '91
Rush Hour '98

Li Ning
*(Lee Ling, Li Ling, Lee
Ning, Michael Ng)*
The Phantom Lover '95
Shaolin Fist of Fury '87
Thunder Ninja Kids:
    The Hunt for the
    Devil Boxer '86/94
Wonder Seven '94

Li, Rain
Goodbye Mr. Cool '01

Li, Rosaline
Ninja in the U.S.A. '88

Li Shiao-hwa
Brave Archer '77

Li Shuang
Beijing Bicycle '01

Li Xida
Her Majesty Is Fine '96

Li Yat-chuen
Killer's Romance '90

Li Yeung-fan
The Deadly Camp '99

Li Ying Ying
(Lee Ying Ying, Li Ying)
Dragon against Vam-
    pire '85
He Has Nothing But
    Kung Fu '77
The Legendary Strike
    '78

Li Zhi Zhou
Deadend of Besiegers
    '92

Li Chi, Nina
(Lei Chi, Li Zhi)
Aces Go Places 5: The
    Terracotta Hit '89
A Chinese Ghost Story
    3 '91
Dragon from Russia
    '90
A Kid from Tibet '91
Pedicab Driver '89
The Seventh Curse '86
Tiger on Beat '88
Twin Dragons '92

Liang, Bruce
*(Leung Siu Leung,
Laing Xiao Long, Hsiao
Liang, Bruce Leung)*
8 Diagram Fighter '91
The Fist, the Kicks and
    the Evils '79
Kung Fu, the Invisible
    Fist '72
Martial Arts Mayhem,
    Vol. 2 '99

My Kung Fu 12 Kicks
    '79
Return of the Deadly
    Blade '81
The Shaolin Kids '77
Ten Tigers of Shaolin
    '78

Liang, Mark
Rage of the Dragon '79

Lim, Burt
Rage of the Dragon '79

Lim Je-eun
Sympathy for Mr.
    Vengeance '01

Lim, Joan
*(Lin Feng Chiao, Lam
Fung Giu, Lin Feng Jiao,
Lin Feng)*
Duel of the Brave Ones
    '78
Revenge of the Zom-
    bies '76

Lim, Mae
Double Dragon in the
    Last Duel '85

Lim, Nancy
Scorpion Thunderbolt
    '85

Lim Ping
Thunder Ninja Kids:
    The Hunt for the
    Devil Boxer '86/94

Limpapat, Korklate
Bangkok Dangerous
    '00

Lin, Andrew
*(Lin Hoi, Lian Kai, Lin
Hai)*
The Blacksheep Affair
    '98
God.com '98
Love au Zen '01
Love Paradox '00
Sunshine Cops '99
2000 A.D. '00
The Vampire Combat
    '01

Lin, Brigitte
*(Lin Ching-Hsia, Lam
Ching Ha, Lin Qing Xia,
Venus Lin)*
Ashes of Time '94
The Bride with White
    Hair '93
The Bride with White
    Hair 2 '93
Chungking Express '94
Deadful Melody '94
Dragon Chronicles:
    Maidens of Heaven-
    ly Mountain '94
Dragon Inn '92
Eagle Shooting Heroes
    '93
The East Is Red '93
Fantasy Mission Force
    '84

The Legend of the
    Swordsman '92
Peking Opera Blues '86
Police Story '85
Royal Tramp '92
Royal Tramp 2 '92
The Three Swordsmen
    '94
Zu: Warriors of the
    Magic Mountain
    '83

Lin, Jimmy
*(Lin Chi-Ying, Lin Chih-
Ying)*
Butterfly and Sword '93
Chivalrous Legend '98

Lin Ke-ming
*(Lam Hak Ming, Ke
Ming, Ku Ming)*
Blind Fist of Bruce '79
Dirty Ho '79
Dirty Tiger, Crazy Frog
    '78
The Eagle's Killer '81
Enter the Fat Dragon
    '78
Executioners from
    Shaolin '77
Fists and Guts '80
The Fists, the Kicks
    and the Evils '79
Hand of Death '76
He Has Nothing But
    Kung Fu '77
Invincible Pole Fighter
    '83
Kung Fu Genius '79
Kung Fu, the Invisible
    Fist '72
The Legendary Strike
    '78
Legendary Weapons of
    China '82
The Magnificent '79
Shaolin Master Killer
    '78
Warrior from Shaolin
    '81

Lin, Kelly
*(Lin Hsi Lei, Lam Hei
Lui, Lin Xi Lei, Kelly
Lam)*
For Bad Boys Only '00
Fulltime Killer '01
The Irresistible Piggies
    '02
Legend of Speed '99
Martial Angels '01
Running out of Time 2
    '01
The Tricky Master '00
Zu Warriors '01

Lin, Lindy
The Bloody Fists '72

Lin, Ruby
*(Lam Sam Yue, Lin Xin
Ru)*
China Strike Force '00
Comic King '00

Lin, Selina
It Takes a Thief '01

Lin, Teddy
Fulltime Killer '01

Lin Ying, Linda
(Lam Ying, Lin Ying)
Dance of the Drunk
    Mantis '79
Drunken Master '78

Lindo, Delroy
The One '01
Romeo Must Die '00

Ling, Lisa
Extreme Challenge '01

Ling-lung, Yu
*(Yu Lin Lung, Yuk Lung,
Yu Long)*
The Killer Meteors '76
To Kill with Intrigue '77

Ling Man Hoi
Shaolin vs. Manchu '80

Ling-wai, Chan
(Chen Ling Wei)
My Kung Fu 12 Kicks
    '79

Ling Yun
(Ling Wan, Lin Yuen)
The Deadly Sword '78
Hong Kong Nocturne
    '67
The Last Duel '82
Militant Eagle '78

Linn, Rex
Rush Hour '98

Linn, Teresa
Lady Ninja: Reflections
    of Darkness '96

Lintan, Sheila
Blowback: Love and
    Death '02

Liu, Annie
Kung Fu Genius '79

Liu Chi-ching
The Shaolin One '83

Liu Fan
(Lu Fen)
Crocodile Hunter '89
Hail the Judge '94
Peace Hotel '95

Liu, Hilda
*(Liu Hao Yi, Liu Hao
Yee, Lau Hiu Yi)*
A Fistful of Talons '83
Shaolin Chastity Kung
    Fu '81

Liu Huai Liang
*(Lau Waai Leung, Liu
Hui Ling)*
Brave Archer '77
The Shaolin Temple '79
Yellow River Fighter '88

Liu, Jackson
(Liu Hseiu-hsien, Lau Hok Yin, Lou Xiao Xian, Jackson Lau)
China Strike Force '00
First Strike '96
Fist of Legend '94
The Last Blood '90
Red Shield '91

Liu, Jimmy
(Lau Ga Yung, Liu Gu Yong, Lau Kar Cheung, Liu Gia Yung, Liu Chia Hsiung) See also sidebar on p. 278.
Dirty Tiger, Crazy Frog '78
Dragon's Claws '79
Duel of the Brave Ones '78
Legend of the Drunken Master '94
The Shaolin Disciple '80
The 36 Crazy Fists '77
Warrior from Shaolin '81

Liu Jing
The Cold Mountain Temple '91

Liu, John
(Liu Chung Liang, Lau Chung Leung, Liu Zhong Liang, John La, Lau Chung-luen)
Death Duel of Kung Fu '79
Dragon on Fire '79
Fighting Ace '79
The Incredible Kung Fu Mission '82
The Invincible Armour '77
The Invincible Kung Fu Trio '78

Liu, Johnny
Iron Monkey 2 '96

Liu Kai-chi
(Liao Qi Zhi)
Dragon Chronicles: Maidens of Heavenly Mountain '94
Funeral March '01
In the Line of Duty 4 '89
Moonlight Express '99

Liu Kat Lin
Doctor No... '01

Liu Lei
Beijing Bicycle '01

Liu Lin
The Phantom Lover '95

Liu, Liu
The Adventures of the Master and His Servant '96

Liu Ping
(Lu Ping)

The Blazing Temple '76
Chinese Iron Man '75
The 8 Masters '77
The 18 Bronzemen '76
The Invincible Kung Fu Trio '78
Militant Eagle '78
Screaming Ninja '73
The Shaolin Kids '77
Snake and Crane Arts of Shaolin '78
Triangular Duel '72

Liu, Rene
A Chinese Ghost Story: The Tsui Hark Animation '97 (V)
A Chinese Ghost Story: The Tsui Hark Animation '97 (V)
Thunder Cop '96 (V)

Liu Shu Hua
(Li Shao Hua)
18 Secrets of Kung Fu '79
Hunted by Royal Decree '00
Rebels under Siege '00

Liu, Terry
(Lau Wai Yue, Liu Hui Ru, Liu Wei Yu, Liu Hui Ju, Liu Hui Juen)
The Invincible Killer '79
Militant Eagle '78
Revenge of the Zombies '76

Liu, Tiffany
(Lau Yuk Ting, Liu Yu Ting)
A Chinese Ghost Story 3 '91

Liu Tingyao
Her Majesty Is Fine '96

Liu, Tony
(Liu Jun Guk, Lu Jun Gu, Lu Chin Ku, Lo Chun Guk, Tony Lo, Lu Chun-ku, Tommy Loo Chun)
The Chinese Connection '71
Dynamo '78
Exit the Dragon, Enter the Tiger '75
Return of the Dragon '72
Tiger over Wall '80

Liu Wai-hung
(Liao Wei Xiaong)
Comic King '00
Iceman Cometh '89
Take 2 in Life '01
Undercover Blues '00

Liu Wu-Chi
The Flying Guillotine '74

Liu Yin Sheung
The Hot, the Cool, and the Vicious '76

Livingston, Richard B.
Reptilian '00

Lo, Candy
(Lo Hau Yam, Lu Qiao Yin)
The Eye '02
Funeral March '01
Happy Family '02
Time and Tide '00
Tiramisu '02

Lo Dik
(Lu Di, Lu Ti)
Chinatown Kid '77
Yoga and Kung Fu Girl '78

Lo Han Ma
The Holy Robe of Shaolin Temple '84

Lo Hoi-pang
(Lu Hai Peng)
The Irresistible Piggies '02
The Longest Nite '98
Losers' Club '01

Lo Hua
The Invincible Killer '79

Lo Hung
(Lu Xiong)
Dragon from Russia '90
Operation Pink Squad '88
Violent Cop '99

Lo, Ken
(Lo Wai-Kwong, Low Houi-Kang, Lo Wei-Gong, Kenneth Houi Kang Low, Lu Wai Kwon, Harold Low)
China Strike Force '00
City Hunter '92
Crime Story '93
Crystal Hunt '91
The Enforcer '95
Final Justice '88
First Strike '96
Gen-X Cops '99
God of Gamblers Returns '94
Gorgeous '99
The Inspector Wears Skirts '88
Kick Boxer's Tears '92
Legend of the Drunken Master '94
Lethal Panther '91
A Man Called Hero '99
Miracles '89
Naked Killer '92
Operation Condor '91
Police Story 2 '88
Project A 2 '87
Runaway '01
Rush Hour '98
Supercop '92
Thunderbolt '95
The Tricky Master '00
2000 A.D. '00

Lo Lieh
(Law Lit, Luo Lie)
Battle of Shaolin '77
Born Invincible '78
City War '88
Dirty Ho '79
Dragons Forever '88
Drunken Arts and Crippled Fist '79
The 18 Jade Arhats '78
Emperor of Shaolin Kung Fu '80
Executioners from Shaolin '77
Fatal Needles vs. Fatal Fists '80
Fists and Guts '79
Fists of Bruce Lee '78
Fists of the White Lotus '80
Five Fingers of Death '72
Glass Tears '01
The Green Dragon Inn '79
In the Line of Duty 5: Middle Man '90
Killer from Above '77
The Kung Fu Master '94
Lady Iron Monkey '83
The Massive '78
The Master of Death '82
Miracles '89
99 Cycling Swords '80
Ninja Supremo '81
Ninja vs. Bruce Lee '82
One Foot Crane '79
On the Run '88
Return of the Deadly Blade '81
Revenge of the Zombies '76
Secret of the Chinese Kung Fu '81
Shaolin Master Killer '78
The Smart Cavalier '78
Supercop '92
Thousand Mile Escort '76
The Tigers '91
Tragic Fantasy: Tiger of Wanchai '94
The Vampire Combat '01

Lo, Lowell
(Lo Koon Ting, Lu Guan Ting)
Aces Go Places 3 '84
Magnificent Warriors '87
Operation Pink Squad '88
Pedicab Driver '89
Rosa '86

Lo, May
(Lo Mei Mei, Law Mei Mei, Luo Mei Mei)
The Last Blood '90
Miracles '89
Picture of a Nymph '88

Pom Pom Strikes Back '86

Lo Meng
(Lo Mang, Johnson Law) See also sidebar on p. 374.
Avenging Warriors of Shaolin '79
Brave Archer '77
Bullets over Summer '99
Chinatown Kid '77
Chinese Super Ninjas '82
The Eternal Evil of Asia '95
Five Deadly Venoms '78
Hard Boiled '91
Kid with the Golden Arm '78
Magnificent Warriors '87
Masked Avengers '81
The Masked Prosecutor '99
The Return of the 5 Deadly Venoms '78
Return to a Better Tomorrow '94
Ten Tigers of Kwangtung '79
Troublesome Night 3 '97

Lo, Money
(Lo Man Yee, Lu Min Yi)
Brother of Darkness '94
Daughter of Darkness '93
Police Story '85
Red to Kill '94

Lo, Monica
(Lo Suk Yee, Lu Shu Yi)
Happy Family '02
Hit Team '00

Lo Ta-yu
A Chinese Ghost Story: The Tsui Hark Animation '97 (V)

Lo, Yoky
Gimme Gimme '01

Loffrede, Phillip
Heroes Shed No Tears '83/86

Loh, Mayu
Record '00

Lok, Cliff
(Goo Lung, Gu Long, Koo Lung, Gam Tung, Chin Tong, Lung Goon Ting, Lung Kuan Ting, Chin Tung)
Killer from Above '77
Kung Fu Genius '79
Ninja Supremo '81
Shadow of the Tiger '79
The Shaolin Kids '77

Lok, Felix
(Lok Ying Kwan, Lok Ying Gwan, Luo Ying Jun)
Born Wild '01
Chinese Orthopedist and the Spice Girls '02

Lone, John
(Juen Lung, Zun Long) See also sidebar on p. 326.
Rush Hour 2 '01
Shanghai 1920 '91
Task Force '97

Long, Johnny
Beast of the Yellow Night '70
Mad Doctor of Blood Island '68

Loong, Loong
Rebels under Siege '00

Lopez, Cecilia
The Walls of Hell '64

Lord, Kris
Rumble in the Bronx '95

Lou, Alexander
(Lo Rei, Law Yui, Luo Rui, Alexander Lo)
The Incredible Kung Fu Mission '82
Ninja Hunter '83
Ninja in the U.S.A. '88
Ninja the Final Duel '85
Ninja vs. Shaolin Guards '84
Shaolin Chastity Kung Fu '81
Shaolin vs. Lama '81
Shaolin vs. Ninja '83
The Super Ninja '84

Louie, Bill
The Bodyguard '73/78
Fist of Fear-Touch of Death '80

Lu Feng
(Luk Fung, Centipede Venom) See also sidebar on p. 374.
Avenging Warriors of Shaolin '79
Brave Archer '77
Chinatown Kid '77
Death Ring '83
Five Deadly Venoms '78
5 Venoms vs. Wu Tang '87
Flag of Iron '80
Kid with the Golden Arm '78
Masked Avengers '81
Nine Demons '83
Ninja in the Deadly Trap '83
The Return of the 5 Deadly Venoms '78

Ten Tigers of Kwang-tung '79

Lu, Peggy
Kung Pow: Enter the Fist '76/2001

Lu Wei
(Liu Wai, Lo Wai)
Blooded Treasury Fight '79
Inheritor of Kung Fu '77
Iron Monkey 2 '77

Lu Yan
The Cold Mountain Temple '91

Lu Yi-ching
What Time Is It There? '01

Lucas, David
Street Fighter 2 '96 (V)

Lui, Bill
(Lui Cho-Hung, Lui Choh Hung, Lei Chu Xiong)
Black Mask '96
The Blade '95
The Bride with White Hair 2 '93
Contract Killer '98
Crime Story '93
Green Snake '93
9413 '98
Pom Pom and Hot Hot '92
Powerful Four '92
Robotrix '91
Twin Dragons '92
You Shoot, I Shoot '01

Lui, Crystal
Comeuppance '00

Lui, Elaine
(Lui Siu Ling, Lu Shao Ling)
Angel '87
Angel 2 '88
The Bride with White Hair '93
The Red Wolf '95

Lui Fong
(Lu Fang)
Miracles '89
New Mr. Vampire '86
Project A 2 '87
Shogun and Little Kitchen '92
Venom Warrior '83

Lui, Jackie
(Lui Chung Yin, Lu Song Xian, Jacky Lui)
The Blood Rules '00
The Final Winner '01
Goodbye Mr. Cool '01
The Mission '99
The Vampire Combat '01

Lui, Kevin
Thunder Ninja Kids: The Hunt for the Devil Boxer '86/94

Lui, Michael
(Lui Mai Go, Lu Mi Gao, Michael Lieu)
Armageddon '97
Beast Cops '98
Hit Team '00

Lui Ming
(Lei Ming, Kui Ming)
Hong Kong Nocturne '67
The Massive '78
Screaming Ninja '73
The Shaolin Brothers '77
Snake-Crane Secret '78

Lui Ngai
Victim '99

Lui, Ray
(Lui Leung-Wai, Lu Liang Wei, Raymond Lui)
Flash Future Kung Fu '83
God of Gamblers 3: Back to Shanghai '91
Miracles '89
Project A 2 '87
The Suspect '98
2000 A.D. '00
Undercover Blues '00

Lui, Raymond
(Lui Shing Gung, Lei Cheng Gong)
Brutal Boxer '72
Hard as a Dragon '80

Lui, Simon
(Lui Yu-Yeung, Lui Yue Yeung, Lei Yu Yang, Simon Loui)
All's Well End's Well '97 '97
Ballistic Kiss '98
The Cheaters '01
F*** / Off '98
Happy Family '02
Headlines '01
Killer '99
Last Ghost Standing '99
Lawyer Lawyer '97
Paramount Motel '00
The Replacement Suspects '01
Sunshine Cops '99
Super Car Criminals '99
Troublesome Night '97
Troublesome Night 3 '97
Troublesome Night 4 '98
Troublesome Night 8 '00

Troublesome Night 9 '00
Undercover Blues '00
Young and Dangerous 5 '98

Luk Chuen
(Luk Chuen Tai Cheung, Lu Cun Tai Xiang, Yasuyoshi Shikamura)
Casino Raiders '89
God of Gamblers '89
God of Gamblers 2 '90
Killer's Romance '87
Shaolin Fist of Fury '87

Luk, Jamie
(Luk Kim Ming, Liu Jian Ming, Lu Chien-ming)
Avenging Eagle '78
Brave Archer '77
C'est la Vie, Mon Cheri '93
Chinatown Kid '77
Dirty Ho '79
Five Superfighters '78
Kid with the Golden Arm '78
Lee Rock '91
Red Shield '91
The Return of the 5 Deadly Venoms '78
Rumble in the Bronx '95
Ten Tigers of Kwang-tung '79
Twin Dragons '92
The Untold Story 2 '98

Luk Yat-lung
(Liu Yi Long, Lu I Lung)
The Killer Meteors '76
New Fist of Fury '75

Lum Ken-ming
BloodFight '89

Lun, Kelly
Magnificent Natural Fist '80

Lung Chuan
(Lung Suen, Long Xuan)
Lady Wu Tang '77
The Six Directions of Boxing '79

Lung, Doris
(Lung Chun Erh, Lung Gwan Ngai, Long Jun Er, Lung Chung Erh, Mabel Lung, Lung Gwan Yi, Doris Chen, Lung Kwan Yee, Lung Chyung-er, Lung Chun Ie)
The 8 Masters '77
Fighting Ace '79
Golden Killah '80
Half a Loaf of Kung Fu '77
The Magnificent '78
Master of the Flying Guillotine '74
Moonlight Sword and Jade Lion '79

The Shaolin Invincibles '79
Shaolin Wooden Men '76
The Silver Spear '79
The Smart Cavalier '78

Lung Fei
(Long Fei, Lung Fai, Long Fuei, Lung Pei)
Blood of the Dragon '71
Born Invincible '78
Bruce Lee We Miss You '77
The Buddha Assassinator '79
Dreaming Fists with Slender Hands '80
The 18 Jade Arhats '78
Exit the Dragon, Enter the Tiger '75
Killer from Above '77
Kung Pow: Enter the Fist '76/2001
Master of the Flying Guillotine '74
The New Game of Death '75
Rage of the Masters '74
Return of the Chinese Boxer '75
Return of the Tiger '79
Revenge of the Patriots '76
Screaming Ninja '73
Secret of the Chinese Kung Fu '81
7 Commandments of Kung Fu '79
The 72 Desperate Rebels '76
The Smart Cavalier '78
The Story in Temple Red Lily '79
A Touch of Zen '69
The World of the Drunken Master '79

Lung Fong
(Long Fang, Jimmy Lee, Lee Kin man, Li Chien Man, Li Chien Min, Lee Jian Min)
Casino Raiders '89
Challenge of Death '78
Crocodile Hunter '89
Dragon in Jail '90
Eagle's Claw '77
Fatal Needles vs. Fatal Fists '80
God of Gamblers '89
God of Gamblers 3: Back to Shanghai '91
H.K. Adams Family '92
The Hot, the Cool, and the Vicious '76
Kick Boxer's Tears '92
Lawyer Lawyer '97
Lee Rock '91
Legend of the Dragon '91
The Longest Nite '98

Master of the Flying
  Guillotine '74
The Shaolin Kids '77

Lung, Jack
*(Lung Sai Ga, Long Shi
Gu, Jack Long, Lung
Shih Chia, Wang Chi-
ang, Lung Si Kar, Wong
Keung, Long Hsu Chia)*
Born Invincible '78
Master of the Flying
  Guillotine '76
Ninja Checkmate '79
Ninja Hunter '83
Return of the Chinese
  Boxer '75
Revenge of the Patriots
  '76
Secret of the Chinese
  Kung Fu '81
The Shaolin Invincibles
  '79
The Six Directions of
  Boxing '79
The Super Ninja '84
The 36 Deadly Styles
  '79
The Unbeaten 28 '80
The World of the Drunk-
  en Master '79

Lung, Mark
*(Lung Goon Mo, Lung
Goon Miu, Long Guan
Wu, Mark Long, Lung
Kuan Wu)*
Born Invincible '78
Ninja Checkmate '79
The 36 Deadly Styles
  '79
The Unbeaten 28 '80
War of the Shaolin Tem-
  ple '80
The World of the Drunk-
  en Master '79

Lung Ming-yan
(Long Ming En)
A Better Tomorrow '86
A Better Tomorrow 2
  '87
Code of Honor '87
Skinny Tiger and Fatty
  Dragon '90

Lung, Patrick
*(Lung Kong, Lung Gong,
Long Gang)*
Black Mask '96
Once upon a Time in
  China and America
  '97
The Wesley's Mysteri-
  ous File '01

Lung, Sihung
Crouching Tiger, Hidden
  Dragon '00
The Touch '02

Lung Tin Cheung
*(Lung Tien Hsiang,
Long Tian Xiang, Lung
Tung Sheng, Lung Tin
Sang, Nung Tien*

Hsiang, Lung Tien
Shang, Lung Tin Cheng)
Angel '87
Chinese Super Ninjas
  '82
Dragon Kid '90
Drunken Art and Crip-
  pled Fist '79
Flag of Iron '80
99 Cycling Swords '80
The Six Directions of
  Boxing '79
Ten Tigers of Kwang-
  tung '79
Two Dragons Fight
  against Tiger '75
The World of the Drunk-
  en Master '79

Lung Woo Yiu
Duel of the Tao Tough
  '82

Lung Yuen
Magnificent Natural
  Fist '80

Lutes, Eric
Fatal Blade '00

Ly, Bruce
Martial Arts Mayhem,
  Vol. 2 '99

Lye, James
2000 A.D. '00

Lyn, Vincent
Blonde Fury '89
Operation Condor '91
Tiger Cage '88

Ma, Anita
Thunder Ninja Kids:
  The Hunt for the
  Devil Boxer '86/94

Ma, Carrie
Thunder Ninja Kids:
  The Hunt for the
  Devil Boxer '86/94

Ma Cheung
*(Ma Chang, Tattooed
Ma)*
Challenge of Death '78
Crippled Masters '80
The Deadly Sword '78
Eagle's Claw '77
Exit the Dragon, Enter
  the Tiger '76
Fatal Needles vs. Fatal
  Fists '78
Fearless Hyena '79
Fearless Hyena 2 '83
Five Elements of Kung
  Fu '78
5 Lady Venoms '78
Iron Neck Li '81
The Killer Meteors '76
Mask of Death '76
Ninja Hunter '84
Raiders of Wu Tang '82
The Unbeaten 28 '80
Ways of Kung Fu '80

Ma Chin-ku
*(Ma Gam Guk, Ma Jin
Gu, Ma Chiu Ku, Xiao
Kao Shan, Siu Ko San,
Hsiao Kao Shan)*
Cantonen Iron Kung Fu
  '79
Dragon Lord '82
A Fistful of Talons '83
Incredible Kung Fu Mis-
  sion '79
Master of the Flying
  Guillotine '76
Militant Eagle '78
Ninja in the Deadly Trap
  '81
Ninja Supremo '81
Raiders of Wu Tang '82
7 Commandments of
  Kung Fu '79

Ma Ching-tao
(Ma Jin Tao, Ma Juntao)
Legend of the Dragon-
  slayer Sword '90
Legend of the Dragon-
  slayer Sword 2-The
  Rising Son '90
Legend of the Dragon-
  slayer Sword 3-The
  Rage of Gina '90

Ma, David
Dragon against Vam-
  pire '85

Ma Fat-yan
*(Ma Bat Yan, Ma Fo
Ren, Frank De Maria)*
Fatal Needles vs. Fatal
  Fists '80

Ma Hok-ming
*(Ma Xiao Ming, Jackie
Ma)*
Happy Family '02
Super Car Criminals
  '99

Ma, James
Legend of the 7 Golden
  Vampires '74

Ma, Joe
*(Ma Chung Tak, Ma
Zhong De)*
Body Weapon '99
Clean My Name, Mr.
  Coroner! '00
Cop Shop Babes '01
The Hero of Swallow
  '96
The 36 Deadly Styles
  '79

Ma Kei
(Ma Ji, Ma Chi)
The Deadly Sword '78
Fearless Fighters '73
Fury of King Boxer '72
The Iron Monkey '77
The Killer Meteors '76
Kung Pow: Enter the
  Fist '76/2001
Lady Whirlwind and the
  Rangers '74

Return of the Chinese
  Boxer '75
Revenge of the Patriots
  '76
Screaming Ninja '73
Sorrowful to a Ghost
  '70
The Story in Temple
  Red Lily '79
Swordsman with an
  Umbrella '70
To Kill with Intrigue '77

Ma Kim-tong
Cantonen Iron Kung Fu
  '79

Ma Lau
Flash Future Kung Fu
  '83

Ma Qian-shan
Flyin Dance '01

Ma, Season
*(Ma Si-San, Ma See
San)*
In the Line of Duty 3
  '88
The Owl vs. Bombo '84
Twinkle Twinkle Lucky
  Stars '85

Ma, Stephen
Doctor No... '01

Ma Sze-Peng
Kid with the Golden
  Arm '78

Ma Tien Long
Ninja vs. Bruce Lee '82

Ma Tzi-chin
Mask of Death '76

Ma Xiaoqing
Frozen '96

Maang Fai
Gold Fingers '01
Young and Dangerous
  5 '98

Macaulay, Charles
Twilight People '72

**Machan, "Little
Man"**
All Monsters Attack '70
Son of Godzilla '67

Machida, Kyosuke
Zatoichi and the Fugi-
  tives '68

Mack, Gilbert
Astro Boy '63 (V)

MacKay, Robin
Robo Vampire '88

Madhoo
Elaan '94

Madhubala
Mahal '48

Maeda, Ai
Battle Royale '00

Gamera 3: The
  Revenge of Irys '99
Godzilla, Mothra and
  King Ghidorah: Bat-
  tle on Fire '01

Maeda, Aki
Battle Royale '00
Gamera 3: The
  Revenge of Irys '99
Godzilla, Mothra and
  King Ghidorah: Bat-
  tle on Fire '01

Maeda, Bibari
Son of Godzilla '67

Mah, Bobby
Champ against Champ
  '83

Mah Ji Leung
The Law and the Out-
  law '95

Maher, Eddie
City War '88
Crocodile Hunter '89
Don't Give a Damn '95
In the Line of Duty 4
  '89
Pedicab Driver '89
Yes, Madam '85

Maheubani, Rashma
Visible Secret '01

Mahmood
Gumnaam '65

Mahoney, Jock
The Walls of Hell '64

Mai Kei
(Mi Ji, Mei Chi)
The Eagle's Killer '81
Fist of Fury 1991 '91
Inspector Wears Skirts
  '88
Leopard Hunting '98
Miracles '89
Peace Hotel '95
Pedicab Driver '89
Police Story 2 '88
Project A 2 '87
Scared Stiff '87
Yes, Madam '85

Mai Taichira
Zero Woman: The
  Accused '96

Mak Cheung-ching
God.com '98

Mak, Marco
Happy Family '02

Mak, Robert
Invincible Pole Fighter
  '83
Ten Tigers of Kwang-
  tung '79

Mak, Shirley
Invincible Obsessed
  Fighter '82

Mak, Steve
Bruce Lee Fights Back from the Grave '76
Duel of the Tao Tough '82

Mak, Teresa
(Mak Ga Kei, Mai Gu Qi, Maggie Mak)
House of the Damned '99
Love Me, Love My Money '01
Martial Angels '01
Troublesome Night '97

Mak, Thomson
Rage of the Dragon '79
The Snake Strikes Back '81

Mak, Walter
Lethal Panther '91

Maka, Karl
(Kais Mak, Jia Mai, Carl Mak, Mak Ka)
Aces Go Places '82
Aces Go Places 2 '83
Aces Go Places 3 '84
Aces Go Places 4 '86
Aces Go Places 5: The Terracotta Hit '89
Crazy Crooks '80
Dirty Kung Fu '78
Dirty Tiger, Crazy Frog '78
Eighth Happiness '88
He Has Nothing But Kung Fu '77
His Name Is Nobody '79
Knockabout '79
The Magnificent Scoundrels '91
Odd Couple '79
Shaolin King Boxer '79
Skinny Tiger and Fatty Dragon '90
The Victim '80

Maki, Chitose
Blind Swordsman: The Tale of Zatoichi '62

Maki, Fuyukichi
Legend of the Dinosaurs '77

Maki, Kuroudo
Brother '00

Maki, Yuko
Princess Blade '02

Mako
The Big Brawl '80
The Green Hornet '74

Malalene
Fists of Fury '71

Malini, Hema
Sholay '75

Mallow, Dave
Tokyo Decameron: Three Tales of Mad-ness and Sensuali-ty '96 (U.S.) (N)

Malonzo, Rhea
Leopard Hunting '98

Mamood, Ricardo
Gen-Y Cops '00

Man, Alex
(Man Chi-Leung, Man Jin Leung)
Casino Tycoon 2 '92
Crocodile Hunter '89
Long Arm of the Law 2 '87
Rich and Famous '87
Young and Dangerous 5 '98
Young and Dangerous 6: Born to Be King '00

Man, Cheng Yuen
(Jeng Yuen Man, Zheng Wan Wen)
Iron Monkey 2 '96
Nightmare Zone '98

Man, Chik King
(Zhi Jing Wen, Noel Chik)
Erotic Ghost Story 2 '91
Forbidden City Cop '96
Her Name Is Cat '98
Young and Dangerous '96

Man Chung-han
Wishful Milenio '01

Man Chung-san
(Wen Song Xian)
The Hot, the Cool, and the Vicious '76
Militant Eagle '78
Moonlight Sword and Jade Lion '79
Thunderbolt '95
A Touch of Zen '69

Man, Fung Ging
(Feng Jing Wen, Louis Feng, Feng Chin Wen)
Aces Go Places 4 '86
Bolo '80
Bruce Lee: The Man, the Myth '76
Dirty Tiger, Crazy Frog '78
Dreadnaught '81
Drunken Master '78
Duel of the Brave Ones '78
Encounter of the Spooky Kind '81
Enter the Fat Dragon '78
Five Superfighters '78
Flag of Iron '80
The Haunted Cop Shop '87
Heart of Dragon '85
The Imp '81
The Legend of Bruce Lee '80

The Magnificent Butch-er '79
New Mr. Vampire '86
The Owl vs. Bombo '84
Pedicab Driver '89
Pom Pom '84
Pom Pom Strikes Back '86
Project A '83
Rosa '86
Shaolin Master Killer '78
Snake in the Eagle's Shadow '78
Ten Tigers of Kwang-tung '79
Warrior from Shaolin '81
Winners and Sinners '83
The Young Avenger '79

Man, Joey
(Man Yee-man, Wan Qi Wen, Joey Meng)
The Bride with White Hair 2 '93
Century of the Dragon '99
Fist of Fury '95
Sound from the Dark '00
Vampire Controller '00
A Wicked Ghost 2: The Fear '00

Man Kong Lung
(Wen Jiang Long, Wen Chiang Long, Chiang Long Wen, Jackie Wen)
Battle of Shaolin '77
Chinese Iron Man '75
18 Fatal Strikes '78
Killer Priest '81
Lady Wu Tang '77
Moonlight Sword and Jade Lion '79
Revengeful Sword-women '79
Triangular Duel '72

Man, Lee Kin
The Hot, the Cool, and the Vicious '76

Man Lee-pang
Kung Fu on Sale '79

Man, Man
(Min min, Min Ming, Min Min)
Challenge of Death '78
Fury of King Boxer '72
The Killer Meteors '76
The Master of Death '82
The Story in Temple Red Lily '79
Thousand Mile Escort '76

Man So
(Man Siu, Wen Su, Man Su)
Erotic Ghost Story '90

Erotic Ghost Story 2 '91

Man, Tony
Scorpion Thunderbolt '85

Man Wun-hsia
Killer of Snake, Fox of Shaolin '78

Manda, Hisako
Parasite Eve '97

Mang Hoi
(Meng Hoi, Hoi Man, Randy Mang) See also sidebar on p. 326.
The Art of Action: Mar-tial Arts in the Movies '02
Blonde Fury '89
The Buddha Assassina-tor '79
Dirty Tiger, Crazy Frog '78
Enter the Fat Dragon '78
Executioners from Shaolin '77
Fatal Flying Guillotine '77
Heart of Dragon '85
Legacy of Rage '86
The Millionaires' Express '86
Pedicab Driver '89
Twinkle Twinkle Lucky Stars '85
Yes, Madam '85
Zu: Warriors of the Magic Mountain '83

Mang Ling-ming
The Master of Death '82

Mang, Suzy
(Mang Lee, Sucy Mang, Meng Li)
The Awaken Punch '73
From China with Death '74

Manmohan
Gumnaam '65

Mann, Larry D.
The Green Hornet '74

Mano, Kirina
Adrenaline Drive '99

Mao, Angela
(Mao Ying, Maau Ying)
Battle of Shaolin '77
Enter the Dragon '73
The Invincible Kung Fu Trio '78
The Legendary Strike '78
Martial Arts Mayhem, Vol. 1 '99
Moonlight Sword and Jade Lion '79
Return of the Tiger '79

Snake Deadly Act '79
Sting of the Dragon Masters '73

Mao, Fredric
(Mao Chun Fai, Mo Jun Fai, Mao Jun Hui, Mo Chun-fai)
9413 '98

Marchent, Jean
Aces Go Places 3 '84

Marchini, Ron
Murder in the Orient '74

Mari, Keiko
Godzilla vs. Hedorah '71

Marie
Leopard Hunting '98

Maro, Akaji
The Haunted Lantern '98
Kikujiro '99
Postman Blues '97

Marquez, Melanie
Angel on Fire '95

Marriott, Alan
Devil Man '87 (V)

Mars
(Feng Sing, Huo Xing, Fwa Sing, Huo Hsing)
See also sidebar on p. 326.
The Awaken Punch '73
Bruce Lee: The Man, the Myth '76
Brutal Boxer '72
The Chinese Connec-tion '71
Crime Story '93
Dirty Tiger, Crazy Frog '78
Dragon Lord '82
Dragon on Fire '79
Enter the Dragon '73
Enter the Fat Dragon '78
Fists and Guts '8
Game of Death '78
He Has Nothing But Kung Fu '77
His Name Is Nobody '79
The Inspector Wears Skirts '88
Knockabout '79
Last Hurrah for Chivalry '78
The Legendary Strike '78
Legend of the Drunken Master '94
The Millionaires' Express '86
Miracles '89
Moonlight Express '99
Odd Couple '79
Police Story '85
Police Story 2 '88

Pom Pom '84
The Private Eyes '76
Project A '83
Project A 2 '87
Return of the Deadly
    Blade '81
Super Kung Fu Kid '74
Supercop '92
Supercop 2 '93
Super Kung Fu Kid '74
Thunder Kick '73
Twin Dragons '92
Wheels on Meals '84
Winners and Sinners
    '83
Yes, Madam '85
The Young Tiger '73

Martin, Dean
Cannonball Run '81

Marui, Taro
Wrath of Daimajin '66

Maruyama, Kenichiro
Ebirah, Horror of the
    Deep '66
Son of Godzilla '67

Masako
Ring '98
Ring 2 '99
Ring 0: Birthday '00

Mash
I.K.U. '00

Masu, Takeshi
The Hypnotist '99

**Masumoto, Shoichi-
ro**
Versus '00

Matalon, Adam
Devil Man '87 (V)

Matsubara, Chieko
Black Tight Killers '66
Tokyo Drifter '66

Matsuda, Kenji
Versus '00

Matsuda, Miyuki
Audition '99

Matsuda, Naofumi
Terminatrix '95

Matsuda, Seiko
Fatal Blade '00

Matsuda, Yasunori
Terminatrix '95

Matsui, Kenzo
Sanjuro '63

Matsui, Norio
Ran '85

Matsui, Tetsuya
(Chung Cheng Chit
Wun, Song Jing Zhe Ye)
Magnificent Warriors
    '87
The Ninja Dragon '90

Matsukata, Hiroki
Fatal Blade '00
The Magic Serpent '66
Renegade Ninjas '79

Matsumoto, Kappei
Invasion of the Nep-
    tune Men '61

**Matsumoto, Kat-
suhei**
Lone Wolf and Cub 2:
    Baby Cart at the
    River Styx '72
Stray Dog '49

Matsumoto, Marina
Big Boobs Buster '90

Matsumoto, Minoru
Versus '00

**Matsumoto,
Somesho**
Ghidorah the Three-
    Headed Monster
    '64
The Human Vapor '60
Invasion of Astro-Mon-
    ster '65
King Kong vs. Godzilla
    '62

Matsumura, Tatsuo
The Human Vapor '60
King Kong vs. Godzilla
    '62
Madadayo '92
The Secret of the
    Telegian '60
Zatuichi Challenged
    '67

Matsuo, Fumito
The Secret of the
    Telegian '60
Varan the Unbelievable
    '58

Matsuo, Kayo
Lone Wolf and Cub 2:
    Baby Cart at the
    River Styx '72
Shogun Assassin '80

Matsuo, Masatoshi
Pulse '01

Matsuo, Suzuki
Ichi the Killer '01

Matsuoka, Shunsuke
Freeze Me '00

Matsushige, Yutaka
Adrenaline Drive '99
Godzilla 2000 '99
Princess Blade '02
Ring '98

Matsushima, Nanako
Ring '98
Ring 2 '99

Matsuyama, Takashi
Blowback: Love and
    Death '90

Matsuyama, Teruo
The Razor 1: Sword of
    Justice '72

Matsuyuki, Yasuko
Another Heaven '00

Matsuzaka, Keiko
The Happiness of the
    Katakuris '01
Sakuya: Slayer of
    Demons '00

Mayama, Tomoko
Lone Wolf and Cub 1:
    Sword of
    Vengeance '72
Notorious Concubines
    '69

Maysuzaki, Yoji
Taboo '97

Mazar, Debi
The Tuxedo '02

McCally
Ninja vs. Ninja '87

McGee, Jack
Fatal Blade '00

McKenzie, Mike
Vampire Hunter D:
    Bloodlust '01 (V)

McKenzie, Nicolette
Roujin Z '91 (V)

McLymont, Karen
Mr. Nice Guy '97

Medel, Aya
Troublesome Night 4
    '98

**Meersbergen,
Matthew**
Mr. Nice Guy '97

Meguro, Yuki
Legend of the Eight
    Samurai '84
Shogun '80

Mehra, Vinod
Aakhri Adalat '88

Mei Chowai
Legend of the Dragon-
    slayer Sword 3-The
    Rage of Gina '90

Mei, Lou
The Super Ninja '84

Mei-fan, Wong
Love on a Diet '01

Mei-yee, Cheung
(Zhang Mei Yi)
Blazing Temple '76
Born Invincible '78
The 18 Bronzemen Part
    2 '76

Meiken, Hidari
Contract Killer '98

Mendoza, Quiel
Brides of Blood '68

Curse of the Vampires
    '70
Mad Doctor of Blood
    Island '68

Meneghetti, Leo
Godzilla vs.
    MechaGodzilla 2
    '93

Meng Fei
(Mang Fei, Ming Fei,
Mong Fei)
The Invincible Kung Fu
    Trio '78
Prodigal Boxer '73
Shaolin King Boxer '79
The Silver Spear '79
Snake-Crane Secret
    '78
The Unbeaten 28 '80
Ways of Kung Fu '80

Meng Kuang-mei
Undercover Blues '00

Merlin, Jan
Twilight People '72

Messuri, Loridawn
Fatal Blade '00

Metcalfe, Ken
Beast of the Yellow
    Night '70
Twilight People '72

Mew, Danton
Once upon a Time in
    China and America
    '97

Miao, Nora
(Miao Ke Hsiu, Miu Hoh
Sau, Miao Ke Xiu, Miao
Ker Siu)
Bruce Lee, The Legend
    '84
The Chinese Connec-
    tion '71
Dragon Fist '78
Fists of Fury '71
The Last Duel '82
New Fist of Fury '76
Return of the Dragon
    '72
Snake and Crane Arts
    of Shaolin '78

Midori, Mako
Blind Beast '69
The Razor 3: Who's Got
    the Gold? '74

Miemachi, Koji
Terror beneath the Sea
    '66

Mifune, Rikiya
Extreme Crisis '98

Mifune, Shiro
Extreme Crisis '98

Mifune, Toshiro
Chushingura '62
The Hidden Fortress
    '58

High and Low '63
Rashomon '50
Samurai 1: Musashi
    Miyamoto '54
Samurai 2: Duel at Ichi-
    joji Temple '55
Samurai 3: Duel at
    Ganryu Island '56
Sanjuro '63
Seven Samurai '54
Shogun '80
Stray Dog '49
Throne of Blood '57
Yojimbo '61

Mihashi, Ko
Samurai 2: Duel at Ichi-
    joji Temple '55

Mihashi, Tatsuya
High and Low '63
The Human Vapor '60
What's Up, Tiger Lily?
    '66

Mikami, Hiroshi
Parasite Eve '97
The Peacock King '89

Miki, Norihei
Zatoichi's Revenge '64

Mikimoto, Kayo
Zatoichi and the Fugi-
    tives '68

Mikimoto, Shinsuke
Atomic Rulers of the
    World '57
Attack from Space '58
Evil Brain from Outer
    Space '58/59

Mikune, Rentaro
(Rentaro Mikumi,
Masao Sato)
Kwaidan '64
Samurai 1: Musashi
    Miyamoto '54
Zatoichi the Outlaw '67

Miller, David G.
Astro Boy '80 (V)

Miller, Linda
King Kong Escapes '67

Miller, Stephen
Lethal Panther '91

Milne, Gordon
Extreme Challenge '01

Milo
The Adventures of Milo
    and Otis '86

Min Choi
The Snake Strikes Back
    '81

Minakami, Ryuko
Invasion of the Nep-
    tune Men '61

Minakata, Eiji
Sonatine '93

788

Minami, Hiroshi
Branded to Kill '67
Mighty Jack '68

Minami, Kaho
Godzilla, Mothra and
  King Ghidorah: Bat-
  tle on Fire '01

Minatsu, Shin
Gamera vs. Barugon
  '66
Gamera vs. Gyaos '67
Gamera vs. Zigra '71
Giant Monster Gamera
  '65

Mine, Hiroko
Prince of Space '59

Mine, Kazuko
Violated Paradise '63

Minegishi, Toru
(Ryunosuke Minegish)
Big Boobs Buster '90
Godzilla vs. Biollante
  '89

Ming Lo
Kung Pow: Enter the
  Fist '76/2001

Ming-Na
Final Fantasy: The Spir-
  its Within '01 (V)

Mintz, Daniel
Operation Condor '91

Mirei
Guinea Pig: Android of
  Notre Dame '88

Misaka, Chieko
Versus '00

Misaya, Haruki
The Hypnotist '99
Parasite Eve '97

Mishima, Ko
The H-Man '58
Mothra '61

Mishima, Yutaka
Wild Zero '99

Mita, Yoshiko
Samaritan Zatoichi '68

Mitamura, Kenji
Beautiful Hunter '94

Mitamura, Kunihiko
Gamera 3: The
  Revenge of Irys '99
Godzilla vs. Biollante
  '89

Mitani, Noboro
(Noboru Mitani)
Evil Dead Trap '88
Message from Space
  '78
Parasite Eve '97

Mito, Mitsuko
Samurai 1: Musashi
  Miyamoto '54

Samurai 2: Duel at Ichi-
  joji Temple '55

Mitsui, Koji
The Hidden Fortress
  '58
High and Low '63
Woman in the Dunes
  '64

Mitsuishi, Ken
Audition '99
Hiruko the Goblin '90

Mitsuya, Utako
Atomic Rulers of the
  World '57
Attack from Space '58
Evil Brain from Outer
  Space '58/59
Invaders from Space
  '58

Miu Fei-Iam
You Shoot, I Shoot '01

Miu Kiu-wai
(Miao Qiao Wei)
Don't Give a Damn '95
The Dragon Family '88
Eastern Condors '86
Scared Stiff '86
The Tigers '91
Twinkle Twinkle Lucky
  Stars '85

Miu Tak San
(Wu De Shan, Mo Tak
San)
Filthy Guy '80
Five Elements of Kung
  Fu '78
Moonlight Sword and
  Jade Lion '79
Shaolin Wooden Men
  '76
Snake and Crane Arts
  of Shaolin '78
Spiritual Kung Fu '78
Succubare '77
Ways of Kung Fu '78

Miwa
Junk '99

Miwa, Asumi
Gamera 3: The
  Revenge of Irys '99
Spiral '00

Miyagi, Yukio
Legend of the
  Dinosaurs '77

Miyaguchi, Jiro
Lone Wolf and Cub 6:
  White Heaven in
  Hell '74

Miyaguchi, Seiji
Kwaidan '64
Seven Samurai '54
Shogun '80
Throne of Blood '57

Miyake, Bontaro
Warning from Space
  '56

Miyake, Kuniko
Good Morning '59

Miyako, Chocho
Samaritan Zatoichi '68

Miyamoto, Nobuko
The Funeral '84
Tampopo '87

Miyamoto, Yoko
Lethal Panther '91

Miyamura, Yuko
Battle Royale '00

Miyata, Fumiko
Atomic Rulers of the
  World '57
Attack from Space '58
Evil Brain from Outer
  Space '58/59

Miyauchi, Hiroshi
Reborn from Hell:
  Samurai Armaged-
  don '96
Sister Street Fighter
  '74
Tokyo Mafia: Yakuza
  Wars '95
Tokyo Mafia 2: Wrath of
  the Yakuza '95

Miyazaki, Yoshiko
Ran '85

Miyoshi, Eiko
Good Morning '59
The Hidden Fortress
  '58
Samurai 1: Musashi
  Miyamoto '54
Stray Dog '49

Mizuhara, Koichi
Wrath of Daimajin '66
Zatoichi and the
  Doomed Man '65

Mizuhashi, Kenji
Pulse '01

Mizuno, Kumi
(Maya Igarashi)
Attack of the Mush-
  room People '63
Chushingura '62
Ebirah, Horror of the
  Deep '66
Frankenstein vs.
  Baragon '65
Invasion of Astro-Mon-
  ster '65
War of the Gargantuas
  '66
What's Up, Tiger Lily?
  '66

Mizuno, Miki
Gamera 2: Advent of
  Legion '96

Mizushima, Michi-
taro
Lone Wolf and Cub 3:
  Baby Cart to Hades
  '72

Mizutani, Kei
(Saori Fukuda)
Kei Mizutani:
  Undressed for Suc-
  cess '94
The Ladies' Phone Sex
  Club '96
Sumo Vixens '96
Terminatrix '95
Tokyo Decameron:
  Three Tales of Mad-
  ness and Sensuali-
  ty '96
Weather Woman '95

Mizutani, Yoshie
The Tale of Zatoichi
  Continues '62

Mo, Allan
(Mo Kei, Wu Ji, Allan
Moo)
Hit Team '00
Task Force '97

Mo, Eric
Gold Fingers '01
The Suspect '98

Mo Sa-sung
Masters of Martial Arts
  '74

Mo, Teresa
(Mo Sun-Kwan)
All's Well End's Well '92
Hard Boiled '91
Legend of the Dragon
  '91
The Magnificent
  Scoundrels '91
Red Shield '91

Mok, Edward
(Mok Ga Yiu, Mo Gu
Yao)
The Final Winner '01
A Wicked Ghost '99

Mok, Karen
(Mok Man-Wai, Mo Wen
Wei, Karen Joy Morris)
The Best of the Best
  '96
Black Mask '96
A Chinese Odyssey Part
  1: Pandora's Box
  '95
A Chinese Odyssey Part
  2: Cinderella '95
Fallen Angels '95
God of Cookery '96
Goodbye Mr. Cool '01
The Irresistible Piggies
  '02
King of Comedy '99
Lawyer Lawyer '97
Shaolin Soccer '01
Task Force '97

Mok, Max
(Mok Siu Chung, Mo
Shao Cong, Benny
Mok)
The Assassin '93
The Dragon Family '88
Eastern Condors '86

Nightmare Zone '98
Once upon a Time in
  China 2 '92
Once upon a Time in
  China 3 '93
Once upon a Time in
  China 4 '93
Pedicab Driver '89

Mok Mei Lam
Shaolin Soccer '01

Momoi, Kaori
Cross Fire '00

Mon, Lawrence Ah
(Lau Gwok Cheong, Liu
Guo Chang, Lawrence
Lau, Larry Lau)
Black Mask '96
Task Force '97

Mongkolpisit,
Pawalit
Bangkok Dangerous
  '00

Monteiro, Johnny
Curse of the Vampires
  '70

Montenegro, Mario
Brides of Blood '68

Montes, Eva
The Blood Drinkers '64

Monty, Mike
Blowback: Love and
  Death '90

Moo, Kelly
Visible Secret '01

Moon Kang
Yongary, Monster from
  the Deep '67

Moore, Roger
Cannonball Run '81

Moorehouse, Mark
C.
Junk '99

Morena, Mona
Twilight People '72

Morgan, André
Sting of the Dragon
  Masters '73

Mori, Ise
(Kazunari Mori)
Godzilla vs.
  MechaGodzilla '74
Terror of MechaGodzilla
  '75

Mori, Masayuki
Men Who Tread on the
  Tiger's Tail '43
Rashomon '50

Mori, Shoji
Lone Wolf and Cub 1:
  Sword of
  Vengeance '72

Lone Wolf and Cub 6:
    White Heaven in
    Hell '74

Morisawa, Yasufumi
Reborn from Hell:
    Samurai Armaged-
    don '96

Morishita, Noko
Ichi the Killer '01

Morishita, Yoshiyuki
Shark Skin Man and
    Peach Hip Girl '98
Wild Zero '00

Morita, Gakuya
Lone Wolf and Cub 4:
    Baby Cart in Peril
    '72
Lone Wolf and Cub 5:
    Baby Cart in the
    Land of Demons
    '73
Lone Wolf and Cub 6:
    White Heaven in
    Hell '74

Morita, Kensaku
Renegade Ninjas '79

Moriya, Yuji
Gamera vs. Gyaos '67

Moriyama, Yuko
Reborn from Hell:
    Samurai Armaged-
    don '96
Tokyo Raiders '00
Zeram '91

Morizuka, Bin
Black Tight Killers '66

Morrison, James
The One '01

Morrow, Vic
Message from Space
    '78

Motoki, Masahiro
Gonin '95

Mui, Anita
(Mui Yim-Fong, Mei Yan-
Fang)
A Better Tomorrow 3
    '89
Dance of a Dream '01
The Enforcer '95
Executioners '93
Fight Back to School 3
    '93
The Heroic Trio '93
Justice, My Foot! '92
Legend of the Drunken
    Master '94
The Magic Crane '93
Midnight Fly '01
Miracles '89
The Moon Warriors '92
100 Ways to Murder
    Your Wife '86
Rumble in the Bronx
    '95
Savior of the Soul '91

Scared Stiff '86
Venom Warrior '83

Mui, Ann
(Mooi Oi Fong, Mei Ai
Fang)
Dragon from Russia
    '90
Iceman Cometh '89
Police Story 2 '88

Mui, Anthony
Thunder Ninja Kids:
    The Hunt for the
    Devil Boxer '86/94

Multan, Peter
Devil Woman '70

Muneta, Masami
The Razor 2: The Snare
    '73

Mung, Yoyo
(Mung Ka-Wai, Mung Ga
Wai, Meng Jia Hui, Yoyo
Mong)
Doctor No... '01
Expect the Unexpected
    '98
Killer '00
Running out of Time
    '99
Super Car Criminals
    '99
Ultimatum '01
Wishful Milenio '01

Munoz, Tita
Mad Doctor of Blood
    Island '68

Munzak, Maxim
Dersu Uzala '74

Murai, Kunio
Godzilla 1985 '84
Godzilla vs. Gigan '72
Godzilla, Mothra and
    King Ghidorah: Bat-
    tle on Fire '01

Murakami, Fuyuki
Battle in Outer Space
    '59
Godzilla, King of the
    Monsters '54
The Human Vapor '60
Invasion of Astro-Mon-
    ster '65
The Mysterians '57
Rodan '56
The Secret of the
    Telegian '60
The Street Fighter's
    Last Revenge '74

Muramatsu, Katsumi
Ring '98
Ring 2 '99

Murase, Sachiko
Zatoichi the Fugitive
    '63

Murata, Takehiro
Godzilla 2000 '99

Godzilla vs. Destroyah
    '95
Godzilla vs. Mothra '92
Godzilla, Mothra and
    King Ghidorah: Bat-
    tle on Fire '01

Murota, Hideo
Hiruko the Goblin '90
Terror beneath the Sea
    '66

Murphy, Christopher
Gamera vs. Guiron '69

Musaka, Naomasa
Another Heaven '00
Brother '00
Princess Blade '02
Tetsuo: The Iron Man
    '89
Tokyo Fist '96

Mutsumi, Goro
(Kiyoji Nakanishi, Goro
Mutsu)
Godzilla vs.
    MechaGodzilla '74
Lone Wolf and Cub 6:
    White Heaven in
    Hell '74
Terror of MechaGodzilla
    '75

Myles, Harry
Robo Vampire '88

Myojo, Masako
Zatoichi and the
    Doomed Man '65

Na, Shiri
Legend of the Flying
    Swordsman '00

Naag, Anant
Raat '91

Nadeki, Fujimi
(Go Shing Foo Si Mei,
Gao Cheng Fu Shi Mei,
Fujimi Takajo)
Crystal Hunt '91

Nagai, Mieko
Warning from Space
    '56

Nagaoka, Teruko
Good Morning '59

Nagasawa, Masami
Cross Fire '00

**Nagashima, Toshiyu-
ki**
Cross Fire '00
Gamera 2: Advent of
    Legion '96
Godzilla vs. Biollante
    '89
Godzilla vs. Megaguirus
    '00
Gonin '95

**Nagatomo, Muneyu-
ki**
Return of Daimajin '66

Nagino, Matoko
Godzilla vs. Megaguirus
    '00

Nagisa, Mayumi
Zatoichi's Flashing
    Sword '64

Nai An
Suzhou River '00

Nai Yen Ne
The Killer Elephants
    '76

Naina
Gumnaam '65

Naito, Takashi
After Life '98
Maborosi '95

Naito, Taketoshi
After Life '98
Godzilla 1985 '84
Lone Wolf and Cub 1:
    Sword of
    Vengeance '72
Lone Wolf and Cub 5:
    Baby Cart in the
    Land of Demons
    '73

Najja, Ahmed
Ninja the Final Duel '85

Naka, Machiko
All Monsters Attack '70

Nakada, Kei
Extreme Crisis '98

Nakadai, Tatsuya
High and Low '63
Kwaidan '64
Ran '85
Sanjuro '63
Seven Samurai '54
Wicked City '92
Yojimbo '61

Nakagawa, Anna
Cure '97
Godzilla vs. King Ghido-
    rah '91

Nakagawa, Eriko
Evil Dead Trap '88

Nakahara, Ken
Gamera vs. Viras '68
Gamera vs. Zigra '71
Giant Monster Gamera
    '65

Nakajima, Doris
(Yutaka Nakajima,
Doris Nakashima)
The Executioner '74
The Street Fighter '74
The Street Fighter's
    Last Revenge '74

Nakajima, Haruo
All Monsters Attack '70
Destroy All Monsters
    '68
Ebirah, Horror of the
    Deep '66

Frankenstein vs.
    Baragon '65
Ghidorah the Three-
    Headed Monster
    '64
Godzilla, King of the
    Monsters '54
Godzilla Raids Again
    '55
Godzilla vs. Gigan '72
Godzilla vs. Hedorah
    '71
The H-Man '58
The Human Vapor '60
Invasion of Astro-Mon-
    ster '65
King Kong Escapes '67
King Kong vs. Godzilla
    '62
Mothra vs. Godzilla '64
The Mysterians '57
Rodan '56
Seven Samurai '54
Son of Godzilla '67
War of the Gargantuas
    '66
Yog: Monster from
    Space '70

Nakajima, Hiromi
Nobody '99

Nakajima, Tomoko
Parasite Eve '97

Nakajimi, Donald
(Yoshio Nakajimi)
Return of the Street
    Fighter '74

Nakajo, Kiyoshi
Fatal Blade '00

Nakajo, Naruka
Wild Zero '99

Nakakita, Chieko
Chushingura '62
Ebirah, Horror of the
    Deep '66
The Last War '61

Nakama, Yukie
Gamera 3: Revenge of
    Iris '99
Ring 0: Birthday '00

Nakamaru, Tadao
The H-Man '58
The Hidden Fortress
    '58
The Hypnotist '99
The Mysterians '57
Secret of the Telegian
    '60
Terror of MechaGodzilla
    '75
What's Up, Tiger Lily?
    '66

Nakamura, Isamu
Return of the Deadly
    Blade '81

Nakamura, Kanemon
Kwaidan '64

790

Nakamura, Katsuo
Godzilla, Mothra and King Ghidorah: Battle on Fire '01
Godzilla vs. Megaguirus '00
Kwaidan '64
Warm Water under a Red Bridge '01

Nakamura, Kinji
Legend of the Dinosaurs '77
Violent Cop '89

Nakamura, Kinnosuke
(Kinnosuke Yorozuya, Nakamura Yorozuya)
Renegade Ninjas '79

Nakamura, Kyoko
Sumo Vixens '96

Nakamura, Nobuo
Dagora the Space Monster '64
Frankenstein vs. Baragon '65
Half Human '55/1957
The Last War '61
Throne of Blood '57
War of the Gargantuas '66

Nakamura, Takashi
Gamera vs. Gyaos '67
Return of Daimajin '66

Nakamura, Tetsu
(Satoshi Nakamura)
The H-Man '58
The Human Vapor '60
The Manster '60
Mothra '61
The Mysterians '57
What's Up, Tiger Lily? '66
Yog: Monster from Space '70

Nakamura, Toru
(Chung Chuen Hang, Zhong Cun Heng)
Gen-X Cops '99
Tokyo Raiders '00

Nakamura, Yutaka
The H-Man '58
Lone Wolf and Cub 1: Sword of Vengeance '72
Lone Wolf and Cub 5: Baby Cart in the Land of Demons '73
Ninja: Band of Assassins '62
The Tale of Zatoichi Continues '62
Zatoichi on the Road '63
Zatoichi's Flashing Sword '64

Nakano, Hideo
Nobody '99

Nakano, Seiya
Postman Blues '97

Nakano, Toshiko
Akira Kurosawa's Dreams '90

Nakao, Akira
Godzilla vs. Destroyah '95
Godzilla vs. MechaGodzilla 2 '93
Godzilla vs. Space Godzilla '94

Nakao, Mie
Zatoichi Challenged '67

Nakata, Tsutomu
Gamera vs. Barugon '66
Giant Monster Gamera '65

Nakata, Yasuko
Rodan '56

Nakatani, Miki
Ring '98
Ring 2 '99

Nakaya, Noboru
Kwaidan '64
Time of the Apes '75

Nakayama, Shinobu
Fist of Legend '94
Gamera 3: The Revenge of Irys '99
Gamera, Guardian of the Universe '95
Godzilla vs. MechaGodzilla 2 '93

Nakayama, Shoji
Atomic Rulers of the World '57
Attack from Space '58
Evil Brain from Outer Space '58/59

Nakayama, Yutaka
All Monsters Attack '69
Dagora the Space Monster '66
Frankenstein vs. Baragon '66
Ghidorah the Three-Headed Monster '66
The H-Man '58
Mothra vs. Godzilla '64
The Secret of the Telegian '60

Nam Cheong-im
Yongary, Monster from the Deep '67

Nam, James
(Nam Gung Fan, Nan Gong Xun, Nan Kung Hsun)
Five Fingers of Death '72

Ninja vs. Bruce Lee '82
Super Kung Fu Kid '74
Thunder Kick '73

Nam, Yammie
(Nam Kit-ying, Laam Git Ying, Lan Jie Ying)
The Bride with White Hair '93
A Chinese Odyssey Part 1: Pandora's Box '95
A Chinese Odyssey Part 2: Cinderella '95
Flirting Scholar '93
The Tigers '91
The Witch from Nepal '85

Nam Yin
The Adventurers '95
Full Contact '92

Namiki, Shiro
Beautiful Beast '95
Godzilla 2000 '99
Ring 2 '99
Wild Zero '99

Nan Yu-li
The Killer Meteors '76

Nanbara, Koji
(Koji Nambara)
Branded to Kill '67

Nanbu, Shozo
The Razor 1: Sword of Justice '72
Return of Daimajin '66
The Tale of Zatoichi Continues '62
Warning from Space '56
Zatoichi and the Fugitives '68

Nanda
Gumnaam '65

Naniwa, Cheiko
Throne of Blood '57

Narita, Junachiro
Zatoichi the Fugitive '63

Narita, Mikio
Legend of the Eight Samurai '84
Message from Space '78
The Razor 3: Who's Got the Gold? '74
Sure Death: Revenge '87
Zatoichi and the Chess Expert '65

Naruse, Chisato
Lady Ninja: Reflections of Darkness '96

Nasa, Kenji
(Kenjin Nasa, Takeomi Nasa)
Organ '96

Nataf, Zachary
I.K.U. '00

Natsuki, Akira
Gamera vs. Barugon '66

Natsuki, Isao
Shogun's Ninja '82

Natsuki, Junpei
Akira Kurosawa's Dreams '90
Godzilla, King of the Monsters '54
Godzilla Raids Again '55
The H-Man '60
Seven Samurai '54

Natsuki, Mari
Legend of the Eight Samurai '84

Natsuki, Sho
Gamera vs. Barugon '66
Gamera vs. Gyaos '67
Gamera vs. Viras '68
Gamera vs. Zigra '71

Natsuki, Yosuke
Chushingura '62
Dagora the Space Monster '64
Ghidorah the Three-Headed Monster '64
Godzilla 1985 '84
The H-Man '58
Shogun '80
Yojimbo '61

Natsuo, Yuna
The Haunted Lantern '98

Natsuyagi, Isao
Warm Water under a Red Bridge '01

Naval, Deepti
Hum Paanch '80

Navarro, Pedro
Brides of Blood '68
The Walls of Hell '64

Nawa, Hiroshi
Legend of the Dinosaurs '77
Lone Wolf and Cub 3: Baby Cart to Hades '72
Return of Daimajin '66
Zatoichi the Fugitive '63

Nazir
Mahal '48

Neal, Peggy
Terror beneath the Sea '66
The X from Outer Space '67

Negishi, Akemi
Half Human '55/1957

King Kong vs. Godzilla '62

Negishi, Toshie
Akira Kurosawa's Dreams '90
Audition '99
Gamera 3: The Revenge of Irys '99
Ghost Actress '96
Warm Water under a Red Bridge '01

Neilson, Erik
Terror beneath the Sea '66

Nelson, Ed
Who Am I? '98

Nelson, Noah
Jackie Chan Adventures 1: The Search for the Talismans '00 (V)
Jackie Chan Adventures 3: The Shadow of Shendu '00 (V)

Nelson, Paul M.
Astro Boy '80 (V)

Nelsson, Anders
Bruce Lee: The Man, the Myth '76
Miracles '89

Nezu, Jinpachi
Gonin '95
Nobody '99
Ran '85

Ng An-ya
Cop on a Mission '01

Ng, Ben
(Ng Ngai-Cheung, Wu Yi Jiang)
The Adventurers '95
City Cop '95
Clueless '01
The Conman '98
The Eternal Evil of Asia '95
Gold Fingers '01
Her Name Is Cat 2: Journey to Death '01
The Kung Fu Master '94
Millennium Dragon '99
Red to Kill '94
Thunder Cop '96

Ng, Carrie
(Ng Ka-Lai, Ng Ga Lai, Wu Gu Li)
C'est la Vie, Mon Cheri '93
City on Fire '87
Crystal Hunt '91
Dragon from Russia '90
Faces of Horror '98
Glass Tears '01
Gunmen '88

Justice, My Foot! '92
Naked Killer '92
Rock 'n' Roll Cop '94
Skinny Tiger and Fatty
  Dragon '90
Thunder Cop '96

Ng, Christine
*(Ng Wing-Mei, Wu Yong
Wei)*
All's Well End's Well '97
  '97
The Cat '91
Combo Cops '96
Crime Story '93
9413 '98
The Replacement Sus-
  pects '01
Rush Hour '98
A Taste of Killing and
  Romance '94
Troublesome Night '97
Troublesome Night 3
  '97

Ng Chun-fung
The Bride with White
  Hair 2 '93

Ng, Francis
*(Ng Chun-Yu, Ng Jan
Yue, Wu Zhen Yu)*
All's Well End's Well '97
  '97
Bakery Amour '01
Beauty and the Breast
  '02
Big Bullet '96
The Bride with White
  Hair '93
Bullets over Summer
  '99
Clean My Name, Mr.
  Coroner! '00
Fall for You '01
Flirting Scholar '93
Full Alert '97
A Gambler's Story '01
Gen-X Cops '99
Horror Hotline...Big
  Head Monster '01
Juliet in Love '00
Last Ghost Standing
  '99
Lord of the Wu Tang
  '93
Losers' Club '01
A Man Called Hero '99
The Mission '99
9413 '98
Too Many Ways to Be
  No. 1 '97
2000 A.D. '00
A War Named Desire
  '00
A Wicked Ghost '99
Young and Dangerous
  '96

Ng, Frankie
*(Ng Chi-Hung, Wu Zhi
Xiong, Ng Kin Hung)*
The Best of the Best
  '96
Bio-Cops '00

Bullets of Love '01
Century of the Dragon
  '99
The Cheaters '01
The Conman '98
Contract Killer '98
Cop on a Mission '01
The Duel '00
For Bad Boys Only '00
Full Alert '97
Iceman Cometh '89
Last Ghost Standing
  '99
The Masked Prosecutor
  '99
Master Q 2001 '01
My School Mate, the
  Barbarian '01
Prison on Fire '87
Prison on Fire 2 '91
Troublesome Night '97
Troublesome Night 3
  '97
Young and Dangerous
  '96

Ng Ho
*(Ng Hoh, Wu Ke, Wu
Ho)*
The Blazing Temple '76
Bruce Lee We Miss You
  '76
Triangular Duel '72

Ng Hoi-tin
(Wu Hai Tian)
Long Arm of the Law
  '84
Long Arm of the Law 2
  '87
Rich and Famous '87

Ng Hong-ling
*(Wu Kang Ning, Ng
Hong Ning)*
God of Gamblers 2 '90
Rich and Famous '87

Ng Hong Song
*(Wu Hang Sheng, Ng
Hong Sang)*
City War '88
Dirty Ho '79
The Kid with the Golden
  Arm '79
Mighty Peking Man '77
Shaolin Master Killer
  '78
Super Gang '78

Ng, Hugo
*(Ng Doy Yung, Ng Toi-
Yung)*
Brother of Darkness
  '94
Daughter of Darkness
  '93

Ng Kwan-lung
Snake Deadly Act '79

Ng, Lawrence
(Ng Kai Wa, Wu Qi Hua)
A Chinese Torture
  Chamber Story '94
Dragon Inn '92

Every Dog Has His
  Date '01
Hail the Judge '94
Lethal Panther '91
The Magic Crane '93
Peace Hotel '95
Picture of a Nymph '88

Ng Man-Tat
*(Wu Meng Da, Ng Mang
Tat)*
All About Ah-Long '89
Best of the Best '92
A Better Tomorrow 2
  '87
The Big Sting '82
A Chinese Odyssey Part
  1: Pandora's Box
  '95
A Chinese Odyssey Part
  2: Cinderella '95
Everyday Is Valentine
  '01
Fight Back to School
  '91
Fight Back to School 2
  '92
Fist of Fury 1991 '91
God of Cookery '96
God of Gamblers '89
God of Gamblers 2 '90
God of Gamblers 3:
  Back to Shanghai
  '91
Hail the Judge '94
Justice, My Foot! '92
King of Beggars '92
King of Comedy '99
Lee Rock '91
Legacy of Rage '86
Love on Delivery '94
A Moment of Romance
  '90
Operation Pink Squad
  '88
Royal Tramp '92
Shaolin Soccer '01
Shogun and Little
  Kitchen '92
Sixty Million Dollar Man
  '95
The Sword Stained with
  Royal Blood '93
Tiger Cage '88
With or Without You '92

Ng, Mark
Eat My Dust '93

Ng, Mickey
Peace Hotel '95

Ng Min Kan
(Wu Mian Qin)
Heart of Dragon '85
The Owl vs. Bombo '84
Pom Pom '84
Pom Pom Strikes Back
  '86
Project A '83
Winners and Sinners
  '83

Ng Ming Choi
*(Wu Ming Cai, Wu Ming
Hsia, Yuen Ting) See
also sidebar on p. 142.*
Beauty Investigator '92
The Chinese Connec-
  tion '71
Enter the Dragon '73
Fearless Fighters '69
Legend of the Mountain
  '79
Rage of the Masters
  '74
Super Gang '78
A Touch of Zen '69

Ng, Natalie
Crime of a Beast '01
Everyday Is Valentine
  '01

Ng, Richard
*(Ng Yiu-Hon, Wu Yao
Han)*
Beijing Rocks '01
Don't Give a Damn '95
In the Line of Duty 3
  '88
Jiang Hu-"The Triad
  Zone" '00
Lord of the Wu Tang
  '93
Magnificent Warriors
  '87
The Millionaires'
  Express '86
Miracles '89
Mr. Boo Meets Pom
  Pom '85
My Lucky Stars '85
Once upon a Time in
  China and America
  '97
Pom Pom '84
Pom Pom Strikes Back
  '86
The Private Eyes '76
Savior of the Soul 2
  '92
Twinkle Twinkle Lucky
  Stars '85
Wheels on Meals '84
Winners and Sinners
  '83
Yes, Madam '85

Ng, Sandra
*(Ng Kwan-Yue, Ng
Kwun-Yu, Ng Sun Kwan)*
All's Well End's Well '92
Casino Tycoon 2 '92
City of Desire '01
Crocodile Hunter '89
Dance of a Dream '01
The Demon's Baby '98
God of Gamblers 3:
  Back to Shanghai
  '91
In the Line of Duty 3
  '88
The Inspector Wears
  Skirts '88
Jiang Hu-"The Triad
  Zone" '00
Juliet in Love '00

The Magnificent
  Scoundrels '91
Martial Angels '01
Operation Pink Squad
  '88
Royal Tramp '92
Royal Tramp 2 '92
Scared Stiff '86
She Shoots Straight
  '90
The Tricky Master '00
Twinkle Twinkle Lucky
  Stars '85
Vampire Kids '91
Young and Dangerous
  5 '98
Young and Dangerous
  6: Born to Be King
  '00

Ng See Yuen
Twin Dragons '92

Ng, Shirley
(Ng Ling, Wu Ling)
Tiger on Beat '88

Ng Shui-ting
(Wu Rui Ting)
The Eternal Evil of Asia
  '95
Hard Boiled '91

Ng Sing Sze
The Red Wolf '95

Ng Ting-yip
Operation Billionaires
  '98

Ng Tung-kiu
*(Ng Dung Kiu, Wu Dong
Qiao)*
Chinese Iron Man '75
Fury of King Boxer '72
Macho Man '72
Screaming Ninja '73
Triangular Duel '72

Ng Wai-Kwok
*(Ng Wai Gwok, Wu Wei
Guo)*
The Defender '94

Ng Yin
Dragon Kid '90

Ng Yuen-yee
Dragon Lord '82

Ngai Chau-wa
Last Hurrah for Chivalry
  '78
Super Gang '78

Ngai Hong
*(Ni Kuang, I Kuang Ni
Kuang)*
Doctor Vampire '90
Miracles '89
The Seventh Curse '86
Skinny Tiger and Fatty
  Dragon '90

Ngai, Joyce
The Chinese Feast '95
Dragon Kid '90

Ngai, Marco
Nightmare Zone '98

Ngai Sing
(Collin Chou Siu Lung,
Ni Sing)
Ashes of Time '94
The Defender '94
Don't Give a Damn '95
The Enforcer '95
Hail the Judge '94
Lord of the Wu Tang
'93
The Red Wolf '95
Return to a Better
Tomorrow '94
Victim '99

Ngai So
Sorrowful to a Ghost
'70

Ngai Suet
(Ni Xue)
Saga of the Phoenix
'90
Vampire Kids '91

Ngai Tai-wang
The Assassin '93

Ngan Lung
Real Kung Fu of
Shaolin, Part 1 '81

Ngan, Rachel
(Ngan Wing Sze, Aan
Wing Si, Yan Ying Si)
Gen-Y Cops '00
Martial Angels '01

Ngan, Sophie
Beauty and the Breast
'02

Ngor, Dr. Haing S.
Eastern Condors '86

Ngor, Peter
On the Run '88

Nguyen Nhu Quynh
Cyclo '95

Nic, Liccy
Para Para Sakura '01

Nicholson, James B.
Bruce Lee, The Legend
'84 (N)

Nickel, Thorsten
Thunderbolt '95

Nicol, Alex
A*P*E '76

Nigake, Taruo
Destroy All Monsters
'68

Nihei, Masanori
(Masanari Jihei,
Masaya Nihei)
Mighty Jack '68

Nihonyanagi, Kan
Black Tight Killers '66

Niizuma, Satoshi
Ichi the Killer '01

Nimiamoto, Katsumi
Terror of MechaGodzilla
'75

Ninagawa, Yuki
Shogun's Ninja '82

Nine, Mr.
(Kau Man Lung, Gau
Man Lung, Jiu Wen
Long)
Troublesome Night 8
'00
Troublesome Night 9
'00
Troublesome Night 14
'02

Ninh Cao, Jason
Shaolin: Wheel of Life
'00

Ninomiya, Hideki
Daimajin '66
Return of Daimajin '66

Nishida, Naomi
Godzilla 2000 '99
The Happiness of the
Katakuris '01

Nishimoto, Hiroyuki
Body Snatcher from
Hell '68
Woman in the Dunes
'64

Nishimura, Ko
(Kou Nishimura, Akira
Nishimura)
The Razor 1: Sword of
Justice '72
The Razor 2: The Snare
'73
The Razor 3: Who's Got
the Gold? '74
Samaritan Zatoichi '68
Yojimbo '61
Zatoichi the Outlaw '67

Nishimura, Masaki
Lady Ninja: Reflections
of Darkness '96

Nishina, Takashi
Godzilla, Mothra and
King Ghidorah: Bat-
tle on Fire '01

Nishio, Mieko
Black Tight Killers '66

Nishioka, Tokuma
Godzilla vs. King Ghido-
rah '91

Nishiwaki, Michiko
(Sai Hip Mei Chi Ji, Xi
Xie Mei Zhi Zi)
City on Fire '93
God of Gamblers '89
In the Line of Duty 3
'88
My Lucky Stars '85

Nishiyama, Yumi
Nobody '99

Nishizawa, Toshiaki
Godzilla vs. Gigan '72

Nitani, Hideaki
Frankenstein vs.
Baragon '65
Mighty Jack '68
Tokyo Drifter '66

Niwa, Matasaburo
Zatoichi on the Road
'63

Niwa, Reiko
Royal Warriors '86

Niyama, Chiharu
(Chiharu Niiyama)
The Dimension Travel-
ers '98
Godzilla, Mothra and
King Ghidorah: Bat-
tle on Fire '01

Nogami, Masayoshi
Naked Pursuit '68

Nogawa, Yumiko
Zatoichi and the Fugi-
tives '68

Nogiwa, Yoko
Shogun's Ninja '82

Noguchi, Masahiro
Gamera 3: The
Revenge of Irys '99
The Hypnotist '99

Nomoto, Miho
Lady Ninja: Reflections
of Darkness '96

Nomura, Kozo
(Terunobu Nomura)
Battle in Outer Space
'59
Frankenstein vs.
Baragon '65
Ghidorah the Three-
Headed Monster
'64
The Human Vapor '60
The Last War '61
Mothra vs. Godzilla '64
Varan the Unbelievable
'58
War of the Gargantuas
'66

Norman, Nick
Robo Vampire '88

Norris, Chuck
Game of Death '78
Martial Arts Mayhem,
Vol. 1 '99
Return of the Dragon
'72

Norton, Richard
City Hunter '92
The Millionaires'
Express '86
Mr. Nice Guy '97

**Twinkle Twinkle Lucky
Stars '85**

Novak, Mel
Game of Death '78

Nozoe, Hitomi
Giants and Toys '58

Nu Yen-Khe, Tran
Cyclo '95

Numata, Yoichi
Princess Blade '02
Ring '98
Ring 2 '99

O Chun Hung
(O Chun-Hung, Oh Jun
Hung, Ke Jun Xiong, Ko
Chun-hsiang, Ko Chuen-
hsiang)
Code of Honor '87
The Dragon Family '88
Generation Consultant
'90
Generation Pendragon
'90
Miracles '89
Rich and Famous '87

O, Henry
Romeo Must Die '00

O Yau-man
(Oh Yau Man, Ke You
Min, Ho Yu Ming, Lung
Siu, Lung Hsiao, Lung
Se)
The Blazing Temple '76
Chinese Iron Man '75
The 8 Masters '77
The 18 Bronzemen '76
The 18 Bronzemen Part
2 '76
The 18 Jade Arhats '78
Five Elements of Kung
Fu '78
Green Dragon Inn '79
Hand of Death '75
Iron Neck Li '81
Killer from Above '77
One Foot Crane '79
The Shaolin Kids '77
Sorrowful to a Ghost
'70
The Unbeaten 28 '80

Obata, Toshiro
Teenage Mutant Ninja
Turtles '90

Obayashi, Takeshi
Godzilla, Mothra and
King Ghidorah: Bat-
tle on Fire '01
Shogun '80

O'Brian, Hugh
Game of Death '78

O'Brien, Robert
Armour of God '86

Oda, Erika
After Life '98

Odaka, Megumi
Godzilla vs. Biollante
'89
Godzilla vs. Destroyah
'95
Godzilla vs. King Ghido-
rah '91
Godzilla vs.
MechaGodzilla 2
'93
Godzilla vs. Mothra '92
Godzilla vs. Space
Godzilla '94

Odashi, Hideto
Godzilla vs. Megalon
'73

Oedekerk, Steve
Kung Pow: Enter the
Fist '76/2001

Ogata, Ken
(Sui Ying Kuen, Xu Xing
Quan)
The Peacock King '89

Ogata, Rinsaku
Battle in Outer Space
'59
The Hidden Fortress
'58
The Mysterians '57
Rodan '56
Yog: Monster from
Space '70

Ogawa, Mariko
Branded to Kill '67

Ogawa, Mayumi
Zatoichi's Vengeance
'66

Ogawa, Minako
Beautiful Beast '95
The Ladies' Phone Sex
Club '96

Ogawa, Tomoko
The Magic Serpent '66

Ogawa, Toranosuke
Godzilla, King of the
Monsters '54
Seven Samurai '54

Ogawa, Yasuzo
Terror of MechaGodzilla
'75

Ogi, Shigemitsu
Dark Water '02
The Hypnotist '99

Ogiwara, Kenzo
Godzilla vs. Biollante
'89
Godzilla vs. King Ghido-
rah '91
Godzilla vs. Mothra '92

Oguchi, Mirei
Dark Water '02

Ogunsanya, Tony
Blowback: Love and
Death '90

Oh Yeong-Il
Yongary, Monster from the Deep '67

Ohashi, Akira
Godzilla, Mothra and King Ghidorah: Battle on Fire '01

Ohba, Kazuhito
Versus '00

Ohba, Kenji
Legend of the Eight Samurai '84
Sister Street Fighter '74

Ohhara, Johji
(Joe Ohara)
Atomic Rulers of the World '57
Attack from Space '58
Evil Brain from Outer Space '58/59
Gamera vs. Barugon '66

Ohki, Minoru
Lone Wolf and Cub 2: Baby Cart at the River Styx '72
Lone Wolf and Cub 5: Baby Cart in the Land of Demons '74
Lone Wolf and Cub 6: White Heaven in Hell '74
Shogun Assassin '80

Ohkura, Johnny
(Johnny Okura)
Boiling Point '90

Ohnaka, Kiyoharu
Rodan '56

Ohsawa, Sachihiro
Atomic Rulers of the World '57
Attack from Space '58
Evil Brain from Outer Space '58/59

Ohtani, Tomohiko
Atomic Rulers of the World '57
Attack from Space '58
Evil Brain from Outer Space '58/59

Ohya, Mitsubo
Mighty Jack '68

Oikawa, Takeo
Godzilla Raids Again '55
The Mysterians '57

Oka, Johji
Prince of Space '59

Oka, Yutaka
All Monsters Attack '68
Attack of the Mushroom People '63

Battle in Outer Space '59
Dagora the Space Monster '64
Ghidorah the Three-Headed Monster '64
Invasion of Astro-Monster '65
The Last War '61
Rodan '56
Samurai 3: Duel on Ganryu Island '56

Okabe, Susumu
Godzilla vs. Hedorah '71

Okabe, Tadashi
Battle in Outer Space '59
Ebirah, Horror of the Deep '66
Godzilla, King of the Monsters '54
Godzilla vs. Hedorah '71
King Kong Escapes '67
The Secret of the Telegian '60

Okada, Eiji
Lone Wolf and Cub 5: Baby Cart in the Land of Demons '73
Woman in the Dunes '64
The X from Outer Space '67

Okada, Mariko
Samurai 1: Musashi Miyamoto '54
Samurai 2: Duel at Ichijoji Temple '55
Samurai 3: Duel at Ganryu Island '56

Okamoto, Yukiko
Another Heaven '00

Okawa, Hashizo
King of the Mongols '60

Okawa, Heihachiro
(Henry Okawa)
Ghidorah the Three-Headed Monster '64
The Mysterians '57

Oki, Goro
Lady Ninja: Reflections of Darkness '96
Legend of the Dinosaurs '77

Oki, Ryojiro
Akira Kurosawa's Dreams '90
Ran '85

Oki, Tamio
Ghost in the Shell '95 (V)

Oki, Tokio
Lone Wolf and Cub 1: Sword of Vengeance '72
Lone Wolf and Cub 4: Baby Cart in Peril '72
Lone Wolf and Cub 6: White Heaven in Hell '74
Ninja: Band of Assassins Continued '63

Okochi, Denjiro
Men Who Tread on the Tiger's Tail '43
Sanshiro Sugata '43

Okubo, Ryu
(Satoru Okubo)
Organ '96

Okunuki, Kaoru
Godzilla, Mothra and King Ghidorah: Battle on Fire '01
Ring 0: Birthday '00

Okura, Johnny
Beautiful Hunter '94

Omae, Hitoshi
Time of the Apes '75

Omae, Wataru
Ebirah, Horror of the Deep '66
Godzilla vs. Gigan '72
Godzilla vs. Hedorah '71
The Last War '61
Son of Godzilla '67
Time of the Apes '75
Yog: Monster from Space '70

Omiya, Koetsu
Godzilla vs. Gigan '72

Omori, Nao
Ichi the Killer '01

Omori, Yoshio
The Razor 2: The Snare '73

Omura, Ayako
Parasite Eve '97

Omura, Kon
Gamera vs. Guiron '69

Omura, Senkichi
Chushingura '62
Ghidorah the Three-Headed Monster '64
Godzilla Raids Again '55
The H-Man '58
The Mysterians '57
The Secret of the Telegian '60
Seven Samurai '54
Throne of Blood '57

On Ping
(An Ping)

Exit the Dragon, Enter the Tiger '75
Fury of King Boxer '72

Onda, Seijiro
Godzilla Raids Again '55

Ong, Alannah
Victim '99

Ong, Jaymee
Gen-X Cops '99

Ong, Stuart
(Yung Sai-kit, Weng Shi Jie, Steven Yung)
The Big Heat '88
Evil Cat '86
In the Line of Duty 3 '88
Legendary Couple '95
Mr. Boo Meets Pom Pom '85
Sex and the Emperor '94

Ongg, Judy
Zu: Warriors of the Magic Mountain '83

Onishi, Yuka
Lady Ninja: Reflections of Darkness '96

Onitsuka
God.com '98

Ono, Masahiko
Ring '98

Ono, Michiko
Giants and Toys '58

Ono, Miyuki
Evil Dead Trap '88

Ono, Shinya
BloodFight '89

Onodera, Akira
Gamera, Guardian of the Universe '95

Onodera, Joh
Ultraman Tiga and Ultraman Dyna: The Warriors of the Lightning Star '98

Onoe, Kuroemon
Samurai 1: Musashi Miyamoto '54
Samurai 2: Duel at Ichijoji Temple '55
Samurai 3: Duel at Ganryu Island '56

Oppenheimer, Alen
Giant Monster Gamera '65 (U.S.)

Orimoto, Junkichi
Godzilla 1985 '84
Message from Space '78

Oropesa, Elizabeth
The Killing of Satan '83

Orr, Corrine
Speed Racer: The Movie(V) '67

Osawa, Sayaka
Godzilla vs. Destroyah '95
Godzilla vs. MechaGodzilla 2 '93
Godzilla vs. Mothra '92

Oshima, Yoko
Another Heaven '00
Gamera, Guardian of the Universe '95
Ring '98

Oshima, Yukari
(Dai Do Yau Ga Lei, Da Dao You Jia Li, Dai Do, Cynthia Luster, Yukari Tsunara)
Angel '87
Beauty Investigator '92
Guardian Angel '96
Kick Boxer's Tears '92
Leopard Hunting '98
Lethal Panther 2 '93
The Millionaires' Express '86
Riki-Oh: The Story of Ricky '89
Supercop 2 '93

Osugi, Ren
(Takashi Osugi, Ren Ohsugi)
Audition '99
Brother '00
Cure '97
Fireworks '97
Ghost Actress '96
The Hypnotist '99
Maborosi '95
Postman Blues '97
Sonatine '93
Spiral '00
Tokyo Mafia 2: Wrath of the Yakuza '95
Tokyo Mafia: Yakuza Wars '95
Weather Woman '96

Ota, Rie
Godzilla, Mothra and King Ghidorah: Battle on Fire '01

Otabe, Michima
Lone Wolf and Cub 4: Baby Cart in Peril '72
Lone Wolf and Cub 5: Baby Cart in the Land of Demons '73

Otaka, Akira
Cure '97
The Hypnotist '99

Otaka, Rikiya
Ring '98
Ring 2 '99

Otake, Hitoe
Tokyo Decameron:
Three Tales of Madness and Sensuality '96

Otaki, Shuji
(Shoji Otake)
The Funeral '84
Lone Wolf and Cub 5:
Baby Cart in the Land of Demons '73
Tampopo '87

Otis
The Adventures of Milo and Otis '86

Otomo, Ryutaro
The Magic Serpent '66
Tampopo '85

Otomo, Shin
Ghidorah the Three-Headed Monster '64
Godzilla Raids Again '55
The H-Man '58
The Mysterians '57
The Secret of the Telegian '60
Throne of Blood '57

Otonashi, Mikiko
Violent Cop '89

Otowa, Nobuko
The Last War '61

Otsubo, Naomi
Aces Go Places 3 '84

Otsuka, Akio
Ghost in the Shell '95 (V)

Otsuka, Ko
Dragon Princess '81

Otsuki, Kenji
The Ninja Dragon '90

Otsuru, Gitan
The Haunted Lantern '98

Otto, Barry
Mr. Nice Guy '97

Owens, Gary
The Green Hornet '74

Owens, Ray
Astro Boy '63 (V)

Oyama, Kenji
Gamera vs. Gyaos '67
Giant Monster Gamera '65

Ozaki, Mayumi
The Ninja Dragon '90

Ozawa, Eitaro
(Sakae Ozawa)
Godzilla 1985 '84
The H-Man '58

Ozawa, Kazuyoshi
Tokyo Mafia 2: Wrath of the Yakuza '95
Tokyo Mafia: Yakuza Wars '95

Ozawa, Sayako
Godzilla vs. Space Godzilla '94

Pa Hung
Prodigal Boxer '73

Padilca, Rommel
Leopard Hunting '98

Pai, Jason
(Pai Piao, Baak Biu, Bai Biao, Pak Piu)
Avenging Warriors of Shaolin '79
Bolo '80
Death Mask of the Ninja '82
Dirty Tiger, Crazy Frog '78
Killer's Romance '90
Lightning Kung Fu '80
Ten Tigers of Shaolin '78
Twinkle Twinkle Lucky Stars '85

Pai Ying
(Baak Ying, Bai Ying)
Bloody Fight '72
Born Wild '01
Dragon from Russia '90
A Fistful of Talons '83
Fists Like Lee '74
Militant Eagle '78
Raiders of Wu Tang '82
The 72 Desperate Rebels '76
SuperManChu '73
Thousand Mile Escort '76
A Touch of Zen '69
Yoga and Kung Fu Girl '78

Pai Yu
Swordsman with an Umbrella '70

Pais, Josh
Teenage Mutant Ninja Turtles '90

Pak Fen
Rage of the Dragon '79

Pak, Ho Sung
(Pak Ho-Sung)
Legend of the Drunken Master '94

Pak, James
(Pak Chin-Shek, Baak Chin Sak, Bai Qian Dan, Bak Chin Sek, James Pax)
Dragon Chronicles: Maidens of Heavenly Mountain '94
The Heroic Trio '93

Pak Kar-sin
(Bak Ka-Sin, Bai Jia Qian)
Everyday Is Valentine '01
Expect the Unexpected '98
Moonlight Express '99
Troublesome Night '97

Pak Sha-lik
(Baak Qui Lik, Bai Sha Li, Pai Sa Leh)
The Bloody Fists '72
Kung Fu Zombie '81
Super Gang '78

Pak Yan
(Baak Yan, Bai Yin)
Legend of the Drunken Master '94
Miracles '89

Pak Yong-hok
Pulgasari '85

Pal, Amrit
Aakhri Adalat '88

Pal, Surender
Champion '00

Palmer, Jonathan
Lethal Panther 2 '93

Pan Ching Fu
The Secrets of the Warrior's Power '97

Pan Jie
The Adventures of the Master and His Servant '96

Pan Ping-chang
(Poon Bing Seung, Pan Bing Chang, Pan Ping Chang, Portia Poon)
Dirty Ho '79
Kid with the Golden Arm '78
Love Me, Love My Money '01
My School Mate, the Barbarian '01
The Return of the 5 Deadly Venoms '78
Troublesome Night 3 '97

Pan Qingfu
(Pan Quing Fu, Iron Fist)
The Shaolin Temple '79
Shaolin Temple 2: Kids from Shaolin '84

Pan, Rebecca
Days of Being Wild '90
In the Mood for Love '00

Pan Ya Kan
Doctor No... '01

Pan Yue-ming
A Love of Blueness '00

Pandey, Leela
Mahal '48

Pang, Bennett
Armour of God '86

Pang, Samuel
(Pang King-Chi, Paang Ging Tsz, Peng Jing Ci)
Hit Team '00
Jiang Hu-"The Triad Zone" '00
My School Mate, the Barbarian '01
Runaway '01
The Wesley's Mysterious File '01

Pang, Wallis
Troublesome Night 3 '97

Pang Yan
Beijing Bicycle '01

Pao Fong
(Bao Fang, Baau Fong, Paul Fong)
The Bride with White Hair '93
Legend of the Drunken Master '94
The Phantom Lover '95

Pao, Ko Saio
(Ko Saio Po, Got Siu Bo, Ge Xiao Boa, Ker Hsiao Po, Ge Shao Bao, Ko Hsiao Pao)
Battle of Shaolin '77
Blood of the Dragon '71
Blooded Treasury Fight '79
The Deadly Sword '78
Eagle's Claw '77
18 Secrets of Kung Fu '79
Exit the Dragon, Enter the Tiger '75
Fatal Needles vs. Fatal Fists '80
Filthy Guy '80
A Fistful of Talons '83
Killer Priest '81
Lady Iron Monkey '83
The Last Duel '82
Ninja Supremo '81
Screaming Ninja '73
The Shaolin Brothers '77
Shaolin Mantis '78
Succubare '77
Ways of Kung Fu '80

Parasher, Deepak
Champion '00

Park Eun-hye
Record '00

Park Joong-hoon
Nowhere to Hide '99

Park Ju-chun
Born Wild '01

Park Jum-soon
Double Dragon in the Last Duel '85

Park, Max
Magnificent Natural Fist '80

Park Sang-myun
(Park Sang-myeon)
The Foul King '00
Hi! Dharma! '01
My Wife Is a Gangster '01
Nowhere to Hide '99

Park Ye-jin
Memento Mori '99

Park Yeong-gyu
Attack the Gas Station! '99

Park Yong-woo
Shiri '99

Parr, Vince
Thunder Ninja Kids: The Hunt for the Devil Boxer '86/94

Parry, Brian
Astro Boy '80 (V)

Parsons, Mike
The Walls of Hell '64

Pasdar, Adrian
Shanghai 1920 '91

Pathak, Dina
Champion '00

Pau Hei-ching
(Bau Hei Jing, Bao Qi Jing)
Bullet in the Head '90
Century of the Dragon '99
Eagle Shooting Heroes '93

Pau Hon-lam
(Baau Hon Lam, Bao Han Lin)
God of Gamblers '89
God of Gamblers 2 '90
God of Gamblers Returns '94

Pau, Peter
The Chinese Feast '95

Pau, Sai Gwa
(Sai Gwa Paau, Xi Gua Bao)
Avenging Warriors of Shaolin '79
Bolo '80
Dirty Kung Fu '78
Dreadnaught '81
Enter the Fat Dragon '78
Erotic Ghost Story '90
Golden Dragon Silver Snake '79
He Has Nothing But Kung Fu '77

The Magnificent Butcher '79
The New Marvelous Double '93
Ten Tigers of Shaolin '78
Winners and Sinners '83

Peacock, Maureen
Legend of the Dinosaurs '77

Pena, Elizabeth
Rush Hour '98

Peng Kang
(Peng Kong, Perng Gang)
The Leg Fighters '80
A Life of Ninja '83

Penn, Chris
Rush Hour '98

Penn, Kim
(Kim Maree Penn)
Armageddon '97
In the Line of Duty 5: Middle Man '90
Queen's High '91
Supercop '92
Supercop 2 '93

Perlman, Ron
Blade 2 '02
Jackie Chan Adventures 2: The Dark Hand Returns '00 (V)

Perrine, Valerie
Cannonball Run '81

Perry, Joe
Ultraman 2 '01 (V)

Perry, Manny
Rush Hour '98

Peter
Ran '85

Petit, Francois
Mortal Kombat '95

Petrov, Jouri
First Strike '96

Pettersson, Kurt Roland
Born to Defence '88

Pettyjohn, Angelique
Mad Doctor of Blood Island '68

Philipson, Donna
Reptilian '00

Philpot, Andrew
Vampire Hunter D: Bloodlust '01 (V)

Pholdee, Jesdaporn
Fear Faith Revenge 303 '98

Pilar, Rosario del
Curse of the Vampires '70

Piven, Jeremy
Rush Hour 2 '01

Png, Pierre
The Eye '02

Po Fu Mei
Fists of Bruce Lee '78

Po Ming-nam
Love on a Diet '01

Po Siu-yee
Sharp Guns '01

Po Yip Dung
Shaolin Soccer '01

Poe, Fernando Jr.
The Walls of Hell '64

Poletto, Vince
Mr. Nice Guy '97

Polida, Sam
Snaker '01

Pong, Joe
Magnificent Natural Fist '80

Pool-sang, Cheung
Killer of Snake, Fox of Shaolin '78

Poon Chan-leung
Love au Zen '01

Poon Chi-man
The Kung Fu Master '94

Poon, Edmond
Horror Hotline...Big Head Monster '01

Poon, Fletcher
(Poon Yiu Ming, Pan Yao Ming)
The Accidental Spy '01
Bullets of Love '01
Forbidden City Cop '96

Poon Hing
Generation Consultant '90

Poon, Jazz
Hit Team '00

Poon, Maggie
(Poon Mei Kei, Pan Mei Qi)
Inner Senses '01
Spacked Out '00

Poon, Tom
(Poon Jan Wai, Pan Zhen Wei)
Evil Cat '86
On the Run '88

Portevy, Om
Snaker '01

Poyer, Jude
(Wong Ji Hung, Huang Zi Hong)
Bio-Cops '00
The Blacksheep Affair '98
Downtown Torpedoes '97
Gen-Y Cops '00
Hot War '98
A Man Called Hero '99
Moonlight Express '99
Vampire Controller '00

Pran
Gumnaam '65

Prochnow, Jurgen
The Replacement Killers '97

Pukkavesh, Siri-yakorn
Mon-Rak Transistor '01

Punzalan, Bruno
Brides of Blood '68
Mad Doctor of Blood Island '68

Pupart, Michael
Fear Faith Revenge 303 '98

Puri, Amrish
Elaan '94
Hum Paanch '80

Puri, Madan
Gumnaam '65

Puri, Om
Raat '91

Q, Maggie
(Maggie Quigley)
Gen-Y Cops '00
Model from Hell '99
Rush Hour 2 '01

Quek, Phyllis
(Gwok Fei Lai, Guo Fei Li)
Born Wild '01
2000 A.D. '00

Raffaelli, Cyril
Kiss of the Dragon '01

Ramos, Ely
Brides of Blood '68
The Walls of Hell '64

Ramos, Kim
Twilight People '72

Ramos, Travador
Fists Like Lee '74

Rapovski, Paul
(Paul Rapouski, Paul Rapowski)
Contract Killer '98
Extreme Challenge '01
Thunderbolt '95

Ratanasopha, Prem-sinee
Bangkok Dangerous '00

Rawal, Paresh
Aakhri Adalat '88

Raymond
Murder in the Orient '74

Reason, Rhodes
King Kong Escapes '67

Reddy, Ramml
Elaan '94

Reedus, Norman
Blade 2 '02

Reis, Michelle
(Lee Ka-Yan, Michelle Lee, Jiaxin Lee, Michele Monique Reis)
Armageddon '97
Bakery Amour '01
Beauty and the Breast '02
Casino Tycoon 2 '92
A Chinese Ghost Story 2 '90
Drunken Master Killer '94
Every Dog Has His Date '01
Fallen Angels '95
The Irresistible Piggies '02
A Kid from Tibet '91
The Legend '92
The Legend 2 '93
The Legend of the Swordsman '92
Royal Tramp 2 '92
Wicked City '92

Remotigue, Couto
Time and Tide '00

Remy, Ronald
The Blood Drinkers '64
Mad Doctor of Blood Island '68

Ren, Richie
Gorgeous '99
Marry a Rich Man '02

Revathi
Raat '91

Revilla, Ramon
The Killing of Satan '83

Reyes, Ernie Jr.
Rush Hour 2 '01

Reyes, Eva
Murder in the Orient '74

Reyes, Randy
Gunhed '89 (V)

Reynolds, Burt
Cannonball Run '81

Reynolds, Patrick
Golden Dragon Silver Snake '79

Rhys-Davies, John
Shogun '80

Ri Gwon
Pulgasari '85

Ri Jong-uk
Pulgasari '85

Ricketts, Ronnie
Angel on Fire '95

Rijyu, Go
Guinea Pig: Mermaid in a Manhole '88

Rindaro, Tep
Snaker '01

Rivera, Linda
Curse of the Vampires '70

Rivers, Victor
Fatal Blade '00

Rivilla, Ramona
Leopard Hunting '98

Riyonun, Ri
Pulgasari '85

Robles, Renato
The Blood Drinkers '64

Rockwell, Sam
Teenage Mutant Ninja Turtles '90

Rodriguez, Celia
The Blood Drinkers '64

Rogers, Taya
Fear Faith Revenge 303 '98

Rojo, Danny
Murder in the Orient '74

Rojo, Max
Devil Woman '70

Rolston, Mark
Rush Hour '98

Romano, Rino
Godzilla the Series: Monster War '99 (V)

Romersa, Joe
Blood: The Last Vampire '00 (V)

Roncal, Oscar
The Walls of Hell '64

Rongguang, Yu
(Yu Rong Guang, Rongguang Yu, Yu Wing-Kwong, Yu Yung Kang)
Ballistic Kiss '98
Big Bullet '96
Combo Cops '96
Deadend of Besiegers '92

The East Is Red '93
The Enforcer '95
From Beijing with Love
'94
The Holy Robe of
Shaolin Temple '84
Iron Monkey '93
Leopard Hunting '98
Man Wanted '95
Rock 'n' Roll Cop '94
Shanghai Affairs '98
The Storm Riders '98
Supercop 2 '93

Rooker, Michael
The Replacement
Killers '97

Roonnak, Piya
Bangkok Dangerous
'00

Roth, Louis
A Better Tomorrow 2
'87
Black Cat '91
City Hunter '92
Legend of the Drunken
Master '94
Miracles '89
Naked Killer '92
Once upon a Time in
China 4 '93
Police Story 2 '88
Robo Vampire '88

Rothrock, Cynthia
(Law Foo Lok, Luo Fu
Luo)
The Art of Action: Mar-
tial Arts in the
Movies '02
Blonde Fury '89
The Inspector Wears
Skirts '88
The Millionaires'
Express '86
Prince of the Sun '90
Righting Wrongs '86
Yes, Madam '85

Roxburgh, Richard
The Touch '02

Roy, Kanu
Mahal '48

Rubinek, Saul
Rush Hour 2 '01

Rudd, Paul
Gen-Y Cops '00

Rujinanon, Chutcha
The Eye '02

Rustla, Ruben
Beast of the Yellow
Night '70

Ruth
Horror Hotline...Big
Head Monster '01

Ryan, James
Martial Arts Mayhem,
Vol. 1 '99

Ryan, Max
Kiss of the Dragon '01

Ryan, Michael
Crystal Hunt '91

Ryder, Irene
Kung Fu, the Invisible
Fist '72

Ryoo Hyoun-kyoung
Bichunmoo '99

Ryu, Artld
Fear Faith Revenge 303
'98

Ryu, Chishu
Akira Kurosawa's
Dreams '90
The Funeral '84
Good Morning '59

Ryu, Daisuke
Ran '85

Sada, Keiji
Good Morning '59

Sada, Yutaka
All Monsters Attack '70
Destroy All Monsters
'68
Ebirah, Horror of the
Deep '66
Frankenstein vs.
Baragon '65
High and Low '63
The Mysterians '57
The Secret of the
Telegian '60
Throne of Blood '57

Saeki, Hinako
Godzilla, Mothra and
King Ghidorah: Bat-
tle on Fire '01
Spiral '00

Saeki, Isamu
Gamera vs. Zigra '71

Saga, Michiko
Samurai 3: Duel at
Ganryu Island '56

Saga, Zembe
The Razor 1: Sword of
Justice '72

Sagara, Haruko
Sure Death: Revenge
'87

Sahara, Kenji
All Monsters Attack '70
Attack of the Mush-
room People '63
Chushingura '62
Contract Killer '98
Destroy All Monsters
'68
Frankenstein vs.
Baragon '65
Ghidorah the Three-
Headed Monster
'64
Godzilla vs. King Ghido-
rah '91

Godzilla vs.
MechaGodzilla '74
Godzilla vs.
MechaGodzilla 2
'93
Godzilla vs. Mothra '92
Godzilla vs. Space
Godzilla '94
The H-Man '58
Half Human '55/1957
King Kong vs. Godzilla
'62
Mothra '61
Mothra vs. Godzilla '64
The Mysterians '57
Rodan '56
Son of Godzilla '67
Terror of MechaGodzilla
'75
War of the Gargantuas
'66
Yog: Monster from
Space '70

Saijo, Hideki
Angel '87

Saijo, Yasuhiko
Godzilla vs. Gigan '72
Son of Godzilla '67

Saiki, Shigeru
Audition '99
Guinea Pig: Mermaid in
a Manhole '88

Saito, Hiroko
Time of the Apes '75

Saito, James
Teenage Mutant Ninja
Turtles '90

Saito, Mai
Ultraman Gaia: The
Battle in Hyper-
space '98

Saito, Noritake
Godzilla vs. Gigan '72
Yog: Monster from
Space '70

Saito, Risa
Ultraman Tiga and
Ultraman Dyna: The
Warriors of the
Lightning Star '98

Saito, Toshiko
Black Tight Killers '66

Saito, Yosuke
Godzilla vs. Space
Godzilla '94
Gunhed '89

Sakagami, Kaori
Sugar-Howling of Angel
'96

Sakagami, Yasushi
Gamera vs. Zigra '71

Sakagi, Keiichiro
Sakuya: Slayer of
Demons '00

Sakaguchi, Tak
Versus '00

Sakai, Frankie
Chushingura '62
The Last War '61
Mothra '61
Shogun '80

Sakai, Sachio
Akira Kurosawa's
Dreams '90
All Monsters Attack '70
Chushingura '62
Godzilla, King of the
Monsters '54
Half Human '55/1957
King Kong Escapes '67
King Kong vs. Godzilla
'62
Samurai 2: Duel at Ichi-
joji Temple '55
Samurai 3: Duel at
Ganryu Island '56
The Secret of the
Telegian '60
Throne of Blood '57
What's Up, Tiger Lily?
'66
Yog: Monster from
Space '70

Sakaki, Hideo
Versus '00

Sakakida, Keiji
Godzilla, King of the
Monsters '54

Sakashi, Ushio
Prince of Space '59

Sakdikul, Somlek
Mon-Rak Transistor '01

Sakura, Asako
Big Boobs Buster '90

Sakura, Mutsuko
Maborosi '95

Sakurai, Masaru
Akira Kurosawa's
Dreams '90

Sakurako, Akino
Sadistic City '93

Salcedo, Felisa
Mad Doctor of Blood
Island '68

Salcedo, Leopoldo
Beast of the Yellow
Night '70

Salcedo, Paquito
The Blood Drinkers '64
Curse of the Vampires
'70
Mad Doctor of Blood
Island '68

Salvitti, John
(Juen Qui Wai Dak, Zun
Sha Wei Te)
Crystal Hunt '91
In the Line of Duty 4
'89

Sam, Sam
Needing You... '00

Sambrell, Aldo
Operation Condor '91

Sammy
Dummy Mommy, with-
out a Baby '01
Fighting for Love '01

Samuels, Bobby
(Robert Samuels)
Don't Give a Damn '95
Red Wolf '95

San Kwal
(San Kuai, Saan Gwai,
Shan Guai, San Kuei,
Sun Kuay, Shan Kwai)
The Awaken Punch '73
The Bloody Fists '72
Bolo '80
The Buddhist Fist '79
Crack Shadow Boxers
'77
Dreadnaught '81
Drunken Master '78
Heart of Dragon '85
Kung Fu's Hero '73
Lightning Kung Fu '80
My Kung Fu 12 Kicks
'79
Shadow of the Tiger
'79
10 Magnificent Killers
'77
Ten Tigers of Shaolin
'78
The 36 Crazy Fists '77
We're Going to Eat You!
'80
Winners and Sinners
'83

San Naai
Leopard Hunting '98

San Sin
(Shen Xian, Sheng Se,
Hsin Hsien)
Code of Honor '87
Dirty Ho '79
Duel of the Brave Ones
'78
Executioners from
Shaolin '77
Kung Fu Genius '79
Warrior from Shaolin
'81

Sanada, Henry
(Duke Sanada, Harry
Sanada, Hiroyuki Sana-
da)
The Executioner '74
Legend of the Eight
Samurai '84
Message from Space
'78
Renegade Ninjas '79
Ring '98
Ring 2 '99
Royal Warriors '86
Shogun's Ninja '82
Spiral '98

Sure Death: Revenge
'87

Sanches, Sylvia
Lethal Panther '91

Sanchez, Ben
Brides of Blood '68
The Walls of Hell '64

Sanchez, Roselyn
Rush Hour 2 '01

Sanders, Steve
Dynamo '78
Enter the Dragon '73

Sands, Julian
Jackie Chan Adven-
tures 1: The Search
for the Talismans
'00 (V)
Jackie Chan Adven-
tures 2: The Dark
Hand Returns '00
(V)
Jackie Chan Adven-
tures 3: The Shad-
ow of Shendu '00
(V)

Sang, Chin Yuet
(Qian Yue Sheng, Chien
Yueh Sheng, Tom Chin,
Chieh Hsueh Shang,
Guo Rong Sheng, Chin
Yet Sun) See also side-
bar on p. 326.
Bolo '80
Buddha Assassinator
'80
Chinese Hercules '73
Dance of the Drunk
Mantis '79
Dirty Tiger, Crazy Frog
'78
Dynamo '78
Enter the Fat Dragon
'78
Executioners from
Shaolin '77
Faces of Horror '98
He Has Nothing But
Kung Fu '77
Heroes Shed No Tears
'83/86
Kung Fu, the Invisible
Fist '72
Last Hurrah for Chivalry
'78
New Mr. Vampire '86
Pom Pom '84
The Prodigal Son '81
Righting Wrongs '86
Shaolin Master Killer
'78
Sting of the Dragon
Masters '73
Super Kung Fu Kid '74

Sang-hyun
Lies '99

Sang-kawes, Charlie
Fear Faith Revenge 303
'98

Sano, Ryoko
Godzilla vs.
MechaGodzilla 2
'93

Sano, Shiro
Godzilla 2000 '99
Godzilla, Mothra and
King Ghidorah: Bat-
tle on Fire '01
Princess Blade '02
Violent Cop '89

**Saram, Michelle Ali-
cia**
Bullets over Summer
'99

Sargent, Lia
Black Magic M-66 '87
(V)

Sasaki, Katsuhiko
Godzilla vs. Biollante
'89
Godzilla vs. King Ghido-
rah '91
Godzilla vs. Megalon
'73
Terror of MechaGodzilla
'75

Sasaki, Nozomu
Akira '88 (V)

Sasaki, Takamaru
The Human Vapor '60
Invasion of Astro-Mon-
ster '65
The Secret of the
Telegian '60
Throne of Blood '57

Sasaki, Yumeka
I.K.U. '00

Sata, Keiko
The Human Vapor '60

Sato, Hitomi
Ring '98
Ring 2 '99

Sato, Jimmy
Bruce Lee Fights Back
from the Grave '76

Sato, Kei
Godzilla 1985 '84
The Razor 2: The Snare
'73
Zatoichi's Vengeance
'66

Sato, Keiji
Contract Killer '98

Sato, Koichi
Battle in Outer Space
'59
Gonin '95
Lone Wolf and Cub 5:
Baby Cart in the
Land of Demons
'73
Lone Wolf and Cub 6:
White Heaven in
Hell '74

Sato, Makoto
Chushingura '62
The Eel '97
The Executioner '74
The H-Man '58
Message from Space
'78
Samaritan Zatoichi '68
Shogun's Ninja '82

Sato, Masahiro
Guinea Pig: He Never
Dies '86
Guinea Pig: The Making
of Guinea Pig '86

Sato, Masao
Wild Zero '99

Sato, Tomomi
Body Snatcher from
Hell '68
Lone Wolf and Cub 5:
Baby Cart in the
Land of Demons
'73

Sato, Yasue
The Dimension Travel-
ers '98

**Satsuma, Kenpa-
chiro**
(Kengo Nakayama)
Godzilla 1985 '84
Godzilla vs. Biollante
'89
Godzilla vs. Destroyah
'95
Godzilla vs. Gigan '72
Godzilla vs. Hedorah
'71
Godzilla vs. King Ghido-
rah '91
Godzilla vs.
MechaGodzilla 2
'93
Godzilla vs. Megalon
'73
Godzilla vs. Mothra '92
Godzilla vs. Space
Godzilla '94
Pulgasari '85

Sattels, Barry
Fatal Blade '00

Saunders, David
Sixty Million Dollar Man
'95

Sawa, Nobiko
Legend of the
Dinosaurs '77

Sawada, Kenji
(Ken Sawada)
The Happiness of the
Katakuris '01
Hiruko the Goblin '90

Sawada, Kenya
(Chak Tin Him Wun; Ze
Tian Qian Ye)
Color of Pain '02
Extreme Crisis '98
Thunderbolt '95

Sawaguchi, Yasuko
Godzilla 1985 '84
Godzilla vs. Biollante
'89

Sawai, Keiko
Frankenstein vs.
Baragon '65
Invasion of Astro-Mon-
ster '65

Sawaki, Asami
Tokyo Mafia 3: Battle
for Shinjuku '96

Sawaki, Tetsu
Audition '99

Sawamura, Ikio
All Monsters Attack '70
Battle in Outer Space
'59
Chushingura '62
Ebirah, Horror of the
Deep '66
Frankenstein vs.
Baragon '65
Ghidorah the Three-
Headed Monster
'64
The Hidden Fortress
'58
King Kong Escapes '67
Terror of MechaGodzilla
'75
Throne of Blood '57
War of the Gargantuas
'66
Yojimbo '61

Sawamura, Sadako
Good Morning '59

**Sawamura, Sono-
suke**
Godzilla Raids Again
'55
Samurai 3: Duel on
Ganryu Island '56
The Tale of Zatoichi
Continues '62
Zatoichi on the Road
'63

Saxena, Sharat
Aakhri Adalat '88

Saxon, John
(Carmen Orrico, Juen
Saat Shun, Zun Sa
Xun)
Enter the Dragon '73
Martial Arts Mayhem,
Vol. 1 '99

Sayah, Joseph
(Joe Sayah)
Mr. Nice Guy '97
Once upon a Time in
China and America
'97

Sazanka, Kyu
Giants and Toys '58

Scarstead, Vance
The Walls of Hell '64

Schultz, Dwight
Vampire Hunter D:
Bloodlust '01 (V)

Schweiger, Til
The Replacement
Killers '97

Scorsese, Martin
Akira Kurosawa's
Dreams '90

Scott, Linda Gaye
The Green Hornet '74

Scott, Mark
Lethal Panther '91

See, Robin
Dragon against Vam-
pire '85

Segall, Pamela
Vampire Hunter D:
Bloodlust '01 (V)

Sek Yin Ji
(Dan Yan Zi)
A Better Tomorrow '86

Seki, Yoshie
Sakuya: Slayer of
Demons '00

Sekiguchi, Kinzo
Woman in the Dunes
'64

Sekiguchi, Yusuke
Kikujiro '99

Sekine, Daigaku
Kikujiro '99
Shark Skin Man and
Peach Hip Girl '98

Sekita, Hiroshi
All Monsters Attack '70
Destroy All Monsters
'68
Ebirah, Horror of the
Deep '66
King Kong Escapes '67
War of the Gargantuas
'66

Sekiyama, Koji
Lone Wolf and Cub 4:
Baby Cart in Peril
'72

Senda, Koreya
Battle in Outer Space
'59
The H-Man '58

Sengoku, Noriko
Blind Beast '69
Invasion of Astro-Mon-
ster '65
Kwaidan '64
Seven Samurai '54
Stray Dog '49

Sera, Akira
The H-Man '58
Half Human '55/1957
The Secret of the
Telegian '60

Shogun '80
Varan the Unbelievable
'58

Sergi, Brad
Reptilian '00

Serizawa, Reita
Ghost Actress '96
Ring 2 '99

Seth, Sushma
Aakhri Adalat '88

Seto, Asaka
Bullets of Love '01

Seto, Reiko
Atomic Rulers of the
World '57
Attack from Space '58
Evil Brain from Outer
Space '58/59

Seung Fung
(Chang Feng)
Kung Fu on Sale '79
The Shaolin Brothers
'77
The Shaolin Kids '77

Shah, Kashmira
Champion '00

Shah, Mahaveer
Aakhri Adalat '88

Shah, Nasiruddin
Hum Paanch '80

Shahlavi, Darren
Angel on Fire '95
Sixty Million Dollar Man
'95

Shaku, Yumiko
Princess Blade '02

Sham Chin-bo
(Sam Chim Boh, Cen
Qian Bo, Sham Tsim
Po, Chen Chien Po,
Ts'en Ch'ieh Pao,
Cheng Chin Pao)
The Bloody Fists '72
Bruce Lee: The Man,
the Myth '76
The Chinese Connec-
tion '72
Dragon Lord '82
Dragon's Claws '79
Fists of Bruce Lee '78
God of Gamblers 2 '90
Kung Fu, the Invisible
Fist '72
Master of the Flying
Guillotine '74
Ninja Supremo '81
The Owl vs. Bombo '84
Return of the Chinese
Boxer '75
The Shaolin Kids '77
The 36 Crazy Fists '77
The 36 Deadly Styles
'79
Winners and Sinners
'83
The Young Master '80

Sham, John
(Sham Kin-fun, Sam Gin
Fan, Cen Jian Xun,
Shum Kin Fun, John
Shum)
Aces Go Places 3 '84
Curry & Pepper '90
Eighth Happiness '88
I Love Maria '88
Miracles '89
Mr. Boo Meets Pom
Pom '85
Painted Faces '88
Pedicab Driver '89
Pom Pom '84
Pom Pom Strikes Back
'86
Twinkle Twinkle Lucky
Stars '85
Wheels on Meals '84
Where's Officer Tuba?
'86
Winners and Sinners
'83
Yes, Madam '85

Shan Mao
(Saan Maau, San Mao,
San Moo, San Mou)
Bruce Lee We Miss You
'76
Exit the Dragon, Enter
the Tiger '75
Fury of King Boxer '72
Master of the Flying
Guillotine '74
Rage of the Masters
'74
Screaming Ninja '73

Shan Yeh
Flash Future Kung Fu
'83

Shang Kwan, Polly
(Seung Goon Leung
Fung, Shang Guan Ling
Feng, Polly Kuan, Sang
Gwan, Polly Shian
Kuan, Shang Kwan Ling
Fung)
The 18 Bronzemen '76
The 18 Bronzemen Part
2 '76
The 18 Jade Arhats '78
Five Elements of Kung
Fu '78
The Green Dragon Inn
'79
Lady Whirlwind and the
Rangers '74
Lady Wu Tang '77
99 Cycling Swords '80
The Shaolin Kids '77
Shaolin Traitorous '76

Shao Bing
Crash Landing '00

Shao Kao Shan
Master of the Flying
Guillotine '74

Sharma, Abishek
Champion '00

Shauq, Vivek
Champion '00

Shaw Luo-hui
(Siu Law Fai, Shao Luo
Hui, Siu Law Fai, Show
Lo Fai, Law Lo FayShaw
Luo Hoi)
The Blazing Temple '76
Chinese Iron Man '75
The 8 Masters '77
The 18 Bronzemen '76
The 18 Bronzemen Part
2 '76
Five Elements of Kung
Fu '78
Golden Killah '80
Lady Whirlwind and the
Rangers '74
Moonlight Sword and
Jade Lion '79
The Shaolin Kids '77
Triangular Duel '72

Shaw, Maggie
(Siu Mei Kei, Shao Mei
Qi, Siao Mei Kei, Mag-
gie Siu)
The Longest Nite '98
Losers' Club '01
Shogun and Little
Kitchen '92

Shaw Yin-Yin
(Siu Yam Yam, Shao
Yin Yin)
Chinatown Kid '77
The Killer '89
You Shoot, I Shoot '01

Shek, Dean
(Sek Tin, Dan Tian,
Shih Tien, Shia Tien,
Shek Tin, Charlie Shek,
Dean Saki)
Aces Go Places '82
A Better Tomorrow 2
'87
Breakout from Oppres-
sion '72
Crazy Crooks '80
Dance of the Drunk
Mantis '79
Dirty Kung Fu '78
Dirty Tiger, Crazy Frog
'78
Dragon from Russia
'90
Drunken Master '78
18 Fatal Strikes '78
Emperor of Shaolin
Kung Fu '80
Fearless Hyena '79
Fearless Hyena 2 '80
Filthy Guy '80
Half a Loaf of Kung Fu
'77
His Name Is Nobody
'79
Kung Fu on Sale '79
Odd Couple '79
Snake-Crane Secret
'78
Snake in the Eagle's
Shadow '78

Spiritual Kung Fu '78

Shen Hai Yung
18 Fatal Strikes '78

Shen Mung Shang
Hunted by Royal Decree
'00

Shepard, Sam
Great Performances:
Kurosawa '02 (N)

Sheperd, Karen
(Karen Shepherd)
Righting Wrongs '86

Sheung, Simon
Eat My Dust '93

Shi Po-hua
Iron Man '86

Shi, Pomson
(Sin Lam Yuk, Sheng
Lin Yu)
Aces Go Places 4 '86
I Love Maria '86
Shadow of the Tiger
'79
Young and Dangerous
5 '98

Shi Yan-Ming
The Secrets of the War-
rior's Power '97

Shia Lin-Lin
Lone Ninja Warrior '81

Shiba, Toshio
(Toshio Shibaki)
Godzilla vs. Hedorah
'71

Shibasaki, Kou
Battle Royale '00

Shibata, Yoshiyuki
Lady Ninja: Reflections
of Darkness '96

Shie, James
Jackie Chan Adven-
tures 1: The Search
for the Talismans
'00 (V)
Jackie Chan Adven-
tures 2: The Dark
Hand Returns '00
(V)
Jackie Chan Adven-
tures 3: The Shad-
ow of Shendu '00
(V)

Shiga, Masaru
Lone Wolf and Cub 3:
Baby Cart to Hades
'72
Lone Wolf and Cub 5:
Baby Cart in the
Land of Demons
'73

Shigaragi, Koji
Good Morning '59

Shigemura, Keishi
Junk '99

Shigenobu, Yasuhiro
The H-Man '58

Shigeta, James
Brother '00

Shih Chun
(Sek Jun, Dan Juan, Shi
Jun, Shih Jun)
Legend of the Mountain
'79
A Touch of Zen '69

Shih Chung Tien
(Shut Chung Tin, Shi
Zhong Tian, Se Chun
Tin)
Chinese Iron Man '75
18 Fatal Strikes '78
The Iron Monkey '77
Iron Monkey 2 '77
Triangular Duel '72

Shih Feng
(Sek Fung, Dan Feng)
Five Elements of Kung
Fu '78

Shih Kien
(Shek Kin, Sek Kin,
Shih Kien, Siak Kin,
Sheek Kin)
Aces Go Places 4 '86
A Better Tomorrow 3
'89
Enter the Dragon '73
From China with Death
'74
H.K. Adams Family '92
The Legend of Bruce
Lee '80
The Millionaires'
Express '86
The Private Eyes '76
The Young Master '80

Shih Kwan-li
(Shiah Guen Lih, Hsia
Kwan Li, Ha Kwong Li,
Ha Gwong Lee, Jia
Guang Li)
The Butterfly Murders
'80
The Leg Fighters '80
Zu: Warriors of the
Magic Mountain
'83

Shih Kwong-li
The Butterfly Murders
'79

Shih, Lu
A Touch of Zen '69

Shih Ting Ken
(Shut Ting Gan, Shi Tin
Gen, Shi Ting Kan, Shi
Shing Gung, Shi Cheng
Kung)
Battle of Shaolin '77
Challenge of Death '78
Dreaming Fists with
Slender Hands '80

Eagle's Claw '77
18 Fatal Strikes '78
Fatal Needles vs. Fatal
    Fists '80
Golden Killah '77
Invincible Armour '77
The Iron Monkey '77
Killer from Above '77
The Killer Meteors '76
The Leg Fighters '80
The Massive '78
Master of the Flying
    Guillotine '75
New Fist of Fury '76
Revengeful Sword-
    women '79
Snake-Crane Secret
    '78
The 36 Deadly Styles
    '79

Shihodo, Wataru
Postman Blues '97

Shihomi, Etsuko
Message from Space
    '78

Shiina, Eihi
Audition '99

Shiina, Kippei
Gonin '95

Shikeharo, Teijo
The Street Fighter '74

Shim Eun-ha
Tell Me Something '99

Shim Won-chul
My Wife Is a Gangster
    '01

Shimada, Go
Another Heaven '00
Gamera 3: The
    Revenge of Irys '99
Ring 0: Birthday '00

Shimada, Kyusaku
Princess Blade '02
Sakuya: Slayer of
    Demons '00

Shimada, Ryuzo
Blind Swordsman: The
    Tale of Zatoichi '62
Daimajin '66
Zatoichi on the Road
    '63

Shimada, Shogo
Zatoichi and the Chest
    of Gold '64

Shimada, Yoko
Shogun '80

Shimamura, Kaori
(Kaori Matsumoto)
Beautiful Beast '95
Junk '99

Shimazu, Masahiko
Good Morning '59

Shimizu, Gen
Godzilla vs. Gigan '72

Invasion of Astro-Mon-
    ster '65
Seven Samurai '54
Stray Dog '49

Shimizu, Hiroshi
Evil Dead Trap '88
Postman Blues '97

Shimizu, Hitomi
Reborn from Hell:
    Samurai Armaged-
    don '96

Shimizu, Isamu
Message from Space
    '78

Shimizu, Kentaro
Fatal Blade '00

Shimizu, Koji
Beautiful Hunter '94

Shimizu, Masao
Godzilla Raids Again
    '55
Sanjuro '63
Stray Dog '49

Shimizu, Misa
The Eel '97
Warm Water under a
    Red Bridge '01

Shimono, Sab
Jackie Chan Adven-
    tures 1: The Search
    for the Talismans
    '00 (V)
Jackie Chan Adven-
    tures 2: The Dark
    Hand Returns '00
    (V)
Jackie Chan Adven-
    tures 3: The Shad-
    ow of Shendu '00
    (V)

Shimura, Takashi
(Shoji Shimazaki)
Bullet Train '75
Chushingura '62
Frankenstein vs.
    Baragon '65
Ghidorah the Three-
    Headed Monster
    '64
Godzilla Raids Again
    '55
Godzilla, King of the
    Monsters '54
The Hidden Fortress
    '58
High and Low '63
Kwaidan '64
Men Who Tread on the
    Tiger's Tail '43
Mothra '61
The Mysterians '57
Rashomon '50
Samurai 3: Duel at
    Ganryu Island '56
Sanjuro '63
Sanshiro Sugata '43
Seven Samurai '54
Stray Dog '49

Throne of Blood '57
Yojimbo '61
Zatoichi and the Fugi-
    tives '68

Shin Eun-kyung
(Shin Eun-kyoung)
My Wife Is a Gangster
    '01
Ring Virus '99
Spiral '00

Shin, George
Golden Dragon Silver
    Snake '79

Shin Ha-kyun
(Shin Ha Gyun)
Dream of Garuda '94
The Foul King '00
Joint Security Area '00
Sympathy for Mr.
    Vengeance '01

Shin Hyun-joon
Bichunmoo '99

Shin Min-ah
Volcano High School
    '01

Shin, Niko
Magnificent Natural
    Fist '80

Shin-yang, Park
Hi! Dharma! '01

Shindo, Eisaku
Taboo '97
Tokyo Decameron:
    Three Tales of Mad-
    ness and Sensuali-
    ty '96
Zero Woman: The
    Accused '96

Shingyoji, Kimie
Shark Skin Man and
    Peach Hip Girl '98

Shinoda, Saburo
Gamera vs. Viras '68
Godzilla vs. Destroyah
    '95
Godzilla vs. Mothra '92

Shinohara, Masashi
Attack of the Mush-
    room People '63
Ghidorah the Three-
    Headed Monster
    '64
Invasion of Astro-Mon-
    ster '65
Varan the Unbelievable
    '58

Shinohara, Yoshiko
Grave of the Fireflies
    '88 (V)

Shioji, Akira
The Street Fighter '74
The Street Fighter's
    Last Revenge '74

Shiomi, Sue
*(Etsuko Shihomi,
Etsuko Shiomi)*
The Bodyguard '73/78
Bullet Train '75
Dragon Princess '81
Legend of the Eight
    Samurai '84
Martial Arts Mayhem,
    Vol. 1 '99
Shogun's Ninja '82
Sister Street Fighter
    '74
The Street Fighter '74
The Street Fighter's
    Last Revenge '74

Shionoya, Masayuki
Pulse '01

Shirai, Akira
The Hypnotist '99

Shiraishi, Ayano
Grave of the Fireflies
    '88 (V)

Shiraishi, Hitomi
Tokyo Decameron:
    Three Tales of Mad-
    ness and Sensuali-
    ty '96

Shiraishi, Kayoko
Female Convict Scorpi-
    on: Jailhouse 41
    '72

Shirakawa, Yumi
Chushingura '62
The H-Man '58
The Last War '61
The Mysterians '57
Rodan '56
The Secret of the
    Telegian '60

Shirichal, Kwancharu
Wild Zero '99

Shiroshima, Yasuyo
Ghost Actress '96
Weather Woman '95

Shishido, Joe
Branded to Kill '67
Fugitive Alien
    '78/1986
Star Force: Fugitive
    Alien 2 '78/86

Shit Pai
Shaolin Fist of Fury '87

Shou, Robin
*(Shou Wan-bo, Chau
Wan Boh, Chou Yun Bo,
Wai Lung)*
The Big Heat '88
Casino Raiders '89
City War '88
In the Line of Duty 3
    '88
Mortal Kombat '95
The Most Wanted '94

Shozo, Tojima
Organ '96

Shroff, Jackie
Aakhri Adalat '88

Shu Qi
*(Shu Kei, Hsu Chi, Li
Lin-Hui)*
Beijing Rocks '01
The Blacksheep Affair
    '98
Extreme Crisis '98
Flyin Dance '01
For Bad Boys Only '00
Gorgeous '99
Love Me, Love My
    Money '01
A Man Called Hero '99
Martial Angels '01
The Storm Riders '98
Visible Secret '01
The Wesley's Mysteri-
    ous File '01
Young and Dangerous
    5 '98
Young and Dangerous
    6: Born to Be King
    '00

Shum, Frankie
Crippled Masters '80
Raiders of Wu Tang '82

Shum Hoi-yung
War of the Shaolin Tem-
    ple '80

Shum Lo
(Sam Liu, Shen Lao)
Dirty Ho '79
Executioners from
    Shaolin '77
Five Deadly Venoms
    '78
Shaolin Master Killer
    '78
Ten Tigers of Kwang-
    tung '79

Shum, Lydia
*(Shum Tin-Ha, Lydia
Sun, Lydia Shun, Lydia
Sham)*
Drunken Tai Chi '84
The Millionaires'
    Express '86
Monkey Fist Floating
    Snake '79
Tiger on Beat '88

Shum Wai
(Sam Wai, Shen Wei)
Beauty Investigator '92
The Bloody Fists '72
Casino Raiders '89
Code of Honor '87
Dragons Forever '88
H.K. Adams Family '92
Kick Boxer's Tears '92
Long Arm of the Law
    '84
Miracles '89
New Mr. Vampire '86
The Protector '85
Queen's High '91
The Victim '80
Yes, Madam '85

Shut Ma Wa Lung
(Si Ma Hua Long, Suma Hua Lung, Suma Wah Lung)
Eagle Shooting Heroes '93
Fist of Fury 1991 '91
A Gambler's Story '01
Last Hero in China '93
Legend of the Drunken Master '94
Prodigal Boxer '73

Shut Ma-yin
(Si Ma Yan)
The Haunted Cop Shop '87
Scared Stiff '86

Si-ho, Leung
(Liang Si Hao)
From Beijing with Love '94
Miracles '89
Sex and the Emperor '94
The Three Swordsmen '94

Si Wai
(Si Wei)
Lone Ninja Warrior '81

Siabkuntod, Somchai
Extreme Challenge '01

Siao, Josephine
(Siao Fong-Fong, Siu Fong Fong, Xiao Fang Fang, Siao Liang) See also sidebar on p. 326.
The Legend '92
The Legend 2 '93

Siao Yuk
(Siu Yuk, Xiao Yu)
Masked Avengers '81
Ten Tigers of Kwangtung '79

Siddharth, Geetha
Hum Paanch '80

Sieou, Antonio
Champ against Champ '83

Sik Chi-wan
Shaolin Soccer '01

Sik Siu-long
(Hsi Hsiao-long, Shieh Sihao Long, Tommy Shik)
Chivalrous Legend '98
Dragon from Shaolin '96

Simon, Glory
The Accidental Spy '01
Who Am I? '98

Sin, Pal
(Tan Lap Man, Daan Laap Man, Chan Li Wen, Sin Lap Man)

All Men Are Brothers: Blood of the Leopard '93
City Hunter '92
Erotic Ghost Story '90
God of Gamblers 2 '90
Iceman Cometh '89
Operation Pink Squad '88

Sing, Chan
(Chen Xing, Chen Sing, Chen Hsing, Henry Xing, Ringo Chan, Chen Shing)
Aces Go Places '82
The Bloody Fists '72
Brutal Boxer '72
Death Ring '83
Fatal Flying Guillotine '77
Iron Monkey 2 '77
Killer Priest '81
Kung Fu, the Invisible Fist '72
Lady Iron Monkey '83
The Legendary Strike '78
Lone Ninja Warrior '81
The Magnificent '78
Mantis Combat '81
Mask of Death '76
The Master of Death '82
Monkey Fist Floating Snake '79
New Fist of Fury '76
Revenge of the Patriots '76
The 72 Desperate Rebels '76
The Silver Spear '79

Sing Lung
Real Kung Fu of Shaolin, Part 1 '81

Sisti, Michelan
Teenage Mutant Ninja Turtles '90

Sit, Allen
(Sit Chun Wai, Xue Chun Wei, Alan Sit, Allan Chun)
First Strike '96
Rumble in the Bronx '95
Supercop 2 '93

Sit Cheung-man
(Hsieh Chang Wen, Shieh Yin Man, Xue Chang Wen, Xue Zhang Wen)
Eagle's Claw '77
Fatal Needles vs. Fatal Fists '80
The Hot, the Cool and the Vicious '76
The Leg Fighters '78
Ways of Kung Fu '78

Sit Chi-lun
(Xue Zhilun, Fanny Sit)

A Chinese Ghost Story '87
Miracles '89
Picture of a Nymph '70

Sit Hon
(Xue Han, Hsieh Han, Shieh Hou, Shit Hong, Hsued Han, Hsueh Han)
Battle of Shaolin '77
Challenge of Death '78
Fatal Needles vs. Fatal Fists '80
Fury of King Boxer '72
The Heroes '80
The Hot, the Cool, and the Vicious '76
The Killer Meteors '76
Master of the Flying Guillotine '74
Militant Eagle '78
Rage of the Masters '74
Return of the Chinese Boxer '75
Return of the Tiger '79
Screaming Ninja '73
The 72 Desperate Rebels '76
The Shaolin Brothers '77
A Touch of Zen '69

Sit, Nancy
(Sit Ka-Yin, Sit Ga Yin, Xue Gu Yan)
The Awaken Punch '73
God of Cookery '96

Siu-fan, Luk
Rosa '86

Siu-foo, Lam
(Lin Hsiao Hu, Lin Xiao Hu, Lam Siu Fu, Lin Hsiao Fu)
Battle of Shaolin '77
The 8 Masters '77
Shaolin Traitorous '76
The Smart Cavalier '76

Siu Foo-dau
(Xiao Hu Dou, Hsiao Hou Tao, Siu Foo-dao)
18 Secrets of Kung Fu '79
Ninja Checkmate '79
7 Commandments of Kung Fu '79

Siu Gam
(Xiao Jin, Hsiao Chin, Siu Kam)
Fearless Dragons '79
Militant Eagle '78
The 72 Desperate Rebels '76
The Silver Spear '79
We're Going to Eat You '80

Siu, Gary
(Siu Yuk Lung, Xiao Yu Long)
Angel 2 '88

Killer's Romance '90

Siu Hon-sung
Bruce Lee, The Legend '84

Siu Leong, Robert
Shadow '01

Siu Suet
Clueless '01

Siu Tak-foo
(Siu Tak Fu, Xiao De Hu)
Ashes of Time '94
Fatal Flying Guillotines '77
Heart of Dragon '85
Kick Boxer's Tears '92
The Millionaires' Express '86
Peacock King '89
Pedicab Driver '89
Righting Wrongs '86
Royal Warriors '86
She Shoots Straight '90
Where's Officer Tuba? '86

Siu Yu-wah
Gimme Gimme '01

Siu Yuk-yin
Hong Kong X-File '98

Smerczak, Ron
Who Am I? '98

Smiljanic, Bozidar
Armour of God '86
Operation Condor '91
Project A 2 '87

Smith, Paul
Extreme Challenge '01
Return of the Tiger '79

Smoorenburg, Ron
The Avenging Fist '01
Born Wild '01
Gen-Y Cops '00
Martial Angels '01
Who Am I? '98

Snipes, Wesley
Blade 2 '02

So, Edmond
(So Chi-Wai, Su Zhi Wei)
Shadow '01
Task Force '97

So Gam-lung
Fearless Fighters '73
Sorrowful to a Ghost '70

So Hang Suen
(Su Xing Xuan)
Bullet in the Head '90
Crocodile Hunter '89
Inner Senses '01

So, Phillip
Masters of Tiger Crane '83

So, Tommy
A Chinese Ghost Story: The Tsui Hark Animation '97 (V)

So, William
(So Wing Hong, Su Yong Kang)
Bakery Amour '01
A Taste of Killing and Romance '94

Sogiyama, Tsunehara
Aces Go Places 3 '84

Solomin, Yuri
Dersu Uzala '74

Somel, Mari
Guinea Pig: Mermaid in a Manhole '88

Someno, Yukio
Devil Woman '70
Thunder Kick '73

Sonam
Aakhri Adalat '88

Song Jia
Born to Defence '88

Song Kang-ho
Dream of Garuda '94
The Foul King '00
Joint Security Area '00
Shiri '99
Sympathy for Mr. Vengeance '01

Song Lei
The Blade '95

Song Wok-suk
My Sassy Girl '01

Song Young-chang
The Foul King '00

Sonoda, Ayumi
The H-Man '58

Sonoi, Keisuke
The X from Outer Space '67

Sonooka, Shintaro
Princess Blade '02

Soo Chun Bay
Double Dragon in the Last Duel '85

Sop Han Gi
Pulgasari '85

Sorimachi, Takashi
Fulltime Killer '01

Sorvino, Mira
The Replacement Killers '97

Soto, Joseph
Dynamo '78

Soto, Talisa
Mortal Kombat '95

Sparks, Carrie Cain
Rumble in the Bronx '95

Sparks, Robert
Running out of Time '99

Spencer, Carl
Extreme Challenge '01

Sricherdchutm, Songwut
Fear Faith Revenge 303 '98

Stanford, Leonard
Battle in Outer Space '59

Steinmetz, Richard
The One '01

Stewart, Robin
Legend of the 7 Golden Vampires '74

Stone, Bruce
Lethal Panther '91

Stone, Doug
Black Magic M-66 '87 (V)

Stone, King
The Street Fighter '74

Stormare, Peter
The Tuxedo '02

Strang, Amanda
Beauty and the Breast '02
Final Romance '01
Martial Angels '01

Stratham, Jason
The One '01

Su Chen Ping
(Siu Chan Ping, Su Zhen Ping, Chen Ping, Shu Chen Ping, Su Jen)
Born Invincible '78
Chinese Iron Man '75
The 18 Bronzemen '76
The 8 Masters '77
Iron Neck Li '81
Kung Fu on Sale '79
Macho Man '72
Master of the Flying Guillotine '75
Moonlight Sword and Jade Lion '79
Raiders of Wu Tang '84
Sorrowful to a Ghost '70
The Story in Temple Red Lily '79

Suchao Pong-wilai
Fear Faith Revenge 303 '98

Sudoh, Ken
Prince of Space '59

Suen Gwok-ming
(Sun Guo Ming)

Martial Arts Master Wong Fei Hung '92
Queen's High '91

Suen Hing
(Sun Xing)
Dragon from Russia '90

Suen King Kal
18 Secrets of Kung Fu '79

Suen Lam
(Sun Lan, Sum Nam, San Lau)
The Bloody Fists '72
Drunken Art and Crippled Fist '79
Five Fingers of Death '71
Incredible Kung Fu Mission '79
Militant Eagle '78
New Fist of Fury '75
Prodigal Boxer '72
Thunder Kick '73

Suen, Richard
(Suen Gwok Ho, Sun Guo Hao, Richard Sun)
The Bride with White Hair 2 '93
Bullets of Love '01
Gen-Y Cops '00

Suen Shu-pau
(Sun Shu Pei, Suen Shu-rau, Suen Shu-peu, Shuen Chuen Po)
Brave Archer '77
Chinatown Kid '77
Five Deadly Venoms '78
7 Commandments of Kung Fu '79

Suet Lee
Dragon Lord '82

Suga, Fujio
Lone Wolf and Cub 5: Baby Cart in the Land of Demons '73
Ninja: Band of Assassins Continued '63
Zatoichi's Cane Sword '67

Sugal, Ichiro
Gamera vs. Barugon '66
Sanshiro Sugata '43
Stray Dog '49

Sugai, Kin
The Funeral '84
Godzilla, King of the Monsters '54
High and Low '63
Kwaidan '64

Sugata, Shun
Blowback: Love and Death '90
Ichi the Killer '01

Organ '96
Pulse '01

Sugawara, Madoka
Naked Killer '92

Sugihara, Yuko
Yog: Monster from Space '70

Sugimoto, Aya
Ultraman Tiga and Ultraman Dyna: The Warriors of the Lightning Star '98

Sugimura, Haruko
Good Morning '59
Kwaidan '64

Sugisaki, Kouichi
Tokyo Mafia 3: Battle for Shinjuku '96

Sugita, Koh
Zatoichi's Flashing Sword '64

Sugiyama, Shosaku
Zatoichi on the Road '63

Suh, Alex
Golden Dragon Silver Snake '79

Suh Tai-wha
Bichunmoo '99

Suizenji, Kiyoko
Zatoichi's Cane Sword '66

Sumida, Takashi
Weather Woman '95

Sun Chien
(Suen Gin, Sun Jian, Scorpion Venom) See also sidebar on p. 374.
Avenging Warriors of Shaolin '79
Chinatown Kid '77
Five Deadly Venoms '78
Kid with the Golden Arm '78
The Return of the 5 Deadly Venoms '78
Robo Vampire '88
Ten Tigers of Kwang-tung '79

Sun Honglei
The Road Home '99

Sun Jung-chi
(Suen Wing Chi, Sun Rong Zhi, Sun Wing Chi, Suen Rong Chi, Suen Rong Jvi)
The Iron Monkey '77
The Leg Fighters '80
A Life of Ninja '83
The Lost Kung Fu Secrets '80
Monkey Fist Floating Snake '79

Return of the Chinese Boxer '75
Shaolin vs. Lama '81

Sun, Karen
(Suen Ga Lam, Sun Jia Lin, Sun Chia Lin)
5 Lady Venoms '78
The Hot, the Cool, and the Vicious '76
The Iron Monkey '77

Sun Kui Hin
Shaolin vs. Manchu '80

Sun Nan
Prodigal Boxer '73

Sun, Paulyn
(Suen Kai-kwan, Suen Gaai Gwan, Sun Jia Jun, Pauline Suen, Alien Sun)
The Accidental Spy '01
Every Dog Has His Date '01
Ichi the Killer '01
Last Ghost Standing '99
Sixty Million Dollar Man '95
Troublesome Night 4 '98
Troublesome Night 9 '00
The Untold Story 2 '98

Sun, William Oscar
Code of Honor '87

Sun Yueh
(Suen Yuet, Sun Yue, Sum Yuen, Sun Yuen, Sun Yuih, Sung Yueh)
City on Fire '87
Crazy Crooks '80
Fantasy Mission Force '84
Legend of the Mountain '79
Ninja Supremo '81
Pedicab Driver '89
Swordsman with an Umbrella '70

Sunazuka, Hideo
Ebirah, Horror of the Deep '66

Sung Lai
Lady Whirlwind and the Rangers '74

Sung Pa
The Killer Elephants '76

Sung, Tilly
Snake Fist Dynamo '84

Sung, Tony
Invincible Obsessed Fighter '82

Sutherland, Donald
Final Fantasy: The Spirits Within '01 (V)

Suwa, Taro
Another Heaven '00
Cure '97
Ring 2 '99
Spiral '00

Suzukawa, Norioko
Lady Ninja: Reflections of Darkness '96

Suzuki, Cutie
The Ninja Dragon '90

Suzuki, Junna
The Haunted Lantern '98

Suzuki, Kazuo
All Monsters Attack '70
Ebirah, Horror of the Deep '66
Ghidorah the Three-Headed Monster '64
Invasion of Astro-Monster '65
King Kong Escapes '67
Son of Godzilla '67
Terror of MechaGodzilla '75

Suzuki, Masafumi
Bronson Lee, Champion '78
Return of the Street Fighter '74
The Street Fighter '74
The Street Fighter's Last Revenge '74

Suzuki, Mayu
Godzilla 2000 '99

Suzuki, Mizuho
Godzilla 1985 '84

Sze, Celia
(Sze Lim Tsz, Si Lim Tsz, Shi Nian Ci, Celia Sie)
A Wicked Ghost '99

Sze, Lot
(Si Gaai Keung, Shi Jie Jiang)
Clueless '01
Love Paradox '00

Sze Ma Lung
(Shut Ma Lung, Si Ma Long, Se-Ma Hung, Shaking Eagle, Yang Kong, Sei Ma Loung)
18 Fatal Strikes '78
Five Elements of Kung Fu '78
The Green Dragon Inn '79
Kung Fu on Sale '79
Lady Wu Tang '77
The Master of Death '82
One Foot Crane '79
Secret of the Chinese Kung Fu '81
The Smart Cavalier '78

Szeto, Roy
(Szeto Wai-Cheuk, Shut Tiu Wai Cheuk, Si Tu Hui Zhou)
Horror Hotline...Big Head Monster '01
The Phantom Lover '95

Szu, Shih
(Si Si, Shi Si, Shy Sy, She Sha)
Avenging Eagle '78
Duel of the Brave Ones '78
The Heroes '80
Legend of the 7 Golden Vampires '74
Lone Ninja Warrior '81

Tabu, Kenzo
Frankenstein vs. Baragon '65
Invasion of Astro-Monster '65
King Kong vs. Godzilla '62
Mothra vs. Godzilla '64

Tachikawa, Hiroshi
(Yoichi Tachikawa)
Attack of the Mushroom People '63
Sanjuro '63
Throne of Blood '57
Yojimbo '61

Tagawa, Cary-Hiroyuli
Mortal Kombat '95

Taguchi, Tomoro
(Tomoroh Taguchi, Tomorowo Taguchi, Tomorrow Taguchi, Tochiro Taguchi)
The Eel '97
Gamera 2: Advent of Legion '96
Gamera 3: The Revenge of Irys '99
Guinea Pig: Android of Notre Dame '88
Postman Blues '97
Reborn from Hell: Samurai Armageddon '96
Sadistic City '93
Tetsuo: The Iron Man '89
Tetsuo 2: Body Hammer '91
Tokyo Mafia 3: Battle for Shinjuku '96

Tahara, Chisako
Atomic Rulers of the World '57
Attack from Space '58
Evil Brain from Outer Space '58/59

Tahil, Dalip
Elaan '94

Tai Bik Chi
Juliet in Love '00

Tai Bo
(Tai Po, Tai Biu, Tai Bao)
Beauty Investigator '92
Blonde Fury '89
City on Fire '93
Dragon Lord '82
Dragons Forever '88
Encounter of the Spooky Kind '81
Enter the Dragon '73
Fist of Fury 1991 '91
Guardian Angel '96
Her Name is Cat 2: Journey to Death '01
Heart of Dragon '85
Iceman Cometh '89
Legend of the Drunken Master '94
The Millionaires' Express '86
Miracles '89
New Mr. Vampire '86
The Owl vs. Bombo '84
Police Story '85
Police Story 2 '88
Pom Pom '84
Prince of the Sun '90
Project A '83
Project A 2 '87
Righting Wrongs '86
Rosa '86
Skinny Tiger and Fatty Dragon '90
Sword Stained with Royal Blood '93
Twinkle Twinkle Lucky Stars '85
The Vampire Combat '01
We're Going to Eat You! '80
Where's Officer Tuba? '86
Winners and Sinners '83
Yes, Madam '85
The Young Master '80

Tai Leung
Dreaming Fists with Slender Hands '80
The Story in Temple Red Lily '79
Swordsman with an Umbrella '70

Tai, Paul
Eat My Dust '93

Tai-ping, Yu
(Chui Tai Ping, Tu Tai Ping)
Avenging Warriors of Shaolin '79
Chinatown Kid '77
Chinese Super Ninjas '82
Five Deadly Venoms '78
Flag of Iron '80
Kid with the Golden Arm '78
Masked Avengers '81
Nine Demons '83

The Return of the 5 Deadly Venoms '78
Ten Tigers of Kwang-tung '79

Tai, Robert
(Daai Chit, Dai Che, Tai Chi Tsien, Tai Chi Hsien, Tai Che, Tai Chi, Tai Yee Tin, Tai Chit)
Chinatown Kid '77
The Incredible Kung Fu Mission '82
Killer from Above '77
Master of the Flying Guillotine '77
Ninja the Final Duel '85
Ninja vs. Shaolin Guards '84
Shaolin vs. Ninja '83
The Smart Cavalier '78

Tai San
(Taai Saan, Tai Shan, Tarzan)
Code of Honor '87
Crazy Crooks '80
Enter the Fat Dragon '78
Fatal Flying Guillotines '77
5 Superfighters '79
Game of Death '78
Heart of Dragon '85
His Name Is Nobody '79
Knockabout '79
Last Hurrah for Chivalry '78
Miracles '89
My Lucky Stars '85
Odd Couple '79
The Owl vs. Bombo '84
Pom Pom '84
Rosa '86
The 36 Deadly Styles '79
Winners and Sinners '83
The Young Master '80

Tai Yee-ha
Five Elements of Kung Fu '78

Taira, Saori
Weather Woman '95

Tajima, Reiko
Godzilla vs. MechaGodzilla '74

Tajima, Yoshifumi
All Monsters Attack '70
Dagora the Space Monster '64
Destroy All Monsters '68
Frankenstein vs. Baragon '65
Ghidorah the Three-Headed Monster '64
Godzilla 1985 '84
The H-Man '58
The Human Vapor '60

Invasion of Astro-Monster '65
King Kong Escapes '67
Mothra '61
Mothra vs. Godzilla '64
Rodan '56
The Secret of the Telegian '60
Varan the Unbelievable '58
War of the Gargantuas '66

Takachiho, Hizuro
Fight, Zatoichi, Fight! '64

Takada, Minoru
Atomic Rulers of the World '57
Attack from Space '58
Battle in Outer Space '59
Evil Brain from Outer Space '58/59
Ghidorah the Three-Headed Monster '64
Invaders from Space '58
The Last War '61

Takada, Miwa
Adventures of a Blind Man '64
Daimajin '66
Zatoichi Challenged '67
Zatoichi the Fugitive '63

Takada, Munehiko
Gamera vs. Viras '68
Giant Monster Gamera '65

Takagi, Hitoshi
My Neighbor Totoro '88 (V)
The Razor 2: The Snare '73
Tampopo '85

Takagi, Mio
(Mio Takaki)
Guinea Pig: Android of Notre Dame '88
Ultraman Tiga and Ultraman Dyna: The Warriors of the Lightning Star '98

Takagi, Shinji
Godzilla vs. Megalon '73

Takagi, Shinpei
The Manster '60
Seven Samurai '54

Takahashi, Akira
Ghost Actress '96

Takahashi, Atsuko
Yog: Monster from Space '70

Takahashi, Choei
Fugitive Alien '78/1986
Star Force: Fugitive Alien 2 '78/86
Tampopo '85

Takahashi, Etsushi
The Razor 3: Who's Got the Gold? '74

Takahashi, Hideki
Entrails of the Virgin '86

Takahashi, Katsumi
The Hypnotist '99

Takahashi, Keiko
Spiral '00

Takahashi, Koji
Godzilla vs. Biollante '89

Takahashi, Masaya
Body Snatcher from Hell '68
Godzilla, Mothra and King Ghidorah: Battle on Fire '01

Takahashi, Toyo
Good Morning '59

Takakura, Ken
Bullet Train '75

Takamatsu, Hideo
Giants and Toys '58
Shogun '80

Takano, Hassel
Pulse '01
Spiral '00

Takarada, Akira
Chushingura '62
Ebirah, Horror of the Deep '66
Frankenstein vs. Baragon '65
Godzilla, King of the Monsters '54
Godzilla vs. Mothra '92
Half Human '55/1957
Invasion of Astro-Monster '65
King Kong Escapes '67
The Last War '61
Mothra vs. Godzilla '64

Takase, Haruna
The Funeral '84

Takashima, Masahiro
Godzilla vs. Destroyah '95
Godzilla vs. MechaGodzilla 2 '93
Gunhed '89

Takashima, Masanobu
Extreme Crisis '98
Godzilla vs. Biollante '89

Takashima, Minoru
Godzilla vs. Gigan '72

Takashima, Shikyoku
Notorious Concubines '69

Takashima, Tadao
(Tadeo Takashima)
Chushingura '62
Frankenstein vs. Baragon '65
Godzilla vs. MechaGodzilla 2 '93
King Kong vs. Godzilla '62
Son of Godzilla '67

Takashina, Kaku
Black Tight Killers '66

Takasugi, Koh
Shark Skin Man and Peach Hip Girl '98

Takasugi, Shinbei
Reborn from Hell: Samurai Armageddon '96

Takatani, Ichiro
Lone Wolf and Cub 3: Baby Cart to Hades '72

Takatsuka, Toru
Gamera vs. Viras '68

Takechi, Toyoko
The Manster '60

Takeda, Shinji
The Happiness of the Katakuris '01
Pulse '01

Takehatsu, Shiro
Postman Blues '97

Takei, Mitsugi
Lady Ninja: Reflections of Darkness '96

Takenaka, Naoto
Freeze Me '00
Gonin '95
Hiruko the Goblin '90
Sakuya: Slayer of Demons '00
Tokyo Fist '96

Takeuchi, Riki
(Chikara Takeuchi)
Blowback: Love and Death '90
Nobody '99
Tokyo Mafia 2: Wrath of the Yakuza '95
Tokyo Mafia 3: Battle for Shinjuku '96
Tokyo Mafia: Yakuza Wars '95

Takeuchi, Yuko
Ring '98

Taki, Eiko
Adventures of a Blind Man '64
Zatoichi and the Doomed Man '65

Takita, Kazue
Time of the Apes '75

Takito, Saburo
A Better Tomorrow 3 '89

Takizawa, Osamu
(Shu Takizawa)
Kwaidan '64

Takizawa, Ryoko
Postman Blues '97

Takuma, Shin
Godzilla 1985 '84
Shogun '80

Takuro, Tatsumi
Godzilla vs. Destroyah '95

Tam, Alan
(Tam Wing Lun, Tan Yong Lin)
Armour of God '86
Casino Raiders '89
The Dragon Family '88
The Last Blood '90
Rich and Famous '87

Tam, Debbie
Spacked Out '00

Tam, Halina
(Tam Siu Wan, Tan Xiao Huan)
Beauty and the Breast '02
Dance of a Dream '01
Troublesome Night 8 '00
Troublesome Night 9 '00

Tam, Patrick
(Tam Yiu-Man, Tan Yao Wen)
Beast Cops '98
Born Wild '01
Century of the Dragon '99
Comeuppance '00
The Duel '00
Legend of Speed '99
Operation Billionaires '98
Zu Warriors '01

Tam, Rebecca
Victim '99

Tam, Shaun
Midnight Fly '01

Tam Suk-mool
Legendary Couple '95

Tam Tak Sing
Shaolin vs. Manchu '80

Tam Wai-ha
Goodbye Mr. Cool '01

Tam, Zoie
Chinese Orthopedist and the Spice Girls '02

Tamagawa, Isao
Branded to Kill '67

Tamba, Tetsuro
(Tetsuro Tanba)
Bullet Train '75
The Happiness of the Katakuris '01
Kwaidan '64
Renegade Ninjas '79
Riki-Oh: The Story of Ricky '89
Sakuya: Slayer of Demons '00
Shogun's Ninja '82

Tamblyn, Russ
War of the Gargantuas '66

Tamura, Akira
Atomic Rulers of the World '57
Attack from Space '58
Evil Brain from Outer Space '58/59

Tamura, Hiroshi
Guinea Pig: Flower of Flesh and Blood '85
Guinea Pig: The Making of Guinea Pig '86

Tamura, Takahiro
The Razor 1: Sword of Justice '72

Tan Chun-tao
(Tam Jan Dung, Tan Zhen Dong, Tan Chen Tu, Tan Jun Tao, Tan Chun To)
Avenging Warriors of Shaolin '79
Crystal Hunt '91

Tan, Delon
(Tan Tao Liang, Taam Diy Leung, Tan Dao Liang, Flash Legs, Delung Tam, Delon Tam, Dorian Tan, Tarn Daw Liang)
Blooded Treasury Fight '79
Challenge of Death '78
Hand of Death '75
The Heroes '80
The Hot, the Cool, and the Vicious '76
The Leg Fighters '80
The Shaolin Invincibles '79
Snake-Crane Secret '78
The Story in Temple Red Lily '79

Tan, Joey
Trust Me U Die '99

Tan Kheng Seong
Para Para Sakura '01

Tan Lee
(Dan Li, Tan Li, Tan Ri)
Ghost Actress '96

Tan, Oliver
Second Time Around '02

Tan, Sally
Chinese Orthopedist and the Spice Girls '02

Tan Sin-hung
Lee Rock '91

Tanabe, Seiichi
Ring 0: Birthday '00

Tanaka, Atsuko
Ghost in the Shell '95 (V)

Tanaka, Haruo
Samurai 3: Duel at Ganryu Island '56

Tanaka, Hiroshi
Lone Wolf and Cub 4: Baby Cart in Peril '72
Lone Wolf and Cub 5: Baby Cart in the Land of Demons '73

Tanaka, Hiroyuki
(Sabu)
Ghost Actress '96
Ichi the Killer '01
Postman Blues '97

Tanaka, Ken
Godzilla 1985 '84

Tanaka, Kotaro
Junk '99

Tanaka, Kunie
Bullet Train '75
Kwaidan '64
Sanjuro '62

Tanaka, Misato
Godzilla vs. Megaguirus '00

Tanaka, Yoji
(Boba)
Adrenaline Drive '99
Kikujiro '99
Shark Skin Man and Peach Hip Girl '98

Tanaka, Yoshiko
Godzilla vs. Biollante '89
Godzilla vs. Mothra '92
Ring 0: Birthday '00

Tanaka, Yoshitaka
Mighty Jack '68

Tang, Alan
(Tang Kwong-Wing, Dang Gwong Wing, Deng Guang Rong)

Bloody Fight '72
The Haunted Cop Shop '87

Tang, Anthony
(Tang Ho Kwong. Dang Ho Gwong, Deng Hao Guang)
The Kung Fu Master '94

Tang Chia
(Tong Gaai, Tang Jia)
Avenging Eagle '78
Death Mask of the Ninja '82

Tang, Joann
Evil Cat '86

Tang, Johnny
(Dang Siu Juen, Deng Zhao Zun, Tang Siu Chuen)
From Beijing with Love '94
A Taste of Killing and Romance '94
Tragic Fantasy: Tiger of Wanchai '94

Tang, Lee
Beautiful Beast '95

Tang Pik-wan
She Shoots Straight '90

Tang, Stephen
From the Queen to the Chief Executive '01

Tang Yim-chan
(Tang Yen-tsan, Tong Yim Chan, Bruce Tong, Tang Hou Yun)
Avenging Eagle '78
Blind Fist of Bruce '79
Dragon Lord '82
The Shaolin Disciple '80
The Young Master '81

Tang Yin-chan
The Young Master '80

Tang Lee, Alex
Devil Woman '70

Tani, Akira
Kwaidan '64
Mothra vs. Godzilla '64
Seven Samurai '54
Throne of Blood '57

Tani, Kei
After Life '98

Tani, Kenichi
Gamera vs. Barugon '66
Giant Monster Gamera '65

Tanigawa, Miyuki
Fugitive Alien '78/1986
Star Force: Fugitive Alien 2 '78/86

Tanihara, Shosuke
Godzilla vs. Megaguirus '00

Tanikado, Yukihito
Versus '00

Tanno, Yoshiyuki
Spiral '00

Tao, David
(Tao Da Wei, Tao Da Way)
Fantasy Mission Force '84
Ninja Supremo '81

Tao, Ruth Winona
(Tao Kwun-mei, Tiu Gwan Mei, Tao Jun Wei)
The Bride with White Hair 2 '93

Tarapore, Eruch
Mahal '48

Tarlton, Alan
The Manster '60

Tartalia, Steve
Once upon a Time in China '91
Operation Condor '91

Tarzan the Monkey
The Six Directions of Boxing '79

Tashiro, Masashi
Ultraman Gaia: The Battle in Hyperspace '98

Tate, Misato
Akira Kurosawa's Dreams '90

Tateyama, Hiro
Fugitive Alien '78/1986
Star Force: Fugitive Alien 2 '78/86

Tatsumi, Tsutomu
Grave of the Fireflies '88 (V)

Tayama, Akihiro
Mothra '61

Taylor, Kent
Brides of Blood '68

Taylor, Lily
Rivals of the Dragon '83

Tazaki, Jun
(Minoru Tanaka)
Chushingura '62
Dagora the Space Monster '64
Destroy All Monsters '68
Ebirah, Horror of the Deep '66
Frankenstein vs. Baragon '65

Invasion of Astro-Monster '65
King Kong vs. Godzilla '62
King of the Mongols '60
Kwaidan '64
Mothra vs. Godzilla '64
Ran '85
Seven Samurai '54
War of the Gargantuas '66

Teduka, Toru
Gamera 3: The Revenge of Irys '99
Spiral '00

Tee, Steven
Thunder Ninja Kids: The Hunt for the Devil Boxer '86/94

Teng Kun Chang
Master of the Flying Guillotine '74

Teng Rujun
A Love of Blueness '00

Terada, Minori
(Nou Terada, Takashi Terada)
Legend of the Eight Samurai '84
Renegade Ninjas '79
Tokyo Decameron: Three Tales of Madness and Sensuality (N) '96

Terajima, Susumu
(Susuma Terashima)
After Life '98
Brother '00
Fireworks '97
Ichi the Killer '01
Postman Blues '97
Shark Skin Man and Peach Hip Girl '98
Sonatine '93
Violent Cop '89

Terajima, Yusaku
Lone Wolf and Cub 1: Sword of Vengeance '72
Lone Wolf and Cub 4: Baby Cart in Peril '72
Zatoichi and the Chest of Gold '64
Zatoichi's Cane Sword '67

Terao, Akira
Akira Kurosawa's Dreams '90
Madadayo '92
Ran '85

Teruko, Ooe
The Razor 2: The Snare '73

Tezuka, Katsumi
Battle in Outer Space '59
Ghidorah the Three-Headed Monster '64
Godzilla Raids Again '55
Rodan '56
Varan the Unbelievable '58

Thanatthanapong, Apichaya
A Fighter's Blues '00

Thomas, Damien
Shogun '80

Thomas, Eugene
Ninja in the U.S.A. '88

Thomas, Rob
Street Fighter 2 '96 (V)

Thomas, Ted
Mighty Peking Man '77

Thompson, Ian
Roujin Z '91 (V)

Thompson, James Brewster
Gunhed '89

Thomson, Ken
Rivals of the Dragon '83

Thor, Alfred
Street Fighter 2 '96 (V)

Thornton, Billy Bob
Princess Mononoke '97 (V)

Thyssen, Greta
Terror Is a Man '59

Ti Lung
(Dyi Long, Dik Lung, Di Long, Sick Loong, Din Lung, Di Long)
Avenging Eagle '78
A Better Tomorrow '86
A Better Tomorrow 2 '87
Brave Archer '77
City War '88
Clean My Name, Mr. Coroner! '00
Death Mask of the Ninja '82
Death Ring '83
The Heroes '80
Inheritor of Kung Fu '77
Legend of the Drunken Master '94
Ninja in the Deadly Trap '83
Paramount Motel '00
Revenge of the Zombies '76
Ten Tigers of Kwangtung '79
Tiger on Beat '88

Tien Ho
(Tin Hok, Tian Hao)
Lone Ninja Warrior '81

Tien, James
(Tien Chun, Tin Jun, Tian Jun, Paul Tien, James Tyan, James Tin Jun)
Blonde Fury '89
Bruce Lee: A Warrior's Journey '00
The Chinese Connection '71
Dragon Fist '78
Dragons Forever '88
Eastern Condors '86
Fearless Hyena '79
Fearless Hyena 2 '80
Fists of Fury '71
Game of Death '78
Half a Loaf of Kung Fu '77
Hand of Death '75
Heart of Dragon '85
Lee Rock '91
The Millionaires' Express '86
Mr. Vampire 2 '86
My Lucky Stars '85
The Owl vs. Bombo '84
Pom Pom '84
The Prodigal Son '81
Righting Wrongs '86
Rosa '86
Shaolin vs. Ninja '83
Spiritual Kung Fu '78
Twinkle Twinkle Lucky Stars '85
Winners and Sinners '83
Yes, Madam '85

Tien Niu
(Tim Nau, Tian Niu, Nau Nau)
Brave Archer '77
City War '88
The Magnificent Scoundrels '91
Para Para Sakura '01

Tilden, Leif
Teenage Mutant Ninja Turtles '90

Tillis, Mel
Cannonball Run '81

Tim Lei
(Tian Ni, Tan Nei, Tanny, Tanny Chu)
Brutal Boxer '72
Revenge of the Zombies '76

Timkul, Patharawarin
Bangkok Dangerous '00

Tin Ching
Crystal Hunt '91
Deadly Snail vs. Kung Fu Killer '77
Eighth Happiness '88

Executioners from Shaolin '77
Goose Boxer '78
Miracles '89
Peking Opera Blues '86
Where's Officer Tuba? '86

Tin Kai-man
(Tian Qi Wen)
A Chinese Ghost Story 2 '90
King of Comedy '99
Project A '83
Shaolin Soccer '01

Tin Mat
(Tian Mi, Tien Mi)
Inheritor of Kung Fu '73
Seeding of a Ghost '83
SuperManChu '73

Tin Ming
(Tian Ming, Tien Ming)
Five Elements of Kung Fu '78
Green Dragon Inn '79
Sorrowful to a Ghost '70
Swordsman with an Umbrella '70

Tin, Miu
(Mu Tien, Miao Tian, Miao Tien)
Blood of the Dragon '71
Half a Loaf of Kung Fu '77
Lady Iron Monkey '83
The Massive '78
Macho Man '72
Militant Eagle '78
One Foot Crane '79
The 72 Desperate Rebels '76
Snake and Crane Arts of Shaolin '78
Thousand Mile Escort '76
A Touch of Zen '69
Triangular Duel '72
What Time Is It There? '01

Tin Peng
(Tian Peng, Tin Pang, Tien Pang, Tien Pen, Roc Tien)
The 18 Bronzemen '76
The 18 Bronzemen Part 2 '76
5 Lady Venoms '78
Lone Ninja Warrior '81
The Shaolin Kids '77
The Silver Spear '79
A Touch of Zen '69

Tin Sum
The Duel '00

Tin Yau
(Tian Ye, Tien Yeh)
Blood of the Dragon '71
The Deadly Sword '78

805

Fury of King Boxer '72
Iron Monkey 2 '77
Rage of the Masters
'74

Tin Yue-lai
*(Tin Yui Lei, Tin Yui-lee,
Tian Rui Ni)*
The Blood Rules '00
Clean My Name, Mr.
Coroner! '00

Ting, Allen
*(Ting Chi-Chun, Ding Ji
Chun, Ding Zi Jun)*
Troublesome Night '97
Troublesome Night 3
'97

Ting, Jerry
Magnificent Natural
Fist '80

Ting Wa-chung
*(Ding Wa Chung, Ding
Hua Chong)*
Cantonen Iron Kung Fu
'79
The Incredible Kung Fu
Mission '82
The Massive '78

Ting Pei, Betty
(Ding Pooi, Ding Pei)
Bruce Lee, The Legend
'84

Tiu Lung
(Tu Long, Tu Lung)
Lightning Kung Fu '80
Masked Avengers '81
Ten Tigers of Kwang-
tung '79

Tiu, Michael
Devil Touch '02

To, Alex
*(To Tak-wai, Do Tak Wai,
Du De Wei)*
Hit Team '00
The Inspector Wears
Skirts '88
The Irresistible Piggies
'02
On the Run '88
Rumble in the Bronx
'95

To, Chapman
*(To Man-chat, Do Man
Chak, Du Wen Ze, Chat-
man To, To Man Zak)*
The Cheaters '01
Goodbye Mr. Cool '01
House of the Damned
'99
The Irresistible Piggies
'02
Paramount Motel '00
Undercover Blues '00

To Chow Kwan
Devil Woman '70

To, Orlando
Task Force '97

To Pak Kwong
Legend of the Drunken
Master '94

To Siu-chun
*(Do Siu Chun, Du Shao
Jin)*
A Chinese Ghost Story
2 '90
One Arm Hero '94
Sam the Iron Bridge:
Champion of Mar-
tial Arts '93
White Lotus Cult '93

To Siu Ming
*(Do Siu Ming, Du Shao
Ming, Tu Shiao Ming, To
Shiao Ming, Dao Shiao
Ming, Tog Siew Meng)*
Bolo '80
Dirty Kung Fu '78
Dirty Tiger, Crazy Frog
'78
Encounter of the
Spooky Kind '81
His Name Is Nobody
'79
Hit-Man in the Hand of
Buddha '80
The Invincible Killer '79
Odd Couple '79
Project A '83
The Victim '80
We're Going to Eat You!
'80
The Young Master '80

To Wai-wo
*(Do Wai Who, Du Wei
Han)*
God of Gamblers 3:
Back to Shanghai
'91
The Master '92
99 Cycling Swords '78
Raiders of Wu Tang '84
Return of the Tiger '77
Shaolin Wooden Men
'76
Snake and Crane Art of
Shaolin '78
A Touch of Zen '69
Tower of Death '81

Tobita, Kisao
Gamera vs. Gyaos '67

Tocha, Paulo
Born to Defence '88

Tochino, Yukitomo
Zeram '91

Toda, Masahiro
Cure '97

Todoroki, Yukiko
Sanshiro Sugata '43

Togashi, Makoto
Cure '97

Togin, Chotaro
All Monsters Attack '70
Destroy All Monsters
'68

Ebirah, Horror of the
Deep '66
Yog: Monster from
Space '70

Togo, Haruko
Akira Kurosawa's
Dreams '90
Ran '85
Stray Dog '49

Tok Chung-wah
*(Tok Chung Wa, Tuo
Zong Hua, Tou Chung
Wah)*
Butterfly and Sword '93

Tokashiki, Katsuo
Beautiful Hunter '94
Boiling Point '90

Tokitho, Ayumi
I.K.U. '00

Tokiwa, Takako
*(Seung Poon Gwai Ji,
Chang Pan Gui Zi)*
A Fighter's Blues '00
Moonlight Express '99

Tokoro, George
Madadayo '92

Tokui, Yu
Adrenaline Drive '99
Dark Water '02

Tokunaga, Reiko
Time of the Apes '75

Tokuyama, Hidenori
Cross Fire '00

Tom, Tom
Angel on Fire '95

Tomikawa, Akihiro
(Masahiro Tomikawa)
Lone Wolf and Cub 1:
Sword of
Vengeance '72
Lone Wolf and Cub 2:
Baby Cart at the
River Styx '72
Lone Wolf and Cub 3:
Baby Cart to Hades
'72
Lone Wolf and Cub 4:
Baby Cart in Peril
'72
Lone Wolf and Cub 5:
Baby Cart in the
Land of Demons
'73
Lone Wolf and Cub 6:
White Heaven in
Hell '74
Shogun Assassin '80

Tomita, Kotaro
Ghidorah the Three-
Headed Monster
'64
Godzilla vs. Megalon
'73
Terror of MechaGodzilla
'75

Tong, Angela
(Tong Ying-Ying)
Beauty and the Breast
'02
Bio Zombie '98
F*** / Off '98
Juliet in Love '00
Last Ghost Standing
'99
You Shoot, I Shoot '01

Tong Hoi-lun
Losers' Club '01

Tong Ka-fai
*(Tong Ga Fai, Tang Gu
Hui)*
Troublesome Night 14
'02
Troublesome Night 8
'00
Troublesome Night 9
'00

Tong Kar-chun
*(Tong Ga Kuen, Tang Gu
Quan, Tang Chia
Chuan)*
Bruce Lee We Miss You
'76
The Story in Temple
Red Lily '79

Tong, Karen
*(Tong Bo Yue, Shang
Bao Ru)*
Ballistic Kiss '98
Faces of Horror '98
Troublesome Night 4
'98

Tong, Kenneth
*(Tong Jan Yip, Shang
Zhen Ye, Ken Tong)*
The Dragon Family '88
Eastern Condors '86
Police Story '85
Royal Tramp 2 '92
The Tigers '91

Tong Lung
*(Tang Long, Tang Lung,
Tin Lung, Kim Tai Long,
Kim Tai Chong, Kim Tai
Chung)*
Chinese Hercules '73
Fists of Bruce Lee '78
Game of Death '78
The Invincible Kung Fu
Trio '78
Romeo Must Die '00
Shaolin Chastity Kung
Fu '81
Tower of Death '81

Tong, Mulo
Ninja vs. Bruce Lee '82

Tong Tin-hei
*(Tang Tian Xi, Tong Tien
Chi)*
Kung Fu's Hero '73
Super Kung Fu Kid '74

Tong Wai
(Tang Wei)
The Blazing Temple '76

The Shaolin Brothers
'77
The Silver Spear '79
The Smart Cavalier '78

Tong, Wilson
*(Tong Wai Shing, Tang
Wei Cheng, Tong Wai
Sang, The Foot Doctor,
Tong San)*
Brutal Boxer '72
Dirty Ho '79
Dirty Kung Fu '78
Duel of the Brave Ones
'78
The End of the Wicked
Tiger '81
Enter the Dragon '73
Executioners from
Shaolin '77
Hand of Death '75
He Has Nothing But
Kung Fu '77
The Iron Monkey '77
Killer from Above '77
Kung Fu Genius '79
Ninja vs. Ninja '87
Shaolin King Boxer '79
Shaolin Mantis '78
Shaolin Master Killer
'78
Snake Deadly Act '79
Sting of the Dragon
Masters '73
The Victim '80
The Young Avenger '79

Tono, Eijiro
Good Morning '59
The Last War '61
Ninja: Band of Assas-
sins Continued '63
Samurai 2: Duel at Ichi-
joji Temple '55
Samurai 3: Duel at
Ganryu Island '56
Seven Samurai '54
Stray Dog '49
Yojimbo '61
Zatoichi's Cane Sword
'66

Toura, Rokko
(Mutsohiro Toura)
Lone Wolf and Cub 5:
Baby Cart in the
Land of Demons
'73
Samaritan Zatoichi '68
Zatoichi and the Chess
Expert '65

Toyama, Haruko
Samurai 3: Duel at
Ganryu Island '56
Seven Samurai '54
Stray Dog '49

Toyama, Kyoko
Postman Blues '97

Toyohara, Kosuke
Godzilla vs. King Ghido-
rah '91

806

Trammel, Eugene
(Tomas Yau, Eugene Thomas)
Ninja in the U.S.A. '85
Ninja the Final Duel '85
The Super Ninja '84

Trejo, Danny
The Replacement Killers '97

Trimble, Jerry
The Master '89

Trimble, Tony
Gen-Y Cops '00

Tripos, George
Robo Vampire '88

Tsang, Andy
The Deadly Camp '99

Tsang Chiu
(Chang Chiu, Ceng Chao)
Battle of Shaolin '79
Fighting Ace '79
Kung Fu on Sale '79
The Secret of Chinese Kung Fu '81
The Shaolin Brothers '77
Two Dragons Fight Against Tiger '77

Tsang Choh-lam
(Chang Choh Lam, Ceng Chu Lin, Tsang Tsor Lam, Tseng Chiu-lin)
Brave Archer '77
Crazy Crooks '80
Dirty Tiger, Crazy Frog '78
Five Fingers of Death '72
His Name Is Nobody '79
Kung Fu Genius '79
The Magnificent Butcher '79
The Owl vs. Bombo '84
Police Story '85
The Private Eyes '76
Righting Wrongs '86
Snake Fist Dynamo '84
Sting of the Dragon Masters '73
Thunder Kick '73
We're Going to Eat You! '80
Winners and Sinners '83
Young Master '80

Tsang, Derek
Shadow '01

Tsang, Eric
(Tsang Chi-Wai, Chang Chi Wai, Ceng Zhi Wei)
The Accidental Spy '01
Aces Go Places 2 '83
Anna Magdalena '98
Bolo '80

Comrades, Almost a Love Story '96
Contract Killer '98
Cop on a Mission '01
Curry & Pepper '90
The End of the Wicked Tiger '81
Enter the Fat Dragon '78
Executioners from Shaolin '77
Gen-X Cops '99
He's a Woman, She's a Man '94
In the Line of Duty 3 '88
Jiang Hu-"The Triad Zone" '00
The Last Blood '90
Losers' Club '01
Merry-Go-Round '01
The Millionaires' Express '86
My Lucky Stars '85
Pedicab Driver '89
Scared Stiff '86
Supercop 2 '93
Take 2 in Life '01
Task Force '97
Twin Dragons '92
Twinkle Twinkle Lucky Stars '85
Warrior from Shaolin '81

Tsang, Kenneth
(Tsang Kong, Chang Kong, Ceng Jiang, Kent Tsang, Ken Tsang, Tzeng Jiang)
The Awaken Punch '73
A Better Tomorrow '86
A Better Tomorrow 2 '87
The Blacksheep Affair '98
Funeral March '01
The Killer '89
Once a Thief '91
Peking Opera Blues '86
Queen's High '91
The Replacement Killers '97
Rush Hour 2 '01
Supercop '92
The Touch '02

Tsang, Michael
Eat My Dust '93

Tsang Sze-Man
(Chang Si Man, Ceng Shi Min, Chan Sze Man)
Iron Monkey '93
Legend of the Drunken Tiger '92

Tsao, Albert
Bronson Lee, Champion '78

Tse, Andy
(Tse Hau Sai, Che Hau Sei, Xie Xiao Si)
The Adventurers '95

The Mission '99
Needing You... '00

Tse Kwan Ho
(Tze Kwan Ho, Che Gwan Ho, Xie Jun Hao)
The Lord of Hangzhou '98

Tse Ling-Ling
(Che Ling Ling, Xie Ling Ling, Hsieh Lin Lin, Sha Ling Ling, O'Yang Ling Ling)
Filthy Guy '80
Kung Pow: Enter the Fist '76/2001
Secret of the Chinese Kung Fu '81
The Story in Temple Red Lily '79

Tse, Michael
(Tse Tin Wah, Che Tin Wa, Xie Tian Hua, Tse Hing Wah)
The Best of the Best '96
The Blade '95
Bullets of Love '01
The Final Winner '01
Losers' Club '01
The Masked Prosecutor '99
The Storm Riders '98
Troublesome Night 3 '97
Young and Dangerous '96
Young and Dangerous 6: Born to Be King '00

Tse Miu
(Tze Miu, Che Miu, Xie Miao)
The Enforcer '95
God of Gamblers Returns '94
The New Legend of Shaolin '94

Tse, Nicholas
(Tse Ting Fung, Xie Ting Feng, Te Hou Sha)
Comic King '00
Gen-X Cops '99
A Man Called Hero '99
Master Q 2001 '01
My School Mate, the Barbarian '01
Time and Tide '00
Tiramisu '02

Tse, Patrick
Shaolin Soccer '01

Tseng, Alice
Ninja the Final Duel '85

Tseng Gen Wing
Brother of Darkness '94

Tseng, Jenny
Chinatown Kid '77

Tsing Yuan-pao
Dreaming Fists with Slender Hands '80

Tso Yen Yung
(Tso Yen Jung)
Revenge of the Patriots '76

Tsoi Chung Chow
5 Lady Venoms '78

Tsoi Wing Wah
5 Lady Venoms '78

Tsousie
I.K.U. '00

Tsu, Hilary
Wonder Seven '94

Tsu, Irene
Comrades, Almost a Love Story '96

Tsubouchi, Kamayuki
The H-Man '58

Tsubouchi, Mikiko
(Mikiko Tsubuchi)
Gamera vs. Zigra '71
New Tale of Zatoichi '63
Ninja: Band of Assassins Continued '63
Zatoichi Challenged '67
Zatoichi and the Chest of Gold '64
Zatoichi's Revenge '64

Tsuchiya, Shinpei
The Last War '61

Tsuchiya, Yoshio
Attack of the Mushroom People '63
Battle in Outer Space '59
Chushingura '62
Destroy All Monsters '68
Frankenstein vs. Baragon '65
Godzilla Raids Again '55
Godzilla vs. King Ghidorah '91
High and Low '63
The H-Man '58
The Human Vapor '60
Invasion of Astro-Monster '65
The Mysterians '57
Sanjuro '63
The Secret of the Telegian '60
Seven Samurai '54
Son of Godzilla '67
Throne of Blood '57
Varan the Unbelievable '58
Yog: Monster from Space '70
Yojimbo '61

Tsuda, Kanji
Audition '99
Fireworks '97
Gonin '95
Shark Skin Man and Peach Hip Girl '98
Sonatine '93

Tsuda, Mitsuo
Battle in Outer Space '59
The H-Man '58
Mothra '61
The Mysterians '57

Tsugawa, Masahiko
Godzilla, Mothra and King Ghidorah: Battle on Fire '01
The Funeral '84
Tampopo '87

Tsui, Benny
Masters of Tiger Crane '83

Tsui, Bernard
Scorpion Thunderbolt '85

Tsui, Danny
Rage of the Dragon '79
The Snake Strikes Back '81

Tsui, Doris
Champ against Champ '83

Tsui, Elvis
(Tsui Kam-Kong, Jinjiang Xu, Chui Kam Kong)
All Men Are Brothers: Blood of the Leopard '93
Body Weapon '99
Butterfly and Sword '93
A Chinese Torture Chamber Story '94
City on Fire '87
Clueless '01
Deadful Melody '94
Death Mask of the Ninja '82
The Demon's Baby '98
Dragon from Shaolin '96
The Duel '00
The Eternal Evil of Asia '95
Faces of Horror '98
Flash Future Kung Fu '83
Full Throttle '95
God of Gamblers Returns '94
Gunmen '88
Hail the Judge '94
The Hero of Swallow '96
Iceman Cometh '89
Long Arm of the Law 2 '87
Lord of the Wu Tang '93

A Man Called Hero '99
Prison on Fire 2 '91
Royal Tramp '92
The Seventh Curse '86
Sixty Million Dollar Man '95
The Storm Riders '98
The Three Swordsmen '94
Too Many Ways to Be No. 1 '97
Wonder Seven '94

Tsui Hark
(Chui Hak, Xu Ke)
Aces Go Places '82
Aces Go Places 2 '83
Aces Go Places 3 '84
A Better Tomorrow '86
A Chinese Ghost Story: The Tsui Hark Animation '97 (V)
I Love Maria '88
Twin Dragons '92
Yes, Madam '85
Zu: Warriors of the Magic Mountain '83

Tsui, Lily
Thunder Ninja Kids: The Hunt for the Devil Boxer '86/94

Tsui, Norman
(Tsui Siu Keung, Chiu Siu Keung, Xu Shao Jiang, Norman Chu, Norman Xu, Norman Chu)
City War '88
The Descendant of Wing Chun '78
Dirty Kung Fu '78
Dragon Chronicles: Maidens of Heavenly Mountain '94
The Dragon Family '88
The Duel '00
Duel to the Death '82
The Flying Guillotine '75
Inner Senses '01
King of Beggars '92
The Magic Crane '93
Mighty Peking Man '77
Ninja vs. Ninja '87
Return of the Deadly Blade '81
Seeding of a Ghost '83
Shaolin Mantis '78
Shaolin Master Killer '78
Tiger on Beat '88
We're Going to Eat You! '80
Wing Chun '94
The Young Avenger '79
Zu: Warriors of the Magic Mountain '83

Tsui, Ridley
(Tsui Bo Wah, Chui Bo Wa, Xu Bao Hua)

Fight Back to School '91
God of Gamblers '89
Skinny Tiger and Fatty Dragon '90
Thunder Ninja Kids: The Hunt for the Devil Boxer '86/94

Tsui Siu-ling
The Butterfly Murders '79

Tsui Siu-ming
(Xiaomin Xu)
The Buddhist Fist '79
Bury Me High '90

Tsuji, Shinmei
Another Heaven '00

Tsujitani, Koji
Street Fighter 2 '96 (V)

Tsukamoto, Kohji
(Koji Tsukamoto)
Postman Blues '97
Tokyo Fist '96

Tsukamoto, Shinya
Ichi the Killer '01
Sakuya: Slayer of Demons '00
Tetsuo 2: Body Hammer '91
Tetsuo: The Iron Man '89
Tokyo Fist '96

Tsukamoto, Takashi
Battle Royale '99
Princess Blade '02

Tsukasa, Yoko
(Yoko Shoji)
Chushingura '62
Yojimbo '61

Tsukasa, Yusuke
Legend of the Dinosaurs '77

Tsukigata, Ryunosuke
Sanshiro Sugata '43

Tsukimiya, Otome
Daimajin '66
Kwaidan '64

Tsukumoto, Hajime
Zero Woman: The Accused '96

Tsumabuki, Satoshi
The Dimension Travelers '98

Tsumura, Takashi
The Funeral '84

Tsuneta, Fujio
The Eel '97

Tsunogae, Kazue
Adrenaline Drive '99
Gamera 2: Advent of Legion '96

Tsurumi, Shingo
Freeze Me '00
Gonin '95
Shark Skin Man and Peach Hip Girl '98

Tsuruno, Takeshi
Ultraman Tiga and Ultraman Dyna: The Warriors of the Lightning Star '98

Tsuruoka, Osamu
Entrails of the Virgin '86

Tsuruta, Koji
Samurai 2: Duel at Ichijoji Temple '55
Samurai 3: Duel at Ganryu Island '56
The Secret of the Telegian '60

Tsutsumi, Daijiro
Sure Death: Revenge '87

Tsutsumi, Shinichi
Postman Blues '97

Tsutsumi, Yasuhisa
Battle in Outer Space '59
Dagora the Space Monster '64
Invasion of Astro-Monster '64
King Kong Escapes '67
Mothra vs. Godzilla '64
Rodan '64
The Secret of the Telegian '60
Seven Samurai '54

Tsuyuguchi, Shigeru
Lone Wolf and Cub 1: Sword of Vengeance '72

Tu Chia-cheng
Fists of Fury '71

Tu Lung
Avenging Eagle '78

Tuchida, Etsuyo
I.K.U. '00

Tucker, Chris
Rush Hour '98
Rush Hour 2 '01

Tuen, William
Ultimatum '01

Tung, Bill
(Tung Piu)
First Strike '96
The Inspector Wears Skirts '88
Legend of the Drunken Master '94
Miracles '89
Police Story '85
Police Story 2 '88
Project A 2 '87

Rumble in the Bronx '95
Supercop '92
Supercop 2 '93

Tung Choi-po
Prodigal Boxer '73

Tung, Eileen
(Tung Oi-ling, Tong Ai Ling)
Don't Give a Damn '95
Man Wanted '95
The Most Wanted '94
Sunshine Cops '99
Your Place or Mine! '98

Tung, Jennifer
Kung Pow: Enter the Fist '76/2001

Tung Lam
(Tong Lin, Tung Lin)
Five Fingers of Death '72
The Killer Meteors '76
Legend of the Mountain '79
Snake and Crane Arts of Shaolin '78
To Kill with Intrigue '77

Tung Li
(Dung Lik, Dong Li, Tong Lik, Dong Le)
The 18 Jade Arhats '78
Five Elements of Kung Fu '78
Moonlight Sword and Jade Lion '79
Revengeful Swordwomen '79
The Shaolin Brothers '77
The Smart Cavalier '78
Snake-Crane Secret '78
The Story in Temple Red Lily '79

Tung, Liza
Masters of Tiger Crane '83

Tung, Stephen
(Tung Wai, Dung Wei, Dong Wei, Tung Wei)
See also sidebar on p. 326.
18 Fatal Strikes '78
Enter the Dragon '73
Golden Killah '80
Hard Boiled '91
Mask of Death '76
No More Love, No More Death '92
Pom Pom and Hot Hot '92
Task Force '97
Twin Dragons '92

Tung Wai Wai
(Dung Wai Wai, Dong Wei Wei)
The Three Swordsmen '94

Turney, Michael
Teenage Mutant Ninja Turtles '90

Tushima, Keiko
Seven Samurai '54

Tze Lin
Prodigal Boxer '73

Tzi Ma
Rush Hour '98

Uchida, Katsumasa
Shogun's Ninja '82

Uchida, Tomoo
Lone Wolf and Cub 1: Sword of Vengeance '72

Uchida, Yoshiro
Giant Monster Gamera '65

Ueda, Kichijiro
Gamera vs. Gyaos '67
The Hidden Fortress '58
Rashomon '50
Seven Samurai '54

Ueda, Koichi
Adrenaline Drive '99
The Eel '97
Godzilla, Mothra and King Ghidorah: Battle on Fire '01
Godzilla 2000 '01
Godzilla vs. Biollante '89
Godzilla vs. Destroyah '95
Godzilla vs. King Ghidorah '91
Godzilla vs. MechaGodzilla 2 '93
Godzilla vs. Megaguirus '00
Godzilla vs. Mothra '92
Godzilla vs. Space Godzilla '94

Uehara, Ken
The Last War '61
Mothra '61

Uehara, Misa
The Hidden Fortress '58

Ueno, Megumi
Hiruko the Goblin '90

Ujiki, Tsuyoshi
Cure '97
The Haunted Lantern '98

Umali, Erlyn
The Killing of Satan '83

Umeda, Masaki
Fatal Blade '00

Umeda, Tomoko
Godzilla vs. Gigan '72

Umemiya, Tatsuo
(Tatsuya Umemiya)
Prince of Space '59

Umezu, Sakai
Lone Wolf and Cub 3:
Baby Cart to Hades
'72

Uno, Koji
Invasion of Astro-Monster '65
The Last War '61
Mothra vs. Godzilla '64
The Secret of the
Telegian '60

Unoyama, Koichi
Wrath of Daimajin '66

Urquidez, Benny
Dragons Forever '88
Wheels on Meals '84

Ushida, Tetsuya
Time of the Apes '75

Utsui, Ken
Atomic Rulers of the
World '57
Attack from Space '58
Bullet Train '75
Evil Brain from Outer
Space '58/59
The Hypnotist '99
Invaders from Space
'58

Utsumi, Sisumi
Destroy All Monsters
'68

Uy, Mahler
Duel of the Tao Tough
'82

Uzaki, Ryudo
Godzilla, Mothra and
King Ghidorah: Battle on Fire '01

Van Clief, Ron
Fist of Fear-Touch of
Death '80

Van Day Nguyen
Cyclo '95

Van Hawley, Norman
The Manster '60

Vandebroucke, Rosemary
Brassiere '01
Martial Angels '01

Varela, Leonor
Blade 2 '02

Vasquez, Romeo
Curse of the Vampires
'70

Veluso, Via
Troublesome Night 4
'98

Verma, Deven
Elaan '94

Villafranca, Jose
Murder in the Orient
'74

Vitali, Keith
Wheels on Meals '84

Volante, Vicki
Horror of the Blood
Monsters '70

Wa, Chung
*(Zong Hua, Tsung Hua,
Chung Hwa)*
The 18 Jade Arhats '78
Kung Fu on Sale '79
The 72 Desperate
Rebels '76
Ways of Kung Fu '80

Wada, Koji
Gappa: The Triphibian
Monster '67
The Street Fighter's
Last Revenge '74

Wagner, Robert
Dragon: The Bruce Lee
Story '93

Wagner, Wende
The Green Hornet '74

Wah, Yuen
*(Yu Wah, Yuen Wa) See
also sidebar on p. 142.*
The Awaken Punch '73
Bury Me High '90
Death Mask of the
Ninja '82
Dragon from Russia
'90
Dragons Forever '88
Eastern Condors '86
Enter the Dragon '73
Game of Death '78
Hand of Death '75
Heart of Dragon '85
Iceman Cometh '89
A Kid from Tibet '91
Legend of the Dragon
'91
Leopard Hunting '98
Lightning Kung Fu '80
The Magnificent
Scoundrels '91
The Master '89
The Millionaires'
Express '86
Mr. Vampire '85
Mr. Vampire Saga 4 '88
My Lucky Stars '85
On the Run '88
Red Shield '91
Scared Stiff '86
She Shoots Straight
'90
Supercop '92
Swordsman '90
Ultimatum '01
Vampire Controller '00
Where's Officer Tuba?
'86

Wai, Austin
*(Wai Tin-Chi, Wai Tin
Tsz, Hui Tian Ci, Hui*

*Tien Chi, Hui Tien Tzu)
See also sidebar on p.
326.*
All Men Are Brothers:
Blood of the Leopard '93
The Blade '95
Fearless Hyena 2 '80
Five Superfighters '78
Generation Consultant
'90
Moonlight Express '99
Pom Pom and Hot Hot
'92
Shaolin Master Killer
'78
Twinkle Twinkle Lucky
Stars '85

Wai Gei-shun
*(Wei Gei-shun, Wei Ji
Shun)*
Dragon in Jail '90
In the Line of Duty 4
'89
Sunshine Cops '99

Wai, Lam
(Lin Wei)
All Men Are Brothers:
Blood of the Leopard '93
A Chinese Ghost Story
'87
Code of Honor '87
Deadful Melody '94
Dragons Forever '88
Flirting Scholar '93
King of Beggars '92
Long Arm of the Law
'84
Picture of a Nymph '88
Project A 2 '87
Royal Warriors '86
Shaolin Master Killer
'78
Ten Tigers of Kwangtung '79
Twinkle Twinkle Lucky
Stars '85
Yes, Madam '85

Wai Lit
(Wei Lie)
The Blood Rules '00
The Kung Fu Master
'94
Queen's High '91

Wakabayashi, Akiko
(Eiko Wakabayashi)
Dagora the Space Monster '64
Ghidorah the Three-
Headed Monster
'64
King Kong vs. Godzilla
'62
What's Up, Tiger Lily?
'66

Wakamatsu, Takeshi
Ring 0: Birthday '00

Wakayama, Setsuko
Godzilla Raids Again
'55

**Wakayama, Tomis-
aburo**
Lone Wolf and Cub 1:
Sword of
Vengeance '72
Lone Wolf and Cub 2:
Baby Cart at the
River Styx '72
Lone Wolf and Cub 3:
Baby Cart to Hades
'72
Lone Wolf and Cub 4:
Baby Cart in Peril
'72
Lone Wolf and Cub 5:
Baby Cart in the
Land of Demons
'73
Lone Wolf and Cub 6:
White Heaven in
Hell '74
New Tale of Zatoichi
'63
Ninja: Band of Assassins '62
Ninja: Band of Assassins Continued '63
Shogun Assassin '80
The Tale of Zatoichi
Continues '63
Zatoichi and the Chest
of Gold '64

Wakayama, Yukari
Lone Wolf and Cub 2:
Baby Cart at the
River Styx '72
Lone Wolf and Cub 4:
Baby Cart in Peril
'72

Wakefield, John
Once upon a Time in
China 3 '93

Wall, Bob
(Robert Wall)
Enter the Dragon '73
Game of Death '78
Return of the Dragon
'72

Wallace, Bill
The Protector '85

Walter, Mary
The Blood Drinkers '64
Curse of the Vampires
'70

Wan, Beau
Magnificent Natural
Fist '80

Wan, Deric
*(Wan Siu Lun, Wen
Zhao Lun)*
Royal Tramp '92
Royal Tramp 2 '92

Wan, Eric
*(Wan Tin Chiu, Yin Tian
Zhao)*

Century of the Dragon
'99
House of the Damned
'99
Sharp Guns '01

Wan Fat
(Yin Fa, Wan Faat)
Chinese Hercules '73
Crime Story '93
Dragons Forever '88
Five Superfighters '78
Police Story '85
Project A '83

Wan Fei
Invincible Obsessed
Fighter '82

Wan, Irene
*(Wan Pik Ha, Wan Bik
Ha, Wen Bi Xia)*
Pom Pom '84
Tiger Cage '88
The Tigers '91

Wan, Pauline
A Life of Ninja '83

Wan Seung-lam
(Yin Xiang Lin)
Chinese Super Ninjas
'82
Crime Story '93

Wan, Vincent
*(Wan Yeung-Ming, Yin
Yang Ming, Wen Yeung
Ming)*
Cold War '00
Fist of Fury 1991 '91
Legendary Couple '95
Powerful Four '91
Prison on Fire 2 '91
The Storm Riders '98
Tragic Fantasy: Tiger of
Wanchai '94
Young and Dangerous
5 '98
Young and Dangerous
6: Born to Be King
'00

Wang Bing
The Phantom Lover '95

Wang Chen-chao
Legend of the Drunken
Tiger '92

Wang Chieh
Casino Raiders 2 '91

Wang Ching-liang
Brave Archer '77

Wang Chu Liang
Born Invincible '78

Wang Chuen
Dragons of the Orient
'88

Wang, Fanny
(Fan Lei)
Death Duel of Kung Fu
'79
The Victim '80

Wang Fu Quen
18 Secrets of Kung Fu
'79

Wang, Gaston
Scorpion Thunderbolt
'85

Wang, George
(Wang Kuo, Wang Gok,
Wang Jue, Wong Gok,
George Wang Jue, Hang
Jui)
The Hot, the Cool, and
the Vicious '76
Iron Neck Li '81
The Prisoner of Five
Boulders '89
The Shaolin Temple '79
To Kill with Intrigue '77

Wang Guang Kuan
The Shaolin Temple '79

Wang Han-chen
(Wong Ham Chan)
Brave Archer '77
Chinatown Kid '77
Dirty Ho '79
Drunken Master '77
Flag of Iron '80
The Flying Guillotine
'74
Legend of the 7 Golden
Vampires '74
Return of the Five
Deadly Venoms '74
Shaolin Master Killer
'78

Wang, Jean
(Wang Ching-Ying,
Wong Jing Yin, Wang
Jing Ying)
The East Is Red '93
Iron Monkey '93
Once upon a Time in
China 4 '93
Once upon a Time in
China and America
'97

Wang, John
Second Time Around
'02

Wang, Johnny
(Wang Lung Wei, Wong
Lung Wai, Wong Leung-
wei)
Avenging Eagle '78
Brave Archer '77
Chinatown Kid '77
Dirty Ho '79
Fearless Dragons '79
Fists of the White
Lotus '80
Five Deadly Venoms
'78
Flash Future Kung Fu
'83
Invincible Pole Fighter
'83
Kid with the Golden
Arm '78
Project A 2 '87

The Return of the 5
Deadly Venoms '78
Return of the Master
Killer '80
Run and Kill '93
The Seventh Curse '86
Ten Tigers of Kwang-
tung '79
3 Evil Masters '80
Tiger Cage '88
Twin Dragons '92
Young and Dangerous
'96

Wang Ki San
18 Secrets of Kung Fu
'79

Wang Kin Chuen
Dragons of the Orient
'88

Wang Li
(Wong Lik)
Avenging Warriors of
Shaolin '79
Brave Archer '77
Chinatown Kid '77
Chinese Super Ninjas
'82
Flag of Iron '80
Masked Avengers '81
The Master of Death
'82
Master of the Flying
Guillotine '76
Nine Demons '83
Revenge of the Patriots
'76
The Secret of Chinese
Kung Fu '81
The Story in Temple
Red Lily '79
Ten Tigers of Kwang-
tung '79

Wang, Maggie
Para Para Sakura '01

Wang, Margaret
The Touch '02

Wang Mawan
Dragon from Shaolin
'96

Wang Meiling
The Swordswoman in
White '92

Wang Pei-chi
(Huang Pei Chi, Wang
Pei-chi)
Avenging Eagle '78

Wang, Roger
Dragon against Vam-
pire '85

Wang Suit
5 Lady Venoms '78

Wang Tai-lang
(Wong Tai-lung, Wong
Tai Long)
Fighting Ace '79
Macho Man '72

Master of the Flying
Guillotine '85
Militant Eagle '78
Screaming Ninja '73

Wang Tao
(Wong Diy, Wang Dao,
Wang Tao, Wang Do,
Don Wong)
Battle of Shaolin '77
Challenge of Death '78
Death Duel of Kung Fu
'79
Drunken Tai Chi '84
Eagle's Claw '77
Fatal Needles vs. Fatal
Fists '80
The Hot, the Cool, and
the Vicious '76
Lady Wu Tang '77
The Leg Fighters '80
Mask of Death '76
Moonlight Sword and
Jade Lion '79

Wang, Wilson
Guardian Angel '96

Wang Yu, Jimmy
(Wong Yue, Wang Yu,
Wang Yue)
Blood of the Dragon
'71
Fantasy Mission Force
'84
Fury of King Boxer '72
The Killer Meteors '76
Martial Arts Mayhem,
Vol. 1 '99
Martial Arts Mayhem,
Vol. 2 '99
Master of the Flying
Guillotine '74
The Millionaires'
Express '86
Once upon a Time in
China '91
The Prisoner '90
Rage of the Masters
'74
Return of the Chinese
Boxer '75
Screaming Ninja '73
Shogun and Little
Kitchen '92

Wang Zhigang
Shaolin: Wheel of Life
'00

Wang Zhonliang
The Cold Mountain
Temple '91

Warhol, Sophia
Thunder Ninja Kids:
The Hunt for the
Devil Boxer '86/94

Washington, Isiaiah
Romeo Must Die '00

Watabe, Ryosuke
Versus '00

Watanabe, Atsushi
Seven Samurai '54

Yojimbo '61

Watanabe, Fumio
Bullet Train '75
Female Convict Scorpi-
on: Jailhouse 41
'72
Lone Wolf and Cub 1:
Sword of
Vengeance '72
The Street Fighter '74

Watanabe, Hiroyuke
Ring '98

Watanabe, Hiroyuki
Gamera 2: Advent of
Legion '96
Gamera 3: The
Revenge of Irys '99
Godzilla, Mothra and
King Ghidorah: Bat-
tle on Fire '01
Ring '98
Reborn from Hell:
Samurai Armaged-
don '96
Ultraman Gaia: The
Battle in Hyper-
space '98

Watanabe, Ken
Tampopo '87

Watanabe, Minoru
Godzilla vs. Megaguirus
'00

Watanabe, Misako
Kwaidan '64

Watanabe, Tetsu
Akira Kurosawa's
Dreams '90
Godzilla vs. King Ghido-
rah '91
Godzilla vs. Mothra '92
The Ladies' Phone Sex
Club '96
Sonatine '93
Zero Woman: The
Accused '96

Watanabe, Toru
Ebirah, Horror of the
Deep '66

Watanabe, Yuki
The Hypnotist '99

Watari, Tetsuya
Brother '00
Tokyo Drifter '66

Watase, Tsunehiko
Legend of the
Dinosaurs '77

Watt, Billie Lou
Astro Boy '63 (V)

Watts, Nian
Robo Vampire '88

Wazaki, Toshiya
Lone Wolf and Cub 3:
Baby Cart to Hades
'72

The X from Outer Space
'67

Weeks, Geoffrey
Enter the Dragon '73

Wei, Dick
(Dik Wai, Di Wei)
Brave Archer '77
Chinatown Kid '77
Code of Honor '87
Dragons Forever '88
Eastern Condors '86
Five Deadly Venoms
'78
Guardian Angel '96
Heart of Dragon '85
In the Line of Duty 3
'88
Kid with the Golden
Arm '78
Lightning Kung Fu '80
The Millionaires'
Express '86
Miracles '89
My Lucky Stars '85
The Owl vs. Bombo '84
Pedicab Driver '89
Pom Pom '84
The Prodigal Son '81
Project A '83
The Return of the 5
Deadly Venoms '78
Rosa '86
The Seventh Curse '86
Supercop 2 '93
Ten Tigers of Kwang-
tung '79
Twinkle Twinkle Lucky
Stars '85
Winners and Sinners
'83
The Witch from Nepal
'85
Yes, Madam '85
Zu: Warriors of the
Magic Mountain
'83

Wei, Frankie
(Wei Hung, Wai Wang,
Wei Hong)
Dirty Ho '79
The Flying Guillotine
'74
The Master of Death
'82
Revenge of the Zom-
bies '76
Shaolin Mantis '78
Shaolin Master Killer
'78

Wei, Lo
(Law Wai, Luo Wei)
The Chinese Connec-
tion '71
Legend of the 7 Golden
Vampires '74
New Fist of Fury '76

Wei, Newton
Snake Fist Dynamo '84

Wei Pai
(Wai Pak, Wai Baak, Wei Bai, Snake Venom)
See also sidebar on p. 374.
Five Deadly Venoms '78
Kid with the Golden Arm '78
Last Hurrah for Chivalry '78
The Magnificent Butcher '79
The Prodigal Son '81
Return of the Master Killer '80
Ten Tigers of Kwangtung '79
The Young Master '80

Wei, Paul
(Wei Ping Ao, Ng Ping Ngo, Ngai Ping Ngo, Yi Pin Our, Yue Ping Au)
The Chinese Connection '71
Drunken Art and Crippled Fist '79
Filthy Guy '80
Fists of Bruce Lee '78
The Incredible Kung Fu Mission '82
Return of the Dragon '72
Snake Fist Dynamo '84
Story of the Dragon '76

Wei Ye
Frozen '96

Wei-tu, Lin
(Lam Wai Tiu)
Mighty Peking Man '77
Revenge of the Zombies '76

Weiner, Michael
The Secrets of the Warrior's Power '97 (N)

Weiner, Tom
Ultraman 2 '01 (V)

Wells, Eric Briant
Reptilian '00

Wen, Candy
(Wen Xue Er, Man Suety Ngai, Man Suet Yi, Wen Hsueh Erh)
3 Evil Masters '80
Tiger over Wall '80

Wen Chou-yen
The Shaolin One '83

Wencheng, Sung
The Road Home '99

Weng Hsiao Hu
(Yung Siu Foo, Weng Xiao Hu, Yung Hsiao Fu)
18 Secrets of Kung Fu '79
Filthy Guy '80
The Killer Meteors '76

Killer Priest '81
Killer from Above '77
Lady Wu Tang '77
The Lost Kung Fu Secrets '80
New Fist of Fury '76
To Kill with Intrigue '77

Wenger, Allan
Roujin Z '91 (V)

Whang In Shik
(Wong Yan Chik, Huang Ren Zhi, Whang Ing Sik, I.S. Wong, Hwang In Shik)
Dragon Lord '82
A Fistful of Talons '83
Game of Death '78
Return of the Dragon '72
Sting of the Dragon Masters '73
The Young Master '80

White, Caryn
Bruce Lee: The Man, the Myth '76

White, Jimmy
Legend of the Dragon '91

White, Wrath
Born Wild '01

Wilcox, Mary
Beast of the Yellow Night '70

Wilkinson, Tom
Rush Hour '98

Williams, Van
Dragon: The Bruce Lee Story '93
The Green Hornet '74

Williamson, Fred
Fist of Fear-Touch of Death '80

Williamson, Melissa
Street Fighter 2 '96 (V)

Wilson, Bridgette
Mortal Kombat '95

Wilson, Claude
The Walls of Hell '64

Wing Pui-Shan
Eagle vs. Silver Fox '83

Winston, Ellis
Angel on Fire '95

Winton, Anne
Sting of the Dragon Masters '73

Wisamon, Rerng-rit
Fear Faith Revenge 303 '98

Wolf, Bass
Wild Zero '99

Wolf, Drum
Wild Zero '99

Wolf, Guitar
Wild Zero '99

Wolfe, Jeff
Once upon a Time in China and America '97

Wong, Albert
Rush Hour '98

Wong, Almen
(Wong Pui-Ha, Wong Rooi Ha, Huang Pei Xia)
Happy Family '02
Her Name Is Cat '98
Her Name Is Cat 2: Journey to Death '01
The Wesley's Mysterious File '01

Wong, Angel
(Wong Chui Ling, Wang Cui Ling)
Armageddon '97

Wong, Anthony
(Wong Chau-Sun, Wong Chau-Sang, Wong Chow-Sun)
Armageddon '97
Beast Cops '98
Big Bullet '96
Black Mask '96
Brother of Darkness '94
Casino Raiders 2 '91
Century of the Dragon '99
City of Desire '01
Daughter of Darkness '93
The Deadly Camp '99
The Demon's Baby '98
Erotic Ghost Story 2 '91
Executioners '93
Fight Back to School 3 '93
Fist Power '99
Full Contact '92
Gen-Y Cops '00
God.com '98
Hard Boiled '91
Haunted Mansion '98
The Heroic Trio '93
Iceman Cometh '89
Jiang Hu-"The Triad Zone" '00
The Legend of a Professional '00
A Man Called Hero '99
The Mission '99
Option Zero '97
Organized Crime and Triad Bureau '94
Rock 'n' Roll Cop '94
Runaway '01
The Storm Riders '98
Time and Tide '00
U-Man '02
United We Stand, and Swim '01
The Untold Story '92
The Untold Story 2 '98

Violent Cop '99
Visible Secret '01
Young and Dangerous 5 '98

Wong, Arthur
(Wong Ngok Tai, Huang Yue Tai)
Beast Cops '98
Born Wild '01

Wong, Barry
(Wong Ping-yiu, Wong Bing Yiu, Huang Bing Yao)
Curry & Pepper '90
Fight Back to School '91
God of Gamblers 3: Back to Shanghai '91
The Killer '89
The Prisoner '90
Winners and Sinners '83

Wong Biu Chan
(Wang Bao Zhen, Wang Pao Chien)
Blind Fist of Bruce '79
The Bloody Fists '72
Dragon on Fire '79
Dragon's Claws '79
Kung Fu Zombie '81
The 36 Crazy Fists '77
The 36 Deadly Styles '79
Tiger Over Wall '80

Wong, Bonnie
(Wong Ping-yiu, Wong Bing Yiu, Huang Bing Yao)
Help!!! '00
Horror Hotline...Big Head Monster '01
Shadow '01
Young and Dangerous 5 '98

Wong, Carter
(Hwang Kah Tah, Wang Ka Ta, Wong Ka Tat, Wong Ga Daat, Huang Gu Da, Wang Chie Ta)
The Blazing Temple '76
Born Invincible '78
The 8 Masters '77
The 18 Bronzemen '76
The 18 Bronzemen Part 2 '76
Emperor of Shaolin Kung Fu '80
Fatal Flying Guillotine '77
Filthy Guy '80
Killer from Above '77
Killer of Snake, Fox of Shaolin '78
The Legendary Strike '78
The Magnificent '78
Rage of the Dragon '79
Revenge of the Patriots '76

The Shaolin Brothers '77
The Shaolin Invincibles '79
The Shaolin Kids '77
Shaolin Traitorous '76
Sting of the Dragon Masters '73
Story of the Dragon '76
Succubare '77

Wong, Casanova
(Sa Fa Ka, Chu Kwong, Human Tornado)
Duel to the Death '82
Game of Death '78
The Legendary Strike '78
The Magnificent '78
Shadow of the Tiger '79
Tower of Death '81

Wong Chi-cheung
Angel '87

Wong Chi Sang
(Wong Au Sang, Wang Qi Sheng, Wang Chi Sang, Wang Chi Sheng, Wang Hsueh K'un)
Battle of Shaolin '77
Drunken Art and Crippled Fist '79
Fearless Hyena '79
Golden Killah '80
The Incredible Kung Fu Mission '82
The Iron Monkey '77
Killer from Above '77
A Life of Ninja '83
Ninja Checkmate '79
Revengeful Swordwomen '79
Shaolin vs. Ninja '83
Snake and Crane Arts of Shaolin '78
War of the Shaolin Temple '80

Wong Chin-chung
The Shaolin One '83

Wong Ching
(Wang Qing, Wang Ching, Wang Ching Lung)
Blooded Treasury Fight '79
The Heroes '80
The Imp '81
Master of the Flying Guillotine '74
Ninja Hunter '83
Prodigal Boxer '73
Return of the Deadly Blade '81
Spiritual Kung Fu '78
The Super Ninja '84
Swordsman with an Umbrella '70

Wong Ching Ho
(Wang Qing He, Wang Ching Ho)

Avenging Warriors of
Shaolin '79
Chinatown Kid '77
Dirty Ho '79
Five Deadly Venoms
'78
Five Fingers of Death
'72
Flag of Iron '80
Invincible Pole Fighter
'83
Killer Snakes '74
Legendary Weapons of
China '82
Return of the Master
Killer '80
Shaolin Mantis '78
Shaolin Master Killer
'78
Ten Tigers of Kwang-
tung '79

Wong Ching-wai
Angel '87

Wong Chiu Yin
Shaolin Temple 2: Kids
from Shaolin '84

Wong Cho-shut
(Huang Zao Shi)
8 Diagram Fighter '91

Wong Chun-kong
Victim '99

Wong Chun Tong
God.com '98
The Legend of a Profes-
sional '00

Wong Chung
(Wang Zhong, Wang
Chung, Wong Jung)
Blooded Treasury Fight
'79
Cantonen Iron Kung Fu
'79
The Green Dragon Inn
'79
The Heroes '80
The Imp '81

Wong, Clint
Snake Fist Dynamo '84

Wong, Dave
(Wong Kit, Wong Git,
Wang Jie, Wang Chieh,
Dave Wang)
Legend of the Flying
Swordsman '00
A War Named Desire
'00

Wong, Dayo
(Wong Chi-wah, Wong Ji
Wa, Huang Zi Hua)
Big Bullet '96
F*** / Off '98
Thunderbolt '95

Wong, Dennis
Magnificent Natural
Fist '80

Wong, Dickson
Rivals of the Dragon
'83

Wong, Eva
Shadow '01

Wong Fan
(Wang Fan)
Blazing Temple '76
The 18 Bronzemen '76
Swordsman with an
Umbrella '70

Wong, Faye
(Faye Wong Fei, Wong
Jing Man, Wang Jing
Wen, Shirley Wong)
Chungking Express '94
Okinawa Rendez-vous
'00

Wong Fei
(Wang Fei)
5 Lady Venoms '78
Exit the Dragon, Enter
the Tiger '76
Lady Whirlwind and the
Rangers '74
Return of the Tiger '79
The Smart Cavalier '78

Wong Fei-lung
(Huang Fei Long, Wong
Fan Long, Nam Siu Foo,
Wong Lung)
The Blazing Temple '76
The 8 Masters '77
The 18 Bronzemen '76
The 18 Bronzemen Part
2 '76
Fists of Bruce Lee '79
Master of the Flying
Guillotine '76
Ninja vs. Shaolin
Guards '84
Screaming Ninja '73
Secret of the Chinese
Kung Fu '81
The Shaolin Kids '77
Shaolin Traitorous '76
The Smart Cavalier '78
Snake-Crane Secret
'78
Two Dragons Fight
against Tiger '75
War of the Shaolin Tem-
ple '80

Wong, Felix
(Wong Yat-Wah)
Legend of the Drunken
Master '94
The Tigers '91

Wong, Frank
(Wong Goon Hung,
Wang Guan Xiong,
Wang Kuan Hsiung,
Wang Kuan Hsing,
Wang Koon Hung,
Champ Wang)
Abbot White '82
Five Elements of Kung
Fu '78
Golden Killah '80

Two Dragons Fight
against Tiger '75

Wong Fung
(Huang Feng, Hwang
Feng)
Sting of the Dragon
Masters '73

Wong, Gabriel
(Wong Yat San, Huang
Yi Shan, Turtle Wong)
Fight Back to School
'91
Fight Back to School 2
'92
Flirting Scholar '93
Hail the Judge '94
Kick Boxer's Tears '92
Love on Delivery '94
The Magnificent
Scoundrels '91
Prince of the Sun '90

Wong Gam-fung
(Wang Jin Feng, Wang
Chin Fung)
Five Fingers of Death
'72
Return of the Master
Killer '80

Wong, Gregory Alan
First Option '96

Wong Hang-sau
(Huang Xing Xiu, Huang
Hsing Hsu, Cecelia
Wong)
Dirty Kung Fu '78
Shaolin Mantis '78
The Young Avenger '79

Wong Hap
(Wang Xia, Wang Hsieh,
Wang Hsia, Wang Ya,
Wang Hsieh, Wang
Shya)
Battle of Shaolin '77
A Better Tomorrow '86
Cantonen Iron Kung Fu
'79
Crippled Masters '80
Emperor of Shaolin
Kung Fu '80
5 Lady Venoms '78
The Leg Fighters '80
Last Hero in China '84
Legend of the Drunken
Tiger '90
The Lost Kung Fu
Secrets '80
Mantis Combat '81
Mask of Death '76
The Prodigal Son '81
Revengeful
Swordswoman '79
Shaolin vs. Ninja '83
Snake-Crane Secret
'78

Wong Hei
Undercover Blues '00

**Wong Ho-yin, Ray-
mond**
(Wong Ho-Yin, Wang
Hao Ran)
Color of Pain '02
Expect the Unexpected
'98
The Irresistible Piggies
'02
Needing You... '00
Where a Good Man
Goes '99

Wong Hoi
18 Fatal Strikes '78

Wong Hung
(Huang Xiong)
A Chinese Ghost Story
2 '90
Gunmen '88

Wong Hung-cheung
(Wang Hong Zhang,
Wang Han Chen)
Drunken Art and Crip-
pled Fist '79
Sorrowful to a Ghost
'70
Swordsman with an
Umbrella '70

Wong, Jackie
Gen-X Cops '99

Wong, James
(Wong Jim, James
Wong Jim, Huang Zhan,
Jim Wong)
Chinatown Kid '77
A Chinese Ghost Story:
The Tsui Hark Ani-
mation '97 (V)
Doctor Vampire '90
Fight Back to School 2
'92
Flirting Scholar '93
Iron Monkey '93
Love Paradox '00
Miracles '89
Return to a Better
Tomorrow '94
Tiger on Beat '88
Twin Dragons '92
Venom Warrior '83
Visible Secret '01

Wong, Jimmy
(Wong Ga Lok, Wong
Kar Lok, Huang Gu
Nuo)
Ballistic Kiss '98
Moonlight Express '99
Sex and the Emperor
'94

Wong Jing
(Wang Jing)
Aces Go Places 2 '83
A Chinese Ghost Story
'87
The Conman '98
Cop Shop Babes '01
Evil Cat '86
God of Gamblers '89
God of Gamblers 2 '90

God of Gamblers 3:
Back to Shanghai
'91
The Iceman Cometh
'89
Martial Angels '01
The New Legend of
Shaolin '94
100 Ways to Murder
Your Wife '86
The Seventh Curse '86
The Tricky Master '00
Twin Dragons '92
Twinkle Twinkle Lucky
Stars '85
The Wesley's Mysteri-
ous File '01

Wong, Joey
(Wong Joe-Hin, Joi
Wang, Wang Tsu-Hsien,
Zuxian Wang, Wong
Cho-Yin, Joey Wang)
All Men Are Brothers:
Blood of the Leop-
ard '93
The Big Heat '88
Butterfly and Sword '93
Casino Tycoon 2 '92
A Chinese Ghost Story
'87
A Chinese Ghost Story
2 '90
A Chinese Ghost Story
3 '91
City Hunter '92
Eagle Shooting Heroes
'93
The East Is Red '93
God of Gamblers '89
Green Snake '93
Killer's Romance '90
100 Ways to Murder
Your Wife '86
Painted Skin '92
Picture of a Nymph '88
Where's Officer Tuba?
'86

Wong Kam-Kong
(Wong Gam Kong,
Huang Jin Jiang)
The Adventurers '95
Burning Paradise '94
The Defender '94
From Beijing with Love
'94
God of Gamblers
Returns '94
Gunmen '88
One Arm Hero '94
Sam the Iron Bridge:
Champion of Mar-
tial Arts '93
Shanghai 1920 '91
Wonder Seven '94

Wong, Karel
(Wong Chi Yeung, Wong
Ji Yeung, Huang Zi
Yang, Karel Ng, Wong
Tze Yeung)
Chinese Orthopedist
and the Spice Girls
'02

The Conman '98
Cop Shop Babes '01
Cop on a Mission '01
Fight Back to School '91
H.K. Adams Family '92
The Legend of a Professional '00
The Legend of the Swordsman '92
Once upon a Time in China '91
Super Car Criminals '99
Undercover Blues '00
Young and Dangerous 5 '98

Wong, Kelvin
(Wong Siu, Wang Xiao)
Casino Raiders 2 '91
Don't Give a Damn '95
High Risk '95
The Moon Warriors '92
Supercop '92

Wong, Ken
(Wong Hop Hey, Wong Gap Choi, Wang He Xi)
The Blacksheep Affair '98
The Cheaters '01
Devil Touch '02
Downtown Torpedoes '97
Killer '00
Sharp Guns '01
Sunshine Cops '99
A Wicked Ghost 2: The Fear '00
You Shoot, I Shoot '01

Wong Kin-mi
(Wong Gan, Huang Gen)
Fearless Hyena '79
A Life of Ninja '83
Shaolin Chastity Kung Fu '81

Wong, Kirk
(Wong Che-kirk, Huang Zhi qiang, Wong Chi Keung)
The Art of Action: Martial Arts in the Movies '02
The Big Heat '88
Casino Raiders '89
Final Justice '88
God of Gamblers 2 '90
I Love Maria '88
Legacy of Rage '86
Long Arm of the Law 2 '87
Shanghai 1920 '91
Twin Dragons '92

Wong Kwan-yuen
(Huang Kun Xuan)
All About Ah-Long '89
Eighth Happiness '88

Wong, Linda
A Chinese Ghost Story: The Tsui Hark Animation '97 (V)

Wong Ling
Filthy Guy '80

Wong Ma Lee
(Wong Lut Lee, Wang Ma Li)
Fantasy Mission Force '84

Wong Man Bao
Masters of Tiger Crane '83

Wong Man-chuen
(Wang Man Chuan, Wang Man Chao)
Battle of Shaolin '77
Fighting Ace '79

Wong Man Ting
Project A '83

Wong, Manfred
(Wong Man Jun, Wen Juan)
Combo Cops '96
Erotic Ghost Story '90
Forbidden City Cop '96
Pedicab Driver '89
Pom Pom '84
Sixty Million Dollar Man '95

Wong, Matthew
(Wong Hin Mung, Huang Yan Meng)
The Big Heat '88

Wong Mei
(Wong Mooi, Huang Mei)
Five Fingers of Death '71
Kung Fu's Hero '73
The Legend of Bruce Lee '80
Prodigal Boxer '73
The Shaolin Disciple '80

Wong Mei-Mei
(Huang Wei Wei, Huang Mei Mei, New Mei Mei)
Five Superfighters '78
Moonlight Sword and Jade Lion '79

Wong, Melvin
(Wong Kam-Sen, Wong Gam San, Huang Jin Shen, Melbourne Wang)
Aces Go Places 5: The Terracotta Hit '89
Beauty Investigator '92
Blonde Fury '89
The Descendant of Wing Chun '78
Don't Give a Damn '95
Dragon in Jail '90
Eastern Condors '86
Heart of Dragon '85
In the Line of Duty 3 '88
Miracles '89
Righting Wrongs '86
Run and Kill '93

Twinkle Twinkle Lucky Stars '85
The Untold Story 2 '98
We're Going to Eat You! '80
Where's Officer Tuba? '86
Yes, Madam '85

Wong, Michael
(Wong Man-Tak, Michael Fitzgerald)
Beast Cops '98
The Blood Rules '00
City Hunter '92
Combo Cops '96
Could You Kill My Husband Please? '01
First Option '96
Her Name Is Cat '98
In the Line of Duty 4 '89
Legacy of Rage '86
Option Zero '97
The Replacement Suspects '01
Return to a Better Tomorrow '94
Royal Warriors '86
Super Car Criminals '99
Thunderbolt '95
Ultimatum '01
Violent Cop '99

Wong, Michelle
(Wong Man, Huang Wen)
F*** / Off '98

Wong, Mike
Champ against Champ '83
Duel of the Tao Tough '82
Invincible Obsessed Fighter '82
Magnificent Natural Fist '80
The Snake Strikes Back '81

Wong Ming-sing
(Huang Ming Sheng)
City Hunter '93
Dragon from Russia '90
Legend of the Drunken Master '94
New Mr. Vampire '86
Supercop '92
Supercop 2 '93
Thunderbolt '95

Wong, Mona
Shaolin Fist of Fury '87

Wong, Natalie
(Wong Gei Ying, Huang Ji Ying)
Troublesome Night 3 '97

Wong, Olivia
Inner Senses '01

Wong, Parkman
(Wong Pak-Man, Wong Paak Man, Huang Bo Wen)
The Adventurers '95
City Cop '95
City on Fire '87
Dr. Lamb '92
Final Justice '88
The Killer '89
Legend of the Dragon '91
Man Wanted '95
Operation Billionaires '98
Organized Crime and Triad Bureau '94
Return to a Better Tomorrow '94
The Untold Story '92

Wong Pau-gel
(Huang Pei Ji, Huang Pei Chih, Wong Pei Tsi, Wong Pen Tsi)
Death Mask of the Ninja '82
Legend of the 7 Golden Vampires '74
Prodigal Boxer '73
Thunder Kick '73

Wong, Paul
(Wong Kwan, Wang Kun)
Avenging Warriors of Shaolin '79
The Dragon Family '88
God of Gamblers '89
In the Line of Duty 4 '89
Police Story '85
Project A '83
Tiger Cage '88
The Young Master '80

Wong, Pauline
(Wong Siu-Fung)
Long Arm of the Law 2 '87
Mr. Vampire '85
New Mr. Vampire '86
The Peacock King '89
Rich and Famous '87
Twinkle Twinkle Lucky Stars '85

Wong Ping
(Wang Ping)
Five Fingers of Death '72
Killer from Above '77
The New Game of Death '75
The Silver Spear '79

Wong, Raymond
(Wong Pak Ming, Wong Baak Ming, Huang Bai Ming)
Aces Go Places '82
Aces Go Places 2 '83
All's Well End's Well '92
All's Well End's Well '97 '97

A Chinese Ghost Story: The Tsui Hark Animation '97 (V)
Eighth Happiness '88
Help!!! '00
Legendary Couple '95
Lethal Panther '91
Paramount Motel '00
Troublesome Night 4 '98

Wong, Ringo
(Wong Chi Ming, Huang Zhi Ming)
Chinese Hercules '73
Dragon on Fire '79
Last Hurrah for Chivalry '78

Wong, Roger
Rage of the Dragon '79

Wong, Ronald
(Wong Ban, Huang Bin)
Bio-Cops '00
Casino Raiders '89
Crocodile Hunter '89
The Demon's Baby '98
God of Gamblers '89
God of Gamblers 2 '90
A Man Called Hero '99
The Owl vs. Bombo '84
Young and Dangerous 5 '98

Wong, Ruby
(Wong Cheuk-Ling)
Double Tap '00
Expect the Unexpected '98
Hit Team '00
Losers' Club '01
Needing You... '00
Runaway '01
Running out of Time '99
Running out of Time 2 '01
Too Many Ways to Be No. 1 '97
U-Man '02
Where a Good Man Goes '99

Wong, Russel
Romeo Must Die '00
Satin Steel '94

Wong, Sally
Beyond Hypothermia '96

Wong Sam
(Wang Chen, Wang Sun)
Body Weapon '99
From China with Death '74

Wong San
(Huang Xin)
A Chinese Torture Chamber Story 2 '98
God of Gamblers '89
Legend of the Drunken Master '94

Wong, Sherman
(Wong Jing Wa, Huang Jing Hua)
C'est la Vie, Mon Cheri '93
Happy Family '02

Wong Shu-kei, Jimmy
(Wong Shu Kei, Wang Shu Qi)
Crocodile Hunter '89
Sex and the Emperor '94

Wong Shu Tong
(Wong Siu Tong, Huang Shu Tang)
The Butterfly Murders '79
Cop on a Mission '01
Death Ring '83
Inner Senses '01
Thunder Kick '73

Wong Siu-ching
Fist of Fury '95

Wong Tak-ban
(Huang De Bin, Wong Dak Ban, Wong Tat Ban)
The Best of the Best '96
A Chinese Torture Chamber Story '94
A Gambler's Story '01

Wong Tin Lam
(Wang Tian Lin)
All About Ah-Long '89
Beauty and the Breast '02
The Blood Rules '00
Justice, My Foot! '92
Last Hero in China '93
The Longest Nite '98
Love on a Diet '01
The Mission '99
The Private Eye Blues '94
Young and Dangerous 5 '98

Wong, Tino
(Wong Cheung, Wang Jiang, Wang Chiang)
The Butterfly Murders '79
Dragon on Fire '79
Drunken Master '78
Hit-Man in the Hand of Buddha '80
The Invincible Armour '77
Legend of the 7 Golden Vampires '74
The Miracle Fighters '82
Prodigal Boxer '73
Snake in the Eagle's Shadow '78

Wong, Tommy
(Wong Kwong-leung, Wong Gwong Leung, Huang Guang Liang)

All's Well End's Well '92
A Chinese Ghost Story 3 '91
A Chinese Torture Chamber Story '94
City on Fire '87
Final Justice '88
The Killer '89
Long Arm of the Law '84
A Moment of Romance '90
Prison on Fire '87
Prison on Fire 2 '91

Wong, Tony
(Wong Yuen San, Huang Yuan Shan)
Deadly Snail vs. Kung Fu Killer '77
Golden Dragon Silver Snake '79
Kung Fu, the Invisible Fist '72
Super Gang '78
Ten Tigers of Shaolin '78

Wong, Victor
(Wong Chi Keung, Huang Zhi Jiang)
The Adventurers '95
I Love Maria '88

Wong Wai
(Wang Wei)
Enter the Fat Dragon '78
In the Line of Duty 5: Middle Man '90
Miracles '89
Police Story 2 '88
Project A '83
Tiger Cage '88

Wong Wai-fai
Hit Team '00

Wong Wan-si
God of Gamblers 3: Back to Shanghai '91

Wong Wing-fong
(Wang Yong Fang, Dassey Wong, Usang Yeong Fang)
Dr. Lamb '92

Wong Wing Sheng
(Wong Wing Sang, Wang Yong Sheng, Wang Yung Hseng, Wang Yung Sheng)
Incredible Kung Fu Mission '79
Master of the Flying Guillotine '75
New Fist of Fury '76
Ninja Checkmate '76
Return of the Tiger '77
The 36 Deadly Styles '79
World of the Drunken Master '79

Wong, Wyman
(Wong Wai Man, Huang Wei Wen)
Dummy Mommy, without a Baby '01
United We Stand, and Swim '01

Wong Yak-ho
Fist of Fury '95

Wong Yat-Fei
(Wong Yat Fei, Huang Yi-fei)
Beauty and the Breast '02
The Chinese Feast '95
Crime of a Beast '01
The Duel '00
Extreme Crisis '98
Forbidden City Cop '96
From Beijing with Love '94
H.K. Adams Family '92
Hail the Judge '94
The Heroic Trio '93
Justice, My Foot! '92
Lee Rock '91
Love Me, Love My Money '01
Love on Delivery '94
Sex and the Emperor '94
Shaolin Soccer '01
Sixty Million Dollar Man '95

Wong Yat-tung
(Wong Tung, Huang Yi Tong)
A Gambler's Story '01
Take 2 in Life '01

Wong Yee-tin
Prodigal Boxer '73

Wong Yeuk-ping
(Wang Re Ping, Wang Jo Ping)
The Heroes '80
Hong Kong Nocturne '67
The Killer Meteors '76
Ninja in the Deadly Trap '81
The Shaolin Kids '77
Snake-Crane Secret '78
Swordsman with an Umbrella '70
Yoga and Kung Fu Girl '78

Wong Yu
(Wong Yue, Wang Yu, Young Wong Yu, Yung Wong Yue, Wang Yue)
The Big Sting '82
The Bloody Fists '72
Dance of a Dream '01
Dirty Ho '79
Dirty Kung Fu '78
Executioners from Shaolin '77
He Has Nothing But Kung Fu '77

Invincible Pole Fighter '83
The Seventh Curse '86
Shaolin Master Killer '78
The World of the Drunken Master '79
The Young Avenger '79

Wong Yuk-wan
(Wang Yu Huan)
Dragons Forever '88
Mr. Vampire 2 '86
Mr. Vampire Saga 4 '88

Wong Yung
(Wang Rong)
Queen's High '91
Seeding of a Ghost '83

Woo Chau-ping
Sorrowful to a Ghost '70

Woo, George
It Takes a Thief '01

Woo Gwong
(Hu Guang)
The Blazing Temple '76
Bruce Lee We Miss You '76
Chinese Iron Man '75
The 18 Bronzemen Part 2 '76
The Shaolin Kids '77

Woo, John
(Ng Yue Sam, Wu Yu Sen, Wu Yu-Sheng)
The Art of Action: Martial Arts in the Movies '02
A Better Tomorrow '86
Bullet in the Head '89
Hand of Death '75
Hard Boiled '91
Once a Thief '91
Task Force '97
Twin Dragons '92

Woo, Terry
First Strike '96

Woo Wai
(Hu Wei)
The Blazing Temple '76
The 18 Bronzemen '76
The Killer Meteors '76
The Master of Death '82

Woo Yiu-chung
Prison on Fire 2 '91

Woo Yoin-jang
A*P*E '76

Woodell, Pat
Twilight People '72

Woods, James
Final Fantasy: The Spirits Within '01 (V)

Woods, Michael
(Mai Go Wood Shut, Mi Gao Huo Si)

Crystal Hunt '91
First Option '96
In the Line of Duty 4 '89
Tiger Cage '88

Woodside, D.B.
Romeo Must Die '00

Wu, Annie
(Ng San-Kwan, Wu Chen Chun)
Ballistic Kiss '98
The Best of the Best '96
The Demon's Baby '98
Faces of Horror '98
First Strike '96
Love Paradox '00
Love au Zen '01

Wu Bai
(Ng Bak, Wu Jun-Lin)
Time and Tide '00

Wu Chia Hsiang
(Wu Jiaxiang, Ng Ga Seung, Wu Chia-shiang, Wu Gu Xiang, Ng Ka-seung, Ng Ka Yan)
Battle of Shaolin '77
Death Duel of Kung Fu '79
Dragon Lord '82
Dreaming Fists with Slender Hands '80
The Iron Monkey '77
Legend of the Mountain '79
The Massive '78
The Master of Death '82
Moonlight Sword and Jade Lion '79
Return of the Tiger '79

Wu, Daisy
(Woo Hoi-yan, Hu Kai Xin, Daisy Woo)
Beast Cops '98
Thunderbolt '95

Wu, Daniel
(Wu Yin-Joe, Daniel Ng)
Beauty and the Breast '02
Beijing Rocks '01
Born Wild '01
Cop on a Mission '01
Gen-X Cops '99
Headlines '01
Hit Team '00
2000 A.D. '00
Undercover Blues '00

Wu, David
(Ng Daai Wai, Wu Da Wei, David Ng, Woo Dai Wai, David Woo)
The Buddhist Fist '79
C'est la Vie, Mon Cheri '93
A Chinese Ghost Story '87
Dance of the Drunk Mantis '79

Doctor Vampire '90
Dragon on Fire '79
Full Throttle '95
Gunmen '88
In the Line of Duty 5: Middle Man '90
Jade Claw '79
Once a Thief '91
Peking Opera Blues '86
Robotrix '91
We're Going to Eat You! '80

Wu Fung
(Woo Fung, Hu Feng)
City Cops '89
Dragons Forever '88
Fist of Fury 1991 '91
H.K. Adams Family '92
The Haunted Cop Shop '87
Heart of Dragon '85
The Millionaires' Express '86
Miracles '89
Mr. Vampire 2 '86
Once a Thief '91
Operation Pink Squad '88
Police Story '85
Prince of the Sun '90
Red Wolf '95
Robotrix '91
Royal Warriors '86
Scared Stiff '86
Skinny Tiger and Fatty Dragon '90
Tricky Master '99
Where's Officer Tuba? '86

Wu Hsing-kuo
(Ng Hing Gwok, Wu Xing Guo, Wu Hsing-guo)
The Accidental Spy '01
Comeuppance '00
God of Gamblers Returns '94
Green Snake '93
Rock 'n' Roll Cop '94

Wu, Jacky
(Ng Ging, Wu Jing)
Zu Warriors '01

Wu, Jacqueline
(Ng Sin Lin, Wu Qian Lian, Wu Chien Lien, Jacqueline Ng)
The Adventurers '95
All's Well End's Well '97 '97
Beyond Hypothermia '96
Casino Raiders 2 '91
God of Gamblers Returns '94
Martial Arts Master Wong Fei Hung '92
A Moment of Romance '90
Peace Hotel '95
The Phantom Lover '95

Wu Kam-Bo
Eagle vs. Silver Fox '83

Wu Lo-yee
Five Elements of Kung Fu '78

Wu Ma
(Fung Ng Ma, Ng Ma)
All Men Are Brothers: Blood of the Leopard '93
Blonde Fury '89
Blooded Treasury Fight '79
A Chinese Ghost Story '87
A Chinese Ghost Story 2 '90
Deadful Melody '94
Don't Give a Damn '95
Eastern Condors '86
Encounter of the Spooky Kind '81
Fighting Ace '79
From China with Death '74
Generation Pendragon '90
Half a Loaf of Kung Fu '77
Heart of Dragon '85
The Heroes '80
High Risk '95
The Iron Monkey '77
Iron Monkey 2 '96
A Kid from Tibet '91
The Magnificent Scoundrels '91
The Master of Death '82
The Millionaires' Express '86
Miracles '89
Mr. Vampire '85
Mr. Vampire 2 '86
Mr. Vampire Saga 4 '88
My Lucky Stars '85
New Mr. Vampire '86
Once upon a Time in China '91
100 Ways to Murder Your Wife '86
The Owl vs. Bombo '84
Painted Faces '88
Painted Skin '92
Peking Opera Blues '86
Picture of a Nymph '88
Police Story 2 '88
Pom Pom '84
Pom Pom Strikes Back '86
The Prodigal Son '81
Project A '83
Righting Wrongs '86
Scared Stiff '86
Snake-Crane Secret '78
The Sword Stained with Royal Blood '93
Swordsman '90
Twinkle Twinkle Lucky Stars '85
Ways of Kung Fu '80
Wheels on Meals '84
Winners and Sinners '83

Yes, Madam '85

Wu, Nicky
(Ng Kei-Lung, Wu Ji Long)
A Chinese Ghost Story: The Tsui Hark Animation '97 (V)
Thunder Cop '96

Wu, Pace
(Wu Pei Ci, Ng Pooi Tsz)
United We Stand, and Swim '97
A War Named Desire '00

Wu Yanxing
Shaolin: Wheel of Life '00

Wu Yuan-chun
(Ng Yuen Jun, Wu Yuan Chun)
Five Superfighters '78

Xinxin, Xiong
(Hung Yan Yan, Xiong Xin Xin)
Black Mask '96
The Blacksheep Affair '98
The Blade '95
The Chinese Feast '95
Dragon Inn '92
Once upon a Time in China 2 '92
Once upon a Time in China 3 '93
Once upon a Time in China 4 '93
Once upon a Time in China and America '97
Wonder Seven '94

Xu Fan
Crash Landing '00

Xu Liying
Shaolin: Wheel of Life '00

Xue Zhilun
Picture of a Nymph '88

Xun, Zhou
Beijing Bicycle '01
Suzhou River '00

Yachi, Zulu
Return of the Street Fighter '74

Yachigusa, Kaoru
The Human Vapor '60
Samurai 1: Musashi Miyamoto '54
Samurai 2: Duel at Ichi-joji Temple '55
Samurai 3: Duel at Ganryu Island '56

Yada, Akiko
Cross Fire '00

Yaegaki, Michiko
Gamera vs. Viras '68

Yahiro, Junko
Gamera vs. Viras '68

Yajima, Kenichi
Sonatine '93

Yakushimaru, Hiroko
Legend of the Eight Samurai '84

Yakusho, Koji
(Koji Hashimoto)
Cure '97
The Eel '97
Pulse '01
Tampopo '87
Warm Water under a Red Bridge '01

Yam, Chan
(Chen Ren)
The Private Eyes '76
Sunshine Cops '99

Yam Ho
Heart of Dragon '85

Yam Kong-sou
Her Name Is Cat 2: Journey to Death '01

Yam, Pauline
(Yam Bo Lam, Yam Biu Lam, Ren Bao Lin, Pauline Lam)
The Blood Rules '00
Dummy Mommy, without a Baby '01
Every Dog Has His Date '01
Funeral March '01

Yam Sai-kwoon
(Yen Shi-Kwan, Yam Sai Goon, Ren Shi Guan, Yam Sai-kun, Yan Yee Kwan, Jen Shin Kuan, Yam Sai Kuun)
Breakout from Oppression '78
Dance of the Drunk Mantis '79
Dragon Fist '78
Dragon Inn '92
Fearless Hyena '79
Fearless Hyena 2 '80
From China with Death '74
Gold Fingers '01
The Heroic Trio '93
Iron Monkey '93
Legend of the 7 Golden Vampires '74
The Legend of the Swordsman '92
Once upon a Time in China '91
Once upon a Time in China 2 '92
Royal Tramp 2 '92
The 36 Crazy Fists '77
Thunder Kick '73

Yam, Simon
(Yam Tat-Wah, Simon Yau)
Black Cat '91
BloodFight '89
Bullet in the Head '90
Cold War '00
Contract Killer '98
Dr. Lamb '92
Dragon Killer '95
Drunken Master Killer '94
Expect the Unexpected '98
Final Romance '01
Full Contact '92
Fulltime Killer '01
Juliet in Love '00
Killer's Romance '90
Legend of Speed '99
Legendary Couple '95
Man Wanted '95
Midnight Fly '01
Miracles '89
The Mission '99
Model from Hell '99
Naked Killer '92
Operation Billionaires '98
Powerful Four '91
Queen's High '91
Run and Kill '93
The Suspect '98
Tiger Cage '88
Tragic Fantasy: Tiger of Wanchai '94
Trust Me U Die '99
Young and Dangerous '96

Yamada, Akira
The H-Man '58
Half Human '55/1957
Mothra '61

Yamada, Gerald
(Waichi Yamada)
The Street Fighter '74
The Street Fighter's Last Revenge '74

Yamada, Isuzu
Throne of Blood '57
Yojimbo '61

Yamada, Mariya
Ultraman Tiga and Ultraman Dyna: The Warriors of the Lightning Star '98

Yamada, Minako
Atomic Rulers of the World '57
Attack from Space '58
Evil Brain from Outer Space '58/59

Yamada, Minosuke
Godzilla Raids Again '55
The H-Man '58
The Human Vapor '60
Rodan '56
Varan the Unbelievable '58

815

Yamagata, Isao
Lone Wolf and Cub 3: Baby Cart to Hades '72
Seven Samurai '54
Warning from Space '56

Yamaguchi, Sayaka
Rebirth of Mothra '96
Rebirth of Mothra 2 '97

Yamamoto, Ichiro
The Razor 1: Sword of Justice '72
The Razor 2: The Snare '73

Yamamoto, Kei
Bullet Train '75

Yamamoto, Mirai
Who Am I? '98

Yamamoto, Ren
Chushingura '62
Frankenstein vs. Baragon '65
Godzilla Raids Again '55
Godzilla, King of the Monsters '54
Half Human '55/1957
The Human Vapor '60
Mothra '61
Rodan '56
The Secret of the Telegian '60
War of the Gargantuas '66

Yamamoto, Ryo
Postman Blues '97

Yamamoto, Ryuji
Weather Woman '95

Yamamoto, Shohei
Reborn from Hell: Samurai Armageddon '96
Tokyo Mafia 2: Wrath of the Yakuza '95
Tokyo Mafia: Yakuza Wars '95

Yamamoto, Taro
Battle Royale '00

Yamamoto, Yoko
Gappa: The Triphibian Monster '67

Yamamura, So
(Hirosada Koga, Satoshi Yamamura, Soh Yamamura)
Godzilla vs. King Ghidorah '91
Lone Wolf and Cub 4: Baby Cart in Peril '72
Ninja: Band of Assassins Continued '63

Yamashiko, Junichiro
Giant Monster Gamera '65

Yamashiro, Jimmy
Bronson Lee, Champion '78

Yamashiro, Shingo
Lone Wolf and Cub 5: Baby Cart in the Land of Demons '73
The Street Fighter's Last Revenge '74

Yamashita, Junichiro
Return of Daimajin '66

Yamashita, Shinji
Zero Woman: The Accused '96

Yamashita, Tadashi
Bronson Lee, Champion '78

Yamatani, Hatsuo
Lone Wolf and Cub 3: Baby Cart to Hades '73
Notorious Concubines '69

Yamato, Takeshi
Beautiful Beast '95

Yamauchi, Akira
Godzilla vs. Hedorah '71
Lone Wolf and Cub 5: Baby Cart in the Land of Demons '73
The Razor 1: Sword of Justice '72
The Razor 3: Who's Got the Gold? '74

Yamauchi, Shuichi
Sakuya: Slayer of Demons '00

Yamazaki, Senri
Gamera 3: The Revenge of Irys '99

Yamazaki, Tsutomu
The Funeral '84
High and Low '63
Tampopo '87

Yan, Ga Chen
Deadend of Besiegers '92

Yan, Lawrence
The Kung Fu Master '94

Yan Yi Shek
Shanghai Affairs '98

Yan, Yolinda
(Yan Choh Sin, Zhen Chu Qian)
Bullet in the Head '90
A Chinese Torture Chamber Story 2 '98
Powerful Four '91

Yanagi, Eijiro
Blind Swordsman: The Tale of Zatoichi '62
Mighty Jack '68
The Tale of Zatoichi Continues '62

Yanagi, Yurei
(Masahiko Ono)
Boiling Point '90
Fireworks '97
Ghost Actress '96
Ring '98
Ring 2 '99

Yanami, Eiko
Gamera vs. Zigra '71

Yang Chih-ching
(Yang Chih-hsing, Yeung Chi Hing, Yang Zhi Qing, Yang Chih Ching, Yeung Chi Hing, Yang Shih Kun)
Avenging Eagle '78
Avenging Warriors of Shaolin '79
Chinatown Kid '77
Dirty Ho '79
Invincible Pole Fighter '83
Revenge of the Zombies '76

Yang Chun Hoi
Shaolin Fist of Fury '87

Yang Chung-hsien
High Risk '95

Yang Dezhi
The Prisoner of Five Boulders '89

Yang Kuang
18 Fatal Strikes '78

Yang Ni-chiu
Brave Archer '77

Yang, Peter
(Yang Kwan, Yang Chun, Yang Qun, Yeung Kwun, Yeung Kwan, Peter K. Yang)
Angel '87
Beauty Investigator '92
Enter the Fat Dragon '78
Fearless Fighters '69
The Protector '85
Rich and Famous '87
Twinkle Twinkle Lucky Stars '85

Yang Ping An
(An Ping)
Shaolin King Boxer '79

Yang, Robinson
Ninja in the U.S.A. '88

Yang Sha-fei
(Yang Sha Fei Au, Ouyang Sha-fei)
Avenging Eagle '78
A Chinese Ghost Story 2 '90

Dragon Fist '78
Fatal Flying Guillotine '77
Hong Kong Nocturne '67
Iron Monkey 2 '77

Yang Song
The Super Ninja '84

Yang, Tiger
(Tiger Yeung)
Blind Fist of Bruce '79

Yang, Tom
Shaolin: Wheel of Life '00

Yank, Big
Supercop 2 '93

Yanyang, Shi
Shaolin: Wheel of Life '00

Yao, Kelly
Naked Killer '92

Yashiro, Miki
Attack of the Mushroom People '63

Yasuda, Michiyo
Lone Wolf and Cub 5: Baby Cart in the Land of Demons '73

Yasuda, Narumi
(Narumi Kinashi, On Tin Shing Mei, An Tian Cheng Mei)
The Peacock King '89

Yasuhara, Reiko
Tokyo Mafia 2: Wrath of the Yakuza '95
Tokyo Mafia: Yakuza Wars '95

Yasuoka, Rikiya
The Ninja Dragon '90
Tampopo '87

Yatsu, Isao
Dark Water '02

Yatsuma, Nobu
Prince of Space '59

Yau, Chingmy
(Yau Suk-Ching, Yiu Suk Ching)
Casino Tycoon 2 '92
City Hunter '92
God of Gamblers Returns '94
High Risk '95
Lawyer Lawyer '97
Lee Rock '91
Legendary Couple '95
Lord of the Wu Tang '93
Naked Killer '92
The New Legend of Shaolin '94
Return to a Better Tomorrow '94
Royal Tramp '92

Royal Tramp 2 '92

Yau, David
Devil Woman '70

Yau, Herman
(Yau Lai To, Qiu Li Tao)
The Best of the Best '96
C'est la Vie, Mon Cheri '93
Happy Family '02

Yau Man-shing
Visible Secret '01

Yau Shui-ling
Fists and Guts '79

Yau Tsui-ling
(Yu Tsui-ling, Yau Chui Ling, You Cui Ling)
Avenging Eagle '78
Dirty Ho '79
Lightning Kung Fu '80
Return of the Master Killer '80

Yazaki, Tomonori
All Monsters Attack '70

Yee, Derek
(Yee Yung Sing, Yi Dung Sing, Er Dong Sheng, Erh Tung Sheng)
Death Mask of the Ninja '82
Magnificent Warriors '87
The Seventh Curse '86

Yee, Eric
Snake Fist Dynamo '84

Yee Tin-hung
(Yi Tian Xiong, Paco Yick)
The Best of the Best '96
Bullet in the Head '90
The Mission '99
Running out of Time '99

Yee Yuen
(Yi Yuan, Yi Tuen, I Yuan, Ei Yuan)
The Blazing Temple '76
Blood of the Dragon '71
Chinese Iron Man '75
The 18 Bronzemen '76
Fearless Fighters '69
Fury of King Boxer '72
The Massive '78
The Shaolin Invincibles '79
The Shaolin Kids '77
The Smart Cavalier '78
Sorrowful to a Ghost '70
The Story in Temple Red Lily '79

Yeh, Sally
(Yip Sin Man, She Qian Wen, Sally Yip)
Aces Go Places 4 '86

I Love Maria '88
The Killer '89
Peking Opera Blues '86
The Protector '85 (HK)

Yeh Shao-im
Lady Whirlwind and the Rangers '74

Yen, Alan
The Killer Elephants '76

Yen, Donnie
(Yen Ji-Dan, Yen Chi-Tan, Yan Che Dan) See also sidebar on p. 152.
The Art of Action: Martial Arts in the Movies '02
Ballistic Kiss '98
Blade 2 '02
Butterfly and Sword '93
Crystal Hunt '91
Dragon Inn '92
Drunken Tai Chi '84
Fist of Fury '95
In the Line of Duty 4 '89
Iron Monkey '93
Iron Monkey 2 '96
The Kung Fu Master '94
Once upon a Time in China 2 '92
Shanghai Affairs '98
Tiger Cage '88
Wing Chun '94

Yen, Nancy
(Yin Naam Hei, Yan Nan-xi, Yan Nan His, Nan Shi Yun, Nancy Yan, Yen Nan See)
Born Invincible '78
Chinese Iron Man '75
Emperor of Shaolin Kung Fu '80
Killer Priest '81
Militant Eagle '78
The Six Directions of Boxing '79
The Smart Cavalier '78
Triangular Duel '72
The Unbeaten 28 '80

Yen, William
Ninja Hunter '83
Ninja the Final Duel '85
Shaolin vs. Lama '81
Shaolin vs. Ninja '83
The Super Ninja '84

Yeoh, Michelle
(Yeoh Chu-Kheng, Michelle Khan, Yang Ziqiong, Yeung Chi-King) See also sidebar on p. 306.
Butterfly and Sword '93
Crouching Tiger, Hidden Dragon '00
Executioners '93
The Heroic Trio '93
Magnificent Warriors '87

Moonlight Express '99
The Owl vs. Bombo '84
Royal Warriors '86
Supercop '92
Supercop 2 '93
The Touch '02
Twin Warriors '93
Twinkle Twinkle Lucky Stars '85
Wing Chun '94
Wonder Seven '94
Yes, Madam '85

Yeow, Gordon
Eat My Dust '93

Yeung, Bolo
(Yeung Shut, Yang Sze, Yang Si)
BloodFight '89
Bolo '80
Chinese Hercules '73
Chinese Samson '79
Dragon on Fire '79
Enter the Dragon '73
The Fist, the Kicks and the Evils '79
Five Fingers of Death '72
Goose Boxer '78
Kung Fu's Hero '73
Legacy of Rage '86
The Legend of Bruce Lee '80
Martial Arts Mayhem, Vol. 1 '99
Martial Arts Mayhem, Vol. 2 '99
The Millionaires' Express '86
My Lucky Stars '85
Snake Deadly Act '79
Super Gang '78
Super Kung Fu Kid '74
10 Magnificent Killers '77
The 36 Deadly Styles '79
Thunder Kick '73

Yeung Chak Lam
(Yeung Chak-Lam, Yang Chak Lam, Yang Ze Lin, Yang Tze Lin)
Five Fingers of Death '72
God of Gamblers '89
Return of the Deadly Blade '81
The 36 Deadly Styles '79

Yeung, Charlie
(Yeung Choi-Nei, Yeung Choi Lei, Yang Cai Ni, Charlie Young)
Ashes of Time '94
A Chinese Ghost Story: The Tsui Hark Animation '97 (V)
Downtown Torpedoes '97
Fallen Angels '95
High Risk '95
Task Force '97

Yeung, Cher
Twinkle Twinkle Lucky Stars '85

Yeung Chong Hon
Shanghai 1920 '91

Yeung Chuen-ngai
Extreme Challenge '01

Yeung, Elsa
(Yeung Wai San, Yang Hui Shan, Yang Hui Sang, Queenie Yang, Yeung Hui Shan)
5 Lady Venoms '78
Kung Fu's Hero '73
A Life of Ninja '83
Snake-Crane Secret '78

Yeung Fan
(Yeung Faan, Yang Fan, Yang Fang)
A Chinese Torture Chamber Story 2 '98
The Untold Story 2 '98

Yeung Gam-yuk
(Yang Jin Yu, Yeung Kuei Yu)
The Blazing Temple '76
The Hot, the Cool, and the Vicious '76

Yeung Hung
(Yang Xiong, Yang Hsi-ung, Ma Tze Pang, Yang Hsiun, Yang Shun, Yang Hung)
Avenging Warriors of Shaolin '79
The Blood Rules '00
A Chinese Torture Chamber Story 2 '98
Dragon Kid '90
A Fistful of Talons '83
Lone Ninja Warrior '81
The Prisoner '90
Raiders of the Wu Tang '84
Return of the 5 Deadly Venoms '78
Scorpion Thunderbolt '85
Shaolin Chastity Kung Fu '81
Shaolin vs. Lama '83
Ten Tigers of Kwang-tung '79
Young Tiger '73

Yeung, Joseph
Rivals of the Dragon '83

Yeung Ka-mun
Take 2 in Life '01

Yeung Kin Wai
Kung Fu Genius '79
The Legend of a Professional '00

Yeung, Kristy
(Yeung Kung-Yu, Yeung Gung Yue, Yang Gong Ru, Christie Yeung, Kristy Yang)
The Avenging Fist '01
City of Desire '01
Comrades, Almost a Love Story '96
The Duel '00
Everyday Is Valentine '01
Fall for You '01
For Bad Boys Only '00
A Man Called Hero '99
The Storm Riders '98

Yeung Lit
(Yang Lie)
Dreaming Fists with Slender Hands '80
Fearless Fighters '73
The Six Directions of Boxing '79

Yeung, Miriam
Dummy Mommy, without a Baby '01

Yeung On-tung
Cold War '00

Yeung, Pauline
All's Well End's Well '97 '97
Dragons Forever '88

Yeung Sau-guen
(Yang Xiu Juan, Yang Hsiu Chian)
Militant Eagle '78
The 72 Desperate Rebels '76

Yeung, Sharon
(Yeung Pan Pan, Pamela Yang, Yang Pan Pan)
Angel on Fire '95
Return of the Deadly Blade '81
Shadow of the Tiger '79

Yeung Shing-lam
Merry-Go-Round '01

Yeung Sing
(Yang Sheng)
Burning Paradise '94
The Killer '89
The Peacock King '89

Yeung Tak-ngai
(Yang De Yi)
The Bride with White Hair 2 '93

Yeung, Vanessa
Hot War '98

Yeung Wai
(Yeung Wei, Yang Wai)
Enter the Fat Dragon '78
Hand of Death '75
Hit-Man in the Hand of Buddha '80

The Legendary Strike '78
The Postman Fights Back '82

Yi Lui, James
Operation Pink Squad '88

Yi, Maria
The Chinese Connection '71
Fists of Fury '71

Yi, Ricky
(Yi Fan Wai, Yi Fan Wei, Ricky Yee)
City War '88
Crocodile Hunter '89
Final Justice '88
The Killer '89
Legend of the Dragon '91
Organized Crime and Triad Bureau '94

Yim, Andy
Option Zero '97

Yin Ping Ko
The Eye '02

Yin, Terence
(Yin Chi-wai, Wan Ji Wai, Yin Zi Wei, Wan Zi Wai)
Bullets of Love '01
Color of Pain '02
Final Romance '01
Gen-X Cops '99
Gold Fingers '01
Hot War '98
Martial Angels '01

Ying, Cherrie
(Ying Choi Ngai, Ying Cai Er)
Dance of a Dream '01
Fulltime Killer '01

Ying-yat, Gam
(Jin Ying Yi)
Dragon Fist '78
Fearless Hyena '79

Yingzi, Pan
Abbot White '82

Yip, Alex
Ninja in the U.S.A. '88

Yip, Amy
(Yip Chi-Mei, Amy Ip)
Erotic Ghost Story '90
Erotic Ghost Story 2 '91
The Inspector Wears Skirts '88
Legend of the Dragon '91
The Magnificent Scoundrels '91
Miracles '89
Robotrix '91
She Shoots Straight '90
Vampire Kids '91

817

Yip, Bobby
(Yip King Sang, Baat Leung Gam, Ba Liang Jin, Bobby Yip King Sang)
The Eternal Evil of Asia '95
F*** / Off '98
God of Cookery '96
God of Gamblers Returns '94
High Risk '95
King of Comedy '99
Lawyer Lawyer '97
Red to Kill '94
The Tricky Master '00

Yip, Cecilia
(Yip Tung, She Tong)
The Avenging Fist '01
Chinese Orthopedist and the Spice Girls '02
Happy Family '02
The Law and the Outlaw '95
Legend of the Dragonslayer Sword '90
Legend of the Dragonslayer Sword 2-The Rising Son '90
Legend of the Dragonslayer Sword 3-The Rage of Gina '90
Organized Crime and Triad Bureau '94
Peace Hotel '95
Swordsman '90
What Time Is It There? '01
Winners and Sinners '83

Yip Chuen Chan
(She Quan Zhen, Yeh Chuan Chen)
Butterfly and Sword '93
One Arm Hero '94
The Prisoner '90
Sam the Iron Bridge: Champion of Martial Arts '93
The Sword Stained with Royal Blood '93
White Lotus Cult '93

Yip Chun
(She Jin)
Bruce Lee: The Man, the Myth '76
Dragon from Russia '90

Yip, Danny
Armour of God '86

Yip, Deanie
(Yip Tak-Han, Deanie Ip, She De Xian, Deannie Yip)
Dragons Forever '88
Fight Back to School 2 '92
Mr. Boo Meets Pom Pom '85

The New Legend of Shaolin '94
The Owl vs. Bombo '84
Pom Pom '84
Pom Pom Strikes Back '86
Twinkle Twinkle Lucky Stars '85

Yip, Frances
It Takes a Thief '01

Yip, Francoise
(Yip Fong Wa, She Fang Hua, Francoise C.J. Yip)
Black Mask '96
Romeo Must Die '00
Rumble in the Bronx '95

Yip, Gloria
(Yip Wan-Yee)
The Cat '91
Miracles '89
The New Marvelous Double '92
The Peacock King '89
Riki-Oh: The Story of Ricky '89
Saga of the Phoenix '90
Savior of the Soul '91

Yip, Grace
(Yip Pooi Man, She Pei Wen, Grace Ip)
Gen-X Cops '99
Headlines '01
Love Paradox '00
A Man Called Hero '99
The Masked Prosecutor '99

Yip Ha-lei
(She Jia Li)
Aces Go Places 2 '83

Yip, Kim
(Yip Kwong-kim, Yip Gong Gim, She Guang Jian)
Armageddon '97
Contract Killer '98
First Option '96

Yip Mau
(She Mau)
The Blazing Temple '76
Chinese Iron Man '75
Triangular Duel '72

Yip, Michelle
Pedicab Driver '89

Yip San
(She Chen)
Iceman Cometh '89
Long Arm of the Law 2 '87
Miracles '89
Red Shield '91

Yip, Stephan
(Yip Tin Hang, She Tian Hang, Yeh Tien Heng, Yip Tin Sing)
Brave Archer '77

The Master of Death '82

Yip, Veronica
(Yip Yuk Hing, She Yu Qing)
Eagle Shooting Heroes '93

Yip, Wilson
(Yip Wai Shun, Yip Wai San, She Wei Shen)
Happy Family '02
Horror Hotline...Big Head Monster '01

Yip Wing-cho
(Ip Wing Cho, Yip Wing Jo, She Rong Zu)
Blonde Fury '89
Don't Give a Damn '95
Heart of Dragon '85
The Killer '89
Legacy of Rage '86
Mr. Boo Meets Pom Pom '85
My Lucky Stars '85
Police Story 2 '88
Pom Pom Strikes Back '86
She Shoots Straight '90
Thunder Kick '73
Twin Dragons '92
Where's Officer Tuba? '86

Yirikian, George
(George V. Yirikian)
Dynamo '78
Return of the Street Fighter '74

Yiu, Claire
(Yiu Ka-Lai, Yu Ga Lei, Yao Jia Ni)
Killer '00

Yiu, Helen
Brave Archer '77

Yiu, Sherming
(Yiu Lok Yi, Yao Le Yi)
Day Off '01
Last Ghost Standing '99
Operation Billionaires '98
Super Car Criminals '99
Troublesome Night 9 '00

Yiu, Siu
(Xiao Yao)
Battle of Shaolin '77
Eagle's Claw '77
Mighty Peking Man '77
Shaolin Traitorous '76

Yo, Kimiko
Hiruko the Goblin '90

Yokoyama, Chisa
Street Fighter 2 '96 (V)

Yokoyama, Rie
Ecstasy of the Angels '72

Yoneyama, Zenkichi
Godzilla vs. Space Godzilla '94

Yong Chol
The Korean Connection '77

Yoo-jung, Choi
Bichunmoo '99

Yoo-jung, Hong
Double Dragon in the Last Duel '85

Yoon Joo-sang
Shiri '99

Yoshida, Kataro
Reborn from Hell: Samurai Armageddon '96

Yoshida, Keiko
Sakuya: Slayer of Demons '00

Yoshida, Mie
Blowback: Love and Death '90

Yoshida, Mizuho
Gamera 2: Advent of Legion '96
Sakuya: Slayer of Demons '00
Zeram '91

Yoshida, Teruo
Body Snatcher from Hell '68

Yoshida, Tsuyoshi
Tokyo Drifter '66

Yoshida, Yoshio
Gamera vs. Zigra '71
King of the Mongols '60
Zatoichi on the Road '63

Yoshihara, Ayumi
Versus '00

Yoshikawa, Towako
Godzilla vs. Space Godzilla '94

Yoshinaga, Minori
Big Boobs Buster '90

Yoshino, Sayaka
After Life '98

Yoshioka, Takeshi
Ultraman Gaia: The Battle in Hyperspace '98

Yoshiyuki, Kazuko
Kikujiro '99

Yoshizawa, Ken
Ecstasy of the Angels '72

Violent Cop '89

Yoshizawa, Yu
Cross Fire '00

You Yong
Crash Landing '00

Young, Gig
Bruce Lee, The Legend '84
Game of Death '78

Young, Harrison
Reptilian '00

Young, Lily
Shaolin Fist of Fury '87

Young, Ric
Dragon: The Bruce Lee Story '93
Kiss of the Dragon '01

Yu, Candy
(Chui On On, Tu An An, Tsui On On, Hu An An, Yu An-An)
Chinese Samson '79
Deadly Snail vs. Kung Fu Killer '77
The Deadly Sword '78
The Legend of the Swordsman '92

Yu Cheng Hui
(Yue Sing Wai)
The Shaolin Temple '79
Shaolin Temple 2: Kids from Shaolin '84
Yellow River Fighter '88

Yu Chien
The Killer Elephants '76

Yu, Dorothy
(Chui Yee Ha, Tu Qi Xia, Yu Yi Ha)
The Imp '81

Yu Hai
(Yue Hoi)
Deadend of Besiegers '92
One Arm Hero '94
Sam the Iron Bridge: Champion of Martial Arts '93
Shaolin Fist of Fury '87
The Shaolin Temple '79
Shaolin Temple 2: Kids from Shaolin '84
Twin Warriors '93
White Lotus Cult '93
Yellow River Fighter '88

Yu Ho-kit
It Takes a Thief '01

Yu Ji-tae
Attack the Gas Station! '99

Yu Jin-bao
The Super Ninja '84

Yu Jun-sang
Tell Me Something '99

Yu Ka-ho
(Chui Ga Ho, Tu Gu Hao, Tsui Ga Ho)
The Avenging Fist '01
Bullets of Love '01
A Man Called Hero '99
My School Mate, the Barbarian '01

Yu Li
(Yue Lee, Yu Liu)
Prison on Fire 2 '91
The Three Swordsmen '94

Yu, Mark
Ninja in the U.S.A. '88

Yu, May
F*** / Off '98

Yu Oh-seong
Attack the Gas Station! '99

Yu, Ronny
The Art of Action: Martial Arts in the Movies '02
Blonde Fury '89

Yu, Shirley
Chinatown Kid '77

Yu Shung-chao
Mask of Death '76

Yu Tien-lung
Snake-Crane Secret '78
Ways of Kung Fu '80

Yu Xiao-ping
The Shaolin One '83

Yu Xiaohui
The Adventures of the Master and His Servant '96

Yu Yung, Henry
(Yue Yeung, Yu Yang, Bruce Lye, Kenny Kung)
The Awaken Punch '73
The Bloody Fists '72
Brave Archer '77
From China with Death '74
Needing You... '00
Shaolin Master Killer '78

Yu Yung, Jenny
Avenging Eagle '78

Yu Yung-yong
Masters of Martial Arts '74

Yuan Quan
A Love of Blueness '00

Yuan, Roger
The Art of Action: Martial Arts in the Movies '02
Once upon a Time in China and America '97

Yue Chun Sin
Ninja in the Deadly Trap '83

Yue Daai Luk
The Holy Robe of Shaolin Temple '84

Yue, Faye
Beijing Rocks '01

Yue Feng
(Ngok Fung, Yueh Feng)
Blazing Temple '76
The 18 Jade Arhats '78
Swordsman with an Umbrella '70

Yue Hang
(Yu Heng)
Drunken Art and Crippled Fist '79
The Shaolin Kids '77

Yue, Raymond
9413 '98

Yue, Sonny
(Sonny Yu)
Raiders of Wu Tang '82

Yue Tau Wan
(Yu Tou Yun, Mu Chao, Chui Tau Wan, Yu His Yen)
Bolo '80
Crazy Crooks '80
Death Mask of the Ninja '82
Dirty Ho '79
Dirty Kung Fu '78
Dreadnaught '81
Duel of the Brave Ones '78
The Fist, the Kicks and the Evils '79
His Name Is Nobody '79
Knockabout '79
My Kung Fu 12 Kicks '79
Pom Pom Strikes Back '86
Project A '83
Shadow of the Tiger '79
Ten Tigers of Shaolin '78
The Victim '80
The Young Master '80

Yueh Hua
(Ngok Wa, Yue Hua, Yo Hua, Ngok Wah, Yuen Hwa, Yao Hwa, Yues Hua)
Filthy Guy '80
The Green Dragon Inn '79
Hong Kong Nocturne '67
The Imp '81
In the Line of Duty 3 '88
Lightning Kung Fu '80
The Massive '78

Monkey Fist Floating Snake '79
99 Cycling Swords '80
Ninja Supremo '81
Rumble in the Bronx '95
The Six Directions of Boxing '79

Yuen, Anita
(Yuen Wing-Yee, Yuan Yong Yi)
Anna Magdalena '98
C'est la Vie, Mon Cheri '93
The Chinese Feast '95
A Chinese Ghost Story: The Tsui Hark Animation '97 (V)
From Beijing with Love '94
He's a Woman, She's a Man '94
Last Hero in China '93
The Sword Stained with Royal Blood '93
A Taste of Killing and Romance '94
Thunderbolt '95

Yuen, Benjamin
(Yuen Wai Ho)
The Avenging Fist '01
Bullets of Love '01
Legend of Speed '99
A Man Called Hero '99

Yuen, Brandy
(Yuen Chun Wei, Yuan Zhen Wei, Yuen Jan Wei) See also sidebar on p. 186.
The Bloody Fists '72
The Buddhist Fist '79
Chinese Hercules '73
Dance of the Drunk Mantis '79
Dreadnaught '81
Drunken Master '78
Jade Claw '79
The Miracle Fighters '82
The Six Directions of Boxing '79
Thunder Kick '73

Yuen Bun
(Yuen Ban, Yuan Bin, Yuen Bing, Yuen Pih, To Chau Kwan)
Avenging Eagle '82
Death Mask of the Ninja '82
Dragon Inn '92
God of Gamblers 2 '90
Gunmen '88
The Longest Nite '98
A Moment of Romance '90
Ninja Supremo '81
The Peacock King '89

Yuen, Che
(Xie Yuan, Hsieh Yuan, Gai Yuen)
The Blazing Temple '76

The 8 Msasters '77
The Hot, the Cool, and the Vicious '76
Invincible Armor '77
Kung Fu, the Invisible Fist '72
The Private Eyes '76
The Shaolin Brothers '77

Yuen Cheung-yan
(Yuan Xiang Ren) See also sidebar on p. 186.
The Buddhist Fist '79
Dragon Inn '92
Dreadnaught '81
Drunken Tai Chi '84
Dynamo '78
Fist of Legend '94
Forbidden City Cop '96
The Invincible Armour '77
The Miracle Fighters '82
Once upon a Time in China '92
Operation Pink Squad '88
Prodigal Boxer '73
The Red Wolf '95
The Six Directions of Boxing '79
Tiger Cage '88
Twin Warriors '93

Yuen Ching Kee
Devil Woman '70

Yuen, Chor
(Choh Yuen, Chu Yuan)
Dummy Mommy, without a Baby '01
Miracles '89
Police Story '85
Police Story 2 '88
The Seventh Curse '86
Thunderbolt '95
Twin Dragons '92

Yuen, Chuen
(Chuan Yuan)
The 18 Jade Arhats '78
Killer Priest '81
Revengeful Swordwomen '79

Yuen, Corey
(Yuen Kwai, Yuen Fui, Yuen Fooi, Yuan Kui, Yuen Kuei, Yuan Feng) See also sidebar on p. 142.
The Art of Action: Martial Arts in the Movies '02
Born Invincible '78
Brutal Boxer '72
The Buddha Assassinator '79
Bury Me High '90
The Chinese Connection '71
Chinese Hercules '73
Dance of the Drunk Mantis '79
Eastern Condors '86

Fist of Fury 1991 '91
From China with Death '74
Heart of Dragon '85
Hit-Man in the Hand of Buddha '80
Iceman Cometh '89
The Invincible Armour '77
The Last Blood '90
The Legend 2 '93
Legend of the Dragon '91
The Millionaires' Express '86
The Most Wanted '94
Pedicab Driver '89
Righting Wrongs '86
Savior of the Soul '91
Savior of the Soul 2 '92
She Shoots Straight '90
The Six Directions of Boxing '79
Thunderbolt '95
We're Going to Eat You! '80
Yes, Madam '85
Zu: Warriors of the Magic Mountain '83

Yuen, David
Champ against Champ '83

Yuen, Fennie
(Yuen Kit-Ying, Yuen Git Ying, Yuan Jie Ying, Fanny Yuen)
Aces Go Places 5: The Terracotta Hit '89
Bullet in the Head '90
Eighth Happiness '88
Happy Family '02
The Legend of the Swordsman '92
One Arm Hero '94
Paramount Motel '00
Pedicab Driver '89
Royal Tramp '92
Royal Tramp 2 '92
Sam the Iron Bridge: Champion of Martial Arts '93
Shanghai 1920 '91
Swordsman '90
Troublesome Night 3 '97
Twin Warriors '93
White Lotus Cult '93

Yuen Jung
China Strike Force '00

Yuen Kam-fai
(Tony Yuen, Yuen Gam Fai, Yuan Jin Hui)
Burning Paradise '94
Once upon a Time in China '91

Yuen, Kitty
United We Stand, and Swim '01

Yuen Miu
(Yuan Wu, Yuen Mo, Yuen Moa, Chow Yuen Miu) See also sidebar on p. 142.
Chinese Hercules '73
Dragons Forever '88
Encounter of the Spooky Kind '81
His Name Is Nobody '79
Knockabout '79
Last Hero in China '93
Leopard Hunting '98
The Magnificent Butcher '79
Millionaire's Express '86
Mr. Vampire '85
Mr. Vampire 2 '86
Odd Couple '79
The Owl vs. Bombo '84
The Prodigal Son '81
Righting Wrongs '86
Rosa '86
Scared Stiff '87
Super Kung Fu Kid '74
The Victim '80
Where's Officer Tuba? '86
Winners and Sinners '83
Zu: Warriors from the Magic Mountain Kid '83

Yuen Po
The Victim '80

Yuen Sam
(Yuan Sen, Yuen Sum, Yuan Wu, Yuen Sun, Yan Shen, Yuan Shen)
Battle of Shaolin '77
Born Invincible '78
The 18 Bronzemen '76
The 18 Bronzemen Part 2 '76
5 Lady Venoms '78
The Invincible Kung Fu Trio '78
Killer from Above '77
The Lost Kung Fu Secrets '80
Moonlight Sword and Jade Lion '79
The Shaolin Brothers '77
The Shaolin Kids '77

Yuen Se Wu
Lady Iron Monkey '83

Yuen, Simon
(Yuen Siu Tin, Yuan Xioa Tian, Yuen Hsiao-Tien, Yuen Shui Tin, Sam the Seed) See also sidebar on p. 186.
Blind Fist of Bruce '79
The Buddhist Fist '79
Dance of the Drunk Mantis '79
Deadly Snail vs. Kung Fu Killer '77

Drunken Art and Crippled Fist '79
Drunken Master '78
Jade Claw '79
Ninja Checkmate '79
Shaolin Master Killer '78
Shaolin Wooden Men '76
The Six Directions of Boxing '79
Snake in the Eagle's Shadow '78
The World of the Drunken Master '79

Yuen, Simpson
Eagle vs. Silver Fox '83

Yuen Siu-yee
(Ruan Xiao Yi)
Everyday Is Valentine '01
For Bad Boys Only '00

Yuen, Stan
Champ against Champ '83
Masters of Tiger Crane '83

Yuen, Sunny
(Yuen Shun-Yi, Yuen San Yee, Yuan Shen Yi, Eagle Yuen, Armstrong Yuen, Yuen Hsun Yi, Ugly Yuen) See also sidebar on p. 186.
The Awaken Punch '73
The Buddhist Fist '79
Chinese Hercules '73
Dance of the Drunk Mantis '79
Dreadnaught '81
Drunken Master '78
Drunken Tai Chi '84
Forbidden City Cop '96
From China with Death '74
In the Line of Duty 4 '89
The Invincible Armour '77
Iron Monkey '93
The Miracle Fighters '82
Once upon a Time in China '91
Prodigal Boxer '73
The Shaolin Drunken Monk '83
Thunder Kick '73
Tiger Cage '88
Tower of Death '81

Yuen Tak
(Yuan De, Yuan Te, Chi-ang Lin, Richard Hung) See also sidebar on p. 142.
Dragon from Russia '90
Fist of Fury 1991 '91
Invincible Pole Fighter '83
Knockabout '79
The Millionaires' Express '86

Pedicab Driver '89
Rivals of the Dragon '83
3 Evil Masters '80

Yuen Tin Wan
Flash Future Kung Fu '83

Yuen Woo-ping
(Yuen Ho Ping, Yuen Wo Ping, Yuan Heping, Yuen Wu Ping) See also sidebar on p. 186.
The Bloody Fists '72
Born Invincible '78
Drunken Master '78
Eastern Condors '86
King of Beggars '92
Tiger Cage '88
Wicked City '92

Yuen Yan Wei
Devil Woman '70

Yuen Yat-chor
(Yuen Yat Choh, Yuen Yen Chu) See also sidebar on p. 186.
The Buddhist Fist '79
Chinese Hercules '73
Drunken Tai Chi '84
In the Line of Duty 4 '89
Long Arm of the Law 2 '87
The Miracle Fighters '82
The Postman Fights Back '82
The Six Directions of Boxing '79

Yuen, Yorky
Gimme Gimme '01

Yugao, Kirara
Guinea Pig: Flower of Flesh and Blood '85
Guinea Pig: The Making of Guinea Pig '86

Yui, Masayaki
(Masayuki Yui)
Akira Kurosawa's Dreams '90
Madadayo '92
Ran '85

Yuk, Cheung Bing
(Zhang Bing Yu, Chang Bing Yue, Chang Ping Yu)
Rage of the Masters '74
A Touch of Zen '69

Yukawa, Tsutomu
Star Force: Fugitive Alien 2 '78/86

Yuki Lai
Merry-Go-Round '01

Yukioka, Keisuke
Gappa: The Triphibian Monster '67

Yulin, Harris
Rush Hour 2 '01

Yum Jung-ah
Tell Me Something '99

Yumeno, Maria
I.K.U. '00

Yun-sang, Baan
(Ban Run Sheng, Baan Ma Chi, Ban Me Tsai)
His Name Is Nobody '79
Last Hurrah for Chivalry '78
Pom Pom Strikes Back '86
Rosa '86

Yune, Johnny
Cannonball Run '81

Yung, Joey
My School Mate, the Barbarian '01

Yung Lu Sam
Real Kung Fu of Shaolin, Part 1 '81

Yung, Peter
(Yung Kam-Cheung, Yueng Kam Cheong, Rong Jin Chang)
City Cop '95
Full Alert '97
Thunderbolt '95

Yung, Wanda
(Wanda Jessica Yung, Yung Wai Tak, Weng Hui De)
Skinny Tiger and Fatty Dragon '90

Yung, Yvonne
(Yung Hung, Weng Hong, Ewong Yueng)
A Chinese Torture Chamber Story '94
Don't Give a Damn '95
The Hero of Swallow '96
Legend of the Drunken Master '94
Nightmare Zone '98
Sex and the Emperor '94
Thunder Cops '98
Tragic Fantasy: Tiger of Wanchai '94

Yusuf, Osman
(Johnny Osman, Yuseph Osman, Johnny Yuseph, Osman Yusef)
Battle in Outer Space '59
King Kong Escapes '67
King Kong vs. Godzilla '62
The Last War '61
Mothra '61
Mothra vs. Godzilla '64
Son of Godzilla '67
The Street Fighter '74

The Street Fighter's Last Revenge '74
What's Up, Tiger Lily? '66

Yut Lai So
The Eye '02

Zaitsu, Ichiro
The Funeral '84

Zao, Timothy
(Siu Chuen Yung, Shao Chuen Yong, Tim Shaw)
Doctor No... '01
A Gambler's Story '01
The Replacement Suspects '01

Zeiring, Ian
Godzilla the Series: Monster War '99 (V)

Zeng, Li Fa
Crouching Tiger, Hidden Dragon '00

Zhang Dongsheng
The Prisoner of Five Boulders '89

Zhang Fengyi
The Assassin '93

Zhang Jibo
The Adventures of the Master and His Servant '96

Zhang, Michelle
Horror Hotline...Big Head Monster '01

Zhang Shuyu
The Cold Mountain Temple '91

Zhang Yongning
Frozen '96

Zhang Zhen
Flyin Dance '01

Zhang Zheng-yuan
The Phantom Lover '95

Zhang Ziyi
(Cheung Ji Yi, Zhang Zi Yi)
Crouching Tiger, Hidden Dragon '00
Dragons of the Orient '88
The Road Home '99
Rush Hour 2 '01
Zu Warriors '01

Zhao Er-kang
Born to Defence '88

Zhao Lei
Succubare '77

Zhao, Vicki
(Zhao Wei, Chiu Mei, Zao Wei)
The Duel '00
Shaolin Soccer '01

Zhao, Vincent
(Zhao Wen-Zhou, Vincent Zhou, Chiu Man Cheuk)
The Blacksheep Affair '98
The Blade '95
Body Weapon '99
The Chinese Feast '95
Fist Power '99
Green Snake '93
The Legend '92

Once upon a Time in China 4 '93

Zhao Yiwei
Beijing Bicycle '01

Zhao Yulian
The Road Home '99

Zhao Zheng
The Phantom Lover '95

Zheng Hao
The Road Home '99

Zhing Jian Wen
Deadend of Besiegers '92

Zhu Mu
(Jue Muk, Chu Muk)
The Private Eyes '76
Young Tiger '72

Zi Lan
(Tza Lan, Chi Lan, Chi Laan)
Screaming Ninja '73
Two Dragons Fight against Tiger '75

Zimmern, Terri
The Manster '60

Zoellner, Arlene
Gamera vs. Zigra '71

Zoellner, Gloria
Gamera vs. Zigra '71

Zushi, Isao
Godzilla vs. MechaGodzilla '74

Zushi, Tonbo
Sonatine '93

Zushi, Yoshitaka
Akira Kurosawa's Dreams '90

Director Index

The Director Index provides a listing for all directors cited in the credits of the movies covered in this book. The names of the directors are listed alphabetically, and their corresponding filmographies are also arranged alphabetically. (Note that only movies covered in this book are listed in the filmographies.) When applicable, one or more pseudonyms are provided (in parentheses) following the directors' names.

Adamson, Al
(Rick Adams, Denver Dixon, Jr., Lyle Felice, Lyle Felisse, George Sheaffer, Albert Victor)
Horror of the Blood Monsters '70

Ah Mon, Lawrence
(Lawrence Lau, Lau Kwok Cheong, Liu Guo Chang, Larry Lau)
Gimme Gimme '01
Lee Rock '91
Spacked Out '00

Akasaka, Koreyoshi
Atomic Rulers of the World '57
Attack from Space '58
Evil Brain from Outer Space '58/59

Akiyama, Katsuhito
Bubblegum Crisis '85

Akiyuki Shimbo
Twilight of the Dark Master '97

Allen, Woody
What's Up, Tiger Lily? '66

Amamiya, Keita
Zeram '91

Amrohi, Kamal
Mahal '48

Anderson, Paul W.S.
Mortal Kombat '95

Andrews, Bryan
Jackie Chan Adventures 1: The Search for the Talismans '00

Jackie Chan Adventures 2: The Dark Hand Returns '00
Jackie Chan Adventures 3: The Shadow of Shendu '00

Ang Lee
Crouching Tiger, Hidden Dragon '00

Aoki, Tetsuro
Devil Hunter Yohko '91

Ashida, Toyoo
(Yutaka Ekoda)
Vampire Hunter D '85

Au, Ulysses
(Au Yeung Jun, Ou Yang Jun, Au Yeung Chun)
Revenge of the Patriots '76
The Shaolin Drunken Monk '83

Baerwitz, Jerry A.
Varan the Unbelievable '58 (U.S.)

Baker, Roy Ward
Legend of the 7 Golden Vampires '74

Banno, Yoshimitsu
Godzilla vs. Hedorah '71

Bapu
Hum Paanch '80

Barron, Steve
Teenage Mutant Ninja Turtles '90

Bartkowiak, Andrej
Romeo Must Die '00

Bau Hok-lai
(Bao Xiao Li, Pao Hsieh Li, H.L. Pao, Bao Hsueh Lee)
Blooded Treasury Fight '79
Inheritor of Kung Fu '77
Iron Monkey 2 '77

Beaudine, William
The Green Hornet '74

Bee, Kenny
100 Ways to Murder Your Wife '86

Bergese, Micha
Shaolin: Wheel of Life '00

Berkeley, Christopher
Godzilla the Series: Monster War '99

Breakston, George P.
The Manster '60

Caldwell, Alan
Godzilla the Series: Monster War '99

Carmen, Rick Del
Jackie Chan Adventures 2: The Dark Hand Returns '00
Jackie Chan Adventures 3: The Shadow of Shendu '00

Carter, John T.
Robo Vampire '88

Cha Chuen-yee
(Cha Chuan Yi)
Fall for You '01

In the Line of Duty 5: Middle Man '90

Chai Yang-Ming
(Choi Yeung Ming, Tsai Yang-Ming, Chai Ying Min)
Chivalrous Legend '98
Prodigal Boxer '73

Chan, Andrew
A Chinese Ghost Story: The Tsui Hark Animation '97

Chan, Benny
(Chan Muk Sing, Chen Mu Sheng)
Big Bullet '96
Fist of Fury '95
Gen-X Cops '99
Gen-Y Cops '00
The Kung Fu Master '94
The Magic Crane '93
Man Wanted '95
A Moment of Romance '90
Who Am I? '98

Chan, Billy
(Chan Wui-Ngai, Chan Kooi Ngai, Chen Hui Ni, Chan Fu Yee)
All Men Are Brothers: Blood of the Leopard '93
Code of Honor '87
The Legend of a Professional '00
New Mr. Vampire '86

Chan Chuen
(Chen Quan, Chen Chuan, Chen Chun)
Fearless Hyena 2 '80

It Takes a Thief '01

Chan, David
Hero's Blood '91

Chan, Frankie
(Chan Fan-Kei, Mandingo)
Operation Condor '91

Chan, Gordon
(Chan Ka-Seung, Chan Ga Seung, Chen Jia Shang)
Armageddon '97
Beast Cops '98
Fight Back to School '91
Fight Back to School 2 '92
First Option '96
Fist of Legend '94
King of Beggars '92
Okinawa Rendez-vous '00
Thunderbolt '95
2000 A.D. '00

Chan Hing-Kar
Brassiere '01

Chan, Jackie
(Chan Kong-Sang, Jacky Chan, Chan Yuen-Lung, Long Cheng, Sing Lung)
See also sidebars on pp. 142, 162, and 596.
Armour of God '86
Crime Story '93
Dragon Lord '82
Fearless Hyena '79
Legend of the Drunken Master '94
Miracles '89
Operation Condor '91
Police Story '85

823

Police Story 2 '88
Project A '83
Project A 2 '87
The Protector '85 (HK)
Who Am I? '98
The Young Master '80

Chan, Peter
(Chan Hoh San, Chen Ke Xin)
Comrades, Almost a Love Story '96
He's a Woman, She's a Man '94

Chan, Phillip
(Chan Yan-Kin, Chen Xin Jian)
Where's Officer Tuba? '86

Chan, Teddy
(Chan Tak Sum)
The Accidental Spy '01
Downtown Torpedoes '97

Chan, Veronica
A Taste of Killing and Romance '94

Chan Wai On
(Chen Wei An)
Temptress of a Thousand Faces '98
Thunder Cops '98

Chang, Aman
(Cheung Man, Zhang Min, Chang Wai-yee)
Body Weapon '99
Cop Shop Babes '01
Fist Power '99

Chang Cheh
(Chang Che, Cheung Chit, Zhang Che, Cheung Kit)
Avenging Warriors of Shaolin '79
Brave Archer '77
Chinatown Kid '77
Chinese Super Ninjas '82
Death Ring '83
Five Deadly Venoms '78
Flag of Iron '80
Kid with the Golden Arm '78
Masked Avengers '81
Nine Demons '83
The Return of the 5 Deadly Venoms '78
Ten Tigers of Kwangtung '79
Venom Warrior '83

Chang Jen-chieh
Iron Neck Li '81

Chang Peng-I
Lone Ninja Warrior '81

Chang Seng-yi
(Cheung San Yee, Chang Hsin Yi, Cheung Xin Yi)

The Incredible Kung Fu Mission '82

Chang Yam Yim
(Cheung Sing Yim)
The Shaolin Temple '79
Shaolin Temple 2: Kids from Shaolin '84

Chang Yoon-hyun
(Cheung Youn-Hyun)
Tell Me Something '99

Chen Chi-hwa
(Chan Che Hwa, Chan Jeung Wa, Chen Zhi Hua, Chen Chi Hua)
Half a Loaf of Kung Fu '77
Lady Iron Monkey '83
Shaolin Wooden Men '76
Snake and Crane Arts of Shaolin '78
The 36 Crazy Fists '77

Chen Hung-man
18 Secrets of Kung Fu '79

Chen Kan-chuan
Swordsman with an Umbrella '70

Chen Kuan-tai
(Chan Goon Tai, Chen Guan Tai, Chen Kwan Tai, Chen Guan Tay, Chan Koon Tai)
The Iron Monkey '77

Chen, Richard
(Cheung Chi Chiu, Zhang Zhi Chao, Chang Chih Chao)
Fighting Ace '79

Chen Shao-Peng
(Chan Siu Pang)
The Magnificent '78

Cheng, Bob
(Cheang Pou-Soi, Jeng Biu Shui, Zheng Bao Rui, Cheng Poi Shui, Soi Cheang)
Horror Hotline Big Head Monster '01

Cheng Chang Ho
(Jeng Cheong Who, Zheng Chang Han)
Five Fingers of Death '72

Cheng Chi Chiu
5 Lady Venoms '78

Cheng, Kent
(Cheng Jak Si, Jeng Jak Si, Zheng Ze Shi)
Dragon in Jail '90

Cheng Siu-keung
White Lotus Cult '93

Cheng, Steve
(Cheng Wai Man, Jeng Wai Man, Zheng Wei Wen)
Bio-Cops '00
Troublesome Night '97
Violent Cop '99

Cheng Wai-man
Fist of Fury '95

Cheng Wing-keung
The Shaolin Disciple '80

Cheung, Alfred
(Cheung Kin-ting, Cheung Gin Ting, Zhang Jian Ting)
All's Well End's Well '97 '97
On the Run '88

Cheung Chi-Sing
U-Man '02

Cheung Chieh
The 18 Jade Arhats '78

Cheung Hoi-Ching
(Cheung Hoi Jing, Zhang Hai Jing)
The Sword Stained with Royal Blood '93

Cheung, Jacob
Midnight Fly '01

Cheung Ji
(Xiang Zi)
Young Tiger '72

Cheung, Joe
(Cheung Chi-leung, Cheung Ji Leung, Zhang Zhi Liang)
Mask of Death '76
Pom Pom '84
Pom Pom and Hot Hot '92
Rosa '86

Cheung Kei, William
(Cheung Kei, Zhang Qi, Chang Chi, Cheung Kay, William Chang Key, William Chang Lee, Cheung Sum)
Death Duel of Kung Fu '79
The Eagle's Killer '81
Ninja vs. Shaolin Guards '84

Cheung, Mabel
(Cheung Yuen Ting, Zhang Wan Ting)
Beijing Rocks '01

Cheung Siu Wal
Deadend of Besiegers '92

Cheung Yam Yim
(Zhang Xin Yan, Chang Hsin Yen)
Yellow River Fighter '88

Chi, Joseph
Tragic Fantasy: Tiger of Wanchai '94

Chin, Andy
(Chin Wing Keung)
Dragon Chronicles: Maidens of Heavenly Mountain '94
The Lord of Hangzhou '98

Chin Man-kei
(Qian Wen Qi)
The Eternal Evil of Asia '95

Chin, Wellson
(Chin Sing Wai, Qian Sheng Wei)
The Inspector Wears Skirts '88
Prince of the Sun '90

Ching Siu-Tung
(Cheng Xiaodong, Tony Ching)
A Chinese Ghost Story '87
A Chinese Ghost Story 2 '90
A Chinese Ghost Story 3 '91
Conman in Tokyo '00
Duel to the Death '82
The East Is Red '93
Executioners '93
The Legend of the Swordsman '92
Swordsman '90
The Witch from Nepal '85
Wonder Seven '94

Chiu Chan-keung
(Chiu Jun Keung, Zhao Zhen Jiang)
Model from Hell '99

Chiu, Derek
(Chiu Sung Kei, Chiu Shung Gei, Zhao Chong Ji)
Comeuppance '00
Love au Zen '01

Chiu Liu Kong
(Zhao Lu Jiang, Cho Lo Kong)
Iron Monkey 2 '96

Cho Chung-sing
(Joh Chung Sing, Zuo Song Sheng)
Fist of Fury 1991 '91

Chong Gon Jo
Pulgasari '85

Chow, Cindy
(Chow Fung)
Lethal Panther 2 '93

Chow Jan-wing
Chinese Orthopedist and the Spice Girls '02

Chow, Matt
United We Stand, and Swim '01

Chow, Stephen
(Chow Sing-chi, Zhou Xing Chi, Stephen Chiau, Stephen Chau)
See also sidebar on p. 258.
Forbidden City Cop '96
From Beijing with Love '94
God of Cookery '96
King of Comedy '99
Shaolin Soccer '01

Chow, Thomas
Merry-Go-Round '01

Choy Tak
Chinese Hercules '73

Chu Ka Liang
Hunted by Royal Decree '00
Rebels under Siege '00

Chu Yen-ping
(Jue Yin Ping, Zhu Yan Ping, Lawrence Full)
Fantasy Mission Force '84
The Prisoner '90

Chui Chang-wang
(Xu Zeng Hong, Hsu Tseng Hung, Sui Jang Hung)
Thousand Mile Escort '76

Chui Hon-cheung
(Tu Han Xiang, Yu Hon Sang)
The Master of Death '82

Chui Pak-lam
(Xu Bo Lin, Tsui Pak Lam)
Crystal Hunt '91

Chung, Billy
(Chung Siu Hung, Zhong Shao Xiong)
The Assassin '93
The Cheaters '01
Killer '00
Last Ghost Standing '99
My School Mate, the Barbarian '01
Paramount Motel '00
Trust Me U Die '99
Undercover Blues '00

Chung, David
(Chung Chi Man)
I Love Maria '88
Magnificent Warriors '87
Royal Warriors '86

Chung Ji-woo
Happy End '99

Chung Yee
The Shaolin One '83

Clarke, Keith
The Art of Action: Martial Arts in the Movies '02

Clouse, Robert
The Big Brawl '80
Enter the Dragon '73
Game of Death '78

Cohen, Rob
Dragon: The Bruce Lee Story '93

Crane, Kenneth G.
Half Human '55 (U.S.)
The Manster '60

de Leon, Gerardo
(Gerry de Leon)
The Blood Drinkers '64
Brides of Blood '68
Curse of the Vampires '70
Mad Doctor of Blood Island '68
Terror Is a Man '59
The Walls of Hell '64

Del Toro, Guillermo
Blade 2 '02

Dezaki, Osamu
Black Jack '96

Dhanoa, Guddu
Elaan '94

Dik Sang
A Chinese Torture Chamber Story 2 '98

Do Gong-yue
8 Diagram Fighter '91

Donovan, Kevin
The Tuxedo '02

Fai Samang
(Fai Sam Ang)
Snaker '01

Fok, Clarence
(Clarence Ford, Foh Yiu Leung, Huo Yao Liang)
Century of the Dragon '99
Cheap Killers '98
Dragon from Russia '90
Her Name Is Cat '98
Iceman Cometh '89
Martial Angels '01
Naked Killer '92
Thunder Cop '96

Fong, Eddie
The Private Eye Blues '94

Fong Lung-seung
The Awaken Punch '73

Fong Yeh
(Fong Yau, Fang Ye, Fang Yeh)

10 Magnificent Killers '77

Foster, Norman
The Green Hornet '74

Fujiwara, Kei
Organ '96

Fukasaku, Kinji
Battle Royale '00
Legend of the Eight Samurai '84
Message from Space '78
Sure Death: Revenge '87

Fukazawa Kiyosumi
Star Force: Fugitive Alien 2 '78/86
Time of the Apes '75

Fukuda, Jun
Ebirah, Horror of the Deep '66
Godzilla vs. Gigan '72
Godzilla vs. MechaGodzilla '74
Godzilla vs. Megalon '73
The Secret of the Telegian '60
Son of Godzilla '67

Fukushima Hiroyuki
Gatchaman '94

Fung Pak-yung
Sam the Iron Bridge: Champion of Martial Arts '93

Fuqua, Antoine
The Replacement Killers '97

Gam Gwok-chiu
Flyin Dance '01

Gam Sing-yan
(Jin Sheng En, Cheng Sheng En)
Two Dragons Fight against Tiger '75

Gering, Marion
Violated Paradise '63

Goda, Hiroaki
Bubblegum Crisis '85

Goto, Daisuke
(Daisuke Gotoh)
Zero Woman: The Accused '96

Goto, Shuji
BloodFight '89

Grapek, Jim
The Secrets of the Warrior's Power '97

Ha, Kenny
(Ha Sau Hin, Jia Xiu Xuan)
Dragon from Shaolin '96

Hai Chung-man
Anna Magdalena '98

Hallenbeck, Darrel
The Green Hornet '74

Harada, Masato
Gunhed '89

Haraguchi Tomoo
Sakuya: Slayer of Demons '00

Hasebe, Yasukaru
(Takashi Fuji)
Black Tight Killers '66

Hashimoto Koji
Godzilla 1985 '84

Hata Masanori
The Adventures of Milo and Otis '86

Hau Chang
(Hou Zheng, Ho Chang, Hou Cheng, Hour Jeng)
Lady Whirlwind and the Rangers '74
Lady Wu Tang '77
The Shaolin Invincibles '79

Hayashi Hiroki
Bubblegum Crisis '85

Heung, Leo
Headlines '01

Heung Ling
Deadly Snail vs. Kung Fu Killer '77

Hideshi Hino
Guinea Pig: Flower of Flesh and Blood '85
Guinea Pig: Mermaid in a Manhole '88

Higuchinsky
Spiral '00

Hiroki, Ryuichi
(Go Ijuin)
Sadistic City '93

Hirota, Mikio
Terminatrix '95

Ho, Godfrey
(Hoh Jeung Keung, He Zhi Jiang, Ho Chi-keung, Godfrey Hall, Zhi Jiang He, Benny Ho, Ho Chi-Mou, Ho Chun-Sing, Charles Lee, Fong Shi-hou, Fang Hao, Fung Ho, Fong Ho, Fung How, Alton Cheung, Cheung Nick, Tomas Tang, Richard Philips, Mark Coston, Daniel Wells, Mick Stuard, Bob Poe, Ken Ashley, Carmen Heller, Bert Brooks, Edgar Jere, Victor

Sears, Bruce Lambert, Ted King, Burt Petersen) See also sidebar on p. 522.
Champ against Champ '83
The Deadly Sword '78
Dragon on Fire '79
Duel of the Tao Tough '82
Eagle vs. Silver Fox '83
Fury in Shaolin Temple '82
Golden Dragon Silver Snake '79
Invincible Obsessed Fighter '82
Lethal Panther '91
Magnificent Natural Fist '80
Masters of Tiger Crane '83
Ninja vs. Ninja '87
Rage of the Dragon '79
Raiders of Wu Tang '82
Robo Vampire '88
Scorpion Thunderbolt '85
The Snake Strikes Back '81
Thunder Ninja Kids: The Hunt for the Devil Boxer '86/94

Ho, Leonard
Bruce Lee, The Legend '84

Ho Meng-Hua
(Hoh Mung Wa, He Meng Hua, Ho Meng-Hwa)
The Flying Guillotine '74
Mighty Peking Man '77
Revenge of the Zombies '76

Honda, Ishiro
(Inoshiro Honda)
Akira Kurosawa's Dreams '90
All Monsters Attack '70
Attack of the Mushroom People '63
Battle in Outer Space '59
Dagora the Space Monster '64
Destroy All Monsters '68
Frankenstein vs. Baragon '65
Ghidorah the Three-Headed Monster '64
Godzilla, King of the Monsters '54
The H-Man '58
Half Human '55/1957
The Human Vapor '60
Invasion of Astro-Monster '65
King Kong Escapes '67

King Kong vs. Godzilla '62
Mothra '61
Mothra vs. Godzilla '64
The Mysterians '57
Rodan '56
Terror of MechaGodzilla '75
Varan the Unbelievable '58
War of the Gargantuas '66
Yog: Monster from Space '70

Hosoyama, Tomoaki
Weather Woman '95

Howard, Sandy
Giant Monster Gamera '65 (U.S.)

Hsu, Sherman
(Chui Dai Chuen, Xu Da Chuen)
Fists Like Lee '74

Hsu, Talun
Fatal Blade '00

Hsu, Tyrone
(Chui Tin Wing, Xu Tian Rong, Chu Tien Yun)
99 Cycling Swords '80
The Six Directions of Boxing '79

Huang Ha
(Wong Guong, Wong Gwong, Huang Ha, Wang Hai, Wang Ha, Wong Ha, Yang Wa)
Breakout from Oppression '78
The Descendant of Wing Chun '78

Hui, Ann
(Hui On-Wah, Hui Ngon Wa, Hu An Hua)
Swordsman '90
Visible Secret '01

Hui Keung
(Hu Jiang)
Emperor of Shaolin Kung Fu '80

Hui Mei Kwan
990714.com '00

Hui, Michael
(Hui Koon Man, Hui Goon Man, Hu Guan Wen)
The Private Eyes '76

Hung, Sammo
(Hung Kam-Bo, Hong Chin-pao, Hong Jinbao, James Hung, Hung Kam-po, Samo Hung, Yuanlong Zhu, Yuen Chu) See also sidebars on p. 142, 182, and 492.
Don't Give a Damn '95
Dragons Forever '88

Eastern Condors '86
Encounter of the Spooky Kind '81
Enter the Fat Dragon '78
Heart of Dragon '85
Knockabout '79
Lord of the Wu Tang '93
The Millionaires' Express '86
The Moon Warriors '92
Mr. Nice Guy '97
My Lucky Stars '85
Once upon a Time in China and America '97
The Owl vs. Bombo '84
Pedicab Driver '89
The Prodigal Son '81
Twinkle Twinkle Lucky Stars '85
The Victim '80
Wheels on Meals '84
Winners and Sinners '83

Huo Jianqi
A Love of Blueness '00

Hwa Yi Hung
(Wa Yat Wang, Hua Yi Hong, Hua I-Jung, Hua I Hung)
Dynamo '78
Jade Claw '79
Kung Fu Zombie '81

Hwang Jang Lee
(Whong Cheng-Li, Wang Chang-Li, Huang Cheng-Li, Wong Cheng-Li, Wang Chang-Li, Wang Ching-Li, Wang Cheng Li, Wong Jing Lei, Huang Zheng Li, Wong Ching Lee)
Hit-Man in the Hand of Buddha '80

Iida, Joji
(George Iida)
Another Heaven '00

Iida, Tsutomu
Devil Man '87

Ikeda, Toshiharu
Beautiful Beast '95
Evil Dead Trap '88

Ikehiro, Kazuo
Zatoichi and the Chest of Gold '64
Zatoichi's Flashing Sword '64

Imamura, Shohei
The Eel '97
Warm Water under a Red Bridge '01

Inagaki, Hiroshi
Chushingura '62
Samurai 1: Musashi Miyamoto '54

Samurai 2: Duel at Ichijoji Temple '55
Samurai 3: Duel at Ganryu Island '56

Inoue, Akira
Zatoichi's Revenge '64

Inoue, Yoshio
The Razor 3: Who's Got the Gold? '74

Ishiguro, Noboru
Astro Boy '80

Ishii, Katsuhito
Shark Skin Man and Peach Hip Girl '98

Ishii, Takashi
Freeze Me '00
Gonin '95

Ishii, Teruo
Atomic Rulers of the World '57
Attack from Space '58
Evil Brain from Outer Space '58/59
The Executioner '74
Invaders from Space '58
The Street Fighter's Last Revenge '74

Ishiyama, Akinobu
Sugar-Howling of Angel '96

Itami, Juzo
The Funeral '84
Tampopo '87

Itano, Ichiro
Violence Jack '88

Ito, Shunya
Female Convict Scorpion: Jailhouse 41 '72

Jang Sun-woo
Lies '99

Jenkins, Gloria
Jackie Chan Adventures 3: The Shadow of Shendu '00

Jin Tao
Her Majesty Is Fine '96

Jo Jin-gyu
My Wife Is a Gangster '01

Kadokawa, Haruki
Legend of the Eight Samurai '84

Kam, Andrew
(Kam Yeung Wa, Gam Yeung Wah, Jin Yang Hua)
The Big Heat '88
Swordsman '90

Kam Bo
Blind Fist of Bruce '79

Kam Lung
(Kim Lung, Jian Long)
Filthy Guy '80
Screaming Ninja '73

Kamijo Osamu
Violence Jack '88

Kanaya Minoru
Fugitive Alien '78/1986
Star Force: Fugitive Alien 2 '78/86

Kaneko, Shusuke
(Shu Keneko)
Cross Fire '00
Gamera 2: Advent of Legion '96
Gamera 3: The Revenge of Irys '99
Gamera, Guardian of the Universe '95
Godzilla, Mothra and King Ghidorah: Battle on Fire '01

Kang Je-gyu
Shiri '99

Kao Pao Shu
(Go Bo Shu, Gao Bao Shu)
Battle of Shaolin '77
Blood of the Dragon '71

Kar Kar
(Ga Ga, Jia Jia)
Hong Kong X-File '98

Katayama, Kazuyoshi
Appleseed '88

Kato, Yasushi
(Tai Kato)
King of the Mongols '60

Kawajiri, Yoshiaki
Ninja Scroll '93
Vampire Hunter D: Bloodlust '01
Wicked City '87

Kim Dong-bin
Ring Virus '99

Kim Gi-hun
Record '00

Kim In-soo
Bloody Beach '00

Kim Ji-woon
The Foul King '00

Kim Jong-seok
Record '00

Kim Ki-duk
Yongary, Monster from the Deep '67

Kim Sang-jin
Attack the Gas Station! '99

Kim See-hyun
Masters of Martial Arts '74

Kim Tae-gyun
Volcano High School '01

Kim Tae-yong
Memento Mori '99

Kim Young-jun
Bichunmoo '99

King Hu
(Woo Gam Chuen, Hu Jin Quan)
Legend of the Mountain '79
Painted Skin '92
Swordsman '90
A Touch of Zen '69

Kitakubo, Hiroyuki
Black Magic M-66 '87
Blood: The Last Vampire '00
Roujin Z '91

Kitamura, Ryuhei
Versus '00

Kitano, Takeshi
("Beat" Takeshi)
Boiling Point '90
Brother '00
Fireworks '97
Kikujiro '99
Sonatine '93
Violent Cop '89

Ko, Blackie
(Ko Shou-Liang, Blacky Ko)
Curry & Pepper '90

Ko, Clifton
(Ko Chi-sum, Go Chi Sam, Gao Zhi Sen)
All's Well End's Well '92
Love Paradox '00

Ko, Phillip
(Ko Fei, Ko Fai, Philip Koa, Gan Fei, Phillip Ku)
Angel on Fire '95
Guardian Angel '96
Killer's Romance '90
Millennium Dragon '99

Ko Saio Pao
7 Commandments of Kung Fu '79

Ko Yeung
Real Kung Fu of Shaolin, Part 1 '81

Kobayashi, Koichi
Tokyo Decameron: Three Tales of Madness and Sensuality '96

Kobayashi, Masaki
Kwaidan '64

Kodaira, Yutaka
Dragon Princess '81

Kodama, Kenji
City Hunter: Secret Service '96

Kohira, Yutaka
Taboo '97

Koji Shima
Warning from Space '56

Kok, Vincent
(Kok Tak-Chiu, De Zhou Gu)
Forbidden City Cop '96
Gorgeous '99
Marry a Rich Man '02

Komizu, Kazuo
(Gaira)
Entrails of the Virgin '86

Konaku, Kazuya
The Dimension Travelers '98
Ultraman Gaia: The Battle in Hyperspace '98
Ultraman Tiga and Ultraman Dyna: The Warriors of the Lightning Star '98

Kong, Joseph
(Kuo Nan-hong, Gwok Naam Wang, Guo Nan Hong, Joseph Poon, Jiang Bin Han)
Kung Fu's Hero '73

Konuma, Masaru
Beautiful Hunter '94

Koreeda, Hirokazu
After Life '98
Maborosi '95

Kumar Padam
Champion '00

Kuo, Joseph
(Kuo Nan-hong, Gwok Naam Wang, Guo Nan Hong, Joseph Poon, Jiang Bin Han)
The Blazing Temple '76
Born Invincible '78
Chinese Iron Man '75
Dragon's Claws '79
The 8 Masters '77
The 18 Bronzemen '76
The 18 Bronzemen Part 2 '76
Ninja Checkmate '79
The Shaolin Brothers '77
The Shaolin Kids '77
The Smart Cavalier '78
Sorrowful to a Ghost '70
The 36 Deadly Styles '79
Triangular Duel '72
The Unbeaten 28 '80
The World of the Drunken Master '79

Kuramoto, Kazuhito
Guinea Pig: Android of
Notre Dame '88

Kurata Junji
Legend of the
Dinosaurs '77

Kurosawa, Akira
*See also sidebar on p.
616.*
Akira Kurosawa's
Dreams '90
Dersu Uzala '74
The Hidden Fortress
'58
High and Low '63
Madadayo '92
Men Who Tread on the
Tiger's Tail '43
Ran '85
Rashomon '50
Sanjuro '63
Sanshiro Sugata '43
Seven Samurai '54
Stray Dog '49
Throne of Blood '57
Yojimbo '61

Kurosawa, Kiyoshi
Cure '97
Pulse '01

Kuzakawa, Kiyosumi
Fugitive Alien
'78/1986

Kuzumi, Masayuki
Guinea Pig: He Never
Dies '86

Kwai Chih-hung
*(Gwai Chi Hung, Gui Zhi
Hong, Kuei Chih Hung)*
Killer Snakes '74
Lightning Kung Fu '80

Kwak Jae-yong
My Sassy Girl '01

Kwan San
*(Guan Shan, Gwaan
Saan)*
Brutal Boxer '72

Kwok, Phillip
*(Gwok Jan Fung, Guo
Zhen Feng, Kuo Chui)*
Ninja in the Deadly Trap
'83

Kwong, Abe
*(Kwong Man Wai,
Kuang Wen Wei)*
F*** / Off '98

Kwong Kam Wang
990714.com '00

Lai, Carol
Glass Tears '01

Lai, David
(Lai Dai Wai)
Savior of the Soul '91
Savior of the Soul 2
'92

Lai, Ivan
*(Lai Kai Ming, Lai Gai
Ming, Li Ji Ming)*
Daughter of Darkness
'93
God.com '98
Troublesome Night 9
'00

Lai, Joseph
Rivals of the Dragon
'83
Snake Fist Dynamo '84

Lam, Ailun
*(Lam Wai Lun, Lin Wei
Lun, Ah Lun)*
The Blacksheep Affair
'98

Lam, Bosco
(Lam Hing-Lung)
A Chinese Torture
Chamber Story '94
H.K. Adams Family '92
House of the Damned
'99
Legend of the Flying
Swordsman '00
Wishful Milenio '01

Lam Chin-wai
Faces of Horror '98
Leopard Hunting '98

Lam, Dante
*(Lam Chiu Yin, Lin
Chao Xian)*
Beast Cops '98
Hit Team '00
Jiang Hu-"The Triad
Zone" '00
Option Zero '97
Runaway '01
Tiramisu '02

Lam, David
*(Lam Tak Luk, Lin De
Lu)*
Powerful Four '91

Lam Fook-dei
(Lin Fu Di, Lin Fu-ti)
Killer Priest '81

Lam, New Kwong
Moonlight Sword and
Jade Lion '79

Lam, Ringo
*(Lam Ling-Tung, Ling-
dong Lin)*
Aces Go Places 4 '86
The Adventurers '95
Burning Paradise '94
City on Fire '87
Full Alert '97
Full Contact '92
Prison on Fire '87
Prison on Fire 2 '91
The Suspect '98
Twin Dragons '92
Victim '99

Lau, Andrew
*(Lau Wai-Keung, Liu Wei
Jiang)*
The Avenging Fist '01
The Best of the Best
'96
Bullets of Love '01
Dance of a Dream '01
The Duel '00
Legend of Speed '99
A Man Called Hero '99
The Storm Riders '98
The Wesley's Mysteri-
ous File '01
Young and Dangerous
'96
Young and Dangerous
5 '98
Young and Dangerous
6: Born to Be King
'00

Lau, Anthony
Dragon Killer '95

Lau, Bowie
The Deadly Camp '99

Lau, Daniel
The Legend of Bruce
Lee '80

Lau, David
Crime of a Beast '01

Lau, Jeff
*(Lau Chun-wai, Lau Jan
Wai, Liu Zhen Wei, Jef-
frey Lau)*
A Chinese Odyssey Part
1: Pandora's Box
'95
A Chinese Odyssey Part
2: Cinderella '95
Eagle Shooting Heroes
'93
The Haunted Cop Shop
'87
Operation Pink Squad
'88
Second Time Around
'02

Lau Kar-Leung
*(Liu Chia-Liang, Kung
Fu Leung, Atachia Liang
Liu) See also sidebar
on p. 278.*
Aces Go Places 5: The
Terracotta Hit '89
Dirty Ho '79
Drunken Master Killer
'94
Executioners from
Shaolin '77
Invincible Pole Fighter
'83
Legend of the Drunken
Master '94
Legendary Weapons of
China '82
Return of the Master
Killer '80
Shaolin Mantis '78
Shaolin Master Killer
'78
Tiger on Beat '88

Lau Kar-Wing
*(Lau Ga Wing, Liu Gu
Rong, Bruce Lau, Liu
Chia Yung, Liu Chia
Jen, Liu Chia Rong) See
also sidebar on p. 278.*
Dirty Kung Fu '78
The Dragon Family '88
Fists and Guts '79
He Has Nothing But
Kung Fu '77
Odd Couple '79
Scared Stiff '86
Skinny Tiger and Fatty
Dragon '90
Warrior from Shaolin
'81

Lau, Ricky
*(Lau Koon Wai, Liu
Guanwei, Eric Lau)*
Mr. Vampire '85
Mr. Vampire 2 '86
Mr. Vampire Saga 4 '88
Super Car Criminals
'99
Where's Officer Tuba?
'86

Lau See-yu
Saga of the Phoenix
'90

Law, Alex
*(Law Kai Yui, Luo Qi
Rui)*
Painted Faces '88

Law, Bruce
*(Law Lai-yin, Luo Li
Xian)*
Extreme Crisis '98

Law Chi-leung
*(Luo Zhi Liang, Lo Chi
Leung)*
Double Tap '00
Inner Senses '01

Law, Joe
*(Law Chi, Luo Chi, Lo
Chie, Lo Chi)*
Crippled Masters '80
The Invincible Kung Fu
Trio '78
Killer from Above '77
The Lost Kung Fu
Secrets '80
Monkey Fist Floating
Snake '79

Law Kei
*(Luo Qi, Law Chi, Law
Kee)*
The End of the Wicked
Tiger '81

Law Ma
(Lo Mar)
Five Superfighters '78

Law, Norman
Legend of the Dragon-
slayer Sword '90
Legend of the Dragon-
slayer Sword 3-The
Rage of Gina '90

Law, Rocky
Dragons of the Orient
'88

Law Wing-cheong
*(Law Wing Cheong, Lam
Wing-cheong, Luo Yong
Chang)*
Running out of Time 2
'01

Le, Bruce
*(Lui Siu Lung, Lu Xiao
Long, Huang Kin Lung,
Wong Kum Hung, Bruce
K.L. Lea, Jun Chong)*
The Legend of Bruce
Lee '80
Shaolin Fist of Fury '87

Leder, Paul
A*P*E '76

Lee, Bruce
*(Little Dragon Lee, Lee
Siu-Lung, Li Xiaolong)
See also sidebars on
pp. 72, 182, 214, and
224.*
Bruce Lee: A Warrior's
Journey '00
Game of Death '78
Return of the Dragon
'72

Lee Chiu
(Lee Chuen, Lei Chiu)
Cantonen Iron Kung Fu
'79
Fearless Dragons '79
Martial Arts Master
Wong Fei Hung '92
Ninja Supremo '81
Ways of Kung Fu '80

Lee, Chris
*(Lee Kin Sang, Lee Gin
Sang, Li Jian Sheng)*
Queen's High '91

Lee Chuen Chun
Shaolin vs. Manchu '80

Lee, Daniel
*(Lee Yan Gong, Li Ren
Gang)*
Black Mask '96
A Fighter's Blues '00
Moonlight Express '99

Lee, Danny
*(Lee Sau-Yin, Li Xiu
Xian, Li Hsiu Hsien)*
Dr. Lamb '92
Legend of the Dragon
'91
The Untold Story '92

Lee, Dick
Take 2 in Life '01

Lee Koon-chung
Bruce Lee We Miss You
'76

Lee Kyoung-young
Gate of Destiny '96

Lee Lik-Chi
(Li Li Chi, Lee Lik Chee)
Flirting Scholar '93
From Beijing with Love
'94
God of Cookery '96
King of Comedy '99
Love on Delivery '94
The Magnificent
Scoundrels '91

Lee Myung-se
Nowhere to Hide '99

Lee Pak-ling
(Li Bo Ling)
Vampire Kids '91

Lee, Raymond
((Lee Wai Man, Li Hui
Min)
Dragon Inn '92
The East Is Red '93

Lee Tso Nam
(Lee Chok Laam, Li Zuo
Nan, To Lo Po, Lee Jua
Nan, Tu Lu Po, Lii Tzvoh
Nan, Do Liu Boh)
Beauty Investigator '92
Challenge of Death '78
Eagle's Claw '77
Exit the Dragon, Enter
the Tiger '75
Fatal Needles vs. Fatal
Fists '80
The Fist, the Kicks and
the Evils '79
The Hot, the Cool, and
the Vicious '76
The Leg Fighters '80
A Life of Ninja '83
My Kung Fu 12 Kicks
'79
Shaolin vs. Lama '81

Lee Yuk-chun
Nightmare Zone '98

Lenzi, Umberto
Bruce Lee Fights Back
from the Grave '76

**Leung Hung-wah,
Tony**
(Leung Hung Wa, Liang
Hong Hua)
Sound from the Dark
'00
Vampire Controller '00
A Wicked Ghost '99

Leung, Kant
(Leung Wang Fat, Liang
Hing Fa)
The Demon's Baby '98
Ultimatum '01

Leung Kar-yan
(Leung Kar Yan, Liang
Jairen, Brian Leung)
Cold War '00

Leung, Lionel
Dragon against Vam-
pire '85

Leung, Patrick
(Leung Pak-kin, Leung
Pak Gin, Liang Bo Jian)
Beyond Hypothermia
'96
Born Wild '01
Brassiere '01
Task Force '97

Leung Po-chi
(Liang Pu Zhi)
Shanghai 1920 '91

Leung, Raymond
Angel '87
Day Off '01

Leung, Sam
Color of Pain '02

Leung Siu-hung, Tony
(Leung Siu Hung, Liang
Xiao Xiong, Hsiung
Kuang, Alex Leung Siu
Hung)
Satin Steel '94

Leung Yun-chuen
Fist of Fury '95

Li, Bruce
(Ho Chung Tao, Lee
Shao-Lung, Lei Hsiao-
Lung, Lee Roy Lung, Ho
Tsung Tao, James Ho)
Fists of Bruce Lee '78

Li Chia Chi
Militant Eagle '78

Li, Jet
(Li Lian-Jie, Jet Lee)
See also sidebar on p.
564.
Born to Defence '88

Liang Shen
The Invincible Killer '79

Liao, Karl
Dreaming Fists with
Slender Hands '80
The Story in Temple
Red Lily '79

Lin Bin
(Lin Bing, Lin Pin)
The New Game of
Death '75
The 72 Desperate
Rebels '76

Lin, David
War of the Shaolin Tem-
ple '80

Ling Yun
The Last Duel '82

Little, John
Bruce Lee: A Warrior's
Journey '00

Liu Kim-wah
(Liu Kim Wa, Lao Jian
Hua, Lo Kim-wah, K.W.
Lo, Liu Kim Wa, Lao
Jian Hua)

The Irresistible Piggies
'02
Sunshine Cops '99

Liu, Sam
Godzilla the Series:
Monster War '99

Liu, Tony
(Liu Jun Guk, Lu Jun
Gu, Lu Chin Ku, Lo
Chun Guk, Tony Lo, Lu
Chun-ku, Tommy Loo
Chun, Loo Chun Kok,
Anthony Lau)
The Big Sting '82
3 Evil Masters '80
Tiger over Wall '80

Liu Yueh-lin
Dragon Lee vs. the Five
Brothers '78

Lo, Alan
(Law Shun Chuen, Luo
Shun Quan)
Her Name Is Cat 2:
Journey to Death
'01

Lo Kim-wah
Shadow '01

Lo Lieh
(Law Lit, Luo Lie)
Fists of the White
Lotus '80

Lo, Steven
(Lo Kit Sing, Lo Git
Sing, Luo Jie Cheng)
Bakery Amour '01
Tragic Fantasy: Tiger of
Wanchai '94

Lo Wei
(Law Wai, Luo Wei)
The Chinese Connec-
tion '71
Dragon Fist '78
Fearless Hyena 2 '80
Fists of Fury '71
The Killer Meteors '76
New Fist of Fury '76
Spiritual Kung Fu '78
To Kill with Intrigue '77

London, Jerry
Shogun '80

Low, Adam
Great Performances:
Kurosawa '02

Lu Feng
(Luk Fung, Centipede
Venom)
Death Ring '83

Lui, Raymond
(Lui Shing Gung, Lei
Cheng Gong)
Fatal Flying Guillotine
'77
Hard as a Dragon '80

Luk, Jamie
(Luk Ken-Ming, Luk Kim
Ming)

Doctor Vampire '90
Robotrix '91

Lung Shiu-kee
Fist of Fury '95

Ma, Jingle
(Ma Choh Sing, Ma Chu
Cheng)
Goodbye Mr. Cool '01
Hot War '98
Para Para Sakura '01
Tokyo Raiders '00

Ma, Joe
(Ma Wai Ho, Ma Wei
Hao)
Dummy Mommy, with-
out a Baby '01
Fighting for Love '01
Funeral March '01
Lawyer Lawyer '97

Mak, Alan
Final Romance '01
A War Named Desire
'00

Mak, Johnny
(Mak Tong-Hung, Mak
Dong Hung, Mai Dang
Xiong)
Long Arm of the Law
'84

Mak Kai-gwong
(Mai Qi Guang, Mak
Kwoi Gwong, Albert
Mak)
Doctor No... '01
Dummy Mommy, with-
out a Baby '01

Mak, Marco
(Mak Chi-Sin)
The Blood Rules '00
Cop on a Mission '01
A Gambler's Story '01
Love Correction '00
The Replacement Sus-
pects '01

Mak, Michael
(Mak Dong Git, Mai
Dang Jie)
Butterfly and Sword '93
Long Arm of the Law 2
'87

Mak, Peter
Wicked City '92

Maka, Karl
(Kais Mak, Jia Mai, Carl
Mak, Mak Ka)
Crazy Crooks '80
Dirty Tiger, Crazy Frog
'78
His Name Is Nobody
'79
Shaolin King Boxer '79

Mallinson, Matthew
Fist of Fear-Touch of
Death '80

Man Man
The Shaolin Disciple
'80

Man Wah
Killer of Snake, Fox of
Shaolin '78

Mang Hoi
(Meng Hoi, Hoi Man,
Randy Mang)
Blonde Fury '89

Markovic, Jim
The Real Bruce Lee '79

Masami Oobari
Bubblegum Crisis '85

Masamura, Yasuzo
Blind Beast '69
Giants and Toys '58
The Razor 2: The Snare
'73

Matsubayashi, Shuei
The Last War '61

Mehra, Rajiv
Aakhri Adalat '88

Miike, Takashi
Audition '99
The Happiness of the
Katakuris '01
Ichi the Killer '01

Min Kyu-dong
Memento Mori '99

Misumi, Kenji
Blind Swordsman: The
Tale of Zatoichi '62
Fight, Zatoichi, Fight!
'64
Lone Wolf and Cub 1:
Sword of
Vengeance '72
Lone Wolf and Cub 2:
Baby Cart at the
River Styx '72
Lone Wolf and Cub 3:
Baby Cart to Hades
'72
Lone Wolf and Cub 5:
Baby Cart in the
Land of Demons
'73
The Razor 1: Sword of
Justice '72
Samaritan Zatoichi '68
Shogun Assassin '80
Wrath of Daimajin '66
Zatoichi Challenged
'67
Zatoichi and the Chess
Expert '65

Mitsuta Kazuho
Mighty Jack '68

Mitsuwa, Akira
Atomic Rulers of the
World '57
Attack from Space '58
Evil Brain from Outer
Space '58/59

Miyasaka, Takeshi
(Takeshi Miyazaka)
Tokyo Mafia 3: Battle for Shinjuku '96

Miyazaki, Hayao
Castle of Cagliostro '79
My Neighbor Totoro '88
Princess Mononoke '97
Spirited Away '01

Miyoshi, Kunio
Rebirth of Mothra 2 '97

Mori, Kazuo
(Issei Mori)
Return of Daimajin '66
The Tale of Zatoichi Continues '62
Zatoichi and the Doomed Man '65

Mori, Masaki
Barefoot Gen '83

Morse, Terry
Godzilla, King of the Monsters '54 (U.S.)

Muroga, Atsushi
Blowback: Love and Death '90
Junk '99

Nagai, Go
The Ninja Dragon '90

Nahon, Chris
Kiss of the Dragon '01

Nakajima, Sadao
Renegade Ninjas '79

Nakano, Takao
Sumo Vixens '96

Nakata, Hideo
Dark Water '02
Ghost Actress '96
Ring '98
Ring 2 '99

Nam, Francis
A Wicked Ghost 2: The Fear '00

Nam Key-nam
Double Dragon in the Last Duel '85

Nam, Simon
(Nam Nai-choi, Nam Ngai Kai Lam, Nam Lai Choi, Nam Ngai Kai, Lam Nai Choi, Lan Nai Cai)
The Cat '91
Erotic Ghost Story '90
The Peacock King '89
Riki-Oh: The Story of Ricky '89
Saga of the Phoenix '90
The Seventh Curse '86

Nawathe, Raja
Gumnaam '65

Needham, Hal
Cannonball Run '81

Ng, Andy
(Ng Yiu-kuen, Wu Yao Quan)
Operation Billionaires '98
The Untold Story 2 '98

Ng, Francis
(Ng Chun-Yu, Ng Jan Yue, Wu Zhen Yu)
9413 '98

Ng Min-kan
(Wu Mian Qin)
Deadful Melody '94

Ng See-yuen
(Ng Si Yuen, Wu Si Yuan, Wu Sye Yeuan)
The Bloody Fists '72
Bruce Lee: The Man, the Myth '76
The Invincible Armour '77
Kung Fu, the Invisible Fist '72
Tower of Death '81

Ng Tin-chi
(Wu Tian Chi, Ng Tien-tsu)
Bloody Fight '72

Ngai Hoi-fung
(Wei Hai Feng, Ye Hoi Fung, Wei Hui Feng)
Iron Man '86
Ten Tigers of Shaolin '78

Ngor, Peter
(Ngor Chi-Kwan, Ngau Chi Gwan, Ao Zhi Jun)
Erotic Ghost Story 2 '91
Legendary Couple '95

Nihonmatsu, Kazui
The X from Outer Space '67

Nishijima, Katsuhiko
Project A-ko '86

Nishiyama, Akihiko
Gatchaman '94

Noda, Yukio
Bronson Lee, Champion '78

Noguchi, Haruyasu
Gappa: The Triphibian Monster '67

O Chung-Hung
(Oh Jun Hung, Ke Jun Xiong)
Generation Consultant '90
Generation Pendragon '90

O Sing-pui
(Oh Sing Pooi, Ke Xing Pei, O Sing Pooi)

Comic King '00

O Yau-man
(Oh Yau Man, Ke You Min, Ho Yu Ming, Lung Siu, Lung Hsiao)
Macho Man '72

Ochiai, Masayuki
The Hypnotist '99
Parasite Eve '97

Oda, Motoyoshi
Godzilla Raids Again '55

Oedekerk, Steve
Kung Pow: Enter the Fist '76/2001

Ohkawa, Shundo
Nobody '99

Ohkawa, Toshimichi
Nobody '99

Okamoto Junko
Guinea Pig: The Making of Guinea Pig '86

Okawara, Takao
Godzilla 2000 '99
Godzilla vs. Destroyah '95
Godzilla vs. MechaGodzilla 2 '93
Godzilla vs. Mothra '92

Okunaka, Atsuo
Time of the Apes '75

Okuwaki, Toshio
Naked Pursuit '68

Olsen, Rolf
(Emerson Fox)
Shocking Asia '75
Shocking Asia 2 '76

Omori, Kazuki
Godzilla vs. Biollante '89
Godzilla vs. King Ghidorah '91

Oshii, Mamoru
Ghost in the Shell '95
Patlabor 1: The Movie '90
Urusei Yatsura Movie 1: Only You '83

Ota, Koji
Invasion of the Neptune Men '61

Otomo, Katsuhiro
Akira '88

Ozawa, Shigehiro
(Sakae Ozawa)
Return of the Street Fighter '74
The Street Fighter '74

Ozu, Yasujiro
Good Morning '59

Pang, Danny
Bangkok Dangerous '00
The Eye '02

Pang, Edmond
You Shoot, I Shoot '01

Pang, Oxide
(Pang Chun)
Bangkok Dangerous '00
The Eye '02

Park Chan-wook
Joint Security Area '00
Sympathy for Mr. Vengeance '01

Park Cheol-kwan
Hi! Dharma! '01

Pau, Peter
The Touch '02

Pen-Ek Ratanaruang
Mon-Rak Transistor '01

Pinon, Efren C.
The Killing of Satan '83

Ratner, Brett
Rush Hour '98
Rush Hour 2 '01

Rintaro
(Shigeyuki Hayashi, Rin Taro)
Metropolis '01
X '96

Romero, Eddie
(Edgar F. Romero)
Beast of the Yellow Night '70
Brides of Blood '68
Mad Doctor of Blood Island '68
Twilight People '72
The Walls of Hell '64

Saito, Buichi
Lone Wolf and Cub 4: Baby Cart in Peril '72

Sakaguchi Hironobu
Final Fantasy: The Spirits Within '01

Sato, Hajime
Body Snatcher from Hell '68
Terror beneath the Sea '66

Sato, Junya
Bullet Train '75

Sato, Shinsuke
Princess Blade '02

Schwartz, Harold B.
The New Game of Death '75

See, Raymond
The New Marvelous Double '92

Sek Bing-chan
Dragons of the Orient '88

Shang Lang
Mantis Combat '81

Shaw, Jimmy
Return of the Tiger '79

Shim Hyung Rae
(Ray Shim)
Reptilian '00

Shin Sang-ok
Pulgasari '85

Shin, Stephen
(Shin Kei Yin, Shin Gei Yin, Sheng Qi Ran)
Black Cat '91

Shin Wee Kyun
Golden Dragon Silver Snake '79

Shirai, Kazumasa
Reborn from Hell: Samurai Armageddon '96

Shirai, Seiichi
Tokyo Mafia 2: Wrath of the Yakuza '95
Tokyo Mafia: Yakuza Wars '95

Shirow Masamune
Black Magic M-66 '87

Shoken Takahashi
Kei Mizutani: Undressed for Success '94

Shu Lea Cheang
I.K.U. '00

Shum Tat-wai
Kick Boxer's Tears '92

Sippy Ramesh
Sholay '75

Siu Sang
(Xiao Sheng)
The Hero of Swallow '96

So, Philip
Eat My Dust '93

Som Kit
The Killer Elephants '76

Songo, Manuel S.
Murder in the Orient '74

Srisupap Somching
Fear Faith Revenge 303 '98

Su Chen Ping
(Siu Chan Ping, Su Zhen Ping, Chen Ping, Shu Chen Ping, Su Jen)
Kung Fu on Sale '79

Sugii, Gisaburo
Street Fighter 2 '96

Sun Chung
(Suen Chung, Sun Zhong)
Avenging Eagle '78
City War '88
A Fistful of Talons '83

Sun Young
Yoga and Kung Fu Girl '78

Sun Zingguo
The Adventures of the Master and His Servant '96

Sung Ting-mei
(Song Ting Mei)
Secret of the Chinese Kung Fu '81
Shaolin Traitorous '76

Suzuki, Norifumi
(Noribumi Suzuki)
Shogun's Ninja '82

Suzuki, Seijun
(Seitaro Suzuki)
Branded to Kill '67
Tokyo Drifter '66

Szeto Ying-kit
Faces of Horror '98

Tai, Robert
(Daai Chit, Dai Che, Tai Chi Tsien, Tai Chi Hsien, Tai Che, Tai Chi, Tai Yee Tin, Tai Chit)
Legend of the Drunken Tiger '92
Ninja the Final Duel '85
Shaolin Chastity Kung Fu '81
Shaolin vs. Ninja '83

Tai See Fu
Goose Boxer '78

Takahata Isao
Grave of the Fireflies '88

Takayama, Fumihiko
Bubblegum Crisis '85

Takayama, Hideri
Urotsukidoji '89

Takeuchi, Tetsuro
Wild Zero '99

Tam Long-cheung
Troublesome Night '97

Tanaka, Hiroyuki
(Sabu)
Postman Blues '97

Tanaka, Shigeo
Gamera vs. Barugon '66

Tanaka, Tokuzo
Fight, Zatoichi, Fight! '64

New Tale of Zatoichi '63
Zatoichi the Fugitive '63
Zatoichi's Vengeance '66

Tang, Billy
(Tang Hin-Sing)
Brother of Darkness '94
Devil Touch '02
Dr. Lamb '92
The Kung Fu Master '94
Red to Kill '94
Run and Kill '93
Sharp Guns '01

Tang Chia
(Tong Gaai)
Death Mask of the Ninja '82

Tang Mau-sing
Fist of Fury '95

Taniguchi, Senkichi
What's Up, Tiger Lily? '66

Teshigahara Hiroshi
Woman in the Dunes '64

Tezuka, Masaaki
Godzilla vs. Megaguirus '00

Tezuka, Osamu
Astro Boy '63

Thom, Andy
Jackie Chan Adventures 1: The Search for the Talismans '00
Jackie Chan Adventures 2: The Dark Hand Returns '00

Tin Peng
(Tian Peng, Tin Pang, Tien Pang, Tien Pen, Roc Tien)
The Silver Spear '79

Ting Chung
(Ding Chung, Ding Chong)
Golden Killah '80

Ting Shan-si
(Ding Shan Xi)
Fury of King Boxer '72

To, Dickson
(Do Lai Chi, Du Li Zi)
Haunted Mansion '98

To, Johnny
(To Kei-Fung, Do Kei Fung, Du Qi Feng)
All About Ah-Long '89
The Big Heat '88
Casino Raiders 2 '91
Eighth Happiness '88
Executioners '93

Fulltime Killer '01
Help!!! '00
The Heroic Trio '93
Justice, My Foot! '92
Love on a Diet '01
The Mission '99
Needing You... '00
Running out of Time '99
Running out of Time 2 '01
Where a Good Man Goes '99

Tong Dik
Drunken Art and Crippled Fist '79

Tong, Stanley
(Tong Gwai Lai, Tang Ji Li)
China Strike Force '00
First Strike '96
Rumble in the Bronx '95
Supercop '92
Supercop 2 '93

Tong, Wilson
(Tong Wai Shing, Tang Wei Cheng, The Foot Doctor)
Kung Fu Genius '79
Snake Deadly Act '79
The Vampire Combat '01
The Young Avenger '79

Tran Anh Hung
Cyclo '95

Trippetti, Vincenzo
Jackie Chan Adventures 1: The Search for the Talismans '00

Tsai Ming-liang
What Time Is It There? '01

Tsang, Eric
(Tsang Chi-Wai, Ceng Zhi Wei)
Aces Go Places '82
Aces Go Places 2 '83
The Tigers '91

Tsui Hark
(Chui Hak, Xu Ke) See also sidebar on p. 94.
Aces Go Places 3 '84
A Better Tomorrow 3 '89
The Blade '95
The Butterfly Murders '79
The Chinese Feast '95
A Chinese Ghost Story 3 '91
Green Snake '93
The Master '89
Once upon a Time in China '91
Once upon a Time in China 2 '92

Once upon a Time in China 3 '93
Peking Opera Blues '86
Swordsman '90
Time and Tide '00
Twin Dragons '92
We're Going to Eat You! '80
Zu Warriors '01
Zu: Warriors of the Magic Mountain '83

Tsui Siu-Ming
(Chui Siu Ming, Xu Xiao Ming, Tu Shiao Ming, Xu Xiaomin)
Bury Me High '90
The Holy Robe of Shaolin Temple '84

Tsukamoto, Shinya
Hiruko the Goblin '90
Tetsuo: The Iron Man '89
Tetsuo 2: Body Hammer '91
Tokyo Fist '96

Tsuruta Norio
Ring 0: Birthday '00

Tsushima Masaru
The Haunted Lantern '98
Lady Ninja: Reflections of Darkness '96

Tung Chin-Woo
(Tung Kar Wu, Tong Chin-Woo)
The Buddha Assassinator '79

Tung, Stephen
(Tung Wai, Dung Wei, Dong Wei, Tung Wei)
See also sidebar on p. 326.
Contract Killer '98
Extreme Challenge '01

Umetsugu Inoue
Hong Kong Nocturne '67

Varma Ramgopal
Raat '91

Velasco, Joseph
Ninja vs. Bruce Lee '82

Villar, Felix
(Albert Yu Villar)
Devil Woman '70

Wada Takuya
Violence Jack '88

Wai Hon-to
One Arm Hero '94

Wai Kar-fai
(Wai Ka-Fai, Wai Ga Fai, Wei Gu Hui)
Fulltime Killer '01
Help!!! '00
Love on a Diet '01

Needing You... '00
Peace Hotel '95
Too Many Ways to Be No. 1 '97

Wai Man
Duel of the Brave Ones '78

Wakabayashi Ejiro
Prince of Space '59

Wakamatsu, Koji
(Takashi Ito)
Ecstasy of the Angels '72
Notorious Concubines '69

Wang Chih-cheng
5 Venoms vs. Wu Tang '87

Wang Xiaoshuai
(Wu Ming)
Beijing Bicycle '01
Frozen '96

Wang Yu, Jimmy
(Wong Yue, Wang Yu, Wang Yue)
Master of the Flying Guillotine '74
Return of the Chinese Boxer '75

Watanabe, Hisashi
(Yota Watabe)
Big Boobs Buster '90
The Ladies' Phone Sex Club '96

Weiner, Tom
Ultraman 2 '01 (English dub)

Wen Yao Hua
Crack Shadow Boxers '77

Wong, Ally
Clueless '01
The Final Winner '01

Wong, Arthur
(Wong Ngok Tai, Huang Yue Tai)
In the Line of Duty 3 '88

Wong, Benny
Gold Fingers '01

Wong Fung
(Huang Feng, Kwang Feng)
The Legendary Strike '78
Sting of the Dragon Masters '73

Wong Gum-miu
Fist of Fury '95

Wong Hung Chang
(Wong Hung Cheung, Wang Hong Zhang, Wang Hung Chang)

Rage of the Masters
'74

Wong, James
The One '01

Wong Jing
(Wang Jing)
Casino Raiders '89
Casino Tycoon 2 '92
City Hunter '92
The Conman '98
Crocodile Hunter '89
Everyday Is Valentine
'01
Fight Back to School 3
'93
God of Gamblers '89
God of Gamblers 2 '90
God of Gamblers 3:
Back to Shanghai
'91
God of Gamblers
Returns '94
Hail the Judge '94
High Risk '95
The Last Blood '90
Last Hero in China '93
Lord of the Wu Tang
'93
Love Me, Love My
Money '01
My School Mate, the
Barbarian '01
The New Legend of
Shaolin '94
Return to a Better
Tomorrow '94
Royal Tramp '92
Royal Tramp 2 '92
The Tricky Master '00

Wong Kam-tin
The Most Wanted '94

Wong Kar-Wai
(Wong Ga Wai, Wang Gu
Wei)
Ashes of Time '94
Chungking Express '94
Days of Being Wild '90
Fallen Angels '95
In the Mood for Love
'00

Wong, Kirk
(Wong Chi Keung,
Huang Zhi Jiang, Che-
Kirk Wong)
Crime Story '93
Flash Future Kung Fu
'83
Gunmen '88
Organized Crime and
Triad Bureau '94
Rock 'n' Roll Cop '94

Wong, Parkman
(Wong Pak-Man, Wong
Paak Man, Huang Bo
Wen)
Final Justice '88
Red Shield '91

Wong, Sherman
(Wong Jing Wa, Huang
Jing Hua, Wong Ching-
Wah)
Sex and the Emperor
'94

Wong Sing-liu
(Wang Xing Lei)
Story of the Dragon '76

Wong Siu-jun
Super Gang '78

Wong Siu Ming
(Wang Ziao Ming)
Combo Cops '96

Wong, Taylor
(Wong Tai-Loi, Wong Tai
Loy, Huang Tai Lai)
Return of the Deadly
Blade '81
Rich and Famous '87
SuperManChu '73
The Three Swordsmen
'94
With or Without You '92

Woo, John
(Ng Yue Sam, Wu Yu
Sen, Wu Yu-Sheng) See
also sidebar on p. 38.
A Better Tomorrow '86
A Better Tomorrow 2
'87
Bullet in the Head '90
Hand of Death '75
Hard Boiled '91
Heroes Shed No Tears
'83/86
The Killer '89
Last Hurrah for Chivalry
'78
Once a Thief '91

Woo, Teresa
(Woo San, Hu Shan)
Angel '87
Angel 2 '88

Wu Chia Chun
Shaolin and Tai Chi '79

Wu, David
(Wu Dai-Wai, Woo Daai
Wai, Hu Da Wei)
The Bride with White
Hair 2 '93

Wu, Dennis
The Imp '81
Ninja in the U.S.A. '88

Wu Kuo-jen
Ninja Hunter '83
The Super Ninja '84

Wu Ma
(Fung Ng Ma, Ng Ma,
Fung Wo-ma)
From China with Death
'74
Generation Consultant
'90
Generation Pendragon
'90
The Heroes '80

The Massive '78
Mr. Boo Meets Pom
Pom '85
Picture of a Nymph '88
Snake-Crane Secret
'78

Wu Ming-hoi
Fist of Fury '95

Wu Ming Hung
(Woo Man Hung, Mo
Ming Hung, Mo Man
Hung, Wu Min Xiong,
Wu Ming Hsiung)
Fearless Fighters '69
Five Elements of Kung
Fu '78
The Green Dragon Inn
'79

Wu Yuen-ling
18 Secrets of Kung Fu
'79

Yaguchi, Shinobu
Adrenaline Drive '99

Yamada, Katsuhisa
Devil Hunter Yohko 2
'92
Devil Hunter Yohko 3
'92

Yamada, Minoru
Voyage into Space '67

Yamaga, Hiroyuki
Royal Space Force: The
Wings of Hon-
neamise '87

**Yamaguchi,
Kazuhiko**
Sister Street Fighter
'74

Yamamoto, Satsuo
Ninja: Band of Assas-
sins '62
Ninja: Band of Assas-
sins Continued '63
Zatoichi the Outlaw '67

Yamashita, Kensho
Godzilla vs. Space
Godzilla '94

Yamauchi, Tetsuya
The Magic Serpent '66

Yang, Bob
One Foot Crane '79

Yang Ching Chen
(Yeung Jing Chan, Yang
Jing Chen, Joseph Che-
ung)
18 Fatal Strikes '78

Yanlin, Tang
The Cold Mountain
Temple '91

Yasuda, Kimiyoshi
Adventures of a Blind
Man '64
Daimajin '66

Zatoichi and the Fugi-
tives '68
Zatoichi on the Road
'63
Zatoichi's Cane Sword
'66

Yasuhiko, Yoshikazu
The Venus Wars '89

Yau, Herman
(Yau Lai To, Qui Li Tao)
City Cop '95
From the Queen to the
Chief Executive '01
Happy Family '02
The Masked Prosecutor
'99
Master Q 2001 '01
No More Love, No More
Death '92
Troublesome Night '97
Troublesome Night 3
'97
Troublesome Night 4
'98
The Untold Story '92

Yau, Patrick
(Yau Tat Chi, Yau Dat
Chi, You Da Zhi)
Expect the Unexpected
'98
The Longest Nite '98
Losers' Club '01
The Odd One Dies '97

Ye, Lou
Suzhou River '00

Yee, Derek
(Yee Yung Sing, Yi Dung
Sing, Er Dong Sheng,
Erh Tung Sheng)
C'est la Vie, Mon Cheri
'93
Full Throttle '95

Yen, Donnie
(Yen Ji-Dan, Yen Chi-
Tan, Yan Che Dan) See
also sidebar on p. 152.
Ballistic Kiss '98
Shanghai Affairs '98

Yeung, Bolo
(Yeung Shut, Yang Sze,
Yang Si)
Bolo '80
Chinese Samson '79

Yeung Kuen
(Yang Chuan, Yang
Quan)
Seeding of a Ghost '83
Shadow of the Tiger
'79

Yip, Raymond
(Yip Wai Man, She Wei
Min)
Beauty and the Breast
'02
City of Desire '01
For Bad Boys Only '00
Sixty Million Dollar Man
'95

Yip, Riley
Lavender '00

Yip Wai-ying
Troublesome Night 14
'02

Yip, Wilson
(Yip Wai-Sun)
Bio Zombie '98
Bullets over Summer
'99
Juliet in Love '00

Yip Wing-cho
(Ip Wing Cho, Yip Wing
Jo, She Rong Zu)
Pom Pom Strikes Back
'86
Thunder Kick '73

Yiu Tin-hung
(Yao Tian Hong)
Could You Kill My Hus-
band Please? '01
Faces of Horror '98

Yoneda, Okihiro
Rebirth of Mothra '96

Yoshida, Hiroaki
Twilight of the Cock-
roaches '87

Yoshiyuki Kuroda
Lone Wolf and Cub 6:
White Heaven in
Hell '74

Yu, Dennis
(Chui Wan Kong, Tu Yun
Kang)
Evil Cat '86

Yu Deshui
The Prisoner of Five
Boulders '89

Yu, Ronny
(Yu Yan-tai, Yue Yan
Taai, Yu Ren Tai)
The Bride with White
Hair '93
Legacy of Rage '86
The Phantom Lover '95
The Postman Fights
Back '82
Shogun and Little
Kitchen '92

Yuasa, Noriaki
Gamera vs. Guiron '69
Gamera vs. Gyaos '67
Gamera vs. Viras '68
Gamera vs. Zigra '71
Giant Monster Gamera
'65

Yuen Biao
(Hsia Ling-Jun, Biao
Yuan, Jimmy Tuen, Yuen
Bill)
A Kid from Tibet '91

Yuen, Brandy
(Yuen Chun Wei, Yuan
Zhen Wei, Yuan Jan
Wei)

In the Line of Duty 3
'88

Yuen Bun
Once upon a Time in
China 4 '93

Yuen Chi-keung
Troublesome Night 8
'00

Yuen, Corey
*(Yuen Kwai, Yuen Fui,
Yuen Fooi, Yuan Kui)*
The Avenging Fist '01
The Defender '94
The Legend '92
The Legend 2 '93

Righting Wrongs '86
Savior of the Soul '91
Savior of the Soul 2
'92
She Shoots Straight
'90
Yes, Madam '85

Yuen, James
*(Yuen Sai Sang, Ruan
Shi Sheng)*
Clean My Name, Mr.
Coroner! '00
Every Dog Has His
Date '01
Your Place or Mine! '98

Yuen Kwai
The Enforcer '95

Yuen Woo-ping
*(Yuen Who Ping, Yuen
Wo Ping, Yuan Han
Ping, Yuen Ho Ping,
Peace Yuen)*
The Buddhist Fist '79
Dance of the Drunk
Mantis '79
Dreadnaught '81
Drunken Master '78
Drunken Tai Chi '84
In the Line of Duty 4
'89
Iron Monkey '93

The Magnificent Butch-
er '79
The Miracle Fighters
'82
The Red Wolf '95
Snake in the Eagle's
Shadow '78
Tiger Cage '88
Twin Warriors '93
Wing Chun '94

Yui Man-Kei
(Wao Min Qi)
Combo Cops '96

Yung Chung-chi
Thunder Cops '98

Zeze, Takahisa
*(South Pole #1, Jean-
Luc Zeze)*
Dream of Garuda '94

Zhang Huaxun
The Swordswoman in
White '92

Zhang Jian-ya
Crash Landing '00

Zhang Yimou
The Road Home '99

Writer Index

The Writer Index contains all screenwriters cited in the credits of the movies covered in this book. The names of the screenwriters are listed alphabetically, and their corresponding videographies are also alphabetically arranged. When applicable, one or more pseudonyms are provided (in parentheses) following the writers' names. If the writing credit is for the film's origin—the story, manga, novel, or adaptation, rather than for the screenplay itself—then this is noted in parentheses.

Abe, Keichi
(Keiiche Abe, Keiichi Abe)
Star Force: Fugitive Alien 2 '78/86
Fugitive Alien '78/1986

Abe, Kobo
Woman in the Dunes '64

Aikawa, Noboru
(Noboro Aikawa)
Urotsukidoji '89
Violence Jack '88

Akhtar, Javed
Sholay '75

Akiyama, Katsuhito
Bubblegum Crisis '85

Allen, Woody
What's Up, Tiger Lily? '66

Allin, Michael
Enter the Dragon '73

Amamiya, Keita
Zeram '91

Amigo, Cesar
The Blood Drinkers '64
The Walls of Hell '64

Aoyagi, Yumiko
Moonlight Express '99

Aoyama, Shinji
Dream of Garuda '94

Araki, Yoshisa
Star Force: Fugitive Alien 2 '78/86

Aramaki, Shinji
Bubblegum Crisis '85

Asai, Shozaburo
Adventures of a Blind Man '64
Zatoichi and the Chest of Gold '64
Zatoichi and the Doomed Man '65
Zatoichi's Flashing Sword '64

Au Kin Yee
Running out of Time 2 '01

Au Shui-lin
Spacked Out '00

Autrey, Steve
Return of the Street Fighter '74
The Street Fighter '74
The Street Fighter's Last Revenge '74

Avellana, Jose Mari
The Killing of Satan '83

Ba Tong
Deadend of Besiegers '92

Baek Seung-jae
Bloody Beach '00

Baker, J.B.
Junk '99

Banno, Yoshimitsu
Godzilla vs. Hedorah '71

Bao Kwok-ian
Kung Fu Zombie '81

Bao Shi
The Road Home '99

Bennett, Julie
What's Up, Tiger Lily? '66

Bercovici, Eric
Shogun '80

Bernt, Eric
Romeo Must Die '00

Besson, Luc
Kiss of the Dragon '01

Bo Ho Writing Team
Pom Pom '84

Breakston, George P. (story)
The Manster '60

Buxton, Frank
What's Up, Tiger Lily? '66

Canoy, Reuben
Mad Doctor of Blood Island '68

Capizzi, Duane
Jackie Chan Adventures 1: The Search for the Talismans '00
Jackie Chan Adventures 2: The Dark Hand Returns '00

Carbon, Julian
Running out of Time '99

Carbourt, Julien
The Touch '02

Cawthorne, Russell
Bruce Lee, The Legend '84

Cha, Louis
Legend of the Dragon-slayer Sword '90
Legend of the Dragon-slayer Sword 3-The Rage of Gina '90
The Legend of the Swordsman '92 (novel)

Chak Ming
Man Wanted '95

Chan, Benny
Gen-X Cops '99

Chan, Billy
The Legend of a Professional '00

Chan Bo-sun
Black Cat '91

Chan, Casey
Erotic Ghost Story 2 '91

Chan, Ella
Dragon from Russia '90

Chan Gam-kuen
Funeral March '01

Chan Gin-tak
Doctor No... '01

Chan, Gordon
Armageddon '97
Beast Cops '98
The Big Heat '88
The Cat '91
The Defender '94
Fight Back to School '91
Fight Back to School 2 '92
First Option '96

Fist of Legend '94
Okinawa Rendez-vous '00
Thunderbolt '95
2000 A.D. '00

Chan Hing-ka
(Chang Hing-kai, Chan Hing-Kar, Chan Hing-kar, Chan Hing Kai, Chan Heng Ka, Chan King-ha)
Beast Cops '98
A Better Tomorrow '86
Born Wild '01
Brassiere '01
The Cat '91
Contract Killer '98
First Option '96
Jiang Hu-"The Triad Zone" '00
Okinawa Rendez-vous '00
Option Zero '97
Task Force '97
Thunderbolt '95

Chan, Jackie
Armour of God '86
Dragon Lord '82
Fearless Hyena '79
Gorgeous '99
Miracles '89
Operation Condor '91
Police Story '85
Police Story 2 '88
Project A '83
Project A 2 '87
Snake in the Eagle's Shadow '78 (story)
Who Am I? '98
The Young Master '80

Chan, Jessica
Ultimatum '01

Chan, Joe
Mr. Boo Meets Pom
Pom '85
Pom Pom Strikes Back
'86

Chan, John
(Chen Jian-zhong)
The Defender '94
Extreme Challenge '01
Fight Back to School 2
'92
King of Beggars '92
The Legend '92
The Legend 2 '93
Savior of the Soul 2
'92

Chan Kiu-ying
(Chan Kui-ying, Chan
Chow-ying)
Final Romance '01
Gen-Y Cops '00
In the Line of Duty 3
'88
The Postman Fights
Back '82

Chan Man-keung
Crime Story '93
Lee Rock '91

Chan Man Kui
Shaolin vs. Manchu '80

Chan Man Yau
Tiramisu '02

Chan, Phillip
Long Arm of the Law
'84
Long Arm of the Law 2
'87

Chan Shu
The Dragon Family '88

Chan, Sunny
Horror Hotline Big Head
Monster '01

Chan, Susan
Goodbye Mr. Cool '01
Para Para Sakura '01
Tokyo Raiders '00
Who Am I? '98

Chan, Susanne
Big Bullet '96
Executioners '93
The Most Wanted '94

Chan, Teddy
Black Mask '96
Crime Story '93

Chan, Thirteen
(Chan Sap Saam, Chen
Shi San, 13 Chan)
The Avenging Fist '01
Bullets of Love '01
The Wesley's Mysteri-
ous File '01

Chan Tin-suen
The Legend of the
Swordsman '92

**Once upon a Time in
China 2 '92**
Once upon a Time in
China 3 '93

Chan Wing-sun
Dummy Mommy, with-
out a Baby '01
Funeral March '01

Chan Yiu-fai
Fist of Fury '95

Chang Jun-il (novel)
Lies '99

Chang, Bryan
City of Desire '01

Chang Cheh
Avenging Warriors of
Shaolin '79
Chinatown Kid '77
Chinese Super Ninjas
'82
Five Deadly Venoms
'78
Flag of Iron '80
Kid with the Golden
Arm '78
Masked Avengers '81
The Return of the 5
Deadly Venoms '78
Ten Tigers of Kwang-
tung '79
Venom Warrior '83

Chang Chien Chih
Shaolin Chastity Kung
Fu '81

Chang Kwan
Erotic Ghost Story '90

Chang Seng-yi
(Chang Hsing-yi, Chang
Hsin Yee, Chang Shun
Yee, Cheung San Yee,
Cheung San-yee, Chang
Seng Yi, Cheung Shan
Yi, Chang Hsin-yee)
Challenge of Death '78
Eagle's Claw '77
Exit the Dragon, Enter
the Tiger '75
Fatal Needles vs. Fatal
Fists '80
The Hot, the Cool, and
the Vicious '76
The Leg Fighters '80
Revenge of the Patriots
'76
Shaolin vs. Lama '81
Snake and Crane Arts
of Shaolin '78
Story of the Dragon '76

Chang Yoon-hyun
Tell Me Something '99

Chatterjee, Dhruva
Gumnaam '65

Chau Ting
No More Love, No More
Death '92
The Storm Riders '98

**Young and Dangerous
5 '98**

Cheang, Shu Lea
I.K.U. '00

Chee Do Hong
Bruce Lee Fights Back
from the Grave '76

Chen, Candy
Legendary Couple '95

Chen Chi-hwa
Shaolin Wooden Men
'76

Chen Wah
Story of the Dragon '76

Cheng, Bob
Horror Hotline Big Head
Monster '01

Cheng, Candy
The Best of the Best
'96
Troublesome Night '97

Cheng, Cary
Sharp Guns '01

Cheng, Clement
A War Named Desire
'00

Cheng, Debbie
One Arm Hero '94

Cheng Kam-fu
(Cheng Kam-fa)
Contract Killer '98
The Inspector Wears
Skirts '88

Cheng Kim-fung
Violent Cop '99

Cheng, Philip
All About Ah-Long '89
The Chinese Feast '95
Eighth Happiness '88

Cheuk Bing
(Zhuo Bing)
A Chinese Torture
Chamber Story '94
Gold Fingers '01
Sex and the Emperor
'94
A Taste of Killing and
Romance '94

Cheung, Alfred
(Cheung Kin-ting, Che-
ung Gin Ting, Zhang
Jian Ting)
The Millionaires'
Express '86
On the Run '88

Cheung, Ben
Bullets over Summer
'99

Cheung, Bryan
Run and Kill '93

Cheung Chi-sing
Crime Story '93

A Fighter's Blues '00
In the Line of Duty 4
'89
U-Man '02

Cheung Hoi-ching
Goose Boxer '78
The Sword Stained with
Royal Blood '93
The Vampire Combat
'01

Cheung, Joe
Mask of Death '76
Pom Pom and Hot Hot
'92
Twin Dragons '92

Cheung Kam-moon
The Imp '81

Cheung Kwok-yuen
Body Weapon '99
Fist of Fury '95
The Kung Fu Master
'94

Cheung Lia-ling
Crime Story '93

Cheung, Mabel
Beijing Rocks '01
Painted Faces '88

Cheung, Peter
Legend of the Flying
Swordsman '00

Cheung, Roman
From Beijing with Love
'94
Satin Steel '94

Cheung Sun
Kung Fu Genius '79

**Cheung Tan, Char-
coal**
The Assassin '93
Dragon Chronicles:
Maidens of Heaven-
ly Mountain '94
Dragon Inn '92
The East Is Red '93
Once upon a Time in
China 2 '92
Once upon a Time in
China 3 '93
Wonder Seven '94

Cheung Wa
The Holy Robe of
Shaolin Temple '84

Cheung Wah Biu
Bury Me High '90

Chia, Louis (story)
Eagle Shooting Heroes
'93

Chiang, P.S. (story)
The Blazing Temple '76
The 8 Masters '77

Chiang Ping-han
Ninja Checkmate '79
The 36 Deadly Styles
'79

Chiang Ping Han
Dragon's Claws '79

Chiang Yang
Five Fingers of Death
'72

Chiao, Peggy
Beijing Bicycle '01

Chiba, Shozo (story)
King of the Mongols
'60

Chim Si
Faces of Horror '98

Chin Hung (novel)
Avenging Eagle '78

Chin, Amy
Born Wild '01
Jiang Hu-"The Triad
Zone" '00

Chin Liang
Emperor of Shaolin
Kung Fu '80

Chin Man-kei
The Eternal Evil of Asia
'95

Chin Shu Mei
Blooded Treasury Fight
'79

Chin Siu-Wai, Amy
Brassiere '01

Chin Yu
Return of the Deadly
Blade '81

Ching Sui-Tung
Duel to the Death '83
Wonder Seven '94

Chiu, Derek
Comeuppance '00

Choi, Clifford
Snake in the Eagle's
Shadow '78

Choi, Tessa
All's Well End's Well '92

Chong Ching, John
Butterfly and Sword '93

Chong, Felix
(Chong Man Keung,
Zhuang Wen Jiang)
Dance of a Dream '01
Final Romance '01
Gen-Y Cops '00
Shadow '01
Sharp Guns '01
Sunshine Cops '99
Tokyo Raiders '00

**Chong Huang (story)
Kuok**
Bruce Lee Fights Back
from the Grave '76

Choo, Kisei
Wicked City '87

Chou Ya Tsu
Killer Priest '81

Chow Jan-wing
Chinese Orthopedist and the Spice Girls '02

Chow, Matt
Bio Zombie '98
Bullets over Summer '99
Juliet in Love '00
Too Many Ways to Be No. 1 '97
United We Stand, and Swim '01

Chow Siu-man
Hot War '98

Chow, Stephen
Forbidden City Cop '96
From Beijing with Love '94
God of Cookery '96
King of Comedy '99
Shaolin Soccer '01

Chow, Taures
(Taurus Chow, Chow Yin Han, Zhou Yan Xian)
Dummy Mommy, without a Baby '01
Expect the Unexpected '98
Fall for You '01
Fighting for Love '01
The Most Wanted '94

Chow Yun-fat
Peace Hotel '95

Chu Yu (story)
Blooded Treasury Fight '79

Chu Hsang Kin
Iron Neck Li '81

Chu Hsiang Kan
Fighting Ace '79

Chu Hsiang-ken
Lady Whirlwind and the Rangers '74

Chui Chung Hei
Mask of Death '76

Chun, Janet
Bullet in the Head '90
Once a Thief '91

Chun Tin-nam
Crime Story '93

Chung Ah-sing
(Chung A Shing, Zhong A Cheng)
Painted Skin '92

Chung, Billy
Code of Honor '87
Killer '00
Last Ghost Standing '99

Chung Fuk Man
Raiders of Wu Tang '82

Chung Ji-woo
Happy End '99

Chung Ling
Legend of the Mountain '79

Chung, Paul
The Cheaters '01

Chung, Rico
(Chung Kai-cheong)
Beauty Investigator '92
City War '88

Chung, Thomas
The Touch '02

Chung Wai-hung
Don't Give a Damn '95

Chung Yao
Dreaming Fists with Slender Hands '80

Chung Yee
The Shaolin One '83

Chung, Yeung
The Shaolin One '83

Clamp
X '96

Clarke, Keith
The Art of Action: Martial Arts in the Movies '02

Clavell, James
Shogun '80

Clouse, Robert
The Big Brawl '80

Cohen, Rob
Dragon: The Bruce Lee Story '93

Courtiaud, Laurent
Running out of Time '99
The Touch '02

Dai Foo-ho
Swordsman '90

Dai, Richard
Ninja vs. Bruce Lee '82

Dak Blu Creative Group
The Owl vs. Bombo '84

Dell'Amico, Duane
Twilight of the Dark Master '97

Dolchin, Lerry
The Real Bruce Lee '79

Droney, Kevin
Mortal Kombat '95

Dung Yen Lyoung
Killer Priest '81

Dyne, Alexx Van
Jackie Chan Adventures 3: The Shadow of Shendu '00

Endo, Akinori
City Hunter: Secret Service '96

Fai Samang
Snaker '01

Fan Chun-fung
The Replacement Suspects '01

Fan Yau-man
Headlines '01

Feleo, Ben
Curse of the Vampires '70

Fok Da-lin
Shaolin Fist of Fury '87

Fong, Eddie
The Private Eye Blues '94

Fong Lung-seung
The Awaken Punch '73

Fong, Simon
Lethal Panther '91

Fong Yeh
10 Magnificent Killers '77

Fu Lee
The Prisoner '90

Fujiwara, Kei
Organ '96

Fukasaku, Kenta
Battle Royale '00

Fukasaku, Kinji
Legend of the Eight Samurai '84
Message from Space '78
Sure Death: Revenge '87

Fukuda, Jun
Godzilla vs. MechaGodzilla '74
Godzilla vs. Megalon '73

Fukuda, Yasushi
The Hypnotist '99

Fukushima, Masami
Attack of the Mushroom People '63
Godzilla vs. MechaGodzilla '74
Terror beneath the Sea '66

Fung, James
Final Justice '88
Red Shield '91
White Lotus Cult '93

Fung Min-hun
King of Comedy '99

Fung, Raymond
Legacy of Rage '86

Fung, Wong
Sting of the Dragon Masters '73

Gai Ming
The Story in Temple Red Lily '79

Gaiman, Neil
Princess Mononoke '97

Gam Sing-yan
Two Dragons Fight against Tiger '75

Gam Yam
Shaolin Wooden Men '76

Glickenhaus, James
The Protector '85

Goo Bi, GC
Merry-Go-Round '01

Goyer, David S.
Blade 2 '02

Grapek, Jim
The Secrets of the Warrior's Power '97

Groff, Ferde Jr.
The Walls of Hell '64

Guo Hong-ting (story)
Sorrowful to a Ghost '70

Guryu, Hachiro
Branded to Kill '67

Han Chang-hak
Record '00

Hanamura, Mangetsu (story)
Beautiful Hunter '94

Hao Jian
Crash Landing '00

Harada, Masato
Gunhed '89

Haraguchi, Tomoo (story)
Sakuya: Slayer of Demons '00

Harber, Harry Paul
Terror Is a Man '59

Harris, Sid
Varan the Unbelievable '58 (U.S.)

Harvey, Ron
Fist of Fear-Touch of Death '80

Hasegawa, Keichi
(Kei'ichi Hasegawa)

Godzilla, Mothra and King Ghidorah: Battle on Fire '01
Ultraman Gaia: The Battle in Hyperspace '98
Ultraman Tiga and Ultraman Dyna: The Warriors of the Lightning Star '98

Hashimoto, Izo
Akira '88

Hashimoto, Kosuke
Tokyo Mafia 3: Battle for Shinjuku '96

Hashimoto, Shinobu
The Hidden Fortress '58
Rashomon '50
Seven Samurai '54
Throne of Blood '57

Hata, Masanori (story)
The Adventures of Milo and Otis '86

Hau Juen
Lady Iron Monkey '83

Haung Tien
Fists of the White Lotus '80

Hay, Phil (story)
The Tuxedo '02

Hearn, Lafcedio (story)
Kwaidan '64

Herbeck, Bobby
Teenage Mutant Ninja Turtles '90

Heung, Jimmy
Casino Raiders '89

Hidaka, Shigeaki
Godzilla Raids Again '55

Hino, Hideshi
Guinea Pig: Flower of Flesh and Blood '85
Guinea Pig: Mermaid in a Manhole '88

Hirano, Yasushi
Vampire Hunter D '85

Hiroki, Ryuichi
Sadistic City '93

Hirota, Mikio
Terminatrix '95

Ho, Godfrey
(Benny Ho, Fong Ho)
Dragon against Vampire '85
Snake Fist Dynamo '84
Scorpion Thunderbolt '85

Thunder Ninja Kids:
The Hunt for the
Devil Boxer '86/94

Ho, Ivy
The Accidental Spy '01
Anna Magdalena '98
Comrades, Almost a
Love Story '96

Ho Man Lung (story)
Victim '99

Ho Shu Hua
Shaolin Temple 2: Kids
from Shaolin '84

**Hodgson, William
Hope (story)**
Attack of the Mush-
room People '63

Hoffman, Charles
The Green Hornet '74

Hoh Cheuk-wing
Code of Honor '87

**Hojo, Hidejo (adapta-
tion)**
Samurai 1: Musashi
Miyamoto '54
Samurai 2: Duel at Ichi-
joji Temple '55
Samurai 3: Duel at
Ganryu Island '56

**Hojo, Tsukasa
(manga)**
City Hunter: Secret Ser-
vice '96

Hon, Rex
Troublesome Night 9
'00

Honcho, Yuka
The Haunted Lantern
'98
Zero Woman: The
Accused '96

Honda, Ishiro
Akira Kurosawa's
Dreams '90
Destroy All Monsters
'68
War of the Gargantuas
'66

Hoshi, Shinchiro
Attack of the Mush-
room People '63

Hoshikawa, Seiji
Fight, Zatoichi, Fight!
'64
Zatoichi the Fugitive
'63

Hosoyama, Tomoaki
Weather Woman '95

Houghton, Don
Legend of the 7 Golden
Vampires '74

Houston, Robert
Shogun Assassin '80

Howard, Bruce
King Kong vs. Godzilla
'62 (U.S.)

Hsiang Yang
Fearless Fighters '69
SuperManChu '73

Hsieh Mo Hung
18 Fatal Strikes '78

Hsu Hsiao-ming
Beijing Bicycle '01

Hsu Li-min
The Eagle's Killer '81

Hsu, Talun (story)
Fatal Blade '00

Hsu, Tyrone
99 Cycling Swords '80

Hsu, William (story)
Angel 2 '88

Hu Yu
Sting of the Dragon
Masters '73

Huang Yin (novel)
The Massive '78

Huang Jo-pe
The Incredible Kung Fu
Mission '82

Hui, Jojo
The Eye '02

Hui, Koan
(Koan Hui-on, Hui Koan)
Black Mask '96
The Blade '95
Gen-X Cops '99
Time and Tide '00

Hui, Michael
The Private Eyes '76

Hui, Sharon
Love Correction '00
Martial Angels '01
Once upon a Time in
China and America
'97

Hung Hin-pang
Crystal Hunt '91

Hung, Richard
Duel of the Tao Tough
'82

Hung, Sammo
Encounter of the
Spooky Kind '81
The Prodigal Son '81
Winners and Sinners
'83

Ide, Masato
Ran '85

Igami, Masaru
Legend of the
Dinosaurs '77
The Magic Serpent '66

**Igami, Masaru
(story)**
Prince of Space '59

Iida, Joji
Another Heaven '00

Iida, Tsutomu
Devil Man '87

Imai, Kenichi
Street Fighter 2 '96

Imamura, Shohei
The Eel '97
Warm Water under a
Red Bridge '01

In Eun-ah
Tell Me Something '99

Inagaki, Hiroshi
Samurai 1: Musashi
Miyamoto '54
Samurai 2: Duel at Ichi-
joji Temple '55
Samurai 3: Duel at
Ganryu Island '56

Inui, Haruka (story)
The Ladies' Phone Sex
Club '96

Inuzuka, Minoru
Blind Swordsman: The
Tale of Zatoichi '62
New Tale of Zatoichi
'63
The Tale of Zatoichi
Continues '62
Zatoichi on the Road
'63
Zatoichi's Revenge '64
Zatoichi's Flashing
Sword '64

Ip Kwong Kim
Fist of Legend '94

Ip, Max
Extreme Challenge '01

Isenberg, Marty
Godzilla the Series:
Monster War '99

Ishi, Takashi
Evil Dead Trap '88

Ishida, Moriyoshi
The X from Outer Space
'67

Ishii, Katsuhito
Shark Skin Man and
Peach Hip Girl '98

Ishii, Takashi
Freeze Me '00
Gonin '95

Ishikawa, Takahito
Shogun's Ninja '82

Ishimura, Masahiro
Bronson Lee, Champi-
on '78

Ishinomori, Shotaro
Message from Space
'78

Itami, Juzo
The Funeral '84
Tampopo '87

Ito, Daisuke
Zatoichi and the Chess
Expert '65

Ito, Junji (manga)
Spiral '00

Itô, Kazunori
Gamera 2: Advent of
Legion '96
Gamera 3: The
Revenge of Irys '99
Gamera, Guardian of
the Universe '95
Ghost in the Shell '95

Ito, Shunya
Female Convict Scorpi-
on: Jailhouse 41
'72

Itoh, Kazunori
Patlabor 1: The Movie
'90

Iwanami, Yoshikazu
Guinea Pig: Android of
Notre Dame '88

Izuchi, Kishu
Dream of Garuda '94

Izuru Deguchi
Ecstasy of the Angels
'72

Jaan Shih-mei
Inheritor of Kung Fu '77

Jang Sun-woo
Lies '99

Jarrell, John
Romeo Must Die '00

Jeong Seong-san
Sympathy for Mr.
Vengeance '01

Jiang Bing-han
Sorrowful to a Ghost
'70

Jiang Dao-hai
Extreme Challenge '01

Jiang Di-An
The Cold Mountain
Temple '91

Jie Er-ge
Born to Defence '88

Jin Yong (story)
(Jin Yung, Yin Yong)
Brave Archer '77
Lord of the Wu Tang
'93
Rebels under Siege '00

Jin Shu-mei
The Heroes '80

Jissouiji, Akio (story)
Tokyo Decameron:
Three Tales of Mad-
ness and Sensuali-
ty '96

Johnson, Leo
The Secrets of the War-
rior's Power '97

Jones, Edmund
Ninja in the U.S.A. '88

Jung Yong-ki
Bichunmoo '99

Kaijo, Hideo
The H-Man '58

Kaiko, Ken (story)
Giants and Toys '58

Kakefuda, Manfred
Sister Street Fighter
'74

Kakinuma, Hideki
Bubblegum Crisis '85

Kam Kam-ming
The Imp '81

Kam-cheung, Chan
A Kid from Tibet '91
Picture of a Nymph '88

Kamata, Toshio
Legend of the Eight
Samurai '84

Kamen, Robert Mark
Kiss of the Dragon '01

Kamiyama, Kenji
Blood: The Last Vam-
pire '00

**Kanagai, S.R. Putan-
na (story)**
Hum Paanch '80

**Kanda, Takeshi
(story)**
The Razor 2: The Snare
'73
The Razor 3: Who's Got
the Gold? '74

Kaneharu, Tomoko
Urusei Yatsura Movie
1: Only You '83

Kaneko, Shusuke
Cross Fire '00
Gamera 3: The
Revenge of Irys '99
Godzilla, Mothra and
King Ghidorah: Bat-
tle on Fire '01

Kang Hyo-jin
My Wife Is a Gangster
'01

Kang Je-gyu
Shiri '99

Kao Pao Shu
(Go Bo Shu)
Battle of Shaolin '77

Blood of the Dragon
'71

Kapner, Mitchell
Romeo Must Die '00

Kapoor, Ravi
Aakhri Adalat '88

Kasahara, Ryozo
Zatoichi Challenged
'67
Zatoichi's Cane Sword
'66

Kashiwabara, Hiroshi
Godzilla 2000 '99
Godzilla vs. Megaguirus
'00
Godzilla vs. Space
Godzilla '94

**Katayama,
Kazuyoshi**
Appleseed '88

Kato, Yasushi
King of the Mongols
'60

Katsumoto, Yoko
Junk '99

Kaul, Mohan (story)
Aakhri Adalat '88

Kawajiri, Yoshiaki
Ninja Scroll '93
Vampire Hunter D:
Bloodlust '01

Kawasaki, Tomoko
Project A-ko '86

Kawauchi, Yasunori
Tokyo Drifter '66

Kayama, Shigeru
Godzilla, King of the
Monsters '54
(story)
Godzilla Raids Again
'55 (story)
Half Human '55/1957
(story)
The Mysterians '57

Khan, Salim
Sholay '75

Khmara, Edward
Dragon: The Bruce Lee
Story '93

Kikuchi, Akinori
Reborn from Hell:
Samurai Armaged-
don '96
Tokyo Mafia 2: Wrath of
the Yakuza '95
Tokyo Mafia: Yakuza
Wars '95

**Kikuchi, Hideyuki
(novel)**
Vampire Hunter D '85
Wicked City '87

Kikushima, Ryuzo
The Hidden Fortress
'58
High and Low '63
Sanjuro '63
Stray Dog '49
Throne of Blood '57
Yojimbo '61

Kim Hye-rin (story)
Bichunmoo '99

Kim Dong-Bin
Ring Virus '99

Kim Ho-sik
My Sassy Girl '01

Kim Hyeon-seok
Sympathy for Mr.
Vengeance '01

Kim Ji-woon
The Foul King '00

Kim Moon-sung
My Wife Is a Gangster
'01

Kim Sang-jin
Attack the Gas Station!
'99

Kim Se Ryun
Pulgasari '85

Kim Tae-gyun
Volcano High School
'01

Kim Young-Jun
Bichunmoo '99

Kimizuka, Ryoichi
Parasite Eve '97

Kimura, Takeo
Branded to Kill '67

Kimura, Takeshi
Attack of the Mush-
room People '63
Destroy All Monsters
'68
Frankenstein vs.
Baragon '65
Godzilla vs. Gigan '72
(story)
Godzilla vs. Hedorah
'71
The Human Vapor '60
King Kong Escapes '67
The Last War '61
The Mysterians '57
Rodan '56
War of the Gargantuas
'66

Kin Tsan
The 72 Desperate
Rebels '76

King Hu
Painted Skin '92
A Touch of Zen '69

Kitamura, Ryuhei
Versus '00

Kitano, Takeshi
Boiling Point '90
Brother '00
Fireworks '97
Kikujiro '99
Sonatine '93

Klein, Greg
Jackie Chan Adven-
tures 3: The Shad-
ow of Shendu '00

Ko Chun-wai
Vampire Kids '91

Ko, Clifton
Legacy of Rage '86
Once a Thief '91

Ko Lung
Return of the Chinese
Boxer '75
Return of the Deadly
Blade '81 (story)

Ko, Paul
Rivals of the Dragon
'83

Ko, Phillip
Angel on Fire '95
Guardian Angel '96
Killer's Romance '90

Kobayashi, Kyuzo
Body Snatcher from
Hell '68

Kodama, Kenji
City Hunter: Secret Ser-
vice '96

Koga, Nobuaki
Guinea Pig: Flower of
Flesh and Blood
'85

Koh, Ko
The Shaolin Drunken
Monk '83

Koike, Kazuo
Lone Wolf and Cub 1:
Sword of
Vengeance '72
Lone Wolf and Cub 2:
Baby Cart at the
River Styx '72
Lone Wolf and Cub 3:
Baby Cart to Hades
'72
Lone Wolf and Cub 4:
Baby Cart in Peril
'72 (also manga)
Lone Wolf and Cub 5:
Baby Cart in the
Land of Demons
'73 (also manga)
Lone Wolf and Cub 6:
White Heaven in
Hell '74 (manga)
The Razor 1: Sword of
Justice '72
The Razor 2: The Snare
'73 (story)
The Razor 3: Who's Got
the Gold? '74
(story)

Shogun Assassin '80
(also manga)

**Kojima, Goseki
(manga)**
Lone Wolf and Cub 4:
Baby Cart in Peril
'72
Lone Wolf and Cub 5:
Baby Cart in the
Land of Demons
'73
Lone Wolf and Cub 6:
White Heaven in
Hell '74
Shogun Assassin '80

Kok, Vincent
All's Well End's Well '92
All's Well End's Well '97
'97
Armageddon '97
Contract Killer '98
Flirting Scholar '93
Forbidden City Cop '96
From Beijing with Love
'94
God of Cookery '96
Gorgeous '99
Love on Delivery '94
Marry a Rich Man '02
Satin Steel '94
You Shoot, I Shoot '01

Komatsu, Sakyo
Time of the Apes '75

Komizu, Kazuo
Entrails of the Virgin
'86

Konami, Norio
Female Convict Scorpi-
on: Jailhouse 41
'72

Kong Heung-sang
Brother of Darkness
'94
The Peacock King '89
Queen's High '91

Kong, Kim
Militant Eagle '78

Kong Lung
Duel to the Death '82

Kong Su-chang
Tell Me Something '99

Koo Bon-han (story)
Tell Me Something '99

Koo Siu-fung
The Postman Fights
Back '82

Koreeda, Hirokazu
After Life '98

Kori, Cher
Fear Faith Revenge 303
'98

Kou, Ryoni
The Ladies' Phone Sex
Club '96

Kouf, Jim
Rush Hour '98

Koyama, Fumio
Shogun's Ninja '82

Ku Long
The Deadly Sword '78
The Last Duel '82
To Kill with Intrigue '77

Ku Lung
The Killer Meteors '76
The Legendary Strike
'78

Kumar, Padam
Champion '00

Kung Yeung
Revenge of the Patriots
'76

Kuni, Kei
Princess Blade '02

Kuo, Joseph
The Blazing Temple '76
Born Invincible '78
The 18 Bronzemen '76
The Shaolin Brothers
'77
The Unbeaten 28 '80

Kuo Wen-shan
Snake-Crane Secret
'78

Kuramoto, Kazuhito
Guinea Pig: Android of
Notre Dame '88

**Kuronuma, Takashi
(story)**
(Ken Kuronuma)
Rodan '56
Varan the Unbelievable
'58

Kurosawa, Akira
Akira Kurosawa's
Dreams '90
Dersu Uzala '74
The Hidden Fortress
'58
High and Low '63
Madadayo '92
Men Who Tread on the
Tiger's Tail '43
Ran '85
Rashomon '50
Sanjuro '63
Sanshiro Sugata '43
Seven Samurai '54
Stray Dog '49
Throne of Blood '57
Yojimbo '61

Kurosawa, Kiyoshi
Cure '97
Pulse '01

Kuzumi, Masayuki
Guinea Pig: He Never
Dies '86

Kwak Jae-yong
My Sassy Girl '01

Kwok, Phillip
Don't Give a Damn '95
Once upon a Time in China and America '97
Thunderbolt '95

Kwon Man-leung
Swordsman '90

Kwong, Abe
Erotic Ghost Story 2 '91
F*** / Off '98
Prince of the Sun '90
Visible Secret '01

Lai, Carol
Glass Tears '01

Lai, David
Duel to the Death '82

Lai, Ivan
Daughter of Darkness '93
God.com '98

Lai Wai-man
Odd Couple '79

Lam, Aubrey
Fighting for Love '01

Lam, Bosco
Legend of the Flying Swordsman '00
Wishful Milenio '01

Lam Cheung Pau
Deadend of Besiegers '92

Lam Chi-ming
The Buddhist Fist '79
The Butterfly Murders '79

Lam Chin-wai
(Lin Chin-wei)
Dynamo '78
Leopard Hunting '98

Lam Chiu-wing
With or Without You '92

Lam, Chris
Thunder Ninja Kids: The Hunt for the Devil Boxer '86/94

Lam, Dante (story)
Hit Team '00

Lam, James
Troublesome Night 14 '02
Troublesome Night 8 '00

Lam Kay Toa
Fist of Legend '94

Lam Kee-to
(Lam Kei-to)
The Bride with White Hair '93
A Chinese Ghost Story 2 '90

Lam, Lam
Ninja Supremo '81

Lam, Ringo
Aces Go Places 4 '86
The Adventurers '95
Full Alert '97
The Suspect '98
Victim '99

Lam Tan-Ping
Black Cat '91

Lam Wa-fan
Chinese Orthopedist and the Spice Girls '02
Leopard Hunting '98

Lam Wai-Lun
Black Cat '91

Lam Wong Kun
5 Lady Venoms '78

Lam Wong-kwan
Filthy Guy '80
The Fist, the Kicks and the Evils '79

Lam Yee-hung
Seeding of a Ghost '83

Langen, Todd W.
Teenage Mutant Ninja Turtles '90

Lasser, Louise
What's Up, Tiger Lily? '66

Lau, Bowie
The Deadly Camp '99

Lau Chi-wah
The Kung Fu Master '94

Lau, Chris
Comic King '00

Lau Chui
Kung Fu on Sale '79

Lau Dai-muk
(Lau Daai Muk, Lau Tai-muk)
A Chinese Ghost Story 2 '90
Iron Monkey '93
The Master '89
Swordsman '90

Lau, Daniel
Dragon Lee vs. the Five Brothers '78
The Legend of Bruce Lee '80

Lau Hau-wai
Troublesome Night '97
Troublesome Night 3 '97

Troublesome Night 4 '98

Lau Ho-leung
Runaway '01

Lau, Jeff
A Chinese Odyssey Part 1: Pandora's Box '95
A Chinese Odyssey Part 2: Cinderella '95
Eagle Shooting Heroes '93
Fist of Fury 1991 '91
The Haunted Cop Shop '87
Operation Pink Squad '88
Savior of the Soul '91

Lau Jun-wai
Prince of the Sun '90

Lau Kar-Leung
Invincible Pole Fighter '83
Legendary Weapons of China '82

Lau, Ricky
Mr. Vampire '85

Lau, W. K.
The Suspect '98

Lau Wing-kin
Full Alert '97

Laughlin, Michael
Shanghai 1920 '91

Law, Alex
Beijing Rocks '01
The Blacksheep Affair '98
The Moon Warriors '92
100 Ways to Murder Your Wife '86
Painted Faces '88

Law, Andy
The Blood Rules '00
Gorgeous '99

Law, Au
Her Name Is Cat 2: Journey to Death '01

Law Chi-leung
Double Tap '00
Full Throttle '95
Hot War '98
Inner Senses '01
Moonlight Express '99

Law Gam-foo
Doctor No... '01

Law Kam-fai
Cold War '00
Dr. Lamb '92
Gunmen '88
Legend of the Dragon '91
Red Shield '91
The Untold Story '92

Law Kam Fai
Trust Me U Die '99

Law Tai-man
In the Line of Duty 3 '88

Leder, Paul
A*P*E '76

Leder, Reuben
A*P*E '76

Lee, Anna
City Cop '95

Lee, Bruce
Bruce Lee: A Warrior's Journey '00
Return of the Dragon '72

Lee, Cindy
Legend of the Drunken Tiger '92

Lee, Clarence
Hit Team '00

Lee, Daniel
A Fighter's Blues '00

Lee, Dick
Kick Boxer's Tears '92

Lee Dun
The Imp '81

Lee, Edward
Eighth Happiness '88
Golden Dragon Silver Snake '79

Lee, Erica
King of Comedy '99
Love Paradox '00

Lee Hyungwoo
Masters of Martial Arts '74

Lee, Johnny
All Men Are Brothers: Blood of the Leopard '93
Deadful Melody '94
Wheels on Meals '84

Lee Kyoung-young
Gate of Destiny '96

Lee Lae-soon
Joint Security Area '00

Lee Lok Wah
Tiramisu '02

Lee Man-chol
Deadful Melody '94
Iron Monkey 2 '96
Master Q 2001 '01
Super Car Criminals '99

Lee Mu-yeong
Sympathy for Mr. Vengeance '01

Lee Myung-se
Nowhere to Hide '99

Lee Ping-wah
Extreme Crisis '98

Lee Po-cheung
Dragon from Shaolin '96

Lee, Raymond
Rivals of the Dragon '83

Lee Sai-hung
The Three Swordsmen '94

Lee, Sean
Lethal Panther 2 '93

Lee Siu-Kei
Operation Billionaires '98

Lee Wai Yee
Supercop '92

Lee Yee Wah
Gen-X Cops '99

Lee Yong-jong
Joint Security Area '00

Leeson, Michael
The Tuxedo '02

Lei Chiu
Cantonen Iron Kung Fu '79

LeManna, Ross
Rush Hour '98

Leung Yiu-sang (novel)
The Bride with White Hair '93
The Bride with White Hair 2 '93

Leung, Canny
Bakery Amour '01

Leung Chi Keung
Shaolin Temple 2: Kids from Shaolin '84

Leung, Edward
(Leung Yiu-ming, Leung Yiu Ming)
A Better Tomorrow 3 '89
A Chinese Ghost Story 2 '90
The Magnificent Scoundrels '91
Once upon a Time in China '91
Saga of the Phoenix '90
Swordsman '90

Leung Hung-wah, Tony
In the Line of Duty 5: Middle Man '90
Sound from the Dark '00
Vampire Controller '00
A Wicked Ghost '99

838

A Wicked Ghost 2: The
Fear '00

Leung, Kant
The Demon's Baby '98
Hong Kong X-File '98
Ultimatum '01

Leung Kar-yan
Cold War '00

Leung, Patrick
Bullet in the Head '90

Leung Po-on
Troublesome Night 9
'00

Leung, Raymond
Day Off '01

Leung, Sam
Color of Pain '02

Leung Suk-wah
A Better Tomorrow '86
A Better Tomorrow 2
'87

Leung Wai
Duel of the Brave Ones
'78

Leung Wai-ting
City War '88

Leung Yan-tung
Tragic Fantasy: Tiger of
Wanchai '94

Li, Benny
Comeuppance '00

Li Chan Wai
Jade Claw '79

Li Chao
Martial Arts Master
Wong Fei Hung '92

Li Chia Chi
Militant Eagle '78

Li, Jet (story)
Kiss of the Dragon '01

Li Man Choi
Zu Warriors '01

Li Ngai Chi
Millennium Dragon '99

Li Tai-hang
Legendary Weapons of
China '82

Lik-Chi, Lee
(Lee Lik-chee, Lee Lik-
chi)
Flirting Scholar '93
From Beijing with Love
'94
The Magnificent
Scoundrels '91

Lin, Lin
Ways of Kung Fu '80

Ling, Ling
The Massive '78

Little, John
Bruce Lee: A Warrior's
Journey '00

Liu, Jerry
Flash Future Kung Fu
'83

Liu Sung-pai
Emperor of Shaolin
Kung Fu '80

Lo Wai (story)
The Young Avenger '79

Lo, Ken
Devil Touch '02

Lo Kin
Armour of God '86

Lo Man-sang
Forbidden City Cop '96
God of Cookery '96

Lo Sing
Tragic Fantasy: Tiger of
Wanchai '94

Lo Tzu
The Lost Kung Fu
Secrets '80

Lo Wei
The Chinese Connec-
tion '71
Fearless Hyena '79
Fists of Fury '71
New Fist of Fury '76

Lo, William C.F.
Ninja vs. Bruce Lee '82

Lo Wing-keung
Mr. Vampire Saga 4 '88

Logan, Bey
Ballistic Kiss '98
Gen-Y Cops '00

Long, Timothy R.
Shanghai 1920 '91

Low, Adam
Great Performances:
Kurosawa '02

Lu Bing
(Liu Bing, Lo Bing)
Organized Crime and
Triad Bureau '94
Rock 'n' Roll Cop '94

Lu Shau Chang
The Shaolin Temple '79

Lui Hok-cheung
Glass Tears '01

Lui Ming
The End of the Wicked
Tiger '81

Lui, Raymond
Fatal Flying Guillotine
'77

Lui, Simon
Killer '00
Last Ghost Standing
'99

Paramount Motel '00
The Replacement Sus-
pects '01
Undercover Blues '00

Luk, Jamie
Doctor Vampire '90
Robotrix '91

Lung Kun
Eagle vs. Silver Fox '83

M.L. Shu
The Blazing Temple '76
The 8 Masters '77

**Ma Wing-shing
(story)**
A Man Called Hero '99

Ma Chi Tsuen
The Lord of Hangzhou
'98

Ma, Fibe
Mr. Nice Guy '97
Rumble in the Bronx
'95
Supercop '92

Ma, George
Ninja vs. Shaolin
Guards '84

Ma, Jack (story)
Killer '00

Ma, Joe
Big Bullet '96
Black Mask '96
Dummy Mommy, with-
out a Baby '01
Fighting for Love '01
Funeral March '01
Lawyer Lawyer '97
Victim '99
A War Named Desire
'00

Ma Wai-pong
Extreme Crisis '98

**Maeda, Toshio
(manga)**
Urotsukidoji '89

Mak, Alan
A War Named Desire
'00

Mak Chi-shing
One Arm Hero '94
Sam the Iron Bridge:
Champion of Mar-
tial Arts '93

Mak, Johnny
Iceman Cometh '89

Mak Kai-chung
Dragon from Shaolin
'96

Mak, Marco
The Replacement Sus-
pects '01

Maka, Karl
Aces Go Places 4 '86

Dirty Tiger, Crazy Frog
'78

Man Cheng
Eat My Dust '93

Man Chun
Duel to the Death '82

Man, Man
The Shaolin Disciple
'80

**Manfredi, Matt
(story)**
The Tuxedo '02

Mao Samnang
Snaker '01

Masamura, Yasuzo
The Razor 3: Who's Got
the Gold? '74

Mason, Paul
King Kong vs. Godzilla
'62 (U.S.)

Masumura, Yasuzo
The Razor 2: The Snare
'73

Matsuda, Hiro
Dragon Princess '81
Female Convict Scorpi-
on: Jailhouse 41
'72
Message from Space
'78

Matsumoto, Hajime
Zeram '91

Matsumoto, Isao
Legend of the
Dinosaurs '77

Matsumoto, Koji
Zatoichi the Outlaw '67

**Matsumura, Masaat-
su**
Fight, Zatoichi, Fight!
'64

**Matsuoka, Keisuke
(novel)**
The Hypnotist '99

Matsushita, Mikio
Violence Jack '88

Matsuzaki, Kenichi
Bubblegum Crisis '85

**Mayumura, Taku
(novel)**
The Dimension Travel-
ers '98

McBain, Ed (story)
High and Low '63

McNair, Sue
Horror of the Blood
Monsters '70

Melching, Steve
Godzilla the Series:
Monster War '99

Mellot, Greg
First Strike '96

**Milkway Creative
Team**
The Mission '99
Running out of Time 2
'01
Where a Good Man
Goes '99

Mimura, Wataru
Godzilla 2000 '99
Godzilla vs.
MechaGodzilla 2
'93
Godzilla vs. Megaguirus
'00

Misumi, Hono
Tokyo Decameron:
Three Tales of Mad-
ness and Sensuali-
ty '96

Mitsui, Juzo (story)
Devil Hunter Yohko '91

Mitsuki, Mitsuo
Guinea Pig: Android of
Notre Dame '88

Mitsumas, Kimiaki
Sakuya: Slayer of
Demons '00

**Miyabe, Miyuki
(novel)**
Cross Fire '00

Miyagawa, Ichiro
Atomic Rulers of the
World '57
Attack from Space '58
Evil Brain from Outer
Space '58/59
Invaders from Space
'58

Miyazaki, Hayao
Castle of Cagliostro
'79
My Neighbor Totoro '88
Princess Mononoke '97
Spirited Away '01

Mizuki, Yoko
Kwaidan '64

Morgan, Glen
The One '01

Mori, Eto
Black Jack '96

Morita, Shin
Invasion of the Nep-
tune Men '61
Prince of Space '59

Moriyama, Yuji
Project A-ko '86

**Moroboshi, Daijiro
(manga)**
Hiruko the Goblin '90

Motomochi, Eibi
The X from Outer Space
'67

Motonaga, Keitaro
Gatchaman '94

Murai, Sadayuki
The Dimension Travelers '98

Murai, Yoshiro
Throne of Blood '57

Murakami, Kazuhiko (story)
Tokyo Mafia 3: Battle for Shinjuku '96

Murakami, Ryu (novel)
Audition '99

Murata, Takeo
Godzilla Raids Again '55
Godzilla, King of the Monsters '54
Half Human '55/1957
Rodan '56

Muroga, Atsushi
Junk '99

Nagahara, Shuichi
Godzilla 1985 '84

Nagai, Go
Devil Man '87
Violence Jack '88 (manga)

Nagibin, Yuri
Dersu Uzala '74

Nakahara, Akira
Sure Death: Revenge '87

Nakajima, Takehiro
Zatoichi the Outlaw '67

Nakamoto, Hiromichi
Lady Ninja: Reflections of Darkness '96

Nakamura, Tsutomu
Lone Wolf and Cub 5: Baby Cart in the Land of Demons '73
Lone Wolf and Cub 6: White Heaven in Hell '74

Nakanishi, Ryuzo
Black Tight Killers '66
Gappa: The Triphibian Monster '67

Nakano, Takao
Sumo Vixens '96

Nakata, Hideo (story)
Ghost Actress '96

Nakazawa, Keiji
Barefoot Gen '83

Nam, Simon
Riki-Oh: The Story of Ricky '89

Nam Yin
Burning Paradise '94
Dragon in Jail '90
Full Contact '92
Legendary Couple '95
The Masked Prosecutor '99
Prison on Fire '87
Prison on Fire 2 '91
The Tigers '91

Naoi, Kinya
Zatoichi and the Fugitives '68

Narutaki, Saburo
Naked Pursuit '68

Nathanson, Jeff
Rush Hour 2 '01

Negishi, Shinsuke (story)
Invaders from Space '58

Ng, Charles
Lethal Panther '91

Ng, Frankie (story)
Last Ghost Standing '99

Ng, Jack
Hit Team '00

Ng Lap-kwong
Tragic Fantasy: Tiger of Wanchai '94

Ng Man-fai
The Chinese Feast '95
Eighth Happiness '88

Ng, Ricky
The Red Wolf '95

Ng See-yuen
(Ng See Yuen)
The Bloody Fists '72
Bruce Lee: The Man, the Myth '76
Dance of the Drunk Mantis '79
Drunken Master '78
The Invincible Armour '78
Snake in the Eagle's Shadow '78

Ng Wai-lun
Runaway '01

Ngai Hoi-fung
Ten Tigers of Shaolin '78
Young Tiger '72

Ngai Hong
Avenging Eagle '78
Avenging Warriors of Shaolin '79
Battle of Shaolin '77
Blood of the Dragon '71

Blooded Treasury Fight '79
Brave Archer '77
The Buddha Assassinator '79
Chinatown Kid '77
Chinese Hercules '73
Chinese Super Ninjas '82
Deadful Melody '94 (novel)
Death Duel of Kung Fu '79
Death Ring '83
Dirty Ho '79
Dirty Kung Fu '78
Enter the Fat Dragon '78
Executioners from Shaolin '77
Five Deadly Venoms '78
Flag of Iron '80
The Flying Guillotine '74
He Has Nothing But Kung Fu '77
The Heroes '80
Inheritor of Kung Fu '77 (novel)
Invincible Pole Fighter '83
The Iron Monkey '77
Kid with the Golden Arm '78
Killer Snakes '74
Masked Avengers '81
Mighty Peking Man '77
Nine Demons '83
Prodigal Boxer '73
The Return of the 5 Deadly Venoms '78
Return of the Master Killer '80
Revenge of the Zombies '76
Shaolin Master Killer '78
Ten Tigers of Kwangtung '79
3 Evil Masters '80
The Wesley's Mysterious File '01 (story)

Ngor, Peter
Erotic Ghost Story 2 '91

Nguyen Trung Binh
Cyclo '95

Nihonmatsu, Kazui
The X from Outer Space '67

Nishijima, Katsuhiko
Project A-ko '86

Nishiyama, Akihiko
Gatchaman '94

Nitta, Takao
Spiral '00

Niu Chung Pa
18 Fatal Strikes '78

Noda, Kogo
Good Morning '59

Noda, Masdahiro (story)
Message from Space '78

Nogami, Tatsuo
Sure Death: Revenge '87

Noh Jin-soo
Bloody Beach '00

Not A Woman
Beauty and the Breast '02
Cop on a Mission '01

Nozawa, Hisashi
Violent Cop '89

O'Bryan, Joey
Fulltime Killer '01

Ochiai, Masayuki
The Hypnotist '99

Oedekerk, Steve
Kung Pow: Enter the Fist '76/2001

Ogawa, Ei
Yog: Monster from Space '70

Ogita, Yoshihisa
Maborosi '95

Oguni, Hideo
The Hidden Fortress '58
High and Low '63
Ran '85
Sanjuro '63
Seven Samurai '54
Warning from Space '56

Ogura, Satoru (story)
Guinea Pig: Android of Notre Dame '88

Oh Kwang-Jay
Double Dragon in the Last Duel '85

Ohkawa, Shundo
Nobody '99

Ohkawa, Toshimichi
Blowback: Love and Death '90

Okamato, Noritaka (story)
Guinea Pig: He Never Dies '86

Okami, Jojiro (story)
(Jotaro Okami)
Battle in Outer Space '59
Dagora the Space Monster '64
The Mysterians '57

Okamoto, Kihachi
Black Jack '96

Okuse, Saki (manga)
Twilight of the Dark Master '97

Olsen, Rolf
Shocking Asia '75

Omagap, Rico Bello (story)
The Blood Drinkers '64

Omori, Kazuki
Godzilla vs. Biollante '89
Godzilla vs. Destroyah '95
Godzilla vs. King Ghidorah '91
Godzilla vs. Mothra '92

On, Kay
The Legend '92
The Legend 2 '93
Second Time Around '02

Ono, Ryunosuke
Bullet Train '75

Or Siu-lun
Crime of a Beast '01

Oshii, Mamoru
Urusei Yatsura Movie 1: Only You '83

Ota, Akikazu
Zatoichi and the Chest of Gold '64

Otomo, Katsuhiro
Akira '88 (manga)
Metropolis '01
Roujin Z '91

Otsu, Ichiro
Legend of the Dinosaurs '77
Shogun's Ninja '82

Ozu, Yasujiro
Good Morning '59

Pak Fei
The Descendant of Wing Chun '78

Palmer, William
Robo Vampire '88

Pan Lei
New Fist of Fury '76

Pang, Danny
Bangkok Dangerous '00
The Eye '02

Pang, Edmond
The Cheaters '01
Killer '00
Undercover Blues '00
You Shoot, I Shoot '01

Pang Ming
Frozen '96

Pang, Oxide
Bangkok Dangerous
'00
The Eye '02

Park Chan-wook
Joint Security Area '00
Sympathy for Mr.
Vengeance '01

Park Gyu-tae
Hi! Dharma! '01

Park Mi-young
Bloody Beach '00

Pascual, Jimmy L.
Devil Woman '70

Pau, Peter (story)
The Touch '02

Peace People, The
Drunken Tai Chi '84

Pettus, Ken
The Green Hornet '74

Poole, Marty
Reptilian '00

Poon, Calvin
Hot War '98

Poon Lui
Spiritual Kung Fu '78

Poon Yuen-leung
Downtown Torpedoes
'97

Pu Songling (story)
A Chinese Ghost Story
'87

Pugsley, Tom
Jackie Chan Adven-
tures 3: The Shad-
ow of Shendu '00

Raffo, John
Dragon: The Bruce Lee
Story '93

Ramana, M.V.
Hum Paanch '80

**Rampo, Edogawa
(story)**
Blind Beast '69

Rat
Spacked Out '00

Ratanaruang, Pen-Ek
Mon-Rak Transistor '01

Reaves, Michael
Godzilla the Series:
Monster War '99

Reinert, Al
Final Fantasy: The Spir-
its Within '01

Rendel, Tony
Godzilla 1985 '84
(U.S.)

**Reyes, Anthony
(story)**
Murder in the Orient
'74

Reynolds, Lee
Who Am I? '98

Rintaro
X '96

Rogers, John
Jackie Chan Adven-
tures 1: The Search
for the Talismans
'00

Romero, Eddie
Beast of the Yellow
Night '70
Twilight People '72
The Walls of Hell '64

Rose, Mickey
What's Up, Tiger Lily?
'66

Roth, Louis
Robo Vampire '88

Rowe, Thomas
Violated Paradise '63

**Ryo, Hanmura
(novel)**
Sadistic City '93

**Saito, Hisashi
(story)**
Tokyo Fist '96

**Sakaguchi, Hironobu
(story)**
Final Fantasy: The Spir-
its Within '01

Sakai, Nao
Fatal Blade '00

Sakai, Naoyuki
Street Fighter 2 '96

Sallas, Pierre L.
Curse of the Vampires
'70

Saltzman, Mark
The Adventures of Milo
and Otis '86

Sam, Richard
Champ against Champ
'83

**Sanyutei, Encho
(story)**
The Haunted Lantern
'98

Sanzel, Ken
The Replacement
Killers '97

Sarangaya, Cony B.
The Awaken Punch '73

Sarizawa, Daisuke
The Ninja Dragon '90

Saruwaka, Kiyokata
Samaritan Zatoichi '68
Zatoichi the Outlaw '67

Sasimoto, Yuichi
The Venus Wars '89

Sato, Junya
Bullet Train '75

Sato, Sakichi
Ichi the Killer '01

Sato, Shinsuke
Princess Blade '02

Sawaguchi, Yoshiaki
BloodFight '89

Schamus, James
Crouching Tiger, Hidden
Dragon '00

See, Raymond
The New Marvelous
Double '92
Take 2 in Life '01

Sek, Charles
Magnificent Natural
Fist '80

Sekizawa, Shenichi
Godzilla vs. Gigan '72

Sekizawa, Shinichi
All Monsters Attack '70
Battle in Outer Space
'59
Dagora the Space Mon-
ster '64
Ebirah, Horror of the
Deep '66
Ghidorah the Three-
Headed Monster
'64
Godzilla vs. Megalon
'73
Invasion of Astro-Mon-
ster '65
King Kong vs. Godzilla
'62
Mighty Jack '68
Mothra '61
Mothra vs. Godzilla '64
The Secret of the
Telegian '60
Son of Godzilla '67
Varan the Unbelievable
'58

**Sekizawa, Shinichi
(story)**
Godzilla vs.
MechaGodzilla '74

**Sena, Hideaki
(novel)**
Parasite Eve '97

Seo Dong-heon
Volcano High School
'01

Seo Yun-sung
Yongary, Monster from
the Deep '67

Sham, Tommy
City on Fire '87

Shang Lang
Mantis Combat '81

Shaw, Sandy
The Adventurers '95
The Enforcer '95
The Heroic Trio '93
Justice, My Foot! '92
Losers' Club '01
9413 '98
Supercop 2 '93

Shaw, Sandy (story)
Executioners '93

Sheldon, William J.
The Manster '60

Sheppard, John
Armour of God '86

Shi Hou
The Shaolin Temple '79

Shi Yang-ping
Born to Defence '88

Shiba, Kazue
Son of Godzilla '67

Shim Hae-won
Bloody Beach '00

**Shimozawa, Kan
(story)**
Adventures of a Blind
Man '64
Blind Swordsman: The
Tale of Zatoichi '62
Fight, Zatoichi, Fight!
'64
New Tale of Zatoichi
'63
Samaritan Zatoichi '68
The Tale of Zatoichi
Continues '62
Zatoichi Challenged
'67
Zatoichi and the Chess
Expert '65
Zatoichi and the Chest
of Gold '64
Zatoichi and the
Doomed Man '65
Zatoichi and the Fugi-
tives '68
Zatoichi on the Road
'63
Zatoichi the Outlaw '67
Zatoichi's Cane Sword
'66
Zatoichi's Flashing
Sword '64
Zatoichi's Revenge '64
Zatoichi's Vengeance
'66

Shing Yang
The 72 Desperate
Rebels '76

Shinohara, Toru
Female Convict Scorpi-
on: Jailhouse 41
'72 (manga)

Zero Woman: The
Accused '96 (story)

Shirasaka, Ishio
Blind Beast '69
Giants and Toys '58

Shirow, Masamune
Ghost in the Shell '95

**Shirow, Masamune
(manga)**
Appleseed '88
Black Magic M-66 '87

Shokh, Charandas
Gumnaam '65

Shui Chung-yuet
Zu: Warriors of the
Magic Mountain
'83

Shukla, Dilip
Elaan '94

Shum Chi-leung
Blonde Fury '89
A Kid from Tibet '91

Shum Wai
Queen's High '91

Siba, Eizaburo
Mighty Jack '68

Siddique, Javed
Aakhri Adalat '88

Sigiura, Hisashi
Samaritan Zatoichi '68

Sit Kar Wah
Bury Me High '90

Sit, Louis
Dragon Lord '82

Siu Lung
Snake in the Eagle's
Shadow '78

Siu, Mickey
A Wicked Ghost 2: The
Fear '00

Siu Sang Workshop
The Hero of Swallow
'96

Siu, Stanley
Drunken Master Killer
'94

Siu, Stephen
Iceman Cometh '89
Rich and Famous '87

Siu Yat-ming
The Final Winner '01

Skir, Robert N.
Godzilla the Series:
Monster War '99

Slack, David
Jackie Chan Adven-
tures 1: The Search
for the Talismans
'00

Jackie Chan Adventures 2: The Dark Hand Returns '00
Jackie Chan Adventures 3: The Shadow of Shendu '00

Sliney, Christopher
The Art of Action: Martial Arts in the Movies '02

Small, Jerome
Twilight People '72

So Jing Man
Combo Cops '96

So Man-sing
(Siu Man Sing)
Bio Zombie '98
The Blade '95
Headlines '01
Once upon a Time in China and America '97
Robotrix '91

So, Stephen
Fury in Shaolin Temple '82

Son Kwang-soo
Bloody Beach '00

Sone, Chusei
Branded to Kill '67

Songo, Manuel S.
Murder in the Orient '74

Spears, Jan
Game of Death '78

Steinbach, Ingeborg Stein
Shocking Asia '75

Suen Ging On
Daughter of Darkness '93

Suetani, Masumi
Rebirth of Mothra 2 '97

Sugii, Susumu
King of the Mongols '60

Sum Sai-shing
Ninja in the Deadly Trap '83

Sung Han-yu
The Six Directions of Boxing '79

Suzuki, Koji
Dark Water '02
Ring '98 (story)
Ring 0: Birthday '00 (story)
Ring 2 '99 (story)

Suzuki, Norifume
Sister Street Fighter '74

Suzuki, Toshimichi
Bubblegum Crisis '85

Sze Mei-yee
Once upon a Time in China and America '97
The Three Swordsmen '94

Szeto Cheuk-hon
(Szeto Cheuk Hon)
Bio-Cops '00
Cop Shop Babes '01
Don't Give a Damn '95
Mr. Vampire '85
My Lucky Stars '85
Righting Wrongs '86
Scared Stiff '86
Zu: Warriors of the Magic Mountain '83

Szeto Kam-yeun
(Szeto Kam Yuen)
Expect the Unexpected '98
The Longest Nite '98
Too Many Ways to Be No. 1 '97

Szeto On
(Szu Tu-an, Szu Tu An, Sze-To On, Shut Tiu On, Si Tu An)
Dragon on Fire '79
The End of the Wicked Tiger '81
Erotic Ghost Story 2 '91
Five Superfighters '78
From China with Death '74
Kick Boxer's Tears '92
A Life of Ninja '83
Lightning Kung Fu '80
Martial Arts Master Wong Fei Hung '92
Shaolin Mantis '78
The 36 Crazy Fists '77

Szeto, Robert
Rage of the Dragon '79
The Snake Strikes Back '81

Szeto, Roy
The Assassin '93
Beyond Hypothermia '96
The Blacksheep Affair '98
A Chinese Ghost Story 3 '91
Dragons Forever '88
The East Is Red '93
Master Q 2001 '01
Once upon a Time in China and America '97
The Phantom Lover '95
We're Going to Eat You! '80
Wicked City '92

Tai Fu-ho
A Better Tomorrow 3 '89

Takabayashi, Hisaya
Devil Hunter Yohko 2 '92

Takada, Koji
Return of the Street Fighter '74
The Street Fighter '74
The Street Fighter's Last Revenge '74

Takagi, Satochi
Wild Zero '99

Takahashi, Fumi
Gamera vs. Gyaos '67

Takahashi, Hiroshi
Beautiful Hunter '94
Ghost Actress '96
Ring '98
Ring 0: Birthday '00
Ring 2 '99

Takahashi, Nisan
Gamera vs. Barugon '66
Gamera vs. Guiron '69
Gamera vs. Viras '68
Gamera vs. Zigra '71
Giant Monster Gamera '65

Takahashi, Rumiko (manga)
Urusei Yatsura Movie 1: Only You '83

Takahata, Isao
Grave of the Fireflies '88

Takaiwa, Hajime
Ninja: Band of Assassins Continued '63

Takaiwa, Hajimi
Zatoichi's Vengeance '66

Takami, Koshun (novel)
Battle Royale '00

Takata, Ken
Bronson Lee, Champion '78

Takayama, Yukiko
Terror of MechaGodzilla '75

Takehashi, Hiroshi
Beautiful Beast '95

Takehashi, Tamiya
Beautiful Beast '95

Takeuchi, Tetsuro
Wild Zero '99

Tam Wai-shing
Could You Kill My Husband Please? '01

Tanaka, Hiroyuki
Postman Blues '97

Tanaka, Koji
Time of the Apes '75

Tanaka, Susumu
Body Snatcher from Hell '68

Tang, Billy
Brother of Darkness '94

Tang Danlan
Beijing Bicycle '01

Tang, Edward
Armour of God '86
Dragon Lord '82
Legend of the Drunken Master '94
The Magnificent Butcher '79
Miracles '89
Mr. Nice Guy '97
Operation Condor '91
The Peacock King '89
Police Story '85
Police Story 2 '88
Project A 2 '87
The Protector '85 (HK)
Rumble in the Bronx '95
Supercop '92
Wheels on Meals '84
The Young Master '80

Tang, Elsa
(Tang Pik-yin)
The Bride with White Hair '93
Iron Monkey '93
The Legend of the Swordsman '92
Once upon a Time in China '91
Once upon a Time in China 4 '93
Wing Chun '94
Wonder Seven '94

Tang Guei-seem
Fist of Fury '95

Tang Min-ji
Half a Loaf of Kung Fu '77

Tani, Kenji (story)
Guinea Pig: Android of Notre Dame '88

Tatsumi, Yuichiro
Tokyo Decameron: Three Tales of Madness and Sensuality '96

Te Man-kan
The World of the Drunken Master '79

Tengan, Daisuke
Audition '99
The Eel '97
Warm Water under a Red Bridge '01

Terao, Emiko
Junk '99

Tezuka, Osamu
Astro Boy '63
Astro Boy '80
Black Jack '96 (manga)
Metropolis '01 (manga)

Thomas, Jerry
The Green Hornet '74

Tin-chi, Lau
Knockabout '79
The Victim '80
The Young Master '80

Tin Ping Group
The Young Avenger '79

To, Dickson
Haunted Mansion '98

To Man-bo
8 Diagram Fighter '91

To, Raymond
The Bride with White Hair 2 '93
Love au Zen '01
Peking Opera Blues '86
Shogun and Little Kitchen '92

To, Stephen
Invincible Obsessed Fighter '82

Tomei, Lisa
Godzilla 1985 '84 (U.S.)

Tomikawa, Motofumi
The Eel '97
Warm Water under a Red Bridge '01

Tomita, Sukehiro
Devil Hunter Yohko 3 '92

Tomita, Tsuneo
Sanshiro Sugata '43

Tomita, Yoshihiro
Devil Hunter Yohko '91

Tong, Elliot
First Strike '96

Tong Man-kit
Crime of a Beast '01

Tong, Man-Ming
Legend of the Drunken Master '94

Tong, Stanley
China Strike Force '00
First Strike '96
Supercop 2 '93

Tong, Zevia
Comeuppance '00

Toyoda, Aritsune (story)
Time of the Apes '75

Tramontaine, Nick
First Strike '96

Tran Anh Hung
Cyclo '95

Tsai Kai-pin
Avenging Warriors of
Shaolin '79

Tsai Kuo Jung
Crouching Tiger, Hidden
Dragon '00

Tsai Ming-liang
What Time Is It There?
'01

Tsang, Eric
Dirty Tiger, Crazy Frog
'78
Shaolin Master Killer
'78

Tsang, John
Kick Boxer's Tears '92

Tsang Kwok-chi
(Tsang Kok-chi)
Aces Go Places 5: The
Terracotta Hit '89
Skinny Tiger and Fatty
Dragon '90
Tiger on Beat '88
Troublesome Night 3
'97
Troublesome Night 4
'98

Tsang, Sammy
(Tsang Kan-cheong,
Tsang Kam-cheong)
Casino Raiders 2 '91
God of Cookery '96
King of Comedy '99
Magnificent Warriors
'87
Royal Warriors '86
Shaolin Soccer '01

Tse Lo
Gimme Gimme '01

Tse, Simon
Fatal Blade '00

Tsi, Peter
Gen-X Cops '99

Tso, Dick
A Chinese Torture
Chamber Story 2
'98

Tsoi Kang Yung
The Legend '92

Tsui Ching-hong
The Witch from Nepal
'85

Tsui Hark
A Better Tomorrow 2
'87
A Better Tomorrow 3
'89
Black Mask '96
The Blade '95
The Chinese Feast '95
A Chinese Ghost Story
3 '91

A Chinese Ghost Story:
The Tsui Hark Ani-
mation '97
Dragon Inn '92
The East Is Red '93
Green Snake '93
Iron Monkey '93
The Legend of the
Swordsman '92
The Magic Crane '93
Master Q 2001 '01
Once upon a Time in
China '91
Once upon a Time in
China 2 '92
Once upon a Time in
China 3 '93
Once upon a Time in
China 4 '93
Time and Tide '00
Twin Dragons '92
We're Going to Eat You!
'80
Wicked City '92
Zu Warriors '01

Tsui, Jobic
Her Name Is Cat 2:
Journey to Death
'01

Tsui, John
Masters of Tiger Crane
'83

Tsui Siu-Ming
The Buddhist Fist '79
Bury Me High '90
The Holy Robe of
Shaolin Temple '84

Tsui Tat-cho
The Magic Crane '93

Tsukamoto, Shinya
Hiruko the Goblin '90
Tetsuo 2: Body Ham-
mer '91
Tetsuo: The Iron Man
'89
Tokyo Fist '96

Tsuzuki, Michio
Black Tight Killers '66

Tu Liang-Ti
The Buddha Assassina-
tor '79

Tung Liu
My Kung Fu 12 Kicks
'79

Tung Lo
City War '88

Tung Lu
The Young Master '80

Umebayashi, Kikuo
New Tale of Zatoichi
'63

Umetsugu, Inoue
Hong Kong Nocturne
'67

Urahata, Tatsuhiko
Twilight of the Dark
Master '97

Varma, Ramgopal
Raat '91

Vintar, Jeff
Final Fantasy: The Spir-
its Within '01

Wada, Takuya
Violence Jack '88

Wai Ka-fai
Love on a Diet '01

Wai Kar-fai
Fulltime Killer '01
Help!!! '00
Needing You... '00
The Odd One Dies '97
Peace Hotel '95
Too Many Ways to Be
No. 1 '97
Where a Good Man
Goes '99 (story)

Wai Man
Duel of the Brave Ones
'78

Wai San
The Sword Stained with
Royal Blood '93

Wai Sen
Monkey Fist Floating
Snake '79

Wakao, Tokuhei
Samurai 1: Musashi
Miyamoto '54
Samurai 2: Duel at Ichi-
joji Temple '55
Samurai 3: Duel at
Ganryu Island '56

Wakatsuki, Bunkou
Fugitive Alien '78
Star Force: Fugitive
Alien 2 '78/86

Wan-fung, Lip
Gunmen '88

Wan Siu-kuen
Shadow of the Tiger
'79

Wang Chi-chi
Martial Arts Master
Wong Fei Hung '92

Wang-gei, Wong
On the Run '88

Wang Hui-Ling
Crouching Tiger, Hidden
Dragon '00

Wang Tsing
Death Mask of the
Ninja '82

Wang Xiaoshuai
Beijing Bicycle '01
Frozen '96

Wang Yu, Jimmy
Master of the Flying
Guillotine '74

**Wanlayangkoon, Wat
(novel)**
Mon-Rak Transistor '01

Watanabe, Hisashi
Big Boobs Buster '90

Wei Hsing
Fantasy Mission Force
'84

Wei Shin
Cantonee Iron Kung Fu
'79

Weingarten, Art
The Green Hornet '74

Weisman, David
Shogun Assassin '80

Wen Shui-on (novel)
The Assassin '93

Whitney, Steven
China Strike Force '00

Wilson, Bryan
What's Up, Tiger Lily?
'66

**Wilson, Michael J.
(also story)**
The Tuxedo '02

**Wing, Wellington
Fung**
Aces Go Places '82

Wong, Anthony
In the Line of Duty 4
'89
Wing Chun '94

Wong, Arthur
Fists and Guts '79

Wong, Barry
Dragon Lord '82
Eastern Condors '86
Fight Back to School
'91
A Fistful of Talons '83
Hard Boiled '91
Heart of Dragon '85
A Kid from Tibet '91
The Millionaires'
Express '86
Mr. Vampire '85
Mr. Vampire 2 '86
My Lucky Stars '85
Pedicab Driver '89
The Prodigal Son '81
Righting Wrongs '86
Rosa '86
She Shoots Straight
'90
Twin Dragons '92
Twinkle Twinkle Lucky
Stars '85
Where's Officer Tuba?
'86
Winners and Sinners
'83

Yes, Madam '85

Wong, Ben
Help!!! '00

Wong Chi
Powerful Four '91

Wong Ching-tai
Mask of Death '76

Wong Chui-wah
Saga of the Phoenix
'90

Wong Chung-ping
Dragon Fist '78

Wong, Eddie
Extreme Crisis '98

Wong Ho-wah
Lawyer Lawyer '97
Red to Kill '94

Wong Hoi-ming
Fists and Guts '79

Wong, James
Chinatown Kid '77
The One '01

Wong Jing
(Wang Jing, Chang Chi)
The Buddhist Fist '79
Casino Raiders '89
Casino Tycoon 2 '92
Century of the Dragon
'99
Cheap Killers '98
City Hunter '92
The Conman '98
Crocodile Hunter '89
The Duel '00
The Eagle's Killer '81
The Enforcer (story) '95
Everyday Is Valentine
'01
Evil Cat '86
Fight Back to School 3
'93
God of Gamblers '89
God of Gamblers 2 '90
God of Gamblers 3:
Back to Shanghai
'91
God of Gamblers
Returns '94
Hail the Judge '94
Her Name Is Cat '98
High Risk '95
The Irresistible Piggies
'02
The Last Blood '90
Last Hero in China '93
Lord of the Wu Tang
'93
Love Me, Love My
Money '01
The Magnificent Butch-
er '79
My School Mate, the
Barbarian '01
Naked Killer '92
The New Legend of
Shaolin '94
New Mr. Vampire '86

Return to a Better
  Tomorrow '94
Royal Tramp '92
Royal Tramp 2 '92
The Seventh Curse '86
Sixty Million Dollar Man
  '95
The Tricky Master '00
The Wesley's Mysteri-
  ous File '01

Wong Kam-ba
Seeding of a Ghost '83

Wong Kar-Wai
(Wong Kar-wei)
Ashes of Time '94
Chungking Express '94
Days of Being Wild '90
Fallen Angels '95
The Haunted Cop Shop
  '87
In the Mood for Love
  '00
Rosa '86

Wong Mak Chuen
Yellow River Fighter '88

Wong, Manfred
The Best of the Best
  '96
City of Desire '01
The Duel '00
Duel to the Death '82
For Bad Boys Only '00
Legend of Speed '99
A Man Called Hero '99
Rich and Famous '87
The Storm Riders '98
Young and Dangerous
  '96
Young and Dangerous
  6: Born to Be King
  '00

Wong, Raymond
Aces Go Places '82
Aces Go Places 2 '83
Aces Go Places 3 '84
All's Well End's Well '92
  (story)
All's Well End's Well '97
  '97
Crazy Crooks '80
Eighth Happiness '88
Odd Couple '79
The Phantom Lover '95

Wong, Sam
Clueless '01

Wong Siu-jun
Armageddon '89
Super Gang '78

**Wong Wing-fai,
Anthony**
Tiger Cage '88

Wong Yeuk-ping
Snake-Crane Secret
  '78

Wong Yik
Twin Dragons '92

Wong Ying
Code of Honor '87
Encounter of the
  Spooky Kind '81
Swordsman '90

Woo, John
A Better Tomorrow '86
A Better Tomorrow 2
  '87
Bullet in the Head '90
Hand of Death '75
Hard Boiled '91
Heroes Shed No Tears
  '83/86
The Killer '89
Last Hurrah for Chivalry
  '78
Once a Thief '91

**Woo Ping Creative
Group**
The Miracle Fighters
  '82

Woo, Shirley
The Peacock King '89

Woo, Teresa
Angel '87
Angel 2 '88

Wu, David
The Bride with White
  Hair '93
The Bride with White
  Hair 2 '93

Wu, Laura
Extreme Crisis '98

Wu Ma
Picture of a Nymph '88

Wu Tien-chi
Shadow of the Tiger
  '79

Wu Tit-yik
Fists Like Lee '74

Yaguchi, Shinobu
Adrenaline Drive '99

**Yamada, Futaroh
(story)**
Reborn from Hell:
  Samurai Armaged-
  don '96

**Yamada, Futaru
(story)**
Lady Ninja: Reflections
  of Darkness '96

Yamada, Kazuo
Chushingura '62
What's Up, Tiger Lily?
  '66

Yamada, Kota
Cross Fire '00

Yamaga, Hiroyuki
Royal Space Force: The
  Wings of Hon-
  neamise '87

Yamagishi, Kikumi
The Happiness of the
  Katakuris '01

Yamaguchi, Yudai
Versus '00

**Yamamoto, Hideo
(manga)**
Ichi the Killer '01

Yamamura, Hiroyasu
Godzilla vs.
  MechaGodzilla '74

Yamatoya, Atsushi
Branded to Kill '67

Yamatoya, Jiku
Notorious Concubines
  '69

Yamaura, Hiroyasu
Star Force: Fugitive
  Alien 2 '78/86
Ultraman 2 '01

Yamazaki, Gan
Gappa: The Triphibian
  Monster '67

Yamazaki, Tadashi
Castle of Cagliostro
  '79

Yang Pi-ying
What Time Is It There?
  '01

Yang Tong
Sorrowful to a Ghost
  '70

Yao Ching-kang
The 18 Jade Arhats '78

Yasuhiko, Yoshikazu
The Venus Wars '89

Yasumi, Toshio
The Last War '61

**Yasunaga, Koichiro
(story)**
Big Boobs Buster '90

Yates, Brock
Cannonball Run '81

Yau Fook-hing
Fist of Fury '95

Yau, Herman
Happy Family '02
Master Q 2001 '01

Yau Nai-hoi
(Yau Nai Hoi)
Expect the Unexpected
  '98
Help!!! '00
The Longest Nite '98
Love on a Diet '01
The Mission '99
Needing You... '00
Running out of Time
  '99
Running out of Time 2
  '01

Where a Good Man
  Goes '99

Ye, Lou
Suzhou River '00

Yee, Derek
C'est la Vie, Mon Cheri
  '93
Double Tap '00
Full Throttle '95
Inner Senses '01

Yee-wah, Lee
Fist of Fury '95

Yeh Yen-chiao
The Prisoner '90

Yeoh, Michelle
The Touch '02

Yeung Chi-hsiao
The Shaolin Invincibles
  '79

Yeung, Elsa
From the Queen to the
  Chief Executive '01

Yeung Hon-ming
Bolo '80

Yeung Sin-ling
(Yeung Shin-ling)
Goodbye Mr. Cool '01
Inner Senses '01
Spacked Out '00

Yeung Wai
Blind Fist of Bruce '79

Yeung Woon-choi
Troublesome Night '97

Yeung Yee-shan
Happy Family '02

Yip, Clarence
The Most Wanted '94

Yip, Kim
(Yip Kwong-kim)
Savior of the Soul 2
  '92
Tiger Cage '88
Twin Warriors '93

Yip Kong-yam
The Adventurers '95

Yip, Riley
Lavender '00

Yip, Wilson
Bio Zombie '98
Bullets over Summer
  '99

Yiu Hing-hong
(Yue Hing-hon)
Born Invincible '78
7 Commandments of
  Kung Fu '79

Yokotani, Masahiro
Cross Fire '00
Godzilla, Mothra and
  King Ghidorah: Bat-
  tle on Fire '01

Yokoyama, Mitsuteru
Voyage into Space '67

Yoneda, Okihiro
Rebirth of Mothra '96

Yoon-chul, Jung
Volcano High School
  '01

Yoshida, Hiroaki
Twilight of the Cock-
  roaches '87

Yoshida, Tatsuo
Speed Racer: The
  Movie '67

Yoshida, Tetsuo
(Tetsuro Yoshida)
Daimajin '66
Fight, Zatoichi, Fight!
  '64
Return of Daimajin '66
Samaritan Zatoichi '68
Wrath of Daimajin '66

**Yoshikawa, Eiji
(novel)**
Samurai 1: Musashi
  Miyamoto '54
Samurai 2: Duel at Ichi-
  joji Temple '55
Samurai 3: Duel at
  Ganryu Island '56

**Yoshimura, Akira
(story)**
The Eel '97

You Yeol
Masters of Martial Arts
  '74

Yu Hon-wing
Sam the Iron Bridge:
  Champion of Mar-
  tial Arts '93

Yu Kan Ping
Shaolin King Boxer '79

Yu, Ronny
The Bride with White
  Hair '93
The Bride with White
  Hair 2 '93
The Phantom Lover '95
The Postman Fights
  Back '82

Yu Wing-chuen
Headlines '01

Yu Wing-man
The Replacement Sus-
  pects '01

Yuen, Brandy
Drunken Tai Chi '84

Yuen Gam Lun
Thunder Cop '96

Yuen, James
The Blood Rules '00
Clean My Name, Mr.
  Coroner! '00
Curry & Pepper '90

Every Dog Has His
  Date '01
He's a Woman, She's a
  Man '94
A Moment of Romance
  '90
Shogun and Little
  Kitchen '92
The Tigers '91
Your Place or Mine! '98

Yuen Kai-chi
*(Tuen Gai Chi, Yuen Gai-
  chi, Yun Kai-Chi)*
A Chinese Ghost Story
  '87
The Dragon Family '88
Dragon Killer '95
Fight Back to School 2
  '92
I Love Maria '88

Legend of the Drunken
  Master '94
Once upon a Time in
  China '91
Pedicab Driver '89
The Seventh Curse '86
She Shoots Straight '90

Yuen, Patrick
In the Line of Duty 5:
  Middle Man '90

Yuen Woo-ping
Dreadnaught '81
Drunken Tai Chi '84

Yuen Yuk-sing
The Kung Fu Master
  '94

Zeik, J.D.
The Touch '02

Zhao Yansen
The Adventures of the
  Master and His
  Servant '96

Zicherman, Stu
2000 A.D. '00

Zide, Bill
Fatal Blade '00

Cinematographer Index

The **Cinematographer Index** lists all cinematographers, or directors of photography (D.P.) credited in at least one movie reviewed in this book. The cinematographer listings are alphabetical, as are their corresponding videographies (note that the videographies only relate to those films covered in this book). When applicable, one or more pseudonyms are provided (in parentheses) following the cinematographers' names.

Abe, Jun
Big Boobs Buster '90

Accion, Mike
Curse of the Vampires '70

Aizawa, Yuzuru
Godzilla vs. MechaGodzilla '74
Godzilla vs. Megalon '73

Andriot, Lucien N.
Half Human '55/1957 (U.S.)

Anwar, S.M.
Aakhri Adalat '88

Arai, Takafumi
Project A-ko '86

Arbogast, Thierry
Kiss of the Dragon '01

Ashida, Isamu
Rodan '56

Atsuta, Yushun
Good Morning '59

Au Chih-chun
Dirty Ho '79
Fists of the White Lotus '80

Au, Jimmy
In the Line of Duty 3 '88
In the Line of Duty 4 '89
The Inspector Wears Skirts '88

Au Wing Sun
Snake Fist Dynamo '84

Au Yang-ying
The Dragon Family '88

Aukema, Dewald
Great Performances: Kurosawa '02

Beiyu, Lu
The Adventures of the Master and His Servant '96

Beristain, Gabriel
Blade 2 '02

Bhuller, Darshan Singh
Shaolin: Wheel of Life '00

Blacksmith, Adam
Rivals of the Dragon '83

Boshi, Nobu
Invaders from Space '58

Butler, Michael
Cannonball Run '81

Byeon Hee-seong
Bichunmoo '99

Byeon In-jib
Yongary, Monster from the Deep '67

Cabrales, Baby
Angel on Fire '95

Casey, Owen
Ninja in the U.S.A. '88

Chamnivikaipong, Chankit
Mon-Rak Transistor '01

Chan Chi-ying
(Chan Chi-Ying, Chen Zhi Ying)
Bakery Amour '01
Final Romance '01
Hot War '98
Tiramisu '02
Tokyo Raiders '00
A War Named Desire '00

Chan Chuen-lai
Crystal Hunt '91

Chan Chun-kau
Pom Pom and Hot Hot '92

Chan Chun Li
Shaolin vs. Manchu '80

Chan Chung
Lady Iron Monkey '83

Chan Chung-yuen
(Chen Zong-yuan, Chan Chung Yun)
A Chinese Torture Chamber Story 2 '98
The Demon's Baby '98
Dragon Lord '82
Snake and Crane Arts of Shaolin '78

Chan, Daniel
The Cheaters '01
Paramount Motel '00
The Replacement Suspects '01
Trust Me U Die '99
Undercover Blues '00

Chan Hang-tiu
The 18 Bronzemen '76

Chan, Henry
Casino Raiders '89
Dragon against Vampire '85
Flash Future Kung Fu '83
He's a Woman, She's a Man '94
Legend of the Mountain '79
The Master '89
Royal Tramp '92
Royal Tramp 2 '92

Chan, Jimmy
(James Chan, Chan Hau Ming)
Legacy of Rage '86
United We Stand, And Swim '86

Chan, Joe
All Men Are Brothers: Blood of the Leopard '93
Bio-Cops '00
Born Wild '01
The Bride with White Hair 2 '93
Color of Pain '02
Cop Shop Babes '01
Eighth Happiness '88
From the Queen to the Chief Executive '01
Full Contact '92
The Masked Prosecutor '99
Mr. Nice Guy '97
A Moment of Romance '90
Organized Crime and Triad Bureau '94
Scared Stiff '86
Shanghai 1920 '91
Thunderbolt '95

Tiger on Beat '88
Troublesome Night '97
Troublesome Night 3 '97
Troublesome Night 4 '98
Wicked City '92

Chan, Paul
Aces Go Places 5: The Terracotta Hit '89

Chan, Sam
Eat My Dust '93

Chan Siu-gwan
Comic King '00

Chan, Tomato
Tiger Cage '88

Chan Tung-chuen
A Kid from Tibet '91
Once upon a Time in China '91

Chan, Wilson
Bullet in the Head '90
Once upon a Time in China '91

Chan Wing Shu
Fearless Hyena '79

Chan Yiu-ming
Clueless '01

Chan Yuen-kai
Fist of Fury 1991 '91

Chang Chee
Story of the Dragon '76

Chang Chi-wing
Crime of a Beast '01

Chang Hai
(Cheung Hon, Chang Hoi)

Dance of the Drunk
	Mantis '79
Drunken Master '78
Hit-Man in the Hand of
	Buddha '80
Snake in the Eagle's
	Shadow '78

Chang Shih-chun
(Chang Shih Chun)
Battle of Shaolin '77
18 Fatal Strikes '78

Chang Te-chuen
The Six Directions of
	Boxing '79

Chang Te-wei
The Eagle's Killer '81

Chang Wei-hung
Battle of Shaolin '77

Chao Hung
(Chiu Hung)
Dirty Kung Fu '78
Kung Fu Genius '79

Chao Yung-sin
Prodigal Boxer '73

Chat, Saray
Snaker '01

Chau Pak-ling
The Shaolin Temple '79
Shaolin Temple 2: Kids
	from Shaolin '84

Cheh Wan
Breakout from Oppres-
	sion '78

Chen Chin-kui
*(Chen Ching-chu, Chen
Ching-chueh, Chan
Ching-kui)*
Dragon Lord '82
Half a Loaf of Kung Fu
	'77
The Iron Monkey '77
Snake-Crane Secret
	'78
The Young Master '80

Chen Ching Cheh
Fists of Fury '71

Chen Ching Chu
The Chinese Connec-
	tion '71

Chen Chong-yuan
(Chen Chung Yuan)
Fighting Ace '79
To Kill with Intrigue '77

Chen Hay-loci
7 Commandments of
	Kung Fu '79

Chen How-chung
Dreaming Fists with
	Slender Hands '80

Chen Jung-shu
Drunken Tai Chi '84

Chen Rong-shu
(Chen Wing Shu)

Butterfly and Sword '93
Mighty Peking Man '77

Chen Sin Lok
The 8 Masters '77

Chen Sing-hoi
Shaolin Fist of Fury '87

Chen Wing
Bruce Lee: The Man,
	the Myth '76

Chen Yung-hsu
Dragon Fist '78

Cheng Chi-wing
The Final Winner '01

Cheng Hui-kung
Ninja Checkmate '79

Cheng Siu-keung
*(Cheng Shiu-keung,
Cheng Siu-Keung,
Chang Siu-keung, Che-
ung Siu-keung, Cheng
Siu Keung)*
Fight Back to School
	'91
Fight Back to School 2
	'92
Fulltime Killer '01
Help!!! '00
In the Line of Duty 5:
	Middle Man '90
Losers' Club '01
Love on a Diet '01
The Mission '99
Needing You... '00
The Odd One Dies '97
Okinawa Rendez-vous
	'00
One Arm Hero '94
Return to a Better
	Tomorrow '94
Running out of Time
	'99
Running out of Time 2
	'01
Sam the Iron Bridge:
	Champion of Mar-
	tial Arts '93
Thunderbolt '95
Where a Good Man
	Goes '99
White Lotus Cult '93

Cheung Jui-lin
Two Dragons Fight
	against Tiger '75

Cheung Man-po
*(Cheung Man Po, Che-
ung Man-bo, Cheung
Man-Po)*
Downtown Torpedoes
	'97
Fighting for Love '01
Gorgeous '99
Jiang Hu-"The Triad
	Zone" '97
Lawyer Lawyer '97
Your Place or Mine! '98

Cheung, Raymond
Scorpion Thunderbolt
	'85

Cheung Tak-wai
Code of Honor '87

Cheung, Tony
(Cheung Tung-leung)
Beast Cops '98
Black Mask '96
Comeuppance '00
Every Dog Has His
	Date '01
F*** / Off '98
Glass Tears '01
Hit Team '00
The Irresistible Piggies
	'02
Legend of the Drunken
	Master '94
Love au Zen '01
Runaway '01

Cheung Yiu-cho
Armour of God '86
Dragons Forever '88
Legend of the Drunken
	Master '94
Leopard Hunting '98
Police Story '85
Police Story 2 '88
The Postman Fights
	Back '82
Prince of the Sun '90
Project A '83
Project A 2 '87
The Protector '85 (HK)

Chi-kan, Kwan
*(Kwan Chi Ken, Kwan
Chi-kun)*
Beauty Investigator '92
God.com '98
Killer '00
The Peacock King '89
Saga of the Phoenix
	'90
Thunderbolt '95

Chiao Yao-xu
Return of the Chinese
	Boxer '75

Chim Pak-hung
*(Chim Ang Hung, Zhan
Ba Xiong)*
Man Wanted '95

Ching Wing Him
Revenge of the Patriots
	'76

Ching Yu
Last Hurrah for Chivalry
	'78

Chiou Yao-hwu
Return of the Tiger '79

Chiu Fei
The Assassin '93

Chiu, Rudolf
The Untold Story '92

Chiu Tao-hu
Master of the Flying
	Guillotine '74

Cho Him
Born to Defence '88

Cho On-sun
Invincible Pole Fighter
	'83
Tiger on Beat '88

Cho Wai-kei
Final Justice '88
The Untold Story '93

Choi Jung-woo
Attack the Gas Station!
	'99

Choi Mojin
Masters of Martial Arts
	'74

Choi Shea Suen
Monkey Fist Floating
	Snake '79

Choi Sung-fai
*(Choi Sung Fai, Choi
Shung Fai, Cai Chong
Hui)*
Body Weapon '99
Fist Power '99
Sunshine Cops '99

Choi Yeong-taek
Volcano High School
	'01

Chong Sun
The Unbeaten 28 '80

Chong Yan Kin
A Life of Ninja '83

Chong Yung-chi
Shaolin vs. Lama '81

Chow Kei-seung
The Three Swordsmen
	'94

Chow Kim-ming
The Three Swordsmen
	'94

Chow Kin-ming
Aces Go Places '82

Chu Chang Yao
Last Hurrah for Chivalry
	'78

Chuang Yin-chien
(Chiang Ying-chien)
Fatal Needles vs. Fatal
	Fists '80
The Incredible Kung Fu
	Mission '82
Kung Pow: Enter the
	Fist '76/2001
The Leg Fighters '80

Chuang Yin-ta
Challenge of Death '78

Chung, David
(Chung Chi-man)
Deadful Melody '94

Flirting Scholar '93
Full Throttle '95
God of Gamblers '89
God of Gamblers 2 '90
Hail the Judge '94
King of Beggars '92
Love on Delivery '94
Once upon a Time in
	China '91
Painted Faces '88
Royal Tramp '92
Royal Tramp 2 '92
Shogun and Little
	Kitchen '92

Chung, E
Bolo '80

Chung Hang
The 18 Bronzemen '76

Chung Shen
The 18 Jade Arhats '78

Clarkson, Ross
Cold War '00
Headlines '01
The Suspect '98
Victim '99

**Collister, Peter
Lyons**
The Replacement
	Killers '97

Conde, Fredy
Twilight People '72

Connor, John J.
Kung Pow: Enter the
	Fist '76/2001

Delhomme, Benoit
Cyclo '95
What Time Is It There?
	'01

Divecha, Dwarka
Sholay '75

Dong Haeng-ki
Nowhere to Hide '99

Doyle, Christopher
Ashes of Time '94
Chungking Express '94
Days of Being Wild '90
Fallen Angels '95
In the Mood for Love
	'00

Dubin, Steve
Godzilla 1985 '84
	(U.S.)

Earnshaw, Phil
The Secrets of the War-
	rior's Power '97

Ebara, Shoji
The Haunted Lantern
	'98
Sakuya: Slayer of
	Demons '00

Eggby, David
Dragon: The Bruce Lee
	Story '93

Endo, Seiichi
Godzilla Raids Again
'55

Erh Don-iung
The Descendant of
Wing Chun '78

Faan Chuen-yam
*(Fan Chuan-lin, Fan
Chuen Lam, Fan Chen-
kam, Fan Chuen-yam,
Fan Chuen-kam)*
Duel of the Brave Ones
'78
Faces of Horror '98
Her Name Is Cat 2:
Journey to Death
'01
Prison on Fire 2 '91
A Taste of Killing and
Romance '94
Troublesome Night 8
'00
The Young Avenger '79

Fan, James
Invincible Obsessed
Fighter '82

Fan Jin-yu
The Butterfly Murders
'79

Fan Shou-fu
Shadow of the Tiger
'79

Fenner, John
Teenage Mutant Ninja
Turtles '90

Finestone, Steven
The Art of Action: Mar-
tial Arts in the
Movies '02

Ford, Roy
Legend of the 7 Golden
Vampires '74

Francis, Tony
A*P*E '76

Fujii, Hideo
The Adventures of Milo
and Otis '86

Fujii, Shizuka
Invasion of the Nep-
tune Men '61

Fujisawa, Junichi
Gunhed '89

Fujishi, Osamu
The Hypnotist '99

Fujiwara, Kei
Organ '96
Tetsuo: The Iron Man
'89

Fujiwara, Saburo
Lady Ninja: Reflections
of Darkness '96

Fukuda, Yojiro
Kei Mizutani:
Undressed for Suc-
cess '94

Fung Yuen-man
The Blood Rules '00
Century of the Dragon
'99
Cheap Killers '98
Clean My Name, Mr.
Coroner! '00
Gold Fingers '01
Her Name is Cat '98
Martial Angels '01
Violent Cop '99

Furuya, Takumi
Versus '00

Gam Sing
The Blade '95

Gantman, Yuri
Dersu Uzala '74

Geung Gwok-man
Beauty and the Breast
'02

Godar, Godfrey A.
Game of Death '78

Goi, Michael
Fatal Blade '00

Greenberg, Adam
Rush Hour '98

Gregg, Walter
Once upon a Time in
China and America
'97
Shanghai 1920 '91

Guthrie, Carl
The Green Hornet '74

Hajime, Koizumi
Varan the Unbeliev-
able '58

Ham Nam-sub
Legend of the Flying
Swordsman '00

Hamada, Takeshi
Adrenaline Drive '99
Ghost Actress '96

Hara, Kazutami
Akira Kurosawa's
Dreams '90
Godzilla 1985 '84

Hasegawa, Hideki
Sumo Vixens '96

Hasegawa, Kiyoshi
Godzilla vs. Gigan '72

Hasegawa, Youichi
City Hunter: Secret Ser-
vice '96

Hashimoto, Naoki
Terminatrix '95

Hayashi, Junichiro
Dark Water '02

Pulse '01
Ring '98

Hayashi, Naoki
Guinea Pig: Mermaid in
a Manhole '88
Guinea Pig: The Making
of Guinea Pig '86

Hazard, John
Fist of Fear-Touch of
Death '80

Herrera, Ricardo
The Killing of Satan '83

Hirase, Shizuo
Body Snatcher from
Hell '68
The X from Outer Space
'67

Ho Bao Yiu
Skinny Tiger and Fatty
Dragon '90

Ho Hak-wai
The Hero of Swallow
'96

Ho Hap-wai
Ninja vs. Bruce Lee '82

Ho Hard Sing
Ninja vs. Ninja '87

Ho Hark-wai
Dragons of the Orient
'88

Ho Lan Shan
Return of the Dragon
'72

Ho Lu Ying
Tiger over Wall '80

Ho Ming
Aces Go Places '82
Crazy Crooks '80
Dirty Tiger, Crazy Frog
'78
Odd Couple '79

Ho Yue
Ten Tigers of Shaolin
'78

Honda, Shozo
Zatoichi on the Road
'63

Hou Yong
The Road Home '99

Hua Hui-ying
A Touch of Zen '69

Huang Chien
Death Mask of the
Ninja '82

Huang Rui-zhang
Sorrowful to a Ghost
'70

Huang Yeh-tai
Shaolin Master Killer
'78

Hubbs, Gilbert
Enter the Dragon '73

Hung Brothers
Picture of a Nymph '88

Hwa San
The Awaken Punch '73
From China with Death
'74

Hwang Chul-hyun
Ring Virus '99

Hyon Cho-myong
Pulgasari '85

Iimura, Masahiko
Bullet Train '75
Prince of Space '59

Iimura, Tadashi
Half Human '55/1957

Im Jin-Whan
Double Dragon in the
Last Duel '85

Imai, Hiroshi
Return of Daimajin '66
Zatoichi and the
Doomed Man '65
Zatoichi's Vengeance
'66

Irwin, Mark
The Protector '85

Isagawa, Hiroshi
Twilight of the Dark
Master '97

Isakawa, Hiroshi
Devil Hunter Yohko 2
'92
Devil Hunter Yohko 3
'92

Ishihara, Shigeru
Sure Death: Revenge
'87

Ishikawa, Kinichi
Barefoot Gen '83
Devil Hunter Yohko '91
Wicked City '87

Ito, Akehiro
Entrails of the Virgin
'86

Ito, Hideo
Notorious Concubines
'69

Ito, Takeo
Men Who Tread on the
Tiger's Tail '43

Ito, Yoshihiro
Reborn from Hell:
Samurai Armaged-
don '96

Itoh, Hideo
Ecstasy of the Angels
'72

Iwaki, Toshio
Blowback: Love and
Death '90

Jang Chyi
Kung Fu, the Invisible
Fist '72

Jeon Jo-myung
My Wife Is a Gangster
'01

Jeong Jeong-hun
Record '00

Jeong Kwang-seok
Nowhere to Hide '99

Jessup, Robert C.
The Big Brawl '80

Junior, Bobby
Guardian Angel '96

Kadwe, Sharad
Hum Paanch '80

Kamoto, Tetsuya
I.K.U. '00

Kankura, Taiichi
Destroy All Monsters
'68
Yog: Monster from
Space '70

Kapadia, K.H.
Gumnaam '65

**Kasamatsu, Norim-
ichi**
Evil Dead Trap '88

Kato, Katsuhiro
Godzilla 2000 '99

Kato, Takanobu
Junk '99

Kato, Yudai
Godzilla vs. Biollante
'89

Kawazu, Taro
Princess Blade '02

Keenan, Glenn
The Tuxedo '02

Kendall, Charles
The Secrets of the War-
rior's Power '96

Keung Kwok-man
Bio Zombie '98
Dragon from Shaolin
'96
A Fighter's Blues '00
Gimme Gimme '01
Moonlight Express '99

Keung, Venus
Double Tap '00
Inner Senses '01

Kidokoro, Hiroshi
Zeram '91

Kikumura, Tokusho
Cure '97

Kim, An Hong
Reptilian '00

Kim Sang-beom
Joint Security Area '00

Kim Sung-bok
Dream of Garuda '94
Gate of Destiny '96
My Sassy Girl '01
Shiri '99
Sympathy for Mr.
  Vengeance '01
Tell Me Something '99

Kim Woo-hyung
Happy End '99
Lies '99

Kim Yoon-soo
Bloody Beach '00
Memento Mori '99

**Kishimoto, Masa-
haru**
Hiruko the Goblin '90

Kishimoto, Masahiro
Godzilla vs.
  MechaGodzilla 2
  '93
Godzilla vs. Megaguirus
  '00
Godzilla vs. Mothra '92
Godzilla vs. Space
  Godzilla '94
Godzilla, Mothra and
  King Ghidorah: Bat-
  tle on Fire '01

Kitazaki, Akira
Gamera vs. Guiron '69
Gamera vs. Viras '68

Kittikun, Somchai
Bullet in the Head '90

Ko Chiu-lam
(Ko Chiu Lam)
The Conman '98
Conman in Tokyo '00
Dance of a Dream '01
Expect the Unexpected
  '98
Funeral March '01
Green Snake '93
Horror Hotline...Big
  Head Monster '01
The Longest Nite '98
Love Correction '00
The Magic Crane '93
Once upon a Time in
  China 4 '93
Operation Billionaires
  '98
Rock 'n' Roll Cop '94
Shadow '01
Time and Tide '00
The Tricky Master '00

Kobayashi, Gen
Spiral '00

Kobayashi, Motoki
Wild Zero '99

Kobayashi, Setsuo
Blind Beast '69

Koizumi, Fuzuko
Sanjuro '63

Koizumi, Hajime
Attack of the Mush-
  room People '63
Battle in Outer Space
  '59
Dagora the Space Mon-
  ster '64
Frankenstein vs.
  Baragon '65
Ghidorah the Three-
  Headed Monster
  '64
The H-Man '58
The Human Vapor '60
Invasion of Astro-Mon-
  ster '65
King Kong Escapes '67
King Kong vs. Godzilla
  '62
Mothra '61
Mothra vs. Godzilla '64
The Mysterians '57
War of the Gargantuas
  '66

**Komatsubara,
Shigeru**
The Eel '97
Warm Water under a
  Red Bridge '01

Kong Sze
The Dragon Family '88

Konishi, Kazuhiro
Bubblegum Crisis '85

Koo, Johnny
Aces Go Places 2 '83
Iceman Cometh '89
Legendary Couple '95
Long Arm of the Law
  '84
Long Arm of the Law 2
  '87
New Mr. Vampire '86
Operation Pink Squad
  '88
The Protector '85
Rich and Famous '87
Second Time Around
  '02
Twinkle Twinkle Lucky
  Stars '85

Kozutsumi, Katsuya
Street Fighter 2 '96

Kumphati, Taweesak
Fear Faith Revenge 303
  '98

Kung Mu-to
Brave Archer '77
Chinatown Kid '77
Five Deadly Venoms
  '78

Kuo Fang Chi
Blood of the Dragon
  '71

Kuramoto, Kazuhito
Guinea Pig: Android of
  Notre Dame '88

Kuriyama, Shuji
Postman Blues '97

Kwan Pun-leung
Lavender '00
Merry-Go-Round '01

Kwen Pak-huen
(Gwan Pak Suen, Park
  Hung-kwen)
The Blacksheep Affair
  '98
Shaolin Soccer '01

Laazlo, Andrew
Shogun '80

Lai, Brian
The Postman Fights
  Back '82

Lai Man-sing
Ninja Supremo '81

Lai Wan Hsiung
Fists of Bruce Lee '78

Lai Wen Shyong
The Massive '78

Lam, Ardy
(Lam Kwok Wa, Lin Guo
  Hua)
The Adventurers '95
Bullet in the Head '90
Crime Story '93
Full Alert '97
Gunmen '88
Iceman Cometh '89
Once upon a Time in
  China '91
The Peacock King '89
The Protector '85
Supercop '92
Supercop 2 '93
Swordsman '90
Thunderbolt '95

Lam Chiu
The Seventh Curse '86

Lam, Ken
Kick Boxer's Tears '92

Lam Li-choi
The Shaolin Disciple
  '80

Lam, Raymond
(Lam Fai Taii)
Mr. Nice Guy '97
Once Upon a Time in
  China and America
  '97
Picture of a Nymph '88

Lam Wah-chuen
Bullets over Summer
  '99
Juliet in Love '00
U-Man '02

Lan Nai-tsai
Avenging Eagle '78

Lau, Andrew
The Best of the Best
  '96
Bullets of Love '01
Chungking Express '94
City on Fire '87
Curry & Pepper '90
Dance of a Dream '01
The Duel '00
Gunmen '88
The Inspector Wears
  Skirts '88
Lee Rock '91
Legend of Speed '99
A Man Called Hero '99
Mr. Vampire 2 '86
Once upon a Time in
  China 3 '93
Sixty Million Dollar Man
  '95
The Storm Riders '98
The Wesley's Mysteri-
  ous File '01
Where's Officer Tuba?
  '86
Wicked City '92
Young and Dangerous
  '96
Young and Dangerous
  6: Born to Be King
  '00

Lau Fung-lam
The Shaolin Temple '79

Lau Hung-chuen
(Lau Hung Cheung)
Duel to the Death '82
Kick Boxer's Tears '92
Return of the Deadly
  Blade '81
Queen's High '91
Sword Stained with
  Royal Blood '93
Thunderbolt '95
We're Going to Eat You!
  '80

Lau, Michael
Lethal Panther '91

Lau, Ricky
Enter the Fat Dragon
  '78
Pom Pom '84
The Prodigal Son '81
Winners and Sinners
  '83

Lau, Tom
(Lau Moon-Tong)
A Chinese Ghost Story
  '87
A Chinese Ghost Story
  3 '91
City Hunter '92
The Defender '94
Dragon Inn '92
The East Is Red '93
The Enforcer '95
The Heroic Trio '93
High Risk '95
The Legend of the
  Swordsman '92
The Magic Crane '93
Mr. Vampire Saga 4 '88

The New Legend of
  Shaolin '94
Pedicab Driver '89
Picture of a Nymph '88
Pom Pom and Hot Hot
  '92
Righting Wrongs '86
Rosa '86
Savior of the Soul 2
  '92
She Shoots Straight
  '90
Twin Warriors '93
The Witch from Nepal
  '85

Lau Yuen-chuen
Don't Give a Damn '95

Lederle, Franz X.
Shocking Asia '75

Lee Chi-wah
One Arm Hero '94
Sam the Iron Bridge:
  Champion of Mar-
  tial Arts '93

Lee Chi-wai
Casino Raiders '89

Lee, Gigo
(Lee Chi-hang)
Casino Tycoon 2 '92
City Hunter '92
Crocodile Hunter '89
Fight Back to School 3
  '93
Lee Rock '91
The Most Wanted '94

Lee Hoo-gon
Bruce Lee: A Warrior's
  Journey '00

Lee, Johnny
Lethal Panther 2 '93

Lee Kin Keung
(Kin Lee, Kin Lee Kin-
  keung, Lee Kin-Keung,
  Lee Kwok Keung)
All's Well End's Well '92
Black Cat '91
Daughter of Darkness
  '93
Forbidden City Cop '96
From Beijing with Love
  '94
Tiger Cage '88
The Tigers '93

Lee, Mark
(Lee Pin Bing, Lee Ping-
  bin, Lee Bing Ban, Li
  Bing Bin)
In the Mood for Love
  '00
The Legend 2 '93
Task Force '97
Wing Chun '94

Lee, Sander
Aces Go Places 4 '86
Angel '87
A Chinese Ghost Story
  '87

850

Satin Steel '94

Lee Tak-wai
Savior of the Soul 2
'92

Lee Yao-tong
Encounter of the
Spooky Kind '81

Leonetti, John R.
Mortal Kombat '95

Leonetti, Matthew F.
Rush Hour 2 '01

Leung, Frank
Devil Woman '70

Leung, Jimmy
Dragons Forever '88
Fist of Fury 1991 '91
100 Ways to Murder
Your Wife '86
Pedicab Driver '89
The Protector '85
Savior of the Soul 2
'92
She Shoots Straight
'90

Leung Lek-chee
One Arm Hero '94
White Lotus Cult '93

Li Chi-keung
Odd Couple '79

Li Hsin-yeh
City War '88
Lightning Kung Fu '80

Li Ming
Deadend of Besiegers
'92

Li, Peter
The New Marvelous
Double '92

Li Shih-chieh
(Lee Shih-jei)
Emperor of Shaolin
Kung Fu '80
Filthy Guy '80
The Fist, the Kicks and
the Evils '79

Li Yu Tang
Duel to the Death '82

Liang Chien
The 36 Deadly Styles
'79

Liang Hung
The Invincible Killer '79

Liang Yung-chi
Hand of Death '75

Liao Ching-song
Fantasy Mission Force
'84

Liao Man Meu
Iron Neck Li '81

Liao Wan Wen
Shaolin King Boxer '79

Lin Chao
Five Superfighters '78

Lin Chi Hsin
SuperManChu '73

Lin Men-kam
Lady Whirlwind and the
Rangers '74

Lin Tsau
Bloody Fight '72

Lin Tse-yung
The Eagle's Killer '81

Ling, Zhou Bai
(Chow Pak Ling)
Deadend of Besiegers
'92
Yellow River Fighter '88

Liu Jie
Beijing Bicycle '01

Liu Man Min
Rage of the Masters
'74

Lo One Win
Killer Priest '81

Lo Wan-shing
(Lai Wen-hsing, Lo Wan
Shing, Law Wan Shing)
Fearless Dragons '79
Goose Boxer '78
I Love Maria '88
Magnificent Warriors
'87
Ways of Kung Fu '80

Lo Yun-cheng
Executioners from
Shaolin '77

Luk Kin-lok
Crystal Hunt '91

Ma Chan-wah
(Ma Chun Wah)
Magnificent Warriors
'87
Royal Warriors '86

Ma, George
(Ma Gam Cheung)
City Hunter '93
Combo Cops '96
Killer's Romance '90
Red Wolf '95
Sword Stained in Royal
Blood '93

Ma, Jingle
Comrades, Almost a
Love Story '96
First Strike '96
Full Throttle '95
God of Cookery '96
Goodbye Mr. Cool '01
Iceman Cometh '89
The Last Blood '90
Last Hero in China '93
The Legend '92
Legend of the Drunken
Master '94
Para Para Sakura '01

Pom Pom and Hot Hot
'92
The Private Eye Blues
'94
Rumble in the Bronx
'95
The Tigers '91
Tokyo Raiders '00

Ma Koon-wah
The Miracle Fighters
'82

Ma Kuan Wah
Tiger over Wall '80

Ma Kuan Wan
Dragon's Claws '79

Ma, Michael
(Ma Kwun-wai)
The Buddhist Fist '79
Dreadnaught '81
In the Line of Duty 4
'89
The Magnificent Butch-
er '79
The Victim '80
Where's Officer Tuba?
'86

Machida, Hiroshi
Shark Skin Man and
Peach Hip Girl '98

MacPherson, Glen
Romeo Must Die '00

Maeda, Yonezo
The Funeral '84

Mah, Joey
Champ against Champ
'83

Mah Kwok Wah
Fury in Shaolin Temple
'82

Mak Hoi-man
The Cat '91
Riki-Oh: The Story of
Ricky '92

Makiura, Chikashi
(Oishi Makiura, Chisi
Makiura, Chishi Makiu-
ra, Chichi Makiura)
Lone Wolf and Cub 1:
Sword of
Vengeance '72
Lone Wolf and Cub 2:
Baby Cart at the
River Styx '72
Lone Wolf and Cub 3:
Baby Cart to Hades
'72
Lone Wolf and Cub 6:
White Heaven in
Hell '74
New Tale of Zatoichi
'63
The Razor 1: Sword of
Justice '72
The Razor 3: Who's Got
the Gold? '74
Shogun Assassin '80

Zatoichi and the Chess
Expert '65
Zatoichi Challenged
'67
Zatoichi the Fugitive
'63

Man Nu
The Killer Elephants
'76

Mang, Anthony
Robo Vampire '88

Manoda, Yoichi
Godzilla vs. Hedorah
'71

**Marquette, Jacques
R.**
Varan the Unbelievable
'58 (U.S.)

Mason, David
The Manster '60

Masuda, Ted
Bronson Lee, Champi-
on '78

McLachlan, Robert
The One '01

Mimura, Akira
Sanshiro Sugata '43

Mine, Shigeyoshi
Tokyo Drifter '66

Misawa, Katsuji
Akira '88

Misumi, Kenji
Twilight of the Cock-
roaches '87

Miu, Tony
(Tony Mui, Tony Mau,
Mau Gin Fai, Miao Jian
Hui, Miu King Fai)
Brother of Darkness
'94
A Chinese Torture
Chamber Story '94
Cop on a Mission '01
Devil Touch '02
Dr. Lamb '92
The Eternal Evil of Asia
'95
A Gambler's Story '01
The Magic Crane '93
Red Shield '91
Red to Kill '94
Run and Kill '93
Sex and the Emperor
'94
Sharp Guns '01

Miyagawa, Kazuo
Rashomon '50
The Razor 2: The Snare
'73
Yojimbo '61
Zatoichi and the Chest
of Gold '64
Zatoichi and the Fugi-
tives '68
Zatoichi the Outlaw '67

Miyajima, Yoshio
Kwaidan '64

Miyaki, Yukio
Ninja vs. Shaolin
Guards '84

Mok Chak-yan
Hong Kong X-File '98

Mori, Yoshihiro
Mighty Jack '68
Time of the Apes '75

Morita, Fujio
(Fukio Morita, Fujiro
Morita)
Daimajin '66
Lone Wolf and Cub 5:
Baby Cart in the
Land of Demons
'73
Return of Daimajin '66
Samaritan Zatoichi '68
Wrath of Daimajin '66
Zatoichi's Revenge '64

Munekawa, Nobuo
Giant Monster Gamera
'65

Murai, Hiroshi
Giants and Toys '58

Murano, Nobuaki
BloodFight '89

Myagawa, Kazuo
Lone Wolf and Cub 4:
Baby Cart in Peril
'72

Mygatt, Jeffrey
China Strike Force '00

Nagatsuka, Kazue
Black Tight Killers '66
Branded to Kill '67

Nai Man-sing
Mask of Death '76

Nakabori, Masao
Maborosi '95

Nakada, Hanjiro
Dragon Princess '81

Nakai, Asaich
Throne of Blood '57

Nakai, Asaichi
Stray Dog '49

Nakai, Asakazu
Dersu Uzala '74
High and Low '63
Ran '85
Seven Samurai '54

Nakajima, Toru
Message from Space
'78

Nakajimi, Yoshio
Sister Street Fighter
'74

Nakajo, Toyomitsu
Gatchaman '94

Nakamoto, Norimasa
Tokyo Decameron: Three Tales of Madness and Sensuality '96

Nam, Simon
Erotic Ghost Story '90

Naragawa, Kenchi
Heroes Shed No Tears '83/86

Natu, Shripad
Elaan '94

Ng Fat-sam
My Kung Fu 12 Kicks '79

Ng Kin-man
9413 '98

Ng Kwok-hwa
Iron Monkey 2 '77

Ng Kwok-yan
(Ng Kwok Yen, Ng Kwok-yun)
Death Ring '83
The Heroes '80
Nine Demons '83

Ng Man-ching
Troublesome Night 14 '02

Ng Man-chuen
Chinese Orthopedist and the Spice Girls '02

Ngor, Peter
(Peter Ngo, Ngor Chi Kwan, Ngo Chi-kwan)
Aces Go Places 2 '83
Armour of God '86
Blonde Fury '89
C'est la Vie, Mon Cheri '93
Dragon Killer '95
Dragon from Russia '90
Drunken Master Killer '94
Erotic Ghost Story 2 '91
Flash Future Kung Fu '83
Full Contact '92
The Haunted Cop Shop '87
The Lord of Hangzhou '98
The Millionaires' Express '86
Mr. Vampire '85
Mr. Vampire 2 '86
My Lucky Stars '85
On the Run '88
Pom Pom and Hot Hot '92
Tragic Fantasy: Tiger of Wanchai '94
Wonder Seven '94

Nishigaki, Rokuro
The Last War '61

O-oka, Shinichi
Ultraman Gaia: The Battle in Hyperspace '98
Ultraman Tiga and Ultraman Dyna: The Warriors of the Lightning Star '98

O Sing-pui
Day Off '01
You Shoot, I Shoot '01

Ogata, Hiroshi
Nobody '99

Okamoto, Junko
Guinea Pig: Flower of Flesh and Blood '85
Guinea Pig: The Making of Guinea Pig '86

Okazaki, Hideo
Roujin Z '91

Okui, Atsushi
Princess Mononoke '97

Osawa, Eiichi
The Ninja Dragon '90

Pan Tai Wai
Drunken Art and Crippled Fist '79

Pan Te-yeh
The 36 Crazy Fists '77

Pang Jun Wai
Haunted Mansion '98

Park Hui-ju
Hi! Dharma! '01

Pau, Peter
Anna Magdalena '98
Beijing Rocks '01
The Bride with White Hair '93
Bury Me High '90
The Chinese Feast '95
Crouching Tiger, Hidden Dragon '00
Eagle Shooting Heroes '93
God of Gamblers '89
God of Gamblers 3: Back to Shanghai '91
Iceman Cometh '89
Justice, My Foot! '92
The Killer '89
Naked Killer '92
The Phantom Lover '95
Savior of the Soul '91
Swordsman '90
The Touch '02

Paulino, Justo
Beast of the Yellow Night '70
Mad Doctor of Blood Island '68

Poon, Fletcher
(Poon Yiu-ming)
Brassiere '01

A Chinese Odyssey Part 1: Pandora's Box '95
A Chinese Odyssey Part 2: Cinderella '95
Gen-Y Cops '00
Once a Thief '91
Who Am I? '98
Wonder Seven '94

Poon Hang-sang
A Chinese Ghost Story '87
Crime Story '93
Dragon Chronicles: Maidens of Heavenly Mountain '94
Everyday Is Valentine '01
Executioners '93
Peking Opera Blues '86
The Heroic Trio '93
Iceman Cometh '89
Zu Warriors '01

Poon Tak-tong
Pedicab Driver '89

Poon Wai-keung
Crime Story '93

Prasad, Rajendra
Raat '91

Riba, Francisco
Wheels on Meals '84

Rojas, Emmanuel I.
Terror Is a Man '59

Rumjahn, Abdul M.
(Lam A Do)
Aces Go Places 2 '83
Dragon in Jail '90
Flash Future Kung Fu '83
Legend of the Dragon '91
The Magnificent Scoundrels '91
Mr. Vampire Saga 4 '88
Picture of a Nymph '88
Rich and Famous '87

Sacdalan, Felipe
The Blood Drinkers '64
The Walls of Hell '64

Sagawa, Kazuo
Mighty Jack '68

Saito, Takao
Akira Kurosawa's Dreams '90
High and Low '63
Madadayo '92
Ran '85
Sanjuro '63

Sakakibara, Moto
Final Fantasy: The Spirits Within '01

Sameer
Raat '91

San Aau Shing Lip Ying Cho
Prison on Fire '87

Sasakibara, Yasushi
Freeze Me '00
Gonin '95
Sadistic City '93
Violent Cop '89

Segara, Hiroshi
Woman in the Dunes '64

Sekiguchi, Yoshinori
Godzilla vs. King Ghidorah '91
Godzilla vs. MechaGodzilla 2 '93

Sengen, Seizo
Beautiful Beast '95
Legend of the Eight Samurai '84

Shang, Tony
The New Game of Death '75

Shen Ming-i
Dragon Lee vs. the Five Brothers '78

Shibanushi, Takahide
Ring 0: Birthday '00

Shibazaki, Kobo
Parasite Eve '97

Shiga, Yoichi
Weather Woman '95
Zero Woman: The Accused '96

Shimizu, Masao
Female Convict Scorpion: Jailhouse 41 '72

Shimomura, Kazuo
Terror beneath the Sea '66

Shiomi, Sakuji
Legend of the Dinosaurs '77

Shirai, Hisao
Ghost in the Shell '95
My Neighbor Totoro '88

Shu Te-li
99 Cycling Swords '80

Shue Kim Tong
Kung Fu on Sale '79

Shyam
Raat '91

Siu, Larry
Flash Future Kung Fu '83

Smith, Sheila
The Secrets of the Warrior's Power '97

Srimantra, Decha
Bangkok Dangerous '00
The Eye '02

Sugaya, Noboyuki
Astro Boy '80

Sun Chang-yi
The Cold Mountain Temple '91

Sun Guangwen
The Adventures of the Master and His Servant '96

Sung Kwong-wah
Nightmare Zone '98

Suzuki, Hiroshi
Invaders from Space '58

Tadashi, Nishimoto
Return of the Dragon '54

Tak-yip, Poon
(Pun Tak Yip, Poon Tak Yip)
The Legend of a Professional '00
Painted Skin '92
Shanghai Affairs '98
Sword Stained with Royal Blood '93

Takahashi, Akihiko
Bubblegum Crisis '85
Gatchaman '94

Takahashi, Michio
Gamera vs. Barugon '66

Takama, Kenji
Cross Fire '00
Gamera, Guardian of the Universe '95

Takase, Hiroshi
Another Heaven '00

Takeda, Senkichiro
Ninja: Band of Assassins Continued '63
Zatoichi's Cane Sword '66

Takeda, Shizuya
Naked Pursuit '68

Takemura, Yasukazu
Zatoichi's Flashing Sword '64

Tam Chi-wai
All's Well End's Well '97 '97
C'est la Vie, Mon Cheri '93
Iron Monkey '93

Tamai, Masao
Godzilla, King of the Monsters '54

Tamura, Masaki
Evil Dead Trap '88

Tampopo '87

Teoh Gay-hian
Take 2 in Life '01

Thiru, S.
Champion '00

Thompson, Bob
Armour of God '86
The Imp '81

Ting-wo, Kwong
(Kwong Ting-ho)
The Deadly Camp '99
Legendary Couple '95
Shaolin Soccer '01

Tomioka, Sokei
All Monsters Attack '70
Terror of MechaGodzilla '75

Tomita, Shinji
The Adventures of Milo and Otis '86

Tong, Tommy
Legend of the Drunken Tiger '92

Tong Yu-tai
Iron Monkey 2 '96

Tozawa, Junichi
Gamera 2: Advent of Legion '96
Gamera 3: The Revenge of Irys '99
Gamera, Guardian of the Universe '95

Tremolet, Laurence
Cyclo '95

Troiano, William G.
Horror of the Blood Monsters '70

Tsang, Rocky
United We Stand, and Swim '01

Tsao Hui-chi
(Tsao Hu-Chi, Tsao Hui Chi)
Avenging Warriors of Shaolin '79
Death Mask of the Ninja '82
Five Deadly Venoms '78
The Flying Guillotine '74
Kid with the Golden Arm '78
Masked Avengers '81
Mighty Peking Man '77
Revenge of the Zombies '76

Tsou, Davy
(Chow Lin-yau)
Dr. No... '01
Dummy Mommy, without a Baby '01

Tsui Hsin Yu
10 Magnificent Killers '77

Tsui Siu-kong
Super Car Criminals '99

Tsukakoshi, Ken
The Street Fighter '74
The Street Fighter's Last Revenge '74

Tsukamoto, Shinya
Tetsuo 2: Body Hammer '91
Tetsuo: The Iron Man '89
Tokyo Fist '96

Tu Tong-show
The 72 Desperate Rebels '76

Tuang Yin Jian
The Hot, the Cool, and the Vicious '76

Tung, Dick
(Tung Wai-keung)
My School Mate, the Barbarian '01
Love Me, Love My Money '01

Ueda, Masaharu
Akira Kurosawa's Dreams '90
Madadayo '92
Ran '85

Ueda, Muneo
Gappa: The Triphibian Monster '67

Uehara, Akira
Gamera vs. Gyaos '67
Gamera vs. Zigra '71

Wakana, Akio
Urusei Yatsura Movie 1: Only You '83

Wan, Derek
(Wan Man Kit)
Fist of Legend '94
Royal Warriors '86

Wang Yu
Suzhou River '00

Wang Yung Lung
Five Fingers of Death '72

Washio, Motoya
The Magic Serpent '66

Watanabe, Kimio
Warning from Space '56

Watanabe, Takashi
Atomic Rulers of the World '57
Attack from Space '58
Evil Brain from Outer Space '58/59

Wilcox, John
Legend of the 7 Golden Vampires '74

Windon, Stephen F.
The Tuxedo '02

Wirsching, Joseph
Mahal '48

Wong, Albert
Bruce Lee Fights Back from the Grave '76

Wong, Ally
(Wong Kai Fei)
Ballistic Kiss '98
A Wicked Ghost '99

Wong, Arthur
Aces Go Places '82
Aces Go Places 2 '83
The Adventurers '95
Armour of God '86
Beyond Hypothermia '96
Big Bullet '96
A Chinese Ghost Story 2 '90
Contract Killer '98
Dirty Ho '79
Dragon Inn '92
Eastern Condors '86
Evil Cat '86
Fists and Guts '79
Flash Future Kung Fu '83
Gen-X Cops '99
Heart of Dragon '85
Hong Kong Nocturne '67
Iron Monkey '93
A Kid from Tibet '91
The Millionaires' Express '86
Miracles '89
The Moon Warriors '92
Mr. Boo Meets Pom Pom '85
Mr. Vampire 2 '86
My Lucky Stars '85
Once upon a Time in China '91
Once upon a Time in China 2 '92
Once upon a Time in China 4 '93
Operation Condor '91
The Owl vs. Bombo '84
Shaolin Mantis '78
Twin Dragons '92
Twinkle Twinkle Lucky Stars '85
2000 A.D. '00
Visible Secret '01

Wong, Bill
Aces Go Places 3 '84
Blonde Fury '89
Lord of the Wu Tang '93
Mr. Vampire Saga 4 '88
Once upon a Time in China '91
Savior of the Soul 2 '92

Yes, Madam '85
Zu: Warriors of the Magic Mountain '83

Wong Chi-wai
Dragon from Russia '90
Iceman Cometh '89

Wong, Horace
(Wong Wing-hang)
The Accidental Spy '01
All About Ah-Long '89
Armageddon '97
A Better Tomorrow '86
A Better Tomorrow 2 '87
A Better Tomorrow 3 '89
The Big Heat '88
Bullet in the Head '90
Casino Raiders 2 '91
A Chinese Ghost Story '87
Extreme Crisis '98
First Option '96
God of Gamblers Returns '94
Hard Boiled '91
The Killer '89
King of Comedy '99
A Moment of Romance '90
Option Zero '97
Organized Crime and Triad Bureau '94
Peace Hotel '95
Thunderbolt '95
Too Many Ways to Be No. 1 '97
Twin Dragons '92

Wong Man Wan
Jade Claw '79

Wong, Nico
(Wong Man-wan)
Angel 2 '88
Fall for You '01
Legend of the Drunken Master '94

Wong Ping-hung
Midnight Fly '01

Wong Po-man
In the Line of Duty 3 '88
Powerful Four '91

Wong Siu-cheung
(Huang Siu-chang)
18 Secrets of Kung Fu '79
5 Lady Venoms '78

Wong, Stephen
A Wicked Ghost '99

Wong Wai-chuen
Goodbye Mr. Cool '01

Wong Wing-fei
The Hero of Swallow '96

Wong Yin-pui
Moonlight Sword and Jade Lion '79

Wong Yue-tai
Warrior from Shaolin '81

Woo Kuo-hsiao
(Wu Kuo Hsiao)
Blooded Treasury Fight '79
Born Invincible '78
The Buddha Assassinator '79
Shaolin Chastity Kung Fu '81

Wu Benli
The Prisoner of Five Boulders '89

Wu Cho-Hua
Mighty Peking Man '77

Wu Chuen-hwa
Killer of Snake, Fox of Shaolin '78

Wu Hoi Shan
Raiders of Wu Tang '82

Xing Pei-xiu
The Cold Mountain Temple '91

Yaginuma, Roy
Violated Paradise '63

Yamada, Kazuo
Ebirah, Horror of the Deep '66
Samurai 3: Duel at Ganryu Island '56
The Secret of the Telegian '60
Son of Godzilla '67
What's Up, Tiger Lily? '66

Yamaguchi, Hitoshi
Ninja Scroll '93

Yamamoto, Hideo
Audition '99
Fireworks '97
The Happiness of the Katakuris '01
Ichi the Killer '01
Ring 2 '99

Yamasaki, Ichio
The Hidden Fortress '58

Yamazaki, Yutaka
After Life '98

Yanagishima, Katsumi
Battle Royale '00
Boiling Point '90
Brother '00
Kikujiro '99
Sonatine '93

Yang Ke-liang
Martial Arts Master Wong Fei Hung '92

Yang Shu
Frozen '96

Yang Tao
Crash Landing '00

Yasumi, Toshio
Chushingura '62

Yasumoto, Jun
Samurai 1: Musashi
Miyamoto '54
Samurai 2: Duel at Ichi-
joji Temple '55

Yau, Herman
9413 '98
Time and Tide '00
With or Without You '92
Zu Warriors '01

Yau Ki
Dragon on Fire '79

Yee, Derek
Pom Pom Strikes Back
'86

Yeung, James
(Yeung Jim)
Doctor Vampire '90
Robotrix '91

Yeung Kwong-leung
The Vampire Combat
'01

Yi Hai-fung
The Shaolin Drunken
Monk '83

Yim, William
Extreme Challenge '01
Naked Killer '92
Once a Thief '91
Zu Warriors '01

Yink Tak-li
Thunder Ninja Kids:
The Hunt for the
Devil Boxer '86/94

Yip Chin Biu
Exit the Dragon, Enter
the Tiger '75

Yip Pak-ying
Aces Go Places '82
Hong Kong X-File '98
Troublesome Night 9
'00

Yip Sing Fook
The Master of Death
'82

Yip Wai-ying
(Yip Wai Ying)
Sound from the Dark
'00
Ultimatum '01
Vampire Controller '00
Violent Cop '00
A Wicked Ghost 2: The
Fear '00

Yip Yau-han
The Dragon Family '88

Yiu-fai, Lai
The Avenging Fist '01
Bullets of Love '01
City of Desire '01
For Bad Boys Only '00
Spacked Out '00

Yiu Yau-hung
Aces Go Places 3 '84

Yoshida, Teiji
King of the Mongols
'60
Return of the Street
Fighter '74

Yoshinori, Sekiguchi
Godzilla vs. Destroyah
'95

Ysai San-chi
Snake-Crane Secret
'78

Yu, Jimmy
Duel of the Tao Tough
'82
Eagle vs. Silver Fox '83
Golden Dragon Silver
Snake '79
Masters of Tiger Crane
'83
Rage of the Dragon '79
The Snake Strikes Back
'81

Yu Kam-chun
Ninja in the Deadly Trap
'83

Yu Kok-ping
Last Ghost Standing
'99

Yu Li-ping
Extreme Challenge '01

Yu, Puccini
(Yu Kwok Bing, Chui
Gwok Bing, Tu Guo
Bing, Kwok Ping-yu)
The Blacksheep Affair
'98

City Cop '95
Happy Family '02
Master Q 2001 '01
Vampire Kids '91

Yu Tang
Sting of the Dragon
Masters '73

Yue Ke
Shaolin Fist of Fury '87

Yue Wu
Militant Eagle '78

Yueng Luen
Spiritual Kung Fu '78

Zhao Lei
A Love of Blueness '00

Zhao Xiaoding
Her Majesty Is Fine '96

Zsigmond, Vilmos
Horror of the Blood
Monsters '70

Composer Index

The Composer Index provides a listing for all composers, arrangers, lyricists, bands, and other musically inclined persons cited in the credits of the movies covered in this book as having contributed to the scores of those flicks. The names of the composers or other musically inclined persons are listed alphabetically, and their corresponding videographies are also alphabetically arranged. When applicable, one or more pseudonyms are provided (in parentheses) following the individuals' names. For a tad bit more musical info, check out the sidebar on p. 268 for more on giant monster music.

Abbado, Marcello
Violated Paradise '63

Abe, Masanari
Blowback: Love and
    Death '90

Amano, Masamichi
Battle Royale '00
Urotsukidoji '89
Urusei Yatsura Movie
    1: Only You '83

Angus
Dragon Killer '95

Anzai, Fumitaka
Urusei Yatsura Movie
    1: Only You '83

Aoyama, Hachiro
Bullet Train '75

Arevalo Jr., Antonio
Eighth Happiness '88

Arevalo, Tito
The Blood Drinkers '64
Curse of the Vampires
    '70
Twilight People '72
The Walls of Hell '64

Armstrong, Craig
Kiss of the Dragon '01

Ashiya, Gary
Cure '97

Ashley, Donald
Tiger Cage '88

Auelino, Ariston
Terror Is a Man '59

Avalon Music
Bruce Lee, The Legend
    '84

Avelino, Ariston
Twilight People '72

Babida, Chris
Blonde Fury '89
Bury Me High '90
Butterfly and Sword '93
C'est la Vie, Mon Cheri
    '93
Operation Condor '91
The Phantom Lover '95
United We Stand, and
    Swim '86
Winners and Sinners
    '83

**Balasubrahmanyam,
P.**
Hum Paanch '80

Bang Jun-seok
Bloody Beach '00
Dream of Garuda '94
Sympathy for Mr.
    Vengeance '01

Barry, John
Game of Death '78

Bassinson, Kevin
Police Story '85
    (export)

Beck, Christophe
The Tuxedo '02

Bee, Kenny
100 Ways to Murder
    Your Wife '86

Bekku, Sadao
Attack of the Mush-
    room People '63

Beltrani, Marco
Blade 2 '02

Bernard, James
Legend of the 7 Golden
    Vampires '74

Bin Lau-lim
Dragon from Shaolin
    '96

Boddicker, Michael
The Adventures of Milo
    and Otis '86 (U.S.)

Bondy, Arpad
The New Game of
    Death '75

Buckethead
Mortal Kombat '95

Burman, Rahul Dev
Sholay '75

Calandrelli, Jorge
Crouching Tiger, Hidden
    Dragon '00

Capps, Al
Cannonball Run '81

Carbone, Joey
Legend of the Eight
    Samurai '84
Project A-ko '86

Carli, Fabio
A Moment of Romance
    '90
Wonder Seven '94

Chan Chun-chi
Encounter of the
    Spooky Kind '81

Chan Chung
Dragon on Fire '79

Chan, Comfort
(Chan Kwok-wing, Ken
Chan, Chan Keong-

wing, Chan Kwong
Wing, Chan Kwong-
wing)
Armageddon '97
Bullets of Love '01
The Duel '00
First Option '96
For Bad Boys Only '00
Goodbye Mr. Cool '01
Legend of Speed '99
Love Me, Love My
    Money '01
A Man Called Hero '99
The Storm Riders '98
The Wesley's Mysteri-
    ous File '01
Young and Dangerous
    5 '98
Young and Dangerous
    6: Born to Be King
    '00

Chan, Edward
9413 '98

Chan, Frankie
(Frankie Chan Fan-Kei,
Chen Shung Chi, Chen
Hsun-chi, Chen Hsun-
Chi, Chen Chen Fang
Chi,
Chan Fan-chi, Fin Kai,
Chen Tsun Chi, Chen
Hsun Chi, Chan Fan-
Kei)
Ashes of Time '94
The Buddha Assassina-
    tor '79
The Buddhist Fist '79
The Butterfly Murders
    '79
Chungking Express '94
Dance of the Drunk
    Mantis '79
Dirty Kung Fu '78

Don't Give a Damn '95
Dragon Fist '78
Dragon Lord '82
Dragon's Claws '79
Dreadnaught '81
Duel of the Brave Ones
    '78
Enter the Fat Dragon
    '78
Fallen Angels '95
From China with Death
    '74
Full Throttle '95
Half a Loaf of Kung Fu
    '77
Jade Claw '79
Last Hurrah for Chivalry
    '79
The Legendary Strike
    '78
The Magnificent Butch-
    er '79
Master of the Flying
    Guillotine '74
Odd Couple '79
The Prodigal Son '81
To Kill with Intrigue '77
Tower of Death '81
The Victim '80
The Young Avenger '79

Chan, Joseph
(Chan Wing Leung)
The Dragon Family '88
Iceman Cometh '89
Magnificent Warriors
    '87
Mr. Boo Meets Pom
    Pom '85
Pom Pom '84
Rich and Famous '87

Chan Kwok-man
Killer of Snake, Fox of
    Shaolin '78

855

Chan, Lawrence
The 36 Deadly Styles
'79

Chan, Phil
(Phillip Chan, Chan Fei-lit)
The Cat '91
Dragon Inn '92
Erotic Ghost Story '90
In the Line of Duty 3
'88
In the Line of Duty 5:
Middle Man '90
Legend of the Dragon
'91
The Prodigal Son '81
Red Shield '91
Riki-Oh: The Story of
Ricky '89
Saga of the Phoenix
'90

Chan, Ricky
Champ against Champ
'83
Eagle vs. Silver Fox '83
Fury in Shaolin Temple
'82
Golden Dragon Silver
Snake '79
Masters of Tiger Crane
'83
Rage of the Dragon '79
The Snake Strikes Back
'81

Chan Tak-kin
Dance of a Dream '01

Chang Ching
Prodigal Boxer '73

Chen Hsua Chi
Blooded Treasury Fight
'79

Chen, Ming Chang
Maborosi '95

Chen Pi Teh
Shaolin Chastity Kung
Fu '81

Chen Yong Tie
Deadend of Besiegers
'92

Chen Yung-yu
(Chuen Yung-Yu)
Avenging Eagle '78
Avenging Warriors of
Shaolin '79
Chinatown Kid '77
Emperor of Shaolin
Kung Fu '80
Executioners from
Shaolin '77
Five Deadly Venoms
'78
Five Fingers of Death
'72
Mighty Peking Man '77
Revenge of the Zom-
bies '76
Shaolin Mantis '78

Shaolin Master Killer
'78

Cheng Chin-rong
Martial Arts Master
Wong Fei Hung '92

Cheng Dazhau
The Prisoner of Five
Boulders '89

Cheung, Leslie
The Phantom Lover '95

Chew, Mac
Supercop '92

Chinn, Jenny
Supercop '92

Chiu Kwai-ping
A Chinese Odyssey Part
1: Pandora's Box
'95
A Chinese Odyssey Part
2: Cinderella '95

Chiu Tsang-Hei
Brassiere '01
Comrades, Almost a
Love Story '96
Second Time Around
'02

Cho Sung-woo
(Jo Sung-woo)
Memento Mori '99
Nowhere to Hide '99
Reptilian '00

Cho Young-ook
Bloody Beach '00
Tell Me Something '99

Chou Fu-liang
(Chow Fu-liang, Chou
Fu-lang, Chow Fu-leung,
Chao Fu-liang, Chow
Fook Leung, Chow Fu
Liang,
Chow Fok Liang, Chou
Fu Liang, Chou Fok
Yeung, Chou Liang,
Chow Fook Leung,
Chou Fok Leung,
Chow Fuk-leung, Chow
Fook-leung, Chow Fook-
lung, Chou Fu-lang,
Chou Fu Jung, Chou-Fu-
liang)
The Awaken Punch '73
Battle of Shaolin '77
The Bloody Fists '72
Bolo '80
Breakout from Oppres-
sion '78
Bruce Lee We Miss You
'76
Devil Woman '70
Drunken Art and Crip-
pled Fist '79
Drunken Master '78
The 8 Masters '77
The 18 Jade Arhats '78
Exit the Dragon, Enter
the Tiger '75

Fatal Needles vs. Fatal
Fists '80
Goose Boxer '78
The Master of Death
'82
Monkey Fist Floating
Snake '79
Fighting Ace '79
The Hot, the Cool, and
the Vicious '76
Iron Monkey 2 '77
Kung Fu, the Invisible
Fist '72
Lady Whirlwind and the
Rangers '74
The Leg Fighters '80
The Massive '78
Moonlight Sword and
Jade Lion '79
Return of the Tiger '79
Revenge of the Patriots
'76
7 Commandments of
Kung Fu '79
Shadow of the Tiger
'79
Shaolin Chastity Kung
Fu '81
Shaolin vs. Lama '81
The Six Directions of
Boxing '79
Snake in the Eagle's
Shadow '78
Snake-Crane Secret
'78
Story of the Dragon '76
Ways of Kung Fu '80
Young Tiger '72

Chow Chi-sang
Miracles '89

Chow, Joseph
Lee Rock '91

Chow Kam-cheung
(Chow Kam Cheung,
Chow Gam Cheung)
Eastern Condors '86
Rosa '86
She Shoots Straight
'90
Trust Me U Die '99
The Witch from Nepal
'85

Chow, Nilson
Lethal Panther 2 '93

Chow, Sherman
Ninja in the U.S.A. '88

Chow, Stanley
5 Lady Venoms '78

Chow, Wilson
Legend of the Drunken
Tiger '92

Chu, Carlton
Clueless '01

Chue, Anthony
(Chu Chun-tung)
Born Wild '01
Brassiere '01
Double Tap '00

Chung, Barry
Wonder Seven '94

Chung Chi-wing
Gimme Gimme '01
Losers' Club '01
The Mission '99

Chung, Danny
(Chung Ding-yat)
Black Cat '91
God.com '98
Gunmen '88
Operation Pink Squad
'88
Pom Pom Strikes Back
'86
Rock 'n' Roll Cop '94
Scared Stiff '86
Where's Officer Tuba?
'86

Clarke, Stanley
Romeo Must Die '00

Clinton, George
Mortal Kombat '95

Cuerco, Ernani
The Killing of Satan '83

Dai-yau, Law
(Law Tai-yau, Lo Tai-yu,
Law Daai-yau)
All About Ah-Long '89
The Big Heat '88
A Moment of Romance
'90
Wonder Seven '94

d'Ambrosio, Marco
Vampire Hunter D:
Bloodlust '01

Dan, Ikuma
The Last War '61
Samurai 1: Musashi
Miyamoto '54
Samurai 2: Duel at Ichi-
joji Temple '55
Samurai 3: Duel at
Ganryu Island '56

Davith, Ben
Snaker '01

Debney, John
The Tuxedo '02

Desmong, Chris
Reptilian '00

Diaz, Romeo
Bullet in the Head '90
Casino Raiders '89
A Chinese Ghost Story
'87
A Chinese Ghost Story
2 '90
A Chinese Ghost Story
3 '91
City Hunter '92
I Love Maria '88
The Legend '92
Righting Wrongs '86
Royal Warriors '86
Swordsman '90
Yes, Madam '85

Dol, Roeland
Frozen '96

Douglas, Robert
Fatal Blade '00

Edelman, Randy
Dragon: The Bruce Lee
Story '93

Edwards, Steve
Fist of Legend '94
(U.S.)
The Legend 2 '93
(U.S.)
Twin Warriors '93 (U.S.)

Egan, Mike
Street Fighter 2 '96

EMP
Body Weapon '99
Cheap Killers '98

Endelman, Stephen
Operation Condor '91
(U.S.)

Endo, Koji
Audition '99
The Happiness of the
Katakuris '01

Fisher, Morgan
Twilight of the Cock-
roaches '87

Flood
Blood of the Dragon
'71

Folk, Robert
Kung Pow: Enter the
Fist '76/2001

Fratelli Brothers
Great Performances:
Kurosawa '02

Fung Kin-shit
Shaolin Fist of Fury '87

Fung, Michael
Beauty Investigator '92

Furusawa, Hideki
Entrails of the Virgin
'86

Galasso, Michael
In the Mood for Love
'00

Garcia, Roel A.
Ashes of Time '94
Chungking Express '94
Fallen Angels '95
Full Throttle '95

Garland, Brian
Godzilla the Series:
Monster War '99

Gei-cheuk, Leung
Spacked Out '00

Gibbs, Michael
Hard Boiled '91

Goldenthal, Elliot
Final Fantasy: The Spirits Within '01

Gregson-Williams, Harry
The Replacement Killers '97

Ha On Chia
Aces Go Places 2 '83

Ha, Sammy
Century of the Dragon '99

Haishima, Kuniaki
The Hypnotist '99

Halletz, Erwin
Shocking Asia '75
Shocking Asia 2 '76

Haneda, Kentaro
Barefoot Gen '83

Hattori, Katsuhisa
Prince of Space '59

Hattori, Tadashi
Men Who Tread on the Tiger's Tail '43

Hattori, Takayuki
Godzilla 2000 '99
Godzilla vs. Space Godzilla '94

Hawkins, Wayne
Bruce Lee: A Warrior's Journey '00

Hayasaka, Fumio
Rashomon '50
Seven Samurai '54
Stray Dog '49

Hayashi, Hikaru
Blind Beast '69

Hinata, Daisuke
King of Comedy '99

Hirao, Masaaki
Sure Death: Revenge '87

Hirose, Kenjiro
Gamera vs. Viras '68

Hisaishi, Jo
(Joe Hisaishi)
Brother '00
Fireworks '97
Kikujiro '99
My Neighbor Totoro '88
Parasite Eve '97
Princess Mononoke '97
Sonatine '93
Spirited Away '01
Venus Wars '89

Ho, Ricky
A Chinese Ghost Story: The Tsui Hark Animation '97
Zu Warriors '01

Honda, Toshiyuki
Gunhed '89

Metropolis '01

Honda, Yasunori
Black Magic M-66 '87

Hou De-jian
Born to Defence '88

Hsun Chi-chen
Knockabout '79

Hui, Clarence
Big Bullet '96
Downtown Torpedoes '97
He's a Woman, She's a Man '94
Young and Dangerous '96

Hui, Sam
(Samuel Hui)
Aces Go Places '82
Aces Go Places 2 '83
The Private Eyes '76

Hung, Brother
City Cop '95
The Masked Prosecutor '99
Troublesome Night 4 '98
Troublesome Night 8 '00
Troublesome Night 9 '00
Troublesome Night 14 '02

Ifukube, Akira
Adventures of a Blind Man '64
Battle in Outer Space '59
Chushingura '62
Dagora the Space Monster '64
Daimajin '66
Destroy All Monsters '68
Fight, Zatoichi, Fight! '64
Frankenstein vs. Baragon '65
Ghidorah the Three-Headed Monster '64
Godzilla vs. Gigan '72
Godzilla 2000 '99
Godzilla vs. Destroyah '95
Godzilla vs. King Ghidorah '91
Godzilla vs. MechaGodzilla 2 '93
Godzilla vs. Mothra '92
Godzilla, King of the Monsters '54
Godzilla, Mothra and King Ghidorah: Battle on Fire '01
Invasion of Astro-Monster '65
King Kong Escapes '67

King Kong vs. Godzilla '62
Mothra vs. Godzilla '64
The Mysterians '57
New Tale of Zatoichi '63
Return of Daimajin '66
The Tale of Zatoichi Continues '62
Terror of MechaGodzilla '75
Varan the Unbelievable '58
War of the Gargantuas '66
Wrath of Daimajin '66
Yog: Monster from Space '70
Zatoichi Challenged '67
Zatoichi and the Chess Expert '65
Zatoichi on the Road '63
Zatoichi the Fugitive '63
Zatoichi's Revenge '64
Zatoichi's Vengeance '66

Ike, Yoshohiro
Blood: The Last Vampire '00

Ikebe, Shinichiro
Akira Kurosawa's Dreams '90
The Eel '97
Madadayo '92
Warm Water under a Red Bridge '01

Ikeno, Sei
Samaritan Zatoichi '68
The Secret of the Telegian '60
Zatoichi the Outlaw '67
Zatoichi's Flashing Sword '64

Il Won
Ring Virus '99

Inoue, Akira
The Young Master '80

Ishikawa, Chu
(Tadashi Ishikawa)
Tetsuo: The Iron Man '89
Tetsuo 2: Body Hammer '91
Tokyo Fist '96

Itakura, Bun
Roujin Z '91

Iwashiro, Taro
Another Heaven '00

Izumi, Taku
The X from Outer Space '67

Jaikishan, Shankar
Gumnaam '65

Jang Dae-sung
My Wife Is a Gangster '01

Jarre, Maurice
Shogun '80

Jeon Jeong-geun
Yongary, Monster from the Deep '67

Jo Yeong-wook
Dream of Garuda '94
Sympathy for Mr. Vengeance '01

Jun Jungkun
Masters of Martial Arts '74

Kaburagi, Kajime
Zatoichi and the Fugitives '68

Kaburagi, So
Tokyo Drifter '66

Kam, Peter
The Accidental Spy '01
Big Bullet '96
Bio Zombie '98
Double Tap '00
Downtown Torpedoes '97
Final Romance '01
Full Alert '97
Gen-Y Cops '00
Hot War '98
Inner Senses '01
Mr. Nice Guy '97
Para Para Sakura '01
Tokyo Raiders '00
You Shoot, I Shoot '01

Karera Musication
Ichi the Killer '01

Kasamatsu, Yasuhiro
After Life '98

Kashibuchi, Tetsuro
Spiral '00

Kawai, Kenji
Dark Water '02
Devil Man '87
Ghost in the Shell '95
Princess Blade '02
Ring '98
Ring 2 '99
Sakuya: Slayer of Demons '00

Kawamura, Akifumi
Ghost Actress '96

Kawamura, Eiji
Black Jack '96

Kikuchi, Shunsuke
(Sid Kikuchi, Juinsuke Kikuchi)
Body Snatcher from Hell '68
Dragon Princess '81
Female Convict Scorpion: Jailhouse 41 '72
Gamera vs. Guiron '69

Gamera vs. Zigra '71
Message from Space '78
Sister Street Fighter '74
Terror beneath the Sea '66

Kim Hyun-seok
My Sassy Girl '01

Kim Jin-ping
Shaolin Fist of Fury '87

Kim Jun-seon
Bichunmoo '99

Kimura, Yumi
Spirited Away '01

King Yong
Crouching Tiger, Hidden Dragon '00

Kinoshita, Chuji
Gamera vs. Barugon '66

Kira, Tomohiko
Evil Dead Trap '88

Kit Cut Club
Guinea Pig: Android of Notre Dame '88
Guinea Pig: Flower of Flesh and Blood '85
Guinea Pig: Mermaid in a Manhole '88

Kitamura, Ken
Final Fantasy: The Spirits Within '01

Kitaro
(Cho To-lung)
Shanghai 1920 '91

Klein, Jim
City on Fire '87 (U.S.)

Ko Yi Dai
The Lord of Hangzhou '98

Kobayashi, Izumi
Urusei Yatsura Movie 1: Only You '83

Komuro, Tetsuya
Vampire Hunter D '85

Koo, Joseph
A Better Tomorrow '86
A Better Tomorrow 2 '87
Fist of Legend '94
Hand of Death '75
King of Beggars '92
Lord of the Wu Tang '93
Return of the Deadly Blade '81
Return of the Dragon '72

Koo Ka-fay
The Heroes '80

Koo Lai Yip
Horror Hotline Big Head
Monster '01

Koroku, Reijiro
Godzilla 1985 '84

Koseki, Yuji
Mothra '61

Koshibe, Nobuyoshi
Speed Racer: The
Movie '67

Ku Chia Hui
The Chinese Connec-
tion '71

Kume, Daisuke
Violent Cop '89

Kwan, Teddy Robin
Aces Go Places '82
Aces Go Places 2 '83
Aces Go Places 5: The
Terracotta Hit '89
The Adventurers '95
Black Mask '96
City on Fire '87
Contract Killer '98
Full Contact '92
The Private Eye Blues
'94
Tiger on Beat '88

Kwok, Alvin
The Three Swordsmen
'94

Lai, Henry
(Lai Wan Man)
Beijing Rocks '01
A Fighter's Blues '00

Lai, Michael
Armour of God '86
City War '88
Duel to the Death '82
My Lucky Stars '85
New Mr. Vampire '86
Police Story '85
Police Story 2 '88
Project A '83
Project A 2 '87

Lam, Violet
All's Well End's Well '92
Dragon Chronicles:
Maidens of Heaven-
ly Mountain '94
Dragon from Russia
'90
Heart of Dragon '85
A Kid from Tibet '91
On the Run '88
Once a Thief '91
The Witch from Nepal
'85

Lam Wah-Chuen
U-Man '02
Time and Tide '00

Lam Yee-tat
The Master '89

Lam-mau, Mooi
Hong Kong Nocturne
'67

Lap Fu
The Prisoner '90

Latham, Jim
Godzilla the Series:
Monster War '99
Jackie Chan Adven-
tures 1: The Search
for the Talismans
'00
Jackie Chan Adven-
tures 2: The Dark
Hand Returns '00
Jackie Chan Adven-
tures 3: The Shad-
ow of Shendu '00

Lau, Tats
(Lau Yee-tat)
Forbidden City Cop '96
The Last Blood '90
The Tigers '91
Tragic Fantasy: Tiger of
Wanchai '94
With or Without You '92

Law, Norman
Legend of the Dragon-
slayer Sword '90
Legend of the Dragon-
slayer Sword 3-The
Rage of Gina '90

Law Wing-fai
Evil Cat '86

Lee, Alan
Last Ghost Standing
'99

Lee, Anthony
Satin Steel '94
Sixty Million Dollar Man
'95

Lee, Charles
9413 '98

Lee Dong-jun
Shiri '99

Lee, Gigo
The Most Wanted '94

Lee Hon-chuen
Return to a Better
Tomorrow '94

Lee, Jonathan
Supercop '92

Lee-on, A
Spacked Out '00

Lemberg, Jorg
Suzhou River '00

Leung, Simon
Sound from the Dark
'00
Vampire Controller '00
A Wicked Ghost '99
A Wicked Ghost 2: The
Fear '00

Leung Wai-kin
Bakery Amour '01

Leung Yiu-pak
Comeuppance '00

Lewis, Jack
What's Up, Tiger Lily?
'66

Lewis, W. Michael
Shogun Assassin '80

Li-ping, Wang
The Shaolin Temple '79

Lin Che-yeung
The Best of the Best
'96

Lindsay, Mark
Shogun Assassin '80

Lip On Tat
Mr. Vampire '85

Lo, Lincoln
(Law Kin, Legend Lo)
Beauty and the Breast
'02
Bio-Cops '00
The Blood Rules '00
The Cheaters '01
A Chinese Torture
Chamber Story 2
'98
City of Desire '01
Clean My Name, Mr.
Coroner! '00
The Conman '98
Cop Shop Babes '01
Cop on a Mission '01
The Demon's Baby '98
Dummy Mommy, with-
out a Baby '01
Every Dog Has His
Date '01
Fighting for Love '01
Funeral March '01
A Gambler's Story '01
Lawyer Lawyer '97
Love Correction '00
Operation Billionaires
'98
The Replacement Sus-
pects '01
Sunshine Cops '99
The Tricky Master '99
Undercover Blues '00
Your Place or Mine! '98

Lo, Lowell
(Lui Koon-ting)
A Better Tomorrow 2
'87
A Better Tomorrow 3
'89
The Chinese Feast '95
Crocodile Hunter '89
Dragon in Jail '90
Fight Back to School 3
'93
Fist of Fury 1991 '91
God of Gamblers '89
God of Gamblers 2 '90

God of Gamblers 3:
Back to Shanghai
'91
God of Gamblers
Returns '94
The Killer '89
The Legend 2 '93
Naked Killer '92
Once upon a Time in
China and America
'97
Painted Faces '88
Pedicab Driver '89
Powerful Four '91
Prison on Fire '87
Prison on Fire 2 '91
She Shoots Straight
'90
Twin Dragons '92

Lo, Richard
Aces Go Places 5: The
Terracotta Hit '89
All About Ah-Long '89
Angel '87
Curry & Pepper '90
The Magnificent
Scoundrels '91
Queen's High '91
Supercop 2 '93

Lo, Tony
Aces Go Places 4 '86

Lo, Wing
9413 '98

Lok-sang, Lau
The Private Eye Blues
'94

Loung, Phe
Twin Dragons '92

Lovin' Spoonful, The
What's Up, Tiger Lily?
'66

Ltd
Ultimatum '01

Luen, Chow
Rage of the Masters
'74

Lui, Mark
Crime Story '93
Deadful Melody '94
Everyday Is Valentine
'01
Green Snake '93
The Legend '92
The Moon Warriors '92
A Taste of Killing and
Romance '94
A War Named Desire
'00

Lui, Patrick
The Tigers '91

Lun, Anthony
Savior of the Soul '91

MacRae, Bruce
A*P*E '76

Maeda, Norio
Star Force: Fugitive
Alien 2 '78/86

Mak Chun-hung
(Mak Jan-hung)
Burning Paradise '94
Chinese Orthopedist
and the Spice Girls
'02
From the Queen to the
Chief Executive '01
Happy Family '02
Headlines '01
Drunken Master Killer
'94
Legendary Couple '95
Master Q 2001 '01
Take 2 in Life '01
Troublesome Night '97
Troublesome Night 3
'97
Troublesome Night 14
'02

Makaino, Koji
The Happiness of the
Katakuris '01

Makaino, Kouji
Bubblegum Crisis '85

Maki, Yoshino
The Peacock King '89

Malik, Anu
Aakhri Adalat '88
Champion '00

Mamiya, Yoshio
Grave of the Fireflies
'88

Man, Ma
Kung Fu Genius '79

Man, Mah
Dragon on Fire '79

Man, Man
The Shaolin Disciple
'80

Manabe, Riichiro
Godzilla vs. Hedorah
'71
Godzilla vs. Megalon
'73
Invaders from Space
'58

Mansfield, Keith
Fist of Fear-Touch of
Death '80

Mao-shan, Huang
Dreaming Fists with
Slender Hands '80

Marquez, Ringgo
Angel on Fire '95

Matsumoto, Akihiko
Extreme Crisis '98

Mau-san, Wang
The Heroes '80

Mau-sen, Huang
Ninja Checkmate '79

Mau-shan, Wang
Kung Pow: Enter the
Fist '76/2001

May, Bill
The Green Hornet '74

Mayazumi, Toshiro
Good Morning '59

McNeely, Joel
Supercop '92 (U.S.)

Melody Bank
Final Justice '88
Mr. Vampire 2 '86
Scared Stiff '86

**Methakunavudh,
Amornbhong**
Mon-Rak Transistor '01

Meyers, Bill
Gatchaman '94

Min
Skinny Tiger and Fatty
Dragon '90

Miyauchi, Kunio
All Monsters Attack '70
The Human Vapor '60

Mo-san, Wang
Militant Eagle '78

Mo-tak, Lam
Long Arm of the Law
'84

Morino, Nobuhiko
Versus '00

Morioka, Ken-Ichiro
Message from Space
'78

Mou-shan, Huang
The Incredible Kung Fu
Mission '82

Mu-hyeon, Son
Attack the Gas Station!
'99

Mu-san, Hang
Iron Neck Li '81

Mu-san, Wang
18 Secrets of Kung Fu
'79
A Life of Ninja '83

Murai, Kunihiko
Lone Wolf and Cub 6:
White Heaven in
Hell '74
The Razor 1: Sword of
Justice '72
Tampopo '87

Nakagawa, Kotoro
The Haunted Lantern
'98

Nakagawa, Takashi
Reborn from Hell:
Samurai Armaged-
don '96
Tokyo Mafia 2: Wrath of
the Yakuza '95
Tokyo Mafia: Yakuza
Wars '95

Nakamoto, Tetsu
Lady Ninja: Reflections
of Darkness '96

Nakanishi, Tatsuo
Terminatrix '95

Nakayama, Takashi
Zero Woman: The
Accused '96

Nanjing Music Group
Ultimatum '01

Nelsson, Anders
The Haunted Cop Shop
'87
Twinkle Twinkle Lucky
Stars '85

**New Note Music Pro-
duction**
The Inspector Wears
Skirts '88

Ng, Ronald
God of Cookery '96
Lavender '00
Merry-Go-Round '01

Ng Tai Hong
Fury of King Boxer '72

Ng-tai, King
Legend of the Mountain
'79

Ng Tai Kong
(Ng Tai Kwong, Wu Ta
Chiang, Wu Ta-chang,
Wu Ta-chiang)
Fearless Dragons '79
Five Fingers of Death
'72
Iron Monkey 2 '96
10 Magnificent Killers
'77
The 36 Crazy Fists '77
Tiger over Wall '80

Nishimura, Yukie
Ballistic Kiss '98

Njo, Johnny
Once upon a Time in
China 2 '92

Ogata, Shinochiro
Ring 0: Birthday '00

Ogawa, Hiroki
The Manster '60

Ogawa, Yoichi
Big Boobs Buster '90

Oguchi, Yuji
BloodFight '89

Ohta, Hirokazu
Zeram '91

Okamoto, Daisuke
Postman Blues '97

Omori, Seitaro
Gappa: The Triphibian
Monster '67
Warning from Space
'56

Omori, Toshiyuki
Devil Hunter Yohko 2
'92
Devil Hunter Yohko 3
'92

Ono, Yuji
Castle of Cagliostro
'79

Orange Music
Bangkok Dangerous
'00
The Eye '02

Oshima, Michiru
Godzilla vs. Megaguirus
'00

Otani, Ko
Cross Fire '00
Gamera 2: Advent of
Legion '96
Gamera 3: The
Revenge of Irys '99
Gamera, Guardian of
the Universe '95
Godzilla, Mothra and
King Ghidorah: Bat-
tle on Fire '01

O'Yang, Gordon
Comeuppance '00

Pa-lan, Dal
Lies '99

Pagoni, Sergio
Violated Paradise '63

Pak, Chong
Spiritual Kung Fu '78

Pan Guoxing
Crash Landing '00

Park Jin-seok
Hi! Dharma! '01

Park, Seneca
The Ladies' Phone Sex
Club '96
Tokyo Decameron:
Three Tales of Mad-
ness and Sensuali-
ty '96

Park Yeong
Volcano High School
'01

**Pheloung, Barring-
ton**
Shaolin: Wheel of Life
'00

Poledouris, Basil
The Touch '02

**Pongprapan,
Chartchai**
Mon-Rak Transistor '01

Poon, Healthy
Peace Hotel '95

Prakash, Kemchan
Mahal '48

Prez, John Du
Teenage Mutant Ninja
Turtles '90

Qing, Liang
The Adventures of the
Master and His
Servant '96

Quinian, Noel
Aces Go Places 3 '84

Rabin, Trevor
The One '01

Rabjohns, Paul
Operation Condor '91
(U.S.)

Rashinban
Adrenaline Drive '99

Rivera, Nicholas
The Defender '94
(U.S.)
The Enforcer '95 (U.S.)
The Legend '92 (U.S.)

Robinson, J. Peter
First Strike '96 (U.S.)
Mr. Nice Guy '97 (U.S.)
Police Story '85 (U.S.)
Police Story 2 '88
(U.S.)
Rumble in the Bronx
'95 (U.S.)

Robles, Nestor
Beast of the Yellow
Night '70

Rodeo, Video
Organ '96

Rucker, Steve
The Art of Action: Mar-
tial Arts in the
Movies '02

Rumjahn, Mahmood
Fight Back to School 2
'92
Pom Pom '84

Ryo, Kunihiko
Thunderbolt '95

Saboten, The
I.K.U. '00

Saegusa, Nariaki
Astro Boy '80

Sahashi, Toshihiko
Ultraman Gaia: The
Battle in Hyper-
space '98

Saito, Ichiro
Zatoichi and the Chest
of Gold '64
Zatoichi's Cane Sword
'66

Sakamoto, Ryuichi
The Adventures of Milo
and Otis '86
Royal Space Force: The
Wings of Hon-
neamise '87

Sakamoto, Yuki
Reborn from Hell:
Samurai Armaged-
don '96
Tokyo Mafia 2: Wrath of
the Yakuza '95
Tokyo Mafia: Yakuza
Wars '95

Sakurai, Eiken
Lone Wolf and Cub 2:
Baby Cart at the
River Styx '72

Sakurai, Hideaki
Lone Wolf and Cub 1:
Sword of
Vengeance '72
Lone Wolf and Cub 3:
Baby Cart to Hades
'72
Lone Wolf and Cub 4:
Baby Cart in Peril
'72
Lone Wolf and Cub 5:
Baby Cart in the
Land of Demons
'73
The Razor 3: Who's Got
the Gold? '74

Sam, Wang Mao
Raiders of Wu Tang '82

Sam-mei, Ha
Martial Angels '01

San, Alex
The Blacksheep Affair
'98

San Bao
The Road Home '99

San, Wang Sat
Lady Iron Monkey '83

Sang, Roman
Invincible Obsessed
Fighter '82

Sang-yun, Lee
Record '00

Sato, Masaru
Ebirah, Horror of the
Deep '66
Godzilla Raids Again
'55
Godzilla vs.
MechaGodzilla '74
The H-Man '58
Half Human '55/1957
The Hidden Fortress
'58

High and Low '63
Sanjuro '63
Son of Godzilla '67
Throne of Blood '57
Yojimbo '61

Sau-pok, Chan
Comeuppance '00

Sau-pok, Wu
Love au Zen '01

Schifrin, Lalo
The Big Brawl '80
Enter the Dragon '73
Rush Hour '98
Rush Hour 2 '01

Seo Young-jin
Gate of Destiny '96

Shan, Huang Mou
Killer Priest '81

Shan, Wang Mao
18 Fatal Strikes '78

Shao-hua
Sting of the Dragon
    Masters '73

Sharma, Mani
Raat '91

Shin Ho-seob
Hi! Dharma! '01

Shing, Stephen
Death Mask of the
    Ninja '82
The New Marvelous
    Double '92

Shiun-chi, Chen
Born Invincible '78

Shrivastava, Aadesh
Champion '00

Shum, Jim
Flash Future Kung Fu
    '83

Shvartz, Isaak
Dersu Uzala '74

Shyam-Surinder
Elaan '94

Sing Kam-wing
Invincible Pole Fighter
    '83
The Millionaires'
    Express '86
The Seventh Curse '86

Sit Jon-ping
Shaolin Fist of Fury '87

Siu-hung, Cheung
Beyond Hypothermia
    '96
Losers' Club '01

Siu-lam, Tang
(Tang Se Lim, Tang Siu
    Lam)
All's Well End's Well '97
    '97
Angel 2 '88

Combo Cops '96
Drunken Tai Chi '84
Heroes Shed No Tears
    '83/86
Queen's High '91
Red Wolf '95
Shaolin vs. Manchu '80

So Chun-hou
(Go Chun Hou)
Death Mask of the
    Ninja '82
Invincible Pole Fighter
    '83

So, Stephen
Snake Fist Dynamo '84

Star East Music Ltd.
Shadow '01

Suga, Shikao
Dark Water '02

Sugiyama, Koichi
Godzilla vs. Biollante
    '89

Sun Chun-lin
Dragon Lee vs. the Five
    Brothers '78

Suzuki, Daisuke
Tokyo Mafia 3: Battle
    for Shinjuku '96

Suzuki, Keichi
Spiral '00

Suzuki, Masakatsu
Shogun's Ninja '82

Suzuki, Seiichi
Sanshiro Sugata '43

Suzuki, Seiji
Astro Boy '80

Takai, Tatsuo
Astro Boy '63
Astro Boy '80

Takarai, Hideto
Final Fantasy: The Spir-
    its Within '01

Takemitsu, Toru
Kwaidan '64
Ran '85
Woman in the Dunes
    '64

Tam, Tony
Vampire Controller '00
A Wicked Ghost 2: The
    Fear '00

Tamagawa, Shizuko
Ultraman Gaia: The
    Battle in Hyper-
    space '98

Tan Dun
Crouching Tiger, Hidden
    Dragon '00

Tang Hin-fai
Doctor No... '01

Tegelman, Jussi
Contract Killer '98

Thorne, Ken
The Protector '85

Tiet Ton-That
Cyclo '95

Timbaland
Romeo Must Die '00

To Chi-chi
Savior of the Soul 2
    '92

Tomita, Isao
Mighty Jack '68
The Razor 2: The Snare
    '73

Tsang Kwong-wah
Her Name Is Cat 2:
    Journey to Death
    '01

Tsang, Roman
Magnificent Natural
    Fist '80

Tsang, Stephen
Dragon against Vam-
    pire '85
Scorpion Thunderbolt
    '85
Thunder Ninja Kids:
    The Hunt for the
    Devil Boxer '86/94

Tsang, Tony
Duel of the Tao Tough
    '82

Tse, Eric
Devil Touch '02

Tse, Michael
Rivals of the Dragon
    '83

Tsui Hark
Once upon a Time in
    China 3 '93

Tsui, Ridley
A Fighter's Blues '00

Tsui Yat-kan
Doctor Vampire '90

Tsukahara, Tetsuo
Giants and Toys '58

Tsushima, Toshiaki
(Tony Tsushima, Tony
    Sushima)
The Bodyguard '73/'78
The Magic Serpent '66
Return of the Street
    Fighter '74
The Street Fighter '74
The Street Fighter's
    Last Revenge '74
Time of the Apes '75
Ultraman 2 '79

T2
Beast Cops '98

Uhuhboo Project
Joint Security Area '00

Umebayashi, Shigeru
2000 A.D. '00
Option Zero '97

Umegaki, Tatsushi
Hiruko the Goblin '90

Urata, Keishi
Twilight of the Dark
    Master '97

Uzaki, Ryudo
The Young Master '80

Vaughn, Ben
Black Mask '96 (U.S.)

Velarde, Mike
Horror of the Blood
    Monsters '70

**Veltz, Kenneth-
Michael**
The Secrets of the War-
    rior's Power '97

Wada, Kaoru
Ninja Scroll '93

Wai, Tommy
(Wai Kai Leung Tommi
    Wai)
Bullets Over Summer
    '99
Day Off '01
The Deadly Camp '99
Extreme Challenge '01
F*** / Off '98
Fist Power '99
Hit Team '00
The Irresistible Piggies
    '02
Jiang Hu-"The Triad
    Zone" '00
Juliet in Love '00
Killer '00
My School Mate, the
    Barbarian '01
Paramount Motel '00
Runaway '01
Sharp Guns '01
Time and Tide '00
Tiramisu '02
Tragic Fantasy: Tiger of
    Wanchai '94
United We Stand, and
    Swim '01
Violent Cop '99
Visible Secret '01

Wai-hung, Kong
Long Arm of the Law 2
    '87

Wan, Marco
Dance of a Dream '01
The Eternal Evil of Asia
    '95
Return to a Better
    Tomorrow '94
Sex and the Emperor
    '94
Sixty Million Dollar Man
    '95

**Wandmacher,
Michael**
The Accidental Spy '01
    (U.S.)
Armour of God '86
    (U.S.)
Legend of the Drunken
    Master '94 (U.S.)
Supercop 2 '93 (U.S.)
Twin Dragons '92 (U.S.)

Wang, Eddie H.
Dirty Ho '79
The Eagle's Killer '81
Fists of the White
    Lotus '80
Five Superfighters '78
Lightning Kung Fu '80
Masked Avengers '81
Return of the Master
    Killer '80
Ten Tigers of Kwang-
    tung '79
3 Evil Masters '80

Wang Feng
Beijing Bicycle '01

Wang Fu-ling
Fists of Fury '71
The Flying Guillotine
    '74

Wang, Nathan
(Wong Chun Yin, Wong
    Chung-yin)
China Strike Force '00
First Strike '96
Gen-X Cops '99
Rumble in the Bronx
    '95
Who Am I? '98

Wang Xiaofeng
A Love of Blueness '00

Watanabe, Hiroya
Devil Hunter Yohko '91

Watanabe, Michiaki
(Chumei Watanabi,
    Chumei Watanabe)
Atomic Rulers of the
    World '57
Attack from Space '58
Evil Brain from Outer
    Space '58/59
Invasion of the Nep-
    tune Men '61
Ninja: Band of Assas-
    sins Continued '63

Watanabe, Toshiyuki
Rebirth of Mothra '96
Rebirth of Mothra 2 '97

Wave Music Works
9413 '98

Wei Hin-kun
Century of the Dragon
    '99

Wilson, Ian
Robo Vampire '88

Wolf, Guitar
Wild Zero '99

Wong, Alan
Doctor No... '01
Last Ghost Standing
    '99

Wong Bon Yin
Fist of Fury '95

Wong Bong
(Jonathan Wong)
The Assassin '93
Brother of Darkness
    '94
Daughter of Darkness
    '93
Dr. Lamb '92
Fight Back to School
    '91
Fist of Legend '94
The Magic Crane '93
Man Wanted '95
New Legend of Shaolin
    '94
Organized Crime and
    Triad Bureau '94
Prince of the Sun '90
Red to Kill '94
Run and Kill '93
The Untold Story '92

Wong, Cacine
Executioners '93
Expect the Unexpected
    '98
Love on a Diet '01
Needing You... '00
Peace Hotel '95
Too Many Ways to Be
    No. 1 '97
Where a Good Man
    Goes '99

Wong Chi-hung
Killer's Romance '90
The Most Wanted '94

Wong Chu-jen
(Wang Chu Jen, Wang
Chu-zen, Wang Chu-jen)
Bloody Fight '72
The Invincible Killer '79
The Shaolin Invincibles
    '79
SuperManChu '73
Two Dragons Fight
    against Tiger '75

Wong, Danny
(Dennie Wong)
Gorgeous '99
Task Force '97

Wong, James
(James Wong Jim)
Bullet in the Head '90
Casino Raiders '89
A Chinese Ghost Story
    '87
A Chinese Ghost Story
    2 '90
A Chinese Ghost Story
    3 '91
City Hunter '92
Crime Story '93
Deadful Melody '94
Dragons Forever '88
Eagle Shooting Heroes
    '93
The Enforcer '95
Green Snake '93
I Love Maria '88
Last Hero in China '93
The Legend '92
The Moon Warriors '92
Once upon a Time in
    China '91
Peking Opera Blues '86
Picture of a Nymph '88
Swordsman '90
Sword Stained with
    Royal Blood '93
Venom Warrior '83

Wong, John
Angel 2 '88

Wong Kuet Yen
Bruce Lee Fights Back
    from the Grave '76

Wong Lai-ping
One Arm Hero '94
Sam the Iron Bridge:
    Champion of Mar-
    tial Arts '93
White Lotus Cult '93

Wong, Raymond
(Wong Ying Wah)
The Blade '95
Help!!! '00
King of Comedy '99
The Longest Nite '98
The Odd One Dies '97

Running out of Time
    '99
Running out of Time 2
    '01
Shaolin Soccer '01
The Suspect '98
A Taste of Killing and
    Romance '94
Victim '99

Woo, William
(William Hu, Hu Wei Li,
William Hu, Wu Wai
Lap, Woo Wai Lap)
All Men Are Brothers:
    Blood of the Leop-
    ard '93
The Blade '95
Casino Raiders 2 '91
C'est la Vie, Mon Cheri
    '93
The Defender '94
The East Is Red '93
Flirting Scholar '93
From Beijing with Love
    '94
Hail the Judge '94
The Heroic Trio '93
Iron Monkey '93
Justice, My Foot! '92
Legend of the Drunken
    Master '94
Love on Delivery '94
Once upon a Time in
    China 3 '93
Once upon a Time in
    China 4 '93
Royal Tramp '92
Royal Tramp 2 '92
Twin Warriors '93

Worboys, Andrew
The Suspect '98

Wu Dai-jiang
(Ng Tai-kong, Wu Dai-
jiang)
Legend of the Mountain
    '79
Painted Skin '92
A Touch of Zen '69

X Japan
X '96

Xiao-song, Qu
Born to Defence '88

Yabunaka, Hiroaki
Sumo Vixens '96

Yagi, Masao
Legend of the
    Dinosaurs '77
Notorious Concubines
    '69

Yamamoto, Naozumi
Black Tight Killers '66
Branded to Kill '67

Yamamoto, Seichi
Adrenaline Drive '99

Yamanaka, Norimasa
Appleseed '88

Yamashiro, Shoji
Akira '88

Yamashita, Takeo
Voyage into Space '67

**Yamashita Trio,
Yosuke**
Ecstasy of the Angels
    '72

Yamauchi, Tadashi
Gamera vs. Gyaos '67
Giant Monster Gamera
    '65

Yang Yilun
Her Majesty Is Fine '96

Yano, Tatemi
Ultraman Tiga and
    Ultraman Dyna: The
    Warriors of the
    Lightning Star '98

Yano, Tatsumi
City Hunter: Secret Ser-
    vice '96

Yasukawa, Goro
Freeze Me '00
Gonin '95
Junk '99

Yeung Jim
Robotrix '91

Yeung, Johnny
(Johnny Young)
Fall for You '01
Iron Monkey '93

Super Car Criminals
    '99

Yeung Siu Hung
Robotrix '91

Yoshikawa, Kiyoshi
Color of Pain '02

Young, Albert
Gold Fingers '01

Yu Feng
Shaolin Temple 2: Kids
    from Shaolin '84

Yuasa, Joji
The Funeral '84

Yue Yat-yiu
Spacked Out '00

Yuen, Bob
Eat My Dust '93

Yuen, Richard
The Bride with White
    Hair '93
The Bride with White
    Hair 2 '93
Code of Honor '87
High Risk '95
In the Line of Duty 4
    '89
Iron Monkey '93
Legacy of Rage '86
The Legend of the
    Swordsman '92
Once upon a Time in
    China 2 '92
Shogun and Little
    Kitchen '92
Wicked City '92

Zerafa, Guy
Fulltime Killer '01

Zhang Shao Tong
Deadend of Besiegers
    '92

Zito, Richie
Legend of the Eight
    Samurai '84
Project A-ko '86

Zorn, John
Sadistic City '93

Category Index

If you're looking for kung fu movies with "that cross-eyed guy," you ought to look at our Cast Index under "Yue Tau Wan" or "To Siu Ming," but what about less personnel-specific queries? Is a turtle your best friend? Peruse "Gamera" for some flicks to watch with that special someone. Check out "Shaolin Temple" (kung fu ground zero) or—one of our favorites—"Porno Emporium." Or go for more straightforward classifications, like "Anime," "Old School Kung Fu," or "Horror." You can also find Asian films listed by country. Or just read the book from cover to cover, to achieve maximum pleasure—preferably aloud and in unison with a large group of people in a public place. If anybody asks, tell 'em where to get their own copy.

Academy Awards
Crouching Tiger, Hidden Dragon '00
Dersu Uzala '74
Ran '85
Rashomon '50
Samurai 1: Musashi Miyamomto '54
Spirited Away '01

Action Comedy
Aces Go Places '82
Aces Go Places 2 '83
Aces Go Places 3 '84
Aces Go Places 4 '86
Aces Go Places 5: The Terracotta Hit '89
The Adventures of the Master and His Servant '96
Beauty Investigator '92
Bio-Cops '00
Cannonball Run '81
City Hunter '92
Cop Shop Babes '01
Crack Shadow Boxers '77
Crazy Crooks '80
Curry & Pepper '90
Dirty Kung Fu '78
Dirty Tiger, Crazy Frog '78
Dragon against Vampire '85
Dragon from Shaolin '96
Dragons Forever '88
Eagle Shooting Heroes '93
Encounter of the Spooky Kind '81
Enter the Fat Dragon '78
Fist of Fury 1991 '91
Forbidden City Cop '96

From Beijing with Love '94
Goose Boxer '78
Gorgeous '99
Half a Loaf of Kung Fu '77
The Haunted Cop Shop '87
He Has Nothing But Kung Fu '77
Invincible Obsessed Fighter '82
Jackie Chan Adventures 1: The Search for the Talismans '00
Jackie Chan Adventures 2: The Dark Hand Returns '00
Jackie Chan Adventures 3: The Shadow of Shendu '00
King of Beggars '92
Knockabout '79
Kung Fu Genius '79
Kung Fu on Sale '79
Kung Fu Zombie '81
Kung Pow: Enter the Fist '76
Legend of the Dragon '91
The Miracle Fighters '82
Mr. Boo Meets Pom Pom '85
Mr. Nice Guy '97
My Lucky Stars '85
Odd Couple '79
The Owl vs. Bombo '84
Pom Pom '84
Pom Pom and Hot Hot '92
Pom Pom Strikes Back '86
Project A 2 '87

Project A-ko '86
Rosa '86
Rush Hour '98
Rush Hour 2 '01
Scared Stiff '86
Shaolin Soccer '01
Sixty Million Dollar Man '95
Skinny Tiger and Fatty Dragon '90
Snake Fist Dynamo '84
Spiritual Kung Fu '78
The Tuxedo '02
Twin Dragons '92
Twinkle Twinkle Lucky Stars '85
Wheels on Meals '84
Where's Officer Tuba? '86
Winners and Sinners '83

Adaptations
See: Comic Books/Manga (Adapted From); Novels (Adapted From); Shakespeare?; TV (Adapted From); also see various authors.

Adventure Drama
Action with more attention to dramatic content.
Aakhri Adalat '88
The Adventurers '95
Battle Royale '00
Beast Cops '98
A Better Tomorrow '86
A Better Tomorrow 2 '87
A Better Tomorrow 3 '89
The Big Heat '88

Blind Swordsman: The Tale of Zatoichi '62
The Blood Rules '00
Boiling Point '90
Born to Defence '88
Born Wild '01
Branded to Kill '67
The Bride with White Hair '93
Brother '00
Bruce Lee: The Man, the Myth '76
Bullet in the Head '90
Bullets of Love '01
Bullets over Summer '99
Casino Raiders '89
Casino Raiders 2 '91
Chinatown Kid '77
City on Fire '87
Cop on a Mission '01
Crime Story '93
Double Tap '00
Dragon: The Bruce Lee Story '93
Expect the Unexpected '98
A Fighter's Blues '00
Fight, Zatoichi, Fight! '64
God of Gamblers '89
Gonin '95
Goodbye Mr. Cool '01
Gorgeous '99
The Heroes '80
Hum Paanch '80
Ichi the Killer '01
Jiang Hu-"The Triad Zone" '00
The Killer '89
Lee Rock '91
The Legend of a Professional '00

Lone Wolf and Cub 1: Sword of Vengeance '72
Lone Wolf and Cub 2: Baby Cart at the River Styx '72
Lone Wolf and Cub 3: Baby Cart to Hades '72
Lone Wolf and Cub 4: Baby Cart in Peril '72
Lone Wolf and Cub 5: Baby Cart in the Land of Demons '73
Lone Wolf and Cub 6: White Heaven in Hell '74
Long Arm of the Law '84
Long Arm of the Law 2 '87
New Tale of Zatoichi '63
Nobody '99
The Odd One Dies '97
Operation Billionaires '98
Prison on Fire '87
Prison on Fire 2 '91
The Prisoner '90
The Private Eye Blues '94
Queen's High '91
Return to a Better Tomorrow '94
Rich and Famous '87
Run and Kill '93
Runaway '01
Running out of Time '99
Samaritan Zatoichi '68
Samurai 1: Musashi Miyamoto '54

863

Samurai 2: Duel at Ichi-
joji Temple '55
Samurai 3: Duel at
Ganryu Island '56
Sanjuro '63
Sanshiro Sugata '43
Shiri '99
Shogun and Little
Kitchen '92
Shogun Assassin '80
Sholay '75
Sonatine '93
The Story in Temple
Red Lily '79
Sugar-Howling of an
Angel '96
Sure Death: Revenge
'87
The Tale of Zatoichi
Continues '62
Task Force '97
A Taste of Killing and
Romance '94
Throne of Blood '57
Time and Tide '00
Tokyo Drifter '66
Tokyo Fist '96
A Touch of Zen '69
Undercover Blues '00
Venom Warrior '83
Victim '99
The Walls of Hell '64
Where a Good Man
Goes '99
Zatoichi and the Chess
Expert '65
Zatoichi and the Chest
of Gold '64
Zatoichi and the
Doomed Man '65
Zatoichi and the Fugi-
tives '68
Zatoichi Challenged
'67
Zatoichi on the Road
'63
Zatoichi the Fugitive
'63
Zatoichi the Outlaw '67
Zatoichi's Cane Sword
'66
Zatoichi's Flashing
Sword '64
Zatoichi's Revenge '65
Zatoichi's Vengeance
'66

Airborne
*Planes, jets & heli-
copters-still the safest
mode of transportation,
unless there's a giant
monster (or John Woo)
nearby.*
Aces Go Places 4 '86
A*P*E '76
Atomic Rulers of the
World '57
Blood: The Last Vam-
pire '00
Body Snatcher from
Hell '68
Cannonball Run '81
Crash Landing '00

Gamera, Guardian of
the Universe '95
Gamera 2: Advent of
Legion '96
Gamera vs. Gyaos '67
Gappa: The Triphibian
Monster '67
Giant Monster Gamera
'65
Godzilla 1985 '84
Godzilla, King of the
Monsters '54
Godzilla Raids Again
'55
Godzilla vs. Biollante
'89
Godzilla vs. King Ghido-
rah '91
Godzilla vs.
MechaGodzilla 2
'93
High Risk '95
King Kong vs. Godzilla
'62
Marry a Rich Man '02
Midnight Fly '01
Mighty Peking Man '77
Reptilian '00
Rodan '56
Royal Warriors '86
Satin Steel '94
Supercop '92
The Suspect '98
Tower of Death '81
Varan the Unbelievable
'58
War of the Gargantuas
'66
Wicked City '87
Wicked City '92

Alcoholism
See: Drunken Masters.

Alien Babes
*See also: Alien Beings-
Benign; Alien Beings-
Vicious.*
Destroy All Monsters
'68
Fugitive Alien '78
Gamera vs. Guillon '69
Gamera vs. Zigra '71
Invasion of Astro-Mon-
ster '65
Message from Space
'78
Star Force: Fugitive
Alien 2 '78/86
Urusei Yatsura Movie
1: Only You '83
Warning from Space
'56
The Wesley's Mysteri-
ous File '01
Zeram '91

Alien Beings-Benign
*Friendly well-meaning
space visitors, includ-
ing Starman. See also:
Alien Babes; Alien
Beings-Vicious.*
Attack from Space '58

Atomic Rulers of the
World '57
The Cat '91
Evil Brain from Outer
Space '58/59
Forbidden City Cop '96
Fugitive Alien
'78/1986
Invaders from Space
'58
Invasion of the Nep-
tune Men '61
Message from Space
'78
Prince of Space '59
Star Force: Fugitive
Alien 2 '78/86
Ultraman 2 '79
Ultraman Gaia: The
Battle in Hyper-
space '98
Ultraman Tiga and
Ultraman Dyna: The
Warriors of the
Lightning Star '98
Urusei Yatsura Movie
1: Only You '83
Warning from Space
'56
Zeram '91

Alien Beings-Vicious
*Not-so-friendly, and,
well, mean space visi-
tors, often bent on
world domination. See
also: Alien Babes; Alien
Beings-Benign.*
Attack from Space '58
Atomic Rulers of the
World '57
Battle in Outer Space
'59
Body Snatcher from
Hell '68
The Cat '91
Dagora the Space Mon-
ster '64
Destroy All Monsters
'68
Evil Brain from Outer
Space '58/59
Final Fantasy: The Spir-
its Within '01
Fugitive Alien '78
Gamera 2: Advent of
Legion '96
Gamera vs. Guillon '69
Gamera vs. Viras '68
Gamera vs. Zigra '71
Gatchaman '94
Ghidorah the Three-
Headed Monster
'64
Godzilla the Series:
Monster War '99
Godzilla 2000 '99
Godzilla vs. Gigan '72
Gamera vs. Guillon
Godzilla vs.
MechaGodzilla '74
Godzilla vs. Megalon
'73

Godzilla vs. Space
Godzilla '94
Invaders from Space
'58
Invasion of Astro-Mon-
ster '65
Invasion of the Nep-
tune Men '61
Kung Pow: Enter the
Fist '76
Message from Space
'78
The Mysterians '57
The Ninja Dragon '90
Prince of Space '59
Project A-ko '86
Reptilian '00
Star Force: Fugitive
Alien 2 '78/86
Terror of MechaGodzilla
'75
Ultraman 2 '79
Ultraman Gaia: The
Battle in Hyper-
space '98
Ultraman Tiga and
Ultraman Dyna: The
Warriors of the
Lightning Star '98
Urusei Yatsura Movie
1: Only You '83
Voyage into Space '67
The Wesley's Mysteri-
ous File '01
The X from Outer Space
'67
Yog: Monster from
Space '70
Zeram '91

Amputations
*See also: Disarmed;
Ears!; Eyeballs!; Pros-
thetic Limbs; Renegade
Body Parts; Where's My
Johnson?*
Audition '99
Champ against Champ
'83
A Chinese Torture
Chamber Story '94
A Chinese Torture
Chamber Story 2
'98
Crippled Masters '80
Dragon Fist '78
Eastern Condors '86
Ebirah, Horror of the
Deep '66
Emperor of Shaolin
Kung Fu '80
Enter the Dragon '73
Evil Brain from Outer
Space '58/59
Fearless Fighters '69
Frankenstein vs.
Baragon '65
Gamera vs. Viras '68
Guinea Pig: Devils
Experiment '85
Guinea Pig: Flower of
Flesh and Blood
'85

Guinea Pig: He Never
Dies '86
Kid with the Golden
Arm '78
The Killer Meteors '76
Lady Ninja: Reflections
of Darkness '96
The Magic Serpent '66
Master of the Flying
Guillotine '74
The Miracle Fighters
'82
Model from Hell '99
Ninja Hunter '83
Ninja the Final Duel '85
Once a Thief '91
One Arm Hero '94
One Foot Crane '79
Organ '96
Raiders of Wu Tang '82
The Return of the 5
Deadly Venoms '78
Revengeful Sword-
women '79
Shaolin King Boxer '79
Shocking Asia 2 '76
Tell Me Something '99

Animals
*See: Birds; Cats; Dogs;
Go Fish; Monkey Busi-
ness; Pigs; Rabbits;
Reptiles; Rodents;
Were-foxes; Were-
snakes; Whales.*

Anime
Akira '88
Appleseed '88
Astro Boy '63
Astro Boy '80
Barefoot Gen '83
Black Jack '96
Black Magic M-66 '87
Blood: The Last Vam-
pire '00
Bubblegum Crisis '85
Castle of Cagliostro
'79
A Chinese Ghost Story:
The Tsui Hark Ani-
mation '97
City Hunter: Secret Ser-
vice '96
Devil Hunter Yohko '91
Devil Hunter Yohko 2
'92
Devil Hunter Yohko 3
'92
Devil Man '87
Final Fantasy: The Spir-
its Within '01
Gatchaman '94
Ghost in the Shell '96
Godzilla the Series:
Monster War '99
Grave of the Fireflies
'88
Jackie Chan Adven-
tures 1: The Search
for the Talismans
'00
Jackie Chan Adven-
tures 2: The Dark
Hand Returns '00

Jackie Chan Adventures 3: The Shadow of Shendu '00
Metropolis '01
My Neighbor Totoro '88
Ninja Scroll '93
Patlabor 1: The Movie '90
Princess Mononoke '97
Project A-ko '86
Roujin Z '91
Royal Space Force: The Wings of Honneamise '87
Speed Racer: The Movie '67
Spirited Away '01
Street Fighter 2 '96
Twilight of the Cockroaches '87
Twilight of the Dark Master '97
Ultraman 2 '79
Urotsukidoji '89
Urusei Yatsura Movie 1: Only You '83
Vampire Hunter D '85
Vampire Hunter D: Bloodlust '01
The Venus Wars '89
Violence Jack '88
Wicked City '87
X '96

Anthologies
When the plot isn't long enough to allow the film to last even an hour and a half. See also: Horror Anthologies.
Akira Kurosawa's Dreams '90
Chungking Express '94
Tokyo Decameron: Three Tales of Madness and Sensuality '96

Anti-Heroes
Bad role models (or relatively good ones, depending upon your criminal record). See also: Rebel with a Cause.
Akira '88
The Assassin '93
Ballistic Kiss '98
Beast Cops '98
Beautiful Beast '95
Beautiful Hunter '94
A Better Tomorrow '86
A Better Tomorrow 2 '87
A Better Tomorrow 3 '89
Black Cat '91
Bloody Fight '72
The Bloody Fists '72
Blowback: Love and Death '90
Boiling Point '90
Branded to Kill '67
The Conman '98

Conman in Tokyo '00
Devil Man '87
The Executioner '74
Fallen Angels '95
Female Convict Scorpion: Jailhouse 41 '72
Full Contact '92
Fulltime Killer '01
Goodbye Mr. Cool '01
The Invincible Killer '79
Jiang Hu-"The Triad Zone" '00
Junk '99
The Killer '89
Killer's Romance '90
The Korean Connection '77
Lady Ninja: Reflections of Darkness '96
Last Hurrah for Chivalry '78
The Legend of a Professional '00
Lightning Kung Fu '80
Lone Wolf and Cub 1: Sword of Vengeance '72
Lone Wolf and Cub 2: Baby Cart at the River Styx '72
Lone Wolf and Cub 3: Baby Cart to Hades '72
Lone Wolf and Cub 4: Baby Cart in Peril '72
Lone Wolf and Cub 5: Baby Cart in the Land of Demons '73
Lone Wolf and Cub 6: White Heaven in Hell '74
Long Arm of the Law '84
Long Arm of the Law 2 '87
Naked Killer '92
Nine Demons '83
No More Love, No More Death '92
Once a Thief '91
Peace Hotel '95
The Phantom Lover '95
Prison on Fire '87
Prison on Fire 2 '91
The Razor 1: Sword of Justice '72
The Razor 2: The Snare '73
The Razor 3: Who's Got the Gold? '74
The Replacement Killers '97
Return of the Street Fighter '74
Return to a Better Tomorrow '94
Running out of Time '99
Running out of Time 2 '01
Sanjuro '63

Seven Samurai '54
Shadow of the Tiger '79
Shogun Assassin '80
Sister Street Fighter '74
The Street Fighter '74
The Street Fighter's Last Revenge '74
Swordsman with an Umbrella '70
Sympathy for Mr. Vengeance '01
Time and Tide '00
Tokyo Drifter '66
Tokyo Mafia: Yakuza Wars '95
Tokyo Mafia 2: Wrath of the Yakuza '95
Tokyo Mafia 3: Battle for Shinjuku '96
Vampire Hunter D '85
Vampire Hunter D: Bloodlust '01
Versus '00
Violence Jack '88
Violent Cop '89
Yojimbo '61
Zero Woman: The Accused '96

Art & Artists
Usually unemployed people seeking alternate means of income. See also: Musicians; Writers.
Blooded Treasury Fight '79
Combo Cops '96
Comic King '00
Crazy Crooks '80
Fall for You '01
Fireworks '97
Flirting Scholar '93
Frozen '96
Great Performances: Kurosawa '02
Hunted by Royal Decree '00
Lone Wolf and Cub 4: Baby Cart in Peril '72
A Love of Blueness '00
Mahal '80
Once a Thief '91
Picture of a Nymph '88
Shocking Asia 2 '76
A Touch of Zen '69
Troublesome Night 4 '98
Zatoichi Challenged '67

Asians in USA
The Art of Action: Martial Arts in the Movies '02
The Big Brawl '80
Blade 2 '02
Cannonball Run '81
Dragon: The Bruce Lee Story '93
Fist of Fear-Touch of Death '80

Godzilla the Series: Monster War '99
The Green Hornet '74
Horror of the Blood Monsters '70
Jackie Chan Adventures 1: The Search for the Talismans '00
Jackie Chan Adventures 2: The Dark Hand Returns '00
Jackie Chan Adventures 3: The Shadow of Shendu '00
Kiss of the Dragon '01
Kung Pow: Enter the Fist '76
Mortal Kombat '95
The One '01
The Protector '85
The Replacement Killers '97
Romeo Must Die '00
Rush Hour '98
Rush Hour 2 '01
Shaolin: Wheel of Life '00
Shogun '80
Teenage Mutant Ninja Turtles '90
The Tuxedo '02
What's Up, Tiger Lily? '66

Asteroids
See: Meteors, Asteroids & Comets.

Astronauts
Battle in Outer Space '59
Destroy All Monsters '68
Fugitive Alien '78
Gamera vs. Zigra '71
Horror of the Blood Monsters '70
Invasion of Astro-Monster '65
Royal Space Force: The Wings of Honneamise '87
Ultraman 2 '79
The X from Outer Space '67
Yongary, Monster from the Deep '67

Atomic Bombs
Atomic Rulers of the World '57
Barefoot Gen '83
Ebirah, Horror of the Deep '66
Frankenstein vs. Baragon '65
Giant Monster Gamera '65
Godzilla 1985 '84
Godzilla vs. King Ghidorah '91
The Green Hornet '74
The Last War '61
Voyage into Space '67

Avant-Garde
Akira Kurosawa's Dreams '90
Ashes of Time '94
Chungking Express '94
Cyclo '95
Ecstasy of the Angels '72
Frozen '96
Guinea Pig: Devils Experiment '85
I.K.U. '00
Lies '99
Tetsuo: The Iron Man '89
Tetsuo 2: Body Hammer '91
Tokyo Drifter '66
Tokyo Fist '96

Babies
See also: Bad Seeds; Just a Little Bit Pregnant; That's a Baby?
Aces Go Places 3 '84
All About Ah-Long '89
Bullets over Summer '99
Combo Cops '96
The Demon's Baby '98
Devil Woman '70
Fight, Zatoichi, Fight! '64
5 Venoms vs. Wu Tang '87
Fury in Shaolin Temple '82
Gappa: The Triphibian Monster '67
Godzilla vs. MechaGodzilla 2 '93
Hard Boiled '91
The Heroic Trio '93
The Imp '81
Juliet in Love '00
Justice, My Foot! '92
Legend of the Dragonslayer Sword '90
Legendary Couple '95
Lone Wolf and Cub 1: Sword of Vengeance '72
Maborosi '95
Mr. Vampire '86
The New Legend of Shaolin '94
Ninja: Band of Assassins Continued '63
Shaolin and Tai Chi '79
Shaolin Temple 2: Kids from Shaolin '84
Shogun Assassin '80
Snaker '01
Son of Godzilla '67
Thousand Mile Escort '76

Bad Dads
Bichunmoo '99
Brother of Darkness '94
Daughter of Darkness '93
The Deadly Camp '99

H.K. Adams Family '92
Hong Kong Nocturne
'67
Hum Paanch '80
Kung Fu Zombie '81
The Magic Serpent '66
Mr. Vampire '85
No More Love, No More
Death '92
The Peacock King '89
Snake Deadly Act '79
Suzhou River '00

Bad Seeds
Naughty children.
Abbot White '82
Battle Royale '00
Blood: The Last Vam-
pire '00
The Deadly Camp '99
The Demon's Baby '98
Eastern Condors '86
Evil Dead Trap '88
5 Venoms vs. Wu Tang
'87
Horror Hotline Big Head
Monster '01
The Imp '81
Mr. Vampire 2 '86
Nine Demons '83
Seeding of a Ghost '83
Snaker '01

Beauty & the Beast
A*P*E '76
Beast of the Yellow
Night '70
Black Magic M-66 '87
Blind Beast '69
Brides of Blood '68
A Chinese Ghost Story
'87
A Chinese Ghost Story:
The Tsui Hark Ani-
mation '97
Daughter of Darkness
'93
Ebirah, Horror of the
Deep '66
Entrails of the Virgin
'86
Evil Dead Trap '88
Frankenstein vs.
Baragon '65
Gamera, Guardian of
the Universe '95
Gamera 3: The
Revenge of Irys '99
Godzilla vs. Biollante
'89
King Kong Escapes '67
King Kong vs. Godzilla
'62
Mighty Peking Man '77
Organ '96
The Peacock King '89
Picture of a Nymph '88
Princess Mononoke '97
Saga of the Phoenix
'90
Savior of the Soul 2
'92
Son of Godzilla '67
Urotsukidoji '89
Vampire Hunter D '85

Vampire Hunter D:
Bloodlust '01
War of the Gargantuas
'66

Beggar So
*The famous Drunken
Master, King of Beg-
gars, and one of the
Ten Tigers of Kwang-
tung. See also: Beg-
gars.*
Drunken Master '78
Drunken Master Killer
'94
King of Beggars '92
Martial Arts Master
Wong Fei Hung '92
Once upon a Time in
China '91
Once upon a Time in
China 2 '92
Ten Tigers of Kwang-
tung '79
Ten Tigers of Shaolin
'78

Beggars
*Got 8 taels for a cup of
tea? See also: Beggar
So.*
Blood of the Dragon
'71
Brave Archer '77
Bullet in the Head '90
Chinese Samson '79
Crazy Crooks '80
Crippled Masters '80
Dirty Ho '79
Dragon Lee vs. the Five
Brothers '78
Drunken Art and Crip-
pled Fist '79
Eagle Shooting Heroes
'93
Flight of the Heroine
'00
Flirting Scholar '93
Godzilla 1985 '84
Grave of the Fireflies
'88
Half a Loaf of Kung Fu
'77
Her Majesty Is Fine '96
Jade Claw '79
Killer from Above '77
Killer Priest '81
Knockabout '79
Kung Fu Genius '79
Kung Fu on Sale '79
Lawyer Lawyer '97
The Lord of Hangzhou
'98
The Magnificent Butch-
er '79
Martial Arts Mayhem,
Vol. 2 '99
Masters of Tiger Crane
'83
My Kung Fu 12 Kicks
'79
Shaolin Soccer '01
Snake and Crane Arts
of Shaolin '78
Snake Deadly Act '79

Snake in the Eagle's
Shadow '78
The Snake Strikes Back
'81
The Storm Riders '98
The 36 Crazy Fists '77

Behind the Scenes
*A peek behind the
show-biz curtain. See
also: Showbiz Comedy;
Showbiz Drama; Show-
biz Thrillers.*
The Art of Action: Mar-
tial Arts in the
Movies '02
Audition '99
Bruce Lee: A Warrior's
Journey '00
Bruce Lee, The Legend
'84
Bruce Lee: The Man,
the Myth '76
Bruce Lee We Miss You
'76
Dynamo '78
Eighth Happiness '88
Executioners from
Shaolin '77
Fist of Fear-Touch of
Death '80
The Foul King '00
Ghost Actress '96
Giants and Toys '58
God of Cookery '96
Guinea Pig: The Making
of Guinea Pig '86
He's a Woman, She's a
Man '94
High Risk '95
Horror Hotline Big Head
Monster '01
House of the Damned
'99
The Hypnotist '99
King Kong vs. Godzilla
'62
King of Comedy '99
Losers' Club '01
Mr. Nice Guy '97
Mothra '61
990714.com '00
Painted Faces '88
Peking Opera Blues '86
The Phantom Lover '95
Ring 0: Birthday '00
The Touch '02
Venom Warrior '83
Weather Woman '95

Bewitched
Abbot White '82
The Bride with White
Hair '93
The Bride with White
Hair 2 '93
A Chinese Ghost Story
3 '91
A Chinese Odyssey Part
1: Pandora's Box
'95
A Chinese Odyssey Part
2: Cinderella '95
Devil Hunter Yohko '91

Encounter of the
Spooky Kind '81
The Eternal Evil of Asia
'95
Green Snake '93
The Killing of Satan '83
The Legend of the
Swordsman '92
The Magic Crane '93
The Magic Serpent '66
The Miracle Fighters
'82
Nine Demons '83
990714.com '00
Painted Skin '92
Picture of a Nymph '88
Reborn from Hell:
Samurai Armaged-
don '96
Revenge of the Zom-
bies '76
Savior of the Soul 2
'92
Seeding of a Ghost '83
Sound from the Dark
'00
The Storm Riders '98
Succubare '77
Throne of Blood '57
Thunder Ninja Kids:
The Hunt for the
Devil Boxer '86/94
Weather Woman '95
The Witch from Nepal
'85

Big Battles
*Big-budget (or least the
illusion of it) clash of
large, opposing military
forces on Earth and
other locales. See
also: Vietnam War;
War; War between the
Sexes.*
A*P*E '76
Battle in Outer Space
'59
Bullet in the Head '90
The Dimension Travel-
ers '98
Eastern Condors '86
Fugitive Alien '78
Generation Consultant
'90
Generation Pendragon
'90
Hard Boiled '91
The Hidden Fortress
'58
King of the Mongols
'60
The Last War '61
Message from Space
'78
The Mysterians '57
Shogun '80
Star Force: Fugitive
Alien 2 '78/86
Throne of Blood '57
War of the Gargantuas
'66

Big Business
All's Well Ends Well '92

The Big Sting '82
The Cheaters '01
China Strike Force '00
City of Desire '01
Code of Honor '87
Could You Kill My Hus-
band Please? '01
Crime Story '93
Dance of a Dream '01
The Defender '94
Devil Touch '02
Downtown Torpedoes
'97
The Dragon Family '88
Dragons Forever '88
Dummy Mommy, with-
out a Baby '01
The Enforcer '95
Fighting for Love '01
Giants and Toys '58
Godzilla vs. Biollante
'89
Godzilla vs. King Ghido-
rah '91
Gorgeous '99
Happy Family '02
Hot War '98
The Irresistible Piggies
'02
King Kong vs. Godzilla
'62
The Ladies' Phone Sex
Club '96
Losers' Club '01
Love Me, Love My
Money '01
Marry a Rich Man '02
Metropolis '01
Operation Billionaires
'98
Powerful Four '91
Romeo Must Die '00
Running out of Time
'99
Running out of Time 2
'01
Rush Hour '98
Rush Hour 2 '01
Shanghai 1920 '91
The Vampire Combat
'01
Your Place or Mine! '98

Bigfoot
See: Yeti/Bigfoot

Bikers
Aakhri Adalat '88
All About Ah-Long '89
Armour of God '86
Cannonball Run '81
China Strike Force '00
5 Lady Venoms '78
Full Contact '92
Full Throttle '95
Legend of Speed '99
A Moment of Romance
'90
No More Love, No More
Death '92
The One '01
Supercop '92
Suzhou River '00
Wonder Seven '94

Biography
See: This Is Your Life.

Birds
Feathered friends and enemies.
Battle of Shaolin '77
Dream of Garuda '94
Eagle's Claw '77
Ebirah, Horror of the Deep '66
A Fistful of Talons '83
Gatchaman '94
Godzilla 1985 '84
Goose Boxer '78
Hard Boiled '91
The Killer '89
Kung Fu Genius '79
The Magic Crane '93
The Magic Serpent '66
Militant Eagle '78
The Peacock King '89
The Private Eyes '76
Return of Daimajin '66
Running out of Time 2 '01
Snake Fist Dynamo '84
The Story in Temple Red Lily '79

Black Comedy
Not everyone gets this kind of humor, but we're sure you do. See also: Comedy Drama; Satire & Parody.
Adrenaline Drive '99
Battle Royale '00
A Chinese Torture Chamber Story '94
The Demon's Baby '98
The Funeral '84
A Gambler's Story '01
Giants and Toys '58
Guinea Pig: He Never Dies '86
The Happiness of the Katakuris '01
Help!!! '00
Jiang Hu-"The Triad Zone" '00
My Wife Is a Gangster '01
Postman Blues '97
Too Many Ways to Be No. 1 '97
Twilight of the Cockroaches '87
We're Going to Eat You! '80
You Shoot, I Shoot '01

Blindness
See: I Can't See.

Blood Island
Brides of Blood '68
Mad Doctor of Blood Island '68
Terror Is a Man '59

Boating
See: Sail Away.

Bodily Functions
See: Chunky Delight; Farts; The Loo.

Bombs
See: Atomic Bombs; Boom!

Boom!
See also: Atomic Bombs
Aces Go Places 2 '83
Aces Go Places 4 '86
Akira '88
Angel '87
Angel 2 '88
Angel on Fire '95
A*P*E '76
Appleseed '88
Barefoot Gen '83
Battle in Outer Space '59
The Best of the Best '96
A Better Tomorrow 3 '89
Black Cat '91
The Blacksheep Affair '98
Boiling Point '90
Breakout from Oppression '78
Bubblegum Crisis '85
Bullet Train '75
Champion '00
China Strike Force '00
Cop Shop Babes '01
Crash Landing '00
Destroy All Monsters '68
Downtown Torpedoes '97
Eastern Condors '86
Eat My Dust '93
Ebirah, Horror of the Deep '66
Ecstasy of the Angels '72
The Enforcer '95
Extreme Crisis '98
Fantasy Mission Force '84
Fireworks '97
Fist Power '99
From Beijing with Love '94
Fugitive Alien '78
Full Alert '97
Full Contact '92
Fulltime Killer '01
Fury of King Boxer '72
Gen-X Cops '99
Gen-Y Cops '00
Godzilla 1985 '84
Godzilla Raids Again '55
Godzilla the Series: Monster War '99
Godzilla 2000 '99
Grave of the Fireflies '88
Hard Boiled '91
Heart of Dragon '85
Heroes Shed No Tears '83/86

High Risk '95
The Inspector Wears Skirts '88
It Takes a Thief '01
Junk '99
The Last Blood '90
The Last War '61
Man Wanted '95
Martial Angels '01
Message from Space '78
Mighty Jack '68
My Lucky Stars '85
Ninja: Band of Assassins '62
Ninja vs. Ninja '87
Once a Thief '91
Patlabor 1: The Movie '90
Police Story 2 '88
The Postman Fights Back '82
The Protector '85
Renegade Ninjas '79
Return of the Chinese Boxer '75
Return of the Deadly Blade '81
Robo Vampire '88
Royal Warriors '86
Running out of Time '99
Rush Hour '98
Rush Hour 2 '01
Satin Steel '94
Savior of the Soul '91
She Shoots Straight '90
Shiri '99
Sonatine '93
Star Force: Fugitive Alien 2 '78/86
Supercop '92
Thunder Cop '96
Time and Tide '00
Voyage into Space '67
The Walls of Hell '64

Bounty Hunters
Blowback: Love and Death '90
Dirty Kung Fu '78
Dreadnaught '81
Five Elements of Kung Fu '78
The Green Dragon Inn '79
The Heroic Trio '93
The Kung Fu Master '94
The Millionaires' Express '86
Ninja vs. Shaolin Guards '84
The Postman Fights Back '82
Rich and Famous '87
10 Magnificent Killers '77
Vampire Hunter D '85
Vampire Hunter D: Bloodlust '01
Zeram '91

Boxing
See also: Kickboxing-Professional.
Born to Defence '88
Born Wild '01
Extreme Challenge '01
A Fighter's Blues '00
Fist of Fear-Touch of Death '80
Flash Future Kung Fu '83
My School Mate, the Barbarian '01
Tokyo Fist '96

Bruceploitation
See sidebars, p. 72 and 224.
Blind Fist of Bruce '79
Bronson Lee, Champion '78
Bruce Lee Fights Back from the Grave '76
Bruce Lee, The Legend '84
Bruce Lee: The Man, the Myth '76
Bruce Lee We Miss You '76
Dragon Lee vs. the Five Brothers '78
Dragon on Fire '79
Dragon: The Bruce Lee Story '93
Dynamo '78
Enter the Fat Dragon '78
Exit the Dragon, Enter the Tiger '75
Fist of Fear-Touch of Death '80
Fist of Fury '95
Fist of Fury 1991 '91
Fist of Legend '94
The Fist, the Kicks and the Evils '79
Fists Like Lee '74
Fists of Bruce Lee '78
Game of Death '78
The Invincible Killer '79
The Legend of Bruce Lee '80
New Fist of Fury '76
The New Game of Death '75
Ninja vs. Bruce Lee '82
The Real Bruce Lee '79
Revenge of the Patriots '76
Story of the Dragon '76
Super Gang '78
Tower of Death '81

Buddies
Heroic pals have adventures.
Aces Go Places '82
Aces Go Places 2 '83
Aces Go Places 3 '84
Aces Go Places 4 '86
Aces Go Places 5: The Terracotta Hit '89
The Adventures of Milo and Otis '86
Angel '87

Angel 2 '88
Angel on Fire '95
Armour of God '86
A Better Tomorrow '86
A Better Tomorrow 2 '87
A Better Tomorrow 3 '89
Bullet in the Head '90
Bullets over Summer '99
Cannonball Run '81
Cheap Killers '98
City Cop '95
Combo Cops '96
Cop Shop Babes '01
Crazy Crooks '80
Crocodile Hunter '89
Curry & Pepper '90
Dirty Tiger, Crazy Frog '78
Downtown Torpedoes '97
Dragons Forever '88
Dreaming Fists with Slender Hands '80
Eat My Dust '93
Expect the Unexpected '98
Fight Back to School '91
Fight Back to School 2 '92
For Bad Boys Only '00
F*** / Off '98
Gen-X Cops '99
Gen-Y Cops '00
Godzilla vs. Gigan '72
Godzilla vs. Megalon '73
Hit Team '00
Hot War '98
I Love Maria '88
The Inspector Wears Skirts '88
In the Line of Duty 3 '88
In the Line of Duty 4 '89
In the Line of Duty 5: Middle Man '90
The Killer '89
Kung Fu Genius '79
Kung Fu on Sale '79
My Kung Fu 12 Kicks '79
My Lucky Stars '85
Ninja vs. Shaolin Guards '84
Ninja in the Deadly Trap '83
Odd Couple '79
Once a Thief '91
The Owl vs. Bombo '84
Pedicab Driver '89
Pom Pom '84
Pom Pom and Hot Hot '92
Pom Pom Strikes Back '86
Project A '83
Project A-ko '86
The Protector '85
Rosa '86

Running out of Time '99
Savior of the Soul '91
Scared Stiff '86
Shanghai Affairs '98
She Shoots Straight '90
Shogun and Little Kitchen '92
Sholay '75
Skinny Tiger and Fatty Dragon '90
Street Fighter 2 '96
Sunshine Cops '99
Supercop '92
Task Force '97
Thunder Cops '98
Tiger Cage '88
Tiger on Beat '88
Tokyo Raiders '00
Twin Dragons '92
Twin Warriors '93
Twinkle Twinkle Lucky Stars '85
Wheels on Meals '84
Winners and Sinners '83
Wonder Seven '94
Zeram '91

Bugs & Slugs
Creepy crawlers. See also: Spiders.
The Butterfly Murders '79
Branded to Kill '67
A Chinese Ghost Story 2 '90
The 18 Jade Arhats '78
Godzilla 1985 '84
Godzilla vs. Gigan '72
Godzilla vs. Megaguirus '00
Grave of the Fireflies '88
Guinea Pig: Mermaid in a Manhole '88
Love on a Diet '01
Martial Arts Master Wong Fei Hung '92
Revenge of the Zombies '76
Seeding of a Ghost '83
Shaolin Mantis '78
Son of Godzilla '67
Succubare '77
The Tricky Master '00
Twilight of the Cockroaches '87

Buried Alive
Deadend of Besiegers '92
Ebirah, Horror of the Deep '66
Godzilla Raids Again '55
Godzilla vs. Mothra '92
Riki-Oh: The Story of Ricky '89
Ring '98
Violence Jack '88

Cabbies
Angel on Fire '95

Dr. Lamb '92
Dynamo '78
Enter the Fat Dragon '78
Gimme Gimme '01
Nightmare Zone '98
Powerful Four '91
Seeding of a Ghost '83
The Tuxedo '02
Where a Good Man Goes '99
Young Tiger '72

Cambodia (Production)
Snaker '01

Cannibalism
See: Eat Me.

Cars
See: Checkered Flag; Motor Vehicle Dept.

Cartoons
See: Anime.

Cats
The Adventures of Milo and Otis '86
Black Cat '91
The Cat '91
Dragon Kid '90
Fear Faith Revenge 303 '98
Godzilla vs. Hedorah '71
Golden Dragon Silver Snake '79
Her Name Is Cat '98
Her Name Is Cat 2: Journey to Death '01
Madadayo '92
My Neighbor Totoro '88
Ninja: Band of Assassins '62
Ninja: Band of Assassins Continued '63
Raat '91
Renegade Ninjas '79
Sakuya: Slayer of Demons '00
Snake in the Eagle's Shadow '78
Who Am I? '98

Cave People
Horror of the Blood Monsters '70
Mighty Peking Man '77
Speed Racer: The Movie '67

Chainsaws
The Deadly Camp '99
Last Ghost Standing '99
Record '00
Red Shield '91
Royal Warriors '86
Tiger on Beat '88

Checkered Flag
See also: Motor Vehicle Dept.
All About Ah-Long '89

Cannonball Run '81
Casino Tycoon 2 '92
Full Throttle '95
Kikujiro '99
Legend of Speed '99
Speed Racer: The Movie '67
Thunderbolt '95
Tragic Fantasy: Tiger of Wanchai '94
Twin Dragons '92
United We Stand, and Swim '01
Who Am I? '98

Child Abuse
Aces Go Places 3 '84
Aces Go Places 4 '86
Battle Royale '00
Brother of Darkness '94
Dr. Lamb '92
High and Low '63
Painted Faces '88
Return of the Deadly Blade '81
Ring '98
Ring 2 '99
Ring Virus '99
Shanghai Affairs '98

Children
See: Babies; Bad Seeds; Child Abuse; Kung Fu Kids; That's a Baby?; Vampire Kids.

China-Mainland (Production)
See sidebar, p. 60.
The Adventures of the Master and His Servant '96
Beijing Bicycle '01
Born to Defence '88
The Cold Mountain Temple '91
Crash Landing '00
Crouching Tiger, Hidden Dragon '00
Deadend of Besiegers '92
Extreme Challenge '01
Flight of the Heroine '00
Frozen '96
Her Majesty Is Fine '96
The Holy Robe of Shaolin Temple '84
Hunted by Royal Decree '00
Kiss of the Dragon '01
Legend of the Dragonslayer Sword '90
Legend of the Dragonslayer Sword 2-The Rising Son '90
Legend of the Dragonslayer Sword 3-The Rage of Gina '90
A Love of Blueness '00
The Phantom Lover '95
The Prisoner of Five Boulders '89

Real Kung Fu of Shaolin, Part 1 '81
Rebels under Siege '00
The Road Home '99
The Shaolin Drunken Monk '83
Shaolin Fist of Fury '87
The Shaolin One '83
The Shaolin Temple '79
Shaolin Temple 2: Kids from Shaolin '84
Shaolin: Wheel of Life '00
Suzhou River '00
The Swordswoman in White '92
The Touch '02
Twin Warriors '93
Yellow River Fighter '88

Chinese Opera
The Art of Action: Martial Arts in the Movies '02
C'est la Vie, Mon Cheri '93
Chivalrous Legend '98
Doctor Vampire '90
Dreadnaught '81
Eighth Happiness '88
Executioners from Shaolin '77
Flirting Scholar '93
Game of Death '78
Hail the Judge '94
The Hero of Swallow '96
In the Line of Duty 3 '88
Iron Monkey 2 '96
A Man Called Hero '99
Odd Couple '79
Once upon a Time in China '91
100 Ways to Murder Your Wife '86
Painted Faces '88
Peking Opera Blues '86
The Prodigal Son '81
The Secrets of the Warrior's Power '97
The Silver Spear '79
Sunshine Cops '99
White Lotus Cult '93

Christmas
Curry & Pepper '90
Executioners '93
The Lord of Hangzhou '98
Troublesome Night 9 '00
Venom Warrior '83

Chunky Delight
Movies that contain our favorite hurling scenes.
Dragon from Shaolin '96
Flirting Scholar '93
My Sassy Girl '01
Naked Killer '92
Seeding of a Ghost '83
Succubare '77

Clowns
Cop Shop Babes '01
Venom Warrior '83

Comedy
See: Action Comedy; Black Comedy; Comedy Drama; Genre Spoofs; Horror Comedy; Kung Fu Comedy; Romantic Comedy; Satire & Parody; Sci-Fi Comedy; Screwball Comedy; Showbiz Comedy; Vampire Spoof.

Comedy Drama
See also: Black Comedy.
Attack the Gas Station! '99
Bullets over Summer '99
Chinese Orthopedist and the Spice Girls '02
Chungking Express '94
Clueless '01
Comeuppance '00
Comic King '00
The Funeral '84
Giants and Toys '58
Good Morning '59
Heart of Dragon
In the Mood for Love '00
Legendary Couple '95
Love au Zen '01
Love Correction '00
Love Me, Love My Money '01
A Love of Blueness '00
Merry-Go-Round '01
My Sassy Girl '01
Para Para Sakura '01
Postman Blues '97
Tampopo '87
Too Many Ways to Be No. 1 '97

Comets
See: Meteors, Asteroids & Comets.

Comic Books/Manga (Adapted From)
Akira '88
Appleseed '88
Astro Boy '63
Astro Boy '80
Barefoot Gen '83
Black Jack '96
Black Magic M-66 '87
Castle of Cagliostro '79
City Hunter '92
City Hunter: Secret Service '96
Devil Man '87
Dragon from Russia '90
Female Convict Scorpion: Jailhouse 41 '72

Ghost in the Shell '96
Guinea Pig: Flower of
   Flesh and Blood
   '85
Guinea Pig: Mermaid in
   a Manhole '88
Hiruko the Goblin '90
Ichi the Killer '01
Killer's Romance '90
Lone Wolf and Cub 1:
   Sword of
   Vengeance '72
Lone Wolf and Cub 2:
   Baby Cart at the
   River Styx '72
Lone Wolf and Cub 3:
   Baby Cart to Hades
   '72
Lone Wolf and Cub 4:
   Baby Cart in Peril
   '72
Lone Wolf and Cub 5:
   Baby Cart in the
   Land of Demons
   '73
Lone Wolf and Cub 6:
   White Heaven in
   Hell '74
Metropolis '01
The Peacock King '89
Riki-Oh: The Story of
   Ricky '89
Saga of the Phoenix
   '90
Shark Skin Man and
   Peach Hip Girl '98
Shogun Assassin '80
Speed Racer: The
   Movie '67
Spiral '00
Twilight of the Dark
   Master '97
Urotsukidoji '89
Urusei Yatsura Movie
   1: Only You '83
Violence Jack '88
Voyage into Space '67
X '96
Zeram '91

Contemporary Noir
See also: Film Noir
Bangkok Dangerous
   '00
Beast Cops '98
Beautiful Beast '95
Beautiful Hunter '94
Bullets of Love '01
Cheap Killers '98
The Cheaters '01
Cop on a Mission '01
Expect the Unexpected
   '98
Happy End '99
Inner Senses '01
Jiang Hu-"The Triad
   Zone" '00
The Longest Nite '98
The Mission '99
Moonlight Express '99
Nobody '99
Sadistic City '93
Suzhou River '00
Tell Me Something '99

Tokyo Fist '96
Victim '99
Visible Secret '01

Cooties
*Diseases, viruses,
plagues, and other
germ warfare.*
The Accidental Spy '01
Bio-Cops '00
Bio Zombie '98
The Bloody Fists '72
Executioners '93
Invaders from Space
   '58
Iron Monkey '93
Killer Priest '81
Ninja Scroll '93
Organ '96
Running out of Time
   '99
Tetsuo: The Iron Man
   '89

Cops & Robbers
*See also: Women
Cops.*
Beast Cops '98
Beauty Investigator '92
The Best of the Best
   '96
Big Bullet '96
The Big Heat '88
Bullets over Summer
   '99
The Cheaters '01
China Strike Force '00
City Cop '95
City on Fire '87
City War '88
Combo Cops '96
Cop Shop Babes '01
Crime Story '93
Crocodile Hunter '89
Downtown Torpedoes
   '97
Eat My Dust '93
Expect the Unexpected
   '98
Final Justice '88
First Option '96
Gen-X Cops '99
Gen-Y Cops '00
Hard Boiled '91
Heart of Dragon '85
High and Low '63
High Risk '95
Hit Team '00
The Inspector Wears
   Skirts '88
In the Line of Duty 3
   '88
In the Line of Duty 4
   '89
In the Line of Duty 5:
   Middle Man '90
Lee Rock '91
Legendary Couple '95
Long Arm of the Law
   '84
Long Arm of the Law 2
   '87
Man Wanted '95
Martial Angels '01

The Masked Prosecutor
   '99
The Most Wanted '94
Nowhere to Hide '99
Once a Thief '91
Operation Billionaires
   '98
Option Zero '97
Organized Crime and
   Triad Bureau '94
Police Story '85
Police Story 2 '88
Pom Pom '84
Pom Pom and Hot Hot
   '92
Pom Pom Strikes Back
   '86
The Protector '85
Red Shield '91
The Replacement Sus-
   pects '01
Rich and Famous '87
Righting Wrongs '86
Royal Warriors '86
Running out of Time
   '99
Running out of Time 2
   '01
Rush Hour '98
Stray Dog '49
Sunshine Cops '99
Super Car Criminals
   '99
Supercop '92
Supercop 2 '93
Task Force '97
The Suspect '98
Thunder Cop '96
Thunder Cops '98
Tiger Cage '88
Tiger on Beat '88
The Tigers '91
Twinkle Twinkle Lucky
   Stars '85
Undercover Blues '00
Victim '99
Violent Cop '89
Violent Cop '99
Where's Officer Tuba?
   '86
Winners and Sinners
   '83
Yes, Madam '85

Creepy Houses
*Scary dwellings in and
out of Amityville. See
also: Horror.*
The Blood Drinkers '64
A Chinese Ghost Story
   '87
A Chinese Ghost Story
   2 '90
A Chinese Ghost Story
   3 '91
A Chinese Ghost Story:
   The Tsui Hark Ani-
   mation '97
The Deadly Camp '99
Death Mask of the
   Ninja '82
Encounter of the
   Spooky Kind '81
Evil Dead Trap '88

Faces of Horror '98
Fantasy Mission Force
   '84
Gumnaam '65
The Haunted Cop Shop
   '87
Haunted Mansion '98
Horror Hotline Big Head
   Monster '01
House of the Damned
   '99
The Imp '81
Last Ghost Standing
   '99
Mahal '48
Raat '91
Revenge of the Zom-
   bies '76
Ring '98
Ring 2 '99
Seeding of a Ghost '83
A Touch of Zen '69
Troublesome Night 3
   '97
Vampire Hunter D '85
Victim '99

Crime & Criminals
*See: Cops & Robbers;
Crime Drama; Disorga-
nized Crime; Escaped
Cons; Fugitives; Heists;
Hit Men & Women;
Organized Crime;
Scams, Stings & Cons;
Serial Killers; Triads;
True Crime; Women
Cops; Yakuza.*

Crime Drama
Adrenaline Drive '99
All About Ah-Long '89
Bangkok Dangerous
   '00
Beast Cops '98
A Better Tomorrow '86
A Better Tomorrow 2
   '87
A Better Tomorrow 3
   '89
Beyond Hypothermia
   '96
Boiling Point '90
Branded to Kill '67
Brother '00
Bullets of Love '01
Bullets over Summer
   '99
Casino Raiders '89
Casino Raiders 2 '91
Casino Tycoon 2 '92
Century of the Dragon
   '99
Chinatown Kid '77
Chungking Express '94
Clean My Name, Mr.
   Coroner! '00
The Conman '98
Conman in Tokyo '00
Cop on a Mission '01
Crime of a Beast '01
Cyclo '95
Dance of a Dream '01
Day Off '01
Days of Being Wild '90

Double Tap '00
The Dragon Family '88
Dragon in Jail '90
Expect the Unexpected
   '98
Fall for You '01
Fallen Angels '95
Fireworks '97
From the Queen to the
   Chief Executive '01
Fulltime Killer '01
A Gambler's Story '01
Gold Fingers '01
Gonin '95
Goodbye Mr. Cool '01
Happy End '99
High and Low '63
Jiang Hu-"The Triad
   Zone" '00
Killer's Romance '90
Lee Rock '91
Legendary Couple '95
Long Arm of the Law
   '84
Long Arm of the Law 2
   '87
The Longest Nite '98
Man Wanted '95
The Mission '99
Moonlight Express '99
The Most Wanted '94
No More Love, No More
   Death '92
The Odd One Dies '97
On the Run '88
Operation Billionaires
   '98
Powerful Four '91
Prison on Fire '87
Prison on Fire 2 '91
The Prisoner '90
The Private Eye Blues
   '94
Queen's High '91
The Replacement Sus-
   pects '01
Return to a Better
   Tomorrow '94
Rich and Famous '87
Run and Kill '93
Sonatine '93
Stray Dog '49
Sugar-Howling of an
   Angel '96
The Suspect '98
Suzhou River '00
Sympathy for Mr.
   Vengeance '01
Task Force '97
A Taste of Killing and
   Romance '94
Tell Me Something '99
The Tigers '91
Time and Tide '00
Tokyo Drifter '66
Tokyo Mafia: Yakuza
   Wars '95
Tokyo Mafia 2: Wrath of
   the Yakuza '95
Tokyo Mafia 3: Battle
   for Shinjuku '96
Tragic Fantasy: Tiger of
   Wanchai '94
Ultimatum '01

Undercover Blues '00
Victim '99
Violent Cop '89
Violent Cop '99
Where a Good Man
 Goes '99
Young and Dangerous
 '96
Young and Dangerous
 5 '98
Young and Dangerous
 6: Born to Be King
 '00

Cults
*Something like a gang
but more intense and
usually governed by a
state of mind similar to
irrationality. See also:
Satan & Satanism.*
Armageddon '97
Armour of God '86
The Bride with White
 Hair '93
The Bride with White
 Hair 2 '93
Deadful Melody '94
Drunken Master Killer
 '94
Extreme Crisis '98
Fists of the White
 Lotus '80
God.com '98
Legend of the Dragon-
 slayer Sword '90
Legend of the 7 Golden
 Vampires '74
The Legend of the
 Swordsman '92
Lord of the Wu Tang
 '93
Once upon a Time in
 China 2 '92
Once upon a Time in
 China 4 '93
Savior of the Soul '91
Savior of the Soul 2
 '92
Shocking Asia
The Sword Stained with
 Royal Blood '93
2000 AD
White Lotus Cult '93

Cyberpunk
Akira '88
Final Fantasy: The Spir-
 its Within '01
Flash Future Kung Fu
 '83
Ghost in the Shell '95
I.K.U. '00
Metropolis '01
Roujin Z '91
Tetsuo: The Iron Man
 '89
Tetsuo 2: Body Ham-
 mer '91

Dads
*See also: Bad Dads;
Moms.*
The Accidental Spy '01
Aces Go Places 3 '84

Aces Go Places 4 '86
Aces Go Places 5: The
 Terracotta Hit '89
The Adventurers '95
Adventures of a Blind
 Man '64
All About Ah-Long '89
All Monsters Attack '70
All's Well End's Well '92
All's Well End's Well '97
 '97
Armour of God '86
The Avenging Fist '01
Blonde Fury '89
Blood of the Dragon
 '71
Boiling Point '90
Chinese Orthopedist
 and the Spice Girls
 '02
Crash Landing '00
Crazy Crooks '80
Crystal Hunt '91
Curse of the Vampires
 '70
The Deadly Camp '99
Drunken Master '78
The Enforcer '95
Fist Power '99
Good Morning '59
Goodbye Mr. Cool '01
Hail the Judge '94
H.K. Adams Family '92
Hong Kong Nocturne
 '67
Iron Monkey '93
Killer of Snake, Fox of
 Shaolin '78
The Korean Connection
 '77
Kung Fu Zombie '81
Last Hero in China '93
Legacy of Rage '86
Legendary Couple '95
Lone Wolf and Cub 1:
 Sword of
 Vengeance '72
Lone Wolf and Cub 2:
 Baby Cart at the
 River Styx '72
Lone Wolf and Cub 3:
 Baby Cart to Hades
 '72
Lone Wolf and Cub 4:
 Baby Cart in Peril
 '72
Lone Wolf and Cub 5:
 Baby Cart in the
 Land of Demons
 '73
Lone Wolf and Cub 6:
 White Heaven in
 Hell '74
Maborosi '95
The Magic Serpent '66
A Man Called Hero '99
Martial Arts Master
 Wong Fei Hung '92
Merry-Go-Round '01
The New Legend of
 Shaolin '94
No More Love, No More
 Death '92

Once upon a Time in
 China 3 '93
Operation Billionaires
 '98
The Peacock King '89
The Phantom Lover '95
The Prisoner '90
The Prodigal Son '81
Raat '91
Shogun Assassin '80
Son of Godzilla '67
Sorrowful to a Ghost
 '70
Spiral '00
The Storm Riders '98
The Touch '02
Triangular Duel '72
Troublesome Night 14
 '02
Young and Dangerous
 6: Born to Be King
 '00

Dance Fever
*Whole lotta foot tappin'
goin' on. See also:
Disco; Dragon Dance;
Lion Dance; Musicals.*
Aakhri Adalat '88
The Blacksheep Affair
 '98
Black Tight Killers '66
Champion '00
Dance of a Dream '01
Days of Being Wild '90
Dragon: The Bruce Lee
 Story '93
Ebirah, Horror of the
 Deep '66
Elaan '94
Flash Future Kung Fu
 '83
Flyin Dance '01
For Bad Boys Only '00
Full Contact '92
Godzilla vs. Hedorah
 '71
Gonin '95
Gumnaam '65
The Happiness of the
 Katakuris '01
Her Name Is Cat '98
Hong Kong Nocturne
 '67
Hum Paanch '80
The Human Vapor '60
Invaders from Space
 '58
The Killer Elephants
 '76
Lethal Panther 2 '93
Love Paradox '00
Mahal '48
Once a Thief '91
The Owl vs. Bombo '84
Para Para Sakura '01
Prison on Fire '87
Red to Kill '94
Romeo Must Die '00
Rumble in the Bronx
 '95
Shaolin Soccer '01
Sholay '75

Skinny Tiger and Fatty
 Dragon '90
Sunshine Cops '99
Tiramisu '02
Troublesome Night 4
 '98
Venom Warrior '83
Violated Paradise '63
What's Up, Tiger Lily?
 '66
Yongary, Monster from
 the Deep '67
Zatoichi's Cane Sword
 '66

Deadly Implants
Battle in Outer Space
 '59
Black Cat '91

Death & the Afterlife
*Dead people, undead
people, walking dead
people, and other dead
issues. See also:
Funerals; Great Death
Scenes; Hell; Paging
Dr. Kevorkian; Reincar-
nation.*
After Life '98
Another Heaven '00
Beast of the Yellow
 Night '70
A Chinese Ghost Story
 '87
A Chinese Ghost Story
 2 '90
A Chinese Ghost Story
 3 '91
A Chinese Ghost Story:
 The Tsui Hark Ani-
 mation '97
Encounter of the
 Spooky Kind '81
Erotic Ghost Story '90
Erotic Ghost Story 2
 '91
The Eternal Evil of Asia
 '95
The Eye '02
Faces of Horror '98
Fear Faith Revenge 303
 '98
Ghost Actress '96
Godzilla vs. Biollante
 '89
The Happiness of the
 Katakuris '01
The Haunted Cop Shop
 '87
The Haunted Lantern
 '98
Haunted Mansion '98
Hong Kong X-File '98
The Imp '81
Kwaidan '64
Last Ghost Standing
 '99
Mahal '48
Memento Mori '99
Nightmare Zone '98
Nine Demons '83
990714.com '00
Picture of a Nymph '88
Pulse '01

Reborn from Hell:
 Samurai Armaged-
 don '96
Ring '98
Ring 2 '99
Ring 0: Birthday '00
Ring Virus '99
Seeding of a Ghost '83
The Seventh Curse '86
Shadow '01
Sound from the Dark
 '00
Victim '99
Visible Secret '01
A Wicked Ghost '99
A Wicked Ghost 2: The
 Fear '00

Death at Weddings
Black Cat '91
Body Weapon '99
Hail the Judge '94
The Hypnotist '99
Lethal Panther '91
Queen's High '91
Rich and Famous '87
Satin Steel '94

Demons
Beast of the Yellow
 Night '70
The Cat '91
A Chinese Ghost Story
 '87
A Chinese Ghost Story
 2 '90
A Chinese Ghost Story
 3 '91
A Chinese Ghost Story:
 The Tsui Hark Ani-
 mation '97
A Chinese Odyssey Part
 1: Pandora's Box
 '95
A Chinese Odyssey Part
 2: Cinderella '95
Daimajin '66
The Demon's Baby '98
Devil Hunter Yohko '91
Devil Hunter Yohko 2
 '92
Devil Hunter Yohko 3
 '92
Devil Man '87
Encounter of the
 Spooky Kind '81
Entrails of the Virgin
 '86
Evil Cat '86
Evil Dead Trap '88
Green Snake '93
Jackie Chan Adven-
 tures 1: The Search
 for the Talismans
 '00
Jackie Chan Adven-
 tures 2: The Dark
 Hand Returns '00
Jackie Chan Adven-
 tures 3: The Shad-
 ow of Shendu '00
The Killing of Satan '83
Last Ghost Standing
 '99

The Miracle Fighters '82
Model from Hell '99
Nine Demons '83
The Peacock King '89
Picture of a Nymph '88
Princess Mononoke '97
Return of Daimajin '66
Ring '98
Ring 2 '99
Ring 0: Birthday '00
Ring Virus '99
Saga of the Phoenix '90
Sakuya: Slayer of Demons '00
Seeding of a Ghost '83
The Seventh Curse '86
The Silver Spear '79
Spiral '00
Spirited Away '01
Spiritual Kung Fu '78
Thunder Ninja Kids: The Hunt for the Devil Boxer '86/94
Urotsukidoji '89
Vampire Hunter D '85
Vampire Hunter D: Bloodlust '00
Wicked City '87
Wicked City '92
Wrath of Daimajin '66
X '96

Deserts
Ashes of Time '94
The Assassin '93
Avenging Eagle '78
Body Snatcher from Hell '68
Cannonball Run '81
Crouching Tiger, Hidden Dragon '00
Dragon Inn '92
Duel to the Death '82
Final Fantasy: The Spirits Within '01
Fugitive Alien '78
Hum Paanch '80
Kung Pow: Enter the Fist '76
Lone Wolf and Cub 2: Baby Cart at the River Styx '72
Lord of the Wu Tang '93
Millennium Dragon '99
Operation Condor '91
Second Time Around '02
Shogun Assassin '80
Sholay '75
The Touch '02
Yellow River Fighter '88

Detectives
See also: Cops & Robbers.
Aces Go Places '82
Aces Go Places 2 '83
Aces Go Places 3 '84
Aces Go Places 4 '86
Aces Go Places 5: The Terracotta Hit '89
Beast Cops '98

Big Bullet '96
Black Mask '96
The Blood Rules '00
Bullets over Summer '99
City Hunter '92
City Hunter: Secret Service '96
Cold War '00
Comeuppance '00
Cross Fire '00
Cure '97
Curry & Pepper '90
Dr. Lamb '92
Double Tap '00
The Executioner '74
Expect the Unexpected '98
Extreme Crisis '98
Fatal Blade '00
First Option '96
For Bad Boys Only '00
Forbidden City Cop '96
The Haunted Cop Shop '87
Her Name Is Cat '98
High and Low '63
In the Line of Duty 3 '88
Lee Rock '91
Legendary Couple '95
A Life of Ninja '83
Metropolis '01
Mr. Boo Meets Pom Pom '85
Naked Killer '92
The New Marvelous Double '92
9413 '98
Nobody '99
No More Love, No More Death '92
Nowhere to Hide '99
Organized Crime and Triad Bureau '94
Patlabor 1: The Movie '90
Police Story '85
Police Story 2 '88
Pom Pom '84
Pom Pom and Hot Hot '92
Pom Pom Strikes Back '86
The Private Eye Blues '94
The Private Eyes '76
The Razor 1: Sword of Justice '72
The Razor 2: The Snare '73
The Razor 3: Who's Got the Gold? '74
Ring 2 '99
Rock 'n' Roll Cop
Rosa '86
Running out of Time '99
Running out of Time 2 '01
Stray Dog '49
Supercop '92
Supercop 2 '93

Sure Death: Revenge '87
Take 2 in Life '01
Tell Me Something '99
Tokyo Raiders '00
The Vampire Combat '01
Victim '99
Violent Cop '89
Violent Cop '99
What's Up, Tiger Lily? '66
Wheels on Meals '84
A Wicked Ghost 2: The Fear '00
With or Without You '92

Dinosaurs
All Monsters Attack '70
All Monsters Attack! '02
Destroy All Monsters '68
Ebirah, Horror of the Deep '66
From Beijing with Love '94
Ghidorah the Three-Headed Monster '64
Godzilla, King of the Monsters '54
Godzilla, Mothra and King Ghidorah: Battle on Fire '01
Godzilla 1985 '84
Godzilla Raids Again '55
Godzilla 2000 '99
Godzilla vs. Biollante '89
Godzilla vs. Destroyah '95
Godzilla vs. Gigan '72
Godzilla vs. Hedorah '71
Godzilla vs. King Ghidorah '91
Godzilla vs. MechaGodzilla '74
Godzilla vs. MechaGodzilla 2 '93
Godzilla vs. Megaguirus '00
Godzilla vs. Megalon '73
Godzilla vs. Mothra '92
Godzilla vs. Space Godzilla '94
Invasion of Astro-Monster '65
King Kong Escapes '67
King Kong vs. Godzilla '62
Legend of the Dinosaurs '77
Mothra vs. Godzilla '64
The Peacock King '89
Reptilian '00
Son of Godzilla '67
Terror of MechaGodzilla '75

Yongary, Monster from the Deep '67

Disabilities
See: Amputations; Disarmed; I Can't See; Prosthetic Limbs; What?

Disarmed
One-Armed (or Un-Armed) Armies. See also: Amputations; Renegade Body Parts.
The Blade '95
Crippled Masters '80
Emperor of Shaolin Kung Fu '80
Enter the Dragon '73
Fearless Fighters '69
Kid with the Golden Arm '78
Master of the Flying Guillotine '74
One Arm Hero '94
Raiders of Wu Tang '82
The Return of the 5 Deadly Venoms '78
Revengeful Swordwomen '79

Disaster Strikes
Natural and man-made. See also: Meltdown.
Akira '88
Akira Kurosawa's Dreams '90
Barefoot Gen '83
Bio-Cops '00
Bio Zombie '98
Crash Landing '00
Executioners '93
Grave of the Fireflies '88
The Happiness of the Katakuris '01
The Last War '61
Legend of the Dinosaurs '77
Metropolis '01
Patlabor 1: The Movie '90
Time of the Apes '75
Violence Jack '88
Warning from Space '56
Yongary, Monster from the Deep '67

Disco
Flash Future Kung Fu '83
For Bad Boys Only '00
Giant Monster Gamera '65
Godzilla vs. Hedorah '71
Gonin '95
Hard as a Dragon '80
Hum Paanch '80
Message from Space '78
100 Ways to Murder Your Wife '86
The Peacock King '89

Troublesome Night 4 '98
Troublesome Night 14 '02
Visible Secret '01

Diseases, Viruses & Plagues
See: Cooties.

Disorganized Crime
Bad guys and gals with inept agendas. See also: Organized Crime.
Attack the Gas Station! '99
Boiling Point '90
Chungking Express '94
City Cop '95
Could You Kill My Husband Please? '01
Crazy Crooks '80
Fantasy Mission Force '84
F*** / Off '98
Gamera vs. Barugon '66
Junk '99
Kung Pow: Enter the Fist '76
Legendary Couple '95
Long Arm of the Law '84
Long Arm of the Law 2 '87
The Magnificent Scoundrels '91
My Lucky Stars '85
The Owl vs. Bombo '84
Postman Blues '97
Project A 2 '87
Sonatine '93
Sunshine Cops '99
Too Many Ways to Be No. 1 '97
Twinkle Twinkle Lucky Stars '85
Versus '00
Winners and Sinners '83

Doctors and/or Nurses
See also: Cooties; Evil Doctors; Hospitals & Medicine; Sanity Check; Shrinks.
Adrenaline Drive '99
The Big Sting '82
Black Jack '96
Blood: The Last Vampire '00
Cure '97
Doctor No... '01
Doctor Vampire '90
Elaan '94
Forbidden City Cop '96
Frozen '96
Guinea Pig: Android of Notre Dame '88
Hard Boiled '91
Help!!! '00
The Last Blood '90
Mad Doctor of Blood Island '68

The Manster '60
Organ '96
Revenge of the Zombies '76
Ring 2 '99
Ring 0: Birthday '00
Roujin Z '91
Running out of Time '99
Samaritan Zatoichi '68
Scared Stiff '86
Shocking Asia '75
Terror Is a Man '59
Trust Me U Die '99
Twilight People '72
Yoga and Kung Fu Girl '78

Docudrama
Somewhat fictionalized documentary-wannabes. See also: Documentaries; True Crime.
Crash Landing '00
Fist of Fear-Touch of Death '80
Gimme Gimme '01
Operation Billionaires '98
The Untold Story '92
Violated Paradise '63

Documentaries
Typically a serious examination of an issue or idea, but don't count on it here. See also: Docudrama; Mockumentaries.
All Monsters Attack! '02
The Art of Action: Martial Arts in the Movies '02
Bruce Lee: A Warrior's Journey '00
Bruce Lee, The Legend '84
Bruce Lee: The Man, the Myth '76
Dragons of the Orient '88
Fist of Fear-Touch of Death '80
Great Performances: Kurosawa '02
Guinea Pig: The Making of Guinea Pig '86
Kei Mizutani: Undressed for Success '94
Martial Arts Mayhem, Vol. 1 '99
Martial Arts Mayhem, Vol. 2 '99
The Real Bruce Lee '79
The Secrets of the Warrior's Power '97
The Shaolin One '83
Shaolin: Wheel of Life '00
Shocking Asia '75
Shocking Asia 2 '76
Violated Paradise '63

Dogs
Man's Best Friend and occasionally dinner.
The Adventures of Milo and Otis '86
The Cat '91
Dragon on Fire '79
Dragon Princess '81
Every Dog Has His Date '01
Fists Like Lee '74
5 Venoms vs. Wu Tang '87
Gamera, Guardian of the Universe '95
Justice, My Foot! '92
Lawyer Lawyer '97
100 Ways to Murder Your Wife '86
The Shaolin Temple '79
The Six Directions of Boxing '79
Tiger over Wall '80
Troublesome Night 8 '00

Domestic Violence
Aces Go Places 3 '84
Combo Cops '96
Cop Shop Babes '01
Son of Godzilla '67

Dracula
Pardon me, your teeth are in my neck. See also: Vampire Babes; Vampire Spoof; Vampires.
Legend of the 7 Golden Vampires '74
Vampire Hunter D
The Victim '80

Dragon Dance
Deadend of Besiegers '92
Iron Man '86
The Killer '89

Dragons
Destroy All Monsters '68
Ebirah, Horror of the Deep '66
Godzilla, King of the Monsters '54
Godzilla, Mothra and King Ghidorah: Battle on Fire '01
Godzilla 1985 '84
Godzilla Raids Again '55
Godzilla the Series: Monster War '99
Godzilla 2000 '99
Godzilla vs. Biollante '89
Godzilla vs. Destroyah '95
Godzilla vs. Gigan '72
Godzilla vs. Hedorah '71
Godzilla vs. King Ghidorah '91

Godzilla vs. MechaGodzilla '74
Godzilla vs. MechaGodzilla 2 '93
Godzilla vs. Megaguirus '00
Godzilla vs. Megalon '73
Godzilla vs. Mothra '92
Godzilla vs. Space Godzilla '94
Green Snake '93
Invasion of Astro-Monster '65
The Magic Serpent '66
Rebirth of Mothra '96
Rebirth of Mothra 2 '97

Drama
See: Adventure Drama; Comedy Drama; Crime Drama; Docudrama; Historical Drama; Melodrama; Romantic Drama; Showbiz Drama.

Drugs
See: This Is Your Brain on Drugs.

Drunken Masters
Adventures of a Blind Man '64
All Men Are Brothers: Blood of the Leopard '93
Bloody Fight '72
Branded to Kill '67
The Buddhist Fist '79
The Chinese Feast '95
Chinese Samson '79
Clean My Name, Mr. Coroner! '00
Could You Kill My Husband Please? '01
Dance of the Drunk Mantis '79
Daughter of Darkness '93
Days of Being Wild '90
The Deadly Sword '78
Dirty Kung Fu '78
Drunken Art and Crippled Fist '79
Drunken Master '78
Drunken Master Killer '94
Drunken Tai Chi '84
Everyday Is Valentine '01
Fighting for Love '01
Fists of Fury '71
Five Superfighters '78
The Funeral '84
Fury in Shaolin Temple '82
Gumnaam '65
Happy Family '02
High Risk '95
Hum Paanch '80
I Love Maria '88
Inheritor of Kung Fu '77

Kid with the Golden Arm '78
King of Beggars '92
The Korean Connection '77
The Kung Fu Master '94
Lady Iron Monkey '83
Last Hero in China '93
Lee Rock '91
The Legend of Bruce Lee '80
Legend of the Drunken Master '94
Legend of the Drunken Tiger '92
Legend of the Mountain '79
The Magnificent Butcher '79
Magnificent Natural Fist '80
The Magnificent Scoundrels '91
The Miracle Fighters '82
My Sassy Girl '01
Ninja in the Deadly Trap '83
100 Ways to Murder Your Wife '86
Postman Blues '97
Raiders of Wu Tang '82
Shaolin and Tai Chi '79
The Shaolin Drunken Monk '83
The Shaolin One '83
The Shaolin Temple '79
Shaolin vs. Manchu '80
Shaolin Wooden Men '76
Snake-Crane Secret '78
Snake Deadly Act '79
Temptress of a Thousand Faces '98
Ten Tigers of Kwangtung '79
The 36 Crazy Fists '77
Time and Tide '00
Troublesome Night 4 '98
United We Stand, and Swim '01
Venom Warrior '83
Ways of Kung Fu '80
With or Without You '92
The World of the Drunken Master '79
Yellow River Fighter '88
Yoga and Kung Fu Girl '78

Ears!
See also: Eyeballs!; Hearts!; Renegade Body Parts; What?
A Chinese Ghost Story 3 '91
The Executioner '74
Ichi the Killer '01
Kwaidan '64

Eat Me
Human Pork Buns and other non-vegetarian scenarios. See also: Edibles; Horror.
Beast of the Yellow Night '70
Bio-Cops '00
Bio Zombie '98
A Chinese Torture Chamber Story 2 '98
The Deadly Camp '99
The Eternal Evil of Asia '95
The Executioner '74
Fantasy Mission Force '84
Gamera vs. Guillon '69
Junk '99
The Seventh Curse '86
Shocking Asia '75
Shocking Asia 2 '76
The Untold Story '92
The Untold Story 2 '98
We're Going to Eat You! '80

Edibles
Chow-time movies. See also: Eat Me.
Attack of the Mushroom People '63
Bakery Amour '01
The Chinese Feast '95
Enter the Fat Dragon '78
The Funeral '84
God of Cookery '96
Half a Loaf of Kung Fu '77
King of Comedy '99
Mr. Nice Guy '97
Spirited Away '01
Tampopo '87
The Untold Story '92
The Untold Story 2 '98
We're Going to Eat You! '80
Wheels on Meals '84

18 Bronzemen
Robotic final exam of the Shaolin Temple, and their mimics.
The Blazing Temple '76
The 8 Masters '77
The 18 Bronzemen '76
The 18 Bronzemen Part 2 '76
Five Elements of Kung Fu '78
Fury in Shaolin Temple '82
Raiders of Wu Tang '82
Shaolin Wooden Men '76
The Unbeaten 28 '80

Emperors
The Blazing Temple '76
Death Mask of the Ninja '82
The Duel '00
8 Diagram Fighter '91

The 18 Bronzemen Part 2 '76
Emperor of Shaolin Kung Fu '80
Filthy Guy '80
Flight of the Heroine '00
The Flying Guillotine '74
Forbidden City Cop '96
Generation Consultant '90
Generation Pendragon '90
Godzilla vs. Megalon '73
Hail the Judge '94
The Heroes '80
The Holy Robe of Shaolin Temple '84
Hunted by Royal Decree '00
Iron Monkey 2 '77
Iron Neck Li '81
King of Beggars '92
King of the Mongols '60
Lady Iron Monkey '83
The Law and the Outlaw '95
The Legend '92
The Legend of the Swordsman '92
The Lord of Hangzhou '98
The Moon Warriors '92
Mortal Kombat '95
Ninja: Band of Assassins '62
Ninja: Band of Assassins Continued '63
Ninja Hunter '83
Ninja the Final Duel '85
Ninja vs. Shaolin Guards '84
The Prisoner of Five Boulders '89
Royal Tramp '92
Royal Tramp 2 '92
Sex and the Emperor '94
The Shaolin Invincibles '79
The Shaolin Kids '77
Shaolin Mantis '78
Shaolin: Wheel of Life '00
Thousand Mile Escort '76
Voyage into Space '67

Erotic Thrillers
The pendulum swings widely between "erotic" and "thriller" in this list. See also: Sex & Sexuality; Sexploitation.
Ballistic Kiss '98
Bangkok Dangerous '00
Beautiful Beast '95
Beautiful Hunter '94
Body Weapon '99

Daughter of Darkness '93
Ecstasy of the Angels '72
Entrails of the Virgin '86
Erotic Ghost Story '90
Erotic Ghost Story 2 '91
Happy End '99
The Ladies' Phone Sex Club '96
Lies '99
Naked Killer '92
Notorious Concubines '69
Sadistic City '93
Taboo '97

Escaped Cons
See also: Fugitives; Great Escapes; Men in Prison.
Dragon against Vampire '85
Female Convict Scorpion: Jailhouse 41 '72
Hail the Judge '94
Hand of Death '75
The Heroes '80
Legacy of Rage '86
Mantis Combat '81
The One '01
The Prisoner '90
Prison on Fire '87
Prison on Fire 2 '91
Supercop '92
Versus '00

Evil Doctors
Turn your head and cough...up blood. See also: Doctors and/or Nurses; Mad Scientists.
The Blood Drinkers '64
Evil Brain from Outer Space '58/59
Game of Death '78
The Green Hornet '74
Guinea Pig: Android of Notre Dame '88
Mad Doctor of Blood Island '68
Organ '96
Reptilian '00
The Shaolin Kids '77
Trust Me U Die '99
Yoga and Kung Fu Girl '78

Exploitation
Often titillating morality tales, rigged to take advantage of the viewer. See also: Sexploitation.
Sex and the Emperor '94
Spacked Out '00
Violated Paradise '63

Eyeballs!
Unnerving scenes involving eyeballs. See also: Ears!; Hearts!
The Assassin '93
Branded to Kill '67
Casino Raiders 2 '91
The Executioner '74
The Eye '02
Female Convict Scorpion: Jailhouse 41 '72
Five Fingers of Death '72
Flight of the Heroine '00
Godzilla vs. Hedorah '71
Heroes Shed No Tears '83/86
Hero's Blood '91
The Killer '89
The Return of the 5 Deadly Venoms '78
Return of the Street Fighter '74
Riki-Oh: The Story of Ricky '89
Savior of the Soul '91
Shaolin Temple 2: Kids from Shaolin '84
Sorrowful to a Ghost '70
The Victim '80
Visible Secret '01

Family Ties
See: Bad Dads; Dads; Kissin' Cousins; Moms; Siamese Twins; That's a Baby?; Twins.

Farts
Beans, beans, the musical fruit....
A Chinese Odyssey Part 2: Cinderella '95
Dragon from Shaolin '96
Good Morning '59

Femme Fatale
She done him and him and him and him wrong. See also: Girls with Guns.
Aces Go Places '82
Aces Go Places 2 '83
Aces Go Places 3 '84
The Adventures of the Master and His Servant '96
Another Heaven '00
Armour of God '86
Beautiful Beast '95
Beautiful Hunter '94
Beauty Investigator '92
Black Cat '91
The Demon's Baby '98
Devil Woman '70
Dirty Tiger, Crazy Frog '78
Doctor Vampire '90
Dragon Chronicles: Maidens of Heavenly Mountain '94

Dragon from Russia '90
Dragon from Shaolin '96
Eastern Condors '86
Erotic Ghost Story '90
Erotic Ghost Story 2 '91
Fallen Angels '95
Fantasy Mission Force '84
Female Convict Scorpion: Jailhouse 41 '72
5 Lady Venoms '78
Flash Future Kung Fu '83
Forbidden City Cop '96
From Beijing with Love '94
Full Contact '92
Ghost in the Shell '95
The Green Hornet '74
Green Snake '93
The Haunted Lantern '98
Her Name Is Cat '98
Her Name Is Cat 2: Journey to Death '01
The Killing of Satan '83
King of Beggars '92
Lady Ninja: Reflections of Darkness '96
Legend of the Eight Samurai '84
Lethal Panther '91
Lone Wolf and Cub 2: Baby Cart at the River Styx '72
The Magnificent Scoundrels '91
The Master of Death '82
Millennium Dragon '99
The Millionaires' Express '86
Mr. Vampire Saga 4 '88
Model from Hell '94
Murder in the Orient '74
Naked Killer '92
Ninja Scroll '93
Notorious Concubines '69
Rush Hour 2 '01
Sadistic City '93
Shiri '99
Snake Fist Dynamo '84
Snaker '01
To Kill with Intrigue '77
Tokyo Decameron: Three Tales of Madness and Sensuality '96
Troublesome Night 4 '98
The Untold Story 2 '98

Feng Shui
Where to put the couch for good luck.
Bury Me High '90
Casino Tycoon 2 '92
Daughter of Darkness '93

Filthy Guy '80
Fists and Guts '79
Haunted Mansion '98
Mr. Vampire '85
Shaolin Temple 2: Kids from Shaolin '84
Troublesome Night '97

Film Noir
Dark and moody or tributes to dark and moody. See also: Contemporary Noir.
Branded to Kill '67
Gumnaam '65
The H-Man '58
Mahal '48
The Odd One Dies '97
On the Run '88
Organized Crime and Triad Bureau '94
Screaming Ninja '73
Stray Dog '49
Terror beneath the Sea '66

Filmmaking
See: Behind the Scenes; Showbiz Comedy; Showbiz Drama; Showbiz Thrillers; Undercover.

Flatulence
See: Farts.

Flying Saucers
See also: Spaceships.
Atomic Rulers of the World '57
Body Snatcher from Hell '68
Destroy All Monsters '68
Gamera vs. Guillon '69
Gamera vs. Zigra '71
Ghidorah the Three-Headed Monster '64
Godzilla vs. King Ghidorah '91
Invaders from Space '58
Invasion of Astro-Monster '65
Prince of Space '59
Thunder Ninja Kids: The Hunt for the Devil Boxer '86/94
Time of the Apes '75
Wild Zero '99
The X from Outer Space '67

Fong Sai-yuk
Burning Paradise '94
The Invincible Kung Fu Trio '78
Iron Man '86
The Legend '92
The Legend 2 '93
Prodigal Boxer '73

Food
See: Edibles.

Four Bones
Our picks.

Akira '88
Armour of God '86
Astro Boy '63
Attack the Gas Station!
    '99
Audition '99
Battle Royale '00
Blood: The Last Vam-
    pire '00
Branded to Kill '67
The Bride with White
    Hair '93
Bruce Lee: A Warrior's
    Journey '00
Bullet in the Head '90
Castle of Cagliostro
    '79
C'est la Vie, Mon Cheri
    '93
The Chinese Connec-
    tion '71
A Chinese Ghost Story:
    The Tsui Hark Ani-
    mation '97
Chungking Express '94
Cross Fire '00
Crouching Tiger, Hidden
    Dragon '00
Destroy All Monsters
    '68
Dragons Forever '88
Dreadnaught '81
Eastern Condors '86
Ecstasy of the Angels
    '72
Enter the Dragon '73
Female Convict Scorpi-
    on: Jailhouse 41
    '72
Fists of the White
    Lotus '80
Five Deadly Venoms
    '78
The Foul King '00
From the Queen to the
    Chief Executive '01
Fulltime Killer '01
Gamera 3: The
    Revenge of Irys '99
Ghost in the Shell '95
God of Gamblers '89
Godzilla, King of the
    Monsters '54
Godzilla vs. Destroyah
    '95
Godzilla vs. King Ghido-
    rah '91
Godzilla vs.
    MechaGodzilla 2
    '93
Godzilla vs. Mothra '92
The Happiness of the
    Katakuris '01
Hard Boiled '91
High and Low '63
Ichi the Killer '01
In the Mood for Love
    '00
Invincible Pole Fighter
    '83

Jackie Chan Adven-
    tures 1: The Search
    for the Talismans
    '00
Jackie Chan Adven-
    tures 2: The Dark
    Hand Returns '00
Joint Security Area '00
The Killer '89
Kwaidan '64
Legend of the Drunken
    Master '94
Lone Wolf and Cub 1:
    Sword of
    Vengeance '72
Lone Wolf and Cub 2:
    Baby Cart at the
    River Styx '72
Master of the Flying
    Guillotine '74
Metropolis '01
The Millionaires'
    Express '86
The Mission '99
Mr. Vampire '85
Mortal Kombat '95
Mothra vs. Godzilla '64
My Neighbor Totoro '88
The One '01
Operation Condor '91
Pedicab Driver '89
Police Story '85
Police Story 2 '88
Princess Mononoke '97
The Private Eyes '76
Project A '83
Project A 2 '87
Project A-ko '86
Ran '85
Rashomon '50
Return of the Dragon
    '72
The Return of the 5
    Deadly Venoms '78
Return of the Master
    Killer '80
Righting Wrongs '86
Ring '88
Royal Space Force: The
    Wings of Hon-
    neamise '87
Samaritan Zatoichi '68
Samurai 3: Duel at
    Ganryu Island '56
The Secrets of the War-
    rior's Power '97
Seven Samurai '54
The Seventh Curse '86
Shaolin Master Killer
    '78
Shaolin Soccer '01
The Shaolin Temple '79
Shaolin Temple 2: Kids
    from Shaolin '84
Shiri '99
Spirited Away '01
The Street Fighter '74
Sympathy for Mr.
    Vengeance '01
Tampopo '87
Throne of Blood '57
A Touch of Zen '69
Vampire Hunter D:
    Bloodlust '01

Violent Cop '89
Volcano High School
    '01
War of the Gargantuas
    '66
Wheels on Meals '84
Yojimbo '61

Foxes
See: Were-foxes.

**Frankenstein and/or
His Monster**
Man-made men.
Frankenstein vs.
    Baragon '65
Terror beneath the Sea
    '66
Terror Is a Man '59
Terror of MechaGodzilla
    '75
Tetsuo: The Iron Man
    '89
Tetsuo 2: Body Ham-
    mer '91
Twilight People '72
War of the Gargantuas
    '66

Front Page
Stop the presses!
Blonde Fury '89
Comeuppance '00
Godzilla, King of the
    Monsters '54
The Green Hornet '74
Headlines '01
In the Mood for Love
    '00
Once upon a Time in
    China 4 '93
Take 2 in Life '01
The Walls of Hell '64

Fugitives
*See also: Escaped
Cons.*
The Assassin '93
Avenging Warriors of
    Shaolin '79
Beast of the Yellow
    Night '70
The Bloody Fists '72
Champion '00
Chivalrous Legend '98
City Cop '95
Crouching Tiger, Hidden
    Dragon '00
Deadend of Besiegers
    '92
Death Duel of Kung Fu
    '79
Dragon Inn '92
Dragon on Fire '79
Dreadnaught '81
Drunken Master Killer
    '94
18 Fatal Strikes '78
The Enforcer '95
Female Convict Scorpi-
    on: Jailhouse 41
    '72
Fugitive Alien '78
Hail the Judge '94

The Hidden Fortress
    '58
High and Low '63
The Invincible Armour
    '77
Invincible Pole Fighter
    '83
Kiss of the Dragon '01
Knockabout '79
The Last Duel '82
Lone Wolf and Cub 1:
    Sword of
    Vengeance '72
Lone Wolf and Cub 2:
    Baby Cart at the
    River Styx '72
Lone Wolf and Cub 3:
    Baby Cart to Hades
    '72
Lone Wolf and Cub 4:
    Baby Cart in Peril
    '72
Lone Wolf and Cub 5:
    Baby Cart in the
    Land of Demons
    '73
Lone Wolf and Cub 6:
    White Heaven in
    Hell '74
Men Who Tread on the
    Tiger's Tail '43
Metropolis '01
Mr. Vampire 2 '86
Naked Killer '92
Nine Demons '83
Ninja: Band of Assas-
    sins '62
Ninja: Band of Assas-
    sins Continued '63
Ninja vs. Shaolin
    Guards '84
No More Love, No More
    Death '92
Notorious Concubines
    '69
Nowhere to Hide '99
On the Run '88
Operation Billionaires
    '98
Organized Crime and
    Triad Bureau '94
Peace Hotel '95
Peking Opera Blues '86
Police Story 2 '88
Postman Blues '97
Prison on Fire '87
Prison on Fire 2 '91
The Prisoner '90
The Replacement
    Killers '97
Revenge of the Patriots
    '76
Rich and Famous '87
Righting Wrongs '86
Robotrix '91
Run and Kill '93
Running out of Time
    '99
Running out of Time 2
    '01
Sanjuro '63
The 72 Desperate
    Rebels '76
Shogun Assassin '80

The Smart Cavalier '78
Star Force: Fugitive
    Alien 2 '78/86
Supercop '92
The Suspect '98
Ten Tigers of Kwang-
    tung '79
The 36 Deadly Styles
    '79
Thousand Mile Escort
    '76
Time and Tide '00
Tokyo Drifter '66
A Touch of Zen '69
War of the Gargantuas
    '66
We're Going to Eat You!
    '80
Where a Good Man
    Goes '99
White Lotus Cult '93
Who Am I? '98
Zatoichi and the Fugi-
    tives '68
Zatoichi the Fugitive
    '63

Funerals
*The final goodbye, usu-
ally over and over
again. See also: Death
& the Afterlife.*
Beast of the Yellow
    Night '70
Brides of Blood '68
Bruce Lee Fights Back
    from the Grave '76
Bruce Lee, The Legend
    '84
The Chinese Connec-
    tion '71
The Dragon Family '88
Dynamo '78
Exit the Dragon, Enter
    the Tiger '75
Final Justice '88
The Funeral '84
Funeral March '01
Mr. Vampire '85
Mr. Vampire 2 '86
Mr. Vampire Saga 4 '88
New Mr. Vampire '86
Powerful Four '91
Ring '98
She Shoots Straight
    '90
Snake Fist Dynamo '84
The Sword Stained with
    Royal Blood '93
Taboo '97
Tower of Death '81
Troublesome Night 3
    '97
Wing Chun '94
The Young Avenger '79

Gambling
*Sometimes it happens
in states other than
Nevada.*
Adventures of a Blind
    Man '64
Beast Cops '98
The Big Sting '82

874

Blind Swordsman: The
Tale of Zatoichi '62
The Blood Rules '00
Bloody Fight '72
Bolo '80
Brother of Darkness
'94
Bruce Lee We Miss You
'76
Bullet in the Head '90
Cannonball Run '81
Casino Raiders '89
Casino Raiders 2 '91
Casino Tycoon 2 '92
Challenge of Death '78
Chinese Orthopedist
and the Spice Girls
'02
Chivalrous Legend '98
City of Desire '01
The Conman '98
Conman in Tokyo '00
Cop on a Mission '01
Crazy Crooks '80
Death Duel of Kung Fu
'79
Death Ring '83
The Defender '94
The Descendant of
Wing Chun '78
Dirty Kung Fu '78
The Dragon Family '88
The East Is Red '93
Encounter of the
Spooky Kind '81
Enter the Dragon '73
Fantasy Mission Force
'84
Fearless Hyena 2 '80
Fight Back to School 2
'92
Fight, Zatoichi, Fight!
'64
Five Deadly Venoms
'78
Five Superfighters '78
A Gambler's Story '01
God of Gamblers '89
God of Gamblers 2 '90
God of Gamblers 3:
Back to Shanghai
'91
God of Gamblers
Returns '94
Goose Boxer '78
The Hero of Swallow
'96
H.K. Adams Family '92
Hum Paanch '80
The Iron Monkey '77
Kikujiro '99
Kung Fu Genius '79
Lee Rock '91
Legend of the Dragon
'91
The Most Wanted '94
The Odd One Dies '97
Pedicab Driver '89
Rage of the Masters
'74
Renegade Ninjas '79
Rich and Famous '87
Rosa '86
Rush Hour 2 '01

Shaolin vs. Lama '81
Super Car Criminals
'99
SuperManChu '73
Thunder Kick '73
The Tigers '91
Tragic Fantasy: Tiger of
Wanchai '94
The Tricky Master '00
Troublesome Night 9
'00
Yoga and Kung Fu Girl
'78
The Young Avenger '79
Zatoichi and the Chess
Expert '65
Zatoichi and the
Doomed Man '65
Zatoichi Challenged
'67
Zatoichi's Cane Sword
'66
Zatoichi's Revenge '64
Zatoichi the Fugitive
'63
Zatoichi's Vengeance
'66

Gamera
See sidebar, p. 244.
Gamera, Guardian of
the Universe '95
Gamera 2: Advent of
Legion '96
Gamera 3: The
Revenge of Irys '99
Gamera vs. Barugon
'66
Gamera vs. Guillon '69
Gamera vs. Gyaos '67
Gamera vs. Viras '68
Gamera vs. Zigra '71
Giant Monster Gamera
'65

Gangs
See: Organized Crime.

Gays
*See also: Gender Bend-
ing; Lesbians.*
All's Well End's Well '92
Body Weapon '99
Cheap Killers '98
Drunken Master Killer
'94
Full Contact '92
Gorgeous '99
He's a Woman, She's a
Man '94
Ichi the Killer '01
Mon-Rak Transistor '01
100 Ways to Murder
Your Wife '86
Shocking Asia '75
Sure Death: Revenge
'87
Vampire Hunter D '85

Gender Bending
*Men who want to be
women and, less often,
vice-versa. See also:
Gays; He's Really a
Girl!; Lesbians; Role
Reversal.*

The Big Sting '82
The Bride with White
Hair '93
Cop Shop Babes '01
Eagle Shooting Heroes
'93
The East Is Red '93
Gatchaman '94
He's a Woman, She's a
Man '94
Ichi the Killer '01
The Incredible Kung Fu
Mission '82
Invincible Obsessed
Fighter '82
Inheritor of Kung Fu '77
The Ladies' Phone Sex
Club '96
Lady Iron Monkey '83
Lady Wu Tang '77
The Legend of the
Swordsman '92
Project A-ko '86
Ring '98
Ring 2 '99
Ring 0: Birthday '00
Ring Virus '99
Shaolin Temple 2: Kids
from Shaolin '84
Shocking Asia '75
Supercop '92
Vampire Hunter D '85
Venom Warrior '83
Yoga and Kung Fu Girl
'78

Genre Spoofs
*Serious looks at film
genres-not! See also:
Satire & Parody; Sci-Fi
Comedy.*
Aces Go Places 3 '84
Aces Go Places 4 '86
Aces Go Places 5: The
Terracotta Hit '89
A Chinese Torture
Chamber Story '94
Combo Cops '96
Cop Shop Babes '01
Doctor Vampire '90
Dragon Kid '90
Fight Back to School
'91
Fight Back to School 2
'92
Fight Back to School 3
'93
Fist of Fury 1991 '91
Flirting Scholar '93
Forbidden City Cop '96
The Foul King '00
From Beijing with Love
'94
God of Cookery '96
God of Gamblers 2 '90
God of Gamblers 3:
Back to Shanghai
'91
Hail the Judge '94
Half a Loaf of Kung Fu
'77
The Happiness of the
Katakuris '01

The Haunted Cop Shop
'87
He's a Woman, She's a
Man '94
High Risk '95
His Name Is Nobody
'79
H.K. Adams Family '92
The Irresistible Piggies
'02
King of Beggars '92
King of Comedy '99
Kung Pow: Enter the
Fist '76
The Ladies' Phone Sex
Club '96
Legend of the Dragon
'91
Love on Delivery '94
The Magnificent
Scoundrels '91
Pedicab Driver '89
Pom Pom Strikes Back
'86
Postman Blues '97
Project A-ko '86
Royal Tramp '92
Royal Tramp 2 '92
Sixty Million Dollar Man
'95
Terminatrix '95
The Tricky Master '00
Yoga and Kung Fu Girl
'78

Germs
See: Cooties.

Giant Monsters
Akira '88
All Monsters Attack '70
All Monsters Attack!
'02
A*P*E '76
The Cat '91
A Chinese Ghost Story
2 '90
A Chinese Odyssey Part
1: Pandora's Box
'95
Dagora the Space Mon-
ster '64
Daimajin '66
Destroy All Monsters
'68
Ebirah, Horror of the
Deep '66
Final Fantasy: The Spir-
its Within '01
Frankenstein vs.
Baragon '65
Gamera, Guardian of
the Universe '95
Gamera 2: Advent of
Legion '96
Gamera 3: The
Revenge of Irys '99
Gamera vs. Barugon
'66
Gamera vs. Guillon '69
Gamera vs. Gyaos '67
Gamera vs. Viras '68
Gamera vs. Zigra '71
Gappa: The Triphibian
Monster '67

Ghidorah the Three-
Headed Monster
'64
Giant Monster Gamera
'65
Godzilla, King of the
Monsters '54
Godzilla, Mothra and
King Ghidorah: Bat-
tle on Fire '01
Godzilla 1985 '84
Godzilla Raids Again
'55
Godzilla the Series:
Monster War '99
Godzilla 2000 '99
Godzilla vs. Biollante
'89
Godzilla vs. Destroyah
'95
Godzilla vs. Gigan '72
Godzilla vs. Hedorah
'71
Godzilla vs. King Ghido-
rah '91
Godzilla vs.
MechaGodzilla '74
Godzilla vs.
MechaGodzilla 2
'93
Godzilla vs. Megaguirus
'00
Godzilla vs. Megalon
'73
Godzilla vs. Mothra '92
Godzilla vs. Space
Godzilla '94
Green Snake '93
Half Human '55
Invasion of Astro-Mon-
ster '65
King Kong Escapes '67
King Kong vs. Godzilla
'62
Legend of the
Dinosaurs '77
The Magic Crane '93
The Magic Serpent '66
Mighty Peking Man '77
Mothra '61
Mothra vs. Godzilla '64
The Mysterians '57
The Peacock King '89
Princess Mononoke '97
Pulgasari '85
Rebirth of Mothra '96
Rebirth of Mothra 2 '97
Reptilian '00
Return of Daimajin '66
Rodan '56
Sakuya: Slayer of
Demons '00
Son of Godzilla '67
Spirited Away '01
Terror of MechaGodzilla
'75
Ultraman 2 '79
Ultraman Gaia: The
Battle in Hyper-
space '98
Ultraman Tiga and
Ultraman Dyna: The
Warriors of the
Lightning Star '98

875

Urotsukidoji '89
Varan the Unbelievable '58
Voyage into Space '67
War of the Gargantuas '66
Wrath of Daimajin '66
The X from Outer Space '67
Yog: Monster from Space '70
Yongary, Monster from the Deep '67

Giants (Humanoid)
Really. Size doesn't matter. I'm telling ya.
Bruce Lee: A Warrior's Journey '00
Daimajin '66
Entrails of the Virgin '86
Exit the Dragon, Enter the Tiger '75
Fearless Dragons '79
Frankenstein vs. Baragon '65
Game of Death '78
Half Human '55
Lone Ninja Warrior '81
Memento Mori '99
Men Who Tread on the Tiger's Tail '43
Mighty Peking Man '77
Militant Eagle '78
Mortal Kombat '95
The Ninja Dragon '90
The Peacock King '89
Return of Daimajin '66
Sakuya: Slayer of Demons '00
The 72 Desperate Rebels '76
The Silver Spear '79
Ultraman 2 '79
Ultraman Gaia: The Battle in Hyper-space '98
Ultraman Tiga and Ultraman Dyna: The Warriors of the Lightning Star '98
Violence Jack '88
War of the Gargantuas '66
Wrath of Daimajin '66

Girls with Guns
Powerful ladies of armed and unarmed combat. See also: Gun Fu.
Angel '87
Angel 2 '88
Angel on Fire '95
Beautiful Beast '95
Beautiful Hunter '94
Beauty Investigator '92
Black Cat '91
Black Tight Killers '66
Blonde Fury '89
Blood: The Last Vampire '00
Body Weapon '99
Bullets of Love '01

Cop Shop Babes '01
Eat My Dust '93
Executioners '93
Ghost in the Shell '95
Guardian Angel '96
Her Name Is Cat '98
Her Name Is Cat 2: Journey to Death '01
The Heroic Trio '93
The Inspector Wears Skirts '88
In the Line of Duty 3 '88
In the Line of Duty 4 '89
In the Line of Duty 5: Middle Man '90
Lethal Panther '91
Lethal Panther 2 '93
Martial Angels '01
Naked Killer '92
Operation Pink Squad '88
Queen's High '91
Righting Wrongs '86
Robotrix '91
Royal Warriors '86
She Shoots Straight '90
Sister Street Fighter '74
Sugar-Howling of an Angel '96
Supercop 2 '93
Temptress of a Thousand Faces '98
Yes, Madam '85
Zero Woman: The Accused '96

Godzilla
See sidebar, p. 262.
All Monsters Attack '70
All Monsters Attack! '02
Destroy All Monsters '68
Ebirah, Horror of the Deep '66
Ghidorah the Three-Headed Monster '64
Godzilla, King of the Monsters '54
Godzilla, Mothra and King Ghidorah: Battle on Fire '01
Godzilla 1985 '84
Godzilla Raids Again '55
Godzilla the Series: Monster War '99
Godzilla 2000 '99
Godzilla vs. Biollante '89
Godzilla vs. Destroyah '95
Godzilla vs. Gigan '72
Godzilla vs. Hedorah '71
Godzilla vs. King Ghidorah '91

Godzilla vs. MechaGodzilla '74
Godzilla vs. MechaGodzilla 2 '93
Godzilla vs. Megaguirus '00
Godzilla vs. Megalon '73
Godzilla vs. Mothra '92
Godzilla vs. Space Godzilla '94
Invasion of Astro-Monster '65
Mothra vs. Godzilla '64
Son of Godzilla '67
Terror of MechaGodzilla '75

Go Fish
See also: Whales.
The Chinese Feast '95
Dragons Forever '88
The Eel '97
Fighting Ace '79
Filthy Guy '80
Gamera vs. Viras '68
Gamera vs. Zigra '71
God of Cookery '96
Godzilla, King of the Monsters '54
Godzilla Raids Again '55
Guinea Pig: Mermaid in a Manhole '88
Hail the Judge '94
The H-Man '58
Legend of the Drunken Master '94
Maborosi '95
The Moon Warriors '92
Ninja Supremo '81
The Private Eyes '76
Secret of the Chinese Kung Fu '81
Shiri '99
Terror beneath the Sea '66
Tiger Cage '88
Violated Paradise '63
Warm Water under a Red Bridge '01
Yog: Monster from Space '70

Grand Hotel
And some not-so-grand.
Adrenaline Drive '99
Adventures of a Blind Man '64
Ashes of Time '94
Dragon Inn '92
18 Fatal Strikes '78
Final Romance '01
First Strike '96
A Fistful of Talons '83
The Green Dragon Inn '79
Gumnaam '65
The Happiness of the Katakuris '01
Kiss of the Dragon '01
Lone Wolf and Cub 3: Baby Cart to Hades '72

Masked Avengers '81
Midnight Fly '01
The Millionaires' Express '86
Moonlight Express '99
My Sassy Girl '01
New Mr. Vampire '86
Once upon a Time in China 2 '92
Paramount Motel '00
Peace Hotel '95
Pom Pom Strikes Back '86
Ring '98
Rush Hour 2 '01
Samaritan Zatoichi '68
Spirited Away '01
Supercop '92
The Tale of Zatoichi Continues '62
Troublesome Night 4 '98
Troublesome Night 14 '02
Twin Dragons '92
Two Dragons Fight against Tiger '75
Victim '99
Where a Good Man Goes '99
Yes, Madam '85
Zatoichi and the Fugitives '68
Zatoichi on the Road '63
Zatoichi the Fugitive '63
Zatoichi's Cane Sword '66

Great Death Scenes
If you gotta go, you might as well make the most of it. See also: Death & the Afterlife; Funerals.
Beast Cops '98
Brother of Darkness '94
Bruce Lee: The Man, the Myth '76
Bullet in the Head '90
Bullets over Summer '99
Dragon in Jail '90
Executioners from Shaolin '77
Expect the Unexpected '98
Flag of Iron '80
The Flying Guillotine '74
Fulltime Killer '01
Godzilla, King of the Monsters '54
Godzilla vs. Destroyah '95
Ichi the Killer '01
Invincible Pole Fighter '83
Iron Neck Li '81
The Killer '89
King of Comedy '99
Kiss of the Dragon '01

Lone Wolf and Cub 1: Sword of Vengeance '72
Lone Wolf and Cub 2: Baby Cart at the River Styx '72
Lone Wolf and Cub 3: Baby Cart to Hades '72
Memento Mori '99
New Fist of Fury '76
Queen's High '91
Raat '72
Return of Daimajin '66
Return of the Dragon '72
Riki-Oh: The Story of Ricky '89
Ring '98
The Shaolin Invincibles '79
Shogun Assassin '80
Spiral '00
The Street Fighter '74
Tiger Cage '88

Great Depression
The era, not the state of mind.
The Big Brawl '80
Drunken Master Killer '94
From China with Death '74
God of Gamblers 3: Back to Shanghai '91
Iron Monkey 2 '96
Kung Fu's Hero '73
Magnificent Warriors '87
Miracles '89
Peking Opera Blues '86
The Phantom Lover '95

Great Escapes
Men and women break out. See also: Escaped Cons; Men in Prison.
Female Convict Scorpion: Jailhouse 41 '72
Godzilla Raids Again '55
Hail the Judge '94
King Kong Escapes '67
Once upon a Time in China 4 '93
The Prisoner '90
Prison on Fire '87
Prison on Fire 2 '91
Sholay '75
Supercop '92
Versus '00
Zeram '91

Growing Older
What happens just seconds after growin' up. See also: Death & the Afterlife.
All's Well End's Well '92
Casino Raiders 2 '91
Curse of the Vampires '70

Dersu Uzala '74
The Dragon Family '88
The Eel '97
The Funeral '84
Glass Tears '01
The Happiness of the
    Katakuris '01
Hong Kong Nocturne
    '67
Madadayo '92
Miracles '89
Painted Faces '88
Ran '85
Roujin Z '91
The Secrets of the War-
    rior's Power '97
Throne of Blood '57
The Tricky Master '00
The World of the Drunk-
    en Master '79

Growing Up
*What happens just sec-
onds before growin'
old.*
Barefoot Gen '83
Battle Royale '00
Big Boobs Buster '90
Boiling Point '90
Cyclo '95
Days of Being Wild '90
Devil Man '87
Dragon Lord '82
Drunken Master '78
Fists of the White
    Lotus '80
Glass Tears '01
Good Morning '59
Goodbye Mr. Cool '01
Grave of the Fireflies
    '88
Memento Mori '99
Merry-Go-Round '01
My Neighbor Totoro '88
My Sassy Girl '01
Painted Faces '88
Project A-ko '86
Spacked Out '00
Spirited Away '01
United We Stand, and
    Swim '01
Urusei Yatsura Movie
    1: Only You '83
The Young Master '80

Gun Fu
*AKA: Bullet Ballet. See
also: Girls with Guns.*
The Best of the Best
    '96
A Better Tomorrow '86
A Better Tomorrow 2
    '87
A Better Tomorrow 3
    '89
Big Bullet '96
The Big Heat '88
Bullet in the Head '90
Bullets of Love '01
Cheap Killers '98
City on Fire '87
Double Tap '00
Eastern Condors '86
Expect the Unexpected
    '98

Full Contact '92
Hard Boiled '91
Heroes Shed No Tears
    '83/86
The Killer '89
The Mission '99
Moonlight Express '99
Naked Killer '92
No More Love, No More
    Death '92
Once a Thief '91
The Replacement
    Killers '97
Sharp Guns '01
Time and Tide '00
Tokyo Mafia: Yakuza
    Wars '95
Tokyo Mafia 2: Wrath of
    the Yakuza '95
Tokyo Mafia 3: Battle
    for Shinjuku '96
Versus '00
Wild Zero '99

Guns
*See: Gun Fu; Girls with
Guns; Lost Guns.*

Gyaos
They're not Rodan!
Gamera, Guardian of
    the Universe '95
Gamera 3: The
    Revenge of Irys '99
Gamera vs. Guillon '69
Gamera vs. Gyaos '67

Hammer Films
Legend of the 7 Golden
    Vampires '74

Hearts!
*See also: Ears!; Eye-
balls!*
The Blood Drinkers '64
Frankenstein vs.
    Baragon '65
The Killing of Satan '83
Lord of the Wu Tang
    '93
The Street Fighter '74
Tell Me Something '99

Heists
*See also: Scams,
Stings & Cons.*
Aces Go Places '82
Aces Go Places 2 '83
Aces Go Places 3 '84
The Blood Rules '00
Castle of Cagliostro
    '79
City on Fire '87
Crocodile Hunter '89
Downtown Torpedoes
    '97
Expect the Unexpected
    '98
From China with Death
    '74
F*** / Off '98
Full Contact '92
Hit Team '00
The Inspector Wears
    Skirts '88
It Takes a Thief '01

Long Arm of the Law
    '84
Long Arm of the Law 2
    '87
Millennium Dragon '99
The Most Wanted '94
Once a Thief '91
Organized Crime and
    Triad Bureau '94
Pom Pom '84
Running out of Time
    '99
Running out of Time 2
    '01
She Shoots Straight
    '90
Supercop 2 '93
Task Force '97
Tokyo Mafia 3: Battle
    for Shinjuku '96
Victim '99

Hell
*The Underworld. See
also: Death & the After-
life; Marriage; Satan &
Satanism.*
Akira Kurosawa's
    Dreams '90
Burning Paradise '94
A Chinese Ghost Story
    '87
A Chinese Ghost Story:
    The Tsui Hark Ani-
    mation '97
The Killing of Satan '83
Nine Demons '83
The Peacock King '89
Saga of the Phoenix
    '90
Urotsukidoji '89
Zu Warriors '01

He's Really a Girl!
*The cast is easily
fooled when a woman
wears the clothes of a
man. The secret usual-
ly comes out when
someone touches her
chest during a fight
scene. See also: Gen-
der Bending.*
Drunken Art and Crip-
    pled Fist '79
Duel of the Tao Tough
    '82
Duel to the Death '82
The East Is Red '93
Filthy Guy '80
He's a Woman, She's a
    Man '94
Iron Monkey '93
Lady Iron Monkey '83
Lady Whirlwind and the
    Rangers '74
Lady Wu Tang '77
The Legend '93
The Legend 2 '93
Legend of the Drunken
    Tiger '92
Legendary Weapons of
    China '82
Magnificent Natural
    Fist '80

99 Cycling Swords '80
Peking Opera Blues '86
Sam the Iron Bridge:
    Champion of Mar-
    tial Arts '93
The Shaolin Kids '77
The Smart Cavalier '78
Snake and Crane Arts
    of Shaolin '78
Swordsman '90

Historical Drama
*Usually at least loosely
based on a real person
or incident.*
The Blazing Temple '76
Cantonen Iron Kung Fu
    '79
Chushingura '62
Dirty Ho '79
8 Diagram Fighter '91
Emperor of Shaolin
    Kung Fu '80
Executioners from
    Shaolin '77
Fists of the White
    Lotus '80
From the Queen to the
    Chief Executive '01
Generation Consultant
    '90
Generation Pendragon
    '90
Grave of the Fireflies
    '88
King of the Mongols
    '60
Ninja: Band of Assas-
    sins '62
Ninja: Band of Assas-
    sins Continued '63
Notorious Concubines
    '69
Powerful Four '91
Sam the Iron Bridge:
    Champion of Mar-
    tial Arts '93
Samurai 1: Musashi
    Miyamoto '54
Samurai 2: Duel at Ichi-
    joji Temple '55
Samurai 3: Duel at
    Ganryu Island '56
Sex and the Emperor
    '94
Shanghai 1920 '91
Shaolin Master Killer
    '78
The Shaolin Temple '79
Shaolin: Wheel of Life
    '00
Zatoichi the Outlaw '67

Hit Men & Women
*Professional assas-
sins. Contract killers.
Hired men and women
armed with silencers.*
Aakhri Adalat '88
Aces Go Places 3 '84
The Assassin '93
Avenging Eagle '78
Ballistic Kiss
Beyond Hypothermia
    '96

Black Cat '91
Branded to Kill '67
Bullet in the Head '90
Bullets of Love '01
City Hunter: Secret Ser-
    vice '96
Cold War '00
Color of Pain '02
Contract Killer '98
Could You Kill My Hus-
    band Please? '01
Cyclo '95
Day Off '01
The Defender '94
Dirty Ho '79
Dragon from Russia
    '90
Dragon Killer '95
Drunken Tai Chi '84
18 Secrets of Kung Fu
    '79
The Executioner '74
Fallen Angels '95
Fatal Blade '00
Fight, Zatoichi, Fight!
    '64
Fulltime Killer '01
Game of Death '78
God of Cookery '96
Golden Killah '80
Gonin '95
Hard Boiled '91
Her Name Is Cat '98
Ichi the Killer '01
In the Line of Duty 4
    '89
Jiang Hu-"The Triad
    Zone" '00
The Killer '89
Kiss of the Dragon '01
The Last Blood '90
The Legend of a Profes-
    sional '00
Lethal Panther '91
Lethal Panther 2 '93
Lone Wolf and Cub 1:
    Sword of
    Vengeance '72
Lone Wolf and Cub 2:
    Baby Cart at the
    River Styx '72
Lone Wolf and Cub 3:
    Baby Cart to Hades
    '72
Lone Wolf and Cub 4:
    Baby Cart in Peril
    '72
Lone Wolf and Cub 5:
    Baby Cart in the
    Land of Demons
    '73
Lone Wolf and Cub 6:
    White Heaven in
    Hell '74
Naked Killer '92
Ninja: Band of Assas-
    sins '62
Ninja: Band of Assas-
    sins Continued '63
No More Love, No More
    Death '92
The Odd One Dies '97
On the Run '88

Pom Pom Strikes Back '86
Postman Blues '97
Princess Blade '02
The Replacement Killers '97
Return to a Better Tomorrow '94
Return of the Chinese Boxer '75
Sharp Guns '01
Shiri '99
Shogun Assassin '80
Skinny Tiger and Fatty Dragon '90
Sure Death: Revenge '87
A Taste of Killing and Romance '94
Thunder Cops '98
Time and Tide '00
Tokyo Drifter '66
Tokyo Mafia 2: Wrath of the Yakuza '95
Twinkle Twinkle Lucky Stars '85
Ultimatum '01
Violent Cop '89
Yes, Madam '85
You Shoot, I Shoot '01
Zero Woman: The Accused '96

Homosexuality
See: Gays; Lesbians.

Hong Kong (Production)
See sidebar, p. 314.
The Accidental Spy '01
Aces Go Places '82
Aces Go Places 2 '83
Aces Go Places 3 '84
Aces Go Places 4 '86
Aces Go Places 5: The Terracotta Hit '89
The Adventurers '95
All About Ah-Long '89
All Men Are Brothers: Blood of the Leopard '93
All's Well End's Well '92
All's Well End's Well '97 '97
Angel 2 '88
Angel on Fire '95
Anna Magdalena '98
Armageddon '97
Armour of God '86
Ashes of Time '94
The Assassin '93
Avenging Eagle '78
The Avenging Fist '01
Avenging Warriors of Shaolin '79
The Awaken Punch '73
Bakery Amour '01
Ballistic Kiss '98
Battle of Shaolin '77
Beast Cops '98
Beautiful Hunter '94
Beauty Investigator '92
Beauty and the Breast '02
Beijing Rocks '01

The Best of the Best '96
A Better Tomorrow '86
A Better Tomorrow 2 '87
A Better Tomorrow 3 '89
Beyond Hypothermia '96
The Big Brawl '80
Big Bullet '96
The Big Heat '88
The Big Sting '82
Bio Zombie '98
Bio-Cops '00
Black Cat '91
Black Mask '96
The Blacksheep Affair '98
The Blade '95
The Blazing Temple '76
Blonde Fury '89
The Blood Rules '00
Blood of the Dragon '71
Blooded Treasury Fight '79
BloodFight '89
Bloody Fight '72
The Bloody Fists '72
Body Weapon '99
Bolo '80
Born Invincible '78
Born to Defence '88
Born Wild '01
Brassiere '01
Brave Archer '77
Breakout from Oppression '78
The Bride with White Hair '93
The Bride with White Hair 2 '93
Brother of Darkness '94
Bruce Lee: A Warrior's Journey '00
Bruce Lee Fights Back from the Grave '76
Bruce Lee, The Legend '84
Bruce Lee: The Man, the Myth '76
Bruce Lee We Miss You '76
Brutal Boxer '72
The Buddha Assassinator '79
The Buddhist Fist '79
Bullet in the Head '90
Bullets of Love '01
Bullets over Summer '99
Burning Paradise '94
Bury Me High '90
Butterfly and Sword '93
The Butterfly Murders '79
Cannonball Run '81
Cantonen Iron Kung Fu '79
Casino Raiders '89
Casino Raiders 2 '91
Casino Tycoon 2 '92

The Cat '91
Century of the Dragon '99
C'est la Vie, Mon Cheri '93
Challenge of Death '78
Champ against Champ '83
Cheap Killers '98
The Cheaters '01
China Strike Force '00
Chinatown Kid '77
The Chinese Connection '71
The Chinese Feast '95
A Chinese Ghost Story '87
A Chinese Ghost Story 2 '90
A Chinese Ghost Story 3 '91
A Chinese Ghost Story: The Tsui Hark Animation '97
Chinese Hercules '73
Chinese Iron Man '75
A Chinese Odyssey Part 1: Pandora's Box '95
A Chinese Odyssey Part 2: Cinderella '95
Chinese Orthopedist and the Spice Girls '02
Chinese Samson '79
Chinese Super Ninjas '82
A Chinese Torture Chamber Story '94
A Chinese Torture Chamber Story 2 '98
Chungking Express '94
City Cop '95
City Hunter '92
City War '88
City of Desire '01
City on Fire '87
Clean My Name, Mr. Coroner! '00
Clueless '01
Code of Honor '87
Cold War '00
Color of Pain '02
Combo Cops '96
Comeuppance '00
Comic King '00
Comrades, Almost a Love Story '96
The Conman '98
Conman in Tokyo '00
Contract Killer '98
Cop Shop Babes '01
Cop on a Mission '01
Could You Kill My Husband Please? '01
Crack Shadow Boxers '77
Crazy Crooks '80
Crime Story '93
Crime of a Beast '01
Crippled Masters '80
Crocodile Hunter '89

Crouching Tiger, Hidden Dragon '00
Crystal Hunt '91
Curry & Pepper '90
Dance of a Dream '01
Dance of the Drunk Mantis '79
Daughter of Darkness '93
Day Off '01
Days of Being Wild '90
Deadful Melody '94
The Deadly Camp '99
Deadly Snail vs. Kung Fu Killer '77
The Deadly Sword '78
Death Duel of Kung Fu '79
Death Mask of the Ninja '82
Death Ring '83
The Defender '94
The Demon's Baby '98
The Descendant of Wing Chun '78
Devil Touch '02
Devil Woman '70
Dirty Ho '79
Dirty Kung Fu '78
Dirty Tiger, Crazy Frog '78
Doctor No... '01
Doctor Vampire '90
Don't Give a Damn '95
Double Tap '00
Downtown Torpedoes '97
Dr. Lamb '92
Dragon Chronicles: Maidens of Heavenly Mountain '94
The Dragon Family '88
Dragon Fist '78
Dragon from Russia '90
Dragon in Jail '90
Dragon Inn '92
Dragon Killer '95
Dragon Lee vs. the Five Brothers '78
Dragon Lord '82
Dragon on Fire '79
Dragon's Claws '79
Dragons Forever '88
Dragons of the Orient '88
Dreadnaught '81
Drunken Art and Crippled Fist '79
Drunken Master '78
Drunken Master Killer '94
Drunken Tai Chi '84
The Duel '00
Duel of the Brave Ones '78
Duel of the Tao Tough '82
Duel to the Death '82
Dummy Mommy, without a Baby '01
Dynamo '78
Eagle Shooting Heroes '93

Eagle's Claw '77
The Eagle's Killer '81
The East Is Red '93
Eastern Condors '86
Eat My Dust '93
8 Diagram Fighter '91
The 18 Bronzemen '76
The 18 Bronzemen Part 2 '76
18 Fatal Strikes '78
The 18 Jade Arhats '78
Eighth Happiness '88
Encounter of the Spooky Kind '81
The End of the Wicked Tiger '81
The Enforcer '95
Enter the Dragon '73
Enter the Fat Dragon '78
Erotic Ghost Story '90
Erotic Ghost Story 2 '91
The Eternal Evil of Asia '95
Every Dog Has His Date '01
Everyday Is Valentine '01
Evil Cat '86
Executioners '93
Executioners from Shaolin '77
Exit the Dragon, Enter the Tiger '75
Expect the Unexpected '98
Extreme Challenge '01
Extreme Crisis '98
The Eye '02
F*** / Off '98
Faces of Horror '98
Fall for You '01
Fallen Angels '95
Fatal Flying Guillotine '77
Fearless Dragons '79
Fearless Hyena '79
Fearless Hyena 2 '80
Fight Back to School '91
Fight Back to School 2 '92
Fight Back to School 3 '93
A Fighter's Blues '00
Fighting Ace '79
Fighting for Love '01
Final Justice '88
Final Romance '01
The Final Winner '01
Fireworks '97
First Option '96
First Strike '96
Fist of Fury '95
Fist of Fury 1991 '91
Fist of Legend '94
Fist Power '99
A Fistful of Talons '83
Fists and Guts '79
Fists Like Lee '74
Fists of Bruce Lee '78
Fists of Fury '71

Fists of the White Lotus '80
Five Deadly Venoms '78
Five Fingers of Death '72
5 Lady Venoms '78
Five Superfighters '78
5 Venoms vs. Wu Tang '87
Flag of Iron '80
Flash Future Kung Fu '83
Flirting Scholar '93
The Flying Guillotine '74
For Bad Boys Only '00
Forbidden City Cop '96
From Beijing with Love '94
From China with Death '74
From the Queen to the Chief Executive '01
Full Alert '97
Full Contact '92
Full Throttle '95
Fulltime Killer '01
Funeral March '01
Fury in Shaolin Temple '82
Fury of King Boxer '72
A Gambler's Story '01
Game of Death '78
Gen-X Cops '99
Gen-Y Cops '00
Generation Consultant '90
Generation Pendragon '90
Gimme Gimme '01
Glass Tears '01
God of Cookery '96
God of Gamblers '89
God of Gamblers 2 '90
God of Gamblers 3: Back to Shanghai '91
God of Gamblers Returns '94
God.com '98
Gold Fingers '01
Golden Dragon Silver Snake '79
Goodbye Mr. Cool '01
Goose Boxer '78
Gorgeous '99
Green Snake '93
Guardian Angel '96
Gunmen '88
H.K. Adams Family '92
Hail the Judge '94
Half a Loaf of Kung Fu '77
Hand of Death '75
Happy Family '02
Hard Boiled '91
The Haunted Cop Shop '87
Haunted Mansion '98
He Has Nothing But Kung Fu '77
Headlines '01
Heart of Dragon '85

Help!!! '00
Her Name Is Cat '98
Her Name Is Cat 2: Journey to Death '01
The Hero of Swallow '96
Heroes Shed No Tears '83/86
The Heroic Trio '93
Hero's Blood '91
He's a Woman, She's a Man '94
High Risk '95
His Name Is Nobody '79
Hit Team '00
Hit-Man in the Hand of Buddha '80
Hong Kong Nocturne '67
Hong Kong X-File '98
Horror Hotline Big Head Monster '01
Hot War '98
The Hot, the Cool, and the Vicious '76
House of the Damned '99
I Love Maria '88
Iceman Cometh '89
Ichi the Killer '01
The Imp '81
In the Line of Duty 3 '88
In the Line of Duty 4 '89
In the Line of Duty 5: Middle Man '90
In the Mood for Love '00
Inner Senses '01
The Inspector Wears Skirts '88
The Invincible Armour '77
The Invincible Killer '79
Invincible Pole Fighter '83
Iron Man '86
The Iron Monkey '77
Iron Monkey '93
Iron Monkey 2 '96
The Irresistible Piggies '02
It Takes a Thief '01
Jackie Chan Adventures 1: The Search for the Talismans '00
Jackie Chan Adventures 2: The Dark Hand Returns '00
Jackie Chan Adventures 3: The Shadow of Shendu '00
Jade Claw '79
Jiang Hu-"The Triad Zone" '00
Juliet in Love '00
Justice, My Foot! '92
Kick Boxer's Tears '92
A Kid from Tibet '91

Kid with the Golden Arm '78
The Killer '89
Killer '00
Killer Priest '81
Killer Snakes '74
Killer's Romance '90
King of Beggars '92
King of Comedy '99
Knockabout '79
Kung Fu Genius '79
The Kung Fu Master '94
Kung Fu on Sale '79
Kung Fu, the Invisible Fist '72
Kung Fu Zombie '81
Kung Fu's Hero '73
Kung Pow: Enter the Fist '76
Lady Whirlwind and the Rangers '74
The Last Blood '90
Last Ghost Standing '99
Last Hero in China '93
Last Hurrah for Chivalry '78
Lavender '00
The Law and the Outlaw '95
Lawyer Lawyer '97
Lee Rock '91
The Leg Fighters '80
Legacy of Rage '86
The Legend '92
The Legend 2 '93
The Legend of Bruce Lee '80
Legend of Speed '99
Legend of a Professional '00
Legend of the 7 Golden Vampires '74
Legend of the Dragon '91
Legend of the Drunken Master '94
Legend of the Flying Swordsman '00
Legend of the Mountain '79
The Legend of the Swordsman '92
Legendary Couple '95
The Legendary Strike '78
Legendary Weapons of China '82
Leopard Hunting '98
Lethal Panther '91
A Life of Ninja '83
Lightning Kung Fu '80
Long Arm of the Law '84
Long Arm of the Law 2 '87
The Longest Nite '98
The Lord of Hangzhou '98
Lord of the Wu Tang '93
Losers' Club '01
Love au Zen '01

Love Correction '00
Love Me, Love My Money '01
Love on a Diet '01
Love on Delivery '94
Love Paradox '00
The Magic Crane '93
The Magnificent '78
The Magnificent Butcher '79
Magnificent Natural Fist '80
The Magnificent Scoundrels '91
Magnificent Warriors '87
A Man Called Hero '99
Man Wanted '95
Mantis Combat '81
Marry a Rich Man '02
Martial Angels '01
Martial Arts Mayhem, Vol. 1 '99
Martial Arts Mayhem, Vol. 2 '99
Mask of Death '76
Masked Avengers '81
The Masked Prosecutor '99
The Massive '78
The Master '89
Master of the Flying Guillotine '74
Master Q 2001 '01
Merry-Go-Round '01
Midnight Fly '01
Mighty Peking Man '77
Militant Eagle '78
Millennium Dragon '99
The Millionaires' Express '86
The Miracle Fighters '82
Miracles '89
The Mission '99
Model from Hell '99
A Moment of Romance '90
Monkey Fist Floating Snake '79
The Moon Warriors '92
Moonlight Express '99
The Most Wanted '94
Mr. Boo Meets Pom Pom '85
Mr. Nice Guy '97
Mr. Vampire '85
Mr. Vampire 2 '86
Mr. Vampire Saga 4 '88
My Kung Fu 12 Kicks '79
My Lucky Stars '85
My School Mate, the Barbarian '01
Naked Killer '92
Needing You... '00
New Fist of Fury '76
The New Game of Death '75
The New Legend of Shaolin '94
The New Marvelous Double '92
New Mr. Vampire '86

Nightmare Zone '98
Nine Demons '83
9413 '98
990714.com '00
Ninja Checkmate '79
Ninja Supremo '81
Ninja the Final Duel '85
Ninja vs. Ninja '87
No More Love, No More Death '92
Odd Couple '79
The Odd One Dies '97
Okinawa Rendez-vous '00
On the Run '88
Once a Thief '91
Once upon a Time in China '91
Once upon a Time in China 2 '92
Once upon a Time in China 3 '93
Once upon a Time in China 4 '93
Once upon a Time in China and America '97
One Arm Hero '94
100 Ways to Murder Your Wife '86
Operation Billionaires '98
Operation Condor '91
Operation Pink Squad '88
Option Zero '97
Organized Crime and Triad Bureau '94
The Owl vs. Bombo '84
Painted Faces '88
Painted Skin '92
Para Para Sakura '01
Paramount Motel '00
Peace Hotel '95
The Peacock King '89
Pedicab Driver '89
Peking Opera Blues '86
The Phantom Lover '95
Picture of a Nymph '88
Police Story '85
Police Story 2 '88
Pom Pom '84
Pom Pom Strikes Back '86
Pom Pom and Hot Hot '92
The Postman Fights Back '82
Powerful Four '91
Prince of the Sun '90
Prison on Fire '87
Prison on Fire 2 '91
The Prisoner '90
The Private Eye Blues '94
The Private Eyes '76
Prodigal Boxer '73
The Prodigal Son '81
Project A '83
Project A 2 '87
The Protector '85
Queen's High '91
Rage of the Masters '74

The Real Bruce Lee '79
Record '00
Red Shield '91
The Red Wolf '95
Red to Kill '94
The Replacement Suspects '01
The Return of the 5 Deadly Venoms '78
Return of the Chinese Boxer '75
Return of the Deadly Blade '81
Return of the Dragon '72
Return of the Master Killer '80
Return of the Tiger '79
Return to a Better Tomorrow '94
Revenge of the Patriots '76
Revenge of the Zombies '76
Rich and Famous '87
Righting Wrongs '86
Riki-Oh: The Story of Ricky '89
Rivals of the Dragon '83
Robotrix '91
Rock 'n' Roll Cop '94
Rosa '86
Royal Tramp '92
Royal Tramp 2 '92
Royal Warriors '86
Rumble in the Bronx '95
Run and Kill '93
Runaway '01
Running out of Time '99
Running out of Time 2 '01
Rush Hour '98
Rush Hour 2 '01
Saga of the Phoenix '90
Sam the Iron Bridge: Champion of Martial Arts '93
Satin Steel '94
Savior of the Soul '91
Savior of the Soul 2 '92
Scared Stiff '86
Scorpion Thunderbolt '85
Screaming Ninja '73
Second Time Around '02
The Secrets of the Warrior's Power '97
Seeding of a Ghost '83
7 Commandments of Kung Fu '79
The Seventh Curse '86
The 72 Desperate Rebels '76
Sex and the Emperor '94
Shadow '01
Shadow of the Tiger '79

Shanghai 1920 '91
Shanghai Affairs '98
The Shaolin Brothers '77
The Shaolin Disciple '80
Shaolin Fist of Fury '87
The Shaolin Invincibles '79
The Shaolin Kids '77
Shaolin King Boxer '79
Shaolin Mantis '78
Shaolin Master Killer '78
The Shaolin One '83
Shaolin Soccer '01
The Shaolin Temple '79
Shaolin Traitorous '76
Shaolin Wooden Men '76
Shaolin and Tai Chi '79
Shaolin vs. Ninja '83
Sharp Guns '01
She Shoots Straight '90
Shocking Asia '75
Shocking Asia 2 '76
Shogun and Little Kitchen '92
The Silver Spear '79
Sixty Million Dollar Man '95
Skinny Tiger and Fatty Dragon '90
The Smart Cavalier '78
Snake Deadly Act '79
The Snake Strikes Back '81
Snake and Crane Arts of Shaolin '78
Snake in the Eagle's Shadow '78
Snake-Crane Secret '78
Son of Godzilla '67
Sound from the Dark '00
Spacked Out '00
Spiritual Kung Fu '78
Sting of the Dragon Masters '73
The Storm Riders '98
The Story in Temple Red Lily '79
Story of the Dragon '76
Succubare '77
Sunshine Cops '99
Super Car Criminals '99
Super Gang '78
Super Kung Fu Kid '74
Supercop '92
Supercop 2 '93
SuperManChu '73
The Suspect '98
The Sword Stained with Royal Blood '93
Swordsman '90
Swordsman with an Umbrella '70
Take 2 in Life '01
The Tale of Zatoichi Continues '62
Task Force '97

A Taste of Killing and Romance '94
Teenage Mutant Ninja Turtles '90
Temptress of a Thousand Faces '98
10 Magnificent Killers '77
Ten Tigers of Kwangtung '79
Ten Tigers of Shaolin '78
The 36 Crazy Fists '77
The 36 Deadly Styles '79
Thousand Mile Escort '76
3 Evil Masters '80
The Three Swordsmen '94
Thunder Cop '96
Thunder Cops '98
Thunder Kick '73
Thunder Ninja Kids: The Hunt for the Devil Boxer '86/94
Thunderbolt '95
Tiger Cage '88
Tiger on Beat '88
Tiger over Wall '80
The Tigers '91
Time and Tide '00
Tiramisu '02
To Kill with Intrigue '77
Tokyo Raiders '00
Too Many Ways to Be No. 1 '97
The Touch '02
Tower of Death '81
Tragic Fantasy: Tiger of Wanchai '94
Triangular Duel '72
The Tricky Master '00
Troublesome Night '97
Troublesome Night 3 '97
Troublesome Night 4 '98
Troublesome Night 8 '00
Troublesome Night 9 '00
Troublesome Night 14 '02
Trust Me U Die '99
Twin Dragons '92
Twin Warriors '93
Twinkle Twinkle Lucky Stars '85
2000 A.D. '00
U-Man '02
Ultimatum '01
The Unbeaten 28 '80
Undercover Blues '00
United We Stand, and Swim '01
The Untold Story '92
The Untold Story 2 '98
The Vampire Combat '01
Vampire Controller '00
Vampire Hunter D: Bloodlust '01
Vampire Kids '91

Venom Warrior '83
The Victim '80
Victim '99
Violent Cop '99
Visible Secret '01
A War Named Desire '00
Warrior from Shaolin '81
Ways of Kung Fu '80
We're Going to Eat You! '80
The Wesley's Mysterious File '01
Wheels on Meals '84
Where a Good Man Goes '99
Where's Officer Tuba? '86
White Lotus Cult '93
Who Am I? '98
Wicked City '92
A Wicked Ghost '99
A Wicked Ghost 2: The Fear '00
Wing Chun '94
Winners and Sinners '83
Wishful Milenio '01
The Witch from Nepal '85
With or Without You '92
Wonder Seven '94
The World of the Drunken Master '79
Yes, Madam '85
Yoga and Kung Fu Girl '78
You Shoot, I Shoot '01
Young and Dangerous '96
Young and Dangerous 5 '98
Young and Dangerous 6: Born to Be King '98
The Young Avenger '79
The Young Master '80
Young Tiger '72
Your Place or Mine! '98
Zu: Warriors of the Magic Mountain '83

Horror
See also: Horror Anthologies; Horror Comedy.
Abbot White '82
Akira '88
Another Heaven '00
Attack of the Mushroom People '63
Audition '99
Beast of the Yellow Night '70
Blade 2 '02
The Blood Drinkers '64
Blood: The Last Vampire '00
Bloody Beach '00
Body Snatcher from Hell '68
Brides of Blood '68

Brother of Darkness '94
The Butterfly Murders '79
The Cat '91
A Chinese Torture Chamber Story '94
A Chinese Torture Chamber Story 2 '98
Crime of a Beast '01
Cross Fire '00
Cure '97
Curse of the Vampires '70
Dagora the Space Monster '64
Daimajin '66
Dark Water '02
Daughter of Darkness '93
The Deadly Camp '99
Devil Man '87
Devil Woman '70
Dr. Lamb '92
Entrails of the Virgin '86
Erotic Ghost Story '90
Erotic Ghost Story 2 '91
The Eternal Evil of Asia '95
Evil Cat '86
Evil Dead Trap '88
The Eye '02
Fear Faith Revenge 303 '98
Ghost Actress '96
Guinea Pig: Android of Notre Dame '88
Guinea Pig: Devils Experiment '85
Guinea Pig: Flower of Flesh and Blood '85
Guinea Pig: He Never Dies '86
Guinea Pig: Mermaid in a Manhole '88
Half Human '55
Happy End '99
The Haunted Lantern '98
Haunted Mansion '98
Hiruko the Goblin '90
The H-Man '58
Hong Kong X-File '98
Horror Hotline Big Head Monster '01
Horror of the Blood Monsters '70
House of the Damned '99
The Human Vapor '60
The Hypnotist '99
Ichi the Killer '01
The Imp '81
Inner Senses '01
Junk '99
Killer Snakes '74
The Killing of Satan '83
Legend of the Dinosaurs '77

Legend of the 7 Golden
    Vampires '74
Mad Doctor of Blood
    Island '68
The Manster '60
Memento Mori '99
Model from Hell '99
Nine Demons '83
9413 '98
Organ '96
Parasite Eve '97
Raat '91
Reborn from Hell:
    Samurai Armaged-
    don '96
Record '00
Red to Kill '94
Revenge of the Zom-
    bies '76
Ring '98
Ring 2 '99
Ring 0: Birthday '00
Ring Virus '99
Robo Vampire '88
Robotrix '91
Scorpion Thunderbolt
    '85
The Secret of the
    Telegian '60
Seeding of a Ghost '83
The Seventh Curse '86
Shadow '01
Sound from the Dark
    '00
Spiral '00
Succubare '77
Terror beneath the Sea
    '66
Terror Is a Man '59
Tetsuo: The Iron Man
    '89
Tetsuo 2: Body Ham-
    mer '91
Trust Me U Die '99
Twilight of the Dark
    Master '97
Twilight People '72
2000 A.D. '00
The Untold Story '92
The Untold Story 2 '98
Urotsukidoji '89
The Vampire Combat
    '01
Vampire Controller '00
Vampire Hunter D '85
Vampire Hunter D:
    Bloodlust '01
Versus '00
Victim '99
Violent Cop '99
Visible Secret '01
The Wesley's Mysteri-
    ous File '01
Wicked City '87
Wicked City '92
A Wicked Ghost '99
A Wicked Ghost 2: The
    Fear '00
Wild Zero '99
The Witch from Nepal
    '85
Wrath of Daimajin '66

Horror Anthologies
Faces of Horror '98
Kwaidan '64
Nightmare Zone '98
990714.com '00
Troublesome Night '97
Troublesome Night 3
    '97
Troublesome Night 4
    '98
Troublesome Night 8
    '00
Troublesome Night 9
    '00
Troublesome Night 14
    '02

Horror Comedy
*Laughing all the way to
the grave.*
A*P*E '76
Bio-Cops '00
Bio Zombie '98
The Demon's Baby '98
Devil Hunter Yohko '91
Devil Hunter Yohko 2
    '92
Devil Hunter Yohko 3
    '92
Doctor Vampire '90
Dragon against Vam-
    pire '85
Dreadnaught '81
Encounter of the
    Spooky Kind '81
Guinea Pig: He Never
    Dies '86
Gumnaam '65
The Happiness of the
    Katakuris '01
The Haunted Cop Shop
    '87
Kung Fu Zombie '81
Last Ghost Standing
    '99
Mr. Vampire '85
Mr. Vampire 2 '86
Mr. Vampire Saga 4 '88
New Mr. Vampire '86
Savior of the Soul 2
    '92
Scared Stiff '86
Troublesome Night '97
Troublesome Night 3
    '97
Troublesome Night 4
    '98
Troublesome Night 8
    '00
Troublesome Night 9
    '00
Troublesome Night 14
    '02
Vampire Kids '91
We're Going to Eat You!
    '80

Hospitals
*Institutions with lots of
sick people-and
patients, too. See also:
Cooties; Doctors
and/or Nurses; Evil
Doctors; Sanity Check;
Shrinks.*

The Accidental Spy '01
Adrenaline Drive '99
Black Jack '96
Casino Tycoon 2 '92
Champion '00
Cold War '00
Cure '97
Doctor Vampire '90
The Eye '02
Fight Back to School 3
    '93
Funeral March '01
Hard Boiled '91
Help!!! '00
Hit Team '00
Horror Hotline Big Head
    Monster '01
The Hypnotist '99
Inner Senses '01
The Killer '89
The Last Blood '90
Legendary Couple '95
A Love of Blueness '00
Man Wanted '95
The Masked Prosecutor
    '99
My Neighbor Totoro '88
Operation Billionaires
    '98
Operation Pink Squad
    '88
Organ '96
Pom Pom Strikes Back
    '86
Raat '91
Ring 2 '99
Rosa '86
Roujin Z '91
Scared Stiff '86
Thunderbolt '95
Twin Dragons '92

Hostage!
*People held against
their will for bargaining
purposes. See also:
Kidnapped!*
Armageddon '97
Attack the Gas Station!
    '99
The Big Heat '88
Casino Tycoon 2 '92
City Cop '95
City Hunter '92
Color of Pain '02
Combo Cops '96
Crocodile Hunter '89
The Enforcer '95
Fist Power '99
Hard as a Dragon '80
Hard Boiled '91
Heart of Dragon '85
Her Name Is Cat '98
High Risk '95
King Kong Escapes '67
Kiss of the Dragon '01
The Legendary Strike
    '78
Lethal Panther 2 '93
Magnificent Warriors
    '87
Martial Angels '01
The Millionaires'
    Express '86

A Moment of Romance
    '90
9413 '98
Ninja Supremo '81
Once upon a Time in
    China '91
Pom Pom Strikes Back
    '86
The Replacement Sus-
    pects '01
Robotrix '91
Run and Kill '93
Rush Hour '98
She Shoots Straight
    '90
Sunshine Cops '99
Thunderbolt '95
Thunder Cops '98
Vampire Hunter D '85
Where a Good Man
    Goes '99
Yes, Madam '85

Hurling
See: Chunky Delight.

I Can't See
*Movies containing
blindness. See also:
Eyeballs!; I Can't See
You; What?*
Adventures of a Blind
    Man '64
Ashes of Time '94
Beast of the Yellow
    Night '70
Beautiful Hunter '94
Blind Beast '69
Blind Fist of Bruce '79
Blind Swordsman: The
    Tale of Zatoichi '62
Brave Archer '77
Breakout from Oppres-
    sion '78
Casino Raiders 2 '91
City Hunter: Secret Ser-
    vice '96
The Conman '98
The Eagle's Killer '81
Ecstasy of the Angels
    '72
Emperor of Shaolin
    Kung Fu '80
Fight, Zatoichi, Fight!
    '64
Iron Monkey 2 '96
Jade Claw '79
The Killer '89
King of the Mongols
    '60
Kwaidan '64
The Legend of Bruce
    Lee '80
Lightning Kung Fu '80
Master of the Flying
    Guillotine '74
New Tale of Zatoichi
    '63
Operation Pink Squad
    '88
Para Para Sakura '01
The Return of the 5
    Deadly Venoms '78
Samaritan Zatoichi '68

Scorpion Thunderbolt
    '85
The 72 Desperate
    Rebels '76
The Sword Stained with
    Royal Blood '93
The Tale of Zatoichi
    Continues '62
The Vampire Combat
    '01
Yellow River Fighter '88
Zatoichi and the Chess
    Expert '65
Zatoichi and the Chest
    of Gold '64
Zatoichi and the
    Doomed Man '65
Zatoichi and the Fugi-
    tives '68
Zatoichi Challenged
    '67
Zatoichi on the Road
    '63
Zatoichi the Fugitive
    '63
Zatoichi the Outlaw '67
Zatoichi's Cane Sword
    '66
Zatoichi's Flashing
    Sword '64
Zatoichi's Revenge '64
Zatoichi's Vengeance
    '66

I Can't See You
*Movies containing invis-
ibility.*
Abbot White '82
A Chinese Torture
    Chamber Story '94
The Eternal Evil of Asia
    '95
Evil Brain from Outer
    Space '58/59
Final Fantasy: The Spir-
    its Within '01
5 Venoms vs. Wu Tang
    '87
The Heroic Trio '93
The Human Vapor '60
Jackie Chan Adven-
    tures 2: The Dark
    Hand Returns '00
Lady Ninja: Reflections
    of Darkness '96
Lady Wu Tang '77
Winners and Sinners
    '83

I Spy
*Trench coats, fedoras,
dark glasses, and often
martinis (shaken, not
stirred).*
The Accidental Spy '01
Aces Go Places 3 '84
Downtown Torpedoes
    '97
First Strike '96
From Beijing with Love
    '94
Gen-X Cops '99
Gen-Y Cops '00
Godzilla vs. Megalon
    '73

881

In the Line of Duty 5: Middle Man '90
Jackie Chan Adventures 1: The Search for the Talismans '00
Jackie Chan Adventures 2: The Dark Hand Returns '00
Jackie Chan Adventures 3: The Shadow of Shendu '00
Kung Fu, the Invisible Fist '72
Mighty Jack '68
Millennium Dragon '99
Peking Opera Blues '86
The Tuxedo '02
2000 A.D. '00
What's Up, Tiger Lily? '66

Incest
See: Kissin' Cousins.

India (Production)
See sidebar, p. 320.
Aakhri Adalat '88
Champion '00
Elaan '94
Gumnaam '65
Hum Paanch '80
Mahal '48
Raat '91
Sholay '75

Inventors & Inventions
See also: Mad Scientists.
Aces Go Places '82
Aces Go Places 2 '83
Aces Go Places 3 '84
Aces Go Places 4 '86
Aces Go Places 5: The Terracotta Hit '89
All Monsters Attack '70
Armageddon '97
Astro Boy '63
Astro Boy '80
Battle in Outer Space '59
Crazy Crooks '80
Dragons Forever '88
Executioners '93
The Flying Guillotine '74
Forbidden City Cop '96
From Beijing with Love '94
Godzilla, King of the Monsters '54
Godzilla vs. Biollante '89
Godzilla vs. Destroyah '95
Godzilla vs. King Ghidorah '91
Godzilla vs. MechaGodzilla '74
Godzilla vs. Megaguirus '00
Godzilla vs. Megalon '73
The Heroic Trio '93

Hiruko the Goblin '90
The Human Vapor '60
Invasion of the Neptune Men '61
Junk '99
King Kong Escapes '67
King Kong vs. Godzilla '62
Parasite Eve '97
Patlabor 1: The Movie '90
Saga of the Phoenix '90
Savior of the Soul '91
Savior of the Soul 2 '92
The Secret of the Telegian '60
Shaolin Master Killer '78
Sixty Million Dollar Man '95
Son of Godzilla '67
Star Force: Fugitive Alien 2 '78/86
Terror beneath the Sea '66
Terror of MechaGodzilla '75
Tetsuo 2: Body Hammer '91

Invisibility
See: I Can't See You.

Islands
Not counting Japan, Hong Kong, Taiwan, Manhattan, nor Tai 0 Island (see also), Blood Island (see also), or Uncharted Desert Isles (see also).
All Monsters Attack '70
Battle Royale '00
The Best of the Best '96
The Deadly Camp '99
Destroy All Monsters '68
Enter the Dragon '73
First Option '96
Glass Tears '01
Godzilla, King of the Monsters '54
Godzilla Raids Again '55
Godzilla vs. Destroyah '95
Godzilla vs. Gigan '72
Godzilla vs. King Ghidorah '91
Godzilla vs. MechaGodzilla 2 '93
Godzilla vs. Space Godzilla '94
Gorgeous '99
Gumnaam '65
Gunhed '89
The Killing of Satan '83
King Kong Escapes '67
King Kong vs. Godzilla '62
Marry a Rich Man '02

Mortal Kombat '95
Mothra '61
Mothra vs. Godzilla '64
Project A '83
Ring '98
Ring 2 '99
Samurai 3: Duel at Ganryu Island '56
Son of Godzilla '67
Twilight People '72
Ultraman Tiga and Ultraman Dyna: The Warriors of the Lightning Star '98
Varan the Unbelievable '58
Violated Paradise '63
Voyage into Space '67
We're Going to Eat You! '80
Wrath of Daimajin '66
Yog: Monster from Space '70

It's a Conspiracy, Man!
See also: Mystery & Suspense.
The Accidental Spy '01
Akira '88
Atomic Rulers of the World '57
The Dimension Travelers '98
Final Fantasy: The Spirits Within '01
Game of Death '78
Ghost in the Shell '95
Godzilla vs. King Ghidorah '91
Iron Monkey 2 '77
Junk '99
Killer from Above '77
Kiss of the Dragon '01
Kung Pow: Enter the Fist '76
Lawyer Lawyer '97
Legend of the Drunken Master '94
Metropolis '01
Nobody '99
The Replacement Killers '97
Royal Tramp '92
The Wesley's Mysterious File '01

Japan (Production)
See sidebar, p. 342.
Adrenaline Drive '99
Adventures of a Blind Man '64
The Adventures of Milo and Otis '86
After Life '98
Akira '88
Akira Kurosawa's Dreams '90
All Monsters Attack '70
All Monsters Attack! '02
Another Heaven '00
Appleseed '88
Astro Boy '63
Astro Boy '80

Atomic Rulers of the World '57
Attack from Space '58
Attack of the Mushroom People '63
Audition '99
Barefoot Gen '83
Battle in Outer Space '59
Battle Royale '00
Beautiful Beast '95
Big Boobs Buster '90
Black Jack '96
Black Magic M-66 '87
Black Tight Killers '66
Blind Beast '69
Blind Swordsman: The Tale of Zatoichi '62
Blood: The Last Vampire '00
BloodFight '89
Blowback: Love and Death '90
Body Snatcher from Hell '68
The Bodyguard '73/78
Boiling Point '90
Branded to Kill '67
Bronson Lee, Champion '78
Brother '00
Bubblegum Crisis '85
Bullet Train '75
Castle of Cagliostro '79
Chushingura '62
City Hunter: Secret Service '96
Cross Fire '00
Cure '97
Dagora the Space Monster '64
Daimajin '66
Dark Water '02
Dersu Uzala '74
Destroy All Monsters '68
Devil Hunter Yohko '91
Devil Hunter Yohko 2 '92
Devil Hunter Yohko 3 '92
Devil Man '87
The Dimension Travelers '98
Dragon Princess '81
Ebirah, Horror of the Deep '66
Ecstasy of the Angels '72
The Eel '97
Entrails of the Virgin '86
Evil Brain from Outer Space '58/59
Evil Dead Trap '88
The Executioner '74
Fatal Blade '00
Female Convict Scorpion: Jailhouse 41 '72
Fight, Zatoichi, Fight! '64

Final Fantasy: The Spirits Within '01
Frankenstein vs. Baragon '65
Freeze Me '00
Fugitive Alien '78
The Funeral '84
Gamera, Guardian of the Universe '95
Gamera 2: Advent of Legion '96
Gamera 3: The Revenge of Irys '99
Gamera vs. Barugon '66
Gamera vs. Guiron '69
Gamera vs. Gyaos '67
Gamera vs. Viras '68
Gamera vs. Zigra '71
Gappa: The Triphibian Monster '67
Gatchaman '94
Ghidorah the Three-Headed Monster '64
Ghost Actress '96
Ghost in the Shell '95
Giant Monster Gamera '65
Giants and Toys '58
Godzilla 1985 '84
Godzilla Raids Again '55
Godzilla the Series: Monster War '99
Godzilla 2000 '99
Godzilla vs. Biollante '89
Godzilla vs. Destroyah '95
Godzilla vs. Gigan '72
Godzilla vs. Hedorah '71
Godzilla vs. King Ghidorah '91
Godzilla vs. MechaGodzilla '74
Godzilla vs. MechaGodzilla 2 '93
Godzilla vs. Megaguirus '00
Godzilla vs. Megalon '73
Godzilla vs. Mothra '92
Godzilla vs. Space Godzilla '94
Godzilla, King of the Monsters '54
Godzilla, Mothra and King Ghidorah: Battle on Fire '01
Gonin '95
Good Morning '59
Grave of the Fireflies '88
Great Performances: Kurosawa '02
Guinea Pig: Android of Notre Dame '88
Guinea Pig: Devil's Experiment '85

882

Guinea Pig: Flower of Flesh and Blood '85
Guinea Pig: He Never Dies '86
Guinea Pig: Mermaid in a Manhole '88
Guinea Pig: The Making of Guinea Pig '86
Gunhed '89
The H-Man '58
Half Human '55
The Happiness of the Katakuris '01
The Haunted Lantern '98
The Hidden Fortress '58
High and Low '63
Hiruko the Goblin '90
The Human Vapor '60
The Hypnotist '99
Ichi the Killer '01
I.K.U. '00
Invaders from Space '58
Invasion of Astro-Monster '65
Invasion of the Neptune Men '61
Junk '99
Kei Mizutani: Undressed for Success '94
Kikujiro '99
King Kong Escapes '67
King Kong vs. Godzilla '62
King of the Mongols '60
Kwaidan '64
The Ladies' Phone Sex Club '96
Lady Ninja: Reflections of Darkness '96
The Last War '61
Legend of the Dinosaurs '77
Legend of the Eight Samurai '84
Lone Wolf and Cub 1: Sword of Vengeance '72
Lone Wolf and Cub 2: Baby Cart at the River Styx '72
Lone Wolf and Cub 3: Baby Cart to Hades '72
Lone Wolf and Cub 4: Baby Cart in Peril '72
Lone Wolf and Cub 5: Baby Cart in the Land of Demons '73
Lone Wolf and Cub 6: White Heaven in Hell '74
Maborosi '95
Madadayo '92
The Magic Serpent '66
The Manster '60

Martial Arts Mayhem, Vol. 1 '99
Men Who Tread on the Tiger's Tail '43
Message from Space '78
Metropolis '01
Mighty Jack '68
Mothra '61
Mothra vs. Godzilla '64
My Neighbor Totoro '88
The Mysterians '57
Naked Pursuit '68
New Tale of Zatoichi '63
Ninja: Band of Assassins '62
Ninja: Band of Assassins Continued '63
The Ninja Dragon '90
Ninja Scroll '93
Nobody '99
Notorious Concubines '69
Organ '96
Parasite Eve '97
Patlabor 1: The Movie '90
The Peacock King '89
Postman Blues '97
Prince of Space '59
Princess Blade '02
Princess Mononoke '97
Project A-ko '86
Pulse '01
Ran '85
Rashomon '50
The Razor 1: Sword of Justice '72
The Razor 2: The Snare '73
The Razor 3: Who's Got the Gold? '74
Rebirth of Mothra '96
Rebirth of Mothra 2 '97
Reborn from Hell: Samurai Armageddon '96
Renegade Ninjas '79
Return of Daimajin '66
Return of the Street Fighter '74
Ring '98
Ring 0: Birthday '00
Ring 2 '99
Rodan '56
Roujin Z '91
Royal Space Force: The Wings of Honneamise '87
Sadistic City '93
Sakuya: Slayer of Demons '00
Samaritan Zatoichi '68
Samurai I: Musashi Miyamoto '54
Samurai 2: Duel at Ichijoji Temple '55
Samurai 3: Duel at Ganryu Island '56
Sanjuro '63
Sanshiro Sugata '43
The Secret of the Telegian '60

Seven Samurai '54
Shark Skin Man and Peach Hip Girl '98
Shogun Assassin '80
Shogun's Ninja '82
Sister Street Fighter '74
Sonatine '93
Speed Racer: The Movie '67
Spiral '00
Spirited Away '01
Star Force: Fugitive Alien 2 '78/86
Stray Dog '49
The Street Fighter '74
Street Fighter 2 '96
The Street Fighter's Last Revenge '74
Sugar-Howling of Angel '96
Sumo Vixens '96
Sure Death: Revenge '87
Taboo '97
Tampopo '87
Terminatrix '95
Terror beneath the Sea '66
Terror of MechaGodzilla '75
Tetsuo 2: Body Hammer '91
Tetsuo: The Iron Man '89
Throne of Blood '57
Time of the Apes '75
Tokyo Decameron: Three Tales of Madness and Sensuality '96
Tokyo Drifter '66
Tokyo Fist '96
Tokyo Mafia 2: Wrath of the Yakuza '95
Tokyo Mafia 3: Battle for Shinjuku '96
Tokyo Mafia: Yakuza Wars '95
Tokyo Raiders '00
Twilight of the Cockroaches '87
Twilight of the Dark Master '97
Ultraman 2 '01
Ultraman Gaia: The Battle in Hyperspace '98
Ultraman Tiga and Ultraman Dyna: The Warriors of the Lightning Star '98
Urotsukidoji '89
Urusei Yatsura Movie 1: Only You '83
Vampire Hunter D '85
Vampire Hunter D: Bloodlust '01
Varan the Unbelievable '58
The Venus Wars '89
Versus '00
Violated Paradise '63
Violence Jack '88

Violent Cop '89
Voyage into Space '67
War of the Gargantuas '66
Warm Water under a Red Bridge '01
Warning from Space '56
Weather Woman '95
What's Up, Tiger Lily? '66
Wicked City '87
Wild Zero '99
Woman in the Dunes '64
Wrath of Daimajin '66
X '96
The X from Outer Space '67
Yog: Monster from Space '70
Yojimbo '61
Zatoichi Challenged '67
Zatoichi and the Chess Expert '65
Zatoichi and the Chest of Gold '64
Zatoichi and the Doomed Man '65
Zatoichi and the Fugitives '68
Zatoichi on the Road '63
Zatoichi the Fugitive '63
Zatoichi the Outlaw '67
Zatoichi's Cane Sword '66
Zatoichi's Flashing Sword '64
Zatoichi's Revenge '64
Zatoichi's Vengeance '66
Zeram '91
Zero Woman: The Accused '96
Zu Warriors '01

Japanese Invaders
The Adventures of the Master and His Servant '96
Bloody Fight '72
The Chinese Connection '71
Chinese Iron Man '75
Chinese Super Ninjas '82
Chivalrous Legend '98
Deadend of Besiegers '92
Duel to the Death '82
Fantasy Mission Force '84
Fist of Fury '95
Fist of Fury 1991 '91
Fist of Legend '94
Five Fingers of Death '72
Gate of Destiny '96
The Haunted Cop Shop '87
Iron Monkey 2 '96

Kung Fu, the Invisible Fist '72
The Legend of the Swordsman '92
Macho Man '72
Magnificent Natural Fist '80
Magnificent Warriors '87
Martial Arts Master Wong Fei Hung '92
The Millionaires' Express '86
Murder in the Orient '74
New Fist of Fury '76
Ninja in the Deadly Trap '83
Ninja the Final Duel '85
One Arm Hero '94
Return of the Chinese Boxer '75
Screaming Ninja '73
Secret of the Chinese Kung Fu '81
Shadow of the Tiger '79
Shanghai 1920 '91
Shaolin Fist of Fury '87
Shaolin vs. Ninja '83
Sting of the Dragon Masters '73
Triangular Duel '72
The Walls of Hell '64
Warrior from Shaolin '81

Jungles
Tarzan, tribes, trees, treasure, temperature, temptresses, and tigers. See also: Monkey Business; Treasure Hunt.
Armour of God '86
Attack of the Mushroom People '63
Brides of Blood '68
Crystal Hunt '91
Dragon Kid '90
Eastern Condors '86
Ebirah, Horror of the Deep '66
Godzilla vs. Mothra '92
King Kong vs. Godzilla '62
Mad Doctor of Blood Island '68
Mighty Peking Man '77
Satin Steel '94
The Seventh Curse '86
Snaker '01
Son of Godzilla '67

Just a Little Bit Pregnant
See also: That's a Baby?
All About Ah-Long '89
Blind Swordsman: The Tale of Zatoichi '62
Bullets over Summer '99
Butterfly and Sword '93
The Conman '98

The Demon's Baby '98
Dummy Mommy, without a Baby '01
Faces of Horror '98
Hum Paanch '80
The Imp '81
Justice, My Foot! '92
The Killer Elephants '76
Legendary Couple '95
Mon-Rak Transistor '01
Revenge of the Zombies '76
Seeding of a Ghost '83
Snaker '01
Succubare '77
Time and Tide '00

Kickboxing-Professional
Angel on Fire '95
Death Ring '83
Game of Death '78
Kick Boxer's Tears '92
Venom Warrior '83
Young and Dangerous 5 '98

Kidnapped!
Held for ransom or just for the heck of it. See also: Hostage!
Aces Go Places 4 '86
Angel 2 '88
Appleseed '88
Armour of God '86
The Awaken Punch '73
The Big Brawl '80
Black Jack '96
Black Mask '96
Blind Beast '69
The Bloody Fists '72
The Bride with White Hair 2 '93
Bronson Lee, Champion '78
City Hunter: Secret Service '96
Crime Story '93
For Bad Boys Only '00
Gamera vs. Guillon '69
Gamera vs. Viras '68
Gamera vs. Zigra '71
Godzilla vs. Space Godzilla '94
Guinea Pig: Devils Experiment '85
Guinea Pig: Flower of Flesh and Blood '85
Heart of Dragon '85
Her Name Is Cat '98
The Heroic Trio '93
High and Low '63
The Invincible Killer '79
The Killer Elephants '76
Legendary Couple '95
Mighty Jack '68
Mothra '61
The New Game of Death '75
The New Marvelous Double '92
Odd Couple '79

Operation Billionaires '98
Organ '96
Police Story 2 '88
The Protector '85
Rich and Famous '87
Run and Kill '93
Rush Hour '98
She Shoots Straight '90
Sister Street Fighter '74
The Street Fighter '74
Sunshine Cops '99
Suzhou River '00
Sympathy for Mr. Vengeance '01
Ten Tigers of Shaolin '78
Tetsuo 2: Body Hammer '91
Wheels on Meals '84
Winners and Sinners '83

Killer Brains
Literally, they have a mind of their own. See also: Renegade Body Parts.
Another Heaven '00
Body Snatcher from Hell '68
Evil Brain from Outer Space '58/59
Gamera vs. Zigra '71
Sixty Million Dollar Man '95

Killer Dreams
Way off Elm Street.
Akira '88
Akira Kurosawa's Dreams '90
Bloody Beach '00
Devil Man '87
The Dimension Travelers '98
Gate of Destiny '96
Guinea Pig: Android of Notre Dame '88
The Haunted Lantern '98
The Legend '92
Nightmare Zone '98
Savior of the Soul 2 '92
Scared Stiff '86
Shiri '99
Ultraman Gaia: The Battle in Hyperspace '98
The Vampire Combat '01
X '96
Young and Dangerous 6: Born to Be King '00

Killer Jello
Akira '88
Body Snatcher from Hell '68
Dagora the Space Monster '64

Godzilla vs. Hedorah '71
The H-Man '58
Parasite Eve '97
The X from Outer Space '67

Killer Plants
Including foliage, fruits, and fungi.
Attack of the Mushroom People
Brides of Blood '68
Godzilla vs. Biollante '89

King Ghidorah
See sidebar, p. 250.
Destroy All Monsters '68
Ghidorah the Three-Headed Monster '64
Godzilla, Mothra and King Ghidorah: Battle on Fire '01
Godzilla vs. Gigan '72
Godzilla vs. King Ghidorah '91
Invasion of Astro-Monster '65
Rebirth of Mothra '96
Rebirth of Mothra 2 '97

Kissin' Cousins
Really, really close family ties.
Brother of Darkness '94
Crime of a Beast '01
Daughter of Darkness '93
Happy Family '02

Korea (Production)
See sidebar, p. 368.
A*P*E '76
Attack the Gas Station! '99
Bichunmoo '99
Bloody Beach '00
Bruce Lee: A Warrior's Journey '00
Cold War '00
Double Dragon in the Last Duel '85
Dream of Garuda '94
Eagle vs. Silver Fox '83
The Foul King '00
Fury in Shaolin Temple '82
Gate of Destiny '96
Happy End '99
Hi! Dharma! '01
Ichi the Killer '01
Invincible Obsessed Fighter '82
Jackie Chan Adventures 1: The Search for the Talismans '00
Jackie Chan Adventures 2: The Dark Hand Returns '00

Jackie Chan Adventures 3: The Shadow of Shendu '00
Joint Security Area '00
The Korean Connection '77
Lies '99
Magnificent Natural Fist '80
Masters of Martial Arts '74
Masters of Tiger Crane '83
Memento Mori '99
My Sassy Girl '01
My Wife Is a Gangster '01
Ninja vs. Bruce Lee '82
Nowhere to Hide '99
Pulgasari '85
Reptilian '00
Ring Virus '99
Shiri '99
Sympathy for Mr. Vengeance '01
Tell Me Something '99
Volcano High School '01
Yongary, Monster from the Deep '67

Kung Fu
See: Kung Fu Comedy; Kung Fu Kids; Kung Fu Moms; Kung Fu-New School; Kung Fu-Old School; Kung Fu-Retro Old School; see also sidebar, p. 168.

Kung Fu Comedy
The Adventures of the Master and His Servant '96
The Cat '91
City Hunter '92
Combo Cops '96
Cop Shop Babes '01
Crack Shadow Boxers '77
Crazy Crooks '80
Curry & Pepper '90
Dance of the Drunk Mantis '79
The Descendant of Wing Chun '78
Dirty Ho '79
Dirty Kung Fu '78
Dirty Tiger, Crazy Frog '78
Doctor Vampire '90
Don't Give a Damn '95
Dragon against Vampire '85
Dragon from Shaolin '96
Dragon Lord '82
Dragons Forever '88
Dreadnaught '81
Dreaming Fists with Slender Hands '80
Drunken Master '78
Drunken Tai Chi '84
Eagle Shooting Heroes '93

Eat My Dust '93
Encounter of the Spooky Kind '81
Enter the Fat Dragon '78
Fantasy Mission Force '84
Fearless Dragons '79
Fearless Hyena '79
Fearless Hyena 2 '80
Filthy Guy '80
Fist of Fury 1991 '91
Fists and Guts '79
The Fist, the Kicks and the Evils '79
5 Venoms vs. Wu Tang '87
Flirting Scholar '93
Forbidden City Cop '96
From Beijing with Love '94
God of Cookery '96
Goose Boxer '78
Gorgeous '99
Hail the Judge '94
Half a Loaf of Kung Fu '77
The Haunted Cop Shop '87
He Has Nothing But Kung Fu '77
High Risk '95
His Name Is Nobody '79
H.K. Adams Family '92
I Love Maria '88
The Inspector Wears Skirts '88
Invincible Obsessed Fighter '82
Jackie Chan Adventures 1: The Search for the Talismans '00
Jackie Chan Adventures 2: The Dark Hand Returns '00
Jackie Chan Adventures 3: The Shadow of Shendu '00
Jade Claw '79
Justice, My Foot! '92
King of Beggars '92
King of Comedy '99
Knockabout '79
Kung Fu Genius '79
Kung Fu on Sale '79
Kung Fu Zombie '81
Kung Pow: Enter the Fist '76
Lady Iron Monkey '83
Lady Ninja: Reflections of Darkness '96
Last Ghost Standing '99
Lawyer Lawyer '97
Legend of the Dragon '91
Legend of the Drunken Master '94
Love on Delivery '94
The Magnificent Butcher '79

Magnificent Natural
    Fist '80
Master Q 2001 '01
The Millionaires'
    Express '86
The Miracle Fighters
    '82
Miracles '89
Mr. Nice Guy '97
Mr. Vampire '85
Mr. Vampire 2 '86
Mr. Vampire Saga 4 '88
Monkey Fist Floating
    Snake '79
My Kung Fu 12 Kicks
    '79
My Lucky Stars '85
The New Marvelous
    Double '92
New Mr. Vampire '86
Odd Couple '79
Operation Condor '91
Operation Pink Squad
    '88
The Owl vs. Bombo '84
Pedicab Driver '89
Picture of a Nymph '88
Pom Pom '84
Pom Pom and Hot Hot
    '92
Pom Pom Strikes Back
    '86
The Prodigal Son '81
Project A '83
Project A 2 '87
Return of the Master
    Killer '80
Rivals of the Dragon
    '83
Rosa '86
Royal Tramp '92
Royal Tramp 2 '92
Rush Hour '98
Rush Hour 2 '01
Savior of the Soul 2
    '92
Scared Stiff '86
Shaolin Soccer '01
Shaolin Temple 2: Kids
    from Shaolin '84
Skinny Tiger and Fatty
    Dragon '90
The Smart Cavalier '78
Snake Fist Dynamo '84
Snake in the Eagle's
    Shadow '78
The Snake Strikes Back
    '81
Spiritual Kung Fu '78
Teenage Mutant Ninja
    Turtles '90
Thunder Ninja Kids:
    The Hunt for the
    Devil Boxer '86/94
The Tuxedo '02
Twin Dragons '92
Twinkle Twinkle Lucky
    Stars '85
Vampire Kids '91
The Victim '80
Warrior from Shaolin
    '81
We're Going to Eat You!
    '80

Wheels on Meals '84
Where's Officer Tuba?
    '86
Winners and Sinners
    '83
Yoga and Kung Fu Girl
    '78
The Young Master '80
Young Tiger '72

Kung Fu Kids
*They never walk when
they can do flips. See
also: Child Abuse; Vam-
pire Kids.*
The Cold Mountain
    Temple '91
Dragon from Shaolin
    '96
The Enforcer '95
God of Gamblers
    Returns '94
Hit-Man in the Hand of
    Buddha '80
Inheritor of Kung Fu '77
Iron Monkey '93
Lady Whirlwind and the
    Rangers '74
The Master of Death
    '82
Militant Eagle '78
The New Legend of
    Shaolin '94
Painted Faces '88
Shaolin Chastity Kung
    Fu '81
Shaolin Temple 2: Kids
    from Shaolin '84
Shaolin: Wheel of Life
    '00
Thunder Ninja Kids:
    The Hunt for the
    Devil Boxer '86/94
Yoga and Kung Fu Girl
    '78

Kung Fu Moms
The Avenging Fist '01
Dragon's Claws '79
Eighth Happiness '88
Executioners from
    Shaolin '77
Fist Power '99
Iron Man '86
The Legend '92
The Legend 2 '93
Legend of the Drunken
    Master '94
Lord of the Wu Tang
    '93
The New Legend of
    Shaolin '94
Prodigal Boxer '73
Shaolin Mantis '78

Kung Fu-New School
*Post-Old School gradu-
ate studies. See also:
Kung Fu Comedy; Kung
Fu Kids; Kung Fu
Moms; Kung Fu-Old
School.*
The Accidental Spy '01
Angel '87
Angel 2 '88

Angel on Fire '95
Armour of God '86
The Avenging Fist '01
Ballistic Kiss '98
Beauty Investigator '92
The Best of the Best
    '96
Black Cat '91
Black Mask '96
Blade 2 '02
Blonde Fury '89
BloodFight '89
Body Weapon '99
Born to Defence '88
Bury Me High '90
China Strike Force '00
City Cop '95
City Hunter '92
Cold War '00
Combo Cops '96
Contract Killer '98
Cop Shop Babes '01
Crime Story '93
Crocodile Hunter '89
Crystal Hunt '91
Curry & Pepper '90
The Defender '94
Doctor Vampire '90
Don't Give a Damn '95
Downtown Torpedoes
    '97
Dragon from Russia
    '90
Dragon from Shaolin
    '96
Dragon in Jail '90
Dragon Kid '90
Dragon Killer '95
Dragon: The Bruce Lee
    Story '93
Dragons Forever '88
Dragons of the Orient
    '88
Eastern Condors '86
Eat My Dust '93
The Enforcer '95
Evil Cat '86
Executioners '93
Extreme Challenge '01
Fatal Blade '00
Final Justice '88
First Strike '96
Fist of Fury 1991 '91
Fist Power '99
5 Venoms vs. Wu Tang
    '87
Flash Future Kung Fu
    '83
For Bad Boys Only '00
From Beijing with Love
    '94
Full Contact '92
Fulltime Killer '01
Gen-X Cops '99
Gen-Y Cops '00
God of Cookery '96
Gorgeous '99
Guardian Angel '96
The Haunted Cop Shop
    '87
Heart of Dragon '85
Her Name Is Cat '98

Her Name Is Cat 2:
    Journey to Death
    '01
The Heroic Trio '93
High Risk '95
Hit Team '00
H.K. Adams Family '92
Hot War '98
I Love Maria '88
Iceman Cometh '89
The Inspector Wears
    Skirts '88
In the Line of Duty 3
    '88
In the Line of Duty 4
    '89
In the Line of Duty 5:
    Middle Man '90
Kick Boxer's Tears '92
A Kid from Tibet '91
Killer's Romance '90
King of Comedy '99
Kiss of the Dragon '01
Lady Ninja: Reflections
    of Darkness '96
The Last Blood '90
Legacy of Rage '86
Legend of the Dragon
    '91
Legendary Couple '95
Leopard Hunting '98
Lethal Panther '91
Lethal Panther 2 '93
Love on Delivery '94
Magnificent Warriors
    '87
A Man Called Hero '99
Martial Angels '01
The Masked Prosecutor
    '99
The Master '89
Master Q 2001 '01
Millennium Dragon '99
The Millionaires'
    Express '86
Miracles '89
Mr. Nice Guy '97
Mr. Vampire '85
Mr. Vampire 2 '86
Mr. Vampire Saga 4 '88
Mortal Kombat '95
My Lucky Stars '85
Naked Killer '92
The New Marvelous
    Double '92
New Mr. Vampire '86
Ninja in the U.S.A. '88
Ninja vs. Ninja '87
No More Love, No More
    Death '92
Once a Thief '91
The One '01
On the Run '88
Operation Condor '91
Operation Pink Squad
    '88
The Owl vs. Bombo '84
Painted Faces '88
The Peacock King '89
Pedicab Driver '89
Peking Opera Blues '86
Police Story '85
Police Story 2 '88
Pom Pom '84

Pom Pom and Hot Hot
    '92
Pom Pom Strikes Back
    '86
Prince of the Sun '90
The Prisoner '90
Project A '83
Project A 2 '87
The Protector '85
The Red Wolf '95
Righting Wrongs '86
Riki-Oh: The Story of
    Ricky '89
Robo Vampire '88
Robotrix '91
Romeo Must Die '00
Rosa '86
Royal Warriors '86
Rumble in the Bronx
    '95
Run and Kill '93
Rush Hour '98
Rush Hour 2 '01
Saga of the Phoenix
    '90
Satin Steel '94
Savior of the Soul '91
Savior of the Soul 2
    '92
Scared Stiff '86
Scorpion Thunderbolt
    '85
The Secrets of the War-
    rior's Power '97
The Seventh Curse '86
Shanghai Affairs '98
Shaolin Fist of Fury '87
Shaolin Soccer '01
She Shoots Straight
    '90
Skinny Tiger & Fatty
    Dragon '90
Street Fighter 2 '96
Sunshine Cops '99
Supercop '92
Supercop 2 '93
Teenage Mutant Ninja
    Turtles '90
Temptress of a Thou-
    sand Faces '98
Thunderbolt '95
Thunder Cop '96
Thunder Cops '98
Thunder Ninja Kids:
    The Hunt for the
    Devil Boxer '86/94
Tiger Cage '88
Tiger on Beat '88
Time and Tide '00
The Touch '02
The Tuxedo '02
Twin Dragons '92
Twinkle Twinkle Lucky
    Stars '85
Ultimatum '01
The Vampire Combat
    '01
Vampire Controller '00
Vampire Kids '91
Versus '00
Volcano High School
    '01
Wheels on Meals '84

Where's Officer Tuba? '86
Who Am I? '98
Winners and Sinners '83
The Witch from Nepal '85
Wonder Seven '94
Yes, Madam '85
Zu Warriors '01
Zu: Warriors of the Magic Mountain '83

Kung Fu-Old School
See also: Kung Fu-New School; Kung Fu-Retro Old School.
Avenging Eagle '78
Avenging Warriors of Shaolin '79
The Awaken Punch '73
Battle of Shaolin '77
The Blazing Temple '76
Blind Fist of Bruce '79
Blood of the Dragon '71
Blooded Treasury Fight '79
Bloody Fight '72
The Bloody Fists '72
Bolo '80
Born Invincible '78
Brave Archer '77
Breakout from Oppression '78
Bruce Lee Fights Back from the Grave '76
Bruce Lee: The Man, the Myth '76
Bruce Lee We Miss You '76
Brutal Boxer '72
The Buddha Assassinator '79
The Buddhist Fist '79
Cantonen Iron Kung Fu '79
Challenge of Death '78
Chinatown Kid '77
The Chinese Connection '71
Chinese Hercules '73
Chinese Iron Man '75
Chinese Samson '79
Chinese Super Ninjas '82
Crack Shadow Boxers '77
Crazy Crooks '80
Crippled Masters '80
Dance of the Drunk Mantis '79
Deadly Snail vs. Kung Fu Killer '77
The Deadly Sword '78
Death Duel of Kung Fu '79
Death Mask of the Ninja '82
Death Ring '83
The Descendant of Wing Chun '78
Dirty Ho '79

Dirty Kung Fu '78
Dirty Tiger, Crazy Frog '78
Dragon Fist '78
Dragon Lee vs. the Five Brothers '78
Dragon on Fire '79
Dragon Princess '81
Dragon's Claws '79
Dreadnaught '81
Dreaming Fists with Slender Hands '80
Drunken Art and Crippled Fist '79
Drunken Master '78
Drunken Tai Chi '84
Duel of the Brave Ones '78
Duel of the Tao Tough '82
Duel to the Death '82
Dynamo '78
Eagle vs. Silver Fox '83
Eagle's Claw '77
The Eagle's Killer '81
The 8 Masters '77
The 18 Bronzemen '76
The 18 Bronzemen Part 2 '76
18 Fatal Strikes '78
The 18 Jade Arhats '78
18 Secrets of Kung Fu '79
Emperor of Shaolin Kung Fu '80
Encounter of the Spooky Kind '81
The End of the Wicked Tiger '81
Enter the Dragon '73
Enter the Fat Dragon '78
Executioners from Shaolin '77
Exit the Dragon, Enter the Tiger '75
Fatal Flying Guillotine '77
Fatal Needles vs. Fatal Fists '80
Fearless Dragons '79
Fearless Fighters '69
Fearless Hyena '79
Fearless Hyena 2 '80
Fighting Ace '79
Filthy Guy '80
The Fist, the Kicks and the Evils '79
A Fistful of Talons '83
Fists and Guts '79
Fists Like Lee '74
Fists of Bruce Lee '78
Fists of Fury '71
Fists of the White Lotus '80
Five Deadly Venoms '78
Five Elements of Kung Fu '78
Five Fingers of Death '72
5 Lady Venoms '78
Five Superfighters '78
Flag of Iron '80

The Flying Guillotine '74
From China with Death '74
Fury in Shaolin Temple '82
Game of Death '78
Golden Dragon Silver Snake '79
Golden Killah '80
Goose Boxer '78
The Green Dragon Inn '79
The Green Hornet '74
Half a Loaf of Kung Fu '77
Hand of Death '75
Hard as a Dragon '80
He Has Nothing But Kung Fu '77
The Heroes '80
His Name Is Nobody '79
Hit-Man in the Hand of Buddha '80
The Holy Robe of Shaolin Temple '84
The Hot, the Cool, and the Vicious '76
The Incredible Kung Fu Mission '82
Inheritor of Kung Fu '77
The Invincible Armour '77
The Invincible Killer '79
The Invincible Kung Fu Trio '78
Invincible Obsessed Fighter '82
Invincible Pole Fighter '83
Iron Man '86
The Iron Monkey '77
Iron Monkey 2 '77
Iron Neck Li '81
Jade Claw '79
Kid with the Golden Arm '78
Killer from Above '77
The Killer Meteors '76
Killer of Snake, Fox of Shaolin '78
Killer Priest '81
Knockabout '79
The Korean Connection '77
Kung Fu Genius '79
Kung Fu on Sale '79
Kung Fu, the Invisible Fist '72
Kung Fu Zombie '81
Kung Fu's Hero '73
Lady Iron Monkey '83
Lady Whirlwind and the Rangers '74
Lady Wu Tang '77
Last Hurrah for Chivalry '78
The Leg Fighters '80
The Legend of Bruce Lee '80
Legend of the 7 Golden Vampires '74

The Legend of the Swordsman '92
The Legendary Strike '78
Legendary Weapons of China '82
Lightning Kung Fu '80
The Lost Kung Fu Secrets '80
Macho Man '72
The Magnificent '78
The Magnificent Butcher '79
Magnificent Natural Fist '80
Mantis Combat '81
Mask of Death '76
Masked Avengers '81
The Massive '78
The Master of Death '82
Master of the Flying Guillotine '74
Masters of Martial Arts '74
Masters of Tiger Crane '83
Militant Eagle '78
The Miracle Fighters '82
Monkey Fist Floating Snake '79
Moonlight Sword and Jade Lion '79
Murder in the Orient '74
My Kung Fu 12 Kicks '79
New Fist of Fury '76
The New Game of Death '75
Nine Demons '83
99 Cycling Swords '80
Ninja Checkmate '79
Ninja in the Deadly Trap '83
Ninja Supremo '81
Ninja the Final Duel '85
Ninja vs. Bruce Lee '82
Ninja vs. Shaolin Guards '84
Odd Couple '79
One Foot Crane '79
The Postman Fights Back '82
Prodigal Boxer '73
The Prodigal Son '81
Rage of the Dragon '79
Rage of the Masters '74
Raiders of Wu Tang '82
The Real Bruce Lee '79
Real Kung Fu of Shaolin, Part 1 '81
Return of the Chinese Boxer '75
Return of the Deadly Blade '81
Return of the Dragon '72
The Return of the 5 Deadly Venoms '78
Return of the Master Killer '80

Return of the Tiger '79
Revenge of the Patriots '76
Revengeful Swordwomen '79
Rivals of the Dragon '83
Screaming Ninja '73
Secret of the Chinese Kung Fu '81
7 Commandments of Kung Fu '79
The 72 Desperate Rebels '76
Shadow of the Tiger '79
Shaolin and Tai Chi '79
The Shaolin Brothers '77
Shaolin Chastity Kung Fu '81
The Shaolin Disciple '80
The Shaolin Drunken Monk '83
The Shaolin Invincibles '79
The Shaolin Kids '77
Shaolin King Boxer '79
Shaolin Mantis '78
Shaolin Master Killer '78
The Shaolin One '83
Shaolin Traitorous '76
Shaolin vs. Lama '81
Shaolin vs. Manchu '80
Shaolin vs. Ninja '83
Shaolin Wooden Men '76
The Silver Spear '79
The Six Directions of Boxing '79
The Smart Cavalier '78
Snake and Crane Arts of Shaolin '78
Snake-Crane Secret '78
Snake Deadly Act '79
Snake Fist Dynamo '84
Snake in the Eagle's Shadow '78
The Snake Strikes Back '81
Spiritual Kung Fu '78
Sting of the Dragon Masters '78
The Story in Temple Red Lily '79
Story of the Dragon '76
Super Gang '78
Super Kung Fu Kid '74
The Super Ninja '84
SuperManChu '73
Swordsman with an Umbrella '70
10 Magnificent Killers '77
Ten Tigers of Kwangtung '79
Ten Tigers of Shaolin '78
The 36 Crazy Fists '77
The 36 Deadly Styles '79

Thousand Mile Escort '76
3 Evil Masters '80
Thunder Kick '73
Tiger over Wall '80
To Kill with Intrigue '77
Tower of Death '81
Triangular Duel '72
Two Dragons Fight against Tiger '75
The Unbeaten 28 '80
The Victim '80
War of the Shaolin Temple '80
Warrior from Shaolin '81
Ways of Kung Fu '80
The World of the Drunken Master '79
Yoga and Kung Fu Girl '78
The Young Master '80
Young Tiger '72

Kung Fu-Retro Old School
Same Fu, different era. See also: Kung Fu-New School; Kung Fu-Old School.
The Bride with White Hair '93
The Bride with White Hair 2 '93
Burning Paradise '94
Butterfly and Sword '93
A Chinese Torture Chamber Story '94
Chivalrous Legend '98
Crouching Tiger, Hidden Dragon '00
Deadend of Besiegers '92
Dragon Inn '92
Drunken Master Killer '94
The Duel '00
Eagle Shooting Heroes '93
The East Is Red '93
8 Diagram Fighter '91
Fist of Fury '95
Fist of Legend '94
Flight of the Heroine '00
Flirting Scholar '93
Forbidden City Cop '96
Hail the Judge '94
The Hero of Swallow '96
Hero's Blood '91
Iron Man '86
Iron Monkey '93
Iron Monkey 2 '96
Justice, My Foot! '92
King of Beggars '92
The Kung Fu Master '94
Last Hero in China '93
The Law and the Outlaw '95
Lawyer Lawyer '97
The Legend '92
The Legend 2 '93

Legend of the Drunken Master '94
Legend of the Drunken Tiger '92
The Legend of the Swordsman '92
The Lord of Hangzhou '98
Lord of the Wu Tang '93
The Magic Crane '93
Martial Arts Master Wong Fei Hung '92
The Moon Warriors '92
The New Legend of Shaolin '94
Once upon a Time in China '91
Once upon a Time in China 2 '92
Once upon a Time in China 3 '93
Once upon a Time in China 4 '93
Once upon a Time in China and America '97
One Arm Hero '94
Picture of a Nymph '88
Rebels Under Siege '00
Royal Tramp '92
Royal Tramp 2 '92
Sam the Iron Bridge: Champion of Martial Arts '93
Shaolin: Wheel of Life '00
The Storm Riders '98
The Sword Stained with Royal Blood '93
Swordsman '90
The Swordswoman in White '92
The Three Swordsmen '94
Twin Warriors '93
White Lotus Cult '93
Wing Chun '94
Yellow River Fighter '88

Law & Lawyers
First, kill all the....
The Defender '94
Dragon in Jail '90
Dragon Kid '90
Dragons Forever '88
Hail the Judge '94
H.K. Adams Family '92
Jiang Hu-"The Triad Zone" '00
Justice, My Foot! '92
Lawyer Lawyer '97
Police Story '85
Police Story 2 '88
Prison on Fire '87
Prison on Fire 2 '91
The Prisoner '90
Return to a Better Tomorrow '94
Righting Wrongs '86

Lesbians
See also: Gays; Gender Bending.

All's Well End's Well '92
Big Boobs Buster '90
A Chinese Ghost Story 3 '91
Female Convict Scorpion: Jailhouse 41 '72
He's a Woman, She's a Man '94
I.K.U. '00
The Ladies' Phone Sex Club '96
Naked Killer '92
Notorious Concubines '69
Project A-ko '86
Ring Virus '99
Sex and the Emperor '94
Time and Tide '00
Tokyo Decameron: Three Tales of Madness and Sensuality '96
U-Man '02
Weather Woman '95

Lion Dance
Dreadnaught '81
The Invincible Kung Fu Trio '78
Iron Man '86
Last Hero in China '93
Once upon a Time in China '91
Once upon a Time in China 3 '93
Once upon a Time in China 4 '93
Shaolin vs. Ninja '83
The Young Master '80

Loner Cops
Beast Cops '98
Cop on a Mission '01
Hard Boiled '91
The Razor 1: Sword of Justice '72
The Razor 2: The Snare '73
The Razor 3: Who's Got the Gold? '74
Running out of Time '99
Violent Cop '89

The Loo
The ultimate in wet, porcelain-tainted sequences.
Bio Zombie '98
The Executioner '74
The Foul King '00
From Beijing with Love '94
Last Ghost Standing '99
Lawyer Lawyer '97
Saga of the Phoenix '90
Seeding of a Ghost '83
Sixty Million Dollar Man '95
Sound from the Dark '00

A Wicked Ghost '99

Lost Guns
Disarmed cops.
Stray Dog '49
With or Without You '92

The Loving Dead
Necrophilia, not including zombie love, for zombies are technically the "undead."
Dr. Lamb '92
The Eternal Evil of Asia '95
God of Gamblers '89
Seeding of a Ghost '83

Mad Scientists
Sin in the name of science. See also: Evil Doctors; Inventors & Inventions.
Astro Boy '63
Astro Boy '80
Bio-Cops '00
Cop Shop Babes '01
Evil Brain from Outer Space '58/59
The Green Hornet '74
Guinea Pig: Android of Notre Dame '88
The Human Vapor '60
King Kong Escapes '67
Mad Doctor of Blood Island '68
The Manster '60
Metropolis '01
Organ '96
Robotrix '91
Sixty Million Dollar Man '95
Terror beneath the Sea '66
Terror Is a Man '59
Terror of MechaGodzilla '75

Magic & Magicians
Stage illusionists, show-biz hocus pocus. See also: Bewitched; Demons.
Every Dog Has His Date '01
God of Gamblers '89
God of Gamblers 2 '90
God of Gamblers 3: Back to Shanghai '91
God of Gamblers Returns '94
Hong Kong Nocturne '67
The Hypnotist '99
The Miracle Fighters '82
Running out of Time 2 '01

Manga
See: Anime; Comic Books/Manga (Adapted From).

Marriage
See also: War between the Sexes.
Aces Go Places 3 '84
Aces Go Places 4 '86
Dragon: The Bruce Lee Story '93
Forbidden City Cop '96
Guinea Pig: Mermaid in a Manhole '88
Haunted Mansion '98
In the Mood for Love '00
The Invincible Killer '79
Mahal '48
Midnight Fly '01
The Miracle Fighters '82
Mon-Rak Transistor '01
My Wife Is a Gangster '01
Notorious Concubines '69
100 Ways to Murder Your Wife '86
Pedicab Driver '89
Run and Kill '93
Seeding of a Ghost '83
Snaker '01

Martial Arts
See: Kung Fu Comedy; Kung Fu Kids; Kung Fu Moms; Kung Fu-New School; Kung Fu-Old School; Kung Fu-Retro Old School; Martial Arts World; School-Martial Arts; Supernatural Martial Arts.

Martial Arts World
In a world beyond time. See also: Supernatural Martial Arts.
All Men Are Brothers: Blood of the Leopard '93
Brave Archer '77
The Bride with White Hair '93
The Bride with White Hair 2 '93
Burning Paradise '94
Butterfly and Sword '93
Crouching Tiger, Hidden Dragon '00
Deadly Snail vs. Kung Fu Killer '77
The Deadly Sword '78
The Duel '00
Eagle Shooting Heroes '93
The East Is Red '93
Iceman Cometh '89
Inheritor of Kung Fu '77
The Invincible Armour '77
Killer from Above '77
Killer of Snake, Fox of Shaolin '78
The Last Duel '82
Last Hurrah for Chivalry '78

The Legend of the
    Swordsman '92
Lord of the Wu Tang
    '93
The Magic Crane '93
The Moon Warriors '92
Nine Demons '83
Return of the Deadly
    Blade '81
The Silver Spear '79
The Storm Riders '98
Swordsman '90
The Three Swordsmen
    '94
Zu Warriors '01
Zu: Warriors of the
    Magic Mountain
    '83

Martyred Pop Icons
See: Bruceploitation.

Melodrama
*Maybe "wallowdrama"
would be a better word.*
All About Ah-Long '89
Anna Magdalena '98
Bakery Amour '01
Casino Raiders '89
Casino Raiders 2 '91
Casino Tycoon 2 '92
Champion '00
City of Desire '01
Code of Honor '87
Daughter of Darkness
    '93
Days of Being Wild '90
The Dragon Family '88
Dragon in Jail '90
Elaan '94
Fists Like Lee '74
Frozen '96
Funeral March '01
Goodbye Mr. Cool '01
Gunmen '88
Happy Family '02
Hong Kong Nocturne
    '67
Inner Senses '01
Juliet in Love '00
Killer's Romance '90
Lee Rock '91
Legacy of Rage '86
Love au Zen '01
Love Correction '00
A Love of Blueness '00
Love Paradox '00
Mahal '48
Marry a Rich Man '02
A Moment of Romance
    '90
Mon-Rak Transistor '01
Moonlight Express '99
My Sassy Girl '01
Needing You... '00
No More Love, No More
    Death '92
Notorious Concubines
    '69
The Odd One Dies '97
Okinawa Rendez-vous
    '00
Painted Faces '88
The Phantom Lover '95
Powerful Four '91

The Prisoner '90
Queen's High '91
Red to Kill '94
Return to a Better
    Tomorrow '94
Rich and Famous '87
The Road Home '99
Sholay '75
Snaker '01
Sugar-Howling of an
    Angel '96
Throne of Blood '57
The Tigers '91
Tragic Fantasy: Tiger of
    Wanchai '94
A War Named Desire
    '00
Warm Water under a
    Red Bridge '01
Where a Good Man
    Goes '99
Wishful Milenio '01
With or Without You '92

Meltdown
*Or, how I learned to
stop worrying and love
the bomb. See also:
Disaster Strikes.*
Godzilla vs. Destroyah
    '95
Godzilla vs. King Ghido-
    rah '91

Men in Prison
*See also: Escaped
Cons; Fugitives; Great
Escapes.*
Aces Go Places 5: The
    Terracotta Hit '89
A Better Tomorrow '86
A Better Tomorrow 2
    '87
Bolo '80
Burning Paradise '94
Doctor No... '01
Dragon in Jail '90
Eastern Condors '86
The Eel '97
The Executioner '74
A Fighter's Blues '00
Fists and Guts '79
From the Queen to the
    Chief Executive '01
God.com '98
God of Gamblers 2 '90
The Heroes '80
Legacy of Rage '86
Once upon a Time in
    China '91
Prison on Fire '87
Prison on Fire 2 '91
The Prisoner '90
Riki-Oh: The Story of
    Ricky '89
Romeo Must Die '00
Sholay '75
The Street Fighter '74
Supercop '92
The Tricky Master '00
The Untold Story '92
Winners and Sinners
    '83

Metamorphosis
*Ch-ch-ch-ch-changes.
See also: Were-foxes;
Were-snakes.*
Abbot White '82
Akira '88
Another Heaven '00
Attack from Space '58
Beast of the Yellow
    Night '70
Bio-Cops '00
Bio Zombie '98
Blade 2 '02
The Blood Drinkers '64
Blood: The Last Vam-
    pire '00
Body Snatcher from
    Hell '68
The Bride with White
    Hair '93
The Cat '91
Curse of the Vampires
    '70
Daimajin '66
Deadly Snail vs. Kung
    Fu Killer '77
The Demon's Baby '98
Destroy All Monsters
    '68
Devil Man '87
Doctor Vampire '90
Dragon against Vam-
    pire '85
The Eternal Evil of Asia
    '95
Evil Brain from Outer
    Space '58/59
5 Venoms vs. Wu Tang
    '87
Frankenstein vs.
    Baragon '65
Gamera 2: Advent of
    Legion '96
Gamera 3: The
    Revenge of Irys '99
Godzilla 2000 '99
Godzilla vs. Biollante
    '89
Godzilla vs. Destroyah
    '95
Godzilla vs. Gigan '72
Godzilla vs. Hedorah
    '71
Godzilla vs. King Ghido-
    rah '91
Godzilla vs.
    MechaGodzilla '74
Godzilla vs. Megaguirus
    '00
Godzilla vs. Megalon
    '73
Godzilla vs. Mothra '92
Godzilla vs. Space
    Godzilla '94
Green Snake '93
Gunhed '89
The H-Man '58
The Haunted Cop Shop
    '87
Hiruko the Goblin '90
The Imp '81
Invaders from Space
    '58

Jackie Chan Adven-
    tures 1: The Search
    for the Talismans
    '00
Jackie Chan Adven-
    tures 2: The Dark
    Hand Returns '00
Jackie Chan Adven-
    tures 3: The Shad-
    ow of Shendu '00
Junk '99
Killer of Snake, Fox of
    Shaolin '78
The Killing of Satan '83
Kung Fu Zombie '81
Kwaidan '64
Lady Ninja: Reflections
    of Darkness '96
Last Ghost Standing
    '99
Legend of the 7 Golden
    Vampires '74
Mad Doctor of Blood
    Island '68
The Magic Serpent '66
The Manster '60
The Miracle Fighters
    '82
Model from Hell '99
Mothra '61
Mothra vs. Godzilla '64
My Neighbor Totoro '88
Nine Demons '83
Ninja Scroll '93
Organ '96
Painted Skin '92
Parasite Eve '97
Prince of Space '59
Pulgasari '85
Raat '91
Reborn from Hell:
    Samurai Armaged-
    don '96
Reptilian '00
Return of Daimajin '66
Revenge of the Zom-
    bies '76
Riki-Oh: The Story of
    Ricky '89
Robo Vampire '88
Robotrix '91
Roujin Z '91
Sakuya: Slayer of
    Demons '00
Scorpion Thunderbolt
    '85
Seeding of a Ghost '83
The Seventh Curse '86
Shocking Asia '75
Sixty Million Dollar Man
    '95
Snaker '01
Son of Godzilla '67
Spiral '00
Spirited Away '01
Succubare '77
Teenage Mutant Ninja
    Turtles '90
Terror beneath the Sea
    '66
Terror Is a Man '59
Tetsuo: The Iron Man
    '89

Tetsuo 2: Body Ham-
    mer '91
Ultraman 2 '79
Ultraman Gaia: The
    Battle in Hyper-
    space '98
Ultraman Tiga and
    Ultraman Dyna: The
    Warriors of the
    Lightning Star '98
Urotsukidoji '89
The Vampire Combat
    '01
Vampire Controller '00
Vampire Hunter D '85
Vampire Hunter D:
    Bloodlust '01
Versus '00
Wicked City '87
Wicked City '92
Wild Zero '99
The Witch from Nepal
    '85
Wrath of Daimajin '66
X '96
The X from Outer Space
    '67
Yog: Monster from
    Space '70

**Meteors, Asteroids
& Comets**
*See also: Alien Beings-
Vicious; Disaster
Strikes.*
Attack from Space '58
Battle in Outer Space
    '59
Final Fantasy: The Spir-
    its Within '01
Gamera vs. Barugon
    '66
Gamera vs. Guillon '69
Ghidorah the Three-
    Headed Monster
    '64
Godzilla 2000 '99
Godzilla vs. Mothra '92
The Legend of Bruce
    Lee '80
Project A-ko '86
Renegade Ninjas '79
The Venus Wars '89
Who Am I? '98
Wild Zero '99

Mistaken Identity
*See also: Gender Bend-
ing; He's Really a Girl!;
Role Reversal.*
Aces Go Places 5: The
    Terracotta Hit '89
Breakout from Oppres-
    sion '78
Bruce Lee We Miss You
    '76
A Chinese Ghost Story
    2 '90
Crack Shadow Boxers
    '77
Don't Give a Damn '95
Fearless Dragons '79
Fist of Fear-Touch of
    Death '80
F*** / Off '98

Godzilla vs. MechaGodzilla '74
Half a Loaf of Kung Fu '77
Her Majesty Is Fine '96
High and Low '63
Killer '00
The Magnificent Butcher '79
The Magnificent Scoundrels '91
Royal Tramp '92
Samurai 2: Duel at Ichijoji Temple '55
Super Gang '78
Twin Dragons '92
Wing Chun '94
The Young Master '80

Mockumentaries
Fist of Fear-Touch of Death '80
Guinea Pig: He Never Dies '86
Violated Paradise '63

Moms
See also: Kung Fu Moms.
Aakhri Adalat '88
All About Ah-Long '89
All's Well End's Well '92
Barefoot Gen '83
Big Boobs Buster '90
Blind Beast '69
The Blood Drinkers '64
Brother of Darkness '94
Curse of the Vampires '70
Dark Water '02
Daughter of Darkness '93
The Eel '97
Fighting for Love '01
Fists Like Lee '74
Flirting Scholar '93
The Funeral '84
Gamera vs. Guillon '69
Good Morning '59
Goodbye Mr. Cool '01
The Happiness of the Katakuris '01
Happy Family '02
Haunted Mansion '98
Kikujiro '99
The Ladies' Phone Sex Club '96
The Legend of a Professional '00
A Love of Blueness '00
Maborosi '95
My Neighbor Totoro '88
Para Para Sakura '01
Raat '91
Ring '98
Ring 2 '99
Ring 0: Birthday '00
Ring Virus '99
The Road Home '99
Samurai 1: Musashi Miyamoto '54
Sex and the Emperor '94

She Shoots Straight '90
Snaker '01
Super Kung Fu Kid '74
Thunder Kick '73
A Touch of Zen '69
Tragic Fantasy: Tiger of Wanchai '94
Troublesome Night 8 '00
Troublesome Night 9 '00
Troublesome Night 14 '02

Mondo Movies
Collections of trashy, gratuitous, and shocking scenes without even the pretense of plot for the viewer's amusement. See also: Documentaries; Docudrama; Mockumentaries.
Bruce Lee, The Legend '84
Fist of Fear-Touch of Death '80
Kei Mizutani: Undressed for Success '94
The Real Bruce Lee '79
Shocking Asia '75
Shocking Asia 2 '76
Violated Paradise '63

Monkey Business
Here they come, walking down...oops, wrong monkeys. See also: Yeti/Bigfoot.
The Adventures of the Master and His Servant '96
All Monsters Attack! '02
A*P*E '76
A Chinese Odyssey Part 1: Pandora's Box '95
A Chinese Odyssey Part 2: Cinderella '95
Godzilla vs. MechaGodzilla '74
The Hypnotist '99
The Iron Monkey '77
King Kong Escapes '67
King Kong vs. Godzilla '62
Lady Iron Monkey '83
Mighty Peking Man '77
Ninja Supremo '81
Renegade Ninjas '79
The Shaolin Invincibles '79
The Six Directions of Boxing '79
The Storm Riders '98
Terror of MechaGodzilla '75
Time of the Apes '75
Who Am I? '98

Monks
Abbot White '82
All Men Are Brothers: Blood of the Leopard '93
Angel on Fire '95
Armour of God '86
Avenging Warriors of Shaolin '79
The Blade '95
The Blazing Temple '76
Brave Archer '77
The Buddha Assassinator '79
The Buddhist Fist '79
Burning Paradise '94
A Chinese Ghost Story 2 '90
A Chinese Ghost Story 3 '91
A Chinese Odyssey Part 1: Pandora's Box '95
A Chinese Odyssey Part 2: Cinderella '95
Death Mask of the Ninja '82
The Demon's Baby '98
The Descendant of Wing Chun '78
Dirty Tiger, Crazy Frog '78
Doctor No... '01
Dragon Chronicles: Maidens of Heavenly Mountain '94
Dragon from Shaolin '96
Dragon's Claws '79
Dragons of the Orient '88
Duel of the Tao Tough '82
8 Diagram Fighter '91
The 8 Masters '77
The 18 Bronzemen '76
The 18 Bronzemen Part 2 '76
18 Fatal Strikes '78
Emperor of Shaolin Kung Fu '80
Enter the Dragon '73
Executioners from Shaolin '77
Fatal Flying Guillotine '77
Filthy Guy '80
Fists of the White Lotus '80
Five Elements of Kung Fu '78
The Funeral '84
Fury in Shaolin Temple '82
God of Cookery '96
Golden Killah '80
The Haunted Cop Shop '87
The Haunted Lantern '98
The Heroes '80
Hi! Dharma! '01
Hit-Man in the Hand of Buddha '80

The Holy Robe of Shaolin Temple '84
Hum Paanch '80
Inheritor of Kung Fu '77
The Invincible Kung Fu Trio '78
Invincible Pole Fighter '83
The Iron Monkey '77
Iron Monkey '93
A Kid from Tibet '91
Killer Priest '81
King of Beggars '92
The Kung Fu Master '94
Kwaidan '64
Lady Wu Tang '77
Last Hero in China '93
The Legendary Strike '78
Legend of the Dragonslayer Sword 2 '90
Legend of the Mountain '79
Lone Wolf and Cub 5: Baby Cart in the Land of Demons '73
Lord of the Wu Tang '93
Love au Zen '01
The Magic Crane '93
A Man Called Hero '99
Mantis Combat '81
Mask of Death '76
Master of the Flying Guillotine '74
Mortal Kombat '95
The New Legend of Shaolin '94
Ninja Hunter '83
Ninja the Final Duel '85
Ninja vs. Shaolin Guards '84
Painted Skin '92
The Peacock King '89
Prince of the Sun '90
The Prisoner of Five Boulders '89
Raiders of Wu Tang '82
Real Kung Fu of Shaolin, Part 1 '81
Reborn from Hell: Samurai Armageddon '96
Return of the Chinese Boxer '75
Return of the Master Killer '80
Revengeful Swordwomen '79
Saga of the Phoenix '90
Samurai 1: Musashi Miyamoto '54
Samurai 2: Duel at Ichijoji Temple '55
Samurai 3: Duel at Ganryu Island '56
The Secrets of the Warrior's Power '97
The 72 Desperate Rebels '76

Shadow of the Tiger '79
Shaolin and Tai Chi '79
The Shaolin Brothers '77
Shaolin Chastity Kung Fu '81
The Shaolin Disciple '80
The Shaolin Drunken Monk '83
The Shaolin Invincibles '79
Shaolin Master Killer '78
The Shaolin One '83
Shaolin Soccer '01
The Shaolin Temple '79
Shaolin Traitorous '76
Shaolin vs. Lama '81
Shaolin vs. Manchu '80
Shaolin vs. Ninja '83
Shaolin: Wheel of Life '00
Shaolin Wooden Men '76
Snake and Crane Arts of Shaolin '78
Snake-Crane Secret '78
Snaker '01
Sorrowful to a Ghost '70
Spiritual Kung Fu '78
The Storm Riders '98
The Story in Temple Red Lily '79
Street Fighter 2 '96
10 Magnificent Killers '77
The 36 Crazy Fists '77
The 36 Deadly Styles '79
A Touch of Zen '69
Twin Warriors '93
War of the Shaolin Temple '80
Warrior from Shaolin '81
Ways of Kung Fu '80
Zu: Warriors of the Magic Mountain '83

Monsters
See: Aliens Beings-Vicious; Dracula; Frankenstein and/or His Monster; Giant Monsters; Giants (Humanoid); Killer Brains; Killer Jello; Killer Plants; Robots, Androids & Cyborgs; That's a Baby?; Vampire Babes; Vampire Kids; Vampires-Hopping; Vampires-Other; Were-foxes; Were-snakes; Yeti/Bigfoot; Zombies.

Motor Vehicle Dept.
See also: Bikers; Cabbies; Checkered Flag; Road Trip.
Aakhri Adalat '88
The Accidental Spy '01
Aces Go Places '82
Aces Go Places 2 '83
Aces Go Places 3 '84
Aces Go Places 4 '86
Adrenaline Drive '99
The Adventures of the Master and His Servant '96
All About Ah-Long '89
Armour of God '86
Blade 2 '02
Branded to Kill '67
Bullet in the Head '90
Cannonball Run '81
Castle of Cagliostro '79
Drunken Master Killer '94
Expect the Unexpected '98
Extreme Crisis '98
Fantasy Mission Force '84
5 Lady Venoms '78
Flash Future Kung Fu '83
From China with Death '74
Full Contact '92
Full Throttle '95
Gatchaman '94
Godzilla 2000 '99
Godzilla vs. Megalon '73
Hard Boiled '91
Legend of Speed '99
My Lucky Stars '85
Operation Condor '91
Police Story '85
Rumble in the Bronx '95
Running out of Time '99
Rush Hour '98
Rush Hour 2 '01
Speed Racer: The Movie '67
Super Car Criminals '99
Supercop '92
Tell Me Something '99
Thunderbolt '95
Who Am I? '98
Wonder Seven '94
Yes, Madam '85

Music
See: Disco; Music: Punk; Music: Rock; Musicals; Musicians.

Music: Punk
Beijing Rocks '01
Blade 2 '02
Last Ghost Standing '99
Wild Zero '99

Music: Rock
Beijing Rocks '01
Blade 2 '02
Blood of the Dragon '71
Bubblegum Crisis '85
Bullet in the Head '90
A Chinese Ghost Story: The Tsui Hark Animation '97
Chungking Express '94
Drunken Master Killer '94
Dummy Mommy, without a Baby '01
From the Queen to the Chief Executive '01
Gimme Gimme '01
Gumnaam '65
The Inspector Wears Skirts '88
Last Ghost Standing '99
Odd Couple '79
Rock 'n' Roll Cop
Shark Skin Man and Peach Hip Girl '98
Shogun's Ninja '82
Wild Zero '99

Musicals
Aakhri Adalat '88
Champion '00
Elaan '94
Gumnaam '65
The Happiness of the Katakuris '01
Hong Kong Nocturne '67
Hum Paanch '80
Mahal '48
The Phantom Lover '95
Sholay '75

Musicians
C'est la Vie, Mon Cheri '93
Deadful Melody '94
Love on a Diet '01
Operation Pink Squad '88
Peking Opera Blues '86
Troublesome Night 3 '97
Twin Dragons '92
Wild Zero '99

Mystery & Suspense
Edge-of-the-couch thrillers and whodunits. See also: Erotic Thrillers; Psycho-Thriller; Showbiz Thrillers.
The Accidental Spy '01
Audition '99
Black Tight Killers '66
Blind Beast '69
Bloody Beach '00
Body Weapon '99
Branded to Kill '67
Bullets over Summer '99
Champion '00

Clean My Name, Mr. Coroner! '00
Crime Story '93
The Deadly Camp '99
Double Tap '00
Fear Faith Revenge 303 '98
Ghost Actress '96
Gumnaam '65
High and Low '63
The Hypnotist '99
Inner Senses '01
Mahal '48
Nobody '99
Postman Blues '97
The Private Eyes '76
Rashomon '50
The Razor 1: Sword of Justice '72
The Razor 2: The Snare '73
The Razor 3: Who's Got the Gold? '74
Ring '98
Ring Virus '99
Sure Death: Revenge '87
Tell Me Something '99
Trust Me U Die '99
Victim '99
Violent Cop '99

Mystery Science Theater 3000
See appendix, pp. 703.

Nazis & Other Paramilitary Slugs
Fantasy Mission Force '84
Flash Future Kung Fu '83
Frankenstein vs. Baragon '65
Operation Condor '91

Necrophilia
See: The Loving Dead.

Negative Utopia
Or "dystopia." Things seemed so perfect until.... See also: Post Apocalypse; Technology-Rampant.
Akira '88
The Dimension Travelers '98
Final Fantasy: The Spirits Within '01
Flash Future Kung Fu '83
Gunhed '89

Newspapers
See: Front Page.

Ninja
See sidebar, p. 452
Black Tight Killers '66
Blade 2 '02
Castle of Cagliostro '79
Chinese Super Ninjas '82
Contract Killer '98

Dragon from Russia '90
Dragon Kid '90
Dragon Lee vs. the Five Brothers '78
Duel to the Death '82
The Executioner '74
Gatchaman '94
The Hero of Swallow '96
The Inspector Wears Skirts '88
Invincible Obsessed Fighter '82
Jackie Chan Adventures 1: The Search for the Talismans '00
Jackie Chan Adventures 2: The Dark Hand Returns '00
Jackie Chan Adventures 3: The Shadow of Shendu '00
Lady Ninja: Reflections of Darkness '96
Last Hurrah for Chivalry '78
The Legend of the Swordsman '92
A Life of Ninja '83
Lone Ninja Warrior '81
Lone Wolf and Cub 2: Baby Cart at the River Styx '72
Lone Wolf and Cub 3: Baby Cart to Hades '72
Lone Wolf and Cub 5: Baby Cart in the Land of Demons '73
The Magic Serpent '66
A Man Called Hero '99
The Miracle Fighters '82
My Lucky Stars '85
The New Legend of Shaolin '94
Ninja: Band of Assassins '62
Ninja: Band of Assassins Continued '63
The Ninja Dragon '90
Ninja Hunter '83
Ninja in the Deadly Trap '83
Ninja in the U.S.A. '88
Ninja Scroll '93
Ninja the Final Duel '85
Ninja vs. Bruce Lee '82
Ninja vs. Ninja '87
Ninja vs. Shaolin Guards '84
The Postman Fights Back '82
The Razor 3: Who's Got the Gold? '74
Renegade Ninjas '79
Return of the Deadly Blade '81
Robo Vampire '88
Sakuya: Slayer of Demons '00

Shaolin and Tai Chi '79
The Shaolin Drunken Monk '83
Shaolin Fist of Fury '87
Shaolin vs. Ninja '83
Shogun Assassin '80
Shogun's Ninja '82
The Super Ninja '84
Teenage Mutant Ninja Turtles '90
Temptress of a Thousand Faces '98
To Kill with Intrigue '77
Vampire Controller '00

Nuclear Disaster
See: Disaster Strikes; Meltdown.

Nuns and/or Priests-Catholic
Real and imposters.
Beautiful Hunter '94
The Blood Drinkers '64
Cannonball Run '81
The Razor 2: The Snare '73
Sister Street Fighter '74
Snake in the Eagle's Shadow '78
Sting of the Dragon Masters '73
The Street Fighter '74
Thunder Cops '98
U-Man '02
Young and Dangerous '96

Nurses
See: Doctors and/or Nurses.

Oldest Profession
Happy and not-so-happy hookers.
Battle of Shaolin '77
The Blade '95
The Buddhist Fist '79
Chinese Orthopedist and the Spice Girls '02
City of Desire '01
Cold War '00
Comrades, Almost a Love Story '96
Crack Shadow Boxers '77
Day Off '01
Days of Being Wild '90
Doctor No... '01
Dream of Garuda '94
Duel of the Brave Ones '78
Fists Like Lee '74
Fists of Fury '71
God of Gamblers 2 '90
The Hero of Swallow '96
Hong Kong X-File '98
Iceman Cometh '89
Ichi the Killer '01
Killer Snakes '74
Kiss of the Dragon '01
Kung Fu Genius '79

Last Hurrah for Chivalry '78
The Millionaires' Express '86
9413 '98
Paramount Motel '00
Pedicab Driver '89
Princess Mononoke '97
Robotrix '91
Shocking Asia '75
Shocking Asia 2 '76
Snake Fist Dynamo '84
Sugar-Howling of an Angel '96
Sumo Vixens '96
Task Force '97
Twin Dragons '92
Wicked City '87
Wicked City '92
Zatoichi's Cane Sword '66
Zatoichi's Revenge '64
Zatoichi's Vengeance '66
Zero Woman: The Accused '96

Only the Lonely
See also: Loner Cops.
Anna Magdalena '98
Audition '99
C'est la Vie, Mon Cheri '93
Chungking Express '94
Cop on a Mission '01
Everyday Is Valentine '01
Fallen Angels '95
Female Convict Scorpion: Jailhouse 41 '72
From the Queen to the Chief Executive '01
Glass Tears '01
Green Snake '93
Guinea Pig: Mermaid in a Manhole '88
Lone Ninja Warrior '81
Maborosi '95
A Moment of Romance '90
Mon-Rak Transistor '01
Pulse '01
Return of the Deadly Blade '81
Seeding of a Ghost '83
Temptress of a Thousand Faces '98
Where a Good Man Goes '99
Woman in the Dunes '64

Organized Crime
Gangsters with palm pilots. See also: Disorganized Crime; Yakuza.
Aakhri Adalat '88
The Adventurers '95
Ballistic Kiss '98
Beast Cops '98
A Better Tomorrow '86
A Better Tomorrow 2 '87

A Better Tomorrow 3 '89
Big Bullet '96
The Big Heat '88
Bullets of Love '01
Casino Raiders '89
Casino Raiders 2 '91
Casino Tycoon 2 '92
Century of the Dragon '99
Chinatown Kid '77
City Cop '95
Code of Honor '87
The Conman '98
Cop on a Mission '01
Curry & Pepper '90
Cyclo '95
Days of Being Wild '90
The Dragon Family '88
Dragon from Russia '90
Dragon in Jail '90
Dragon Killer '95
The Enforcer '95
Fallen Angels '95
First Option '96
5 Lady Venoms '78
Fulltime Killer '01
A Gambler's Story '01
Goodbye Mr. Cool '01
Gunmen '88
Hit Team '00
H.K. Adams Family '92
Jiang Hu-"The Triad Zone" '00
The Killer '89
Killer's Romance '90
The Korean Connection '77
The Last Blood '90
Lee Rock '91
The Legend of a Professional '00
The Masked Prosecutor '99
Miracles '89
The Mission '99
Moonlight Express '99
The Most Wanted '94
My Wife Is a Gangster '01
Nowhere to Hide '99
Option Zero '97
Organized Crime and Triad Bureau '94
Powerful Four '91
Queen's High '91
Red Shield '91
The Replacement Killers '97
Return of the Dragon '72
Return to a Better Tomorrow '94
Return of the Tiger '79
Rich and Famous '87
Romeo Must Die '00
Shanghai 1920 '91
Task Force '97
A Taste of Killing and Romance '94
Tiger Cage '88
The Tigers '91
Time and Tide '00

Too Many Ways to Be No. 1 '97
Tragic Fantasy: Tiger of Wanchai '94
The Tricky Master '00
Undercover Blues '00
Where a Good Man Goes '99
Young and Dangerous '96
Young and Dangerous 5 '98

Paging Dr. Kevorkian
Self-inflicted premature ends, either attempted, threatened, faked, or successful. See also: Death & the Afterlife.
Ashes of Time '94
Battle Royale '00
Bloody Beach '00
Brave Archer '77
Champion '00
Chinese Super Ninjas '82
Chushingura '62
Crouching Tiger, Hidden Dragon '00
The Eel '97
The 8 Masters '77
Emperor of Shaolin Kung Fu '80
Funeral March '01
Fury of King Boxer '72
God.com '98
Great Performances: Kurosawa '02
Guinea Pig: He Never Dies '86
The Happiness of the Katakuris '01
Happy Family '02
The Haunted Cop Shop '87
The Haunted Lantern '98
Hit-Man in the Hand of Buddha '80
Horror Hotline Big Head Monster '01
Hum Paanch '80
The Hypnotist '99
Inner Senses '01
Killer '00
Killer Priest '81
Lone Wolf and Cub 1: Sword of Vengeance '72
A Love of Blueness '00
The Magnificent '78
Moonlight Express '99
Naked Pursuit '68
Patlabor 1: The Movie '90
Pom Pom '84
Rashomon '50
Red to Kill '94
Renegade Ninjas '79
Ring 0: Birthday '00
Robo Vampire '88
Shadow '01
Shiri '99
Shogun Assassin '80

The Silver Spear '79
Sonatine '93
Spiral '00
Troublesome Night 14 '02
Vampire Controller '00
Violent Cop '89
Visible Secret '01
Zero Woman: The Accused '96

Parades & Festivals
Adventures of a Blind Man '64
Bruce Lee Fights Back from the Grave '76
Everyday Is Valentine '01
Flyin Dance '01
The Killer '89
The Legend 2 '93
Legend of the Dinosaurs '77
Losers' Club '01
The Magic Serpent '66
The Red Wolf '95
Shaolin vs. Ninja '83
Shocking Asia 2 '76
Troublesome Night '97
Violated Paradise '63
A Wicked Ghost '99
Zatoichi's Cane Sword '66
Zatoichi's Vengeance '66
Zatoichi the Fugitive '63

Parenthood
See: Babies; Bad Dads; Bad Seeds; Dads; Kung Fu Moms; Moms; That's a Baby?

Pedicabs
Foot-powered taxis, also known as rickshaws.
Born to Defence '88
Cyclo '95
Fearless Dragons '79
Pedicab Driver '89
Fist of Fury '95
Golden Dragon Silver Snake '79
Gunmen '88
Miracles '89
My Kung Fu 12 Kicks '79
Once upon a Time in China 3 '93
Triangular Duel '72

Period Pieces
See: The Great Depression; Historical Drama; Vietnam War.

Phillipines (Production)
See sidebar, p. 302.
Angel on Fire '95
Beast of the Yellow Night '70
The Blood Drinkers '64

Blowback: Love and Death '90
Brides of Blood '68
Curse of the Vampires '70
Devil Woman '70
Guardian Angel '96
Horror of the Blood Monsters '70
The Killing of Satan '83
Leopard Hunting '98
Lethal Panther 2 '93
Mad Doctor of Blood Island '68
Martial Arts Mayhem, Vol. 1 '99
Martial Arts Mayhem, Vol. 2 '99
Murder in the Orient '74
Ninja vs. Bruce Lee '82
Ninja vs. Ninja '87
Robo Vampire '88
Terror Is a Man '59
Thunder Ninja Kids: The Hunt for the Devil Boxer '86/94
Twilight People '72
The Walls of Hell '64

Phone Terror
Usually worse than a persistent telemarketer (but not much).
High and Low '63
The Hypnotist '99
Nightmare Zone '98
Nobody '99
Pulse '01
Ring '98
Ring 2 '99
Ring Virus '99

Photography
See: Shutterbugs.

Pigs
Six degrees of Bacon.
The Adventures of Milo and Otis '86
A Chinese Odyssey Part 1: Pandora's Box '95
A Chinese Odyssey Part 2: Cinderella '95
Crippled Masters '80
The Magnificent Butcher '79
Once upon a Time in China '91
Princess Mononoke '97
Revenge of the Patriots '76
Spirited Away '01

Pirates
Deadend of Besiegers '92
The Legend of the Swordsman '92
One Arm Hero '94
Project A '83
Project A 2 '87
Screaming Ninja '73

The 72 Desperate Rebels '76

Pirates-Video
Bio Zombie '98
Century of the Dragon '99
Last Ghost Standing '99

Politics
Sort of like organized crime.
Adventures of a Blind Man '64
Battle Royale '00
The Blacksheep Affair '98
City Hunter: Secret Service '96
Combo Cops '96
Comrades, Almost a Love Story '96
Crime Story '93
Eastern Condors '86
Ecstasy of the Angels '72
Elaan '94
Executioners '93
Fist of Fury '95
Fist of Legend '94
Forbidden City Cop '96
From the Queen to the Chief Executive '01
Full Alert '97
Fury of King Boxer '72
Gamera, Guardian of the Universe '95
Generation Consultant '90
Generation Pendragon '90
Giants and Toys '58
Godzilla, King of the Monsters '54
Godzilla 1985 '84
Gunmen '88
Her Majesty Is Fine '96
The Heroes '80
The Heroic Trio '93
The Hidden Fortress '58
High and Low '63
Hum Paanch '80
In the Line of Duty 3 '88
Joint Security Area '00
King of the Mongols '60
The Last War '61
Lee Rock '91
Metropolis '01
Mothra '61
Ninja: Band of Assassins '62
Notorious Concubines '69
Once upon a Time in China '91
Once upon a Time in China 2 '92
Once upon a Time in China 3 '93
Once upon a Time in China 4 '93

Once upon a Time in China and America '97
One Arm Hero '94
Operation Billionaires '98
Organized Crime and Triad Bureau '94
Peace Hotel '95
Powerful Four '91
Princess Mononoke '97
Project A '83
Project A 2 '87
The Razor 1: Sword of Justice '72
The Razor 2: The Snare '73
The Razor 3: Who's Got the Gold? '74
Rebels under Siege '00
Royal Space Force: The Wings of Honneamise '87
Sam the Iron Bridge: Champion of Martial Arts '93
Sex and the Emperor '94
Shanghai 1920 '91
Shiri '99
Supercop '92
Sympathy for Mr. Vengeance '01
Throne of Blood '57
The Tigers '91
The Venus Wars '89
Zatoichi the Fugitive '63

Porno Emporium
Titles that sound like pornography, but aren't. See also: Sex & Sexuality; Sexploitation.
The Adventures of the Master and His Servant '96
All About Ah-Long '89
Angel on Fire '95
Audition '99
Born Wild '01
Bullets of Love '01
A Chinese Odyssey Part 1: Pandora's Box '95
Comeuppance '00
Crack Shadow Boxers '77
Dirty Ho '79
Dirty Kung Fu '78
The Eel '97
Enter the Dragon '73
Every Dog Has His Date '01
Filthy Guy '80
Fists of Fury '71
For Bad Boys Only '00
The Foul King '00
Full Contact '92
Full Throttle '95
Gold Fingers '01
Happy End '99
Hard as a Dragon '80
Her Majesty Is Fine '96

The Hero of Swallow '96
Hong Kong X-File '98
Horror Hotline Big Head Monster '01
The Hot, the Cool, and the Vicious '76
Iceman Cometh '89
The Inspector Wears Skirts '88
Invincible Pole Fighter '83
Iron Monkey '93
Joint Security Area '00
Lady Wu Tang '77
The Leg Fighters '80
The Lord of Hangzhou '98
Love Me, Love My Money '01
Macho Man '72
Magnificent Natural Fist '80
Man Wanted '95
The Massive '78
Mighty Jack '68
Mr. Boo Meets Pom Pom '85
The Most Wanted '94
One Arm Hero '94
Organ '96
Painted Skin '92
The Peacock King '89
The Phantom Lover '95
Picture of a Nymph '88
Pom Pom and Hot Hot '92
Prison on Fire '87
Project A '83
Queen's High '91
Ring Virus '99
Royal Tramp '92
Scared Stiff '86
Shaolin Chastity Kung Fu '81
Shaolin Wooden Men '76
The Silver Spear '79
Snake Fist Dynamo '84
Tetsuo 2: Body Hammer '91
Tokyo Fist '96
The Touch '02
We're Going to Eat You! '80
Where a Good Man Goes '99
Yes, Madam '85
You Shoot, I Shoot '01
Your Place or Mine! '99
Zatoichi and the Chest of Gold '64
Zatoichi's Flashing Sword '64

Pornography
Sorry...these are movies about *pornography. See also: Sex & Sexuality; Sexploitation.*
Final Justice '88
Guardian Angel '96
I.K.U. '00

Lies '99
Snake-Crane Secret '78
You Shoot, I Shoot '01
Zatoichi Challenged '67

Post Apocalypse
No more convenience stores. See also: Negative Utopia; Technology-Rampant.
Akira '88
Akira Kurosawa's Dreams '90
Body Snatcher from Hell '68
Executioners '93
Final Fantasy: The Spirits Within '01
Flash Future Kung Fu '83
Godzilla vs. King Ghidorah '91
The Heroic Trio '93
Time of the Apes '75
Urotsukidoji '89
Vampire Hunter D '85
Vampire Hunter D: Bloodlust '01
Violence Jack '88

Pregnancy
See: Just a Little Bit Pregnant; That's a Baby?

Prison
See: Great Escapes; Men in Prison.

Prosthetic Limbs
Champ against Champ '83
Dirty Tiger, Crazy Frog '78
Enter the Dragon '73
Godzilla vs. King Ghidorah '91
I Love Maria '88
Kid with the Golden Arm '78
The Return of the 5 Deadly Venoms '78
Robo Vampire '88
Robotrix '91
Sixty Million Dollar Man '95
Tetsuo: The Iron Man '89
Tetsuo 2: Body Hammer '91

Prostitutes
See: Oldest Profession.

Psychiatry
See: Shrinks.

Psychic Powers
Cross Fire '00
Cure '97
The Demon's Baby '98
The Dimension Travelers '98
Doctor No... '01

Evil Dead Trap '88
5 Venoms vs. Wu Tang '87
Gamera, Guardian of the Universe '95
Gamera 2: Advent of Legion '96
Gamera 3: The Revenge of Irys '99
Ghidorah the Three-Headed Monster '64
God.com '98
God.com '98
God of Gamblers '89
God of Gamblers 2 '90
God of Gamblers 3: Back to Shanghai '91
God of Gamblers Returns '94
Godzilla vs. Biollante '89
Godzilla vs. Destroyah '95
Godzilla vs. King Ghidorah '91
Godzilla vs. MechaGodzilla 2 '93
Godzilla vs. Mothra '92
Godzilla vs. Space Godzilla '94
Horror Hotline Big Head Monster '01
The Hypnotist '99
Inner Senses '01
Jackie Chan Adventures 1: The Search for the Talismans '00
Jackie Chan Adventures 2: The Dark Hand Returns '00
Jackie Chan Adventures 3: The Shadow of Shendu '00
The Killing of Satan '83
Memento Mori '99
Mothra '61
Mothra vs. Godzilla '64
My Lucky Stars '85
Organ '96
Raat '91
Rashomon '50
Renegade Ninjas '79
Ring '98
Ring 2 '99
Ring 0: Birthday '00
Ring Virus '99
Shadow '01
The Street Fighter's Last Revenge '74
Tokyo Decameron: Three Tales of Madness and Sensuality '96
Troublesome Night '97
Troublesome Night 3 '97
Troublesome Night 4 '98
Troublesome Night 8 '00

Troublesome Night 9 '00
Troublesome Night 14 '02
Twin Dragons '92
The Wesley's Mysterious File '01

Psycho-Thriller, Qu'est que c'est?
It's all in your mind....
See also: Mystery & Suspense.
Attack of the Mushroom People '63
Body Weapon '99
Branded to Kill '67
Cure '97
The Eye '02
Fear Faith Revenge 303 '98
Guinea Pig: Mermaid in a Manhole '88
Happy End '99
The Hypnotist '99
Inner Senses '01
Nobody '99
Pulse '01
Rashomon '50
Ring '98
Ring 2 '99
Ring 0: Birthday '00
Ring Virus '99
Shadow '01
Stray Dog '49
Tell Me Something '99
Tokyo Decameron: Three Tales of Madness and Sensuality '96
Tokyo Fist '96
Violent Cop '99

Psychotics/Sociopaths
Social deviants without a conscience. See also: Presidents.
Beauty Investigator '92
Blind Beast '69
Body Weapon '99
Brother of Darkness '94
Champion '00
Chinese Samson '79
A Chinese Torture Chamber Story 2 '98
Crazy Crooks '80
Crime of a Beast '01
Daughter of Darkness '93
The Deadly Camp '99
Dr. Lamb '92
Double Tap '00
Dreadnaught '81
The East Is Red '93
Evil Dead Trap '88
Expect the Unexpected '98
Female Convict Scorpion: Jailhouse 41 '72
Full Contact '92
God.com '98

Guinea Pig: Android of Notre Dame '88
Guinea Pig: Devils Experiment '85
Guinea Pig: Flower of Flesh and Blood '85
Guinea Pig: Mermaid in a Manhole '88
The H-Man '58
Hard Boiled '91
The Heroic Trio '93
The Hypnotist '99
Iceman Cometh '89
Ichi the Killer '01
Killer '00
Killer Snakes '74
Nightmare Zone '98
Ninja vs. Ninja '87
The One '01
Organ '96
Record '00
Red to Kill '94
Robotrix '91
Run and Kill '93
Scared Stiff '86
The Street Fighter '74
Succubare '77
Sympathy for Mr. Vengeance '01
Tell Me Something '99
Tetsuo: The Iron Man '89
Tetsuo 2: Body Hammer '91
Ultimatum '01
The Untold Story '92
The Untold Story 2 '98
Violent Cop '99
With or Without You '92

Rabbits
Jackie Chan Adventures 2: The Dark Hand Returns '00
The Moon Warriors '92

Radio Activity
Ballistic Kiss '98
Black Magic M-66 '87
Horror Hotline Big Head Monster '01
The Last War '61
Love Correction '00
Mighty Jack '68
Rush Hour '98
Warning from Space '56

Radioactivity
Akira Kurosawa's Dreams '90
Attack of the Mushroom People '63
Barefoot Gen '83
Destroy All Monsters '68
Ebirah, Horror of the Deep '66
Frankenstein vs. Baragon '65
Ghidorah the Three-Headed Monster '64

Godzilla, Mothra and King Ghidorah: Battle on Fire '01
Godzilla 1985 '84
Godzilla Raids Again '55
Godzilla the Series: Monster War '99
Godzilla 2000 '99
Godzilla vs. Biollante '89
Godzilla vs. Destroyah '95
Godzilla vs. Gigan '72
Godzilla vs. Hedorah '71
Godzilla vs. King Ghidorah '91
Godzilla vs. MechaGodzilla '74
Godzilla vs. MechaGodzilla 2 '93
Godzilla vs. Megaguirus '00
Godzilla vs. Megalon '73
Godzilla vs. Mothra '92
Godzilla vs. Space Godzilla '94
Grave of the Fireflies '88
Gunhed '89
The H-Man '58
Invasion of Astro-Monster '65
King Kong Escapes '67
King Kong vs. Godzilla '62
The Last War '61
Mothra '61
Mothra vs. Godzilla '64
Son of Godzilla '67
Teenage Mutant Ninja Turtles '90
Terror beneath the Sea '66
Terror of MechaGodzilla '75

Rape
Victims and often their revenge. See also: Kissin' Cousins.
Bangkok Dangerous '00
Crime of a Beast '01
Daughter of Darkness '93
Devil Touch '02
Dream of Garuda '94
Ecstasy of the Angels '72
Entrails of the Virgin '86
Evil Dead Trap '88
Female Convict Scorpion: Jailhouse 41 '72
Freeze Me '00
Naked Pursuit '68
Rashomon '50
Red to Kill '94
Robotrix '91

Sadistic City '93
Seeding of a Ghost '83
Snake Deadly Act '79
Trust Me U Die '99
Urotsukidoji '89

Rebel with a Cause
Bucking the establishment for a reason. See also: Rebel without a Cause.
Battle Royale '00
Big Boobs Buster '90
Dragon: The Bruce Lee Story '93
Executioners '93
Extreme Challenge '01
A Fighter's Blues '00
Fist of Fury '95
Fist of Legend '94
God.com '98
Good Morning '59
Goodbye Mr. Cool '01
Gunmen '88
The Heroic Trio '93
Lee Rock '91
The Razor 1: Sword of Justice '72
The Razor 2: The Snare '73
The Razor 3: Who's Got the Gold? '74
Rebels under Siege '00
Renegade Ninjas '79
Righting Wrongs '86

Rebel without a Cause
Bucking the establishment just because it's the establishment. See also: Rebel with a Cause.
Akira '88
Attack the Gas Station! '99
Bullet in the Head '90
Cyclo '95
Days of Being Wild '90
Fallen Angels '95
Female Convict Scorpion: Jailhouse 41 '72
Full Contact '92
Ichi the Killer '01
Junk '99
Legend of Speed '99
Tetsuo: The Iron Man '89
Tetsuo 2: Body Hammer '91
Tokyo Drifter '66
Venom Warrior '83
Versus '00
Violent Cop '89

Recycled and Stock Footage/Redubbed Dialogue
Techniques that made Godfrey Ho and Ed Wood great.
All Monsters Attack '70
Bruce Lee Fights Back from the Grave '76

Exit the Dragon, Enter the Tiger '75
Fist of Fear-Touch of Death '80
Game of Death '78
Gamera vs. Barugon '66
Gamera vs. Guillon '69
Gamera vs. Gyaos '67
Gamera vs. Viras '68
Gamera vs. Zigra '71
God of Gamblers 2 '90
Godzilla, King of the Monsters '54
Godzilla Raids Again '55
Godzilla vs. Gigan '72
Godzilla vs. MechaGodzilla '74
Godzilla vs. Megalon '73
Godzilla vs. Hedorah '71
Horror of the Blood Monsters '70
Invasion of the Neptune Men '61
Kung Pow: Enter the Fist '76
Ninja Hunter '83
Ninja vs. Ninja '87
The Real Bruce Lee '79
Robo Vampire '88
Shaolin Fist of Fury '87
Super Gang '78
Thunder Ninja Kids: The Hunt for the Devil Boxer '86/94
Tower of Death '81
Varan the Unbelievable '58
What's Up, Tiger Lily? '66
The World of the Drunken Master '79
Yes, Madam '85

Reincarnation
See also: Death & the Afterlife.
A Chinese Ghost Story '87
A Chinese Ghost Story 2 '90
A Chinese Ghost Story: The Tsui Hark Animation '97
A Chinese Odyssey Part 1: Pandora's Box '95
A Chinese Odyssey Part 2: Cinderella '95
Erotic Ghost Story 2 '91
Evil Cat '86
Faces of Horror '98
The Haunted Cop Shop '87
The Imp '81
Kung Fu Zombie '81
Legend of the Eight Samurai '84
Mahal '48

Reborn from Hell: Samurai Armageddon '96
Shadow '01
The Vampire Combat '01
Vampire Controller '00
What Time Is It There? '01

Renegade Body Parts
Hands, fingers, eyes, brains, and other appendages with a life of their own. See also: Amputations; Ears!; Eyeballs!; Hearts!; Killer Brains; Where's My Johnson?
Another Heaven '00
Body Snatcher from Hell '68
Evil Brain from Outer Space '58/59
The Eye '02
Frankenstein vs. Baragon '65
Guinea Pig: He Never Dies '86
Lady Ninja: Reflections of Darkness '96
The Magic Serpent '66
Model from Hell '99
Sixty Million Dollar Man '95

Reptiles
See: Dinosaurs; Gamera; Godzilla; King Ghidorah; Rodan; Snakes; Were-snakes.

Rescue Missions
See also: Rescue Missions involving Time Travel
Aces Go Places 4 '86
The Adventures of Milo and Otis '86
Angel 2 '88
Armour of God '86
Atomic Rulers of the World '57
Big Bullet '96
Black Magic M-66 '87
The Blade '95
Blade 2 '02
The Bride with White Hair 2 '93
Bronson Lee, Champion '78
Bullet in the Head '90
Casino Raiders '89
Castle of Cagliostro '79
Champion '00
Chinese Iron Man '75
City Hunter '92
City Hunter: Secret Service '96
Crocodile Hunter '89
Daimajin '66
Deadend of Besiegers '92

The Deadly Camp '99
Dragon Inn '92
Duel to the Death '82
Eagle vs. Silver Fox '83
Ebirah, Horror of the Deep '66
The Enforcer '95
Enter the Fat Dragon '78
Evil Brain from Outer Space '58/59
Exit the Dragon, Enter the Tiger '75
Fantasy Mission Force '84
Fist Power '99
For Bad Boys Only '00
Full Contact '92
Game of Death '78
Gamera vs. Guillon '69
Gappa: The Triphibian Monster '67
God of Gamblers 2 '90
Heart of Dragon '85
Her Name Is Cat 2: Journey to Death '01
Heroes Shed No Tears '83/86
The Heroic Trio '93
The Hero of Swallow '96
Hero's Blood '91
High Risk '95
Hiruko the Goblin '90
Hit Team '00
Hot War '98
The Incredible Kung Fu Mission '82
Invaders from Space '58
Invincible Obsessed Fighter '82
Invincible Pole Fighter '83
Iron Man '86
Iron Monkey 2 '77
Iron Neck Li '81
Killer from Above '77
The Killing of Satan '83
King Kong vs. Godzilla '62
King of Beggars '92
Kiss of the Dragon '01
The Korean Connection '77
Kung Fu Genius '79
Kung Fu's Hero '73
Lawyer Lawyer '97
The Legend 2 '93
The Magic Crane '93
The Magnificent Butcher '79
A Man Called Hero '99
Masters of Tiger Crane '83
Mighty Jack '68
Mothra '61
Mothra vs. Godzilla '64
My Kung Fu 12 Kicks '79
The Ninja Dragon '90
Ninja vs. Bruce Lee '82
Odd Couple '79

Once upon a Time in China '91
Organ '96
Peking Opera Blues '86
Picture of a Nymph '88
Police Story '85
Police Story 2 '88
Pom Pom Strikes Back '86
Project A '83
Project A-ko '86
Return of Daimajin '66
Robotrix '91
Rodan '56
Royal Tramp 2 '92
Rush Hour '98
Sanjuro '63
Secret of the Chinese Kung Fu '81
The Seventh Curse '86
Shaolin Chastity Kung Fu '81
The Shaolin Kids '77
The Shaolin Temple '79
Shaolin vs. Lama '81
Sister Street Fighter '74
The Six Directions of Boxing '79
Son of Godzilla '67
Spirited Away '01
Star Force: Fugitive Alien 2 '78/86
Sting of the Dragon Masters '73
Super Kung Fu Kid '74
Swordsman with an Umbrella '70
Teenage Mutant Ninja Turtles '90
Thunder Ninja Kids: The Hunt for the Devil Boxer '86/94
To Kill with Intrigue '77
The Touch '02
War of the Shaolin Temple '80
What's Up, Tiger Lily? '66
Wheels on Meals '84
Where's Officer Tuba? '86
White Lotus Cult '93
Winners and Sinners '83
Wrath of Daimajin '66
Yoga and Kung Fu Girl '78
The Young Master '80
Zu: Warriors of the Magic Mountain '83

Rescue Missions involving Time Travel
God of Gamblers 3: Back to Shanghai '91
Godzilla vs. King Ghidorah '91
Time of the Apes '75

Road Trip
Escapism courtesy two- and four-wheeled vehi-

cles. See also: Bikers; Checkered Flag; Motor Vehicle Dept.
Adrenaline Drive '99
Cannonball Run '81
Castle of Cagliostro '79
Kikujiro '99
Rush Hour 2 '01

Robots, Androids & Cyborgs
Jet Jaguar! See also: Technology-Rampant.
Aces Go Places 2 '83
Appleseed '88
Astro Boy '63
Astro Boy '80
Black Magic M-66 '87
The 18 Bronzemen '76
The 18 Bronzemen Part 2 '76
Evil Brain from Outer Space '58/59
Fury in Shaolin Temple '82
Gen-Y Cops '00
Ghost in the Shell '95
Godzilla the Series: Monster War '99
Godzilla vs. Gigan '72
Godzilla vs. King Ghidorah '91
Godzilla vs. MechaGodzilla '74
Godzilla vs. MechaGodzilla 2 '93
Godzilla vs. Megalon '73
Godzilla vs. Space Godzilla '94
Gunhed '89
I.K.U. '00
I Love Maria
King Kong Escapes '67
Message from Space '78
Metropolis '01
The Mysterians '57
Patlabor 1: The Movie '90
Project A-ko '86
Raiders of Wu Tang '82
Robotrix '91
Robo Vampire '88
Roujin Z '91
Sixty Million Dollar Man '95
Terminatrix '95
Terror beneath the Sea '66
Terror of MechaGodzilla '75
Ultraman 2 '79
Ultraman Tiga and Ultraman Dyna: The Warriors of the Lightning Star '98
The Unbeaten 28 '80
Voyage into Space '67
Zeram '91

Rodan
Destroy All Monsters '68
Ghidorah the Three-Headed Monster '64
Godzilla vs. MechaGodzilla 2 '93
Invasion of Astro-Monster '65
Rodan '56

Rodents
Blonde Fury '89
Executioners from Shaolin '77
The Postman Fights Back '82
Shaolin Fist of Fury '87
Teenage Mutant Ninja Turtles '90

Role Reversal
Walkin' in another man's shoes for a few reels. See also: Gender Bending; He's Really a Girl!
The Adventures of the Master and His Servant '96
The Cat '91
Giants and Toys '58
God of Gamblers '89
Inner Senses '01
Jackie Chan Adventures 2: The Dark Hand Returns '00
Justice, My Foot! '92
The Legend of the Swordsman '92
Love on a Diet '01
Raat '91
Ring 0: Birthday '00
Shaolin Soccer '01
Sixty Million Dollar Man '95

Romance
See: Romantic Adventure; Romantic Comedy; Romantic Drama.

Romantic Adventure
Adrenaline Drive '99
The Adventurers '95
All About Ah-Long '89
Ballistic Kiss '98
Bangkok Dangerous '00
Black Cat '91
Black Mask '96
Born Wild '01
The Bride with White Hair '93
Bullets of Love '01
Butterfly and Sword '93
A Chinese Ghost Story '87
A Chinese Ghost Story 2 '90
Cop on a Mission '01
Crouching Tiger, Hidden Dragon '00

894

Deadful Melody '94
The Defender '94
Fallen Angels '95
Fireworks '97
For Bad Boys Only '00
From Beijing with Love '94
Gorgeous '99
Green Snake '93
Her Name Is Cat '98
Killer's Romance '90
The Legend of a Professional '00
The Legend of the Swordsman '92
Legendary Couple '95
Love on Delivery '94
The Magic Crane '93
Miracles '89
Moonlight Express '99
Naked Killer '92
Ninja Scroll '93
Once a Thief '91
Peace Hotel '95
Peking Opera Blues '86
Picture of a Nymph '88
Princess Mononoke '97
Romeo Must Die '00
Shiri '99
The Storm Riders '98
A Taste of Killing and Romance '94
Time and Tide '00
The Touch '02
Twin Dragons '92
Twin Warriors '93

Romantic Comedy
Love thing leads to laughs.
Adrenaline Drive '99
All's Well End's Well '92
All's Well End's Well 1997 '97
Beauty and the Breast '02
Brassiere '01
Could You Kill My Husband Please? '01
Dummy Mommy, without a Baby '01
Eighth Happiness '88
Flirting Scholar '93
Forbidden City Cop '96
From Beijing with Love '94
The Funeral '84
Giants and Toys '58
Gorgeous '99
He's a Woman, She's a Man '94
Hi! Dharma! '01
The Irresistible Piggies '02
Legendary Couple '95
Love Me, Love My Money '01
Love on a Diet '01
Love on Delivery '94
Love Paradox '00
Marry a Rich Man '02
My Sassy Girl '01
My Wife Is a Gangster '01

100 Ways to Murder Your Wife '86
Para Para Sakura '01
Shaolin Temple 2: Kids from Shaolin '84
Shark Skin Man and Peach Hip Girl '98
Urusei Yatsura Movie 1: Only You! '83
Your Place or Mine! '98

Romantic Drama
Love thing leads to tension and anxiety.
The Adventurers '95
Anna Magdalena '98
Ashes of Time '94
Audition '99
Bakery Amour '01
Ballistic Kiss '98
Black Cat '91
Body Weapon '99
Branded to Kill '67
The Bride with White Hair '93
The Bride with White Hair 2 '93
Bullets of Love '01
C'est la Vie, Mon Cheri '93
City of Desire '01
Comrades, Almost a Love Story '96
Crouching Tiger, Hidden Dragon '00
Dance of a Dream '01
Days of Being Wild '90
Dragon Inn '92
Ecstasy of the Angels '72
The Eel '97
Fall for You '01
Fallen Angels '95
Fighting for Love '01
Final Romance '01
Fireworks '97
The Funeral '84
Goodbye Mr. Cool '01
Green Snake '93
Happy End '99
The Haunted Lantern '98
Inner Senses '01
Juliet in Love '00
Killer's Romance '90
King of Comedy '99
Lavender '00
Legacy of Rage '86
Legend of the Flying Swordsman '00
Lies '99
Love au Zen '01
Love Correction '00
A Love of Blueness '00
Maborosi '95
The Magic Crane '93
Mahal '48
Memento Mori '99
Merry-Go-Round '01
Midnight Fly '01
Millennium Dragon '99
A Moment of Romance '90
Mon-Rak Transistor '01

Moonlight Express '99
Naked Pursuit '68
Needing You... '00
Notorious Concubines '69
Nowhere to Hide '99
Okinawa Rendez-vous '00
Once a Thief '91
On the Run '88
Peace Hotel '95
The Phantom Lover '95
Picture of a Nymph '88
Romeo Must Die '00
Sadistic City '93
Second Time Around '02
Shanghai 1920 '91
Shiri '99
Sholay '75
Suzhou River '00
Taboo '97
Take 2 in Life '01
A Taste of Killing and Romance '94
Tell Me Something '99
Tokyo Fist
A War Named Desire '00
Warm Water under a Red Bridge '01
What Time Is It There? '01
Where a Good Man Goes '99
With or Without You '92
Woman in the Dunes '64

Royalty
See also: Historical Drama.
Aces Go Places 3 '84
Blood of the Dragon '71
Brave Archer '77
The Duel '71
The East Is Red '93
Emperor of Shaolin Kung Fu '80
Filthy Guy '80
Flight of the Heroine '00
Flirting Scholar '93
The Flying Guillotine '74
Forbidden City Cop '96
From the Queen to the Chief Executive '01
Generation Consultant '90
Generation Pendragon '90
Ghidorah the Three-Headed Monster '64
Godzilla vs. Megalon '73
Her Majesty Is Fine '96
The Hero of Swallow '96
The Hidden Fortress '58

The Holy Robe of Shaolin Temple '84
Hunted by Royal Decree '00
Iceman Cometh '89
Iron Neck Li '81
King of Beggars '92
King of the Mongols '60
Lady Iron Monkey '83
The Law and the Outlaw '95
The Legend '92
The Legend 2 '93
Lightning Kung Fu '80
The Lord of Hangzhou '98
Lord of the Wu Tang '93
The Magic Crane '93
The Magic Serpent '66
The Magnificent '78
Message from Space '78
The Miracle Fighters '82
The Moon Warriors '92
Mortal Kombat '95
Once upon a Time in China 3 '93
One Arm Hero '94
Princess Mononoke '97
Project A-ko '86
Royal Tramp '92
Royal Tramp 2 '92
Sex and the Emperor '94
The Shaolin Invincibles '79
Shaolin: Wheel of Life '00
The Story in Temple Red Lily '79
The Sword Stained with Royal Blood '93
Thousand Mile Escort '76
Voyage into Space '67
White Lotus Cult '93
Yellow River Fighter '88

Russia (Production)
Dersu Uzala '74

Sail Away
See also: Go Fish; Submarines.
Aces Go Places 3 '84
The Adventures of Milo and Otis '86
A*P*E '76
Attack of the Mushroom People '63
City Hunter '92
Deadend of Besiegers '92
The Deadly Camp '99
Dragon Killer '95
Dragons Forever '88
The East Is Red '93
Ebirah, Horror of the Deep '66
The Enforcer '95
First Option '96
Game of Death '78

Gamera, Guardian of the Universe '95
Generation Consultant '90
God of Gamblers '89
Godzilla, King of the Monsters '54
Godzilla 1985 '84
Godzilla Raids Again '55
Godzilla 2000 '99
Godzilla vs. Hedorah '71
Godzilla vs. Megaguirus '00
Godzilla vs. Mothra '92
The H-Man '58
Her Name Is Cat '98
In the Line of Duty 5: Middle Man '90
The Killing of Satan '83
King Kong Escapes '67
King Kong vs. Godzilla '62
King of Beggars '92
King of the Mongols '60
The Last War '61
The Legend '92
The Legend of Bruce Lee '80
Lone Wolf and Cub 2: Baby Cart at the River Styx '72
Mad Doctor of Blood Island '68
The Magic Serpent '66
The Magnificent '78
Mighty Peking Man '77
Model from Hell '99
Mortal Kombat '95
Ninja Scroll '93
Once upon a Time in China '91
Project A '83
The Protector '85
The Red Wolf '95
Ring '98
Rumble in the Bronx '95
Rush Hour 2 '01
Shanghai 1920 '91
Shogun '80
Terror beneath the Sea '66
Troublesome Night 9 '00
Voyage into Space '67
War of the Gargantuas '66
What's Up, Tiger Lily? '66

Samurai
Adventures of a Blind Man '64
Blade 2 '02
Blind Swordsman: The Tale of Zatoichi '62
Daimajin '66
The East Is Red '93
Fight, Zatoichi, Fight! '64
Gate of Destiny '96

895

Guinea Pig: Flower of Flesh and Blood '85
The Haunted Lantern '98
The Hidden Fortress '58
King of the Mongols '60
Kwaidan '64
The Legend 2 '93
Legend of the Eight Samurai '84
The Legendary Strike '78
Lone Wolf and Cub 1: Sword of Vengeance '72
Lone Wolf and Cub 2: Baby Cart at the River Styx '72
Lone Wolf and Cub 3: Baby Cart to Hades '72
Lone Wolf and Cub 4: Baby Cart in Peril '72
Lone Wolf and Cub 5: Baby Cart in the Land of Demons '73
Lone Wolf and Cub 6: White Heaven in Hell '74
The New Game of Death '75
New Tale of Zatoichi '63
Ninja Scroll '93
Ran '85
Rashomon '50
The Razor 1: Sword of Justice '72
The Razor 2: The Snare '73
The Razor 3: Who's Got the Gold? '74
Reborn from Hell: Samurai Armageddon '96
Renegade Ninjas '79
Return of Daimajin '66
Sakuya: Slayer of Demons '00
Samaritan Zatoichi '68
Samurai 1: Musashi Miyamoto '54
Samurai 2: Duel at Ichijoji Temple '55
Samurai 3: Duel at Ganryu Island '56
Sanjuro '63
Seven Samurai '54
Shaolin vs. Ninja '83
Shogun '80
Shogun Assassin '80
Shogun's Ninja '82
Sure Death: Revenge '87
The Tale of Zatoichi Continues '62
Throne of Blood '57
Tokyo Mafia 3: Battle for Shinjuku '96

Versus '00
Wrath of Daimajin '66
Yojimbo '61
Zatoichi and the Chess Expert '65
Zatoichi and the Chest of Gold '64
Zatoichi and the Doomed Man '65
Zatoichi and the Fugitives '68
Zatoichi Challenged '67
Zatoichi on the Road '63
Zatoichi's Cane Sword '66
Zatoichi's Flashing Sword '64
Zatoichi's Revenge '64
Zatoichi's Vengeance '66
Zatoichi the Fugitive '63
Zatoichi the Outlaw '67

Sanity Check
Inmates running the asylum; also deviant states of mind. See also: Doctors and/or Nurses; Hospitals; Psychotics/Sociopaths; Shrinks.
Akira '88
All's Well End's Well '97 '97
Attack of the Mushroom People '63
Audition '99
Beast Cops '98
A Better Tomorrow 2 '87
Black Mask '96
Blind Beast '69
Branded to Kill '67
Brother of Darkness '94
Bullet in the Head '90
Champion '00
Cheap Killers '98
Crazy Crooks '80
Cure '97
Daughter of Darkness '93
The Deadly Camp '99
Devil Man '87
The Dimension Travelers '98
Dr. Lamb '92
Dreadnaught '81
Duel to the Death '82
Eastern Condors '86
The Eel '97
Emperor of Shaolin Kung Fu '80
Evil Dead Trap '88
God.com '98
The Happiness of the Katakuris '01
Hot War '98
The Hypnotist '99
Ichi the Killer '01
Inheritor of Kung Fu '77

Inner Senses '01
Invincible Pole Fighter '83
Killer Snakes '74
The Korean Connection '77
Kung Fu Genius '79
The Shaolin Invincibles '79
Tell Me Something '99
Throne of Blood '57
Tokyo Fist '96
The Untold Story '92
The Untold Story 2 '98
Violent Cop '89
Violent Cop '99
War of the Shaolin Temple '80
Wheels on Meals '84

Satan & Satanism
Speak of the devil....
Armour of God '86
Atomic Rulers of the World '57
Beast of the Yellow Night '70
Burning Paradise '94
Devil Woman '70
The Killing of Satan '83
Last Ghost Standing '99
Nine Demons '83
The Peacock King '89
Reborn from Hell: Samurai Armageddon '96
Saga of the Phoenix '90
The Seventh Curse '86
Thunder Ninja Kids: The Hunt for the Devil Boxer '86/94

Satire & Parody
Biting social comment or genre spoofs. See also: Black Comedy; Genre Spoofs; Mockumentaries.
Aces Go Places '82
Aces Go Places 2 '83
Aces Go Places 3 '84
Aces Go Places 4 '86
Aces Go Places 5: The Terracotta Hit '89
Attack the Gas Station! '99
City Hunter '92
Comic King '00
Doctor Vampire '90
Enter the Fat Dragon '78
Fight Back to School '91
Fight Back to School 2 '92
Fight Back to School 3 '93
Fist of Fury 1991 '91
Flirting Scholar '93
Forbidden City Cop '96
The Foul King '00
From Beijing with Love '94

Giants and Toys '58
God of Gamblers 2 '90
God of Gamblers 3: Back to Shanghai '91
The Happiness of the Katakuris '01
The Haunted Cop Shop '87
He's a Woman, She's a Man '94
High Risk '95
H.K. Adams Family '92
I Love Maria '88
Justice, My Foot! '92
King Kong vs. Godzilla '62
King of Beggars '92
King of Comedy '99
Kung Pow: Enter the Fist '76
Last Ghost Standing '99
Lawyer Lawyer '97
Legend of the Dragon '91
The Magnificent Scoundrels '91
Master Q 2001 '01
Royal Tramp '92
Royal Tramp 2 '92
Shaolin Soccer '01
Shark Skin Man and Peach Hip Girl '98
Sixty Million Dollar Man '95
Teenage Mutant Ninja Turtles '90
Weather Woman '95
We're Going to Eat You! '80
Yoga and Kung Fu Girl '78

Scams, Stings & Cons
See also: Heists.
Aces Go Places '82
Aces Go Places 2 '83
Aces Go Places 3 '84
Aces Go Places 4 '86
Aces Go Places 5: The Terracotta Hit '89
The Big Sting '82
Cannonball Run '81
The Cheaters '01
The Conman '98
Conman in Tokyo '00
Crack Shadow Boxers '77
Crazy Crooks '80
Dummy Mommy, without a Baby '01
God of Gamblers '89
God of Gamblers 2 '90
God of Gamblers 3: Back to Shanghai '91
God of Gamblers Returns '94
He's a Woman, She's a Man '94
High Risk '95

Invincible Obsessed Fighter '82
King of Beggars '92
King of Comedy '99
The Magnificent Scoundrels '91
The Millionaires' Express '86
Miracles '89
The Owl vs. Bombo '84
Peking Opera Blues '86
Return of the Master Killer '80
The Tricky Master '00
Twin Dragons '92
Winners and Sinners '83
Yoga and Kung Fu Girl '78

Scarface
Somebody might have been careless with something hot or sharp.
Bangkok Dangerous '00
Black Jack '96
Curry & Pepper '90
For Bad Boys Only '00
Hard Boiled '91
Kung Fu Zombie '81
The New Legend of Shaolin '94
Odd Couple '79
Pom Pom '84
Prison on Fire '87
Shaolin Soccer '01
The Six Directions of Boxing '79
Snake-Crane Secret '78
Swordsman with an Umbrella '70
To Kill with Intrigue '77
Triangular Duel '72
Violent Cop '99
Ways of Kung Fu '80

School
Battle Royale '00
Big Boobs Buster '90
Blood: The Last Vampire '00
Dark Water '02
The Dimension Travelers '98
Dragon in Jail '90
Fear Faith Revenge 303 '98
Fight Back to School '91
Fight Back to School 2 '92
Fight Back to School 3 '93
Fist Power '99
Hiruko the Goblin '90
My Neighbor Totoro '88
My School Mate, the Barbarian '01
Organ '96
Painted Faces '88
Project A-ko '86
Record '00

Sixty Million Dollar Man
'95
Spiral '00
Sunshine Cops '99
U-Man '02
Volcano High School
'01

School-Martial Arts
Avenging Warriors of
Shaolin '79
Blind Fist of Bruce '79
Bloody Fight '72
The Bloody Fists '72
The Bodyguard '73/78
Born Invincible '78
Bronson Lee, Champi-
on '78
Bruce Lee: The Man,
the Myth '76
The Chinese Connec-
tion '71
Chinese Hercules '73
Chinese Iron Man '75
Chinese Super Ninjas
'82
Dragon Fist '78
Dragon Princess '81
Dragon's Claws '79
Drunken Art and Crip-
pled Fist '79
The Eagle's Killer '81
Fatal Needles vs. Fatal
Fists '80
Fearless Hyena '79
Fist of Fury '95
Fist of Fury 1991 '91
Fist of Legend '94
The Fist, the Kicks and
the Evils '79
Five Fingers of Death
'72
Five Superfighters '78
Flash Future Kung Fu
'83
Flight of the Heroine
'00
Goose Boxer '78
Iron Man '86
Jade Claw '79
Kung Fu Genius '79
The Kung Fu Master
'94
Kung Fu on Sale '79
Kung Pow: Enter the
Fist '76
The Magic Crane '93
The Magnificent Butch-
er '79
Martial Arts Master
Wong Fei Hung '92
Master of the Flying
Guillotine '74
Memento Mori '99
Monkey Fist Floating
Snake '79
My Kung Fu 12 Kicks
'79
New Fist of Fury '76
Ninja Checkmate '79
Once upon a Time in
China '91
Once upon a Time in
China 2 '92

Once upon a Time in
China 3 '93
One Foot Crane '79
Painted Faces '88
Prodigal Boxer '73
The Real Bruce Lee '79
Return of the Street
Fighter '74
Samurai 2: Duel at Ichi-
joji Temple '55
Sanshiro Sugata '43
Screaming Ninja '73
Shadow of the Tiger
'79
Shaolin Fist of Fury '87
Shaolin Soccer '01
The Shaolin Temple '79
Sister Street Fighter
'74
Snake Fist Dynamo '84
Snake in the Eagle's
Shadow '78
Sorrowful to a Ghost
'70
Sting of the Dragon
Masters '73
Story of the Dragon '76
The Street Fighter '74
Ten Tigers of Kwang-
tung '79
Ten Tigers of Shaolin
'78
The 36 Crazy Fists '77
3 Evil Masters '80
Thunder Ninja Kids:
The Hunt for the
Devil Boxer '86/94
Triangular Duel '72
Venom Warrior '83
The Young Master '80

Sci-Fi
*Imagination fueled by
science and a vision of
the future. See also:
Anime; Sci-Fi Comedy.*
Akira '88
All Monsters Attack '70
Appleseed '88
Armageddon '97
Another Heaven '00
Astro Boy '63
Astro Boy '80
Atomic Rulers of the
World '57
Attack from Space '58
The Avenging Fist '01
Battle in Outer Space
'59
Battle Royale '00
Black Jack '96
Black Magic M-66 '87
Black Mask '96
Body Snatcher from
Hell '68
Brides of Blood '68
Bubblegum Crisis '85
Cross Fire '00
Dagora the Space Mon-
ster '64
Destroy All Monsters
'68
The Dimension Travel-
ers '98

Ebirah, Horror of the
Deep '66
Evil Brain from Outer
Space '58/59
Evil Dead Trap '88
Executioners '93
Extreme Challenge '01
Final Fantasy: The Spir-
its Within '01
Flash Future Kung Fu
'83
Frankenstein vs.
Baragon '65
Fugitive Alien '78
Gamera, Guardian of
the Universe '95
Gamera 2: Advent of
Legion '96
Gamera 3: The
Revenge of Irys '99
Gamera vs. Barugon
'66
Gamera vs. Gyaos '67
Gappa: The Triphibian
Monster '67
Gatchaman '94
Ghidorah the Three-
Headed Monster
'64
Ghost in the Shell '95
Giant Monster Gamera
'65
Godzilla, King of the
Monsters '54
Godzilla, Mothra and
King Ghidorah: Bat-
tle on Fire '01
Godzilla 1985 '84
Godzilla Raids Again
'55
Godzilla the Series:
Monster War '99
Godzilla 2000 '99
Godzilla vs. Biollante
'89
Godzilla vs. Destroyah
'95
Godzilla vs. Gigan '72
Godzilla vs. Hedorah
'71
Godzilla vs. King Ghido-
rah '91
Godzilla vs.
MechaGodzilla '74
Godzilla vs.
MechaGodzilla 2
'93
Godzilla vs. Megaguirus
'00
Godzilla vs. Megalon
'73
Godzilla vs. Mothra '92
Godzilla vs. Space
Godzilla '94
Guinea Pig: Android of
Notre Dame '88
Gunhed '89
The H-Man '58
The Heroic Trio '93
Horror of the Blood
Monsters '70
Hot War '98
The Human Vapor '60
I.K.U. '00

Invaders from Space
'58
Invasion of Astro-Mon-
ster '65
Invasion of the Nep-
tune Men '61
Junk '99
King Kong Escapes '67
Mad Doctor of Blood
Island '68
The Manster '60
Message from Space
'78
Metropolis '01
Mighty Jack '68
Mothra vs. Godzilla '64
The Mysterians '57
The One '01
Organ '96
Parasite Eve '97
Patlabor 1: The Movie
'90
Prince of Space '59
Reptilian '00
Robo Vampire '88
Robotrix '91
Rodan '56
Roujin Z '91
Royal Space Force: The
Wings of Hon-
neamise '87
Son of Godzilla '67
Speed Racer: The
Movie '67
Star Force: Fugitive
Alien 2 '78/86
Terror beneath the Sea
'66
Terror Is a Man '59
Terror of MechaGodzilla
'75
Tetsuo: The Iron Man
'89
Tetsuo 2: Body Ham-
mer '91
Time of the Apes '75
Trust Me U Die '99
The Tuxedo '02
Twilight People '72
2000 A.D. '00
Ultraman 2 '79
Ultraman Gaia: The
Battle in Hyper-
space '98
Ultraman Tiga and
Ultraman Dyna: The
Warriors of the
Lightning Star '98
Vampire Hunter D '85
Vampire Hunter D:
Bloodlust '01
Varan the Unbelievable
'58
The Venus Wars '89
Versus '00
Volcano High School
'01
Voyage into Space '67
Warning from Space
'56
War of the Gargantuas
'66
The Wesley's Mysteri-
ous File '01

The X from Outer Space
'67
Yog: Monster from
Space '70
Yongary, Monster from
the Deep '67

Sci-Fi Comedy
*See also: Genre
Spoofs; Satire & Paro-
dy; Sci-Fi.*
Bio-Cops '00
Bio Zombie '98
The Cat '91
Gamera vs. Guillon '69
Gamera vs. Viras '68
Gamera vs. Zigra '71
I Love Maria '88
King Kong vs. Godzilla
'62
Project A-ko '86
Sixty Million Dollar Man
'95
Teenage Mutant Ninja
Turtles '90
Terminatrix '95
Urusei Yatsura Movie
1: Only You '83
The X from Outer Space
'67
Zeram '91

Scientists
*See: Inventors & Inven-
tions; Mad Scientists.*

Screwball Comedy
*Stupid is as stupid
does.*
All's Well End's Well '92
All's Well End's Well
1997 '97
Bakery Amour '01
Beauty and the Breast
'02
The Big Sting '82
Brassiere '01
Eighth Happiness '88
He's a Woman, She's a
Man '94
Love Me, Love My
Money '01
The Magnificent
Scoundrels '91
Marry a Rich Man '02
100 Ways to Murder
Your Wife '86
The Private Eyes '76
The Tricky Master '00
Your Place or Mine! '98

Serial Killers
See also: Stalked!
Abbot White '82
Beauty Investigator '92
Chinese Samson '79
Comeuppance '00
Crime of a Beast '01
The Deadly Camp '99
Dr. Lamb '92
Guinea Pig: Devils
Experiment '85
Guinea Pig: Flower of
Flesh and Blood
'85

The Hypnotist '99
Killer Snakes '74
Lone Ninja Warrior '81
Model from Hell '99
Red to Kill '94
Robotrix '91
Scorpion Thunderbolt '85
Tell Me Something '99
The Untold Story '92
The Untold Story 2 '98
Violent Cop '99

Sex & Sexuality
Focus is on lust, for better or worse. See also: Erotic Thrillers; Pornography; Sexcapades; Sexploitation; Swingers.
Beautiful Beast '95
Beautiful Hunter '94
Beauty and the Breast '02
Big Boobs Buster '90
Blind Beast '69
Body Weapon '99
Brassiere '01
Brother of Darkness '94
A Chinese Torture Chamber Story '94
A Chinese Torture Chamber Story 2 '98
City of Desire '01
Daughter of Darkness '93
Devil Touch '02
Ecstasy of the Angels '72
Entrails of the Virgin '86
Erotic Ghost Story '90
Erotic Ghost Story 2 '91
5 Lady Venoms '78
Freeze Me '00
Green Snake '93
Happy End '99
He's a Woman, She's a Man '94
I.K.U. '00
Kei Mizutani: Undressed for Success '94
The Ladies' Phone Sex Club '96
Lady Ninja: Reflections of Darkness '96
Lies '99
Naked Killer '92
Naked Pursuit '68
Notorious Concubines '69
Red to Kill '94
Robotrix '91
Sadistic City '93
Sex and the Emperor '94
Shocking Asia '75
Shocking Asia 2 '76
Taboo '97
Terminatrix '95

Tokyo Decameron: Three Tales of Madness and Sensuality '96
Urotsukidoji '89
Violated Paradise '63
Weather Woman '95
Zero Woman: The Accused '96

Sexcapades
Beauty and the Breast '02
Big Boobs Buster '90
I.K.U. '00
Kei Mizutani: Undressed for Success '94
The Ladies' Phone Sex Club '96
Terminatrix '95
Weather Woman '95

Sexploitation
Softcore epics usually lacking in plot but not skin. See also: Erotic Thrillers; Exploitation.
Big Boobs Buster '90
A Chinese Torture Chamber Story '94
A Chinese Torture Chamber Story 2 '98
Erotic Ghost Story '90
Erotic Ghost Story 2 '91
I.K.U. '00
Kei Mizutani: Undressed for Success '94
The Ladies' Phone Sex Club '96
Notorious Concubines '69
Robotrix '91
Sex and the Emperor '94
Terminatrix '95
Tokyo Decameron: Three Tales of Madness and Sensuality '96
Violated Paradise '63
Weather Woman '95

Shakespeare?
Sometimes dubious adaptions of the Bard's work.
Ran '85
Romeo Must Die '00
Throne of Blood '57

Shaolin Temple
See sidebar, p. 558
Abbot White '82
Angel '87
Angel on Fire '95
The Art of Action: Martial Arts in the Movies '02
Avenging Warriors of Shaolin '79
The Blazing Temple '76

Burning Paradise '94
Deadend of Besiegers '92
Death Mask of the Ninja '82
Dragon Chronicles: Maidens of Heavenly Mountain '94
Dragon from Shaolin '96
Dragon Kid '90
Dragons of the Orient '88
Duel of the Tao Tough '82
Duel to the Death '82
The 8 Masters '77
The 18 Bronzemen '76
The 18 Bronzemen Part 2 '76
18 Fatal Strikes '78
Emperor of Shaolin Kung Fu '80
Enter the Dragon '73
Executioners from Shaolin '77
Fatal Flying Guillotine '77
Five Elements of Kung Fu '78
Fury in Shaolin Temple '82
God of Cookery '96
The Heroes '80
The Holy Robe of Shaolin Temple '84
The Invincible Kung Fu Trio '78
Iron Man '86
The Iron Monkey '77
Lady Wu Tang '77
Legend of the Dragonslayer Sword 3 '90
The Master of Death '82
The New Legend of Shaolin '94
Ninja Hunter '83
Ninja the Final Duel '85
Ninja vs. Shaolin Guards '84
Raiders of Wu Tang '82
Real Kung Fu of Shaolin, Part 1 '81
Return of the Master Killer '80
The Secrets of the Warrior's Power '97
Shadow of the Tiger '79
Shaolin and Tai Chi '79
The Shaolin Disciple '80
The Shaolin Drunken Monk '83
Shaolin Master Killer '78
The Shaolin One '83
Shaolin Soccer '01
The Shaolin Temple '79
Shaolin Traitorous '76
Shaolin vs. Lama '81
Shaolin vs. Manchu '80

Shaolin: Wheel of Life '00
Shaolin Wooden Men '76
Spiritual Kung Fu '78
The 36 Crazy Fists '77
Twin Warriors '93
War of the Shaolin Temple '80
Warrior from Shaolin '81

Showbiz Comedy
Eighth Happiness '88
The Foul King '00
Giants and Toys '58
God of Cookery '96
He's a Woman, She's a Man '94
High Risk '95
King Kong vs. Godzilla '62
King of Comedy '99
Losers' Club '01
Weather Woman '95

Showbiz Drama
Bruce Lee, The Legend '84
Bruce Lee: The Man, the Myth '76
Bruce Lee We Miss You '76
Dragon: The Bruce Lee Story '93
Dynamo '78
Ghost Actress '96
Giants and Toys '58
He's a Woman, She's a Man '94
The Hypnotist '99
Inner Senses '01
Painted Faces '88
Peking Opera Blues '86
The Phantom Lover '95
Ring 0: Birthday '00
Venom Warrior '83

Showbiz Thrillers
Audition '99
Bruce Lee, The Legend '84
Bruce Lee: The Man, the Myth '76
Bruce Lee We Miss You '76
Dynamo '78
Fist of Fear-Touch of Death '80
Ghost Actress '96
High Risk '95
Horror Hotline Big Head Monster '01
The Hypnotist '99
Mr. Nice Guy '97
Peking Opera Blues '86
The Phantom Lover '95
Ring 0: Birthday '00

Shower & Bath Scenes
See also: The Loo.
The Accidental Spy '01
Armour of God '86
Beauty Investigator '92

Black Cat '91
The Bride with White Hair '93
Cheap Killers '98
A Chinese Ghost Story '87
Conman in Tokyo '00
Daughter of Darkness '93
The Defender '94
Devil Man '87
Double Tap '00
Executioners '93
Fear Faith Revenge 303 '98
First Strike '96
Full Contact '92
Green Snake '93
Guinea Pig: Mermaid in a Manhole '88
Heart of Dragon '85
Lone Wolf and Cub 2: Baby Cart at the River Styx '72
Lone Wolf and Cub 4: Baby Cart in Peril '72
The Millionaires' Express '86
My Neighbor Totoro '88
Naked Killer '92
Notorious Concubines '69
Parasite Eve '97
Peace Hotel '95
Picture of a Nymph '88
Police Story '85
Prodigal Boxer '73
The Razor 1: Sword of Justice '72
The Razor 2: The Snare '73
The Razor 3: Who's Got the Gold? '74
Red to Kill '94
Renegade Ninjas '79
The Replacement Killers '97
Riki-Oh: The Story of Ricky '89
Roujin Z '91
Rush Hour 2 '01
Savior of the Soul 2 '92
The Seventh Curse '86
Shanghai 1920 '91
Son of Godzilla '67
Sonatine '93
Spirited Away '01
Tokyo Decameron: Three Tales of Madness and Sensuality '96
Twin Dragons '92
The Victim '80
Wing Chun '94
Winners and Sinners '83
Zatoichi and the Chess Expert '65

Shrinkage
It happens in places other than swimming pools.

898

All Monsters Attack '70
Mothra '61
Mothra vs. Godzilla '64
Rebirth of Mothra '96
Rebirth of Mothra 2 '97
The X from Outer Space '67

Shrinks
As in head shrinkers (psychiatrists, not witch doctors). See also: Doctors and/or Nurses.
Body Snatcher from Hell '68
Color of Pain '02
Crime of a Beast '01
Cure '97
Horror Hotline Big Head Monster '01
The Hypnotist '99
Inner Senses '01
Love Me, Love My Money '01
9413 '98
Postman Blues '97
Ultimatum '01

Shutterbugs
See also: Front Page.
Beautiful Hunter '94
Black Magic M-66 '87
Black Tight Killers '66
Bullets of Love '01
Dr. Lamb '92
Entrails of the Virgin '86
Extreme Challenge '01
Freeze Me '00
The Funeral '84
Giants and Toys '58
God of Gamblers 2 '90
Guinea Pig: Devils Experiment '85
Guinea Pig: Flower of Flesh and Blood '85
Horror Hotline Big Head Monster '01
Model from Hell '99
Once upon a Time in China '91
Once upon a Time in China 2 '92
Once upon a Time in China 3 '93
Suzhou River '00
Take 2 in Life '01
Thunderbolt '95
The Untold Story 2 '98
A Wicked Ghost 2: The Fear '00
You Shoot, I Shoot '01

Siamese Twins
See also: Two (or Three) Heads Are Better Than One.
The Bride with White Hair '93

'60s-a-Go-Go
Rockers, Mods, and long-haired freaky pinko

peace-luvin' mello-headed hippie types.
Black Tight Killers '66
Blind Beast '69
Branded to Kill '67
Ebirah, Horror of the Deep '66
Frankenstein vs. Baragon '65
Giant Monster Gamera '65
Gumnaam '65
King Kong Escapes '67
Mad Doctor of Blood Island '68
Mighty Jack '68
Naked Pursuit '68
Speed Racer: The Movie '67
Tokyo Drifter '66
War of the Gargantuas '66
What's Up, Tiger Lily? '66
The X from Outer Space '67
Yongary, Monster from the Deep '67

Slavery
Ninja vs. Bruce Lee '82
Once upon a Time in China '91

Snakes
See also: Were-snakes.
The Adventures of Milo and Otis '86
Butterfly and Sword '93
Deadly Snail vs. Kung Fu Killer '77
Devil Woman '70
Dirty Kung Fu '78
Duel of the Tao Tough '82
Green Snake '93
The Hot, the Cool, and the Vicious '76
Killer of Snake, Fox of Shaolin '78
Killer Snakes '74
The Killing of Satan '83
The Last Duel '82
The Legend of Bruce Lee '80
Legend of the Dinosaurs '77
The Legend of the Swordsman '92
The Lord of Hangzhou '98
Mahal '48
Mask of Death '76
Mighty Peking Man '77
The Miracle Fighters '82
Ninja Scroll '93
Revenge of the Zombies '76
Robo Vampire '88
Scorpion Thunderbolt '85
Seeding of a Ghost '83
Shocking Asia '75

The Six Directions of Boxing '79
Snake Fist Dynamo '84
Snaker '01
Succubare '77
The Sword Stained with Royal Blood '93

Soccer
They call it "football."
Eagle Shooting Heroes '93
Jiang Hu-"The Triad Zone" '00
100 Ways to Murder Your Wife '86
Shaolin Soccer '01

Spaceships
Astro Boy '63
Astro Boy '80
Atomic Rulers of the World '57
Attack from Space '58
Battle in Outer Space '59
Body Snatcher from Hell '68
Destroy All Monsters '68
Evil Brain from Outer Space '58/59
Final Fantasy: The Spirits Within '01
Fugitive Alien '78
Gamera vs. Guillon '69
Gamera vs. Viras '68
Gamera vs. Zigra '71
Giant Monster Gamera '65
Godzilla 2000 '99
Godzilla vs. King Ghidorah '91
Godzilla vs. Space Godzilla '94
Invaders from Space '58
Invasion of Astro-Monster '65
Invasion of the Neptune Men '61
Message from Space '78
The Mysterians '57
Prince of Space '59
Project A-ko '86
Reptilian '00
Royal Space Force: The Wings of Honneamise '87
Star Force: Fugitive Alien 2 '78/86
Time of the Apes '75
Ultraman 2 '79
Ultraman Gaia: The Battle in Hyperspace '98
Ultraman Tiga and Ultraman Dyna: The Warriors of the Lightning Star '98
Urusei Yatsura Movie 1: Only You '83
Vampire Hunter D: Bloodlust '01

The Venus Wars '89
Voyage into Space '67
Warning from Space '56
The Wesley's Mysterious File '01
The X from Outer Space '67
Zeram '91

Spiders
Challenge of Death '78
A Chinese Odyssey Part 1: Pandora's Box '95
Destroy All Monsters '68
The 18 Jade Arhats '78
The Magic Serpent '66
Sakuya: Slayer of Demons '00
Son of Godzilla '67
A Touch of Zen '69
The Tricky Master '00
Wicked City '87
Wicked City '92

Stalked!
See also: Serial Killers.
Ballistic Kiss '98
Beast of the Yellow Night '70
Big Boobs Buster '90
Black Cat '91
Black Mask '96
Blade 2 '02
Blind Beast '69
The Blood Drinkers '64
Blood: The Last Vampire '00
Body Weapon '99
Champion '00
Cheap Killers '98
A Chinese Ghost Story '87
A Chinese Ghost Story 2 '90
A Chinese Ghost Story 3 '91
A Chinese Ghost Story: The Tsui Hark Animation '97
City Hunter: Secret Service '96
Cross Fire '00
The Deadly Camp '99
The Demon's Baby '98
Devil Hunter Yohko '91
Devil Hunter Yohko 2 '92
Devil Man '87
Devil Touch '02
Dr. Lamb '92
Dragon from Russia '90
Dreadnaught '81
Entrails of the Virgin '86
Evil Cat '86
Evil Dead Trap '88
Fallen Angels '95
Fear Faith Revenge 303 '98
Fulltime Killer '01
Green Snake '93

Guinea Pig: Flower of Flesh and Blood '85
The Hypnotist '99
Ichi the Killer '01
The Killer '89
Killer Snakes '74
Last Ghost Standing '99
Mad Doctor of Blood Island '68
The Masked Prosecutor '99
Memento Mori '99
Model from Hell '99
Naked Killer '92
The Phantom Lover '95
Picture of a Nymph '88
The Replacement Killers '97
Revenge of the Zombies '76
Robotrix '91
Scorpion Thunderbolt '85
The Secret of the Telegian '60
Tell Me Something '99
Time and Tide '00
Twilight People '72
Ultimatum '01
The Untold Story 2 '98
Vampire Hunter D '85
Vampire Hunter D: Bloodlust '01
A Wicked Ghost 2: The Fear '00
The Witch from Nepal '85
Zeram '91
Zero Woman: The Accused '96

Submarines
The East Is Red '93
Gamera 3: The Revenge of Irys '99
Gamera vs. Viras '68
Godzilla 1985 '84
Godzilla 2000 '99
Godzilla vs. King Ghidorah '91
King Kong Escapes '67
King Kong vs. Godzilla '62
Mighty Jack '68
Terror beneath the Sea '66

Subways
See also: Trains.
Blood: The Last Vampire '00
Dragon from Russia '90
Dragon from Shaolin '96
Gamera 2: Advent of Legion '96
My Sassy Girl '01
Tetsuo: The Iron Man '89

Suicide
See: Paging Dr. Kevorkian.

Superheroes
Men and women of extraordinary strength and/or abilities, sometimes wearing silly-looking costumes.
Akira '88
Astro Boy '63
Astro Boy '80
Atomic Rulers of the World '57
Attack from Space '58
The Avenging Fist '01
Big Boobs Buster '90
Black Mask '96
Blade 2 '02
Blood: The Last Vampire '00
Cross Fire '00
Devil Hunter Yohko '91
Devil Hunter Yohko 2 '92
Devil Hunter Yohko 3 '92
Devil Man '87
Dragon from Russia '90
Evil Brain from Outer Space '58/59
Executioners '93
Gatchaman '94
The Green Hornet '74
Her Name Is Cat '98
The Heroic Trio '93
Ichi the Killer '01
Invaders from Space '58
Invasion of the Neptune Men '61
A Man Called Hero '99
Mortal Kombat '95
The Ninja Dragon '90
The One '01
Prince of Space '59
Project A-ko '86
Shaolin Soccer '01
Teenage Mutant Ninja Turtles '90
Temptress of a Thousand Faces '98
Ultraman 2 '79
Ultraman Gaia: The Battle in Hyperspace '98
Ultraman Tiga and Ultraman Dyna: The Warriors of the Lightning Star '98
Vampire Hunter D '85
Vampire Hunter D: Bloodlust '01
Violence Jack '88
Volcano High School '01
Weather Woman '95
X '96
Zeram '91

Supernatural Martial Arts
Forces from beyond terrorize via head kicking and rib crunching. See also: Superheroes.
Abbot White '82
The Avenging Fist '01
Blade 2 '02
The Bride with White Hair '93
The Bride with White Hair 2 '93
Butterfly and Sword '93
A Chinese Torture Chamber Story '94
Crouching Tiger, Hidden Dragon '00
Deadly Snail vs. Kung Fu Killer '77
Doctor Vampire '90
Dragon against Vampire '85
Dragon from Russia '90
Dragon Inn '92
The Duel '00
Duel to the Death '82
Eagle Shooting Heroes '93
The East Is Red '93
Encounter of the Spooky Kind '81
Evil Cat '86
Executioners '93
Fatal Needles vs. Fatal Fists '80
5 Venoms vs. Wu Tang '87
Flight of the Heroine '00
Flirting Scholar '93
Forbidden City Cop '96
The Heroic Trio '93
Iceman Cometh '89
Inheritor of Kung Fu '77
The Invincible Armour '77
Iron Monkey '93
A Kid from Tibet '91
Killer of Snake, Fox of Shaolin '78
King of Beggars '92
Kung Fu Zombie '81
Kung Pow: Enter the Fist '76
Lady Ninja: Reflections of Darkness '96
Lady Wu Tang '77
Last Hurrah for Chivalry '78
The Legend of the Swordsman '92
A Life of Ninja '83
Lord of the Wu Tang '93
The Magic Crane '93
A Man Called Hero '99
Master of the Flying Guillotine '74
Master Q 2001 '01
The Miracle Fighters '82
The Moon Warriors '92

Mortal Kombat '95
Nine Demons '83
99 Cycling Swords '80
The Ninja Dragon '90
Ninja Hunter '83
Ninja in the Deadly Trap '83
Ninja in the U.S.A. '88
Ninja Scroll '93
Ninja Supremo '81
Ninja the Final Duel '85
Ninja vs. Bruce Lee '82
Ninja vs. Ninja '87
Ninja vs. Shaolin Guards '84
The One '01
Painted Skin '92
The Peacock King '89
Picture of a Nymph '88
Prince of the Sun '90
Return of the Chinese Boxer '75
Return of the Deadly Blade '81
Riki-Oh: The Story of Ricky '89
Saga of the Phoenix '90
Savior of the Soul '91
Savior of the Soul 2 '92
The Seventh Curse '86
Shaolin Soccer '01
The Silver Spear '79
Spiritual Kung Fu '78
The Storm Riders '98
Swordsman '90
Swordsman with an Umbrella '70
The Three Swordsmen '94
A Touch of Zen '69
Twin Warriors '93
The Vampire Combat '01
Volcano High School '01
The Witch from Nepal '85
Zu Warriors '01
Zu: Warriors of the Magic Mountain '83

Survival
People were doing it before it was a TV show. See also: Negative Utopia; Post Apocalypse.
Attack of the Mushroom People '63
Barefoot Gen '83
Battle Royale '00
Bio-Cops '00
Bio Zombie '98
Body Snatcher from Hell '68
Brides of Blood '68
Bullet in the Head '90
The Deadly Camp '99
Eastern Condors '86
Ebirah, Horror of the Deep '66

Female Convict Scorpion: Jailhouse 41 '72
Grave of the Fireflies '88
Gumnaam '65
Mad Doctor of Blood Island '68
Son of Godzilla '67
Time of the Apes '75
Twilight of the Cockroaches '87
Vampire Kids '91
Violence Jack '88
We're Going to Eat You! '80

Swingers
Take my wife...please!
A Chinese Torture Chamber Story '94
A Chinese Torture Chamber Story 2 '98
Ecstasy of the Angels '72
Entrails of the Virgin '86
I.K.U. '00
Lies '99
Notorious Concubines '69
Sadistic City '93
Taboo '97

Swordplay
Old School Swords & Sorcery. See also: Supernatural Martial Arts.
All Men Are Brothers: Blood of the Leopard '93
Ashes of Time '94
Bichunmoo '99
The Bride with White Hair '93
The Bride with White Hair 2 '93
Butterfly and Sword '93
A Chinese Odyssey Part 1: Pandora's Box '95
A Chinese Odyssey Part 2: Cinderella '95
Chivalrous Legend '98
The Cold Mountain Temple '91
Dragon Chronicles: Maidens of Heavenly Mountain '94
Dream of Garuda '94
The Duel '00
Duel to the Death '82
Eagle Shooting Heroes '93
The East Is Red '93
Green Snake '93
Iceman Cometh '89
Killer of Snake, Fox of Shaolin '78
Legend of the Flying Swordsman '00
Legend of the Mountain '79

The Legend of the Swordsman '92
Lord of the Wu Tang '93
The Magic Crane '93
The Magic Serpent '66
The Moon Warriors '92
99 Cycling Swords '80
Painted Skin '92
The Peacock King '89
Picture of a Nymph '88
Princess Blade '02
Reborn from Hell: Samurai Armageddon '96
Revengeful Swordwomen '79
Royal Tramp '92
Royal Tramp 2 '92
Saga of the Phoenix '90
Sakuya: Slayer of Demons '00
Savior of the Soul '91
The Silver Spear '79
The Storm Riders '98
The Sword Stained with Royal Blood '93
Swordsman '90
Swordsman with an Umbrella '70
The Swordswoman in White '92
The Three Swordsmen '94
To Kill with Intrigue '77
A Touch of Zen '69
Yellow River Fighter '88
Zu Warriors '01
Zu: Warriors of the Magic Mountain '83

Tai O Island
Bullets of Love '01
Legend of the Dragon '91

Taiwan (Production)
See sidebar, p. 414.
Abbot White '82
Angel '87
Beijing Bicycle '01
Blind Fist of Bruce '79
Born Invincible '78
Butterfly and Sword '93
Chinese Samson '79
Chivalrous Legend '98
Crouching Tiger, Hidden Dragon '00
Dragon Kid '90
Dragon Lee vs. the Five Brothers '78
Dragon against Vampire '85
Dragon from Shaolin '96
Dreaming Fists with Slender Hands '80
The 8 Masters '77
18 Secrets of Kung Fu '79
Emperor of Shaolin Kung Fu '80

Fantasy Mission Force '84
Fatal Needles vs. Fatal Fists '80
Fearless Fighters '69
Filthy Guy '80
The Fist, the Kicks and the Evils '79
Five Elements of Kung Fu '78
Flyin Dance '01
Golden Killah '80
The Green Dragon Inn '79
Guardian Angel '96
Hard as a Dragon '80
The Heroes '80
The Incredible Kung Fu Mission '82
Inheritor of Kung Fu '77
The Invincible Kung Fu Trio '78
Iron Monkey 2 '77
Iron Neck Li '81
A Kid from Tibet '91
Killer from Above '77
The Killer Meteors '76
Killer of Snake, Fox of Shaolin '78
Lady Iron Monkey '83
Lady Wu Tang '77
The Last Duel '82
Legend of the Drunken Tiger '92
Lethal Panther '91
A Life of Ninja '83
Lone Ninja Warrior '81
The Lost Kung Fu Secrets '80
Macho Man '72
Mantis Combat '81
Martial Arts Master Wong Fei Hung '92
Martial Arts Mayhem, Vol. 1 '99
Martial Arts Mayhem, Vol. 2 '99
The Master of Death '82
Moonlight Sword and Jade Lion '79
99 Cycling Swords '80
Ninja Checkmate '79
Ninja Hunter '83
Ninja in the Deadly Trap '83
Ninja in the U.S.A. '88
Ninja the Final Duel '85
Ninja vs. Shaolin Guards '84
One Foot Crane '79
The Prisoner '90
Rage of the Dragon '79
Raiders of Wu Tang '82
Revengeful Sword-women '79
Secret of the Chinese Kung Fu '81
Shaolin Chastity Kung Fu '81
Shaolin and Tai Chi '79
Shaolin vs. Lama '81
Shaolin vs. Manchu '80

The Six Directions of Boxing '79
Snake Fist Dynamo '84
Sorrowful to a Ghost '70
Story of the Dragon '76
The Super Ninja '84
Swordsman '90
A Touch of Zen '69
Two Dragons Fight against Tiger '75
War of the Shaolin Temple '80
What Time Is It There? '01

Tattoos
Aces Go Places '82
The Blade '95
Blooded Treasury Fight '79
The Deadly Camp '99
Death Duel of Kung Fu '79
Dragon from Russia '90
Female Convict Scorpion: Jailhouse 41 '72
5 Lady Venoms '78
Lone Wolf and Cub 4: Baby Cart in Peril '72
The Masked Prosecutor '99
The Miracle Fighters '82
The New Legend of Shaolin '94
The Ninja Dragon '90
Ninja Scroll '93
Ninja vs. Shaolin Guards '84
The Razor 1: Sword of Justice '72
Riki-Oh: The Story of Ricky '89
Robo Vampire '88
Tokyo Drifter '66
Tokyo Fist '96

Technology-Rampant
See also: Robots, Androids & Cyborgs.
Akira '88
Bio-Cops '00
Bio Zombie '98
Black Magic M-66 '87
Black Mask '96
Final Fantasy: The Spirits Within '01
Flash Future Kung Fu '83
Ghost in the Shell '95
Gunhed '89
Hot War '98
The Human Vapor '60
I Love Maria '88
I.K.U. '00
Metropolis '01
The One '01
Patlabor 1: The Movie '90
Prince of Space '59
Robotrix '91

Roujin Z '91
Sixty Million Dollar Man '95
Terminatrix '95
Tetsuo: The Iron Man '89
Tetsuo 2: Body Hammer '91
Trust Me U Die '99

Television
See: TV (Adapted From); TV Movies; TV Series; TV Tales.

Terror in the Woods
Summer camp isn't what it used to be.
Attack of the Mushroom People '63
Bloody Beach '00
Brides of Blood '68
The Deadly Camp '99
Entrails of the Virgin '86
Gamera, Guardian of the Universe '95
Gamera 3: The Revenge of Irys '99
Gamera vs. Gyaos '67
Godzilla vs. Mothra '92
Half Human '55
Horror of the Blood Monsters '70
King Kong vs. Godzilla '62
Legend of the Dinosaurs '77
Mad Doctor of Blood Island '68
Mighty Peking Man '77
Ninja Scroll '93
Picture of a Nymph '88
Princess Mononoke '97
Record '00
Return of Daimajin '66
The Seventh Curse '86
Son of Godzilla '67
Twilight People '72
Versus '00
War of the Gargantuas '66
We're Going to Eat You! '80

Terrorists
Appleseed '88
Armageddon '97
The Best of the Best '96
The Blacksheep Affair '98
Champion '00
Ebirah, Horror of the Deep '66
Ecstasy of the Angels '72
Extreme Crisis '98
Fight Back to School 2 '92
Godzilla vs. King Ghidorah '91
The Last Blood '90
Mighty Jack '68

She Shoots Straight '90
Shiri '99
The Tuxedo '02

Thailand (Production)
Bangkok Dangerous '00
Fear Faith Revenge 303 '98
The Killer Elephants '76
Mon-Rak Transistor '01
Robo Vampire '88
Snaker '01

That's a Baby?
Faces even a mother can't love. See also: Bad Seeds; Just a Little Bit Pregnant.
The Demon's Baby '98
Devil Woman '70
5 Venoms vs. Wu Tang '87
Gamera 3: The Revenge of Irys '99
Gappa: The Triphibian Monster '67
Godzilla vs. MechaGodzilla 2 '93
Horror Hotline Big Head Monster '01
The Imp '81
Mr. Vampire 2 '86
Seeding of a Ghost '83
Snaker '01
Son of Godzilla '67
Vampire Controller '00
The X from Outer Space '67

That's Showbiz!
See: Behind the Scenes; Showbiz Comedy; Showbiz Drama; Showbiz Thrillers; TV Tales; Undercover.

This Is Your Brain on Drugs
Via pills, weed, or intravenous injection.
Blind Fist of Bruce '79
Blonde Fury '89
Brother of Darkness '94
Chinatown Kid '77
Duel to the Death '82
Gonin '95
Guinea Pig: Flower of Flesh and Blood '85
The Magic Crane '93
Organ '96
Sugar-Howling of an Angel '96
Trust Me U Die '99
Twilight of the Dark Master '97
Wicked City '92

This Is Your Life
Bruce Lee: A Warrior's Journey '00
Bruce Lee, The Legend '84
Bruce Lee: The Man, the Myth '76
Chivalrous Legend '98
Dragon: The Bruce Lee Story '93
Fist of Fear-Touch of Death '80
Great Performances: Kurosawa '02
The Real Bruce Lee '79

The 3 Brothers
Stars of the Seven Little Fortunes Chinese Opera: Jackie Chan, Sammo Hung, Yuen Biao
Dragons Forever '88
Hand of Death '75
Heart of Dragon '85
My Lucky Stars '85
Pom Pom '84
Project A '83
Twinkle Twinkle Lucky Stars '83
Wheels on Meals '84
Winners and Sinners '83

Time Travel
Fast forward or reverse. See also: Rescue Missions involving Time Travel.
The Dimension Travelers '98
God of Gamblers 3: Back to Shanghai '91
Godzilla vs. King Ghidorah '91
Iceman Cometh '89
Time of the Apes '75

Torn In Two (or More)
Akira '88
Black Mask '96
Devil Man '97
Eastern Condors '86
The East Is Red '93
Entrails of the Virgin '86
Gamera 2: Advent of Legion '96
Gamera vs. Guillon '69
Gamera vs. Gyaos '67
Guinea Pig: Devils Experiment '85
Guinea Pig: Flower of Flesh and Blood '85
Guinea Pig: He Never Dies '86
Ichi the Killer '01
Lady Ninja: Reflections of Darkness '96
The Legend of the Swordsman '92
The Manster '60

Riki-Oh: The Story of
    Ricky '89
Robotrix '91
Swordsman '90
Urotsukidoji '89
War of the Gargantuas
    '66

Tournaments
The Avenging Fist '01
Battle Royale '00
The Big Brawl '80
BloodFight '89
Body Weapon '99
Bronson Lee, Champi-
    on '78
The Butterfly Murders
    '79
Double Tap '00
Dragon Princess '81
Dragon: The Bruce Lee
    Story '93
The Enforcer '95
Enter the Dragon '73
Exit the Dragon, Enter
    the Tiger '75
Extreme Challenge '01
Fist of Fury 1991 '91
Five Fingers of Death
    '72
Inheritor of Kung Fu '77
Killer from Above '77
The Legend '92
Legend of the Dragon-
    slayer Sword 3 '90
Master of the Flying
    Guillotine '74
Masters of Martial Arts
    '74
Mortal Kombat '95
Once upon a Time in
    China 3 '93
Postman Blues '97
Real Kung Fu of
    Shaolin, Part 1 '81
Sanshiro Sugata '43
Shadow of the Tiger
    '79
Shaolin Soccer '01
Shaolin vs. Ninja '83

Trailers
*Previews of coming
attractions-or long past
attractions. See also:
Documentaries.*
All Monsters Attack!
    '02
Martial Arts Mayhem,
    Vol. 1 '99
Martial Arts Mayhem,
    Vol. 2 '99

Trains
See also: Subways.
The Awaken Punch '73
Bullet Train '75
Cannonball Run '81
A Chinese Ghost Story:
    The Tsui Hark Ani-
    mation '97
Fulltime Killer '01
High and Low '63
Legend of the Drunken
    Master '94

Maborosi '95
Macho Man '72
The Millionaires'
    Express '86
Once upon a Time in
    China 2 '92
One Arm Hero '94
Return of the Chinese
    Boxer '75
Screaming Ninja '73
Sholay '75
Supercop '92
Thunder Cop '96

**Transvestites &
Transsexuals**
*See: Gender Bending;
He's Really a Girl!*

**Trapped with a
Killer!**
*See also:
Psychotics/Sociopaths.*
Blind Beast '69
Body Weapon '99
Brother of Darkness
    '94
Champion '00
The Deadly Camp '99
Evil Dead Trap '88
Guinea Pig: Devils
    Experiment '85
Guinea Pig: Flower of
    Flesh and Blood
    '85
Organ '96
Red to Kill '94
The Untold Story '92

Treasure Hunt
*Looking for hidden rich-
es.*
Armour of God '86
Blooded Treasury Fight
    '79
Castle of Cagliostro
    '79
Gamera vs. Barugon
    '66
Operation Condor '91
The Razor 3: Who's Got
    the Gold? '74
Revenge of the Patriots
    '76
The Touch '02
Zatoichi and the Chest
    of Gold '64

Triads
See sidebar, p. 688.
Ballistic Kiss '98
Beast Cops '98
A Better Tomorrow '86
A Better Tomorrow 2
    '87
A Better Tomorrow 3
    '89
Big Bullet '96
The Big Heat '88
Bullets of Love '01
Casino Raiders '89
Casino Raiders 2 '91
Casino Tycoon 2 '92
Century of the Dragon
    '99

Chinatown Kid '77
City Cop '95
City War '88
Code of Honor '87
Comic King '00
The Conman '98
Contract Killer '98
Cop on a Mission '01
Curry & Pepper '90
Days of Being Wild '90
The Defender '94
The Dragon Family '88
Dragon from Russia
    '90
Dragon in Jail '90
Dragon Killer '95
The Enforcer '95
Fallen Angels '95
First Option '96
5 Lady Venoms '78
Full Alert '97
Fulltime Killer '01
A Gambler's Story '01
Goodbye Mr. Cool '01
Gunmen '88
Hit Team '00
H.K. Adams Family '92
Jiang Hu-"The Triad
    Zone" '00
The Killer '89
Killer's Romance '90
The Last Blood '90
Lee Rock '91
The Legend of a Profes-
    sional '00
The Masked Prosecutor
    '99
Miracles '89
The Mission '99
Moonlight Express '99
The Most Wanted '94
Naked Killer '92
Nowhere to Hide '99
The Odd One Dies '97
Option Zero '97
Organized Crime and
    Triad Bureau '94
The Owl vs. Bombo '84
Powerful Four '91
Queen's High '91
Red Shield '91
The Replacement
    Killers '97
Return of the Dragon
    '72
Return of the Tiger '79
Return to a Better
    Tomorrow '94
Rich and Famous '87
Romeo Must Die '00
Shanghai 1920 '91
Task Force '97
A Taste of Killing and
    Romance '94
Tiger Cage '88
The Tigers '91
Time and Tide '00
Too Many Ways to Be
    No. 1 '97
Tragic Fantasy: Tiger of
    Wanchai '94
The Tricky Master '00
Undercover Blues '00
Venom Warrior '83

Where a Good Man
    Goes '99
Young and Dangerous
    '96
Young and Dangerous
    5 '98
Young and Dangerous
    6: Born to Be King
    '00

True Crime
*See also: This Is Your
Life; True Stories.*
Brother of Darkness
    '94
Crime Story '93
Daughter of Darkness
    '93
Dr. Lamb '92
God.com '98
Operation Billionaires
    '98
Organized Crime and
    Triad Bureau '94
Red to Kill '94
The Untold Story '92
The Untold Story 2 '98

True Stories
*Approximations of real-
life events, often signif-
icantly fictionalized for
the screen. See also:
Docudrama; This Is
Your Life; True Crime.*
The Blazing Temple '76
Brother of Darkness
    '94
Bruce Lee: A Warrior's
    Journey '00
Bruce Lee, The Legend
    '84
Bruce Lee: The Man,
    the Myth '76
Cantonese Iron Kung Fu
    '79
Chivalrous Legend '98
Chushingura '62
Crime Story '93
Daughter of Darkness
    '93
Dirty Ho '79
Dr. Lamb '92
Dragon: The Bruce Lee
    Story '93
8 Diagram Fighter '91
Emperor of Shaolin
    Kung Fu '80
Executioners from
    Shaolin '77
Fist of Fear-Touch of
    Death '80
Fists of the White
    Lotus '80
The Flying Guillotine
    '74
From the Queen to the
    Chief Executive '01
Fury of King Boxer '72
Generation Consultant
    '90
Generation Pendragon
    '90
God.com '98

Grave of the Fireflies
    '88
Great Performances:
    Kurosawa '02
Invincible Pole Fighter
    '83
Iron Neck Li '81
Killer Priest '81
King of the Mongols
    '60
The Legend '92
The Legend 2 '93
Madadayo '92
The Magnificent '78
The New Legend of
    Shaolin '94
Ninja: Band of Assas-
    sins '62
Ninja: Band of Assas-
    sins Continued '63
Notorious Concubines
    '69
Operation Billionaires
    '98
Organized Crime and
    Triad Bureau '94
Peking Opera Blues '86
Powerful Four '91
The Real Bruce Lee '79
Rebels under Siege '00
Red to Kill '94
Renegade Ninjas '79
Revenge of the Patriots
    '76
Sam the Iron Bridge:
    Champion of Mar-
    tial Arts '93
Samurai 1: Musashi
    Miyamoto '54
Samurai 2: Duel at Ichi-
    joji Temple '55
Samurai 3: Duel at
    Ganryu Island '56
Sanshiro Sugata '43
The Secrets of the War-
    rior's Power '97
Sex and the Emperor
    '94
Shanghai 1920 '91
Shaolin Master Killer
    '78
The Shaolin Temple '79
Shaolin: Wheel of Life
    '00
Ten Tigers of Kwang-
    tung '79
Ten Tigers of Shaolin
    '78
The Untold Story '92
The Untold Story 2 '98
Wing Chun '94
Zatoichi the Outlaw '67

TV (Adapted From)
Another Heaven '00
Dr. Lamb '92
Ninja the Final Duel '85
Patlabor 1: The Movie
    '90
Sure Death: Revenge
    '87
Ultraman Gaia: The
    Battle in Hyper-
    space '98

Ultraman Tiga and Ultraman Dyna: The Warriors of the Lightning Star '98

TV Movies
Movies made for the small screen.
Dragons of the Orient '88
Hunted by Royal Decree '00
It Takes a Thief '01
Legend of the Dragonslayer Sword '90
Legend of the Dragonslayer Sword 2 '90
Legend of the Dragonslayer Sword 3 '90
Shogun '80

TV Series
Astro Boy '63
Astro Boy '80
Fist of Fury '95
Fugitive Alien '78
Godzilla the Series: Monster War '99
Good Morning '59
Great Performances: Kurosawa '02
The Green Hornet '74
Jackie Chan Adventures 1: The Search for the Talismans '00
Jackie Chan Adventures 2: The Dark Hand Returns '00
Jackie Chan Adventures 3: The Shadow of Shendu '00
The Kung Fu Master '94
The Law and the Outlaw '95
Mighty Jack '68
Speed Racer: The Movie '67
Star Force: Fugitive Alien 2 '78/86
Street Fighter 2 '96
Time of the Apes '75
Ultraman 2 '79
Voyage into Space '67

TV Tales
Movies about TV (not to be confused with TV movies).
Eighth Happiness '88
Extreme Crisis '98
God of Cookery '96
God of Gamblers 3: Back to Shanghai '91
King Kong vs. Godzilla '62
Losers' Club '01
Mr. Nice Guy '97
Ring '98
Ring 2 '99
Ring 0: Birthday '00
Ring Virus '99
Weather Woman '95

Twins
Seeing double. See also: Siamese Twins.
A Better Tomorrow 2 '87
The Blood Drinkers '64
Born Wild '01
The Bride with White Hair '93
Dragon Chronicles: Maidens of Heavenly Mountain '94
Ghidorah the Three-Headed Monster '64
God of Gamblers 3: Back to Shanghai '91
Godzilla vs. Mothra '92
Hong Kong X-File '98
Ichi the Killer '01
The Invincible Kung Fu Trio '78
A Man Called Hero '99
Mothra '61
Mothra vs. Godzilla '64
990714.com '00
99 Cycling Swords '80
The One '01
Organ '96
Rebirth of Mothra '96
Rebirth of Mothra 2 '97
Savior of the Soul '91
Spirited Away '01
Take 2 in Life '01
Troublesome Night '97
Twin Dragons '92
War of the Gargantuas '66

Two (or Three) Heads Are Better than One
Ghidorah the Three-Headed Monster '64
The Manster '60
Urotsukidoji '89

Uncharted Desert Isle
Attack of the Mushroom People '63
The Deadly Camp '99
Ebirah, Horror of the Deep '66
Legend of the Dragonslayer Sword '90
Legend of the Dragonslayer Sword 2 '90
Vampire Kids '91

Undercover
Actors acting as actors.
Beauty Investigator '92
A Better Tomorrow 2 '87
Blonde Fury '89
Blood: The Last Vampire '00
Bury Me High '90
Butterfly and Sword '93
The Cat '91
Century of the Dragon '99

City on Fire '87
Clean My Name, Mr. Coroner! '00
Cop on a Mission '01
Curry & Pepper '90
Don't Give a Damn '95
Dragon on Fire '79
The Enforcer '95
Fight Back to School '91
Fight Back to School 2 '92
5 Lady Venoms '78
Fury of King Boxer '72
Gen-X Cops '99
Gold Fingers '01
Hard Boiled '91
The Heroes '80
Hit Team '00
The Holy Robe of Shaolin Temple '84
The Hot, the Cool, and the Vicious '76
It Takes a Thief '01
King of Comedy '99
Kung Fu, the Invisible Fist '72
Long Arm of the Law 2 '87
Mantis Combat '81
Man Wanted '95
Millennium Dragon '99
Moonlight Express '99
The Most Wanted '94
Ninja: Band of Assassins Continued '63
Ninja vs. Bruce Lee '82
Ninja vs. Ninja '87
Police Story 2 '88
Pom Pom and Hot Hot '92
The Prisoner '90
Project A '83
Revenge of the Patriots '76
Robo Vampire '88
Robotrix '91
Royal Tramp '92
Rush Hour 2 '01
Secret of the Chinese Kung Fu '81
Shadow of the Tiger '79
She Shoots Straight '90
Shiri '99
Sister Street Fighter '74
Skinny Tiger and Fatty Dragon '90
Super Car Criminals '99
Supercop '92
Supercop 2 '93
SuperManChu '73
Sure Death: Revenge '87
Thunder Cop '96
Thunder Cops '98
The Tricky Master '00
U-Man '02
Undercover Blues '00
Who Am I? '98
Yes, Madam '85

Zatoichi Challenged '67

Unexplained Phenomena
Ummm, it's hard to define....
After Life '98
Another Heaven '00
Body Snatcher from Hell '68
Cross Fire '00
Cure '97
Dagora the Space Monster '64
Devil Man '87
Devil Woman '70
The Dimension Travelers '98
Dragon Chronicles: Maidens of Heavenly Mountain '94
Ebirah, Horror of the Deep '66
Entrails of the Virgin '86
Evil Brain from Outer Space '58/59
Evil Dead Trap '88
The Eye '02
Gamera, Guardian of the Universe '95
Gamera 2: Advent of Legion '96
Gamera 3: The Revenge of Irys '99
Gamera vs. Barugon '66
Gamera vs. Guillon '69
Gamera vs. Gyaos '67
Gamera vs. Viras '68
Gamera vs. Zigra '71
Ghidorah the Three-Headed Monster '64
Giant Monster Gamera '65
God of Gamblers '89
God of Gamblers 2 '90
God of Gamblers 3: Back to Shanghai '91
God of Gamblers Returns '94
Godzilla vs. Hedorah '71
Godzilla vs. Space Godzilla '94
Guinea Pig: He Never Dies '86
The Happiness of the Katakuris '01
The Heroic Trio '93
Hiruko the Goblin '90
Hong Kong X-File '98
Horror Hotline Big Head Monster '01
Iceman Cometh '89
The Imp '81
Inheritor of Kung Fu '77
Killer of Snake, Fox of Shaolin '78
The Killing of Satan '83
Kung Fu Zombie '81

Kung Pow: Enter the Fist '76
Kwaidan '64
Lady Ninja: Reflections of Darkness '96
Last Ghost Standing '99
The Magic Crane '93
Message from Space '78
The Miracle Fighters '82
Model from Hell '99
Mothra '61
Mothra vs. Godzilla '64
My Neighbor Totoro '88
Nightmare Zone '98
Nine Demons '83
The Ninja Dragon '90
Painted Skin '92
Parasite Eve '97
The Peacock King '89
Prince of the Sun '90
Princess Mononoke '97
Pulgasari '85
Rebirth of Mothra '96
Rebirth of Mothra 2 '97
Reptilian '00
Revenge of the Zombies '76
Riki-Oh: The Story of Ricky '89
Ring '98
Ring 2 '99
Ring 0: Birthday '00
Ring Virus '99
Sakuya: Slayer of Demons '00
Scorpion Thunderbolt '85
Seeding of a Ghost '83
The Seventh Curse '86
Shaolin Soccer '01
Snaker '01
Spiral '00
Spirited Away '01
The Storm Riders '98
Succubare '77
Thunder Ninja Kids: The Hunt for the Devil Boxer '86/94
Time of the Apes '75
The Touch '02
A Touch of Zen '69
Urusei Yatsura Movie 1: Only You '83
Versus '00
Volcano High School '01
Voyage into Space '67
Weather Woman '95
Wicked City '87
Wicked City '92
A Wicked Ghost '99
A Wicked Ghost 2: The Fear '00
Wild Zero '99
The Witch from Nepal '85
X '96
The X from Outer Space '67
Yog: Monster from Space '70

Yonigary, Monster from the Deep '67
Zu Warriors '01
Zu: Warriors of the Magic Mountain '83

U.S. (Production)
See: Asians in USA.

Vampire Babes
No, that's not redundant.
Blade 2 '02
The Blood Drinkers '64
Blood: The Last Vampire '00
The Demon's Baby '98
Doctor Vampire '90
The Haunted Cop Shop '87
New Mr. Vampire '86
The Vampire Combat '01
Vampire Controller '00
Vampire Hunter D '85
Vampire Hunter D: Bloodlust '01

Vampire Kids
Little bloodsuckers.
See also: Child Abuse; Kung Fu Kids.
5 Venoms vs. Wu Tang '87
Mr. Vampire 2 '86
Nine Demons '83
Thunder Ninja Kids: The Hunt for the Devil Boxer '86/94
Vampire Kids '91

Vampire Spoof
Bloodsucking buffoons.
See also: Horror Comedy.
Doctor Vampire '90
Dragon against Vampire '85
Encounter of the Spooky Kind '81
The Haunted Cop Shop '87
Mr. Vampire '85
Mr. Vampire 2 '86
Mr. Vampire Saga 4 '88
New Mr. Vampire '86
Vampire Kids '91

Vampires-Hopping
Chinese Kyonsi. See sidebar, p. 428.
Dragon against Vampire '85
Encounter of the Spooky Kind '81
5 Venoms vs. Wu Tang '87
Mr. Vampire '85
Mr. Vampire 2 '86
Mr. Vampire Saga 4 '88
New Mr. Vampire '86
Robo Vampire '88
Thunder Ninja Kids: The Hunt for the Devil Boxer '86/94

Vampire Controller '00
Vampire Kids '91

Vampires-Other
See also: Vampire Babes; Vampire Children; Vampire Spoof; Vampires-Hopping.
Curse of the Vampires '70
Horror of the Blood Monsters '70
Legend of the 7 Golden Vampires '74

Veterans
They often have trouble re-assimilating.
Eastern Condors '86
Female Convict Scorpion: Jailhouse 41 '72
Gunhed '89
Gunmen '88
The Haunted Cop Shop '87
Joint Security Area '00
Kwaidan '64
Lethal Panther '91
Long Arm of the Law 2 '87
Ninja in the U.S.A. '88
Operation Condor '91
Royal Warriors '86
Samurai 1: Musashi Miyamoto '54

Vietnam (Production)
Cyclo '95

Vietnam War
Technically, a police action.
A Better Tomorrow 3 '89
Bullet in the Head '90
Eastern Condors '86
Heroes Shed No Tears '83/86
Ninja in the U.S.A. '88

Vomit
See: Chunky Delight.

Voodoo
...that you do. See also: Bewitched; Demons; Magic & Magicians; Zombies.
Devil Woman '70
Mad Doctor of Blood Island '68
Revenge of the Zombies '76
Seeding of a Ghost '83
The Seventh Curse '86
Snaker '01
Succubare '77
The Witch from Nepal '85

War
See also: Big Battles; Veterans; Vietnam War.

Akira Kurosawa's Dreams '90
Barefoot Gen '83
Battle in Outer Space '59
A Better Tomorrow 3 '89
Blood: The Last Vampire '00
Bullet in the Head '90
Chivalrous Legend '98
Destroy All Monsters '68
The Dimension Travelers '98
Eastern Condors '86
Fantasy Mission Force '84
Final Fantasy: The Spirits Within '01
Frankenstein vs. Baragon '65
Fugitive Alien '78
Generation Consultant '90
Generation Pendragon '90
Godzilla vs. King Ghidorah '91
Grave of the Fireflies '88
Gunmen '88
Heroes Shed No Tears '83/86
The Hidden Fortress '58
Invasion of Astro-Monster '65
Invasion of the Neptune Men '61
King of the Mongols '60
The Last War '61
Magnificent Warriors '87
Message from Space '78
The Mysterians '57
Ninja: Band of Assassins '62
Ninja: Band of Assassins Continued '63
Notorious Concubines '69
Pulgasari '85
Royal Space Force: The Wings of Honneamise '87
Samurai 1: Musashi Miyamoto '54
Star Force: Fugitive Alien 2 '78/86
The Venus Wars '89
Voyage into Space '67
The Walls of Hell '64
War of the Shaolin Temple '80
Zu: Warriors of the Magic Mountain '83

War between the Sexes
See also: Marriage.

All's Well End's Well '92
All's Well End's Well '97 '97
Audition '99
Blind Beast '69
Brassiere '01
The Bride with White Hair '93
The Bride with White Hair 2 '93
Could You Kill My Husband Please? '01
Dummy Mommy, without a Baby '01
The East Is Red '93
Eighth Happiness '88
Female Convict Scorpion: Jailhouse 41 '72
He's a Woman, She's a Man '94
The Irresistible Piggies '02
Kick Boxer's Tears '92
The Ladies' Phone Sex Club '96
Marry a Rich Man '02
My Sassy Girl '01
Naked Killer '92
Naked Pursuit '68
100 Ways to Murder Your Wife '86
Princess Mononoke '97
Succubare '77
Sugar-Howling of an Angel '96
Sumo Vixens '96
Terminatrix '88
Urusei Yatsura Movie 1: Only You '83
Your Place or Mine! '98

Weddings
See: Death at Weddings; Marriage.

Were-foxes
See also: Were-snakes.
Akira Kurosawa's Dreams '90
Erotic Ghost Story '90
Killer of Snake, Fox of Shaolin '78
Mr. Vampire Saga 4 '88

Were-snakes
See also: Were-foxes.
Deadly Snail vs. Kung Fu Killer '77
Devil Woman '70
Green Snake '93
Killer of Snake, Fox of Shaolin '78
Scorpion Thunderbolt '85
Snaker '01
Succubare '77

Westerns à la Asia
Cowpersons riding and fighting on the plains (and in the saloons).
The Awaken Punch '73
Battle of Shaolin '77
Bloody Fight '72

The Bloody Fists '72
Bolo '80
Challenge of Death '78
Crouching Tiger, Hidden Dragon '00
Five Fingers of Death '72
The Holy Robe of Shaolin Temple '84
The Hot, the Cool, and the Vicious '76
Lightning Kung Fu '80
The Millionaires' Express '86
Once upon a Time in China and America '97
Peace Hotel '95
The Postman Fights Back '82
Rivals of the Dragon '83
Savior of the Soul 2 '92
7 Commandments of Kung Fu '79
Sholay '75
SuperManChu '73
Two Dragons Fight against Tiger '75
Yojimbo '61

Whales
Gamera vs. Viras '68
The Moon Warriors '92

What?
Movies containing deaf people, mute people, or people who just don't talk much. See also: Ears!
Bangkok Dangerous '00
City of Desire '01
Downtown Torpedoes '97
Hero's Blood '91
Jade Claw '79
Raiders of Wu Tang '82
The Return of the 5 Deadly Venoms '78
Runaway '01
Sympathy for Mr. Vengeance '01
Tiramisu '02

Where's My Johnson?
Movies that may have inspired Lorena Bobbit. See also: Amputations; Renegade Body Parts.
Inheritor of Kung Fu '77
The Invincible Kung Fu Trio '78
The Legend of the Swordsman '92
Naked Killer '92
Royal Tramp '92
Sex and the Emperor '94
Shocking Asia '75
The Street Fighter '74
Violent Cop '99

904

White Lotus Cult
The Demon's Baby '98
Drunken Master Killer '94
Fists of the White Lotus '80
Once upon a Time in China 2 '92
The Secrets of the Warrior's Power '97
White Lotus Cult '93

Wisely Wei
Ngai Hong's popular sci-fi author & adventurer.
Bury Me High '90
The Cat '91
The Seventh Curse '86
The Wesley's Mysterious File '01

Witchcraft
See: Bewitched; Magic & Magicians.

Women Cops
The Best of the Best '96
Blonde Fury '89
Body Weapon '99
Bubblegum Crisis '85
Bury Me High '90
City Hunter: Secret Service '96
Combo Cops '96
Cop Shop Babes '01
Cross Fire '00
Crystal Hunt '91
Daughter of Darkness '93
Dr. Lamb '92
Don't Give a Damn '95
Downtown Torpedoes '97
Eat My Dust '93
Expect the Unexpected '98
Extreme Crisis '98
First Option '96
From Beijing with Love '94
F*** / Off '98
Gen-X Cops '99
Gen-Y Cops '00
Guardian Angel '96
Hard Boiled '91

The Haunted Cop Shop '87
Hit Team '00
The Inspector Wears Skirts '88
In the Line of Duty 3 '88
In the Line of Duty 4 '89
In the Line of Duty 5: Middle Man '90
Last Ghost Standing '99
Leopard Hunting '98
Lethal Panther '91
Lethal Panther 2 '93
Mortal Kombat '95
Operation Pink Squad '88
Option Zero '97
Pom Pom '84
Righting Wrongs '86
Robotrix '91
Royal Warriors '86
Satin Steel '94
Sister Street Fighter '74
Sound from the Dark '00
Sunshine Cops '99
Supercop '92
Supercop 2 '93
Task Force '97
Tiger Cage '88
Time and Tide '00
Twinkle Twinkle Lucky Stars '85
The Untold Story '92
The Untold Story 2 '98
A Wicked Ghost 2: The Fear '00
Yes, Madam '85
Young Tiger '72

Wong Fei-Hung
See sidebar, p. 464.
Dreadnaught '81
Drunken Master '78
Drunken Master Killer '94
Iron Monkey '93
Last Hero in China '93
Legend of the Drunken Master '94
The Magnificent Butcher '79
Martial Arts Master Wong Fei Hung '92

The Master '89
Once upon a Time in China '91
Once upon a Time in China 2 '92
Once upon a Time in China 3 '93
Once upon a Time in China 4 '93
Once upon a Time in China and America '97

Worst Ape Costumes
Our candidates for movies most likely to have been snubbed by Roddy McDowall. See also: Monkey Business.
A*P*E '76
King Kong Escapes '67
King Kong vs. Godzilla '62
The Shaolin Invincibles '79

Wrestling
See also: Wrestling-Sumo
The Executioner '74
Extreme Challenge '01
Fantasy Mission Force '84
The Foul King '00
Jackie Chan Adventures 1: The Search for the Talismans '00
A Life of Ninja '83
The Ninja Dragon '90

Wrestling-Sumo
The Happiness of the Katakuris '01
Mr. Boo Meets Pom Pom '85
Sumo Vixens '96
Zatoichi the Fugitive '63

Writers
See also: This Is Your Life.
The Cat '91
Godzilla vs. King Ghidorah '91

Inner Senses '01
King of Beggars '92
990714.com '00
The Seventh Curse '86
The Wesley's Mysterious File '01
Wishful Milenio '01

Yakuza
See sidebar, p. 626.
Adrenaline Drive '99
Black Tight Killers '66
The Bodyguard '73/78
Boiling Point '90
Branded to Kill '67
Brother '00
Conman in Tokyo '00
Contract Killer '98
The Executioner '74
Ichi the Killer '01
My Lucky Stars '85
The Odd One Dies '97
Postman Blues '97
Sonatine '93
Tokyo Drifter '66
Tokyo Mafia: Yakuza Wars '95
Tokyo Mafia 2: Wrath of the Yakuza '95
Tokyo Mafia 3: Battle for Shinjuku '96
Tokyo Raiders '00
Violent Cop '89
Wicked City '87
Wicked City '92
Young and Dangerous 6: Born to Be King '00

Yeti/Bigfoot
Half Human '55
War of the Gargantuas '66

Zatoichi
See sidebar, p. 694.
Adventures of a Blind Man '64
Blind Swordsman: The Tale of Zatoichi '62
Fight, Zatoichi, Fight! '64
New Tale of Zatoichi '63
Samaritan Zatoichi '68
The Tale of Zatoichi Continues '62

Zatoichi and the Chess Expert '65
Zatoichi and the Chest of Gold '64
Zatoichi and the Doomed Man '65
Zatoichi and the Fugitives '68
Zatoichi Challenged '67
Zatoichi on the Road '63
Zatoichi's Cane Sword '66
Zatoichi's Flashing Sword '64
Zatoichi's Revenge '64
Zatoichi's Vengeance '66
Zatoichi the Fugitive '63
Zatoichi the Outlaw '67

Zombies
See also: Death & the Afterlife.
Bio-Cops '00
Bio Zombie '98
The Cat '91
The Eternal Evil of Asia '95
The Happiness of the Katakuris '01
Iron Monkey 2 '77
Junk '99
Kung Fu Zombie '81
Legend of the 7 Golden Vampires '74
New Mr. Vampire '86
Ninja Hunter '83
Reborn from Hell: Samurai Armageddon '96
Return of the Chinese Boxer '75
Revenge of the Zombies '76
Saga of the Phoenix '90
The Seventh Curse '86
Thunder Ninja Kids: The Hunt for the Devil Boxer '86/94
Troublesome Night 4 '98
Vampire Controller '00
Versus '00
Wild Zero '99
The Witch from Nepal '85